MW00597971

SIMPLE

FAITH

BIBLE

NEW REVISED STANDARD VERSION

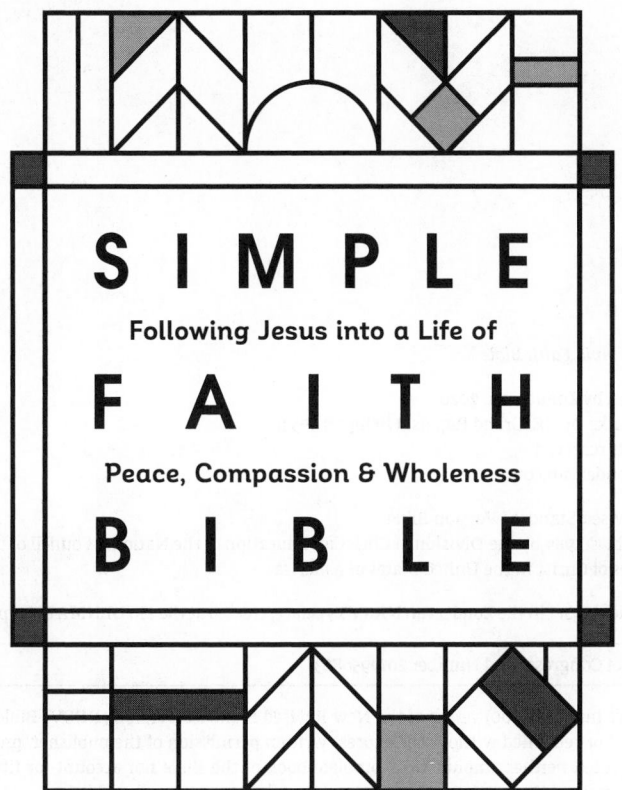

SIMPLE

Following Jesus into a Life of

FAITH

Peace, Compassion & Wholeness

BIBLE

REFLECTIONS FROM

JIMMY CARTER

◆ ◆ ◆

WINNER OF THE *NOBEL PEACE PRIZE*

ZONDERVAN®

NRSV Simple Faith Bible

Published by Zondervan, 2020
3900 Sparks Dr. SE, Grand Rapids, Michigan 49546
All rights reserved
www.Zondervan.com

New Revised Standard Version Bible
Copyright © 1989 by the Division of Christian Education of the National Council of the
Churches of Christ in the United States of America

This Bible was set in the Zondervan NRSV Typeface, created at the 2K/DENMARK type foundry.

Library of Congress Card Number 2019956863

Printed in China

---

20 21 22 23 24 25 26 27 /AMC/ 14 13 12 11 10 9 8 7 6 5 4 3 2 1

TABLE OF CONTENTS

OLD TESTAMENT

NEW TESTAMENT

OLD TESTAMENT

NEW TESTAMENT

ALPHABETICAL ORDER OF THE BOOKS OF THE BIBLE

The books of the New Testament are indicated by *italics*.

Acts...... 1300	Judges...... 277
Amos 1066	1 Kings...... 386
1 Chronicles...... 459	2 Kings...... 424
2 Chronicles...... 491	Lamentations 954
Colossians 1425	Leviticus 117
1 Corinthians 1367	*Luke* 1216
2 Corinthians 1388	Malachi 1129
Daniel...... 1025	*Mark*...... 1185
Deuteronomy 201	*Matthew* 1137
Ecclesiastes 773	Micah 1087
Ephesians 1411	Nahum...... 1097
Esther...... 563	Nehemiah 545
Exodus 65	Numbers 152
Ezekiel 964	Obadiah 1079
Ezra...... 531	*1 Peter* 1483
Galatians...... 1402	*2 Peter* 1491
Genesis......1	*Philemon* 1457
Habakkuk 1101	*Philippians* 1419
Haggai 1112	Proverbs...... 736
Hebrews...... 1461	Psalms 616
Hosea 1046	*Revelation*...... 1510
Isaiah 791	*Romans* 1346
James 1476	Ruth...... 307
Jeremiah 875	1 Samuel 312
Job...... 574	2 Samuel 352
Joel...... 1060	Song of Solomon 784
John 1264	*1 Thessalonians* 1431
1 John...... 1496	*2 Thessalonians* 1437
2 John...... 1503	*1 Timothy* 1441
3 John...... 1505	*2 Timothy* 1448
Jonah 1082	*Titus*...... 1453
Joshua...... 246	Zechariah...... 1117
Jude 1507	Zephaniah...... 1106

ALPHABETICAL ORDER OF THE BOOKS OF THE BIBLE

The books of the New Testament are indicated by italics.

WELCOME TO THE NRSV SIMPLE FAITH BIBLE

———————◁▷———————

Former United States President Jimmy Carter has been teaching Sunday school for over 65 years, many of them at Maranatha Baptist Church in Plains, Georgia. *NRSV Simple Faith* draws on the content of the lessons he has taught, as well as insights he has gained over the years. President Carter has lived these principles throughout his life, private and public. Through his important work in the White House and with The Carter Center and Habitat for Humanity, President Carter and his wife Rosalynn have been active in many capacities promoting peace and justice among people around the world.

President Carter teaches that, 1) our salvation is through the sacrificial death and resurrection of Jesus Christ, and 2) faith in Christ leads to manifesting personal qualities such as love, humility, gentleness, forgiveness and faithfulness. These qualities bear fruit in interpersonal relationships as well as in our public lives in the workplace, school and neighborhood. And faith in Jesus Christ requires us not only to believe but also to act. It means that we obey Jesus' commands and follow his example. It means that we embrace justice, peace, freedom, concern for the poor, the suffering and the oppressed.

President Carter has authored nearly 30 books, and he has now teamed up with Zondervan to incorporate his insights on Scripture into the text of the New Revised Standard Version of the Bible. We hope that these notes and articles will give you a glimpse into the heart of a man who has sought to know God and do his will for many years. More importantly, we hope this Bible helps you understand God's will as revealed through his Word. To help you read, study and contemplate this Bible, we have provided the following features:

- *Bible in Focus* articles illuminate select Biblical principles. Each is one page long and includes a key verse with an inset featuring *Going Deeper* questions for reflection.

⫫ **BIBLE IN FOCUS**

AN ACCEPTABLE OFFERING

The LORD said to Cain, "Why are you angry, and why has your countenance fallen? If you do well, will you not be accepted? And if you do not do well, sin is lurking at the door; its desire is for you, but you must master it."

—Genesis 4.6–7

Exactly why God accepted Abel's offering but didn't accept Cain's is one of the mysteries of the Bible. Within the text, however, there are subtle hints as to why God might have done this. Most notably, it seems that Abel brought his best, the firstborn of his flock, and Cain just brought some of his crops, such as a bushel of wheat. Cain may have come and said, "I have done my work," and Abel may have come with a spirit of seeking God's blessing and his forgiveness. Certainly, God looked within the hearts of Cain and Abel and made his judgment.

This same emphasis upon the heart can be seen in the story that Jesus told in Luke 18. In that story, a Pharisee self-righteously thanked God that he was not as bad as other people, including a tax collector who was standing nearby. In contrast, the tax collector humbly recognized his own sinfulness and asked God for mercy. Jesus concluded that the tax collector, not the Pharisee, went home justified before God.

If we are right that the problem with Cain's offering lay in his heart attitude, then it makes sense why God later instructed him about the dangers of sin (see Genesis 4.6–7). God warned Cain that sin would always lurk at the door of his heart, waiting to overtake him, and that Cain must master sin instead. We are tempted with self-congratulation, complacency, selfishness, resentment and exclusivity. But we do not have to succumb to these sins. We can master them. With God's help, we can overcome when Satan tempts us to depart from God's precepts and neglect the opportunities the Lord gives us to do good.

As we think about this passage, we also need to be careful not to distance ourselves from Cain's sin by saying, "At least I haven't killed anyone." Instead, if we are living up to our obligations and commitments as Christians, we will say, "I'm not going to hate anyone." "I'm not going to despise anyone." "I'm going to forgive those who have injured me or aggravated me in any fashion." We should not even bring an offering to God until we search our own hearts and minds: Have I done anything to anyone to hurt them or to insult them or to ignore them or to betray them? That's a command from Christ himself (see Matthew 5.21–24).

Going Deeper

- What are some ways you can offer your best to God?
- In what ways do you transgress the commands of God? Do you have the desire to overcome your sin with God's help? Do you believe that you can?

BIBLE IN LIFE

God's Call Through Creation
Genesis 1.1–19

God has given human beings a collective ability to explore the grandeur of what he designed—the breathtaking degree of power, knowledge, wisdom, order and creativity with which the universe was formed. God calls us to take increasingly knowledgeable glimpses into its many wonders.

God also gives us individual opportunities to explore in greater depth the truth about ourselves and our spiritual lives. How many of us would dare to think that our intimate knowledge of the life of Christ is adequate, that we have reached the limit of our relationship with God through the Holy Spirit, that we have explored the boundaries of the power of prayer, that we have reached the limit of our spiritual life? It would be foolish for any of us to claim that.

- **Bible in Life** highlights passages of special interest to President Carter with short, application-oriented notes.

PONDER

God blessed Noah and his sons, and said to them, "Be fruitful and multiply, and fill the earth."
—Genesis 9.1

PRAY

Heavenly Father, thank you for showing us how in your greatness you have created a universe. You grant us freedom to use our own hearts and minds to remember lessons from the Old Testament that repeatedly teach us that departing from your commands brings havoc and devastation to our lives. But we can repent of our disobedience; we will be saved by your favor as Noah and his family were saved and given the promise of your faithfulness. We pray that every heart in doubt will turn to you through faith in Jesus Christ and that those of us who have not done so will make a public profession: "I believe in Jesus Christ; I know that I have been and I am a sinner; I know that Christ took the punishment for my sin upon himself, and through my faith in him I will be saved." We ask this in the name of our Savior, Jesus Christ. Amen.

- **Ponder and Pray** provide a specific verse or two and a short prayer of application.

OUR QUESTIONS DO
NOT THREATEN GOD.

- **Reflections** are brief and notable quotations of Jimmy Carter scattered throughout the text.

- The text of the New Revised Standard Version (Protestant canon), vetted by an ecumenical pool of Christian academics and renowned for its beautiful balance of scholarship and readability.

- An Index of Features on page xiii of this Bible lists the various features and tells you where to find them.

May God bless you richly as you read and pray through the *NRSV Simple Faith Bible* with President Carter.

The Editors
November, 2011 (original publication)
November, 2019

FOREWORD

I can tell you that no one works harder on a Habitat for Humanity build site than President and Mrs. Carter. They don hard hats and work together in a rhythm and with an energy that would amaze many half their ages. They are incredible builders and tireless champions for social justice.

Each year the Carters give Habitat a week of their time — and their construction skills — to build or repair homes and to raise awareness of the critical need for affordable housing. Participation in the annual event that bears their names has made Jimmy and Rosalynn Carter our most famous volunteers.

Having a former president of the United States endorse our work certainly put Habitat on the map, but their involvement with our ministry means so much more. They demonstrate so genuinely what it means to put faith into action.

For more than a quarter century, they have shown the world how to reach out to people whose similarities turn out to be so much greater than their differences. They have traveled the world together, working alongside others who share their vision of what the kingdom of heaven can be like here on earth. Their deep and abiding faith beckons them to care for those in need, and their servant leadership has brought hope to families worldwide.

When a Habitat house is completed, we gather for a dedication service in which we pray for the homeowners, the volunteers and all those who have come together in a community of compassion. Often during the Carter Project, President Carter has the honor of presenting a Bible to the family. It is a symbol of the foundation of this ministry and of the love that makes it possible. President and Mrs. Carter remind us that we are builders, not only of houses, but of hope, dignity and community.

While Jimmy Carter has been a leader on the world stage and an internationally recognized face for the ministry of Habitat, he has also remained a Sunday school teacher in Plains, Georgia. I pray that these notes from his lessons will touch your hearts and inspire you to reach out to the least of these and demonstrate the love and teachings of Jesus Christ.

Blessings,
Jonathan T. M. Reckford
Habitat for Humanity International CEO
July, 2011

INDEX OF FEATURES

PRAYERS OF JIMMY CARTER

TO THE READER

———————⊕———————

This preface is addressed to you by the Committee of translators, who wish to explain, as briefly as possible, the origin and character of our work. The publication of our revision is yet another step in the long, continual process of making the Bible available in the form of the English language that is most widely current in our day. To summarize in a single sentence: the New Revised Standard Version of the Bible is an authorized revision of the Revised Standard Version, published in 1952, which was a revision of the American Standard Version, published in 1901, which, in turn, embodied earlier revisions of the King James Version, published in 1611.

In the course of time, the King James Version came to be regarded as "the Authorized Version." With good reason it has been termed "the noblest monument of English prose," and it has entered, as no other book has, into the making of the personal character and the public institutions of the English-speaking peoples. We owe to it an incalculable debt.

Yet the King James Version has serious defects. By the middle of the nineteenth century, the development of biblical studies and the discovery of many biblical manuscripts more ancient than those on which the King James Version was based made it apparent that these defects were so many as to call for revision. The task was begun, by authority of the Church of England, in 1870. The (British) Revised Version of the Bible was published in 1881–1885; and the American Standard Version, its variant embodying the preferences of the American scholars associated with the work, was published, as was mentioned above, in 1901. In 1928 the copyright of the latter was acquired by the International Council of Religious Education and thus passed into the ownership of the Churchesof the United States and Canada that were associated in this Council through their boards of education and publication.

The Council appointed a committee of scholars to have charge of the text of the American Standard Version and to undertake inquiry concerning the need for further revision. After studying the questions whether or not revision should be undertaken, and if so, what its nature and extent should be, in 1937 the Council authorized a revision. The scholars who served as members of the Committee worked in two sections, one dealing with the Old Testament and one with the New Testament. In 1946 the Revised Standard Version of the New Testament was published. The publication of the Revised Standard Version of the Bible, containing the Old and New Testaments, took place on September 30, 1952. A translation of the *Apocryphal/ Deuterocanonical* Books of the Old Testament followed in 1957. In 1977 this collection was issued in an expanded edition, containing three additional texts received by Eastern Orthodox communions (3 and 4 Maccabees and Psalm 151). Thereafter the Revised Standard Version gained the distinction of being officially authorized for use by all major Christian churches: Protestant, Anglican, Roman Catholic, and Eastern Orthodox.

The Revised Standard Version Bible Committee is a continuing body, comprising about thirty members, both men and women. Ecumenical in representation, it includes scholars affiliated with various Protestant denominations, as well as several Roman Catholic members, an Eastern Orthodox member, and a Jewish member who serves in the Old Testament section. For a period of time the Committee included several members from Canada and from England.

Because no translation of the Bible is perfect or is acceptable to all groups of readers, and because discoveries of older manuscripts and further investigation of linguistic features of the text continue to become available, renderings of the Bible have proliferated. During the years following the publication of the Revised Standard Version, twenty-six other English translations and revisions of the Bible were produced by committees and by individual scholars—not to mention twenty-five other translations and revisions of the New Testament alone. One of the latter was the second edition of the RSV New Testament, issued in 1971, twenty-five years after its initial publication.

Following the publication of the RSV Old Testament in 1952, significant advances were made in the discovery and interpretation of documents in Semitic languages related to Hebrew. In addition to the information that had become available in the late 1940s from the Dead Sea texts of Isaiah and Habakkuk, subsequent acquisitions from the same area brought to light many other early copies of all the books of the Hebrew Scriptures (except Esther), though most of these copies are fragmentary. During the same period early Greek manuscript copies of books of the New Testament also became available.

In order to take these discoveries into account, along with recent studies of documents in Semitic languages related to Hebrew, in 1974 the Policies Committee of the Revised Standard Version, which is a standing committee of the National Council of the Churches of Christ in the U.S.A., authorized the preparation of a revision of the entire RSV Bible.

For the Old Testament the Committee has made use of the *Biblia Hebraica Stuttgartensia* (1977; ed. sec. emendata, 1983). This is an edition of the Hebrew and Aramaic text as current early in the Christian era and fixed by Jewish scholars (the "Masoretes") of the sixth to the ninth centuries. The vowel signs, which were added by the Masoretes, are accepted in the main, but where a more probable and convincing reading can be obtained by assuming different vowels, this has been done. No notes are given in such cases, because the vowel points are less ancient and reliable than the consonants. When an alternative reading given by the Masoretes is translated in a footnote, this is identified by the words "Another reading is."

Departures from the consonantal text of the best manuscripts have been made only where it seems clear that errors in copying had been made before the text was standardized. Most of the corrections adopted are based on the ancient versions (translations into Greek, Aramaic, Syriac, and Latin), which were made prior to the time of the work of the Masoretes and which therefore may reflect earlier forms of the Hebrew text. In such instances a footnote specifies the version or versions from which the correction has been derived and also gives a translation of the Masoretic Text. Where it was deemed appropriate to do so, information is supplied in footnotes from subsidiary Jewish traditions concerning other textual readings (the *Tiqqune Sopherim*, "emendations of the scribes"). These are identified in the footnotes as "Ancient Heb tradition."

Occasionally it is evident that the text has suffered in transmission and that none of the versions provides a satisfactory restoration. Here we can only follow the best judgment of competent scholars as to the most probable reconstruction of the original text. Such reconstructions are indicated in footnotes by the abbreviation Cn ("Correction"), and a translation of the Masoretic Text is added.

For the Apocryphal/Deuterocanonical Books of the Old Testament the Committee has made use of a number of texts. For most of these books the basic Greek text from which the present translation was made is the edition of the Septuagint prepared by Alfred Rahlfs and published by the Württemberg Bible Society (Stuttgart, 1935). For several of the books the more recently published individual volumes of the Göttingen Septuagint project were utilized. For the book of Tobit it was decided to follow the form of the Greek text found in codex Sinaiticus (supported as it is by evidence from Qumran); where this text is defective, it was supplemented and corrected by other Greek manuscripts. For the three Additions to Daniel (namely, Susanna, the Prayer of Azariah and the Song of the Three Jews, and Bel and the Dragon) the Committee continued to use the Greek version attributed to Theodotion (the so-called "Theodotion-Daniel"). In translating Ecclesiasticus (Sirach), while constant reference was made to the Hebrew fragments of a large portion of this book (those discovered at Qumran and Masada as well as those recovered from the Cairo Geniza), the Committee generally followed the Greek text (including verse numbers) published by Joseph Ziegler in the Göttingen Septuagint (1965). But in many places the Committee has translated the Hebrew text when this provides a reading that is clearly superior to the Greek; the Syriac and Latin versions were also consulted throughout and occasionally adopted. The basic text adopted in rendering 2 Esdras is the Latin version given in *Biblia Sacra*, edited by Robert Weber (Stuttgart, 1971). This was supplemented by consulting the Latin text as edited by R. L. Bensly (1895) and by Bruno Violet (1910), as well as by taking into account the several Oriental versions of 2 Esdras, namely, the Syriac, Ethiopic, Arabic (two forms, referred to as Arabic 1 and Arabic 2), Armenian, and Georgian versions. Finally, since the Additions to the Book of Esther are disjointed and quite unintelligible as they stand in most editions of the Apocrypha, we have provided them with their original context by translating the whole of the Greek version of Esther from Robert Hanhart's Göttingen edition (1983).

For the New Testament the Committee has based its work on the most recent edition of *The Greek New Testament*, prepared by an interconfessional and international committee and published by the United Bible Societies (1966; 3rd ed. corrected, 1983; information concerning changes to be introduced into the critical apparatus of the forthcoming 4th edition was available to the Committee). As in that edition, double brackets are used to enclose a few passages that are generally regarded to be later additions to the text, but which we have retained because of their evident antiquity and their importance in the textual tradition. Only in very rare instances have we replaced the text or the punctuation of the Bible Societies' edition by an alternative that seemed to us to be superior. Here and there in the footnotes the phrase, "Other ancient authorities read," identifies alternative readings preserved by Greek manuscripts and early versions. In both Testaments, alternative renderings of the text are indicated by the word "Or."

As for the style of English adopted for the present revision, among the mandates given to the Committee in 1980 by the Division of Education and Ministry of the National Council of Churches of Christ (which now holds the copyright of the RSV Bible) was the directive to continue in the tradition of the King James Bible, but to introduce such changes as are warranted on the basis of accuracy, clarity, euphony, and current English usage. Within the constraints set by the original texts and by the mandates of the Division, the Committee has followed the maxim, "As literal as possible, as free as necessary." As a consequence, the New Revised Standard Version (NRSV) remains essentially a literal translation. Paraphrastic renderings have been adopted only sparingly, and then chiefly to compensate for a deficiency in the English language—the lack of a common gender third person singular pronoun.

During the almost half a century since the publication of the RSV, many in the churches have become sensitive to the danger of linguistic sexism arising from the inherent bias of the English language towards the masculine gender, a bias that in the case of the Bible has often restricted or obscured the meaning of the original text. The mandates from the Division specified that, in references to men and women, masculine-oriented language should be eliminated as far as this can be done without altering passages that reflect the historical situation of ancient patriarchal culture. As can be appreciated, more than once the Committee found that the several mandates stood in tension and even in conflict. The various concerns had to be balanced case by case in order to provide a faithful and acceptable rendering without using contrived English. Only very occasionally has the pronoun "he" or "him" been retained in passages where the reference may have been to a woman as well as to a man; for example, in several legal texts in Leviticus and Deuteronomy. In such instances of formal, legal language, the options of either putting the passage in the plural or of introducing additional nouns to avoid masculine pronouns in English seemed to the Committee to obscure the historic structure and literary character of the original. In the vast majority of cases, however, inclusiveness has been attained by simple rephrasing or by introducing plural forms when this does not distort the meaning of the passage. Of course, in narrative and in parable no attempt was made to generalize the sex of individual persons.

Another aspect of style will be detected by readers who compare the more stately English rendering of the Old Testament with the less formal rendering adopted for the New Testament. For example, the traditional distinction between *shall* and *will* in English has been retained in the Old Testament as appropriate in rendering a document that embodies what may be termed the classic form of Hebrew, while in the New Testament the abandonment of such distinctions in the usage of the future tense in English reflects the more colloquial nature of the koine Greek used by most New Testament authors except when they are quoting the Old Testament.

Careful readers will notice that here and there in the Old Testament the word LORD (or in certain cases GOD) is printed in capital letters. This represents the traditional manner in English versions of rendering the Divine Name, the "Tetragrammaton" (see the notes on Exodus 3.14, 15), following the precedent of the ancient Greek and Latin translators and the long established practice in the reading of the Hebrew Scriptures in the synagogue. While it is almost if not quite certain that the Name was originally pronounced "Yahweh," this pronunciation was not indicated when the Masoretes added vowel sounds to the consonantal Hebrew text. To the four consonants YHWH of the Name, which had come to be regarded as too sacred to be pronounced, they attached vowel signs indicating that in its place should be read the Hebrew word *Adonai* meaning "Lord" (or *Elohim* meaning "God"). Ancient Greek translators employed the word *Kyrios* ("Lord") for the Name. The Vulgate likewise used the Latin word *Dominus* ("Lord"). The form "Jehovah" is of late medieval origin; it is a combination of the consonants of the Divine Name and the vowels attached to it by the Masoretes but belonging to an entirely different word. Although the American Standard Version (1901) had used "Jehovah" to render the Tetragrammaton (the sound of Y being represented by J and the sound of W by V, as in Latin), for two reasons the Committees that produced the RSV and the NRSV returned to the more familiar usage of the King James Version. (1) The word "Jehovah" does not accurately represent any form of the Name ever used in Hebrew. (2) The use of any proper name for the one and only God, as though there were other gods from whom the true God had to be distinguished, began to be discontinued in Judaism before the Christian era and is inappropriate for the universal faith of the Christian Church.

It will be seen that in the Psalms and in other prayers addressed to God the archaic second person singular pronouns *(thee, thou, thine)* and verb forms *(art, hast, hadst)* are no longer used. Although some readers may regret this change, it should be pointed out that in the original languages neither the Old Testament nor the New makes any linguistic distinction between addressing a human being and addressing the Deity. Furthermore, in the tradition of the King James Version one will not expect to find the use of capital letters for pronouns that refer to the Deity—such capitalization is an unnecessary innovation that has only recently been introduced into a few English translations of the Bible. Finally, we have left to the discretion of the licensed publishers such matters as section headings, cross-references, and clues to the pronunciation of proper names.

This new version seeks to preserve all that is best in the English Bible as it has been known and used through the years. It is intended for use in public reading and congregational worship, as well as in private study, instruction, and meditation. We have resisted the temptation to introduce terms and phrases that merely reflect current moods, and have tried to put the message of the Scriptures in simple, enduring words and expressions that are worthy to stand in the great tradition of the King James Bible and its predecessors.

In traditional Judaism and Christianity, the Biblehas been more than a historical document to be preserved or a classic of literature to be cherished and admired; it is recognized as the unique record of God's dealings with people over the ages. The Old Testament sets forth the call of a special people to enter into covenant relation with the God of justice and steadfast love and to bring God's law to the nations. The New Testament records the life and work of Jesus Christ, the one in whom "the Word became flesh," as well as describes the rise and spread of the early Christian Church. The Bible carries its full message, not to those who regard it simply as a noble literary heritage of the past or who wish to use it to enhance political purposes and advance otherwise desirable goals, but to all persons and communities who read it so that they may discern and understand what God is saying to them. That message must not be disguised in phrases that are no longer clear, or hidden under words that have changed or lost their meaning; it must be presented in language that is direct and plain and meaningful to people today. It is the hope and prayer of the translators that this version of the Bible may continue to hold a large place in congregational life and to speak to all readers, young and old alike, helping them to understand and believe and respond to its message.

For the Committee,
BRUCE M. METZGER

THE OLD TESTAMENT

GENESIS

The question of when and how the world began has intrigued us since, well, since the beginning. The book of Genesis is about many beginnings—the beginning of the universe, the beginning of people, the beginning of sin, and the beginning of God's promises and plan for salvation. It's a book about why we began and where God wants to take us. It's about relationships—between God and the creation, between God and all people, between one person and another. The book of Genesis recounts how God designed a covenant with the Israelites and how the Lord pledged love and faithfulness to them.

SIX DAYS OF CREATION AND THE SABBATH

1 In the beginning when God created[a] the heavens and the earth, ²the earth was a formless void and darkness covered the face of the deep, while a wind from God[b] swept over the face of the waters. ³Then God said, "Let there be light"; and there was light. ⁴And God saw that the light was good; and God separated the light from the darkness. ⁵God called the light Day, and the darkness he called Night. And there was evening and there was morning, the first day.

6 And God said, "Let there be a dome in the midst of the waters, and let it separate the waters from the waters." ⁷So God made the dome and separated the waters that were under the dome from the waters that were above the dome. And it was so. ⁸God called the dome Sky. And there was evening and there was morning, the second day.

9 And God said, "Let the waters under the sky be gathered together into one place, and let the dry land appear." And it was so. ¹⁰God called the dry land Earth, and the waters that were gathered together he called Seas. And God saw that it was good. ¹¹Then God said, "Let the earth put forth vegetation: plants yielding seed, and fruit trees of every kind on earth that bear fruit with the seed in it." And it was so. ¹²The earth brought forth vegetation: plants yielding seed of every kind, and trees of every kind bearing fruit with the seed in it. And God saw that it was good. ¹³And there was evening and there was morning, the third day.

14 And God said, "Let there be lights in the dome of the sky to separate the day from the night; and let them be for signs and for seasons and for days and years, ¹⁵and let them be lights in the dome of the sky to give light upon the earth." And it was so. ¹⁶God made the two great lights—the greater light to rule the day and the lesser light to rule the night—and the stars. ¹⁷God set them in the dome of the sky to give light upon the earth, ¹⁸to rule over the day and over the night, and to separate the light from the darkness. And God saw that it was good. ¹⁹And there was evening and there was morning, the fourth day.

20 And God said, "Let the waters bring forth swarms of living creatures, and let birds fly above the earth across the dome of the sky." ²¹So God created the great sea monsters and every living creature that moves, of every kind, with which the waters swarm, and every winged bird of every kind. And God saw that it was good. ²²God blessed them, saying, "Be fruitful and multiply and fill the waters in the seas, and let birds multiply on the earth." ²³And there was evening and there was morning, the fifth day.

[a] 1.1 Or *when God began to create* or *In the beginning God created*   [b] 1.2 Or *while the spirit of God* or *while a mighty wind*

⊣⊢ BIBLE IN LIFE ▷   ⊖

God's Call Through Creation   *Genesis 1.1–19*

God has given human beings a collective ability to explore the grandeur of what he designed—the breathtaking degree of power, knowledge, wisdom, order and creativity with which the universe was formed. God calls us to take increasingly knowledgeable glimpses into its many wonders.

God also gives us individual opportunities to explore in greater depth the truth about ourselves and our spiritual lives. How many of us would dare to think that our intimate knowledge of the life of Christ is adequate, that we have reached the limit of our relationship with God through the Holy Spirit, that we have explored the boundaries of the power of prayer, that we have reached the limit of our spiritual life? It would be foolish for any of us to claim that.

24 And God said, "Let the earth bring forth living creatures of every kind: cattle and creeping things and wild animals of the earth of every kind." And it was so. 25God made the wild animals of the earth of every kind, and the cattle of every kind, and everything that creeps upon the ground of every kind. And God saw that it was good.

26 Then God said, "Let us make humankind[a] in our image, according to our likeness; and let them have dominion over the fish of the sea, and over the birds of the air, and over the cattle, and over all the wild animals of the earth,[b] and over every creeping thing that creeps upon the earth."

27 So God created humankind[a]
    in his image,
  in the image of God he
    created them;[c]
  male and female he
    created them.

28God blessed them, and God said to them, "Be fruitful and multiply, and fill the earth and subdue it; and have dominion over the fish of the sea and over the birds of the air and over every living thing that moves upon the earth." 29God said, "See, I have given you every plant yielding seed that is upon the face of all the earth, and every tree with seed in its fruit; you shall have them for food. 30And to every beast of the earth, and to every bird of the air, and to everything that creeps on the earth, everything that has the breath of life, I have given every green plant for food." And it was so. 31God saw everything that he had made, and indeed, it was very good. And there was evening and there was morning, the sixth day.

2 Thus the heavens and the earth were finished, and all their multitude. 2And on the seventh day God finished the work that he had done, and he rested on the seventh day from all the work that he had done. 3So God blessed the seventh day and hallowed it, because on it God rested from all the work that he had done in creation.

4 These are the generations of the heavens and the earth when they were created.

ANOTHER ACCOUNT OF THE CREATION

In the day that the LORD[d] God made the earth and the heavens, 5when no plant of the field was yet in the earth and no herb of the field had yet sprung up—for the LORD God had not caused it to rain upon the earth, and there was no one to till the ground; 6but a stream would rise from the earth, and water the

[a] 1.26,27 Heb adam [b] 1.26 Syr: Heb and over all the earth [c] 1.27 Heb him [d] 2.4 Heb YHWH, as in other places where "LORD" is spelled with capital letters (see also Ex 3.14–15 with notes).

⊦ BIBLE IN LIFE ▷

Walking With God
Genesis 1.27–31

Genesis describes the unique nature of our relationship with God our Creator. In John 4.24, Jesus says that "God is spirit, and those who worship him must worship in spirit and truth." Christ was completely human and also completely divine. Humans, created in God's image, are spiritual creatures. We have the potential for a complete spiritual relationship with God through Christ. God created us with a unique capability of communicating with our Creator and being able to question the reason for our own existence. There is no limit on us concerning how intimately we can relate to God, how much we can be aware of God's presence in our lives, how much we can open our hearts to the influence of the Holy Spirit. We have the potential to have exalted, liberated, adventurous lives filled with "indescribable joy." Christ himself confirmed that God has given us the potential for expansive lives, or to "have [life] abundantly" (John 10.10).

whole face of the ground— ⁷then the LORD God formed man from the dust of the ground,ᵃ and breathed into his nostrils the breath of life; and the man became a living being. ⁸And the LORD God planted a garden in Eden, in the east; and there he put the man whom he had formed. ⁹Out of the ground the LORD God made to grow every tree that is pleasant to the sight and good for food, the tree of life also in the midst of the garden, and the tree of the knowledge of good and evil.

10 A river flows out of Eden to water the garden, and from there it divides and becomes four branches. ¹¹The name of the first is Pishon; it is the one that flows around the whole land of Havilah, where there is gold; ¹²and the gold of that land is good; bdellium and onyx stone are there. ¹³The name of the second river is Gihon; it is the one that flows around the whole land of Cush. ¹⁴The name of the third river is Tigris, which flows east of Assyria. And the fourth river is the Euphrates.

15 The LORD God took the man and put him in the garden of Eden to till it and keep it. ¹⁶And the LORD God commanded the man, "You may freely eat of every tree of the garden; ¹⁷but of the tree of the knowledge of good and evil you shall not eat, for in the day that you eat of it you shall die."

18 Then the LORD God said, "It is not good that the man should be alone; I will make him a helper as his partner." ¹⁹So out of the ground the LORD God formed every animal of the field and every bird of the air, and brought them to the man to see what he would call them; and whatever the man called every living creature, that was its name. ²⁰The man gave names to all cattle, and to the birds of the air, and to every animal of the field; but for the manᵇ there was not found a helper as his partner. ²¹So the LORD God caused a deep sleep to fall upon the man, and he slept; then he took one of his ribs and closed up its place with flesh. ²²And the rib that the LORD God had taken from the man he made into a woman and brought her to the man. ²³Then the man said,

"This at last is bone of my bones
    and flesh of my flesh;
this one shall be called Woman,ᶜ
    for out of Manᵈ this one
        was taken."

²⁴Therefore a man leaves his father and his mother and clings to his wife, and they become one flesh. ²⁵And the man and his wife were both naked, and were not ashamed.

THE FIRST SIN AND ITS PUNISHMENT

3 Now the serpent was more crafty than any other wild animal that the LORD God had made. He said to the woman, "Did God say,

ᵃ **2.7** Or *formed a man* (Heb *adam*) *of dust from the ground* (Heb *adamah*) ᵇ **2.20** Or *for Adam* ᶜ **2.23** Heb *ishshah* ᵈ **2.23** Heb *ish*

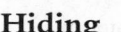 **BIBLE IN LIFE**

Hiding   Genesis 3.1–24

Adam and Eve's sin separated them from God and from each other. This was immediately evident when God asked, "Where are you?" (verse 9). For the first time, they experienced suspicion, guilt, embarrassment, disobedience and distrust.

God has given us freedom to make our own choices. How do we use that freedom? Do we choose to obey God, or do we rationalize our departure from the standards that Christ set for us? Our conscience probes our mind and heart and reminds us to live like Christ, but we often avoid our conscience. We don't want to face our failure to live up to Christ's standards, so we do nothing to correct our sinful behavior. By avoiding a confrontation with our sin, we hide in fear from the judgment of God, just as Adam and Eve did.

'You shall not eat from any tree in the garden'?" ²The woman said to the serpent, "We may eat of the fruit of the trees in the garden; ³but God said, 'You shall not eat of the fruit of the tree that is in the middle of the garden, nor shall you touch it, or you shall die.' " ⁴But the serpent said to the woman, "You will not die; ⁵for God knows that when you eat of it your eyes will be opened, and you will be like God,ᵃ knowing good and evil." ⁶So when the woman saw that the tree was good for food, and that it was a delight to the eyes, and that the tree was to be desired to make one wise, she took of its fruit and ate; and she also gave some to her husband, who was with her, and he ate. ⁷Then the eyes of both were opened, and they knew that they were naked; and they sewed fig leaves together and made loincloths for themselves.

8 They heard the sound of the Lᴏʀᴅ God walking in the garden at the time of the evening breeze, and the man and his wife hid themselves from the presence of the Lᴏʀᴅ God among the trees of the garden. ⁹But the Lᴏʀᴅ God called to the man, and said to him, "Where are you?" ¹⁰He said, "I heard the sound of you in the garden, and I was afraid, because I was naked; and I hid myself." ¹¹He said, "Who told you that you were naked? Have you eaten from the tree of which I commanded you not to eat?" ¹²The man said, "The woman whom you gave to be with me, she gave me fruit from the tree, and I ate." ¹³Then the Lᴏʀᴅ God said to the woman, "What is this that you have done?" The woman said, "The serpent tricked me, and I ate." ¹⁴The Lᴏʀᴅ God said to the serpent,
"Because you have done this,
    cursed are you among
        all animals
    and among all wild creatures;
upon your belly you shall go,
    and dust you shall eat
    all the days of your life.
¹⁵ I will put enmity between
        you and the woman,
    and between your
        offspring and hers;

he will strike your head,
    and you will strike his heel."
¹⁶To the woman he said,
"I will greatly increase your
        pangs in childbearing;
    in pain you shall bring
        forth children,
yet your desire shall be for
        your husband,
    and he shall rule over you."
¹⁷And to the manᵇ he said,
"Because you have listened to
        the voice of your wife,
    and have eaten of the tree
    about which I commanded you,
    'You shall not eat of it,'
cursed is the ground
        because of you;
    in toil you shall eat of it all
        the days of your life;
¹⁸ thorns and thistles it shall
        bring forth for you;
    and you shall eat the
        plants of the field.
¹⁹ By the sweat of your face
        you shall eat bread
until you return to the ground,
    for out of it you were taken;
you are dust,
    and to dust you shall return."

20 The man named his wife Eve,ᶜ because she was the mother of all living. ²¹And the Lᴏʀᴅ God made garments of skins for the manᵈ and for his wife, and clothed them. 22 Then the Lᴏʀᴅ God said, "See, the man has become like one of us, knowing good and evil; and now, he might reach out his hand and take also from the tree of life, and eat, and live forever"— ²³therefore the Lᴏʀᴅ God sent him forth from the garden of Eden, to till the ground from which he was taken. ²⁴He drove out the man; and at the east of the garden of Eden he placed the cherubim, and a sword flaming and turning to guard the way to the tree of life.

CAIN MURDERS ABEL

4 Now the man knew his wife Eve, and she conceived and bore Cain, saying, "I have producedᵉ

ᵃ 3.5 Or gods   ᵇ 3.17 Or to Adam   ᶜ 3.20 In Heb Eve resembles the word for living   ᵈ 3.21 Or for Adam   ᵉ 4.1 The verb in Heb resembles the word for Cain

a man with the help of the LORD." ²Next she bore his brother Abel. Now Abel was a keeper of sheep, and Cain a tiller of the ground. ³In the course of time Cain brought to the LORD an offering of the fruit of the ground, ⁴and Abel for his part brought of the firstlings of his flock, their fat portions. And the LORD had regard for Abel and his offering, ⁵but for Cain and his offering he had no regard. So Cain was very angry, and his countenance fell. ⁶The LORD said to Cain, "Why are you angry, and why has your countenance fallen? ⁷If you do well, will you not be accepted? And if you do not do well, sin is lurking at the door; its desire is for you, but you must master it."

8 Cain said to his brother Abel, "Let us go out to the field."ᵃ And when they were in the field, Cain rose up against his brother Abel, and killed him. ⁹Then the LORD said to Cain, "Where is your brother Abel?" He said, "I do not know; am I my brother's keeper?" ¹⁰And the LORD said, "What have you done? Listen; your brother's blood is crying out to me from the ground! ¹¹And now you are cursed from the ground, which has opened its mouth to receive your brother's blood from your hand. ¹²When you till the ground, it will no longer yield to you its strength; you will be a fugitive and a wanderer on the earth." ¹³Cain said to the LORD, "My punishment is greater than I can bear! ¹⁴Today you have driven me away from the soil, and I shall be hidden from your face; I shall be a fugitive and a wanderer on the earth, and anyone who meets me may kill me." ¹⁵Then the LORD said to him, "Not so!ᵇ Whoever kills Cain will suffer a sevenfold vengeance." And the LORD put a mark on Cain, so that no one who came upon him would kill him. ¹⁶Then Cain went away from the presence of the LORD, and settled in the land of Nod,ᶜ east of Eden.

BEGINNINGS OF CIVILIZATION

17 Cain knew his wife, and she conceived and bore Enoch; and he built a city, and named it Enoch after his son Enoch. ¹⁸To Enoch was born Irad; and Irad was the father of Mehujael, and Mehujael the father of Methushael, and Methushael the father of Lamech. ¹⁹Lamech took two wives; the name of the one was Adah, and the name of the other Zillah. ²⁰Adah bore Jabal; he was the ancestor of those who live in tents and have livestock. ²¹His brother's name was Jubal; he was the ancestor of all those who play the lyre and pipe. ²²Zillah bore Tubal-cain, who made all kinds of bronze and iron tools. The sister of Tubal-cain was Naamah.

23 Lamech said to his wives:
"Adah and Zillah, hear my voice;
    you wives of Lamech,
    listen to what I say:

ᵃ 4.8 Sam Gk Syr Compare Vg: MT lacks Let us go out to the field   ᵇ 4.15 Gk Syr Vg: Heb Therefore   ᶜ 4.16 That is Wandering

BIBLE IN LIFE

Sibling Rivalry   Genesis 4.1–8

The story of Cain and Abel is the first of many famous sibling rivals found throughout the Bible. Jealousy and anger seem to be common themes among many of these siblings: Jacob and Esau, Rachel and Leah, Joseph and his brothers, Moses and Aaron and Miriam, Absalom and Amnon, even Mary and Martha.

Within a family, the sibling relationship is vital and sometimes volatile. We learn from our brothers and sisters the basic elements of life: love, animosity, how to fight, how to protect ourselves, how to relate to other people, how to give and take. No two siblings are alike, and sometimes the differences (and similarities) can create tension. Perhaps we have let the symptoms of divisiveness—jealousy, envy or the struggle for ascendancy—become factors in our lives, and we have put off reconciliation with a brother or sister. Now may be the time for reconciliation.

BIBLE IN FOCUS

AN ACCEPTABLE OFFERING

The LORD said to Cain, "Why are you angry, and why has your countenance fallen? If you do well, will you not be accepted? And if you do not do well, sin is lurking at the door; its desires is for you, but you must master it."

—Genesis 4.6–7

Exactly why God accepted Abel's offering but didn't accept Cain's is one of the mysteries of the Bible. Within the text, however, there are subtle hints as to why God might have done this. Most notably, it seems that Abel brought his best, the firstborn of his flock, and Cain just brought some of his crops, such as a bushel of wheat. Cain may have come and said, "I have done my work," and Abel may have come with a spirit of seeking God's blessing and his forgiveness. Certainly, God looked within the hearts of Cain and Abel and made his judgment.

This same emphasis upon the heart can be seen in the story that Jesus told in Luke 18. In that story, a Pharisee self-righteously thanked God that he was not as bad as other people, including a tax collector who was standing nearby. In contrast, the tax collector humbly recognized his own sinfulness and asked God for mercy. Jesus concluded that the tax collector, not the Pharisee, went home justified before God.

If we are right that the problem with Cain's offering lay in his heart attitude, then it makes sense why God later instructed him about the dangers of sin (see Genesis 4.6–7). God warned Cain that sin would always lurk at the door of his heart, waiting to overtake him, and that Cain must master sin instead. We are tempted with self-congratulation, complacency, selfishness, resentment and exclusivity. But we do not have to succumb to these sins. We can master them. With God's help, we can overcome when Satan tempts us to depart from God's precepts and neglect the opportunities the Lord gives us to do good.

As we think about this passage, we also need to be careful not to distance ourselves from Cain's sin by saying, "At least I haven't killed anyone." Instead, if we are living up to our obligations and commitments as Christians, we will say, "I'm not going to hate anyone." "I'm not going to despise anyone." "I'm going to forgive those who have injured me or aggravated me in any fashion." We should not even bring an offering to God until we search our own hearts and minds: Have I done anything to anyone to hurt them or to insult them or to ignore them or to betray them? That's a command from Christ himself (see Matthew 5.21–24).

Going Deeper

- What are some ways you can offer your best to God?
- In what ways do you transgress the commands of God? Do you have the desire to overcome your sin with God's help? Do you believe that you can?

I have killed a man for
  wounding me,
  a young man for striking me.
²⁴ If Cain is avenged sevenfold,
  truly Lamech
    seventy-sevenfold."

25 Adam knew his wife again, and she bore a son and named him Seth, for she said, "God has appointed[a] for me another child instead of Abel, because Cain killed him." **26**To Seth also a son was born, and he named him Enosh. At that time people began to invoke the name of the LORD.

$$\bigoplus$$

PONDER

At that time people began to invoke the name of the LORD.
—Genesis 4.26

PRAY

Lord, we look back with wonder on the lives of people who lived many thousands of years ago: Adam, Eve, Cain, Abel, Seth, Noah, Abraham and others. As the ancient people did, help us to remember to call on your name. Help us to be brave with our questions and receptive to your answers. Help us to apply the ideas in your Holy Word, realizing that these are not just entertaining historical stories, but that there are lessons there to be learned from them. Teach us what your will is and open up our hearts to receive the presence of the Holy Spirit as a guide. In the name of Jesus, we pray. Amen.

ADAM'S DESCENDANTS TO NOAH AND HIS SONS

5 This is the list of the descendants of Adam. When God created humankind,[b] he made them[c] in the likeness of God. **2**Male and female he created them, and he blessed them and named them "Humankind"[b] when they were created. **3**When Adam had lived one hundred thirty years, he became the father of a son in his likeness, according to his image, and named him Seth. **4**The days of Adam after he became the father of Seth were eight hundred years; and he had other sons and daughters. **5**Thus all the days that Adam lived were nine hundred thirty years; and he died.

6When Seth had lived one hundred five years, he became the father of Enosh. **7**Seth lived after the birth of Enosh eight hundred seven years, and had other sons and daughters. **8**Thus all the days of Seth were nine hundred twelve years; and he died.

9When Enosh had lived ninety years, he became the father of Kenan. **10**Enosh lived after the birth of Kenan eight hundred fifteen years, and had other sons and daughters. **11**Thus all the days of Enosh were nine hundred five years; and he died.

12When Kenan had lived seventy years, he became the father of Mahalalel. **13**Kenan lived after the birth of Mahalalel eight hundred and forty years, and had other sons and daughters. **14**Thus all the days of Kenan were nine hundred and ten years; and he died.

15When Mahalalel had lived sixty-five years, he became the father of Jared. **16**Mahalalel lived after the birth of Jared eight hundred thirty years, and had other sons and daughters. **17**Thus all the days of Mahalalel were eight hundred ninety-five years; and he died.

18When Jared had lived one hundred sixty-two years he became the father of Enoch. **19**Jared lived after the birth of Enoch eight hundred years, and had other sons and daughters. **20**Thus all the days of Jared were nine hundred sixty-two years; and he died.

21When Enoch had lived sixty-five years, he became the father of Methuselah. **22**Enoch walked with God after the birth of Methuselah three hundred years, and had other sons and daughters. **23**Thus all the days of Enoch were three hundred sixty-five years. **24**Enoch walked

---

[a] 4.25 The verb in Heb resembles the word for *Seth*   [b] 5.1,2 Heb *adam*   [c] 5.1 Heb *him*

with God; then he was no more, because God took him.

25 When Methuselah had lived one hundred eighty-seven years, he became the father of Lamech. 26 Methuselah lived after the birth of Lamech seven hundred eighty-two years, and had other sons and daughters. 27 Thus all the days of Methuselah were nine hundred sixty-nine years; and he died.

28 When Lamech had lived one hundred eighty-two years, he became the father of a son; 29 he named him Noah, saying, "Out of the ground that the LORD has cursed this one shall bring us relief from our work and from the toil of our hands." 30 Lamech lived after the birth of Noah five hundred ninety-five years, and had other sons and daughters. 31 Thus all the days of Lamech were seven hundred seventy-seven years; and he died. 32 After Noah was five hundred years old, Noah became the father of Shem, Ham, and Japheth.

THE WICKEDNESS OF HUMANKIND

6 When people began to multiply on the face of the ground, and daughters were born to them, 2 the sons of God saw that they were fair; and they took wives for themselves of all that they chose. 3 Then the LORD said, "My spirit shall not abide[a] in mortals forever, for they are flesh; their days shall be one hundred twenty years." 4 The Nephilim were on the earth in those days—and also afterward—when the sons of God went in to the daughters of humans, who bore children to them. These were the heroes that were of old, warriors of renown.

5 The LORD saw that the wickedness of humankind was great in the earth, and that every inclination of the thoughts of their hearts was only evil continually. 6 And the LORD was sorry that he had made humankind on the earth, and it grieved him to his heart. 7 So the LORD said, "I will blot out from the earth the human beings I have created—people together with animals and creeping things and birds of the air, for I am sorry that I have made them." 8 But Noah found favor in the sight of the LORD.

NOAH PLEASES GOD

9 These are the descendants of Noah. Noah was a righteous man, blameless in his generation; Noah walked with God. 10 And Noah had three sons, Shem, Ham, and Japheth.

11 Now the earth was corrupt in God's sight, and the earth was filled with violence. 12 And God saw that the earth was corrupt; for all flesh had corrupted its ways upon the earth. 13 And God said to Noah, "I have determined to make an end of all flesh, for the earth is filled with violence because of them; now I am going to destroy them along with the earth. 14 Make yourself an ark of cypress[a] wood; make rooms in the ark, and cover it inside and out with pitch. 15 This is how you are to make it: the length of the ark three hundred cubits, its width fifty cubits, and its height thirty cubits. 16 Make a roof[b] for the ark, and finish it to a cubit above; and put the door of the ark in its side; make it with lower, second, and third decks. 17 For my part, I am going to bring a flood of waters on the earth, to destroy from under heaven all flesh in which is the breath of life; everything that is on the earth shall die. 18 But I will establish my covenant with you; and you shall come into the ark, you, your sons, your wife, and your sons' wives with you. 19 And of every living thing, of all flesh, you shall bring two of every kind into the ark, to keep them alive with you; they shall be male and female. 20 Of the birds according to their kinds, and of the animals according to their kinds, of every creeping thing of the ground according to its kind, two of every kind shall come in to you, to keep them alive. 21 Also take with you every kind of food that is eaten, and store it up; and it shall serve as food

[a] 6.3,14 Meaning of Heb uncertain
[b] 6.16 Or window

for you and for them." ²²Noah did this; he did all that God commanded him.

THE GREAT FLOOD

7 Then the LORD said to Noah, "Go into the ark, you and all your household, for I have seen that you alone are righteous before me in this generation. ²Take with you seven pairs of all clean animals, the male and its mate; and a pair of the animals that are not clean, the male and its mate; ³and seven pairs of the birds of the air also, male and female, to keep their kind alive on the face of all the earth. ⁴For in seven days I will send rain on the earth for forty days and forty nights; and every living thing that I have made I will blot out from the face of the ground." ⁵And Noah did all that the LORD had commanded him.

6 Noah was six hundred years old when the flood of waters came on the earth. ⁷And Noah with his sons and his wife and his sons' wives went into the ark to escape the waters of the flood. ⁸Of clean animals, and of animals that are not clean, and of birds, and of everything that creeps on the ground, ⁹two and two, male and female, went into the ark with Noah, as God had commanded Noah. ¹⁰And after seven days the waters of the flood came on the earth.

11 In the six hundredth year of Noah's life, in the second month, on the seventeenth day of the month, on that day all the fountains of the great deep burst forth, and the windows of the heavens were opened. ¹²The rain fell on the earth forty days and forty nights. ¹³On the very same day Noah with his sons, Shem and Ham and Japheth, and Noah's wife and the three wives of his sons entered the ark, ¹⁴they and every wild animal of every kind, and all domestic animals of every kind, and every creeping thing that creeps on the earth, and every bird of every kind—every bird, every winged creature. ¹⁵They went into the ark with Noah, two and two of all flesh in which there was the breath of life. ¹⁶And those that entered, male and female of all flesh, went in as God had commanded him; and the LORD shut him in.

17 The flood continued forty days on the earth; and the waters increased, and bore up the ark, and it rose high above the earth. ¹⁸The waters swelled and increased greatly on the earth; and the ark floated on the face of the waters. ¹⁹The waters swelled so mightily on the earth that all the high mountains under the whole heaven were covered; ²⁰the waters swelled above the mountains, covering them fifteen cubits deep. ²¹And all flesh died that moved on the earth, birds, domestic animals, wild animals, all swarming creatures that swarm on the earth, and all human beings; ²²ev-

---

⊣⊢ BIBLE IN LIFE ▷

A New Beginning

God's standard is perfection, and when we sin, there is an inevitable punishment. The demands of a perfect God are absolute; God cannot accept evil. Yet God is filled with grace, love and forgiveness. Through Noah, God redeemed human beings and perpetuated the human race. Through Jesus, God redeemed us: "There is therefore now no condemnation for those who are in Christ Jesus" (Romans 8.1). Someday we will experience a glorious universe without fear, without sorrow, without evil . . . and even without a fearsome ocean: "Then I saw a new heaven and a new earth; for the first heaven and the first earth had passed away, and the sea was no more" (Revelation 21.1). In ancient cultures, people feared the sea and the power of water to inundate an area, as it did in Noah's day. Those who are in Christ can live without fear of anything—flood, pain or punishment—and can look forward to a new beginning.

erything on dry land in whose nostrils was the breath of life died. ²³He blotted out every living thing that was on the face of the ground, human beings and animals and creeping things and birds of the air; they were blotted out from the earth. Only Noah was left, and those that were with him in the ark. ²⁴And the waters swelled on the earth for one hundred fifty days.

THE FLOOD SUBSIDES

8 But God remembered Noah and all the wild animals and all the domestic animals that were with him in the ark. And God made a wind blow over the earth, and the waters subsided; ²the fountains of the deep and the windows of the heavens were closed, the rain from the heavens was restrained, ³and the waters gradually receded from the earth. At the end of one hundred fifty days the waters had abated; ⁴and in the seventh month, on the seventeenth day of the month, the ark came to rest on the mountains of Ararat. ⁵The waters continued to abate until the tenth month; in the tenth month, on the first day of the month, the tops of the mountains appeared.

6 At the end of forty days Noah opened the window of the ark that he had made ⁷and sent out the raven; and it went to and fro until the waters were dried up from the earth. ⁸Then he sent out the dove from him, to see if the waters had subsided from the face of the ground; ⁹but the dove found no place to set its foot, and it returned to him to the ark, for the waters were still on the face of the whole earth. So he put out his hand and took it and brought it into the ark with him. ¹⁰He waited another seven days, and again he sent out the dove from the ark; ¹¹and the dove came back to him in the evening, and there in its beak was a freshly plucked olive leaf; so Noah knew that the waters had subsided from the earth. ¹²Then he waited another seven days, and sent out the dove; and it did not return to him any more.

13 In the six hundred first year, in the first month, on the first day of the month, the waters were dried up from the earth; and Noah removed the covering of the ark, and looked, and saw that the face of the ground was drying. ¹⁴In the second month, on the twenty-seventh day of the month, the earth was dry. ¹⁵Then God said to Noah, ¹⁶"Go out of the ark, you and your wife, and your sons and your sons' wives with you. ¹⁷Bring out with you every living thing that is with you of all flesh—birds and animals and every creeping thing that creeps on the earth—so that they may abound on the earth, and be fruitful and multiply on the earth." ¹⁸So Noah went out with his sons and his wife and his sons' wives. ¹⁹And every animal, every creeping thing, and every bird, everything that moves on the earth, went out of the ark by families.

GOD'S PROMISE TO NOAH

20 Then Noah built an altar to the LORD, and took of every clean animal and of every clean bird, and offered burnt offerings on the altar. ²¹And when the LORD smelled the pleasing odor, the LORD said in his heart, "I will never again curse the ground because of humankind, for the inclination of the human heart is evil from youth; nor will I ever again destroy every living creature as I have done.
²² As long as the earth endures,
seedtime and harvest,
cold and heat,
summer and winter, day
and night,
shall not cease."

THE COVENANT WITH NOAH

9 God blessed Noah and his sons, and said to them, "Be fruitful and multiply, and fill the earth. ²The fear and dread of you shall rest on every animal of the earth, and on every bird of the air, on everything that creeps on the ground, and on all the fish of the sea; into your hand they are delivered. ³Every moving thing that lives shall be food for you; and just as I gave you the green

PONDER

God blessed Noah and his sons, and said to them, "Be fruitful and multiply, and fill the earth."
—Genesis 9.1

PRAY

Heavenly Father, thank you for showing us how in your greatness you have created a universe. You grant us freedom to use our own hearts and minds to remember lessons from the Old Testament that repeatedly teach us that departing from your commands brings havoc and devastation to our lives. But we can repent of our disobedience; we will be saved by your favor as Noah and his family were saved and given the promise of your faithfulness. We pray that every heart in doubt will turn to you through faith in Jesus Christ and that those of us who have not done so will make a public profession: "I believe in Jesus Christ; I know that I have been and I am a sinner; I know that Christ took the punishment for my sin upon himself, and through my faith in him I will be saved." We ask this in the name of our Savior, Jesus Christ. Amen.

plants, I give you everything. 4Only, you shall not eat flesh with its life, that is, its blood. 5For your own life-blood I will surely require a reckoning: from every animal I will require it and from human beings, each one for the blood of another, I will require a reckoning for human life.

6   Whoever sheds the blood
        of a human,
   by a human shall that
        person's blood be shed;
   for in his own image
        God made humankind.

7And you, be fruitful and multiply, abound on the earth and multiply in it."

8 Then God said to Noah and to his sons with him, 9"As for me, I am establishing my covenant with you and your descendants after you, 10and with every living creature that is with you, the birds, the domestic animals, and every animal of the earth with you, as many as came out of the ark.ᵃ 11I establish my covenant with you, that never again shall all flesh be cut off by the waters of a flood, and never again shall there be a flood to destroy the earth." 12God said, "This is the sign of the covenant that I make between me and you and every living creature that is with you, for all future generations: 13I have set my bow in the clouds, and it shall be a sign of the covenant between me and the earth. 14When I bring clouds over the earth and the bow is seen in the clouds, 15I will remember my covenant that is between me and you and every living creature of all flesh; and the waters shall never again become a flood to destroy all flesh. 16When the bow is in the clouds, I will see it and remember the everlasting covenant between God and every living creature of all flesh that is on the earth." 17God said to Noah, "This is the sign of the covenant that I have established between me and all flesh that is on the earth."

NOAH AND HIS SONS

18 The sons of Noah who went out of the ark were Shem, Ham, and Japheth. Ham was the father of Canaan. 19These three were the sons of Noah; and from these the whole earth was peopled.

20 Noah, a man of the soil, was the first to plant a vineyard. 21He drank some of the wine and became drunk, and he lay uncovered in his tent. 22And Ham, the father of Canaan, saw the nakedness of his father, and told his two brothers outside. 23Then Shem and Japheth took a garment, laid it on both their shoulders, and walked backward and covered the nakedness of their father; their faces were turned away, and they did not see their father's

ᵃ 9.10 Gk: Heb adds *every animal of the earth*

nakedness. 24When Noah awoke from his wine and knew what his youngest son had done to him, 25he said,

"Cursed be Canaan;
lowest of slaves shall he
be to his brothers."

26He also said,

"Blessed by the LORD my
God be Shem;
and let Canaan be his slave.
27 May God make space for[a] Japheth,
and let him live in the
tents of Shem;
and let Canaan be his slave."

28 After the flood Noah lived three hundred fifty years. 29All the days of Noah were nine hundred fifty years; and he died.

NATIONS DESCENDED
FROM NOAH

10 These are the descendants of Noah's sons, Shem, Ham, and Japheth; children were born to them after the flood.

2 The descendants of Japheth: Gomer, Magog, Madai, Javan, Tubal, Meshech, and Tiras. 3The descendants of Gomer: Ashkenaz, Riphath, and Togarmah. 4The descendants of Javan: Elishah, Tarshish, Kittim, and Rodanim.[b] 5From these the coastland peoples spread. These are the descendants of Japheth[c] in their lands, with their own language, by their families, in their nations.

6 The descendants of Ham: Cush, Egypt, Put, and Canaan. 7The descendants of Cush: Seba, Havilah, Sabtah, Raamah, and Sabteca. The descendants of Raamah: Sheba and Dedan. 8Cush became the father of Nimrod; he was the first on earth to become a mighty warrior. 9He was a mighty hunter before the LORD; therefore it is said, "Like Nimrod a mighty hunter before the LORD." 10The beginning of his kingdom was Babel, Erech, and Accad, all of them in the land of Shinar. 11From that land he went into Assyria, and built Nineveh, Rehoboth-ir, Calah, and 12Resen between Nineveh and Calah; that is the great city. 13Egypt became the father of Ludim, Anamim, Lehabim, Naphtuhim, 14Path-

rusim, Casluhim, and Caphtorim, from which the Philistines come.[d]

15 Canaan became the father of Sidon his firstborn, and Heth, 16and the Jebusites, the Amorites, the Girgashites, 17the Hivites, the Arkites, the Sinites, 18the Arvadites, the Zemarites, and the Hamathites. Afterward the families of the Canaanites spread abroad. 19And the territory of the Canaanites extended from Sidon, in the direction of Gerar, as far as Gaza, and in the direction of Sodom, Gomorrah, Admah, and Zeboiim, as far as Lasha. 20These are the descendants of Ham, by their families, their languages, their lands, and their nations.

21 To Shem also, the father of all the children of Eber, the elder brother of Japheth, children were born. 22The descendants of Shem: Elam, Asshur, Arpachshad, Lud, and Aram. 23The descendants of Aram: Uz, Hul, Gether, and Mash. 24Arpachshad became the father of Shelah; and Shelah became the father of Eber. 25To Eber were born two sons: the name of the one was Peleg,[e] for in his days the earth was divided, and his brother's name was Joktan. 26Joktan became the father of Almodad, Sheleph, Hazarmaveth, Jerah, 27Hadoram, Uzal, Diklah, 28Obal, Abimael, Sheba, 29Ophir, Havilah, and Jobab; all these were the descendants of Joktan. 30The territory in which they lived extended from Mesha in the direction of Sephar, the hill country of the east. 31These are the descendants of Shem, by their families, their languages, their lands, and their nations.

32 These are the families of Noah's sons, according to their genealogies, in their nations; and from these the nations spread abroad on the earth after the flood.

a 9.27 Heb *yapht*, a play on *Japheth*
b 10.4 Heb Mss Sam Gk See 1 Chr 1.7: MT *Dodanim*   c 10.5 Compare verses 20, 31. Heb lacks *These are the descendants of Japheth*   d 10.14 Cn: Heb *Casluhim, from which the Philistines come, and Caphtorim*
e 10.25 That is *Division*

THE TOWER OF BABEL

11 Now the whole earth had one language and the same words. ²And as they migrated from the east,ᵃ they came upon a plain in the land of Shinar and settled there. ³And they said to one another, "Come, let us make bricks, and burn them thoroughly." And they had brick for stone, and bitumen for mortar. ⁴Then they said, "Come, let us build ourselves a city, and a tower with its top in the heavens, and let us make a name for ourselves; otherwise we shall be scattered abroad upon the face of the whole earth." ⁵The LORD came down to see the city and the tower, which mortals had built. ⁶And the LORD said, "Look, they are one people, and they have all one language; and this is only the beginning of what they will do; nothing that they propose to do will now be impossible for them. ⁷Come, let us go down, and confuse their language there, so that they will not understand one another's speech." ⁸So the LORD scattered them abroad from there over the face of all the earth, and they left off building the city. ⁹Therefore it was called Babel, because there the LORD confusedᵇ the language of all the earth; and from there the LORD scattered them abroad over the face of all the earth.

DESCENDANTS OF SHEM

10 These are the descendants of Shem. When Shem was one hundred years old, he became the father of Arpachshad two years after the flood; ¹¹and Shem lived after the birth of Arpachshad five hundred years, and had other sons and daughters.

12 When Arpachshad had lived thirty-five years, he became the father of Shelah; ¹³and Arpachshad lived after the birth of Shelah four hundred three years, and had other sons and daughters.

14 When Shelah had lived thirty years, he became the father of Eber; ¹⁵and Shelah lived after the birth of Eber four hundred three years, and had other sons and daughters.

16 When Eber had lived thirty-four years, he became the father of Peleg; ¹⁷and Eber lived after the birth of Peleg four hundred thirty years, and had other sons and daughters.

18 When Peleg had lived thirty years, he became the father of Reu; ¹⁹and Peleg lived after the birth of Reu two hundred nine years, and had other sons and daughters.

20 When Reu had lived thirty-two years, he became the father of Serug; ²¹and Reu lived after the birth of Serug two hundred seven years, and had other sons and daughters.

22 When Serug had lived thirty years, he became the father of Nahor; ²³and Serug lived after the birth of Nahor two hundred years, and had other sons and daughters.

24 When Nahor had lived twenty-nine years, he became the father of Terah; ²⁵and Nahor lived after the birth of Terah one hundred nineteen years, and had other sons and daughters.

26 When Terah had lived seventy years, he became the father of Abram, Nahor, and Haran.

DESCENDANTS OF TERAH

27 Now these are the descendants of Terah. Terah was the father of Abram, Nahor, and Haran; and Haran was the father of Lot. ²⁸Haran died before his father Terah in the land of his birth, in Ur of the Chaldeans. ²⁹Abram and Nahor took wives; the name of Abram's wife was Sarai, and the name of Nahor's wife was Milcah. She was the daughter of Haran the father of Milcah and Iscah. ³⁰Now Sarai was barren; she had no child.

31 Terah took his son Abram and his grandson Lot son of Haran, and his daughter-in-law Sarai, his son Abram's wife, and they went out together from Ur of the Chaldeans to go into the land of Canaan; but when they came to Haran, they settled there. ³²The days of Terah were two hundred five years; and Terah died in Haran.

ᵃ **11.2** Or *migrated eastward*   ᵇ **11.9** Heb *balal*, meaning *to confuse*

THE CALL OF ABRAM

12 Now the LORD said to Abram, "Go from your country and your kindred and your father's house to the land that I will show you. ²I will make of you a great nation, and I will bless you, and make your name great, so that you will be a blessing. ³I will bless those who bless you, and the one who curses you I will curse; and in you all the families of the earth shall be blessed."ᵃ

4 So Abram went, as the LORD had told him; and Lot went with him. Abram was seventy-five years old when he departed from Haran. ⁵Abram took his wife Sarai and his brother's son Lot, and all the possessions that they had gathered, and the persons whom they had acquired in Haran; and they set forth to go to the land of Canaan. When they had come to the land of Canaan, ⁶Abram passed through the land to the place at Shechem, to the oakᵇ of Moreh. At that time the Canaanites were in the land. ⁷Then the LORD appeared to Abram, and said, "To your offspringᶜ I will give this land." So he built there an altar to the LORD, who had appeared to him. ⁸From there he moved on to the hill country on the east of Bethel, and pitched his tent, with Bethel on the west and Ai on the east; and there he built an altar to the LORD and invoked the name of the LORD. ⁹And Abram journeyed on by stages toward the Negeb.

ABRAM AND SARAI IN EGYPT

10 Now there was a famine in the land. So Abram went down to Egypt to reside there as an alien, for the famine was severe in the land. ¹¹When he was about to enter Egypt, he said to his wife Sarai, "I know well that you are a woman beautiful in appearance; ¹²and when the Egyptians see you, they will say, 'This is his wife'; then they will kill me, but they will let you live. ¹³Say you are my sister, so that it may go well with me because of you, and that my life may be spared on your account." ¹⁴When Abram entered Egypt the Egyptians saw that the woman was very beautiful. ¹⁵When the officials of Pharaoh saw her, they praised her to Pharaoh. And the woman was taken into Pharaoh's house. ¹⁶And for her sake he dealt well with Abram; and he had sheep, oxen, male donkeys, male and female slaves, female donkeys, and camels.

17 But the LORD afflicted Pharaoh and his house with great plagues because of Sarai, Abram's wife. ¹⁸So Pharaoh called Abram, and said, "What is this you have done to me?

ᵃ 12.3 Or *by you all the families of the earth shall bless themselves*   ᵇ 12.6 Or *terebinth*   ᶜ 12.7 Heb *seed*

BIBLE IN LIFE

Measuring Success   Genesis 12.1–9

By human standards, Abraham was enormously successful. He owned vast quantities of cattle, sheep and goats and lived with his extended family. He was happily married. Yet these things did not bring him success. Perhaps he considered himself to be a failure because he didn't have any children. God called him to leave his secure place and go to an unknown place. And when Abraham obeyed, he discovered a new purpose. All of us on occasion feel a sense of frustration or disappointment. But there is a call from God for each one of us, and that call is very similar to the call Abraham heard. God says, "Why don't you take upon yourself a greater responsibility in my name?" Look about you—there are vast opportunities for a more exalted life, not as measured by power and wealth and prestige and fame, but measured by compatibility with the life and teachings of Jesus Christ. Our call is to be transformed into the image of Jesus Christ, who exemplified peace, humility, service, compassion, gentleness, forgiveness and love. Those are the measurements of success in a Christian's life.

Why did you not tell me that she was your wife? [19]Why did you say, 'She is my sister,' so that I took her for my wife? Now then, here is your wife, take her, and be gone." [20]And Pharaoh gave his men orders concerning him; and they set him on the way, with his wife and all that he had.

ABRAM AND LOT SEPARATE

13 So Abram went up from Egypt, he and his wife, and all that he had, and Lot with him, into the Negeb. [2]Now Abram was very rich in livestock, in silver, and in gold. [3]He journeyed on by stages from the Negeb as far as Bethel, to the place where his tent had been at the beginning, between Bethel and Ai, [4]to the place where he had made an altar at the first; and there Abram called on the name of the LORD. [5]Now Lot, who went with Abram, also had flocks and herds and tents, [6]so that the land could not support both of them living together; for their possessions were so great that they could not live together, [7]and there was strife between the herders of Abram's livestock and the herders of Lot's livestock. At that time the Canaanites and the Perizzites lived in the land. [8]Then Abram said to Lot, "Let there be no strife between you and me, and between your herders and my herders; for we are kindred. [9]Is not the whole land before you? Separate yourself from me. If you take the left hand, then I will go to the right; or if you take the right hand, then I will go to the left." [10]Lot looked about him, and saw that the plain of the Jordan was well watered everywhere like the garden of the LORD, like the land of Egypt, in the direction of Zoar; this was before the LORD had destroyed Sodom and Gomorrah. [11]So Lot chose for himself all the plain of the Jordan, and Lot journeyed eastward; thus they separated from each other. [12]Abram settled in the land of Canaan, while Lot settled among the cities of the Plain and moved his tent as far as Sodom. [13]Now the people of Sodom were wicked, great sinners against the LORD.

[14] The LORD said to Abram, after Lot had separated from him, "Raise your eyes now, and look from the place where you are, northward and southward and eastward and westward; [15]for all the land that you see I will give to you and to your offspring[a] forever. [16]I will make your offspring like the dust of the earth; so that if one can count the dust of the earth, your offspring also can be counted. [17]Rise up, walk through the length and the breadth of the land, for I will give it to you." [18]So Abram moved his tent, and came and settled by the oaks[b] of Mamre, which are at Hebron; and there he built an altar to the LORD.

LOT'S CAPTIVITY AND RESCUE

14 In the days of King Amraphel of Shinar, King Arioch of Ellasar, King Chedorlaomer of Elam, and King Tidal of Goiim, [2]these kings made war with King Bera of Sodom, King Birsha of Gomorrah, King Shinab of Admah, King Shemeber of Zeboiim, and the king of Bela (that is, Zoar). [3]All these joined forces in the Valley of Siddim (that is, the Dead Sea).[c] [4]Twelve years they had served Chedorlaomer, but in the thirteenth year they rebelled. [5]In the fourteenth year Chedorlaomer and the kings who were with him came and subdued the Rephaim in Ashteroth-karnaim, the Zuzim in Ham, the Emim in Shaveh-kiriathaim, [6]and the Horites in the hill country of Seir as far as El-paran on the edge of the wilderness; [7]then they turned back and came to En-mishpat (that is, Kadesh), and subdued all the country of the Amalekites, and also the Amorites who lived in Hazazon-tamar. [8]Then the king of Sodom, the king of Gomorrah, the king of Admah, the king of Zeboiim, and the king of Bela (that is, Zoar) went out, and they joined battle in the Valley of Siddim [9]with King Chedorlaomer

---

[a] 13.15 Heb seed   [b] 13.18 Or terebinths
[c] 14.3 Heb Salt Sea

of Elam, King Tidal of Goiim, King Amraphel of Shinar, and King Arioch of Ellasar, four kings against five. ¹⁰Now the Valley of Siddim was full of bitumen pits; and as the kings of Sodom and Gomorrah fled, some fell into them, and the rest fled to the hill country. ¹¹So the enemy took all the goods of Sodom and Gomorrah, and all their provisions, and went their way; ¹²they also took Lot, the son of Abram's brother, who lived in Sodom, and his goods, and departed.

13 Then one who had escaped came and told Abram the Hebrew, who was living by the oaksᵃ of Mamre the Amorite, brother of Eshcol and of Aner; these were allies of Abram. ¹⁴When Abram heard that his nephew had been taken captive, he led forth his trained men, born in his house, three hundred eighteen of them, and went in pursuit as far as Dan. ¹⁵He divided his forces against them by night, he and his servants, and routed them and pursued them to Hobah, north of Damascus. ¹⁶Then he brought back all the goods, and also brought back his nephew Lot with his goods, and the women and the people.

ABRAM BLESSED BY MELCHIZEDEK

17 After his return from the defeat of Chedorlaomer and the kings who were with him, the king of Sodom went out to meet him at the Valley of Shaveh (that is, the King's Valley). ¹⁸And King Melchizedek of Salem brought out bread and wine; he was priest of God Most High.ᵇ ¹⁹He blessed him and said,

"Blessed be Abram by God
      Most High,ᵇ
    maker of heaven and earth;
²⁰ and blessed be God Most High,ᵇ
    who has delivered your
        enemies into your hand!"

And Abram gave him one-tenth of everything. ²¹Then the king of Sodom said to Abram, "Give me the persons, but take the goods for yourself." ²²But Abram said to the king of Sodom, "I have sworn to the LORD, God Most High,ᵇ maker of heaven and earth, ²³that I would not take a thread or a sandal-thong or anything that is yours, so that you might not say, 'I have made Abram rich.' ²⁴I will take nothing but what the young men have eaten, and the share of the men who went with me—Aner, Eshcol, and Mamre. Let them take their share."

GOD'S COVENANT WITH ABRAM

15 After these things the word of the LORD came to Abram in a vision, "Do not be afraid, Abram, I am your shield; your reward shall be very great." ²But

ᵃ 14.13 Or *terebinths*   ᵇ 14.18,19,20,22 Heb *El Elyon*

╫ **BIBLE IN LIFE** ▷ ⊖

Justified by Faith   Genesis 15.1–7

Abraham was a very good man, arguably an outstanding man. But his belief in God's promises, not his actions, justified him before God. "For if Abraham was justified by works, he has something to boast about, but not before God. For what does the scripture say? 'Abraham believed God, and it was reckoned to him as righteousness'" (Romans 4.2–3). What do we learn from Abraham? We may consider ourselves outstanding people. We may spend half our time building houses for the homeless; give half of everything we earn to the church, to missions programs or to the poor; spend two afternoons a week visiting prisoners in jail. Even then, we cannot save ourselves. Good works are admirable, but we cannot earn our way into heaven. No matter how many good things we do, we are still guilty of sin and thus separated from God. We cannot save ourselves. Abraham knew he could not save himself. Salvation comes only through faith in God.

Abram said, "O Lord GOD, what will you give me, for I continue childless, and the heir of my house is Eliezer of Damascus?"[a] 3And Abram said, "You have given me no offspring, and so a slave born in my house is to be my heir." 4But the word of the LORD came to him, "This man shall not be your heir; no one but your very own issue shall be your heir." 5He brought him outside and said, "Look toward heaven and count the stars, if you are able to count them." Then he said to him, "So shall your descendants be." 6And he believed the LORD; and the LORD[b] reckoned it to him as righteousness.

7 Then he said to him, "I am the LORD who brought you from Ur of the Chaldeans, to give you this land to possess." 8But he said, "O Lord GOD, how am I to know that I shall possess it?" 9He said to him, "Bring me a heifer three years old, a female goat three years old, a ram three years old, a turtledove, and a young pigeon." 10He brought him all these and cut them in two, laying each half over against the other; but he did not cut the birds in two. 11And when birds of prey came down on the carcasses, Abram drove them away.

12 As the sun was going down, a deep sleep fell upon Abram, and a deep and terrifying darkness descended upon him. 13Then the LORD[b] said to Abram, "Know this for certain, that your offspring shall be aliens in a land that is not theirs, and shall be slaves there, and they shall be oppressed for four hundred years; 14but I will bring judgment on the nation that they serve, and afterward they shall come out with great possessions. 15As for yourself, you shall go to your ancestors in peace; you shall be buried in a good old age. 16And they shall come back here in the fourth generation; for the iniquity of the Amorites is not yet complete."

17 When the sun had gone down and it was dark, a smoking fire pot and a flaming torch passed between these pieces. 18On that day the LORD made a covenant with Abram, saying, "To your descendants I give this land, from the river of Egypt to the great river, the river Euphrates, 19the land of the Kenites, the Kenizzites, the Kadmonites, 20the Hittites, the Perizzites, the Rephaim, 21the Amorites, the Canaanites, the Girgashites, and the Jebusites."

THE BIRTH OF ISHMAEL

16 Now Sarai, Abram's wife, bore him no children. She had an Egyptian slave-girl whose name was Hagar, 2and Sarai said to Abram, "You see that the LORD has prevented me from bearing children; go in to my slave-girl; it may be that I shall obtain children by her." And Abram listened to the voice of Sarai. 3So, after Abram had lived ten years in the land of Canaan, Sarai, Abram's wife, took Hagar the Egyptian, her slave-girl, and gave her to her husband Abram as a wife. 4He went in to Hagar, and she conceived; and when she saw that she had conceived, she looked with contempt on her mistress. 5Then Sarai said to Abram, "May the wrong done to me be on you! I gave my slave-girl to your embrace, and when she saw that she had conceived, she looked on me with contempt. May the LORD judge between you and me!" 6But Abram said to Sarai, "Your slave-girl is in your power; do to her as you please." Then Sarai dealt harshly with her, and she ran away from her.

7 The angel of the LORD found her by a spring of water in the wilderness, the spring on the way to Shur. 8And he said, "Hagar, slave-girl of Sarai, where have you come from and where are you going?" She said, "I am running away from my mistress Sarai." 9The angel of the LORD said to her, "Return to your mistress, and submit to her." 10The angel of the LORD also said to her, "I will so greatly multiply your offspring that they cannot be counted for multitude." 11And the angel of the LORD said to her,

---

[a] 15.2 Meaning of Heb uncertain
[b] 15.6,13 Heb he

"Now you have conceived and
shall bear a son;
you shall call him Ishmael,ᵃ
for the LORD has given heed
to your affliction.
¹² He shall be a wild ass of a man,
with his hand against everyone,
and everyone's hand
against him;
and he shall live at odds
with all his kin."
¹³So she named the LORD who spoke
to her, "You are El-roi";ᵇ for she
said, "Have I really seen God and
remained alive after seeing him?"ᶜ
¹⁴Therefore the well was called Beer-
lahai-roi;ᵈ it lies between Kadesh
and Bered.

¹⁵ Hagar bore Abram a son; and
Abram named his son, whom Hagar
bore, Ishmael. ¹⁶Abram was eighty-
six years old when Hagar bore himᵉ
Ishmael.

THE SIGN OF THE COVENANT

17 When Abram was ninety-
nine years old, the LORD appeared to Abram, and said to him, "I
am God Almighty;ᶠ walk before me,
and be blameless. ²And I will make
my covenant between me and you,
and will make you exceedingly numerous." ³Then Abram fell on his
face; and God said to him, ⁴"As for
me, this is my covenant with you:
You shall be the ancestor of a multitude of nations. ⁵No longer shall
your name be Abram,ᵍ but your
name shall be Abraham;ʰ for I have
made you the ancestor of a multitude of nations. ⁶I will make you
exceedingly fruitful; and I will make
nations of you, and kings shall come
from you. ⁷I will establish my covenant between me and you, and
your offspring after you throughout
their generations, for an everlasting
covenant, to be God to you and to
your offspringⁱ after you. ⁸And I will
give to you, and to your offspring after you, the land where you are now
an alien, all the land of Canaan, for a
perpetual holding; and I will be their
God."

⁹ God said to Abraham, "As for
you, you shall keep my covenant,
you and your offspring after you

throughout their generations. ¹⁰This
is my covenant, which you shall
keep, between me and you and your
offspring after you: Every male
among you shall be circumcised.
¹¹You shall circumcise the flesh of
your foreskins, and it shall be a sign
of the covenant between me and
you. ¹²Throughout your generations
every male among you shall be circumcised when he is eight days old,
including the slave born in your
house and the one bought with your
money from any foreigner who is
not of your offspring. ¹³Both the
slave born in your house and the one
bought with your money must be
circumcised. So shall my covenant
be in your flesh an everlasting covenant. ¹⁴Any uncircumcised male
who is not circumcised in the flesh
of his foreskin shall be cut off from
his people; he has broken my covenant."

¹⁵ God said to Abraham, "As for
Sarai your wife, you shall not call
her Sarai, but Sarah shall be her
name. ¹⁶I will bless her, and moreover I will give you a son by her. I
will bless her, and she shall give rise
to nations; kings of peoples shall
come from her." ¹⁷Then Abraham
fell on his face and laughed, and said
to himself, "Can a child be born to
a man who is a hundred years old?
Can Sarah, who is ninety years old,
bear a child?" ¹⁸And Abraham said
to God, "O that Ishmael might live
in your sight!" ¹⁹God said, "No, but
your wife Sarah shall bear you a son,
and you shall name him Isaac.ʲ I will
establish my covenant with him as
an everlasting covenant for his offspring after him. ²⁰As for Ishmael, I
have heard you; I will bless him and
make him fruitful and exceedingly
numerous; he shall be the father of
twelve princes, and I will make him
a great nation. ²¹But my covenant

ᵃ 16.11 That is God hears   ᵇ 16.13 Perhaps
God of seeing or God who sees
ᶜ 16.13 Meaning of Heb uncertain
ᵈ 16.14 That is the Well of the Living
One who sees me   ᵉ 16.16 Heb Abram
ᶠ 17.1 Traditional rendering of Heb El Shaddai
ᵍ 17.5 That is exalted ancestor   ʰ 17.5 Here
taken to mean ancestor of a multitude
ⁱ 17.7 Heb seed   ʲ 17.19 That is he laughs

I will establish with Isaac, whom Sarah shall bear to you at this season next year." ²²And when he had finished talking with him, God went up from Abraham.

23 Then Abraham took his son Ishmael and all the slaves born in his house or bought with his money, every male among the men of Abraham's house, and he circumcised the flesh of their foreskins that very day, as God had said to him. ²⁴Abraham was ninety-nine years old when he was circumcised in the flesh of his foreskin. ²⁵And his son Ishmael was thirteen years old when he was circumcised in the flesh of his foreskin. ²⁶That very day Abraham and his son Ishmael were circumcised; ²⁷and all the men of his house, slaves born in the house and those bought with money from a foreigner, were circumcised with him.

A SON PROMISED TO ABRAHAM AND SARAH

18 The LORD appeared to Abraham[a] by the oaks[b] of Mamre, as he sat at the entrance of his tent in the heat of the day. ²He looked up and saw three men standing near him. When he saw them, he ran from the tent entrance to meet them, and bowed down to the ground. ³He said, "My lord, if I find favor with you, do not pass by your servant. ⁴Let a little water be brought, and wash your feet, and rest yourselves under the tree. ⁵Let me bring a little bread, that you may refresh yourselves, and after that you may pass on—since you have come to your servant." So they said, "Do as you have said." ⁶And Abraham hastened into the tent to Sarah, and said, "Make ready quickly three measures[c] of choice flour, knead it, and make cakes." ⁷Abraham ran to the herd, and took a calf, tender and good, and gave it to the servant, who hastened to prepare it. ⁸Then he took curds and milk and the calf that he had prepared, and set it before them; and he stood by them under the tree while they ate.

9 They said to him, "Where is your wife Sarah?" And he said, "There,

in the tent." ¹⁰Then one said, "I will surely return to you in due season, and your wife Sarah shall have a son." And Sarah was listening at the tent entrance behind him. ¹¹Now Abraham and Sarah were old, advanced in age; it had ceased to be with Sarah after the manner of women. ¹²So Sarah laughed to herself, saying, "After I have grown old, and my husband is old, shall I have pleasure?" ¹³The LORD said to Abraham, "Why did Sarah laugh, and say, 'Shall I indeed bear a child, now that I am old?' ¹⁴Is anything too wonderful for the LORD? At the set time I will return to you, in due season, and Sarah shall have a son." ¹⁵But Sarah denied, saying, "I did not laugh"; for she was afraid. He said, "Oh yes, you did laugh."

PONDER

"Is anything too wonderful for the LORD?"
—Genesis 18.14

PRAY

Father, as we study these ancient scriptures, open our hearts to search for the truth we can derive from your Word in our modern-day lives. As you were faithful to keep your promises to Abraham, you will be faithful to us; nothing is impossible for you. Having faith is just as important to us in our relationship with you as it was to those ancient people Abraham, Sarah, Isaac, Jacob and Joseph. Strengthen our faith. Forgive our sins. Bring us together in the service of our Savior, Jesus Christ. In his name we pray. Amen.

JUDGMENT PRONOUNCED ON SODOM

16 Then the men set out from there, and they looked toward Sodom; and

a **18.1** Heb *him*   b **18.1** Or *terebinths*   c **18.6** Heb *seahs*

Abraham went with them to set them on their way. ¹⁷The LORD said, "Shall I hide from Abraham what I am about to do, ¹⁸seeing that Abraham shall become a great and mighty nation, and all the nations of the earth shall be blessed in him?ᵃ ¹⁹No, for I have chosenᵇ him, that he may charge his children and his household after him to keep the way of the LORD by doing righteousness and justice; so that the LORD may bring about for Abraham what he has promised him." ²⁰Then the LORD said, "How great is the outcry against Sodom and Gomorrah and how very grave their sin! ²¹I must go down and see whether they have done altogether according to the outcry that has come to me; and if not, I will know."

22 So the men turned from there, and went toward Sodom, while Abraham remained standing before the LORD.ᶜ ²³Then Abraham came near and said, "Will you indeed sweep away the righteous with the wicked? ²⁴Suppose there are fifty righteous within the city; will you then sweep away the place and not forgive it for the fifty righteous who are in it? ²⁵Far be it from you to do such a thing, to slay the righteous with the wicked, so that the righteous fare as the wicked! Far be that from you! Shall not the Judge of all the earth do what is just?" ²⁶And the LORD said, "If I find at Sodom fifty righteous in the city, I will forgive the whole place for their sake." ²⁷Abraham answered, "Let me take it upon myself to speak to the Lord, I who am but dust and ashes. ²⁸Suppose five of the fifty righteous are lacking? Will you destroy the whole city for lack of five?" And he said, "I will not destroy it if I find forty-five there." ²⁹Again he spoke to him, "Suppose forty are found there." He answered, "For the sake of forty I will not do it." ³⁰Then he said, "Oh do not let the Lord be angry if I speak. Suppose thirty are found there." He answered, "I will not do it, if I find thirty there." ³¹He said, "Let me take it upon myself to speak to the Lord. Suppose twenty are found there." He

answered, "For the sake of twenty I will not destroy it." ³²Then he said, "Oh do not let the Lord be angry if I speak just once more. Suppose ten are found there." He answered, "For the sake of ten I will not destroy it." ³³And the LORD went his way, when he had finished speaking to Abraham; and Abraham returned to his place.

OUR QUESTIONS DO

NOT THREATEN GOD.

THE DEPRAVITY OF SODOM

19 The two angels came to Sodom in the evening, and Lot was sitting in the gateway of Sodom. When Lot saw them, he rose to meet them, and bowed down with his face to the ground. ²He said, "Please, my lords, turn aside to your servant's house and spend the night, and wash your feet; then you can rise early and go on your way." They said, "No; we will spend the night in the square." ³But he urged them strongly; so they turned aside to him and entered his house; and he made them a feast, and baked unleavened bread, and they ate. ⁴But before they lay down, the men of the city, the men of Sodom, both young and old, all the people to the last man, surrounded the house; ⁵and they called to Lot, "Where are the men who came to you tonight? Bring them out to us, so that we may know them." ⁶Lot went out of the door to the men, shut the door after him, ⁷and said, "I beg you, my brothers, do not act so wickedly. ⁸Look, I have two daughters who have not known a man; let me bring them out to you, and do to them as you please; only do nothing to these

ᵃ 18.18 Or *and all the nations of the earth shall bless themselves by him*   ᵇ 18.19 Heb *known*   ᶜ 18.22 Another ancient tradition reads *while the LORD remained standing before Abraham*

men, for they have come under the shelter of my roof." 9But they replied, "Stand back!" And they said, "This fellow came here as an alien, and he would play the judge! Now we will deal worse with you than with them." Then they pressed hard against the man Lot, and came near the door to break it down. 10But the men inside reached out their hands and brought Lot into the house with them, and shut the door. 11And they struck with blindness the men who were at the door of the house, both small and great, so that they were unable to find the door.

SODOM AND GOMORRAH DESTROYED

12 Then the men said to Lot, "Have you anyone else here? Sons-in-law, sons, daughters, or anyone you have in the city—bring them out of the place. 13For we are about to destroy this place, because the outcry against its people has become great before the LORD, and the LORD has sent us to destroy it." 14So Lot went out and said to his sons-in-law, who were to marry his daughters, "Up, get out of this place; for the LORD is about to destroy the city." But he seemed to his sons-in-law to be jesting.

15 When morning dawned, the angels urged Lot, saying, "Get up, take your wife and your two daughters who are here, or else you will be consumed in the punishment of the city." 16But he lingered; so the men seized him and his wife and his two daughters by the hand, the LORD being merciful to him, and they brought him out and left him outside the city. 17When they had brought them outside, theya said, "Flee for your life; do not look back or stop anywhere in the Plain; flee to the hills, or else you will be consumed." 18And Lot said to them, "Oh, no, my lords; 19your servant has found favor with you, and you have shown me great kindness in saving my life; but I cannot flee to the hills, for fear the disaster will overtake me and I die. 20Look, that city is near enough to flee to, and it is a

little one. Let me escape there—is it not a little one?—and my life will be saved!" 21He said to him, "Very well, I grant you this favor too, and will not overthrow the city of which you have spoken. 22Hurry, escape there, for I can do nothing until you arrive there." Therefore the city was called Zoar.b 23The sun had risen on the earth when Lot came to Zoar.

24 Then the LORD rained on Sodom and Gomorrah sulfur and fire from the LORD out of heaven; 25and he overthrew those cities, and all the Plain, and all the inhabitants of the cities, and what grew on the ground. 26But Lot's wife, behind him, looked back, and she became a pillar of salt.

27 Abraham went early in the morning to the place where he had stood before the LORD; 28and he looked down toward Sodom and Gomorrah and toward all the land of the Plain and saw the smoke of the land going up like the smoke of a furnace.

29 So it was that, when God destroyed the cities of the Plain, God remembered Abraham, and sent Lot out of the midst of the overthrow, when he overthrew the cities in which Lot had settled.

THE SHAMEFUL ORIGIN OF MOAB AND AMMON

30 Now Lot went up out of Zoar and settled in the hills with his two daughters, for he was afraid to stay in Zoar; so he lived in a cave with his two daughters. 31And the firstborn said to the younger, "Our father is old, and there is not a man on earth to come in to us after the manner of all the world. 32Come, let us make our father drink wine, and we will lie with him, so that we may preserve offspring through our father." 33So they made their father drink wine that night; and the firstborn went in, and lay with her father; he did not know when she lay down or when she rose. 34On the next day, the firstborn said to

a 19.17 Gk Syr Vg: Heb *he*   b 19.22 That is *Little*

the younger, "Look, I lay last night with my father; let us make him drink wine tonight also; then you go in and lie with him, so that we may preserve offspring through our father." 35 So they made their father drink wine that night also; and the younger rose, and lay with him; and he did not know when she lay down or when she rose. 36 Thus both the daughters of Lot became pregnant by their father. 37 The firstborn bore a son, and named him Moab; he is the ancestor of the Moabites to this day. 38 The younger also bore a son and named him Ben-ammi; he is the ancestor of the Ammonites to this day.

ABRAHAM AND SARAH AT GERAR

20 From there Abraham journeyed toward the region of the Negeb, and settled between Kadesh and Shur. While residing in Gerar as an alien, 2 Abraham said of his wife Sarah, "She is my sister." And King Abimelech of Gerar sent and took Sarah. 3 But God came to Abimelech in a dream by night, and said to him, "You are about to die because of the woman whom you have taken; for she is a married woman." 4 Now Abimelech had not approached her; so he said, "Lord, will you destroy an innocent people? 5 Did he not himself say to me, 'She is my sister'? And she herself said, 'He is my brother.' I did this in the integrity of my heart and the innocence of my hands." 6 Then God said to him in the dream, "Yes, I know that you did this in the integrity of your heart; furthermore it was I who kept you from sinning against me. Therefore I did not let you touch her. 7 Now then, return the man's wife; for he is a prophet, and he will pray for you and you shall live. But if you do not restore her, know that you shall surely die, you and all that are yours."

8 So Abimelech rose early in the morning, and called all his servants and told them all these things; and the men were very much afraid. 9 Then Abimelech called Abraham, and said to him, "What have you done to us? How have I sinned against you, that you have brought such great guilt on me and my kingdom? You have done things to me that ought not to be done." 10 And Abimelech said to Abraham, "What were you thinking of, that you did this thing?" 11 Abraham said, "I did it because I thought, There is no fear of God at all in this place, and they will kill me because of my wife. 12 Besides, she is indeed my sister, the daughter of my father but not the daughter of my mother; and she became my wife. 13 And when God caused me to wander from my father's house, I said to her, 'This is the kindness you must do me: at every place to which we come, say of me, He is my brother.' " 14 Then Abimelech took sheep and oxen, and male and female slaves, and gave them to Abraham, and restored his wife Sarah to him. 15 Abimelech said, "My land is before you; settle where it pleases you." 16 To Sarah he said, "Look, I have given your brother a thousand pieces of silver; it is your exoneration before all who are with you; you are completely vindicated." 17 Then Abraham prayed to God; and God healed Abimelech, and also healed his wife and female slaves so that they bore children. 18 For the LORD had closed fast all the wombs of the house of Abimelech because of Sarah, Abraham's wife.

THE BIRTH OF ISAAC

21 The LORD dealt with Sarah as he had said, and the LORD did for Sarah as he had promised. 2 Sarah conceived and bore Abraham a son in his old age, at the time of which God had spoken to him. 3 Abraham gave the name Isaac to his son whom Sarah bore him. 4 And Abraham circumcised his son Isaac when he was eight days old, as God had commanded him. 5 Abraham was a hundred years old when his son Isaac was born to him. 6 Now Sarah said, "God has brought laughter for me; everyone who hears will laugh with me." 7 And she said, "Who would ever have said to Abraham that Sarah would nurse children?

Yet I have borne him a son in his old age."

HAGAR AND ISHMAEL
SENT AWAY

8 The child grew, and was weaned; and Abraham made a great feast on the day that Isaac was weaned. 9 But Sarah saw the son of Hagar the Egyptian, whom she had borne to Abraham, playing with her son Isaac.[a] 10 So she said to Abraham, "Cast out this slave woman with her son; for the son of this slave woman shall not inherit along with my son Isaac." 11 The matter was very distressing to Abraham on account of his son. 12 But God said to Abraham, "Do not be distressed because of the boy and because of your slave woman; whatever Sarah says to you, do as she tells you, for it is through Isaac that offspring shall be named for you. 13 As for the son of the slave woman, I will make a nation of him also, because he is your offspring." 14 So Abraham rose early in the morning, and took bread and a skin of water, and gave it to Hagar, putting it on her shoulder, along with the child, and sent her away. And she departed, and wandered about in the wilderness of Beer-sheba.

15 When the water in the skin was gone, she cast the child under one of the bushes. 16 Then she went and sat down opposite him a good way off, about the distance of a bowshot; for she said, "Do not let me look on the death of the child." And as she sat opposite him, she lifted up her voice and wept. 17 And God heard the voice of the boy; and the angel of God called to Hagar from heaven, and said to her, "What troubles you, Hagar? Do not be afraid; for God has heard the voice of the boy where he is. 18 Come, lift up the boy and hold him fast with your hand, for I will make a great nation of him." 19 Then God opened her eyes and she saw a well of water. She went, and filled the skin with water, and gave the boy a drink.

20 God was with the boy, and he grew up; he lived in the wilderness, and became an expert with the bow.

21 He lived in the wilderness of Paran; and his mother got a wife for him from the land of Egypt.

ABRAHAM AND ABIMELECH
MAKE A COVENANT

22 At that time Abimelech, with Phicol the commander of his army, said to Abraham, "God is with you in all that you do; 23 now therefore swear to me here by God that you will not deal falsely with me or with my offspring or with my posterity, but as I have dealt loyally with you, you will deal with me and with the land where you have resided as an alien." 24 And Abraham said, "I swear it."

25 When Abraham complained to Abimelech about a well of water that Abimelech's servants had seized, 26 Abimelech said, "I do not know who has done this; you did not tell me, and I have not heard of it until today." 27 So Abraham took sheep and oxen and gave them to Abimelech, and the two men made a covenant. 28 Abraham set apart seven ewe lambs of the flock. 29 And Abimelech said to Abraham, "What is the meaning of these seven ewe lambs that you have set apart?" 30 He said, "These seven ewe lambs you shall accept from my hand, in order that you may be a witness for me that I dug this well." 31 Therefore that place was called Beer-sheba;[b] because there both of them swore an oath. 32 When they had made a covenant at Beer-sheba, Abimelech, with Phicol the commander of his army, left and returned to the land of the Philistines. 33 Abraham[c] planted a tamarisk tree in Beer-sheba, and called there on the name of the LORD, the Everlasting God.[d] 34 And Abraham resided as an alien many days in the land of the Philistines.

THE COMMAND TO
SACRIFICE ISAAC

22 After these things God tested Abraham. He said to him,

---

[a] 21.9 Gk Vg: Heb lacks *with her son Isaac*
[b] 21.31 That is *Well of seven* or *Well of the oath*   [c] 21.33 Heb *He*   [d] 21.33 Or *the LORD, El Olam*

"Abraham!" And he said, "Here I am." ²He said, "Take your son, your only son Isaac, whom you love, and go to the land of Moriah, and offer him there as a burnt offering on one of the mountains that I shall show you." ³So Abraham rose early in the morning, saddled his donkey, and took two of his young men with him, and his son Isaac; he cut the wood for the burnt offering, and set out and went to the place in the distance that God had shown him. ⁴On the third day Abraham looked up and saw the place far away. ⁵Then Abraham said to his young men, "Stay here with the donkey; the boy and I will go over there; we will worship, and then we will come back to you." ⁶Abraham took the wood of the burnt offering and laid it on his son Isaac, and he himself carried the fire and the knife. So the two of them walked on together. ⁷Isaac said to his father Abraham, "Father!" And he said, "Here I am, my son." He said, "The fire and the wood are here, but where is the lamb for a burnt offering?" ⁸Abraham said, "God himself will provide the lamb for a burnt offering, my son." So the two of them walked on together.

9 When they came to the place that God had shown him, Abraham built an altar there and laid the wood in order. He bound his son Isaac, and laid him on the altar, on top of the wood. ¹⁰Then Abraham reached out his hand and took the knife to kill[a] his son. ¹¹But the an-gel of the LORD called to him from heaven, and said, "Abraham, Abraham!" And he said, "Here I am." ¹²He said, "Do not lay your hand on the boy or do anything to him; for now I know that you fear God, since you have not withheld your son, your only son, from me." ¹³And Abraham looked up and saw a ram, caught in a thicket by its horns. Abraham went and took the ram and offered it up as a burnt offering instead of his son. ¹⁴So Abraham called that place "The LORD will provide";[b] as it is said to this day, "On the mount of the LORD it shall be provided."[c]

15 The angel of the LORD called to Abraham a second time from heaven, ¹⁶and said, "By myself I have sworn, says the LORD: Because you have done this, and have not withheld your son, your only son, ¹⁷I will indeed bless you, and I will make your offspring as numerous as the stars of heaven and as the sand that is on the seashore. And your offspring shall possess the gate of their enemies, ¹⁸and by your offspring shall all the nations of the earth gain blessing for themselves, because you have obeyed my voice." ¹⁹So Abraham returned to his young men, and they arose and went together to Beer-sheba; and Abraham lived at Beer-sheba.

---

[a] **22.10** Or *to slaughter* [b] **22.14** Or *will see*; Heb traditionally transliterated *Jehovah Jireh* [c] **22.14** Or *he shall be seen*

BIBLE IN LIFE

Willing to Sacrifice   Genesis 22.1–18

In the most vivid and courageous fashion, Abraham demonstrated his willingness to sacrifice his long-expected son, his *only* child, the son who represented the fulfillment of the promise that God had made about his offspring. God said, "Offer [Isaac] there as a burnt offering on one of the mountains that I shall show you" (verse 2). And Abraham, ever faithful, was willing to make the sacrifice. Compared to Abraham's sacrifice, any sacrifice that is asked of us seems relatively insignificant. But its insignificant nature doesn't mean that we shouldn't be willing or eager to let go of those things that we cherish. What are the sacrifices God is asking us to make? Can we have faith that God will give us hope and purpose as we let go of the cherished things we cling to in this life?

THE CHILDREN OF NAHOR

20 Now after these things it was told Abraham, "Milcah also has borne children, to your brother Nahor: ²¹Uz the firstborn, Buz his brother, Kemuel the father of Aram, ²²Chesed, Hazo, Pildash, Jidlaph, and Bethuel." ²³Bethuel became the father of Rebekah. These eight Milcah bore to Nahor, Abraham's brother. ²⁴Moreover, his concubine, whose name was Reumah, bore Tebah, Gaham, Tahash, and Maacah.

SARAH'S DEATH AND BURIAL

23 Sarah lived one hundred twenty-seven years; this was the length of Sarah's life. ²And Sarah died at Kiriath-arba (that is, Hebron) in the land of Canaan; and Abraham went in to mourn for Sarah and to weep for her. ³Abraham rose up from beside his dead, and said to the Hittites, ⁴"I am a stranger and an alien residing among you; give me property among you for a burying place, so that I may bury my dead out of my sight." ⁵The Hittites answered Abraham, ⁶"Hear us, my lord; you are a mighty prince among us. Bury your dead in the choicest of our burial places; none of us will withhold from you any burial ground for burying your dead." ⁷Abraham rose and bowed to the Hittites, the people of the land. ⁸He said to them, "If you are willing that I should bury my dead out of my sight, hear me, and entreat for me Ephron son of Zohar, ⁹so that he may give me the cave of Machpelah, which he owns; it is at the end of his field. For the full price let him give it to me in your presence as a possession for a burying place." ¹⁰Now Ephron was sitting among the Hittites; and Ephron the Hittite answered Abraham in the hearing of the Hittites, of all who went in at the gate of his city, ¹¹"No, my lord, hear me; I give you the field, and I give you the cave that is in it; in the presence of my people I give it to you; bury your dead." ¹²Then Abraham bowed down before the people of the land. ¹³He said to Ephron in the hearing of the people of the land, "If you only will listen to me! I will give the price of the field; accept it from me, so that I may bury my dead there." ¹⁴Ephron answered Abraham, ¹⁵"My lord, listen to me; a piece of land worth four hundred shekels of silver—what is that between you and me? Bury your dead." ¹⁶Abraham agreed with Ephron; and Abraham weighed out for Ephron the silver that he had named in the hearing of the Hittites, four hundred shekels of silver, according to the weights current among the merchants.

17 So the field of Ephron in Machpelah, which was to the east of Mamre, the field with the cave that was in it and all the trees that were in the field, throughout its whole area, passed ¹⁸to Abraham as a possession in the presence of the Hittites, in the presence of all who went in at the gate of his city. ¹⁹After this, Abraham buried Sarah his wife in the cave of the field of Machpelah facing Mamre (that is, Hebron) in the land of Canaan. ²⁰The field and the cave that is in it passed from the Hittites into Abraham's possession as a burying place.

THE MARRIAGE OF ISAAC AND REBEKAH

24 Now Abraham was old, well advanced in years; and the LORD had blessed Abraham in all things. ²Abraham said to his servant, the oldest of his house, who had charge of all that he had, "Put your hand under my thigh ³and I will make you swear by the LORD, the God of heaven and earth, that you will not get a wife for my son from the daughters of the Canaanites, among whom I live, ⁴but will go to my country and to my kindred and get a wife for my son Isaac." ⁵The servant said to him, "Perhaps the woman may not be willing to follow me to this land; must I then take your son back to the land from which you came?" ⁶Abraham said to him, "See to it that you do not take my son back there. ⁷The LORD, the God of heaven, who took me from my father's house and from the land of my birth, and who spoke to me and swore to me, 'To your offspring I will give this land,' he will send his angel before you, and you shall take a wife for my son from there. 8But if the woman is not willing to follow you, then you will be free from this oath of mine; only you must not take my son back there." 9So the servant put his hand under the thigh of Abraham his master and swore to him concerning this matter.

10 Then the servant took ten of his master's camels and departed, taking all kinds of choice gifts from his master; and he set out and went to Aramnaharaim, to the city of Nahor. 11He made the camels kneel down outside the city by the well of water; it was toward evening, the time when women go out to draw water. 12And he said, "O LORD, God of my master Abraham, please grant me success today and show steadfast love to my master Abraham. 13I am standing here by the spring of water, and the daughters of the townspeople are coming out to draw water. 14Let the girl to whom I shall say, 'Please offer your jar that I may drink,' and who shall say, 'Drink, and I will water your camels'—let her be the one whom you have appointed for your servant Isaac. By this I shall know that you have shown steadfast love to my master."

15 Before he had finished speaking, there was Rebekah, who was born to Bethuel son of Milcah, the wife of Nahor, Abraham's brother, coming out with her water jar on her shoulder. 16The girl was very fair to look upon, a virgin, whom no man had known. She went down to the spring, filled her jar, and came up. 17Then the servant ran to meet her and said, "Please let me sip a little water from your jar." 18"Drink, my lord," she said, and quickly lowered her jar upon her hand and gave him a drink. 19When she had finished giving him a drink, she said, "I will draw for your camels also, until they have finished drinking." 20So she quickly emptied her jar into the trough and ran again to the well to draw, and she drew for all his camels. 21The man gazed at her in silence to learn

whether or not the LORD had made his journey successful.

22 When the camels had finished drinking, the man took a gold nosering weighing a half shekel, and two bracelets for her arms weighing ten gold shekels, 23and said, "Tell me whose daughter you are. Is there room in your father's house for us to spend the night?" 24She said to him, "I am the daughter of Bethuel son of Milcah, whom she bore to Nahor." 25She added, "We have plenty of straw and fodder and a place to spend the night." 26The man bowed his head and worshiped the LORD 27and said, "Blessed be the LORD, the God of my master Abraham, who has not forsaken his steadfast love and his faithfulness toward my master. As for me, the LORD has led me on the way to the house of my master's kin."

28 Then the girl ran and told her mother's household about these things. 29Rebekah had a brother whose name was Laban; and Laban ran out to the man, to the spring. 30As soon as he had seen the nosering, and the bracelets on his sister's arms, and when he heard the words of his sister Rebekah, "Thus the man spoke to me," he went to the man; and there he was, standing by the camels at the spring. 31He said, "Come in, O blessed of the LORD. Why do you stand outside when I have prepared the house and a place for the camels?" 32So the man came into the house; and Laban unloaded the camels, and gave him straw and fodder for the camels, and water to wash his feet and the feet of the men who were with him. 33Then food was set before him to eat; but he said, "I will not eat until I have told my errand." He said, "Speak on."

34 So he said, "I am Abraham's servant. 35The LORD has greatly blessed my master, and he has become wealthy; he has given him flocks and herds, silver and gold, male and female slaves, camels and donkeys. 36And Sarah my master's wife bore a son to my master when she was old; and he has given him all that he has. 37My master made me swear, saying, 'You shall not take a wife for my son

from the daughters of the Canaanites, in whose land I live; ³⁸but you shall go to my father's house, to my kindred, and get a wife for my son.' ³⁹I said to my master, 'Perhaps the woman will not follow me.' ⁴⁰But he said to me, 'The LORD, before whom I walk, will send his angel with you and make your way successful. You shall get a wife for my son from my kindred, from my father's house. ⁴¹Then you will be free from my oath, when you come to my kindred; even if they will not give her to you, you will be free from my oath.'

42 "I came today to the spring, and said, 'O LORD, the God of my master Abraham, if now you will only make successful the way I am going! ⁴³I am standing here by the spring of water; let the young woman who comes out to draw, to whom I shall say, "Please give me a little water from your jar to drink," ⁴⁴and who will say to me, "Drink, and I will draw for your camels also"—let her be the woman whom the LORD has appointed for my master's son.'

45 "Before I had finished speaking in my heart, there was Rebekah coming out with her water jar on her shoulder; and she went down to the spring, and drew. I said to her, 'Please let me drink.' ⁴⁶She quickly let down her jar from her shoulder, and said, 'Drink, and I will also water your camels.' So I drank, and she also watered the camels. ⁴⁷Then I asked her, 'Whose daughter are you?' She said, 'The daughter of Bethuel, Nahor's son, whom Milcah bore to him.' So I put the ring on her nose, and the bracelets on her arms. ⁴⁸Then I bowed my head and worshiped the LORD, and blessed the LORD, the God of my master Abraham, who had led me by the right way to obtain the daughter of my master's kinsman for his son. ⁴⁹Now then, if you will deal loyally and truly with my master, tell me; and if not, tell me, so that I may turn either to the right hand or to the left."

50 Then Laban and Bethuel answered, "The thing comes from the LORD; we cannot speak to you anything bad or good. ⁵¹Look, Rebekah is before you, take her and go, and let her be the wife of your master's son, as the LORD has spoken."

52 When Abraham's servant heard their words, he bowed himself to the ground before the LORD. ⁵³And the servant brought out jewelry of silver and of gold, and garments, and gave them to Rebekah; he also gave to her brother and to her mother costly ornaments. ⁵⁴Then he and the men who were with him ate and drank, and they spent the night there. When they rose in the morning, he said, "Send me back to my master." ⁵⁵Her brother and her mother said, "Let the girl remain with us a while, at least ten days; after that she may go." ⁵⁶But he said to them, "Do not delay me, since the LORD has made my journey successful; let me go that I may go to my master." ⁵⁷They said, "We will call the girl, and ask her." ⁵⁸And they called Rebekah, and said to her, "Will you go with this man?" She said, "I will." ⁵⁹So they sent away their sister Rebekah and her nurse along with Abraham's servant and his men. ⁶⁰And they blessed Rebekah and said to her,

"May you, our sister, become
thousands of myriads;
may your offspring gain
possession
of the gates of their foes."

⁶¹Then Rebekah and her maids rose up, mounted the camels, and followed the man; thus the servant took Rebekah, and went his way.

OUR CHALLENGE IS TO
PUT OUR OWN LIVES INTO
PERSPECTIVE—COMMITMENTS
AND OBJECTIVES, MAINTAINING
FAITH, PATIENCE AND
ENDURANCE—AS A MEANS
TO MEETING LIFE'S GOALS.

62 Now Isaac had come from[a] Beer-lahai-roi, and was settled in the Negeb. 63 Isaac went out in the evening to walk[b] in the field; and looking up, he saw camels coming. 64 And Rebekah looked up, and when she saw Isaac, she slipped quickly from the camel, 65 and said to the servant, "Who is the man over there, walking in the field to meet us?" The servant said, "It is my master." So she took her veil and covered herself. 66 And the servant told Isaac all the things that he had done. 67 Then Isaac brought her into his mother Sarah's tent. He took Rebekah, and she became his wife; and he loved her. So Isaac was comforted after his mother's death.

ABRAHAM MARRIES KETURAH

25 Abraham took another wife, whose name was Keturah. 2 She bore him Zimran, Jokshan, Medan, Midian, Ishbak, and Shuah. 3 Jokshan was the father of Sheba and Dedan. The sons of Dedan were Asshurim, Letushim, and Leummim. 4 The sons of Midian were Ephah, Epher, Hanoch, Abida, and Eldaah. All these were the children of Keturah. 5 Abraham gave all he had to Isaac. 6 But to the sons of his concubines Abraham gave gifts, while he was still living, and he sent them away from his son Isaac, eastward to the east country.

THE DEATH OF ABRAHAM

7 This is the length of Abraham's life, one hundred seventy-five years. 8 Abraham breathed his last and died in a good old age, an old man and full of years, and was gathered to his people. 9 His sons Isaac and Ishmael buried him in the cave of Machpelah, in the field of Ephron son of Zohar the Hittite, east of Mamre, 10 the field that Abraham purchased from the Hittites. There Abraham was buried, with his wife Sarah. 11 After the death of Abraham God blessed his son Isaac. And Isaac settled at Beer-lahai-roi.

ISHMAEL'S DESCENDANTS

12 These are the descendants of Ishmael, Abraham's son, whom Ha-

gar the Egyptian, Sarah's slave-girl, bore to Abraham. 13 These are the names of the sons of Ishmael, named in the order of their birth: Nebaioth, the firstborn of Ishmael; and Kedar, Adbeel, Mibsam, 14 Mishma, Dumah, Massa, 15 Hadad, Tema, Jetur, Naphish, and Kedemah. 16 These are the sons of Ishmael and these are their names, by their villages and by their encampments, twelve princes according to their tribes. 17 (This is the length of the life of Ishmael, one hundred thirty-seven years; he breathed his last and died, and was gathered to his people.) 18 They settled from Havilah to Shur, which is opposite Egypt in the direction of Assyria; he settled down[c] alongside of[d] all his people.

THE BIRTH AND YOUTH OF ESAU AND JACOB

19 These are the descendants of Isaac, Abraham's son: Abraham was the father of Isaac, 20 and Isaac was forty years old when he married Rebekah, daughter of Bethuel the Aramean of Paddan-aram, sister of Laban the Aramean. 21 Isaac prayed to the LORD for his wife, because she was barren; and the LORD granted his prayer, and his wife Rebekah conceived. 22 The children struggled together within her; and she said, "If it is to be this way, why do I live?"[e] So she went to inquire of the LORD. 23 And the LORD said to her,

"Two nations are in your womb,
    and two peoples born of
        you shall be divided;
the one shall be stronger
        than the other,
    the elder shall serve
        the younger."

24 When her time to give birth was at hand, there were twins in her womb. 25 The first came out red, all his body like a hairy mantle; so they named him Esau. 26 Afterward his brother came out, with his hand gripping Esau's heel; so he was named Jacob.[f]

---

[a] 24.62 Syr Tg: Heb *from coming to*
[b] 24.63 Meaning of Heb word is uncertain
[c] 25.18 Heb *he fell*   [d] 25.18 Or *down in opposition to*   [e] 25.22 Syr: Meaning of Heb uncertain   [f] 25.26 That is *He takes by the heel* or *He supplants*

Isaac was sixty years old when she bore them.

27 When the boys grew up, Esau was a skillful hunter, a man of the field, while Jacob was a quiet man, living in tents. 28 Isaac loved Esau, because he was fond of game; but Rebekah loved Jacob.

ESAU SELLS HIS BIRTHRIGHT

29 Once when Jacob was cooking a stew, Esau came in from the field, and he was famished. 30 Esau said to Jacob, "Let me eat some of that red stuff, for I am famished!" (Therefore he was called Edom.ᵃ) 31 Jacob said, "First sell me your birthright." 32 Esau said, "I am about to die; of what use is a birthright to me?" 33 Jacob said, "Swear to me first."ᵇ So he swore to him, and sold his birthright to Jacob. 34 Then Jacob gave Esau bread and lentil stew, and he ate and drank, and rose and went his way. Thus Esau despised his birthright.

ISAAC AND ABIMELECH

26 Now there was a famine in the land, besides the former famine that had occurred in the days of Abraham. And Isaac went to Gerar, to King Abimelech of the Philistines. 2 The LORD appeared to Isaacᶜ and said, "Do not go down to Egypt; settle in the land that I shall show you. 3 Reside in this land as an alien, and I will be with you, and will bless you; for to you and to your descendants I will give all these lands, and I will fulfill the oath that I swore to your father Abraham. 4 I will make your offspring as numerous as the stars of heaven, and will give to your offspring all these lands; and all the nations of the earth shall gain blessing for themselves through your offspring, 5 because Abraham obeyed my voice and kept my charge, my commandments, my statutes, and my laws."

6 So Isaac settled in Gerar. 7 When the men of the place asked him about his wife, he said, "She is my sister"; for he was afraid to say, "My wife," thinking, "or else the men of the place might kill me for the sake of Rebekah, because she is attractive in appearance." 8 When Isaac had been there a long time, King Abimelech of the Philistines looked out of a window and saw him fondling his wife Rebekah. 9 So Abimelech called for Isaac, and said, "So she is your wife! Why then did you say, 'She is my sister'?" Isaac said to him, "Because I thought I might die because of her." 10 Abimelech said, "What is this you have done to us? One of the people might easily have lain with your wife, and you would have brought guilt upon us." 11 So Abimelech warned all the people, saying, "Whoever touches this man or his wife shall be put to death."

12 Isaac sowed seed in that land, and in the same year reaped a hundredfold. The LORD blessed him, 13 and the man became rich; he prospered more and more until he became very wealthy. 14 He had possessions of flocks and herds, and a great household, so that the Philistines envied him. 15 (Now the Philistines had stopped up and filled with earth all the wells that his father's servants had dug in the days of his father Abraham.) 16 And Abimelech said to Isaac, "Go away from us; you have become too powerful for us."

17 So Isaac departed from there and camped in the valley of Gerar and settled there. 18 Isaac dug again the wells of water that had been dug in the days of his father Abraham; for the Philistines had stopped them up after the death of Abraham; and he gave them the names that his father had given them. 19 But when Isaac's servants dug in the valley and found there a well of spring water, 20 the herders of Gerar quarreled with Isaac's herders, saying, "The water is ours." So he called the well Esek,ᵈ because they contended with him. 21 Then they dug another well, and they quarreled over that one also; so he called it Sitnah.ᵉ 22 He moved from there and dug another well, and they did not quarrel over

ᵃ 25.30 That is Red   ᵇ 25.33 Heb today
ᶜ 26.2 Heb him   ᵈ 26.20 That is Contention
ᵉ 26.21 That is Enmity

it; so he called it Rehoboth,[a] saying, "Now the LORD has made room for us, and we shall be fruitful in the land."

23 From there he went up to Beersheba. 24And that very night the LORD appeared to him and said, "I am the God of your father Abraham; do not be afraid, for I am with you and will bless you and make your offspring numerous for my servant Abraham's sake." 25So he built an altar there, called on the name of the LORD, and pitched his tent there. And there Isaac's servants dug a well.

26 Then Abimelech went to him from Gerar, with Ahuzzath his adviser and Phicol the commander of his army. 27Isaac said to them, "Why have you come to me, seeing that you hate me and have sent me away from you?" 28They said, "We see plainly that the LORD has been with you; so we say, let there be an oath between you and us, and let us make a covenant with you 29so that you will do us no harm, just as we have not touched you and have done to you nothing but good and have sent you away in peace. You are now the blessed of the LORD." 30So he made them a feast, and they ate and drank. 31In the morning they rose early and exchanged oaths; and Isaac set them on their way, and they departed from him in peace. 32That same day Isaac's servants came and told him about the well

that they had dug, and said to him, "We have found water!" 33He called it Shibah;[b] therefore the name of the city is Beer-sheba[c] to this day.

ESAU'S HITTITE WIVES

34 When Esau was forty years old, he married Judith daughter of Beeri the Hittite, and Basemath daughter of Elon the Hittite; 35and they made life bitter for Isaac and Rebekah.

ISAAC BLESSES JACOB

27 When Isaac was old and his eyes were dim so that he could not see, he called his elder son Esau and said to him, "My son"; and he answered, "Here I am." 2He said, "See, I am old; I do not know the day of my death. 3Now then, take your weapons, your quiver and your bow, and go out to the field, and hunt game for me. 4Then prepare for me savory food, such as I like, and bring it to me to eat, so that I may bless you before I die."

5 Now Rebekah was listening when Isaac spoke to his son Esau. So when Esau went to the field to hunt for game and bring it, 6Rebekah said to her son Jacob, "I heard your father say to your brother Esau, 7'Bring me game, and prepare for me savory food to eat, that I may bless you before the LORD before I die.' 8Now

[a] 26.22 That is Broad places or Room
[b] 26.33 A word resembling the word for oath   [c] 26.33 That is Well of the oath or Well of seven

---

BIBLE IN LIFE

Ambitious Mothering   Genesis 27.1–10

We often think of Rebekah as an example of a bad or manipulative mother because of her favoritism, deception and overprotection, but she is not the only mother in history to crave power, prestige or success for her child. In Matthew 20.20–28, the mother of James and John wanted something special for her sons—places of authority alongside Jesus. The problem was not that she or Rebekah wanted to help their sons; it was that they wanted something measured in human terms. They were thinking about an earthly kingdom, not the things that matter to God. While there is nothing wrong with having positions of authority or success, when we anoint these as being preeminent in our lives, as these mothers did for their children, we are at odds with the basic standards of Jesus Christ. As Jesus said, "The last will be first, and the first will be last" (Matthew 20.16).

therefore, my son, obey my word as I command you. ⁹Go to the flock, and get me two choice kids, so that I may prepare from them savory food for your father, such as he likes; ¹⁰and you shall take it to your father to eat, so that he may bless you before he dies." ¹¹But Jacob said to his mother Rebekah, "Look, my brother Esau is a hairy man, and I am a man of smooth skin. ¹²Perhaps my father will feel me, and I shall seem to be mocking him, and bring a curse on myself and not a blessing." ¹³His mother said to him, "Let your curse be on me, my son; only obey my word, and go, get them for me." ¹⁴So he went and got them and brought them to his mother; and his mother prepared savory food, such as his father loved. ¹⁵Then Rebekah took the best garments of her elder son Esau, which were with her in the house, and put them on her younger son Jacob; ¹⁶and she put the skins of the kids on his hands and on the smooth part of his neck. ¹⁷Then she handed the savory food, and the bread that she had prepared, to her son Jacob.

18 So he went in to his father, and said, "My father"; and he said, "Here I am; who are you, my son?" ¹⁹Jacob said to his father, "I am Esau your firstborn. I have done as you told me; now sit up and eat of my game, so that you may bless me." ²⁰But Isaac said to his son, "How is it that you have found it so quickly, my son?" He answered, "Because the LORD your God granted me success." ²¹Then Isaac said to Jacob, "Come near, that I may feel you, my son, to know whether you are really my son Esau or not." ²²So Jacob went up to his father Isaac, who felt him and said, "The voice is Jacob's voice, but the hands are the hands of Esau." ²³He did not recognize him, because his hands were hairy like his brother Esau's hands; so he blessed him. ²⁴He said, "Are you really my son Esau?" He answered, "I am." ²⁵Then he said, "Bring it to me, that I may eat of my son's game and bless you." So he brought it to him, and he ate; and he brought him wine, and he drank. ²⁶Then his father Isaac said

to him, "Come near and kiss me, my son." ²⁷So he came near and kissed him; and he smelled the smell of his garments, and blessed him, and said,

"Ah, the smell of my son
   is like the smell of a field that
      the LORD has blessed.
²⁸ May God give you of the
      dew of heaven,
   and of the fatness of the earth,
      and plenty of grain and wine.
²⁹ Let peoples serve you,
   and nations bow down to you.
Be lord over your brothers,
   and may your mother's sons
      bow down to you.
Cursed be everyone who
      curses you,
   and blessed be everyone
      who blesses you!"

ESAU'S LOST BLESSING

30 As soon as Isaac had finished blessing Jacob, when Jacob had scarcely gone out from the presence of his father Isaac, his brother Esau came in from his hunting. ³¹He also prepared savory food, and brought it to his father. And he said to his father, "Let my father sit up and eat of his son's game, so that you may bless me." ³²His father Isaac said to him, "Who are you?" He answered, "I am your firstborn son, Esau." ³³Then Isaac trembled violently, and said, "Who was it then that hunted game and brought it to me, and I ate it all[a] before you came, and I have blessed him?—yes, and blessed he shall be!" ³⁴When Esau heard his father's words, he cried out with an exceedingly great and bitter cry, and said to his father, "Bless me, me also, father!" ³⁵But he said, "Your brother came deceitfully, and he has taken away your blessing." ³⁶Esau said, "Is he not rightly named Jacob?[b] For he has supplanted me these two times. He took away my birthright; and look, now he has taken away my blessing." Then he said, "Have you not reserved a blessing for me?" ³⁷Isaac answered Esau, "I have already made

---

[a] 27.33 Cn: Heb of all   [b] 27.36 That is He supplants or He takes by the heel

him your lord, and I have given him all his brothers as servants, and with grain and wine I have sustained him. What then can I do for you, my son?" ³⁸Esau said to his father, "Have you only one blessing, father? Bless me, me also, father!" And Esau lifted up his voice and wept.

PONDER

Isaac answered Esau, "I have already made him your lord, and I have given him all his brothers as servants." . . . Esau said to his father, "Have you only one blessing, father? Bless me, me also, father!"
—Genesis 27.37–38

PRAY

Father God, we are taught from childhood to succeed. We want to be successful. We want to be leaders, and there is nothing wrong with being a leader if we accept the definition Jesus gave us, that leaders are to be servants. Help us set aside any sense of superiority and domination over others. Let us not grasp for things for ourselves as Jacob grasped for his brother's birthright and blessing. Mold our lives according to the perfect example of humility and submission to you set for us by our Savior, Jesus Christ. Help us realize this is not impossible; it is not impractical. In his name we pray. Amen.

---

39 Then his father Isaac answered him:
"See, away from ᵃ the fatness
    of the earth shall
    your home be,
and away from ᵇ the dew
    of heaven on high.
⁴⁰ By your sword you shall live,
    and you shall serve
        your brother;
but when you break loose, ᶜ
    you shall break his yoke
        from your neck."

JACOB ESCAPES ESAU'S FURY

41 Now Esau hated Jacob because of the blessing with which his father had blessed him, and Esau said to himself, "The days of mourning for my father are approaching; then I will kill my brother Jacob." ⁴²But the words of her elder son Esau were told to Rebekah; so she sent and called her younger son Jacob and said to him, "Your brother Esau is consoling himself by planning to kill you. ⁴³Now therefore, my son, obey my voice; flee at once to my brother Laban in Haran, ⁴⁴and stay with him a while, until your brother's fury turns away— ⁴⁵until your brother's anger against you turns away, and he forgets what you have done to him; then I will send, and bring you back from there. Why should I lose both of you in one day?" ⁴⁶Then Rebekah said to Isaac, "I am weary of my life because of the Hittite women. If Jacob marries one of the Hittite women such as these, one of the women of the land, what good will my life be to me?"

28 Then Isaac called Jacob and blessed him, and charged him, "You shall not marry one of the Canaanite women. ²Go at once to Paddan-aram to the house of Bethuel, your mother's father; and take as wife from there one of the daughters of Laban, your mother's brother. ³May God Almightyᵈ bless you and make you fruitful and numerous, that you may become a company of peoples. ⁴May he give to you the blessing of Abraham, to you and to your offspring with you, so that you may take possession of the land where you now live as an alien—land that God gave to Abraham." ⁵Thus Isaac sent Jacob away; and he went to Paddan-aram, to Laban son of Bethuel the Aramean, the brother of Rebekah, Jacob's and Esau's mother.

ᵃ **27.39** Or *See, of* ᵇ **27.39** Or *and of* ᶜ **27.40** Meaning of Heb uncertain ᵈ **28.3** Traditional rendering of Heb *El Shaddai*

ESAU MARRIES ISHMAEL'S DAUGHTER

6 Now Esau saw that Isaac had blessed Jacob and sent him away to Paddan-aram to take a wife from there, and that as he blessed him he charged him, "You shall not marry one of the Canaanite women," 7and that Jacob had obeyed his father and his mother and gone to Paddan-aram. 8So when Esau saw that the Canaanite women did not please his father Isaac, 9Esau went to Ishmael and took Mahalath daughter of Abraham's son Ishmael, and sister of Nebaioth, to be his wife in addition to the wives he had.

JACOB'S DREAM AT BETHEL

10 Jacob left Beer-sheba and went toward Haran. 11He came to a certain place and stayed there for the night, because the sun had set. Taking one of the stones of the place, he put it under his head and lay down in that place. 12And he dreamed that there was a ladder[a] set up on the earth, the top of it reaching to heaven; and the angels of God were ascending and descending on it. 13And the LORD stood beside him[b] and said, "I am the LORD, the God of Abraham your father and the God of Isaac; the land on which you lie I will give to you and to your offspring; 14and your offspring shall be like the dust of the earth, and you shall spread abroad to the west and to the east and to the north and to the south; and all the families of the earth shall be blessed[c] in you and in your offspring. 15Know that I am with you and will keep you wherever you go, and will bring you back to this land; for I will not leave you until I have done what I have promised you." 16Then Jacob woke from his sleep and said, "Surely the LORD is in this place—and I did not know it!" 17And he was afraid, and said, "How awesome is this place! This is none other than the house of God, and this is the gate of heaven."

18 So Jacob rose early in the morning, and he took the stone that he had put under his head and set it up for a pillar and poured oil on the top of it. 19He called that place Bethel;[d]

PONDER

"All the families of the earth shall be blessed in you and in your offspring." —Genesis 28.14

PRAY

Lord, we have read about one of the most interesting characters in your Holy Word. In spite of Jacob's failings, you lifted him up and gave him a mission and a promise. Thank you for the blessing of the covenant that you gave to Noah, Abraham, Moses, Isaac, Jacob, and later to David and through Jesus Christ to us. Help us remember the deep roots and rich history—your story—you have given us and show each of us how we can serve you. We ask all this in the name of our Savior, Jesus Christ. Amen.

but the name of the city was Luz at the first. 20Then Jacob made a vow, saying, "If God will be with me, and will keep me in this way that I go, and will give me bread to eat and clothing to wear, 21so that I come again to my father's house in peace, then the LORD shall be my God, 22and this stone, which I have set up for a pillar, shall be God's house; and of all that you give me I will surely give one-tenth to you."

JACOB MEETS RACHEL

29 Then Jacob went on his journey, and came to the land of the people of the east. 2As he looked, he saw a well in the field and three flocks of sheep lying there beside it; for out of that well the flocks were watered. The stone on the well's mouth was large, 3and when all the flocks were gathered there, the shepherds would roll the stone from the mouth of the well, and water the

a 28.12 Or stairway or ramp   b 28.13 Or stood above it   c 28.14 Or shall bless themselves   d 28.19 That is House of God sheep, and put the stone back in its place on the mouth of the well.

4 Jacob said to them, "My brothers, where do you come from?" They said, "We are from Haran." 5 He said to them, "Do you know Laban son of Nahor?" They said, "We do." 6 He said to them, "Is it well with him?" "Yes," they replied, "and here is his daughter Rachel, coming with the sheep." 7 He said, "Look, it is still broad daylight; it is not time for the animals to be gathered together. Water the sheep, and go, pasture them." 8 But they said, "We cannot until all the flocks are gathered together, and the stone is rolled from the mouth of the well; then we water the sheep."

9 While he was still speaking with them, Rachel came with her father's sheep; for she kept them. 10 Now when Jacob saw Rachel, the daughter of his mother's brother Laban, and the sheep of his mother's brother Laban, Jacob went up and rolled the stone from the well's mouth, and watered the flock of his mother's brother Laban. 11 Then Jacob kissed Rachel, and wept aloud. 12 And Jacob told Rachel that he was her father's kinsman, and that he was Rebekah's son; and she ran and told her father.

13 When Laban heard the news about his sister's son Jacob, he ran to meet him; he embraced him and kissed him, and brought him to his house. Jacob[a] told Laban all these things, 14 and Laban said to him, "Surely you are my bone and my flesh!" And he stayed with him a month.

JACOB MARRIES LABAN'S DAUGHTERS

15 Then Laban said to Jacob, "Because you are my kinsman, should you therefore serve me for nothing? Tell me, what shall your wages be?" 16 Now Laban had two daughters; the name of the elder was Leah, and the name of the younger was Rachel. 17 Leah's eyes were lovely,[b] and Rachel was graceful and beautiful. 18 Jacob loved Rachel; so he said, "I will serve you seven years for your younger daughter Rachel." 19 Laban said, "It is better that I give her to you than that I should give her to any other man; stay with me." 20 So Jacob served seven years for Rachel, and they seemed to him but a few days because of the love he had for her.

21 Then Jacob said to Laban, "Give me my wife that I may go in to her, for my time is completed." 22 So Laban gathered together all the people of the place, and made a feast. 23 But in the evening he took his daughter Leah and brought her to Jacob; and he went in to her. 24 (Laban gave his maid Zilpah to his daughter Leah to be her maid.) 25 When morning came, it was Leah! And Jacob said to Laban, "What is this you have done to me? Did I not serve with you for Rachel? Why then have you deceived me?" 26 Laban said, "This is not done in our country—giving the younger before the firstborn. 27 Complete the week of this one, and we will give you the other also in return for serving me another seven years." 28 Jacob did so, and completed her week; then Laban gave him his daughter Rachel as a wife. 29 (Laban gave his maid Bilhah to his daughter Rachel to be her maid.) 30 So Jacob went in to Rachel also, and he loved Rachel more than Leah. He served Laban[c] for another seven years.

31 When the LORD saw that Leah was unloved, he opened her womb; but Rachel was barren. 32 Leah conceived and bore a son, and she named him Reuben;[d] for she said, "Because the LORD has looked on my affliction; surely now my husband will love me." 33 She conceived again and bore a son, and said, "Because the LORD has heard[e] that I am hated, he has given me this son also"; and she named him Simeon. 34 Again she conceived and bore a son, and said, "Now this time my husband will be joined[f] to me, because I have borne him three sons"; therefore he was named Levi. 35 She conceived again and bore a son, and said, "This

---

[a] 29.13 Heb He [b] 29.17 Meaning of Heb uncertain [c] 29.30 Heb him [d] 29.32 That is See, a son [e] 29.33 Heb shama [f] 29.34 Heb lawah

time I will praise[a] the LORD"; therefore she named him Judah; then she ceased bearing.

30 When Rachel saw that she bore Jacob no children, she envied her sister; and she said to Jacob, "Give me children, or I shall die!" [2]Jacob became very angry with Rachel and said, "Am I in the place of God, who has withheld from you the fruit of the womb?" [3]Then she said, "Here is my maid Bilhah; go in to her, that she may bear upon my knees and that I too may have children through her." [4]So she gave him her maid Bilhah as a wife; and Jacob went in to her. [5]And Bilhah conceived and bore Jacob a son. [6]Then Rachel said, "God has judged me, and has also heard my voice and given me a son"; therefore she named him Dan.[b] [7]Rachel's maid Bilhah conceived again and bore Jacob a second son. [8]Then Rachel said, "With mighty wrestlings I have wrestled[c] with my sister, and have prevailed"; so she named him Naphtali.

[9]When Leah saw that she had ceased bearing children, she took her maid Zilpah and gave her to Jacob as a wife. [10]Then Leah's maid Zilpah bore Jacob a son. [11]And Leah said, "Good fortune!" so she named him Gad.[d] [12]Leah's maid Zilpah bore Jacob a second son. [13]And Leah said, "Happy am I! For the women will call me happy"; so she named him Asher.[e]

[14]In the days of wheat harvest Reuben went and found mandrakes in the field, and brought them to his mother Leah. Then Rachel said to Leah, "Please give me some of your son's mandrakes." [15]But she said to her, "Is it a small matter that you have taken away my husband? Would you take away my son's mandrakes also?" Rachel said, "Then he may lie with you tonight for your son's mandrakes." [16]When Jacob came from the field in the evening, Leah went out to meet him, and said, "You must come in to me; for I have hired you with my son's mandrakes." So he lay with her that night. [17]And God heeded Leah, and she conceived and bore Jacob a fifth son. [18]Leah said, "God has given me my hire[f] because I gave my maid to my husband"; so she named him Issachar. [19]And Leah conceived again, and she bore Jacob a sixth son. [20]Then Leah said, "God has endowed me with a good dowry; now my husband will honor[g] me, because I have borne him six sons"; so she named him Zebulun. [21]Afterwards she bore a daughter, and named her Dinah.

[22]Then God remembered Rachel, and God heeded her and opened her womb. [23]She conceived and bore a son, and said, "God has taken away my reproach"; [24]and she named him Joseph,[h] saying, "May the LORD add to me another son!"

JACOB PROSPERS AT LABAN'S EXPENSE

[25]When Rachel had borne Joseph, Jacob said to Laban, "Send me away, that I may go to my own home and country. [26]Give me my wives and my children for whom I have served you, and let me go; for you know very well the service I have given you." [27]But Laban said to him, "If you will allow me to say so, I have learned by divination that the LORD has blessed me because of you; [28]name your wages, and I will give it." [29]Jacob said to him, "You yourself know how I have served you, and how your cattle have fared with me. [30]For you had little before I came, and it has increased abundantly; and the LORD has blessed you wherever I turned. But now when shall I provide for my own household also?" [31]He said, "What shall I give you?" Jacob said, "You shall not give me anything; if you will do this for me, I will again feed your flock and keep it: [32]let me pass through all your flock today, removing from it every speckled and spotted sheep and every black lamb, and the spotted and speckled among the goats; and such shall be my wages. [33]So my honesty will answer for me

[a] 29.35 Heb hodah [b] 30.6 That is He judged [c] 30.8 Heb niphtal [d] 30.11 That is Fortune [e] 30.13 That is Happy [f] 30.18 Heb sakar [g] 30.20 Heb zabal [h] 30.24 That is He adds

later, when you come to look into my wages with you. Every one that is not speckled and spotted among the goats and black among the lambs, if found with me, shall be counted stolen." ³⁴Laban said, "Good! Let it be as you have said." ³⁵But that day Laban removed the male goats that were striped and spotted, and all the female goats that were speckled and spotted, every one that had white on it, and every lamb that was black, and put them in charge of his sons; ³⁶and he set a distance of three days' journey between himself and Jacob, while Jacob was pasturing the rest of Laban's flock.

37 Then Jacob took fresh rods of poplar and almond and plane, and peeled white streaks in them, exposing the white of the rods. ³⁸He set the rods that he had peeled in front of the flocks in the troughs, that is, the watering places, where the flocks came to drink. And since they bred when they came to drink, ³⁹the flocks bred in front of the rods, and so the flocks produced young that were striped, speckled, and spotted. ⁴⁰Jacob separated the lambs, and set the faces of the flocks toward the striped and the completely black animals in the flock of Laban; and he put his own droves apart, and did not put them with Laban's flock. ⁴¹Whenever the stronger of the flock were breeding, Jacob laid the rods in the troughs before the eyes of the flock, that they might breed among the rods, ⁴²but for the feebler of the flock he did not lay them there; so the feebler were Laban's, and the stronger Jacob's. ⁴³Thus the man grew exceedingly rich, and had large flocks, and male and female slaves, and camels and donkeys.

JACOB FLEES WITH FAMILY AND FLOCKS

31 Now Jacob heard that the sons of Laban were saying, "Jacob has taken all that was our father's; he has gained all this wealth from what belonged to our father." ²And Jacob saw that Laban did not regard him as favorably as he did before. ³Then the LORD said to Jacob,

"Return to the land of your ancestors and to your kindred, and I will be with you." ⁴So Jacob sent and called Rachel and Leah into the field where his flock was, ⁵and said to them, "I see that your father does not regard me as favorably as he did before. But the God of my father has been with me. ⁶You know that I have served your father with all my strength; ⁷yet your father has cheated me and changed my wages ten times, but God did not permit him to harm me. ⁸If he said, 'The speckled shall be your wages,' then all the flock bore speckled; and if he said, 'The striped shall be your wages,' then all the flock bore striped. ⁹Thus God has taken away the livestock of your father, and given them to me.

10 "During the mating of the flock I once had a dream in which I looked up and saw that the male goats that leaped upon the flock were striped, speckled, and mottled. ¹¹Then the angel of God said to me in the dream, 'Jacob,' and I said, 'Here I am!' ¹²And he said, 'Look up and see that all the goats that leap on the flock are striped, speckled, and mottled; for I have seen all that Laban is doing to you. ¹³I am the God of Bethel,ᵃ where you anointed a pillar and made a vow to me. Now leave this land at once and return to the land of your birth.' " ¹⁴Then Rachel and Leah answered him, "Is there any portion or inheritance left to us in our father's house? ¹⁵Are we not regarded by him as foreigners? For he has sold us, and he has been using up the money given for us. ¹⁶All the property that God has taken away from our father belongs to us and to our children; now then, do whatever God has said to you."

17 So Jacob arose, and set his children and his wives on camels; ¹⁸and he drove away all his livestock, all the property that he had gained, the livestock in his possession that he had acquired in Paddan-aram, to go to his father Isaac in the land of Canaan.

19 Now Laban had gone to shear his sheep, and Rachel stole her father's

ᵃ 31.13 Cn: Meaning of Heb uncertain

household gods. 20 And Jacob deceived Laban the Aramean, in that he did not tell him that he intended to flee. 21 So he fled with all that he had; starting out he crossed the Euphrates,ᵃ and set his face toward the hill country of Gilead.

LABAN OVERTAKES JACOB

22 On the third day Laban was told that Jacob had fled. 23 So he took his kinsfolk with him and pursued him for seven days until he caught up with him in the hill country of Gilead. 24 But God came to Laban the Aramean in a dream by night, and said to him, "Take heed that you say not a word to Jacob, either good or bad."

25 Laban overtook Jacob. Now Jacob had pitched his tent in the hill country, and Laban with his kinsfolk camped in the hill country of Gilead. 26 Laban said to Jacob, "What have you done? You have deceived me, and carried away my daughters like captives of the sword. 27 Why did you flee secretly and deceive me and not tell me? I would have sent you away with mirth and songs, with tambourine and lyre. 28 And why did you not permit me to kiss my sons and my daughters farewell? What you have done is foolish. 29 It is in my power to do you harm; but the God of your father spoke to me last night, saying, 'Take heed that you speak to Jacob neither good nor bad.' 30 Even though you had to go because you longed greatly for your father's house, why did you steal my gods?" 31 Jacob answered Laban, "Because I was afraid, for I thought that you would take your daughters from me by force. 32 But anyone with whom you find your gods shall not live. In the presence of our kinsfolk, point out what I have that is yours, and take it." Now Jacob did not know that Rachel had stolen the gods.ᵇ

33 So Laban went into Jacob's tent, and into Leah's tent, and into the tent of the two maids, but he did not find them. And he went out of Leah's tent, and entered Rachel's. 34 Now Rachel had taken the household gods and put them in the camel's saddle, and sat on them. Laban felt all about in the tent, but did not find them. 35 And she said to her father, "Let not my lord be angry that I cannot rise before you, for the way of women is upon me." So he searched, but did not find the household gods.

36 Then Jacob became angry, and upbraided Laban. Jacob said to Laban, "What is my offense? What is my sin, that you have hotly pursued me? 37 Although you have felt about through all my goods, what have you found of all your household goods? Set it here before my kinsfolk and your kinsfolk, so that they may decide between us two. 38 These twenty years I have been with you; your ewes and your female goats have not miscarried, and I have not eaten the rams of your flocks. 39 That which was torn by wild beasts I did not bring to you; I bore the loss of it myself; of my hand you required it, whether stolen by day or stolen by night. 40 It was like this with me: by day the heat consumed me, and the cold by night, and my sleep fled from my eyes. 41 These twenty years I have been in your house; I served you fourteen years for your two daughters, and six years for your flock, and you have changed my wages ten times. 42 If the God of my father, the God of Abraham and the Fearᶜ of Isaac, had not been on my side, surely now you would have sent me away empty-handed. God saw my affliction and the labor of my hands, and rebuked you last night."

LABAN AND JACOB MAKE A COVENANT

43 Then Laban answered and said to Jacob, "The daughters are my daughters, the children are my children, the flocks are my flocks, and all that you see is mine. But what can I do today about these daughters of mine, or about their children whom they have borne? 44 Come now, let us make a covenant, you and I; and let it be a witness between you and me." 45 So Jacob took a stone, and set it up as a pillar. 46 And Jacob said to his

ᵃ 31.21 Heb the river   ᵇ 31.32 Heb them
ᶜ 31.42 Meaning of Heb uncertain

kinsfolk, "Gather stones," and they took stones, and made a heap; and they ate there by the heap. ⁴⁷Laban called it Jegar-sahadutha:ᵃ but Jacob called it Galeed.ᵇ ⁴⁸Laban said, "This heap is a witness between you and me today." Therefore he called it Galeed, ⁴⁹and the pillarᶜ Mizpah,ᵈ for he said, "The LORD watch between you and me, when we are absent one from the other. ⁵⁰If you ill-treat my daughters, or if you take wives in addition to my daughters, though no one else is with us, remember that God is witness between you and me."

⁵¹Then Laban said to Jacob, "See this heap and see the pillar, which I have set between you and me. ⁵²This heap is a witness, and the pillar is a witness, that I will not pass beyond this heap to you, and you will not pass beyond this heap and this pillar to me, for harm. ⁵³May the God of Abraham and the God of Nahor"— the God of their father—"judge between us." So Jacob swore by the Fearᵉ of his father Isaac, ⁵⁴and Jacob offered a sacrifice on the height and called his kinsfolk to eat bread; and they ate bread and tarried all night in the hill country.

⁵⁵ᶠ Early in the morning Laban rose up, and kissed his grandchildren and his daughters and blessed them; then he departed and returned home.

32 Jacob went on his way and the angels of God met him; ²and when Jacob saw them he said, "This is God's camp!" So he called that place Mahanaim.ᵍ

JACOB SENDS PRESENTS TO APPEASE ESAU

3 Jacob sent messengers before him to his brother Esau in the land of Seir, the country of Edom, ⁴instructing them, "Thus you shall say to my lord Esau: Thus says your servant Jacob, 'I have lived with Laban as an alien, and stayed until now; ⁵and I have oxen, donkeys, flocks, male and female slaves; and I have sent to tell my lord, in order that I may find favor in your sight.'"

6 The messengers returned to Jacob, saying, "We came to your brother Esau, and he is coming to meet you, and four hundred men are with him." ⁷Then Jacob was greatly afraid and distressed; and he divided the people that were with him, and the flocks and herds and camels, into two companies, ⁸thinking, "If Esau comes to the one company and destroys it, then the company that is left will escape."

9 And Jacob said, "O God of my father Abraham and God of my father Isaac, O LORD who said to me, 'Return to your country and to your kindred, and I will do you good,' ¹⁰I am not worthy of the least of all the steadfast love and all the faithfulness that you have shown to your servant, for with only my staff I crossed this Jordan; and now I have become two companies. ¹¹Deliver me, please, from the hand of my brother, from the hand of Esau, for I am afraid of him; he may come and kill us all, the mothers with the children. ¹²Yet you have said, 'I will surely do you good, and make your offspring as the sand of the sea, which cannot be counted because of their number.'"

13 So he spent that night there, and from what he had with him he took a present for his brother Esau, ¹⁴two hundred female goats and twenty male goats, two hundred ewes and twenty rams, ¹⁵thirty milch camels and their colts, forty cows and ten bulls, twenty female donkeys and ten male donkeys. ¹⁶These he delivered into the hand of his servants, every drove by itself, and said to his servants, "Pass on ahead of me, and put a space between drove and drove." ¹⁷He instructed the foremost, "When Esau my brother meets you, and asks you, 'To whom do you belong? Where are you going? And whose are these ahead of you?' ¹⁸then you shall say, 'They belong to your servant Jacob; they are a present sent to my lord Esau; and moreover he is behind

ᵃ 31.47 In Aramaic *The heap of witness*
ᵇ 31.47 In Hebrew *The heap of witness*
ᶜ 31.49 Compare Sam: MT lacks *the pillar*
ᵈ 31.49 That is *Watchpost*   ᵉ 31.53 Meaning of Heb uncertain   ᶠ 31.55 Ch 32.1 in Heb
ᵍ 32.2 Here taken to mean *Two camps*

us.' " ¹⁹He likewise instructed the second and the third and all who followed the droves, "You shall say the same thing to Esau when you meet him, ²⁰and you shall say, 'Moreover your servant Jacob is behind us.' " For he thought, "I may appease him with the present that goes ahead of me, and afterwards I shall see his face; perhaps he will accept me." ²¹So the present passed on ahead of him; and he himself spent that night in the camp.

JACOB WRESTLES AT PENIEL

22 The same night he got up and took his two wives, his two maids, and his eleven children, and crossed the ford of the Jabbok. ²³He took them and sent them across the stream, and likewise everything that he had. ²⁴Jacob was left alone; and a man wrestled with him until daybreak. ²⁵When the man saw that he did not prevail against Jacob, he struck him on the hip socket; and Jacob's hip was put out of joint as he wrestled with him. ²⁶Then he said, "Let me go, for the day is breaking." But Jacob said, "I will not let you go, unless you bless me." ²⁷So he said to him, "What is your name?" And he said, "Jacob." ²⁸Then the man[a] said, "You shall no longer be called Jacob, but Israel,[b] for you have striven with God and with humans,[c] and have prevailed." ²⁹Then Jacob asked him, "Please tell me your name." But he said, "Why is it that you ask my name?" And there he blessed him. ³⁰So Jacob called the place Peniel,[d] saying, "For I have seen God face to face, and yet my life is preserved." ³¹The sun rose upon him as he passed Penuel, limping because of his hip. ³²Therefore to this day the Israelites do not eat the thigh muscle that is on the hip socket, because he struck Jacob on the hip socket at the thigh muscle.

JACOB AND ESAU MEET

33 Now Jacob looked up and saw Esau coming, and four hundred men with him. So he divided the children among Leah and Rachel and the two maids. ²He put the maids with their children in front, then Leah with her children, and Rachel and Joseph last of all. ³He himself went on ahead of them, bowing himself to the ground seven times, until he came near his brother.

HUMILITY AND

RECONCILIATION ARE GOD'S

WAY FOR OUR LIVES.

4 But Esau ran to meet him, and embraced him, and fell on his neck and kissed him, and they wept. ⁵When Esau looked up and saw the women and children, he said, "Who are these with you?" Jacob said, "The children whom God has graciously given your servant." ⁶Then the maids drew near, they and their children, and bowed down; ⁷Leah likewise and her children drew near and bowed down; and finally Joseph and Rachel drew near, and they bowed down. ⁸Esau said, "What do you mean by all this company that I met?" Jacob answered, "To find favor with my lord." ⁹But Esau said, "I have enough, my brother; keep what you have for yourself." ¹⁰Jacob said, "No, please; if I find favor with you, then accept my present from my hand; for truly to see your face is like seeing the face of God—since you have received me with such favor. ¹¹Please accept my gift that is brought to you, because God has dealt graciously with me, and because I have everything I want." So he urged him, and he took it.

12 Then Esau said, "Let us journey on our way, and I will go alongside you." ¹³But Jacob said to him, "My lord knows that the children are frail and that the flocks and herds, which

---

[a] 32.28 Heb *he*   [b] 32.28 That is *The one who strives with God* or *God strives*
[c] 32.28 Or *with divine and human beings*
[d] 32.30 That is *The face of God*

A NEW NAME

"You shall no longer be called Jacob, but Israel, for you have striven with God and with humans, and have prevailed."

—Genesis 32.28

In Genesis 32, we read of Jacob's travels as he continued his journey to Canaan from Haran. While he traveled, he kept a watchful eye out for his brother, Esau. The last time Jacob had seen his brother, he had swindled Esau out of their father's blessing (see Genesis 27). As he approached Canaan, Jacob sent messengers ahead of him to discover the strength of his brother's convoy and even brag a bit about his own.

But when Jacob's messengers returned, they told him that Esau was coming, and he had four hundred men with him! Jacob changed his strategy, and, fearing Esau was coming to kill him, tried to appease his brother by sending Esau rich gifts of livestock. Jacob also divided everything he had into two groups, so that if Esau did attack, Jacob would still have some belongings.

After sending all of his family and flocks across the river, Jacob prepared to spend the night alone. But instead, he spent the night wrestling with "a man" who was none other than a personification of God himself. At some point in the struggle, the man touched Jacob's hip and threw it out of joint. Finally, as dawn approached, the man said, "Let me go, for the day is breaking" (verse 26), but Jacob wouldn't let him go until he had received his blessing. The man blessed him and even changed Jacob's name to Israel, showing that Jacob had become a new person. The "supplanter" (the meaning of *Jacob*)—the person who steals the blessings of others—was now blessed by God. By relentlessly struggling for God's blessing, Jacob was, in a sense, reminding God of God's promise to be with him (see Genesis 28.10–17).

This same idea is reiterated in the New Testament. Out of his great love for his people, God has promised to remove the punishment for our sins if we put our faith in Christ. When we turn to God in repentance, we do so trusting in his promise and calling on him to fulfill it for us. If we didn't know that God would forgive us, we would probably never admit that we are sinful. But the gospel frees us from the fear of punishment, and we can simply turn to God in faith. Christ paid the penalty of sin for us; our sins are washed clean "like snow" (Isaiah 1.18), just as though we had never committed them. It's just as though we had never been selfish, or looked the other way when somebody was in need, or told a lie, or despised someone and didn't forgive them.

And like Jacob, as we call upon God to carry out his promises to us, the Lord grants us a new identity. We are no longer slaves to sin; instead we are children of our loving Father in heaven (see 1 John 3.1).

Going Deeper

- How have you grown impatient to waiting for God's promised blessings? In what ways do you wrongly struggle to work things out for yourself?
- What sins have you been afraid to confess to God because you feared his punishment?

are nursing, are a care to me; and if they are overdriven for one day, all the flocks will die. ¹⁴Let my lord pass on ahead of his servant, and I will lead on slowly, according to the pace of the cattle that are before me and according to the pace of the children, until I come to my lord in Seir."

15 So Esau said, "Let me leave with you some of the people who are with me." But he said, "Why should my lord be so kind to me?" ¹⁶So Esau returned that day on his way to Seir. ¹⁷But Jacob journeyed to Succoth,ᵃ and built himself a house, and made booths for his cattle; therefore the place is called Succoth.

JACOB REACHES SHECHEM

18 Jacob came safely to the city of Shechem, which is in the land of Canaan, on his way from Paddan-aram; and he camped before the city. ¹⁹And from the sons of Hamor, Shechem's father, he bought for one hundred pieces of moneyᵇ the plot of land on which he had pitched his tent. ²⁰There he erected an altar and called it El-Elohe-Israel.ᶜ

THE RAPE OF DINAH

34 Now Dinah the daughter of Leah, whom she had borne to Jacob, went out to visit the women of the region. ²When Shechem son of Hamor the Hivite, prince of the region, saw her, he seized her and lay with her by force. ³And his soul was drawn to Dinah daughter of Jacob; he loved the girl, and spoke tenderly to her. ⁴So Shechem spoke to his father Hamor, saying, "Get me this girl to be my wife."

5 Now Jacob heard that Shechemᵈ had defiled his daughter Dinah; but his sons were with his cattle in the field, so Jacob held his peace until they came. ⁶And Hamor the father of Shechem went out to Jacob to speak with him, ⁷just as the sons of Jacob came in from the field. When they heard of it, the men were indignant and very angry, because he had committed an outrage in Israel by lying with Jacob's daughter, for such a thing ought not to be done.

8 But Hamor spoke with them, saying, "The heart of my son Shechem longs for your daughter; please give her to him in marriage. ⁹Make marriages with us; give your daughters to us, and take our daughters for yourselves. ¹⁰You shall live with us; and the land shall be open to you; live and trade in it, and get property in it." ¹¹Shechem also said to her father and to her brothers, "Let me find favor with you, and whatever you say to me I will give. ¹²Put the marriage present and gift as high as you like, and I will give whatever you ask me; only give me the girl to be my wife."

13 The sons of Jacob answered Shechem and his father Hamor deceitfully, because he had defiled their sister Dinah. ¹⁴They said to them, "We cannot do this thing, to give our sister to one who is uncircumcised, for that would be a disgrace to us. ¹⁵Only on this condition will we consent to you: that you will become as we are and every male among you be circumcised. ¹⁶Then we will give our daughters to you, and we will take your daughters for ourselves, and we will live among you and become one people. ¹⁷But if you will not listen to us and be circumcised, then we will take our daughter and be gone."

18 Their words pleased Hamor and Hamor's son Shechem. ¹⁹And the young man did not delay to do the thing, because he was delighted with Jacob's daughter. Now he was the most honored of all his family. ²⁰So Hamor and his son Shechem came to the gate of their city and spoke to the men of their city, saying, ²¹"These people are friendly with us; let them live in the land and trade in it, for the land is large enough for them; let us take their daughters in marriage, and let us give them our daughters. ²²Only on this condition will they agree to live among us, to become one people: that every male among us be circumcised as they are circumcised. ²³Will not their livestock, their prop-

ᵃ 33.17 That is Booths   ᵇ 33.19 Heb one hundred qesitah   ᶜ 33.20 That is God, the God of Israel   ᵈ 34.5 Heb he

erty, and all their animals be ours? Only let us agree with them, and they will live among us." ²⁴And all who went out of the city gate heeded Hamor and his son Shechem; and every male was circumcised, all who went out of the gate of his city.

DINAH'S BROTHERS AVENGE THEIR SISTER

25 On the third day, when they were still in pain, two of the sons of Jacob, Simeon and Levi, Dinah's brothers, took their swords and came against the city unawares, and killed all the males. ²⁶They killed Hamor and his son Shechem with the sword, and took Dinah out of Shechem's house, and went away. ²⁷And the other sons of Jacob came upon the slain, and plundered the city, because their sister had been defiled. ²⁸They took their flocks and their herds, their donkeys, and whatever was in the city and in the field. ²⁹All their wealth, all their little ones and their wives, all that was in the houses, they captured and made their prey. ³⁰Then Jacob said to Simeon and Levi, "You have brought trouble on me by making me odious to the inhabitants of the land, the Canaanites and the Perizzites; my numbers are few, and if they gather themselves against me and attack me, I shall be destroyed, both I and my household." ³¹But they said, "Should our sister be treated like a whore?"

JACOB RETURNS TO BETHEL

35 God said to Jacob, "Arise, go up to Bethel, and settle there. Make an altar there to the God who appeared to you when you fled from your brother Esau." ²So Jacob said to his household and to all who were with him, "Put away the foreign gods that are among you, and purify yourselves, and change your clothes; ³then come, let us go up to Bethel, that I may make an altar there to the God who answered me in the day of my distress and has been with me wherever I have gone." ⁴So they gave to Jacob all the foreign gods that they had, and the rings that were in

their ears; and Jacob hid them under the oak that was near Shechem.

5 As they journeyed, a terror from God fell upon the cities all around them, so that no one pursued them. ⁶Jacob came to Luz (that is, Bethel), which is in the land of Canaan, he and all the people who were with him, ⁷and there he built an altar and called the place El-bethel,ᵃ because it was there that God had revealed himself to him when he fled from his brother. ⁸And Deborah, Rebekah's nurse, died, and she was buried under an oak below Bethel. So it was called Allon-bacuth.ᵇ

9 God appeared to Jacob again when he came from Paddan-aram, and he blessed him. ¹⁰God said to him, "Your name is Jacob; no longer shall you be called Jacob, but Israel shall be your name." So he was called Israel. ¹¹God said to him, "I am God Almighty:ᶜ be fruitful and multiply; a nation and a company of nations shall come from you, and kings shall spring from you. ¹²The land that I gave to Abraham and Isaac I will give to you, and I will give the land to your offspring after you." ¹³Then God went up from him at the place where he had spoken with him. ¹⁴Jacob set up a pillar in the place where he had spoken with him, a pillar of stone; and he poured out a drink offering on it, and poured oil on it. ¹⁵So Jacob called the place where God had spoken with him Bethel.

THE BIRTH OF BENJAMIN AND THE DEATH OF RACHEL

16 Then they journeyed from Bethel; and when they were still some distance from Ephrath, Rachel was in childbirth, and she had hard labor. ¹⁷When she was in her hard labor, the midwife said to her, "Do not be afraid; for now you will have another son." ¹⁸As her soul was departing (for she died), she named him Ben-oni;ᵈ but his father called him Benjamin.ᵉ ¹⁹So Rachel died,

ᵃ 35.7 That is God of Bethel   ᵇ 35.8 That is Oak of weeping   ᶜ 35.11 Traditional rendering of Heb El Shaddai   ᵈ 35.18 That is Son of my sorrow   ᵉ 35.18 That is Son of the right hand or Son of the South and she was buried on the way to Ephrath (that is, Bethlehem), 20and Jacob set up a pillar at her grave; it is the pillar of Rachel's tomb, which is there to this day. 21Israel journeyed on, and pitched his tent beyond the tower of Eder.

22 While Israel lived in that land, Reuben went and lay with Bilhah his father's concubine; and Israel heard of it.

Now the sons of Jacob were twelve. 23The sons of Leah: Reuben (Jacob's firstborn), Simeon, Levi, Judah, Issachar, and Zebulun. 24The sons of Rachel: Joseph and Benjamin. 25The sons of Bilhah, Rachel's maid: Dan and Naphtali. 26The sons of Zilpah, Leah's maid: Gad and Asher. These were the sons of Jacob who were born to him in Paddan-aram.

THE DEATH OF ISAAC

27 Jacob came to his father Isaac at Mamre, or Kiriath-arba (that is, Hebron), where Abraham and Isaac had resided as aliens. 28Now the days of Isaac were one hundred eighty years. 29And Isaac breathed his last; he died and was gathered to his people, old and full of days; and his sons Esau and Jacob buried him.

ESAU'S DESCENDANTS

36 These are the descendants of Esau (that is, Edom). 2Esau took his wives from the Canaanites: Adah daughter of Elon the Hittite, Oholibamah daughter of Anah sona of Zibeon the Hivite, 3and Basemath, Ishmael's daughter, sister of Nebaioth. 4Adah bore Eliphaz to Esau; Basemath bore Reuel; 5and Oholibamah bore Jeush, Jalam, and Korah. These are the sons of Esau who were born to him in the land of Canaan.

6 Then Esau took his wives, his sons, his daughters, and all the members of his household, his cattle, all his livestock, and all the property he had acquired in the land of Canaan; and he moved to a land some distance from his brother Jacob. 7For their possessions were too great for them to live together; the land where they were staying could

not support them because of their livestock. 8So Esau settled in the hill country of Seir; Esau is Edom.

9 These are the descendants of Esau, ancestor of the Edomites, in the hill country of Seir. 10These are the names of Esau's sons: Eliphaz son of Adah the wife of Esau; Reuel, the son of Esau's wife Basemath. 11The sons of Eliphaz were Teman, Omar, Zepho, Gatam, and Kenaz. 12(Timna was a concubine of Eliphaz, Esau's son; she bore Amalek to Eliphaz.) These were the sons of Adah, Esau's wife. 13These were the sons of Reuel: Nahath, Zerah, Shammah, and Mizzah. These were the sons of Esau's wife, Basemath. 14These were the sons of Esau's wife Oholibamah, daughter of Anah sonb of Zibeon: she bore to Esau Jeush, Jalam, and Korah.

CLANS AND KINGS OF EDOM

15 These are the clansc of the sons of Esau. The sons of Eliphaz the firstborn of Esau: the clansc Teman, Omar, Zepho, Kenaz, 16Korah, Gatam, and Amalek; these are the clansc of Eliphaz in the land of Edom; they are the sons of Adah. 17These are the sons of Esau's son Reuel: the clansc Nahath, Zerah, Shammah, and Mizzah; these are the clansc of Reuel in the land of Edom; they are the sons of Esau's wife Basemath. 18These are the sons of Esau's wife Oholibamah: the clansc Jeush, Jalam, and Korah; these are the clansc born of Esau's wife Oholibamah, the daughter of Anah. 19These are the sons of Esau (that is, Edom), and these are their clans.c

20 These are the sons of Seir the Horite, the inhabitants of the land: Lotan, Shobal, Zibeon, Anah, 21Dishon, Ezer, and Dishan; these are the clansc of the Horites, the sons of Seir in the land of Edom. 22The sons of Lotan were Hori and Heman; and Lotan's sister was Timna. 23These are the sons of Shobal: Alvan, Manahath, Ebal, Shepho, and Onam. 24These are the sons of Zib-

a 36.2 Sam Gk Syr: Heb daughter b 36.14 Gk Syr: Heb daughter c 36.15,16,17,18,19,21 Or chiefs

eon: Aiah and Anah; he is the Anah who found the springs^a in the wilderness, as he pastured the donkeys of his father Zibeon. ²⁵These are the children of Anah: Dishon and Oholibamah daughter of Anah. ²⁶These are the sons of Dishon: Hemdan, Eshban, Ithran, and Cheran. ²⁷These are the sons of Ezer: Bilhan, Zaavan, and Akan. ²⁸These are the sons of Dishan: Uz and Aran. ²⁹These are the clans^b of the Horites: the clans^b Lotan, Shobal, Zibeon, Anah, ³⁰Dishon, Ezer, and Dishan; these are the clans^b of the Horites, clan by clan^c in the land of Seir.

³¹These are the kings who reigned in the land of Edom, before any king reigned over the Israelites. ³²Bela son of Beor reigned in Edom, the name of his city being Dinhabah. ³³Bela died, and Jobab son of Zerah of Bozrah succeeded him as king. ³⁴Jobab died, and Husham of the land of the Temanites succeeded him as king. ³⁵Husham died, and Hadad son of Bedad, who defeated Midian in the country of Moab, succeeded him as king, the name of his city being Avith. ³⁶Hadad died, and Samlah of Masrekah succeeded him as king. ³⁷Samlah died, and Shaul of Rehoboth on the Euphrates succeeded him as king. ³⁸Shaul died, and Baal-hanan son of Achbor succeeded him as king. ³⁹Baal-hanan son of Achbor died, and Hadar succeeded him as king, the name of his city being Pau; his wife's name was Mehetabel, the daughter of Matred, daughter of Me-zahab.

⁴⁰These are the names of the clans^b of Esau, according to their families and their localities by their names: the clans^b Timna, Alvah, Jetheth, ⁴¹Oholibamah, Elah, Pinon, ⁴²Kenaz, Teman, Mibzar, ⁴³Magdiel, and Iram; these are the clans^b of Edom (that is, Esau, the father of Edom), according to their settlements in the land that they held.

JOSEPH DREAMS OF GREATNESS

37 Jacob settled in the land where his father had lived as an alien, the land of Canaan. ²This is the story of the family of Jacob.

Joseph, being seventeen years old, was shepherding the flock with his brothers; he was a helper to the sons of Bilhah and Zilpah, his father's wives; and Joseph brought a bad report of them to their father. ³Now Israel loved Joseph more than any other of his children, because he was the son of his old age; and he had made him a long robe with sleeves.^d ⁴But when his brothers saw that their father loved him more than all his brothers, they hated him, and could not speak peaceably to him.

⁵Once Joseph had a dream, and when he told it to his brothers, they hated him even more. ⁶He said to them, "Listen to this dream that I dreamed. ⁷There we were, binding sheaves in the field. Suddenly my sheaf rose and stood upright; then your sheaves gathered around it, and bowed down to my sheaf." ⁸His brothers said to him, "Are you indeed to reign over us? Are you indeed to have dominion over us?" So they hated him even more because of his dreams and his words.

⁹He had another dream, and told it to his brothers, saying, "Look, I have had another dream: the sun, the moon, and eleven stars were bowing down to me." ¹⁰But when he told it to his father and to his brothers, his father rebuked him, and said to him, "What kind of dream is this that you have had? Shall we indeed come, I and your mother and your brothers, and bow to the ground before you?" ¹¹So his brothers were jealous of him, but his father kept the matter in mind.

JOSEPH IS SOLD BY HIS BROTHERS

¹²Now his brothers went to pasture their father's flock near Shechem. ¹³And Israel said to Joseph, "Are not your brothers pasturing the flock at Shechem? Come, I will send you to them." He answered, "Here I am." ¹⁴So he said to him, "Go now,

^a 36.24 Meaning of Heb uncertain
^b 36.29,30,40,43 Or chiefs ^c 36.30 Or chief by chief ^d 37.3 Traditional rendering (compare Gk): a coat of many colors; meaning of Heb uncertain

see if it is well with your brothers and with the flock; and bring word back to me." So he sent him from the valley of Hebron.

He came to Shechem, [15]and a man found him wandering in the fields; the man asked him, "What are you seeking?" [16]"I am seeking my brothers," he said; "tell me, please, where they are pasturing the flock." [17]The man said, "They have gone away, for I heard them say, 'Let us go to Dothan.'" So Joseph went after his brothers, and found them at Dothan. [18]They saw him from a distance, and before he came near to them, they conspired to kill him. [19]They said to one another, "Here comes this dreamer. [20]Come now, let us kill him and throw him into one of the pits; then we shall say that a wild animal has devoured him, and we shall see what will become of his dreams." [21]But when Reuben heard it, he delivered him out of their hands, saying, "Let us not take his life." [22]Reuben said to them, "Shed no blood; throw him into this pit here in the wilderness, but lay no hand on him"—that he might rescue him out of their hand and restore him to his father. [23]So when Joseph came to his brothers, they stripped him of his robe, the long robe with sleeves[a] that he wore; [24]and they took him and threw him into a pit. The pit was empty; there was no water in it.

25 Then they sat down to eat; and looking up they saw a caravan of Ishmaelites coming from Gilead, with their camels carrying gum, balm, and resin, on their way to carry it down to Egypt. [26]Then Judah said to his brothers, "What profit is it if we kill our brother and conceal his blood? [27]Come, let us sell him to the Ishmaelites, and not lay our hands on him, for he is our brother, our own flesh." And his brothers agreed. [28]When some Midianite traders passed by, they drew Joseph up, lifting him out of the pit, and sold him to the Ishmaelites for twenty pieces of silver. And they took Joseph to Egypt.

29 When Reuben returned to the pit and saw that Joseph was not in the pit, he tore his clothes. [30]He returned to his brothers, and said, "The boy is gone; and I, where can I turn?" [31]Then they took Joseph's robe, slaughtered a goat, and dipped the robe in the blood. [32]They had the long robe with sleeves[a] taken to their father, and they said, "This we have found; see now whether it is your son's robe or not." [33]He recognized it, and said, "It is my son's robe! A wild animal has devoured him; Joseph is without doubt torn to pieces." [34]Then Jacob tore his garments, and put sackcloth on his loins, and mourned for his son many days. [35]All his sons and all his daughters sought to comfort him; but he refused to be comforted, and said, "No, I shall go down to Sheol to my son, mourning." Thus his father bewailed him. [36]Meanwhile the Midianites had sold him in Egypt to Potiphar, one of Pharaoh's officials, the captain of the guard.

JUDAH AND TAMAR

38 It happened at that time that Judah went down from his brothers and settled near a certain Adullamite whose name was Hirah. [2]There Judah saw the daughter of a certain Canaanite whose name was Shua; he married her and went in to her. [3]She conceived and bore a son; and he named him Er. [4]Again she conceived and bore a son whom she named Onan. [5]Yet again she bore a son, and she named him Shelah. She[b] was in Chezib when she bore him. [6]Judah took a wife for Er his firstborn; her name was Tamar. [7]But Er, Judah's firstborn, was wicked in the sight of the LORD, and the LORD put him to death. [8]Then Judah said to Onan, "Go in to your brother's wife and perform the duty of a brother-in-law to her; raise up offspring for your brother." [9]But since Onan knew that the offspring would not be his, he spilled his semen on the ground whenever he went in to his brother's wife, so that he would not give offspring to his brother. [10]What he did was displeasing in the sight of the LORD, and he put him to death also.

[a] 37.23,32 See note on 37.3   [b] 38.5 Gk: Heb He

[11]Then Judah said to his daughter-in-law Tamar, "Remain a widow in your father's house until my son Shelah grows up"—for he feared that he too would die, like his brothers. So Tamar went to live in her father's house.

12 In course of time the wife of Judah, Shua's daughter, died; when Judah's time of mourning was over,[a] he went up to Timnah to his sheep-shearers, he and his friend Hirah the Adullamite. [13]When Tamar was told, "Your father-in-law is going up to Timnah to shear his sheep," [14]she put off her widow's garments, put on a veil, wrapped herself up, and sat down at the entrance to Enaim, which is on the road to Timnah. She saw that Shelah was grown up, yet she had not been given to him in marriage. [15]When Judah saw her, he thought her to be a prostitute, for she had covered her face. [16]He went over to her at the roadside, and said, "Come, let me come in to you," for he did not know that she was his daughter-in-law. She said, "What will you give me, that you may come in to me?" [17]He answered, "I will send you a kid from the flock." And she said, "Only if you give me a pledge, until you send it." [18]He said, "What pledge shall I give you?" She replied, "Your signet and your cord, and the staff that is in your hand." So he gave them to her, and went in to her, and she conceived by him. [19]Then she got up and went away, and taking off her veil she put on the garments of her widowhood.

20 When Judah sent the kid by his friend the Adullamite, to recover the pledge from the woman, he could not find her. [21]He asked the townspeople, "Where is the temple prostitute who was at Enaim by the wayside?" But they said, "No prostitute has been here." [22]So he returned to Judah, and said, "I have not found her; moreover the townspeople said, 'No prostitute has been here.'" [23]Judah replied, "Let her keep the things as her own, otherwise we will be laughed at; you see, I sent this kid, and you could not find her."

24 About three months later Judah was told, "Your daughter-in-law Tamar has played the whore; more-over she is pregnant as a result of whoredom." And Judah said, "Bring her out, and let her be burned." [25]As she was being brought out, she sent word to her father-in-law, "It was the owner of these who made me pregnant." And she said, "Take note, please, whose these are, the signet and the cord and the staff." [26]Then Judah acknowledged them and said, "She is more in the right than I, since I did not give her to my son Shelah." And he did not lie with her again.

27 When the time of her delivery came, there were twins in her womb. [28]While she was in labor, one put out a hand; and the midwife took and bound on his hand a crimson thread, saying, "This one came out first." [29]But just then he drew back his hand, and out came his brother; and she said, "What a breach you have made for yourself!" Therefore he was named Perez.[b] [30]Afterward his brother came out with the crimson thread on his hand; and he was named Zerah.[c]

SIN SOMETIMES LOOKS

LIKE GLORY AND HONOR,

BUT ENDS IN SHAME,

FEAR AND LONELINESS.

JOSEPH AND POTIPHAR'S WIFE

39 Now Joseph was taken down to Egypt, and Potiphar, an officer of Pharaoh, the captain of the guard, an Egyptian, bought him from the Ishmaelites who had brought him down there. [2]The LORD was with Joseph, and he became a successful man; he was in the house of his Egyptian master. [3]His master saw that the LORD was with him, and that the LORD caused all that he did to prosper in his hands. [4]So

[a] 38.12 Heb *when Judah was comforted*
[b] 38.29 That is *A breach* [c] 38.30 That is *Brightness*; perhaps alluding to the crimson thread

FAVOR

His master saw that the LORD was with him, and that the LORD
caused all that he did to prosper in his hands.

—Genesis 39.3

Joseph, Jacob's son, is one of the most highly regarded heroes in the Bible. He endured great hardship and mistreatment; his life was also marked by great success and blessings. What was it about him that resulted in these achievements and good fortune? Undoubtedly, much of it came from his clear commitments to those who trusted him with responsibility, but even more important was his commitment to follow the ways of God.

Joseph's commitment to his superiors is seen in the way he faithfully managed Potiphar's household. Moreover, he refused to submit to the overtures of Potiphar's wife and commit adultery with her. Then, when Joseph was imprisoned, he demonstrated loyalty to his superiors by managing the prison for them. Finally, when Joseph was given responsibility as second-in-command for all Egypt, he faithfully oversaw the stockpiling of grain for the years of famine that were to come. His commitment to God is evident in his dedication to obey regardless of the temptations placed in his path or the consequences he suffered for his faithfulness.

The examination of Joseph's life lends itself to reflecting on our own. Every day we lay foundations for our lives. We establish standards for ourselves that will guide our actions and decisions for years to come. What are those values, and where did they originate? For most of us, our parents provided the first and most significant source of standards for life. Church and Bible study are other important sources of beliefs that guide us in our decisions amid life's many ups and downs. Educators, laws and the collective attitude of our society also affect how we think and act.

Earthly standards are fallible and subject to change. Our parents, well-meaning as they may be, sometimes hold beliefs incompatible with the teachings of Jesus Christ and pass them on to us. The same is true of our teachers. Some of the laws of our nation, such as the laws permitting slavery and later enforcing racial segregation, were incredibly flawed and needed to be changed. Even pastors can have wrong perceptions about life that could unintentionally mislead their congregations. Ultimately, our greatest source of principles should come from Jesus Christ himself. He represented God perfectly for us on earth, and we are called to imitate him in our own journeys. All other sources of standards are imperfect, but Christ's ideals are absolute and unwavering. All who build their lives on the teachings of Jesus lay a firm foundation that will never fail (see Matthew 7.24–27).

Going Deeper

- Can you think of moral or ethical standards you used to hold that now you believe to be erroneous? What led you to realize those ideas were in error?
- What are some important and practical standards Jesus has taught you that guide you in tough or uncertain times?

Joseph found favor in his sight and attended him; he made him overseer of his house and put him in charge of all that he had. 5From the time that he made him overseer in his house and over all that he had, the LORD blessed the Egyptian's house for Joseph's sake; the blessing of the LORD was on all that he had, in house and field. 6So he left all that he had in Joseph's charge; and, with him there, he had no concern for anything but the food that he ate.

Now Joseph was handsome and good-looking. 7And after a time his master's wife cast her eyes on Joseph and said, "Lie with me." 8But he refused and said to his master's wife, "Look, with me here, my master has no concern about anything in the house, and he has put everything that he has in my hand. 9He is not greater in this house than I am, nor has he kept back anything from me except yourself, because you are his wife. How then could I do this great wickedness, and sin against God?" 10And although she spoke to Joseph day after day, he would not consent to lie beside her or to be with her. 11One day, however, when he went into the house to do his work, and while no one else was in the house, 12she caught hold of his garment, saying, "Lie with me!" But he left his garment in her hand, and fled and ran outside. 13When she saw that he had left his garment in her hand and had fled outside, 14she called out to the members of her household and said to them, "See, my husbanda has brought among us a Hebrew to insult us! He came in to me to lie with me, and I cried out with a loud voice; 15and when he heard me raise my voice and cry out, he left his garment beside me, and fled outside." 16Then she kept his garment by her until his master came home, 17and she told him the same story, saying, "The Hebrew servant, whom you have brought among us, came in to me to insult me; 18but as soon as I raised my voice and cried out, he left his garment beside me, and fled outside."

19 When his master heard the words that his wife spoke to him, saying,

"This is the way your servant treated me," he became enraged. 20And Joseph's master took him and put him into the prison, the place where the king's prisoners were confined; he remained there in prison. 21But the LORD was with Joseph and showed him steadfast love; he gave him favor in the sight of the chief jailer. 22The chief jailer committed to Joseph's care all the prisoners who were in the prison, and whatever was done there, he was the one who did it. 23The chief jailer paid no heed to anything that was in Joseph's care, because the LORD was with him; and whatever he did, the LORD made it prosper.

THE DREAMS OF TWO PRISONERS

40 Some time after this, the cupbearer of the king of Egypt and his baker offended their lord the king of Egypt. 2Pharaoh was angry with his two officers, the chief cupbearer and the chief baker, 3and he put them in custody in the house of the captain of the guard, in the prison where Joseph was confined. 4The captain of the guard charged Joseph with them, and he waited on them; and they continued for some time in custody. 5One night they both dreamed—the cupbearer and the baker of the king of Egypt, who were confined in the prison—each his own dream, and each dream with its own meaning. 6When Joseph came to them in the morning, he saw that they were troubled. 7So he asked Pharaoh's officers, who were with him in custody in his master's house, "Why are your faces downcast today?" 8They said to him, "We have had dreams, and there is no one to interpret them." And Joseph said to them, "Do not interpretations belong to God? Please tell them to me."

9 So the chief cupbearer told his dream to Joseph, and said to him, "In my dream there was a vine before me, 10and on the vine there were three branches. As soon as it budded, its blossoms came out and the clusters

a 39.14 Heb he

ripened into grapes. [11]Pharaoh's cup was in my hand; and I took the grapes and pressed them into Pharaoh's cup, and placed the cup in Pharaoh's hand." [12]Then Joseph said to him, "This is its interpretation: the three branches are three days; [13]within three days Pharaoh will lift up your head and restore you to your office; and you shall place Pharaoh's cup in his hand, just as you used to do when you were his cupbearer. [14]But remember me when it is well with you; please do me the kindness to make mention of me to Pharaoh, and so get me out of this place. [15]For in fact I was stolen out of the land of the Hebrews; and here also I have done nothing that they should have put me into the dungeon."

[16]When the chief baker saw that the interpretation was favorable, he said to Joseph, "I also had a dream: there were three cake baskets on my head, [17]and in the uppermost basket there were all sorts of baked food for Pharaoh, but the birds were eating it out of the basket on my head." [18]And Joseph answered, "This is its interpretation: the three baskets are three days; [19]within three days Pharaoh will lift up your head—from you!—and hang you on a pole; and the birds will eat the flesh from you."

[20]On the third day, which was Pharaoh's birthday, he made a feast for all his servants, and lifted up the head of the chief cupbearer and the head of the chief baker among his servants. [21]He restored the chief cupbearer to his cupbearing, and he placed the cup in Pharaoh's hand; [22]but the chief baker he hanged, just as Joseph had interpreted to them. [23]Yet the chief cupbearer did not remember Joseph, but forgot him.

JOSEPH INTERPRETS PHARAOH'S DREAM

41 After two whole years, Pharaoh dreamed that he was standing by the Nile, [2]and there came up out of the Nile seven sleek and fat cows, and they grazed in the reed grass. [3]Then seven other cows, ugly and thin, came up out of the Nile after them, and stood by the other cows on the bank of the Nile. [4]The ugly and thin cows ate up the seven sleek and fat cows. And Pharaoh awoke. [5]Then he fell asleep and dreamed a second time; seven ears of grain, plump and good, were growing on one stalk. [6]Then seven ears, thin and blighted by the east wind, sprouted after them. [7]The thin ears swallowed up the seven plump and full ears. Pharaoh awoke, and it was a dream. [8]In the morning his spirit was troubled; so he sent and called for all the magicians of Egypt and all its wise men. Pharaoh told them his dreams, but there was no one who could interpret them to Pharaoh.

[9]Then the chief cupbearer said to Pharaoh, "I remember my faults today. [10]Once Pharaoh was angry with his servants, and put me and the chief baker in custody in the house of the captain of the guard. [11]We dreamed on the same night, he and I, each having a dream with its own meaning. [12]A young Hebrew was there with us, a servant of the captain of the guard. When we told him, he interpreted our dreams to us, giving an interpretation to each according to his dream. [13]As he interpreted to us, so it turned out; I was restored to my office, and the baker was hanged."

[14]Then Pharaoh sent for Joseph, and he was hurriedly brought out of the dungeon. When he had shaved himself and changed his clothes, he came in before Pharaoh. [15]And Pharaoh said to Joseph, "I have had a dream, and there is no one who can interpret it. I have heard it said of you that when you hear a dream you can interpret it." [16]Joseph answered Pharaoh, "It is not I; God will give Pharaoh a favorable answer." [17]Then Pharaoh said to Joseph, "In my dream I was standing on the banks of the Nile; [18]and seven cows, fat and sleek, came up out of the Nile and fed in the reed grass. [19]Then seven other cows came up after them, poor, very ugly, and thin. Never had I seen such ugly ones in all the land of Egypt. [20]The thin and ugly cows ate up the first seven fat cows, [21]but when they had eaten them no one would have known that they had

done so, for they were still as ugly as before. Then I awoke. [22]I fell asleep a second time[a] and I saw in my dream seven ears of grain, full and good, growing on one stalk, [23]and seven ears, withered, thin, and blighted by the east wind, sprouting after them; [24]and the thin ears swallowed up the seven good ears. But when I told it to the magicians, there was no one who could explain it to me."

[25] Then Joseph said to Pharaoh, "Pharaoh's dreams are one and the same; God has revealed to Pharaoh what he is about to do. [26]The seven good cows are seven years, and the seven good ears are seven years; the dreams are one. [27]The seven lean and ugly cows that came up after them are seven years, as are the seven empty ears blighted by the east wind. They are seven years of famine. [28]It is as I told Pharaoh; God has shown to Pharaoh what he is about to do. [29]There will come seven years of great plenty throughout all the land of Egypt. [30]After them there will arise seven years of famine, and all the plenty will be forgotten in the land of Egypt; the famine will consume the land. [31]The plenty will no longer be known in the land because of the famine that will follow, for it will be very grievous. [32]And the doubling of Pharaoh's dream means that the thing is fixed by God, and God will shortly bring it about. [33]Now therefore let Pharaoh select a man who is discerning and wise, and set him over the land of Egypt. [34]Let Pharaoh proceed to appoint overseers over the land, and take one-fifth of the produce of the land of Egypt during the seven plenteous years. [35]Let them gather all the food of these good years that are coming, and lay up grain under the authority of Pharaoh for food in the cities, and let them keep it. [36]That food shall be a reserve for the land against the seven years of famine that are to befall the land of Egypt, so that the land may not perish through the famine."

JOSEPH'S RISE TO POWER

[37] The proposal pleased Pharaoh and all his servants. [38]Pharaoh said to his servants, "Can we find anyone else like this—one in whom is the spirit of God?" [39]So Pharaoh said to Joseph, "Since God has shown you all this, there is no one so discerning and wise as you. [40]You shall be over my house, and all my people shall order themselves as you command; only with regard to the throne will I be greater than you." [41]And Pharaoh said to Joseph, "See, I have set you over all the land of Egypt." [42]Removing his signet ring from his hand, Pharaoh put it on Joseph's hand; he arrayed him in garments of fine linen, and put a gold chain around his neck. [43]He had him ride in the chariot of his second-in-command; and they cried out in front of him, "Bow the knee!"[b] Thus he set him over all the land of Egypt. [44]Moreover Pharaoh said to Joseph, "I am Pharaoh, and without your consent no one shall lift up hand or foot in all the land of Egypt." [45]Pharaoh gave Joseph the name Zaphenath-paneah; and he gave him Asenath daughter of Potiphera, priest of On, as his wife. Thus Joseph gained authority over the land of Egypt.

[46] Joseph was thirty years old when he entered the service of Pharaoh king of Egypt. And Joseph went out from the presence of Pharaoh, and went through all the land of Egypt. [47]During the seven plenteous years the earth produced abundantly. [48]He gathered up all the food of the seven years when there was plenty[c] in the land of Egypt, and stored up food in the cities; he stored up in every city the food from the fields around it. [49]So Joseph stored up grain in such abundance—like the sand of the sea—that he stopped measuring it; it was beyond measure.

[50] Before the years of famine came, Joseph had two sons, whom Asenath daughter of Potiphera, priest of On, bore to him. [51]Joseph

[a] 41.22 Gk Syr Vg: Heb lacks *I fell asleep a second time* [b] 41.43 *Abrek*, apparently an Egyptian word similar in sound to the Hebrew word meaning *to kneel* [c] 41.48 Sam Gk: MT *the seven years that were*

POSITIVE POWER

Pharaoh said to Joseph, "Since God has shown you all this, there is no one so discerning and wise as you . . . all my people shall order themselves as you command."

—Genesis 41.39–40

As former President of the United States, I have known tremendous power. But how should power like that be used? To dominate other nations and impose our will on them? To promote our own interests? No, power always should be used to promote peace and justice and to help others. Whether a person is the CEO of a Fortune 500 company or a peanut farmer from South Georgia, they should always strive to use the power and influence that they possess to treat others fairly, to alleviate suffering and to stop people from harming others.

Joseph had a tremendous amount of authority after Pharaoh elevated him to a governing position in Egypt, the superpower nation of the time. Joseph could have used his influence selfishly, but instead he chose to save many lives throughout the world (see Genesis 50.20). God enabled Joseph to interpret Pharaoh's dream and foresee the coming years of plenty and the years of famine that were to follow. Then God empowered Joseph to supervise the storage of grain for the difficult times ahead. When the shortage finally did come and many people—including his brothers— were begging for food, Joseph could have chosen to avenge himself for the terrible mistreatment he had suffered at his sibling's hands. But Joseph chose to provide his brothers with food, and more significantly, he chose to reconcile with them and forgive them. In all of this, Joseph recognized that God is sovereign and can use less than ideal situations for good.

Joseph was not perfect. For instance, while Joseph was in Egypt, he renounced his heritage altogether. He married the daughter of an Egyptian priest and gave one of his sons a name to commemorate the fact that he had forgotten all his troubles and "all [his] father's house" (Genesis 41.51). Apparently, during those days he never inquired if his father was still alive. Yet God still used Joseph, an imperfect person, to do great things to help others.

Like Joseph, with God's Spirit present within us, we can promote justice and alleviate the suffering of our fellow humans. Instead of using whatever power we have to serve ourselves and exploit others, we can promote fairness. Even more, we can extend ourselves in agape love—that is, self-sacrificial, dedicated love for others, regardless of who they are or how they treat us. In doing so, we emulate the love of our Savior, Jesus Christ, who gave his life for us.

Going Deeper

- Name three areas in which you possess power or influence. What are some ways you use that influence to benefit others? How can you do so even more?
- What are some excuses you give for why God cannot use you to work good things in others' lives? How do those objections match up against examples of God's willingness to use imperfect people to do good things for others?

named the firstborn Manasseh,[a] "For," he said, "God has made me forget all my hardship and all my father's house." 52The second he named Ephraim,[b] "For God has made me fruitful in the land of my misfortunes."

53 The seven years of plenty that prevailed in the land of Egypt came to an end; 54and the seven years of famine began to come, just as Joseph had said. There was famine in every country, but throughout the land of Egypt there was bread. 55When all the land of Egypt was famished, the people cried to Pharaoh for bread. Pharaoh said to all the Egyptians, "Go to Joseph; what he says to you, do." 56And since the famine had spread over all the land, Joseph opened all the storehouses,[c] and sold to the Egyptians, for the famine was severe in the land of Egypt. 57Moreover, all the world came to Joseph in Egypt to buy grain, because the famine became severe throughout the world.

JOSEPH'S BROTHERS GO TO EGYPT

42 When Jacob learned that there was grain in Egypt, he said to his sons, "Why do you keep looking at one another? 2I have heard," he said, "that there is grain in Egypt; go down and buy grain for us there, that we may live and not die." 3So ten of Joseph's brothers went down to buy grain in Egypt. 4But Jacob did not send Joseph's brother Benjamin with his brothers, for he feared that harm might come to him. 5Thus the sons of Israel were among the other people who came to buy grain, for the famine had reached the land of Canaan.

6 Now Joseph was governor over the land; it was he who sold to all the people of the land. And Joseph's brothers came and bowed themselves before him with their faces to the ground. 7When Joseph saw his brothers, he recognized them, but he treated them like strangers and spoke harshly to them. "Where do you come from?" he said. They said, "From the land of Canaan, to buy food." 8Although Joseph had recognized his brothers, they did not recognize him. 9Joseph also remembered the dreams that he had dreamed about them. He said to them, "You are spies; you have come to see the nakedness of the land!" 10They said to him, "No, my lord; your servants have come to buy food. 11We are all sons of one man; we are honest men; your servants have never been spies." 12But he said to them, "No, you have come to see the nakedness of the land!" 13They said, "We, your servants, are twelve brothers, the sons of a certain man in the land of Canaan; the youngest, however, is now with our father, and one is no more." 14But Joseph said to them, "It is just as I have said to you; you are spies! 15Here is how you shall be tested: as Pharaoh lives, you shall not leave this place unless your youngest brother comes here! 16Let one of you go and bring your brother, while the rest of you remain in prison, in order that your words may be tested, whether there is truth in you; or else, as Pharaoh lives, surely you are spies." 17And he put them all together in prison for three days.

18 On the third day Joseph said to them, "Do this and you will live, for I fear God: 19if you are honest men, let one of your brothers stay here where you are imprisoned. The rest of you shall go and carry grain for the famine of your households, 20and bring your youngest brother to me. Thus your words will be verified, and you shall not die." And they agreed to do so. 21They said to one another, "Alas, we are paying the penalty for what we did to our brother; we saw his anguish when he pleaded with us, but we would not listen. That is why this anguish has come upon us." 22Then Reuben answered them, "Did I not tell you not to wrong the boy? But you would not listen. So now there comes a reckoning for his blood." 23They did not know that Joseph

[a] 41.51 That is *Making to forget*
[b] 41.52 From a Hebrew word meaning *to be fruitful*   [c] 41.56 Gk Vg Compare Syr: Heb *opened all that was in* (or, *among*) *them*

understood them, since he spoke with them through an interpreter. 24He turned away from them and wept; then he returned and spoke to them. And he picked out Simeon and had him bound before their eyes. 25Joseph then gave orders to fill their bags with grain, to return every man's money to his sack, and to give them provisions for their journey. This was done for them.

JOSEPH'S BROTHERS RETURN TO CANAAN

26 They loaded their donkeys with their grain, and departed. 27When one of them opened his sack to give his donkey fodder at the lodging place, he saw his money at the top of the sack. 28He said to his brothers, "My money has been put back; here it is in my sack!" At this they lost heart and turned trembling to one another, saying, "What is this that God has done to us?"

29 When they came to their father Jacob in the land of Canaan, they told him all that had happened to them, saying, 30"The man, the lord of the land, spoke harshly to us, and charged us with spying on the land. 31But we said to him, 'We are honest men, we are not spies. 32We are twelve brothers, sons of our father; one is no more, and the youngest is now with our father in the land of Canaan.' 33Then the man, the lord of the land, said to us, 'By this I shall know that you are honest men: leave one of your brothers with me, take grain for the famine of your households, and go your way. 34Bring your youngest brother to me, and I shall know that you are not spies but honest men. Then I will release your brother to you, and you may trade in the land.'"

35 As they were emptying their sacks, there in each one's sack was his bag of money. When they and their father saw their bundles of money, they were dismayed. 36And their father Jacob said to them, "I am the one you have bereaved of children: Joseph is no more, and Simeon is no more, and now you would take Benjamin. All this has happened to me!" 37Then Reuben said to his father, "You may kill my two sons if I do not bring him back to you. Put him in my hands, and I will bring him back to you." 38But he said, "My son shall not go down with you, for his brother is dead, and he alone is left. If harm should come to him on the journey that you are to make, you would bring down my gray hairs with sorrow to Sheol."

THE BROTHERS COME AGAIN, BRINGING BENJAMIN

43 Now the famine was severe in the land. 2And when they had eaten up the grain that they had brought from Egypt, their father said to them, "Go again, buy us a little more food." 3But Judah said to him, "The man solemnly warned us, saying, 'You shall not see my face unless your brother is with you.' 4If you will send our brother with us, we will go down and buy you food; 5but if you will not send him, we will not go down, for the man said to us, 'You shall not see my face, unless your brother is with you.' " 6Israel said, "Why did you treat me so badly as to tell the man that you had another brother?" 7They replied, "The man questioned us carefully about ourselves and our kindred, saying, 'Is your father still alive? Have you another brother?' What we told him was in answer to these questions. Could we in any way know that he would say, 'Bring your brother down'?" 8Then Judah said to his father Israel, "Send the boy with me, and let us be on our way, so that we may live and not die—you and we and also our little ones. 9I myself will be surety for him; you can hold me accountable for him. If I do not bring him back to you and set him before you, then let me bear the blame forever. 10If we had not delayed, we would now have returned twice."

11 Then their father Israel said to them, "If it must be so, then do this: take some of the choice fruits of the land in your bags, and carry them down as a present to the man—a little balm and a little honey, gum,

resin, pistachio nuts, and almonds. ¹²Take double the money with you. Carry back with you the money that was returned in the top of your sacks; perhaps it was an oversight. ¹³Take your brother also, and be on your way again to the man; ¹⁴may God Almighty[a] grant you mercy before the man, so that he may send back your other brother and Benjamin. As for me, if I am bereaved of my children, I am bereaved." ¹⁵So the men took the present, and they took double the money with them, as well as Benjamin. Then they went on their way down to Egypt, and stood before Joseph.

16 When Joseph saw Benjamin with them, he said to the steward of his house, "Bring the men into the house, and slaughter an animal and make ready, for the men are to dine with me at noon." ¹⁷The man did as Joseph said, and brought the men to Joseph's house. ¹⁸Now the men were afraid because they were brought to Joseph's house, and they said, "It is because of the money, replaced in our sacks the first time, that we have been brought in, so that he may have an opportunity to fall upon us, to make slaves of us and take our donkeys." ¹⁹So they went up to the steward of Joseph's house and spoke with him at the entrance to the house. ²⁰They said, "Oh, my lord, we came down the first time to buy food; ²¹and when we came to the lodging place we opened our sacks, and there was each one's money in the top of his sack, our money in full weight. So we have brought it back with us. ²²Moreover we have brought down with us additional money to buy food. We do not know who put our money in our sacks." ²³He replied, "Rest assured, do not be afraid; your God and the God of your father must have put treasure in your sacks for you; I received your money." Then he brought Simeon out to them. ²⁴When the steward[b] had brought the men into Joseph's house, and given them water, and they had washed their feet, and when he had given their donkeys fodder, ²⁵they made the present

ready for Joseph's coming at noon, for they had heard that they would dine there.

26 When Joseph came home, they brought him the present that they had carried into the house, and bowed to the ground before him. ²⁷He inquired about their welfare, and said, "Is your father well, the old man of whom you spoke? Is he still alive?" ²⁸They said, "Your servant our father is well; he is still alive." And they bowed their heads and did obeisance. ²⁹Then he looked up and saw his brother Benjamin, his mother's son, and said, "Is this your youngest brother, of whom you spoke to me? God be gracious to you, my son!" ³⁰With that, Joseph hurried out, because he was overcome with affection for his brother, and he was about to weep. So he went into a private room and wept there. ³¹Then he washed his face and came out; and controlling himself he said, "Serve the meal." ³²They served him by himself, and them by themselves, and the Egyptians who ate with him by themselves, because the Egyptians could not eat with the Hebrews, for that is an abomination to the Egyptians. ³³When they were seated before him, the firstborn according to his birthright and the youngest according to his youth, the men looked at one another in amazement. ³⁴Portions were taken to them from Joseph's table, but Benjamin's portion was five times as much as any of theirs. So they drank and were merry with him.

JOSEPH DETAINS BENJAMIN

44 Then he commanded the steward of his house, "Fill the men's sacks with food, as much as they can carry, and put each man's money in the top of his sack. ²Put my cup, the silver cup, in the top of the sack of the youngest, with his money for the grain." And he did as Joseph told him. ³As soon as the morning was light, the men

---

[a] 43.14 Traditional rendering of Heb *El Shaddai*   [b] 43.24 Heb *the man*

were sent away with their donkeys. 4When they had gone only a short distance from the city, Joseph said to his steward, "Go, follow after the men; and when you overtake them, say to them, 'Why have you returned evil for good? Why have you stolen my silver cup?ᵃ 5Is it not from this that my lord drinks? Does he not indeed use it for divination? You have done wrong in doing this.' "

6When he overtook them, he repeated these words to them. 7They said to him, "Why does my lord speak such words as these? Far be it from your servants that they should do such a thing! 8Look, the money that we found at the top of our sacks, we brought back to you from the land of Canaan; why then would we steal silver or gold from your lord's house? 9Should it be found with any one of your servants, let him die; moreover the rest of us will become my lord's slaves." 10He said, "Even so; in accordance with your words, let it be: he with whom it is found shall become my slave, but the rest of you shall go free." 11Then each one quickly lowered his sack to the ground, and each opened his sack. 12He searched, beginning with the eldest and ending with the youngest; and the cup was found in Benjamin's sack. 13At this they tore their clothes. Then each one loaded his donkey, and they returned to the city.

14Judah and his brothers came to Joseph's house while he was still there; and they fell to the ground before him. 15Joseph said to them, "What deed is this that you have done? Do you not know that one such as I can practice divination?" 16And Judah said, "What can we say to my lord? What can we speak? How can we clear ourselves? God has found out the guilt of your servants; here we are then, my lord's slaves, both we and also the one in whose possession the cup has been found." 17But he said, "Far be it from me that I should do so! Only the one in whose possession the cup was found shall be my slave; but as for you, go up in peace to your father."

JUDAH PLEADS FOR BENJAMIN'S RELEASE

18Then Judah stepped up to him and said, "O my lord, let your servant please speak a word in my lord's ears, and do not be angry with your servant; for you are like Pharaoh himself. 19My lord asked his servants, saying, 'Have you a father or a brother?' 20And we said to my lord, 'We have a father, an old man, and a young brother, the child of his old age. His brother is dead; he alone is left of his mother's children, and his father loves him.' 21Then you said to your servants, 'Bring him down to me, so that I may set my eyes on him.' 22We said to my lord, 'The boy cannot leave his father, for if he should leave his father, his father would die.' 23Then you said to your servants, 'Unless your youngest brother comes down with you, you shall see my face no more.' 24When we went back to your servant my father we told him the words of my lord. 25And when our father said, 'Go again, buy us a little food,' 26we said, 'We cannot go down. Only if our youngest brother goes with us, will we go down; for we cannot see the man's face unless our youngest brother is with us.' 27Then your servant my father said to us, 'You know that my wife bore me two sons; 28one left me, and I said, Surely he has been torn to pieces; and I have never seen him since. 29If you take this one also from me, and harm comes to him, you will bring down my gray hairs in sorrow to Sheol.' 30Now therefore, when I come to your servant my father and the boy is not with us, then, as his life is bound up in the boy's life, 31when he sees that the boy is not with us, he will die; and your servants will bring down the gray hairs of your servant our father with sorrow to Sheol. 32For your servant became surety for the boy to my father, saying, 'If I do not bring him back to you, then I will bear the blame in the sight of my father all my life.' 33Now there-

ᵃ 44.4 Gk Compare Vg: Heb lacks *Why have you stolen my silver cup?*

fore, please let your servant remain as a slave to my lord in place of the boy; and let the boy go back with his brothers. 34For how can I go back to my father if the boy is not with me? I fear to see the suffering that would come upon my father."

JOSEPH REVEALS HIMSELF TO HIS BROTHERS

45 Then Joseph could no longer control himself before all those who stood by him, and he cried out, "Send everyone away from me." So no one stayed with him when Joseph made himself known to his brothers. 2And he wept so loudly that the Egyptians heard it, and the household of Pharaoh heard it. 3Joseph said to his brothers, "I am Joseph. Is my father still alive?" But his brothers could not answer him, so dismayed were they at his presence.

4 Then Joseph said to his brothers, "Come closer to me." And they came closer. He said, "I am your brother, Joseph, whom you sold into Egypt. 5And now do not be distressed, or angry with yourselves, because you sold me here; for God sent me before you to preserve life. 6For the famine has been in the land these two years; and there are five more years in which there will be neither plowing nor harvest. 7God sent me before you to preserve for you a remnant on earth, and to keep alive for you many survivors. 8So it was not you who sent me here, but God; he has made me a father to Pharaoh, and lord of all his house and ruler over all the land of Egypt. 9Hurry and go up to my father and say to him, 'Thus says your son Joseph, God has made me lord of all Egypt; come down to me, do not delay. 10You shall settle in the land of Goshen, and you shall be near me, you and your children and your children's children, as well as your flocks, your herds, and all that you have. 11I will provide for you there—since there are five more years of famine to come—so that you and your household, and all that you have, will not come to poverty.' 12And now your eyes and the eyes

PONDER

"God sent me before you to preserve for you a remnant on earth, and to keep alive for you many survivors."
—Genesis 45.7

PRAY

Lord God, as we encounter your Holy Word, we are disturbed, educated and inspired, given new hope and determination. Encourage us to take a stern look at ourselves—to orient our priorities toward you, as Joseph did. And as he forgave, teach us to forgive those from whom we are alienated: a spouse, a co-worker or a friend. We know that you can use even hard challenges for our good and for the good of others. Encourage us to look at the blessings you have given us and see how we might use them in the name of Christ to further your kingdom. In the name of our perfect Savior, Jesus Christ. Amen.

of my brother Benjamin see that it is my own mouth that speaks to you. 13You must tell my father how greatly I am honored in Egypt, and all that you have seen. Hurry and bring my father down here." 14Then he fell upon his brother Benjamin's neck and wept, while Benjamin wept upon his neck. 15And he kissed all his brothers and wept upon them; and after that his brothers talked with him.

16 When the report was heard in Pharaoh's house, "Joseph's brothers have come," Pharaoh and his servants were pleased. 17Pharaoh said to Joseph, "Say to your brothers, 'Do this: load your animals and go back to the land of Canaan. 18Take your father and your households and come to me, so that I may give you the best of the land of Egypt, and you may enjoy the fat of the land.' 19You are further charged to say, 'Do this: take wagons from the land

of Egypt for your little ones and for your wives, and bring your father, and come. 20 Give no thought to your possessions, for the best of all the land of Egypt is yours.' "

21 The sons of Israel did so. Joseph gave them wagons according to the instruction of Pharaoh, and he gave them provisions for the journey. 22 To each one of them he gave a set of garments; but to Benjamin he gave three hundred pieces of silver and five sets of garments. 23 To his father he sent the following: ten donkeys loaded with the good things of Egypt, and ten female donkeys loaded with grain, bread, and provision for his father on the journey. 24 Then he sent his brothers on their way, and as they were leaving he said to them, "Do not quarrel[a] along the way."

25 So they went up out of Egypt and came to their father Jacob in the land of Canaan. 26 And they told him, "Joseph is still alive! He is even ruler over all the land of Egypt." He was stunned; he could not believe them. 27 But when they told him all the words of Joseph that he had said to them, and when he saw the wagons that Joseph had sent to carry him, the spirit of their father Jacob revived. 28 Israel said, "Enough! My son Joseph is still alive. I must go and see him before I die."

JACOB BRINGS HIS WHOLE FAMILY TO EGYPT

46 When Israel set out on his journey with all that he had and came to Beer-sheba, he offered sacrifices to the God of his father Isaac. 2 God spoke to Israel in visions of the night, and said, "Jacob, Jacob." And he said, "Here I am." 3 Then he said, "I am God,[b] the God of your father; do not be afraid to go down to Egypt, for I will make of you a great nation there. 4 I myself will go down with you to Egypt, and I will also bring you up again; and Joseph's own hand shall close your eyes."

5 Then Jacob set out from Beer-sheba; and the sons of Israel carried their father Jacob, their little ones, and their wives, in the wagons that Pharaoh had sent to carry him. 6 They also took their livestock and the goods that they had acquired in the land of Canaan, and they came into Egypt, Jacob and all his offspring with him, 7 his sons, and his sons' sons with him, his daughters, and his sons' daughters; all his offspring he brought with him into Egypt.

8 Now these are the names of the Israelites, Jacob and his offspring, who came to Egypt. Reuben, Jacob's firstborn, 9 and the children of Reuben: Hanoch, Pallu, Hezron, and Carmi. 10 The children of Simeon: Jemuel, Jamin, Ohad, Jachin, Zohar, and Shaul,[c] the son of a Canaanite woman. 11 The children of Levi: Gershon, Kohath, and Merari. 12 The children of Judah: Er, Onan, Shelah, Perez, and Zerah (but Er and Onan died in the land of Canaan); and the children of Perez were Hezron and Hamul. 13 The children of Issachar: Tola, Puvah, Jashub,[d] and Shimron. 14 The children of Zebulun: Sered, Elon, and Jahleel 15 (these are the sons of Leah, whom she bore to Jacob in Paddan-aram, together with his daughter Dinah; in all his sons and his daughters numbered thirty-three). 16 The children of Gad: Ziphion, Haggi, Shuni, Ezbon, Eri, Arodi, and Areli. 17 The children of Asher: Imnah, Ishvah, Ishvi, Beriah, and their sister Serah. The children of Beriah: Heber and Malchiel 18 (these are the children of Zilpah, whom Laban gave to his daughter Leah; and these she bore to Jacob—sixteen persons). 19 The children of Jacob's wife Rachel: Joseph and Benjamin. 20 To Joseph in the land of Egypt were born Manasseh and Ephraim, whom Asenath daughter of Potiphera, priest of On, bore to him. 21 The children of Benjamin: Bela, Becher, Ashbel, Gera, Naaman, Ehi, Rosh, Muppim, Huppim, and Ard 22 (these are the children of Rachel, who were born to Jacob—fourteen persons in all). 23 The children of Dan: Hashum.[e]

---

[a] 45.24 Or be agitated   [b] 46.3 Heb the God
[c] 46.10 Or Saul   [d] 46.13 Compare Sam Gk
Num 26.24; 1 Chr 7.1: MT Iob   [e] 46.23 Gk:
Heb Hushim

24The children of Naphtali: Jahzeel, Guni, Jezer, and Shillem 25(these are the children of Bilhah, whom Laban gave to his daughter Rachel, and these she bore to Jacob—seven persons in all). 26All the persons belonging to Jacob who came into Egypt, who were his own offspring, not including the wives of his sons, were sixty-six persons in all. 27The children of Joseph, who were born to him in Egypt, were two; all the persons of the house of Jacob who came into Egypt were seventy.

JACOB SETTLES IN GOSHEN

28 Israel[a] sent Judah ahead to Joseph to lead the way before him into Goshen. When they came to the land of Goshen, 29Joseph made ready his chariot and went up to meet his father Israel in Goshen. He presented himself to him, fell on his neck, and wept on his neck a good while. 30Israel said to Joseph, "I can die now, having seen for myself that you are still alive." 31Joseph said to his brothers and to his father's household, "I will go up and tell Pharaoh, and will say to him, 'My brothers and my father's household, who were in the land of Canaan, have come to me. 32The men are shepherds, for they have been keepers of livestock; and they have brought their flocks, and their herds, and all that they have.' 33When Pharaoh calls you, and says, 'What is your occupation?' 34you shall say, 'Your servants have been keepers of livestock from our youth even until now, both we and our ancestors'—in order that you may settle in the land of Goshen, because all shepherds are abhorrent to the Egyptians."

47 So Joseph went and told Pharaoh, "My father and my brothers, with their flocks and herds and all that they possess, have come from the land of Canaan; they are now in the land of Goshen." 2From among his brothers he took five men and presented them to Pharaoh. 3Pharaoh said to his brothers, "What is your occupation?" And they said to Pharaoh, "Your servants are shepherds, as our ancestors

were." 4They said to Pharaoh, "We have come to reside as aliens in the land; for there is no pasture for your servants' flocks because the famine is severe in the land of Canaan. Now, we ask you, let your servants settle in the land of Goshen." 5Then Pharaoh said to Joseph, "Your father and your brothers have come to you. 6The land of Egypt is before you; settle your father and your brothers in the best part of the land; let them live in the land of Goshen; and if you know that there are capable men among them, put them in charge of my livestock."

7 Then Joseph brought in his father Jacob, and presented him before Pharaoh, and Jacob blessed Pharaoh. 8Pharaoh said to Jacob, "How many are the years of your life?" 9Jacob said to Pharaoh, "The years of my earthly sojourn are one hundred thirty; few and hard have been the years of my life. They do not compare with the years of the life of my ancestors during their long sojourn." 10Then Jacob blessed Pharaoh, and went out from the presence of Pharaoh. 11Joseph settled his father and his brothers, and granted them a holding in the land of Egypt, in the best part of the land, in the land of Rameses, as Pharaoh had instructed. 12And Joseph provided his father, his brothers, and all his father's household with food, according to the number of their dependents.

THE FAMINE IN EGYPT

13 Now there was no food in all the land, for the famine was very severe. The land of Egypt and the land of Canaan languished because of the famine. 14Joseph collected all the money to be found in the land of Egypt and in the land of Canaan, in exchange for the grain that they bought; and Joseph brought the money into Pharaoh's house. 15When the money from the land of Egypt and from the land of Canaan was spent, all the Egyptians came to Joseph, and said, "Give us food! Why should we die before your eyes? For our money

a 46.28 Heb He

is gone." 16And Joseph answered, "Give me your livestock, and I will give you food in exchange for your livestock, if your money is gone." 17So they brought their livestock to Joseph; and Joseph gave them food in exchange for the horses, the flocks, the herds, and the donkeys. That year he supplied them with food in exchange for all their livestock. 18When that year was ended, they came to him the following year, and said to him, "We can not hide from my lord that our money is all spent; and the herds of cattle are my lord's. There is nothing left in the sight of my lord but our bodies and our lands. 19Shall we die before your eyes, both we and our land? Buy us and our land in exchange for food. We with our land will become slaves to Pharaoh; just give us seed, so that we may live and not die, and that the land may not become desolate."

20 So Joseph bought all the land of Egypt for Pharaoh. All the Egyptians sold their fields, because the famine was severe upon them; and the land became Pharaoh's. 21As for the people, he made slaves of them[a] from one end of Egypt to the other. 22Only the land of the priests he did not buy; for the priests had a fixed allowance from Pharaoh, and lived on the allowance that Pharaoh gave them; therefore they did not sell their land. 23Then Joseph said to the people, "Now that I have this day bought you and your land for Pharaoh, here is seed for you; sow the land. 24And at the harvests you shall give one-fifth to Pharaoh, and four-fifths shall be your own, as seed for the field and as food for yourselves and your households, and as food for your little ones." 25They said, "You have saved our lives; may it please my lord, we will be slaves to Pharaoh." 26So Joseph made it a statute concerning the land of Egypt, and it stands to this day, that Pharaoh should have the fifth. The land of the priests alone did not become Pharaoh's.

THE LAST DAYS OF JACOB

27 Thus Israel settled in the land of Egypt, in the region of Goshen; and they gained possessions in it, and were fruitful and multiplied exceedingly. 28Jacob lived in the land of Egypt seventeen years; so the days of Jacob, the years of his life, were one hundred forty-seven years.

29 When the time of Israel's death drew near, he called his son Joseph and said to him, "If I have found favor with you, put your hand under my thigh and promise to deal loyally and truly with me. Do not bury me in Egypt. 30When I lie down with my ancestors, carry me out of Egypt and bury me in their burial place." He answered, "I will do as you have said." 31And he said, "Swear to me"; and he swore to him. Then Israel bowed himself on the head of his bed.

JACOB BLESSES JOSEPH'S SONS

48 After this Joseph was told, "Your father is ill." So he took with him his two sons, Manasseh and Ephraim. 2When Jacob was told, "Your son Joseph has come to you," he[b] summoned his strength and sat up in bed. 3And Jacob said to Joseph, "God Almighty[c] appeared to me at Luz in the land of Canaan, and he blessed me, 4and said to me, 'I am going to make you fruitful and increase your numbers; I will make of you a company of peoples, and will give this land to your offspring after you for a perpetual holding.' 5Therefore your two sons, who were born to you in the land of Egypt before I came to you in Egypt, are now mine; Ephraim and Manasseh shall be mine, just as Reuben and Simeon are. 6As for the offspring born to you after them, they shall be yours. They shall be recorded under the names of their brothers with regard to their inheritance. 7For when I came from Paddan, Rachel, alas, died in the land of Canaan on the way, while there was still some distance to go to Ephrath; and I buried her there on the way to Ephrath" (that is, Bethlehem).

a 47.21 Sam Gk Compare Vg: MT *He removed them to the cities*   b 48.2 Heb *Israel*   c 48.3 Traditional rendering of Heb *El Shaddai*

8 When Israel saw Joseph's sons, he said, "Who are these?" 9 Joseph said to his father, "They are my sons, whom God has given me here." And he said, "Bring them to me, please, that I may bless them." 10 Now the eyes of Israel were dim with age, and he could not see well. So Joseph brought them near him; and he kissed them and embraced them. 11 Israel said to Joseph, "I did not expect to see your face; and here God has let me see your children also." 12 Then Joseph removed them from his father's knees,[a] and he bowed himself with his face to the earth. 13 Joseph took them both, Ephraim in his right hand toward Israel's left, and Manasseh in his left hand toward Israel's right, and brought them near him. 14 But Israel stretched out his right hand and laid it on the head of Ephraim, who was the younger, and his left hand on the head of Manasseh, crossing his hands, for Manasseh was the firstborn. 15 He blessed Joseph, and said,
"The God before whom my
      ancestors Abraham
      and Isaac walked,
   the God who has been my
      shepherd all my
      life to this day,
16   the angel who has redeemed
      me from all harm,
      bless the boys;
   and in them let my name be
      perpetuated, and the
      name of my ancestors
      Abraham and Isaac;
   and let them grow into a
      multitude on the earth."
17 When Joseph saw that his father laid his right hand on the head of Ephraim, it displeased him; so he took his father's hand, to remove it from Ephraim's head to Manasseh's head. 18 Joseph said to his father, "Not so, my father! Since this one is the firstborn, put your right hand on his head." 19 But his father refused, and said, "I know, my son, I know; he also shall become a people, and he also shall be great. Nevertheless his younger brother shall be greater than he, and his offspring shall become a multitude of nations." 20 So he blessed them that day, saying,

"By you[b] Israel will invoke
      blessings, saying,
   'God make you[b] like Ephraim
      and like Manasseh.' "
So he put Ephraim ahead of Manasseh. 21 Then Israel said to Joseph, "I am about to die, but God will be with you and will bring you again to the land of your ancestors. 22 I now give to you one portion[c] more than to your brothers, the portion[c] that I took from the hand of the Amorites with my sword and with my bow."

JACOB'S LAST WORDS TO HIS SONS

49 Then Jacob called his sons, and said: "Gather around, that I may tell you what will happen to you in days to come.
2   Assemble and hear, O sons
         of Jacob;
      listen to Israel your father.

3   Reuben, you are my firstborn,
         my might and the first
            fruits of my vigor,
      excelling in rank and
         excelling in power.
4   Unstable as water, you shall
            no longer excel
      because you went up onto
         your father's bed;
      then you defiled it—you[d]
         went up onto my couch!

5   Simeon and Levi are brothers;
      weapons of violence are
         their swords.
6   May I never come into
         their council;
      may I not be joined to
         their company—
      for in their anger they killed men,
         and at their whim they
            hamstrung oxen.
7   Cursed be their anger,
         for it is fierce,
      and their wrath, for it is cruel!
      I will divide them in Jacob,
         and scatter them in Israel.

[a] 48.12 Heb *from his knees*   [b] 48.20 *you* here is singular in Heb   [c] 48.22 Or *mountain slope* (Heb *shekem*, a play on the name of the town and district of Shechem)   [d] 49.4 Gk Syr Tg: Heb *he*

8 Judah, your brothers shall
  praise you;
  your hand shall be on the
    neck of your enemies;
  your father's sons shall bow
    down before you.
9 Judah is a lion's whelp;
  from the prey, my son,
    you have gone up.
  He crouches down, he stretches
    out like a lion,
  like a lioness—who dares
    rouse him up?
10 The scepter shall not depart
    from Judah,
  nor the ruler's staff from
    between his feet,
  until tribute comes to him;ᵃ
  and the obedience of the
    peoples is his.
11 Binding his foal to the vine
  and his donkey's colt to
    the choice vine,
  he washes his garments in wine
  and his robe in the
    blood of grapes;
12 his eyes are darker than wine,
  and his teeth whiter than milk.

13 Zebulun shall settle at the
    shore of the sea;
  he shall be a haven for ships,
  and his border shall be at Sidon.

14 Issachar is a strong donkey,
  lying down between
    the sheepfolds;
15 he saw that a resting place
    was good,
  and that the land was pleasant;
  so he bowed his shoulder
    to the burden,
  and became a slave at
    forced labor.

16 Dan shall judge his people
  as one of the tribes of Israel.
17 Dan shall be a snake by
    the roadside,
  a viper along the path,
  that bites the horse's heels
  so that its rider falls backward.

18 I wait for your salvation, O LORD.

19 Gad shall be raided by raiders,
  but he shall raid at their heels.

20 Asher'sᵇ food shall be rich,
  and he shall provide
    royal delicacies.

21 Naphtali is a doe let loose
  that bears lovely fawns.ᶜ

22 Joseph is a fruitful bough,
  a fruitful bough by a spring;
  his branches run over the wall.ᵈ
23 The archers fiercely attacked him;
  they shot at him and
    pressed him hard.
24 Yet his bow remained taut,
  and his armsᵉ were made agile
  by the hands of the Mighty
    One of Jacob,
  by the name of the Shepherd,
    the Rock of Israel,
25 by the God of your father,
    who will help you,
  by the Almightyᶠ who
    will bless you
  with blessings of heaven above,
  blessings of the deep that
    lies beneath,
  blessings of the breasts
    and of the womb.
26 The blessings of your father
  are stronger than the blessings
    of the eternal mountains,
  the bountiesᵍ of the
    everlasting hills;
  may they be on the head
    of Joseph,
  on the brow of him who
    was set apart from
    his brothers.

27 Benjamin is a ravenous wolf,
  in the morning devouring
    the prey,
  and at evening dividing
    the spoil."

28 All these are the twelve tribes
of Israel, and this is what their father said to them when he blessed

ᵃ 49.10 Or until Shiloh comes or until he
comes to Shiloh or (with Syr) until he comes
to whom it belongs   ᵇ 49.20 Gk Vg Syr:
Heb From Asher   ᶜ 49.21 Or that gives
beautiful words   ᵈ 49.22 Meaning of Heb
uncertain   ᵉ 49.24 Heb the arms of his
hands   ᶠ 49.25 Traditional rendering of
Heb Shaddai   ᵍ 49.26 Cn Compare Gk: Heb
of my progenitors to the boundaries

them, blessing each one of them with a suitable blessing.

JACOB'S DEATH AND BURIAL

29 Then he charged them, saying to them, "I am about to be gathered to my people. Bury me with my ancestors—in the cave in the field of Ephron the Hittite, 30 in the cave in the field at Machpelah, near Mamre, in the land of Canaan, in the field that Abraham bought from Ephron the Hittite as a burial site. 31 There Abraham and his wife Sarah were buried; there Isaac and his wife Rebekah were buried; and there I buried Leah— 32 the field and the cave that is in it were purchased from the Hittites." 33 When Jacob ended his charge to his sons, he drew up his feet into the bed, breathed his last, and was gathered to his people.

50 Then Joseph threw himself on his father's face and wept over him and kissed him. 2 Joseph commanded the physicians in his service to embalm his father. So the physicians embalmed Israel; 3 they spent forty days in doing this, for that is the time required for embalming. And the Egyptians wept for him seventy days.

4 When the days of weeping for him were past, Joseph addressed the household of Pharaoh, "If now I have found favor with you, please speak to Pharaoh as follows: 5 My father made me swear an oath; he said, 'I am about to die. In the tomb that I hewed out for myself in the land of Canaan, there you shall bury me.' Now therefore let me go up, so that I may bury my father; then I will return." 6 Pharaoh answered, "Go up, and bury your father, as he made you swear to do."

7 So Joseph went up to bury his father. With him went up all the servants of Pharaoh, the elders of his household, and all the elders of the land of Egypt, 8 as well as all the household of Joseph, his brothers, and his father's household. Only their children, their flocks, and their herds were left in the land of Goshen. 9 Both chariots and charioteers went up with him. It was a very great company. 10 When they came to the threshing floor of Atad, which is beyond the Jordan, they held there a very great and sorrowful lamentation; and he observed a time of mourning for his father seven days. 11 When the Canaanite inhabitants of the land saw the mourning on the threshing floor of Atad, they said, "This is a grievous mourning on the part of the Egyptians." Therefore the place was named Abel-mizraim;[a] it is beyond the Jordan. 12 Thus his sons did for him as he had instructed them. 13 They carried him to the land of Canaan and buried him in the cave of the field at Machpelah, the field near Mamre, which Abraham bought as a burial site from Ephron the Hittite. 14 After he had buried his father, Joseph returned to Egypt with his brothers and all who had gone up with him to bury his father.

JOSEPH FORGIVES HIS BROTHERS

15 Realizing that their father was dead, Joseph's brothers said, "What if Joseph still bears a grudge against us and pays us back in full for all the wrong that we did to him?" 16 So they approached[b] Joseph, saying, "Your father gave this instruction before he died, 17 'Say to Joseph: I beg you, forgive the crime of your brothers and the wrong they did in harming you.' Now therefore please forgive the crime of the servants of the God of your father." Joseph wept when they spoke to him. 18 Then his brothers also wept,[c] fell down before him, and said, "We are here as your slaves." 19 But Joseph said to them, "Do not be afraid! Am I in the place of God? 20 Even though you intended to do harm to me, God intended it for good, in order to preserve a numerous people, as he is doing today. 21 So have no fear; I myself will provide for you and your little ones." In this way he reassured them, speaking kindly to them.

a 50.11 That is *mourning* (or *meadow*) *of Egypt*   b 50.16 Gk Syr: Heb *they commanded*   c 50.18 Cn: Heb *also came*

JOSEPH'S LAST DAYS AND DEATH

22 So Joseph remained in Egypt, he and his father's household; and Joseph lived one hundred ten years. 23 Joseph saw Ephraim's children of the third generation; the children of Machir son of Manasseh were also born on Joseph's knees.

24 Then Joseph said to his brothers, "I am about to die; but God will surely come to you, and bring you up out of this land to the land that he swore to Abraham, to Isaac, and to Jacob." 25 So Joseph made the Israelites swear, saying, "When God comes to you, you shall carry up my bones from here." 26 And Joseph died, being one hundred ten years old; he was embalmed and placed in a coffin in Egypt.

⊣ BIBLE IN LIFE ▷

Seeking Reconciliation

Genesis 50.15–21

Are there people in your past to whom you once felt close, but now some difference has come between you? Perhaps it was due to some wrongdoing on their part or yours, causing you to no longer want to be around them. Whatever the cause, consider now whether God might be leading you to reconcile with them. I've had to do this at various times in my life, and I have often found it to be very cleansing and gratifying. It doesn't require that much to start the process of reconciliation—a brief postcard or note, a quick call to say hello, a simple invitation to share a cup of coffee. However we choose to initiate it, the ultimate goal is simply to communicate that we've been thinking about them lately and want to see if it is possible to reconcile and renew our friendship. We may need to admit where we have been wrong, to see a situation from their perspective, to be willing to forgive others where they have been wrong, but this is a small price to pay for the joy of reconciliation and renewed friendship. We should take some time today to consider how to initiate the process—and then be sure to follow through.

EXODUS

Ever wonder what it would be like to witness the parting of the Red Sea? To hear God speak from a burning bush? To see the glory of the Lord? Moses and the Israelites experienced this and more as recorded in the book of Exodus. The author Moses narrates these incredible stories and tells how God freed the Israelites from Egyptian slavery. Moses tells how God established the law—our foundation for worship and life.

1 These are the names of the sons of Israel who came to Egypt with Jacob, each with his household: 2Reuben, Simeon, Levi, and Judah, 3Issachar, Zebulun, and Benjamin, 4Dan and Naphtali, Gad and Asher. 5The total number of people born to Jacob was seventy. Joseph was already in Egypt. 6Then Joseph died, and all his brothers, and that whole generation. 7But the Israelites were fruitful and prolific; they multiplied and grew exceedingly strong, so that the land was filled with them.

THE ISRAELITES ARE OPPRESSED

8 Now a new king arose over Egypt, who did not know Joseph. 9He said to his people, "Look, the Israelite people are more numerous and more powerful than we. 10Come, let us deal shrewdly with them, or they will increase and, in the event of war, join our enemies and fight against us and escape from the land." 11Therefore they set taskmasters over them to oppress them with forced labor. They built supply cities, Pithom and Rameses, for Pharaoh. 12But the more they were oppressed, the more they multiplied and spread, so that the Egyptians came to dread the Israelites. 13The Egyptians became ruthless in imposing tasks on the Israelites, 14and made their lives bitter with hard service in mortar and brick and in every kind of field labor. They were ruthless in all the tasks that they imposed on them.

15 The king of Egypt said to the Hebrew midwives, one of whom was named Shiphrah and the other Puah, 16"When you act as midwives to the Hebrew women, and see them on the birthstool, if it is a boy, kill him; but if it is a girl, she shall live." 17But the midwives feared God; they did not do as the king of Egypt commanded them, but they let the boys live. 18So the king of Egypt summoned the midwives and said to them, "Why have you done this, and allowed the boys to live?" 19The midwives said to Pharaoh, "Because the Hebrew women are not like the Egyptian women; for they are vigorous and give birth before the midwife comes to them." 20So God dealt well with the midwives; and the people multiplied and became very strong. 21And because the midwives feared God, he gave them families. 22Then Pharaoh commanded all his people, "Every boy that is born to the Hebrews[a] you shall throw into the Nile, but you shall let every girl live."

PONDER

And because the midwives feared God, he gave them families.
—Exodus 1.21

PRAY

Almighty God, we are surprised that these two midwives, Shiphrah and Puah, have been singled out as examples to us. Perhaps they were tempted to obey the pharaoh, but then they would have had to disobey you, the King of the world. God Almighty, strengthen us so that we might be able to distinguish, courageously and persistently, the accepted premises of a secular world and try to follow, aggressively, individually and courageously, the teachings of your son Jesus in all aspects of our dealings with other people. We are thankful for your many blessings, and we pray we might build upon them to be effective servants in your kingdom through our faith in Jesus Christ. Amen.

BIRTH AND YOUTH OF MOSES

2 Now a man from the house of Levi went and married a Levite woman. 2The woman conceived and bore a son; and when she saw that he was a fine baby, she hid him three months. 3When she could hide him no longer she got a papyrus basket for him, and plastered it with bitu-

a 1.22 Sam Gk Tg: Heb lacks *to the Hebrews*

men and pitch; she put the child in it and placed it among the reeds on the bank of the river. 4His sister stood at a distance, to see what would happen to him.

5 The daughter of Pharaoh came down to bathe at the river, while her attendants walked beside the river. She saw the basket among the reeds and sent her maid to bring it. 6When she opened it, she saw the child. He was crying, and she took pity on him. "This must be one of the Hebrews' children," she said. 7Then his sister said to Pharaoh's daughter, "Shall I go and get you a nurse from the Hebrew women to nurse the child for you?" 8Pharaoh's daughter said to her, "Yes." So the girl went and called the child's mother. 9Pharaoh's daughter said to her, "Take this child and nurse it for me, and I will give you your wages." So the woman took the child and nursed it. 10When the child grew up, she brought him to Pharaoh's daughter, and she took him as her son. She named him Moses,a "because," she said, "I drew him outb of the water."

MOSES FLEES TO MIDIAN

11 One day, after Moses had grown up, he went out to his people and saw their forced labor. He saw an Egyptian beating a Hebrew, one of his kinsfolk. 12He looked this way and that, and seeing no one he killed the Egyptian and hid him in the sand. 13When he went out the next day, he saw two Hebrews fighting; and he said to the one who was in the wrong, "Why do you strike your fellow Hebrew?" 14He answered, "Who made you a ruler and judge over us? Do you mean to kill me as you killed the Egyptian?" Then Moses was afraid and thought, "Surely the thing is known." 15When Pharaoh heard of it, he sought to kill Moses.

But Moses fled from Pharaoh. He settled in the land of Midian, and sat down by a well. 16The priest of Midian had seven daughters. They came to draw water, and filled the troughs to water their father's flock. 17But some shepherds came and drove

them away. Moses got up and came to their defense and watered their flock. 18When they returned to their father Reuel, he said, "How is it that you have come back so soon today?" 19They said, "An Egyptian helped us against the shepherds; he even drew water for us and watered the flock." 20He said to his daughters, "Where is he? Why did you leave the man? Invite him to break bread." 21Moses agreed to stay with the man, and he gave Moses his daughter Zipporah in marriage. 22She bore a son, and he named him Gershom; for he said, "I have been an alienc residing in a foreign land."

23 After a long time the king of Egypt died. The Israelites groaned under their slavery, and cried out. Out of the slavery their cry for help rose up to God. 24God heard their groaning, and God remembered his covenant with Abraham, Isaac, and Jacob. 25God looked upon the Israelites, and God took notice of them.

MOSES AT THE BURNING BUSH

3 Moses was keeping the flock of his father-in-law Jethro, the priest of Midian; he led his flock beyond the wilderness, and came to Horeb, the mountain of God. 2There the angel of the LORD appeared to him in a flame of fire out of a bush; he looked, and the bush was blazing, yet it was not consumed. 3Then Moses said, "I must turn aside and look at this great sight, and see why the bush is not burned up." 4When the LORD saw that he had turned aside to see, God called to him out of the bush, "Moses, Moses!" And he said, "Here I am." 5Then he said, "Come no closer! Remove the sandals from your feet, for the place on which you are standing is holy ground." 6He said further, "I am the God of your father, the God of Abraham, the God of Isaac, and the God of Jacob." And Moses hid his face, for he was afraid to look at God.

7 Then the LORD said, "I have observed the misery of my people who

a 2.10 Heb Mosheh   b 2.10 Heb mashah
c 2.22 Heb ger

are in Egypt; I have heard their cry on account of their taskmasters. Indeed, I know their sufferings, [8]and I have come down to deliver them from the Egyptians, and to bring them up out of that land to a good and broad land, a land flowing with milk and honey, to the country of the Canaanites, the Hittites, the Amorites, the Perizzites, the Hivites, and the Jebusites. [9]The cry of the Israelites has now come to me; I have also seen how the Egyptians oppress them. [10]So come, I will send you to Pharaoh to bring my people, the Israelites, out of Egypt." [11]But Moses said to God, "Who am I that I should go to Pharaoh, and bring the Israelites out of Egypt?" [12]He said, "I will be with you; and this shall be the sign for you that it is I who sent you: when you have brought the people out of Egypt, you shall worship God on this mountain."

THE DIVINE NAME REVEALED

[13] But Moses said to God, "If I come to the Israelites and say to them, 'The God of your ancestors has sent me to you,' and they ask me, 'What is his name?' what shall I say to them?" [14]God said to Moses, "I AM WHO I AM."[a] He said further, "Thus you shall say to the Israelites, 'I AM has sent me to you.'" [15]God also said to Moses, "Thus you shall say to the Israelites, 'The LORD,[b] the God of your ancestors, the God of Abraham, the God of Isaac, and the God of Jacob, has sent me to you':

This is my name forever,
  and this my title for all
    generations.

[16]Go and assemble the elders of Israel, and say to them, 'The LORD, the God of your ancestors, the God of Abraham, of Isaac, and of Jacob, has appeared to me, saying: I have given heed to you and to what has been done to you in Egypt. [17]I declare that I will bring you up out of the misery of Egypt, to the land of the Canaanites, the Hittites, the Amorites, the Perizzites, the Hivites, and the Jebusites, a land flowing with milk and honey.' [18]They will listen to your voice; and you and the elders of Israel shall go to the king of Egypt and say to him, 'The LORD, the God of the Hebrews, has met with us; let us now go a three days' journey into the wilderness, so that we may sacrifice to the LORD our God.' [19]I know, however, that the king of Egypt will not let you go unless compelled by a mighty hand.[c] [20]So I will stretch out my hand and strike Egypt with all my wonders that I will perform in it; after that he will let you go. [21]I will bring this people into such favor with the Egyptians that, when you go, you will not go empty-handed; [22]each woman shall ask her neighbor

[a] 3.14 Or I AM WHAT I AM or I WILL BE WHAT I WILL BE [b] 3.15 The word "LORD" when spelled with capital letters stands for the divine name, YHWH, which is here connected with the verb hayah, "to be"
[c] 3.19 Gk Vg: Heb no, not by a mighty hand

BIBLE IN LIFE

Our Mission   *Exodus 3.11–15*

A *missionary* is defined as someone who has a mission that is endorsed or inspired by God. Though we don't often think of Moses as a missionary, by this definition, he certainly was. At age 80, Moses received his mission from God at Mount Sinai. Moses was human—fallible, selfish and sinful. He had murdered a man. He was not an eloquent or confident speaker. But empowered by God, Moses became a great servant of God. Just like every other missionary in the past and present, Moses was unable to be truly successful in life until he went outside himself and began to serve others in the name of God. That is true for all of us. No matter how ambitious we may be, we will not succeed if we are preoccupied with ourselves. Success comes when we invest in the well-being of other people. Christ calls us to have a mission in life that is transcendent—above and beyond the normal.

THROUGH GOD'S POWER

*"Who am I that I should go to Pharaoh, and bring the Israel-
ites out of Egypt?" [God] said, "I will be with you."*

—Exodus 3.11–12

"Who am I?"

Moses' question to God at the burning bush is a question we are all tempted to ask as we each consider our place in life: "With so much strife and suffering in the world, who am I to do anything about it? I am inadequate. I am sinful. I'm not an eloquent speaker. I don't have much money. I don't have much influence. Who am I to carry out the plans of God Almighty?"

But God does not need perfect people to carry out his purposes. Moses had trouble speaking. Jacob, one of Moses' ancestors, was a liar and a cheat (see Genesis 27). David was an adulterer and the murderer of his lover's husband (see 2 Samuel 11). In the New Testament, Peter, who had followed Jesus for three years and witnessed countless miracles he performed, denied even knowing Jesus at his most difficult hour (see Matthew 26.69–75). Paul (also called Saul) was a persecutor of Christians before the Lord appeared to him on the road to Damascus (see Acts 8–9). But God was with each of these men, and he used them to carry out his purposes for his people.

God can use anyone—even if we're weak, even if we're sinful, even if we're not eloquent, even if we don't have much money to give away, even if we aren't very influential. God can use each one of us to carry out his will if we are willing to depend on him for the strength and ability to do it.

In fact, if we strive to do God's work on our own, we are likely to be headed down a dead-end street. We cannot carry out God's work by our own power. We are not capable of carving out a successful plan for our lives. If we believe we are self-sufficient, that we don't need God, that we know what's good for us, that we can handle things just fine without God's help, we are mistaken. We are no more able to handle things on our own than the rich fool of Luke 12.15–21 was able to ensure his own security by his great riches.

When we sense that God might be calling us to do something for him, instead of asking, "Who am I to take on this task?" we should simply say, "Here am I" like the prophet Isaiah (Isaiah 6.8). We can do this because we can be fully confident that God will always be with us and will empower us to do whatever he is calling us to do (see Exodus 3.12).

Going Deeper

· What do you try to do by your own strength rather than by God's help?
· What might God be calling you to do for his kingdom today?

and any woman living in the neighbor's house for jewelry of silver and of gold, and clothing, and you shall put them on your sons and on your daughters; and so you shall plunder the Egyptians."

MOSES' MIRACULOUS POWER

4 Then Moses answered, "But suppose they do not believe me or listen to me, but say, 'The LORD did not appear to you.' " ²The LORD said to him, "What is that in your hand?" He said, "A staff." ³And he said, "Throw it on the ground." So he threw the staff on the ground, and it became a snake; and Moses drew back from it. ⁴Then the LORD said to Moses, "Reach out your hand, and seize it by the tail"—so he reached out his hand and grasped it, and it became a staff in his hand— ⁵"so that they may believe that the LORD, the God of their ancestors, the God of Abraham, the God of Isaac, and the God of Jacob, has appeared to you."

6 Again, the LORD said to him, "Put your hand inside your cloak." He put his hand into his cloak; and when he took it out, his hand was leprous,ᵃ as white as snow. ⁷Then God said, "Put your hand back into your cloak"—so he put his hand back into his cloak, and when he took it out, it was restored like the rest of his body— ⁸"If they will not believe you or heed the first sign, they may believe the second sign. ⁹If they will not believe even these two signs or heed you, you shall take some water from the Nile and pour it on the dry ground; and the water that you shall take from the Nile will become blood on the dry ground."

10 But Moses said to the LORD, "O my Lord, I have never been eloquent, neither in the past nor even now that you have spoken to your servant; but I am slow of speech and slow of tongue." ¹¹Then the LORD said to him, "Who gives speech to mortals? Who makes them mute or deaf, seeing or blind? Is it not I, the LORD? ¹²Now go, and I will be with your mouth and teach you what you are to speak." ¹³But he said, "O my Lord, please send someone else." ¹⁴Then the anger of the LORD was kindled against Moses and he said, "What of your brother Aaron the Levite? I know that he can speak fluently; even now he is coming out to meet you, and when he sees you his heart will be glad. ¹⁵You shall speak to him and put the words in his mouth; and I will be with your mouth and with his mouth, and will teach you what you shall do. ¹⁶He indeed shall speak for you to the people; he shall serve as a mouth for you, and you shall serve as God for him. ¹⁷Take in your hand this staff, with which you shall perform the signs."

ᵃ 4.6 A term for several skin diseases; precise meaning uncertain

---

BIBLE IN LIFE ▷

Potential for Greatness
Exodus 4.4–16

Moses could not understand why God chose him to deliver the Israelites from Pharaoh. He openly asked God, "Who am I that I should go to Pharaoh?" (3.11). Countless other men and women throughout history have asked God this same question—even Jesus' own disciples. The disciples were a bunch of failures in many ways. They weren't bold; they weren't courageous; they weren't loyal; they weren't educated or especially intelligent. They couldn't even comprehend Jesus' sermons, which were directed personally to them. They had no confidence in themselves or even in Jesus. However, Jesus saw within each of them a potential for greatness, just as God had seen in Moses. Within each of us, no matter who we are or where we're from, there is a potential for greatness *with* God. With the presence of the Holy Spirit in us, we can find the courage to take a chance for God, to grow and to expand our lives. God has placed no limits on us. The only limits we have are self-imposed.

MOSES RETURNS TO EGYPT

18 Moses went back to his father-in-law Jethro and said to him, "Please let me go back to my kindred in Egypt and see whether they are still living." And Jethro said to Moses, "Go in peace." 19 The LORD said to Moses in Midian, "Go back to Egypt; for all those who were seeking your life are dead." 20 So Moses took his wife and his sons, put them on a donkey, and went back to the land of Egypt; and Moses carried the staff of God in his hand.

21 And the LORD said to Moses, "When you go back to Egypt, see that you perform before Pharaoh all the wonders that I have put in your power; but I will harden his heart, so that he will not let the people go. 22 Then you shall say to Pharaoh, 'Thus says the LORD: Israel is my firstborn son. 23 I said to you, "Let my son go that he may worship me." But you refused to let him go; now I will kill your firstborn son.'"

24 On the way, at a place where they spent the night, the LORD met him and tried to kill him. 25 But Zipporah took a flint and cut off her son's foreskin, and touched Moses'[a] feet with it, and said, "Truly you are a bridegroom of blood to me!" 26 So he let him alone. It was then she said, "A bridegroom of blood by circumcision."

27 The LORD said to Aaron, "Go into the wilderness to meet Moses." So he went; and he met him at the mountain of God and kissed him. 28 Moses told Aaron all the words of the LORD with which he had sent him, and all the signs with which he had charged him. 29 Then Moses and Aaron went and assembled all the elders of the Israelites. 30 Aaron spoke all the words that the LORD had spoken to Moses, and performed the signs in the sight of the people. 31 The people believed; and when they heard that the LORD had given heed to the Israelites and that he had seen their misery, they bowed down and worshiped.

BRICKS WITHOUT STRAW

5 Afterward Moses and Aaron went to Pharaoh and said, "Thus says the LORD, the God of Israel, 'Let my people go, so that they may celebrate a festival to me in the wilderness.'" 2 But Pharaoh said, "Who is the LORD, that I should heed him and let Israel go? I do not know the LORD, and I will not let Israel go." 3 Then they said, "The God of the Hebrews has revealed himself to us; let us go a three days' journey into the wilderness to sacrifice to the LORD our God, or he will fall upon us with pestilence or sword." 4 But the king of Egypt said to them, "Moses and Aaron, why are you taking the people away from their work? Get to your labors!" 5 Pharaoh continued, "Now they are more numerous than the people of the land[b] and yet you want them to stop working!" 6 That same day Pharaoh commanded the taskmasters of the people, as well as their supervisors, 7 "You shall no longer give the people straw to make bricks, as before; let them go and gather straw for themselves. 8 But you shall require of them the same quantity of bricks as they have made previously; do not diminish it, for they are lazy; that is why they cry, 'Let us go and offer sacrifice to our God.' 9 Let heavier work be laid on them; then they will labor at it and pay no attention to deceptive words."

10 So the taskmasters and the supervisors of the people went out and said to the people, "Thus says Pharaoh, 'I will not give you straw. 11 Go and get straw yourselves, wherever you can find it; but your work will not be lessened in the least.'" 12 So the people scattered throughout the land of Egypt, to gather stubble for straw. 13 The taskmasters were urgent, saying, "Complete your work, the same daily assignment as when you were given straw." 14 And the supervisors of the Israelites, whom Pharaoh's taskmasters had set over them, were beaten, and were asked, "Why did you not finish the required quantity of bricks yesterday and today, as you did before?"

a 4.25 Heb his   b 5.5 Sam: Heb The people of the land are now many

15 Then the Israelite supervisors came to Pharaoh and cried, "Why do you treat your servants like this? **16** No straw is given to your servants, yet they say to us, 'Make bricks!' Look how your servants are beaten! You are unjust to your own people."[a] **17** He said, "You are lazy, lazy; that is why you say, 'Let us go and sacrifice to the LORD.' **18** Go now, and work; for no straw shall be given you, but you shall still deliver the same number of bricks." **19** The Israelite supervisors saw that they were in trouble when they were told, "You shall not lessen your daily number of bricks." **20** As they left Pharaoh, they came upon Moses and Aaron who were waiting to meet them. **21** They said to them, "The LORD look upon you and judge! You have brought us into bad odor with Pharaoh and his officials, and have put a sword in their hand to kill us."

22 Then Moses turned again to the LORD and said, "O LORD, why have you mistreated this people? Why did you ever send me? **23** Since I first came to Pharaoh to speak in your name, he has mistreated this people, and you have done nothing at all to deliver your people."

ISRAEL'S DELIVERANCE ASSURED

6 Then the LORD said to Moses, "Now you shall see what I will do to Pharaoh: Indeed, by a mighty hand he will let them go; by a mighty hand he will drive them out of his land."

2 God also spoke to Moses and said to him: "I am the LORD. **3** I appeared to Abraham, Isaac, and Jacob as God Almighty,[b] but by my name 'The LORD'[c] I did not make myself known to them. **4** I also established my covenant with them, to give them the land of Canaan, the land in which they resided as aliens. **5** I have also heard the groaning of the Israelites whom the Egyptians are holding as slaves, and I have remembered my covenant. **6** Say therefore to the Israelites, 'I am the LORD, and I will free you from the burdens of the Egyptians and deliver you from slavery

to them. I will redeem you with an outstretched arm and with mighty acts of judgment. **7** I will take you as my people, and I will be your God. You shall know that I am the LORD your God, who has freed you from the burdens of the Egyptians. **8** I will bring you into the land that I swore to give to Abraham, Isaac, and Jacob; I will give it to you for a possession. I am the LORD.' " **9** Moses told this to the Israelites; but they would not listen to Moses, because of their broken spirit and their cruel slavery.

PONDER

"I am the LORD, and I will free you from the burdens of the Egyptians and deliver you from slavery to them. I will redeem you with an outstretched arm and with mighty acts of judgment."
—Exodus 6.6

PRAY

Father, Moses had shortcomings, but you entrusted him with the leadership of your people. Let us each examine our own hearts and minds concerning our relationship to you. Give us confidence, working through your power, to reach for great things and to do wonderful deeds for your kingdom. Help us to take advantage of the opportunities you show us, to realize that with you anything is possible, and that with you and some friends here on earth we can do great things in Jesus' name. Amen.

---

10 Then the LORD spoke to Moses, **11** "Go and tell Pharaoh king of Egypt to let the Israelites go out of his land." **12** But Moses spoke to the LORD, "The Israelites have not listened to me; how then shall Pharaoh listen to me, poor speaker that

a 5.16 Gk Compare Syr Vg: Heb *beaten, and the sin of your people*   b 6.3 Traditional rendering of Heb *El Shaddai*   c 6.3 Heb *YHWH*; see note at 3.15

I am?"[a] [13]Thus the LORD spoke to Moses and Aaron, and gave them orders regarding the Israelites and Pharaoh king of Egypt, charging them to free the Israelites from the land of Egypt.

THE GENEALOGY OF MOSES AND AARON

[14]The following are the heads of their ancestral houses: the sons of Reuben, the firstborn of Israel: Hanoch, Pallu, Hezron, and Carmi; these are the families of Reuben. [15]The sons of Simeon: Jemuel, Jamin, Ohad, Jachin, Zohar, and Shaul,[b] the son of a Canaanite woman; these are the families of Simeon. [16]The following are the names of the sons of Levi according to their genealogies: Gershon,[c] Kohath, and Merari, and the length of Levi's life was one hundred thirty-seven years. [17]The sons of Gershon:[c] Libni and Shimei, by their families. [18]The sons of Kohath: Amram, Izhar, Hebron, and Uzziel, and the length of Kohath's life was one hundred thirty-three years. [19]The sons of Merari: Mahli and Mushi. These are the families of the Levites according to their genealogies. [20]Amram married Jochebed his father's sister and she bore him Aaron and Moses, and the length of Amram's life was one hundred thirty-seven years. [21]The sons of Izhar: Korah, Nepheg, and Zichri. [22]The sons of Uzziel: Mishael, Elzaphan, and Sithri. [23]Aaron married Elisheba, daughter of Amminadab and sister of Nahshon, and she bore him Nadab, Abihu, Eleazar, and Ithamar. [24]The sons of Korah: Assir, Elkanah, and Abiasaph; these are the families of the Korahites. [25]Aaron's son Eleazar married one of the daughters of Putiel, and she bore him Phinehas. These are the heads of the ancestral houses of the Levites by their families.

[26]It was this same Aaron and Moses to whom the LORD said, "Bring the Israelites out of the land of Egypt, company by company." [27]It was they who spoke to Pharaoh king of Egypt to bring the Israelites out of Egypt, the same Moses and Aaron.

MOSES AND AARON OBEY GOD'S COMMANDS

[28]On the day when the LORD spoke to Moses in the land of Egypt, [29]he said to him, "I am the LORD; tell Pharaoh king of Egypt all that I am speaking to you." [30]But Moses said in the LORD's presence, "Since I am a poor speaker,[d] why would Pharaoh listen to me?"

7 The LORD said to Moses, "See, I have made you like God to Pharaoh, and your brother Aaron shall be your prophet. [2]You shall speak all that I command you, and your brother Aaron shall tell Pharaoh to let the Israelites go out of his land. [3]But I will harden Pharaoh's heart, and I will multiply my signs and wonders in the land of Egypt. [4]When Pharaoh does not listen to you, I will lay my hand upon Egypt and bring my people the Israelites, company by company, out of the land of Egypt by great acts of judgment. [5]The Egyptians shall know that I am the LORD, when I stretch out my hand against Egypt and bring the Israelites out from among them." [6]Moses and Aaron did so; they did just as the LORD commanded them. [7]Moses was eighty years old and Aaron eighty-three when they spoke to Pharaoh.

AARON'S MIRACULOUS ROD

8 The LORD said to Moses and Aaron, [9]"When Pharaoh says to you, 'Perform a wonder,' then you shall say to Aaron, 'Take your staff and throw it down before Pharaoh, and it will become a snake.'" [10]So Moses and Aaron went to Pharaoh and did as the LORD had commanded; Aaron threw down his staff before Pharaoh and his officials, and it became a snake. [11]Then Pharaoh summoned the wise men and the sorcerers; and they also, the magicians of Egypt, did the same by their secret arts. [12]Each one threw down his staff, and they became snakes; but Aaron's staff swallowed up theirs. [13]Still

[a] 6.12 Heb me? I am uncircumcised of lips   [b] 6.15 Or Saul   [c] 6.16,17 Also spelled Gershom; see 2.22   [d] 6.30 Heb am uncircumcised of lips; see 6.12

Pharaoh's heart was hardened, and he would not listen to them, as the LORD had said.

THE FIRST PLAGUE: WATER TURNED TO BLOOD

14 Then the LORD said to Moses, "Pharaoh's heart is hardened; he refuses to let the people go. 15Go to Pharaoh in the morning, as he is going out to the water; stand by at the river bank to meet him, and take in your hand the staff that was turned into a snake. 16Say to him, 'The LORD, the God of the Hebrews, sent me to you to say, "Let my people go, so that they may worship me in the wilderness." But until now you have not listened. 17Thus says the LORD, "By this you shall know that I am the LORD." See, with the staff that is in my hand I will strike the water that is in the Nile, and it shall be turned to blood. 18The fish in the river shall die, the river itself shall stink, and the Egyptians shall be unable to drink water from the Nile.' " 19The LORD said to Moses, "Say to Aaron, 'Take your staff and stretch out your hand over the waters of Egypt—over its rivers, its canals, and its ponds, and all its pools of water—so that they may become blood; and there shall be blood throughout the whole land of Egypt, even in vessels of wood and in vessels of stone.' "

20 Moses and Aaron did just as the LORD commanded. In the sight of Pharaoh and of his officials he lifted up the staff and struck the water in the river, and all the water in the river was turned into blood, 21and the fish in the river died. The river stank so that the Egyptians could not drink its water, and there was blood throughout the whole land of Egypt. 22But the magicians of Egypt did the same by their secret arts; so Pharaoh's heart remained hardened, and he would not listen to them, as the LORD had said. 23Pharaoh turned and went into his house, and he did not take even this to heart. 24And all the Egyptians had to dig along the Nile for water to drink, for they could not drink the water of the river.

25 Seven days passed after the LORD had struck the Nile.

THE SECOND PLAGUE: FROGS

8 [a] Then the LORD said to Moses, "Go to Pharaoh and say to him, 'Thus says the LORD: Let my people go, so that they may worship me. 2If you refuse to let them go, I will plague your whole country with frogs. 3The river shall swarm with frogs; they shall come up into your palace, into your bedchamber and your bed, and into the houses of your officials and of your people,[b] and into your ovens and your kneading bowls. 4The frogs shall come up on you and on your people and on all your officials.' " 5[c]And the LORD said to Moses, "Say to Aaron, 'Stretch out your hand with your staff over the rivers, the canals, and the pools, and make frogs come up on the land of Egypt.' " 6So Aaron stretched out his hand over the waters of Egypt; and the frogs came up and covered the land of Egypt. 7But the magicians did the same by their secret arts, and brought frogs up on the land of Egypt.

8 Then Pharaoh called Moses and Aaron, and said, "Pray to the LORD to take away the frogs from me and my people, and I will let the people go to sacrifice to the LORD." 9Moses said to Pharaoh, "Kindly tell me when I am to pray for you and for your officials and for your people, that the frogs may be removed from you and your houses and be left only in the Nile." 10And he said, "Tomorrow." Moses said, "As you say! So that you may know that there is no one like the LORD our God, 11the frogs shall leave you and your houses and your officials and your people; they shall be left only in the Nile." 12Then Moses and Aaron went out from Pharaoh; and Moses cried out to the LORD concerning the frogs that he had brought upon Pharaoh.[d] 13And the LORD did as Moses requested: the frogs died in the houses, the courtyards, and the

[a] 8.1 Ch 7.26 in Heb   [b] 8.3 Gk: Heb upon your people   [c] 8.5 Ch 8.1 in Heb   [d] 8.12 Or frogs, as he had agreed with Pharaoh

PONDER

Then the LORD said to Moses, "Go to Pharaoh and say to him, 'Thus says the LORD: Let my people go, so that they may worship me.'"
—Exodus 8.1

PRAY

Heavenly Father, let us carry in our hearts the lessons of this leader Moses, and help us realize that, like Moses, we have a mission waiting for us: to further your kingdom, to alleviate suffering in the world, to do away with racism and strife, to help combat the prevalence of selfishness and to bridge the division between those who have riches and security and those who don't. Thank you for the freedom we have to worship you in spirit and in truth. During this coming week, help us resolve to find one hour, just one hour in our busy lives, to be by ourselves and kneel down, be patient and let your message come to us. We look forward to a glorious life in the presence of our Savior. In his name we pray. Amen.

fields. ¹⁴And they gathered them together in heaps, and the land stank. ¹⁵But when Pharaoh saw that there was a respite, he hardened his heart, and would not listen to them, just as the LORD had said.

THE THIRD PLAGUE: GNATS

16 Then the LORD said to Moses, "Say to Aaron, 'Stretch out your staff and strike the dust of the earth, so that it may become gnats throughout the whole land of Egypt.'" ¹⁷And they did so; Aaron stretched out his hand with his staff and struck the dust of the earth, and gnats came on humans and animals alike; all the dust of the earth turned into gnats throughout the whole land of Egypt. ¹⁸The magicians tried to produce gnats by their secret arts, but they could not. There were gnats on both humans and animals. ¹⁹And the magicians said to Pharaoh, "This is the finger of God!" But Pharaoh's heart was hardened, and he would not listen to them, just as the LORD had said.

THE FOURTH PLAGUE: FLIES

20 Then the LORD said to Moses, "Rise early in the morning and present yourself before Pharaoh, as he goes out to the water, and say to him, 'Thus says the LORD: Let my people go, so that they may worship me. ²¹For if you will not let my people go, I will send swarms of flies on you, your officials, and your people, and into your houses; and the houses of the Egyptians shall be filled with swarms of flies; so also the land where they live. ²²But on that day I will set apart the land of Goshen, where my people live, so that no swarms of flies shall be there, that you may know that I the LORD am in this land. ²³Thus I will make a distinctionª between my people and your people. This sign shall appear tomorrow.'" ²⁴The LORD did so, and great swarms of flies came into the house of Pharaoh and into his officials' houses; in all of Egypt the land was ruined because of the flies.

25 Then Pharaoh summoned Moses and Aaron, and said, "Go, sacrifice to your God within the land." ²⁶But Moses said, "It would not be right to do so; for the sacrifices that we offer to the LORD our God are offensive to the Egyptians. If we offer in the sight of the Egyptians sacrifices that are offensive to them, will they not stone us? ²⁷We must go a three days' journey into the wilderness and sacrifice to the LORD our God as he commands us." ²⁸So Pharaoh said, "I will let you go to sacrifice to the LORD your God in the wilderness, provided you do not go very far away. Pray for me." ²⁹Then Moses said, "As soon as I leave you, I will pray to the LORD that the swarms of flies may depart tomorrow from Pharaoh, from his officials, and from his people; only do not let Pharaoh

ª 8.23 Gk Vg: Heb *will set redemption*

again deal falsely by not letting the people go to sacrifice to the LORD."

30 So Moses went out from Pharaoh and prayed to the LORD. ³¹And the LORD did as Moses asked: he removed the swarms of flies from Pharaoh, from his officials, and from his people; not one remained. ³²But Pharaoh hardened his heart this time also, and would not let the people go.

THE FIFTH PLAGUE: LIVESTOCK DISEASED

9 Then the LORD said to Moses, "Go to Pharaoh, and say to him, 'Thus says the LORD, the God of the Hebrews: Let my people go, so that they may worship me. ²For if you refuse to let them go and still hold them, ³the hand of the LORD will strike with a deadly pestilence your livestock in the field: the horses, the donkeys, the camels, the herds, and the flocks. ⁴But the LORD will make a distinction between the livestock of Israel and the livestock of Egypt, so that nothing shall die of all that belongs to the Israelites.' " ⁵The LORD set a time, saying, "Tomorrow the LORD will do this thing in the land." ⁶And on the next day the LORD did so; all the livestock of the Egyptians died, but of the livestock of the Israelites not one died. ⁷Pharaoh inquired and found that not one of the livestock of the Israelites was dead. But the heart of Pharaoh was hardened, and he would not let the people go.

THE SIXTH PLAGUE: BOILS

8 Then the LORD said to Moses and Aaron, "Take handfuls of soot from the kiln, and let Moses throw it in the air in the sight of Pharaoh. ⁹It shall become fine dust all over the land of Egypt, and shall cause festering boils on humans and animals throughout the whole land of Egypt." ¹⁰So they took soot from the kiln, and stood before Pharaoh, and Moses threw it in the air, and it caused festering boils on humans and animals. ¹¹The magicians could not stand before Moses because of the boils, for the boils afflicted the

magicians as well as all the Egyptians. ¹²But the LORD hardened the heart of Pharaoh, and he would not listen to them, just as the LORD had spoken to Moses.

WE SHOULD REJOICE IN THE

PLACE WHERE GOD HAS PUT

US AND IN THE PURPOSE

GOD HAS GIVEN US.

THE SEVENTH PLAGUE: THUNDER AND HAIL

13 Then the LORD said to Moses, "Rise up early in the morning and present yourself before Pharaoh, and say to him, 'Thus says the LORD, the God of the Hebrews: Let my people go, so that they may worship me. ¹⁴For this time I will send all my plagues upon you yourself, and upon your officials, and upon your people, so that you may know that there is no one like me in all the earth. ¹⁵For by now I could have stretched out my hand and struck you and your people with pestilence, and you would have been cut off from the earth. ¹⁶But this is why I have let you live: to show you my power, and to make my name resound through all the earth. ¹⁷You are still exalting yourself against my people, and will not let them go. ¹⁸Tomorrow at this time I will cause the heaviest hail to fall that has ever fallen in Egypt from the day it was founded until now. ¹⁹Send, therefore, and have your livestock and everything that you have in the open field brought to a secure place; every human or animal that is in the open field and is not brought under shelter will die when the hail comes down upon them.' " ²⁰Those officials of Pharaoh who feared the word of the LORD hurried their slaves and livestock off to a secure place. ²¹Those who did not regard the word of the LORD left

their slaves and livestock in the open field.

22 The LORD said to Moses, "Stretch out your hand toward heaven so that hail may fall on the whole land of Egypt, on humans and animals and all the plants of the field in the land of Egypt." 23 Then Moses stretched out his staff toward heaven, and the LORD sent thunder and hail, and fire came down on the earth. And the LORD rained hail on the land of Egypt; 24 there was hail with fire flashing continually in the midst of it, such heavy hail as had never fallen in all the land of Egypt since it became a nation. 25 The hail struck down everything that was in the open field throughout all the land of Egypt, both human and animal; the hail also struck down all the plants of the field, and shattered every tree in the field. 26 Only in the land of Goshen, where the Israelites were, there was no hail.

27 Then Pharaoh summoned Moses and Aaron, and said to them, "This time I have sinned; the LORD is in the right, and I and my people are in the wrong. 28 Pray to the LORD! Enough of God's thunder and hail! I will let you go; you need stay no longer." 29 Moses said to him, "As soon as I have gone out of the city, I will stretch out my hands to the LORD; the thunder will cease, and there will be no more hail, so that you may know that the earth is the LORD's. 30 But as for you and your officials, I know that you do not yet fear the LORD God." 31 (Now the flax

and the barley were ruined, for the barley was in the ear and the flax was in bud. 32 But the wheat and the spelt were not ruined, for they are late in coming up.) 33 So Moses left Pharaoh, went out of the city, and stretched out his hands to the LORD; then the thunder and the hail ceased, and the rain no longer poured down on the earth. 34 But when Pharaoh saw that the rain and the hail and the thunder had ceased, he sinned once more and hardened his heart, he and his officials. 35 So the heart of Pharaoh was hardened, and he would not let the Israelites go, just as the LORD had spoken through Moses.

THE EIGHTH PLAGUE: LOCUSTS

10 Then the LORD said to Moses, "Go to Pharaoh; for I have hardened his heart and the heart of his officials, in order that I may show these signs of mine among them, 2 and that you may tell your children and grandchildren how I have made fools of the Egyptians and what signs I have done among them—so that you may know that I am the LORD."

3 So Moses and Aaron went to Pharaoh, and said to him, "Thus says the LORD, the God of the Hebrews, 'How long will you refuse to humble yourself before me? Let my people go, so that they may worship me. 4 For if you refuse to let my people go, tomorrow I will bring locusts into your country. 5 They shall cover the surface of the land, so that no

---

─┤ BIBLE IN LIFE ▷───────⊕

Demonstrating God's Supremacy   Exodus 9.16

God used the relative weakness and impotence of Pharaoh to demonstrate the overwhelming heavenly power that would be marshaled in support of the Israelites as they threw off the shackles of slavery and became free under the leadership of Moses. This demonstration of God's supremacy was similar to when Elijah contended with the prophets of Baal at the end of the three-year drought, as described in 1 Kings 18. The plagues that afflicted Egypt and the death of the Baal worshipers were the harsh consequences of opposing God's will.

For Christians, the triumph of God over death with the resurrection of Jesus Christ is an event of profound and personal meaning.

one will be able to see the land. They shall devour the last remnant left you after the hail, and they shall devour every tree of yours that grows in the field. 6They shall fill your houses, and the houses of all your officials and of all the Egyptians—something that neither your parents nor your grandparents have seen, from the day they came on earth to this day.' " Then he turned and went out from Pharaoh.

7 Pharaoh's officials said to him, "How long shall this fellow be a snare to us? Let the people go, so that they may worship the LORD their God; do you not yet understand that Egypt is ruined?" 8So Moses and Aaron were brought back to Pharaoh, and he said to them, "Go, worship the LORD your God! But which ones are to go?" 9Moses said, "We will go with our young and our old; we will go with our sons and daughters and with our flocks and herds, because we have the LORD's festival to celebrate." 10He said to them, "The LORD indeed will be with you, if ever I let your little ones go with you! Plainly, you have some evil purpose in mind. 11No, never! Your men may go and worship the LORD, for that is what you are asking." And they were driven out from Pharaoh's presence.

12 Then the LORD said to Moses, "Stretch out your hand over the land of Egypt, so that the locusts may come upon it and eat every plant in the land, all that the hail has left." 13So Moses stretched out his staff over the land of Egypt, and the LORD brought an east wind upon the land all that day and all that night; when morning came, the east wind had brought the locusts. 14The locusts came upon all the land of Egypt and settled on the whole country of Egypt, such a dense swarm of locusts as had never been before, nor ever shall be again. 15They covered the surface of the whole land, so that the land was black; and they ate all the plants in the land and all the fruit of the trees that the hail had left; nothing green was left, no tree, no plant in the field, in all the land of Egypt. 16Pharaoh hurriedly sum-

moned Moses and Aaron and said, "I have sinned against the LORD your God, and against you. 17Do forgive my sin just this once, and pray to the LORD your God that at the least he remove this deadly thing from me." 18So he went out from Pharaoh and prayed to the LORD. 19The LORD changed the wind into a very strong west wind, which lifted the locusts and drove them into the Red Sea;ª not a single locust was left in all the country of Egypt. 20But the LORD hardened Pharaoh's heart, and he would not let the Israelites go.

THE NINTH PLAGUE: DARKNESS

21 Then the LORD said to Moses, "Stretch out your hand toward heaven so that there may be darkness over the land of Egypt, a darkness that can be felt." 22So Moses stretched out his hand toward heaven, and there was dense darkness in all the land of Egypt for three days. 23People could not see one another, and for three days they could not move from where they were; but all the Israelites had light where they lived. 24Then Pharaoh summoned Moses, and said, "Go, worship the LORD. Only your flocks and your herds shall remain behind. Even your children may go with you." 25But Moses said, "You must also let us have sacrifices and burnt offerings to sacrifice to the LORD our God. 26Our livestock also must go with us; not a hoof shall be left behind, for we must choose some of them for the worship of the LORD our God, and we will not know what to use to worship the LORD until we arrive there." 27But the LORD hardened Pharaoh's heart, and he was unwilling to let them go. 28Then Pharaoh said to him, "Get away from me! Take care that you do not see my face again, for on the day you see my face you shall die." 29Moses said, "Just as you say! I will never see your face again."

WARNING OF THE FINAL PLAGUE

11 The LORD said to Moses, "I will bring one more plague

ª 10.19 Or *Sea of Reeds*

upon Pharaoh and upon Egypt; afterwards he will let you go from here; indeed, when he lets you go, he will drive you away. ²Tell the people that every man is to ask his neighbor and every woman is to ask her neighbor for objects of silver and gold." ³The LORD gave the people favor in the sight of the Egyptians. Moreover, Moses himself was a man of great importance in the land of Egypt, in the sight of Pharaoh's officials and in the sight of the people.

4 Moses said, "Thus says the LORD: About midnight I will go out through Egypt. ⁵Every firstborn in the land of Egypt shall die, from the firstborn of Pharaoh who sits on his throne to the firstborn of the female slave who is behind the handmill, and all the firstborn of the livestock. ⁶Then there will be a loud cry throughout the whole land of Egypt, such as has never been or will ever be again. ⁷But not a dog shall growl at any of the Israelites—not at people, not at animals—so that you may know that the LORD makes a distinction between Egypt and Israel. ⁸Then all these officials of yours shall come down to me, and bow low to me, saying, 'Leave us, you and all the people who follow you.' After that I will leave." And in hot anger he left Pharaoh.

9 The LORD said to Moses, "Pharaoh will not listen to you, in order that my wonders may be multiplied in the land of Egypt." ¹⁰Moses and Aaron performed all these wonders before Pharaoh; but the LORD hardened Pharaoh's heart, and he did not let the people of Israel go out of his land.

THE FIRST PASSOVER INSTITUTED

12 The LORD said to Moses and Aaron in the land of Egypt: ²This month shall mark for you the beginning of months; it shall be the first month of the year for you. ³Tell the whole congregation of Israel that on the tenth of this month they are to take a lamb for each family, a lamb for each household. ⁴If a household is too small for a whole lamb,

it shall join its closest neighbor in obtaining one; the lamb shall be divided in proportion to the number of people who eat of it. ⁵Your lamb shall be without blemish, a year-old male; you may take it from the sheep or from the goats. ⁶You shall keep it until the fourteenth day of this month; then the whole assembled congregation of Israel shall slaughter it at twilight. ⁷They shall take some of the blood and put it on the two doorposts and the lintel of the houses in which they eat it. ⁸They shall eat the lamb that same night; they shall eat it roasted over the fire with unleavened bread and bitter herbs. ⁹Do not eat any of it raw or boiled in water, but roasted over the fire, with its head, legs, and inner organs. ¹⁰You shall let none of it remain until the morning; anything that remains until the morning you shall burn. ¹¹This is how you shall eat it: your loins girded, your sandals on your feet, and your staff in your hand; and you shall eat it hurriedly. It is the passover of the LORD. ¹²For I will pass through the land of Egypt that night, and I will strike down every firstborn in the land of Egypt, both human beings and animals; on all the gods of Egypt I will execute judgments: I am the LORD. ¹³The blood shall be a sign for you on the houses where you live: when I see the blood, I will pass over you, and no plague shall destroy you when I strike the land of Egypt.

14 This day shall be a day of remembrance for you. You shall celebrate it as a festival to the LORD; throughout your generations you shall observe it as a perpetual ordinance. ¹⁵Seven days you shall eat unleavened bread; on the first day you shall remove leaven from your houses, for whoever eats leavened bread from the first day until the seventh day shall be cut off from Israel. ¹⁶On the first day you shall hold a solemn assembly, and on the seventh day a solemn assembly; no work shall be done on those days; only what everyone must eat, that alone may be prepared by you. ¹⁷You shall observe the festival of

unleavened bread, for on this very day I brought your companies out of the land of Egypt: you shall observe this day throughout your generations as a perpetual ordinance. 18In the first month, from the evening of the fourteenth day until the evening of the twenty-first day, you shall eat unleavened bread. 19For seven days no leaven shall be found in your houses; for whoever eats what is leavened shall be cut off from the congregation of Israel, whether an alien or a native of the land. 20You shall eat nothing leavened; in all your settlements you shall eat unleavened bread.

21 Then Moses called all the elders of Israel and said to them, "Go, select lambs for your families, and slaughter the passover lamb. 22Take a bunch of hyssop, dip it in the blood that is in the basin, and touch the lintel and the two doorposts with the blood in the basin. None of you shall go outside the door of your house until morning. 23For the LORD will pass through to strike down the Egyptians; when he sees the blood on the lintel and on the two doorposts, the LORD will pass over that door and will not allow the destroyer to enter your houses to strike you down. 24You shall observe this rite as a perpetual ordinance for you and your children. 25When you come to the land that the LORD will give you, as he has promised, you shall keep this observance. 26And when your children ask you, 'What do you mean by this observance?' 27you shall say, 'It is the passover sacrifice to the LORD, for he passed over the houses of the Israelites in Egypt, when he struck down the Egyptians but spared our houses.' " And the people bowed down and worshiped.

28 The Israelites went and did just as the LORD had commanded Moses and Aaron.

THE TENTH PLAGUE: DEATH
OF THE FIRSTBORN

29 At midnight the LORD struck down all the firstborn in the land of Egypt, from the firstborn of Pha-raoh who sat on his throne to the firstborn of the prisoner who was in the dungeon, and all the firstborn of the livestock. 30Pharaoh arose in the night, he and all his officials and all the Egyptians; and there was a loud cry in Egypt, for there was not a house without someone dead. 31Then he summoned Moses and Aaron in the night, and said, "Rise up, go away from my people, both you and the Israelites! Go, worship the LORD, as you said. 32Take your flocks and your herds, as you said, and be gone. And bring a blessing on me too!"

THE EXODUS: FROM RAMESES
TO SUCCOTH

33 The Egyptians urged the people to hasten their departure from the land, for they said, "We shall all be dead." 34So the people took their dough before it was leavened, with their kneading bowls wrapped up in their cloaks on their shoulders. 35The Israelites had done as Moses told them; they had asked the Egyptians for jewelry of silver and gold, and for clothing, 36and the LORD had given the people favor in the sight of the Egyptians, so that they let them have what they asked. And so they plundered the Egyptians.

37 The Israelites journeyed from Rameses to Succoth, about six hundred thousand men on foot, besides children. 38A mixed crowd also went up with them, and livestock in great numbers, both flocks and herds. 39They baked unleavened cakes of the dough that they had brought out of Egypt; it was not leavened, because they were driven out of Egypt and could not wait, nor had they prepared any provisions for themselves.

40 The time that the Israelites had lived in Egypt was four hundred thirty years. 41At the end of four hundred thirty years, on that very day, all the companies of the LORD went out from the land of Egypt. 42That was for the LORD a night of vigil, to bring them out of the land of Egypt. That same night is a vigil to be kept for the LORD by all the

Israelites throughout their generations.

DIRECTIONS FOR THE PASSOVER

43 The LORD said to Moses and Aaron: This is the ordinance for the passover: no foreigner shall eat of it, 44but any slave who has been purchased may eat of it after he has been circumcised; 45no bound or hired servant may eat of it. 46It shall be eaten in one house; you shall not take any of the animal outside the house, and you shall not break any of its bones. 47The whole congregation of Israel shall celebrate it. 48If an alien who resides with you wants to celebrate the passover to the LORD, all his males shall be circumcised; then he may draw near to celebrate it; he shall be regarded as a native of the land. But no uncircumcised person shall eat of it; 49there shall be one law for the native and for the alien who resides among you. 50 All the Israelites did just as the LORD had commanded Moses and Aaron. 51That very day the LORD brought the Israelites out of the land of Egypt, company by company.

13 The LORD said to Moses: 2Consecrate to me all the firstborn; whatever is the first to open the womb among the Israelites, of human beings and animals, is mine.

THE FESTIVAL OF UNLEAVENED BREAD

3 Moses said to the people, "Remember this day on which you came out of Egypt, out of the house of slavery, because the LORD brought you out from there by strength of hand; no leavened bread shall be eaten. 4Today, in the month of Abib, you are going out. 5When the LORD brings you into the land of the Canaanites, the Hittites, the Amorites, the Hivites, and the Jebusites, which he swore to your ancestors to give you, a land flowing with milk and honey, you shall keep this observance in this month. 6Seven days you shall eat unleavened bread, and on the seventh day there shall be a festival to the LORD. 7Unleavened

bread shall be eaten for seven days; no leavened bread shall be seen in your possession, and no leaven shall be seen among you in all your territory. 8You shall tell your child on that day, 'It is because of what the LORD did for me when I came out of Egypt.' 9It shall serve for you as a sign on your hand and as a reminder on your forehead, so that the teaching of the LORD may be on your lips; for with a strong hand the LORD brought you out of Egypt. 10You shall keep this ordinance at its proper time from year to year.

THE CONSECRATION OF THE FIRSTBORN

11 "When the LORD has brought you into the land of the Canaanites, as he swore to you and your ancestors, and has given it to you, 12you shall set apart to the LORD all that first opens the womb. All the firstborn of your livestock that are males shall be the LORD's. 13But every firstborn donkey you shall redeem with a sheep; if you do not redeem it, you must break its neck. Every firstborn male among your children you shall redeem. 14When in the future your child asks you, 'What does this mean?' you shall answer, 'By strength of hand the LORD brought us out of Egypt, from the house of slavery. 15When Pharaoh stubbornly refused to let us go, the LORD killed all the firstborn in the land of Egypt, from human firstborn to the firstborn of animals. Therefore I sacrifice to the LORD every male that first opens the womb, but every firstborn of my sons I redeem.' 16It shall serve as a sign on your hand and as an emblema on your forehead that by strength of hand the LORD brought us out of Egypt."

THE PILLARS OF CLOUD AND FIRE

17 When Pharaoh let the people go, God did not lead them by way of the land of the Philistines, although that was nearer; for God thought,

a 13.16 Or as a frontlet; meaning of Heb uncertain

"If the people face war, they may change their minds and return to Egypt." 18So God led the people by the roundabout way of the wilderness toward the Red Sea.ª The Israelites went up out of the land of Egypt prepared for battle. 19And Moses took with him the bones of Joseph who had required a solemn oath of the Israelites, saying, "God will surely take notice of you, and then you must carry my bones with you from here." 20They set out from Succoth, and camped at Etham, on the edge of the wilderness. 21The LORD went in front of them in a pillar of cloud by day, to lead them along the way, and in a pillar of fire by night, to give them light, so that they might travel by day and by night. 22Neither the pillar of cloud by day nor the pillar of fire by night left its place in front of the people.

CROSSING THE RED SEA

14 Then the LORD said to Moses: 2Tell the Israelites to turn back and camp in front of Pi-hahiroth, between Migdol and the sea, in front of Baal-zephon; you shall camp opposite it, by the sea. 3Pharaoh will say of the Israelites, "They are wandering aimlessly in the land; the wilderness has closed in on them." 4I will harden Pharaoh's heart, and he will pursue them, so that I will gain glory for myself over Pharaoh and all his army; and the Egyptians shall know that I am the LORD. And they did so.

5 When the king of Egypt was told that the people had fled, the minds of Pharaoh and his officials were changed toward the people, and they said, "What have we done, letting Israel leave our service?" 6So he had his chariot made ready, and took his army with him; 7he took six hundred picked chariots and all the other chariots of Egypt with officers over all of them. 8The LORD hardened the heart of Pharaoh king of Egypt and he pursued the Israelites, who were going out boldly. 9The Egyptians pursued them, all Pharaoh's horses and chariots, his chariot drivers and his army; they over-

took them camped by the sea, by Pi-hahiroth, in front of Baal-zephon.

10 As Pharaoh drew near, the Israelites looked back, and there were the Egyptians advancing on them. In great fear the Israelites cried out to the LORD. 11They said to Moses, "Was it because there were no graves in Egypt that you have taken us away to die in the wilderness? What have you done to us, bringing us out of Egypt? 12Is this not the very thing we told you in Egypt, 'Let us alone and let us serve the Egyptians'? For it would have been better for us to serve the Egyptians than to die in the wilderness." 13But Moses said to the people, "Do not be afraid, stand firm, and see the deliverance that the LORD will accomplish for you today; for the Egyptians whom you see today you shall never see again. 14The LORD will fight for you, and you have only to keep still."

15 Then the LORD said to Moses, "Why do you cry out to me? Tell the Israelites to go forward. 16But you lift up your staff, and stretch out your hand over the sea and divide it, that the Israelites may go into the sea on dry ground. 17Then I will harden the hearts of the Egyptians so that they will go in after them; and so I will gain glory for myself over Pharaoh and all his army, his chariots, and his chariot drivers. 18And the Egyptians shall know that I am the LORD, when I have gained glory for myself over Pharaoh, his chariots, and his chariot drivers."

19 The angel of God who was going before the Israelite army moved and went behind them; and the pillar of cloud moved from in front of them and took its place behind them. 20It came between the army of Egypt and the army of Israel. And so the cloud was there with the darkness, and it lit up the night; one did not come near the other all night.

21 Then Moses stretched out his hand over the sea. The LORD drove the sea back by a strong east wind all night, and turned the sea into dry land; and the waters were

ª 13.18 Or Sea of Reeds

BE STILL

"The LORD will fight for you, and you have only to keep still."

—Exodus 14.14

In this pivotal moment in Israelite history, a moment in which the Israelites' very existence as a people hung in the balance, the Lord answered the people's cries with three phrases: *Do not be afraid. Be still. Go forward.* The key to each of these commands was the recognition that God is all-powerful and sovereign over all things and would act on behalf of his people. These profound truths were decisively demonstrated by God's miraculous rescue of the Israelites when the sea parted for them to pass through.

The Lord told the people not to be afraid because he promised to deliver them from the Egyptians, who were seeking to destroy them. Though the situation looked bleak, the Israelites could trust that they were safe in God's care.

The Lord told the people to be still because he would fight for them. Their salvation was not contingent upon their ability to handle the situation. They needed only to rest in God's power and open their minds to greater understanding of God.

Finally, the Lord told the people to move forward. At first this may seem at odds with the command to be still, but it is not. Instead, it was a command to step out in faith to do great things for God and rest in God's unchanging promises. God was essentially telling the Israelites, "What are you waiting for? I have promised to save you, so trust me and move forward to see it all take place!"

God speaks these same words to people today. He calls us to take a chance, to risk bold things for him, to test the limits that we have placed on ourselves (see Ecclesiastes 11.4–6). God is still sovereign over all things and acts on behalf of all people. We do not need to be afraid. We need not be locked up by uncertainty. Instead, we can be still, rest in God's power, and trust our Lord. God gives us the opportunity to expand our understanding of him and of ourselves. We can move ahead in faith boldly, confident that God will keep his promises. As the apostle James says, we should "consider it nothing but joy" when we are faced with difficulty because we know that trials can help us to grow in our walk with God (James 1.2–3).

Going Deeper

- What situations have you faced that seemed hopeless? Were there any promises of God that inspired hope and assurance in those situations?
- Consider one of the specific, difficult situations you face now. What would "moving forward" in faith look like in that situation?

divided. 22The Israelites went into the sea on dry ground, the waters forming a wall for them on their right and on their left. 23The Egyptians pursued, and went into the sea after them, all of Pharaoh's horses, chariots, and chariot drivers. 24At the morning watch the LORD in the pillar of fire and cloud looked down upon the Egyptian army, and threw the Egyptian army into panic. 25He clogged[a] their chariot wheels so that they turned with difficulty. The Egyptians said, "Let us flee from the Israelites, for the LORD is fighting for them against Egypt."

THE PURSUERS DROWNED

26 Then the LORD said to Moses, "Stretch out your hand over the sea, so that the water may come back upon the Egyptians, upon their chariots and chariot drivers." 27So Moses stretched out his hand over the sea, and at dawn the sea returned to its normal depth. As the Egyptians fled before it, the LORD tossed the Egyptians into the sea. 28The waters returned and covered the chariots and the chariot drivers, the entire army of Pharaoh that had followed them into the sea; not one of them remained. 29But the Israelites walked on dry ground through the sea, the waters forming a wall for them on their right and on their left.

30 Thus the LORD saved Israel that day from the Egyptians; and Israel saw the Egyptians dead on the seashore. 31Israel saw the great work that the LORD did against the Egyptians. So the people feared the LORD and believed in the LORD and in his servant Moses.

THE SONG OF MOSES

15 Then Moses and the Israelites sang this song to the LORD:

"I will sing to the LORD, for he
    has triumphed gloriously;
    horse and rider he has
        thrown into the sea.
2 The LORD is my strength
        and my might,[b]
    and he has become
        my salvation;

this is my God, and I will
        praise him,
    my father's God, and I
        will exalt him.
3 The LORD is a warrior;
    the LORD is his name.

4 "Pharaoh's chariots and his army
        he cast into the sea;
    his picked officers were sunk
        in the Red Sea.[c]
5 The floods covered them;
    they went down into the
        depths like a stone.
6 Your right hand, O LORD,
        glorious in power—
    your right hand, O LORD,
        shattered the enemy.
7 In the greatness of your
        majesty you overthrew
        your adversaries;
    you sent out your fury,
        it consumed them
        like stubble.
8 At the blast of your nostrils
        the waters piled up,
    the floods stood up in a heap;
        the deeps congealed in the
        heart of the sea.
9 The enemy said, 'I will pursue,
        I will overtake,
    I will divide the spoil, my desire
        shall have its fill of them.
    I will draw my sword, my hand
        shall destroy them.'
10 You blew with your wind, the
        sea covered them;
    they sank like lead in the
        mighty waters.

11 "Who is like you, O LORD,
        among the gods?
    Who is like you, majestic
        in holiness,
    awesome in splendor,
        doing wonders?
12 You stretched out your right hand,
    the earth swallowed them.

13 "In your steadfast love you
        led the people whom
        you redeemed;
    you guided them by your
        strength to your holy abode.

---

[a] 14.25 Sam Gk Syr: MT removed   [b] 15.2 Or song   [c] 15.4 Or Sea of Reeds

14 The peoples heard, they trembled;
  pangs seized the inhabitants
    of Philistia.
15 Then the chiefs of Edom
    were dismayed;
  trembling seized the
    leaders of Moab;
  all the inhabitants of
    Canaan melted away.
16 Terror and dread fell upon them;
  by the might of your arm, they
    became still as a stone
  until your people, O LORD,
    passed by,
  until the people whom you
    acquired passed by.
17 You brought them in and planted
    them on the mountain
  of your own possession,
  the place, O LORD, that you
    made your abode,
  the sanctuary, O LORD,
    that your hands
    have established.
18 The LORD will reign forever
    and ever."
19 When the horses of Pharaoh
with his chariots and his chariot
drivers went into the sea, the LORD
brought back the waters of the sea
upon them; but the Israelites walked
through the sea on dry ground.

THE SONG OF MIRIAM

20 Then the prophet Miriam,
Aaron's sister, took a tambourine in
her hand; and all the women went
out after her with tambourines and
with dancing. 21And Miriam sang to
them:
"Sing to the LORD, for he has
    triumphed gloriously;
  horse and rider he has thrown
    into the sea."

BITTER WATER MADE SWEET

22 Then Moses ordered Israel to
set out from the Red Sea,ª and they
went into the wilderness of Shur.
They went three days in the wilderness and found no water. 23When
they came to Marah, they could
not drink the water of Marah because it was bitter. That is why it
was called Marah.ᵇ 24And the people complained against Moses, saying, "What shall we drink?" 25He

cried out to the LORD; and the LORD
showed him a piece of wood;ᶜ he
threw it into the water, and the water became sweet.

There the LORDᵈ made for them a
statute and an ordinance and there
he put them to the test. 26He said, "If
you will listen carefully to the voice
of the LORD your God, and do what
is right in his sight, and give heed to
his commandments and keep all his
statutes, I will not bring upon you
any of the diseases that I brought
upon the Egyptians; for I am the
LORD who heals you."

27 Then they came to Elim, where
there were twelve springs of water
and seventy palm trees; and they
camped there by the water.

WHEN GOD CALLS US TO

PERFORM A TASK, GOD

PROVIDES THE MEANS.

BREAD FROM HEAVEN

16 The whole congregation of
the Israelites set out from
Elim; and Israel came to the wilderness of Sin, which is between Elim
and Sinai, on the fifteenth day of
the second month after they had departed from the land of Egypt. 2The
whole congregation of the Israelites complained against Moses and
Aaron in the wilderness. 3The Israelites said to them, "If only we had
died by the hand of the LORD in the
land of Egypt, when we sat by the
fleshpots and ate our fill of bread;
for you have brought us out into this
wilderness to kill this whole assembly with hunger."

4 Then the LORD said to Moses, "I
am going to rain bread from heaven
for you, and each day the people shall
go out and gather enough for that
day. In that way I will test them,

ª 15.22 Or Sea of Reeds   ᵇ 15.23 That is
Bitterness   ᶜ 15.25 Or a tree
ᵈ 15.25 Heb he

whether they will follow my instruction or not. ⁵On the sixth day, when they prepare what they bring in, it will be twice as much as they gather on other days." ⁶So Moses and Aaron said to all the Israelites, "In the evening you shall know that it was the LORD who brought you out of the land of Egypt, ⁷and in the morning you shall see the glory of the LORD, because he has heard your complaining against the LORD. For what are we, that you complain against us?" ⁸And Moses said, "When the LORD gives you meat to eat in the evening and your fill of bread in the morning, because the LORD has heard the complaining that you utter against him—what are we? Your complaining is not against us but against the LORD."

9 Then Moses said to Aaron, "Say to the whole congregation of the Israelites, 'Draw near to the LORD, for he has heard your complaining.' " ¹⁰And as Aaron spoke to the whole congregation of the Israelites, they looked toward the wilderness, and the glory of the LORD appeared in the cloud. ¹¹The LORD spoke to Moses and said, ¹²"I have heard the complaining of the Israelites; say to them, 'At twilight you shall eat meat, and in the morning you shall have your fill of bread; then you shall know that I am the LORD your God.' "

13 In the evening quails came up and covered the camp; and in the morning there was a layer of dew around the camp. ¹⁴When the layer of dew lifted, there on the surface of the wilderness was a fine flaky substance, as fine as frost on the ground. ¹⁵When the Israelites saw it, they said to one another, "What is it?"ᵃ For they did not know what it was. Moses said to them, "It is the bread that the LORD has given you to eat. ¹⁶This is what the LORD has commanded: 'Gather as much of it as each of you needs, an omer to a person according to the number of persons, all providing for those in their own tents.' " ¹⁷The Israelites did so, some gathering more, some less. ¹⁸But when they measured it with

an omer, those who gathered much had nothing over, and those who gathered little had no shortage; they gathered as much as each of them needed. ¹⁹And Moses said to them, "Let no one leave any of it over until morning." ²⁰But they did not listen to Moses; some left part of it until morning, and it bred worms and became foul. And Moses was angry with them. ²¹Morning by morning they gathered it, as much as each needed; but when the sun grew hot, it melted.

22 On the sixth day they gathered twice as much food, two omers apiece. When all the leaders of the congregation came and told Moses, ²³he said to them, "This is what the LORD has commanded: 'Tomorrow is a day of solemn rest, a holy sabbath to the LORD; bake what you want to bake and boil what you want to boil, and all that is left over put aside to be kept until morning.' " ²⁴So they put it aside until morning, as Moses commanded them; and it did not become foul, and there were no worms in it. ²⁵Moses said, "Eat it today, for today is a sabbath to the LORD; today you will not find it in the field. ²⁶Six days you shall gather it; but on the seventh day, which is a sabbath, there will be none."

27 On the seventh day some of the people went out to gather, and they found none. ²⁸The LORD said to Moses, "How long will you refuse to keep my commandments and instructions? ²⁹See! The LORD has given you the sabbath, therefore on the sixth day he gives you food for two days; each of you stay where you are; do not leave your place on the seventh day." ³⁰So the people rested on the seventh day.

31 The house of Israel called it manna; it was like coriander seed, white, and the taste of it was like wafers made with honey. ³²Moses said, "This is what the LORD has commanded: 'Let an omer of it be kept throughout your generations, in order that they may see the food

ᵃ 16.15 Or "It is manna" (Heb man hu, see verse 31)

with which I fed you in the wilderness, when I brought you out of the land of Egypt.'" 33And Moses said to Aaron, "Take a jar, and put an omer of manna in it, and place it before the LORD, to be kept throughout your generations." 34As the LORD commanded Moses, so Aaron placed it before the covenant,a for safekeeping. 35The Israelites ate manna forty years, until they came to a habitable land; they ate manna, until they came to the border of the land of Canaan. 36An omer is a tenth of an ephah.

WATER FROM THE ROCK

17 From the wilderness of Sin the whole congregation of the Israelites journeyed by stages, as the LORD commanded. They camped at Rephidim, but there was no water for the people to drink. 2The people quarreled with Moses, and said, "Give us water to drink." Moses said to them, "Why do you quarrel with me? Why do you test the LORD?" 3But the people thirsted there for water; and the people complained against Moses and said, "Why did you bring us out of Egypt, to kill us and our children and livestock with thirst?" 4So Moses cried out to the LORD, "What shall I do with this people? They are almost ready to stone me." 5The LORD said to Moses, "Go on ahead of the people, and take some of the elders of Israel with you; take in your hand the staff with which you struck the Nile, and go. 6I will be standing there in front of you on the rock at Horeb. Strike the rock, and water will come out of it, so that the people may drink." Moses did so, in the sight of the elders of Israel. 7He called the place Massahb and Meribah,c because the Israelites quarreled and tested the LORD, saying, "Is the LORD among us or not?"

AMALEK ATTACKS ISRAEL AND IS DEFEATED

8 Then Amalek came and fought with Israel at Rephidim. 9Moses said to Joshua, "Choose some men for us and go out, fight with Amalek. Tomorrow I will stand on the top of the hill with the staff of God in my hand." 10So Joshua did as Moses told him, and fought with Amalek, while Moses, Aaron, and Hur went up to the top of the hill. 11Whenever Moses held up his hand, Israel prevailed; and whenever he lowered his hand, Amalek prevailed. 12But Moses' hands grew weary; so they took a stone and put it under him, and he sat on it. Aaron and Hur held up his hands, one on one side, and the other on the other side; so his hands were steady until the sun set. 13And Joshua defeated Amalek and his people with the sword.

14 Then the LORD said to Moses, "Write this as a reminder in a book and recite it in the hearing of Joshua: I will utterly blot out the remembrance of Amalek from under heaven." 15And Moses built an altar and called it, The LORD is my banner. 16He said, "A hand upon the banner of the LORD!d The LORD will have war with Amalek from generation to generation."

JETHRO'S ADVICE

18 Jethro, the priest of Midian, Moses' father-in-law, heard of all that God had done for Moses and for his people Israel, how the LORD had brought Israel out of Egypt. 2After Moses had sent away his wife Zipporah, his father-in-law Jethro took her back, 3along with her two sons. The name of the one was Gershom (for he said, "I have been an aliene in a foreign land"), 4and the name of the other, Eliezerf (for he said, "The God of my father was my help, and delivered me from the sword of Pharaoh"). 5Jethro, Moses' father-in-law, came into the wilderness where Moses was encamped at the mountain of God, bringing Moses' sons and wife to him. 6He sent word to Moses, "I, your father-in-law Jethro, am coming to you, with your wife and her two sons." 7Moses went out to meet his father-in-law;

a 16.34 Or treaty or testimony; Heb eduth
b 17.7 That is Test   c 17.7 That is Quarrel
d 17.16 Cn: Meaning of Heb uncertain
e 18.3 Heb ger   f 18.4 Heb Eli, my God; ezer, help

he bowed down and kissed him; each asked after the other's welfare, and they went into the tent. ⁸Then Moses told his father-in-law all that the LORD had done to Pharaoh and to the Egyptians for Israel's sake, all the hardship that had beset them on the way, and how the LORD had delivered them. ⁹Jethro rejoiced for all the good that the LORD had done to Israel, in delivering them from the Egyptians.

10 Jethro said, "Blessed be the LORD, who has delivered you from the Egyptians and from Pharaoh. ¹¹Now I know that the LORD is greater than all gods, because he delivered the people from the Egyptians,ᵃ when they dealt arrogantly with them." ¹²And Jethro, Moses' father-in-law, brought a burnt offering and sacrifices to God; and Aaron came with all the elders of Israel to eat bread with Moses' father-in-law in the presence of God.

13 The next day Moses sat as judge for the people, while the people stood around him from morning until evening. ¹⁴When Moses' father-in-law saw all that he was doing for the people, he said, "What is this that you are doing for the people? Why do you sit alone, while all the people stand around you from morning until evening?" ¹⁵Moses said to his father-in-law, "Because the people come to me to inquire of God. ¹⁶When they have a dispute, they come to me and I decide between one person and another, and I make known to them the statutes and instructions of God." ¹⁷Moses' father-in-law said to him, "What you are doing is not good. ¹⁸You will surely wear yourself out, both you and these people with you. For the task is too heavy for you; you cannot do it alone. ¹⁹Now listen to me. I will give you counsel, and God be with you! You should represent the people before God, and you should bring their cases before God; ²⁰teach them the statutes and instructions and make known to them the way they are to go and the things they are to do. ²¹You should also look for able men among all the people, men who fear God, are trust-worthy, and hate dishonest gain; set such men over them as officers over thousands, hundreds, fifties, and tens. ²²Let them sit as judges for the people at all times; let them bring every important case to you, but decide every minor case themselves. So it will be easier for you, and they will bear the burden with you. ²³If you do this, and God so commands you, then you will be able to endure, and all these people will go to their home in peace."

24 So Moses listened to his father-in-law and did all that he had said. ²⁵Moses chose able men from all Israel and appointed them as heads over the people, as officers over thousands, hundreds, fifties, and tens. ²⁶And they judged the people at all times; hard cases they brought to Moses, but any minor case they decided themselves. ²⁷Then Moses let his father-in-law depart, and he went off to his own country.

THE ISRAELITES REACH MOUNT SINAI

19 On the third new moon after the Israelites had gone out of the land of Egypt, on that very day, they came into the wilderness of Sinai. ²They had journeyed from Rephidim, entered the wilderness of Sinai, and camped in the wilderness; Israel camped there in front of the mountain. ³Then Moses went up to God; the LORD called to him from the mountain, saying, "Thus you shall say to the house of Jacob, and tell the Israelites: ⁴You have seen what I did to the Egyptians, and how I bore you on eagles' wings and brought you to myself. ⁵Now therefore, if you obey my voice and keep my covenant, you shall be my treasured possession out of all the peoples. Indeed, the whole earth is mine, ⁶but you shall be for me a priestly kingdom and a holy nation. These are the words that you shall speak to the Israelites."

7 So Moses came, summoned the elders of the people, and set before

ᵃ **18.11** The clause *because... Egyptians* has been transposed from verse 10

PONDER

"Now therefore, if you obey my voice and keep my covenant, you shall be my treasured possession out of all the peoples. Indeed, the whole earth is mine, but you shall be for me a priestly kingdom and a holy nation."
—Exodus 19.5–6

PRAY

O Lord our God, may these commandments be embedded in our hearts and minds and become a part of our existence—our thoughts, actions and relationships with you and with our fellow human beings. Let them guide us in what we say and do as we live in harmony with your commands, but also in the freedom of the Spirit and our Savior, Jesus Christ. In his name we pray. Amen.

them all these words that the LORD had commanded him. 8The people all answered as one: "Everything that the LORD has spoken we will do." Moses reported the words of the people to the LORD. 9Then the LORD said to Moses, "I am going to come to you in a dense cloud, in order that the people may hear when I speak with you and so trust you ever after."

THE PEOPLE CONSECRATED

When Moses had told the words of the people to the LORD, 10the LORD said to Moses: "Go to the people and consecrate them today and tomorrow. Have them wash their clothes 11and prepare for the third day, because on the third day the LORD will come down upon Mount Sinai in the sight of all the people. 12You shall set limits for the people all around, saying, 'Be careful not to go up the mountain or to touch the edge of it. Any who touch the mountain shall be put to death. 13No hand shall touch them, but they shall be stoned

or shot with arrows;[a] whether animal or human being, they shall not live.' When the trumpet sounds a long blast, they may go up on the mountain." 14So Moses went down from the mountain to the people. He consecrated the people, and they washed their clothes. 15And he said to the people, "Prepare for the third day; do not go near a woman."

16 On the morning of the third day there was thunder and lightning, as well as a thick cloud on the mountain, and a blast of a trumpet so loud that all the people who were in the camp trembled. 17Moses brought the people out of the camp to meet God. They took their stand at the foot of the mountain. 18Now Mount Sinai was wrapped in smoke, because the LORD had descended upon it in fire; the smoke went up like the smoke of a kiln, while the whole mountain shook violently. 19As the blast of the trumpet grew louder and louder, Moses would speak and God would answer him in thunder. 20When the LORD descended upon Mount Sinai, to the top of the mountain, the LORD summoned Moses to the top of the mountain, and Moses went up. 21Then the LORD said to Moses, "Go down and warn the people not to break through to the LORD to look; otherwise many of them will perish. 22Even the priests who approach the LORD must consecrate themselves or the LORD will break out against them." 23Moses said to the LORD, "The people are not permitted to come up to Mount Sinai; for you yourself warned us, saying, 'Set limits around the mountain and keep it holy.' " 24The LORD said to him, "Go down, and come up bringing Aaron with you; but do not let either the priests or the people break through to come up to the LORD; otherwise he will break out against them." 25So Moses went down to the people and told them.

THE TEN COMMANDMENTS

20 Then God spoke all these words:

---

a 19.13 Heb lacks with arrows

2 I am the LORD your God, who brought you out of the land of Egypt, out of the house of slavery; ³you shall have no other gods before[a] me.

4 You shall not make for yourself an idol, whether in the form of anything that is in heaven above, or that is on the earth beneath, or that is in the water under the earth. ⁵You shall not bow down to them or worship them; for I the LORD your God am a jealous God, punishing children for the iniquity of parents, to the third and the fourth generation of those who reject me, ⁶but showing steadfast love to the thousandth generation[b] of those who love me and keep my commandments.

7 You shall not make wrongful use of the name of the LORD your God, for the LORD will not acquit anyone who misuses his name.

8 Remember the sabbath day, and keep it holy. ⁹Six days you shall labor and do all your work. ¹⁰But the seventh day is a sabbath to the LORD your God; you shall not do any work—you, your son or your daughter, your male or female slave, your livestock, or the alien resident in your towns. ¹¹For in six days the LORD made heaven and earth, the sea, and all that is in them, but rested the seventh day; therefore the LORD blessed the sabbath day and consecrated it.

12 Honor your father and your mother, so that your days may be long in the land that the LORD your God is giving you.

13 You shall not murder.[c]

14 You shall not commit adultery.

15 You shall not steal.

16 You shall not bear false witness against your neighbor.

17 You shall not covet your neighbor's house; you shall not covet your neighbor's wife, or male or female slave, or ox, or donkey, or anything that belongs to your neighbor.

18 When all the people witnessed the thunder and lightning, the sound of the trumpet, and the mountain smoking, they were afraid[d] and trembled and stood at a distance, ¹⁹and said to Moses, "You speak to us, and we will listen; but do not let God speak to us, or we will die." ²⁰Moses said to the people, "Do not be afraid; for God has come only to test you and to put the fear of him upon you so that you do not sin." ²¹Then the people stood at a distance, while Moses drew near to the thick darkness where God was.

THE LAW CONCERNING THE ALTAR

22 The LORD said to Moses: Thus you shall say to the Israelites: "You

[a] 20.3 Or besides [b] 20.6 Or to thousands [c] 20.13 Or kill [d] 20.18 Sam Gk Syr Vg: MT they saw

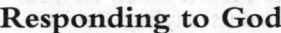

BIBLE IN LIFE

Responding to God *Exodus 20.1–21*

The Israelites stood at the foot of Mount Sinai, listening to the thunder, and trembling at the sight of smoke and lightning. This event inspired awe and convinced the people of God's all-powerful nature. Not surprisingly, the people reacted with fear—not with thanksgiving, praise, worship or a willingness to form an intimate relationship with God. They knew God had saved them. They had seen the Egyptian army perish in the Red Sea; they had seen a pillar of cloud by day and a pillar of fire by night showing the presence of God. Yet they did not want to hear from God directly anymore.

How do we respond to awe-inspiring events that cause us consternation, wonder, worry or fear? The truths that we know now from studying the universe—from astronomy to subnuclear physics, for example—have increasingly shown us a God who is even more powerful than the Israelites had grasped at that time. Yes, we should have a healthy fear of and respect for a God this powerful. Yet in the new covenant with Christ, "we act with great boldness" (2 Corinthians 3.12), and we need not remain at a distance from God. We are invited into intimacy with God.

have seen for yourselves that I spoke with you from heaven. 23 You shall not make gods of silver alongside me, nor shall you make for yourselves gods of gold. 24 You need make for me only an altar of earth and sacrifice on it your burnt offerings and your offerings of well-being, your sheep and your oxen; in every place where I cause my name to be remembered I will come to you and bless you. 25 But if you make for me an altar of stone, do not build it of hewn stones; for if you use a chisel upon it you profane it. 26 You shall not go up by steps to my altar, so that your nakedness may not be exposed on it."

THE LAW CONCERNING SLAVES

21 These are the ordinances that you shall set before them:

2 When you buy a male Hebrew slave, he shall serve six years, but in the seventh he shall go out a free person, without debt. 3 If he comes in single, he shall go out single; if he comes in married, then his wife shall go out with him. 4 If his master gives him a wife and she bears him sons or daughters, the wife and her children shall be her master's and he shall go out alone. 5 But if the slave declares, "I love my master, my wife, and my children; I will not go out a free person," 6 then his master shall bring him before God. a He shall be brought to the door or the doorpost; and his master shall pierce his ear with an awl; and he shall serve him for life.

7 When a man sells his daughter as a slave, she shall not go out as the male slaves do. 8 If she does not please her master, who designated her for himself, then he shall let her be redeemed; he shall have no right to sell her to a foreign people, since he has dealt unfairly with her. 9 If he designates her for his son, he shall deal with her as with a daughter. 10 If he takes another wife to himself, he shall not diminish the food, clothing, or marital rights of the first wife. b 11 And if he does not do these three things for her, she shall go out

without debt, without payment of money.

THE LAW CONCERNING VIOLENCE

12 Whoever strikes a person mortally shall be put to death. 13 If it was not premeditated, but came about by an act of God, then I will appoint for you a place to which the killer may flee. 14 But if someone willfully attacks and kills another by treachery, you shall take the killer from my altar for execution.

15 Whoever strikes father or mother shall be put to death.

16 Whoever kidnaps a person, whether that person has been sold or is still held in possession, shall be put to death.

17 Whoever curses father or mother shall be put to death.

18 When individuals quarrel and one strikes the other with a stone or fist so that the injured party, though not dead, is confined to bed, 19 but recovers and walks around outside with the help of a staff, then the assailant shall be free of liability, except to pay for the loss of time, and to arrange for full recovery.

20 When a slaveowner strikes a male or female slave with a rod and the slave dies immediately, the owner shall be punished. 21 But if the slave survives a day or two, there is no punishment; for the slave is the owner's property.

22 When people who are fighting injure a pregnant woman so that there is a miscarriage, and yet no further harm follows, the one responsible shall be fined what the woman's husband demands, paying as much as the judges determine. 23 If any harm follows, then you shall give life for life, 24 eye for eye, tooth for tooth, hand for hand, foot for foot, 25 burn for burn, wound for wound, stripe for stripe.

26 When a slaveowner strikes the eye of a male or female slave, destroying it, the owner shall let the slave go, a free person, to compensate for the eye. 27 If the owner

a 21.6 Or to the judges   b 21.10 Heb of her

knocks out a tooth of a male or female slave, the slave shall be let go, a free person, to compensate for the tooth.

LAWS CONCERNING PROPERTY

28 When an ox gores a man or a woman to death, the ox shall be stoned, and its flesh shall not be eaten; but the owner of the ox shall not be liable. 29 If the ox has been accustomed to gore in the past, and its owner has been warned but has not restrained it, and it kills a man or a woman, the ox shall be stoned, and its owner also shall be put to death. 30 If a ransom is imposed on the owner, then the owner shall pay whatever is imposed for the redemption of the victim's life. 31 If it gores a boy or a girl, the owner shall be dealt with according to this same rule. 32 If the ox gores a male or female slave, the owner shall pay to the slaveowner thirty shekels of silver, and the ox shall be stoned.

33 If someone leaves a pit open, or digs a pit and does not cover it, and an ox or a donkey falls into it, 34 the owner of the pit shall make restitution, giving money to its owner, but keeping the dead animal. 35 If someone's ox hurts the ox of another, so that it dies, then they shall sell the live ox and divide the price of it; and the dead animal they shall also divide. 36 But if it was known that the ox was accustomed to gore in the past, and its owner has not restrained it, the owner shall restore ox for ox, but keep the dead animal.

LAWS OF RESTITUTION

22 [a] When someone steals an ox or a sheep, and slaughters it or sells it, the thief shall pay five oxen for an ox, and four sheep for a sheep. [b] The thief shall make restitution, but if unable to do so, shall be sold for the theft. 4 When the animal, whether ox or donkey or sheep, is found alive in the thief's possession, the thief shall pay double.

2 [c] If a thief is found breaking in, and is beaten to death, no bloodguilt is incurred; 3 but if it happens after sunrise, bloodguilt is incurred.

5 When someone causes a field or vineyard to be grazed over, or lets livestock loose to graze in someone else's field, restitution shall be made from the best in the owner's field or vineyard.

6 When fire breaks out and catches in thorns so that the stacked grain or the standing grain or the field is consumed, the one who started the fire shall make full restitution.

7 When someone delivers to a neighbor money or goods for safekeeping, and they are stolen from the neighbor's house, then the thief, if caught, shall pay double. 8 If the thief is not caught, the owner of the house shall be brought before God,[d] to determine whether or not the owner had laid hands on the neighbor's goods.

9 In any case of disputed ownership involving ox, donkey, sheep, clothing, or any other loss, of which one party says, "This is mine," the case of both parties shall come before God;[d] the one whom God condemns[e] shall pay double to the other.

10 When someone delivers to another a donkey, ox, sheep, or any other animal for safekeeping, and it dies or is injured or is carried off, without anyone seeing it, 11 an oath before the LORD shall decide between the two of them that the one has not laid hands on the property of the other; the owner shall accept the oath, and no restitution shall be made. 12 But if it was stolen, restitution shall be made to its owner. 13 If it was mangled by beasts, let it be brought as evidence; restitution shall not be made for the mangled remains.

14 When someone borrows an animal from another and it is injured or dies, the owner not being present, full restitution shall be made. 15 If the owner was present, there shall be no restitution; if it was hired, only the hiring fee is due.

[a] 22.1 Ch 21.37 in Heb   [b] 22.1 Verses 2, 3, and 4 rearranged thus: 3b, 4, 2, 3a   [c] 22.2 Ch 22.1 in Heb   [d] 22.8,9 Or *before the judges*   [e] 22.9 Or *the judges condemn*

SOCIAL AND RELIGIOUS LAWS

16 When a man seduces a virgin who is not engaged to be married, and lies with her, he shall give the bride-price for her and make her his wife. **17** But if her father refuses to give her to him, he shall pay an amount equal to the bride-price for virgins.

18 You shall not permit a female sorcerer to live.

19 Whoever lies with an animal shall be put to death.

20 Whoever sacrifices to any god, other than the LORD alone, shall be devoted to destruction.

21 You shall not wrong or oppress a resident alien, for you were aliens in the land of Egypt. **22** You shall not abuse any widow or orphan. **23** If you do abuse them, when they cry out to me, I will surely heed their cry; **24** my wrath will burn, and I will kill you with the sword, and your wives shall become widows and your children orphans.

25 If you lend money to my people, to the poor among you, you shall not deal with them as a creditor; you shall not exact interest from them. **26** If you take your neighbor's cloak in pawn, you shall restore it before the sun goes down; **27** for it may be your neighbor's only clothing to use as cover; in what else shall that person sleep? And if your neighbor cries out to me, I will listen, for I am compassionate.

28 You shall not revile God, or curse a leader of your people.

29 You shall not delay to make offerings from the fullness of your harvest and from the outflow of your presses.ᵃ The firstborn of your sons you shall give to me. **30** You shall do the same with your oxen and with your sheep: seven days it shall remain with its mother; on the eighth day you shall give it to me.

31 You shall be people consecrated to me; therefore you shall not eat any meat that is mangled by beasts in the field; you shall throw it to the dogs.

JUSTICE FOR ALL

23 You shall not spread a false report. You shall not join hands with the wicked to act as a malicious witness. **2** You shall not follow a majority in wrongdoing; when you bear witness in a lawsuit, you shall not side with the majority so as to pervert justice; **3** nor shall you be partial to the poor in a lawsuit.

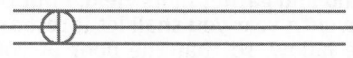

PONDER

"You shall be people consecrated to me . . . you shall not side with the majority so as to pervert justice."
—Exodus 22.31; 23.2

PRAY

Father, help us to have open hearts, to realize that your inspired words apply not only to those who first heard them thousands of years ago but to us today. Let them guide us and help us to emphasize the principles that never change: justice, truth, peace, servanthood, humility, compassion and unselfish love. These are the qualities by which our lives should be lived. Give us the wisdom and courage to be self-critical, with ambition to apply the truth to our own lives. We ask these things in your name. Amen.

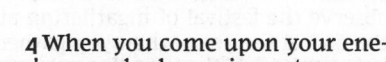

4 When you come upon your enemy's ox or donkey going astray, you shall bring it back.

5 When you see the donkey of one who hates you lying under its burden and you would hold back from setting it free, you must help to set it free.ᵃ

6 You shall not pervert the justice due to your poor in their lawsuits. **7** Keep far from a false charge, and do not kill the innocent and those in the right, for I will not acquit the guilty. **8** You shall take no bribe, for a bribe blinds the officials, and subverts the cause of those who are in the right.

ᵃ 22.29; 23.5 Meaning of Heb uncertain

9 You shall not oppress a resident alien; you know the heart of an alien, for you were aliens in the land of Egypt.

SABBATICAL YEAR AND SABBATH

10 For six years you shall sow your land and gather in its yield; 11but the seventh year you shall let it rest and lie fallow, so that the poor of your people may eat; and what they leave the wild animals may eat. You shall do the same with your vineyard, and with your olive orchard.

12 Six days you shall do your work, but on the seventh day you shall rest, so that your ox and your donkey may have relief, and your homeborn slave and the resident alien may be refreshed. 13Be attentive to all that I have said to you. Do not invoke the names of other gods; do not let them be heard on your lips.

THE ANNUAL FESTIVALS

14 Three times in the year you shall hold a festival for me. 15You shall observe the festival of unleavened bread; as I commanded you, you shall eat unleavened bread for seven days at the appointed time in the month of Abib, for in it you came out of Egypt. No one shall appear before me empty-handed.

16 You shall observe the festival of harvest, of the first fruits of your labor, of what you sow in the field. You shall observe the festival of ingathering at the end of the year, when you gather in from the field the fruit of your labor. 17Three times in the year all your males shall appear before the Lord GOD.

18 You shall not offer the blood of my sacrifice with anything leavened, or let the fat of my festival remain until the morning.

19 The choicest of the first fruits of your ground you shall bring into the house of the LORD your God. You shall not boil a kid in its mother's milk.

THE CONQUEST OF CANAAN PROMISED

20 I am going to send an angel in front of you, to guard you on the way and to bring you to the place that I have prepared. 21Be attentive to him and listen to his voice; do not rebel against him, for he will not pardon your transgression; for my name is in him.

22 But if you listen attentively to his voice and do all that I say, then I will be an enemy to your enemies and a foe to your foes.

23 When my angel goes in front of you, and brings you to the Amorites, the Hittites, the Perizzites, the Canaanites, the Hivites, and the Jebusites, and I blot them out, 24you shall not bow down to their gods, or worship them, or follow their practices, but you shall utterly demolish them and break their pillars in pieces. 25You shall worship the LORD your God, and Iᵃ will bless your bread and your water; and I will take sickness away from among you. 26No one shall miscarry or be barren in your land; I will fulfill the number of your days. 27I will send my terror in front of you, and will throw into confusion all the people against whom you shall come, and I will make all your enemies turn their backs to you. 28And I will send the pestilenceᵇ in front of you, which shall drive out the Hivites, the Canaanites, and the Hittites from before you. 29I will not drive them out from before you in one year, or the land would become desolate and the wild animals would multiply against you. 30Little by little I will drive them out from before you, until you have increased and possess the land. 31I will set your borders from the Red Seaᶜ to the sea of the Philistines, and from the wilderness to the Euphrates; for I will hand over to you the inhabitants of the land, and you shall drive them out before you. 32You shall make no covenant with them and their gods. 33They shall not live in your land, or they will make you sin against me; for if you worship their gods, it will surely be a snare to you.

ᵃ 23.25 Gk Vg: Heb *he*   ᵇ 23.28 Or *hornets:* Meaning of Heb uncertain   ᶜ 23.31 Or *Sea of Reeds*

THE BLOOD OF THE COVENANT

24 Then he said to Moses, "Come up to the LORD, you and Aaron, Nadab, and Abihu, and seventy of the elders of Israel, and worship at a distance. ²Moses alone shall come near the LORD; but the others shall not come near, and the people shall not come up with him."

3 Moses came and told the people all the words of the LORD and all the ordinances; and all the people answered with one voice, and said, "All the words that the LORD has spoken we will do." ⁴And Moses wrote down all the words of the LORD. He rose early in the morning, and built an altar at the foot of the mountain, and set up twelve pillars, corresponding to the twelve tribes of Israel. ⁵He sent young men of the people of Israel, who offered burnt offerings and sacrificed oxen as offerings of well-being to the LORD. ⁶Moses took half of the blood and put it in basins, and half of the blood he dashed against the altar. ⁷Then he took the book of the covenant, and read it in the hearing of the people; and they said, "All that the LORD has spoken we will do, and we will be obedient." ⁸Moses took the blood and dashed it on the people, and said, "See the blood of the covenant that the LORD has made with you in accordance with all these words."

EACH OF US NEEDS TO MAKE

A POSITIVE COMMITMENT

TO CHRIST. THIS IS FOR OUR

OWN HAPPINESS, PEACE AND

SENSE OF PERSONAL WORTH.

BEING PART OF A CHRISTIAN

COMMUNITY STRENGTHENS

OUR COMMITMENT.

ON THE MOUNTAIN WITH GOD

9 Then Moses and Aaron, Nadab, and Abihu, and seventy of the elders of Israel went up, ¹⁰and they saw the God of Israel. Under his feet there was something like a pavement of sapphire stone, like the very heaven for clearness. ¹¹God[a] did not lay his hand on the chief men of the people of Israel; also they beheld God, and they ate and drank.

12 The LORD said to Moses, "Come up to me on the mountain, and wait there; and I will give you the tablets of stone, with the law and the commandment, which I have written for their instruction." ¹³So Moses set out with his assistant Joshua, and Moses went up into the mountain of God. ¹⁴To the elders he had said, "Wait here for us, until we come to you again; for Aaron and Hur are with you; whoever has a dispute may go to them."

15 Then Moses went up on the mountain, and the cloud covered the mountain. ¹⁶The glory of the LORD settled on Mount Sinai, and the cloud covered it for six days; on the seventh day he called to Moses out of the cloud. ¹⁷Now the appearance of the glory of the LORD was like a devouring fire on the top of the mountain in the sight of the people of Israel. ¹⁸Moses entered the cloud, and went up on the mountain. Moses was on the mountain for forty days and forty nights.

OFFERINGS FOR THE TABERNACLE

25 The LORD said to Moses: ²Tell the Israelites to take for me an offering; from all whose hearts prompt them to give you shall receive the offering for me. ³This is the offering that you shall receive from them: gold, silver, and bronze, ⁴blue, purple, and crimson yarns and fine linen, goats' hair, ⁵tanned rams' skins, fine leather,[b] acacia wood, ⁶oil for the lamps, spices for the anointing oil and for the fragrant incense, ⁷onyx stones and gems to be set in the ephod and for the breastpiece. ⁸And have them make me a sanctuary,

a 24.11 Heb *He*   b 25.5 Meaning of Heb uncertain

so that I may dwell among them. ⁹In accordance with all that I show you concerning the pattern of the tabernacle and of all its furniture, so you shall make it.

THE ARK OF THE COVENANT

10 They shall make an ark of acacia wood; it shall be two and a half cubits long, a cubit and a half wide, and a cubit and a half high. ¹¹You shall overlay it with pure gold, inside and outside you shall overlay it, and you shall make a molding of gold upon it all around. ¹²You shall cast four rings of gold for it and put them on its four feet, two rings on the one side of it, and two rings on the other side. ¹³You shall make poles of acacia wood, and overlay them with gold. ¹⁴And you shall put the poles into the rings on the sides of the ark, by which to carry the ark. ¹⁵The poles shall remain in the rings of the ark; they shall not be taken from it. ¹⁶You shall put into the ark the covenantᵃ that I shall give you.

17 Then you shall make a mercy seatᵇ of pure gold; two cubits and a half shall be its length, and a cubit and a half its width. ¹⁸You shall make two cherubim of gold; you shall make them of hammered work, at the two ends of the mercy seat.ᶜ ¹⁹Make one cherub at the one end, and one cherub at the other; of one piece with the mercy seatᶜ you shall make the cherubim at its two ends. ²⁰The cherubim shall spread out their wings above, overshadowing the mercy seatᶜ with their wings. They shall face one to another; the faces of the cherubim shall be turned toward the mercy seat.ᶜ ²¹You shall put the mercy seatᶜ on the top of the ark; and in the ark you shall put the covenantᵈ that I shall give you. ²²There I will meet with you, and from above the mercy seat,ᶜ from between the two cherubim that are on the ark of the covenant,ᵈ I will deliver to you all my commands for the Israelites.

THE TABLE FOR THE BREAD OF THE PRESENCE

23 You shall make a table of acacia wood, two cubits long, one cubit wide, and a cubit and a half high. ²⁴You shall overlay it with pure gold, and make a molding of gold around it. ²⁵You shall make around it a rim a handbreadth wide, and a molding of gold around the rim. ²⁶You shall make for it four rings of gold, and fasten the rings to the four corners at its four legs. ²⁷The rings that hold the poles used for carrying the table shall be close to the rim. ²⁸You shall make the poles of acacia wood, and overlay them with gold, and the table shall be carried with these. ²⁹You shall make its plates and dishes for incense, and its flagons and bowls with which to pour drink offerings; you shall make them of pure gold. ³⁰And you shall set the bread of the Presence on the table before me always.

THE LAMPSTAND

31 You shall make a lampstand of pure gold. The base and the shaft of the lampstand shall be made of hammered work; its cups, its calyxes, and its petals shall be of one piece with it; ³²and there shall be six branches going out of its sides, three branches of the lampstand out of one side of it and three branches of the lampstand out of the other side of it; ³³three cups shaped like almond blossoms, each with calyx and petals, on one branch, and three cups shaped like almond blossoms, each with calyx and petals, on the other branch—so for the six branches going out of the lampstand. ³⁴On the lampstand itself there shall be four cups shaped like almond blossoms, each with its calyxes and petals. ³⁵There shall be a calyx of one piece with it under the first pair of branches, a calyx of one piece with it under the next pair of branches, and a calyx of one piece with it under the last pair of branches—so for the six branches that go out of the lampstand. ³⁶Their calyxes and their branches shall be of one piece with it, the whole of it one hammered piece of pure gold. ³⁷You

ᵃ 25.16 Or *treaty,* or *testimony;* Heb *eduth*
ᵇ 25.17 Or *a cover*   ᶜ 25.18,19,20,21,22 Or *the cover*   ᵈ 25.21,22 Or *treaty,* or *testimony;* Heb *eduth*

shall make the seven lamps for it; and the lamps shall be set up so as to give light on the space in front of it. [38]Its snuffers and trays shall be of pure gold. [39]It, and all these utensils, shall be made from a talent of pure gold. [40]And see that you make them according to the pattern for them, which is being shown you on the mountain.

THE TABERNACLE

26 Moreover you shall make the tabernacle with ten curtains of fine twisted linen, and blue, purple, and crimson yarns; you shall make them with cherubim skillfully worked into them. [2]The length of each curtain shall be twenty-eight cubits, and the width of each curtain four cubits; all the curtains shall be of the same size. [3]Five curtains shall be joined to one another; and the other five curtains shall be joined to one another. [4]You shall make loops of blue on the edge of the outermost curtain in the first set; and likewise you shall make loops on the edge of the outermost curtain in the second set. [5]You shall make fifty loops on the one curtain, and you shall make fifty loops on the edge of the curtain that is in the second set; the loops shall be opposite one another. [6]You shall make fifty clasps of gold, and join the curtains to one another with the clasps, so that the tabernacle may be one whole.

7 You shall also make curtains of goats' hair for a tent over the tabernacle; you shall make eleven curtains. [8]The length of each curtain shall be thirty cubits, and the width of each curtain four cubits; the eleven curtains shall be of the same size. [9]You shall join five curtains by themselves, and six curtains by themselves, and the sixth curtain you shall double over at the front of the tent. [10]You shall make fifty loops on the edge of the curtain that is outermost in one set, and fifty loops on the edge of the curtain that is outermost in the second set.

11 You shall make fifty clasps of bronze, and put the clasps into the loops, and join the tent together, so

that it may be one whole. [12]The part that remains of the curtains of the tent, the half curtain that remains, shall hang over the back of the tabernacle. [13]The cubit on the one side, and the cubit on the other side, of what remains in the length of the curtains of the tent, shall hang over the sides of the tabernacle, on this side and that side, to cover it. [14]You shall make for the tent a covering of tanned rams' skins and an outer covering of fine leather.[a]

THE FRAMEWORK

15 You shall make upright frames of acacia wood for the tabernacle. [16]Ten cubits shall be the length of a frame, and a cubit and a half the width of each frame. [17]There shall be two pegs in each frame to fit the frames together; you shall make these for all the frames of the tabernacle. [18]You shall make the frames for the tabernacle: twenty frames for the south side; [19]and you shall make forty bases of silver under the twenty frames, two bases under the first frame for its two pegs, and two bases under the next frame for its two pegs; [20]and for the second side of the tabernacle, on the north side twenty frames, [21]and their forty bases of silver, two bases under the first frame, and two bases under the next frame; [22]and for the rear of the tabernacle westward you shall make six frames. [23]You shall make two frames for corners of the tabernacle in the rear; [24]they shall be separate beneath, but joined at the top, at the first ring; it shall be the same with both of them; they shall form the two corners. [25]And so there shall be eight frames, with their bases of silver, sixteen bases; two bases under the first frame, and two bases under the next frame.

26 You shall make bars of acacia wood, five for the frames of the one side of the tabernacle, [27]and five bars for the frames of the other side of the tabernacle, and five bars for the frames of the side of the tabernacle at the rear westward. [28]The middle

[a] 26.14 Meaning of Heb uncertain

bar, halfway up the frames, shall pass through from end to end. 29You shall overlay the frames with gold, and shall make their rings of gold to hold the bars; and you shall overlay the bars with gold. 30Then you shall erect the tabernacle according to the plan for it that you were shown on the mountain.

THE CURTAIN

31You shall make a curtain of blue, purple, and crimson yarns, and of fine twisted linen; it shall be made with cherubim skillfully worked into it. 32You shall hang it on four pillars of acacia overlaid with gold, which have hooks of gold and rest on four bases of silver. 33You shall hang the curtain under the clasps, and bring the ark of the covenant[a] in there, within the curtain; and the curtain shall separate for you the holy place from the most holy. 34You shall put the mercy seat[b] on the ark of the covenant[a] in the most holy place. 35You shall set the table outside the curtain, and the lampstand on the south side of the tabernacle opposite the table; and you shall put the table on the north side.

36You shall make a screen for the entrance of the tent, of blue, purple, and crimson yarns, and of fine twisted linen, embroidered with needlework. 37You shall make for the screen five pillars of acacia, and overlay them with gold; their hooks shall be of gold, and you shall cast five bases of bronze for them.

THE ALTAR OF BURNT OFFERING

27 You shall make the altar of acacia wood, five cubits long and five cubits wide; the altar shall be square, and it shall be three cubits high. 2You shall make horns for it on its four corners; its horns shall be of one piece with it, and you shall overlay it with bronze. 3You shall make pots for it to receive its ashes, and shovels and basins and forks and firepans; you shall make all its utensils of bronze. 4You shall also make for it a grating, a network of bronze; and on the net you shall make four bronze rings at its four corners. 5You shall set it under the ledge of the altar so that the net shall extend halfway down the altar. 6You shall make poles for the altar, poles of acacia wood, and overlay them with bronze; 7the poles shall be put through the rings, so that the poles shall be on the two sides of the altar when it is carried. 8You shall make it hollow, with boards. They shall be made just as you were shown on the mountain.

THE COURT AND ITS HANGINGS

9You shall make the court of the tabernacle. On the south side the court shall have hangings of fine twisted linen one hundred cubits long for that side; 10its twenty pillars and their twenty bases shall be of bronze, but the hooks of the pillars and their bands shall be of silver. 11Likewise for its length on the north side there shall be hangings one hundred cubits long, their pillars twenty and their bases twenty, of bronze, but the hooks of the pillars and their bands shall be of silver. 12For the width of the court on the west side there shall be fifty cubits of hangings, with ten pillars and ten bases. 13The width of the court on the front to the east shall be fifty cubits. 14There shall be fifteen cubits of hangings on the one side, with three pillars and three bases. 15There shall be fifteen cubits of hangings on the other side, with three pillars and three bases. 16For the gate of the court there shall be a screen twenty cubits long, of blue, purple, and crimson yarns, and of fine twisted linen, embroidered with needlework; it shall have four pillars and with them four bases. 17All the pillars around the court shall be banded with silver; their hooks shall be of silver, and their bases of bronze. 18The length of the court shall be one hundred cubits, the width fifty, and the height five cubits, with hangings of fine twisted linen and bases of bronze. 19All the utensils of the tabernacle for every

---

a 26.33,34 Or *treaty,* or *testimony;* Heb *eduth*   b 26.34 Or *the cover* use, and all its pegs and all the pegs of the court, shall be of bronze.

THE OIL FOR THE LAMP

20 You shall further command the Israelites to bring you pure oil of beaten olives for the light, so that a lamp may be set up to burn regularly. 21 In the tent of meeting, outside the curtain that is before the covenant,ᵃ Aaron and his sons shall tend it from evening to morning before the LORD. It shall be a perpetual ordinance to be observed throughout their generations by the Israelites.

VESTMENTS FOR THE PRIESTHOOD

28 Then bring near to you your brother Aaron, and his sons with him, from among the Israelites, to serve me as priests—Aaron and Aaron's sons, Nadab and Abihu, Eleazar and Ithamar. 2 You shall make sacred vestments for the glorious adornment of your brother Aaron. 3 And you shall speak to all who have ability, whom I have endowed with skill, that they make Aaron's vestments to consecrate him for my priesthood. 4 These are the vestments that they shall make: a breastpiece, an ephod, a robe, a checkered tunic, a turban, and a sash. When they make these sacred vestments for your brother Aaron and his sons to serve me as priests, 5 they shall use gold, blue, purple, and crimson yarns, and fine linen.

THE EPHOD

6 They shall make the ephod of gold, of blue, purple, and crimson yarns, and of fine twisted linen, skillfully worked. 7 It shall have two shoulder-pieces attached to its two edges, so that it may be joined together. 8 The decorated band on it shall be of the same workmanship and materials, of gold, of blue, purple, and crimson yarns, and of fine twisted linen. 9 You shall take two onyx stones, and engrave on them the names of the sons of Israel, 10 six of their names on the one stone, and the names of the remaining six on

the other stone, in the order of their birth. 11 As a gem-cutter engraves signets, so you shall engrave the two stones with the names of the sons of Israel; you shall mount them in settings of gold filigree. 12 You shall set the two stones on the shoulder-pieces of the ephod, as stones of remembrance for the sons of Israel; and Aaron shall bear their names before the LORD on his two shoulders for remembrance. 13 You shall make settings of gold filigree, 14 and two chains of pure gold, twisted like cords; and you shall attach the corded chains to the settings.

WORSHIP IS NOT A GRIM DUTY, BUT A JOYOUS, EXPANSIVE, EXHILARATING RESPONSIBILITY THAT SHOULD BE SHARED WITH OTHERS.

THE BREASTPLATE

15 You shall make a breastpiece of judgment, in skilled work; you shall make it in the style of the ephod; of gold, of blue and purple and crimson yarns, and of fine twisted linen you shall make it. 16 It shall be square and doubled, a span in length and a span in width. 17 You shall set in it four rows of stones. A row of carnelian,ᵇ chrysolite, and emerald shall be the first row; 18 and the second row a turquoise, a sapphire,ᶜ and a moonstone; 19 and the third row a jacinth, an agate, and an amethyst; 20 and the fourth row a beryl, an onyx, and a jasper; they shall be set in gold filigree. 21 There shall be twelve stones with names corresponding to the names of the sons of Israel; they shall be like signets, each engraved with its name, for the

ᵃ 27.21 Or treaty, or testimony; Heb eduth
ᵇ 28.17 The identity of several of these stones is uncertain   ᶜ 28.18 Or lapis lazuli

twelve tribes. 22You shall make for the breastpiece chains of pure gold, twisted like cords; 23and you shall make for the breastpiece two rings of gold, and put the two rings on the two edges of the breastpiece. 24You shall put the two cords of gold in the two rings at the edges of the breastpiece; 25the two ends of the two cords you shall attach to the two settings, and so attach it in front to the shoulder-pieces of the ephod. 26You shall make two rings of gold, and put them at the two ends of the breastpiece, on its inside edge next to the ephod. 27You shall make two rings of gold, and attach them in front to the lower part of the two shoulder-pieces of the ephod, at its joining above the decorated band of the ephod. 28The breastpiece shall be bound by its rings to the rings of the ephod with a blue cord, so that it may lie on the decorated band of the ephod, and so that the breastpiece shall not come loose from the ephod. 29So Aaron shall bear the names of the sons of Israel in the breastpiece of judgment on his heart when he goes into the holy place, for a continual remembrance before the LORD. 30In the breastpiece of judgment you shall put the Urim and the Thummim, and they shall be on Aaron's heart when he goes in before the LORD; thus Aaron shall bear the judgment of the Israelites on his heart before the LORD continually.

OTHER PRIESTLY VESTMENTS

31 You shall make the robe of the ephod all of blue. 32It shall have an opening for the head in the middle of it, with a woven binding around the opening, like the opening in a coat of mail,ᵃ so that it may not be torn. 33On its lower hem you shall make pomegranates of blue, purple, and crimson yarns, all around the lower hem, with bells of gold between them all around— 34a golden bell and a pomegranate alternating all around the lower hem of the robe. 35Aaron shall wear it when he ministers, and its sound shall be heard when he goes into the holy place be-

fore the LORD, and when he comes out, so that he may not die.

36 You shall make a rosette of pure gold, and engrave on it, like the engraving of a signet, "Holy to the LORD." 37You shall fasten it on the turban with a blue cord; it shall be on the front of the turban. 38It shall be on Aaron's forehead, and Aaron shall take on himself any guilt incurred in the holy offering that the Israelites consecrate as their sacred donations; it shall always be on his forehead, in order that they may find favor before the LORD.

39 You shall make the checkered tunic of fine linen, and you shall make a turban of fine linen, and you shall make a sash embroidered with needlework.

40 For Aaron's sons you shall make tunics and sashes and headdresses; you shall make them for their glorious adornment. 41You shall put them on your brother Aaron, and on his sons with him, and shall anoint them and ordain them and consecrate them, so that they may serve me as priests. 42You shall make for them linen undergarments to cover their naked flesh; they shall reach from the hips to the thighs; 43Aaron and his sons shall wear them when they go into the tent of meeting, or when they come near the altar to minister in the holy place; or they will bring guilt on themselves and die. This shall be a perpetual ordinance for him and for his descendants after him.

THE ORDINATION OF THE PRIESTS

29 Now this is what you shall do to them to consecrate them, so that they may serve me as priests. Take one young bull and two rams without blemish, 2and unleavened bread, unleavened cakes mixed with oil, and unleavened wafers spread with oil. You shall make them of choice wheat flour. 3You shall put them in one basket and bring them in the basket, and bring the bull and the two rams. 4You shall bring

ᵃ 28.32 Meaning of Heb uncertain

Aaron and his sons to the entrance of the tent of meeting, and wash them with water. 5Then you shall take the vestments, and put on Aaron the tunic and the robe of the ephod, and the ephod, and the breastpiece, and gird him with the decorated band of the ephod; 6and you shall set the turban on his head, and put the holy diadem on the turban. 7You shall take the anointing oil, and pour it on his head and anoint him. 8Then you shall bring his sons, and put tunics on them, 9and you shall gird them with sashes^a and tie headdresses on them; and the priesthood shall be theirs by a perpetual ordinance. You shall then ordain Aaron and his sons.

10 You shall bring the bull in front of the tent of meeting. Aaron and his sons shall lay their hands on the head of the bull, 11and you shall slaughter the bull before the LORD, at the entrance of the tent of meeting, 12and shall take some of the blood of the bull and put it on the horns of the altar with your finger, and all the rest of the blood you shall pour out at the base of the altar. 13You shall take all the fat that covers the entrails, and the appendage of the liver, and the two kidneys with the fat that is on them, and turn them into smoke on the altar. 14But the flesh of the bull, and its skin, and its dung, you shall burn with fire outside the camp; it is a sin offering.

15 Then you shall take one of the rams, and Aaron and his sons shall lay their hands on the head of the ram, 16and you shall slaughter the ram, and shall take its blood and dash it against all sides of the altar. 17Then you shall cut the ram into its parts, and wash its entrails and its legs, and put them with its parts and its head, 18and turn the whole ram into smoke on the altar; it is a burnt offering to the LORD; it is a pleasing odor, an offering by fire to the LORD.

19 You shall take the other ram; and Aaron and his sons shall lay their hands on the head of the ram, 20and you shall slaughter the ram, and take some of its blood and put it on the lobe of Aaron's right ear and

on the lobes of the right ears of his sons, and on the thumbs of their right hands, and on the big toes of their right feet, and dash the rest of the blood against all sides of the altar. 21Then you shall take some of the blood that is on the altar, and some of the anointing oil, and sprinkle it on Aaron and his vestments and on his sons and his sons' vestments with him; then he and his vestments shall be holy, as well as his sons and his sons' vestments.

22 You shall also take the fat of the ram, the fat tail, the fat that covers the entrails, the appendage of the liver, the two kidneys with the fat that is on them, and the right thigh (for it is a ram of ordination), 23and one loaf of bread, one cake of bread made with oil, and one wafer, out of the basket of unleavened bread that is before the LORD; 24and you shall place all these on the palms of Aaron and on the palms of his sons, and raise them as an elevation offering before the LORD. 25Then you shall take them from their hands, and turn them into smoke on the altar on top of the burnt offering of pleasing odor before the LORD; it is an offering by fire to the LORD.

26 You shall take the breast of the ram of Aaron's ordination and raise it as an elevation offering before the LORD; and it shall be your portion. 27You shall consecrate the breast that was raised as an elevation offering and the thigh that was raised as an elevation offering from the ram of ordination, from that which belonged to Aaron and his sons. 28These things shall be a perpetual ordinance for Aaron and his sons from the Israelites, for this is an offering; and it shall be an offering by the Israelites from their sacrifice of offerings of well-being, their offering to the LORD.

29 The sacred vestments of Aaron shall be passed on to his sons after him; they shall be anointed in them and ordained in them. 30The son who is priest in his place shall wear them seven days, when he comes

^a 29.9 Gk: Heb sashes, Aaron and his sons

into the tent of meeting to minister in the holy place. 31 You shall take the ram of ordination, and boil its flesh in a holy place; 32and Aaron and his sons shall eat the flesh of the ram and the bread that is in the basket, at the entrance of the tent of meeting. 33They themselves shall eat the food by which atonement is made, to ordain and consecrate them, but no one else shall eat of them, because they are holy. 34If any of the flesh for the ordination, or of the bread, remains until the morning, then you shall burn the remainder with fire; it shall not be eaten, because it is holy. 35 Thus you shall do to Aaron and to his sons, just as I have commanded you; through seven days you shall ordain them. 36Also every day you shall offer a bull as a sin offering for atonement. Also you shall offer a sin offering for the altar, when you make atonement for it, and shall anoint it, to consecrate it. 37Seven days you shall make atonement for the altar, and consecrate it, and the altar shall be most holy; whatever touches the altar shall become holy.

THE DAILY OFFERINGS

38 Now this is what you shall offer on the altar: two lambs a year old regularly each day. 39One lamb you shall offer in the morning, and the other lamb you shall offer in the evening; 40and with the first lamb one-tenth of a measure of choice flour mixed with one-fourth of a hin of beaten oil, and one-fourth of a hin of wine for a drink offering. 41And the other lamb you shall offer in the evening, and shall offer with it a grain offering and its drink offering, as in the morning, for a pleasing odor, an offering by fire to the LORD. 42It shall be a regular burnt offering throughout your generations at the entrance of the tent of meeting before the LORD, where I will meet with you, to speak to you there. 43I will meet with the Israelites there, and it shall be sanctified by my glory; 44I will consecrate the tent of meeting and the altar; Aaron also and his

sons I will consecrate, to serve me as priests. 45I will dwell among the Israelites, and I will be their God. 46And they shall know that I am the LORD their God, who brought them out of the land of Egypt that I might dwell among them; I am the LORD their God.

THE ALTAR OF INCENSE

30 You shall make an altar on which to offer incense; you shall make it of acacia wood. 2It shall be one cubit long, and one cubit wide; it shall be square, and shall be two cubits high; its horns shall be of one piece with it. 3You shall overlay it with pure gold, its top, and its sides all around and its horns; and you shall make for it a molding of gold all around. 4And you shall make two golden rings for it; under its molding on two opposite sides of it you shall make them, and they shall hold the poles with which to carry it. 5You shall make the poles of acacia wood, and overlay them with gold. 6You shall place it in front of the curtain that is above the ark of the covenant,a in front of the mercy seatb that is over the covenant,a where I will meet with you. 7Aaron shall offer fragrant incense on it; every morning when he dresses the lamps he shall offer it, 8and when Aaron sets up the lamps in the evening, he shall offer it, a regular incense offering before the LORD throughout your generations. 9You shall not offer unholy incense on it, or a burnt offering, or a grain offering; and you shall not pour a drink offering on it. 10Once a year Aaron shall perform the rite of atonement on its horns. Throughout your generations he shall perform the atonement for it once a year with the blood of the atoning sin offering. It is most holy to the LORD.

THE HALF SHEKEL FOR THE SANCTUARY

11 The LORD spoke to Moses: 12When you take a census of the

a 30.6 Or treaty, or testimony; Heb eduth
b 30.6 Or the cover

Israelites to register them, at registration all of them shall give a ransom for their lives to the LORD, so that no plague may come upon them for being registered. 13This is what each one who is registered shall give: half a shekel according to the shekel of the sanctuary (the shekel is twenty gerahs), half a shekel as an offering to the LORD. 14Each one who is registered, from twenty years old and upward, shall give the LORD's offering. 15The rich shall not give more, and the poor shall not give less, than the half shekel, when you bring this offering to the LORD to make atonement for your lives. 16You shall take the atonement money from the Israelites and shall designate it for the service of the tent of meeting; before the LORD it will be a reminder to the Israelites of the ransom given for your lives.

THE BRONZE BASIN

17 The LORD spoke to Moses: 18You shall make a bronze basin with a bronze stand for washing. You shall put it between the tent of meeting and the altar, and you shall put water in it; 19with the watera Aaron and his sons shall wash their hands and their feet. 20When they go into the tent of meeting, or when they come near the altar to minister, to make an offering by fire to the LORD, they shall wash with water, so that they may not die. 21They shall wash their hands and their feet, so that they may not die: it shall be a perpetual ordinance for them, for him and for his descendants throughout their generations.

THE ANOINTING OIL AND INCENSE

22 The LORD spoke to Moses: 23Take the finest spices: of liquid myrrh five hundred shekels, and of sweet-smelling cinnamon half as much, that is, two hundred fifty, and two hundred fifty of aromatic cane, 24and five hundred of cassia— measured by the sanctuary shekel— and a hin of olive oil; 25and you shall make of these a sacred anointing oil blended as by the perfumer; it shall

be a holy anointing oil. 26With it you shall anoint the tent of meeting and the ark of the covenant,b 27and the table and all its utensils, and the lampstand and its utensils, and the altar of incense, 28and the altar of burnt offering with all its utensils, and the basin with its stand; 29you shall consecrate them, so that they may be most holy; whatever touches them will become holy. 30You shall anoint Aaron and his sons, and consecrate them, in order that they may serve me as priests. 31You shall say to the Israelites, "This shall be my holy anointing oil throughout your generations. 32It shall not be used in any ordinary anointing of the body, and you shall make no other like it in composition; it is holy, and it shall be holy to you. 33Whoever compounds any like it or whoever puts any of it on an unqualified person shall be cut off from the people."

34 The LORD said to Moses: Take sweet spices, stacte, and onycha, and galbanum, sweet spices with pure frankincense (an equal part of each), 35and make an incense blended as by the perfumer, seasoned with salt, pure and holy; 36and you shall beat some of it into powder, and put part of it before the covenantb in the tent of meeting where I shall meet with you; it shall be for you most holy. 37When you make incense according to this composition, you shall not make it for yourselves; it shall be regarded by you as holy to the LORD. 38Whoever makes any like it to use as perfume shall be cut off from the people.

BEZALEL AND OHOLIAB

31 The LORD spoke to Moses: 2See, I have called by name Bezalel son of Uri son of Hur, of the tribe of Judah: 3and I have filled him with divine spirit,c with ability, intelligence, and knowledge in every kind of craft, 4to devise artistic designs, to work in gold, silver, and bronze, 5in cutting stones for setting, and in carving wood, in every

a 30.19 Heb it   b 30.26,36 Or treaty, or testimony; Heb eduth   c 31.3 Or with the spirit of God kind of craft. ⁶Moreover, I have appointed with him Oholiab son of Ahisamach, of the tribe of Dan; and I have given skill to all the skillful, so that they may make all that I have commanded you: ⁷the tent of meeting, and the ark of the covenant,ª and the mercy seatᵇ that is on it, and all the furnishings of the tent, ⁸the table and its utensils, and the pure lampstand with all its utensils, and the altar of incense, ⁹and the altar of burnt offering with all its utensils, and the basin with its stand, ¹⁰and the finely worked vestments, the holy vestments for the priest Aaron and the vestments of his sons, for their service as priests, ¹¹and the anointing oil and the fragrant incense for the holy place. They shall do just as I have commanded you.

THE SABBATH LAW

12 The LORD said to Moses: ¹³You yourself are to speak to the Israelites: "You shall keep my sabbaths, for this is a sign between me and you throughout your generations, given in order that you may know that I, the LORD, sanctify you. ¹⁴You shall keep the sabbath, because it is holy for you; everyone who profanes it shall be put to death; whoever does any work on it shall be cut off from among the people. ¹⁵Six days shall work be done, but the seventh day is a sabbath of solemn rest, holy to the LORD; whoever does any work on the sabbath day shall be put to death. ¹⁶Therefore the Israelites shall keep the sabbath, observing the sabbath throughout their generations, as a perpetual covenant. ¹⁷It is a sign forever between me and the people of Israel that in six days the LORD made heaven and earth, and on the seventh day he rested, and was refreshed."

THE TWO TABLETS OF THE COVENANT

18 When Godᶜ finished speaking with Moses on Mount Sinai, he gave him the two tablets of the covenant,ª tablets of stone, written with the finger of God.

PONDER

"I have given skill to all the skillful, so that they may make all that I have commanded you."
—Exodus 31.6

PRAY

Lord God, help us to realize that you are ever present and willing to answer our questions about what is needed in our lives, about our achievements and our goals. Help us to understand how we can use our talents to serve you, to build your kingdom, to serve others. Guide us as we look inside our hearts to see who we are, who we want to be and who you want us to be. Show us more opportunities to serve and relate more intimately to our Savior, Jesus Christ, whom we profess as the foundation for our very existence. Amen.

THE GOLDEN CALF

32 When the people saw that Moses delayed to come down from the mountain, the people gathered around Aaron, and said to him, "Come, make gods for us, who shall go before us; as for this Moses, the man who brought us up out of the land of Egypt, we do not know what has become of him." ²Aaron said to them, "Take off the gold rings that are on the ears of your wives, your sons, and your daughters, and bring them to me." ³So all the people took off the gold rings from their ears, and brought them to Aaron. ⁴He took the gold from them, formed it in a mold,ᵈ and cast an image of a calf; and they said, "These are your gods, O Israel, who brought you up out of the land of Egypt!" ⁵When Aaron saw this, he built an altar before it; and Aaron made proclamation and said, "Tomorrow shall be

ª 31.7,18 Or treaty, or testimony; Heb eduth   ᵇ 31.7 Or the cover   ᶜ 31.18 Heb he   ᵈ 32.4 Or fashioned it with a graving tool; Meaning of Heb uncertain

a festival to the LORD." 6They rose early the next day, and offered burnt offerings and brought sacrifices of well-being; and the people sat down to eat and drink, and rose up to revel.

7 The LORD said to Moses, "Go down at once! Your people, whom you brought up out of the land of Egypt, have acted perversely; 8they have been quick to turn aside from the way that I commanded them; they have cast for themselves an image of a calf, and have worshiped it and sacrificed to it, and said, 'These are your gods, O Israel, who brought you up out of the land of Egypt!'" 9The LORD said to Moses, "I have seen this people, how stiff-necked they are. 10Now let me alone, so that my wrath may burn hot against them and I may consume them; and of you I will make a great nation."

11 But Moses implored the LORD his God, and said, "O LORD, why does your wrath burn hot against your people, whom you brought out of the land of Egypt with great power and with a mighty hand? 12Why should the Egyptians say, 'It was with evil intent that he brought them out to kill them in the mountains, and to consume them from the face of the earth'? Turn from your fierce wrath; change your mind and do not bring disaster on your people. 13Remember Abraham, Isaac, and Israel, your servants, how you swore to them by your own self, saying to them, 'I will multiply your descendants like the stars of heaven, and all this land that I have promised I will give to your descendants, and they shall inherit it forever.'" 14And the LORD changed his mind about the disaster that he planned to bring on his people.

15 Then Moses turned and went down from the mountain, carrying the two tablets of the covenanta in his hands, tablets that were written on both sides, written on the front and on the back. 16The tablets were the work of God, and the writing was the writing of God, engraved upon the tablets. 17When Joshua heard the noise of the people as they shouted, he said to Moses, "There is a noise of war in the camp." 18But he said,

"It is not the sound made
    by victors,
or the sound made by losers;
it is the sound of revelers
    that I hear."

19As soon as he came near the camp and saw the calf and the dancing, Moses' anger burned hot, and he threw the tablets from his hands and broke them at the foot of the mountain. 20He took the calf that they had made, burned it with fire, ground it to powder, scattered it on the water, and made the Israelites drink it.

a 32.15 Or treaty, or testimony; Heb eduth

BIBLE IN LIFE

Spiritual Adultery   Exodus 32.1–24

The backdrop of this story is that the Israelites had just received the covenantal invitation from God, and they were to be faithful to God alone. However, because "Moses delayed to come down from the mountain" (verse 1), the people prostituted themselves. They committed spiritual adultery by worshiping other gods. When Moses came down from Sinai, he found that they had melted down their gold earrings and made them into a calf, which they were worshiping instead of God.

How does that resonate with us today? We know God's all-powerful nature, the benefits we receive from fellowship, the sense of reassurance that we have from worshiping God. But sometimes, instead of pursuing an intimacy with and full commitment to God, we substitute the acquisition of things—money, beautiful homes, new cars or exotic vacations. These things are not inherently evil, but when we substitute them for intimacy with God, then we too commit the sin of idolatry.

21 Moses said to Aaron, "What did this people do to you that you have brought so great a sin upon them?" 22And Aaron said, "Do not let the anger of my lord burn hot; you know the people, that they are bent on evil. 23They said to me, 'Make us gods, who shall go before us; as for this Moses, the man who brought us up out of the land of Egypt, we do not know what has become of him.' 24So I said to them, 'Whoever has gold, take it off'; so they gave it to me, and I threw it into the fire, and out came this calf!"

25 When Moses saw that the people were running wild (for Aaron had let them run wild, to the derision of their enemies), 26then Moses stood in the gate of the camp, and said, "Who is on the LORD's side? Come to me!" And all the sons of Levi gathered around him. 27He said to them, "Thus says the LORD, the God of Israel, 'Put your sword on your side, each of you! Go back and forth from gate to gate throughout the camp, and each of you kill your brother, your friend, and your neighbor.'" 28The sons of Levi did as Moses commanded, and about three thousand of the people fell on that day. 29Moses said, "Today you have ordained yourselves[a] for the service of the LORD, each one at the cost of a son or a brother, and so have brought a blessing on yourselves this day."

30 On the next day Moses said to the people, "You have sinned a great sin. But now I will go up to the LORD; perhaps I can make atonement for your sin." 31So Moses returned to the LORD and said, "Alas, this people has sinned a great sin; they have made for themselves gods of gold. 32But now, if you will only forgive their sin—but if not, blot me out of the book that you have written." 33But the LORD said to Moses, "Whoever has sinned against me I will blot out of my book. 34But now go, lead the people to the place about which I have spoken to you; see, my angel shall go in front of you. Nevertheless, when the day comes for punishment, I will punish them for their sin."

35 Then the LORD sent a plague on the people, because they made the calf—the one that Aaron made.

THE COMMAND TO LEAVE SINAI

33 The LORD said to Moses, "Go, leave this place, you and the people whom you have brought up out of the land of Egypt, and go to the land of which I swore to Abraham, Isaac, and Jacob, saying, 'To your descendants I will give it.' 2I will send an angel before you, and I will drive out the Canaanites, the Amorites, the Hittites, the Perizzites, the Hivites, and the Jebusites. 3Go up to a land flowing with milk and honey; but I will not go up among you, or I would consume you on the way, for you are a stiff-necked people."

4When the people heard these harsh words, they mourned, and no one put on ornaments. 5For the LORD had said to Moses, "Say to the Israelites, 'You are a stiff-necked people; if for a single moment I should go up among you, I would consume you. So now take off your ornaments, and I will decide what to do to you.'" 6Therefore the Israelites stripped themselves of their ornaments, from Mount Horeb onward.

THE TENT OUTSIDE THE CAMP

7 Now Moses used to take the tent and pitch it outside the camp, far off from the camp; he called it the tent of meeting. And everyone who sought the LORD would go out to the tent of meeting, which was outside the camp. 8Whenever Moses went out to the tent, all the people would rise and stand, each of them, at the entrance of their tents and watch Moses until he had gone into the tent. 9When Moses entered the tent, the pillar of cloud would descend and stand at the entrance of the tent, and the LORD would speak with Moses. 10When all the people saw the pillar of cloud standing at the entrance of the tent, all the people would rise and bow down, all of them, at the entrance of their tent. 11Thus the

[a] 32.29 Gk Vg Compare Tg: Heb *Today ordain yourselves*

LORD used to speak to Moses face to face, as one speaks to a friend. Then he would return to the camp; but his young assistant, Joshua son of Nun, would not leave the tent.

MOSES' INTERCESSION

12 Moses said to the LORD, "See, you have said to me, 'Bring up this people'; but you have not let me know whom you will send with me. Yet you have said, 'I know you by name, and you have also found favor in my sight.' 13Now if I have found favor in your sight, show me your ways, so that I may know you and find favor in your sight. Consider too that this nation is your people." 14He said, "My presence will go with you, and I will give you rest." 15And he said to him, "If your presence will not go, do not carry us up from here. 16For how shall it be known that I have found favor in your sight, I and your people, unless you go with us? In this way, we shall be distinct, I and your people, from every people on the face of the earth."

17 The LORD said to Moses, "I will do the very thing that you have asked; for you have found favor in my sight, and I know you by name." 18Moses said, "Show me your glory, I pray." 19And he said, "I will make all my goodness pass before you, and will proclaim before you the name, 'The LORD';a and I will be gracious to whom I will be gracious, and will show mercy on whom I will show mercy. 20But," he said, "you cannot see my face; for no one shall see me and live." 21And the LORD continued, "See, there is a place by me where you shall stand on the rock; 22and while my glory passes by I will put you in a cleft of the rock, and I will cover you with my hand until I have passed by; 23then I will take away my hand, and you shall see my back; but my face shall not be seen."

MOSES MAKES NEW TABLETS

34 The LORD said to Moses, "Cut two tablets of stone like the former ones, and I will write on the tablets the words that were on the former tablets, which you broke. 2Be ready in the morning, and come up in the morning to Mount Sinai and present yourself there to me, on the top of the mountain. 3No one shall come up with you, and do not let anyone be seen throughout all the mountain; and do not let flocks or herds graze in front of that mountain." 4So Moses cut two tablets of stone like the former ones; and he rose early in the morning and went up on Mount Sinai, as the LORD had commanded him, and took in his hand the two tablets of stone. 5The LORD descended in the cloud and stood with him there, and proclaimed the name, "The LORD."a

a 33.19; 34.5 Heb YHWH; see note at 3.15

BIBLE IN LIFE

Our View of God   Exodus 33.12–23

No one has ever seen God. Because no physical description is available to us, we struggle to visualize God. We might envision God as a man with a long beard and white hair, or we might view God as an exacting judge keeping tabs on us. Yet Christ is God, and Christ gives us an actual picture of God the Father. When the disciples asked Jesus to show them the Father, he replied, "Whoever has seen me has seen the Father" (John 14.9). We may not see a physical God, but we can see God's attributes embodied in Jesus, and we can see God's love displayed through people who follow Jesus. "God is love" (1 John 4.8)—a godly love, a forgiving love, a love for those who don't deserve to be loved, a love for those who don't love us back, a love for unattractive, abrasive people, a love for our neighbors whom we don't want to acknowledge, love in its purest and most exalted and most exciting and challenging and difficult meanings. God is love.

6 The LORD passed before him, and proclaimed,

"The LORD, the LORD,
a God merciful and gracious,
slow to anger,
and abounding in steadfast
love and faithfulness,
7 keeping steadfast love for the
thousandth generation,[a]
forgiving iniquity and
transgression and sin,
yet by no means clearing
the guilty,
but visiting the iniquity
of the parents
upon the children
and the children's children,
to the third and the fourth
generation."

8 And Moses quickly bowed his head toward the earth, and worshiped. 9 He said, "If now I have found favor in your sight, O Lord, I pray, let the Lord go with us. Although this is a stiff-necked people, pardon our iniquity and our sin, and take us for your inheritance."

THE COVENANT RENEWED

10 He said: I hereby make a covenant. Before all your people I will perform marvels, such as have not been performed in all the earth or in any nation; and all the people among whom you live shall see the work of the LORD; for it is an awesome thing that I will do with you. 11 Observe what I command you today. See, I will drive out before you the Amorites, the Canaanites, the Hittites, the Perizzites, the Hivites, and the Jebusites. 12 Take care not to make a covenant with the inhabitants of the land to which you are going, or it will become a snare among you. 13 You shall tear down their altars, break their pillars, and cut down their sacred poles[b] 14(for you shall worship no other god, because the LORD, whose name is Jealous, is a jealous God). 15 You shall not make a covenant with the inhabitants of the land, for when they prostitute themselves to their gods and sacrifice to their gods, someone among them will invite you, and you will eat of the sacrifice. 16 And you will take wives from among their daughters for your sons, and their daughters who prostitute themselves to their gods will make your sons also prostitute themselves to their gods.

17 You shall not make cast idols.

18 You shall keep the festival of unleavened bread. Seven days you shall eat unleavened bread, as I commanded you, at the time appointed in the month of Abib; for in the month of Abib you came out from Egypt.

19 All that first opens the womb is mine, all your male[c] livestock, the firstborn of cow and sheep. 20 The firstborn of a donkey you shall redeem with a lamb, or if you will not redeem it you shall break its neck. All the firstborn of your sons you shall redeem.

No one shall appear before me empty-handed.

OUR SINS ALWAYS AFFECT
OTHERS, ESPECIALLY
OUR LOVED ONES.

21 Six days you shall work, but on the seventh day you shall rest; even in plowing time and in harvest time you shall rest. 22 You shall observe the festival of weeks, the first fruits of wheat harvest, and the festival of ingathering at the turn of the year. 23 Three times in the year all your males shall appear before the LORD God, the God of Israel. 24 For I will cast out nations before you, and enlarge your borders; no one shall covet your land when you go up to appear before the LORD your God three times in the year.

25 You shall not offer the blood of my sacrifice with leaven, and the sac-

a 34.7 Or *for thousands*   b 34.13 Heb *Asherim*   c 34.19 Gk Theodotion Vg Tg: Meaning of Heb uncertain

rifice of the festival of the passover shall not be left until the morning. 26 The best of the first fruits of your ground you shall bring to the house of the LORD your God. You shall not boil a kid in its mother's milk.

27 The LORD said to Moses: Write these words; in accordance with these words I have made a covenant with you and with Israel. 28 He was there with the LORD forty days and forty nights; he neither ate bread nor drank water. And he wrote on the tablets the words of the covenant, the ten commandments.ᵃ

THE SHINING FACE OF MOSES

29 Moses came down from Mount Sinai. As he came down from the mountain with the two tablets of the covenantᵇ in his hand, Moses did not know that the skin of his face shone because he had been talking with God. 30 When Aaron and all the Israelites saw Moses, the skin of his face was shining, and they were afraid to come near him. 31 But Moses called to them; and Aaron and all the leaders of the congregation returned to him, and Moses spoke with them. 32 Afterward all the Israelites came near, and he gave them in commandment all that the LORD had spoken with him on Mount Sinai. 33 When Moses had finished speaking with them, he put a veil on his face; 34 but whenever Moses went in before the LORD to speak with him, he would take the veil off, until he came out; and when he came out, and told the Israelites what he had been commanded, 35 the Israelites would see the face of Moses, that the skin of his face was shining; and Moses would put the veil on his face again, until he went in to speak with him.

SABBATH REGULATIONS

35 Moses assembled all the congregation of the Israelites and said to them: These are the things that the LORD has commanded you to do: 2 Six days shall work be done, but on the seventh day you shall have a holy sabbath of solemn rest to the LORD; whoever does any work on it shall be put to death. 3 You shall kindle no fire in all your dwellings on the sabbath day.

PREPARATIONS FOR MAKING THE TABERNACLE

4 Moses said to all the congregation of the Israelites: This is the thing that the LORD has commanded: 5 Take from among you an offering to the LORD; let whoever is of a generous heart bring the LORD's offering: gold, silver, and bronze; 6 blue, purple, and crimson yarns, and fine linen; goats' hair, 7 tanned rams' skins, and fine leather;ᶜ acacia wood, 8 oil for the light, spices for the anointing oil and for the fragrant incense, 9 and onyx stones and gems to be set in the ephod and the breastpiece.

10 All who are skillful among you shall come and make all that the LORD has commanded: the tabernacle, 11 its tent and its covering, its clasps and its frames, its bars, its pillars, and its bases; 12 the ark with its poles, the mercy seat,ᵈ and the curtain for the screen; 13 the table with its poles and all its utensils, and the bread of the Presence; 14 the lampstand also for the light, with its utensils and its lamps, and the oil for the light; 15 and the altar of incense, with its poles, and the anointing oil and the fragrant incense, and the screen for the entrance, the entrance of the tabernacle; 16 the altar of burnt offering, with its grating of bronze, its poles, and all its utensils, the basin with its stand; 17 the hangings of the court, its pillars and its bases, and the screen for the gate of the court; 18 the pegs of the tabernacle and the pegs of the court, and their cords; 19 the finely worked vestments for ministering in the holy place, the holy vestments for the priest Aaron, and the vestments of his sons, for their service as priests.

ᵃ 34.28 Heb *words*   ᵇ 34.29 Or *treaty,* or *testimony*; Heb *eduth*   ᶜ 35.7 Meaning of Heb uncertain   ᵈ 35.12 Or *the cover*

OFFERINGS FOR THE TABERNACLE

20 Then all the congregation of the Israelites withdrew from the presence of Moses. 21And they came, everyone whose heart was stirred, and everyone whose spirit was willing, and brought the LORD's offering to be used for the tent of meeting, and for all its service, and for the sacred vestments. 22So they came, both men and women; all who were of a willing heart brought brooches and earrings and signet rings and pendants, all sorts of gold objects, everyone bringing an offering of gold to the LORD. 23And everyone who possessed blue or purple or crimson yarn or fine linen or goats' hair or tanned rams' skins or fine leather,a brought them. 24Everyone who could make an offering of silver or bronze brought it as the LORD's offering; and everyone who possessed acacia wood of any use in the work, brought it. 25All the skillful women spun with their hands, and brought what they had spun in blue and purple and crimson yarns and fine linen; 26all the women whose hearts moved them to use their skill spun the goats' hair. 27And the leaders brought onyx stones and gems to be set in the ephod and the breastpiece, 28and spices and oil for the light, and for the anointing oil, and for the fragrant incense. 29All the Israelite men and women whose hearts made them willing to bring anything for the work that the LORD had commanded by Moses to be done, brought it as a freewill offering to the LORD.

BEZALEL AND OHOLIAB

30 Then Moses said to the Israelites: See, the LORD has called by name Bezalel son of Uri son of Hur, of the tribe of Judah; 31he has filled him with divine spirit,b with skill, intelligence, and knowledge in every kind of craft, 32to devise artistic designs, to work in gold, silver, and bronze, 33in cutting stones for setting, and in carving wood, in every kind of craft. 34And he has inspired him to teach, both him and Oholiab son of Ahisamach, of the tribe of Dan. 35He has filled them with skill to do every kind of work done by an artisan or by a designer or by an embroiderer in blue, purple, and crimson yarns, and in fine linen, or by a weaver—by any sort of artisan or skilled designer.

OUR PERSONAL GIVING OF

TIME AND RESOURCES IS A

TEST OF OUR COMPLETENESS

AS HUMAN BEINGS AND

AS CHRISTIANS.

36 Bezalel and Oholiab and every skillful one to whom the LORD has given skill and understanding to know how to do any work in the construction of the sanctuary shall work in accordance with all that the LORD has commanded.

2 Moses then called Bezalel and Oholiab and every skillful one to whom the LORD had given skill, everyone whose heart was stirred to come to do the work; 3and they received from Moses all the freewill offerings that the Israelites had brought for doing the work on the sanctuary. They still kept bringing him freewill offerings every morning, 4so that all the artisans who were doing every sort of task on the sanctuary came, each from the task being performed, 5and said to Moses, "The people are bringing much more than enough for doing the work that the LORD has commanded us to do." 6So Moses gave command, and word was proclaimed throughout the camp: "No man or woman is to make anything else as an offering for the sanctuary." So the people were restrained from bringing; 7for what they had already brought was more than enough to do all the work.

a 35.23 Meaning of Heb uncertain
b 35.31 Or the spirit of God

CONSTRUCTION OF
THE TABERNACLE

8 All those with skill among the workers made the tabernacle with ten curtains; they were made of fine twisted linen, and blue, purple, and crimson yarns, with cherubim skillfully worked into them. 9 The length of each curtain was twenty-eight cubits, and the width of each curtain four cubits; all the curtains were of the same size. 10 He joined five curtains to one another, and the other five curtains he joined to one another. 11 He made loops of blue on the edge of the outermost curtain of the first set; likewise he made them on the edge of the outermost curtain of the second set; 12 he made fifty loops on the one curtain, and he made fifty loops on the edge of the curtain that was in the second set; the loops were opposite one another. 13 And he made fifty clasps of gold, and joined the curtains one to the other with clasps; so the tabernacle was one whole.

14 He also made curtains of goats' hair for a tent over the tabernacle; he made eleven curtains. 15 The length of each curtain was thirty cubits, and the width of each curtain four cubits; the eleven curtains were of the same size. 16 He joined five curtains by themselves, and six curtains by themselves. 17 He made fifty loops on the edge of the outermost curtain of the one set, and fifty loops on the edge of the other connecting curtain. 18 He made fifty clasps of bronze to join the tent together so that it might be one whole. 19 And he made for the tent a covering of tanned rams' skins and an outer covering of fine leather.[a]

20 Then he made the upright frames for the tabernacle of acacia wood. 21 Ten cubits was the length of a frame, and a cubit and a half the width of each frame. 22 Each frame had two pegs for fitting together; he did this for all the frames of the tabernacle. 23 The frames for the tabernacle he made in this way: twenty frames for the south side; 24 and he made forty bases of silver under the twenty frames, two bases under the

first frame for its two pegs, and two bases under the next frame for its two pegs. 25 For the second side of the tabernacle, on the north side, he made twenty frames 26 and their forty bases of silver, two bases under the first frame and two bases under the next frame. 27 For the rear of the tabernacle westward he made six frames. 28 He made two frames for corners of the tabernacle in the rear. 29 They were separate beneath, but joined at the top, at the first ring; he made two of them in this way, for the two corners. 30 There were eight frames with their bases of silver: sixteen bases, under every frame two bases.

31 He made bars of acacia wood, five for the frames of the one side of the tabernacle, 32 and five bars for the frames of the other side of the tabernacle, and five bars for the frames of the tabernacle at the rear westward. 33 He made the middle bar to pass through from end to end halfway up the frames. 34 And he overlaid the frames with gold, and made rings of gold for them to hold the bars, and overlaid the bars with gold.

35 He made the curtain of blue, purple, and crimson yarns, and fine twisted linen, with cherubim skillfully worked into it. 36 For it he made four pillars of acacia, and overlaid them with gold; their hooks were of gold, and he cast for them four bases of silver. 37 He also made a screen for the entrance to the tent, of blue, purple, and crimson yarns, and fine twisted linen, embroidered with needlework; 38 and its five pillars with their hooks. He overlaid their capitals and their bases with gold, but their five bases were of bronze.

MAKING THE ARK OF
THE COVENANT

37 Bezalel made the ark of acacia wood; it was two and a half cubits long, a cubit and a half wide, and a cubit and a half high. 2 He overlaid it with pure gold inside

a 36.19 Meaning of Heb uncertain

and outside, and made a molding of gold around it. ³He cast for it four rings of gold for its four feet, two rings on its one side and two rings on its other side. ⁴He made poles of acacia wood, and overlaid them with gold, ⁵and put the poles into the rings on the sides of the ark, to carry the ark. ⁶He made a mercy seat[a] of pure gold; two cubits and a half was its length, and a cubit and a half its width. ⁷He made two cherubim of hammered gold; at the two ends of the mercy seat[b] he made them, ⁸one cherub at the one end, and one cherub at the other end; of one piece with the mercy seat[b] he made the cherubim at its two ends. ⁹The cherubim spread out their wings above, overshadowing the mercy seat[b] with their wings. They faced one another; the faces of the cherubim were turned toward the mercy seat.[b]

MAKING THE TABLE FOR THE BREAD OF THE PRESENCE

10 He also made the table of acacia wood, two cubits long, one cubit wide, and a cubit and a half high. ¹¹He overlaid it with pure gold, and made a molding of gold around it. ¹²He made around it a rim a handbreadth wide, and made a molding of gold around the rim. ¹³He cast for it four rings of gold, and fastened the rings to the four corners at its four legs. ¹⁴The rings that held the poles used for carrying the table were close to the rim. ¹⁵He made the poles of acacia wood to carry the table, and overlaid them with gold. ¹⁶And he made the vessels of pure gold that were to be on the table, its plates and dishes for incense, and its bowls and flagons with which to pour drink offerings.

MAKING THE LAMPSTAND

17 He also made the lampstand of pure gold. The base and the shaft of the lampstand were made of hammered work; its cups, its calyxes, and its petals were of one piece with it. ¹⁸There were six branches going out of its sides, three branches of the lampstand out of one side of it and three branches of the lampstand out of the other side of it; ¹⁹three cups shaped like almond blossoms, each with calyx and petals, on one branch, and three cups shaped like almond blossoms, each with calyx and petals, on the other branch—so for the six branches going out of the lampstand. ²⁰On the lampstand itself there were four cups shaped like almond blossoms, each with its calyxes and petals. ²¹There was a calyx of one piece with it under the first pair of branches, a calyx of one piece with it under the next pair of branches, and a calyx of one piece with it under the last pair of branches. ²²Their calyxes and their branches were of one piece with it, the whole of it one hammered piece of pure gold. ²³He made its seven lamps and its snuffers and its trays of pure gold. ²⁴He made it and all its utensils of a talent of pure gold.

MAKING THE ALTAR OF INCENSE

25 He made the altar of incense of acacia wood, one cubit long, and one cubit wide; it was square, and was two cubits high; its horns were of one piece with it. ²⁶He overlaid it with pure gold, its top, and its sides all around, and its horns; and he made for it a molding of gold all around, ²⁷and made two golden rings for it under its molding, on two opposite sides of it, to hold the poles with which to carry it. ²⁸And he made the poles of acacia wood, and overlaid them with gold.

MAKING THE ANOINTING OIL AND THE INCENSE

29 He made the holy anointing oil also, and the pure fragrant incense, blended as by the perfumer.

MAKING THE ALTAR OF BURNT OFFERING

38 He made the altar of burnt offering also of acacia wood; it was five cubits long, and five cubits wide; it was square, and three cubits high. ²He made horns for it on

[a] 37.6 Or *a cover* [b] 37.7,8,9 Or *the cover*

its four corners; its horns were of one piece with it, and he overlaid it with bronze. ³He made all the utensils of the altar, the pots, the shovels, the basins, the forks, and the firepans: all its utensils he made of bronze. ⁴He made for the altar a grating, a network of bronze, under its ledge, extending halfway down. ⁵He cast four rings on the four corners of the bronze grating to hold the poles; ⁶he made the poles of acacia wood, and overlaid them with bronze. ⁷And he put the poles through the rings on the sides of the altar, to carry it with them; he made it hollow, with boards.

8 He made the basin of bronze with its stand of bronze, from the mirrors of the women who served at the entrance to the tent of meeting.

MAKING THE COURT OF THE TABERNACLE

9 He made the court; for the south side the hangings of the court were of fine twisted linen, one hundred cubits long; ¹⁰its twenty pillars and their twenty bases were of bronze, but the hooks of the pillars and their bands were of silver. ¹¹For the north side there were hangings one hundred cubits long; its twenty pillars and their twenty bases were of bronze, but the hooks of the pillars and their bands were of silver. ¹²For the west side there were hangings fifty cubits long, with ten pillars and ten bases; the hooks of the pillars and their bands were of silver. ¹³And for the front to the east, fifty cubits. ¹⁴The hangings for one side of the gate were fifteen cubits, with three pillars and three bases. ¹⁵And so for the other side; on each side of the gate of the court were hangings of fifteen cubits, with three pillars and three bases. ¹⁶All the hangings around the court were of fine twisted linen. ¹⁷The bases for the pillars were of bronze, but the hooks of the pillars and their bands were of silver; the overlaying of their capitals was also of silver, and all the pillars of the court were banded with silver. ¹⁸The screen for the entrance to the court was em-broidered with needlework in blue, purple, and crimson yarns and fine twisted linen. It was twenty cubits long and, along the width of it, five cubits high, corresponding to the hangings of the court. ¹⁹There were four pillars; their four bases were of bronze, their hooks of silver, and the overlaying of their capitals and their bands of silver. ²⁰All the pegs for the tabernacle and for the court all around were of bronze.

MATERIALS OF THE TABERNACLE

21 These are the records of the tabernacle, the tabernacle of the covenant,ᵃ which were drawn up at the commandment of Moses, the work of the Levites being under the direction of Ithamar son of the priest Aaron. ²²Bezalel son of Uri son of Hur, of the tribe of Judah, made all that the LORD commanded Moses; ²³and with him was Oholiab son of Ahisamach, of the tribe of Dan, engraver, designer, and embroiderer in blue, purple, and crimson yarns, and in fine linen.

24 All the gold that was used for the work, in all the construction of the sanctuary, the gold from the offering, was twenty-nine talents and seven hundred thirty shekels, measured by the sanctuary shekel. ²⁵The silver from those of the congregation who were counted was one hundred talents and one thousand seven hundred seventy-five shekels, measured by the sanctuary shekel; ²⁶a beka a head (that is, half a shekel, measured by the sanctuary shekel), for everyone who was counted in the census, from twenty years old and upward, for six hundred three thousand, five hundred fifty men. ²⁷The hundred talents of silver were for casting the bases of the sanctuary, and the bases of the curtain; one hundred bases for the hundred talents, a talent for a base. ²⁸Of the thousand seven hundred seventy-five shekels he made hooks for the pillars, and overlaid their capitals and made bands for them. ²⁹The bronze that was contributed was seventy talents, and

ᵃ 38.21 Or *treaty*, or *testimony*; Heb *eduth*

two thousand four hundred shekels; 30with it he made the bases for the entrance of the tent of meeting, the bronze altar and the bronze grating for it and all the utensils of the altar, 31the bases all around the court, and the bases of the gate of the court, all the pegs of the tabernacle, and all the pegs around the court.

MAKING THE VESTMENTS FOR THE PRIESTHOOD

39 Of the blue, purple, and crimson yarns they made finely worked vestments, for ministering in the holy place; they made the sacred vestments for Aaron; as the LORD had commanded Moses.

2 He made the ephod of gold, of blue, purple, and crimson yarns, and of fine twisted linen. 3Gold leaf was hammered out and cut into threads to work into the blue, purple, and crimson yarns and into the fine twisted linen, in skilled design. 4They made for the ephod shoulder-pieces, joined to it at its two edges. 5The decorated band on it was of the same materials and workmanship, of gold, of blue, purple, and crimson yarns, and of fine twisted linen; as the LORD had commanded Moses.

6 The onyx stones were prepared, enclosed in settings of gold filigree and engraved like the engravings of a signet, according to the names of the sons of Israel. 7He set them on the shoulder-pieces of the ephod, to be stones of remembrance for the sons of Israel; as the LORD had commanded Moses.

8 He made the breastpiece, in skilled work, like the work of the ephod, of gold, of blue, purple, and crimson yarns, and of fine twisted linen. 9It was square; the breastpiece was made double, a span in length and a span in width when doubled. 10They set in it four rows of stones. A row of carnelian,a chrysolite, and emerald was the first row; 11and the second row, a turquoise, a sapphire,b and a moonstone; 12and the third row, a jacinth, an agate, and an amethyst; 13and the fourth row, a beryl, an onyx, and a jasper; they were enclosed in settings of gold filigree. 14There were twelve stones with

names corresponding to the names of the sons of Israel; they were like signets, each engraved with its name, for the twelve tribes. 15They made on the breastpiece chains of pure gold, twisted like cords; 16and they made two settings of gold filigree and two gold rings, and put the two rings on the two edges of the breastpiece; 17and they put the two cords of gold in the two rings at the edges of the breastpiece. 18Two ends of the two cords they had attached to the two settings of filigree; in this way they attached it in front to the shoulder-pieces of the ephod. 19Then they made two rings of gold, and put them at the two ends of the breastpiece, on its inside edge next to the ephod. 20They made two rings of gold, and attached them in front to the lower part of the two shoulder-pieces of the ephod, at its joining above the decorated band of the ephod. 21They bound the breastpiece by its rings to the rings of the ephod with a blue cord, so that it should lie on the decorated band of the ephod, and that the breastpiece should not come loose from the ephod; as the LORD had commanded Moses.

22 He also made the robe of the ephod woven all of blue yarn; 23and the opening of the robe in the middle of it was like the opening in a coat of mail,c with a binding around the opening, so that it might not be torn. 24On the lower hem of the robe they made pomegranates of blue, purple, and crimson yarns, and of fine twisted linen. 25They also made bells of pure gold, and put the bells between the pomegranates on the lower hem of the robe all around, between the pomegranates; 26a bell and a pomegranate, a bell and a pomegranate all around on the lower hem of the robe for ministering; as the LORD had commanded Moses.

27 They also made the tunics, woven of fine linen, for Aaron and his sons, 28and the turban of fine linen, and the headdresses of fine linen, and the linen undergarments of fine

a 39.10 The identification of several of these stones is uncertain b 39.11 Or lapis lazuli
c 39.23 Meaning of Heb uncertain

twisted linen, 29and the sash of fine twisted linen, and of blue, purple, and crimson yarns, embroidered with needlework; as the LORD had commanded Moses.

30 They made the rosette of the holy diadem of pure gold, and wrote on it an inscription, like the engraving of a signet, "Holy to the LORD." 31They tied to it a blue cord, to fasten it on the turban above; as the LORD had commanded Moses.

THE WORK COMPLETED

32 In this way all the work of the tabernacle of the tent of meeting was finished; the Israelites had done everything just as the LORD had commanded Moses. 33Then they brought the tabernacle to Moses, the tent and all its utensils, its hooks, its frames, its bars, its pillars, and its bases; 34the covering of tanned rams' skins and the covering of fine leather,[a] and the curtain for the screen; 35the ark of the covenant[b] with its poles and the mercy seat;[c] 36the table with all its utensils, and the bread of the Presence; 37the pure lampstand with its lamps set on it and all its utensils, and the oil for the light; 38the golden altar, the anointing oil and the fragrant incense, and the screen for the entrance of the tent; 39the bronze altar, and its grating of bronze, its poles, and all its utensils; the basin with its stand; 40the hangings of the court, its pillars, and its bases, and the screen for the gate of the court, its cords, and its pegs; and all the utensils for the service of the tabernacle, for the tent of meeting; 41the finely worked vestments for ministering in the holy place, the sacred vestments for the priest Aaron, and the vestments of his sons to serve as priests. 42The Israelites had done all of the work just as the LORD had commanded Moses. 43When Moses saw that they had done all the work just as the LORD had commanded, he blessed them.

THE TABERNACLE ERECTED AND ITS EQUIPMENT INSTALLED

40 The LORD spoke to Moses: 2On the first day of the first month you shall set up the taberna-cle of the tent of meeting. 3You shall put in it the ark of the covenant,[b] and you shall screen the ark with the curtain. 4You shall bring in the table, and arrange its setting; and you shall bring in the lampstand, and set up its lamps. 5You shall put the golden altar for incense before the ark of the covenant,[b] and set up the screen for the entrance of the tabernacle. 6You shall set the altar of burnt offering before the entrance of the tabernacle of the tent of meeting, 7and place the basin between the tent of meeting and the altar, and put water in it. 8You shall set up the court all around, and hang up the screen for the gate of the court. 9Then you shall take the anointing oil, and anoint the tabernacle and all that is in it, and consecrate it and all its furniture, so that it shall become holy. 10You shall also anoint the altar of burnt offering and all its utensils, and consecrate the altar, so that the altar shall be most holy. 11You shall also anoint the basin with its stand, and consecrate it. 12Then you shall bring Aaron and his sons to the entrance of the tent of meeting, and shall wash them with water, 13and put on Aaron the sacred vestments, and you shall anoint him and consecrate him, so that he may serve me as priest. 14You shall bring his sons also and put tunics on them, 15and anoint them, as you anointed their father, that they may serve me as priests: and their anointing shall admit them to a perpetual priesthood throughout all generations to come.

16 Moses did everything just as the LORD had commanded him. 17In the first month in the second year, on the first day of the month, the tabernacle was set up. 18Moses set up the tabernacle; he laid its bases, and set up its frames, and put in its poles, and raised up its pillars; 19and he spread the tent over the tabernacle, and put the covering of the tent over it; as the LORD had commanded Moses. 20He took the covenant[b] and put it into the ark,

a 39.34 Meaning of Heb uncertain   b 39.35; 40.3,5,20 Or *treaty*, or *testimony*; Heb *eduth*   c 39.35 Or *the cover*

and put the poles on the ark, and set the mercy seat[a] above the ark; [21]and he brought the ark into the tabernacle, and set up the curtain for screening, and screened the ark of the covenant;[b] as the LORD had commanded Moses. [22]He put the table in the tent of meeting, on the north side of the tabernacle, outside the curtain, [23]and set the bread in order on it before the LORD; as the LORD had commanded Moses. [24]He put the lampstand in the tent of meeting, opposite the table on the south side of the tabernacle, [25]and set up the lamps before the LORD; as the LORD had commanded Moses. [26]He put the golden altar in the tent of meeting before the curtain, [27]and offered fragrant incense on it; as the LORD had commanded Moses. [28]He also put in place the screen for the entrance of the tabernacle. [29]He set the altar of burnt offering at the entrance of the tabernacle of the tent of meeting, and offered on it the burnt offering and the grain offering as the LORD had commanded Moses. [30]He set the basin between the tent of meeting and the altar, and put water in it for washing, [31]with which Moses and Aaron and his sons washed their hands and their feet. [32]When they went into the tent of meeting, and when they approached the altar, they washed; as the LORD had commanded Mo-

ses. [33]He set up the court around the tabernacle and the altar, and put up the screen at the gate of the court. So Moses finished the work.

LIFE IS MEANINGFUL WHEN THE
RISEN CHRIST IS WITH US.

THE CLOUD AND THE GLORY

34 Then the cloud covered the tent of meeting, and the glory of the LORD filled the tabernacle. [35]Moses was not able to enter the tent of meeting because the cloud settled upon it, and the glory of the LORD filled the tabernacle. [36]Whenever the cloud was taken up from the tabernacle, the Israelites would set out on each stage of their journey; [37]but if the cloud was not taken up, then they did not set out until the day that it was taken up. [38]For the cloud of the LORD was on the tabernacle by day, and fire was in the cloud[c] by night, before the eyes of all the house of Israel at each stage of their journey.

a 40.20 Or the cover   b 40.21 Or treaty, or testimony; Heb eduth   c 40.38 Heb it

LEVITICUS

At first Leviticus may seem like an endless list of rules and regulations.
The book catalogs the instructions God gave to Moses for the Israelites,
including such things as sacrifices, moral laws and special holidays. But
the book of Leviticus isn't about rules; it's about holiness—as it is unveiled
in the name, attributes and redemptive work of God. Leviticus is about
God's heart for the Israelites—and for all God's followers today: "Be holy,
for I am holy" (Leviticus 11.45).

THE BURNT OFFERING

1 The LORD summoned Moses and spoke to him from the tent of meeting, saying: ²Speak to the people of Israel and say to them: When any of you bring an offering of livestock to the LORD, you shall bring your offering from the herd or from the flock.

3 If the offering is a burnt offering from the herd, you shall offer a male without blemish; you shall bring it to the entrance of the tent of meeting, for acceptance in your behalf before the LORD. ⁴You shall lay your hand on the head of the burnt offering, and it shall be acceptable in your behalf as atonement for you. ⁵The bull shall be slaughtered before the LORD; and Aaron's sons the priests shall offer the blood, dashing the blood against all sides of the altar that is at the entrance of the tent of meeting. ⁶The burnt offering shall be flayed and cut up into its parts. ⁷The sons of the priest Aaron shall put fire on the altar and arrange wood on the fire. ⁸Aaron's sons the priests shall arrange the parts, with the head and the suet, on the wood that is on the fire on the altar; ⁹but its entrails and its legs shall be washed with water. Then the priest shall turn the whole into smoke on the altar as a burnt offering, an offering by fire of pleasing odor to the LORD.

10 If your gift for a burnt offering is from the flock, from the sheep or goats, your offering shall be a male without blemish. ¹¹It shall be slaughtered on the north side of the altar before the LORD, and Aaron's sons the priests shall dash its blood against all sides of the altar. ¹²It shall be cut up into its parts, with its head and its suet, and the priest shall arrange them on the wood that is on the fire on the altar; ¹³but the entrails and the legs shall be washed with water. Then the priest shall offer the whole and turn it into smoke on the altar; it is a burnt offering, an offering by fire of pleasing odor to the LORD.

14 If your offering to the LORD is a burnt offering of birds, you shall choose your offering from turtle-doves or pigeons. ¹⁵The priest shall bring it to the altar and wring off its head, and turn it into smoke on the altar; and its blood shall be drained out against the side of the altar. ¹⁶He shall remove its crop with its contentsª and throw it at the east side of the altar, in the place for ashes. ¹⁷He shall tear it open by its wings without severing it. Then the priest shall turn it into smoke on the altar, on the wood that is on the fire; it is a burnt offering, an offering by fire of pleasing odor to the LORD.

GRAIN OFFERINGS

2 When anyone presents a grain offering to the LORD, the offering shall be of choice flour; the worshiper shall pour oil on it, and put frankincense on it, ²and bring it to Aaron's sons the priests. After taking from it a handful of the choice flour and oil, with all its frankincense, the priest shall turn this token portion into smoke on the altar, an offering by fire of pleasing odor to the LORD. ³And what is left of the grain offering shall be for Aaron and his sons, a most holy part of the offerings by fire to the LORD.

4 When you present a grain offering baked in the oven, it shall be of choice flour: unleavened cakes mixed with oil, or unleavened wafers spread with oil. ⁵If your offering is grain prepared on a griddle, it shall be of choice flour mixed with oil, unleavened; ⁶break it in pieces, and pour oil on it; it is a grain offering. ⁷If your offering is grain prepared in a pan, it shall be made of choice flour in oil. ⁸You shall bring to the LORD the grain offering that is prepared in any of these ways; and when it is presented to the priest, he shall take it to the altar. ⁹The priest shall remove from the grain offering its token portion and turn this into smoke on the altar, an offering by fire of pleasing odor to the LORD. ¹⁰And what is left of the grain offering shall be for Aaron and his sons; it is a most holy part of the offerings by fire to the LORD.

ª 1.16 Meaning of Heb uncertain

11 No grain offering that you bring to the LORD shall be made with leaven, for you must not turn any leaven or honey into smoke as an offering by fire to the LORD. 12 You may bring them to the LORD as an offering of choice products, but they shall not be offered on the altar for a pleasing odor. 13 You shall not omit from your grain offerings the salt of the covenant with your God; with all your offerings you shall offer salt.

14 If you bring a grain offering of first fruits to the LORD, you shall bring as the grain offering of your first fruits coarse new grain from fresh ears, parched with fire. 15 You shall add oil to it and lay frankincense on it; it is a grain offering. 16 And the priest shall turn a token portion of it into smoke—some of the coarse grain and oil with all its frankincense; it is an offering by fire to the LORD.

OFFERINGS OF WELL-BEING

3 If the offering is a sacrifice of well-being, if you offer an animal of the herd, whether male or female, you shall offer one without blemish before the LORD. 2 You shall lay your hand on the head of the offering and slaughter it at the entrance of the tent of meeting; and Aaron's sons the priests shall dash the blood against all sides of the altar. 3 You shall offer from the sacrifice of well-being, as an offering by fire to the LORD, the fat that covers the entrails and all the fat that is around the entrails; 4 the two kidneys with the fat that is on them at the loins, and the appendage of the liver, which he shall remove with the kidneys. 5 Then Aaron's sons shall turn these into smoke on the altar, with the burnt offering that is on the wood on the fire, as an offering by fire of pleasing odor to the LORD.

6 If your offering for a sacrifice of well-being to the LORD is from the flock, male or female, you shall offer one without blemish. 7 If you present a sheep as your offering, you shall bring it before the LORD 8 and lay your hand on the head of the of-

fering. It shall be slaughtered before the tent of meeting, and Aaron's sons shall dash its blood against all sides of the altar. 9 You shall present its fat from the sacrifice of well-being, as an offering by fire to the LORD: the whole broad tail, which shall be removed close to the backbone, the fat that covers the entrails, and all the fat that is around the entrails; 10 the two kidneys with the fat that is on them at the loins, and the appendage of the liver, which you shall remove with the kidneys. 11 Then the priest shall turn these into smoke on the altar as a food offering by fire to the LORD.

12 If your offering is a goat, you shall bring it before the LORD 13 and lay your hand on its head; it shall be slaughtered before the tent of meeting; and the sons of Aaron shall dash its blood against all sides of the altar. 14 You shall present as your offering from it, as an offering by fire to the LORD, the fat that covers the entrails, and all the fat that is around the entrails; 15 the two kidneys with the fat that is on them at the loins, and the appendage of the liver, which you shall remove with the kidneys. 16 Then the priest shall turn these into smoke on the altar as a food offering by fire for a pleasing odor.

All fat is the LORD's. 17 It shall be a perpetual statute throughout your generations, in all your settlements: you must not eat any fat or any blood.

SIN OFFERINGS

4 The LORD spoke to Moses, saying, 2 Speak to the people of Israel, saying: When anyone sins unintentionally in any of the LORD's commandments about things not to be done, and does any one of them:

3 If it is the anointed priest who sins, thus bringing guilt on the people, he shall offer for the sin that he has committed a bull of the herd without blemish as a sin offering to the LORD. 4 He shall bring the bull to the entrance of the tent of meeting before the LORD and lay his hand on the head of the bull; the bull shall be

slaughtered before the LORD. ⁵The anointed priest shall take some of the blood of the bull and bring it into the tent of meeting. ⁶The priest shall dip his finger in the blood and sprinkle some of the blood seven times before the LORD in front of the curtain of the sanctuary. ⁷The priest shall put some of the blood on the horns of the altar of fragrant incense that is in the tent of meeting before the LORD; and the rest of the blood of the bull he shall pour out at the base of the altar of burnt offering, which is at the entrance of the tent of meeting. ⁸He shall remove all the fat from the bull of sin offering: the fat that covers the entrails and all the fat that is around the entrails; ⁹the two kidneys with the fat that is on them at the loins; and the appendage of the liver, which he shall remove with the kidneys, ¹⁰just as these are removed from the ox of the sacrifice of well-being. The priest shall turn them into smoke upon the altar of burnt offering. ¹¹But the skin of the bull and all its flesh, as well as its head, its legs, its entrails, and its dung— ¹²all the rest of the bull—he shall carry out to a clean place outside the camp, to the ash heap, and shall burn it on a wood fire; at the ash heap it shall be burned.

13 If the whole congregation of Israel errs unintentionally and the matter escapes the notice of the assembly, and they do any one of the things that by the LORD's commandments ought not to be done and incur guilt; ¹⁴when the sin that they have committed becomes known, the assembly shall offer a bull of the herd for a sin offering and bring it before the tent of meeting. ¹⁵The elders of the congregation shall lay their hands on the head of the bull before the LORD, and the bull shall be slaughtered before the LORD. ¹⁶The anointed priest shall bring some of the blood of the bull into the tent of meeting, ¹⁷and the priest shall dip his finger in the blood and sprinkle it seven times before the LORD, in front of the curtain. ¹⁸He shall put some of the blood on the horns of the altar that is before the

LORD in the tent of meeting; and the rest of the blood he shall pour out at the base of the altar of burnt offering that is at the entrance of the tent of meeting. ¹⁹He shall remove all its fat and turn it into smoke on the altar. ²⁰He shall do with the bull just as is done with the bull of sin offering; he shall do the same with this. The priest shall make atonement for them, and they shall be forgiven. ²¹He shall carry the bull outside the camp, and burn it as he burned the first bull; it is the sin offering for the assembly.

22 When a ruler sins, doing unintentionally any one of all the things that by commandments of the LORD his God ought not to be done and incurs guilt, ²³once the sin that he has committed is made known to him, he shall bring as his offering a male goat without blemish. ²⁴He shall lay his hand on the head of the goat; it shall be slaughtered at the spot where the burnt offering is slaughtered before the LORD; it is a sin offering. ²⁵The priest shall take some of the blood of the sin offering with his finger and put it on the horns of the altar of burnt offering, and pour out the rest of its blood at the base of the altar of burnt offering. ²⁶All its fat he shall turn into smoke on the altar, like the fat of the sacrifice of well-being. Thus the priest shall make atonement on his behalf for his sin, and he shall be forgiven.

27 If anyone of the ordinary people among you sins unintentionally in doing any one of the things that by the LORD's commandments ought not to be done and incurs guilt, ²⁸when the sin that you have committed is made known to you, you shall bring a female goat without blemish as your offering, for the sin that you have committed. ²⁹You shall lay your hand on the head of the sin offering; and the sin offering shall be slaughtered at the place of the burnt offering. ³⁰The priest shall take some of its blood with his finger and put it on the horns of the altar of burnt offering, and he shall pour out the rest of its blood at the base of the altar. ³¹He shall remove all its fat, as

the fat is removed from the offering of well-being, and the priest shall turn it into smoke on the altar for a pleasing odor to the LORD. Thus the priest shall make atonement on your behalf, and you shall be forgiven. 32 If the offering you bring as a sin offering is a sheep, you shall bring a female without blemish. 33 You shall lay your hand on the head of the sin offering; and it shall be slaughtered as a sin offering at the spot where the burnt offering is slaughtered. 34 The priest shall take some of the blood of the sin offering with his finger and put it on the horns of the altar of burnt offering, and pour out the rest of its blood at the base of the altar. 35 You shall remove all its fat, as the fat of the sheep is removed from the sacrifice of well-being, and the priest shall turn it into smoke on the altar, with the offerings by fire to the LORD. Thus the priest shall make atonement on your behalf for the sin that you have committed, and you shall be forgiven.

5 When any of you sin in that you have heard a public adjuration to testify and—though able to testify as one who has seen or learned of the matter—do not speak up, you are subject to punishment. 2 Or when any of you touch any unclean thing—whether the carcass of an unclean beast or the carcass of unclean livestock or the carcass of an unclean swarming thing—and are unaware of it, you have become unclean, and are guilty. 3 Or when you touch human uncleanness—any uncleanness by which one can become unclean—and are unaware of it, when you come to know it, you shall be guilty. 4 Or when any of you utter aloud a rash oath for a bad or a good purpose, whatever people utter in an oath, and are unaware of it, when you come to know it, you shall in any of these be guilty. 5 When you realize your guilt in any of these, you shall confess the sin that you have committed. 6 And you shall bring to the LORD, as your penalty for the sin that you have committed, a female from the flock, a sheep or a goat, as a sin offering; and the priest shall make atonement on your behalf for your sin.

7 But if you cannot afford a sheep, you shall bring to the LORD, as your penalty for the sin that you have committed, two turtledoves or two pigeons, one for a sin offering and the other for a burnt offering. 8 You shall bring them to the priest, who shall offer first the one for the sin offering, wringing its head at the nape without severing it. 9 He shall sprinkle some of the blood of the sin offering on the side of the altar, while the rest of the blood shall be drained out at the base of the altar; it is a sin offering. 10 And the second he shall offer for a burnt offering according to the regulation. Thus the priest shall make atonement on your behalf for the sin that you have committed, and you shall be forgiven. 11 But if you cannot afford two turtledoves or two pigeons, you shall

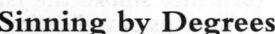

BIBLE IN LIFE

Sinning by Degrees

Leviticus 4.27–35

We tend to measure the severity of sins for our own convenience. We escalate certain faults or habits that we don't have to a more severe level of sin. For example, if we don't drink, we equate drinking with being un-Christian. We convince ourselves that "lesser" sins such as selfishness, envy or gossip are not as important. We may lie a little every now and then for our own benefit, or we may cheat occasionally, or we may walk coldly by someone lying on the street. To admit we are guilty of these sins is difficult, and we would rather talk about the things that we don't find difficult in our lives. God does not separate the "lesser" sins from the "greater." They are all equally sinful and equally "unclean" in the presence of God. Like other sinners, we need to repent and ask forgiveness.

bring as your offering for the sin that you have committed one-tenth of an ephah of choice flour for a sin offering; you shall not put oil on it or lay frankincense on it, for it is a sin offering. ¹²You shall bring it to the priest, and the priest shall scoop up a handful of it as its memorial portion, and turn this into smoke on the altar, with the offerings by fire to the LORD; it is a sin offering. ¹³Thus the priest shall make atonement on your behalf for whichever of these sins you have committed, and you shall be forgiven. Like the grain offering, the rest shall be for the priest.

OFFERINGS WITH RESTITUTION

14 The LORD spoke to Moses, saying: ¹⁵When any of you commit a trespass and sin unintentionally in any of the holy things of the LORD, you shall bring, as your guilt offering to the LORD, a ram without blemish from the flock, convertible into silver by the sanctuary shekel; it is a guilt offering. ¹⁶And you shall make restitution for the holy thing in which you were remiss, and shall add one-fifth to it and give it to the priest. The priest shall make atonement on your behalf with the ram of the guilt offering, and you shall be forgiven.

17 If any of you sin without knowing it, doing any of the things that by the LORD's commandments ought not to be done, you have incurred guilt, and are subject to punishment. ¹⁸You shall bring to the priest a ram without blemish from the flock, or the equivalent, as a guilt offering; and the priest shall make atonement on your behalf for the error that you committed unintentionally, and you shall be forgiven. ¹⁹It is a guilt offering; you have incurred guilt before the LORD.

6 ᵃ The LORD spoke to Moses, saying: ²When any of you sin and commit a trespass against the LORD by deceiving a neighbor in a matter of a deposit or a pledge, or by robbery, or if you have defrauded a neighbor, ³or have found something lost and lied about it—if you swear falsely regarding any of the vari-

ous things that one may do and sin thereby— ⁴when you have sinned and realize your guilt, and would restore what you took by robbery or by fraud or the deposit that was committed to you, or the lost thing that you found, ⁵or anything else about which you have sworn falsely, you shall repay the principal amount and shall add one-fifth to it. You shall pay it to its owner when you realize your guilt. ⁶And you shall bring to the priest, as your guilt offering to the LORD, a ram without blemish from the flock, or its equivalent, for a guilt offering. ⁷The priest shall make atonement on your behalf before the LORD, and you shall be forgiven for any of the things that one may do and incur guilt thereby.

INSTRUCTIONS CONCERNING SACRIFICES

8ᵇ The LORD spoke to Moses, saying: ⁹Command Aaron and his sons, saying: This is the ritual of the burnt offering. The burnt offering itself shall remain on the hearth upon the altar all night until the morning, while the fire on the altar shall be kept burning. ¹⁰The priest shall put on his linen vestments after putting on his linen undergarments next to his body; and he shall take up the ashes to which the fire has reduced the burnt offering on the altar, and place them beside the altar. ¹¹Then he shall take off his vestments and put on other garments, and carry the ashes out to a clean place outside the camp. ¹²The fire on the altar shall be kept burning; it shall not go out. Every morning the priest shall add wood to it, lay out the burnt offering on it, and turn into smoke the fat pieces of the offerings of well-being. ¹³A perpetual fire shall be kept burning on the altar; it shall not go out.

14 This is the ritual of the grain offering: The sons of Aaron shall offer it before the LORD, in front of the altar. ¹⁵They shall take from it a handful of the choice flour and oil of the grain offering, with all the frankincense that is on the offering, and

ᵃ 6.1 Ch 5.20 in Heb   ᵇ 6.8 Ch 6.1 in Heb

they shall turn its memorial portion into smoke on the altar as a pleasing odor to the LORD. 16Aaron and his sons shall eat what is left of it; it shall be eaten as unleavened cakes in a holy place; in the court of the tent of meeting they shall eat it. 17It shall not be baked with leaven. I have given it as their portion of my offerings by fire; it is most holy, like the sin offering and the guilt offering. 18Every male among the descendants of Aaron shall eat of it, as their perpetual due throughout your generations, from the LORD's offerings by fire; anything that touches them shall become holy.

19 The LORD spoke to Moses, saying: 20This is the offering that Aaron and his sons shall offer to the LORD on the day when he is anointed: onetenth of an ephah of choice flour as a regular offering, half of it in the morning and half in the evening. 21It shall be made with oil on a griddle; you shall bring it well soaked, as a grain offering of baked[a] pieces, and you shall present it as a pleasing odor to the LORD. 22And so the priest, anointed from among Aaron's descendants as a successor, shall prepare it; it is the LORD's—a perpetual due—to be turned entirely into smoke. 23Every grain offering of a priest shall be wholly burned; it shall not be eaten.

24 The LORD spoke to Moses, saying: 25Speak to Aaron and his sons, saying: This is the ritual of the sin offering. The sin offering shall be slaughtered before the LORD at the spot where the burnt offering is slaughtered; it is most holy. 26The priest who offers it as a sin offering shall eat of it; it shall be eaten in a holy place, in the court of the tent of meeting. 27Whatever touches its flesh shall become holy; and when any of its blood is spattered on a garment, you shall wash the bespattered part in a holy place. 28An earthen vessel in which it was boiled shall be broken; but if it is boiled in a bronze vessel, that shall be scoured and rinsed in water. 29Every male among the priests shall eat of it; it is most holy. 30But no sin offering

shall be eaten from which any blood is brought into the tent of meeting for atonement in the holy place; it shall be burned with fire.

7 This is the ritual of the guilt offering. It is most holy; 2at the spot where the burnt offering is slaughtered, they shall slaughter the guilt offering, and its blood shall be dashed against all sides of the altar. 3All its fat shall be offered: the broad tail, the fat that covers the entrails, 4the two kidneys with the fat that is on them at the loins, and the appendage of the liver, which shall be removed with the kidneys. 5The priest shall turn them into smoke on the altar as an offering by fire to the LORD; it is a guilt offering. 6Every male among the priests shall eat of it; it shall be eaten in a holy place; it is most holy.

7 The guilt offering is like the sin offering, there is the same ritual for them; the priest who makes atonement with it shall have it. 8So, too, the priest who offers anyone's burnt offering shall keep the skin of the burnt offering that he has offered. 9And every grain offering baked in the oven, and all that is prepared in a pan or on a griddle, shall belong to the priest who offers it. 10But every other grain offering, mixed with oil or dry, shall belong to all the sons of Aaron equally.

FURTHER INSTRUCTIONS

11 This is the ritual of the sacrifice of the offering of well-being that one may offer to the LORD. 12If you offer it for thanksgiving, you shall offer with the thank offering unleavened cakes mixed with oil, unleavened wafers spread with oil, and cakes of choice flour well soaked in oil. 13With your thanksgiving sacrifice of well-being you shall bring your offering with cakes of leavened bread. 14From this you shall offer one cake from each offering, as a gift to the LORD; it shall belong to the priest who dashes the blood of the offering of well-being. 15And the flesh of your thanksgiving sacrifice of well-being

a 6.21 Meaning of Heb uncertain

shall be eaten on the day it is offered; you shall not leave any of it until morning. ¹⁶But if the sacrifice you offer is a votive offering or a freewill offering, it shall be eaten on the day that you offer your sacrifice, and what is left of it shall be eaten the next day; ¹⁷but what is left of the flesh of the sacrifice shall be burned up on the third day. ¹⁸If any of the flesh of your sacrifice of well-being eaten on the third day, it shall not be acceptable, nor shall it be credited to the one who offers it; it shall be an abomination, and the one who eats of it shall incur guilt.

19 Flesh that touches any unclean thing shall not be eaten; it shall be burned up. As for other flesh, all who are clean may eat such flesh. ²⁰But those who eat flesh from the LORD's sacrifice of well-being while in a state of uncleanness shall be cut off from their kin. ²¹When any one of you touches any unclean thing— human uncleanness or an unclean animal or any unclean creature— and then eats flesh from the LORD's sacrifice of well-being, you shall be cut off from your kin.

22 The LORD spoke to Moses, saying: ²³Speak to the people of Israel, saying: You shall eat no fat of ox or sheep or goat. ²⁴The fat of an animal that died or was torn by wild animals may be put to any other use, but you must not eat it. ²⁵If any one of you eats the fat from an animal

of which an offering by fire may be made to the LORD, you who eat it shall be cut off from your kin. ²⁶You must not eat any blood whatever, either of bird or of animal, in any of your settlements. ²⁷Any one of you who eats any blood shall be cut off from your kin.

28 The LORD spoke to Moses, saying: ²⁹Speak to the people of Israel, saying: Any one of you who would offer to the LORD your sacrifice of well-being must yourself bring to the LORD your offering from your sacrifice of well-being. ³⁰Your own hands shall bring the LORD's offering by fire; you shall bring the fat with the breast, so that the breast may be raised as an elevation offering before the LORD. ³¹The priest shall turn the fat into smoke on the altar, but the breast shall belong to Aaron and his sons. ³²And the right thigh from your sacrifices of well-being you shall give to the priest as an offering; ³³the one among the sons of Aaron who offers the blood and fat of the offering of well-being shall have the right thigh for a portion. ³⁴For I have taken the breast of the elevation offering, and the thigh that is offered, from the people of Israel, from their sacrifices of well-being, and have given them to Aaron the priest and to his sons, as a perpetual due from the people of Israel. ³⁵This is the portion allotted to Aaron and to his sons from the offer-

---

⊢ BIBLE IN LIFE ▷ ⊕

Giving Thanks
Leviticus 7.12–16

God requires thankfulness from all people. In 1 Chronicles 16, David appointed specific Levites to the role of giving thanks and charged the people "to invoke, to thank, and to praise the LORD" (verse 4). In the same way, thankfulness should be a way of life for all of us. Yet how often do we devote even one minute to genuinely expressing our thanks to God? Generally, we thank God when a crisis that we face is resolved. Or when tragedy occurs, we're thankful we escaped unharmed. A lot of our thanks center on how events directly affect us. Too often we hardly acknowledge God, let alone express our thanks. In Romans 1.21, Paul says that because of the incomprehensible things we see around us in creation, even people who have not heard about God have no excuse for ignoring our Creator. Do we who know God look with awe upon creation? Do we trace God's active hand in our lives? Do we pause to give thanks? We have so much for which to be thankful.

ings made by fire to the LORD, once they have been brought forward to serve the LORD as priests; 36these the LORD commanded to be given them, when he anointed them, as a perpetual due from the people of Israel throughout their generations. 37 This is the ritual of the burnt offering, the grain offering, the sin offering, the guilt offering, the offering of ordination, and the sacrifice of well-being, 38which the LORD commanded Moses on Mount Sinai, when he commanded the people of Israel to bring their offerings to the LORD, in the wilderness of Sinai.

THE RITES OF ORDINATION

8 The LORD spoke to Moses, saying: 2Take Aaron and his sons with him, the vestments, the anointing oil, the bull of sin offering, the two rams, and the basket of unleavened bread; 3and assemble the whole congregation at the entrance of the tent of meeting. 4And Moses did as the LORD commanded him. When the congregation was assembled at the entrance of the tent of meeting, 5Moses said to the congregation, "This is what the LORD has commanded to be done." 6 Then Moses brought Aaron and his sons forward, and washed them with water. 7He put the tunic on him, fastened the sash around him, clothed him with the robe, and put the ephod on him. He then put the decorated band of the ephod around him, tying the ephod to him with it. 8He placed the breastpiece on him, and in the breastpiece he put the Urim and the Thummim. 9And he set the turban on his head, and on the turban, in front, he set the golden ornament, the holy crown, as the LORD commanded Moses. 10 Then Moses took the anointing oil and anointed the tabernacle and all that was in it, and consecrated them. 11He sprinkled some of it on the altar seven times, and anointed the altar and all its utensils, and the basin and its base, to consecrate them. 12He poured some of the anointing oil on Aaron's head and anointed him, to consecrate

him. 13And Moses brought forward Aaron's sons, and clothed them with tunics, and fastened sashes around them, and tied headdresses on them, as the LORD commanded Moses. 14 He led forward the bull of sin offering; and Aaron and his sons laid their hands upon the head of the bull of sin offering, 15and it was slaughtered. Moses took the blood and with his finger put some on each of the horns of the altar, purifying the altar; then he poured out the blood at the base of the altar. Thus he consecrated it, to make atonement for it. 16Moses took all the fat that was around the entrails, and the appendage of the liver, and the two kidneys with their fat, and turned them into smoke on the altar. 17But the bull itself, its skin and flesh and its dung, he burned with fire outside the camp, as the LORD commanded Moses. 18 Then he brought forward the ram of burnt offering. Aaron and his sons laid their hands on the head of the ram, 19and it was slaughtered. Moses dashed the blood against all sides of the altar. 20The ram was cut into its parts, and Moses turned into smoke the head and the parts and the suet. 21And after the entrails and the legs were washed with water, Moses turned into smoke the whole ram on the altar; it was a burnt offering for a pleasing odor, an offering by fire to the LORD, as the LORD commanded Moses. 22 Then he brought forward the second ram, the ram of ordination. Aaron and his sons laid their hands on the head of the ram, 23and it was slaughtered. Moses took some of its blood and put it on the lobe of Aaron's right ear and on the thumb of his right hand and on the big toe of his right foot. 24After Aaron's sons were brought forward, Moses put some of the blood on the lobes of their right ears and on the thumbs of their right hands and on the big toes of their right feet; and Moses dashed the rest of the blood against all sides of the altar. 25He took the fat— the broad tail, all the fat that was around the entrails, the appendage of the liver, and the two kidneys with their fat—and the right thigh. 26From the basket of unleavened bread that was before the LORD, he took one cake of unleavened bread, one cake of bread with oil, and one wafer, and placed them on the fat and on the right thigh. 27He placed all these on the palms of Aaron and on the palms of his sons, and raised them as an elevation offering before the LORD. 28Then Moses took them from their hands and turned them into smoke on the altar with the burnt offering. This was an ordination offering for a pleasing odor, an offering by fire to the LORD. 29Moses took the breast and raised it as an elevation offering before the LORD; it was Moses' portion of the ram of ordination, as the LORD commanded Moses.

30 Then Moses took some of the anointing oil and some of the blood that was on the altar and sprinkled them on Aaron and his vestments, and also on his sons and their vestments. Thus he consecrated Aaron and his vestments, and also his sons and their vestments.

31 And Moses said to Aaron and his sons, "Boil the flesh at the entrance of the tent of meeting, and eat it there with the bread that is in the basket of ordination offerings, as I was commanded, 'Aaron and his sons shall eat it'; 32and what remains of the flesh and the bread you shall burn with fire. 33You shall not go outside the entrance of the tent of meeting for seven days, until the day when your period of ordination is completed. For it will take seven days to ordain you; 34as has been done today, the LORD has commanded to be done to make atonement for you. 35You shall remain at the entrance of the tent of meeting day and night for seven days, keeping the LORD's charge so that you do not die; for so I am commanded." 36Aaron and his sons did all the things that the LORD commanded through Moses.

AARON'S PRIESTHOOD INAUGURATED

9 On the eighth day Moses summoned Aaron and his sons and the elders of Israel. 2He said to Aaron, "Take a bull calf for a sin offering and a ram for a burnt offering, without blemish, and offer them before the LORD. 3And say to the people of Israel, 'Take a male goat for a sin offering; a calf and a lamb, yearlings without blemish, for a burnt offering; 4and an ox and a ram for an offering of well-being to sacrifice before the LORD; and a grain offering mixed with oil. For today the LORD will appear to you.' " 5They brought what Moses commanded to the front of the tent of meeting; and the whole congregation drew near and stood before the LORD. 6And Moses said, "This is the thing that the LORD commanded you to do, so that the glory of the LORD may appear to you." 7Then Moses said to Aaron, "Draw near to the altar and sacrifice your sin offering and your burnt offering, and make atonement for yourself and for the people; and sacrifice the offering of the people, and make atonement for them; as the LORD has commanded."

⊢ **BIBLE IN LIFE** ▷━━━━━━

True Sacrifice   Leviticus 9.1–7

In Old Testament times, the Hebrew people sacrificed animals for the propitiation of their sins. Later, Christ died as the ultimate sacrifice for our sins. In the New Testament, Paul points out that we should offer our bodies as *living* sacrifices (see Romans 12.1). In offering ourselves to God, we are not giving up lives of freedom, excitement, adventure, joy or peace; the more we submit to Jesus Christ and align ourselves with him, the more we are expanding our lives. Through the presence of the Holy Spirit in our bodies, we become a living sacrifice—full of life! And the more we dedicate ourselves to Jesus Christ, the more alive we are.

8 Aaron drew near to the altar, and slaughtered the calf of the sin offering, which was for himself. 9The sons of Aaron presented the blood to him, and he dipped his finger in the blood and put it on the horns of the altar; and the rest of the blood he poured out at the base of the altar. 10But the fat, the kidneys, and the appendage of the liver from the sin offering he turned into smoke on the altar, as the LORD commanded Moses; 11and the flesh and the skin he burned with fire outside the camp. 12 Then he slaughtered the burnt offering. Aaron's sons brought him the blood, and he dashed it against all sides of the altar. 13And they brought him the burnt offering piece by piece, and the head, which he turned into smoke on the altar. 14He washed the entrails and the legs and, with the burnt offering, turned them into smoke on the altar. 15 Next he presented the people's offering. He took the goat of the sin offering that was for the people, and slaughtered it, and presented it as a sin offering like the first one. 16He presented the burnt offering, and sacrificed it according to regulation. 17He presented the grain offering, and, taking a handful of it, he turned it into smoke on the altar, in addition to the burnt offering of the morning. 18 He slaughtered the ox and the ram as a sacrifice of well-being for the people. Aaron's sons brought him the blood, which he dashed against all sides of the altar, 19and the fat of the ox and of the ram—the broad tail, the fat that covers the entrails, the two kidneys and the fat on them,[a] and the appendage of the liver. 20They first laid the fat on the breasts, and the fat was turned into smoke on the altar; 21and the breasts and the right thigh Aaron raised as an elevation offering before the LORD, as Moses had commanded. 22 Aaron lifted his hands toward the people and blessed them; and he came down after sacrificing the sin offering, the burnt offering, and the offering of well-being. 23Moses and Aaron entered the tent of meeting, and then came out and blessed the people; and the glory of the LORD appeared to all the people. 24Fire came out from the LORD and consumed the burnt offering and the fat on the altar; and when all the people saw it, they shouted and fell on their faces.

NADAB AND ABIHU

10 Now Aaron's sons, Nadab and Abihu, each took his censer, put fire in it, and laid incense on it; and they offered unholy fire before the LORD, such as he had not commanded them. 2And fire came out from the presence of the LORD and consumed them, and they died before the LORD. 3Then Moses said to Aaron, "This is what the LORD meant when he said,

"Through those who are near me
    I will show myself holy,
and before all the people
    I will be glorified.'"

And Aaron was silent.

4 Moses summoned Mishael and Elzaphan, sons of Uzziel the uncle of Aaron, and said to them, "Come forward, and carry your kinsmen away from the front of the sanctuary to a place outside the camp." 5They came forward and carried them by their tunics out of the camp, as Moses had ordered. 6And Moses said to Aaron and to his sons Eleazar and Ithamar, "Do not dishevel your hair, and do not tear your vestments, or you will die and wrath will strike all the congregation; but your kindred, the whole house of Israel, may mourn the burning that the LORD has sent. 7You shall not go outside the entrance of the tent of meeting, or you will die; for the anointing oil of the LORD is on you." And they did as Moses had ordered.

8 And the LORD spoke to Aaron: 9Drink no wine or strong drink, neither you nor your sons, when you enter the tent of meeting, that you may not die; it is a statute forever throughout your generations. 10You

a 9.19 Gk: Heb *the broad tail, and that which covers, and the kidneys*

are to distinguish between the holy and the common, and between the unclean and the clean; [11]and you are to teach the people of Israel all the statutes that the LORD has spoken to them through Moses.

[12] Moses spoke to Aaron and to his remaining sons, Eleazar and Ithamar: Take the grain offering that is left from the LORD's offerings by fire, and eat it unleavened beside the altar, for it is most holy; [13]you shall eat it in a holy place, because it is your due and your sons' due, from the offerings by fire to the LORD; for so I am commanded. [14]But the breast that is elevated and the thigh that is raised, you and your sons and daughters as well may eat in any clean place; for they have been assigned to you and your children from the sacrifices of the offerings of well-being of the people of Israel. [15]The thigh that is raised and the breast that is elevated they shall bring, together with the offerings by fire of the fat, to raise for an elevation offering before the LORD; they are to be your due and that of your children forever, as the LORD has commanded.

[16] Then Moses made inquiry about the goat of the sin offering, and—it had already been burned! He was angry with Eleazar and Ithamar, Aaron's remaining sons, and said, [17]"Why did you not eat the sin offering in the sacred area? For it is most holy, and God[a] has given it to you that you may remove the guilt of the congregation, to make atonement on their behalf before the LORD. [18]Its blood was not brought into the inner part of the sanctuary. You should certainly have eaten it in the sanctuary, as I commanded." [19]And Aaron spoke to Moses, "See, today they offered their sin offering and their burnt offering before the LORD; and yet such things as these have befallen me! If I had eaten the sin offering today, would it have been agreeable to the LORD?" [20]And when Moses heard that, he agreed.

CLEAN AND UNCLEAN FOODS

11 The LORD spoke to Moses and Aaron, saying to them:

[2]Speak to the people of Israel, saying:

From among all the land animals, these are the creatures that you may eat. [3]Any animal that has divided hoofs and is cleft-footed and chews the cud—such you may eat. [4]But among those that chew the cud or have divided hoofs, you shall not eat the following: the camel, for even though it chews the cud, it does not have divided hoofs; it is unclean for you. [5]The rock badger, for even though it chews the cud, it does not have divided hoofs; it is unclean for you. [6]The hare, for even though it chews the cud, it does not have divided hoofs; it is unclean for you. [7]The pig, for even though it has divided hoofs and is cleft-footed, it does not chew the cud; it is unclean for you. [8]Of their flesh you shall not eat, and their carcasses you shall not touch; they are unclean for you.

[9] These you may eat, of all that are in the waters. Everything in the waters that has fins and scales, whether in the seas or in the streams—such you may eat. [10]But anything in the seas or the streams that does not have fins and scales, of the swarming creatures in the waters and among all the other living creatures that are in the waters—they are detestable to you [11]and detestable they shall remain. Of their flesh you shall not eat, and their carcasses you shall regard as detestable. [12]Everything in the waters that does not have fins and scales is detestable to you.

[13] These you shall regard as detestable among the birds. They shall not be eaten; they are an abomination: the eagle, the vulture, the osprey, [14]the buzzard, the kite of any kind; [15]every raven of any kind; [16]the ostrich, the nighthawk, the sea gull, the hawk of any kind; [17]the little owl, the cormorant, the great owl, [18]the water hen, the desert owl,[b] the carrion vulture, [19]the stork, the heron of any kind, the hoopoe, and the bat.[c]

---

[a] 10.17 Heb *he*   [b] 11.18 Or *pelican*
[c] 11.19 Identification of several of the birds in verses 13–19 is uncertain

20 All winged insects that walk upon all fours are detestable to you. **21**But among the winged insects that walk on all fours you may eat those that have jointed legs above their feet, with which to leap on the ground. **22**Of them you may eat: the locust according to its kind, the bald locust according to its kind, the cricket according to its kind, and the grasshopper according to its kind. **23**But all other winged insects that have four feet are detestable to you.

UNCLEAN ANIMALS

24 By these you shall become unclean; whoever touches the carcass of any of them shall be unclean until the evening, **25**and whoever carries any part of the carcass of any of them shall wash his clothes and be unclean until the evening. **26**Every animal that has divided hoofs but is not cleft-footed or does not chew the cud is unclean for you; everyone who touches one of them shall be unclean. **27**All that walk on their paws, among the animals that walk on all fours, are unclean for you; whoever touches the carcass of any of them shall be unclean until the evening, **28**and the one who carries the carcass shall wash his clothes and be unclean until the evening; they are unclean for you.

29 These are unclean for you among the creatures that swarm upon the earth: the weasel, the mouse, the great lizard according to its kind, **30**the gecko, the land crocodile, the lizard, the sand lizard, and the chameleon. **31**These are unclean for you among all that swarm; whoever touches one of them when they are dead shall be unclean until the evening. **32**And anything upon which any of them falls when they are dead shall be unclean, whether an article of wood or cloth or skin or sacking, any article that is used for any purpose; it shall be dipped into water, and it shall be unclean until the evening, and then it shall be clean. **33**And if any of them falls into any earthen vessel, all that is in it shall be unclean, and you shall break the vessel. **34**Any food that could be eaten shall be unclean if water from any such vessel comes upon it; and any liquid that could be drunk shall be unclean if it was in any such vessel. **35**Everything on which any part of the carcass falls shall be unclean; whether an oven or stove, it shall be broken in pieces; they are unclean, and shall remain unclean for you. **36**But a spring or a cistern holding water shall be clean, while whatever touches the carcass in it shall be unclean. **37**If any part of their carcass falls upon any seed set aside for sowing, it is clean; **38**but if water is put on the seed and any part of their carcass falls on it, it is unclean for you.

39 If an animal of which you may eat dies, anyone who touches its carcass shall be unclean until the evening. **40**Those who eat of its carcass shall wash their clothes and be unclean until the evening; and those who carry the carcass shall wash their clothes and be unclean until the evening.

41 All creatures that swarm upon the earth are detestable; they shall not be eaten. **42**Whatever moves on its belly, and whatever moves on all fours, or whatever has many feet, all the creatures that swarm upon the earth, you shall not eat; for they are detestable. **43**You shall not make yourselves detestable with any creature that swarms; you shall not defile yourselves with them, and so become unclean. **44**For I am the LORD your God; sanctify yourselves therefore, and be holy, for I am holy. You shall not defile yourselves with any swarming creature that moves on the earth. **45**For I am the LORD who brought you up from the land of Egypt, to be your God; you shall be holy, for I am holy.

46 This is the law pertaining to land animal and bird and every living creature that moves through the waters and every creature that swarms upon the earth, **47**to make a distinction between the unclean and the clean, and between the living creature that may be eaten and the living creature that may not be eaten.

PURIFICATION OF WOMEN
AFTER CHILDBIRTH

12 The LORD spoke to Moses, saying: [2]Speak to the people of Israel, saying:

If a woman conceives and bears a male child, she shall be ceremonially unclean seven days; as at the time of her menstruation, she shall be unclean. [3]On the eighth day the flesh of his foreskin shall be circumcised. [4]Her time of blood purification shall be thirty-three days; she shall not touch any holy thing, or come into the sanctuary, until the days of her purification are completed. [5]If she bears a female child, she shall be unclean two weeks, as in her menstruation; her time of blood purification shall be sixty-six days.

6 When the days of her purification are completed, whether for a son or for a daughter, she shall bring to the priest at the entrance of the tent of meeting a lamb in its first year for a burnt offering, and a pigeon or a turtledove for a sin offering. [7]He shall offer it before the LORD, and make atonement on her behalf; then she shall be clean from her flow of blood. This is the law for her who bears a child, male or female. [8]If she cannot afford a sheep, she shall take two turtledoves or two pigeons, one for a burnt offering and the other for a sin offering; and the priest shall make atonement on her behalf, and she shall be clean.

LEPROSY, VARIETIES
AND SYMPTOMS

13 The LORD spoke to Moses and Aaron, saying:

2 When a person has on the skin of his body a swelling or an eruption or a spot, and it turns into a leprous[a] disease on the skin of his body, he shall be brought to Aaron the priest or to one of his sons the priests. [3]The priest shall examine the disease on the skin of his body, and if the hair in the diseased area has turned white and the disease appears to be deeper than the skin of his body, it is a leprous[a] disease; after the priest has examined him he shall pronounce him ceremonially unclean. [4]But if the spot is white in the skin of his body, and appears no deeper than the skin, and the hair in it has not turned white, the priest shall confine the diseased person for seven days. [5]The priest shall examine him on the seventh day, and if he sees that the disease is checked and the disease has not spread in the skin, then the priest shall confine him seven days more. [6]The priest shall examine him again on the seventh day, and if the disease has abated and the disease has not spread in the skin, the priest shall pronounce him clean; it is only an eruption; and he shall wash his clothes, and be clean. [7]But if the eruption spreads in the skin after he has shown himself to the priest for his cleansing, he shall appear again before the priest. [8]The priest shall make an examination, and if the eruption has spread in the skin, the priest shall pronounce him unclean; it is a leprous[a] disease.

9 When a person contracts a leprous[a] disease, he shall be brought to the priest. [10]The priest shall make an examination, and if there is a white swelling in the skin that has turned the hair white, and there is quick raw flesh in the swelling, [11]it is a chronic leprous[a] disease in the skin of his body. The priest shall pronounce him unclean; he shall not confine him, for he is unclean. [12]But if the disease breaks out in the skin, so that it covers all the skin of the diseased person from head to foot, so far as the priest can see, [13]then the priest shall make an examination, and if the disease has covered all his body, he shall pronounce him clean of the disease; since it has all turned white, he is clean. [14]But if raw flesh ever appears on him, he shall be unclean; [15]the priest shall examine the raw flesh and pronounce him unclean. Raw flesh is unclean, for it is a leprous[a] disease. [16]But if the raw flesh again turns white, he shall come to the priest; [17]the priest shall examine him, and if the disease has turned white, the priest shall pro-

---

[a] 13.2,3,8,9,11,15 A term for several skin diseases; precise meaning uncertain

nounce the diseased person clean. He is clean.

18 When there is on the skin of one's body a boil that has healed, [19] and in the place of the boil there appears a white swelling or a reddish-white spot, it shall be shown to the priest. [20] The priest shall make an examination, and if it appears deeper than the skin and its hair has turned white, the priest shall pronounce him unclean; this is a leprous[a] disease, broken out in the boil. [21] But if the priest examines it and the hair on it is not white, nor is it deeper than the skin but has abated, the priest shall confine him seven days. [22] If it spreads in the skin, the priest shall pronounce him unclean; it is diseased. [23] But if the spot remains in one place and does not spread, it is the scar of the boil; the priest shall pronounce him clean.

24 Or, when the body has a burn on the skin and the raw flesh of the burn becomes a spot, reddish-white or white, [25] the priest shall examine it. If the hair in the spot has turned white and it appears deeper than the skin, it is a leprous[a] disease; it has broken out in the burn, and the priest shall pronounce him unclean. This is a leprous[a] disease. [26] But if the priest examines it and the hair in the spot is not white, and it is no deeper than the skin but has abated, the priest shall confine him seven days. [27] The priest shall examine him the seventh day; if it is spreading in the skin, the priest shall pronounce him unclean. This is a leprous[a] disease. [28] But if the spot remains in one place and does not spread in the skin but has abated, it is a swelling from the burn, and the priest shall pronounce him clean; for it is the scar of the burn.

29 When a man or woman has a disease on the head or in the beard, [30] the priest shall examine the disease. If it appears deeper than the skin and the hair in it is yellow and thin, the priest shall pronounce him unclean; it is an itch, a leprous[a] disease of the head or the beard. [31] If the priest examines the itching disease, and it appears no deeper than

the skin and there is no black hair in it, the priest shall confine the person with the itching disease for seven days. [32] On the seventh day the priest shall examine the itch; if the itch has not spread, and there is no yellow hair in it, and the itch appears to be no deeper than the skin, [33] he shall shave, but the itch he shall not shave. The priest shall confine the person with the itch for seven days more. [34] On the seventh day the priest shall examine the itch; if the itch has not spread in the skin and it appears to be no deeper than the skin, the priest shall pronounce him clean. He shall wash his clothes and be clean. [35] But if the itch spreads in the skin after he was pronounced clean, [36] the priest shall examine him. If the itch has spread in the skin, the priest need not seek for the yellow hair; he is unclean. [37] But if in his eyes the itch is checked, and black hair has grown in it, the itch is healed, he is clean; and the priest shall pronounce him clean.

38 When a man or a woman has spots on the skin of the body, white spots, [39] the priest shall make an examination, and if the spots on the skin of the body are of a dull white, it is a rash that has broken out on the skin; he is clean.

40 If anyone loses the hair from his head, he is bald but he is clean. [41] If he loses the hair from his forehead and temples, he has baldness of the forehead but he is clean. [42] But if there is on the bald head or the bald forehead a reddish-white diseased spot, it is a leprous[a] disease breaking out on his bald head or his bald forehead. [43] The priest shall examine him; if the diseased swelling is reddish-white on his bald head or on his bald forehead, which resembles a leprous[a] disease in the skin of the body, [44] he is leprous,[a] he is unclean. The priest shall pronounce him unclean; the disease is on his head.

45 The person who has the leprous[a] disease shall wear torn clothes and let the hair of his head be disheveled;

---

[a] 13.20,25,27,30,42,43,44,45 A term for several skin diseases; precise meaning uncertain

and he shall cover his upper lip and cry out, "Unclean, unclean." 46He shall remain unclean as long as he has the disease; he is unclean. He shall live alone; his dwelling shall be outside the camp.

47 Concerning clothing: when a leprous[a] disease appears in it, in woolen or linen cloth, 48in warp or woof of linen or wool, or in a skin or in anything made of skin, 49if the disease shows greenish or reddish in the garment, whether in warp or woof or in skin or in anything made of skin, it is a leprous[a] disease and shall be shown to the priest. 50The priest shall examine the disease, and put the diseased article aside for seven days. 51He shall examine the disease on the seventh day. If the disease has spread in the cloth, in warp or woof, or in the skin, whatever be the use of the skin, this is a spreading leprous[a] disease; it is unclean. 52He shall burn the clothing, whether diseased in warp or woof, woolen or linen, or anything of skin, for it is a spreading leprous[a] disease; it shall be burned in fire.

53 If the priest makes an examination, and the disease has not spread in the clothing, in warp or woof or in anything of skin, 54the priest shall command them to wash the article in which the disease appears, and he shall put it aside seven days more. 55The priest shall examine the diseased article after it has been washed. If the diseased spot has not changed color, though the disease has not spread, it is unclean; you shall burn it in fire, whether the leprous[a] spot is on the inside or on the outside.

56 If the priest makes an examination, and the disease has abated after it is washed, he shall tear the spot out of the cloth, in warp or woof, or out of skin. 57If it appears again in the garment, in warp or woof, or in anything of skin, it is spreading; you shall burn with fire that in which the disease appears. 58But the cloth, warp or woof, or anything of skin from which the disease disappears when you have washed it, shall then be washed a second time, and it shall be clean.

59 This is the ritual for a leprous[a] disease in a cloth of wool or linen, either in warp or woof, or in anything of skin, to decide whether it is clean or unclean.

PURIFICATION OF LEPERS AND LEPROUS HOUSES

14 The LORD spoke to Moses, saying: 2This shall be the ritual for the leprous[a] person at the time of his cleansing:

He shall be brought to the priest; 3the priest shall go out of the camp, and the priest shall make an examination. If the disease is healed in the leprous[a] person, 4the priest shall command that two living clean birds and cedarwood and crimson yarn and hyssop be brought for the one who is to be cleansed. 5The priest shall command that one of the birds be slaughtered over fresh water in an earthen vessel. 6He shall take the living bird with the cedarwood and the crimson yarn and the hyssop, and dip them and the living bird in the blood of the bird that was slaughtered over the fresh water. 7He shall sprinkle it seven times upon the one who is to be cleansed of the leprous[a] disease; then he shall pronounce him clean, and he shall let the living bird go into the open field. 8The one who is to be cleansed shall wash his clothes, and shave off all his hair, and bathe himself in water, and he shall be clean. After that he shall come into the camp, but shall live outside his tent seven days. 9On the seventh day he shall shave all his hair: of head, beard, eyebrows; he shall shave all his hair. Then he shall wash his clothes, and bathe his body in water, and he shall be clean.

10 On the eighth day he shall take two male lambs without blemish, and one ewe lamb in its first year without blemish, and a grain offering of three-tenths of an ephah of choice flour mixed with oil, and one log[b] of oil. 11The priest who cleanses shall set the person to be cleansed, along with these things, before the

[a] 13.47,49,51,52,55,59; 14.2,3,7 A term for several skin diseases; precise meaning uncertain   [b] 14.10 A liquid measure

LORD, at the entrance of the tent of meeting. ¹²The priest shall take one of the lambs, and offer it as a guilt offering, along with the log^a of oil, and raise them as an elevation offering before the LORD. ¹³He shall slaughter the lamb in the place where the sin offering and the burnt offering are slaughtered in the holy place; for the guilt offering, like the sin offering, belongs to the priest: it is most holy. ¹⁴The priest shall take some of the blood of the guilt offering and put it on the lobe of the right ear of the one to be cleansed, and on the thumb of the right hand, and on the big toe of the right foot. ¹⁵The priest shall take some of the log^a of oil and pour it into the palm of his own left hand, ¹⁶and dip his right finger in the oil that is in his left hand and sprinkle some oil with his finger seven times before the LORD. ¹⁷Some of the oil that remains in his hand the priest shall put on the lobe of the right ear of the one to be cleansed, and on the thumb of the right hand, and on the big toe of the right foot, on top of the blood of the guilt offering. ¹⁸The rest of the oil that is in the priest's hand he shall put on the head of the one to be cleansed. Then the priest shall make atonement on his behalf before the LORD: ¹⁹the priest shall offer the sin offering, to make atonement for the one to be cleansed from his uncleanness. Afterward he shall slaughter the burnt offering; ²⁰and the priest shall offer the burnt offering and the grain offering on the altar. Thus the priest shall make atonement on his behalf and he shall be clean.

²¹ But if he is poor and cannot afford so much, he shall take one male lamb for a guilt offering to be elevated, to make atonement on his behalf, and one-tenth of an ephah of choice flour mixed with oil for a grain offering and a log^a of oil; ²²also two turtledoves or two pigeons, such as he can afford, one for a sin offering and the other for a burnt offering. ²³On the eighth day he shall bring them for his cleansing to the priest, to the entrance of the tent of meeting, before the LORD; ²⁴and the priest shall take the lamb of the guilt offering and the log^a of oil, and the priest shall raise them as an elevation offering before the LORD. ²⁵The priest shall slaughter the lamb of the guilt offering and shall take some of the blood of the guilt offering, and put it on the lobe of the right ear of the one to be cleansed, and on the thumb of the right hand, and on the big toe of the right foot. ²⁶The priest shall pour some of the oil into the palm of his own left hand, ²⁷and shall sprinkle with his right finger some of the oil that is in his left hand seven times before the LORD. ²⁸The priest shall put some of the oil that is in his hand on the lobe of the right ear of the one to be cleansed, and on the thumb of the right hand, and the big toe of the right foot, where the blood of the guilt offering was placed. ²⁹The rest of the oil that is in the priest's hand he shall put on the head of the one to be cleansed, to make atonement on his behalf before the LORD. ³⁰And he shall offer, of the turtledoves or pigeons such as he can afford, ³¹one^b for a sin offering and the other for a burnt offering, along with a grain offering; and the priest shall make atonement before the LORD on behalf of the one being cleansed. ³²This is the ritual for the one who has a leprous^c disease, who cannot afford the offerings for his cleansing.

³³ The LORD spoke to Moses and Aaron, saying:

³⁴ When you come into the land of Canaan, which I give you for a possession, and I put a leprous^c disease in a house in the land of your possession, ³⁵the owner of the house shall come and tell the priest, saying, "There seems to me to be some sort of disease in my house." ³⁶The priest shall command that they empty the house before the priest goes to examine the disease, or all that is in the house will become unclean; and afterward the priest shall go in to inspect the house. ³⁷He shall

^a 14.12,15,21,24 A liquid measure   ^b 14.31 Gk Syr: Heb afford, ³¹such as he can afford, one   ^c 14.32,34 A term for several skin diseases; precise meaning uncertain

examine the disease; if the disease is in the walls of the house with greenish or reddish spots, and if it appears to be deeper than the surface, 38the priest shall go outside to the door of the house and shut up the house seven days. 39The priest shall come again on the seventh day and make an inspection; if the disease has spread in the walls of the house, 40the priest shall command that the stones in which the disease appears be taken out and thrown into an unclean place outside the city. 41He shall have the inside of the house scraped thoroughly, and the plaster that is scraped off shall be dumped in an unclean place outside the city. 42They shall take other stones and put them in the place of those stones, and take other plaster and plaster the house.

43 If the disease breaks out again in the house, after he has taken out the stones and scraped the house and plastered it, 44the priest shall go and make inspection; if the disease has spread in the house, it is a spreading leprousa disease in the house; it is unclean. 45He shall have the house torn down, its stones and timber and all the plaster of the house, and taken outside the city to an unclean place. 46All who enter the house while it is shut up shall be unclean until the evening; 47and all who sleep in the house shall wash their clothes; and all who eat in the house shall wash their clothes.

48 If the priest comes and makes an inspection, and the disease has not spread in the house after the house was plastered, the priest shall pronounce the house clean; the disease is healed. 49For the cleansing of the house he shall take two birds, with cedarwood and crimson yarn and hyssop, 50and shall slaughter one of the birds over fresh water in an earthen vessel, 51and shall take the cedarwood and the hyssop and the crimson yarn, along with the living bird, and dip them in the blood of the slaughtered bird and the fresh water, and sprinkle the house seven times. 52Thus he shall cleanse the house with the blood of the bird,

and with the fresh water, and with the living bird, and with the cedarwood and hyssop and crimson yarn; 53and he shall let the living bird go out of the city into the open field; so he shall make atonement for the house, and it shall be clean.

54 This is the ritual for any leprousa disease: for an itch, 55for leprousa diseases in clothing and houses, 56and for a swelling or an eruption or a spot, 57to determine when it is unclean and when it is clean. This is the ritual for leprousa diseases.

CONCERNING BODILY DISCHARGES

15 The LORD spoke to Moses and Aaron, saying: 2Speak to the people of Israel and say to them: When any man has a discharge from his member,b his discharge makes him ceremonially unclean. 3The uncleanness of his discharge is this: whether his memberb flows with his discharge, or his memberb is stopped from discharging, it is uncleanness for him. 4Every bed on which the one with the discharge lies shall be unclean; and everything on which he sits shall be unclean. 5Anyone who touches his bed shall wash his clothes, and bathe in water, and be unclean until the evening. 6All who sit on anything on which the one with the discharge has sat shall wash their clothes, and bathe in water, and be unclean until the evening. 7All who touch the body of the one with the discharge shall wash their clothes, and bathe in water, and be unclean until the evening. 8If the one with the discharge spits on persons who are clean, then they shall wash their clothes, and bathe in water, and be unclean until the evening. 9Any saddle on which the one with the discharge rides shall be unclean. 10All who touch anything that was under him shall be unclean until the evening, and all who carry such a thing shall wash their clothes, and bathe in water,

a 14.44,54,55,57 A term for several skin diseases; precise meaning uncertain
b 15.2,3 Heb *flesh*

and be unclean until the evening. ¹¹All those whom the one with the discharge touches without his having rinsed his hands in water shall wash their clothes, and bathe in water, and be unclean until the evening. ¹²Any earthen vessel that the one with the discharge touches shall be broken; and every vessel of wood shall be rinsed in water.

¹³When the one with a discharge is cleansed of his discharge, he shall count seven days for his cleansing; he shall wash his clothes and bathe his body in fresh water, and he shall be clean. ¹⁴On the eighth day he shall take two turtledoves or two pigeons and come before the LORD to the entrance of the tent of meeting and give them to the priest. ¹⁵The priest shall offer them, one for a sin offering and the other for a burnt offering; and the priest shall make atonement on his behalf before the LORD for his discharge.

¹⁶If a man has an emission of semen, he shall bathe his whole body in water, and be unclean until the evening. ¹⁷Everything made of cloth or of skin on which the semen falls shall be washed with water, and be unclean until the evening. ¹⁸If a man lies with a woman and has an emission of semen, both of them shall bathe in water, and be unclean until the evening.

¹⁹When a woman has a discharge of blood that is her regular discharge from her body, she shall be in her impurity for seven days, and whoever touches her shall be unclean until the evening. ²⁰Everything upon which she lies during her impurity shall be unclean; everything also upon which she sits shall be unclean. ²¹Whoever touches her bed shall wash his clothes, and bathe in water, and be unclean until the evening. ²²Whoever touches anything upon which she sits shall wash his clothes, and bathe in water, and be unclean until the evening; ²³whether it is the bed or anything upon which she sits, when he touches it he shall be unclean until the evening. ²⁴If any man lies with her, and her impurity falls on him, he shall be unclean

seven days; and every bed on which he lies shall be unclean.

²⁵If a woman has a discharge of blood for many days, not at the time of her impurity, or if she has a discharge beyond the time of her impurity, all the days of the discharge she shall continue in uncleanness; as in the days of her impurity, she shall be unclean. ²⁶Every bed on which she lies during all the days of her discharge shall be treated as the bed of her impurity; and everything on which she sits shall be unclean, as in the uncleanness of her impurity. ²⁷Whoever touches these things shall be unclean, and shall wash his clothes, and bathe in water, and be unclean until the evening. ²⁸If she is cleansed of her discharge, she shall count seven days, and after that she shall be clean. ²⁹On the eighth day she shall take two turtledoves or two pigeons and bring them to the priest at the entrance of the tent of meeting. ³⁰The priest shall offer one for a sin offering and the other for a burnt offering; and the priest shall make atonement on her behalf before the LORD for her unclean discharge.

³¹Thus you shall keep the people of Israel separate from their uncleanness, so that they do not die in their uncleanness by defiling my tabernacle that is in their midst.

³²This is the ritual for those who have a discharge: for him who has an emission of semen, becoming unclean thereby, ³³for her who is in the infirmity of her period, for anyone, male or female, who has a discharge, and for the man who lies with a woman who is unclean.

THE DAY OF ATONEMENT

16 The LORD spoke to Moses after the death of the two sons of Aaron, when they drew near before the LORD and died. ²The LORD said to Moses:

Tell your brother Aaron not to come just at any time into the sanctuary inside the curtain before the mercy seat[a] that is upon the ark, or he will die; for I appear in the cloud

---

ᵃ 16.2 Or *the cover*

upon the mercy seat.[a] 3Thus shall Aaron come into the holy place: with a young bull for a sin offering and a ram for a burnt offering. 4He shall put on the holy linen tunic, and shall have the linen undergarments next to his body, fasten the linen sash, and wear the linen turban; these are the holy vestments. He shall bathe his body in water, and then put them on. 5He shall take from the congregation of the people of Israel two male goats for a sin offering, and one ram for a burnt offering.

6 Aaron shall offer the bull as a sin offering for himself, and shall make atonement for himself and for his house. 7He shall take the two goats and set them before the LORD at the entrance of the tent of meeting; 8and Aaron shall cast lots on the two goats, one lot for the LORD and the other lot for Azazel.[b] 9Aaron shall present the goat on which the lot fell for the LORD, and offer it as a sin offering; 10but the goat on which the lot fell for Azazel[b] shall be presented alive before the LORD to make atonement over it, that it may be sent away into the wilderness to Azazel.[b]

11 Aaron shall present the bull as a sin offering for himself, and shall make atonement for himself and for his house; he shall slaughter the bull as a sin offering for himself. 12He shall take a censer full of coals of fire from the altar before the LORD, and two handfuls of crushed sweet incense, and he shall bring it inside the curtain 13and put the incense on the fire before the LORD, that the cloud of the incense may cover the mercy seat[a] that is upon the covenant,[c] or he will die. 14He shall take some of the blood of the bull, and sprinkle it with his finger on the front of the mercy seat,[a] and before the mercy seat[a] he shall sprinkle the blood with his finger seven times.

15 He shall slaughter the goat of the sin offering that is for the people and bring its blood inside the curtain, and do with its blood as he did with the blood of the bull, sprinkling it upon the mercy seat[a] and before the mercy seat.[a] 16Thus he shall make atonement for the sanctuary,

because of the uncleannesses of the people of Israel, and because of their transgressions, all their sins; and so he shall do for the tent of meeting, which remains with them in the midst of their uncleannesses. 17No one shall be in the tent of meeting from the time he enters to make atonement in the sanctuary until he comes out and has made atonement for himself and for his house and for all the assembly of Israel. 18Then he shall go out to the altar that is before the LORD and make atonement on its behalf, and shall take some of the blood of the bull and of the blood of the goat, and put it on each of the horns of the altar. 19He shall sprinkle some of the blood on it with his finger seven times, and cleanse it and hallow it from the uncleannesses of the people of Israel.

20 When he has finished atoning for the holy place and the tent of meeting and the altar, he shall present the live goat. 21Then Aaron shall lay both his hands on the head of the live goat, and confess over it all the iniquities of the people of Israel, and all their transgressions, all their sins, putting them on the head of the goat, and sending it away into the wilderness by means of someone designated for the task.[d] 22The goat shall bear on itself all their iniquities to a barren region; and the goat shall be set free in the wilderness.

23 Then Aaron shall enter the tent of meeting, and shall take off the linen vestments that he put on when he went into the holy place, and shall leave them there. 24He shall bathe his body in water in a holy place, and put on his vestments; then he shall come out and offer his burnt offering and the burnt offering of the people, making atonement for himself and for the people. 25The fat of the sin offering he shall turn into smoke on the altar. 26The one who sets the goat free for Azazel[b] shall wash his clothes and bathe

[a] 16.2,13,14,15 Or the cover
[b] 16.8,10,26 Traditionally rendered a scapegoat [c] 16.13 Or treaty, or testament; Heb eduth [d] 16.21 Meaning of Heb uncertain

his body in water, and afterward may come into the camp. ²⁷The bull of the sin offering and the goat of the sin offering, whose blood was brought in to make atonement in the holy place, shall be taken outside the camp; their skin and their flesh and their dung shall be consumed in fire. ²⁸The one who burns them shall wash his clothes and bathe his body in water, and afterward may come into the camp.

29 This shall be a statute to you forever: In the seventh month, on the tenth day of the month, you shall deny yourselves,ᵃ and shall do no work, neither the citizen nor the alien who resides among you. ³⁰For on this day atonement shall be made for you, to cleanse you; from all your sins you shall be clean before the LORD. ³¹It is a sabbath of complete rest to you, and you shall deny yourselves;ᵃ it is a statute forever. ³²The priest who is anointed and consecrated as priest in his father's place shall make atonement, wearing the linen vestments, the holy vestments. ³³He shall make atonement for the sanctuary, and he shall make atonement for the tent of meeting and for the altar, and he shall make atonement for the priests and for all the people of the assembly. ³⁴This shall be an everlasting statute for you, to make atonement for the people of Israel once in the year for all their sins. And Moses did as the LORD had commanded him.

THE SLAUGHTERING OF ANIMALS

17 The LORD spoke to Moses: 2 Speak to Aaron and his sons and to all the people of Israel and say to them: This is what the LORD has commanded. ³If anyone of the house of Israel slaughters an ox or a lamb or a goat in the camp, or slaughters it outside the camp, ⁴and does not bring it to the entrance of the tent of meeting, to present it as an offering to the LORD before the tabernacle of the LORD, he shall be held guilty of bloodshed; he has shed blood, and he shall be cut off from the people. ⁵This is in order that the

people of Israel may bring their sacrifices that they offer in the open field, that they may bring them to the LORD, to the priest at the entrance of the tent of meeting, and offer them as sacrifices of well-being to the LORD. ⁶The priest shall dash the blood against the altar of the LORD at the entrance of the tent of meeting, and turn the fat into smoke as a pleasing odor to the LORD, ⁷so that they may no longer offer their sacrifices for goat-demons, to whom they prostitute themselves. This shall be a statute forever to them throughout their generations.

8 And say to them further: Anyone of the house of Israel or of the aliens who reside among them who offers a burnt offering or sacrifice, ⁹and does not bring it to the entrance of the tent of meeting, to sacrifice it to the LORD, shall be cut off from the people.

EATING BLOOD PROHIBITED

10 If anyone of the house of Israel or of the aliens who reside among them eats any blood, I will set my face against that person who eats blood, and will cut that person off from the people. ¹¹For the life of the flesh is in the blood; and I have given it to you for making atonement for your lives on the altar; for, as life, it is the blood that makes atonement. ¹²Therefore I have said to the people of Israel: No person among you shall eat blood, nor shall any alien who resides among you eat blood. ¹³And anyone of the people of Israel, or of the aliens who reside among them, who hunts down an animal or bird that may be eaten shall pour out its blood and cover it with earth.

14 For the life of every creature— its blood is its life; therefore I have said to the people of Israel: You shall not eat the blood of any creature, for the life of every creature is its blood; whoever eats it shall be cut off. ¹⁵All persons, citizens or aliens, who eat what dies of itself or what has been torn by wild animals, shall wash their clothes, and bathe themselves

ᵃ 16.29,31 Or *shall fast*

in water, and be unclean until the evening; then they shall be clean. [16]But if they do not wash themselves or bathe their body, they shall bear their guilt.

SEXUAL RELATIONS

18 The LORD spoke to Moses, saying:

2 Speak to the people of Israel and say to them: I am the LORD your God. [3]You shall not do as they do in the land of Egypt, where you lived, and you shall not do as they do in the land of Canaan, to which I am bringing you. You shall not follow their statutes. [4]My ordinances you shall observe and my statutes you shall keep, following them: I am the LORD your God. [5]You shall keep my statutes and my ordinances; by doing so one shall live: I am the LORD.

6 None of you shall approach anyone near of kin to uncover nakedness: I am the LORD. [7]You shall not uncover the nakedness of your father, which is the nakedness of your mother; she is your mother, you shall not uncover her nakedness. [8]You shall not uncover the nakedness of your father's wife; it is the nakedness of your father. [9]You shall not uncover the nakedness of your sister, your father's daughter or your mother's daughter, whether born at home or born abroad. [10]You shall not uncover the nakedness of your son's daughter or of your daughter's daughter, for their nakedness is your own nakedness. [11]You shall not uncover the nakedness of your father's wife's daughter, begotten by your father, since she is your sister. [12]You shall not uncover the nakedness of your father's sister; she is your father's flesh. [13]You shall not uncover the nakedness of your mother's sister, for she is your mother's flesh. [14]You shall not uncover the nakedness of your father's brother, that is, you shall not approach his wife; she is your aunt. [15]You shall not uncover the nakedness of your daughter-in-law: she is your son's wife; you shall not uncover her nakedness. [16]You shall not uncover the nakedness of your brother's wife; it is your brother's nakedness. [17]You

shall not uncover the nakedness of a woman and her daughter, and you shall not take[a] her son's daughter or her daughter's daughter to uncover her nakedness; they are your[b] flesh; it is depravity. [18]And you shall not take[a] a woman as a rival to her sister, uncovering her nakedness while her sister is still alive.

19 You shall not approach a woman to uncover her nakedness while she is in her menstrual uncleanness. [20]You shall not have sexual relations with your kinsman's wife, and defile yourself with her. [21]You shall not give any of your offspring to sacrifice them[c] to Molech, and so profane the name of your God: I am the LORD. [22]You shall not lie with a male as with a woman; it is an abomination. [23]You shall not have sexual relations with any animal and defile yourself with it, nor shall any woman give herself to an animal to have sexual relations with it: it is perversion.

24 Do not defile yourselves in any of these ways, for by all these practices the nations I am casting out before you have defiled themselves. [25]Thus the land became defiled; and I punished it for its iniquity, and the land vomited out its inhabitants. [26]But you shall keep my statutes and my ordinances and commit none of these abominations, either the citizen or the alien who resides among you [27](for the inhabitants of the land, who were before you, committed all of these abominations, and the land became defiled); [28]otherwise the land will vomit you out for defiling it, as it vomited out the nation that was before you. [29]For whoever commits any of these abominations shall be cut off from their people. [30]So keep my charge not to commit any of these abominations that were done before you, and not to defile yourselves by them: I am the LORD your God.

RITUAL AND MORAL HOLINESS

19 The LORD spoke to Moses, saying:

---

a 18.17,18 Or *marry*   b 18.17 Gk: Heb lacks *your*   c 18.21 Heb *to pass them over*

2 Speak to all the congregation of the people of Israel and say to them: You shall be holy, for I the LORD your God am holy. ³You shall each revere your mother and father, and you shall keep my sabbaths: I am the LORD your God. ⁴Do not turn to idols or make cast images for yourselves: I am the LORD your God.

5 When you offer a sacrifice of well-being to the LORD, offer it in such a way that it is acceptable in your behalf. ⁶It shall be eaten on the same day you offer it, or on the next day; and anything left over until the third day shall be consumed in fire. ⁷If it is eaten at all on the third day, it is an abomination; it will not be acceptable. ⁸All who eat it shall be subject to punishment, because they have profaned what is holy to the LORD; and any such person shall be cut off from the people.

9 When you reap the harvest of your land, you shall not reap to the very edges of your field, or gather the gleanings of your harvest. ¹⁰You shall not strip your vineyard bare, or gather the fallen grapes of your vineyard; you shall leave them for the poor and the alien: I am the LORD your God.

11 You shall not steal; you shall not deal falsely; and you shall not lie to one another. ¹²And you shall not swear falsely by my name, profaning the name of your God: I am the LORD.

13 You shall not defraud your neighbor; you shall not steal; and you shall not keep for yourself the wages of a laborer until morning. ¹⁴You shall not revile the deaf or put a stumbling block before the blind; you shall fear your God: I am the LORD.

15 You shall not render an unjust judgment; you shall not be partial to the poor or defer to the great: with justice you shall judge your neighbor. ¹⁶You shall not go around as a slanderer[a] among your people, and you shall not profit by the blood[b] of your neighbor: I am the LORD.

17 You shall not hate in your heart anyone of your kin; you shall reprove your neighbor, or you will incur

guilt yourself. ¹⁸You shall not take vengeance or bear a grudge against any of your people, but you shall love your neighbor as yourself: I am the LORD.

19 You shall keep my statutes. You shall not let your animals breed with a different kind; you shall not sow your field with two kinds of seed; nor shall you put on a garment made of two different materials.

20 If a man has sexual relations with a woman who is a slave, designated for another man but not ransomed or given her freedom, an inquiry shall be held. They shall not be put to death, since she has not been freed; ²¹but he shall bring a guilt offering for himself to the LORD, at the entrance of the tent of meeting, a ram as guilt offering. ²²And the priest shall make atonement for him with the ram of guilt offering before the LORD for his sin that he committed; and the sin he committed shall be forgiven him.

23 When you come into the land and plant all kinds of trees for food, then you shall regard their fruit as forbidden;[c] three years it shall be forbidden[d] to you, it must not be eaten. ²⁴In the fourth year all their fruit shall be set apart for rejoicing in the LORD. ²⁵But in the fifth year you may eat of their fruit, that their yield may be increased for you: I am the LORD your God.

26 You shall not eat anything with its blood. You shall not practice augury or witchcraft. ²⁷You shall not round off the hair on your temples or mar the edges of your beard. ²⁸You shall not make any gashes in your flesh for the dead or tattoo any marks upon you: I am the LORD.

29 Do not profane your daughter by making her a prostitute, that the land not become prostituted and full of depravity. ³⁰You shall keep my sabbaths and reverence my sanctuary: I am the LORD.

31 Do not turn to mediums or wizards; do not seek them out, to be

a 19.16 Meaning of Heb uncertain
b 19.16 Heb *stand against the blood*
c 19.23 Heb *as their uncircumcision*
d 19.23 Heb *uncircumcision*

defiled by them: I am the LORD your God.

32 You shall rise before the aged, and defer to the old; and you shall fear your God: I am the LORD.

33 When an alien resides with you in your land, you shall not oppress the alien. 34 The alien who resides with you shall be to you as the citizen among you; you shall love the alien as yourself, for you were aliens in the land of Egypt: I am the LORD your God.

35 You shall not cheat in measuring length, weight, or quantity. 36 You shall have honest balances, honest weights, an honest ephah, and an honest hin: I am the LORD your God, who brought you out of the land of Egypt. 37 You shall keep all my statutes and all my ordinances, and observe them: I am the LORD.

PENALTIES FOR VIOLATIONS OF HOLINESS

20 The LORD spoke to Moses, saying: 2 Say further to the people of Israel:

Any of the people of Israel, or of the aliens who reside in Israel, who give any of their offspring to Molech shall be put to death; the people of the land shall stone them to death. 3 I myself will set my face against them, and will cut them off from the people, because they have given of their offspring to Molech, defiling my sanctuary and profaning my holy name. 4 And if the people of the land should ever close their eyes to them, when they give of their offspring to Molech, and do not put them to death, 5 I myself will set my face against them and against their family, and will cut them off from among their people, them and all who follow them in prostituting themselves to Molech.

6 If any turn to mediums and wizards, prostituting themselves to them, I will set my face against them, and will cut them off from the people. 7 Consecrate yourselves therefore, and be holy; for I am the LORD your God. 8 Keep my statutes, and observe them; I am the LORD; I sanctify you. 9 All who curse father or mother shall be put to death; having cursed father or mother, their blood is upon them.

10 If a man commits adultery with the wife of[a] his neighbor, both the adulterer and the adulteress shall be put to death. 11 The man who lies with his father's wife has uncovered his father's nakedness; both of them shall be put to death; their blood is upon them. 12 If a man lies with his daughter-in-law, both of them shall be put to death; they have commit-

a 20.10 Heb repeats *if a man commits adultery with the wife of*

⊣ BIBLE IN LIFE ▷

Caring for the Elderly   *Leviticus 19.32*

God calls us to show respect for the elderly. One of the ways we can do this is simply by getting to know them. Nearly everybody knows of older people, maybe living alone as widows or widowers, who probably live nearby. Some of them are not very friendly or attractive; they may act quite differently or perhaps are even of a different race. How many of us have the willingness, in a very quiet way, to find elderly or lonely people around us and then visit them? We may need look no further than half a mile. We need do nothing more than knock on the door, get to know them, take a cake to them or something simple like that. We could ask about their background and needs, perhaps call every morning at a set time to make sure they're okay. We could invite them to our house, to a movie or for a nice drive. We can imagine ourselves as a lonely person, partially crippled or unable to drive, living in a house that we shared with our spouse for decades. How would we feel if a friendly neighbor knocked on our door? What kind of difference would that make?

ted perversion, their blood is upon them. ¹³If a man lies with a male as with a woman, both of them have committed an abomination; they shall be put to death; their blood is upon them. ¹⁴If a man takes a wife and her mother also, it is depravity; they shall be burned to death, both he and they, that there may be no depravity among you. ¹⁵If a man has sexual relations with an animal, he shall be put to death; and you shall kill the animal. ¹⁶If a woman approaches any animal and has sexual relations with it, you shall kill the woman and the animal; they shall be put to death, their blood is upon them.

17 If a man takes his sister, a daughter of his father or a daughter of his mother, and sees her nakedness, and she sees his nakedness, it is a disgrace, and they shall be cut off in the sight of their people; he has uncovered his sister's nakedness, he shall be subject to punishment. ¹⁸If a man lies with a woman having her sickness and uncovers her nakedness, he has laid bare her flow and she has laid bare her flow of blood; both of them shall be cut off from their people. ¹⁹You shall not uncover the nakedness of your mother's sister or of your father's sister, for that is to lay bare one's own flesh; they shall be subject to punishment. ²⁰If a man lies with his uncle's wife, he has uncovered his uncle's nakedness; they shall be subject to punishment; they shall die childless. ²¹If a man takes his brother's wife, it is impurity; he has uncovered his brother's nakedness; they shall be childless.

22 You shall keep all my statutes and all my ordinances, and observe them, so that the land to which I bring you to settle in may not vomit you out. ²³You shall not follow the practices of the nation that I am driving out before you. Because they did all these things, I abhorred them. ²⁴But I have said to you: You shall inherit their land, and I will give it to you to possess, a land flowing with milk and honey. I am the LORD your God; I have separated you from the peoples. ²⁵You shall there-

fore make a distinction between the clean animal and the unclean, and between the unclean bird and the clean; you shall not bring abomination on yourselves by animal or by bird or by anything with which the ground teems, which I have set apart for you to hold unclean. ²⁶You shall be holy to me; for I the LORD am holy, and I have separated you from the other peoples to be mine.

27 A man or a woman who is a medium or a wizard shall be put to death; they shall be stoned to death, their blood is upon them.

LIFE IS BOTH A GIFT AND A RESPONSIBILITY. WE ARE FREE TO CHOOSE, BUT WE CANNOT AVOID THE CONSEQUENCES OF OUR CHOICES.

THE HOLINESS OF PRIESTS

21 The LORD said to Moses: Speak to the priests, the sons of Aaron, and say to them:

No one shall defile himself for a dead person among his relatives, ²except for his nearest kin: his mother, his father, his son, his daughter, his brother; ³likewise, for a virgin sister, close to him because she has had no husband, he may defile himself for her. ⁴But he shall not defile himself as a husband among his people and so profane himself. ⁵They shall not make bald spots upon their heads, or shave off the edges of their beards, or make any gashes in their flesh. ⁶They shall be holy to their God, and not profane the name of their God; for they offer the LORD's offerings by fire, the food of their God; therefore they shall be holy. ⁷They shall not marry a prostitute or a woman who has been defiled; neither shall they marry a woman divorced from her husband. For they are holy to their God, ⁸and you shall treat them as holy, since they offer the food of your God; they shall be holy to you, for I the LORD, I who sanctify you, am holy. ⁹When the daughter of a priest profanes herself through prostitution, she profanes her father; she shall be burned to death.

10 The priest who is exalted above his fellows, on whose head the anointing oil has been poured and who has been consecrated to wear the vestments, shall not dishevel his hair, nor tear his vestments. ¹¹He shall not go where there is a dead body; he shall not defile himself even for his father or mother. ¹²He shall not go outside the sanctuary and thus profane the sanctuary of his God; for the consecration of the anointing oil of his God is upon him: I am the LORD. ¹³He shall marry only a woman who is a virgin. ¹⁴A widow, or a divorced woman, or a woman who has been defiled, a prostitute, these he shall not marry. He shall marry a virgin of his own kin, ¹⁵that he may not profane his offspring among his kin; for I am the LORD; I sanctify him.

16 The LORD spoke to Moses, saying: ¹⁷Speak to Aaron and say: No one of your offspring throughout their generations who has a blemish may approach to offer the food of his God. ¹⁸For no one who has a blemish shall draw near, one who is blind or lame, or one who has a mutilated face or a limb too long, ¹⁹or one who has a broken foot or a broken hand, ²⁰or a hunchback, or a dwarf, or a man with a blemish in his eyes or an itching disease or scabs or crushed testicles. ²¹No descendant of Aaron the priest who has a blemish shall come near to offer the LORD's offerings by fire; since he has a blemish, he shall not come near to offer the food of his God. ²²He may eat the food of his God, of the most holy as well as of the holy. ²³But he shall not come near the curtain or approach the altar, because he has a blemish, that he may not profane my sanctuaries; for I am the LORD; I sanctify them. ²⁴Thus Moses spoke to Aaron and to his sons and to all the people of Israel.

THE USE OF HOLY OFFERINGS

22 The LORD spoke to Moses, saying: ²Direct Aaron and his sons to deal carefully with the sacred donations of the people of Israel, which they dedicate to me, so that they may not profane my holy name; I am the LORD. ³Say to them: If anyone among all your offspring throughout your generations comes near the sacred donations, which the people of Israel dedicate to the LORD, while he is in a state of uncleanness, that person shall be cut off from my presence: I am the LORD. ⁴No one of Aaron's offspring who has a leprousᵃ disease or suffers a discharge may eat of the sacred donations until he is clean. Whoever touches anything made unclean by a corpse or a man who has had an emission of semen, ⁵and whoever touches any swarming thing by which he may be made unclean or any human being by whom he may be made unclean—whatever his uncleanness may be— ⁶the person who touches any such shall be unclean until evening and shall not eat of the sacred donations unless he has washed his body in water. ⁷When the sun sets he shall be clean; and afterward he may eat of the sacred donations, for they are his food. ⁸That which died or was torn by wild animals he shall not eat, becoming unclean by it: I am the LORD. ⁹They shall keep my charge, so that they may not incur guilt and die in the sanctuaryᵇ for having profaned it: I am the LORD; I sanctify them.

10 No lay person shall eat of the sacred donations. No bound or hired servant of the priest shall eat of the sacred donations; ¹¹but if a priest acquires anyone by purchase, the person may eat of them; and those that are born in his house may eat of his food. ¹²If a priest's daughter marries a layman, she shall not eat of the offering of the sacred donations; ¹³but if a priest's daughter is widowed or divorced, without offspring, and returns to her father's house, as in her

ᵃ 22.4 A term for several skin diseases; precise meaning uncertain   ᵇ 22.9 Vg: Heb *incur guilt for it and die in it*

youth, she may eat of her father's food. No lay person shall eat of it. ¹⁴If a man eats of the sacred donation unintentionally, he shall add one-fifth of its value to it, and give the sacred donation to the priest. ¹⁵No one shall profane the sacred donations of the people of Israel, which they offer to the LORD, ¹⁶causing them to bear guilt requiring a guilt offering, by eating their sacred donations: for I am the LORD; I sanctify them.

ACCEPTABLE OFFERINGS

17 The LORD spoke to Moses, saying: ¹⁸Speak to Aaron and his sons and all the people of Israel and say to them: When anyone of the house of Israel or of the aliens residing in Israel presents an offering, whether in payment of a vow or as a freewill offering that is offered to the LORD as a burnt offering, ¹⁹to be acceptable in your behalf it shall be a male without blemish, of the cattle or the sheep or the goats. ²⁰You shall not offer anything that has a blemish, for it will not be acceptable in your behalf.

21 When anyone offers a sacrifice of well-being to the LORD, in fulfillment of a vow or as a freewill offering, from the herd or from the flock, to be acceptable it must be perfect; there shall be no blemish in it. ²²Anything blind, or injured, or maimed, or having a discharge or an itch or scabs—these you shall not offer to the LORD or put any of them on the altar as offerings by fire to the LORD. ²³An ox or a lamb that has a limb too long or too short you may present for a freewill offering; but it will not be accepted for a vow. ²⁴Any animal that has its testicles bruised or crushed or torn or cut, you shall not offer to the LORD; such you shall not do within your land, ²⁵nor shall you accept any such animals from a foreigner to offer as food to your God; since they are mutilated, with a blemish in them, they shall not be accepted in your behalf.

26 The LORD spoke to Moses, saying: ²⁷When an ox or a sheep or a goat is born, it shall remain seven days with its mother, and from the eighth day on it shall be acceptable as the LORD's offering by fire. ²⁸But you shall not slaughter, from the herd or the flock, an animal with its young on the same day. ²⁹When you sacrifice a thanksgiving offering to the LORD, you shall sacrifice it so that it may be acceptable in your behalf. ³⁰It shall be eaten on the same day; you shall not leave any of it until morning: I am the LORD.

31 Thus you shall keep my commandments and observe them: I am the LORD. ³²You shall not profane my holy name, that I may be sanctified among the people of Israel: I am the LORD; I sanctify you, ³³I who brought you out of the land of Egypt to be your God: I am the LORD.

APPOINTED FESTIVALS

23 The LORD spoke to Moses, saying: ²Speak to the people of Israel and say to them: These are the appointed festivals of the LORD that you shall proclaim as holy convocations, my appointed festivals.

THE SABBATH, PASSOVER, AND UNLEAVENED BREAD

3 Six days shall work be done; but the seventh day is a sabbath of complete rest, a holy convocation; you shall do no work: it is a sabbath to the LORD throughout your settlements.

4 These are the appointed festivals of the LORD, the holy convocations, which you shall celebrate at the time appointed for them. ⁵In the first month, on the fourteenth day of the month, at twilight,ᵃ there shall be a passover offering to the LORD, ⁶and on the fifteenth day of the same month is the festival of unleavened bread to the LORD; seven days you shall eat unleavened bread. ⁷On the first day you shall have a holy convocation; you shall not work at your occupations. ⁸For seven days you shall present the LORD's offerings by fire; on the seventh day there shall be a holy convocation: you shall not work at your occupations.

ᵃ 23.5 Heb *between the two evenings*

THE OFFERING OF FIRST FRUITS

9 The LORD spoke to Moses: 10Speak to the people of Israel and say to them: When you enter the land that I am giving you and you reap its harvest, you shall bring the sheaf of the first fruits of your harvest to the priest. 11He shall raise the sheaf before the LORD, that you may find acceptance; on the day after the sabbath the priest shall raise it. 12On the day when you raise the sheaf, you shall offer a lamb a year old, without blemish, as a burnt offering to the LORD. 13And the grain offering with it shall be two-tenths of an ephah of choice flour mixed with oil, an offering by fire of pleasing odor to the LORD; and the drink offering with it shall be of wine, one-fourth of a hin. 14You shall eat no bread or parched grain or fresh ears until that very day, until you have brought the offering of your God: it is a statute forever throughout your generations in all your settlements.

THE FESTIVAL OF WEEKS

15 And from the day after the sabbath, from the day on which you bring the sheaf of the elevation offering, you shall count off seven weeks; they shall be complete. 16You shall count until the day after the seventh sabbath, fifty days; then you shall present an offering of new grain to the LORD. 17You shall bring from your settlements two loaves of bread as an elevation offering, each made of two-tenths of an ephah; they shall be of choice flour, baked with leaven, as first fruits to the LORD. 18You shall present with the bread seven lambs a year old without blemish, one young bull, and two rams; they shall be a burnt offering to the LORD, along with their grain offering and their drink offerings, an offering by fire of pleasing odor to the LORD. 19You shall also offer one male goat for a sin offering, and two male lambs a year old as a sacrifice of well-being. 20The priest shall raise them with the bread of the first fruits as an elevation offering before the LORD, together with the two lambs; they shall be holy to

the LORD for the priest. 21On that same day you shall make proclamation; you shall hold a holy convocation; you shall not work at your occupations. This is a statute forever in all your settlements throughout your generations.

22 When you reap the harvest of your land, you shall not reap to the very edges of your field, or gather the gleanings of your harvest; you shall leave them for the poor and for the alien: I am the LORD your God.

THE FESTIVAL OF TRUMPETS

23 The LORD spoke to Moses, saying: 24Speak to the people of Israel, saying: In the seventh month, on the first day of the month, you shall observe a day of complete rest, a holy convocation commemorated with trumpet blasts. 25You shall not work at your occupations; and you shall present the LORD's offering by fire.

THE DAY OF ATONEMENT

26 The LORD spoke to Moses, saying: 27Now, the tenth day of this seventh month is the day of atonement; it shall be a holy convocation for you: you shall deny yourselves[a] and present the LORD's offering by fire; 28and you shall do no work during that entire day; for it is a day of atonement, to make atonement on your behalf before the LORD your God. 29For anyone who does not practice self-denial[b] during that entire day shall be cut off from the people. 30And anyone who does any work during that entire day, such a one I will destroy from the midst of the people. 31You shall do no work: it is a statute forever throughout your generations in all your settlements. 32It shall be to you a sabbath of complete rest, and you shall deny yourselves;[a] on the ninth day of the month at evening, from evening to evening you shall keep your sabbath.

THE FESTIVAL OF BOOTHS

33 The LORD spoke to Moses, saying: 34Speak to the people of Israel,

a 23.27,32 Or shall fast   b 23.29 Or does not fast

saying: On the fifteenth day of this seventh month, and lasting seven days, there shall be the festival of booths[a] to the LORD. 35The first day shall be a holy convocation; you shall not work at your occupations. 36Seven days you shall present the LORD's offerings by fire; on the eighth day you shall observe a holy convocation and present the LORD's offerings by fire; it is a solemn assembly; you shall not work at your occupations.

37 These are the appointed festivals of the LORD, which you shall celebrate as times of holy convocation, for presenting to the LORD offerings by fire—burnt offerings and grain offerings, sacrifices and drink offerings, each on its proper day— 38apart from the sabbaths of the LORD, and apart from your gifts, and apart from all your votive offerings, and apart from all your freewill offerings, which you give to the LORD.

39 Now, the fifteenth day of the seventh month, when you have gathered in the produce of the land, you shall keep the festival of the LORD, lasting seven days; a complete rest on the first day, and a complete rest on the eighth day. 40On the first day you shall take the fruit of majestic[b] trees, branches of palm trees, boughs of leafy trees, and willows of the brook; and you shall rejoice before the LORD your God for seven days. 41You shall keep it as a festival to the LORD seven days in the year; you shall keep it in the seventh month as a statute forever throughout your generations. 42You shall live in booths for seven days; all that are citizens in Israel shall live in booths, 43so that your generations may know that I made the people of Israel live in booths when I brought them out of the land of Egypt: I am the LORD your God.

44 Thus Moses declared to the people of Israel the appointed festivals of the LORD.

THE LAMP

24 The LORD spoke to Moses, saying: 2Command the people of Israel to bring you pure oil of beaten olives for the lamp, that a light may be kept burning regularly. 3Aaron shall set it up in the tent of meeting, outside the curtain of the covenant,[c] to burn from evening to morning before the LORD regularly; it shall be a statute forever throughout your generations. 4He shall set up the lamps on the lampstand of pure gold[d] before the LORD regularly.

THE BREAD FOR THE TABERNACLE

5 You shall take choice flour, and bake twelve loaves of it; two-tenths of an ephah shall be in each loaf. 6You shall place them in two rows, six in a row, on the table of pure gold.[e] 7You shall put pure frankincense with each row, to be a token offering for the bread, as an offering by fire to the LORD. 8Every sabbath day Aaron shall set them in order before the LORD regularly as a commitment of the people of Israel, as a covenant forever. 9They shall be for Aaron and his descendants, who shall eat them in a holy place, for they are most holy portions for him from the offerings by fire to the LORD, a perpetual due.

BLASPHEMY AND ITS PUNISHMENT

10 A man whose mother was an Israelite and whose father was an Egyptian came out among the people of Israel; and the Israelite woman's son and a certain Israelite began fighting in the camp. 11The Israelite woman's son blasphemed the Name in a curse. And they brought him to Moses—now his mother's name was Shelomith, daughter of Dibri, of the tribe of Dan— 12and they put him in custody, until the decision of the LORD should be made clear to them.

13 The LORD said to Moses, saying: 14Take the blasphemer outside the camp; and let all who were within hearing lay their hands on his head, and let the whole congregation stone

---

[a] 23.34 Or *tabernacles*: Heb *succoth*
[b] 23.40 Meaning of Heb uncertain
[c] 24.3 Or *treaty*, or *testament*; Heb *eduth*
[d] 24.4 Heb *pure lampstand*   [e] 24.6 Heb *pure table*

him. 15 And speak to the people of Israel, saying: Anyone who curses God shall bear the sin. 16 One who blasphemes the name of the LORD shall be put to death; the whole congregation shall stone the blasphemer. Aliens as well as citizens, when they blaspheme the Name, shall be put to death. 17 Anyone who kills a human being shall be put to death. 18 Anyone who kills an animal shall make restitution for it, life for life. 19 Anyone who maims another shall suffer the same injury in return: 20 fracture for fracture, eye for eye, tooth for tooth; the injury inflicted is the injury to be suffered. 21 One who kills an animal shall make restitution for it; but one who kills a human being shall be put to death. 22 You shall have one law for the alien and for the citizen: for I am the LORD your God. 23 Moses spoke thus to the people of Israel; and they took the blasphemer outside the camp, and stoned him to death. The people of Israel did as the LORD had commanded Moses.

THE SABBATICAL YEAR

25 The LORD spoke to Moses on Mount Sinai, saying: 2 Speak to the people of Israel and say to them: When you enter the land that I am giving you, the land shall observe a sabbath for the LORD. 3 Six years you shall sow your field, and six years you shall prune your vineyard, and gather in their yield; 4 but in the seventh year there shall be a sabbath of complete rest for the land, a sabbath for the LORD: you shall not sow your field or prune your vineyard. 5 You shall not reap the aftergrowth of your harvest or gather the grapes of your unpruned vine: it shall be a year of complete rest for the land. 6 You may eat what the land yields during its sabbath—you, your male and female slaves, your hired and your bound laborers who live with you; 7 for your livestock also, and for the wild animals in your land all its yield shall be for food.

THE YEAR OF JUBILEE

8 You shall count off seven weeks[a] of years, seven times seven years,

so that the period of seven weeks of years gives forty-nine years. 9 Then you shall have the trumpet sounded loud; on the tenth day of the seventh month—on the day of atonement—you shall have the trumpet sounded throughout all your land. 10 And you shall hallow the fiftieth year and you shall proclaim liberty throughout the land to all its inhabitants. It shall be a jubilee for you: you shall return, every one of you, to your property and every one of you to your family. 11 That fiftieth year shall be a jubilee for you: you shall not sow, or reap the aftergrowth, or harvest the unpruned vines. 12 For it is a jubilee; it shall be holy to you: you shall eat only what the field itself produces.

13 In this year of jubilee you shall return, every one of you, to your property. 14 When you make a sale to your neighbor or buy from your neighbor, you shall not cheat one another. 15 When you buy from your neighbor, you shall pay only for the number of years since the jubilee; the seller shall charge you only for the remaining crop years. 16 If the years are more, you shall increase the price, and if the years are fewer, you shall diminish the price; for it is a certain number of harvests that are being sold to you. 17 You shall not cheat one another, but you shall fear your God; for I am the LORD your God.

18 You shall observe my statutes and faithfully keep my ordinances, so that you may live on the land securely. 19 The land will yield its fruit, and you will eat your fill and live on it securely. 20 Should you ask, "What shall we eat in the seventh year, if we may not sow or gather in our crop?" 21 I will order my blessing for you in the sixth year, so that it will yield a crop for three years. 22 When you sow in the eighth year, you will be eating from the old crop; until the ninth year, when its produce comes in, you shall eat the old. 23 The land shall not be sold in perpetuity, for the land is mine; with me you are but aliens and tenants. 24 Through-

a 25.8 Or *sabbaths*

out the land that you hold, you shall provide for the redemption of the land.

25 If anyone of your kin falls into difficulty and sells a piece of property, then the next of kin shall come and redeem what the relative has sold. 26If the person has no one to redeem it, but then prospers and finds sufficient means to do so, 27the years since its sale shall be computed and the difference shall be refunded to the person to whom it was sold, and the property shall be returned. 28But if there are not sufficient means to recover it, what was sold shall remain with the purchaser until the year of jubilee; in the jubilee it shall be released, and the property shall be returned.

29 If anyone sells a dwelling house in a walled city, it may be redeemed until a year has elapsed since its sale; the right of redemption shall be one year. 30If it is not redeemed before a full year has elapsed, a house that is in a walled city shall pass in perpetuity to the purchaser, throughout the generations; it shall not be released in the jubilee. 31But houses in villages that have no walls around them shall be classed as open country; they may be redeemed, and they shall be released in the jubilee. 32As for the cities of the Levites, the Levites shall forever have the right of redemption of the houses in the cities belonging to them. 33Such property as may be redeemed from the Levites—houses sold in a city belonging to them—shall be released in the jubilee; because the houses in the cities of the Levites are their possession among the people of Israel. 34But the open land around their cities may not be sold; for that is their possession for all time.

35 If any of your kin fall into difficulty and become dependent on you,ᵃ you shall support them; they shall live with you as though resident aliens. 36Do not take interest in advance or otherwise make a profit from them, but fear your God; let them live with you. 37You shall not lend them your money at interest taken in advance, or provide them

food at a profit. 38I am the LORD your God, who brought you out of the land of Egypt, to give you the land of Canaan, to be your God.

39 If any who are dependent on you become so impoverished that they sell themselves to you, you shall not make them serve as slaves. 40They shall remain with you as hired or bound laborers. They shall serve with you until the year of the jubilee. 41Then they and their children with them shall be free from your authority; they shall go back to their own family and return to their ancestral property. 42For they are my servants, whom I brought out of the land of Egypt; they shall not be sold as slaves are sold. 43You shall not rule over them with harshness, but shall fear your God. 44As for the male and female slaves whom you may have, it is from the nations around you that you may acquire male and female slaves. 45You may also acquire them from among the aliens residing with you, and from their families that are with you, who have been born in your land; and they may be your property. 46You may keep them as a possession for your children after you, for them to inherit as property. These you may treat as slaves, but as for your fellow Israelites, no one shall rule over the other with harshness.

EACH DAY IS GOD'S GIFT, TO

BE USED TO HONOR OUR

CREATOR BY OUR ACTIONS,

DECISIONS AND WORDS.

47 If resident aliens among you prosper, and if any of your kin fall into difficulty with one of them and sell themselves to an alien, or to a branch of the alien's family, 48after

ᵃ 25.35 Meaning of Heb uncertain

they have sold themselves they shall have the right of redemption; one of their brothers may redeem them, ⁴⁹or their uncle or their uncle's son may redeem them, or anyone of their family who is of their own flesh may redeem them; or if they prosper they may redeem themselves. ⁵⁰They shall compute with the purchaser the total from the year when they sold themselves to the alien until the jubilee year; the price of the sale shall be applied to the number of years: the time they were with the owner shall be rated as the time of a hired laborer. ⁵¹If many years remain, they shall pay for their redemption in proportion to the purchase price; ⁵²and if few years remain until the jubilee year, they shall compute thus: according to the years involved they shall make payment for their redemption. ⁵³As a laborer hired by the year they shall be under the alien's authority, who shall not, however, rule with harshness over them in your sight. ⁵⁴And if they have not been redeemed in any of these ways, they and their children with them shall go free in the jubilee year. ⁵⁵For to me the people of Israel are servants; they are my servants whom I brought out from the land of Egypt: I am the LORD your God.

REWARDS FOR OBEDIENCE

26 You shall make for yourselves no idols and erect no carved images or pillars, and you shall not place figured stones in your land, to worship at them; for I am the LORD your God. ²You shall keep my sabbaths and reverence my sanctuary: I am the LORD.

3 If you follow my statutes and keep my commandments and observe them faithfully, ⁴I will give you your rains in their season, and the land shall yield its produce, and the trees of the field shall yield their fruit. ⁵Your threshing shall overtake the vintage, and the vintage shall overtake the sowing; you shall eat your bread to the full, and live securely in your land. ⁶And I will grant peace in the land, and

PONDER

"If you follow my statutes and keep my commandments and observe them faithfully, I will give you your rains in their season, and the land shall yield its produce, and the trees of the field shall yield their fruit."
—Leviticus 26.3–4

PRAY

Gracious Lord, sometimes it isn't easy to extract your truths for our daily lives from the writings of Moses. Often we feel that these ancient scriptures don't really apply to our fast-changing, technological existence. But these verses help us learn what you value, that which is precious and holy and unchanging. We pray that we might have the courage to examine our own characters, actions, and priorities and reorder them in accordance with these verses from Leviticus, that we might live in obedience to your holy will. We acknowledge you as our Redeemer, our one and only True God. Help us to honor your name in everything we say and do. Amen.

you shall lie down, and no one shall make you afraid; I will remove dangerous animals from the land, and no sword shall go through your land. ⁷You shall give chase to your enemies, and they shall fall before you by the sword. ⁸Five of you shall give chase to a hundred, and a hundred of you shall give chase to ten thousand; your enemies shall fall before you by the sword. ⁹I will look with favor upon you and make you fruitful and multiply you; and I will maintain my covenant with you. ¹⁰You shall eat old grain long stored, and you shall have to clear out the old to make way for the new. ¹¹I will place my dwelling in your midst, and I shall not abhor you. ¹²And I will walk among you, and will be your God, and you shall be my people. ¹³I am the LORD your God who brought you out of the land of Egypt, to be their slaves no more; I have broken the bars of your yoke and made you walk erect.

PENALTIES FOR DISOBEDIENCE

14 But if you will not obey me, and do not observe all these commandments, 15if you spurn my statutes, and abhor my ordinances, so that you will not observe all my commandments, and you break my covenant, 16I in turn will do this to you: I will bring terror on you; consumption and fever that waste the eyes and cause life to pine away. You shall sow your seed in vain, for your enemies shall eat it. 17I will set my face against you, and you shall be struck down by your enemies; your foes shall rule over you, and you shall flee though no one pursues you. 18And if in spite of this you will not obey me, I will continue to punish you sevenfold for your sins. 19I will break your proud glory, and I will make your sky like iron and your earth like copper. 20Your strength shall be spent to no purpose: your land shall not yield its produce, and the trees of the land shall not yield their fruit.

21 If you continue hostile to me, and will not obey me, I will continue to plague you sevenfold for your sins. 22I will let loose wild animals against you, and they shall bereave you of your children and destroy your livestock; they shall make you few in number, and your roads shall be deserted.

23 If in spite of these punishments you have not turned back to me, but continue hostile to me, 24then I too will continue hostile to you: I myself will strike you sevenfold for your sins. 25I will bring the sword against you, executing vengeance for the covenant; and if you withdraw within your cities, I will send pestilence among you, and you shall be delivered into enemy hands. 26When I break your staff of bread, ten women shall bake your bread in a single oven, and they shall dole out your bread by weight; and though you eat, you shall not be satisfied.

27 But if, despite this, you disobey me, and continue hostile to me, 28I will continue hostile to you in fury; I in turn will punish you myself sevenfold for your sins. 29You shall eat the flesh of your sons, and you shall eat the flesh of your daughters. 30I will destroy your high places and cut down your incense altars; I will heap your carcasses on the carcasses of your idols. I will abhor you. 31I will lay your cities waste, will make your sanctuaries desolate, and I will not smell your pleasing odors. 32I will devastate the land, so that your enemies who come to settle in it shall be appalled at it. 33And you I will scatter among the nations, and I will unsheathe the sword against you; your land shall be a desolation, and your cities a waste.

34 Then the land shall enjoya its sabbath years as long as it lies desolate, while you are in the land of your enemies; then the land shall rest, and enjoya its sabbath years. 35As long as it lies desolate, it shall have the rest it did not have on your sabbaths when you were living on it. 36And as for those of you who survive, I will send faintness into their hearts in the lands of their enemies; the sound of a driven leaf shall put them to flight, and they shall flee as one flees from the sword, and they shall fall though no one pursues. 37They shall stumble over one another, as if to escape a sword, though no one pursues; and you shall have no power to stand against your enemies. 38You shall perish among the nations, and the land of your enemies shall devour you. 39And those of you who survive shall languish in the land of your enemies because of their iniquities; also they shall languish because of the iniquities of their ancestors.

40 But if they confess their iniquity and the iniquity of their ancestors, in that they committed treachery against me and, moreover, that they continued hostile to me— 41so that I, in turn, continued hostile to them and brought them into the

a 26.34 Or make up for

land of their enemies; if then their uncircumcised heart is humbled and they make amends for their iniquity, ⁴²then will I remember my covenant with Jacob; I will remember also my covenant with Isaac and also my covenant with Abraham, and I will remember the land. ⁴³For the land shall be deserted by them, and enjoy[a] its sabbath years by lying desolate without them, while they shall make amends for their iniquity, because they dared to spurn my ordinances, and they abhorred my statutes. ⁴⁴Yet for all that, when they are in the land of their enemies, I will not spurn them, or abhor them so as to destroy them utterly and break my covenant with them; for I am the LORD their God; ⁴⁵but I will remember in their favor the covenant with their ancestors whom I brought out of the land of Egypt in the sight of the nations, to be their God: I am the LORD.

46 These are the statutes and ordinances and laws that the LORD established between himself and the people of Israel on Mount Sinai through Moses.

VOTIVE OFFERINGS

27 The LORD spoke to Moses, saying: ²Speak to the people of Israel and say to them: When a person makes an explicit vow to the LORD concerning the equivalent for a human being, ³the equivalent for a male shall be: from twenty to sixty years of age the equivalent shall be fifty shekels of silver by the sanctuary shekel. ⁴If the person is a female, the equivalent is thirty shekels. ⁵If the age is from five to twenty years of age, the equivalent is twenty shekels for a male and ten shekels for a female. ⁶If the age is from one month to five years, the equivalent for a male is five shekels of silver, and for a female the equivalent is three shekels of silver. ⁷And if the person is sixty years old or over, then the equivalent for a male is fifteen shekels, and for a female ten shekels. ⁸If any cannot afford the equivalent, they shall be brought before the priest and the priest shall assess them; the priest shall assess them according to what each one making a vow can afford.

9 If it concerns an animal that may be brought as an offering to the LORD, any such that may be given to the LORD shall be holy. ¹⁰Another shall not be exchanged or substituted for it, either good for bad or bad for good; and if one animal is substituted for another, both that one and its substitute shall be holy. ¹¹If it concerns any unclean animal that may not be brought as an offering to the LORD, the animal shall be presented before the priest. ¹²The priest shall assess it: whether good or bad, according to the assessment of the priest, so it shall be. ¹³But if it is to be redeemed, one-fifth must be added to the assessment.

14 If a person consecrates a house to the LORD, the priest shall assess it: whether good or bad, as the priest assesses it, so it shall stand. ¹⁵And if the one who consecrates the house wishes to redeem it, one-fifth shall be added to its assessed value, and it shall revert to the original owner.

16 If a person consecrates to the LORD any inherited landholding, its assessment shall be in accordance with its seed requirements: fifty shekels of silver to a homer of barley seed. ¹⁷If the person consecrates the field as of the year of jubilee, that assessment shall stand; ¹⁸but if the field is consecrated after the jubilee, the priest shall compute the price for it according to the years that remain until the year of jubilee, and the assessment shall be reduced. ¹⁹And if the one who consecrates the field wishes to redeem it, then one-fifth shall be added to its assessed value, and it shall revert to the original owner; ²⁰but if the field is not redeemed, or if it has been sold to someone else, it shall no longer be redeemable. ²¹But when the field is released in the jubilee, it shall be holy to the LORD as a devoted field; it becomes the priest's holding. ²²If someone consecrates to the LORD a field that has been purchased, which

[a] 26.43 Or *make up for*

is not a part of the inherited land-holding, ²³the priest shall compute for it the proportionate assessment up to the year of jubilee, and the assessment shall be paid as of that day, a sacred donation to the LORD. ²⁴In the year of jubilee the field shall return to the one from whom it was bought, whose holding the land is. ²⁵All assessments shall be by the sanctuary shekel: twenty gerahs shall make a shekel.

26 A firstling of animals, however, which as a firstling belongs to the LORD, cannot be consecrated by anyone; whether ox or sheep, it is the LORD's. ²⁷If it is an unclean animal, it shall be ransomed at its assessment, with one-fifth added; if it is not redeemed, it shall be sold at its assessment.

28 Nothing that a person owns that has been devoted to destruction for the LORD, be it human or animal, or inherited landholding, may be sold or redeemed; every devoted thing is most holy to the LORD. ²⁹No human beings who have been devoted to destruction can be ransomed; they shall be put to death.

30 All tithes from the land, whether the seed from the ground or the fruit from the tree, are the LORD's; they are holy to the LORD. ³¹If persons wish to redeem any of their tithes, they must add one-fifth to them. ³²All tithes of herd and flock, every tenth one that passes under the shepherd's staff, shall be holy to the LORD. ³³Let no one inquire whether it is good or bad, or make substitution for it; if one makes substitution for it, then both it and the substitute shall be holy and cannot be redeemed.

34 These are the commandments that the LORD gave to Moses for the people of Israel on Mount Sinai.

NUMBERS

We might think of the book of Numbers as a census, a Gallup poll and a social commentary all rolled into one. The Israelites were counted twice during their 38 years of wandering in the wilderness, hence the book's name. Numbers describes the complaining and rebellion of the Israelites and how their attitude resulted in punishment—a life of exile in the wilderness—rather than enjoyment of God's promised blessings. But throughout the wilderness years, it became clear to the Israelites that God's presence was always with them, and that God loved, forgave and provided for them—even when they wandered.

THE FIRST CENSUS OF ISRAEL

1 The LORD spoke to Moses in the wilderness of Sinai, in the tent of meeting, on the first day of the second month, in the second year after they had come out of the land of Egypt, saying: ²Take a census of the whole congregation of Israelites, in their clans, by ancestral houses, according to the number of names, every male individually; ³from twenty years old and upward, everyone in Israel able to go to war. You and Aaron shall enroll them, company by company. ⁴A man from each tribe shall be with you, each man the head of his ancestral house. ⁵These are the names of the men who shall assist you:

From Reuben, Elizur son of Shedeur.
⁶ From Simeon, Shelumiel son of Zurishaddai.
⁷ From Judah, Nahshon son of Amminadab.
⁸ From Issachar, Nethanel son of Zuar.
⁹ From Zebulun, Eliab son of Helon.
¹⁰ From the sons of Joseph:
from Ephraim, Elishama son of Ammihud;
from Manasseh, Gamaliel son of Pedahzur.
¹¹ From Benjamin, Abidan son of Gideoni.
¹² From Dan, Ahiezer son of Ammishaddai.
¹³ From Asher, Pagiel son of Ochran.
¹⁴ From Gad, Eliasaph son of Deuel.
¹⁵ From Naphtali, Ahira son of Enan.

¹⁶These were the ones chosen from the congregation, the leaders of their ancestral tribes, the heads of the divisions of Israel.

¹⁷ Moses and Aaron took these men who had been designated by name, ¹⁸and on the first day of the second month they assembled the whole congregation together. They registered themselves in their clans, by their ancestral houses, according to the number of names from twenty years old and upward, individually, ¹⁹as the LORD commanded Moses. So he enrolled them in the wilderness of Sinai.

20 The descendants of Reuben, Israel's firstborn, their lineage, in their clans, by their ancestral houses, according to the number of names, individually, every male from twenty years old and upward, everyone able to go to war: ²¹those enrolled of the tribe of Reuben were forty-six thousand five hundred.

22 The descendants of Simeon, their lineage, in their clans, by their ancestral houses, those of them that were numbered, according to the number of names, individually, every male from twenty years old and upward, everyone able to go to war: ²³those enrolled of the tribe of Simeon were fifty-nine thousand three hundred.

24 The descendants of Gad, their lineage, in their clans, by their ancestral houses, according to the number of the names, from twenty years old and upward, everyone able to go to war: ²⁵those enrolled of the tribe of Gad were forty-five thousand six hundred fifty.

26 The descendants of Judah, their lineage, in their clans, by their ancestral houses, according to the number of names, from twenty years old and upward, everyone able to go to war: ²⁷those enrolled of the tribe of Judah were seventy-four thousand six hundred.

28 The descendants of Issachar, their lineage, in their clans, by their ancestral houses, according to the number of names, from twenty years old and upward, everyone able to go to war: ²⁹those enrolled of the tribe of Issachar were fifty-four thousand four hundred.

30 The descendants of Zebulun, their lineage, in their clans, by their ancestral houses, according to the number of names, from twenty years old and upward, everyone able to go to war: ³¹those enrolled of the tribe of Zebulun were fifty-seven thousand four hundred.

32 The descendants of Joseph, namely, the descendants of Ephraim, their lineage, in their clans, by their ancestral houses, according to the

number of names, from twenty years old and upward, everyone able to go to war: ³³those enrolled of the tribe of Ephraim were forty thousand five hundred.

34 The descendants of Manasseh, their lineage, in their clans, by their ancestral houses, according to the number of names, from twenty years old and upward, everyone able to go to war: ³⁵those enrolled of the tribe of Manasseh were thirty-two thousand two hundred.

36 The descendants of Benjamin, their lineage, in their clans, by their ancestral houses, according to the number of names, from twenty years old and upward, everyone able to go to war: ³⁷those enrolled of the tribe of Benjamin were thirty-five thousand four hundred.

38 The descendants of Dan, their lineage, in their clans, by their ancestral houses, according to the number of names, from twenty years old and upward, everyone able to go to war: ³⁹those enrolled of the tribe of Dan were sixty-two thousand seven hundred.

40 The descendants of Asher, their lineage, in their clans, by their ancestral houses, according to the number of names, from twenty years old and upward, everyone able to go to war: ⁴¹those enrolled of the tribe of Asher were forty-one thousand five hundred.

42 The descendants of Naphtali, their lineage, in their clans, by their ancestral houses, according to the number of names, from twenty years old and upward, everyone able to go to war: ⁴³those enrolled of the tribe of Naphtali were fifty-three thousand four hundred.

44 These are those who were enrolled, whom Moses and Aaron enrolled with the help of the leaders of Israel, twelve men, each representing his ancestral house. ⁴⁵So the whole number of the Israelites, by their ancestral houses, from twenty years old and upward, everyone able to go to war in Israel— ⁴⁶their whole number was six hundred three thousand five hundred fifty. ⁴⁷The Levites, however, were not numbered by their ancestral tribe along with them.

48 The LORD had said to Moses: ⁴⁹Only the tribe of Levi you shall not enroll, and you shall not take a census of them with the other Israelites. ⁵⁰Rather you shall appoint the Levites over the tabernacle of the covenant,^a and over all its equipment, and over all that belongs to it; they are to carry the tabernacle and all its equipment, and they shall tend it, and shall camp around the tabernacle. ⁵¹When the tabernacle is to set out, the Levites shall take it down; and when the tabernacle is to be pitched, the Levites shall set it up. And any outsider who comes near shall be put to death. ⁵²The other Israelites shall camp in their respective regimental camps, by companies; ⁵³but the Levites shall camp around the tabernacle of the covenant,^a that there may be no wrath on the congregation of the Israelites; and the Levites shall perform the guard duty of the tabernacle of the covenant.^a ⁵⁴The Israelites did so; they did just as the LORD commanded Moses.

THE ORDER OF ENCAMPMENT AND MARCHING

2 The LORD spoke to Moses and Aaron, saying: ²The Israelites shall camp each in their respective regiments, under ensigns by their ancestral houses; they shall camp facing the tent of meeting on every side. ³Those to camp on the east side toward the sunrise shall be of the regimental encampment of Judah by companies. The leader of the people of Judah shall be Nahshon son of Amminadab, ⁴with a company as enrolled of seventy-four thousand six hundred. ⁵Those to camp next to him shall be the tribe of Issachar. The leader of the Issacharites shall be Nethanel son of Zuar, ⁶with a company as enrolled of fifty-four thousand four hundred. ⁷Then the tribe of Zebulun: The leader of the Zebulunites shall be Eliab son of Helon, ⁸with a company as enrolled of

^a 1.50,53 Or *treaty*, or *testimony*; Heb *eduth*

fifty-seven thousand four hundred. 9The total enrollment of the camp of Judah, by companies, is one hundred eighty-six thousand four hundred. They shall set out first on the march.

10 On the south side shall be the regimental encampment of Reuben by companies. The leader of the Reubenites shall be Elizur son of Shedeur, 11with a company as enrolled of forty-six thousand five hundred. 12And those to camp next to him shall be the tribe of Simeon. The leader of the Simeonites shall be Shelumiel son of Zurishaddai, 13with a company as enrolled of fifty-nine thousand three hundred. 14Then the tribe of Gad: The leader of the Gadites shall be Eliasaph son of Reuel, 15with a company as enrolled of forty-five thousand six hundred fifty. 16The total enrollment of the camp of Reuben, by companies, is one hundred fifty-one thousand four hundred fifty. They shall set out second.

17 The tent of meeting, with the camp of the Levites, shall set out in the center of the camps; they shall set out just as they camp, each in position, by their regiments.

18 On the west side shall be the regimental encampment of Ephraim by companies. The leader of the people of Ephraim shall be Elishama son of Ammihud, 19with a company as enrolled of forty thousand five hundred. 20Next to him shall be the tribe of Manasseh. The leader of the people of Manasseh shall be Gamaliel son of Pedahzur, 21with a company as enrolled of thirty-two thousand two hundred. 22Then the tribe of Benjamin: The leader of the Benjaminites shall be Abidan son of Gideoni, 23with a company as enrolled of thirty-five thousand four hundred. 24The total enrollment of the camp of Ephraim, by companies, is one hundred eight thousand one hundred. They shall set out third on the march.

25 On the north side shall be the regimental encampment of Dan by companies. The leader of the Danites shall be Ahiezer son of Ammishad-

dai, 26with a company as enrolled of sixty-two thousand seven hundred. 27Those to camp next to him shall be the tribe of Asher. The leader of the Asherites shall be Pagiel son of Ochran, 28with a company as enrolled of forty-one thousand five hundred. 29Then the tribe of Naphtali: The leader of the Naphtalites shall be Ahira son of Enan, 30with a company as enrolled of fifty-three thousand four hundred. 31The total enrollment of the camp of Dan is one hundred fifty-seven thousand six hundred. They shall set out last, by companies.[a]

32 This was the enrollment of the Israelites by their ancestral houses; the total enrollment in the camps by their companies was six hundred three thousand five hundred fifty. 33Just as the LORD had commanded Moses, the Levites were not enrolled among the other Israelites.

34 The Israelites did just as the LORD had commanded Moses: They camped by regiments, and they set out the same way, everyone by clans, according to ancestral houses.

THE SONS OF AARON

3 This is the lineage of Aaron and Moses at the time when the LORD spoke with Moses on Mount Sinai. 2These are the names of the sons of Aaron: Nadab the firstborn, and Abihu, Eleazar, and Ithamar; 3these are the names of the sons of Aaron, the anointed priests, whom he ordained to minister as priests. 4Nadab and Abihu died before the LORD when they offered unholy fire before the LORD in the wilderness of Sinai, and they had no children. Eleazar and Ithamar served as priests in the lifetime of their father Aaron.

THE DUTIES OF THE LEVITES

5 Then the LORD spoke to Moses, saying: 6Bring the tribe of Levi near, and set them before Aaron the priest, so that they may assist him. 7They shall perform duties for him and for the whole congregation

[a] 2.31 Compare verses 9, 16, 24: Heb by their regiments

in front of the tent of meeting, doing service at the tabernacle; 8they shall be in charge of all the furnishings of the tent of meeting, and attend to the duties for the Israelites as they do service at the tabernacle. 9You shall give the Levites to Aaron and his descendants; they are unreservedly given to him from among the Israelites. 10But you shall make a register of Aaron and his descendants; it is they who shall attend to the priesthood, and any outsider who comes near shall be put to death.

11 Then the LORD spoke to Moses, saying: 12I hereby accept the Levites from among the Israelites as substitutes for all the firstborn that open the womb among the Israelites. The Levites shall be mine, 13for all the firstborn are mine; when I killed all the firstborn in the land of Egypt, I consecrated for my own all the firstborn in Israel, both human and animal; they shall be mine. I am the LORD.

A CENSUS OF THE LEVITES

14 Then the LORD spoke to Moses in the wilderness of Sinai, saying: 15Enroll the Levites by ancestral houses and by clans. You shall enroll every male from a month old and upward. 16So Moses enrolled them according to the word of the LORD, as he was commanded. 17The following were the sons of Levi, by their names: Gershon, Kohath, and Merari. 18These are the names of the sons of Gershon by their clans: Libni and Shimei. 19The sons of Kohath by their clans: Amram, Izhar, Hebron, and Uzziel. 20The sons of Merari by their clans: Mahli and Mushi. These are the clans of the Levites, by their ancestral houses.

21 To Gershon belonged the clan of the Libnites and the clan of the Shimeites; these were the clans of the Gershonites. 22Their enrollment, counting all the males from a month old and upward, was seven thousand five hundred. 23The clans of the Gershonites were to camp behind the tabernacle on the west, 24with Eliasaph son of Lael as head of the ancestral house of the Gershonites. 25The responsibility of the sons of Gershon in the tent of meeting was to be the tabernacle, the tent with its covering, the screen for the entrance of the tent of meeting, 26the hangings of the court, the screen for the entrance of the court that is around the tabernacle and the altar, and its cords—all the service pertaining to these.

27 To Kohath belonged the clan of the Amramites, the clan of the Izharites, the clan of the Hebronites, and the clan of the Uzzielites; these are the clans of the Kohathites. 28Counting all the males, from a month old and upward, there were eight thousand six hundred, attending to the duties of the sanctuary. 29The clans of the Kohathites were to camp on the south side of the tabernacle, 30with Elizaphan son of Uzziel as head of the ancestral house of the clans of the Kohathites. 31Their responsibility was to be the ark, the table, the lampstand, the altars, the vessels of the sanctuary with which the priests minister, and the screen—all the service pertaining to these. 32Eleazar son of Aaron the priest was to be chief over the leaders of the Levites, and to have oversight of those who had charge of the sanctuary.

WE HAVE TWO BASIC NEEDS:

SOMEONE TO LOVE AND

SOMETHING TO DO. GOD

OFFERS THE FULFILLMENT

OF THESE NEEDS.

33 To Merari belonged the clan of the Mahlites and the clan of the Mushites: these are the clans of Merari. 34Their enrollment, counting all the males from a month old and upward, was six thousand two hundred. 35The head of the ances-

tral house of the clans of Merari was Zuriel son of Abihail; they were to camp on the north side of the tabernacle. ³⁶The responsibility assigned to the sons of Merari was to be the frames of the tabernacle, the bars, the pillars, the bases, and all their accessories—all the service pertaining to these; ³⁷also the pillars of the court all around, with their bases and pegs and cords.

38 Those who were to camp in front of the tabernacle on the east—in front of the tent of meeting toward the east—were Moses and Aaron and Aaron's sons, having charge of the rites within the sanctuary, whatever had to be done for the Israelites; and any outsider who came near was to be put to death. ³⁹The total enrollment of the Levites whom Moses and Aaron enrolled at the commandment of the LORD, by their clans, all the males from a month old and upward, was twenty-two thousand.

THE REDEMPTION OF THE FIRSTBORN

40 Then the LORD said to Moses: Enroll all the firstborn males of the Israelites, from a month old and upward, and count their names. ⁴¹But you shall accept the Levites for me— I am the LORD—as substitutes for all the firstborn among the Israelites, and the livestock of the Levites as substitutes for all the firstborn among the livestock of the Israelites. ⁴²So Moses enrolled all the firstborn among the Israelites, as the LORD commanded him. ⁴³The total enrollment, all the firstborn males from a month old and upward, counting the number of names, was twenty-two thousand two hundred seventy-three.

44 Then the LORD spoke to Moses, saying: ⁴⁵Accept the Levites as substitutes for all the firstborn among the Israelites, and the livestock of the Levites as substitutes for their livestock; and the Levites shall be mine. I am the LORD. ⁴⁶As the price of redemption of the two hundred seventy-three of the firstborn of the Israelites, over and above the number of the Levites, ⁴⁷you shall accept five shekels apiece, reckoning by the shekel of the sanctuary, a shekel of twenty gerahs. ⁴⁸Give to Aaron and his sons the money by which the excess number of them is redeemed. ⁴⁹So Moses took the redemption money from those who were over and above those redeemed by the Levites; ⁵⁰from the firstborn of the Israelites he took the money, one thousand three hundred sixty-five shekels, reckoned by the shekel of the sanctuary; ⁵¹and Moses gave the redemption money to Aaron and his sons, according to the word of the LORD, as the LORD had commanded Moses.

THE KOHATHITES

4 The LORD spoke to Moses and Aaron, saying: ²Take a census of the Kohathites separate from the other Levites, by their clans and their ancestral houses, ³from thirty years old up to fifty years old, all who qualify to do work relating to the tent of meeting. ⁴The service of the Kohathites relating to the tent of meeting concerns the most holy things.

5 When the camp is to set out, Aaron and his sons shall go in and take down the screening curtain, and cover the ark of the covenantᵃ with it; ⁶then they shall put on it a covering of fine leather,ᵇ and spread over that a cloth all of blue, and shall put its poles in place. ⁷Over the table of the bread of the Presence they shall spread a blue cloth, and put on it the plates, the dishes for incense, the bowls, and the flagons for the drink offering; the regular bread also shall be on it; ⁸then they shall spread over them a crimson cloth, and cover it with a covering of fine leather,ᵇ and shall put its poles in place. ⁹They shall take a blue cloth, and cover the lampstand for the light, with its lamps, its snuffers, its trays, and all the vessels for oil with which it is supplied; ¹⁰and they shall put it with all its utensils in a covering

ᵃ 4.5 Or treaty, or testimony; Heb eduth
ᵇ 4.6,8 Meaning of Heb uncertain

of fine leather,[a] and put it on the carrying frame. [11]Over the golden altar they shall spread a blue cloth, and cover it with a covering of fine leather,[a] and shall put its poles in place; [12]and they shall take all the utensils of the service that are used in the sanctuary, and put them in a blue cloth, and cover them with a covering of fine leather,[a] and put them on the carrying frame. [13]They shall take away the ashes from the altar, and spread a purple cloth over it; [14]and they shall put on it all the utensils of the altar, which are used for the service there, the firepans, the forks, the shovels, and the basins, all the utensils of the altar; and they shall spread on it a covering of fine leather,[a] and shall put its poles in place. [15]When Aaron and his sons have finished covering the sanctuary and all the furnishings of the sanctuary, as the camp sets out, after that the Kohathites shall come to carry these, but they must not touch the holy things, or they will die. These are the things of the tent of meeting that the Kohathites are to carry.

16 Eleazar son of Aaron the priest shall have charge of the oil for the light, the fragrant incense, the regular grain offering, and the anointing oil, the oversight of all the tabernacle and all that is in it, in the sanctuary and in its utensils.

17 Then the LORD spoke to Moses and Aaron, saying: [18]You must not let the tribe of the clans of the Kohathites be destroyed from among the Levites. [19]This is how you must deal with them in order that they may live and not die when they come near to the most holy things: Aaron and his sons shall go in and assign each to a particular task or burden. [20]But the Kohathites[b] must not go in to look on the holy things even for a moment; otherwise they will die.

THE GERSHONITES AND MERARITES

21 Then the LORD spoke to Moses, saying: [22]Take a census of the Gershonites also, by their ancestral houses and by their clans; [23]from thirty years old up to fifty years old you shall enroll them, all who qualify to do work in the tent of meeting. [24]This is the service of the clans of the Gershonites, in serving and bearing burdens: [25]They shall carry the curtains of the tabernacle, and the tent of meeting with its covering, and the outer covering of fine leather[a] that is on top of it, and the screen for the entrance of the tent of meeting, [26]and the hangings of the court, and the screen for the entrance of the gate of the court that is around the tabernacle and the altar, and their cords, and all the equipment for their service; and they shall do all that needs to be done with regard to them. [27]All the service of the Gershonites shall be at the command of Aaron and his sons, in all that they are to carry, and in all that they have to do; and you shall assign to their charge all that they are to carry. [28]This is the service of the clans of the Gershonites relating to the tent of meeting, and their responsibilities are to be under the oversight of Ithamar son of Aaron the priest.

29 As for the Merarites, you shall enroll them by their clans and their ancestral houses; [30]from thirty years old up to fifty years old you shall enroll them, everyone who qualifies to do the work of the tent of meeting. [31]This is what they are charged to carry, as the whole of their service in the tent of meeting: the frames of the tabernacle, with its bars, pillars, and bases, [32]and the pillars of the court all around with their bases, pegs, and cords, with all their equipment and all their related service; and you shall assign by name the objects that they are required to carry. [33]This is the service of the clans of the Merarites, the whole of their service relating to the tent of meeting, under the hand of Ithamar son of Aaron the priest.

CENSUS OF THE LEVITES

34 So Moses and Aaron and the leaders of the congregation enrolled

[a] 4.10,11,12,14,25 Meaning of Heb uncertain
[b] 4.20 Heb they

the Kohathites, by their clans and their ancestral houses, ³⁵from thirty years old up to fifty years old, everyone who qualified for work relating to the tent of meeting; ³⁶and their enrollment by clans was two thousand seven hundred fifty. ³⁷This was the enrollment of the clans of the Kohathites, all who served at the tent of meeting, whom Moses and Aaron enrolled according to the commandment of the LORD by Moses.

38 The enrollment of the Gershonites, by their clans and their ancestral houses, ³⁹from thirty years old up to fifty years old, everyone who qualified for work relating to the tent of meeting— ⁴⁰their enrollment by their clans and their ancestral houses was two thousand six hundred thirty. ⁴¹This was the enrollment of the clans of the Gershonites, all who served at the tent of meeting, whom Moses and Aaron enrolled according to the commandment of the LORD.

42 The enrollment of the clans of the Merarites, by their clans and their ancestral houses, ⁴³from thirty years old up to fifty years old, everyone who qualified for work relating to the tent of meeting— ⁴⁴their enrollment by their clans was three thousand two hundred. ⁴⁵This is the enrollment of the clans of the Merarites, whom Moses and Aaron enrolled according to the commandment of the LORD by Moses.

46 All those who were enrolled of the Levites, whom Moses and Aaron and the leaders of Israel enrolled, by their clans and their ancestral houses, ⁴⁷from thirty years old up to fifty years old, everyone who qualified to do the work of service and the work of bearing burdens relating to the tent of meeting, ⁴⁸their enrollment was eight thousand five hundred eighty. ⁴⁹According to the commandment of the LORD through Moses they were appointed to their several tasks of serving or carrying; thus they were enrolled by him, as the LORD commanded Moses.

UNCLEAN PERSONS

5 The LORD spoke to Moses, saying: ²Command the Israelites to put out of the camp everyone who is leprous,ª or has a discharge, and everyone who is unclean through contact with a corpse; ³you shall put out both male and female, putting them outside the camp; they must not defile their camp, where I dwell among them. ⁴The Israelites did so, putting them outside the camp; as the LORD had spoken to Moses, so the Israelites did.

CONFESSION AND RESTITUTION

5 The LORD spoke to Moses, saying: ⁶Speak to the Israelites: When a man or a woman wrongs another, breaking faith with the LORD, that person incurs guilt ⁷and shall confess the sin that has been committed. The person shall make full restitution for the wrong, adding one-fifth to it, and giving it to the one who was wronged. ⁸If the injured party has no next of kin to whom restitution may be made for the wrong, the restitution for wrong shall go to the LORD for the priest, in addition to the ram of atonement with which atonement is made for the guilty party. ⁹Among all the sacred donations of the Israelites, every gift that they bring to the priest shall be his. ¹⁰The sacred donations of all are their own; whatever anyone gives to the priest shall be his.

CONCERNING AN UNFAITHFUL WIFE

11 The LORD spoke to Moses, saying: ¹²Speak to the Israelites and say to them: If any man's wife goes astray and is unfaithful to him, ¹³if a man has had intercourse with her but it is hidden from her husband, so that she is undetected though she has defiled herself, and there is no witness against her since she was not caught in the act; ¹⁴if a spirit of jealousy comes on him, and he is jealous of his wife who has defiled herself; or if a spirit of jealousy comes on him, and he is jealous of his wife, though she has not defiled herself; ¹⁵then the man shall

ª 5.2 A term for several skin diseases; precise meaning uncertain bring his wife to the priest. And he shall bring the offering required for her, one-tenth of an ephah of barley flour. He shall pour no oil on it and put no frankincense on it, for it is a grain offering of jealousy, a grain offering of remembrance, bringing iniquity to remembrance.

16 Then the priest shall bring her near, and set her before the LORD; 17the priest shall take holy water in an earthen vessel, and take some of the dust that is on the floor of the tabernacle and put it into the water. 18The priest shall set the woman before the LORD, dishevel the woman's hair, and place in her hands the grain offering of remembrance, which is the grain offering of jealousy. In his own hand the priest shall have the water of bitterness that brings the curse. 19Then the priest shall make her take an oath, saying, "If no man has lain with you, if you have not turned aside to uncleanness while under your husband's authority, be immune to this water of bitterness that brings the curse. 20But if you have gone astray while under your husband's authority, if you have defiled yourself and some man other than your husband has had intercourse with you," 21—let the priest make the woman take the oath of the curse and say to the woman— "the LORD make you an execration and an oath among your people, when the LORD makes your uterus drop, your womb discharge; 22now may this water that brings the curse enter your bowels and make your womb discharge, your uterus drop!" And the woman shall say, "Amen. Amen."

23 Then the priest shall put these curses in writing, and wash them off into the water of bitterness. 24He shall make the woman drink the water of bitterness that brings the curse, and the water that brings the curse shall enter her and cause bitter pain. 25The priest shall take the grain offering of jealousy out of the woman's hand, and shall elevate the grain offering before the LORD and bring it to the altar; 26and the priest shall take a handful of the grain offering, as its memorial portion, and turn it into smoke on the altar, and afterward shall make the woman drink the water. 27When he has made her drink the water, then, if she has defiled herself and has been unfaithful to her husband, the water that brings the curse shall enter into her and cause bitter pain, and her womb shall discharge, her uterus drop, and the woman shall become an execration among her people. 28But if the woman has not defiled herself and is clean, then she shall be immune and be able to conceive children.

29 This is the law in cases of jealousy, when a wife, while under her husband's authority, goes astray and defiles herself, 30or when a spirit of jealousy comes on a man and he is jealous of his wife; then he shall set the woman before the LORD, and the priest shall apply this entire law to her. 31The man shall be free from iniquity, but the woman shall bear her iniquity.

THE NAZIRITES

6 The LORD spoke to Moses, saying: 2Speak to the Israelites and say to them: When either men or women make a special vow, the vow of a nazirite,[a] to separate themselves to the LORD, 3they shall separate themselves from wine and strong drink; they shall drink no wine vinegar or other vinegar, and shall not drink any grape juice or eat grapes, fresh or dried. 4All their days as nazirites[b] they shall eat nothing that is produced by the grapevine, not even the seeds or the skins.

5 All the days of their nazirite vow no razor shall come upon the head; until the time is completed for which they separate themselves to the LORD, they shall be holy; they shall let the locks of the head grow long.

6 All the days that they separate themselves to the LORD they shall not go near a corpse. 7Even if their father or mother, brother or sis-

a 6.2 That is one separated or one consecrated   b 6.4 That is those separated or those consecrated

ter, should die, they may not defile themselves; because their consecration to God is upon the head. ⁸All their days as nazirites[a] they are holy to the LORD.

9 If someone dies very suddenly nearby, defiling the consecrated head, then they shall shave the head on the day of their cleansing; on the seventh day they shall shave it. ¹⁰On the eighth day they shall bring two turtledoves or two young pigeons to the priest at the entrance of the tent of meeting, ¹¹and the priest shall offer one as a sin offering and the other as a burnt offering, and make atonement for them, because they incurred guilt by reason of the corpse. They shall sanctify the head that same day, ¹²and separate themselves to the LORD for their days as nazirites,[a] and bring a male lamb a year old as a guilt offering. The former time shall be void, because the consecrated head was defiled.

INGRATITUDE CAUSES

SOME PEOPLE TO FIND

FAULT WITH ALMOST ALL

OF LIFE'S EXPERIENCES.

13 This is the law for the nazirites[a] when the time of their consecration has been completed: they shall be brought to the entrance of the tent of meeting, ¹⁴and they shall offer their gift to the LORD, one male lamb a year old without blemish as a burnt offering, one ewe lamb a year old without blemish as a sin offering, one ram without blemish as an offering of well-being, ¹⁵and a basket of unleavened bread, cakes of choice flour mixed with oil and unleavened wafers spread with oil, with their grain offering and their drink offerings. ¹⁶The priest shall present them before the LORD and offer their sin offering and burnt offering, ¹⁷and shall offer the ram as a sacri-

fice of well-being to the LORD, with the basket of unleavened bread; the priest also shall make the accompanying grain offering and drink offering. ¹⁸Then the nazirites[a] shall shave the consecrated head at the entrance of the tent of meeting, and shall take the hair from the consecrated head and put it on the fire under the sacrifice of well-being. ¹⁹The priest shall take the shoulder of the ram, when it is boiled, and one unleavened cake out of the basket, and one unleavened wafer, and shall put them in the palms of the nazirites,[a] after they have shaved the consecrated head. ²⁰Then the priest shall elevate them as an elevation offering before the LORD; they are a holy portion for the priest, together with the breast that is elevated and the thigh that is offered. After that the nazirites[a] may drink wine.

21 This is the law for the nazirites[a] who take a vow. Their offering to the LORD must be in accordance with the nazirite[b] vow, apart from what else they can afford. In accordance with whatever vow they take, so they shall do, following the law for their consecration.

THE PRIESTLY BENEDICTION

22 The LORD spoke to Moses, saying: ²³Speak to Aaron and his sons, saying, Thus you shall bless the Israelites: You shall say to them,
²⁴ The LORD bless you and keep you;
²⁵ the LORD make his face to
shine upon you, and
be gracious to you;
²⁶ the LORD lift up his countenance
upon you, and
give you peace.
27 So they shall put my name on the Israelites, and I will bless them.

OFFERINGS OF THE LEADERS

7 On the day when Moses had finished setting up the tabernacle, and had anointed and consecrated it with all its furnishings, and had anointed and consecrated the altar with all its utensils, ²the leaders

a 6.8,12,13,18,19,20,21 That is *those separated* or *those consecrated* b 6.21 That is *one separated* or *one consecrated*

of Israel, heads of their ancestral houses, the leaders of the tribes, who were over those who were enrolled, made offerings. ³They brought their offerings before the LORD, six covered wagons and twelve oxen, a wagon for every two of the leaders, and for each one an ox; they presented them before the tabernacle. ⁴Then the LORD said to Moses: ⁵Accept these from them, that they may be used in doing the service of the tent of meeting, and give them to the Levites, to each according to his service. ⁶So Moses took the wagons and the oxen, and gave them to the Levites. ⁷Two wagons and four oxen he gave to the Gershonites, according to their service; ⁸and four wagons and eight oxen he gave to the Merarites, according to their service, under the direction of Ithamar son of Aaron the priest. ⁹But to the Kohathites he gave none, because they were charged with the care of the holy things that had to be carried on the shoulders.

10 The leaders also presented offerings for the dedication of the altar at the time when it was anointed; the leaders presented their offering before the altar. ¹¹The LORD said to Moses: They shall present their offerings, one leader each day, for the dedication of the altar.

12 The one who presented his offering the first day was Nahshon son of Amminadab, of the tribe of Judah; ¹³his offering was one silver plate weighing one hundred thirty shekels, one silver basin weighing seventy shekels, according to the shekel of the sanctuary, both of them full of choice flour mixed with oil for a grain offering; ¹⁴one golden dish weighing ten shekels, full of incense; ¹⁵one young bull, one ram, one male lamb a year old, for a burnt offering; ¹⁶one male goat for a sin offering; ¹⁷and for the sacrifice of well-being, two oxen, five rams, five male goats, and five male lambs a year old. This was the offering of Nahshon son of Amminadab.

18 On the second day Nethanel son of Zuar, the leader of Issachar, presented an offering; ¹⁹he presented for his offering one silver plate weighing one hundred thirty shekels, one silver basin weighing seventy shekels, according to the shekel of the sanctuary, both of them full of choice flour mixed with oil for a grain offering; ²⁰one golden dish weighing ten shekels, full of incense; ²¹one young bull, one ram, one male lamb a year old, as a burnt offering; ²²one male goat as a sin offering; ²³and for the sacrifice of well-being, two oxen, five rams, five male goats, and five male lambs a year old. This was the offering of Nethanel son of Zuar.

24 On the third day Eliab son of Helon, the leader of the Zebulunites: ²⁵his offering was one silver plate weighing one hundred thirty shekels, one silver basin weighing seventy shekels, according to the shekel of the sanctuary, both of them full of choice flour mixed with oil for a grain offering; ²⁶one golden dish weighing ten shekels, full of incense; ²⁷one young bull, one ram, one male lamb a year old, for a burnt offering; ²⁸one male goat for a sin offering; ²⁹and for the sacrifice of well-being, two oxen, five rams, five male goats, and five male lambs a year old. This was the offering of Eliab son of Helon.

30 On the fourth day Elizur son of Shedeur, the leader of the Reubenites: ³¹his offering was one silver plate weighing one hundred thirty shekels, one silver basin weighing seventy shekels, according to the shekel of the sanctuary, both of them full of choice flour mixed with oil for a grain offering; ³²one golden dish weighing ten shekels, full of incense; ³³one young bull, one ram, one male lamb a year old, for a burnt offering; ³⁴one male goat for a sin offering; ³⁵and for the sacrifice of well-being, two oxen, five rams, five male goats, and five male lambs a year old. This was the offering of Elizur son of Shedeur.

36 On the fifth day Shelumiel son of Zurishaddai, the leader of the Simeonites: ³⁷his offering was one silver plate weighing one hundred thirty shekels, one silver basin

weighing seventy shekels, according to the shekel of the sanctuary, both of them full of choice flour mixed with oil for a grain offering; 38one golden dish weighing ten shekels, full of incense; 39one young bull, one ram, one male lamb a year old, for a burnt offering; 40one male goat for a sin offering; 41and for the sacrifice of well-being, two oxen, five rams, five male goats, and five male lambs a year old. This was the offering of Shelumiel son of Zurishaddai.

42 On the sixth day Eliasaph son of Deuel, the leader of the Gadites: 43his offering was one silver plate weighing one hundred thirty shekels, one silver basin weighing seventy shekels, according to the shekel of the sanctuary, both of them full of choice flour mixed with oil for a grain offering; 44one golden dish weighing ten shekels, full of incense; 45one young bull, one ram, one male lamb a year old, for a burnt offering; 46one male goat for a sin offering; 47and for the sacrifice of well-being, two oxen, five rams, five male goats, and five male lambs a year old. This was the offering of Eliasaph son of Deuel.

48 On the seventh day Elishama son of Ammihud, the leader of the Ephraimites: 49his offering was one silver plate weighing one hundred thirty shekels, one silver basin weighing seventy shekels, according to the shekel of the sanctuary, both of them full of choice flour mixed with oil for a grain offering; 50one golden dish weighing ten shekels, full of incense; 51one young bull, one ram, one male lamb a year old, for a burnt offering; 52one male goat for a sin offering; 53and for the sacrifice of well-being, two oxen, five rams, five male goats, and five male lambs a year old. This was the offering of Elishama son of Ammihud.

54 On the eighth day Gamaliel son of Pedahzur, the leader of the Manassites: 55his offering was one silver plate weighing one hundred thirty shekels, one silver basin weighing seventy shekels, according to the shekel of the sanctuary, both of them full of choice flour mixed

with oil for a grain offering; 56one golden dish weighing ten shekels, full of incense; 57one young bull, one ram, one male lamb a year old, for a burnt offering; 58one male goat for a sin offering; 59and for the sacrifice of well-being, two oxen, five rams, five male goats, and five male lambs a year old. This was the offering of Gamaliel son of Pedahzur.

60 On the ninth day Abidan son of Gideoni, the leader of the Benjaminites: 61his offering was one silver plate weighing one hundred thirty shekels, one silver basin weighing seventy shekels, according to the shekel of the sanctuary, both of them full of choice flour mixed with oil for a grain offering; 62one golden dish weighing ten shekels, full of incense; 63one young bull, one ram, one male lamb a year old, for a burnt offering; 64one male goat for a sin offering; 65and for the sacrifice of well-being, two oxen, five rams, five male goats, and five male lambs a year old. This was the offering of Abidan son of Gideoni.

66 On the tenth day Ahiezer son of Ammishaddai, the leader of the Danites: 67his offering was one silver plate weighing one hundred thirty shekels, one silver basin weighing seventy shekels, according to the shekel of the sanctuary, both of them full of choice flour mixed with oil for a grain offering; 68one golden dish weighing ten shekels, full of incense; 69one young bull, one ram, one male lamb a year old, for a burnt offering; 70one male goat for a sin offering; 71and for the sacrifice of well-being, two oxen, five rams, five male goats, and five male lambs a year old. This was the offering of Ahiezer son of Ammishaddai.

72 On the eleventh day Pagiel son of Ochran, the leader of the Asherites: 73his offering was one silver plate weighing one hundred thirty shekels, one silver basin weighing seventy shekels, according to the shekel of the sanctuary, both of them full of choice flour mixed with oil for a grain offering; 74one golden dish weighing ten shekels, full of incense; 75one young bull, one ram,

one male lamb a year old, for a burnt offering; 76one male goat for a sin offering; 77and for the sacrifice of well-being, two oxen, five rams, five male goats, and five male lambs a year old. This was the offering of Pagiel son of Ochran.

78 On the twelfth day Ahira son of Enan, the leader of the Naphtalites: 79his offering was one silver plate weighing one hundred thirty shekels, one silver basin weighing seventy shekels, according to the shekel of the sanctuary, both of them full of choice flour mixed with oil for a grain offering; 80one golden dish weighing ten shekels, full of incense; 81one young bull, one ram, one male lamb a year old, for a burnt offering; 82one male goat for a sin offering; 83and for the sacrifice of well-being, two oxen, five rams, five male goats, and five male lambs a year old. This was the offering of Ahira son of Enan.

84 This was the dedication offering for the altar, at the time when it was anointed, from the leaders of Israel: twelve silver plates, twelve silver basins, twelve golden dishes, 85each silver plate weighing one hundred thirty shekels and each basin seventy, all the silver of the vessels two thousand four hundred shekels according to the shekel of the sanctuary, 86the twelve golden dishes, full of incense, weighing ten shekels apiece according to the shekel of the sanctuary, all the gold of the dishes being one hundred twenty shekels; 87all the livestock for the burnt offering twelve bulls, twelve rams, twelve male lambs a year old, with their grain offering; and twelve male goats for a sin offering; 88and all the livestock for the sacrifice of well-being twenty-four bulls, the rams sixty, the male goats sixty, the male lambs a year old sixty. This was the dedication offering for the altar, after it was anointed.

89 When Moses went into the tent of meeting to speak with the LORD,a he would hear the voice speaking to him from above the mercy seatb that was on the ark of the covenantc from between the two cherubim; thus it spoke to him.

THE SEVEN LAMPS

8 The LORD spoke to Moses, saying: 2Speak to Aaron and say to him: When you set up the lamps, the seven lamps shall give light in front of the lampstand. 3Aaron did so; he set up its lamps to give light in front of the lampstand, as the LORD had commanded Moses. 4Now this was how the lampstand was made, out of hammered work of gold. From its base to its flowers, it was hammered work; according to the pattern that the LORD had shown Moses, so he made the lampstand.

CONSECRATION AND SERVICE OF THE LEVITES

5 The LORD spoke to Moses, saying: 6Take the Levites from among the Israelites and cleanse them. 7Thus you shall do to them, to cleanse them: sprinkle the water of purification on them, have them shave their whole body with a razor and wash their clothes, and so cleanse themselves. 8Then let them take a young bull and its grain offering of choice flour mixed with oil, and you shall take another young bull for a sin offering. 9You shall bring the Levites before the tent of meeting, and assemble the whole congregation of the Israelites. 10When you bring the Levites before the LORD, the Israelites shall lay their hands on the Levites, 11and Aaron shall present the Levites before the LORD as an elevation offering from the Israelites, that they may do the service of the LORD. 12The Levites shall lay their hands on the heads of the bulls, and he shall offer the one for a sin offering and the other for a burnt offering to the LORD, to make atonement for the Levites. 13Then you shall have the Levites stand before Aaron and his sons, and you shall present them as an elevation offering to the LORD. 14 Thus you shall separate the Levites from among the other Israelites, and the Levites shall be mine. 15Thereafter the Levites may go in to do service at the tent of meeting,

a 7.89 Heb him   b 7.89 Or the cover
c 7.89 Or treaty, or testimony; Heb eduth

once you have cleansed them and presented them as an elevation offering. ¹⁶For they are unreservedly given to me from among the Israelites; I have taken them for myself, in place of all that open the womb, the firstborn of all the Israelites. ¹⁷For all the firstborn among the Israelites are mine, both human and animal. On the day that I struck down all the firstborn in the land of Egypt I consecrated them for myself, ¹⁸but I have taken the Levites in place of all the firstborn among the Israelites. ¹⁹Moreover, I have given the Levites as a gift to Aaron and his sons from among the Israelites, to do the service for the Israelites at the tent of meeting, and to make atonement for the Israelites, in order that there may be no plague among the Israelites for coming too close to the sanctuary.

20 Moses and Aaron and the whole congregation of the Israelites did with the Levites accordingly; the Israelites did with the Levites just as the LORD had commanded Moses concerning them. ²¹The Levites purified themselves from sin and washed their clothes; then Aaron presented them as an elevation offering before the LORD, and Aaron made atonement for them to cleanse them. ²²Thereafter the Levites went in to do their service in the tent of meeting in attendance on Aaron and his sons. As the LORD had commanded Moses concerning the Levites, so they did with them.

23 The LORD spoke to Moses, saying: ²⁴This applies to the Levites: from twenty-five years old and upward they shall begin to do duty in the service of the tent of meeting; ²⁵and from the age of fifty years they shall retire from the duty of the service and serve no more. ²⁶They may assist their brothers in the tent of meeting in carrying out their duties, but they shall perform no service. Thus you shall do with the Levites in assigning their duties.

THE PASSOVER AT SINAI

9 The LORD spoke to Moses in the wilderness of Sinai, in the first month of the second year after they had come out of the land of Egypt, saying: ²Let the Israelites keep the passover at its appointed time. ³On the fourteenth day of this month, at twilight,ᵃ you shall keep it at its appointed time; according to all its statutes and all its regulations you shall keep it. ⁴So Moses told the Israelites that they should keep the passover. ⁵They kept the passover in the first month, on the fourteenth day of the month, at twilight,ᵃ in the wilderness of Sinai. Just as the LORD had commanded Moses, so the Israelites did. ⁶Now there were certain people who were unclean through touching a corpse, so that they could not keep the passover on that day. They came before Moses and Aaron on that day, ⁷and said to him, "Although we are unclean through touching a corpse, why must we be kept from presenting the LORD's offering at its appointed time among the Israelites?" ⁸Moses spoke to them, "Wait, so that I may hear what the LORD will command concerning you."

9 The LORD spoke to Moses, saying: ¹⁰Speak to the Israelites, saying: Anyone of you or your descendants who is unclean through touching a corpse, or is away on a journey, shall still keep the passover to the LORD. ¹¹In the second month on the fourteenth day, at twilight,ᵃ they shall keep it; they shall eat it with unleavened bread and bitter herbs. ¹²They shall leave none of it until morning, nor break a bone of it; according to all the statute for the passover they shall keep it. ¹³But anyone who is clean and is not on a journey, and yet refrains from keeping the passover, shall be cut off from the people for not presenting the LORD's offering at its appointed time; such a one shall bear the consequences for the sin. ¹⁴Any alien residing among you who wishes to keep the passover to the LORD shall do so according to the statute of the passover and according to its regulation; you shall have one statute for both the resident alien and the native.

ᵃ 9.3,5,11 Heb *between the two evenings*

THE CLOUD AND THE FIRE

15 On the day the tabernacle was set up, the cloud covered the tabernacle, the tent of the covenant;[a] and from evening until morning it was over the tabernacle, having the appearance of fire. **16**It was always so: the cloud covered it by day[b] and the appearance of fire by night. **17**Whenever the cloud lifted from over the tent, then the Israelites would set out; and in the place where the cloud settled down, there the Israelites would camp. **18**At the command of the LORD the Israelites would set out, and at the command of the LORD they would camp. As long as the cloud rested over the tabernacle, they would remain in camp. **19**Even when the cloud continued over the tabernacle many days, the Israelites would keep the charge of the LORD, and would not set out. **20**Sometimes the cloud would remain a few days over the tabernacle, and according to the command of the LORD they would remain in camp; then according to the command of the LORD they would set out. **21**Sometimes the cloud would remain from evening until morning; and when the cloud lifted in the morning, they would set out, or if it continued for a day and a night, when the cloud lifted they would set out. **22**Whether it was two days, or a month, or a longer time, that the cloud continued over the tabernacle, resting upon it, the Israelites would remain in camp

GOD HAS NEVER FORSAKEN

HIS PEOPLE. IN THE SAME

WAY, WE CHRISTIANS MUST

REMAIN FAITHFUL IN OUR

LOVE FOR OTHERS, EVEN

WHEN IT SEEMS THAT WE HAVE

NOT BEEN TREATED FAIRLY.

and would not set out; but when it lifted they would set out. **23**At the command of the LORD they would camp, and at the command of the LORD they would set out. They kept the charge of the LORD, at the command of the LORD by Moses.

THE SILVER TRUMPETS

10 The LORD spoke to Moses, saying: **2**Make two silver trumpets; you shall make them of hammered work; and you shall use them for summoning the congregation, and for breaking camp. **3**When both are blown, the whole congregation shall assemble before you at the entrance of the tent of meeting. **4**But if only one is blown, then the leaders, the heads of the tribes of Israel, shall assemble before you. **5**When you blow an alarm, the camps on the east side shall set out; **6**when you blow a second alarm, the camps on the south side shall set out. An alarm is to be blown whenever they are to set out. **7**But when the assembly is to be gathered, you shall blow, but you shall not sound an alarm. **8**The sons of Aaron, the priests, shall blow the trumpets; this shall be a perpetual institution for you throughout your generations. **9**When you go to war in your land against the adversary who oppresses you, you shall sound an alarm with the trumpets, so that you may be remembered before the LORD your God and be saved from your enemies. **10**Also on your days of rejoicing, at your appointed festivals, and at the beginnings of your months, you shall blow the trumpets over your burnt offerings and over your sacrifices of well-being; they shall serve as a reminder on your behalf before the LORD your God: I am the LORD your God.

DEPARTURE FROM SINAI

11 In the second year, in the second month, on the twentieth day of the month, the cloud lifted from over the tabernacle of the covenant.[a] **12**Then the Israelites set out by

[a] 9.15; 10.11 Or *treaty*, or *testimony*; Heb *eduth* [b] 9.16 Gk Syr Vg: Heb lacks *by day*

stages from the wilderness of Sinai, and the cloud settled down in the wilderness of Paran. ¹³They set out for the first time at the command of the LORD by Moses. ¹⁴The standard of the camp of Judah set out first, company by company, and over the whole company was Nahshon son of Amminadab. ¹⁵Over the company of the tribe of Issachar was Nethanel son of Zuar; ¹⁶and over the company of the tribe of Zebulun was Eliab son of Helon.

17 Then the tabernacle was taken down, and the Gershonites and the Merarites, who carried the tabernacle, set out. ¹⁸Next the standard of the camp of Reuben set out, company by company; and over the whole company was Elizur son of Shedeur. ¹⁹Over the company of the tribe of Simeon was Shelumiel son of Zurishaddai, ²⁰and over the company of the tribe of Gad was Eliasaph son of Deuel.

21 Then the Kohathites, who carried the holy things, set out; and the tabernacle was set up before their arrival. ²²Next the standard of the Ephraimite camp set out, company by company, and over the whole company was Elishama son of Ammihud. ²³Over the company of the tribe of Manasseh was Gamaliel son of Pedahzur, ²⁴and over the company of the tribe of Benjamin was Abidan son of Gideoni.

25 Then the standard of the camp of Dan, acting as the rear guard of all the camps, set out, company by company, and over the whole company was Ahiezer son of Ammishaddai. ²⁶Over the company of the tribe of Asher was Pagiel son of Ochran, ²⁷and over the company of the tribe of Naphtali was Ahira son of Enan. ²⁸This was the order of march of the Israelites, company by company, when they set out.

29 Moses said to Hobab son of Reuel the Midianite, Moses' father-in-law, "We are setting out for the place of which the LORD said, 'I will give it to you'; come with us, and we will treat you well; for the LORD has promised good to Israel." ³⁰But he said to him, "I will not go, but I will

go back to my own land and to my kindred." ³¹He said, "Do not leave us, for you know where we should camp in the wilderness, and you will serve as eyes for us. ³²Moreover, if you go with us, whatever good the LORD does for us, the same we will do for you."

33 So they set out from the mount of the LORD three days' journey with the ark of the covenant of the LORD going before them three days' journey, to seek out a resting place for them, ³⁴the cloud of the LORD being over them by day when they set out from the camp. ³⁵Whenever the ark set out, Moses would say,

"Arise, O LORD, let your
    enemies be scattered,
and your foes flee before you."
³⁶And whenever it came to rest, he would say,
"Return, O LORD of the ten
    thousand thousands
    of Israel."ᵃ

COMPLAINING IN THE DESERT

11 Now when the people complained in the hearing of the LORD about their misfortunes, the LORD heard it and his anger was kindled. Then the fire of the LORD burned against them, and consumed some outlying parts of the camp. ²But the people cried out to Moses; and Moses prayed to the LORD, and the fire abated. ³So that place was called Taberah,ᵇ because the fire of the LORD burned against them.

4 The rabble among them had a strong craving; and the Israelites also wept again, and said, "If only we had meat to eat! ⁵We remember the fish we used to eat in Egypt for nothing, the cucumbers, the melons, the leeks, the onions, and the garlic; ⁶but now our strength is dried up, and there is nothing at all but this manna to look at."

7 Now the manna was like coriander seed, and its color was like the color of gum resin. ⁸The people went around and gathered it, ground it

ᵃ 10.36 Meaning of Heb uncertain
ᵇ 11.3 That is Burning

in mills or beat it in mortars, then boiled it in pots and made cakes of it; and the taste of it was like the taste of cakes baked with oil. 9When the dew fell on the camp in the night, the manna would fall with it.

10 Moses heard the people weeping throughout their families, all at the entrances of their tents. Then the LORD became very angry, and Moses was displeased. 11So Moses said to the LORD, "Why have you treated your servant so badly? Why have I not found favor in your sight, that you lay the burden of all this people on me? 12Did I conceive all this people? Did I give birth to them, that you should say to me, 'Carry them in your bosom, as a nurse carries a sucking child, to the land that you promised on oath to their ancestors'? 13Where am I to get meat to give to all this people? For they come weeping to me and say, 'Give us meat to eat!' 14I am not able to carry all this people alone, for they are too heavy for me. 15If this is the way you are going to treat me, put me to death at once—if I have found favor in your sight—and do not let me see my misery."

THE SEVENTY ELDERS

16 So the LORD said to Moses, "Gather for me seventy of the elders of Israel, whom you know to be the elders of the people and officers over them; bring them to the tent of meeting, and have them take their place there with you. 17I will come down and talk with you there; and I will take some of the spirit that is on you and put it on them; and they shall bear the burden of the people along with you so that you will not bear it all by yourself. 18And say to the people: Consecrate yourselves for tomorrow, and you shall eat meat; for you have wailed in the hearing of the LORD, saying, 'If only we had meat to eat! Surely it was better for us in Egypt.' Therefore the LORD will give you meat, and you shall eat. 19You shall eat not only one day, or two days, or five days, or ten days, or twenty days, 20but for a whole month—until it comes out of your

nostrils and becomes loathsome to you—because you have rejected the LORD who is among you, and have wailed before him, saying, 'Why did we ever leave Egypt?' " 21But Moses said, "The people I am with number six hundred thousand on foot; and you say, 'I will give them meat, that they may eat for a whole month'! 22Are there enough flocks and herds to slaughter for them? Are there enough fish in the sea to catch for them?" 23The LORD said to Moses, "Is the LORD's power limited?a Now you shall see whether my word will come true for you or not."

24 So Moses went out and told the people the words of the LORD; and he gathered seventy elders of the people, and placed them all around the tent. 25Then the LORD came down in the cloud and spoke to him, and took some of the spirit that was on him and put it on the seventy elders; and when the spirit rested upon them, they prophesied. But they did not do so again.

26 Two men remained in the camp, one named Eldad, and the other named Medad, and the spirit rested on them; they were among those registered, but they had not gone out to the tent, and so they prophesied in the camp. 27And a young man ran and told Moses, "Eldad and Medad are prophesying in the camp." 28And Joshua son of Nun, the assistant of Moses, one of his chosen men,b said, "My lord Moses, stop them!" 29But Moses said to him, "Are you jealous for my sake? Would that all the LORD's people were prophets, and that the LORD would put his spirit on them!" 30And Moses and the elders of Israel returned to the camp.

THE QUAILS

31 Then a wind went out from the LORD, and it brought quails from the sea and let them fall beside the camp, about a day's journey on this side and a day's journey on the other side, all around the camp, about two

---

a 11.23 Heb LORD's hand too short?
b 11.28 Or of Moses from his youth

HONEST WITH GOD

"If this is the way you are going to treat me, put me to death at once—if I have found favor in your sight—and do not let me see my misery."

—Numbers 11.15

When we read Moses' prayer to God (verses 11–15), we might be uncomfortable with its brutal honesty. Moses was straining under the heavy burden of leading God's people in the wilderness, and he openly and honestly expressed his frustrations to God. He complained that he was only trying to carry out the commission that God had given him. Why was God not helping him? How was Moses supposed to satisfy the people's demand for meat to eat? Moses even seemed to be despairing of his very life, for he asked God to put him to death rather than abandon him to face this daunting task all by himself.

Moses was not the only person in scripture who bluntly expressed frustration to God. Soon after he witnessed God's victory over the prophets of Baal on Mount Carmel, Elijah fled for his life into the wilderness. At one point he was in such despair that he sat under a tree and asked God to let him die (see 1 Kings 19). Likewise, when Job experienced terrible loss, he cursed the day of his birth and wished that he had been stillborn (see Job 3). Even Jesus himself offered prayers of deep distress to his Father in heaven. The night before he was crucified, Jesus became very troubled and asked God to spare him from the suffering that lay in store for him (see Matthew 26). The next day, as Jesus was being crucified, he cried out from the cross, "My God, my God, why have you forsaken me?" (Matthew 27.46). Can there be a more honest prayer of personal distress?

Clearly, God is not offended by honest and open distress. In Moses' case, God honored Moses' prayer and miraculously provided food for the people—as well as help for Moses himself. God placed his Spirit on 70 other men to help Moses lead the people.

Just like Moses and others in the Bible, we too can be candid with God regarding our troubles and frustrations; God will hear us. Whether we are feeling overwhelmed, confused, disappointed or angry, we can come to God in honesty and sincerity and expect to receive help. Though God's answers may not always be what we would hope for or expect, we can be certain that our God will always give us what is best (see Matthew 7.7–11).

Going Deeper

- What are some troubles or concerns you have been reluctant to express to God?
- What do you fear might happen if you are open and honest with God about your thoughts? What do the examples of Moses and others suggest about these fears?

cubits deep on the ground. [32]So the people worked all that day and night and all the next day, gathering the quails; the least anyone gathered was ten homers; and they spread them out for themselves all around the camp. [33]But while the meat was still between their teeth, before it was consumed, the anger of the LORD was kindled against the people, and the LORD struck the people with a very great plague. [34]So that place was called Kibroth-hattaavah,[a] because there they buried the people who had the craving. [35]From Kibroth-hattaavah the people journeyed to Hazeroth.

AARON AND MIRIAM JEALOUS OF MOSES

12 While they were at Hazeroth, Miriam and Aaron spoke against Moses because of the Cushite woman whom he had married (for he had indeed married a Cushite woman); [2]and they said, "Has the LORD spoken only through Moses? Has he not spoken through us also?" And the LORD heard it. [3]Now the man Moses was very humble,[b] more so than anyone else on the face of the earth. [4]Suddenly the LORD said to Moses, Aaron, and Miriam, "Come out, you three, to the tent of meeting." So the three of them came out. [5]Then the LORD came down in a pillar of cloud, and stood at the entrance of the tent, and called Aaron and Miriam; and they both came forward. [6]And he said, "Hear my words:

When there are prophets
    among you,
I the LORD make myself
    known to them in visions;
I speak to them in dreams.
[7] Not so with my servant Moses;
    he is entrusted with
        all my house.
[8] With him I speak face to face—
        clearly, not in riddles;
    and he beholds the form
        of the LORD.

Why then were you not afraid to speak against my servant Moses?" [9]And the anger of the LORD was kindled against them, and he departed.

[10]When the cloud went away from over the tent, Miriam had become leprous,[c] as white as snow. And Aaron turned towards Miriam and saw that she was leprous. [11]Then Aaron said to Moses, "Oh, my lord, do not punish us[d] for a sin that we have so foolishly committed. [12]Do not let her be like one stillborn, whose flesh is half consumed when it comes out of its mother's womb." [13]And Moses cried to the LORD, "O God, please heal her." [14]But the LORD said to Moses, "If her father had but spit in her face, would she not bear her shame for seven days? Let her be shut out of the camp for seven days, and after that she may be brought in again." [15]So Miriam was shut out of the camp for seven days; and the people did not set out on the march until Miriam had been brought in again. [16]After that the people set out from Hazeroth, and camped in the wilderness of Paran.

SPIES SENT INTO CANAAN

13 The LORD said to Moses, [2]"Send men to spy out the land of Canaan, which I am giving to the Israelites; from each of their ancestral tribes you shall send a man, every one a leader among them." [3]So Moses sent them from the wilderness of Paran, according to the command of the LORD, all of them leading men among the Israelites. [4]These were their names: From the tribe of Reuben, Shammua son of Zaccur; [5]from the tribe of Simeon, Shaphat son of Hori; [6]from the tribe of Judah, Caleb son of Jephunneh; [7]from the tribe of Issachar, Igal son of Joseph; [8]from the tribe of Ephraim, Hoshea son of Nun; [9]from the tribe of Benjamin, Palti son of Raphu; [10]from the tribe of Zebulun, Gaddiel son of Sodi; [11]from the tribe of Joseph (that is, from the tribe of Manasseh), Gaddi son of Susi; [12]from the tribe of Dan, Ammiel son of Gemalli; [13]from the tribe of Asher, Sethur son of Michael; [14]from the tribe of Naphtali,

[a] 11.34 That is *Graves of craving*   [b] 12.3 Or *devout*   [c] 12.10 A term for several skin diseases; precise meaning uncertain   [d] 12.11 Heb *do not lay sin upon us*

Nahbi son of Vophsi; ¹⁵from the tribe of Gad, Geuel son of Machi. ¹⁶These were the names of the men whom Moses sent to spy out the land. And Moses changed the name of Hoshea son of Nun to Joshua.

17 Moses sent them to spy out the land of Canaan, and said to them, "Go up there into the Negeb, and go up into the hill country, ¹⁸and see what the land is like, and whether the people who live in it are strong or weak, whether they are few or many, ¹⁹and whether the land they live in is good or bad, and whether the towns that they live in are unwalled or fortified, ²⁰and whether the land is rich or poor, and whether there are trees in it or not. Be bold, and bring some of the fruit of the land." Now it was the season of the first ripe grapes.

21 So they went up and spied out the land from the wilderness of Zin to Rehob, near Lebo-hamath. ²²They went up into the Negeb, and came to Hebron; and Ahiman, Sheshai, and Talmai, the Anakites, were there. (Hebron was built seven years before Zoan in Egypt.) ²³And they came to the Wadi Eshcol, and cut down from there a branch with a single cluster of grapes, and they carried it on a pole between two of them. They also brought some pomegranates and figs. ²⁴That place was called the Wadi Eshcol,ᵃ because of the cluster that the Israelites cut down from there.

THE REPORT OF THE SPIES

25 At the end of forty days they returned from spying out the land. ²⁶And they came to Moses and Aaron and to all the congregation of the Israelites in the wilderness of Paran, at Kadesh; they brought back word to them and to all the congregation, and showed them the fruit of the land. ²⁷And they told him, "We came to the land to which you sent us; it flows with milk and honey, and this is its fruit. ²⁸Yet the people who live in the land are strong, and the towns are fortified and very large; and besides, we saw the descendants of Anak there. ²⁹The Amalekites live in the land of the Negeb; the Hittites, the Jebusites, and the Amorites live in the hill country; and the Canaanites live by the sea, and along the Jordan."

30 But Caleb quieted the people before Moses, and said, "Let us go up at once and occupy it, for we are well able to overcome it." ³¹Then the men who had gone up with him said, "We are not able to go up against this people, for they are stronger than we." ³²So they brought to the Israelites an unfavorable report of the land that they had spied out, saying, "The land that we have gone through as spies is a land that devours its inhabitants; and all the people that we saw in it are of great size. ³³There we saw

ᵃ 13.24 That is *Cluster*

BIBLE IN LIFE

Fear of Failure   *Numbers 13.26–33*

Other than Caleb and Joshua, the spies Moses sent to explore Canaan were afraid and unwilling to face the challenge that God put before them. They were afraid of being defeated and afraid to fail, but in their fear, they rebelled against Almighty God. The spies admitted that they looked like grasshoppers in their own eyes and in the eyes of their enemies (verse 33), but in God's eyes they looked like victorious warriors.

In our human weakness, one of the things we fear most is failure. We sometimes lower our goals, so we can be sure we won't fail. We want to avoid the scorn of others. We think it's better to be a safe, mediocre nonentity than to be a highly publicized failure. Like the spies, because of our faulty vision, we avoid good opportunities God places in front of us. As we face challenges in life, do we fixate on our human limitations or on God's limitless power? Are we so afraid to fail that we forfeit the promised land?

the Nephilim (the Anakites come from the Nephilim); and to ourselves we seemed like grasshoppers, and so we seemed to them."

THE PEOPLE REBEL

14 Then all the congregation raised a loud cry, and the people wept that night. ²And all the Israelites complained against Moses and Aaron; the whole congregation said to them, "Would that we had died in the land of Egypt! Or would that we had died in this wilderness! ³Why is the LORD bringing us into this land to fall by the sword? Our wives and our little ones will become booty; would it not be better for us to go back to Egypt?" ⁴So they said to one another, "Let us choose a captain, and go back to Egypt."

5 Then Moses and Aaron fell on their faces before all the assembly of the congregation of the Israelites. ⁶And Joshua son of Nun and Caleb son of Jephunneh, who were among those who had spied out the land, tore their clothes ⁷and said to all the congregation of the Israelites, "The land that we went through as spies is an exceedingly good land. ⁸If the LORD is pleased with us, he will bring us into this land and give it to us, a land that flows with milk and honey. ⁹Only, do not rebel against the LORD; and do not fear the people of the land, for they are no more than bread for us; their protection is removed from them, and the LORD is with us; do not fear them." ¹⁰But the whole congregation threatened to stone them.

Then the glory of the LORD appeared at the tent of meeting to all the Israelites. ¹¹And the LORD said to Moses, "How long will this people despise me? And how long will they refuse to believe in me, in spite of all the signs that I have done among them? ¹²I will strike them with pestilence and disinherit them, and I will make of you a nation greater and mightier than they."

MOSES INTERCEDES
FOR THE PEOPLE

13 But Moses said to the LORD, "Then the Egyptians will hear of it, for in your might you brought up this people from among them, ¹⁴and they will tell the inhabitants of this land. They have heard that you, O LORD, are in the midst of this people; for you, O LORD, are seen face to face, and your cloud stands over them and you go in front of them, in a pillar of cloud by day and in a pillar of fire by night. ¹⁵Now if you kill this people all at one time, then the nations who have heard about you will say, ¹⁶'It is because the LORD was not able to bring this people into the land he swore to give them that he has slaughtered them in the wilderness.' ¹⁷And now, therefore, let the power of the LORD be great in the way that you promised when you spoke, saying,
¹⁸ 'The LORD is slow to anger,
    and abounding in steadfast love,
    forgiving iniquity and
        transgression,
    but by no means clearing
        the guilty,
    visiting the iniquity of the parents
    upon the children
    to the third and the fourth
        generation.'
¹⁹Forgive the iniquity of this people according to the greatness of your steadfast love, just as you have pardoned this people, from Egypt even until now."

20 Then the LORD said, "I do forgive, just as you have asked; ²¹nevertheless—as I live, and as all the earth shall be filled with the glory of the LORD— ²²none of the people who have seen my glory and the signs that I did in Egypt and in the wilderness, and yet have tested me these ten times and have not obeyed my voice, ²³shall see the land that I swore to give to your ancestors; none of those who despised me shall see it. ²⁴But my servant Caleb, because he has a different spirit and has followed me wholeheartedly, I will bring into the land into which he went, and his descendants shall possess it. ²⁵Now, since the Amalekites and the Canaanites live in the valleys, turn tomorrow and set out for the wilderness by the way to the Red Sea."ᵃ

ᵃ 14.25 Or *Sea of Reeds*

AN ATTEMPTED INVASION IS REPULSED

26 And the LORD spoke to Moses and to Aaron, saying: 27How long shall this wicked congregation complain against me? I have heard the complaints of the Israelites, which they complain against me. 28Say to them, "As I live," says the LORD, "I will do to you the very things I heard you say: 29your dead bodies shall fall in this very wilderness; and of all your number, included in the census, from twenty years old and upward, who have complained against me, 30not one of you shall come into the land in which I swore to settle you, except Caleb son of Jephunneh and Joshua son of Nun. 31But your little ones, who you said would become booty, I will bring in, and they shall know the land that you have despised. 32But as for you, your dead bodies shall fall in this wilderness. 33And your children shall be shepherds in the wilderness for forty years, and shall suffer for your faithlessness, until the last of your dead bodies lies in the wilderness. 34According to the number of the days in which you spied out the land, forty days, for every day a year, you shall bear your iniquity, forty years, and you shall know my displeasure." 35I the LORD have spoken; surely I will do thus to all this wicked congregation gathered together against me: in this wilderness they shall come to a full end, and there they shall die.

GOD'S PARDON PREPARES

US FOR GREATER

SERVICE IN HIS NAME.

36 And the men whom Moses sent to spy out the land, who returned and made all the congregation complain against him by bringing a bad report about the land— 37the men who brought an unfavorable report about the land died by a plague before the LORD. 38But Joshua son of Nun and Caleb son of Jephunneh alone remained alive, of those men who went to spy out the land.

39 When Moses told these words to all the Israelites, the people mourned greatly. 40They rose early in the morning and went up to the heights of the hill country, saying, "Here we are. We will go up to the place that the LORD has promised, for we have sinned." 41But Moses said, "Why do you continue to transgress the command of the LORD? That will not succeed. 42Do not go up, for the LORD is not with you; do not let yourselves be struck down before your enemies. 43For the Amalekites and the Canaanites will confront you there, and you shall fall by the sword; because you have turned back from following the LORD, the LORD will not be with you." 44But they presumed to go up to the heights of the hill country, even though the ark of the covenant of the LORD, and Moses, had not left the camp. 45Then the Amalekites and the Canaanites who lived in that hill country came down and defeated them, pursuing them as far as Hormah.

VARIOUS OFFERINGS

15 The LORD spoke to Moses, saying: 2Speak to the Israelites and say to them: When you come into the land you are to inhabit, which I am giving you, 3and you make an offering by fire to the LORD from the herd or from the flock—whether a burnt offering or a sacrifice, to fulfill a vow or as a freewill offering or at your appointed festivals—to make a pleasing odor for the LORD, 4then whoever presents such an offering to the LORD shall present also a grain offering, one-tenth of an ephah of choice flour, mixed with one-fourth of a hin of oil. 5Moreover, you shall offer one-fourth of a hin of wine as a drink offering with the burnt offering or the sacrifice, for each lamb. 6For a ram, you shall offer a grain offering, two-tenths of an ephah of choice flour mixed with one-third of a hin of oil; 7and as a drink offering you shall offer one-third of a hin of wine, a pleasing odor to the LORD. 8When you offer a bull as a burnt offering or a sacrifice, to fulfill a vow or as an offering of well-being to the LORD, 9then you shall present with the bull a grain offering, three-tenths of an ephah of choice flour, mixed with half a hin of oil, 10and you shall present as a drink offering half a hin of wine, as an offering by fire, a pleasing odor to the LORD. 11 Thus it shall be done for each ox or ram, or for each of the male lambs or the kids. 12According to the number that you offer, so you shall do with each and every one. 13Every native Israelite shall do these things in this way, in presenting an offering by fire, a pleasing odor to the LORD. 14An alien who lives with you, or who takes up permanent residence among you, and wishes to offer an offering by fire, a pleasing odor to the LORD, shall do as you do. 15As for the assembly, there shall be for both you and the resident alien a single statute, a perpetual statute throughout your generations; you and the alien shall be alike before the LORD. 16You and the alien who resides with you shall have the same law and the same ordinance.

17 The LORD spoke to Moses, saying: 18Speak to the Israelites and say to them: After you come into the land to which I am bringing you, 19whenever you eat of the bread of the land, you shall present a donation to the LORD. 20From your first batch of dough you shall present a loaf as a donation; you shall present it just as you present a donation from the threshing floor. 21Throughout your generations you shall give to the LORD a donation from the first of your batch of dough.

22 But if you unintentionally fail to observe all these commandments that the LORD has spoken to Moses— 23everything that the LORD has commanded you by Moses, from the day the LORD gave commandment and thereafter, throughout your generations— 24then if it was done unintentionally without the knowledge of the congregation, the whole congregation shall offer one young bull for a burnt offering, a pleasing odor to the LORD, together with its grain offering and its drink offering, according to the ordinance, and one male goat for a sin offering. 25The priest shall make atonement for all the congregation of the Israelites, and they shall be forgiven; it was unintentional, and they have brought their offering, an offering by fire to the LORD, and their sin offering before the LORD, for their error. 26All the congregation of the Israelites shall be forgiven, as well as the aliens residing among them, because the whole people was involved in the error.

27 An individual who sins unintentionally shall present a female goat a year old for a sin offering. 28And the priest shall make atonement before the LORD for the one who commits an error, when it is unintentional, to make atonement for the person, who then shall be forgiven. 29For both the native among the Israelites and the alien residing among them—you shall have the same law for anyone who acts in error. 30But whoever acts high-handedly, whether a native or an alien, affronts the LORD, and shall be cut off from among the people. 31Because of having despised the word of the LORD and broken his commandment, such a person shall be utterly cut off and bear the guilt.

PENALTY FOR VIOLATING THE SABBATH

32 When the Israelites were in the wilderness, they found a man gathering sticks on the sabbath day. 33Those who found him gathering sticks brought him to Moses, Aaron, and to the whole congregation. 34They put him in custody, because it was not clear what should be done to him. 35Then the LORD said to Moses, "The man shall be put to death; all the congregation shall stone him outside the camp." 36The whole congregation brought him outside the camp and stoned him to death, just as the LORD had commanded Moses.

FRINGES ON GARMENTS

37 The LORD said to Moses: 38Speak to the Israelites, and tell them to make fringes on the corners of their garments throughout their generations and to put a blue cord on the fringe at each corner. 39You have the fringe so that, when you see it, you will remember all the commandments of the LORD and do them, and not follow the lust of your own heart and your own eyes. 40So you shall remember and do all my commandments, and you shall be holy to your God. 41I am the LORD your God, who brought you out of the land of Egypt, to be your God: I am the LORD your God.

REVOLT OF KORAH, DATHAN, AND ABIRAM

16 Now Korah son of Izhar son of Kohath son of Levi, along with Dathan and Abiram sons of Eliab, and On son of Peleth— descendants of Reuben—took 2two hundred fifty Israelite men, leaders of the congregation, chosen from the assembly, well-known men,ª and they confronted Moses. 3They assembled against Moses and against Aaron, and said to them, "You have gone too far! All the congregation are holy, every one of them, and the LORD is among them. So why then do you exalt yourselves above the assembly of the LORD?" 4When Moses heard it, he fell on his face. 5Then he said to Korah and all his company, "In the morning the LORD will make known who is his, and who is holy, and who will be allowed to approach him; the one whom he will choose he will allow to approach him. 6Do this: take censers, Korah and all yourᵇ company, 7and tomorrow put fire in them, and lay incense on them before the LORD; and the man whom the LORD chooses shall be the holy one. You Levites have gone too far!" 8Then Moses said to Korah, "Hear now, you Levites! 9Is it too little for you that the God of Israel has separated you from the congregation of Israel, to allow you to approach him in order to perform the duties of the LORD's tabernacle, and

to stand before the congregation and serve them? 10He has allowed you to approach him, and all your brother Levites with you; yet you seek the priesthood as well! 11Therefore you and all your company have gathered together against the LORD. What is Aaron that you rail against him?"

12 Moses sent for Dathan and Abiram sons of Eliab; but they said, "We will not come! 13Is it too little that you have brought us up out of a land flowing with milk and honey to kill us in the wilderness, that you must also lord it over us? 14It is clear you have not brought us into a land flowing with milk and honey, or given us an inheritance of fields and vineyards. Would you put out the eyes of these men? We will not come!"

15 Moses was very angry and said to the LORD, "Pay no attention to their offering. I have not taken one donkey from them, and I have not harmed any one of them." 16And Moses said to Korah, "As for you and all your company, be present tomorrow before the LORD, you and they and Aaron; 17and let each one of you take his censer, and put incense on it, and each one of you present his censer before the LORD, two hundred fifty censers; you also, and Aaron, each his censer." 18So each man took his censer, and they put fire in the censers and laid incense on them, and they stood at the entrance of the tent of meeting with Moses and Aaron. 19Then Korah assembled the whole congregation against them at the entrance of the tent of meeting. And the glory of the LORD appeared to the whole congregation.

20 Then the LORD spoke to Moses and to Aaron, saying: 21Separate yourselves from this congregation, so that I may consume them in a moment. 22They fell on their faces, and said, "O God, the God of the spirits of all flesh, shall one person sin and you become angry with the whole congregation?"

23 And the LORD spoke to Moses, saying: 24Say to the congregation:

ª 16.2 Cn: Heb and they confronted Moses, and two hundred fifty men… well-known men ᵇ 16.6 Heb his

Get away from the dwellings of Korah, Dathan, and Abiram. 25So Moses got up and went to Dathan and Abiram; the elders of Israel followed him. 26He said to the congregation, "Turn away from the tents of these wicked men, and touch nothing of theirs, or you will be swept away for all their sins." 27So they got away from the dwellings of Korah, Dathan, and Abiram; and Dathan and Abiram came out and stood at the entrance of their tents, together with their wives, their children, and their little ones. 28And Moses said, "This is how you shall know that the LORD has sent me to do all these works; it has not been of my own accord: 29If these people die a natural death, or if a natural fate comes on them, then the LORD has not sent me. 30But if the LORD creates something new, and the ground opens its mouth and swallows them up, with all that belongs to them, and they go down alive into Sheol, then you shall know that these men have despised the LORD."

WHEN WE EXPERIENCE

SPIRITUAL FAMINE, WE

NEED TO TRUST THE LORD

GOD TO LET THE HOLY

SPIRIT FILL US WITH THE

PRESENCE OF JESUS CHRIST.

31 As soon as he finished speaking all these words, the ground under them was split apart. 32The earth opened its mouth and swallowed them up, along with their households—everyone who belonged to Korah and all their goods. 33So they with all that belonged to them went down alive into Sheol; the earth closed over them, and they perished from the midst of the assembly. 34All Israel around them fled at their outcry, for they said, "The earth will swallow us too!" 35And fire came out

from the LORD and consumed the two hundred fifty men offering the incense.

36a Then the LORD spoke to Moses, saying: 37Tell Eleazar son of Aaron the priest to take the censers out of the blaze; then scatter the fire far and wide. 38For the censers of these sinners have become holy at the cost of their lives. Make them into hammered plates as a covering for the altar, for they presented them before the LORD and they became holy. Thus they shall be a sign to the Israelites. 39So Eleazar the priest took the bronze censers that had been presented by those who were burned; and they were hammered out as a covering for the altar— 40a reminder to the Israelites that no outsider, who is not of the descendants of Aaron, shall approach to offer incense before the LORD, so as not to become like Korah and his company—just as the LORD had said to him through Moses.

41 On the next day, however, the whole congregation of the Israelites rebelled against Moses and against Aaron, saying, "You have killed the people of the LORD." 42And when the congregation had assembled against them, Moses and Aaron turned toward the tent of meeting; the cloud had covered it and the glory of the LORD appeared. 43Then Moses and Aaron came to the front of the tent of meeting, 44and the LORD spoke to Moses, saying, 45"Get away from this congregation, so that I may consume them in a moment." And they fell on their faces. 46Moses said to Aaron, "Take your censer, put fire on it from the altar and lay incense on it, and carry it quickly to the congregation and make atonement for them. For wrath has gone out from the LORD; the plague has begun." 47So Aaron took it as Moses had ordered, and ran into the middle of the assembly, where the plague had already begun among the people. He put on the incense, and made atonement for people. 48He stood between the dead and the living; and the plague was stopped. 49Those who died by the

a 16.36 Ch 17.1 in Heb

plague were fourteen thousand seven hundred, besides those who died in the affair of Korah. ⁵⁰When the plague was stopped, Aaron returned to Moses at the entrance of the tent of meeting.

THE BUDDING OF AARON'S ROD

17 ᵃThe LORD spoke to Moses, saying: ²Speak to the Israelites, and get twelve staffs from them, one for each ancestral house, from all the leaders of their ancestral houses. Write each man's name on his staff, ³and write Aaron's name on the staff of Levi. For there shall be one staff for the head of each ancestral house. ⁴Place them in the tent of meeting before the covenant,ᵇ where I meet with you. ⁵And the staff of the man whom I choose shall sprout; thus I will put a stop to the complaints of the Israelites that they continually make against you. ⁶Moses spoke to the Israelites; and all their leaders gave him staffs, one for each leader, according to their ancestral houses, twelve staffs; and the staff of Aaron was among theirs. ⁷So Moses placed the staffs before the LORD in the tent of the covenant.ᵇ

8 When Moses went into the tent of the covenantᵇ on the next day, the staff of Aaron for the house of Levi had sprouted. It put forth buds, produced blossoms, and bore ripe almonds. ⁹Then Moses brought out all the staffs from before the LORD to all the Israelites; and they looked, and each man took his staff. ¹⁰And the LORD said to Moses, "Put back the staff of Aaron before the covenant,ᵇ to be kept as a warning to rebels, so that you may make an end of their complaints against me, or else they will die." ¹¹Moses did so; just as the LORD commanded him, so he did.

12 The Israelites said to Moses, "We are perishing; we are lost, all of us are lost! ¹³Everyone who approaches the tabernacle of the LORD will die. Are we all to perish?"

RESPONSIBILITY OF PRIESTS AND LEVITES

18 The LORD said to Aaron: You and your sons and your an-cestral house with you shall bear responsibility for offenses connected with the sanctuary, while you and your sons alone shall bear responsibility for offenses connected with the priesthood. ²So bring with you also your brothers of the tribe of Levi, your ancestral tribe, in order that they may be joined to you, and serve you while you and your sons with you are in front of the tent of the covenant.ᵇ ³They shall perform duties for you and for the whole tent. But they must not approach either the utensils of the sanctuary or the altar, otherwise both they and you will die. ⁴They are attached to you in order to perform the duties of the tent of meeting, for all the service of the tent; no outsider shall approach you. ⁵You yourselves shall perform the duties of the sanctuary and the duties of the altar, so that wrath may never again come upon the Israelites. ⁶It is I who now take your brother Levites from among the Israelites; they are now yours as a gift, dedicated to the LORD, to perform the service of the tent of meeting. ⁷But you and your sons with you shall diligently perform your priestly duties in all that concerns the altar and the area behind the curtain. I give your priesthood as a gift;ᶜ any outsider who approaches shall be put to death.

THE PRIESTS' PORTION

8 The LORD spoke to Aaron: I have given you charge of the offerings made to me, all the holy gifts of the Israelites; I have given them to you and your sons as a priestly portion due you in perpetuity. ⁹This shall be yours from the most holy things, reserved from the fire: every offering of theirs that they render to me as a most holy thing, whether grain offering, sin offering, or guilt offering, shall belong to you and your sons. ¹⁰As a most holy thing you shall eat it; every male may eat it; it shall be holy to you. ¹¹This also is yours: I have given to you, together

---

ᵃ 17.1 Ch 17.16 in Heb   ᵇ 17.4,7,8,10; 18.2 Or *treaty*, or *testimony*; Heb *eduth*   ᶜ 18.7 Heb *as a service of gift*

with your sons and daughters, as a perpetual due, whatever is set aside from the gifts of all the elevation offerings of the Israelites; everyone who is clean in your house may eat them. 12 All the best of the oil and all the best of the wine and of the grain, the choice produce that they give to the LORD, I have given to you. 13 The first fruits of all that is in their land, which they bring to the LORD, shall be yours; everyone who is clean in your house may eat of it. 14 Every devoted thing in Israel shall be yours. 15 The first issue of the womb of all creatures, human and animal, which is offered to the LORD, shall be yours; but the firstborn of human beings you shall redeem, and the firstborn of unclean animals you shall redeem. 16 Their redemption price, reckoned from one month of age, you shall fix at five shekels of silver, according to the shekel of the sanctuary (that is, twenty gerahs). 17 But the firstborn of a cow, or the firstborn of a sheep, or the firstborn of a goat, you shall not redeem; they are holy. You shall dash their blood on the altar, and shall turn their fat into smoke as an offering by fire for a pleasing odor to the LORD; 18 but their flesh shall be yours, just as the breast that is elevated and as the right thigh are yours. 19 All the holy offerings that the Israelites present to the LORD I have given to you, together with your sons and daughters, as a perpetual due; it is a covenant of salt forever before the LORD for you and your descendants as well. 20 Then the LORD said to Aaron: You shall have no allotment in their land, nor shall you have any share among them; I am your share and your possession among the Israelites.

21 To the Levites I have given every tithe in Israel for a possession in return for the service that they perform, the service in the tent of meeting. 22 From now on the Israelites shall no longer approach the tent of meeting, or else they will incur guilt and die. 23 But the Levites shall perform the service of the tent of meeting, and they shall bear responsibility for their own offenses; it shall be a perpetual statute throughout your generations. But among the Israelites they shall have no allotment, 24 because I have given to the Levites as their portion the tithe of the Israelites, which they set apart as an offering to the LORD. Therefore I have said of them that they shall have no allotment among the Israelites.

25 Then the LORD spoke to Moses, saying: 26 You shall speak to the Levites, saying: When you receive from the Israelites the tithe that I have given you from them for your portion, you shall set apart an offering from it to the LORD, a tithe of the tithe. 27 It shall be reckoned to you as your gift, the same as the grain of the threshing floor and the fullness of the wine press. 28 Thus you also shall set apart an offering to the LORD from all the tithes that you receive from the Israelites; and from them you shall give the LORD's offering to the priest Aaron. 29 Out of all the gifts to you, you shall set apart every offering due to the LORD; the best of all of them is the part to be consecrated. 30 Say also to them: When you have set apart the best of it, then the rest shall be reckoned to the Levites as produce of the threshing floor, and as produce of the wine press. 31 You may eat it in any place, you and your households; for it is your payment for your service in the tent of meeting. 32 You shall incur no guilt by reason of it, when you have offered the best of it. But you shall not profane the holy gifts of the Israelites, on pain of death.

CEREMONY OF THE RED HEIFER

19 The LORD spoke to Moses and Aaron, saying: 2 This is a statute of the law that the LORD has commanded: Tell the Israelites to bring you a red heifer without defect, in which there is no blemish and on which no yoke has been laid. 3 You shall give it to the priest Eleazar, and it shall be taken outside the camp and slaughtered in his presence. 4 The priest Eleazar shall take some of its blood with his finger and sprinkle it seven times towards the

front of the tent of meeting. ⁵Then the heifer shall be burned in his sight; its skin, its flesh, and its blood, with its dung, shall be burned. ⁶The priest shall take cedarwood, hyssop, and crimson material, and throw them into the fire in which the heifer is burning. ⁷Then the priest shall wash his clothes and bathe his body in water, and afterwards he may come into the camp; but the priest shall remain unclean until evening. ⁸The one who burns the heiferᵃ shall wash his clothes in water and bathe his body in water; he shall remain unclean until evening. ⁹Then someone who is clean shall gather up the ashes of the heifer, and deposit them outside the camp in a clean place; and they shall be kept for the congregation of the Israelites for the water for cleansing. It is a purification offering. ¹⁰The one who gathers the ashes of the heifer shall wash his clothes and be unclean until evening.

This shall be a perpetual statute for the Israelites and for the alien residing among them. ¹¹Those who touch the dead body of any human being shall be unclean seven days. ¹²They shall purify themselves with the water on the third day and on the seventh day, and so be clean; but if they do not purify themselves on the third day and on the seventh day, they will not become clean. ¹³All who touch a corpse, the body of a human being who has died, and do not purify themselves, defile the tabernacle of the LORD; such persons shall be cut off from Israel. Since water for cleansing was not dashed on them, they remain unclean; their uncleanness is still on them.

14 This is the law when someone dies in a tent: everyone who comes into the tent, and everyone who is in the tent, shall be unclean seven days. ¹⁵And every open vessel with no cover fastened on it is unclean. ¹⁶Whoever in the open field touches one who has been killed by a sword, or who has died naturally,ᵇ or a human bone, or a grave, shall be unclean seven days. ¹⁷For the unclean they shall take some ashes of the burnt purification offering, and running water shall be added in a vessel; ¹⁸then a clean person shall take hyssop, dip it in the water, and sprinkle it on the tent, on all the furnishings, on the persons who were there, and on whoever touched the bone, the slain, the corpse, or the grave. ¹⁹The clean person shall sprinkle the unclean ones on the third day and on the seventh day, thus purifying them on the seventh day. Then they shall wash their clothes and bathe themselves in water, and at evening they shall be clean. ²⁰Any who are unclean but do not purify themselves, those persons shall be cut off from the assembly, for they have defiled the sanctuary of the LORD. Since the water for cleansing has not been dashed on them, they are unclean.

21 It shall be a perpetual statute for them. The one who sprinkles the water for cleansing shall wash his clothes, and whoever touches the water for cleansing shall be unclean until evening. ²²Whatever the unclean person touches shall be unclean, and anyone who touches it shall be unclean until evening.

THE WATERS OF MERIBAH

20 The Israelites, the whole congregation, came into the wilderness of Zin in the first month, and the people stayed in Kadesh. Miriam died there, and was buried there.

2 Now there was no water for the congregation; so they gathered together against Moses and against Aaron. ³The people quarreled with Moses and said, "Would that we had died when our kindred died before the LORD! ⁴Why have you brought the assembly of the LORD into this wilderness for us and our livestock to die here? ⁵Why have you brought us up out of Egypt, to bring us to this wretched place? It is no place for grain, or figs, or vines, or pomegranates; and there is no water to drink." ⁶Then Moses and Aaron went away from the assembly to the entrance of

ᵃ 19.8 Heb it ᵇ 19.16 Heb lacks *naturally*

the tent of meeting; they fell on their faces, and the glory of the LORD appeared to them. [7] The LORD spoke to Moses, saying: [8] Take the staff, and assemble the congregation, you and your brother Aaron, and command the rock before their eyes to yield its water. Thus you shall bring water out of the rock for them; thus you shall provide drink for the congregation and their livestock.

GOD CANNOT USE THE

SELF-SUFFICIENT.

[9] So Moses took the staff from before the LORD, as he had commanded him. [10] Moses and Aaron gathered the assembly together before the rock, and he said to them, "Listen, you rebels, shall we bring water for you out of this rock?" [11] Then Moses lifted up his hand and struck the rock twice with his staff; water came out abundantly, and the congregation and their livestock drank. [12] But the LORD said to Moses and Aaron, "Because you did not trust in me, to show my holiness before the eyes of the Israelites, therefore you shall not bring this assembly into the land that I have given them." [13] These are the waters of Meribah, [a] where the people of Israel quarreled with the LORD, and by which he showed his holiness.

PASSAGE THROUGH
EDOM REFUSED

[14] Moses sent messengers from Kadesh to the king of Edom, "Thus says your brother Israel: You know all the adversity that has befallen us: [15] how our ancestors went down to Egypt, and we lived in Egypt a long time; and the Egyptians oppressed us and our ancestors; [16] and when we cried to the LORD, he heard our voice, and sent an angel and brought us out of Egypt; and here we are in Kadesh, a town on the edge of your territory. [17] Now let us pass through your land. We will not pass through field or vineyard, or drink water from any well; we will go along the King's Highway, not turning aside to the right hand or to the left until we have passed through your territory." [18] But Edom said to him, "You shall not pass through, or we will come out with the sword against you." [19] The Israelites said to him, "We will stay on the highway; and if we drink of your water, we and our livestock, then we will pay for it. It is only a small matter; just let us pass through on foot." [20] But he said, "You shall not pass through." And Edom came out against them with a large force, heavily armed. [21] Thus Edom refused to give Israel passage through their territory; so Israel turned away from them.

THE DEATH OF AARON

[22] They set out from Kadesh, and the Israelites, the whole congregation, came to Mount Hor. [23] Then the LORD said to Moses and Aaron at Mount Hor, on the border of the land of Edom, [24] "Let Aaron be gathered to his people. For he shall not enter the land that I have given to the Israelites, because you rebelled against my command at the waters of Meribah. [25] Take Aaron and his son Eleazar, and bring them up Mount Hor; [26] strip Aaron of his vestments, and put them on his son Eleazar. But Aaron shall be gathered to his people, [b] and shall die there." [27] Moses did as the LORD had commanded; they went up Mount Hor in the sight of the whole congregation. [28] Moses stripped Aaron of his vestments, and put them on his son Eleazar; and Aaron died there on the top of the mountain. Moses and Eleazar came down from the mountain. [29] When all the congregation saw that Aaron had died, all the house of Israel mourned for Aaron thirty days.

[a] 20.13 That is *Quarrel*   [b] 20.26 Heb lacks *to his people*

THE BRONZE SERPENT

21 When the Canaanite, the king of Arad, who lived in the Negeb, heard that Israel was coming by the way of Atharim, he fought against Israel and took some of them captive. ²Then Israel made a vow to the LORD and said, "If you will indeed give this people into our hands, then we will utterly destroy their towns." ³The LORD listened to the voice of Israel, and handed over the Canaanites; and they utterly destroyed them and their towns; so the place was called Hormah.ᵃ

4 From Mount Hor they set out by the way to the Red Sea,ᵇ to go around the land of Edom; but the people became impatient on the way. ⁵The people spoke against God and against Moses, "Why have you brought us up out of Egypt to die in the wilderness? For there is no food and no water, and we detest this miserable food." ⁶Then the LORD sent poisonousᶜ serpents among the people, and they bit the people, so that many Israelites died. ⁷The people came to Moses and said, "We have sinned by speaking against the LORD and against you; pray to the LORD to take away the serpents from us." So Moses prayed for the people. ⁸And the LORD said to Moses, "Make a poisonousᵈ serpent, and set it on a pole; and everyone who is bitten shall look at it and live." ⁹So Moses made a serpent of bronze, and put it upon a pole; and whenever a serpent bit someone, that person would look at the serpent of bronze and live.

THE JOURNEY TO MOAB

10 The Israelites set out, and camped in Oboth. ¹¹They set out from Oboth, and camped at Iye-abarim, in the wilderness bordering Moab toward the sunrise. ¹²From there they set out, and camped in the Wadi Zered. ¹³From there they set out, and camped on the other side of the Arnon, inᵉ the wilderness that extends from the boundary of the Amorites; for the Arnon is the boundary of Moab, between Moab and the Amorites. ¹⁴Wherefore it is said in the Book of the Wars of the LORD,

"Waheb in Suphah and the wadis. The Arnon ¹⁵and the slopes of the wadis that extend to the seat of Ar, and lie along the border of Moab."ᶠ

16 From there they continued to Beer;ᵍ that is the well of which the LORD said to Moses, "Gather the people together, and I will give them water." ¹⁷Then Israel sang this song: "Spring up, O well!—Sing to it!— ¹⁸ the well that the leaders sank, that the nobles of the people dug, with the scepter, with the staff." From the wilderness to Mattanah, ¹⁹from Mattanah to Nahaliel, from Nahaliel to Bamoth, ²⁰and from Bamoth to the valley lying in the region of Moab by the top of Pisgah that overlooks the wasteland.ʰ

THE CROSS WAS THE FULFILLMENT OF GOD'S TRANSCENDENT PLAN FOR THE WORLD—A BRIDGE BETWEEN GOD AND PEOPLE WHO ARE IN NEED OF LOVE, FORGIVENESS, MERCY AND A FULL LIFE.

KING SIHON DEFEATED

21 Then Israel sent messengers to King Sihon of the Amorites, saying, ²²"Let me pass through your land; we will not turn aside into field or vineyard; we will not drink the water of any well; we will go by the King's Highway until we have passed through your territory." ²³But Sihon would not allow Israel to pass through his territory. Sihon

---

ᵃ 21.3 Heb Destruction   ᵇ 21.4 Or Sea of Reeds   ᶜ 21.6 Or fiery; Heb seraphim   ᵈ 21.8 Or fiery; Heb seraph   ᵉ 21.13 Gk: Heb which is in   ᶠ 21.15 Meaning of Heb uncertain   ᵍ 21.16 That is Well   ʰ 21.20 Or Jeshimon

gathered all his people together, and went out against Israel to the wilderness; he came to Jahaz, and fought against Israel. 24Israel put him to the sword, and took possession of his land from the Arnon to the Jabbok, as far as to the Ammonites; for the boundary of the Ammonites was strong. 25Israel took all these towns, and Israel settled in all the towns of the Amorites, in Heshbon, and in all its villages. 26For Heshbon was the city of King Sihon of the Amorites, who had fought against the former king of Moab and captured all his land as far as the Arnon. 27Therefore the ballad singers say,

"Come to Heshbon, let it be built;
    let the city of Sihon be
        established.
28 For fire came out
        from Heshbon,
    flame from the city of Sihon.
It devoured Ar of Moab,
    and swallowed upᵃ the
        heights of the Arnon.
29 Woe to you, O Moab!
You are undone, O people
        of Chemosh!
He has made his sons fugitives,
    and his daughters captives,
    to an Amorite king, Sihon.
30 So their posterity perished
    from Heshbonᵇ to Dibon,
    and we laid waste until fire
        spread to Medeba."ᶜ

31 Thus Israel settled in the land of the Amorites. 32Moses sent to spy out Jazer; and they captured its villages, and dispossessed the Amorites who were there.

KING OG DEFEATED

33 Then they turned and went up the road to Bashan; and King Og of Bashan came out against them, he and all his people, to battle at Edrei. 34But the LORD said to Moses, "Do not be afraid of him; for I have given him into your hand, with all his people, and all his land. You shall do to him as you did to King Sihon of the Amorites, who ruled in Heshbon." 35So they killed him, his sons, and all his people, until there was no survivor left; and they took possession of his land.

BALAK SUMMONS BALAAM TO CURSE ISRAEL

22 The Israelites set out, and camped in the plains of Moab across the Jordan from Jericho. 2Now Balak son of Zippor saw all that Israel had done to the Amorites. 3Moab was in great dread of the people, because they were so numerous; Moab was overcome with fear of the people of Israel. 4And Moab said to the elders of Midian, "This horde will now lick up all that is around us, as an ox licks up the grass of the field." Now Balak son of Zippor was king of Moab at that time. 5He sent messengers to Balaam son of Beor at Pethor, which is on the Euphrates, in the land of Amaw,ᵈ to summon him, saying, "A people has come out of Egypt; they have spread over the face of the earth, and they have settled next to me. 6Come now, curse this people for me, since they are stronger than I; perhaps I shall be able to defeat them and drive them from the land; for I know that whomever you bless is blessed, and whomever you curse is cursed."

7 So the elders of Moab and the elders of Midian departed with the fees for divination in their hand; and they came to Balaam, and gave him Balak's message. 8He said to them, "Stay here tonight, and I will bring back word to you, just as the LORD speaks to me"; so the officials of Moab stayed with Balaam. 9God came to Balaam and said, "Who are these men with you?" 10Balaam said to God, "King Balak son of Zippor of Moab, has sent me this message: 11'A people has come out of Egypt and has spread over the face of the earth; now come, curse them for me; perhaps I shall be able to fight against them and drive them out.'" 12God said to Balaam, "You shall not go with them; you shall not curse the people, for they are blessed." 13So Balaam rose in the morning, and said

ᵃ 21.28 Gk: Heb and the lords of
ᵇ 21.30 Gk: Heb we have shot at them; Heshbon has perished   ᶜ 21.30 Compare Sam Gk: Meaning of MT uncertain
ᵈ 22.5 Or land of his kinsfolk

to the officials of Balak, "Go to your own land, for the LORD has refused to let me go with you." ¹⁴So the officials of Moab rose and went to Balak, and said, "Balaam refuses to come with us."

15 Once again Balak sent officials, more numerous and more distinguished than these. ¹⁶They came to Balaam and said to him, "Thus says Balak son of Zippor: 'Do not let anything hinder you from coming to me; ¹⁷for I will surely do you great honor, and whatever you say to me I will do; come, curse this people for me.' " ¹⁸But Balaam replied to the servants of Balak, "Although Balak were to give me his house full of silver and gold, I could not go beyond the command of the LORD my God, to do less or more. ¹⁹You remain here, as the others did, so that I may learn what more the LORD may say to me." ²⁰That night God came to Balaam and said to him, "If the men have come to summon you, get up and go with them; but do only what I tell you to do." ²¹So Balaam got up in the morning, saddled his donkey, and went with the officials of Moab.

BALAAM, THE DONKEY, AND THE ANGEL

22 God's anger was kindled because he was going, and the angel of the LORD took his stand in the road as his adversary. Now he was riding on the donkey, and his two servants were with him. ²³The donkey saw the angel of the LORD standing in the road, with a drawn sword in his hand; so the donkey turned off the road, and went into the field; and Balaam struck the donkey, to turn it back onto the road. ²⁴Then the angel of the LORD stood in a narrow path between the vineyards, with a wall on either side. ²⁵When the donkey saw the angel of the LORD, it scraped against the wall, and scraped Balaam's foot against the wall; so he struck it again. ²⁶Then the angel of the LORD went ahead, and stood in a narrow place, where there was no way to turn either to the right or to the left. ²⁷When the donkey saw the angel of the LORD, it lay down

under Balaam; and Balaam's anger was kindled, and he struck the donkey with his staff. ²⁸Then the LORD opened the mouth of the donkey, and it said to Balaam, "What have I done to you, that you have struck me these three times?" ²⁹Balaam said to the donkey, "Because you have made a fool of me! I wish I had a sword in my hand! I would kill you right now!" ³⁰But the donkey said to Balaam, "Am I not your donkey, which you have ridden all your life to this day? Have I been in the habit of treating you this way?" And he said, "No."

31 Then the LORD opened the eyes of Balaam, and he saw the angel of the LORD standing in the road, with his drawn sword in his hand; and he bowed down, falling on his face. ³²The angel of the LORD said to him, "Why have you struck your donkey these three times? I have come out as an adversary, because your way is perverse[a] before me. ³³The donkey saw me, and turned away from me these three times. If it had not turned away from me, surely just now I would have killed you and let it live." ³⁴Then Balaam said to the angel of the LORD, "I have sinned, for I did not know that you were standing in the road to oppose me. Now therefore, if it is displeasing to you, I will return home." ³⁵The angel of the LORD said to Balaam, "Go with the men; but speak only what I tell you to speak." So Balaam went on with the officials of Balak.

36 When Balak heard that Balaam had come, he went out to meet him at Ir-moab, on the boundary formed by the Arnon, at the farthest point of the boundary. ³⁷Balak said to Balaam, "Did I not send to summon you? Why did you not come to me? Am I not able to honor you?" ³⁸Balaam said to Balak, "I have come to you now, but do I have power to say just anything? The word God puts in my mouth, that is what I must say." ³⁹Then Balaam went with Balak, and they came to Kiriath-huzoth. ⁴⁰Balak sacrificed oxen and sheep,

---

a 22.32 Meaning of Heb uncertain

and sent them to Balaam and to the officials who were with him.

BALAAM'S FIRST ORACLE

41 On the next day Balak took Balaam and brought him up to Bamoth-baal; and from there he could see part of the people of
23 Israel.ᵃ ¹Then Balaam said to Balak, "Build me seven altars here, and prepare seven bulls and seven rams for me." ²Balak did as Balaam had said; and Balak and Balaam offered a bull and a ram on each altar. ³Then Balaam said to Balak, "Stay here beside your burnt offerings while I go aside. Perhaps the LORD will come to meet me. Whatever he shows me I will tell you." And he went to a bare height.

4 Then God met Balaam; and Balaam said to him, "I have arranged the seven altars, and have offered a bull and a ram on each altar." ⁵The LORD put a word in Balaam's mouth, and said, "Return to Balak, and this is what you must say." ⁶So he returned to Balak,ᵇ who was standing beside his burnt offerings with all the officials of Moab. ⁷Then Balaamᶜ uttered his oracle, saying:

"Balak has brought me
        from Aram,
    the king of Moab from the
        eastern mountains:
'Come, curse Jacob for me;
    Come, denounce Israel!'
8 How can I curse whom God
        has not cursed?
    How can I denounce those
        whom the LORD has
        not denounced?
9 For from the top of the
        crags I see him,
    from the hills I behold him.
Here is a people living alone,
    and not reckoning itself
        among the nations!
10 Who can count the dust of Jacob,
    or number the dust-cloudᵈ
        of Israel?
Let me die the death of
        the upright,
    and let my end be like his!"

11 Then Balak said to Balaam, "What have you done to me? I brought you to curse my enemies, but now

you have done nothing but bless them." ¹²He answered, "Must I not take care to say what the LORD puts into my mouth?"

BALAAM'S SECOND ORACLE

13 So Balak said to him, "Come with me to another place from which you may see them; you shall see only part of them, and shall not see them all; then curse them for me from there." ¹⁴So he took him to the field of Zophim, to the top of Pisgah. He built seven altars, and offered a bull and a ram on each altar. ¹⁵Balaam said to Balak, "Stand here beside your burnt offerings, while I meet the LORD over there." ¹⁶The LORD met Balaam, put a word into his mouth, and said, "Return to Balak, and this is what you shall say." ¹⁷When he came to him, he was standing beside his burnt offerings with the officials of Moab. Balak said to him, "What has the LORD said?" ¹⁸Then Balaam uttered his oracle, saying:

"Rise, Balak, and hear;
    listen to me, O son of Zippor:
19 God is not a human being,
        that he should lie,
    or a mortal, that he should
        change his mind.
Has he promised, and will
        he not do it?
Has he spoken, and will
        he not fulfill it?
20 See, I received a command
        to bless;
    he has blessed, and I
        cannot revoke it.
21 He has not beheld misfortune
        in Jacob;
    nor has he seen trouble
        in Israel.
The LORD their God is
        with them,
    acclaimed as a king
        among them.
22 God, who brings them
        out of Egypt,
    is like the horns of a wild
        ox for them.

ᵃ 22.41 Heb lacks *of Israel*   ᵇ 23.6 Heb *him*
ᶜ 23.7 Heb *he*   ᵈ 23.10 Or *fourth part*

23 Surely there is no enchantment
   against Jacob,
   no divination against Israel;
   now it shall be said of Jacob
   and Israel,
   'See what God has done!'
24 Look, a people rising up
   like a lioness,
   and rousing itself like a lion!
It does not lie down until it
   has eaten the prey
   and drunk the blood
   of the slain."
25 Then Balak said to Balaam,
"Do not curse them at all, and do
not bless them at all." 26But Balaam
answered Balak, "Did I not tell you,
'Whatever the LORD says, that is
what I must do'?"
27 So Balak said to Balaam, "Come
now, I will take you to another place;
perhaps it will please God that you
may curse them for me from there."
28So Balak took Balaam to the top
of Peor, which overlooks the waste-
land.ᵃ 29Balaam said to Balak, "Build
me seven altars here, and prepare
seven bulls and seven rams for me."
30So Balak did as Balaam had said,
and offered a bull and a ram on each
altar.

BALAAM'S THIRD ORACLE

24 Now Balaam saw that it
pleased the LORD to bless
Israel, so he did not go, as at other
times, to look for omens, but set his
face toward the wilderness. 2Balaam
looked up and saw Israel camping
tribe by tribe. Then the spirit of God
came upon him, 3and he uttered his
oracle, saying:
"The oracle of Balaam
   son of Beor,
   the oracle of the man
   whose eye is clear,ᵇ
4 the oracle of one who hears
   the words of God,
   who sees the vision of
   the Almighty,ᶜ
   who falls down, but with
   eyes uncovered:
5 how fair are your tents, O Jacob,
   your encampments, O Israel!
6 Like palm groves that
   stretch far away,
   like gardens beside a river,

like aloes that the LORD
   has planted,
   like cedar trees beside
   the waters.
7 Water shall flow from his buckets,
   and his seed shall have
   abundant water,
   his king shall be higher
   than Agag,
   and his kingdom shall
   be exalted.
8 God who brings him out of Egypt,
   is like the horns of a
   wild ox for him;
he shall devour the nations
   that are his foes
   and break their bones.
He shall strike with
   his arrows.ᵈ
9 He crouched, he lay down
   like a lion,
   and like a lioness; who
   will rouse him up?
Blessed is everyone who
   blesses you,
   and cursed is everyone
   who curses you."
10 Then Balak's anger was kindled
against Balaam, and he struck his
hands together. Balak said to Balaam,
"I summoned you to curse my enemies, but instead you have blessed
them these three times. 11Now be
off with you! Go home! I said, 'I will
reward you richly,' but the LORD
has denied you any reward." 12And
Balaam said to Balak, "Did I not tell
your messengers whom you sent to
me, 13'If Balak should give me his
house full of silver and gold, I would
not be able to go beyond the word of
the LORD, to do either good or bad
of my own will; what the LORD says,
that is what I will say'? 14So now, I
am going to my people; let me advise
you what this people will do to your
people in days to come."

BALAAM'S FOURTH ORACLE

15 So he uttered his oracle, saying:
"The oracle of Balaam son of Beor,
   the oracle of the man
   whose eye is clear,ᵇ

ᵃ 23.28 Or *overlooks Jeshimon*   ᵇ 24.3,15 Or
closed or open   ᶜ 24.4 Traditional
rendering of Heb *Shaddai*   ᵈ 24.8 Meaning
of Heb uncertain

16 the oracle of one who hears
the words of God,
and knows the knowledge
of the Most High,ᵃ
who sees the vision of the
Almighty,ᵇ
who falls down, but with
his eyes uncovered:
17 I see him, but not now;
I behold him, but not near—
a star shall come out of Jacob,
and a scepter shall rise
out of Israel;
it shall crush the borderlandsᶜ
of Moab,
and the territoryᵈ of all
the Shethites.
18 Edom will become a possession,
Seir a possession of
its enemies,ᵉ
while Israel does valiantly.
19 One out of Jacob shall rule,
and destroy the survivors of Ir."
20 Then he looked on Amalek, and
uttered his oracle, saying:
"First among the nations
was Amalek,
but its end is to perish forever."
21 Then he looked on the Kenite,
and uttered his oracle, saying:
"Enduring is your dwelling place,
and your nest is set in the rock;
22 yet Kain is destined for burning.
How long shall Asshur take
you away captive?"
23 Again he uttered his oracle,
saying:
"Alas, who shall live when
God does this?
24 But ships shall come
from Kittim
and shall afflict Asshur and Eber;
and he also shall perish
forever."
25 Then Balaam got up and went
back to his place, and Balak also
went his way.

WORSHIP OF BAAL OF PEOR

25 While Israel was staying at
Shittim, the people began
to have sexual relations with the
women of Moab. 2 These invited the
people to the sacrifices of their gods,
and the people ate and bowed down
to their gods. 3 Thus Israel yoked
itself to the Baal of Peor, and the
LORD's anger was kindled against Israel. 4 The LORD said to Moses, "Take
all the chiefs of the people, and impale them in the sun before the
LORD, in order that the fierce anger
of the LORD may turn away from Israel." 5 And Moses said to the judges
of Israel, "Each of you shall kill any of
your people who have yoked themselves to the Baal of Peor."

6 Just then one of the Israelites came and brought a Midianite woman into his family, in the
sight of Moses and in the sight of
the whole congregation of the Israelites, while they were weeping at
the entrance of the tent of meeting.
7 When Phinehas son of Eleazar, son
of Aaron the priest, saw it, he got up
and left the congregation. Taking
a spear in his hand, 8 he went after
the Israelite man into the tent, and
pierced the two of them, the Israelite and the woman, through the
belly. So the plague was stopped
among the people of Israel. 9 Nevertheless those that died by the plague
were twenty-four thousand.

10 The LORD spoke to Moses, saying: 11 "Phinehas son of Eleazar, son
of Aaron the priest, has turned back
my wrath from the Israelites by
manifesting such zeal among them
on my behalf that in my jealousy
I did not consume the Israelites.
12 Therefore say, 'I hereby grant him
my covenant of peace. 13 It shall be
for him and for his descendants after
him a covenant of perpetual priesthood, because he was zealous for his
God, and made atonement for the Israelites.' "

14 The name of the slain Israelite
man, who was killed with the Midianite woman, was Zimri son of Salu,
head of an ancestral house belonging to the Simeonites. 15 The name
of the Midianite woman who was
killed was Cozbi daughter of Zur,
who was the head of a clan, an ancestral house in Midian.

16 The LORD said to Moses, 17 "Harass the Midianites, and defeat

ᵃ 24.16 Or of Elyon ᵇ 24.16 Traditional
rendering of Heb Shaddai ᶜ 24.17 Or
forehead ᵈ 24.17 Some Mss read skull
ᵉ 24.18 Heb Seir, its enemies, a possession

them; 18for they have harassed you by the trickery with which they deceived you in the affair of Peor, and in the affair of Cozbi, the daughter of a leader of Midian, their sister; she was killed on the day of the plague that resulted from Peor."

A CENSUS OF THE NEW GENERATION

26 After the plague the LORD said to Moses and to Eleazar son of Aaron the priest, 2"Take a census of the whole congregation of the Israelites, from twenty years old and upward, by their ancestral houses, everyone in Israel able to go to war." 3Moses and Eleazar the priest spoke with them in the plains of Moab by the Jordan opposite Jericho, saying, 4"Take a census of the people,ª from twenty years old and upward," as the LORD commanded Moses.

The Israelites, who came out of the land of Egypt, were:

5 Reuben, the firstborn of Israel. The descendants of Reuben: of Hanoch, the clan of the Hanochites; of Pallu, the clan of the Palluites; 6of Hezron, the clan of the Hezronites; of Carmi, the clan of the Carmites. 7These are the clans of the Reubenites; the number of those enrolled was forty-three thousand seven hundred thirty. 8And the descendants of Pallu: Eliab. 9The descendants of Eliab: Nemuel, Dathan, and Abiram. These are the same Dathan and Abiram, chosen from the congregation, who rebelled against Moses and Aaron in the company of Korah, when they rebelled against the LORD, 10and the earth opened its mouth and swallowed them up along with Korah, when that company died, when the fire devoured two hundred fifty men; and they became a warning. 11Notwithstanding, the sons of Korah did not die.

12 The descendants of Simeon by their clans: of Nemuel, the clan of the Nemuelites; of Jamin, the clan of the Jaminites; of Jachin, the clan of the Jachinites; 13of Zerah, the clan of the Zerahites; of Shaul, the clan of the Shaulites.b 14These are the clans

of the Simeonites, twenty-two thousand two hundred.

15 The children of Gad by their clans: of Zephon, the clan of the Zephonites; of Haggi, the clan of the Haggites; of Shuni, the clan of the Shunites; 16of Ozni, the clan of the Oznites; of Eri, the clan of the Erites; 17of Arod, the clan of the Arodites; of Areli, the clan of the Arelites. 18These are the clans of the Gadites: the number of those enrolled was forty thousand five hundred.

19 The sons of Judah: Er and Onan; Er and Onan died in the land of Canaan. 20The descendants of Judah by their clans were: of Shelah, the clan of the Shelanites; of Perez, the clan of the Perezites; of Zerah, the clan of the Zerahites. 21The descendants of Perez were: of Hezron, the clan of the Hezronites; of Hamul, the clan of the Hamulites. 22These are the clans of Judah: the number of those enrolled was seventy-six thousand five hundred.

23 The descendants of Issachar by their clans: of Tola, the clan of the Tolaites; of Puvah, the clan of the Punites; 24of Jashub, the clan of the Jashubites; of Shimron, the clan of the Shimronites. 25These are the clans of Issachar: sixty-four thousand three hundred enrolled.

26 The descendants of Zebulun by their clans: of Sered, the clan of the Seredites; of Elon, the clan of the Elonites; of Jahleel, the clan of the Jahleelites. 27These are the clans of the Zebulunites; the number of those enrolled was sixty thousand five hundred.

28 The sons of Joseph by their clans: Manasseh and Ephraim. 29The descendants of Manasseh: of Machir, the clan of the Machirites; and Machir was the father of Gilead; of Gilead, the clan of the Gileadites. 30These are the descendants of Gilead: of Iezer, the clan of the Iezerites; of Helek, the clan of the Helekites; 31and of Asriel, the clan of the Asrielites; and of Shechem, the clan of the Shechemites; 32and of Shemida,

ª 26.4 Heb lacks take a census of the people: Compare verse 2   b 26.13 Or Saul... Saulites

the clan of the Shemidaites; and of Hepher, the clan of the Hepherites. ³³Now Zelophehad son of Hepher had no sons, but daughters: and the names of the daughters of Zelophehad were Mahlah, Noah, Hoglah, Milcah, and Tirzah. ³⁴These are the clans of Manasseh; the number of those enrolled was fifty-two thousand seven hundred.

35 These are the descendants of Ephraim according to their clans: of Shuthelah, the clan of the Shuthelahites; of Becher, the clan of the Becherites; of Tahan, the clan of the Tahanites. ³⁶And these are the descendants of Shuthelah: of Eran, the clan of the Eranites. ³⁷These are the clans of the Ephraimites: the number of those enrolled was thirty-two thousand five hundred. These are the descendants of Joseph by their clans.

38 The descendants of Benjamin by their clans: of Bela, the clan of the Belaites; of Ashbel, the clan of the Ashbelites; of Ahiram, the clan of the Ahiramites; ³⁹of Shephupham, the clan of the Shuphamites; of Hupham, the clan of the Huphamites. ⁴⁰And the sons of Bela were Ard and Naaman: of Ard, the clan of the Ardites; of Naaman, the clan of the Naamites. ⁴¹These are the descendants of Benjamin by their clans; the number of those enrolled was forty-five thousand six hundred.

42 These are the descendants of Dan by their clans: of Shuham, the clan of the Shuhamites. These are the clans of Dan by their clans. ⁴³All the clans of the Shuhamites: sixty-four thousand four hundred enrolled.

44 The descendants of Asher by their families: of Imnah, the clan of the Imnites; of Ishvi, the clan of the Ishvites; of Beriah, the clan of the Beriites. ⁴⁵Of the descendants of Beriah: of Heber, the clan of the Heberites; of Malchiel, the clan of the Malchielites. ⁴⁶And the name of the daughter of Asher was Serah. ⁴⁷These are the clans of the Asherites: the number of those enrolled was fifty-three thousand four hundred.

48 The descendants of Naphtali by their clans: of Jahzeel, the clan of the Jahzeelites; of Guni, the clan of the Gunites; ⁴⁹of Jezer, the clan of the Jezerites; of Shillem, the clan of the Shillemites. ⁵⁰These are the Naphtalites[a] by their clans: the number of those enrolled was forty-five thousand four hundred.

51 This was the number of the Israelites enrolled: six hundred and one thousand seven hundred thirty.

52 The LORD spoke to Moses, saying: ⁵³To these the land shall be apportioned for inheritance according to the number of names. ⁵⁴To a large tribe you shall give a large inheritance, and to a small tribe you shall give a small inheritance; every tribe shall be given its inheritance according to its enrollment. ⁵⁵But the land shall be apportioned by lot; according to the names of their ancestral tribes they shall inherit. ⁵⁶Their inheritance shall be apportioned according to lot between the larger and the smaller.

57 This is the enrollment of the Levites by their clans: of Gershon, the clan of the Gershonites; of Kohath, the clan of the Kohathites; of Merari, the clan of the Merarites. ⁵⁸These are the clans of Levi: the clan of the Libnites, the clan of the Hebronites, the clan of the Mahlites, the clan of the Mushites, the clan of the Korahites. Now Kohath was the father of Amram. ⁵⁹The name of Amram's wife was Jochebed daughter of Levi, who was born to Levi in Egypt; and she bore to Amram: Aaron, Moses, and their sister Miriam. ⁶⁰To Aaron were born Nadab, Abihu, Eleazar, and Ithamar. ⁶¹But Nadab and Abihu died when they offered unholy fire before the LORD. ⁶²The number of those enrolled was twenty-three thousand, every male one month old and upward; for they were not enrolled among the Israelites because there was no allotment given to them among the Israelites.

63 These were those enrolled by Moses and Eleazar the priest, who enrolled the Israelites in the plains

---

[a] 26.50 Heb clans of Naphtali

of Moab by the Jordan opposite Jericho. ⁶⁴Among these there was not one of those enrolled by Moses and Aaron the priest, who had enrolled the Israelites in the wilderness of Sinai. ⁶⁵For the LORD had said of them, "They shall die in the wilderness." Not one of them was left, except Caleb son of Jephunneh and Joshua son of Nun.

THE DAUGHTERS OF ZELOPHEHAD

27 Then the daughters of Zelophehad came forward. Zelophehad was son of Hepher son of Gilead son of Machir son of Manasseh son of Joseph, a member of the Manassite clans. The names of his daughters were: Mahlah, Noah, Hoglah, Milcah, and Tirzah. ²They stood before Moses, Eleazar the priest, the leaders, and all the congregation, at the entrance of the tent of meeting, and they said, ³"Our father died in the wilderness; he was not among the company of those who gathered themselves together against the LORD in the company of Korah, but died for his own sin; and he had no sons. ⁴Why should the name of our father be taken away from his clan because he had no son? Give to us a possession among our father's brothers."

⁵Moses brought their case before the LORD. ⁶And the LORD spoke to Moses, saying: ⁷The daughters of Zelophehad are right in what they are saying; you shall indeed let them possess an inheritance among their father's brothers and pass the inheritance of their father on to them. ⁸You shall also say to the Israelites, "If a man dies, and has no son, then you shall pass his inheritance on to his daughter. ⁹If he has no daughter, then you shall give his inheritance to his brothers. ¹⁰If he has no brothers, then you shall give his inheritance to his father's brothers. ¹¹And if his father has no brothers, then you shall give his inheritance to the nearest kinsman of his clan, and he shall possess it. It shall be for the Israelites a statute and ordinance, as the LORD commanded Moses."

JOSHUA APPOINTED MOSES' SUCCESSOR

¹²The LORD said to Moses, "Go up this mountain of the Abarim range, and see the land that I have given to the Israelites. ¹³When you have seen it, you also shall be gathered to your people, as your brother Aaron was, ¹⁴because you rebelled against my word in the wilderness of Zin when the congregation quarreled with me.^a You did not show my holiness before their eyes at the waters." (These are the waters of Meribath-kadesh in the wilderness of Zin.) ¹⁵Moses spoke to the LORD, saying, ¹⁶"Let the LORD, the God of the spirits of all flesh, appoint someone over the congregation ¹⁷who shall go out before them and come in before them, who shall lead them out and bring them in, so that the congregation of the LORD may not be like sheep without a shepherd." ¹⁸So the LORD said to Moses, "Take Joshua son of Nun, a man in whom is the spirit, and lay your hand upon him; ¹⁹have him stand before Eleazar the priest and all the congregation, and commission him in their sight. ²⁰You shall give him some of your authority, so that all the congregation of the Israelites may obey. ²¹But he shall stand before Eleazar the priest, who shall inquire for him by the decision of the Urim before the LORD; at his word they shall go out, and at his word they shall come in, both he and all the Israelites with him, the whole congregation." ²²So Moses did as the LORD commanded him. He took Joshua and had him stand before Eleazar the priest and the whole congregation; ²³he laid his hands on him and commissioned him—as the LORD had directed through Moses.

DAILY OFFERINGS

28 The LORD spoke to Moses, saying: ²Command the Israelites, and say to them: My offering, the food for my offerings by fire, my pleasing odor, you shall take care to offer to me at its appointed time.

^a 27.14 Heb lacks *with me*

³And you shall say to them, This is the offering by fire that you shall offer to the LORD: two male lambs a year old without blemish, daily, as a regular offering. ⁴One lamb you shall offer in the morning, and the other lamb you shall offer at twilight;ᵃ ⁵also one-tenth of an ephah of choice flour for a grain offering, mixed with one-fourth of a hin of beaten oil. ⁶It is a regular burnt offering, ordained at Mount Sinai for a pleasing odor, an offering by fire to the LORD. ⁷Its drink offering shall be one-fourth of a hin for each lamb; in the sanctuary you shall pour out a drink offering of strong drink to the LORD. ⁸The other lamb you shall offer at twilightᵃ with a grain offering and a drink offering like the one in the morning; you shall offer it as an offering by fire, a pleasing odor to the LORD.

SABBATH OFFERINGS

9 On the sabbath day: two male lambs a year old without blemish, and two-tenths of an ephah of choice flour for a grain offering, mixed with oil, and its drink offering— ¹⁰this is the burnt offering for every sabbath, in addition to the regular burnt offering and its drink offering.

MONTHLY OFFERINGS

11 At the beginnings of your months you shall offer a burnt offering to the LORD: two young bulls, one ram, seven male lambs a year old without blemish; ¹²also three-tenths of an ephah of choice flour for a grain offering, mixed with oil, for each bull; and two-tenths of choice flour for a grain offering, mixed with oil, for the one ram; ¹³and one-tenth of choice flour mixed with oil as a grain offering for every lamb—a burnt offering of pleasing odor, an offering by fire to the LORD. ¹⁴Their drink offerings shall be half a hin of wine for a bull, one-third of a hin for a ram, and one-fourth of a hin for a lamb. This is the burnt offering of every month throughout the months of the year. ¹⁵And there shall be one male goat for a sin offering to the LORD; it shall be offered in addition to the regular burnt offering and its drink offering.

OFFERINGS AT PASSOVER

16 On the fourteenth day of the first month there shall be a passover offering to the LORD. ¹⁷And on the fifteenth day of this month is a festival; seven days shall unleavened bread be eaten. ¹⁸On the first day there shall be a holy convocation. You shall not work at your occupations. ¹⁹You shall offer an offering by fire, a burnt offering to the LORD: two young bulls, one ram, and seven male lambs a year old; see that they are without blemish. ²⁰Their grain offering shall be of choice flour mixed with oil: three-tenths of an ephah shall you offer for a bull, and two-tenths for a ram; ²¹one-tenth shall you offer for each of the seven lambs; ²²also one male goat for a sin offering, to make atonement for you. ²³You shall offer these in addition to the burnt offering of the morning, which belongs to the regular burnt offering. ²⁴In the same way you shall offer daily, for seven days, the food of an offering by fire, a pleasing odor to the LORD; it shall be offered in addition to the regular burnt offering and its drink offering. ²⁵And on the seventh day you shall have a holy convocation; you shall not work at your occupations.

OFFERINGS AT THE FESTIVAL OF WEEKS

26 On the day of the first fruits, when you offer a grain offering of new grain to the LORD at your festival of weeks, you shall have a holy convocation; you shall not work at your occupations. ²⁷You shall offer a burnt offering, a pleasing odor to the LORD: two young bulls, one ram, seven male lambs a year old. ²⁸Their grain offering shall be of choice flour mixed with oil, three-tenths of an ephah for each bull, two-tenths for one ram, ²⁹one-tenth for each of the seven lambs; ³⁰with one male goat, to make atonement for you. ³¹In addition to the regular burnt offering

ᵃ 28.4,8 Heb *between the two evenings*

with its grain offering, you shall offer them and their drink offering. They shall be without blemish.

OFFERINGS AT THE FESTIVAL OF TRUMPETS

29 On the first day of the seventh month you shall have a holy convocation; you shall not work at your occupations. It is a day for you to blow the trumpets, ²and you shall offer a burnt offering, a pleasing odor to the LORD: one young bull, one ram, seven male lambs a year old without blemish. ³Their grain offering shall be of choice flour mixed with oil, three-tenths of one ephah for the bull, two-tenths for the ram, ⁴and one-tenth for each of the seven lambs; ⁵with one male goat for a sin offering, to make atonement for you. ⁶These are in addition to the burnt offering of the new moon and its grain offering, and the regular burnt offering and its grain offering, and their drink offerings, according to the ordinance for them, a pleasing odor, an offering by fire to the LORD.

OFFERINGS ON THE DAY OF ATONEMENT

7 On the tenth day of this seventh month you shall have a holy convocation, and deny yourselves;ᵃ you shall do no work. ⁸You shall offer a burnt offering to the LORD, a pleasing odor: one young bull, one ram, seven male lambs a year old. They shall be without blemish. ⁹Their grain offering shall be of choice flour mixed with oil, three-tenths of an ephah for the bull, two-tenths for the one ram, ¹⁰one-tenth for each of the seven lambs; ¹¹with one male goat for a sin offering, in addition to the sin offering of atonement, and the regular burnt offering and its grain offering, and their drink offerings.

OFFERINGS AT THE FESTIVAL OF BOOTHS

12 On the fifteenth day of the seventh month you shall have a holy convocation; you shall not work at your occupations. You shall cele-

brate a festival to the LORD seven days. ¹³You shall offer a burnt offering, an offering by fire, a pleasing odor to the LORD: thirteen young bulls, two rams, fourteen male lambs a year old. They shall be without blemish. ¹⁴Their grain offering shall be of choice flour mixed with oil, three-tenths of an ephah for each of the thirteen bulls, two-tenths for each of the two rams, ¹⁵and one-tenth for each of the fourteen lambs; ¹⁶also one male goat for a sin offering, in addition to the regular burnt offering, its grain offering and its drink offering.

17 On the second day: twelve young bulls, two rams, fourteen male lambs a year old without blemish, ¹⁸with the grain offering and the drink offerings for the bulls, for the rams, and for the lambs, as prescribed in accordance with their number; ¹⁹also one male goat for a sin offering, in addition to the regular burnt offering and its grain offering, and their drink offerings.

20 On the third day: eleven bulls, two rams, fourteen male lambs a year old without blemish, ²¹with the grain offering and the drink offerings for the bulls, for the rams, and for the lambs, as prescribed in accordance with their number; ²²also one male goat for a sin offering, in addition to the regular burnt offering and its grain offering and its drink offering.

23 On the fourth day: ten bulls, two rams, fourteen male lambs a year old without blemish, ²⁴with the grain offering and the drink offerings for the bulls, for the rams, and for the lambs, as prescribed in accordance with their number; ²⁵also one male goat for a sin offering, in addition to the regular burnt offering, its grain offering and its drink offering.

26 On the fifth day: nine bulls, two rams, fourteen male lambs a year old without blemish, ²⁷with the grain offering and the drink offerings for the bulls, for the rams, and for the lambs, as prescribed

ᵃ 29.7 Or and fast

in accordance with their number; 28also one male goat for a sin offering, in addition to the regular burnt offering and its grain offering and its drink offering.

29 On the sixth day: eight bulls, two rams, fourteen male lambs a year old without blemish, 30with the grain offering and the drink offerings for the bulls, for the rams, and for the lambs, as prescribed in accordance with their number; 31also one male goat for a sin offering, in addition to the regular burnt offering, its grain offering, and its drink offerings.

32 On the seventh day: seven bulls, two rams, fourteen male lambs a year old without blemish, 33with the grain offering and the drink offerings for the bulls, for the rams, and for the lambs, as prescribed in accordance with their number; 34also one male goat for a sin offering, besides the regular burnt offering, its grain offering, and its drink offering.

35 On the eighth day you shall have a solemn assembly; you shall not work at your occupations. 36You shall offer a burnt offering, an offering by fire, a pleasing odor to the LORD: one bull, one ram, seven male lambs a year old without blemish, 37and the grain offering and the drink offerings for the bull, for the ram, and for the lambs, as prescribed in accordance with their number; 38also one male goat for a sin offering, in addition to the regular burnt offering and its grain offering and its drink offering.

39 These you shall offer to the LORD at your appointed festivals, in addition to your votive offerings and your freewill offerings, as your burnt offerings, your grain offerings, your drink offerings, and your offerings of well-being.

40a So Moses told the Israelites everything just as the LORD had commanded Moses.

VOWS MADE BY WOMEN

30 Then Moses said to the heads of the tribes of the Israelites: This is what the LORD has commanded. 2When a man makes a vow to the LORD, or swears an oath to bind himself by a pledge, he shall not break his word; he shall do according to all that proceeds out of his mouth.

3 When a woman makes a vow to the LORD, or binds herself by a pledge, while within her father's house, in her youth, 4and her father hears of her vow or her pledge by which she has bound herself, and says nothing to her; then all her vows shall stand, and any pledge by which she has bound herself shall stand. 5But if her father expresses disapproval to her at the time that he hears of it, no vow of hers, and no pledge by which she has bound herself, shall stand; and the LORD will forgive her, because her father had expressed to her his disapproval.

6 If she marries, while obligated by her vows or any thoughtless utterance of her lips by which she has bound herself, 7and her husband hears of it and says nothing to her at the time that he hears, then her vows shall stand, and her pledges by which she has bound herself shall stand. 8But if, at the time that her husband hears of it, he expresses disapproval to her, then he shall nullify the vow by which she was obligated, or the thoughtless utterance of her lips, by which she bound herself; and the LORD will forgive her. 9(But every vow of a widow or of a divorced woman, by which she has bound herself, shall be binding upon her.) 10And if she made a vow in her husband's house, or bound herself by a pledge with an oath, 11and her husband heard it and said nothing to her, and did not express disapproval to her, then all her vows shall stand, and any pledge by which she bound herself shall stand. 12But if her husband nullifies them at the time that he hears them, then whatever proceeds out of her lips concerning her vows, or concerning her pledge of herself, shall not stand. Her husband has nullified them, and the LORD will forgive her. 13Any vow or any binding oath to deny herself,b

a 29.40 Ch 30.1 in Heb   b 30.13 Or to fast

her husband may allow to stand, or her husband may nullify. ¹⁴But if her husband says nothing to her from day to day,ᵃ then he validates all her vows, or all her pledges, by which she is obligated; he has validated them, because he said nothing to her at the time that he heard of them. ¹⁵But if he nullifies them some time after he has heard of them, then he shall bear her guilt.

16 These are the statutes that the LORD commanded Moses concerning a husband and his wife, and a father and his daughter while she is still young and in her father's house.

WAR AGAINST MIDIAN

31 The LORD spoke to Moses, saying, ²"Avenge the Israelites on the Midianites; afterward you shall be gathered to your people." ³So Moses said to the people, "Arm some of your number for the war, so that they may go against Midian, to execute the LORD's vengeance on Midian. ⁴You shall send a thousand from each of the tribes of Israel to the war." ⁵So out of the thousands of Israel, a thousand from each tribe were conscripted, twelve thousand armed for battle. ⁶Moses sent them to the war, a thousand from each tribe, along with Phinehas son of Eleazar the priest,ᵇ with the vessels of the sanctuary and the trumpets for sounding the alarm in his hand. ⁷They did battle against Midian, as the LORD had commanded Moses, and killed every male. ⁸They killed the kings of Midian: Evi, Rekem, Zur, Hur, and Reba, the five kings of Midian, in addition to others who were slain by them; and they also killed Balaam son of Beor with the sword. ⁹The Israelites took the women of Midian and their little ones captive; and they took all their cattle, their flocks, and all their goods as booty. ¹⁰All their towns where they had settled, and all their encampments, they burned, ¹¹but they took all the spoil and all the booty, both people and animals. ¹²Then they brought the captives and the booty and the spoil to Moses, to Eleazar the priest, and to the congregation of the Israelites, at the camp on the plains of Moab by the Jordan at Jericho.

RETURN FROM THE WAR

13 Moses, Eleazar the priest, and all the leaders of the congregation went to meet them outside the camp. ¹⁴Moses became angry with the officers of the army, the commanders of thousands and the commanders of hundreds, who had come from service in the war. ¹⁵Moses said to them, "Have you allowed all the women to live? ¹⁶These women here, on Balaam's advice, made the Israelites act treacherously against the LORD in the affair of Peor, so that the plague came among the congregation of the LORD. ¹⁷Now therefore, kill every male among the little ones, and kill every woman who has known a man by sleeping with him. ¹⁸But all the young girls who have not known a man by sleeping with him, keep alive for yourselves. ¹⁹Camp outside the camp seven days; whoever of you has killed any person or touched a corpse, purify yourselves and your captives on the third and on the seventh day. ²⁰You shall purify every garment, every article of skin, everything made of goats' hair, and every article of wood."

21 Eleazar the priest said to the troops who had gone to battle: "This is the statute of the law that the LORD has commanded Moses: ²²gold, silver, bronze, iron, tin, and lead— ²³everything that can withstand fire, shall be passed through fire, and it shall be clean. Nevertheless it shall also be purified with the water for purification; and whatever cannot withstand fire, shall be passed through the water. ²⁴You must wash your clothes on the seventh day, and you shall be clean; afterward you may come into the camp."

DISPOSITION OF CAPTIVES AND BOOTY

25 The LORD spoke to Moses, saying, ²⁶"You and Eleazar the priest

---

ᵃ 30.14 Or *from that day to the next*
ᵇ 31.6 Gk: Heb adds *to the war*

and the heads of the ancestral houses of the congregation make an inventory of the booty captured, both human and animal. 27Divide the booty into two parts, between the warriors who went out to battle and all the congregation. 28From the share of the warriors who went out to battle, set aside as tribute for the LORD, one item out of every five hundred, whether persons, oxen, donkeys, sheep, or goats. 29Take it from their half and give it to Eleazar the priest as an offering to the LORD. 30But from the Israelites' half you shall take one out of every fifty, whether persons, oxen, donkeys, sheep, or goats—all the animals—and give them to the Levites who have charge of the tabernacle of the LORD."

JESUS DID NOT CONDEMN
WEALTH, AS SUCH, OR EXALT
POVERTY. HE DEMANDS THE
COMPLETE ABANDONMENT OF
ANY DESIRES NOT COINCIDING
WITH HIS WILL FOR US.

31 Then Moses and Eleazar the priest did as the LORD had commanded Moses:

32 The booty remaining from the spoil that the troops had taken totaled six hundred seventy-five thousand sheep, 33seventy-two thousand oxen, 34sixty-one thousand donkeys, 35and thirty-two thousand persons in all, women who had not known a man by sleeping with him.

36 The half-share, the portion of those who had gone out to war, was in number three hundred thirty-seven thousand five hundred sheep and goats, 37and the LORD's tribute of sheep and goats was six hundred seventy-five. 38The oxen were thirty-six thousand, of which the LORD's tribute was seventy-two. 39The donkeys were thirty thousand

five hundred, of which the LORD's tribute was sixty-one. 40The persons were sixteen thousand, of which the LORD's tribute was thirty-two persons. 41Moses gave the tribute, the offering for the LORD, to Eleazar the priest, as the LORD had commanded Moses.

42 As for the Israelites' half, which Moses separated from that of the troops, 43the congregation's half was three hundred thirty-seven thousand five hundred sheep and goats, 44thirty-six thousand oxen, 45thirty thousand five hundred donkeys, 46and sixteen thousand persons. 47From the Israelites' half Moses took one of every fifty, both of persons and of animals, and gave them to the Levites who had charge of the tabernacle of the LORD; as the LORD had commanded Moses.

48 Then the officers who were over the thousands of the army, the commanders of thousands and the commanders of hundreds, approached Moses, 49and said to Moses, "Your servants have counted the warriors who are under our command, and not one of us is missing. 50And we have brought the LORD's offering, what each of us found, articles of gold, armlets and bracelets, signet rings, earrings, and pendants, to make atonement for ourselves before the LORD." 51Moses and Eleazar the priest received the gold from them, all in the form of crafted articles. 52And all the gold of the offering that they offered to the LORD, from the commanders of thousands and the commanders of hundreds, was sixteen thousand seven hundred fifty shekels. 53(The troops had all taken plunder for themselves.) 54So Moses and Eleazar the priest received the gold from the commanders of thousands and of hundreds, and brought it into the tent of meeting as a memorial for the Israelites before the LORD.

CONQUEST AND DIVISION OF TRANSJORDAN

32 Now the Reubenites and the Gadites owned a very great number of cattle. When they saw

that the land of Jazer and the land of Gilead was a good place for cattle, ²the Gadites and the Reubenites came and spoke to Moses, to Eleazar the priest, and to the leaders of the congregation, saying, ³"Ataroth, Dibon, Jazer, Nimrah, Heshbon, Elealeh, Sebam, Nebo, and Beon— ⁴the land that the LORD subdued before the congregation of Israel—is a land for cattle; and your servants have cattle." ⁵They continued, "If we have found favor in your sight, let this land be given to your servants for a possession; do not make us cross the Jordan."

6 But Moses said to the Gadites and to the Reubenites, "Shall your brothers go to war while you sit here? ⁷Why will you discourage the hearts of the Israelites from going over into the land that the LORD has given them? ⁸Your fathers did this, when I sent them from Kadeshbarnea to see the land. ⁹When they went up to the Wadi Eshcol and saw the land, they discouraged the hearts of the Israelites from going into the land that the LORD had given them. ¹⁰The LORD's anger was kindled on that day and he swore, saying, ¹¹"Surely none of the people who came up out of Egypt, from twenty years old and upward, shall see the land that I swore to give to Abraham, to Isaac, and to Jacob, because they have not unreservedly followed me— ¹²none except Caleb son of Jephunneh the Kenizzite and Joshua son of Nun, for they have unreservedly followed the LORD.' ¹³And the LORD's anger was kindled against Israel, and he made them wander in the wilderness for forty years, until all the generation that had done evil in the sight of the LORD had disappeared. ¹⁴And now you, a brood of sinners, have risen in place of your fathers, to increase the LORD's fierce anger against Israel! ¹⁵If you turn away from following him, he will again abandon them in the wilderness; and you will destroy all this people."

16 Then they came up to him and said, "We will build sheepfolds here for our flocks, and towns for our little ones, ¹⁷but we will take up arms as a vanguardᵃ before the Israelites, until we have brought them to their place. Meanwhile our little ones will stay in the fortified towns because of the inhabitants of the land. ¹⁸We will not return to our homes until all the Israelites have obtained their inheritance. ¹⁹We will not inherit with them on the other side of the Jordan and beyond, because our inheritance has come to us on this side of the Jordan to the east."

20 So Moses said to them, "If you do this—if you take up arms to go before the LORD for the war, ²¹and all those of you who bear arms cross the Jordan before the LORD, until he has driven out his enemies from before him ²²and the land is subdued before the LORD—then after that you may return and be free of obligation to the LORD and to Israel, and this land shall be your possession before the LORD. ²³But if you do not do this, you have sinned against the LORD; and be sure your sin will find you out. ²⁴Build towns for your little ones, and folds for your flocks; but do what you have promised."

25 Then the Gadites and the Reubenites said to Moses, "Your servants will do as my lord commands. ²⁶Our little ones, our wives, our flocks, and all our livestock shall remain there in the towns of Gilead; ²⁷but your servants will cross over, everyone armed for war, to do battle for the LORD, just as my lord orders."

28 So Moses gave command concerning them to Eleazar the priest, to Joshua son of Nun, and to the heads of the ancestral houses of the Israelite tribes. ²⁹And Moses said to them, "If the Gadites and the Reubenites, everyone armed for battle before the LORD, will cross over the Jordan with you and the land shall be subdued before you, then you shall give them the land of Gilead for a possession; ³⁰but if they will not cross over with you armed, they shall have possessions among you in the land of Canaan." ³¹The Gadites and the Reubenites answered, "As

ᵃ 32.17 Cn: Heb *hurrying*

the LORD has spoken to your servants, so we will do. ³²We will cross over armed before the LORD into the land of Canaan, but the possession of our inheritance shall remain with us on this side of[a] the Jordan."

33 Moses gave to them—to the Gadites and to the Reubenites and to the half-tribe of Manasseh son of Joseph—the kingdom of King Sihon of the Amorites and the kingdom of King Og of Bashan, the land and its towns, with the territories of the surrounding towns. ³⁴And the Gadites rebuilt Dibon, Ataroth, Aroer, ³⁵Atroth-shophan, Jazer, Jogbehah, ³⁶Beth-nimrah, and Beth-haran, fortified cities, and folds for sheep. ³⁷And the Reubenites rebuilt Heshbon, Elealeh, Kiriathaim, ³⁸Nebo, and Baal-meon (some names being changed), and Sibmah; and they gave names to the towns that they rebuilt. ³⁹The descendants of Machir son of Manasseh went to Gilead, captured it, and dispossessed the Amorites who were there; ⁴⁰so Moses gave Gilead to Machir son of Manasseh, and he settled there. ⁴¹Jair son of Manasseh went and captured their villages, and renamed them Havvoth-jair.[b] ⁴²And Nobah went and captured Kenath and its villages, and renamed it Nobah after himself.

THE STAGES OF ISRAEL'S JOURNEY FROM EGYPT

33 These are the stages by which the Israelites went out of the land of Egypt in military formation under the leadership of Moses and Aaron. ²Moses wrote down their starting points, stage by stage, by command of the LORD; and these are their stages according to their starting places. ³They set out from Rameses in the first month, on the fifteenth day of the first month; on the day after the passover the Israelites went out boldly in the sight of all the Egyptians, ⁴while the Egyptians were burying all their firstborn, whom the LORD had struck down among them. The LORD executed judgments even against their gods.

5 So the Israelites set out from Rameses, and camped at Succoth. ⁶They set out from Succoth, and camped at Etham, which is on the edge of the wilderness. ⁷They set out from Etham, and turned back to Pi-hahiroth, which faces Baal-zephon; and they camped before Migdol. ⁸They set out from Pi-hahiroth, passed through the sea into the wilderness, went a three days' journey in the wilderness of Etham, and camped at Marah. ⁹They set out from Marah and came to Elim; at Elim there were twelve springs of water and seventy palm trees, and they camped there. ¹⁰They set out from Elim and camped by the Red Sea.[c] ¹¹They set out from the Red Sea[c] and camped in the wilderness of Sin. ¹²They set out from the wilderness of Sin and camped at Dophkah. ¹³They set out from Dophkah and camped at Alush. ¹⁴They set out from Alush and camped at Rephidim, where there was no water for the people to drink. ¹⁵They set out from Rephidim and camped in the wilderness of Sinai. ¹⁶They set out from the wilderness of Sinai and camped at Kibroth-hattaavah. ¹⁷They set out from Kibroth-hattaavah and camped at Hazeroth. ¹⁸They set out from Hazeroth and camped at Rithmah. ¹⁹They set out from Rithmah and camped at Rimmon-perez. ²⁰They set out from Rimmon-perez and camped at Libnah. ²¹They set out from Libnah and camped at Rissah. ²²They set out from Rissah and camped at Kehelathah. ²³They set out from Kehelathah and camped at Mount Shepher. ²⁴They set out from Mount Shepher and camped at Haradah. ²⁵They set out from Haradah and camped at Makheloth. ²⁶They set out from Makheloth and camped at Tahath. ²⁷They set out from Tahath and camped at Terah. ²⁸They set out from Terah and camped at Mithkah. ²⁹They set out from Mithkah and camped at Hashmonah. ³⁰They set out from Hashmonah and camped at Moseroth. ³¹They set out from Mo-

a 32.32 Heb beyond   b 32.41 That is the villages of Jair   c 33.10,11 Or Sea of Reeds

seroth and camped at Bene-jaakan. ³²They set out from Bene-jaakan and camped at Hor-haggidgad. ³³They set out from Hor-haggidgad and camped at Jotbathah. ³⁴They set out from Jotbathah and camped at Abronah. ³⁵They set out from Abronah and camped at Ezion-geber. ³⁶They set out from Ezion-geber and camped in the wilderness of Zin (that is, Kadesh). ³⁷They set out from Kadesh and camped at Mount Hor, on the edge of the land of Edom.

38 Aaron the priest went up Mount Hor at the command of the LORD and died there in the fortieth year after the Israelites had come out of the land of Egypt, on the first day of the fifth month. ³⁹Aaron was one hundred twenty-three years old when he died on Mount Hor.

40 The Canaanite, the king of Arad, who lived in the Negeb in the land of Canaan, heard of the coming of the Israelites.

41 They set out from Mount Hor and camped at Zalmonah. ⁴²They set out from Zalmonah and camped at Punon. ⁴³They set out from Punon and camped at Oboth. ⁴⁴They set out from Oboth and camped at Iye-abarim, in the territory of Moab. ⁴⁵They set out from Iyim and camped at Dibon-gad. ⁴⁶They set out from Dibon-gad and camped at Almon-diblathaim. ⁴⁷They set out from Almon-diblathaim and camped in the mountains of Abarim, before Nebo. ⁴⁸They set out from the mountains of Abarim and camped in the plains of Moab by the Jordan at Jericho; ⁴⁹they camped by the Jordan from Beth-jeshimoth as far as Abel-shittim in the plains of Moab.

DIRECTIONS FOR THE CONQUEST OF CANAAN

50 In the plains of Moab by the Jordan at Jericho, the LORD spoke to Moses, saying: ⁵¹Speak to the Israelites, and say to them: When you cross over the Jordan into the land of Canaan, ⁵²you shall drive out all the inhabitants of the land from before you, destroy all their figured stones, destroy all their cast images, and de-

molish all their high places. ⁵³You shall take possession of the land and settle in it, for I have given you the land to possess. ⁵⁴You shall apportion the land by lot according to your clans; to a large one you shall give a large inheritance, and to a small one you shall give a small inheritance; the inheritance shall belong to the person on whom the lot falls; according to your ancestral tribes you shall inherit. ⁵⁵But if you do not drive out the inhabitants of the land from before you, then those whom you let remain shall be as barbs in your eyes and thorns in your sides; they shall trouble you in the land where you are settling. ⁵⁶And I will do to you as I thought to do to them.

THE BOUNDARIES OF THE LAND

34 The LORD spoke to Moses, saying: ²Command the Israelites, and say to them: When you enter the land of Canaan (this is the land that shall fall to you for an inheritance, the land of Canaan, defined by its boundaries), ³your south sector shall extend from the wilderness of Zin along the side of Edom. Your southern boundary shall begin from the end of the Dead Sea[a] on the east; ⁴your boundary shall turn south of the ascent of Akrabbim, and cross to Zin, and its outer limit shall be south of Kadesh-barnea; then it shall go on to Hazar-addar, and cross to Azmon; ⁵the boundary shall turn from Azmon to the Wadi of Egypt, and its termination shall be at the Sea.

6 For the western boundary, you shall have the Great Sea and its[b] coast; this shall be your western boundary.

7 This shall be your northern boundary: from the Great Sea you shall mark out your line to Mount Hor; ⁸from Mount Hor you shall mark it out to Lebo-hamath, and the outer limit of the boundary shall be at Zedad; ⁹then the boundary shall extend to Ziphron, and its end shall

---

[a] 34.3 Heb Salt Sea [b] 34.6 Syr: Heb lacks its

be at Hazar-enan; this shall be your northern boundary.

10 You shall mark out your eastern boundary from Hazar-enan to Shepham; [11]and the boundary shall continue down from Shepham to Riblah on the east side of Ain; and the boundary shall go down, and reach the eastern slope of the sea of Chinnereth; [12]and the boundary shall go down to the Jordan, and its end shall be at the Dead Sea.[a] This shall be your land with its boundaries all around.

13 Moses commanded the Israelites, saying: This is the land that you shall inherit by lot, which the LORD has commanded to give to the nine tribes and to the half-tribe; [14]for the tribe of the Reubenites by their ancestral houses and the tribe of the Gadites by their ancestral houses have taken their inheritance, and also the half-tribe of Manasseh; [15]the two tribes and the half-tribe have taken their inheritance beyond the Jordan at Jericho eastward, toward the sunrise.

TRIBAL LEADERS

16 The LORD spoke to Moses, saying: [17]These are the names of the men who shall apportion the land to you for inheritance: the priest Eleazar and Joshua son of Nun. [18]You shall take one leader of every tribe to apportion the land for inheritance. [19]These are the names of the men: Of the tribe of Judah, Caleb son of Jephunneh. [20]Of the tribe of the Simeonites, Shemuel son of Ammihud. [21]Of the tribe of Benjamin, Elidad son of Chislon. [22]Of the tribe of the Danites a leader, Bukki son of Jogli. [23]Of the Josephites: of the tribe of the Manassites a leader, Hanniel son of Ephod, [24]and of the tribe of the Ephraimites a leader, Kemuel son of Shiphtan. [25]Of the tribe of the Zebulunites a leader, Eli-zaphan son of Parnach. [26]Of the tribe of the Issacharites a leader, Paltiel son of Azzan. [27]And of the tribe of the Asherites a leader, Ahihud son of Shelomi. [28]Of the tribe of the Naphtalites a leader, Pedahel son of Ammihud. [29]These were the ones whom the LORD commanded to apportion the inheritance for the Israelites in the land of Canaan.

CITIES FOR THE LEVITES

35 In the plains of Moab by the Jordan at Jericho, the LORD spoke to Moses, saying: [2]Command the Israelites to give, from the inheritance that they possess, towns for the Levites to live in; you shall also give to the Levites pasture lands surrounding the towns. [3]The towns shall be theirs to live in, and their pasture lands shall be for their cattle, for their livestock, and for all their animals. [4]The pasture lands of the towns, which you shall give to the Levites, shall reach from the wall of the town outward a thousand cubits all around. [5]You shall measure, outside the town, for the east side two thousand cubits, for the south side two thousand cubits, for the west side two thousand cubits, and for the north side two thousand cubits, with the town in the middle; this shall belong to them as pasture land for their towns.

6 The towns that you give to the Levites shall include the six cities of refuge, where you shall permit a slayer to flee, and in addition to them you shall give forty-two towns. [7]The towns that you give to the Levites shall total forty-eight, with their pasture lands. [8]And as for the towns that you shall give from the possession of the Israelites, from the larger tribes you shall take many, and from the smaller tribes you shall take few; each, in proportion to the inheritance that it obtains, shall give of its towns to the Levites.

CITIES OF REFUGE

9 The LORD spoke to Moses, saying: [10]Speak to the Israelites, and say to them: When you cross the Jordan into the land of Canaan, [11]then you shall select cities to be cities of refuge for you, so that a slayer who kills a person without intent may flee there. [12]The cities shall be for you a refuge from the avenger, so that the

[a] 34.12 Heb Salt Sea

slayer may not die until there is a trial before the congregation.

13 The cities that you designate shall be six cities of refuge for you: 14you shall designate three cities beyond the Jordan, and three cities in the land of Canaan, to be cities of refuge. 15These six cities shall serve as refuge for the Israelites, for the resident or transient alien among them, so that anyone who kills a person without intent may flee there.

CONCERNING MURDER AND BLOOD REVENGE

16 But anyone who strikes another with an iron object, and death ensues, is a murderer; the murderer shall be put to death. 17Or anyone who strikes another with a stone in hand that could cause death, and death ensues, is a murderer; the murderer shall be put to death. 18Or anyone who strikes another with a weapon of wood in hand that could cause death, and death ensues, is a murderer; the murderer shall be put to death. 19The avenger of blood is the one who shall put the murderer to death; when they meet, the avenger of blood shall execute the sentence. 20Likewise, if someone pushes another from hatred, or hurls something at another, lying in wait, and death ensues, 21or in enmity strikes another with the hand, and death ensues, then the one who struck the blow shall be put to death; that person is a murderer; the avenger of blood shall put the murderer to death, when they meet.

22 But if someone pushes another suddenly without enmity, or hurls any object without lying in wait, 23or, while handling any stone that could cause death, unintentionally[a] drops it on another and death ensues, though they were not enemies, and no harm was intended, 24then the congregation shall judge between the slayer and the avenger of blood, in accordance with these ordinances; 25and the congregation shall rescue the slayer from the avenger of blood. Then the congregation shall send the slayer back to the original city of refuge. The slayer shall live in it until the death of the high priest who was anointed with the holy oil. 26But if the slayer shall at any time go outside the bounds of the original city of refuge, 27and is found by the avenger of blood outside the bounds of the city of refuge, and is killed by the avenger, no bloodguilt shall be incurred. 28For the slayer must remain in the city of refuge until the death of the high priest; but after the death of the high priest the slayer may return home.

29 These things shall be a statute and ordinance for you throughout your generations wherever you live.

30 If anyone kills another, the murderer shall be put to death on the evidence of witnesses; but no one shall be put to death on the testimony of a single witness. 31Moreover you shall accept no ransom for the life of a murderer who is subject to the death penalty; a murderer must be put to death. 32Nor shall you accept ransom for one who has fled to a city of refuge, enabling the fugitive to return to live in the land before the death of the high priest. 33You shall not pollute the land in which you live; for blood pollutes the land, and no expiation can be made for the land, for the blood that is shed in it, except by the blood of the one who shed it. 34You shall not defile the land in which you live, in which I also dwell; for I the LORD dwell among the Israelites.

WE CANNOT CHANGE THE
WORLD, BUT WE CAN,
IN JESUS' NAME, CHANGE
SOMEONE'S WORLD.

MARRIAGE OF FEMALE HEIRS

36 The heads of the ancestral houses of the clans of the

[a] 35.23 Heb *without seeing*

descendants of Gilead son of Machir son of Manasseh, of the Josephite clans, came forward and spoke in the presence of Moses and the leaders, the heads of the ancestral houses of the Israelites; 2they said, "The LORD commanded my lord to give the land for inheritance by lot to the Israelites; and my lord was commanded by the LORD to give the inheritance of our brother Zelophehad to his daughters. 3But if they are married into another Israelite tribe, then their inheritance will be taken from the inheritance of our ancestors and added to the inheritance of the tribe into which they marry; so it will be taken away from the allotted portion of our inheritance. 4And when the jubilee of the Israelites comes, then their inheritance will be added to the inheritance of the tribe into which they have married; and their inheritance will be taken from the inheritance of our ancestral tribe."

5 Then Moses commanded the Israelites according to the word of the LORD, saying, "The descendants of the tribe of Joseph are right in what they are saying. 6This is what the LORD commands concerning the daughters of Zelophehad, 'Let them marry whom they think best; only it must be into a clan of their father's tribe that they are married, 7so that no inheritance of the Israelites shall be transferred from one tribe to another; for all Israelites shall retain the inheritance of their ancestral tribes. 8Every daughter who possesses an inheritance in any tribe of the Israelites shall marry one from the clan of her father's tribe, so that all Israelites may continue to possess their ancestral inheritance. 9No inheritance shall be transferred from one tribe to another; for each of the tribes of the Israelites shall retain its own inheritance.'"

10 The daughters of Zelophehad did as the LORD had commanded Moses. 11Mahlah, Tirzah, Hoglah, Milcah, and Noah, the daughters of Zelophehad, married sons of their father's brothers. 12They were married into the clans of the descendants of Manasseh son of Joseph, and their inheritance remained in the tribe of their father's clan.

13 These are the commandments and the ordinances that the LORD commanded through Moses to the Israelites in the plains of Moab by the Jordan at Jericho.

DEUTERONOMY

Reminders. We all need them, and the most important ones often come at crossroads in our lives. In Deuteronomy, Moses and the Israelites were at a crossroads. Forty years of wilderness wandering were behind them. A land of promise and opportunity stretched before them. At this key moment, Moses reminded them to obey the laws God had established. He reminded them how God loved and cared for them and that they were to return the love of the awesome God they served.

EVENTS AT HOREB RECALLED

1 These are the words that Moses spoke to all Israel beyond the Jordan—in the wilderness, on the plain opposite Suph, between Paran and Tophel, Laban, Hazeroth, and Di-zahab. ²(By the way of Mount Seir it takes eleven days to reach Kadesh-barnea from Horeb.) ³In the fortieth year, on the first day of the eleventh month, Moses spoke to the Israelites just as the LORD had commanded him to speak to them. ⁴This was after he had defeated King Sihon of the Amorites, who reigned in Heshbon, and King Og of Bashan, who reigned in Ashtaroth and[a] in Edrei. ⁵Beyond the Jordan in the land of Moab, Moses undertook to expound this law as follows:

6 The LORD our God spoke to us at Horeb, saying, "You have stayed long enough at this mountain. ⁷Resume your journey, and go into the hill country of the Amorites as well as into the neighboring regions—the Arabah, the hill country, the Shephelah, the Negeb, and the seacoast—the land of the Canaanites and the Lebanon, as far as the great river, the river Euphrates. ⁸See, I have set the land before you; go in and take possession of the land that I[b] swore to your ancestors, to Abraham, to Isaac, and to Jacob, to give to them and to their descendants after them."

APPOINTMENT OF TRIBAL LEADERS

9 At that time I said to you, "I am unable by myself to bear you. ¹⁰The LORD your God has multiplied you, so that today you are as numerous as the stars of heaven. ¹¹May the LORD, the God of your ancestors, increase you a thousand times more and bless you, as he has promised you! ¹²But how can I bear the heavy burden of your disputes all by myself? ¹³Choose for each of your tribes individuals who are wise, discerning, and reputable to be your leaders." ¹⁴You answered me, "The plan you have proposed is a good one." ¹⁵So I took the leaders of your tribes, wise and reputable individuals, and installed them as leaders over you, commanders of thousands, commanders of hundreds, commanders of fifties, commanders of tens, and officials, throughout your tribes. ¹⁶I charged your judges at that time: "Give the members of your community a fair hearing, and judge rightly between one person and another, whether citizen or resident alien. ¹⁷You must not be partial in judging: hear out the small and the great alike; you shall not be intimidated by anyone, for the judgment is God's. Any case that is too hard for you, bring to me, and I will hear it." ¹⁸So I charged you at that time with all the things that you should do.

ISRAEL'S REFUSAL TO ENTER THE LAND

19 Then, just as the LORD our God had ordered us, we set out from Ho-

---

a 1.4 Gk Syr Vg Compare Josh 12.4: Heb lacks and   b 1.8 Sam Gk: MT the LORD

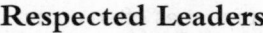

╫ BIBLE IN LIFE ▷

Respected Leaders   Deuteronomy 1.9–18

Following the wise advice of his father-in-law, Moses appointed respected men to lead in authority under him (see Exodus 18.24–26). We cannot underestimate the importance of good, solid leadership. Consider those in the church who are eloquent, attractive or socially prominent, who might even be serving as pastors, but who have an air of arrogance and who use their position to divide. Effective, respectable leaders are not the same ones as those who cause divisions. Good leaders follow the advice of Paul to "[b]e at peace among yourselves" (1 Thessalonians 5.13). They find ways to resolve differences and bring harmony within the church. A good leader is worthy of our deepest respect.

reb and went through all that great and terrible wilderness that you saw, on the way to the hill country of the Amorites, until we reached Kadesh-barnea. 20I said to you, "You have reached the hill country of the Amorites, which the LORD our God is giving us. 21See, the LORD your God has given the land to you; go up, take possession, as the LORD, the God of your ancestors, has promised you; do not fear or be dismayed."

22 All of you came to me and said, "Let us send men ahead of us to explore the land for us and bring back a report to us regarding the route by which we should go up and the cities we will come to." 23The plan seemed good to me, and I selected twelve of you, one from each tribe. 24They set out and went up into the hill country, and when they reached the Valley of Eshcol they spied it out 25and gathered some of the land's produce, which they brought down to us. They brought back a report to us, and said, "It is a good land that the LORD our God is giving us."

26 But you were unwilling to go up. You rebelled against the command of the LORD your God; 27you grumbled in your tents and said, "It is because the LORD hates us that he has brought us out of the land of Egypt, to hand us over to the Amorites to destroy us. 28Where are we headed? Our kindred have made our hearts melt by reporting, 'The people are stronger and taller than we; the cities are large and fortified up to heaven! We actually saw there the offspring of the Anakim!' " 29I said to you, "Have no dread or fear of them. 30The LORD your God, who goes before you, is the one who will fight for you, just as he did for you in Egypt before your very eyes, 31and in the wilderness, where you saw how the LORD your God carried you, just as one carries a child, all the way that you traveled until you reached this place. 32But in spite of this, you have no trust in the LORD your God, 33who goes before you on the way to seek out a place for you to camp, in fire by night, and in the cloud by day, to show you the route you should take."

THE PENALTY FOR ISRAEL'S REBELLION

34 When the LORD heard your words, he was wrathful and swore: 35"Not one of these—not one of this evil generation—shall see the good land that I swore to give to your ancestors, 36except Caleb son of Jephunneh. He shall see it, and to him and to his descendants I will give the land on which he set foot, because of his complete fidelity to the LORD." 37Even with me the LORD was angry on your account, saying, "You also shall not enter there. 38Joshua son of Nun, your assistant, shall enter there; encourage him, for he is the one who will secure Israel's possession of it. 39And as for your little ones, who you thought would become booty, your children, who today do not yet know right from wrong, they shall enter there; to them I will give it, and they shall take possession of it. 40But as for you, journey back into the wilderness, in the direction of the Red Sea."[a]

41 You answered me, "We have sinned against the LORD! We are ready to go up and fight, just as the LORD our God commanded us." So all of you strapped on your battle gear, and thought it easy to go up into the hill country. 42The LORD said to me, "Say to them, 'Do not go up and do not fight, for I am not in the midst of you; otherwise you will be defeated by your enemies.' " 43Although I told you, you would not listen. You rebelled against the command of the LORD and presumptuously went up into the hill country. 44The Amorites who lived in that hill country then came out against you and chased you as bees do. They beat you down in Seir as far as Hormah. 45When you returned and wept before the LORD, the LORD would neither heed your voice nor pay you any attention.

THE DESERT YEARS

46 After you had stayed at Kadesh as many days as you did, 1we journeyed back into the wilderness, in the direction of the Red

a 1.40 Or Sea of Reeds

Sea,ᵃ as the LORD had told me and skirted Mount Seir for many days. ²Then the LORD said to me: ³"You have been skirting this hill country long enough. Head north, ⁴and charge the people as follows: You are about to pass through the territory of your kindred, the descendants of Esau, who live in Seir. They will be afraid of you, so, be very careful ⁵not to engage in battle with them, for I will not give you even so much as a foot's length of their land, since I have given Mount Seir to Esau as a possession. ⁶You shall purchase food from them for money, so that you may eat; and you shall also buy water from them for money, so that you may drink. ⁷Surely the LORD your God has blessed you in all your undertakings; he knows your going through this great wilderness. These forty years the LORD your God has been with you; you have lacked nothing." ⁸So we passed by our kin, the descendants of Esau who live in Seir, leaving behind the route of the Arabah, and leaving behind Elath and Ezion-geber.

When we had headed out along the route of the wilderness of Moab, ⁹the LORD said to me: "Do not harass Moab or engage them in battle, for I will not give you any of its land as a possession, since I have given Ar as a possession to the descendants of Lot." ¹⁰(The Emim—a large and numerous people, as tall as the Anakim—had formerly inhabited it. ¹¹Like the Anakim, they are usually reckoned as Rephaim, though the Moabites call them Emim. ¹²Moreover, the Horim had formerly inhabited Seir, but the descendants of Esau dispossessed them, destroying them and settling in their place, as Israel has done in the land that the LORD gave them as a possession.) ¹³"Now then, proceed to cross over the Wadi Zered."

So we crossed over the Wadi Zered. ¹⁴And the length of time we had traveled from Kadesh-barnea until we crossed the Wadi Zered was thirty-eight years, until the entire generation of warriors had perished from the camp, as the LORD had

---

PONDER

"Surely the LORD your God has blessed you in all your undertakings; he knows your going through this great wilderness. These forty years the LORD your God has been with you; you have lacked nothing."
—Deuteronomy 2.7

PRAY

Almighty God, we are grateful to read these ancient scriptures written for ancient people but still applicable to us. Help us take them into our own hearts, to understand the consequences of disobeying you and the blessings of heeding your guidance. Help us increase the number of people we love and decrease the number of people to whom we are indifferent and even those we hate, because that is what Jesus Christ would have us do. Receive this entreaty in the name of our Savior. Amen.

---

sworn concerning them. ¹⁵Indeed, the LORD's own hand was against them, to root them out from the camp, until all had perished.

16 Just as soon as all the warriors had died off from among the people, ¹⁷the LORD spoke to me, saying, ¹⁸"Today you are going to cross the boundary of Moab at Ar. ¹⁹When you approach the frontier of the Ammonites, do not harass them or engage them in battle, for I will not give the land of the Ammonites to you as a possession, because I have given it to the descendants of Lot." ²⁰(It also is usually reckoned as a land of Rephaim. Rephaim formerly inhabited it, though the Ammonites call them Zamzummim, ²¹a strong and numerous people, as tall as the Anakim. But the LORD destroyed them from before the Ammonites so that they could dispossess them

ᵃ 2.1 Or Sea of Reeds

and settle in their place. 22He did the same for the descendants of Esau, who live in Seir, by destroying the Horim before them so that they could dispossess them and settle in their place even to this day. 23As for the Avvim, who had lived in settlements in the vicinity of Gaza, the Caphtorim, who came from Caphtor, destroyed them and settled in their place.) 24"Proceed on your journey and cross the Wadi Arnon. See, I have handed over to you King Sihon the Amorite of Heshbon, and his land. Begin to take possession by engaging him in battle. 25This day I will begin to put the dread and fear of you upon the peoples everywhere under heaven; when they hear report of you, they will tremble and be in anguish because of you."

DEFEAT OF KING SIHON

26 So I sent messengers from the wilderness of Kedemoth to King Sihon of Heshbon with the following terms of peace: 27"If you let me pass through your land, I will travel only along the road; I will turn aside neither to the right nor to the left. 28You shall sell me food for money, so that I may eat, and supply me water for money, so that I may drink. Only allow me to pass through on foot— 29just as the descendants of Esau who live in Seir have done for me and likewise the Moabites who live in Ar—until I cross the Jordan into the land that the LORD our God is giving us." 30But King Sihon of Heshbon was not willing to let us pass through, for the LORD your God had hardened his spirit and made his heart defiant in order to hand him over to you, as he has now done. 31The LORD said to me, "See, I have begun to give Sihon and his land over to you. Begin now to take possession of his land." 32So when Sihon came out against us, he and all his people for battle at Jahaz, 33the LORD our God gave him over to us; and we struck him down, along with his offspring and all his people. 34At that time we captured all his towns, and in each town we utterly destroyed men, women, and

children. We left not a single survivor. 35Only the livestock we kept as spoil for ourselves, as well as the plunder of the towns that we had captured. 36From Aroer on the edge of the Wadi Arnon (including the town that is in the wadi itself) as far as Gilead, there was no citadel too high for us. The LORD our God gave everything to us. 37You did not encroach, however, on the land of the Ammonites, avoiding the whole upper region of the Wadi Jabbok as well as the towns of the hill country, just as[a] the LORD our God had charged.

DEFEAT OF KING OG

3 When we headed up the road to Bashan, King Og of Bashan came out against us, he and all his people, for battle at Edrei. 2The LORD said to me, "Do not fear him, for I have handed him over to you, along with his people and his land. Do to him as you did to King Sihon of the Amorites, who reigned in Heshbon." 3So the LORD our God also handed over to us King Og of Bashan and all his people. We struck him down until not a single survivor was left. 4At that time we captured all his towns; there was no citadel that we did not take from them—sixty towns, the whole region of Argob, the kingdom of Og in Bashan. 5All these were fortress towns with high walls, double gates, and bars, besides a great many villages. 6And we utterly destroyed them, as we had done to King Sihon of Heshbon, in each city utterly destroying men, women, and children. 7But all the livestock and the plunder of the towns we kept as spoil for ourselves.

8 So at that time we took from the two kings of the Amorites the land beyond the Jordan, from the Wadi Arnon to Mount Hermon 9(the Sidonians call Hermon Sirion, while the Amorites call it Senir), 10all the towns of the tableland, the whole of Gilead, and all of Bashan, as far as Salecah and Edrei, towns of Og's kingdom in Bashan. 11(Now only King Og of Bashan was left of the

---

[a] 2.37 Gk Tg: Heb and all

remnant of the Rephaim. In fact his bed, an iron bed, can still be seen in Rabbah of the Ammonites. By the common cubit it is nine cubits long and four cubits wide.) ¹²As for the land that we took possession of at that time, I gave to the Reubenites and Gadites the territory north of Aroer,ᵃ that is on the edge of the Wadi Arnon, as well as half the hill country of Gilead with its towns, ¹³and I gave to the half-tribe of Manasseh the rest of Gilead and all of Bashan, Og's kingdom. (The whole region of Argob: all that portion of Bashan used to be called a land of Rephaim; ¹⁴Jair the Manassite acquired the whole region of Argob as far as the border of the Geshurites and the Maacathites, and he named them—that is, Bashan—after himself, Havvoth-jair,ᵇ as it is to this day.) ¹⁵To Machir I gave Gilead. ¹⁶And to the Reubenites and the Gadites I gave the territory from Gilead as far as the Wadi Arnon, with the middle of the wadi as a boundary, and up to the Jabbok, the wadi being boundary of the Ammonites; ¹⁷the Arabah also, with the Jordan and its banks, from Chinnereth down to the sea of the Arabah, the Dead Sea,ᶜ with the lower slopes of Pisgah on the east.

18 At that time, I charged you as follows: "Although the LORD your God has given you this land to occupy, all your troops shall cross over armed as the vanguard of your Israelite kin. ¹⁹Only your wives, your children, and your livestock—I know that you have much livestock—shall stay behind in the towns that I have given to you. ²⁰When the LORD gives rest to your kindred, as to you, and they too have occupied the land that the LORD your God is giving them beyond the Jordan, then each of you may return to the property that I have given to you." ²¹And I charged Joshua as well at that time, saying: "Your own eyes have seen everything that the LORD your God has done to these two kings; so the LORD will do to all the kingdoms into which you are about to cross. ²²Do not fear them, for it is the LORD your God who fights for you."

MOSES VIEWS CANAAN FROM PISGAH

23 At that time, too, I entreated the LORD, saying: ²⁴"O Lord GOD, you have only begun to show your servant your greatness and your might; what god in heaven or on earth can perform deeds and mighty acts like yours! ²⁵Let me cross over to see the good land beyond the Jordan, that good hill country and the Lebanon." ²⁶But the LORD was angry with me on your account and would not heed me. The LORD said to me, "Enough from you! Never speak to me of this matter again! ²⁷Go up to the top of Pisgah and look around you to the west, to the north, to the south, and to the east. Look well, for you shall not cross over this Jordan.

ᵃ 3.12 Heb territory from Aroer   ᵇ 3.14 That is Settlement of Jair   ᶜ 3.17 Heb Salt Sea

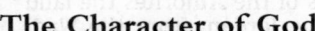

BIBLE IN LIFE

The Character of God   Deuteronomy 3.1–7

If our entire view of God were shaped by a few violent episodes lifted from the Old Testament, we would have a very different image of God: a stern judge, punishing those who disobey; ordering the Israelites to kill every man, woman and child in a village; heaping judgment on nations. These scenes are very disturbing to us, and many people see only a skewed view of God because of these violent stories. However, the Bible paints a fuller picture of God: Though just and holy, God is also faithful, loving, patient, compassionate and full of grace. Whenever we want a clear glimpse of God's character, we need only to study the life of Jesus, who affirmed, "Whoever has seen me has seen the Father" (John 14.9).

28But charge Joshua, and encourage and strengthen him, because it is he who shall cross over at the head of this people and who shall secure their possession of the land that you will see." 29So we remained in the valley opposite Beth-peor.

MOSES COMMANDS OBEDIENCE

4 So now, Israel, give heed to the statutes and ordinances that I am teaching you to observe, so that you may live to enter and occupy the land that the LORD, the God of your ancestors, is giving you. 2You must neither add anything to what I command you nor take away anything from it, but keep the commandments of the LORD your God with which I am charging you. 3You have seen for yourselves what the LORD did with regard to the Baal of Peor—how the LORD your God destroyed from among you everyone who followed the Baal of Peor, 4while those of you who held fast to the LORD your God are all alive today.

5 See, just as the LORD my God has charged me, I now teach you statutes and ordinances for you to observe in the land that you are about to enter and occupy. 6You must observe them diligently, for this will show your wisdom and discernment to the peoples, who, when they hear all these statutes, will say, "Surely this great nation is a wise and discerning people!" 7For what other great nation has a god so near to it as the LORD our God is whenever we call to him? 8And what other great nation has statutes and ordinances as just as this entire law that I am setting before you today?

9 But take care and watch yourselves closely, so as neither to forget the things that your eyes have seen nor to let them slip from your mind all the days of your life; make them known to your children and your children's children— 10how you once stood before the LORD your God at Horeb, when the LORD said to me, "Assemble the people for me, and I will let them hear my words, so that they may learn to fear me as long as they live on the earth, and

may teach their children so"; 11you approached and stood at the foot of the mountain while the mountain was blazing up to the very heavens, shrouded in dark clouds. 12Then the LORD spoke to you out of the fire. You heard the sound of words but saw no form; there was only a voice. 13He declared to you his covenant, which he charged you to observe, that is, the ten commandments;a and he wrote them on two stone tablets. 14And the LORD charged me at that time to teach you statutes and ordinances for you to observe in the land that you are about to cross into and occupy.

15 Since you saw no form when the LORD spoke to you at Horeb out of the fire, take care and watch yourselves closely, 16so that you do not act corruptly by making an idol for yourselves, in the form of any figure—the likeness of male or female, 17the likeness of any animal that is on the earth, the likeness of any winged bird that flies in the air, 18the likeness of anything that creeps on the ground, the likeness of any fish that is in the water under the earth. 19And when you look up to the heavens and see the sun, the moon, and the stars, all the host of heaven, do not be led astray and bow down to them and serve them, things that the LORD your God has allotted to all the peoples everywhere under heaven. 20But the LORD has taken you and brought you out of the iron-smelter, out of Egypt, to become a people of his very own possession, as you are now.

21 The LORD was angry with me because of you, and he vowed that I should not cross the Jordan and that I should not enter the good land that the LORD your God is giving for your possession. 22For I am going to die in this land without crossing over the Jordan, but you are going to cross over to take possession of that good land. 23So be careful not to forget the covenant that the LORD your God made with you, and not to make for yourselves an idol in the form of

a 4.13 Heb the ten words

anything that the LORD your God has forbidden you. 24For the LORD your God is a devouring fire, a jealous God.

25 When you have had children and children's children, and become complacent in the land, if you act corruptly by making an idol in the form of anything, thus doing what is evil in the sight of the LORD your God, and provoking him to anger, 26I call heaven and earth to witness against you today that you will soon utterly perish from the land that you are crossing the Jordan to occupy; you will not live long on it, but will be utterly destroyed. 27The LORD will scatter you among the peoples; only a few of you will be left among the nations where the LORD will lead you. 28There you will serve other gods made by human hands, objects of wood and stone that neither see, nor hear, nor eat, nor smell. 29From there you will seek the LORD your God, and you will find him if you search after him with all your heart and soul. 30In your distress, when all these things have happened to you in time to come, you will return to the LORD your God and heed him. 31Because the LORD your God is a merciful God, he will neither abandon you nor destroy you; he will not forget the covenant with your ancestors that he swore to them.

32 For ask now about former ages, long before your own, ever since the day that God created human beings on the earth; ask from one end of heaven to the other: has anything so great as this ever happened or has its like ever been heard of? 33Has any people ever heard the voice of a god speaking out of a fire, as you have heard, and lived? 34Or has any god ever attempted to go and take a nation for himself from the midst of another nation, by trials, by signs and wonders, by war, by a mighty hand and an outstretched arm, and by terrifying displays of power, as the LORD your God did for you in Egypt before your very eyes? 35To you it was shown so that you would acknowledge that the LORD is God; there is no other besides him.

36From heaven he made you hear his voice to discipline you. On earth he showed you his great fire, while you heard his words coming out of the fire. 37And because he loved your ancestors, he chose their descendants after them. He brought you out of Egypt with his own presence, by his great power, 38driving out before you nations greater and mightier than yourselves, to bring you in, giving you their land for a possession, as it is still today. 39So acknowledge today and take to heart that the LORD is God in heaven above and on the earth beneath; there is no other. 40Keep his statutes and his commandments, which I am commanding you today for your own well-being and that of your descendants after you, so that you may long remain in the land that the LORD your God is giving you for all time.

CITIES OF REFUGE EAST OF THE JORDAN

41 Then Moses set apart on the east side of the Jordan three cities 42to which a homicide could flee, someone who unintentionally kills another person, the two not having been at enmity before; the homicide could flee to one of these cities and live: 43Bezer in the wilderness on the tableland belonging to the Reubenites, Ramoth in Gilead belonging to the Gadites, and Golan in Bashan belonging to the Manassites.

TRANSITION TO THE SECOND ADDRESS

44 This is the law that Moses set before the Israelites. 45These are the decrees and the statutes and ordinances that Moses spoke to the Israelites when they had come out of Egypt, 46beyond the Jordan in the valley opposite Beth-peor, in the land of King Sihon of the Amorites, who reigned at Heshbon, whom Moses and the Israelites defeated when they came out of Egypt. 47They occupied his land and the land of King Og of Bashan, the two kings of the Amorites on the eastern side of the Jordan: 48from Aroer, which is on

the edge of the Wadi Arnon, as far as Mount Sirion[a] (that is, Hermon), [49]together with all the Arabah on the east side of the Jordan as far as the Sea of the Arabah, under the slopes of Pisgah.

THE TEN COMMANDMENTS

5 Moses convened all Israel, and said to them:

Hear, O Israel, the statutes and ordinances that I am addressing to you today; you shall learn them and observe them diligently. [2]The LORD our God made a covenant with us at Horeb. [3]Not with our ancestors did the LORD make this covenant, but with us, who are all of us here alive today. [4]The LORD spoke with you face to face at the mountain, out of the fire. [5](At that time I was standing between the LORD and you to declare to you the words[b] of the LORD; for you were afraid because of the fire and did not go up the mountain.) And he said:

[6]I am the LORD your God, who brought you out of the land of Egypt, out of the house of slavery; [7]you shall have no other gods before[c] me.

[8]You shall not make for yourself an idol, whether in the form of anything that is in heaven above, or that is on the earth beneath, or that is in the water under the earth. [9]You shall not bow down to them or worship them; for I the LORD your God am a jealous God, punishing children for the iniquity of parents, to the third and fourth generation of those who reject me, [10]but showing steadfast love to the thousandth generation[d] of those who love me and keep my commandments.

[11]You shall not make wrongful use of the name of the LORD your God, for the LORD will not acquit anyone who misuses his name.

[12]Observe the sabbath day and keep it holy, as the LORD your God commanded you. [13]Six days you shall labor and do all your work. [14]But the seventh day is a sabbath to the LORD your God; you shall not do any work—you, or your son or your daughter, or your male or female slave, or your ox or your donkey, or any of your livestock, or the resident alien in your towns, so that your male and female slave may rest as well as you. [15]Remember that you were a slave in the land of Egypt, and the LORD your God brought you out from there with a mighty hand and an outstretched arm; therefore the LORD your God commanded you to keep the sabbath day.

[16]Honor your father and your mother, as the LORD your God commanded you, so that your days may be long and that it may go well with you in the land that the LORD your God is giving you.

[17]You shall not murder.[e]

a 4.48 Syr: Heb *Sion*   b 5.5 Q Mss Sam Gk Syr Vg Tg: MT *word*   c 5.7 Or *besides*   d 5.10 Or *to thousands*   e 5.17 Or *kill*

BIBLE IN LIFE

Misusing God's Name
Deuteronomy 5.11

When God gave the Israelites the third commandment (see Exodus 20.7), they understood the personal nature of God's name. God prefaced the ten commandments with this statement to the people of Israel: "I am the LORD your God, who brought you out of the land of Egypt, out of the house of slavery" (Exodus 20.2). God had saved and redeemed them. God's name was to be honored above all other names. We too are to honor God's name and not misuse it. Every day, we hear God's name used countless times in inappropriate and meaningless ways. Even some Christians use the name of our Creator, our personal Redeemer and Savior, in a careless or non-reverential way. We must avoid this temptation. Sometimes it occurs through habit; sometimes it occurs through carelessness; sometimes it occurs because we forget, downplay or willfully ignore this third commandment. May we revere the name of God.

18 Neither shall you commit adultery. **19** Neither shall you steal. **20** Neither shall you bear false witness against your neighbor. **21** Neither shall you covet your neighbor's wife.

Neither shall you desire your neighbor's house, or field, or male or female slave, or ox, or donkey, or anything that belongs to your neighbor.

MOSES THE MEDIATOR
OF GOD'S WILL

22 These words the LORD spoke with a loud voice to your whole assembly at the mountain, out of the fire, the cloud, and the thick darkness, and he added no more. He wrote them on two stone tablets, and gave them to me. **23** When you heard the voice out of the darkness, while the mountain was burning with fire, you approached me, all the heads of your tribes and your elders; **24** and you said, "Look, the LORD our God has shown us his glory and greatness, and we have heard his voice out of the fire. Today we have seen that God may speak to someone and the person may still live. **25** So now why should we die? For this great fire will consume us; if we hear the voice of the LORD our God any longer, we shall die. **26** For who is there of all flesh that has heard the voice of the living God speaking out of fire, as we have, and remained alive? **27** Go near, you yourself, and hear all that the LORD our God will say. Then tell us everything that the LORD our God tells you, and we will listen and do it."

28 The LORD heard your words when you spoke to me, and the LORD said to me: "I have heard the words of this people, which they have spoken to you; they are right in all that they have spoken. **29** If only they had such a mind as this, to fear me and to keep all my commandments always, so that it might go well with them and with their children forever! **30** Go say to them, 'Return to your tents.' **31** But you, stand here by me, and I will tell you all the commandments, the statutes and

the ordinances, that you shall teach them, so that they may do them in the land that I am giving them to possess." **32** You must therefore be careful to do as the LORD your God has commanded you; you shall not turn to the right or to the left. **33** You must follow exactly the path that the LORD your God has commanded you, so that you may live, and that it may go well with you, and that you may live long in the land that you are to possess.

THE GREAT COMMANDMENT

6 Now this is the commandment—the statutes and the ordinances—that the LORD your God charged me to teach you to observe in the land that you are about to cross into and occupy, **2** so that you and your children and your children's children may fear the LORD your God all the days of your life, and keep all his decrees and his commandments that I am commanding you, so that your days may be long. **3** Hear therefore, O Israel, and observe them diligently, so that it may go well with you, and so that you may multiply greatly in a land flowing with milk and honey, as the LORD, the God of your ancestors, has promised you.

4 Hear, O Israel: The LORD is our God, the LORD alone.[a] **5** You shall love the LORD your God with all your heart, and with all your soul, and with all your might. **6** Keep these words that I am commanding you today in your heart. **7** Recite them to your children and talk about them when you are at home and when you are away, when you lie down and when you rise. **8** Bind them as a sign on your hand, fix them as an emblem[b] on your forehead, **9** and write them on the doorposts of your house and on your gates.

CAUTION AGAINST
DISOBEDIENCE

10 When the LORD your God has brought you into the land that he

a 6.4 Or *The LORD our God is one LORD,* or *The LORD our God, the LORD is one,* or *The LORD is our God, the LORD is one*   b 6.8 Or *as a frontlet*

swore to your ancestors, to Abraham, to Isaac, and to Jacob, to give you—a land with fine, large cities that you did not build, 11houses filled with all sorts of goods that you did not fill, hewn cisterns that you did not hew, vineyards and olive groves that you did not plant—and when you have eaten your fill, 12take care that you do not forget the LORD, who brought you out of the land of Egypt, out of the house of slavery. 13The LORD your God you shall fear; him you shall serve, and by his name alone you shall swear. 14Do not follow other gods, any of the gods of the peoples who are all around you, 15because the LORD your God, who is present with you, is a jealous God. The anger of the LORD your God would be kindled against you and he would destroy you from the face of the earth.

16 Do not put the LORD your God to the test, as you tested him at Massah. 17You must diligently keep the commandments of the LORD your God, and his decrees, and his statutes that he has commanded you. 18Do what is right and good in the sight of the LORD, so that it may go well with you, and so that you may go in and occupy the good land that the LORD swore to your ancestors to give you, 19thrusting out all your enemies from before you, as the LORD has promised.

20 When your children ask you in time to come, "What is the meaning of the decrees and the statutes and the ordinances that the LORD our God has commanded you?" 21then you shall say to your children, "We were Pharaoh's slaves in Egypt, but the LORD brought us out of Egypt with a mighty hand. 22The LORD displayed before our eyes great and awesome signs and wonders against Egypt, against Pharaoh and all his household. 23He brought us out from there in order to bring us in, to give us the land that he promised on oath to our ancestors. 24Then the LORD commanded us to observe all these statutes, to fear the LORD our God, for our lasting good, so as to keep us alive, as is now the case.

25If we diligently observe this entire commandment before the LORD our God, as he has commanded us, we will be in the right."

A CHOSEN PEOPLE

7 When the LORD your God brings you into the land that you are about to enter and occupy, and he clears away many nations before you—the Hittites, the Girgashites, the Amorites, the Canaanites, the Perizzites, the Hivites, and the Jebusites, seven nations mightier and more numerous than you— 2and when the LORD your God gives them over to you and you defeat them, then you must utterly destroy them. Make no covenant with them and show them no mercy. 3Do not intermarry with them, giving your daughters to their sons or taking their daughters for your sons, 4for that would turn away your children from following me, to serve other gods. Then the anger of the LORD would be kindled against you, and he would destroy you quickly. 5But this is how you must deal with them: break down their altars, smash their pillars, hew down their sacred poles,a and burn their idols with fire. 6For you are a people holy to the LORD your God; the LORD your God has chosen you out of all the peoples on earth to be his people, his treasured possession.

7 It was not because you were more numerous than any other people that the LORD set his heart on you and chose you—for you were the fewest of all peoples. 8It was because the LORD loved you and kept the oath that he swore to your ancestors, that the LORD has brought you out with a mighty hand, and redeemed you from the house of slavery, from the hand of Pharaoh king of Egypt. 9Know therefore that the LORD your God is God, the faithful God who maintains covenant loyalty with those who love him and keep his commandments, to a thousand generations, 10and who repays in their own person those who reject

a 7.5 Heb Asherim

PONDER

Know therefore that the LORD your God is God, the faithful God who maintains covenant loyalty with those who love him and keep his commandments, to a thousand generations.
—Deuteronomy 7.9

PRAY

O Lord, thank you for showing us the trials, sorrows and recoveries of the Hebrew people. We see how they often struggled with their temptations and often failed to prevail, how they turned away from you, received your forgiveness and grace and then learned from their mistakes. Help us learn from their example; strengthen us in our resolve to uphold our share of the covenant that we have with you, our Creator, through love of our Savior, Jesus Christ. Amen.

him. He does not delay but repays in their own person those who reject him. [11]Therefore, observe diligently the commandment—the statutes and the ordinances—that I am commanding you today.

BLESSINGS FOR OBEDIENCE

12 If you heed these ordinances, by diligently observing them, the LORD your God will maintain with you the covenant loyalty that he swore to your ancestors; [13]he will love you, bless you, and multiply you; he will bless the fruit of your womb and the fruit of your ground, your grain and your wine and your oil, the increase of your cattle and the issue of your flock, in the land that he swore to your ancestors to give you. [14]You shall be the most blessed of peoples, with neither sterility nor barrenness among you or your livestock. [15]The LORD will turn away from you every illness; all the dread diseases of Egypt that you ex-

perienced, he will not inflict on you, but he will lay them on all who hate you. [16]You shall devour all the peoples that the LORD your God is giving over to you, showing them no pity; you shall not serve their gods, for that would be a snare to you.

17 If you say to yourself, "These nations are more numerous than I; how can I dispossess them?" [18]do not be afraid of them. Just remember what the LORD your God did to Pharaoh and to all Egypt, [19]the great trials that your eyes saw, the signs and wonders, the mighty hand and the outstretched arm by which the LORD your God brought you out. The LORD your God will do the same to all the peoples of whom you are afraid. [20]Moreover, the LORD your God will send the pestilence[a] against them, until even the survivors and the fugitives are destroyed. [21]Have no dread of them, for the LORD your God, who is present with you, is a great and awesome God. [22]The LORD your God will clear away these nations before you little by little; you will not be able to make a quick end of them, otherwise the wild animals would become too numerous for you. [23]But the LORD your God will give them over to you, and throw them into great panic, until they are destroyed. [24]He will hand their kings over to you and you shall blot out their name from under heaven; no one will be able to stand against you, until you have destroyed them. [25]The images of their gods you shall burn with fire. Do not covet the silver or the gold that is on them and take it for yourself, because you could be ensnared by it; for it is abhorrent to the LORD your God. [26]Do not bring an abhorrent thing into your house, or you will be set apart for destruction like it. You must utterly detest and abhor it, for it is set apart for destruction.

A WARNING NOT TO FORGET GOD IN PROSPERITY

8 This entire commandment that I command you today you must

[a] 7.20 Or *hornets*: Meaning of Heb uncertain

diligently observe, so that you may live and increase, and go in and occupy the land that the LORD promised on oath to your ancestors. ²Remember the long way that the LORD your God has led you these forty years in the wilderness, in order to humble you, testing you to know what was in your heart, whether or not you would keep his commandments. ³He humbled you by letting you hunger, then by feeding you with manna, with which neither you nor your ancestors were acquainted, in order to make you understand that one does not live by bread alone, but by every word that comes from the mouth of the LORD.ᵃ ⁴The clothes on your back did not wear out and your feet did not swell these forty years. ⁵Know then in your heart that as a parent disciplines a child so the LORD your God disciplines you. ⁶Therefore keep the commandments of the LORD your God, by walking in his ways and by fearing him. ⁷For the LORD your God is bringing you into a good land, a land with flowing streams, with springs and underground waters welling up in valleys and hills, ⁸a land of wheat and barley, of vines and fig trees and pomegranates, a land of olive trees and honey, ⁹a land where you may eat bread without scarcity, where you will lack nothing, a land whose stones are iron and from whose hills you may mine copper. ¹⁰You shall eat your fill and bless the LORD your God for the good land that he has given you.

¹¹ Take care that you do not forget the LORD your God, by failing to keep his commandments, his ordinances, and his statutes, which I am commanding you today. ¹²When you have eaten your fill and have built fine houses and live in them, ¹³and when your herds and flocks have multiplied, and your silver and gold is multiplied, and all that you have is multiplied, ¹⁴then do not exalt yourself, forgetting the LORD your God, who brought you out of the land of Egypt, out of the house of slavery, ¹⁵who led you through the great and terrible wilderness, an arid wasteland with poisonousᵇ snakes and scorpions. He made water flow for you from flint rock, ¹⁶and fed you in the wilderness with manna that your ancestors did not know, to humble you and to test you, and in the end to do you good. ¹⁷Do not say to yourself, "My power and the might of my own hand have gotten me this wealth." ¹⁸But remember the LORD your God, for it is he who gives you power to get wealth, so that he may confirm his covenant that he swore to your ancestors, as he is doing today. ¹⁹If you do forget the LORD your God and follow other gods to serve and worship them, I solemnly warn you today that you shall surely perish. ²⁰Like the nations that the LORD is destroying before you, so shall you perish, because you would not obey the voice of the LORD your God.

GOD'S DISCIPLINE YIELDS

FRUITFUL LIVES.

THE CONSEQUENCES OF REBELLING AGAINST GOD

9 Hear, O Israel! You are about to cross the Jordan today, to go in and dispossess nations larger and mightier than you, great cities, fortified to the heavens, ²a strong and tall people, the offspring of the Anakim, whom you know. You have heard it said of them, "Who can stand up to the Anakim?" ³Know then today that the LORD your God is the one who crosses over before you as a devouring fire; he will defeat them and subdue them before you, so that you may dispossess and destroy them quickly, as the LORD has promised you.

⁴When the LORD your God thrusts them out before you, do not

ᵃ 8.3 Or by anything that the LORD decrees
ᵇ 8.15 Or fiery; Heb seraph

say to yourself, "It is because of my righteousness that the LORD has brought me in to occupy this land"; it is rather because of the wickedness of these nations that the LORD is dispossessing them before you. 5It is not because of your righteousness or the uprightness of your heart that you are going in to occupy their land; but because of the wickedness of these nations the LORD your God is dispossessing them before you, in order to fulfill the promise that the LORD made on oath to your ancestors, to Abraham, to Isaac, and to Jacob.

6 Know, then, that the LORD your God is not giving you this good land to occupy because of your righteousness; for you are a stubborn people. 7Remember and do not forget how you provoked the LORD your God to wrath in the wilderness; you have been rebellious against the LORD from the day you came out of the land of Egypt until you came to this place.

8 Even at Horeb you provoked the LORD to wrath, and the LORD was so angry with you that he was ready to destroy you. 9When I went up the mountain to receive the stone tablets, the tablets of the covenant that the LORD made with you, I remained on the mountain forty days and forty nights; I neither ate bread nor drank water. 10And the LORD gave me the two stone tablets written with the finger of God; on them were all the words that the LORD had spoken to you at the mountain out of the fire on the day of the assembly. 11At the end of forty days and forty nights the LORD gave me the two stone tablets, the tablets of the covenant. 12Then the LORD said to me, "Get up, go down quickly from here, for your people whom you have brought from Egypt have acted corruptly. They have been quick to turn from the way that I commanded them; they have cast an image for themselves." 13Furthermore the LORD said to me, "I have seen that this people is indeed a stubborn people. 14Let me alone that I may destroy them and blot out

their name from under heaven; and I will make of you a nation mightier and more numerous than they."

15 So I turned and went down from the mountain, while the mountain was ablaze; the two tablets of the covenant were in my two hands. 16Then I saw that you had indeed sinned against the LORD your God, by casting for yourselves an image of a calf; you had been quick to turn from the way that the LORD had commanded you. 17So I took hold of the two tablets and flung them from my two hands, smashing them before your eyes. 18Then I lay prostrate before the LORD as before, forty days and forty nights; I neither ate bread nor drank water, because of all the sin you had committed, provoking the LORD by doing what was evil in his sight. 19For I was afraid that the anger that the LORD bore against you was so fierce that he would destroy you. But the LORD listened to me that time also. 20The LORD was so angry with Aaron that he was ready to destroy him, but I interceded also on behalf of Aaron at that same time. 21Then I took the sinful thing you had made, the calf, and burned it with fire and crushed it, grinding it thoroughly, until it was reduced to dust; and I threw the dust of it into the stream that runs down the mountain.

22 At Taberah also, and at Massah, and at Kibroth-hattaavah, you provoked the LORD to wrath. 23And when the LORD sent you from Kadesh-barnea, saying, "Go up and occupy the land that I have given you," you rebelled against the command of the LORD your God, neither trusting him nor obeying him. 24You have been rebellious against the LORD as long as he hasᵃ known you.

25 Throughout the forty days and forty nights that I lay prostrate before the LORD when the LORD intended to destroy you, 26I prayed to the LORD and said, "Lord GOD, do not destroy the people who are your very own possession, whom you re-

ᵃ 9.24 Sam Gk: MT *I have*

deemed in your greatness, whom you brought out of Egypt with a mighty hand. ²⁷Remember your servants, Abraham, Isaac, and Jacob; pay no attention to the stubbornness of this people, their wickedness and their sin, ²⁸otherwise the land from which you have brought us might say, 'Because the LORD was not able to bring them into the land that he promised them, and because he hated them, he has brought them out to let them die in the wilderness.' ²⁹For they are the people of your very own possession, whom you brought out by your great power and by your outstretched arm."

THE SECOND PAIR OF TABLETS

10 At that time the LORD said to me, "Carve out two tablets of stone like the former ones, and come up to me on the mountain, and make an ark of wood. ²I will write on the tablets the words that were on the former tablets, which you smashed, and you shall put them in the ark." ³So I made an ark of acacia wood, cut two tablets of stone like the former ones, and went up the mountain with the two tablets in my hand. ⁴Then he wrote on the tablets the same words as before, the ten commandmentsᵃ that the LORD had spoken to you on the mountain out of the fire on the day of the assembly; and the LORD gave them to me. ⁵So I turned and came down from the mountain, and put the tablets in the ark that I had made; and there they are, as the LORD commanded me.

6 (The Israelites journeyed from Beeroth-bene-jaakanᵇ to Moserah. There Aaron died, and there he was buried; his son Eleazar succeeded him as priest. ⁷From there they journeyed to Gudgodah, and from Gudgodah to Jotbathah, a land with flowing streams. ⁸At that time the LORD set apart the tribe of Levi to carry the ark of the covenant of the LORD, to stand before the LORD to minister to him, and to bless in his name, to this day. ⁹Therefore Levi has no allotment or inheritance with his kindred; the LORD is his inheritance, as the LORD your God promised him.)

10 I stayed on the mountain forty days and forty nights, as I had done the first time. And once again the LORD listened to me. The LORD was unwilling to destroy you. ¹¹The LORD said to me, "Get up, go on your journey at the head of the people, that they may go in and occupy the land that I swore to their ancestors to give them."

THE ESSENCE OF THE LAW

12 So now, O Israel, what does the LORD your God require of you? Only to fear the LORD your God, to walk in all his ways, to love him, to serve the LORD your God with all your heart and with all your soul, ¹³and to keep the commandments of the LORD your Godᶜ and his decrees that I am commanding you today, for your own well-being. ¹⁴Although heaven and the heaven of heavens belong to the LORD your God, the earth with all that is in it, ¹⁵yet the LORD set his heart in love on your ancestors alone and chose you, their descendants after them, out of all the peoples, as it is today. ¹⁶Circumcise, then, the foreskin of your heart, and do not be stubborn any longer. ¹⁷For the LORD your God is God of gods and Lord of lords, the great God, mighty and awesome, who is not partial and takes no bribe, ¹⁸who executes justice for the orphan and the widow, and who loves the strangers, providing them food and clothing. ¹⁹You shall also love the stranger, for you were strangers in the land of Egypt. ²⁰You shall fear the LORD your God; him alone you shall worship; to him you shall hold fast, and by his name you shall swear. ²¹He is your praise; he is your God, who has done for you these great and awesome things that your own eyes have seen. ²²Your ancestors went down to Egypt seventy persons; and now the LORD your God has made you as numerous as the stars in heaven.

ᵃ **10.4** Heb *the ten words*   ᵇ **10.6** Or *the wells of the Bene-jaakan*   ᶜ **10.13** Q Ms Gk Syr: MT lacks *your God*

REWARDS FOR OBEDIENCE

11 You shall love the LORD your God, therefore, and keep his charge, his decrees, his ordinances, and his commandments always. ²Remember today that it was not your children (who have not known or seen the discipline of the LORD your God), but it is you who must acknowledge his greatness, his mighty hand and his outstretched arm, ³his signs and his deeds that he did in Egypt to Pharaoh, the king of Egypt, and to all his land; ⁴what he did to the Egyptian army, to their horses and chariots, how he made the water of the Red Seaª flow over them as they pursued you, so that the LORD has destroyed them to this day; ⁵what he did to you in the wilderness, until you came to this place; ⁶and what he did to Dathan and Abiram, sons of Eliab son of Reuben, how in the midst of all Israel the earth opened its mouth and swallowed them up, along with their households, their tents, and every living being in their company; ⁷for it is your own eyes that have seen every great deed that the LORD did.

8 Keep, then, this entire commandment that I am commanding you today, so that you may have strength to go in and occupy the land that you are crossing over to occupy, ⁹and so that you may live long in the land that the LORD swore to your ancestors to give them and to their descendants, a land flowing with milk and honey. ¹⁰For the land that you are about to enter to occupy is not like the land of Egypt, from which you have come, where you sow your seed and irrigate by foot like a vegetable garden. ¹¹But the land that you are crossing over to occupy is a land of hills and valleys, watered by rain from the sky, ¹²a land that the LORD your God looks after. The eyes of the LORD your God are always on it, from the beginning of the year to the end of the year.

13 If you will only heed his every commandmentᵇ that I am commanding you today—loving the LORD your God, and serving him with all your heart and with all your soul— ¹⁴then heᶜ will give the rain for your land in its season, the early rain and the later rain, and you will gather in your grain, your wine, and your oil; ¹⁵and heᶜ will give grass in your fields for your livestock, and you will eat your fill. ¹⁶Take care, or you will be seduced into turning away, serving other gods and worshiping them, ¹⁷for then the anger of the LORD will be kindled against you and he will shut up the heavens, so that there will be no rain and the land will yield no fruit; then you will perish quickly off the good land that the LORD is giving you.

18 You shall put these words of mine in your heart and soul, and you shall bind them as a sign on your hand, and fix them as an emblemᵈ on your forehead. ¹⁹Teach them to

ª 11.4 Or *Sea of Reeds* ᵇ 11.13 Compare Gk: Heb *my commandments* ᶜ 11.14,15 Sam Gk Vg: MT *I* ᵈ 11.18 Or *as a frontlet*

BIBLE IN LIFE

Love and Obey
Deuteronomy 11.1–25

Loving God and keeping his commandments go hand in hand. Jesus said, "If you love me, you will keep my commandments" (John 14.15). If we don't keep his commands, we demonstrate an absence of love for him. There is a constant interplay between two things: the demands of God on us and the grace of God for us. The demands of God are quite stringent. Christ said, "Be perfect" (Matthew 5.48), yet none of us can obey that command entirely. By the grace of God, however, regardless of our sin, we are forgiven. We are able to obey and to love because of what Christ has done for us. We're weak, we're sinful, we're doubtful, we're anxious, we're lonely, we're insecure, but through Christ and his Holy Spirit, we receive adequate strength to meet the responsibility put on us by God.

your children, talking about them when you are at home and when you are away, when you lie down and when you rise. 20Write them on the doorposts of your house and on your gates, 21so that your days and the days of your children may be multiplied in the land that the LORD swore to your ancestors to give them, as long as the heavens are above the earth.

22 If you will diligently observe this entire commandment that I am commanding you, loving the LORD your God, walking in all his ways, and holding fast to him, 23then the LORD will drive out all these nations before you, and you will dispossess nations larger and mightier than yourselves. 24Every place on which you set foot shall be yours; your territory shall extend from the wilderness to the Lebanon and from the River, the river Euphrates, to the Western Sea. 25No one will be able to stand against you; the LORD your God will put the fear and dread of you on all the land on which you set foot, as he promised you.

26 See, I am setting before you today a blessing and a curse: 27the blessing, if you obey the commandments of the LORD your God that I am commanding you today; 28and the curse, if you do not obey the commandments of the LORD your God, but turn from the way that I am commanding you today, to follow other gods that you have not known.

29 When the LORD your God has brought you into the land that you are entering to occupy, you shall set the blessing on Mount Gerizim and the curse on Mount Ebal. 30As you know, they are beyond the Jordan, some distance to the west, in the land of the Canaanites who live in the Arabah, opposite Gilgal, beside the oak[a] of Moreh. 31When you cross the Jordan to go in to occupy the land that the LORD your God is giving you, and when you occupy it and live in it, 32you must diligently observe all the statutes and ordinances that I am setting before you today.

PAGAN SHRINES TO BE DESTROYED

12 These are the statutes and ordinances that you must diligently observe in the land that the LORD, the God of your ancestors, has given you to occupy all the days that you live on the earth.

2 You must demolish completely all the places where the nations whom you are about to dispossess served their gods, on the mountain heights, on the hills, and under every leafy tree. 3Break down their altars, smash their pillars, burn their sacred poles[b] with fire, and hew down the idols of their gods, and thus blot out their name from their places. 4You shall not worship the LORD your God in such ways. 5But you shall seek the place that the LORD your God will choose out of all your tribes as his habitation to put his name there. You shall go there, 6bringing there your burnt offerings and your sacrifices, your tithes and your donations, your votive gifts, your freewill offerings, and the firstlings of your herds and flocks. 7And you shall eat there in the presence of the LORD your God, you and your households together, rejoicing in all the undertakings in which the LORD your God has blessed you.

8 You shall not act as we are acting here today, all of us according to our own desires, 9for you have not yet come into the rest and the possession that the LORD your God is giving you. 10When you cross over the Jordan and live in the land that the LORD your God is allotting to you, and when he gives you rest from your enemies all around so that you live in safety, 11then you shall bring everything that I command you to the place that the LORD your God will choose as a dwelling for his name: your burnt offerings and your sacrifices, your tithes and your donations, and all your choice votive gifts that you vow to the LORD. 12And you shall rejoice before the LORD your God, you together

a 11.30 Gk Syr: Compare Gen 12.6; Heb oaks or terebinths   b 12.3 Heb Asherim

with your sons and your daughters, your male and female slaves, and the Levites who reside in your towns (since they have no allotment or inheritance with you).

A PRESCRIBED PLACE OF WORSHIP

13 Take care that you do not offer your burnt offerings at any place you happen to see. 14But only at the place that the LORD will choose in one of your tribes—there you shall offer your burnt offerings and there you shall do everything I command you. 15 Yet whenever you desire you may slaughter and eat meat within any of your towns, according to the blessing that the LORD your God has given you; the unclean and the clean may eat of it, as they would of gazelle or deer. 16The blood, however, you must not eat; you shall pour it out on the ground like water. 17Nor may you eat within your towns the tithe of your grain, your wine, and your oil, the firstlings of your herds and your flocks, any of your votive gifts that you vow, your freewill offerings, or your donations; 18these you shall eat in the presence of the LORD your God at the place that the LORD your God will choose, you together with your son and your daughter, your male and female slaves, and the Levites resident in your towns, rejoicing in the presence of the LORD your God in all your undertakings. 19Take care that you do not neglect the Levite as long as you live in your land.

20 When the LORD your God enlarges your territory, as he has promised you, and you say, "I am going to eat some meat," because you wish to eat meat, you may eat meat whenever you have the desire. 21If the place where the LORD your God will choose to put his name is too far from you, and you slaughter as I have commanded you any of your herd or flock that the LORD has given you, then you may eat within your towns whenever you desire. 22Indeed, just as gazelle or deer is eaten, so you may eat it; the unclean and the clean alike may eat it. 23Only

be sure that you do not eat the blood; for the blood is the life, and you shall not eat the life with the meat. 24Do not eat it; you shall pour it out on the ground like water. 25Do not eat it, so that all may go well with you and your children after you, because you do what is right in the sight of the LORD. 26But the sacred donations that are due from you, and your votive gifts, you shall bring to the place that the LORD will choose. 27You shall present your burnt offerings, both the meat and the blood, on the altar of the LORD your God; the blood of your other sacrifices shall be poured out besidea the altar of the LORD your God, but the meat you may eat.

28 Be careful to obey all these words that I command you today,b so that it may go well with you and with your children after you forever, because you will be doing what is good and right in the sight of the LORD your God.

WARNING AGAINST IDOLATRY

29 When the LORD your God has cut off before you the nations whom you are about to enter to dispossess them, when you have dispossessed them and live in their land, 30take care that you are not snared into imitating them, after they have been destroyed before you: do not inquire concerning their gods, saying, "How did these nations worship their gods? I also want to do the same." 31You must not do the same for the LORD your God, because every abhorrent thing that the LORD hates they have done for their gods. They would even burn their sons and their daughters in the fire to their gods. 32cYou must diligently observe everything that I command you; do not add to it or take anything from it.

13d If prophets or those who divine by dreams appear among you and promise you omens or portents, 2and the omens or the portents declared by them take place,

a 12.27 Or on   b 12.28 Gk Sam Syr: MT lacks today   c 12.32 Ch 13.1 in Heb   d 13.1 Ch 13.2 in Heb and they say, "Let us follow other gods" (whom you have not known) "and let us serve them," ³you must not heed the words of those prophets or those who divine by dreams; for the LORD your God is testing you, to know whether you indeed love the LORD your God with all your heart and soul. ⁴The LORD your God you shall follow, him alone you shall fear, his commandments you shall keep, his voice you shall obey, him you shall serve, and to him you shall hold fast. ⁵But those prophets or those who divine by dreams shall be put to death for having spoken treason against the LORD your God—who brought you out of the land of Egypt and redeemed you from the house of slavery—to turn you from the way in which the LORD your God commanded you to walk. So you shall purge the evil from your midst.

6 If anyone secretly entices you— even if it is your brother, your father's son orᵃ your mother's son, or your own son or daughter, or the wife you embrace, or your most intimate friend—saying, "Let us go worship other gods," whom neither you nor your ancestors have known, ⁷any of the gods of the peoples that are around you, whether near you or far away from you, from one end of the earth to the other, ⁸you must not yield to or heed any such persons. Show them no pity or compassion and do not shield them. ⁹But you shall surely kill them; your own hand shall be first against them to execute them, and afterwards the hand of all the people. ¹⁰Stone them to death for trying to turn you away from the LORD your God, who brought you out of the land of Egypt, out of the house of slavery. ¹¹Then all Israel shall hear and be afraid, and never again do any such wickedness.

12 If you hear it said about one of the towns that the LORD your God is giving you to live in, ¹³that scoundrels from among you have gone out and led the inhabitants of the town astray, saying, "Let us go and worship other gods," whom you have not known, ¹⁴then you shall inquire and make a thorough investigation. If the charge is established that such an abhorrent thing has been done among you, ¹⁵you shall put the inhabitants of that town to the sword, utterly destroying it and everything in it—even putting its livestock to the sword. ¹⁶All of its spoil you shall gather into its public square; then burn the town and all its spoil with fire, as a whole burnt offering to the LORD your God. It shall remain a perpetual ruin, never to be rebuilt. ¹⁷Do not let anything devoted to destruction stick to your hand, so that the LORD may turn from his fierce anger and show you compassion, and in his compassion multiply you, as he swore to your ancestors, ¹⁸if you obey the voice of the LORD your God by keeping all his commandments that I am commanding you today, doing what is right in the sight of the LORD your God.

REPENTANCE IS NOT JUST "FEELING SORRY," BUT RATHER A COMMITMENT TO REMOVE ONESELF FROM THE CIRCUMSTANCES OF SIN.

PAGAN PRACTICES FORBIDDEN

14 You are children of the LORD your God. You must not lacerate yourselves or shave your forelocks for the dead. ²For you are a people holy to the LORD your God; it is you the LORD has chosen out of all the peoples on earth to be his people, his treasured possession.

CLEAN AND UNCLEAN FOODS

3 You shall not eat any abhorrent thing. ⁴These are the animals you may eat: the ox, the sheep, the goat,

ᵃ 13.6 Sam Gk Compare Tg: MT lacks *your father's son or*

⁵the deer, the gazelle, the roebuck, the wild goat, the ibex, the antelope, and the mountain-sheep. ⁶Any animal that divides the hoof and has the hoof cleft in two, and chews the cud, among the animals, you may eat. ⁷Yet of those that chew the cud or have the hoof cleft you shall not eat these: the camel, the hare, and the rock badger, because they chew the cud but do not divide the hoof; they are unclean for you. ⁸And the pig, because it divides the hoof but does not chew the cud, is unclean for you. You shall not eat their meat, and you shall not touch their carcasses.

9 Of all that live in water you may eat these: whatever has fins and scales you may eat. ¹⁰And whatever does not have fins and scales you shall not eat; it is unclean for you.

11 You may eat any clean birds. ¹²But these are the ones that you shall not eat: the eagle, the vulture, the osprey, ¹³the buzzard, the kite of any kind; ¹⁴every raven of any kind; ¹⁵the ostrich, the nighthawk, the sea gull, the hawk of any kind; ¹⁶the little owl and the great owl, the water hen ¹⁷and the desert owl,ᵃ the carrion vulture and the cormorant, ¹⁸the stork, the heron of any kind; the hoopoe and the bat.ᵇ ¹⁹And all winged insects are unclean for you; they shall not be eaten. ²⁰You may eat any clean winged creature.

21 You shall not eat anything that dies of itself; you may give it to aliens residing in your towns for them to eat, or you may sell it to a foreigner. For you are a people holy to the LORD your God.

You shall not boil a kid in its mother's milk.

REGULATIONS CONCERNING TITHES

22 Set apart a tithe of all the yield of your seed that is brought in yearly from the field. ²³In the presence of the LORD your God, in the place that he will choose as a dwelling for his name, you shall eat the tithe of your grain, your wine, and your oil, as well as the firstlings of your herd and flock, so that you may learn

to fear the LORD your God always. ²⁴But if, when the LORD your God has blessed you, the distance is so great that you are unable to transport it, because the place where the LORD your God will choose to set his name is too far away from you, ²⁵then you may turn it into money. With the money secure in hand, go to the place that the LORD your God will choose; ²⁶spend the money for whatever you wish—oxen, sheep, wine, strong drink, or whatever you desire. And you shall eat there in the presence of the LORD your God, you and your household rejoicing together. ²⁷As for the Levites resident in your towns, do not neglect them, because they have no allotment or inheritance with you.

28 Every third year you shall bring out the full tithe of your produce for that year, and store it within your towns; ²⁹the Levites, because they have no allotment or inheritance with you, as well as the resident aliens, the orphans, and the widows in your towns, may come and eat their fill so that the LORD your God may bless you in all the work that you undertake.

LAWS CONCERNING THE SABBATICAL YEAR

15 Every seventh year you shall grant a remission of debts. ²And this is the manner of the remission: every creditor shall remit the claim that is held against a neighbor, not exacting it of a neighbor who is a member of the community, because the LORD's remission has been proclaimed. ³Of a foreigner you may exact it, but you must remit your claim on whatever any member of your community owes you. ⁴There will, however, be no one in need among you, because the LORD is sure to bless you in the land that the LORD your God is giving you as a possession to occupy, ⁵if only you will obey the LORD your God by diligently observing this entire commandment that I command you today. ⁶When

ᵃ 14.17 Or pelican ᵇ 14.18 Identification of several of the birds in verses 12–18 is uncertain

the LORD your God has blessed you, as he promised you, you will lend to many nations, but you will not borrow; you will rule over many nations, but they will not rule over you.

7 If there is among you anyone in need, a member of your community in any of your towns within the land that the LORD your God is giving you, do not be hard-hearted or tightfisted toward your needy neighbor. 8 You should rather open your hand, willingly lending enough to meet the need, whatever it may be. 9 Be careful that you do not entertain a mean thought, thinking, "The seventh year, the year of remission, is near," and therefore view your needy neighbor with hostility and give nothing; your neighbor might cry to the LORD against you, and you would incur guilt. 10 Give liberally and be ungrudging when you do so, for on this account the LORD your God will bless you in all your work and in all that you undertake. 11 Since there will never cease to be some in need on the earth, I therefore command you, "Open your hand to the poor and needy neighbor in your land."

12 If a member of your community, whether a Hebrew man or a Hebrew woman, is sold[a] to you and works for you six years, in the seventh year you shall set that person free. 13 And when you send a male slave[b] out from you a free person, you shall not send him out empty-handed. 14 Provide liberally out of your flock, your threshing floor, and your wine press, thus giving to him some of the bounty with which the LORD your God has blessed you. 15 Remember that you were a slave in the land of Egypt, and the LORD your God redeemed you; for this reason I lay this command upon you today. 16 But if he says to you, "I will not go out from you," because he loves you and your household, since he is well off with you, 17 then you shall take an awl and thrust it through his earlobe into the door, and he shall be your slave[c] forever.

You shall do the same with regard to your female slave.[d]

18 Do not consider it a hardship when you send them out from you free persons, because for six years they have given you services worth the wages of hired laborers; and the LORD your God will bless you in all that you do.

THE FIRSTBORN OF LIVESTOCK

19 Every firstling male born of your herd and flock you shall consecrate to the LORD your God; you shall not do work with your firstling ox nor shear the firstling of your flock. 20 You shall eat it, you together with your household, in the presence of the LORD your God year by year at the place that the LORD will choose. 21 But if it has any defect—any serious defect, such as lameness or blindness—you shall not sacrifice it to the LORD your God; 22 within your towns you may eat it, the unclean and the clean alike, as you would a gazelle or deer. 23 Its blood, however, you must not eat; you shall pour it out on the ground like water.

THE PASSOVER REVIEWED

16 Observe the month[e] of Abib by keeping the passover to the LORD your God, for in the month of Abib the LORD your God brought you out of Egypt by night. 2 You shall offer the passover sacrifice to the LORD your God, from the flock and the herd, at the place that the LORD will choose as a dwelling for his name. 3 You must not eat with it anything leavened. For seven days you shall eat unleavened bread with it— the bread of affliction—because you came out of the land of Egypt in great haste, so that all the days of your life you may remember the day of your departure from the land of Egypt. 4 No leaven shall be seen with you in all your territory for seven days; and none of the meat of what you slaughter on the evening of the first day shall remain until morning. 5 You are not permitted to offer the passover sacrifice within any of your towns that the LORD your God is giving

---

[a] 15.12 Or sells himself or herself
[b] 15.13 Heb him   [c] 15.17 Or bondman
[d] 15.17 Or bondwoman   [e] 16.1 Or new moon

you. 6But at the place that the LORD your God will choose as a dwelling for his name, only there shall you offer the passover sacrifice, in the evening at sunset, the time of day when you departed from Egypt. 7You shall cook it and eat it at the place that the LORD your God will choose; the next morning you may go back to your tents. 8For six days you shall continue to eat unleavened bread, and on the seventh day there shall be a solemn assembly for the LORD your God, when you shall do no work.

THE FESTIVAL OF WEEKS REVIEWED

9 You shall count seven weeks; begin to count the seven weeks from the time the sickle is first put to the standing grain. 10Then you shall keep the festival of weeks to the LORD your God, contributing a freewill offering in proportion to the blessing that you have received from the LORD your God. 11Rejoice before the LORD your God—you and your sons and your daughters, your male and female slaves, the Levites resident in your towns, as well as the strangers, the orphans, and the widows who are among you—at the place that the LORD your God will choose as a dwelling for his name. 12Remember that you were a slave in Egypt, and diligently observe these statutes.

THE FESTIVAL OF BOOTHS REVIEWED

13 You shall keep the festival of boothsa for seven days, when you have gathered in the produce from your threshing floor and your wine press. 14Rejoice during your festival, you and your sons and your daughters, your male and female slaves, as well as the Levites, the strangers, the orphans, and the widows resident in your towns. 15Seven days you shall keep the festival to the LORD your God at the place that the LORD will choose; for the LORD your God will bless you in all your produce and in all your undertakings, and you shall surely celebrate.

16 Three times a year all your males shall appear before the LORD your God at the place that he will choose: at the festival of unleavened bread, at the festival of weeks, and at the festival of booths.a They shall not appear before the LORD emptyhanded; 17all shall give as they are able, according to the blessing of the LORD your God that he has given you.

MUNICIPAL JUDGES AND OFFICERS

18 You shall appoint judges and officials throughout your tribes, in all your towns that the LORD your God is giving you, and they shall render just decisions for the people. 19You must not distort justice; you must not show partiality; and you must not accept bribes, for a bribe blinds the eyes of the wise and subverts the cause of those who are in the right. 20Justice, and only justice, you shall pursue, so that you may live and occupy the land that the LORD your God is giving you.

a 16.13,16 Or tabernacles; Heb succoth

⊢ BIBLE IN LIFE ▷

Favoritism
Deuteronomy 16.18

One of the challenges of life is dealing with difficult people. We all know unpleasant, unattractive, sometimes aggravating people who engender uncertainty or even resentment in us. We naturally tend to close them out of our lives and concentrate our attention and affection on those who are just like us. The more we resent or avoid other kinds of people, the more we close our hearts to love and to understanding Christ and his example. God sternly warns us not to show bias and to treat all people fairly—even those who are unlike us (Leviticus 19.15; James 2.1–4). We are all the same before God; none of us is distinctive or superior.

FORBIDDEN FORMS OF WORSHIP

21 You shall not plant any tree as a sacred pole[a] beside the altar that you make for the LORD your God; 22nor shall you set up a stone pillar—things that the LORD your God hates.

17 You must not sacrifice to the LORD your God an ox or a sheep that has a defect, anything seriously wrong; for that is abhorrent to the LORD your God.

2 If there is found among you, in one of your towns that the LORD your God is giving you, a man or woman who does what is evil in the sight of the LORD your God, and transgresses his covenant 3by going to serve other gods and worshiping them—whether the sun or the moon or any of the host of heaven, which I have forbidden— 4and if it is reported to you or you hear of it, and you make a thorough inquiry, and the charge is proved true that such an abhorrent thing has occurred in Israel, 5then you shall bring out to your gates that man or that woman who has committed this crime and you shall stone the man or woman to death. 6On the evidence of two or three witnesses the death sentence shall be executed; a person must not be put to death on the evidence of only one witness. 7The hands of the witnesses shall be the first raised against the person to execute the death penalty, and afterward the hands of all the people. So you shall purge the evil from your midst.

LEGAL DECISIONS BY PRIESTS AND JUDGES

8 If a judicial decision is too difficult for you to make between one kind of bloodshed and another, one kind of legal right and another, or one kind of assault and another— any such matters of dispute in your towns—then you shall immediately go up to the place that the LORD your God will choose, 9where you shall consult with the levitical priests and the judge who is in office in those days; they shall announce to you the decision in the case. 10Carry out exactly the decision that they announce to you from the place that the LORD will choose, diligently observing everything they instruct you. 11You must carry out fully the law that they interpret for you or the ruling that they announce to you; do not turn aside from the decision that they announce to you, either to the right or to the left. 12As for anyone who presumes to disobey the priest appointed to minister there to the LORD your God, or the judge, that person shall die. So you shall purge the evil from Israel. 13All the people will hear and be afraid, and will not act presumptuously again.

LIMITATIONS OF ROYAL AUTHORITY

14 When you have come into the land that the LORD your God is giving you, and have taken possession of it and settled in it, and you say, "I will set a king over me, like all the nations that are around me," 15you may indeed set over you a king whom the LORD your God will choose. One of your own community you may set as king over you; you are not permitted to put a foreigner over you, who is not of your own community. 16Even so, he must not acquire many horses for himself, or return the people to Egypt in order to acquire more horses, since the LORD has said to you, "You must never return that way again." 17And he must not acquire many wives for himself, or else his heart will turn away; also silver and gold he must not acquire in great quantity for himself. 18When he has taken the throne of his kingdom, he shall have a copy of this law written for him in the presence of the levitical priests. 19It shall remain with him and he shall read in it all the days of his life, so that he may learn to fear the LORD his God, diligently observing all the words of this law and these statutes, 20neither exalting himself above other members of the community nor turning aside from the commandment, either to the right or to the left, so that he and his

a 16.21 Heb Asherah

descendants may reign long over his kingdom in Israel.

PRIVILEGES OF PRIESTS AND LEVITES

18 The levitical priests, the whole tribe of Levi, shall have no allotment or inheritance within Israel. They may eat the sacrifices that are the LORD's portion[a] ²but they shall have no inheritance among the other members of the community; the LORD is their inheritance, as he promised them.

3 This shall be the priests' due from the people, from those offering a sacrifice, whether an ox or a sheep: they shall give to the priest the shoulder, the two jowls, and the stomach. ⁴The first fruits of your grain, your wine, and your oil, as well as the first of the fleece of your sheep, you shall give him. ⁵For the LORD your God has chosen Levi[b] out of all your tribes, to stand and minister in the name of the LORD, him and his sons for all time.

6 If a Levite leaves any of your towns, from wherever he has been residing in Israel, and comes to the place that the LORD will choose (and he may come whenever he wishes), ⁷then he may minister in the name of the LORD his God, like all his fellow-Levites who stand to minister there before the LORD. ⁸They shall have equal portions to eat, even though they have income from the sale of family possessions.[a]

CHILD-SACRIFICE, DIVINATION, AND MAGIC PROHIBITED

9 When you come into the land that the LORD your God is giving you, you must not learn to imitate the abhorrent practices of those nations. ¹⁰No one shall be found among you who makes a son or daughter pass through fire, or who practices divination, or is a soothsayer, or an augur, or a sorcerer, ¹¹or one who casts spells, or who consults ghosts or spirits, or who seeks oracles from the dead. ¹²For whoever does these things is abhorrent to the LORD; it is because of such abhorrent practices that the LORD your God is

driving them out before you. ¹³You must remain completely loyal to the LORD your God. ¹⁴Although these nations that you are about to dispossess do give heed to soothsayers and diviners, as for you, the LORD your God does not permit you to do so.

A NEW PROPHET LIKE MOSES

15 The LORD your God will raise up for you a prophet[c] like me from among your own people; you shall heed such a prophet.[d] ¹⁶This is what you requested of the LORD your God at Horeb on the day of the assembly when you said: "If I hear the voice of the LORD my God any more, or ever again see this great fire, I will die." ¹⁷Then the LORD replied to me: "They are right in what they have said. ¹⁸I will raise up for them a prophet[c] like you from among their own people; I will put my words in the mouth of the prophet,[e] who shall speak to them everything that I command. ¹⁹Anyone who does not heed the words that the prophet[f] shall speak in my name, I myself will hold accountable. ²⁰But any prophet who speaks in the name of other gods, or who presumes to speak in my name a word that I have not commanded the prophet to speak—that prophet shall die." ²¹You may say to yourself, "How can we recognize a word that the LORD has not spoken?" ²²If a prophet speaks in the name of the LORD but the thing does not take place or prove true, it is a word that the LORD has not spoken. The prophet has spoken it presumptuously; do not be frightened by it.

LAWS CONCERNING THE CITIES OF REFUGE

19 When the LORD your God has cut off the nations whose land the LORD your God is giving you, and you have dispossessed them and settled in their towns and in their houses, ²you shall set apart three cities in the land that

---

[a] 18.1,8 Meaning of Heb uncertain
[b] 18.5 Heb him [c] 18.15,18 Or prophets
[d] 18.15 Or such prophets [e] 18.18 Or mouths of the prophets [f] 18.19 Heb he

the LORD your God is giving you to possess. ³You shall calculate the distances[a] and divide into three regions the land that the LORD your God gives you as a possession, so that any homicide can flee to one of them.

4 Now this is the case of a homicide who might flee there and live, that is, someone who has killed another person unintentionally when the two had not been at enmity before: ⁵Suppose someone goes into the forest with another to cut wood, and when one of them swings the ax to cut down a tree, the head slips from the handle and strikes the other person who then dies; the killer may flee to one of these cities and live. ⁶But if the distance is too great, the avenger of blood in hot anger might pursue and overtake and put the killer to death, although a death sentence was not deserved, since the two had not been at enmity before. ⁷Therefore I command you: You shall set apart three cities.

8 If the LORD your God enlarges your territory, as he swore to your ancestors—and he will give you all the land that he promised your ancestors to give you, ⁹provided you diligently observe this entire commandment that I command you today, by loving the LORD your God and walking always in his ways—then you shall add three more cities to these three, ¹⁰so that the blood

of an innocent person may not be shed in the land that the LORD your God is giving you as an inheritance, thereby bringing bloodguilt upon you.

11 But if someone at enmity with another lies in wait and attacks and takes the life of that person, and flees into one of these cities, ¹²then the elders of the killer's city shall send to have the culprit taken from there and handed over to the avenger of blood to be put to death. ¹³Show no pity; you shall purge the guilt of innocent blood from Israel, so that it may go well with you.

PROPERTY BOUNDARIES

14 You must not move your neighbor's boundary marker, set up by former generations, on the property that will be allotted to you in the land that the LORD your God is giving you to possess.

LAW CONCERNING WITNESSES

15 A single witness shall not suffice to convict a person of any crime or wrongdoing in connection with any offense that may be committed. Only on the evidence of two or three witnesses shall a charge be sustained. ¹⁶If a malicious witness comes forward to accuse someone of wrongdoing, ¹⁷then both parties

a 19.3 Or *prepare roads to them*

⊢ BIBLE IN LIFE ▷

Resolving Problems   *Deuteronomy 19.15–19*

We find good, solid advice in the words of Deuteronomy 19.15. Jesus taught this same principle: "If another member of the church sins against you, go and point out the fault when the two of you are alone. If the member listens to you, you have regained that one. But if you are not listened to, take one or two others along with you, so that every word may be confirmed by the evidence of two or three witnesses. If the member refuses to listen to them, tell it to the church" (Matthew 18.15–17). One of the most difficult steps in resolving a dispute is getting the two sides to communicate with each other. That's what a mediator sometimes has to do—this could be a pastor, a mutual friend, a counselor. If we have a problem with someone, we should be willing to confront that person with respect. If that proves unsuccessful, we should selectively involve other people. Ultimately, the problem must be placed in the presence of Christ, who is the mediator between God and us (see 1 Timothy 2.5). In this way, we start the process of forgiveness and reconciliation.

to the dispute shall appear before the LORD, before the priests and the judges who are in office in those days, ¹⁸and the judges shall make a thorough inquiry. If the witness is a false witness, having testified falsely against another, ¹⁹then you shall do to the false witness just as the false witness had meant to do to the other. So you shall purge the evil from your midst. ²⁰The rest shall hear and be afraid, and a crime such as this shall never again be committed among you. ²¹Show no pity: life for life, eye for eye, tooth for tooth, hand for hand, foot for foot.

RULES OF WARFARE

20 When you go out to war against your enemies, and see horses and chariots, an army larger than your own, you shall not be afraid of them; for the LORD your God is with you, who brought you up from the land of Egypt. ²Before you engage in battle, the priest shall come forward and speak to the troops, ³and shall say to them: "Hear, O Israel! Today you are drawing near to do battle against your enemies. Do not lose heart, or be afraid, or panic, or be in dread of them; ⁴for it is the LORD your God who goes with you, to fight for you against your enemies, to give you victory." ⁵Then the officials shall address the troops, saying, "Has anyone built a new house but not dedicated it? He should go back to his house, or he might die in the battle and another dedicate it. ⁶Has anyone planted a vineyard but not yet enjoyed its fruit? He should go back to his house, or he might die in the battle and another be first to enjoy its fruit. ⁷Has anyone become engaged to a woman but not yet married her? He should go back to his house, or he might die in the battle and another marry her." ⁸The officials shall continue to address the troops, saying, "Is anyone afraid or disheartened? He should go back to his house, or he might cause the heart of his comrades to melt like his own." ⁹When the officials have finished addressing the troops, then

the commanders shall take charge of them. ¹⁰When you draw near to a town to fight against it, offer it terms of peace. ¹¹If it accepts your terms of peace and surrenders to you, then all the people in it shall serve you at forced labor. ¹²If it does not submit to you peacefully, but makes war against you, then you shall besiege it; ¹³and when the LORD your God gives it into your hand, you shall put all its males to the sword. ¹⁴You may, however, take as your booty the women, the children, livestock, and everything else in the town, all its spoil. You may enjoy the spoil of your enemies, which the LORD your God has given you. ¹⁵Thus you shall treat all the towns that are very far from you, which are not towns of the nations here. ¹⁶But as for the towns of these peoples that the LORD your God is giving you as an inheritance, you must not let anything that breathes remain alive. ¹⁷You shall annihilate them—the Hittites and the Amorites, the Canaanites and the Perizzites, the Hivites and the Jebusites—just as the LORD your God has commanded, ¹⁸so that they may not teach you to do all the abhorrent things that they do for their gods, and you thus sin against the LORD your God.

¹⁹ If you besiege a town for a long time, making war against it in order to take it, you must not destroy its trees by wielding an ax against them. Although you may take food from them, you must not cut them down. Are trees in the field human beings that they should come under siege from you? ²⁰You may destroy only the trees that you know do not produce food; you may cut them down for use in building siegeworks against the town that makes war with you, until it falls.

LAW CONCERNING MURDER BY PERSONS UNKNOWN

21 If, in the land that the LORD your God is giving you to possess, a body is found lying in open country, and it is not known who struck the person down, ²then your elders and your judges shall come out to measure the distances to the towns that are near the body. ³The elders of the town nearest the body shall take a heifer that has never been worked, one that has not pulled in the yoke; ⁴the elders of that town shall bring the heifer down to a wadi with running water, which is neither plowed nor sown, and shall break the heifer's neck there in the wadi. ⁵Then the priests, the sons of Levi, shall come forward, for the LORD your God has chosen them to minister to him and to pronounce blessings in the name of the LORD, and by their decision all cases of dispute and assault shall be settled. ⁶All the elders of that town nearest the body shall wash their hands over the heifer whose neck was broken in the wadi, ⁷and they shall declare: "Our hands did not shed this blood, nor were we witnesses to it. ⁸Absolve, O LORD, your people Israel, whom you redeemed; do not let the guilt of innocent blood remain in the midst of your people Israel." Then they will be absolved of bloodguilt. ⁹So you shall purge the guilt of innocent blood from your midst, because you must do what is right in the sight of the LORD.

FEMALE CAPTIVES

10 When you go out to war against your enemies, and the LORD your God hands them over to you and you take them captive, ¹¹suppose you see among the captives a beautiful woman whom you desire and want to marry, ¹²and so you bring her home to your house: she shall shave her head, pare her nails, ¹³discard her captive's garb, and shall remain in your house a full month, mourning for her father and mother; after that you may go in to her and be her husband, and she shall be your wife. ¹⁴But if you are not satisfied with her, you shall let her go free and not sell her for money. You must not treat her as a slave, since you have dishonored her.

THE RIGHT OF THE FIRSTBORN

15 If a man has two wives, one of them loved and the other disliked, and if both the loved and the disliked have borne him sons, the firstborn being the son of the one who is disliked, ¹⁶then on the day when he wills his possessions to his sons, he is not permitted to treat the son of the loved as the firstborn in preference to the son of the disliked, who is the firstborn. ¹⁷He must acknowledge as firstborn the son of the one who is disliked, giving him a double portionª of all that he has; since he is the first issue of his virility, the right of the firstborn is his.

REBELLIOUS CHILDREN

18 If someone has a stubborn and rebellious son who will not obey his father and mother, who does not heed them when they discipline him, ¹⁹then his father and his mother shall take hold of him and bring him out to the elders of his town at the gate of that place. ²⁰They shall say to the elders of his town, "This son of ours is stubborn and rebellious. He will not obey us. He is a glutton and a drunkard." ²¹Then all the men of the town shall stone him to death. So you shall purge the evil from your midst; and all Israel will hear, and be afraid.

MISCELLANEOUS LAWS

22 When someone is convicted of a crime punishable by death and is executed, and you hang him on a tree, ²³his corpse must not remain all night upon the tree; you shall bury him that same day, for anyone hung on a tree is under God's curse. You must not defile the land that the LORD your God is giving you for possession.

22 You shall not watch your neighbor's ox or sheep straying away and ignore them; you shall take them back to their owner. ²If the owner does not reside near you or you do not know who the owner is, you shall bring it to your own house, and it shall remain with you until the owner claims it; then you shall return it. ³You shall do the same with a neighbor's donkey; you

ª 21.17 Heb *two-thirds*

shall do the same with a neighbor's garment; and you shall do the same with anything else that your neighbor loses and you find. You may not withhold your help.

4 You shall not see your neighbor's donkey or ox fallen on the road and ignore it; you shall help to lift it up.

5 A woman shall not wear a man's apparel, nor shall a man put on a woman's garment; for whoever does such things is abhorrent to the LORD your God.

6 If you come on a bird's nest, in any tree or on the ground, with fledglings or eggs, with the mother sitting on the fledglings or on the eggs, you shall not take the mother with the young. 7 Let the mother go, taking only the young for yourself, in order that it may go well with you and you may live long.

8 When you build a new house, you shall make a parapet for your roof; otherwise you might have bloodguilt on your house, if anyone should fall from it.

9 You shall not sow your vineyard with a second kind of seed, or the whole yield will have to be forfeited, both the crop that you have sown and the yield of the vineyard itself.

10 You shall not plow with an ox and a donkey yoked together.

11 You shall not wear clothes made of wool and linen woven together.

12 You shall make tassels on the four corners of the cloak with which you cover yourself.

LAWS CONCERNING SEXUAL RELATIONS

13 Suppose a man marries a woman, but after going in to her, he dislikes her 14 and makes up charges against her, slandering her by saying, "I married this woman; but when I lay with her, I did not find evidence of her virginity." 15 The father of the young woman and her mother shall then submit the evidence of the young woman's virginity to the elders of the city at the gate. 16 The father of the young woman shall say to the elders: "I gave my daughter in marriage to this man but he dislikes

her; 17 now he has made up charges against her, saying, 'I did not find evidence of your daughter's virginity.' But here is the evidence of my daughter's virginity." Then they shall spread out the cloth before the elders of the town. 18 The elders of that town shall take the man and punish him; 19 they shall fine him one hundred shekels of silver (which they shall give to the young woman's father) because he has slandered a virgin of Israel. She shall remain his wife; he shall not be permitted to divorce her as long as he lives.

20 If, however, this charge is true, that evidence of the young woman's virginity was not found, 21 then they shall bring the young woman out to the entrance of her father's house and the men of her town shall stone her to death, because she committed a disgraceful act in Israel by prostituting herself in her father's house. So you shall purge the evil from your midst.

THE LAW OF GOD IS NOT

SOMETHING TO DEBATE,

BUT TO DEMONSTRATE.

22 If a man is caught lying with the wife of another man, both of them shall die, the man who lay with the woman as well as the woman. So you shall purge the evil from Israel.

23 If there is a young woman, a virgin already engaged to be married, and a man meets her in the town and lies with her, 24 you shall bring both of them to the gate of that town and stone them to death, the young woman because she did not cry for help in the town and the man because he violated his neighbor's wife. So you shall purge the evil from your midst.

25 But if the man meets the engaged woman in the open country, and the man seizes her and lies with

her, then only the man who lay with her shall die. 26 You shall do nothing to the young woman; the young woman has not committed an offense punishable by death, because this case is like that of someone who attacks and murders a neighbor. 27 Since he found her in the open country, the engaged woman may have cried for help, but there was no one to rescue her.

28 If a man meets a virgin who is not engaged, and seizes her and lies with her, and they are caught in the act, 29 the man who lay with her shall give fifty shekels of silver to the young woman's father, and she shall become his wife. Because he violated her he shall not be permitted to divorce her as long as he lives.

30 a A man shall not marry his father's wife, thereby violating his father's rights. b

THOSE EXCLUDED FROM THE ASSEMBLY

23 No one whose testicles are crushed or whose penis is cut off shall be admitted to the assembly of the LORD.

2 Those born of an illicit union shall not be admitted to the assembly of the LORD. Even to the tenth generation, none of their descendants shall be admitted to the assembly of the LORD.

3 No Ammonite or Moabite shall be admitted to the assembly of the LORD. Even to the tenth generation, none of their descendants shall be admitted to the assembly of the LORD, 4 because they did not meet you with food and water on your journey out of Egypt, and because they hired against you Balaam son of Beor, from Pethor of Mesopotamia, to curse you. 5 (Yet the LORD your God refused to heed Balaam; the LORD your God turned the curse into a blessing for you, because the LORD your God loved you.) 6 You shall never promote their welfare or their prosperity as long as you live.

7 You shall not abhor any of the Edomites, for they are your kin. You shall not abhor any of the Egyptians, because you were an alien residing in their land. 8 The children of the third generation that are born to them may be admitted to the assembly of the LORD.

SANITARY, RITUAL, AND HUMANITARIAN PRECEPTS

9 When you are encamped against your enemies you shall guard against any impropriety.

10 If one of you becomes unclean because of a nocturnal emission, then he shall go outside the camp; he must not come within the camp. 11 When evening comes, he shall wash himself with water, and when the sun has set, he may come back into the camp.

12 You shall have a designated area outside the camp to which you shall go. 13 With your utensils you shall have a trowel; when you relieve yourself outside, you shall dig a hole with it and then cover up your excrement. 14 Because the LORD your God travels along with your camp, to save you and to hand over your enemies to you, therefore your camp must be holy, so that he may not see anything indecent among you and turn away from you.

15 Slaves who have escaped to you from their owners shall not be given back to them. 16 They shall reside with you, in your midst, in any place they choose in any one of your towns, wherever they please; you shall not oppress them.

17 None of the daughters of Israel shall be a temple prostitute; none of the sons of Israel shall be a temple prostitute. 18 You shall not bring the fee of a prostitute or the wages of a male prostitute c into the house of the LORD your God in payment for any vow, for both of these are abhorrent to the LORD your God.

19 You shall not charge interest on loans to another Israelite, interest on money, interest on provisions, interest on anything that is lent. 20 On loans to a foreigner you may charge interest, but on loans to another

a 22.30 Ch 23.1 in Heb   b 22.30 Heb
uncovering his father's skirt   c 23.18 Heb
a dog

Israelite you may not charge interest, so that the LORD your God may bless you in all your undertakings in the land that you are about to enter and possess.

21 If you make a vow to the LORD your God, do not postpone fulfilling it; for the LORD your God will surely require it of you, and you would incur guilt. 22But if you refrain from vowing, you will not incur guilt. 23Whatever your lips utter you must diligently perform, just as you have freely vowed to the LORD your God with your own mouth.

24 If you go into your neighbor's vineyard, you may eat your fill of grapes, as many as you wish, but you shall not put any in a container.

25 If you go into your neighbor's standing grain, you may pluck the ears with your hand, but you shall not put a sickle to your neighbor's standing grain.

LAWS CONCERNING MARRIAGE AND DIVORCE

24 Suppose a man enters into marriage with a woman, but she does not please him because he finds something objectionable about her, and so he writes her a certificate of divorce, puts it in her hand, and sends her out of his house; she then leaves his house 2and goes off to become another man's wife. 3Then suppose the second man dislikes her, writes her a bill of divorce, puts it in her hand, and sends her out of his house (or the second man who married her dies); 4her first husband, who sent her away, is not permitted to take her again to be his wife after she has been defiled; for that would be abhorrent to the LORD, and you shall not bring guilt on the land that the LORD your God is giving you as a possession.

MISCELLANEOUS LAWS

5 When a man is newly married, he shall not go out with the army or be charged with any related duty. He shall be free at home one year, to be happy with the wife whom he has married.

6 No one shall take a mill or an upper millstone in pledge, for that would be taking a life in pledge.

7 If someone is caught kidnaping another Israelite, enslaving or selling the Israelite, then that kidnaper shall die. So you shall purge the evil from your midst.

8 Guard against an outbreak of a leprous[a] skin disease by being very careful; you shall carefully observe whatever the levitical priests instruct you, just as I have commanded them. 9Remember what the LORD your God did to Miriam on your journey out of Egypt.

10 When you make your neighbor a loan of any kind, you shall not go into the house to take the pledge. 11You shall wait outside, while the person to whom you are making the loan brings the pledge out to you. 12If the person is poor, you shall not sleep in the garment given you as[b] the pledge. 13You shall give the pledge back by sunset, so that your neighbor may sleep in the cloak and bless you; and it will be to your credit before the LORD your God.

14 You shall not withhold the wages of poor and needy laborers, whether other Israelites or aliens who reside in your land in one of your towns. 15You shall pay them their wages daily before sunset, because they are poor and their livelihood depends on them; otherwise they might cry to the LORD against you, and you would incur guilt.

16 Parents shall not be put to death for their children, nor shall children be put to death for their parents; only for their own crimes may persons be put to death.

17 You shall not deprive a resident alien or an orphan of justice; you shall not take a widow's garment in pledge. 18Remember that you were a slave in Egypt and the LORD your God redeemed you from there; therefore I command you to do this.

19 When you reap your harvest in your field and forget a sheaf in the field, you shall not go back to get it;

[a] 24.8 A term for several skin diseases; precise meaning uncertain   [b] 24.12 Heb lacks the garment given you as

it shall be left for the alien, the orphan, and the widow, so that the LORD your God may bless you in all your undertakings. 20When you beat your olive trees, do not strip what is left; it shall be for the alien, the orphan, and the widow.

21When you gather the grapes of your vineyard, do not glean what is left; it shall be for the alien, the orphan, and the widow. 22Remember that you were a slave in the land of Egypt; therefore I am commanding you to do this.

25 Suppose two persons have a dispute and enter into litigation, and the judges decide between them, declaring one to be in the right and the other to be in the wrong. 2If the one in the wrong deserves to be flogged, the judge shall make that person lie down and be beaten in his presence with the number of lashes proportionate to the offense. 3Forty lashes may be given but not more; if more lashes than these are given, your neighbor will be degraded in your sight.

4You shall not muzzle an ox while it is treading out the grain.

EACH OF US HAS A DIVINELY

APPOINTED MISSION: TO

UPHOLD JUSTICE AND LET

PEOPLE KNOW OF GOD'S LOVE.

LEVIRATE MARRIAGE

5When brothers reside together, and one of them dies and has no son, the wife of the deceased shall not be married outside the family to a stranger. Her husband's brother shall go in to her, taking her in marriage, and performing the duty of a husband's brother to her, 6and the firstborn whom she bears shall succeed to the name of the deceased brother, so that his name may not be blotted out of Israel. 7But if the man has no desire

to marry his brother's widow, then his brother's widow shall go up to the elders at the gate and say, "My husband's brother refuses to perpetuate his brother's name in Israel; he will not perform the duty of a husband's brother to me." 8Then the elders of his town shall summon him and speak to him. If he persists, saying, "I have no desire to marry her," 9then his brother's wife shall go up to him in the presence of the elders, pull his sandal off his foot, spit in his face, and declare, "This is what is done to the man who does not build up his brother's house." 10Throughout Israel his family shall be known as "the house of him whose sandal was pulled off."

VARIOUS COMMANDS

11 If men get into a fight with one another, and the wife of one intervenes to rescue her husband from the grip of his opponent by reaching out and seizing his genitals, 12you shall cut off her hand; show no pity.

13 You shall not have in your bag two kinds of weights, large and small. 14You shall not have in your house two kinds of measures, large and small. 15You shall have only a full and honest weight; you shall have only a full and honest measure, so that your days may be long in the land that the LORD your God is giving you. 16For all who do such things, all who act dishonestly, are abhorrent to the LORD your God.

17 Remember what Amalek did to you on your journey out of Egypt, 18how he attacked you on the way, when you were faint and weary, and struck down all who lagged behind you; he did not fear God. 19Therefore when the LORD your God has given you rest from all your enemies on every hand, in the land that the LORD your God is giving you as an inheritance to possess, you shall blot out the remembrance of Amalek from under heaven; do not forget.

FIRST FRUITS AND TITHES

26 When you have come into the land that the LORD your God is giving you as an inheritance to possess, and you possess it, and

settle in it, ²you shall take some of the first of all the fruit of the ground, which you harvest from the land that the LORD your God is giving you, and you shall put it in a basket and go to the place that the LORD your God will choose as a dwelling for his name. ³You shall go to the priest who is in office at that time, and say to him, "Today I declare to the LORD your God that I have come into the land that the LORD swore to our ancestors to give us." ⁴When the priest takes the basket from your hand and sets it down before the altar of the LORD your God, ⁵you shall make this response before the LORD your God: "A wandering Aramean was my ancestor; he went down into Egypt and lived there as an alien, few in number, and there he became a great nation, mighty and populous. ⁶When the Egyptians treated us harshly and afflicted us, by imposing hard labor on us, ⁷we cried to the LORD, the God of our ancestors; the LORD heard our voice and saw our affliction, our toil, and our oppression. ⁸The LORD brought us out of Egypt with a mighty hand and an outstretched arm, with a terrifying display of power, and with signs and wonders; ⁹and he brought us into this place and gave us this land, a land flowing with milk and honey. ¹⁰So now I bring the first of the fruit of the ground that you, O LORD, have given me." You shall set it down before the LORD your God and bow down before the LORD your God. ¹¹Then you, together with the Levites and the aliens who reside among you, shall celebrate with all the bounty that the LORD your God has given to you and to your house.

12 When you have finished paying all the tithe of your produce in the third year (which is the year of the tithe), giving it to the Levites, the aliens, the orphans, and the widows, so that they may eat their fill within your towns, ¹³then you shall say before the LORD your God: "I have removed the sacred portion from the house, and I have given it to the Levites, the resident aliens, the orphans, and the widows, in accordance with your entire commandment that you commanded me; I have neither transgressed nor forgotten any of your commandments: ¹⁴I have not eaten of it while in mourning; I have not removed any of it while I was unclean; and I have not offered any of it to the dead. I have obeyed the LORD my God, doing just as you commanded me. ¹⁵Look down from your holy habitation, from heaven, and bless your people Israel and the ground that you have given us, as you swore to our ancestors—a land flowing with milk and honey."

OUR SERVICE SHOULD BE
MOTIVATED BY OUR LOVE
FOR GOD, NOT BY ANY
EXPECTATION OF REWARDS.

CONCLUDING EXHORTATION

16 This very day the LORD your God is commanding you to observe these statutes and ordinances; so observe them diligently with all your heart and with all your soul. ¹⁷Today you have obtained the LORD's agreement: to be your God; and for you to walk in his ways, to keep his statutes, his commandments, and his ordinances, and to obey him. ¹⁸Today the LORD has obtained your agreement: to be his treasured people, as he promised you, and to keep his commandments; ¹⁹for him to set you high above all nations that he has made, in praise and in fame and in honor; and for you to be a people holy to the LORD your God, as he promised.

THE INSCRIBED STONES AND ALTAR ON MOUNT EBAL

27 Then Moses and the elders of Israel charged all the people as follows: Keep the entire commandment that I am commanding

you today. ²On the day that you cross over the Jordan into the land that the LORD your God is giving you, you shall set up large stones and cover them with plaster. ³You shall write on them all the words of this law when you have crossed over, to enter the land that the LORD your God is giving you, a land flowing with milk and honey, as the LORD, the God of your ancestors, promised you. ⁴So when you have crossed over the Jordan, you shall set up these stones, about which I am commanding you today, on Mount Ebal, and you shall cover them with plaster. ⁵And you shall build an altar there to the LORD your God, an altar of stones on which you have not used an iron tool. ⁶You must build the altar of the LORD your God of un-hewnᵃ stones. Then offer up burnt offerings on it to the LORD your God, ⁷make sacrifices of well-being, and eat them there, rejoicing before the LORD your God. ⁸You shall write on the stones all the words of this law very clearly.

9 Then Moses and the levitical priests spoke to all Israel, saying: Keep silence and hear, O Israel! This very day you have become the people of the LORD your God. ¹⁰Therefore obey the LORD your God, observing his commandments and his statutes that I am commanding you today.

TWELVE CURSES

11 The same day Moses charged the people as follows: ¹²When you have crossed over the Jordan, these shall stand on Mount Gerizim for the blessing of the people: Simeon, Levi, Judah, Issachar, Joseph, and Benjamin. ¹³And these shall stand on Mount Ebal for the curse: Reuben, Gad, Asher, Zebulun, Dan, and Naphtali. ¹⁴Then the Levites shall declare in a loud voice to all the Israelites:

15 "Cursed be anyone who makes an idol or casts an image, anything abhorrent to the LORD, the work of an artisan, and sets it up in secret." All the people shall respond, saying, "Amen!"

16 "Cursed be anyone who dishonors father or mother." All the people shall say, "Amen!"
17 "Cursed be anyone who moves a neighbor's boundary marker." All the people shall say, "Amen!"
18 "Cursed be anyone who misleads a blind person on the road." All the people shall say, "Amen!"
19 "Cursed be anyone who deprives the alien, the orphan, and the widow of justice." All the people shall say, "Amen!"
20 "Cursed be anyone who lies with his father's wife, because he has violated his father's rights."ᵇ All the people shall say, "Amen!"
21 "Cursed be anyone who lies with any animal." All the people shall say, "Amen!"
22 "Cursed be anyone who lies with his sister, whether the daughter of his father or the daughter of his mother." All the people shall say, "Amen!"
23 "Cursed be anyone who lies with his mother-in-law." All the people shall say, "Amen!"
24 "Cursed be anyone who strikes down a neighbor in secret." All the people shall say, "Amen!"
25 "Cursed be anyone who takes a bribe to shed innocent blood." All the people shall say, "Amen!"
26 "Cursed be anyone who does not uphold the words of this law by observing them." All the people shall say, "Amen!"

BLESSINGS FOR OBEDIENCE

28 If you will only obey the LORD your God, by diligently observing all his commandments that I am commanding you today, the LORD your God will set you high above all the nations of the earth; ²all these blessings shall come upon you and overtake you, if you obey the LORD your God:
3 Blessed shall you be in the city, and blessed shall you be in the field.
4 Blessed shall be the fruit of your womb, the fruit of your ground, and the fruit of your livestock, both the

ᵃ 27.6 Heb *whole*   ᵇ 27.20 Heb *uncovered his father's skirt*

increase of your cattle and the issue of your flock.

5 Blessed shall be your basket and your kneading bowl.

6 Blessed shall you be when you come in, and blessed shall you be when you go out.

7 The LORD will cause your enemies who rise against you to be defeated before you; they shall come out against you one way, and flee before you seven ways. 8 The LORD will command the blessing upon you in your barns, and in all that you undertake; he will bless you in the land that the LORD your God is giving you. 9 The LORD will establish you as his holy people, as he has sworn to you, if you keep the commandments of the LORD your God and walk in his ways. 10 All the peoples of the earth shall see that you are called by the name of the LORD, and they shall be afraid of you. 11 The LORD will make you abound in prosperity, in the fruit of your womb, in the fruit of your livestock, and in the fruit of your ground in the land that the LORD swore to your ancestors to give you. 12 The LORD will open for you his rich storehouse, the heavens, to give the rain of your land in its season and to bless all your undertakings. You will lend to many nations, but you will not borrow. 13 The LORD will make you the head, and not the tail; you shall be only at the top, and not at the bottom—if you obey the commandments of the LORD your God, which I am commanding you today,

by diligently observing them, 14 and if you do not turn aside from any of the words that I am commanding you today, either to the right or to the left, following other gods to serve them.

WARNINGS AGAINST DISOBEDIENCE

15 But if you will not obey the LORD your God by diligently observing all his commandments and decrees, which I am commanding you today, then all these curses shall come upon you and overtake you:

16 Cursed shall you be in the city, and cursed shall you be in the field.

17 Cursed shall be your basket and your kneading bowl.

18 Cursed shall be the fruit of your womb, the fruit of your ground, the increase of your cattle and the issue of your flock.

19 Cursed shall you be when you come in, and cursed shall you be when you go out.

20 The LORD will send upon you disaster, panic, and frustration in everything you attempt to do, until you are destroyed and perish quickly, on account of the evil of your deeds, because you have forsaken me. 21 The LORD will make the pestilence cling to you until it has consumed you off the land that you are entering to possess. 22 The LORD will afflict you with consumption, fever, inflammation, with fiery heat and drought, and with blight and mildew; they shall pursue you until you perish. 23 The sky over your head

---

┤ BIBLE IN LIFE ▷

God's Commandments
Deuteronomy 28.1–26

Obedience is a consistent theme of scripture. As described in Deuteronomy 28, the chosen people of Israel were to follow God's laws in order to receive God's rewards. Obedience yielded blessing, and disobedience yielded suffering.

We know that our choices also have consequences. Yet we are saved by grace through faith, not because we earn God's favor through right choices. This shifts the motivation of our obedience. We do not obey for fear of a punitive God or to avoid suffering. We obey because our love for God compels us to comply with the Bible's commandments, as exemplified by Jesus. God has already rewarded us with salvation, and we know that the rules of scripture are meant for our good, not to constrain us from a fuller life.

shall be bronze, and the earth under you iron. ²⁴The LORD will change the rain of your land into powder, and only dust shall come down upon you from the sky until you are destroyed.

25 The LORD will cause you to be defeated before your enemies; you shall go out against them one way and flee before them seven ways. You shall become an object of horror to all the kingdoms of the earth. ²⁶Your corpses shall be food for every bird of the air and animal of the earth, and there shall be no one to frighten them away. ²⁷The LORD will afflict you with the boils of Egypt, with ulcers, scurvy, and itch, of which you cannot be healed. ²⁸The LORD will afflict you with madness, blindness, and confusion of mind; ²⁹you shall grope about at noon as blind people grope in darkness, but you shall be unable to find your way; and you shall be continually abused and robbed, without anyone to help. ³⁰You shall become engaged to a woman, but another man shall lie with her. You shall build a house, but not live in it. You shall plant a vineyard, but not enjoy its fruit. ³¹Your ox shall be butchered before your eyes, but you shall not eat of it. Your donkey shall be stolen in front of you, and shall not be restored to you. Your sheep shall be given to your enemies, without anyone to help you. ³²Your sons and daughters shall be given to another people, while you look on; you will strain your eyes looking for them all day but be powerless to do anything. ³³A people whom you do not know shall eat up the fruit of your ground and of all your labors; you shall be continually abused and crushed, ³⁴and driven mad by the sight that your eyes shall see. ³⁵The LORD will strike you on the knees and on the legs with grievous boils of which you cannot be healed, from the sole of your foot to the crown of your head. ³⁶The LORD will bring you, and the king whom you set over you, to a nation that neither you nor your ancestors have known, where you shall serve other gods, of wood and stone. ³⁷You shall become an object of horror, a proverb, and a byword among all the peoples where the LORD will lead you.

38 You shall carry much seed into the field but shall gather little in, for the locust shall consume it. ³⁹You shall plant vineyards and dress them, but you shall neither drink the wine nor gather the grapes, for the worm shall eat them. ⁴⁰You shall have olive trees throughout all your territory, but you shall not anoint yourself with the oil, for your olives shall drop off. ⁴¹You shall have sons and daughters, but they shall not remain yours, for they shall go into captivity. ⁴²All your trees and the fruit of your ground the cicada shall take over. ⁴³Aliens residing among you shall ascend above you higher and higher, while you shall descend lower and lower. ⁴⁴They shall lend to you but you shall not lend to them; they shall be the head and you shall be the tail.

45 All these curses shall come upon you, pursuing and overtaking you until you are destroyed, because you did not obey the LORD your God, by observing the commandments and the decrees that he commanded you. ⁴⁶They shall be among you and your descendants as a sign and a portent forever.

47 Because you did not serve the LORD your God joyfully and with gladness of heart for the abundance of everything, ⁴⁸therefore you shall serve your enemies whom the LORD will send against you, in hunger and thirst, in nakedness and lack of everything. He will put an iron yoke on your neck until he has destroyed you. ⁴⁹The LORD will bring a nation from far away, from the end of the earth, to swoop down on you like an eagle, a nation whose language you do not understand, ⁵⁰a grim-faced nation showing no respect to the old or favor to the young. ⁵¹It shall consume the fruit of your livestock and the fruit of your ground until you are destroyed, leaving you neither grain, wine, and oil, nor the increase of your cattle and the issue of your flock, until it has made you perish. ⁵²It shall besiege you in all

your towns until your high and fortified walls, in which you trusted, come down throughout your land; it shall besiege you in all your towns throughout the land that the LORD your God has given you. ⁵³In the desperate straits to which the enemy siege reduces you, you will eat the fruit of your womb, the flesh of your own sons and daughters whom the LORD your God has given you. ⁵⁴Even the most refined and gentle of men among you will begrudge food to his own brother, to the wife whom he embraces, and to the last of his remaining children, ⁵⁵giving to none of them any of the flesh of his children whom he is eating, because nothing else remains to him, in the desperate straits to which the enemy siege will reduce you in all your towns. ⁵⁶She who is the most refined and gentle among you, so gentle and refined that she does not venture to set the sole of her foot on the ground, will begrudge food to the husband whom she embraces, to her own son, and to her own daughter, ⁵⁷begrudging even the afterbirth that comes out from between her thighs, and the children that she bears, because she is eating them in secret for lack of anything else, in the desperate straits to which the enemy siege will reduce you in your towns.

⁵⁸ If you do not diligently observe all the words of this law that are written in this book, fearing this glorious and awesome name, the LORD your God, ⁵⁹then the LORD will overwhelm both you and your offspring with severe and lasting afflictions and grievous and lasting maladies. ⁶⁰He will bring back upon you all the diseases of Egypt, of which you were in dread, and they shall cling to you. ⁶¹Every other malady and affliction, even though not recorded in the book of this law, the LORD will inflict on you until you are destroyed. ⁶²Although once you were as numerous as the stars in heaven, you shall be left few in number, because you did not obey the LORD your God. ⁶³And just as the LORD took delight in making you prosperous and numerous, so the LORD will take delight in bringing you to ruin and destruction; you shall be plucked off the land that you are entering to possess. ⁶⁴The LORD will scatter you among all peoples, from one end of the earth to the other; and there you shall serve other gods, of wood and stone, which neither you nor your ancestors have known. ⁶⁵Among those nations you shall find no ease, no resting place for the sole of your foot. There the LORD will give you a trembling heart, failing eyes, and a languishing spirit. ⁶⁶Your life shall hang in doubt before you; night and day you shall be in dread, with no assurance of your life. ⁶⁷In the morning you shall say, "If only it were evening!" and at evening you shall say, "If only it were morning!"—because of the dread that your heart shall feel and the sights that your eyes shall see. ⁶⁸The LORD will bring you back in ships to Egypt, by a route that I promised you would never see again; and there you shall offer yourselves for sale to your enemies as male and female slaves, but there will be no buyer.

29 ᵃ These are the words of the covenant that the LORD commanded Moses to make with the Israelites in the land of Moab, in addition to the covenant that he had made with them at Horeb.

THE COVENANT RENEWED IN MOAB

2ᵇ Moses summoned all Israel and said to them: You have seen all that the LORD did before your eyes in the land of Egypt, to Pharaoh and to all his servants and to all his land, ³the great trials that your eyes saw, the signs, and those great wonders. ⁴But to this day the LORD has not given you a mind to understand, or eyes to see, or ears to hear. ⁵I have led you forty years in the wilderness. The clothes on your back have not worn out, and the sandals on your feet have not worn out; ⁶you have not eaten bread, and you have not

ᵃ 29.1 Ch 28.69 in Heb   ᵇ 29.2 Ch 29.1 in Heb

drunk wine or strong drink—so that you may know that I am the LORD your God. ⁷When you came to this place, King Sihon of Heshbon and King Og of Bashan came out against us for battle, but we defeated them. ⁸We took their land and gave it as an inheritance to the Reubenites, the Gadites, and the half-tribe of Manasseh. ⁹Therefore diligently observe the words of this covenant, in order that you may succeedᵃ in everything that you do.

10 You stand assembled today, all of you, before the LORD your God— the leaders of your tribes,ᵇ your elders, and your officials, all the men of Israel, ¹¹your children, your women, and the aliens who are in your camp, both those who cut your wood and those who draw your water— ¹²to enter into the covenant of the LORD your God, sworn by an oath, which the LORD your God is making with you today; ¹³in order that he may establish you today as his people, and that he may be your God, as he promised you and as he swore to your ancestors, to Abraham, to Isaac, and to Jacob. ¹⁴I am making this covenant, sworn by an oath, not only with you who stand here with us today before the LORD our God, ¹⁵but also with those who are not here with us today. ¹⁶You know how we lived in the land of Egypt, and how we came through the midst of the nations through which you passed. ¹⁷You have seen their detestable things, the filthy idols of wood and stone, of silver and gold, that were among them. ¹⁸It may be that there is among you a man or woman, or a family or tribe, whose heart is already turning away from the LORD our God to serve the gods of those nations. It may be that there is among you a root sprouting poisonous and bitter growth. ¹⁹All who hear the words of this oath and bless themselves, thinking in their hearts, "We are safe even though we go our own stubborn ways" (thus bringing disaster on moist and dry alike)ᶜ— ²⁰the LORD will be unwilling to pardon them, for the LORD's anger and passion will smoke

against them. All the curses written in this book will descend on them, and the LORD will blot out their names from under heaven. ²¹The LORD will single them out from all the tribes of Israel for calamity, in accordance with all the curses of the covenant written in this book of the law. ²²The next generation, your children who rise up after you, as well as the foreigner who comes from a distant country, will see the devastation of that land and the afflictions with which the LORD has afflicted it— ²³all its soil burned out by sulfur and salt, nothing planted, nothing sprouting, unable to support any vegetation, like the destruction of Sodom and Gomorrah, Admah and Zeboiim, which the LORD destroyed in his fierce anger— ²⁴they and indeed all the nations will wonder, "Why has the LORD done thus to this land? What caused this great display of anger?" ²⁵They will conclude, "It is because they abandoned the covenant of the LORD, the God of their ancestors, which he made with them when he brought them out of the land of Egypt. ²⁶They turned and served other gods, worshiping them, gods whom they had not known and whom he had not allotted to them; ²⁷so the anger of the LORD was kindled against that land, bringing on it every curse written in this book. ²⁸The LORD uprooted them from their land in anger, fury, and great wrath, and cast them into another land, as is now the case." ²⁹The secret things belong to the LORD our God, but the revealed things belong to us and to our children forever, to observe all the words of this law.

GOD'S FIDELITY ASSURED

30 When all these things have happened to you, the blessings and the curses that I have set before you, if you call them to mind among all the nations where the LORD your God has driven you, ²and return to the LORD your God,

ᵃ **29.9** Or *deal wisely* ᵇ **29.10** Gk Syr: Heb *your leaders, your tribes* ᶜ **29.19** Meaning of Heb uncertain and you and your children obey him with all your heart and with all your soul, just as I am commanding you today, ³then the LORD your God will restore your fortunes and have compassion on you, gathering you again from all the peoples among whom the LORD your God has scattered you. ⁴Even if you are exiled to the ends of the world,ᵃ from there the LORD your God will gather you, and from there he will bring you back. ⁵The LORD your God will bring you into the land that your ancestors possessed, and you will possess it; he will make you more prosperous and numerous than your ancestors.

6 Moreover, the LORD your God will circumcise your heart and the heart of your descendants, so that you will love the LORD your God with all your heart and with all your soul, in order that you may live. ⁷The LORD your God will put all these curses on your enemies and on the adversaries who took advantage of you. ⁸Then you shall again obey the LORD, observing all his commandments that I am commanding you today, ⁹and the LORD your God will make you abundantly prosperous in all your undertakings, in the fruit of your body, in the fruit of your livestock, and in the fruit of your soil. For the LORD will again take delight in prospering you, just as he delighted in prospering your ancestors, ¹⁰when you obey the LORD your God by observing his command-

ments and decrees that are written in this book of the law, because you turn to the LORD your God with all your heart and with all your soul.

EXHORTATION TO CHOOSE LIFE

11 Surely, this commandment that I am commanding you today is not too hard for you, nor is it too far away. ¹²It is not in heaven, that you should say, "Who will go up to heaven for us, and get it for us so that we may hear it and observe it?" ¹³Neither is it beyond the sea, that you should say, "Who will cross to the other side of the sea for us, and get it for us so that we may hear it and observe it?" ¹⁴No, the word is very near to you; it is in your mouth and in your heart for you to observe.

15 See, I have set before you today life and prosperity, death and adversity. ¹⁶If you obey the commandments of the LORD your Godᵇ that I am commanding you today, by loving the LORD your God, walking in his ways, and observing his commandments, decrees, and ordinances, then you shall live and become numerous, and the LORD your God will bless you in the land that you are entering to possess. ¹⁷But if your heart turns away and you do not hear, but are led astray to bow down to other gods and serve them,

ᵃ **30.4** Heb of heaving   ᵇ **30.16** Gk: Heb lacks If you obey the commandments of the LORD your God

---

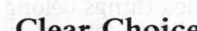 **BIBLE IN LIFE**

A Clear Choice   *Deuteronomy 30.11–20*

God gave the Israelites a clear choice between obedience and disobedience, between life and death. They were commanded to love and obey God (see Deuteronomy 30.16), but the decision was left entirely up to them. We often wonder why God permits sin. We are not robots or puppets controlled by God. We are given minds and hearts and feelings of our own. We are the ones who make decisions about our actions and habits. That's what makes us transcendent above the animals. We are given evidence and proof of God's omniscience, omnipresence and power. But we are not protected from our own sinful nature or from turning away from God. God gave us the ability—and the responsibility—to choose. We have to choose. Will we choose to visit someone who's unattractive, forgive someone who has harmed us, share what we have (our money and our time) with somebody who's a neighbor? What is our choice?

18 I declare to you today that you shall perish; you shall not live long in the land that you are crossing the Jordan to enter and possess. 19 I call heaven and earth to witness against you today that I have set before you life and death, blessings and curses. Choose life so that you and your descendants may live, 20 loving the LORD your God, obeying him, and holding fast to him; for that means life to you and length of days, so that you may live in the land that the LORD swore to give to your ancestors, to Abraham, to Isaac, and to Jacob.

JOSHUA BECOMES MOSES' SUCCESSOR

31 When Moses had finished speaking all[a] these words to all Israel, 2 he said to them: "I am now one hundred twenty years old. I am no longer able to get about, and the LORD has told me, 'You shall not cross over this Jordan.' 3 The LORD your God himself will cross over before you. He will destroy these nations before you, and you shall dispossess them. Joshua also will cross over before you, as the LORD promised. 4 The LORD will do to them as he did to Sihon and Og, the kings of the Amorites, and to their land, when he destroyed them. 5 The LORD will give them over to you and you shall deal with them in full accord with the command that I have given to you. 6 Be strong and bold; have no fear or dread of them, because it is the LORD your God who goes with you; he will not fail you or forsake you."

7 Then Moses summoned Joshua and said to him in the sight of all Israel: "Be strong and bold, for you are the one who will go with this people into the land that the LORD has sworn to their ancestors to give them; and you will put them in possession of it. 8 It is the LORD who goes before you. He will be with you; he will not fail you or forsake you. Do not fear or be dismayed."

THE LAW TO BE READ EVERY SEVENTH YEAR

9 Then Moses wrote down this law, and gave it to the priests, the sons of Levi, who carried the ark of the covenant of the LORD, and to all the elders of Israel. 10 Moses commanded them: "Every seventh year, in the scheduled year of remission, during the festival of booths,[b] 11 when all Israel comes to appear before the LORD your God at the place that he will choose, you shall read this law before all Israel in their hearing. 12 Assemble the people—men, women, and children, as well as the aliens residing in your towns—so that they may hear and learn to fear the LORD your God and to observe diligently all the words of this law, 13 and so that their children, who have not known it, may hear and learn to fear the LORD your God, as long as you live in the land that you are crossing over the Jordan to possess."

MOSES AND JOSHUA RECEIVE GOD'S CHARGE

14 The LORD said to Moses, "Your time to die is near; call Joshua and present yourselves in the tent of meeting, so that I may commission him." So Moses and Joshua went and presented themselves in the tent of meeting, 15 and the LORD appeared at the tent in a pillar of cloud; the pillar of cloud stood at the entrance to the tent.

16 The LORD said to Moses, "Soon you will lie down with your ancestors. Then this people will begin to prostitute themselves to the foreign gods in their midst, the gods of the land into which they are going; they will forsake me, breaking my covenant that I have made with them. 17 My anger will be kindled against them in that day. I will forsake them and hide my face from them; they will become easy prey, and many terrible troubles will come upon them. In that day they will say, 'Have not these troubles come upon us because our God is not in our midst?' 18 On that day I will surely hide my face on account of all the evil they have done by turning to other gods. 19 Now therefore write

a 31.1 Q Ms Gk: MT Moses went and spoke
b 31.10 Or tabernacles; Heb succoth

this song, and teach it to the Israelites; put it in their mouths, in order that this song may be a witness for me against the Israelites. [20]For when I have brought them into the land flowing with milk and honey, which I promised on oath to their ancestors, and they have eaten their fill and grown fat, they will turn to other gods and serve them, despising me and breaking my covenant. [21]And when many terrible troubles come upon them, this song will confront them as a witness, because it will not be lost from the mouths of their descendants. For I know what they are inclined to do even now, before I have brought them into the land that I promised them on oath." [22]That very day Moses wrote this song and taught it to the Israelites.

[23] Then the LORD commissioned Joshua son of Nun and said, "Be strong and bold, for you shall bring the Israelites into the land that I promised them; I will be with you."

[24] When Moses had finished writing down in a book the words of this law to the very end, [25]Moses commanded the Levites who carried the ark of the covenant of the LORD, saying, [26]"Take this book of the law and put it beside the ark of the covenant of the LORD your God; let it remain there as a witness against you. [27]For I know well how rebellious and stubborn you are. If you already have been so rebellious toward the LORD while I am still alive among you, how much more after my death! [28]Assemble to me all the elders of your tribes and your officials, so that I may recite these words in their hearing and call heaven and earth to witness against them. [29]For I know that after my death you will surely act corruptly, turning aside from the way that I have commanded you. In time to come trouble will befall you, because you will do what is evil in the sight of the LORD, provoking him to anger through the work of your hands."

THE SONG OF MOSES

[30] Then Moses recited the words of this song, to the very end, in the hearing of the whole assembly of Israel:

32 [1] Give ear, O heavens,
and I will speak;
let the earth hear the words
of my mouth.
[2] May my teaching drop
like the rain,
my speech condense
like the dew;
like gentle rain on grass,
like showers on new growth.
[3] For I will proclaim the name
of the LORD;
ascribe greatness to our God!

[4] The Rock, his work is perfect,
and all his ways are just.
A faithful God, without deceit,
just and upright is he;
[5] yet his degenerate children have
dealt falsely with him,[a]
a perverse and crooked
generation.
[6] Do you thus repay the LORD,
O foolish and senseless people?
Is not he your father, who
created you,
who made you and
established you?
[7] Remember the days of old,
consider the years long past;
ask your father, and he
will inform you;
your elders, and they
will tell you.
[8] When the Most High[b]
apportioned the nations,
when he divided humankind,
he fixed the boundaries
of the peoples
according to the number
of the gods;[c]
[9] the LORD's own portion
was his people,
Jacob his allotted share.

[10] He sustained[d] him in a
desert land,
in a howling wilderness waste;
he shielded him, cared for him,
guarded him as the
apple of his eye.

---

[a] 32.5 Meaning of Heb uncertain
[b] 32.8 Traditional rendering of Heb Elyon   [c] 32.8 Q Ms Compare Gk Tg: MT the Israelites   [d] 32.10 Sam Gk Compare Tg: MT found

11 As an eagle stirs up its nest,
 and hovers over its young;
 as it spreads its wings,
  takes them up,
 and bears them aloft
  on its pinions,
12 the LORD alone guided him;
 no foreign god was with him.
13 He set him atop the heights
  of the land,
 and fed him with[a] produce
  of the field;
 he nursed him with honey
  from the crags,
 with oil from flinty rock;
14 curds from the herd, and milk
  from the flock,
 with fat of lambs and rams;
 Bashan bulls and goats,
 together with the
  choicest wheat—
 you drank fine wine from
  the blood of grapes.
15 Jacob ate his fill;[b]
 Jeshurun grew fat, and kicked.
 You grew fat, bloated,
  and gorged!
 He abandoned God who
  made him,
 and scoffed at the Rock
  of his salvation.
16 They made him jealous with
  strange gods,
 with abhorrent things
  they provoked him.
17 They sacrificed to demons,
  not God,
 to deities they had
  never known,
 to new ones recently arrived,
 whom your ancestors
  had not feared.
18 You were unmindful of the
  Rock that bore you;[c]
 you forgot the God who
  gave you birth.

19 The LORD saw it, and was jealous;[d]
 he spurned[e] his sons
  and daughters.
20 He said: I will hide my face
  from them,
 I will see what their end will be;
 for they are a perverse
  generation,
 children in whom there
  is no faithfulness.

21 They made me jealous with
  what is no god,
 provoked me with their idols.
 So I will make them jealous
  with what is no people,
 provoke them with a
  foolish nation.
22 For a fire is kindled by my anger,
 and burns to the depths
  of Sheol;
 it devours the earth and
  its increase,
 and sets on fire the
  foundations of the
  mountains.
23 I will heap disasters upon them,
 spend my arrows against them:
24 wasting hunger,
 burning consumption,
 bitter pestilence.
 The teeth of beasts I will send
  against them,
 with venom of things
  crawling in the dust.
25 In the street the sword
  shall bereave,
 and in the chambers terror,
 for young man and woman alike,
 nursing child and old gray head.
26 I thought to scatter them[f]
 and blot out the memory of
  them from humankind;
27 but I feared provocation
  by the enemy,
 for their adversaries might
  misunderstand
 and say, "Our hand is triumphant;
 it was not the LORD who
  did all this."

28 They are a nation void of sense;
 there is no understanding
  in them.
29 If they were wise, they would
  understand this;
 they would discern what
  the end would be.
30 How could one have routed
  a thousand,
 and two put a myriad to flight,

a 32.13 Sam Gk Syr Tg: MT *he ate*
b 32.15 Q Mss Sam Gk: MT lacks *Jacob ate his fill*   c 32.18 Or *that begot you*
d 32.19 Q Mss Gk: MT lacks *was jealous*
e 32.19 Cn: Heb *he spurned because of provocation*   f 32.26 Gk: Meaning of Heb uncertain

unless their Rock
    had sold them,
    the LORD had given them up?
31 Indeed their rock is not
    like our Rock;
    our enemies are fools.ª
32 Their vine comes from the
    vinestock of Sodom,
    from the vineyards of
    Gomorrah;
    their grapes are grapes of poison,
    their clusters are bitter;
33 their wine is the poison
    of serpents,
    the cruel venom of asps.

34 Is not this laid up in store
    with me,
    sealed up in my treasuries?
35 Vengeance is mine, and
    recompense,
    for the time when their
    foot shall slip;
because the day of their
    calamity is at hand,
    their doom comes swiftly.

36 Indeed the LORD will
    vindicate his people,
    have compassion on
    his servants,
when he sees that their
    power is gone,
    neither bond nor free
    remaining.
37 Then he will say: Where
    are their gods,
    the rock in which they
    took refuge,
38 who ate the fat of
    their sacrifices,
    and drank the wine of
    their libations?
Let them rise up and help you,
    let them be your protection!

39 See now that I, even I, am he;
    there is no god besides me.
I kill and I make alive;
    I wound and I heal;
    and no one can deliver
    from my hand.
40 For I lift up my hand to heaven,
    and swear: As I live forever,
41 when I whet my flashing sword,
    and my hand takes hold
    on judgment;

I will take vengeance on
    my adversaries,
    and will repay those
    who hate me.
42 I will make my arrows
    drunk with blood,
    and my sword shall
    devour flesh—
with the blood of the slain
    and the captives,
    from the long-haired enemy.

43 Praise, O heavens,ᵇ his people,
    worship him, all you gods!ᶜ
For he will avenge the blood
    of his children,ᵈ
    and take vengeance on
    his adversaries;
he will repay those who
    hate him,ᶜ
    and cleanse the land
    for his people.ᵉ

44 Moses came and recited all the words of this song in the hearing of the people, he and Joshuaᶠ son of Nun. 45When Moses had finished reciting all these words to all Israel, 46he said to them: "Take to heart all the words that I am giving in witness against you today; give them as a command to your children, so that they may diligently observe all the words of this law. 47This is no trifling matter for you, but rather your very life; through it you may live long in the land that you are crossing over the Jordan to possess."

MOSES' DEATH FORETOLD

48 On that very day the LORD addressed Moses as follows: 49"Ascend this mountain of the Abarim, Mount Nebo, which is in the land of Moab, across from Jericho, and view the land of Canaan, which I am giving to the Israelites for a possession; 50you shall die there on the mountain that you ascend and shall be gathered to your kin, as your brother Aaron died on Mount Hor and was gathered to

---

ª 32. 31 Gk: Meaning of Heb uncertain
ᵇ 32.43 Q Ms Gk: MT *nations*   ᶜ 32.43 Q Ms
Gk: MT lacks this line   ᵈ 32.43 Q Ms Gk: MT
his servants   ᵉ 32.43 Q Ms Sam Gk Vg: MT
his land his people   ᶠ 32.44 Sam Gk Syr Vg:
MT *Hoshea*

PONDER

"Take to heart all the words that I am giving in witness against you today; give them as a command to your children, so that they may diligently observe all the words of this law. This is no trifling matter for you, but rather your very life."
—Deuteronomy 32.46–47

PRAY

Lord God, we know that in every story in your Holy Scriptures there is something that we are to take to heart. Each of us might say to you: I ask for courage to face my sinfulness, knowing that I need your forgiveness; I confess my sin with absolute certainty that your love and grace will always be available. What should I do to make reparation for my sin against others? How should I act, knowing that I am saved from condemnation? How can I express my deep gratitude to you? How can I make your priorities mine? Stir in us the desire to choose abundant life, to love you and to listen to your voice. Amen.

his kin; 51because both of you broke faith with me among the Israelites at the waters of Meribath-kadesh in the wilderness of Zin, by failing to maintain my holiness among the Israelites. 52Although you may view the land from a distance, you shall not enter it—the land that I am giving to the Israelites."

MOSES' FINAL BLESSING ON ISRAEL

33 This is the blessing with which Moses, the man of God, blessed the Israelites before his death. 2He said:
The LORD came from Sinai,
and dawned from Seir
upon us;[a]
he shone forth from
Mount Paran.

With him were myriads
of holy ones;[b]
at his right, a host of his own.[c]
3 Indeed, O favorite among[d]
peoples,
all his holy ones were
in your charge;
they marched at your heels,
accepted direction from you.
4 Moses charged us with the law,
as a possession for the
assembly of Jacob.
5 There arose a king in Jeshurun,
when the leaders of the
people assembled—
the united tribes of Israel.

6 May Reuben live, and not die out,
even though his numbers
are few.

7 And this he said of Judah:
O LORD, give heed to Judah,
and bring him to his people;
strengthen his hands for him,[e]
and be a help against
his adversaries.

8 And of Levi he said:
Give to Levi[f] your Thummim,
and your Urim to your
loyal one,
whom you tested at Massah,
with whom you contended at
the waters of Meribah;
9 who said of his father
and mother,
"I regard them not";
he ignored his kin,
and did not acknowledge
his children.
For they observed your word,
and kept your covenant.
10 They teach Jacob your ordinances,
and Israel your law;
they place incense before you,
and whole burnt offerings
on your altar.

a 33.2 Gk Syr Vg Compare Tg: Heb *upon them*   b 33.2 Cn Compare Gk Sam Syr Vg: MT *He came from Riboboth-kadesh,*
c 33.2 Cn Compare Gk: Meaning of Heb uncertain   d 33.3 Or *O lover of the*
e 33.7 Cn: Heb *with his hands he contended*
f 33.8 Q Ms Gk: MT lacks *Give to Levi*

11 Bless, O LORD, his substance,
and accept the work
of his hands;
crush the loins of his adversaries,
of those that hate him, so that
they do not rise again.

12 Of Benjamin he said:
The beloved of the LORD
rests in safety—
the High God[a] surrounds
him all day long—
the beloved[b] rests between
his shoulders.

13 And of Joseph he said:
Blessed by the LORD be his land,
with the choice gifts of
heaven above,
and of the deep that
lies beneath;
14 with the choice fruits of the sun,
and the rich yield of
the months;
15 with the finest produce of the
ancient mountains,
and the abundance of the
everlasting hills;
16 with the choice gifts of the
earth and its fullness,
and the favor of the one
who dwells on Sinai.[c]
Let these come on the
head of Joseph,
on the brow of the prince
among his brothers.
17 A firstborn[d] bull—majesty is his!
His horns are the horns
of a wild ox;
with them he gores the peoples,
driving them to[e] the
ends of the earth;
such are the myriads of Ephraim,
such are the thousands of
Manasseh.

18 And of Zebulun he said:
Rejoice, Zebulun, in your
going out;
and Issachar, in your tents.
19 They call peoples to the mountain;
there they offer the
right sacrifices;
for they suck the affluence
of the seas
and the hidden treasures
of the sand.

20 And of Gad he said:
Blessed be the enlargement
of Gad!
Gad lives like a lion;
he tears at arm and scalp.
21 He chose the best for himself,
for there a commander's
allotment was reserved;
he came at the head
of the people,
he executed the justice
of the LORD,
and his ordinances for Israel.

22 And of Dan he said:
Dan is a lion's whelp
that leaps forth from Bashan.

23 And of Naphtali he said:
O Naphtali, sated with favor,
full of the blessing of the LORD,
possess the west and the south.

24 And of Asher he said:
Most blessed of sons be Asher;
may he be the favorite
of his brothers,
and may he dip his foot in oil.
25 Your bars are iron and bronze;
and as your days, so is
your strength.

26 There is none like God,
O Jeshurun,
who rides through the
heavens to your help,
majestic through the skies.
27 He subdues the ancient gods,[f]
shatters[g] the forces of old;[h]
he drove out the enemy
before you,
and said, "Destroy!"
28 So Israel lives in safety,
untroubled is Jacob's abode[i]
in a land of grain and wine,
where the heavens drop
down dew.
29 Happy are you, O Israel!
Who is like you,
a people saved by the LORD,

a 33.12 Heb *above him*   b 33.12 Heb *he*
c 33.16 Cn: Heb *in the bush*   d 33.17 Q Ms
Gk Syr Vg: MT *His firstborn*   e 33.17 Cn:
Heb *the peoples, together*   f 33.27 Or *The
eternal God is a dwelling place*   g 33.27 Cn:
Heb *from underneath*   h 33.27 Or *the
everlasting arms*   i 33.28 Or *fountain*

the shield of your help,
    and the sword of your triumph!
Your enemies shall come
        fawning to you,
    and you shall tread on
        their backs.

MOSES DIES AND IS BURIED IN THE LAND OF MOAB

34 Then Moses went up from the plains of Moab to Mount Nebo, to the top of Pisgah, which is opposite Jericho, and the LORD showed him the whole land: Gilead as far as Dan, ²all Naphtali, the land of Ephraim and Manasseh, all the land of Judah as far as the Western Sea, ³the Negeb, and the Plain—that is, the valley of Jericho, the city of palm trees—as far as Zoar. ⁴The LORD said to him, "This is the land of which I swore to Abraham, to Isaac, and to Jacob, saying, 'I will give it to your descendants'; I have let you see it with your eyes, but you shall not cross over there." ⁵Then Moses, the servant of the LORD, died there in the land of Moab, at the LORD's command. ⁶He was buried in a valley in the land of Moab, opposite Bethpeor, but no one knows his burial place to this day. ⁷Moses was one hundred twenty years old when he died; his sight was unimpaired and his vigor had not abated. ⁸The Isra-elites wept for Moses in the plains of Moab thirty days; then the period of mourning for Moses was ended.

9 Joshua son of Nun was full of the spirit of wisdom, because Moses had laid his hands on him; and the Israelites obeyed him, doing as the LORD had commanded Moses.

EVEN IN OLD AGE,

OUR ENTHUSIASM AND

PURPOSE FOR LIVING CAN

BE RENEWED BY USING

OUR SPIRITUAL GIFTS.

10 Never since has there arisen a prophet in Israel like Moses, whom the LORD knew face to face. ¹¹He was unequaled for all the signs and wonders that the LORD sent him to perform in the land of Egypt, against Pharaoh and all his servants and his entire land, ¹²and for all the mighty deeds and all the terrifying displays of power that Moses performed in the sight of all Israel.

JOSHUA

The book of Joshua documents one of the greatest periods in the history of the Israelites—the establishment of the nation of Israel in the land God had promised them. If you're into war stories, this book is full of them. But you won't find what many would consider brilliant examples of military genius. What you will see is the power of the God who not only promised victory but made it happen in ways that defy human understanding. Behind all the accounts of battles and conquests is the story of a people who believed God and experienced the blessings that came from obedience to the Lord of lords.

GOD'S COMMISSION TO JOSHUA

1 After the death of Moses the servant of the LORD, the LORD spoke to Joshua son of Nun, Moses' assistant, saying, 2"My servant Moses is dead. Now proceed to cross the Jordan, you and all this people, into the land that I am giving to them, to the Israelites. 3Every place that the sole of your foot will tread upon I have given to you, as I promised to Moses. 4From the wilderness and the Lebanon as far as the great river, the river Euphrates, all the land of the Hittites, to the Great Sea in the west shall be your territory. 5No one shall be able to stand against you all the days of your life. As I was with Moses, so I will be with you; I will not fail you or forsake you. 6Be strong and courageous; for you shall put this people in possession of the land that I swore to their ancestors to give them. 7Only be strong and very courageous, being careful to act in accordance with all the law that my servant Moses commanded you; do not turn from it to the right hand or to the left, so that you may be successful wherever you go. 8This book of the law shall not depart out of your mouth; you shall meditate on it day and night, so that you may be careful to act in accordance with all that is written in it. For then you shall make your way prosperous, and then you shall be successful. 9I hereby command you: Be strong and courageous; do not be frightened or dismayed, for the LORD your God is with you wherever you go."

PREPARATIONS FOR THE INVASION

10 Then Joshua commanded the officers of the people, 11"Pass through the camp, and command the people: 'Prepare your provisions; for in three days you are to cross over the Jordan, to go in to take possession of the land that the LORD your God gives you to possess.'"

12 To the Reubenites, the Gadites, and the half-tribe of Manasseh Joshua said, 13"Remember the word that Moses the servant of the LORD commanded you, saying, 'The LORD your God is providing you a place of rest, and will give you this land.' 14Your wives, your little ones, and your livestock shall remain in the land that Moses gave you beyond the Jordan. But all the warriors among you shall cross over armed before your kindred and shall help them, 15until the LORD gives rest to your kindred as well as to you, and they too take possession of the land that the LORD your God is giving them. Then you shall return to your own land and take possession of it, the land that Moses the servant of the LORD gave you beyond the Jordan to the east."

16 They answered Joshua: "All that you have commanded us we will do, and wherever you send us we will go. 17Just as we obeyed Moses in all

---

PONDER

"All that you have commanded us we will do, and wherever you send us we will go."
—Joshua 1.16

PRAY

Father, we don't always know how to reconcile the pressures in our lives—the pressures of a competitive world—with the standards prescribed for us by our Savior, Jesus Christ. We ask you, as we read about Joshua and his faith in you, to give us the same kind of faith so that we can make the right choices as measured not by our peers, not by cultural standards, but by your unchanging holiness. Let us not stay dormant. Let us not be self-satisfied. Let us not ignore the opportunities you give us for adventure and challenge. But let us live constantly expanding lives blessed by the kind of peace that passes understanding, the joy that is indescribable and the knowledge that our lives can be successful in your eyes when we follow you courageously and obediently. We ask these things in the name of Jesus. Amen.

GOD IS WITH YOU

*"Be strong and courageous; do not be frightened or dismayed,
for the LORD your God is with you wherever you go."*

—Joshua 1.9

Change can be frightening. Whether it's starting a new job or moving to a new home or going off to college, few things generate such a mix of feelings within us. On the one hand, we may be excited about new opportunities that change can bring; on the other hand, we fear the unknown that always accompanies change. What difficulties will I face? How will I know what to do?

Sometimes our fear of change can become so powerful that we won't try anything new unless we are absolutely sure we're going to be successful. But this debilitating approach to life can only lead to stagnation and self-centeredness. As we build a protective cage of certainty around ourselves, we refuse to stretch our hearts. We fail to stretch our minds. We become self-satisfied. In the end, we focus much of our energy simply digging in our heels and justifying the way we already are.

When God called Joshua to lead the Israelites into the land promised to them, God knew that Joshua might be tempted to fear what lay ahead. So, God assured Joshua that success would be certain because he, the Lord, would be with him. At the same time, God warned Joshua not to stray from the commands that he had given his people through Moses (see Joshua 1.2–9).

Like Joshua, we have been given assurance of God's constant presence as we go about living and serving him. Before he ascended into heaven, Jesus commissioned us with this assurance: "And remember, I am with you always, to the end of the age." (Matthew 28.20). We can know that, no matter what we may face, nothing is too hard for God, and he will see us through. Such assurance should give us courage, freeing us to do great new things for him. We can go to work knowing that God is ultimately our Provider and Sustainer. We can venture into new avenues of service because our security rests in God's care for us. We can face illness, knowing that in Christ our hope of heaven is sure. At times we may even find that something we thought was going to be a tragedy is actually a blessing from God.

Going Deeper

- What fears are you facing? How does God's promise to be near you help you to overcome those fears?
- What are some examples of things from your past that turned out to be blessings, though you feared they were going to be tragedies?

things, so we will obey you. Only may the LORD your God be with you, as he was with Moses! 18 Whoever rebels against your orders and disobeys your words, whatever you command, shall be put to death. Only be strong and courageous."

SPIES SENT TO JERICHO

2 Then Joshua son of Nun sent two men secretly from Shittim as spies, saying, "Go, view the land, especially Jericho." So they went, and entered the house of a prostitute whose name was Rahab, and spent the night there. 2 The king of Jericho was told, "Some Israelites have come here tonight to search out the land." 3 Then the king of Jericho sent orders to Rahab, "Bring out the men who have come to you, who entered your house, for they have come only to search out the whole land." 4 But the woman took the two men and hid them. Then she said, "True, the men came to me, but I did not know where they came from. 5 And when it was time to close the gate at dark, the men went out. Where the men went I do not know. Pursue them quickly, for you can overtake them." 6 She had, however, brought them up to the roof and hidden them with the stalks of flax that she had laid out on the roof. 7 So the men pursued them on the way to the Jordan as far as the fords. As soon as the pursuers had gone out, the gate was shut.

8 Before they went to sleep, she came up to them on the roof 9 and said to the men: "I know that the LORD has given you the land, and that dread of you has fallen on us, and that all the inhabitants of the land melt in fear before you. 10 For we have heard how the LORD dried up the water of the Red Sea a before you when you came out of Egypt, and what you did to the two kings of the Amorites that were beyond the Jordan, to Sihon and Og, whom you utterly destroyed. 11 As soon as we heard it, our hearts melted, and there was no courage left in any of us because of you. The LORD your God is indeed God in heaven above and on earth below. 12 Now then, since

I have dealt kindly with you, swear to me by the LORD that you in turn will deal kindly with my family. Give me a sign of good faith 13 that you will spare my father and mother, my brothers and sisters, and all who belong to them, and deliver our lives from death." 14 The men said to her, "Our life for yours! If you do not tell this business of ours, then we will deal kindly and faithfully with you when the LORD gives us the land."

15 Then she let them down by a rope through the window, for her house was on the outer side of the city wall and she resided within the wall itself. 16 She said to them, "Go toward the hill country, so that the pursuers may not come upon you. Hide yourselves there three days, until the pursuers have returned; then afterward you may go your way." 17 The men said to her, "We will be released from this oath that you have made us swear to you 18 if we invade the land and you do not tie this crimson cord in the window through which you let us down, and you do not gather into your house your father and mother, your brothers, and all your family. 19 If any of you go out of the doors of your house into the street, they shall be responsible for their own death, and we shall be innocent; but if a hand is laid upon any who are with you in the house, we shall bear the responsibility for their death. 20 But if you tell this business of ours, then we shall be released from this oath that you made us swear to you." 21 She said, "According to your words, so be it." She sent them away and they departed. Then she tied the crimson cord in the window.

22 They departed and went into the hill country and stayed there three days, until the pursuers returned. The pursuers had searched all along the way and found nothing. 23 Then the two men came down again from the hill country. They crossed over, came to Joshua son of Nun, and told him all that had happened to them. 24 They said to

---

a 2.10 Or *Sea of Reeds*

Joshua, "Truly the LORD has given all the land into our hands; moreover all the inhabitants of the land melt in fear before us."

ISRAEL CROSSES THE JORDAN

3 Early in the morning Joshua rose and set out from Shittim with all the Israelites, and they came to the Jordan. They camped there before crossing over. ²At the end of three days the officers went through the camp ³and commanded the people, "When you see the ark of the covenant of the LORD your God being carried by the levitical priests, then you shall set out from your place. Follow it, ⁴so that you may know the way you should go, for you have not passed this way before. Yet there shall be a space between you and it, a distance of about two thousand cubits; do not come any nearer to it." ⁵Then Joshua said to the people, "Sanctify yourselves; for tomorrow the LORD will do wonders among you." ⁶To the priests Joshua said, "Take up the ark of the covenant, and pass on in front of the people." So they took up the ark of the covenant and went in front of the people.

7 The LORD said to Joshua, "This day I will begin to exalt you in the sight of all Israel, so that they may know that I will be with you as I was with Moses. ⁸You are the one who shall command the priests who bear the ark of the covenant, 'When you come to the edge of the waters of the Jordan, you shall stand still in the Jordan.' " ⁹Joshua then said to the Israelites, "Draw near and hear the words of the LORD your God." ¹⁰Joshua said, "By this you shall know that among you is the living God who without fail will drive out from before you the Canaanites, Hittites, Hivites, Perizzites, Girgashites, Amorites, and Jebusites: ¹¹the ark of the covenant of the Lord of all the earth is going to pass before you into the Jordan. ¹²So now select twelve men from the tribes of Israel, one from each tribe. ¹³When the soles of the feet of the priests who bear the ark of the LORD, the Lord of all the earth, rest in the waters of the Jordan, the waters of the Jordan flowing from above shall be cut off; they shall stand in a single heap."

14 When the people set out from their tents to cross over the Jordan, the priests bearing the ark of the covenant were in front of the people. ¹⁵Now the Jordan overflows all its banks throughout the time of harvest. So when those who bore the ark had come to the Jordan, and the feet of the priests bearing the ark were dipped in the edge of the water, ¹⁶the waters flowing from above stood still, rising up in a single heap far off at Adam, the city that is beside Zarethan, while those flowing toward the sea of the Arabah, the Dead Sea,ᵃ were wholly cut off. Then the people crossed over opposite Jericho. ¹⁷While all Israel were crossing over on dry ground, the priests who bore the ark of the covenant of the LORD stood on dry ground in the middle of the Jordan, until the entire nation finished crossing over the Jordan.

TWELVE STONES SET UP AT GILGAL

4 When the entire nation had finished crossing over the Jordan, the LORD said to Joshua: ²"Select twelve men from the people, one from each tribe, ³and command them, 'Take twelve stones from here out of the middle of the Jordan, from the place where the priests' feet stood, carry them over with you, and lay them down in the place where you camp tonight.' " ⁴Then Joshua summoned the twelve men from the Israelites, whom he had appointed, one from each tribe. ⁵Joshua said to them, "Pass on before the ark of the LORD your God into the middle of the Jordan, and each of you take up a stone on his shoulder, one for each of the tribes of the Israelites, ⁶so that this may be a sign among you. When your children ask in time to come, 'What do those stones mean to you?' ⁷then you shall tell them that the waters of the Jordan were cut off in

ᵃ 3.16 Heb Salt Sea

front of the ark of the covenant of the LORD. When it crossed over the Jordan, the waters of the Jordan were cut off. So these stones shall be to the Israelites a memorial forever."

8 The Israelites did as Joshua commanded. They took up twelve stones out of the middle of the Jordan, according to the number of the tribes of the Israelites, as the LORD told Joshua, carried them over with them to the place where they camped, and laid them down there. 9(Joshua set up twelve stones in the middle of the Jordan, in the place where the feet of the priests bearing the ark of the covenant had stood; and they are there to this day.)

10 The priests who bore the ark remained standing in the middle of the Jordan, until everything was finished that the LORD commanded Joshua to tell the people, according to all that Moses had commanded Joshua. The people crossed over in haste. 11As soon as all the people had finished crossing over, the ark of the LORD, and the priests, crossed over in front of the people. 12The Reubenites, the Gadites, and the half-tribe of Manasseh crossed over armed before the Israelites, as Moses had ordered them. 13About forty thousand armed for war crossed over before the LORD to the plains of Jericho for battle.

14 On that day the LORD exalted Joshua in the sight of all Israel; and they stood in awe of him, as they had stood in awe of Moses, all the days of his life.

15 The LORD said to Joshua, 16"Command the priests who bear

the ark of the covenant,[a] to come up out of the Jordan." 17Joshua therefore commanded the priests, "Come up out of the Jordan." 18When the priests bearing the ark of the covenant of the LORD came up from the middle of the Jordan, and the soles of the priests' feet touched dry ground, the waters of the Jordan returned to their place and overflowed all its banks, as before.

19 The people came up out of the Jordan on the tenth day of the first month, and they camped in Gilgal on the east border of Jericho. 20Those twelve stones, which they had taken out of the Jordan, Joshua set up in Gilgal, 21saying to the Israelites, "When your children ask their parents in time to come, 'What do these stones mean?' 22then you shall let your children know, 'Israel crossed over the Jordan here on dry ground.' 23For the LORD your God dried up the waters of the Jordan for you until you crossed over, as the LORD your God did to the Red Sea,[b] which he dried up for us until we crossed over, 24so that all the peoples of the earth may know that the hand of the LORD is mighty, and so that you may fear the LORD your God forever."

THE NEW GENERATION CIRCUMCISED

5 When all the kings of the Amorites beyond the Jordan to the west, and all the kings of the

[a] 4.16 Or treaty, or testimony; Heb eduth
[b] 4.23 Or Sea of Reeds

BIBLE IN LIFE

Fearing God   Joshua 4.1–24

Joshua gave the Israelites a visual reminder to fear God. When they looked at the stones of memorial, they were to remember the awesome power of God that had led them across the Red Sea and across the Jordan River. Throughout the generations, the people were to acknowledge God's purity and holiness. Fearing God is an aspect of reverence that compels us to kneel down rather than run away. Many of us have a distorted fear that causes us to tremble at the thought of being punished and to run away from God. Instead, we should be kneeling, remembering God's awesome deeds and holiness.

Canaanites by the sea, heard that the LORD had dried up the waters of the Jordan for the Israelites until they had crossed over, their hearts melted, and there was no longer any spirit in them, because of the Israelites. 2 At that time the LORD said to Joshua, "Make flint knives and circumcise the Israelites a second time." 3 So Joshua made flint knives, and circumcised the Israelites at Gibeath-haaraloth.a 4 This is the reason why Joshua circumcised them: all the males of the people who came out of Egypt, all the warriors, had died during the journey through the wilderness after they had come out of Egypt. 5 Although all the people who came out had been circumcised, yet all the people born on the journey through the wilderness after they had come out of Egypt had not been circumcised. 6 For the Israelites traveled forty years in the wilderness, until all the nation, the warriors who came out of Egypt, perished, not having listened to the voice of the LORD. To them the LORD swore that he would not let them see the land that he had sworn to their ancestors to give us, a land flowing with milk and honey. 7 So it was their children, whom he raised up in their place, that Joshua circumcised; for they were uncircumcised, because they had not been circumcised on the way.

8 When the circumcising of all the nation was done, they remained in their places in the camp until they were healed. 9 The LORD said to Joshua, "Today I have rolled away from you the disgrace of Egypt." And so that place is called Gilgalb to this day.

THE PASSOVER AT GILGAL

10 While the Israelites were camped in Gilgal they kept the passover in the evening on the fourteenth day of the month in the plains of Jericho. 11 On the day after the passover, on that very day, they ate the produce of the land, unleavened cakes and parched grain. 12 The manna ceased on the day they ate the produce of the land, and the Israelites no longer had manna; they ate the crops of the land of Canaan that year.

JOSHUA'S VISION

13 Once when Joshua was by Jericho, he looked up and saw a man standing before him with a drawn sword in his hand. Joshua went to him and said to him, "Are you one of us, or one of our adversaries?" 14 He replied, "Neither; but as commander of the army of the LORD I have now come." And Joshua fell on his face to the earth and worshiped, and he said to him, "What do you command your servant, my lord?" 15 The commander of the army of the LORD said to Joshua, "Remove the sandals from your feet, for the place where you stand is holy." And Joshua did so.

JERICHO TAKEN AND DESTROYED

6 Now Jericho was shut up inside and out because of the Israelites; no one came out and no one went in. 2 The LORD said to Joshua, "See, I have handed Jericho over to you, along with its king and soldiers. 3 You shall march around the city, all the warriors circling the city once. Thus you shall do for six days, 4 with seven priests bearing seven trumpets of rams' horns before the ark. On the seventh day you shall march around the city seven times, the priests blowing the trumpets. 5 When they make a long blast with the ram's horn, as soon as you hear the sound of the trumpet, then all the people shall shout with a great shout; and the wall of the city will fall down flat, and all the people shall charge straight ahead." 6 So Joshua son of Nun summoned the priests and said to them, "Take up the ark of the covenant, and have seven priests carry seven trumpets of rams' horns in front of the ark of the LORD." 7 To the people he said, "Go forward and march around the city; have the armed men pass on before the ark of the LORD."

---

a 5.3 That is the Hill of the Foreskins
b 5.9 Related to Heb galal to roll

8 As Joshua had commanded the people, the seven priests carrying the seven trumpets of rams' horns before the LORD went forward, blowing the trumpets, with the ark of the covenant of the LORD following them. **9** And the armed men went before the priests who blew the trumpets; the rear guard came after the ark, while the trumpets blew continually. **10** To the people Joshua gave this command: "You shall not shout or let your voice be heard, nor shall you utter a word, until the day I tell you to shout. Then you shall shout." **11** So the ark of the LORD went around the city, circling it once; and they came into the camp, and spent the night in the camp.

12 Then Joshua rose early in the morning, and the priests took up the ark of the LORD. **13** The seven priests carrying the seven trumpets of rams' horns before the ark of the LORD passed on, blowing the trumpets continually. The armed men went before them, and the rear guard came after the ark of the LORD, while the trumpets blew continually. **14** On the second day they marched around the city once and then returned to the camp. They did this for six days.

15 On the seventh day they rose early, at dawn, and marched around the city in the same manner seven times. It was only on that day that they marched around the city seven times. **16** And at the seventh time, when the priests had blown the trumpets, Joshua said to the people, "Shout! For the LORD has given you the city. **17** The city and all that is in it shall be devoted to the LORD for destruction. Only Rahab the prostitute and all who are with her in her house shall live because she hid the messengers we sent. **18** As for you, keep away from the things devoted to destruction, so as not to covet[a] and take any of the devoted things and make the camp of Israel an object for destruction, bringing trouble upon it. **19** But all silver and gold, and vessels of bronze and iron, are sacred to the LORD; they shall go into the treasury of the LORD." **20** So the people shouted, and the trumpets were blown. As soon as the people heard the sound of the trumpets, they raised a great shout, and the wall fell down flat; so the people charged straight ahead into the city and captured it. **21** Then they devoted to destruction by the edge of the sword all in the city, both men and women, young and old, oxen, sheep, and donkeys.

22 Joshua said to the two men who had spied out the land, "Go into the prostitute's house, and bring the woman out of it and all who belong to her, as you swore to her." **23** So the young men who had been spies went in and brought Rahab out, along with her father, her mother, her brothers, and all who belonged to her—they brought all her kindred out—and set them outside the camp of Israel. **24** They burned down the city, and everything in it; only the silver and gold, and the vessels of bronze and iron, they put into the treasury of the house of the LORD. **25** But Rahab the prostitute, with her family and all who belonged to her, Joshua spared. Her family[b] has lived in Israel ever since. For she hid the messengers whom Joshua sent to spy out Jericho.

INDIVIDUAL ACTS CAN HAVE BROAD SOCIAL EFFECTS.

26 Joshua then pronounced this oath, saying,
"Cursed before the LORD be
    anyone who tries
    to build this city—this Jericho!
At the cost of his firstborn he
        shall lay its foundation,
    and at the cost of his youngest
        he shall set up its gates!"
27 So the LORD was with Joshua; and his fame was in all the land.

[a] 6.18 Gk: Heb *devote to destruction* Compare 7.21   [b] 6.25 Heb *She*

THE SIN OF ACHAN AND ITS PUNISHMENT

7 But the Israelites broke faith in regard to the devoted things: Achan son of Carmi son of Zabdi son of Zerah, of the tribe of Judah, took some of the devoted things; and the anger of the LORD burned against the Israelites.

2 Joshua sent men from Jericho to Ai, which is near Beth-aven, east of Bethel, and said to them, "Go up and spy out the land." And the men went up and spied out Ai. ³Then they returned to Joshua and said to him, "Not all the people need go up; about two or three thousand men should go up and attack Ai. Since they are so few, do not make the whole people toil up there." ⁴So about three thousand of the people went up there; and they fled before the men of Ai. ⁵The men of Ai killed about thirty-six of them, chasing them from outside the gate as far as Shebarim and killing them on the slope. The hearts of the people melted and turned to water.

6 Then Joshua tore his clothes, and fell to the ground on his face before the ark of the LORD until the evening, he and the elders of Israel; and they put dust on their heads. ⁷Joshua said, "Ah, Lord GOD! Why have you brought this people across the Jordan at all, to hand us over to the Amorites so as to destroy us? Would that we had been content to settle beyond the Jordan! ⁸O Lord, what can I say, now that Israel has turned their backs to their enemies! ⁹The Canaanites and all the inhabitants of the land will hear of it, and surround us, and cut off our name from the earth. Then what will you do for your great name?"

10 The LORD said to Joshua, "Stand up! Why have you fallen upon your face? ¹¹Israel has sinned; they have transgressed my covenant that I imposed on them. They have taken some of the devoted things; they have stolen, they have acted deceitfully, and they have put them among their own belongings. ¹²Therefore the Israelites are unable to stand before their enemies; they turn their backs to their enemies, because they have become a thing devoted for destruction themselves. I will be with you no more, unless you destroy the devoted things from among you. ¹³Proceed to sanctify the people, and say, 'Sanctify yourselves for tomorrow; for thus says the LORD, the God of Israel, "There are devoted things among you, O Israel; you will be unable to stand before your enemies until you take away the devoted things from among you." ¹⁴In the morning therefore you shall come forward tribe by tribe. The tribe that

---

BIBLE IN LIFE

Obsessed With Wealth

Joshua 7.1–26

Achan exalted wealth. The Israelites were supposed to destroy everything when they captured the city of Jericho, but Achan wrongly kept some valuable loot. Because of his sin, 36 Israelites died as the army tried to capture the small town of Ai.

Like Achan, some of us today—including me on many occasions—have elevated the acquisition of wealth to a top priority in our lives. We become obsessed with possessions. We never have enough. We become greedy and selfish, and we don't want to share. We want to see how much we can improve our property values, how big we can grow our bank accounts, and how fancy we can make our homes. But Christ teaches us that material things should be a very low priority. That doesn't mean it's wrong for us to have nice homes, reliable cars or other possessions. It doesn't mean that we should have a zero bank account or that we shouldn't give any thought to our retirement. But it does mean that our possessions should not dominate our thoughts and lead us to selfish behavior in order to acquire or maintain them. Christ calls us to love God, not our wealth, and we should use our wealth to help others in need.

the LORD takes shall come near by clans, the clan that the LORD takes shall come near by households, and the household that the LORD takes shall come near one by one. ¹⁵And the one who is taken as having the devoted things shall be burned with fire, together with all that he has, for having transgressed the covenant of the LORD, and for having done an outrageous thing in Israel.'"

16 So Joshua rose early in the morning, and brought Israel near tribe by tribe, and the tribe of Judah was taken. ¹⁷He brought near the clans of Judah, and the clan of the Zerahites was taken; and he brought near the clan of the Zerahites, family by family,ᵃ and Zabdi was taken. ¹⁸And he brought near his household one by one, and Achan son of Carmi son of Zabdi son of Zerah, of the tribe of Judah, was taken. ¹⁹Then Joshua said to Achan, "My son, give glory to the LORD God of Israel and make confession to him. Tell me now what you have done; do not hide it from me." ²⁰And Achan answered Joshua, "It is true; I am the one who sinned against the LORD God of Israel. This is what I did: ²¹when I saw among the spoil a beautiful mantle from Shinar, and two hundred shekels of silver, and a bar of gold weighing fifty shekels, then I coveted them and took them. They now lie hidden in the ground inside my tent, with the silver underneath."

22 So Joshua sent messengers, and they ran to the tent; and there it was, hidden in his tent with the silver underneath. ²³They took them out of the tent and brought them to Joshua and all the Israelites; and they spread them out before the LORD. ²⁴Then Joshua and all Israel with him took Achan son of Zerah, with the silver, the mantle, and the bar of gold, with his sons and daughters, with his oxen, donkeys, and sheep, and his tent and all that he had; and they brought them up to the Valley of Achor. ²⁵Joshua said, "Why did you bring trouble on us? The LORD is bringing trouble on you today." And all Israel stoned him to death; they burned them with fire,

cast stones on them, ²⁶and raised over him a great heap of stones that remains to this day. Then the LORD turned from his burning anger. Therefore that place to this day is called the Valley of Achor.ᵇ

AI CAPTURED BY A STRATAGEM AND DESTROYED

8 Then the LORD said to Joshua, "Do not fear or be dismayed; take all the fighting men with you, and go up now to Ai. See, I have handed over to you the king of Ai with his people, his city, and his land. ²You shall do to Ai and its king as you did to Jericho and its king; only its spoil and its livestock you may take as booty for yourselves. Set an ambush against the city, behind it."

3 So Joshua and all the fighting men set out to go up against Ai. Joshua chose thirty thousand warriors and sent them out by night ⁴with the command, "You shall lie in ambush against the city, behind it; do not go very far from the city, but all of you stay alert. ⁵I and all the people who are with me will approach the city. When they come out against us, as before, we shall flee from them. ⁶They will come out after us until we have drawn them away from the city; for they will say, 'They are fleeing from us, as before.' While we flee from them, ⁷you shall rise up from the ambush and seize the city; for the LORD your God will give it into your hand. ⁸And when you have taken the city, you shall set the city on fire, doing as the LORD has ordered; see, I have commanded you." ⁹So Joshua sent them out; and they went to the place of ambush, and lay between Bethel and Ai, to the west of Ai; but Joshua spent that night in the camp.ᶜ

10 In the morning Joshua rose early and mustered the people, and went up, with the elders of Israel, before the people to Ai. ¹¹All the fighting men who were with him went up, and drew near before the city, and camped on the north side of Ai,

---

ᵃ 7.17 Mss Syr: MT man by man   ᵇ 7.26 That is Trouble   ᶜ 8.9 Heb among the people

with a ravine between them and Ai. ¹²Taking about five thousand men, he set them in ambush between Bethel and Ai, to the west of the city. ¹³So they stationed the forces, the main encampment that was north of the city and its rear guard west of the city. But Joshua spent that night in the valley. ¹⁴When the king of Ai saw this, he and all his people, the inhabitants of the city, hurried out early in the morning to the meeting place facing the Arabah to meet Israel in battle; but he did not know that there was an ambush against him behind the city. ¹⁵And Joshua and all Israel made a pretense of being beaten before them, and fled in the direction of the wilderness. ¹⁶So all the people who were in the city were called together to pursue them, and as they pursued Joshua they were drawn away from the city. ¹⁷There was not a man left in Ai or Bethel who did not go out after Israel; they left the city open, and pursued Israel.

18 Then the LORD said to Joshua, "Stretch out the sword that is in your hand toward Ai; for I will give it into your hand." And Joshua stretched out the sword that was in his hand toward the city. ¹⁹As soon as he stretched out his hand, the troops in ambush rose quickly out of their place and rushed forward. They entered the city, took it, and at once set the city on fire. ²⁰So when the men of Ai looked back, the smoke of the city was rising to the sky. They had no power to flee this way or that, for the people who fled to the wilderness turned back against the pursuers. ²¹When Joshua and all Israel saw that the ambush had taken the city and that the smoke of the city was rising, then they turned back and struck down the men of Ai. ²²And the others came out from the city against them; so they were surrounded by Israelites, some on one side, and some on the other; and Israel struck them down until no one was left who survived or escaped. ²³But the king of Ai was taken alive and brought to Joshua.

24 When Israel had finished slaughtering all the inhabitants of Ai in the open wilderness where they pursued them, and when all of them to the very last had fallen by the edge of the sword, all Israel returned to Ai, and attacked it with the edge of the sword. ²⁵The total of those who fell that day, both men and women, was twelve thousand— all the people of Ai. ²⁶For Joshua did not draw back his hand, with which he stretched out the sword, until he had utterly destroyed all the inhabitants of Ai. ²⁷Only the livestock and the spoil of that city Israel took as their booty, according to the word of the LORD that he had issued to Joshua. ²⁸So Joshua burned Ai, and made it forever a heap of ruins, as it is to this day. ²⁹And he hanged the king of Ai on a tree until evening; and at sunset Joshua commanded, and they took his body down from the tree, threw it down at the entrance of the gate of the city, and raised over it a great heap of stones, which stands there to this day.

JOSHUA RENEWS THE COVENANT

30 Then Joshua built on Mount Ebal an altar to the LORD, the God of Israel, ³¹just as Moses the servant of the LORD had commanded the Israelites, as it is written in the book of the law of Moses, "an altar of unhewnª stones, on which no iron tool has been used"; and they offered on it burnt offerings to the LORD, and sacrificed offerings of well-being. ³²And there, in the presence of the Israelites, Joshuaᵇ wrote on the stones a copy of the law of Moses, which he had written. ³³All Israel, alien as well as citizen, with their elders and officers and their judges, stood on opposite sides of the ark in front of the levitical priests who carried the ark of the covenant of the LORD, half of them in front of Mount Gerizim and half of them in front of Mount Ebal, as Moses the servant of the LORD had commanded at the first, that they should bless the people of Israel. ³⁴And afterward he read all the words of the law, blessings and curses, according to all that is writ-

ª 8.31 Heb whole   ᵇ 8.32 Heb he

PONDER

[Joshua] read all the words of the law, blessings and curses, according to all that is written in the book of the law.
—Joshua 8.34

PRAY

Lord, we are grateful to have an opportunity to study the ancient words that you have provided for us. They are still so pertinent to today, tomorrow and every day we live. Remind us daily to seek your face, your voice and your commands in your Word. Forgive us our sins, and bind our hearts in Christian love. Use our voices, our talents and our way of life to strengthen your kingdom on earth. We ask in our Savior's name. Amen.

ten in the book of the law. ³⁵There was not a word of all that Moses commanded that Joshua did not read before all the assembly of Israel, and the women, and the little ones, and the aliens who resided among them.

THE GIBEONITES SAVE THEMSELVES BY TRICKERY

9 Now when all the kings who were beyond the Jordan in the hill country and in the lowland all along the coast of the Great Sea toward Lebanon—the Hittites, the Amorites, the Canaanites, the Perizzites, the Hivites, and the Jebusites—heard of this, ²they gathered together with one accord to fight Joshua and Israel.

3 But when the inhabitants of Gibeon heard what Joshua had done to Jericho and to Ai, ⁴they on their part acted with cunning: they went and prepared provisions,ᵃ and took worn-out sacks for their donkeys, and wineskins, worn-out and torn and mended, ⁵with worn-out, patched sandals on their feet, and worn-out clothes; and all their pro-

visions were dry and moldy. ⁶They went to Joshua in the camp at Gilgal, and said to him and to the Israelites, "We have come from a far country; so now make a treaty with us." ⁷But the Israelites said to the Hivites, "Perhaps you live among us; then how can we make a treaty with you?" ⁸They said to Joshua, "We are your servants." And Joshua said to them, "Who are you? And where do you come from?" ⁹They said to him, "Your servants have come from a very far country, because of the name of the LORD your God; for we have heard a report of him, of all that he did in Egypt, ¹⁰and of all that he did to the two kings of the Amorites who were beyond the Jordan, King Sihon of Heshbon, and King Og of Bashan who lived in Ashtaroth. ¹¹So our elders and all the inhabitants of our country said to us, 'Take provisions in your hand for the journey; go to meet them, and say to them, "We are your servants; come now, make a treaty with us." ' ¹²Here is our bread; it was still warm when we took it from our houses as our food for the journey, on the day we set out to come to you, but now, see, it is dry and moldy; ¹³these wineskins were new when we filled them, and see, they are burst; and these garments and sandals of ours are worn out from the very long journey." ¹⁴So the leadersᵇ partook of their provisions, and did not ask direction from the LORD. ¹⁵And Joshua made peace with them, guaranteeing their lives by a treaty; and the leaders of the congregation swore an oath to them.

16 But when three days had passed after they had made a treaty with them, they heard that they were their neighbors and were living among them. ¹⁷So the Israelites set out and reached their cities on the third day. Now their cities were Gibeon, Chephirah, Beeroth, and Kiriath-jearim. ¹⁸But the Israelites did not attack them, because the leaders of the congregation had sworn to them by the LORD, the

ᵃ 9.4 Cn: Meaning of Heb uncertain
ᵇ 9.14 Gk: Heb *men*

God of Israel. Then all the congregation murmured against the leaders. ¹⁹But all the leaders said to all the congregation, "We have sworn to them by the LORD, the God of Israel, and now we must not touch them. ²⁰This is what we will do to them: We will let them live, so that wrath may not come upon us, because of the oath that we swore to them." ²¹The leaders said to them, "Let them live." So they became hewers of wood and drawers of water for all the congregation, as the leaders had decided concerning them.

22 Joshua summoned them, and said to them, "Why did you deceive us, saying, 'We are very far from you,' while in fact you are living among us? ²³Now therefore you are cursed, and some of you shall always be slaves, hewers of wood and drawers of water for the house of my God." ²⁴They answered Joshua, "Because it was told to your servants for a certainty that the LORD your God had commanded his servant Moses to give you all the land, and to destroy all the inhabitants of the land before you; so we were in great fear for our lives because of you, and did this thing. ²⁵And now we are in your hand: do as it seems good and right in your sight to do to us." ²⁶This is what he did for them: he saved them from the Israelites; and they did not kill them. ²⁷But on that day Joshua made them hewers of wood and drawers of water for the congregation and for the altar of the LORD, to continue to this day, in the place that he should choose.

THE SUN STANDS STILL

10 When King Adoni-zedek of Jerusalem heard how Joshua had taken Ai, and had utterly destroyed it, doing to Ai and its king as he had done to Jericho and its king, and how the inhabitants of Gibeon had made peace with Israel and were among them, ²he[a] became greatly frightened, because Gibeon was a large city, like one of the royal cities, and was larger than Ai, and all its men were warriors. ³So King Adoni-zedek of Jerusalem sent a message

to King Hoham of Hebron, to King Piram of Jarmuth, to King Japhia of Lachish, and to King Debir of Eglon, saying, ⁴"Come up and help me, and let us attack Gibeon; for it has made peace with Joshua and with the Israelites." ⁵Then the five kings of the Amorites—the king of Jerusalem, the king of Hebron, the king of Jarmuth, the king of Lachish, and the king of Eglon—gathered their forces, and went up with all their armies and camped against Gibeon, and made war against it.

6 And the Gibeonites sent to Joshua at the camp in Gilgal, saying, "Do not abandon your servants; come up to us quickly, and save us, and help us; for all the kings of the Amorites who live in the hill country are gathered against us." ⁷So Joshua went up from Gilgal, he and all the fighting force with him, all the mighty warriors. ⁸The LORD said to Joshua, "Do not fear them, for I have handed them over to you; not one of them shall stand before you." ⁹So Joshua came upon them suddenly, having marched up all night from Gilgal. ¹⁰And the LORD threw them into a panic before Israel, who inflicted a great slaughter on them at Gibeon, chased them by the way of the ascent of Beth-horon, and struck them down as far as Azekah and Makkedah. ¹¹As they fled before Israel, while they were going down the slope of Beth-horon, the LORD threw down huge stones from heaven on them as far as Azekah, and they died; there were more who died because of the hailstones than the Israelites killed with the sword.

12 On the day when the LORD gave the Amorites over to the Israelites, Joshua spoke to the LORD; and he said in the sight of Israel,

"Sun, stand still at Gibeon,
    and Moon, in the valley
        of Aijalon."
13 And the sun stood still, and
        the moon stopped,
    until the nation took
        vengeance on
            their enemies.

a 10.2 Heb they

Is this not written in the Book of Jashar? The sun stopped in midheaven, and did not hurry to set for about a whole day. [14]There has been no day like it before or since, when the LORD heeded a human voice; for the LORD fought for Israel.

15 Then Joshua returned, and all Israel with him, to the camp at Gilgal.

FIVE KINGS DEFEATED

16 Meanwhile, these five kings fled and hid themselves in the cave at Makkedah. [17]And it was told Joshua, "The five kings have been found, hidden in the cave at Makkedah." [18]Joshua said, "Roll large stones against the mouth of the cave, and set men by it to guard them; [19]but do not stay there yourselves; pursue your enemies, and attack them from the rear. Do not let them enter their towns, for the LORD your God has given them into your hand." [20]When Joshua and the Israelites had finished inflicting a very great slaughter on them, until they were wiped out, and when the survivors had entered into the fortified towns, [21]all the people returned safe to Joshua in the camp at Makkedah; no one dared to speak[a] against any of the Israelites.

22 Then Joshua said, "Open the mouth of the cave, and bring those five kings out to me from the cave." [23]They did so, and brought the five kings out to him from the cave, the king of Jerusalem, the king of Hebron, the king of Jarmuth, the king of Lachish, and the king of Eglon. [24]When they brought the kings out to Joshua, Joshua summoned all the Israelites, and said to the chiefs of the warriors who had gone with him, "Come near, put your feet on the necks of these kings." Then they came near and put their feet on their necks. [25]And Joshua said to them, "Do not be afraid or dismayed; be strong and courageous; for thus the LORD will do to all the enemies against whom you fight." [26]Afterward Joshua struck them down and put them to death, and he hung them on five trees. And they hung on the trees until evening. [27]At sunset Joshua commanded, and they took them down from the trees and threw them into the cave where they had hidden themselves; they set large stones against the mouth of the cave, which remain to this very day.

28 Joshua took Makkedah on that day, and struck it and its king with the edge of the sword; he utterly destroyed every person in it; he left no one remaining. And he did to the king of Makkedah as he had done to the king of Jericho.

29 Then Joshua passed on from Makkedah, and all Israel with him, to Libnah, and fought against Libnah. [30]The LORD gave it also and its king into the hand of Israel; and he struck it with the edge of the sword, and every person in it; he left no one remaining in it; and he did to its king as he had done to the king of Jericho.

THE GREATEST MIRACLES ARE
THOSE THAT MAKE US WHOLE
DESPITE SUFFERING AND PAIN.

31 Next Joshua passed on from Libnah, and all Israel with him, to Lachish, and laid siege to it, and assaulted it. [32]The LORD gave Lachish into the hand of Israel, and he took it on the second day, and struck it with the edge of the sword, and every person in it, as he had done to Libnah.

33 Then King Horam of Gezer came up to help Lachish; and Joshua struck him and his people, leaving him no survivors.

34 From Lachish Joshua passed on with all Israel to Eglon; and they laid siege to it, and assaulted it; [35]and they took it that day, and struck it with the edge of the sword; and every person in it he utterly destroyed that day, as he had done to Lachish.

[a] 10.21 Heb *moved his tongue*

36 Then Joshua went up with all Israel from Eglon to Hebron; they assaulted it, 37and took it, and struck it with the edge of the sword, and its king and its towns, and every person in it; he left no one remaining, just as he had done to Eglon, and utterly destroyed it with every person in it. 38 Then Joshua, with all Israel, turned back to Debir and assaulted it, 39and he took it with its king and all its towns; they struck them with the edge of the sword, and utterly destroyed every person in it; he left no one remaining; just as he had done to Hebron, and, as he had done to Libnah and its king, so he did to Debir and its king. 40 So Joshua defeated the whole land, the hill country and the Negeb and the lowland and the slopes, and all their kings; he left no one remaining, but utterly destroyed all that breathed, as the LORD God of Israel commanded. 41And Joshua defeated them from Kadesh-barnea to Gaza, and all the country of Goshen, as far as Gibeon. 42Joshua took all these kings and their land at one time, because the LORD God of Israel fought for Israel. 43Then Joshua returned, and all Israel with him, to the camp at Gilgal.

THE UNITED KINGS OF NORTHERN CANAAN DEFEATED

11 When King Jabin of Hazor heard of this, he sent to King Jobab of Madon, to the king of Shimron, to the king of Achshaph, 2and to the kings who were in the northern hill country, and in the Arabah south of Chinneroth, and in the lowland, and in Naphoth-dor on the west, 3to the Canaanites in the east and the west, the Amorites, the Hittites, the Perizzites, and the Jebusites in the hill country, and the Hivites under Hermon in the land of Mizpah. 4They came out, with all their troops, a great army, in number like the sand on the seashore, with very many horses and chariots. 5All these kings joined their forces, and came and camped together at the waters of Merom, to fight with Israel.

6 And the LORD said to Joshua, "Do not be afraid of them, for tomorrow at this time I will hand over all of them, slain, to Israel; you shall hamstring their horses, and burn their chariots with fire." 7So Joshua came suddenly upon them with all his fighting force, by the waters of Merom, and fell upon them. 8And the LORD handed them over to Israel, who attacked them and chased them as far as Great Sidon and Misrephoth-maim, and eastward as far as the valley of Mizpeh. They struck them down, until they had left no one remaining. 9And Joshua did to them as the LORD commanded him; he hamstrung their horses, and burned their chariots with fire.

10 Joshua turned back at that time, and took Hazor, and struck its king down with the sword. Before that time Hazor was the head of all those kingdoms. 11And they put to the sword all who were in it, utterly destroying them; there was no one left who breathed, and he burned Hazor with fire. 12And all the towns of those kings, and all their kings, Joshua took, and struck them with the edge of the sword, utterly destroying them, as Moses the servant of the LORD had commanded. 13But Israel burned none of the towns that stood on mounds except Hazor, which Joshua did burn. 14All the spoil of these towns, and the livestock, the Israelites took for their booty; but all the people they struck down with the edge of the sword, until they had destroyed them, and they did not leave any who breathed. 15As the LORD had commanded his servant Moses, so Moses commanded Joshua, and so Joshua did; he left nothing undone of all that the LORD had commanded Moses.

SUMMARY OF JOSHUA'S CONQUESTS

16 So Joshua took all that land: the hill country and all the Negeb and all the land of Goshen and the lowland and the Arabah and the hill country of Israel and its lowland, 17from Mount Halak, which rises to-

ward Seir, as far as Baal-gad in the valley of Lebanon below Mount Hermon. He took all their kings, struck them down, and put them to death. 18 Joshua made war a long time with all those kings. 19 There was not a town that made peace with the Israelites, except the Hivites, the inhabitants of Gibeon; all were taken in battle. 20 For it was the LORD's doing to harden their hearts so that they would come against Israel in battle, in order that they might be utterly destroyed, and might receive no mercy, but be exterminated, just as the LORD had commanded Moses.

21 At that time Joshua came and wiped out the Anakim from the hill country, from Hebron, from Debir, from Anab, and from all the hill country of Judah, and from all the hill country of Israel; Joshua utterly destroyed them with their towns. 22 None of the Anakim was left in the land of the Israelites; some remained only in Gaza, in Gath, and in Ashdod. 23 So Joshua took the whole land, according to all that the LORD had spoken to Moses; and Joshua gave it for an inheritance to Israel according to their tribal allotments. And the land had rest from war.

THE KINGS CONQUERED BY MOSES

12 Now these are the kings of the land, whom the Israelites defeated, whose land they occupied beyond the Jordan toward the east, from the Wadi Arnon to Mount Hermon, with all the Arabah eastward: 2 King Sihon of the Amorites who lived at Heshbon, and ruled from Aroer, which is on the edge of the Wadi Arnon, and from the middle of the valley as far as the river Jabbok, the boundary of the Ammonites, that is, half of Gilead, 3 and the Arabah to the Sea of Chinneroth eastward, and in the direction of Beth-jeshimoth, to the sea of the Arabah, the Dead Sea,a southward to the foot of the slopes of Pisgah; 4 and King Og b of Bashan, one of the last of the Rephaim, who lived at Ashtaroth and at Edrei 5 and ruled over Mount Hermon and Salecah and all

Bashan to the boundary of the Geshurites and the Maacathites, and over half of Gilead to the boundary of King Sihon of Heshbon. 6 Moses, the servant of the LORD, and the Israelites defeated them; and Moses the servant of the LORD gave their land for a possession to the Reubenites and the Gadites and the half-tribe of Manasseh.

THE KINGS CONQUERED BY JOSHUA

7 The following are the kings of the land whom Joshua and the Israelites defeated on the west side of the Jordan, from Baal-gad in the valley of Lebanon to Mount Halak, that rises toward Seir (and Joshua gave their land to the tribes of Israel as a possession according to their allotments, 8 in the hill country, in the lowland, in the Arabah, in the slopes, in the wilderness, and in the Negeb, the land of the Hittites, Amorites, Canaanites, Perizzites, Hivites, and Jebusites):

9 the king of Jericho	one
the king of Ai, which is next to Bethel	one
10 the king of Jerusalem	one
the king of Hebron	one
11 the king of Jarmuth	one
the king of Lachish	one
12 the king of Eglon	one
the king of Gezer	one
13 the king of Debir	one
the king of Geder	one
14 the king of Hormah	one
the king of Arad	one
15 the king of Libnah	one
the king of Adullam	one
16 the king of Makkedah	one
the king of Bethel	one
17 the king of Tappuah	one
the king of Hepher	one
18 the king of Aphek	one
the king of Lasharon	one
19 the king of Madon	one
the king of Hazor	one
20 the king of Shimron-meron	one
the king of Achshaph	one
21 the king of Taanach	one
the king of Megiddo	one

a 12.3 Heb Salt Sea   b 12.4 Gk: Heb the boundary of King Og

²² the king of Kedesh   one
the king of Jokneam in
    Carmel   one
²³ the king of Dor in
    Naphath-dor   one
the king of Goiim in Galilee,ᵃ one
²⁴ the king of Tirzah   one
thirty-one kings in all.

THE PARTS OF CANAAN
STILL UNCONQUERED

13 Now Joshua was old and advanced in years; and the LORD said to him, "You are old and advanced in years, and very much of the land still remains to be possessed. ²This is the land that still remains: all the regions of the Philistines, and all those of the Geshurites ³(from the Shihor, which is east of Egypt, northward to the boundary of Ekron, it is reckoned as Canaanite; there are five rulers of the Philistines, those of Gaza, Ashdod, Ashkelon, Gath, and Ekron), and those of the Avvim ⁴in the south; all the land of the Canaanites, and Mearah that belongs to the Sidonians, to Aphek, to the boundary of the Amorites, ⁵and the land of the Gebalites, and all Lebanon, toward the east, from Baal-gad below Mount Hermon to Lebo-hamath, ⁶all the inhabitants of the hill country from Lebanon to Misrephoth-maim, even all the Sidonians. I will myself drive them out from before the Israelites; only allot the land to Israel for an inheritance, as I have commanded you. ⁷Now therefore divide this land for an inheritance to the nine tribes and the half-tribe of Manasseh."

THE TERRITORY EAST
OF THE JORDAN

8 With the other half-tribe of Manassehᵇ the Reubenites and the Gadites received their inheritance, which Moses gave them, beyond the Jordan eastward, as Moses the servant of the LORD gave them: ⁹from Aroer, which is on the edge of the Wadi Arnon, and the town that is in the middle of the valley, and all the tableland fromᶜ Medeba as far as Dibon; ¹⁰and all the cities of King Sihon of the Amorites, who reigned in Heshbon,

as far as the boundary of the Ammonites; ¹¹and Gilead, and the region of the Geshurites and Maacathites, and all Mount Hermon, and all Bashan to Salecah; ¹²all the kingdom of Og in Bashan, who reigned in Ashtaroth and in Edrei (he alone was left of the survivors of the Rephaim); these Moses had defeated and driven out. ¹³Yet the Israelites did not drive out the Geshurites or the Maacathites; but Geshur and Maacath live within Israel to this day.

14 To the tribe of Levi alone Moses gave no inheritance; the offerings by fire to the LORD God of Israel are their inheritance, as he said to them.

THE TERRITORY OF REUBEN

15 Moses gave an inheritance to the tribe of the Reubenites according to their clans. ¹⁶Their territory was from Aroer, which is on the edge of the Wadi Arnon, and the town that is in the middle of the valley, and all the tableland by Medeba; ¹⁷with Heshbon, and all its towns that are in the tableland; Dibon, and Bamoth-baal, and Beth-baal-meon, ¹⁸and Jahaz, and Kedemoth, and Mephaath, ¹⁹and Kiriathaim, and Sibmah, and Zereth-shahar on the hill of the valley, ²⁰and Beth-peor, and the slopes of Pisgah, and Beth-jeshimoth, ²¹that is, all the towns of the tableland, and all the kingdom of King Sihon of the Amorites, who reigned in Heshbon, whom Moses defeated with the leaders of Midian, Evi and Rekem and Zur and Hur and Reba, as princes of Sihon, who lived in the land. ²²Along with the rest of those they put to death, the Israelites also put to the sword Balaam son of Beor, who practiced divination. ²³And the border of the Reubenites was the Jordan and its banks. This was the inheritance of the Reubenites according to their families, with their towns and villages.

THE TERRITORY OF GAD

24 Moses gave an inheritance also to the tribe of the Gadites, accord-

---

ᵃ 12.23 Gk: Heb *Gilgal* ᵇ 13.8 Cn: Heb *With it* ᶜ 13.9 Compare Gk: Heb lacks *from*

ing to their families. 25Their territory was Jazer, and all the towns of Gilead, and half the land of the Ammonites, to Aroer, which is east of Rabbah, 26and from Heshbon to Ramath-mizpeh and Betonim, and from Mahanaim to the territory of Debir,a 27and in the valley Beth-haram, Beth-nimrah, Succoth, and Zaphon, the rest of the kingdom of King Sihon of Heshbon, the Jordan and its banks, as far as the lower end of the Sea of Chinnereth, eastward beyond the Jordan. 28This is the inheritance of the Gadites according to their clans, with their towns and villages.

THE TERRITORY OF THE HALF-TRIBE OF MANASSEH (EAST)

29 Moses gave an inheritance to the half-tribe of Manasseh; it was allotted to the half-tribe of the Manassites according to their families. 30Their territory extended from Mahanaim, through all Bashan, the whole kingdom of King Og of Bashan, and all the settlements of Jair, which are in Bashan, sixty towns, 31and half of Gilead, and Ashtaroth, and Edrei, the towns of the kingdom of Og in Bashan; these were allotted to the people of Machir son of Manasseh according to their clans—for half the Machirites.

32 These are the inheritances that Moses distributed in the plains of Moab, beyond the Jordan east of Jericho. 33But to the tribe of Levi Moses gave no inheritance; the LORD God of Israel is their inheritance, as he said to them.

THE DISTRIBUTION OF TERRITORY WEST OF THE JORDAN

14 These are the inheritances that the Israelites received in the land of Canaan, which the priest Eleazar, and Joshua son of Nun, and the heads of the families of the tribes of the Israelites distributed to them. 2Their inheritance was by lot, as the LORD had commanded Moses for the nine and one-half tribes. 3For Moses had given an inheritance to the two and one-half tribes beyond the Jordan; but to the Levites he gave no inheritance among them. 4For the people of Joseph were two tribes, Manasseh and Ephraim; and no portion was given to the Levites in the land, but only towns to live in, with their pasture lands for their flocks and herds. 5The Israelites did as the LORD commanded Moses; they allotted the land.

HEBRON ALLOTTED TO CALEB

6 Then the people of Judah came to Joshua at Gilgal; and Caleb son of Jephunneh the Kenizzite said to him, "You know what the LORD said to Moses the man of God in Kadesh-barnea concerning you and me. 7I was forty years old when Moses the servant of the LORD sent me from Kadesh-barnea to spy out the land; and I brought him an honest report. 8But my companions who went up with me made the heart of the people melt; yet I wholeheartedly followed the LORD my God. 9And Moses swore on that day, saying, 'Surely the land on which your foot has trodden shall be an inheritance for you and your children forever, because you have wholeheartedly followed the LORD my God.' 10And now, as you see, the LORD has kept me alive, as he said, these forty-five years since the time that the LORD spoke this word to Moses, while Israel was journeying through the wilderness; and here I am today, eighty-five years old. 11I am still as strong today as I was on the day that Moses sent me; my strength now is as my strength was then, for war, and for going and coming. 12So now give me this hill country of which the LORD spoke on that day; for you heard on that day how the Anakim were there, with great fortified cities; it may be that the LORD will be with me, and I shall drive them out, as the LORD said."

13 Then Joshua blessed him, and gave Hebron to Caleb son of Jephunneh for an inheritance. 14So Hebron became the inheritance of Caleb son of Jephunneh the Kenizzite to this

a 13.26 Gk Syr Vg: Heb Lidebir

day, because he wholeheartedly followed the LORD, the God of Israel. [15]Now the name of Hebron formerly was Kiriath-arba;[a] this Arba was[b] the greatest man among the Anakim. And the land had rest from war.

THE TERRITORY OF JUDAH

15 The lot for the tribe of the people of Judah according to their families reached southward to the boundary of Edom, to the wilderness of Zin at the farthest south. [2]And their south boundary ran from the end of the Dead Sea,[c] from the bay that faces southward; [3]it goes out southward of the ascent of Akrabbim, passes along to Zin, and goes up south of Kadesh-barnea, along by Hezron, up to Addar, makes a turn to Karka, [4]passes along to Azmon, goes out by the Wadi of Egypt, and comes to its end at the sea. This shall be your south boundary. [5]And the east boundary is the Dead Sea,[c] to the mouth of the Jordan. And the boundary on the north side runs from the bay of the sea at the mouth of the Jordan; [6]and the boundary goes up to Beth-hoglah, and passes along north of Beth-arabah; and the boundary goes up to the Stone of Bohan, Reuben's son; [7]and the boundary goes up to Debir from the Valley of Achor, and so northward, turning toward Gilgal, which is opposite the ascent of Adummim, which is on the south side of the valley; and the boundary passes along to the waters of En-shemesh, and ends at En-rogel; [8]then the boundary goes up by the valley of the son of Hinnom at the southern slope of the Jebusites (that is, Jerusalem); and the boundary goes up to the top of the mountain that lies over against the valley of Hinnom, on the west, at the northern end of the valley of Rephaim; [9]then the boundary extends from the top of the mountain to the spring of the Waters of Nephtoah, and from there to the towns of Mount Ephron; then the boundary bends around to Baalah (that is, Kiriath-jearim); [10]and the boundary circles west of Baalah to Mount Seir,

passes along to the northern slope of Mount Jearim (that is, Chesalon), and goes down to Beth-shemesh, and passes along by Timnah; [11]the boundary goes out to the slope of the hill north of Ekron, then the boundary bends around to Shikkeron, and passes along to Mount Baalah, and goes out to Jabneel; then the boundary comes to an end at the sea. [12]And the west boundary was the Mediterranean with its coast. This is the boundary surrounding the people of Judah according to their families.

PRAYER WELDS US TO SUPREME

WISDOM AND STRENGTH.

CALEB OCCUPIES HIS PORTION

13 According to the commandment of the LORD to Joshua, he gave to Caleb son of Jephunneh a portion among the people of Judah, Kiriath-arba,[a] that is, Hebron (Arba was the father of Anak). [14]And Caleb drove out from there the three sons of Anak: Sheshai, Ahiman, and Talmai, the descendants of Anak. [15]From there he went up against the inhabitants of Debir; now the name of Debir formerly was Kiriath-sepher. [16]And Caleb said, "Whoever attacks Kiriath-sepher and takes it, to him I will give my daughter Achsah as wife." [17]Othniel son of Kenaz, the brother of Caleb, took it; and he gave him his daughter Achsah as wife. [18]When she came to him, she urged him to ask her father for a field. As she dismounted from her donkey, Caleb said to her, "What do you wish?" [19]She said to him, "Give me a present; since you have set me in the land of the Negeb, give me springs of water as well." So Caleb gave her the upper springs and the lower springs.

[a] 14.15; 15.13 That is *the city of Arba*   [b] 14.15 Heb lacks *this Arba was*   [c] 15.2,5 Heb *Salt Sea*

THE TOWNS OF JUDAH

20 This is the inheritance of the tribe of the people of Judah according to their families. 21The towns belonging to the tribe of the people of Judah in the extreme south, toward the boundary of Edom, were Kabzeel, Eder, Jagur, 22Kinah, Dimonah, Adadah, 23Kedesh, Hazor, Ithnan, 24Ziph, Telem, Bealoth, 25Hazor-hadattah, Kerioth-hezron (that is, Hazor), 26Amam, Shema, Moladah, 27Hazar-gaddah, Heshmon, Beth-pelet, 28Hazar-shual, Beer-sheba, Biziothiah, 29Baalah, Iim, Ezem, 30Eltolad, Chesil, Hormah, 31Ziklag, Madmannah, Sansannah, 32Lebaoth, Shilhim, Ain, and Rimmon: in all, twenty-nine towns, with their villages.

33 And in the lowland, Eshtaol, Zorah, Ashnah, 34Zanoah, En-gannim, Tappuah, Enam, 35Jarmuth, Adullam, Socoh, Azekah, 36Shaaraim, Adithaim, Gederah, Gederothaim: fourteen towns with their villages.

37 Zenan, Hadashah, Migdal-gad, 38Dilan, Mizpeh, Jokthe-el, 39Lachish, Bozkath, Eglon, 40Cabbon, Lahmam, Chitlish, 41Gederoth, Beth-dagon, Naamah, and Makkedah: sixteen towns with their villages.

42 Libnah, Ether, Ashan, 43Iphtah, Ashnah, Nezib, 44Keilah, Achzib, and Mareshah: nine towns with their villages.

45 Ekron, with its dependencies and its villages; 46from Ekron to the sea, all that were near Ashdod, with their villages.

47 Ashdod, its towns and its villages; Gaza, its towns and its villages; to the Wadi of Egypt, and the Great Sea with its coast.

48 And in the hill country, Shamir, Jattir, Socoh, 49Dannah, Kiriath-sannah (that is, Debir), 50Anab, Eshtemoh, Anim, 51Goshen, Holon, and Giloh: eleven towns with their villages.

52 Arab, Dumah, Eshan, 53Janim, Beth-tappuah, Aphekah, 54Humtah, Kiriath-arba (that is, Hebron), and Zior: nine towns with their villages.

55 Maon, Carmel, Ziph, Juttah, 56Jezreel, Jokdeam, Zanoah, 57Kain, Gibeah, and Timnah: ten towns with their villages.

58 Halhul, Beth-zur, Gedor, 59Maarath, Beth-anoth, and Eltekon: six towns with their villages.

60 Kiriath-baal (that is, Kiriath-jearim) and Rabbah: two towns with their villages.

61 In the wilderness, Beth-arabah, Middin, Secacah, 62Nibshan, the City of Salt, and En-gedi: six towns with their villages.

63 But the people of Judah could not drive out the Jebusites, the inhabitants of Jerusalem; so the Jebusites live with the people of Judah in Jerusalem to this day.

THE TERRITORY OF EPHRAIM

16 The allotment of the Josephites went from the Jordan by Jericho, east of the waters of Jericho, into the wilderness, going up from Jericho into the hill country to Bethel; 2then going from Bethel to Luz, it passes along to Ataroth, the territory of the Archites; 3then it goes down westward to the territory of the Japhletites, as far as the territory of Lower Beth-horon, then to Gezer, and it ends at the sea.

4 The Josephites—Manasseh and Ephraim—received their inheritance.

5 The territory of the Ephraimites by their families was as follows: the boundary of their inheritance on the east was Ataroth-addar as far as Upper Beth-horon, 6and the boundary goes from there to the sea; on the north is Michmethath; then on the east the boundary makes a turn toward Taanath-shiloh, and passes along beyond it on the east to Janoah, 7then it goes down from Janoah to Ataroth and to Naarah, and touches Jericho, ending at the Jordan. 8From Tappuah the boundary goes westward to the Wadi Kanah, and ends at the sea. Such is the inheritance of the tribe of the Ephraimites by their families, 9together with the towns that were set apart for the Ephraimites within the inheritance of the Manassites, all those towns with their villages. 10They did not, however, drive out

the Canaanites who lived in Gezer: so the Canaanites have lived within Ephraim to this day but have been made to do forced labor.

THE OTHER HALF-TRIBE OF MANASSEH (WEST)

17 Then allotment was made to the tribe of Manasseh, for he was the firstborn of Joseph. To Machir the firstborn of Manasseh, the father of Gilead, were allotted Gilead and Bashan, because he was a warrior. 2 And allotments were made to the rest of the tribe of Manasseh, by their families, Abiezer, Helek, Asriel, Shechem, Hepher, and Shemida; these were the male descendants of Manasseh son of Joseph, by their families.

3 Now Zelophehad son of Hepher son of Gilead son of Machir son of Manasseh had no sons, but only daughters; and these are the names of his daughters: Mahlah, Noah, Hoglah, Milcah, and Tirzah. 4 They came before the priest Eleazar and Joshua son of Nun and the leaders, and said, "The LORD commanded Moses to give us an inheritance along with our male kin." So according to the commandment of the LORD he gave them an inheritance among the kinsmen of their father. 5 Thus there fell to Manasseh ten portions, besides the land of Gilead and Bashan, which is on the other side of the Jordan, 6 because the daughters of Manasseh received an inheritance along with his sons. The land of Gilead was allotted to the rest of the Manassites.

7 The territory of Manasseh reached from Asher to Michmethath, which is east of Shechem; then the boundary goes along southward to the inhabitants of En-tappuah. 8 The land of Tappuah belonged to Manasseh, but the town of Tappuah on the boundary of Manasseh belonged to the Ephraimites. 9 Then the boundary went down to the Wadi Kanah. The towns here, to the south of the wadi, among the towns of Manasseh, belong to Ephraim. Then the boundary of Manasseh goes along the north side of the wadi and ends at the sea. 10 The land to the south is Ephraim's and that to the north is Manasseh's, with the sea forming its boundary; on the north Asher is reached, and on the east Issachar. 11 Within Issachar and Asher, Manasseh had Beth-shean and its villages, Ibleam and its villages, the inhabitants of Dor and its villages, the inhabitants of En-dor and its villages, the inhabitants of Taanach and its villages, and the inhabitants of Megiddo and its villages (the third is Naphath).[a] 12 Yet the Manassites could not take possession of those towns; but the Canaanites continued to live in that land. 13 But when the Israelites grew strong, they put the Canaanites to forced labor, but did not utterly drive them out.

THE TRIBE OF JOSEPH PROTESTS

14 The tribe of Joseph spoke to Joshua, saying, "Why have you given me but one lot and one portion as an inheritance, since we are a numerous people, whom all along the LORD has blessed?" 15 And Joshua said to them, "If you are a numerous people, go up to the forest, and clear ground there for yourselves in the land of the Perizzites and the Rephaim, since the hill country of Ephraim is too narrow for you." 16 The tribe of Joseph said, "The hill country is not enough for us; yet all the Canaanites who live in the plain have chariots of iron, both those in Beth-shean and its villages and those in the Valley of Jezreel." 17 Then Joshua said to the house of Joseph, to Ephraim and Manasseh, "You are indeed a numerous people, and have great power; you shall not have one lot only, 18 but the hill country shall be yours; for though it is a forest, you shall clear it and possess it to its farthest borders; for you shall drive out the Canaanites, though they have chariots of iron, and though they are strong."

THE TERRITORIES OF THE REMAINING TRIBES

18 Then the whole congregation of the Israelites assem-

---

a 17.11 Meaning of Heb uncertain

bled at Shiloh, and set up the tent of meeting there. The land lay subdued before them.

2 There remained among the Israelites seven tribes whose inheritance had not yet been apportioned. ³So Joshua said to the Israelites, "How long will you be slack about going in and taking possession of the land that the LORD, the God of your ancestors, has given you? ⁴Provide three men from each tribe, and I will send them out that they may begin to go throughout the land, writing a description of it with a view to their inheritances. Then come back to me. ⁵They shall divide it into seven portions, Judah continuing in its territory on the south, and the house of Joseph in their territory on the north. ⁶You shall describe the land in seven divisions and bring the description here to me; and I will cast lots for you here before the LORD our God. ⁷The Levites have no portion among you, for the priesthood of the LORD is their heritage; and Gad and Reuben and the half-tribe of Manasseh have received their inheritance beyond the Jordan eastward, which Moses the servant of the LORD gave them."

8 So the men started on their way; and Joshua charged those who went to write the description of the land, saying, "Go throughout the land and write a description of it, and come back to me; and I will cast lots for you here before the LORD in Shiloh." ⁹So the men went and traversed the land and set down in a book a description of it by towns in seven divisions; then they came back to Joshua in the camp at Shiloh, ¹⁰and Joshua cast lots for them in Shiloh before the LORD; and there Joshua apportioned the land to the Israelites, to each a portion.

THE TERRITORY OF BENJAMIN

11 The lot of the tribe of Benjamin according to its families came up, and the territory allotted to it fell between the tribe of Judah and the tribe of Joseph. ¹²On the north side their boundary began at the Jordan; then the boundary goes up to the

PONDER

So Joshua said to the Israelites: "How long will you be slack about going in and taking possession of the land that the LORD, the God of your ancestors, has given you?"
—Joshua 18.3

PRAY

O Father, give us courage to seek out your will. Strip away the barriers that we erect in our lives so that we won't be disturbed by new ideas, new demands, new concepts and new challenges. Let us be adventurous in the name of Christ. Let us be expansive in the name of Christ, realizing that the sacrifices we think we are making often turn out to be blessings. Unite us in true community, taking responsibility for one another. Let us apply the lessons of love and compassion in our lives, in the name of our Savior, Jesus Christ. Amen.

slope of Jericho on the north, then up through the hill country westward; and it ends at the wilderness of Beth-aven. ¹³From there the boundary passes along southward in the direction of Luz, to the slope of Luz (that is, Bethel), then the boundary goes down to Ataroth-addar, on the mountain that lies south of Lower Beth-horon. ¹⁴Then the boundary goes in another direction, turning on the western side southward from the mountain that lies to the south, opposite Beth-horon, and it ends at Kiriath-baal (that is, Kiriath-jearim), a town belonging to the tribe of Judah. This forms the western side. ¹⁵The southern side begins at the outskirts of Kiriath-jearim; and the boundary goes from there to Ephron,ᵃ to the spring of the Waters of Nephtoah; ¹⁶then the boundary goes down to the border of the

ᵃ 18.15 Cn See 15.9. Heb westward

mountain that overlooks the valley of the son of Hinnom, which is at the north end of the valley of Rephaim; and it then goes down the valley of Hinnom, south of the slope of the Jebusites, and downward to En-rogel; 17then it bends in a northerly direction going on to En-shemesh, and from there goes to Geliloth, which is opposite the ascent of Adummim; then it goes down to the Stone of Bohan, Reuben's son; 18and passing on to the north of the slope of Beth-arabah[a] it goes down to the Arabah; 19then the boundary passes on to the north of the slope of Beth-hoglah; and the boundary ends at the northern bay of the Dead Sea,[b] at the south end of the Jordan: this is the southern border. 20The Jordan forms its boundary on the eastern side. This is the inheritance of the tribe of Benjamin, according to its families, boundary by boundary all around.

21 Now the towns of the tribe of Benjamin according to their families were Jericho, Beth-hoglah, Emek-keziz, 22Beth-arabah, Zemaraim, Bethel, 23Avvim, Parah, Ophrah, 24Chephar-ammoni, Ophni, and Geba—twelve towns with their villages: 25Gibeon, Ramah, Beeroth, 26Mizpeh, Chephirah, Mozah, 27Rekem, Irpeel, Taralah, 28Zela, Haeleph, Jebus[c] (that is, Jerusalem), Gibeah[d] and Kiriath-jearim[e]—fourteen towns with their villages. This is the inheritance of the tribe of Benjamin according to its families.

THE TERRITORY OF SIMEON

19 The second lot came out for Simeon, for the tribe of Simeon, according to its families; its inheritance lay within the inheritance of the tribe of Judah. 2It had for its inheritance Beer-sheba, Sheba, Moladah, 3Hazar-shual, Balah, Ezem, 4Eltolad, Bethul, Hormah, 5Ziklag, Beth-marcaboth, Hazar-susah, 6Beth-lebaoth, and Sharuhen—thirteen towns with their villages; 7Ain, Rimmon, Ether, and Ashan—four towns with their villages; 8together with all the villages all around these towns as far as Baalath-beer, Ramah of the Negeb. This was the inheritance of the tribe of Simeon according to its families. 9The inheritance of the tribe of Simeon formed part of the territory of Judah; because the portion of the tribe of Judah was too large for them, the tribe of Simeon obtained an inheritance within their inheritance.

THE TERRITORY OF ZEBULUN

10 The third lot came up for the tribe of Zebulun, according to its families. The boundary of its inheritance reached as far as Sarid; 11then its boundary goes up westward, and on to Maralah, and touches Dabbesheth, then the wadi that is east of Jokneam; 12from Sarid it goes in the other direction eastward toward the sunrise to the boundary of Chisloth-tabor; from there it goes to Daberath, then up to Japhia; 13from there it passes along on the east toward the sunrise to Gath-hepher, to Eth-kazin, and going on to Rimmon it bends toward Neah; 14then on the north the boundary makes a turn to Hannathon, and it ends at the valley of Iphtah-el; 15and Kattath, Nahalal, Shimron, Idalah, and Bethlehem—twelve towns with their villages. 16This is the inheritance of the tribe of Zebulun, according to its families—these towns with their villages.

THE TERRITORY OF ISSACHAR

17 The fourth lot came out for Issachar, for the tribe of Issachar, according to its families. 18Its territory included Jezreel, Chesulloth, Shunem, 19Hapharaim, Shion, Anaharath, 20Rabbith, Kishion, Ebez, 21Remeth, En-gannim, En-haddah, Beth-pazzez; 22the boundary also touches Tabor, Shahazumah, and Beth-shemesh, and its boundary ends at the Jordan—sixteen towns with their villages. 23This is the inheritance of the tribe of Issachar, ac-

a 18.18 Gk: Heb to the slope over against the Arabah   b 18.19 Heb Salt Sea   c 18.28 Gk Syr Vg: Heb the Jebusite   d 18.28 Heb Gibeath   e 18.28 Gk: Heb Kiriath

cording to its families—the towns with their villages.

THE TERRITORY OF ASHER

24 The fifth lot came out for the tribe of Asher according to its families. 25Its boundary included Helkath, Hali, Beten, Achshaph, 26Allammelech, Amad, and Mishal; on the west it touches Carmel and Shihor-libnath, 27then it turns eastward, goes to Beth-dagon, and touches Zebulun and the valley of Iphtah-el northward to Beth-emek and Neiel; then it continues in the north to Cabul, 28Ebron, Rehob, Hammon, Kanah, as far as Great Sidon; 29then the boundary turns to Ramah, reaching to the fortified city of Tyre; then the boundary turns to Hosah, and it ends at the sea; Mahalab,ᵃ Achzib, 30Ummah, Aphek, and Rehob—twenty-two towns with their villages. 31This is the inheritance of the tribe of Asher according to its families—these towns with their villages.

THE TERRITORY OF NAPHTALI

32 The sixth lot came out for the tribe of Naphtali, for the tribe of Naphtali, according to its families. 33And its boundary ran from Heleph, from the oak in Zaanannim, and Adami-nekeb, and Jabneel, as far as Lakkum; and it ended at the Jordan; 34then the boundary turns westward to Aznoth-tabor, and goes from there to Hukkok, touching Zebulun at the south, and Asher on the west, and Judah on the east at the Jordan. 35The fortified towns are Ziddim, Zer, Hammath, Rakkath, Chinnereth, 36Adamah, Ramah, Hazor, 37Kedesh, Edrei, En-hazor, 38Iron, Migdal-el, Horem, Beth-anath, and Beth-shemesh—nineteen towns with their villages. 39This is the inheritance of the tribe of Naphtali according to its families—the towns with their villages.

THE TERRITORY OF DAN

40 The seventh lot came out for the tribe of Dan, according to its families. 41The territory of its inheritance included Zorah, Eshtaol,

Ir-shemesh, 42Shaalabbin, Aijalon, Ithlah, 43Elon, Timnah, Ekron, 44Eltekeh, Gibbethon, Baalath, 45Jehud, Bene-berak, Gath-rimmon, 46Mejarkon, and Rakkon at the border opposite Joppa. 47When the territory of the Danites was lost to them, the Danites went up and fought against Leshem, and after capturing it and putting it to the sword, they took possession of it and settled in it, calling Leshem, Dan, after their ancestor Dan. 48This is the inheritance of the tribe of Dan, according to their families—these towns with their villages.

JOSHUA'S INHERITANCE

49 When they had finished distributing the several territories of the land as inheritances, the Israelites gave an inheritance among them to Joshua son of Nun. 50By command of the LORD they gave him the town that he asked for, Timnath-serah in the hill country of Ephraim; he rebuilt the town, and settled in it.

51 These are the inheritances that the priest Eleazar and Joshua son of Nun and the heads of the families of the tribes of the Israelites distributed by lot at Shiloh before the LORD, at the entrance of the tent of meeting. So they finished dividing the land.

THE CITIES OF REFUGE

20 Then the LORD spoke to Joshua, saying, 2"Say to the Israelites, 'Appoint the cities of refuge, of which I spoke to you through Moses, 3so that anyone who kills a person without intent or by mistake may flee there; they shall be for you a refuge from the avenger of blood. 4The slayer shall flee to one of these cities and shall stand at the entrance of the gate of the city, and explain the case to the elders of that city; then the fugitive shall be taken into the city, and given a place, and shall remain with them. 5And if the avenger of blood is in pursuit, they shall not give up the slayer, because

ᵃ 19.29 Cn Compare Gk: Heb Mehebel

the neighbor was killed by mistake, there having been no enmity between them before. 6 The slayer shall remain in that city until there is a trial before the congregation, until the death of the one who is high priest at the time: then the slayer may return home, to the town in which the deed was done.'"

7 So they set apart Kedesh in Galilee in the hill country of Naphtali, and Shechem in the hill country of Ephraim, and Kiriath-arba (that is, Hebron) in the hill country of Judah. 8 And beyond the Jordan east of Jericho, they appointed Bezer in the wilderness on the tableland, from the tribe of Reuben, and Ramoth in Gilead, from the tribe of Gad, and Golan in Bashan, from the tribe of Manasseh. 9 These were the cities designated for all the Israelites, and for the aliens residing among them, that anyone who killed a person without intent could flee there, so as not to die by the hand of the avenger of blood, until there was a trial before the congregation.

CITIES ALLOTTED TO
THE LEVITES

21 Then the heads of the families of the Levites came to the priest Eleazar and to Joshua son of Nun and to the heads of the families of the tribes of the Israelites; 2 they said to them at Shiloh in the land of Canaan, "The LORD commanded through Moses that we be given towns to live in, along with their pasture lands for our livestock." 3 So by command of the LORD the Israelites gave to the Levites the following towns and pasture lands out of their inheritance.

4 The lot came out for the families of the Kohathites. So those Levites who were descendants of Aaron the priest received by lot thirteen towns from the tribes of Judah, Simeon, and Benjamin.

5 The rest of the Kohathites received by lot ten towns from the families of the tribe of Ephraim, from the tribe of Dan, and the half-tribe of Manasseh.

6 The Gershonites received by lot thirteen towns from the families of the tribe of Issachar, from the tribe of Asher, from the tribe of Naphtali, and from the half-tribe of Manasseh in Bashan.

7 The Merarites according to their families received twelve towns from the tribe of Reuben, the tribe of Gad, and the tribe of Zebulun.

8 These towns and their pasture lands the Israelites gave by lot to the Levites, as the LORD had commanded through Moses.

9 Out of the tribe of Judah and the tribe of Simeon they gave the following towns mentioned by name, 10 which went to the descendants of Aaron, one of the families of the Kohathites who belonged to the Levites, since the lot fell to them first. 11 They gave them Kiriath-arba (Arba being the father of Anak), that is Hebron, in the hill country of Judah, along with the pasture lands around it. 12 But the fields of the town and its villages had been given to Caleb son of Jephunneh as his holding.

13 To the descendants of Aaron the priest they gave Hebron, the city of refuge for the slayer, with its pasture lands, Libnah with its pasture lands, 14 Jattir with its pasture lands, Eshtemoa with its pasture lands, 15 Holon with its pasture lands, Debir with its pasture lands, 16 Ain with its pasture lands, Juttah with its pasture lands, and Beth-shemesh with its pasture lands—nine towns out of these two tribes. 17 Out of the tribe of Benjamin: Gibeon with its pasture lands, Geba with its pasture lands, 18 Anathoth with its pasture lands, and Almon with its pasture lands—four towns. 19 The towns of the descendants of Aaron—the priests—were thirteen in all, with their pasture lands.

20 As to the rest of the Kohathites belonging to the Kohathite families of the Levites, the towns allotted to them were out of the tribe of Ephraim. 21 To them were given Shechem, the city of refuge for the slayer, with its pasture lands in the hill country of Ephraim, Gezer with its pasture lands, 22 Kibzaim with its pasture lands, and Beth-horon with its pasture lands—four towns.

23Out of the tribe of Dan: Elteke with its pasture lands, Gibbethon with its pasture lands, 24Aijalon with its pasture lands, Gath-rimmon with its pasture lands—four towns. 25Out of the half-tribe of Manasseh: Taanach with its pasture lands, and Gath-rimmon with its pasture lands—two towns. 26The towns of the families of the rest of the Kohathites were ten in all, with their pasture lands.

WE MUST DECIDE

WHO OWNS US.

27 To the Gershonites, one of the families of the Levites, were given out of the half-tribe of Manasseh, Golan in Bashan with its pasture lands, the city of refuge for the slayer, and Beeshterah with its pasture lands—two towns. 28Out of the tribe of Issachar: Kishion with its pasture lands, Daberath with its pasture lands, 29Jarmuth with its pasture lands, En-gannim with its pasture lands—four towns. 30Out of the tribe of Asher: Mishal with its pasture lands, Abdon with its pasture lands, 31Helkath with its pasture lands, and Rehob with its pasture lands—four towns. 32Out of the tribe of Naphtali: Kedesh in Galilee with its pasture lands, the city of refuge for the slayer, Hammoth-dor with its pasture lands, and Kartan with its pasture lands—three towns. 33The towns of the several families of the Gershonites were in all thirteen, with their pasture lands.

34 To the rest of the Levites—the Merarite families—were given out of the tribe of Zebulun: Jokneam with its pasture lands, Kartah with its pasture lands, 35Dimnah with its pasture lands, Nahalal with its pasture lands—four towns. 36Out of the tribe of Reuben: Bezer with its pasture lands, Jahzah with its pasture lands, 37Kedemoth with its pasture

lands, and Mephaath with its pasture lands—four towns. 38Out of the tribe of Gad: Ramoth in Gilead with its pasture lands, the city of refuge for the slayer, Mahanaim with its pasture lands, 39Heshbon with its pasture lands, Jazer with its pasture lands—four towns in all. 40As for the towns of the several Merarite families, that is, the remainder of the families of the Levites, those allotted to them were twelve in all.

41 The towns of the Levites within the holdings of the Israelites were in all forty-eight towns with their pasture lands. 42Each of these towns had its pasture lands around it; so it was with all these towns.

43 Thus the LORD gave to Israel all the land that he swore to their ancestors that he would give them; and having taken possession of it, they settled there. 44And the LORD gave them rest on every side just as he had sworn to their ancestors; not one of all their enemies had withstood them, for the LORD had given all their enemies into their hands. 45Not one of all the good promises that the LORD had made to the house of Israel had failed; all came to pass.

THE EASTERN TRIBES RETURN TO THEIR TERRITORY

22 Then Joshua summoned the Reubenites, the Gadites, and the half-tribe of Manasseh, 2and said to them, "You have observed all that Moses the servant of the LORD commanded you, and have obeyed me in all that I have commanded you; 3you have not forsaken your kindred these many days, down to this day, but have been careful to keep the charge of the LORD your God. 4And now the LORD your God has given rest to your kindred, as he promised them; therefore turn and go to your tents in the land where your possession lies, which Moses the servant of the LORD gave you on the other side of the Jordan. 5Take good care to observe the commandment and instruction that Moses the servant of the LORD commanded you, to love the LORD your God, to walk in all his

ways, to keep his commandments, and to hold fast to him, and to serve him with all your heart and with all your soul." 6So Joshua blessed them and sent them away, and they went to their tents.

7 Now to the one half of the tribe of Manasseh Moses had given a possession in Bashan; but to the other half Joshua had given a possession beside their fellow Israelites in the land west of the Jordan. And when Joshua sent them away to their tents and blessed them, 8he said to them, "Go back to your tents with much wealth, and with very much livestock, with silver, gold, bronze, and iron, and with a great quantity of clothing; divide the spoil of your enemies with your kindred." 9So the Reubenites and the Gadites and the half-tribe of Manasseh returned home, parting from the Israelites at Shiloh, which is in the land of Canaan, to go to the land of Gilead, their own land of which they had taken possession by command of the LORD through Moses.

A MEMORIAL ALTAR EAST OF THE JORDAN

10 When they came to the regiona near the Jordan that lies in the land of Canaan, the Reubenites and the Gadites and the half-tribe of Manasseh built there an altar by the Jordan, an altar of great size. 11The Israelites heard that the Reubenites and the Gadites and the half-tribe of Manasseh had built an altar at the frontier of the land of Canaan, in the regionb near the Jordan, on the side that belongs to the Israelites. 12And when the people of Israel heard of it, the whole assembly of the Israelites gathered at Shiloh, to make war against them.

13 Then the Israelites sent the priest Phinehas son of Eleazar to the Reubenites and the Gadites and the half-tribe of Manasseh, in the land of Gilead, 14and with him ten chiefs, one from each of the tribal families of Israel, every one of them the head of a family among the clans of Israel. 15They came to the Reubenites, the Gadites, and the half-tribe of Manas-

seh, in the land of Gilead, and they said to them, 16"Thus says the whole congregation of the LORD, 'What is this treachery that you have committed against the God of Israel in turning away today from following the LORD, by building yourselves an altar today in rebellion against the LORD? 17Have we not had enough of the sin at Peor from which even yet we have not cleansed ourselves, and for which a plague came upon the congregation of the LORD, 18that you must turn away today from following the LORD! If you rebel against the LORD today, he will be angry with the whole congregation of Israel tomorrow. 19But now, if your land is unclean, cross over into the LORD's land where the LORD's tabernacle now stands, and take for yourselves a possession among us; only do not rebel against the LORD, or rebel against usc by building yourselves an altar other than the altar of the LORD our God. 20Did not Achan son of Zerah break faith in the matter of the devoted things, and wrath fell upon all the congregation of Israel? And he did not perish alone for his iniquity!' "

21 Then the Reubenites, the Gadites, and the half-tribe of Manasseh said in answer to the heads of the families of Israel, 22"The LORD, God of gods! The LORD, God of gods! He knows; and let Israel itself know! If it was in rebellion or in breach of faith toward the LORD, do not spare us today 23for building an altar to turn away from following the LORD; or if we did so to offer burnt offerings or grain offerings or offerings of well-being on it, may the LORD himself take vengeance. 24No! We did it from fear that in time to come your children might say to our children, 'What have you to do with the LORD, the God of Israel? 25For the LORD has made the Jordan a boundary between us and you, you Reubenites and Gadites; you have no portion in the LORD.' So your children might make our children cease to worship the LORD.

a 22.10 Or to Geliloth b 22.11 Or at Geliloth
c 22.19 Or make rebels of us

26Therefore we said, 'Let us now build an altar, not for burnt offering, nor for sacrifice, 27but to be a witness between us and you, and between the generations after us, that we do perform the service of the LORD in his presence with our burnt offerings and sacrifices and offerings of well-being; so that your children may never say to our children in time to come, "You have no portion in the LORD."' 28And we thought, If this should be said to us or to our descendants in time to come, we could say, 'Look at this copy of the altar of the LORD, which our ancestors made, not for burnt offerings, nor for sacrifice, but to be a witness between us and you.' 29Far be it from us that we should rebel against the LORD, and turn away this day from following the LORD by building an altar for burnt offering, grain offering, or sacrifice, other than the altar of the LORD our God that stands before his tabernacle!"

30 When the priest Phinehas and the chiefs of the congregation, the heads of the families of Israel who were with him, heard the words that the Reubenites and the Gadites and the Manassites spoke, they were satisfied. 31The priest Phinehas son of Eleazar said to the Reubenites and the Gadites and the Manassites, "Today we know that the LORD is among us, because you have not committed this treachery against the LORD; now you have saved the Israelites from the hand of the LORD."

32 Then the priest Phinehas son of Eleazar and the chiefs returned from the Reubenites and the Gadites in the land of Gilead to the land of Canaan, to the Israelites, and brought back word to them. 33The report pleased the Israelites; and the Israelites blessed God and spoke no more of making war against them, to destroy the land where the Reubenites and the Gadites were settled. 34The Reubenites and the Gadites called the altar Witness;a "For," said they, "it is a witness between us that the LORD is God."

JOSHUA EXHORTS THE PEOPLE

23 A long time afterward, when the LORD had given rest to Israel from all their enemies all around, and Joshua was old and well advanced in years, 2Joshua summoned all Israel, their elders and heads, their judges and officers, and said to them, "I am now old and well advanced in years; 3and you have seen all that the LORD your God has done to all these nations for your sake, for it is the LORD your God who has fought for you. 4I have allotted to you as an inheritance for your tribes those nations that remain, along with all the nations that I have already cut off, from the Jordan to the Great Sea in the west. 5The LORD your God will push them back before you, and drive them out of your sight; and you shall possess their land, as the LORD your God promised you. 6Therefore be very steadfast to observe and do all that is written in the book of the law of Moses, turning aside from it neither to the right nor to the left, 7so that you may not be mixed with these nations left here among you, or make mention of the names of their gods, or swear by them, or serve them, or bow yourselves down to them, 8but hold fast to the LORD your God, as you have done to this day. 9For the LORD has driven out before you great and strong nations; and as for you, no one has been able to withstand you to this day. 10One of you puts to flight a thousand, since it is the LORD your God who fights for you, as he promised you. 11Be very careful, therefore, to love the LORD your God. 12For if you turn back, and join the survivors of these nations left here among you, and intermarry with them, so that you marry their women and they yours, 13know assuredly that the LORD your God will not continue to drive out these nations before you; but they shall be a snare and a trap for you, a scourge on your sides, and thorns in your eyes, until you perish from this good land that the LORD your God has given you.

14 "And now I am about to go the way of all the earth, and you know

a 22.34 Cn Compare Syr: Heb lacks Witness

in your hearts and souls, all of you, that not one thing has failed of all the good things that the LORD your God promised concerning you; all have come to pass for you, not one of them has failed. 15But just as all the good things that the LORD your God promised concerning you have been fulfilled for you, so the LORD will bring upon you all the bad things, until he has destroyed you from this good land that the LORD your God has given you. 16If you transgress the covenant of the LORD your God, which he enjoined on you, and go and serve other gods and bow down to them, then the anger of the LORD will be kindled against you, and you shall perish quickly from the good land that he has given to you."

THE TRIBES RENEW THE COVENANT

24 Then Joshua gathered all the tribes of Israel to Shechem, and summoned the elders, the heads, the judges, and the officers of Israel; and they presented themselves before God. 2And Joshua said to all the people, "Thus says the LORD, the God of Israel: Long ago your ancestors—Terah and his sons Abraham and Nahor—lived beyond the Euphrates and served other gods. 3Then I took your father Abraham from beyond the River and led him through all the land of Canaan and made his offspring many. I gave him Isaac; 4and to Isaac I gave Jacob and Esau. I gave Esau the hill country of Seir to possess, but Jacob and his children went down to Egypt. 5Then I sent Moses and Aaron, and I plagued Egypt with what I did in its midst; and afterwards I brought you out. 6When I brought your ancestors out of Egypt, you came to the sea; and the Egyptians pursued your ancestors with chariots and horsemen to the Red Sea.a 7When they cried out to the LORD, he put darkness between you and the Egyptians, and made the sea come upon them and cover them; and your eyes saw what I did to Egypt. Afterwards you lived in the wilderness a long time. 8Then I brought you to the land of the Am-

orites, who lived on the other side of the Jordan; they fought with you, and I handed them over to you, and you took possession of their land, and I destroyed them before you. 9Then King Balak son of Zippor of Moab, set out to fight against Israel. He sent and invited Balaam son of Beor to curse you, 10but I would not listen to Balaam; therefore he blessed you; so I rescued you out of his hand. 11When you went over the Jordan and came to Jericho, the citizens of Jericho fought against you, and also the Amorites, the Perizzites, the Canaanites, the Hittites, the Girgashites, the Hivites, and the Jebusites; and I handed them over to you. 12I sent the hornetb ahead of you, which drove out before you the two kings of the Amorites; it was not by your sword or by your bow. 13I gave you a land on which you had not labored, and towns that you had not built, and you live in them; you eat the fruit of vineyards and oliveyards that you did not plant.

14 "Now therefore revere the LORD, and serve him in sincerity and in faithfulness; put away the gods that your ancestors served beyond the River and in Egypt, and serve the LORD. 15Now if you are unwilling to serve the LORD, choose this day whom you will serve, whether the gods your ancestors served in the region beyond the River or the gods of the Amorites in whose land you are living; but as for me and my household, we will serve the LORD."

16 Then the people answered, "Far be it from us that we should forsake the LORD to serve other gods; 17for it is the LORD our God who brought us and our ancestors up from the land of Egypt, out of the house of slavery, and who did those great signs in our sight. He protected us along all the way that we went, and among all the peoples through whom we passed; 18and the LORD drove out before us all the peoples, the Amorites who lived in the land. Therefore we also will serve the LORD, for he is our God."

a 24.6 Or Sea of Reeds   b 24.12 Meaning of Heb uncertain

19 But Joshua said to the people, "You cannot serve the LORD, for he is a holy God. He is a jealous God; he will not forgive your transgressions or your sins. **20** If you forsake the LORD and serve foreign gods, then he will turn and do you harm, and consume you, after having done you good." **21** And the people said to Joshua, "No, we will serve the LORD!" **22** Then Joshua said to the people, "You are witnesses against yourselves that you have chosen the LORD, to serve him." And they said, "We are witnesses." **23** He said, "Then put away the foreign gods that are among you, and incline your hearts to the LORD, the God of Israel." **24** The people said to Joshua, "The LORD our God we will serve, and him we will obey." **25** So Joshua made a covenant with the people that day, and made statutes and ordinances for them at Shechem. **26** Joshua wrote these words in the book of the law of God; and he took a large stone, and set it up there under the oak in the sanctuary of the LORD. **27** Joshua said to all the people, "See, this stone shall be a witness against us; for it has heard all the words of the LORD that he spoke to us; therefore it shall be a witness against you, if you deal falsely with your God." **28** So Joshua sent the people away to their inheritances.

DEATH OF JOSHUA AND ELEAZAR

29 After these things Joshua son of Nun, the servant of the LORD,

PONDER

The people said to Joshua, "The LORD our God we will serve, and him we will obey."
—Joshua 24.24

PRAY

Gracious Father, we are blessed in so many ways, as were the Hebrew people when they finally reached the promised land. They had to choose whether to serve other gods or to serve you, who had led them into a land of plenty. We have what we need and much of what we want. Now our responsibility is to decide: Do we or do we not accept the grace of God? Is Christ our guide, our leader, our example? That is the decision we have to make, and we do it many times during our lives. Strengthen us in our resolve to serve you, in the name of our Savior. Amen.

died, being one hundred ten years old. **30** They buried him in his own inheritance at Timnath-serah, which is in the hill country of Ephraim, north of Mount Gaash.

31 Israel served the LORD all the days of Joshua, and all the days of the elders who outlived Joshua and had known all the work that the LORD did for Israel.

BIBLE IN LIFE

Godly Leaders
Joshua 24.15

When we think about godly leaders of the Bible, Joshua's name comes quickly to mind. Joshua set the bar high for leadership. When we choose leaders in general, we want them to represent us fairly and honestly. When we choose our spiritual leaders in particular, we want them to follow the commandments of God. We want leaders who can intercede for us when we don't feel adequate in our own personal relationships with God. We want leaders who will help us reorient our lives if we are afflicted with sorrow, despair, hopelessness or failure. A spiritual leader should be humble and assume the role of servant among us. Jesus exemplified this as he washed the feet of his disciples (see John 13). But the ultimate expectation for leaders is that they bring us closer to God.

32 The bones of Joseph, which the Israelites had brought up from Egypt, were buried at Shechem, in the portion of ground that Jacob had bought from the children of Hamor, the father of Shechem, for one hundred pieces of money;[a] it became an inheritance of the descendants of Joseph.

33 Eleazar son of Aaron died; and they buried him at Gibeah, the town of his son Phinehas, which had been given him in the hill country of Ephraim.

[a] **24.32** Heb *one hundred qesitah*

JUDGES

If the book of Joshua recounts an "up" time for the people of Israel, then Judges recounts some of the "down" times. In fact, this period in Israel's history resembles a roller-coaster ride. Israel repeatedly fell away from God, a situation in which "There was no king in Israel; all the people did what was right in their own eyes" (Judges 17.6). Eventually the Israelites became desperate and begged God to save them. God sent a judge to lead them out of trouble and things went better for a while—then the cycle started again. This book clearly shows what happens when we try to get along without God—and what can happen when we turn around and trust God again.

ISRAEL'S FAILURE TO COMPLETE THE CONQUEST OF CANAAN

1 After the death of Joshua, the Israelites inquired of the LORD, "Who shall go up first for us against the Canaanites, to fight against them?" 2The LORD said, "Judah shall go up. I hereby give the land into his hand." 3Judah said to his brother Simeon, "Come up with me into the territory allotted to me, that we may fight against the Canaanites; then I too will go with you into the territory allotted to you." So Simeon went with him. 4Then Judah went up and the LORD gave the Canaanites and the Perizzites into their hand; and they defeated ten thousand of them at Bezek. 5They came upon Adoni-bezek at Bezek, and fought against him, and defeated the Canaanites and the Perizzites. 6Adoni-bezek fled; but they pursued him, and caught him, and cut off his thumbs and big toes. 7Adoni-bezek said, "Seventy kings with their thumbs and big toes cut off used to pick up scraps under my table; as I have done, so God has paid me back." They brought him to Jerusalem, and he died there.

8 Then the people of Judah fought against Jerusalem and took it. They put it to the sword and set the city on fire. 9Afterward the people of Judah went down to fight against the Canaanites who lived in the hill country, in the Negeb, and in the lowland. 10Judah went against the Canaanites who lived in Hebron (the name of Hebron was formerly Kiriath-arba); and they defeated Sheshai and Ahiman and Talmai.

11 From there they went against the inhabitants of Debir (the name of Debir was formerly Kiriath-sepher). 12Then Caleb said, "Whoever attacks Kiriath-sepher and takes it, I will give him my daughter Achsah as wife." 13And Othniel son of Kenaz, Caleb's younger brother, took it; and he gave him his daughter Achsah as wife. 14When she came to him, she urged her to ask her father for a field. As she dismounted from her donkey, Caleb said to her, "What do you wish?" 15She said to him, "Give me a present; since you have set me in the land of the Negeb, give me also Gulloth-mayim."ᵃ So Caleb gave her Upper Gulloth and Lower Gulloth.

16 The descendants of Hobabᵇ the Kenite, Moses' father-in-law, went up with the people of Judah from the city of palms into the wilderness of Judah, which lies in the Negeb near Arad. Then they went and settled with the Amalekites.ᶜ 17Judah went with his brother Simeon, and they defeated the Canaanites who inhabited Zephath, and devoted it to destruction. So the city was called Hormah. 18Judah took Gaza with its territory, Ashkelon with its territory, and Ekron with its territory. 19The LORD was with Judah, and he took possession of the hill country, but could not drive out the inhabitants of the plain, because they had chariots of iron. 20Hebron was given to Caleb, as Moses had said; and he drove out from it the three sons of Anak. 21But the Benjaminites did not drive out the Jebusites who lived in Jerusalem; so the Jebusites have lived in Jerusalem among the Benjaminites to this day.

22 The house of Joseph also went up against Bethel; and the LORD was with them. 23The house of Joseph sent out spies to Bethel (the name of the city was formerly Luz). 24When the spies saw a man coming out of the city, they said to him, "Show us the way into the city, and we will deal kindly with you." 25So he showed them the way into the city; and they put the city to the sword, but they let the man and all his family go. 26So the man went to the land of the Hittites and built a city, and named it Luz; that is its name to this day.

27 Manasseh did not drive out the inhabitants of Beth-shean and its villages, or Taanach and its villages, or the inhabitants of Dor and its villages, or the inhabitants of Ibleam and its villages, or the inhabitants of Megiddo and its villages; but the

ᵃ 1.15 That is *Basins of Water*   ᵇ 1.16 Gk: Heb lacks *Hobab*   ᶜ 1.16 See 1 Sam 15.6: Heb *people*

Canaanites continued to live in that land. 28When Israel grew strong, they put the Canaanites to forced labor, but did not in fact drive them out.

29 And Ephraim did not drive out the Canaanites who lived in Gezer; but the Canaanites lived among them in Gezer.

30 Zebulun did not drive out the inhabitants of Kitron, or the inhabitants of Nahalol; but the Canaanites lived among them, and became subject to forced labor.

31 Asher did not drive out the inhabitants of Acco, or the inhabitants of Sidon, or of Ahlab, or of Achzib, or of Helbah, or of Aphik, or of Rehob; 32but the Asherites lived among the Canaanites, the inhabitants of the land; for they did not drive them out.

33 Naphtali did not drive out the inhabitants of Beth-shemesh, or the inhabitants of Beth-anath, but lived among the Canaanites, the inhabitants of the land; nevertheless the inhabitants of Beth-shemesh and of Beth-anath became subject to forced labor for them.

34 The Amorites pressed the Danites back into the hill country; they did not allow them to come down to the plain. 35The Amorites continued to live in Har-heres, in Aijalon, and in Shaalbim, but the hand of the house of Joseph rested heavily on them, and they became subject to forced labor. 36The border of the Amorites ran from the ascent of Akrabbim, from Sela and upward.

ISRAEL'S DISOBEDIENCE

2 Now the angel of the LORD went up from Gilgal to Bochim, and said, "I brought you up from Egypt, and brought you into the land that I had promised to your ancestors. I said, 'I will never break my covenant with you. 2For your part, do not make a covenant with the inhabitants of this land; tear down their altars.' But you have not obeyed my command. See what you have done! 3So now I say, I will not drive them out before you; but they shall become adversaries[a] to you, and their

gods shall be a snare to you." 4When the angel of the LORD spoke these words to all the Israelites, the people lifted up their voices and wept. 5So they named that place Bochim,[b] and there they sacrificed to the LORD.

DEATH OF JOSHUA

6 When Joshua dismissed the people, the Israelites all went to their own inheritances to take possession of the land. 7The people worshiped the LORD all the days of Joshua, and all the days of the elders who outlived Joshua, who had seen all the great work that the LORD had done for Israel. 8Joshua son of Nun, the servant of the LORD, died at the age of one hundred ten years. 9So they buried him within the bounds of his inheritance in Timnath-heres, in the hill country of Ephraim, north of Mount Gaash. 10Moreover, that whole generation was gathered to their ancestors, and another generation grew up after them, who did not know the LORD or the work that he had done for Israel.

ISRAEL'S UNFAITHFULNESS

11 Then the Israelites did what was evil in the sight of the LORD and worshiped the Baals; 12and they abandoned the LORD, the God of their ancestors, who had brought them out of the land of Egypt; they followed other gods, from among the gods of the peoples who were all around them, and bowed down to them; and they provoked the LORD to anger. 13They abandoned the LORD, and worshiped Baal and the Astartes. 14So the anger of the LORD was kindled against Israel, and he gave them over to plunderers who plundered them, and he sold them into the power of their enemies all around, so that they could no longer withstand their enemies. 15Whenever they marched out, the hand of the LORD was against them to bring misfortune, as the LORD had warned them and sworn to them; and they were in great distress.

[a] 2.3 OL Vg Compare Gk: Heb *sides*
[b] 2.5 That is *Weepers*

16 Then the LORD raised up judges, who delivered them out of the power of those who plundered them. 17 Yet they did not listen even to their judges; for they lusted after other gods and bowed down to them. They soon turned aside from the way in which their ancestors had walked, who had obeyed the commandments of the LORD; they did not follow their example. 18 Whenever the LORD raised up judges for them, the LORD was with the judge, and he delivered them from the hand of their enemies all the days of the judge; for the LORD would be moved to pity by their groaning because of those who persecuted and oppressed them. 19 But whenever the judge died, they would relapse and behave worse than their ancestors, following other gods, worshiping them and bowing down to them. They would not drop any of their practices or their stubborn ways. 20 So the anger of the LORD was kindled against Israel; and he said, "Because this people have transgressed my covenant that I commanded their ancestors, and have not obeyed my voice, 21 I will no longer drive out before them any of the nations that Joshua left when he died." 22 In order to test Israel, whether or not they would take care to walk in the way of the LORD as their ancestors did, 23 the LORD had left those nations, not driving them out at once, and had not handed them over to Joshua.

NATIONS REMAINING IN THE LAND

3 Now these are the nations that the LORD left to test all those in Israel who had no experience of any war in Canaan 2 (it was only that successive generations of Israelites might know war, to teach those who had no experience of it before): 3 the five lords of the Philistines, and all the Canaanites, and the Sidonians, and the Hivites who lived on Mount Lebanon, from Mount Baal-hermon as far as Lebo-hamath. 4 They were for the testing of Israel, to know whether Israel would obey the commandments of the LORD, which he commanded their ancestors by Moses. 5 So the Israelites lived among the Canaanites, the Hittites, the Amorites, the Perizzites, the Hivites, and the Jebusites; 6 and they took their daughters as wives for themselves, and their own daughters they gave to their sons; and they worshiped their gods.

OTHNIEL

7 The Israelites did what was evil in the sight of the LORD, forgetting the LORD their God, and worshiping the Baals and the Asherahs. 8 Therefore the anger of the LORD was kindled against Israel, and he sold them into the hand of King Cushan-rishathaim of Aram-naharaim; and the Israelites served Cushan-rishathaim eight years. 9 But when the Israelites cried out to the LORD, the LORD raised up a deliverer for

---

├─┤ BIBLE IN LIFE ▷ ─────────── ⊕

No Other Gods
Judges 2.19–20

God explicitly commanded the Israelites not to worship other gods: "You shall have no other gods before me" (Exodus 20.3). In those days, it was uncommon for a group of people to have only one god. People embraced multiple gods, worshiping different gods for different things: They had a god for health, a god for good crops, a god for many children and a god for economic success. The Israelites had seen the success of Egypt and the wealth of the people in the land of Canaan. They were enticed by the gods of the world around them.

We are also enticed by the world. Many "gods" can occupy our thoughts, our minds and our ambitions. What are the things that concern us? What material goals have we set for our lives? Those desires can become gods that we revere or even worship.

the Israelites, who delivered them, Othniel son of Kenaz, Caleb's younger brother. [10] The spirit of the LORD came upon him, and he judged Israel; he went out to war, and the LORD gave King Cushan-rishathaim of Aram into his hand; and his hand prevailed over Cushan-rishathaim. [11] So the land had rest forty years. Then Othniel son of Kenaz died.

EHUD

[12] The Israelites again did what was evil in the sight of the LORD; and the LORD strengthened King Eglon of Moab against Israel, because they had done what was evil in the sight of the LORD. [13] In alliance with the Ammonites and the Amalekites, he went and defeated Israel; and they took possession of the city of palms. [14] So the Israelites served King Eglon of Moab eighteen years.

[15] But when the Israelites cried out to the LORD, the LORD raised up for them a deliverer, Ehud son of Gera, the Benjaminite, a left-handed man. The Israelites sent tribute by him to King Eglon of Moab. [16] Ehud made for himself a sword with two edges, a cubit in length; and he fastened it on his right thigh under his clothes. [17] Then he presented the tribute to King Eglon of Moab. Now Eglon was a very fat man. [18] When Ehud had finished presenting the tribute, he sent the people who carried the tribute on their way. [19] But he himself turned back at the sculptured stones near Gilgal, and said, "I have a secret message for you, O king." So the king said, [a] "Silence!" and all his attendants went out from his presence. [20] Ehud came to him, while he was sitting alone in his cool roof chamber, and said, "I have a message from God for you." So he rose from his seat. [21] Then Ehud reached with his left hand, took the sword from his right thigh, and thrust it into Eglon's [b] belly; [22] the hilt also went in after the blade, and the fat closed over the blade, for he did not draw the sword out of his belly; and the dirt came out. [c] [23] Then Ehud went out into the vestibule, [d] and closed the doors of the roof chamber on him, and locked them.

[24] After he had gone, the servants came. When they saw that the doors of the roof chamber were locked, they thought, "He must be relieving himself [e] in the cool chamber." [25] So they waited until they were embarrassed. When he still did not open the doors of the roof chamber, they took the key and opened them. There was their lord lying dead on the floor.

[26] Ehud escaped while they delayed, and passed beyond the sculptured stones, and escaped to Seirah. [27] When he arrived, he sounded the trumpet in the hill country of Ephraim; and the Israelites went down with him from the hill country, having him at their head. [28] He said to them, "Follow after me; for the LORD has given your enemies the Moabites into your hand." So they went down after him, and seized the fords of the Jordan against the Moabites, and allowed no one to cross over. [29] At that time they killed about ten thousand of the Moabites, all strong, able-bodied men; no one escaped. [30] So Moab was subdued that day under the hand of Israel. And the land had rest eighty years.

SHAMGAR

[31] After him came Shamgar son of Anath, who killed six hundred of the Philistines with an oxgoad. He too delivered Israel.

DEBORAH AND BARAK

4 The Israelites again did what was evil in the sight of the LORD, after Ehud died. [2] So the LORD sold them into the hand of King Jabin of Canaan, who reigned in Hazor; the commander of his army was Sisera, who lived in Harosheth-ha-goiim. [3] Then the Israelites cried out to the LORD for help; for he had nine hundred chariots of iron, and had oppressed the Israelites cruelly twenty years.

---

[a] 3.19 Heb *he said* [b] 3.21 Heb *his*
[c] 3.22 With Tg Vg: Meaning of Heb uncertain
[d] 3.23 Meaning of Heb uncertain
[e] 3.24 Heb *covering his feet*

4 At that time Deborah, a prophetess, wife of Lappidoth, was judging Israel. ⁵She used to sit under the palm of Deborah between Ramah and Bethel in the hill country of Ephraim; and the Israelites came up to her for judgment. ⁶She sent and summoned Barak son of Abinoam from Kedesh in Naphtali, and said to him, "The LORD, the God of Israel, commands you, 'Go, take position at Mount Tabor, bringing ten thousand from the tribe of Naphtali and the tribe of Zebulun. ⁷I will draw out Sisera, the general of Jabin's army, to meet you by the Wadi Kishon with his chariots and his troops; and I will give him into your hand.' " ⁸Barak said to her, "If you will go with me, I will go; but if you will not go with me, I will not go." ⁹And she said, "I will surely go with you; nevertheless, the road on which you are going will not lead to your glory, for the LORD will sell Sisera into the hand of a woman." Then Deborah got up and went with Barak to Kedesh. ¹⁰Barak summoned Zebulun and Naphtali to Kedesh; and ten thousand warriors went up behind him; and Deborah went up with him.

11 Now Heber the Kenite had separated from the other Kenites,ᵃ that is, the descendants of Hobab the father-in-law of Moses, and had encamped as far away as Elon-bezaanannim, which is near Kedesh. 12 When Sisera was told that Barak son of Abinoam had gone up to Mount Tabor, ¹³Sisera called out all his chariots, nine hundred chariots of iron, and all the troops who were with him, from Harosheth-ha-goiim to the Wadi Kishon. ¹⁴Then Deborah said to Barak, "Up! For this is the day on which the LORD has given Sisera into your hand. The LORD is indeed going out before you." So Barak went down from Mount Tabor with ten thousand warriors following him. ¹⁵And the LORD threw Sisera and all his chariots and all his army into a panicᵇ before Barak; Sisera got down from his chariot and fled away on foot, ¹⁶while Barak pursued the chariots and the army to Harosheth-ha-

goiim. All the army of Sisera fell by the sword; no one was left.

17 Now Sisera had fled away on foot to the tent of Jael wife of Heber the Kenite; for there was peace between King Jabin of Hazor and the clan of Heber the Kenite. ¹⁸Jael came out to meet Sisera, and said to him, "Turn aside, my lord, turn aside to me; have no fear." So he turned aside to her into the tent, and she covered him with a rug. ¹⁹Then he said to her, "Please give me a little water to drink; for I am thirsty." So she opened a skin of milk and gave him a drink and covered him. ²⁰He said to her, "Stand at the entrance of the tent, and if anybody comes and asks you, 'Is anyone here?' say, 'No.' " ²¹But Jael wife of Heber took a tent peg, and took a hammer in her hand,

---

PONDER

At that time Deborah, a prophetess, wife of Lappidoth, was judging Israel. She used to sit under the palm of Deborah between Ramah and Bethel in the hill country of Ephraim; and the Israelites came up to her for judgment.
—Judges 4.4–5

PRAY

Lord God, implant these scriptures in our hearts so that we might remember that we are closely bound to you through our covenant faith in Jesus Christ, just as Deborah and Barak were in their covenant with you. Help us to remember that no matter what our own capabilities might be, that even though we may not be brilliant, educated, rich or influential, we can still be blessed and vital in your kingdom. It is a sobering thought for us, but also encouraging and reassuring to know your hand is on us. We pray in your holy name. Amen.

ᵃ 4.11 Heb *from the Kain*   ᵇ 4.15 Heb adds *to the sword*; compare verse 16

and went softly to him and drove the peg into his temple, until it went down into the ground—he was lying fast asleep from weariness—and he died. ²²Then, as Barak came in pursuit of Sisera, Jael went out to meet him, and said to him, "Come, and I will show you the man whom you are seeking." So he went into her tent; and there was Sisera lying dead, with the tent peg in his temple.

23 So on that day God subdued King Jabin of Canaan before the Israelites. ²⁴Then the hand of the Israelites bore harder and harder on King Jabin of Canaan, until they destroyed King Jabin of Canaan.

THE SONG OF DEBORAH

5 Then Deborah and Barak son of Abinoam sang on that day, saying:

2 "When locks are long in Israel,
    when the people offer
        themselves willingly—
    blessᵃ the LORD!

3 "Hear, O kings; give ear,
        O princes;
    to the LORD I will sing,
    I will make melody to the
        LORD, the God of Israel.

4 "LORD, when you went
        out from Seir,
    when you marched from
        the region of Edom,
    the earth trembled,
        and the heavens poured,
    the clouds indeed
        poured water.

5 The mountains quaked before the
        LORD, the One of Sinai,
    before the LORD, the
        God of Israel.

6 "In the days of Shamgar
        son of Anath,
    in the days of Jael,
        caravans ceased
    and travelers kept to
        the byways.

7 The peasantry prospered in Israel,
        they grew fat on plunder,
    because you arose, Deborah,
        arose as a mother in Israel.

8 When new gods were chosen,
        then war was in the gates.
    Was shield or spear to be seen
        among forty thousand
            in Israel?

9 My heart goes out to the
        commanders of Israel
    who offered themselves
        willingly among
            the people.
    Bless the LORD.

OVER THE CENTURIES, THE
CHURCH HAS CHANGED
THE MANDATES OF CHRIST,
DISCOUNTING THE ROLE
OF WOMEN. JESUS MADE
IT CLEAR: THERE IS NO
DISTINCTION AMONG US IN
OUR ABILITIES TO SERVE HIM.

10 "Tell of it, you who ride on
        white donkeys,
    you who sit on rich carpetsᵇ
    and you who walk
        by the way.

11 To the sound of musiciansᵇ at
        the watering places,
    there they repeat the
        triumphs of the LORD,
    the triumphs of his
        peasantry in Israel.

"Then down to the gates marched
        the people of the LORD.

12 "Awake, awake, Deborah!
    Awake, awake, utter a song!
    Arise, Barak, lead away
        your captives,
    O son of Abinoam.

ᵃ 5.2 Or You who offer yourselves willingly among the people, bless   ᵇ 5.10,11 Meaning of Heb uncertain

13 Then down marched the
    remnant of the noble;
the people of the LORD
    marched down for him[a]
    against the mighty.
14 From Ephraim they set out[b]
    into the valley,[c]
following you, Benjamin,
    with your kin;
from Machir marched down
    the commanders,
and from Zebulun those who
    bear the marshal's staff;
15 the chiefs of Issachar came
    with Deborah,
and Issachar faithful to Barak;
    into the valley they rushed
    out at his heels.
Among the clans of Reuben
    there were great searchings
    of heart.
16 Why did you tarry among
    the sheepfolds,
to hear the piping for
    the flocks?
Among the clans of Reuben
    there were great searchings
    of heart.
17 Gilead stayed beyond the Jordan;
    and Dan, why did he abide
    with the ships?
Asher sat still at the coast
    of the sea,
    settling down by his landings.
18 Zebulun is a people that
    scorned death;
Naphtali too, on the
    heights of the field.

19 "The kings came, they fought;
    then fought the kings
    of Canaan,
at Taanach, by the waters
    of Megiddo;
    they got no spoils of silver.
20 The stars fought from heaven,
    from their courses they
    fought against Sisera.
21 The torrent Kishon swept
    them away,
the onrushing torrent, the
    torrent Kishon.
March on, my soul, with might!

22 "Then loud beat the horses' hoofs
    with the galloping, galloping
    of his steeds.

23 "Curse Meroz, says the angel
    of the LORD,
curse bitterly its inhabitants,
because they did not come to
    the help of the LORD,
to the help of the LORD
    against the mighty.

24 "Most blessed of women be Jael,
    the wife of Heber the Kenite,
of tent-dwelling women
    most blessed.
25 He asked water and she
    gave him milk,
she brought him curds
    in a lordly bowl.
26 She put her hand to the tent peg
    and her right hand to the
    workmen's mallet;
she struck Sisera a blow,
    she crushed his head,
she shattered and pierced
    his temple.
27 He sank, he fell,
    he lay still at her feet;
at her feet he sank, he fell;
    where he sank, there
    he fell dead.

28 "Out of the window she peered,
    the mother of Sisera gazed[d]
    through the lattice:
'Why is his chariot so long
    in coming?
Why tarry the hoofbeats
    of his chariots?'
29 Her wisest ladies make answer,
indeed, she answers the
    question herself:
30 'Are they not finding and
    dividing the spoil?—
A girl or two for every man;
spoil of dyed stuffs for Sisera,
    spoil of dyed stuffs embroidered,
two pieces of dyed work
    embroidered for my
    neck as spoil?'

31 "So perish all your enemies,
    O LORD!
But may your friends be like the
    sun as it rises in its might."

And the land had rest forty years.

a 5.13 Gk: Heb *me*   b 5.14 Cn: Heb *From
Ephraim their root*   c 5.14 Gk: Heb *in Amalek*
d 5.28 Gk Compare Tg: Heb *exclaimed*

THE MIDIANITE OPPRESSION

6 The Israelites did what was evil in the sight of the LORD, and the LORD gave them into the hand of Midian seven years. ²The hand of Midian prevailed over Israel; and because of Midian the Israelites provided for themselves hiding places in the mountains, caves and strongholds. ³For whenever the Israelites put in seed, the Midianites and the Amalekites and the people of the east would come up against them. ⁴They would encamp against them and destroy the produce of the land, as far as the neighborhood of Gaza, and leave no sustenance in Israel, and no sheep or ox or donkey. ⁵For they and their livestock would come up, and they would even bring their tents, as thick as locusts; neither they nor their camels could be counted; so they wasted the land as they came in. ⁶Thus Israel was greatly impoverished because of Midian; and the Israelites cried out to the LORD for help.

7 When the Israelites cried to the LORD on account of the Midianites, ⁸the LORD sent a prophet to the Israelites; and he said to them, "Thus says the LORD, the God of Israel: I led you up from Egypt, and brought you out of the house of slavery; ⁹and I delivered you from the hand of the Egyptians, and from the hand of all who oppressed you, and drove them out before you, and gave you their land; ¹⁰and I said to you, 'I am the LORD your God; you shall not pay reverence to the gods of the Amorites, in whose land you live.' But you have not given heed to my voice."

THE CALL OF GIDEON

11 Now the angel of the LORD came and sat under the oak at Ophrah, which belonged to Joash the Abiezrite, as his son Gideon was beating out wheat in the wine press, to hide it from the Midianites. ¹²The angel of the LORD appeared to him and said to him, "The LORD is with you, you mighty warrior." ¹³Gideon answered him, "But sir, if the LORD is with us, why then has all this happened to us? And where are all his wonderful deeds that our ancestors recounted to us, saying, 'Did not the LORD bring us up from Egypt?' But now the LORD has cast us off, and given us into the hand of Midian." ¹⁴Then the LORD turned to him and said, "Go in this might of yours and deliver Israel from the hand of Midian; I hereby commission you." ¹⁵He responded, "But sir, how can I deliver Israel? My clan is the weakest in Manasseh, and I am the least in my family." ¹⁶The LORD said to him, "But I will be with you, and you shall strike down the Midianites, every one of them." ¹⁷Then he said to him, "If now I have found favor with you, then show me a sign that it is you who speak with me. ¹⁸Do not depart from here until I come to you, and bring out my present, and set it before you." And he said, "I will stay until you return."

PONDER

Then the LORD turned to [Gideon] and said, "Go in this might of yours and deliver Israel from the hand of Midian; I hereby commission you."
—Judges 6.14

PRAY

Heavenly Father, again we have been forced to confront some challenging words. We pray for wisdom to see how in our fumbling ways we can apply the lessons of Gideon's challenge to our own lives and respond when you call us. We are thankful that when we are tempted to take the natural escape route of taking care of our own business and postponing everything else, you are present and promise to strengthen us. Forgive us for passing up the many opportunities in which we could have used our talents, great or small. Help us dedicate our hearts and minds to you and to those in need, for that is the essence of a called life. We ask these things in the name of our perfect Savior. Amen.

19 So Gideon went into his house and prepared a kid, and unleavened cakes from an ephah of flour; the meat he put in a basket, and the broth he put in a pot, and brought them to him under the oak and presented them. **20**The angel of God said to him, "Take the meat and the unleavened cakes, and put them on this rock, and pour out the broth." And he did so. **21**Then the angel of the LORD reached out the tip of the staff that was in his hand, and touched the meat and the unleavened cakes; and fire sprang up from the rock and consumed the meat and the unleavened cakes; and the angel of the LORD vanished from his sight. **22**Then Gideon perceived that it was the angel of the LORD; and Gideon said, "Help me, Lord GOD! For I have seen the angel of the LORD face to face." **23**But the LORD said to him, "Peace be to you; do not fear, you shall not die." **24**Then Gideon built an altar there to the LORD, and called it, The LORD is peace. To this day it still stands at Ophrah, which belongs to the Abiezrites.

25 That night the LORD said to him, "Take your father's bull, the second bull seven years old, and pull down the altar of Baal that belongs to your father, and cut down the sacred pole[a] that is beside it; **26**and build an altar to the LORD your God on the top of the stronghold here, in proper order; then take the second bull, and offer it as a burnt offering with the wood of the sacred pole[a] that you shall cut down." **27**So Gideon took ten of his servants, and did as the LORD had told him; but because he was too afraid of his family and the townspeople to do it by day, he did it by night.

GIDEON DESTROYS THE ALTAR OF BAAL

28 When the townspeople rose early in the morning, the altar of Baal was broken down, and the sacred pole[a] beside it was cut down, and the second bull was offered on the altar that had been built. **29**So they said to one another, "Who has done this?" After searching and inquiring, they were told, "Gideon son of Joash did it." **30**Then the townspeople said to Joash, "Bring out your son, so that he may die, for he has pulled down the altar of Baal and cut down the sacred pole[a] beside it." **31**But Joash said to all who were arrayed against him, "Will you contend for Baal? Or will you defend his cause? Whoever contends for him shall be put to death by morning. If he is a god, let him contend for himself, because his altar has been pulled down." **32**Therefore on that day Gideon[b] was called Jerubbaal, that is to say, "Let Baal contend against him," because he pulled down his altar.

33 Then all the Midianites and the Amalekites and the people of the east came together, and crossing the Jordan they encamped in the Valley of Jezreel. **34**But the spirit of the LORD took possession of Gideon; and he sounded the trumpet, and the Abiezrites were called out to follow him. **35**He sent messengers throughout all Manasseh, and they too were called out to follow him. He also sent messengers to Asher, Zebulun, and Naphtali, and they went up to meet them.

THE SIGN OF THE FLEECE

36 Then Gideon said to God, "In order to see whether you will deliver Israel by my hand, as you have said, **37**I am going to lay a fleece of wool on the threshing floor; if there is dew on the fleece alone, and it is dry on all the ground, then I shall know that you will deliver Israel by my hand, as you have said." **38**And it was so. When he rose early next morning and squeezed the fleece, he wrung enough dew from the fleece to fill a bowl with water. **39**Then Gideon said to God, "Do not let your anger burn against me, let me speak one more time; let me, please, make trial with the fleece just once more; let it be dry only on the fleece, and on all the ground let there be dew." **40**And God did so that night. It was dry on the fleece only, and on all the ground there was dew.

[a] 6.25,26,28,30 Heb *Asherah*   [b] 6.32 Heb *he*

GIDEON SURPRISES AND ROUTS THE MIDIANITES

7 Then Jerubbaal (that is, Gideon) and all the troops that were with him rose early and encamped beside the spring of Harod; and the camp of Midian was north of them, below[a] the hill of Moreh, in the valley. 2 The LORD said to Gideon, "The troops with you are too many for me to give the Midianites into their hand. Israel would only take the credit away from me, saying, 'My own hand has delivered me.' 3 Now therefore proclaim this in the hearing of the troops, 'Whoever is fearful and trembling, let him return home.' " Thus Gideon sifted them out;[b] twenty-two thousand returned, and ten thousand remained.

4 Then the LORD said to Gideon, "The troops are still too many; take them down to the water and I will sift them out for you there. When I say, 'This one shall go with you,' he shall go with you; and when I say, 'This one shall not go with you,' he shall not go." 5 So he brought the troops down to the water; and the LORD said to Gideon, "All those who lap the water with their tongues, as a dog laps, you shall put to one side; all those who kneel down to drink, putting their hands to their mouths,[c] you shall put to the other side." 6 The number of those that lapped was three hundred; but all the rest of the troops knelt down to drink water. 7 Then the LORD said to Gideon, "With the three hundred that lapped I will deliver you, and give the Midianites into your hand. Let all the others go to their homes." 8 So he took the jars of the troops from their hands,[d] and their trumpets; and he sent all the rest of Israel back to their own tents, but retained the three hundred. The camp of Midian was below him in the valley.

9 That same night the LORD said to him, "Get up, attack the camp; for I have given it into your hand. 10 But if you fear to attack, go down to the camp with your servant Purah; 11 and you shall hear what they say, and afterward your hands shall be strengthened to attack the camp." Then he went down with his servant Purah to the outposts of the armed men that were in the camp. 12 The Midianites and the Amalekites and all the people of the east lay along the valley as thick as locusts; and their camels were without number, countless as the sand on the seashore. 13 When Gideon arrived, there was a man telling a dream to his comrade; and he said, "I had a dream, and in it a cake of barley bread tumbled into the camp of Midian, and came to the tent, and struck it so that it fell; it turned upside down, and the tent collapsed." 14 And his comrade answered, "This is no other than the sword of Gideon son of Joash, a man of Israel; into his hand God has given Midian and all the army."

15 When Gideon heard the telling of the dream and its interpretation, he worshiped; and he returned to the camp of Israel, and said, "Get up; for the LORD has given the army of Midian into your hand." 16 After he divided the three hundred men into three companies, and put trumpets into the hands of all of them, and empty jars, with torches inside the jars, 17 he said to them, "Look at me, and do the same; when I come to the outskirts of the camp, do as I do. 18 When I blow the trumpet, I and all who are with me, then you also blow the trumpets around the whole camp, and shout, 'For the LORD and for Gideon!' "

19 So Gideon and the hundred who were with him came to the outskirts of the camp at the beginning of the middle watch, when they had just set the watch; and they blew the trumpets and smashed the jars that were in their hands. 20 So the three companies blew the trumpets and broke the jars, holding in their left hands the torches, and in their right hands the trumpets to blow; and

---

[a] 7.1 Heb *from*   [b] 7.3 Cn: Heb *home, and depart from Mount Gilead' "*   [c] 7.5 Heb places the words *putting their hands to their mouths* after the word *lapped* in verse 6   [d] 7.8 Cn: Heb *So the people took provisions in their hands*

they cried, "A sword for the LORD and for Gideon!" 21Every man stood in his place all around the camp, and all the men in camp ran; they cried out and fled. 22When they blew the three hundred trumpets, the LORD set every man's sword against his fellow and against all the army; and the army fled as far as Beth-shittah toward Zererah,[a] as far as the border of Abel-meholah, by Tabbath. 23And the men of Israel were called out from Naphtali and from Asher and from all Manasseh, and they pursued after the Midianites.

24 Then Gideon sent messengers throughout all the hill country of Ephraim, saying, "Come down against the Midianites and seize the waters against them, as far as Beth-barah, and also the Jordan." So all the men of Ephraim were called out, and they seized the waters as far as Beth-barah, and also the Jordan. 25They captured the two captains of Midian, Oreb and Zeeb; they killed Oreb at the rock of Oreb, and Zeeb they killed at the wine press of Zeeb, as they pursued the Midianites. They brought the heads of Oreb and Zeeb to Gideon beyond the Jordan.

GIDEON'S TRIUMPH AND VENGEANCE

8 Then the Ephraimites said to him, "What have you done to us, not to call us when you went to fight against the Midianites?" And they upbraided him violently. 2So he said to them, "What have I done now in comparison with you? Is not the gleaning of the grapes of Ephraim better than the vintage of Abiezer? 3God has given into your hands the captains of Midian, Oreb and Zeeb; what have I been able to do in comparison with you?" When he said this, their anger against him subsided.

4 Then Gideon came to the Jordan and crossed over, he and the three hundred who were with him, exhausted and famished.[b] 5So he said to the people of Succoth, "Please give some loaves of bread to my followers, for they are exhausted, and I am pursuing Zebah and Zalmunna, the kings of Midian." 6But the officials of Succoth said, "Do you already have in your possession the hands of Zebah and Zalmunna, that we should give bread to your army?" 7Gideon replied, "Well then, when the LORD has given Zebah and Zalmunna into my hand, I will trample your flesh on the thorns of the wilderness and on briers." 8From there he went up to Penuel, and made the same request of them; and the people of Penuel answered him as the people of Succoth had answered. 9So he said to the people of Penuel, "When I come back victorious, I will break down this tower."

10 Now Zebah and Zalmunna were in Karkor with their army, about fifteen thousand men, all who were left of all the army of the people of the east; for one hundred twenty thousand men bearing arms had fallen. 11So Gideon went up by the caravan route east of Nobah and Jogbehah, and attacked the army; for the army was off its guard. 12Zebah and Zalmunna fled; and he pursued them and took the two kings of Midian, Zebah and Zalmunna, and threw all the army into a panic.

13 When Gideon son of Joash returned from the battle by the ascent of Heres, 14he caught a young man, one of the people of Succoth, and questioned him; and he listed for him the officials and elders of Succoth, seventy-seven people. 15Then he came to the people of Succoth, and said, "Here are Zebah and Zalmunna, about whom you taunted me, saying, 'Do you already have in your possession the hands of Zebah and Zalmunna, that we should give bread to your troops who are exhausted?' " 16So he took the elders of the city and he took thorns of the wilderness and briers and with them he trampled[c] the people of Succoth. 17He also broke down the tower of Penuel, and killed the men of the city.

18 Then he said to Zebah and Zalmunna, "What about the men whom

a 7.22 Another reading is Zeredah
b 8.4 Gk: Heb pursuing   c 8.16 With verse 7, Compare Gk: Heb he taught

you killed at Tabor?" They answered, "As you are, so were they, every one of them; they resembled the sons of a king." ¹⁹And he replied, "They were my brothers, the sons of my mother; as the LORD lives, if you had saved them alive, I would not kill you." ²⁰So he said to Jether his firstborn, "Go kill them!" But the boy did not draw his sword, for he was afraid, because he was still a boy. ²¹Then Zebah and Zalmunna said, "You come and kill us; for as the man is, so is his strength." So Gideon proceeded to kill Zebah and Zalmunna; and he took the crescents that were on the necks of their camels.

GIDEON'S IDOLATRY

22 Then the Israelites said to Gideon, "Rule over us, you and your son and your grandson also; for you have delivered us out of the hand of Midian." ²³Gideon said to them, "I will not rule over you, and my son will not rule over you; the LORD will rule over you." ²⁴Then Gideon said to them, "Let me make a request of you; each of you give me an earring he has taken as booty." (For the enemy[a] had golden earrings, because they were Ishmaelites.) ²⁵"We will willingly give them," they answered. So they spread a garment, and each threw into it an earring he had taken as booty. ²⁶The weight of the golden earrings that he requested was one thousand seven hundred shekels of gold (apart from the crescents and the pendants and the purple garments worn by the kings of Midian, and the collars that were on the necks of their camels). ²⁷Gideon made an ephod of it and put it in his town, in Ophrah; and all Israel prostituted themselves to it there, and it became a snare to Gideon and to his family. ²⁸So Midian was subdued before the Israelites, and they lifted up their heads no more. So the land had rest forty years in the days of Gideon.

DEATH OF GIDEON

29 Jerubbaal son of Joash went to live in his own house. ³⁰Now Gideon had seventy sons, his own offspring, for he had many wives. ³¹His concubine who was in Shechem also bore him a son, and he named him Abimelech. ³²Then Gideon son of Joash died at a good old age, and was buried in the tomb of his father Joash at Ophrah of the Abiezrites.

33 As soon as Gideon died, the Israelites relapsed and prostituted themselves with the Baals, making Baal-berith their god. ³⁴The Israelites did not remember the LORD their God, who had rescued them from the hand of all their enemies on every side; ³⁵and they did not exhibit loyalty to the house of Jerubbaal (that is, Gideon) in return for all the good that he had done to Israel.

ABIMELECH ATTEMPTS TO ESTABLISH A MONARCHY

9 Now Abimelech son of Jerubbaal went to Shechem to his mother's kinsfolk and said to them and to the whole clan of his mother's family, ²"Say in the hearing of all the lords of Shechem, 'Which is better for you, that all seventy of the sons of Jerubbaal rule over you, or that one rule over you?' Remember also that I am your bone and your flesh." ³So his mother's kinsfolk spoke all these words on his behalf in the hearing of all the lords of Shechem; and their hearts inclined to follow Abimelech, for they said, "He is our brother." ⁴They gave him seventy pieces of silver out of the temple of Baal-berith with which Abimelech hired worthless and reckless fellows, who followed him. ⁵He went to his father's house at Ophrah, and killed his brothers the sons of Jerubbaal, seventy men, on one stone; but Jotham, the youngest son of Jerubbaal, survived, for he hid himself. ⁶Then all the lords of Shechem and all Beth-millo came together, and they went and made Abimelech king, by the oak of the pillar[b] at Shechem.

THE PARABLE OF THE TREES

7 When it was told to Jotham, he went and stood on the top of Mount

---

[a] 8.24 Heb *they* [b] 9.6 Cn: Meaning of Heb uncertain

Gerizim, and cried aloud and said to them, "Listen to me, you lords of Shechem, so that God may listen to you. 8 The trees once went out

to anoint a king over themselves.
So they said to the olive tree,
'Reign over us.'
9 The olive tree answered them,
'Shall I stop producing
my rich oil
by which gods and
mortals are honored,
and go to sway over the trees?'
10 Then the trees said to the fig tree,
'You come and reign over us.'
11 But the fig tree answered them,
'Shall I stop producing
my sweetness
and my delicious fruit,
and go to sway over the trees?'

DOMINANCE OF OTHERS

IS PERVASIVE IN FAMILIES,

IN CHURCHES, AT WORK,

IN OUR NATION AND

INTERNATIONALLY. CLAIMING

GOD TO BE ON OUR SIDE

IS ESPECIALLY TEMPTING

AND DESTRUCTIVE.

12 Then the trees said to the vine,
'You come and reign over us.'
13 But the vine said to them,
'Shall I stop producing my wine
that cheers gods and mortals,
and go to sway over the trees?'
14 So all the trees said to the bramble,
'You come and reign over us.'
15 And the bramble said to the trees,
'If in good faith you
are anointing me
king over you,
then come and take
refuge in my shade;
but if not, let fire come
out of the bramble
and devour the cedars
of Lebanon.'

16 "Now therefore, if you acted in good faith and honor when you made Abimelech king, and if you have dealt well with Jerubbaal and his house, and have done to him as his actions deserved— 17for my father fought for you, and risked his life, and rescued you from the hand of Midian; 18but you have risen up against my father's house this day, and have killed his sons, seventy men on one stone, and have made Abimelech, the son of his slave woman, king over the lords of Shechem, because he is your kinsman— 19if, I say, you have acted in good faith and honor with Jerubbaal and with his house this day, then rejoice in Abimelech, and let him also rejoice in you; 20but if not, let fire come out from Abimelech, and devour the lords of Shechem, and Beth-millo; and let fire come out from the lords of Shechem, and from Beth-millo, and devour Abimelech." 21Then Jotham ran away and fled, going to Beer, where he remained for fear of his brother Abimelech.

THE DOWNFALL OF ABIMELECH

22 Abimelech ruled over Israel three years. 23But God sent an evil spirit between Abimelech and the lords of Shechem; and the lords of Shechem dealt treacherously with Abimelech. 24This happened so that the violence done to the seventy sons of Jerubbaal might be avenged[a] and their blood be laid on their brother Abimelech, who killed them, and on the lords of Shechem, who strengthened his hands to kill his brothers. 25So, out of hostility to him, the lords of Shechem set ambushes on the mountain tops. They robbed all who passed by them along that way; and it was reported to Abimelech.

26 When Gaal son of Ebed moved into Shechem with his kinsfolk, the lords of Shechem put confidence in him. 27They went out into the field and gathered the grapes from their vineyards, trod them, and celebrated. Then they went into the temple of their god, ate and drank,

a 9.24 Heb *might come*

and ridiculed Abimelech. 28Gaal son of Ebed said, "Who is Abimelech, and who are we of Shechem, that we should serve him? Did not the son of Jerubbaal and Zebul his officer serve the men of Hamor father of Shechem? Why then should we serve him? 29If only this people were under my command! Then I would remove Abimelech; I would saya to him, 'Increase your army, and come out.'"

30 When Zebul the ruler of the city heard the words of Gaal son of Ebed, his anger was kindled. 31He sent messengers to Abimelech at Arumah,b saying, "Look, Gaal son of Ebed and his kinsfolk have come to Shechem, and they are stirring upc the city against you. 32Now therefore, go by night, you and the troops that are with you, and lie in wait in the fields. 33Then early in the morning, as soon as the sun rises, get up and rush on the city; and when he and the troops that are with him come out against you, you may deal with them as best you can."

34 So Abimelech and all the troops with him got up by night and lay in wait against Shechem in four companies. 35When Gaal son of Ebed went out and stood in the entrance of the gate of the city, Abimelech and the troops with him rose from the ambush. 36And when Gaal saw them, he said to Zebul, "Look, people are coming down from the mountain tops!" And Zebul said to him, "The shadows on the mountains look like people to you." 37Gaal spoke again and said, "Look, people are coming down from Tabbur-erez, and one company is coming from the direction of Elon-meonenim."d 38Then Zebul said to him, "Where is your boaste now, you who said, 'Who is Abimelech, that we should serve him?' Are not these the troops you made light of? Go out now and fight with them." 39So Gaal went out at the head of the lords of Shechem, and fought with Abimelech. 40Abimelech chased him, and he fled before him. Many fell wounded, up to the entrance of the gate. 41So Abimelech resided at Arumah; and

Zebul drove out Gaal and his kinsfolk, so that they could not live on at Shechem.

42 On the following day the people went out into the fields. When Abimelech was told, 43he took his troops and divided them into three companies, and lay in wait in the fields. When he looked and saw the people coming out of the city, he rose against them and killed them. 44Abimelech and the company that wasf with him rushed forward and stood at the entrance of the gate of the city, while the two companies rushed on all who were in the fields and killed them. 45Abimelech fought against the city all that day; he took the city, and killed the people that were in it; and he razed the city and sowed it with salt.

46 When all the lords of the Tower of Shechem heard of it, they entered the stronghold of the temple of El-berith. 47Abimelech was told that all the lords of the Tower of Shechem were gathered together. 48So Abimelech went up to Mount Zalmon, he and all the troops that were with him. Abimelech took an ax in his hand, cut down a bundle of brushwood, and took it up and laid it on his shoulder. Then he said to the troops with him, "What you have seen me do, do quickly, as I have done." 49So every one of the troops cut down a bundle and following Abimelech put it against the stronghold, and they set the stronghold on fire over them, so that all the people of the Tower of Shechem also died, about a thousand men and women.

50 Then Abimelech went to Thebez, and encamped against Thebez, and took it. 51But there was a strong tower within the city, and all the men and women and all the lords of the city fled to it and shut themselves in; and they went to the roof of the tower. 52Abimelech came to the tower, and fought against it, and came near to the entrance of

a 9.29 Gk: Heb and he said   b 9.31 Cn
See 9.41. Heb Tormah   c 9.31 Cn: Heb are
besieging   d 9.37 That is Diviners' Oak
e 9.38 Heb mouth   f 9.44 Vg and some Gk
Mss: Heb companies that were

the tower to burn it with fire. ⁵³But a certain woman threw an upper millstone on Abimelech's head, and crushed his skull. ⁵⁴Immediately he called to the young man who carried his armor and said to him, "Draw your sword and kill me, so people will not say about me, 'A woman killed him.' " So the young man thrust him through, and he died. ⁵⁵When the Israelites saw that Abimelech was dead, they all went home. ⁵⁶Thus God repaid Abimelech for the crime he committed against his father in killing his seventy brothers; ⁵⁷and God also made all the wickedness of the people of Shechem fall back on their heads, and on them came the curse of Jotham son of Jerubbaal.

TOLA AND JAIR

10 After Abimelech, Tola son of Puah son of Dodo, a man of Issachar, who lived at Shamir in the hill country of Ephraim, rose to deliver Israel. ²He judged Israel twenty-three years. Then he died, and was buried at Shamir.

³After him came Jair the Gileadite, who judged Israel twenty-two years. ⁴He had thirty sons who rode on thirty donkeys; and they had thirty towns, which are in the land of Gilead, and are called Havvoth-jair to this day. ⁵Jair died, and was buried in Kamon.

OPPRESSION BY THE AMMONITES

⁶The Israelites again did what was evil in the sight of the LORD, worshiping the Baals and the Astartes, the gods of Aram, the gods of Sidon, the gods of Moab, the gods of the Ammonites, and the gods of the Philistines. Thus they abandoned the LORD, and did not worship him. ⁷So the anger of the LORD was kindled against Israel, and he sold them into the hand of the Philistines and into the hand of the Ammonites, ⁸and they crushed and oppressed the Israelites that year. For eighteen years they oppressed all the Israelites that were beyond the Jordan in the land of the Amorites, which

is in Gilead. ⁹The Ammonites also crossed the Jordan to fight against Judah and against Benjamin and against the house of Ephraim; so that Israel was greatly distressed.

¹⁰So the Israelites cried to the LORD, saying, "We have sinned against you, because we have abandoned our God and have worshiped the Baals." ¹¹And the LORD said to the Israelites, "Did I not deliver you[a] from the Egyptians and from the Amorites, from the Ammonites and from the Philistines? ¹²The Sidonians also, and the Amalekites, and the Maonites, oppressed you; and you cried to me, and I delivered you out of their hand. ¹³Yet you have abandoned me and worshiped other gods; therefore I will deliver you no more. ¹⁴Go and cry to the gods whom you have chosen; let them deliver you in the time of your distress." ¹⁵And the Israelites said to the LORD, "We have sinned; do to us whatever seems good to you; but deliver us this day!" ¹⁶So they put away the foreign gods from among them and worshiped the LORD; and he could no longer bear to see Israel suffer.

¹⁷Then the Ammonites were called to arms, and they encamped in Gilead; and the Israelites came together, and they encamped at Mizpah. ¹⁸The commanders of the people of Gilead said to one another, "Who will begin the fight against the Ammonites? He shall be head over all the inhabitants of Gilead."

JEPHTHAH

11 Now Jephthah the Gileadite, the son of a prostitute, was a mighty warrior. Gilead was the father of Jephthah. ²Gilead's wife also bore him sons; and when his wife's sons grew up, they drove Jephthah away, saying to him, "You shall not inherit anything in our father's house; for you are the son of another woman." ³Then Jephthah fled from his brothers and lived in the land of Tob. Outlaws collected around Jephthah and went raiding with him.

^a **10.11** Heb lacks *Did I not deliver you*

4 After a time the Ammonites made war against Israel. 5 And when the Ammonites made war against Israel, the elders of Gilead went to bring Jephthah from the land of Tob. 6 They said to Jephthah, "Come and be our commander, so that we may fight with the Ammonites." 7 But Jephthah said to the elders of Gilead, "Are you not the very ones who rejected me and drove me out of my father's house? So why do you come to me now when you are in trouble?" 8 The elders of Gilead said to Jephthah, "Nevertheless, we have now turned back to you, so that you may go with us and fight with the Ammonites, and become head over us, over all the inhabitants of Gilead." 9 Jephthah said to the elders of Gilead, "If you bring me home again to fight with the Ammonites, and the LORD gives them over to me, I will be your head." 10 And the elders of Gilead said to Jephthah, "The LORD will be witness between us; we will surely do as you say." 11 So Jephthah went with the elders of Gilead, and the people made him head and commander over them; and Jephthah spoke all his words before the LORD at Mizpah.

12 Then Jephthah sent messengers to the king of the Ammonites and said, "What is there between you and me, that you have come to me to fight against my land?" 13 The king of the Ammonites answered the messengers of Jephthah, "Because Israel, on coming from Egypt, took away my land from the Arnon to the Jabbok and to the Jordan; now therefore restore it peaceably." 14 Once again Jephthah sent messengers to the king of the Ammonites 15 and said to him: "Thus says Jephthah: Israel did not take away the land of Moab or the land of the Ammonites, 16 but when they came up from Egypt, Israel went through the wilderness to the Red Sea[a] and came to Kadesh. 17 Israel then sent messengers to the king of Edom, saying, 'Let us pass through your land'; but the king of Edom would not listen. They also sent to the king of Moab, but he would not consent. So Israel remained at Kadesh. 18 Then they

journeyed through the wilderness, went around the land of Edom and the land of Moab, arrived on the east side of the land of Moab, and camped on the other side of the Arnon. They did not enter the territory of Moab, for the Arnon was the boundary of Moab. 19 Israel then sent messengers to King Sihon of the Amorites, king of Heshbon; and Israel said to him, 'Let us pass through your land to our country.' 20 But Sihon did not trust Israel to pass through his territory; so Sihon gathered all his people together, and encamped at Jahaz, and fought with Israel. 21 Then the LORD, the God of Israel, gave Sihon and all his people into the hand of Israel, and they defeated them; so Israel occupied all the land of the Amorites, who inhabited that country. 22 They occupied all the territory of the Amorites from the Arnon to the Jabbok and from the wilderness to the Jordan. 23 So now the LORD, the God of Israel, has conquered the Amorites for the benefit of his people Israel. Do you intend to take their place? 24 Should you not possess what your god Chemosh gives you to possess? And should we not be the ones to possess everything that the LORD our God has conquered for our benefit? 25 Now are you any better than King Balak son of Zippor of Moab? Did he ever enter into conflict with Israel, or did he ever go to war with them? 26 While Israel lived in Heshbon and its villages, and in Aroer and its villages, and in all the towns that are along the Arnon, three hundred years, why did you not recover them within that time? 27 It is not I who have sinned against you, but you are the one who does me wrong by making war on me. Let the LORD, who is judge, decide today for the Israelites or for the Ammonites." 28 But the king of the Ammonites did not heed the message that Jephthah sent him.

JEPHTHAH'S VOW

29 Then the spirit of the LORD came upon Jephthah, and he passed through Gilead and Manasseh. He

a 11.16 Or Sea of Reeds

passed on to Mizpah of Gilead, and from Mizpah of Gilead he passed on to the Ammonites. ³⁰And Jephthah made a vow to the LORD, and said, "If you will give the Ammonites into my hand, ³¹then whoever comes out of the doors of my house to meet me, when I return victorious from the Ammonites, shall be the LORD's, to be offered up by me as a burnt offering." ³²So Jephthah crossed over to the Ammonites to fight against them; and the LORD gave them into his hand. ³³He inflicted a massive defeat on them from Aroer to the neighborhood of Minnith, twenty towns, and as far as Abel-keramim. So the Ammonites were subdued before the people of Israel.

JEPHTHAH'S DAUGHTER

34 Then Jephthah came to his home at Mizpah; and there was his daughter coming out to meet him with timbrels and with dancing. She was his only child; he had no son or daughter except her. ³⁵When he saw her, he tore his clothes, and said, "Alas, my daughter! You have brought me very low; you have become the cause of great trouble to me. For I have opened my mouth to the LORD, and I cannot take back my vow." ³⁶She said to him, "My father, if you have opened your mouth to the LORD, do to me according to what has gone out of your mouth, now that the LORD has given you vengeance against your enemies, the Ammonites." ³⁷And she said to her father, "Let this thing be done for me: Grant me two months, so that I may go and wander[a] on the mountains, and bewail my virginity, my companions and I." ³⁸"Go," he said and sent her away for two months. So she departed, she and her companions, and bewailed her virginity on the mountains. ³⁹At the end of two months, she returned to her father, who did with her according to the vow he had made. She had never slept with a man. So there arose an Israelite custom that ⁴⁰for four days every year the daughters of Israel would go out to lament the daughter of Jephthah the Gileadite.

INTERTRIBAL DISSENSION

12 The men of Ephraim were called to arms, and they crossed to Zaphon and said to Jephthah, "Why did you cross over to fight against the Ammonites, and did not call us to go with you? We will burn your house down over you!" ²Jephthah said to them, "My people and I were engaged in conflict with the Ammonites who oppressed us[b] severely. But when I called you, you did not deliver me from their hand. ³When I saw that you would not deliver me, I took my life in my hand, and crossed over against the Ammonites, and the LORD gave them into my hand. Why then have you come up to me this day, to fight against me?" ⁴Then Jephthah gathered all the men of Gilead and fought with Ephraim; and the men of Gilead defeated Ephraim, because they said, "You are fugitives from Ephraim, you Gileadites—in the heart of Ephraim and Manasseh."[c] ⁵Then the Gileadites took the fords of the Jordan against the Ephraimites. Whenever one of the fugitives of Ephraim said, "Let me go over," the men of Gilead would say to him, "Are you an Ephraimite?" When he said, "No," ⁶they said to him, "Then say Shibboleth," and he said, "Sibboleth," for he could not pronounce it right. Then they seized him and killed him at the fords of the Jordan. Forty-two thousand of the Ephraimites fell at that time.

7 Jephthah judged Israel six years. Then Jephthah the Gileadite died, and was buried in his town in Gilead.[d]

IBZAN, ELON, AND ABDON

8 After him Ibzan of Bethlehem judged Israel. ⁹He had thirty sons. He gave his thirty daughters in marriage outside his clan and brought in thirty young women from outside for his sons. He judged Israel seven years. ¹⁰Then Ibzan died, and was buried at Bethlehem.

a 11.37 Cn: Heb go down   b 12.2 Gk
OL, Syr H: Heb lacks who oppressed us
c 12.4 Meaning of Heb uncertain: Gk omits
because... Manasseh   d 12.7 Gk: Heb in the
towns of Gilead

11 After him Elon the Zebulunite judged Israel; and he judged Israel ten years. 12 Then Elon the Zebulunite died, and was buried at Aijalon in the land of Zebulun.

13 After him Abdon son of Hillel the Pirathonite judged Israel. 14 He had forty sons and thirty grandsons, who rode on seventy donkeys; he judged Israel eight years. 15 Then Abdon son of Hillel the Pirathonite died, and was buried at Pirathon in the land of Ephraim, in the hill country of the Amalekites.

THE BIRTH OF SAMSON

13 The Israelites again did what was evil in the sight of the LORD, and the LORD gave them into the hand of the Philistines forty years.

2 There was a certain man of Zorah, of the tribe of the Danites, whose name was Manoah. His wife was barren, having borne no children. 3 And the angel of the LORD appeared to the woman and said to her, "Although you are barren, having borne no children, you shall conceive and bear a son. 4 Now be careful not to drink wine or strong drink, or to eat anything unclean, 5 for you shall conceive and bear a son. No razor is to come on his head, for the boy shall be a nazirite[a] to God from birth. It is he who shall begin to deliver Israel from the hand of the Philistines." 6 Then the woman came and told her husband, "A man of God came to me, and his appearance was like that of an angel[b] of God, most awe-inspiring; I did not ask him where he came from, and he did not tell me his name; 7 but he said to me, 'You shall conceive and bear a son. So then drink no wine or strong drink, and eat nothing unclean, for the boy shall be a nazirite[a] to God from birth to the day of his death.'"

8 Then Manoah entreated the LORD, and said, "O LORD, I pray, let the man of God whom you sent come to us again and teach us what we are to do concerning the boy who will be born." 9 God listened to Manoah, and the angel of God came again to the woman as she sat in the field; but her husband Manoah was not with her. 10 So the woman ran quickly and told her husband, "The man who came to me the other day has appeared to me." 11 Manoah got up and followed his wife, and came to the man and said to him, "Are you the man who spoke to this woman?" And he said, "I am." 12 Then Manoah said, "Now when your words come true, what is to be the boy's rule of life; what is he to do?" 13 The angel of the LORD said to Manoah, "Let the woman give heed to all that I said to her. 14 She may not eat of anything that comes from the vine. She is not to drink wine or strong drink, or eat any unclean thing. She is to observe everything that I commanded her."

15 Manoah said to the angel of the LORD, "Allow us to detain you, and prepare a kid for you." 16 The angel of the LORD said to Manoah, "If you detain me, I will not eat your food; but if you want to prepare a burnt offering, then offer it to the LORD." (For Manoah did not know that he was the angel of the LORD.) 17 Then Manoah said to the angel of the LORD, "What is your name, so that we may honor you when your words come true?" 18 But the angel of the LORD said to him, "Why do you ask my name? It is too wonderful."

19 So Manoah took the kid with the grain offering, and offered it on the rock to the LORD, to him who works[c] wonders.[d] 20 When the flame went up toward heaven from the altar, the angel of the LORD ascended in the flame of the altar while Manoah and his wife looked on; and they fell on their faces to the ground. 21 The angel of the LORD did not appear again to Manoah and his wife. Then Manoah realized that it was the angel of the LORD. 22 And Manoah said to his wife, "We shall surely die, for we have seen God." 23 But his wife said to him, "If the LORD had meant to kill us, he would not have accepted

[a] 13.5,7 That is one separated or one consecrated [b] 13.6 Or the angel
[c] 13.19 Gk Vg: Heb and working
[d] 13.19 Heb wonders, while Manoah and his wife looked on

a burnt offering and a grain offering at our hands, or shown us all these things, or now announced to us such things as these." 24 The woman bore a son, and named him Samson. The boy grew, and the LORD blessed him. 25 The spirit of the LORD began to stir him in Mahaneh-dan, between Zorah and Eshtaol.

PONDER

The woman bore a son, and named him Samson. The boy grew, and the LORD blessed him. The spirit of the LORD began to stir him.

—Judges 13.24–25

PRAY

Lord God, we are grateful to read about Samson's mother and father who, though they may have been humble people in the world's eyes, received a message from you and didn't question it. They accepted the blessings that you gave them and adhered meticulously to your instructions. They were blessed with a fine young son, even though Samson didn't completely succeed in following you. Help us to remember to rely on you regardless of our natural abilities, wealth, influence or fame. Give us the courage to take advantage of the opportunities that you have given us, which are multifold. And may we always perform our tasks and achieve our goals in the name of our Savior, Jesus Christ. Amen.

SAMSON'S MARRIAGE

14 Once Samson went down to Timnah, and at Timnah he saw a Philistine woman. 2 Then he came up, and told his father and mother, "I saw a Philistine woman at Timnah; now get her for me as my wife." 3 But his father and mother said to him, "Is there not a woman among your kin, or among all our[a]

people, that you must go to take a wife from the uncircumcised Philistines?" But Samson said to his father, "Get her for me, because she pleases me." 4 His father and mother did not know that this was from the LORD; for he was seeking a pretext to act against the Philistines. At that time the Philistines had dominion over Israel.

5 Then Samson went down with his father and mother to Timnah. When he came to the vineyards of Timnah, suddenly a young lion roared at him. 6 The spirit of the LORD rushed on him, and he tore the lion apart barehanded as one might tear apart a kid. But he did not tell his father or his mother what he had done. 7 Then he went down and talked with the woman, and she pleased Samson. 8 After a while he returned to marry her, and he turned aside to see the carcass of the lion, and there was a swarm of bees in the body of the lion, and honey. 9 He scraped it out into his hands, and went on, eating as he went. When he came to his father and mother, he gave some to them, and they ate it. But he did not tell them that he had taken the honey from the carcass of the lion.

10 His father went down to the woman, and Samson made a feast there as the young men were accustomed to do. 11 When the people saw him, they brought thirty companions to be with him. 12 Samson said to them, "Let me now put a riddle to you. If you can explain it to me within the seven days of the feast, and find it out, then I will give you thirty linen garments and thirty festal garments. 13 But if you cannot explain it to me, then you shall give me thirty linen garments and thirty festal garments." So they said to him, "Ask your riddle; let us hear it." 14 He said to them,

"Out of the eater came
    something to eat.
Out of the strong came
    something sweet."

---

a 14.3 Cn: Heb my

But for three days they could not explain the riddle.

15 On the fourth[a] day they said to Samson's wife, "Coax your husband to explain the riddle to us, or we will burn you and your father's house with fire. Have you invited us here to impoverish us?" 16 So Samson's wife wept before him, saying, "You hate me; you do not really love me. You have asked a riddle of my people, but you have not explained it to me." He said to her, "Look, I have not told my father or my mother. Why should I tell you?" 17 She wept before him the seven days that their feast lasted; and because she nagged him, on the seventh day he told her. Then she explained the riddle to her people. 18 The men of the town said to him on the seventh day before the sun went down,

"What is sweeter than honey?
What is stronger than a lion?"

And he said to them,

"If you had not plowed
        with my heifer,
    you would not have found
        out my riddle."

19 Then the spirit of the LORD rushed on him, and he went down to Ashkelon. He killed thirty men of the town, took their spoil, and gave the festal garments to those who had explained the riddle. In hot anger he went back to his father's house. 20 And Samson's wife was given to his companion, who had been his best man.

SAMSON DEFEATS THE PHILISTINES

15 After a while, at the time of the wheat harvest, Samson went to visit his wife, bringing along a kid. He said, "I want to go into my wife's room." But her father would not allow him to go in. 2 Her father said, "I was sure that you had rejected her; so I gave her to your companion. Is not her younger sister prettier than she? Why not take her instead?" 3 Samson said to them, "This time, when I do mischief to the Philistines, I will be without blame." 4 So Samson went and caught three hundred foxes, and

took some torches; and he turned the foxes'[b] tail to tail, and put a torch between each pair of tails. 5 When he had set fire to the torches, he let the foxes go into the standing grain of the Philistines, and burned up the shocks and the standing grain, as well as the vineyards and[c] olive groves. 6 Then the Philistines asked, "Who has done this?" And they said, "Samson, the son-in-law of the Timnite, because he has taken Samson's wife and given her to his companion." So the Philistines came up, and burned her and her father. 7 Samson said to them, "If this is what you do, I swear I will not stop until I have taken revenge on you." 8 He struck them down hip and thigh with great slaughter; and he went down and stayed in the cleft of the rock of Etam.

9 Then the Philistines came up and encamped in Judah, and made a raid on Lehi. 10 The men of Judah said, "Why have you come up against us?" They said, "We have come up to bind Samson, to do to him as he did to us." 11 Then three thousand men of Judah went down to the cleft of the rock of Etam, and they said to Samson, "Do you not know that the Philistines are rulers over us? What then have you done to us?" He replied, "As they did to me, so I have done to them." 12 They said to him, "We have come down to bind you, so that we may give you into the hands of the Philistines." Samson answered them, "Swear to me that you yourselves will not attack me." 13 They said to him, "No, we will only bind you and give you into their hands; we will not kill you." So they bound him with two new ropes, and brought him up from the rock.

14 When he came to Lehi, the Philistines came shouting to meet him; and the spirit of the LORD rushed on him, and the ropes that were on his arms became like flax that has caught fire, and his bonds melted off his hands. 15 Then he found a fresh jawbone of a donkey, reached down

a 14.15 Gk Syr: Heb seventh   b 15.4 Heb them   c 15.5 Gk Tg Vg: Heb lacks and

and took it, and with it he killed a thousand men. 16 And Samson said,

"With the jawbone of a donkey,
heaps upon heaps,
with the jawbone of a donkey
I have slain a thousand men."

17 When he had finished speaking, he threw away the jawbone; and that place was called Ramath-lehi.[a]

18 By then he was very thirsty, and he called on the LORD, saying, "You have granted this great victory by the hand of your servant. Am I now to die of thirst, and fall into the hands of the uncircumcised?" 19 So God split open the hollow place that is at Lehi, and water came from it. When he drank, his spirit returned, and he revived. Therefore it was named En-hakkore,[b] which is at Lehi to this day. 20 And he judged Israel in the days of the Philistines twenty years.

SAMSON AND DELILAH

16 Once Samson went to Gaza, where he saw a prostitute and went in to her. 2 The Gazites were told,[c] "Samson has come here." So they circled around and lay in wait for him all night at the city gate. They kept quiet all night, thinking, "Let us wait until the light of the morning; then we will kill him." 3 But Samson lay only until midnight. Then at midnight he rose up, took hold of the doors of the city gate and the two posts, pulled them up, bar and all, put them on his shoulders, and carried them to the top of the hill that is in front of Hebron.

4 After this he fell in love with a woman in the valley of Sorek, whose name was Delilah. 5 The lords of the Philistines came to her and said to her, "Coax him, and find out what makes his strength so great, and how we may overpower him, so that we may bind him in order to subdue him; and we will each give you eleven hundred pieces of silver." 6 So Delilah said to Samson, "Please tell me what makes your strength so great, and how you could be bound, so that one could subdue you." 7 Samson said to her, "If they bind me with seven fresh bowstrings that are not dried out, then I shall become weak, and be like anyone else."

8 Then the lords of the Philistines brought her seven fresh bowstrings that had not dried out, and she bound him with them. 9 While men were lying in wait in an inner chamber, she said to him, "The Philistines are upon you, Samson!" But he snapped the bowstrings, as a strand of fiber snaps when it touches the fire. So the secret of his strength was not known.

10 Then Delilah said to Samson, "You have mocked me and told me lies; please tell me how you could be bound." 11 He said to her, "If they bind me with new ropes that have not been used, then I shall become weak, and be like anyone else." 12 So Delilah took new ropes and bound him with them, and said to him, "The Philistines are upon you, Samson!" (The men lying in wait were in an inner chamber.) But he snapped the ropes off his arms like a thread.

13 Then Delilah said to Samson, "Until now you have mocked me and told me lies; tell me how you could be bound." He said to her, "If you weave the seven locks of my head with the web and make it tight with the pin, then I shall become weak, and be like anyone else." 14 So while he slept, Delilah took the seven locks of his head and wove them into the web,[d] and made them tight with the pin. Then she said to him, "The Philistines are upon you, Samson!" But he awoke from his sleep, and pulled away the pin, the loom, and the web.

15 Then she said to him, "How can you say, 'I love you,' when your heart is not with me? You have mocked me three times now and have not told me what makes your strength so great." 16 Finally, after she had nagged him with her words day after day, and pestered him, he was tired to death. 17 So he told her his whole secret, and said to her, "A razor has never come upon my head; for I have been a nazirite[e] to God

[a] 15.17 That is *The Hill of the Jawbone*
[b] 15.19 That is *The Spring of the One who Called* [c] 16.2 Gk: Heb lacks *were told* [d] 16.14 Compare Gk: in verses 13–14, Heb lacks *and make it tight... into the web* [e] 16.17 That is *one separated* or *one consecrated*

from my mother's womb. If my head were shaved, then my strength would leave me; I would become weak, and be like anyone else."

18 When Delilah realized that he had told her his whole secret, she sent and called the lords of the Philistines, saying, "This time come up, for he has told his whole secret to me." Then the lords of the Philistines came up to her, and brought the money in their hands. 19She let him fall asleep on her lap; and she called a man, and had him shave off the seven locks of his head. He began to weaken,ᵃ and his strength left him. 20Then she said, "The Philistines are upon you, Samson!" When he awoke from his sleep, he thought, "I will go out as at other times, and shake myself free." But he did not know that the LORD had left him. 21So the Philistines seized him and gouged out his eyes. They brought him down to Gaza and bound him with bronze shackles; and he ground at the mill in the prison. 22But the hair of his head began to grow again after it had been shaved.

SAMSON'S DEATH

23 Now the lords of the Philistines gathered to offer a great sacrifice to their god Dagon, and to rejoice; for they said, "Our god has given Samson our enemy into our hand." 24When the people saw him, they praised their god; for they said, "Our god has given our enemy into our hand, the ravager of our country, who has killed many of us." 25And when their hearts were merry, they said, "Call Samson, and let him entertain us." So they called Samson out of the prison, and he performed for them. They made him stand between the pillars; 26and Samson said to the attendant who held him by the hand, "Let me feel the pillars on which the house rests, so that I may lean against them." 27Now the house was full of men and women; all the lords of the Philistines were there, and on the roof there were about three thousand men and women, who looked on while Samson performed.

28 Then Samson called to the LORD and said, "Lord GOD, remember me and strengthen me only this once, O God, so that with this one act of revenge I may pay back the Philistines for my two eyes."ᵇ 29And Samson grasped the two middle pillars on which the house rested, and he leaned his weight against them, his right hand on the one and his left hand on the other. 30Then Samson said, "Let me die with the Philistines." He strained with all his might; and the house fell on the lords and all the people who were in it. So those he killed at his death were more than those he had killed during his life. 31Then his brothers and all his family came down and took him and brought him up and buried him between Zorah and Eshtaol in the tomb of his father Manoah. He had judged Israel twenty years.

ᵃ 16.19 Gk: Heb *She began to torment him*
ᵇ 16.28 Or *so that I may be avenged upon the Philistines for one of my two eyes*

PONDER

Then Samson called to the LORD and said, "Lord GOD, remember me and strengthen me only this once, O God."
—Judges 16.28

PRAY

Father, we are thankful for the blessings that you have given many of us: freedom, adequate food, shelter, clothing, education, health care and the ability to worship you in peace. We pray, after reading about Samson, that you guard us from becoming complacent or self-satisfied. We are thankful that when we face challenges and trials, you are present and promise to strengthen us. We pray that we won't forget the perfect example set for us by Jesus Christ and our pledge as Christians to live accordingly. We ask in the name of our Savior, Jesus Christ. Amen.

MICAH AND THE LEVITE

17 There was a man in the hill country of Ephraim whose name was Micah. ²He said to his mother, "The eleven hundred pieces of silver that were taken from you, about which you uttered a curse, and even spoke it in my hearing,—that silver is in my possession; I took it; but now I will return it to you."ᵃ And his mother said, "May my son be blessed by the LORD!" ³Then he returned the eleven hundred pieces of silver to his mother; and his mother said, "I consecrate the silver to the LORD from my hand for my son, to make an idol of cast metal." ⁴So when he returned the money to his mother, his mother took two hundred pieces of silver, and gave it to the silversmith, who made it into an idol of cast metal; and it was in the house of Micah. ⁵This man Micah had a shrine, and he made an ephod and teraphim, and installed one of his sons, who became his priest. ⁶In those days there was no king in Israel; all the people did what was right in their own eyes.

7 Now there was a young man of Bethlehem in Judah, of the clan of Judah. He was a Levite residing there. ⁸This man left the town of Bethlehem in Judah, to live wherever he could find a place. He came to the house of Micah in the hill country of Ephraim to carry on his work.ᵇ ⁹Micah said to him, "From where do you come?" He replied, "I am a Levite of Bethlehem in Judah, and I am going to live wherever I can find a place." ¹⁰Then Micah said to him, "Stay with me, and be to me a father and a priest, and I will give you ten pieces of silver a year, a set of clothes, and your living."ᶜ ¹¹The Levite agreed to stay with the man; and the young man became to him like one of his sons. ¹²So Micah installed the Levite, and the young man became his priest, and was in the house of Micah. ¹³Then Micah said, "Now I know that the LORD will prosper me, because the Levite has become my priest."

THE MIGRATION OF DAN

18 In those days there was no king in Israel. And in those days the tribe of the Danites was seeking for itself a territory to live in; for until then no territory among the tribes of Israel had been allotted to them. ²So the Danites sent five valiant men from the whole number of their clan, from Zorah and from Eshtaol, to spy out the land and to explore it; and they said to them, "Go, explore the land." When they came to the hill country of Ephraim, to the house of Micah, they stayed there. ³While they were at Micah's house, they recognized the voice of the young Levite; so they went over and asked him, "Who brought you here? What are you doing in this place? What is your business here?" ⁴He said to them, "Micah did such and such for me, and he hired me, and I have become his priest." ⁵Then they said to him, "Inquire of God that we may know whether the mission we are undertaking will succeed." ⁶The priest replied, "Go in peace. The mission you are on is under the eye of the LORD."

7 The five men went on, and when they came to Laish, they observed the people who were there living securely, after the manner of the Sidonians, quiet and unsuspecting, lackingᵈ nothing on earth, and possessing wealth.ᵉ Furthermore, they were far from the Sidonians and had no dealings with Aram.ᶠ ⁸When they came to their kinsfolk at Zorah and Eshtaol, they said to them, "What do you report?" ⁹They said, "Come, let us go up against them; for we have seen the land, and it is very good. Will you do nothing? Do not be slow to go, but enter in and possess the land. ¹⁰When you go, you will come to an unsuspecting people. The land is broad—God has indeed given it into your hands—a place where there is no lack of anything on earth."

ᵃ **17.2** The words *but now I will return it to you* are transposed from the end of verse 3 in Heb   ᵇ **17.8** Or *Ephraim, continuing his journey*   ᶜ **17.10** Heb *living, and the Levite went*   ᵈ **18.7** Cn Compare 18.10: Meaning of Heb uncertain   ᵉ **18.7** Meaning of Heb uncertain   ᶠ **18.7** Symmachus: Heb *with anyone*

11 Six hundred men of the Danite clan, armed with weapons of war, set out from Zorah and Eshtaol, 12and went up and encamped at Kiriath-jearim in Judah. On this account that place is called Mahaneh-dan[a] to this day; it is west of Kiriath-jearim. 13From there they passed on to the hill country of Ephraim, and came to the house of Micah.

14 Then the five men who had gone to spy out the land (that is, Laish) said to their comrades, "Do you know that in these buildings there are an ephod, teraphim, and an idol of cast metal? Now therefore consider what you will do." 15So they turned in that direction and came to the house of the young Levite, at the home of Micah, and greeted him. 16While the six hundred men of the Danites, armed with their weapons of war, stood by the entrance of the gate, 17the five men who had gone to spy out the land proceeded to enter and take the idol of cast metal, the ephod, and the teraphim.[b] The priest was standing by the entrance of the gate with the six hundred men armed with weapons of war. 18When the men went into Micah's house and took the idol of cast metal, the ephod, and the teraphim, the priest said to them, "What are you doing?" 19They said to him, "Keep quiet! Put your hand over your mouth, and come with us, and be to us a father and a priest. Is it better for you to be priest to the house of one person, or to be priest to a tribe and clan in Israel?" 20Then the priest accepted the offer. He took the ephod, the teraphim, and the idol, and went along with the people.

21 So they resumed their journey, putting the little ones, the livestock, and the goods in front of them. 22When they were some distance from the home of Micah, the men who were in the houses near Micah's house were called out, and they overtook the Danites. 23They shouted to the Danites, who turned around and said to Micah, "What is the matter that you come with such a company?" 24He replied, "You take my gods that I made, and the priest, and go away, and what have I left? How then can you ask me, 'What is the matter?' " 25And the Danites said to him, "You had better not let your voice be heard among us or else hot-tempered fellows will attack you, and you will lose your life and the lives of your household." 26Then the Danites went their way. When Micah saw that they were too strong for him, he turned and went back to his home.

MANY TIMES WE ERRONEOUSLY
ANTICIPATE GOD'S WILL AND
ARE FRUSTRATED BECAUSE
OF IMPROPER TIMING OR
SUBSTANTIVE ERROR.

THE DANITES SETTLE IN LAISH

27 The Danites, having taken what Micah had made, and the priest who belonged to him, came to Laish, to a people quiet and unsuspecting, put them to the sword, and burned down the city. 28There was no deliverer, because it was far from Sidon and they had no dealings with Aram.[c] It was in the valley that belongs to Beth-rehob. They rebuilt the city, and lived in it. 29They named the city Dan, after their ancestor Dan, who was born to Israel; but the name of the city was formerly Laish. 30Then the Danites set up the idol for themselves. Jonathan son of Gershom, son of Moses,[d] and his sons were priests to the tribe of the Danites until the time the land went into captivity. 31So they maintained as their own Micah's idol that he had made, as long as the house of God was at Shiloh.

---

[a] 18.12 That is *Camp of Dan*
[b] 18.17 Compare 17.4, 5; 18.14: Heb *teraphim and the cast metal*   [c] 18.28 Cn Compare verse 7: Heb *with anyone*   [d] 18.30 Another reading is *son of Manasseh*

THE LEVITE'S CONCUBINE

19 In those days, when there was no king in Israel, a certain Levite, residing in the remote parts of the hill country of Ephraim, took to himself a concubine from Bethlehem in Judah. 2But his concubine became angry with[a] him, and she went away from him to her father's house at Bethlehem in Judah, and was there some four months. 3Then her husband set out after her, to speak tenderly to her and bring her back. He had with him his servant and a couple of donkeys. When he reached[b] her father's house, the girl's father saw him and came with joy to meet him. 4His father-in-law, the girl's father, made him stay, and he remained with him three days; so they ate and drank, and he[c] stayed there. 5On the fourth day they got up early in the morning, and he prepared to go; but the girl's father said to his son-in-law, "Fortify yourself with a bit of food, and after that you may go." 6So the two men sat and ate and drank together; and the girl's father said to the man, "Why not spend the night and enjoy yourself?" 7When the man got up to go, his father-in-law kept urging him until he spent the night there again. 8On the fifth day he got up early in the morning to leave; and the girl's father said, "Fortify yourself." So they lingered[d] until the day declined, and the two of them ate and drank.[e] 9When the man with his concubine and his servant got up to leave, his father-in-law, the girl's father, said to him, "Look, the day has worn on until it is almost evening. Spend the night. See, the day has drawn to a close. Spend the night here and enjoy yourself. Tomorrow you can get up early in the morning for your journey, and go home."

10 But the man would not spend the night; he got up and departed, and arrived opposite Jebus (that is, Jerusalem). He had with him a couple of saddled donkeys, and his concubine was with him. 11When they were near Jebus, the day was far spent, and the servant said to his master, "Come now, let us turn aside

to this city of the Jebusites, and spend the night in it." 12But his master said to him, "We will not turn aside into a city of foreigners, who do not belong to the people of Israel; but we will continue on to Gibeah." 13Then he said to his servant, "Come, let us try to reach one of these places, and spend the night at Gibeah or at Ramah." 14So they passed on and went their way; and the sun went down on them near Gibeah, which belongs to Benjamin. 15They turned aside there, to go in and spend the night at Gibeah. He went in and sat down in the open square of the city, but no one took them in to spend the night.

16 Then at evening there was an old man coming from his work in the field. The man was from the hill country of Ephraim, and he was residing in Gibeah. (The people of the place were Benjaminites.) 17When the old man looked up and saw the wayfarer in the open square of the city, he said, "Where are you going and where do you come from?" 18He answered him, "We are passing from Bethlehem in Judah to the remote parts of the hill country of Ephraim, from which I come. I went to Bethlehem in Judah; and I am going to my home.[f] Nobody has offered to take me in. 19We your servants have straw and fodder for our donkeys, with bread and wine for me and the woman and the young man along with us. We need nothing more." 20The old man said, "Peace be to you. I will care for all your wants; only do not spend the night in the square." 21So he brought him into his house, and fed the donkeys; they washed their feet, and ate and drank.

GIBEAH'S CRIME

22 While they were enjoying themselves, the men of the city, a perverse lot, surrounded the house,

[a] 19.2 Gk OL: Heb *prostituted herself against*   [b] 19.3 Gk: Heb *she brought him to*
[c] 19.4 Compare verse 7 and Gk: Heb *they*
[d] 19.8 Cn: Heb *Linger*   [e] 19.8 Gk: Heb lacks *and drank*   [f] 19.18 Gk Compare 19.29. Heb *to the house of the* LORD

and started pounding on the door. They said to the old man, the master of the house, "Bring out the man who came into your house, so that we may have intercourse with him." ²³And the man, the master of the house, went out to them and said to them, "No, my brothers, do not act so wickedly. Since this man is my guest, do not do this vile thing. ²⁴Here are my virgin daughter and his concubine; let me bring them out now. Ravish them and do whatever you want to them; but against this man do not do such a vile thing." ²⁵But the men would not listen to him. So the man seized his concubine, and put her out to them. They wantonly raped her, and abused her all through the night until the morning. And as the dawn began to break, they let her go. ²⁶As morning appeared, the woman came and fell down at the door of the man's house where her master was, until it was light. 27 In the morning her master got up, opened the doors of the house, and when he went out to go on his way, there was his concubine lying at the door of the house, with her hands on the threshold. ²⁸"Get up," he said to her, "we are going." But there was no answer. Then he put her on the donkey; and the man set out for his home. ²⁹When he had entered his house, he took a knife, and grasping his concubine he cut her into twelve pieces, limb by limb, and sent her throughout all the territory of Israel. ³⁰Then he commanded the men whom he sent, saying, "Thus shall you say to all the Israelites, 'Has such a thing ever happenedª since the day that the Israelites came up from the land of Egypt until this day? Consider it, take counsel, and speak out.' "

THE OTHER TRIBES ATTACK BENJAMIN

20 Then all the Israelites came out, from Dan to Beer-sheba, including the land of Gilead, and the congregation assembled in one body before the LORD at Mizpah. ²The chiefs of all the people, of all the tribes of Israel, presented themselves in the assembly of the people of God, four hundred thousand foot-soldiers bearing arms. ³(Now the Benjaminites heard that the people of Israel had gone up to Mizpah.) And the Israelites said, "Tell us, how did this criminal act come about?" ⁴The Levite, the husband of the woman who was murdered, answered, "I came to Gibeah that belongs to Benjamin, I and my concubine, to spend the night. ⁵The lords of Gibeah rose up against me, and surrounded the house at night. They intended to kill me, and they raped my concubine until she died. ⁶Then I took my concubine and cut her into pieces, and sent her throughout the whole extent of Israel's territory; for they have committed a vile outrage in Israel. ⁷So now, you Israelites, all of you, give your advice and counsel here."

8 All the people got up as one, saying, "We will not any of us go to our tents, nor will any of us return to our houses. ⁹But now this is what we will do to Gibeah: we will go upᵇ against it by lot. ¹⁰We will take ten men of a hundred throughout all the tribes of Israel, and a hundred of a thousand, and a thousand of ten thousand, to bring provisions for the troops, who are going to repayᶜ Gibeah of Benjamin for all the disgrace that they have done in Israel." ¹¹So all the men of Israel gathered against the city, united as one. 12 The tribes of Israel sent men through all the tribe of Benjamin, saying, "What crime is this that has been committed among you? ¹³Now then, hand over those scoundrels in Gibeah, so that we may put them to death, and purge the evil from Israel." But the Benjaminites would not listen to their kinsfolk, the Israelites. ¹⁴The Benjaminites came together out of the towns to Gibeah, to go out to battle against the Israelites. ¹⁵On that day the Benjaminites

ª 19.30 Compare Gk: Heb ³⁰And all who saw it said, "Such a thing has not happened or been seen ᵇ 20.9 Gk: Heb lacks we will go up ᶜ 20.10 Compare Gk: Meaning of Heb uncertain

mustered twenty-six thousand armed men from their towns, besides the inhabitants of Gibeah. 16Of all this force, there were seven hundred picked men who were left-handed; every one could sling a stone at a hair, and not miss. 17And the Israelites, apart from Benjamin, mustered four hundred thousand armed men, all of them warriors.

18 The Israelites proceeded to go up to Bethel, where they inquired of God, "Which of us shall go up first to battle against the Benjaminites?" And the LORD answered, "Judah shall go up first."

19 Then the Israelites got up in the morning, and encamped against Gibeah. 20The Israelites went out to battle against Benjamin; and the Israelites drew up the battle line against them at Gibeah. 21The Benjaminites came out of Gibeah, and struck down on that day twenty-two thousand of the Israelites. 23a The Israelites went up and wept before the LORD until the evening; and they inquired of the LORD, "Shall we again draw near to battle against our kinsfolk the Benjaminites?" And the LORD said, "Go up against them." 22The Israelites took courage, and again formed the battle line in the same place where they had formed it on the first day.

24 So the Israelites advanced against the Benjaminites the second day. 25Benjamin moved out against them from Gibeah the second day, and struck down eighteen thousand of the Israelites, all of them armed men. 26Then all the Israelites, the whole army, went back to Bethel and wept, sitting there before the LORD; they fasted that day until evening. Then they offered burnt offerings and sacrifices of well-being before the LORD. 27And the Israelites inquired of the LORD (for the ark of the covenant of God was there in those days, 28and Phinehas son of Eleazar, son of Aaron, ministered before it in those days), saying, "Shall we go out once more to battle against our kinsfolk the Benjaminites, or shall we desist?" The LORD answered, "Go up, for tomorrow I will give them into your hand."

29 So Israel stationed men in ambush around Gibeah. 30Then the Israelites went up against the Benjaminites on the third day, and set themselves in array against Gibeah, as before. 31When the Benjaminites went out against the army, they were drawn away from the city. As before they began to inflict casualties on the troops, along the main roads, one of which goes up to Bethel and the other to Gibeah, as well as in the open country, killing about thirty men of Israel. 32The Benjaminites thought, "They are being routed before us, as previously." But the Israelites said, "Let us retreat and draw them away from the city toward the roads." 33The main body of the Israelites drew back its battle line to Baal-tamar, while those Israelites who were in ambush rushed out of their place westb of Geba. 34There came against Gibeah ten thousand picked men out of all Israel, and the battle was fierce. But the Benjaminites did not realize that disaster was close upon them.

35 The LORD defeated Benjamin before Israel; and the Israelites destroyed twenty-five thousand one hundred men of Benjamin that day, all of them armed.

36 Then the Benjaminites saw that they were defeated.c

The Israelites gave ground to Benjamin, because they trusted to the troops in ambush that they had stationed against Gibeah. 37The troops in ambush rushed quickly upon Gibeah. Then they put the whole city to the sword. 38Now the agreement between the main body of Israel and the men in ambush was that when they sent up a cloud of smoke out of the city 39the main body of Israel should turn in battle. But Benjamin had begun to inflict casualties on the Israelites, killing about thirty of them; so they thought, "Surely they are defeated before us, as in the first battle." 40But when the cloud, a column of smoke, began to rise out of the city, the Benjaminites looked

---

a 20.23 Verses 22 and 23 are transposed
b 20.33 Gk Vg: Heb in the plain   c 20.36 This sentence is continued by verse 45.

behind them—and there was the whole city going up in smoke toward the sky! 41Then the main body of Israel turned, and the Benjaminites were dismayed, for they saw that disaster was close upon them. 42Therefore they turned away from the Israelites in the direction of the wilderness; but the battle overtook them, and those who came out of the city[a] were slaughtering them in between.[b] 43Cutting down[c] the Benjaminites, they pursued them from Nohah[d] and trod them down as far as a place east of Gibeah. 44Eighteen thousand Benjaminites fell, all of them courageous fighters. 45When they turned and fled toward the wilderness to the rock of Rimmon, five thousand of them were cut down on the main roads, and they were pursued as far as Gidom, and two thousand of them were slain. 46So all who fell that day of Benjamin were twenty-five thousand arms-bearing men, all of them courageous fighters. 47But six hundred turned and fled toward the wilderness to the rock of Rimmon, and remained at the rock of Rimmon for four months. 48Meanwhile, the Israelites turned back against the Benjaminites, and put them to the sword—the city, the people, the animals, and all that remained. Also the remaining towns they set on fire.

THE BENJAMINITES SAVED FROM EXTINCTION

21 Now the Israelites had sworn at Mizpah, "No one of us shall give his daughter in marriage to Benjamin." 2And the people came to Bethel, and sat there until evening before God, and they lifted up their voices and wept bitterly. 3They said, "O LORD, the God of Israel, why has it come to pass that today there should be one tribe lacking in Israel?" 4On the next day, the people got up early, and built an altar there, and offered burnt offerings and sacrifices of well-being. 5Then the Israelites said, "Which of all the tribes of Israel did not come up in the assembly to the LORD?" For a solemn oath had been taken concerning whoever

did not come up to the LORD to Mizpah, saying, "That one shall be put to death." 6But the Israelites had compassion for Benjamin their kin, and said, "One tribe is cut off from Israel this day. 7What shall we do for wives for those who are left, since we have sworn by the LORD that we will not give them any of our daughters as wives?"

8 Then they said, "Is there anyone from the tribes of Israel who did not come up to the LORD to Mizpah?" It turned out that no one from Jabesh-gilead had come to the camp, to the assembly. 9For when the roll was called among the people, not one of the inhabitants of Jabesh-gilead was there. 10So the congregation sent twelve thousand soldiers there and commanded them, "Go, put the inhabitants of Jabesh-gilead to the sword, including the women and the little ones. 11This is what you shall do; every male and every woman that has lain with a male you shall devote to destruction." 12And they found among the inhabitants of Jabesh-gilead four hundred young virgins who had never slept with a man and brought them to the camp at Shiloh, which is in the land of Canaan.

13 Then the whole congregation sent word to the Benjaminites who were at the rock of Rimmon, and proclaimed peace to them. 14Benjamin returned at that time; and they gave them the women whom they had saved alive of the women of Jabesh-gilead; but they did not suffice for them.

15 The people had compassion on Benjamin because the LORD had made a breach in the tribes of Israel. 16So the elders of the congregation said, "What shall we do for wives for those who are left, since there are no women left in Benjamin?" 17And they said, "There must be heirs for the survivors of Benjamin, in order that a tribe may not be blotted out

---

[a] 20.42 Compare Vg and some Gk Mss: Heb cities [b] 20.42 Compare Syr: Meaning of Heb uncertain [c] 20.43 Gk: Heb Surrounding [d] 20.43 Gk: Heb pursued them at their resting place

from Israel. ¹⁸Yet we cannot give any of our daughters to them as wives." For the Israelites had sworn, "Cursed be anyone who gives a wife to Benjamin." ¹⁹So they said, "Look, the yearly festival of the LORD is taking place at Shiloh, which is north of Bethel, on the east of the highway that goes up from Bethel to Shechem, and south of Lebonah." ²⁰And they instructed the Benjaminites, saying, "Go and lie in wait in the vineyards, ²¹and watch; when the young women of Shiloh come out to dance in the dances, then come out of the vineyards and each of you carry off a wife for himself from the young women of Shiloh, and go to the land of Benjamin. ²²Then if their

fathers or their brothers come to complain to us, we will say to them, 'Be generous and allow us to have them; because we did not capture in battle a wife for each man. But neither did you incur guilt by giving your daughters to them.' " ²³The Benjaminites did so; they took wives for each of them from the dancers whom they abducted. Then they went and returned to their territory, and rebuilt the towns, and lived in them. ²⁴So the Israelites departed from there at that time by tribes and families, and they went out from there to their own territories.

²⁵ In those days there was no king in Israel; all the people did what was right in their own eyes.

RUTH

God often uses difficult or confusing times in our lives to fulfill his purposes, and often goes about that work in ways that surprise us. Take Ruth's story, for example. This short book gives us an intimate glimpse into the lives of Ruth, Naomi and Boaz. We see how, in the midst of grief and loss, their true faith and devotion to God led them into self-giving love for each other. In this ancient love story, God responded to the needs of ordinary people and unfolded an extraordinary design for their salvation.

ELIMELECH'S FAMILY
GOES TO MOAB

1 In the days when the judges ruled, there was a famine in the land, and a certain man of Bethlehem in Judah went to live in the country of Moab, he and his wife and two sons. ²The name of the man was Elimelech and the name of his wife Naomi, and the names of his two sons were Mahlon and Chilion; they were Ephrathites from Bethlehem in Judah. They went into the country of Moab and remained there. ³But Elimelech, the husband of Naomi, died, and she was left with her two sons. ⁴These took Moabite wives; the name of the one was Orpah and the name of the other Ruth. When they had lived there about ten years, ⁵both Mahlon and Chilion also died, so that the woman was left without her two sons and her husband.

NAOMI AND HER MOABITE
DAUGHTERS-IN-LAW

6 Then she started to return with her daughters-in-law from the country of Moab, for she had heard in the country of Moab that the LORD had considered his people and given them food. ⁷So she set out from the place where she had been living, she and her two daughters-in-law, and they went on their way to go back to the land of Judah. ⁸But Naomi said to her two daughters-in-law, "Go back each of you to your mother's house. May the LORD deal kindly with you, as you have dealt with the dead and with me. ⁹The LORD grant that you may find security, each of you in the house of your husband." Then she kissed them, and they wept aloud. ¹⁰They said to her, "No, we will return with you to your people." ¹¹But Naomi said, "Turn back, my daughters, why will you go with me? Do I still have sons in my womb that they may become your husbands? ¹²Turn back, my daughters, go your way, for I am too old to have a husband. Even if I thought there was hope for me, even if I should have a husband tonight and bear sons, ¹³would you then wait until they were grown?

Would you then refrain from marrying? No, my daughters, it has been far more bitter for me than for you, because the hand of the LORD has turned against me." ¹⁴Then they wept aloud again. Orpah kissed her mother-in-law, but Ruth clung to her.

15 So she said, "See, your sister-in-law has gone back to her people and to her gods; return after your sister-in-law." ¹⁶But Ruth said,
"Do not press me to leave you
    or to turn back from
    following you!
Where you go, I will go;
    where you lodge, I will lodge;
your people shall be my people,
    and your God my God.
¹⁷ Where you die, I will die—
    there will I be buried.
May the LORD do thus
    and so to me,
    and more as well,
if even death parts me from you!"
¹⁸When Naomi saw that she was determined to go with her, she said no more to her.

19 So the two of them went on until they came to Bethlehem. When they came to Bethlehem, the whole town was stirred because of them; and the women said, "Is this Naomi?" ²⁰She said to them,
"Call me no longer Naomi,ᵃ
    call me Mara,ᵇ
for the Almightyᶜ has dealt
    bitterly with me.
²¹ I went away full,
    but the LORD has brought
    me back empty;
why call me Naomi
    when the LORD has dealt
    harshly withᵈ me,
    and the Almightyᶜ has brought
    calamity upon me?"
22 So Naomi returned together with Ruth the Moabite, her daughter-in-law, who came back with her from the country of Moab. They came to Bethlehem at the beginning of the barley harvest.

ᵃ 1.20 That is *Pleasant*   ᵇ 1.20 That is *Bitter*
ᶜ 1.20,21 Traditional rendering of Heb *Shaddai*   ᵈ 1.21 Or *has testified against*

PONDER

But Ruth said, "Do not press me to leave you or to turn back from following you! Where you go, I will go; where you lodge, I will lodge; your people shall be my people, and your God my God."
—Ruth 1.16

PRAY

Lord of all, as we read these verses and the beautiful story of Ruth's love and commitment to Naomi, we are reminded that you extend your grace and love to people without regard to their station in life, their position or nationality. Help us to overcome the limitations we place on ourselves, to live with open hearts and inquiring minds, and to expansively reach out as Christ did to those who are poor, despised, ignored, criticized or afflicted. Give us love to help and support our brothers and sisters in the name of our Savior, Jesus Christ. Amen.

RUTH MEETS BOAZ

2 Now Naomi had a kinsman on her husband's side, a prominent rich man, of the family of Elimelech, whose name was Boaz. ²And Ruth the Moabite said to Naomi, "Let me go to the field and glean among the ears of grain, behind someone in whose sight I may find favor." She said to her, "Go, my daughter." ³So she went. She came and gleaned in the field behind the reapers. As it happened, she came to the part of the field belonging to Boaz, who was of the family of Elimelech. ⁴Just then Boaz came from Bethlehem. He said to the reapers, "The LORD be with you." They answered, "The LORD bless you." ⁵Then Boaz said to his servant who was in charge of the reapers, "To whom does this young woman belong?" ⁶The servant who was in charge of the reapers answered, "She is the Moabite who came back with Naomi from the country of Moab. ⁷She said, 'Please, let me glean and gather among the sheaves behind the reapers.' So she came, and she has been on her feet from early this morning until now, without resting even for a moment."[a]

8 Then Boaz said to Ruth, "Now listen, my daughter, do not go to glean in another field or leave this one, but keep close to my young women. ⁹Keep your eyes on the field that is being reaped, and follow behind them. I have ordered the young men not to bother you. If you get thirsty, go to the vessels and drink from what the young men have drawn." ¹⁰Then she fell prostrate, with her face to the ground, and said to him, "Why have I found favor in your sight, that you should take notice of me, when I am a foreigner?" ¹¹But Boaz answered her, "All that you have done for your mother-in-law since the death of your husband has been fully told me, and how you left your father and mother and your native land and came to a people that you did not know before. ¹²May the LORD reward you for your deeds, and may you have a full reward from the LORD, the God of Israel, under whose wings you have come for refuge!" ¹³Then she said, "May I continue to find favor in your sight, my lord, for you have comforted me and spoken kindly to your servant, even though I am not one of your servants."

14 At mealtime Boaz said to her, "Come here, and eat some of this bread, and dip your morsel in the sour wine." So she sat beside the reapers, and he heaped up for her some parched grain. She ate until she was satisfied, and she had some left over. ¹⁵When she got up to glean, Boaz instructed his young men, "Let her glean even among the standing sheaves, and do not reproach her. ¹⁶You must also pull out some handfuls for her from the bundles, and leave them for her to glean, and do not rebuke her."

ª 2.7 Compare Gk Vg: Meaning of Heb uncertain

17 So she gleaned in the field until evening. Then she beat out what she had gleaned, and it was about an ephah of barley. **18** She picked it up and came into the town, and her mother-in-law saw how much she had gleaned. Then she took out and gave her what was left over after she herself had been satisfied. **19** Her mother-in-law said to her, "Where did you glean today? And where have you worked? Blessed be the man who took notice of you." So she told her mother-in-law with whom she had worked, and said, "The name of the man with whom I worked today is Boaz." **20** Then Naomi said to her daughter-in-law, "Blessed be he by the LORD, whose kindness has not forsaken the living or the dead!" Naomi also said to her, "The man is a relative of ours, one of our nearest kin."[a] **21** Then Ruth the Moabite said, "He even said to me, 'Stay close by my servants, until they have finished all my harvest.'" **22** Naomi said to Ruth, her daughter-in-law, "It is better, my daughter, that you go out with his young women, otherwise you might be bothered in another field." **23** So she stayed close to the young women of Boaz, gleaning until the end of the barley and wheat harvests; and she lived with her mother-in-law.

RUTH AND BOAZ AT THE THRESHING FLOOR

3 Naomi her mother-in-law said to her, "My daughter, I need to seek some security for you, so that it may be well with you. **2** Now here is our kinsman Boaz, with whose young women you have been working. See, he is winnowing barley tonight at the threshing floor. **3** Now wash and anoint yourself, and put on your best clothes and go down to the threshing floor; but do not make yourself known to the man until he has finished eating and drinking. **4** When he lies down, observe the place where he lies; then, go and uncover his feet and lie down; and he will tell you what to do." **5** She said to her, "All that you tell me I will do."

6 So she went down to the threshing floor and did just as her mother-in-law had instructed her. **7** When Boaz had eaten and drunk, and he was in a contented mood, he went to lie down at the end of the heap of grain. Then she came stealthily and uncovered his feet, and lay down. **8** At midnight the man was startled, and turned over, and there, lying at his feet, was a woman! **9** He said, "Who are you?" And she answered, "I am Ruth, your servant; spread your cloak over your servant, for you are next-of-kin."[a] **10** He said, "May you be blessed by the LORD, my daughter; this last instance of your loyalty is better than the first; you have not gone after young men, whether poor or rich. **11** And now, my daughter, do not be afraid, I will do for you all that you ask, for all the assembly of my people know that you are a worthy woman. **12** But now, though it is true that I am a near kinsman, there is another kinsman more closely related than I. **13** Remain this night, and in the morning, if he will act as next-of-kin[a] for you, good; let him do it. If he is not willing to act as next-of-kin[a] for you, then, as the LORD lives, I will act as next-of-kin[a] for you. Lie down until the morning."

14 So she lay at his feet until morning, but got up before one person could recognize another; for he said, "It must not be known that the woman came to the threshing floor." **15** Then he said, "Bring the cloak you are wearing and hold it out." So she held it, and he measured out six measures of barley, and put it on her back; then he went into the city. **16** She came to her mother-in-law, who said, "How did things go with you,[b] my daughter?" Then she told her all that the man had done for her, **17** saying, "He gave me these six measures of barley, for he said, 'Do not go back to your mother-in-law empty-handed.'" **18** She replied, "Wait, my daughter, until you learn how the matter turns out, for the man will not rest, but will settle the matter today."

[a] 2.20; 3.9,13 Or one with the right to redeem
[b] 3.16 Or "Who are you,

THE MARRIAGE OF BOAZ AND RUTH

4 No sooner had Boaz gone up to the gate and sat down there than the next-of-kin,[a] of whom Boaz had spoken, came passing by. So Boaz said, "Come over, friend; sit down here." And he went over and sat down. ²Then Boaz took ten men of the elders of the city, and said, "Sit down here"; so they sat down. ³He then said to the next-of-kin,[a] "Naomi, who has come back from the country of Moab, is selling the parcel of land that belonged to our kinsman Elimelech. ⁴So I thought I would tell you of it, and say: Buy it in the presence of those sitting here, and in the presence of the elders of my people. If you will redeem it, redeem it; but if you will not, tell me, so that I may know; for there is no one prior to you to redeem it, and I come after you." So he said, "I will redeem it." ⁵Then Boaz said, "The day you acquire the field from the hand of Naomi, you are also acquiring Ruth[b] the Moabite, the widow of the dead man, to maintain the dead man's name on his inheritance." ⁶At this, the next-of-kin[a] said, "I cannot redeem it for myself without damaging my own inheritance. Take my right of redemption yourself, for I cannot redeem it."

THERE IS AN INTERWEAVING

OF DIVINE PURPOSE AND

HUMAN PLANNING IN ALMOST

EVERY BIBLICAL STORY.

⁷Now this was the custom in former times in Israel concerning redeeming and exchanging: to confirm a transaction, the one took off a sandal and gave it to the other; this was the manner of attesting in Israel. ⁸So when the next-of-kin[a] said to Boaz, "Acquire it for yourself," he took off his sandal. ⁹Then Boaz said to the elders and all the people, "Today you are witnesses that I have acquired from the hand of Naomi all that belonged to Elimelech and all that belonged to Chilion and Mahlon. ¹⁰I have also acquired Ruth the Moabite, the wife of Mahlon, to be my wife, to maintain the dead man's name on his inheritance, in order that the name of the dead may not be cut off from his kindred and from the gate of his native place; today you are witnesses." ¹¹Then all the people who were at the gate, along with the elders, said, "We are witnesses. May the LORD make the woman who is coming into your house like Rachel and Leah, who together built up the house of Israel. May you produce children in Ephrathah and bestow a name in Bethlehem; ¹²and, through the children that the LORD will give you by this young woman, may your house be like the house of Perez, whom Tamar bore to Judah."

THE GENEALOGY OF DAVID

13 So Boaz took Ruth and she became his wife. When they came together, the LORD made her conceive, and she bore a son. ¹⁴Then the women said to Naomi, "Blessed be the LORD, who has not left you this day without next-of-kin;[a] and may his name be renowned in Israel! ¹⁵He shall be to you a restorer of life and a nourisher of your old age; for your daughter-in-law who loves you, who is more to you than seven sons, has borne him." ¹⁶Then Naomi took the child and laid him in her bosom, and became his nurse. ¹⁷The women of the neighborhood gave him a name, saying, "A son has been born to Naomi." They named him Obed; he became the father of Jesse, the father of David.

18 Now these are the descendants of Perez: Perez became the father of Hezron, ¹⁹Hezron of Ram, Ram of Amminadab, ²⁰Amminadab of Nahshon, Nahshon of Salmon, ²¹Salmon of Boaz, Boaz of Obed, ²²Obed of Jesse, and Jesse of David.

[a] 4.1,3,6,8,14 Or one with the right to redeem
[b] 4.5 OL Vg: Heb from the hand of Naomi and from Ruth

1 SAMUEL

First Samuel is a story of contrast between a man who abandoned
God and a man who abandoned his life to God. Written by the prophet
Samuel, the book focuses on Israel's first two kings, Saul and David. Saul,
the first anointed king of Israel, chose to disobey God's directions. He
was tormented by his guilt, and later God rejected him as ruler of Israel.
In contrast, his successor, David, dedicated himself to the Lord, and God
blessed his reign. As we read 1 Samuel, the stirring stories of David and
Saul can inspire us to follow God wholeheartedly.

SAMUEL'S BIRTH AND DEDICATION

1 There was a certain man of Ramathaim, a Zuphite[a] from the hill country of Ephraim, whose name was Elkanah son of Jeroham son of Elihu son of Tohu son of Zuph, an Ephraimite. [2]He had two wives; the name of the one was Hannah, and the name of the other Peninnah. Peninnah had children, but Hannah had no children.

3 Now this man used to go up year by year from his town to worship and to sacrifice to the LORD of hosts at Shiloh, where the two sons of Eli, Hophni and Phinehas, were priests of the LORD. [4]On the day when Elkanah sacrificed, he would give portions to his wife Peninnah and to all her sons and daughters; [5]but to Hannah he gave a double portion,[b] because he loved her, though the LORD had closed her womb. [6]Her rival used to provoke her severely, to irritate her, because the LORD had closed her womb. [7]So it went on year by year; as often as she went up to the house of the LORD, she used to provoke her. Therefore Hannah wept and would not eat. [8]Her husband Elkanah said to her, "Hannah, why do you weep? Why do you not eat? Why is your heart sad? Am I not more to you than ten sons?"

9 After they had eaten and drunk at Shiloh, Hannah rose and presented herself before the LORD.[c] Now Eli the priest was sitting on the seat beside the doorpost of the temple of the LORD. [10]She was deeply distressed and prayed to the LORD, and wept bitterly. [11]She made this vow: "O LORD of hosts, if only you will look on the misery of your servant, and remember me, and not forget your servant, but will give to your servant a male child, then I will set him before you as a nazirite[d] until the day of his death. He shall drink neither wine nor intoxicants,[e] and no razor shall touch his head."

12 As she continued praying before the LORD, Eli observed her mouth. [13]Hannah was praying silently; only her lips moved, but her voice was not heard; therefore Eli thought she was drunk. [14]So Eli said to her, "How long will you make a drunken spectacle of yourself? Put away your wine." [15]But Hannah answered, "No, my lord, I am a woman deeply troubled; I have drunk neither wine nor strong drink, but I have been pouring out my soul before the LORD. [16]Do not regard your servant as a worthless woman, for I have been speaking out of my great anxiety and vexation all this time." [17]Then Eli answered, "Go in peace; the God of Israel grant the petition you have made to him." [18]And she said, "Let your servant find favor in your sight." Then the woman went to her quarters,[f] ate and drank with her husband,[g] and her countenance was sad no longer.[h]

19 They rose early in the morning and worshiped before the LORD; then they went back to their house at Ramah. Elkanah knew his wife Hannah, and the LORD remembered her. [20]In due time Hannah conceived and bore a son. She named him Samuel, for she said, "I have asked him of the LORD."

PRAYER IS NOT A PASSIVE ACT.

21 The man Elkanah and all his household went up to offer to the LORD the yearly sacrifice, and to pay his vow. [22]But Hannah did not go up, for she said to her husband, "As soon as the child is weaned, I will bring him, that he may appear in the presence of the LORD, and remain there forever; I will offer him as a nazirite[d] for all time."[i] [23]Her husband

---

[a] 1.1 Compare Gk and 1 Chr 6.35–36: Heb *Ramathaim-zophim*   [b] 1.5 Syr: Meaning of Heb uncertain   [c] 1.9 Gk: Heb lacks *and presented herself before the LORD*
[d] 1.11,22 That is *one separated* or *one consecrated*   [e] 1.11 Cn Compare Gk Q Ms 1.22: MT *then I will give him to the LORD all the days of his life*   [f] 1.18 Gk: Heb *went her way*   [g] 1.18 Gk: Heb lacks *and drank with her husband*   [h] 1.18 Gk: Meaning of Heb uncertain   [i] 1.22 Cn Compare Q Ms: MT lacks *I will offer him as a nazirite for all time*

Elkanah said to her, "Do what seems
best to you, wait until you have
weaned him; only—may the LORD
establish his word."[a] So the woman
remained and nursed her son, until
she weaned him. 24 When she had
weaned him, she took him up with
her, along with a three-year-old
bull,[b] an ephah of flour, and a skin of
wine. She brought him to the house
of the LORD at Shiloh; and the child
was young. 25 Then they slaughtered the bull, and they brought the
child to Eli. 26 And she said, "Oh, my
lord! As you live, my lord, I am the
woman who was standing here in
your presence, praying to the LORD.
27 For this child I prayed; and the
LORD has granted me the petition
that I made to him. 28 Therefore I
have lent him to the LORD; as long
as he lives, he is given to the LORD."
She left him there for[c] the LORD.

HANNAH'S PRAYER

2 Hannah prayed and said,
"My heart exults in the LORD;
my strength is exalted
in my God.[d]
My mouth derides my enemies,
because I rejoice in my[e] victory.

2 "There is no Holy One
like the LORD,
no one besides you;
there is no Rock like our God.
3 Talk no more so very proudly,
let not arrogance come
from your mouth;
for the LORD is a God of
knowledge,
and by him actions
are weighed.
4 The bows of the mighty
are broken,
but the feeble gird on strength.
5 Those who were full have hired
themselves out for bread,
but those who were hungry
are fat with spoil.
The barren has borne seven,
but she who has many
children is forlorn.
6 The LORD kills and brings to life;
he brings down to Sheol
and raises up.
7 The LORD makes poor and
makes rich;
he brings low, he also exalts.
8 He raises up the poor
from the dust;
he lifts the needy from
the ash heap,
to make them sit with princes
and inherit a seat of honor.[f]
For the pillars of the earth
are the LORD's,
and on them he has
set the world.

9 "He will guard the feet of
his faithful ones,
but the wicked shall be
cut off in darkness;
for not by might does
one prevail.
10 The LORD! His adversaries
shall be shattered;
the Most High[g] will
thunder in heaven.
The LORD will judge the
ends of the earth;
he will give strength
to his king,
and exalt the power of
his anointed."

ELI'S WICKED SONS

11 Then Elkanah went home to
Ramah, while the boy remained to
minister to the LORD, in the presence of the priest Eli.
12 Now the sons of Eli were
scoundrels; they had no regard for
the LORD 13 or for the duties of the
priests to the people. When anyone
offered sacrifice, the priest's servant
would come, while the meat was
boiling, with a three-pronged fork
in his hand, 14 and he would thrust it
into the pan, or kettle, or caldron, or
pot; all that the fork brought up the
priest would take for himself.[h] This
is what they did at Shiloh to all the

[a] 1.23 MT: Q Ms Gk Compare Syr *that which goes out of your mouth* [b] 1.24 Q Ms Gk Syr: MT *three bulls* [c] 1.28 Gk (Compare Q Ms) and Gk at 2.11: MT *And he* (that is, Elkanah) *worshiped there before* [d] 2.1 Gk: Heb *the LORD* [e] 2.1 Q Ms: MT *your* [f] 2.8 Gk (Compare Q Ms) adds *He grants the vow of the one who vows, and blesses the years of the just* [g] 2.10 Cn Heb *against him he* [h] 2.14 Gk Syr Vg: Heb *with it*

Israelites who came there. [15]Moreover, before the fat was burned, the priest's servant would come and say to the one who was sacrificing, "Give meat for the priest to roast; for he will not accept boiled meat from you, but only raw." [16]And if the man said to him, "Let them burn the fat first, and then take whatever you wish," he would say, "No, you must give it now; if not, I will take it by force." [17]Thus the sin of the young men was very great in the sight of the LORD; for they treated the offerings of the LORD with contempt.

THE CHILD SAMUEL AT SHILOH

[18] Samuel was ministering before the LORD, a boy wearing a linen ephod. [19]His mother used to make for him a little robe and take it to him each year, when she went up with her husband to offer the yearly sacrifice. [20]Then Eli would bless Elkanah and his wife, and say, "May the LORD repay[a] you with children by this woman for the gift that she made to[b] the LORD"; and then they would return to their home.

[21] And[c] the LORD took note of Hannah; she conceived and bore three sons and two daughters. And the boy Samuel grew up in the presence of the LORD.

PROPHECY AGAINST ELI'S HOUSEHOLD

[22] Now Eli was very old. He heard all that his sons were doing to all Israel, and how they lay with the women who served at the entrance to the tent of meeting. [23]He said to them, "Why do you do such things? For I hear of your evil dealings from all these people. [24]No, my sons; it is not a good report that I hear the people of the LORD spreading abroad. [25]If one person sins against another, someone can intercede for the sinner with the LORD;[d] but if someone sins against the LORD, who can make intercession?" But they would not listen to the voice of their father; for it was the will of the LORD to kill them.

[26] Now the boy Samuel continued to grow both in stature and in favor with the LORD and with the people.

[27] A man of God came to Eli and said to him, "Thus the LORD has said, 'I revealed[e] myself to the family of your ancestor in Egypt when they were slaves[f] to the house of Pharaoh. [28]I chose him out of all the tribes of Israel to be my priest, to go up to my altar, to offer incense, to wear an ephod before me; and I gave to the family of your ancestor all my offerings by fire from the people of Israel. [29]Why then look with greedy eye[g] at my sacrifices and my offerings that I commanded, and honor your sons more than me by fattening yourselves on the choicest parts of every offering of my people Israel?' [30]Therefore the LORD the God of Israel declares: 'I promised that your family and the family of your ancestor should go in and out before me forever'; but now the LORD declares: 'Far be it from me; for those who honor me I will honor, and those who despise me shall be treated with contempt. [31]See, a time is coming when I will cut off your strength and the strength of your ancestor's family, so that no one in your family will live to old age. [32]Then in distress you will look with greedy eye[h] on all the prosperity that shall be bestowed upon Israel; and no one in your family shall ever live to old age. [33]The only one of you whom I shall not cut off from my altar shall be spared to weep out his[i] eyes and grieve his[j] heart; all the members of your household shall die by the sword.[k] [34]The fate of your two sons, Hophni and Phinehas, shall be the sign to you—both of them shall die on the same day. [35]I will raise up for myself a faithful priest, who shall do according to what is in my heart and in my mind. I will build him a

---

[a] 2.20 Q Ms Gk: MT give   [b] 2.20 Q Ms Gk: MT for the petition that she asked of   [c] 2.21 Q Ms Gk: MT When   [d] 2.25 Gk Compare Q Ms: MT another, God will mediate for him   [e] 2.27 Gk Tg Syr: Heb Did I reveal   [f] 2.27 Q Ms Gk: MT lacks slaves   [g] 2.29 Q Ms Gk: MT then kick   [h] 2.32 Q Ms Gk: MT will kick   [i] 2.33 Q Ms Gk: MT your   [j] 2.33 Q Ms Gk: Heb your   [k] 2.33 Q Ms See Gk: MT die like mortals

sure house, and he shall go in and out before my anointed one forever. 36 Everyone who is left in your family shall come to implore him for a piece of silver or a loaf of bread, and shall say, Please put me in one of the priest's places, that I may eat a morsel of bread.' "

SAMUEL'S CALLING AND PROPHETIC ACTIVITY

3 Now the boy Samuel was ministering to the LORD under Eli. The word of the LORD was rare in those days; visions were not widespread.

2 At that time Eli, whose eyesight had begun to grow dim so that he could not see, was lying down in his room; 3 the lamp of God had not yet gone out, and Samuel was lying down in the temple of the LORD, where the ark of God was. 4 Then the LORD called, "Samuel! Samuel!"a and he said, "Here I am!" 5 and ran to Eli, and said, "Here I am, for you called me." But he said, "I did not call; lie down again." So he went and lay down. 6 The LORD called again, "Samuel!" Samuel got up and went to Eli, and said, "Here I am, for you called me." But he said, "I did not call, my son; lie down again." 7 Now Samuel did not yet know the LORD, and the word of the LORD had not yet been revealed to him. 8 The LORD called Samuel again, a third time. And he got up and went to Eli, and said, "Here I am, for you called me." Then Eli perceived that the LORD was calling the boy. 9 Therefore Eli said to Samuel, "Go, lie down; and if he calls you, you shall say, 'Speak, LORD, for your servant is listening.' " So Samuel went and lay down in his place.

10 Now the LORD came and stood there, calling as before, "Samuel! Samuel!" And Samuel said, "Speak, for your servant is listening." 11 Then the LORD said to Samuel, "See, I am about to do something in Israel that will make both ears of anyone who hears of it tingle. 12 On that day I will fulfill against Eli all that I have spoken concerning his house, from beginning to end. 13 For I have told

him that I am about to punish his house forever, for the iniquity that he knew, because his sons were blaspheming God,b and he did not restrain them. 14 Therefore I swear to the house of Eli that the iniquity of Eli's house shall not be expiated by sacrifice or offering forever."

15 Samuel lay there until morning; then he opened the doors of the house of the LORD. Samuel was afraid to tell the vision to Eli. 16 But Eli called Samuel and said, "Samuel, my son." He said, "Here I am." 17 Eli said, "What was it that he told you? Do not hide it from me. May God do so to you and more also, if you hide anything from me of all that he told you." 18 So Samuel told him everything and hid nothing from him. Then he said, "It is the LORD; let him do what seems good to him."

19 As Samuel grew up, the LORD was with him and let none of his words fall to the ground. 20 And all Israel from Dan to Beer-sheba knew that Samuel was a trustworthy prophet of the LORD. 21 The LORD continued to appear at Shiloh, for the LORD revealed himself to Samuel at Shiloh by the word of the LORD. 1 And the word of Samuel came to all Israel.

THE ARK OF GOD CAPTURED

In those days the Philistines mustered for war against Israel,c and Israel went out to battle against them;d they encamped at Ebenezer, and the Philistines encamped at Aphek. 2 The Philistines drew up in line against Israel, and when the battle was joined,e Israel was defeated by the Philistines, who killed about four thousand men on the field of battle. 3 When the troops came to the camp, the elders of Israel said, "Why has the LORD put us to rout today before the Philistines? Let us bring the ark of the covenant of the LORD here from Shiloh, so that he may

a 3.4 Q Ms Gk See 3.10: MT the LORD called Samuel   b 3.13 Another reading is for themselves   c 4.1 Gk: Heb lacks In those days the Philistines mustered for war against Israel   d 4.1 Gk: Heb against the Philistines   e 4.2 Meaning of Heb uncertain

FAITHFUL

As Samuel grew up, the LORD was with him and let none of his words fall to the ground.

—1 Samuel 3.19

Samuel was one of the most important leaders in Israel during the time of the judges. He led Israel during a difficult time of oppression by the Philistines and helped the nation progress from a loose confederation of tribes into a unified monarchy. What was it about Samuel that made him able to persevere and guide the nation through such tough times? The secret of Samuel's success as a judge of Israel was his unswerving faith in God.

Samuel demonstrated his faithfulness to God early in life. When he was a young boy, he was sent to live and serve in the temple of the Lord. One night, Samuel heard God calling him, and the boy willingly responded.

Though faced with many hardships, Samuel held fast to his faith. God granted Samuel wisdom and sound judgment as a judge in Israel. Samuel traveled as a circuit judge, deciding difficult cases and leading the people. Later, when the Israelites wanted a king to help them fight against the Philistines, Samuel listened to God and anointed Saul to lead them. Eventually Samuel had to rebuke Saul for his sinful actions and tell him that God was going to tear the kingdom away from him. After that God led Samuel to anoint David as the next king.

Through all of this, Samuel's faith in God gave him a solid foundation, an unfailing anchor that held firm through the many storms he faced. We never read of Samuel floundering in the face of difficulty or failing to provide guidance when the community needed his help. Even when many people were turning to idols and abandoning God, Samuel remained rooted in his devotion to God and called upon the people to do the same, "If you are returning to the LORD with all your heart, then . . . direct your heart to the LORD, and serve him only, and he will deliver you" (1 Samuel 7.3).

Like Samuel, we need to place our faith in God, who will never fail. We can depend on God when it seems that nothing else can be trusted. God is the all-powerful, the all-knowing Lord, who loves us so much that he sent his son Jesus to die for us. As we build our lives on Christ, we can be sure that he will see us through all that we will face.

Going Deeper

- Describe a time when someone or something you thought you could trust failed you.
- In what ways does faith in God give you a firm foundation for weathering life's storms?

come among us and save us from the power of our enemies." [4]So the people sent to Shiloh, and brought from there the ark of the covenant of the LORD of hosts, who is enthroned on the cherubim. The two sons of Eli, Hophni and Phinehas, were there with the ark of the covenant of God.

[5]When the ark of the covenant of the LORD came into the camp, all Israel gave a mighty shout, so that the earth resounded. [6]When the Philistines heard the noise of the shouting, they said, "What does this great shouting in the camp of the Hebrews mean?" When they learned that the ark of the LORD had come to the camp, [7]the Philistines were afraid; for they said, "Gods have[a] come into the camp." They also said, "Woe to us! For nothing like this has happened before. [8]Woe to us! Who can deliver us from the power of these mighty gods? These are the gods who struck the Egyptians with every sort of plague in the wilderness. [9]Take courage, and be men, O Philistines, in order not to become slaves to the Hebrews as they have been to you; be men and fight."

[10]So the Philistines fought; Israel was defeated, and they fled, everyone to his home. There was a very great slaughter, for there fell of Israel thirty thousand foot soldiers. [11]The ark of God was captured; and the two sons of Eli, Hophni and Phinehas, died.

DEATH OF ELI

[12]A man of Benjamin ran from the battle line, and came to Shiloh the same day, with his clothes torn and with earth upon his head. [13]When he arrived, Eli was sitting upon his seat by the road watching, for his heart trembled for the ark of God. When the man came into the city and told the news, all the city cried out. [14]When Eli heard the sound of the outcry, he said, "What is this uproar?" Then the man came quickly and told Eli. [15]Now Eli was ninety-eight years old and his eyes were set, so that he could not see. [16]The man said to Eli, "I have just come from the battle; I fled from the battle today." He said, "How did it go, my son?" [17]The messenger replied, "Israel has fled before the Philistines, and there has also been a great slaughter among the troops; your two sons also, Hophni and Phinehas, are dead, and the ark of God has been captured." [18]When he mentioned the ark of God, Eli[b] fell over backward from his seat by the side of the gate; and his neck was broken and he died, for he was an old man, and heavy. He had judged Israel forty years.

[19]Now his daughter-in-law, the wife of Phinehas, was pregnant, about to give birth. When she heard the news that the ark of God was captured, and that her father-in-law and her husband were dead, she bowed and gave birth; for her labor pains overwhelmed her. [20]As she was about to die, the women attending her said to her, "Do not be afraid, for you have borne a son." But she did not answer or give heed. [21]She named the child Ichabod, meaning, "The glory has departed from Israel," because the ark of God had been captured and because of her father-in-law and her husband. [22]She said, "The glory has departed from Israel, for the ark of God has been captured."

THE PHILISTINES AND THE ARK

5 When the Philistines captured the ark of God, they brought it from Ebenezer to Ashdod; [2]then the Philistines took the ark of God and brought it into the house of Dagon and placed it beside Dagon. [3]When the people of Ashdod rose early the next day, there was Dagon, fallen on his face to the ground before the ark of the LORD. So they took Dagon and put him back in his place. [4]But when they rose early on the next morning, Dagon had fallen on his face to the ground before the ark of the LORD, and the head of Dagon and both his hands were lying cut off upon the threshold; only the trunk of[c] Dagon was left to him. [5]This is why the priests of Dagon and all who enter

[a] 4.7 Or A god has   [b] 4.18 Heb he
[c] 5.4 Heb lacks the trunk of

the house of Dagon do not step on the threshold of Dagon in Ashdod to this day.

6 The hand of the LORD was heavy upon the people of Ashdod, and he terrified and struck them with tumors, both in Ashdod and in its territory. 7And when the inhabitants of Ashdod saw how things were, they said, "The ark of the God of Israel must not remain with us; for his hand is heavy on us and on our god Dagon." 8So they sent and gathered together all the lords of the Philistines, and said, "What shall we do with the ark of the God of Israel?" The inhabitants of Gath replied, "Let the ark of God be moved on to us."a So they moved the ark of the God of Israel to Gath.b 9But after they had brought it to Gath,c the hand of the LORD was against the city, causing a very great panic; he struck the inhabitants of the city, both young and old, so that tumors broke out on them. 10So they sent the ark of the God of Israeld to Ekron. But when the ark of God came to Ekron, the people of Ekron cried out, "Whye have they brought around to usf the ark of the God of Israel to kill usf and ourg people?" 11They sent therefore and gathered together all the lords of the Philistines, and said, "Send away the ark of the God of Israel, and let it return to its own place, that it may not kill us and our people." For there was a deathly panich throughout the whole city. The hand of God was very heavy there; 12those who did not die were stricken with tumors, and the cry of the city went up to heaven.

THE CONSEQUENCES OF SIN

ARE NOT PREDICTABLE.

THE ARK RETURNED TO ISRAEL

6 The ark of the LORD was in the country of the Philistines seven months. 2Then the Philistines called for the priests and the diviners and said, "What shall we do with the ark of the LORD? Tell us what we should send with it to its place." 3They said, "If you send away the ark of the God of Israel, do not send it empty, but by all means return him a guilt offering. Then you will be healed and will be ransomed;i will not his hand then turn from you?" 4And they said, "What is the guilt offering that we shall return to him?" They answered, "Five gold tumors and five gold mice, according to the number of the lords of the Philistines; for the same plague was upon all of you and upon your lords. 5So you must make images of your tumors and images of your mice that ravage the land, and give glory to the God of Israel; perhaps he will lighten his hand on you and your gods and your land. 6Why should you harden your hearts as the Egyptians and Pharaoh hardened their hearts? After he had made fools of them, did they not let the people go, and they departed? 7Now then, get ready a new cart and two milch cows that have never borne a yoke, and yoke the cows to the cart, but take their calves home, away from them. 8Take the ark of the LORD and place it on the cart, and put in a box at its side the figures of gold, which you are returning to him as a guilt offering. Then send it off, and let it go its way. 9And watch; if it goes up on the way to its own land, to Beth-shemesh, then it is he who has done us this great harm; but if not, then we shall know that it is not his hand that struck us; it happened to us by chance."

10 The men did so; they took two milch cows and yoked them to the cart, and shut up their calves at home. 11They put the ark of the LORD on the cart, and the box with the gold mice and the images of their

---

a 5.8 Gk Compare Q Ms: MT They answered, "Let the ark of the God of Israel be brought around to Gath." b 5.8 Gk: Heb lacks to Gath c 5.9 Q Ms: MT lacks to Gath d 5.10 Q Ms Gk: MT lacks of Israel e 5.10 Q Ms Gk: MT lacks Why f 5.10 Heb me g 5.10 Heb my h 5.11 Q Ms reads a panic from the LORD i 6.3 Q Ms Gk: MT and it will be known to you

tumors. [12]The cows went straight in the direction of Beth-shemesh along one highway, lowing as they went; they turned neither to the right nor to the left, and the lords of the Philistines went after them as far as the border of Beth-shemesh.

[13] Now the people of Beth-shemesh were reaping their wheat harvest in the valley. When they looked up and saw the ark, they went with rejoicing to meet it.[a] [14]The cart came into the field of Joshua of Beth-shemesh, and stopped there. A large stone was there; so they split up the wood of the cart and offered the cows as a burnt offering to the LORD. [15]The Levites took down the ark of the LORD and the box that was beside it, in which were the gold objects, and set them upon the large stone. Then the people of Beth-shemesh offered burnt offerings and presented sacrifices on that day to the LORD. [16]When the five lords of the Philistines saw it, they returned that day to Ekron.

[17] These are the gold tumors, which the Philistines returned as a guilt offering to the LORD: one for Ashdod, one for Gaza, one for Ashkelon, one for Gath, one for Ekron; [18]also the gold mice, according to the number of all the cities of the Philistines belonging to the five lords, both fortified cities and unwalled villages. The great stone, beside which they set down the ark of the LORD, is a witness to this day in the field of Joshua of Beth-shemesh.

THE ARK AT KIRIATH-JEARIM

[19] The descendants of Jeconiah did not rejoice with the people of Beth-shemesh when they greeted[b] the ark of the LORD; and he killed seventy men of them.[c] The people mourned because the LORD had made a great slaughter among the people. [20]Then the people of Beth-shemesh said, "Who is able to stand before the LORD, this holy God? To whom shall he go so that we may be rid of him?" [21]So they sent messengers to the inhabitants of Kiriath-jearim, saying, "The Philistines have returned the ark of the LORD. Come

7 down and take it up to you." [1]And the people of Kiriath-jearim came and took up the ark of the LORD, and brought it to the house of Abinadab on the hill. They consecrated his son, Eleazar, to have charge of the ark of the LORD.

[2] From the day that the ark was lodged at Kiriath-jearim, a long time passed, some twenty years, and all the house of Israel lamented[d] after the LORD.

SAMUEL AS JUDGE

[3] Then Samuel said to all the house of Israel, "If you are returning to the LORD with all your heart, then put away the foreign gods and the Astartes from among you. Direct your heart to the LORD, and serve him only, and he will deliver you out of the hand of the Philistines." [4]So Israel put away the Baals and the Astartes, and they served the LORD only.

[5] Then Samuel said, "Gather all Israel at Mizpah, and I will pray to the LORD for you." [6]So they gathered at Mizpah, and drew water and poured it out before the LORD. They fasted that day, and said, "We have sinned against the LORD." And Samuel judged the people of Israel at Mizpah.

[7] When the Philistines heard that the people of Israel had gathered at Mizpah, the lords of the Philistines went up against Israel. And when the people of Israel heard of it they were afraid of the Philistines. [8]The people of Israel said to Samuel, "Do not cease to cry out to the LORD our God for us, and pray that he may save us from the hand of the Philistines." [9]So Samuel took a sucking lamb and offered it as a whole burnt offering to the LORD; Samuel cried out to the LORD for Israel, and the LORD answered him. [10]As Samuel was offering up the burnt offering, the Philistines drew near to attack Israel; but the LORD thundered with

[a] 6.13 Gk: Heb *rejoiced to see it*   [b] 6.19 Gk: Heb *And he killed some of the people of Beth-shemesh, because they looked into*   [c] 6.19 Heb *killed seventy men, fifty thousand men*   [d] 7.2 Meaning of Heb uncertain

a mighty voice that day against the Philistines and threw them into confusion; and they were routed before Israel. ¹¹And the men of Israel went out of Mizpah and pursued the Philistines, and struck them down as far as beyond Beth-car.

12 Then Samuel took a stone and set it up between Mizpah and Jeshanah,ᵃ and named it Ebenezer;ᵇ for he said, "Thus far the LORD has helped us." ¹³So the Philistines were subdued and did not again enter the territory of Israel; the hand of the LORD was against the Philistines all the days of Samuel. ¹⁴The towns that the Philistines had taken from Israel were restored to Israel, from Ekron to Gath; and Israel recovered their territory from the hand of the Philistines. There was peace also between Israel and the Amorites.

15 Samuel judged Israel all the days of his life. ¹⁶He went on a circuit year by year to Bethel, Gilgal, and Mizpah; and he judged Israel in all these places. ¹⁷Then he would come back to Ramah, for his home was there; he administered justice there to Israel, and built there an altar to the LORD.

ISRAEL DEMANDS A KING

8 When Samuel became old, he made his sons judges over Israel. ²The name of his firstborn son was Joel, and the name of his second, Abijah; they were judges in Beer-sheba. ³Yet his sons did not follow in his ways, but turned aside after gain; they took bribes and perverted justice.

4 Then all the elders of Israel gathered together and came to Samuel at Ramah, ⁵and said to him, "You are old and your sons do not follow in your ways; appoint for us, then, a king to govern us, like other nations." ⁶But the thing displeased Samuel when they said, "Give us a king to govern us." Samuel prayed to the LORD, ⁷and the LORD said to Samuel, "Listen to the voice of the people in all that they say to you; for they have not rejected you, but they have rejected me from being king over them. ⁸Just as they have done

to me,ᶜ from the day I brought them up out of Egypt to this day, forsaking me and serving other gods, so also they are doing to you. ⁹Now then, listen to their voice; only—you shall solemnly warn them, and show them the ways of the king who shall reign over them."

10 So Samuel reported all the words of the LORD to the people who were asking him for a king. ¹¹He said, "These will be the ways of the king who will reign over you: he will take your sons and appoint them to his chariots and to be his horsemen, and to run before his chariots; ¹²and he will appoint for himself commanders of thousands and commanders of fifties, and some to plow his ground and to reap his harvest, and to make his implements of war and the equipment of his chariots.

THE RESURRECTION FULFILLS
THE DEEPEST LONGINGS OF THE
HUMAN SPIRIT: FORGIVENESS,
REDEMPTION, PURPOSE,
RELATIONSHIP AND A FUTURE
THAT CANNOT BE DISRUPTED.

¹³He will take your daughters to be perfumers and cooks and bakers. ¹⁴He will take the best of your fields and vineyards and olive orchards and give them to his courtiers. ¹⁵He will take one-tenth of your grain and of your vineyards and give it to his officers and his courtiers. ¹⁶He will take your male and female slaves, and the best of your cattleᵈ and donkeys, and put them to his work. ¹⁷He will take one-tenth of your flocks, and you shall be his slaves. ¹⁸And in that day you will cry out because of your king, whom you have chosen

ᵃ 7.12 Gk Syr: Heb *Shen*   ᵇ 7.12 That is *Stone of Help*   ᶜ 8.8 Gk: Heb lacks *to me*   ᵈ 8.16 Gk: Heb *young men*

for yourselves; but the LORD will not answer you in that day."

ISRAEL'S REQUEST FOR A KING GRANTED

19 But the people refused to listen to the voice of Samuel; they said, "No! but we are determined to have a king over us, 20 so that we also may be like other nations, and that our king may govern us and go out before us and fight our battles." 21 When Samuel had heard all the words of the people, he repeated them in the ears of the LORD. 22 The LORD said to Samuel, "Listen to their voice and set a king over them." Samuel then said to the people of Israel, "Each of you return home."

SAUL CHOSEN TO BE KING

9 There was a man of Benjamin whose name was Kish son of Abiel son of Zeror son of Becorath son of Aphiah, a Benjaminite, a man of wealth. 2 He had a son whose name was Saul, a handsome young man. There was not a man among the people of Israel more handsome than he; he stood head and shoulders above everyone else.

3 Now the donkeys of Kish, Saul's father, had strayed. So Kish said to his son Saul, "Take one of the boys with you; go and look for the donkeys." 4 He passed through the hill country of Ephraim and passed through the land of Shalishah, but they did not find them. And they passed through the land of Shaalim, but they were not there. Then he passed through the land of Benjamin, but they did not find them.

5 When they came to the land of Zuph, Saul said to the boy who was with him, "Let us turn back, or my father will stop worrying about the donkeys and worry about us." 6 But he said to him, "There is a man of God in this town; he is a man held in honor. Whatever he says always comes true. Let us go there now; perhaps he will tell us about the journey on which we have set out." 7 Then Saul replied to the boy, "But if we go, what can we bring the man? For the bread in our sacks is gone, and there

is no present to bring to the man of God. What have we?" 8 The boy answered Saul again, "Here, I have with me a quarter shekel of silver; I will give it to the man of God, to tell us our way." 9 (Formerly in Israel, anyone who went to inquire of God would say, "Come, let us go to the seer"; for the one who is now called a prophet was formerly called a seer.) 10 Saul said to the boy, "Good; come, let us go." So they went to the town where the man of God was.

11 As they went up the hill to the town, they met some girls coming out to draw water, and said to them, "Is the seer here?" 12 They answered, "Yes, there he is just ahead of you. Hurry; he has come just now to the town, because the people have a sacrifice today at the shrine. 13 As soon as you enter the town, you will find him, before he goes up to the shrine to eat. For the people will not eat until he comes, since he must bless the sacrifice; afterward those eat who are invited. Now go up, for you will meet him immediately." 14 So they went up to the town. As they were entering the town, they saw Samuel coming out toward them on his way up to the shrine.

15 Now the day before Saul came, the LORD had revealed to Samuel: 16 "Tomorrow about this time I will send to you a man from the land of Benjamin, and you shall anoint him to be ruler over my people Israel. He shall save my people from the hand of the Philistines; for I have seen the suffering of[a] my people, because their outcry has come to me." 17 When Samuel saw Saul, the LORD told him, "Here is the man of whom I spoke to you. He it is who shall rule over my people." 18 Then Saul approached Samuel inside the gate, and said, "Tell me, please, where is the house of the seer?" 19 Samuel answered Saul, "I am the seer; go up before me to the shrine, for today you shall eat with me, and in the morning I will let you go and will tell you all that is on your mind. 20 As for your donkeys that were lost three

[a] 9.16 Gk: Heb lacks *the suffering of*

⊖

PONDER

When Samuel saw Saul, the LORD
told him, "Here is the man of
whom I spoke to you. He it is who
shall rule over my people."
—1 Samuel 9.17

PRAY

O Father, we might feel that we are fairly
well off and that we are adequately
successful in life. But sometimes we
forget the aspirations that you have for
us. Open our hearts to this passage
about leaders such as Samuel and
Saul, whom you called and blessed.
Help us remember that we are also
called. Give us wisdom to serve and
lead in whatever positions of authority
we find ourselves. Help us to keep the
covenant we made when we accepted
Jesus Christ as our Savior, knowing
that in you we can find joy, peace
and guidance as well as eternal life.
In our Savior's name we pray. Amen.

◿

days ago, give no further thought to
them, for they have been found. And
on whom is all Israel's desire fixed, if
not on you and on all your ancestral
house?" 21Saul answered, "I am only
a Benjaminite, from the least of the
tribes of Israel, and my family is the
humblest of all the families of the
tribe of Benjamin. Why then have
you spoken to me in this way?"

22 Then Samuel took Saul and his
servant-boy and brought them into
the hall, and gave them a place at the
head of those who had been invited,
of whom there were about thirty.
23And Samuel said to the cook,
"Bring the portion I gave you, the
one I asked you to put aside." 24The
cook took up the thigh and what
went with it[a] and set them before
Saul. Samuel said, "See, what was
kept is set before you. Eat; for it is set[b]
before you at the appointed time, so
that you might eat with the guests."[c]

So Saul ate with Samuel that
day. 25When they came down from
the shrine into the town, a bed was
spread for Saul[d] on the roof, and he
lay down to sleep.[e] 26Then at the
break of dawn[f] Samuel called to Saul
upon the roof, "Get up, so that I may
send you on your way." Saul got up,
and both he and Samuel went out
into the street.

SAMUEL ANOINTS SAUL

27 As they were going down to
the outskirts of the town, Samuel
said to Saul, "Tell the boy to go on
before us, and when he has passed
on, stop here yourself for a while,
that I may make known to you the
10 word of God." 1Samuel took
a vial of oil and poured it on
his head, and kissed him; he said,
"The LORD has anointed you ruler
over his people Israel. You shall
reign over the people of the LORD
and you will save them from the
hand of their enemies all around.
Now this shall be the sign to you
that the LORD has anointed you
ruler[g] over his heritage: 2When you
depart from me today you will meet
two men by Rachel's tomb in the
territory of Benjamin at Zelzah; they
will say to you, 'The donkeys that
you went to seek are found, and now
your father has stopped worrying
about them and is worrying about
you, saying: What shall I do about
my son?' 3Then you shall go on from
there further and come to the oak of
Tabor; three men going up to God at
Bethel will meet you there, one carrying three kids, another carrying
three loaves of bread, and another
carrying a skin of wine. 4They will
greet you and give you two loaves of
bread, which you shall accept from
them. 5After that you shall come to
Gibeath-elohim,[h] at the place where
the Philistine garrison is; there, as

a 9.24 Meaning of Heb uncertain
b 9.24 Q Ms Gk: MT it was kept   c 9.24 Cn:
Heb it was kept for you, saying, I have invited
the people   d 9.25 Gk: Heb and he spoke
with Saul   e 9.25 Gk: Heb lacks and he lay
down to sleep   f 9.26 Gk: Heb and they
arose early and at break of dawn   g 10.1 Gk:
Heb lacks over his people Israel. You shall...
anointed you ruler   h 10.5 Or the Hill of God

you come to the town, you will meet a band of prophets coming down from the shrine with harp, tambourine, flute, and lyre playing in front of them; they will be in a prophetic frenzy. 6Then the spirit of the LORD will possess you, and you will be in a prophetic frenzy along with them and be turned into a different person. 7Now when these signs meet you, do whatever you see fit to do, for God is with you. 8And you shall go down to Gilgal ahead of me; then I will come down to you to present burnt offerings and offer sacrifices of well-being. Seven days you shall wait, until I come to you and show you what you shall do."

SAUL PROPHESIES

9 As he turned away to leave Samuel, God gave him another heart; and all these signs were fulfilled that day. 10When they were going from there[a] to Gibeah,[b] a band of prophets met him; and the spirit of God possessed him, and he fell into a prophetic frenzy along with them. 11When all who knew him before saw how he prophesied with the prophets, the people said to one another, "What has come over the son of Kish? Is Saul also among the prophets?" 12A man of the place answered, "And who is their father?" Therefore it became a proverb, "Is Saul also among the prophets?" 13When his prophetic frenzy had ended, he went home.[c]

14 Saul's uncle said to him and to the boy, "Where did you go?" And he replied, "To seek the donkeys; and when we saw they were not to be found, we went to Samuel." 15Saul's uncle said, "Tell me what Samuel said to you." 16Saul said to his uncle, "He told us that the donkeys had been found." But about the matter of the kingship, of which Samuel had spoken, he did not tell him anything.

SAUL PROCLAIMED KING

17 Samuel summoned the people to the LORD at Mizpah 18and said to them,[d] "Thus says the LORD, the God of Israel, 'I brought up Israel out of Egypt, and I rescued you from the hand of the Egyptians and from the hand of all the kingdoms that were oppressing you.' 19But today you have rejected your God, who saves you from all your calamities and your distresses; and you have said, 'No! but set a king over us.' Now therefore present yourselves before the LORD by your tribes and by your clans."

20 Then Samuel brought all the tribes of Israel near, and the tribe of Benjamin was taken by lot. 21He brought the tribe of Benjamin near by its families, and the family of the Matrites was taken by lot. Finally he brought the family of the Matrites near man by man,[e] and Saul the son of Kish was taken by lot. But when they sought him, he could not be found. 22So they inquired again of the LORD, "Did the man come here?"[f] and the LORD said, "See, he has hidden himself among the baggage." 23Then they ran and brought him from there. When he took his stand among the people, he was head and shoulders taller than any of them. 24Samuel said to all the people, "Do you see the one whom the LORD has chosen? There is no one like him among all the people." And all the people shouted, "Long live the king!"

25 Samuel told the people the rights and duties of the kingship; and he wrote them in a book and laid it up before the LORD. Then Samuel sent all the people back to their homes. 26Saul also went to his home at Gibeah, and with him went warriors whose hearts God had touched. 27But some worthless fellows said, "How can this man save us?" They despised him and brought him no present. But he held his peace.

Now Nahash, king of the Ammonites, had been grievously oppressing the Gadites and the Reubenites. He would gouge out the right eye of each of them and would not grant Israel a deliverer. No one was left

---

[a] 10.10 Gk: Heb *they came there*   [b] 10.10 Or *the hill*   [c] 10.13 Cn: Heb *he came to the shrine*   [d] 10.18 Heb *to the people of Israel*   [e] 10.21 Gk: Heb lacks *Finally … man by man*   [f] 10.22 Gk: Heb *Is there yet a man to come here?*

of the Israelites across the Jordan whose right eye Nahash, king of the Ammonites, had not gouged out. But there were seven thousand men who had escaped from the Ammonites and had entered Jabesh-gilead.[a]

SAUL DEFEATS THE AMMONITES

11 About a month later,[b] Nahash the Ammonite went up and besieged Jabesh-gilead; and all the men of Jabesh said to Nahash, "Make a treaty with us, and we will serve you." 2But Nahash the Ammonite said to them, "On this condition I will make a treaty with you, namely that I gouge out everyone's right eye, and thus put disgrace upon all Israel." 3The elders of Jabesh said to him, "Give us seven days' respite that we may send messengers through all the territory of Israel. Then, if there is no one to save us, we will give ourselves up to you." 4When the messengers came to Gibeah of Saul, they reported the matter in the hearing of the people; and all the people wept aloud.

5 Now Saul was coming from the field behind the oxen; and Saul said, "What is the matter with the people, that they are weeping?" So they told him the message from the inhabitants of Jabesh. 6And the spirit of God came upon Saul in power when he heard these words, and his anger was greatly kindled. 7He took a yoke of oxen, and cut them in pieces and sent them throughout all the territory of Israel by messengers, saying, "Whoever does not come out after Saul and Samuel, so shall it be done to his oxen!" Then the dread of the LORD fell upon the people, and they came out as one. 8When he mustered them at Bezek, those from Israel were three hundred thousand, and those from Judah seventy[c] thousand. 9They said to the messengers who had come, "Thus shall you say to the inhabitants of Jabesh-gilead: 'Tomorrow, by the time the sun is hot, you shall have deliverance.'" When the messengers came and told the inhabitants of Jabesh, they rejoiced. 10So the inhabitants of Jabesh said, "Tomorrow we will give ourselves up to you, and you may do to us whatever seems good to you." 11The next day Saul put the people in three companies. At the morning watch they came into the camp and cut down the Ammonites until the heat of the day; and those who survived were scattered, so that no two of them were left together.

12 The people said to Samuel, "Who is it that said, 'Shall Saul reign over us?' Give them to us so that we may put them to death." 13But Saul said, "No one shall be put to death this day, for today the LORD has brought deliverance to Israel."

14 Samuel said to the people, "Come, let us go to Gilgal and there renew the kingship." 15So all the people went to Gilgal, and there they made Saul king before the LORD in Gilgal. There they sacrificed offerings of well-being before the LORD, and there Saul and all the Israelites rejoiced greatly.

SAMUEL'S FAREWELL ADDRESS

12 Samuel said to all Israel, "I have listened to you in all that you have said to me, and have set a king over you. 2See, it is the king who leads you now; I am old and gray, but my sons are with you. I have led you from my youth until this day. 3Here I am; testify against me before the LORD and before his anointed. Whose ox have I taken? Or whose donkey have I taken? Or whom have I defrauded? Whom have I oppressed? Or from whose hand have I taken a bribe to blind my eyes with it? Testify against me[d] and I will restore it to you." 4They said, "You have not defrauded us or oppressed us or taken anything from the hand of anyone." 5He said to them, "The LORD is witness against you, and his anointed is witness this day, that you have not found anything in my hand." And they said, "He is witness."

---

a **10.27** Q Ms Compare Josephus, *Antiquities* VI.v.1 (68–71): MT lacks *Now Nahash... entered Jabesh-gilead.* b **11.1** Q Ms Gk: MT lacks *About a month later* c **11.8** Q Ms Gk: MT *thirty* d **12.3** Gk: Heb lacks *Testify against me*

6 Samuel said to the people, "The LORD is witness, who[a] appointed Moses and Aaron and brought your ancestors up out of the land of Egypt. 7Now therefore take your stand, so that I may enter into judgment with you before the LORD, and I will declare to you[b] all the saving deeds of the LORD that he performed for you and for your ancestors. 8When Jacob went into Egypt and the Egyptians oppressed them,[c] then your ancestors cried to the LORD and the LORD sent Moses and Aaron, who brought forth your ancestors out of Egypt, and settled them in this place. 9But they forgot the LORD their God; and he sold them into the hand of Sisera, commander of the army of King Jabin of[d] Hazor, and into the hand of the Philistines, and into the hand of the king of Moab; and they fought against them. 10Then they cried to the LORD, and said, 'We have sinned, because we have forsaken the LORD, and have served the Baals and the Astartes; but now rescue us out of the hand of our enemies, and we will serve you.' 11And the LORD sent Jerubbaal and Barak,[e] and Jephthah, and Samson,[f] and rescued you out of the hand of your enemies on every side; and you lived in safety. 12But when you saw that King Nahash of the Ammonites came against you, you said to me, 'No, but a king shall reign over us,' though the LORD your God was your king. 13See, here is the king whom you have chosen, for whom you have asked; see, the LORD has set a king over you. 14If you will fear the LORD and serve him and heed his voice and not rebel against the commandment of the LORD, and if both you and the king who reigns over you will follow the LORD your God, it will be well; 15but if you will not heed the voice of the LORD, but rebel against the commandment of the LORD, then the hand of the LORD will be against you and your king.[g] 16Now therefore take your stand and see this great thing that the LORD will do before your eyes. 17Is it not the wheat harvest today? I will call upon the LORD, that he may send thunder and rain; and you shall know and see that the wickedness that you have done in the sight of the LORD is great in demanding a king for yourselves." 18So Samuel called upon the LORD, and the LORD sent thunder and rain that day; and all the people greatly feared the LORD and Samuel.

19 All the people said to Samuel, "Pray to the LORD your God for your servants, so that we may not die; for we have added to all our sins the evil of demanding a king for ourselves." 20And Samuel said to the people, "Do not be afraid; you have done all this evil, yet do not turn aside from following the LORD, but serve the LORD with all your heart; 21and do not turn aside after useless things that cannot profit or save, for they are useless. 22For the LORD will not cast away his people, for his great name's sake, because it has pleased the LORD to make you a people for himself. 23Moreover as for me, far be it from me that I should sin against the LORD by ceasing to pray for you; and I will instruct you in the good and the right way. 24Only fear the LORD, and serve him faithfully with all your heart; for consider what great things he has done for you. 25But if you still do wickedly, you shall be swept away, both you and your king."

SAUL'S UNLAWFUL SACRIFICE

13 Saul was . . .[h] years old when he began to reign; and he reigned . . . and two[i] years over Israel.

2 Saul chose three thousand out of Israel; two thousand were with Saul in Michmash and the hill country of Bethel, and a thousand were with Jonathan in Gibeah of Benjamin; the rest of the people he sent home to their tents. 3Jonathan defeated

---

[a] 12.6 Gk: Heb lacks *is witness, who*
[b] 12.7 Gk: Heb lacks *and I will declare to you* [c] 12.8 Gk: Heb lacks *and the Egyptians oppressed them* [d] 12.9 Gk: Heb lacks *King Jabin of* [e] 12.11 Gk Syr: Heb *Bedan*
[f] 12.11 Gk: Heb *Samuel* [g] 12.15 Gk: Heb *and your ancestors* [h] 13.1 The number is lacking in the Heb text (the verse is lacking in the Septuagint). [i] 13.1 *Two* is not the entire number; something has dropped out.

the garrison of the Philistines that was at Geba; and the Philistines heard of it. And Saul blew the trumpet throughout all the land, saying, "Let the Hebrews hear!" ⁴When all Israel heard that Saul had defeated the garrison of the Philistines, and also that Israel had become odious to the Philistines, the people were called out to join Saul at Gilgal.

5 The Philistines mustered to fight with Israel, thirty thousand chariots, and six thousand horsemen, and troops like the sand on the seashore in multitude; they came up and encamped at Michmash, to the east of Beth-aven. ⁶When the Israelites saw that they were in distress (for the troops were hard pressed), the people hid themselves in caves and in holes and in rocks and in tombs and in cisterns. ⁷Some Hebrews crossed the Jordan to the land of Gad and Gilead. Saul was still at Gilgal, and all the people followed him trembling.

8 He waited seven days, the time appointed by Samuel; but Samuel did not come to Gilgal, and the people began to slip away from Saul.ᵃ ⁹So Saul said, "Bring the burnt offering here to me, and the offerings of well-being." And he offered the burnt offering. ¹⁰As soon as he had finished offering the burnt offering, Samuel arrived; and Saul went out to meet him and salute him. ¹¹Samuel said, "What have you done?" Saul replied, "When I saw that the people were slipping away from me, and that you did not come within the days appointed, and that the Philistines were mustering at Michmash, ¹²I said, 'Now the Philistines will come down upon me at Gilgal, and I have not entreated the favor of the Lord'; so I forced myself, and offered the burnt offering." ¹³Samuel said to Saul, "You have done foolishly; you have not kept the commandment of the Lord your God, which he commanded you. The Lord would have established your kingdom over Israel forever, ¹⁴but now your kingdom will not continue; the Lord has sought out a man after his own heart; and the Lord has appointed him to be

ruler over his people, because you have not kept what the Lord commanded you." ¹⁵And Samuel left and went on his way from Gilgal.ᵇ The rest of the people followed Saul to join the army; they went up from Gilgal toward Gibeah of Benjamin.ᶜ

WE SHOULD REACT WITH HUMILITY TOWARD THE SIN OF OTHERS, WITH REPENTANCE TOWARD OUR SINS, WITH GRATITUDE TO GOD FOR GRACE.

PREPARATIONS FOR BATTLE
Saul counted the people who were present with him, about six hundred men. ¹⁶Saul, his son Jonathan, and the people who were present with them stayed in Geba of Benjamin; but the Philistines encamped at Michmash. ¹⁷And raiders came out of the camp of the Philistines in three companies; one company turned toward Ophrah, to the land of Shual, ¹⁸another company turned toward Beth-horon, and another company turned toward the mountainᵈ that looks down upon the valley of Zeboim toward the wilderness.

19 Now there was no smith to be found throughout all the land of Israel; for the Philistines said, "The Hebrews must not make swords or spears for themselves"; ²⁰so all the Israelites went down to the Philistines to sharpen their plowshares, mattocks, axes, or sickles;ᵉ ²¹The charge was two-thirds of a shekelᶠ for the plowshares and for the mattocks, and one-third of a shekel for

ᵃ 13.8 Heb him   ᵇ 13.15 Gk: Heb went up from Gilgal to Gibeah of Benjamin   ᶜ 13.15 Gk: Heb lacks The rest ... of Benjamin   ᵈ 13.18 Cn Compare Gk: Heb toward the border   ᵉ 13.20 Gk: Heb plowshare   ᶠ 13.21 Heb was a pim

sharpening the axes and for setting the goads.ᵃ ²²So on the day of the battle neither sword nor spear was to be found in the possession of any of the people with Saul and Jonathan; but Saul and his son Jonathan had them.

JONATHAN SURPRISES AND ROUTS THE PHILISTINES

23 Now a garrison of the Philistines had gone out to the pass of **14** Michmash. ¹One day Jonathan son of Saul said to the young man who carried his armor, "Come, let us go over to the Philistine garrison on the other side." But he did not tell his father. ²Saul was staying in the outskirts of Gibeah under the pomegranate tree that is at Migron; the troops that were with him were about six hundred men, ³along with Ahijah son of Ahitub, Ichabod's brother, son of Phinehas son of Eli, the priest of the LORD in Shiloh, carrying an ephod. Now the people did not know that Jonathan had gone. ⁴In the pass,ᵇ by which Jonathan tried to go over to the Philistine garrison, there was a rocky crag on one side and a rocky crag on the other; the name of the one was Bozez, and the name of the other Seneh. ⁵One crag rose on the north in front of Michmash, and the other on the south in front of Geba.

6 Jonathan said to the young man who carried his armor, "Come, let us go over to the garrison of these uncircumcised; it may be that the LORD will act for us; for nothing can hinder the LORD from saving by many or by few." ⁷His armor-bearer said to him, "Do all that your mind inclines to.ᶜ I am with you; as your mind is, so is mine."ᵈ ⁸Then Jonathan said, "Now we will cross over to those men and will show ourselves to them. ⁹If they say to us, 'Wait until we come to you,' then we will stand still in our place, and we will not go up to them. ¹⁰But if they say, 'Come up to us,' then we will go up; for the LORD has given them into our hand. That will be the sign for us." ¹¹So both of them showed themselves to the garrison of the Philistines; and the

Philistines said, "Look, Hebrews are coming out of the holes where they have hidden themselves." ¹²The men of the garrison hailed Jonathan and his armor-bearer, saying, "Come up to us, and we will show you something." Jonathan said to his armor-bearer, "Come up after me; for the LORD has given them into the hand of Israel." ¹³Then Jonathan climbed up on his hands and feet, with his armor-bearer following after him. The Philistinesᵉ fell before Jonathan, and his armor-bearer, coming after him, killed them. ¹⁴In that first slaughter Jonathan and his armor-bearer killed about twenty men within an area about half a furrow long in an acreᶠ of land. ¹⁵There was a panic in the camp, in the field, and among all the people; the garrison and even the raiders trembled; the earth quaked; and it became a very great panic.

16 Saul's lookouts in Gibeah of Benjamin were watching as the multitude was surging back and forth.ᵍ ¹⁷Then Saul said to the troops that were with him, "Call the roll and see who has gone from us." When they had called the roll, Jonathan and his armor-bearer were not there. ¹⁸Saul said to Ahijah, "Bring the arkʰ of God here." For at that time the arkʰ of God went with the Israelites. ¹⁹While Saul was talking to the priest, the tumult in the camp of the Philistines increased more and more; and Saul said to the priest, "Withdraw your hand." ²⁰Then Saul and all the people who were with him rallied and went into the battle; and every sword was against the other, so that there was very great confusion. ²¹Now the Hebrews who previously had been with the Philistines and had gone up with them into the camp turned and joined the Israelites who were with Saul and Jonathan. ²²Likewise, when all the Israelites who had gone into hiding

ᵃ 13.21 Cn: Meaning of Heb uncertain
ᵇ 14.4 Heb *Between the passes*   ᶜ 14.7 Gk: Heb *Do all that is in your mind. Turn*
ᵈ 14.7 Gk: Heb lacks *so is mine*   ᵉ 14.13 Heb *They*   ᶠ 14.14 Heb *yoke*   ᵍ 14.16 Gk: Heb *they went and there*   ʰ 14.18 Gk *the ephod*

in the hill country of Ephraim heard that the Philistines were fleeing, they too followed closely after them in the battle. 23So the LORD gave Israel the victory that day.

The battle passed beyond Bethaven, and the troops with Saul numbered altogether about ten thousand men. The battle spread out over the hill country of Ephraim.

SAUL'S RASH OATH

24 Now Saul committed a very rash act on that day.[a] He had laid an oath on the troops, saying, "Cursed be anyone who eats food before it is evening and I have been avenged on my enemies." So none of the troops tasted food. 25All the troops[b] came upon a honeycomb; and there was honey on the ground. 26When the troops came upon the honeycomb, the honey was dripping out; but they did not put their hands to their mouths, for they feared the oath. 27But Jonathan had not heard his father charge the troops with the oath; so he extended the staff that was in his hand, and dipped the tip of it in the honeycomb, and put his hand to his mouth; and his eyes brightened. 28Then one of the soldiers said, "Your father strictly charged the troops with an oath, saying, 'Cursed be anyone who eats food this day.' And so the troops are faint." 29Then Jonathan said, "My father has troubled the land; see how my eyes have brightened because I tasted a little of this honey. 30How much better if today the troops had eaten freely of the spoil taken from their enemies; for now the slaughter among the Philistines has not been great."

31 After they had struck down the Philistines that day from Michmash to Aijalon, the troops were very faint; 32so the troops flew upon the spoil, and took sheep and oxen and calves, and slaughtered them on the ground; and the troops ate them with the blood. 33Then it was reported to Saul, "Look, the troops are sinning against the LORD by eating with the blood." And he said, "You have dealt treacherously; roll a large stone before me here."[c] 34Saul

said, "Disperse yourselves among the troops, and say to them, 'Let all bring their oxen or their sheep, and slaughter them here, and eat; and do not sin against the LORD by eating with the blood.' " So all of the troops brought their oxen with them that night, and slaughtered them there. 35And Saul built an altar to the LORD; it was the first altar that he built to the LORD.

JONATHAN IN DANGER OF DEATH

36 Then Saul said, "Let us go down after the Philistines by night and despoil them until the morning light; let us not leave one of them." They said, "Do whatever seems good to you." But the priest said, "Let us draw near to God here." 37So Saul inquired of God, "Shall I go down after the Philistines? Will you give them into the hand of Israel?" But he did not answer him that day. 38Saul said, "Come here, all you leaders of the people; and let us find out how this sin has arisen today. 39For as the LORD lives who saves Israel, even if it is in my son Jonathan, he shall surely die!" But there was no one among all the people who answered him. 40He said to all Israel, "You shall be on one side, and I and my son Jonathan will be on the other side." The people said to Saul, "Do what seems good to you." 41Then Saul said, "O LORD God of Israel, why have you not answered your servant today? If this guilt is in me or in my son Jonathan, O LORD God of Israel, give Urim; but if this guilt is in your people Israel,[d] give Thummim." And Jonathan and Saul were indicated by the lot, but the people were cleared. 42Then Saul said, "Cast the lot between me and my son Jonathan." And Jonathan was taken.

43 Then Saul said to Jonathan, "Tell me what you have done." Jonathan told him, "I tasted a little honey with the tip of the staff that

---

a 14.24 Gk: Heb The Israelites were distressed that day   b 14.25 Heb land   c 14.33 Gk: Heb me this day   d 14.41 Vg Compare Gk: Heb 41Saul said to the LORD, the God of Israel

was in my hand; here I am, I will die." ⁴⁴Saul said, "God do so to me and more also; you shall surely die, Jonathan!" ⁴⁵Then the people said to Saul, "Shall Jonathan die, who has accomplished this great victory in Israel? Far from it! As the LORD lives, not one hair of his head shall fall to the ground; for he has worked with God today." So the people ransomed Jonathan, and he did not die. ⁴⁶Then Saul withdrew from pursuing the Philistines; and the Philistines went to their own place.

SAUL'S CONTINUING WARS

⁴⁷When Saul had taken the kingship over Israel, he fought against all his enemies on every side—against Moab, against the Ammonites, against Edom, against the kings of Zobah, and against the Philistines; wherever he turned he routed them. ⁴⁸He did valiantly, and struck down the Amalekites, and rescued Israel out of the hands of those who plundered them.

⁴⁹Now the sons of Saul were Jonathan, Ishvi, and Malchishua; and the names of his two daughters were these: the name of the firstborn was Merab, and the name of the younger, Michal. ⁵⁰The name of Saul's wife was Ahinoam daughter of Ahimaaz. And the name of the commander of his army was Abner son of Ner, Saul's uncle; ⁵¹Kish was the father of Saul, and Ner the father of Abner was the son of Abiel.

⁵²There was hard fighting against the Philistines all the days of Saul; and when Saul saw any strong or valiant warrior, he took him into his service.

SAUL DEFEATS THE AMALEKITES BUT SPARES THEIR KING

15 Samuel said to Saul, "The LORD sent me to anoint you king over his people Israel; now therefore listen to the words of the LORD. ²Thus says the LORD of hosts, 'I will punish the Amalekites for what they did in opposing the Israelites when they came up out of Egypt. ³Now go and attack Amalek, and utterly destroy all that they have; do not spare them, but kill both man and woman, child and infant, ox and sheep, camel and donkey.'"

⁴So Saul summoned the people, and numbered them in Telaim, two hundred thousand foot soldiers, and ten thousand soldiers of Judah. ⁵Saul came to the city of the Amalekites and lay in wait in the valley. ⁶Saul said to the Kenites, "Go! Leave! Withdraw from among the Amalekites, or I will destroy you with them; for you showed kindness to all the people of Israel when they came up out of Egypt." So the Kenites withdrew from the Amalekites. ⁷Saul defeated the Amalekites, from Havilah as far as Shur, which is east of Egypt. ⁸He took King Agag of the Amalekites alive, but utterly destroyed all the people with the edge of the sword. ⁹Saul and the people spared Agag, and the best of the sheep and of the cattle and of the fatlings, and the lambs, and all that was valuable, and would not utterly destroy them; all that was despised and worthless they utterly destroyed.

SAUL REJECTED AS KING

¹⁰The word of the LORD came to Samuel: ¹¹"I regret that I made Saul king, for he has turned back from following me, and has not carried out my commands." Samuel was angry; and he cried out to the LORD all night. ¹²Samuel rose early in the morning to meet Saul, and Samuel was told, "Saul went to Carmel, where he set up a monument for himself, and on returning he passed on down to Gilgal." ¹³When Samuel came to Saul, Saul said to him, "May you be blessed by the LORD; I have carried out the command of the LORD." ¹⁴But Samuel said, "What then is this bleating of sheep in my ears, and the lowing of cattle that I hear?" ¹⁵Saul said, "They have brought them from the Amalekites; for the people spared the best of the sheep and the cattle, to sacrifice to the LORD your God; but the rest we have utterly destroyed." ¹⁶Then Samuel said to Saul, "Stop! I will tell you what the LORD said to me last night." He replied, "Speak."

17 Samuel said, "Though you are little in your own eyes, are you not the head of the tribes of Israel? The LORD anointed you king over Israel. **18**And the LORD sent you on a mission, and said, 'Go, utterly destroy the sinners, the Amalekites, and fight against them until they are consumed.' **19**Why then did you not obey the voice of the LORD? Why did you swoop down on the spoil, and do what was evil in the sight of the LORD?" **20**Saul said to Samuel, "I have obeyed the voice of the LORD, I have gone on the mission on which the LORD sent me, I have brought Agag the king of Amalek, and I have utterly destroyed the Amalekites. **21**But from the spoil the people took sheep and cattle, the best of the things devoted to destruction, to sacrifice to the LORD your God in Gilgal." **22**And Samuel said,

"Has the LORD as great delight
　　in burnt offerings
　　　and sacrifices,
　as in obedience to the
　　voice of the LORD?
Surely, to obey is better
　　than sacrifice,
　and to heed than the
　　fat of rams.
23 For rebellion is no less a sin
　　than divination,
　and stubbornness is like
　　iniquity and idolatry.
Because you have rejected the
　　word of the LORD,
　he has also rejected you
　　from being king."

24 Saul said to Samuel, "I have sinned; for I have transgressed the commandment of the LORD and your words, because I feared the people and obeyed their voice. **25**Now therefore, I pray, pardon my sin, and return with me, so that I may worship the LORD." **26**Samuel said to Saul, "I will not return with you; for you have rejected the word of the LORD, and the LORD has rejected you from being king over Israel." **27**As Samuel turned to go away, Saul caught hold of the hem of his robe, and it tore. **28**And Samuel said to him, "The LORD has torn the kingdom of Israel from you this

very day, and has given it to a neighbor of yours, who is better than you. **29**Moreover the Glory of Israel will not recant[a] or change his mind; for he is not a mortal, that he should change his mind." **30**Then Saul[b] said, "I have sinned; yet honor me now before the elders of my people and before Israel, and return with me, so that I may worship the LORD your God." **31**So Samuel turned back after Saul; and Saul worshiped the LORD.

32 Then Samuel said, "Bring Agag king of the Amalekites here to me." And Agag came to him haltingly.[c] Agag said, "Surely this is the bitterness of death."[d] **33**But Samuel said,

"As your sword has made
　　women childless,
　so your mother shall be
　　childless among women."

And Samuel hewed Agag in pieces before the LORD in Gilgal.

34 Then Samuel went to Ramah; and Saul went up to his house in Gibeah of Saul. **35**Samuel did not see Saul again until the day of his death, but Samuel grieved over Saul. And the LORD was sorry that he had made Saul king over Israel.

DAVID ANOINTED AS KING

16 The LORD said to Samuel, "How long will you grieve over Saul? I have rejected him from being king over Israel. Fill your horn with oil and set out; I will send you to Jesse the Bethlehemite, for I have provided for myself a king among his sons." **2**Samuel said, "How can I go? If Saul hears of it, he will kill me." And the LORD said, "Take a heifer with you, and say, 'I have come to sacrifice to the LORD.' **3**Invite Jesse to the sacrifice, and I will show you what you shall do; and you shall anoint for me the one whom I name to you." **4**Samuel did what the LORD commanded, and came to Bethlehem. The elders of the city came to meet him trembling, and said, "Do you come peaceably?" **5**He said, "Peaceably; I have come to sacrifice

---

[a] **15.29** Q Ms Gk: MT *deceive*　[b] **15.30** Heb *he*　[c] **15.32** Cn Compare Gk: Meaning of Heb uncertain　[d] **15.32** Q Ms Gk: MT *Surely the bitterness of death is past*

to the LORD; sanctify yourselves and come with me to the sacrifice." And he sanctified Jesse and his sons and invited them to the sacrifice.

6 When they came, he looked on Eliab and thought, "Surely the LORD's anointed is now before the LORD."[a] 7 But the LORD said to Samuel, "Do not look on his appearance or on the height of his stature, because I have rejected him; for the LORD does not see as mortals see; they look on the outward appearance, but the LORD looks on the heart." 8 Then Jesse called Abinadab, and made him pass before Samuel. He said, "Neither has the LORD chosen this one." 9 Then Jesse made Shammah pass by. And he said, "Neither has the LORD chosen this one." 10 Jesse made seven of his sons pass before Samuel, and Samuel said to Jesse, "The LORD has not chosen any of these." 11 Samuel said to Jesse, "Are all your sons here?" And he said, "There remains yet the youngest, but he is keeping the sheep." And Samuel said to Jesse, "Send and bring him; for we will not sit down until he comes here." 12 He sent and brought him in. Now he was ruddy, and had beautiful eyes, and was handsome. The LORD said, "Rise and anoint him; for this is the one." 13 Then Samuel took the horn of oil, and anointed him in the presence of his brothers; and the spirit of the LORD came mightily upon David from that day forward. Samuel then set out and went to Ramah.

DAVID PLAYS THE LYRE FOR SAUL

14 Now the spirit of the LORD departed from Saul, and an evil spirit from the LORD tormented him. 15 And Saul's servants said to him, "See now, an evil spirit from God is tormenting you. 16 Let our lord now command the servants who attend you to look for someone who is skillful in playing the lyre; and when the evil spirit from God is upon you, he will play it, and you will feel better." 17 So Saul said to his servants, "Provide for me someone who can play

PONDER

But the LORD said to Samuel, "Do not look on his appearance or on the height of his stature, because I have rejected him; for the LORD does not see as mortals see; they look on the outward appearance, but the LORD looks on the heart."
—1 Samuel 16.7

PRAY

Sovereign Lord, we are grateful for these transforming words. You looked beyond David's youth, beyond his stature, and saw his heart, a heart that was turned toward you. Search our hearts also, Lord, and beckon them to you, Lord, so that we become people open to the leading of your Holy Spirit. And just as David made mistakes and sinned, so also do we. Thank you for offering us forgiveness and grace. Amen.

well, and bring him to me." 18 One of the young men answered, "I have seen a son of Jesse the Bethlehemite who is skillful in playing, a man of valor, a warrior, prudent in speech, and a man of good presence; and the LORD is with him." 19 So Saul sent messengers to Jesse, and said, "Send me your son David who is with the sheep." 20 Jesse took a donkey loaded with bread, a skin of wine, and a kid, and sent them by his son David to Saul. 21 And David came to Saul, and entered his service. Saul loved him greatly, and he became his armorbearer. 22 Saul sent to Jesse, saying, "Let David remain in my service, for he has found favor in my sight." 23 And whenever the evil spirit from God came upon Saul, David took the lyre and played it with his hand, and Saul would be relieved and feel better, and the evil spirit would depart from him.

[a] 16.6 Heb *him*

DAVID AND GOLIATH

17 Now the Philistines gathered their armies for battle; they were gathered at Socoh, which belongs to Judah, and encamped between Socoh and Azekah, in Ephes-dammim. ²Saul and the Israelites gathered and encamped in the valley of Elah, and formed ranks against the Philistines. ³The Philistines stood on the mountain on the one side, and Israel stood on the mountain on the other side, with a valley between them. ⁴And there came out from the camp of the Philistines a champion named Goliath, of Gath, whose height was six[a] cubits and a span. ⁵He had a helmet of bronze on his head, and he was armed with a coat of mail; the weight of the coat was five thousand shekels of bronze. ⁶He had greaves of bronze on his legs and a javelin of bronze slung between his shoulders. ⁷The shaft of his spear was like a weaver's beam, and his spear's head weighed six hundred shekels of iron; and his shield-bearer went before him. ⁸He stood and shouted to the ranks of Israel, "Why have you come out to draw up for battle? Am I not a Philistine, and are you not servants of Saul? Choose a man for yourselves, and let him come down to me. ⁹If he is able to fight with me and kill me, then we will be your servants; but if I prevail against him and kill him, then you shall be our servants and serve us." ¹⁰And the Philistine said, "Today I defy the ranks of Israel! Give me a man, that we may fight together." ¹¹When Saul and all Israel heard these words of the Philistine, they were dismayed and greatly afraid.

12 Now David was the son of an Ephrathite of Bethlehem in Judah, named Jesse, who had eight sons. In the days of Saul the man was already old and advanced in years.[b] ¹³The three eldest sons of Jesse had followed Saul to the battle; the names of his three sons who went to the battle were Eliab the firstborn, and next to him Abinadab, and the third Shammah. ¹⁴David was the youngest; the three eldest followed Saul, ¹⁵but David went back and forth from Saul to feed his father's sheep at Bethlehem. ¹⁶For forty days the Philistine came forward and took his stand, morning and evening.

17 Jesse said to his son David, "Take for your brothers an ephah of this parched grain and these ten loaves, and carry them quickly to the camp to your brothers; ¹⁸also take these ten cheeses to the commander of their thousand. See how your brothers fare, and bring some token from them."

19 Now Saul, and they, and all the men of Israel, were in the valley of Elah, fighting with the Philistines. ²⁰David rose early in the morning, left the sheep with a keeper, took the provisions, and went as Jesse had commanded him. He came to the encampment as the army was going forth to the battle line, shouting the war cry. ²¹Israel and the Philistines drew up for battle, army against army. ²²David left the things in charge of the keeper of the baggage, ran to the ranks, and went and greeted his brothers. ²³As he talked with them, the champion, the Philistine of Gath, Goliath by name, came up out of the ranks of the Philistines, and spoke the same words as before. And David heard him.

24 All the Israelites, when they saw the man, fled from him and were very much afraid. ²⁵The Israelites said, "Have you seen this man who has come up? Surely he has come up to defy Israel. The king will greatly enrich the man who kills him, and will give him his daughter and make his family free in Israel." ²⁶David said to the men who stood by him, "What shall be done for the man who kills this Philistine, and takes away the reproach from Israel? For who is this uncircumcised Philistine that he should defy the armies of the living God?" ²⁷The people answered him in the same way, "So shall it be done for the man who kills him."

---

[a] 17.4 MT: Q Ms Gk *four*   [b] 17.12 Gk Syr: Heb *among men*

28 His eldest brother Eliab heard him talking to the men; and Eliab's anger was kindled against David. He said, "Why have you come down? With whom have you left those few sheep in the wilderness? I know your presumption and the evil of your heart; for you have come down just to see the battle." 29David said, "What have I done now? It was only a question." 30He turned away from him toward another and spoke in the same way; and the people answered him again as before.

31When the words that David spoke were heard, they repeated them before Saul; and he sent for him. 32David said to Saul, "Let no one's heart fail because of him; your servant will go and fight with this Philistine." 33Saul said to David, "You are not able to go against this Philistine to fight with him; for you are just a boy, and he has been a warrior from his youth." 34But David said to Saul, "Your servant used to keep sheep for his father; and whenever a lion or a bear came, and took a lamb from the flock, 35I went after it and struck it down, rescuing the lamb from its mouth; and if it turned against me, I would catch it by the jaw, strike it down, and kill it. 36Your servant has killed both lions and bears; and this uncircumcised Philistine shall be like one of them, since he has defied the armies of the living God." 37David said, "The LORD, who saved me from the paw of the lion and from the paw of the bear, will save me from the hand of this Philistine." So Saul said to David, "Go, and may the LORD be with you!"

38 Saul clothed David with his armor; he put a bronze helmet on his head and clothed him with a coat of mail. 39David strapped Saul's sword over the armor, and he tried in vain to walk, for he was not used to them. Then David said to Saul, "I cannot walk with these; for I am not used to them." So David removed them. 40Then he took his staff in his hand, and chose five smooth stones from the wadi, and put them in his shepherd's bag, in the pouch; his sling was in his hand, and he drew near to the Philistine.

41 The Philistine came on and drew near to David, with his shield-bearer in front of him. 42When the Philistine looked and saw David, he disdained him, for he was only a youth, ruddy and handsome in appearance. 43The Philistine said to David, "Am I a dog, that you come to me with sticks?" And the Philistine cursed David by his gods. 44The Philistine said to David, "Come to me, and I will give your flesh to the birds of the air and to the wild animals of the field." 45But David said to the Philistine, "You come to me with sword and spear and javelin; but I come to you in the name of the LORD of hosts, the God of the armies of Israel, whom you have defied. 46This very day the LORD will deliver you into my hand, and I will strike you down and cut off your head; and I will give the dead bodies of the Philistine army this very day to the birds of the air and to the wild animals of the earth, so that all the earth may know that there is a God in Israel, 47and that all this assembly may know that the LORD does not save by sword and spear; for the battle is the LORD's and he will give you into our hand."

48 When the Philistine drew nearer to meet David, David ran quickly toward the battle line to meet the Philistine. 49David put his hand in his bag, took out a stone, slung it, and struck the Philistine on his forehead; the stone sank into his forehead, and he fell face down on the ground.

50 So David prevailed over the Philistine with a sling and a stone, striking down the Philistine and killing him; there was no sword in David's hand. 51Then David ran and stood over the Philistine; he grasped his sword, drew it out of its sheath, and killed him; then he cut off his head with it.

When the Philistines saw that their champion was dead, they fled. 52The troops of Israel and Judah rose up with a shout and pursued the Philistines as far as Gath[a] and the gates of Ekron, so that the wounded Philistines fell on the way from Shaaraim as far as Gath and Ekron. 53The Israelites came back from chasing the Philistines, and they plundered their camp. 54David took the head of the Philistine and brought it to Jerusalem; but he put his armor in his tent.

55 When Saul saw David go out against the Philistine, he said to Abner, the commander of the army, "Abner, whose son is this young man?" Abner said, "As your soul lives, O king, I do not know." 56The king said, "Inquire whose son the stripling is." 57On David's return from killing the Philistine, Abner took him and brought him before Saul, with the head of the Philistine in his hand. 58Saul said to him, "Whose son are you, young man?" And David answered, "I am the son of your servant Jesse the Bethlehemite."

JONATHAN'S COVENANT WITH DAVID

18 When David[b] had finished speaking to Saul, the soul of Jonathan was bound to the soul of David, and Jonathan loved him as his own soul. 2Saul took him that day and would not let him return to his father's house. 3Then Jonathan made a covenant with David, because he loved him as his own soul. 4Jonathan stripped himself of the robe that he was wearing, and gave it to David, and his armor, and even his sword and his bow and his belt. 5David went out and was successful wherever Saul sent him; as a result, Saul set him over the army. And all the people, even the servants of Saul, approved.

6 As they were coming home, when David returned from killing the Philistine, the women came out of all the towns of Israel, singing and dancing, to meet King Saul, with tambourines, with songs of joy, and with musical instruments.[c] 7And the women sang to one another as they made merry,

"Saul has killed his thousands,
and David his ten thousands."

8Saul was very angry, for this saying displeased him. He said, "They have ascribed to David ten thousands, and to me they have ascribed thousands; what more can he have but the kingdom?" 9So Saul eyed David from that day on.

[a] 17.52 Gk Syr: Heb *Gai* [b] 18.1 Heb *he* [c] 18.6 Or *triangles,* or *three-stringed instruments*

⊢⊣ **BIBLE IN LIFE** ▷ ⊖⊣

Bonds of Friendship
1 Samuel 18.1–4

How many true friends do you have with whom you can let down your guard and share your shortcomings, doubts and fears? I have a few friends of whom I'm very proud and whom I cherish, but how many of them would I trust with my life or my darkest secrets? Like many people, I often feel reticent about sharing my inner thoughts and plans, my secret frustrations and failures. In contrast, my brother Billy had many friends with whom he felt very close. The difference between our personalities was quite noticeable. You could argue that I have been more successful in life politically or financially, but I would claim that in some ways, Billy was more successful than I was because he demonstrated this ability to reach out to others in an intimate way. In the same way, Saul's son Jonathan formed a very strong bond of friendship with David, a friendship that endured even through the most trying circumstances. Long after Jonathan was killed in battle and David took the throne of Israel, David continued to honor Jonathan and his descendants. We have opportunities to form strong bonds of friendship, but how often do we capitalize on these opportunities? When we emulate Jonathan and form bonds of friendship with others, we establish powerful alliances that help us stand strong through the many challenges we face.

JEALOUSY OR GRATITUDE?

Saul was very angry, for this saying displeased him. He said, "They have as-cribed to David ten thousands, and to me they have ascribed thousands."

—1 Samuel 18.8

Jealousy seems intrinsic to human nature. We envy the neighbor whose children are more academically distinguished than ours, whose home is nicer than ours or whose career is more prestigious than ours. Instead of appreciating and admiring them for their accomplishments, we grow resentful toward them. We may even resort to tearing that person down or sharing rumors we've heard about them.

When we meet David in 1 Samuel 18, he is faithfully serving his king (Saul) and his God. David had no ambition to acquire Saul's position as leader of the nation. In fact, as Saul continued to try to hunt him down, David remained loyal to Saul (see 1 Samuel 24–26). David's success as a warrior and his great popularity galled Saul, however, who grew jealous and soon wanted him gone. In stark contrast, Saul's son Jonathan—the heir apparent to the throne of Israel—displayed no jealousy at all toward David. Instead, he loved David as he loved himself. Jonathan even presented David with the very symbols of his royal position, saying, in essence, "I give you the right to the throne" (see 1 Samuel 18.1–5).

What can lead one person to jealousy and another to appreciation? It comes from two things: 1) measuring our success in terms of Jesus' priorities and 2) trusting in the promises of God. When we make Christ's love the measure of our worth, we will no longer need to compare ourselves with others and be jealous of them. At the same time, we can trust in the wonderful promises of God's love, which free us from the need to reach for acceptance, significance or security. Romans 8.38–39 assures us that "neither death, nor life, nor angels, nor rulers, nor things present, nor things to come, nor powers, nor height, nor depth, nor anything else in all creation, will be able to separate us from the love of God in Christ Jesus our Lord." No failure, no tragedy, no outside force, nothing that we can ever experience can separate us from God's infinite love for us in Christ Jesus. That's a wonderful promise.

We must look to God for our significance and know that the Lord loves us more than we can possibly imagine—not because of anything we have done but simply because of who God is. Then, instead of being jealous of others' accomplishments and relationships, we will be free to rejoice in them and even admire them.

Going Deeper

- What kinds of things make you jealous of others? What does that say about where you are finding your significance?
- Why does God love you? How does your answer match up with what the Bible says about God's love for you?

SAUL TRIES TO KILL DAVID

10 The next day an evil spirit from God rushed upon Saul, and he raved within his house, while David was playing the lyre, as he did day by day. Saul had his spear in his hand; 11and Saul threw the spear, for he thought, "I will pin David to the wall." But David eluded him twice. 12 Saul was afraid of David, because the LORD was with him but had departed from Saul. 13 So Saul removed him from his presence, and made him a commander of a thousand; and David marched out and came in, leading the army. 14David had success in all his undertakings; for the LORD was with him. 15When Saul saw that he had great success, he stood in awe of him. 16But all Israel and Judah loved David; for it was he who marched out and came in leading them.

DAVID MARRIES MICHAL

17 Then Saul said to David, "Here is my elder daughter Merab; I will give her to you as a wife; only be valiant for me and fight the LORD's battles." For Saul thought, "I will not raise a hand against him; let the Philistines deal with him." 18David said to Saul, "Who am I and who are my kinsfolk, my father's family in Israel, that I should be son-in-law to the king?" 19But at the time when Saul's daughter Merab should have been given to David, she was given to Adriel the Meholathite as a wife. 20 Now Saul's daughter Michal loved David. Saul was told, and the thing pleased him. 21Saul thought, "Let me give her to him that she may be a snare for him and that the hand of the Philistines may be against him." Therefore Saul said to David a second time,a "You shall now be my son-in-law." 22Saul commanded his servants, "Speak to David in private and say, 'See, the king is delighted with you, and all his servants love you; now then, become the king's son-in-law.' " 23So Saul's servants reported these words to David in private. And David said, "Does it seem to you a little thing to become the king's son-in-law,

seeing that I am a poor man and of no repute?" 24The servants of Saul told him, "This is what David said." 25Then Saul said, "Thus shall you say to David, 'The king desires no marriage present except a hundred foreskins of the Philistines, that he may be avenged on the king's enemies.' " Now Saul planned to make David fall by the hand of the Philistines. 26When his servants told David these words, David was well pleased to be the king's son-in-law. Before the time had expired, 27David rose and went, along with his men, and killed one hundredb of the Philistines; and David brought their foreskins, which were given in full number to the king, that he might become the king's son-in-law. Saul gave him his daughter Michal as a wife. 28But when Saul realized that the LORD was with David, and that Saul's daughter Michal loved him, 29Saul was still more afraid of David. So Saul was David's enemy from that time forward.

30 Then the commanders of the Philistines came out to battle; and as often as they came out, David had more success than all the servants of Saul, so that his fame became very great.

JONATHAN INTERCEDES FOR DAVID

19 Saul spoke with his son Jonathan and with all his servants about killing David. But Saul's son Jonathan took great delight in David. 2Jonathan told David, "My father Saul is trying to kill you; therefore be on guard tomorrow morning; stay in a secret place and hide yourself. 3I will go out and stand beside my father in the field where you are, and I will speak to my father about you; if I learn anything I will tell you." 4Jonathan spoke well of David to his father Saul, saying to him, "The king should not sin against his servant David, because he has not sinned against you, and because his deeds have been of good service to you; 5for he took his

a 18.21 Heb by two   b 18.27 Gk Compare 2 Sam 3.14: Heb two hundred

life in his hand when he attacked the Philistine, and the LORD brought about a great victory for all Israel. You saw it, and rejoiced; why then will you sin against an innocent person by killing David without cause?" ⁶Saul heeded the voice of Jonathan; Saul swore, "As the LORD lives, he shall not be put to death." ⁷So Jonathan called David and related all these things to him. Jonathan then brought David to Saul, and he was in his presence as before.

MICHAL HELPS DAVID ESCAPE FROM SAUL

8 Again there was war, and David went out to fight the Philistines. He launched a heavy attack on them, so that they fled before him. ⁹Then an evil spirit from the LORD came upon Saul, as he sat in his house with his spear in his hand, while David was playing music. ¹⁰Saul sought to pin David to the wall with the spear; but he eluded Saul, so that he struck the spear into the wall. David fled and escaped that night.

11 Saul sent messengers to David's house to keep watch over him, planning to kill him in the morning. David's wife Michal told him, "If you do not save your life tonight, tomorrow you will be killed." ¹²So Michal let David down through the window; he fled away and escaped. ¹³Michal took an idolᵃ and laid it on the bed; she put a netᵇ of goats' hair on its head, and covered it with the clothes. ¹⁴When Saul sent messengers to take David, she said, "He is sick." ¹⁵Then Saul sent the messengers to see David for themselves. He said, "Bring him up to me in the bed, that I may kill him." ¹⁶When the messengers came in, the idolᶜ was in the bed, with the coveringᵇ of goats' hair on its head. ¹⁷Saul said to Michal, "Why have you deceived me like this, and let my enemy go, so that he has escaped?" Michal answered Saul, "He said to me, 'Let me go; why should I kill you?'"

DAVID JOINS SAMUEL IN RAMAH

18 Now David fled and escaped; he came to Samuel at Ramah, and told

him all that Saul had done to him. He and Samuel went and settled at Naioth. ¹⁹Saul was told, "David is at Naioth in Ramah." ²⁰Then Saul sent messengers to take David. When they saw the company of the prophets in a frenzy, with Samuel standing in charge ofᵇ them, the spirit of God came upon the messengers of Saul, and they also fell into a prophetic frenzy. ²¹When Saul was told, he sent other messengers, and they also fell into a frenzy. Saul sent messengers again the third time, and they also fell into a frenzy. ²²Then he himself went to Ramah. He came to the great well that is in Secu;ᵈ he asked, "Where are Samuel and David?" And someone said, "They are at Naioth in Ramah." ²³He went there, toward Naioth in Ramah; and the spirit of God came upon him. As he was going, he fell into a prophetic frenzy, until he came to Naioth in Ramah. ²⁴He too stripped off his clothes, and he too fell into a frenzy before Samuel. He lay naked all that day and all that night. Therefore it is said, "Is Saul also among the prophets?"

THE FRIENDSHIP OF DAVID AND JONATHAN

20 David fled from Naioth in Ramah. He came before Jonathan and said, "What have I done? What is my guilt? And what is my sin against your father that he is trying to take my life?" ²He said to him, "Far from it! You shall not die. My father does nothing either great or small without disclosing it to me; and why should my father hide this from me? Never!" ³But David also swore, "Your father knows well that you like me; and he thinks, 'Do not let Jonathan know this, or he will be grieved.' But truly, as the LORD lives and as you yourself live, there is but a step between me and death." ⁴Then Jonathan said to David, "Whatever you say, I will do for you."

ᵃ 19.13 Heb took the teraphim
ᵇ 19.13,16,20 Meaning of Heb uncertain
ᶜ 19.16 Heb the teraphim   ᵈ 19.22 Gk reads to the well of the threshing floor on the bare height

5David said to Jonathan, "Tomorrow is the new moon, and I should not fail to sit with the king at the meal; but let me go, so that I may hide in the field until the third evening. 6If your father misses me at all, then say, 'David earnestly asked leave of me to run to Bethlehem his city; for there is a yearly sacrifice there for all the family.' 7If he says, 'Good!' it will be well with your servant; but if he is angry, then know that evil has been determined by him. 8Therefore deal kindly with your servant, for you have brought your servant into a sacred covenanta with you. But if there is guilt in me, kill me yourself; why should you bring me to your father?" 9Jonathan said, "Far be it from you! If I knew that it was decided by my father that evil should come upon you, would I not tell you?" 10Then David said to Jonathan, "Who will tell me if your father answers you harshly?" 11Jonathan replied to David, "Come, let us go out into the field." So they both went out into the field.

12Jonathan said to David, "By the LORD, the God of Israel! When I have sounded out my father, about this time tomorrow, or on the third day, if he is well disposed toward David, shall I not then send and disclose it to you? 13But if my father intends to do you harm, the LORD do so to Jonathan, and more also, if I do not disclose it to you, and send you away, so that you may go in safety. May the LORD be with you, as he has been with my father. 14If I am still alive, show me the faithful love of the LORD; but if I die,b 15never cut off your faithful love from my house, even if the LORD were to cut off every one of the enemies of David from the face of the earth." 16Thus Jonathan made a covenant with the house of David, saying, "May the LORD seek out the enemies of David." 17Jonathan made David swear again by his love for him; for he loved him as he loved his own life.

18Jonathan said to him, "Tomorrow is the new moon; you will be missed, because your place will be empty. 19On the day after tomorrow, you shall go a long way down; go to the place where you hid yourself earlier, and remain beside the stone there.b 20I will shoot three arrows to the side of it, as though I shot at a mark. 21Then I will send the boy, saying, 'Go, find the arrows.' If I say to the boy, 'Look, the arrows are on this side of you, collect them,' then you are to come, for, as the LORD lives, it is safe for you and there is no danger. 22But if I say to the young man, 'Look, the arrows are beyond you,' then go; for the LORD has sent you away. 23As for the matter about which you and I have spoken, the LORD is witnessc between you and me forever."

24 So David hid himself in the field. When the new moon came, the king sat at the feast to eat. 25The king sat upon his seat, as at other times, upon the seat by the wall. Jonathan stood, while Abner sat by Saul's side; but David's place was empty. 26 Saul did not say anything that day; for he thought, "Something has befallen him; he is not clean, surely he is not clean." 27But on the second day, the day after the new moon, David's place was empty. And Saul said to his son Jonathan, "Why has the son of Jesse not come to the feast, either yesterday or today?" 28Jonathan answered Saul, "David earnestly asked leave of me to go to Bethlehem; 29he said, 'Let me go; for our family is holding a sacrifice in the city, and my brother has commanded me to be there. So now, if I have found favor in your sight, let me get away, and see my brothers.' For this reason he has not come to the king's table."

30 Then Saul's anger was kindled against Jonathan. He said to him, "You son of a perverse, rebellious woman! Do I not know that you have chosen the son of Jesse to your own shame, and to the shame of your mother's nakedness? 31For as long as the son of Jesse lives upon the earth, neither you nor your kingdom shall be established. Now send and bring

a 20.8 Heb a covenant of the LORD
b 20.14,19 Meaning of Heb uncertain
c 20.23 Gk: Heb lacks witness

him to me, for he shall surely die." ³²Then Jonathan answered his father Saul, "Why should he be put to death? What has he done?" ³³But Saul threw his spear at him to strike him; so Jonathan knew that it was the decision of his father to put David to death. ³⁴Jonathan rose from the table in fierce anger and ate no food on the second day of the month, for he was grieved for David, and because his father had disgraced him.

³⁵ In the morning Jonathan went out into the field to the appointment with David, and with him was a little boy. ³⁶He said to the boy, "Run and find the arrows that I shoot." As the boy ran, he shot an arrow beyond him. ³⁷When the boy came to the place where Jonathan's arrow had fallen, Jonathan called after the boy and said, "Is the arrow not beyond you?" ³⁸Jonathan called after the boy, "Hurry, be quick, do not linger." So Jonathan's boy gathered up the arrows and came to his master. ³⁹But the boy knew nothing; only Jonathan and David knew the arrangement. ⁴⁰Jonathan gave his weapons to the boy and said to him, "Go and carry them to the city." ⁴¹As soon as the boy had gone, David rose from beside the stone heap[a] and prostrated himself with his face to the ground. He bowed three times, and they kissed each other, and wept with each other; David wept the more.[b] ⁴²Then Jonathan said to David, "Go in peace, since both of us have sworn in the name of the LORD, saying, 'The LORD shall be between me and you, and between my descendants and your descendants, forever.' " He got up and left; and Jonathan went into the city.[c]

DAVID AND THE HOLY BREAD

21[d] David came to Nob to the priest Ahimelech. Ahimelech came trembling to meet David, and said to him, "Why are you alone, and no one with you?" ²David said to the priest Ahimelech, "The king has charged me with a matter, and said to me, 'No one must know anything of the matter about which I send you, and with which I have charged you.'

PONDER

Then Jonathan said to David, "Go in peace, since both of us have sworn in the name of the LORD, saying, 'The LORD shall be between me and you, and between my descendants and your descendants, forever.'"
—1 Samuel 20.42

PRAY

O Father, we pray that we can be a friend to others like Jonathan was to David, that we will exceed your challenge to reach out to others and therefore to enrich their lives and our own. Give us the wisdom to know how to do this. Give us your Holy Spirit to be with us. Receive our thanks for this challenging and adventurous story of kings, bows and arrows and a friendship that you blessed. Let us see the parallels between Jonathan's life and our own and apply these words as we serve Jesus Christ our Savior and your kingdom. In his name we pray. Amen.

I have made an appointment[e] with the young men for such and such a place. ³Now then, what have you at hand? Give me five loaves of bread, or whatever is here." ⁴The priest answered David, "I have no ordinary bread at hand, only holy bread—provided that the young men have kept themselves from women." ⁵David answered the priest, "Indeed women have been kept from us as always when I go on an expedition; the vessels of the young men are holy even when it is a common journey; how much more today will their vessels be holy?" ⁶So the priest gave him the holy bread; for there was no bread there except the bread of the

[a] 20.41 Gk: Heb *from beside the south*   [b] 20.41 Vg: Meaning of Heb uncertain   [c] 20.42 This sentence is 21.1 in Heb   [d] 21.1 Ch 21.2 in Heb   [e] 21.2 Q Ms Vg Compare Gk: Meaning of MT uncertain

Presence, which is removed from before the LORD, to be replaced by hot bread on the day it is taken away.

7 Now a certain man of the servants of Saul was there that day, detained before the LORD; his name was Doeg the Edomite, the chief of Saul's shepherds.

8 David said to Ahimelech, "Is there no spear or sword here with you? I did not bring my sword or my weapons with me, because the king's business required haste." 9 The priest said, "The sword of Goliath the Philistine, whom you killed in the valley of Elah, is here wrapped in a cloth behind the ephod; if you will take that, take it, for there is none here except that one." David said, "There is none like it; give it to me."

DAVID FLEES TO GATH

10 David rose and fled that day from Saul; he went to King Achish of Gath. 11 The servants of Achish said to him, "Is this not David the king of the land? Did they not sing to one another of him in dances,

'Saul has killed his thousands,
and David his ten thousands'?"

12 David took these words to heart and was very much afraid of King Achish of Gath. 13 So he changed his behavior before them; he pretended to be mad when in their presence.[a] He scratched marks on the doors of the gate, and let his spittle run down his beard. 14 Achish said to his servants, "Look, you see the man is mad; why then have you brought him to me? 15 Do I lack madmen, that you have brought this fellow to play the madman in my presence? Shall this fellow come into my house?"

DAVID AND HIS FOLLOWERS AT ADULLAM

22 David left there and escaped to the cave of Adullam; when his brothers and all his father's house heard of it, they went down there to him. 2 Everyone who was in distress, and everyone who was in debt, and everyone who was discontented gathered to him; and he became captain over them. Those who were with him numbered about four hundred.

3 David went from there to Mizpeh of Moab. He said to the king of Moab, "Please let my father and mother come[b] to you, until I know what God will do for me." 4 He left them with the king of Moab, and they stayed with him all the time that David was in the stronghold. 5 Then the prophet Gad said to David, "Do not remain in the stronghold; leave, and go into the land of Judah." So David left, and went into the forest of Hereth.

SAUL SLAUGHTERS THE PRIESTS AT NOB

6 Saul heard that David and those who were with him had been located. Saul was sitting at Gibeah, under the tamarisk tree on the height, with his spear in his hand, and all his servants were standing around him. 7 Saul said to his servants who stood around him, "Hear now, you Benjaminites; will the son of Jesse give every one of you fields and vineyards, will he make you all commanders of thousands and commanders of hundreds? 8 Is that why all of you have conspired against me? No one discloses to me when my son makes a league with the son of Jesse, none of you is sorry for me or discloses to me that my son has stirred up my servant against me, to lie in wait, as he is doing today." 9 Doeg the Edomite, who was in charge of Saul's servants, answered, "I saw the son of Jesse coming to Nob, to Ahimelech son of Ahitub; 10 he inquired of the LORD for him, gave him provisions, and gave him the sword of Goliath the Philistine."

11 The king sent for the priest Ahimelech son of Ahitub and for all his father's house, the priests who were at Nob; and all of them came to the king. 12 Saul said, "Listen now, son of Ahitub." He answered, "Here I am, my lord." 13 Saul said to him, "Why have you conspired against me, you and the son of Jesse, by giving him bread and a sword, and by inquiring of God for him, so that he

---

[a] 21.13 Heb *in their hands*   [b] 22.3 Syr Vg: Heb *come out*

has risen against me, to lie in wait, as he is doing today?" 14 Then Ahimelech answered the king, "Who among all your servants is so faithful as David? He is the king's son-in-law, and is quick[a] to do your bidding, and is honored in your house. 15 Is today the first time that I have inquired of God for him? By no means! Do not let the king impute anything to his servant or to any member of my father's house; for your servant has known nothing of all this, much or little." 16 The king said, "You shall surely die, Ahimelech, you and all your father's house." 17 The king said to the guard who stood around him, "Turn and kill the priests of the LORD, because their hand also is with David; they knew that he fled, and did not disclose it to me." But the servants of the king would not raise their hand to attack the priests of the LORD. 18 Then the king said to Doeg, "You, Doeg, turn and attack the priests." Doeg the Edomite turned and attacked the priests; on that day he killed eighty-five who wore the linen ephod. 19 Nob, the city of the priests, he put to the sword; men and women, children and infants, oxen, donkeys, and sheep, he put to the sword.

20 But one of the sons of Ahimelech son of Ahitub, named Abiathar, escaped and fled after David. 21 Abiathar told David that Saul had killed the priests of the LORD. 22 David said to Abiathar, "I knew on that day, when Doeg the Edomite was there, that he would surely tell Saul. I am responsible[b] for the lives of all your father's house. 23 Stay with me, and do not be afraid; for the one who seeks my life seeks your life; you will be safe with me."

DAVID SAVES THE CITY OF KEILAH

23 Now they told David, "The Philistines are fighting against Keilah, and are robbing the threshing floors." 2 David inquired of the LORD, "Shall I go and attack these Philistines?" The LORD said to David, "Go and attack the Philistines and save Keilah." 3 But David's men said to him, "Look, we are afraid here in Judah; how much more then if we go to Keilah against the armies of the Philistines?" 4 Then David inquired of the LORD again. The LORD answered him, "Yes, go down to Keilah; for I will give the Philistines into your hand." 5 So David and his men went to Keilah, fought with the Philistines, brought away their livestock, and dealt them a heavy defeat. Thus David rescued the inhabitants of Keilah.

6 When Abiathar son of Ahimelech fled to David at Keilah, he came down with an ephod in his hand. 7 Now it was told Saul that David had come to Keilah. And Saul said, "God has given[c] him into my hand; for he has shut himself in by entering a town that has gates and bars." 8 Saul summoned all the people to war, to go down to Keilah, to besiege David and his men. 9 When David learned that Saul was plotting evil against him, he said to the priest Abiathar, "Bring the ephod here." 10 David said, "O LORD, the God of Israel, your servant has heard that Saul seeks to come to Keilah, to destroy the city on my account. 11 And now, will[d] Saul come down as your servant has heard? O LORD, the God of Israel, I beseech you, tell your servant." The LORD said, "He will come down." 12 Then David said, "Will the men of Keilah surrender me and my men into the hand of Saul?" The LORD said, "They will surrender you." 13 Then David and his men, who were about six hundred, set out and left Keilah; they wandered wherever they could go. When Saul was told that David had escaped from Keilah, he gave up the expedition. 14 David remained in the strongholds in the wilderness, in the hill country of the Wilderness of Ziph. Saul sought him every day, but the LORD[e] did not give him into his hand.

a 22.14 Heb *and turns aside*   b 22.22 Gk Vg: Meaning of Heb uncertain   c 23.7 Gk Tg: Heb *made a stranger of*   d 23.11 Q Ms Compare Gk: MT *Will the men of Keilah surrender me into his hand? Will*   e 23.14 Q Ms Gk: MT *God*

DAVID ELUDES SAUL IN THE WILDERNESS

15 David was in the Wilderness of Ziph at Horesh when he learned that[a] Saul had come out to seek his life. [16]Saul's son Jonathan set out and came to David at Horesh; there he strengthened his hand through the LORD.[b] [17]He said to him, "Do not be afraid; for the hand of my father Saul shall not find you; you shall be king over Israel, and I shall be second to you; my father Saul also knows that this is so." [18]Then the two of them made a covenant before the LORD; David remained at Horesh, and Jonathan went home.

19 Then some Ziphites went up to Saul at Gibeah and said, "David is hiding among us in the strongholds of Horesh, on the hill of Hachilah, which is south of Jeshimon. [20]Now, O king, whenever you wish to come down, do so; and our part will be to surrender him into the king's hand." [21]Saul said, "May you be blessed by the LORD for showing me compassion! [22]Go and make sure once more; find out exactly where he is, and who has seen him there; for I am told that he is very cunning. [23]Look around and learn all the hiding places where he lurks, and come back to me with sure information. Then I will go with you; and if he is in the land, I will search him out among all the thousands of Judah." [24]So they set out and went to Ziph ahead of Saul.

David and his men were in the wilderness of Maon, in the Arabah to the south of Jeshimon. [25]Saul and his men went to search for him. When David was told, he went down to the rock and stayed in the wilderness of Maon. When Saul heard that, he pursued David into the wilderness of Maon. [26]Saul went on one side of the mountain, and David and his men on the other side of the mountain. David was hurrying to get away from Saul, while Saul and his men were closing in on David and his men to capture them. [27]Then a messenger came to Saul, saying, "Hurry and come; for the Philistines have made a raid on the

land." [28]So Saul stopped pursuing David, and went against the Philistines; therefore that place was called the Rock of Escape.[c] [29d]David then went up from there, and lived in the strongholds of En-gedi.

DAVID SPARES SAUL'S LIFE

24 When Saul returned from following the Philistines, he was told, "David is in the wilderness of En-gedi." [2]Then Saul took three thousand chosen men out of all Israel, and went to look for David and his men in the direction of the Rocks of the Wild Goats. [3]He came to the sheepfolds beside the road, where there was a cave; and Saul went in to relieve himself.[e] Now David and his men were sitting in the innermost parts of the cave. [4]The men of David said to him, "Here is the day of which the LORD said to you, 'I will give your enemy into your hand, and you shall do to him as it seems good to you.'" Then David went and stealthily cut off a corner of Saul's cloak. [5]Afterward David was stricken to the heart because he had cut off a corner of Saul's cloak. [6]He said to his men, "The LORD forbid that I should do this thing to my lord, the LORD's anointed, to raise my hand against him; for he is the LORD's anointed." [7]So David scolded his men severely and did not permit them to attack Saul. Then Saul got up and left the cave, and went on his way.

8 Afterwards David also rose up and went out of the cave and called after Saul, "My lord the king!" When Saul looked behind him, David bowed with his face to the ground, and did obeisance. [9]David said to Saul, "Why do you listen to the words of those who say, 'David seeks to do you harm'? [10]This very day your eyes have seen how the LORD gave you into my hand in the cave; and some urged me to kill you, but I spared[f] you. I said, 'I will not raise my hand

---

[a] 23.15 Or *saw that* [b] 23.16 Compare Q Ms Gk: MT *God* [c] 23.28 Or *Rock of Division*; meaning of Heb uncertain [d] 23.29 Ch 24.1 in Heb [e] 24.3 Heb *to cover his feet* [f] 24.10 Gk Syr Tg Vg: Heb *it* (my eye) *spared*

against my lord; for he is the LORD's anointed.' 11See, my father, see the corner of your cloak in my hand; for by the fact that I cut off the corner of your cloak, and did not kill you, you may know for certain that there is no wrong or treason in my hands. I have not sinned against you, though you are hunting me to take my life. 12May the LORD judge between me and you! May the LORD avenge me on you; but my hand shall not be against you. 13As the ancient proverb says, 'Out of the wicked comes forth wickedness'; but my hand shall not be against you. 14Against whom has the king of Israel come out? Whom do you pursue? A dead dog? A single flea? 15May the LORD therefore be judge, and give sentence between me and you. May he see to it, and plead my cause, and vindicate me against you."

16 When David had finished speaking these words to Saul, Saul said, "Is this your voice, my son David?" Saul lifted up his voice and wept. 17He said to David, "You are more righteous than I; for you have repaid me good, whereas I have repaid you evil. 18Today you have explained how you have dealt well with me, in that you did not kill me when the LORD put me into your hands. 19For who has ever found an enemy, and sent the enemy safely away? So may the LORD reward you with good for what you have done to me this day. 20Now I know that you shall surely be king, and that the kingdom of Israel shall be established in your hand. 21Swear to me therefore by the LORD that you will not cut off my descendants after me, and that you will not wipe out my name from my father's house." 22So David swore this to Saul. Then Saul went home; but David and his men went up to the stronghold.

DEATH OF SAMUEL

25 Now Samuel died; and all Israel assembled and mourned for him. They buried him at his home in Ramah.

Then David got up and went down to the wilderness of Paran.

DAVID AND THE WIFE OF NABAL

2 There was a man in Maon, whose property was in Carmel. The man was very rich; he had three thousand sheep and a thousand goats. He was shearing his sheep in Carmel. 3Now the name of the man was Nabal, and the name of his wife Abigail. The woman was clever and beautiful, but the man was surly and mean; he was a Calebite. 4David heard in the wilderness that Nabal was shearing his sheep. 5So David sent ten young men; and David said to the young men, "Go up to Carmel, and go to Nabal, and greet him in my name. 6Thus you shall salute him: 'Peace be to you, and peace be to your house, and peace be to all that you have. 7I hear that you have shearers; now your shepherds have been with us, and we did them no harm, and they missed nothing, all the time they were in Carmel. 8Ask your young men, and they will tell you. Therefore let my young men find favor in your sight; for we have come on a feast day. Please give whatever you have at hand to your servants and to your son David.' "

REAL WISDOM COMES

FROM GOD, REFLECTS

GOD, HONORS GOD.

9 When David's young men came, they said all this to Nabal in the name of David; and then they waited. 10But Nabal answered David's servants, "Who is David? Who is the son of Jesse? There are many servants today who are breaking away from their masters. 11Shall I take my bread and my water and the meat that I have butchered for my shearers, and give it to men who come from I do not know where?" 12So David's young men turned away, and came back and told him all this. 13David said to his men, "Ev-

ery man strap on his sword!" And every one of them strapped on his sword; David also strapped on his sword; and about four hundred men went up after David, while two hundred remained with the baggage.

14 But one of the young men told Abigail, Nabal's wife, "David sent messengers out of the wilderness to salute our master; and he shouted insults at them. 15 Yet the men were very good to us, and we suffered no harm, and we never missed anything when we were in the fields, as long as we were with them; 16 they were a wall to us both by night and by day, all the while we were with them keeping the sheep. 17 Now therefore know this and consider what you should do; for evil has been decided against our master and against all his house; he is so ill-natured that no one can speak to him."

18 Then Abigail hurried and took two hundred loaves, two skins of wine, five sheep ready dressed, five measures of parched grain, one hundred clusters of raisins, and two hundred cakes of figs. She loaded them on donkeys 19 and said to her young men, "Go on ahead of me; I am coming after you." But she did not tell her husband Nabal. 20 As she rode on the donkey and came down under cover of the mountain, David and his men came down toward her; and she met them. 21 Now David had said, "Surely it was in vain that I protected all that this fellow has in the wilderness, so that nothing was missed of all that belonged to him; but he has returned me evil for good. 22 God do so to David[a] and more also, if by morning I leave so much as one male of all who belong to him."

23 When Abigail saw David, she hurried and alighted from the donkey, and fell before David on her face, bowing to the ground. 24 She fell at his feet and said, "Upon me alone, my lord, be the guilt; please let your servant speak in your ears, and hear the words of your servant. 25 My lord, do not take seriously this ill-natured fellow, Nabal; for as his name is, so is he; Nabal[b] is his name,

and folly is with him; but I, your servant, did not see the young men of my lord, whom you sent.

26 "Now then, my lord, as the LORD lives, and as you yourself live, since the LORD has restrained you from bloodguilt and from taking vengeance with your own hand, now let your enemies and those who seek to do evil to my lord be like Nabal. 27 And now let this present that your servant has brought to my lord be given to the young men who follow my lord. 28 Please forgive the trespass of your servant; for the LORD will certainly make my lord a sure house, because my lord is fighting the battles of the LORD; and evil shall not be found in you so long as you live. 29 If anyone should rise up to pursue you and to seek your life, the life of my lord shall be bound in the bundle of the living under the care of the LORD your God; but the lives of your enemies he shall sling out as from the hollow of a sling. 30 When the LORD has done to my lord according to all the good that he has spoken concerning you, and has appointed you prince over Israel, 31 my lord shall have no cause of grief, or pangs of conscience, for having shed blood without cause or for having saved himself. And when the LORD has dealt well with my lord, then remember your servant."

32 David said to Abigail, "Blessed be the LORD, the God of Israel, who sent you to meet me today! 33 Blessed be your good sense, and blessed be you, who have kept me today from bloodguilt and from avenging myself by my own hand! 34 For as surely as the LORD the God of Israel lives, who has restrained me from hurting you, unless you had hurried and come to meet me, truly by morning there would not have been left to Nabal so much as one male." 35 Then David received from her hand what she had brought him; he said to her, "Go up to your house in peace; see, I have heeded your voice, and I have granted your petition."

---

[a] 25.22 Gk Compare Syr: Heb *the enemies of David*   [b] 25.25 That is *Fool*

36 Abigail came to Nabal; he was holding a feast in his house, like the feast of a king. Nabal's heart was merry within him, for he was very drunk; so she told him nothing at all until the morning light. **37** In the morning, when the wine had gone out of Nabal, his wife told him these things, and his heart died within him; he became like a stone. **38** About ten days later the LORD struck Nabal, and he died.

39 When David heard that Nabal was dead, he said, "Blessed be the LORD who has judged the case of Nabal's insult to me, and has kept back his servant from evil; the LORD has returned the evildoing of Nabal upon his own head." Then David sent and wooed Abigail, to make her his wife. **40** When David's servants came to Abigail at Carmel, they said to her, "David has sent us to you to take you to him as his wife." **41** She rose and bowed down, with her face to the ground, and said, "Your servant is a slave to wash the feet of the servants of my lord." **42** Abigail got up hurriedly and rode away on a donkey; her five maids attended her. She went after the messengers of David and became his wife.

43 David also married Ahinoam of Jezreel; both of them became his wives. **44** Saul had given his daughter Michal, David's wife, to Palti son of Laish, who was from Gallim.

DAVID SPARES SAUL'S LIFE A SECOND TIME

26 Then the Ziphites came to Saul at Gibeah, saying, "David is in hiding on the hill of Hachilah, which is opposite Jeshimon."[a] **2** So Saul rose and went down to the Wilderness of Ziph, with three thousand chosen men of Israel, to seek David in the Wilderness of Ziph. **3** Saul encamped on the hill of Hachilah, which is opposite Jeshimon[a] beside the road. But David remained in the wilderness. When he learned that Saul had come after him into the wilderness, **4** David sent out spies, and learned that Saul had indeed arrived. **5** Then David set out and came to the place where Saul had encamped; and David saw the place where Saul lay, with Abner son of Ner, the commander of his army. Saul was lying within the encampment, while the army was encamped around him.

6 Then David said to Ahimelech the Hittite, and to Joab's brother Abishai son of Zeruiah, "Who will go down with me into the camp to Saul?" Abishai said, "I will go down with you." **7** So David and Abishai went to the army by night; there Saul lay sleeping within the encampment, with his spear stuck in the ground at his head; and Abner and the army lay around him. **8** Abishai said to David, "God has given your enemy into your hand today; now therefore let me pin him to the ground with one stroke of the spear; I will not strike him twice." **9** But David said to Abishai, "Do not destroy him; for who can raise his hand against the LORD's anointed, and be guiltless?" **10** David said, "As the LORD lives, the LORD will strike him down; or his day will come to die; or he will go down into battle and perish. **11** The LORD forbid that I should raise my hand against the LORD's anointed; but now take the spear that is at his head, and the water jar, and let us go." **12** So David took the spear that was at Saul's head and the water jar, and they went away. No one saw it, or knew it, nor did anyone awake; for they were all asleep, because a deep sleep from the LORD had fallen upon them.

13 Then David went over to the other side, and stood on top of a hill far away, with a great distance between them. **14** David called to the army and to Abner son of Ner, saying, "Abner! Will you not answer?" Then Abner replied, "Who are you that calls to the king?" **15** David said to Abner, "Are you not a man? Who is like you in Israel? Why then have you not kept watch over your lord the king? For one of the people came in to destroy your lord the king. **16** This thing that you have done is not good. As the LORD lives, you deserve to

[a] 26.1,3 Or *opposite the wasteland*

die, because you have not kept watch over your lord, the LORD's anointed. See now, where is the king's spear, or the water jar that was at his head?" 17 Saul recognized David's voice, and said, "Is this your voice, my son David?" David said, "It is my voice, my lord, O king." 18 And he added, "Why does my lord pursue his servant? For what have I done? What guilt is on my hands? 19 Now therefore let my lord the king hear the words of his servant. If it is the LORD who has stirred you up against me, may he accept an offering; but if it is mortals, may they be cursed before the LORD, for they have driven me out today from my share in the heritage of the LORD, saying, 'Go, serve other gods.' 20 Now therefore, do not let my blood fall to the ground, away from the presence of the LORD; for the king of Israel has come out to seek a single flea, like one who hunts a partridge in the mountains."

21 Then Saul said, "I have done wrong; come back, my son David, for I will never harm you again, because my life was precious in your sight today; I have been a fool, and have made a great mistake." 22 David replied, "Here is the spear, O king! Let one of the young men come over and get it. 23 The LORD rewards everyone for his righteousness and his faithfulness; for the LORD gave you into my hand today, but I would not raise my hand against the LORD's anointed. 24 As your life was precious today in my sight, so may my life be precious in the sight of the LORD, and may he rescue me from all tribulation." 25 Then Saul said to David, "Blessed be you, my son David! You will do many things and will succeed in them." So David went his way, and Saul returned to his place.

DAVID SERVES KING ACHISH OF GATH

27 David said in his heart, "I shall now perish one day by the hand of Saul; there is nothing better for me than to escape to the land of the Philistines; then Saul will despair of seeking me any longer within the borders of Israel, and I shall escape out of his hand." 2 So David set out and went over, he and the six hundred men who were with him, to King Achish son of Maoch of Gath. 3 David stayed with Achish at Gath, he and his troops, every man with his household, and David with his two wives, Ahinoam of Jezreel, and Abigail of Carmel, Nabal's widow. 4 When Saul was told that David had fled to Gath, he no longer sought for him.

5 Then David said to Achish, "If I have found favor in your sight, let a place be given me in one of the country towns, so that I may live there; for why should your servant live in the royal city with you?" 6 So that day Achish gave him Ziklag; therefore Ziklag has belonged to the kings of Judah to this day. 7 The length of time that David lived in the country of the Philistines was one year and four months.

WE ARE GIVEN A CLEAR
PICTURE OF PROPER LIFE
IN THE PERFECT EXAMPLE
SET BY JESUS. THE PROOF
IS HOW WE TREAT OTHER
PEOPLE—TO MAKE THE
INVISIBLE GOD VISIBLE.

8 Now David and his men went up and made raids on the Geshurites, the Girzites, and the Amalekites; for these were the landed settlements from Telam[a] on the way to Shur and on to the land of Egypt. 9 David struck the land, leaving neither man nor woman alive, but took away the sheep, the oxen, the donkeys, the camels, and the clothing, and came back to Achish. 10 When Achish asked, "Against whom[b] have

a 27.8 Compare Gk 15.4: Heb *from of old*
b 27.10 Q Ms Gk Vg: MT lacks *whom*

you made a raid today?" David would say, "Against the Negeb of Judah," or "Against the Negeb of the Jerahmeelites," or, "Against the Negeb of the Kenites." [11]David left neither man nor woman alive to be brought back to Gath, thinking, "They might tell about us, and say, 'David has done so and so.' " Such was his practice all the time he lived in the country of the Philistines. [12]Achish trusted David, thinking, "He has made himself utterly abhorrent to his people Israel; therefore he shall always be my servant."

28 In those days the Philistines gathered their forces for war, to fight against Israel. Achish said to David, "You know, of course, that you and your men are to go out with me in the army." [2]David said to Achish, "Very well, then you shall know what your servant can do." Achish said to David, "Very well, I will make you my bodyguard for life."

SAUL CONSULTS A MEDIUM

[3]Now Samuel had died, and all Israel had mourned for him and buried him in Ramah, his own city. Saul had expelled the mediums and the wizards from the land. [4]The Philistines assembled, and came and encamped at Shunem. Saul gathered all Israel, and they encamped at Gilboa. [5]When Saul saw the army of the Philistines, he was afraid, and his heart trembled greatly. [6]When Saul inquired of the LORD, the LORD did not answer him, not by dreams, or by Urim, or by prophets. [7]Then Saul said to his servants, "Seek out for me a woman who is a medium, so that I may go to her and inquire of her." His servants said to him, "There is a medium at Endor."

[8]So Saul disguised himself and put on other clothes and went there, he and two men with him. They came to the woman by night. And he said, "Consult a spirit for me, and bring up for me the one whom I name to you." [9]The woman said to him, "Surely you know what Saul has done, how he has cut off the mediums and the wizards from

the land. Why then are you laying a snare for my life to bring about my death?" [10]But Saul swore to her by the LORD, "As the LORD lives, no punishment shall come upon you for this thing." [11]Then the woman said, "Whom shall I bring up for you?" He answered, "Bring up Samuel for me." [12]When the woman saw Samuel, she cried out with a loud voice; and the woman said to Saul, "Why have you deceived me? You are Saul!" [13]The king said to her, "Have no fear; what do you see?" The woman said to Saul, "I see a divine being[a] coming up out of the ground." [14]He said to her, "What is his appearance?" She said, "An old man is coming up; he is wrapped in a robe." So Saul knew that it was Samuel, and he bowed with his face to the ground, and did obeisance.

FEAR AND DISBELIEF ARE

THE ENEMIES OF LIFE.

[15]Then Samuel said to Saul, "Why have you disturbed me by bringing me up?" Saul answered, "I am in great distress, for the Philistines are warring against me, and God has turned away from me and answers me no more, either by prophets or by dreams; so I have summoned you to tell me what I should do." [16]Samuel said, "Why then do you ask me, since the LORD has turned from you and become your enemy? [17]The LORD has done to you just as he spoke by me; for the LORD has torn the kingdom out of your hand, and given it to your neighbor, David. [18]Because you did not obey the voice of the LORD, and did not carry out his fierce wrath against Amalek, therefore the LORD has done this thing to you today. [19]Moreover the LORD will give Israel along with you into the hands of the Philistines; and

---

[a] **28.13** Or *a god*; or *gods*

tomorrow you and your sons shall be with me; the LORD will also give the army of Israel into the hands of the Philistines."

20 Immediately Saul fell full length on the ground, filled with fear because of the words of Samuel; and there was no strength in him, for he had eaten nothing all day and all night. 21The woman came to Saul, and when she saw that he was terrified, she said to him, "Your servant has listened to you; I have taken my life in my hand, and have listened to what you have said to me. 22Now therefore, you also listen to your servant; let me set a morsel of bread before you. Eat, that you may have strength when you go on your way." 23He refused, and said, "I will not eat." But his servants, together with the woman, urged him; and he listened to their words. So he got up from the ground and sat on the bed. 24Now the woman had a fatted calf in the house. She quickly slaughtered it, and she took flour, kneaded it, and baked unleavened cakes. 25She put them before Saul and his servants, and they ate. Then they rose and went away that night.

THE PHILISTINES REJECT DAVID

29 Now the Philistines gathered all their forces at Aphek, while the Israelites were encamped by the fountain that is in Jezreel. 2As the lords of the Philistines were passing on by hundreds and by thousands, and David and his men were passing on in the rear with Achish, 3the commanders of the Philistines said, "What are these Hebrews doing here?" Achish said to the commanders of the Philistines, "Is this not David, the servant of King Saul of Israel, who has been with me now for days and years? Since he deserted to me I have found no fault in him to this day." 4But the commanders of the Philistines were angry with him; and the commanders of the Philistines said to him, "Send the man back, so that he may return to the place that you have assigned to him; he shall not go down with us to battle, or else he may become an ad-

versary to us in the battle. For how could this fellow reconcile himself to his lord? Would it not be with the heads of the men here? 5Is this not David, of whom they sing to one another in dances,

'Saul has killed his thousands,
    and David his ten thousands'?"

6 Then Achish called David and said to him, "As the LORD lives, you have been honest, and to me it seems right that you should march out and in with me in the campaign; for I have found nothing wrong in you from the day of your coming to me until today. Nevertheless the lords do not approve of you. 7So go back now; and go peaceably; do nothing to displease the lords of the Philistines." 8David said to Achish, "But what have I done? What have you found in your servant from the day I entered your service until now, that I should not go and fight against the enemies of my lord the king?" 9Achish replied to David, "I know that you are as blameless in my sight as an angel of God; nevertheless, the commanders of the Philistines have said, 'He shall not go up with us to the battle.' 10Now then rise early in the morning, you and the servants of your lord who came with you, and go to the place that I appointed for you. As for the evil report, do not take it to heart, for you have done well before me.a Start early in the morning, and leave as soon as you have light." 11So David set out with his men early in the morning, to return to the land of the Philistines. But the Philistines went up to Jezreel.

DAVID AVENGES THE DESTRUCTION OF ZIKLAG

30 Now when David and his men came to Ziklag on the third day, the Amalekites had made a raid on the Negeb and on Ziklag. They had attacked Ziklag, burned it down, 2and taken captive the women and allb who were in it, both small and great; they killed none of

a 29.10 Gk: Heb lacks *and go to the place… done well before me*   b 30.2 Gk: Heb lacks *and all* them, but carried them off, and went their way. ³When David and his men came to the city, they found it burned down, and their wives and sons and daughters taken captive. ⁴Then David and the people who were with him raised their voices and wept, until they had no more strength to weep. ⁵David's two wives also had been taken captive, Ahinoam of Jezreel, and Abigail the widow of Nabal of Carmel. ⁶David was in great danger; for the people spoke of stoning him, because all the people were bitter in spirit for their sons and daughters. But David strengthened himself in the LORD his God.

7 David said to the priest Abiathar son of Ahimelech, "Bring me the ephod." So Abiathar brought the ephod to David. ⁸David inquired of the LORD, "Shall I pursue this band? Shall I overtake them?" He answered him, "Pursue; for you shall surely overtake and shall surely rescue." ⁹So David set out, he and the six hundred men who were with him. They came to the Wadi Besor, where those stayed who were left behind. ¹⁰But David went on with the pursuit, he and four hundred men; two hundred stayed behind, too exhausted to cross the Wadi Besor.

11 In the open country they found an Egyptian, and brought him to David. They gave him bread and he ate; they gave him water to drink; ¹²they also gave him a piece of fig cake and two clusters of raisins. When he had eaten, his spirit revived; for he had not eaten bread or drunk water for three days and three nights. ¹³Then David said to him, "To whom do you belong? Where are you from?" He said, "I am a young man of Egypt, servant to an Amalekite. My master left me behind because I fell sick three days ago. ¹⁴We had made a raid on the Negeb of the Cherethites and on that which belongs to Judah and on the Negeb of Caleb; and we burned Ziklag down." ¹⁵David said to him, "Will you take me down to this raiding party?" He said, "Swear to me by God that you will not kill me, or hand me over to my master, and I will take you down to them."

PONDER

But David strengthened himself in the LORD his God.
—1 Samuel 30.6

PRAY

Lord, sometimes it is very difficult for us to read these harsh stories of warfare and death in the Old Testament and apply them to our own lives. As we read about this vivid series of events in the lives of Saul, David and Jonathan, we pray that you give us the courage to apply the lesson you show us here. As David found strength in you, so we rely on you because there is no other help on earth or in heaven. May these words penetrate our tense and strained hearts and minds so that we can rest in a future and live in your presence. Lead us closer to our Savior, Jesus Christ. In his name we pray. Amen.

16 When he had taken him down, they were spread out all over the ground, eating and drinking and dancing, because of the great amount of spoil they had taken from the land of the Philistines and from the land of Judah. ¹⁷David attacked them from twilight until the evening of the next day. Not one of them escaped, except four hundred young men, who mounted camels and fled. ¹⁸David recovered all that the Amalekites had taken; and David rescued his two wives. ¹⁹Nothing was missing, whether small or great, sons or daughters, spoil or anything that had been taken; David brought back everything. ²⁰David also captured all the flocks and herds, which were driven ahead of the other cattle; people said, "This is David's spoil."

21 Then David came to the two hundred men who had been too exhausted to follow David, and who had been left at the Wadi Besor.

They went out to meet David and to meet the people who were with him. When David drew near to the people he saluted them. ²²Then all the corrupt and worthless fellows among the men who had gone with David said, "Because they did not go with us, we will not give them any of the spoil that we have recovered, except that each man may take his wife and children, and leave." ²³But David said, "You shall not do so, my brothers, with what the LORD has given us; he has preserved us and handed over to us the raiding party that attacked us. ²⁴Who would listen to you in this matter? For the share of the one who goes down into the battle shall be the same as the share of the one who stays by the baggage; they shall share alike." ²⁵From that day forward he made it a statute and an ordinance for Israel; it continues to the present day.

26 When David came to Ziklag, he sent part of the spoil to his friends, the elders of Judah, saying, "Here is a present for you from the spoil of the enemies of the LORD"; ²⁷it was for those in Bethel, in Ramoth of the Negeb, in Jattir, ²⁸in Aroer, in Siphmoth, in Eshtemoa, ²⁹in Racal, in the towns of the Jerahmeelites, in the towns of the Kenites, ³⁰in Hormah, in Bor-ashan, in Athach, ³¹in Hebron, all the places where David and his men had roamed.

THE DEATH OF SAUL AND HIS SONS

31 Now the Philistines fought against Israel; and the men of Israel fled before the Philistines, and many fellᵃ on Mount Gilboa. ²The Philistines overtook Saul and his sons; and the Philistines killed Jonathan and Abinadab and Malchishua, the sons of Saul. ³The battle pressed

hard upon Saul; the archers found him, and he was badly wounded by them. ⁴Then Saul said to his armor-bearer, "Draw your sword and thrust me through with it, so that these uncircumcised may not come and thrust me through, and make sport of me." But his armor-bearer was unwilling; for he was terrified. So Saul took his own sword and fell upon it. ⁵When his armor-bearer saw that Saul was dead, he also fell upon his sword and died with him. ⁶So Saul and his three sons and his armor-bearer and all his men died together on the same day. ⁷When the men of Israel who were on the other side of the valley and those beyond the Jordan saw that the men of Israel had fled and that Saul and his sons were dead, they forsook their towns and fled; and the Philistines came and occupied them.

8 The next day, when the Philistines came to strip the dead, they found Saul and his three sons fallen on Mount Gilboa. ⁹They cut off his head, stripped off his armor, and sent messengers throughout the land of the Philistines to carry the good news to the houses of their idols and to the people. ¹⁰They put his armor in the temple of Astarte;ᵇ and they fastened his body to the wall of Beth-shan. ¹¹But when the inhabitants of Jabesh-gilead heard what the Philistines had done to Saul, ¹²all the valiant men set out, traveled all night long, and took the body of Saul and the bodies of his sons from the wall of Beth-shan. They came to Jabesh and burned them there. ¹³Then they took their bones and buried them under the tamarisk tree in Jabesh, and fasted seven days.

ᵃ **31.1** Heb *and they fell slain*   ᵇ **31.10** Heb plural

2 SAMUEL

What does it mean to be a person "after [God's] own heart"? (1 Samuel 13.14). To find out, look at David's life. David's greatness resided in his response to his failures, as well as to his many successes. Even after he had sinned with Bathsheba, David turned back to God with honesty and humility. From David we learn that God's favor doesn't depend on our perfection but on God's. As we read 2 Samuel, we can follow David's example: We can go to the Lord, regardless of our imperfection, lay down our lives before the Sovereign Lord and watch God's redeeming power at work.

DAVID MOURNS FOR SAUL AND JONATHAN

After the death of Saul, when David had returned from defeating the Amalekites, David remained two days in Ziklag. ²On the third day, a man came from Saul's camp, with his clothes torn and dirt on his head. When he came to David, he fell to the ground and did obeisance. ³David said to him, "Where have you come from?" He said to him, "I have escaped from the camp of Israel." ⁴David said to him, "How did things go? Tell me!" He answered, "The army fled from the battle, but also many of the army fell and died; and Saul and his son Jonathan also died." ⁵Then David asked the young man who was reporting to him, "How do you know that Saul and his son Jonathan died?" ⁶The young man reporting to him said, "I happened to be on Mount Gilboa; and there was Saul leaning on his spear, while the chariots and the horsemen drew close to him. ⁷When he looked behind him, he saw me, and called to me. I answered, 'Here sir.' ⁸And he said to me, 'Who are you?' I answered him, 'I am an Amalekite.' ⁹He said to me, 'Come, stand over me and kill me; for convulsions have seized me, and yet my life still lingers.' ¹⁰So I stood over him, and killed him, for I knew that he could not live after he had fallen. I took the crown that was on his head and the armlet that was on his arm, and I have brought them here to my lord."

¹¹Then David took hold of his clothes and tore them; and all the men who were with him did the same. ¹²They mourned and wept, and fasted until evening for Saul and for his son Jonathan, and for the army of the LORD and for the house of Israel, because they had fallen by the sword. ¹³David said to the young man who had reported to him, "Where do you come from?" He answered, "I am the son of a resident alien, an Amalekite." ¹⁴David said to him, "Were you not afraid to lift your hand to destroy the LORD's anointed?" ¹⁵Then David called one of the young men and said, "Come here and strike him down." So he struck him down and he died. ¹⁶David said to him, "Your blood be on your head; for your own mouth has testified against you, saying, 'I have killed the LORD's anointed.'"

¹⁷David intoned this lamentation over Saul and his son Jonathan. ¹⁸(He ordered that The Song of the Bowᵃ be taught to the people of Judah; it is written in the Book of Jashar.) He said:

¹⁹ Your glory, O Israel, lies slain
    upon your high places!
  How the mighty have fallen!
²⁰ Tell it not in Gath,
    proclaim it not in the
      streets of Ashkelon;
  or the daughters of the
      Philistines will rejoice,
    the daughters of the
      uncircumcised will exult.

²¹ You mountains of Gilboa,
    let there be no dew or
      rain upon you,
    nor bounteous fields!ᵇ
  For there the shield of the
      mighty was defiled,
    the shield of Saul, anointed
      with oil no more.

²² From the blood of the slain,
    from the fat of the mighty,
  the bow of Jonathan did
      not turn back,
    nor the sword of Saul
      return empty.

²³ Saul and Jonathan, beloved
      and lovely!
  In life and in death they
      were not divided;
  they were swifter than eagles,
    they were stronger than lions.

²⁴ O daughters of Israel,
      weep over Saul,
  who clothed you with
      crimson, in luxury,
  who put ornaments of gold
      on your apparel.

²⁵ How the mighty have fallen
      in the midst of the battle!

ᵃ 1.18 Heb *that The Bow*   ᵇ 1.21 Meaning of Heb uncertain

Jonathan lies slain upon
your high places.
26 I am distressed for you, my
brother Jonathan;
greatly beloved were you to me;
your love to me was wonderful,
passing the love of women.
27 How the mighty have fallen,
and the weapons of
war perished!

DAVID ANOINTED KING OF JUDAH

2 After this David inquired of the LORD, "Shall I go up into any of the cities of Judah?" The LORD said to him, "Go up." David said, "To which shall I go up?" He said, "To Hebron." 2So David went up there, along with his two wives, Ahinoam of Jezreel, and Abigail the widow of Nabal of Carmel. 3David brought up the men who were with him, every one with his household; and they settled in the towns of Hebron. 4Then the people of Judah came, and there they anointed David king over the house of Judah.

When they told David, "It was the people of Jabesh-gilead who buried Saul," 5David sent messengers to the people of Jabesh-gilead, and said to them, "May you be blessed by the LORD, because you showed this loyalty to Saul your lord, and buried him! 6Now may the LORD show steadfast love and faithfulness to you! And I too will reward you because you have done this thing. 7Therefore let your hands be strong, and be valiant; for Saul your lord is dead, and the house of Judah has anointed me king over them."

ISHBAAL KING OF ISRAEL

8 But Abner son of Ner, commander of Saul's army, had taken Ishbaal[a] son of Saul, and brought him over to Mahanaim. 9He made him king over Gilead, the Ashurites, Jezreel, Ephraim, Benjamin, and over all Israel. 10Ishbaal,[a] Saul's son, was forty years old when he began to reign over Israel, and he reigned two years. But the house of Judah followed David. 11The time that David

was king in Hebron over the house of Judah was seven years and six months.

THE BATTLE OF GIBEON

12 Abner son of Ner, and the servants of Ishbaal[a] son of Saul, went out from Mahanaim to Gibeon. 13Joab son of Zeruiah, and the servants of David, went out and met them at the pool of Gibeon. One group sat on one side of the pool, while the other sat on the other side of the pool. 14Abner said to Joab, "Let the young men come forward and have a contest before us." Joab said, "Let them come forward." 15So they came forward and were counted as they passed by, twelve for Benjamin and Ishbaal[a] son of Saul, and twelve of the servants of David. 16Each grasped his opponent by the head, and thrust his sword in his opponent's side; so they fell down together. Therefore that place was called Helkath-hazzurim,[b] which is at Gibeon. 17The battle was very fierce that day; and Abner and the men of Israel were beaten by the servants of David.

18 The three sons of Zeruiah were there, Joab, Abishai, and Asahel. Now Asahel was as swift of foot as a wild gazelle. 19Asahel pursued Abner, turning neither to the right nor to the left as he followed him. 20Then Abner looked back and said, "Is it you, Asahel?" He answered, "Yes, it is." 21Abner said to him, "Turn to your right or to your left, and seize one of the young men, and take his spoil." But Asahel would not turn away from following him. 22Abner said again to Asahel, "Turn away from following me; why should I strike you to the ground? How then could I show my face to your brother Joab?" 23But he refused to turn away. So Abner struck him in the stomach with the butt of his spear, so that the spear came out at his back. He fell there, and died where he lay. And all those who came to the place where

a 2.8,10,12,15 Gk Compare 1 Chr 8.33; 9.39: Heb *Ish-bosheth*, "man of shame"
b 2.16 That is *Field of Sword-edges*

Asahel had fallen and died, stood
still.

24 But Joab and Abishai pursued
Abner. As the sun was going down
they came to the hill of Ammah,
which lies before Giah on the way to
the wilderness of Gibeon. 25 The Benjaminites rallied around Abner and
formed a single band; they took their
stand on the top of a hill. 26 Then Abner called to Joab, "Is the sword to
keep devouring forever? Do you not
know that the end will be bitter?
How long will it be before you order
your people to turn from the pursuit of their kinsmen?" 27 Joab said,
"As God lives, if you had not spoken,
the people would have continued to
pursue their kinsmen, not stopping
until morning." 28 Joab sounded the
trumpet and all the people stopped;
they no longer pursued Israel or engaged in battle any further.

29 Abner and his men traveled all
that night through the Arabah; they
crossed the Jordan, and, marching
the whole forenoon,[a] they came to
Mahanaim. 30 Joab returned from
the pursuit of Abner; and when he
had gathered all the people together,
there were missing of David's servants nineteen men besides Asahel. 31 But the servants of David had
killed of Benjamin three hundred
sixty of Abner's men. 32 They took up
Asahel and buried him in the tomb
of his father, which was at Bethlehem. Joab and his men marched all
night, and the day broke upon them
at Hebron.

ABNER DEFECTS TO DAVID

3 There was a long war between
the house of Saul and the house
of David; David grew stronger and
stronger, while the house of Saul became weaker and weaker.

2 Sons were born to David at Hebron: his firstborn was Amnon, of
Ahinoam of Jezreel; 3 his second,
Chileab, of Abigail the widow of Nabal of Carmel; the third, Absalom
son of Maacah, daughter of King
Talmai of Geshur; 4 the fourth, Adonijah son of Haggith; the fifth,
Shephatiah son of Abital; 5 and
the sixth, Ithream, of David's wife

Eglah. These were born to David in
Hebron.

6 While there was war between
the house of Saul and the house of
David, Abner was making himself
strong in the house of Saul. 7 Now
Saul had a concubine whose name
was Rizpah daughter of Aiah. And
Ishbaal[b] said to Abner, "Why have
you gone in to my father's concubine?" 8 The words of Ishbaal[c] made
Abner very angry; he said, "Am I a
dog's head for Judah? Today I keep
showing loyalty to the house of your
father Saul, to his brothers, and to
his friends, and have not given you
into the hand of David; and yet you
charge me now with a crime concerning this woman. 9 So may God
do to Abner and so may he add to it!
For just what the LORD has sworn
to David, that will I accomplish for
him, 10 to transfer the kingdom from
the house of Saul, and set up the
throne of David over Israel and over
Judah, from Dan to Beer-sheba."
11 And Ishbaal[b] could not answer Abner another word, because he feared
him.

CHRISTIANITY IS A RELIGION
OF RELATIONSHIPS—BETWEEN
US AND GOD AND AMONG
OURSELVES. EACH OF US HAS
A RESPONSIBILITY TO HEAL
BROKEN RELATIONSHIPS.

12 Abner sent messengers to David at Hebron,[d] saying, "To whom
does the land belong? Make your
covenant with me, and I will give
you my support to bring all Israel
over to you." 13 He said, "Good; I will

---

[a] 2.29 Meaning of Heb uncertain
[b] 3.7,11 Heb And he [c] 3.8 Gk Compare 1 Chr
8.33; 9.39: Heb Ish-bosheth, "man of shame"
[d] 3.12 Gk: Heb where he was

make a covenant with you. But one thing I require of you: you shall never appear in my presence unless you bring Saul's daughter Michal when you come to see me." [14]Then David sent messengers to Saul's son Ishbaal,[a] saying, "Give me my wife Michal, to whom I became engaged at the price of one hundred foreskins of the Philistines." [15]Ishbaal[a] sent and took her from her husband Paltiel the son of Laish. [16]But her husband went with her, weeping as he walked behind her all the way to Bahurim. Then Abner said to him, "Go back home!" So he went back.

[17]Abner sent word to the elders of Israel, saying, "For some time past you have been seeking David as king over you. [18]Now then bring it about; for the LORD has promised David: Through my servant David I will save my people Israel from the hand of the Philistines, and from all their enemies." [19]Abner also spoke directly to the Benjaminites; then Abner went to tell David at Hebron all that Israel and the whole house of Benjamin were ready to do.

[20]When Abner came with twenty men to David at Hebron, David made a feast for Abner and the men who were with him. [21]Abner said to David, "Let me go and rally all Israel to my lord the king, in order that they may make a covenant with you, and that you may reign over all that your heart desires." So David dismissed Abner, and he went away in peace.

ABNER IS KILLED BY JOAB

[22]Just then the servants of David arrived with Joab from a raid, bringing much spoil with them. But Abner was not with David at Hebron, for David[b] had dismissed him, and he had gone away in peace. [23]When Joab and all the army that was with him came, it was told Joab, "Abner son of Ner came to the king, and he has dismissed him, and he has gone away in peace." [24]Then Joab went to the king and said, "What have you done? Abner came to you; why did you dismiss him, so that he got away? [25]You know that Abner son of Ner came to deceive you, and to learn your comings and goings and to learn all that you are doing."

[26]When Joab came out from David's presence, he sent messengers after Abner, and they brought him back from the cistern of Sirah; but David did not know about it. [27]When Abner returned to Hebron, Joab took him aside in the gateway to speak with him privately, and there he stabbed him in the stomach. So he died for shedding[c] the blood of Asahel, Joab's[d] brother. [28]Afterward, when David heard of it, he said, "I and my kingdom are forever guiltless before the LORD for the blood of Abner son of Ner. [29]May the guilt[e] fall on the head of Joab, and on all his father's house; and may the house of Joab never be without one who has a discharge, or who is leprous,[f] or who holds a spindle, or who falls by the sword, or who lacks food!" [30]So Joab and his brother Abishai murdered Abner because he had killed their brother Asahel in the battle at Gibeon.

[31]Then David said to Joab and to all the people who were with him, "Tear your clothes, and put on sackcloth, and mourn over Abner." And King David followed the bier. [32]They buried Abner at Hebron. The king lifted up his voice and wept at the grave of Abner, and all the people wept. [33]The king lamented for Abner, saying,

"Should Abner die as a fool dies?
[34] Your hands were not bound,
your feet were not fettered;
as one falls before the wicked
you have fallen."

And all the people wept over him again. [35]Then all the people came to persuade David to eat something while it was still day; but David swore, saying, "So may God do to me, and more, if I taste bread or anything else before the sun goes down!" [36]All the people took notice of it, and it pleased them; just as everything the king did pleased all the

[a] 3.14,15 Heb Ish-bosheth [b] 3.22 Heb he
[c] 3.27 Heb lacks shedding [d] 3.27 Heb his
[e] 3.29 Heb May it [f] 3.29 A term for several skin diseases; precise meaning uncertain

people. [37]So all the people and all Israel understood that day that the king had no part in the killing of Abner son of Ner. [38]And the king said to his servants, "Do you not know that a prince and a great man has fallen this day in Israel? [39]Today I am powerless, even though anointed king; these men, the sons of Zeruiah, are too violent for me. The LORD pay back the one who does wickedly in accordance with his wickedness!"

ISHBAAL ASSASSINATED

4 When Saul's son Ishbaal[a] heard that Abner had died at Hebron, his courage failed, and all Israel was dismayed. [2]Saul's son had two captains of raiding bands; the name of the one was Baanah, and the name of the other Rechab. They were sons of Rimmon a Benjaminite from Beeroth—for Beeroth is considered to belong to Benjamin. [3](Now the people of Beeroth had fled to Gittaim and are there as resident aliens to this day).

[4]Saul's son Jonathan had a son who was crippled in his feet. He was five years old when the news about Saul and Jonathan came from Jezreel. His nurse picked him up and fled; and, in her haste to flee, it happened that he fell and became lame. His name was Mephibosheth.[b]

[5]Now the sons of Rimmon the Beerothite, Rechab and Baanah, set out, and about the heat of the day they came to the house of Ishbaal,[c] while he was taking his noonday rest. [6]They came inside the house as though to take wheat, and they struck him in the stomach; then Rechab and his brother Baanah escaped.[d] [7]Now they had come into the house while he was lying on his couch in his bedchamber; they attacked him, killed him, and beheaded him. Then they took his head and traveled by way of the Arabah all night long. [8]They brought the head of Ishbaal[c] to David at Hebron and said to the king, "Here is the head of Ishbaal,[c] son of Saul, your enemy, who sought your life; the LORD has avenged my lord the king this day on Saul and on his offspring."

[9]David answered Rechab and his brother Baanah, the sons of Rimmon the Beerothite, "As the LORD lives, who has redeemed my life out of every adversity, [10]when the one who told me, 'See, Saul is dead,' thought he was bringing good news, I seized him and killed him at Ziklag—this was the reward I gave him for his news. [11]How much more then, when wicked men have killed a righteous man on his bed in his own house! And now shall I not require his blood at your hand, and destroy you from the earth?" [12]So David commanded the young men, and they killed them; they cut off their hands and feet, and hung their bodies beside the pool at Hebron. But the head of Ishbaal[c] they took and buried in the tomb of Abner at Hebron.

DAVID ANOINTED KING
OF ALL ISRAEL

5 Then all the tribes of Israel came to David at Hebron, and said, "Look, we are your bone and flesh. [2]For some time, while Saul was king over us, it was you who led out Israel and brought it in. The LORD said to you: It is you who shall be shepherd of my people Israel, you who shall be ruler over Israel." [3]So all the elders of Israel came to the king at Hebron; and King David made a covenant with them at Hebron before the LORD, and they anointed David king over Israel. [4]David was thirty years old when he began to reign, and he reigned forty years. [5]At Hebron he reigned over Judah seven years and six months; and at Jerusalem he reigned over all Israel and Judah thirty-three years.

JERUSALEM MADE CAPITAL
OF THE UNITED KINGDOM

[6]The king and his men marched to Jerusalem against the Jebusites, the inhabitants of the land, who said to David, "You will not come in here, even the blind and the lame will

[a] 4.1 Heb lacks *Ishbaal*   [b] 4.4 In 1 Chr 8.34 and 9.40, *Merib-baal*   [c] 4.5,8,12 Heb *Ish-bosheth*   [d] 4.6 Meaning of Heb of verse 6 uncertain

turn you back"—thinking, "David cannot come in here." [7]Nevertheless David took the stronghold of Zion, which is now the city of David. [8]David had said on that day, "Whoever would strike down the Jebusites, let him get up the water shaft to attack the lame and the blind, those whom David hates."[a] Therefore it is said, "The blind and the lame shall not come into the house." [9]David occupied the stronghold, and named it the city of David. David built the city all around from the Millo inward. [10]And David became greater and greater, for the LORD, the God of hosts, was with him.

[11] King Hiram of Tyre sent messengers to David, along with cedar trees, and carpenters and masons who built David a house. [12]David then perceived that the LORD had established him king over Israel, and that he had exalted his kingdom for the sake of his people Israel.

[13] In Jerusalem, after he came from Hebron, David took more concubines and wives; and more sons and daughters were born to David. [14]These are the names of those who were born to him in Jerusalem: Shammua, Shobab, Nathan, Solomon, [15]Ibhar, Elishua, Nepheg, Japhia, [16]Elishama, Eliada, and Eliphelet.

PHILISTINE ATTACK REPULSED

[17] When the Philistines heard that David had been anointed king over Israel, all the Philistines went up in search of David; but David heard about it and went down to the stronghold. [18]Now the Philistines had come and spread out in the valley of Rephaim. [19]David inquired of the LORD, "Shall I go up against the Philistines? Will you give them into my hand?" The LORD said to David, "Go up; for I will certainly give the Philistines into your hand." [20]So David came to Baal-perazim, and David defeated them there. He said, "The LORD has burst forth against[b] my enemies before me, like a bursting flood." Therefore that place is called Baal-perazim.[c] [21]The Philistines abandoned their idols there, and David and his men carried them away.

PONDER

David then perceived that the LORD had established him king over Israel, and that he had exalted his kingdom for the sake of his people Israel.
—2 Samuel 5.12

PRAY

Sovereign Lord, as we confront these stories of bloodshed, abuse and betrayal in your Holy Bible, we find ourselves in a quandary: We don't quite understand what it all means. But we know in all the history of Israel, your purpose was unchanging. When we consider how Jesus Christ descended from David, it is all made clear. We don't have to look further than the life, death and resurrection of Christ, who brought redemption to give us joy, peace and eternal life. Help us to be strong in our faith, to be courageous enough to see the truth about ourselves. Bestow on us the spirit of love as given to us in words and deeds of our Savior. In his name we pray. Amen.

[22] Once again the Philistines came up, and were spread out in the valley of Rephaim. [23]When David inquired of the LORD, he said, "You shall not go up; go around to their rear, and come upon them opposite the balsam trees. [24]When you hear the sound of marching in the tops of the balsam trees, then be on the alert; for then the LORD has gone out before you to strike down the army of the Philistines." [25]David did just as the LORD had commanded him; and he struck down the Philistines from Geba all the way to Gezer.

DAVID BRINGS THE ARK TO JERUSALEM

6 David again gathered all the chosen men of Israel, thirty

[a] 5.8 Another reading is those who hate David [b] 5.20 Heb paraz [c] 5.20 That is Lord of Bursting Forth

thousand. 2David and all the people with him set out and went from Baale-judah, to bring up from there the ark of God, which is called by the name of the LORD of hosts who is enthroned on the cherubim. 3They carried the ark of God on a new cart, and brought it out of the house of Abinadab, which was on the hill. Uzzah and Ahio,ª the sons of Abinadab, were driving the new cart 4with the ark of God;ᵇ and Ahioª went in front of the ark. 5David and all the house of Israel were dancing before the LORD with all their might, with songsᶜ and lyres and harps and tambourines and castanets and cymbals.

6 When they came to the threshing floor of Nacon, Uzzah reached out his hand to the ark of God and took hold of it, for the oxen shook it. 7The anger of the LORD was kindled against Uzzah; and God struck him there because he reached out his hand to the ark;ᵈ and he died there beside the ark of God. 8David was angry because the LORD had burst forth with an outburst upon Uzzah; so that place is called Perez-uzzah,ᵉ to this day. 9David was afraid of the LORD that day; he said, "How can the ark of the LORD come into my care?" 10So David was unwilling to take the ark of the LORD into his care in the city of David; instead David took it to the house of Obed-edom the Gittite. 11The ark of the LORD remained in the house of Obed-edom the Gittite three months; and the LORD blessed Obed-edom and all his household.

12 It was told King David, "The LORD has blessed the household of Obed-edom and all that belongs to him, because of the ark of God." So David went and brought up the ark of God from the house of Obed-edom to the city of David with rejoicing; 13and when those who bore the ark of the LORD had gone six paces, he sacrificed an ox and a fatling. 14David danced before the LORD with all his might; David was girded with a linen ephod. 15So David and all the house of Israel brought up the ark of the LORD with shouting, and with the sound of the trumpet.

16 As the ark of the LORD came into the city of David, Michal daughter of Saul looked out of the window, and saw King David leaping and dancing before the LORD; and she despised him in her heart.

17 They brought in the ark of the LORD, and set it in its place, inside the tent that David had pitched for it; and David offered burnt offerings and offerings of well-being before the LORD. 18When David had finished offering the burnt offerings and the offerings of well-being, he blessed the people in the name of the LORD of hosts, 19and distributed food among all the people, the whole multitude of Israel, both men and women, to each a cake of bread, a portion of meat,ᶠ and a cake of raisins. Then all the people went back to their homes.

20 David returned to bless his household. But Michal the daughter of Saul came out to meet David, and said, "How the king of Israel honored himself today, uncovering himself today before the eyes of his servants' maids, as any vulgar fellow might shamelessly uncover himself!" 21David said to Michal, "It was before the LORD, who chose me in place of your father and all his household, to appoint me as prince over Israel, the people of the LORD, that I have danced before the LORD. 22I will make myself yet more contemptible than this, and I will be abased in my own eyes; but by the maids of whom you have spoken, by them I shall be held in honor." 23And Michal the daughter of Saul had no child to the day of her death.

GOD'S COVENANT WITH DAVID

7 Now when the king was settled in his house, and the LORD had given him rest from all his enemies around him, 2the king said to the

---

ª 6.3,4 Or and his brother   ᵇ 6.4 Compare Gk: Heb and brought it out of the house of Abinadab, which was on the hill with the ark of God   ᶜ 6.5 Q Ms Gk 1 Chr 13.8: Heb fir trees   ᵈ 6.7 1 Chr 13.10 Compare Q Ms: Meaning of Heb uncertain   ᵉ 6.8 That is Bursting Out Against Uzzah   ᶠ 6.19 Vg: Meaning of Heb uncertain

prophet Nathan, "See now, I am living in a house of cedar, but the ark of God stays in a tent." [3]Nathan said to the king, "Go, do all that you have in mind; for the LORD is with you."

4 But that same night the word of the LORD came to Nathan: [5]Go and tell my servant David: Thus says the LORD: Are you the one to build me a house to live in? [6]I have not lived in a house since the day I brought up the people of Israel from Egypt to this day, but I have been moving about in a tent and a tabernacle. [7]Wherever I have moved about among all the people of Israel, did I ever speak a word with any of the tribal leaders[a] of Israel, whom I commanded to shepherd my people Israel, saying, "Why have you not built me a house of cedar?" [8]Now therefore thus you shall say to my servant David: Thus says the LORD of hosts: I took you from the pasture, from following the sheep to be prince over my people Israel; [9]and I have been with you wherever you went, and have cut off all your enemies from before you; and I will make for you a great name, like the name of the great ones of the earth. [10]And I will appoint a place for my people Israel and will plant them, so that they may live in their own place, and be disturbed no more; and evildoers shall afflict them no more, as formerly, [11]from the time that I appointed judges over my people Israel; and I will give you rest from all your enemies. Moreover the LORD declares to you that the LORD will make you a house. [12]When your days are fulfilled and you lie down with your ancestors, I will raise up your offspring after you, who shall come forth from your body, and I will establish his kingdom. [13]He shall build a house for my name, and I will establish the throne of his kingdom forever. [14]I will be a father to him, and he shall be a son to me. When he commits iniquity, I will punish him with a rod such as mortals use, with blows inflicted by human beings. [15]But I will not take[b] my steadfast love from him, as I took it from Saul, whom I put away from before you. [16]Your house and your kingdom shall be made sure forever before me;[c] your throne shall be established forever. [17]In accordance with all these words and with all this vision, Nathan spoke to David.

DAVID'S PRAYER

18 Then King David went in and sat before the LORD, and said, "Who am I, O Lord GOD, and what is my house, that you have brought me thus far? [19]And yet this was a small thing in your eyes, O Lord GOD; you have spoken also of your servant's house for a great while to come. May this be instruction for the people,[d] O Lord GOD! [20]And what more can David say to you? For you know your servant, O Lord GOD! [21]Because of your promise, and according to your own heart, you have wrought all this greatness, so that your servant may know it. [22]Therefore you are great, O LORD God; for there is no one like you, and there is no God besides you, according to all that we have heard with our ears. [23]Who is like your people, like Israel? Is there another[e] nation on earth whose God went to redeem it as a people, and to make a name for himself, doing great and awesome things for them,[f] by driving out[g] before his people nations and their gods?[h] [24]And you established your people Israel for yourself to be your people forever; and you, O LORD, became their God. [25]And now, O LORD God, as for the word that you have spoken concerning your servant and concerning his house, confirm it forever; do as you have promised. [26]Thus your name will be magnified forever in the saying, 'The LORD of hosts is God over Israel'; and the house of your servant David will be established before you. [27]For you, O LORD of hosts, the God of Israel, have made this revelation

a 7.7 Or any of the tribes   b 7.15 Gk Syr Vg 1 Chr 17.13: Heb shall not depart   c 7.16 Gk Heb Mss: MT before you; Compare 2 Sam 7.26, 29 d 7.19 Meaning of Heb uncertain   e 7.23 Gk: Heb one   f 7.23 Heb you   g 7.23 Gk 1 Chr 17.21: Heb for your land   h 7.23 Cn: Heb before your people, whom you redeemed for yourself from Egypt, nations and its gods

to your servant, saying, 'I will build you a house'; therefore your servant has found courage to pray this prayer to you. 28And now, O Lord GOD, you are God, and your words are true, and you have promised this good thing to your servant; 29now therefore may it please you to bless the house of your servant, so that it may continue forever before you; for you, O Lord GOD, have spoken, and with your blessing shall the house of your servant be blessed forever."

DAVID'S WARS

8 Some time afterward, David attacked the Philistines and subdued them; David took Methegammah out of the hand of the Philistines.

2 He also defeated the Moabites and, making them lie down on the ground, measured them off with a cord; he measured two lengths of cord for those who were to be put to death, and one length[a] for those who were to be spared. And the Moabites became servants to David and brought tribute.

3 David also struck down King Hadadezer son of Rehob of Zobah, as he went to restore his monument[b] at the river Euphrates. 4David took from him one thousand seven hundred horsemen, and twenty thousand foot soldiers. David hamstrung all the chariot horses, but left enough for a hundred chariots. 5When the Arameans of Damascus came to help King Hadadezer of Zobah, David killed twenty-two thousand men of the Arameans. 6Then David put garrisons among the Arameans of Damascus; and the Arameans became servants to David and brought tribute. The LORD gave victory to David wherever he went. 7David took the gold shields that were carried by the servants of Hadadezer, and brought them to Jerusalem. 8From Betah and from Berothai, towns of Hadadezer, King David took a great amount of bronze.

9 When King Toi of Hamath heard that David had defeated the whole army of Hadadezer, 10Toi sent his son Joram to King David, to greet him and to congratulate him because he had fought against Hadadezer and defeated him. Now Hadadezer had often been at war with Toi. Joram brought with him articles of silver, gold, and bronze; 11these also King David dedicated to the LORD, together with the silver and gold that he dedicated from all the nations he subdued, 12from Edom, Moab, the Ammonites, the Philistines, Amalek, and from the spoil of King Hadadezer son of Rehob of Zobah.

13 David won a name for himself. When he returned, he killed eighteen thousand Edomites[c] in the Valley of Salt. 14He put garrisons in Edom; throughout all Edom he put garrisons, and all the Edomites became David's servants. And the LORD gave victory to David wherever he went.

DAVID'S OFFICERS

15 So David reigned over all Israel; and David administered justice and equity to all his people. 16Joab son of Zeruiah was over the army; Jehoshaphat son of Ahilud was recorder; 17Zadok son of Ahitub and Ahimelech son of Abiathar were priests; Seraiah was secretary; 18Benaiah son of Jehoiada was over[d] the Cherethites and the Pelethites; and David's sons were priests.

DAVID'S KINDNESS TO MEPHIBOSHETH

9 David asked, "Is there still anyone left of the house of Saul to whom I may show kindness for Jonathan's sake?" 2Now there was a servant of the house of Saul whose name was Ziba, and he was summoned to David. The king said to him, "Are you Ziba?" And he said, "At your service!" 3The king said, "Is there anyone remaining of the house of Saul to whom I may show the kindness of God?" Ziba said to

---

[a] 8.2 Heb one full length [b] 8.3 Compare 1 Sam 15.12 and 2 Sam 18.18 [c] 8.13 Gk: Heb returned from striking down eighteen thousand Arameans [d] 8.18 Syr Tg Vg 20.23; 1 Chr 18.17: Heb lacks was over

AN ANSWERED PRAYER

"And now, O Lord GOD, you are God, and your words are true, and you have promised this good thing to your servant; now therefore may it please you to bless the house of your servant."

—2 Samuel 7.28–29

When we look at David's prayer asking God for permission to build a temple, we aren't told exactly what was in David's heart and mind. Because God had given him victory over his enemies, David wanted to provide a glorious, permanent resting place for the ark of the covenant, where God's glory could reside. But could David also have wanted to emulate the surrounding nations, such as Egypt, that had built grand temples for their gods? Perhaps David wanted to build a temple to demonstrate to all who visited Jerusalem that Israel was powerful and prosperous. It's hard to know for sure, but these may have been the motivations behind David's desire to build a grand temple for God. Maybe that was part of the reason God declined David's offer and told him that Solomon, David's son, would build the temple instead.

There is a saying that God typically answers our prayers in one of three ways: "Yes," "No" and "You've got to be kidding!" God knows our motives when we are asking for something, whether those motives are pure, mixed, or selfish and self-serving. God knows that sometimes it is best for us if our prayers are not answered positively even when it seems as if we are praying for something we think is beneficial. Nevertheless, we are always to bring our requests to God with the understanding that the answers will be in conformity with God's will. And it's always a legitimate prayer that asks God what his will is. We should not expect to receive what we ask for when our requests are primarily self-serving: "You do not have, because you do not ask. You ask and do not receive, because you ask wrongly, in order to spend what you get on your pleasures." (James 4.2–3). Our requests should reflect a desire to do God's will, not just a desire to serve ourselves. Regardless, we should seek to glorify God in all things.

Though God said no to David's request to build a temple, in the end God offered David something far greater: God established David's dynasty forever as the rulers of Israel. This promise was fully realized in Jesus Christ, David's descendant.

Going Deeper

• Describe a time when you earnestly asked God for something, and God's response was no. How did you respond to God's answer?
• Name something you once prayed for, that, looking back later, you were glad that God did not give you. What might that say about God's wisdom and love?

the king, "There remains a son of Jonathan; he is crippled in his feet." ⁴The king said to him, "Where is he?" Ziba said to the king, "He is in the house of Machir son of Ammiel, at Lo-debar." ⁵Then King David sent and brought him from the house of Machir son of Ammiel, at Lo-debar. ⁶Mephiboshethᵃ son of Jonathan son of Saul came to David, and fell on his face and did obeisance. David said, "Mephibosheth!"ᵃ He answered, "I am your servant." ⁷David said to him, "Do not be afraid, for I will show you kindness for the sake of your father Jonathan; I will restore to you all the land of your grandfather Saul, and you yourself shall eat at my table always." ⁸He did obeisance and said, "What is your servant, that you should look upon a dead dog such as I?"

A TRUE TEST OF CHARACTER

IS HOW WE TREAT PEOPLE

WHO CAN DO NOTHING

TO US OR FOR US.

⁹ Then the king summoned Saul's servant Ziba, and said to him, "All that belonged to Saul and to all his house I have given to your master's grandson. ¹⁰You and your sons and your servants shall till the land for him, and shall bring in the produce, so that your master's grandson may have food to eat; but your master's grandson Mephiboshethᵃ shall always eat at my table." Now Ziba had fifteen sons and twenty servants. ¹¹Then Ziba said to the king, "According to all that my lord the king commands his servant, so your servant will do." Mephiboshethᵃ ate at David'sᵇ table, like one of the king's sons. ¹²Mephiboshethᵃ had a young son whose name was Mica. And all who lived in Ziba's house became Mephibosheth'sᶜ servants. ¹³Mephiboshethᵃ lived in Jerusalem, for

he always ate at the king's table. Now he was lame in both his feet.

THE AMMONITES AND ARAMEANS ARE DEFEATED

10 Some time afterward, the king of the Ammonites died, and his son Hanun succeeded him. ²David said, "I will deal loyally with Hanun son of Nahash, just as his father dealt loyally with me." So David sent envoys to console him concerning his father. When David's envoys came into the land of the Ammonites, ³the princes of the Ammonites said to their lord Hanun, "Do you really think that David is honoring your father just because he has sent messengers with condolences to you? Has not David sent his envoys to you to search the city, to spy it out, and to overthrow it?" ⁴So Hanun seized David's envoys, shaved off half the beard of each, cut off their garments in the middle at their hips, and sent them away. ⁵When David was told, he sent to meet them, for the men were greatly ashamed. The king said, "Remain at Jericho until your beards have grown, and then return."

⁶ When the Ammonites saw that they had become odious to David, the Ammonites sent and hired the Arameans of Beth-rehob and the Arameans of Zobah, twenty thousand foot soldiers, as well as the king of Maacah, one thousand men, and the men of Tob, twelve thousand men. ⁷When David heard of it, he sent Joab and all the army with the warriors. ⁸The Ammonites came out and drew up in battle array at the entrance of the gate; but the Arameans of Zobah and of Rehob, and the men of Tob and Maacah, were by themselves in the open country.

⁹ When Joab saw that the battle was set against him both in front and in the rear, he chose some of the picked men of Israel, and arrayed them against the Arameans; ¹⁰the rest of his men he put in the charge of his brother Abishai, and he arrayed

ᵃ 9.6,10,11,12,13 Or *Merib-baal*: See 4.4 note
ᵇ 9.11 Gk: Heb *my*   ᶜ 9.12 Or *Merib-baal's*: See 4.4 note

them against the Ammonites. [11]He said, "If the Arameans are too strong for me, then you shall help me; but if the Ammonites are too strong for you, then I will come and help you. [12]Be strong, and let us be courageous for the sake of our people, and for the cities of our God; and may the LORD do what seems good to him." [13]So Joab and the people who were with him moved forward into battle against the Arameans; and they fled before him. [14]When the Ammonites saw that the Arameans fled, they likewise fled before Abishai, and entered the city. Then Joab returned from fighting against the Ammonites, and came to Jerusalem.

[15] But when the Arameans saw that they had been defeated by Israel, they gathered themselves together. [16]Hadadezer sent and brought out the Arameans who were beyond the Euphrates; and they came to Helam, with Shobach the commander of the army of Hadadezer at their head. [17]When it was told David, he gathered all Israel together, and crossed the Jordan, and came to Helam. The Arameans arrayed themselves against David and fought with him. [18]The Arameans fled before Israel; and David killed of the Arameans seven hundred chariot teams, and forty thousand horsemen,[a] and wounded Shobach the commander of their army, so that he died there. [19]When all the kings who were servants of Hadadezer saw that they had been defeated by Israel, they made peace with Israel, and became subject to them. So the Arameans were afraid to help the Ammonites any more.

DAVID COMMITS ADULTERY WITH BATHSHEBA

11 In the spring of the year, the time when kings go out to battle, David sent Joab with his officers and all Israel with him; they ravaged the Ammonites, and besieged Rabbah. But David remained at Jerusalem.

[2] It happened, late one afternoon, when David rose from his couch and was walking about on the roof of the king's house, that he saw from the roof a woman bathing; the woman was very beautiful. [3]David sent someone to inquire about the woman. It was reported, "This is Bathsheba daughter of Eliam, the wife of Uriah the Hittite." [4]So David sent messengers to get her, and she came to him, and he lay with her. (Now she was purifying herself after her period.) Then she returned to her house. [5]The woman conceived; and she sent and told David, "I am pregnant."

[6] So David sent word to Joab, "Send me Uriah the Hittite." And Joab sent Uriah to David. [7]When Uriah came to him, David asked how Joab and the people fared, and how the war was going. [8]Then David said to Uriah, "Go down to your house, and wash your feet." Uriah went out of the king's house, and there followed him a present from the king. [9]But Uriah slept at the entrance of the king's house with all the servants of his lord, and did not go down to his house. [10]When they told David, "Uriah did not go down to his house," David said to Uriah, "You have just come from a journey. Why did you not go down to your house?" [11]Uriah said to David, "The ark and Israel and Judah remain in booths;[b] and my lord Joab and the servants of my lord are camping in the open field; shall I then go to my house, to eat and to drink, and to lie with my wife? As you live, and as your soul lives, I will not do such a thing." [12]Then David said to Uriah, "Remain here today also, and tomorrow I will send you back." So Uriah remained in Jerusalem that day. On the next day, [13]David invited him to eat and drink in his presence and made him drunk; and in the evening he went out to lie on his couch with the servants of his lord, but he did not go down to his house.

DAVID HAS URIAH KILLED

[14] In the morning David wrote a letter to Joab, and sent it by the

---

[a] 10.18 1 Chr 19.18 and some Gk Mss read foot soldiers   [b] 11.11 Or at Succoth

hand of Uriah. 15In the letter he wrote, "Set Uriah in the forefront of the hardest fighting, and then draw back from him, so that he may be struck down and die." 16As Joab was besieging the city, he assigned Uriah to the place where he knew there were valiant warriors. 17The men of the city came out and fought with Joab; and some of the servants of David among the people fell. Uriah the Hittite was killed as well. 18Then Joab sent and told David all the news about the fighting; 19and he instructed the messenger, "When you have finished telling the king all the news about the fighting, 20then, if the king's anger rises, and if he says to you, 'Why did you go so near the city to fight? Did you not know that they would shoot from the wall? 21Who killed Abimelech son of Jerubbaal?a Did not a woman throw an upper millstone on him from the wall, so that he died at Thebez? Why did you go so near the wall?' then you shall say, 'Your servant Uriah the Hittite is dead too.' "

22 So the messenger went, and came and told David all that Joab had sent him to tell. 23The messenger said to David, "The men gained an advantage over us, and came out against us in the field; but we drove them back to the entrance of the gate. 24Then the archers shot at your servants from the wall; some of the king's servants are dead; and your servant Uriah the Hittite is dead also." 25David said to the messenger, "Thus you shall say to Joab, 'Do not let this matter trouble you, for the sword devours now one and now another; press your attack on the city, and overthrow it.' And encourage him."

26 When the wife of Uriah heard that her husband was dead, she made lamentation for him. 27When the mourning was over, David sent and brought her to his house, and she became his wife, and bore him a son.

NATHAN CONDEMNS DAVID

12 But the thing that David had done displeased the LORD, 1and the LORD sent Nathan to David. He came to him, and said to him, "There were two men in a certain city, the one rich and the other poor. 2The rich man had very many flocks and herds; 3but the poor man had nothing but one little ewe lamb, which he had bought. He brought it up, and it grew up with him and with his children; it used to eat of his meager fare, and drink from his cup, and lie in his bosom, and it was like a daughter to him. 4Now there came a traveler to the rich man, and he was loath to take one of his own flock or herd to prepare for the wayfarer who had come to him, but he took the poor man's lamb, and prepared that for the guest who had come to him." 5Then David's anger was greatly kindled against the man. He said to Nathan, "As the LORD lives, the man who has done this deserves to die; 6he shall restore the lamb fourfold, because he did this thing, and because he had no pity."

7 Nathan said to David, "You are the man! Thus says the LORD, the God of Israel: I anointed you king over Israel, and I rescued you from the hand of Saul; 8I gave you your master's house, and your master's wives into your bosom, and gave you the house of Israel and of Judah; and if that had been too little, I would have added as much more. 9Why have you despised the word of the LORD, to do what is evil in his sight? You have struck down Uriah the Hittite with the sword, and have taken his wife to be your wife, and have killed him with the sword of the Ammonites. 10Now therefore the sword shall never depart from your house, for you have despised me, and have taken the wife of Uriah the Hittite to be your wife. 11Thus says the LORD: I will raise up trouble against you from within your own house; and I will take your wives before your eyes, and give them to your neighbor, and he shall lie with your wives in the sight of this very sun. 12For you did it secretly; but I will do this thing before all Israel,

a 11.21 Gk Syr Judg 7.1: Heb *Jerubbesheth*

and before the sun." [13]David said to Nathan, "I have sinned against the LORD." Nathan said to David, "Now the LORD has put away your sin; you shall not die. [14]Nevertheless, because by this deed you have utterly scorned the LORD,[a] the child that is born to you shall die." [15]Then Nathan went to his house.

BATHSHEBA'S CHILD DIES

The LORD struck the child that Uriah's wife bore to David, and it became very ill. [16]David therefore pleaded with God for the child; David fasted, and went in and lay all night on the ground. [17]The elders of his house stood beside him, urging him to rise from the ground; but he would not, nor did he eat food with them. [18]On the seventh day the child died. And the servants of David were afraid to tell him that the child was dead; for they said, "While the child was still alive, we spoke to him, and he did not listen to us; how then can we tell him the child is dead? He may do himself some harm." [19]But when David saw that his servants were whispering together, he perceived that the child was dead; and David said to his servants, "Is the child dead?" They said, "He is dead."

[20]Then David rose from the ground, washed, anointed himself, and changed his clothes. He went into the house of the LORD, and worshiped; he then went to his own house; and when he asked, they set food before him and he ate. [21]Then his servants said to him, "What is this thing that you have done? You fasted and wept for the child while it was alive; but when the child died, you rose and ate food." [22]He said, "While the child was still alive, I fasted and wept; for I said, 'Who knows? The LORD may be gracious to me, and the child may live.' [23]But now he is dead; why should I fast? Can I bring him back again? I shall go to him, but he will not return to me."

SOLOMON IS BORN

24 Then David consoled his wife Bathsheba, and went to her, and lay with her; and she bore a son, and he named him Solomon. The LORD loved him, [25]and sent a message by the prophet Nathan; so he named him Jedidiah,[b] because of the LORD.

THE AMMONITES CRUSHED

26 Now Joab fought against Rabbah of the Ammonites, and took the royal city. [27]Joab sent messengers to David, and said, "I have fought against Rabbah; moreover, I have taken the water city. [28]Now, then, gather the rest of the people together, and encamp against the city, and take it; or I myself will take the city, and it will be called by my name." [29]So David gathered all the people together and went to Rabbah, and fought against it and took it. [30]He took the crown of Milcom[c] from his head; the weight of it was a talent of gold, and in it was a precious stone; and it was placed on David's head. He also brought forth the spoil of the city, a very great amount. [31]He brought out the people who were in it, and set them to work with saws and iron picks and iron axes, or sent them to the brickworks. Thus he did to all the cities of the Ammonites. Then David and all the people returned to Jerusalem.

AMNON AND TAMAR

13 Some time passed. David's son Absalom had a beautiful sister whose name was Tamar; and David's son Amnon fell in love with her. [2]Amnon was so tormented that he made himself ill because of his sister Tamar, for she was a virgin and it seemed impossible to Amnon to do anything to her. [3]But Amnon had a friend whose name was Jonadab, the son of David's brother Shimeah; and Jonadab was a very crafty man. [4]He said to him, "O son of the king, why are you so haggard morning after morning? Will you not tell me?" Amnon said to him, "I love Tamar, my brother Absalom's

---

[a] 12.14 Ancient scribal tradition: Compare 1 Sam 25.22 note: Heb *scorned the enemies of the LORD*   [b] 12.25 That is *Beloved of the LORD*   [c] 12.30 Gk See 1 Kings 11.5, 33: Heb *their kings*

HAVE MERCY ON ME

David said to Nathan, "I have sinned against the LORD."

—2 Samuel 12.13

When we read this story of how David sinned with Bathsheba and murdered her husband Uriah, we might be angry or repulsed by his actions. How could a man "after God's own heart" do something so despicable, so wicked? The truth is that when we take a hard look at our own hearts, we realize that perhaps we are not so different from David. We want what belongs to others. We try to hide our misdeeds from others. We harbor hatred. We act selfishly and callously. We refuse to forgive those who have wronged us. All human sin is rooted in the same selfishness and alienation from God.

Once we realize that we are sinful, we are faced with the same choices as David. We can try to hide our sins so that others will never suspect us of wrongdoing, or we can delude ourselves into thinking our sin isn't so bad. But just as God judged David's actions, our actions are not hidden from the Lord, even if they are hidden from others, and disobedience to his commands displeases him and separates us from his grace.

There is no way we can be reconciled with God unless we are willing to take the same steps that David took: experiencing true sorrow and acknowledging the sins before God. He wrote, "Have mercy on me, O God, according to your steadfast love; according to your abundant mercy blot out my transgressions. Wash me thoroughly from my iniquity, and cleanse me from my sin . . . Against you, you alone, have I sinned" (Psalm 51.1–2,4). When we sin, it is only when we confess our sin that we can receive God's forgiveness and be restored to fellowship with our Creator: "If we say that we have no sin, we deceive ourselves, and the truth is not in us. If we confess our sins, he who is faithful and just will forgive us our sins and cleanse us from all unrighteousness" (1 John 1.8–9).

Another story of failure, repentance and restoration occurs in the New Testament: Jesus' disciple Peter was foremost among the Twelve and even vowed that he would be willing to die for Jesus (see Matthew 26.35). Yet when Jesus was arrested and people began to suspect Peter of being one of his followers, Peter denied even knowing Jesus. Later, however, Jesus restored Peter as his disciple and made him an apostle; Peter did many great things for God before he was martyred.

We can be certain of forgiveness when we repent and ask God to reconcile us to him. And not only does he restore us, he also enables us to do great acts of service.

Going Deeper

- How do you react when you read about David's sins of adultery and murder? How you feel when you read David's prayer in Psalm 51?
- Have you ever chosen to ignore or even hide a grave sin rather than confessing it? When?

sister." ⁵Jonadab said to him, "Lie down on your bed, and pretend to be ill; and when your father comes to see you, say to him, 'Let my sister Tamar come and give me something to eat, and prepare the food in my sight, so that I may see it and eat it from her hand.'" ⁶So Amnon lay down, and pretended to be ill; and when the king came to see him, Amnon said to the king, "Please let my sister Tamar come and make a couple of cakes in my sight, so that I may eat from her hand."

7 Then David sent home to Tamar, saying, "Go to your brother Amnon's house, and prepare food for him." ⁸So Tamar went to her brother Amnon's house, where he was lying down. She took dough, kneaded it, made cakes in his sight, and baked the cakes. ⁹Then she took the pan and set themᵃ out before him, but he refused to eat. Amnon said, "Send out everyone from me." So everyone went out from him. ¹⁰Then Amnon said to Tamar, "Bring the food into the chamber, so that I may eat from your hand." So Tamar took the cakes she had made, and brought them into the chamber to Amnon her brother. ¹¹But when she brought them near him to eat, he took hold of her, and said to her, "Come, lie with me, my sister." ¹²She answered him, "No, my brother, do not force me; for such a thing is not done in Israel; do not do anything so vile! ¹³As for me, where could I carry my shame? And as for you, you would be as one of the scoundrels in Israel. Now therefore, I beg you, speak to the king; for he will not withhold me from you." ¹⁴But he would not listen to her; and being stronger than she, he forced her and lay with her.

15 Then Amnon was seized with a very great loathing for her; indeed, his loathing was even greater than the lust he had felt for her. Amnon said to her, "Get out!" ¹⁶But she said to him, "No, my brother;ᵇ for this wrong in sending me away is greater than the other that you did to me." But he would not listen to her. ¹⁷He called the young man who served him and said, "Put this woman out

of my presence, and bolt the door after her." ¹⁸(Now she was wearing a long robe with sleeves; for this is how the virgin daughters of the king were clothed in earlier times.ᶜ) So his servant put her out, and bolted the door after her. ¹⁹But Tamar put ashes on her head, and tore the long robe that she was wearing; she put her hand on her head, and went away, crying aloud as she went.

20 Her brother Absalom said to her, "Has Amnon your brother been with you? Be quiet for now, my sister; he is your brother; do not take this to heart." So Tamar remained, a desolate woman, in her brother Absalom's house. ²¹When King David heard of all these things, he became very angry, but he would not punish his son Amnon, because he loved him, for he was his firstborn.ᵈ ²²But Absalom spoke to Amnon neither good nor bad; for Absalom hated Amnon, because he had raped his sister Tamar.

ABSALOM AVENGES THE VIOLATION OF HIS SISTER

23 After two full years Absalom had sheepshearers at Baal-hazor, which is near Ephraim, and Absalom invited all the king's sons. ²⁴Absalom came to the king, and said, "Your servant has sheepshearers; will the king and his servants please go with your servant?" ²⁵But the king said to Absalom, "No, my son, let us not all go, or else we will be burdensome to you." He pressed him, but he would not go but gave him his blessing. ²⁶Then Absalom said, "If not, please let my brother Amnon go with us." The king said to him, "Why should he go with you?" ²⁷But Absalom pressed him until he let Amnon and all the king's sons go with him. Absalom made a feast like a king's feast.ᵉ ²⁸Then Absalom commanded his servants, "Watch when

ᵃ 13.9 Heb and poured   ᵇ 13.16 Cn
Compare Gk Vg: Meaning of Heb uncertain
ᶜ 13.18 Cn: Heb were clothed in robes
ᵈ 13.21 Q Ms Gk: MT lacks but he would not punish... firstborn   ᵉ 13.27 Gk Compare Q Ms: MT lacks Absalom made a feast like a king's feast

Amnon's heart is merry with wine, and when I say to you, 'Strike Amnon,' then kill him. Do not be afraid; have I not myself commanded you? Be courageous and valiant." 29 So the servants of Absalom did to Amnon as Absalom had commanded. Then all the king's sons rose, and each mounted his mule and fled.

30 While they were on the way, the report came to David that Absalom had killed all the king's sons, and not one of them was left. 31 The king rose, tore his garments, and lay on the ground; and all his servants who were standing by tore their garments. 32 But Jonadab, the son of David's brother Shimeah, said, "Let not my lord suppose that they have killed all the young men the king's sons; Amnon alone is dead. This has been determined by Absalom from the day Amnon^a raped his sister Tamar. 33 Now therefore, do not let my lord the king take it to heart, as if all the king's sons were dead; for Amnon alone is dead."

34 But Absalom fled. When the young man who kept watch looked up, he saw many people coming from the Horonaim road^b by the side of the mountain. 35 Jonadab said to the king, "See, the king's sons have come; as your servant said, so it has come about." 36 As soon as he had finished speaking, the king's sons arrived, and raised their voices and wept; and the king and all his servants also wept very bitterly.

37 But Absalom fled, and went to Talmai son of Ammihud, king of Geshur. David mourned for his son day after day. 38 Absalom, having fled to Geshur, stayed there three years. 39 And the heart of^c the king went out, yearning for Absalom; for he was now consoled over the death of Amnon.

ABSALOM RETURNS TO JERUSALEM

14 Now Joab son of Zeruiah perceived that the king's mind was on Absalom. 2 Joab sent to Tekoa and brought from there a wise woman. He said to her, "Pretend to be a mourner; put on mourning garments, do not anoint yourself with oil, but behave like a woman who has been mourning many days for the dead. 3 Go to the king and speak to him as follows." And Joab put the words into her mouth.

4 When the woman of Tekoa came to the king, she fell on her face to the ground and did obeisance, and said, "Help, O king!" 5 The king asked her, "What is your trouble?" She answered, "Alas, I am a widow; my husband is dead. 6 Your servant had two sons, and they fought with one another in the field; there was no one to part them, and one struck the other and killed him. 7 Now the whole family has risen against your servant. They say, 'Give up the man who struck his brother, so that we may kill him for the life of his brother whom he murdered, even if we destroy the heir as well.' Thus they would quench my one remaining ember, and leave to my husband neither name nor remnant on the face of the earth."

8 Then the king said to the woman, "Go to your house, and I will give orders concerning you." 9 The woman of Tekoa said to the king, "On me be the guilt, my lord the king, and on my father's house; let the king and his throne be guiltless." 10 The king said, "If anyone says anything to you, bring him to me, and he shall never touch you again." 11 Then she said, "Please, may the king keep the LORD your God in mind, so that the avenger of blood may kill no more, and my son not be destroyed." He said, "As the LORD lives, not one hair of your son shall fall to the ground."

12 Then the woman said, "Please let your servant speak a word to my lord the king." He said, "Speak." 13 The woman said, "Why then have you planned such a thing against the people of God? For in giving this decision the king convicts himself, inasmuch as the king does not bring his banished one home again. 14 We must all die; we are like water

a 13.32 Heb he   b 13.34 Cn Compare Gk: Heb the road behind him   c 13.39 Q Ms Gk: MT And David spilled on the ground, which cannot be gathered up. But God will not take away a life; he will devise plans so as not to keep an outcast banished forever from his presence.[a] 15 Now I have come to say this to my lord the king because the people have made me afraid; your servant thought, 'I will speak to the king; it may be that the king will perform the request of his servant. 16 For the king will hear, and deliver his servant from the hand of the man who would cut both me and my son off from the heritage of God.' 17 Your servant thought, 'The word of my lord the king will set me at rest'; for my lord the king is like the angel of God, discerning good and evil. The LORD your God be with you!"

18 Then the king answered the woman, "Do not withhold from me anything I ask you." The woman said, "Let my lord the king speak." 19 The king said, "Is the hand of Joab with you in all this?" The woman answered and said, "As surely as you live, my lord the king, one cannot turn right or left from anything that my lord the king has said. For it was your servant Joab who commanded me; it was he who put all these words into the mouth of your servant. 20 In order to change the course of affairs your servant Joab did this. But my lord has wisdom like the wisdom of the angel of God to know all things that are on the earth."

21 Then the king said to Joab, "Very well, I grant this; go, bring back the young man Absalom." 22 Joab prostrated himself with his face to the ground and did obeisance, and blessed the king; and Joab said, "Today your servant knows that I have found favor in your sight, my lord the king, in that the king has granted the request of his servant." 23 So Joab set off, went to Geshur, and brought Absalom to Jerusalem. 24 The king said, "Let him go to his own house; he is not to come into my presence." So Absalom went to his own house, and did not come into the king's presence.

DAVID FORGIVES ABSALOM

25 Now in all Israel there was no one to be praised so much for his beauty as Absalom; from the sole of his foot to the crown of his head there was no blemish in him. 26 When he cut the hair of his head (for at the end of every year he used to cut it; when it was heavy on him, he cut it), he weighed the hair of his head, two hundred shekels by the king's weight. 27 There were born to Absalom three sons, and one daughter whose name was Tamar; she was a beautiful woman.

28 So Absalom lived two full years in Jerusalem, without coming into the king's presence. 29 Then Absalom sent for Joab to send him to the king; but Joab would not come to him. He sent a second time, but Joab would not come. 30 Then he said to his servants, "Look, Joab's field is next to mine, and he has barley there; go and set it on fire." So Absalom's servants set the field on fire. 31 Then Joab rose and went to Absalom at his house, and said to him, "Why have your servants set my field on fire?" 32 Absalom answered Joab, "Look, I sent word to you: Come here, that I may send you to the king with the question, 'Why have I come from Geshur? It would be better for me to be there still.' Now let me go into the king's presence; if there is guilt in me, let him kill me!" 33 Then Joab went to the king and told him; and he summoned Absalom. So he came to the king and prostrated himself with his face to the ground before the king; and the king kissed Absalom.

ABSALOM USURPS THE THRONE

15 After this Absalom got himself a chariot and horses, and fifty men to run ahead of him. 2 Absalom used to rise early and stand beside the road into the gate; and when anyone brought a suit before the king for judgment, Absalom would call out and say, "From what city are you?" When the person said, "Your servant is of such and such a tribe in Israel," 3 Absalom would say, "See, your claims are good and right; but there is no one deputed

[a] 14.14 Meaning of Heb uncertain

by the king to hear you." 4Absalom said moreover, "If only I were judge in the land! Then all who had a suit or cause might come to me, and I would give them justice." 5Whenever people came near to do obeisance to him, he would put out his hand and take hold of them, and kiss them. 6Thus Absalom did to every Israelite who came to the king for judgment; so Absalom stole the hearts of the people of Israel.

7 At the end of four[a] years Absalom said to the king, "Please let me go to Hebron and pay the vow that I have made to the LORD. 8For your servant made a vow while I lived at Geshur in Aram: If the LORD will indeed bring me back to Jerusalem, then I will worship the LORD in Hebron."[b] 9The king said to him, "Go in peace." So he got up, and went to Hebron. 10But Absalom sent secret messengers throughout all the tribes of Israel, saying, "As soon as you hear the sound of the trumpet, then shout: Absalom has become king at Hebron!" 11Two hundred men from Jerusalem went with Absalom; they were invited guests, and they went in their innocence, knowing nothing of the matter. 12While Absalom was offering the sacrifices, he sent for[c] Ahithophel the Gilonite, David's counselor, from his city Giloh. The conspiracy grew in strength, and the people with Absalom kept increasing.

DAVID FLEES FROM JERUSALEM

13 A messenger came to David, saying, "The hearts of the Israelites have gone after Absalom." 14Then David said to all his officials who were with him at Jerusalem, "Get up! Let us flee, or there will be no escape for us from Absalom. Hurry, or he will soon overtake us, and bring disaster down upon us, and attack the city with the edge of the sword." 15The king's officials said to the king, "Your servants are ready to do whatever our lord the king decides." 16So the king left, followed by all his household, except ten concubines whom he left behind to look after the house. 17The king left, followed

by all the people; and they stopped at the last house. 18All his officials passed by him; and all the Cherethites, and all the Pelethites, and all the six hundred Gittites who had followed him from Gath, passed on before the king.

19 Then the king said to Ittai the Gittite, "Why are you also coming with us? Go back, and stay with the king; for you are a foreigner, and also an exile from your home. 20You came only yesterday, and shall I today make you wander about with us, while I go wherever I can? Go back, and take your kinsfolk with you; and may the LORD show[d] steadfast love and faithfulness to you." 21But Ittai answered the king, "As the LORD lives, and as my lord the king lives, wherever my lord the king may be, whether for death or for life, there also your servant will be." 22David said to Ittai, "Go then, march on." So Ittai the Gittite marched on, with all his men and all the little ones who were with him. 23The whole country wept aloud as all the people passed by; the king crossed the Wadi Kidron, and all the people moved on toward the wilderness.

24 Abiathar came up, and Zadok also, with all the Levites, carrying the ark of the covenant of God. They set down the ark of God, until the people had all passed out of the city. 25Then the king said to Zadok, "Carry the ark of God back into the city. If I find favor in the eyes of the LORD, he will bring me back and let me see both it and the place where it stays. 26But if he says, 'I take no pleasure in you,' here I am, let him do to me what seems good to him." 27The king also said to the priest Zadok, "Look,[e] go back to the city in peace, you and Abiathar,[f] with your two sons, Ahimaaz your son, and Jonathan son of Abiathar. 28See, I will wait at the fords of the wilderness until word comes from you to

[a] 15.7 Gk Syr: Heb forty [b] 15.8 Gk Mss: Heb lacks in Hebron [c] 15.12 Or he sent [d] 15.20 Gk Compare 2.6: Heb lacks may the LORD show [e] 15.27 Gk: Heb Are you a seer or Do you see? [f] 15.27 Cn: Heb lacks and Abiathar

inform me." 29So Zadok and Abiathar carried the ark of God back to Jerusalem, and they remained there.

30 But David went up the ascent of the Mount of Olives, weeping as he went, with his head covered and walking barefoot; and all the people who were with him covered their heads and went up, weeping as they went. 31David was told that Ahithophel was among the conspirators with Absalom. And David said, "O LORD, I pray you, turn the counsel of Ahithophel into foolishness."

HUSHAI BECOMES DAVID'S SPY

32 When David came to the summit, where God was worshiped, Hushai the Archite came to meet him with his coat torn and earth on his head. 33David said to him, "If you go on with me, you will be a burden to me. 34But if you return to the city and say to Absalom, 'I will be your servant, O king; as I have been your father's servant in time past, so now I will be your servant,' then you will defeat for me the counsel of Ahithophel. 35The priests Zadok and Abiathar will be with you there. So whatever you hear from the king's house, tell it to the priests Zadok and Abiathar. 36Their two sons are with them there, Zadok's son Ahimaaz and Abiathar's son Jonathan; and by them you shall report to me everything you hear." 37So Hushai, David's friend, came into the city, just as Absalom was entering Jerusalem.

DAVID'S ADVERSARIES

16 When David had passed a little beyond the summit, Ziba the servant of Mephibosheth[a] met him, with a couple of donkeys saddled, carrying two hundred loaves of bread, one hundred bunches of raisins, one hundred of summer fruits, and one skin of wine. 2The king said to Ziba, "Why have you brought these?" Ziba answered, "The donkeys are for the king's household to ride, the bread and summer fruit for the young men to eat, and the wine is for those to drink who faint in the wilderness." 3The king said, "And where is your master's son?"

Ziba said to the king, "He remains in Jerusalem; for he said, 'Today the house of Israel will give me back my grandfather's kingdom.'" 4Then the king said to Ziba, "All that belonged to Mephibosheth[a] is now yours." Ziba said, "I do obeisance; let me find favor in your sight, my lord the king."

SHIMEI CURSES DAVID

5 When King David came to Bahurim, a man of the family of the house of Saul came out whose name was Shimei son of Gera; he came out cursing. 6He threw stones at David and at all the servants of King David; now all the people and all the warriors were on his right and on his left. 7Shimei shouted while he cursed, "Out! Out! Murderer! Scoundrel! 8The LORD has avenged on all of you the blood of the house of Saul, in whose place you have reigned; and the LORD has given the kingdom into the hand of your son Absalom. See, disaster has overtaken you; for you are a man of blood."

9 Then Abishai son of Zeruiah said to the king, "Why should this dead dog curse my lord the king? Let me go over and take off his head." 10But the king said, "What have I to do with you, you sons of Zeruiah? If he is cursing because the LORD has said to him, 'Curse David,' who then shall say, 'Why have you done so?'" 11David said to Abishai and to all his servants, "My own son seeks my life; how much more now may this Benjaminite! Let him alone, and let him curse; for the LORD has bidden him. 12It may be that the LORD will look on my distress,[b] and the LORD will repay me with good for this cursing of me today." 13So David and his men went on the road, while Shimei went along on the hillside opposite him and cursed as he went, throwing stones and flinging dust at him. 14The king and all the people who were with him arrived weary at the Jordan;[c] and there he refreshed himself.

THE COUNSEL OF AHITHOPHEL

15 Now Absalom and all the Israelites[a] came to Jerusalem; Ahithophel was with him. 16When Hushai the Archite, David's friend, came to Absalom, Hushai said to Absalom, "Long live the king! Long live the king!" 17Absalom said to Hushai, "Is this your loyalty to your friend? Why did you not go with your friend?" 18Hushai said to Absalom, "No; but the one whom the LORD and this people and all the Israelites have chosen, his I will be, and with him I will remain. 19Moreover, whom should I serve? Should it not be his son? Just as I have served your father, so I will serve you."

WE SHOULD BASE OUR

LIFE'S WORK ON OUR

RELATIONSHIP TO CHRIST

AND LET JESUS BE THE FOCUS

OF OUR GOOD WORKS.

20 Then Absalom said to Ahithophel, "Give us your counsel; what shall we do?" 21Ahithophel said to Absalom, "Go in to your father's concubines, the ones he has left to look after the house; and all Israel will hear that you have made yourself odious to your father, and the hands of all who are with you will be strengthened." 22So they pitched a tent for Absalom upon the roof; and Absalom went in to his father's concubines in the sight of all Israel. 23Now in those days the counsel that Ahithophel gave was as if one consulted the oracle[b] of God; so all the counsel of Ahithophel was esteemed, both by David and by Absalom.

17 Moreover Ahithophel said to Absalom, "Let me choose twelve thousand men, and I will set out and pursue David tonight. 2I will come upon him while he is weary and discouraged, and throw him into a panic; and all the people who are with him will flee. I will strike down only the king, 3and I will bring all the people back to you as a bride comes home to her husband. You seek the life of only one man,[c] and all the people will be at peace." 4The advice pleased Absalom and all the elders of Israel.

THE COUNSEL OF HUSHAI

5 Then Absalom said, "Call Hushai the Archite also, and let us hear too what he has to say." 6When Hushai came to Absalom, Absalom said to him, "This is what Ahithophel has said; shall we do as he advises? If not, you tell us." 7Then Hushai said to Absalom, "This time the counsel that Ahithophel has given is not good." 8Hushai continued, "You know that your father and his men are warriors, and that they are enraged, like a bear robbed of her cubs in the field. Besides, your father is expert in war; he will not spend the night with the troops. 9Even now he has hidden himself in one of the pits, or in some other place. And when some of our troops[d] fall at the first attack, whoever hears it will say, 'There has been a slaughter among the troops who follow Absalom.' 10Then even the valiant warrior, whose heart is like the heart of a lion, will utterly melt with fear; for all Israel knows that your father is a warrior, and that those who are with him are valiant warriors. 11But my counsel is that all Israel be gathered to you, from Dan to Beer-sheba, like the sand by the sea for multitude, and that you go to battle in person. 12So we shall come upon him in whatever place he may be found, and we shall light on him as the dew falls on the ground; and he will not survive, nor will any of those with him. 13If he withdraws into a city, then all Israel will bring ropes to that city, and we shall drag it into the valley, until not even a

pebble is to be found there." ¹⁴Absalom and all the men of Israel said, "The counsel of Hushai the Archite is better than the counsel of Ahithophel." For the LORD had ordained to defeat the good counsel of Ahithophel, so that the LORD might bring ruin on Absalom.

HUSHAI WARNS DAVID TO ESCAPE

15 Then Hushai said to the priests Zadok and Abiathar, "Thus and so did Ahithophel counsel Absalom and the elders of Israel; and thus and so I have counseled. ¹⁶Therefore send quickly and tell David, 'Do not lodge tonight at the fords of the wilderness, but by all means cross over; otherwise the king and all the people who are with him will be swallowed up.'" ¹⁷Jonathan and Ahimaaz were waiting at En-rogel; a servant-girl used to go and tell them, and they would go and tell King David; for they could not risk being seen entering the city. ¹⁸But a boy saw them, and told Absalom; so both of them went away quickly, and came to the house of a man at Bahurim, who had a well in his courtyard; and they went down into it. ¹⁹The man's wife took a covering, stretched it over the well's mouth, and spread out grain on it; and nothing was known of it. ²⁰When Absalom's servants came to the woman at the house, they said, "Where are Ahimaaz and Jonathan?" The woman said to them, "They have crossed over the brookᵃ of water." And when they had searched and could not find them, they returned to Jerusalem.

21 After they had gone, the men came up out of the well, and went and told King David. They said to David, "Go and cross the water quickly; for thus and so has Ahithophel counseled against you." ²²So David and all the people who were with him set out and crossed the Jordan; by daybreak not one was left who had not crossed the Jordan.

23 When Ahithophel saw that his counsel was not followed, he saddled his donkey and went off home to his own city. He set his house in order, and hanged himself; he died and was buried in the tomb of his father.

24 Then David came to Mahanaim, while Absalom crossed the Jordan with all the men of Israel. ²⁵Now Absalom had set Amasa over the army in the place of Joab. Amasa was the son of a man named Ithra the Ishmaelite,ᵇ who had married Abigal daughter of Nahash, sister of Zeruiah, Joab's mother. ²⁶The Israelites and Absalom encamped in the land of Gilead.

27 When David came to Mahanaim, Shobi son of Nahash from Rabbah of the Ammonites, and Machir son of Ammiel from Lodebar, and Barzillai the Gileadite from Rogelim, ²⁸brought beds, basins, and earthen vessels, wheat, barley, meal, parched grain, beans and lentils,ᶜ ²⁹honey and curds, sheep, and cheese from the herd, for David and the people with him to eat; for they said, "The troops are hungry and weary and thirsty in the wilderness."

THE DEFEAT AND DEATH OF ABSALOM

18 Then David mustered the men who were with him, and set over them commanders of thousands and commanders of hundreds. ²And David divided the army into three groups:ᵈ one third under the command of Joab, one third under the command of Abishai son of Zeruiah, Joab's brother, and one third under the command of Ittai the Gittite. The king said to the men, "I myself will also go out with you." ³But the men said, "You shall not go out. For if we flee, they will not care about us. If half of us die, they will not care about us. But you are worth ten thousand of us;ᵉ therefore it is better that you send us help from the city." ⁴The king said to them, "Whatever seems best to you I will do." So the king stood at the side of

---

ᵃ 17.20 Meaning of Heb uncertain
ᵇ 17.25 1 Chr 2.17: Heb *Israelite*   ᶜ 17.28 Heb *and lentils and parched grain*   ᵈ 18.2 Gk: Heb *sent forth the army*   ᵉ 18.3 Gk Vg Symmachus: Heb *for now there are ten thousand such as we*

the gate, while all the army marched out by hundreds and by thousands. [5]The king ordered Joab and Abishai and Ittai, saying, "Deal gently for my sake with the young man Absalom." And all the people heard when the king gave orders to all the commanders concerning Absalom.

[6] So the army went out into the field against Israel; and the battle was fought in the forest of Ephraim. [7]The men of Israel were defeated there by the servants of David, and the slaughter there was great on that day, twenty thousand men. [8]The battle spread over the face of all the country; and the forest claimed more victims that day than the sword.

WE CAN ALLOW SUFFERING

AND LOSS TO DEFEAT US—

OR WE CAN GAIN STRENGTH

BY EMBRACING GOD.

[9] Absalom happened to meet the servants of David. Absalom was riding on his mule, and the mule went under the thick branches of a great oak. His head caught fast in the oak, and he was left hanging[a] between heaven and earth, while the mule that was under him went on. [10]A man saw it, and told Joab, "I saw Absalom hanging in an oak." [11]Joab said to the man who told him, "What, you saw him! Why then did you not strike him there to the ground? I would have been glad to give you ten pieces of silver and a belt." [12]But the man said to Joab, "Even if I felt in my hand the weight of a thousand pieces of silver, I would not raise my hand against the king's son; for in our hearing the king commanded you and Abishai and Ittai, saying: For my sake protect the young man Absalom! [13]On the other hand, if I had dealt treacherously against his life[b] (and there is nothing hid-

den from the king), then you yourself would have stood aloof." [14]Joab said, "I will not waste time like this with you." He took three spears in his hand, and thrust them into the heart of Absalom, while he was still alive in the oak. [15]And ten young men, Joab's armor-bearers, surrounded Absalom and struck him, and killed him.

[16] Then Joab sounded the trumpet, and the troops came back from pursuing Israel, for Joab restrained the troops. [17]They took Absalom, threw him into a great pit in the forest, and raised over him a very great heap of stones. Meanwhile all the Israelites fled to their homes. [18]Now Absalom in his lifetime had taken and set up for himself a pillar that is in the King's Valley, for he said, "I have no son to keep my name in remembrance"; he called the pillar by his own name. It is called Absalom's Monument to this day.

DAVID HEARS OF ABSALOM'S DEATH

[19] Then Ahimaaz son of Zadok said, "Let me run, and carry tidings to the king that the LORD has delivered him from the power of his enemies." [20]Joab said to him, "You are not to carry tidings today; you may carry tidings another day, but today you shall not do so, because the king's son is dead." [21]Then Joab said to a Cushite, "Go, tell the king what you have seen." The Cushite bowed before Joab, and ran. [22]Then Ahimaaz son of Zadok said again to Joab, "Come what may, let me also run after the Cushite." And Joab said, "Why will you run, my son, seeing that you have no reward[c] for the tidings?" [23]"Come what may," he said, "I will run." So he said to him, "Run." Then Ahimaaz ran by the way of the Plain, and outran the Cushite.

[24] Now David was sitting between the two gates. The sentinel went up to the roof of the gate by the wall, and when he looked up, he saw a man running alone. [25]The sentinel

[a] 18.9 Gk Syr Tg: Heb *was put*
[b] 18.13 Another reading is *at the risk of my life*   [c] 18.22 Meaning of Heb uncertain

shouted and told the king. The king said, "If he is alone, there are tidings in his mouth." He kept coming, and drew near. 26Then the sentinel saw another man running; and the sentinel called to the gatekeeper and said, "See, another man running alone!" The king said, "He also is bringing tidings." 27The sentinel said, "I think the running of the first one is like the running of Ahimaaz son of Zadok." The king said, "He is a good man, and comes with good tidings."

28 Then Ahimaaz cried out to the king, "All is well!" He prostrated himself before the king with his face to the ground, and said, "Blessed be the LORD your God, who has delivered up the men who raised their hand against my lord the king." 29The king said, "Is it well with the young man Absalom?" Ahimaaz answered, "When Joab sent your servant,a I saw a great tumult, but I do not know what it was." 30The king said, "Turn aside, and stand here." So he turned aside, and stood still.

31 Then the Cushite came; and the Cushite said, "Good tidings for my lord the king! For the LORD has vindicated you this day, delivering you from the power of all who rose up against you." 32The king said to the Cushite, "Is it well with the young man Absalom?" The Cushite answered, "May the enemies of my lord the king, and all who rise up to do you harm, be like that young man."

DAVID MOURNS FOR ABSALOM

33b The king was deeply moved, and went up to the chamber over the gate, and wept; and as he went, he said, "O my son Absalom, my son, my son Absalom! Would I had died instead of you, O Absalom, my son, my son!"

19 It was told Joab, "The king is weeping and mourning for Absalom." 2So the victory that day was turned into mourning for all the troops; for the troops heard that day, "The king is grieving for his son." 3The troops stole into the city that day as soldiers steal in who are ashamed when they flee in battle.

4The king covered his face, and the king cried with a loud voice, "O my son Absalom, O Absalom, my son, my son!" 5Then Joab came into the house to the king, and said, "Today you have covered with shame the faces of all your officers who have saved your life today, and the lives of your sons and your daughters, and the lives of your wives and your concubines, 6for love of those who hate you and for hatred of those who love you. You have made it clear today that commanders and officers are nothing to you; for I perceive that if Absalom were alive and all of us were dead today, then you would be pleased. 7So go out at once and speak kindly to your servants; for I swear by the LORD, if you do not go, not a man will stay with you this night; and this will be worse for you than any disaster that has come upon you from your youth until now." 8Then the king got up and took his seat in the gate. The troops were all told, "See, the king is sitting in the gate"; and all the troops came before the king.

DAVID RECALLED TO JERUSALEM

Meanwhile, all the Israelites had fled to their homes. 9All the people were disputing throughout all the tribes of Israel, saying, "The king delivered us from the hand of our enemies, and saved us from the hand of the Philistines; and now he has fled out of the land because of Absalom. 10But Absalom, whom we anointed over us, is dead in battle. Now therefore why do you say nothing about bringing the king back?"

11 King David sent this message to the priests Zadok and Abiathar, "Say to the elders of Judah, 'Why should you be the last to bring the king back to his house? The talk of all Israel has come to the king.c 12You are my kin, you are my bone and my flesh; why then should you be the last to bring back the king?' 13And say to Amasa, 'Are you not my bone and my flesh? So may God do to me,

a 18.29 Heb *the king's servant, your servant*
b 18.33 Ch 19.1 in Heb   c 19.11 Gk: Heb *to the king, to his house*

and more, if you are not the commander of my army from now on, in place of Joab.' " [14]Amasa[a] swayed the hearts of all the people of Judah as one, and they sent word to the king, "Return, both you and all your servants." [15]So the king came back to the Jordan; and Judah came to Gilgal to meet the king and to bring him over the Jordan.

[16] Shimei son of Gera, the Benjaminite, from Bahurim, hurried to come down with the people of Judah to meet King David; [17]with him were a thousand people from Benjamin. And Ziba, the servant of the house of Saul, with his fifteen sons and his twenty servants, rushed down to the Jordan ahead of the king, [18]while the crossing was taking place,[b] to bring over the king's household, and to do his pleasure.

DAVID'S MERCY TO SHIMEI

Shimei son of Gera fell down before the king, as he was about to cross the Jordan, [19]and said to the king, "May my lord not hold me guilty or remember how your servant did wrong on the day my lord the king left Jerusalem; may the king not bear it in mind. [20]For your servant knows that I have sinned; therefore, see, I have come this day, the first of all the house of Joseph to come down to meet my lord the king." [21]Abishai son of Zeruiah answered, "Shall not Shimei be put to death for this, because he cursed the LORD's anointed?" [22]But David said, "What have I to do with you, you sons of Zeruiah, that you should today become an adversary to me? Shall anyone be put to death in Israel this day? For do I not know that I am this day king over Israel?" [23]The king said to Shimei, "You shall not die." And the king gave him his oath.

DAVID AND MEPHIBOSHETH
MEET

[24] Mephibosheth[c] grandson of Saul came down to meet the king; he had not taken care of his feet, or trimmed his beard, or washed his clothes, from the day the king left until the day he came back in safety. [25]When he came from Jerusalem to meet the king, the king said to him, "Why did you not go with me, Mephibosheth?"[c] [26]He answered, "My lord, O king, my servant deceived me; for your servant said to him, 'Saddle a donkey for me,[d] so that I may ride on it and go with the king.' For your servant is lame. [27]He has slandered your servant to my lord the king. But my lord the king is like the angel of God; do therefore what seems good to you. [28]For all my father's house were doomed to death before my lord the king; but you set your servant among those who eat at your table. What further right have I, then, to appeal to the king?" [29]The king said to him, "Why speak any more of your affairs? I have decided: you and Ziba shall divide the land." [30]Mephibosheth[c] said to the king, "Let him take it all, since my lord the king has arrived home safely."

DAVID'S KINDNESS
TO BARZILLAI

[31] Now Barzillai the Gileadite had come down from Rogelim; he went on with the king to the Jordan, to escort him over the Jordan. [32]Barzillai was a very aged man, eighty years old. He had provided the king with food while he stayed at Mahanaim, for he was a very wealthy man. [33]The king said to Barzillai, "Come over with me, and I will provide for you in Jerusalem at my side." [34]But Barzillai said to the king, "How many years have I still to live, that I should go up with the king to Jerusalem? [35]Today I am eighty years old; can I discern what is pleasant and what is not? Can your servant taste what he eats or what he drinks? Can I still listen to the voice of singing men and singing women? Why then should your servant be an added burden to my lord the king? [36]Your servant will go a little way over the Jordan with the king. Why should the king

---

[a] 19.14 Heb *He*   [b] 19.18 Cn: Heb *the ford crossed*   [c] 19.24,25,30 Or *Merib-baal*: See 4.4 note   [d] 19.26 Gk Syr Vg: Heb *said, 'I will saddle a donkey for myself*

recompense me with such a reward? [37]Please let your servant return, so that I may die in my own town, near the graves of my father and my mother. But here is your servant Chimham; let him go over with my lord the king; and do for him whatever seems good to you." [38]The king answered, "Chimham shall go over with me, and I will do for him whatever seems good to you; and all that you desire of me I will do for you." [39]Then all the people crossed over the Jordan, and the king crossed over; the king kissed Barzillai and blessed him, and he returned to his own home. [40]The king went on to Gilgal, and Chimham went on with him; all the people of Judah, and also half the people of Israel, brought the king on his way.

[41]Then all the people of Israel came to the king, and said to him, "Why have our kindred the people of Judah stolen you away, and brought the king and his household over the Jordan, and all David's men with him?" [42]All the people of Judah answered the people of Israel, "Because the king is near of kin to us. Why then are you angry over this matter? Have we eaten at all at the king's expense? Or has he given us any gift?" [43]But the people of Israel answered the people of Judah, "We have ten shares in the king, and in David also we have more than you. Why then did you despise us? Were we not the first to speak of bringing back our king?" But the words of the people of Judah were fiercer than the words of the people of Israel.

THE REBELLION OF SHEBA

20 Now a scoundrel named Sheba son of Bichri, a Benjaminite, happened to be there. He sounded the trumpet and cried out,
"We have no portion in David,
no share in the son of Jesse!
Everyone to your tents, O Israel!"
[2]So all the people of Israel withdrew from David and followed Sheba son of Bichri; but the people of Judah followed their king steadfastly from the Jordan to Jerusalem.

[3]David came to his house at Jerusalem; and the king took the ten concubines whom he had left to look after the house, and put them in a house under guard, and provided for them, but did not go in to them. So they were shut up until the day of their death, living as if in widowhood.

[4]Then the king said to Amasa, "Call the men of Judah together to me within three days, and be here yourself." [5]So Amasa went to summon Judah; but he delayed beyond the set time that had been appointed him. [6]David said to Abishai, "Now Sheba son of Bichri will do us more harm than Absalom; take your lord's servants and pursue him, or he will find fortified cities for himself, and escape from us." [7]Joab's men went out after him, along with the Cherethites, the Pelethites, and all the warriors; they went out from Jerusalem to pursue Sheba son of Bichri. [8]When they were at the large stone that is in Gibeon, Amasa came to meet them. Now Joab was wearing a soldier's garment and over it was a belt with a sword in its sheath fastened at his waist; as he went forward it fell out. [9]Joab said to Amasa, "Is it well with you, my brother?" And Joab took Amasa by the beard with his right hand to kiss him. [10]But Amasa did not notice the sword in Joab's hand; Joab struck him in the belly so that his entrails poured out on the ground, and he died. He did not strike a second blow.

Then Joab and his brother Abishai pursued Sheba son of Bichri. [11]And one of Joab's men took his stand by Amasa, and said, "Whoever favors Joab, and whoever is for David, let him follow Joab." [12]Amasa lay wallowing in his blood on the highway, and the man saw that all the people were stopping. Since he saw that all who came by him were stopping, he carried Amasa from the highway into a field, and threw a garment over him. [13]Once he was removed from the highway, all the people went on after Joab to pursue Sheba son of Bichri.

[14]Sheba[a] passed through all the tribes of Israel to Abel of Beth-

---

[a] 20.14 Heb *He*

maacah;[a] and all the Bichrites[b] assembled, and followed him inside. [15]Joab's forces[c] came and besieged him in Abel of Beth-maacah; they threw up a siege ramp against the city, and it stood against the rampart. Joab's forces were battering the wall to break it down. [16]Then a wise woman called from the city, "Listen! Listen! Tell Joab, 'Come here, I want to speak to you.' " [17]He came near her; and the woman said, "Are you Joab?" He answered, "I am." Then she said to him, "Listen to the words of your servant." He answered, "I am listening." [18]Then she said, "They used to say in the old days, 'Let them inquire at Abel'; and so they would settle a matter. [19]I am one of those who are peaceable and faithful in Israel; you seek to destroy a city that is a mother in Israel; why will you swallow up the heritage of the LORD?" [20]Joab answered, "Far be it from me, far be it, that I should swallow up or destroy! [21]That is not the case! But a man of the hill country of Ephraim, called Sheba son of Bichri, has lifted up his hand against King David; give him up alone, and I will withdraw from the city." The woman said to Joab, "His head shall be thrown over the wall to you." [22]Then the woman went to all the people with her wise plan. And they cut off the head of Sheba son of Bichri, and threw it out to Joab. So he blew the trumpet, and they dispersed from the city, and all went to their homes, while Joab returned to Jerusalem to the king.

[23] Now Joab was in command of all the army of Israel;[d] Benaiah son of Jehoiada was in command of the Cherethites and the Pelethites; [24]Adoram was in charge of the forced labor; Jehoshaphat son of Ahilud was the recorder; [25]Sheva was secretary; Zadok and Abiathar were priests; [26]and Ira the Jairite was also David's priest.

DAVID AVENGES THE GIBEONITES

21 Now there was a famine in the days of David for three years, year after year; and David in-

quired of the LORD. The LORD said, "There is bloodguilt on Saul and on his house, because he put the Gibeonites to death." [2]So the king called the Gibeonites and spoke to them. (Now the Gibeonites were not of the people of Israel, but of the remnant of the Amorites; although the people of Israel had sworn to spare them, Saul had tried to wipe them out in his zeal for the people of Israel and Judah.) [3]David said to the Gibeonites, "What shall I do for you? How shall I make expiation, that you may bless the heritage of the LORD?" [4]The Gibeonites said to him, "It is not a matter of silver or gold between us and Saul or his house; neither is it for us to put anyone to death in Israel." He said, "What do you say that I should do for you?" [5]They said to the king, "The man who consumed us and planned to destroy us, so that we should have no place in all the territory of Israel— [6]let seven of his sons be handed over to us, and we will impale them before the LORD at Gibeon on the mountain of the LORD."[e] The king said, "I will hand them over."

[7] But the king spared Mephibosheth,[f] the son of Saul's son Jonathan, because of the oath of the LORD that was between them, between David and Jonathan son of Saul. [8]The king took the two sons of Rizpah daughter of Aiah, whom she bore to Saul, Armoni and Mephibosheth;[f] and the five sons of Merab[g] daughter of Saul, whom she bore to Adriel son of Barzillai the Meholathite; [9]he gave them into the hands of the Gibeonites, and they impaled them on the mountain before the LORD. The seven of them perished together. They were put to death in the first days of harvest, at the beginning of barley harvest.

a **20.14** Compare 20.15: Heb *and Beth-maacah*   b **20.14** Compare Gk Vg: Heb *Berites*   c **20.15** Heb *They*   d **20.23** Cn: Heb *Joab to all the army, Israel*   e **21.6** Cn Compare Gk and 21.9: Heb *at Gibeah of Saul, the chosen of the LORD*   f **21.7,8** Or *Merib-baal*: See 4.4 note   g **21.8** Two Heb Mss Syr Compare Gk: MT *Michal*

10 Then Rizpah the daughter of Aiah took sackcloth, and spread it on a rock for herself, from the beginning of harvest until rain fell on them from the heavens; she did not allow the birds of the air to come on the bodies[a] by day, or the wild animals by night. 11 When David was told what Rizpah daughter of Aiah, the concubine of Saul, had done, 12 David went and took the bones of Saul and the bones of his son Jonathan from the people of Jabesh-gilead, who had stolen them from the public square of Beth-shan, where the Philistines had hung them up, on the day the Philistines killed Saul on Gilboa. 13 He brought up from there the bones of Saul and the bones of his son Jonathan; and they gathered the bones of those who had been impaled. 14 They buried the bones of Saul and of his son Jonathan in the land of Benjamin in Zela, in the tomb of his father Kish; they did all that the king commanded. After that, God heeded supplications for the land.

EXPLOITS OF DAVID'S MEN

15 The Philistines went to war again with Israel, and David went down together with his servants. They fought against the Philistines, and David grew weary. 16 Ishbi-benob, one of the descendants of the giants, whose spear weighed three hundred shekels of bronze, and who was fitted out with new weapons,[b] said he would kill David. 17 But Abishai son of Zeruiah came to his aid, and attacked the Philistine and killed him. Then David's men swore to him, "You shall not go out with us to battle any longer, so that you do not quench the lamp of Israel."

18 After this a battle took place with the Philistines, at Gob; then Sibbecai the Hushathite killed Saph, who was one of the descendants of the giants. 19 Then there was another battle with the Philistines at Gob; and Elhanan son of Jaare-oregim, the Bethlehemite, killed Goliath the Gittite, the shaft of whose spear was like a weaver's beam. 20 There was again war at Gath, where there was

a man of great size, who had six fingers on each hand, and six toes on each foot, twenty-four in number; he too was descended from the giants. 21 When he taunted Israel, Jonathan son of David's brother Shimei, killed him. 22 These four were descended from the giants in Gath; they fell by the hands of David and his servants.

DAVID'S SONG OF THANKSGIVING

22 David spoke to the LORD the words of this song on the day when the LORD delivered him from the hand of all his enemies, and from the hand of Saul. 2 He said:
The LORD is my rock, my fortress, and my deliverer,
3   my God, my rock, in whom I take refuge,
my shield and the horn of my salvation,
my stronghold and my refuge,
my savior; you save me from violence.
4 I call upon the LORD, who is worthy to be praised, and I am saved from my enemies.

5 For the waves of death encompassed me, the torrents of perdition assailed me;
6 the cords of Sheol entangled me, the snares of death confronted me.

7 In my distress I called upon the LORD; to my God I called. From his temple he heard my voice, and my cry came to his ears.

8 Then the earth reeled and rocked; the foundations of the heavens trembled and quaked, because he was angry.

PONDER

"The LORD is my rock, my fortress,
and my deliverer, my God, my rock,
in whom I take refuge, my shield
and the horn of my salvation."
—2 Samuel 22.2–3

PRAY

O Father, we are thankful for the blessings we may have, to have breath and life, to live in freedom, to travel around the world, to get to know other people, and to live in security. But we are grateful more than anything else for the simple plan of salvation, knowing that we are personally loved by the Creator of the universe. In that knowledge we find our strength. And as David sang your praises, we also praise you for your love, your glory and your mighty power, our Rock and our Savior. Amen.

9 Smoke went up from his nostrils,
  and devouring fire from
    his mouth;
  glowing coals flamed
    forth from him.
10 He bowed the heavens, and
    came down;
  thick darkness was
    under his feet.
11 He rode on a cherub, and flew;
  he was seen upon the
    wings of the wind.
12 He made darkness around
    him a canopy,
  thick clouds, a gathering
    of water.
13 Out of the brightness before him
  coals of fire flamed forth.
14 The LORD thundered from heaven;
  the Most High uttered his voice.
15 He sent out arrows, and
    scattered them
  —lightning, and routed them.
16 Then the channels of the
    sea were seen,
  the foundations of the
    world were laid bare

at the rebuke of the LORD,
  at the blast of the breath
    of his nostrils.

17 He reached from on high,
    he took me,
  he drew me out of
    mighty waters.
18 He delivered me from my
    strong enemy,
  from those who hated me;
  for they were too
    mighty for me.
19 They came upon me in the
    day of my calamity,
  but the LORD was my stay.
20 He brought me out into
    a broad place;
  he delivered me, because
    he delighted in me.

21 The LORD rewarded me according
    to my righteousness;
  according to the cleanness
    of my hands he
    recompensed me.
22 For I have kept the ways
    of the LORD,
  and have not wickedly
    departed from my God.
23 For all his ordinances were
    before me,
  and from his statutes I
    did not turn aside.
24 I was blameless before him,
  and I kept myself
    from guilt.
25 Therefore the LORD has
    recompensed me
  according to my
    righteousness,
  according to my cleanness
    in his sight.

26 With the loyal you show
    yourself loyal;
  with the blameless you show
    yourself blameless;
27 with the pure you show
    yourself pure,
  and with the crooked you
    show yourself perverse.
28 You deliver a humble
    people,
  but your eyes are upon
    the haughty to bring
    them down.

29 Indeed, you are my lamp, O LORD,
   the LORD lightens my
      darkness.
30 By you I can crush a troop,
   and by my God I can
      leap over a wall.
31 This God—his way is perfect;
   the promise of the LORD
      proves true;
   he is a shield for all who
      take refuge in him.

OUR FAITH IS ROOTED IN
GOD'S FAITHFULNESS

32 For who is God, but the LORD?
   And who is a rock,
      except our God?
33 The God who has girded me
      with strength[a]
   has opened wide my path.[b]
34 He made my[c] feet like the
      feet of deer,
   and set me secure on
      the heights.
35 He trains my hands for war,
   so that my arms can bend
      a bow of bronze.
36 You have given me the shield
      of your salvation,
   and your help[d] has
      made me great.
37 You have made me stride freely,
   and my feet do not slip;
38 I pursued my enemies and
      destroyed them,
   and did not turn back until
      they were consumed.
39 I consumed them; I struck
      them down, so that
         they did not rise;
   they fell under my feet.
40 For you girded me with
      strength for the battle;
   you made my assailants
      sink under me.
41 You made my enemies turn
      their backs to me,
   those who hated me, and
      I destroyed them.

42 They looked, but there was no
      one to save them;
   they cried to the LORD, but he
      did not answer them.
43 I beat them fine like the
      dust of the earth,
   I crushed them and stamped
      them down like the
         mire of the streets.

44 You delivered me from strife
      with the peoples;[e]
   you kept me as the head
      of the nations;
   people whom I had not
      known served me.
45 Foreigners came cringing to me;
   as soon as they heard of
      me, they obeyed me.
46 Foreigners lost heart,
   and came trembling out of
      their strongholds.

47 The LORD lives! Blessed
      be my rock,
   and exalted be my God, the
      rock of my salvation,
48 the God who gave me vengeance
   and brought down
      peoples under me,
49 who brought me out from
      my enemies;
   you exalted me above
      my adversaries,
   you delivered me from
      the violent.

50 For this I will extol you, O LORD,
      among the nations,
   and sing praises to your name.
51 He is a tower of salvation
      for his king,
   and shows steadfast love
      to his anointed,
   to David and his
      descendants forever.

THE LAST WORDS OF DAVID

23 Now these are the last words
   of David:

---

a 22.33 Q Ms Gk Syr Vg Compare Ps
18.32: MT *God is my strong refuge*
b 22.33 Meaning of Heb uncertain
c 22.34 Another reading is *his*
d 22.36 Q Ms: MT *your answering*
e 22.44 Gk: Heb *from strife with my people*

The oracle of David, son of Jesse,
  the oracle of the man
    whom God exalted,ᵃ
the anointed of the God of Jacob,
  the favorite of the Strong
    One of Israel:

2 The spirit of the LORD speaks
    through me,
  his word is upon my tongue.
3 The God of Israel has spoken,
  the Rock of Israel has
    said to me:
One who rules over people justly,
  ruling in the fear of God,
4 is like the light of morning,
  like the sun rising on a
    cloudless morning,
  gleaming from the rain
    on the grassy land.

5 Is not my house like this
    with God?
  For he has made with me an
    everlasting covenant,
  ordered in all things
    and secure.
Will he not cause to prosper
  all my help and my desire?
6 But the godless areᵇ all like thorns
    that are thrown away;
  for they cannot be picked
    up with the hand;
7 to touch them one uses
    an iron bar
  or the shaft of a spear.
And they are entirely
    consumed in fire
  on the spot.ᶜ

DAVID'S MIGHTY MEN

8 These are the names of the
warriors whom David had: Josheb-
basshebeth a Tahchemonite; he was
chief of the Three;ᵈ he wielded his
spearᵉ against eight hundred whom
he killed at one time.
9 Next to him among the three
warriors was Eleazar son of Dodo
son of Ahohi. He was with David
when they defied the Philistines
who were gathered there for battle.
The Israelites withdrew, 10but he
stood his ground. He struck down
the Philistines until his arm grew
weary, though his hand clung to the
sword. The LORD brought about a

great victory that day. Then the people came back to him—but only to
strip the dead.

11 Next to him was Shammah
son of Agee, the Hararite. The Philistines gathered together at Lehi,
where there was a plot of ground full
of lentils; and the army fled from the
Philistines. 12But he took his stand
in the middle of the plot, defended
it, and killed the Philistines; and the
LORD brought about a great victory.

13 Towards the beginning of harvest three of the thirtyᶠ chiefs went
down to join David at the cave of
Adullam, while a band of Philistines was encamped in the valley
of Rephaim. 14David was then in
the stronghold; and the garrison of
the Philistines was then at Bethlehem. 15David said longingly, "O that
someone would give me water to
drink from the well of Bethlehem
that is by the gate!" 16Then the three
warriors broke through the camp of
the Philistines, drew water from the
well of Bethlehem that was by the
gate, and brought it to David. But
he would not drink of it; he poured
it out to the LORD, 17for he said, "The
LORD forbid that I should do this.
Can I drink the blood of the men
who went at the risk of their lives?"
Therefore he would not drink it. The
three warriors did these things.

18 Now Abishai son of Zeruiah,
the brother of Joab, was chief of the
Thirty.ᵍ With his spear he fought
against three hundred men and
killed them, and won a name beside
the Three. 19He was the most renowned of the Thirty,ʰ and became
their commander; but he did not attain to the Three.

20 Benaiah son of Jehoiada was a
valiant warriorⁱ from Kabzeel, a doer
of great deeds; he struck down two
sons of Arielʲ of Moab. He also went

ᵃ 23.1 Q Ms: MT *who was raised on high*
ᵇ 23.6 Heb *But worthlessness*   ᶜ 23.7 Heb
in sitting   ᵈ 23.8 Gk Vg Compare 1 Chr 11.11:
Meaning of Heb uncertain   ᵉ 23.8 1 Chr
11.11: Meaning of Heb uncertain   ᶠ 23.13 Heb
adds *head*   ᵍ 23.18 Two Heb Mss Syr: MT
Three   ʰ 23.19 Syr Compare 1 Chr 11.25: Heb
Was he the most renowned of the Three?
ⁱ 23.20 Another reading is *the son of Ish-hai*
ʲ 23.20 Gk: Heb lacks *sons of*

down and killed a lion in a pit on a day when snow had fallen. 21And he killed an Egyptian, a handsome man. The Egyptian had a spear in his hand; but Benaiah went against him with a staff, snatched the spear out of the Egyptian's hand, and killed him with his own spear. 22Such were the things Benaiah son of Jehoiada did, and won a name beside the three warriors. 23He was renowned among the Thirty, but he did not attain to the Three. And David put him in charge of his bodyguard.

24 Among the Thirty were Asahel brother of Joab; Elhanan son of Dodo of Bethlehem; 25Shammah of Harod; Elika of Harod; 26Helez the Paltite; Ira son of Ikkesh of Tekoa; 27Abiezer of Anathoth; Mebunnai the Hushathite; 28Zalmon the Ahohite; Maharai of Netophah; 29Heleb son of Baanah of Netophah; Ittai son of Ribai of Gibeah of the Benjaminites; 30Benaiah of Pirathon; Hiddai of the torrents of Gaash; 31Abi-albon the Arbathite; Azmaveth of Bahurim; 32Eliahba of Shaalbon; the sons of Jashen: Jonathan 33son of[a] Shammah the Hararite; Ahiam son of Sharar the Hararite; 34Eliphelet son of Ahasbai of Maacah; Eliam son of Ahithophel the Gilonite; 35Hezro[b] of Carmel; Paarai the Arbite; 36Igal son of Nathan of Zobah; Bani the Gadite; 37Zelek the Ammonite; Naharai of Beeroth, the armor-bearer of Joab son of Zeruiah; 38Ira the Ithrite; Gareb the Ithrite; 39Uriah the Hittite—thirty-seven in all.

DAVID'S CENSUS OF ISRAEL AND JUDAH

24 Again the anger of the LORD was kindled against Israel, and he incited David against them, saying, "Go, count the people of Israel and Judah." 2So the king said to Joab and the commanders of the army,[c] who were with him, "Go through all the tribes of Israel, from Dan to Beer-sheba, and take a census of the people, so that I may know how many there are." 3But Joab said to the king, "May the LORD your God increase the number of the peo-

ple a hundredfold, while the eyes of my lord the king can still see it! But why does my lord the king want to do this?" 4But the king's word prevailed against Joab and the commanders of the army. So Joab and the commanders of the army went out from the presence of the king to take a census of the people of Israel. 5They crossed the Jordan, and began from[d] Aroer and from the city that is in the middle of the valley, toward Gad and on to Jazer. 6Then they came to Gilead, and to Kadesh in the land of the Hittites;[e] and they came to Dan, and from Dan[f] they went around to Sidon, 7and came to the fortress of Tyre and to all the cities of the Hivites and Canaanites; and they went out to the Negeb of Judah at Beer-sheba. 8So when they had gone through all the land, they came back to Jerusalem at the end of nine months and twenty days. 9Joab reported to the king the number of those who had been recorded: in Israel there were eight hundred thousand soldiers able to draw the sword, and those of Judah were five hundred thousand.

JUDGMENT ON DAVID'S SIN

10 But afterward, David was stricken to the heart because he had numbered the people. David said to the LORD, "I have sinned greatly in what I have done. But now, O LORD, I pray you, take away the guilt of your servant; for I have done very foolishly." 11When David rose in the morning, the word of the LORD came to the prophet Gad, David's seer, saying, 12"Go and say to David: Thus says the LORD: Three things I offer[g] you; choose one of them, and I will do it to you." 13So Gad came to David and told him; he asked him, "Shall three[h] years of famine come to you on your land? Or will you flee

[a] 23.33 Gk: Heb lacks son of
[b] 23.35 Another reading is Hezrai
[c] 24.2 1 Chr 21.2 Gk: Heb to Joab the commander of the army   [d] 24.5 Gk
Mss: Heb encamped in Aroer south of
[e] 24.6 Gk: Heb to the land of Tahtim-hodshi
[f] 24.6 Cn Compare Gk: Heb they came to Dan-jaan and   [g] 24.12 Or hold over
[h] 24.13 1 Chr 21.12 Gk: Heb seven

three months before your foes while they pursue you? Or shall there be three days' pestilence in your land? Now consider, and decide what answer I shall return to the one who sent me." ¹⁴Then David said to Gad, "I am in great distress; let us fall into the hand of the LORD, for his mercy is great; but let me not fall into human hands."

15 So the LORD sent a pestilence on Israel from that morning until the appointed time; and seventy thousand of the people died, from Dan to Beer-sheba. ¹⁶But when the angel stretched out his hand toward Jerusalem to destroy it, the LORD relented concerning the evil, and said to the angel who was bringing destruction among the people, "It is enough; now stay your hand." The angel of the LORD was then by the threshing floor of Araunah the Jebusite. ¹⁷When David saw the angel who was destroying the people, he said to the LORD, "I alone have sinned, and I alone have done wickedly; but these sheep, what have they done? Let your hand, I pray, be against me and against my father's house."

DAVID'S ALTAR ON THE THRESHING FLOOR

18 That day Gad came to David and said to him, "Go up and erect an altar to the LORD on the threshing floor of Araunah the Jebusite." ¹⁹Following Gad's instructions, David went up, as the LORD had commanded. ²⁰When Araunah looked down, he saw the king and his servants coming toward him; and Araunah went out and prostrated himself before the king with his face to the ground. ²¹Araunah said, "Why has my lord the king come to his servant?" David said, "To buy the threshing floor from you in order to build an altar to the LORD, so that the plague may be averted from the people." ²²Then Araunah said to David, "Let my lord the king take and offer up what seems good to him; here are the oxen for the burnt offering, and the threshing sledges and the yokes of the oxen for the wood. ²³All this, O king, Araunah gives to the king." And Araunah said to the king, "May the LORD your God respond favorably to you."

24 But the king said to Araunah, "No, but I will buy them from you for a price; I will not offer burnt offerings to the LORD my God that cost me nothing." So David bought the threshing floor and the oxen for fifty shekels of silver. ²⁵David built there an altar to the LORD, and offered burnt offerings and offerings of well-being. So the LORD answered his supplication for the land, and the plague was averted from Israel.

1 KINGS

First Kings evaluates the kings of Israel and Judah and how faithfully they served God. Some kings worshiped the Lord; others completely disregarded God. Probably the highest standards for leadership were set by King Solomon and the prophet Elijah. Solomon is known as the wisest man who ever lived; in 1 Kings we see the impact of his leadership on the entire ancient world. And Elijah's total dedication to God distinguished him as a model leader for all times. We might consider their positive examples as we serve God.

THE STRUGGLE FOR
THE SUCCESSION

1 King David was old and advanced in years; and although they covered him with clothes, he could not get warm. ²So his servants said to him, "Let a young virgin be sought for my lord the king, and let her wait on the king, and be his attendant; let her lie in your bosom, so that my lord the king may be warm." ³So they searched for a beautiful girl throughout all the territory of Israel, and found Abishag the Shunammite, and brought her to the king. ⁴The girl was very beautiful. She became the king's attendant and served him, but the king did not know her sexually.

5 Now Adonijah son of Haggith exalted himself, saying, "I will be king"; he prepared for himself chariots and horsemen, and fifty men to run before him. ⁶His father had never at any time displeased him by asking, "Why have you done thus and so?" He was also a very handsome man, and he was born next after Absalom. ⁷He conferred with Joab son of Zeruiah and with the priest Abiathar, and they supported Adonijah. ⁸But the priest Zadok, and Benaiah son of Jehoiada, and the prophet Nathan, and Shimei, and Rei, and David's own warriors did not side with Adonijah.

9 Adonijah sacrificed sheep, oxen, and fatted cattle by the stone Zoheleth, which is beside En-rogel, and he invited all his brothers, the king's sons, and all the royal officials of Judah, ¹⁰but he did not invite the prophet Nathan or Benaiah or the warriors or his brother Solomon.

11 Then Nathan said to Bathsheba, Solomon's mother, "Have you not heard that Adonijah son of Haggith has become king and our lord David does not know it? ¹²Now therefore come, let me give you advice, so that you may save your own life and the life of your son Solomon. ¹³Go in at once to King David, and say to him, 'Did you not, my lord the king, swear to your servant, saying: Your son Solomon shall succeed me as king, and he shall sit on my throne?

Why then is Adonijah king?' ¹⁴Then while you are still there speaking with the king, I will come in after you and confirm your words."

15 So Bathsheba went to the king in his room. The king was very old; Abishag the Shunammite was attending the king. ¹⁶Bathsheba bowed and did obeisance to the king, and the king said, "What do you wish?" ¹⁷She said to him, "My lord, you swore to your servant by the LORD your God, saying: Your son Solomon shall succeed me as king, and he shall sit on my throne. ¹⁸But now suddenly Adonijah has become king, though you, my lord the king, do not know it. ¹⁹He has sacrificed oxen, fatted cattle, and sheep in abundance, and has invited all the children of the king, the priest Abiathar, and Joab the commander of the army; but your servant Solomon he has not invited. ²⁰But you, my lord the king—the eyes of all Israel are on you to tell them who shall sit on the throne of my lord the king after him. ²¹Otherwise it will come to pass, when my lord the king sleeps with his ancestors, that my son Solomon and I will be counted offenders."

22 While she was still speaking with the king, the prophet Nathan came in. ²³The king was told, "Here is the prophet Nathan." When he came in before the king, he did obeisance to the king, with his face to the ground. ²⁴Nathan said, "My lord the king, have you said, 'Adonijah shall succeed me as king, and he shall sit on my throne'? ²⁵For today he has gone down and has sacrificed oxen, fatted cattle, and sheep in abundance, and has invited all the king's children, Joab the commander[a] of the army, and the priest Abiathar, who are now eating and drinking before him, and saying, 'Long live King Adonijah!' ²⁶But he did not invite me, your servant, and the priest Zadok, and Benaiah son of Jehoiada, and your servant Solomon. ²⁷Has this thing been brought about by my lord the king and you have not let your servants

---

[a] 1.25 Gk: Heb *the commanders*

know who should sit on the throne of my lord the king after him?"

THE ACCESSION OF SOLOMON

28 King David answered, "Summon Bathsheba to me." So she came into the king's presence, and stood before the king. 29The king swore, saying, "As the LORD lives, who has saved my life from every adversity, 30as I swore to you by the LORD, the God of Israel, 'Your son Solomon shall succeed me as king, and he shall sit on my throne in my place,' so will I do this day." 31Then Bathsheba bowed with her face to the ground, and did obeisance to the king, and said, "May my lord King David live forever!"

32 King David said, "Summon to me the priest Zadok, the prophet Nathan, and Benaiah son of Jehoiada." When they came before the king, 33the king said to them, "Take with you the servants of your lord, and have my son Solomon ride on my own mule, and bring him down to Gihon. 34There let the priest Zadok and the prophet Nathan anoint him king over Israel; then blow the trumpet, and say, 'Long live King Solomon!' 35You shall go up following him. Let him enter and sit on my throne; he shall be king in my place; for I have appointed him to be ruler over Israel and over Judah." 36Benaiah son of Jehoiada answered the king, "Amen! May the LORD, the God of my lord the king, so ordain. 37As the LORD has been with my lord the king, so may he be with Solomon, and make his throne greater than the throne of my lord King David."

38 So the priest Zadok, the prophet Nathan, and Benaiah son of Jehoiada, and the Cherethites and the Pelethites, went down and had Solomon ride on King David's mule, and led him to Gihon. 39There the priest Zadok took the horn of oil from the tent and anointed Solomon. Then they blew the trumpet, and all the people said, "Long live King Solomon!" 40And all the people went up following him, playing on pipes and rejoicing with great joy, so that the earth quaked at their noise.

41 Adonijah and all the guests who were with him heard it as they finished feasting. When Joab heard the sound of the trumpet, he said, "Why is the city in an uproar?" 42While he was still speaking, Jonathan son of the priest Abiathar arrived. Adonijah said, "Come in, for you are a worthy man and surely you bring good news." 43Jonathan answered Adonijah, "No, for our lord King David has made Solomon king; 44the king has sent with him the priest Zadok, the prophet Nathan, and Benaiah son of Jehoiada, and the Cherethites and the Pelethites; and they had him ride on the king's mule; 45the priest Zadok and the prophet Nathan have anointed him king at Gihon; and they have gone up from there rejoicing, so that the city is in an uproar. This is the noise that you heard. 46Solomon now sits on the royal throne. 47Moreover the king's servants came to congratulate our lord King David, saying, 'May God make the name of Solomon more famous than yours, and make his throne greater than your throne.' The king bowed in worship on the bed 48and went on to pray thus, 'Blessed be the LORD, the God of Israel, who today has granted one of my offspringa to sit on my throne and permitted me to witness it.'"

49 Then all the guests of Adonijah got up trembling and went their own ways. 50Adonijah, fearing Solomon, got up and went to grasp the horns of the altar. 51Solomon was informed, "Adonijah is afraid of King Solomon; see, he has laid hold of the horns of the altar, saying, 'Let King Solomon swear to me first that he will not kill his servant with the sword.'" 52So Solomon responded, "If he proves to be a worthy man, not one of his hairs shall fall to the ground; but if wickedness is found in him, he shall die." 53Then King Solomon sent to have him brought down from the altar. He came to do obeisance to King Solomon; and Solomon said to him, "Go home."

a 1.48 Gk: Heb one

DAVID'S INSTRUCTION TO SOLOMON

2 When David's time to die drew near, he charged his son Solomon, saying: ²"I am about to go the way of all the earth. Be strong, be courageous, ³and keep the charge of the LORD your God, walking in his ways and keeping his statutes, his commandments, his ordinances, and his testimonies, as it is written in the law of Moses, so that you may prosper in all that you do and wherever you turn. ⁴Then the LORD will establish his word that he spoke concerning me: 'If your heirs take heed to their way, to walk before me in faithfulness with all their heart and with all their soul, there shall not fail you a successor on the throne of Israel.'

⁵ "Moreover you know also what Joab son of Zeruiah did to me, how he dealt with the two commanders of the armies of Israel, Abner son of Ner, and Amasa son of Jether, whom he murdered, retaliating in time of peace for blood that had been shed in war, and putting the blood of war on the belt around his waist, and on the sandals on his feet. ⁶Act therefore according to your wisdom, but do not let his gray head go down to Sheol in peace. ⁷Deal loyally, however, with the sons of Barzillai the Gileadite, and let them be among those who eat at your table; for with such loyalty they met me when I fled from your brother Absalom. ⁸There is also with you Shimei son of Gera, the Benjaminite from Bahurim, who cursed me with a terrible curse on the day when I went to Mahanaim; but when he came down to meet me at the Jordan, I swore to him by the LORD, 'I will not put you to death with the sword.' ⁹Therefore do not hold him guiltless, for you are a wise man; you will know what you ought to do to him, and you must bring his gray head down with blood to Sheol."

DEATH OF DAVID

10 Then David slept with his ancestors, and was buried in the city of David. ¹¹The time that David reigned over Israel was forty years; he reigned seven years in Hebron, and thirty-three years in Jerusalem. ¹²So Solomon sat on the throne of his father David; and his kingdom was firmly established.

SOLOMON CONSOLIDATES HIS REIGN

13 Then Adonijah son of Haggith came to Bathsheba, Solomon's mother. She asked, "Do you come peaceably?" He said, "Peaceably." ¹⁴Then he said, "May I have a word with you?" She said, "Go on." ¹⁵He said, "You know that the kingdom was mine, and that all Israel expected me to reign; however, the kingdom has turned about and become my brother's, for it was his from the LORD. ¹⁶And now I have one request to make of you; do not refuse me." She said to him, "Go on." ¹⁷He said, "Please ask King Solomon—he will not refuse you—to give me Abishag the Shunammite as my wife." ¹⁸Bathsheba said, "Very well; I will speak to the king on your behalf."

19 So Bathsheba went to King Solomon, to speak to him on behalf of Adonijah. The king rose to meet her, and bowed down to her; then he sat on his throne, and had a throne brought for the king's mother, and she sat on his right. ²⁰Then she said, "I have one small request to make of you; do not refuse me." And the king said to her, "Make your request, my mother; for I will not refuse you." ²¹She said, "Let Abishag the Shunammite be given to your brother Adonijah as his wife." ²²King Solomon answered his mother, "And why do you ask Abishag the Shunammite for Adonijah? Ask for him the kingdom as well! For he is my elder brother; ask not only for him but also for the priest Abiathar and for Joab son of Zeruiah!" ²³Then King Solomon swore by the LORD, "So may God do to me, and more also, for Adonijah has devised this scheme at the risk of his life! ²⁴Now therefore as the LORD lives, who has established me and placed me on the throne of my father David, and who has made me a house as he promised,

LOVE THAT COVERS

"Keep the charge of the LORD your God, walking in his ways and keeping his statutes, his commandments, his ordinances, and his testimonies, as it is written in the law of Moses . . . you must bring [Shimei's] gray head down with blood to Sheol."

—1 Kings 2.3,9

When we read this account of David's final words to his son Solomon, David's character becomes more evident. He tells Solomon, in no uncertain terms, to stand tall and obey the Lord's commandments, yet in the same breath he also instructs Solomon to carry out vengeance on two of his enemies. This dichotomy illustrates the complexity of David's character: He was a man after God's own heart and wrote dozens of poignant psalms, yet he also committed adultery and murder. It serves to underscore the wonderful truth that God can and does use all kinds of people to do his will, and he is always ready to forgive and restore those who confess their sins.

There is no question that David did some terrible things in his life. Some of his sins seem so despicable that we might even wonder how God could still have regarded him as a chosen king. Why didn't God tear the kingdom away from him as he had Saul? Perhaps it is because for all of David's inconsistencies, his most distinctive, consistent characteristics seem to have been his love for God and his penitent heart. There were times when he sinned very deeply, yet when he was confronted with his sins, he always repented equally and asked for God's forgiveness. No doubt this is what made him a man "after [God's] own heart." At the same time, God continued to show David favor despite his many transgressions.

When we think of David's sins and God's unfailing love toward him, it is exhilarating to realize that God loves us just as deeply. Likewise, God's mercy and forgiveness are as strong for us as they were for David. We may not have committed adultery or murder with our own hands, but we have done so with our hearts, which is just as sinful before God. We need forgiveness just as much as David did. And by God's grace, we can be confident that God always will be ready to forgive us when we repent.

David was a flawed human being, but God commissioned him to do remarkable things. David was a man of extraordinary faith in God, and God was faithful in his promises to the shepherd boy, the warrior and the king. The key to David's character was that he loved God with an amazing passion, a love that covered a multitude of sins: "How lovely is your dwelling place, O LORD of hosts! My soul longs, indeed it faints for the courts of the LORD; my heart and my flesh sing for joy to the living God . . . O LORD of hosts, happy is everyone who trusts in you" (Psalm 84.1–2,12).

Going Deeper

- Are there other people whom you have regarded as unworthy of God's forgiveness and restoration?
- Is your love for God passionate? If not, how can you fan the flame?

today Adonijah shall be put to death." 25So King Solomon sent Benaiah son of Jehoiada; he struck him down, and he died.

26 The king said to the priest Abiathar, "Go to Anathoth, to your estate; for you deserve death. But I will not at this time put you to death, because you carried the ark of the Lord GOD before my father David, and because you shared in all the hardships my father endured." 27So Solomon banished Abiathar from being priest to the LORD, thus fulfilling the word of the LORD that he had spoken concerning the house of Eli in Shiloh.

28 When the news came to Joab—for Joab had supported Adonijah though he had not supported Absalom—Joab fled to the tent of the LORD and grasped the horns of the altar. 29When it was told King Solomon, "Joab has fled to the tent of the LORD and now is beside the altar," Solomon sent Benaiah son of Jehoiada, saying, "Go, strike him down." 30So Benaiah came to the tent of the LORD and said to him, "The king commands, 'Come out.' " But he said, "No, I will die here." Then Benaiah brought the king word again, saying, "Thus said Joab, and thus he answered me." 31The king replied to him, "Do as he has said, strike him down and bury him; and thus take away from me and from my father's house the guilt for the blood that Joab shed without cause. 32The LORD will bring back his bloody deeds on his own head, because, without the knowledge of my father David, he attacked and killed with the sword two men more righteous and better than himself, Abner son of Ner, commander of the army of Israel, and Amasa son of Jether, commander of the army of Judah. 33So shall their blood come back on the head of Joab and on the head of his descendants forever; but to David, and to his descendants, and to his house, and to his throne, there shall be peace from the LORD forevermore." 34Then Benaiah son of Jehoiada went up and struck him down and killed him; and he was buried at his own house near the

wilderness. 35The king put Benaiah son of Jehoiada over the army in his place, and the king put the priest Zadok in the place of Abiathar.

36 Then the king sent and summoned Shimei, and said to him, "Build yourself a house in Jerusalem, and live there, and do not go out from there to any place whatever. 37For on the day you go out, and cross the Wadi Kidron, know for certain that you shall die; your blood shall be on your own head." 38And Shimei said to the king, "The sentence is fair; as my lord the king has said, so will your servant do." So Shimei lived in Jerusalem many days.

39 But it happened at the end of three years that two of Shimei's slaves ran away to King Achish son of Maacah of Gath. When it was told Shimei, "Your slaves are in Gath," 40Shimei arose and saddled a donkey, and went to Achish in Gath, to search for his slaves; Shimei went and brought his slaves from Gath. 41When Solomon was told that Shimei had gone from Jerusalem to Gath and returned, 42the king sent and summoned Shimei, and said to him, "Did I not make you swear by the LORD, and solemnly adjure you, saying, 'Know for certain that on the day you go out and go to any place whatever, you shall die'? And you said to me, 'The sentence is fair; I accept.' 43Why then have you not kept your oath to the LORD and the commandment with which I charged you?" 44The king also said to Shimei, "You know in your own heart all the evil that you did to my father David; so the LORD will bring back your evil on your own head. 45But King Solomon shall be blessed, and the throne of David shall be established before the LORD forever." 46Then the king commanded Benaiah son of Jehoiada; and he went out and struck him down, and he died.

So the kingdom was established in the hand of Solomon.

SOLOMON'S PRAYER FOR WISDOM

3 Solomon made a marriage alliance with Pharaoh king of

Egypt; he took Pharaoh's daughter and brought her into the city of David, until he had finished building his own house and the house of the LORD and the wall around Jerusalem. ²The people were sacrificing at the high places, however, because no house had yet been built for the name of the LORD.

3 Solomon loved the LORD, walking in the statutes of his father David; only, he sacrificed and offered incense at the high places. ⁴The king went to Gibeon to sacrifice there, for that was the principal high place; Solomon used to offer a thousand burnt offerings on that altar. ⁵At Gibeon the LORD appeared to Solomon in a dream by night; and God said, "Ask what I should give you." ⁶And Solomon said, "You have shown great and steadfast love to your servant my father David, because he walked before you in faithfulness, in righteousness, and in uprightness of heart toward you; and you have kept for him this great and steadfast love, and have given him a son to sit on his throne today. ⁷And now, O LORD my God, you have made your servant king in place of my father David, although I am only a little child; I do not know how to go out or come in. ⁸And your servant is in the midst of the people whom you have chosen, a great people, so numerous they cannot be numbered or counted. ⁹Give your servant therefore an understanding mind to govern your people, able to discern between good and evil; for who can govern this your great people?"

10 It pleased the Lord that Solomon had asked this. ¹¹God said to him, "Because you have asked this, and have not asked for yourself long life or riches, or for the life of your enemies, but have asked for yourself understanding to discern what is right, ¹²I now do according to your word. Indeed I give you a wise and discerning mind; no one like you has been before you and no one like you shall arise after you. ¹³I give you also what you have not asked, both riches and honor all your life; no other king shall compare with you.

¹⁴If you will walk in my ways, keeping my statutes and my commandments, as your father David walked, then I will lengthen your life."

15 Then Solomon awoke; it had been a dream. He came to Jerusalem where he stood before the ark of the covenant of the LORD. He offered up burnt offerings and offerings of well-being, and provided a feast for all his servants.

THE SOURCE OF WISDOM FOR

CHRISTIANS IS THE WORDS

AND ACTIONS OF JESUS CHRIST.

THIS IS THE PREEMINENT

ISSUE OF OUR LIVES.

SOLOMON'S WISDOM IN JUDGMENT

16 Later, two women who were prostitutes came to the king and stood before him. ¹⁷The one woman said, "Please, my lord, this woman and I live in the same house; and I gave birth while she was in the house. ¹⁸Then on the third day after I gave birth, this woman also gave birth. We were together; there was no one else with us in the house, only the two of us were in the house. ¹⁹Then this woman's son died in the night, because she lay on him. ²⁰She got up in the middle of the night and took my son from beside me while your servant slept. She laid him at her breast, and laid her dead son at my breast. ²¹When I rose in the morning to nurse my son, I saw that he was dead; but when I looked at him closely in the morning, clearly it was not the son I had borne." ²²But the other woman said, "No, the living son is mine, and the dead son is yours." The first said, "No, the dead son is yours, and the living son is mine." So they argued before the king.

23 Then the king said, "The one says, 'This is my son that is alive, and

your son is dead'; while the other says, 'Not so! Your son is dead, and my son is the living one.' " 24So the king said, "Bring me a sword," and they brought a sword before the king. 25The king said, "Divide the living boy in two; then give half to the one, and half to the other." 26But the woman whose son was alive said to the king—because compassion for her son burned within her—"Please, my lord, give her the living boy; certainly do not kill him!" The other said, "It shall be neither mine nor yours; divide it." 27Then the king responded: "Give the first woman the living boy; do not kill him. She is his mother." 28All Israel heard of the judgment that the king had rendered; and they stood in awe of the king, because they perceived that the wisdom of God was in him, to execute justice.

SOLOMON'S ADMINISTRATIVE OFFICERS

4 King Solomon was king over all Israel, 2and these were his high officials: Azariah son of Zadok was the priest; 3Elihoreph and Ahijah sons of Shisha were secretaries; Jehoshaphat son of Ahilud was recorder; 4Benaiah son of Jehoiada was in command of the army; Zadok and Abiathar were priests; 5Azariah son of Nathan was over the officials; Zabud son of Nathan was priest and king's friend; 6Ahishar was in charge of the palace; and Adoniram son of Abda was in charge of the forced labor.

7 Solomon had twelve officials over all Israel, who provided food for the king and his household; each one had to make provision for one month in the year. 8These were their names: Ben-hur, in the hill country of Ephraim; 9Ben-deker, in Makaz, Shaalbim, Beth-shemesh, and Elon-beth-hanan; 10Ben-hesed, in Arubboth (to him belonged Socoh and all the land of Hepher); 11Ben-abinadab, in all Naphath-dor (he had Taphath, Solomon's daughter, as his wife); 12Baana son of Ahilud, in Taanach, Megiddo, and all Beth-shean, which is beside Zarethan below Jezreel, and from Beth-shean to Abel-meholah, as far as the other side of Jokmeam; 13Ben-geber, in Ramoth-gilead (he had the villages of Jair son of Manasseh, which are in Gilead, and he had the region of Argob, which is in Bashan, sixty great cities with walls and bronze bars); 14Ahinadab son of Iddo, in Mahanaim; 15Ahimaaz, in Naphtali (he had taken Basemath, Solomon's daughter, as his wife); 16Baana son of Hushai, in Asher and Bealoth; 17Jehoshaphat son of Paruah, in Issachar; 18Shimei son of Ela, in Benjamin; 19Geber son of Uri, in the land of Gilead, the country of King Sihon of the Amorites and of King Og of Bashan. And there was one official in the land of Judah.

MAGNIFICENCE OF SOLOMON'S RULE

20 Judah and Israel were as numerous as the sand by the sea; they ate and drank and were happy. 21aSolomon was sovereign over all the kingdoms from the Euphrates to the land of the Philistines, even to the border of Egypt; they brought tribute and served Solomon all the days of his life.

22 Solomon's provision for one day was thirty cors of choice flour, and sixty cors of meal, 23ten fat oxen, and twenty pasture-fed cattle, one hundred sheep, besides deer, gazelles, roebucks, and fatted fowl. 24For he had dominion over all the region west of the Euphrates from Tiphsah to Gaza, over all the kings west of the Euphrates; and he had peace on all sides. 25During Solomon's lifetime Judah and Israel lived in safety, from Dan even to Beer-sheba, all of them under their vines and fig trees. 26Solomon also had forty thousand stalls of horses for his chariots, and twelve thousand horsemen. 27Those officials supplied provisions for King Solomon and for all who came to King Solomon's table, each one in his month; they let nothing be lacking. 28They also brought to the required place barley

ᵃ 4.21 Ch 5.1 in Heb

and straw for the horses and swift steeds, each according to his charge.

FAME OF SOLOMON'S WISDOM

29 God gave Solomon very great wisdom, discernment, and breadth of understanding as vast as the sand on the seashore, 30so that Solomon's wisdom surpassed the wisdom of all the people of the east, and all the wisdom of Egypt. 31He was wiser than anyone else, wiser than Ethan the Ezrahite, and Heman, Calcol, and Darda, children of Mahol; his fame spread throughout all the surrounding nations. 32He composed three thousand proverbs, and his songs numbered a thousand and five. 33He would speak of trees, from the cedar that is in the Lebanon to the hyssop that grows in the wall; he would speak of animals, and birds, and reptiles, and fish. 34People came from all the nations to hear the wisdom of Solomon; they came from all the kings of the earth who had heard of his wisdom.

PREPARATIONS AND MATERIALS FOR THE TEMPLE

5 [a] Now King Hiram of Tyre sent his servants to Solomon, when he heard that they had anointed him king in place of his father; for Hiram had always been a friend to David. 2Solomon sent word to Hiram, saying, 3"You know that my father David could not build a house for the name of the LORD his God because of the warfare with which his enemies surrounded him, until the LORD put them under the soles of his feet.[b] 4But now the LORD my God has given me rest on every side; there is neither adversary nor misfortune. 5So I intend to build a house for the name of the LORD my God, as the LORD said to my father David, 'Your son, whom I will set on your throne in your place, shall build the house for my name.' 6Therefore command that cedars from the Lebanon be cut for me. My servants will join your servants, and I will give you whatever wages you set for your servants; for you know that there is no one among us who knows how to cut timber like the Sidonians."

7When Hiram heard the words of Solomon, he rejoiced greatly, and said, "Blessed be the LORD today, who has given to David a wise son to be over this great people." 8Hiram sent word to Solomon, "I have heard the message that you have sent to me; I will fulfill all your needs in the matter of cedar and cypress timber. 9My servants shall bring it down to the sea from the Lebanon; I will make it into rafts to go by sea to the place you indicate. I will have them broken up there for you to take away. And you shall meet my needs by providing food for my household." 10So Hiram supplied Solomon's every need for timber of cedar and cypress. 11Solomon in turn gave Hiram twenty thousand cors of wheat as food for his household, and twenty cors of fine oil. Solomon gave this to Hiram year by year. 12So the LORD gave Solomon wisdom, as he promised him. There was peace between Hiram and Solomon; and the two of them made a treaty.

13 King Solomon conscripted forced labor out of all Israel; the levy numbered thirty thousand men. 14He sent them to the Lebanon, ten thousand a month in shifts; they would be a month in the Lebanon and two months at home; Adoniram was in charge of the forced labor. 15Solomon also had seventy thousand laborers and eighty thousand stonecutters in the hill country, 16besides Solomon's three thousand three hundred supervisors who were over the work, having charge of the people who did the work. 17At the king's command, they quarried out great, costly stones in order to lay the foundation of the house with dressed stones. 18So Solomon's builders and Hiram's builders and the Gebalites did the stonecutting and prepared the timber and the stone to build the house.

SOLOMON BUILDS THE TEMPLE

6 In the four hundred eightieth year after the Israelites came

[a] 5.1 Ch 5.15 in Heb   [b] 5.3 Gk Tg Vg: Heb *my feet* or *his feet*

out of the land of Egypt, in the fourth year of Solomon's reign over Israel, in the month of Ziv, which is the second month, he began to build the house of the LORD. ²The house that King Solomon built for the LORD was sixty cubits long, twenty cubits wide, and thirty cubits high. ³The vestibule in front of the nave of the house was twenty cubits wide, across the width of the house. Its depth was ten cubits in front of the house. ⁴For the house he made windows with recessed frames.ᵃ ⁵He also built a structure against the wall of the house, running around the walls of the house, both the nave and the inner sanctuary; and he made side chambers all around. ⁶The lowest storyᵇ was five cubits wide, the middle one was six cubits wide, and the third was seven cubits wide; for around the outside of the house he made offsets on the wall in order that the supporting beams should not be inserted into the walls of the house.

7 The house was built with stone finished at the quarry, so that neither hammer nor ax nor any tool of iron was heard in the temple while it was being built.

8 The entrance for the middle story was on the south side of the house: one went up by winding stairs to the middle story, and from the middle story to the third. ⁹So he built the house, and finished it; he roofed the house with beams and planks of cedar. ¹⁰He built the structure against the whole house, each storyᶜ five cubits high, and it was joined to the house with timbers of cedar.

11 Now the word of the LORD came to Solomon, ¹²"Concerning this house that you are building, if you will walk in my statutes, obey my ordinances, and keep all my commandments by walking in them, then I will establish my promise with you, which I made to your father David. ¹³I will dwell among the children of Israel, and will not forsake my people Israel."

14 So Solomon built the house, and finished it. ¹⁵He lined the walls of the house on the inside with boards of cedar; from the floor of the house to the rafters of the ceiling, he covered them on the inside with wood; and he covered the floor of the house with boards of cypress. ¹⁶He built twenty cubits of the rear of the house with boards of cedar from the floor to the rafters, and he built this within as an inner sanctuary, as the most holy place. ¹⁷The house, that is, the nave in front of the inner sanctuary, was forty cubits long. ¹⁸The cedar within the house had carvings of gourds and open flowers; all was cedar, no stone was seen. ¹⁹The inner sanctuary he prepared in the innermost part of the house, to set there the ark of the covenant of the LORD. ²⁰The interior of the inner sanctuary was twenty cubits long, twenty cubits wide, and twenty cubits high; he overlaid it with pure gold. He also overlaid the altar with cedar.ᵈ ²¹Solomon overlaid the inside of the house with pure gold, then he drew chains of gold across, in front of the inner sanctuary, and overlaid it with gold. ²²Next he overlaid the whole house with gold, in order that the whole house might be perfect; even the whole altar that belonged to the inner sanctuary he overlaid with gold.

THE FURNISHINGS OF THE TEMPLE

23 In the inner sanctuary he made two cherubim of olivewood, each ten cubits high. ²⁴Five cubits was the length of one wing of the cherub, and five cubits the length of the other wing of the cherub; it was ten cubits from the tip of one wing to the tip of the other. ²⁵The other cherub also measured ten cubits; both cherubim had the same measure and the same form. ²⁶The height of one cherub was ten cubits, and so was that of the other cherub. ²⁷He put the cherubim in the innermost part of the house; the wings of the cherubim were spread out so that a wing of one was touching the

ᵃ 6.4 Gk: Meaning of Heb uncertain
ᵇ 6.6 Gk: Heb *structure*   ᶜ 6.10 Heb lacks *each story*   ᵈ 6.20 Meaning of Heb uncertain

one wall, and a wing of the other cherub was touching the other wall; their other wings toward the center of the house were touching wing to wing. 28 He also overlaid the cherubim with gold.

29 He carved the walls of the house all around about with carved engravings of cherubim, palm trees, and open flowers, in the inner and outer rooms. 30 The floor of the house he overlaid with gold, in the inner and outer rooms.

31 For the entrance to the inner sanctuary he made doors of olivewood; the lintel and the doorposts were five-sided.a 32 He covered the two doors of olivewood with carvings of cherubim, palm trees, and open flowers; he overlaid them with gold, and spread gold on the cherubim and on the palm trees.

33 So also he made for the entrance to the nave doorposts of olivewood, four-sided each, 34 and two doors of cypress wood; the two leaves of the one door were folding, and the two leaves of the other door were folding. 35 He carved cherubim, palm trees, and open flowers, overlaying them with gold evenly applied upon the carved work. 36 He built the inner court with three courses of dressed stone to one course of cedar beams.

37 In the fourth year the foundation of the house of the LORD was laid, in the month of Ziv. 38 In the eleventh year, in the month of Bul, which is the eighth month, the house was finished in all its parts, and according to all its specifications. He was seven years in building it.

SOLOMON'S PALACE AND OTHER BUILDINGS

7 Solomon was building his own house thirteen years, and he finished his entire house.

2 He built the House of the Forest of the Lebanon one hundred cubits long, fifty cubits wide, and thirty cubits high, built on four rows of cedar pillars, with cedar beams on the pillars. 3 It was roofed with cedar on the forty-five rafters, fifteen in each row, which were on the pillars.

4 There were window frames in the three rows, facing each other in the three rows. 5 All the doorways and doorposts had four-sided frames, opposite, facing each other in the three rows.

6 He made the Hall of Pillars fifty cubits long and thirty cubits wide. There was a porch in front with pillars, and a canopy in front of them.

7 He made the Hall of the Throne where he was to pronounce judgment, the Hall of Justice, covered with cedar from floor to floor.

8 His own house where he would reside, in the other court back of the hall, was of the same construction. Solomon also made a house like this hall for Pharaoh's daughter, whom he had taken in marriage.

SELF-INDULGENCE MAY

SEEM OKAY, BUT IT

SEPARATES US FROM GOD.

9 All these were made of costly stones, cut according to measure, sawed with saws, back and front, from the foundation to the coping, and from outside to the great court. 10 The foundation was of costly stones, huge stones, stones of eight and ten cubits. 11 There were costly stones above, cut to measure, and cedarwood. 12 The great court had three courses of dressed stone to one layer of cedar beams all around; so had the inner court of the house of the LORD, and the vestibule of the house.

PRODUCTS OF HIRAM THE BRONZEWORKER

13 Now King Solomon invited and received Hiram from Tyre. 14 He was the son of a widow of the tribe of Naphtali, whose father, a man of Tyre, had been an artisan in bronze;

a 6.31 Meaning of Heb uncertain

he was full of skill, intelligence, and knowledge in working bronze. He came to King Solomon, and did all his work.

15 He cast two pillars of bronze. Eighteen cubits was the height of the one, and a cord of twelve cubits would encircle it; the second pillar was the same.[a] 16He also made two capitals of molten bronze, to set on the tops of the pillars; the height of the one capital was five cubits, and the height of the other capital was five cubits. 17There were nets of checker work with wreaths of chain work for the capitals on the tops of the pillars; seven[b] for the one capital, and seven[b] for the other capital. 18He made the columns with two rows around each latticework to cover the capitals that were above the pomegranates; he did the same with the other capital. 19Now the capitals that were on the tops of the pillars in the vestibule were of lily-work, four cubits high. 20The capitals were on the two pillars and also above the rounded projection that was beside the latticework; there were two hundred pomegranates in rows all around; and so with the other capital. 21He set up the pillars at the vestibule of the temple; he set up the pillar on the south and called it Jachin; and he set up the pillar on the north and called it Boaz. 22On the tops of the pillars was lily-work. Thus the work of the pillars was finished.

23 Then he made the molten sea; it was round, ten cubits from brim to brim, and five cubits high. A line of thirty cubits would encircle it completely. 24Under its brim were panels all around it, each of ten cubits, surrounding the sea; there were two rows of panels, cast when it was cast. 25It stood on twelve oxen, three facing north, three facing west, three facing south, and three facing east; the sea was set on them. The hindquarters of each were toward the inside. 26Its thickness was a handbreadth; its brim was made like the brim of a cup, like the flower of a lily; it held two thousand baths.[c]

27 He also made the ten stands of bronze; each stand was four cubits long, four cubits wide, and three cubits high. 28This was the construction of the stands: they had borders; the borders were within the frames; 29on the borders that were set in the frames were lions, oxen, and cherubim. On the frames, both above and below the lions and oxen, there were wreaths of beveled work. 30Each stand had four bronze wheels and axles of bronze; at the four corners were supports for a basin. The supports were cast with wreaths at the side of each. 31Its opening was within the crown whose height was one cubit; its opening was round, as a pedestal is made; it was a cubit and a half wide. At its opening there were carvings; its borders were four-sided, not round. 32The four wheels were underneath the borders; the axles of the wheels were in the stands; and the height of a wheel was a cubit and a half. 33The wheels were made like a chariot wheel; their axles, their rims, their spokes, and their hubs were all cast. 34There were four supports at the four corners of each stand; the supports were of one piece with the stands. 35On the top of the stand there was a round band half a cubit high; on the top of the stand, its stays and its borders were of one piece with it. 36On the surfaces of its stays and on its borders he carved cherubim, lions, and palm trees, where each had space, with wreaths all around. 37In this way he made the ten stands; all of them were cast alike, with the same size and the same form.

38 He made ten basins of bronze; each basin held forty baths,[c] each basin measured four cubits; there was a basin for each of the ten stands. 39He set five of the stands on the south side of the house, and five on the north side of the house; he set the sea on the southeast corner of the house.

40 Hiram also made the pots, the shovels, and the basins. So Hiram finished all the work that he

---

[a] 7.15 Cn: Heb *and a cord of twelve cubits encircled the second pillar*; Compare Jer 52.21   [b] 7.17 Heb: Gk *a net*   [c] 7.26,38 A Heb measure of volume

did for King Solomon on the house of the LORD: 41the two pillars, the two bowls of the capitals that were on the tops of the pillars, the two latticeworks to cover the two bowls of the capitals that were on the tops of the pillars; 42the four hundred pomegranates for the two latticeworks, two rows of pomegranates for each latticework, to cover the two bowls of the capitals that were on the pillars; 43the ten stands, the ten basins on the stands; 44the one sea, and the twelve oxen underneath the sea.

45 The pots, the shovels, and the basins, all these vessels that Hiram made for King Solomon for the house of the LORD were of burnished bronze. 46In the plain of the Jordan the king cast them, in the clay ground between Succoth and Zarethan. 47Solomon left all the vessels unweighed, because there were so many of them; the weight of the bronze was not determined.

48 So Solomon made all the vessels that were in the house of the LORD: the golden altar, the golden table for the bread of the Presence, 49the lampstands of pure gold, five on the south side and five on the north, in front of the inner sanctuary; the flowers, the lamps, and the tongs, of gold; 50the cups, snuffers, basins, dishes for incense, and firepans, of pure gold; the sockets for the doors of the innermost part of the house, the most holy place, and for the doors of the nave of the temple, of gold.

51 Thus all the work that King Solomon did on the house of the LORD was finished. Solomon brought in the things that his father David had dedicated, the silver, the gold, and the vessels, and stored them in the treasuries of the house of the LORD.

DEDICATION OF THE TEMPLE

8 Then Solomon assembled the elders of Israel and all the heads of the tribes, the leaders of the ancestral houses of the Israelites, before King Solomon in Jerusalem, to bring up the ark of the covenant of the LORD out of the city of David, which

is Zion. 2All the people of Israel assembled to King Solomon at the festival in the month Ethanim, which is the seventh month. 3And all the elders of Israel came, and the priests carried the ark. 4So they brought up the ark of the LORD, the tent of meeting, and all the holy vessels that were in the tent; the priests and the Levites brought them up. 5King Solomon and all the congregation of Israel, who had assembled before him, were with him before the ark, sacrificing so many sheep and oxen that they could not be counted or numbered. 6Then the priests brought the ark of the covenant of the LORD to its place, in the inner sanctuary of the house, in the most holy place, underneath the wings of the cherubim. 7For the cherubim spread out their wings over the place of the ark, so that the cherubim made a covering above the ark and its poles. 8The poles were so long that the ends of the poles were seen from the holy place in front of the inner sanctuary; but they could not be seen from outside; they are there to this day. 9There was nothing in the ark except the two tablets of stone that Moses had placed there at Horeb, where the LORD made a covenant with the Israelites, when they came out of the land of Egypt. 10And when the priests came out of the holy place, a cloud filled the house of the LORD, 11so that the priests could not stand to minister because of the cloud; for the glory of the LORD filled the house of the LORD.

12 Then Solomon said,
"The LORD has said that he would
　　dwell in thick darkness.
13 I have built you an exalted house,
　　a place for you to dwell
　　　in forever."

SOLOMON'S SPEECH

14 Then the king turned around and blessed all the assembly of Israel, while all the assembly of Israel stood. 15He said, "Blessed be the LORD, the God of Israel, who with his hand has fulfilled what he promised with his mouth to my father David, saying, 16'Since the day that

I brought my people Israel out of Egypt, I have not chosen a city from any of the tribes of Israel in which to build a house, that my name might be there; but I chose David to be over my people Israel.' 17My father David had it in mind to build a house for the name of the LORD, the God of Israel. 18But the LORD said to my father David, 'You did well to consider building a house for my name; 19nevertheless you shall not build the house, but your son who shall be born to you shall build the house for my name.' 20Now the LORD has upheld the promise that he made; for I have risen in the place of my father David; I sit on the throne of Israel, as the LORD promised, and have built the house for the name of the LORD, the God of Israel. 21There I have provided a place for the ark, in which is the covenant of the LORD that he made with our ancestors when he brought them out of the land of Egypt."

SOLOMON'S PRAYER OF DEDICATION

22 Then Solomon stood before the altar of the LORD in the presence of all the assembly of Israel, and spread out his hands to heaven. 23He said, "O LORD, God of Israel, there is no God like you in heaven above or on earth beneath, keeping covenant and steadfast love for your servants who walk before you with all their heart, 24the covenant that you kept for your servant my father David as you declared to him; you promised with your mouth and have this day fulfilled with your hand. 25Therefore, O LORD, God of Israel, keep for your servant my father David that which you promised him, saying, 'There shall never fail you a successor before me to sit on the throne of Israel, if only your children look to their way, to walk before me as you have walked before me.' 26Therefore, O God of Israel, let your word be confirmed, which you promised to your servant my father David.

27 "But will God indeed dwell on the earth? Even heaven and the highest heaven cannot contain you,

PONDER

"O LORD, God of Israel, there is no God like you in heaven above or on earth beneath, keeping covenant and steadfast love for your servants who walk before you with all their heart."
—1 Kings 8.23

PRAY

Lord, often we don't quite know how to follow up on what we learn in the scriptures; we don't quite know what every passage should mean to us. As we read these few verses, implant them in our hearts so that we can learn how to stretch the boundaries of our spirits, the boundaries of our love for you. Guide us in the self-examination that leads to repentance and transformation, showing us how to "walk before you with all [our] heart." Forgive our sins of ungodliness, wickedness and insensitivity to others, and join our hearts in the kind of love that you have for us. Amen.

much less this house that I have built! 28Regard your servant's prayer and his plea, O LORD my God, heeding the cry and the prayer that your servant prays to you today; 29that your eyes may be open night and day toward this house, the place of which you said, 'My name shall be there,' that you may heed the prayer that your servant prays toward this place. 30Hear the plea of your servant and of your people Israel when they pray toward this place; O hear in heaven your dwelling place; heed and forgive.

31 "If someone sins against a neighbor and is given an oath to swear, and comes and swears before your altar in this house, 32then hear in heaven, and act, and judge your servants, condemning the guilty by bringing their conduct on their own head, and vindicating the righteous

by rewarding them according to their righteousness.

33 "When your people Israel, having sinned against you, are defeated before an enemy but turn again to you, confess your name, pray and plead with you in this house, 34then hear in heaven, forgive the sin of your people Israel, and bring them again to the land that you gave to their ancestors.

35 "When heaven is shut up and there is no rain because they have sinned against you, and then they pray toward this place, confess your name, and turn from their sin, because you punish[a] them, 36then hear in heaven, and forgive the sin of your servants, your people Israel, when you teach them the good way in which they should walk; and grant rain on your land, which you have given to your people as an inheritance.

37 "If there is famine in the land, if there is plague, blight, mildew, locust, or caterpillar; if their enemy besieges them in any[b] of their cities; whatever plague, whatever sickness there is; 38whatever prayer, whatever plea there is from any individual or from all your people Israel, all knowing the afflictions of their own hearts so that they stretch out their hands toward this house; 39then hear in heaven your dwelling place, forgive, act, and render to all whose hearts you know—according to all their ways, for only you know what is in every human heart— 40so that they may fear you all the days that they live in the land that you gave to our ancestors.

41 "Likewise when a foreigner, who is not of your people Israel, comes from a distant land because of your name 42—for they shall hear of your great name, your mighty hand, and your outstretched arm—when a foreigner comes and prays toward this house, 43then hear in heaven your dwelling place, and do according to all that the foreigner calls to you, so that all the peoples of the earth may know your name and fear you, as do your people Israel, and so that they may know that your name has been invoked on this house that I have built.

44 "If your people go out to battle against their enemy, by whatever way you shall send them, and they pray to the LORD toward the city that you have chosen and the house that I have built for your name, 45then hear in heaven their prayer and their plea, and maintain their cause.

46 "If they sin against you—for there is no one who does not sin—and you are angry with them and give them to an enemy, so that they are carried away captive to the land of the enemy, far off or near; 47yet if they come to their senses in the land to which they have been taken captive, and repent, and plead with you in the land of their captors, saying, 'We have sinned, and have done wrong; we have acted wickedly'; 48if they repent with all their heart and soul in the land of their enemies, who took them captive, and pray to you toward their land, which you gave to their ancestors, the city that you have chosen, and the house that I have built for your name; 49then hear in heaven your dwelling place their prayer and their plea, maintain their cause 50and forgive your people who have sinned against you, and all their transgressions that they have committed against you; and grant them compassion in the sight of their captors, so that they may have compassion on them 51(for they are your people and heritage, which you brought out of Egypt, from the midst of the iron-smelter); 52Let your eyes be open to the plea of your servant, and to the plea of your people Israel, listening to them whenever they call to you. 53For you have separated them from among all the peoples of the earth, to be your heritage, just as you promised through Moses, your servant, when you brought our ancestors out of Egypt, O Lord GOD."

SOLOMON BLESSES THE ASSEMBLY

54 Now when Solomon finished offering all this prayer and this plea

a 8.35 Or when you answer   b 8.37 Gk Syr: Heb in the land

to the LORD, he arose from facing the altar of the LORD, where he had knelt with hands outstretched toward heaven; 55he stood and blessed all the assembly of Israel with a loud voice:

56 "Blessed be the LORD, who has given rest to his people Israel according to all that he promised; not one word has failed of all his good promise, which he spoke through his servant Moses. 57The LORD our God be with us, as he was with our ancestors; may he not leave us or abandon us, 58but incline our hearts to him, to walk in all his ways, and to keep his commandments, his statutes, and his ordinances, which he commanded our ancestors. 59Let these words of mine, with which I pleaded before the LORD, be near to the LORD our God day and night, and may he maintain the cause of his servant and the cause of his people Israel, as each day requires; 60so that all the peoples of the earth may know that the LORD is God; there is no other. 61Therefore devote yourselves completely to the LORD our God, walking in his statutes and keeping his commandments, as at this day."

SOLOMON OFFERS SACRIFICES

62 Then the king, and all Israel with him, offered sacrifice before the LORD. 63Solomon offered as sacrifices of well-being to the LORD twenty-two thousand oxen and one hundred twenty thousand sheep. So the king and all the people of Israel dedicated the house of the LORD. 64The same day the king consecrated the middle of the court that was in front of the house of the LORD; for there he offered the burnt offerings and the grain offerings and the fat pieces of the sacrifices of well-being, because the bronze altar that was before the LORD was too small to receive the burnt offerings and the grain offerings and the fat pieces of the sacrifices of well-being. 65 So Solomon held the festival at that time, and all Israel with him—a great assembly, people from Lebo-hamath to the Wadi of Egypt—before the LORD our God, seven days.[a] 66On the eighth day he sent the people away; and they blessed the king, and went to their tents, joyful and in good spirits because of all the goodness that the LORD had shown to his servant David and to his people Israel.

JOY IS AN UNDERSTANDING

OF EXISTENCE.

GOD APPEARS AGAIN TO SOLOMON

9 When Solomon had finished building the house of the LORD and the king's house and all that Solomon desired to build, 2the LORD appeared to Solomon a second time, as he had appeared to him at Gibeon. 3The LORD said to him, "I have heard your prayer and your plea, which you made before me; I have consecrated this house that you have built, and put my name there forever; my eyes and my heart will be there for all time. 4As for you, if you will walk before me, as David your father walked, with integrity of heart and uprightness, doing according to all that I have commanded you, and keeping my statutes and my ordinances, 5then I will establish your royal throne over Israel forever, as I promised your father David, saying, 'There shall not fail you a successor on the throne of Israel.'

6 "If you turn aside from following me, you or your children, and do not keep my commandments and my statutes that I have set before you, but go and serve other gods and worship them, 7then I will cut Israel off from the land that I have given them; and the house that I have consecrated for my name I will cast out of my sight; and Israel will become a proverb and a taunt among all peoples. 8This house will become a

<hr />

a **8.65** Compare Gk: Heb *seven days and seven days, fourteen days*

heap of ruins;[a] everyone passing by it will be astonished, and will hiss; and they will say, 'Why has the LORD done such a thing to this land and to this house?' 9 Then they will say, 'Because they have forsaken the LORD their God, who brought their ancestors out of the land of Egypt, and embraced other gods, worshiping them and serving them; therefore the LORD has brought this disaster upon them.' "

10 At the end of twenty years, in which Solomon had built the two houses, the house of the LORD and the king's house, 11 King Hiram of Tyre having supplied Solomon with cedar and cypress timber and gold, as much as he desired, King Solomon gave to Hiram twenty cities in the land of Galilee. 12 But when Hiram came from Tyre to see the cities that Solomon had given him, they did not please him. 13 Therefore he said, "What kind of cities are these that you have given me, my brother?" So they are called the land of Cabul[b] to this day. 14 But Hiram had sent to the king one hundred twenty talents of gold.

OTHER ACTS OF SOLOMON

15 This is the account of the forced labor that King Solomon conscripted to build the house of the LORD and his own house, the Millo and the wall of Jerusalem, Hazor, Megiddo, Gezer 16 (Pharaoh king of Egypt had gone up and captured Gezer and burned it down, had killed the Canaanites who lived in the city, and had given it as dowry to his daughter, Solomon's wife; 17 so Solomon rebuilt Gezer), Lower Beth-horon, 18 Baalath, Tamar in the wilderness, within the land, 19 as well as all of Solomon's storage cities, the cities for his chariots, the cities for his cavalry, and whatever Solomon desired to build, in Jerusalem, in Lebanon, and in all the land of his dominion. 20 All the people who were left of the Amorites, the Hittites, the Perizzites, the Hivites, and the Jebusites, who were not of the people of Israel— 21 their descendants who were still left in the land, whom the Israelites were unable to destroy completely—these Solomon conscripted for slave labor, and so they are to this day. 22 But of the Israelites Solomon made no slaves; they were the soldiers, they were his officials, his commanders, his captains, and the commanders of his chariotry and cavalry.

23 These were the chief officers who were over Solomon's work: five hundred fifty, who had charge of the people who carried on the work.

24 But Pharaoh's daughter went up from the city of David to her own house that Solomon had built for her; then he built the Millo.

25 Three times a year Solomon used to offer up burnt offerings and sacrifices of well-being on the altar that he built for the LORD, offering incense[c] before the LORD. So he completed the house.

SOLOMON'S COMMERCIAL ACTIVITY

26 King Solomon built a fleet of ships at Ezion-geber, which is near Eloth on the shore of the Red Sea,[d] in the land of Edom. 27 Hiram sent his servants with the fleet, sailors who were familiar with the sea, together with the servants of Solomon. 28 They went to Ophir, and imported from there four hundred twenty talents of gold, which they delivered to King Solomon.

VISIT OF THE QUEEN OF SHEBA

10 When the queen of Sheba heard of the fame of Solomon (fame due to[e] the name of the LORD), she came to test him with hard questions. 2 She came to Jerusalem with a very great retinue, with camels bearing spices, and very much gold, and precious stones; and when she came to Solomon, she told him all that was on her mind. 3 Solomon answered all her questions; there was nothing hidden from the king that he could not explain to her. 4 When

a 9.8 Syr Old Latin: Heb will become high
b 9.13 Perhaps meaning a land good for nothing   c 9.25 Gk: Heb offering incense with it that was   d 9.26 Or Sea of Reeds
e 10.1 Meaning of Heb uncertain

the queen of Sheba had observed all the wisdom of Solomon, the house that he had built, 5the food of his table, the seating of his officials, and the attendance of his servants, their clothing, his valets, and his burnt offerings that he offered at the house of the LORD, there was no more spirit in her.

6 So she said to the king, "The report was true that I heard in my own land of your accomplishments and of your wisdom, 7but I did not believe the reports until I came and my own eyes had seen it. Not even half had been told me; your wisdom and prosperity far surpass the report that I had heard. 8Happy are your wives!a Happy are these your servants, who continually attend you and hear your wisdom! 9Blessed be the LORD your God, who has delighted in you and set you on the throne of Israel! Because the LORD loved Israel forever, he has made you king to execute justice and righteousness." 10Then she gave the king one hundred twenty talents of gold, a great quantity of spices, and precious stones; never again did spices come in such quantity as that which the queen of Sheba gave to King Solomon.

11 Moreover, the fleet of Hiram, which carried gold from Ophir, brought from Ophir a great quantity of almug wood and precious stones. 12From the almug wood the king made supports for the house of the LORD, and for the king's house, lyres also and harps for the singers; no such almug wood has come or been seen to this day.

13 Meanwhile King Solomon gave to the queen of Sheba every desire that she expressed, as well as what he gave her out of Solomon's royal bounty. Then she returned to her own land, with her servants.

14 The weight of gold that came to Solomon in one year was six hundred sixty-six talents of gold, 15besides that which came from the traders and from the business of the merchants, and from all the kings of Arabia and the governors of the land. 16King Solomon made two hundred large shields of beaten gold; six hundred shekels of gold went into each large shield. 17He made three hundred shields of beaten gold; three minas of gold went into each shield; and the king put them in the House of the Forest of Lebanon. 18The king also made a great ivory throne, and overlaid it with the finest gold. 19The throne had six steps. The top of the throne was rounded in the back, and on each side of the seat were arm rests and two lions standing beside the arm rests, 20while twelve lions were standing, one on each end of a step on the six steps. Nothing like it was ever made in any kingdom. 21All King Solomon's drinking vessels were of gold, and all the vessels of the House of the Forest of Lebanon were of pure gold; none were of silver—it was not considered as anything in the days of Solomon. 22For the king had a fleet of ships of Tarshish at sea with the fleet of Hiram. Once every three years the fleet of ships of Tarshish used to come bringing gold, silver, ivory, apes, and peacocks.b

23 Thus King Solomon excelled all the kings of the earth in riches and in wisdom. 24The whole earth sought the presence of Solomon to hear his wisdom, which God had put into his mind. 25Every one of them brought a present, objects of silver and gold, garments, weaponry, spices, horses, and mules, so much year by year.

26 Solomon gathered together chariots and horses; he had fourteen hundred chariots and twelve thousand horses, which he stationed in the chariot cities and with the king in Jerusalem. 27The king made silver as common in Jerusalem as stones, and he made cedars as numerous as the sycamores of the Shephelah. 28Solomon's import of horses was from Egypt and Kue, and the king's traders received them from Kue at a price. 29A chariot could be imported from Egypt for six hundred shekels of silver, and a horse for one

a 10.8 Gk Syr: Heb men   b 10.22 Or baboons

hundred fifty; so through the king's traders they were exported to all the kings of the Hittites and the kings of Aram.

SOLOMON'S ERRORS

11 King Solomon loved many foreign women along with the daughter of Pharaoh: Moabite, Ammonite, Edomite, Sidonian, and Hittite women, ²from the nations concerning which the LORD had said to the Israelites, "You shall not enter into marriage with them, neither shall they with you; for they will surely incline your heart to follow their gods"; Solomon clung to these in love. ³Among his wives were seven hundred princesses and three hundred concubines; and his wives turned away his heart. ⁴For when Solomon was old, his wives turned away his heart after other gods; and his heart was not true to the LORD his God, as was the heart of his father David. ⁵For Solomon followed Astarte the goddess of the Sidonians, and Milcom the abomination of the Ammonites. ⁶So Solomon did what was evil in the sight of the LORD, and did not completely follow the LORD, as his father David had done. ⁷Then Solomon built a high place for Chemosh the abomination of Moab, and for Molech the abomination of the Ammonites, on the mountain east of Jerusalem. ⁸He did the same for all his foreign wives, who offered incense and sacrificed to their gods.

9 Then the LORD was angry with Solomon, because his heart had turned away from the LORD, the God of Israel, who had appeared to him twice, ¹⁰and had commanded him concerning this matter, that he should not follow other gods; but he did not observe what the LORD commanded. ¹¹Therefore the LORD said to Solomon, "Since this has been your mind and you have not kept my covenant and my statutes that I have commanded you, I will surely tear the kingdom from you and give it to your servant. ¹²Yet for the sake of your father David I will not do it in your lifetime; I will tear it out of the hand of your son. ¹³I will not, however, tear away the entire kingdom; I will give one tribe to your son, for the sake of my servant David and for the sake of Jerusalem, which I have chosen."

ADVERSARIES OF SOLOMON

14 Then the LORD raised up an adversary against Solomon, Hadad the Edomite; he was of the royal house in Edom. ¹⁵For when David was in Edom, and Joab the commander of the army went up to bury the dead, he killed every male in Edom ¹⁶(for Joab and all Israel remained there six months, until he had eliminated every male in Edom); ¹⁷but Hadad fled to Egypt with some Edomites who were servants of his father. He was a young boy at that time. ¹⁸They set out from Midian and came to Paran; they took people with them from Paran and came to Egypt, to Pharaoh king of Egypt, who gave him a house, assigned him an allowance of food, and gave him land. ¹⁹Hadad found great favor in the sight of Pharaoh, so that he gave him his sister-in-law for a wife, the sister of Queen Tahpenes. ²⁰The sister of Tahpenes gave birth by him to his son Genubath, whom Tahpenes weaned in Pharaoh's house; Genubath was in Pharaoh's house among the children of Pharaoh. ²¹When Hadad heard in Egypt that David slept with his ancestors and that Joab the commander of the army was dead, Hadad said to Pharaoh, "Let me depart, that I may go to my own country." ²²But Pharaoh said to him, "What do you lack with me that you now seek to go to your own country?" And he said, "No, do let me go."

23 God raised up another adversary against Solomon,ᵃ Rezon son of Eliada, who had fled from his master, King Hadadezer of Zobah. ²⁴He gathered followers around him and became leader of a marauding band, after the slaughter by David; they went to Damascus, settled there, and made him king in Damascus. ²⁵He was an adversary of Israel all

ᵃ 11.23 Heb *him*

LITTLE BY LITTLE

*The LORD was angry with Solomon, because his heart had turned away
from the LORD, the God of Israel, who had appeared to him twice.*

—1 Kings 11.9

Solomon was an interesting person. He appears to have started his life well: he was given great wisdom by God, and he built a glorious temple for the Lord. He had God on his side and everything going for him. Later, however, Solomon's heart was led astray into idolatry by his many pagan wives, and he even built sanctuaries for their gods. And unlike his father, David, Solomon didn't sin in a fleeting moment of passion or anger; his relationship with God seems to have gradually deteriorated as he compromised his allegiance to the True God.

Solomon did not decide to abandon his faith in the True God hastily, but rather, he rationalized his sins little by little until he eventually wound up in a difficult position. He acquired 700 wives to seal political alliances with neighboring nations and tribes, which in turn gained peace for his nation. Undoubtedly Solomon considered his actions justified because they protected his people, the Israelites. However, Solomon likely figured that he couldn't convert all these wives to the Israelite faith, so instead he allowed them to worship as they always did. Eventually his wives promoted idolatry within Israel and even within Solomon's own heart. No doubt many in Israel assumed that if pagan worship was okay with King Solomon, then it must not be so bad after all.

If we take a good look at ourselves, we may see that we practice idolatry, though it may look different from Solomon's. Like Solomon, we might slip into its practice slowly and without awareness. We may move toward sin for what we think are good reasons, as Solomon did, even though we may know we are walking a fine line.

Our idolatry usually takes the form of evil desires and greed, as Paul pointed out in Colossians 3.5. Greed is the desire for material things that someone else has, rather than being content with what God has given us. The apostle John made it very clear just how serious greed is: "Do not love the world or the things in the world. The love of the Father is not in those who love the world" (1 John 2.15). Does that mean we can never desire anything other than what we already have? Not exactly. It has a lot more to do with our hearts. Are our hearts captivated by things of the world? By wealth or a comfortable lifestyle? Do the things of God take a backseat to our worldly interests? These are good indicators that our hearts might have evolved into the love for the world that John describes. We must be on guard that we don't slowly, almost imperceptibly, slide into a life of idolatry and let our relationship with God suffer as a result.

Going Deeper

- What are some "idols" that subtly tempt your heart away from God?
- What are some practical ways you can guard against letting your heart drift away from God?

the days of Solomon, making trouble as Hadad did; he despised Israel and reigned over Aram.

JEROBOAM'S REBELLION

26 Jeroboam son of Nebat, an Ephraimite of Zeredah, a servant of Solomon, whose mother's name was Zeruah, a widow, rebelled against the king. 27The following was the reason he rebelled against the king. Solomon built the Millo, and closed up the gap in the walla of the city of his father David. 28The man Jeroboam was very able, and when Solomon saw that the young man was industrious he gave him charge over all the forced labor of the house of Joseph. 29About that time, when Jeroboam was leaving Jerusalem, the prophet Ahijah the Shilonite found him on the road. Ahijah had clothed himself with a new garment. The two of them were alone in the open country 30when Ahijah laid hold of the new garment he was wearing and tore it into twelve pieces. 31He then said to Jeroboam: Take for yourself ten pieces; for thus says the LORD, the God of Israel, "See, I am about to tear the kingdom from the hand of Solomon, and will give you ten tribes. 32One tribe will remain his, for the sake of my servant David and for the sake of Jerusalem, the city that I have chosen out of all the tribes of Israel. 33This is because he hasb forsaken me, worshiped Astarte the goddess of the Sidonians, Chemosh the god of Moab, and Milcom the god of the Ammonites, and hasb not walked in my ways, doing what is right in my sight and keeping my statutes and my ordinances, as his father David did. 34Nevertheless I will not take the whole kingdom away from him but will make him ruler all the days of his life, for the sake of my servant David whom I chose and who did keep my commandments and my statutes; 35but I will take the kingdom away from his son and give it to you—that is, the ten tribes. 36Yet to his son I will give one tribe, so that my servant David may always have a lamp before me in Jerusalem, the city where I have

chosen to put my name. 37I will take you, and you shall reign over all that your soul desires; you shall be king over Israel. 38If you will listen to all that I command you, walk in my ways, and do what is right in my sight by keeping my statutes and my commandments, as David my servant did, I will be with you, and will build you an enduring house, as I built for David, and I will give Israel to you. 39For this reason I will punish the descendants of David, but not forever." 40Solomon sought therefore to kill Jeroboam; but Jeroboam promptly fled to Egypt, to King Shishak of Egypt, and remained in Egypt until the death of Solomon.

DEATH OF SOLOMON

41 Now the rest of the acts of Solomon, all that he did as well as his wisdom, are they not written in the Book of the Acts of Solomon? 42The time that Solomon reigned in Jerusalem over all Israel was forty years. 43Solomon slept with his ancestors and was buried in the city of his father David; and his son Rehoboam succeeded him.

THE NORTHERN TRIBES SECEDE

12 Rehoboam went to Shechem, for all Israel had come to Shechem to make him king. 2When Jeroboam son of Nebat heard of it (for he was still in Egypt, where he had fled from King Solomon), then Jeroboam returned fromc Egypt. 3And they sent and called him; and Jeroboam and all the assembly of Israel came and said to Rehoboam, 4"Your father made our yoke heavy. Now therefore lighten the hard service of your father and his heavy yoke that he placed on us, and we will serve you." 5He said to them, "Go away for three days, then come again to me." So the people went away.

6 Then King Rehoboam took counsel with the older men who had attended his father Solomon while he was still alive, saying, "How do

a 11.27 Heb lacks *in the wall*   b 11.33 Gk Syr Vg: Heb *they have*   c 12.2 Gk Vg Compare 2 Chr 10.2: Heb *lived in* you advise me to answer this people?" 7They answered him, "If you will be a servant to this people today and serve them, and speak good words to them when you answer them, then they will be your servants forever." 8But he disregarded the advice that the older men gave him, and consulted with the young men who had grown up with him and now attended him. 9He said to them, "What do you advise that we answer this people who have said to me, 'Lighten the yoke that your father put on us'?" 10The young men who had grown up with him said to him, "Thus you should say to this people who spoke to you, 'Your father made our yoke heavy, but you must lighten it for us'; thus you should say to them, 'My little finger is thicker than my father's loins. 11Now, whereas my father laid on you a heavy yoke, I will add to your yoke. My father disciplined you with whips, but I will discipline you with scorpions.'"

12 So Jeroboam and all the people came to Rehoboam the third day, as the king had said, "Come to me again the third day." 13The king answered the people harshly. He disregarded the advice that the older men had given him 14and spoke to them according to the advice of the young men, "My father made your yoke heavy, but I will add to your yoke; my father disciplined you with whips, but I will discipline you with scorpions." 15So the king did not listen to the people, because it was a turn of affairs brought about by the LORD that he might fulfill his word, which the LORD had spoken by Ahijah the Shilonite to Jeroboam son of Nebat.

16 When all Israel saw that the king would not listen to them, the people answered the king,

"What share do we have in David?
We have no inheritance
     in the son of Jesse.
To your tents, O Israel!
Look now to your own
     house, O David."

So Israel went away to their tents. 17But Rehoboam reigned over the Israelites who were living in the towns of Judah. 18When King Rehoboam sent Adoram, who was taskmaster over the forced labor, all Israel stoned him to death. King Rehoboam then hurriedly mounted his chariot to flee to Jerusalem. 19So Israel has been in rebellion against the house of David to this day.

FIRST DYNASTY: JEROBOAM REIGNS OVER ISRAEL

20 When all Israel heard that Jeroboam had returned, they sent and called him to the assembly and made him king over all Israel. There was no one who followed the house of David, except the tribe of Judah alone.

21 When Rehoboam came to Jerusalem, he assembled all the house of Judah and the tribe of Benjamin, one hundred eighty thousand chosen troops to fight against the house of Israel, to restore the kingdom to Rehoboam son of Solomon. 22But the word of God came to Shemaiah the man of God: 23Say to King Rehoboam of Judah, son of Solomon, and to all the house of Judah and Benjamin, and to the rest of the people, 24"Thus says the LORD, You shall not go up or fight against your kindred the people of Israel. Let everyone go home, for this thing is from me." So they heeded the word of the LORD and went home again, according to the word of the LORD.

JEROBOAM'S GOLDEN CALVES

25 Then Jeroboam built Shechem in the hill country of Ephraim, and resided there; he went out from there and built Penuel. 26Then Jeroboam said to himself, "Now the kingdom may well revert to the house of David. 27If this people continues to go up to offer sacrifices in the house of the LORD at Jerusalem, the heart of this people will turn again to their master, King Rehoboam of Judah; they will kill me and return to King Rehoboam of Judah." 28So the king took counsel, and made two calves of gold. He said to the people,[a] "You have gone up to

a 12.28 Gk: Heb to them

Jerusalem long enough. Here are your gods, O Israel, who brought you up out of the land of Egypt." ²⁹He set one in Bethel, and the other he put in Dan. ³⁰And this thing became a sin, for the people went to worship before the one at Bethel and before the other as far as Dan.^a ³¹He also made houses^b on high places, and appointed priests from among all the people, who were not Levites. ³²Jeroboam appointed a festival on the fifteenth day of the eighth month like the festival that was in Judah, and he offered sacrifices on the altar; so he did in Bethel, sacrificing to the calves that he had made. And he placed in Bethel the priests of the high places that he had made. ³³He went up to the altar that he had made in Bethel on the fifteenth day in the eighth month, in the month that he alone had devised; he appointed a festival for the people of Israel, and he went up to the altar to offer incense.

A MAN OF GOD FROM JUDAH

13 While Jeroboam was standing by the altar to offer incense, a man of God came out of Judah by the word of the LORD to Bethel ²and proclaimed against the altar by the word of the LORD, and said, "O altar, altar, thus says the LORD: 'A son shall be born to the house of David, Josiah by name; and he shall sacrifice on you the priests of the high places who offer incense on you, and human bones shall be burned on you.'" ³He gave a sign the same day, saying, "This is the sign that the LORD has spoken: 'The altar shall be torn down, and the ashes that are on it shall be poured out.'" ⁴When the king heard what the man of God cried out against the altar at Bethel, Jeroboam stretched out his hand from the altar, saying, "Seize him!" But the hand that he stretched out against him withered so that he could not draw it back to himself. ⁵The altar also was torn down, and the ashes poured out from the altar, according to the sign that the man of God had given by the word of the LORD. ⁶The king said to the man of

God, "Entreat now the favor of the LORD your God, and pray for me, so that my hand may be restored to me." So the man of God entreated the LORD; and the king's hand was restored to him, and became as it was before. ⁷Then the king said to the man of God, "Come home with me and dine, and I will give you a gift." ⁸But the man of God said to the king, "If you give me half your kingdom, I will not go in with you; nor will I eat food or drink water in this place. ⁹For thus I was commanded by the word of the LORD: You shall not eat food, or drink water, or return by the way that you came." ¹⁰So he went another way, and did not return by the way that he had come to Bethel.

¹¹Now there lived an old prophet in Bethel. One of his sons came and told him all that the man of God had done that day in Bethel; the words also that he had spoken to the king, they told to their father. ¹²Their father said to them, "Which way did he go?" And his sons showed him the way that the man of God who came from Judah had gone. ¹³Then he said to his sons, "Saddle a donkey for me." So they saddled a donkey for him, and he mounted it. ¹⁴He went after the man of God, and found him sitting under an oak tree. He said to him, "Are you the man of God who came from Judah?" He answered, "I am." ¹⁵Then he said to him, "Come home with me and eat some food." ¹⁶But he said, "I cannot return with you, or go in with you; nor will I eat food or drink water with you in this place; ¹⁷for it was said to me by the word of the LORD: You shall not eat food or drink water there, or return by the way that you came." ¹⁸Then the other^c said to him, "I also am a prophet as you are, and an angel spoke to me by the word of the LORD: Bring him back with you into your house so that he may eat food and drink water." But he was deceiving him. ¹⁹Then the man of God^c went back with him, and ate food and drank water in his house.

a 12.30 Compare Gk: Heb *went to the one as far as Dan*   b 12.31 Gk Vg Compare 13.32: Heb *a house*   c 13.18,19 Heb *he*

20 As they were sitting at the table, the word of the LORD came to the prophet who had brought him back; **21**and he proclaimed to the man of God who came from Judah, "Thus says the LORD: Because you have disobeyed the word of the LORD, and have not kept the commandment that the LORD your God commanded you, **22**but have come back and have eaten food and drunk water in the place of which he said to you, 'Eat no food, and drink no water,' your body shall not come to your ancestral tomb." **23**After the man of God[a] had eaten food and had drunk, they saddled for him a donkey belonging to the prophet who had brought him back. **24**Then as he went away, a lion met him on the road and killed him. His body was thrown in the road, and the donkey stood beside it; the lion also stood beside the body. **25**People passed by and saw the body thrown in the road, with the lion standing by the body. And they came and told it in the town where the old prophet lived.

26 When the prophet who had brought him back from the way heard of it, he said, "It is the man of God who disobeyed the word of the LORD; therefore the LORD has given him to the lion, which has torn him and killed him according to the word that the LORD spoke to him." **27**Then he said to his sons, "Saddle a donkey for me." So they saddled one, **28**and he went and found the body thrown in the road, with the donkey and the lion standing beside the body. The lion had not eaten the body or attacked the donkey. **29**The prophet took up the body of the man of God, laid it on the donkey, and brought it back to the city,[b] to mourn and to bury him. **30**He laid the body in his own grave; and they mourned over him, saying, "Alas, my brother!" **31**After he had buried him, he said to his sons, "When I die, bury me in the grave in which the man of God is buried; lay my bones beside his bones. **32**For the saying that he proclaimed by the word of the LORD against the altar in Bethel, and

against all the houses of the high places that are in the cities of Samaria, shall surely come to pass."

33 Even after this event Jeroboam did not turn from his evil way, but made priests for the high places again from among all the people; any who wanted to be priests he consecrated for the high places. **34**This matter became sin to the house of Jeroboam, so as to cut it off and to destroy it from the face of the earth.

JUDGMENT ON THE HOUSE OF JEROBOAM

14 At that time Abijah son of Jeroboam fell sick. **2**Jeroboam said to his wife, "Go, disguise yourself, so that it will not be known that you are the wife of Jeroboam, and go to Shiloh; for the prophet Ahijah is there, who said of me that I should be king over this people. **3**Take with you ten loaves, some cakes, and a jar of honey, and go to him; he will tell you what shall happen to the child."

4 Jeroboam's wife did so; she set out and went to Shiloh, and came to the house of Ahijah. Now Ahijah could not see, for his eyes were dim because of his age. **5**But the LORD said to Ahijah, "The wife of Jeroboam is coming to inquire of you concerning her son; for he is sick. Thus and thus you shall say to her."

When she came, she pretended to be another woman. **6**But when Ahijah heard the sound of her feet, as she came in at the door, he said, "Come in, wife of Jeroboam; why do you pretend to be another? For I am charged with heavy tidings for you. **7**Go, tell Jeroboam, 'Thus says the LORD, the God of Israel: Because I exalted you from among the people, made you leader over my people Israel, **8**and tore the kingdom away from the house of David to give it to you; yet you have not been like my servant David, who kept my commandments and followed me with all his heart, doing only that which was right in my sight, **9**but you have

---

[a] 13.23 Heb *he*   [b] 13.29 Gk: Heb *he came to the town of the old prophet*

done evil above all those who were before you and have gone and made for yourself other gods, and cast images, provoking me to anger, and have thrust me behind your back; [10]therefore, I will bring evil upon the house of Jeroboam. I will cut off from Jeroboam every male, both bond and free in Israel, and will consume the house of Jeroboam, just as one burns up dung until it is all gone. [11]Anyone belonging to Jeroboam who dies in the city, the dogs shall eat; and anyone who dies in the open country, the birds of the air shall eat; for the LORD has spoken.' [12]Therefore set out, go to your house. When your feet enter the city, the child shall die. [13]All Israel shall mourn for him and bury him; for he alone of Jeroboam's family shall come to the grave, because in him there is found something pleasing to the LORD, the God of Israel, in the house of Jeroboam. [14]Moreover the LORD will raise up for himself a king over Israel, who shall cut off the house of Jeroboam today, even right now![a]

[15] "The LORD will strike Israel, as a reed is shaken in the water; he will root up Israel out of this good land that he gave to their ancestors, and scatter them beyond the Euphrates, because they have made their sacred poles,[b] provoking the LORD to anger. [16]He will give Israel up because of the sins of Jeroboam, which he sinned and which he caused Israel to commit."

[17] Then Jeroboam's wife got up and went away, and she came to Tirzah. As she came to the threshold of the house, the child died. [18]All Israel buried him and mourned for him, according to the word of the LORD, which he spoke by his servant the prophet Ahijah.

DEATH OF JEROBOAM

[19] Now the rest of the acts of Jeroboam, how he warred and how he reigned, are written in the Book of the Annals of the Kings of Israel. [20]The time that Jeroboam reigned was twenty-two years; then he slept with his ancestors, and his son Nadab succeeded him.

REHOBOAM REIGNS OVER JUDAH

[21] Now Rehoboam son of Solomon reigned in Judah. Rehoboam was forty-one years old when he began to reign, and he reigned seventeen years in Jerusalem, the city that the LORD had chosen out of all the tribes of Israel, to put his name there. His mother's name was Naamah the Ammonite. [22]Judah did what was evil in the sight of the LORD; they provoked him to jealousy with their sins that they committed, more than all that their ancestors had done. [23]For they also built for themselves high places, pillars, and sacred poles[b] on every high hill and under every green tree; [24]there were also male temple prostitutes in the land. They committed all the abominations of the nations that the LORD drove out before the people of Israel.

FEAR COMES WHEN WE
DEPART FROM TRUTH, SERVICE,
PEACE, FREEDOM AND LOVE.

[25] In the fifth year of King Rehoboam, King Shishak of Egypt came up against Jerusalem; [26]he took away the treasures of the house of the LORD and the treasures of the king's house; he took everything. He also took away all the shields of gold that Solomon had made; [27]so King Rehoboam made shields of bronze instead, and committed them to the hands of the officers of the guard, who kept the door of the king's house. [28]As often as the king went into the house of the LORD, the guard carried them and brought them back to the guardroom.

[29] Now the rest of the acts of Rehoboam, and all that he did, are they not written in the Book of the Annals of the Kings of Judah? [30]There was war between Rehoboam and

[a] 14.14 Meaning of Heb uncertain
[b] 14.15,23 Heb Asherim

Jeroboam continually. ³¹Rehoboam slept with his ancestors and was buried with his ancestors in the city of David. His mother's name was Naamah the Ammonite. His son Abijam succeeded him.

ABIJAM REIGNS OVER JUDAH: IDOLATRY AND WAR

15 Now in the eighteenth year of King Jeroboam son of Nebat, Abijam began to reign over Judah. ²He reigned for three years in Jerusalem. His mother's name was Maacah daughter of Abishalom. ³He committed all the sins that his father did before him; his heart was not true to the LORD his God, like the heart of his father David. ⁴Nevertheless for David's sake the LORD his God gave him a lamp in Jerusalem, setting up his son after him, and establishing Jerusalem; ⁵because David did what was right in the sight of the LORD, and did not turn aside from anything that he commanded him all the days of his life, except in the matter of Uriah the Hittite. ⁶The war begun between Rehoboam and Jeroboam continued all the days of his life. ⁷The rest of the acts of Abijam, and all that he did, are they not written in the Book of the Annals of the Kings of Judah? There was war between Abijam and Jeroboam. ⁸Abijam slept with his ancestors, and they buried him in the city of David. Then his son Asa succeeded him.

ASA REIGNS OVER JUDAH

⁹In the twentieth year of King Jeroboam of Israel, Asa began to reign over Judah; ¹⁰he reigned forty-one years in Jerusalem. His mother's name was Maacah daughter of Abishalom. ¹¹Asa did what was right in the sight of the LORD, as his father David had done. ¹²He put away the male temple prostitutes out of the land, and removed all the idols that his ancestors had made. ¹³He also removed his mother Maacah from being queen mother, because she had made an abominable image for Asherah; Asa cut down her image and burned it

at the Wadi Kidron. ¹⁴But the high places were not taken away. Nevertheless the heart of Asa was true to the LORD all his days. ¹⁵He brought into the house of the LORD the votive gifts of his father and his own votive gifts—silver, gold, and utensils.

ALLIANCE WITH ARAM AGAINST ISRAEL

¹⁶There was war between Asa and King Baasha of Israel all their days. ¹⁷King Baasha of Israel went up against Judah, and built Ramah, to prevent anyone from going out or coming in to King Asa of Judah. ¹⁸Then Asa took all the silver and the gold that were left in the treasures of the house of the LORD and the treasures of the king's house, and gave them into the hands of his servants. King Asa sent them to King Ben-hadad son of Tabrimmon son of Hezion of Aram, who resided in Damascus, saying, ¹⁹"Let there be an alliance between me and you, like that between my father and your father: I am sending you a present of silver and gold; go, break your alliance with King Baasha of Israel, so that he may withdraw from me." ²⁰Ben-hadad listened to King Asa, and sent the commanders of his armies against the cities of Israel. He conquered Ijon, Dan, Abel-beth-maacah, and all Chinneroth, with all the land of Naphtali. ²¹When Baasha heard of it, he stopped building Ramah and lived in Tirzah. ²²Then King Asa made a proclamation to all Judah, none was exempt: they carried away the stones of Ramah and its timber, with which Baasha had been building; with them King Asa built Geba of Benjamin and Mizpah. ²³Now the rest of all the acts of Asa, all his power, all that he did, and the cities that he built, are they not written in the Book of the Annals of the Kings of Judah? But in his old age he was diseased in his feet. ²⁴Then Asa slept with his ancestors, and was buried with his ancestors in the city of his father David; his son Jehoshaphat succeeded him.

NADAB REIGNS OVER ISRAEL

25 Nadab son of Jeroboam began to reign over Israel in the second year of King Asa of Judah; he reigned over Israel two years. 26He did what was evil in the sight of the LORD, walking in the way of his ancestor and in the sin that he caused Israel to commit.

27 Baasha son of Ahijah, of the house of Issachar, conspired against him; and Baasha struck him down at Gibbethon, which belonged to the Philistines; for Nadab and all Israel were laying siege to Gibbethon. 28So Baasha killed Nadab[a] in the third year of King Asa of Judah, and succeeded him. 29As soon as he was king, he killed all the house of Jeroboam; he left to the house of Jeroboam not one that breathed, until he had destroyed it, according to the word of the LORD that he spoke by his servant Ahijah the Shilonite— 30because of the sins of Jeroboam that he committed and that he caused Israel to commit, and because of the anger to which he provoked the LORD, the God of Israel.

31 Now the rest of the acts of Nadab, and all that he did, are they not written in the Book of the Annals of the Kings of Israel? 32There was war between Asa and King Baasha of Israel all their days.

SECOND DYNASTY: BAASHA REIGNS OVER ISRAEL

33 In the third year of King Asa of Judah, Baasha son of Ahijah began to reign over all Israel at Tirzah; he reigned twenty-four years. 34He did what was evil in the sight of the LORD, walking in the way of Jeroboam and in the sin that he caused Israel to commit.

16 The word of the LORD came to Jehu son of Hanani against Baasha, saying, 2"Since I exalted you out of the dust and made you leader over my people Israel, and you have walked in the way of Jeroboam, and have caused my people Israel to sin, provoking me to anger with their sins, 3therefore, I will consume Baasha and his house, and I will make your house like the house of Jeroboam son of Nebat. 4Anyone belonging to Baasha who dies in the city the dogs shall eat; and anyone of his who dies in the field the birds of the air shall eat."

5 Now the rest of the acts of Baasha, what he did, and his power, are they not written in the Book of the Annals of the Kings of Israel? 6Baasha slept with his ancestors, and was buried at Tirzah; and his son Elah succeeded him. 7Moreover the word of the LORD came by the prophet Jehu son of Hanani against Baasha and his house, both because of all the evil that he did in the sight of the LORD, provoking him to anger with the work of his hands, in being like the house of Jeroboam, and also because he destroyed it.

IT IS DIFFICULT TO SEPARATE CORPORATE GUILT FROM INDIVIDUAL GUILT. WE CONTRIBUTE TO BOTH AND ARE AFFECTED BY BOTH.

ELAH REIGNS OVER ISRAEL

8 In the twenty-sixth year of King Asa of Judah, Elah son of Baasha began to reign over Israel in Tirzah; he reigned two years. 9But his servant Zimri, commander of half his chariots, conspired against him. When he was at Tirzah, drinking himself drunk in the house of Arza, who was in charge of the palace at Tirzah, 10Zimri came in and struck him down and killed him, in the twenty-seventh year of King Asa of Judah, and succeeded him.

11When he began to reign, as soon as he had seated himself on his throne, he killed all the house of Baasha; he did not leave him a single male of his kindred or his friends. 12Thus Zimri destroyed all the house

a 15.28 Heb *him*

of Baasha, according to the word of the LORD, which he spoke against Baasha by the prophet Jehu— [13]because of all the sins of Baasha and the sins of his son Elah that they committed, and that they caused Israel to commit, provoking the LORD God of Israel to anger with their idols. [14]Now the rest of the acts of Elah, and all that he did, are they not written in the Book of the Annals of the Kings of Israel?

THIRD DYNASTY: ZIMRI REIGNS OVER ISRAEL

15 In the twenty-seventh year of King Asa of Judah, Zimri reigned seven days in Tirzah. Now the troops were encamped against Gibbethon, which belonged to the Philistines, [16]and the troops who were encamped heard it said, "Zimri has conspired, and he has killed the king"; therefore all Israel made Omri, the commander of the army, king over Israel that day in the camp. [17]So Omri went up from Gibbethon, and all Israel with him, and they besieged Tirzah. [18]When Zimri saw that the city was taken, he went into the citadel of the king's house; he burned down the king's house over himself with fire, and died— [19]because of the sins that he committed, doing evil in the sight of the LORD, walking in the way of Jeroboam, and for the sin that he committed, causing Israel to sin. [20]Now the rest of the acts of Zimri, and the conspiracy that he made, are they not written in the Book of the Annals of the Kings of Israel?

FOURTH DYNASTY: OMRI REIGNS OVER ISRAEL

21 Then the people of Israel were divided into two parts; half of the people followed Tibni son of Ginath, to make him king, and half followed Omri. [22]But the people who followed Omri overcame the people who followed Tibni son of Ginath; so Tibni died, and Omri became king. [23]In the thirty-first year of King Asa of Judah, Omri began to reign over Israel; he reigned for twelve years, six of them in Tirzah.

SAMARIA THE NEW CAPITAL

24 He bought the hill of Samaria from Shemer for two talents of silver; he fortified the hill, and called the city that he built, Samaria, after the name of Shemer, the owner of the hill.

25 Omri did what was evil in the sight of the LORD; he did more evil than all who were before him. [26]For he walked in all the way of Jeroboam son of Nebat, and in the sins that he caused Israel to commit, provoking the LORD, the God of Israel, to anger by their idols. [27]Now the rest of the acts of Omri that he did, and the power that he showed, are they not written in the Book of the Annals of the Kings of Israel? [28]Omri slept with his ancestors, and was buried in Samaria; his son Ahab succeeded him.

AHAB REIGNS OVER ISRAEL

29 In the thirty-eighth year of King Asa of Judah, Ahab son of Omri began to reign over Israel; Ahab son of Omri reigned over Israel in Samaria twenty-two years. [30]Ahab son of Omri did evil in the sight of the LORD more than all who were before him.

AHAB MARRIES JEZEBEL AND WORSHIPS BAAL

31 And as if it had been a light thing for him to walk in the sins of Jeroboam son of Nebat, he took as his wife Jezebel daughter of King Ethbaal of the Sidonians, and went and served Baal, and worshiped him. [32]He erected an altar for Baal in the house of Baal, which he built in Samaria. [33]Ahab also made a sacred pole.[a] Ahab did more to provoke the anger of the LORD, the God of Israel, than had all the kings of Israel who were before him. [34]In his days Hiel of Bethel built Jericho; he laid its foundation at the cost of Abiram his firstborn, and set up its gates at the cost of his youngest son Segub, according to the word of the LORD, which he spoke by Joshua son of Nun.

[a] 16.33 Heb *Asherah*

ELIJAH PREDICTS A DROUGHT

17 Now Elijah the Tishbite, of Tishbe[a] in Gilead, said to Ahab, "As the LORD the God of Israel lives, before whom I stand, there shall be neither dew nor rain these years, except by my word." ²The word of the LORD came to him, saying, ³"Go from here and turn eastward, and hide yourself by the Wadi Cherith, which is east of the Jordan. ⁴You shall drink from the wadi, and I have commanded the ravens to feed you there." ⁵So he went and did according to the word of the LORD; he went and lived by the Wadi Cherith, which is east of the Jordan. ⁶The ravens brought him bread and meat in the morning, and bread and meat in the evening; and he drank from the wadi. ⁷But after a while the wadi dried up, because there was no rain in the land.

THE WIDOW OF ZAREPHATH

8 Then the word of the LORD came to him, saying, ⁹"Go now to Zarephath, which belongs to Sidon, and live there; for I have commanded a widow there to feed you." ¹⁰So he set out and went to Zarephath. When he came to the gate of the town, a widow was there gathering sticks; he called to her and said, "Bring me a little water in a vessel, so that I may drink." ¹¹As she was going to bring it, he called to her and said, "Bring me a morsel of bread in your hand." ¹²But she said, "As the LORD your God lives, I have nothing baked, only a handful of meal in a jar, and a little oil in a jug; I am now gathering a couple of sticks, so that I may go home and prepare it for myself and my son, that we may eat it, and die." ¹³Elijah said to her, "Do not be afraid; go and do as you have said; but first make me a little cake of it and bring it to me, and afterwards make something for yourself and your son. ¹⁴For thus says the LORD the God of Israel: The jar of meal will not be emptied and the jug of oil will not fail until the day that the LORD sends rain on the earth." ¹⁵She went and did as Elijah said, so that she as well as he and her household ate for many days. ¹⁶The jar of meal was not emptied, neither did the jug of oil fail, according to the word of the LORD that he spoke by Elijah.

ELIJAH REVIVES THE WIDOW'S SON

17 After this the son of the woman, the mistress of the house, became ill; his illness was so severe that there was no breath left in him. ¹⁸She then said to Elijah, "What have you against me, O man

a **17.1** Gk: Heb *of the settlers*

BIBLE IN LIFE

Generous Giving

1 Kings 17.1–16

We are asked to give generously to others, just as the widow at Zarephath was asked to give all she had to feed Elijah. We are asked to give money, or material items, or food, or our time or our talents. It is not the *amount* that is important, though. Many of us don't have much money to give, but Christ has blessed us with adequate talent, opportunities and resources to do transcendent things. Following the metaphor of this story, we shouldn't carry around what we are and what we have in a closed jar, using a medicine dropper to expend it. Unfortunately, that's the way we ordinarily share our resources. We don't want to risk giving away too much, so we pass it out a little at a time, making sure we always have more than we need, on which we can depend in an emergency. We should be reminded of this story and consider what God has done and can do through us. We underestimate the gifts that we have received from God: life, talents, abilities, knowledge, freedom and influence. All that we have comes from God. We must be sensitive to God's call to give extravagantly, to give what we have for God's glory and not for our own.

of God? You have come to me to bring my sin to remembrance, and to cause the death of my son!" ¹⁹But he said to her, "Give me your son." He took him from her bosom, carried him up into the upper chamber where he was lodging, and laid him on his own bed. ²⁰He cried out to the LORD, "O LORD my God, have you brought calamity even upon the widow with whom I am staying, by killing her son?" ²¹Then he stretched himself upon the child three times, and cried out to the LORD, "O LORD my God, let this child's life come into him again." ²²The LORD listened to the voice of Elijah; the life of the child came into him again, and he revived. ²³Elijah took the child, brought him down from the upper chamber into the house, and gave him to his mother; then Elijah said, "See, your son is alive." ²⁴So the woman said to Elijah, "Now I know that you are a man of God, and that the word of the LORD in your mouth is truth."

ELIJAH'S MESSAGE TO AHAB

18 After many days the word of the LORD came to Elijah, in the third year of the drought,ᵃ saying, "Go, present yourself to Ahab; I will send rain on the earth." ²So Elijah went to present himself to Ahab. The famine was severe in Samaria. ³Ahab summoned Obadiah, who was in charge of the palace. (Now Obadiah revered the LORD greatly; ⁴when Jezebel was killing off the prophets of the LORD, Obadiah took a hundred prophets, hid them fifty to a cave, and provided them with bread and water.) ⁵Then Ahab said to Obadiah, "Go through the land to all the springs of water and to all the wadis; perhaps we may find grass to keep the horses and mules alive, and not lose some of the animals." ⁶So they divided the land between them to pass through it; Ahab went in one direction by himself, and Obadiah went in another direction by himself.

⁷As Obadiah was on the way, Elijah met him; Obadiah recognized him, fell on his face, and said, "Is it you, my lord Elijah?" ⁸He answered

him, "It is I. Go, tell your lord that Elijah is here." ⁹And he said, "How have I sinned, that you would hand your servant over to Ahab, to kill me? ¹⁰As the LORD your God lives, there is no nation or kingdom to which my lord has not sent to seek you; and when they would say, 'He is not here,' he would require an oath of the kingdom or nation, that they had not found you. ¹¹But now you say, 'Go, tell your lord that Elijah is here.' ¹²As soon as I have gone from you, the spirit of the LORD will carry you I know not where; so, when I come and tell Ahab and he cannot find you, he will kill me, although I your servant have revered the LORD from my youth. ¹³Has it not been told my lord what I did when Jezebel killed the prophets of the LORD, how I hid a hundred of the LORD's prophets fifty to a cave, and provided them with bread and water? ¹⁴Yet now you say, 'Go, tell your lord that Elijah is here'; he will surely kill me." ¹⁵Elijah said, "As the LORD of hosts lives, before whom I stand, I will surely show myself to him today." ¹⁶So Obadiah went to meet Ahab, and told him; and Ahab went to meet Elijah.

¹⁷When Ahab saw Elijah, Ahab said to him, "Is it you, you troubler of Israel?" ¹⁸He answered, "I have not troubled Israel; but you have, and your father's house, because you have forsaken the commandments of the LORD and followed the Baals. ¹⁹Now therefore have all Israel assemble for me at Mount Carmel, with the four hundred fifty prophets of Baal and the four hundred prophets of Asherah, who eat at Jezebel's table."

ELIJAH'S TRIUMPH OVER THE PRIESTS OF BAAL

20 So Ahab sent to all the Israelites, and assembled the prophets at Mount Carmel. ²¹Elijah then came near to all the people, and said, "How long will you go limping with two different opinions? If the LORD is God, follow him; but if Baal, then follow him." The people did not answer him a word. ²²Then Elijah

---

ᵃ **18.1** Heb lacks *of the drought*

said to the people, "I, even I only, am left a prophet of the LORD; but Baal's prophets number four hundred fifty. 23Let two bulls be given to us; let them choose one bull for themselves, cut it in pieces, and lay it on the wood, but put no fire to it; I will prepare the other bull and lay it on the wood, but put no fire to it. 24Then you call on the name of your god and I will call on the name of the LORD; the god who answers by fire is indeed God." All the people answered, "Well spoken!" 25Then Elijah said to the prophets of Baal, "Choose for yourselves one bull and prepare it first, for you are many; then call on the name of your god, but put no fire to it." 26So they took the bull that was given them, prepared it, and called on the name of Baal from morning until noon, crying, "O Baal, answer us!" But there was no voice, and no answer. They limped about the altar that they had made. 27At noon Elijah mocked them, saying, "Cry aloud! Surely he is a god; either he is meditating, or he has wandered away, or he is on a journey, or perhaps he is asleep and must be awakened." 28Then they cried aloud and, as was their custom, they cut themselves with swords and lances until the blood gushed out over them. 29As midday passed, they raved on until the time of the offering of the oblation, but there was no voice, no answer, and no response.

30 Then Elijah said to all the people, "Come closer to me"; and all the people came closer to him. First he repaired the altar of the LORD that had been thrown down; 31Elijah took twelve stones, according to the number of the tribes of the sons of Jacob, to whom the word of the LORD came, saying, "Israel shall be your name"; 32with the stones he built an altar in the name of the LORD. Then he made a trench around the altar, large enough to contain two measures of seed. 33Next he put the wood in order, cut the bull in pieces, and laid it on the wood. He said, "Fill four jars with water and pour it on the burnt offering and on the wood." 34Then he said, "Do it a second

time"; and they did it a second time. Again he said, "Do it a third time"; and they did it a third time, 35so that the water ran all around the altar, and filled the trench also with water.

36 At the time of the offering of the oblation, the prophet Elijah came near and said, "O LORD, God of Abraham, Isaac, and Israel, let it be known this day that you are God in Israel, that I am your servant, and that I have done all these things at your bidding. 37Answer me, O LORD, answer me, so that this people may know that you, O LORD, are God, and that you have turned their hearts back." 38Then the fire of the LORD fell and consumed the burnt offering, the wood, the stones, and the dust, and even licked up the water that was in the trench. 39When all the people saw it, they fell on their faces and said, "The LORD indeed is God; the LORD indeed is God." 40Elijah said to them, "Seize the prophets of Baal; do not

PONDER

When all the people saw it, they fell on their faces and said, "The LORD indeed is God; the LORD indeed is God."
—1 Kings 18.39

PRAY

Father, give us the courage, strength and wisdom to understand how we might meet the challenges life brings us in the bold and faithful way that Elijah did. We know that we are not strong enough to do this on our own and that we need to submit ourselves completely to your guidance and direction. Help us to orient our thoughts, commitments and priorities toward being your true followers. Forgive us our many sins. We put ourselves in your hands, in the wonderful and exhilarating grace and love of our Savior, Jesus Christ. In his name we pray. Amen.

let one of them escape." Then they seized them; and Elijah brought them down to the Wadi Kishon, and killed them there.

THE DROUGHT ENDS

41 Elijah said to Ahab, "Go up, eat and drink; for there is a sound of rushing rain." 42So Ahab went up to eat and to drink. Elijah went up to the top of Carmel; there he bowed himself down upon the earth and put his face between his knees. 43He said to his servant, "Go up now, look toward the sea." He went up and looked, and said, "There is nothing." Then he said, "Go again seven times." 44At the seventh time he said, "Look, a little cloud no bigger than a person's hand is rising out of the sea." Then he said, "Go say to Ahab, 'Harness your chariot and go down before the rain stops you.' " 45In a little while the heavens grew black with clouds and wind; there was a heavy rain. Ahab rode off and went to Jezreel. 46But the hand of the LORD was on Elijah; he girded up his loins and ran in front of Ahab to the entrance of Jezreel.

ELIJAH FLEES FROM JEZEBEL

19 Ahab told Jezebel all that Elijah had done, and how he had killed all the prophets with the sword. 2Then Jezebel sent a messenger to Elijah, saying, "So may the gods do to me, and more also, if I do not make your life like the life of one of them by this time tomorrow." 3Then he was afraid; he got up and fled for his life, and came to Beersheba, which belongs to Judah; he left his servant there.

4 But he himself went a day's journey into the wilderness, and came and sat down under a solitary broom tree. He asked that he might die: "It is enough; now, O LORD, take away my life, for I am no better than my ancestors." 5Then he lay down under the broom tree and fell asleep. Suddenly an angel touched him and said to him, "Get up and eat." 6He looked, and there at his head was a cake baked on hot stones, and a jar of water. He ate and drank, and lay down again. 7The angel of the LORD came a second time, touched him, and said, "Get up and eat, otherwise the journey will be too much for you." 8He got up, and ate and drank; then he went in the strength of that food forty days and forty nights to Horeb the mount of God. 9At that place he came to a cave, and spent the night there.

Then the word of the LORD came to him, saying, "What are you doing here, Elijah?" 10He answered, "I have been very zealous for the LORD, the God of hosts; for the Israelites have forsaken your covenant, thrown down your altars, and killed your prophets with the sword. I alone am left, and they are seeking my life, to take it away."

ELIJAH MEETS GOD AT HOREB

11 He said, "Go out and stand on the mountain before the LORD, for the LORD is about to pass by." Now there was a great wind, so strong that it was splitting mountains and breaking rocks in pieces before the LORD, but the LORD was not in the wind; and after the wind an earthquake, but the LORD was not in the earthquake; 12and after the earthquake a fire, but the LORD was not in the fire; and after the fire a sound of sheer silence. 13When Elijah heard it, he wrapped his face in his mantle and went out and stood at the entrance of the cave. Then there came a voice to him that said, "What are you doing here, Elijah?" 14He answered, "I have been very zealous for the LORD, the God of hosts; for the Israelites have forsaken your covenant, thrown down your altars, and killed your prophets with the sword. I alone am left, and they are seeking my life, to take it away." 15Then the LORD said to him, "Go, return on your way to the wilderness of Damascus; when you arrive, you shall anoint Hazael as king over Aram. 16Also you shall anoint Jehu son of Nimshi as king over Israel; and you shall anoint Elisha son of Shaphat of Abel-meholah as prophet in your place. 17Whoever escapes from the sword of Hazael, Jehu shall kill; and

whoever escapes from the sword of Jehu, Elisha shall kill. ¹⁸ Yet I will leave seven thousand in Israel, all the knees that have not bowed to Baal, and every mouth that has not kissed him."

───────⊕───────

PONDER

After the fire [there was] a sound of sheer silence. When Elijah heard it, he wrapped his face in his mantle and went out and stood at the entrance of the cave.
—1 Kings 19.12–13

PRAY

O Father, we struggle with doubt and questions as we search for truth in the Bible. Help us to listen for your gentle whisper calling us to listen to you and commune with you. We ask that you give us wisdom, insight, and above all, humility. Give us the desire to eagerly follow you. And let us realize that we are bound to our brothers and sisters in the kind of love that glorifies you because you are love. These things we pray in the name of our Savior, Jesus Christ. Amen.

───────⊘───────

ELISHA BECOMES ELIJAH'S DISCIPLE

19 So he set out from there, and found Elisha son of Shaphat, who was plowing. There were twelve yoke of oxen ahead of him, and he was with the twelfth. Elijah passed by him and threw his mantle over him. ²⁰ He left the oxen, ran after Elijah, and said, "Let me kiss my father and my mother, and then I will follow you." Then Elijah[a] said to him, "Go back again; for what have I done to you?" ²¹ He returned from following him, took the yoke of oxen, and slaughtered them; using the equipment from the oxen, he boiled their flesh, and gave it to the people, and they ate. Then he set out and followed Elijah, and became his servant.

AHAB'S WARS WITH THE ARAMEANS

20 King Ben-hadad of Aram gathered all his army together; thirty-two kings were with him, along with horses and chariots. He marched against Samaria, laid siege to it, and attacked it. ² Then he sent messengers into the city to King Ahab of Israel, and said to him: "Thus says Ben-hadad: ³ Your silver and gold are mine; your fairest wives and children also are mine." ⁴ The king of Israel answered, "As you say, my lord, O king, I am yours, and all that I have." ⁵ The messengers came again and said: "Thus says Ben-hadad: I sent to you, saying, 'Deliver to me your silver and gold, your wives and children'; ⁶ nevertheless I will send my servants to you tomorrow about this time, and they shall search your house and the houses of your servants, and lay hands on whatever pleases them,[b] and take it away."

⁷ Then the king of Israel called all the elders of the land, and said, "Look now! See how this man is seeking trouble; for he sent to me for my wives, my children, my silver, and my gold; and I did not refuse him." ⁸ Then all the elders and all the people said to him, "Do not listen or consent." ⁹ So he said to the messengers of Ben-hadad, "Tell my lord the king: All that you first demanded of your servant I will do; but this thing I cannot do." The messengers left and brought him word again. ¹⁰ Ben-hadad sent to him and said, "The gods do so to me, and more also, if the dust of Samaria will provide a handful for each of the people who follow me." ¹¹ The king of Israel answered, "Tell him: One who puts on armor should not brag like one who takes it off." ¹² When Ben-hadad heard this message—now he had been drinking with the kings in the booths—he said to his men, "Take your positions!" And they took positions against the city.

[a] **19.20** Heb *he*   [b] **20.6** Gk Syr Vg: Heb *you*

PROPHETIC OPPOSITION TO AHAB

13 Then a certain prophet came up to King Ahab of Israel and said, "Thus says the LORD, Have you seen all this great multitude? Look, I will give it into your hand today; and you shall know that I am the LORD." 14 Ahab said, "By whom?" He said, "Thus says the LORD, By the young men who serve the district governors." Then he said, "Who shall begin the battle?" He answered, "You." 15 Then he mustered the young men who served the district governors, two hundred thirty-two; after them he mustered all the people of Israel, seven thousand.

16 They went out at noon, while Ben-hadad was drinking himself drunk in the booths, he and the thirty-two kings allied with him. 17 The young men who served the district governors went out first. Ben-hadad had sent out scouts,[a] and they reported to him, "Men have come out from Samaria." 18 He said, "If they have come out for peace, take them alive; if they have come out for war, take them alive."

ON WHAT OCCASIONS DO

WE PASS UNAWARE OF THE

PRESENCE OF CHRIST?

19 But these had already come out of the city: the young men who served the district governors, and the army that followed them. 20 Each killed his man; the Arameans fled and Israel pursued them, but King Ben-hadad of Aram escaped on a horse with the cavalry. 21 The king of Israel went out, attacked the horses and chariots, and defeated the Arameans with a great slaughter.

22 Then the prophet approached the king of Israel and said to him, "Come, strengthen yourself, and consider well what you have to do; for in the spring the king of Aram will come up against you."

THE ARAMEANS ARE DEFEATED

23 The servants of the king of Aram said to him, "Their gods are gods of the hills, and so they were stronger than we; but let us fight against them in the plain, and surely we shall be stronger than they. 24 Also do this: remove the kings, each from his post, and put commanders in place of them; 25 and muster an army like the army that you have lost, horse for horse, and chariot for chariot; then we will fight against them in the plain, and surely we shall be stronger than they." He heeded their voice, and did so.

26 In the spring Ben-hadad mustered the Arameans and went up to Aphek to fight against Israel. 27 After the Israelites had been mustered and provisioned, they went out to engage them; the people of Israel encamped opposite them like two little flocks of goats, while the Arameans filled the country. 28 A man of God approached and said to the king of Israel, "Thus says the LORD: Because the Arameans have said, 'The LORD is a god of the hills but he is not a god of the valleys,' therefore I will give all this great multitude into your hand, and you shall know that I am the LORD." 29 They encamped opposite one another seven days. Then on the seventh day the battle began; the Israelites killed one hundred thousand Aramean foot soldiers in one day. 30 The rest fled into the city of Aphek; and the wall fell on twenty-seven thousand men that were left.

Ben-hadad also fled, and entered the city to hide. 31 His servants said to him, "Look, we have heard that the kings of the house of Israel are merciful kings; let us put sackcloth around our waists and ropes on our heads, and go out to the king of Israel; perhaps he will spare your life." 32 So they tied sackcloth around their waists, put ropes on their

a 20.17 Heb lacks scouts

heads, went to the king of Israel, and said, "Your servant Ben-hadad says, 'Please let me live.' " And he said, "Is he still alive? He is my brother." ³³Now the men were watching for an omen; they quickly took it up from him and said, "Yes, Ben-hadad is your brother." Then he said, "Go and bring him." So Ben-hadad came out to him; and he had him come up into the chariot. ³⁴Ben-hadadᵃ said to him, "I will restore the towns that my father took from your father; and you may establish bazaars for yourself in Damascus, as my father did in Samaria." The king of Israel responded,ᵇ "I will let you go on those terms." So he made a treaty with him and let him go.

A PROPHET CONDEMNS AHAB

35 At the command of the LORD a certain member of a company of prophetsᶜ said to another, "Strike me!" But the man refused to strike him. ³⁶Then he said to him, "Because you have not obeyed the voice of the LORD, as soon as you have left me, a lion will kill you." And when he had left him, a lion met him and killed him. ³⁷Then he found another man and said, "Strike me!" So the man hit him, striking and wounding him. ³⁸Then the prophet departed, and waited for the king along the road, disguising himself with a bandage over his eyes. ³⁹As the king passed by, he cried to the king and said, "Your servant went out into the thick of the battle; then a soldier turned and brought a man to me, and said, 'Guard this man; if he is missing, your life shall be given for his life, or else you shall pay a talent of silver.' ⁴⁰While your servant was busy here and there, he was gone." The king of Israel said to him, "So shall your judgment be; you yourself have decided it." ⁴¹Then he quickly took the bandage away from his eyes. The king of Israel recognized him as one of the prophets. ⁴²Then he said to him, "Thus says the LORD, 'Because you have let the man go whom I had devoted to destruction, therefore your life shall be for his life, and your people for his

people.' " ⁴³The king of Israel set out toward home, resentful and sullen, and came to Samaria.

NABOTH'S VINEYARD

21 Later the following events took place: Naboth the Jezreelite had a vineyard in Jezreel, beside the palace of King Ahab of Samaria. ²And Ahab said to Naboth, "Give me your vineyard, so that I may have it for a vegetable garden, because it is near my house; I will give you a better vineyard for it; or, if it seems good to you, I will give you its value in money." ³But Naboth said to Ahab, "The LORD forbid that I should give you my ancestral inheritance." ⁴Ahab went home resentful and sullen because of what Naboth the Jezreelite had said to him; for he had said, "I will not give you my ancestral inheritance." He lay down on his bed, turned away his face, and would not eat.

AVARICE COMES FROM WANTING MORE. ANXIETY COMES WHEN WE THINK WE REALLY NEED MORE.

⁵His wife Jezebel came to him and said, "Why are you so depressed that you will not eat?" ⁶He said to her, "Because I spoke to Naboth the Jezreelite and said to him, 'Give me your vineyard for money; or else, if you prefer, I will give you another vineyard for it'; but he answered, 'I will not give you my vineyard.' " ⁷His wife Jezebel said to him, "Do you now govern Israel? Get up, eat some food, and be cheerful; I will give you the vineyard of Naboth the Jezreelite."

ᵃ **20.34** Heb *He*   ᵇ **20.34** Heb lacks *The king of Israel responded*   ᶜ **20.35** Heb *of the sons of the prophets*

8 So she wrote letters in Ahab's name and sealed them with his seal; she sent the letters to the elders and the nobles who lived with Naboth in his city. **9** She wrote in the letters, "Proclaim a fast, and seat Naboth at the head of the assembly; **10** seat two scoundrels opposite him, and have them bring a charge against him, saying, 'You have cursed God and the king.' Then take him out, and stone him to death." **11** The men of his city, the elders and the nobles who lived in his city, did as Jezebel had sent word to them. Just as it was written in the letters that she had sent to them, **12** they proclaimed a fast and seated Naboth at the head of the assembly. **13** The two scoundrels came in and sat opposite him; and the scoundrels brought a charge against Naboth, in the presence of the people, saying, "Naboth cursed God and the king." So they took him outside the city, and stoned him to death. **14** Then they sent to Jezebel, saying, "Naboth has been stoned; he is dead."

15 As soon as Jezebel heard that Naboth had been stoned and was dead, Jezebel said to Ahab, "Go, take possession of the vineyard of Naboth the Jezreelite, which he refused to give you for money; for Naboth is not alive, but dead." **16** As soon as Ahab heard that Naboth was dead, Ahab set out to go down to the vineyard of Naboth the Jezreelite, to take possession of it.

ELIJAH PRONOUNCES GOD'S SENTENCE

17 Then the word of the LORD came to Elijah the Tishbite, saying: **18** Go down to meet King Ahab of Israel, who rules[a] in Samaria; he is now in the vineyard of Naboth, where he has gone to take possession. **19** You shall say to him, "Thus says the LORD: Have you killed, and also taken possession?" You shall say to him, "Thus says the LORD: In the place where dogs licked up the blood of Naboth, dogs will also lick up your blood."

20 Ahab said to Elijah, "Have you found me, O my enemy?" He an-

swered, "I have found you. Because you have sold yourself to do what is evil in the sight of the LORD, **21** I will bring disaster on you; I will consume you, and will cut off from Ahab every male, bond or free, in Israel; **22** and I will make your house like the house of Jeroboam son of Nebat, and like the house of Baasha son of Ahijah, because you have provoked me to anger and have caused Israel to sin. **23** Also concerning Jezebel the LORD said, 'The dogs shall eat Jezebel within the bounds of Jezreel.' **24** Anyone belonging to Ahab who dies in the city the dogs shall eat; and anyone of his who dies in the open country the birds of the air shall eat."

25 (Indeed, there was no one like Ahab, who sold himself to do what was evil in the sight of the LORD, urged on by his wife Jezebel. **26** He acted most abominably in going after idols, as the Amorites had done, whom the LORD drove out before the Israelites.)

27 When Ahab heard those words, he tore his clothes and put sackcloth over his bare flesh; he fasted, lay in the sackcloth, and went about dejectedly. **28** Then the word of the LORD came to Elijah the Tishbite: **29** "Have you seen how Ahab has humbled himself before me? Because he has humbled himself before me, I will not bring the disaster in his days; but in his son's days I will bring the disaster on his house."

JOINT CAMPAIGN WITH JUDAH AGAINST ARAM

22 For three years Aram and Israel continued without war. **2** But in the third year King Jehoshaphat of Judah came down to the king of Israel. **3** The king of Israel said to his servants, "Do you know that Ramoth-gilead belongs to us, yet we are doing nothing to take it out of the hand of the king of Aram?" **4** He said to Jehoshaphat, "Will you go with me to battle at Ramoth-gilead?" Jehoshaphat replied to the king of Israel, "I am as you are; my

[a] 21.18 Heb *who is*

people are your people, my horses are your horses."

5 But Jehoshaphat also said to the king of Israel, "Inquire first for the word of the LORD." 6Then the king of Israel gathered the prophets together, about four hundred of them, and said to them, "Shall I go to battle against Ramoth-gilead, or shall I refrain?" They said, "Go up; for the LORD will give it into the hand of the king." 7But Jehoshaphat said, "Is there no other prophet of the LORD here of whom we may inquire?" 8The king of Israel said to Jehoshaphat, "There is still one other by whom we may inquire of the LORD, Micaiah son of Imlah; but I hate him, for he never prophesies anything favorable about me, but only disaster." Jehoshaphat said, "Let the king not say such a thing." 9Then the king of Israel summoned an officer and said, "Bring quickly Micaiah son of Imlah." 10Now the king of Israel and King Jehoshaphat of Judah were sitting on their thrones, arrayed in their robes, at the threshing floor at the entrance of the gate of Samaria; and all the prophets were prophesying before them. 11Zedekiah son of Chenaanah made for himself horns of iron, and he said, "Thus says the LORD: With these you shall gore the Arameans until they are destroyed." 12All the prophets were prophesying the same and saying, "Go up to Ramoth-gilead and triumph; the LORD will give it into the hand of the king."

MICAIAH PREDICTS FAILURE

13 The messenger who had gone to summon Micaiah said to him, "Look, the words of the prophets with one accord are favorable to the king; let your word be like the word of one of them, and speak favorably." 14But Micaiah said, "As the LORD lives, whatever the LORD says to me, that I will speak."

15 When he had come to the king, the king said to him, "Micaiah, shall we go to Ramoth-gilead to battle, or shall we refrain?" He answered him, "Go up and triumph; the LORD will give it into the hand of the king." 16But the king said to him, "How many times must I make you swear to tell me nothing but the truth in the name of the LORD?" 17Then Micaiah[a] said, "I saw all Israel scattered on the mountains, like sheep that have no shepherd; and the LORD said, 'These have no master; let each one go home in peace.'" 18The king of Israel said to Jehoshaphat, "Did I not tell you that he would not prophesy anything favorable about me, but only disaster?"

19 Then Micaiah[a] said, "Therefore hear the word of the LORD: I saw the LORD sitting on his throne, with all the host of heaven standing beside him to the right and to the left of him. 20And the LORD said, 'Who will entice Ahab, so that he may go up and fall at Ramoth-gilead?' Then one said one thing, and another said another, 21until a spirit came forward and stood before the LORD, saying, 'I will entice him.' 22'How?' the LORD asked him. He replied, 'I will go out and be a lying spirit in the mouth of all his prophets.' Then the LORD[a] said, 'You are to entice him, and you shall succeed; go out and do it.' 23So you see, the LORD has put a lying spirit in the mouth of all these your prophets; the LORD has decreed disaster for you."

24 Then Zedekiah son of Chenaanah came up to Micaiah, slapped him on the cheek, and said, "Which way did the spirit of the LORD pass from me to speak to you?" 25Micaiah replied, "You will find out on that day when you go in to hide in an inner chamber." 26The king of Israel then ordered, "Take Micaiah, and return him to Amon the governor of the city and to Joash the king's son, 27and say, 'Thus says the king: Put this fellow in prison, and feed him on reduced rations of bread and water until I come in peace.'" 28Micaiah said, "If you return in peace, the LORD has not spoken by me." And he said, "Hear, you peoples, all of you!"

DEFEAT AND DEATH OF AHAB

29 So the king of Israel and King Jehoshaphat of Judah went up to

[a] 22.17,19,22 Heb *he*

Ramoth-gilead. [30]The king of Israel said to Jehoshaphat, "I will disguise myself and go into battle, but you wear your robes." So the king of Israel disguised himself and went into battle. [31]Now the king of Aram had commanded the thirty-two captains of his chariots, "Fight with no one small or great, but only with the king of Israel." [32]When the captains of the chariots saw Jehoshaphat, they said, "It is surely the king of Israel." So they turned to fight against him; and Jehoshaphat cried out. [33]When the captains of the chariots saw that it was not the king of Israel, they turned back from pursuing him. [34]But a certain man drew his bow and unknowingly struck the king of Israel between the scale armor and the breastplate; so he said to the driver of his chariot, "Turn around, and carry me out of the battle, for I am wounded." [35]The battle grew hot that day, and the king was propped up in his chariot facing the Arameans, until at evening he died; the blood from the wound had flowed into the bottom of the chariot. [36]Then about sunset a shout went through the army, "Every man to his city, and every man to his country!"

[37]So the king died, and was brought to Samaria; they buried the king in Samaria. [38]They washed the chariot by the pool of Samaria; the dogs licked up his blood, and the prostitutes washed themselves in it,[a] according to the word of the LORD that he had spoken. [39]Now the rest of the acts of Ahab, and all that he did, and the ivory house that he built, and all the cities that he built, are they not written in the Book of the Annals of the Kings of Israel? [40]So Ahab slept with his ancestors; and his son Ahaziah succeeded him.

JEHOSHAPHAT REIGNS OVER JUDAH

[41]Jehoshaphat son of Asa began to reign over Judah in the fourth year of King Ahab of Israel. [42]Jehoshaphat was thirty-five years old when he began to reign, and he reigned twenty-five years in Jerusalem. His mother's name was Azubah daughter of Shilhi. [43]He walked in all the way of his father Asa; he did not turn aside from it, doing what was right in the sight of the LORD; yet the high places were not taken away, and the people still sacrificed and offered incense on the high places. [44]Jehoshaphat also made peace with the king of Israel.

[45]Now the rest of the acts of Jehoshaphat, and his power that he showed, and how he waged war, are they not written in the Book of the Annals of the Kings of Judah? [46]The remnant of the male temple prostitutes who were still in the land in the days of his father Asa, he exterminated.

[47]There was no king in Edom; a deputy was king. [48]Jehoshaphat made ships of the Tarshish type to go to Ophir for gold; but they did not go, for the ships were wrecked at Ezion-geber. [49]Then Ahaziah son of Ahab said to Jehoshaphat, "Let my servants go with your servants in the ships," but Jehoshaphat was not willing. [50]Jehoshaphat slept with his ancestors and was buried with his ancestors in the city of his father David; his son Jehoram succeeded him.

AHAZIAH REIGNS OVER ISRAEL

[51]Ahaziah son of Ahab began to reign over Israel in Samaria in the seventeenth year of King Jehoshaphat of Judah; he reigned two years over Israel. [52]He did what was evil in the sight of the LORD, and walked in the way of his father and mother, and in the way of Jeroboam son of Nebat, who caused Israel to sin. [53]He served Baal and worshiped him; he provoked the LORD, the God of Israel, to anger, just as his father had done.

[a] 22.38 Heb lacks in it

2 KINGS

Sometimes a nation's downfall is due more to inner corruption than to outside domination. Second Kings shows how the Israelites' stubborn refusal to listen to the warnings from God's chosen prophets led to their destruction. While most of the book details this downward slide, there are some bright spots. Though many bad rulers led their people into lawlessness and ruin, a few kings and prophets—lights that shone in the dark ages of Israel and Judah—"Walked before [God] in faithfulness with a whole heart" (2 Kings 20.3). Hezekiah, Josiah and a few other kings had moments of devotion to the Lord.

ELIJAH DENOUNCES AHAZIAH

1 After the death of Ahab, Moab rebelled against Israel.

2 Ahaziah had fallen through the lattice in his upper chamber in Samaria, and lay injured; so he sent messengers, telling them, "Go, inquire of Baal-zebub, the god of Ekron, whether I shall recover from this injury." 3But the angel of the LORD said to Elijah the Tishbite, "Get up, go to meet the messengers of the king of Samaria, and say to them, 'Is it because there is no God in Israel that you are going to inquire of Baal-zebub, the god of Ekron?' 4Now therefore thus says the LORD, 'You shall not leave the bed to which you have gone, but you shall surely die.'" So Elijah went.

5 The messengers returned to the king, who said to them, "Why have you returned?" 6They answered him, "There came a man to meet us, who said to us, 'Go back to the king who sent you, and say to him: Thus says the LORD: Is it because there is no God in Israel that you are sending to inquire of Baal-zebub, the god of Ekron? Therefore you shall not leave the bed to which you have gone, but shall surely die.'" 7He said to them, "What sort of man was he who came to meet you and told you these things?" 8They answered him, "A hairy man, with a leather belt around his waist." He said, "It is Elijah the Tishbite."

9 Then the king sent to him a captain of fifty with his fifty men. He went up to Elijah, who was sitting on the top of a hill, and said to him, "O man of God, the king says, 'Come down.'" 10But Elijah answered the captain of fifty, "If I am a man of God, let fire come down from heaven and consume you and your fifty." Then fire came down from heaven, and consumed him and his fifty.

11 Again the king sent to him another captain of fifty with his fifty. He went up[a] and said to him, "O man of God, this is the king's order: Come down quickly!" 12But Elijah answered them, "If I am a man of God, let fire come down from heaven and consume you and your fifty." Then the fire of God came down from heaven and consumed him and his fifty.

THE ULTIMATE HUMAN

FAILURE IS IDOLATRY—

REFUSING TO ACKNOWLEDGE

GOD AS SUPREME.

13 Again the king sent the captain of a third fifty with his fifty. So the third captain of fifty went up, and came and fell on his knees before Elijah, and entreated him, "O man of God, please let my life, and the life of these fifty servants of yours, be precious in your sight. 14Look, fire came down from heaven and consumed the two former captains of fifty men with their fifties; but now let my life be precious in your sight." 15Then the angel of the LORD said to Elijah, "Go down with him; do not be afraid of him." So he set out and went down with him to the king, 16and said to him, "Thus says the LORD: Because you have sent messengers to inquire of Baal-zebub, the god of Ekron,—is it because there is no God in Israel to inquire of his word?—therefore you shall not leave the bed to which you have gone, but you shall surely die."

DEATH OF AHAZIAH

17 So he died according to the word of the LORD that Elijah had spoken. His brother,[b] Jehoram succeeded him as king in the second year of King Jehoram son of Jehoshaphat of Judah, because Ahaziah had no son. 18Now the rest of the acts of Ahaziah that he did, are they not written in the Book of the Annals of the Kings of Israel?

a 1.11 Gk Compare verses 9, 13: Heb *He answered*   b 1.17 Gk Syr: Heb lacks *His brother*

ELIJAH ASCENDS TO HEAVEN

2 Now when the LORD was about to take Elijah up to heaven by a whirlwind, Elijah and Elisha were on their way from Gilgal. [2]Elijah said to Elisha, "Stay here; for the LORD has sent me as far as Bethel." But Elisha said, "As the LORD lives, and as you yourself live, I will not leave you." So they went down to Bethel. [3]The company of prophets[a] who were in Bethel came out to Elisha, and said to him, "Do you know that today the LORD will take your master away from you?" And he said, "Yes, I know; keep silent."

[4]Elijah said to him, "Elisha, stay here; for the LORD has sent me to Jericho." But he said, "As the LORD lives, and as you yourself live, I will not leave you." So they came to Jericho. [5]The company of prophets[a] who were at Jericho drew near to Elisha, and said to him, "Do you know that today the LORD will take your master away from you?" And he answered, "Yes, I know; be silent."

[6]Then Elijah said to him, "Stay here; for the LORD has sent me to the Jordan." But he said, "As the LORD lives, and as you yourself live, I will not leave you." So the two of them went on. [7]Fifty men of the company of prophets[a] also went, and stood at some distance from them, as they both were standing by the Jordan. [8]Then Elijah took his mantle and rolled it up, and struck the water; the water was parted to the one side and to the other, until the two of them crossed on dry ground.

[9]When they had crossed, Elijah said to Elisha, "Tell me what I may do for you, before I am taken from you." Elisha said, "Please let me inherit a double share of your spirit." [10]He responded, "You have asked a hard thing; yet, if you see me as I am being taken from you, it will be granted you; if not, it will not." [11]As they continued walking and talking, a chariot of fire and horses of fire separated the two of them, and Elijah ascended in a whirlwind into heaven. [12]Elisha kept watching and crying out, "Father, father! The chariots of Israel and its horsemen!" But when he could no longer see him, he grasped his own clothes and tore them in two pieces.

ELISHA SUCCEEDS ELIJAH

[13]He picked up the mantle of Elijah that had fallen from him, and went back and stood on the bank of the Jordan. [14]He took the mantle of Elijah that had fallen from him, and struck the water, saying, "Where is the LORD, the God of Elijah?" When he had struck the water, the water was parted to the one side and to the other, and Elisha went over.

[15]When the company of prophets[a] who were at Jericho saw him at a distance, they declared, "The spirit of Elijah rests on Elisha." They came to meet him and bowed to the ground before him. [16]They said to him, "See now, we have fifty strong men among your servants; please let them go and seek your master; it may be that the spirit of the LORD has caught him up and thrown him down on some mountain or into some valley." He responded, "No, do not send them." [17]But when they urged him until he was ashamed, he said, "Send them." So they sent fifty men who searched for three days but did not find him. [18]When they came back to him (he had remained at Jericho), he said to them, "Did I not say to you, Do not go?"

ELISHA PERFORMS MIRACLES

[19]Now the people of the city said to Elisha, "The location of this city is good, as my lord sees; but the water is bad, and the land is unfruitful." [20]He said, "Bring me a new bowl, and put salt in it." So they brought it to him. [21]Then he went to the spring of water and threw the salt into it, and said, "Thus says the LORD, I have made this water wholesome; from now on neither death nor miscarriage shall come from it." [22]So the water has been wholesome to this day, according to the word that Elisha spoke.

[23]He went up from there to Bethel; and while he was going up

---

[a] 2.3,5,7,15 Heb sons of the prophets

on the way, some small boys came out of the city and jeered at him, saying, "Go away, baldhead! Go away, baldhead!" 24When he turned around and saw them, he cursed them in the name of the LORD. Then two she-bears came out of the woods and mauled forty-two of the boys. 25From there he went on to Mount Carmel, and then returned to Samaria.

JEHORAM REIGNS OVER ISRAEL

3 In the eighteenth year of King Jehoshaphat of Judah, Jehoram son of Ahab became king over Israel in Samaria; he reigned twelve years. 2He did what was evil in the sight of the LORD, though not like his father and mother, for he removed the pillar of Baal that his father had made. 3Nevertheless he clung to the sin of Jeroboam son of Nebat, which he caused Israel to commit; he did not depart from it.

WAR WITH MOAB

4 Now King Mesha of Moab was a sheep breeder, who used to deliver to the king of Israel one hundred thousand lambs, and the wool of one hundred thousand rams. 5But when Ahab died, the king of Moab rebelled against the king of Israel. 6So King Jehoram marched out of Samaria at that time and mustered all Israel. 7As he went he sent word to King Jehoshaphat of Judah, "The king of Moab has rebelled against me; will you go with me to battle against Moab?" He answered, "I will; I am with you, my people are your people, my horses are your horses." 8Then he asked, "By which way shall we march?" Jehoram answered, "By the way of the wilderness of Edom."

9 So the king of Israel, the king of Judah, and the king of Edom set out; and when they had made a roundabout march of seven days, there was no water for the army or for the animals that were with them. 10Then the king of Israel said, "Alas! The LORD has summoned us, three kings, only to be handed over to Moab." 11But Jehoshaphat said, "Is there no prophet of the LORD here, through whom we may inquire of the LORD?" Then one of the servants of the king of Israel answered, "Elisha son of Shaphat, who used to pour water on the hands of Elijah, is here." 12Jehoshaphat said, "The word of the LORD is with him." So the king of Israel and Jehoshaphat and the king of Edom went down to him.

13 Elisha said to the king of Israel, "What have I to do with you? Go to your father's prophets or to your mother's." But the king of Israel said to him, "No; it is the LORD who has summoned us, three kings, only to be handed over to Moab." 14Elisha said, "As the LORD of hosts lives, whom I serve, were it not that I have regard for King Jehoshaphat of Judah, I would give you neither a look nor a glance. 15But get me a musician." And then, while the musician was playing, the power of the LORD came on him. 16And he said, "Thus says the LORD, 'I will make this wadi full of pools.' 17For thus says the LORD, 'You shall see neither wind nor rain, but the wadi shall be filled with water, so that you shall drink, you, your cattle, and your animals.' 18This is only a trifle in the sight of the LORD, for he will also hand Moab over to you. 19You shall conquer every fortified city and every choice city; every good tree you shall fell, all springs of water you shall stop up, and every good piece of land you shall ruin with stones." 20The next day, about the time of the morning offering, suddenly water began to flow from the direction of Edom, until the country was filled with water.

21 When all the Moabites heard that the kings had come up to fight against them, all who were able to put on armor, from the youngest to the oldest, were called out and were drawn up at the frontier. 22When they rose early in the morning, and the sun shone upon the water, the Moabites saw the water opposite them as red as blood. 23They said, "This is blood; the kings must have fought together, and killed one another. Now then, Moab, to the spoil!" 24But when they came to the camp

of Israel, the Israelites rose up and attacked the Moabites, who fled before them; as they entered Moab they continued the attack.[a] 25The cities they overturned, and on every good piece of land everyone threw a stone, until it was covered; every spring of water they stopped up, and every good tree they felled. Only at Kir-hareseth did the stone walls remain, until the slingers surrounded and attacked it. 26When the king of Moab saw that the battle was going against him, he took with him seven hundred swordsmen to break through, opposite the king of Edom; but they could not. 27Then he took his firstborn son who was to succeed him, and offered him as a burnt offering on the wall. And great wrath came upon Israel, so they withdrew from him and returned to their own land.

ELISHA AND THE WIDOW'S OIL

4 Now the wife of a member of the company of prophets[b] cried to Elisha, "Your servant my husband is dead; and you know that your servant feared the LORD, but a creditor has come to take my two children as slaves." 2Elisha said to her, "What shall I do for you? Tell me, what do you have in the house?" She answered, "Your servant has nothing in the house, except a jar of oil." 3He said, "Go outside, borrow vessels from all your neighbors, empty vessels and not just a few. 4Then go in, and shut the door behind you and your children, and start pouring into all these vessels; when each is full, set it aside." 5So she left him and shut the door behind her and her children; they kept bringing vessels to her, and she kept pouring. 6When the vessels were full, she said to her son, "Bring me another vessel." But he said to her, "There are no more." Then the oil stopped flowing. 7She came and told the man of God, and he said, "Go sell the oil and pay your debts, and you and your children can live on the rest."

ELISHA RAISES THE SHUNAMMITE'S SON

8 One day Elisha was passing through Shunem, where a wealthy woman lived, who urged him to have a meal. So whenever he passed that way, he would stop there for a meal. 9She said to her husband, "Look, I am sure that this man who regularly passes our way is a holy man of God. 10Let us make a small roof chamber with walls, and put there for him a bed, a table, a chair, and a lamp, so that he can stay there whenever he comes to us."

PONDER

One day Elisha was passing through Shunem, where a wealthy woman lived, who urged him to have a meal. So whenever he passed that way, he would stop there for a meal. She said to her husband, "Look, I am sure that this man who regularly passes our way is a holy man of God."
—2 Kings 4.8–9

PRAY

Lord God, we read here about a woman who showed generosity, kindness and friendship to a great prophet, Elisha. Although she didn't ask for any reward, she was rewarded because of her faithfulness to you.
Let us remember that we, too, are rewarded for our faithfulness to Jesus Christ, who has loved us, forgiven our sins and reconciled us to your gracious self. Teach us that we have an obligation and an opportunity to encourage and support those who minister in your kingdom. In Jesus' name we pray. Amen.

11 One day when he came there, he went up to the chamber and lay down there. 12He said to his servant Gehazi, "Call the Shunammite woman." When he had called her, she stood before him. 13He said to

---

[a] 3.24 Compare Gk Syr: Meaning of Heb uncertain   [b] 4.1 Heb *the sons of the prophets*

him, "Say to her, Since you have taken all this trouble for us, what may be done for you? Would you have a word spoken on your behalf to the king or to the commander of the army?" She answered, "I live among my own people." ¹⁴He said, "What then may be done for her?" Gehazi answered, "Well, she has no son, and her husband is old." ¹⁵He said, "Call her." When he had called her, she stood at the door. ¹⁶He said, "At this season, in due time, you shall embrace a son." She replied, "No, my lord, O man of God; do not deceive your servant."

17 The woman conceived and bore a son at that season, in due time, as Elisha had declared to her.

18 When the child was older, he went out one day to his father among the reapers. ¹⁹He complained to his father, "Oh, my head, my head!" The father said to his servant, "Carry him to his mother." ²⁰He carried him and brought him to his mother; the child sat on her lap until noon, and he died. ²¹She went up and laid him on the bed of the man of God, closed the door on him, and left. ²²Then she called to her husband, and said, "Send me one of the servants and one of the donkeys, so that I may quickly go to the man of God and come back again." ²³He said, "Why go to him today? It is neither new moon nor sabbath." She said, "It will be all right." ²⁴Then she saddled the donkey and said to her servant, "Urge the animal on; do not hold back for me unless I tell you." ²⁵So she set out, and came to the man of God at Mount Carmel.

When the man of God saw her coming, he said to Gehazi his servant, "Look, there is the Shunammite woman; ²⁶run at once to meet her, and say to her, Are you all right? Is your husband all right? Is the child all right?" She answered, "It is all right." ²⁷When she came to the man of God at the mountain, she caught hold of his feet. Gehazi approached to push her away. But the man of God said, "Let her alone, for she is in bitter distress; the LORD has hidden it from me and has not

told me." ²⁸Then she said, "Did I ask my lord for a son? Did I not say, Do not mislead me?" ²⁹He said to Gehazi, "Gird up your loins, and take my staff in your hand, and go. If you meet anyone, give no greeting, and if anyone greets you, do not answer; and lay my staff on the face of the child." ³⁰Then the mother of the child said, "As the LORD lives, and as you yourself live, I will not leave without you." So he rose up and followed her. ³¹Gehazi went on ahead and laid the staff on the face of the child, but there was no sound or sign of life. He came back to meet him and told him, "The child has not awakened."

32 When Elisha came into the house, he saw the child lying dead on his bed. ³³So he went in and closed the door on the two of them, and prayed to the LORD. ³⁴Then he got up on the bed[a] and lay upon the child, putting his mouth upon his mouth, his eyes upon his eyes, and his hands upon his hands; and while he lay bent over him, the flesh of the child became warm. ³⁵He got down, walked once to and fro in the room, then got up again and bent over him; the child sneezed seven times, and the child opened his eyes. ³⁶Elisha[b] summoned Gehazi and said, "Call the Shunammite woman." So he called her. When she came to him, he said, "Take your son." ³⁷She came and fell at his feet, bowing to the ground; then she took her son and left.

ELISHA PURIFIES THE POT OF STEW

38 When Elisha returned to Gilgal, there was a famine in the land. As the company of prophets was[c] sitting before him, he said to his servant, "Put the large pot on, and make some stew for the company of prophets."[d] ³⁹One of them went out into the field to gather herbs; he found a wild vine and gathered from it a lapful of wild gourds, and came and cut them up into the pot of

---

[a] 4.34 Heb lacks *on the bed*   [b] 4.36 Heb *he*   [c] 4.38 Heb *sons of the prophets were*   [d] 4.38 Heb *sons of the prophets*

stew, not knowing what they were. 40They served some for the men to eat. But while they were eating the stew, they cried out, "O man of God, there is death in the pot!" They could not eat it. 41He said, "Then bring some flour." He threw it into the pot, and said, "Serve the people and let them eat." And there was nothing harmful in the pot.

ELISHA FEEDS ONE HUNDRED MEN

42 A man came from Baal-shalishah, bringing food from the first fruits to the man of God: twenty loaves of barley and fresh ears of grain in his sack. Elisha said, "Give it to the people and let them eat." 43But his servant said, "How can I set this before a hundred people?" So he repeated, "Give it to the people and let them eat, for thus says the LORD, 'They shall eat and have some left.' " 44He set it before them, they ate, and had some left, according to the word of the LORD.

THE HEALING OF NAAMAN

5 Naaman, commander of the army of the king of Aram, was a great man and in high favor with his master, because by him the LORD had given victory to Aram. The man, though a mighty warrior, suffered from leprosy.[a] 2Now the Arameans on one of their raids had taken a young girl captive from the land of Israel, and she served Naaman's wife. 3She said to her mistress, "If only my lord were with the prophet who is in Samaria! He would cure him of his leprosy."[a] 4So Naaman[b] went in and told his lord just what the girl from the land of Israel had said. 5And the king of Aram said, "Go then, and I will send along a letter to the king of Israel."

He went, taking with him ten talents of silver, six thousand shekels of gold, and ten sets of garments. 6He brought the letter to the king of Israel, which read, "When this letter reaches you, know that I have sent to you my servant Naaman, that you may cure him of his leprosy."[a] 7When the king of Israel read the letter, he tore his clothes and said, "Am I God, to give death or life, that this man sends word to me to cure a man of his leprosy?[a] Just look and see how he is trying to pick a quarrel with me."

8 But when Elisha the man of God heard that the king of Israel had torn his clothes, he sent a message to the king, "Why have you torn your clothes? Let him come to me, that he

[a] 5.1,3,6,7 A term for several skin diseases; precise meaning uncertain   [b] 5.4 Heb he

---

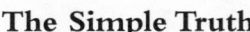

BIBLE IN LIFE

The Simple Truth
2 Kings 5.1–14

Naaman, a powerful commander in the Syrian army, had a problem—he was afflicted with leprosy. He was advised to go to Elisha, a prophet in Israel, who told him to bathe himself in the Jordan River. But Naaman thought that solution was too simple, even stupid. There were much better rivers in Syria. Only when he humbled himself and bathed in the Jordan was his leprosy healed.

Quite often we assume the attitude that afflicted Naaman. We have the problem of sin, and we are given simple instructions to find healing: "If you confess with your lips that Jesus is Lord and believe in your heart that God raised him from the dead, you will be saved" (Romans 10.9). Because this command is so simple and clear, many people feel it must not be enough. They suspect there must be more to it than this. *Surely my life can't be changed; surely I cannot receive eternal life just by following these simple verses in the Bible.* But God Almighty says this is true. Jesus Christ affirms that this is true. We can have salvation, eternal life and forgiveness of sin—when we humble ourselves and accept God's simple plan. Simple, yes, but also profound. And it is the single most important fact that we can ever learn.

may learn that there is a prophet in Israel." 9So Naaman came with his horses and chariots, and halted at the entrance of Elisha's house. 10Elisha sent a messenger to him, saying, "Go, wash in the Jordan seven times, and your flesh shall be restored and you shall be clean." 11But Naaman became angry and went away, saying, "I thought that for me he would surely come out, and stand and call on the name of the LORD his God, and would wave his hand over the spot, and cure the leprosy!ᵃ 12Are not Abanaᵇ and Pharpar, the rivers of Damascus, better than all the waters of Israel? Could I not wash in them, and be clean?" He turned and went away in a rage. 13But his servants approached and said to him, "Father, if the prophet had commanded you to do something difficult, would you not have done it? How much more, when all he said to you was, 'Wash, and be clean'?" 14So he went down and immersed himself seven times in the Jordan, according to the word of the man of God; his flesh was restored like the flesh of a young boy, and he was clean.

15 Then he returned to the man of God, he and all his company; he came and stood before him and said, "Now I know that there is no God in all the earth except in Israel; please accept a present from your servant." 16But he said, "As the LORD lives, whom I serve, I will accept nothing!" He urged him to accept, but he refused. 17Then Naaman said, "If not, please let two mule-loads of earth be given to your servant; for your servant will no longer offer burnt offering or sacrifice to any god except the LORD. 18But may the LORD pardon your servant on one count: when my master goes into the house of Rimmon to worship there, leaning on my arm, and I bow down in the house of Rimmon, when I do bow down in the house of Rimmon, may the LORD pardon your servant on this one count." 19He said to him, "Go in peace."

GEHAZI'S GREED

But when Naaman had gone from him a short distance, 20Gehazi, the servant of Elisha the man of God, thought, "My master has let that Aramean Naaman off too lightly by not accepting from him what he offered. As the LORD lives, I will run after him and get something out of him." 21So Gehazi went after Naaman. When Naaman saw someone running after him, he jumped down from the chariot to meet him and said, "Is everything all right?" 22He replied, "Yes, but my master has sent me to say, 'Two members of a company of prophetsᶜ have just come to me from the hill country of Ephraim; please give them a talent of silver and two changes of clothing.'" 23Naaman said, "Please accept two talents." He urged him, and tied up two talents of silver in two bags, with two changes of clothing, and gave them to two of his servants, who carried them in front of Gehazi.ᵈ 24When he came to the citadel, he took the bagsᵉ from them, and stored them inside; he dismissed the men, and they left.

25 He went in and stood before his master; and Elisha said to him, "Where have you been, Gehazi?" He answered, "Your servant has not gone anywhere at all." 26But he said to him, "Did I not go with you in spirit when someone left his chariot to meet you? Is this a time to accept money and to accept clothing, olive orchards and vineyards, sheep and oxen, and male and female slaves? 27Therefore the leprosyᵃ of Naaman shall cling to you, and to your descendants forever." So he left his presence leprous,ᵃ as white as snow.

THE MIRACLE OF THE AX HEAD

6 Now the company of prophetsᶜ said to Elisha, "As you see, the place where we live under your charge is too small for us. 2Let us go to the Jordan, and let us collect logs there, one for each of us, and build a place there for us to live." He answered, "Do so." 3Then one of them

---

ᵃ 5.11,27 A term for several skin diseases; precise meaning uncertain   ᵇ 5.12 Another reading is *Amana*   ᶜ 5.22; 6.1 Heb *sons of the prophets*   ᵈ 5.23 Heb *him*   ᵉ 5.24 Heb lacks *the bags*

said, "Please come with your servants." And he answered, "I will." 4So he went with them. When they came to the Jordan, they cut down trees. 5But as one was felling a log, his ax head fell into the water; he cried out, "Alas, master! It was borrowed." 6Then the man of God said, "Where did it fall?" When he showed him the place, he cut off a stick, and threw it in there, and made the iron float. 7He said, "Pick it up." So he reached out his hand and took it.

THE ARAMEAN ATTACK IS THWARTED

8 Once when the king of Aram was at war with Israel, he took counsel with his officers. He said, "At such and such a place shall be my camp." 9But the man of God sent word to the king of Israel, "Take care not to pass this place, because the Arameans are going down there." 10The king of Israel sent word to the place of which the man of God spoke. More than once or twice he warned such a place[a] so that it was on the alert.

11 The mind of the king of Aram was greatly perturbed because of this; he called his officers and said to them, "Now tell me who among us sides with the king of Israel?" 12Then one of his officers said, "No one, my lord king. It is Elisha, the prophet in Israel, who tells the king of Israel the words that you speak in your bedchamber." 13He said, "Go and find where he is; I will send and seize him." He was told, "He is in Dothan." 14So he sent horses and chariots there and a great army; they came by night, and surrounded the city.

15 When an attendant of the man of God rose early in the morning and went out, an army with horses and chariots was all around the city. His servant said, "Alas, master! What shall we do?" 16He replied, "Do not be afraid, for there are more with us than there are with them." 17Then Elisha prayed: "O LORD, please open his eyes that he may see." So the LORD opened the eyes of the servant, and he saw; the mountain was full of horses and chariots of fire all around Elisha. 18When the Arameans[b] came down against him, Elisha prayed to the LORD, and said, "Strike this people, please, with blindness." So he struck them with blindness as Elisha had asked. 19Elisha said to them, "This is not the way, and this is not the city; follow me, and I will bring you to the man whom you seek." And he led them to Samaria.

20 As soon as they entered Samaria, Elisha said, "O LORD, open the eyes of these men so that they may see." The LORD opened their eyes, and they saw that they were inside Samaria. 21When the king of Israel saw them he said to Elisha, "Father, shall I kill them? Shall I kill them?" 22He answered, "No! Did you capture with your sword and your bow those whom you want to kill? Set food and water before them so that they may eat and drink; and let them go to their master." 23So he prepared for them a great feast; after they ate and drank, he sent them on their way, and they went to their master. And the Arameans no longer came raiding into the land of Israel.

BEN-HADAD'S SIEGE OF SAMARIA

24 Some time later King Benhadad of Aram mustered his entire army; he marched against Samaria and laid siege to it. 25As the siege continued, famine in Samaria became so great that a donkey's head was sold for eighty shekels of silver, and one-fourth of a kab of dove's dung for five shekels of silver. 26Now as the king of Israel was walking on the city wall, a woman cried out to him, "Help, my lord king!" 27He said, "No! Let the LORD help you. How can I help you? From the threshing floor or from the wine press?" 28But then the king asked her, "What is your complaint?" She answered, "This woman said to me, 'Give up your son; we will eat him today, and we will eat my son tomorrow.' 29So we cooked my son and ate him. The next day I said to her, 'Give up your

---

[a] 6.10 Heb *warned it*   [b] 6.18 Heb *they*

son and we will eat him.' But she has hidden her son." 30When the king heard the words of the woman he tore his clothes—now since he was walking on the city wall, the people could see that he had sackcloth on his body underneath— 31and he said, "So may God do to me, and more, if the head of Elisha son of Shaphat stays on his shoulders today." 32So he dispatched a man from his presence.

Now Elisha was sitting in his house, and the elders were sitting with him. Before the messenger arrived, Elisha said to the elders, "Are you aware that this murderer has sent someone to take off my head? When the messenger comes, see that you shut the door and hold it closed against him. Is not the sound of his master's feet behind him?" 33While he was still speaking with them, the king[a] came down to him and said, "This trouble is from the LORD! Why should I hope in the LORD any longer?" 1But Elisha said, "Hear the word of the LORD: thus says the LORD, Tomorrow about this time a measure of choice meal shall be sold for a shekel, and two measures of barley for a shekel, at the gate of Samaria." 2Then the captain on whose hand the king leaned said to the man of God, "Even if the LORD were to make windows in the sky, could such a thing happen?" But he said, "You shall see it with your own eyes, but you shall not eat from it."

THE ARAMEANS FLEE

3 Now there were four leprous[b] men outside the city gate, who said to one another, "Why should we sit here until we die? 4If we say, 'Let us enter the city,' the famine is in the city, and we shall die there; but if we sit here, we shall also die. Therefore, let us desert to the Aramean camp; if they spare our lives, we shall live; and if they kill us, we shall but die." 5So they arose at twilight to go to the Aramean camp; but when they came to the edge of the Aramean camp, there was no one there at all. 6For the Lord had caused the Aramean army to hear the sound of chariots, and of horses, the sound of a great army, so that they said to one another, "The king of Israel has hired the kings of the Hittites and the kings of Egypt to fight against us." 7So they fled away in the twilight and abandoned their tents, their horses, and their donkeys leaving the camp just as it was, and fled for their lives. 8When these leprous[b] men had come to the edge of the camp, they went into a tent, ate and drank, carried off silver, gold, and clothing, and went and hid them. Then they came back, entered another tent, carried off things from it, and went and hid them.

9 Then they said to one another, "What we are doing is wrong. This is a day of good news; if we are silent and wait until the morning light, we will be found guilty; therefore let us go and tell the king's household." 10So they came and called to the gatekeepers of the city, and told them, "We went to the Aramean camp, but there was no one to be seen or heard there, nothing but the horses tied, the donkeys tied, and the tents as they were." 11Then the gatekeepers called out and proclaimed it to the king's household. 12The king got up in the night, and said to his servants, "I will tell you what the Arameans have prepared against us. They know that we are starving; so they have left the camp to hide themselves in the open country, thinking, 'When they come out of the city, we shall take them alive and get into the city.' " 13One of his servants said, "Let some men take five of the remaining horses, since those left here will suffer the fate of the whole multitude of Israel that have perished already;[c] let us send and find out." 14So they took two mounted men, and the king sent them after the Aramean army, saying, "Go and find out." 15So they went after them as far as the Jordan; the whole way was littered with garments and equipment that the

[a] 6.33 See 7.2: Heb *messenger*   [b] 7.3,8 A term for several skin diseases; precise meaning uncertain   [c] 7.13 Compare Gk Syr Vg: Meaning of Heb uncertain

Arameans had thrown away in their haste. So the messengers returned, and told the king.

WE ALWAYS PAY FOR

DISOBEYING GOD.

16 Then the people went out, and plundered the camp of the Arameans. So a measure of choice meal was sold for a shekel, and two measures of barley for a shekel, according to the word of the LORD. 17 Now the king had appointed the captain on whose hand he leaned to have charge of the gate; the people trampled him to death in the gate, just as the man of God had said when the king came down to him. 18 For when the man of God had said to the king, "Two measures of barley shall be sold for a shekel, and a measure of choice meal for a shekel, about this time tomorrow in the gate of Samaria," 19 the captain had answered the man of God, "Even if the LORD were to make windows in the sky, could such a thing happen?" And he had answered, "You shall see it with your own eyes, but you shall not eat from it." 20 It did indeed happen to him; the people trampled him to death in the gate.

THE SHUNAMMITE WOMAN'S LAND RESTORED

8 Now Elisha had said to the woman whose son he had restored to life, "Get up and go with your household, and settle wherever you can; for the LORD has called for a famine, and it will come on the land for seven years." 2 So the woman got up and did according to the word of the man of God; she went with her household and settled in the land of the Philistines seven years. 3 At the end of the seven years, when the woman returned from the land of the Philistines, she set out to appeal to the king for her house and her land. 4 Now the king was talking

with Gehazi the servant of the man of God, saying, "Tell me all the great things that Elisha has done." 5 While he was telling the king how Elisha had restored a dead person to life, the woman whose son he had restored to life appealed to the king for her house and her land. Gehazi said, "My lord king, here is the woman, and here is her son whom Elisha restored to life." 6 When the king questioned the woman, she told him. So the king appointed an official for her, saying, "Restore all that was hers, together with all the revenue of the fields from the day that she left the land until now."

DEATH OF BEN-HADAD

7 Elisha went to Damascus while King Ben-hadad of Aram was ill. When it was told him, "The man of God has come here," 8 the king said to Hazael, "Take a present with you and go to meet the man of God. Inquire of the LORD through him, whether I shall recover from this illness." 9 So Hazael went to meet him, taking a present with him, all kinds of goods of Damascus, forty camel loads. When he entered and stood before him, he said, "Your son King Ben-hadad of Aram has sent me to you, saying, 'Shall I recover from this illness?'" 10 Elisha said to him, "Go, say to him, 'You shall certainly recover'; but the LORD has shown me that he shall certainly die." 11 He fixed his gaze and stared at him, until he was ashamed. Then the man of God wept. 12 Hazael asked, "Why does my lord weep?" He answered, "Because I know the evil that you will do to the people of Israel; you will set their fortresses on fire, you will kill their young men with the sword, dash in pieces their little ones, and rip up their pregnant women." 13 Hazael said, "What is your servant, who is a mere dog, that he should do this great thing?" Elisha answered, "The LORD has shown me that you are to be king over Aram." 14 Then he left Elisha,[a] and went to his master Ben-hadad,[a] who said to him, "What

---

a 8.14 Heb lacks Ben-hadad

did Elisha say to you?" And he answered, "He told me that you would certainly recover." ¹⁵But the next day he took the bed-cover and dipped it in water and spread it over the king's face, until he died. And Hazael succeeded him.

JEHORAM REIGNS OVER JUDAH

16 In the fifth year of King Joram son of Ahab of Israel,ᵃ Jehoram son of King Jehoshaphat of Judah began to reign. ¹⁷He was thirty-two years old when he became king, and he reigned eight years in Jerusalem. ¹⁸He walked in the way of the kings of Israel, as the house of Ahab had done, for the daughter of Ahab was his wife. He did what was evil in the sight of the LORD. ¹⁹Yet the LORD would not destroy Judah, for the sake of his servant David, since he had promised to give a lamp to him and to his descendants forever.

20 In his days Edom revolted against the rule of Judah, and set up a king of their own. ²¹Then Joram crossed over to Zair with all his chariots. He set out by night and attacked the Edomites and their chariot commanders who had surrounded him;ᵇ but his army fled home. ²²So Edom has been in revolt against the rule of Judah to this day. Libnah also revolted at the same time. ²³Now the rest of the acts of Joram, and all that he did, are they not written in the Book of the Annals of the Kings of Judah? ²⁴So Joram slept with his ancestors, and was buried with them in the city of David; his son Ahaziah succeeded him.

AHAZIAH REIGNS OVER JUDAH

25 In the twelfth year of King Joram son of Ahab of Israel, Ahaziah son of King Jehoram of Judah began to reign. ²⁶Ahaziah was twenty-two years old when he began to reign; he reigned one year in Jerusalem. His mother's name was Athaliah, a granddaughter of King Omri of Israel. ²⁷He also walked in the way of the house of Ahab, doing what was evil in the sight of the LORD, as the house of Ahab had done, for he was son-in-law to the house of Ahab.

28 He went with Joram son of Ahab to wage war against King Hazael of Aram at Ramoth-gilead, where the Arameans wounded Joram. ²⁹King Joram returned to be healed in Jezreel of the wounds that the Arameans had inflicted on him at Ramah, when he fought against King Hazael of Aram. King Ahaziah son of Jehoram of Judah went down to see Joram son of Ahab in Jezreel, because he was wounded.

ANOINTING OF JEHU

9 Then the prophet Elisha called a member of the company of prophetsᶜ and said to him, "Gird up your loins; take this flask of oil in your hand, and go to Ramoth-gilead. ²When you arrive, look there for Jehu son of Jehoshaphat, son of Nimshi; go in and get him to leave his companions, and take him into an inner chamber. ³Then take the flask of oil, pour it on his head, and say, 'Thus says the LORD: I anoint you king over Israel.' Then open the door and flee; do not linger."

4 So the young man, the young prophet, went to Ramoth-gilead. ⁵He arrived while the commanders of the army were in council, and he announced, "I have a message for you, commander." "For which one of us?" asked Jehu. "For you, commander." ⁶So Jehuᵈ got up and went inside; the young man poured the oil on his head, saying to him, "Thus says the LORD the God of Israel: I anoint you king over the people of the LORD, over Israel. ⁷You shall strike down the house of your master Ahab, so that I may avenge on Jezebel the blood of my servants the prophets, and the blood of all the servants of the LORD. ⁸For the whole house of Ahab shall perish; I will cut off from Ahab every male, bond or free, in Israel. ⁹I will make the house of Ahab like the house of Jeroboam son of Nebat, and like the house of Baasha son of Ahijah. ¹⁰The dogs shall eat Jezebel in the territory

ᵃ **8.16** Gk Syr: Heb adds *Jehoshaphat being king of Judah,*   ᵇ **8.21** Meaning of Heb uncertain   ᶜ **9.1** Heb *sons of the prophets*   ᵈ **9.6** Heb *he*

of Jezreel, and no one shall bury her."
Then he opened the door and fled.

11 When Jehu came back to his master's officers, they said to him, "Is everything all right? Why did that madman come to you?" He answered them, "You know the sort and how they babble." 12 They said, "Liar! Come on, tell us!" So he said, "This is just what he said to me: 'Thus says the LORD, I anoint you king over Israel.'" 13 Then hurriedly they all took their cloaks and spread them for him on the bare[a] steps; and they blew the trumpet, and proclaimed, "Jehu is king."

WHAT IS EXPECTED OF

CHRISTIANS? WE ARE

NOT SAVED JUST TO BE

BLESSED, BUT TO BE USED.

JORAM OF ISRAEL KILLED

14 Thus Jehu son of Jehoshaphat son of Nimshi conspired against Joram. Joram with all Israel had been on guard at Ramoth-gilead against King Hazael of Aram; 15 but King Joram had returned to be healed in Jezreel of the wounds that the Arameans had inflicted on him, when he fought against King Hazael of Aram. So Jehu said, "If this is your wish, then let no one slip out of the city to go and tell the news in Jezreel." 16 Then Jehu mounted his chariot and went to Jezreel, where Joram was lying ill. King Ahaziah of Judah had come down to visit Joram.

17 In Jezreel, the sentinel standing on the tower spied the company of Jehu arriving, and said, "I see a company." Joram said, "Take a horseman; send him to meet them, and let him say, 'Is it peace?'" 18 So the horseman went to meet him; he said, "Thus says the king, 'Is it peace?'" Jehu responded, "What have you to do with peace? Fall in behind me." The sentinel reported, saying, "The messenger reached them, but he is not coming back." 19 Then he sent out a second horseman, who came to them and said, "Thus says the king, 'Is it peace?'" Jehu answered, "What have you to do with peace? Fall in behind me." 20 Again the sentinel reported, "He reached them, but he is not coming back. It looks like the driving of Jehu son of Nimshi; for he drives like a maniac."

21 Joram said, "Get ready." And they got his chariot ready. Then King Joram of Israel and King Ahaziah of Judah set out, each in his chariot, and went to meet Jehu; they met him at the property of Naboth the Jezreelite. 22 When Joram saw Jehu, he said, "Is it peace, Jehu?" He answered, "What peace can there be, so long as the many whoredoms and sorceries of your mother Jezebel continue?" 23 Then Joram reined about and fled, saying to Ahaziah, "Treason, Ahaziah!" 24 Jehu drew his bow with all his strength, and shot Joram between the shoulders, so that the arrow pierced his heart; and he sank in his chariot. 25 Jehu said to his aide Bidkar, "Lift him out, and throw him on the plot of ground belonging to Naboth the Jezreelite; for remember, when you and I rode side by side behind his father Ahab how the LORD uttered this oracle against him: 26 'For the blood of Naboth and for the blood of his children that I saw yesterday, says the LORD, I swear I will repay you on this very plot of ground.' Now therefore lift him out and throw him on the plot of ground, in accordance with the word of the LORD."

AHAZIAH OF JUDAH KILLED

27 When King Ahaziah of Judah saw this, he fled in the direction of Beth-haggan. Jehu pursued him, saying, "Shoot him also!" And they shot him[b] in the chariot at the ascent to Gur, which is by Ibleam. Then he fled to Megiddo, and died there. 28 His officers carried him in a chariot to Jerusalem, and buried

[a] 9.13 Meaning of Heb uncertain [b] 9.27 Syr Vg Compare Gk: Heb lacks *and they shot him*

him in his tomb with his ancestors in the city of David.

29 In the eleventh year of Joram son of Ahab, Ahaziah began to reign over Judah.

JEZEBEL'S VIOLENT DEATH

30 When Jehu came to Jezreel, Jezebel heard of it; she painted her eyes, and adorned her head, and looked out of the window. 31As Jehu entered the gate, she said, "Is it peace, Zimri, murderer of your master?" 32He looked up to the window and said, "Who is on my side? Who?" Two or three eunuchs looked out at him. 33He said, "Throw her down." So they threw her down; some of her blood spattered on the wall and on the horses, which trampled on her. 34Then he went in and ate and drank; he said, "See to that cursed woman and bury her; for she is a king's daughter." 35But when they went to bury her, they found no more of her than the skull and the feet and the palms of her hands. 36When they came back and told him, he said, "This is the word of the LORD, which he spoke by his servant Elijah the Tishbite, 'In the territory of Jezreel the dogs shall eat the flesh of Jezebel; 37the corpse of Jezebel shall be like dung on the field in the territory of Jezreel, so that no one can say, This is Jezebel.'"

MASSACRE OF AHAB'S DESCENDANTS

10 Now Ahab had seventy sons in Samaria. So Jehu wrote letters and sent them to Samaria, to the rulers of Jezreel,[a] to the elders, and to the guardians of the sons of[b] Ahab, saying, 2"Since your master's sons are with you and you have at your disposal chariots and horses, a fortified city, and weapons, 3select the son of your master who is the best qualified, set him on his father's throne, and fight for your master's house." 4But they were utterly terrified and said, "Look, two kings could not withstand him; how then can we stand?" 5So the steward of the palace, and the governor of the city, along with the elders and the guardians, sent word to Jehu: "We are your servants; we will do anything you say. We will not make anyone king; do whatever you think right." 6Then he wrote them a second letter, saying, "If you are on my side, and if you are ready to obey me, take the heads of your master's sons and come to me at Jezreel tomorrow at this time." Now the king's sons, seventy persons, were with the leaders of the city, who were charged with their upbringing. 7When the letter reached them, they took the king's sons and killed them, seventy persons; they put their heads in baskets and sent them to him at Jezreel. 8When the messenger came and told him, "They have brought the heads of the king's sons," he said, "Lay them in two heaps at the entrance of the gate until the morning." 9Then in the morning when he went out, he stood and said to all the people, "You are innocent. It was I who conspired against my master and killed him; but who struck down all these? 10Know then that there shall fall to the earth nothing of the word of the LORD, which the LORD spoke concerning the house of Ahab; for the LORD has done what he said through his servant Elijah." 11So Jehu killed all who were left of the house of Ahab in Jezreel, all his leaders, close friends, and priests, until he left him no survivor.

12 Then he set out and went to Samaria. On the way, when he was at Beth-eked of the Shepherds, 13Jehu met relatives of King Ahaziah of Judah and said, "Who are you?" They answered, "We are kin of Ahaziah; we have come down to visit the royal princes and the sons of the queen mother." 14He said, "Take them alive." They took them alive, and slaughtered them at the pit of Beth-eked, forty-two in all; he spared none of them.

15 When he left there, he met Jehonadab son of Rechab coming to meet him; he greeted him, and said to him, "Is your heart as true to

---

a **10.1** Or *of the city*; Vg Compare Gk
b **10.1** Gk: Heb lacks *of the sons of*

mine as mine is to yours?"[a] Jehonadab answered, "It is." Jehu said,[b] "If it is, give me your hand." So he gave him his hand. Jehu took him up with him into the chariot. [16]He said, "Come with me, and see my zeal for the LORD." So he[c] had him ride in his chariot. [17]When he came to Samaria, he killed all who were left to Ahab in Samaria, until he had wiped them out, according to the word of the LORD that he spoke to Elijah.

SLAUGHTER OF WORSHIPERS OF BAAL

[18] Then Jehu assembled all the people and said to them, "Ahab offered Baal small service; but Jehu will offer much more. [19]Now therefore summon to me all the prophets of Baal, all his worshipers, and all his priests; let none be missing, for I have a great sacrifice to offer to Baal; whoever is missing shall not live." But Jehu was acting with cunning in order to destroy the worshipers of Baal. [20]Jehu decreed, "Sanctify a solemn assembly for Baal." So they proclaimed it. [21]Jehu sent word throughout all Israel; all the worshipers of Baal came, so that there was no one left who did not come. They entered the temple of Baal, until the temple of Baal was filled from wall to wall. [22]He said to the keeper of the wardrobe, "Bring out the vestments for all the worshipers of Baal." So he brought out the vestments for them. [23]Then Jehu entered the temple of Baal with Jehonadab son of Rechab; he said to the worshipers of Baal, "Search and see that there is no worshiper of the LORD here among you, but only worshipers of Baal." [24]Then they proceeded to offer sacrifices and burnt offerings.

Now Jehu had stationed eighty men outside, saying, "Whoever allows any of those to escape whom I deliver into your hands shall forfeit his life." [25]As soon as he had finished presenting the burnt offering, Jehu said to the guards and to the officers, "Come in and kill them; let no one escape." So they put them to the sword. The guards and the officers threw them out, and then went into the

citadel of the temple of Baal. [26]They brought out the pillar[d] that was in the temple of Baal, and burned it. [27]Then they demolished the pillar of Baal, and destroyed the temple of Baal, and made it a latrine to this day.

[28] Thus Jehu wiped out Baal from Israel. [29]But Jehu did not turn aside from the sins of Jeroboam son of Nebat, which he caused Israel to commit—the golden calves that were in Bethel and in Dan. [30]The LORD said to Jehu, "Because you have done well in carrying out what I consider right, and in accordance with all that was in my heart have dealt with the house of Ahab, your sons of the fourth generation shall sit on the throne of Israel." [31]But Jehu was not careful to follow the law of the LORD the God of Israel with all his heart; he did not turn from the sins of Jeroboam, which he caused Israel to commit.

DEATH OF JEHU

[32] In those days the LORD began to trim off parts of Israel. Hazael defeated them throughout the territory of Israel: [33]from the Jordan eastward, all the land of Gilead, the Gadites, the Reubenites, and the Manassites, from Aroer, which is by the Wadi Arnon, that is, Gilead and Bashan. [34]Now the rest of the acts of Jehu, all that he did, and all his power, are they not written in the Book of the Annals of the Kings of Israel? [35]So Jehu slept with his ancestors, and they buried him in Samaria. His son Jehoahaz succeeded him. [36]The time that Jehu reigned over Israel in Samaria was twenty-eight years.

ATHALIAH REIGNS OVER JUDAH

11 Now when Athaliah, Ahaziah's mother, saw that her son was dead, she set about to destroy all the royal family. [2]But Jehosheba, King Joram's daughter, Ahaziah's sister, took Joash son of Ahaziah, and stole him away from among the

---

[a] 10.15 Gk: Heb *Is it right with your heart, as my heart is with your heart?* [b] 10.15 Gk: Heb lacks *Jehu said* [c] 10.16 Gk Syr Tg: Heb *they* [d] 10.26 Gk Vg Syr Tg: Heb *pillars*

king's children who were about to be killed; she put[a] him and his nurse in a bedroom. Thus she[b] hid him from Athaliah, so that he was not killed; ³he remained with her six years, hidden in the house of the LORD, while Athaliah reigned over the land.

JEHOIADA ANOINTS THE CHILD JOASH

4 But in the seventh year Jehoiada summoned the captains of the Carites and of the guards and had them come to him in the house of the LORD. He made a covenant with them and put them under oath in the house of the LORD; then he showed them the king's son. ⁵He commanded them, "This is what you are to do: one-third of you, those who go off duty on the sabbath and guard the king's house ⁶(another third being at the gate Sur and a third at the gate behind the guards), shall guard the palace; ⁷and your two divisions that come on duty in force on the sabbath and guard the house of the LORD[c] ⁸shall surround the king, each with weapons in hand; and whoever approaches the ranks is to be killed. Be with the king in his comings and goings."

9 The captains did according to all that the priest Jehoiada commanded; each brought his men who were to go off duty on the sabbath, with those who were to come on duty on the sabbath, and came to the priest Jehoiada. ¹⁰The priest delivered to the captains the spears and shields that had been King David's, which were in the house of the LORD; ¹¹the guards stood, every man with his weapons in his hand, from the south side of the house to the north side of the house, around the altar and the house, to guard the king on every side. ¹²Then he brought out the king's son, put the crown on him, and gave him the covenant;[d] they proclaimed him king, and anointed him; they clapped their hands and shouted, "Long live the king!"

DEATH OF ATHALIAH

13 When Athaliah heard the noise of the guard and of the people, she went into the house of the LORD to the people; ¹⁴when she looked, there was the king standing by the pillar, according to custom, with the captains and the trumpeters beside the king, and all the people of the land rejoicing and blowing trumpets. Athaliah tore her clothes and cried, "Treason! Treason!" ¹⁵Then the priest Jehoiada commanded the captains who were set over the army, "Bring her out between the ranks, and kill with the sword anyone who follows her." For the priest said, "Let her not be killed in the house of the LORD." ¹⁶So they laid hands on her; she went through the horses' entrance to the king's house, and there she was put to death.

17 Jehoiada made a covenant between the LORD and the king and people, that they should be the LORD's people; also between the king and the people. ¹⁸Then all the people of the land went to the house of Baal, and tore it down; his altars and his images they broke in pieces, and they killed Mattan, the priest of Baal, before the altars. The priest posted guards over the house of the LORD. ¹⁹He took the captains, the Carites, the guards, and all the people of the land; then they brought the king down from the house of the LORD, marching through the gate of the guards to the king's house. He took his seat on the throne of the kings. ²⁰So all the people of the land rejoiced; and the city was quiet after Athaliah had been killed with the sword at the king's house.

21[e] Jehoash[f] was seven years old when he began to reign.

THE TEMPLE REPAIRED

12 In the seventh year of Jehu, Jehoash began to reign; he reigned forty years in Jerusalem. His mother's name was Zibiah of Beer-sheba. ²Jehoash did what was right in the sight of the LORD all his

a 11.2 With 2 Chr 22.11: Heb lacks *she put*
b 11.2 Gk Syr Vg Compare 2 Chr 22.11: Heb *they* c 11.7 Heb *the LORD to the king*
d 11.12 Or *treaty* or *testimony*; Heb *eduth*
e 11.21 Ch 12.1 in Heb f 11.21 Another spelling is *Joash*; see verse 19

days, because the priest Jehoiada instructed him. ³Nevertheless the high places were not taken away; the people continued to sacrifice and make offerings on the high places.

4 Jehoash said to the priests, "All the money offered as sacred donations that is brought into the house of the LORD, the money for which each person is assessed—the money from the assessment of persons—and the money from the voluntary offerings brought into the house of the LORD, ⁵let the priests receive from each of the donors; and let them repair the house wherever any need of repairs is discovered." ⁶But by the twenty-third year of King Jehoash the priests had made no repairs on the house. ⁷Therefore King Jehoash summoned the priest Jehoiada with the other priests and said to them, "Why are you not repairing the house? Now therefore do not accept any more money from your donors but hand it over for the repair of the house." ⁸So the priests agreed that they would neither accept more money from the people nor repair the house.

9 Then the priest Jehoiada took a chest, made a hole in its lid, and set it beside the altar on the right side as one entered the house of the LORD; the priests who guarded the threshold put in it all the money that was brought into the house of the LORD. ¹⁰Whenever they saw that there was a great deal of money in the chest, the king's secretary and the high priest went up, counted the money that was found in the house of the LORD, and tied it up in bags. ¹¹They would give the money that was weighed out into the hands of the workers who had the oversight of the house of the LORD; then they paid it out to the carpenters and the builders who worked on the house of the LORD, ¹²to the masons and the stonecutters, as well as to buy timber and quarried stone for making repairs on the house of the LORD, as well as for any outlay for repairs of the house. ¹³But for the house of the LORD no basins of silver, snuffers, bowls, trumpets, or any vessels of gold, or of silver, were made from the money that was brought into the house of the LORD, ¹⁴for that was given to the workers who were repairing the house of the LORD with it. ¹⁵They did not ask an accounting from those into whose hand they delivered the money to pay out to the workers, for they dealt honestly. ¹⁶The money from the guilt offerings and the money from the sin offerings was not brought into the house of the LORD; it belonged to the priests.

WHAT ARE THE TOP PRIORITIES IN OUR LIVES? OUR CALENDARS AND CHECKBOOKS ARE THE BEST INDICATORS.

HAZAEL THREATENS JERUSALEM

17 At that time King Hazael of Aram went up, fought against Gath, and took it. But when Hazael set his face to go up against Jerusalem, ¹⁸King Jehoash of Judah took all the votive gifts that Jehoshaphat, Jehoram, and Ahaziah, his ancestors, the kings of Judah, had dedicated, as well as his own votive gifts, all the gold that was found in the treasuries of the house of the LORD and of the king's house, and sent these to King Hazael of Aram. Then Hazael withdrew from Jerusalem.

DEATH OF JOASH

19 Now the rest of the acts of Joash, and all that he did, are they not written in the Book of the Annals of the Kings of Judah? ²⁰His servants arose, devised a conspiracy, and killed Joash in the house of Millo, on the way that goes down to Silla. ²¹It was Jozacar son of Shimeath and Jehozabad son of Shomer, his servants, who struck him down, so that he died. He was buried with his ancestors in the city of David; then his son Amaziah succeeded him.

JEHOAHAZ REIGNS OVER ISRAEL

13 In the twenty-third year of King Joash son of Ahaziah of Judah, Jehoahaz son of Jehu began to reign over Israel in Samaria; he reigned seventeen years. 2He did what was evil in the sight of the LORD, and followed the sins of Jeroboam son of Nebat, which he caused Israel to sin; he did not depart from them. 3The anger of the LORD was kindled against Israel, so that he gave them repeatedly into the hand of King Hazael of Aram, then into the hand of Ben-hadad son of Hazael. 4But Jehoahaz entreated the LORD, and the LORD heeded him; for he saw the oppression of Israel, how the king of Aram oppressed them. 5Therefore the LORD gave Israel a savior, so that they escaped from the hand of the Arameans; and the people of Israel lived in their homes as formerly. 6Nevertheless they did not depart from the sins of the house of Jeroboam, which he caused Israel to sin, but walked[a] in them; the sacred pole[b] also remained in Samaria. 7So Jehoahaz was left with an army of not more than fifty horsemen, ten chariots and ten thousand footmen; for the king of Aram had destroyed them and made them like the dust at threshing. 8Now the rest of the acts of Jehoahaz and all that he did, including his might, are they not written in the Book of the Annals of the Kings of Israel? 9So Jehoahaz slept with his ancestors, and they buried him in Samaria; then his son Joash succeeded him.

JEHOASH REIGNS OVER ISRAEL

10 In the thirty-seventh year of King Joash of Judah, Jehoash son of Jehoahaz began to reign over Israel in Samaria; he reigned sixteen years. 11He also did what was evil in the sight of the LORD; he did not depart from all the sins of Jeroboam son of Nebat, which he caused Israel to sin, but he walked in them. 12Now the rest of the acts of Joash, and all that he did, as well as the might with which he fought against King Amaziah of Judah, are they not written in the Book of the Annals of the Kings of Israel? 13So Joash slept with his ancestors, and Jeroboam sat upon his throne; Joash was buried in Samaria with the kings of Israel.

DEATH OF ELISHA

14 Now when Elisha had fallen sick with the illness of which he was to die, King Joash of Israel went down to him, and wept before him, crying, "My father, my father! The chariots of Israel and its horsemen!" 15Elisha said to him, "Take a bow and arrows"; so he took a bow and arrows. 16Then he said to the king of Israel, "Draw the bow"; and he drew it. Elisha laid his hands on the king's hands. 17Then he said, "Open the window eastward"; and he opened it. Elisha said, "Shoot"; and he shot. Then he said, "The LORD's arrow of victory, the arrow of victory over Aram! For you shall fight the Arameans in Aphek until you have made an end of them." 18He continued, "Take the arrows"; and he took them. He said to the king of Israel, "Strike the ground with them"; he struck three times, and stopped. 19Then the man of God was angry with him, and said, "You should have struck five or six times; then you would have struck down Aram until you had made an end of it, but now you will strike down Aram only three times."

20 So Elisha died, and they buried him. Now bands of Moabites used to invade the land in the spring of the year. 21As a man was being buried, a marauding band was seen and the man was thrown into the grave of Elisha; as soon as the man touched the bones of Elisha, he came to life and stood on his feet.

ISRAEL RECAPTURES CITIES FROM ARAM

22 Now King Hazael of Aram oppressed Israel all the days of Jehoahaz. 23But the LORD was gracious to them and had compassion on them; he turned toward them, because of

---

[a] 13.6 Gk Syr Tg Vg: Heb *he walked*
[b] 13.6 Heb *Asherah*

his covenant with Abraham, Isaac, and Jacob, and would not destroy them; nor has he banished them from his presence until now.

24 When King Hazael of Aram died, his son Ben-hadad succeeded him. 25 Then Jehoash son of Jehoahaz took again from Ben-hadad son of Hazael the towns that he had taken from his father Jehoahaz in war. Three times Joash defeated him and recovered the towns of Israel.

AMAZIAH REIGNS OVER JUDAH

14 In the second year of King Joash son of Joahaz of Israel, King Amaziah son of Joash of Judah, began to reign. 2 He was twenty-five years old when he began to reign, and he reigned twenty-nine years in Jerusalem. His mother's name was Jehoaddin of Jerusalem. 3 He did what was right in the sight of the LORD, yet not like his ancestor David; in all things he did as his father Joash had done. 4 But the high places were not removed; the people still sacrificed and made offerings on the high places. 5 As soon as the royal power was firmly in his hand he killed his servants who had murdered his father the king. 6 But he did not put to death the children of the murderers; according to what is written in the book of the law of Moses, where the LORD commanded, "The parents shall not be put to death for the children, or the children be put to death for the parents; but all shall be put to death for their own sins."

7 He killed ten thousand Edomites in the Valley of Salt and took Sela by storm; he called it Jokthe-el, which is its name to this day.

8 Then Amaziah sent messengers to King Jehoash son of Jehoahaz, son of Jehu, of Israel, saying, "Come, let us look one another in the face." 9 King Jehoash of Israel sent word to King Amaziah of Judah, "A thornbush on Lebanon sent to a cedar on Lebanon, saying, 'Give your daughter to my son for a wife'; but a wild animal of Lebanon passed by and trampled down the thornbush. 10 You have indeed defeated Edom,

and your heart has lifted you up. Be content with your glory, and stay at home; for why should you provoke trouble so that you fall, you and Judah with you?"

11 But Amaziah would not listen. So King Jehoash of Israel went up; he and King Amaziah of Judah faced one another in battle at Beth-shemesh, which belongs to Judah. 12 Judah was defeated by Israel; everyone fled home. 13 King Jehoash of Israel captured King Amaziah of Judah son of Jehoash, son of Ahaziah, at Beth-shemesh; he came to Jerusalem, and broke down the wall of Jerusalem from the Ephraim Gate to the Corner Gate, a distance of four hundred cubits. 14 He seized all the gold and silver, and all the vessels that were found in the house of the LORD and in the treasuries of the king's house, as well as hostages; then he returned to Samaria.

DIFFERENCES OF OPINION

ARE INEVITABLE, BUT

DIVISION AND ANTAGONISM

AMONG CHRISTIANS STRIKE

AT THE ROOTS OF OUR

EVANGELICAL CALL.

15 Now the rest of the acts that Jehoash did, his might, and how he fought with King Amaziah of Judah, are they not written in the Book of the Annals of the Kings of Israel? 16 Jehoash slept with his ancestors, and was buried in Samaria with the kings of Israel; then his son Jeroboam succeeded him.

17 King Amaziah son of Joash of Judah lived fifteen years after the death of King Jehoash son of Jehoahaz of Israel. 18 Now the rest of the deeds of Amaziah, are they not written in the Book of the Annals of the Kings of Judah? 19 They made

a conspiracy against him in Jerusalem, and he fled to Lachish. But they sent after him to Lachish, and killed him there. 20They brought him on horses; he was buried in Jerusalem with his ancestors in the city of David. 21All the people of Judah took Azariah, who was sixteen years old, and made him king to succeed his father Amaziah. 22He rebuilt Elath and restored it to Judah, after King Amaziah[a] slept with his ancestors.

JEROBOAM II REIGNS OVER ISRAEL

23 In the fifteenth year of King Amaziah son of Joash of Judah, King Jeroboam son of Joash of Israel began to reign in Samaria; he reigned forty-one years. 24He did what was evil in the sight of the LORD; he did not depart from all the sins of Jeroboam son of Nebat, which he caused Israel to sin. 25He restored the border of Israel from Lebo-hamath as far as the Sea of the Arabah, according to the word of the LORD, the God of Israel, which he spoke by his servant Jonah son of Amittai, the prophet, who was from Gath-hepher. 26For the LORD saw that the distress of Israel was very bitter; there was no one left, bond or free, and no one to help Israel. 27But the LORD had not said that he would blot out the name of Israel from under heaven, so he saved them by the hand of Jeroboam son of Joash.

28 Now the rest of the acts of Jeroboam, and all that he did, and his might, how he fought, and how he recovered for Israel Damascus and Hamath, which had belonged to Judah, are they not written in the Book of the Annals of the Kings of Israel? 29Jeroboam slept with his ancestors, the kings of Israel; his son Zechariah succeeded him.

AZARIAH REIGNS OVER JUDAH

15 In the twenty-seventh year of King Jeroboam of Israel King Azariah son of Amaziah of Judah began to reign. 2He was sixteen years old when he began to reign, and he reigned fifty-two years in Jerusalem. His mother's name was Jecoliah of Jerusalem. 3He did what was right in the sight of the LORD, just as his father Amaziah had done. 4Nevertheless the high places were not taken away; the people still sacrificed and made offerings on the high places. 5The LORD struck the king, so that he was leprous[b] to the day of his death, and lived in a separate house. Jotham the king's son was in charge of the palace, governing the people of the land. 6Now the rest of the acts of Azariah, and all that he did, are they not written in the Book of the Annals of the Kings of Judah? 7Azariah slept with his ancestors; they buried him with his ancestors in the city of David; his son Jotham succeeded him.

ZECHARIAH REIGNS OVER ISRAEL

8 In the thirty-eighth year of King Azariah of Judah, Zechariah son of Jeroboam reigned over Israel in Samaria six months. 9He did what was evil in the sight of the LORD, as his ancestors had done. He did not depart from the sins of Jeroboam son of Nebat, which he caused Israel to sin. 10Shallum son of Jabesh conspired against him, and struck him down in public and killed him, and reigned in place of him. 11Now the rest of the deeds of Zechariah are written in the Book of the Annals of the Kings of Israel. 12This was the promise of the LORD that he gave to Jehu, "Your sons shall sit on the throne of Israel to the fourth generation." And so it happened.

SHALLUM REIGNS OVER ISRAEL

13 Shallum son of Jabesh began to reign in the thirty-ninth year of King Uzziah of Judah; he reigned one month in Samaria. 14Then Menahem son of Gadi came up from Tirzah and came to Samaria; he struck down Shallum son of Jabesh in Samaria and killed him; he reigned in place of him. 15Now the rest of the deeds of Shallum, including the conspiracy that he made, are written in

a 14.22 Heb *the king*   b 15.5 A term for several skin diseases; precise meaning uncertain

the Book of the Annals of the Kings of Israel. [16] At that time Menahem sacked Tiphsah, all who were in it and its territory from Tirzah on; because they did not open it to him, he sacked it. He ripped open all the pregnant women in it.

MENAHEM REIGNS OVER ISRAEL

17 In the thirty-ninth year of King Azariah of Judah, Menahem son of Gadi began to reign over Israel; he reigned ten years in Samaria. [18] He did what was evil in the sight of the LORD; he did not depart all his days from any of the sins of Jeroboam son of Nebat, which he caused Israel to sin. [19] King Pul of Assyria came against the land; Menahem gave Pul a thousand talents of silver, so that he might help him confirm his hold on the royal power. [20] Menahem exacted the money from Israel, that is, from all the wealthy, fifty shekels of silver from each one, to give to the king of Assyria. So the king of Assyria turned back, and did not stay there in the land. [21] Now the rest of the deeds of Menahem, and all that he did, are they not written in the Book of the Annals of the Kings of Israel? [22] Menahem slept with his ancestors, and his son Pekahiah succeeded him.

PEKAHIAH REIGNS OVER ISRAEL

23 In the fiftieth year of King Azariah of Judah, Pekahiah son of Menahem began to reign over Israel in Samaria; he reigned two years. [24] He did what was evil in the sight of the LORD; he did not turn away from the sins of Jeroboam son of Nebat, which he caused Israel to sin. [25] Pekah son of Remaliah, his captain, conspired against him with fifty of the Gileadites, and attacked him in Samaria, in the citadel of the palace along with Argob and Arieh; he killed him, and reigned in place of him. [26] Now the rest of the deeds of Pekahiah, and all that he did, are written in the Book of the Annals of the Kings of Israel.

PEKAH REIGNS OVER ISRAEL

27 In the fifty-second year of King Azariah of Judah, Pekah son of Remaliah began to reign over Israel in Samaria; he reigned twenty years. [28] He did what was evil in the sight of the LORD; he did not depart from the sins of Jeroboam son of Nebat, which he caused Israel to sin.

29 In the days of King Pekah of Israel, King Tiglath-pileser of Assyria came and captured Ijon, Abel-beth-maacah, Janoah, Kedesh, Hazor, Gilead, and Galilee, all the land of Naphtali; and he carried the people captive to Assyria. [30] Then Hoshea son of Elah made a conspiracy against Pekah son of Remaliah, attacked him, and killed him; he reigned in place of him, in the twentieth year of Jotham son of Uzziah. [31] Now the rest of the acts of Pekah, and all that he did, are written in the Book of the Annals of the Kings of Israel.

JOTHAM REIGNS OVER JUDAH

32 In the second year of King Pekah son of Remaliah of Israel, King Jotham son of Uzziah of Judah began to reign. [33] He was twenty-five years old when he began to reign and reigned sixteen years in Jerusalem. His mother's name was Jerusha daughter of Zadok. [34] He did what was right in the sight of the LORD, just as his father Uzziah had done. [35] Nevertheless the high places were not removed; the people still sacrificed and made offerings on the high places. He built the upper gate of the house of the LORD. [36] Now the rest of the acts of Jotham, and all that he did, are they not written in the Book of the Annals of the Kings of Judah? [37] In those days the LORD began to send King Rezin of Aram and Pekah son of Remaliah against Judah. [38] Jotham slept with his ancestors, and was buried with his ancestors in the city of David, his ancestor; his son Ahaz succeeded him.

AHAZ REIGNS OVER JUDAH

16 In the seventeenth year of Pekah son of Remaliah, King Ahaz son of Jotham of Judah began to reign. [2] Ahaz was twenty years old when he began to reign; he reigned sixteen years in Jerusalem. He did

not do what was right in the sight of the LORD his God, as his ancestor David had done, ³but he walked in the way of the kings of Israel. He even made his son pass through fire, according to the abominable practices of the nations whom the LORD drove out before the people of Israel. ⁴He sacrificed and made offerings on the high places, on the hills, and under every green tree.

5 Then King Rezin of Aram and King Pekah son of Remaliah of Israel came up to wage war on Jerusalem; they besieged Ahaz but could not conquer him. ⁶At that time the king of Edom[a] recovered Elath for Edom,[b] and drove the Judeans from Elath; and the Edomites came to Elath, where they live to this day. ⁷Ahaz sent messengers to King Tiglath-pileser of Assyria, saying, "I am your servant and your son. Come up, and rescue me from the hand of the king of Aram and from the hand of the king of Israel, who are attacking me." ⁸Ahaz also took the silver and gold found in the house of the LORD and in the treasures of the king's house, and sent a present to the king of Assyria. ⁹The king of Assyria listened to him; the king of Assyria marched up against Damascus, and took it, carrying its people captive to Kir; then he killed Rezin.

10 When King Ahaz went to Damascus to meet King Tiglath-pileser of Assyria, he saw the altar that was at Damascus. King Ahaz sent to the priest Uriah a model of the altar, and its pattern, exact in all its details. ¹¹The priest Uriah built the altar; in accordance with all that King Ahaz had sent from Damascus, just so did the priest Uriah build it, before King Ahaz arrived from Damascus. ¹²When the king came from Damascus, the king viewed the altar. Then the king drew near to the altar, went up on it, ¹³and offered his burnt offering and his grain offering, poured his drink offering, and dashed the blood of his offerings of well-being against the altar. ¹⁴The bronze altar that was before the LORD he removed from the front of the house, from the place between his altar and the house of the LORD, and put it on the north side of his altar. ¹⁵King Ahaz commanded the priest Uriah, saying, "Upon the great altar offer the morning burnt offering, and the evening grain offering, and the king's burnt offering, and his grain offering, with the burnt offering of all the people of the land, their grain offering, and their drink offering; then dash against it all the blood of the burnt offering, and all the blood of the sacrifice; but the bronze altar shall be for me to inquire by." ¹⁶The priest Uriah did everything that King Ahaz commanded.

17 Then King Ahaz cut off the frames of the stands, and removed the laver from them; he removed the sea from the bronze oxen that were under it, and put it on a pediment of stone. ¹⁸The covered portal for use on the sabbath that had been built inside the palace, and the outer entrance for the king he removed from[c] the house of the LORD. He did this because of the king of Assyria. ¹⁹Now the rest of the acts of Ahaz that he did, are they not written in the Book of the Annals of the Kings of Judah? ²⁰Ahaz slept with his ancestors, and was buried with his ancestors in the city of David; his son Hezekiah succeeded him.

HOSHEA REIGNS OVER ISRAEL

17 In the twelfth year of King Ahaz of Judah, Hoshea son of Elah began to reign in Samaria over Israel; he reigned nine years. ²He did what was evil in the sight of the LORD, yet not like the kings of Israel who were before him. ³King Shalmaneser of Assyria came up against him; Hoshea became his vassal, and paid him tribute. ⁴But the king of Assyria found treachery in Hoshea; for he had sent messengers to King So of Egypt, and offered no tribute to the king of Assyria, as he had done year by year; therefore the king of Assyria confined him and imprisoned him.

---

[a] 16.6 Cn: Heb *King Rezin of Aram*
[b] 16.6 Cn: Heb *Aram*   [c] 16.18 Cn: Heb lacks *from*

ISRAEL CARRIED CAPTIVE
TO ASSYRIA

5 Then the king of Assyria invaded all the land and came to Samaria; for three years he besieged it. 6 In the ninth year of Hoshea the king of Assyria captured Samaria; he carried the Israelites away to Assyria. He placed them in Halah, on the Habor, the river of Gozan, and in the cities of the Medes.

7 This occurred because the people of Israel had sinned against the LORD their God, who had brought them up out of the land of Egypt from under the hand of Pharaoh king of Egypt. They had worshiped other gods 8 and walked in the customs of the nations whom the LORD drove out before the people of Israel, and in the customs that the kings of Israel had introduced.ª 9 The people of Israel secretly did things that were not right against the LORD their God. They built for themselves high places at all their towns, from watchtower to fortified city; 10 they set up for themselves pillars and sacred poles^b on every high hill and under every green tree; 11 there they made offerings on all the high places, as the nations did whom the LORD carried away before them. They did wicked things, provoking the LORD to anger; 12 they served idols, of which the LORD had said to them, "You shall not do this." 13 Yet the LORD warned Israel and Judah by every prophet and every seer, saying, "Turn from your evil ways and keep my commandments and my statutes, in accordance with all the law that I commanded your ancestors and that I sent to you by my servants the prophets." 14 They would not listen but were stubborn, as their ancestors had been, who did not believe in the LORD their God. 15 They despised his statutes, and his covenant that he made with their ancestors, and the warnings that he gave them. They went after false idols and became false; they followed the nations that were around them, concerning whom the LORD had commanded them that they should not do as they did. 16 They rejected all the commandments of the LORD their God and made for themselves cast images of two calves; they made a sacred pole,^c worshiped all the host of heaven, and served Baal. 17 They made their sons and their daughters pass through fire; they used divination and augury; and they sold themselves to do evil in the sight of the LORD, provoking him to anger. 18 Therefore the LORD was very angry with Israel and removed them out of his sight; none was left but the tribe of Judah alone.

19 Judah also did not keep the commandments of the LORD their God but walked in the customs that Israel had introduced. 20 The LORD rejected all the descendants of Israel; he punished them and gave them into the hand of plunderers, until he had banished them from his presence.

21 When he had torn Israel from the house of David, they made Jeroboam son of Nebat king. Jeroboam drove Israel from following the LORD and made them commit great sin. 22 The people of Israel continued in all the sins that Jeroboam committed; they did not depart from them 23 until the LORD removed Israel out of his sight, as he had foretold through all his servants the prophets. So Israel was exiled from their own land to Assyria until this day.

ASSYRIA RESETTLES SAMARIA

24 The king of Assyria brought people from Babylon, Cuthah, Avva, Hamath, and Sepharvaim, and placed them in the cities of Samaria in place of the people of Israel; they took possession of Samaria, and settled in its cities. 25 When they first settled there, they did not worship the LORD; therefore the LORD sent lions among them, which killed some of them. 26 So the king of Assyria was told, "The nations that you have carried away and placed in the cities of Samaria do not know the law of the god of the land; therefore

ª 17.8 Meaning of Heb uncertain
^b 17.10 Heb Asherim   ^c 17.16 Heb Asherah

he has sent lions among them; they are killing them, because they do not know the law of the god of the land." ²⁷Then the king of Assyria commanded, "Send there one of the priests whom you carried away from there; let him[a] go and live there, and teach them the law of the god of the land." ²⁸So one of the priests whom they had carried away from Samaria came and lived in Bethel; he taught them how they should worship the LORD.

²⁹ But every nation still made gods of its own and put them in the shrines of the high places that the people of Samaria had made, every nation in the cities in which they lived; ³⁰the people of Babylon made Succoth-benoth, the people of Cuth made Nergal, the people of Hamath made Ashima; ³¹the Avvites made Nibhaz and Tartak; the Sepharvites burned their children in the fire to Adrammelech and Anammelech, the gods of Sepharvaim. ³²They also worshiped the LORD and appointed from among themselves all sorts of people as priests of the high places, who sacrificed for them in the shrines of the high places. ³³So they worshiped the LORD but also served their own gods, after the manner of the nations from among whom they had been carried away. ³⁴To this day they continue to practice their former customs.

They do not worship the LORD and they do not follow the statutes or the ordinances or the law or the commandment that the LORD commanded the children of Jacob, whom he named Israel. ³⁵The LORD had made a covenant with them and commanded them, "You shall not worship other gods or bow yourselves to them or serve them or sacrifice to them, ³⁶but you shall worship the LORD, who brought you out of the land of Egypt with great power and with an outstretched arm; you shall bow yourselves to him, and to him you shall sacrifice. ³⁷The statutes and the ordinances and the law and the commandment that he wrote for you, you shall always be careful to observe. You

shall not worship other gods; ³⁸you shall not forget the covenant that I have made with you. You shall not worship other gods, ³⁹but you shall worship the LORD your God; he will deliver you out of the hand of all your enemies." ⁴⁰They would not listen, however, but they continued to practice their former custom.

41 So these nations worshiped the LORD, but also served their carved images; to this day their children and their children's children continue to do as their ancestors did.

HEZEKIAH'S REIGN OVER JUDAH

18 In the third year of King Hoshea son of Elah of Israel, Hezekiah son of King Ahaz of Judah began to reign. ²He was twenty-five years old when he began to reign; he reigned twenty-nine years in Jerusalem. His mother's name was Abi daughter of Zechariah. ³He did what was right in the sight of the LORD just as his ancestor David had done. ⁴He removed the high places, broke down the pillars, and cut down the sacred pole.[b] He broke in pieces the bronze serpent that Moses had made, for until those days the people of Israel had made offerings to it; it was called Nehushtan. ⁵He trusted in the LORD the God of Israel; so that there was no one like him among all the kings of Judah after him, or among those who were before him. ⁶For he held fast to the LORD; he did not depart from following him but kept the commandments that the LORD commanded Moses. ⁷The LORD was with him; wherever he went, he prospered. He rebelled against the king of Assyria and would not serve him. ⁸He attacked the Philistines as far as Gaza and its territory, from watchtower to fortified city.

9 In the fourth year of King Hezekiah, which was the seventh year of King Hoshea son of Elah of Israel, King Shalmaneser of Assyria came up against Samaria, besieged it, ¹⁰and at the end of three years,

---

[a] 17.27 Syr Vg: Heb them   [b] 18.4 Heb Asherah

took it. In the sixth year of Hezekiah, which was the ninth year of King Hoshea of Israel, Samaria was taken. ¹¹The king of Assyria carried the Israelites away to Assyria, settled them in Halah, on the Habor, the river of Gozan, and in the cities of the Medes, ¹²because they did not obey the voice of the LORD their God but transgressed his covenant—all that Moses the servant of the LORD had commanded; they neither listened nor obeyed.

SENNACHERIB INVADES JUDAH

13 In the fourteenth year of King Hezekiah, King Sennacherib of Assyria came up against all the fortified cities of Judah and captured them. ¹⁴King Hezekiah of Judah sent to the king of Assyria at Lachish, saying, "I have done wrong; withdraw from me; whatever you impose on me I will bear." The king of Assyria demanded of King Hezekiah of Judah three hundred talents of silver and thirty talents of gold. ¹⁵Hezekiah gave him all the silver that was found in the house of the LORD and in the treasuries of the king's house. ¹⁶At that time Hezekiah stripped the gold from the doors of the temple of the LORD, and from the doorposts that King Hezekiah of Judah had overlaid and gave it to the king of Assyria. ¹⁷The king of Assyria sent the Tartan, the Rabsaris, and the Rabshakeh with a great army from Lachish to King Hezekiah at Jerusalem. They went up and came to Jerusalem. When they arrived, they came and stood by the conduit of the upper pool, which is on the highway to the Fuller's Field. ¹⁸When they called for the king, there came out to them Eliakim son of Hilkiah, who was in charge of the palace, and Shebnah the secretary, and Joah son of Asaph, the recorder.

19 The Rabshakeh said to them, "Say to Hezekiah: Thus says the great king, the king of Assyria: On what do you base this confidence of yours? ²⁰Do you think that mere words are strategy and power for war? On whom do you now rely, that you have rebelled against me? ²¹See, you are relying now on Egypt, that broken reed of a staff, which will pierce the hand of anyone who leans on it. Such is Pharaoh king of Egypt to all who rely on him. ²²But if you say to me, 'We rely on the LORD our God,' is it not he whose high places and altars Hezekiah has removed, saying to Judah and to Jerusalem, 'You shall worship before this altar in Jerusalem'? ²³Come now, make a wager with my master the king of Assyria: I will give you two thousand horses, if you are able on your part to set riders on them. ²⁴How then can you repulse a single captain among the least of my master's servants, when you rely on Egypt for chariots and for horsemen? ²⁵Moreover, is it without the LORD that I have come up against this place to destroy it? The LORD said to me, Go up against this land, and destroy it."

26 Then Eliakim son of Hilkiah, and Shebnah, and Joah said to the Rabshakeh, "Please speak to your servants in the Aramaic language, for we understand it; do not speak to us in the language of Judah within the hearing of the people who are on the wall." ²⁷But the Rabshakeh said to them, "Has my master sent me to speak these words to your master and to you, and not to the people sitting on the wall, who are doomed with you to eat their own dung and to drink their own urine?"

28 Then the Rabshakeh stood and called out in a loud voice in the language of Judah, "Hear the word of the great king, the king of Assyria! ²⁹Thus says the king: 'Do not let Hezekiah deceive you, for he will not be able to deliver you out of my hand. ³⁰Do not let Hezekiah make you rely on the LORD by saying, The LORD will surely deliver us, and this city will not be given into the hand of the king of Assyria.' ³¹Do not listen to Hezekiah; for thus says the king of Assyria: 'Make your peace with me and come out to me; then every one of you will eat from your own vine and your own fig tree, and drink water from your own cistern, ³²until I come and take you away to a land like your own land, a land of grain and wine, a land of bread and vineyards, a land of olive oil and honey, that you may live and not die. Do not listen to Hezekiah when he misleads you by saying, The LORD will deliver us. 33Has any of the gods of the nations ever delivered its land out of the hand of the king of Assyria? 34Where are the gods of Hamath and Arpad? Where are the gods of Sepharvaim, Hena, and Ivvah? Have they delivered Samaria out of my hand? 35Who among all the gods of the countries have delivered their countries out of my hand, that the LORD should deliver Jerusalem out of my hand?'"

36 But the people were silent and answered him not a word, for the king's command was, "Do not answer him." 37Then Eliakim son of Hilkiah, who was in charge of the palace, and Shebna the secretary, and Joah son of Asaph, the recorder, came to Hezekiah with their clothes torn and told him the words of the Rabshakeh.

HEZEKIAH CONSULTS ISAIAH

19 When King Hezekiah heard it, he tore his clothes, covered himself with sackcloth, and went into the house of the LORD. 2And he sent Eliakim, who was in charge of the palace, and Shebna the secretary, and the senior priests, covered with sackcloth, to the prophet Isaiah son of Amoz. 3They said to him, "Thus says Hezekiah, This day is a day of distress, of rebuke, and of disgrace; children have come to the birth, and there is no strength to bring them forth. 4It may be that the LORD your God heard all the words of the Rabshakeh, whom his master the king of Assyria has sent to mock the living God, and will rebuke the words that the LORD your God has heard; therefore lift up your prayer for the remnant that is left." 5When the servants of King Hezekiah came to Isaiah, 6Isaiah said to them, "Say to your master, 'Thus says the LORD: Do not be afraid because of the words that you have heard, with which the servants of the king of Assyria have reviled me. 7I myself

will put a spirit in him, so that he shall hear a rumor and return to his own land; I will cause him to fall by the sword in his own land.'"

SENNACHERIB'S THREAT

8 The Rabshakeh returned, and found the king of Assyria fighting against Libnah; for he had heard that the king had left Lachish. 9When the kinga heard concerning King Tirhakah of Ethiopia,b "See, he has set out to fight against you," he sent messengers again to Hezekiah, saying, 10"Thus shall you speak to King Hezekiah of Judah: Do not let your God on whom you rely deceive you by promising that Jerusalem will not be given into the hand of the king of Assyria. 11See, you have heard what the kings of Assyria have done to all lands, destroying them utterly. Shall you be delivered? 12Have the gods of the nations delivered them, the nations that my predecessors destroyed, Gozan, Haran, Rezeph, and the people of Eden who were in Telassar? 13Where is the king of Hamath, the king of Arpad, the king of the city of Sepharvaim, the king of Hena, or the king of Ivvah?"

HEZEKIAH'S PRAYER

14 Hezekiah received the letter from the hand of the messengers and read it; then Hezekiah went up to the house of the LORD and spread it before the LORD. 15And Hezekiah prayed before the LORD, and said: "O LORD the God of Israel, who are enthroned above the cherubim, you are God, you alone, of all the kingdoms of the earth; you have made heaven and earth. 16Incline your ear, O LORD, and hear; open your eyes, O LORD, and see; hear the words of Sennacherib, which he has sent to mock the living God. 17Truly, O LORD, the kings of Assyria have laid waste the nations and their lands, 18and have hurled their gods into the fire, though they were no gods but the work of human hands—wood and stone—and so they were destroyed. 19So now, O LORD our God, save us,

a 19.9 Heb *he*   b 19.9 Or Nubia; Heb *Cush*

I pray you, from his hand, so that all
the kingdoms of the earth may know
that you, O LORD, are God alone."

20 Then Isaiah son of Amoz sent
to Hezekiah, saying, "Thus says the
LORD, the God of Israel: I have heard
your prayer to me about King Sennacherib of Assyria. 21This is the word
that the LORD has spoken concerning
him:

She despises you, she scorns you—
    virgin daughter Zion;
she tosses her head—behind
    your back,
    daughter Jerusalem.

22 "Whom have you mocked
    and reviled?
Against whom have you
    raised your voice
and haughtily lifted your eyes?
    Against the Holy One of Israel!
23 By your messengers you have
    mocked the Lord,
and you have said, 'With
    my many chariots
I have gone up the heights of
    the mountains,
    to the far recesses of Lebanon;
I felled its tallest cedars,
    its choicest cypresses;
I entered its farthest retreat,
    its densest forest.
24 I dug wells
    and drank foreign waters,
I dried up with the sole of my foot
    all the streams of Egypt.'

25 "Have you not heard
    that I determined it long ago?
I planned from days of old
    what now I bring to pass,
that you should make fortified cities
    crash into heaps of ruins,
26 while their inhabitants,
    shorn of strength,
    are dismayed and confounded;
they have become like plants
    of the field
and like tender grass,
like grass on the housetops,
    blighted before it is grown.

27 "But I know your rising[a]
    and your sitting,
    your going out and coming in,
    and your raging against me.

28 Because you have raged
    against me
and your arrogance has
    come to my ears,
I will put my hook in your nose
    and my bit in your mouth;
I will turn you back on the way
    by which you came.

29 "And this shall be the sign for
you: This year you shall eat what
grows of itself, and in the second year
what springs from that; then in the
third year sow, reap, plant vineyards,
and eat their fruit. 30The surviving
remnant of the house of Judah shall
again take root downward, and bear
fruit upward; 31for from Jerusalem
a remnant shall go out, and from
Mount Zion a band of survivors. The
zeal of the LORD of hosts will do this.

32 "Therefore thus says the LORD
concerning the king of Assyria: He
shall not come into this city, shoot
an arrow there, come before it with
a shield, or cast up a siege ramp
against it. 33By the way that he
came, by the same he shall return;
he shall not come into this city, says
the LORD. 34For I will defend this
city to save it, for my own sake and
for the sake of my servant David."

SENNACHERIB'S DEFEAT AND DEATH

35 That very night the angel of
the LORD set out and struck down
one hundred eighty-five thousand
in the camp of the Assyrians; when
morning dawned, they were all dead
bodies. 36Then King Sennacherib of
Assyria left, went home, and lived
at Nineveh. 37As he was worshiping in the house of his god Nisroch,
his sons Adrammelech and Sharezer
killed him with the sword, and they
escaped into the land of Ararat. His
son Esar-haddon succeeded him.

HEZEKIAH'S ILLNESS

20 In those days Hezekiah became sick and was at the
point of death. The prophet Isaiah
son of Amoz came to him, and said

a 19.27 Gk Compare Isa 37.27 Q Ms: MT lacks
rising

to him, "Thus says the LORD: Set your house in order, for you shall die; you shall not recover." ²Then Hezekiah turned his face to the wall and prayed to the LORD: ³"Remember now, O LORD, I implore you, how I have walked before you in faithfulness with a whole heart, and have done what is good in your sight." Hezekiah wept bitterly. ⁴Before Isaiah had gone out of the middle court, the word of the LORD came to him: ⁵"Turn back, and say to Hezekiah prince of my people, Thus says the LORD, the God of your ancestor David: I have heard your prayer, I have seen your tears; indeed, I will heal you; on the third day you shall go up to the house of the LORD. ⁶I will add fifteen years to your life. I will deliver you and this city out of the hand of the king of Assyria; I will defend this city for my own sake and for my servant David's sake." ⁷Then Isaiah said, "Bring a lump of figs. Let them take it and apply it to the boil, so that he may recover."

PONDER

"I have heard your prayer, I have seen your tears; indeed, I will heal you."
—2 Kings 20.5

PRAY

O Lord of life and healing, we are inspired by how Hezekiah called on you to heal him. We know that his prayer was answered because it was your will. Help us stretch our minds to equate Isaiah's experience with ours, to ask in faith for your healing touch for others and for ourselves, to have the innovation to reach out and find the imprisoned, the blind, the leper, the abandoned, the lonely or the inarticulate. Help us to realize that from this kind of innovation comes the realization that our lives will be pleasing to you. In the spirit of our Savior, Jesus Christ, in whose name we pray. Amen.

⁸Hezekiah said to Isaiah, "What shall be the sign that the LORD will heal me, and that I shall go up to the house of the LORD on the third day?" ⁹Isaiah said, "This is the sign to you from the LORD, that the LORD will do the thing that he has promised: the shadow has now advanced ten intervals; shall it retreat ten intervals?" ¹⁰Hezekiah answered, "It is normal for the shadow to lengthen ten intervals; rather let the shadow retreat ten intervals." ¹¹The prophet Isaiah cried to the LORD; and he brought the shadow back the ten intervals, by which the sunᵃ had declined on the dial of Ahaz.

ENVOYS FROM BABYLON

12 At that time King Merodach-baladan son of Baladan of Babylon sent envoys with letters and a present to Hezekiah, for he had heard that Hezekiah had been sick. ¹³Hezekiah welcomed them;ᵇ he showed them all his treasure house, the silver, the gold, the spices, the precious oil, his armory, all that was found in his storehouses; there was nothing in his house or in all his realm that Hezekiah did not show them. ¹⁴Then the prophet Isaiah came to King Hezekiah, and said to him, "What did these men say? From where did they come to you?" Hezekiah answered, "They have come from a far country, from Babylon." ¹⁵He said, "What have they seen in your house?" Hezekiah answered, "They have seen all that is in my house; there is nothing in my storehouses that I did not show them."

16 Then Isaiah said to Hezekiah, "Hear the word of the LORD: ¹⁷Days are coming when all that is in your house, and that which your ancestors have stored up until this day, shall be carried to Babylon; nothing shall be left, says the LORD. ¹⁸Some of your own sons who are born to you shall be taken away; they shall be eunuchs in the palace of the king of Babylon." ¹⁹Then Hezekiah said to Isaiah, "The word of the LORD that

ᵃ **20.11** Syr See Isa 38.8 and Tg: Heb *it*
ᵇ **20.13** Gk Vg Syr: Heb *When Hezekiah heard about them*

you have spoken is good." For he thought, "Why not, if there will be peace and security in my days?"

DEATH OF HEZEKIAH

20 The rest of the deeds of Hezekiah, all his power, how he made the pool and the conduit and brought water into the city, are they not written in the Book of the Annals of the Kings of Judah? 21Hezekiah slept with his ancestors; and his son Manasseh succeeded him.

MANASSEH REIGNS OVER JUDAH

21 Manasseh was twelve years old when he began to reign; he reigned fifty-five years in Jerusalem. His mother's name was Hephzibah. 2He did what was evil in the sight of the LORD, following the abominable practices of the nations that the LORD drove out before the people of Israel. 3For he rebuilt the high places that his father Hezekiah had destroyed; he erected altars for Baal, made a sacred pole,a as King Ahab of Israel had done, worshiped all the host of heaven, and served them. 4He built altars in the house of the LORD, of which the LORD had said, "In Jerusalem I will put my name." 5He built altars for all the host of heaven in the two courts of the house of the LORD. 6He made his son pass through fire; he practiced soothsaying and augury, and dealt with mediums and with wizards. He did much evil in the sight of the LORD, provoking him to anger. 7The carved image of Asherah that he had made he set in the house of which the LORD said to David and to his son Solomon, "In this house, and in Jerusalem, which I have chosen out of all the tribes of Israel, I will put my name forever; 8I will not cause the feet of Israel to wander any more out of the land that I gave to their ancestors, if only they will be careful to do according to all that I have commanded them, and according to all the law that my servant Moses commanded them." 9But they did not listen; Manasseh misled them to do more evil than the nations had done that the LORD destroyed before the people of Israel.

10 The LORD said by his servants the prophets, 11"Because King Manasseh of Judah has committed these abominations, has done things more wicked than all that the Amorites did, who were before him, and has caused Judah also to sin with his idols; 12therefore thus says the LORD, the God of Israel, I am bringing upon Jerusalem and Judah such evil that the ears of everyone who hears of it will tingle. 13I will stretch over Jerusalem the measuring line for Samaria, and the plummet for the house of Ahab; I will wipe Jerusalem as one wipes a dish, wiping it and turning it upside down. 14I will cast off the remnant of my heritage, and give them into the hand of their enemies; they shall become a prey and a spoil to all their enemies, 15because they have done what is evil in my sight and have provoked me to anger, since the day their ancestors came out of Egypt, even to this day."

16 Moreover Manasseh shed very much innocent blood, until he had filled Jerusalem from one end to another, besides the sin that he caused Judah to sin so that they did what was evil in the sight of the LORD.

17 Now the rest of the acts of Manasseh, all that he did, and the sin that he committed, are they not written in the Book of the Annals of the Kings of Judah? 18Manasseh slept with his ancestors, and was buried in the garden of his house, in the garden of Uzza. His son Amon succeeded him.

AMON REIGNS OVER JUDAH

19 Amon was twenty-two years old when he began to reign; he reigned two years in Jerusalem. His mother's name was Meshullemeth daughter of Haruz of Jotbah. 20He did what was evil in the sight of the LORD, as his father Manasseh had done. 21He walked in all the way in which his father walked, served the idols that his father served, and worshiped them; 22he abandoned the LORD, the God of his ancestors, and did not walk in the way of the

a 21.3 Heb Asherah

LORD. 23The servants of Amon conspired against him, and killed the king in his house. 24But the people of the land killed all those who had conspired against King Amon, and the people of the land made his son Josiah king in place of him. 25Now the rest of the acts of Amon that he did, are they not written in the Book of the Annals of the Kings of Judah? 26He was buried in his tomb in the garden of Uzza; then his son Josiah succeeded him.

JOSIAH REIGNS OVER JUDAH

22 Josiah was eight years old when he began to reign; he reigned thirty-one years in Jerusalem. His mother's name was Jedidah daughter of Adaiah of Bozkath. 2He did what was right in the sight of the LORD, and walked in all the way of his father David; he did not turn aside to the right or to the left.

HILKIAH FINDS THE
BOOK OF THE LAW

3 In the eighteenth year of King Josiah, the king sent Shaphan son of Azaliah, son of Meshullam, the secretary, to the house of the LORD, saying, 4"Go up to the high priest Hilkiah, and have him count the entire sum of the money that has been brought into the house of the LORD, which the keepers of the threshold have collected from the people; 5let it be given into the hand of the workers who have the oversight of the house of the LORD; let them give it to the workers who are at the house of the LORD, repairing the house, 6that is, to the carpenters, to the builders, to the masons; and let them use it to buy timber and quarried stone to repair the house. 7But no accounting shall be asked from them for the money that is delivered into their hand, for they deal honestly."

8 The high priest Hilkiah said to Shaphan the secretary, "I have found the book of the law in the house of the LORD." When Hilkiah gave the book to Shaphan, he read it. 9Then Shaphan the secretary came to the king, and reported to the king, "Your servants have emptied out the money that was found in the house, and have delivered it into the hand of the workers who have oversight of the house of the LORD." 10Shaphan the secretary informed the king, "The priest Hilkiah has given me a book." Shaphan then read it aloud to the king.

11 When the king heard the words of the book of the law, he tore his clothes. 12Then the king commanded the priest Hilkiah, Ahikam son of Shaphan, Achbor son of Micaiah, Shaphan the secretary, and the king's servant Asaiah, saying, 13"Go, inquire of the LORD for me, for the people, and for all Judah, concerning the words of this book that has been found; for great is the wrath of the LORD that is kindled against us, because our ancestors did not obey the words of this book, to do according to all that is written concerning us."

WHEN WE DISTANCE

OURSELVES FROM THE WORD

OF GOD, WE INEVITABLY

ABANDON GOD'S WILL.

14 So the priest Hilkiah, Ahikam, Achbor, Shaphan, and Asaiah went to the prophetess Huldah the wife of Shallum son of Tikvah, son of Harhas, keeper of the wardrobe; she resided in Jerusalem in the Second Quarter, where they consulted her. 15She declared to them, "Thus says the LORD, the God of Israel: Tell the man who sent you to me, 16Thus says the LORD, I will indeed bring disaster on this place and on its inhabitants—all the words of the book that the king of Judah has read. 17Because they have abandoned me and have made offerings to other gods, so that they have provoked me to anger with all the work of their hands, therefore my wrath will be kindled against this place, and it will not be quenched. 18But as to

PONDER

"Go, inquire of the LORD for me,
for the people, and for all Judah,
concerning the words of this book
that has been found; for great is
the wrath of the LORD that is kindled
against us, because our ancestors did
not obey the words of this book."
—2 Kings 22.13

PRAY

Father God, King Josiah's reaction
on finding the book of the law shows
us how blessed we are to have your
Word so readily available to us. Open
our hearts and minds to receive your
message, and give us the courage
to commit ourselves to apply what
you tell us through these pages. Let
these unequivocal and demanding
words serve as the guiding light in our
lives. Let us be courageous enough
to let them shape our existence in
the years remaining to us. We ask
in the name of our Savior. Amen.

the king of Judah, who sent you to
inquire of the LORD, thus shall you
say to him, Thus says the LORD, the
God of Israel: Regarding the words
that you have heard, 19because your
heart was penitent, and you humbled yourself before the LORD, when
you heard how I spoke against this
place, and against its inhabitants,
that they should become a desolation and a curse, and because you
have torn your clothes and wept before me, I also have heard you, says
the LORD. 20Therefore, I will gather
you to your ancestors, and you shall
be gathered to your grave in peace;
your eyes shall not see all the disaster
that I will bring on this place." They
took the message back to the king.

JOSIAH'S REFORMATION

23 Then the king directed that
all the elders of Judah and Jerusalem should be gathered to him.
2The king went up to the house of
the LORD, and with him went all
the people of Judah, all the inhabitants of Jerusalem, the priests, the
prophets, and all the people, both
small and great; he read in their
hearing all the words of the book of
the covenant that had been found
in the house of the LORD. 3The king
stood by the pillar and made a covenant before the LORD, to follow the
LORD, keeping his commandments,
his decrees, and his statutes, with all
his heart and all his soul, to perform
the words of this covenant that were
written in this book. All the people
joined in the covenant.

4 The king commanded the high
priest Hilkiah, the priests of the second order, and the guardians of the
threshold, to bring out of the temple of the LORD all the vessels made
for Baal, for Asherah, and for all the
host of heaven; he burned them outside Jerusalem in the fields of the
Kidron, and carried their ashes to
Bethel. 5He deposed the idolatrous
priests whom the kings of Judah
had ordained to make offerings in
the high places at the cities of Judah
and around Jerusalem; those also
who made offerings to Baal, to the
sun, the moon, the constellations,
and all the host of the heavens. 6He
brought out the image of[a] Asherah
from the house of the LORD, outside Jerusalem, to the Wadi Kidron,
burned it at the Wadi Kidron, beat it
to dust and threw the dust of it upon
the graves of the common people.
7He broke down the houses of the
male temple prostitutes that were
in the house of the LORD, where the
women did weaving for Asherah.
8He brought all the priests out of the
towns of Judah, and defiled the high
places where the priests had made
offerings, from Geba to Beer-sheba;
he broke down the high places of
the gates that were at the entrance
of the gate of Joshua the governor
of the city, which were on the left
at the gate of the city. 9The priests
of the high places, however, did not

a 23.6 Heb lacks image of

come up to the altar of the LORD in Jerusalem, but ate unleavened bread among their kindred. ¹⁰He defiled Topheth, which is in the valley of Ben-hinnom, so that no one would make a son or a daughter pass through fire as an offering to Molech. ¹¹He removed the horses that the kings of Judah had dedicated to the sun, at the entrance to the house of the LORD, by the chamber of the eunuch Nathan-melech, which was in the precincts;ᵃ then he burned the chariots of the sun with fire. ¹²The altars on the roof of the upper chamber of Ahaz, which the kings of Judah had made, and the altars that Manasseh had made in the two courts of the house of the LORD, he pulled down from there and broke in pieces, and threw the rubble into the Wadi Kidron. ¹³The king defiled the high places that were east of Jerusalem, to the south of the Mount of Destruction, which King Solomon of Israel had built for Astarte the abomination of the Sidonians, for Chemosh the abomination of Moab, and for Milcom the abomination of the Ammonites. ¹⁴He broke the pillars in pieces, cut down the sacred poles,ᵇ and covered the sites with human bones.

15 Moreover, the altar at Bethel, the high place erected by Jeroboam son of Nebat, who caused Israel to sin—he pulled down that altar along with the high place. He burned the high place, crushing it to dust; he also burned the sacred pole.ᶜ ¹⁶As Josiah turned, he saw the tombs there on the mount; and he sent and took the bones out of the tombs, and burned them on the altar, and defiled it, according to the word of the LORD that the man of God proclaimed,ᵈ when Jeroboam stood by the altar at the festival; he turned and looked up at the tomb of the man of God who predicted these things. ¹⁷Then he said, "What is that monument that I see?" The people of the city told him, "It is the tomb of the man of God who came from Judah and predicted these things that you have done against the altar at Bethel." ¹⁸He said, "Let him rest; let no one move his bones."

So they let his bones alone, with the bones of the prophet who came out of Samaria. ¹⁹Moreover, Josiah removed all the shrines of the high places that were in the towns of Samaria, which kings of Israel had made, provoking the LORD to anger; he did to them just as he had done at Bethel. ²⁰He slaughtered on the altars all the priests of the high places who were there, and burned human bones on them. Then he returned to Jerusalem.

THE PASSOVER CELEBRATED

21 The king commanded all the people, "Keep the passover to the LORD your God as prescribed in this book of the covenant." ²²No such passover had been kept since the days of the judges who judged Israel, even during all the days of the kings of Israel and of the kings of Judah; ²³but in the eighteenth year of King Josiah this passover was kept to the LORD in Jerusalem.

24 Moreover Josiah put away the mediums, wizards, teraphim,ᵉ idols, and all the abominations that were seen in the land of Judah and in Jerusalem, so that he established the words of the law that were written in the book that the priest Hilkiah had found in the house of the LORD. ²⁵Before him there was no king like him, who turned to the LORD with all his heart, with all his soul, and with all his might, according to all the law of Moses; nor did any like him arise after him.

26 Still the LORD did not turn from the fierceness of his great wrath, by which his anger was kindled against Judah, because of all the provocations with which Manasseh had provoked him. ²⁷The LORD said, "I will remove Judah also out of my sight, as I have removed Israel; and I will reject this city that I have chosen, Jerusalem, and the house of which I said, My name shall be there."

ᵃ 23.11 Meaning of Heb uncertain ᵇ 23.14 Heb *Asherim* ᶜ 23.15 Heb *Asherah* ᵈ 23.16 Gk: Heb *proclaimed, who had predicted these things* ᵉ 23.24 Or *household gods*

JOSIAH DIES IN BATTLE

28 Now the rest of the acts of Josiah, and all that he did, are they not written in the Book of the Annals of the Kings of Judah? **29**In his days Pharaoh Neco king of Egypt went up to the king of Assyria to the river Euphrates. King Josiah went to meet him; but when Pharaoh Neco met him at Megiddo, he killed him. **30**His servants carried him dead in a chariot from Megiddo, brought him to Jerusalem, and buried him in his own tomb. The people of the land took Jehoahaz son of Josiah, anointed him, and made him king in place of his father.

REIGN AND CAPTIVITY OF JEHOAHAZ

31 Jehoahaz was twenty-three years old when he began to reign; he reigned three months in Jerusalem. His mother's name was Hamutal daughter of Jeremiah of Libnah. **32**He did what was evil in the sight of the LORD, just as his ancestors had done. **33**Pharaoh Neco confined him at Riblah in the land of Hamath, so that he might not reign in Jerusalem, and imposed tribute on the land of one hundred talents of silver and a talent of gold. **34**Pharaoh Neco made Eliakim son of Josiah king in place of his father Josiah, and changed his name to Jehoiakim. But he took Jehoahaz away; he came to Egypt, and died there. **35**Jehoiakim gave the silver and the gold to Pharaoh, but he taxed the land in order to meet Pharaoh's demand for money. He exacted the silver and the gold from the people of the land, from all according to their assessment, to give it to Pharaoh Neco.

JEHOIAKIM REIGNS OVER JUDAH

36 Jehoiakim was twenty-five years old when he began to reign; he reigned eleven years in Jerusalem. His mother's name was Zebidah daughter of Pedaiah of Rumah. **37**He did what was evil in the sight of the LORD, just as all his ancestors had done.

JUDAH OVERRUN BY ENEMIES

24 In his days King Nebuchadnezzar of Babylon came up;

Jehoiakim became his servant for three years; then he turned and rebelled against him. **2**The LORD sent against him bands of the Chaldeans, bands of the Arameans, bands of the Moabites, and bands of the Ammonites; he sent them against Judah to destroy it, according to the word of the LORD that he spoke by his servants the prophets. **3**Surely this came upon Judah at the command of the LORD, to remove them out of his sight, for the sins of Manasseh, for all that he had committed, **4**and also for the innocent blood that he had shed; for he filled Jerusalem with innocent blood, and the LORD was not willing to pardon. **5**Now the rest of the deeds of Jehoiakim, and all that he did, are they not written in the Book of the Annals of the Kings of Judah? **6**So Jehoiakim slept with his ancestors; then his son Jehoiachin succeeded him. **7**The king of Egypt did not come again out of his land, for the king of Babylon had taken over all that belonged to the king of Egypt from the Wadi of Egypt to the River Euphrates.

REIGN AND CAPTIVITY OF JEHOIACHIN

8 Jehoiachin was eighteen years old when he began to reign; he reigned three months in Jerusalem. His mother's name was Nehushta daughter of Elnathan of Jerusalem. **9**He did what was evil in the sight of the LORD, just as his father had done.

10 At that time the servants of King Nebuchadnezzar of Babylon came up to Jerusalem, and the city was besieged. **11**King Nebuchadnezzar of Babylon came to the city, while his servants were besieging it; **12**King Jehoiachin of Judah gave himself up to the king of Babylon, himself, his mother, his servants, his officers, and his palace officials. The king of Babylon took him prisoner in the eighth year of his reign.

CAPTURE OF JERUSALEM

13 He carried off all the treasures of the house of the LORD, and the treasures of the king's house; he cut in pieces all the vessels of gold in the temple of the LORD, which King Solomon of Israel had made, all this as the LORD had foretold. ¹⁴He carried away all Jerusalem, all the officials, all the warriors, ten thousand captives, all the artisans and the smiths; no one remained, except the poorest people of the land. ¹⁵He carried away Jehoiachin to Babylon; the king's mother, the king's wives, his officials, and the elite of the land, he took into captivity from Jerusalem to Babylon. ¹⁶The king of Babylon brought captive to Babylon all the men of valor, seven thousand, the artisans and the smiths, one thousand, all of them strong and fit for war. ¹⁷The king of Babylon made Mattaniah, Jehoiachin's uncle, king in his place, and changed his name to Zedekiah.

ZEDEKIAH REIGNS OVER JUDAH

¹⁸ Zedekiah was twenty-one years old when he began to reign; he reigned eleven years in Jerusalem. His mother's name was Hamutal daughter of Jeremiah of Libnah. ¹⁹He did what was evil in the sight of the LORD, just as Jehoiakim had done. ²⁰Indeed, Jerusalem and Judah so angered the LORD that he expelled them from his presence.

THE FALL AND CAPTIVITY OF JUDAH

25 Zedekiah rebelled against the king of Babylon. ¹And in the ninth year of his reign, in the tenth month, on the tenth day of the month, King Nebuchadnezzar of Babylon came with all his army against Jerusalem, and laid siege to it; they built siegeworks against it all around. ²So the city was besieged until the eleventh year of King Zedekiah. ³On the ninth day of the fourth month the famine became so severe in the city that there was no food for the people of the land. ⁴Then a breach was made in the city wall;^a the king with all the soldiers fled^b by night by the way of the gate between the two walls, by the king's garden, though the Chaldeans were all around the city. They went in

the direction of the Arabah. ⁵But the army of the Chaldeans pursued the king, and overtook him in the plains of Jericho; all his army was scattered, deserting him. ⁶Then they captured the king and brought him up to the king of Babylon at Riblah, who passed sentence on him. ⁷They slaughtered the sons of Zedekiah before his eyes, then put out the eyes of Zedekiah; they bound him in fetters and took him to Babylon.

8 In the fifth month, on the seventh day of the month—which was the nineteenth year of King Nebuchadnezzar, king of Babylon—Nebuzaradan, the captain of the bodyguard, a servant of the king of Babylon, came to Jerusalem. ⁹He burned the house of the LORD, the king's house, and all the houses of Jerusalem; every great house he burned down. ¹⁰All the army of the Chaldeans who were with the captain of the guard broke down the walls around Jerusalem. ¹¹Nebuzaradan the captain of the guard carried into exile the rest of the people who were left in the city and the deserters who had defected to the king of Babylon—all the rest of the population. ¹²But the captain of the guard left some of the poorest people of the land to be vinedressers and tillers of the soil.

13 The bronze pillars that were in the house of the LORD, as well as the stands and the bronze sea that were in the house of the LORD, the Chaldeans broke in pieces, and carried the bronze to Babylon. ¹⁴They took away the pots, the shovels, the snuffers, the dishes for incense, and all the bronze vessels used in the temple service, ¹⁵as well as the firepans and the basins. What was made of gold the captain of the guard took away for the gold, and what was made of silver, for the silver. ¹⁶As for the two pillars, the one sea, and the stands, which Solomon had made for the house of the LORD, the bronze of all these vessels was beyond weighing. ¹⁷The height of the one pillar was eighteen cubits,

^a 25.4 Heb lacks *wall* ^b 25.4 Gk Compare Jer 39.4; 52.7: Heb lacks *the king* and lacks *fled*

and on it was a bronze capital; the height of the capital was three cubits; latticework and pomegranates, all of bronze, were on the capital all around. The second pillar had the same, with the latticework.

18 The captain of the guard took the chief priest Seraiah, the second priest Zephaniah, and the three guardians of the threshold; 19from the city he took an officer who had been in command of the soldiers, and five men of the king's council who were found in the city; the secretary who was the commander of the army who mustered the people of the land; and sixty men of the people of the land who were found in the city. 20Nebuzaradan the captain of the guard took them, and brought them to the king of Babylon at Riblah. 21The king of Babylon struck them down and put them to death at Riblah in the land of Hamath. So Judah went into exile out of its land.

GEDALIAH MADE GOVERNOR OF JUDAH

22 He appointed Gedaliah son of Ahikam son of Shaphan as governor over the people who remained in the land of Judah, whom King Nebuchadnezzar of Babylon had left. 23Now when all the captains of the forces and their men heard that the king of Babylon had appointed Gedaliah as governor, they came with their men to Gedaliah at Mizpah, namely, Ishmael son of Nethaniah, Johanan son of Kareah, Seraiah

son of Tanhumeth the Netophathite, and Jaazaniah son of the Maacathite. 24Gedaliah swore to them and their men, saying, "Do not be afraid because of the Chaldean officials; live in the land, serve the king of Babylon, and it shall be well with you." 25But in the seventh month, Ishmael son of Nethaniah son of Elishama, of the royal family, came with ten men; they struck down Gedaliah so that he died, along with the Judeans and Chaldeans who were with him at Mizpah. 26Then all the people, high and low,a and the captains of the forces set out and went to Egypt; for they were afraid of the Chaldeans.

JEHOIACHIN RELEASED FROM PRISON

27 In the thirty-seventh year of the exile of King Jehoiachin of Judah, in the twelfth month, on the twenty-seventh day of the month, King Evil-merodach of Babylon, in the year that he began to reign, released King Jehoiachin of Judah from prison; 28he spoke kindly to him, and gave him a seat above the other seats of the kings who were with him in Babylon. 29So Jehoiachin put aside his prison clothes. Every day of his life he dined regularly in the king's presence. 30For his allowance, a regular allowance was given him by the king, a portion every day, as long as he lived.

a 25.26 Or *young and old*

1 CHRONICLES

When we get discouraged with ourselves because of our sin, it's easy to lose sight of God's love for us. Sometimes we need to be reminded that God is always with us and that God is faithful. The books of Chronicles were written to reconnect the Israelites in Babylonian exile with their history as a people beloved and chosen by God. There may be a point in our lives when we ask the same question the exiles must have asked: Is God still interested in us?

FROM ADAM TO ABRAHAM

1 Adam, Seth, Enosh; ²Kenan, Mahalalel, Jared; ³Enoch, Methuselah, Lamech; ⁴Noah, Shem, Ham, and Japheth.

5 The descendants of Japheth: Gomer, Magog, Madai, Javan, Tubal, Meshech, and Tiras. ⁶The descendants of Gomer: Ashkenaz, Diphath,ᵃ and Togarmah. ⁷The descendants of Javan: Elishah, Tarshish, Kittim, and Rodanim.ᵇ

8 The descendants of Ham: Cush, Egypt, Put, and Canaan. ⁹The descendants of Cush: Seba, Havilah, Sabta, Raama, and Sabteca. The descendants of Raamah: Sheba and Dedan. ¹⁰Cush became the father of Nimrod; he was the first to be a mighty one on the earth.

11 Egypt became the father of Ludim, Anamim, Lehabim, Naphtuhim, ¹²Pathrusim, Casluhim, and Caphtorim, from whom the Philistines come.ᶜ

13 Canaan became the father of Sidon his firstborn, and Heth, ¹⁴and the Jebusites, the Amorites, the Girgashites, ¹⁵the Hivites, the Arkites, the Sinites, ¹⁶the Arvadites, the Zemarites, and the Hamathites.

17 The descendants of Shem: Elam, Asshur, Arpachshad, Lud, Aram, Uz, Hul, Gether, and Meshech.ᵈ ¹⁸Arpachshad became the father of Shelah; and Shelah became the father of Eber. ¹⁹To Eber were born two sons: the name of the one was Peleg (for in his days the earth was divided), and the name of his brother Joktan. ²⁰Joktan became the father of Almodad, Sheleph, Hazarmaveth, Jerah, ²¹Hadoram, Uzal, Diklah, ²²Ebal, Abimael, Sheba, ²³Ophir, Havilah, and Jobab; all these were the descendants of Joktan.

24 Shem, Arpachshad, Shelah; ²⁵Eber, Peleg, Reu; ²⁶Serug, Nahor, Terah; ²⁷Abram, that is, Abraham.

FROM ABRAHAM TO JACOB

28 The sons of Abraham: Isaac and Ishmael. ²⁹These are their genealogies: the firstborn of Ishmael, Nebaioth; and Kedar, Adbeel, Mibsam, ³⁰Mishma, Dumah, Massa, Hadad, Tema, ³¹Jetur, Naphish, and Kedemah. These are the sons of Ishmael.

32 The sons of Keturah, Abraham's concubine: she bore Zimran, Jokshan, Medan, Midian, Ishbak, and Shuah. The sons of Jokshan: Sheba and Dedan. ³³The sons of Midian: Ephah, Epher, Hanoch, Abida, and Eldaah. All these were the descendants of Keturah.

34 Abraham became the father of Isaac. The sons of Isaac: Esau and Israel. ³⁵The sons of Esau: Eliphaz, Reuel, Jeush, Jalam, and Korah. ³⁶The sons of Eliphaz: Teman, Omar, Zephi, Gatam, Kenaz, Timna, and Amalek. ³⁷The sons of Reuel: Nahath, Zerah, Shammah, and Mizzah.

38 The sons of Seir: Lotan, Shobal, Zibeon, Anah, Dishon, Ezer, and Dishan. ³⁹The sons of Lotan: Hori and Homam; and Lotan's sister was Timna. ⁴⁰The sons of Shobal: Alian, Manahath, Ebal, Shephi, and Onam. The sons of Zibeon: Aiah and Anah. ⁴¹The sons of Anah: Dishon. The sons of Dishon: Hamran, Eshban, Ithran, and Cheran. ⁴²The sons of Ezer: Bilhan, Zaavan, and Jaakan.ᵉ The sons of Dishan:ᶠ Uz and Aran.

43 These are the kings who reigned in the land of Edom before any king reigned over the Israelites: Bela son of Beor, whose city was called Dinhabah. ⁴⁴When Bela died, Jobab son of Zerah of Bozrah succeeded him. ⁴⁵When Jobab died, Husham of the land of the Temanites succeeded him. ⁴⁶When Husham died, Hadad son of Bedad, who defeated Midian in the country of Moab, succeeded him; and the name of his city was Avith. ⁴⁷When Hadad died, Samlah of Masrekah succeeded him. ⁴⁸When Samlah died, Shaulᵍ of Rehoboth on the Euphrates succeeded him. ⁴⁹When Shaulᵍ died, Baal-hanan son of Achbor succeeded him. ⁵⁰When Baal-hanan died, Hadad succeeded him; the name of his city was Pai, and his wife's name

---

ᵃ 1.6 Gen 10.3 *Ripath*; see Gk Vg   ᵇ 1.7 Gen 10.4 *Dodanim*; see Syr Vg   ᶜ 1.12 Heb *Casluhim, from which the Philistines come, Caphtorim*; see Am 9.7, Jer 47.4   ᵈ 1.17 *Mash* in Gen 10.23   ᵉ 1.42 Or *and Akan*; see Gen 36.27   ᶠ 1.42 See 1.38: Heb *Dishon*   ᵍ 1.48,49 Or *Saul*

Mehetabel daughter of Matred, daughter of Me-zahab. [51]And Hadad died.

The clans[a] of Edom were: clans[a] Timna, Aliah,[b] Jetheth, [52]Oholibamah, Elah, Pinon, [53]Kenaz, Teman, Mibzar, [54]Magdiel, and Iram; these are the clans[a] of Edom.

THE SONS OF ISRAEL AND THE DESCENDANTS OF JUDAH

2 These are the sons of Israel: Reuben, Simeon, Levi, Judah, Issachar, Zebulun, [2]Dan, Joseph, Benjamin, Naphtali, Gad, and Asher. [3]The sons of Judah: Er, Onan, and Shelah; these three the Canaanite woman Bath-shua bore to him. Now Er, Judah's firstborn, was wicked in the sight of the LORD, and he put him to death. [4]His daughter-in-law Tamar also bore him Perez and Zerah. Judah had five sons in all.

[5]The sons of Perez: Hezron and Hamul. [6]The sons of Zerah: Zimri, Ethan, Heman, Calcol, and Dara,[c] five in all. [7]The sons of Carmi: Achar, the troubler of Israel, who transgressed in the matter of the devoted thing; [8]and Ethan's son was Azariah.

[9]The sons of Hezron, who were born to him: Jerahmeel, Ram, and Chelubai. [10]Ram became the father of Amminadab, and Amminadab became the father of Nahshon, prince of the sons of Judah. [11]Nahshon became the father of Salma, Salma of Boaz, [12]Boaz of Obed, Obed of Jesse. [13]Jesse became the father of Eliab his firstborn, Abinadab the second, Shimea the third, [14]Nethanel the fourth, Raddai the fifth, [15]Ozem the sixth, David the seventh; [16]and their sisters were Zeruiah and Abigail. The sons of Zeruiah: Abishai, Joab, and Asahel, three. [17]Abigail bore Amasa, and the father of Amasa was Jether the Ishmaelite.

[18]Caleb son of Hezron had children by his wife Azubah, and by Jerioth; these were her sons: Jesher, Shobab, and Ardon. [19]When Azubah died, Caleb married Ephrath, who bore him Hur. [20]Hur became the father of Uri, and Uri became the father of Bezalel.

[21]Afterward Hezron went in to the daughter of Machir father of Gilead, whom he married when he was sixty years old; and she bore him Segub; [22]and Segub became the father of Jair, who had twenty-three towns in the land of Gilead. [23]But Geshur and Aram took from them Havvoth-jair, Kenath and its villages, sixty towns. All these were descendants of Machir, father of Gilead. [24]After the death of Hezron, in Caleb-ephrathah, Abijah wife of Hezron bore him Ashhur, father of Tekoa.

[25]The sons of Jerahmeel, the firstborn of Hezron: Ram his firstborn, Bunah, Oren, Ozem, and Ahijah. [26]Jerahmeel also had another wife, whose name was Atarah; she was the mother of Onam. [27]The sons of Ram, the firstborn of Jerahmeel: Maaz, Jamin, and Eker. [28]The sons of Onam: Shammai and Jada. The sons of Shammai: Nadab and Abishur. [29]The name of Abishur's wife was Abihail, and she bore him Ahban and Molid. [30]The sons of Nadab: Seled and Appaim; and Seled died childless. [31]The son[d] of Appaim: Ishi. The son[d] of Ishi: Sheshan. The son[d] of Sheshan: Ahlai. [32]The sons of Jada, Shammai's brother: Jether and Jonathan; and Jether died childless. [33]The sons of Jonathan: Peleth and Zaza. These were the descendants of Jerahmeel. [34]Now Sheshan had no sons, only daughters; but Sheshan had an Egyptian slave, whose name was Jarha. [35]So Sheshan gave his daughter in marriage to his slave Jarha; and she bore him Attai. [36]Attai became the father of Nathan, and Nathan of Zabad. [37]Zabad became the father of Ephlal, and Ephlal of Obed. [38]Obed became the father of Jehu, and Jehu of Azariah. [39]Azariah became the father of Helez, and Helez of Eleasah. [40]Eleasah became the father of Sismai, and Sismai of Shallum. [41]Shallum became the father of Jekamiah, and Jekamiah of Elishama.

---

[a] 1.51,54 Or *chiefs*   [b] 1.51 Or *Alvah*; see Gen 36.40   [c] 2.6 Or *Darda*; Compare Syr Tg some Gk Mss; see 1 Kings 4.31
[d] 2.31 Heb *sons*

42 The sons of Caleb brother of Jerahmeel: Mesha[a] his firstborn, who was father of Ziph. The sons of Mareshah father of Hebron. **43** The sons of Hebron: Korah, Tappuah, Rekem, and Shema. **44** Shema became father of Raham, father of Jorkeam; and Rekem became the father of Shammai. **45** The son of Shammai: Maon; and Maon was the father of Beth-zur. **46** Ephah also, Caleb's concubine, bore Haran, Moza, and Gazez; and Haran became the father of Gazez. **47** The sons of Jahdai: Regem, Jotham, Geshan, Pelet, Ephah, and Shaaph. **48** Maacah, Caleb's concubine, bore Sheber and Tirhanah. **49** She also bore Shaaph father of Madmannah, Sheva father of Machbenah and father of Gibea; and the daughter of Caleb was Achsah. **50** These were the descendants of Caleb.

The sons[b] of Hur the firstborn of Ephrathah: Shobal father of Kiriath-jearim, **51** Salma father of Bethlehem, and Hareph father of Beth-gader. **52** Shobal father of Kiriath-jearim had other sons: Haroeh, half of the Menuhoth. **53** And the families of Kiriath-jearim: the Ithrites, the Puthites, the Shumathites, and the Mishraites; from these came the Zorathites and the Eshtaolites. **54** The sons of Salma: Bethlehem, the Netophathites, Atroth-beth-joab, and half of the Manahathites, the Zorites. **55** The families also of the scribes that lived at Jabez: the Tirathites, the Shimeathites, and the Sucathites. These are the Kenites who came from Hammath, father of the house of Rechab.

DESCENDANTS OF DAVID AND SOLOMON

3 These are the sons of David who were born to him in Hebron: the firstborn Amnon, by Ahinoam the Jezreelite; the second Daniel, by Abigail the Carmelite; **2** the third Absalom, son of Maacah, daughter of King Talmai of Geshur; the fourth Adonijah, son of Haggith; **3** the fifth Shephatiah, by Abital; the sixth Ithream, by his wife Eglah; **4** six were born to him in Hebron, where he reigned for seven years and six

months. And he reigned thirty-three years in Jerusalem. **5** These were born to him in Jerusalem: Shimea, Shobab, Nathan, and Solomon, four by Bath-shua, daughter of Ammiel; **6** then Ibhar, Elishama, Eliphelet, **7** Nogah, Nepheg, Japhia, **8** Elishama, Eliada, and Eliphelet, nine. **9** All these were David's sons, besides the sons of the concubines; and Tamar was their sister.

GOD'S CALL CAN BE VIVID AND DRAMATIC—OR QUIET AND PRIVATE.

10 The descendants of Solomon: Rehoboam, Abijah his son, Asa his son, Jehoshaphat his son, **11** Joram his son, Ahaziah his son, Joash his son, **12** Amaziah his son, Azariah his son, Jotham his son, **13** Ahaz his son, Hezekiah his son, Manasseh his son, **14** Amon his son, Josiah his son. **15** The sons of Josiah: Johanan the firstborn, the second Jehoiakim, the third Zedekiah, the fourth Shallum. **16** The descendants of Jehoiakim: Jeconiah his son, Zedekiah his son; **17** and the sons of Jeconiah, the captive: Shealtiel his son, **18** Malchiram, Pedaiah, Shenazzar, Jekamiah, Hoshama, and Nedabiah; **19** The sons of Pedaiah: Zerubbabel and Shimei; and the sons of Zerubbabel: Meshullam and Hananiah, and Shelomith was their sister; **20** and Hashubah, Ohel, Berechiah, Hasadiah, and Jushab-hesed, five. **21** The sons of Hananiah: Pelatiah and Jeshaiah, his son[c] Rephaiah, his son[c] Arnan, his son[c] Obadiah, his son[c] Shecaniah. **22** The son[d] of Shecaniah: Shemaiah. And the sons of Shemaiah: Hattush, Igal, Bariah, Neariah, and Shaphat, six. **23** The sons of Neariah: Elioenai, Hizkiah, and Azrikam,

a **2.42** Gk reads *Mareshah* b **2.50** GkVg: Heb *son* c **3.21** Gk Compare SyrVg: Heb *sons of* d **3.22** Heb *sons*

three. ²⁴The sons of Elioenai: Hodaviah, Eliashib, Pelaiah, Akkub, Johanan, Delaiah, and Anani, seven.

DESCENDANTS OF JUDAH

4 The sons of Judah: Perez, Hezron, Carmi, Hur, and Shobal. ²Reaiah son of Shobal became the father of Jahath, and Jahath became the father of Ahumai and Lahad. These were the families of the Zorathites. ³These were the sons^a of Etam: Jezreel, Ishma, and Idbash; and the name of their sister was Hazzelelponi, ⁴and Penuel was the father of Gedor, and Ezer the father of Hushah. These were the sons of Hur, the firstborn of Ephrathah, the father of Bethlehem. ⁵Ashhur father of Tekoa had two wives, Helah and Naarah; ⁶Naarah bore him Ahuzzam, Hepher, Temeni, and Haahashtari.^b These were the sons of Naarah. ⁷The sons of Helah: Zereth, Izhar,^c and Ethnan. ⁸Koz became the father of Anub, Zobebah, and the families of Aharhel son of Harum. ⁹Jabez was honored more than his brothers; and his mother named him Jabez, saying, "Because I bore him in pain." ¹⁰Jabez called on the God of Israel, saying, "Oh that you would bless me and enlarge my border, and that your hand might be with me, and that you would keep me from hurt and harm!" And God granted what he asked. ¹¹Chelub the brother of Shuhah became the father of Mehir, who was the father of Eshton. ¹²Eshton became the father of Beth-rapha, Paseah, and Tehinnah the father of Ir-nahash. These are the men of Recah. ¹³The sons of Kenaz: Othniel and Seraiah; and the sons of Othniel: Hathath and Meonothai.^d ¹⁴Meonothai became the father of Ophrah; and Seraiah became the father of Joab father of Ge-harashim,^e so-called because they were artisans. ¹⁵The sons of Caleb son of Jephunneh: Iru, Elah, and Naam; and the son^f of Elah: Kenaz. ¹⁶The sons of Jehallelel: Ziph, Ziphah, Tiria, and Asarel. ¹⁷The sons of Ezrah: Jether, Mered, Epher, and Jalon. These are the sons of Bithiah, daughter of Pharaoh, whom Mered married;^g and she

conceived and bore^h Miriam, Shammai, and Ishbah father of Eshtemoa. ¹⁸And his Judean wife bore Jered father of Gedor, Heber father of Soco, and Jekuthiel father of Zanoah. ¹⁹The sons of the wife of Hodiah, the sister of Naham, were the fathers of Keilah the Garmite and Eshtemoa the Maacathite. ²⁰The sons of Shimon: Amnon, Rinnah, Ben-hanan, and Tilon. The sons of Ishi: Zoheth and Ben-zoheth. ²¹The sons of Shelah son of Judah: Er father of Lecah, Laadah father of Mareshah, and the families of the guild of linen workers at Beth-ashbea; ²²and Jokim, and the men of Cozeba, and Joash, and Saraph, who married into Moab but returned to Lehemⁱ (now the records^j are ancient). ²³These were the potters and inhabitants of Netaim and Gederah; they lived there with the king in his service.

DESCENDANTS OF SIMEON

24 The sons of Simeon: Nemuel, Jamin, Jarib, Zerah, Shaul;^k ²⁵Shallum was his son, Mibsam his son, Mishma his son. ²⁶The sons of Mishma: Hammuel his son, Zaccur his son, Shimei his son. ²⁷Shimei had sixteen sons and six daughters; but his brothers did not have many children, nor did all their family multiply like the Judeans. ²⁸They lived in Beer-sheba, Moladah, Hazar-shual, ²⁹Bilhah, Ezem, Tolad, ³⁰Bethuel, Hormah, Ziklag, ³¹Bethmarcaboth, Hazar-susim, Beth-biri, and Shaaraim. These were their towns until David became king. ³²And their villages were Etam, Ain, Rimmon, Tochen, and Ashan, five towns, ³³along with all their villages that were around these towns as far as Baal. These were their settlements. And they kept a genealogical record.

^a 4.3 Gk Compare Vg: Heb the father
^b 4.6 Or Ahashtari   ^c 4.7 Another reading is Zohar   ^d 4.13 Gk Vg: Heb lacks and Meonothai   ^e 4.14 That is Valley of artisans
^f 4.15 Heb sons   ^g 4.17 The clause: These are... married is transposed from verse 18
^h 4.17 Heb lacks and bore   ⁱ 4.22 Vg Compare Gk: Heb and Jashubi-lahem
^j 4.22 Or matters   ^k 4.24 Or Saul

34 Meshobab, Jamlech, Joshah son of Amaziah, 35Joel, Jehu son of Joshibiah son of Seraiah son of Asiel, 36Elioenai, Jaakobah, Jeshohaiah, Asaiah, Adiel, Jesimiel, Benaiah, 37Ziza son of Shiphi son of Allon son of Jedaiah son of Shimri son of Shemaiah— 38these mentioned by name were leaders in their families, and their clans increased greatly. 39They journeyed to the entrance of Gedor, to the east side of the valley, to seek pasture for their flocks, 40where they found rich, good pasture, and the land was very broad, quiet, and peaceful; for the former inhabitants there belonged to Ham. 41These, registered by name, came in the days of King Hezekiah of Judah, and attacked their tents and the Meunim who were found there, and exterminated them to this day, and settled in their place, because there was pasture there for their flocks. 42And some of them, five hundred men of the Simeonites, went to Mount Seir, having as their leaders Pelatiah, Neariah, Rephaiah, and Uzziel, sons of Ishi; 43they destroyed the remnant of the Amalekites that had escaped, and they have lived there to this day.

DESCENDANTS OF REUBEN

5 The sons of Reuben the first-born of Israel. (He was the firstborn, but because he defiled his father's bed his birthright was given to the sons of Joseph son of Israel, so that he is not enrolled in the genealogy according to the birthright; 2though Judah became prominent among his brothers and a ruler came from him, yet the birthright belonged to Joseph.) 3The sons of Reuben, the firstborn of Israel: Hanoch, Pallu, Hezron, and Carmi. 4The sons of Joel: Shemaiah his son, Gog his son, Shimei his son, 5Micah his son, Reaiah his son, Baal his son, 6Beerah his son, whom King Tilgath-pilneser of Assyria carried away into exile; he was a chieftain of the Reubenites. 7And his kindred by their families, when the genealogy of their generations was reckoned: the chief, Jeiel, and Zechariah, 8and

Bela son of Azaz, son of Shema, son of Joel, who lived in Aroer, as far as Nebo and Baal-meon. 9He also lived to the east as far as the beginning of the desert this side of the Euphrates, because their cattle had multiplied in the land of Gilead. 10And in the days of Saul they made war on the Hagrites, who fell by their hand; and they lived in their tents throughout all the region east of Gilead.

DESCENDANTS OF GAD

11 The sons of Gad lived beside them in the land of Bashan as far as Salecah: 12Joel the chief, Shapham the second, Janai, and Shaphat in Bashan. 13And their kindred according to their clans: Michael, Meshullam, Sheba, Jorai, Jacan, Zia, and Eber, seven. 14These were the sons of Abihail son of Huri, son of Jaroah, son of Gilead, son of Michael, son of Jeshishai, son of Jahdo, son of Buz; 15Ahi son of Abdiel, son of Guni, was chief in their clan; 16and they lived in Gilead, in Bashan and in its towns, and in all the pasture lands of Sharon to their limits. 17All of these were enrolled by genealogies in the days of King Jotham of Judah, and in the days of King Jeroboam of Israel.

18 The Reubenites, the Gadites, and the half-tribe of Manasseh had valiant warriors, who carried shield and sword, and drew the bow, expert in war, forty-four thousand seven hundred sixty, ready for service. 19They made war on the Hagrites, Jetur, Naphish, and Nodab; 20and when they received help against them, the Hagrites and all who were with them were given into their hands, for they cried to God in the battle, and he granted their entreaty because they trusted in him. 21They captured their livestock: fifty thousand of their camels, two hundred fifty thousand sheep, two thousand donkeys, and one hundred thousand captives. 22Many fell slain, because the war was of God. And they lived in their territory until the exile.

THE HALF-TRIBE OF MANASSEH

23 The members of the half-tribe of Manasseh lived in the land; they

were very numerous from Bashan to Baal-hermon, Senir, and Mount Hermon. 24These were the heads of their clans: Epher,[a] Ishi, Eliel, Azriel, Jeremiah, Hodaviah, and Jahdiel, mighty warriors, famous men, heads of their clans. 25But they transgressed against the God of their ancestors, and prostituted themselves to the gods of the peoples of the land, whom God had destroyed before them. 26So the God of Israel stirred up the spirit of King Pul of Assyria, the spirit of King Tilgath-pilneser of Assyria, and he carried them away, namely, the Reubenites, the Gadites, and the half-tribe of Manasseh, and brought them to Halah, Habor, Hara, and the river Gozan, to this day.

DESCENDANTS OF LEVI

6[b] The sons of Levi: Gershom,[c] Kohath, and Merari. 2The sons of Kohath: Amram, Izhar, Hebron, and Uzziel. 3The children of Amram: Aaron, Moses, and Miriam. The sons of Aaron: Nadab, Abihu, Eleazar, and Ithamar. 4Eleazar became the father of Phinehas, Phinehas of Abishua, 5Abishua of Bukki, Bukki of Uzzi, 6Uzzi of Zerahiah, Zerahiah of Meraioth, 7Meraioth of Amariah, Amariah of Ahitub, 8Ahitub of Zadok, Zadok of Ahimaaz, 9Ahimaaz of Azariah, Azariah of Johanan, 10and Johanan of Azariah (it was he who served as priest in the house that Solomon built in Jerusalem). 11Azariah became the father of Amariah, Amariah of Ahitub, 12Ahitub of Zadok, Zadok of Shallum, 13Shallum of Hilkiah, Hilkiah of Azariah, 14Azariah of Seraiah, Seraiah of Jehozadak; 15and Jehozadak went into exile when the LORD sent Judah and Jerusalem into exile by the hand of Nebuchadnezzar.

16[d] The sons of Levi: Gershom, Kohath, and Merari. 17These are the names of the sons of Gershom: Libni and Shimei. 18The sons of Kohath: Amram, Izhar, Hebron, and Uzziel. 19The sons of Merari: Mahli and Mushi. These are the clans of the Levites according to their ancestry. 20Of Gershom: Libni his son, Jahath his son, Zimmah his son, 21Joah his

son, Iddo his son, Zerah his son, Jeatherai his son. 22The sons of Kohath: Amminadab his son, Korah his son, Assir his son, 23Elkanah his son, Ebiasaph his son, Assir his son, 24Tahath his son, Uriel his son, Uzziah his son, and Shaul his son. 25The sons of Elkanah: Amasai and Ahimoth, 26Elkanah his son, Zophai his son, Nahath his son, 27Eliab his son, Jeroham his son, Elkanah his son. 28The sons of Samuel: Joel[e] his firstborn, the second Abijah.[f] 29The sons of Merari: Mahli, Libni his son, Shimei his son, Uzzah his son, 30Shimea his son, Haggiah his son, and Asaiah his son.

MUSICIANS APPOINTED BY DAVID

31 These are the men whom David put in charge of the service of song in the house of the LORD, after the ark came to rest there. 32They ministered with song before the tabernacle of the tent of meeting, until Solomon had built the house of the LORD in Jerusalem; and they performed their service in due order. 33These are the men who served; and their sons were: Of the Kohathites: Heman, the singer, son of Joel, son of Samuel, 34son of Elkanah, son of Jeroham, son of Eliel, son of Toah, 35son of Zuph, son of Elkanah, son of Mahath, son of Amasai, 36son of Elkanah, son of Joel, son of Azariah, son of Zephaniah, 37son of Tahath, son of Assir, son of Ebiasaph, son of Korah, 38son of Izhar, son of Kohath, son of Levi, son of Israel; 39and his brother Asaph, who stood on his right, namely, Asaph son of Berechiah, son of Shimea, 40son of Michael, son of Baaseiah, son of Malchijah, 41son of Ethni, son of Zerah, son of Adaiah, 42son of Ethan, son of Zimmah, son of Shimei, 43son of Jahath, son of Gershom, son of Levi. 44On the left were their kindred the

a 5.24 Gk Vg: Heb and Epher   b 6.1 Ch 5.27 in Heb   c 6.1 Heb Gershon, variant of Gershom; see 6.16   d 6.16 Ch 6.1 in Heb   e 6.28 Gk Syr Compare verse 33 and 1 Sam 8.2: Heb lacks Joel   f 6.28 Heb reads Vashni, and Abijah for the second Abijah, taking the second as a proper name

sons of Merari: Ethan son of Kishi, son of Abdi, son of Malluch, 45son of Hashabiah, son of Amaziah, son of Hilkiah, 46son of Amzi, son of Bani, son of Shemer, 47son of Mahli, son of Mushi, son of Merari, son of Levi; 48and their kindred the Levites were appointed for all the service of the tabernacle of the house of God.

49 But Aaron and his sons made offerings on the altar of burnt offering and on the altar of incense, doing all the work of the most holy place, to make atonement for Israel, according to all that Moses the servant of God had commanded. 50These are the sons of Aaron: Eleazar his son, Phinehas his son, Abishua his son, 51Bukki his son, Uzzi his son, Zerahiah his son, 52Meraioth his son, Amariah his son, Ahitub his son, 53Zadok his son, Ahimaaz his son.

SETTLEMENTS OF THE LEVITES

54 These are their dwelling places according to their settlements within their borders: to the sons of Aaron of the families of Kohathites—for the lot fell to them first— 55to them they gave Hebron in the land of Judah and its surrounding pasture lands, 56but the fields of the city and its villages they gave to Caleb son of Jephunneh. 57To the sons of Aaron they gave the cities of refuge: Hebron, Libnah with its pasture lands, Jattir, Eshtemoa with its pasture lands, 58Hilena with its pasture lands, Debir with its pasture lands, 59Ashan with its pasture lands, and Beth-shemesh with its pasture lands. 60From the tribe of Benjamin, Geba with its pasture lands, Alemeth with its pasture lands, and Anathoth with its pasture lands. All their towns throughout their families were thirteen.

61 To the rest of the Kohathites were given by lot out of the family of the tribe, out of the half-tribe, the half of Manasseh, ten towns. 62To the Gershomites according to their families were allotted thirteen towns out of the tribes of Issachar, Asher, Naphtali, and Manasseh in Bashan. 63To the Merarites according to their families were allotted twelve towns out of the tribes of Reuben, Gad, and Zebulun. 64So the people of Israel gave the Levites the towns with their pasture lands. 65They also gave them by lot out of the tribes of Judah, Simeon, and Benjamin these towns that are mentioned by name.

66 And some of the families of the sons of Kohath had towns of their territory out of the tribe of Ephraim. 67They were given the cities of refuge: Shechem with its pasture lands in the hill country of Ephraim, Gezer with its pasture lands, 68Jokmeam with its pasture lands, Beth-horon with its pasture lands, 69Aijalon with its pasture lands, Gath-rimmon with its pasture lands; 70and out of the half-tribe of Manasseh, Aner with its pasture lands, and Bileam with its pasture lands, for the rest of the families of the Kohathites.

71 To the Gershomites: out of the half-tribe of Manasseh: Golan in Bashan with its pasture lands and Ashtaroth with its pasture lands; 72and out of the tribe of Issachar: Kedesh with its pasture lands, Daberathb with its pasture lands, 73Ramoth with its pasture lands, and Anem with its pasture lands; 74out of the tribe of Asher: Mashal with its pasture lands, Abdon with its pasture lands, 75Hukok with its pasture lands, and Rehob with its pasture lands; 76and out of the tribe of Naphtali: Kedesh in Galilee with its pasture lands, Hammon with its pasture lands, and Kiriathaim with its pasture lands. 77To the rest of the Merarites out of the tribe of Zebulun: Rimmono with its pasture lands, Tabor with its pasture lands, 78and across the Jordan from Jericho, on the east side of the Jordan, out of the tribe of Reuben: Bezer in the steppe with its pasture lands, Jahzah with its pasture lands, 79Kedemoth with its pasture lands, and Mephaath with its pasture lands; 80and out of the tribe of Gad: Ramoth in Gilead with its pasture lands, Mahanaim with its pasture lands, 81Heshbon with its pasture lands, and Jazer with its pasture lands.

a 6.58 Other readings Hilez, Holon; see Josh 21.15   b 6.72 Or Dobrath

DESCENDANTS OF ISSACHAR

7 The sons[a] of Issachar: Tola, Puah, Jashub, and Shimron, four. 2The sons of Tola: Uzzi, Rephaiah, Jeriel, Jahmai, Ibsam, and Shemuel, heads of their ancestral houses, namely of Tola, mighty warriors of their generations, their number in the days of David being twenty-two thousand six hundred. 3The son[b] of Uzzi: Izrahiah. And the sons of Izrahiah: Michael, Obadiah, Joel, and Isshiah, five, all of them chiefs; 4and along with them, by their generations, according to their ancestral houses, were units of the fighting force, thirty-six thousand, for they had many wives and sons. 5Their kindred belonging to all the families of Issachar were in all eighty-seven thousand mighty warriors, enrolled by genealogy.

DESCENDANTS OF BENJAMIN

6 The sons of Benjamin: Bela, Becher, and Jediael, three. 7The sons of Bela: Ezbon, Uzzi, Uzziel, Jerimoth, and Iri, five, heads of ancestral houses, mighty warriors; and their enrollment by genealogies was twenty-two thousand thirty-four. 8The sons of Becher: Zemirah, Joash, Eliezer, Elioenai, Omri, Jeremoth, Abijah, Anathoth, and Alemeth. All these were the sons of Becher; 9and their enrollment by genealogies, according to their generations, as heads of their ancestral houses, mighty warriors, was twenty thousand two hundred. 10The sons of Jediael: Bilhan. And the sons of Bilhan: Jeush, Benjamin, Ehud, Chenaanah, Zethan, Tarshish, and Ahishahar. 11All these were the sons of Jediael according to the heads of their ancestral houses, mighty warriors, seventeen thousand two hundred, ready for service in war. 12And Shuppim and Huppim were the sons of Ir, Hushim the son[b] of Aher.

DESCENDANTS OF NAPHTALI

13 The descendants of Naphtali: Jahziel, Guni, Jezer, and Shallum, the descendants of Bilhah.

DESCENDANTS OF MANASSEH

14 The sons of Manasseh: Asriel, whom his Aramean concubine bore; she bore Machir the father of Gilead. 15And Machir took a wife for Huppim and for Shuppim. The name of his sister was Maacah. And the name of the second was Zelophehad; and Zelophehad had daughters. 16Maacah the wife of Machir bore a son, and she named him Peresh; the name of his brother was Sheresh; and his sons were Ulam and Rekem. 17The son[b] of Ulam: Bedan. These were the sons of Gilead son of Machir, son of Manasseh. 18And his sister Hammolecheth bore Ishhod, Abiezer, and Mahlah. 19The sons of Shemida were Ahian, Shechem, Likhi, and Aniam.

DESCENDANTS OF EPHRAIM

20 The sons of Ephraim: Shuthelah, and Bered his son, Tahath his son, Eleadah his son, Tahath his son, 21Zabad his son, Shuthelah his son, and Ezer and Elead. Now the people of Gath, who were born in the land, killed them, because they came down to raid their cattle. 22And their father Ephraim mourned many days, and his brothers came to comfort him. 23Ephraim[c] went in to his wife, and she conceived and bore a son; and he named him Beriah, because disaster[d] had befallen his house. 24His daughter was Sheerah, who built both Lower and Upper Bethhoron, and Uzzen-sheerah. 25Rephah was his son, Resheph his son, Telah his son, Tahan his son, 26Ladan his son, Ammihud his son, Elishama his son, 27Nun[e] his son, Joshua his son. 28Their possessions and settlements were Bethel and its towns, and eastward Naaran, and westward Gezer and its towns, Shechem and its towns, as far as Ayyah and its towns; 29also along the borders of the Manassites, Beth-shean and its towns, Taanach and its towns, Megiddo and its towns, Dor and its towns. In these lived the sons of Joseph son of Israel.

DESCENDANTS OF ASHER

30 The sons of Asher: Imnah, Ishvah, Ishvi, Beriah, and their sister

[a] 7.1 Syr Compare Vg: Heb *And to the sons* [b] 7.3,12,17 Heb *sons* [c] 7.23 Heb *He* [d] 7.23 Heb *beraah* [e] 7.27 Here spelled *Non*; see Ex 33.11

Serah. 31The sons of Beriah: Heber and Malchiel, who was the father of Birzaith. 32Heber became the father of Japhlet, Shomer, Hotham, and their sister Shua. 33The sons of Japhlet: Pasach, Bimhal, and Ashvath. These are the sons of Japhlet. 34The sons of Shemer: Ahi, Rohgah, Hubbah, and Aram. 35The sons of Helema his brother: Zophah, Imna, Shelesh, and Amal. 36The sons of Zophah: Suah, Harnepher, Shual, Beri, Imrah, 37Bezer, Hod, Shamma, Shilshah, Ithran, and Beera. 38The sons of Jether: Jephunneh, Pispa, and Ara. 39The sons of Ulla: Arah, Hanniel, and Rizia. 40All of these were men of Asher, heads of ancestral houses, select mighty warriors, chief of the princes. Their number enrolled by genealogies, for service in war, was twenty-six thousand men.

DESCENDANTS OF BENJAMIN

8 Benjamin became the father of Bela his firstborn, Ashbel the second, Aharah the third, 2Nohah the fourth, and Rapha the fifth. 3And Bela had sons: Addar, Gera, Abihud,b 4Abishua, Naaman, Ahoah, 5Gera, Shephuphan, and Huram. 6These are the sons of Ehud (they were heads of ancestral houses of the inhabitants of Geba, and they were carried into exile to Manahath): 7Naaman,c Ahijah, and Gera, that is, Heglam,d who became the father of Uzza and Ahihud. 8And Shaharaim had sons in the country of Moab after he had sent away his wives Hushim and Baara. 9He had sons by his wife Hodesh: Jobab, Zibia, Mesha, Malcam, 10Jeuz, Sachia, and Mirmah. These were his sons, heads of ancestral houses. 11He also had sons by Hushim: Abitub and Elpaal. 12The sons of Elpaal: Eber, Misham, and Shemed, who built Ono and Lod with its towns, 13and Beriah and Shema (they were heads of ancestral houses of the inhabitants of Aijalon, who put to flight the inhabitants of Gath); 14and Ahio, Shashak, and Jeremoth. 15Zebadiah, Arad, Eder, 16Michael, Ishpah, and Joha were sons of Beriah. 17Zebadiah, Meshullam, Hizki, Heber, 18Ishmerai, Iz-

liah, and Jobab were the sons of Elpaal. 19Jakim, Zichri, Zabdi, 20Elienai, Zillethai, Eliel, 21Adaiah, Beraiah, and Shimrath were the sons of Shimei. 22Ishpan, Eber, Eliel, 23Abdon, Zichri, Hanan, 24Hananiah, Elam, Anthothijah, 25Iphdeiah, and Penuel were the sons of Shashak. 26Shamsherai, Shehariah, Athaliah, 27Jaareshiah, Elijah, and Zichri were the sons of Jeroham. 28These were the heads of ancestral houses, according to their generations, chiefs. These lived in Jerusalem.

29 Jeiele the father of Gibeon lived in Gibeon, and the name of his wife was Maacah. 30His firstborn son: Abdon, then Zur, Kish, Baal,f Nadab, 31Gedor, Ahio, Zecher, 32and Mikloth, who became the father of Shimeah. Now these also lived opposite their kindred in Jerusalem, with their kindred. 33Ner became the father of Kish, Kish of Saul,g Saulg of Jonathan, Malchishua, Abinadab, and Esh-baal; 34and the son of Jonathan was Merib-baal; and Meribbaal became the father of Micah. 35The sons of Micah: Pithon, Melech, Tarea, and Ahaz. 36Ahaz became the father of Jehoaddah; and Jehoaddah became the father of Alemeth, Azmaveth, and Zimri; Zimri became the father of Moza. 37Moza became the father of Binea; Raphah was his son, Eleasah his son, Azel his son. 38Azel had six sons, and these are their names: Azrikam, Bocheru, Ishmael, Sheariah, Obadiah, and Hanan; all these were the sons of Azel. 39The sons of his brother Eshek: Ulam his firstborn, Jeush the second, and Eliphelet the third. 40The sons of Ulam were mighty warriors, archers, having many children and grandchildren, one hundred fifty. All these were Benjaminites.

9 So all Israel was enrolled by genealogies; and these are written in the Book of the Kings of Israel. And Judah was taken into exile in Babylon

---

a 7.35 Or *Hotham*; see 7.32   b 8.3 Or *father of Ehud*; see 8.6   c 8.7 Heb and *Naaman*   d 8.7 Or *he carried them into exile*   e 8.29 Compare 9.35: Heb lacks *Jeiel* f 8.30 Gk Ms adds *Ner*; Compare 8.33 and 9.36   g 8.33 Or *Shaul*

because of their unfaithfulness. ²Now the first to live again in their possessions in their towns were Israelites, priests, Levites, and temple servants.

SHARING LOVE DOES

NOT DEPLETE IT, BUT

RATHER ENHANCES IT.

INHABITANTS OF JERUSALEM AFTER THE EXILE

3 And some of the people of Judah, Benjamin, Ephraim, and Manasseh lived in Jerusalem: ⁴Uthai son of Ammihud, son of Omri, son of Imri, son of Bani, from the sons of Perez son of Judah. ⁵And of the Shilonites: Asaiah the firstborn, and his sons. ⁶Of the sons of Zerah: Jeuel and their kin, six hundred ninety. ⁷Of the Benjaminites: Sallu son of Meshullam, son of Hodaviah, son of Hassenuah, ⁸Ibneiah son of Jeroham, Elah son of Uzzi, son of Michri, and Meshullam son of Shephatiah, son of Reuel, son of Ibnijah; ⁹and their kindred according to their generations, nine hundred fifty-six. All these were heads of families according to their ancestral houses.

PRIESTLY FAMILIES

10 Of the priests: Jedaiah, Jehoiarib, Jachin, ¹¹and Azariah son of Hilkiah, son of Meshullam, son of Zadok, son of Meraioth, son of Ahitub, the chief officer of the house of God; ¹²and Adaiah son of Jeroham, son of Pashhur, son of Malchijah, and Maasai son of Adiel, son of Jahzerah, son of Meshullam, son of Meshillemith, son of Immer; ¹³besides their kindred, heads of their ancestral houses, one thousand seven hundred sixty, qualified for the work of the service of the house of God.

LEVITICAL FAMILIES

14 Of the Levites: Shemaiah son of Hasshub, son of Azrikam, son of Hashabiah, of the sons of Merari; ¹⁵and Bakbakkar, Heresh, Galal, and Mattaniah son of Mica, son of Zichri, son of Asaph; ¹⁶and Obadiah son of Shemaiah, son of Galal, son of Jeduthun, and Berechiah son of Asa, son of Elkanah, who lived in the villages of the Netophathites.

17 The gatekeepers were: Shallum, Akkub, Talmon, Ahiman; and their kindred Shallum was the chief, ¹⁸stationed previously in the king's gate on the east side. These were the gatekeepers of the camp of the Levites. ¹⁹Shallum son of Kore, son of Ebiasaph, son of Korah, and his kindred of his ancestral house, the Korahites, were in charge of the work of the service, guardians of the thresholds of the tent, as their ancestors had been in charge of the camp of the LORD, guardians of the entrance. ²⁰And Phinehas son of Eleazar was chief over them in former times; the LORD was with him. ²¹Zechariah son of Meshelemiah was gatekeeper at the entrance of the tent of meeting. ²²All these, who were chosen as gatekeepers at the thresholds, were two hundred twelve. They were enrolled by genealogies in their villages. David and the seer Samuel established them in their office of trust. ²³So they and their descendants were in charge of the gates of the house of the LORD, that is, the house of the tent, as guards. ²⁴The gatekeepers were on the four sides, east, west, north, and south; ²⁵and their kindred who were in their villages were obliged to come in every seven days, in turn, to be with them; ²⁶for the four chief gatekeepers, who were Levites, were in charge of the chambers and the treasures of the house of God. ²⁷And they would spend the night near the house of God; for on them lay the duty of watching, and they had charge of opening it every morning.

28 Some of them had charge of the utensils of service, for they were required to count them when they were brought in and taken out. ²⁹Others of them were appointed over the furniture, and over all the holy utensils, also over the choice

flour, the wine, the oil, the incense, and the spices. 30Others, of the sons of the priests, prepared the mixing of the spices, 31and Mattithiah, one of the Levites, the firstborn of Shallum the Korahite, was in charge of making the flat cakes. 32Also some of their kindred of the Kohathites had charge of the rows of bread, to prepare them for each sabbath.

33 Now these are the singers, the heads of ancestral houses of the Levites, living in the chambers of the temple free from other service, for they were on duty day and night. 34These were heads of ancestral houses of the Levites, according to their generations; these leaders lived in Jerusalem.

THE FAMILY OF KING SAUL

35 In Gibeon lived the father of Gibeon, Jeiel, and the name of his wife was Maacah. 36His firstborn son was Abdon, then Zur, Kish, Baal, Ner, Nadab, 37Gedor, Ahio, Zechariah, and Mikloth; 38and Mikloth became the father of Shimeam; and these also lived opposite their kindred in Jerusalem, with their kindred. 39Ner became the father of Kish, Kish of Saul, Saul of Jonathan, Malchishua, Abinadab, and Esh-baal; 40and the son of Jonathan was Merib-baal; and Merib-baal became the father of Micah. 41The sons of Micah: Pithon, Melech, Tahrea, and Ahaz;a 42and Ahaz became the father of Jarah, and Jarah of Alemeth, Azmaveth, and Zimri; and Zimri became the father of Moza. 43Moza became the father of Binea; and Rephaiah was his son, Eleasah his son, Azel his son. 44Azel had six sons, and these are their names: Azrikam, Bocheru, Ishmael, Sheariah, Obadiah, and Hanan; these were the sons of Azel.

DEATH OF SAUL AND HIS SONS

10 Now the Philistines fought against Israel; and the men of Israel fled before the Philistines, and fell slain on Mount Gilboa. 2The Philistines overtook Saul and his sons; and the Philistines killed Jonathan and Abinadab and Malchishua,

sons of Saul. 3The battle pressed hard on Saul; and the archers found him, and he was wounded by the archers. 4Then Saul said to his armor-bearer, "Draw your sword, and thrust me through with it, so that these uncircumcised may not come and make sport of me." But his armor-bearer was unwilling, for he was terrified. So Saul took his own sword and fell on it. 5When his armor-bearer saw that Saul was dead, he also fell on his sword and died. 6Thus Saul died; he and his three sons and all his house died together. 7When all the men of Israel who were in the valley saw that the armyb had fled and that Saul and his sons were dead, they abandoned their towns and fled; and the Philistines came and occupied them.

8 The next day when the Philistines came to strip the dead, they found Saul and his sons fallen on Mount Gilboa. 9They stripped him and took his head and his armor, and sent messengers throughout the land of the Philistines to carry the good news to their idols and to the people. 10They put his armor in the temple of their gods, and fastened his head in the temple of Dagon. 11But when all Jabesh-gilead heard everything that the Philistines had done to Saul, 12all the valiant warriors got up and took away the body of Saul and the bodies of his sons, and brought them to Jabesh. Then they buried their bones under the oak in Jabesh, and fasted seven days.

13 So Saul died for his unfaithfulness; he was unfaithful to the LORD in that he did not keep the command of the LORD; moreover, he had consulted a medium, seeking guidance, 14and did not seek guidance from the LORD. Therefore the LORDc put him to death and turned the kingdom over to David son of Jesse.

DAVID ANOINTED KING OF ALL ISRAEL

11 Then all Israel gathered together to David at Hebron

a 9.41 Compare 8.35: Heb lacks and Ahaz
b 10.7 Heb they   c 10.14 Heb he

and said, "See, we are your bone and flesh. ²For some time now, even while Saul was king, it was you who commanded the army of Israel. The LORD your God said to you: It is you who shall be shepherd of my people Israel, you who shall be ruler over my people Israel." ³So all the elders of Israel came to the king at Hebron, and David made a covenant with them at Hebron before the LORD. And they anointed David king over Israel, according to the word of the LORD by Samuel.

JERUSALEM CAPTURED

4 David and all Israel marched to Jerusalem, that is Jebus, where the Jebusites were, the inhabitants of the land. ⁵The inhabitants of Jebus said to David, "You will not come in here." Nevertheless David took the stronghold of Zion, now the city of David. ⁶David had said, "Whoever attacks the Jebusites first shall be chief and commander." And Joab son of Zeruiah went up first, so he became chief. ⁷David resided in the stronghold; therefore it was called the city of David. ⁸He built the city all around, from the Millo in complete circuit; and Joab repaired the rest of the city. ⁹And David became greater and greater, for the LORD of hosts was with him.

DAVID'S MIGHTY MEN AND THEIR EXPLOITS

10 Now these are the chiefs of David's warriors, who gave him strong support in his kingdom, together with all Israel, to make him king, according to the word of the LORD concerning Israel. ¹¹This is an account of David's mighty warriors: Jashobeam, son of Hachmoni,ᵃ was chief of the Three;ᵇ he wielded his spear against three hundred whom he killed at one time.

12 And next to him among the three warriors was Eleazar son of Dodo, the Ahohite. ¹³He was with David at Pas-dammim when the Philistines were gathered there for battle. There was a plot of ground full of barley. Now the people had fled from the Philistines, ¹⁴but he

and David took their stand in the middle of the plot, defended it, and killed the Philistines; and the LORD saved them by a great victory.

15 Three of the thirty chiefs went down to the rock to David at the cave of Adullam, while the army of Philistines was encamped in the valley of Rephaim. ¹⁶David was then in the stronghold; and the garrison of the Philistines was then at Bethlehem. ¹⁷David said longingly, "O that someone would give me water to drink from the well of Bethlehem that is by the gate!" ¹⁸Then the Three broke through the camp of the Philistines, and drew water from the well of Bethlehem that was by the gate, and they brought it to David. But David would not drink of it; he poured it out to the LORD, ¹⁹and said, "My God forbid that I should do this. Can I drink the blood of these men? For at the risk of their lives they brought it." Therefore he would not drink it. The three warriors did these things.

20 Now Abishai,ᶜ the brother of Joab, was chief of the Thirty.ᵈ With his spear he fought against three hundred and killed them, and won a name beside the Three. ²¹He was the most renownedᵉ of the Thirty,ᵈ and became their commander; but he did not attain to the Three.

22 Benaiah son of Jehoiada was a valiant manᶠ of Kabzeel, a doer of great deeds; he struck down two sons ofᵍ Ariel of Moab. He also went down and killed a lion in a pit on a day when snow had fallen. ²³And he killed an Egyptian, a man of great stature, five cubits tall. The Egyptian had in his hand a spear like a weaver's beam; but Benaiah went against him with a staff, snatched the spear out of the Egyptian's hand, and killed him with his own spear. ²⁴Such were the things Benaiah son

ᵃ 11.11 Or *a Hachmonite* ᵇ 11.11 Compare 2 Sam 23.8: Heb *Thirty* or *captains*
ᶜ 11.20 Gk Vg Tg Compare 2 Sam 23.18: Heb *Abshai* ᵈ 11.20,21 Syr: Heb *Three*
ᵉ 11.21 Compare 2 Sam 23.19: Heb *more renowned among the two* ᶠ 11.22 Syr: Heb *the son of a valiant man* ᵍ 11.22 See 2 Sam 23.20: Heb lacks *sons of*

of Jehoiada did, and he won a name beside the three warriors. 25He was renowned among the Thirty, but he did not attain to the Three. And David put him in charge of his bodyguard.

26 The warriors of the armies were Asahel brother of Joab, Elhanan son of Dodo of Bethlehem, 27Shammoth of Harod,a Helez the Pelonite, 28Ira son of Ikkesh of Tekoa, Abiezer of Anathoth, 29Sibbecai the Hushathite, Ilai the Ahohite, 30Maharai of Netophah, Heled son of Baanah of Netophah, 31Ithai son of Ribai of Gibeah of the Benjaminites, Benaiah of Pirathon, 32Hurai of the wadis of Gaash, Abiel the Arbathite, 33Azmaveth of Baharum, Eliahba of Shaalbon, 34Hashemb the Gizonite, Jonathan son of Shagee the Hararite, 35Ahiam son of Sachar the Hararite, Eliphal son of Ur, 36Hepher the Mecherathite, Ahijah the Pelonite, 37Hezro of Carmel, Naarai son of Ezbai, 38Joel the brother of Nathan, Mibhar son of Hagri, 39Zelek the Ammonite, Naharai of Beeroth, the armor-bearer of Joab son of Zeruiah, 40Ira the Ithrite, Gareb the Ithrite, 41Uriah the Hittite, Zabad son of Ahlai, 42Adina son of Shiza the Reubenite, a leader of the Reubenites, and thirty with him, 43Hanan son of Maacah, and Joshaphat the Mithnite, 44Uzzia the Ashterathite, Shama and Jeiel sons of Hotham the Aroerite, 45Jediael son of Shimri, and his brother Joha the Tizite, 46Eliel the Mahavite, and Jeribai and Joshaviah sons of Elnaam, and Ithmah the Moabite, 47Eliel, and Obed, and Jaasiel the Mezobaite.

DAVID'S FOLLOWERS IN THE WILDERNESS

12 The following are those who came to David at Ziklag, while he could not move about freely because of Saul son of Kish; they were among the mighty warriors who helped him in war. 2They were archers, and could shoot arrows and sling stones with either the right hand or the left; they were Benjaminites, Saul's kindred. 3The chief was Ahiezer, then Joash, both sons of Shemaah of Gibeah; also Jeziel and Pelet sons of Azmaveth; Beracah, Jehu of Anathoth, 4Ishmaiah of Gibeon, a warrior among the Thirty and a leader over the Thirty; Jeremiah,c Jahaziel, Johanan, Jozabad of Gederah, 5Eluzai,d Jerimoth, Bealiah, Shemariah, Shephatiah the Haruphite; 6Elkanah, Isshiah, Azarel, Joezer, and Jashobeam, the Korahites; 7and Joelah and Zebadiah, sons of Jeroham of Gedor.

8 From the Gadites there went over to David at the stronghold in the wilderness mighty and experienced warriors, expert with shield and spear, whose faces were like the faces of lions, and who were swift as gazelles on the mountains: 9Ezer the chief, Obadiah second, Eliab third, 10Mishmannah fourth, Jeremiah fifth, 11Attai sixth, Eliel seventh, 12Johanan eighth, Elzabad ninth, 13Jeremiah tenth, Machbannai eleventh. 14These Gadites were officers of the army, the least equal to a hundred and the greatest to a thousand. 15These are the men who crossed the Jordan in the first month, when it was overflowing all its banks, and put to flight all those in the valleys, to the east and to the west.

16 Some Benjaminites and Judahites came to the stronghold to David. 17David went out to meet them and said to them, "If you have come to me in friendship, to help me, then my heart will be knit to you; but if you have come to betray me to my adversaries, though my hands have done no wrong, then may the God of our ancestors see and give judgment." 18Then the spirit came upon Amasai, chief of the Thirty, and he said,

"We are yours, O David;
    and with you, O son of Jesse!
Peace, peace to you,
    and peace to the one
        who helps you!
For your God is the one
    who helps you."

---

a 11.27 Compare 2 Sam 23.25: Heb the Harorite   b 11.34 Compare Gk and 2 Sam 23.32: Heb the sons of Hashem   c 12.4 Heb verse 5   d 12.5 Heb verse 6

Then David received them, and made them officers of his troops.

19 Some of the Manassites deserted to David when he came with the Philistines for the battle against Saul. (Yet he did not help them, for the rulers of the Philistines took counsel and sent him away, saying, "He will desert to his master Saul at the cost of our heads.") 20 As he went to Ziklag these Manassites deserted to him: Adnah, Jozabad, Jediael, Michael, Jozabad, Elihu, and Zillethai, chiefs of the thousands in Manasseh. 21 They helped David against the band of raiders,[a] for they were all warriors and commanders in the army. 22 Indeed from day to day people kept coming to David to help him, until there was a great army, like an army of God.

DAVID'S ARMY AT HEBRON

23 These are the numbers of the divisions of the armed troops who came to David in Hebron to turn the kingdom of Saul over to him, according to the word of the LORD. 24 The people of Judah bearing shield and spear numbered six thousand eight hundred armed troops. 25 Of the Simeonites, mighty warriors, seven thousand one hundred. 26 Of the Levites four thousand six hundred. 27 Jehoiada, leader of the house of Aaron, and with him three thousand seven hundred. 28 Zadok, a young warrior, and twenty-two commanders from his own ancestral house. 29 Of the Benjaminites, the kindred of Saul, three thousand, of whom the majority had continued to keep their allegiance to the house of Saul. 30 Of the Ephraimites, twenty thousand eight hundred, mighty warriors, notables in their ancestral houses. 31 Of the half-tribe of Manasseh, eighteen thousand, who were expressly named to come and make David king. 32 Of Issachar, those who had understanding of the times, to know what Israel ought to do, two hundred chiefs, and all their kindred under their command. 33 Of Zebulun, fifty thousand seasoned troops, equipped for battle with all the weapons of war, to help

David[b] with singleness of purpose. 34 Of Naphtali, a thousand commanders, with whom there were thirty-seven thousand armed with shield and spear. 35 Of the Danites, twenty-eight thousand six hundred equipped for battle. 36 Of Asher, forty thousand seasoned troops ready for battle. 37 Of the Reubenites and Gadites and the half-tribe of Manasseh from beyond the Jordan, one hundred twenty thousand armed with all the weapons of war.

38 All these, warriors arrayed in battle order, came to Hebron with full intent to make David king over all Israel; likewise all the rest of Israel were of a single mind to make David king. 39 They were there with David for three days, eating and drinking, for their kindred had provided for them. 40 And also their neighbors, from as far away as Issachar and Zebulun and Naphtali, came bringing food on donkeys, camels, mules, and oxen—abundant provisions of meal, cakes of figs, clusters of raisins, wine, oil, oxen, and sheep, for there was joy in Israel.

THE ARK BROUGHT FROM KIRIATH-JEARIM

13 David consulted with the commanders of the thousands and of the hundreds, with every leader. 2 David said to the whole assembly of Israel, "If it seems good to you, and if it is the will of the LORD our God, let us send abroad to our kindred who remain in all the land of Israel, including the priests and Levites in the cities that have pasture lands, that they may come together to us. 3 Then let us bring again the ark of our God to us; for we did not turn to it in the days of Saul." 4 The whole assembly agreed to do so, for the thing pleased all the people.

5 So David assembled all Israel from the Shihor of Egypt to Lebo-hamath, to bring the ark of God from Kiriath-jearim. 6 And David and all Israel went up to Baalah, that is, to Kiriath-jearim, which belongs to

a 12.21 Or *as officers of his troops*
b 12.33 Gk: Heb lacks *David*

Judah, to bring up from there the ark of God, the LORD, who is enthroned on the cherubim, which is called by his[a] name. [7]They carried the ark of God on a new cart, from the house of Abinadab, and Uzzah and Ahio[b] were driving the cart. [8]David and all Israel were dancing before God with all their might, with song and lyres and harps and tambourines and cymbals and trumpets.

[9]When they came to the threshing floor of Chidon, Uzzah put out his hand to hold the ark, for the oxen shook it. [10]The anger of the LORD was kindled against Uzzah; he struck him down because he put out his hand to the ark; and he died there before God. [11]David was angry because the LORD had burst out against Uzzah; so that place is called Perez-uzzah[c] to this day. [12]David was afraid of God that day; he said, "How can I bring the ark of God into my care?" [13]So David did not take the ark into his care into the city of David; he took it instead to the house of Obed-edom the Gittite. [14]The ark of God remained with the household of Obed-edom in his house three months, and the LORD blessed the household of Obed-edom and all that he had.

DAVID ESTABLISHED AT JERUSALEM

14 King Hiram of Tyre sent messengers to David, along with cedar logs, and masons and carpenters to build a house for him. [2]David then perceived that the LORD had established him as king over Israel, and that his kingdom was highly exalted for the sake of his people Israel.

[3]David took more wives in Jerusalem, and David became the father of more sons and daughters. [4]These are the names of the children whom he had in Jerusalem: Shammua, Shobab, and Nathan; Solomon, [5]Ibhar, Elishua, and Elpelet; [6]Nogah, Nepheg, and Japhia; [7]Elishama, Beeliada, and Eliphelet.

DEFEAT OF THE PHILISTINES

[8]When the Philistines heard that David had been anointed king over all Israel, all the Philistines went up in search of David; and David heard of it and went out against them. [9]Now the Philistines had come and made a raid in the valley of Rephaim. [10]David inquired of God, "Shall I go up against the Philistines? Will you give them into my hand?" The LORD said to him, "Go up, and I will give them into your hand." [11]So he went up to Baal-perazim, and David defeated them there. David said, "God has burst out[d] against my enemies by my hand, like a bursting flood." Therefore that place is called Baal-perazim.[e] [12]They abandoned their gods there, and at David's command they were burned.

[13]Once again the Philistines made a raid in the valley. [14]When David again inquired of God, God said to him, "You shall not go up after them; go around and come on them opposite the balsam trees. [15]When you hear the sound of marching in the tops of the balsam trees, then go out to battle; for God has gone out before you to strike down the army of the Philistines." [16]David did as God had commanded him, and they struck down the Philistine army from Gibeon to Gezer. [17]The fame of David went out into all lands, and the LORD brought the fear of him on all nations.

THE ARK BROUGHT TO JERUSALEM

15 David[f] built houses for himself in the city of David, and he prepared a place for the ark of God and pitched a tent for it. [2]Then David commanded that no one but the Levites were to carry the ark of God, for the LORD had chosen them to carry the ark of the LORD and to minister to him forever. [3]David assembled all Israel in Jerusalem to bring up the ark of the LORD to its place, which he had prepared for it. [4]Then David gathered together the descendants of Aaron and the Levites: [5]of the sons of Kohath, Uriel the chief, with

[a] 13.6 Heb lacks *his*   [b] 13.7 Or *and his brother*   [c] 13.11 That is *Bursting Out Against Uzzah*   [d] 14.11 Heb *paraz*   [e] 14.11 That is *Lord of Bursting Out*   [f] 15.1 Heb *He*

one hundred twenty of his kindred; 6of the sons of Merari, Asaiah the chief, with two hundred twenty of his kindred; 7of the sons of Gershom, Joel the chief, with one hundred thirty of his kindred; 8of the sons of Elizaphan, Shemaiah the chief, with two hundred of his kindred; 9of the sons of Hebron, Eliel the chief, with eighty of his kindred; 10of the sons of Uzziel, Amminadab the chief, with one hundred twelve of his kindred.

11 David summoned the priests Zadok and Abiathar, and the Levites Uriel, Asaiah, Joel, Shemaiah, Eliel, and Amminadab. 12He said to them, "You are the heads of families of the Levites; sanctify yourselves, you and your kindred, so that you may bring up the ark of the LORD, the God of Israel, to the place that I have prepared for it. 13Because you did not carry it the first time,a the LORD our God burst out against us, because we did not give it proper care." 14So the priests and the Levites sanctified themselves to bring up the ark of the LORD, the God of Israel. 15And the Levites carried the ark of God on their shoulders with the poles, as Moses had commanded according to the word of the LORD.

16 David also commanded the chiefs of the Levites to appoint their kindred as the singers to play on musical instruments, on harps and lyres and cymbals, to raise loud sounds of joy. 17So the Levites appointed Heman son of Joel; and of his kindred Asaph son of Berechiah; and of the sons of Merari, their kindred, Ethan son of Kushaiah; 18and with them their kindred of the second order, Zechariah, Jaaziel, Shemiramoth, Jehiel, Unni, Eliab, Benaiah, Maaseiah, Mattithiah, Eliphelehu, and Mikneiah, and the gatekeepers Obed-edom and Jeiel. 19The singers Heman, Asaph, and Ethan were to sound bronze cymbals; 20Zechariah, Aziel, Shemiramoth, Jehiel, Unni, Eliab, Maaseiah, and Benaiah were to play harps according to Alamoth; 21but Mattithiah, Eliphelehu, Mikneiah, Obed-edom, Jeiel, and Azaziah were to lead with lyres according to the Sheminith. 22Chenaniah,

leader of the Levites in music, was to direct the music, for he understood it. 23Berechiah and Elkanah were to be gatekeepers for the ark. 24Shebaniah, Joshaphat, Nethanel, Amasai, Zechariah, Benaiah, and Eliezer, the priests, were to blow the trumpets before the ark of God. Obed-edom and Jehiah also were to be gatekeepers for the ark.

25 So David and the elders of Israel, and the commanders of the thousands, went to bring up the ark of the covenant of the LORD from the house of Obed-edom with rejoicing. 26And because God helped the Levites who were carrying the ark of the covenant of the LORD, they sacrificed seven bulls and seven rams. 27David was clothed with a robe of fine linen, as also were all the Levites who were carrying the ark, and the singers, and Chenaniah the leader of the music of the singers; and David wore a linen ephod. 28So all Israel brought up the ark of the covenant of the LORD with shouting, to the sound of the horn, trumpets, and cymbals, and made loud music on harps and lyres.

29 As the ark of the covenant of the LORD came to the city of David, Michal daughter of Saul looked out of the window, and saw King David leaping and dancing; and she despised him in her heart.

THE ARK PLACED IN THE TENT

16 They brought in the ark of God, and set it inside the tent that David had pitched for it; and they offered burnt offerings and offerings of well-being before God. 2When David had finished offering the burnt offerings and the offerings of well-being, he blessed the people in the name of the LORD; 3and he distributed to every person in Israel—man and woman alike— to each a loaf of bread, a portion of meat,b and a cake of raisins.

4 He appointed certain of the Levites as ministers before the ark of the LORD, to invoke, to thank, and

a 15.13 Meaning of Heb uncertain
b 16.3 Compare Gk Syr Vg: Meaning of Heb uncertain

to praise the LORD, the God of Israel. ⁵Asaph was the chief, and second to him Zechariah, Jeiel, Shemiramoth, Jehiel, Mattithiah, Eliab, Benaiah, Obed-edom, and Jeiel, with harps and lyres; Asaph was to sound the cymbals, ⁶and the priests Benaiah and Jahaziel were to blow trumpets regularly, before the ark of the covenant of God.

DAVID'S PSALM OF THANKSGIVING

7 Then on that day David first appointed the singing of praises to the LORD by Asaph and his kindred.

8 O give thanks to the LORD,
   call on his name,
   make known his deeds
   among the peoples.
9 Sing to him, sing praises to him,
   tell of all his wonderful works.
10 Glory in his holy name;
   let the hearts of those who
   seek the LORD rejoice.
11 Seek the LORD and his strength,
   seek his presence continually.
12 Remember the wonderful
   works he has done,
   his miracles, and the
   judgments he uttered,
13 O offspring of his servant Israel,ᵃ
   children of Jacob, his
   chosen ones.

14 He is the LORD our God;
   his judgments are in
   all the earth.

15 Remember his covenant forever,
   the word that he commanded,
   for a thousand generations,
16 the covenant that he made
   with Abraham,
   his sworn promise to Isaac,
17 which he confirmed to Jacob
   as a statute,
   to Israel as an everlasting
   covenant,
18 saying, "To you I will give
   the land of Canaan
   as your portion for an
   inheritance."

19 When they were few in number,
   of little account, and
   strangers in the land,ᵇ
20 wandering from nation to nation,
   from one kingdom to
   another people,
21 he allowed no one to oppress them;
   he rebuked kings on
   their account,
22 saying, "Do not touch my
   anointed ones;
   do my prophets no harm."

23 Sing to the LORD, all the earth.
   Tell of his salvation from
   day to day.
24 Declare his glory among
   the nations,
   his marvelous works among
   all the peoples.

ᵃ **16.13** Another reading is *Abraham* (compare Ps 105.6)   ᵇ **16.19** Heb *in it*

BIBLE IN LIFE

Miracles

1 Chronicles 16.12

In his exuberant song of praise to God after the ark was moved to Jerusalem, David charges his people to remember the mighty acts of God. The Israelites were witnesses of God's miraculous acts. In the same way, the people of Jesus' time witnessed his miracles, but the writers of the Gospels didn't recount the stories just so we would remember them. They understood the transforming nature of Jesus' miracles. Christ performed these miracles for two reasons: 1) to show that he was the Son of God, the promised Messiah (see Acts 2.22,36); and 2) to give us evidence for belief, that by believing, we may have life (see John 20.31). When we look to the miracles performed by our Savior, we are challenged to get out of our own narrow, self-contained, self-centered lives and learn how to reach out to others as Christ did. We can minister to those who are in need and show the same kind of love that Jesus exhibited. In doing so, we can give others the opportunity to believe in Jesus and receive life.

²⁵ For great is the LORD, and
           greatly to be praised;
     he is to be revered
           above all gods.
²⁶ For all the gods of the
           peoples are idols,
     but the LORD made
           the heavens.
²⁷ Honor and majesty are
           before him;
     strength and joy are
           in his place.

²⁸ Ascribe to the LORD, O families
           of the peoples,
     ascribe to the LORD glory
           and strength.
²⁹ Ascribe to the LORD the glory
           due his name;
     bring an offering, and
           come before him.
     Worship the LORD in
           holy splendor;
³⁰   tremble before him,
           all the earth.
     The world is firmly established;
           it shall never be moved.
³¹ Let the heavens be glad, and
           let the earth rejoice,
     and let them say among
           the nations, "The
           LORD is king!"
³² Let the sea roar, and all
           that fills it;
     let the field exult, and
           everything in it.
³³ Then shall the trees of the
           forest sing for joy
     before the LORD, for he comes
           to judge the earth.
³⁴ O give thanks to the LORD,
           for he is good;
     for his steadfast love
           endures forever.

³⁵Say also:
     "Save us, O God of our salvation,
           and gather and rescue us from
                among the nations,
     that we may give thanks to
           your holy name,
           and glory in your praise.
³⁶ Blessed be the LORD, the
           God of Israel,
     from everlasting to everlasting."
Then all the people said "Amen!" and
praised the LORD.

REGULAR WORSHIP MAINTAINED

37 David left Asaph and his kinsfolk there before the ark of the covenant of the LORD to minister regularly before the ark as each day required, **38**and also Obed-edom and hisᵃ sixty-eight kinsfolk; while Obed-edom son of Jeduthun and Hosah were to be gatekeepers. **39**And he left the priest Zadok and his kindred the priests before the tabernacle of the LORD in the high place that was at Gibeon, **40**to offer burnt offerings to the LORD on the altar of burnt offering regularly, morning and evening, according to all that is written in the law of the LORD that he commanded Israel. **41**With them were Heman and Jeduthun, and the rest of those chosen and expressly named to render thanks to the LORD, for his steadfast love endures

ᵃ **16.38** Gk Syr Vg: Heb *their*

PONDER

[David] left the priest Zadok and his
kindred the priests before the tabernacle
of the LORD . . . to offer burnt offerings
to the LORD on the altar of burnt
offering regularly, morning and evening,
according to all that is written in the law
of the LORD that he commanded Israel.
—1 Chronicles 16.39–40

PRAY

Father, we pray that you will transform
us and turn us more constantly to
you in prayer, as David did, so the
things we do today or next week will
be in compliance with your will. And
help us to seek your will so we do not
go from one crisis to another, one
disappointment to another, one hope
to another, even one achievement
to another, without your direction,
guidance and blessing. Let our
lives be lived in awareness of your
holiness and mighty power. Amen.

forever. 42Heman and Jeduthun had with them trumpets and cymbals for the music, and instruments for sacred song. The sons of Jeduthun were appointed to the gate.

43 Then all the people departed to their homes, and David went home to bless his household.

GOD'S COVENANT WITH DAVID

17 Now when David settled in his house, David said to the prophet Nathan, "I am living in a house of cedar, but the ark of the covenant of the LORD is under a tent." 2Nathan said to David, "Do all that you have in mind, for God is with you."

3 But that same night the word of the LORD came to Nathan, saying: 4Go and tell my servant David: Thus says the LORD: You shall not build me a house to live in. 5For I have not lived in a house since the day I brought out Israel to this very day, but I have lived in a tent and a tabernacle.ᵃ 6Wherever I have moved about among all Israel, did I ever speak a word with any of the judges of Israel, whom I commanded to shepherd my people, saying, Why have you not built me a house of cedar? 7Now therefore thus you shall say to my servant David: Thus says the LORD of hosts: I took you from the pasture, from following the sheep, to be ruler over my people Israel; 8and I have been with you wherever you went, and have cut off all your enemies before you; and I will make for you a name, like the name of the great ones of the earth. 9I will appoint a place for my people Israel, and will plant them, so that they may live in their own place, and be disturbed no more; and evildoers shall wear them down no more, as they did formerly, 10from the time that I appointed judges over my people Israel; and I will subdue all your enemies.

Moreover I declare to you that the LORD will build you a house. 11When your days are fulfilled to go to be with your ancestors, I will raise up your offspring after you, one of your own sons, and I will estab-lish his kingdom. 12He shall build a house for me, and I will establish his throne forever. 13I will be a father to him, and he shall be a son to me. I will not take my steadfast love from him, as I took it from him who was before you, 14but I will confirm him in my house and in my kingdom forever, and his throne shall be established forever. 15In accordance with all these words and all this vision, Nathan spoke to David.

DAVID'S PRAYER

16 Then King David went in and sat before the LORD, and said, "Who am I, O LORD God, and what is my house, that you have brought me thus far? 17And even this was a small thing in your sight, O God; you have also spoken of your servant's house for a great while to come. You regard me as someone of high rank,ᵇ O LORD God! 18And what more can David say to you for honoring your servant? You know your servant. 19For your servant's sake, O LORD, and according to your own heart, you have done all these great deeds, making known all these great things. 20There is no one like you, O LORD, and there is no God besides you, according to all that we have heard with our ears. 21Who is like your people Israel, one nation on the earth whom God went to redeem to be his people, making for yourself a name for great and terrible things, in driving out nations before your people whom you redeemed from Egypt? 22And you made your people Israel to be your people forever; and you, O LORD, became their God.

23 "And now, O LORD, as for the word that you have spoken concerning your servant and concerning his house, let it be established forever, and do as you have promised. 24Thus your name will be established and magnified forever in the saying, 'The LORD of hosts, the God of Israel, is Israel's God'; and the house of your servant David will be established in your presence. 25For you, my God,

---

ᵃ 17.5 Gk 2 Sam 7.6: Heb *but I have been from tent to tent and from tabernacle*
ᵇ 17.17 Meaning of Heb uncertain

have revealed to your servant that you will build a house for him; therefore your servant has found it possible to pray before you. 26 And now, O LORD, you are God, and you have promised this good thing to your servant; 27 therefore may it please you to bless the house of your servant, that it may continue forever before you. For you, O LORD, have blessed and are blessed[a] forever."

DAVID'S KINGDOM ESTABLISHED AND EXTENDED

18 Some time afterward, David attacked the Philistines and subdued them; he took Gath and its villages from the Philistines.

2 He defeated Moab, and the Moabites became subject to David and brought tribute.

3 David also struck down King Hadadezer of Zobah, toward Hamath,[b] as he went to set up a monument at the river Euphrates. 4 David took from him one thousand chariots, seven thousand cavalry, and twenty thousand foot soldiers. David hamstrung all the chariot horses, but left one hundred of them. 5 When the Arameans of Damascus came to help King Hadadezer of Zobah, David killed twenty-two thousand Arameans. 6 Then David put garrisons[c] in Aram of Damascus; and the Arameans became subject to David, and brought tribute. The LORD gave victory to David wherever he went. 7 David took the gold shields that were carried by the servants of Hadadezer, and brought them to Jerusalem. 8 From Tibhath and from Cun, cities of Hadadezer, David took a vast quantity of bronze; with it Solomon made the bronze sea and the pillars and the vessels of bronze.

9 When King Tou of Hamath heard that David had defeated the whole army of King Hadadezer of Zobah, 10 he sent his son Hadoram to King David, to greet him and to congratulate him, because he had fought against Hadadezer and defeated him. Now Hadadezer had often been at war with Tou. He sent all sorts of articles of gold, of silver,

and of bronze; 11 these also King David dedicated to the LORD, together with the silver and gold that he had carried off from all the nations, from Edom, Moab, the Ammonites, the Philistines, and Amalek.

12 Abishai son of Zeruiah killed eighteen thousand Edomites in the Valley of Salt. 13 He put garrisons in Edom; and all the Edomites became subject to David. And the LORD gave victory to David wherever he went.

DAVID'S ADMINISTRATION

14 So David reigned over all Israel; and he administered justice and equity to all his people. 15 Joab son of Zeruiah was over the army; Jehoshaphat son of Ahilud was recorder; 16 Zadok son of Ahitub and Ahimelech son of Abiathar were priests; Shavsha was secretary; 17 Benaiah son of Jehoiada was over the Cherethites and the Pelethites; and David's sons were the chief officials in the service of the king.

DEFEAT OF THE AMMONITES AND ARAMEANS

19 Some time afterward, King Nahash of the Ammonites died, and his son succeeded him. 2 David said, "I will deal loyally with Hanun son of Nahash, for his father dealt loyally with me." So David sent messengers to console him concerning his father. When David's servants came to Hanun in the land of the Ammonites, to console him, 3 the officials of the Ammonites said to Hanun, "Do you think, because David has sent consolers to you, that he is honoring your father? Have not his servants come to you to search and to overthrow and to spy out the land?" 4 So Hanun seized David's servants, shaved them, cut off their garments in the middle at their hips, and sent them away; 5 and they departed. When David was told about the men, he sent messengers to them, for they felt greatly humiliated. The king said, "Remain at Jericho

[a] 17.27 Or *and it is blessed*   [b] 18.3 Meaning of Heb uncertain   [c] 18.6 Gk Vg 2 Sam 8.6 Compare Syr: Heb lacks *garrisons*

until your beards have grown, and then return."

6 When the Ammonites saw that they had made themselves odious to David, Hanun and the Ammonites sent a thousand talents of silver to hire chariots and cavalry from Mesopotamia, from Aram-maacah and from Zobah. 7 They hired thirty-two thousand chariots and the king of Maacah with his army, who came and camped before Medeba. And the Ammonites were mustered from their cities and came to battle. 8 When David heard of it, he sent Joab and all the army of the warriors. 9 The Ammonites came out and drew up in battle array at the entrance of the city, and the kings who had come were by themselves in the open country.

10 When Joab saw that the line of battle was set against him both in front and in the rear, he chose some of the picked men of Israel and arrayed them against the Arameans; 11 the rest of his troops he put in the charge of his brother Abishai, and they were arrayed against the Ammonites. 12 He said, "If the Arameans are too strong for me, then you shall help me; but if the Ammonites are too strong for you, then I will help you. 13 Be strong, and let us be courageous for our people and for the cities of our God; and may the LORD do what seems good to him." 14 So Joab and the troops who were with him advanced toward the Arameans for battle; and they fled before him. 15 When the Ammonites saw that the Arameans fled, they likewise fled before Abishai, Joab's brother, and entered the city. Then Joab came to Jerusalem.

16 But when the Arameans saw that they had been defeated by Israel, they sent messengers and brought out the Arameans who were beyond the Euphrates, with Shophach the commander of the army of Hadadezer at their head. 17 When David was informed, he gathered all Israel together, crossed the Jordan, came to them, and drew up his forces against them. When David set the battle in array against the Arameans, they

fought with him. 18 The Arameans fled before Israel; and David killed seven thousand Aramean charioteers and forty thousand foot soldiers, and also killed Shophach the commander of their army. 19 When the servants of Hadadezer saw that they had been defeated by Israel, they made peace with David, and became subject to him. So the Arameans were not willing to help the Ammonites any more.

SIEGE AND CAPTURE OF RABBAH

20 In the spring of the year, the time when kings go out to battle, Joab led out the army, ravaged the country of the Ammonites, and came and besieged Rabbah. But David remained at Jerusalem. Joab attacked Rabbah, and overthrew it. 2 David took the crown of Milcom[a] from his head; he found that it weighed a talent of gold, and in it was a precious stone; and it was placed on David's head. He also brought out the booty of the city, a very great amount. 3 He brought out the people who were in it, and set them to work[b] with saws and iron picks and axes.[c] Thus David did to all the cities of the Ammonites. Then David and all the people returned to Jerusalem.

PRAYERS SHOULD BE DESIGNED TO LEARN GOD'S WILL, TO REEXAMINE OUR DESIRES AND TO SUBSTITUTE GOD'S PRIORITIES FOR OUR OWN.

EXPLOITS AGAINST THE PHILISTINES

4 After this, war broke out with the Philistines at Gezer; then Sib-

a 20.2 Gk Vg See 1 Kings 11.5, 33: MT of their king   b 20.3 Compare 2 Sam 12.31: Heb and he sawed   c 20.3 Compare 2 Sam 12.31: Heb saws

becai the Hushathite killed Sippai, who was one of the descendants of the giants; and the Philistines were subdued. ⁵Again there was war with the Philistines; and El-hanan son of Jair killed Lahmi the brother of Goliath the Gittite, the shaft of whose spear was like a weaver's beam. ⁶Again there was war at Gath, where there was a man of great size, who had six fingers on each hand, and six toes on each foot, twenty-four in number; he also was descended from the giants. ⁷When he taunted Israel, Jonathan son of Shimea, David's brother, killed him. ⁸These were descended from the giants in Gath; they fell by the hand of David and his servants.

THE CENSUS AND PLAGUE

21 Satan stood up against Is-rael, and incited David to count the people of Israel. ²So David said to Joab and the commanders of the army, "Go, number Israel, from Beer-sheba to Dan, and bring me a report, so that I may know their number." ³But Joab said, "May the LORD increase the number of his people a hundredfold! Are they not, my lord the king, all of them my lord's servants? Why then should my lord require this? Why should he bring guilt on Israel?" ⁴But the king's word prevailed against Joab. So Joab departed and went through-out all Israel, and came back to Je-rusalem. ⁵Joab gave the total count of the people to David. In all Israel there were one million one hundred thousand men who drew the sword, and in Judah four hundred seventy thousand who drew the sword. ⁶But he did not include Levi and Benja-min in the numbering, for the king's command was abhorrent to Joab.

⁷ But God was displeased with this thing, and he struck Israel. ⁸David said to God, "I have sinned greatly in that I have done this thing. But now, I pray you, take away the guilt of your servant; for I have done very foolishly." ⁹The LORD spoke to Gad, David's seer, saying, ¹⁰"Go and say to David, 'Thus says the LORD: Three things I offer you; choose one of them, so that I may do it to you.' "
¹¹So Gad came to David and said to him, "Thus says the LORD, 'Take your choice: ¹²either three years of famine; or three months of devasta-tion by your foes, while the sword of your enemies overtakes you; or three days of the sword of the LORD, pes-tilence on the land, and the angel of the LORD destroying throughout all the territory of Israel.' Now decide what answer I shall return to the one who sent me." ¹³Then David said to Gad, "I am in great distress; let me fall into the hand of the LORD, for his mercy is very great; but let me not fall into human hands."

¹⁴ So the LORD sent a pestilence on Israel; and seventy thousand per-sons fell in Israel. ¹⁵And God sent an angel to Jerusalem to destroy it; but when he was about to destroy it, the LORD took note and relented concerning the calamity; he said to the destroying angel, "Enough! Stay your hand." The angel of the LORD was then standing by the threshing floor of Ornan the Jebusite. ¹⁶David looked up and saw the angel of the LORD standing between earth and heaven, and in his hand a drawn sword stretched out over Jerusalem. Then David and the elders, clothed in sackcloth, fell on their faces. ¹⁷And David said to God, "Was it not I who gave the command to count the people? It is I who have sinned and done very wickedly. But these sheep, what have they done? Let your hand, I pray, O LORD my God, be against me and against my fa-ther's house; but do not let your peo-ple be plagued!"

DAVID'S ALTAR AND SACRIFICE

¹⁸ Then the angel of the LORD commanded Gad to tell David that he should go up and erect an altar to the LORD on the threshing floor of Ornan the Jebusite. ¹⁹So David went up following Gad's instructions, which he had spoken in the name of the LORD. ²⁰Ornan turned and saw the angel; and while his four sons who were with him hid themselves, Ornan continued to thresh wheat. ²¹As David came to Ornan, Ornan

looked and saw David; he went out from the threshing floor, and did obeisance to David with his face to the ground. 22David said to Ornan, "Give me the site of the threshing floor that I may build on it an altar to the LORD—give it to me at its full price—so that the plague may be averted from the people." 23Then Ornan said to David, "Take it; and let my lord the king do what seems good to him; see, I present the oxen for burnt offerings, and the threshing sledges for the wood, and the wheat for a grain offering. I give it all." 24But King David said to Ornan, "No; I will buy them for the full price. I will not take for the LORD what is yours, nor offer burnt offerings that cost me nothing." 25So David paid Ornan six hundred shekels of gold by weight for the site. 26David built there an altar to the LORD and presented burnt offerings and offerings of well-being. He called upon the LORD, and he answered him with fire from heaven on the altar of burnt offering. 27Then the LORD commanded the angel, and he put his sword back into its sheath.

THE PLACE CHOSEN
FOR THE TEMPLE

28 At that time, when David saw that the LORD had answered him at the threshing floor of Ornan the Jebusite, he made his sacrifices there. 29For the tabernacle of the LORD, which Moses had made in the wilderness, and the altar of burnt offering were at that time in the high place at Gibeon; 30but David could not go before it to inquire of God, for he was afraid of the sword of the angel of the LORD. 1Then David said, "Here shall be the house of the LORD God and here the altar of burnt offering for Israel."

DAVID PREPARES TO
BUILD THE TEMPLE

2 David gave orders to gather together the aliens who were residing in the land of Israel, and he set stonecutters to prepare dressed stones for building the house of God. 3David also provided great stores of iron

for nails for the doors of the gates and for clamps, as well as bronze in quantities beyond weighing, 4and cedar logs without number—for the Sidonians and Tyrians brought great quantities of cedar to David. 5For David said, "My son Solomon is young and inexperienced, and the house that is to be built for the LORD must be exceedingly magnificent, famous and glorified throughout all lands; I will therefore make preparation for it." So David provided materials in great quantity before his death.

DAVID'S CHARGE TO SOLOMON
AND THE LEADERS

6 Then he called for his son Solomon and charged him to build a house for the LORD, the God of Israel. 7David said to Solomon, "My son, I had planned to build a house to the name of the LORD my God. 8But the word of the LORD came to me, saying, 'You have shed much blood and have waged great wars; you shall not build a house to my name, because you have shed so much blood in my sight on the earth. 9See, a son shall be born to you; he shall be a man of peace. I will give him peace from all his enemies on every side; for his name shall be Solomon,[a] and I will give peace[b] and quiet to Israel in his days. 10He shall build a house for my name. He shall be a son to me, and I will be a father to him, and I will establish his royal throne in Israel forever.' 11Now, my son, the LORD be with you, so that you may succeed in building the house of the LORD your God, as he has spoken concerning you. 12Only, may the LORD grant you discretion and understanding, so that when he gives you charge over Israel you may keep the law of the LORD your God. 13Then you will prosper if you are careful to observe the statutes and the ordinances that the LORD commanded Moses for Israel. Be strong and of good courage. Do not be afraid or dismayed. 14With great pains I have provided for the house of the LORD one hun-

a 22.9 Heb Shelomoh   b 22.9 Heb shalom

dred thousand talents of gold, one million talents of silver, and bronze and iron beyond weighing, for there is so much of it; timber and stone too I have provided. To these you must add more. 15 You have an abundance of workers: stonecutters, masons, carpenters, and all kinds of artisans without number, skilled in working 16 gold, silver, bronze, and iron. Now begin the work, and the LORD be with you."

17 David also commanded all the leaders of Israel to help his son Solomon, saying, 18 "Is not the LORD your God with you? Has he not given you peace on every side? For he has delivered the inhabitants of the land into my hand; and the land is subdued before the LORD and his people. 19 Now set your mind and heart to seek the LORD your God. Go and build the sanctuary of the LORD God so that the ark of the covenant of the LORD and the holy vessels of God may be brought into a house built for the name of the LORD."

FAMILIES OF THE LEVITES AND THEIR FUNCTIONS

23 When David was old and full of days, he made his son Solomon king over Israel.

2 David assembled all the leaders of Israel and the priests and the Levites. 3 The Levites, thirty years old and upward, were counted, and the total was thirty-eight thousand. 4 "Twenty-four thousand of these," David said, "shall have charge of the work in the house of the LORD, six thousand shall be officers and judges, 5 four thousand gatekeepers, and four thousand shall offer praises to the LORD with the instruments that I have made for praise." 6 And David organized them in divisions corresponding to the sons of Levi: Gershon,[a] Kohath, and Merari.

7 The sons of Gershon[b] were Ladan and Shimei. 8 The sons of Ladan: Jehiel the chief, Zetham, and Joel, three. 9 The sons of Shimei: Shelomoth, Haziel, and Haran, three. These were the heads of families of Ladan. 10 And the sons of Shimei: Jahath, Zina, Jeush, and Beriah. These

four were the sons of Shimei. 11 Jahath was the chief, and Zizah the second; but Jeush and Beriah did not have many sons, so they were enrolled as a single family.

12 The sons of Kohath: Amram, Izhar, Hebron, and Uzziel, four. 13 The sons of Amram: Aaron and Moses. Aaron was set apart to consecrate the most holy things, so that he and his sons forever should make offerings before the LORD, and minister to him and pronounce blessings in his name forever; 14 but as for Moses the man of God, his sons were to be reckoned among the tribe of Levi. 15 The sons of Moses: Gershom and Eliezer. 16 The sons of Gershom: Shebuel the chief. 17 The sons of Eliezer: Rehabiah the chief; Eliezer had no other sons, but the sons of Rehabiah were very numerous. 18 The sons of Izhar: Shelomith the chief. 19 The sons of Hebron: Jeriah the chief, Amariah the second, Jahaziel the third, and Jekameam the fourth. 20 The sons of Uzziel: Micah the chief and Isshiah the second.

21 The sons of Merari: Mahli and Mushi. The sons of Mahli: Eleazar and Kish. 22 Eleazar died having no sons, but only daughters; their kindred, the sons of Kish, married them. 23 The sons of Mushi: Mahli, Eder, and Jeremoth, three.

24 These were the sons of Levi by their ancestral houses, the heads of families as they were enrolled according to the number of the names of the individuals from twenty years old and upward who were to do the work for the service of the house of the LORD. 25 For David said, "The LORD, the God of Israel, has given rest to his people; and he resides in Jerusalem forever. 26 And so the Levites no longer need to carry the tabernacle or any of the things for its service"— 27 for according to the last words of David these were the number of the Levites from twenty years old and upward— 28 "but their duty shall be to assist the descendants of Aaron for the service of the

a 23.6 Or *Gershom*; see 1 Chr 6.1, note, and 23.15 b 23.7 Vg Compare Gk Syr: Heb *to the Gershonite* house of the LORD, having the care of the courts and the chambers, the cleansing of all that is holy, and any work for the service of the house of God; 29to assist also with the rows of bread, the choice flour for the grain offering, the wafers of unleavened bread, the baked offering, the offering mixed with oil, and all measures of quantity or size. 30And they shall stand every morning, thanking and praising the LORD, and likewise at evening, 31and whenever burnt offerings are offered to the LORD on sabbaths, new moons, and appointed festivals, according to the number required of them, regularly before the LORD. 32Thus they shall keep charge of the tent of meeting and the sanctuary, and shall attend the descendants of Aaron, their kindred, for the service of the house of the LORD."

DIVISIONS OF THE PRIESTS

24 The divisions of the descendants of Aaron were these. The sons of Aaron: Nadab, Abihu, Eleazar, and Ithamar. 2But Nadab and Abihu died before their father, and had no sons; so Eleazar and Ithamar became the priests. 3Along with Zadok of the sons of Eleazar, and Ahimelech of the sons of Ithamar, David organized them according to the appointed duties in their service. 4Since more chief men were found among the sons of Eleazar than among the sons of Ithamar, they organized them under sixteen heads of ancestral houses of the sons of Eleazar, and eight of the sons of Ithamar. 5They organized them by lot, all alike, for there were officers of the sanctuary and officers of God among both the sons of Eleazar and the sons of Ithamar. 6The scribe Shemaiah son of Nethanel, a Levite, recorded them in the presence of the king, and the officers, and Zadok the priest, and Ahimelech son of Abiathar, and the heads of ancestral houses of the priests and of the Levites; one ancestral house being chosen for Eleazar and one chosen for Ithamar.

7 The first lot fell to Jehoiarib, the second to Jedaiah, 8the third to Ha-rim, the fourth to Seorim, 9the fifth to Malchijah, the sixth to Mijamin, 10the seventh to Hakkoz, the eighth to Abijah, 11the ninth to Jeshua, the tenth to Shecaniah, 12the eleventh to Eliashib, the twelfth to Jakim, 13the thirteenth to Huppah, the fourteenth to Jeshebeab, 14the fifteenth to Bilgah, the sixteenth to Immer, 15the seventeenth to Hezir, the eighteenth to Happizzez, 16the nineteenth to Pethahiah, the twentieth to Jehezkel, 17the twenty-first to Jachin, the twenty-second to Gamul, 18the twenty-third to Delaiah, the twenty-fourth to Maaziah. 19These had as their appointed duty in their service to enter the house of the LORD according to the procedure established for them by their ancestor Aaron, as the LORD God of Israel had commanded him.

OTHER LEVITES

20 And of the rest of the sons of Levi: of the sons of Amram, Shubael; of the sons of Shubael, Jehdeiah. 21Of Rehabiah: of the sons of Rehabiah, Isshiah the chief. 22Of the Izharites, Shelomoth; of the sons of Shelomoth, Jahath. 23The sons of Hebron:[a] Jeriah the chief,[b] Amariah the second, Jahaziel the third, Jekameam the fourth. 24The sons of Uzziel, Micah; of the sons of Micah, Shamir. 25The brother of Micah, Isshiah; of the sons of Isshiah, Zechariah. 26The sons of Merari: Mahli and Mushi. The sons of Jaaziah: Beno.[c] 27The sons of Merari: of Jaaziah, Beno,[c] Shoham, Zaccur, and Ibri. 28Of Mahli: Eleazar, who had no sons. 29Of Kish, the sons of Kish: Jerahmeel. 30The sons of Mushi: Mahli, Eder, and Jerimoth. These were the sons of the Levites according to their ancestral houses. 31These also cast lots corresponding to their kindred, the descendants of Aaron, in the presence of King David, Zadok, Ahimelech, and the heads of ancestral houses of the priests and of the Levites, the chief as well as the youngest brother.

[a] 24.23 See 23.19: Heb lacks *Hebron*
[b] 24.23 See 23.19: Heb lacks *the chief*
[c] 24.26,27 Or *his son*: Meaning of Heb uncertain

THE TEMPLE MUSICIANS

25 David and the officers of the army also set apart for the service the sons of Asaph, and of Heman, and of Jeduthun, who should prophesy with lyres, harps, and cymbals. The list of those who did the work and of their duties was: ²Of the sons of Asaph: Zaccur, Joseph, Nethaniah, and Asarelah, sons of Asaph, under the direction of Asaph, who prophesied under the direction of the king. ³Of Jeduthun, the sons of Jeduthun: Gedaliah, Zeri, Jeshaiah, Shimei,ᵃ Hashabiah, and Mattithiah, six, under the direction of their father Jeduthun, who prophesied with the lyre in thanksgiving and praise to the LORD. ⁴Of Heman, the sons of Heman: Bukkiah, Mattaniah, Uzziel, Shebuel, and Jerimoth, Hananiah, Hanani, Eliathah, Giddalti, and Romamti-ezer, Joshbekashah, Mallothi, Hothir, Mahazioth. ⁵All these were the sons of Heman the king's seer, according to the promise of God to exalt him; for God had given Heman fourteen sons and three daughters. ⁶They were all under the direction of their father for the music in the house of the LORD with cymbals, harps, and lyres for the service of the house of God. Asaph, Jeduthun, and Heman were under the order of the king. ⁷They and their kindred, who were trained in singing to the LORD, all of whom were skillful, numbered two hundred eighty-eight. ⁸And they cast lots for their duties, small and great, teacher and pupil alike.

⁹The first lot fell for Asaph to Joseph; the second to Gedaliah, to him and his brothers and his sons, twelve; ¹⁰the third to Zaccur, his sons and his brothers, twelve; ¹¹the fourth to Izri, his sons and his brothers, twelve; ¹²the fifth to Nethaniah, his sons and his brothers, twelve; ¹³the sixth to Bukkiah, his sons and his brothers, twelve; ¹⁴the seventh to Jesarelah,ᵇ his sons and his brothers, twelve; ¹⁵the eighth to Jeshaiah, his sons and his brothers, twelve; ¹⁶the ninth to Mattaniah, his sons and his brothers, twelve; ¹⁷the tenth to Shimei, his sons and his brothers, twelve; ¹⁸the eleventh to Azarel, his sons and his brothers, twelve; ¹⁹the twelfth to Hashabiah, his sons and his brothers, twelve; ²⁰to the thirteenth, Shubael, his sons and his brothers, twelve; ²¹to the fourteenth, Mattithiah, his sons and his brothers, twelve; ²²to the fifteenth, to Jeremoth, his sons and his brothers, twelve; ²³to the sixteenth, to Hananiah, his sons and his brothers, twelve; ²⁴to the seventeenth, to Joshbekashah, his sons and his brothers, twelve; ²⁵to the eighteenth, to Hanani, his sons and his brothers, twelve; ²⁶to the nineteenth, to Mallothi, his sons and his brothers, twelve; ²⁷to the twentieth, to Eliathah, his sons and his brothers, twelve; ²⁸to the twenty-first, to Hothir, his sons and his brothers, twelve; ²⁹to the twenty-second, to Giddalti, his sons and his brothers, twelve; ³⁰to the twenty-third, to Mahazioth, his sons and his brothers, twelve; ³¹to the twenty-fourth, to Romamti-ezer, his sons and his brothers, twelve.

THE GATEKEEPERS

26 As for the divisions of the gatekeepers: of the Korahites, Meshelemiah son of Kore, of the sons of Asaph. ²Meshelemiah had sons: Zechariah the firstborn, Jediael the second, Zebadiah the third, Jathniel the fourth, ³Elam the fifth, Jehohanan the sixth, Eliehoenai the seventh. ⁴Obed-edom had sons: Shemaiah the firstborn, Jehozabad the second, Joah the third, Sachar the fourth, Nethanel the fifth, ⁵Ammiel the sixth, Issachar the seventh, Peullethai the eighth; for God blessed him. ⁶Also to his son Shemaiah sons were born who exercised authority in their ancestral houses, for they were men of great ability. ⁷The sons of Shemaiah: Othni, Rephael, Obed, and Elzabad, whose brothers were able men, Elihu and Semachiah. ⁸All these, sons of Obed-edom with their sons and brothers, were able men qualified for the service;

ᵃ 25.3 One Ms: Gk: MT lacks *Shimei*
ᵇ 25.14 Or *Asarelah*; see 25.2

sixty-two of Obed-edom. [9]Meshelemiah had sons and brothers, able men, eighteen. [10]Hosah, of the sons of Merari, had sons: Shimri the chief (for though he was not the firstborn, his father made him chief), [11]Hilkiah the second, Tebaliah the third, Zechariah the fourth: all the sons and brothers of Hosah totaled thirteen.

[12] These divisions of the gatekeepers, corresponding to their leaders, had duties, just as their kindred did, ministering in the house of the LORD; [13]and they cast lots by ancestral houses, small and great alike, for their gates. [14]The lot for the east fell to Shelemiah. They cast lots also for his son Zechariah, a prudent counselor, and his lot came out for the north. [15]Obed-edom's came out for the south, and to his sons was allotted the storehouse. [16]For Shuppim and Hosah it came out for the west, at the gate of Shallecheth on the ascending road. Guard corresponded to guard. [17]On the east there were six Levites each day,[a] on the north four each day, on the south four each day, as well as two and two at the storehouse; [18]and for the colonnade[b] on the west there were four at the road and two at the colonnade.[b] [19]These were the divisions of the gatekeepers among the Korahites and the sons of Merari.

THE TREASURERS, OFFICERS, AND JUDGES

[20] And of the Levites, Ahijah had charge of the treasuries of the house of God and the treasuries of the dedicated gifts. [21]The sons of Ladan, the sons of the Gershonites belonging to Ladan, the heads of families belonging to Ladan the Gershonite: Jehieli.[c]

[22] The sons of Jehieli, Zetham and his brother Joel, were in charge of the treasuries of the house of the LORD. [23]Of the Amramites, the Izharites, the Hebronites, and the Uzzielites: [24]Shebuel son of Gershom, son of Moses, was chief officer in charge of the treasuries. [25]His brothers: from Eliezer were his son Rehabiah, his son Jeshaiah, his son Joram, his son Zichri, and his son Shelomoth. [26]This Shelomoth and his brothers were in charge of all the treasuries of the dedicated gifts that King David, and the heads of families, and the officers of the thousands and the hundreds, and the commanders of the army, had dedicated. [27]From booty won in battles they dedicated gifts for the maintenance of the house of the LORD. [28]Also all that Samuel the seer, and Saul son of Kish, and Abner son of Ner, and Joab son of Zeruiah had dedicated—all dedicated gifts were in the care of Shelomoth[d] and his brothers.

[29] Of the Izharites, Chenaniah and his sons were appointed to outside duties for Israel, as officers and judges. [30]Of the Hebronites, Hashabiah and his brothers, one thousand seven hundred men of ability, had the oversight of Israel west of the Jordan for all the work of the LORD and for the service of the king. [31]Of the Hebronites, Jerijah was chief of the Hebronites. (In the fortieth year of David's reign search was made, of whatever genealogy or family, and men of great ability among them were found at Jazer in Gilead.) [32]King David appointed him and his brothers, two thousand seven hundred men of ability, heads of families, to have the oversight of the Reubenites, the Gadites, and the half-tribe of the Manassites for everything pertaining to God and for the affairs of the king.

THE MILITARY DIVISIONS

27 This is the list of the people of Israel, the heads of families, the commanders of the thousands and the hundreds, and their officers who served the king in all matters concerning the divisions that came and went, month after month throughout the year, each division numbering twenty-four thousand:

[2] Jashobeam son of Zabdiel was in charge of the first division in the first month; in his division were twenty-four thousand. [3]He was a

---

[a] 26.17 Gk: Heb lacks *each day*   [b] 26.18 Heb *parbar*: Meaning uncertain   [c] 26.21 The Hebrew text of verse 21 is confused   [d] 26.28 Gk Compare 26.28: Heb *Shelomith*

descendant of Perez, and was chief of all the commanders of the army for the first month. 4Dodai the Ahohite was in charge of the division of the second month; Mikloth was the chief officer of his division. In his division were twenty-four thousand. 5The third commander, for the third month, was Benaiah son of the priest Jehoiada, as chief; in his division were twenty-four thousand. 6This is the Benaiah who was a mighty man of the Thirty and in command of the Thirty; his son Ammizabad was in charge of his division.[a] 7Asahel brother of Joab was fourth, for the fourth month, and his son Zebadiah after him; in his division were twenty-four thousand. 8The fifth commander, for the fifth month, was Shamhuth, the Izrahite; in his division were twenty-four thousand. 9Sixth, for the sixth month, was Ira son of Ikkesh the Tekoite; in his division were twenty-four thousand. 10Seventh, for the seventh month, was Helez the Pelonite, of the Ephraimites; in his division were twenty-four thousand. 11Eighth, for the eighth month, was Sibbecai the Hushathite, of the Zerahites; in his division were twenty-four thousand. 12Ninth, for the ninth month, was Abiezer of Anathoth, a Benjaminite; in his division were twenty-four thousand. 13Tenth, for the tenth month, was Maharai of Netophah, of the Zerahites; in his division were twenty-four thousand. 14Eleventh, for the eleventh month, was Benaiah of Pirathon, of the Ephraimites; in his division were twenty-four thousand. 15Twelfth, for the twelfth month, was Heldai the Netophathite, of Othniel; in his division were twenty-four thousand.

LEADERS OF TRIBES

16 Over the tribes of Israel, for the Reubenites, Eliezer son of Zichri was chief officer; for the Simeonites, Shephatiah son of Maacah; 17for Levi, Hashabiah son of Kemuel; for Aaron, Zadok; 18for Judah, Elihu, one of David's brothers; for Issachar, Omri son of Michael; 19for Zebulun, Ishmaiah son of Obadiah; for Naphtali, Jerimoth son of Azriel; 20for the Ephraimites, Hoshea son of Azaziah; for the half-tribe of Manasseh, Joel son of Pedaiah; 21for the half-tribe of Manasseh in Gilead, Iddo son of Zechariah; for Benjamin, Jaasiel son of Abner; 22for Dan, Azarel son of Jeroham. These were the leaders of the tribes of Israel. 23David did not count those below twenty years of age, for the LORD had promised to make Israel as numerous as the stars of heaven. 24Joab son of Zeruiah began to count them, but did not finish; yet wrath came upon Israel for this, and the number was not entered into the account of the Annals of King David.

OTHER CIVIC OFFICIALS

25 Over the king's treasuries was Azmaveth son of Adiel. Over the treasuries in the country, in the cities, in the villages and in the towers, was Jonathan son of Uzziah. 26Over those who did the work of the field, tilling the soil, was Ezri son of Chelub. 27Over the vineyards was Shimei the Ramathite. Over the produce of the vineyards for the wine cellars was Zabdi the Shiphmite. 28Over the olive and sycamore trees in the Shephelah was Baal-hanan the Gederite. Over the stores of oil was Joash. 29Over the herds that pastured in Sharon was Shitrai the Sharonite. Over the herds in the valleys was Shaphat son of Adlai. 30Over the camels was Obil the Ishmaelite. Over the donkeys was Jehdeiah the Meronothite. Over the flocks was Jaziz the Hagrite. 31All these were stewards of King David's property.

32 Jonathan, David's uncle, was a counselor, being a man of understanding and a scribe; Jehiel son of Hachmoni attended the king's sons. 33Ahithophel was the king's counselor, and Hushai the Archite was the king's friend. 34After Ahithophel came Jehoiada son of Benaiah, and Abiathar. Joab was commander of the king's army.

a 27.6 Gk Vg: Heb Ammizabad was his division

SOLOMON INSTRUCTED TO BUILD THE TEMPLE

28 David assembled at Jerusalem all the officials of Israel, the officials of the tribes, the officers of the divisions that served the king, the commanders of the thousands, the commanders of the hundreds, the stewards of all the property and cattle of the king and his sons, together with the palace officials, the mighty warriors, and all the warriors. ²Then King David rose to his feet and said: "Hear me, my brothers and my people. I had planned to build a house of rest for the ark of the covenant of the LORD, for the footstool of our God; and I made preparations for building. ³But God said to me, 'You shall not build a house for my name, for you are a warrior and have shed blood.' ⁴Yet the LORD God of Israel chose me from all my ancestral house to be king over Israel forever; for he chose Judah as leader, and in the house of Judah my father's house, and among my father's sons he took delight in making me king over all Israel. ⁵And of all my sons, for the LORD has given me many, he has chosen my son Solomon to sit upon the throne of the kingdom of the LORD over Israel. ⁶He said to me, 'It is your son Solomon who shall build my house and my courts, for I have chosen him to be a son to me, and I will be a father to him. ⁷I will establish his kingdom forever if he continues resolute in keeping my commandments and my ordinances, as he is today.' ⁸Now therefore in the sight of all Israel, the assembly of the LORD, and in the hearing of our God, observe and search out all the commandments of the LORD your God; that you may possess this good land, and leave it for an inheritance to your children after you forever.

⁹"And you, my son Solomon, know the God of your father, and serve him with single mind and willing heart; for the LORD searches every mind, and understands every plan and thought. If you seek him, he will be found by you; but if you forsake him, he will abandon you forever. ¹⁰Take heed now, for the LORD has chosen you to build a house as the sanctuary; be strong, and act."

¹¹Then David gave his son Solomon the plan of the vestibule of the temple, and of its houses, its treasuries, its upper rooms, and its inner chambers, and of the room for the mercy seat;ᵃ ¹²and the plan of all that he had in mind: for the courts of the house of the LORD, all the surrounding chambers, the treasuries of the house of God, and the treasuries for dedicated gifts; ¹³for the divisions of the priests and of the Levites, and all the work of the service in the house of the LORD; for all the vessels for the service in the house of the LORD, ¹⁴the weight of gold for all golden vessels for each service, the weight of silver vessels for each service, ¹⁵the weight of the golden lampstands and their lamps, the weight of gold for each lampstand and its lamps, the weight of silver for a lampstand and its lamps, according to the use of each in the service, ¹⁶the weight of gold for each table for the rows of bread, the silver for the silver tables, ¹⁷and pure gold for the forks, the basins, and the cups; for the golden bowls and the weight of each; for the silver bowls and the weight of each; ¹⁸for the altar of incense made of refined gold, and its weight; also his plan for the golden chariot of the cherubim that spread their wings and covered the ark of the covenant of the LORD.

¹⁹"All this, in writing at the LORD's direction, he made clear to me—the plan of all the works."

²⁰David said further to his son Solomon, "Be strong and of good courage, and act. Do not be afraid or dismayed; for the LORD God, my God, is with you. He will not fail you or forsake you, until all the work for the service of the house of the LORD is finished. ²¹Here are the divisions of the priests and the Levites for all the service of the house of God; and with you in all the work will be every volunteer who has skill for any kind of service; also the officers and

ᵃ 28.11 Or *the cover*

all the people will be wholly at your command."

OFFERINGS FOR BUILDING THE TEMPLE

29 King David said to the whole assembly, "My son Solomon, whom alone God has chosen, is young and inexperienced, and the work is great; for the temple[a] will not be for mortals but for the LORD God. ²So I have provided for the house of my God, so far as I was able, the gold for the things of gold, the silver for the things of silver, and the bronze for the things of bronze, the iron for the things of iron, and wood for the things of wood, besides great quantities of onyx and stones for setting, antimony, colored stones, all sorts of precious stones, and marble in abundance. ³Moreover, in addition to all that I have provided for the holy house, I have a treasure of my own of gold and silver, and because of my devotion to the house of my God I give it to the house of my God: ⁴three thousand talents of gold, of the gold of Ophir, and seven thousand talents of refined silver, for overlaying the walls of the house, ⁵and for all the work to be done by artisans, gold for the things of gold and silver for the things of silver. Who then will offer willingly, consecrating themselves today to the LORD?"

6 Then the leaders of ancestral houses made their freewill offerings, as did also the leaders of the tribes, the commanders of the thousands and of the hundreds, and the officers over the king's work. ⁷They gave for the service of the house of God five thousand talents and ten thousand darics of gold, ten thousand talents of silver, eighteen thousand talents of bronze, and one hundred thousand talents of iron. ⁸Whoever had precious stones gave them to the treasury of the house of the LORD, into the care of Jehiel the Gershonite. ⁹Then the people rejoiced because these had given willingly, for with single mind they had offered freely to the LORD; King David also rejoiced greatly.

PONDER

Then the people rejoiced because these had given willingly, for with single mind they had offered freely to the LORD; King David also rejoiced greatly.
—1 Chronicles 29.9

PRAY

Father God, we are grateful again for some words in the Bible that we quite often read but perhaps do not apply to our own lives. Help us to resolve in our hearts to consider the opportunities, challenges and responsibilities your scripture offers to us: to refrain from husbanding what we have for ourselves and to instead return our bounty to you by sharing freely with others. In doing so, we pray that we will represent the humility, forgiveness, compassion and most important of all, the love of Jesus Christ. We ask these things in his name. Amen.

DAVID'S PRAISE TO GOD

10 Then David blessed the LORD in the presence of all the assembly; David said: "Blessed are you, O LORD, the God of our ancestor Israel, forever and ever. ¹¹Yours, O LORD, are the greatness, the power, the glory, the victory, and the majesty; for all that is in the heavens and on the earth is yours; yours is the kingdom, O LORD, and you are exalted as head above all. ¹²Riches and honor come from you, and you rule over all. In your hand are power and might; and it is in your hand to make great and to give strength to all. ¹³And now, our God, we give thanks to you and praise your glorious name.

14 "But who am I, and what is my people, that we should be able to make this freewill offering? For all things come from you, and of your own have we given you. ¹⁵For we

---

[a] **29.1** Heb *fortress*

are aliens and transients before you, as were all our ancestors; our days on the earth are like a shadow, and there is no hope. ¹⁶O LORD our God, all this abundance that we have provided for building you a house for your holy name comes from your hand and is all your own. ¹⁷I know, my God, that you search the heart, and take pleasure in uprightness; in the uprightness of my heart I have freely offered all these things, and now I have seen your people, who are present here, offering freely and joyously to you. ¹⁸O LORD, the God of Abraham, Isaac, and Israel, our ancestors, keep forever such purposes and thoughts in the hearts of your people, and direct their hearts toward you. ¹⁹Grant to my son Solomon that with single mind he may keep your commandments, your decrees, and your statutes, performing all of them, and that he may build the temple[a] for which I have made provision."

20 Then David said to the whole assembly, "Bless the LORD your God." And all the assembly blessed the LORD, the God of their ancestors, and bowed their heads and prostrated themselves before the LORD and the king. ²¹On the next day they offered sacrifices and burnt offerings to the LORD, a thousand bulls, a thousand rams, and a thousand lambs, with their libations, and sacrifices in abundance for all Israel; ²²and they ate and drank

before the LORD on that day with great joy.

SOLOMON ANOINTED KING

They made David's son Solomon king a second time; they anointed him as the LORD's prince, and Zadok as priest. ²³Then Solomon sat on the throne of the LORD, succeeding his father David as king; he prospered, and all Israel obeyed him. ²⁴All the leaders and the mighty warriors, and also all the sons of King David, pledged their allegiance to King Solomon. ²⁵The LORD highly exalted Solomon in the sight of all Israel, and bestowed upon him such royal majesty as had not been on any king before him in Israel.

SUMMARY OF DAVID'S REIGN

26 Thus David son of Jesse reigned over all Israel. ²⁷The period that he reigned over Israel was forty years; he reigned seven years in Hebron, and thirty-three years in Jerusalem. ²⁸He died in a good old age, full of days, riches, and honor; and his son Solomon succeeded him. ²⁹Now the acts of King David, from first to last, are written in the records of the seer Samuel, and in the records of the prophet Nathan, and in the records of the seer Gad, ³⁰with accounts of all his rule and his might and of the events that befell him and Israel and all the kingdoms of the earth.

a 29.19 Heb fortress

2 CHRONICLES

In Matthew 6.21, Jesus said, "Where your treasure is, there your heart will be also." Our priorities—where we spend our time, attention and energy—reveal where our minds and hearts are focused. While the book repeats many of the historical facts of 1 and 2 Kings, this chronicle is much more than history. It's a critique of the careers of Judah's kings. Notice that each king's merit is assessed not on his diplomatic abilities, military accomplishments or wealth, but on whether or not his heart was focused on God. As we read 2 Chronicles, we can think about our priorities from this perspective.

SOLOMON REQUESTS WISDOM

1 Solomon son of David established himself in his kingdom; the LORD his God was with him and made him exceedingly great.

2 Solomon summoned all Israel, the commanders of the thousands and of the hundreds, the judges, and all the leaders of all Israel, the heads of families. 3 Then Solomon, and the whole assembly with him, went to the high place that was at Gibeon; for God's tent of meeting, which Moses the servant of the LORD had made in the wilderness, was there. 4 (But David had brought the ark of God up from Kiriath-jearim to the place that David had prepared for it; for he had pitched a tent for it in Jerusalem.) 5 Moreover the bronze altar that Bezalel son of Uri, son of Hur, had made, was there in front of the tabernacle of the LORD. And Solomon and the assembly inquired at it. 6 Solomon went up there to the bronze altar before the LORD, which was at the tent of meeting, and offered a thousand burnt offerings on it.

7 That night God appeared to Solomon, and said to him, "Ask what I should give you." 8 Solomon said to God, "You have shown great and steadfast love to my father David, and have made me succeed him as king. 9 O LORD God, let your promise to my father David now be fulfilled, for you have made me king over a people as numerous as the dust of the earth. 10 Give me now wisdom and knowledge to go out and come in before this people, for who can rule this great people of yours?" 11 God answered Solomon, "Because this was in your heart, and you have not asked for possessions, wealth, honor, or the life of those who hate you, and have not even asked for long life, but have asked for wisdom and knowledge for yourself that you may rule my people over whom I have made you king, 12 wisdom and knowledge are granted to you. I will also give you riches, possessions, and honor, such as none of the kings had who were before you, and none after you shall have the like." 13 So

Solomon came from[a] the high place at Gibeon, from the tent of meeting, to Jerusalem. And he reigned over Israel.

SOLOMON'S MILITARY AND COMMERCIAL ACTIVITY

14 Solomon gathered together chariots and horses; he had fourteen hundred chariots and twelve thousand horses, which he stationed in the chariot cities and with the king in Jerusalem. 15 The king made silver and gold as common in Jerusalem as stone, and he made cedar as plentiful as the sycamore of the Shephelah. 16 Solomon's horses were imported from Egypt and Kue; the king's traders received them from Kue at the prevailing price. 17 They imported from Egypt, and then exported, a chariot for six hundred shekels of silver, and a horse for one hundred fifty; so through them these were exported to all the kings of the Hittites and the kings of Aram.

PREPARATIONS FOR BUILDING THE TEMPLE

2[b] Solomon decided to build a temple for the name of the LORD, and a royal palace for himself. 2[c] Solomon conscripted seventy thousand laborers and eighty thousand stonecutters in the hill country, with three thousand six hundred to oversee them.

ALLIANCE WITH HURAM OF TYRE

3 Solomon sent word to King Huram of Tyre: "Once you dealt with my father David and sent him cedar to build himself a house to live in. 4 I am now about to build a house for the name of the LORD my God and dedicate it to him for offering fragrant incense before him, and for the regular offering of the rows of bread, and for burnt offerings morning and evening, on the sabbaths and the new moons and the appointed festivals of the LORD our God, as ordained forever for Israel. 5 The house that I am about to build

---

[a] 1.13 Gk Vg: Heb to   [b] 2.1 Ch 1.18 in Heb
[c] 2.2 Ch 2.1 in Heb

will be great, for our God is greater than other gods. 6But who is able to build him a house, since heaven, even highest heaven, cannot contain him? Who am I to build a house for him, except as a place to make offerings before him? 7So now send me an artisan skilled to work in gold, silver, bronze, and iron, and in purple, crimson, and blue fabrics, trained also in engraving, to join the skilled workers who are with me in Judah and Jerusalem, whom my father David provided. 8Send me also cedar, cypress, and algum timber from Lebanon, for I know that your servants are skilled in cutting Lebanon timber. My servants will work with your servants 9to prepare timber for me in abundance, for the house I am about to build will be great and wonderful. 10I will provide for your servants, those who cut the timber, twenty thousand cors of crushed wheat, twenty thousand cors of barley, twenty thousand baths[a] of wine, and twenty thousand baths of oil."

11 Then King Huram of Tyre answered in a letter that he sent to Solomon, "Because the LORD loves his people he has made you king over them." 12Huram also said, "Blessed be the LORD God of Israel, who made heaven and earth, who has given King David a wise son, endowed with discretion and understanding, who will build a temple for the LORD, and a royal palace for himself. 13 "I have dispatched Huram-abi, a skilled artisan, endowed with understanding, 14the son of one of the Danite women, his father a Tyrian. He is trained to work in gold, silver, bronze, iron, stone, and wood, and in purple, blue, and crimson fabrics and fine linen, and to do all sorts of engraving and execute any design that may be assigned him, with your artisans, the artisans of my lord, your father David. 15Now, as for the wheat, barley, oil, and wine, of which my lord has spoken, let him send them to his servants. 16We will cut whatever timber you need from Lebanon, and bring it to you as rafts by sea to Joppa; you will take it up to Jerusalem."

17 Then Solomon took a census of all the aliens who were residing in the land of Israel, after the census that his father David had taken; and there were found to be one hundred fifty-three thousand six hundred. 18Seventy thousand of them he assigned as laborers, eighty thousand as stonecutters in the hill country, and three thousand six hundred as overseers to make the people work.

SOLOMON BUILDS THE TEMPLE

3 Solomon began to build the house of the LORD in Jerusalem on Mount Moriah, where the LORD had appeared to his father David, at the place that David had designated, on the threshing floor of Ornan the Jebusite. 2He began to build on the second day of the second month of the fourth year of his reign. 3These are Solomon's measurements[b] for building the house of God: the length, in cubits of the old standard, was sixty cubits, and the width twenty cubits. 4The vestibule in front of the nave of the house was twenty cubits long, across the width of the house;[c] and its height was one hundred twenty cubits. He overlaid it on the inside with pure gold. 5The nave he lined with cypress, covered it with fine gold, and made palms and chains on it. 6He adorned the house with settings of precious stones. The gold was gold from Parvaim. 7So he lined the house with gold—its beams, its thresholds, its walls, and its doors; and he carved cherubim on the walls.

8 He made the most holy place; its length, corresponding to the width of the house, was twenty cubits, and its width was twenty cubits; he overlaid it with six hundred talents of fine gold. 9The weight of the nails was fifty shekels of gold. He overlaid the upper chambers with gold.

10 In the most holy place he made two carved cherubim and overlaid[d] them with gold. 11The wings of the cherubim together extended

a 2.10 A Hebrew measure of volume
b 3.3 Syr: Heb *foundations*   c 3.4 Compare
1 Kings 6.3: Meaning of Heb uncertain
d 3.10 Heb *they overlaid*

twenty cubits: one wing of the one, five cubits long, touched the wall of the house, and its other wing, five cubits long, touched the wing of the other cherub; 12and of this cherub, one wing, five cubits long, touched the wall of the house, and the other wing, also five cubits long, was joined to the wing of the first cherub. 13The wings of these cherubim extended twenty cubits; the cherubim[a] stood on their feet, facing the nave. 14And Solomon[b] made the curtain of blue and purple and crimson fabrics and fine linen, and worked cherubim into it.

15 In front of the house he made two pillars thirty-five cubits high, with a capital of five cubits on the top of each. 16He made encircling[c] chains and put them on the tops of the pillars; and he made one hundred pomegranates, and put them on the chains. 17He set up the pillars in front of the temple, one on the right, the other on the left; the one on the right he called Jachin, and the one on the left, Boaz.

FURNISHINGS OF THE TEMPLE

4 He made an altar of bronze, twenty cubits long, twenty cubits wide, and ten cubits high. 2Then he made the molten sea; it was round, ten cubits from rim to rim, and five cubits high. A line of thirty cubits would encircle it completely. 3Under it were panels all around, each of ten cubits, surrounding the sea; there were two rows of panels, cast when it was cast. 4It stood on twelve oxen, three facing north, three facing west, three facing south, and three facing east; the sea was set on them. The hindquarters of each were toward the inside. 5Its thickness was a handbreadth; its rim was made like the rim of a cup, like the flower of a lily; it held three thousand baths.[d] 6He also made ten basins in which to wash, and set five on the right side, and five on the left. In these they were to rinse what was used for the burnt offering. The sea was for the priests to wash in.

7 He made ten golden lampstands as prescribed, and set them in the temple, five on the south side and five on the north. 8He also made ten tables and placed them in the temple, five on the right side and five on the left. And he made one hundred basins of gold. 9He made the court of the priests, and the great court, and doors for the court; he overlaid their doors with bronze. 10He set the sea at the southeast corner of the house.

11 And Huram made the pots, the shovels, and the basins. Thus Huram finished the work that he did for King Solomon on the house of God: 12the two pillars, the bowls, and the two capitals on the top of the pillars; and the two latticeworks to cover the two bowls of the capitals that were on the top of the pillars; 13the four hundred pomegranates for the two latticeworks, two rows of pomegranates for each latticework, to cover the two bowls of the capitals that were on the pillars. 14He made the stands, the basins on the stands, 15the one sea, and the twelve oxen underneath it. 16The pots, the shovels, the forks, and all the equipment for these Huram-abi made of burnished bronze for King Solomon for the house of the LORD. 17In the plain of the Jordan the king cast them, in the clay ground between Succoth and Zeredah. 18Solomon made all these things in great quantities, so that the weight of the bronze was not determined.

19 So Solomon made all the things that were in the house of God: the golden altar, the tables for the bread of the Presence, 20the lampstands and their lamps of pure gold to burn before the inner sanctuary, as prescribed; 21the flowers, the lamps, and the tongs, of purest gold; 22the snuffers, basins, ladles, and firepans, of pure gold. As for the entrance to the temple: the inner doors to the most holy place and the doors of the nave of the temple were of gold.

5 Thus all the work that Solomon did for the house of the LORD was finished. Solomon brought in the things that his father David had

a 3.13 Heb they   b 3.14 Heb he   c 3.16 Cn: Heb in the inner sanctuary   d 4.5 A Hebrew measure of volume dedicated, and stored the silver, the gold, and all the vessels in the treasuries of the house of God.

THE ARK BROUGHT INTO THE TEMPLE

2 Then Solomon assembled the elders of Israel and all the heads of the tribes, the leaders of the ancestral houses of the people of Israel, in Jerusalem, to bring up the ark of the covenant of the LORD out of the city of David, which is Zion. ³And all the Israelites assembled before the king at the festival that is in the seventh month. ⁴And all the elders of Israel came, and the Levites carried the ark. ⁵So they brought up the ark, the tent of meeting, and all the holy vessels that were in the tent; the priests and the Levites brought them up. ⁶King Solomon and all the congregation of Israel, who had assembled before him, were before the ark, sacrificing so many sheep and oxen that they could not be numbered or counted. ⁷Then the priests brought the ark of the covenant of the LORD to its place, in the inner sanctuary of the house, in the most holy place, underneath the wings of the cherubim. ⁸For the cherubim spread out their wings over the place of the ark, so that the cherubim made a covering above the ark and its poles. ⁹The poles were so long that the ends of the poles were seen from the holy place in front of the inner sanctuary; but they could not be seen from outside; they are there to this day. ¹⁰There was nothing in the ark except the two tablets that Moses put there at Horeb, where the LORD made a covenant[a] with the people of Israel after they came out of Egypt.

11 Now when the priests came out of the holy place (for all the priests who were present had sanctified themselves, without regard to their divisions), ¹²all the levitical singers, Asaph, Heman, and Jeduthun, their sons and kindred, arrayed in fine linen, with cymbals, harps, and lyres, stood east of the altar with one hundred twenty priests who were trumpeters. ¹³It was the duty of the trumpeters and singers to make themselves heard in unison in praise and thanksgiving to the LORD, and when the song was raised, with trumpets and cymbals and other musical instruments, in praise to the LORD,

"For he is good,
    for his steadfast love
        endures forever,"

the house, the house of the LORD, was filled with a cloud, ¹⁴so that the priests could not stand to minister because of the cloud; for the glory of the LORD filled the house of God.

DEDICATION OF THE TEMPLE

6 Then Solomon said, "The LORD has said that he would reside in thick darkness. ²I have built you an exalted house, a place for you to reside in forever."

3 Then the king turned around and blessed all the assembly of Israel, while all the assembly of Israel stood. ⁴And he said, "Blessed be the LORD, the God of Israel, who with his hand has fulfilled what he promised with his mouth to my father David, saying, ⁵'Since the day that I brought my people out of the land of Egypt, I have not chosen a city from any of the tribes of Israel in which to build a house, so that my name might be there, and I chose no one as ruler over my people Israel; ⁶but I have chosen Jerusalem in order that my name may be there, and I have chosen David to be over my people Israel.' ⁷My father David had it in mind to build a house for the name of the LORD, the God of Israel. ⁸But the LORD said to my father David, 'You did well to consider building a house for my name; ⁹nevertheless you shall not build the house, but your son who shall be born to you shall build the house for my name.' ¹⁰Now the LORD has fulfilled his promise that he made; for I have succeeded my father David, and sit on the throne of Israel, as the LORD promised, and have built the house for the name of the LORD, the God of Israel. ¹¹There I have set the ark, in which is the covenant of the LORD

[a] 5.10 Heb lacks *a covenant*

that he made with the people of Israel."

SOLOMON'S PRAYER OF DEDICATION

12 Then Solomon[a] stood before the altar of the LORD in the presence of the whole assembly of Israel, and spread out his hands. 13Solomon had made a bronze platform five cubits long, five cubits wide, and three cubits high, and had set it in the court; and he stood on it. Then he knelt on his knees in the presence of the whole assembly of Israel, and spread out his hands toward heaven. 14He said, "O LORD, God of Israel, there is no God like you, in heaven or on earth, keeping covenant in steadfast love with your servants who walk before you with all their heart— 15you who have kept for your servant, my father David, what you promised to him. Indeed, you promised with your mouth and this day have fulfilled with your hand. 16Therefore, O LORD, God of Israel, keep for your servant, my father David, that which you promised him, saying, 'There shall never fail you a successor before me to sit on the throne of Israel, if only your children keep to their way, to walk in my law as you have walked before me.' 17Therefore, O LORD, God of Israel, let your word be confirmed, which you promised to your servant David.

18 "But will God indeed reside with mortals on earth? Even heaven and the highest heaven cannot contain you, how much less this house that I have built! 19Regard your servant's prayer and his plea, O LORD my God, heeding the cry and the prayer that your servant prays to you. 20May your eyes be open day and night toward this house, the place where you promised to set your name, and may you heed the prayer that your servant prays toward this place. 21And hear the plea of your servant and of your people Israel, when they pray toward this place; may you hear from heaven your dwelling place; hear and forgive.

22 "If someone sins against another and is required to take an oath

and comes and swears before your altar in this house, 23may you hear from heaven, and act, and judge your servants, repaying the guilty by bringing their conduct on their own head, and vindicating those who are in the right by rewarding them in accordance with their righteousness.

24 "When your people Israel, having sinned against you, are defeated before an enemy but turn again to you, confess your name, pray and plead with you in this house, 25may you hear from heaven, and forgive the sin of your people Israel, and bring them again to the land that you gave to them and to their ancestors.

26 "When heaven is shut up and there is no rain because they have sinned against you, and then they pray toward this place, confess your name, and turn from their sin, because you punish them, 27may you hear in heaven, forgive the sin of your servants, your people Israel, when you teach them the good way in which they should walk; and send down rain upon your land, which you have given to your people as an inheritance.

28 "If there is famine in the land, if there is plague, blight, mildew, locust, or caterpillar; if their enemies besiege them in any of the settlements of the lands; whatever suffering, whatever sickness there is; 29whatever prayer, whatever plea from any individual or from all your people Israel, all knowing their own suffering and their own sorrows so that they stretch out their hands toward this house; 30may you hear from heaven, your dwelling place, forgive, and render to all whose heart you know, according to all their ways, for only you know the human heart. 31Thus may they fear you and walk in your ways all the days that they live in the land that you gave to our ancestors.

32 "Likewise when foreigners, who are not of your people Israel, come from a distant land because of

a 6.12 Heb he

your great name, and your mighty hand, and your outstretched arm, when they come and pray toward this house, [33]may you hear from heaven your dwelling place, and do whatever the foreigners ask of you, in order that all the peoples of the earth may know your name and fear you, as do your people Israel, and that they may know that your name has been invoked on this house that I have built.

34 "If your people go out to battle against their enemies, by whatever way you shall send them, and they pray to you toward this city that you have chosen and the house that I have built for your name, [35]then hear from heaven their prayer and their plea, and maintain their cause.

36 "If they sin against you—for there is no one who does not sin—and you are angry with them and give them to an enemy, so that they are carried away captive to a land far or near; [37]then if they come to their senses in the land to which they have been taken captive, and repent, and plead with you in the land of their captivity, saying, 'We have sinned, and have done wrong; we have acted wickedly'; [38]if they repent with all their heart and soul in the land of their captivity, to which they were taken captive, and pray toward their land, which you gave to their ancestors, the city that you have chosen, and the house that I have built for your name, [39]then hear from heaven your dwelling place their prayer and their pleas, maintain their cause and forgive your people who have sinned against you. [40]Now, O my God, let your eyes be open and your ears attentive to prayer from this place.

[41] "Now rise up, O LORD God, and
go to your resting place,
you and the ark of your might.
Let your priests, O LORD God, be
clothed with salvation,
and let your faithful rejoice
in your goodness.
[42] O LORD God, do not reject
your anointed one.
Remember your steadfast love
for your servant David."

SOLOMON DEDICATES THE TEMPLE

7 When Solomon had ended his prayer, fire came down from heaven and consumed the burnt offering and the sacrifices; and the glory of the LORD filled the temple. [2]The priests could not enter the house of the LORD, because the glory of the LORD filled the LORD's house. [3]When all the people of Israel saw the fire come down and the glory of the LORD on the temple, they bowed down on the pavement with their faces to the ground, and worshiped and gave thanks to the LORD, saying,

"For he is good,
for his steadfast love
endures forever."

4 Then the king and all the people offered sacrifice before the LORD. [5]King Solomon offered as a sacrifice twenty-two thousand oxen and one hundred twenty thousand sheep. So the king and all the people dedicated the house of God. [6]The priests stood at their posts; the Levites also, with the instruments for music to the LORD that King David had made for giving thanks to the LORD—for his steadfast love endures forever—whenever David offered praises by their ministry. Opposite them the priests sounded trumpets; and all Israel stood.

7 Solomon consecrated the middle of the court that was in front of the house of the LORD; for there he offered the burnt offerings and the fat of the offerings of well-being because the bronze altar Solomon had made could not hold the burnt offering and the grain offering and the fat parts.

8 At that time Solomon held the festival for seven days, and all Israel with him, a very great congregation, from Lebo-hamath to the Wadi of Egypt. [9]On the eighth day they held a solemn assembly; for they had observed the dedication of the altar seven days and the festival seven days. [10]On the twenty-third day of the seventh month he sent the people away to their homes, joyful and in good spirits because of the

goodness that the LORD had shown to David and to Solomon and to his people Israel.

11 Thus Solomon finished the house of the LORD and the king's house; all that Solomon had planned to do in the house of the LORD and in his own house he successfully accomplished.

GOD'S SECOND APPEARANCE TO SOLOMON

12 Then the LORD appeared to Solomon in the night and said to him: "I have heard your prayer, and have chosen this place for myself as a house of sacrifice. 13 When I shut up the heavens so that there is no rain, or command the locust to devour the land, or send pestilence among my people, 14 if my people who are called by my name humble themselves, pray, seek my face, and turn from their wicked ways, then I will hear from heaven, and will forgive their sin and heal their land. 15 Now my eyes will be open and my ears attentive to the prayer that is made in this place. 16 For now I have chosen and consecrated this house so that my name may be there forever; my eyes and my heart will be there for all time. 17 As for you, if you walk before me, as your father David walked, doing according to all that I have commanded you and keeping my

statutes and my ordinances, 18 then I will establish your royal throne, as I made covenant with your father David saying, 'You shall never lack a successor to rule over Israel.'

19 "But if youª turn aside and forsake my statutes and my commandments that I have set before you, and go and serve other gods and worship them, 20 then I will pluck youᵇ up from the land that I have given you;ᵇ and this house, which I have consecrated for my name, I will cast out of my sight, and will make it a proverb and a byword among all peoples. 21 And regarding this house, now exalted, everyone passing by will be astonished, and say, 'Why has the LORD done such a thing to this land and to this house?' 22 Then they will say, 'Because they abandoned the LORD the God of their ancestors who brought them out of the land of Egypt, and they adopted other gods, and worshiped them and served them; therefore he has brought all this calamity upon them.'"

VARIOUS ACTIVITIES OF SOLOMON

8 At the end of twenty years, during which Solomon had built the house of the LORD and his own

ª 7.19 The word you in this verse is plural
ᵇ 7.20 Heb them

BIBLE IN LIFE

Humility   *2 Chronicles 7.13–15*

God's people are called to humble themselves. Having humility means we don't exalt ourselves or think that we're better than others (see Matthew 23.12). Humility is accompanied by gentleness, kindness, patience and love. Jesus modeled humility for us, setting aside his rightful place in heaven to assume human flesh, "taking the form of a slave, being born in human likeness. And being found in human form, he humbled himself and became obedient to the point of death—even death on a cross" (Philippians 2.7–8). In contrast to humility are the attitudes of superiority and divisiveness—attitudes that separate us from other human beings and prevent us from realizing in our own lives the essence of Jesus' love. Usually people don't leave the church or reject Christianity because of a deep theological issue. Almost invariably, people turn against Christianity after observing Christians who fail to demonstrate the humility, love and forgiveness that Jesus Christ expressed in his life. If we claim to be Christians, yet are filled with pride, envy and spite or are inclined toward gossip and tearing others down, then we alienate others from the church or from belief in our Savior.

house, [2]Solomon rebuilt the cities that Huram had given to him, and settled the people of Israel in them.

[3] Solomon went to Hamath-zobah, and captured it. [4]He built Tadmor in the wilderness and all the storage towns that he built in Hamath. [5]He also built Upper Beth-horon and Lower Beth-horon, fortified cities, with walls, gates, and bars, [6]and Baalath, as well as all Solomon's storage towns, and all the towns for his chariots, the towns for his cavalry, and whatever Solomon desired to build, in Jerusalem, in Lebanon, and in all the land of his dominion. [7]All the people who were left of the Hittites, the Amorites, the Perizzites, the Hivites, and the Jebusites, who were not of Israel, [8]from their descendants who were still left in the land, whom the people of Israel had not destroyed—these Solomon conscripted for forced labor, as is still the case today. [9]But of the people of Israel Solomon made no slaves for his work; they were soldiers, and his officers, the commanders of his chariotry and cavalry. [10]These were the chief officers of King Solomon, two hundred fifty of them, who exercised authority over the people.

[11] Solomon brought Pharaoh's daughter from the city of David to the house that he had built for her, for he said, "My wife shall not live in the house of King David of Israel, for the places to which the ark of the LORD has come are holy."

[12] Then Solomon offered up burnt offerings to the LORD on the altar of the LORD that he had built in front of the vestibule, [13]as the duty of each day required, offering according to the commandment of Moses for the sabbaths, the new moons, and the three annual festivals—the festival of unleavened bread, the festival of weeks, and the festival of booths. [14]According to the ordinance of his father David, he appointed the divisions of the priests for their service, and the Levites for their offices of praise and ministry alongside the priests as the duty of each day required, and the gatekeepers in their divisions for the several gates; for

so David the man of God had commanded. [15]They did not turn away from what the king had commanded the priests and Levites regarding anything at all, or regarding the treasuries.

[16] Thus all the work of Solomon was accomplished from[a] the day the foundation of the house of the LORD was laid until the house of the LORD was finished completely.

[17] Then Solomon went to Ezion-geber and Eloth on the shore of the sea, in the land of Edom. [18]Huram sent him, in the care of his servants, ships and servants familiar with the sea. They went to Ophir, together with the servants of Solomon, and imported from there four hundred fifty talents of gold and brought it to King Solomon.

VISIT OF THE QUEEN OF SHEBA

9 When the queen of Sheba heard of the fame of Solomon, she came to Jerusalem to test him with hard questions, having a very great retinue and camels bearing spices and very much gold and precious stones. When she came to Solomon, she discussed with him all that was on her mind. [2]Solomon answered all her questions; there was nothing hidden from Solomon that he could not explain to her. [3]When the queen of Sheba had observed the wisdom of Solomon, the house that he had built, [4]the food of his table, the seating of his officials, and the attendance of his servants, and their clothing, his valets, and their clothing, and his burnt offerings[b] that he offered at the house of the LORD, there was no more spirit left in her.

[5] So she said to the king, "The report was true that I heard in my own land of your accomplishments and of your wisdom, [6]but I did not believe the[c] reports until I came and my own eyes saw it. Not even half of the greatness of your wisdom had been told to me; you far surpass the report that I had heard. [7]Happy are your people! Happy are these your

---

[a] 8.16 Gk Syr Vg: Heb to   [b] 9.4 Gk Syr Vg
1 Kings 10.5: Heb *ascent*   [c] 9.6 Heb *their*

servants, who continually attend you and hear your wisdom! [8]Blessed be the LORD your God, who has delighted in you and set you on his throne as king for the LORD your God. Because your God loved Israel and would establish them forever, he has made you king over them, that you may execute justice and righteousness." [9]Then she gave the king one hundred twenty talents of gold, a very great quantity of spices, and precious stones: there were no spices such as those that the queen of Sheba gave to King Solomon.

[10] Moreover the servants of Huram and the servants of Solomon who brought gold from Ophir brought algum wood and precious stones. [11]From the algum wood, the king made steps[a] for the house of the LORD and for the king's house, lyres also and harps for the singers; there never was seen the like of them before in the land of Judah.

[12] Meanwhile King Solomon granted the queen of Sheba every desire that she expressed, well beyond what she had brought to the king. Then she returned to her own land, with her servants.

SOLOMON'S GREAT WEALTH

[13] The weight of gold that came to Solomon in one year was six hundred sixty-six talents of gold, [14]besides that which the traders and merchants brought; and all the kings of Arabia and the governors of the land brought gold and silver to Solomon. [15]King Solomon made two hundred large shields of beaten gold; six hundred shekels of beaten gold went into each large shield. [16]He made three hundred shields of beaten gold; three hundred shekels of gold went into each shield; and the king put them in the House of the Forest of Lebanon. [17]The king also made a great ivory throne, and overlaid it with pure gold. [18]The throne had six steps and a footstool of gold, which were attached to the throne, and on each side of the seat were arm rests and two lions standing beside the arm rests, [19]while twelve lions were standing, one on each end of a step on the six steps. The like of it was never made in any kingdom. [20]All King Solomon's drinking vessels were of gold, and all the vessels of the House of the Forest of Lebanon were of pure gold; silver was not considered as anything in the days of Solomon. [21]For the king's ships went to Tarshish with the servants of Huram; once every three years the ships of Tarshish used to come bringing gold, silver, ivory, apes, and peacocks.[b]

[22] Thus King Solomon excelled all the kings of the earth in riches and in wisdom. [23]All the kings of the earth sought the presence of Solomon to hear his wisdom, which God had put into his mind. [24]Every one of them brought a present, objects of silver and gold, garments, weaponry, spices, horses, and mules, so much year by year. [25]Solomon had four thousand stalls for horses and chariots, and twelve thousand horses, which he stationed in the chariot cities and with the king in Jerusalem. [26]He ruled over all the kings from the Euphrates to the land of the Philistines, and to the border of Egypt. [27]The king made silver as common in Jerusalem as stone, and cedar as plentiful as the sycamore of the Shephelah. [28]Horses were imported for Solomon from Egypt and from all lands.

DEATH OF SOLOMON

[29] Now the rest of the acts of Solomon, from first to last, are they not written in the history of the prophet Nathan, and in the prophecy of Ahijah the Shilonite, and in the visions of the seer Iddo concerning Jeroboam son of Nebat? [30]Solomon reigned in Jerusalem over all Israel forty years. [31]Solomon slept with his ancestors and was buried in the city of his father David; and his son Rehoboam succeeded him.

THE REVOLT AGAINST REHOBOAM

10 Rehoboam went to Shechem, for all Israel had come

---

[a] 9.11 Gk Vg: Meaning of Heb uncertain
[b] 9.21 Or *baboons*

to Shechem to make him king. ²When Jeroboam son of Nebat heard of it (for he was in Egypt, where he had fled from King Solomon), then Jeroboam returned from Egypt. ³They sent and called him; and Jeroboam and all Israel came and said to Rehoboam, ⁴"Your father made our yoke heavy. Now therefore lighten the hard service of your father and his heavy yoke that he placed on us, and we will serve you." ⁵He said to them, "Come to me again in three days." So the people went away.

6 Then King Rehoboam took counsel with the older men who had attended his father Solomon while he was still alive, saying, "How do you advise me to answer this people?" ⁷They answered him, "If you will be kind to this people and please them, and speak good words to them, then they will be your servants forever." ⁸But he rejected the advice that the older men gave him, and consulted the young men who had grown up with him and now attended him. ⁹He said to them, "What do you advise that we answer this people who have said to me, 'Lighten the yoke that your father put on us'?" ¹⁰The young men who had grown up with him said to him, "Thus should you speak to the people who said to you, 'Your father made our yoke heavy, but you must lighten it for us'; tell them, 'My little finger is thicker than my father's loins. ¹¹Now, whereas my father laid on you a heavy yoke, I will add to your yoke. My father disciplined you with whips, but I will discipline you with scorpions.'"

12 So Jeroboam and all the people came to Rehoboam the third day, as the king had said, "Come to me again the third day." ¹³The king answered them harshly. King Rehoboam rejected the advice of the older men; ¹⁴he spoke to them in accordance with the advice of the young men, "My father made your yoke heavy, but I will add to it; my father disciplined you with whips, but I will discipline you with scorpions." ¹⁵So the king did not listen to the people, because it was a turn of affairs brought about by God so that the LORD might fulfill his word, which he had spoken by Ahijah the Shilonite to Jeroboam son of Nebat.

16 When all Israel saw that the king would not listen to them, the people answered the king,

"What share do we have in David?
We have no inheritance
    in the son of Jesse.
Each of you to your tents,
    O Israel!
Look now to your own
    house, O David."

So all Israel departed to their tents. ¹⁷But Rehoboam reigned over the people of Israel who were living in the cities of Judah. ¹⁸When King Rehoboam sent Hadoram, who was taskmaster over the forced labor, the people of Israel stoned him to death. King Rehoboam hurriedly mounted his chariot to flee to Jerusalem. ¹⁹So Israel has been in rebellion against the house of David to this day.

JUDAH AND BENJAMIN FORTIFIED

11 When Rehoboam came to Jerusalem, he assembled one hundred eighty thousand chosen troops of the house of Judah and Benjamin to fight against Israel, to restore the kingdom to Rehoboam. ²But the word of the LORD came to Shemaiah the man of God: ³Say to King Rehoboam of Judah, son of Solomon, and to all Israel in Judah and Benjamin, ⁴"Thus says the LORD: You shall not go up or fight against your kindred. Let everyone return home, for this thing is from me." So they heeded the word of the LORD and turned back from the expedition against Jeroboam.

5 Rehoboam resided in Jerusalem, and he built cities for defense in Judah. ⁶He built up Bethlehem, Etam, Tekoa, ⁷Beth-zur, Soco, Adullam, ⁸Gath, Mareshah, Ziph, ⁹Adoraim, Lachish, Azekah, ¹⁰Zorah, Aijalon, and Hebron, fortified cities that are in Judah and in Benjamin. ¹¹He made the fortresses strong, and put commanders in them, and stores of food, oil, and wine. ¹²He also put large shields and spears in all the cities,

and made them very strong. So he held Judah and Benjamin.

PRIESTS AND LEVITES SUPPORT REHOBOAM

13 The priests and the Levites who were in all Israel presented themselves to him from all their territories. 14The Levites had left their common lands and their holdings and had come to Judah and Jerusalem, because Jeroboam and his sons had prevented them from serving as priests of the LORD, 15and had appointed his own priests for the high places, and for the goat-demons, and for the calves that he had made. 16Those who had set their hearts to seek the LORD God of Israel came after them from all the tribes of Israel to Jerusalem to sacrifice to the LORD, the God of their ancestors. 17They strengthened the kingdom of Judah, and for three years they made Rehoboam son of Solomon secure, for they walked for three years in the way of David and Solomon.

REHOBOAM'S MARRIAGES

18 Rehoboam took as his wife Mahalath daughter of Jerimoth son of David, and of Abihail daughter of Eliab son of Jesse. 19She bore him sons: Jeush, Shemariah, and Zaham. 20After her he took Maacah daughter of Absalom, who bore him Abijah, Attai, Ziza, and Shelomith. 21Rehoboam loved Maacah daughter of Absalom more than all his other wives and concubines (he took eighteen wives and sixty concubines, and became the father of twenty-eight sons and sixty daughters). 22Rehoboam appointed Abijah son of Maacah as chief prince among his brothers, for he intended to make him king. 23He dealt wisely, and distributed some of his sons through all the districts of Judah and Benjamin, in all the fortified cities; he gave them abundant provisions, and found many wives for them.

EGYPT ATTACKS JUDAH

12 When the rule of Rehoboam was established and he grew strong, he abandoned the law of the LORD, he and all Israel with him. 2In the fifth year of King Rehoboam, because they had been unfaithful to the LORD, King Shishak of Egypt came up against Jerusalem 3with twelve hundred chariots and sixty thousand cavalry. A countless army came with him from Egypt—Libyans, Sukkiim, and Ethiopians.[a] 4He took the fortified cities of Judah and came as far as Jerusalem. 5Then the prophet Shemaiah came to Rehoboam and to the officers of Judah, who had gathered at Jerusalem because of Shishak, and said to them, "Thus says the LORD: You abandoned me, so I have abandoned you to the hand of Shishak." 6Then the officers of Israel and the king humbled themselves and said, "The LORD is in the right." 7When the LORD saw that they humbled themselves, the word of the LORD came to Shemaiah, saying: "They have humbled themselves; I will not destroy them, but I will grant them some deliverance, and my wrath shall not be poured out on Jerusalem by the hand of Shishak. 8Nevertheless they shall be his servants, so that they may know the difference between serving me and serving the kingdoms of other lands."

9 So King Shishak of Egypt came up against Jerusalem; he took away the treasures of the house of the LORD and the treasures of the king's house; he took everything. He also took away the shields of gold that Solomon had made; 10but King Rehoboam made in place of them shields of bronze, and committed them to the hands of the officers of the guard, who kept the door of the king's house. 11Whenever the king went into the house of the LORD, the guard would come along bearing them, and would then bring them back to the guardroom. 12Because he humbled himself the wrath of the LORD turned from him, so as not to destroy them completely; moreover, conditions were good in Judah.

DEATH OF REHOBOAM

13 So King Rehoboam established himself in Jerusalem and reigned.

a 12.3 Or *Nubians*; Heb *Cushites*

Rehoboam was forty-one years old when he began to reign; he reigned seventeen years in Jerusalem, the city that the LORD had chosen out of all the tribes of Israel to put his name there. His mother's name was Naamah the Ammonite. ¹⁴He did evil, for he did not set his heart to seek the LORD.

15 Now the acts of Rehoboam, from first to last, are they not written in the records of the prophet Shemaiah and of the seer Iddo, recorded by genealogy? There were continual wars between Rehoboam and Jeroboam. ¹⁶Rehoboam slept with his ancestors and was buried in the city of David; and his son Abijah succeeded him.

ABIJAH REIGNS OVER JUDAH

13 In the eighteenth year of King Jeroboam, Abijah began to reign over Judah. ²He reigned for three years in Jerusalem. His mother's name was Micaiah daughter of Uriel of Gibeah.

Now there was war between Abijah and Jeroboam. ³Abijah engaged in battle, having an army of valiant warriors, four hundred thousand picked men; and Jeroboam drew up his line of battle against him with eight hundred thousand picked mighty warriors. ⁴Then Abijah stood on the slope of Mount Zemaraim that is in the hill country of Ephraim, and said, "Listen to me, Jeroboam and all Israel! ⁵Do you not know that the LORD God of Israel gave the kingship over Israel forever to David and his sons by a covenant of salt? ⁶Yet Jeroboam son of Nebat, a servant of Solomon son of David, rose up and rebelled against his lord; ⁷and certain worthless scoundrels gathered around him and defied Rehoboam son of Solomon, when Rehoboam was young and irresolute and could not withstand them.

8 "And now you think that you can withstand the kingdom of the LORD in the hand of the sons of David, because you are a great multitude and have with you the golden calves that Jeroboam made as gods for you. ⁹Have you not driven out

the priests of the LORD, the descendants of Aaron, and the Levites, and made priests for yourselves like the peoples of other lands? Whoever comes to be consecrated with a young bull or seven rams becomes a priest of what are no gods. ¹⁰But as for us, the LORD is our God, and we have not abandoned him. We have priests ministering to the LORD who are descendants of Aaron, and Levites for their service. ¹¹They offer to the LORD every morning and every evening burnt offerings and fragrant incense, set out the rows of bread on the table of pure gold, and care for the golden lampstand so that its lamps may burn every evening; for we keep the charge of the LORD our God, but you have abandoned him. ¹²See, God is with us at our head, and his priests have their battle trumpets to sound the call to battle against you. O Israelites, do not fight against the LORD, the God of your ancestors; for you cannot succeed."

13 Jeroboam had sent an ambush around to come on them from behind; thus his troops[a] were in front of Judah, and the ambush was behind them. ¹⁴When Judah turned, the battle was in front of them and behind them. They cried out to the LORD, and the priests blew the trumpets. ¹⁵Then the people of Judah raised the battle shout. And when the people of Judah shouted, God defeated Jeroboam and all Israel before Abijah and Judah. ¹⁶The Israelites fled before Judah, and God gave them into their hands. ¹⁷Abijah and his army defeated them with great slaughter; five hundred thousand picked men of Israel fell slain. ¹⁸Thus the Israelites were subdued at that time, and the people of Judah prevailed, because they relied on the LORD, the God of their ancestors. ¹⁹Abijah pursued Jeroboam, and took cities from him: Bethel with its villages and Jeshanah with its villages and Ephron[b] with its villages. ²⁰Jeroboam did not recover

a 13.13 Heb *they*   b 13.19 Another reading is *Ephrain*

his power in the days of Abijah; the LORD struck him down, and he died. ²¹But Abijah grew strong. He took fourteen wives, and became the father of twenty-two sons and sixteen daughters. ²²The rest of the acts of Abijah, his behavior and his deeds, are written in the story of the prophet Iddo.

ASA REIGNS

14 ᵃ So Abijah slept with his ancestors, and they buried him in the city of David. His son Asa succeeded him. In his days the land had rest for ten years. ²ᵇAsa did what was good and right in the sight of the LORD his God. ³He took away the foreign altars and the high places, broke down the pillars, hewed down the sacred poles,ᶜ ⁴and commanded Judah to seek the LORD, the God of their ancestors, and to keep the law and the commandment. ⁵He also removed from all the cities of Judah the high places and the incense altars. And the kingdom had rest under him. ⁶He built fortified cities in Judah while the land had rest. He had no war in those years, for the LORD gave him peace. ⁷He said to Judah, "Let us build these cities, and surround them with walls and towers, gates and bars; the land is still ours because we have sought the LORD our God; we have sought him, and he has given us peace on every side." So they built and prospered. ⁸Asa had an army of three hundred thousand from Judah, armed with large shields and spears, and two hundred eighty thousand troops from Benjamin who carried shields and drew bows; all these were mighty warriors.

ETHIOPIAN INVASION REPULSED

⁹ Zerah the Ethiopianᵈ came out against them with an army of a million men and three hundred chariots, and came as far as Mareshah. ¹⁰Asa went out to meet him, and they drew up their lines of battle in the valley of Zephathah at Mareshah. ¹¹Asa cried to the LORD his God, "O LORD, there is no difference for you between helping the mighty and the weak. Help us, O LORD our God, for we rely on you, and in your name we have come against this multitude. O LORD, you are our God; let no mortal prevail against you." ¹²So the LORD defeated the Ethiopiansᵉ before Asa and before Judah, and the Ethiopiansᵉ fled. ¹³Asa and the army with him pursued them as far as Gerar, and the Ethiopiansᵉ fell until no one remained alive; for they were broken before the LORD and his army. The people of Judahᶠ carried away a great quantity of booty. ¹⁴They defeated all the cities around Gerar, for the fear of the LORD was on them. They plundered all the cities; for there was much plunder in them. ¹⁵They also attacked the tents of those who had livestock,ᵍ and carried away sheep and goats in abundance, and camels. Then they returned to Jerusalem.

15 The spirit of God came upon Azariah son of Oded. ²He went out to meet Asa and said to him, "Hear me, Asa, and all Judah and Benjamin: The LORD is with you, while you are with him. If you seek him, he will be found by you, but if you abandon him, he will abandon you. ³For a long time Israel was without the true God, and without a teaching priest, and without law; ⁴but when in their distress they turned to the LORD, the God of Israel, and sought him, he was found by them. ⁵In those times it was not safe for anyone to go or come, for great disturbances afflicted all the inhabitants of the lands. ⁶They were broken in pieces, nation against nation and city against city, for God troubled them with every sort of distress. ⁷But you, take courage! Do not let your hands be weak, for your work shall be rewarded."

⁸When Asa heard these words, the prophecy of Azariah son of Oded,ʰ he took courage, and put

---

ᵃ **14.1** Ch 13.23 in Heb   ᵇ **14.2** Ch 14.1 in Heb   ᶜ **14.3** Heb *Asherim*   ᵈ **14.9** Or *Nubian*; Heb *Cushite*   ᵉ **14.12,13** Or *Nubians*; Heb *Cushites*   ᶠ **14.13** Heb *They*   ᵍ **14.15** Meaning of Heb uncertain   ʰ **15.8** Compare Syr Vg: Heb *the prophecy, the prophet Obed*

away the abominable idols from all the land of Judah and Benjamin and from the towns that he had taken in the hill country of Ephraim. He repaired the altar of the LORD that was in front of the vestibule of the house of the LORD.[a] 9He gathered all Judah and Benjamin, and those from Ephraim, Manasseh, and Simeon who were residing as aliens with them, for great numbers had deserted to him from Israel when they saw that the LORD his God was with him. 10They were gathered at Jerusalem in the third month of the fifteenth year of the reign of Asa. 11They sacrificed to the LORD on that day, from the booty that they had brought, seven hundred oxen and seven thousand sheep. 12They entered into a covenant to seek the LORD, the God of their ancestors, with all their heart and with all their soul. 13Whoever would not seek the LORD, the God of Israel, should be put to death, whether young or old, man or woman. 14They took an oath to the LORD with a loud voice, and with shouting, and with trumpets, and with horns. 15All Judah rejoiced over the oath; for they had sworn with all their heart, and had sought him with their whole desire, and he was found by them, and the LORD gave them rest all around.

16 King Asa even removed his mother Maacah from being queen mother because she had made an abominable image for Asherah. Asa cut down her image, crushed it, and burned it at the Wadi Kidron. 17But the high places were not taken out of Israel. Nevertheless the heart of Asa was true all his days. 18He brought into the house of God the votive gifts of his father and his own votive gifts—silver, gold, and utensils. 19And there was no more war until the thirty-fifth year of the reign of Asa.

ALLIANCE WITH ARAM CONDEMNED

16 In the thirty-sixth year of the reign of Asa, King Baasha of Israel went up against Judah, and built Ramah, to prevent any-

---

PONDER

All Judah rejoiced over the oath; for they had sworn with all their heart, and had sought him with their whole desire, and he was found by them, and the LORD gave them rest all around.
—2 Chronicles 15.15

PRAY

Almighty Father, we are thankful for all parts of the Bible, some of which are troubling, some of which may cause us concern. We are thankful for the purity of its message. Help us understand these verses and apply them to our own lives. Give us the desire to seek you eagerly. Help us to acknowledge our doubts and face those doubts courageously. Forgive us our sins as we forgive those against whom we might have a grudge. Let us act always in the pattern of our Savior, in whom you give us peace and rest. In his name we pray. Amen.

---

one from going out or coming into the territory of[b] King Asa of Judah. 2Then Asa took silver and gold from the treasures of the house of the LORD and the king's house, and sent them to King Ben-hadad of Aram, who resided in Damascus, saying, 3"Let there be an alliance between me and you, like that between my father and your father; I am sending to you silver and gold; go, break your alliance with King Baasha of Israel, so that he may withdraw from me." 4Ben-hadad listened to King Asa, and sent the commanders of his armies against the cities of Israel. They conquered Ijon, Dan, Abel-maim, and all the store-cities of Naphtali. 5When Baasha heard of it, he stopped building Ramah, and let his work cease. 6Then King Asa

[a] 15.8 Heb *the vestibule of the LORD*
[b] 16.1 Heb lacks *the territory of*

brought all Judah, and they carried away the stones of Ramah and its timber, with which Baasha had been building, and with them he built up Geba and Mizpah.

7 At that time the seer Hanani came to King Asa of Judah, and said to him, "Because you relied on the king of Aram, and did not rely on the LORD your God, the army of the king of Aram has escaped you. 8 Were not the Ethiopians[a] and the Libyans a huge army with exceedingly many chariots and cavalry? Yet because you relied on the LORD, he gave them into your hand. 9 For the eyes of the LORD range throughout the entire earth, to strengthen those whose heart is true to him. You have done foolishly in this; for from now on you will have wars." 10 Then Asa was angry with the seer, and put him in the stocks, in prison, for he was in a rage with him because of this. And Asa inflicted cruelties on some of the people at the same time.

ASA'S DISEASE AND DEATH

11 The acts of Asa, from first to last, are written in the Book of the Kings of Judah and Israel. 12 In the thirty-ninth year of his reign Asa was diseased in his feet, and his disease became severe; yet even in his disease he did not seek the LORD, but sought help from physicians. 13 Then Asa slept with his ancestors, dying in the forty-first year of his reign. 14 They buried him in the tomb that he had hewn out for himself in the city of David. They laid him on a bier that had been filled with various kinds of spices prepared by the perfumer's art; and they made a very great fire in his honor.

JEHOSHAPHAT'S REIGN

17 His son Jehoshaphat succeeded him, and strengthened himself against Israel. 2 He placed forces in all the fortified cities of Judah, and set garrisons in the land of Judah, and in the cities of Ephraim that his father Asa had taken. 3 The LORD was with Jehoshaphat, because he walked in the earlier ways of his father;[b] he did not seek the Baals, 4 but sought the God of his father and walked in his commandments, and not according to the ways of Israel. 5 Therefore the LORD established the kingdom in his hand. All Judah brought tribute to Jehoshaphat, and he had great riches and honor. 6 His heart was courageous in the ways of the LORD; and furthermore he removed the high places and the sacred poles[c] from Judah.

7 In the third year of his reign he sent his officials, Ben-hail, Obadiah, Zechariah, Nethanel, and Micaiah, to teach in the cities of Judah. 8 With them were the Levites, Shemaiah, Nethaniah, Zebadiah, Asahel, Shemiramoth, Jehonathan, Adonijah, Tobijah, and Tob-adonijah; and with these Levites, the priests Elishama and Jehoram. 9 They taught in Judah, having the book of the law of the LORD with them; they went around through all the cities of Judah and taught among the people.

10 The fear of the LORD fell on all the kingdoms of the lands around Judah, and they did not make war against Jehoshaphat. 11 Some of the Philistines brought Jehoshaphat presents, and silver for tribute; and the Arabs also brought him seven thousand seven hundred rams and seven thousand seven hundred male goats. 12 Jehoshaphat grew steadily greater. He built fortresses and storage cities in Judah. 13 He carried out great works in the cities of Judah. He had soldiers, mighty warriors, in Jerusalem. 14 This was the muster of them by ancestral houses: Of Judah, the commanders of the thousands: Adnah the commander, with three hundred thousand mighty warriors, 15 and next to him Jehohanan the commander, with two hundred eighty thousand, 16 and next to him Amasiah son of Zichri, a volunteer for the service of the LORD, with two hundred thousand mighty warriors. 17 Of Benjamin: Eliada, a mighty warrior, with two hundred thousand armed with bow and shield,

a 16.8 Or *Nubians*; Heb *Cushites*
b 17.3 Another reading is *his father David*
c 17.6 Heb *Asherim*

¹⁸and next to him Jehozabad with one hundred eighty thousand armed for war. ¹⁹These were in the service of the king, besides those whom the king had placed in the fortified cities throughout all Judah.

MICAIAH PREDICTS FAILURE

18 Now Jehoshaphat had great riches and honor; and he made a marriage alliance with Ahab. ²After some years he went down to Ahab in Samaria. Ahab slaughtered an abundance of sheep and oxen for him and for the people who were with him, and induced him to go up against Ramoth-gilead. ³King Ahab of Israel said to King Jehoshaphat of Judah, "Will you go with me to Ramoth-gilead?" He answered him, "I am with you, my people are your people. We will be with you in the war."

⁴ But Jehoshaphat also said to the king of Israel, "Inquire first for the word of the LORD." ⁵Then the king of Israel gathered the prophets together, four hundred of them, and said to them, "Shall we go to battle against Ramoth-gilead, or shall I refrain?" They said, "Go up; for God will give it into the hand of the king." ⁶But Jehoshaphat said, "Is there no other prophet of the LORD here of whom we may inquire?" ⁷The king of Israel said to Jehoshaphat, "There is still one other by whom we may inquire of the LORD, Micaiah son of Imlah; but I hate him, for he never prophesies anything favorable about me, but only disaster." Jehoshaphat said, "Let the king not say such a thing." ⁸Then the king of Israel summoned an officer and said, "Bring quickly Micaiah son of Imlah." ⁹Now the king of Israel and King Jehoshaphat of Judah were sitting on their thrones, arrayed in their robes; and they were sitting at the threshing floor at the entrance of the gate of Samaria; and all the prophets were prophesying before them. ¹⁰Zedekiah son of Chenaanah made for himself horns of iron, and he said, "Thus says the LORD: With these you shall gore the Arameans until they are destroyed." ¹¹All the prophets were prophesying the same and saying, "Go up to Ramoth-gilead and triumph; the LORD will give it into the hand of the king."

¹² The messenger who had gone to summon Micaiah said to him, "Look, the words of the prophets with one accord are favorable to the king; let your word be like the word of one of them, and speak favorably." ¹³But Micaiah said, "As the LORD lives, whatever my God says, that I will speak."

¹⁴ When he had come to the king, the king said to him, "Micaiah, shall we go to Ramoth-gilead to battle, or shall I refrain?" He answered, "Go up and triumph; they will be given into your hand." ¹⁵But the king said to him, "How many times must I make you swear to tell me nothing but the truth in the name of the LORD?" ¹⁶Then Micaiah[a] said, "I saw all Israel scattered on the mountains, like sheep without a shepherd; and the LORD said, 'These have no master; let each one go home in peace.' " ¹⁷The king of Israel said to Jehoshaphat, "Did I not tell you that he would not prophesy anything favorable about me, but only disaster?"

¹⁸ Then Micaiah[a] said, "Therefore hear the word of the LORD: I saw the LORD sitting on his throne, with all the host of heaven standing to the right and to the left of him. ¹⁹And the LORD said, 'Who will entice King Ahab of Israel, so that he may go up and fall at Ramoth-gilead?' Then one said one thing, and another said another, ²⁰until a spirit came forward and stood before the LORD, saying, 'I will entice him.' The LORD asked him, 'How?' ²¹He replied, 'I will go out and be a lying spirit in the mouth of all his prophets.' Then the LORD[a] said, 'You are to entice him, and you shall succeed; go out and do it.' ²²So you see, the LORD has put a lying spirit in the mouth of these your prophets; the LORD has decreed disaster for you."

²³ Then Zedekiah son of Chenaanah came up to Micaiah, slapped him on the cheek, and said, "Which

[a] 18.16,18,21 Heb *he*

way did the spirit of the LORD pass from me to speak to you?" 24Micaiah replied, "You will find out on that day when you go in to hide in an inner chamber." 25The king of Israel then ordered, "Take Micaiah, and return him to Amon the governor of the city and to Joash the king's son; 26and say, 'Thus says the king: Put this fellow in prison, and feed him on reduced rations of bread and water until I return in peace.' " 27Micaiah said, "If you return in peace, the LORD has not spoken by me." And he said, "Hear, you peoples, all of you!"

DEFEAT AND DEATH OF AHAB

28 So the king of Israel and King Jehoshaphat of Judah went up to Ramoth-gilead. 29The king of Israel said to Jehoshaphat, "I will disguise myself and go into battle, but you wear your robes." So the king of Israel disguised himself, and they went into battle. 30Now the king of Aram had commanded the captains of his chariots, "Fight with no one small or great, but only with the king of Israel." 31When the captains of the chariots saw Jehoshaphat, they said, "It is the king of Israel." So they turned to fight against him; and Jehoshaphat cried out, and the LORD helped him. God drew them away from him, 32for when the captains of the chariots saw that it was not the king of Israel, they turned back from pursuing him. 33But a certain man drew his bow and unknowingly struck the king of Israel between the scale armor and the breastplate; so he said to the driver of his chariot, "Turn around, and carry me out of the battle, for I am wounded." 34The battle grew hot that day, and the king of Israel propped himself up in his chariot facing the Arameans until evening; then at sunset he died.

19 King Jehoshaphat of Judah returned in safety to his house in Jerusalem. 2Jehu son of Hanani the seer went out to meet him and said to King Jehoshaphat, "Should you help the wicked and love those who hate the LORD? Because of this, wrath has gone out against you from the LORD. 3Never-

theless, some good is found in you, for you destroyed the sacred poles[a] out of the land, and have set your heart to seek God."

THE REFORMS OF JEHOSHAPHAT

4 Jehoshaphat resided at Jerusalem; then he went out again among the people, from Beer-sheba to the hill country of Ephraim, and brought them back to the LORD, the God of their ancestors. 5He appointed judges in the land in all the fortified cities of Judah, city by city, 6and said to the judges, "Consider what you are doing, for you judge not on behalf of human beings but on the LORD's behalf; he is with you in giving judgment. 7Now, let the fear of the LORD be upon you; take care what you do, for there is no perversion of justice with the LORD our God, or partiality, or taking of bribes."

8 Moreover in Jerusalem Jehoshaphat appointed certain Levites and priests and heads of families of Israel, to give judgment for the LORD and to decide disputed cases. They had their seat at Jerusalem. 9He charged them: "This is how you shall act: in the fear of the LORD, in faithfulness, and with your whole heart; 10whenever a case comes to you from your kindred who live in their cities, concerning bloodshed, law or commandment, statutes or ordinances, then you shall instruct them, so that they may not incur guilt before the LORD and wrath may not come on you and your kindred. Do so, and you will not incur guilt. 11See, Amariah the chief priest is over you in all matters of the LORD; and Zebadiah son of Ishmael, the governor of the house of Judah, in all the king's matters; and the Levites will serve you as officers. Deal courageously, and may the LORD be with the good!"

INVASION FROM THE EAST

20 After this the Moabites and Ammonites, and with them some of the Meunites,[b] came against

a 19.3 Heb *Asheroth*   b 20.1 Compare 26.7: Heb *Ammonites*

Jehoshaphat for battle. [2]Messengers[a] came and told Jehoshaphat, "A great multitude is coming against you from Edom,[b] from beyond the sea; already they are at Hazazon-tamar" (that is, En-gedi). [3]Jehoshaphat was afraid; he set himself to seek the LORD, and proclaimed a fast throughout all Judah. [4]Judah assembled to seek help from the LORD; from all the towns of Judah they came to seek the LORD.

JEHOSHAPHAT'S PRAYER AND VICTORY

[5]Jehoshaphat stood in the assembly of Judah and Jerusalem, in the house of the LORD, before the new court, [6]and said, "O LORD, God of our ancestors, are you not God in heaven? Do you not rule over all the kingdoms of the nations? In your hand are power and might, so that no one is able to withstand you. [7]Did you not, O our God, drive out the inhabitants of this land before your people Israel, and give it forever to the descendants of your friend Abraham? [8]They have lived in it, and in it have built you a sanctuary for your name, saying, [9]'If disaster comes upon us, the sword, judgment,[c] or pestilence, or famine, we will stand before this house, and before you, for your name is in this house, and cry to you in our distress, and you will hear and save.' [10]See now, the people of Ammon, Moab, and Mount Seir, whom you would not let Israel invade when they came from the land of Egypt, and whom they avoided and did not destroy— [11]they reward us by coming to drive us out of your possession that you have given us to inherit. [12]O our God, will you not execute judgment upon them? For we are powerless against this great multitude that is coming against us. We do not know what to do, but our eyes are on you."

[13]Meanwhile all Judah stood before the LORD, with their little ones, their wives, and their children. [14]Then the spirit of the LORD came upon Jahaziel son of Zechariah, son of Benaiah, son of Jeiel, son of Mattaniah, a Levite of the sons of Asaph, in the middle of the assembly. [15]He said, "Listen, all Judah and inhabitants of Jerusalem, and King Jehoshaphat: Thus says the LORD to you: 'Do not fear or be dismayed at this great multitude; for the battle is not yours but God's. [16]Tomorrow go down against them; they will come up by the ascent of Ziz; you will find them at the end of the valley, before the wilderness of Jeruel. [17]This battle is not for you to fight; take your position, stand still, and see the victory of the LORD on your behalf, O Judah and Jerusalem.' Do not fear or be dismayed; tomorrow go out against them, and the LORD will be with you."

[18]Then Jehoshaphat bowed down with his face to the ground, and all Judah and the inhabitants of Jerusalem fell down before the LORD, worshiping the LORD. [19]And the Levites, of the Kohathites and the Korahites, stood up to praise the LORD, the God of Israel, with a very loud voice.

[20]They rose early in the morning and went out into the wilderness of Tekoa; and as they went out, Jehoshaphat stood and said, "Listen to me, O Judah and inhabitants of Jerusalem! Believe in the LORD your God and you will be established; believe his prophets." [21]When he had taken counsel with the people, he appointed those who were to sing to the LORD and praise him in holy splendor, as they went before the army, saying,

"Give thanks to the LORD,
    for his steadfast love
        endures forever."

[22]As they began to sing and praise, the LORD set an ambush against the Ammonites, Moab, and Mount Seir, who had come against Judah, so that they were routed. [23]For the Ammonites and Moab attacked the inhabitants of Mount Seir, destroying them utterly; and when they had made an end of the inhabitants of Seir, they all helped to destroy one another.

---

[a] **20.2** Heb *They*　　[b] **20.2** One Ms: MT *Aram*
[c] **20.9** Or *the sword of judgment*

24 When Judah came to the watchtower of the wilderness, they looked toward the multitude; they were corpses lying on the ground; no one had escaped. 25 When Jehoshaphat and his people came to take the booty from them, they found livestock[a] in great numbers, goods, clothing, and precious things, which they took for themselves until they could carry no more. They spent three days taking the booty, because of its abundance. 26 On the fourth day they assembled in the Valley of Beracah, for there they blessed the LORD; therefore that place has been called the Valley of Beracah[b] to this day. 27 Then all the people of Judah and Jerusalem, with Jehoshaphat at their head, returned to Jerusalem with joy, for the LORD had enabled them to rejoice over their enemies. 28 They came to Jerusalem, with harps and lyres and trumpets, to the house of the LORD. 29 The fear of God came on all the kingdoms of the countries when they heard that the LORD had fought against the enemies of Israel. 30 And the realm of Jehoshaphat was quiet, for his God gave him rest all around.

THE END OF JEHOSHAPHAT'S REIGN

31 So Jehoshaphat reigned over Judah. He was thirty-five years old when he began to reign; he reigned twenty-five years in Jerusalem. His mother's name was Azubah daughter of Shilhi. 32 He walked in the way of his father Asa and did not turn aside from it, doing what was right in the sight of the LORD. 33 Yet the high places were not removed; the people had not yet set their hearts upon the God of their ancestors.

34 Now the rest of the acts of Jehoshaphat, from first to last, are written in the Annals of Jehu son of Hanani, which are recorded in the Book of the Kings of Israel. 35 After this King Jehoshaphat of Judah joined with King Ahaziah of Israel, who did wickedly. 36 He joined him in building ships to go to Tarshish; they built the ships in Ezion-geber. 37 Then Eliezer son of Dodavahu of Mareshah prophesied against Jehoshaphat, saying, "Because you have joined with Ahaziah, the LORD will destroy what you have made." And the ships were wrecked and were not able to go to Tarshish.

JEHORAM'S REIGN

21 Jehoshaphat slept with his ancestors and was buried with his ancestors in the city of David; his son Jehoram succeeded him. 2 He had brothers, the sons of Jehoshaphat: Azariah, Jehiel, Zechariah, Azariah, Michael, and Shephatiah; all these were the sons of King Jehoshaphat of Judah.[c] 3 Their father gave them many gifts, of silver, gold, and valuable possessions, together with fortified cities in Judah; but he gave the kingdom to Jehoram, because he was the firstborn. 4 When Jehoram had ascended the throne of his father and was established, he put all his brothers to the sword, and also some of the officials of Israel. 5 Jehoram was thirty-two years old when he began to reign; he reigned eight years in Jerusalem. 6 He walked in the way of the kings of Israel, as the house of Ahab had done; for the daughter of Ahab was his wife. He did what was evil in the sight of the LORD. 7 Yet the LORD would not destroy the house of David because of the covenant that he had made with David, and since he had promised to give a lamp to him and to his descendants forever.

REVOLT OF EDOM

8 In his days Edom revolted against the rule of Judah and set up a king of their own. 9 Then Jehoram crossed over with his commanders and all his chariots. He set out by night and attacked the Edomites, who had surrounded him and his chariot commanders. 10 So Edom has been in revolt against the rule of Judah to this day. At that time Libnah also revolted against his rule, because he had forsaken the LORD, the God of his ancestors.

ELIJAH'S LETTER

11 Moreover he made high places in the hill country of Judah, and led the inhabitants of Jerusalem into unfaithfulness, and made Judah go astray. **12** A letter came to him from the prophet Elijah, saying: "Thus says the LORD, the God of your father David: Because you have not walked in the ways of your father Jehoshaphat or in the ways of King Asa of Judah, **13** but have walked in the way of the kings of Israel, and have led Judah and the inhabitants of Jerusalem into unfaithfulness, as the house of Ahab led Israel into unfaithfulness, and because you also have killed your brothers, members of your father's house, who were better than yourself, **14** see, the LORD will bring a great plague on your people, your children, your wives, and all your possessions, **15** and you yourself will have a severe sickness with a disease of your bowels, until your bowels come out, day after day, because of the disease."

16 The LORD aroused against Jehoram the anger of the Philistines and of the Arabs who are near the Ethiopians.[a] **17** They came up against Judah, invaded it, and carried away all the possessions they found that belonged to the king's house, along with his sons and his wives, so that no son was left to him except Jehoahaz, his youngest son.

DISEASE AND DEATH OF JEHORAM

18 After all this the LORD struck him in his bowels with an incurable disease. **19** In course of time, at the end of two years, his bowels came out because of the disease, and he died in great agony. His people made no fire in his honor, like the fires made for his ancestors. **20** He was thirty-two years old when he began to reign; he reigned eight years in Jerusalem. He departed with no one's regret. They buried him in the city of David, but not in the tombs of the kings.

AHAZIAH'S REIGN

22 The inhabitants of Jerusalem made his youngest son

Ahaziah king as his successor; for the troops who came with the Arabs to the camp had killed all the older sons. So Ahaziah son of Jehoram reigned as king of Judah. **2** Ahaziah was forty-two years old when he began to reign; he reigned one year in Jerusalem. His mother's name was Athaliah, a granddaughter of Omri. **3** He also walked in the ways of the house of Ahab, for his mother was his counselor in doing wickedly. **4** He did what was evil in the sight of the LORD, as the house of Ahab had done; for after the death of his father they were his counselors, to his ruin. **5** He even followed their advice, and went with Jehoram son of King Ahab of Israel to make war against King Hazael of Aram at Ramoth-gilead. The Arameans wounded Joram, **6** and he returned to be healed in Jezreel of the wounds that he had received at Ramah, when he fought King Hazael of Aram. And Ahaziah son of King Jehoram of Judah went down to see Joram son of Ahab in Jezreel, because he was sick.

7 But it was ordained by God that the downfall of Ahaziah should come about through his going to visit Joram. For when he came there he went out with Jehoram to meet Jehu son of Nimshi, whom the LORD had anointed to destroy the house of Ahab. **8** When Jehu was executing judgment on the house of Ahab, met the officials of Judah and the sons of Ahaziah's brothers, who attended Ahaziah, and he killed them. **9** He searched for Ahaziah, who was captured while hiding in Samaria and was brought to Jehu, and put to death. They buried him, for they said, "He is the grandson of Jehoshaphat, who sought the LORD with all his heart." And the house of Ahaziah had no one able to rule the kingdom.

ATHALIAH SEIZES THE THRONE

10 Now when Athaliah, Ahaziah's mother, saw that her son was dead, she set about to destroy all the royal family of the house of Judah. **11** But Jehoshabeath, the king's daughter,

[a] **21.16** Or *Nubians*; Heb *Cushites*

took Joash son of Ahaziah, and stole him away from among the king's children who were about to be killed; she put him and his nurse in a bedroom. Thus Jehoshabeath, daughter of King Jehoram and wife of the priest Jehoiada—because she was a sister of Ahaziah—hid him from Athaliah, so that she did not kill him; [12] he remained with them six years, hidden in the house of God, while Athaliah reigned over the land.

LIFE IS PRECIOUS. A GIFT OF

GOD. IT IS TOO VALUABLE TO

WASTE ON SELFISH GOALS.

23 But in the seventh year Jehoiada took courage, and entered into a compact with the commanders of the hundreds, Azariah son of Jeroham, Ishmael son of Jehohanan, Azariah son of Obed, Maaseiah son of Adaiah, and Elishaphat son of Zichri. [2] They went around through Judah and gathered the Levites from all the towns of Judah, and the heads of families of Israel, and they came to Jerusalem. [3] Then the whole assembly made a covenant with the king in the house of God. Jehoiada[a] said to them, "Here is the king's son! Let him reign, as the LORD promised concerning the sons of David. [4] This is what you are to do: one-third of you, priests and Levites, who come on duty on the sabbath, shall be gatekeepers, [5] one-third shall be at the king's house, and one-third at the Gate of the Foundation; and all the people shall be in the courts of the house of the LORD. [6] Do not let anyone enter the house of the LORD except the priests and ministering Levites; they may enter, for they are holy, but all the other[b] people shall observe the instructions of the LORD. [7] The Levites shall surround the king, each with his weapons in his hand; and whoever enters

the house shall be killed. Stay with the king in his comings and goings."

JOASH CROWNED KING

[8] The Levites and all Judah did according to all that the priest Jehoiada commanded; each brought his men, who were to come on duty on the sabbath, with those who were to go off duty on the sabbath; for the priest Jehoiada did not dismiss the divisions. [9] The priest Jehoiada delivered to the captains the spears and the large and small shields that had been King David's, which were in the house of God; [10] and he set all the people as a guard for the king, everyone with weapon in hand, from the south side of the house to the north side of the house, around the altar and the house. [11] Then he brought out the king's son, put the crown on him, and gave him the covenant;[c] they proclaimed him king, and Jehoiada and his sons anointed him; and they shouted, "Long live the king!"

ATHALIAH MURDERED

[12] When Athaliah heard the noise of the people running and praising the king, she went into the house of the LORD to the people; [13] and when she looked, there was the king standing by his pillar at the entrance, and the captains and the trumpeters beside the king, and all the people of the land rejoicing and blowing trumpets, and the singers with their musical instruments leading in the celebration. Athaliah tore her clothes, and cried, "Treason! Treason!" [14] Then the priest Jehoiada brought out the captains who were set over the army, saying to them, "Bring her out between the ranks; anyone who follows her is to be put to the sword." For the priest said, "Do not put her to death in the house of the LORD." [15] So they laid hands on her; she went into the entrance of the Horse Gate of the king's house, and there they put her to death.

[a] **23.3** Heb *He*   [b] **23.6** Heb lacks *other*   [c] **23.11** Or *treaty*, or *testimony*; Heb *eduth*

16 Jehoiada made a covenant between himself and all the people and the king that they should be the LORD's people. 17Then all the people went to the house of Baal, and tore it down; his altars and his images they broke in pieces, and they killed Mattan, the priest of Baal, in front of the altars. 18Jehoiada assigned the care of the house of the LORD to the levitical priests whom David had organized to be in charge of the house of the LORD, to offer burnt offerings to the LORD, as it is written in the law of Moses, with rejoicing and with singing, according to the order of David. 19He stationed the gatekeepers at the gates of the house of the LORD so that no one should enter who was in any way unclean. 20And he took the captains, the nobles, the governors of the people, and all the people of the land, and they brought the king down from the house of the LORD, marching through the upper gate to the king's house. They set the king on the royal throne. 21So all the people of the land rejoiced, and the city was quiet after Athaliah had been killed with the sword.

JOASH REPAIRS THE TEMPLE

24 Joash was seven years old when he began to reign; he reigned forty years in Jerusalem; his mother's name was Zibiah of Beersheba. 2Joash did what was right in the sight of the LORD all the days of the priest Jehoiada. 3Jehoiada got two wives for him, and he became the father of sons and daughters.

4 Some time afterward Joash decided to restore the house of the LORD. 5He assembled the priests and the Levites and said to them, "Go out to the cities of Judah and gather money from all Israel to repair the house of your God, year by year; and see that you act quickly." But the Levites did not act quickly. 6So the king summoned Jehoiada the chief, and said to him, "Why have you not required the Levites to bring in from Judah and Jerusalem the tax levied by Moses, the servant of the LORD, on[a] the congregation of Israel for the tent of the covenant?"[b]

7For the children of Athaliah, that wicked woman, had broken into the house of God, and had even used all the dedicated things of the house of the LORD for the Baals.

8 So the king gave command, and they made a chest, and set it outside the gate of the house of the LORD. 9A proclamation was made throughout Judah and Jerusalem to bring in for the LORD the tax that Moses the servant of God laid on Israel in the wilderness. 10All the leaders and all the people rejoiced and brought their tax and dropped it into the chest until it was full. 11Whenever the chest was brought to the king's officers by the Levites, when they saw that there was a large amount of money in it, the king's secretary and the officer of the chief priest would come and empty the chest and take it and return it to its place. So they did day after day, and collected money in abundance. 12The king and Jehoiada gave it to those who had charge of the work of the house of the LORD, and they hired masons and carpenters to restore the house of the LORD, and also workers in iron and bronze to repair the house of the LORD. 13So those who were engaged in the work labored, and the repairing went forward at their hands, and they restored the house of God to its proper condition and strengthened it. 14When they had finished, they brought the rest of the money to the king and Jehoiada, and with it were made utensils for the house of the LORD, utensils for the service and for the burnt offerings, and ladles, and vessels of gold and silver. They offered burnt offerings in the house of the LORD regularly all the days of Jehoiada.

APOSTASY OF JOASH

15 But Jehoiada grew old and full of days, and died; he was one hundred thirty years old at his death. 16And they buried him in the city of David among the kings, because he had done good in Israel, and for God and his house.

a 24.6 Compare Vg: Heb and   b 24.6 Or treaty, or testimony; Heb eduth

17 Now after the death of Jehoiada the officials of Judah came and did obeisance to the king; then the king listened to them. 18 They abandoned the house of the LORD, the God of their ancestors, and served the sacred poles[a] and the idols. And wrath came upon Judah and Jerusalem for this guilt of theirs. 19 Yet he sent prophets among them to bring them back to the LORD; they testified against them, but they would not listen.

20 Then the spirit of God took possession of[b] Zechariah son of the priest Jehoiada; he stood above the people and said to them, "Thus says God: Why do you transgress the commandments of the LORD, so that you cannot prosper? Because you have forsaken the LORD, he has also forsaken you." 21 But they conspired against him, and by command of the king they stoned him to death in the court of the house of the LORD. 22 King Joash did not remember the kindness that Jehoiada, Zechariah's father, had shown him, but killed his son. As he was dying, he said, "May the LORD see and avenge!"

DEATH OF JOASH

23 At the end of the year the army of Aram came up against Joash. They came to Judah and Jerusalem, and destroyed all the officials of the people from among them, and sent all the booty they took to the king of Damascus. 24 Although the army of Aram had come with few men, the LORD delivered into their hand a very great army, because they had abandoned the LORD, the God of their ancestors. Thus they executed judgment on Joash.

25 When they had withdrawn, leaving him severely wounded, his servants conspired against him because of the blood of the son[c] of the priest Jehoiada, and they killed him on his bed. So he died; and they buried him in the city of David, but they did not bury him in the tombs of the kings. 26 Those who conspired against him were Zabad son of Shimeath the Ammonite, and Jehozabad son of Shimrith the Mo-

abite. 27 Accounts of his sons, and of the many oracles against him, and of the rebuilding[d] of the house of God are written in the Commentary on the Book of the Kings. And his son Amaziah succeeded him.

REIGN OF AMAZIAH

25 Amaziah was twenty-five years old when he began to reign, and he reigned twenty-nine years in Jerusalem. His mother's name was Jehoaddan of Jerusalem. 2 He did what was right in the sight of the LORD, yet not with a true heart. 3 As soon as the royal power was firmly in his hand he killed his servants who had murdered his father the king. 4 But he did not put their children to death, according to what is written in the law, in the book of Moses, where the LORD commanded, "The parents shall not be put to death for the children, or the children be put to death for the parents; but all shall be put to death for their own sins."

SLAUGHTER OF THE EDOMITES

5 Amaziah assembled the people of Judah, and set them by ancestral houses under commanders of the thousands and of the hundreds for all Judah and Benjamin. He mustered those twenty years old and upward, and found that they were three hundred thousand picked troops fit for war, able to handle spear and shield. 6 He also hired one hundred thousand mighty warriors from Israel for one hundred talents of silver. 7 But a man of God came to him and said, "O king, do not let the army of Israel go with you, for the LORD is not with Israel—all these Ephraimites. 8 Rather, go by yourself and act; be strong in battle, or God will fling you down before the enemy; for God has power to help or to overthrow." 9 Amaziah said to the man of God, "But what shall we do about the hundred talents that I have given to the army of Israel?" The man of God answered, "The LORD is able to give

[a] 24.18 Heb Asherim   [b] 24.20 Heb clothed itself with   [c] 24.25 Gk Vg: Heb sons
[d] 24.27 Heb founding

you much more than this." ¹⁰Then Amaziah discharged the army that had come to him from Ephraim, letting them go home again. But they became very angry with Judah, and returned home in fierce anger.

11 Amaziah took courage, and led out his people; he went to the Valley of Salt, and struck down ten thousand men of Seir. ¹²The people of Judah captured another ten thousand alive, took them to the top of Sela, and threw them down from the top of Sela, so that all of them were dashed to pieces. ¹³But the men of the army whom Amaziah sent back, not letting them go with him to battle, fell on the cities of Judah from Samaria to Beth-horon; they killed three thousand people in them, and took much booty.

14 Now after Amaziah came from the slaughter of the Edomites, he brought the gods of the people of Seir, set them up as his gods, and worshiped them, making offerings to them. ¹⁵The LORD was angry with Amaziah and sent to him a prophet, who said to him, "Why have you resorted to a people's gods who could not deliver their own people from your hand?" ¹⁶But as he was speaking the king[a] said to him, "Have we made you a royal counselor? Stop! Why should you be put to death?" So the prophet stopped, but said, "I know that God has determined to destroy you, because you have done this and have not listened to my advice."

ISRAEL DEFEATS JUDAH

17 Then King Amaziah of Judah took counsel and sent to King Joash son of Jehoahaz son of Jehu of Israel, saying, "Come, let us look one another in the face." ¹⁸King Joash of Israel sent word to King Amaziah of Judah, "A thornbush on Lebanon sent to a cedar on Lebanon, saying, 'Give your daughter to my son for a wife'; but a wild animal of Lebanon passed by and trampled down the thornbush. ¹⁹You say, 'See, I have defeated Edom,' and your heart has lifted you up in boastfulness. Now stay at home; why should you provoke trouble so that you fall, you and Judah with you?"

20 But Amaziah would not listen—it was God's doing, in order to hand them over, because they had sought the gods of Edom. ²¹So King Joash of Israel went up; he and King Amaziah of Judah faced one another in battle at Beth-shemesh, which belongs to Judah. ²²Judah was defeated by Israel; everyone fled home. ²³King Joash of Israel captured King Amaziah of Judah, son of Joash, son of Ahaziah, at Beth-shemesh; he brought him to Jerusalem, and broke down the wall of Jerusalem from the Ephraim Gate to the Corner Gate, a distance of four hundred cubits. ²⁴He seized all the gold and silver, and all the vessels that were found in the house of God, and Obed-edom with them; he seized also the treasuries of the king's house, also hostages; then he returned to Samaria.

DEATH OF AMAZIAH

25 King Amaziah son of Joash of Judah, lived fifteen years after the death of King Joash son of Jehoahaz of Israel. ²⁶Now the rest of the deeds of Amaziah, from first to last, are they not written in the Book of the Kings of Judah and Israel? ²⁷From the time that Amaziah turned away from the LORD they made a conspiracy against him in Jerusalem, and he fled to Lachish. But they sent after him to Lachish, and killed him there. ²⁸They brought him back on horses; he was buried with his ancestors in the city of David.

REIGN OF UZZIAH

26 Then all the people of Judah took Uzziah, who was sixteen years old, and made him king to succeed his father Amaziah. ²He rebuilt Eloth and restored it to Judah, after the king slept with his ancestors. ³Uzziah was sixteen years old when he began to reign, and he reigned fifty-two years in Jerusalem. His mother's name was Jecoliah of Jerusalem. ⁴He did what was right in the sight of the LORD, just

[a] 25.16 Heb *he*

as his father Amaziah had done. [5]He set himself to seek God in the days of Zechariah, who instructed him in the fear of God; and as long as he sought the LORD, God made him prosper.

6 He went out and made war against the Philistines, and broke down the wall of Gath and the wall of Jabneh and the wall of Ashdod; he built cities in the territory of Ashdod and elsewhere among the Philistines. [7]God helped him against the Philistines, against the Arabs who lived in Gur-baal, and against the Meunites. [8]The Ammonites paid tribute to Uzziah, and his fame spread even to the border of Egypt, for he became very strong. [9]Moreover Uzziah built towers in Jerusalem at the Corner Gate, at the Valley Gate, and at the Angle, and fortified them. [10]He built towers in the wilderness and hewed out many cisterns, for he had large herds, both in the Shephelah and in the plain, and he had farmers and vinedressers in the hills and in the fertile lands, for he loved the soil. [11]Moreover Uzziah had an army of soldiers, fit for war, in divisions according to the numbers in the muster made by the secretary Jeiel and the officer Maaseiah, under the direction of Hananiah, one of the king's commanders. [12]The whole number of the heads of ancestral houses of mighty warriors was two thousand six hundred. [13]Under their command was an army of three hundred seven thousand five hundred, who could make war with mighty power, to help the king against the enemy. [14]Uzziah provided for all the army the shields, spears, helmets, coats of mail, bows, and stones for slinging. [15]In Jerusalem he set up machines, invented by skilled workers, on the towers and the corners for shooting arrows and large stones. And his fame spread far, for he was marvelously helped until he became strong.

PRIDE AND APOSTASY

16 But when he had become strong he grew proud, to his destruction. For he was false to the LORD his God, and entered the temple of the LORD to make offering on the altar of incense. [17]But the priest Azariah went in after him, with eighty priests of the LORD who were men of valor; [18]they withstood King Uzziah, and said to him, "It is not for you, Uzziah, to make offering to the LORD, but for the priests the descendants of Aaron, who are consecrated to make offering. Go out of the sanctuary; for you have done wrong, and it will bring you no honor from the LORD God." [19]Then Uzziah was angry. Now he had a censer in his hand to make offering, and when he became angry with the priests a leprous[a] disease broke out on his forehead, in the presence of the priests in the house of the LORD, by the altar of incense. [20]When the chief priest Azariah, and all the priests, looked at him, he was leprous[a] in his forehead. They hurried him out, and he himself hurried to get out, because the LORD had struck him. [21]King Uzziah was leprous[a] to the day of his death, and being leprous[a] lived in a separate house, for he was excluded from the house of the LORD. His son Jotham was in charge of the palace of the king, governing the people of the land.

22 Now the rest of the acts of Uzziah, from first to last, the prophet Isaiah son of Amoz wrote. [23]Uzziah slept with his ancestors; they buried him near his ancestors in the burial field that belonged to the kings, for they said, "He is leprous."[a] His son Jotham succeeded him.

REIGN OF JOTHAM

27 Jotham was twenty-five years old when he began to reign; he reigned sixteen years in Jerusalem. His mother's name was Jerushah daughter of Zadok. [2]He did what was right in the sight of the LORD just as his father Uzziah had done—only he did not invade the temple of the LORD. But the people still followed corrupt practices. [3]He built the upper gate of the house of

---

[a] 26.19,20,21,23 A term for several skin diseases; precise meaning uncertain

the LORD, and did extensive building on the wall of Ophel. ⁴Moreover he built cities in the hill country of Judah, and forts and towers on the wooded hills. ⁵He fought with the king of the Ammonites and prevailed against them. The Ammonites gave him that year one hundred talents of silver, ten thousand cors of wheat and ten thousand of barley. The Ammonites paid him the same amount in the second and the third years. ⁶So Jotham became strong because he ordered his ways before the LORD his God. ⁷Now the rest of the acts of Jotham, and all his wars and his ways, are written in the Book of the Kings of Israel and Judah. ⁸He was twenty-five years old when he began to reign; he reigned sixteen years in Jerusalem. ⁹Jotham slept with his ancestors, and they buried him in the city of David; and his son Ahaz succeeded him.

REIGN OF AHAZ

28 Ahaz was twenty years old when he began to reign; he reigned sixteen years in Jerusalem. He did not do what was right in the sight of the LORD, as his ancestor David had done, ²but he walked in the ways of the kings of Israel. He even made cast images for the Baals; ³and he made offerings in the valley of the son of Hinnom, and made his sons pass through fire, according to the abominable practices of the nations whom the LORD drove out before the people of Israel. ⁴He sacrificed and made offerings on the high places, on the hills, and under every green tree.

ARAM AND ISRAEL
DEFEAT JUDAH

⁵Therefore the LORD his God gave him into the hand of the king of Aram, who defeated him and took captive a great number of his people and brought them to Damascus. He was also given into the hand of the king of Israel, who defeated him with great slaughter. ⁶Pekah son of Remaliah killed one hundred twenty thousand in Judah in one day, all of them valiant warriors, because they had abandoned the LORD, the God of their ancestors. ⁷And Zichri, a mighty warrior of Ephraim, killed the king's son Maaseiah, Azrikam the commander of the palace, and Elkanah the next in authority to the king.

INTERVENTION OF ODED

⁸The people of Israel took captive two hundred thousand of their kin, women, sons, and daughters; they also took much booty from them and brought the booty to Samaria. ⁹But a prophet of the LORD was there, whose name was Oded; he went out to meet the army that came to Samaria, and said to them, "Because the LORD, the God of your ancestors, was angry with Judah, he gave them into your hand, but you have killed them in a rage that has reached up to heaven. ¹⁰Now you intend to subjugate the people of Judah and Jerusalem, male and female, as your slaves. But what have you except sins against the LORD your God? ¹¹Now hear me, and send back the captives whom you have taken from your kindred, for the fierce wrath of the LORD is upon you." ¹²Moreover, certain chiefs of the Ephraimites, Azariah son of Johanan, Berechiah son of Meshillemoth, Jehizkiah son of Shallum, and Amasa son of Hadlai, stood up against those who were coming from the war, ¹³and said to them, "You shall not bring the captives in here, for you propose to bring on us guilt against the LORD in addition to our present sins and guilt. For our guilt is already great, and there is fierce wrath against Israel." ¹⁴So the warriors left the captives and the booty before the officials and all the assembly. ¹⁵Then those who were mentioned by name got up and took the captives, and with the booty they clothed all that were naked among them; they clothed them, gave them sandals, provided them with food and drink, and anointed them; and carrying all the feeble among them on donkeys, they brought them to their kindred at Jericho, the city of palm trees. Then they returned to Samaria.

ASSYRIA REFUSES TO HELP JUDAH

16 At that time King Ahaz sent to the king[a] of Assyria for help. 17For the Edomites had again invaded and defeated Judah, and carried away captives. 18And the Philistines had made raids on the cities in the Shephelah and the Negeb of Judah, and had taken Beth-shemesh, Aijalon, Gederoth, Soco with its villages, Timnah with its villages, and Gimzo with its villages; and they settled there. 19For the LORD brought Judah low because of King Ahaz of Israel, for he had behaved without restraint in Judah and had been faithless to the LORD. 20So King Tilgath-pilneser of Assyria came against him, and oppressed him instead of strengthening him. 21For Ahaz plundered the house of the LORD and the houses of the king and of the officials, and gave tribute to the king of Assyria; but it did not help him.

APOSTASY AND DEATH OF AHAZ

22 In the time of his distress he became yet more faithless to the LORD—this same King Ahaz. 23For he sacrificed to the gods of Damascus, which had defeated him, and said, "Because the gods of the kings of Aram helped them, I will sacrifice to them so that they may help me." But they were the ruin of him, and of all Israel. 24Ahaz gathered together the utensils of the house of God, and cut in pieces the utensils of the house of God. He shut up the doors of the house of the LORD and made himself altars in every corner of Jerusalem. 25In every city of Judah he made high places to make offerings to other gods, provoking to anger the LORD, the God of his ancestors. 26Now the rest of his acts and all his ways, from first to last, are written in the Book of the Kings of Judah and Israel. 27Ahaz slept with his ancestors, and they buried him in the city, in Jerusalem; but they did not bring him into the tombs of the kings of Israel. His son Hezekiah succeeded him.

REIGN OF HEZEKIAH

29 Hezekiah began to reign when he was twenty-five years old; he reigned twenty-nine years in Jerusalem. His mother's name was Abijah daughter of Zechariah. 2He did what was right in the sight of the LORD, just as his ancestor David had done.

THE TEMPLE CLEANSED

3 In the first year of his reign, in the first month, he opened the doors of the house of the LORD and repaired them. 4He brought in the priests and the Levites and assembled them in the square on the east. 5He said to them, "Listen to me, Levites! Sanctify yourselves, and sanctify the house of the LORD, the God of your ancestors, and carry out the filth from the holy place. 6For our ancestors have been unfaithful and have done what was evil in the sight of the LORD our God; they have forsaken him, and have turned away their faces from the dwelling of the LORD, and turned their backs. 7They also shut the doors of the vestibule and put out the lamps, and have not offered incense or made burnt offerings in the holy place to the God of Israel. 8Therefore the wrath of the LORD came upon Judah and Jerusalem, and he has made them an object of horror, of astonishment, and of hissing, as you see with your own eyes. 9Our fathers have fallen by the sword and our sons and our daughters and our wives are in captivity for this. 10Now it is in my heart to make a covenant with the LORD, the God of Israel, so that his fierce anger may turn away from us. 11My sons, do not now be negligent, for the LORD has chosen you to stand in his presence to minister to him, and to be his ministers and make offerings to him."

12 Then the Levites arose, Mahath son of Amasai, and Joel son of Azariah, of the sons of the Kohathites; and of the sons of Merari, Kish son of Abdi, and Azariah son of Jehal-

a 28.16 Gk Syr Vg Compare 2 Kings 16.7: Heb kings

lelel; and of the Gershonites, Joah son of Zimmah, and Eden son of Joah; 13and of the sons of Elizaphan, Shimri and Jeuel; and of the sons of Asaph, Zechariah and Mattaniah; 14and of the sons of Heman, Jehuel and Shimei; and of the sons of Jeduthun, Shemaiah and Uzziel. 15They gathered their brothers, sanctified themselves, and went in as the king had commanded, by the words of the LORD, to cleanse the house of the LORD. 16The priests went into the inner part of the house of the LORD to cleanse it, and they brought out all the unclean things that they found in the temple of the LORD into the court of the house of the LORD; and the Levites took them and carried them out to the Wadi Kidron. 17They began to sanctify on the first day of the first month, and on the eighth day of the month they came to the vestibule of the LORD; then for eight days they sanctified the house of the LORD, and on the sixteenth day of the first month they finished. 18Then they went inside to King Hezekiah and said, "We have cleansed all the house of the LORD, the altar of burnt offering and all its utensils, and the table for the rows of bread and all its utensils. 19All the utensils that King Ahaz repudiated during his reign when he was faithless, we have made ready and sanctified; see, they are in front of the altar of the LORD."

TEMPLE WORSHIP RESTORED

20 Then King Hezekiah rose early, assembled the officials of the city, and went up to the house of the LORD. 21They brought seven bulls, seven rams, seven lambs, and seven male goats for a sin offering for the kingdom and for the sanctuary and for Judah. He commanded the priests the descendants of Aaron to offer them on the altar of the LORD. 22So they slaughtered the bulls, and the priests received the blood and dashed it against the altar; they slaughtered the rams and their blood was dashed against the altar; they also slaughtered the lambs and their blood was dashed against the altar.

23Then the male goats for the sin offering were brought to the king and the assembly; they laid their hands on them, 24and the priests slaughtered them and made a sin offering with their blood at the altar, to make atonement for all Israel. For the king commanded that the burnt offering and the sin offering should be made for all Israel.

25 He stationed the Levites in the house of the LORD with cymbals, harps, and lyres, according to the commandment of David and of Gad the king's seer and of the prophet Nathan, for the commandment was from the LORD through his prophets. 26The Levites stood with the instruments of David, and the priests with the trumpets. 27Then Hezekiah commanded that the burnt offering be offered on the altar. When the burnt offering began, the song to the LORD began also, and the trumpets, accompanied by the instruments of King David of Israel. 28The whole assembly worshiped, the singers sang, and the trumpeters sounded; all this continued until the burnt offering was finished. 29When the offering was finished, the king and all who were present with him bowed down and worshiped. 30King Hezekiah and the officials commanded the Levites to sing praises to the LORD with the words of David and of the seer Asaph. They sang praises with gladness, and they bowed down and worshiped.

31 Then Hezekiah said, "You have now consecrated yourselves to the LORD; come near, bring sacrifices and thank offerings to the house of the LORD." The assembly brought sacrifices and thank offerings; and all who were of a willing heart brought burnt offerings. 32The number of the burnt offerings that the assembly brought was seventy bulls, one hundred rams, and two hundred lambs; all these were for a burnt offering to the LORD. 33The consecrated offerings were six hundred bulls and three thousand sheep. 34But the priests were too few and could not skin all the burnt offerings, so, until other priests had sanctified

themselves, their kindred, the Levites, helped them until the work was finished—for the Levites were more conscientious[a] than the priests in sanctifying themselves. 35 Besides the great number of burnt offerings there was the fat of the offerings of well-being, and there were the drink offerings for the burnt offerings. Thus the service of the house of the LORD was restored. 36 And Hezekiah and all the people rejoiced because of what God had done for the people; for the thing had come about suddenly.

THE GREAT PASSOVER

30 Hezekiah sent word to all Israel and Judah, and wrote letters also to Ephraim and Manasseh, that they should come to the house of the LORD at Jerusalem, to keep the passover to the LORD the God of Israel. 2 For the king and his officials and all the assembly in Jerusalem had taken counsel to keep the passover in the second month 3 (for they could not keep it at its proper time because the priests had not sanctified themselves in sufficient number, nor had the people assembled in Jerusalem). 4 The plan seemed right to the king and all the assembly. 5 So they decreed to make a proclamation throughout all Israel, from Beer-sheba to Dan, that the people should come and keep the passover to the LORD the God of Israel, at Jerusalem; for they had not kept it in great numbers as prescribed. 6 So couriers went throughout all Israel and Judah with letters from the king and his officials, as the king had commanded, saying, "O people of Israel, return to the LORD, the God of Abraham, Isaac, and Israel, so that he may turn again to the remnant of you who have escaped from the hand of the kings of Assyria. 7 Do not be like your ancestors and your kindred, who were faithless to the LORD God of their ancestors, so that he made them a desolation, as you see. 8 Do not now be stiff-necked as your ancestors were, but yield yourselves to the LORD and come to his sanctuary, which he has sanctified forever,

and serve the LORD your God, so that his fierce anger may turn away from you. 9 For as you return to the LORD, your kindred and your children will find compassion with their captors, and return to this land. For the LORD your God is gracious and merciful, and will not turn away his face from you, if you return to him."

10 So the couriers went from city to city through the country of Ephraim and Manasseh, and as far as Zebulun; but they laughed them to scorn, and mocked them. 11 Only a few from Asher, Manasseh, and Zebulun humbled themselves and came to Jerusalem. 12 The hand of God was also on Judah to give them one heart to do what the king and the officials commanded by the word of the LORD.

13 Many people came together in Jerusalem to keep the festival of unleavened bread in the second month, a very large assembly. 14 They set to work and removed the altars that were in Jerusalem, and all the altars for offering incense they took away and threw into the Wadi Kidron. 15 They slaughtered the passover lamb on the fourteenth day of the second month. The priests and the Levites were ashamed, and they sanctified themselves and brought burnt offerings into the house of the LORD. 16 They took their accustomed posts according to the law of Moses the man of God; the priests dashed the blood that they received[b] from the hands of the Levites. 17 For there were many in the assembly who had not sanctified themselves; therefore the Levites had to slaughter the passover lamb for everyone who was not clean, to make it holy to the LORD. 18 For a multitude of the people, many of them from Ephraim, Manasseh, Issachar, and Zebulun, had not cleansed themselves, yet they ate the passover otherwise than as prescribed. But Hezekiah prayed for them, saying, "The good LORD pardon all 19 who set their hearts to seek God, the LORD the

a 29.34 Heb *upright in heart*   b 30.16 Heb lacks *that they received*

God of their ancestors, even though not in accordance with the sanctuary's rules of cleanness." 20 The LORD heard Hezekiah, and healed the people. 21 The people of Israel who were present at Jerusalem kept the festival of unleavened bread seven days with great gladness; and the Levites and the priests praised the LORD day by day, accompanied by loud instruments for the LORD. 22 Hezekiah spoke encouragingly to all the Levites who showed good skill in the service of the LORD. So the people ate the food of the festival for seven days, sacrificing offerings of well-being and giving thanks to the LORD the God of their ancestors.

23 Then the whole assembly agreed together to keep the festival for another seven days; so they kept it for another seven days with gladness. 24 For King Hezekiah of Judah gave the assembly a thousand bulls and seven thousand sheep for offerings, and the officials gave the assembly a thousand bulls and ten thousand sheep. The priests sanctified themselves in great numbers. 25 The whole assembly of Judah, the priests and the Levites, and the whole assembly that came out of Israel, and the resident aliens who came out of the land of Israel, and the resident aliens who lived in Judah, rejoiced. 26 There was great joy in Jerusalem, for since the time of Solomon son of King David of Israel there had been nothing like this in Jerusalem. 27 Then the priests and the Levites stood up and blessed the people, and their voice was heard; their prayer came to his holy dwelling in heaven.

PAGAN SHRINES DESTROYED

31 Now when all this was finished, all Israel who were present went out to the cities of Judah and broke down the pillars, hewed down the sacred poles,[a] and pulled down the high places and the altars throughout all Judah and Benjamin, and in Ephraim and Manasseh, until they had destroyed them all. Then all the people of Israel returned to their cities, all to their individual properties.

2 Hezekiah appointed the divisions of the priests and of the Levites, division by division, everyone according to his service, the priests and the Levites, for burnt offerings and offerings of well-being, to minister in the gates of the camp of the LORD and to give thanks and praise. 3 The contribution of the king from his own possessions was for the burnt offerings: the burnt offerings of morning and evening, and the burnt offerings for the sabbaths, the new moons, and the appointed festivals, as it is written in the law of the LORD. 4 He commanded the people who lived in Jerusalem to give the portion due to the priests and the Levites, so that they might devote themselves to the law of the LORD. 5 As soon as the word spread, the people of Israel gave in abundance the first fruits of grain, wine, oil, honey, and of all the produce of the field; and they brought in abundantly the tithe of everything. 6 The people of Israel and Judah who lived in the cities of Judah also brought in the tithe of cattle and sheep, and the tithe of the dedicated things that had been consecrated to the LORD their God, and laid them in heaps. 7 In the third month they began to pile up the heaps, and finished them in the seventh month. 8 When Hezekiah and the officials came and saw the heaps, they blessed the LORD and his people Israel. 9 Hezekiah questioned the priests and the Levites about the heaps. 10 The chief priest Azariah, who was of the house of Zadok, answered him, "Since they began to bring the contributions into the house of the LORD, we have had enough to eat and have plenty to spare; for the LORD has blessed his people, so that we have this great supply left over."

REORGANIZATION OF PRIESTS AND LEVITES

11 Then Hezekiah commanded them to prepare store-chambers in the house of the LORD; and they prepared them. 12 Faithfully they brought in the contributions, the tithes and

a 31.1 Heb *Asherim*

the dedicated things. The chief officer in charge of them was Conaniah the Levite, with his brother Shimei as second; [13] while Jehiel, Azaziah, Nahath, Asahel, Jerimoth, Jozabad, Eliel, Ismachiah, Mahath, and Benaiah were overseers assisting Conaniah and his brother Shimei, by the appointment of King Hezekiah and of Azariah the chief officer of the house of God. [14] Kore son of Imnah the Levite, keeper of the east gate, was in charge of the freewill offerings to God, to apportion the contribution reserved for the LORD and the most holy offerings. [15] Eden, Miniamin, Jeshua, Shemaiah, Amariah, and Shecaniah were faithfully assisting him in the cities of the priests, to distribute the portions to their kindred, old and young alike, by divisions, [16] except those enrolled by genealogy, males from three years old and upwards, all who entered the house of the LORD as the duty of each day required, for their service according to their offices, by their divisions. [17] The enrollment of the priests was according to their ancestral houses; that of the Levites from twenty years old and upwards was according to their offices, by their divisions. [18] The priests were enrolled with all their little children, their wives, their sons, and their daughters, the whole multitude; for they were faithful in keeping themselves holy. [19] And for the descendants of Aaron, the priests, who were in the fields of common land belonging to their towns, town by town, the people designated by name were to distribute portions to every male among the priests and to everyone among the Levites who was enrolled.

20 Hezekiah did this throughout all Judah; he did what was good and right and faithful before the LORD his God. [21] And every work that he undertook in the service of the house of God, and in accordance with the law and the commandments, to seek his God, he did with all his heart; and he prospered.

SENNACHERIB'S INVASION

32 After these things and these acts of faithfulness, King Sennacherib of Assyria came and invaded Judah and encamped against the fortified cities, thinking to win them for himself. [2] When Hezekiah saw that Sennacherib had come and intended to fight against Jerusalem, [3] he planned with his officers and his warriors to stop the flow of the springs that were outside the city; and they helped him. [4] A great many people were gathered, and they stopped all the springs and the wadi that flowed through the land, saying, "Why should the Assyrian kings come and find water in abundance?" [5] Hezekiah[a] set to work resolutely and built up the entire wall that was broken down, and raised towers on it,[b] and outside it he built another wall; he also strengthened the Millo in the city of David, and made weapons and shields in abundance. [6] He appointed combat commanders over the people, and gathered them together to him in the square at the gate of the city and spoke encouragingly to them, saying, [7] "Be strong and of good courage. Do not be afraid or dismayed before the king of Assyria and all the horde that is with him; for there is one greater with us than with him. [8] With him is an arm of flesh; but with us is the LORD our God, to help us and to fight our battles." The people were encouraged by the words of King Hezekiah of Judah.

9 After this, while King Sennacherib of Assyria was at Lachish with all his forces, he sent his servants to Jerusalem to King Hezekiah of Judah and to all the people of Judah that were in Jerusalem, saying, [10] "Thus says King Sennacherib of Assyria: On what are you relying, that you undergo the siege of Jerusalem? [11] Is not Hezekiah misleading you, handing you over to die by famine and by thirst, when he tells you, 'The LORD our God will save us from the hand of the king of Assyria'? [12] Was it not this same Hezekiah who took away his high places and his altars and commanded Judah and

a 32.5 Heb He   b 32.5 Vg: Heb and raised on the towers

Jerusalem, saying, 'Before one altar you shall worship, and upon it you shall make your offerings'? 13Do you not know what I and my ancestors have done to all the peoples of other lands? Were the gods of the nations of those lands at all able to save their lands out of my hand? 14Who among all the gods of those nations that my ancestors utterly destroyed was able to save his people from my hand, that your God should be able to save you from my hand? 15Now therefore do not let Hezekiah deceive you or mislead you in this fashion, and do not believe him, for no god of any nation or kingdom has been able to save his people from my hand or from the hand of my ancestors. How much less will your God save you out of my hand!"

16 His servants said still more against the Lord GOD and against his servant Hezekiah. 17He also wrote letters to throw contempt on the LORD the God of Israel and to speak against him, saying, "Just as the gods of the nations in other lands did not rescue their people from my hands, so the God of Hezekiah will not rescue his people from my hand." 18They shouted it with a loud voice in the language of Judah to the people of Jerusalem who were on the wall, to frighten and terrify them, in order that they might take the city. 19They spoke of the God of Jerusalem as if he were like the gods of the peoples of the earth, which are the work of human hands.

SENNACHERIB'S DEFEAT AND DEATH

20 Then King Hezekiah and the prophet Isaiah son of Amoz prayed because of this and cried to heaven. 21And the LORD sent an angel who cut off all the mighty warriors and commanders and officers in the camp of the king of Assyria. So he returned in disgrace to his own land. When he came into the house of his god, some of his own sons struck him down there with the sword. 22So the LORD saved Hezekiah and the inhabitants of Jerusalem from the hand of King Sennacherib of

Assyria and from the hand of all his enemies; he gave them resta on every side. 23Many brought gifts to the LORD in Jerusalem and precious things to King Hezekiah of Judah, so that he was exalted in the sight of all nations from that time onward.

HEZEKIAH'S SICKNESS

24 In those days Hezekiah became sick and was at the point of death. He prayed to the LORD, and he answered him and gave him a sign. 25But Hezekiah did not respond according to the benefit done to him, for his heart was proud. Therefore wrath came upon him and upon Judah and Jerusalem. 26Then Hezekiah humbled himself for the pride of his heart, both he and the inhabitants of Jerusalem, so that the wrath of the LORD did not come upon them in the days of Hezekiah.

HEZEKIAH'S PROSPERITY AND ACHIEVEMENTS

27 Hezekiah had very great riches and honor; and he made for himself treasuries for silver, for gold, for precious stones, for spices, for shields, and for all kinds of costly objects; 28storehouses also for the yield of grain, wine, and oil; and stalls for all kinds of cattle, and sheepfolds.b 29He likewise provided cities for himself, and flocks and herds in abundance; for God had given him very great possessions. 30This same Hezekiah closed the upper outlet of the waters of Gihon and directed them down to the west side of the city of David. Hezekiah prospered in all his works. 31So also in the matter of the envoys of the officials of Babylon, who had been sent to him to inquire about the sign that had been done in the land, God left him to himself, in order to test him and to know all that was in his heart.

32 Now the rest of the acts of Hezekiah, and his good deeds, are written in the vision of the prophet Isaiah son of Amoz in the Book of the Kings of Judah and Israel. 33Hezekiah

a 32.22 Gk Vg: Heb *guided them*
b 32.28 Gk Vg: Heb *flocks for folds*

slept with his ancestors, and they buried him on the ascent to the tombs of the descendants of David; and all Judah and the inhabitants of Jerusalem did him honor at his death. His son Manasseh succeeded him.

REIGN OF MANASSEH

33 Manasseh was twelve years old when he began to reign; he reigned fifty-five years in Jerusalem. ²He did what was evil in the sight of the LORD, according to the abominable practices of the nations whom the LORD drove out before the people of Israel. ³For he rebuilt the high places that his father Hezekiah had pulled down, and erected altars to the Baals, made sacred poles,ᵃ worshiped all the host of heaven, and served them. ⁴He built altars in the house of the LORD, of which the LORD had said, "In Jerusalem shall my name be forever." ⁵He built altars for all the host of heaven in the two courts of the house of the LORD. ⁶He made his son pass through fire in the valley of the son of Hinnom, practiced soothsaying and augury and sorcery, and dealt with mediums and with wizards. He did much evil in the sight of the LORD, provoking him to anger. ⁷The carved image of the idol that he had made he set in the house of God, of which God said to David and to his son Solomon, "In this house, and in Jerusalem, which I have chosen out of all the tribes of Israel, I will put my name forever; ⁸I will never again remove the feet of Israel from the land that I appointed for your ancestors, if only they will be careful to do all that I have commanded them, all the law, the statutes, and the ordinances given through Moses." ⁹Manasseh misled Judah and the inhabitants of Jerusalem, so that they did more evil than the nations whom the LORD had destroyed before the people of Israel.

MANASSEH RESTORED
AFTER REPENTANCE

10 The LORD spoke to Manasseh and to his people, but they gave no heed. ¹¹Therefore the LORD brought against them the commanders of the army of the king of Assyria, who took Manasseh captive in manacles, bound him with fetters, and brought him to Babylon. ¹²While he was in distress he entreated the favor of the LORD his God and humbled himself greatly before the God of his ancestors. ¹³He prayed to him, and God received his entreaty, heard his plea, and restored him again to Jerusalem and to his kingdom. Then Manasseh knew that the LORD indeed was God.

14 Afterward he built an outer wall for the city of David west of Gihon, in the valley, reaching the entrance at the Fish Gate; he carried it around Ophel, and raised it to a very great height. He also put commanders of the army in all the fortified cities in Judah. ¹⁵He took away the foreign gods and the idol from the house of the LORD, and all the altars that he had built on the mountain of the house of the LORD and in Jerusalem, and he threw them out of the city. ¹⁶He also restored the altar of the LORD and offered on it sacrifices of well-being and of thanksgiving; and he commanded Judah to serve the LORD the God of Israel. ¹⁷The people, however, still sacrificed at the high places, but only to the LORD their God.

DEATH OF MANASSEH

18 Now the rest of the acts of Manasseh, his prayer to his God, and the words of the seers who spoke to him in the name of the LORD God of Israel, these are in the Annals of the Kings of Israel. ¹⁹His prayer, and how God received his entreaty, all his sin and his faithlessness, the sites on which he built high places and set up the sacred polesᵇ and the images, before he humbled himself, these are written in the records of the seers.ᶜ ²⁰So Manasseh slept with his ancestors, and they buried him in his house. His son Amon succeeded him.

AMON'S REIGN AND DEATH

21 Amon was twenty-two years old when he began to reign; he

ᵃ 33.3 Heb *Asheroth*   ᵇ 33.19 Heb *Asherim*
ᶜ 33.19 One Ms Gk: MT *of Hozai*

reigned two years in Jerusalem. [22]He did what was evil in the sight of the LORD, as his father Manasseh had done. Amon sacrificed to all the images that his father Manasseh had made, and served them. [23]He did not humble himself before the LORD, as his father Manasseh had humbled himself, but this Amon incurred more and more guilt. [24]His servants conspired against him and killed him in his house. [25]But the people of the land killed all those who had conspired against King Amon; and the people of the land made his son Josiah king to succeed him.

REIGN OF JOSIAH

34 Josiah was eight years old when he began to reign; he reigned thirty-one years in Jerusalem. [2]He did what was right in the sight of the LORD, and walked in the ways of his ancestor David; he did not turn aside to the right or to the left. [3]For in the eighth year of his reign, while he was still a boy, he began to seek the God of his ancestor David, and in the twelfth year he began to purge Judah and Jerusalem of the high places, the sacred poles,[a] and the carved and the cast images. [4]In his presence they pulled down the altars of the Baals; he demolished the incense altars that stood above them. He broke down the sacred poles[a] and the carved and the cast images; he made dust of them and scattered it over the graves of those who had sacrificed to them. [5]He also burned the bones of the priests on their altars, and purged Judah and Jerusalem. [6]In the towns of Manasseh, Ephraim, and Simeon, and as far as Naphtali, in their ruins[b] all around, [7]he broke down the altars, beat the sacred poles[a] and the images into powder, and demolished all the incense altars throughout all the land of Israel. Then he returned to Jerusalem.

DISCOVERY OF THE BOOK OF THE LAW

8 In the eighteenth year of his reign, when he had purged the land and the house, he sent Shaphan son of Azaliah, Maaseiah the governor of the city, and Joah son of Joahaz, the recorder, to repair the house of the LORD his God. [9]They came to the high priest Hilkiah and delivered the money that had been brought into the house of God, which the Levites, the keepers of the threshold, had collected from Manasseh and Ephraim and from all the remnant of Israel and from all Judah and Benjamin and from the inhabitants of Jerusalem. [10]They delivered it to the workers who had the oversight of the house of the LORD, and the workers who were working in the house of the LORD gave it for repairing and restoring the house. [11]They gave it to the carpenters and the builders to buy quarried stone, and timber for binders, and beams for the buildings that the kings of Judah had let go to ruin. [12]The people did the work faithfully. Over them were appointed the Levites Jahath and Obadiah, of the sons of Merari, along with Zechariah and Meshullam, of the sons of the Kohathites, to have oversight. Other Levites, all skillful with instruments of music, [13]were over the burden bearers and directed all who did work in every kind of service; and some of the Levites were scribes, and officials, and gatekeepers.

14 While they were bringing out the money that had been brought into the house of the LORD, the priest Hilkiah found the book of the law of the LORD given through Moses. [15]Hilkiah said to the secretary Shaphan, "I have found the book of the law in the house of the LORD"; and Hilkiah gave the book to Shaphan. [16]Shaphan brought the book to the king, and further reported to the king, "All that was committed to your servants they are doing. [17]They have emptied out the money that was found in the house of the LORD and have delivered it into the hand of the overseers and the workers." [18]The secretary Shaphan informed the king, "The priest Hilkiah has

---

[a] 34.3,4,7 Heb *Asherim*   [b] 34.6 Meaning of Heb uncertain

given me a book." Shaphan then read it aloud to the king.

19 When the king heard the words of the law he tore his clothes. 20 Then the king commanded Hilkiah, Ahikam son of Shaphan, Abdon son of Micah, the secretary Shaphan, and the king's servant Asaiah: 21 "Go, inquire of the LORD for me and for those who are left in Israel and in Judah, concerning the words of the book that has been found; for the wrath of the LORD that is poured out on us is great, because our ancestors did not keep the word of the LORD, to act in accordance with all that is written in this book."

THE PROPHET HULDAH CONSULTED

22 So Hilkiah and those whom the king had sent went to the prophet Huldah, the wife of Shallum son of Tokhath son of Hasrah, keeper of the wardrobe (who lived in Jerusalem in the Second Quarter) and spoke to her to that effect. 23 She declared to them, "Thus says the LORD, the God of Israel: Tell the man who sent you to me, 24 Thus says the LORD: I will indeed bring disaster upon this place and upon its inhabitants, all the curses that are written in the book that was read before the king of Judah. 25 Because they have forsaken me and have made offerings to other gods, so that they have provoked me to anger with all the works of their hands, my wrath will be poured out on this place and will not be quenched. 26 But as to the king of Judah, who sent you to inquire of the LORD, thus shall you say to him: Thus says the LORD, the God of Israel: Regarding the words that you have heard, 27 because your heart was penitent and you humbled yourself before God when you heard his words against this place and its inhabitants, and you have humbled yourself before me, and have torn your clothes and wept before me, I also have heard you, says the LORD. 28 I will gather you to your ancestors and you shall be gathered to your grave in peace; your eyes shall not see all the disaster that I will bring

on this place and its inhabitants." They took the message back to the king.

THE COVENANT RENEWED

29 Then the king sent word and gathered together all the elders of Judah and Jerusalem. 30 The king went up to the house of the LORD, with all the people of Judah, the inhabitants of Jerusalem, the priests and the Levites, all the people both great and small; he read in their hearing all the words of the book of the covenant that had been found in the house of the LORD. 31 The king stood in his place and made a covenant before the LORD, to follow the LORD, keeping his commandments, his decrees, and his statutes, with all his heart and all his soul, to perform the words of the covenant that were written in this book. 32 Then he made all who were present in Jerusalem and in Benjamin pledge themselves to it. And the inhabitants of Jerusalem acted according to the covenant of God, the God of their ancestors. 33 Josiah took away all the abominations from all the territory that belonged to the people of Israel, and made all who were in Israel worship the LORD their God. All his days they did not turn away from following the LORD the God of their ancestors.

CELEBRATION OF THE PASSOVER

35 Josiah kept a passover to the LORD in Jerusalem; they slaughtered the passover lamb on the fourteenth day of the first month. 2 He appointed the priests to their offices and encouraged them in the service of the house of the LORD. 3 He said to the Levites who taught all Israel and who were holy to the LORD, "Put the holy ark in the house that Solomon son of David, king of Israel, built; you need no longer carry it on your shoulders. Now serve the LORD your God and his people Israel. 4 Make preparations by your ancestral houses by your divisions, following the written directions of King David of Israel and the written directions of his

son Solomon. 5Take position in the holy place according to the groupings of the ancestral houses of your kindred the people, and let there be Levites for each division of an ancestral house.ª 6Slaughter the passover lamb, sanctify yourselves, and on behalf of your kindred make preparations, acting according to the word of the Lord by Moses."

7 Then Josiah contributed to the people, as passover offerings for all that were present, lambs and kids from the flock to the number of thirty thousand, and three thousand bulls; these were from the king's possessions. 8His officials contributed willingly to the people, to the priests, and to the Levites. Hilkiah, Zechariah, and Jehiel, the chief officers of the house of God, gave to the priests for the passover offerings two thousand six hundred lambs and kids and three hundred bulls. 9Conaniah also, and his brothers Shemaiah and Nethanel, and Hashabiah and Jeiel and Jozabad, the chiefs of the Levites, gave to the Levites for the passover offerings five thousand lambs and kids and five hundred bulls.

10 When the service had been prepared for, the priests stood in their place, and the Levites in their divisions according to the king's command. 11They slaughtered the passover lamb, and the priests dashed the blood that they receivedᵇ from them, while the Levites did the skinning. 12They set aside the burnt offerings so that they might distribute them according to the groupings of the ancestral houses of the people, to offer to the Lord, as it is written in the book of Moses. And they did the same with the bulls. 13They roasted the passover lamb with fire according to the ordinance; and they boiled the holy offerings in pots, in caldrons, and in pans, and carried them quickly to all the people. 14Afterward they made preparations for themselves and for the priests, because the priests the descendants of Aaron were occupied in offering the burnt offerings and the fat parts until night; so the Levites made preparations for them-

selves and for the priests, the descendants of Aaron. 15The singers, the descendants of Asaph, were in their place according to the command of David, and Asaph, and Heman, and the king's seer Jeduthun. The gatekeepers were at each gate; they did not need to interrupt their service, for their kindred the Levites made preparations for them.

16 So all the service of the Lord was prepared that day, to keep the passover and to offer burnt offerings on the altar of the Lord, according to the command of King Josiah. 17The people of Israel who were present kept the passover at that time, and the festival of unleavened bread seven days. 18No passover like it had been kept in Israel since the days of the prophet Samuel; none of the kings of Israel had kept such a passover as was kept by Josiah, by the priests and the Levites, by all Judah and Israel who were present, and by the inhabitants of Jerusalem. 19In the eighteenth year of the reign of Josiah this passover was kept.

DEFEAT BY PHARAOH NECO AND DEATH OF JOSIAH

20 After all this, when Josiah had set the temple in order, King Neco of Egypt went up to fight at Carchemish on the Euphrates, and Josiah went out against him. 21But Necoᶜ sent envoys to him, saying, "What have I to do with you, king of Judah? I am not coming against you today, but against the house with which I am at war; and God has commanded me to hurry. Cease opposing God, who is with me, so that he will not destroy you." 22But Josiah would not turn away from him, but disguised himself in order to fight with him. He did not listen to the words of Neco from the mouth of God, but joined battle in the plain of Megiddo. 23The archers shot King Josiah; and the king said to his servants, "Take me away, for I am badly wounded." 24So his servants took him out of the chariot and carried him in his second

ª 35.5 Meaning of Heb uncertain
ᵇ 35.11 Heb lacks *that they received*
ᶜ 35.21 Heb *he*

chariot[a] and brought him to Jerusalem. There he died, and was buried in the tombs of his ancestors. All Judah and Jerusalem mourned for Josiah. 25Jeremiah also uttered a lament for Josiah, and all the singing men and singing women have spoken of Josiah in their laments to this day. They made these a custom in Israel; they are recorded in the Laments. 26Now the rest of the acts of Josiah and his faithful deeds in accordance with what is written in the law of the LORD, 27and his acts, first and last, are written in the Book of the Kings of Israel and Judah.

REIGN OF JEHOAHAZ

36 The people of the land took Jehoahaz son of Josiah and made him king to succeed his father in Jerusalem. 2Jehoahaz was twenty-three years old when he began to reign; he reigned three months in Jerusalem. 3Then the king of Egypt deposed him in Jerusalem and laid on the land a tribute of one hundred talents of silver and one talent of gold. 4The king of Egypt made his brother Eliakim king over Judah and Jerusalem, and changed his name to Jehoiakim; but Neco took his brother Jehoahaz and carried him to Egypt.

REIGN AND CAPTIVITY OF JEHOIAKIM

5Jehoiakim was twenty-five years old when he began to reign; he reigned eleven years in Jerusalem. He did what was evil in the sight of the LORD his God. 6Against him King Nebuchadnezzar of Babylon came up, and bound him with fetters to take him to Babylon. 7Nebuchadnezzar also carried some of the vessels of the house of the LORD to Babylon and put them in his palace in Babylon. 8Now the rest of the acts of Jehoiakim, and the abominations that he did, and what was found against him, are written in the Book of the Kings of Israel and Judah; and his son Jehoiachin succeeded him.

REIGN AND CAPTIVITY OF JEHOIACHIN

9Jehoiachin was eight years old when he began to reign; he reigned

three months and ten days in Jerusalem. He did what was evil in the sight of the LORD. 10In the spring of the year King Nebuchadnezzar sent and brought him to Babylon, along with the precious vessels of the house of the LORD, and made his brother Zedekiah king over Judah and Jerusalem.

REIGN OF ZEDEKIAH

11Zedekiah was twenty-one years old when he began to reign; he reigned eleven years in Jerusalem. 12He did what was evil in the sight of the LORD his God. He did not humble himself before the prophet Jeremiah who spoke from the mouth of the LORD. 13He also rebelled against King Nebuchadnezzar, who had made him swear by God; he stiffened his neck and hardened his heart against turning to the LORD, the God of Israel. 14All the leading priests and the people also were exceedingly unfaithful, following all the abominations of the nations; and they polluted the house of the LORD that he had consecrated in Jerusalem.

THE FALL OF JERUSALEM

15The LORD, the God of their ancestors, sent persistently to them by his messengers, because he had compassion on his people and on his dwelling place; 16but they kept mocking the messengers of God, despising his words, and scoffing at his prophets, until the wrath of the LORD against his people became so great that there was no remedy. 17Therefore he brought up against them the king of the Chaldeans, who killed their youths with the sword in the house of their sanctuary, and had no compassion on young man or young woman, the aged or the feeble; he gave them all into his hand. 18All the vessels of the house of God, large and small, and the treasures of the house of the LORD, and the treasures of the king and of his officials, all these he brought to Babylon. 19They burned the house of God, broke down the wall of Jerusalem,

a 35.24 Or *the chariot of his deputy*

A GRACIOUS GOD

*They kept mocking the messengers of God, despising his words, and
scoffing at his prophets, until the wrath of the LORD against his
people became so great that there was no remedy.*

—2 Chronicles 36.16

Every human being is inclined to think that if they are favored with long life, wealth, security or some other good thing, they must somehow be more deserving than others who are not as well off, that they must be superior in God's eyes. They may even consider themselves more righteous before God and less sinful than other people. Perhaps this is how the people of Judah felt—just before the nation fell to the Babylonians.

To understand the events described in this chapter, it is important to learn about a few things that had happened in Israel's history up to this point. After the death of King Solomon, the nation of Israel split into two kingdoms: the northern kingdom of Israel (with ten Israelite tribes) and the southern kingdom of Judah (with two tribes). Over time, the northern kingdom became so wicked that around 722 BC, the Lord allowed the Assyrian Empire to capture Israel's capital city, Samaria, and exile many Israelites into faraway places. Those living in the southern kingdom of Judah, however, remained in their homeland under their own king. They continued to disobey the Lord too, and he sent prophets to warn them to turn away from their sin, but the people mocked them and continued in their wicked ways. By the time King Zedekiah was made king over Judah, it had been over 130 years since the northern kingdom had fallen to the Assyrians—almost the same length of time between the Civil War and our day. No doubt the people of Judah were thinking that they must have special favor with God and that disaster would never strike them. But as we see in this chapter, the sins of the people finally did catch up with them, and the nation of Judah fell to the Babylonian Empire. The Babylonians leveled the city of Jerusalem, including the temple of the Lord, and exiled numerous Israelites to Babylonia.

When we experience good health, financial well-being or some other blessing from God, does this mean that we are more deserving or loved by God than others who are undergoing difficulty? Does it mean we are less sinful than others? Not at all. In fact, God may simply be acting graciously toward us, giving us good things in spite of our unfaithfulness to him in many ways. Instead of becoming arrogant and proud about the good things we have, we should seek to use them to help others who are experiencing hardship. In this way, we are following the example of Christ himself, who freely chose to surrender the glories of heaven to bestow eternal life and blessings to his people on earth.

Going Deeper

- What are some specific ways you are tempted to become arrogant about things that are actually gracious gifts from God?
- How can you use the blessings God has given you to help others?

burned all its palaces with fire, and destroyed all its precious vessels. ²⁰He took into exile in Babylon those who had escaped from the sword, and they became servants to him and to his sons until the establishment of the kingdom of Persia, ²¹to fulfill the word of the LORD by the mouth of Jeremiah, until the land had made up for its sabbaths. All the days that it lay desolate it kept sabbath, to fulfill seventy years.

CYRUS PROCLAIMS LIBERTY FOR THE EXILES

22 In the first year of King Cyrus of Persia, in fulfillment of the word of the LORD spoken by Jeremiah, the LORD stirred up the spirit of King Cyrus of Persia so that he sent a herald throughout all his kingdom and also declared in a written edict: ²³"Thus says King Cyrus of Persia: The LORD, the God of heaven, has given me all the kingdoms of the earth, and he has charged me to build him a house at Jerusalem, which is in Judah. Whoever is among you of all his people, may the LORD his God be with him! Let him go up."

EZRA

In the book of Ezra, the Israelites' situation took an upward swing. After a long exile in Babylon, they were allowed to return to Judah and rebuild the temple. What's more, God raised up a new leader in Ezra, a man devoted to studying and teaching the law. While under Ezra's dynamic leadership, the temple was rebuilt and dedicated, and the people celebrated and renewed their commitment to faithfulness and purity. The Israelites rejoiced in the God who always gives people a second chance to trust and follow him. So can we!

END OF THE BABYLONIAN CAPTIVITY

1 In the first year of King Cyrus of Persia, in order that the word of the LORD by the mouth of Jeremiah might be accomplished, the LORD stirred up the spirit of King Cyrus of Persia so that he sent a herald throughout all his kingdom, and also in a written edict declared:

2 "Thus says King Cyrus of Persia: The LORD, the God of heaven, has given me all the kingdoms of the earth, and he has charged me to build him a house at Jerusalem in Judah. 3 Any of those among you who are of his people—may their God be with them!—are now permitted to go up to Jerusalem in Judah, and rebuild the house of the LORD, the God of Israel—he is the God who is in Jerusalem; 4 and let all survivors, in whatever place they reside, be assisted by the people of their place with silver and gold, with goods and with animals, besides freewill offerings for the house of God in Jerusalem."

5 The heads of the families of Judah and Benjamin, and the priests and the Levites—everyone whose spirit God had stirred—got ready to go up and rebuild the house of the LORD in Jerusalem. 6 All their neighbors aided them with silver vessels, with gold, with goods, with animals, and with valuable gifts, besides all that was freely offered. 7 King Cyrus himself brought out the vessels of the house of the LORD that Nebuchadnezzar had carried away from Jerusalem and placed in the house of his gods. 8 King Cyrus of Persia had them released into the charge of Mithredath the treasurer, who counted them out to Sheshbazzar the prince of Judah. 9 And this was the inventory: gold basins, thirty; silver basins, one thousand; knives,[a] twenty-nine; 10 gold bowls, thirty; other silver bowls, four hundred ten; other vessels, one thousand; 11 the total of the gold and silver vessels was five thousand four hundred. All these Sheshbazzar brought up, when the exiles were brought up from Babylonia to Jerusalem.

LIST OF THE RETURNED EXILES

2 Now these were the people of the province who came from those captive exiles whom King Nebuchadnezzar of Babylon had carried captive to Babylonia; they returned to Jerusalem and Judah, all to their own towns. 2 They came with Zerubbabel, Jeshua, Nehemiah, Seraiah, Reelaiah, Mordecai, Bilshan, Mispar, Bigvai, Rehum, and Baanah.

The number of the Israelite people: 3 the descendants of Parosh, two thousand one hundred seventy-two. 4 Of Shephatiah, three hundred seventy-two. 5 Of Arah, seven hundred seventy-five. 6 Of Pahath-moab, namely the descendants of Jeshua and Joab, two thousand eight hundred twelve. 7 Of Elam, one thousand two hundred fifty-four. 8 Of Zattu, nine hundred forty-five. 9 Of Zaccai, seven hundred sixty. 10 Of Bani, six hundred forty-two. 11 Of Bebai, six hundred twenty-three. 12 Of Azgad, one thousand two hundred twenty-two. 13 Of Adonikam, six hundred sixty-six. 14 Of Bigvai, two thousand fifty-six. 15 Of Adin, four hundred fifty-four. 16 Of Ater, namely of Hezekiah, ninety-eight. 17 Of Bezai, three hundred twenty-three. 18 Of Jorah, one hundred twelve. 19 Of Hashum, two hundred twenty-three. 20 Of Gibbar, ninety-five. 21 Of Bethlehem, one hundred twenty-three. 22 The people of Netophah, fifty-six. 23 Of Anathoth, one hundred twenty-eight. 24 The descendants of Azmaveth, forty-two. 25 Of Kiriatharim, Chephirah, and Beeroth, seven hundred forty-three. 26 Of Ramah and Geba, six hundred twenty-one. 27 The people of Michmas, one hundred twenty-two. 28 Of Bethel and Ai, two hundred twenty-three. 29 The descendants of Nebo, fifty-two. 30 Of Magbish, one hundred fifty-six. 31 Of the other Elam, one thousand two hundred fifty-four. 32 Of Harim, three hundred twenty. 33 Of Lod, Hadid, and Ono, seven hundred twenty-five. 34 Of Jericho, three hundred forty-five. 35 Of Se-

---

a 1.9 Vg: Meaning of Heb uncertain

naah, three thousand six hundred thirty.

36 The priests: the descendants of Jedaiah, of the house of Jeshua, nine hundred seventy-three. **37**Of Immer, one thousand fifty-two. **38**Of Pashhur, one thousand two hundred forty-seven. **39**Of Harim, one thousand seventeen.

40 The Levites: the descendants of Jeshua and Kadmiel, of the descendants of Hodaviah, seventy-four. **41**The singers: the descendants of Asaph, one hundred twenty-eight. **42**The descendants of the gatekeepers: of Shallum, of Ater, of Talmon, of Akkub, of Hatita, and of Shobai, in all one hundred thirty-nine.

43 The temple servants: the descendants of Ziha, Hasupha, Tabbaoth, **44**Keros, Siaha, Padon, **45**Lebanah, Hagabah, Akkub, **46**Hagab, Shamlai, Hanan, **47**Giddel, Gahar, Reaiah, **48**Rezin, Nekoda, Gazzam, **49**Uzza, Paseah, Besai, **50**Asnah, Meunim, Nephisim, **51**Bakbuk, Hakupha, Harhur, **52**Bazluth, Mehida, Harsha, **53**Barkos, Sisera, Temah, **54**Neziah, and Hatipha.

55 The descendants of Solomon's servants: Sotai, Hassophereth, Peruda, **56**Jaalah, Darkon, Giddel, **57**Shephatiah, Hattil, Pochereth-hazzebaim, and Ami.

58 All the temple servants and the descendants of Solomon's servants were three hundred ninety-two.

59 The following were those who came up from Tel-melah, Tel-harsha, Cherub, Addan, and Immer, though they could not prove their families or their descent, whether they belonged to Israel: **60**the descendants of Delaiah, Tobiah, and Nekoda, six hundred fifty-two. **61**Also, of the descendants of the priests: the descendants of Habaiah, Hakkoz, and Barzillai (who had married one of the daughters of Barzillai the Gileadite, and was called by their name). **62**These looked for their entries in the genealogical records, but they were not found there, and so they were excluded from the priesthood as unclean; **63**the governor told them that they were not to partake of the

most holy food, until there should be a priest to consult Urim and Thummim.

64 The whole assembly together was forty-two thousand three hundred sixty, **65**besides their male and female servants, of whom there were seven thousand three hundred thirty-seven; and they had two hundred male and female singers. **66**They had seven hundred thirty-six horses, two hundred forty-five mules, **67**four hundred thirty-five camels, and six thousand seven hundred twenty donkeys.

68 As soon as they came to the house of the LORD in Jerusalem, some of the heads of families made freewill offerings for the house of God, to erect it on its site. **69**According to their resources they gave to the building fund sixty-one thousand darics of gold, five thousand minas of silver, and one hundred priestly robes.

70 The priests, the Levites, and some of the people lived in Jerusalem and its vicinity;[a] and the singers, the gatekeepers, and the temple servants lived in their towns, and all Israel in their towns.

WORSHIP RESTORED AT JERUSALEM

3 When the seventh month came, and the Israelites were in the towns, the people gathered together in Jerusalem. **2**Then Jeshua son of Jozadak, with his fellow priests, and Zerubbabel son of Shealtiel with his kin set out to build the altar of the God of Israel, to offer burnt offerings on it, as prescribed in the law of Moses the man of God. **3**They set up the altar on its foundation, because they were in dread of the neighboring peoples, and they offered burnt offerings upon it to the LORD, morning and evening. **4**And they kept the festival of booths,[b] as prescribed, and offered the daily burnt offerings by number according to the ordinance, as required for each day, **5**and after that the regular burnt offerings, the

---

a **2.70** 1 Esdras 5.46: Heb lacks *lived in Jerusalem and its vicinity*   b **3.4** Or *tabernacles*; Heb *succoth*

offerings at the new moon and at all the sacred festivals of the LORD, and the offerings of everyone who made a freewill offering to the LORD. ⁶From the first day of the seventh month they began to offer burnt offerings to the LORD. But the foundation of the temple of the LORD was not yet laid. ⁷So they gave money to the masons and the carpenters, and food, drink, and oil to the Sidonians and the Tyrians to bring cedar trees from Lebanon to the sea, to Joppa, according to the grant that they had from King Cyrus of Persia.

FOUNDATION LAID
FOR THE TEMPLE

8 In the second year after their arrival at the house of God at Jerusalem, in the second month, Zerubbabel son of Shealtiel and Jeshua son of Jozadak made a beginning, together with the rest of their people, the priests and the Levites and all who had come to Jerusalem from the captivity. They appointed the Levites, from twenty years old and upward, to have the oversight of the work on the house of the LORD. ⁹And Jeshua with his sons and his kin, and Kadmiel and his sons, Binnui and Hodaviahᵃ along with the sons of Henadad, the Levites, their sons and kin, together took charge of the workers in the house of God.

¹⁰When the builders laid the foundation of the temple of the LORD, the priests in their vestments were stationed to praise the LORD with trumpets, and the Levites, the sons of Asaph, with cymbals, according to the directions of King David of Israel; ¹¹and they sang responsively, praising and giving thanks to the LORD,

"For he is good,
for his steadfast love endures
forever toward Israel."

And all the people responded with a great shout when they praised the LORD, because the foundation of the house of the LORD was laid. ¹²But many of the priests and Levites and heads of families, old people who had seen the first house on its foundations, wept with a loud voice when they saw this house, though many shouted aloud for joy, ¹³so that the people could not distinguish the sound of the joyful shout from the sound of the people's weeping, for the people shouted so loudly that the sound was heard far away.

RESISTANCE TO REBUILDING
THE TEMPLE

4 When the adversaries of Judah and Benjamin heard that the

ᵃ 3.9 Compare 2.40; Neh 7.43; 1 Esdras 5.58: Heb *sons of Judah*

BIBLE IN LIFE

More Than a Building

Ezra 3.8–13

The temple served as a place for the entire Jewish nation to come together, to worship, and to give their offerings. The temple rebuilding under the leadership of Ezra and Nehemiah was important in reminding the Hebrews of their new-found freedom from captivity and their need to unite as God's chosen people. Its completion was delayed more than 60 years, and it was not very ornate or beautiful when finished, but the temple was still a crucial factor in reasserting the Israelites' nationhood and their loyalty to God.

We know that the focus of our worship should be on God, who is omnipresent—not confined to any building or place. In more general terms, we should not invest our hopes, our status, our future or our confidence in material things, even things as beautiful or as religious as a temple or a modern-day church. As in Biblical times, however, these buildings provide us with havens from the secular world, precious places set aside for worship—where fellowship and unity can be enhanced as we concentrate intimately on the blessings that come from our Creator.

returned exiles were building a temple to the LORD, the God of Israel, 2they approached Zerubbabel and the heads of families and said to them, "Let us build with you, for we worship your God as you do, and we have been sacrificing to him ever since the days of King Esar-haddon of Assyria who brought us here." 3But Zerubbabel, Jeshua, and the rest of the heads of families in Israel said to them, "You shall have no part with us in building a house to our God; but we alone will build to the LORD, the God of Israel, as King Cyrus of Persia has commanded us."

4 Then the people of the land discouraged the people of Judah, and made them afraid to build, 5and they bribed officials to frustrate their plan throughout the reign of King Cyrus of Persia and until the reign of King Darius of Persia.

REBUILDING OF JERUSALEM OPPOSED

6 In the reign of Ahasuerus, in his accession year, they wrote an accusation against the inhabitants of Judah and Jerusalem.

7 And in the days of Artaxerxes, Bishlam and Mithredath and Tabeel and the rest of their associates wrote to King Artaxerxes of Persia; the letter was written in Aramaic and translated.[a] 8Rehum the royal deputy and Shimshai the scribe wrote a letter against Jerusalem to King Artaxerxes as follows 9(then Rehum the royal deputy, Shimshai the scribe, and the rest of their associates, the judges, the envoys, the officials, the Persians, the people of Erech, the Babylonians, the people of Susa, that is, the Elamites, 10and the rest of the nations whom the great and noble Osnappar deported and settled in the cities of Samaria and in the rest of the province Beyond the River wrote—and now 11this is a copy of the letter that they sent):

"To King Artaxerxes: Your servants, the people of the province Beyond the River, send greeting. And now 12may it be known to the king that the Jews who came up from you to us have gone to Jerusalem. They are rebuilding that rebellious and wicked city; they are finishing the walls and repairing the foundations. 13Now may it be known to the king that, if this city is rebuilt and the walls finished, they will not pay tribute, custom, or toll, and the royal revenue will be reduced. 14Now because we share the salt of the palace and it is not fitting for us to witness the king's dishonor, therefore we send and inform the king, 15so that a search may be made in the annals of your ancestors. You will discover in the annals that this is a rebellious city, hurtful to kings and provinces, and that sedition was stirred up in it from long ago. On that account this city was laid waste. 16We make known to the king that, if this city is rebuilt and its walls finished, you will then have no possession in the province Beyond the River."

17 The king sent an answer: "To Rehum the royal deputy and Shimshai the scribe and the rest of their associates who live in Samaria and in the rest of the province Beyond the River, greeting. And now 18the letter that you sent to us has been read in translation before me. 19So I made a decree, and someone searched and discovered that this city has risen against kings from long ago, and that rebellion and sedition have been made in it. 20Jerusalem has had mighty kings who ruled over the whole province Beyond the River, to whom tribute, custom, and toll were paid. 21Therefore issue an order that these people be made to cease, and that this city not be rebuilt, until I make a decree. 22Moreover, take care not to be slack in this matter; why should damage grow to the hurt of the king?"

23 Then when the copy of King Artaxerxes' letter was read before Rehum and the scribe Shimshai and their associates, they hurried to the Jews in Jerusalem and by force and

[a] 4.7 Heb adds in Aramaic, indicating that 4.8–6.18 is in Aramaic. Another interpretation is *The letter was written in the Aramaic script and set forth in the Aramaic language*

power made them cease. ²⁴At that time the work on the house of God in Jerusalem stopped and was discontinued until the second year of the reign of King Darius of Persia.

RESTORATION OF THE TEMPLE RESUMED

5 Now the prophets, Haggai[a] and Zechariah son of Iddo, prophesied to the Jews who were in Judah and Jerusalem, in the name of the God of Israel who was over them. ²Then Zerubbabel son of Shealtiel and Jeshua son of Jozadak set out to rebuild the house of God in Jerusalem; and with them were the prophets of God, helping them.

PONDER

Then Zerubbabel son of Shealtiel and Jeshua son of Jozadak set out to rebuild the house of God in Jerusalem; and with them were the prophets of God, helping them.
—Ezra 5.2

PRAY

O Father, although this ancient history may seem to have relatively little significance for our own lives, we are thankful that this message of Ezra and Nehemiah and the chosen people has application to us, for it is a message of commitment, renewal, hope and joy. We pray that we might retain it in our minds and hearts. We pray in the name of our Savior, Jesus Christ. Amen.

---

³At the same time Tattenai the governor of the province Beyond the River and Shethar-bozenai and their associates came to them and spoke to them thus, "Who gave you a decree to build this house and to finish this structure?" ⁴They[b] also asked them this, "What are the names of the men who are building this building?" ⁵But the eye of their God

was upon the elders of the Jews, and they did not stop them until a report reached Darius and then answer was returned by letter in reply to it.

⁶The copy of the letter that Tattenai the governor of the province Beyond the River and Shethar-bozenai and his associates the envoys who were in the province Beyond the River sent to King Darius; ⁷they sent him a report, in which was written as follows: "To Darius the king, all peace! ⁸May it be known to the king that we went to the province of Judah, to the house of the great God. It is being built of hewn stone, and timber is laid in the walls; this work is being done diligently and prospers in their hands. ⁹Then we spoke to those elders and asked them, 'Who gave you a decree to build this house and to finish this structure?' ¹⁰We also asked them their names, for your information, so that we might write down the names of the men at their head. ¹¹This was their reply to us: 'We are the servants of the God of heaven and earth, and we are rebuilding the house that was built many years ago, which a great king of Israel built and finished. ¹²But because our ancestors had angered the God of heaven, he gave them into the hand of King Nebuchadnezzar of Babylon, the Chaldean, who destroyed this house and carried away the people to Babylonia. ¹³However, King Cyrus of Babylon, in the first year of his reign, made a decree that this house of God should be rebuilt. ¹⁴Moreover, the gold and silver vessels of the house of God, which Nebuchadnezzar had taken out of the temple in Jerusalem and had brought into the temple of Babylon, these King Cyrus took out of the temple of Babylon, and they were delivered to a man named Sheshbazzar, whom he had made governor. ¹⁵He said to him, "Take these vessels; go and put them in the temple in Jerusalem, and let the house of God be rebuilt on its site." ¹⁶Then this Sheshbazzar came and laid the foun-

[a] 5.1 Aram adds *the prophet*   [b] 5.4 Gk Syr: Aram *We*

dations of the house of God in Jerusalem; and from that time until now it has been under construction, and it is not yet finished.' [17]And now, if it seems good to the king, have a search made in the royal archives there in Babylon, to see whether a decree was issued by King Cyrus for the rebuilding of this house of God in Jerusalem. Let the king send us his pleasure in this matter."

THE DECREE OF DARIUS

6 Then King Darius made a decree, and they searched the archives where the documents were stored in Babylon. [2]But it was in Ecbatana, the capital in the province of Media, that a scroll was found on which this was written: "A record. [3]In the first year of his reign, King Cyrus issued a decree: Concerning the house of God at Jerusalem, let the house be rebuilt, the place where sacrifices are offered and burnt offerings are brought;[a] its height shall be sixty cubits and its width sixty cubits, [4]with three courses of hewn stones and one course of timber; let the cost be paid from the royal treasury. [5]Moreover, let the gold and silver vessels of the house of God, which Nebuchadnezzar took out of the temple in Jerusalem and brought to Babylon, be restored and brought back to the temple in Jerusalem, each to its place; you shall put them in the house of God."

[6] "Now you, Tattenai, governor of the province Beyond the River, Shethar-bozenai, and you, their associates, the envoys in the province Beyond the River, keep away; [7]let the work on this house of God alone; let the governor of the Jews and the elders of the Jews rebuild this house of God on its site. [8]Moreover I make a decree regarding what you shall do for these elders of the Jews for the rebuilding of this house of God: the cost is to be paid to these people, in full and without delay, from the royal revenue, the tribute of the province Beyond the River. [9]Whatever is needed—young bulls, rams, or sheep for burnt offerings to the God of heaven, wheat, salt, wine, or oil,

as the priests in Jerusalem require— let that be given to them day by day without fail, [10]so that they may offer pleasing sacrifices to the God of heaven, and pray for the life of the king and his children. [11]Furthermore I decree that if anyone alters this edict, a beam shall be pulled out of the house of the perpetrator, who then shall be impaled on it. The house shall be made a dunghill. [12]May the God who has established his name there overthrow any king or people that shall put forth a hand to alter this, or to destroy this house of God in Jerusalem. I, Darius, make a decree; let it be done with all diligence."

COMPLETION AND DEDICATION OF THE TEMPLE

[13] Then, according to the word sent by King Darius, Tattenai, the governor of the province Beyond the River, Shethar-bozenai, and their associates did with all diligence what King Darius had ordered. [14]So the elders of the Jews built and prospered, through the prophesying of the prophet Haggai and Zechariah son of Iddo. They finished their building by command of the God of Israel and by decree of Cyrus, Darius, and King Artaxerxes of Persia; [15]and this house was finished on the third day of the month of Adar, in the sixth year of the reign of King Darius.

[16] The people of Israel, the priests and the Levites, and the rest of the returned exiles, celebrated the dedication of this house of God with joy. [17]They offered at the dedication of this house of God one hundred bulls, two hundred rams, four hundred lambs, and as a sin offering for all Israel, twelve male goats, according to the number of the tribes of Israel. [18]Then they set the priests in their divisions and the Levites in their courses for the service of God at Jerusalem, as it is written in the book of Moses.

THE PASSOVER CELEBRATED

[19] On the fourteenth day of the first month the returned exiles kept the passover. [20]For both the priests

---

[a] 6.3 Meaning of Aram uncertain

and the Levites had purified themselves; all of them were clean. So they killed the passover lamb for all the returned exiles, for their fellow priests, and for themselves. 21It was eaten by the people of Israel who had returned from exile, and also by all who had joined them and separated themselves from the pollutions of the nations of the land to worship the LORD, the God of Israel. 22With joy they celebrated the festival of unleavened bread seven days; for the LORD had made them joyful, and had turned the heart of the king of Assyria to them, so that he aided them in the work on the house of God, the God of Israel.

THE COMING AND WORK OF EZRA

7 After this, in the reign of King Artaxerxes of Persia, Ezra son of Seraiah, son of Azariah, son of Hilkiah, 2son of Shallum, son of Zadok, son of Ahitub, 3son of Amariah, son of Azariah, son of Meraioth, 4son of Zerahiah, son of Uzzi, son of Bukki, 5son of Abishua, son of Phinehas, son of Eleazar, son of the chief priest Aaron— 6this Ezra went up from Babylonia. He was a scribe skilled in the law of Moses that the LORD the God of Israel had given; and the king granted him all that he asked, for the hand of the LORD his God was upon him.

7 Some of the people of Israel, and some of the priests and Levites, the singers and gatekeepers, and the temple servants also went up to Jerusalem, in the seventh year of King Artaxerxes. 8They came to Jerusalem in the fifth month, which was in the seventh year of the king. 9On the first day of the first month the journey up from Babylon was begun, and on the first day of the fifth month he came to Jerusalem, for the gracious hand of his God was upon him. 10For Ezra had set his heart to study the law of the LORD, and to do it, and to teach the statutes and ordinances in Israel.

THE LETTER OF ARTAXERXES TO EZRA

11 This is a copy of the letter that King Artaxerxes gave to the priest Ezra, the scribe, a scholar of the text of the commandments of the LORD and his statutes for Israel: 12"Artaxerxes, king of kings, to the priest Ezra, the scribe of the law of the God of heaven: Peace.ª And now 13I decree that any of the people of Israel or their priests or Levites in my kingdom who freely offers to go to Jerusalem may go with you. 14For you are sent by the king and his seven counselors to make inquiries about Judah and Jerusalem according to the law of your God, which is in your hand, 15and also to convey the silver and gold that the king and his counselors have freely offered to the God of Israel, whose dwelling is in Jerusalem, 16with all the silver and gold that you shall find in the whole province of Babylonia, and with the freewill offerings of the people and the priests, given willingly for the house of their God in Jerusalem. 17With this money, then, you shall with all diligence buy bulls, rams, and lambs, and their grain offerings and their drink offerings, and you shall offer them on the altar of the house of your God in Jerusalem. 18Whatever seems good to you and your colleagues to do with the rest of the silver and gold, you may do, according to the will of your God. 19The vessels that have been given you for the service of the house of your God, you shall deliver before the God of Jerusalem. 20And whatever else is required for the house of your God, which you are responsible for providing, you may provide out of the king's treasury.

21 "I, King Artaxerxes, decree to all the treasurers in the province Beyond the River: Whatever the priest Ezra, the scribe of the law of the God of heaven, requires of you, let it be done with all diligence, 22up to one hundred talents of silver, one hundred cors of wheat, one hundred bathsᵇ of wine, one hundred bathsᵇ of oil, and unlimited salt. 23Whatever is commanded by the God of heaven, let it be done with zeal for

---

ª 7.12 Syr Vg 1 Esdras 8.9: Aram *Perfect*
ᵇ 7.22 A Heb measure of volume

BIBLE IN FOCUS

BEDROCK

[The passover lamb] was eaten by the people of Israel who had returned from exile . . . to worship the LORD, the God of Israel. With joy they celebrated the festival of unleavened bread seven days; for the LORD had made them joyful.

—Ezra 6:21–22

We live in a world that is constantly changing. Technological change continually pushes us to adopt new ways of doing things faster. Economic change keeps us on our toes about our ability to work and live well. Social change often challenges our very familiar lifestyle. In a world where nothing seems to stay the same from one day to the next, how do we keep from losing our way? How do we stay centered on what is really important?

Just before Ezra arrived in Judea, the Jews had fairly recently returned from exile in Babylon, and they were told to go and rebuild the temple of the Lord. They started out well, but soon they grew discouraged. Foreign leaders opposed the work, and the people became sidetracked with other concerns—for a long time. Then the Lord sent prophets and other leaders to remind the people of what was truly important, and the Jews began work on the temple once again. When the temple was finally completed, the people joyfully celebrated the Passover.

When our relentlessly changing and challenging world threatens to undermine the bedrock values of our lives, and our hopes for the future seem dim, how should we respond? Many people respond by simply readjusting their standards and aiming lower in life. That way they can continue to feel like they are okay because they measure up to their revised standards of greatness. But that is not a very good way to cope with life.

Instead, we should do what the people of Judah did—center ourselves on the bedrock of God's values. As Christians we can look to Jesus to see what he considered important. When we do, we will inevitably be led to ask questions of ourselves like, "How can I be closer to God?" "How can I be closer to my neighbors?" "How can I demonstrate sacrificial love?" "How can I demonstrate justice or truth or concern or compassion?" "How can I reach out to people who are different from me and show them Christianity?"

In the end, we must accommodate changing times but cling to unchanging principles. No matter how frozen we may feel by all the changes taking place in the world, we can always keep our eyes fixed on Jesus and strive to live by his values.

Going Deeper

- How do you respond when the world feels like it is changing faster than you can cope?
- What are some of the unchanging principles that you need to cling to while you accommodate constantly changing times?

the house of the God of heaven, or wrath will come upon the realm of the king and his heirs. 24We also notify you that it shall not be lawful to impose tribute, custom, or toll on any of the priests, the Levites, the singers, the doorkeepers, the temple servants, or other servants of this house of God.

25 "And you, Ezra, according to the God-given wisdom you possess, appoint magistrates and judges who may judge all the people in the province Beyond the River who know the laws of your God; and you shall teach those who do not know them. 26All who will not obey the law of your God and the law of the king, let judgment be strictly executed on them, whether for death or for banishment or for confiscation of their goods or for imprisonment."

27 Blessed be the LORD, the God of our ancestors, who put such a thing as this into the heart of the king to glorify the house of the LORD in Jerusalem, 28and who extended to me steadfast love before the king and his counselors, and before all the king's mighty officers. I took courage, for the hand of the LORD my God was upon me, and I gathered leaders from Israel to go up with me.

HEADS OF FAMILIES WHO RETURNED WITH EZRA

8 These are their family heads, and this is the genealogy of those who went up with me from Babylonia, in the reign of King Artaxerxes: 2Of the descendants of Phinehas, Gershom. Of Ithamar, Daniel. Of David, Hattush, 3of the descendants of Shecaniah. Of Parosh, Zechariah, with whom were registered one hundred fifty males. 4Of the descendants of Pahath-moab, Eliehoenai son of Zerahiah, and with him two hundred males. 5Of the descendants of Zattu,a Shecaniah son of Jahaziel, and with him three hundred males. 6Of the descendants of Adin, Ebed son of Jonathan, and with him fifty males. 7Of the descendants of Elam, Jeshaiah son of Athaliah, and with him seventy males. 8Of the descendants of Shephatiah, Zebadiah son of

Michael, and with him eighty males. 9Of the descendants of Joab, Obadiah son of Jehiel, and with him two hundred eighteen males. 10Of the descendants of Bani,b Shelomith son of Josiphiah, and with him one hundred sixty males. 11Of the descendants of Bebai, Zechariah son of Bebai, and with him twenty-eight males. 12Of the descendants of Azgad, Johanan son of Hakkatan, and with him one hundred ten males. 13Of the descendants of Adonikam, those who came later, their names being Eliphelet, Jeuel, and Shemaiah, and with them sixty males. 14Of the descendants of Bigvai, Uthai and Zaccur, and with them seventy males.

SERVANTS FOR THE TEMPLE

15 I gathered them by the river that runs to Ahava, and there we camped three days. As I reviewed the people and the priests, I found there none of the descendants of Levi. 16Then I sent for Eliezer, Ariel, Shemaiah, Elnathan, Jarib, Elnathan, Nathan, Zechariah, and Meshullam, who were leaders, and for Joiarib and Elnathan, who were wise, 17and sent them to Iddo, the leader at the place called Casiphia, telling them what to say to Iddo and his colleagues the temple servants at Casiphia, namely, to send us ministers for the house of our God. 18Since the gracious hand of our God was upon us, they brought us a man of discretion, of the descendants of Mahli son of Levi son of Israel, namely Sherebiah, with his sons and kin, eighteen; 19also Hashabiah and with him Jeshaiah of the descendants of Merari, with his kin and their sons, twenty; 20besides two hundred twenty of the temple servants, whom David and his officials had set apart to attend the Levites. These were all mentioned by name.

FASTING AND PRAYER FOR PROTECTION

21 Then I proclaimed a fast there, at the river Ahava, that we might

a 8.5 Gk 1 Esdras 8.32: Heb lacks *of Zattu*
b 8.10 Gk 1 Esdras 8.36: Heb lacks *Bani*

deny ourselves[a] before our God, to seek from him a safe journey for ourselves, our children, and all our possessions. 22For I was ashamed to ask the king for a band of soldiers and cavalry to protect us against the enemy on our way, since we had told the king that the hand of our God is gracious to all who seek him, but his power and his wrath are against all who forsake him. 23So we fasted and petitioned our God for this, and he listened to our entreaty.

GIFTS FOR THE TEMPLE

24 Then I set apart twelve of the leading priests: Sherebiah, Hashabiah, and ten of their kin with them. 25And I weighed out to them the silver and the gold and the vessels, the offering for the house of our God that the king, his counselors, his lords, and all Israel there present had offered; 26I weighed out into their hand six hundred fifty talents of silver, and one hundred silver vessels worth . . . talents,[b] and one hundred talents of gold, 27twenty gold bowls worth a thousand darics, and two vessels of fine polished bronze as precious as gold. 28And I said to them, "You are holy to the LORD, and the vessels are holy; and the silver and the gold are a freewill offering to the LORD, the God of your ancestors. 29Guard them and keep them until you weigh them before the chief priests and the Levites and the heads of families in Israel at Jerusalem, within the chambers of the house of the LORD." 30So the priests and the Levites took over the silver, the gold, and the vessels as they were weighed out, to bring them to Jerusalem, to the house of our God.

THE RETURN TO JERUSALEM

31 Then we left the river Ahava on the twelfth day of the first month, to go to Jerusalem; the hand of our God was upon us, and he delivered us from the hand of the enemy and from ambushes along the way. 32We came to Jerusalem and remained there three days. 33On the fourth day, within the house of our God, the silver, the gold, and the vessels

were weighed into the hands of the priest Meremoth son of Uriah, and with him was Eleazar son of Phinehas, and with them were the Levites, Jozabad son of Jeshua and Noadiah son of Binnui. 34The total was counted and weighed, and the weight of everything was recorded.

35 At that time those who had come from captivity, the returned exiles, offered burnt offerings to the God of Israel, twelve bulls for all Israel, ninety-six rams, seventy-seven lambs, and as a sin offering twelve male goats; all this was a burnt offering to the LORD. 36They also delivered the king's commissions to the king's satraps and to the governors of the province Beyond the River; and they supported the people and the house of God.

DENUNCIATION OF MIXED MARRIAGES

9 After these things had been done, the officials approached me and said, "The people of Israel, the priests, and the Levites have not separated themselves from the peoples of the lands with their abominations, from the Canaanites, the Hittites, the Perizzites, the Jebusites, the Ammonites, the Moabites, the Egyptians, and the Amorites. 2For they have taken some of their daughters as wives for themselves and for their sons. Thus the holy seed has mixed itself with the peoples of the lands, and in this faithlessness the officials and leaders have led the way." 3When I heard this, I tore my garment and my mantle, and pulled hair from my head and beard, and sat appalled. 4Then all who trembled at the words of the God of Israel, because of the faithlessness of the returned exiles, gathered around me while I sat appalled until the evening sacrifice.

EZRA'S PRAYER

5 At the evening sacrifice I got up from my fasting, with my garments and my mantle torn, and fell on my

a 8.21 Or *might fast*   b 8.26 The number of talents is lacking

knees, spread out my hands to the LORD my God, [6]and said,

"O my God, I am too ashamed and embarrassed to lift my face to you, my God, for our iniquities have risen higher than our heads, and our guilt has mounted up to the heavens. [7]From the days of our ancestors to this day we have been deep in guilt, and for our iniquities we, our kings, and our priests have been handed over to the kings of the lands, to the sword, to captivity, to plundering, and to utter shame, as is now the case. [8]But now for a brief moment favor has been shown by the LORD our God, who has left us a remnant, and given us a stake in his holy place, in order that he[a] may brighten our eyes and grant us a little sustenance in our slavery. [9]For we are slaves; yet our God has not forsaken us in our slavery, but has extended to us his steadfast love before the kings of Persia, to give us new life to set up the house of our God, to repair its ruins, and to give us a wall in Judea and Jerusalem.

[10] "And now, our God, what shall we say after this? For we have forsaken your commandments, [11]which you commanded by your servants the prophets, saying, 'The land that you are entering to possess is a land unclean with the pollutions of the peoples of the lands, with their abominations. They have filled it from end to end with their uncleanness. [12]Therefore do not give your daughters to their sons, neither take their daughters for your sons, and never seek their peace or prosperity, so that you may be strong and eat the good of the land and leave it for an inheritance to your children forever.' [13]After all that has come upon us for our evil deeds and for our great guilt, seeing that you, our God, have punished us less than our iniquities deserved and have given us such a remnant as this, [14]shall we break your commandments again and intermarry with the peoples who practice these abominations? Would you not be angry with us until you destroy us without remnant or survivor? [15]O LORD, God of Israel, you

are just, but we have escaped as a remnant, as is now the case. Here we are before you in our guilt, though no one can face you because of this."

WHAT IS FREEDOM? FREEDOM IS VOLUNTARY SUBMISSION TO CHRIST. REAL FREEDOM IS LIBERATION FROM FEAR, TIMIDITY, PRIDE, SELFISHNESS AND LACK OF CONFIDENCE.

THE PEOPLE'S RESPONSE

10 While Ezra prayed and made confession, weeping and throwing himself down before the house of God, a very great assembly of men, women, and children gathered to him out of Israel; the people also wept bitterly. [2]Shecaniah son of Jehiel, of the descendants of Elam, addressed Ezra, saying, "We have broken faith with our God and have married foreign women from the peoples of the land, but even now there is hope for Israel in spite of this. [3]So now let us make a covenant with our God to send away all these wives and their children, according to the counsel of my lord and of those who tremble at the commandment of our God; and let it be done according to the law. [4]Take action, for it is your duty, and we are with you; be strong, and do it." [5]Then Ezra stood up and made the leading priests, the Levites, and all Israel swear that they would do as had been said. So they swore.

FOREIGN WIVES AND THEIR CHILDREN REJECTED

[6] Then Ezra withdrew from before the house of God, and went to the chamber of Jehohanan son of Eliashib, where he spent the night.[b]

---

[a] 9.8 Heb *our God*   [b] 10.6 1 Esdras 9.2: Heb *where he went*

He did not eat bread or drink water, for he was mourning over the faithlessness of the exiles. [7]They made a proclamation throughout Judah and Jerusalem to all the returned exiles that they should assemble at Jerusalem, [8]and that if any did not come within three days, by order of the officials and the elders all their property should be forfeited, and they themselves banned from the congregation of the exiles.

9 Then all the people of Judah and Benjamin assembled at Jerusalem within the three days; it was the ninth month, on the twentieth day of the month. All the people sat in the open square before the house of God, trembling because of this matter and because of the heavy rain. [10]Then Ezra the priest stood up and said to them, "You have trespassed and married foreign women, and so increased the guilt of Israel. [11]Now make confession to the LORD the God of your ancestors, and do his will; separate yourselves from the peoples of the land and from the foreign wives." [12]Then all the assembly answered with a loud voice, "It is so; we must do as you have said. [13]But the people are many, and it is a time of heavy rain; we cannot stand in the open. Nor is this a task for one day or for two, for many of us have transgressed in this matter. [14]Let our officials represent the whole assembly, and let all in our towns who have taken foreign wives come at appointed times, and with them the elders and judges of every town, until the fierce wrath of our God on this account is averted from us." [15]Only Jonathan son of Asahel and Jahzeiah son of Tikvah opposed this, and Meshullam and Shabbethai the Levites supported them.

16 Then the returned exiles did so. Ezra the priest selected men,[a] heads of families, according to their families, each of them designated by name. On the first day of the tenth month they sat down to examine the matter. [17]By the first day of the first month they had come to the end of all the men who had married foreign women.

18 There were found of the descendants of the priests who had married foreign women, of the descendants of Jeshua son of Jozadak and his brothers: Maaseiah, Eliezer, Jarib, and Gedaliah. [19]They pledged themselves to send away their wives, and their guilt offering was a ram of the flock for their guilt. [20]Of the descendants of Immer: Hanani and Zebadiah. [21]Of the descendants of Harim: Maaseiah, Elijah, Shemaiah, Jehiel, and Uzziah. [22]Of the descendants of Pashhur: Elioenai, Maaseiah, Ishmael, Nethanel, Jozabad, and Elasah.

23 Of the Levites: Jozabad, Shimei, Kelaiah (that is, Kelita), Pethahiah, Judah, and Eliezer. [24]Of the singers: Eliashib. Of the gatekeepers: Shallum, Telem, and Uri.

25 And of Israel: of the descendants of Parosh: Ramiah, Izziah, Malchijah, Mijamin, Eleazar, Hashabiah,[b] and Benaiah. [26]Of the descendants of Elam: Mattaniah, Zechariah, Jehiel, Abdi, Jeremoth, and Elijah. [27]Of the descendants of Zattu: Elioenai, Eliashib, Mattaniah, Jeremoth, Zabad, and Aziza. [28]Of the descendants of Bebai: Jehohanan, Hananiah, Zabbai, and Athlai. [29]Of the descendants of Bani: Meshullam, Malluch, Adaiah, Jashub, Sheal, and Jeremoth. [30]Of the descendants of Pahath-moab: Adna, Chelal, Benaiah, Maaseiah, Mattaniah, Bezalel, Binnui, and Manasseh. [31]Of the descendants of Harim: Eliezer, Isshijah, Malchijah, Shemaiah, Shimeon, [32]Benjamin, Malluch, and Shemariah. [33]Of the descendants of Hashum: Mattenai, Mattattah, Zabad, Eliphelet, Jeremai, Manasseh, and Shimei. [34]Of the descendants of Bani: Maadai, Amram, Uel, [35]Benaiah, Bedeiah, Cheluhi, [36]Vaniah, Meremoth, Eliashib, [37]Mattaniah, Mattenai, and Jaasu. [38]Of the descendants of Binnui:[c] Shimei, [39]Shelemiah, Nathan, Adaiah, [40]Machnadebai, Shashai, Sharai, [41]Azarel, Shelemiah,

Shemariah, 42Shallum, Amariah, and Joseph. 43Of the descendants of Nebo: Jeiel, Mattithiah, Zabad, Zebina, Jaddai, Joel, and Benaiah. 44All these had married foreign women,

and they sent them away with their children.[a]

---

[a] 10.44 1 Esdras 9.36; meaning of Heb uncertain

NEHEMIAH

In very simple terms, the second law of thermodynamics essentially states that matter is in a steady state of decline. Unless an outside force is applied, matter will break down and generally become useless. That's what happened to the walls surrounding Jerusalem. Enter Nehemiah; he arrives in Jerusalem in 445 BC and leads the people in rebuilding Jerusalem's walls. In this book, we see the power behind Nehemiah's leadership: prayer. We can learn a lot from Nehemiah's example. He balanced his spiritual sensitivity with down-to-earth action—a forceful combination!

NEHEMIAH PRAYS FOR HIS PEOPLE

1 The words of Nehemiah son of Hacaliah. In the month of Chislev, in the twentieth year, while I was in Susa the capital, 2one of my brothers, Hanani, came with certain men from Judah; and I asked them about the Jews that survived, those who had escaped the captivity, and about Jerusalem. 3They replied, "The survivors there in the province who escaped captivity are in great trouble and shame; the wall of Jerusalem is broken down, and its gates have been destroyed by fire."

4 When I heard these words I sat down and wept, and mourned for days, fasting and praying before the God of heaven. 5I said, "O LORD God of heaven, the great and awesome God who keeps covenant and steadfast love with those who love him and keep his commandments; 6let your ear be attentive and your eyes open to hear the prayer of your servant that I now pray before you day and night for your servants, the people of Israel, confessing the sins of the people of Israel, which we have sinned against you. Both I and my family have sinned. 7We have offended you deeply, failing to keep the commandments, the statutes, and the ordinances that you commanded your servant Moses. 8Remember the word that you commanded your servant Moses, 'If you are unfaithful, I will scatter you among the peoples; 9but if you return to me and keep my commandments and do them, though your outcasts are under the farthest skies, I will gather them from there and bring them to the place at which I have chosen to establish my name.' 10They are your servants and your people, whom you redeemed by your great power and your strong hand. 11O Lord, let your ear be attentive to the prayer of your servant, and to the prayer of your servants who delight in revering your name. Give success to your servant today, and grant him mercy in the sight of this man!"

At the time, I was cupbearer to the king.

NEHEMIAH SENT TO JUDAH

2 In the month of Nisan, in the twentieth year of King Artaxerxes, when wine was served him, I carried the wine and gave it to the king. Now, I had never been sad in his presence before. 2So the king said to me, "Why is your face sad, since you are not sick? This can only be sadness of the heart." Then I was very much afraid. 3I said to the king, "May the king live forever! Why should my face not be sad, when the city, the place of my ancestors' graves, lies waste, and its gates have been destroyed by fire?" 4Then the king said to me, "What do you request?" So I prayed to the God of heaven. 5Then I said to the king, "If it pleases the king, and if your servant has found favor with you, I ask that you send me to Judah, to the city of my ancestors' graves, so that I may rebuild it." 6The king said to me (the queen also was sitting beside him), "How long will you be gone, and when will you return?" So it pleased the king to send me, and I set him a date. 7Then I said to the king, "If it pleases the king, let letters be given me to the governors of the province Beyond the River, that they may grant me passage until I arrive in Judah; 8and a letter to Asaph, the keeper of the king's forest, directing him to give me timber to make beams for the gates of the temple fortress, and for the wall of the city, and for the house that I shall occupy." And the king granted me what I asked, for the gracious hand of my God was upon me.

9 Then I came to the governors of the province Beyond the River, and gave them the king's letters. Now the king had sent officers of the army and cavalry with me. 10When Sanballat the Horonite and Tobiah the Ammonite official heard this, it displeased them greatly that someone had come to seek the welfare of the people of Israel.

NEHEMIAH'S INSPECTION OF THE WALLS

11 So I came to Jerusalem and was there for three days. 12Then I got up

BIBLE IN FOCUS

PRAYER AND MORE PRAYER

So I prayed to the God of heaven. Then I said to the king ...

—Nehemiah 2.4–5

When we read the story of Nehemiah and many other episodes in the Bible, it is easy to overlook the significance of Nehemiah's prayers in all these events. Nehemiah did not simply pray about his concerns and wait for God to drop the answers in his lap with little or no effort on his part. Nehemiah both prayed and acted after he received word that Jerusalem was in ruins (see Nehemiah 1.4). He prayed that God would give him success in his plans to rebuild Jerusalem. Then he went ahead and carried out his strategy as he approached the king of Persia for a favor. Even as he was speaking with the king, he prayed for God to work in the situation (2.4). And God, through the king, granted Nehemiah's request.

But that is not the end of the story. Nehemiah requested and received letters of permission from the king to restore Jerusalem, including rebuilding the walls. After he arrived in Jerusalem, Nehemiah was faced with opposition from leaders of neighboring regions, and he had to act to ensure the safety of the people of Jerusalem. All the while, he asked God to be involved in all that was happening (4.9; 6.9). At the end of the project, he prayed that God would bless his work and count it worthy: "Remember me, O my God, concerning this, and do not wipe out my good deeds that I have done for the house of my God and for his service" (13.14).

Nehemiah's approach to the challenges he faced should be ours as well. When we are making plans, it is tempting to rush ahead with them, forgetting to consult God. But we need to make sure that our strategy is in keeping with God's. We can discern what God desires of us through prayer and by reading the Bible, which focuses our minds and hearts on his will. The apostle Paul writes: "Do not be conformed to this world, but be transformed by the renewing of your minds, so that you may discern what is the will of God—what is good and acceptable and perfect" (Romans 12.2). We should ask God to direct and help us at the start and continue to pray and seek the Lord's guidance throughout the process. All the while, though, it's up to us to act on what God is leading us to do. Whatever we are thinking about doing—what career path to follow, whom to marry, how to raise our children, and so on—we must be sure to seek God's will, and then do it!

Going Deeper

- On what occasion did you rush ahead with plans without praying and seeking God's will?
- What do you think you might gain by praying about your plans and goals?

during the night, I and a few men with me; I told no one what my God had put into my heart to do for Jerusalem. The only animal I took was the animal I rode. [13] I went out by night by the Valley Gate past the Dragon's Spring and to the Dung Gate, and I inspected the walls of Jerusalem that had been broken down and its gates that had been destroyed by fire. [14] Then I went on to the Fountain Gate and to the King's Pool; but there was no place for the animal I was riding to continue. [15] So I went up by way of the valley by night and inspected the wall. Then I turned back and entered by the Valley Gate, and so returned. [16] The officials did not know where I had gone or what I was doing; I had not yet told the Jews, the priests, the nobles, the officials, and the rest that were to do the work.

DECISION TO RESTORE THE WALLS

[17] Then I said to them, "You see the trouble we are in, how Jerusalem lies in ruins with its gates burned. Come, let us rebuild the wall of Jerusalem, so that we may no longer suffer disgrace." [18] I told them that the hand of my God had been gracious upon me, and also the words that the king had spoken to me. Then they said, "Let us start building!" So they committed themselves to the common good. [19] But when Sanballat the Horonite and Tobiah the Ammonite official, and Geshem the Arab heard of it, they mocked and ridiculed us, saying, "What is this that you are doing? Are you rebelling against the king?" [20] Then I replied to them, "The God of heaven is the one who will give us success, and we his servants are going to start building; but you have no share or claim or historic right in Jerusalem."

ORGANIZATION OF THE WORK

3 Then the high priest Eliashib set to work with his fellow priests and rebuilt the Sheep Gate. They consecrated it and set up its doors; they consecrated it as far as the Tower of the Hundred and as far as the Tower

of Hananel. [2] And the men of Jericho built next to him. And next to them[a] Zaccur son of Imri built.

[3] The sons of Hassenaah built the Fish Gate; they laid its beams and set up its doors, its bolts, and its bars. [4] Next to them Meremoth son of Uriah son of Hakkoz made repairs. Next to them Meshullam son of Berechiah son of Meshezabel made repairs. Next to them Zadok son of Baana made repairs. [5] Next to them the Tekoites made repairs; but their nobles would not put their shoulders to the work of their Lord.[b]

[6] Joiada son of Paseah and Meshullam son of Besodeiah repaired the Old Gate; they laid its beams and set up its doors, its bolts, and

[a] 3.2 Heb him   [b] 3.5 Or lords

its bars. [7]Next to them repairs were made by Melatiah the Gibeonite and Jadon the Meronothite—the men of Gibeon and of Mizpah—who were under the jurisdiction of[a] the governor of the province Beyond the River. [8]Next to them Uzziel son of Harhaiah, one of the goldsmiths, made repairs. Next to him Hananiah, one of the perfumers, made repairs; and they restored Jerusalem as far as the Broad Wall. [9]Next to them Rephaiah son of Hur, ruler of half the district of[b] Jerusalem, made repairs. [10]Next to them Jedaiah son of Harumaph made repairs opposite his house; and next to him Hattush son of Hashabneiah made repairs. [11]Malchijah son of Harim and Hasshub son of Pahath-moab repaired another section and the Tower of the Ovens. [12]Next to him Shallum son of Hallohesh, ruler of half the district of[b] Jerusalem, made repairs, he and his daughters.

[13] Hanun and the inhabitants of Zanoah repaired the Valley Gate; they rebuilt it and set up its doors, its bolts, and its bars, and repaired a thousand cubits of the wall, as far as the Dung Gate.

[14] Malchijah son of Rechab, ruler of the district of[c] Beth-haccherem, repaired the Dung Gate; he rebuilt it and set up its doors, its bolts, and its bars.

[15] And Shallum son of Col-hozeh, ruler of the district of[c] Mizpah, repaired the Fountain Gate; he rebuilt it and covered it and set up its doors, its bolts, and its bars; and he built the wall of the Pool of Shelah of the king's garden, as far as the stairs that go down from the City of David. [16]After him Nehemiah son of Azbuk, ruler of half the district of[b] Beth-zur, repaired from a point opposite the graves of David, as far as the artificial pool and the house of the warriors. [17]After him the Levites made repairs: Rehum son of Bani; next to him Hashabiah, ruler of half the district of[b] Keilah, made repairs for his district. [18]After him their kin made repairs: Binnui,[d] son of Henadad, ruler of half the district of[b] Keilah; [19]next to him Ezer son of Jeshua,

ruler[e] of Mizpah, repaired another section opposite the ascent to the armory at the Angle. [20]After him Baruch son of Zabbai repaired another section from the Angle to the door of the house of the high priest Eliashib. [21]After him Meremoth son of Uriah son of Hakkoz repaired another section from the door of the house of Eliashib to the end of the house of Eliashib. [22]After him the priests, the men of the surrounding area, made repairs. [23]After them Benjamin and Hasshub made repairs opposite their house. After them Azariah son of Maaseiah son of Ananiah made repairs beside his own house. [24]After him Binnui son of Henadad repaired another section, from the house of Azariah to the Angle and to the corner. [25]Palal son of Uzai repaired opposite the Angle and the tower projecting from the upper house of the king at the court of the guard. After him Pedaiah son of Parosh [26]and the temple servants living[f] on Ophel made repairs up to a point opposite the Water Gate on the east and the projecting tower. [27]After him the Tekoites repaired another section opposite the great projecting tower as far as the wall of Ophel.

THE QUALITY OF OUR

LIVES IS REVEALED BY THE

QUALITY OF OUR PRAYER.

[28] Above the Horse Gate the priests made repairs, each one opposite his own house. [29]After them Zadok son of Immer made repairs opposite his own house. After him Shemaiah son of Shecaniah, the

[a] 3.7 Meaning of Heb uncertain
[b] 3.9,12,16,17,18 Or supervisor of half the portion assigned to   [c] 3.14,15 Or supervisor of the portion assigned to   [d] 3.18 Gk Syr Compare verse 24, 10.9: Heb Bavvai
[e] 3.19 Or supervisor   [f] 3.26 Cn: Heb were living

keeper of the East Gate, made repairs. 30 After him Hananiah son of Shelemiah and Hanun sixth son of Zalaph repaired another section. After him Meshullam son of Berechiah made repairs opposite his living quarters. 31 After him Malchijah, one of the goldsmiths, made repairs as far as the house of the temple servants and of the merchants, opposite the Muster Gate,[a] and to the upper room of the corner. 32 And between the upper room of the corner and the Sheep Gate the goldsmiths and the merchants made repairs.

HOSTILE PLOTS THWARTED

4[b] Now when Sanballat heard that we were building the wall, he was angry and greatly enraged, and he mocked the Jews. 2 He said in the presence of his associates and of the army of Samaria, "What are these feeble Jews doing? Will they restore things? Will they sacrifice? Will they finish it in a day? Will they revive the stones out of the heaps of rubbish—and burned ones at that?" 3 Tobiah the Ammonite was beside him, and he said, "That stone wall they are building—any fox going up on it would break it down!" 4 Hear, O our God, for we are despised; turn their taunt back on their own heads, and give them over as plunder in a land of captivity. 5 Do not cover their guilt, and do not let their sin be blotted out from your sight; for they have hurled insults in the face of the builders.

6 So we rebuilt the wall, and all the wall was joined together to half its height; for the people had a mind to work.

7[c] But when Sanballat and Tobiah and the Arabs and the Ammonites and the Ashdodites heard that the repairing of the walls of Jerusalem was going forward and the gaps were beginning to be closed, they were very angry, 8 and all plotted together to come and fight against Jerusalem and to cause confusion in it. 9 So we prayed to our God, and set a guard as a protection against them day and night.

10 But Judah said, "The strength of the burden bearers is failing, and

there is too much rubbish so that we are unable to work on the wall." 11 And our enemies said, "They will not know or see anything before we come upon them and kill them and stop the work." 12 When the Jews who lived near them came, they said to us ten times, "From all the places where they live[d] they will come up against us."[e] 13 So in the lowest parts of the space behind the wall, in open places, I stationed the people according to their families,[f] with their swords, their spears, and their bows. 14 After I looked these things over, I stood up and said to the nobles and the officials and the rest of the people, "Do not be afraid of them. Remember the LORD, who is great and awesome, and fight for your kin, your sons, your daughters, your wives, and your homes."

15 When our enemies heard that their plot was known to us, and that God had frustrated it, we all returned to the wall, each to his work. 16 From that day on, half of my servants worked on construction, and half held the spears, shields, bows, and body-armor; and the leaders posted themselves behind the whole house of Judah, 17 who were building the wall. The burden bearers carried their loads in such a way that each labored on the work with one hand and with the other held a weapon. 18 And each of the builders had his sword strapped at his side while he built. The man who sounded the trumpet was beside me. 19 And I said to the nobles, the officials, and the rest of the people, "The work is great and widely spread out, and we are separated far from one another on the wall. 20 Rally to us wherever you hear the sound of the trumpet. Our God will fight for us."

21 So we labored at the work, and half of them held the spears from break of dawn until the stars came out. 22 I also said to the people at that time, "Let every man and his

a 3.31 Or *Hammiphkad Gate*   b 4.1 Ch 3.33 in Heb   c 4.7 Ch 4.1 in Heb   d 4.12 Cn: Heb *you return*   e 4.12 Compare Gk Syr: Meaning of Heb uncertain   f 4.13 Meaning of Heb uncertain

servant pass the night inside Jerusalem, so that they may be a guard for us by night and may labor by day." 23So neither I nor my brothers nor my servants nor the men of the guard who followed me ever took off our clothes; each kept his weapon in his right hand.ª

NEHEMIAH DEALS WITH OPPRESSION

5 Now there was a great outcry of the people and of their wives against their Jewish kin. 2For there were those who said, "With our sons and our daughters, we are many; we must get grain, so that we may eat and stay alive." 3There were also those who said, "We are having to pledge our fields, our vineyards, and our houses in order to get grain during the famine." 4And there were those who said, "We are having to borrow money on our fields and vineyards to pay the king's tax. 5Now our flesh is the same as that of our kindred; our children are the same as their children; and yet we are forcing our sons and daughters to be slaves, and some of our daughters have been ravished; we are powerless, and our fields and vineyards now belong to others."

6 I was very angry when I heard their outcry and these complaints. 7After thinking it over, I brought charges against the nobles and the officials; I said to them, "You are all taking interest from your own people." And I called a great assembly to deal with them, 8and said to them, "As far as we were able, we have bought back our Jewish kindred who had been sold to other nations; but now you are selling your own kin, who must then be bought back by us!" They were silent, and could not find a word to say. 9So I said, "The thing that you are doing is not good. Should you not walk in the fear of our God, to prevent the taunts of the nations our enemies? 10Moreover I and my brothers and my servants are lending them money and grain. Let us stop this taking of interest. 11Restore to them, this very day, their fields, their vineyards, their ol-

ive orchards, and their houses, and the interest on money, grain, wine, and oil that you have been exacting from them." 12Then they said, "We will restore everything and demand nothing more from them. We will do as you say." And I called the priests, and made them take an oath to do as they had promised. 13I also shook out the fold of my garment and said, "So may God shake out everyone from house and from property who does not perform this promise. Thus may they be shaken out and emptied." And all the assembly said, "Amen," and praised the LORD. And the people did as they had promised.

THE GENEROSITY OF NEHEMIAH

14 Moreover from the time that I was appointed to be their governor in the land of Judah, from the twentieth year to the thirty-second year of King Artaxerxes, twelve years, neither I nor my brothers ate the food allowance of the governor. 15The former governors who were before me laid heavy burdens on the people, and took food and wine from them, besides forty shekels of silver. Even their servants lorded it over the people. But I did not do so, because of the fear of God. 16Indeed, I devoted myself to the work on this wall, and acquired no land; and all my servants were gathered there for the work. 17Moreover there were at my table one hundred fifty people, Jews and officials, besides those who came to us from the nations around us. 18Now that which was prepared for one day was one ox and six choice sheep; also fowls were prepared for me, and every ten days skins of wine in abundance; yet with all this I did not demand the food allowance of the governor, because of the heavy burden of labor on the people. 19Remember for my good, O my God, all that I have done for this people.

INTRIGUES OF ENEMIES FOILED

6 Now when it was reported to Sanballat and Tobiah and to Geshem the Arab and to the rest

ª 4.23 Cn: Heb *each his weapon the water*

of our enemies that I had built the wall and that there was no gap left in it (though up to that time I had not set up the doors in the gates), [2]Sanballat and Geshem sent to me, saying, "Come and let us meet together in one of the villages in the plain of Ono." But they intended to do me harm. [3]So I sent messengers to them, saying, "I am doing a great work and I cannot come down. Why should the work stop while I leave it to come down to you?" [4]They sent to me four times in this way, and I answered them in the same manner. [5]In the same way Sanballat for the fifth time sent his servant to me with an open letter in his hand. [6]In it was written, "It is reported among the nations—and Geshem[a] also says it—that you and the Jews intend to rebel; that is why you are building the wall; and according to this report you wish to become their king. [7]You have also set up prophets to proclaim in Jerusalem concerning you, 'There is a king in Judah!' And now it will be reported to the king according to these words. So come, therefore, and let us confer together." [8]Then I sent to him, saying, "No such things as you say have been done; you are inventing them out of your own mind" [9]—for they all wanted to frighten us, thinking, "Their hands will drop from the work, and it will not be done." But now, O God, strengthen my hands.

[10] One day when I went into the house of Shemaiah son of Delaiah son of Mehetabel, who was confined to his house, he said, "Let us meet together in the house of God, within the temple, and let us close the doors of the temple, for they are coming to kill you; indeed, tonight they are coming to kill you." [11]But I said, "Should a man like me run away? Would a man like me go into the temple to save his life? I will not go in!" [12]Then I perceived and saw that God had not sent him at all, but he had pronounced the prophecy against me because Tobiah and Sanballat had hired him. [13]He was hired for this purpose, to intimidate me and make me sin by acting in this way, and so they could give me a bad name, in order to taunt me. [14]Remember Tobiah and Sanballat, O my God, according to these things that they did, and also the prophetess Noadiah and the rest of the prophets who wanted to make me afraid.

THE WALL COMPLETED

[15] So the wall was finished on the twenty-fifth day of the month Elul, in fifty-two days. [16]And when all our enemies heard of it, all the nations around us were afraid[b] and fell greatly in their own esteem; for they perceived that this work had been accomplished with the help of our God. [17]Moreover in those days the

[a] 6.6 Heb *Gashmu*   [b] 6.16 Another reading is *saw*

✙

PONDER

And when all our enemies heard of it, all the nations around us were afraid and fell greatly in their own esteem; for they perceived that this work had been accomplished with the help of our God.
—Nehemiah 6.16

PRAY

O Father, thank you for this story about Nehemiah, who was a hero in his own time. Though his biggest accomplishment was building a stone wall and repairing burnt gates, he helped unify your chosen people to prepare them for the birth of our Savior, Jesus Christ, a few centuries later. He set for us an example of persistence and courage through faith in you. Bless us as we go about our day, and let our hearts be filled with thanksgiving, with the confidence and courage to examine our own lives with wisdom and to discern how we can perform the work you have given us to do. In the name of our Savior, Jesus Christ, we pray. Amen.

nobles of Judah sent many letters to Tobiah, and Tobiah's letters came to them. ¹⁸For many in Judah were bound by oath to him, because he was the son-in-law of Shecaniah son of Arah: and his son Jehohanan had married the daughter of Meshullam son of Berechiah. ¹⁹Also they spoke of his good deeds in my presence, and reported my words to him. And Tobiah sent letters to intimidate me.

7 Now when the wall had been built and I had set up the doors, and the gatekeepers, the singers, and the Levites had been appointed, ²I gave my brother Hanani charge over Jerusalem, along with Hananiah the commander of the citadel— for he was a faithful man and feared God more than many. ³And I said to them, "The gates of Jerusalem are not to be opened until the sun is hot; while the gatekeepersᵃ are still standing guard, let them shut and bar the doors. Appoint guards from among the inhabitants of Jerusalem, some at their watch posts, and others before their own houses." ⁴The city was wide and large, but the people within it were few and no houses had been built.

LISTS OF THE RETURNED EXILES

⁵Then my God put it into my mind to assemble the nobles and the officials and the people to be enrolled by genealogy. And I found the book of the genealogy of those who were the first to come back, and I found the following written in it:

⁶These are the people of the province who came up out of the captivity of those exiles whom King Nebuchadnezzar of Babylon had carried into exile; they returned to Jerusalem and Judah, each to his town. ⁷They came with Zerubbabel, Jeshua, Nehemiah, Azariah, Raamiah, Nahamani, Mordecai, Bilshan, Mispereth, Bigvai, Nehum, Baanah.

The number of the Israelite people: ⁸the descendants of Parosh, two thousand one hundred seventy-two. ⁹Of Shephatiah, three hundred seventy-two. ¹⁰Of Arah, six hundred fifty-two. ¹¹Of Pahath-moab, namely the descendants of Jeshua and Joab, two thousand eight hundred eighteen. ¹²Of Elam, one thousand two hundred fifty-four. ¹³Of Zattu, eight hundred forty-five. ¹⁴Of Zaccai, seven hundred sixty. ¹⁵Of Binnui, six hundred forty-eight. ¹⁶Of Bebai, six hundred twenty-eight. ¹⁷Of Azgad, two thousand three hundred twenty-two. ¹⁸Of Adonikam, six hundred sixty-seven. ¹⁹Of Bigvai, two thousand sixty-seven. ²⁰Of Adin, six hundred fifty-five. ²¹Of Ater, namely of Hezekiah, ninety-eight. ²²Of Hashum, three hundred twenty-eight. ²³Of Bezai, three hundred twenty-four. ²⁴Of Hariph, one hundred twelve. ²⁵Of Gibeon, ninety-five. ²⁶The people of Bethlehem and Netophah, one hundred eighty-eight. ²⁷Of Anathoth, one hundred twenty-eight. ²⁸Of Bethazmaveth, forty-two. ²⁹Of Kiriathjearim, Chephirah, and Beeroth, seven hundred forty-three. ³⁰Of Ramah and Geba, six hundred twenty-one. ³¹Of Michmas, one hundred twenty-two. ³²Of Bethel and Ai, one hundred twenty-three. ³³Of the other Nebo, fifty-two. ³⁴The descendants of the other Elam, one thousand two hundred fifty-four. ³⁵Of Harim, three hundred twenty. ³⁶Of Jericho, three hundred forty-five. ³⁷Of Lod, Hadid, and Ono, seven hundred twenty-one. ³⁸Of Senaah, three thousand nine hundred thirty.

³⁹The priests: the descendants of Jedaiah, namely the house of Jeshua, nine hundred seventy-three. ⁴⁰Of Immer, one thousand fifty-two. ⁴¹Of Pashhur, one thousand two hundred forty-seven. ⁴²Of Harim, one thousand seventeen.

⁴³The Levites: the descendants of Jeshua, namely of Kadmiel of the descendants of Hodevah, seventy-four. ⁴⁴The singers: the descendants of Asaph, one hundred forty-eight. ⁴⁵The gatekeepers: the descendants of Shallum, of Ater, of Talmon, of Akkub, of Hatita, of Shobai, one hundred thirty-eight.

⁴⁶The temple servants: the descendants of Ziha, of Hasupha, of

ᵃ 7.3 Heb *while they*

Tabbaoth, 47of Keros, of Sia, of Padon, 48of Lebana, of Hagaba, of Shalmai, 49of Hanan, of Giddel, of Gahar, 50of Reaiah, of Rezin, of Nekoda, 51of Gazzam, of Uzza, of Paseah, 52of Besai, of Meunim, of Nephushesim, 53of Bakbuk, of Hakupha, of Harhur, 54of Bazlith, of Mehida, of Harsha, 55of Barkos, of Sisera, of Temah, 56of Neziah, of Hatipha.

57 The descendants of Solomon's servants: of Sotai, of Sophereth, of Perida, 58of Jaala, of Darkon, of Giddel, 59of Shephatiah, of Hattil, of Pochereth-hazzebaim, of Amon.

60 All the temple servants and the descendants of Solomon's servants were three hundred ninety-two.

61 The following were those who came up from Tel-melah, Tel-harsha, Cherub, Addon, and Immer, but they could not prove their ancestral houses or their descent, whether they belonged to Israel: 62the descendants of Delaiah, of Tobiah, of Nekoda, six hundred forty-two. 63Also, of the priests: the descendants of Hobaiah, of Hakkoz, of Barzillai (who had married one of the daughters of Barzillai the Gileadite and was called by their name). 64These sought their registration among those enrolled in the genealogies, but it was not found there, so they were excluded from the priesthood as unclean; 65the governor told them that they were not to partake of the most holy food, until a priest with Urim and Thummim should come.

66 The whole assembly together was forty-two thousand three hundred sixty, 67besides their male and female slaves, of whom there were seven thousand three hundred thirty-seven; and they had two hundred forty-five singers, male and female. 68They had seven hundred thirty-six horses, two hundred forty-five mules,[a] 69four hundred thirty-five camels, and six thousand seven hundred twenty donkeys.

70 Now some of the heads of ancestral houses contributed to the work. The governor gave to the treasury one thousand darics of gold, fifty basins, and five hundred thirty priestly robes. 71And some of the heads of ancestral houses gave into the building fund twenty thousand darics of gold and two thousand two hundred minas of silver. 72And what the rest of the people gave was twenty thousand darics of gold, two thousand minas of silver, and sixty-seven priestly robes.

73 So the priests, the Levites, the gatekeepers, the singers, some of the people, the temple servants, and all Israel settled in their towns.

EZRA SUMMONS THE PEOPLE TO OBEY THE LAW

When the seventh month came— the people of Israel being settled in **8** their towns— 1all the people gathered together into the square before the Water Gate. They told the scribe Ezra to bring the book of the law of Moses, which the LORD had given to Israel. 2Accordingly, the priest Ezra brought the law before the assembly, both men and women and all who could hear with understanding. This was on the first day of the seventh month. 3He read from it facing the square before the Water Gate from early morning until midday, in the presence of the men and the women and those who could understand; and the ears of all the people were attentive to the book of the law. 4The scribe Ezra stood on a wooden platform that had been made for the purpose; and beside him stood Mattithiah, Shema, Anaiah, Uriah, Hilkiah, and Maaseiah on his right hand; and Pedaiah, Mishael, Malchijah, Hashum, Hash-baddanah, Zechariah, and Meshullam on his left hand. 5And Ezra opened the book in the sight of all the people, for he was standing above all the people; and when he opened it, all the people stood up. 6Then Ezra blessed the LORD, the great God, and all the people answered, "Amen, Amen," lifting up their hands. Then they bowed their heads and worshiped the LORD

a 7.68 Ezra 2.66 and the margins of some Hebrew Mss: MT lacks They had . . . forty-five mules with their faces to the ground. ⁷Also Jeshua, Bani, Sherebiah, Jamin, Akkub, Shabbethai, Hodiah, Maaseiah, Kelita, Azariah, Jozabad, Hanan, Pelaiah, the Levites,ᵃ helped the people to understand the law, while the people remained in their places. ⁸So they read from the book, from the law of God, with interpretation. They gave the sense, so that the people understood the reading.

9 And Nehemiah, who was the governor, and Ezra the priest and scribe, and the Levites who taught the people said to all the people, "This day is holy to the LORD your God; do not mourn or weep." For all the people wept when they heard the words of the law. ¹⁰Then he said to them, "Go your way, eat the fat and drink sweet wine and send portions of them to those for whom nothing is prepared, for this day is holy to our LORD; and do not be grieved, for the joy of the LORD is your strength." ¹¹So the Levites stilled all the people, saying, "Be quiet, for this day is holy; do not be grieved." ¹²And all the people went their way to eat and drink and to send portions and to make great rejoicing, because they had understood the words that were declared to them.

THE FESTIVAL OF BOOTHS CELEBRATED

13 On the second day the heads of ancestral houses of all the people, with the priests and the Levites, came together to the scribe Ezra in order to study the words of the law. ¹⁴And they found it written in the law, which the LORD had commanded by Moses, that the people of Israel should live in boothsᵇ during the festival of the seventh month, ¹⁵and that they should publish and proclaim in all their towns and in Jerusalem as follows, "Go out to the hills and bring branches of olive, wild olive, myrtle, palm, and other leafy trees to make booths,ᵇ as it is written." ¹⁶So the people went out and brought them, and made boothsᵇ for themselves, each on the roofs of their houses, and in their courts and in the courts of the house

of God, and in the square at the Water Gate and in the square at the Gate of Ephraim. ¹⁷And all the assembly of those who had returned from the captivity made boothsᵇ and lived in them; for from the days of Jeshua son of Nun to that day the people of Israel had not done so. And there was very great rejoicing. ¹⁸And day by day, from the first day to the last day, he read from the book of the law of God. They kept the festival seven days; and on the eighth day there was a solemn assembly, according to the ordinance.

NATIONAL CONFESSION

9 Now on the twenty-fourth day of this month the people of Israel were assembled with fasting and in sackcloth, and with earth on their heads.ᶜ ²Then those of Israelite descent separated themselves from all foreigners, and stood and confessed their sins and the iniquities of their ancestors. ³They stood up in their place and read from the book of the law of the LORD their God for a fourth part of the day, and for another fourth they made confession and worshiped the LORD their God. ⁴Then Jeshua, Bani, Kadmiel, Shebaniah, Bunni, Sherebiah, Bani, and Chenani stood on the stairs of the Levites and cried out with a loud voice to the LORD their God. ⁵Then the Levites, Jeshua, Kadmiel, Bani, Hashabneiah, Sherebiah, Hodiah, Shebaniah, and Pethahiah, said, "Stand up and bless the LORD your God from everlasting to everlasting. Blessed be your glorious name, which is exalted above all blessing and praise."

6 And Ezra said:ᵈ "You are the LORD, you alone; you have made heaven, the heaven of heavens, with all their host, the earth and all that is on it, the seas and all that is in them. To all of them you give life, and the host of heaven worships you. ⁷You are the LORD, the God who chose Abram and brought him out of Ur

ᵃ 8.7 1 Esdras 9.48 Vg: Heb *and the Levites*
ᵇ 8.14,15,16,17 Or *tabernacles*; Heb *succoth*
ᶜ 9.1 Heb *on them*   ᵈ 9.6 Gk: Heb lacks *And Ezra said*

of the Chaldeans and gave him the name Abraham; 8and you found his heart faithful before you, and made with him a covenant to give to his descendants the land of the Canaanite, the Hittite, the Amorite, the Perizzite, the Jebusite, and the Girgashite; and you have fulfilled your promise, for you are righteous.

9 "And you saw the distress of our ancestors in Egypt and heard their cry at the Red Sea.ᵃ 10You performed signs and wonders against Pharaoh and all his servants and all the people of his land, for you knew that they acted insolently against our ancestors. You made a name for yourself, which remains to this day. 11And you divided the sea before them, so that they passed through the sea on dry land, but you threw their pursuers into the depths, like a stone into mighty waters. 12Moreover, you led them by day with a pillar of cloud, and by night with a pillar of fire, to give them light on the way in which they should go. 13You came down also upon Mount Sinai, and spoke with them from heaven, and gave them right ordinances and true laws, good statutes and commandments, 14and you made known your holy sabbath to them and gave them commandments and statutes and a law through your servant Moses. 15For their hunger you gave them bread from heaven, and for their thirst you brought water for them out of the rock, and you told them to go in to possess the land that you swore to give them.

16 "But they and our ancestors acted presumptuously and stiffened their necks and did not obey your commandments; 17they refused to obey, and were not mindful of the wonders that you performed among them; but they stiffened their necks and determined to return to their slavery in Egypt. But you are a God ready to forgive, gracious and merciful, slow to anger and abounding in steadfast love, and you did not forsake them. 18Even when they had cast an image of a calf for themselves and said, 'This is your God who brought you up out of Egypt,'

and had committed great blasphemies, 19you in your great mercies did not forsake them in the wilderness; the pillar of cloud that led them in the way did not leave them by day, nor the pillar of fire by night that gave them light on the way by which they should go. 20You gave your good spirit to instruct them, and did not withhold your manna from their mouths, and gave them water for their thirst. 21Forty years you sustained them in the wilderness so that they lacked nothing; their clothes did not wear out and their feet did not swell. 22And you gave them kingdoms and peoples, and allotted to them every corner,ᵇ so they took possession of the land of King Sihon of Heshbon and the land of King Og of Bashan. 23You multiplied their descendants like the stars of heaven, and brought them into the land that you had told their ancestors to enter and possess. 24So the descendants went in and possessed the land, and you subdued before them the inhabitants of the land, the Canaanites, and gave them into their hands, with their kings and the peoples of the land, to do with them as they pleased. 25And they captured fortress cities and a rich land, and took possession of houses filled with all sorts of goods, hewn cisterns, vineyards, olive orchards, and fruit trees in abundance; so they ate, and were filled and became fat, and delighted themselves in your great goodness.

26 "Nevertheless they were disobedient and rebelled against you and cast your law behind their backs and killed your prophets, who had warned them in order to turn them back to you, and they committed great blasphemies. 27Therefore you gave them into the hands of their enemies, who made them suffer. Then in the time of their suffering they cried out to you and you heard them from heaven, and according to your great mercies you gave them saviors who saved them from the

ᵃ 9.9 Or Sea of Reeds   ᵇ 9.22 Meaning of Heb uncertain

hands of their enemies. [28]But after they had rest, they again did evil before you, and you abandoned them to the hands of their enemies, so that they had dominion over them; yet when they turned and cried to you, you heard from heaven, and many times you rescued them according to your mercies. [29]And you warned them in order to turn them back to your law. Yet they acted presumptuously and did not obey your commandments, but sinned against your ordinances, by the observance of which a person shall live. They turned a stubborn shoulder and stiffened their neck and would not obey. [30]Many years you were patient with them, and warned them by your spirit through your prophets; yet they would not listen. Therefore you handed them over to the peoples of the lands. [31]Nevertheless, in your great mercies you did not make an end of them or forsake them, for you are a gracious and merciful God.

[32] "Now therefore, our God—the great and mighty and awesome God, keeping covenant and steadfast love—do not treat lightly all the hardship that has come upon us, upon our kings, our officials, our priests, our prophets, our ancestors, and all your people, since the time of the kings of Assyria until today. [33]You have been just in all that has come upon us, for you have dealt faithfully and we have acted wickedly; [34]our kings, our officials, our priests, and our ancestors have not kept your law or heeded the commandments and the warnings that you gave them. [35]Even in their own kingdom, and in the great goodness you bestowed on them, and in the large and rich land that you set before them, they did not serve you and did not turn from their wicked works. [36]Here we are, slaves to this day—slaves in the land that you gave to our ancestors to enjoy its fruit and its good gifts. [37]Its rich yield goes to the kings whom you have set over us because of our sins; they have power also over our bodies and over our livestock at their pleasure, and we are in great distress."

THOSE WHO SIGNED THE COVENANT

[38][a] Because of all this we make a firm agreement in writing, and on that sealed document are inscribed the names of our officials, our Levites, and our priests.

10[b] Upon the sealed document are the names of Nehemiah the governor, son of Hacaliah, and Zedekiah; [2]Seraiah, Azariah, Jeremiah, [3]Pashhur, Amariah, Malchijah, [4]Hattush, Shebaniah, Malluch, [5]Harim, Meremoth, Obadiah, [6]Daniel, Ginnethon, Baruch, [7]Meshullam, Abijah, Mijamin, [8]Maaziah, Bilgai, Shemaiah; these are the priests. [9]And the Levites: Jeshua son of Azaniah, Binnui of the sons of Henadad, Kadmiel; [10]and their associates, Shebaniah, Hodiah, Kelita, Pelaiah, Hanan, [11]Mica, Rehob, Hashabiah, [12]Zaccur, Sherebiah, Shebaniah, [13]Hodiah, Bani, Beninu. [14]The leaders of the people: Parosh, Pahath-moab, Elam, Zattu, Bani, [15]Bunni, Azgad, Bebai, [16]Adonijah, Bigvai, Adin, [17]Ater, Hezekiah, Azzur, [18]Hodiah, Hashum, Bezai, [19]Hariph, Anathoth, Nebai, [20]Magpiash, Meshullam, Hezir, [21]Meshezabel, Zadok, Jaddua, [22]Pelatiah, Hanan, Anaiah, [23]Hoshea, Hananiah, Hasshub, [24]Hallohesh, Pilha, Shobek, [25]Rehum, Hashabnah, Maaseiah, [26]Ahiah, Hanan, Anan, [27]Malluch, Harim, and Baanah.

SUMMARY OF THE COVENANT

[28] The rest of the people, the priests, the Levites, the gatekeepers, the singers, the temple servants, and all who have separated themselves from the peoples of the lands to adhere to the law of God, their wives, their sons, their daughters, all who have knowledge and understanding, [29]join with their kin, their nobles, and enter into a curse and an oath to walk in God's law, which was given by Moses the servant of God, and to observe and do all the commandments of the LORD our Lord and his ordinances and his statutes. [30]We will not give our

[a] **9.38** Ch 10.1 in Heb   [b] **10.1** Ch 10.2 in Heb

daughters to the peoples of the land or take their daughters for our sons; 31and if the peoples of the land bring in merchandise or any grain on the sabbath day to sell, we will not buy it from them on the sabbath or on a holy day; and we will forego the crops of the seventh year and the exaction of every debt.

32 We also lay on ourselves the obligation to charge ourselves yearly one-third of a shekel for the service of the house of our God: 33for the rows of bread, the regular grain offering, the regular burnt offering, the sabbaths, the new moons, the appointed festivals, the sacred donations, and the sin offerings to make atonement for Israel, and for all the work of the house of our God. 34We have also cast lots among the priests, the Levites, and the people, for the wood offering, to bring it into the house of our God, by ancestral houses, at appointed times, year by year, to burn on the altar of the LORD our God, as it is written in the law. 35We obligate ourselves to bring the first fruits of our soil and the first fruits of all fruit of every tree, year by year, to the house of the LORD; 36also to bring to the house of our God, to the priests who minister in the house of our God, the firstborn of our sons and of our livestock, as it is written in the law, and the firstlings of our herds and of our flocks; 37and to bring the first of our dough, and our contributions, the fruit of every tree, the wine and the oil, to the priests, to the chambers of the house of our God; and to bring to the Levites the tithes from our soil, for it is the Levites who collect the tithes in all our rural towns. 38And the priest, the descendant of Aaron, shall be with the Levites when the Levites receive the tithes; and the Levites shall bring up a tithe of the tithes to the house of our God, to the chambers of the storehouse. 39For the people of Israel and the sons of Levi shall bring the contribution of grain, wine, and oil to the storerooms where the vessels of the sanctuary are, and where the priests that minister, and the gatekeepers and the singers are. We will not neglect the house of our God.

POPULATION OF THE CITY INCREASED

11 Now the leaders of the people lived in Jerusalem; and the rest of the people cast lots to bring one out of ten to live in the holy city Jerusalem, while nine-tenths remained in the other towns. 2And the people blessed all those who willingly offered to live in Jerusalem.

3 These are the leaders of the province who lived in Jerusalem; but in the towns of Judah all lived on their property in their towns: Israel, the priests, the Levites, the temple servants, and the descendants of Solomon's servants. 4And in Jerusalem lived some of the Judahites and of the Benjaminites. Of the Judahites: Athaiah son of Uzziah son of Zechariah son of Amariah son of Shephatiah son of Mahalalel, of the descendants of Perez; 5and Maaseiah son of Baruch son of Col-hozeh son of Hazaiah son of Adaiah son of Joiarib son of Zechariah son of the Shilonite. 6All the descendants of Perez who lived in Jerusalem were four hundred sixty-eight valiant warriors.

7 And these are the Benjaminites: Sallu son of Meshullam son of Joed son of Pedaiah son of Kolaiah son of Maaseiah son of Ithiel son of Jeshaiah. 8And his brothers[a] Gabbai, Sallai: nine hundred twenty-eight. 9Joel son of Zichri was their overseer; and Judah son of Hassenuah was second in charge of the city.

10 Of the priests: Jedaiah son of Joiarib, Jachin, 11Seraiah son of Hilkiah son of Meshullam son of Zadok son of Meraioth son of Ahitub, officer of the house of God, 12and their associates who did the work of the house, eight hundred twenty-two; and Adaiah son of Jeroham son of Pelaliah son of Amzi son of Zechariah son of Pashhur son of Malchijah, 13and his associates, heads of ancestral houses, two hundred forty-

a 11.8 Gk Mss: Heb And after him

two; and Amashsai son of Azarel son of Ahzai son of Meshillemoth son of Immer, 14and their associates, valiant warriors, one hundred twenty-eight; their overseer was Zabdiel son of Haggedolim.

15 And of the Levites: Shemaiah son of Hasshub son of Azrikam son of Hashabiah son of Bunni; 16and Shabbethai and Jozabad, of the leaders of the Levites, who were over the outside work of the house of God; 17and Mattaniah son of Mica son of Zabdi son of Asaph, who was the leader to begin the thanksgiving in prayer, and Bakbukiah, the second among his associates; and Abda son of Shammua son of Galal son of Jeduthun. 18All the Levites in the holy city were two hundred eighty-four.

19 The gatekeepers, Akkub, Talmon and their associates, who kept watch at the gates, were one hundred seventy-two. 20And the rest of Israel, and of the priests and the Levites, were in all the towns of Judah, all of them in their inheritance. 21But the temple servants lived on Ophel; and Ziha and Gishpa were over the temple servants.

22 The overseer of the Levites in Jerusalem was Uzzi son of Bani son of Hashabiah son of Mattaniah son of Mica, of the descendants of Asaph, the singers, in charge of the work of the house of God. 23For there was a command from the king concerning them, and a settled provision for the singers, as was required every day. 24And Pethahiah son of Meshezabel, of the descendants of Zerah son of Judah, was at the king's hand in all matters concerning the people.

VILLAGES OUTSIDE JERUSALEM

25 And as for the villages, with their fields, some of the people of Judah lived in Kiriath-arba and its villages, and in Dibon and its villages, and in Jekabzeel and its villages, 26and in Jeshua and in Moladah and Beth-pelet, 27in Hazar-shual, in Beer-sheba and its villages, 28in Ziklag, in Meconah and its villages, 29in En-rimmon, in Zorah, in Jarmuth, 30Zanoah, Adullam, and their villages, Lachish and its fields,

and Azekah and its villages. So they camped from Beer-sheba to the valley of Hinnom. 31The people of Benjamin also lived from Geba onward, at Michmash, Aija, Bethel and its villages, 32Anathoth, Nob, Ananiah, 33Hazor, Ramah, Gittaim, 34Hadid, Zeboim, Neballat, 35Lod, and Ono, the valley of artisans. 36And certain divisions of the Levites in Judah were joined to Benjamin.

A LIST OF PRIESTS AND LEVITES

12 These are the priests and the Levites who came up with Zerubbabel son of Shealtiel, and Jeshua: Seraiah, Jeremiah, Ezra, 2Amariah, Malluch, Hattush, 3Shecaniah, Rehum, Meremoth, 4Iddo, Ginnethoi, Abijah, 5Mijamin, Maadiah, Bilgah, 6Shemaiah, Joiarib, Jedaiah, 7Sallu, Amok, Hilkiah, Jedaiah. These were the leaders of the priests and of their associates in the days of Jeshua.

8 And the Levites: Jeshua, Binnui, Kadmiel, Sherebiah, Judah, and Mattaniah, who with his associates was in charge of the songs of thanksgiving. 9And Bakbukiah and Unno their associates stood opposite them in the service. 10Jeshua was the father of Joiakim, Joiakim the father of Eliashib, Eliashib the father of Joiada, 11Joiada the father of Jonathan, and Jonathan the father of Jaddua.

12 In the days of Joiakim the priests, heads of ancestral houses, were: of Seraiah, Meraiah; of Jeremiah, Hananiah; 13of Ezra, Meshullam; of Amariah, Jehohanan; 14of Malluchi, Jonathan; of Shebaniah, Joseph; 15of Harim, Adna; of Meraioth, Helkai; 16of Iddo, Zechariah; of Ginnethon, Meshullam; 17of Abijah, Zichri; of Miniamin, of Moadiah, Piltai; 18of Bilgah, Shammua; of Shemaiah, Jehonathan; 19of Joiarib, Mattenai; of Jedaiah, Uzzi; 20of Sallai, Kallai; of Amok, Eber; 21of Hilkiah, Hashabiah; of Jedaiah, Nethanel.

22 As for the Levites, in the days of Eliashib, Joiada, Johanan, and Jaddua, there were recorded the heads of ancestral houses; also the priests until the reign of Darius the Persian.

23The Levites, heads of ancestral houses, were recorded in the Book of the Annals until the days of Johanan son of Eliashib. 24And the leaders of the Levites: Hashabiah, Sherebiah, and Jeshua son of Kadmiel, with their associates over against them, to praise and to give thanks, according to the commandment of David the man of God, section opposite to section. 25Mattaniah, Bakbukiah, Obadiah, Meshullam, Talmon, and Akkub were gatekeepers standing guard at the storehouses of the gates. 26These were in the days of Joiakim son of Jeshua son of Jozadak, and in the days of the governor Nehemiah and of the priest Ezra, the scribe.

DEDICATION OF THE CITY WALL

27 Now at the dedication of the wall of Jerusalem they sought out the Levites in all their places, to bring them to Jerusalem to celebrate the dedication with rejoicing, with thanksgivings and with singing, with cymbals, harps, and lyres. 28The companies of the singers gathered together from the circuit around Jerusalem and from the villages of the Netophathites; 29also from Beth-gilgal and from the region of Geba and Azmaveth; for the singers had built for themselves villages around Jerusalem. 30And the priests and the Levites purified themselves; and they purified the people and the gates and the wall.

31 Then I brought the leaders of Judah up onto the wall, and appointed two great companies that gave thanks and went in procession. One went to the right on the wall to the Dung Gate; 32and after them went Hoshaiah and half the officials of Judah, 33and Azariah, Ezra, Meshullam, 34Judah, Benjamin, Shemaiah, and Jeremiah, 35and some of the young priests with trumpets: Zechariah son of Jonathan son of Shemaiah son of Mattaniah son of Micaiah son of Zaccur son of Asaph; 36and his kindred, Shemaiah, Azarel, Milalai, Gilalai, Maai, Nethanel, Judah, and Hanani, with the musical instruments of David the man of God; and the scribe Ezra went in front of them. 37At the Fountain Gate, in front of them, they went straight up by the stairs of the city of David, at the ascent of the wall, above the house of David, to the Water Gate on the east.

38 The other company of those who gave thanks went to the left,a and I followed them with half of the people on the wall, above the Tower of the Ovens, to the Broad Wall, 39and above the Gate of Ephraim, and by the Old Gate, and by the Fish Gate and the Tower of Hananel and the Tower of the Hundred, to the Sheep Gate; and they came to a halt at the Gate of the Guard. 40So both companies of those who gave thanks stood in the house of God, and I and half of the officials with me; 41and the priests Eliakim, Maaseiah, Miniamin, Micaiah, Elioenai, Zechariah, and Hananiah, with trumpets; 42and Maaseiah, Shemaiah, Eleazar, Uzzi, Jehohanan, Malchijah, Elam, and Ezer. And the singers sang with Jezrahiah as their leader. 43They offered great sacrifices that day and rejoiced, for God had made them rejoice with great joy; the women and children also rejoiced. The joy of Jerusalem was heard far away.

TEMPLE RESPONSIBILITIES

44 On that day men were appointed over the chambers for the stores, the contributions, the first fruits, and the tithes, to gather into them the portions required by the law for the priests and for the Levites from the fields belonging to the towns; for Judah rejoiced over the priests and the Levites who ministered. 45They performed the service of their God and the service of purification, as did the singers and the gatekeepers, according to the command of David and his son Solomon. 46For in the days of David and Asaph long ago there was a leader of the singers, and there were songs of praise and thanksgiving to God. 47In the days of Zerubbabel and in the days of Nehemiah all Israel

a 12.38 Cn: Heb *opposite*

gave the daily portions for the singers and the gatekeepers. They set apart that which was for the Levites; and the Levites set apart that which was for the descendants of Aaron.

FOREIGNERS SEPARATED FROM ISRAEL

13 On that day they read from the book of Moses in the hearing of the people; and in it was found written that no Ammonite or Moabite should ever enter the assembly of God, 2because they did not meet the Israelites with bread and water, but hired Balaam against them to curse them—yet our God turned the curse into a blessing. 3When the people heard the law, they separated from Israel all those of foreign descent.

THE REFORMS OF NEHEMIAH

4 Now before this, the priest Eliashib, who was appointed over the chambers of the house of our God, and who was related to Tobiah, 5prepared for Tobiah a large room where they had previously put the grain offering, the frankincense, the vessels, and the tithes of grain, wine, and oil, which were given by commandment to the Levites, singers, and gatekeepers, and the contributions for the priests. 6While this was taking place I was not in Jerusalem, for in the thirty-second year of King Artaxerxes of Babylon I went to the king. After some time I asked leave of the king 7and returned to Jerusalem. I then discovered the wrong that Eliashib had done on behalf of Tobiah, preparing a room for him in the courts of the house of God. 8And I was very angry, and I threw all the household furniture of Tobiah out of the room. 9Then I gave orders and they cleansed the chambers, and I brought back the vessels of the house of God, with the grain offering and the frankincense.

10 I also found out that the portions of the Levites had not been given to them; so that the Levites and the singers, who had conducted the service, had gone back to their fields. 11So I remonstrated with the officials and said, "Why is the house of God forsaken?" And I gathered them together and set them in their stations. 12Then all Judah brought the tithe of the grain, wine, and oil into the storehouses. 13And I appointed as treasurers over the storehouses the priest Shelemiah, the scribe Zadok, and Pedaiah of the Levites, and as their assistant Hanan son of Zaccur son of Mattaniah, for they were considered faithful; and their duty was to distribute to their associates. 14Remember me, O my God, concerning this, and do not wipe out my good deeds that I have done for the house of my God and for his service.

SABBATH REFORMS BEGUN

15 In those days I saw in Judah people treading wine presses on the sabbath, and bringing in heaps of grain and loading them on donkeys; and also wine, grapes, figs, and all kinds of burdens, which they brought into Jerusalem on the sabbath day; and I warned them at that time against selling food. 16Tyrians also, who lived in the city, brought in fish and all kinds of merchandise and sold them on the sabbath to the people of Judah, and in Jerusalem. 17Then I remonstrated with the nobles of Judah and said to them, "What is this evil thing that you are doing, profaning the sabbath day? 18Did not your ancestors act in this way, and did not our God bring all this disaster on us and on this city? Yet you bring more wrath on Israel by profaning the sabbath."

19 When it began to be dark at the gates of Jerusalem before the sabbath, I commanded that the doors should be shut and gave orders that they should not be opened until after the sabbath. And I set some of my servants over the gates, to prevent any burden from being brought in on the sabbath day. 20Then the merchants and sellers of all kinds of merchandise spent the night outside Jerusalem once or twice. 21But I warned them and said to them, "Why do you spend the night in front of the wall? If you do so again,

I will lay hands on you." From that time on they did not come on the sabbath. 22And I commanded the Levites that they should purify themselves and come and guard the gates, to keep the sabbath day holy. Remember this also in my favor, O my God, and spare me according to the greatness of your steadfast love.

MIXED MARRIAGES CONDEMNED

23 In those days also I saw Jews who had married women of Ashdod, Ammon, and Moab; 24and half of their children spoke the language of Ashdod, and they could not speak the language of Judah, but spoke the language of various peoples. 25And I contended with them and cursed them and beat some of them and pulled out their hair; and I made them take an oath in the name of God, saying, "You shall not give your daughters to their sons, or take their daughters for your sons or

for yourselves. 26Did not King Solomon of Israel sin on account of such women? Among the many nations there was no king like him, and he was beloved by his God, and God made him king over all Israel; nevertheless, foreign women made even him to sin. 27Shall we then listen to you and do all this great evil and act treacherously against our God by marrying foreign women?"

28 And one of the sons of Jehoiada, son of the high priest Eliashib, was the son-in-law of Sanballat the Horonite; I chased him away from me. 29Remember them, O my God, because they have defiled the priesthood, the covenant of the priests and the Levites.

30 Thus I cleansed them from everything foreign, and I established the duties of the priests and Levites, each in his work; 31and I provided for the wood offering, at appointed times, and for the first fruits. Remember me, O my God, for good.

ESTHER

Intrigue. Deception. Romance. Power struggles. All these can be found in the book of Esther. Esther was a beautiful young Jewish woman chosen by King Ahasuerus of Persia to be his queen. The book of Esther vividly recounts the deliverance of the Jewish people after they were sentenced to annihilation. It highlights the courage and effectiveness of the queen and her steadfast cousin, Mordecai, as they took a stand against the forces of hatred and bigotry. Although God's name isn't mentioned in the book, the events of this fascinating story clearly reveal God's power and providence.

KING AHASUERUS DEPOSES QUEEN VASHTI

1 This happened in the days of Ahasuerus, the same Ahasuerus who ruled over one hundred twenty-seven provinces from India to Ethiopia.[a] 2 In those days when King Ahasuerus sat on his royal throne in the citadel of Susa, 3 in the third year of his reign, he gave a banquet for all his officials and ministers. The army of Persia and Media and the nobles and governors of the provinces were present, 4 while he displayed the great wealth of his kingdom and the splendor and pomp of his majesty for many days, one hundred eighty days in all.

5 When these days were completed, the king gave for all the people present in the citadel of Susa, both great and small, a banquet lasting for seven days, in the court of the garden of the king's palace. 6 There were white cotton curtains and blue hangings tied with cords of fine linen and purple to silver rings[b] and marble pillars. There were couches of gold and silver on a mosaic pavement of porphyry, marble, mother-of-pearl, and colored stones. 7 Drinks were served in golden goblets, goblets of different kinds, and the royal wine was lavished according to the bounty of the king. 8 Drinking was by flagons, without restraint; for the king had given orders to all the officials of his palace to do as each one desired. 9 Furthermore, Queen Vashti gave a banquet for the women in the palace of King Ahasuerus.

10 On the seventh day, when the king was merry with wine, he commanded Mehuman, Biztha, Harbona, Bigtha and Abagtha, Zethar and Carkas, the seven eunuchs who attended him, 11 to bring Queen Vashti before the king, wearing the royal crown, in order to show the peoples and the officials her beauty; for she was fair to behold. 12 But Queen Vashti refused to come at the king's command conveyed by the eunuchs. At this the king was enraged, and his anger burned within him.

13 Then the king consulted the sages who knew the laws[c] (for this was the king's procedure toward all who were versed in law and custom, 14 and those next to him were Carshena, Shethar, Admatha, Tarshish, Meres, Marsena, and Memucan, the seven officials of Persia and Media, who had access to the king, and sat first in the kingdom): 15 "According to the law, what is to be done to Queen Vashti because she has not performed the command of King Ahasuerus conveyed by the eunuchs?" 16 Then Memucan said in the presence of the king and the officials, "Not only has Queen Vashti done wrong to the king, but also to all the officials and all the peoples who are in all the provinces of King Ahasuerus. 17 For this deed of the queen will be made known to all women, causing them to look with contempt on their husbands, since they will say, 'King Ahasuerus commanded Queen Vashti to be brought before him, and she did not come.' 18 This very day the noble ladies of Persia and Media who have heard of the queen's behavior will rebel against[d] the king's officials, and there will be no end of contempt and wrath! 19 If it pleases the king, let a royal order go out from him, and let it be written among the laws of the Persians and the Medes so that it may not be altered, that Vashti is never again to come before King Ahasuerus; and let the king give her royal position to another who is better than she. 20 So when the decree made by the king is proclaimed throughout all his kingdom, vast as it is, all women will give honor to their husbands, high and low alike."

21 This advice pleased the king and the officials, and the king did as Memucan proposed; 22 he sent letters to all the royal provinces, to every province in its own script and to every people in its own language, declaring that every man should be master in his own house.[e]

---

[a] 1.1 Or Nubia; Heb Cush   [b] 1.6 Or rods
[c] 1.13 Cn: Heb times   [d] 1.18 Cn: Heb will tell
[e] 1.22 Heb adds and speak according to the language of his people

ESTHER BECOMES QUEEN

2 After these things, when the anger of King Ahasuerus had abated, he remembered Vashti and what she had done and what had been decreed against her. ²Then the king's servants who attended him said, "Let beautiful young virgins be sought out for the king. ³And let the king appoint commissioners in all the provinces of his kingdom to gather all the beautiful young virgins to the harem in the citadel of Susa under custody of Hegai, the king's eunuch, who is in charge of the women; let their cosmetic treatments be given them. ⁴And let the girl who pleases the king be queen instead of Vashti." This pleased the king, and he did so.

5 Now there was a Jew in the citadel of Susa whose name was Mordecai son of Jair son of Shimei son of Kish, a Benjaminite. ⁶Kishª had been carried away from Jerusalem among the captives carried away with King Jeconiah of Judah, whom King Nebuchadnezzar of Babylon had carried away. ⁷Mordecaiᵇ had brought up Hadassah, that is Esther, his cousin, for she had neither father nor mother; the girl was fair and beautiful, and when her father and her mother died, Mordecai adopted her as his own daughter. ⁸So when the king's order and his edict were proclaimed, and when many young women were gathered in the citadel of Susa in custody of Hegai, Esther also was taken into the king's palace and put in custody of Hegai, who had charge of the women. ⁹The girl pleased him and won his favor, and he quickly provided her with her cosmetic treatments and her portion of food, and with seven chosen maids from the king's palace, and advanced her and her maids to the best place in the harem. ¹⁰Esther did not reveal her people or kindred, for Mordecai had charged her not to tell. ¹¹Every day Mordecai would walk around in front of the court of the harem, to learn how Esther was and how she fared.

12 The turn came for each girl to go in to King Ahasuerus, after be-ing twelve months under the regulations for the women, since this was the regular period of their cosmetic treatment, six months with oil of myrrh and six months with perfumes and cosmetics for women. ¹³When the girl went in to the king she was given whatever she asked for to take with her from the harem to the king's palace. ¹⁴In the evening she went in; then in the morning she came back to the second harem in custody of Shaashgaz, the king's eunuch, who was in charge of the concubines; she did not go in to the king again, unless the king delighted in her and she was summoned by name.

15 When the turn came for Esther daughter of Abihail the uncle of Mordecai, who had adopted her as his own daughter, to go in to the king, she asked for nothing except what Hegai the king's eunuch, who had charge of the women, advised. Now Esther was admired by all who saw her. ¹⁶When Esther was taken to King Ahasuerus in his royal palace in the tenth month, which is the month of Tebeth, in the seventh year of his reign, ¹⁷the king loved Esther more than all the other women; of all the virgins she won his favor and devotion, so that he set the royal crown on her head and made her queen instead of Vashti. ¹⁸Then the king gave a great banquet to all his officials and ministers—"Esther's banquet." He also granted a holidayᶜ to the provinces, and gave gifts with royal liberality.

MORDECAI DISCOVERS A PLOT

19 When the virgins were being gathered together,ᵈ Mordecai was sitting at the king's gate. ²⁰Now Esther had not revealed her kindred or her people, as Mordecai had charged her; for Esther obeyed Mordecai just as when she was brought up by him. ²¹In those days, while Mordecai was sitting at the king's gate, Bigthan and Teresh, two of the king's eunuchs, who guarded the threshold,

---

ª 2.6 Heb *a Benjaminite* ⁶*who*   ᵇ 2.7 Heb *He*   ᶜ 2.18 Or *an amnesty*   ᵈ 2.19 Heb adds *a second time*

became angry and conspired to assassinate[a] King Ahasuerus. 22But the matter came to the knowledge of Mordecai, and he told it to Queen Esther, and Esther told the king in the name of Mordecai. 23When the affair was investigated and found to be so, both the men were hanged on the gallows. It was recorded in the book of the annals in the presence of the king.

HAMAN UNDERTAKES TO DESTROY THE JEWS

3 After these things King Ahasuerus promoted Haman son of Hammedatha the Agagite, and advanced him and set his seat above all the officials who were with him. 2And all the king's servants who were at the king's gate bowed down and did obeisance to Haman; for the king had so commanded concerning him. But Mordecai did not bow down or do obeisance. 3Then the king's servants who were at the king's gate said to Mordecai, "Why do you disobey the king's command?" 4When they spoke to him day after day and he would not listen to them, they told Haman, in order to see whether Mordecai's words would avail; for he had told them that he was a Jew. 5When Haman saw that Mordecai did not bow down or do obeisance to him, Haman was infuriated. 6But he thought it beneath him to lay hands on Mordecai alone. So, having been told who Mordecai's people were, Haman plotted to destroy all the Jews, the people of Mordecai, throughout the whole kingdom of Ahasuerus.

7 In the first month, which is the month of Nisan, in the twelfth year of King Ahasuerus, they cast Pur—which means "the lot"—before Haman for the day and for the month, and the lot fell on the thirteenth day[b] of the twelfth month, which is the month of Adar. 8Then Haman said to King Ahasuerus, "There is a certain people scattered and separated among the peoples in all the provinces of your kingdom; their laws are different from those of every other people, and they do not

keep the king's laws, so that it is not appropriate for the king to tolerate them. 9If it pleases the king, let a decree be issued for their destruction, and I will pay ten thousand talents of silver into the hands of those who have charge of the king's business, so that they may put it into the king's treasuries." 10So the king took his signet ring from his hand and gave it to Haman son of Hammedatha the Agagite, the enemy of the Jews. 11The king said to Haman, "The money is given to you, and the people as well, to do with them as it seems good to you."

12 Then the king's secretaries were summoned on the thirteenth day of the first month, and an edict, according to all that Haman commanded, was written to the king's satraps and to the governors over all the provinces and to the officials of all the peoples, to every province in its own script and every people in its own language; it was written in the name of King Ahasuerus and sealed with the king's ring. 13Letters were sent by couriers to all the king's provinces, giving orders to destroy, to kill, and to annihilate all Jews, young and old, women and children, in one day, the thirteenth day of the twelfth month, which is the month of Adar, and to plunder their goods. 14A copy of the document was to be issued as a decree in every province by proclamation, calling on all the peoples to be ready for that day. 15The couriers went quickly by order of the king, and the decree was issued in the citadel of Susa. The king and Haman sat down to drink; but the city of Susa was thrown into confusion.

ESTHER AGREES TO HELP THE JEWS

4 When Mordecai learned all that had been done, Mordecai tore his clothes and put on sackcloth and ashes, and went through the city, wailing with a loud and bitter cry; 2he went up to the entrance of the

a 2.21 Heb to lay hands on   b 3.7 Cn Compare Gk and verse 13 below: Heb the twelfth month king's gate, for no one might enter the king's gate clothed with sackcloth. ³In every province, wherever the king's command and his decree came, there was great mourning among the Jews, with fasting and weeping and lamenting, and most of them lay in sackcloth and ashes.

4 When Esther's maids and her eunuchs came and told her, the queen was deeply distressed; she sent garments to clothe Mordecai, so that he might take off his sackcloth; but he would not accept them. ⁵Then Esther called for Hathach, one of the king's eunuchs, who had been appointed to attend her, and ordered him to go to Mordecai to learn what was happening and why. ⁶Hathach went out to Mordecai in the open square of the city in front of the king's gate, ⁷and Mordecai told him all that had happened to him, and the exact sum of money that Haman had promised to pay into the king's treasuries for the destruction of the Jews. ⁸Mordecai also gave him a copy of the written decree issued in Susa for their destruction, that he might show it to Esther, explain it to her, and charge her to go to the king to make supplication to him and entreat him for her people.

9 Hathach went and told Esther what Mordecai had said. ¹⁰Then Esther spoke to Hathach and gave him a message for Mordecai, saying, ¹¹"All the king's servants and the people of the king's provinces know that if any man or woman goes to the king inside the inner court without being called, there is but one law—all alike are to be put to death. Only if the king holds out the golden scepter to someone, may that person live. I myself have not been called to come in to the king for thirty days." ¹²When they told Mordecai what Esther had said, ¹³Mordecai told them to reply to Esther, "Do not think that in the king's palace you will escape any more than all the other Jews. ¹⁴For if you keep silence at such a time as this, relief and deliverance will rise for the Jews from another quarter, but you and your father's family will perish. Who knows? Per-

haps you have come to royal dignity for just such a time as this." ¹⁵Then Esther said in reply to Mordecai, ¹⁶"Go, gather all the Jews to be found in Susa, and hold a fast on my behalf, and neither eat nor drink for three days, night or day. I and my maids will also fast as you do. After that I will go to the king, though it is against the law; and if I perish, I perish." ¹⁷Mordecai then went away and did everything as Esther had ordered him.

PONDER

"For if you keep silence at such a time as this, relief and deliverance will rise for the Jews from another quarter, but you and your father's family will perish. Who knows? Perhaps you have come to royal dignity for just such a time as this."
—Esther 4.14

PRAY

Sovereign God, we are intrigued, inspired and perhaps disturbed by the stories of the Old Testament—such as this one about Esther, Mordecai and Haman. We pray that you show us what you would have us see. We offer our renewed commitment to be Christlike in our daily lives, and that each of us might strive to spread Christianity through our words and actions in a courageous and effective fashion. We ask in the name of the epitome of love, our Savior, Jesus Christ. Amen.

ESTHER'S BANQUET

5 On the third day Esther put on her royal robes and stood in the inner court of the king's palace, opposite the king's hall. The king was sitting on his royal throne inside the palace opposite the entrance to the palace. ²As soon as the king saw Queen Esther standing in the court, she won his favor and he held out to her the golden scepter that was in

FOR SUCH A TIME

"For if you keep silence at such a time as this, relief and deliverance will rise for the Jews from another quarter, but you and your father's family will perish. Who knows? Perhaps you have come to royal dignity for just such a time as this."

—Esther 4.14

The book of Esther is an intriguing read. It always has been somewhat controversial, primarily because of its lack of any direct reference to God or prayer. Martin Luther suggested that it should not be included in the canon of authoritative scripture. Despite its maligned reputation, however, the book of Esther has an important message for believers today.

First of all, the events of the book of Esther highlight the dangers and destructive effects of ethnocentrism—the belief that our own society or way of thinking is superior to another. Haman's hatred for the Jews, combined with his significant influence in the Persian government, led him to attempt to exterminate the Jews; he would have largely succeeded if it were not for Esther's courageous efforts. Our world still is plagued with ethnocentrism. It is sometimes manifest in outright conflict between groups of people and sometimes results in war and terrible suffering. Other forms of ethnocentrism are not so easy to recognize, like the superiority we sometimes feel toward people who are different from us. Whether it is the color of their skin, the social stratum to which they belong or whatever artificial distinction, we often perceive others as inferior to us or less deserving of God's blessing.

Another lesson from the book of Esther is the responsibility we bear to help others and alleviate suffering wherever we can. Esther risked her life to help her fellow Jews, who were facing extermination at the hands of Haman. We too are called to give of ourselves and our resources to help those who are suffering. Perhaps we are in a position of influence, from which we can speak for those who don't have a voice. We don't have to be financially rich—or politically influential or intellectually gifted—to help someone. Sometimes we help by lending a listening ear to someone who is hurting or offering to check in on an elderly neighbor from time to time.

Although Mordecai was clearly urging Esther to act on behalf of the Jews, he fully believed that God was sovereign whether Esther rose to the occasion or not. In other words, Esther was responsible to help, but ultimately the people were in God's hands. Likewise, we are responsible to do what we can to help others, but those who are suffering can always know they are never out of God's all-knowing and all-powerful care.

Going Deeper

- When have you felt completely at the mercy of another person or of circumstances beyond your control? How does the book of Esther speak to that situation?
- Who are some people in your sphere of knowledge or influence who are suffering? What are some ways you can reach out to help them?

his hand. Then Esther approached and touched the top of the scepter. ³The king said to her, "What is it, Queen Esther? What is your request? It shall be given you, even to the half of my kingdom." ⁴Then Esther said, "If it pleases the king, let the king and Haman come today to a banquet that I have prepared for the king." ⁵Then the king said, "Bring Haman quickly, so that we may do as Esther desires." So the king and Haman came to the banquet that Esther had prepared. ⁶While they were drinking wine, the king said to Esther, "What is your petition? It shall be granted you. And what is your request? Even to the half of my kingdom, it shall be fulfilled." ⁷Then Esther said, "This is my petition and request: ⁸If I have won the king's favor, and if it pleases the king to grant my petition and fulfill my request, let the king and Haman come tomorrow to the banquet that I will prepare for them, and then I will do as the king has said."

WE NEED TO ASK GOD FOR COURAGE TO ESPOUSE CAUSES THAT ARE RIGHT BUT UNPOPULAR.

HAMAN PLANS TO HAVE MORDECAI HANGED

9 Haman went out that day happy and in good spirits. But when Haman saw Mordecai in the king's gate, and observed that he neither rose nor trembled before him, he was infuriated with Mordecai; ¹⁰nevertheless Haman restrained himself and went home. Then he sent and called for his friends and his wife Zeresh, ¹¹and Haman recounted to them the splendor of his riches, the number of his sons, all the promotions with which the king had honored him, and how he had advanced him

above the officials and the ministers of the king. ¹²Haman added, "Even Queen Esther let no one but myself come with the king to the banquet that she prepared. Tomorrow also I am invited by her, together with the king. ¹³Yet all this does me no good so long as I see the Jew Mordecai sitting at the king's gate." ¹⁴Then his wife Zeresh and all his friends said to him, "Let a gallows fifty cubits high be made, and in the morning tell the king to have Mordecai hanged on it; then go with the king to the banquet in good spirits." This advice pleased Haman, and he had the gallows made.

THE KING HONORS MORDECAI

6 On that night the king could not sleep, and he gave orders to bring the book of records, the annals, and they were read to the king. ²It was found written how Mordecai had told about Bigthana and Teresh, two of the king's eunuchs, who guarded the threshold, and who had conspired to assassinate[a] King Ahasuerus. ³Then the king said, "What honor or distinction has been bestowed on Mordecai for this?" The king's servants who attended him said, "Nothing has been done for him." ⁴The king said, "Who is in the court?" Now Haman had just entered the outer court of the king's palace to speak to the king about having Mordecai hanged on the gallows that he had prepared for him. ⁵So the king's servants told him, "Haman is there, standing in the court." The king said, "Let him come in." ⁶So Haman came in, and the king said to him, "What shall be done for the man whom the king wishes to honor?" Haman said to himself, "Whom would the king wish to honor more than me?" ⁷So Haman said to the king, "For the man whom the king wishes to honor, ⁸let royal robes be brought, which the king has worn, and a horse that the king has ridden, with a royal crown on its head. ⁹Let the robes and the horse be handed over to one of the king's most noble

a **6.2** Heb *to lay hands on*

officials; let him[a] robe the man whom the king wishes to honor, and let him[a] conduct the man on horseback through the open square of the city, proclaiming before him: 'Thus shall it be done for the man whom the king wishes to honor.' " [10]Then the king said to Haman, "Quickly, take the robes and the horse, as you have said, and do so to the Jew Mordecai who sits at the king's gate. Leave out nothing that you have mentioned." [11]So Haman took the robes and the horse and robed Mordecai and led him riding through the open square of the city, proclaiming, "Thus shall it be done for the man whom the king wishes to honor."

[12]Then Mordecai returned to the king's gate, but Haman hurried to his house, mourning and with his head covered. [13]When Haman told his wife Zeresh and all his friends everything that had happened to him, his advisers and his wife Zeresh said to him, "If Mordecai, before whom your downfall has begun, is of the Jewish people, you will not prevail against him, but will surely fall before him."

HAMAN'S DOWNFALL AND MORDECAI'S ADVANCEMENT

[14]While they were still talking with him, the king's eunuchs arrived and hurried Haman off to the banquet that Esther had prepared. **7** [1]So the king and Haman went in to feast with Queen Esther. [2]On the second day, as they were drinking wine, the king again said to Esther, "What is your petition, Queen Esther? It shall be granted you. And what is your request? Even to the half of my kingdom, it shall be fulfilled." [3]Then Queen Esther answered, "If I have won your favor, O king, and if it pleases the king, let my life be given me—that is my petition—and the lives of my people—that is my request. [4]For we have been sold, I and my people, to be destroyed, to be killed, and to be annihilated. If we had been sold merely as slaves, men and women, I would have held my peace; but

PONDER

"If I have won your favor, O king, and if it pleases the king, let my life be given me—that is my petition—and the lives of my people—that is my request." —Esther 7.3

PRAY

O Father, these Biblical characters were courageous in defending your people. Help us to learn this lesson for ourselves, to be courageous in standing firm in our faith, defending it and your people, the church, from those who seek to destroy them. And when we have a question about your will, we know we have access to you through your Son Jesus and the Holy Spirit who teaches us justice, humility, service to others, forgiveness, compassion and love. Implant those characteristics in our hearts as we go about the tasks you give us. We ask in the name of Jesus. Amen.

no enemy can compensate for this damage to the king."[b] [5]Then King Ahasuerus said to Queen Esther, "Who is he, and where is he, who has presumed to do this?" [6]Esther said, "A foe and enemy, this wicked Haman!" Then Haman was terrified before the king and the queen. [7]The king rose from the feast in wrath and went into the palace garden, but Haman stayed to beg his life from Queen Esther, for he saw that the king had determined to destroy him. [8]When the king returned from the palace garden to the banquet hall, Haman had thrown himself on the couch where Esther was reclining; and the king said, "Will he even assault the queen in my presence, in my own house?" As the words left the mouth of the king, they covered

[a] 6.9 Heb *them* [b] 7.4 Meaning of Heb uncertain

Haman's face. 9Then Harbona, one of the eunuchs in attendance on the king, said, "Look, the very gallows that Haman has prepared for Mordecai, whose word saved the king, stands at Haman's house, fifty cubits high." And the king said, "Hang him on that." 10So they hanged Haman on the gallows that he had prepared for Mordecai. Then the anger of the king abated.

8 On that day King Ahasuerus gave to Queen Esther the house of Haman, the enemy of the Jews; and Mordecai came before the king, for Esther had told what he was to her. 2Then the king took off his signet ring, which he had taken from Haman, and gave it to Mordecai. So Esther set Mordecai over the house of Haman.

ESTHER SAVES THE JEWS

3 Then Esther spoke again to the king; she fell at his feet, weeping and pleading with him to avert the evil design of Haman the Agagite and the plot that he had devised against the Jews. 4The king held out the golden scepter to Esther, 5and Esther rose and stood before the king. She said, "If it pleases the king, and if I have won his favor, and if the thing seems right before the king, and I have his approval, let an order be written to revoke the letters devised by Haman son of Hammedatha the Agagite, which he wrote giving orders to destroy the Jews who are in all the provinces of the king. 6For how can I bear to see the calamity that is coming on my people? Or how can I bear to see the destruction of my kindred?" 7Then King Ahasuerus said to Queen Esther and to the Jew Mordecai, "See, I have given Esther the house of Haman, and they have hanged him on the gallows, because he plotted to lay hands on the Jews. 8You may write as you please with regard to the Jews, in the name of the king, and seal it with the king's ring; for an edict written in the name of the king and sealed with the king's ring cannot be revoked."

9 The king's secretaries were summoned at that time, in the third month, which is the month of Sivan, on the twenty-third day; and an edict was written, according to all that Mordecai commanded, to the Jews and to the satraps and the governors and the officials of the provinces from India to Ethiopia,ª one hundred twenty-seven provinces, to every province in its own script and to every people in its own language, and also to the Jews in their script and their language. 10He wrote letters in the name of King Ahasuerus, sealed them with the king's ring, and sent them by mounted couriers riding on fast steeds bred from the royal herd.ᵇ 11By these letters the king allowed the Jews who were in every city to assemble and defend their lives, to destroy, to kill, and to annihilate any armed force of any people or province that might attack them, with their children and women, and to plunder their goods 12on a single day throughout all the provinces of King Ahasuerus, on the thirteenth day of the twelfth month, which is the month of Adar. 13A copy of the writ was to be issued as a decree in every province and published to all peoples, and the Jews were to be ready on that day to take revenge on their enemies. 14So the couriers, mounted on their swift royal steeds, hurried out, urged by the king's command. The decree was issued in the citadel of Susa.

15 Then Mordecai went out from the presence of the king, wearing royal robes of blue and white, with a great golden crown and a mantle of fine linen and purple, while the city of Susa shouted and rejoiced. 16For the Jews there was light and gladness, joy and honor. 17In every province and in every city, wherever the king's command and his edict came, there was gladness and joy among the Jews, a festival and a holiday. Furthermore, many of the peoples of the country professed to be Jews, because the fear of the Jews had fallen upon them.

ª 8.9 Or Nubia; Heb Cush   ᵇ 8.10 Meaning of Heb uncertain

DESTRUCTION OF THE ENEMIES OF THE JEWS

9 Now in the twelfth month, which is the month of Adar, on the thirteenth day, when the king's command and edict were about to be executed, on the very day when the enemies of the Jews hoped to gain power over them, but which had been changed to a day when the Jews would gain power over their foes, ²the Jews gathered in their cities throughout all the provinces of King Ahasuerus to lay hands on those who had sought their ruin; and no one could withstand them, because the fear of them had fallen upon all peoples. ³All the officials of the provinces, the satraps and the governors, and the royal officials were supporting the Jews, because the fear of Mordecai had fallen upon them. ⁴For Mordecai was powerful in the king's house, and his fame spread throughout all the provinces as the man Mordecai grew more and more powerful. ⁵So the Jews struck down all their enemies with the sword, slaughtering, and destroying them, and did as they pleased to those who hated them. ⁶In the citadel of Susa the Jews killed and destroyed five hundred people. ⁷They killed Parshandatha, Dalphon, Aspatha, ⁸Poratha, Adalia, Aridatha, ⁹Parmashta, Arisai, Aridai, Vaizatha, ¹⁰the ten sons of Haman son of Hammedatha, the enemy of the Jews; but they did not touch the plunder.

11 That very day the number of those killed in the citadel of Susa was reported to the king. ¹²The king said to Queen Esther, "In the citadel of Susa the Jews have killed five hundred people and also the ten sons of Haman. What have they done in the rest of the king's provinces? Now what is your petition? It shall be granted you. And what further is your request? It shall be fulfilled." ¹³Esther said, "If it pleases the king, let the Jews who are in Susa be allowed tomorrow also to do according to this day's edict, and let the ten sons of Haman be hanged on the gallows." ¹⁴So the king commanded this to be done; a decree was issued in Susa, and the ten sons of Haman were hanged. ¹⁵The Jews who were in Susa gathered also on the fourteenth day of the month of Adar and they killed three hundred persons in Susa; but they did not touch the plunder.

16 Now the other Jews who were in the king's provinces also gathered to defend their lives, and gained relief from their enemies, and killed seventy-five thousand of those who hated them; but they laid no hands on the plunder. ¹⁷This was on the thirteenth day of the month of Adar, and on the fourteenth day they rested and made that a day of feasting and gladness.

THE FEAST OF PURIM INAUGURATED

18 But the Jews who were in Susa gathered on the thirteenth day and on the fourteenth, and rested on the fifteenth day, making that a day of feasting and gladness. ¹⁹Therefore the Jews of the villages, who live in the open towns, hold the fourteenth day of the month of Adar as a day for gladness and feasting, a holiday on which they send gifts of food to one another.

20 Mordecai recorded these things, and sent letters to all the Jews who were in all the provinces of King Ahasuerus, both near and far, ²¹enjoining them that they should keep the fourteenth day of the month Adar and also the fifteenth day of the same month, year by year, ²²as the days on which the Jews gained relief from their enemies, and as the month that had been turned for them from sorrow into gladness and from mourning into a holiday; that they should make them days of feasting and gladness, days for sending gifts of food to one another and presents to the poor. ²³So the Jews adopted as a custom what they had begun to do, as Mordecai had written to them.

24 Haman son of Hammedatha the Agagite, the enemy of all the Jews, had plotted against the Jews to destroy them, and had cast Pur—that is "the lot"—to crush and de-

stroy them; 25but when Esther came before the king, he gave orders in writing that the wicked plot that he had devised against the Jews should come upon his own head, and that he and his sons should be hanged on the gallows. 26Therefore these days are called Purim, from the word Pur. Thus because of all that was written in this letter, and of what they had faced in this matter, and of what had happened to them, 27the Jews established and accepted as a custom for themselves and their descendants and all who joined them, that without fail they would continue to observe these two days every year, as it was written and at the time appointed. 28These days should be remembered and kept throughout every generation, in every family, province, and city; and these days of Purim should never fall into disuse among the Jews, nor should the commemoration of these days cease among their descendants.

29 Queen Esther daughter of Abihail, along with the Jew Mordecai, gave full written authority, confirming this second letter about Purim.

30Letters were sent wishing peace and security to all the Jews, to the one hundred twenty-seven provinces of the kingdom of Ahasuerus, 31and giving orders that these days of Purim should be observed at their appointed seasons, as the Jew Mordecai and Queen Esther enjoined on the Jews, just as they had laid down for themselves and for their descendants regulations concerning their fasts and their lamentations. 32The command of Queen Esther fixed these practices of Purim, and it was recorded in writing.

10 King Ahasuerus laid tribute on the land and on the islands of the sea. 2All the acts of his power and might, and the full account of the high honor of Mordecai, to which the king advanced him, are they not written in the annals of the kings of Media and Persia? 3For Mordecai the Jew was next in rank to King Ahasuerus, and he was powerful among the Jews and popular with his many kindred, for he sought the good of his people and interceded for the welfare of all his descendants.

JOB

Where is God when we hurt? Why would a wise, just, loving God allow suffering to stalk a man who seemed to do all the right things? Because Job lost everything—wealth, family and health—he wondered about these same questions and struggled to make sense of his own misery in the light of God's justice. But after the crying, the reasoning and the questioning, he still trusted God. Although we may never fully understand Job's suffering or our own, God is always in control. And God restored Job's health, blessed him materially and gave him a new family.

JOB AND HIS FAMILY

1 There was once a man in the land of Uz whose name was Job. That man was blameless and upright, one who feared God and turned away from evil. ²There were born to him seven sons and three daughters. ³He had seven thousand sheep, three thousand camels, five hundred yoke of oxen, five hundred donkeys, and very many servants; so that this man was the greatest of all the people of the east. ⁴His sons used to go and hold feasts in one another's houses in turn; and they would send and invite their three sisters to eat and drink with them. ⁵And when the feast days had run their course, Job would send and sanctify them, and he would rise early in the morning and offer burnt offerings according to the number of them all; for Job said, "It may be that my children have sinned, and cursed God in their hearts." This is what Job always did.

ATTACK ON JOB'S CHARACTER

6 One day the heavenly beings[a] came to present themselves before the LORD, and Satan[b] also came among them. ⁷The LORD said to Satan,[b] "Where have you come from?" Satan[b] answered the LORD, "From going to and fro on the earth, and from walking up and down on it." ⁸The LORD said to Satan,[b] "Have you considered my servant Job? There is no one like him on the earth, a blameless and upright man who fears God and turns away from evil." ⁹Then Satan[b] answered the LORD, "Does Job fear God for nothing? ¹⁰Have you not put a fence around him and his house and all that he has, on every side? You have blessed the work of his hands, and his possessions have increased in the land. ¹¹But stretch out your hand now, and touch all that he has, and he will curse you to your face." ¹²The LORD said to Satan,[b] "Very well, all that he has is in your power; only do not stretch out your hand against him!" So Satan[b] went out from the presence of the LORD.

JOB LOSES PROPERTY AND CHILDREN

13 One day when his sons and daughters were eating and drinking wine in the eldest brother's house, ¹⁴a messenger came to Job and said, "The oxen were plowing and the donkeys were feeding beside them, ¹⁵and the Sabeans fell on them and carried them off, and killed the servants with the edge of the sword; I alone have escaped to tell you." ¹⁶While he was still speaking, another came and said, "The fire of God fell from heaven and burned up the sheep and the servants, and consumed them; I alone have escaped to tell you." ¹⁷While he was still speaking, another came and said, "The Chaldeans formed three columns, made a raid on the camels and carried them off, and killed the servants with the edge of the sword; I alone have escaped to tell you." ¹⁸While he was still speaking, another came and said, "Your sons and daughters were eating and drinking wine in their eldest brother's house, ¹⁹and suddenly a great wind came across the desert, struck the four corners of the house, and it fell on the young people, and they are dead; I alone have escaped to tell you."

20 Then Job arose, tore his robe, shaved his head, and fell on the ground and worshiped. ²¹He said, "Naked I came from my mother's womb, and naked shall I return there; the LORD gave, and the LORD has taken away; blessed be the name of the LORD."

22 In all this Job did not sin or charge God with wrongdoing.

ATTACK ON JOB'S HEALTH

2 One day the heavenly beings[a] came to present themselves before the LORD, and Satan[b] also came among them to present himself before the LORD. ²The LORD said to Satan,[b] "Where have you come from?" Satan[b] answered the LORD, "From going to and fro on the earth, and from walking up and down on it." ³The LORD said to Satan,[b] "Have you

[a] 1.6; 2.1 Heb *sons of God*   [b] 1.6,7,8,9,12; 2.1,2,3 Or *the Accuser*; Heb *ha-satan*

considered my servant Job? There is no one like him on the earth, a blameless and upright man who fears God and turns away from evil. He still persists in his integrity, although you incited me against him, to destroy him for no reason." ⁴Then Satanᵃ answered the LORD, "Skin for skin! All that people have they will give to save their lives.ᵇ ⁵But stretch out your hand now and touch his bone and his flesh, and he will curse you to your face." ⁶The LORD said to Satan,ᵃ "Very well, he is in your power; only spare his life."

⁷ So Satanᵃ went out from the presence of the LORD, and inflicted loathsome sores on Job from the sole of his foot to the crown of his head. ⁸Jobᶜ took a potsherd with which to scrape himself, and sat among the ashes.

⁹ Then his wife said to him, "Do you still persist in your integrity? Curseᵈ God, and die." ¹⁰But he said to her, "You speak as any foolish woman would speak. Shall we receive the good at the hand of God, and not receive the bad?" In all this Job did not sin with his lips.

JOB'S THREE FRIENDS

¹¹ Now when Job's three friends heard of all these troubles that had come upon him, each of them set out from his home—Eliphaz the Teman-

---

PONDER

The LORD said to Satan, "Have you considered my servant Job? There is no one like him on the earth, a blameless and upright man who fears God and turns away from evil. He still persists in his integrity, although you incited me against him, to destroy him for no reason."
—Job 2.3

PRAY

Lord, sometimes we have to think deeply, not only to comprehend the depth of Job's sufferings, but also to realize the depth of the relationship this admirable man had with you. We are thankful for his loyalty and his fidelity to you, and we pray that we might realize that, though we all have ups and downs, the goal of our lives is to worship you and ultimately serve you and Jesus Christ, our Savior, and gratefully receive the blessings of faith in him. In his name we pray. Amen.

ᵃ **2.4,6,7** Or *the Accuser*; Heb *ha-satan*
ᵇ **2.4** Or *All that the man has he will give for his life*   ᶜ **2.8** Heb *He*   ᵈ **2.9** Heb *Bless*

BIBLE IN LIFE

Praising God When It Hurts   *Job 1.20–22*

How do we respond to hardship? When we are afflicted with great hardship, we tend to blame God. *Why did God let this happen to me? Why does God allow tragedy to strike innocent people? Why does God permit sin?* God is indeed sovereign over all things and able to prevent evil and even to change people's hearts. At the same time, however, God has granted freedom to human beings to think and act as they will. Ever since sin entered the world through Adam and Eve, tragedy and hardship have afflicted people, who respond in different ways. Some are driven away from God because they see an all-powerful being who does not care enough to stop the suffering of innocent people. Others respond by clinging to God as a constant source of compassion, love, mercy and forgiveness. Whether we are experiencing blessing or suffering, our response should be like Job's—we should praise God for all we have been given, including our very lives. We must not believe that God is somehow being unloving toward us or wronging us by what has been allowed to come into our lives. God always loves us. But often, like Job, we cannot understand all that God is doing behind the scenes of our experiences.

ite, Bildad the Shuhite, and Zophar the Naamathite. They met together to go and console and comfort him. ¹²When they saw him from a distance, they did not recognize him, and they raised their voices and wept aloud; they tore their robes and threw dust in the air upon their heads. ¹³They sat with him on the ground seven days and seven nights, and no one spoke a word to him, for they saw that his suffering was very great.

JOB CURSES THE DAY
HE WAS BORN

3 After this Job opened his mouth and cursed the day of his birth. ²Job said:

³ "Let the day perish in which
    I was born,
  and the night that said,
    'A man-child is conceived.'
⁴ Let that day be darkness!
  May God above not seek it,
  or light shine on it.
⁵ Let gloom and deep
    darkness claim it.
  Let clouds settle upon it;
  let the blackness of the
    day terrify it.
⁶ That night—let thick
    darkness seize it!
  let it not rejoice among the
    days of the year;
  let it not come into the
    number of the months.
⁷ Yes, let that night be barren;
  let no joyful cry be heard^a in it.
⁸ Let those curse it who
    curse the Sea,^b
  those who are skilled to
    rouse up Leviathan.
⁹ Let the stars of its dawn be dark;
  let it hope for light, but
    have none;
  may it not see the eyelids
    of the morning—
¹⁰ because it did not shut the doors
    of my mother's womb,
  and hide trouble from my eyes.

¹¹ "Why did I not die at birth,
  come forth from the
    womb and expire?
¹² Why were there knees to
    receive me,
  or breasts for me to suck?

¹³ Now I would be lying
    down and quiet;
  I would be asleep; then I
    would be at rest
¹⁴ with kings and counselors
    of the earth
  who rebuild ruins for
    themselves,
¹⁵ or with princes who have gold,
  who fill their houses
    with silver.
¹⁶ Or why was I not buried like
    a stillborn child,
  like an infant that never
    sees the light?
¹⁷ There the wicked cease
    from troubling,
  and there the weary are at rest.
¹⁸ There the prisoners are at
    ease together;
  they do not hear the voice
    of the taskmaster.
¹⁹ The small and the great are there,
  and the slaves are free
    from their masters.

OUR THEOLOGY SHOULD

ACKNOWLEDGE THAT THE

RIGHTEOUS CAN SUFFER.

²⁰ "Why is light given to
    one in misery,
  and life to the bitter in soul,
²¹ who long for death, but it
    does not come,
  and dig for it more than for
    hidden treasures;
²² who rejoice exceedingly,
  and are glad when they
    find the grave?
²³ Why is light given to one who
    cannot see the way,
  whom God has fenced in?
²⁴ For my sighing comes
    like^c my bread,
  and my groanings are
    poured out like water.

^a 3.7 Heb *come* ^b 3.8 Cn: Heb *day*
^c 3.24 Heb *before*

25 Truly the thing that I fear
        comes upon me,
    and what I dread befalls me.
26 I am not at ease, nor am I quiet;
    I have no rest; but
        trouble comes."

ELIPHAZ SPEAKS: JOB HAS SINNED

4 Then Eliphaz the Temanite answered:
2 "If one ventures a word with you,
        will you be offended?
    But who can keep from
        speaking?
3 See, you have instructed many;
    you have strengthened
        the weak hands.
4 Your words have supported those
        who were stumbling,
    and you have made firm
        the feeble knees.
5 But now it has come to you,
        and you are impatient;
    it touches you, and you
        are dismayed.
6 Is not your fear of God your
        confidence,
    and the integrity of your
        ways your hope?

7 "Think now, who that was
        innocent ever perished?
    Or where were the
        upright cut off?
8 As I have seen, those who
        plow iniquity
    and sow trouble reap the same.
9 By the breath of God they perish,
    and by the blast of his anger
        they are consumed.
10 The roar of the lion, the voice
        of the fierce lion,
    and the teeth of the young
        lions are broken.
11 The strong lion perishes
        for lack of prey,
    and the whelps of the
        lioness are scattered.

12 "Now a word came stealing to me,
    my ear received the
        whisper of it.
13 Amid thoughts from visions
        of the night,
    when deep sleep falls
        on mortals,

14 dread came upon me, and
        trembling,
    which made all my
        bones shake.
15 A spirit glided past my face;
    the hair of my flesh bristled.
16 It stood still,
    but I could not discern
        its appearance.
    A form was before my eyes;
        there was silence, then
    I heard a voice:
17 'Can mortals be righteous
        before[a] God?
    Can human beings be pure
        before[a] their Maker?
18 Even in his servants he
        puts no trust,
    and his angels he charges
        with error;
19 how much more those who
        live in houses of clay,
    whose foundation is
        in the dust,
    who are crushed like a moth.
20 Between morning and evening
        they are destroyed;
    they perish forever without
        any regarding it.
21 Their tent-cord is plucked
        up within them,
    and they die devoid of wisdom.'

JOB IS CORRECTED BY GOD

5 "Call now; is there anyone
        who will answer you?
    To which of the holy ones
        will you turn?
2 Surely vexation kills the fool,
    and jealousy slays the simple.
3 I have seen fools taking root,
    but suddenly I cursed
        their dwelling.
4 Their children are far from safety,
    they are crushed in the gate,
    and there is no one to
        deliver them.
5 The hungry eat their harvest,
    and they take it even out
        of the thorns;[b]
    and the thirsty[c] pant after
        their wealth.

---

a 4.17 Or more than   b 5.5 Meaning of Heb
uncertain   c 5.5 Aquila Symmachus Syr Vg:
Heb snare

6 For misery does not come
  from the earth,
  nor does trouble sprout
  from the ground;
7 but human beings are
  born to trouble
  just as sparks[a] fly upward.

8 "As for me, I would seek God,
  and to God I would
  commit my cause.
9 He does great things and
  unsearchable,
  marvelous things
  without number.
10 He gives rain on the earth
  and sends waters on the fields;
11 he sets on high those who
  are lowly,
  and those who mourn are
  lifted to safety.
12 He frustrates the devices
  of the crafty,
  so that their hands achieve
  no success.
13 He takes the wise in their
  own craftiness;
  and the schemes of the wily are
  brought to a quick end.
14 They meet with darkness
  in the daytime,
  and grope at noonday
  as in the night.
15 But he saves the needy from the
  sword of their mouth,
  from the hand of the mighty.
16 So the poor have hope,
  and injustice shuts its mouth.

17 "How happy is the one whom
  God reproves;
  therefore do not despise the
  discipline of the Almighty.[b]
18 For he wounds, but he binds up;
  he strikes, but his hands heal.
19 He will deliver you from
  six troubles;
  in seven no harm shall
  touch you.
20 In famine he will redeem
  you from death,
  and in war from the power
  of the sword.
21 You shall be hidden from the
  scourge of the tongue,
  and shall not fear destruction
  when it comes.

22 At destruction and famine
  you shall laugh,
  and shall not fear the wild
  animals of the earth.
23 For you shall be in league with
  the stones of the field,
  and the wild animals shall
  be at peace with you.
24 You shall know that your
  tent is safe,
  you shall inspect your fold
  and miss nothing.
25 You shall know that your
  descendants will be many,
  and your offspring like the
  grass of the earth.
26 You shall come to your grave
  in ripe old age,
  as a shock of grain comes
  up to the threshing
  floor in its season.
27 See, we have searched this
  out; it is true.
  Hear, and know it for yourself."

JOB REPLIES: MY COMPLAINT IS JUST

6 Then Job answered:
2 "O that my vexation
  were weighed,
  and all my calamity laid
  in the balances!
3 For then it would be heavier
  than the sand of the sea;
  therefore my words
  have been rash.
4 For the arrows of the
  Almighty[b] are in me;
  my spirit drinks their poison;
  the terrors of God are
  arrayed against me.
5 Does the wild ass bray
  over its grass,
  or the ox low over its fodder?
6 Can that which is tasteless be
  eaten without salt,
  or is there any flavor in the
  juice of mallows?[c]
7 My appetite refuses to
  touch them;
  they are like food that is
  loathsome to me.[c]

---

a 5.7 Or *birds*; Heb *sons of Resheph*
b 5.17; 6.4 Traditional rendering of Heb
Shaddai   c 6.6,7 Meaning of Heb uncertain

8 "O that I might have
      my request,
   and that God would
      grant my desire;
9 that it would please God
      to crush me,
   that he would let loose his
      hand and cut me off!
10 This would be my consolation;
   I would even exult[a] in
      unrelenting pain;
   for I have not denied the
      words of the Holy One.
11 What is my strength, that
      I should wait?
   And what is my end, that
      I should be patient?
12 Is my strength the strength
      of stones,
   or is my flesh bronze?
13 In truth I have no help in me,
   and any resource is
      driven from me.

14 "Those who withhold[b] kindness
      from a friend
   forsake the fear of the
      Almighty.[c]
15 My companions are treacherous
      like a torrent-bed,
   like freshets that pass away,
16 that run dark with ice,
   turbid with melting snow.
17 In time of heat they disappear;
   when it is hot, they vanish
      from their place.
18 The caravans turn aside
      from their course;
   they go up into the waste,
      and perish.
19 The caravans of Tema look,
   the travelers of Sheba hope.
20 They are disappointed because
      they were confident;
   they come there and are
      confounded.
21 Such you have now
      become to me;[d]
   you see my calamity,
      and are afraid.
22 Have I said, 'Make me a gift'?
   Or, 'From your wealth offer
      a bribe for me'?
23 Or, 'Save me from an
      opponent's hand'?
   Or, 'Ransom me from the
      hand of oppressors'?

24 "Teach me, and I will be silent;
   make me understand how
      I have gone wrong.
25 How forceful are honest words!
   But your reproof, what
      does it reprove?
26 Do you think that you can
      reprove words,
   as if the speech of the
      desperate were wind?
27 You would even cast lots
      over the orphan,
   and bargain over your friend.

28 "But now, be pleased to
      look at me;
   for I will not lie to your face.
29 Turn, I pray, let no wrong
      be done.
   Turn now, my vindication
      is at stake.
30 Is there any wrong on my tongue?
   Cannot my taste discern
      calamity?

JOB: MY SUFFERING IS WITHOUT END

7 "Do not human beings have a
      hard service on earth,
   and are not their days like
      the days of a laborer?
2 Like a slave who longs for
      the shadow,
   and like laborers who look
      for their wages,
3 so I am allotted months
      of emptiness,
   and nights of misery are
      apportioned to me.
4 When I lie down I say, 'When
      shall I rise?'
   But the night is long,
   and I am full of tossing
      until dawn.
5 My flesh is clothed with
      worms and dirt;
   my skin hardens, then
      breaks out again.
6 My days are swifter than a
      weaver's shuttle,
   and come to their end
      without hope.[e]

a 6.10 Meaning of Heb uncertain b 6.14 Syr
Vg Compare Tg: Meaning of Heb uncertain
c 6.14 Traditional rendering of Heb Shaddai
d 6.21 Cn Compare Gk Syr: Meaning of Heb
uncertain e 7.6 Or as the thread runs out

7 "Remember that my life
is a breath;
my eye will never again
see good.
8 The eye that beholds me will
see me no more;
while your eyes are upon
me, I shall be gone.
9 As the cloud fades and vanishes,
so those who go down to
Sheol do not come up;
10 they return no more to
their houses,
nor do their places know
them any more.

11 "Therefore I will not restrain
my mouth;
I will speak in the anguish
of my spirit;
I will complain in the
bitterness of my soul.
12 Am I the Sea, or the Dragon,
that you set a guard over me?
13 When I say, 'My bed will
comfort me,
my couch will ease my
complaint,'
14 then you scare me with dreams
and terrify me with visions,
15 so that I would
choose strangling
and death rather than
this body.
16 I loathe my life; I would
not live forever.
Let me alone, for my days
are a breath.
17 What are human beings, that you
make so much of them,
that you set your mind
on them,
18 visit them every morning,
test them every moment?
19 Will you not look away from
me for a while,
let me alone until I swallow
my spittle?
20 If I sin, what do I do to you, you
watcher of humanity?
Why have you made me
your target?
Why have I become a
burden to you?
21 Why do you not pardon my
transgression
and take away my iniquity?

For now I shall lie in the earth;
you will seek me, but I
shall not be."

BILDAD SPEAKS: JOB SHOULD REPENT

8 Then Bildad the Shuhite answered:
2 "How long will you say
these things,
and the words of your mouth
be a great wind?
3 Does God pervert justice?
Or does the Almighty[a]
pervert the right?
4 If your children sinned
against him,
he delivered them into
the power of their
transgression.
5 If you will seek God
and make supplication
to the Almighty,[a]
6 if you are pure and upright,
surely then he will rouse
himself for you
and restore to you your
rightful place.
7 Though your beginning
was small,
your latter days will be
very great.

8 "For inquire now of bygone
generations,
and consider what their
ancestors have found;
9 for we are but of yesterday, and
we know nothing,
for our days on earth are
but a shadow.
10 Will they not teach you
and tell you
and utter words out of their
understanding?

11 "Can papyrus grow where
there is no marsh?
Can reeds flourish where
there is no water?
12 While yet in flower and
not cut down,
they wither before any
other plant.

---

a 8.3,5 Traditional rendering of Heb *Shaddai*

13 Such are the paths of all
who forget God;
the hope of the godless
shall perish.
14 Their confidence is gossamer,
a spider's house their trust.
15 If one leans against its house,
it will not stand;
if one lays hold of it, it
will not endure.
16 The wicked thrive[a] before the sun,
and their shoots spread
over the garden.
17 Their roots twine around
the stoneheap;
they live among the rocks.[b]
18 If they are destroyed from
their place,
then it will deny them, saying,
'I have never seen you.'
19 See, these are their happy ways,[c]
and out of the earth still
others will spring.

20 "See, God will not reject a
blameless person,
nor take the hand of evildoers.
21 He will yet fill your mouth
with laughter,
and your lips with
shouts of joy.
22 Those who hate you will be
clothed with shame,
and the tent of the wicked
will be no more."

JOB REPLIES: THERE IS NO MEDIATOR

9 Then Job answered:
2 "Indeed I know that this is so;
but how can a mortal be
just before God?
3 If one wished to contend
with him,
one could not answer him
once in a thousand.
4 He is wise in heart, and
mighty in strength
—who has resisted him,
and succeeded?—
5 he who removes mountains, and
they do not know it,
when he overturns them
in his anger;
6 who shakes the earth out
of its place,
and its pillars tremble;

7 who commands the sun, and
it does not rise;
who seals up the stars;
8 who alone stretched out
the heavens
and trampled the waves
of the Sea;[d]
9 who made the Bear and Orion,
the Pleiades and the
chambers of the south;
10 who does great things beyond
understanding,
and marvelous things
without number.
11 Look, he passes by me, and
I do not see him;
he moves on, but I do not
perceive him.
12 He snatches away; who
can stop him?
Who will say to him, 'What
are you doing?'
13 "God will not turn back his anger;
the helpers of Rahab bowed
beneath him.
14 How then can I answer him,
choosing my words with him?
15 Though I am innocent, I
cannot answer him;
I must appeal for mercy
to my accuser.[e]
16 If I summoned him and he
answered me,
I do not believe that he would
listen to my voice.
17 For he crushes me with
a tempest,
and multiplies my wounds
without cause;
18 he will not let me get my breath,
but fills me with bitterness.
19 If it is a contest of strength,
he is the strong one!
If it is a matter of justice, who
can summon him?[f]
20 Though I am innocent, my
own mouth would
condemn me;
though I am blameless, he
would prove me perverse.

[a] 8.16 Heb He thrives   [b] 8.17 Gk Vg:
Meaning of Heb uncertain   [c] 8.19 Meaning
of Heb uncertain   [d] 9.8 Or trampled the
back of the sea dragon   [e] 9.15 Or for my
right   [f] 9.19 Compare Gk: Heb me

21 I am blameless; I do not
know myself;
I loathe my life.
22 It is all one; therefore I say,
he destroys both the blameless
and the wicked.
23 When disaster brings
sudden death,
he mocks at the calamity[a]
of the innocent.
24 The earth is given into the
hand of the wicked;
he covers the eyes of its judges—
if it is not he, who then is it?

25 "My days are swifter than
a runner;
they flee away, they see no good.
26 They go by like skiffs of reed,
like an eagle swooping
on the prey.
27 If I say, 'I will forget my complaint;
I will put off my sad
countenance and be
of good cheer,'
28 I become afraid of all my suffering,
for I know you will not
hold me innocent.
29 I shall be condemned;
why then do I labor in vain?
30 If I wash myself with soap
and cleanse my hands with lye,
31 yet you will plunge me into filth,
and my own clothes
will abhor me.
32 For he is not a mortal, as I am,
that I might answer him,
that we should come to
trial together.
33 There is no umpire[b] between us,
who might lay his hand
on us both.
34 If he would take his rod
away from me,
and not let dread of him
terrify me,
35 then I would speak without
fear of him,
for I know I am not what I
am thought to be.[c]

JOB: I LOATHE MY LIFE

10 "I loathe my life;
I will give free utterance
to my complaint;
I will speak in the bitterness
of my soul.

2 I will say to God, Do not
condemn me;
let me know why you
contend against me.
3 Does it seem good to you
to oppress,
to despise the work of
your hands
and favor the schemes
of the wicked?
4 Do you have eyes of flesh?
Do you see as humans see?
5 Are your days like the days
of mortals,
or your years like human years,
6 that you seek out my iniquity
and search for my sin,
7 although you know that I
am not guilty,
and there is no one to deliver
out of your hand?
8 Your hands fashioned
and made me;
and now you turn and
destroy me.[d]
9 Remember that you fashioned
me like clay;
and will you turn me
to dust again?
10 Did you not pour me out like milk
and curdle me like cheese?
11 You clothed me with skin
and flesh,
and knit me together with
bones and sinews.
12 You have granted me life
and steadfast love,
and your care has preserved
my spirit.
13 Yet these things you hid
in your heart;
I know that this was
your purpose.
14 If I sin, you watch me,
and do not acquit me
of my iniquity.
15 If I am wicked, woe to me!
If I am righteous, I cannot
lift up my head,
for I am filled with disgrace
and look upon my affliction.

[a] 9.23 Meaning of Heb uncertain
[b] 9.33 Another reading is *Would that there
were an umpire*   [c] 9.35 Cn: Heb *for I am
not so in myself*   [d] 10.8 Cn Compare Gk
Syr: Heb *made me together all around, and
you destroy me*

16 Bold as a lion you hunt me;
    you repeat your exploits
        against me.
17 You renew your witnesses
        against me,
    and increase your vexation
        toward me;
    you bring fresh troops
        against me.ᵃ

18 "Why did you bring me forth
        from the womb?
    Would that I had died before
        any eye had seen me,
19 and were as though I had not been,
    carried from the womb
        to the grave.
20 Are not the days of my life few?ᵇ
    Let me alone, that I may
        find a little comfortᶜ
21 before I go, never to return,
    to the land of gloom and
        deep darkness,
22 the land of gloomᵈ and chaos,
    where light is like darkness."

ZOPHAR SPEAKS: JOB'S GUILT DESERVES PUNISHMENT

11 Then Zophar the Naama-
    thite answered:
2 "Should a multitude of words
        go unanswered,
    and should one full of talk
        be vindicated?
3 Should your babble put
        others to silence,
    and when you mock, shall
        no one shame you?
4 For you say, 'My conductᵉ is pure,
    and I am clean in God'sᶠ sight.'
5 But O that God would speak,
    and open his lips to you,
6 and that he would tell you the
        secrets of wisdom!
    For wisdom is many-sided.ᵍ
    Know then that God exacts
        of you less than your
        guilt deserves.

7 "Can you find out the deep
        things of God?
    Can you find out the limit
        of the Almighty?ʰ
8 It is higher than heavenⁱ—what
        can you do?
    Deeper than Sheol—what
        can you know?

9 Its measure is longer than
        the earth,
    and broader than the sea.
10 If he passes through, and
        imprisons,
    and assembles for judgment,
        who can hinder him?
11 For he knows those who
        are worthless;
    when he sees iniquity, will
        he not consider it?
12 But a stupid person will get
        understanding,
    when a wild ass is
        born human.ᵍ

13 "If you direct your heart rightly,
    you will stretch out your
        hands toward him.
14 If iniquity is in your hand,
        put it far away,
    and do not let wickedness
        reside in your tents.
15 Surely then you will lift up your
        face without blemish;
    you will be secure, and
        will not fear.
16 You will forget your misery;
    you will remember it as waters
        that have passed away.
17 And your life will be brighter
        than the noonday;
    its darkness will be like
        the morning.
18 And you will have confidence,
        because there is hope;
    you will be protectedʲ and
        take your rest in safety.
19 You will lie down, and no one
        will make you afraid;
    many will entreat your favor.
20 But the eyes of the wicked
        will fail;
    all way of escape will be
        lost to them,
    and their hope is to
        breathe their last."

ᵃ 10.17 Cn Compare Gk: Heb *toward me; changes and a troop are with me* ᵇ 10.20 Cn Compare Gk Syr: Heb *Are not my days few? Let him cease!* ᶜ 10.20 Heb *that I may brighten up a little* ᵈ 10.22 Heb *gloom as darkness, deep darkness* ᵉ 11.4 Gk: Heb *teaching* ᶠ 11.4 Heb *your* ᵍ 11.6,12 Meaning of Heb uncertain ʰ 11.7 Traditional rendering of Heb *Shaddai* ⁱ 11.8 Heb *The heights of heaven* ʲ 11.18 Or *you will look around*

JOB REPLIES: I AM A LAUGHINGSTOCK

12 Then Job answered:
² "No doubt you are
the people,
and wisdom will die with you.
³ But I have understanding
as well as you;
I am not inferior to you.
Who does not know such
things as these?
⁴ I am a laughingstock to
my friends;
I, who called upon God and
he answered me,
a just and blameless man, I
am a laughingstock.
⁵ Those at ease have contempt
for misfortune,ᵃ
but it is ready for those whose
feet are unstable.
⁶ The tents of robbers are at peace,
and those who provoke
God are secure,
who bring their god in
their hands.ᵇ

⁷ "But ask the animals, and
they will teach you;
the birds of the air, and
they will tell you;
⁸ ask the plants of the earth,ᶜ and
they will teach you;
and the fish of the sea will
declare to you.
⁹ Who among all these does
not know
that the hand of the LORD
has done this?
¹⁰ In his hand is the life of
every living thing
and the breath of every
human being.
¹¹ Does not the ear test words
as the palate tastes food?
¹² Is wisdom with the aged,
and understanding in
length of days?

¹³ "With Godᵈ are wisdom
and strength;
he has counsel and
understanding.
¹⁴ If he tears down, no one
can rebuild;
if he shuts someone in, no
one can open up.

¹⁵ If he withholds the waters,
they dry up;
if he sends them out, they
overwhelm the land.
¹⁶ With him are strength
and wisdom;
the deceived and the
deceiver are his.
¹⁷ He leads counselors away stripped,
and makes fools of judges.
¹⁸ He looses the sash of kings,
and binds a waistcloth
on their loins.
¹⁹ He leads priests away stripped,
and overthrows the mighty.
²⁰ He deprives of speech those
who are trusted,
and takes away the
discernment of the elders.
²¹ He pours contempt on princes,
and looses the belt of the strong.
²² He uncovers the deeps out
of darkness,
and brings deep darkness
to light.
²³ He makes nations great, then
destroys them;
he enlarges nations, then
leads them away.
²⁴ He strips understanding from
the leadersᵉ of the earth,
and makes them wander
in a pathless waste.
²⁵ They grope in the dark
without light;
he makes them stagger
like a drunkard.

13 "Look, my eye has
seen all this,
my ear has heard and
understood it.
² What you know, I also know;
I am not inferior to you.
³ But I would speak to the Almighty,ᶠ
and I desire to argue my
case with God.
⁴ As for you, you whitewash
with lies;
all of you are worthless
physicians.

ᵃ **12.5** Meaning of Heb uncertain ᵇ **12.6** Or
whom God brought forth by his hand;
Meaning of Heb uncertain ᶜ **12.8** Or *speak
to the earth* ᵈ **12.13** Heb *him* ᵉ **12.24** Heb
adds *of the people* ᶠ **13.3** Traditional
rendering of Heb *Shaddai*

5 If you would only keep silent,
    that would be your wisdom!
6 Hear now my reasoning,
    and listen to the pleadings
        of my lips.
7 Will you speak falsely for God,
    and speak deceitfully for him?
8 Will you show partiality
    toward him,
    will you plead the case for God?
9 Will it be well with you when
        he searches you out?
    Or can you deceive him, as one
        person deceives another?
10 He will surely rebuke you
    if in secret you show partiality.
11 Will not his majesty terrify you,
    and the dread of him
        fall upon you?
12 Your maxims are proverbs
    of ashes,
    your defenses are
        defenses of clay.

13 "Let me have silence, and
    I will speak,
    and let come on me what may.
14 I will take my flesh in my teeth,
    and put my life in my hand.[a]
15 See, he will kill me; I have
    no hope;[b]
    but I will defend my
        ways to his face.
16 This will be my salvation,
    that the godless shall not
        come before him.
17 Listen carefully to my words,
    and let my declaration
        be in your ears.
18 I have indeed prepared my case;
    I know that I shall be
        vindicated.
19 Who is there that will
    contend with me?
    For then I would be
        silent and die.

JOB'S DESPONDENT PRAYER

20 Only grant two things to me,
    then I will not hide myself
        from your face:
21 withdraw your hand far from me,
    and do not let dread of
        you terrify me.
22 Then call, and I will answer;
    or let me speak, and you
        reply to me.

PONDER

"Will it be well with you when he searches you out? Or can you deceive him, as one person deceives another?"
—Job 13.9

PRAY

O Father, Job was being urged to examine, in your presence, his shortcomings, mistakes and transgressions. We often need to do so ourselves. Give us the courage to open our hearts to you as you urge us to reach for greatness, transcendence, purity, honesty and truth. Bind us in more intimate communion with you. We ask that these trenchant thoughts be made more permanent and become an integral part of our lives so that we can live a truly liberated existence, always exploring new ways and new ideas. We ask for lives full of abundance and joy, knowing that in your love and your mercy, your forgiveness to us is complete. We give you praise and thanksgiving in the name of Jesus Christ. Amen.

23 How many are my iniquities
    and my sins?
    Make me know my
        transgression and my sin.
24 Why do you hide your face,
    and count me as your enemy?
25 Will you frighten a
        windblown leaf
    and pursue dry chaff?
26 For you write bitter things
    against me,
    and make me reap[c] the
        iniquities of my youth.
27 You put my feet in the stocks,
    and watch all my paths;
    you set a bound to the
        soles of my feet.

[a] 13.14 Gk: Heb *Why should I take ... in my hand?* [b] 13.15 Or *Though he kill me, yet I will trust in him* [c] 13.26 Heb *inherit*

28 One wastes away like a
  rotten thing,
  like a garment that is
  moth-eaten.

14

"A mortal, born of
  woman, few of days
  and full of trouble,
2 comes up like a flower
  and withers,
  flees like a shadow and
  does not last.
3 Do you fix your eyes on such a one?
  Do you bring me into
  judgment with you?
4 Who can bring a clean thing
  out of an unclean?
  No one can.
5 Since their days are determined,
  and the number of their
  months is known to you,
  and you have appointed
  the bounds that
  they cannot pass,
6 look away from them, and desist,[a]
  that they may enjoy, like
  laborers, their days.

7 "For there is hope for a tree,
  if it is cut down, that it
  will sprout again,
  and that its shoots will
  not cease.
8 Though its root grows old
  in the earth,
  and its stump dies in
  the ground,

9 yet at the scent of water it will bud
  and put forth branches
  like a young plant.
10 But mortals die, and are laid low;
  humans expire, and
  where are they?
11 As waters fail from a lake,
  and a river wastes away
  and dries up,
12 so mortals lie down and do
  not rise again;
  until the heavens are no more,
  they will not awake
  or be roused out of their sleep.
13 O that you would hide
  me in Sheol,
  that you would conceal me
  until your wrath is past,
  that you would appoint
  me a set time, and
  remember me!
14 If mortals die, will they
  live again?
  All the days of my service
  I would wait
  until my release should come.
15 You would call, and I would
  answer you;
  you would long for the
  work of your hands.
16 For then you would not[b]
  number my steps,
  you would not keep watch
  over my sin;

a 14.6 Cn: Heb that they may desist
b 14.16 Syr: Heb lacks not

⊦ BIBLE IN LIFE ▷

Accepting Death

Job 14.1–5

One of the intriguing qualities about human beings is that we alone, of all God's creatures, have the certain knowledge of our own inevitable deaths. This is a very sobering fact for us to face, and it causes us anxiety. Much of what we do or say is subconsciously affected by the necessity of our accepting our brief life on earth. People who can't accept it, who try to confine it to the recesses of their minds, can become traumatized or overwhelmed by the tragedy of death. The Bible gives us premises we must accept in order to deal with the inevitability of death: 1) Our time on earth is limited; 2) we can't change the physical laws that result in earthly death; 3) we should never judge others by claiming that their deaths are the result of sin (see Job 36.17; Luke 13.1–9), for we are all sinners. When we are able to accept the reality of death, we can then focus on doing the things in life that have permanent significance: loving God, promoting peace and justice, helping others, spending time with family, forming new friendships and forgiving enemies.

17 my transgression would be
       sealed up in a bag,
   and you would cover over
       my iniquity.

18 "But the mountain falls and
       crumbles away,
   and the rock is removed
       from its place;

19 the waters wear
       away the stones;
   the torrents wash away the
       soil of the earth;
   so you destroy the hope
       of mortals.

20 You prevail forever against them,
       and they pass away;
   you change their countenance,
       and send them away.

21 Their children come to honor,
       and they do not know it;
   they are brought low, and
       it goes unnoticed.

22 They feel only the pain of
       their own bodies,
   and mourn only for
       themselves."

ELIPHAZ SPEAKS: JOB UNDERMINES RELIGION

15 Then Eliphaz the Temanite
       answered:

2 "Should the wise answer with
       windy knowledge,
   and fill themselves with
       the east wind?

3 Should they argue in
       unprofitable talk,
   or in words with which
       they can do no good?

4 But you are doing away with
       the fear of God,
   and hindering meditation
       before God.

5 For your iniquity teaches
       your mouth,
   and you choose the tongue
       of the crafty.

6 Your own mouth condemns
       you, and not I;
   your own lips testify
       against you.

7 "Are you the firstborn of
       the human race?
   Were you brought forth
       before the hills?

8 Have you listened in the
       council of God?
   And do you limit wisdom
       to yourself?

9 What do you know that we
       do not know?
   What do you understand
       that is not clear to us?

10 The gray-haired and the aged
       are on our side,
   those older than your father.

11 Are the consolations of God
       too small for you,
   or the word that deals
       gently with you?

12 Why does your heart carry
       you away,
   and why do your eyes flash,[a]

13 so that you turn your spirit
       against God,
   and let such words go out
       of your mouth?

14 What are mortals, that they
       can be clean?
   Or those born of woman, that
       they can be righteous?

15 God puts no trust even in
       his holy ones,
   and the heavens are not
       clean in his sight;

16 how much less one who is
       abominable and corrupt,
   one who drinks iniquity
       like water!

17 "I will show you; listen to me;
   what I have seen I will
       declare—

18 what sages have told,
   and their ancestors have
       not hidden,

19 to whom alone the land
       was given,
   and no stranger passed
       among them.

20 The wicked writhe in pain
       all their days,
   through all the years that are
       laid up for the ruthless.

21 Terrifying sounds are in
       their ears;
   in prosperity the destroyer
       will come upon them.

a 15.12 Meaning of Heb uncertain

22 They despair of returning
 from darkness,
 and they are destined
 for the sword.
23 They wander abroad for bread,
 saying, 'Where is it?'
 They know that a day of
 darkness is ready at hand;
24 distress and anguish
 terrify them;
 they prevail against them, like
 a king prepared for battle.
25 Because they stretched out their
 hands against God,
 and bid defiance to the
 Almighty,[a]
26 running stubbornly against him
 with a thick-bossed shield;
27 because they have covered their
 faces with their fat,
 and gathered fat upon
 their loins,
28 they will live in desolate cities,
 in houses that no one
 should inhabit,
 houses destined to become
 heaps of ruins;
29 they will not be rich, and their
 wealth will not endure,
 nor will they strike root
 in the earth;[b]
30 they will not escape from
 darkness;
 the flame will dry up
 their shoots,
 and their blossom[c] will be
 swept away[d] by the wind.
31 Let them not trust in emptiness,
 deceiving themselves;
 for emptiness will be
 their recompense.
32 It will be paid in full before
 their time,
 and their branch will
 not be green.
33 They will shake off their unripe
 grape, like the vine,
 and cast off their blossoms,
 like the olive tree.
34 For the company of the
 godless is barren,
 and fire consumes the
 tents of bribery.
35 They conceive mischief and
 bring forth evil
 and their heart prepares
 deceit."

JOB REAFFIRMS HIS INNOCENCE

16 Then Job answered:
2 "I have heard many
 such things;
 miserable comforters
 are you all.
3 Have windy words no limit?
 Or what provokes you that
 you keep on talking?
4 I also could talk as you do,
 if you were in my place;
 I could join words together
 against you,
 and shake my head at you.
5 I could encourage you with
 my mouth,
 and the solace of my lips would
 assuage your pain.

6 "If I speak, my pain is
 not assuaged,
 and if I forbear, how much
 of it leaves me?
7 Surely now God has worn me out;
 he has[e] made desolate
 all my company.
8 And he has[e] shriveled me up,
 which is a witness against me;
 my leanness has risen up
 against me,
 and it testifies to my face.
9 He has torn me in his wrath,
 and hated me;
 he has gnashed his teeth at me;
 my adversary sharpens his
 eyes against me.
10 They have gaped at me with
 their mouths;
 they have struck me insolently
 on the cheek;
 they mass themselves
 together against me.
11 God gives me up to the ungodly,
 and casts me into the hands
 of the wicked.
12 I was at ease, and he broke
 me in two;
 he seized me by the neck and
 dashed me to pieces;
 he set me up as his target;
13 his archers surround me.

[a] 15.25 Traditional rendering of Heb *Shaddai*
[b] 15.29 Vg: Meaning of Heb uncertain
[c] 15.30 Gk: Heb *mouth* [d] 15.30 Cn: Heb *will depart* [e] 16.7,8 Heb *you have*

He slashes open my kidneys,
and shows no mercy;
he pours out my gall
on the ground.

14 He bursts upon me again
and again;
he rushes at me like a warrior.

15 I have sewed sackcloth
upon my skin,
and have laid my strength
in the dust.

16 My face is red with weeping,
and deep darkness is
on my eyelids,

17 though there is no violence
in my hands,
and my prayer is pure.

18 "O earth, do not
cover my blood;
let my outcry find no
resting place.

19 Even now, in fact, my witness
is in heaven,
and he that vouches for
me is on high.

20 My friends scorn me;
my eye pours out
tears to God,

21 that he would maintain the right
of a mortal with God,
as[a] one does for a neighbor.

22 For when a few years have come,
I shall go the way from which
I shall not return.

JOB PRAYS FOR RELIEF

17 My spirit is broken, my
days are extinct,
the grave is ready for me.

2 Surely there are mockers
around me,
and my eye dwells on
their provocation.

3 "Lay down a pledge for me
with yourself;
who is there that will give
surety for me?

4 Since you have closed their
minds to understanding,
therefore you will not let
them triumph.

5 Those who denounce friends
for reward—
the eyes of their children
will fail.

6 "He has made me a byword
of the peoples,
and I am one before whom
people spit.

7 My eye has grown dim from grief,
and all my members are
like a shadow.

8 The upright are appalled at this,
and the innocent stir themselves
up against the godless.

9 Yet the righteous hold
to their way,
and they that have clean
hands grow stronger
and stronger.

10 But you, come back now, all of you,
and I shall not find a sensible
person among you.

11 My days are past, my plans
are broken off,
the desires of my heart.

12 They make night into day;
'The light,' they say, 'is near
to the darkness.'[b]

13 If I look for Sheol as my house,
if I spread my couch in darkness,

14 if I say to the Pit, 'You are
my father,'
and to the worm, 'My
mother,' or 'My sister,'

15 where then is my hope?
Who will see my hope?

16 Will it go down to the
bars of Sheol?
Shall we descend together
into the dust?"

BILDAD SPEAKS: GOD PUNISHES THE WICKED

18 Then Bildad the Shuhite answered:

2 "How long will you hunt
for words?
Consider, and then we
shall speak.

3 Why are we counted as cattle?
Why are we stupid in
your sight?

4 You who tear yourself in
your anger—
shall the earth be forsaken
because of you,
or the rock be removed
out of its place?

---

[a] 16.21 Syr Vg Tg: Heb *and*   [b] 17.12 Meaning
of Heb uncertain

5 "Surely the light of the
    wicked is put out,
  and the flame of their fire
    does not shine.
6 The light is dark in their tent,
  and the lamp above
    them is put out.
7 Their strong steps are shortened,
  and their own schemes
    throw them down.
8 For they are thrust into a net
    by their own feet,
  and they walk into a pitfall.
9 A trap seizes them by the heel;
  a snare lays hold of them.
10 A rope is hid for them in
    the ground,
  a trap for them in the path.
11 Terrors frighten them on
    every side,
  and chase them at their heels.
12 Their strength is consumed
    by hunger,ᵃ
  and calamity is ready for
    their stumbling.
13 By disease their skin is consumed,ᵇ
  the firstborn of Death
    consumes their limbs.
14 They are torn from the tent in
    which they trusted,
  and are brought to the
    king of terrors.
15 In their tents nothing remains;
  sulfur is scattered upon
    their habitations.
16 Their roots dry up beneath,
  and their branches wither above.
17 Their memory perishes
    from the earth,
  and they have no name
    in the street.
18 They are thrust from light
    into darkness,
  and driven out of the world.
19 They have no offspring or
    descendant among
    their people,
  and no survivor where
    they used to live.
20 They of the west are appalled
    at their fate,
  and horror seizes those
    of the east.
21 Surely such are the dwellings
    of the ungodly,
  such is the place of those who
    do not know God."

JOB REPLIES: I KNOW THAT MY REDEEMER LIVES

19 Then Job answered:
2 "How long will you
    torment me,
  and break me in pieces
    with words?
3 These ten times you have cast
    reproach upon me;
  are you not ashamed
    to wrong me?
4 And even if it is true that
    I have erred,
  my error remains with me.
5 If indeed you magnify
    yourselves against me,
  and make my humiliation an
    argument against me,
6 know then that God has put
    me in the wrong,
  and closed his net around me.
7 Even when I cry out, 'Violence!'
    I am not answered;
  I call aloud, but there
    is no justice.
8 He has walled up my way so
    that I cannot pass,
  and he has set darkness
    upon my paths.
9 He has stripped my glory
    from me,
  and taken the crown
    from my head.
10 He breaks me down on every
    side, and I am gone,
  he has uprooted my
    hope like a tree.
11 He has kindled his wrath
    against me,
  and counts me as his adversary.
12 His troops come on together;
  they have thrown up
    siegeworksᶜ against me,
  and encamp around my tent.

13 "He has put my family
    far from me,
  and my acquaintances are
    wholly estranged from me.
14 My relatives and my close
    friends have failed me;
15   the guests in my house
    have forgotten me;

ᵃ 18.12 Or *Disaster is hungry for them*
ᵇ 18.13 Cn: Heb *It consumes the limbs of his skin*   ᶜ 19.12 Cn: Heb *their way*

my serving girls count me
as a stranger;
I have become an alien
in their eyes.
16 I call to my servant, but he
gives me no answer;
I must myself plead with him.
17 My breath is repulsive to my wife;
I am loathsome to my
own family.
18 Even young children despise me;
when I rise, they talk
against me.
19 All my intimate friends
abhor me,
and those whom I loved have
turned against me.
20 My bones cling to my skin
and to my flesh,
and I have escaped by the
skin of my teeth.
21 Have pity on me, have pity on
me, O you my friends,
for the hand of God has
touched me!
22 Why do you, like God, pursue me,
never satisfied with my flesh?

23 "O that my words were
written down!
O that they were inscribed
in a book!
24 O that with an iron pen
and with lead
they were engraved on
a rock forever!
25 For I know that my
Redeemer[a] lives,
and that at the last he[b] will
stand upon the earth;[c]
26 and after my skin has been
thus destroyed,
then in[d] my flesh I
shall see God,[e]
27 whom I shall see on my side,[f]
and my eyes shall behold,
and not another.
My heart faints within me!
28 If you say, 'How we will
persecute him!'
and, 'The root of the matter
is found in him';
29 be afraid of the sword,
for wrath brings the
punishment of the sword,
so that you may know there
is a judgment."

PONDER

"For I know that my Redeemer lives,
and that at the last he will stand upon
the earth; and after my skin has been
thus destroyed, then in my flesh I shall
see God, whom I shall see on my side,
and my eyes shall behold, and not
another. My heart faints within me!"
—Job 19.25–27

PRAY

O Father, we are always blessed to read
the scriptures, which you have given us
for contemplation and enlightenment,
and to stimulate us to aspire to a closer
walk with you. We pray that we might
absorb the truth that, though Job lost
everything, he did not turn against you.
And even after suffering great losses,
he bowed down and worshiped you.
Help us place our own priorities in life
into proper perspective, and as we do,
help us leave behind animosity and
scorn toward others. Guide our search
for the truth about our relationships
with you and our fellow human beings,
and help us to find answers from
the close observation of the words
and actions of our Savior, Jesus
Christ. In his name we pray. Amen.

ZOPHAR SPEAKS: WICKEDNESS RECEIVES JUST RETRIBUTION

20 Then Zophar the Naama-
thite answered:
2 "Pay attention! My thoughts
urge me to answer,
because of the agitation
within me.
3 I hear censure that insults me,
and a spirit beyond my
understanding
answers me.

a 19.25 Or *Vindicator*   b 19.25 Or *that he
the Last*   c 19.25 Heb *dust*   d 19.26 Or
without   e 19.26 Meaning of Heb of this
verse uncertain   f 19.27 Or *for myself*

4 Do you not know
 this from of old,
 ever since mortals were
 placed on earth,
5 that the exulting of the
 wicked is short,
 and the joy of the godless is
 but for a moment?
6 Even though they mount up
 high as the heavens,
 and their head reaches
 to the clouds,
7 they will perish forever like
 their own dung;
 those who have seen them will
 say, 'Where are they?'
8 They will fly away like a dream,
 and not be found;
 they will be chased away like
 a vision of the night.
9 The eye that saw them will
 see them no more,
 nor will their place behold
 them any longer.
10 Their children will seek the
 favor of the poor,
 and their hands will give
 back their wealth.
11 Their bodies, once
 full of youth,
 will lie down in the dust
 with them.

12 "Though wickedness is sweet
 in their mouth,
 though they hide it under
 their tongues,
13 though they are
 loath to let it go,
 and hold it in their mouths,
14 yet their food is turned in
 their stomachs;
 it is the venom of asps
 within them.
15 They swallow down riches and
 vomit them up again;
 God casts them out of
 their bellies.
16 They will suck the poison of asps;
 the tongue of a viper
 will kill them.
17 They will not look on the rivers,
 the streams flowing with
 honey and curds.
18 They will give back the
 fruit of their toil,
 and will not swallow it down;
 from the profit of
 their trading
 they will get no enjoyment.
19 For they have crushed and
 abandoned the poor,
 they have seized a house that
 they did not build.

20 "They knew no quiet in
 their bellies;
 in their greed they let
 nothing escape.
21 There was nothing left after
 they had eaten;
 therefore their prosperity
 will not endure.
22 In full sufficiency they will
 be in distress;
 all the force of misery will
 come upon them.
23 To fill their belly to the full
 God[a] will send his fierce
 anger into them,
 and rain it upon them
 as their food.[b]
24 They will flee from an
 iron weapon;
 a bronze arrow will strike
 them through.
25 It is drawn forth and comes
 out of their body,
 and the glittering point
 comes out of their gall;
 terrors come upon them.
26 Utter darkness is laid up for
 their treasures;
 a fire fanned by no one
 will devour them;
 what is left in their tent
 will be consumed.
27 The heavens will reveal
 their iniquity,
 and the earth will rise
 up against them.
28 The possessions of their house
 will be carried away,
 dragged off in the day
 of God's[c] wrath.
29 This is the portion of the
 wicked from God,
 the heritage decreed for
 them by God."

a **20.23** Heb *he* b **20.23** Cn: Meaning of
Heb uncertain c **20.28** Heb *his*

JOB REPLIES: THE WICKED OFTEN GO UNPUNISHED

21 Then Job answered:
² "Listen carefully
    to my words,
and let this be your
    consolation.
³ Bear with me, and I will speak;
    then after I have spoken,
    mock on.
⁴ As for me, is my complaint
    addressed to mortals?
Why should I not be
    impatient?
⁵ Look at me, and be appalled,
    and lay your hand upon
    your mouth.
⁶ When I think of it I am dismayed,
    and shuddering seizes
    my flesh.
⁷ Why do the wicked live on,
    reach old age, and grow
    mighty in power?
⁸ Their children are established
    in their presence,
and their offspring
    before their eyes.
⁹ Their houses are safe from fear,
    and no rod of God is
    upon them.
¹⁰ Their bull breeds without fail;
    their cow calves and
    never miscarries.
¹¹ They send out their little
    ones like a flock,
and their children
    dance around.
¹² They sing to the tambourine
    and the lyre,
and rejoice to the sound
    of the pipe.
¹³ They spend their days in
    prosperity,
and in peace they go
    down to Sheol.
¹⁴ They say to God,
    'Leave us alone!
We do not desire to know
    your ways.
¹⁵ What is the Almighty,ᵃ that
    we should serve him?
And what profit do we get
    if we pray to him?'
¹⁶ Is not their prosperity indeed
    their own achievement?ᵇ
The plans of the wicked are
    repugnant to me.

¹⁷ "How often is the lamp of the
    wicked put out?
How often does calamity
    come upon them?
How often does Godᶜ distribute
    pains in his anger?
¹⁸ How often are they like straw
    before the wind,
and like chaff that the
    storm carries away?
¹⁹ You say, 'God stores up their
    iniquity for their children.'
Let it be paid back to them, so
    that they may know it.
²⁰ Let their own eyes see their
    destruction,
and let them drink of the
    wrath of the Almighty.ᵃ
²¹ For what do they care for their
    household after them,
when the number of their
    months is cut off?
²² Will any teach God knowledge,
    seeing that he judges those
    that are on high?
²³ One dies in full prosperity,
    being wholly at ease
    and secure,
²⁴ his loins full of milk
    and the marrow of his
    bones moist.
²⁵ Another dies in bitterness of soul,
    never having tasted of good.
²⁶ They lie down alike in the dust,
    and the worms cover them.

²⁷ "Oh, I know your thoughts,
    and your schemes to wrong me.
²⁸ For you say, 'Where is the
    house of the prince?
Where is the tent in which
    the wicked lived?'
²⁹ Have you not asked those who
    travel the roads,
and do you not accept
    their testimony,
³⁰ that the wicked are spared in
    the day of calamity,
and are rescued in the
    day of wrath?
³¹ Who declares their way
    to their face,
and who repays them for
    what they have done?

ᵃ 21.15,20 Traditional rendering of Heb
Shaddai ᵇ 21.16 Heb *in their hand*
ᶜ 21.17 Heb *he*

32 When they are carried
    to the grave,
  a watch is kept over their tomb.
33 The clods of the valley are
    sweet to them;
  everyone will follow after,
  and those who went before
    are innumerable.
34 How then will you comfort me
    with empty nothings?
  There is nothing left of your
    answers but falsehood."

ELIPHAZ SPEAKS: JOB'S WICKEDNESS IS GREAT

22 Then Eliphaz the Temanite answered:
2 "Can a mortal be of use to God?
  Can even the wisest be of
    service to him?
3 Is it any pleasure to the
    Almighty[a] if you
    are righteous,
  or is it gain to him if you make
    your ways blameless?
4 Is it for your piety that he
    reproves you,
  and enters into judgment
    with you?
5 Is not your wickedness great?
  There is no end to your
    iniquities.
6 For you have exacted pledges
    from your family
    for no reason,
  and stripped the naked
    of their clothing.

7 You have given no water to
    the weary to drink,
  and you have withheld bread
    from the hungry.
8 The powerful possess the land,
  and the favored live in it.
9 You have sent widows away
    empty-handed,
  and the arms of the orphans
    you have crushed.[b]
10 Therefore snares are around you,
  and sudden terror
    overwhelms you,
11 or darkness so that you
    cannot see;
  a flood of water covers you.

12 "Is not God high in the heavens?
  See the highest stars, how
    lofty they are!
13 Therefore you say, 'What
    does God know?
  Can he judge through the
    deep darkness?
14 Thick clouds enwrap him, so
    that he does not see,
  and he walks on the
    dome of heaven.'
15 Will you keep to the old way
    that the wicked have trod?
16 They were snatched away
    before their time;
  their foundation was washed
    away by a flood.

[a] 22.3 Traditional rendering of Heb *Shaddai*
[b] 22.9 Gk Syr Tg Vg: Heb *were crushed*

⊣ BIBLE IN LIFE ▷

Self–Righteousness

Job 22.4–5

Job was a godly man. He followed the laws of God; he was generous to the poor; he made righteous choices; yet bad things happened to him. His self-righteous friends accused him of not repenting of his sin, which they believed was the reason for his suffering. The common assumption in the time of the Old Testament was that people who suffered deserved their punishment; their sin was linked directly to their pain. This faulty thinking persists today. We often assume that there must be something sinful about others if they are suffering, but we forget to look at ourselves. Concluding that others suffer because of their sin betrays our own self-righteousness. Luke 13.1–5 describes a scene in which Jesus was confronted with this issue. Some Galileans had been praying and offering sacrifices, and Pilate had them assassinated by his troops. Were these murdered Galileans worse sinners than others because they suffered so terribly? Jesus answers, "No, I tell you; but unless you repent, you will all perish just as they did" (verse 5). We are all sinners; we all need to repent.

17 They said to God, 'Leave us alone,'
and 'What can the Almighty[a]
do to us?'[b]
18 Yet he filled their houses
with good things—
but the plans of the wicked
are repugnant to me.
19 The righteous see it and are glad;
the innocent laugh
them to scorn,
20 saying, 'Surely our adversaries
are cut off,
and what they left, the
fire has consumed.'

21 "Agree with God,[c] and be at peace;
in this way good will
come to you.
22 Receive instruction from
his mouth,
and lay up his words
in your heart.
23 If you return to the Almighty,[a]
you will be restored,
if you remove unrighteousness
from your tents,
24 if you treat gold like dust,
and gold of Ophir like the
stones of the torrent-bed,
25 and if the Almighty[a] is your gold
and your precious silver,
26 then you will delight yourself
in the Almighty,[a]
and lift up your face to God.
27 You will pray to him, and
he will hear you,
and you will pay your vows.
28 You will decide on a matter,
and it will be
established for you,
and light will shine on
your ways.
29 When others are humiliated,
you say it is pride;
for he saves the humble.
30 He will deliver even those
who are guilty;
they will escape because of the
cleanness of your hands."[d]

JOB REPLIES: MY COMPLAINT IS BITTER

23

Then Job answered:
2 "Today also my
complaint is bitter;[e]
his[f] hand is heavy despite
my groaning.

3 Oh, that I knew where I
might find him,
that I might come even
to his dwelling!
4 I would lay my case before him,
and fill my mouth with
arguments.
5 I would learn what he would
answer me,
and understand what he
would say to me.
6 Would he contend with me in the
greatness of his power?
No; but he would give
heed to me.
7 There an upright person could
reason with him,
and I should be acquitted
forever by my judge.

8 "If I go forward, he is not there;
or backward, I cannot
perceive him;
9 on the left he hides, and I
cannot behold him;
I turn[g] to the right, but I
cannot see him.
10 But he knows the way that I take;
when he has tested me, I shall
come out like gold.
11 My foot has held fast to his steps;
I have kept his way and have
not turned aside.
12 I have not departed from the
commandment of his lips;
I have treasured in[h] my bosom
the words of his mouth.
13 But he stands alone and who
can dissuade him?
What he desires, that he does.
14 For he will complete what he
appoints for me;
and many such things
are in his mind.
15 Therefore I am terrified at
his presence;
when I consider, I am
in dread of him.
16 God has made my heart faint;
the Almighty[a] has terrified me;

[a] 22.17,23,25,26; 23.16 Traditional rendering
of Heb *Shaddai*   [b] 22.17 Gk Syr: Heb *them*
[c] 22.21 Heb *him*   [d] 22.30 Meaning of Heb
uncertain   [e] 23.2 Syr Vg Tg: Heb *rebellious*
[f] 23.2 Gk Syr: Heb *my*   [g] 23.9 Syr Vg: Heb
he turns   [h] 23.12 Gk Vg: Heb *from*

17 If only I could vanish in darkness,
  and thick darkness would
    cover my face![a]

JOB COMPLAINS OF VIOLENCE
ON THE EARTH

24 "Why are times not kept
  by the Almighty,[b]
and why do those who know
  him never see his days?
2 The wicked[c] remove
    landmarks;
  they seize flocks and
    pasture them.
3 They drive away the donkey
    of the orphan;
  they take the widow's
    ox for a pledge.
4 They thrust the needy
    off the road;
  the poor of the earth all
    hide themselves.
5 Like wild asses in the desert
    they go out to their toil,
scavenging in the wasteland
  food for their young.
6 They reap in a field
    not their own
  and they glean in the
    vineyard of the wicked.
7 They lie all night naked,
    without clothing,
  and have no covering
    in the cold.
8 They are wet with the rain
    of the mountains,
  and cling to the rock for
    want of shelter.

9 "There are those who snatch
    the orphan child
    from the breast,
  and take as a pledge the
    infant of the poor.
10 They go about naked,
    without clothing;
  though hungry, they
    carry the sheaves;
11 between their terraces[d]
    they press out oil;
  they tread the wine presses,
    but suffer thirst.
12 From the city the dying groan,
    and the throat of the
      wounded cries for help;
  yet God pays no attention
    to their prayer.

13 "There are those who rebel
    against the light,
  who are not acquainted
    with its ways,
  and do not stay in its paths.
14 The murderer rises at dusk
    to kill the poor and needy,
  and in the night
    is like a thief.
15 The eye of the adulterer also
    waits for the twilight,
  saying, 'No eye will see me';
  and he disguises his face.
16 In the dark they dig
    through houses;
  by day they shut
    themselves up;
  they do not know the light.
17 For deep darkness is morning
    to all of them;
  for they are friends with the
    terrors of deep darkness.

18 "Swift are they on the face
    of the waters;
  their portion in the
    land is cursed;
  no treader turns toward
    their vineyards.
19 Drought and heat snatch away
    the snow waters;
  so does Sheol those who
    have sinned.
20 The womb forgets them;
    the worm finds them sweet;
  they are no longer remembered;
  so wickedness is broken
    like a tree.

21 "They harm[e] the
    childless woman,
  and do no good to the widow.
22 Yet God[f] prolongs the life of the
    mighty by his power;
  they rise up when they
    despair of life.
23 He gives them security, and
    they are supported;
  his eyes are upon their ways.

[a] 23.17 Or *But I am not destroyed by the
darkness; he has concealed the thick
darkness from me*   [b] 24.1 Traditional
rendering of Heb *Shaddai*   [c] 24.2 Gk: Heb
they   [d] 24.11 Meaning of Heb uncertain
[e] 24.21 Gk Tg: Heb *feed on* or *associate with*
[f] 24.22 Heb *he*

24 They are exalted a little while,
  and then are gone;
  they wither and fade like
    the mallow;[a]
  they are cut off like the
    heads of grain.
25 If it is not so, who will
    prove me a liar,
  and show that there is
    nothing in what I say?"

BILDAD SPEAKS: HOW CAN A MORTAL BE RIGHTEOUS BEFORE GOD?

25 Then Bildad the Shuhite answered:
2 "Dominion and fear are
    with God;[b]
  he makes peace in his
    high heaven.
3 Is there any number to
    his armies?
  Upon whom does his
    light not arise?
4 How then can a mortal be
    righteous before God?
  How can one born of
    woman be pure?
5 If even the moon
    is not bright
  and the stars are not
    pure in his sight,
6 how much less a mortal,
    who is a maggot,
  and a human being,
    who is a worm!"

JOB REPLIES: GOD'S MAJESTY IS UNSEARCHABLE

26 Then Job answered:
2 "How you have helped
    one who has no power!
  How you have assisted the arm
    that has no strength!
3 How you have counseled one
    who has no wisdom,
  and given much good advice!
4 With whose help have you
    uttered words,
  and whose spirit has come
    forth from you?
5 The shades below tremble,
    the waters and their
    inhabitants.
6 Sheol is naked before God,
    and Abaddon has
    no covering.

7 He stretches out Zaphon[c]
    over the void,
  and hangs the earth
    upon nothing.
8 He binds up the waters in
    his thick clouds,
  and the cloud is not torn
    open by them.
9 He covers the face of the
    full moon,
  and spreads over it his cloud.
10 He has described a circle on
    the face of the waters,
  at the boundary between
    light and darkness.
11 The pillars of heaven tremble,
    and are astounded at
    his rebuke.
12 By his power he stilled the Sea;
  by his understanding he
    struck down Rahab.
13 By his wind the heavens
    were made fair;
  his hand pierced the
    fleeing serpent.
14 These are indeed but the
    outskirts of his ways;
  and how small a whisper
    do we hear of him!
  But the thunder of his power
    who can understand?"

JOB MAINTAINS HIS INTEGRITY

27 Job again took up his discourse and said:
2 "As God lives, who has taken
    away my right,
  and the Almighty,[d] who has
    made my soul bitter,
3 as long as my breath is in me
  and the spirit of God is
    in my nostrils,
4 my lips will not speak falsehood,
  and my tongue will not
    utter deceit.
5 Far be it from me to say that
    you are right;
  until I die I will not put away
    my integrity from me.
6 I hold fast my righteousness,
    and will not let it go;
  my heart does not reproach
    me for any of my days.

---

a 24.24 Gk: Heb like all others
b 25.2 Heb him   c 26.7 Or the North
d 27.2 Traditional rendering of Heb Shaddai

7 "May my enemy be like
        the wicked,
    and may my opponent be
        like the unrighteous.
8 For what is the hope of the
        godless when God
        cuts them off,
    when God takes away
        their lives?
9 Will God hear their cry
    when trouble comes
        upon them?
10 Will they take delight in
        the Almighty?[a]
    Will they call upon God
        at all times?
11 I will teach you concerning
        the hand of God;
    that which is with the
        Almighty[a] I will
        not conceal.
12 All of you have seen it yourselves;
    why then have you become
        altogether vain?

GOD IS THE REAL DEFENSE

AGAINST OUR ENEMIES.

13 "This is the portion of the
        wicked with God,
    and the heritage that
        oppressors receive
        from the Almighty:[a]
14 If their children are multiplied,
        it is for the sword;
    and their offspring have
        not enough to eat.
15 Those who survive them the
        pestilence buries,
    and their widows make
        no lamentation.
16 Though they heap up
        silver like dust,
    and pile up clothing like clay—
17 they may pile it up, but the
        just will wear it,
    and the innocent will
        divide the silver.
18 They build their houses like nests,
    like booths made by sentinels
        of the vineyard.

19 They go to bed with wealth, but
        will do so no more;
    they open their eyes,
        and it is gone.
20 Terrors overtake them
        like a flood;
    in the night a whirlwind
        carries them off.
21 The east wind lifts them up
        and they are gone;
    it sweeps them out of
        their place.
22 It[b] hurls at them without pity;
    they flee from its[c] power
        in headlong flight.
23 It[b] claps its[c] hands at them,
    and hisses at them
        from its[c] place.

INTERLUDE: WHERE WISDOM IS FOUND

28 "Surely there is a
        mine for silver,
    and a place for gold to
        be refined.
2 Iron is taken out of the earth,
    and copper is smelted from ore.
3 Miners put[d] an end to darkness,
    and search out to the
        farthest bound
    the ore in gloom and
        deep darkness.
4 They open shafts in a valley away
        from human habitation;
    they are forgotten by travelers,
    they sway suspended,
        remote from people.
5 As for the earth, out of it
        comes bread;
    but underneath it is turned
        up as by fire.
6 Its stones are the place
        of sapphires,[e]
    and its dust contains gold.

7 "That path no bird of prey knows,
    and the falcon's eye has
        not seen it.
8 The proud wild animals have
        not trodden it;
    the lion has not passed over it.

---

[a] **27.10,11,13** Traditional rendering of Heb
Shaddai   [b] **27.22,23** Or *He* (that is God)
[c] **27.22,23** Or *his*   [d] **28.3** Heb *He puts*
[e] **28.6** Or *lapis lazuli*

9 "They put their hand to
        the flinty rock,
    and overturn mountains
        by the roots.
10 They cut out channels
        in the rocks,
    and their eyes see every
        precious thing.
11 The sources of the rivers
        they probe;[a]
    hidden things they
        bring to light.

12 "But where shall wisdom
        be found?
    And where is the place of
        understanding?
13 Mortals do not know the
        way to it,[b]
    and it is not found in the
        land of the living.
14 The deep says, 'It is not in me,'
    and the sea says, 'It is
        not with me.'
15 It cannot be gotten for gold,
    and silver cannot be weighed
        out as its price.
16 It cannot be valued in the
        gold of Ophir,
    in precious onyx or sapphire.[c]
17 Gold and glass cannot equal it,
    nor can it be exchanged for
        jewels of fine gold.
18 No mention shall be made of
        coral or of crystal;
    the price of wisdom is
        above pearls.
19 The chrysolite of Ethiopia[d]
        cannot compare with it,
    nor can it be valued
        in pure gold.

20 "Where then does wisdom
        come from?
    And where is the place of
        understanding?
21 It is hidden from the eyes
        of all living,
    and concealed from the
        birds of the air.
22 Abaddon and Death say,
    'We have heard a rumor
        of it with our ears.'

23 "God understands
        the way to it,
    and he knows its place.

24 For he looks to the ends
        of the earth,
    and sees everything under
        the heavens.
25 When he gave to the wind
        its weight,
    and apportioned out the
        waters by measure;
26 when he made a decree
        for the rain,
    and a way for the thunderbolt;
27 then he saw it and declared it;
    he established it, and
        searched it out.
28 And he said to humankind,
    'Truly, the fear of the Lord,
        that is wisdom;
    and to depart from evil is
        understanding.'"

JOB FINISHES HIS DEFENSE

29 Job again took up his dis-
        course and said:
2 "O that I were as in the
        months of old,
    as in the days when God
        watched over me;
3 when his lamp shone
        over my head,
    and by his light I walked
        through darkness;
4 when I was in my prime,
    when the friendship of God
        was upon my tent;
5 when the Almighty[e] was
        still with me,
    when my children were
        around me;
6 when my steps were washed
        with milk,
    and the rock poured out for
        me streams of oil!
7 When I went out to the
        gate of the city,
    when I took my seat
        in the square,
8 the young men saw me
        and withdrew,
    and the aged rose up and stood;
9 the nobles refrained from talking,
    and laid their hands on
        their mouths;

[a] 28.11 Gk Vg: Heb *bind*   [b] 28.13 Gk: Heb *its
price*   [c] 28.16 Or *lapis lazuli*   [d] 28.19 Or
Nubia; Heb *Cush*   [e] 29.5 Traditional
rendering of Heb *Shaddai*

10 the voices of princes were hushed,
   and their tongues stuck to the
      roof of their mouths.
11 When the ear heard, it
      commended me,
   and when the eye saw,
      it approved;
12 because I delivered the
      poor who cried,
   and the orphan who
      had no helper.
13 The blessing of the wretched
      came upon me,
   and I caused the widow's
      heart to sing for joy.
14 I put on righteousness, and
      it clothed me;
   my justice was like a robe
      and a turban.
15 I was eyes to the blind,
      and feet to the lame.
16 I was a father to the needy,
   and I championed the cause
      of the stranger.
17 I broke the fangs of the
      unrighteous,
   and made them drop their
      prey from their teeth.
18 Then I thought, 'I shall die
      in my nest,
   and I shall multiply my days
      like the phoenix;[a]
19 my roots spread out to the waters,
   with the dew all night
      on my branches;
20 my glory was fresh with me,
   and my bow ever new
      in my hand.'

21 "They listened to me, and waited,
   and kept silence for my counsel.
22 After I spoke they did not
      speak again,
   and my word dropped upon
      them like dew.[b]
23 They waited for me as for the rain;
   they opened their mouths
      as for the spring rain.
24 I smiled on them when they
      had no confidence;
   and the light of my countenance
      they did not extinguish.[c]
25 I chose their way, and sat as chief,
   and I lived like a king
      among his troops,
   like one who comforts
      mourners.

30 "But now they make
      sport of me,
   those who are younger than I,
   whose fathers I would
      have disdained
   to set with the dogs
      of my flock.
2 What could I gain from the
      strength of their hands?
   All their vigor is gone.
3 Through want and hard hunger
   they gnaw the dry and
      desolate ground,
4 they pick mallow and the
      leaves of bushes,
   and to warm themselves
      the roots of broom.
5 They are driven out from society;
   people shout after them
      as after a thief.
6 In the gullies of wadis
      they must live,
   in holes in the ground,
      and in the rocks.
7 Among the bushes they bray;
   under the nettles they
      huddle together.
8 A senseless, disreputable brood,
   they have been whipped
      out of the land.

9 "And now they mock me in song;
   I am a byword to them.
10 They abhor me, they keep
      aloof from me;
   they do not hesitate to spit
      at the sight of me.
11 Because God has loosed
      my bowstring and
      humbled me,
   they have cast off restraint
      in my presence.
12 On my right hand the
      rabble rise up;
   they send me sprawling,
   and build roads for my ruin.
13 They break up my path,
   they promote my calamity;
   no one restrains[d] them.
14 As through a wide breach
      they come;
   amid the crash they roll on.

a 29.18 Or like sand   b 29.22 Heb lacks like
dew   c 29.24 Meaning of Heb uncertain
d 30.13 Cn: Heb helps

15 Terrors are turned upon me;
    my honor is pursued as
       by the wind,
    and my prosperity has passed
       away like a cloud.

16 "And now my soul is poured
       out within me;
    days of affliction have
       taken hold of me.
17 The night racks my bones,
    and the pain that gnaws
       me takes no rest.
18 With violence he seizes
       my garment;[a]
    he grasps me by[b] the
       collar of my tunic.
19 He has cast me into the mire,
    and I have become like
       dust and ashes.
20 I cry to you and you do
       not answer me;
    I stand, and you merely
       look at me.
21 You have turned cruel to me;
    with the might of your hand
       you persecute me.
22 You lift me up on the wind, you
       make me ride on it,
    and you toss me about in
       the roar of the storm.
23 I know that you will bring
       me to death,
    and to the house appointed
       for all living.

24 "Surely one does not turn
       against the needy,[c]
    when in disaster they
       cry for help.[d]
25 Did I not weep for those whose
       day was hard?
    Was not my soul grieved
       for the poor?
26 But when I looked for
       good, evil came;
    and when I waited for light,
       darkness came.
27 My inward parts are in turmoil,
       and are never still;
    days of affliction come
       to meet me.
28 I go about in sunless gloom;
    I stand up in the assembly
       and cry for help.
29 I am a brother of jackals,
    and a companion of ostriches.

30 My skin turns black and
       falls from me,
    and my bones burn with heat.
31 My lyre is turned to mourning,
    and my pipe to the voice
       of those who weep.

31

"I have made a covenant
    with my eyes;
how then could I look
    upon a virgin?
2 What would be my portion
       from God above,
    and my heritage from the
       Almighty[e] on high?
3 Does not calamity befall
       the unrighteous,
    and disaster the workers
       of iniquity?
4 Does he not see my ways,
    and number all my steps?

5 "If I have walked with falsehood,
    and my foot has hurried
       to deceit—
6 let me be weighed in a
       just balance,
    and let God know my
       integrity!—
7 if my step has turned aside
       from the way,
    and my heart has followed
       my eyes,
    and if any spot has clung
       to my hands;
8 then let me sow, and another eat;
    and let what grows for
       me be rooted out.

9 "If my heart has been enticed
       by a woman,
    and I have lain in wait at
       my neighbor's door;
10 then let my wife grind for another,
    and let other men kneel
       over her.
11 For that would be a heinous crime;
    that would be a criminal
       offense;
12 for that would be a fire consuming
       down to Abaddon,
    and it would burn to the
       root all my harvest.

a 30.18 Gk: Heb *my garment is disfigured*
b 30.18 Heb *like*   c 30.24 Heb *ruin*
d 30.24 Cn: Meaning of Heb uncertain
e 31.2 Traditional rendering of Heb *Shaddai*

13 "If I have rejected the cause of my
      male or female slaves,
  when they brought a
      complaint against me;
14 what then shall I do when
      God rises up?
  When he makes inquiry, what
      shall I answer him?
15 Did not he who made me in the
      womb make them?
  And did not one fashion
      us in the womb?

16 "If I have withheld anything
      that the poor desired,
  or have caused the eyes of
      the widow to fail,
17 or have eaten my morsel alone,
  and the orphan has not
      eaten from it—
18 for from my youth I reared the
      orphan[a] like a father,
  and from my mother's womb
      I guided the widow[b]—
19 if I have seen anyone perish
      for lack of clothing,
  or a poor person without
      covering,
20 whose loins have not blessed me,
  and who was not warmed with
      the fleece of my sheep;
21 if I have raised my hand
      against the orphan,
  because I saw I had supporters
      at the gate;
22 then let my shoulder blade fall
      from my shoulder,
  and let my arm be broken
      from its socket.
23 For I was in terror of calamity
      from God,
  and I could not have faced
      his majesty.

24 "If I have made gold my trust,
  or called fine gold my confidence;
25 if I have rejoiced because my
      wealth was great,
  or because my hand had
      gotten much;
26 if I have looked at the sun[c]
      when it shone,
  or the moon moving in splendor,
27 and my heart has been
      secretly enticed,
  and my mouth has
      kissed my hand;

28 this also would be an iniquity to
      be punished by the judges,
  for I should have been
      false to God above.

29 "If I have rejoiced at the ruin of
      those who hated me,
  or exulted when evil
      overtook them—
30 I have not let my mouth sin
  by asking for their lives
      with a curse—
31 if those of my tent ever said,
  'O that we might be sated
      with his flesh!'[d]—
32 the stranger has not lodged
      in the street;
  I have opened my doors
      to the traveler—
33 if I have concealed my
      transgressions as
      others do,[e]
  by hiding my iniquity
      in my bosom,
34 because I stood in great fear
      of the multitude,
  and the contempt of families
      terrified me,
  so that I kept silence, and did
      not go out of doors—
35 O that I had one to hear me!
  (Here is my signature! Let the
      Almighty[f] answer me!)
  O that I had the indictment
      written by my adversary!
36 Surely I would carry it on
      my shoulder;
  I would bind it on me
      like a crown;
37 I would give him an account
      of all my steps;
  like a prince I would
      approach him.

38 "If my land has cried out
      against me,
  and its furrows have
      wept together;
39 if I have eaten its yield
      without payment,
  and caused the death
      of its owners;

---

a 31.18 Heb *him*   b 31.18 Heb *her*
c 31.26 Heb *the light*   d 31.31 Meaning of
Heb uncertain   e 31.33 Or *as Adam did*
f 31.35 Traditional rendering of Heb *Shaddai*

40 let thorns grow instead of wheat,
and foul weeds instead
of barley."

The words of Job are ended.

ELIHU REBUKES JOB'S FRIENDS

32 So these three men ceased to answer Job, because he was righteous in his own eyes. 2Then Elihu son of Barachel the Buzite, of the family of Ram, became angry. He was angry at Job because he justified himself rather than God; 3he was angry also at Job's three friends because they had found no answer, though they had declared Job to be in the wrong.[a] 4Now Elihu had waited to speak to Job, because they were older than he. 5But when Elihu saw that there was no answer in the mouths of these three men, he became angry.

6 Elihu son of Barachel the Buzite answered:
"I am young in years,
and you are aged;
therefore I was timid and afraid
to declare my opinion to you.
7 I said, 'Let days speak,
and many years teach wisdom.'
8 But truly it is the spirit in a mortal,
the breath of the Almighty,[b]
that makes for
understanding.
9 It is not the old[c] that are wise,
nor the aged that understand
what is right.
10 Therefore I say, 'Listen to me;
let me also declare my opinion.'

11 "See, I waited for your words,
I listened for your wise sayings,
while you searched out
what to say.
12 I gave you my attention,
but there was in fact no one
that confuted Job,
no one among you that
answered his words.
13 Yet do not say, 'We have
found wisdom;
God may vanquish him,
not a human.'
14 He has not directed his
words against me,
and I will not answer him
with your speeches.

15 "They are dismayed, they
answer no more;
they have not a word to say.
16 And am I to wait, because
they do not speak,
because they stand there,
and answer no more?
17 I also will give my answer;
I also will declare my opinion.
18 For I am full of words;
the spirit within me
constrains me.
19 My heart is indeed like wine
that has no vent;
like new wineskins, it is
ready to burst.
20 I must speak, so that I
may find relief;
I must open my lips
and answer.
21 I will not show partiality
to any person
or use flattery toward anyone.
22 For I do not know how
to flatter—
or my Maker would soon
put an end to me!

ELIHU REBUKES JOB

33 "But now, hear my speech, O Job,
and listen to all my words.
2 See, I open my mouth;
the tongue in my
mouth speaks.
3 My words declare the uprightness
of my heart,
and what my lips know
they speak sincerely.
4 The spirit of God has made me,
and the breath of the
Almighty[b] gives me life.
5 Answer me, if you can;
set your words in order before
me; take your stand.
6 See, before God I am as you are;
I too was formed from
a piece of clay.
7 No fear of me need terrify you;
my pressure will not be
heavy on you.

---

[a] 32.3 Another ancient tradition reads *answer, and had put God in the wrong*
[b] 32.8; 33.4 Traditional rendering of Heb *Shaddai*   [c] 32.9 Gk Syr Vg: Heb *many*

8 "Surely, you have spoken
in my hearing,
and I have heard the sound
of your words.
9 You say, 'I am clean, without
transgression;
I am pure, and there is no
iniquity in me.
10 Look, he finds occasions
against me,
he counts me as his enemy;
11 he puts my feet in the stocks,
and watches all my paths.'

12 "But in this you are not right.
I will answer you:
God is greater than
any mortal.
13 Why do you contend against him,
saying, 'He will answer
none of my[a] words'?
14 For God speaks in one way,
and in two, though people
do not perceive it.
15 In a dream, in a vision
of the night,
when deep sleep falls
on mortals,
while they slumber on
their beds,
16 then he opens their ears,
and terrifies them with
warnings,
17 that he may turn them aside
from their deeds,
and keep them from pride,
18 to spare their souls from the Pit,
their lives from traversing
the River.
19 They are also chastened with
pain upon their beds,
and with continual strife
in their bones,
20 so that their lives loathe bread,
and their appetites dainty food.
21 Their flesh is so wasted away
that it cannot be seen;
and their bones, once
invisible, now stick out.
22 Their souls draw near the Pit,
and their lives to those
who bring death.
23 Then, if there should be for one
of them an angel,
a mediator, one of a thousand,
one who declares a
person upright,

24 and he is gracious to that
person, and says,
'Deliver him from going
down into the Pit;
I have found a ransom;
25 let his flesh become fresh
with youth;
let him return to the days of
his youthful vigor';
26 then he prays to God, and is
accepted by him,
he comes into his presence
with joy,
and God[b] repays him for his
righteousness.
27 That person sings to
others and says,
'I sinned, and perverted
what was right,
and it was not paid back to me.
28 He has redeemed my soul from
going down to the Pit,
and my life shall see the light.'

29 "God indeed does all these things,
twice, three times,
with mortals,
30 to bring back their souls
from the Pit,
so that they may see the
light of life.[c]
31 Pay heed, Job, listen to me;
be silent, and I will speak.
32 If you have anything to
say, answer me;
speak, for I desire to
justify you.
33 If not, listen to me;
be silent, and I will teach
you wisdom."

ELIHU PROCLAIMS
GOD'S JUSTICE

34 Then Elihu continued and
said:
2 "Hear my words, you wise men,
and give ear to me, you
who know;
3 for the ear tests words
as the palate tastes food.
4 Let us choose what is right;
let us determine among
ourselves what is good.

[a] 33.13 Compare Gk: Heb *his* [b] 33.26 Heb
he [c] 33.30 Syr: Heb *to be lighted with the
light of life*

5 For Job has said, 'I am innocent,
    and God has taken away
        my right;
6 in spite of being right I am
        counted a liar;
    my wound is incurable, though I
        am without transgression.'
7 Who is there like Job,
    who drinks up scoffing
        like water,
8 who goes in company
    with evildoers
    and walks with the wicked?
9 For he has said, 'It profits
    one nothing
    to take delight in God.'

10 "Therefore, hear me, you
        who have sense,
    far be it from God that he
        should do wickedness,
    and from the Almighty[a] that
        he should do wrong.
11 For according to their deeds
    he will repay them,
    and according to their ways he
        will make it befall them.
12 Of a truth, God will not
        do wickedly,
    and the Almighty[a] will not
        pervert justice.
13 Who gave him charge
        over the earth
    and who laid on him[b] the
        whole world?
14 If he should take back his
        spirit[c] to himself,
    and gather to himself his breath,
15 all flesh would perish together,
    and all mortals return to dust.

16 "If you have understanding,
        hear this;
    listen to what I say.
17 Shall one who hates justice
        govern?
    Will you condemn one who is
        righteous and mighty,
18 who says to a king, 'You scoundrel!'
    and to princes, 'You
        wicked men!';
19 who shows no partiality
        to nobles,
    nor regards the rich more
        than the poor,
    for they are all the work
        of his hands?

20 In a moment they die;
    at midnight the people are
        shaken and pass away,
    and the mighty are taken away
        by no human hand.

21 "For his eyes are upon the
        ways of mortals,
    and he sees all their steps.
22 There is no gloom or deep
        darkness
    where evildoers may
        hide themselves.
23 For he has not appointed a
        time[d] for anyone
    to go before God in judgment.
24 He shatters the mighty without
        investigation,
    and sets others in their place.
25 Thus, knowing their works,
    he overturns them in
        the night, and they
        are crushed.
26 He strikes them for their
        wickedness
    while others look on,
27 because they turned aside
        from following him,
    and had no regard for
        any of his ways,
28 so that they caused the cry of the
        poor to come to him,
    and he heard the cry of
        the afflicted—
29 When he is quiet, who
        can condemn?
    When he hides his face,
        who can behold him,
    whether it be a nation or
        an individual?—
30 so that the godless should
        not reign,
    or those who ensnare
        the people.

31 "For has anyone said to God,
    'I have endured punishment; I
        will not offend any more;
32 teach me what I do not see;
    if I have done iniquity, I
        will do it no more'?

a 34.10,12 Traditional rendering of Heb
Shaddai   b 34.13 Heb lacks on him
c 34.14 Heb his heart his spirit   d 34.23 Cn:
Heb yet

33 Will he then pay back to suit you,
  because you reject it?
For you must choose, and not I;
  therefore declare what
    you know.[a]
34 Those who have sense
    will say to me,
  and the wise who hear
    me will say,
35 'Job speaks without knowledge,
  his words are without insight.'
36 Would that Job were tried
    to the limit,
  because his answers are
    those of the wicked.
37 For he adds rebellion to his sin;
  he claps his hands among us,
  and multiplies his words
    against God."

ELIHU CONDEMNS
SELF-RIGHTEOUSNESS

35 Elihu continued and said:
2"Do you think this
    to be just?
You say, 'I am in the
  right before God.'
3 If you ask, 'What advantage have I?
  How am I better off than
    if I had sinned?'
4 I will answer you
  and your friends with you.
5 Look at the heavens and see;
  observe the clouds, which
    are higher than you.
6 If you have sinned, what do you
    accomplish against him?
  And if your transgressions
    are multiplied, what
    do you do to him?
7 If you are righteous, what do
    you give to him;
  or what does he receive
    from your hand?
8 Your wickedness affects
    others like you,
  and your righteousness,
    other human beings.

9 "Because of the multitude of
    oppressions people cry out;
  they call for help because of
    the arm of the mighty.
10 But no one says, 'Where is
    God my Maker,
  who gives strength
    in the night,

11 who teaches us more than the
    animals of the earth,
  and makes us wiser than
    the birds of the air?'
12 There they cry out, but he
    does not answer,
  because of the pride
    of evildoers.
13 Surely God does not hear
    an empty cry,
  nor does the Almighty[b]
    regard it.
14 How much less when you say
    that you do not see him,
  that the case is before him, and
    you are waiting for him!
15 And now, because his anger
    does not punish,
  and he does not greatly
    heed transgression,[c]
16 Job opens his mouth in
    empty talk,
  he multiplies words without
    knowledge."

ELIHU EXALTS GOD'S GOODNESS

36 Elihu continued and said:
2"Bear with me a little,
    and I will show you,
  for I have yet something to
    say on God's behalf.
3 I will bring my knowledge
    from far away,
  and ascribe righteousness
    to my Maker.
4 For truly my words are not false;
  one who is perfect in
    knowledge is with you.

5 "Surely God is mighty and
    does not despise any;
  he is mighty in strength
    of understanding.
6 He does not keep the
    wicked alive,
  but gives the afflicted
    their right.
7 He does not withdraw his eyes
    from the righteous,
  but with kings on the throne
    he sets them forever, and
    they are exalted.

a 34.33 Meaning of Heb of verses 29–33
uncertain   b 35.13 Traditional rendering
of Heb *Shaddai*   c 35.15 Theodotion
Symmachus Compare Vg: Meaning of Heb
uncertain

8 And if they are bound in fetters
    and caught in the cords
        of affliction,
9 then he declares to them
        their work
    and their transgressions,
        that they are behaving
            arrogantly.
10 He opens their ears to instruction,
    and commands that they
        return from iniquity.
11 If they listen, and serve him,
    they complete their days
        in prosperity,
    and their years in pleasantness.
12 But if they do not listen, they shall
        perish by the sword,
    and die without knowledge.

13 "The godless in heart
        cherish anger;
    they do not cry for help
        when he binds them.
14 They die in their youth,
    and their life ends in shame.[a]
15 He delivers the afflicted by
        their affliction,
    and opens their ear by adversity.
16 He also allured you out of distress
    into a broad place where there
        was no constraint,
    and what was set on your
        table was full of fatness.

17 "But you are obsessed with the
        case of the wicked;
    judgment and justice seize you.
18 Beware that wrath does not
        entice you into scoffing,
    and do not let the greatness of
        the ransom turn you aside.
19 Will your cry avail to keep
        you from distress,
    or will all the force of
        your strength?
20 Do not long for the night,
    when peoples are cut off
        in their place.
21 Beware! Do not turn to iniquity;
    because of that you have been
        tried by affliction.
22 See, God is exalted in his power;
    who is a teacher like him?
23 Who has prescribed for
        him his way,
    or who can say, 'You have
        done wrong'?

ELIHU PROCLAIMS GOD'S MAJESTY

24 "Remember to extol his work,
    of which mortals have sung.
25 All people have looked on it;
    everyone watches it
        from far away.
26 Surely God is great, and we
        do not know him;
    the number of his years
        is unsearchable.
27 For he draws up the drops of water;
    he distills[b] his mist in rain,
28 which the skies pour down
    and drop upon mortals
        abundantly.
29 Can anyone understand the
        spreading of the clouds,
    the thunderings of his pavilion?
30 See, he scatters his lightning
        around him
    and covers the roots of the sea.
31 For by these he governs peoples;
    he gives food in abundance.
32 He covers his hands with
        the lightning,
    and commands it to
        strike the mark.
33 Its crashing[c] tells about him;
    he is jealous[c] with anger
        against iniquity.

37 "At this also my
        heart trembles,
    and leaps out of its place.
2 Listen, listen to the thunder
        of his voice
    and the rumbling that comes
        from his mouth.
3 Under the whole heaven
        he lets it loose,
    and his lightning to the
        corners of the earth.
4 After it his voice roars;
    he thunders with his
        majestic voice
    and he does not restrain
        the lightnings[d] when
            his voice is heard.
5 God thunders wondrously
        with his voice;
    he does great things that we
        cannot comprehend.

a 36.14 Heb ends among the temple
prostitutes   b 36.27 Cn: Heb they
distill   c 36.33 Meaning of Heb uncertain
d 37.4 Heb them

6 For to the snow he says,
'Fall on the earth';
and the shower of rain, his
heavy shower of rain,
7 serves as a sign on
everyone's hand,
so that all whom he has
made may know it.[a]
8 Then the animals go into
their lairs
and remain in their dens.
9 From its chamber comes
the whirlwind,
and cold from the
scattering winds.
10 By the breath of God ice is given,
and the broad waters
are frozen fast.
11 He loads the thick cloud
with moisture;
the clouds scatter his lightning.
12 They turn round and round
by his guidance,
to accomplish all that he
commands them
on the face of the
habitable world.
13 Whether for correction,
or for his land,
or for love, he causes
it to happen.

14 "Hear this, O Job;
stop and consider the
wondrous works of God.
15 Do you know how God lays his
command upon them,
and causes the lightning of
his cloud to shine?
16 Do you know the balancings
of the clouds,
the wondrous works
of the one whose
knowledge is perfect,
17 you whose garments are hot
when the earth is still because
of the south wind?
18 Can you, like him, spread
out the skies,
hard as a molten mirror?
19 Teach us what we shall say to him;
we cannot draw up our case
because of darkness.
20 Should he be told that I
want to speak?
Did anyone ever wish to
be swallowed up?

21 Now, no one can look on the light
when it is bright in the skies,
when the wind has passed
and cleared them.
22 Out of the north comes
golden splendor;
around God is awesome
majesty.
23 The Almighty[b]—we cannot
find him;
he is great in power
and justice,
and abundant righteousness
he will not violate.
24 Therefore mortals fear him;
he does not regard any who are
wise in their own conceit."

THE LORD ANSWERS JOB

38 Then the LORD answered Job
out of the whirlwind:
2 "Who is this that darkens
counsel by words
without knowledge?
3 Gird up your loins like a man,
I will question you, and you
shall declare to me.

4 "Where were you when I laid the
foundation of the earth?
Tell me, if you have
understanding.
5 Who determined its
measurements—
surely you know!
Or who stretched the
line upon it?
6 On what were its bases sunk,
or who laid its cornerstone
7 when the morning stars
sang together
and all the heavenly beings[c]
shouted for joy?

8 "Or who shut in the sea
with doors
when it burst out from
the womb?—
9 when I made the clouds
its garment,
and thick darkness its
swaddling band,
10 and prescribed bounds for it,
and set bars and doors,

a 37.7 Meaning of Heb of verse 7 uncertain
b 37.23 Traditional rendering of Heb *Shaddai*
c 38.7 Heb *sons of God*

11 and said, 'Thus far shall you
        come, and no farther,
    and here shall your proud
        waves be stopped'?

12 "Have you commanded
        the morning since
        your days began,
    and caused the dawn to
        know its place,
13 so that it might take hold of the
        skirts of the earth,
    and the wicked be
        shaken out of it?
14 It is changed like clay
        under the seal,
    and it is dyed[a] like a garment.
15 Light is withheld from the wicked,
    and their uplifted arm
        is broken.

16 "Have you entered into the
        springs of the sea,
    or walked in the recesses
        of the deep?
17 Have the gates of death been
        revealed to you,
    or have you seen the gates
        of deep darkness?
18 Have you comprehended the
        expanse of the earth?
    Declare, if you know all this.

19 "Where is the way to the
        dwelling of light,
    and where is the place
        of darkness,
20 that you may take it to its territory
    and that you may discern
        the paths to its home?
21 Surely you know, for you
        were born then,
    and the number of your
        days is great!

22 "Have you entered the
        storehouses of the snow,
    or have you seen the
        storehouses of the hail,
23 which I have reserved for the
        time of trouble,
    for the day of battle and war?
24 What is the way to the place
        where the light is
        distributed,
    or where the east wind is
        scattered upon the earth?

25 "Who has cut a channel for
        the torrents of rain,
    and a way for the thunderbolt,
26 to bring rain on a land where
        no one lives,
    on the desert, which is
        empty of human life,
27 to satisfy the waste and
        desolate land,
    and to make the ground
        put forth grass?

28 "Has the rain a father,
    or who has begotten the
        drops of dew?
29 From whose womb did the
        ice come forth,
    and who has given birth to
        the hoarfrost of heaven?
30 The waters become hard
        like stone,
    and the face of the
        deep is frozen.

WHEN WE LOOK UPON THE
WORLD AND KNOW THERE
MUST BE MORE THAN WE CAN
SEE, THE ETERNAL POWER
OF GOD IS REVEALED.

31 "Can you bind the chains
        of the Pleiades,
    or loose the cords of Orion?
32 Can you lead forth the Mazzaroth
        in their season,
    or can you guide the Bear
        with its children?
33 Do you know the ordinances
        of the heavens?
    Can you establish their
        rule on the earth?

34 "Can you lift up your voice
        to the clouds,
    so that a flood of waters
        may cover you?

a 38.14 Cn: Heb *and they stand forth*

35 Can you send forth lightnings,
  so that they may go
  and say to you, 'Here we are'?
36 Who has put wisdom in the
  inward parts,ᵃ
  or given understanding
  to the mind?ᵃ
37 Who has the wisdom to
  number the clouds?
  Or who can tilt the waterskins
  of the heavens,
38 when the dust runs into a mass
  and the clods cling together?

39 "Can you hunt the prey
  for the lion,
  or satisfy the appetite of
  the young lions,
40 when they crouch in their dens,
  or lie in wait in their covert?
41 Who provides for the
  raven its prey,
  when its young ones cry to God,
  and wander about for
  lack of food?

39 "Do you know when the
  mountain goats give birth?
  Do you observe the calving
  of the deer?
2 Can you number the months
  that they fulfill,
  and do you know the time
  when they give birth,
3 when they crouch to give birth
  to their offspring,
  and are delivered of
  their young?
4 Their young ones become strong,
  they grow up in the open;
  they go forth, and do not
  return to them.

5 "Who has let the wild ass go free?
  Who has loosed the bonds
  of the swift ass,
6 to which I have given the
  steppe for its home,
  the salt land for its
  dwelling place?
7 It scorns the tumult of the city;
  it does not hear the shouts
  of the driver.
8 It ranges the mountains
  as its pasture,
  and it searches after every
  green thing.

9 "Is the wild ox willing
  to serve you?
  Will it spend the night
  at your crib?
10 Can you tie it in the furrow
  with ropes,
  or will it harrow the
  valleys after you?
11 Will you depend on it because
  its strength is great,
  and will you hand over
  your labor to it?
12 Do you have faith in it that
  it will return,
  and bring your grain to your
  threshing floor?ᵇ

13 "The ostrich's wings flap wildly,
  though its pinions lack
  plumage.ᵃ
14 For it leaves its eggs to the earth,
  and lets them be warmed
  on the ground,
15 forgetting that a foot may
  crush them,
  and that a wild animal
  may trample them.
16 It deals cruelly with its young, as
  if they were not its own;
  though its labor should be in
  vain, yet it has no fear;
17 because God has made it
  forget wisdom,
  and given it no share in
  understanding.
18 When it spreads its plumes aloft,ᵃ
  it laughs at the horse
  and its rider.

19 "Do you give the horse its might?
  Do you clothe its neck
  with mane?
20 Do you make it leap like
  the locust?
  Its majestic snorting is terrible.
21 It pawsᶜ violently, exults
  mightily;
  it goes out to meet the
  weapons.
22 It laughs at fear, and is
  not dismayed;
  it does not turn back
  from the sword.

ᵃ 38.36; 39.13,18 Meaning of Heb uncertain
ᵇ 39.12 Heb *your grain and your threshing floor* ᶜ 39.21 Gk Syr Vg: Heb *they dig*

23 Upon it rattle the quiver,
    the flashing spear, and
        the javelin.
24 With fierceness and rage it
        swallows the ground;
    it cannot stand still at the
        sound of the trumpet.
25 When the trumpet sounds,
        it says 'Aha!'
    From a distance it smells
        the battle,
    the thunder of the captains,
        and the shouting.

26 "Is it by your wisdom that
        the hawk soars,
    and spreads its wings
        toward the south?
27 Is it at your command that
        the eagle mounts up
    and makes its nest on high?
28 It lives on the rock and
        makes its home
    in the fastness of the rocky crag.
29 From there it spies the prey;
    its eyes see it from far away.
30 Its young ones suck up blood;
    and where the slain
        are, there it is."

40 And the LORD said to Job:
2   "Shall a faultfinder
    contend with the
    Almighty?[a]
    Anyone who argues with
    God must respond."

JOB'S RESPONSE TO GOD

3 Then Job answered the LORD:
4 "See, I am of small account; what
        shall I answer you?
    I lay my hand on my mouth.
5 I have spoken once, and I
        will not answer;
    twice, but will proceed
        no further."

GOD'S CHALLENGE TO JOB

6 Then the LORD answered Job
out of the whirlwind:
7 "Gird up your loins like a man;
    I will question you, and
        you declare to me.
8 Will you even put me in
        the wrong?
    Will you condemn me that
        you may be justified?

9 Have you an arm like God,
    and can you thunder with
        a voice like his?

10 "Deck yourself with majesty
        and dignity;
    clothe yourself with glory
        and splendor.
11 Pour out the overflowings
        of your anger,
    and look on all who are proud,
        and abase them.
12 Look on all who are proud,
        and bring them low;
    tread down the wicked
        where they stand.
13 Hide them all in the dust
        together;
    bind their faces in the
        world below.[b]
14 Then I will also acknowledge
        to you
    that your own right hand
        can give you victory.

15 "Look at Behemoth,
    which I made just as
        I made you;
    it eats grass like an ox.
16 Its strength is in its loins,
    and its power in the
        muscles of its belly.
17 It makes its tail stiff like a cedar;
    the sinews of its thighs
        are knit together.
18 Its bones are tubes of bronze,
    its limbs like bars of iron.

19 "It is the first of the great
        acts of God—
    only its Maker can approach
        it with the sword.
20 For the mountains yield
        food for it
    where all the wild
        animals play.
21 Under the lotus plants it lies,
    in the covert of the reeds
        and in the marsh.
22 The lotus trees cover it for shade;
    the willows of the wadi
        surround it.

[a] 40.2 Traditional rendering of Heb Shaddai
[b] 40.13 Heb the hidden place

23 Even if the river is turbulent,
     it is not frightened;
   it is confident though Jordan
     rushes against its mouth.
24 Can one take it with hooks[a]
     or pierce its nose with a snare?

41[b] "Can you draw out
       Leviathan[c] with
       a fishhook,
     or press down its tongue
       with a cord?
2 Can you put a rope in its nose,
     or pierce its jaw with a hook?
3 Will it make many
       supplications to you?
     Will it speak soft words to you?
4 Will it make a covenant with you
     to be taken as your
       servant forever?
5 Will you play with it as
       with a bird,
     or will you put it on leash
       for your girls?
6 Will traders bargain over it?
     Will they divide it up among
       the merchants?
7 Can you fill its skin with
       harpoons,
     or its head with fishing spears?
8 Lay hands on it;
     think of the battle; you
       will not do it again!
9[d] Any hope of capturing it[e] will
       be disappointed;
     were not even the gods[f]
       overwhelmed at
       the sight of it?
10 No one is so fierce as to
       dare to stir it up.
     Who can stand before it?[g]
11 Who can confront it[g] and be safe?[h]
     —under the whole
       heaven, who?[i]

12 "I will not keep silence
       concerning its limbs,
     or its mighty strength, or
       its splendid frame.
13 Who can strip off its outer
       garment?
     Who can penetrate its
       double coat of mail?[j]
14 Who can open the doors
       of its face?
     There is terror all around
       its teeth.

15 Its back[k] is made of shields
       in rows,
     shut up closely as with a seal.
16 One is so near to another
     that no air can come
       between them.
17 They are joined one to another;
     they clasp each other and
       cannot be separated.
18 Its sneezes flash forth light,
     and its eyes are like the
       eyelids of the dawn.
19 From its mouth go flaming
       torches;
     sparks of fire leap out.
20 Out of its nostrils comes smoke,
     as from a boiling pot and
       burning rushes.
21 Its breath kindles coals,
     and a flame comes out
       of its mouth.
22 In its neck abides strength,
     and terror dances before it.
23 The folds of its flesh cling
       together;
     it is firmly cast and
       immovable.
24 Its heart is as hard as stone,
     as hard as the lower millstone.
25 When it raises itself up the
       gods are afraid;
     at the crashing they are
       beside themselves.
26 Though the sword reaches it,
       it does not avail,
     nor does the spear, the
       dart, or the javelin.
27 It counts iron as straw,
     and bronze as rotten wood.
28 The arrow cannot make it flee;
     slingstones, for it, are
       turned to chaff.
29 Clubs are counted as chaff;
     it laughs at the rattle
       of javelins.
30 Its underparts are like
       sharp potsherds;
     it spreads itself like a threshing
       sledge on the mire.

a 40.24 Cn: Heb *in his eyes*   b 41.1 Ch 40.25
in Heb   c 41.1 Or *the crocodile*   d 41.9 Ch
41.1 in Heb   e 41.9 Heb *of it*   f 41.9 Cn
Compare Symmachus Syr: Heb *one is*
g 41.10,11 Heb *me*   h 41.11 Gk: Heb *that I
shall repay*   i 41.11 Heb *to me*   j 41.13 Gk:
Heb *bridle*   k 41.15 Cn Compare Gk Vg: Heb
pride

31 It makes the deep boil like a pot;
    it makes the sea like a
        pot of ointment.
32 It leaves a shining wake behind it;
    one would think the deep
        to be white-haired.
33 On earth it has no equal,
    a creature without fear.
34 It surveys everything
        that is lofty;
    it is king over all that
        are proud."

JOB IS HUMBLED AND SATISFIED

42 Then Job answered the LORD:
2 "I know that you can do
        all things,
    and that no purpose of yours
        can be thwarted.
3 'Who is this that hides counsel
        without knowledge?'
    Therefore I have uttered what
        I did not understand,
    things too wonderful for me,
        which I did not know.
4 'Hear, and I will speak;
    I will question you, and
        you declare to me.'
5 I had heard of you by the
        hearing of the ear,
    but now my eye sees you;
6 therefore I despise myself,
    and repent in dust
        and ashes."

JOB'S FRIENDS ARE HUMILIATED

7 After the LORD had spoken these words to Job, the LORD said to Eliphaz the Temanite: "My wrath is kindled against you and against your two friends; for you have not spoken of me what is right, as my servant Job has. 8 Now therefore take seven bulls and seven rams, and go to my servant Job, and offer up for yourselves a burnt offering; and my servant Job shall pray for you, for I will accept his prayer not to deal with you according to your folly; for you have not spoken of me what is right, as my servant Job has done." 9 So Eliphaz the Temanite and Bildad the Shuhite and Zophar the Naamathite went and did what the LORD had told them; and the LORD accepted Job's prayer.

PONDER

"I know that you can do all things, and that no purpose of yours can be thwarted. 'Who is this that hides counsel without knowledge?' Therefore I have uttered what I did not understand, things too wonderful for me, which I did not know."
—Job 42.2–3

PRAY

Almighty God, it is awe-inspiring to us to be confronted with so much evidence of your powerful and majestic nature. And even more marvelous, you have offered to be our Father, in whom our troubles, doubts, trials, fears and sorrows are taken away. Through your Son Jesus Christ and the Holy Spirit, your power, strength, wisdom and knowledge are always available to us. Cleanse us from the egocentricity that makes us think we don't need you. In our approach to you, let us be humble as brothers and sisters of our Savior, Jesus Christ. In his name we pray. Amen.

JOB'S FORTUNES ARE RESTORED TWOFOLD

10 And the LORD restored the fortunes of Job when he had prayed for his friends; and the LORD gave Job twice as much as he had before. 11 Then there came to him all his brothers and sisters and all who had known him before, and they ate bread with him in his house; they showed him sympathy and comforted him for all the evil that the LORD had brought upon him; and each of them gave him a piece of money[a] and a gold ring. 12 The LORD blessed the latter days of Job more than his beginning; and he had fourteen thousand sheep, six thousand camels, a thousand yoke of oxen, and a thousand donkeys.

[a] **42.11** Heb *a qesitah*

¹³He also had seven sons and three daughters. ¹⁴He named the first Jemimah, the second Keziah, and the third Keren-happuch. ¹⁵In all the land there were no women so beautiful as Job's daughters; and their father gave them an inheritance along with their brothers. ¹⁶After this Job lived one hundred and forty years, and saw his children, and his children's children, four generations. ¹⁷And Job died, old and full of days.

The

PSALMS

Perhaps nothing reflects who we are as much as the way in which we express our most intimate thoughts about the God who deserves our most honest and sincere worship. Psalms is a collection of prayers and songs written by a variety of authors who voice their praise, fears and questions. The psalms help us discover what it means to be honest with God, for we often hear our own emotions reflected in these timeless songs. Through the psalms, we discover what it means to "worship in spirit and truth" (John 4.24).

BOOK I

(PSALMS 1–41)

PSALM 1

THE TWO WAYS

1 Happy are those
who do not follow the advice
of the wicked,
or take the path that sinners tread,
or sit in the seat of scoffers;
2 but their delight is in the
law of the LORD,
and on his law they meditate
day and night.
3 They are like trees
planted by streams of water,
which yield their fruit in its season,
and their leaves do not wither.
In all that they do, they prosper.

4 The wicked are not so,
but are like chaff that the
wind drives away.
5 Therefore the wicked will not
stand in the judgment,
nor sinners in the congregation
of the righteous;
6 for the LORD watches over the
way of the righteous,
but the way of the wicked
will perish.

PSALM 2

GOD'S PROMISE TO
HIS ANOINTED

1 Why do the nations conspire,
and the peoples plot in vain?

2 The kings of the earth set
themselves,
and the rulers take
counsel together,
against the LORD and his
anointed, saying,
3 "Let us burst their
bonds asunder,
and cast their
cords from us."

WALKING WITH THE SPIRIT

IS A MATTER OF CONSTANT

FAITHFULNESS TO CHRIST

IN EVERY ACT AND

DECISION OF OUR LIVES.

4 He who sits in the heavens
laughs;
the LORD has them
in derision.
5 Then he will speak to them
in his wrath,
and terrify them in his
fury, saying,
6 "I have set my king on Zion,
my holy hill."

7 I will tell of the decree
of the LORD:
He said to me, "You
are my son;
today I have begotten you.

⊣| BIBLE IN LIFE |▷

The Delightful Law

Psalm 1.1–6

The psalmist is not extolling a cold and sterile observance of the multiple laws later emphasized by the Pharisees during the time of Jesus. The emphasis here is on the much broader concept of righteousness, which includes principles of justice, fair treatment of the poor and weak, humility, service of others and forgiveness. It includes a total commitment to these finer aspects of life, from which a worshiper derives "delight" and "meditate[s] day and night" on God's laws.

8 Ask of me, and I will make the
    nations your heritage,
  and the ends of the earth
    your possession.
9 You shall break them with
    a rod of iron,
  and dash them in pieces
    like a potter's vessel."

10 Now therefore, O kings, be wise;
  be warned, O rulers
    of the earth.
11 Serve the LORD with fear,
  with trembling 12kiss his feet,[a]
or he will be angry, and you
    will perish in the way;
  for his wrath is quickly kindled.

Happy are all who take
  refuge in him.

PSALM 3

TRUST IN GOD UNDER
ADVERSITY

A Psalm of David, when he fled
from his son Absalom.

1 O LORD, how many are my foes!
  Many are rising against me;
2 many are saying to me,
  "There is no help for you[b] in
    God."   *Selah*

3 But you, O LORD, are a
    shield around me,
  my glory, and the one who
    lifts up my head.
4 I cry aloud to the LORD,
  and he answers me from his
    holy hill.   *Selah*

5 I lie down and sleep;
  I wake again, for the
    LORD sustains me.
6 I am not afraid of ten
    thousands of people
  who have set themselves
    against me all around.

7 Rise up, O LORD!
  Deliver me, O my God!
  For you strike all my enemies
    on the cheek;
  you break the teeth of
    the wicked.

8 Deliverance belongs to the LORD;
  may your blessing be on your
    people!   *Selah*

PSALM 4

CONFIDENT PLEA FOR
DELIVERANCE FROM ENEMIES

To the leader: with stringed instruments.
A Psalm of David.

1 Answer me when I call,
  O God of my right!
  You gave me room when
    I was in distress.
  Be gracious to me, and
    hear my prayer.

2 How long, you people, shall my
    honor suffer shame?
  How long will you love vain
    words, and seek after
    lies?   *Selah*
3 But know that the LORD
    has set apart the
    faithful for himself;
  the LORD hears when
    I call to him.

4 When you are disturbed,[c]
    do not sin;
  ponder it on your beds, and be
    silent.   *Selah*
5 Offer right sacrifices,
  and put your trust in
    the LORD.

6 There are many who say, "O that
    we might see some good!
  Let the light of your face
    shine on us, O LORD!"
7 You have put gladness
    in my heart
  more than when their grain
    and wine abound.

8 I will both lie down and
    sleep in peace;
  for you alone, O LORD, make
    me lie down in safety.

[a] 2.12 Cn: Meaning of Heb of verses 11b
and 12a is uncertain   [b] 3.2 Syr: Heb *him*
[c] 4.4 Or *are angry*

PSALM 5

TRUST IN GOD FOR DELIVERANCE FROM ENEMIES

To the leader: for the flutes.
A Psalm of David.

1 Give ear to my words,
    O LORD;
  give heed to my
    sighing.
2 Listen to the sound
    of my cry,
  my King and my God,
    for to you I pray.
3 O LORD, in the morning you
    hear my voice;
  in the morning I plead my
    case to you, and watch.

4 For you are not a God who
    delights in wickedness;
  evil will not sojourn
    with you.
5 The boastful will not stand
    before your eyes;
  you hate all evildoers.
6 You destroy those
    who speak lies;
  the LORD abhors the
    bloodthirsty and deceitful.

7 But I, through the abundance
    of your steadfast love,
  will enter your house,
    I will bow down toward
      your holy temple
    in awe of you.
8 Lead me, O LORD, in your
    righteousness
  because of my enemies;
    make your way straight
      before me.

9 For there is no truth in
    their mouths;
  their hearts are destruction;
  their throats are open graves;
    they flatter with their
      tongues.
10 Make them bear their guilt, O God;
  let them fall by their
    own counsels;
  because of their many
    transgressions
      cast them out,
  for they have rebelled
    against you.

11 But let all who take refuge
    in you rejoice;
  let them ever sing for joy.
  Spread your protection
    over them,
  so that those who love your
    name may exult in you.
12 For you bless the righteous,
    O LORD;
  you cover them with favor
    as with a shield.

BIBLE IN LIFE

Peace That Transcends Understanding   *Psalm 4.1–8*

When was the last time you felt totally at peace? I recall one Memorial Day when I was out on a little two-person fishing boat with my grandson, Joshua. He wanted to be the captain of the ship, so he sat in the front seat steering the boat. Every now and then, we'd catch a nice bass. We were enjoying a beautiful day fishing on the pond, just me and my grandson. This was a time for us of true peace. But what about the times that have not been so tranquil? When someone in our family has died, or we've been unsure of what life was going to bring next? When we were in debt or in danger of losing our business? We have experienced all these things. Can we have peace in the turmoil of our daily existence? The answer is "yes." God has promised that we can have peace even in the midst of difficult times in life. The key to finding this peace is trusting that God will indeed take care of us, that God hears our prayers (see Philippians 4.6) and has the will and the power to answer them for our good. God is always with us, whether we are fishing on a tranquil lake or struggling with a long-term illness. We never need to fear (see John 14.27), and we can rest in the "peace of God, which surpasses all understanding" (Philippians 4.7).

PSALM 6

PRAYER FOR RECOVERY FROM GRAVE ILLNESS

To the leader: with stringed instruments; according to The Sheminith. A Psalm of David.

1 O LORD, do not rebuke me
in your anger,
or discipline me in your wrath.
2 Be gracious to me, O LORD, for
I am languishing;
O LORD, heal me, for my bones
are shaking with terror.
3 My soul also is struck with terror,
while you, O LORD—how long?

4 Turn, O LORD, save my life;
deliver me for the sake of
your steadfast love.
5 For in death there is no
remembrance of you;
in Sheol who can give you praise?

6 I am weary with my moaning;
every night I flood my
bed with tears;
I drench my couch with
my weeping.
7 My eyes waste away because of grief;
they grow weak because
of all my foes.

8 Depart from me, all you
workers of evil,
for the LORD has heard the
sound of my weeping.
9 The LORD has heard my
supplication;
the LORD accepts my prayer.
10 All my enemies shall be ashamed
and struck with terror;
they shall turn back, and in a
moment be put to shame.

PSALM 7

PLEA FOR HELP AGAINST PERSECUTORS

A Shiggaion of David, which he sang to the LORD concerning Cush, a Benjaminite.

1 O LORD my God, in you
I take refuge;
save me from all my pursuers,
and deliver me,

2 or like a lion they will
tear me apart;
they will drag me away,
with no one to rescue.

3 O LORD my God, if I have
done this,
if there is wrong in my hands,
4 if I have repaid my ally
with harm
or plundered my foe
without cause,
5 then let the enemy pursue
and overtake me,
trample my life to the ground,
and lay my soul in the
dust.   *Selah*

6 Rise up, O LORD,
in your anger;
lift yourself up against the
fury of my enemies;
awake, O my God;[a] you have
appointed a judgment.
7 Let the assembly of the peoples
be gathered around you,
and over it take your
seat[b] on high.
8 The LORD judges the peoples;
judge me, O LORD, according
to my righteousness
and according to the integrity
that is in me.

9 O let the evil of the wicked
come to an end,
but establish the righteous,
you who test the minds
and hearts,
O righteous God.
10 God is my shield,
who saves the upright in heart.
11 God is a righteous judge,
and a God who has
indignation every day.

12 If one does not repent, God[c]
will whet his sword;
he has bent and strung
his bow;
13 he has prepared his deadly
weapons,
making his arrows fiery shafts.

a 7.6 Or *awake for me*   b 7.7 Cn: Heb *return*
c 7.12 Heb *he*

14 See how they conceive evil,
   and are pregnant with
      mischief,
   and bring forth lies.
15 They make a pit,
      digging it out,
   and fall into the hole that
      they have made.
16 Their mischief returns upon
      their own heads,
   and on their own heads their
      violence descends.

17 I will give to the LORD the thanks
      due to his righteousness,
   and sing praise to the name of
      the LORD, the Most High.

PSALM 8

DIVINE MAJESTY AND HUMAN DIGNITY

To the leader: according to The Gittith. A Psalm of David.

1 O LORD, our Sovereign,
   how majestic is your name
      in all the earth!

You have set your glory
   above the heavens.
2   Out of the mouths of
      babes and infants
you have founded a bulwark
   because of your foes,
   to silence the enemy and
      the avenger.

3 When I look at your heavens, the
      work of your fingers,
   the moon and the stars that
      you have established;
4 what are human beings that you
      are mindful of them,
   mortals[a] that you care
      for them?

5 Yet you have made them a
      little lower than God,[b]
   and crowned them with
      glory and honor.
6 You have given them
      dominion over the
      works of your hands;
   you have put all things
      under their feet,

PONDER

When I look at your heavens, the work of your fingers, the moon and the stars that you have established; what are human beings that you are mindful of them, mortals that you care for them?
—Psalm 8.3–4

PRAY

Creator God, this psalm reminds us of your glory, beauty and majesty in creating the universe. You gave us the mental capabilities and scientific tools to ascertain facts about your creation. Help us not to be fearful to face scientific truth, because it does not infringe upon or damage our faith; in fact, it can strengthen it. We are grateful that you created us just a little lower than the angels; you have crowned us with glory and honor and put us over your creation. We are grateful that by your grace we have been given salvation through our faith in Jesus Christ, in whose name we pray. Amen.

---

7   all sheep and oxen,
      and also the beasts of the field,
8   the birds of the air, and the
         fish of the sea,
      whatever passes along the
         paths of the seas.

9 O LORD, our Sovereign,
   how majestic is your name
      in all the earth!

PSALM 9

GOD'S POWER AND JUSTICE

To the leader: according to Muth-labben. A Psalm of David.

1   I will give thanks to the LORD
         with my whole heart;
      I will tell of all your
         wonderful deeds.

a **8.4** Heb *ben adam*, lit. *son of man*
b **8.5** Or *than the divine beings* or *angels*: Heb *elohim*

² I will be glad and exult in you;
   I will sing praise to your
      name, O Most High.

³ When my enemies turned back,
   they stumbled and perished
      before you.
⁴ For you have maintained
      my just cause;
   you have sat on the throne
      giving righteous
         judgment.

⁵ You have rebuked the nations,
   you have destroyed
      the wicked;
   you have blotted out their
      name forever and ever.
⁶ The enemies have vanished
      in everlasting ruins;
   their cities you have rooted out;
   the very memory of them
      has perished.

⁷ But the LORD sits enthroned
      forever,
   he has established his
      throne for judgment.
⁸ He judges the world with
      righteousness;
   he judges the peoples
      with equity.

⁹ The LORD is a stronghold
      for the oppressed,
   a stronghold in times
      of trouble.
¹⁰ And those who know your name
      put their trust in you,
   for you, O LORD, have
      not forsaken those
         who seek you.

¹¹ Sing praises to the LORD,
      who dwells in Zion.
   Declare his deeds among
      the peoples.
¹² For he who avenges blood is
      mindful of them;
   he does not forget the cry
      of the afflicted.

¹³ Be gracious to me, O LORD.
   See what I suffer from
      those who hate me;
   you are the one who lifts me up
      from the gates of death,

¹⁴ so that I may recount all
      your praises,
   and, in the gates of
      daughter Zion,
   rejoice in your deliverance.

¹⁵ The nations have sunk in the
      pit that they made;
   in the net that they hid
      has their own foot
         been caught.
¹⁶ The LORD has made himself
      known, he has
      executed judgment;
   the wicked are snared in
      the work of their own
      hands.   *Higgaion. Selah*

¹⁷ The wicked shall
      depart to Sheol,
   all the nations
      that forget God.

¹⁸ For the needy shall not always
      be forgotten,
   nor the hope of the poor
      perish forever.

¹⁹ Rise up, O LORD! Do not let
      mortals prevail;
   let the nations be judged
      before you.
²⁰ Put them in fear, O LORD;
   let the nations
      know that they
      are only human.   *Selah*

PSALM 10

PRAYER FOR DELIVERANCE
FROM ENEMIES

¹ Why, O LORD, do you
      stand far off?
   Why do you hide yourself
      in times of trouble?
² In arrogance the wicked
      persecute the poor—
   let them be caught in
      the schemes they
      have devised.

³ For the wicked boast of the
      desires of their heart,
   those greedy for gain curse
      and renounce the LORD.

4 In the pride of their countenance
   the wicked say, "God
   will not seek it out";
all their thoughts are,
   "There is no God."

5 Their ways prosper
   at all times;
your judgments are on high,
   out of their sight;
as for their foes, they
   scoff at them.
6 They think in their heart, "We
   shall not be moved;
throughout all generations we
   shall not meet adversity."

PRIDE AND PERSONAL

SECURITY LEAD TO

ARROGANCE AND THE

EXCLUSION OF OTHERS.

IMAGINE HOW PERSECUTION

WOULD BRING AMERICAN

CHRISTIANS TOGETHER.

7 Their mouths are filled with
   cursing and deceit
   and oppression;
under their tongues are
   mischief and iniquity.
8 They sit in ambush
   in the villages;
in hiding places they murder
   the innocent.

Their eyes stealthily watch
   for the helpless;
9 they lurk in secret like a
   lion in its covert;
they lurk that they may
   seize the poor;
they seize the poor and drag
   them off in their net.

10 They stoop, they crouch,
   and the helpless fall by
   their might.

11 They think in their heart,
   "God has forgotten,
   he has hidden his face, he
   will never see it."

12 Rise up, O LORD; O God, lift
   up your hand;
   do not forget the oppressed.
13 Why do the wicked renounce God,
   and say in their hearts, "You
   will not call us to account"?

14 But you do see! Indeed you note
   trouble and grief,
   that you may take it into
   your hands;
the helpless commit
   themselves to you;
you have been the helper
   of the orphan.

15 Break the arm of the wicked
   and evildoers;
   seek out their wickedness
   until you find none.
16 The LORD is king forever and ever;
   the nations shall perish
   from his land.

17 O LORD, you will hear the
   desire of the meek;
   you will strengthen their heart,
   you will incline your ear
18 to do justice for the orphan
   and the oppressed,
   so that those from earth may
   strike terror no more.[a]

PSALM 11

SONG OF TRUST IN GOD

To the leader. Of David.

1 In the LORD I take refuge; how
   can you say to me,
"Flee like a bird to the
   mountains;[b]
2 for look, the wicked bend
   the bow,
they have fitted their
   arrow to the string,
to shoot in the dark at the
   upright in heart.

a **10.18** Meaning of Heb uncertain   b **11.1** Gk
Syr Jerome Tg: Heb *flee to your mountain,*
O bird

3 If the foundations are destroyed,
    what can the righteous do?"

4 The LORD is in his holy temple;
    the LORD's throne is in heaven.
    His eyes behold, his gaze
        examines humankind.
5 The LORD tests the righteous
        and the wicked,
    and his soul hates the
        lover of violence.
6 On the wicked he will rain coals
        of fire and sulfur;
    a scorching wind shall be the
        portion of their cup.
7 For the LORD is righteous;
    he loves righteous deeds;
        the upright shall behold his face.

PSALM 12

PLEA FOR HELP IN EVIL TIMES

*To the leader: according to The
Sheminith. A Psalm of David.*

1 Help, O LORD, for there is no longer
        anyone who is godly;
    the faithful have disappeared
        from humankind.
2 They utter lies to each other;
    with flattering lips and a
        double heart they speak.

3 May the LORD cut off all
        flattering lips,
    the tongue that makes
        great boasts,
4 those who say, "With our tongues
        we will prevail;
    our lips are our own—who
        is our master?"

5 "Because the poor are despoiled,
        because the needy groan,
    I will now rise up," says the LORD;
    "I will place them in the safety
        for which they long."
6 The promises of the LORD are
        promises that are pure,
    silver refined in a furnace
        on the ground,
    purified seven times.

7 You, O LORD, will protect us;
    you will guard us from this
        generation forever.

8 On every side the wicked prowl,
    as vileness is exalted among
        humankind.

PSALM 13

PRAYER FOR DELIVERANCE
FROM ENEMIES

To the leader. A Psalm of David.

1 How long, O LORD? Will you
        forget me forever?
    How long will you hide
        your face from me?
2 How long must I bear pain[a]
        in my soul,
    and have sorrow in my
        heart all day long?
    How long shall my enemy be
        exalted over me?

3 Consider and answer me,
        O LORD my God!
    Give light to my eyes, or I will
        sleep the sleep of death,
4 and my enemy will say, "I
        have prevailed";
    my foes will rejoice because
        I am shaken.

5 But I trusted in your steadfast love;
    my heart shall rejoice in
        your salvation.
6 I will sing to the LORD,
    because he has dealt
        bountifully with me.

PSALM 14

DENUNCIATION OF GODLESSNESS

To the leader. Of David.

1 Fools say in their hearts,
        "There is no God."
    They are corrupt, they do
        abominable deeds;
    there is no one who does good.

2 The LORD looks down from
        heaven on humankind
    to see if there are any
        who are wise,
    who seek after God.

a 13.2 Syr: Heb *hold counsels*

3 They have all gone astray, they
    are all alike perverse;
    there is no one who does good,
    no, not one.

4 Have they no knowledge,
    all the evildoers
  who eat up my people as
    they eat bread,
  and do not call upon the LORD?

5 There they shall be in great terror,
  for God is with the company
    of the righteous.
6 You would confound the
    plans of the poor,
  but the LORD is their refuge.

7 O that deliverance for Israel
    would come from Zion!
  When the LORD restores the
    fortunes of his people,
  Jacob will rejoice; Israel
    will be glad.

PSALM 15

WHO SHALL ABIDE IN GOD'S SANCTUARY?

A Psalm of David.

1 O LORD, who may abide
    in your tent?
  Who may dwell on
    your holy hill?

2 Those who walk blamelessly,
    and do what is right,
  and speak the truth from
    their heart;
3 who do not slander with
    their tongue,
  and do no evil to their friends,
  nor take up a reproach against
    their neighbors;
4 in whose eyes the wicked
    are despised,
  but who honor those who
    fear the LORD;
  who stand by their oath
    even to their hurt;
5 who do not lend money at interest,
  and do not take a bribe
    against the innocent.

Those who do these things
    shall never be moved.

PSALM 16

SONG OF TRUST AND SECURITY IN GOD

A Miktam of David.

1 Protect me, O God, for in
    you I take refuge.
2 I say to the LORD, "You
    are my Lord;
  I have no good apart from you."[a]

a 16.2 Jerome Tg: Meaning of Heb uncertain

⊦ BIBLE IN LIFE ▷

Worthy to Worship
Psalm 15.1–5

Who is worthy to worship? This penetrating question opens Psalm 15, a song for those approaching the temple of the Lord and preparing to worship. This song was intended to lead worshipers to reflect on what God calls people to be and how their lives measure up against this calling. How often do we ask ourselves this same question when we prepare to worship God? Quite often we approach God without any preparation, thinking: *God cares for me, and I expect God to listen when I ask for things.* We do not humble ourselves or assume an attitude of self-assessment. Instead, we project pride, superiority or confidence that we are worthy to be in God's presence. By failing to ask who is worthy to worship, we are ultimately failing to acknowledge that we have sinned, for the standards of holiness described in the psalm show that none of us is worthy. All of us have lied, slandered others, broken our promises and failed to care for others. Yet by God's grace through Christ, we have been sanctified, *made* worthy to worship God (see Hebrews 10.10). At the same time, we are called to live in a way that is worthy of the gospel—that is, in a way that reflects the holiness given to us in Jesus Christ (see Ephesians 4.1; Philippians 1.27).

3 As for the holy ones in the land,
    they are the noble,
  in whom is all my delight.

4 Those who choose another god
    multiply their sorrows;[a]
  their drink offerings of blood
    I will not pour out
  or take their names upon my lips.

5 The LORD is my chosen portion
    and my cup;
  you hold my lot.

6 The boundary lines have fallen for
    me in pleasant places;
  I have a goodly heritage.

7 I bless the LORD who gives
    me counsel;
  in the night also my heart
    instructs me.

8 I keep the LORD always before me;
  because he is at my right hand,
    I shall not be moved.

9 Therefore my heart is glad, and
    my soul rejoices;
  my body also rests secure.

10 For you do not give me up to Sheol,
  or let your faithful one
    see the Pit.

11 You show me the path of life.
  In your presence there is
    fullness of joy;
  in your right hand are
    pleasures forevermore.

PSALM 17

PRAYER FOR DELIVERANCE
FROM PERSECUTORS

A Prayer of David.

1 Hear a just cause, O LORD;
    attend to my cry;
  give ear to my prayer from
    lips free of deceit.

2 From you let my vindication come;
  let your eyes see the right.

3 If you try my heart, if you
    visit me by night,
  if you test me, you will find
    no wickedness in me;
  my mouth does not transgress.

4 As for what others do, by the
    word of your lips
  I have avoided the ways
    of the violent.

5 My steps have held fast
    to your paths;
  my feet have not slipped.

6 I call upon you, for you will
    answer me, O God;
  incline your ear to me,
    hear my words.

7 Wondrously show your
    steadfast love,
  O savior of those who
    seek refuge
  from their adversaries at
    your right hand.

8 Guard me as the
    apple of the eye;
  hide me in the shadow
    of your wings,

9 from the wicked
    who despoil me,
  my deadly enemies who
    surround me.

10 They close their hearts to pity;
  with their mouths they
    speak arrogantly.

11 They track me down;[b] now
    they surround me;
  they set their eyes to cast
    me to the ground.

12 They are like a lion eager to tear,
  like a young lion lurking
    in ambush.

13 Rise up, O LORD, confront them,
    overthrow them!
  By your sword deliver my
    life from the wicked,

14 from mortals—by your
    hand, O LORD—
  from mortals whose portion
    in life is in this world.
  May their bellies be filled
    with what you have
    stored up for them;
  may their children have
    more than enough;
  may they leave something
    over to their little ones.

---

a 16.4 Cn: Meaning of Heb uncertain
b 17.11 One Ms Compare Syr: MT *Our steps*

15 As for me, I shall behold your
    face in righteousness;
when I awake I shall be
    satisfied, beholding
    your likeness.

PSALM 18

ROYAL THANKSGIVING
FOR VICTORY

*To the leader. A Psalm of David the
servant of the LORD, who addressed
the words of this song to the LORD
on the day when the LORD delivered
him from the hand of all his enemies,
and from the hand of Saul. He said:*

1 I love you, O LORD,
    my strength.
2 The LORD is my rock, my fortress,
    and my deliverer,
my God, my rock in whom
    I take refuge,
my shield, and the horn of my
    salvation, my stronghold.
3 I call upon the LORD, who is
    worthy to be praised,
so I shall be saved from
    my enemies.

4 The cords of death
    encompassed me;
the torrents of perdition
    assailed me;
5 the cords of Sheol entangled me;
the snares of death
    confronted me.

6 In my distress I called
    upon the LORD;
to my God I cried for help.
From his temple he heard
    my voice,
and my cry to him
    reached his ears.

7 Then the earth reeled and rocked;
the foundations also of the
    mountains trembled
and quaked, because
    he was angry.
8 Smoke went up from his nostrils,
and devouring fire from
    his mouth;
glowing coals flamed
    forth from him.

9 He bowed the heavens,
    and came down;
thick darkness was
    under his feet.
10 He rode on a cherub, and flew;
he came swiftly upon the
    wings of the wind.
11 He made darkness his covering
    around him,
his canopy thick clouds
    dark with water.
12 Out of the brightness before him
    there broke through his clouds
    hailstones and coals of fire.
13 The LORD also thundered
    in the heavens,
and the Most High
    uttered his voice.[a]
14 And he sent out his arrows,
    and scattered them;
he flashed forth lightnings,
    and routed them.
15 Then the channels of the
    sea were seen,
and the foundations of the
    world were laid bare
at your rebuke, O LORD,
    at the blast of the breath
    of your nostrils.

16 He reached down from on
    high, he took me;
he drew me out of
    mighty waters.
17 He delivered me from my
    strong enemy,
and from those who hated me;
for they were too
    mighty for me.
18 They confronted me in the
    day of my calamity;
but the LORD was
    my support.
19 He brought me out into
    a broad place;
he delivered me, because
    he delighted in me.

20 The LORD rewarded me according
    to my righteousness;
according to the cleanness
    of my hands he
    recompensed me.

a **18.13** Gk See 2 Sam 22.14: Heb adds
hailstones and coals of fire

21 For I have kept the ways
    of the LORD,
  and have not wickedly
    departed from my God.
22 For all his ordinances were
    before me,
  and his statutes I did not
    put away from me.
23 I was blameless before him,
  and I kept myself from guilt.
24 Therefore the LORD has
    recompensed me according
    to my righteousness,
  according to the cleanness of
    my hands in his sight.

25 With the loyal you show
    yourself loyal;
  with the blameless you show
    yourself blameless;
26 with the pure you show
    yourself pure;
  and with the crooked you
    show yourself perverse.
27 For you deliver a humble people,
  but the haughty eyes
    you bring down.
28 It is you who light my lamp;
  the LORD, my God, lights
    up my darkness.
29 By you I can crush a troop,
  and by my God I can
    leap over a wall.
30 This God—his way is perfect;
  the promise of the LORD
    proves true;
  he is a shield for all who
    take refuge in him.

31 For who is God except the LORD?
  And who is a rock besides
    our God?—
32 the God who girded me
    with strength,
  and made my way safe.
33 He made my feet like the
    feet of a deer,
  and set me secure on
    the heights.
34 He trains my hands for war,
  so that my arms can bend
    a bow of bronze.
35 You have given me the shield
    of your salvation,
  and your right hand has
    supported me;
  your help[a] has made me great.

36 You gave me a wide place for
    my steps under me,
  and my feet did not slip.
37 I pursued my enemies and
    overtook them;
  and did not turn back until
    they were consumed.
38 I struck them down, so that they
    were not able to rise;
  they fell under my feet.
39 For you girded me with
    strength for the battle;
  you made my assailants
    sink under me.
40 You made my enemies turn
    their backs to me,
  and those who hated
    me I destroyed.
41 They cried for help, but there was
    no one to save them;
  they cried to the LORD, but he
    did not answer them.
42 I beat them fine, like dust
    before the wind;
  I cast them out like the
    mire of the streets.

43 You delivered me from strife
    with the peoples;[b]
  you made me head of
    the nations;
  people whom I had not
    known served me.
44 As soon as they heard of me
    they obeyed me;
  foreigners came
    cringing to me.
45 Foreigners lost heart,
  and came trembling out of
    their strongholds.

46 The LORD lives! Blessed
    be my rock,
  and exalted be the God
    of my salvation,
47 the God who gave me vengeance
  and subdued peoples under me;
48 who delivered me from
    my enemies;
  indeed, you exalted me
    above my adversaries;
  you delivered me from
    the violent.

[a] 18.35 Or gentleness   [b] 18.43 Gk Tg: Heb
people

⁴⁹ For this I will extol you, O LORD,
       among the nations,
    and sing praises
       to your name.
⁵⁰ Great triumphs he gives
       to his king,
    and shows steadfast love
       to his anointed,
    to David and his
       descendants forever.

PSALM 19

GOD'S GLORY IN CREATION
AND THE LAW

To the leader. A Psalm of David.

¹ The heavens are telling the
       glory of God;
    and the firmamentᵃ proclaims
       his handiwork.
² Day to day pours forth speech,
       and night to night declares
       knowledge.
³ There is no speech, nor are
       there words;
    their voice is not heard;
⁴ yet their voiceᵇ goes out
       through all the earth,
    and their words to the
       end of the world.

In the heavensᶜ he has set a
       tent for the sun,
⁵ which comes out like a
       bridegroom from his
       wedding canopy,
    and like a strong man runs
       its course with joy.
⁶ Its rising is from the end
       of the heavens,
    and its circuit to the
       end of them;
    and nothing is hid
       from its heat.

⁷ The law of the LORD is perfect,
       reviving the soul;
    the decrees of the LORD are sure,
       making wise the simple;
⁸ the precepts of the LORD
       are right,
    rejoicing the heart;
    the commandment of the
       LORD is clear,
    enlightening the eyes;

⁹ the fear of the LORD is pure,
       enduring forever;
    the ordinances of the
       LORD are true
    and righteous altogether.
¹⁰ More to be desired are
       they than gold,
    even much fine gold;
    sweeter also than honey,
       and drippings of the
       honeycomb.

¹¹ Moreover by them is your
       servant warned;
    in keeping them there
       is great reward.
¹² But who can detect
       their errors?
    Clear me from hidden faults.
¹³ Keep back your servant also
       from the insolent;ᵈ
    do not let them have
       dominion over me.
    Then I shall be blameless,
       and innocent of great
       transgression.

¹⁴ Let the words of my mouth
       and the meditation
       of my heart
    be acceptable to you,
    O LORD, my rock and
       my redeemer.

PSALM 20

PRAYER FOR VICTORY

To the leader. A Psalm of David.

¹ The LORD answer you in the
       day of trouble!
    The name of the God of
       Jacob protect you!
² May he send you help from
       the sanctuary,
    and give you support
       from Zion.
³ May he remember all
       your offerings,
    and regard with favor your
       burnt sacrifices.   *Selah*

ᵃ 19.1 Or *dome*   ᵇ 19.4 Gk Jerome Compare
Syr: Heb *line*   ᶜ 19.4 Heb *In them*
ᵈ 19.13 Or *from proud thoughts*

4 May he grant you your
 heart's desire,
 and fulfill all your plans.
5 May we shout for joy over
 your victory,
 and in the name of our God
 set up our banners.
May the LORD fulfill all
 your petitions.

6 Now I know that the LORD will
 help his anointed;
 he will answer him from
 his holy heaven
 with mighty victories by
 his right hand.
7 Some take pride in chariots,
 and some in horses,
 but our pride is in the name
 of the LORD our God.
8 They will collapse and fall,
 but we shall rise and
 stand upright.

9 Give victory to the king, O LORD;
 answer us when we call. [a]

PSALM 21

THANKSGIVING FOR VICTORY

To the leader. A Psalm of David.

1 In your strength the king
 rejoices, O LORD,
 and in your help how
 greatly he exults!
2 You have given him his
 heart's desire,
 and have not withheld the
 request of his lips. *Selah*
3 For you meet him with
 rich blessings;
 you set a crown of fine
 gold on his head.
4 He asked you for life; you
 gave it to him—
 length of days
 forever and ever.
5 His glory is great through
 your help;
 splendor and majesty you
 bestow on him.
6 You bestow on him
 blessings forever;
 you make him glad with the
 joy of your presence.

7 For the king trusts in the LORD,
 and through the steadfast
 love of the Most High
 he shall not be moved.

8 Your hand will find out all
 your enemies;
 your right hand will find out
 those who hate you.
9 You will make them like
 a fiery furnace
 when you appear.
The LORD will swallow them
 up in his wrath,
 and fire will consume them.
10 You will destroy their offspring
 from the earth,
 and their children from
 among humankind.
11 If they plan evil against you,
 if they devise mischief, they
 will not succeed.
12 For you will put them to flight;
 you will aim at their faces
 with your bows.

13 Be exalted, O LORD, in
 your strength!
 We will sing and praise
 your power.

PSALM 22

PLEA FOR DELIVERANCE FROM SUFFERING AND HOSTILITY

*To the leader: according to The Deer
of the Dawn. A Psalm of David.*

1 My God, my God, why have
 you forsaken me?
 Why are you so far from
 helping me, from the
 words of my groaning?
2 O my God, I cry by day, but
 you do not answer;
 and by night, but find no rest.

3 Yet you are holy,
 enthroned on the
 praises of Israel.
4 In you our ancestors trusted;
 they trusted, and you
 delivered them.

[a] 20.9 Gk: Heb *give victory, O LORD; let the
King answer us when we call*

5 To you they cried, and were saved;
in you they trusted, and were
not put to shame.

6 But I am a worm, and
not human;
scorned by others, and
despised by the people.
7 All who see me mock at me;
they make mouths at me,
they shake their heads;
8 "Commit your cause to the
LORD; let him deliver—
let him rescue the one in
whom he delights!"

9 Yet it was you who took me
from the womb;
you kept me safe on my
mother's breast.
10 On you I was cast from my birth,
and since my mother bore me
you have been my God.
11 Do not be far from me,
for trouble is near
and there is no one to help.

12 Many bulls encircle me,
strong bulls of Bashan
surround me;
13 they open wide their
mouths at me,
like a ravening and
roaring lion.

14 I am poured out like water,
and all my bones are
out of joint;
my heart is like wax;
it is melted within my breast;
15 my mouth[a] is dried up
like a potsherd,
and my tongue sticks
to my jaws;
you lay me in the dust of death.

16 For dogs are all around me;
a company of evildoers
encircles me.
My hands and feet have
shriveled;[b]
17 I can count all my bones.
They stare and gloat over me;
18 they divide my clothes
among themselves,
and for my clothing
they cast lots.

19 But you, O LORD, do not
be far away!
O my help, come quickly
to my aid!
20 Deliver my soul from the sword,
my life[c] from the power
of the dog!
21 Save me from the mouth
of the lion!

From the horns of the wild oxen
you have rescued[d] me.
22 I will tell of your name to my
brothers and sisters;[e]
in the midst of the congregation
I will praise you:
23 You who fear the LORD, praise him!
All you offspring of Jacob,
glorify him;
stand in awe of him, all you
offspring of Israel!
24 For he did not despise or abhor
the affliction of the afflicted;
he did not hide his face from me,[f]
but heard when I[g] cried to him.

25 From you comes my praise in
the great congregation;
my vows I will pay before
those who fear him.
26 The poor[h] shall eat and be satisfied;
those who seek him shall
praise the LORD.
May your hearts live forever!

27 All the ends of the earth
shall remember
and turn to the LORD;
and all the families of the nations
shall worship before him.[i]
28 For dominion belongs to the LORD,
and he rules over the nations.

29 To him,[j] indeed, shall all
who sleep in[k] the
earth bow down;
before him shall bow all who
go down to the dust,
and I shall live for him.[l]

a 22.15 Cn: Heb *strength*   b 22.16 Meaning
of Heb uncertain   c 22.20 Heb *my only
one*   d 22.21 Heb *answered*   e 22.22 Or
kindred   f 22.24 Heb *him*   g 22.24 Heb *he*
h 22.26 Or *afflicted*   i 22.27 Gk Syr Jerome:
Heb *you*   j 22.29 Cn: Heb *They have eaten
and*   k 22.29 Cn: Heb *all the fat ones*
l 22.29 Compare Gk Syr Vg: Heb *and he who
cannot keep himself alive*

30 Posterity will serve him;
    future generations will be
        told about the Lord,
31 and[a] proclaim his deliverance
        to a people yet unborn,
    saying that he has done it.

PSALM 23

THE DIVINE SHEPHERD

A Psalm of David.

1 The LORD is my shepherd,
    I shall not want.
2   He makes me lie down in
        green pastures;
  he leads me beside still waters;[b]
3   he restores my soul.[c]
  He leads me in right paths[d]
    for his name's sake.

4 Even though I walk through
        the darkest valley,[e]
    I fear no evil;
  for you are with me;
    your rod and your staff—
        they comfort me.

5 You prepare a table before me
    in the presence of my enemies;
  you anoint my head with oil;
    my cup overflows.
6 Surely[f] goodness and mercy[g]
        shall follow me
    all the days of my life,
  and I shall dwell in the
        house of the LORD
    my whole life long.[h]

PSALM 24

ENTRANCE INTO THE TEMPLE

Of David. A Psalm.

1 The earth is the LORD's and
    all that is in it,
  the world, and those
    who live in it;
2 for he has founded it on the seas,
    and established it on the rivers.

3 Who shall ascend the hill
    of the LORD?
  And who shall stand in
    his holy place?

PONDER

The LORD is my shepherd, I shall not want. He makes me lie down in green pastures; he leads me beside still waters; he restores my soul. He leads me in right paths for his name's sake.
—Psalm 23.1–3

PRAY

Sovereign God, we are thankful that we can turn to these ancient psalms that never change, even though our circumstances in life might. We know that we can always go back to these verses and be reminded of our proper relationship with you. We are thankful that a few centuries after these songs were collected, you sent your only Son, Jesus Christ, to be our Savior and give us a new glimpse, a new image, a new description and a new knowledge about your character of love, forgiveness and grace. We pray in the name of our Savior, Jesus Christ. Amen.

---

4 Those who have clean hands
        and pure hearts,
    who do not lift up their
        souls to what is false,
    and do not swear
        deceitfully.
5 They will receive blessing
        from the LORD,
    and vindication from the
        God of their salvation.
6 Such is the company of those
        who seek him,
    who seek the face of
        the God of Jacob.[i]   *Selah*

---

[a] 22.31 Compare Gk: Heb *it will be told about the Lord to the generation,* 31*they will come and*   [b] 23.2 Heb *waters of rest*   [c] 23.3 Or *life*   [d] 23.3 Or *paths of righteousness*   [e] 23.4 Or *the valley of the shadow of death*   [f] 23.6 Or *Only*   [g] 23.6 Or *kindness*   [h] 23.6 Heb *for length of days*   [i] 24.6 Gk Syr: Heb *your face, O Jacob*

7 Lift up your heads, O gates!
    and be lifted up, O ancient doors!
    that the King of glory
        may come in.
8 Who is the King of glory?
    The LORD, strong and mighty,
    the LORD, mighty in battle.
9 Lift up your heads, O gates!
    and be lifted up, O ancient doors!
    that the King of glory
        may come in.
10 Who is this King of glory?
    The LORD of hosts,
    he is the King of glory.   *Selah*

PSALM 25

PRAYER FOR GUIDANCE AND FOR DELIVERANCE

Of David.

1 To you, O LORD, I lift up my soul.
2 O my God, in you I trust;
    do not let me be put to shame;
    do not let my enemies
        exult over me.
3 Do not let those who wait for
        you be put to shame;
    let them be ashamed who are
        wantonly treacherous.

4 Make me to know your
        ways, O LORD;
    teach me your paths.
5 Lead me in your truth,
    and teach me,
    for you are the God of
        my salvation;
    for you I wait all day long.

6 Be mindful of your mercy, O LORD,
    and of your steadfast love,
    for they have been from of old.
7 Do not remember the sins
        of my youth or my
        transgressions;
    according to your steadfast
        love remember me,
    for your goodness'
        sake, O LORD!

8 Good and upright is the LORD;
    therefore he instructs
        sinners in the way.
9 He leads the humble in
        what is right,
    and teaches the humble his way.
10 All the paths of the LORD
        are steadfast love
        and faithfulness,
    for those who keep his covenant
        and his decrees.

11 For your name's sake, O LORD,
    pardon my guilt, for it is great.
12 Who are they that fear the LORD?
    He will teach them the way
        that they should choose.

13 They will abide in prosperity,
    and their children shall
        possess the land.
14 The friendship of the LORD is for
        those who fear him,
    and he makes his covenant
        known to them.
15 My eyes are ever toward
        the LORD,
    for he will pluck my feet
        out of the net.

⊢ BIBLE IN LIFE ▷

Preparing for Worship   *Psalm 24.1–10*

Psalm 24 was likely sung by the ancient Israelites on their way to the temple. The words guide us to reflect on what God has done for us and to seek the presence of God through worship. Before worshiping God, we must recognize the power of God: "The earth is the LORD's, and all that is in it, the world, and those who live in it" (verse 1). Before worshiping God, we must shift our focus from ourselves to God. We are often self-centered. We think we know so much about the world around us. Scientific discoveries have taught us much about this universe, but God has known every detail all along, for God created everything, and everything belongs to God—including our hearts, souls and minds. In order to properly worship God, we must first humble ourselves.

16 Turn to me and be
     gracious to me,
   for I am lonely and afflicted.
17 Relieve the troubles of my heart,
   and bring me[a] out of
     my distress.
18 Consider my affliction and
     my trouble,
   and forgive all my sins.

19 Consider how many are my foes,
   and with what violent
     hatred they hate me.
20 O guard my life, and deliver me;
   do not let me be put to shame,
   for I take refuge in you.
21 May integrity and uprightness
     preserve me,
   for I wait for you.

22 Redeem Israel, O God,
   out of all its troubles.

PSALM 26

PLEA FOR JUSTICE
AND DECLARATION OF
RIGHTEOUSNESS

Of David.

1 Vindicate me, O LORD,
   for I have walked in
     my integrity,
   and I have trusted in the LORD
     without wavering.
2 Prove me, O LORD, and try me;
   test my heart and mind.
3 For your steadfast love is
     before my eyes,
   and I walk in faithfulness
     to you.[b]

4 I do not sit with the worthless,
   nor do I consort with
     hypocrites;
5 I hate the company of evildoers,
   and will not sit with
     the wicked.
6 I wash my hands in innocence,
   and go around your
     altar, O LORD,
7 singing aloud a song of
     thanksgiving,
   and telling all your
     wondrous deeds.

8 O LORD, I love the house in
     which you dwell,
   and the place where your
     glory abides.
9 Do not sweep me away
     with sinners,
   nor my life with the
     bloodthirsty,
10 those in whose hands are
     evil devices,
   and whose right hands
     are full of bribes.

11 But as for me, I walk in
     my integrity;
   redeem me, and be
     gracious to me.
12 My foot stands on level ground;
   in the great congregation I
     will bless the LORD.

PSALM 27

TRIUMPHANT SONG
OF CONFIDENCE

Of David.

1 The LORD is my light and
     my salvation;
   whom shall I fear?
   The LORD is the stronghold[c]
     of my life;
   of whom shall I be afraid?

2 When evildoers assail me
   to devour my flesh—
   my adversaries and foes—
   they shall stumble and fall.

3 Though an army encamp
     against me,
   my heart shall not fear;
   though war rise up against me,
   yet I will be confident.

4 One thing I asked of the LORD,
   that I will seek after:
   to live in the house of the LORD
   all the days of my life,
   to behold the beauty of the LORD,
   and to inquire in his temple.

a 25.17 Or *The troubles of my heart are
enlarged; bring me*   b 26.3 Or *in your
faithfulness*   c 27.1 Or *refuge*

5 For he will hide me in his shelter
  in the day of trouble;
  he will conceal me under the
    cover of his tent;
  he will set me high on a rock.

6 Now my head is lifted up
  above my enemies all
    around me,
  and I will offer in his tent
  sacrifices with shouts of joy;
  I will sing and make melody
    to the LORD.

7 Hear, O LORD, when I cry aloud,
  be gracious to me and
    answer me!
8 "Come," my heart says,
    "seek his face!"
  Your face, LORD, do I seek.
9 Do not hide your face from me.

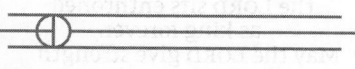

PONDER

"Come," my heart says, "seek his face!"
Your face, LORD, do I seek . . . Wait
for the LORD; be strong, and let your
heart take courage; wait for the LORD!
—Psalm 27.8,14

PRAY

Father, give us an open heart as
we read these verses, so that you
can make them part of us. Thank
you for giving us the desire to seek
you, to wait for you as the psalmist
did. We know that you do all things
in your perfect timing, that you
will reveal yourself at just the right
times. Through Christ you have
given us your Spirit. Because of the
presence of the Holy Spirit within us,
we need not live lives of timidity or
inadequacy but rather of courage,
tenacity, gratification, peace, joy
and love. Help us remember that
Christ offers us these things as we
experience eternal life with him. We
ask in the name of our Savior. Amen.

Do not turn your servant
    away in anger,
  you who have been my help.
Do not cast me off, do not
    forsake me,
  O God of my salvation!
10 If my father and mother
    forsake me,
  the LORD will take me up.

11 Teach me your way, O LORD,
  and lead me on a level path
  because of my enemies.
12 Do not give me up to the will
    of my adversaries,
  for false witnesses have
    risen against me,
  and they are breathing
    out violence.

13 I believe that I shall see the
    goodness of the LORD
  in the land of the living.
14 Wait for the LORD;
  be strong, and let your
    heart take courage;
  wait for the LORD!

PSALM 28

PRAYER FOR HELP AND
THANKSGIVING FOR IT

Of David.

1 To you, O LORD, I call;
  my rock, do not refuse
    to hear me,
  for if you are silent to me,
  I shall be like those who
    go down to the Pit.
2 Hear the voice of my supplication,
  as I cry to you for help,
  as I lift up my hands
    toward your most holy
    sanctuary.[a]

3 Do not drag me away with
    the wicked,
  with those who are
    workers of evil,
  who speak peace with
    their neighbors,
  while mischief is in
    their hearts.

---

[a] **28.2** Heb *your innermost sanctuary*

4 Repay them according to
        their work,
    and according to the evil
        of their deeds;
    repay them according to the
        work of their hands;
    render them their due reward.
5 Because they do not regard the
        works of the LORD,
    or the work of his hands,
    he will break them down and
        build them up no more.

6 Blessed be the LORD,
    for he has heard the sound
        of my pleadings.
7 The LORD is my strength
        and my shield;
    in him my heart trusts;
    so I am helped, and my
        heart exults,
    and with my song I give
        thanks to him.

8 The LORD is the strength
        of his people;
    he is the saving refuge
        of his anointed.
9 O save your people, and bless
        your heritage;
    be their shepherd, and
        carry them forever.

PSALM 29

THE VOICE OF GOD IN
A GREAT STORM

A Psalm of David.

1 Ascribe to the LORD,
        O heavenly beings,[a]
    ascribe to the LORD glory
        and strength.
2 Ascribe to the LORD the
        glory of his name;
    worship the LORD in
        holy splendor.

3 The voice of the LORD is
        over the waters;
    the God of glory thunders,
    the LORD, over mighty waters.
4 The voice of the LORD
        is powerful;
    the voice of the LORD is
        full of majesty.

5 The voice of the LORD
        breaks the cedars;
    the LORD breaks the
        cedars of Lebanon.
6 He makes Lebanon skip like a calf,
    and Sirion like a young wild ox.

7 The voice of the LORD flashes
        forth flames of fire.
8 The voice of the LORD shakes
        the wilderness;
    the LORD shakes the
        wilderness of Kadesh.

9 The voice of the LORD causes
        the oaks to whirl,[b]
    and strips the forest bare;
    and in his temple all
        say, "Glory!"

10 The LORD sits enthroned
        over the flood;
    the LORD sits enthroned
        as king forever.
11 May the LORD give strength
        to his people!
    May the LORD bless his
        people with peace!

PSALM 30

THANKSGIVING FOR RECOVERY
FROM GRAVE ILLNESS

*A Psalm. A Song at the dedication
of the temple. Of David.*

1 I will extol you, O LORD, for you
        have drawn me up,
    and did not let my foes
        rejoice over me.
2 O LORD my God, I cried to
        you for help,
    and you have healed me.
3 O LORD, you brought up my
        soul from Sheol,
    restored me to life from
        among those gone
        down to the Pit.[c]

4 Sing praises to the LORD, O you
        his faithful ones,
    and give thanks to his
        holy name.

a **29.1** Heb *sons of gods*   b **29.9** Or *causes
the deer to calve*   c **30.3** Or *that I should
not go down to the Pit*

5 For his anger is but for a moment;
   his favor is for a lifetime.
Weeping may linger for the night,
   but joy comes with the morning.

6 As for me, I said in my prosperity,
   "I shall never be moved."
7 By your favor, O LORD,
   you had established me as
      a strong mountain;
you hid your face;
   I was dismayed.

8 To you, O LORD, I cried,
   and to the LORD I made
      supplication:
9 "What profit is there in my death,
   if I go down to the Pit?
Will the dust praise you?
   Will it tell of your faithfulness?
10 Hear, O LORD, and be
      gracious to me!
   O LORD, be my helper!"

11 You have turned my mourning
      into dancing;
   you have taken off my sackcloth
   and clothed me with joy,
12 so that my soul[a] may praise
      you and not be silent.
   O LORD my God, I will give
      thanks to you forever.

PSALM 31

PRAYER AND PRAISE FOR DELIVERANCE FROM ENEMIES

To the leader. A Psalm of David.

1 In you, O LORD, I seek refuge;
   do not let me ever be
      put to shame;
   in your righteousness
      deliver me.
2 Incline your ear to me;
   rescue me speedily.
Be a rock of refuge for me,
   a strong fortress to save me.

3 You are indeed my rock
      and my fortress;
   for your name's sake lead
      me and guide me,
4 take me out of the net that
      is hidden for me,
   for you are my refuge.

5 Into your hand I commit
      my spirit;
   you have redeemed me,
      O LORD, faithful God.

6 You hate[b] those who pay regard
      to worthless idols,
   but I trust in the LORD.
7 I will exult and rejoice in
      your steadfast love,
   because you have seen
      my affliction;
   you have taken heed of
      my adversities,
8 and have not delivered me into
      the hand of the enemy;
   you have set my feet in
      a broad place.

9 Be gracious to me, O LORD,
      for I am in distress;
   my eye wastes away from grief,
   my soul and body also.
10 For my life is spent with sorrow,
   and my years with sighing;
my strength fails because
      of my misery,[c]
   and my bones waste away.

11 I am the scorn of all my
      adversaries,
   a horror[d] to my neighbors,
an object of dread to my
      acquaintances;
   those who see me in the
      street flee from me.
12 I have passed out of mind like
      one who is dead;
   I have become like a
      broken vessel.
13 For I hear the whispering
      of many—
   terror all around!—
as they scheme together
      against me,
   as they plot to take my life.

14 But I trust in you, O LORD;
   I say, "You are my God."
15 My times are in your hand;
   deliver me from the hand of my
      enemies and persecutors.

[a] 30.12 Heb *that glory* [b] 31.6 One Heb
Ms Gk Syr Jerome: MT *I hate* [c] 31.10 Gk
Syr: Heb *my iniquity* [d] 31.11 Cn: Heb
exceedingly

16 Let your face shine upon
    your servant;
    save me in your steadfast love.
17 Do not let me be put to
    shame, O LORD,
    for I call on you;
    let the wicked be put to shame;
    let them go dumbfounded
    to Sheol.
18 Let the lying lips be stilled
    that speak insolently against
    the righteous
    with pride and contempt.

GOD'S PRIORITIES AND

MORAL VALUES NEVER

CHANGE. THEY APPLY TO

ALL HUMAN EXPERIENCES.

19 O how abundant is your goodness
    that you have laid up for
    those who fear you,
    and accomplished for those who
    take refuge in you,
    in the sight of everyone!
20 In the shelter of your presence
    you hide them
    from human plots;
    you hold them safe under
    your shelter
    from contentious tongues.

21 Blessed be the LORD,
    for he has wondrously shown
    his steadfast love to me
    when I was beset as a
    city under siege.
22 I had said in my alarm,
    "I am driven far[a] from
    your sight."
    But you heard my supplications
    when I cried out to
    you for help.

23 Love the LORD, all you his saints.
    The LORD preserves
    the faithful,
    but abundantly repays the
    one who acts haughtily.

24 Be strong, and let your heart
    take courage,
    all you who wait for the LORD.

PSALM 32

THE JOY OF FORGIVENESS

Of David. A Maskil.

1 Happy are those whose
    transgression is forgiven,
    whose sin is covered.
2 Happy are those to whom the
    LORD imputes no iniquity,
    and in whose spirit there
    is no deceit.

3 While I kept silence, my
    body wasted away
    through my groaning
    all day long.
4 For day and night your hand
    was heavy upon me;
    my strength was dried
    up[b] as by the heat of
    summer.   *Selah*

5 Then I acknowledged my
    sin to you,
    and I did not hide my iniquity;
    I said, "I will confess my
    transgressions to
    the LORD,"
    and you forgave the guilt of my
    sin.   *Selah*

6 Therefore let all who are faithful
    offer prayer to you;
    at a time of distress,[c] the rush
    of mighty waters
    shall not reach them.
7 You are a hiding place for me;
    you preserve me from trouble;
    you surround me with
    glad cries of
    deliverance.   *Selah*

8 I will instruct you and teach you
    the way you should go;
    I will counsel you with
    my eye upon you.

---

a 31.22 Another reading is *cut off*
b 32.4 Meaning of Heb uncertain
c 32.6 Cn: Heb *at a time of finding only*

9 Do not be like a horse or a mule,
    without understanding,
  whose temper must be curbed
    with bit and bridle,
  else it will not stay near you.

10 Many are the torments
    of the wicked,
  but steadfast love surrounds
    those who trust
    in the LORD.
11 Be glad in the LORD and
    rejoice, O righteous,
  and shout for joy, all you
    upright in heart.

PSALM 33

THE GREATNESS AND
GOODNESS OF GOD

1 Rejoice in the LORD, O you
    righteous.
  Praise befits the upright.
2 Praise the LORD with the lyre;
  make melody to him with
    the harp of ten strings.
3 Sing to him a new song;
  play skillfully on the strings,
    with loud shouts.

4 For the word of the LORD
    is upright,
  and all his work is done
    in faithfulness.

5 He loves righteousness
    and justice;
  the earth is full of the steadfast
    love of the LORD.

6 By the word of the LORD the
    heavens were made,
  and all their host by the
    breath of his mouth.
7 He gathered the waters of the
    sea as in a bottle;
  he put the deeps in storehouses.

8 Let all the earth fear the LORD;
  let all the inhabitants of the
    world stand in awe of him.
9 For he spoke, and it came to be;
  he commanded, and
    it stood firm.

10 The LORD brings the counsel of
    the nations to nothing;
  he frustrates the plans
    of the peoples.
11 The counsel of the LORD
    stands forever,
  the thoughts of his heart
    to all generations.
12 Happy is the nation whose
    God is the LORD,
  the people whom he has
    chosen as his heritage.

13 The LORD looks down
    from heaven;
  he sees all humankind.

BIBLE IN LIFE

Confessing Our Sins   Psalm 32.1–11

The Bible makes it clear that confessing our sins is an integral part of receiving God's forgiveness, but many of us prefer to bypass this part of our relationship with Christ. We would rather not face the fact that we have done things that have indebted us to God and others. We may go many days without confessing sin, and soon the days become weeks, months and then years. We may go to the grave without knowing the true intimacy that Christ offers us. Rather than avoiding confession, we should embrace it as an opportunity to relieve ourselves of our burdensome guilt and receive God's forgiveness. Perhaps we have spread gossip about another person. Perhaps we have harbored animosity or bitterness in our hearts. Perhaps we are ignoring someone who needs our help. Whatever our sin, we need not be afraid to acknowledge where we have been wrong, because God is always ready to forgive us when we confess and repent. We need no longer condemn ourselves for wrong choices. Through Jesus Christ we can face our sin, confess it to God and rest in his forgiveness. And then we can carry out Jesus' command to extend this same forgiveness to others (see Matthew 6.12).

14 From where he sits enthroned
   he watches
   all the inhabitants of
   the earth—
15 he who fashions the hearts
   of them all,
   and observes all their deeds.
16 A king is not saved by his
   great army;
   a warrior is not delivered by
   his great strength.
17 The war horse is a vain
   hope for victory,
   and by its great might
   it cannot save.

18 Truly the eye of the LORD is on
   those who fear him,
   on those who hope in his
   steadfast love,
19 to deliver their soul from death,
   and to keep them alive
   in famine.

20 Our soul waits for the LORD;
   he is our help and shield.
21 Our heart is glad in him,
   because we trust in his
   holy name.
22 Let your steadfast love,
   O LORD, be upon us,
   even as we hope in you.

PSALM 34

PRAISE FOR DELIVERANCE
FROM TROUBLE

Of David, when he feigned madness
before Abimelech, so that he drove
him out, and he went away.

1 I will bless the LORD at all times;
   his praise shall continually
   be in my mouth.
2 My soul makes its boast
   in the LORD;
   let the humble hear
   and be glad.
3 O magnify the LORD with me,
   and let us exalt his
   name together.
4 I sought the LORD, and he
   answered me,
   and delivered me from
   all my fears.

5 Look to him, and be radiant;
   so your[a] faces shall never
   be ashamed.
6 This poor soul cried, and was
   heard by the LORD,
   and was saved from
   every trouble.
7 The angel of the
   LORD encamps
   around those who fear him,
   and delivers them.
8 O taste and see that the
   LORD is good;
   happy are those who take
   refuge in him.
9 O fear the LORD, you his
   holy ones,
   for those who fear him
   have no want.
10 The young lions suffer want
   and hunger,
   but those who seek the LORD
   lack no good thing.

11 Come, O children,
   listen to me;
   I will teach you the fear
   of the LORD.
12 Which of you desires life,
   and covets many days
   to enjoy good?
13 Keep your tongue from evil,
   and your lips from
   speaking deceit.
14 Depart from evil, and do good;
   seek peace, and pursue it.

DO WE BELIEVE THAT
CHRIST IS ABLE WITH HIS
POWER TO TRANSCEND ANY
FEARS WE MIGHT HAVE?

15 The eyes of the LORD are on
   the righteous,
   and his ears are open
   to their cry.

a **34.5** Gk Syr Jerome: Heb *their*

16 The face of the LORD is
    against evildoers,
    to cut off the remembrance of
    them from the earth.
17 When the righteous cry for
    help, the LORD hears,
    and rescues them from
    all their troubles.
18 The LORD is near to the
    brokenhearted,
    and saves the crushed in spirit.

19 Many are the afflictions of
    the righteous,
    but the LORD rescues them
    from them all.
20 He keeps all their bones;
    not one of them will be broken.
21 Evil brings death to the wicked,
    and those who hate the
    righteous will be
    condemned.
22 The LORD redeems the life
    of his servants;
    none of those who take
    refuge in him will
    be condemned.

PSALM 35

PRAYER FOR DELIVERANCE FROM ENEMIES

Of David.

1 Contend, O LORD, with those
    who contend with me;
    fight against those who
    fight against me!
2 Take hold of shield and buckler,
    and rise up to help me!

3 Draw the spear and javelin
    against my pursuers;
    say to my soul,
    "I am your salvation."

4 Let them be put to shame
    and dishonor
    who seek after my life.
    Let them be turned back
    and confounded
    who devise evil against me.
5 Let them be like chaff
    before the wind,
    with the angel of the LORD
    driving them on.
6 Let their way be dark
    and slippery,
    with the angel of the LORD
    pursuing them.

7 For without cause they hid
    their net[a] for me;
    without cause they dug
    a pit[b] for my life.
8 Let ruin come on
    them unawares.
    And let the net that they
    hid ensnare them;
    let them fall in it—
    to their ruin.

9 Then my soul shall rejoice
    in the LORD,
    exulting in his
    deliverance.
10 All my bones shall say,
    "O LORD, who is like you?

[a] **35.7** Heb *a pit, their net*   [b] **35.7** The word *pit* is transposed from the preceding line

---

BIBLE IN LIFE ▷

Eager to Do Good   *Psalm 34.14*

Goodness is more than just the absence of evil in our lives. Though refraining from evil is wise, we should actively seek to do good. Psalm 34.14 advises us to "Depart from evil, and do good." First Peter 3.13 echoes that: "Who will harm you if you are eager to do what is good?" Both verses require that the reader *do* something. Why is *doing* so important? Because it's active. How many of us shape our lives by actively searching for ways to *do* good things in the name of Christ? It's not enough to just refrain from doing evil. We are to be eager or excited to make a habit of performing acts that glorify God and benefit others—not because we are forced to do it, but because we are inspired to do it out of love for our Savior, Jesus Christ.

You deliver the weak
   from those too strong for them,
   the weak and needy from those
    who despoil them."

11 Malicious witnesses rise up;
   they ask me about things
    I do not know.
12 They repay me evil for good;
   my soul is forlorn.
13 But as for me, when they were sick,
   I wore sackcloth;
   I afflicted myself with fasting.
I prayed with head bowed[a]
   on my bosom,
14   as though I grieved for a
    friend or a brother;
I went about as one who
   laments for a mother,
   bowed down and in mourning.

15 But at my stumbling they
    gathered in glee,
   they gathered together
    against me;
ruffians whom I did not know
   tore at me without ceasing;
16 they impiously mocked
    more and more,[b]
   gnashing at me with their teeth.

17 How long, O LORD, will
    you look on?
Rescue me from their ravages,
   my life from the lions!
18 Then I will thank you in the
    great congregation;
in the mighty throng I
   will praise you.

19 Do not let my treacherous
   enemies rejoice over me,
or those who hate me without
   cause wink the eye.
20 For they do not speak peace,
   but they conceive
    deceitful words
   against those who are
    quiet in the land.
21 They open wide their mouths
    against me;
they say, "Aha, Aha,
   our eyes have seen it."

22 You have seen, O LORD; do
    not be silent!
O Lord, do not be far from me!

23 Wake up! Bestir yourself
    for my defense,
   for my cause, my God
    and my Lord!
24 Vindicate me, O LORD, my God,
   according to your
    righteousness,
   and do not let them
    rejoice over me.
25 Do not let them say to
    themselves,
   "Aha, we have our
    heart's desire."
Do not let them say, "We have
   swallowed you[c] up."

26 Let all those who rejoice
    at my calamity
   be put to shame and confusion;
let those who exalt themselves
    against me
   be clothed with shame
    and dishonor.

27 Let those who desire my
    vindication
   shout for joy and be glad,
   and say evermore,
"Great is the LORD,
   who delights in the welfare
   of his servant."
28 Then my tongue shall tell of
    your righteousness
   and of your praise all day long.

PSALM 36

HUMAN WICKEDNESS AND DIVINE GOODNESS

*To the leader. Of David, the
servant of the LORD.*

1 Transgression speaks to
    the wicked
   deep in their hearts;
there is no fear of God
   before their eyes.
2 For they flatter themselves
   in their own eyes
   that their iniquity cannot be
    found out and hated.

a 35.13 Or *My prayer turned back*
b 35.16 Cn Compare Gk: Heb *like the
profanest of mockers of a cake*
c 35.25 Heb *him*

³ The words of their mouths are
             mischief and deceit;
    they have ceased to act
             wisely and do good.
⁴ They plot mischief while
             on their beds;
    they are set on a way
             that is not good;
    they do not reject evil.

⁵ Your steadfast love, O LORD,
             extends to the heavens,
    your faithfulness
             to the clouds.
⁶ Your righteousness is like the
             mighty mountains,
    your judgments are like
             the great deep;
    you save humans and
             animals alike, O LORD.

⁷ How precious is your steadfast
             love, O God!
    All people may take refuge in
             the shadow of your wings.
⁸ They feast on the abundance
             of your house,
    and you give them drink from
             the river of your delights.
⁹ For with you is the
             fountain of life;
    in your light we see light.

¹⁰ O continue your steadfast love
             to those who know you,
    and your salvation to the
             upright of heart!
¹¹ Do not let the foot of the
             arrogant tread on me,
    or the hand of the wicked
             drive me away.
¹² There the evildoers lie prostrate;
    they are thrust down,
             unable to rise.

GOD IS ALWAYS READY TO

LISTEN TO US AND WILL

ANSWER OUR PRAYERS IN

AN APPROPRIATE WAY.

PSALM 37

EXHORTATION TO PATIENCE
AND TRUST

Of David.

¹ Do not fret because
             of the wicked;
    do not be envious of
             wrongdoers,
² for they will soon fade
             like the grass,
    and wither like the green herb.

³ Trust in the LORD, and do good;
    so you will live in the land,
             and enjoy security.
⁴ Take delight in the LORD,
    and he will give you the
             desires of your heart.

⁵ Commit your way to the LORD;
    trust in him, and he will act.
⁶ He will make your vindication
             shine like the light,
    and the justice of your cause
             like the noonday.

⁷ Be still before the LORD, and
             wait patiently for him;
    do not fret over those who
             prosper in their way,
    over those who carry
             out evil devices.

⁸ Refrain from anger, and
             forsake wrath.
    Do not fret—it leads
             only to evil.
⁹ For the wicked shall be cut off,
    but those who wait for
             the LORD shall
             inherit the land.

¹⁰ Yet a little while,
             and the wicked
             will be no more;
    though you look diligently
             for their place, they
             will not be there.
¹¹ But the meek shall inherit
             the land,
    and delight themselves in
             abundant prosperity.

¹² The wicked plot against
             the righteous,
    and gnash their teeth at them;

13 but the LORD laughs at
the wicked,
for he sees that their
day is coming.

14 The wicked draw the sword
and bend their bows
to bring down the poor
and needy,
to kill those who walk
uprightly;
15 their sword shall enter
their own heart,
and their bows
shall be broken.

16 Better is a little that the
righteous person has
than the abundance of
many wicked.
17 For the arms of the wicked
shall be broken,
but the LORD upholds
the righteous.

18 The LORD knows the days
of the blameless,
and their heritage will
abide forever;
19 they are not put to shame
in evil times,
in the days of famine they
have abundance.

20 But the wicked perish,
and the enemies of the
LORD are like the glory
of the pastures;
they vanish—like smoke
they vanish away.

21 The wicked borrow, and do
not pay back,
but the righteous are generous
and keep giving;
22 for those blessed by the LORD
shall inherit the land,
but those cursed by him
shall be cut off.

23 Our steps[a] are made firm
by the LORD,
when he delights in our[b] way;
24 though we stumble,[c] we[d] shall
not fall headlong,
for the LORD holds us[e]
by the hand.

25 I have been young, and
now am old,
yet I have not seen the
righteous forsaken
or their children
begging bread.
26 They are ever giving liberally
and lending,
and their children become
a blessing.

27 Depart from evil, and do good;
so you shall abide forever.
28 For the LORD loves justice;
he will not forsake his
faithful ones.

The righteous shall be kept
safe forever,
but the children of the
wicked shall be cut off.
29 The righteous shall inherit
the land,
and live in it forever.

30 The mouths of the righteous
utter wisdom,
and their tongues speak justice.
31 The law of their God is in
their hearts;
their steps do not slip.

32 The wicked watch for the
righteous,
and seek to kill them.
33 The LORD will not abandon
them to their power,
or let them be condemned
when they are
brought to trial.

34 Wait for the LORD, and
keep to his way,
and he will exalt you to
inherit the land;
you will look on the
destruction of the wicked.

35 I have seen the wicked
oppressing,
and towering like a cedar
of Lebanon.[f]

a 37.23 Heb A man's steps   b 37.23 Heb
his   c 37.24 Heb he stumbles   d 37.24 Heb
he   e 37.24 Heb him   f 37.35 Gk: Meaning
of Heb uncertain

36 Again I[a] passed by, and they
	were no more;
	though I sought them, they
		could not be found.

37 Mark the blameless, and
		behold the upright,
	for there is posterity for
		the peaceable.
38 But transgressors shall be
		altogether destroyed;
	the posterity of the wicked
		shall be cut off.

39 The salvation of the righteous
		is from the LORD;
	he is their refuge in the
		time of trouble.
40 The LORD helps them and
		rescues them;
	he rescues them from the
		wicked, and saves them,
	because they take
		refuge in him.

PSALM 38

A PENITENT SUFFERER'S PLEA FOR HEALING

A Psalm of David, for the memorial offering.

1 O LORD, do not rebuke me
		in your anger,
	or discipline me in your wrath.
2 For your arrows have
		sunk into me,
	and your hand has come
		down on me.

3 There is no soundness
		in my flesh
	because of your indignation;
	there is no health in my bones
		because of my sin.
4 For my iniquities have gone
		over my head;
	they weigh like a burden
		too heavy for me.

5 My wounds grow foul and fester
	because of my foolishness;
6 I am utterly bowed down
		and prostrate;
	all day long I go around
		mourning.

7 For my loins are filled
		with burning,
	and there is no soundness
		in my flesh.
8 I am utterly spent and crushed;
	I groan because of the
		tumult of my heart.

9 O Lord, all my longing is
		known to you;
	my sighing is not hidden
		from you.
10 My heart throbs, my
		strength fails me;
	as for the light of my eyes—it
		also has gone from me.
11 My friends and companions stand
		aloof from my affliction,
	and my neighbors stand far off.

12 Those who seek my life lay
		their snares;
	those who seek to hurt
		me speak of ruin,
	and meditate treachery
		all day long.

13 But I am like the deaf, I
		do not hear;
	like the mute, who
		cannot speak.
14 Truly, I am like one who
		does not hear,
	and in whose mouth
		is no retort.

15 But it is for you, O LORD,
		that I wait;
	it is you, O Lord my God,
		who will answer.
16 For I pray, "Only do not let
		them rejoice over me,
	those who boast against me
		when my foot slips."

17 For I am ready to fall,
	and my pain is ever with me.
18 I confess my iniquity;
	I am sorry for my sin.
19 Those who are my foes without
		cause[b] are mighty,
	and many are those who
		hate me wrongfully.

---

[a] 37.36 Gk Syr Jerome: Heb *he*
[b] 38.19 Q Ms: MT *my living foes*

20 Those who render me
   evil for good
are my adversaries because
   I follow after good.

21 Do not forsake me, O LORD;
   O my God, do not be
      far from me;
22 make haste to help me,
   O Lord, my salvation.

PSALM 39

PRAYER FOR WISDOM
AND FORGIVENESS

To the leader: to Jeduthun.
A Psalm of David.

1 I said, "I will guard my ways
   that I may not sin with
      my tongue;
I will keep a muzzle on my mouth
   as long as the wicked are
      in my presence."
2 I was silent and still;
   I held my peace to no avail;
my distress grew worse,
3   my heart became hot within me.
While I mused, the fire burned;
   then I spoke with my tongue:

4 "LORD, let me know my end,
   and what is the measure
      of my days;
   let me know how fleeting
      my life is.
5 You have made my days a
      few handbreadths,
   and my lifetime is as nothing
      in your sight.
Surely everyone stands as a mere
      breath. *Selah*
6   Surely everyone goes about
      like a shadow.
Surely for nothing they
      are in turmoil;
   they heap up, and do not
      know who will gather.

7 "And now, O Lord, what
      do I wait for?
   My hope is in you.
8 Deliver me from all my
      transgressions.
   Do not make me the
      scorn of the fool.

9 I am silent; I do not open
      my mouth,
   for it is you who have done it.
10 Remove your stroke from me;
   I am worn down by the
      blows[a] of your hand.

11 "You chastise mortals
   in punishment for sin,
consuming like a moth what
      is dear to them;
   surely everyone is a mere
      breath. *Selah*

12 "Hear my prayer, O LORD,
   and give ear to my cry;
   do not hold your peace
      at my tears.
For I am your passing guest,
   an alien, like all my forebears.
13 Turn your gaze away from me,
   that I may smile again,
   before I depart and
      am no more."

PSALM 40

THANKSGIVING FOR
DELIVERANCE AND
PRAYER FOR HELP

To the leader. Of David. A Psalm.

1 I waited patiently for the LORD;
   he inclined to me and
      heard my cry.
2 He drew me up from the
      desolate pit,[b]
   out of the miry bog,
and set my feet upon a rock,
   making my steps secure.
3 He put a new song in my mouth,
   a song of praise to our God.
Many will see and fear,
   and put their trust in
      the LORD.

4 Happy are those who make
   the LORD their trust,
who do not turn to the proud,
   to those who go astray
      after false gods.

a **39.10** Heb *hostility*   b **40.2** Cn: Heb *pit of tumult*

BUT A BREATH

"LORD, let me know my end, and what is the measure of my days; let me know how fleeting my life is. You have made my days a few handbreadths, and my lifetime is as nothing in your sight. Surely everyone stands as a mere breath."

—Psalm 39.4–5

We will all die someday, unless Jesus returns first. A day is coming for each of us when our earthly life will come to an end, and all our activity will cease. For many of us, this stark reality leads to deep anxiety and fear. But we do not need to fear because when we gave our lives to Christ, we received the unshakable promise of eternal life with God in heaven. Not even death can separate us from God's love (see Romans 8.38–39).

These verses in Psalms also make it clear that our lifespan on earth is relatively insignificant in the totality of time. But does that mean that we ourselves are insignificant? Not at all. Jesus Christ said that God knows each of us intimately, even keeping track of the very number of hairs on our heads (see Matthew 10.29–31). God knows us completely and is always watching over us and working for our good.

None of us knows exactly when the end of our existence will occur. Our hearts might be beating today, and we might be free of disease, but we could very well be gone tomorrow. We need to be prepared for that day and to live as though it could come at any time—whether it's 20 years or two months from now. Nevertheless, because we are all given a limited amount of time to live, we must decide how we will make the most of those days.

Are we using our time to serve God and others? Are we making sure all members of our family know that we love them? Are we taking steps to reconcile with those who are at odds with us? Are we telling others what Christ means to us? Ultimately, it will be up to us to decide what is truly important to us, and that is how we should spend our time on earth. It would be a shame to come to the end of our lives and realize that we wasted our time and effort on things that don't really last, on things that don't matter very much. We must ask God to help us discern what our highest priorities should be and then follow through to make sure we are living in a way that is in accordance with those priorities.

Going Deeper

- When you think about dying, do you feel fearful? Why or why not? If so, what verses of scripture speak to your fears?
- On what important things should you be spending your time on earth? How does that match up with how you are spending your time right now?

⁵ You have multiplied,
    O LORD my God,
    your wondrous deeds and your
        thoughts toward us;
    none can compare with you.
Were I to proclaim and
        tell of them,
    they would be more than
        can be counted.

WE NEED TO ASSESS OUR

OWN PERSONAL EXPERIENCES

AND SOLEMNLY REFLECT

ON THE GIFTS OF GOD

IN OUR OWN LIVES.

⁶ Sacrifice and offering you
        do not desire,
    but you have given me
        an open ear.ᵃ
Burnt offering and sin offering
        you have not required.
⁷ Then I said, "Here I am;
        in the scroll of the book it
        is written of me.ᵇ
⁸ I delight to do your will,
        O my God;
    your law is within my heart."

⁹ I have told the glad news
        of deliverance
    in the great congregation;
    see, I have not restrained my lips,
        as you know, O LORD.
¹⁰ I have not hidden your saving
        help within my heart,
    I have spoken of your
        faithfulness and
        your salvation;
    I have not concealed your
        steadfast love and
        your faithfulness
    from the great congregation.

¹¹ Do not, O LORD, withhold
        your mercy from me;
    let your steadfast love and
        your faithfulness
        keep me safe forever.

¹² For evils have encompassed
        me
    without number;
my iniquities have
        overtaken me,
    until I cannot see;
they are more than the
        hairs of my head,
    and my heart fails me.

¹³ Be pleased, O LORD,
        to deliver me;
    O LORD, make haste
        to help me.
¹⁴ Let all those be put to shame
        and confusion
    who seek to snatch
        away my life;
    let those be turned back and
        brought to dishonor
    who desire my hurt.
¹⁵ Let those be appalled because
        of their shame
    who say to me, "Aha, Aha!"

¹⁶ But may all who seek you
        rejoice and be
        glad in you;
    may those who love your
        salvation
    say continually, "Great
        is the LORD!"
¹⁷ As for me, I am poor
        and needy,
    but the Lord takes
        thought for me.
You are my help and my
        deliverer;
    do not delay, O my God.

PSALM 41

ASSURANCE OF GOD'S HELP AND A PLEA FOR HEALING

To the leader. A Psalm of David.

¹ Happy are those who
        consider the poor;ᶜ
    the LORD delivers them in
        the day of trouble.

ᵃ 40.6 Heb *ears you have dug for me*
ᵇ 40.7 Meaning of Heb uncertain   ᶜ 41.1 Or
weak

2 The LORD protects them and
    keeps them alive;
they are called happy
    in the land.
You do not give them up to
    the will of their enemies.
3 The LORD sustains them
    on their sickbed;
in their illness you heal all
    their infirmities.[a]

4 As for me, I said, "O LORD,
    be gracious to me;
heal me, for I have sinned
    against you."
5 My enemies wonder
    in malice
when I will die, and my
    name perish.
6 And when they come to see me,
    they utter empty words,
while their hearts gather
    mischief;
when they go out, they
    tell it abroad.
7 All who hate me whisper
    together about me;
they imagine the
    worst for me.

8 They think that a deadly thing
    has fastened on me,
that I will not rise again
    from where I lie.
9 Even my bosom friend in
    whom I trusted,
who ate of my bread, has lifted
    the heel against me.
10 But you, O LORD, be
    gracious to me,
and raise me up, that I
    may repay them.

11 By this I know that you are
    pleased with me;
because my enemy has not
    triumphed over me.
12 But you have upheld me because
    of my integrity,
and set me in your
    presence forever.

13 Blessed be the LORD, the
    God of Israel,
from everlasting to
    everlasting.
    Amen and Amen.

BOOK II

(PSALMS 42–72)

PSALM 42

LONGING FOR GOD AND HIS HELP IN DISTRESS

To the leader. A Maskil of the Korahites.

1 As a deer longs for flowing
    streams,
so my soul longs for you, O God.
2 My soul thirsts for God,
    for the living God.
When shall I come and behold
    the face of God?
3 My tears have been my food
    day and night,
while people say to me
    continually,
    "Where is your God?"

[a] 41.3 Heb *you change all his bed*

PONDER

As a deer longs for flowing streams,
so my soul longs for you, O God.
My soul thirsts for God, for the
living God. When shall I come
and behold the face of God?
—Psalm 42.1–2

PRAY

Father, give us hunger and thirst for
you that equals that of this psalmist.
Strengthen our belief and eliminate our
doubt. We praise you for lifting us up
when we are down and giving us hope
when ours is burning low. Let us realize
that no matter what our human doubts,
fears, failures or sorrows might be,
fellowship with you gives us the strength
to face any elements of life. Help us grow
in our intimacy with Christ. We do this
with joy, happiness and the peace that
passes understanding. We thank you
for these blessings through our Savior,
Jesus Christ. In his name we pray. Amen.

4 These things I remember,
    as I pour out my soul:
how I went with the throng,[a]
    and led them in procession
        to the house of God,
with glad shouts and songs
        of thanksgiving,
    a multitude keeping festival.
5 Why are you cast down, O my soul,
    and why are you disquieted
        within me?
Hope in God; for I shall
        again praise him,
    my help 6and my God.

My soul is cast down within me;
    therefore I remember you
from the land of Jordan
    and of Hermon,
    from Mount Mizar.
7 Deep calls to deep
    at the thunder of your cataracts;
all your waves and your billows
    have gone over me.
8 By day the LORD commands
        his steadfast love,
    and at night his song is with me,
    a prayer to the God of my life.

9 I say to God, my rock,
    "Why have you forgotten me?
Why must I walk about
        mournfully
    because the enemy
        oppresses me?"
10 As with a deadly wound
        in my body,
    my adversaries taunt me,
while they say to me continually,
    "Where is your God?"

11 Why are you cast down, O my soul,
    and why are you disquieted
        within me?
Hope in God; for I shall
        again praise him,
    my help and my God.

PSALM 43

PRAYER TO GOD IN
TIME OF TROUBLE

1 Vindicate me, O God, and
        defend my cause
    against an ungodly people;

from those who are deceitful
        and unjust
    deliver me!
2 For you are the God in whom
        I take refuge;
    why have you cast me off?
Why must I walk about
        mournfully
    because of the oppression
        of the enemy?

3 O send out your light and
        your truth;
    let them lead me;
let them bring me to your holy hill
    and to your dwelling.
4 Then I will go to the altar of God,
    to God my exceeding joy;
and I will praise you with the harp,
    O God, my God.

5 Why are you cast down, O my soul,
    and why are you disquieted
        within me?
Hope in God; for I shall
        again praise him,
    my help and my God.

PSALM 44

NATIONAL LAMENT AND
PRAYER FOR HELP

To the leader. Of the Korahites. A Maskil.

1 We have heard with our
        ears, O God,
    our ancestors have told us,
what deeds you performed
        in their days,
    in the days of old:
2 you with your own hand drove
        out the nations,
    but them you planted;
you afflicted the peoples,
    but them you set free;
3 for not by their own sword did
        they win the land,
    nor did their own arm
        give them victory;
but your right hand, and
        your arm,
    and the light of your
        countenance,
    for you delighted in them.

a 42.4 Meaning of Heb uncertain

4 You are my King and my God;
 you command[a] victories
  for Jacob.
5 Through you we push
   down our foes;
  through your name we tread
   down our assailants.
6 For not in my bow do I trust,
  nor can my sword save me.
7 But you have saved us
   from our foes,
  and have put to confusion
   those who hate us.
8 In God we have boasted
   continually,
  and we will give thanks to your
   name forever.   *Selah*

9 Yet you have rejected us
   and abased us,
  and have not gone out
   with our armies.
10 You made us turn back
    from the foe,
   and our enemies have
    gotten spoil.
11 You have made us like sheep
    for slaughter,
   and have scattered us
    among the nations.
12 You have sold your people
    for a trifle,
   demanding no high
    price for them.

13 You have made us the taunt
    of our neighbors,
   the derision and scorn of
    those around us.
14 You have made us a byword
    among the nations,
   a laughingstock[b] among
    the peoples.
15 All day long my disgrace
    is before me,
   and shame has covered my face
16 at the words of the taunters
    and revilers,
   at the sight of the enemy
    and the avenger.

17 All this has come upon us,
   yet we have not forgotten you,
    or been false to your covenant.
18 Our heart has not turned back,
   nor have our steps departed
    from your way,

19 yet you have broken us in the
    haunt of jackals,
   and covered us with
    deep darkness.

20 If we had forgotten the
    name of our God,
   or spread out our hands
    to a strange god,
21 would not God discover this?
   For he knows the secrets
    of the heart.
22 Because of you we are being
    killed all day long,
   and accounted as sheep
    for the slaughter.

23 Rouse yourself! Why do you
    sleep, O Lord?
   Awake, do not cast us
    off forever!
24 Why do you hide your face?
   Why do you forget our
    affliction and oppression?
25 For we sink down to the dust;
   our bodies cling to the ground.
26 Rise up, come to our help.
   Redeem us for the sake of
    your steadfast love.

PSALM 45

ODE FOR A ROYAL WEDDING

To the leader: according to Lilies. Of the Korahites. A Maskil. A love song.

1 My heart overflows with a
   goodly theme;
  I address my verses to the king;
  my tongue is like the pen
   of a ready scribe.

2 You are the most handsome
   of men;
  grace is poured upon your lips;
  therefore God has blessed
   you forever.
3 Gird your sword on your
   thigh, O mighty one,
  in your glory and majesty.

---

a **44.4** Gk Syr: Heb *You are my King, O God;
command*   b **44.14** Heb *a shaking of
the head*

4 In your majesty ride on
        victoriously
    for the cause of truth and
        to defend[a] the right;
    let your right hand teach
        you dread deeds.
5 Your arrows are sharp
        in the heart of the
        king's enemies;
    the peoples fall under you.

6 Your throne, O God,[b] endures
        forever and ever.
    Your royal scepter is a
        scepter of equity;
7 you love righteousness and
        hate wickedness.
    Therefore God, your God,
        has anointed you
    with the oil of
        gladness beyond
        your companions;
8 your robes are all fragrant
        with myrrh and
        aloes and cassia.
    From ivory palaces stringed
        instruments make
        you glad;
9   daughters of kings are among
        your ladies of honor;
    at your right hand stands the
        queen in gold of Ophir.

10 Hear, O daughter, consider
        and incline your ear;
    forget your people and
        your father's house,
11   and the king will desire
        your beauty.
    Since he is your lord,
        bow to him;
12   the people[c] of Tyre will seek
        your favor with gifts,
    the richest of the people [13]with
        all kinds of wealth.

    The princess is decked in
        her chamber with
        gold-woven robes;[d]
14   in many-colored robes she
        is led to the king;
    behind her the virgins, her
        companions, follow.
15 With joy and gladness they
        are led along
    as they enter the palace
        of the king.

16 In the place of ancestors you,
        O king,[e] shall have sons;
    you will make them princes
        in all the earth.
17 I will cause your name to
        be celebrated in all
        generations;
    therefore the peoples
        will praise you
        forever and ever.

PSALM 46

GOD'S DEFENSE OF HIS CITY AND PEOPLE

To the leader. Of the Korahites.
According to Alamoth. A Song.

1 God is our refuge and strength,
        a very present[f] help in trouble.
2 Therefore we will not fear, though
        the earth should change,
    though the mountains shake
        in the heart of the sea;
3 though its waters roar and foam,
        though the mountains tremble
        with its tumult.   *Selah*

WE MUST HONOR GOD WITH

PERSISTENCE, FAITH AND JOY.

4 There is a river whose streams
        make glad the city of God,
    the holy habitation of
        the Most High.
5 God is in the midst of the city;[g]
        it shall not be moved;
    God will help it when the
        morning dawns.
6 The nations are in an uproar,
        the kingdoms totter;
    he utters his voice, the
        earth melts.

a **45.4** Cn: Heb *and the meekness of*
b **45.6** Or *Your throne is a throne of God, it*
c **45.12** Heb *daughter*   d **45.13** Or *people.*
[13]*All glorious is the princess within, gold*
embroidery is her clothing   e **45.16** Heb
lacks *O king*   f **46.1** Or *well proved*
g **46.5** Heb *of it*

7 The LORD of hosts is with us;
   the God of Jacob is our
      refuge.[a]   *Selah*

8 Come, behold the works
      of the LORD;
   see what desolations he has
      brought on the earth.
9 He makes wars cease to the
      end of the earth;
   he breaks the bow, and
      shatters the spear;
   he burns the shields with fire.
10 "Be still, and know that I am God!
   I am exalted among
      the nations,
   I am exalted in the earth."
11 The LORD of hosts is with us;
   the God of Jacob is our
      refuge.[a]   *Selah*

PSALM 47

GOD'S RULE OVER THE NATIONS
To the leader. Of the Korahites. A Psalm.

1 Clap your hands, all you peoples;
   shout to God with loud
      songs of joy.
2 For the LORD, the Most
      High, is awesome,
   a great king over all the earth.
3 He subdued peoples under us,
   and nations under our feet.
4 He chose our heritage for us,
   the pride of Jacob whom he
      loves.   *Selah*

5 God has gone up with a shout,
   the LORD with the sound
      of a trumpet.
6 Sing praises to God, sing praises;
   sing praises to our King,
      sing praises.
7 For God is the king of all
      the earth;
   sing praises with a psalm.[b]

8 God is king over the nations;
   God sits on his holy throne.
9 The princes of the peoples gather
   as the people of the God
      of Abraham.
   For the shields of the earth
      belong to God;
   he is highly exalted.

PSALM 48

THE GLORY AND STRENGTH
OF ZION
A Song. A Psalm of the Korahites.

1 Great is the LORD and greatly
      to be praised
   in the city of our God.
   His holy mountain, 2beautiful
      in elevation,
   is the joy of all the earth,
   Mount Zion, in the far north,
      the city of the great King.
3 Within its citadels God
   has shown himself a
      sure defense.

4 Then the kings assembled,
   they came on together.
5 As soon as they saw it, they
      were astounded;
   they were in panic, they
      took to flight;
6 trembling took hold of
      them there,
   pains as of a woman in labor,
7 as when an east wind shatters
   the ships of Tarshish.
8 As we have heard, so
      have we seen
   in the city of the LORD of hosts,
   in the city of our God,
      which God establishes
      forever.   *Selah*

9 We ponder your steadfast
      love, O God,
   in the midst of your temple.
10 Your name, O God, like
      your praise,
   reaches to the ends of
      the earth.
   Your right hand is filled
      with victory.
11   Let Mount Zion be glad,
   let the towns[c] of Judah rejoice
   because of your judgments.

12 Walk about Zion, go
      all around it,
      count its towers,
13 consider well its ramparts;
   go through its citadels,

---

[a] 46.7,11 Or *fortress*   [b] 47.7 Heb *Maskil*
[c] 48.11 Heb *daughters*

that you may tell the next
generation

14 that this is God,
our God forever and ever.
He will be our guide forever.

PSALM 49

THE FOLLY OF TRUST IN RICHES

*To the leader. Of the Korahites.
A Psalm.*

1 Hear this, all you peoples;
give ear, all inhabitants
of the world,

2 both low and high,
rich and poor together.

3 My mouth shall speak wisdom;
the meditation of my heart
shall be understanding.

4 I will incline my ear to a proverb;
I will solve my riddle to the
music of the harp.

5 Why should I fear in times
of trouble,
when the iniquity of my
persecutors surrounds me,

6 those who trust in their wealth
and boast of the abundance
of their riches?

7 Truly, no ransom avails
for one's life,[a]
there is no price one can
give to God for it.

8 For the ransom of life is costly,
and can never suffice,

9 that one should live on forever
and never see the grave.[b]

10 When we look at the
wise, they die;
fool and dolt perish together
and leave their wealth
to others.

11 Their graves[c] are their
homes forever,
their dwelling places to
all generations,
though they named
lands their own.

12 Mortals cannot abide in
their pomp;
they are like the animals
that perish.

13 Such is the fate of the foolhardy,
the end of those[d] who are
pleased with their
lot.   *Selah*

14 Like sheep they are appointed
for Sheol;
Death shall be their shepherd;
straight to the grave they
descend,[e]
and their form shall
waste away;
Sheol shall be their home.[f]

15 But God will ransom my soul
from the power of Sheol,
for he will receive me.   *Selah*

16 Do not be afraid when some
become rich,
when the wealth of their
houses increases.

17 For when they die they will
carry nothing away;
their wealth will not go
down after them.

18 Though in their lifetime they
count themselves happy
—for you are praised when you
do well for yourself—

19 they[g] will go to the company
of their ancestors,
who will never again
see the light.

20 Mortals cannot abide in
their pomp;
they are like the animals
that perish.

PSALM 50

THE ACCEPTABLE SACRIFICE

A Psalm of Asaph.

1 The mighty one, God the LORD,
speaks and summons the earth
from the rising of the
sun to its setting.

2 Out of Zion, the perfection
of beauty,
God shines forth.

a **49.7** Another reading is *no one can ransom
a brother*   b **49.9** Heb *the pit*   c **49.11** Gk
Syr Compare Tg: Heb *their inward* (thought)
d **49.13** Tg: Heb *after them*   e **49.14** Cn: Heb
*the upright shall have dominion over them
in the morning*   f **49.14** Meaning of Heb
uncertain   g **49.19** Cn: Heb *you*

3 Our God comes and does
      not keep silence,
    before him is a devouring fire,
    and a mighty tempest
      all around him.
4 He calls to the heavens above
    and to the earth, that he
      may judge his people:
5 "Gather to me my faithful ones,
    who made a covenant with
      me by sacrifice!"
6 The heavens declare his
      righteousness,
    for God himself is judge. *Selah*

7 "Hear, O my people, and
      I will speak,
    O Israel, I will testify
      against you.
    I am God, your God.
8 Not for your sacrifices do
      I rebuke you;
    your burnt offerings are
      continually before me.
9 I will not accept a bull from
      your house,
    or goats from your folds.
10 For every wild animal of the
      forest is mine,
    the cattle on a thousand hills.
11 I know all the birds of the air,[a]
    and all that moves in the
      field is mine.

12 "If I were hungry, I would
      not tell you,
    for the world and all that
      is in it is mine.
13 Do I eat the flesh of bulls,
    or drink the blood of goats?
14 Offer to God a sacrifice of
      thanksgiving,[b]
    and pay your vows to
      the Most High.
15 Call on me in the
      day of trouble;
    I will deliver you, and you
      shall glorify me."

16 But to the wicked God says:
    "What right have you to
      recite my statutes,
    or take my covenant
      on your lips?
17 For you hate discipline,
    and you cast my words
      behind you.

18 You make friends with a thief
      when you see one,
    and you keep company
      with adulterers.

19 "You give your mouth free
      rein for evil,
    and your tongue
      frames deceit.
20 You sit and speak against
      your kin;
    you slander your own
      mother's child.
21 These things you have done
      and I have been silent;
    you thought that I was one
      just like yourself.
    But now I rebuke you, and lay
      the charge before you.

22 "Mark this, then, you who
      forget God,
    or I will tear you apart,
      and there will be no
      one to deliver.
23 Those who bring thanksgiving as
      their sacrifice honor me;
    to those who go
      the right way[c]
    I will show the salvation
      of God."

PSALM 51

PRAYER FOR CLEANSING AND PARDON

To the leader. A Psalm of David, when the prophet Nathan came to him, after he had gone in to Bathsheba.

1 Have mercy on me, O God,
    according to your
      steadfast love;
    according to your abundant
      mercy
    blot out my transgressions.
2 Wash me thoroughly from
      my iniquity,
    and cleanse me from my sin.

3 For I know my transgressions,
    and my sin is ever
      before me.

a 50.11 Gk Syr Tg: Heb *mountains*
b 50.14 Or *make thanksgiving your sacrifice to God*   c 50.23 Heb *who set a way*

4 Against you, you alone,
    have I sinned,
  and done what is evil
    in your sight,
  so that you are justified in
    your sentence
  and blameless when you
    pass judgment.
5 Indeed, I was born guilty,
    a sinner when my mother
    conceived me.

6 You desire truth in the
    inward being;[a]
  therefore teach me wisdom
    in my secret heart.
7 Purge me with hyssop, and
    I shall be clean;
  wash me, and I shall be
    whiter than snow.
8 Let me hear joy and gladness;
  let the bones that you have
    crushed rejoice.
9 Hide your face from my sins,
  and blot out all
    my iniquities.

10 Create in me a clean
    heart, O God,
  and put a new and right[b]
    spirit within me.
11 Do not cast me away from
    your presence,
  and do not take your holy
    spirit from me.
12 Restore to me the joy of
    your salvation,
  and sustain in me a
    willing[c] spirit.

13 Then I will teach transgressors
    your ways,
  and sinners will
    return to you.
14 Deliver me from bloodshed,
    O God,
  O God of my salvation,
  and my tongue will sing aloud
    of your deliverance.

15 O Lord, open my lips,
  and my mouth will declare
    your praise.
16 For you have no delight
    in sacrifice;
  if I were to give a burnt
    offering, you would
    not be pleased.
17 The sacrifice acceptable to God[d]
    is a broken spirit;
  a broken and contrite
    heart, O God, you
    will not despise.

18 Do good to Zion in your
    good pleasure;
  rebuild the walls
    of Jerusalem,
19 then you will delight in
    right sacrifices,
  in burnt offerings and whole
    burnt offerings;
  then bulls will be offered
    on your altar.

a 51.6 Meaning of Heb uncertain   b 51.10 Or
steadfast   c 51.12 Or generous   d 51.17 Or
My sacrifice, O God,

BIBLE IN LIFE

Confession   Psalm 51.1–19

David was a lot like the rest of us: a broken person and an unworthy sinner. Through his feelings of guilt, his confession, his turning to God and his repentance, however, his relationship with God was reconciled. As soon as he confessed and repented of his sin, God immediately removed it. In addition to what David had, we have something more: faith in Christ. And we can confidently confess, knowing we will be totally forgiven because Christ has taken the punishment for our sins. When we confess, our debt is paid. Once we have reconciliation with God, we should make our most earnest effort to continue in that sense of reconciliation with God through Christ. By looking at the life of Jesus as a pattern, we can take upon ourselves a new set of standards by which we live in intimacy with God.

PSALM 52

JUDGMENT ON THE DECEITFUL

To the leader. A Maskil of David,
when Doeg the Edomite came to
Saul and said to him, "David has
come to the house of Ahimelech."

1 Why do you boast, O mighty one,
    of mischief done against
        the godly?[a]
    All day long 2you are
        plotting destruction.
    Your tongue is like a sharp razor,
        you worker of treachery.
3 You love evil more than good,
    and lying more than speaking
        the truth.   *Selah*
4 You love all words that devour,
    O deceitful tongue.

5 But God will break you
        down forever;
    he will snatch and tear you
        from your tent;
    he will uproot you from the
        land of the living.   *Selah*
6 The righteous will see, and fear,
    and will laugh at the
        evildoer,[b] saying,
7 "See the one who would not take
        refuge in God,
    but trusted in abundant riches,
        and sought refuge in wealth!"[c]

8 But I am like a green olive tree
        in the house of God.
    I trust in the steadfast love of God
        forever and ever.
9 I will thank you forever,
        because of what you have done.

In the presence of the faithful
    I will proclaim[d] your name,
        for it is good.

PSALM 53

DENUNCIATION OF GODLESSNESS

To the leader: according to
Mahalath. A Maskil of David.

1 Fools say in their hearts,
        "There is no God."
    They are corrupt, they commit
        abominable acts;
    there is no one who does good.

2 God looks down from heaven
        on humankind
    to see if there are any
        who are wise,
    who seek after God.

3 They have all fallen away, they
        are all alike perverse;
    there is no one
        who does good,
    no, not one.

4 Have they no knowledge,
        those evildoers,
    who eat up my people as
        they eat bread,
    and do not call upon God?

a **52.1** Cn Compare Syr: Heb *the kindness of*
God   b **52.6** Heb *him*   c **52.7** Syr Tg: Heb *in*
his destruction   d **52.9** Cn: Heb *wait for*

⊣ BIBLE IN LIFE ▷ ⊕

A True Worshiper   Psalm 51.10

The Israelites had to follow strict rules and purification rites before they were permitted to enter the temple to worship (see Leviticus 14). There was an element of outward distinction, a kind of "pecking order" among those who worshiped God. We should also meet certain requirements before we worship, but these involve attitudes of the heart and not a desire for personal benefits for ourselves in the eyes of others. We should come before God with a desire for a pure heart, with an openness to the presence of the Holy Spirit, asking, "Create in me a clean heart, O God, and put a new and right spirit within me" (Psalm 51.10). With a clean heart, we can be free of resentment against other human beings, and we can desire and enjoy an even closer intimacy with God.

⁵ There they shall be
 in great terror,
  in terror such as
   has not been.
For God will scatter the bones
 of the ungodly;ᵃ
 they will be put to shame,ᵇ for
  God has rejected them.

⁶ O that deliverance for Israel
  would come from Zion!
When God restores the
  fortunes of his people,
Jacob will rejoice; Israel
  will be glad.

PSALM 54

PRAYER FOR VINDICATION

*To the leader: with stringed
instruments. A Maskil of David,
when the Ziphites went and
told Saul, "David is in hiding
among us."*

¹ Save me, O God,
 by your name,
 and vindicate me by
  your might.
² Hear my prayer, O God;
 give ear to the words
  of my mouth.

³ For the insolent have risen
  against me,
 the ruthless seek my life;
 they do not set God before
  them.   *Selah*

⁴ But surely, God is my helper;
 the Lord is the upholder
  ofᶜ my life.
⁵ He will repay my enemies
 for their evil.
In your faithfulness, put
 an end to them.

⁶ With a freewill offering I will
  sacrifice to you;
 I will give thanks to your
  name, O LORD,
  for it is good.
⁷ For he has delivered me from
  every trouble,
 and my eye has looked in
  triumph on my enemies.

PSALM 55

COMPLAINT ABOUT A FRIEND'S TREACHERY

*To the leader: with stringed
instruments. A Maskil of David.*

¹ Give ear to my prayer, O God;
 do not hide yourself from
  my supplication.
² Attend to me, and answer me;
 I am troubled in my complaint.
I am distraught ³by the noise
 of the enemy,
 because of the clamor
  of the wicked.
For they bringᵈ trouble upon me,
 and in anger they cherish
  enmity against me.

⁴ My heart is in anguish
  within me,
 the terrors of death have
  fallen upon me.
⁵ Fear and trembling come
  upon me,
 and horror overwhelms me.
⁶ And I say, "O that I had
  wings like a dove!
 I would fly away and be at rest;
⁷ truly, I would flee far away;
 I would lodge in the
  wilderness;   *Selah*
⁸ I would hurry to find a
  shelter for myself
 from the raging wind
  and tempest."

⁹ Confuse, O Lord, confound
  their speech;
 for I see violence and
  strife in the city.
¹⁰ Day and night they go around it
  on its walls,
 and iniquity and trouble
  are within it;
¹¹ ruin is in its midst;
 oppression and fraud
  do not depart from its
   marketplace.

ᵃ 53.5 Cn Compare Gk Syr: Heb *him who
encamps against you* ᵇ 53.5 Gk: Heb *you
have put (them) to shame* ᶜ 54.4 Gk Syr
Jerome: Heb *is of those who uphold* or *is
with those who uphold* ᵈ 55.3 Cn Compare
Gk: Heb *they cause to totter*

12 It is not enemies who taunt me—
    I could bear that;
  it is not adversaries who deal
        insolently with me—
    I could hide from them.
13 But it is you, my equal,
    my companion, my
        familiar friend,
14 with whom I kept pleasant
        company;
    we walked in the house of
        God with the throng.
15 Let death come upon them;
    let them go down alive to Sheol;
  for evil is in their homes
        and in their hearts.

16 But I call upon God,
    and the LORD will save me.
17 Evening and morning
        and at noon
    I utter my complaint and moan,
    and he will hear my voice.
18 He will redeem me unharmed
    from the battle that I wage,
  for many are arrayed
        against me.
19 God, who is enthroned from of
        old,   Selah
    will hear, and will
        humble them—
  because they do not change,
    and do not fear God.

20 My companion laid hands
        on a friend
    and violated a covenant
        with me[a]
21 with speech smoother
        than butter,
    but with a heart set on war;
  with words that were
        softer than oil,
    but in fact were drawn swords.

22 Cast your burden[b] on the LORD,
    and he will sustain you;
  he will never permit
        the righteous to be moved.

23 But you, O God, will cast
        them down
    into the lowest pit;
  the bloodthirsty and treacherous
        shall not live out half
        their days.
  But I will trust in you.

PSALM 56

TRUST IN GOD UNDER PERSECUTION

To the leader: according to The Dove on Far-off Terebinths. *Of David. A Miktam, when the Philistines seized him in Gath.*

1 Be gracious to me, O God, for
        people trample on me;
    all day long foes oppress me;
2 my enemies trample on
        me all day long,
    for many fight against me.
  O Most High, ³when I am afraid,
    I put my trust in you.
4 In God, whose word I praise,
    in God I trust; I am not afraid;
    what can flesh do to me?

5 All day long they seek to
        injure my cause;
    all their thoughts are
        against me for evil.
6 They stir up strife, they lurk,
    they watch my steps.
  As they hoped to have my life,
7   so repay[c] them for their crime;
    in wrath cast down the
        peoples, O God!

8 You have kept count of
        my tossings;
    put my tears in your bottle.
    Are they not in your record?
9 Then my enemies will retreat
    in the day when I call.
    This I know, that[d] God
        is for me.
10 In God, whose word I praise,
    in the LORD, whose
        word I praise,
11 in God I trust; I am not afraid.
    What can a mere mortal
        do to me?

12 My vows to you I must
        perform, O God;
    I will render thank
        offerings to you.
13 For you have delivered my
        soul from death,
    and my feet from falling,
  so that I may walk before God
    in the light of life.

---

a 55.20 Heb lacks *with me*   b 55.22 Or *Cast what he has given you*   c 56.7 Cn: Heb *rescue*   d 56.9 Or *because*

PSALM 57

PRAISE AND ASSURANCE UNDER PERSECUTION

To the leader: Do Not Destroy. Of David. A Miktam, when he fled from Saul, in the cave.

1 Be merciful to me, O God,
      be merciful to me,
      for in you my soul takes refuge;
   in the shadow of your wings
      I will take refuge,
      until the destroying
         storms pass by.
2 I cry to God Most High,
   to God who fulfills his
      purpose for me.
3 He will send from heaven
      and save me,
   he will put to shame those who
      trample on me.   *Selah*

PONDER

Be merciful to me, O God, be merciful to me, for in you my soul takes refuge; in the shadow of your wings I will take refuge, until the destroying streams pass by.
—Psalm 57.1

PRAY

O God, our Help, as we contemplate the afflictions of our lives, let us remember that we have a source of strength in your power, your grace, your love for us, and your confidence in us to reach for greatness in our own ways. We take refuge in you. May we not be concerned about the opinions of others or the standards of our culture, but rather adhere to the standards of our Savior, Jesus Christ, who epitomized peace, love, compassion, service, humility and forgiveness. Let us elevate these traits in our own consciousnesses and our own ambitions for the future—and in so doing find joy. We ask these things in the name of our Savior. Amen.

God will send forth his steadfast
      love and his faithfulness.
4 I lie down among lions
   that greedily devour[a]
      human prey;
   their teeth are spears and arrows,
      their tongues sharp swords.
5 Be exalted, O God, above
      the heavens.
   Let your glory be over
      all the earth.

6 They set a net for my steps;
   my soul was bowed down.
   They dug a pit in my path,
      but they have fallen into it
         themselves.   *Selah*
7 My heart is steadfast, O God,
   my heart is steadfast.
   I will sing and make melody.
8   Awake, my soul!
   Awake, O harp and lyre!
   I will awake the dawn.
9 I will give thanks to you, O Lord,
      among the peoples;
   I will sing praises to you
      among the nations.
10 For your steadfast love is as
      high as the heavens;
   your faithfulness extends
      to the clouds.

11 Be exalted, O God, above
      the heavens.
   Let your glory be over
      all the earth.

PSALM 58

PRAYER FOR VENGEANCE

To the leader: Do Not Destroy. Of David. A Miktam.

1 Do you indeed decree what
      is right, you gods?[b]
   Do you judge people fairly?
2 No, in your hearts you
      devise wrongs;
   your hands deal out
      violence on earth.

[a] **57.4** Cn: Heb *are aflame for*   [b] **58.1** Or *mighty lords*

3 The wicked go astray from
        the womb;
    they err from their birth,
        speaking lies.
4 They have venom like the
        venom of a serpent,
    like the deaf adder that
        stops its ear,
5 so that it does not hear the
        voice of charmers
    or of the cunning
        enchanter.

6 O God, break the teeth in
        their mouths;
    tear out the fangs of the
        young lions, O LORD!
7 Let them vanish like water
        that runs away;
    like grass let them be trodden
        down[a] and wither.
8 Let them be like the snail that
        dissolves into slime;
    like the untimely birth that
        never sees the sun.
9 Sooner than your pots can feel
        the heat of thorns,
    whether green or ablaze, may
        he sweep them away!

10 The righteous will rejoice
        when they see
        vengeance done;
    they will bathe their feet in
        the blood of the wicked.
11 People will say, "Surely there is a
        reward for the righteous;
    surely there is a God who
        judges on earth."

PSALM 59

PRAYER FOR DELIVERANCE
FROM ENEMIES

*To the leader: Do Not Destroy. Of David.
A Miktam, when Saul ordered his house
to be watched in order to kill him.*

1 Deliver me from my enemies,
        O my God;
    protect me from those who
        rise up against me.
2 Deliver me from those
        who work evil;
    from the bloodthirsty
        save me.

3 Even now they lie in wait
        for my life;
    the mighty stir up strife
        against me.
For no transgression or sin
        of mine, O LORD,
4   for no fault of mine, they
        run and make ready.

Rouse yourself, come to
        my help and see!
5   You, LORD God of hosts,
        are God of Israel.
Awake to punish all the nations;
    spare none of those who
        treacherously plot
        evil.   *Selah*

6 Each evening they come back,
        howling like dogs
    and prowling about the city.
7 There they are, bellowing
        with their mouths,
    with sharp words[b] on
        their lips—
    for "Who," they think,[c]
        "will hear us?"

8 But you laugh at them, O LORD;
        you hold all the nations
        in derision.
9 O my strength, I will
        watch for you;
    for you, O God, are my fortress.
10 My God in his steadfast love
        will meet me;
    my God will let me look in
        triumph on my enemies.

11 Do not kill them, or my
        people may forget;
    make them totter by your
        power, and bring
        them down,
    O Lord, our shield.
12 For the sin of their mouths, the
        words of their lips,
    let them be trapped in
        their pride.
For the cursing and lies
        that they utter,
13   consume them in wrath;
    consume them until they
        are no more.

a 58.7 Cn: Meaning of Heb uncertain
b 59.7 Heb *with swords*   c 59.7 Heb lacks
they think

Then it will be known to the
    ends of the earth
    that God rules over Jacob. *Selah*

14 Each evening they come back,
    howling like dogs
    and prowling about the city.
15 They roam about for food,
    and growl if they do not
      get their fill.

16 But I will sing of your might;
    I will sing aloud of your steadfast
      love in the morning.
    For you have been a fortress for me
    and a refuge in the day
      of my distress.
17 O my strength, I will sing
      praises to you,
    for you, O God, are my fortress,
    the God who shows me
      steadfast love.

PSALM 60

PRAYER FOR NATIONAL VICTORY AFTER DEFEAT

*To the leader: according to the Lily of
the Covenant. A Miktam of David; for
instruction; when he struggled with
Aram-naharaim and with Aram-zobah,
and when Joab on his return killed twelve
thousand Edomites in the Valley of Salt.*

1 O God, you have rejected us,
      broken our defenses;
    you have been angry;
      now restore us!
2 You have caused the land
      to quake; you have
      torn it open;
    repair the cracks in it,
      for it is tottering.
3 You have made your people
      suffer hard things;
    you have given us wine to
      drink that made us reel.

4 You have set up a banner for
      those who fear you,
    to rally to it out of
      bowshot.[a]   *Selah*
5 Give victory with your right
      hand, and answer us,[b]
    so that those whom you
      love may be rescued.

6 God has promised in his
      sanctuary:[c]
    "With exultation I will
      divide up Shechem,
    and portion out the
      Vale of Succoth.
7 Gilead is mine, and
      Manasseh is mine;
    Ephraim is my helmet;
      Judah is my scepter.
8 Moab is my washbasin;
    on Edom I hurl my shoe;
    over Philistia I shout
      in triumph."

9 Who will bring me to the
      fortified city?
    Who will lead me to Edom?
10 Have you not rejected us, O God?
    You do not go out, O God,
      with our armies.
11 O grant us help against the foe,
    for human help is worthless.
12 With God we shall do valiantly;
    it is he who will tread
      down our foes.

PSALM 61

ASSURANCE OF GOD'S PROTECTION

*To the leader: with stringed
instruments. Of David.*

1 Hear my cry, O God;
    listen to my prayer.
2 From the end of the earth
      I call to you,
    when my heart is faint.

Lead me to the rock
    that is higher than I;
3 for you are my refuge,
    a strong tower against
      the enemy.

4 Let me abide in your
      tent forever,
    find refuge under
      the shelter of your
      wings.   *Selah*

---

a **60.4** Gk Syr Jerome: Heb *because of
the truth*   b **60.5** Another reading is *me*
c **60.6** Or *by his holiness*

5 For you, O God, have heard
     my vows;
  you have given me the
     heritage of those who
     fear your name.

6 Prolong the life of the king;
     may his years endure to
     all generations!
7 May he be enthroned forever
     before God;
  appoint steadfast love
     and faithfulness to
     watch over him!

8 So I will always sing praises
     to your name,
  as I pay my vows day after day.

PSALM 62

SONG OF TRUST IN GOD ALONE

*To the leader: according to
Jeduthun. A Psalm of David.*

1 For God alone my soul
     waits in silence;
  from him comes my salvation.
2 He alone is my rock and
     my salvation,
  my fortress; I shall never
     be shaken.

3 How long will you assail a person,
  will you batter your
     victim, all of you,
  as you would a leaning wall,
     a tottering fence?
4 Their only plan is to bring down
     a person of prominence.
  They take pleasure in
     falsehood;
  they bless with their mouths,
     but inwardly they curse. *Selah*

5 For God alone my soul
     waits in silence,
  for my hope is from him.
6 He alone is my rock and
     my salvation,
  my fortress; I shall not
     be shaken.
7 On God rests my deliverance
     and my honor;
  my mighty rock, my
     refuge is in God.

8 Trust in him at all times,
     O people;
  pour out your heart
     before him;
  God is a refuge for us.   *Selah*

9 Those of low estate are
     but a breath,
  those of high estate are
     a delusion;
  in the balances they go up;
  they are together lighter
     than a breath.
10 Put no confidence in extortion,
  and set no vain hopes
     on robbery;
  if riches increase, do not set
     your heart on them.

11 Once God has spoken;
  twice have I heard this:
  that power belongs to God,
12   and steadfast love belongs
     to you, O Lord.
  For you repay to all
     according to their work.

WE SHOULD REJOICE TO

KNOW THAT, ULTIMATELY,

GOD IS IN CONTROL.

PSALM 63

COMFORT AND ASSURANCE
IN GOD'S PRESENCE

*A Psalm of David, when he was
in the Wilderness of Judah.*

1 O God, you are my God,
     I seek you,
  my soul thirsts for you;
  my flesh faints for you,
     as in a dry and weary land
     where there is no water.
2 So I have looked upon you
     in the sanctuary,
  beholding your power
     and glory.
3 Because your steadfast love
     is better than life,
  my lips will praise you.

4 So I will bless you as long as I live;
    I will lift up my hands and
        call on your name.

5 My soul is satisfied as with
        a rich feast,[a]
    and my mouth praises you
        with joyful lips
6 when I think of you on my bed,
    and meditate on you in the
        watches of the night;
7 for you have been my help,
    and in the shadow of your
        wings I sing for joy.
8 My soul clings to you;
    your right hand upholds me.

9 But those who seek to
        destroy my life
    shall go down into the
        depths of the earth;
10 they shall be given over to the
        power of the sword,
    they shall be prey for jackals.
11 But the king shall
        rejoice in God;
    all who swear by him
        shall exult,
    for the mouths of liars
        will be stopped.

OUR SECURITY IS NOT

INDEPENDENT OF GOD.

PSALM 64

PRAYER FOR PROTECTION
FROM ENEMIES

To the leader. A Psalm of David.

1 Hear my voice, O God, in
        my complaint;
    preserve my life from the
        dread enemy.
2 Hide me from the secret
        plots of the wicked,
    from the scheming
        of evildoers,
3 who whet their tongues
        like swords,
    who aim bitter words
        like arrows,

4 shooting from ambush at
        the blameless;
    they shoot suddenly and
        without fear.
5 They hold fast to their evil purpose;
    they talk of laying
        snares secretly,
thinking, "Who can see us?[b]
6   Who can search out our crimes?[c]
We have thought out a cunningly
        conceived plot."
    For the human heart and
        mind are deep.

7 But God will shoot his
        arrow at them;
    they will be wounded suddenly.
8 Because of their tongue he will
        bring them to ruin;[d]
    all who see them will
        shake with horror.
9 Then everyone will fear;
    they will tell what God has
        brought about,
    and ponder what he has done.

10 Let the righteous rejoice
        in the LORD
    and take refuge in him.
    Let all the upright in heart glory.

PSALM 65

THANKSGIVING FOR
EARTH'S BOUNTY

To the leader. A Psalm of David. A Song.

1 Praise is due to you,
        O God, in Zion;
    and to you shall vows be
        performed,
2   O you who answer prayer!
    To you all flesh shall come.
3 When deeds of iniquity
        overwhelm us,
    you forgive our transgressions.
4 Happy are those whom you
        choose and bring near
    to live in your courts.
    We shall be satisfied with the
        goodness of your house,
    your holy temple.

a 63.5 Heb *with fat and fatness*   b 64.5 Syr:
Heb *them*   c 64.6 Cn: Heb *They search out
crimes*   d 64.8 Cn: Heb *They will bring him
to ruin, their tongue being against them*

⁵ By awesome deeds you answer
us with deliverance,
O God of our salvation;
you are the hope of all the
ends of the earth
and of the farthest seas.
⁶ By your[a] strength you established
the mountains;
you are girded with might.
⁷ You silence the roaring
of the seas,
the roaring of their waves,
the tumult of the peoples.
⁸ Those who live at earth's
farthest bounds are
awed by your signs;
you make the gateways of
the morning and the
evening shout for joy.

⁹ You visit the earth and water it,
you greatly enrich it;
the river of God is full of water;
you provide the people
with grain,
for so you have prepared it.
¹⁰ You water its furrows
abundantly,
settling its ridges,
softening it with showers,
and blessing its growth.
¹¹ You crown the year with
your bounty;
your wagon tracks overflow
with richness.
¹² The pastures of the wilderness
overflow,
the hills gird themselves
with joy,
¹³ the meadows clothe themselves
with flocks,
the valleys deck themselves
with grain,
they shout and sing
together for joy.

PSALM 66

PRAISE FOR GOD'S GOODNESS TO ISRAEL

To the leader. A Song. A Psalm.

¹ Make a joyful noise to God,
all the earth;
² sing the glory of his name;
give to him glorious praise.

³ Say to God, "How awesome
are your deeds!
Because of your great
power, your enemies
cringe before you.
⁴ All the earth worships you;
they sing praises to you,
sing praises to your
name."   *Selah*

⁵ Come and see what God has done:
he is awesome in his deeds
among mortals.
⁶ He turned the sea into dry land;
they passed through the
river on foot.
There we rejoiced in him,
⁷ who rules by his might forever,
whose eyes keep watch on
the nations—
let the rebellious not exalt
themselves.   *Selah*

⁸ Bless our God, O peoples,
let the sound of his
praise be heard,
⁹ who has kept us among
the living,
and has not let our feet slip.
¹⁰ For you, O God, have tested us;
you have tried us as
silver is tried.
¹¹ You brought us into the net;
you laid burdens on our backs;
¹² you let people ride over our heads;
we went through fire and
through water;
yet you have brought us out
to a spacious place.[b]

¹³ I will come into your house
with burnt offerings;
I will pay you my vows,
¹⁴ those that my lips uttered
and my mouth promised
when I was in trouble.
¹⁵ I will offer to you burnt
offerings of fatlings,
with the smoke of the
sacrifice of rams;
I will make an offering of bulls
and goats.   *Selah*

[a] 65.6 Gk Jerome: Heb *his*   [b] 66.12 Cn
Compare Gk Syr Jerome Tg: Heb *to a
saturation*

16 Come and hear, all you
who fear God,
and I will tell what he
has done for me.
17 I cried aloud to him,
and he was extolled with
my tongue.
18 If I had cherished iniquity
in my heart,
the Lord would not
have listened.
19 But truly God has listened;
he has given heed to the
words of my prayer.

20 Blessed be God,
because he has not
rejected my prayer
or removed his steadfast
love from me.

PSALM 67

THE NATIONS CALLED
TO PRAISE GOD

*To the leader: with stringed
instruments. A Psalm. A Song.*

1 May God be gracious to
us and bless us
and make his face to shine
upon us, *Selah*
2 that your way may be known
upon earth,
your saving power among
all nations.
3 Let the peoples praise
you, O God;
let all the peoples praise you.

4 Let the nations be glad
and sing for joy,
for you judge the peoples
with equity
and guide the nations upon
earth. *Selah*
5 Let the peoples praise
you, O God;
let all the peoples praise you.

6 The earth has yielded
its increase;
God, our God, has blessed us.
7 May God continue to bless us;
let all the ends of the
earth revere him.

PSALM 68

PRAISE AND THANKSGIVING

*To the leader. Of David.
A Psalm. A Song.*

1 Let God rise up, let his enemies
be scattered;
let those who hate him
flee before him.
2 As smoke is driven away, so
drive them away;
as wax melts before the fire,
let the wicked perish
before God.
3 But let the righteous be joyful;
let them exult before God;
let them be jubilant
with joy.

4 Sing to God, sing praises
to his name;
lift up a song to him who rides
upon the clouds[a]—
his name is the LORD—
be exultant before him.

5 Father of orphans and
protector of widows
is God in his holy habitation.
6 God gives the desolate a
home to live in;
he leads out the prisoners
to prosperity,
but the rebellious live in
a parched land.

7 O God, when you went out
before your people,
when you marched through
the wilderness, *Selah*
8 the earth quaked, the heavens
poured down rain
at the presence of God,
the God of Sinai,
at the presence of God,
the God of Israel.
9 Rain in abundance, O God, you
showered abroad;
you restored your heritage
when it languished;
10 your flock found a dwelling in it;
in your goodness, O God, you
provided for the needy.

a 68.4 Or *cast up a highway for him who
rides through the deserts*

11 The Lord gives the command;
    great is the company of those[a]
        who bore the tidings:
12   "The kings of the armies,
        they flee, they flee!"
The women at home divide
    the spoil,
13   though they stay among
        the sheepfolds—
the wings of a dove covered
    with silver,
    its pinions with green gold.
14 When the Almighty[b] scattered
    kings there,
    snow fell on Zalmon.

15 O mighty mountain, mountain
    of Bashan;
    O many-peaked mountain,
        mountain of Bashan!
16 Why do you look with envy,
    O many-peaked
        mountain,
    at the mount that God
        desired for his abode,
    where the LORD will
        reside forever?

17 With mighty chariotry, twice
    ten thousand,
    thousands upon thousands,
    the Lord came from Sinai
        into the holy place.[c]
18 You ascended the high mount,
    leading captives
        in your train
    and receiving gifts
        from people,
even from those who rebel
    against the LORD
        God's abiding there.
19 Blessed be the Lord,
    who daily bears us up;
    God is our salvation.   Selah
20 Our God is a God of salvation,
    and to GOD, the Lord, belongs
        escape from death.

21 But God will shatter the heads
    of his enemies,
    the hairy crown of those who
        walk in their guilty ways.
22 The Lord said,
    "I will bring them back
        from Bashan,
I will bring them back from
    the depths of the sea,

23 so that you may bathe[d] your
    feet in blood,
    so that the tongues of your
        dogs may have their
        share from the foe."

24 Your solemn processions
    are seen,[e] O God,
    the processions of my
        God, my King, into
        the sanctuary—
25 the singers in front, the
    musicians last,
    between them girls playing
        tambourines:
26 "Bless God in the great
    congregation,
    the LORD, O you who are
        of Israel's fountain!"
27 There is Benjamin, the least
    of them, in the lead,
    the princes of Judah in a body,
    the princes of Zebulun, the
        princes of Naphtali.

28 Summon your might, O God;
    show your strength,
        O God, as you have
        done for us before.
29 Because of your temple
    at Jerusalem
    kings bear gifts to you.
30 Rebuke the wild animals that
    live among the reeds,
    the herd of bulls with the
        calves of the peoples.
Trample[f] under foot those who
    lust after tribute;
    scatter the peoples who
        delight in war.[g]
31 Let bronze be brought
    from Egypt;
    let Ethiopia[h] hasten to stretch
        out its hands to God.

32 Sing to God, O kingdoms
    of the earth;
    sing praises to the Lord,   Selah

a **68.11** Or *company of the women*
b **68.14** Traditional rendering of Heb
Shaddai   c **68.17** Cn: Heb *The Lord among
them Sinai in the holy* (place)   d **68.23** Gk
Syr Tg: Heb *shatter*   e **68.24** Or *have
been seen*   f **68.30** Cn: Heb *Trampling*
g **68.30** Meaning of Heb of verse 30 is
uncertain   h **68.31** Or *Nubia*; Heb *Cush*

33 O rider in the heavens, the
    ancient heavens;
  listen, he sends out his voice,
    his mighty voice.
34 Ascribe power to God,
    whose majesty is over Israel;
  and whose power is
    in the skies.
35 Awesome is God in his[a]
    sanctuary,
  the God of Israel;
  he gives power and strength
    to his people.

Blessed be God!

PSALM 69

PRAYER FOR DELIVERANCE
FROM PERSECUTION

To the leader: according to Lilies. Of David.

1 Save me, O God,
    for the waters have come
      up to my neck.
2 I sink in deep mire,
    where there is no foothold;
  I have come into deep waters,
    and the flood sweeps
      over me.
3 I am weary with my crying;
    my throat is parched.
My eyes grow dim
    with waiting for my God.

4 More in number than the
    hairs of my head
  are those who hate me
    without cause;
many are those who would
    destroy me,
  my enemies who accuse
    me falsely.
What I did not steal
    must I now restore?
5 O God, you know my folly;
    the wrongs I have done are
      not hidden from you.

6 Do not let those who hope in
    you be put to shame
      because of me,
  O Lord GOD of hosts;
do not let those who seek you be
    dishonored because of me,
  O God of Israel.

7 It is for your sake that I have
    borne reproach,
  that shame has covered
    my face.
8 I have become a stranger
    to my kindred,
  an alien to my mother's
    children.

9 It is zeal for your house that
    has consumed me;
  the insults of those who insult
    you have fallen on me.
10 When I humbled my soul
    with fasting,[b]
  they insulted me for doing so.
11 When I made sackcloth
    my clothing,
  I became a byword to them.
12 I am the subject of gossip for
    those who sit in the gate,
  and the drunkards make
    songs about me.

13 But as for me, my prayer is
    to you, O LORD.
  At an acceptable time, O God,
  in the abundance of your
    steadfast love, answer me.
With your faithful help
    14rescue me
  from sinking in the mire;
  let me be delivered from
    my enemies
  and from the deep waters.
15 Do not let the flood sweep
    over me,
  or the deep swallow me up,
  or the Pit close its
    mouth over me.

16 Answer me, O LORD, for your
    steadfast love is good;
  according to your abundant
    mercy, turn to me.
17 Do not hide your face from
    your servant,
  for I am in distress—make
    haste to answer me.
18 Draw near to me, redeem me,
  set me free because of
    my enemies.

---

a **68.35** Gk: Heb *from your* b **69.10** Gk Syr:
Heb *I wept, with fasting my soul,* or *I made
my soul mourn with fasting*

19 You know the insults I receive,
    and my shame and dishonor;
    my foes are all known to you.
20 Insults have broken my heart,
    so that I am in despair.
  I looked for pity, but there
        was none;
    and for comforters, but
        I found none.
21 They gave me poison for food,
    and for my thirst they gave
        me vinegar to drink.

22 Let their table be a trap for them,
    a snare for their allies.
23 Let their eyes be darkened so
        that they cannot see,
    and make their loins
        tremble continually.
24 Pour out your indignation
        upon them,
    and let your burning anger
        overtake them.
25 May their camp be
        a desolation;
    let no one live in their tents.
26 For they persecute those whom
        you have struck down,
    and those whom you
        have wounded, they
        attack still more.[a]
27 Add guilt to their guilt;
    may they have no acquittal
        from you.
28 Let them be blotted out of the
        book of the living;
    let them not be enrolled
        among the righteous.
29 But I am lowly and in pain;
    let your salvation, O God,
        protect me.

30 I will praise the name of
        God with a song;
    I will magnify him with
        thanksgiving.
31 This will please the LORD
        more than an ox
    or a bull with horns
        and hoofs.
32 Let the oppressed see it
        and be glad;
    you who seek God, let
        your hearts revive.
33 For the LORD hears the needy,
    and does not despise his own
        that are in bonds.

34 Let heaven and earth praise him,
    the seas and everything
        that moves in them.
35 For God will save Zion
    and rebuild the cities of Judah;
  and his servants shall live[b]
        there and possess it;
36   the children of his servants
        shall inherit it,
    and those who love his
        name shall live in it.

PSALM 70

PRAYER FOR DELIVERANCE FROM ENEMIES

*To the leader. Of David, for
the memorial offering.*

1 Be pleased, O God, to deliver me.
   O LORD, make haste
        to help me!

[a] **69.26** Gk Syr: Heb *recount the pain of*
[b] **69.35** Syr: Heb *and they shall live*

PONDER

But I am lowly and in pain; let your
salvation, O God, protect me.
—Psalm 69.29

PRAY

O Father, we pray that this psalm and
its essence be embedded in us forever,
whatever our circumstances: "I will praise
the name of God with a song; I will
magnify him with thanksgiving" (Psalm
69.30). This psalm brings to mind your
Son Jesus, who was "a man of suffering
and acquainted with infirmity" (Isaiah
53.3), and who walked a lonely road. He
experienced hunger, cold and temptation
as we do. But he gives us the image
of a life that is truly transcendent, truly
exalted. Let us always turn to you and
call on your name when trials threaten
to overcome us, even as Jesus always
turned to you. In his name we pray. Amen.

2 Let those be put to shame
    and confusion
  who seek my life.
  Let those be turned back and
    brought to dishonor
  who desire to hurt me.
3 Let those who say, "Aha, Aha!"
  turn back because of
    their shame.

4 Let all who seek you
  rejoice and be glad in you.
  Let those who love your salvation
    say evermore, "God is great!"
5 But I am poor and needy;
  hasten to me, O God!
  You are my help and my
    deliverer;
  O LORD, do not delay!

DEALING WITH A

DIFFICULT PERSON CAN

BE A GOOD OPPORTUNITY

TO DEMONSTRATE

CHRISTLIKE LOVE.

PSALM 71

PRAYER FOR LIFELONG
PROTECTION AND HELP

1 In you, O LORD, I take refuge;
  let me never be put to shame.
2 In your righteousness deliver
    me and rescue me;
  incline your ear to me
    and save me.
3 Be to me a rock of refuge,
  a strong fortress,[a] to save me,
  for you are my rock and
    my fortress.

4 Rescue me, O my God, from the
    hand of the wicked,
  from the grasp of the
    unjust and cruel.
5 For you, O Lord, are my hope,
  my trust, O LORD, from
    my youth.

6 Upon you I have leaned
    from my birth;
  it was you who took me from
    my mother's womb.
  My praise is continually of you.

7 I have been like a portent
    to many,
  but you are my strong refuge.
8 My mouth is filled with
    your praise,
  and with your glory
    all day long.
9 Do not cast me off in the
    time of old age;
  do not forsake me when my
    strength is spent.
10 For my enemies speak
    concerning me,
  and those who watch for my
    life consult together.
11 They say, "Pursue and seize
    that person
  whom God has forsaken,
  for there is no one to deliver."

12 O God, do not be far from me;
  O my God, make haste
    to help me!
13 Let my accusers be put to
    shame and consumed;
  let those who seek to hurt me
  be covered with scorn
    and disgrace.
14 But I will hope continually,
  and will praise you yet
    more and more.
15 My mouth will tell of your
    righteous acts,
  of your deeds of salvation
    all day long,
  though their number is
    past my knowledge.
16 I will come praising the mighty
    deeds of the Lord GOD,
  I will praise your
    righteousness,
    yours alone.

17 O God, from my youth you
    have taught me,
  and I still proclaim your
    wondrous deeds.

[a] 71.3 Gk Compare 31.3: Heb *to come
continually you have commanded*

18 So even to old age and gray hairs,
   O God, do not forsake me,
until I proclaim your might
   to all the generations to come.[a]
Your power 19and your
   righteousness, O God,
   reach the high heavens.

You who have done great things,
   O God, who is like you?
20 You who have made me see many
   troubles and calamities
will revive me again;
from the depths of the earth
   you will bring me up again.
21 You will increase my honor,
   and comfort me once again.

22 I will also praise you
   with the harp
for your faithfulness,
   O my God;
I will sing praises to you
   with the lyre,
   O Holy One of Israel.
23 My lips will shout for joy
   when I sing praises to you;
my soul also, which you
   have rescued.
24 All day long my tongue will talk
   of your righteous help,
for those who tried to
   do me harm
have been put to shame,
   and disgraced.

PSALM 72

PRAYER FOR GUIDANCE AND SUPPORT FOR THE KING

Of Solomon.

1 Give the king your
      justice, O God,
   and your righteousness
      to a king's son.
2 May he judge your people
      with righteousness,
   and your poor with justice.
3 May the mountains yield
      prosperity for the people,
   and the hills, in righteousness.
4 May he defend the cause of the
      poor of the people,
   give deliverance to the needy,
   and crush the oppressor.

5 May he live[b] while the
      sun endures,
   and as long as the moon,
      throughout all
      generations.
6 May he be like rain that falls
      on the mown grass,
   like showers that water
      the earth.
7 In his days may righteousness
      flourish
   and peace abound, until the
      moon is no more.

8 May he have dominion
      from sea to sea,
   and from the River to the
      ends of the earth.
9 May his foes[c] bow down
      before him,
   and his enemies
      lick the dust.
10 May the kings of Tarshish
      and of the isles
   render him tribute,
   may the kings of
      Sheba and Seba
   bring gifts.
11 May all kings fall down
      before him,
   all nations give him service.

12 For he delivers the needy
      when they call,
   the poor and those who
      have no helper.
13 He has pity on the weak
      and the needy,
   and saves the lives of
      the needy.
14 From oppression and violence
      he redeems their life;
   and precious is their
      blood in his sight.

15 Long may he live!
   May gold of Sheba be
      given to him.
May prayer be made for
   him continually,
   and blessings invoked for
      him all day long.

[a] 71.18 Gk Compare Syr: Heb *to a generation, to all that come* [b] 72.5 Gk: Heb *may they fear you* [c] 72.9 Cn: Heb *those who live in the wilderness*

WHAT KIND OF KING?

May [the king] defend the cause of the poor of the people, give
deliverance to the needy, and crush the oppressor.

—Psalm 72.4

Psalm 72 is an example of what is often called a royal psalm. Royal psalms were written about a particular Israelite king, even perhaps for his coronation. The king played an important role in ancient Israel, not just because he had ultimate power over the people, but also because he represented the nation before God. When the king violated God's covenant, the nation lost battles or even experienced plagues and other difficulties. There was a strong association in the Israelites' minds between the king's relationship to God and the way things were going for the nation. In that sense, the king personified Israel, and it was very important for the Israelites to be ruled by a king who honored God.

The psalmist here wrote a coronation song that detailed the kind of king the people wanted. Note the kinds of attributes they were looking for. They weren't merely looking for a tall and muscular, stalwart and courageous leader to take their nation forward economically and politically. They were also looking for someone who was committed to keeping God's laws, to promoting justice, to defending the poor and stopping oppression.

In many ways, this description of the Israelites' desires for their earthly king also anticipates the characteristics to be even more fully realized in another King, the Messiah. The prophet Isaiah spoke about the character traits of this King in Isaiah 61.1: "The spirit of the Lord GOD is upon me, because the LORD has anointed me; he has sent me to bring good news to the oppressed, to bind up the brokenhearted, to proclaim liberty to the captives, and release to the prisoners." Similar to the king described in Psalm 72, the ruler envisioned by Isaiah would be humble, eager to learn, compassionate and just.

When the Messiah did finally come, he exhibited the characteristics that Isaiah had listed, the marks of God's true King (see Luke 4.16–21). We could say they were the planks of God's "political agenda." This agenda ran directly counter to the hopes and expectations of many Jews in Jesus' day who were seeking a powerful leader who would expel the hated Romans from Israel. This agenda—to promote justice and care for the poor and oppressed—is still God's "political" agenda for his people today. If we are truly followers of our King, Jesus Christ, then we are compelled to take up his agenda for ourselves and promote his values in our communities and our world.

Going Deeper

- What would you list as the characteristics and concerns of a great political leader?
- What is your political agenda? How does it compare to what you know about God's agenda?

16 May there be abundance of
    grain in the land;
  may it wave on the tops
    of the mountains;
  may its fruit be like Lebanon;
and may people blossom
    in the cities
  like the grass of the field.
17 May his name endure forever,
  his fame continue as
    long as the sun.
May all nations be blessed
    in him;[a]
  may they pronounce
    him happy.

18 Blessed be the LORD, the
    God of Israel,
  who alone does wondrous
    things.
19 Blessed be his glorious
    name forever;
  may his glory fill the
    whole earth.
    Amen and Amen.

20 The prayers of David son of
    Jesse are ended.

BOOK III

(PSALMS 73–89)

PSALM 73

PLEA FOR RELIEF FROM OPPRESSORS

A Psalm of Asaph.

1 Truly God is good to the upright,[b]
  to those who are pure in heart.

2 But as for me, my feet had
    almost stumbled;
  my steps had nearly slipped.
3 For I was envious of the arrogant;
  I saw the prosperity of
    the wicked.

4 For they have no pain;
  their bodies are sound
    and sleek.
5 They are not in trouble
    as others are;
  they are not plagued like
    other people.
6 Therefore pride is their necklace;
  violence covers them
    like a garment.
7 Their eyes swell out with fatness;
  their hearts overflow
    with follies.
8 They scoff and speak with malice;
  loftily they threaten
    oppression.
9 They set their mouths
    against heaven,
  and their tongues range
    over the earth.

10 Therefore the people turn
    and praise them,[c]
  and find no fault in them.[d]
11 And they say, "How can
    God know?
  Is there knowledge in
    the Most High?"
12 Such are the wicked;
  always at ease, they
    increase in riches.

[a] **72.17** Or *bless themselves by him*
[b] **73.1** Or *good to Israel*   [c] **73.10** Cn: Heb *his people return here*   [d] **73.10** Cn: Heb *abundant waters are drained by them*

BIBLE IN LIFE

Envying the "Successful"   *Psalm 73.1–12*

Why is it that good people suffer and bad people seem to succeed or prosper? We can easily get caught up in wanting what others have, to the point of envying people who gain wealth or advantages by unchristian means. The problem is that we often define success by material standards—how rich people are, how handsome they appear, how impressive their jobs are, how much publicity they receive. When we use these measures to define success in life, we become envious of the wrong people. Success in the eyes of Christ is the degree to which we commit ourselves to peace, truth, justice, freedom in the Spirit, humility, service, sharing, compassion and love.

13 All in vain I have kept my
        heart clean
    and washed my hands
        in innocence.
14 For all day long I have
        been plagued,
    and am punished every
        morning.

15 If I had said, "I will talk
        on in this way,"
    I would have been untrue to
        the circle of your children.
16 But when I thought how to
        understand this,
    it seemed to me a
        wearisome task,
17 until I went into the
        sanctuary of God;
    then I perceived their end.
18 Truly you set them in
        slippery places;
    you make them fall to ruin.
19 How they are destroyed
        in a moment,
    swept away utterly by terrors!
20 They are[a] like a dream when
        one awakes;
    on awaking you despise
        their phantoms.

21 When my soul was embittered,
        when I was pricked in heart,
22 I was stupid and ignorant;
    I was like a brute beast
        toward you.
23 Nevertheless I am continually
        with you;
    you hold my right hand.
24 You guide me with your counsel,
    and afterward you will receive
        me with honor.[b]
25 Whom have I in
        heaven but you?
    And there is nothing on
        earth that I desire
        other than you.
26 My flesh and my
        heart may fail,
    but God is the strength[c]
        of my heart and my
        portion forever.

27 Indeed, those who are far
        from you will perish;
    you put an end to those
        who are false to you.

28 But for me it is good to
        be near God;
    I have made the Lord
    GOD my refuge,
    to tell of all your works.

PSALM 74

PLEA FOR HELP IN TIME OF NATIONAL HUMILIATION

A Maskil of Asaph.

1 O God, why do you cast
        us off forever?
    Why does your anger smoke
        against the sheep
        of your pasture?
2 Remember your congregation,
        which you acquired
        long ago,
    which you redeemed to be the
        tribe of your heritage.
    Remember Mount Zion, where
        you came to dwell.
3 Direct your steps to the
        perpetual ruins;
    the enemy has destroyed
        everything in the
        sanctuary.

4 Your foes have roared within
        your holy place;
    they set up their
        emblems there.
5 At the upper entrance they hacked
        the wooden trellis with axes.[d]
6 And then, with hatchets
        and hammers,
    they smashed all its
        carved work.
7 They set your sanctuary on fire;
    they desecrated the dwelling
        place of your name,
    bringing it to the ground.
8 They said to themselves, "We will
        utterly subdue them";
    they burned all the meeting
        places of God in the land.

9 We do not see our emblems;
    there is no longer any prophet,
    and there is no one among us
        who knows how long.

a 73.20 Cn: Heb *Lord*   b 73.24 Or *to glory*
c 73.26 Heb *rock*   d 74.5 Cn Compare Gk
Syr: Meaning of Heb uncertain

10 How long, O God, is the
       foe to scoff?
   Is the enemy to revile your
       name forever?
11 Why do you hold back your hand;
   why do you keep your hand
       in[a] your bosom?

12 Yet God my King is from of old,
       working salvation in the earth.
13 You divided the sea by
       your might;
   you broke the heads of the
       dragons in the waters.
14 You crushed the heads
       of Leviathan;
   you gave him as food[b]
       for the creatures of
       the wilderness.
15 You cut openings for springs
       and torrents;
   you dried up ever-flowing
       streams.
16 Yours is the day, yours
       also the night;
   you established the luminaries[c]
       and the sun.
17 You have fixed all the bounds
       of the earth;
   you made summer
       and winter.

18 Remember this, O LORD, how
       the enemy scoffs,
   and an impious people
       reviles your name.
19 Do not deliver the soul of your
       dove to the wild animals;
   do not forget the life of
       your poor forever.

20 Have regard for your[d] covenant,
       for the dark places of the
       land are full of the
       haunts of violence.
21 Do not let the downtrodden
       be put to shame;
   let the poor and needy
       praise your name.
22 Rise up, O God, plead
       your cause;
   remember how the impious
       scoff at you all day long.
23 Do not forget the clamor
       of your foes,
   the uproar of your adversaries
       that goes up continually.

PSALM 75

THANKSGIVING FOR GOD'S WONDROUS DEEDS

To the leader: Do Not Destroy.
A Psalm of Asaph. A Song.

1 We give thanks to you, O God;
   we give thanks; your
       name is near.
   People tell of your
       wondrous deeds.

2 At the set time that I appoint
       I will judge with equity.
3 When the earth totters, with
       all its inhabitants,
   it is I who keep its pillars
       steady. *Selah*
4 I say to the boastful, "Do
       not boast,"
   and to the wicked, "Do not
       lift up your horn;
5 do not lift up your
       horn on high,
   or speak with insolent neck."

6 For not from the east or
       from the west
   and not from the wilderness
       comes lifting up;
7 but it is God who executes
       judgment,
   putting down one and
       lifting up another.
8 For in the hand of the LORD
       there is a cup
   with foaming wine,
       well mixed;
   he will pour a draught from it,
   and all the wicked
       of the earth
   shall drain it down to
       the dregs.
9 But I will rejoice[e] forever;
   I will sing praises to the
       God of Jacob.

10 All the horns of the wicked
       I will cut off,
   but the horns of the righteous
       shall be exalted.

[a] 74.11 Cn: Heb *do you consume your right hand from*   [b] 74.14 Heb *food for the people*   [c] 74.16 Or *moon*; Heb *light*   [d] 74.20 Gk Syr: Heb *the*   [e] 75.9 Gk: Heb *declare*

PSALM 76

ISRAEL'S GOD—JUDGE OF ALL THE EARTH

To the leader: with stringed instruments.
A Psalm of Asaph. A Song.

1 In Judah God is known,
    his name is great in Israel.
2 His abode has been established
        in Salem,
    his dwelling place in Zion.
3 There he broke the flashing
        arrows,
    the shield, the sword, and the
        weapons of war.   *Selah*

4 Glorious are you, more majestic
    than the everlasting
        mountains.[a]
5 The stouthearted were stripped
        of their spoil;
    they sank into sleep;
none of the troops
    was able to lift a hand.
6 At your rebuke, O God of Jacob,
    both rider and horse
        lay stunned.

7 But you indeed are awesome!
    Who can stand before you
    when once your anger is roused?
8 From the heavens you
        uttered judgment;
    the earth feared and was still
9 when God rose up to establish
        judgment,
    to save all the oppressed of the
        earth.   *Selah*

10 Human wrath serves only
        to praise you,
    when you bind the last bit of
        your[b] wrath around you.

WE MUST LEARN TO LIVE

WITHOUT ALL THE ANSWERS,

BUT WITH EAGERNESS TO

TAKE OUR QUESTIONS TO

GOD WITHOUT RESTRAINT.

11 Make vows to the LORD your
        God, and perform them;
    let all who are around
        him bring gifts
    to the one who is awesome,
12 who cuts off the spirit of princes,
    who inspires fear in the
        kings of the earth.

PSALM 77

GOD'S MIGHTY DEEDS RECALLED

To the leader: according to
Jeduthun. Of Asaph. A Psalm.

1 I cry aloud to God,
    aloud to God, that he
        may hear me.
2 In the day of my trouble I
        seek the Lord;
    in the night my hand
        is stretched out
        without wearying;
    my soul refuses to be
        comforted.
3 I think of God, and I moan;
    I meditate, and my spirit
        faints.   *Selah*

4 You keep my eyelids from closing;
    I am so troubled that I
        cannot speak.
5 I consider the days of old,
    and remember the years
        of long ago.
6 I commune[c] with my heart
        in the night;
    I meditate and search
        my spirit:[d]
7 "Will the Lord spurn forever,
    and never again be favorable?
8 Has his steadfast love
        ceased forever?
    Are his promises at an
        end for all time?
9 Has God forgotten to be gracious?
    Has he in anger shut up his
        compassion?"   *Selah*
10 And I say, "It is my grief
    that the right hand of the
        Most High has changed."

---

a 76.4 Gk: Heb *the mountains of prey*
b 76.10 Heb lacks *your*   c 77.6 Gk Syr: Heb
My music   d 77.6 Syr Jerome: Heb *my spirit*
searches

11 I will call to mind the deeds
    of the LORD;
    I will remember your
        wonders of old.
12 I will meditate on all your work,
    and muse on your
        mighty deeds.
13 Your way, O God, is holy.
    What god is so great
        as our God?
14 You are the God who
        works wonders;
    you have displayed your might
        among the peoples.
15 With your strong arm you
        redeemed your people,
    the descendants of Jacob and
        Joseph.   *Selah*

16 When the waters
        saw you, O God,
    when the waters saw you,
        they were afraid;
    the very deep trembled.
17 The clouds poured out water;
    the skies thundered;
    your arrows flashed
        on every side.
18 The crash of your thunder was
        in the whirlwind;
    your lightnings lit up
        the world;
    the earth trembled and shook.
19 Your way was through the sea,
    your path, through the
        mighty waters;
    yet your footprints
        were unseen.
20 You led your people like a flock
    by the hand of Moses
        and Aaron.

PSALM 78

GOD'S GOODNESS AND ISRAEL'S INGRATITUDE

A Maskil of Asaph.

1 Give ear, O my people, to
        my teaching;
    incline your ears to the
        words of my mouth.
2 I will open my mouth
        in a parable;
    I will utter dark sayings
        from of old,

3 things that we have heard
        and known,
    that our ancestors have told us.
4 We will not hide them from
        their children;
    we will tell to the coming
        generation
    the glorious deeds of the
        LORD, and his might,
    and the wonders that
        he has done.

5 He established a
        decree in Jacob,
    and appointed a law in Israel,
    which he commanded
        our ancestors
    to teach to their children;
6 that the next generation
        might know them,
    the children yet unborn,

PONDER

[The LORD] established a decree in
Jacob, and appointed a law in Israel,
which he commanded our ancestors
to teach to their children; that the
next generation might know them,
the children yet unborn, and rise up
and tell them to their children.
—Psalm 78.5–6

PRAY

Everlasting Father, we are grateful for
these thoughts from the Old Testament
psalms that teach us so much about
who you are and what you expect
from us as your covenant people. Give
us the boldness and the courage to
share—depending on our unique talents,
opportunities and environment—with
those who need to hear about you and
about our Savior, Jesus Christ, especially
with the children within our sphere of
influence. We know people may be
depending on us to tell them of your
love so that you can give them a life of
joy. In the peace of our Savior. Amen.

and rise up and tell them to
their children,
7 so that they should set
their hope in God,
and not forget the works of God,
but keep his commandments;
8 and that they should not be
like their ancestors,
a stubborn and rebellious
generation,
a generation whose heart
was not steadfast,
whose spirit was not
faithful to God.

9 The Ephraimites, armed
with[a] the bow,
turned back on the day of battle.
10 They did not keep
God's covenant,
but refused to walk
according to his law.
11 They forgot what he had done,
and the miracles that he
had shown them.
12 In the sight of their ancestors
he worked marvels
in the land of Egypt, in
the fields of Zoan.
13 He divided the sea and let
them pass through it,
and made the waters
stand like a heap.
14 In the daytime he led them
with a cloud,
and all night long with
a fiery light.
15 He split rocks open in the
wilderness,
and gave them drink
abundantly as
from the deep.
16 He made streams come
out of the rock,
and caused waters to flow
down like rivers.

17 Yet they sinned still more
against him,
rebelling against the Most
High in the desert.
18 They tested God in their heart
by demanding the food
they craved.
19 They spoke against God, saying,
"Can God spread a table
in the wilderness?

20 Even though he struck the rock
so that water gushed out
and torrents overflowed,
can he also give bread,
or provide meat for his people?"

21 Therefore, when the LORD heard,
he was full of rage;
a fire was kindled
against Jacob,
his anger mounted
against Israel,
22 because they had no faith in God,
and did not trust his
saving power.
23 Yet he commanded the
skies above,
and opened the doors
of heaven;
24 he rained down on them
manna to eat,
and gave them the grain
of heaven.
25 Mortals ate of the bread of angels;
he sent them food in
abundance.
26 He caused the east wind to
blow in the heavens,
and by his power he led
out the south wind;
27 he rained flesh upon them
like dust,
winged birds like the
sand of the seas;
28 he let them fall within
their camp,
all around their dwellings.
29 And they ate and were well filled,
for he gave them what
they craved.
30 But before they had satisfied
their craving,
while the food was still
in their mouths,
31 the anger of God rose
against them
and he killed the strongest
of them,
and laid low the flower
of Israel.

32 In spite of all this they
still sinned;
they did not believe in
his wonders.

a 78.9 Heb armed with shooting

33 So he made their days vanish
      like a breath,
   and their years in terror.
34 When he killed them, they
      sought for him;
   they repented and sought
      God earnestly.
35 They remembered that God
      was their rock,
   the Most High God
      their redeemer.
36 But they flattered him with
      their mouths;
   they lied to him with
      their tongues.
37 Their heart was not steadfast
      toward him;
   they were not true to
      his covenant.
38 Yet he, being compassionate,
      forgave their iniquity,
   and did not destroy them;
   often he restrained his anger,
      and did not stir up all his wrath.
39 He remembered that they
      were but flesh,
   a wind that passes and does
      not come again.
40 How often they rebelled against
      him in the wilderness
   and grieved him in the desert!
41 They tested God again and again,
   and provoked the Holy
      One of Israel.
42 They did not keep in mind
      his power,
   or the day when he redeemed
      them from the foe;
43 when he displayed his
      signs in Egypt,
   and his miracles in the
      fields of Zoan.
44 He turned their rivers to blood,
   so that they could not drink
      of their streams.
45 He sent among them swarms
      of flies, which
      devoured them,
   and frogs, which
      destroyed them.
46 He gave their crops to the
      caterpillar,
   and the fruit of their labor
      to the locust.
47 He destroyed their vines
      with hail,
   and their sycamores with frost.

48 He gave over their cattle
      to the hail,
   and their flocks to
      thunderbolts.
49 He let loose on them his
      fierce anger,
   wrath, indignation,
      and distress,
   a company of destroying angels.
50 He made a path for his anger;
   he did not spare them
      from death,
   but gave their lives over
      to the plague.
51 He struck all the firstborn
      in Egypt,
   the first issue of their strength
      in the tents of Ham.
52 Then he led out his people
      like sheep,
   and guided them in the
      wilderness like a flock.
53 He led them in safety, so that
      they were not afraid;
   but the sea overwhelmed
      their enemies.
54 And he brought them to
      his holy hill,
   to the mountain that his
      right hand had won.
55 He drove out nations before them;
   he apportioned them
      for a possession
   and settled the tribes of
      Israel in their tents.
56 Yet they tested the Most
      High God,
   and rebelled against him.
   They did not observe
      his decrees,
57 but turned away and were
      faithless like their
      ancestors;
   they twisted like a
      treacherous bow.
58 For they provoked him to anger
      with their high places;
   they moved him to jealousy
      with their idols.
59 When God heard, he was
      full of wrath,
   and he utterly rejected Israel.
60 He abandoned his dwelling
      at Shiloh,
   the tent where he dwelt
      among mortals,

61 and delivered his power
        to captivity,
    his glory to the
        hand of the foe.
62 He gave his people to the sword,
    and vented his wrath
        on his heritage.
63 Fire devoured their
        young men,
    and their girls had no
        marriage song.
64 Their priests fell by the sword,
    and their widows made
        no lamentation.
65 Then the Lord awoke as
        from sleep,
    like a warrior shouting
        because of wine.
66 He put his adversaries to rout;
    he put them to everlasting
        disgrace.

67 He rejected the tent of Joseph,
    he did not choose the
        tribe of Ephraim;
68 but he chose the tribe of Judah,
    Mount Zion, which he loves.
69 He built his sanctuary like
        the high heavens,
    like the earth, which he
        has founded forever.
70 He chose his servant David,
    and took him from the
        sheepfolds;
71 from tending the nursing
        ewes he brought him
    to be the shepherd of his
        people Jacob,
    of Israel, his inheritance.
72 With upright heart he
        tended them,
    and guided them with
        skillful hand.

PSALM 79

PLEA FOR MERCY
FOR JERUSALEM

A Psalm of Asaph.

1   O God, the nations have come
        into your inheritance;
    they have defiled your
        holy temple;
    they have laid Jerusalem
        in ruins.

2   They have given the bodies
        of your servants
    to the birds of the air for food,
    the flesh of your faithful to the
        wild animals of the earth.
3   They have poured out their
        blood like water
    all around Jerusalem,
    and there was no one
        to bury them.
4   We have become a taunt to
        our neighbors,
    mocked and derided by
        those around us.

5   How long, O LORD? Will you
        be angry forever?
    Will your jealous wrath
        burn like fire?
6   Pour out your anger on the nations
        that do not know you,
    and on the kingdoms
        that do not call on your name.
7   For they have devoured Jacob
    and laid waste his habitation.

8   Do not remember against us the
        iniquities of our ancestors;
    let your compassion come
        speedily to meet us,
    for we are brought very low.
9   Help us, O God of our salvation,
        for the glory of your name;
    deliver us, and forgive our sins,
        for your name's sake.
10 Why should the nations say,
        "Where is their God?"
    Let the avenging of the outpoured
        blood of your servants
    be known among the nations
        before our eyes.

11 Let the groans of the prisoners
        come before you;
    according to your great
        power preserve those
        doomed to die.
12 Return sevenfold into the bosom
        of our neighbors
    the taunts with which they
        taunted you, O Lord!
13 Then we your people, the flock
        of your pasture,
    will give thanks to you forever;
    from generation to
        generation we will
        recount your praise.

PSALM 80

PRAYER FOR ISRAEL'S RESTORATION

To the leader: on Lilies, a Covenant. Of Asaph. A Psalm.

1 Give ear, O Shepherd of Israel,
   you who lead Joseph
      like a flock!
You who are enthroned upon the
      cherubim, shine forth
2   before Ephraim and Benjamin
      and Manasseh.
Stir up your might,
   and come to save us!

3 Restore us, O God;
   let your face shine, that
      we may be saved.

4 O Lord God of hosts,
   how long will you be
      angry with your
      people's prayers?
5 You have fed them with the
      bread of tears,
   and given them tears to
      drink in full measure.
6 You make us the scorn[a] of
      our neighbors;
   our enemies laugh among
      themselves.

7 Restore us, O God of hosts;
   let your face shine, that
      we may be saved.

8 You brought a vine out of Egypt;
   you drove out the nations
      and planted it.
9 You cleared the ground for it;
   it took deep root and
      filled the land.
10 The mountains were covered
      with its shade,
   the mighty cedars with
      its branches;
11 it sent out its branches to the sea,
   and its shoots to the River.
12 Why then have you broken
      down its walls,
   so that all who pass along the
      way pluck its fruit?
13 The boar from the forest
      ravages it,
   and all that move in the
      field feed on it.

14 Turn again, O God of hosts;
   look down from heaven,
      and see;
have regard for this vine,
15   the stock that your right
      hand planted.[b]
16 They have burned it with fire,
   they have cut it down;[c]
   may they perish at the rebuke
      of your countenance.
17 But let your hand be upon the
      one at your right hand,
   the one whom you made
      strong for yourself.
18 Then we will never turn
      back from you;
   give us life, and we will
      call on your name.

19 Restore us, O Lord God of hosts;
   let your face shine, that
      we may be saved.

SUBMISSION MAY BE

ONE OF OUR GREATEST

TESTS AS CHRISTIANS.

PSALM 81

GOD'S APPEAL TO STUBBORN ISRAEL

To the leader: according to The Gittith. Of Asaph.

1 Sing aloud to God our strength;
   shout for joy to the
      God of Jacob.
2 Raise a song, sound the
      tambourine,
   the sweet lyre with the harp.
3 Blow the trumpet at the
      new moon,
   at the full moon, on
      our festal day.
4 For it is a statute for Israel,
   an ordinance of the
      God of Jacob.

a **80.6** Syr: Heb *strife*   b **80.15** Heb adds from verse 17 *and upon the one whom you made strong for yourself*   c **80.16** Cn: Heb *it is cut down*

5 He made it a decree
        in Joseph,
    when he went out over[a]
        the land of Egypt.

    I hear a voice I had
        not known:
6 "I relieved your[b] shoulder
        of the burden;
    your[e] hands were freed
        from the basket.
7 In distress you called, and
        I rescued you;
    I answered you in the secret
        place of thunder;
    I tested you at the waters of
        Meribah.   *Selah*
8 Hear, O my people, while I
        admonish you;
    O Israel, if you would
        but listen to me!
9 There shall be no strange
        god among you;
    you shall not bow down
        to a foreign god.
10 I am the LORD your God,
    who brought you up out of
        the land of Egypt.
    Open your mouth wide
        and I will fill it.

11 "But my people did not
        listen to my voice;
    Israel would not
        submit to me.
12 So I gave them over to their
        stubborn hearts,
    to follow their
        own counsels.
13 O that my people would
        listen to me,
    that Israel would walk
        in my ways!
14 Then I would quickly subdue
        their enemies,
    and turn my hand against
        their foes.
15 Those who hate
        the LORD would
        cringe before him,
    and their doom would
        last forever.
16 I would feed you[c] with the
        finest of the wheat,
    and with honey from
        the rock I would
        satisfy you."

PSALM 82

A PLEA FOR JUSTICE

A Psalm of Asaph.

1 God has taken his place in
        the divine council;
    in the midst of the gods he
        holds judgment:
2 "How long will you
        judge unjustly
    and show partiality to the
        wicked?   *Selah*
3 Give justice to the weak
        and the orphan;
    maintain the right of the
        lowly and the destitute.
4 Rescue the weak
        and the needy;
    deliver them from the hand
        of the wicked."

GOD HELPS THOSE

WHO ARE NOT ABLE TO

HELP THEMSELVES.

5 They have neither knowledge
        nor understanding,
    they walk around
        in darkness;
    all the foundations of the
        earth are shaken.

6 I say, "You are gods,
        children of the Most
        High, all of you;
7 nevertheless, you shall die
        like mortals,
    and fall like any prince."[d]

8 Rise up, O God,
        judge the earth;
    for all the nations
        belong to you!

---

a 81.5 Or *against*   b 81.6 Heb *his*
c 81.16 Cn Compare verse 16b: Heb *he
would feed him*   d 82.7 Or *fall as one man,
O princes*

PSALM 83

PRAYER FOR JUDGMENT ON ISRAEL'S FOES

A Song. A Psalm of Asaph.

1 O God, do not keep silence;
   do not hold your peace
      or be still, O God!
2 Even now your enemies
      are in tumult;
   those who hate you have
      raised their heads.
3 They lay crafty plans against
      your people;
   they consult together against
      those you protect.
4 They say, "Come, let us wipe
      them out as a nation;
   let the name of Israel be
      remembered no more."
5 They conspire with one accord;
      against you they make
      a covenant—
6 the tents of Edom and the
      Ishmaelites,
   Moab and the Hagrites,
7 Gebal and Ammon and Amalek,
      Philistia with the
      inhabitants of Tyre;
8 Assyria also has joined them;
   they are the strong arm of the
      children of Lot.   *Selah*

9 Do to them as you
      did to Midian,
   as to Sisera and Jabin at
      the Wadi Kishon,
10 who were destroyed at En-dor,
   who became dung for
      the ground.
11 Make their nobles like
      Oreb and Zeeb,
   all their princes like Zebah
      and Zalmunna,
12 who said, "Let us take the
      pastures of God
   for our own possession."

13 O my God, make them like
      whirling dust,[a]
   like chaff before the wind.
14 As fire consumes the forest,
      as the flame sets the
      mountains ablaze,
15 so pursue them with your tempest
   and terrify them with
      your hurricane.

16 Fill their faces with shame,
   so that they may seek your
      name, O LORD.
17 Let them be put to shame and
      dismayed forever;
   let them perish in disgrace.
18 Let them know that you alone,
      whose name is the LORD,
   are the Most High over
      all the earth.

PSALM 84

THE JOY OF WORSHIP IN THE TEMPLE

To the leader: according to The Gittith. Of the Korahites. A Psalm.

1 How lovely is your dwelling place,
      O LORD of hosts!
2 My soul longs, indeed it faints
   for the courts of the LORD;
   my heart and my flesh sing for joy
      to the living God.

3 Even the sparrow finds a home,
   and the swallow a nest
      for herself,
   where she may lay her young,
   at your altars, O LORD of hosts,
      my King and my God.
4 Happy are those who live
      in your house,
   ever singing your
      praise.   *Selah*

5 Happy are those whose
      strength is in you,
   in whose heart are the
      highways to Zion.[b]
6 As they go through the
      valley of Baca
   they make it a place of springs;
   the early rain also covers
      it with pools.
7 They go from strength
      to strength;
   the God of gods will be
      seen in Zion.

8 O LORD God of hosts, hear
      my prayer;
   give ear, O God of Jacob! *Selah*

[a] 83.13 Or *a tumbleweed*   [b] 84.5 Heb lacks *to Zion*

9 Behold our shield, O God;
    look on the face of your
        anointed.

10 For a day in your
        courts is better
    than a thousand elsewhere.
    I would rather be a doorkeeper
        in the house of my God
    than live in the tents
        of wickedness.
11 For the LORD God is a sun
        and shield;
    he bestows favor and honor.
    No good thing does the
        LORD withhold
    from those who
        walk uprightly.
12 O LORD of hosts,
    happy is everyone who
        trusts in you.

PSALM 85

PRAYER FOR THE RESTORATION OF GOD'S FAVOR

To the leader. Of the Korahites.
A Psalm.

1 LORD, you were favorable
        to your land;
    you restored the fortunes
        of Jacob.
2 You forgave the iniquity
        of your people;
    you pardoned all their
        sin.   *Selah*
3 You withdrew all your wrath;
    you turned from your
        hot anger.

4 Restore us again, O God of
        our salvation,
    and put away your
        indignation toward us.
5 Will you be angry with
        us forever?
    Will you prolong your anger
        to all generations?
6 Will you not revive us again,
    so that your people may
        rejoice in you?
7 Show us your steadfast
        love, O LORD,
    and grant us your salvation.

8 Let me hear what God the
        LORD will speak,
    for he will speak peace
        to his people,
    to his faithful, to those
        who turn to him
        in their hearts.[a]
9 Surely his salvation is at hand
        for those who fear him,
    that his glory may dwell
        in our land.

10 Steadfast love and faithfulness
        will meet;
    righteousness and peace
        will kiss each other.
11 Faithfulness will spring up
        from the ground,
    and righteousness will look
        down from the sky.
12 The LORD will give what is good,
    and our land will yield
        its increase.

a 85.8 Gk: Heb *but let them not turn back to folly*

⊨ BIBLE IN LIFE ▷

In God's Presence

Psalm 84.1–12

As we read this psalm, we can consider what it means for us to prepare to be in the presence of God. Our religious experience should not be limited to a church sanctuary. It involves a direct relationship with God through a commitment to daily prayer, self-examination and studying the scriptures—and not just on Sundays or when we're in trouble or really want a favor. Sadly, that's what many of us do. We might wait until it's too late to fully commit to God. We must not get to the end of our life without intensifying our relationship with God, but instead should joyfully prepare for being in heaven someday by living in a dynamic and committed relationship with God now.

13 Righteousness will go before him,
and will make a path
for his steps.

PSALM 86

SUPPLICATION FOR HELP
AGAINST ENEMIES

A Prayer of David.

1 Incline your ear, O LORD,
and answer me,
for I am poor and needy.
2 Preserve my life, for I am
devoted to you;
save your servant who
trusts in you.
You are my God; 3be gracious
to me, O Lord,
for to you do I cry all day long.
4 Gladden the soul of
your servant,
for to you, O Lord, I lift
up my soul.
5 For you, O Lord, are good
and forgiving,
abounding in steadfast love
to all who call on you.
6 Give ear, O LORD, to my prayer;
listen to my cry of supplication.
7 In the day of my trouble
I call on you,
for you will answer me.

8 There is none like you among
the gods, O Lord,
nor are there any works
like yours.

9 All the nations you have
made shall come
and bow down before
you, O Lord,
and shall glorify your name.
10 For you are great and do
wondrous things;
you alone are God.
11 Teach me your way, O LORD,
that I may walk in your truth;
give me an undivided heart
to revere your name.
12 I give thanks to you, O Lord
my God, with my
whole heart,
and I will glorify your
name forever.
13 For great is your steadfast
love toward me;
you have delivered my soul
from the depths of Sheol.

14 O God, the insolent rise
up against me;
a band of ruffians
seeks my life,
and they do not set you
before them.
15 But you, O Lord, are a God
merciful and gracious,
slow to anger and abounding
in steadfast love
and faithfulness.
16 Turn to me and be
gracious to me;
give your strength to
your servant;
save the child of your
serving girl.

▷ BIBLE IN LIFE ◁

The Peace of God
Psalm 85.8

The psalmist reminds us that God promised peace to us. The peace of God is so magnificent that, as human beings, we cannot describe it in words or envision it in our minds. In the New Testament, Paul describes peace as something that "surpasses all understanding" (Philippians 4.7). It's more than we could ever expect or imagine. Books written on the topic of peace sell millions of copies and convince readers that if they will do certain things, such as think positively, they can somehow attain peace. This is as misleading as the concept of earning salvation through good works, another impossible feat. Peace is a free gift. We don't earn it by being good or by being dormant or by being dynamic. We get it because God loves us. All of us have times of stress and doubt in our lives. We can pray and accept God's free gift of peace at any time.

17 Show me a sign of your favor,
     so that those who hate me may
       see it and be put to shame,
   because you, LORD, have
     helped me and
     comforted me.

PSALM 87

THE JOY OF LIVING IN ZION

Of the Korahites. A Psalm. A Song.

1 On the holy mount stands
     the city he founded;
2   the LORD loves the
       gates of Zion
   more than all the
     dwellings of Jacob.
3 Glorious things are spoken of you,
   O city of God.   *Selah*

4 Among those who know
     me I mention Rahab
     and Babylon;
   Philistia too, and Tyre,
     with Ethiopia[a]—
   "This one was born
     there," they say.

5 And of Zion it shall be said,
   "This one and that one
     were born in it";
   for the Most High himself
     will establish it.
6 The LORD records, as he
     registers the peoples,
   "This one was born
     there."   *Selah*

7 Singers and dancers alike say,
   "All my springs are in you."

PSALM 88

PRAYER FOR HELP IN
DESPONDENCY

*A Song. A Psalm of the Korahites. To the
leader: according to Mahalath Leannoth.
A Maskil of Heman the Ezrahite.*

1 O LORD, God of my salvation,
   when, at night, I cry out
     in your presence,
2 let my prayer come before you;
   incline your ear to my cry.

3 For my soul is full of troubles,
   and my life draws near to Sheol.
4 I am counted among those who
     go down to the Pit;
   I am like those who
     have no help,
5 like those forsaken among
     the dead,
   like the slain that lie
     in the grave,
   like those whom you
     remember no more,
   for they are cut off from
     your hand.
6 You have put me in the
     depths of the Pit,
   in the regions dark and deep.
7 Your wrath lies heavy upon me,
   and you overwhelm me with all
     your waves.   *Selah*

8 You have caused my companions
     to shun me;
   you have made me a thing
     of horror to them.
   I am shut in so that I
     cannot escape;
9   my eye grows dim
       through sorrow.
   Every day I call on you, O LORD;
   I spread out my hands to you.
10 Do you work wonders
     for the dead?
   Do the shades rise up to praise
     you?   *Selah*
11 Is your steadfast love declared
     in the grave,
   or your faithfulness in
     Abaddon?
12 Are your wonders known
     in the darkness,
   or your saving help in the
     land of forgetfulness?

13 But I, O LORD, cry out to you;
   in the morning my prayer
     comes before you.
14 O LORD, why do you cast me off?
   Why do you hide your
     face from me?
15 Wretched and close to death
     from my youth up,
   I suffer your terrors; I
     am desperate.[b]

a 87.4 Or *Nubia*; Heb *Cush*
b 88.15 Meaning of Heb uncertain

16 Your wrath has swept over me;
　　your dread assaults destroy me.
17 They surround me like a
　　　flood all day long;
　　from all sides they close
　　　in on me.
18 You have caused friend and
　　　neighbor to shun me;
　　my companions are
　　　in darkness.

PSALM 89

GOD'S COVENANT WITH DAVID

A Maskil of Ethan the Ezrahite.

1 I will sing of your steadfast
　　　love, O LORD,[a] forever;
　　with my mouth I will proclaim
　　　your faithfulness to
　　　all generations.
2 I declare that your steadfast love
　　　is established forever;
　　your faithfulness is as firm
　　　as the heavens.

3 You said, "I have made
　　　a covenant with
　　　my chosen one,
　　I have sworn to my
　　　servant David:
4 'I will establish your
　　　descendants forever,
　　and build your throne for all
　　　generations.' "   *Selah*

5 Let the heavens praise your
　　　wonders, O LORD,
　　your faithfulness in the
　　　assembly of the holy ones.
6 For who in the skies can be
　　　compared to the LORD?
　　Who among the heavenly
　　　beings is like the LORD,
7 a God feared in the council
　　　of the holy ones,
　　great and awesome[b] above all
　　　that are around him?
8 O LORD God of hosts,
　　who is as mighty as
　　　you, O LORD?
　　Your faithfulness
　　　surrounds you.
9 You rule the raging of the sea;
　　when its waves rise,
　　　you still them.

10 You crushed Rahab like a carcass;
　　you scattered your enemies
　　　with your mighty arm.
11 The heavens are yours, the
　　　earth also is yours;
　　the world and all that is in it—
　　　you have founded them.
12 The north and the south[c]—you
　　　created them;
　　Tabor and Hermon joyously
　　　praise your name.
13 You have a mighty arm;
　　strong is your hand, high
　　　your right hand.
14 Righteousness and justice are the
　　　foundation of your throne;
　　steadfast love and faithfulness
　　　go before you.
15 Happy are the people who
　　　know the festal shout,
　　who walk, O LORD, in the light
　　　of your countenance;
16 they exult in your name
　　　all day long,
　　and extol[d] your righteousness.
17 For you are the glory of
　　　their strength;
　　by your favor our horn
　　　is exalted.
18 For our shield belongs
　　　to the LORD,
　　our king to the Holy
　　　One of Israel.

19 Then you spoke in a vision to your
　　　faithful one, and said:
　　"I have set the crown[e] on
　　　one who is mighty,
　　I have exalted one chosen
　　　from the people.
20 I have found my servant David;
　　with my holy oil I have
　　　anointed him;
21 my hand shall always
　　　remain with him;
　　my arm also shall
　　　strengthen him.
22 The enemy shall not outwit him,
　　the wicked shall not
　　　humble him.
23 I will crush his foes before him
　　and strike down those
　　　who hate him.

[a] 89.1 Gk: Heb *the steadfast love of the*
LORD   [b] 89.7 Gk Syr: Heb *greatly awesome*
[c] 89.12 Or *Zaphon and Yamin*   [d] 89.16 Cn:
Heb *are exalted in*   [e] 89.19 Cn: Heb *help*

24 My faithfulness and steadfast
     love shall be with him;
   and in my name his horn
     shall be exalted.
25 I will set his hand on the sea
   and his right hand on
     the rivers.
26 He shall cry to me, 'You
     are my Father,
   my God, and the Rock of
     my salvation!'
27 I will make him the firstborn,
   the highest of the kings
     of the earth.
28 Forever I will keep my steadfast
     love for him,
   and my covenant with him
     will stand firm.
29 I will establish his line forever,
   and his throne as long as
     the heavens endure.
30 If his children forsake my law
   and do not walk according
     to my ordinances,
31 if they violate my statutes
   and do not keep my
     commandments,
32 then I will punish their
     transgression
     with the rod
   and their iniquity with
     scourges;
33 but I will not remove from him
     my steadfast love,
   or be false to my faithfulness.
34 I will not violate my covenant,
   or alter the word that went
     forth from my lips.
35 Once and for all I have sworn
     by my holiness;
   I will not lie to David.
36 His line shall continue forever,
   and his throne endure before
     me like the sun.
37 It shall be established forever
     like the moon,
   an enduring witness in the
     skies."   *Selah*

38 But now you have spurned
     and rejected him;
   you are full of wrath against
     your anointed.
39 You have renounced the covenant
     with your servant;
   you have defiled his
     crown in the dust.

40 You have broken through
     all his walls;
   you have laid his strongholds
     in ruins.
41 All who pass by plunder him;
   he has become the scorn
     of his neighbors.
42 You have exalted the right
     hand of his foes;
   you have made all his
     enemies rejoice.
43 Moreover, you have turned back
     the edge of his sword,
   and you have not supported
     him in battle.
44 You have removed the scepter
     from his hand,[a]
   and hurled his throne
     to the ground.
45 You have cut short the days
     of his youth;
   you have covered him with
     shame.   *Selah*

46 How long, O LORD? Will you
     hide yourself forever?
   How long will your wrath
     burn like fire?
47 Remember how short
     my time is—[b]
   for what vanity you have
     created all mortals!
48 Who can live and
     never see death?
   Who can escape the power of
     Sheol?   *Selah*

49 Lord, where is your steadfast
     love of old,
   which by your faithfulness
     you swore to David?
50 Remember, O Lord, how your
     servant is taunted;
   how I bear in my bosom the
     insults of the peoples,[c]
51 with which your enemies
     taunt, O LORD,
   with which they taunted the
     footsteps of your anointed.

52 Blessed be the LORD forever.
     Amen and Amen.

---

[a] 89.44 Cn: Heb *removed his cleanness*
[b] 89.47 Meaning of Heb uncertain
[c] 89.50 Cn: Heb *bosom all of many peoples*

BOOK IV

(PSALMS 90–106)

PSALM 90

GOD'S ETERNITY AND HUMAN FRAILTY

A Prayer of Moses, the man of God.

1 Lord, you have been our
        dwelling place[a]
    in all generations.
2 Before the mountains were
        brought forth,
    or ever you had formed the
        earth and the world,
    from everlasting to everlasting
        you are God.

3 You turn us[b] back to dust,
    and say, "Turn back,
        you mortals."
4 For a thousand years in
        your sight
    are like yesterday when
        it is past,
    or like a watch in the night.

5 You sweep them away; they
        are like a dream,
    like grass that is renewed
        in the morning;
6 in the morning it flourishes
        and is renewed;
    in the evening it fades
        and withers.

7 For we are consumed by
        your anger;
    by your wrath we are
        overwhelmed.
8 You have set our iniquities
        before you,
    our secret sins in the light
        of your countenance.

9 For all our days pass away
        under your wrath;
    our years come to an
        end[c] like a sigh.
10 The days of our life are
        seventy years,
    or perhaps eighty, if
        we are strong;
    even then their span[d] is only
        toil and trouble;
    they are soon gone, and
        we fly away.

11 Who considers the power
        of your anger?
    Your wrath is as great as the
        fear that is due you.
12 So teach us to count our days
        that we may gain
        a wise heart.

13 Turn, O LORD! How long?
    Have compassion on
        your servants!

a **90.1** Another reading is *our refuge*
b **90.3** Heb *humankind*   c **90.9** Syr: Heb
we bring our years to an end   d **90.10** Cn
Compare Gk Syr Jerome Tg: Heb *pride*

BIBLE IN LIFE

Unpopular

Psalm 89.50–51

Being a true, dedicated Christian is not always going to be popular. Following Christ may subject us to ridicule. Even some people we respect may see us as naïve, foolish, nonconformist or strange. We know that almost all of Jesus' disciples were killed, died in prison or suffered in other ways. Though we may not suffer to that degree, if we act in the name of Christ, we have to be ready for ridicule and perhaps suffering. We have to be able to face tragedy with equanimity. We may lose our status among people who are close to us, we may suffer loss and we may have disappointments and setbacks, but our eternal reward is great. Joy fills our lives when we reach out in compassion to others who are lonely or abandoned, when we refrain from gossip, when we heal wounds between us and other people, when we live a life patterned after our Savior, Jesus Christ.

14 Satisfy us in the morning with
    your steadfast love,
  so that we may rejoice and
    be glad all our days.
15 Make us glad as many days as
    you have afflicted us,
  and as many years as we
    have seen evil.
16 Let your work be manifest
    to your servants,
  and your glorious power
    to their children.
17 Let the favor of the Lord our
    God be upon us,
  and prosper for us the work
    of our hands—
  O prosper the work of
    our hands!

PSALM 91

ASSURANCE OF GOD'S
PROTECTION

1 You who live in the shelter
    of the Most High,
  who abide in the shadow
    of the Almighty,[a]
2 will say to the LORD, "My refuge
    and my fortress;
  my God, in whom I trust."
3 For he will deliver you from the
    snare of the fowler
  and from the deadly pestilence;
4 he will cover you with
    his pinions,
  and under his wings you
    will find refuge;
  his faithfulness is a shield
    and buckler.
5 You will not fear the terror
    of the night,
  or the arrow that flies by day,
6 or the pestilence that stalks
    in darkness,
  or the destruction that
    wastes at noonday.
7 A thousand may fall at your side,
  ten thousand at your
    right hand,
  but it will not come near you.
8 You will only look
    with your eyes
  and see the punishment
    of the wicked.

9 Because you have made the
    LORD your refuge,[b]
  the Most High your
    dwelling place,
10 no evil shall befall you,
  no scourge come near
    your tent.

11 For he will command his angels
    concerning you
  to guard you in all your ways.
12 On their hands they will
    bear you up,
  so that you will not dash your
    foot against a stone.
13 You will tread on the lion
    and the adder,
  the young lion and the
    serpent you will
    trample under foot.

14 Those who love me, I will deliver;
  I will protect those who
    know my name.
15 When they call to me, I will
    answer them;
  I will be with them in trouble,
  I will rescue them and
    honor them.
16 With long life I will satisfy them,
  and show them my salvation.

PSALM 92

THANKSGIVING FOR
VINDICATION

A Psalm. A Song for the Sabbath Day.

1 It is good to give thanks
    to the LORD,
  to sing praises to your
    name, O Most High;
2 to declare your steadfast love
    in the morning,
  and your faithfulness by night,
3 to the music of the lute
    and the harp,
  to the melody of the lyre.
4 For you, O LORD, have made
    me glad by your work;
  at the works of your hands
    I sing for joy.

[a] 91.1 Traditional rendering of Heb *Shaddai*
[b] 91.9 Cn: Heb *Because you, LORD, are my
refuge; you have made*

5 How great are your works,
    O Lord!
  Your thoughts are very deep!
6 The dullard cannot know,
    the stupid cannot
      understand this:
7 though the wicked sprout
    like grass
  and all evildoers flourish,
they are doomed to
    destruction forever,
8 but you, O Lord, are on
    high forever.
9 For your enemies, O Lord,
    for your enemies shall perish;
  all evildoers shall be scattered.

10 But you have exalted my horn
    like that of the wild ox;
  you have poured over
    me[a] fresh oil.
11 My eyes have seen the downfall
    of my enemies;
  my ears have heard the doom
    of my evil assailants.

12 The righteous flourish like
    the palm tree,
  and grow like a cedar
    in Lebanon.
13 They are planted in the
    house of the Lord;
  they flourish in the
    courts of our God.
14 In old age they still
    produce fruit;
  they are always green
    and full of sap,
15 showing that the Lord
    is upright;
  he is my rock, and there is no
    unrighteousness in him.

PSALM 93

THE MAJESTY OF GOD'S RULE

1 The Lord is king, he is
    robed in majesty;
  the Lord is robed, he is
    girded with strength.
He has established the world; it
    shall never be moved;
2   your throne is established
    from of old;
  you are from everlasting.

3 The floods have lifted up, O Lord,
    the floods have lifted
      up their voice;
  the floods lift up their roaring.
4 More majestic than the thunders
    of mighty waters,
  more majestic than the
    waves[b] of the sea,
  majestic on high is the Lord!

5 Your decrees are very sure;
    holiness befits your house,
  O Lord, forevermore.

PSALM 94

GOD THE AVENGER OF
THE RIGHTEOUS

1 O Lord, you God of vengeance,
    you God of vengeance,
      shine forth!
2 Rise up, O judge of the earth;
    give to the proud what
      they deserve!
3 O Lord, how long shall
    the wicked,
  how long shall the
    wicked exult?

4 They pour out their
    arrogant words;
  all the evildoers boast.
5 They crush your
    people, O Lord,
  and afflict your heritage.
6 They kill the widow and
    the stranger,
  they murder the orphan,
7 and they say, "The Lord
    does not see;
  the God of Jacob does
    not perceive."

8 Understand, O dullest of
    the people;
  fools, when will
    you be wise?
9 He who planted the ear,
    does he not hear?
  He who formed the eye,
    does he not see?
10 He who disciplines the nations,

---

[a] 92.10 Syr: Meaning of Heb uncertain
[b] 93.4 Cn: Heb *majestic are the waves*

he who teaches knowledge
to humankind,
does he not chastise?
11 The LORD knows our thoughts,[a]
that they are but an
empty breath.

12 Happy are those whom you
discipline, O LORD,
and whom you teach
out of your law,
13 giving them respite from
days of trouble,
until a pit is dug for the wicked.
14 For the LORD will not
forsake his people;
he will not abandon
his heritage;
15 for justice will return to
the righteous,
and all the upright in
heart will follow it.

16 Who rises up for me against
the wicked?
Who stands up for me
against evildoers?
17 If the LORD had not been
my help,
my soul would soon have lived
in the land of silence.
18 When I thought, "My foot
is slipping,"
your steadfast love, O LORD,
held me up.
19 When the cares of my
heart are many,
your consolations
cheer my soul.
20 Can wicked rulers be allied
with you,
those who contrive
mischief by statute?
21 They band together against the
life of the righteous,
and condemn the
innocent to death.
22 But the LORD has become
my stronghold,
and my God the rock
of my refuge.
23 He will repay them for
their iniquity
and wipe them out for
their wickedness;
the LORD our God will
wipe them out.

PSALM 95

A CALL TO WORSHIP AND OBEDIENCE

1 O come, let us sing
to the LORD;
let us make a joyful noise to
the rock of our salvation!
2 Let us come into his presence
with thanksgiving;
let us make a joyful noise to
him with songs of praise!
3 For the LORD is a great God,
and a great King above
all gods.
4 In his hand are the depths
of the earth;
the heights of the mountains
are his also.
5 The sea is his, for he made it,
and the dry land, which his
hands have formed.

6 O come, let us worship
and bow down,
let us kneel before the
LORD, our Maker!
7 For he is our God,
and we are the people
of his pasture,
and the sheep of his hand.

O that today you would
listen to his voice!
8   Do not harden your hearts,
as at Meribah,
as on the day at Massah
in the wilderness,
9 when your ancestors
tested me,
and put me to the proof,
though they had
seen my work.
10 For forty years I loathed
that generation
and said, "They are a people
whose hearts go astray,
and they do not regard
my ways."
11 Therefore in my
anger I swore,
"They shall not
enter my rest."

a **94.11** Heb *the thoughts of humankind*

PONDER

O come, let us worship and bow
down, let us kneel before the LORD,
our Maker! For he is our God, and
we are the people of his pasture,
and the sheep of his hand.
—Psalm 95.6–7

PRAY

Sovereign Lord, there are so many ways
we can learn about you, though we do
not fully comprehend the greatness of
your nature. We simply realize that you
are Spirit—a creative Spirit, a healing
Spirit, a Spirit of love and forgiveness,
charity and grace—who is all-powerful
in creation and in our own lives. Reveal
the presence of your transforming
Spirit in every aspect of our lives.
Remind us to reach for you without
ceasing. Give us strength and courage
to examine our own lives and to see
how we might be greater examples of
faith in you and so bless those around
us. In your name we pray. Amen.

PSALM 96

PRAISE TO GOD WHO
COMES IN JUDGMENT

1 O sing to the LORD a new song;
sing to the LORD,
all the earth.
2 Sing to the LORD,
bless his name;
tell of his salvation from
day to day.
3 Declare his glory among
the nations,
his marvelous works among
all the peoples.
4 For great is the LORD, and
greatly to be praised;
he is to be revered
above all gods.
5 For all the gods of the
peoples are idols,
but the LORD made
the heavens.

6 Honor and majesty are
before him;
strength and beauty are
in his sanctuary.
7 Ascribe to the LORD, O families
of the peoples,
ascribe to the LORD glory
and strength.
8 Ascribe to the LORD the glory
due his name;
bring an offering, and come
into his courts.
9 Worship the LORD in
holy splendor;
tremble before him,
all the earth.

10 Say among the nations,
"The LORD is king!
The world is firmly established;
it shall never be moved.
He will judge the peoples
with equity."
11 Let the heavens be glad, and
let the earth rejoice;
let the sea roar, and all
that fills it;
12 let the field exult, and
everything in it.
Then shall all the trees of the
forest sing for joy
13 before the LORD; for
he is coming,
for he is coming to judge
the earth.
He will judge the world with
righteousness,
and the peoples with his truth.

PSALM 97

THE GLORY OF GOD'S REIGN

1 The LORD is king! Let the
earth rejoice;
let the many coastlands
be glad!
2 Clouds and thick darkness
are all around him;
righteousness and justice
are the foundation
of his throne.
3 Fire goes before him,
and consumes his adversaries
on every side.

4 His lightnings light up the world;
   the earth sees and trembles.
5 The mountains melt like wax
      before the LORD,
   before the Lord of all the earth.
6 The heavens proclaim his
      righteousness;
   and all the peoples
      behold his glory.
7 All worshipers of images
   are put to shame,
   those who make their boast
      in worthless idols;
   all gods bow down
      before him.
8 Zion hears and is glad,
   and the towns[a] of
      Judah rejoice,
   because of your judgments,
      O God.
9 For you, O LORD, are most high
      over all the earth;
   you are exalted far
      above all gods.
10 The LORD loves those
      who hate[b] evil;
   he guards the lives of
      his faithful;
   he rescues them from the
      hand of the wicked.
11 Light dawns[c] for the righteous,
   and joy for the upright
      in heart.
12 Rejoice in the LORD, O you
      righteous,
   and give thanks to his
      holy name!

PSALM 98

PRAISE THE JUDGE
OF THE WORLD

A Psalm.

1 O sing to the LORD a new song,
   for he has done marvelous
      things.
   His right hand and
      his holy arm
   have gotten him victory.
2 The LORD has made known
      his victory;
   he has revealed his vindication
   in the sight of the nations.

3 He has remembered his steadfast
      love and faithfulness
   to the house of Israel.
   All the ends of the earth
      have seen
   the victory of our God.
4 Make a joyful noise to the
      LORD, all the earth;
   break forth into joyous song
      and sing praises.
5 Sing praises to the LORD
      with the lyre,
   with the lyre and the
      sound of melody.
6 With trumpets and the
      sound of the horn
   make a joyful noise before
      the King, the LORD.
7 Let the sea roar, and all
      that fills it;
   the world and those
      who live in it.
8 Let the floods clap their hands;
   let the hills sing together for joy
9 at the presence of the LORD,
      for he is coming
   to judge the earth.
   He will judge the world with
      righteousness,
   and the peoples with equity.

PSALM 99

PRAISE TO GOD FOR
HIS HOLINESS

1 The LORD is king; let the
      peoples tremble!
   He sits enthroned upon
      the cherubim; let
      the earth quake!
2 The LORD is great in Zion;
   he is exalted over all the peoples.
3 Let them praise your great
      and awesome name.
   Holy is he!
4 Mighty King,[d] lover of justice,
   you have established equity;
   you have executed justice
   and righteousness in Jacob.

a 97.8 Heb *daughters*   b 97.10 Cn: Heb *You
who love the LORD hate*   c 97.11 Gk Syr
Jerome: Heb *is sown*   d 99.4 Cn: Heb *And a
king's strength*

5 Extol the LORD our God;
    worship at his footstool.
    Holy is he!

6 Moses and Aaron were
        among his priests,
    Samuel also was among those
        who called on his name.
    They cried to the LORD, and
        he answered them.

7 He spoke to them in the
        pillar of cloud;
    they kept his decrees,
    and the statutes that
        he gave them.

8 O LORD our God, you
        answered them;
    you were a forgiving
        God to them,
    but an avenger of their
        wrongdoings.

9 Extol the LORD our God,
    and worship at his holy
        mountain;
    for the LORD our God is holy.

PSALM 100

ALL LANDS SUMMONED
TO PRAISE GOD

A Psalm of thanksgiving.

1 Make a joyful noise to the
        LORD, all the earth.

2 Worship the LORD with gladness;
    come into his presence
        with singing.

3 Know that the LORD is God.
    It is he that made us,
        and we are his;[a]
    we are his people, and the
        sheep of his pasture.

4 Enter his gates with
        thanksgiving,
    and his courts with praise.
    Give thanks to him,
        bless his name.

5 For the LORD is good;
    his steadfast love
        endures forever,
    and his faithfulness to
        all generations.

PSALM 101

A SOVEREIGN'S PLEDGE OF
INTEGRITY AND JUSTICE

Of David. A Psalm.

1 I will sing of loyalty
        and of justice;
    to you, O LORD, I will sing.

2 I will study the way that
        is blameless.
    When shall I attain it?

    I will walk with integrity of heart
        within my house;

3 I will not set before my eyes
    anything that is base.

[a] 100.3 Another reading is *and not we
ourselves*

▷ BIBLE IN LIFE

A Rare Virtue
Psalm 100.1–5

Gratitude is a rare virtue. We're not naturally inclined to be grateful. We are inclined to be self-sufficient, to stand on our own feet, to make our own way, to heal our own wounds. We don't like to be dependent on others. And we fail to see that the totality of what we are and what we have is dependent on God. Quite often we don't even remember to thank God for life itself—for our existence, freedom, security, wealth, friends, opportunities to serve others, joy, peace, satisfaction and love. We don't often thank God for those who have forgiven us or for opportunities to forgive others. We don't thank God for salvation, for eternal life, for God's only Son, who took upon himself our sins so that we could be totally forgiven and embraced constantly in the intense, personal love of our Creator. This psalm is an invitation to glorify God constantly—God who is the source of life—and offer thanksgiving. And to do it with gladness!

I hate the work of those
who fall away;
it shall not cling to me.
4 Perverseness of heart shall
be far from me;
I will know nothing of evil.

5 One who secretly slanders
a neighbor
I will destroy.
A haughty look and an
arrogant heart
I will not tolerate.

6 I will look with favor on the
faithful in the land,
so that they may live with me;
whoever walks in the way
that is blameless
shall minister to me.

7 No one who practices deceit
shall remain in my house;
no one who utters lies
shall continue in
my presence.

8 Morning by morning I
will destroy
all the wicked in the land,
cutting off all evildoers
from the city of the LORD.

PSALM 102

PRAYER TO THE ETERNAL
KING FOR HELP

*A prayer of one afflicted, when faint
and pleading before the LORD.*

1 Hear my prayer, O LORD;
let my cry come to you.
2 Do not hide your face from me
in the day of my distress.
Incline your ear to me;
answer me speedily in the
day when I call.

3 For my days pass away
like smoke,
and my bones burn
like a furnace.
4 My heart is stricken and
withered like grass;
I am too wasted to eat
my bread.

5 Because of my loud groaning
my bones cling to my skin.
6 I am like an owl of the wilderness,
like a little owl of the
waste places.
7 I lie awake;
I am like a lonely bird on
the housetop.
8 All day long my enemies
taunt me;
those who deride me use
my name for a curse.
9 For I eat ashes like bread,
and mingle tears with
my drink,
10 because of your indignation
and anger;
for you have lifted me up
and thrown me aside.
11 My days are like an evening
shadow;
I wither away like grass.

12 But you, O LORD, are
enthroned forever;
your name endures to
all generations.
13 You will rise up and have
compassion on Zion,
for it is time to favor it;
the appointed time has come.
14 For your servants hold its
stones dear,
and have pity on its dust.
15 The nations will fear the
name of the LORD,
and all the kings of the
earth your glory.
16 For the LORD will build up Zion;
he will appear in his glory.
17 He will regard the prayer
of the destitute,
and will not despise
their prayer.

18 Let this be recorded for a
generation to come,
so that a people yet unborn
may praise the LORD:
19 that he looked down from
his holy height,
from heaven the LORD
looked at the earth,
20 to hear the groans of the
prisoners,
to set free those who were
doomed to die;

21 so that the name of the LORD
        may be declared in Zion,
    and his praise in Jerusalem,
22 when peoples gather together,
    and kingdoms, to worship
        the LORD.

23 He has broken my strength
        in midcourse;
    he has shortened my days.
24 "O my God," I say, "do not
        take me away
    at the midpoint of my life,
    you whose years endure
        throughout all generations."

25 Long ago you laid the foundation
        of the earth,
    and the heavens are the
        work of your hands.
26 They will perish, but
        you endure;
    they will all wear out
        like a garment.
    You change them like clothing,
        and they pass away;
27   but you are the same, and
        your years have no end.
28 The children of your servants
        shall live secure;
    their offspring shall
        be established in
        your presence.

PSALM 103

THANKSGIVING FOR GOD'S GOODNESS

Of David.

1 Bless the LORD, O my soul,
    and all that is within me,
        bless his holy name.
2 Bless the LORD, O my soul,
    and do not forget all
        his benefits—
3 who forgives all your iniquity,
    who heals all your diseases,
4 who redeems your life
        from the Pit,
    who crowns you with steadfast
        love and mercy,
5 who satisfies you with good
        as long as you live[a]
    so that your youth is renewed
        like the eagle's.

6 The LORD works vindication
    and justice for all who
        are oppressed.
7 He made known his ways
        to Moses,
    his acts to the people of Israel.
8 The LORD is merciful
        and gracious,
    slow to anger and abounding
        in steadfast love.
9 He will not always accuse,
    nor will he keep his
        anger forever.
10 He does not deal with us
        according to our sins,
    nor repay us according
        to our iniquities.
11 For as the heavens are high
        above the earth,
    so great is his steadfast
        love toward those
        who fear him;
12 as far as the east is from the west,
    so far he removes our
        transgressions from us.
13 As a father has compassion
        for his children,
    so the LORD has compassion
        for those who fear him.
14 For he knows how we were made;
    he remembers that
        we are dust.

15 As for mortals, their days
        are like grass;
    they flourish like a flower
        of the field;
16 for the wind passes over it,
        and it is gone,
    and its place knows it no more.
17 But the steadfast love of the
        LORD is from everlasting
        to everlasting
    on those who fear him,
    and his righteousness to
        children's children,
18 to those who keep his covenant
    and remember to do his
        commandments.

19 The LORD has established his
        throne in the heavens,
    and his kingdom rules over all.

---

[a] 103.5 Meaning of Heb uncertain

20 Bless the LORD, O you his angels,
    you mighty ones who
      do his bidding,
    obedient to his spoken word.
21 Bless the LORD, all his hosts,
    his ministers that do his will.
22 Bless the LORD, all his works,
    in all places of his dominion.
    Bless the LORD, O my soul.

PSALM 104

GOD THE CREATOR AND PROVIDER

1 Bless the LORD, O my soul.
    O LORD my God, you
      are very great.
    You are clothed with honor
      and majesty,
2   wrapped in light as with
      a garment.
    You stretch out the heavens
      like a tent,
3   you set the beams of your[a]
      chambers on the waters,
  you make the clouds
      your[a] chariot,
  you ride on the wings
      of the wind,
4 you make the winds your[a]
      messengers,
    fire and flame your[a]
      ministers.

5 You set the earth on its
      foundations,
    so that it shall never be shaken.
6 You cover it with the deep as
      with a garment;
    the waters stood above
      the mountains.
7 At your rebuke they flee;
    at the sound of your thunder
      they take to flight.
8 They rose up to the mountains,
    ran down to the valleys
    to the place that you
      appointed for them.
9 You set a boundary that
      they may not pass,
    so that they might not again
      cover the earth.

10 You make springs gush forth
      in the valleys;
    they flow between the hills,
11 giving drink to every
      wild animal;
    the wild asses quench
      their thirst.
12 By the streams[b] the birds of the
      air have their habitation;
    they sing among the branches.
13 From your lofty abode you
      water the mountains;
    the earth is satisfied with
      the fruit of your work.

[a] **104.3,4** Heb *his*   [b] **104.12** Heb *By them*

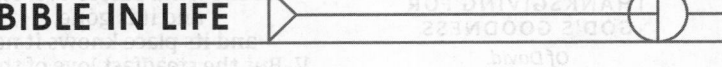

BIBLE IN LIFE

Praising God for Our Blessings   Psalm 103.1–22

How often do we bless God in the way this psalm calls us to—with all our hearts, with all our souls? Usually we are too consumed by our everyday concerns to reflect on our lives and thank God for our blessings. At best, our modest thanks are expressed in a brief comment during a mealtime prayer. When we pause to consider our lives, though, we can recognize so many ways that God has blessed us. We should give to God heartfelt, grateful praise for all God has done for us. For example, we have all been granted life up to this point, and God has spared many of us from great danger or serious illness. When I was four years old, I had colitis, and the doctors thought I was going to die. Yet God spared my life. When I was in the US Navy submarine force, on three different occasions a slight change in the course of events could have ended my life. How rarely I pause to say, "God, thank you for saving my life." Such blessings, however, should evoke deep praise from our total beings—heart, mind and soul—and foster a spirit of humility within us as we recognize that it is only by God's grace that we are what we are.

14 You cause the grass to grow
        for the cattle,
    and plants for people to use,ᵃ
    to bring forth food from the earth,
15 and wine to gladden the
        human heart,
    oil to make the face shine,
    and bread to strengthen
        the human heart.
16 The trees of the LORD are
        watered abundantly,
    the cedars of Lebanon
        that he planted.
17 In them the birds build
        their nests;
    the stork has its home
        in the fir trees.
18 The high mountains are for
        the wild goats;
    the rocks are a refuge
        for the coneys.
19 You have made the moon to
        mark the seasons;
    the sun knows its time
        for setting.
20 You make darkness, and
        it is night,
    when all the animals of the
        forest come creeping out.
21 The young lions roar for
        their prey,
    seeking their food from God.
22 When the sun rises, they
        withdraw
    and lie down in their dens.
23 People go out to their work
    and to their labor until
        the evening.

24 O LORD, how manifold are
        your works!
    In wisdom you have
        made them all;
    the earth is full of your
        creatures.
25 Yonder is the sea, great and wide,
    creeping things innumerable
        are there,
    living things both small
        and great.
26 There go the ships,
    and Leviathan that you
        formed to sport in it.

27 These all look to you
        to give them their food
        in due season;

28 when you give to them,
        they gather it up;
    when you open your
        hand, they are filled
        with good things.
29 When you hide your face,
        they are dismayed;
    when you take away their
        breath, they die
    and return to their dust.
30 When you send forth your
        spirit,ᵇ they are created;
    and you renew the face
        of the ground.

31 May the glory of the LORD
        endure forever;
    may the LORD rejoice
        in his works—
32 who looks on the earth
        and it trembles,
    who touches the mountains
        and they smoke.
33 I will sing to the LORD as
        long as I live;
    I will sing praise to my God
        while I have being.
34 May my meditation be
        pleasing to him,
    for I rejoice in the LORD.
35 Let sinners be consumed
        from the earth,
    and let the wicked be no more.
    Bless the LORD, O my soul.
    Praise the LORD!

PSALM 105

GOD'S FAITHFULNESS TO ISRAEL

1 O give thanks to the LORD,
        call on his name,
    make known his deeds
        among the peoples.
2 Sing to him, sing praises to him;
    tell of all his wonderful works.
3 Glory in his holy name;
    let the hearts of those who
        seek the LORD rejoice.
4 Seek the LORD and
        his strength;
    seek his presence continually.

ᵃ 104.14 Or to *cultivate*   ᵇ 104.30 Or *your breath*

5 Remember the wonderful
        works he has done,
    his miracles, and the judgments
        he has uttered,
6 O offspring of his servant
        Abraham,[a]
    children of Jacob, his
        chosen ones.

7 He is the LORD our God;
    his judgments are in
        all the earth.
8 He is mindful of his
        covenant forever,
    of the word that he
        commanded, for a
        thousand generations,
9 the covenant that he made
        with Abraham,
    his sworn promise to Isaac,
10 which he confirmed to Jacob
        as a statute,
    to Israel as an everlasting
        covenant,
11 saying, "To you I will give
        the land of Canaan
    as your portion for an
        inheritance."

12 When they were few in number,
    of little account, and
        strangers in it,
13 wandering from nation to nation,
    from one kingdom to
        another people,
14 he allowed no one to oppress them;
    he rebuked kings on
        their account,
15 saying, "Do not touch my
        anointed ones;
    do my prophets no harm."

16 When he summoned famine
        against the land,
    and broke every staff of bread,
17 he had sent a man ahead of them,
    Joseph, who was sold as a slave.
18 His feet were hurt with fetters,
    his neck was put in a
        collar of iron;
19 until what he had said
        came to pass,
    the word of the LORD
        kept testing him.
20 The king sent and released him;
    the ruler of the peoples
        set him free.

21 He made him lord of his house,
    and ruler of all his possessions,
22 to instruct[b] his officials at
        his pleasure,
    and to teach his elders wisdom.

23 Then Israel came to Egypt;
    Jacob lived as an alien in
        the land of Ham.
24 And the LORD made his
        people very fruitful,
    and made them stronger
        than their foes,
25 whose hearts he then turned
        to hate his people,
    to deal craftily with
        his servants.

26 He sent his servant Moses,
    and Aaron whom he
        had chosen.
27 They performed his signs
        among them,
    and miracles in the
        land of Ham.
28 He sent darkness, and made
        the land dark;
    they rebelled[c] against
        his words.
29 He turned their waters
        into blood,
    and caused their fish to die.
30 Their land swarmed with frogs,
    even in the chambers
        of their kings.
31 He spoke, and there came
        swarms of flies,
    and gnats throughout
        their country.
32 He gave them hail for rain,
    and lightning that flashed
        through their land.
33 He struck their vines
        and fig trees,
    and shattered the trees
        of their country.
34 He spoke, and the locusts came,
    and young locusts
        without number;
35 they devoured all the vegetation
        in their land,
    and ate up the fruit of
        their ground.

a 105.6 Another reading is *Israel* (compare
1 Chr 16.13)   b 105.22 Gk Syr Jerome: Heb
to bind   c 105.28 Cn Compare Gk Syr: Heb
they did not rebel

36 He struck down all the firstborn
in their land,
the first issue of all
their strength.

37 Then he brought Israel[a] out
with silver and gold,
and there was no one among
their tribes who stumbled.
38 Egypt was glad when
they departed,
for dread of them had
fallen upon it.
39 He spread a cloud
for a covering,
and fire to give light by night.
40 They asked, and he
brought quails,
and gave them food from
heaven in abundance.
41 He opened the rock, and
water gushed out;
it flowed through the
desert like a river.
42 For he remembered his
holy promise,
and Abraham, his servant.

43 So he brought his people
out with joy,
his chosen ones with singing.
44 He gave them the lands
of the nations,
and they took possession of the
wealth of the peoples,
45 that they might keep his statutes
and observe his laws.
Praise the LORD!

PSALM 106

A CONFESSION OF
ISRAEL'S SINS

1 Praise the LORD!
O give thanks to the LORD,
for he is good;
for his steadfast love
endures forever.
2 Who can utter the mighty
doings of the LORD,
or declare all his praise?
3 Happy are those who
observe justice,
who do righteousness
at all times.

4 Remember me, O LORD,
when you show favor
to your people;
help me when you
deliver them;
5 that I may see the prosperity
of your chosen ones,
that I may rejoice in the
gladness of your nation,
that I may glory in
your heritage.

6 Both we and our ancestors
have sinned;
we have committed iniquity,
have done wickedly.
7 Our ancestors, when they
were in Egypt,
did not consider your
wonderful works;
they did not remember the
abundance of your
steadfast love,
but rebelled against the Most
High[b] at the Red Sea.[c]
8 Yet he saved them for his
name's sake,
so that he might make known
his mighty power.
9 He rebuked the Red Sea,[c]
and it became dry;
he led them through the deep
as through a desert.
10 So he saved them from the
hand of the foe,
and delivered them from the
hand of the enemy.
11 The waters covered their
adversaries;
not one of them was left.
12 Then they believed his words;
they sang his praise.

13 But they soon forgot his works;
they did not wait for
his counsel.
14 But they had a wanton craving
in the wilderness,
and put God to the test
in the desert;
15 he gave them what they asked,
but sent a wasting disease
among them.

a 105.37 Heb *them*   b 106.7 Cn Compare
78.17, 56: Heb *rebelled at the sea*
c 106.7,9 Or *Sea of Reeds*

16 They were jealous of Moses
    in the camp,
  and of Aaron, the holy
    one of the LORD.
17 The earth opened and swallowed
    up Dathan,
  and covered the faction
    of Abiram.
18 Fire also broke out in their
    company;
  the flame burned up the wicked.

19 They made a calf at Horeb
  and worshiped a cast image.
20 They exchanged the glory of God[a]
    for the image of an ox
    that eats grass.
21 They forgot God, their Savior,
    who had done great
    things in Egypt,
22 wondrous works in the
    land of Ham,
  and awesome deeds by
    the Red Sea.[b]
23 Therefore he said he would
    destroy them—
  had not Moses, his chosen one,
  stood in the breach before him,
  to turn away his wrath from
    destroying them.

24 Then they despised the
    pleasant land,
  having no faith in his promise.
25 They grumbled in their tents,
  and did not obey the voice
    of the LORD.
26 Therefore he raised his hand
    and swore to them
  that he would make them
    fall in the wilderness,
27 and would disperse[c] their
    descendants among
    the nations,
  scattering them over the lands.

28 Then they attached themselves
    to the Baal of Peor,
  and ate sacrifices offered
    to the dead;
29 they provoked the LORD to
    anger with their deeds,
  and a plague broke out
    among them.
30 Then Phinehas stood up
    and interceded,
  and the plague was stopped.

31 And that has been reckoned to
    him as righteousness
  from generation to
    generation forever.

32 They angered the LORD[d] at the
    waters of Meribah,
  and it went ill with Moses
    on their account;
33 for they made his spirit bitter,
  and he spoke words
    that were rash.

34 They did not destroy the peoples,
  as the LORD commanded them,
35 but they mingled with
    the nations
  and learned to do as they did.
36 They served their idols,
  which became a snare to them.
37 They sacrificed their sons
  and their daughters to
    the demons;
38 they poured out innocent blood,
  the blood of their sons
    and daughters,
  whom they sacrificed to the
    idols of Canaan;
  and the land was polluted
    with blood.
39 Thus they became unclean
    by their acts,
  and prostituted themselves
    in their doings.

40 Then the anger of the LORD
    was kindled against
    his people,
  and he abhorred his heritage;
41 he gave them into the hand
    of the nations,
  so that those who hated
    them ruled over them.
42 Their enemies oppressed them,
  and they were brought
    into subjection under
    their power.
43 Many times he delivered them,
  but they were rebellious
    in their purposes,
  and were brought low
    through their iniquity.

---

a 106.20 Compare Gk Mss: Heb *exchanged
their glory* b 106.22 Or *Sea of Reeds*
c 106.27 Syr Compare Ezek 20.23: Heb *cause
to fall* d 106.32 Heb *him*

44 Nevertheless he regarded
    their distress
  when he heard their cry.
45 For their sake he remembered
    his covenant,
  and showed compassion
    according to the
    abundance of his
    steadfast love.
46 He caused them to be pitied
  by all who held them captive.

47 Save us, O LORD our God,
  and gather us from among
    the nations,
  that we may give thanks to
    your holy name
  and glory in your praise.

48 Blessed be the LORD, the
    God of Israel,
  from everlasting to everlasting.
  And let all the people
    say, "Amen."
  Praise the LORD!

BOOK V

(PSALMS 107–150)

PSALM 107

THANKSGIVING FOR DELIVERANCE FROM MANY TROUBLES

1 O give thanks to the LORD,
    for he is good;
  for his steadfast love
    endures forever.
2 Let the redeemed of the
    LORD say so,
  those he redeemed
    from trouble
3 and gathered in from the lands,
  from the east and from
    the west,
  from the north and from
    the south.[a]

4 Some wandered in
    desert wastes,
  finding no way to an
    inhabited town;
5 hungry and thirsty,
    their soul fainted within them.

6 Then they cried to the LORD
    in their trouble,
  and he delivered them
    from their distress;
7 he led them by a
    straight way,
  until they reached an
    inhabited town.
8 Let them thank the LORD for
    his steadfast love,
  for his wonderful works
    to humankind.
9 For he satisfies the thirsty,
  and the hungry he fills
    with good things.

PONDER

Let them thank the LORD for his steadfast love, for his wonderful works to humankind. For he satisfies the thirsty, and the hungry he fills with good things. —Psalm 107.8–9

PRAY

O Father, we realize we are a people blessed with homes, food, education, health care and security, and we thank you. Remind us of the admonition of Christ to share what we have with others, either in our own communities or perhaps even in more distant places. Help us to be aware of the fact that we can live transcendent lives without ever going far from where we live. Help us align ourselves with Jesus as we pledged to do when we accepted him. Help us remember that our prayers are answered when we ask sincerely and are sincerely committed. Transform us in the name of our Savior, Jesus Christ. Amen.

---

10 Some sat in darkness and
    in gloom,
  prisoners in misery
    and in irons,

a 107.3 Cn: Heb *sea*

11 for they had rebelled against
        the words of God,
    and spurned the counsel
        of the Most High.
12 Their hearts were bowed down
        with hard labor;
    they fell down, with no
        one to help.
13 Then they cried to the LORD
        in their trouble,
    and he saved them from
        their distress;
14 he brought them out of
        darkness and gloom,
    and broke their bonds asunder.
15 Let them thank the LORD for
        his steadfast love,
    for his wonderful works
        to humankind.
16 For he shatters the doors
        of bronze,
    and cuts in two the bars of iron.

17 Some were sick[a] through
        their sinful ways,
    and because of their iniquities
        endured affliction;
18 they loathed any kind of food,
    and they drew near to the
        gates of death.
19 Then they cried to the LORD
        in their trouble,
    and he saved them from
        their distress;
20 he sent out his word and
        healed them,
    and delivered them from
        destruction.
21 Let them thank the LORD for
        his steadfast love,
    for his wonderful works
        to humankind.
22 And let them offer thanksgiving
        sacrifices,
    and tell of his deeds with
        songs of joy.

23 Some went down to the
        sea in ships,
    doing business on the
        mighty waters;
24 they saw the deeds of the LORD,
    his wondrous works in the deep.
25 For he commanded and raised
        the stormy wind,
    which lifted up the
        waves of the sea.

26 They mounted up to heaven, they
        went down to the depths;
    their courage melted away
        in their calamity;
27 they reeled and staggered
        like drunkards,
    and were at their wits' end.
28 Then they cried to the LORD
        in their trouble,
    and he brought them out
        from their distress;
29 he made the storm be still,
    and the waves of the sea
        were hushed.
30 Then they were glad because
        they had quiet,
    and he brought them to
        their desired haven.
31 Let them thank the LORD for
        his steadfast love,
    for his wonderful works
        to humankind.
32 Let them extol him in
        the congregation
        of the people,
    and praise him in the
        assembly of the elders.

33 He turns rivers into a desert,
    springs of water into
        thirsty ground,
34 a fruitful land into a salty waste,
    because of the wickedness
        of its inhabitants.
35 He turns a desert into
        pools of water,
    a parched land into
        springs of water.
36 And there he lets
        the hungry live,
    and they establish a
        town to live in;
37 they sow fields, and plant
        vineyards,
    and get a fruitful yield.
38 By his blessing they
        multiply greatly,
    and he does not let their
        cattle decrease.

39 When they are diminished
        and brought low
    through oppression,
        trouble, and sorrow,

a 107.17 Cn: Heb *fools*

40 he pours contempt on princes
     and makes them wander
        in trackless wastes;
41 but he raises up the needy
        out of distress,
     and makes their families
        like flocks.
42 The upright see it and are glad;
     and all wickedness stops
        its mouth.
43 Let those who are wise give
        heed to these things,
     and consider the steadfast
        love of the LORD.

PSALM 108

PRAISE AND PRAYER
FOR VICTORY

A Song. A Psalm of David.

1 My heart is steadfast, O God,
        my heart is steadfast;[a]
   I will sing and make melody.
     Awake, my soul![b]
2 Awake, O harp and lyre!
     I will awake the dawn.
3 I will give thanks to
        you, O LORD, among
        the peoples,
     and I will sing praises to you
        among the nations.
4 For your steadfast love is higher
        than the heavens,
     and your faithfulness
        reaches to the clouds.

5 Be exalted, O God, above
        the heavens,
     and let your glory be over
        all the earth.
6 Give victory with your right
        hand, and answer me,
     so that those whom you
        love may be rescued.

7 God has promised in his
        sanctuary:[c]
   "With exultation I will
        divide up Shechem,
     and portion out the
        Vale of Succoth.
8 Gilead is mine; Manasseh
        is mine;
     Ephraim is my helmet;
        Judah is my scepter.

9 Moab is my washbasin;
        on Edom I hurl my shoe;
     over Philistia I shout
        in triumph."

10 Who will bring me to the
        fortified city?
     Who will lead me to Edom?
11 Have you not rejected us, O God?
     You do not go out, O God,
        with our armies.
12 O grant us help against the foe,
     for human help is worthless.
13 With God we shall do valiantly;
     it is he who will tread
        down our foes.

NONE OF US IS SELF-

SUFFICIENT, BUT WE ARE

INCLINED TO PRIDE OURSELVES

ON SELF-RELIANCE.

PSALM 109

PRAYER FOR VINDICATION
AND VENGEANCE

To the leader. Of David. A Psalm.

1 Do not be silent, O God
     of my praise.
2 For wicked and deceitful mouths
        are opened against me,
     speaking against me with
        lying tongues.
3 They beset me with
        words of hate,
     and attack me without cause.
4 In return for my love they
        accuse me,
     even while I make prayer
        for them.[d]
5 So they reward me
        evil for good,
     and hatred for my love.

<hr>

a **108.1** Heb Mss Gk Syr: MT lacks *my heart
is steadfast*   b **108.1** Compare 57.8: Heb
also my soul   c **108.7** Or *by his holiness*
d **109.4** Syr: Heb *I prayer*

6 They say,[a] "Appoint a wicked
    man against him;
    let an accuser stand on his right.
7 When he is tried, let him
    be found guilty;
    let his prayer be counted as sin.
8 May his days be few;
    may another seize his position.
9 May his children be orphans,
    and his wife a widow.
10 May his children wander
    about and beg;
    may they be driven out of[b]
    the ruins they inhabit.
11 May the creditor seize all
    that he has;
    may strangers plunder the
    fruits of his toil.
12 May there be no one to do
    him a kindness,
    nor anyone to pity his
    orphaned children.
13 May his posterity be cut off;
    may his name be blotted out in
    the second generation.
14 May the iniquity of his father[c]
    be remembered
    before the LORD,
    and do not let the sin of his
    mother be blotted out.
15 Let them be before the LORD
    continually,
    and may his[d] memory be cut
    off from the earth.
16 For he did not remember to
    show kindness,
    but pursued the poor and needy
    and the brokenhearted
    to their death.
17 He loved to curse; let curses
    come on him.
    He did not like blessing; may
    it be far from him.
18 He clothed himself with
    cursing as his coat,
    may it soak into his
    body like water,
    like oil into his bones.
19 May it be like a garment that he
    wraps around himself,
    like a belt that he wears
    every day."

20 May that be the reward of my
    accusers from the LORD,
    of those who speak evil
    against my life.

21 But you, O LORD my Lord,
    act on my behalf for your
    name's sake;
    because your steadfast love
    is good, deliver me.
22 For I am poor and needy,
    and my heart is pierced
    within me.
23 I am gone like a shadow at evening;
    I am shaken off like a locust.
24 My knees are weak through fasting;
    my body has become gaunt.
25 I am an object of scorn to
    my accusers;
    when they see me, they
    shake their heads.

26 Help me, O LORD my God!
    Save me according to your
    steadfast love.
27 Let them know that this
    is your hand;
    you, O LORD, have done it.
28 Let them curse, but you will bless.
    Let my assailants be put
    to shame;[e] may your
    servant be glad.
29 May my accusers be clothed
    with dishonor;
    may they be wrapped in their
    own shame as in a mantle.
30 With my mouth I will give great
    thanks to the LORD;
    I will praise him in the
    midst of the throng.
31 For he stands at the right
    hand of the needy,
    to save them from those
    who would condemn
    them to death.

PSALM 110

ASSURANCE OF VICTORY
FOR GOD'S PRIEST-KING

Of David. A Psalm.

1 The LORD says to my lord,
    "Sit at my right hand
    until I make your enemies
    your footstool."

---

a 109.6 Heb lacks *They say* b 109.10 Gk:
Heb *and seek* c 109.14 Cn: Heb *fathers*
d 109.15 Gk: Heb *their* e 109.28 Gk: Heb *They
have risen up and have been put to shame*

2 The LORD sends out from Zion
    your mighty scepter.
    Rule in the midst of your foes.
3 Your people will offer
        themselves willingly
    on the day you lead your forces
    on the holy mountains.[a]
    From the womb of the morning,
    like dew, your youth[b] will
        come to you.
4 The LORD has sworn and will
        not change his mind,
    "You are a priest forever
        according to the order
        of Melchizedek."[c]

5 The Lord is at your right hand;
    he will shatter kings on the
        day of his wrath.
6 He will execute judgment
        among the nations,
    filling them with corpses;
    he will shatter heads
        over the wide earth.
7 He will drink from the stream
        by the path;
    therefore he will lift up his head.

PSALM 111
PRAISE FOR GOD'S
WONDERFUL WORKS

1 Praise the LORD!
    I will give thanks to the LORD
        with my whole heart,
    in the company of the upright,
        in the congregation.
2 Great are the works of the LORD,
    studied by all who delight
        in them.
3 Full of honor and majesty
        is his work,
    and his righteousness
        endures forever.
4 He has gained renown by his
        wonderful deeds;
    the LORD is gracious
        and merciful.
5 He provides food for those
        who fear him;
    he is ever mindful of his covenant.
6 He has shown his people the
        power of his works,
    in giving them the heritage
        of the nations.

7 The works of his hands are
        faithful and just;
    all his precepts are
        trustworthy.
8 They are established forever
        and ever,
    to be performed with
        faithfulness and
        uprightness.
9 He sent redemption to his people;
    he has commanded his
        covenant forever.
    Holy and awesome is his name.
10 The fear of the LORD is the
        beginning of wisdom;
    all those who practice it[d] have
        a good understanding.
    His praise endures forever.

---

[a] 110.3 Another reading is *in holy splendor*
[b] 110.3 Cn: Heb *the dew of your youth*
[c] 110.4 Or *forever, a rightful king by my edict*
[d] 111.10 Gk Syr: Heb *them*

PONDER

The fear of the LORD is the beginning
of wisdom; all those who practice
it have a good understanding.
—Psalm 111.10

PRAY

Holy Father, your Word has intriguing
significance for us—a deep and
penetrating impact on our lives—if
we are willing to open our minds and
hearts to you, the source of all wisdom
and knowledge. Forgive us for self-
centeredness when we are reluctant to
reach out to others. Let us realize that
what made your Son's own ministry so
significant was that he reached out to
those who were most in need, those who
were lonely and those who suffered. We
admit that it is very difficult to do these
things, but we also know that you said
that with you, nothing is impossible (see
Matthew 17.20). We ask these things
in the name of our Savior. Amen.

PSALM 112

BLESSINGS OF THE RIGHTEOUS

1 Praise the LORD!
   Happy are those who
      fear the LORD,
   who greatly delight in his
      commandments.
2 Their descendants will be
      mighty in the land;
   the generation of the upright
      will be blessed.
3 Wealth and riches are in
      their houses,
   and their righteousness
      endures forever.
4 They rise in the darkness as a
      light for the upright;
   they are gracious, merciful,
      and righteous.
5 It is well with those who deal
      generously and lend,
   who conduct their affairs
      with justice.
6 For the righteous will
      never be moved;
   they will be remembered
      forever.
7 They are not afraid
      of evil tidings;
   their hearts are firm,
      secure in the LORD.
8 Their hearts are steady, they
      will not be afraid;
   in the end they will look in
      triumph on their foes.
9 They have distributed freely, they
      have given to the poor;
   their righteousness
      endures forever;
   their horn is exalted in honor.

10 The wicked see it and are angry;
   they gnash their teeth
      and melt away;
   the desire of the wicked
      comes to nothing.

PSALM 113

GOD THE HELPER OF THE NEEDY

1 Praise the LORD!
   Praise, O servants of the LORD;
      praise the name of the LORD.

2 Blessed be the name of the LORD
      from this time on and
         forevermore.
3 From the rising of the sun
      to its setting
   the name of the LORD
      is to be praised.
4 The LORD is high above
      all nations,
   and his glory above
      the heavens.

5 Who is like the LORD our God,
      who is seated on high,
6 who looks far down
      on the heavens and the earth?
7 He raises the poor from the dust,
   and lifts the needy from
      the ash heap,
8 to make them sit with princes,
   with the princes of his people.
9 He gives the barren
      woman a home,
   making her the joyous
      mother of children.
Praise the LORD!

BIBLE IN LIFE

Unbelief

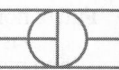
Psalm 112.4

Out of the darkness of unbelief and doubt comes the light of truth. It's okay for us to ask questions and to have doubts. It's okay for us to search for the truth. God can withstand our sharpest questions, our darkest doubts and our persistent search for the truth. God wants to be revealed to us. If we just sit back and say we believe but are afraid to expose our lack of belief or our questions to God, then we stunt our faith. When we claim that our way is right, quit searching for truth and think we're self-sufficient and know it all, then we remain in the dark (see John 9). We should be willing to admit our doubt or unbelief and ask God, "I believe; help my unbelief!" (Mark 9.24).

PSALM 114

GOD'S WONDERS AT THE EXODUS

1 When Israel went out
    from Egypt,
  the house of Jacob from
    a people of strange
    language,
2 Judah became God's[a] sanctuary,
  Israel his dominion.

3 The sea looked and fled;
  Jordan turned back.
4 The mountains skipped like rams,
  the hills like lambs.

5 Why is it, O sea, that you flee?
  O Jordan, that you turn back?
6 O mountains, that you
    skip like rams?
  O hills, like lambs?

7 Tremble, O earth, at the
    presence of the LORD,
  at the presence of the
    God of Jacob,
8 who turns the rock into a
    pool of water,
  the flint into a spring of water.

PSALM 115

THE IMPOTENCE OF IDOLS AND THE GREATNESS OF GOD

1 Not to us, O LORD, not to us, but
    to your name give glory,
  for the sake of your steadfast
    love and your faithfulness.
2 Why should the nations say,
  "Where is their God?"

3 Our God is in the heavens;
  he does whatever he pleases.
4 Their idols are silver and gold,
  the work of human hands.
5 They have mouths, but
    do not speak;
  eyes, but do not see.
6 They have ears, but do not hear;
  noses, but do not smell.
7 They have hands, but do not feel;
  feet, but do not walk;
  they make no sound in
    their throats.

8 Those who make them
    are like them;
  so are all who trust in them.

9 O Israel, trust in the LORD!
  He is their help and
    their shield.
10 O house of Aaron, trust
    in the LORD!
  He is their help and
    their shield.
11 You who fear the LORD,
    trust in the LORD!
  He is their help and
    their shield.

12 The LORD has been mindful of
    us; he will bless us;
  he will bless the house of Israel;
  he will bless the house
    of Aaron;
13 he will bless those who
    fear the LORD,
  both small and great.

14 May the LORD give you increase,
  both you and your children.
15 May you be blessed by the LORD,
  who made heaven and earth.

16 The heavens are the LORD'S
    heavens,
  but the earth he has given
    to human beings.
17 The dead do not praise the LORD,
  nor do any that go down
    into silence.
18 But we will bless the LORD
  from this time on and
    forevermore.
Praise the LORD!

PSALM 116

THANKSGIVING FOR RECOVERY FROM ILLNESS

1 I love the LORD, because
    he has heard
  my voice and my supplications.
2 Because he inclined his ear to me,
  therefore I will call on him
    as long as I live.

a 114.2 Heb *his*

3 The snares of death
        encompassed me;
    the pangs of Sheol laid
        hold on me;
    I suffered distress and anguish.
4 Then I called on the name
        of the LORD:
    "O LORD, I pray, save my life!"

5 Gracious is the LORD, and
        righteous;
    our God is merciful.
6 The LORD protects the simple;
    when I was brought low,
        he saved me.
7 Return, O my soul, to your rest,
    for the LORD has dealt
        bountifully with you.

8 For you have delivered my
        soul from death,
    my eyes from tears,
    my feet from stumbling.
9 I walk before the LORD
    in the land of the living.
10 I kept my faith, even when I said,
    "I am greatly afflicted";
11 I said in my consternation,
    "Everyone is a liar."

GOD DOES NOT PROMISE AN

ABSENCE OF SUFFERING, BUT

THE ABILITY TO BEAR IT AND

GROW IN THE PROCESS.

12 What shall I return to the LORD
    for all his bounty to me?
13 I will lift up the cup of salvation
    and call on the name
        of the LORD,
14 I will pay my vows to the LORD
    in the presence of all
        his people.
15 Precious in the sight of the LORD
    is the death of his faithful ones.
16 O LORD, I am your servant;
    I am your servant, the child
        of your serving girl.
    You have loosed my bonds.

17 I will offer to you a thanksgiving
        sacrifice
    and call on the name
        of the LORD.
18 I will pay my vows to the LORD
    in the presence of all
        his people,
19 in the courts of the house
        of the LORD,
    in your midst, O Jerusalem.
Praise the LORD!

PSALM 117

UNIVERSAL CALL TO WORSHIP

1 Praise the LORD, all you nations!
    Extol him, all you peoples!
2 For great is his steadfast
        love toward us,
    and the faithfulness of the
        LORD endures forever.
Praise the LORD!

PSALM 118

A SONG OF VICTORY

1 O give thanks to the LORD,
        for he is good;
    his steadfast love
        endures forever!

2 Let Israel say,
    "His steadfast love
        endures forever."
3 Let the house of Aaron say,
    "His steadfast love
        endures forever."
4 Let those who fear
        the LORD say,
    "His steadfast love
        endures forever."
5 Out of my distress I called
        on the LORD;
    the LORD answered me and
        set me in a broad place.
6 With the LORD on my side
    I do not fear.
    What can mortals do to me?
7 The LORD is on my side
        to help me;
    I shall look in triumph on
        those who hate me.

8 It is better to take refuge
    in the LORD
        than to put confidence
        in mortals.
9 It is better to take refuge
    in the LORD
        than to put confidence
        in princes.

10 All nations surrounded me;
        in the name of the LORD
        I cut them off!
11 They surrounded me, surrounded
        me on every side;
        in the name of the LORD
        I cut them off!
12 They surrounded me like bees;
        they blazed[a] like a fire of thorns;
        in the name of the LORD
        I cut them off!
13 I was pushed hard,[b] so that
        I was falling,
        but the LORD helped me.
14 The LORD is my strength
        and my might;
        he has become my salvation.

15 There are glad songs of victory in
        the tents of the righteous:
    "The right hand of the LORD
        does valiantly;
16   the right hand of the
        LORD is exalted;
        the right hand of the LORD
        does valiantly."
17 I shall not die, but I shall live,
        and recount the deeds
        of the LORD.
18 The LORD has punished
        me severely,
        but he did not give me
        over to death.

19 Open to me the gates of
        righteousness,
        that I may enter through them
        and give thanks to the LORD.

20 This is the gate of the LORD;
        the righteous shall enter
        through it.

21 I thank you that you have
        answered me
        and have become my salvation.
22 The stone that the builders rejected
        has become the chief cornerstone.

23 This is the LORD's doing;
        it is marvelous in our eyes.
24 This is the day that the
        LORD has made;
        let us rejoice and be glad in it.[c]
25 Save us, we beseech you, O LORD!
        O LORD, we beseech you,
        give us success!

26 Blessed is the one who comes in
        the name of the LORD.[d]
    We bless you from the
        house of the LORD.
27 The LORD is God,
        and he has given us light.
    Bind the festal procession
        with branches,
        up to the horns of the altar.[e]

28 You are my God, and I will
        give thanks to you;
        you are my God, I will extol you.

29 O give thanks to the LORD,
        for he is good,
        for his steadfast love
        endures forever.

WHEN WE LOOK TO HUMANS

INSTEAD OF GOD FOR

HONOR AND PRAISE, EVEN

IN DOING GOOD DEEDS,

WHAT WE GAIN IS USELESS.

PSALM 119

THE GLORIES OF GOD'S LAW

1   Happy are those whose
        way is blameless,
        who walk in the law
        of the LORD.

a 118.12 Gk: Heb *were extinguished*
b 118.13 Gk Syr Jerome: Heb *You pushed
me hard*   c 118.24 Or *in him*   d 118.26 Or
*Blessed in the name of the LORD is the one
who comes*   e 118.27 Meaning of Heb
uncertain

2 Happy are those who keep
    his decrees,
  who seek him with their
    whole heart,
3 who also do no wrong,
  but walk in his ways.
4 You have commanded
    your precepts
  to be kept diligently.
5 O that my ways may be steadfast
  in keeping your statutes!
6 Then I shall not be put to shame,
  having my eyes fixed on all
    your commandments.
7 I will praise you with an
    upright heart,
  when I learn your righteous
    ordinances.
8 I will observe your statutes;
  do not utterly forsake me.

9 How can young people keep
    their way pure?
  By guarding it according
    to your word.
10 With my whole heart I seek you;
  do not let me stray from your
    commandments.
11 I treasure your word in my heart,
  so that I may not sin
    against you.
12 Blessed are you, O LORD;
  teach me your statutes.
13 With my lips I declare
  all the ordinances of
    your mouth.
14 I delight in the way of your decrees
  as much as in all riches.
15 I will meditate on your precepts,
  and fix my eyes on your ways.
16 I will delight in your statutes;
  I will not forget your word.

17 Deal bountifully with
    your servant,
  so that I may live and
    observe your word.
18 Open my eyes, so that I
    may behold
  wondrous things out
    of your law.
19 I live as an alien in the land;
  do not hide your
    commandments from me.
20 My soul is consumed
    with longing
  for your ordinances at all times.

21 You rebuke the insolent,
    accursed ones,
  who wander from your
    commandments;
22 take away from me their
    scorn and contempt,
  for I have kept your decrees.
23 Even though princes sit
    plotting against me,
  your servant will meditate
    on your statutes.
24 Your decrees are my delight,
  they are my counselors.

25 My soul clings to the dust;
  revive me according
    to your word.
26 When I told of my ways, you
    answered me;
  teach me your statutes.
27 Make me understand the way
    of your precepts,
  and I will meditate on your
    wondrous works.
28 My soul melts away for sorrow;
  strengthen me according
    to your word.
29 Put false ways far from me;
  and graciously teach
    me your law.
30 I have chosen the way of
    faithfulness;
  I set your ordinances
    before me.
31 I cling to your decrees, O LORD;
  let me not be put to shame.
32 I run the way of your
    commandments,
  for you enlarge my
    understanding.

33 Teach me, O LORD, the way
    of your statutes,
  and I will observe
    it to the end.
34 Give me understanding, that
    I may keep your law
  and observe it with my
    whole heart.
35 Lead me in the path of your
    commandments,
  for I delight in it.
36 Turn my heart to your decrees,
  and not to selfish gain.
37 Turn my eyes from looking
    at vanities;
  give me life in your ways.

38 Confirm to your servant
      your promise,
   which is for those who
      fear you.
39 Turn away the disgrace
      that I dread,
   for your ordinances are good.
40 See, I have longed for
      your precepts;
   in your righteousness
      give me life.

41 Let your steadfast love come
      to me, O LORD,
   your salvation according
      to your promise.
42 Then I shall have an answer for
      those who taunt me,
   for I trust in your word.
43 Do not take the word of truth
      utterly out of my mouth,
   for my hope is in your
      ordinances.
44 I will keep your law continually,
      forever and ever.
45 I shall walk at liberty,
   for I have sought your precepts.
46 I will also speak of your
      decrees before kings,
   and shall not be put to shame;
47 I find my delight in your
      commandments,
   because I love them.
48 I revere your commandments,
      which I love,
   and I will meditate on
      your statutes.

49 Remember your word to
      your servant,
   in which you have
      made me hope.
50 This is my comfort
      in my distress,
   that your promise
      gives me life.
51 The arrogant utterly deride me,
   but I do not turn away
      from your law.
52 When I think of your ordinances
      from of old,
   I take comfort, O LORD.
53 Hot indignation seizes me
      because of the wicked,
   those who forsake your law.
54 Your statutes have been my songs
   wherever I make my home.

55 I remember your name in
      the night, O LORD,
   and keep your law.
56 This blessing has fallen to me,
   for I have kept your precepts.

57 The LORD is my portion;
   I promise to keep your words.
58 I implore your favor with
      all my heart;
   be gracious to me according
      to your promise.
59 When I think of your ways,
   I turn my feet to your decrees;
60 I hurry and do not delay
   to keep your commandments.
61 Though the cords of the
      wicked ensnare me,
   I do not forget your law.
62 At midnight I rise to praise you,
   because of your righteous
      ordinances.
63 I am a companion of all
      who fear you,
   of those who keep your
      precepts.
64 The earth, O LORD, is full of
      your steadfast love;
   teach me your statutes.

65 You have dealt well with
      your servant,
   O LORD, according to
      your word.
66 Teach me good judgment
      and knowledge,
   for I believe in your
      commandments.
67 Before I was humbled I
      went astray,
   but now I keep your word.
68 You are good and do good;
   teach me your statutes.
69 The arrogant smear
      me with lies,
   but with my whole heart I
      keep your precepts.
70 Their hearts are fat and gross,
   but I delight in your law.
71 It is good for me that I
      was humbled,
   so that I might learn
      your statutes.
72 The law of your mouth is
      better to me
   than thousands of gold
      and silver pieces.

73 Your hands have made and
       fashioned me;
   give me understanding
       that I may learn your
       commandments.
74 Those who fear you shall see
       me and rejoice,
   because I have hoped
       in your word.
75 I know, O LORD, that your
       judgments are right,
   and that in faithfulness you
       have humbled me.
76 Let your steadfast love
       become my comfort
   according to your promise
       to your servant.
77 Let your mercy come to me,
       that I may live;
   for your law is my delight.
78 Let the arrogant be put to shame,
       because they have subverted
       me with guile;
   as for me, I will meditate
       on your precepts.
79 Let those who fear you
       turn to me,
   so that they may know
       your decrees.
80 May my heart be blameless
       in your statutes,
   so that I may not be
       put to shame.

81 My soul languishes for
       your salvation;
   I hope in your word.
82 My eyes fail with watching
       for your promise;
   I ask, "When will you
       comfort me?"
83 For I have become like a
       wineskin in the smoke,
   yet I have not forgotten
       your statutes.
84 How long must your
       servant endure?
   When will you judge those
       who persecute me?
85 The arrogant have dug
       pitfalls for me;
   they flout your law.
86 All your commandments
       are enduring;
   I am persecuted without
       cause; help me!
87 They have almost made an
       end of me on earth;
   but I have not forsaken
       your precepts.
88 In your steadfast love spare my life,
   so that I may keep the decrees
       of your mouth.
89 The LORD exists forever;
   your word is firmly fixed
       in heaven.
90 Your faithfulness endures to
       all generations;
   you have established the
       earth, and it stands fast.
91 By your appointment they
       stand today,
   for all things are your servants.

BIBLE IN LIFE

Now . . .

Psalm 119.60

When we sense God calling us to action, to tangibly show love to others by serving them, do we ever fall into the procrastination trap? Though we know what we should do, we harden our hearts against God and decide not to do it just yet. Perhaps we figure that we will wait for a more convenient time—until we finish college or settle into a comfortable job. Or perhaps we wait until we pay off a few bills or buy a house. Maybe we'll do it after we get our kids through school. Then we have to consider our grandchildren and make sure we are financially secure in our old age. Maybe when we retire, at 65 or so, will be the time to do what God is calling us to do. Of course, after retirement we'll need to work around the house a bit first and take up some hobbies. Before we know it, our life is over, and we've never even begun to carry out God's call to serve him and others. We must not fall prey to the deceptive idea that a more convenient time to serve God and others lies just around the corner. The best time to obey is today, before the opportunity passes us by.

92 If your law had not been
    my delight,
  I would have perished
    in my misery.
93 I will never forget your precepts,
  for by them you have
    given me life.
94 I am yours; save me,
  for I have sought your precepts.
95 The wicked lie in wait to
    destroy me,
  but I consider your decrees.
96 I have seen a limit to all
    perfection,
  but your commandment is
    exceedingly broad.

97 Oh, how I love your law!
  It is my meditation
    all day long.
98 Your commandment makes me
    wiser than my enemies,
  for it is always with me.
99 I have more understanding
    than all my teachers,
  for your decrees are my
    meditation.
100 I understand more than
    the aged,
  for I keep your precepts.
101 I hold back my feet from
    every evil way,
  in order to keep your word.
102 I do not turn away from
    your ordinances,
  for you have taught me.
103 How sweet are your words
    to my taste,
  sweeter than honey to
    my mouth!
104 Through your precepts I get
    understanding;
  therefore I hate every
    false way.

105 Your word is a lamp to my feet
  and a light to my path.
106 I have sworn an oath and
    confirmed it,
  to observe your righteous
    ordinances.
107 I am severely afflicted;
  give me life, O LORD,
    according to your word.
108 Accept my offerings of
    praise, O LORD,
  and teach me your ordinances.

109 I hold my life in my hand
    continually,
  but I do not forget your law.
110 The wicked have laid a
    snare for me,
  but I do not stray from
    your precepts.
111 Your decrees are my
    heritage forever;
  they are the joy of my heart.
112 I incline my heart to perform
    your statutes
  forever, to the end.

113 I hate the double-minded,
  but I love your law.
114 You are my hiding place
    and my shield;
  I hope in your word.
115 Go away from me,
    you evildoers,
  that I may keep the
    commandments
    of my God.
116 Uphold me according to your
    promise, that I may live,
  and let me not be put to
    shame in my hope.
117 Hold me up, that I may be safe
  and have regard for your
    statutes continually.
118 You spurn all who go astray
    from your statutes;
  for their cunning is in vain.
119 All the wicked of the earth
    you count as dross;
  therefore I love your decrees.
120 My flesh trembles
    for fear of you,
  and I am afraid of your
    judgments.

121 I have done what is just
    and right;
  do not leave me to my
    oppressors.
122 Guarantee your servant's
    well-being;
  do not let the godless
    oppress me.
123 My eyes fail from watching
    for your salvation,
  and for the fulfillment of your
    righteous promise.
124 Deal with your servant according
    to your steadfast love,
  and teach me your statutes.

125 I am your servant; give me
     understanding,
   so that I may know
     your decrees.
126 It is time for the LORD to act,
   for your law has been broken.
127 Truly I love your
     commandments
   more than gold, more
     than fine gold.
128 Truly I direct my steps by
     all your precepts;[a]
   I hate every false way.

129 Your decrees are wonderful;
   therefore my soul keeps them.
130 The unfolding of your
     words gives light;
   it imparts understanding
     to the simple.
131 With open mouth I pant,
   because I long for your
     commandments.
132 Turn to me and be
     gracious to me,
   as is your custom toward those
     who love your name.
133 Keep my steps steady according
     to your promise,
   and never let iniquity have
     dominion over me.
134 Redeem me from human
     oppression,
   that I may keep your precepts.
135 Make your face shine upon
     your servant,
   and teach me your statutes.
136 My eyes shed streams of tears
   because your law is not kept.

137 You are righteous, O LORD,
   and your judgments
     are right.
138 You have appointed your decrees
     in righteousness
   and in all faithfulness.
139 My zeal consumes me
   because my foes forget
     your words.
140 Your promise is well tried,
   and your servant loves it.
141 I am small and despised,
   yet I do not forget your
     precepts.
142 Your righteousness is an
     everlasting righteousness,
   and your law is the truth.

143 Trouble and anguish have
     come upon me,
   but your commandments
     are my delight.
144 Your decrees are righteous
     forever;
   give me understanding
     that I may live.

145 With my whole heart I cry;
     answer me, O LORD.
   I will keep your statutes.
146 I cry to you; save me,
   that I may observe
     your decrees.
147 I rise before dawn and
     cry for help;
   I put my hope in your words.
148 My eyes are awake before each
     watch of the night,
   that I may meditate on
     your promise.
149 In your steadfast love
     hear my voice;
   O LORD, in your justice
     preserve my life.
150 Those who persecute me with
     evil purpose draw near;
   they are far from your law.
151 Yet you are near, O LORD,
   and all your commandments
     are true.
152 Long ago I learned from
     your decrees
   that you have established
     them forever.

153 Look on my misery and
     rescue me,
   for I do not forget your law.
154 Plead my cause and redeem me;
   give me life according to
     your promise.
155 Salvation is far from the wicked,
   for they do not seek
     your statutes.
156 Great is your mercy, O LORD;
   give me life according
     to your justice.
157 Many are my persecutors
     and my adversaries,
   yet I do not swerve from
     your decrees.

a 119.128 Gk Jerome: Meaning of Heb
uncertain

158 I look at the faithless
 with disgust,
   because they do not keep
    your commands.
159 Consider how I love your
  precepts;
   preserve my life according
    to your steadfast love.
160 The sum of your word is truth;
  and every one of your
   righteous ordinances
    endures forever.

161 Princes persecute me
  without cause,
   but my heart stands in
    awe of your words.
162 I rejoice at your word
  like one who finds great spoil.
163 I hate and abhor falsehood,
  but I love your law.
164 Seven times a day I praise you
  for your righteous ordinances.
165 Great peace have those who
   love your law;
  nothing can make
    them stumble.
166 I hope for your salvation,
   O Lord,
  and I fulfill your
    commandments.
167 My soul keeps your decrees;
  I love them exceedingly.
168 I keep your precepts and decrees,
  for all my ways
    are before you.

169 Let my cry come before
   you, O Lord;
  give me understanding
    according to your word.

170 Let my supplication come
   before you;
  deliver me according to
    your promise.
171 My lips will pour forth praise,
   because you teach me
    your statutes.
172 My tongue will sing of
    your promise,
  for all your commandments
    are right.
173 Let your hand be ready to help me,
  for I have chosen your precepts.
174 I long for your salvation, O Lord,
  and your law is my delight.
175 Let me live that I may praise you,
  and let your ordinances
    help me.
176 I have gone astray like a
    lost sheep; seek out
    your servant,
  for I do not forget your
    commandments.

PSALM 120

PRAYER FOR DELIVERANCE FROM SLANDERERS

A Song of Ascents.

1 In my distress I cry to the Lord,
   that he may answer me:
2 "Deliver me, O Lord,
    from lying lips,
    from a deceitful tongue."

3 What shall be given to you?
   And what more shall
    be done to you,
    you deceitful tongue?

⊢‖ BIBLE IN LIFE ▷

Wandering   *Psalm 119.176*

The imagery of God's people as sheep appears throughout the Bible. How easily we stray from the protection of our shepherd, our Savior. The preoccupation with daily tasks and with our own selfish ambitions—the accumulation of money, social standing, earthly success—can lead us astray and separate us from a proper relationship with Christ. All of these kinds of distractions are like the thieves that come in and steal away the essence of our relationship with Christ (see John 10.9–11). Our intimacy with Christ will prevent us from following someone or something that comes into our lives by subterfuge, promising benefits but leading us to an empty life. With Jesus as our Shepherd, we will find redemption, hope and peace.

4 A warrior's sharp arrows,
   with glowing coals of
      the broom tree!

5 Woe is me, that I am an
      alien in Meshech,
   that I must live among
      the tents of Kedar.
6 Too long have I had my dwelling
   among those who hate peace.
7 I am for peace;
   but when I speak,
      they are for war.

PSALM 121

ASSURANCE OF GOD'S PROTECTION

A Song of Ascents.

1 I lift up my eyes to the hills—
   from where will my help come?
2 My help comes from the LORD,
   who made heaven and earth.

3 He will not let your foot
      be moved;
   he who keeps you will
      not slumber.

PONDER

I lift up my eyes to the hills—from
where will my help come?
—Psalm 121.1

PRAY

Creator God, Maker of heaven and
earth, we pause for a few minutes and
look more deeply into the messages
of the psalms. And we pray that
through the blessings of these words,
our hearts might be permanently
impressed with the truth of your
abiding love and protection, for your
majesty and grace. Thank you for
watching over our lives. We extend
our thanks, our praise and our faith
in our Savior, Jesus Christ. Amen.

---

4 He who keeps Israel
   will neither slumber nor sleep.

5 The LORD is your keeper;
   the LORD is your shade at
      your right hand.
6 The sun shall not strike
      you by day,
   nor the moon by night.

7 The LORD will keep you
      from all evil;
   he will keep your life.
8 The LORD will keep
   your going out and
      your coming in
   from this time on and
      forevermore.

PSALM 122

SONG OF PRAISE AND PRAYER FOR JERUSALEM

A Song of Ascents. Of David.

1 I was glad when they said to me,
   "Let us go to the house
      of the LORD!"
2 Our feet are standing
   within your gates, O Jerusalem.

3 Jerusalem—built as a city
   that is bound firmly together.
4 To it the tribes go up,
   the tribes of the LORD,
   as was decreed for Israel,
   to give thanks to the
      name of the LORD.
5 For there the thrones for
      judgment were set up,
   the thrones of the house
      of David.

6 Pray for the peace of Jerusalem:
   "May they prosper
      who love you.
7 Peace be within your walls,
   and security within
      your towers."
8 For the sake of my relatives
      and friends
   I will say, "Peace be
      within you."
9 For the sake of the house of
      the LORD our God,
   I will seek your good.

PEACE WITHIN

Pray for the peace of Jerusalem: "May they prosper who love you. Peace be within your walls, and security within your towers." For the sake of my relatives and friends I will say, "Peace be within you."

—Psalm 122.6–8

This psalm is called a song of ascents because it was written for those who were making a pilgrimage to Jerusalem to offer their sacrifices at the temple built on a hill above the city. All Israelites, regardless of their tribe, were required to go to Jerusalem at certain times throughout the year to offer sacrifices to God, so this song, indeed the whole experience, would have been familiar to each of them.

As we read this psalm, one word that likely stands out is peace. In Old Testament times this word meant much more than the absence of conflict, although it certainly encompassed that. It referred to wholeness in general—to health, moral integrity and a sense of security. Pilgrims were to pray for the peace of Jerusalem because it was the religious and political heart of the nation. If Jerusalem was not at peace, the nation could not truly be at peace.

Peace is a word that is still crucial to Christians today. Though we may not all be threatened with political or physical conflict, we experience turmoil and personal conflict in all kinds of situations. We may fear that we will not get an adequate job or that we will not make enough money. We may fear that we will not find a good spouse or that we might lose someone we love. We deal with interpersonal conflict with people in our families, at work, and in our communities. All these conflicts and fears rob our hearts of peace and demonstrate a lack of trust in God.

But it doesn't have to be that way. Paul assures believers: "Do not worry about anything, but in everything by prayer and supplication with thanksgiving let your requests be made known to God. And the peace of God, which surpasses all understanding, will guard your hearts and your minds in Christ Jesus" (Philippians 4.6–7). We don't need to fear what may happen to us, because we know that God is all-powerful and loves us more than we comprehend. We can bring our conflicts, our anger and our struggles to him. Since we can be confident that God hears our requests and will answer them in a way that is best for us, we can cast aside our anxiety. Just as the peace of Jerusalem was dependent on prayer, so our true peace comes from our willingness to pray to God about all things.

Going Deeper

- What kinds of concerns most frequently occupy your mind?
- If you had absolute assurance that your concerns would be assuaged, how would that change your life? How does this relate to God's giving you this exact promise?

PSALM 123

SUPPLICATION FOR MERCY

A Song of Ascents.

1 To you I lift up my eyes,
   O you who are enthroned
      in the heavens!
2 As the eyes of servants
      look to the hand of
         their master,
   as the eyes of a maid
      to the hand of her mistress,
   so our eyes look to the
      LORD our God,
   until he has mercy upon us.

3 Have mercy upon us, O LORD,
      have mercy upon us,
   for we have had more than
      enough of contempt.
4 Our soul has had more
         than its fill
      of the scorn of those
   who are at ease,
      of the contempt of the proud.

PSALM 124

THANKSGIVING FOR ISRAEL'S DELIVERANCE

A Song of Ascents. Of David.

1 If it had not been the LORD
      who was on our side
   —let Israel now say—
2 if it had not been the LORD
      who was on our side,
   when our enemies attacked us,
3 then they would have
      swallowed us up alive,
   when their anger was
      kindled against us;
4 then the flood would have
      swept us away,
   the torrent would have
      gone over us;
5 then over us would have gone
      the raging waters.

6 Blessed be the LORD,
   who has not given us
      as prey to their teeth.
7 We have escaped like a bird
      from the snare of the fowlers;
   the snare is broken,
      and we have escaped.

8 Our help is in the name
      of the LORD,
   who made heaven and earth.

PSALM 125

THE SECURITY OF GOD'S PEOPLE

A Song of Ascents.

1 Those who trust in the LORD
      are like Mount Zion,
   which cannot be moved,
      but abides forever.
2 As the mountains surround
         Jerusalem,
   so the LORD surrounds
         his people,
   from this time on and
         forevermore.
3 For the scepter of wickedness
      shall not rest
   on the land allotted to
      the righteous,
   so that the righteous might
      not stretch out
   their hands to do wrong.
4 Do good, O LORD, to those
      who are good,
   and to those who are upright
      in their hearts.
5 But those who turn aside to
      their own crooked ways
   the LORD will lead away
      with evildoers.
   Peace be upon Israel!

WE MUST REMEMBER THAT

THERE IS NO OBSTACLE

WE CANNOT OVERCOME,

NO PROBLEM WE CANNOT

SOLVE, NO GOAL WE

CANNOT REACH—PROVIDED

IT IS COMPATIBLE WITH

THE WILL OF GOD.

PSALM 126

A HARVEST OF JOY

A Song of Ascents.

1 When the LORD restored the
fortunes of Zion,[a]
we were like those who dream.
2 Then our mouth was filled
with laughter,
and our tongue with
shouts of joy;
then it was said among
the nations,
"The LORD has done great
things for them."
3 The LORD has done great
things for us,
and we rejoiced.

4 Restore our fortunes, O LORD,
like the watercourses
in the Negeb.
5 May those who sow in tears
reap with shouts of joy.
6 Those who go out weeping,
bearing the seed for sowing,
shall come home with
shouts of joy,
carrying their sheaves.

PSALM 127

GOD'S BLESSINGS IN THE HOME

A Song of Ascents. Of Solomon.

1 Unless the LORD builds
the house,
those who build it
labor in vain.
Unless the LORD guards the city,
the guard keeps watch in vain.
2 It is in vain that you
rise up early
and go late to rest,
eating the bread of anxious toil;
for he gives sleep to
his beloved.[b]

3 Sons are indeed a heritage
from the LORD,
the fruit of the womb a reward.
4 Like arrows in the hand
of a warrior
are the sons of one's youth.
5 Happy is the man who has
his quiver full of them.

He shall not be put to shame
when he speaks with his
enemies in the gate.

PSALM 128

THE HAPPY HOME OF THE FAITHFUL

A Song of Ascents.

1 Happy is everyone who
fears the LORD,
who walks in his ways.
2 You shall eat the fruit of the
labor of your hands;
you shall be happy, and it
shall go well with you.

3 Your wife will be like a
fruitful vine
within your house;
your children will be like
olive shoots
around your table.
4 Thus shall the man be blessed
who fears the LORD.

5 The LORD bless you from Zion.
May you see the prosperity
of Jerusalem
all the days of your life.
6 May you see your children's
children.
Peace be upon Israel!

PSALM 129

PRAYER FOR THE DOWNFALL OF ISRAEL'S ENEMIES

A Song of Ascents.

1 "Often have they attacked me
from my youth"
—let Israel now say—
2 "often have they attacked me
from my youth,
yet they have not prevailed
against me.
3 The plowers plowed on my back;
they made their furrows long."

a 126.1 Or *brought back those who returned
to Zion* b 127.2 Or *for he provides for his
beloved during sleep*

⁴ The LORD is righteous;
    he has cut the cords of
        the wicked.
⁵ May all who hate Zion
    be put to shame and
        turned backward.
⁶ Let them be like the grass
        on the housetops
    that withers before
        it grows up,
⁷ with which reapers do not
        fill their hands
    or binders of sheaves their arms,
⁸ while those who pass by do not say,
    "The blessing of the LORD
        be upon you!
    We bless you in the name
        of the LORD!"

PSALM 130

WAITING FOR DIVINE REDEMPTION

A Song of Ascents.

¹ Out of the depths I cry to
        you, O LORD.
² Lord, hear my voice!
    Let your ears be attentive
    to the voice of my supplications!

³ If you, O LORD, should
        mark iniquities,
    Lord, who could stand?
⁴ But there is forgiveness with you,
    so that you may be revered.

⁵ I wait for the LORD, my soul waits,
    and in his word I hope;

⁶ my soul waits for the Lord
    more than those who watch
        for the morning,
    more than those who watch
        for the morning.

⁷ O Israel, hope in the LORD!
    For with the LORD there
        is steadfast love,
    and with him is great
        power to redeem.
⁸ It is he who will redeem Israel
    from all its iniquities.

PSALM 131

SONG OF QUIET TRUST

A Song of Ascents. Of David.

¹ O LORD, my heart is not lifted up,
    my eyes are not raised
        too high;
    I do not occupy myself
        with things
    too great and too
        marvelous for me.
² But I have calmed and
        quieted my soul,
    like a weaned child with
        its mother;
    my soul is like the weaned
        child that is with me.ᵃ

³ O Israel, hope in the LORD
    from this time on and
        forevermore.

ᵃ **131.2** Or *my soul within me is like a weaned child*

⊣ **BIBLE IN LIFE** ▷

Forgiven   Psalm 130.1–8

We cannot have true spiritual or emotional health unless we believe that God forgives us. If we live with permanent guilt, feeling that we cannot be forgiven, then we are spiritually and emotionally crippled. When we confess and receive God's forgiveness, we have hope, as Psalm 130 tells us. God demonstrated forgiveness in a vivid and beautiful way by sending Christ to take the punishment for our sins. He broke down the barriers between us and God so we can renew our relationship with God and be reconciled with God, trusting we are forgiven no matter how badly we may have acted. God loves us in spite of all our defects and doesn't keep track of our iniquities (see verse 3). And we are to do the same—to love and forgive others.

PSALM 132

THE ETERNAL DWELLING OF GOD IN ZION

A Song of Ascents.

1 O LORD, remember in
        David's favor
    all the hardships he endured;
2 how he swore to the LORD
        and vowed to the Mighty
            One of Jacob,
3 "I will not enter my house
        or get into my bed;
4 I will not give sleep to my eyes
        or slumber to my eyelids,
5 until I find a place for the LORD,
        a dwelling place for the
            Mighty One of Jacob."

6 We heard of it in Ephrathah;
        we found it in the
            fields of Jaar.
7 "Let us go to his dwelling place;
        let us worship at
            his footstool."

8 Rise up, O LORD, and go to
        your resting place,
    you and the ark of
        your might.
9 Let your priests be clothed
        with righteousness,
    and let your faithful
        shout for joy.
10 For your servant David's sake
        do not turn away the face of
            your anointed one.

11 The LORD swore to David
        a sure oath
    from which he will not
        turn back:
    "One of the sons of your body
        I will set on your throne.
12 If your sons keep my covenant
        and my decrees that I
            shall teach them,
    their sons also, forevermore,
        shall sit on your throne."

13 For the LORD has chosen Zion;
        he has desired it for his
            habitation:
14 "This is my resting
        place forever;
    here I will reside, for I
        have desired it.

15 I will abundantly bless
        its provisions;
    I will satisfy its poor
        with bread.
16 Its priests I will clothe
        with salvation,
    and its faithful will
        shout for joy.
17 There I will cause a horn to
        sprout up for David;
    I have prepared a lamp for
        my anointed one.
18 His enemies I will clothe
        with disgrace,
    but on him, his crown
        will gleam."

PSALM 133

THE BLESSEDNESS OF UNITY

A Song of Ascents.

1 How very good and pleasant it is
        when kindred live
            together in unity!
2 It is like the precious oil
        on the head,
    running down
        upon the beard,
    on the beard of Aaron,
        running down over the
            collar of his robes.
3 It is like the dew of Hermon,
        which falls on the
            mountains of Zion.
    For there the LORD ordained
        his blessing,
    life forevermore.

PSALM 134

PRAISE IN THE NIGHT

A Song of Ascents.

1 Come, bless the LORD, all you
        servants of the LORD,
    who stand by night in the
        house of the LORD!
2 Lift up your hands to the
        holy place,
    and bless the LORD.

3 May the LORD, maker of
        heaven and earth,
    bless you from Zion.

PSALM 135

PRAISE FOR GOD'S GOODNESS AND MIGHT

1 Praise the LORD!
   Praise the name of the LORD;
   give praise, O servants
      of the LORD,
2 you that stand in the house
      of the LORD,
   in the courts of the house
      of our God.
3 Praise the LORD, for the
      LORD is good;
   sing to his name, for
      he is gracious.
4 For the LORD has chosen
      Jacob for himself,
   Israel as his own possession.

5 For I know that the LORD is great;
   our Lord is above all gods.
6 Whatever the LORD
      pleases he does,
   in heaven and on earth,
   in the seas and all deeps.
7 He it is who makes the clouds rise
      at the end of the earth;
   he makes lightnings
      for the rain
   and brings out the wind
      from his storehouses.

8 He it was who struck down the
      firstborn of Egypt,
   both human beings
      and animals;

9 he sent signs and wonders
      into your midst, O Egypt,
   against Pharaoh and all
      his servants.
10 He struck down many nations
      and killed mighty kings—
11 Sihon, king of the Amorites,
   and Og, king of Bashan,
   and all the kingdoms
      of Canaan—
12 and gave their land
      as a heritage,
   a heritage to his people Israel.

13 Your name, O LORD,
      endures forever,
   your renown, O LORD,
      throughout all ages.
14 For the LORD will vindicate
      his people,
   and have compassion
      on his servants.

15 The idols of the nations are
      silver and gold,
   the work of human hands.
16 They have mouths, but they
      do not speak;
   they have eyes, but they
      do not see;
17 they have ears, but they
      do not hear,
   and there is no breath
      in their mouths.
18 Those who make them
   and all who trust them
      shall become like them.

┤ BIBLE IN LIFE ▷

Living in Unity

Psalm 133.1

It is "good and pleasant" for God's people to live in unity. The psalmist knew this; we know it too. But of all the historic failures of the Christian church, disunity is one of the most prevalent. We have failed to embrace the life, hope and unity that Christ offers us. Because of our inability—through weakness, lack of courage, lack of strength—to control our own tendency toward divisiveness, selfishness and lack of forgiveness, we have deprived ourselves of unity. It can be difficult for us to create a spirit of unity with those who are different from us, with those who disagree with us or with those who have injured us in some way. But because of God's free gift to us and Christ's sacrifice to save us from our own sinfulness, we should recognize that we are one (see John 17.20–23). Through the Spirit, we are to be unified in the body of Christ. No material or substantial differences among us should keep us from being filled with Christian love and a desire to cooperate with one another in Jesus' name.

19 O house of Israel, bless the LORD!
    O house of Aaron, bless
        the LORD!
20 O house of Levi,
        bless the LORD!
    You that fear the LORD,
        bless the LORD!
21 Blessed be the LORD
        from Zion,
    he who resides in Jerusalem.
    Praise the LORD!

PSALM 136

GOD'S WORK IN CREATION
AND IN HISTORY

1 O give thanks to the LORD,
    for he is good,
    for his steadfast love
        endures forever.
2 O give thanks to the
        God of gods,
    for his steadfast love
        endures forever.
3 O give thanks to the
        Lord of lords,
    for his steadfast love
        endures forever;

4 who alone does great wonders,
    for his steadfast love
        endures forever;
5 who by understanding made
        the heavens,
    for his steadfast love
        endures forever;
6 who spread out the earth
        on the waters,
    for his steadfast love
        endures forever;
7 who made the great lights,
    for his steadfast love
        endures forever;
8 the sun to rule over the day,
    for his steadfast love
        endures forever;
9 the moon and stars to rule
        over the night,
    for his steadfast love
        endures forever;

10 who struck Egypt through
        their firstborn,
    for his steadfast love
        endures forever;

11 and brought Israel out from
        among them,
    for his steadfast love
        endures forever;
12 with a strong hand and an
        outstretched arm,
    for his steadfast love
        endures forever;
13 who divided the Red
        Sea[a] in two,
    for his steadfast love
        endures forever;
14 and made Israel pass through
        the midst of it,
    for his steadfast love
        endures forever;
15 but overthrew Pharaoh and his
        army in the Red Sea,[a]
    for his steadfast love
        endures forever;
16 who led his people through
        the wilderness,
    for his steadfast love
        endures forever;
17 who struck down
        great kings,
    for his steadfast love
        endures forever;
18 and killed famous kings,
    for his steadfast love
        endures forever;
19 Sihon, king of the Amorites,
    for his steadfast love
        endures forever;
20 and Og, king of Bashan,
    for his steadfast love
        endures forever;
21 and gave their land
        as a heritage,
    for his steadfast love
        endures forever;
22 a heritage to his
        servant Israel,
    for his steadfast love
        endures forever.

23 It is he who remembered us
        in our low estate,
    for his steadfast love
        endures forever;
24 and rescued us from
        our foes,
    for his steadfast love
        endures forever;

a 136.13,15 Or *Sea of Reeds*

25 who gives food to all flesh,
for his steadfast love
endures forever.

26 O give thanks to the God
of heaven,
for his steadfast love
endures forever.

PSALM 137

LAMENT OVER THE DESTRUCTION OF JERUSALEM

1 By the rivers of Babylon—
there we sat down and
there we wept
when we remembered Zion.
2 On the willows[a] there
we hung up our harps.
3 For there our captors
asked us for songs,
and our tormentors asked
for mirth, saying,
"Sing us one of the
songs of Zion!"

4 How could we sing the
Lord's song
in a foreign land?
5 If I forget you, O Jerusalem,
let my right
hand wither!
6 Let my tongue cling to the
roof of my mouth,
if I do not remember you,
if I do not set Jerusalem
above my highest joy.

7 Remember, O Lord, against
the Edomites
the day of Jerusalem's fall,
how they said, "Tear it down!
Tear it down!
Down to its foundations!"
8 O daughter Babylon, you
devastator![b]
Happy shall they be who
pay you back
what you have
done to us!
9 Happy shall they be who take
your little ones
and dash them against
the rock!

PSALM 138

THANKSGIVING AND PRAISE

Of David.

1 I give you thanks, O Lord,
with my whole heart;
before the gods I sing
your praise;
2 I bow down toward your
holy temple
and give thanks to your name
for your steadfast love
and your faithfulness;
for you have exalted your
name and your word
above everything.[c]
3 On the day I called, you
answered me,
you increased my
strength of soul.[d]

4 All the kings of the earth shall
praise you, O Lord,
for they have heard the
words of your mouth.
5 They shall sing of the ways
of the Lord,
for great is the glory
of the Lord.
6 For though the Lord is high,
he regards the lowly;
but the haughty he perceives
from far away.

7 Though I walk in the midst
of trouble,
you preserve me against the
wrath of my enemies;
you stretch out
your hand,
and your right hand
delivers me.
8 The Lord will fulfill his
purpose for me;
your steadfast love, O Lord,
endures forever.
Do not forsake the work
of your hands.

---

a 137.2 Or *poplars*   b 137.8 Or *you who
are devastated*   c 138.2 Cn: Heb *you have
exalted your word above all your name*
d 138.3 Syr Compare Gk Tg: Heb *you made
me arrogant in my soul with strength*

PSALM 139

THE INESCAPABLE GOD

To the leader. Of David. A Psalm.

1 O LORD, you have searched
      me and known me.
2 You know when I sit down
      and when I rise up;
   you discern my thoughts
      from far away.
3 You search out my path and
      my lying down,
   and are acquainted with
      all my ways.
4 Even before a word is on
      my tongue,
   O LORD, you know it
      completely.
5 You hem me in, behind
      and before,
   and lay your hand upon me.
6 Such knowledge is too
      wonderful for me;
   it is so high that I
      cannot attain it.

7 Where can I go from your spirit?
   Or where can I flee from
      your presence?
8 If I ascend to heaven,
      you are there;
   if I make my bed in Sheol,
      you are there.
9 If I take the wings of the morning
   and settle at the farthest
      limits of the sea,
10 even there your hand
      shall lead me,
   and your right hand shall
      hold me fast.
11 If I say, "Surely the darkness
      shall cover me,
   and the light around me
      become night,"
12 even the darkness is not
      dark to you;
   the night is as bright
      as the day,
   for darkness is as light to you.

13 For it was you who formed
      my inward parts;
   you knit me together in
      my mother's womb.
14 I praise you, for I am fearfully
      and wonderfully made.
   Wonderful are your works;

that I know very well.
15 My frame was not hidden
      from you,
   when I was being made in secret,
      intricately woven in the
      depths of the earth.
16 Your eyes beheld my unformed
      substance.
   In your book were written
      all the days that were
      formed for me,
   when none of them as
      yet existed.
17 How weighty to me are your
      thoughts, O God!
   How vast is the sum of them!
18 I try to count them—they are
      more than the sand;
   I come to the end[a]—I am
      still with you.

OUR MOST MEANINGFUL

SOURCE OF STRENGTH IS

THE REALITY OF GOD'S

PRESENCE. WE NEED NEVER

FEEL ALONE OR HELPLESS.

19 O that you would kill the
      wicked, O God,
   and that the bloodthirsty
      would depart from me—
20 those who speak of you
      maliciously,
   and lift themselves up
      against you for evil![b]
21 Do I not hate those who hate
      you, O LORD?
   And do I not loathe those who
      rise up against you?
22 I hate them with perfect hatred;
   I count them my enemies.
23 Search me, O God, and
      know my heart;
   test me and know my
      thoughts.

a 139.18 Or *I awake*   b 139.20 Cn: Meaning
of Heb uncertain

24 See if there is any wicked[a]
    way in me,
  and lead me in the way
    everlasting.[b]

PSALM 140

PRAYER FOR DELIVERANCE
FROM ENEMIES

To the leader. A Psalm of David.

1 Deliver me, O LORD, from
    evildoers;
  protect me from those
    who are violent,
2 who plan evil things in
    their minds
  and stir up wars continually.
3 They make their tongue
    sharp as a snake's,
  and under their lips is the
    venom of vipers.   *Selah*

4 Guard me, O LORD, from the
    hands of the wicked;
  protect me from the violent
  who have planned my
    downfall.
5 The arrogant have hidden
    a trap for me,
  and with cords they have
    spread a net,[c]
  along the road they have set
    snares for me.   *Selah*

6 I say to the LORD, "You
    are my God;
  give ear, O LORD, to the voice
    of my supplications."
7 O LORD, my Lord, my
    strong deliverer,
  you have covered my head
    in the day of battle.
8 Do not grant, O LORD, the
    desires of the wicked;
  do not further their evil
    plot.[d]   *Selah*

9 Those who surround me lift
    up their heads;[e]
  let the mischief of their lips
    overwhelm them!
10 Let burning coals
    fall on them!
  Let them be flung into pits,
    no more to rise!

11 Do not let the slanderer be
    established in the land;
  let evil speedily hunt
    down the violent!

12 I know that the LORD maintains
    the cause of the needy,
  and executes justice
    for the poor.
13 Surely the righteous shall give
    thanks to your name;
  the upright shall live in
    your presence.

PSALM 141

PRAYER FOR PRESERVATION
FROM EVIL

A Psalm of David.

1 I call upon you, O LORD; come
    quickly to me;
  give ear to my voice when
    I call to you.
2 Let my prayer be counted as
    incense before you,
  and the lifting up of my hands
    as an evening sacrifice.

3 Set a guard over my mouth,
    O LORD;
  keep watch over the
    door of my lips.
4 Do not turn my heart to any evil,
    to busy myself with
      wicked deeds
  in company with those who
    work iniquity;
  do not let me eat of
    their delicacies.

5 Let the righteous strike me;
    let the faithful correct me.
  Never let the oil of the wicked
    anoint my head,[f]
  for my prayer is continually[g]
    against their wicked deeds.

---

a 139.24 Heb *hurtful*   b 139.24 Or
the ancient way. Compare Jer 6.16
c 140.5 Or *they have spread cords as a
net*   d 140.8 Heb adds *they are exalted*
e 140.9 Cn Compare Gk: Heb *those
who surround me are uplifted in head*;
Heb divides verses 8 and 9 differently
f 141.5 Gk: Meaning of Heb uncertain
g 141.5 Cn: Heb *for continually and my prayer*

6 When they are given over
    to those who shall
    condemn them,
    then they shall learn that my
    words were pleasant.
7 Like a rock that one breaks apart
    and shatters on the land,
    so shall their bones be strewn
    at the mouth of Sheol.[a]

8 But my eyes are turned toward
    you, O GOD, my Lord;
    in you I seek refuge; do not
    leave me defenseless.
9 Keep me from the trap that
    they have laid for me,
    and from the snares
    of evildoers.
10 Let the wicked fall into
    their own nets,
    while I alone escape.

PSALM 142

PRAYER FOR DELIVERANCE
FROM PERSECUTORS

*A Maskil of David. When he
was in the cave. A Prayer.*

1 With my voice I cry to the LORD;
    with my voice I make
    supplication to the LORD.
2 I pour out my complaint
    before him;
    I tell my trouble before him.
3 When my spirit is faint,
    you know my way.

In the path where I walk
    they have hidden a trap for me.
4 Look on my right hand and see—
    there is no one who takes
    notice of me;
no refuge remains to me;
    no one cares for me.

5 I cry to you, O LORD;
    I say, "You are my refuge,
    my portion in the land
    of the living."
6 Give heed to my cry,
    for I am brought very low.

Save me from my persecutors,
    for they are too
    strong for me.

7 Bring me out of prison,
    so that I may give thanks
    to your name.
The righteous will surround me,
    for you will deal bountifully
    with me.

GOD KNOWS THAT THE

RIGHTEOUS EXPERIENCE PAIN.

PSALM 143

PRAYER FOR DELIVERANCE
FROM ENEMIES

A Psalm of David.

1 Hear my prayer, O LORD;
    give ear to my supplications
    in your faithfulness;
    answer me in your
    righteousness.
2 Do not enter into judgment
    with your servant,
    for no one living is righteous
    before you.

3 For the enemy has pursued me,
    crushing my life to the ground,
    making me sit in darkness
    like those long dead.
4 Therefore my spirit faints
    within me;
    my heart within me
    is appalled.

5 I remember the days of old,
    I think about all your deeds,
    I meditate on the works
    of your hands.
6 I stretch out my hands to you;
    my soul thirsts for you like a
    parched land.   *Selah*

7 Answer me quickly, O LORD;
    my spirit fails.
Do not hide your face from me,
    or I shall be like those who
    go down to the Pit.

[a] **141.7** Meaning of Heb of verses 5–7 is
uncertain

8 Let me hear of your steadfast
        love in the morning,
    for in you I put my trust.
    Teach me the way I should go,
        for to you I lift up my soul.

9 Save me, O LORD, from
        my enemies;
    I have fled to you for refuge.[a]
10 Teach me to do your will,
        for you are my God.
    Let your good spirit lead me
        on a level path.

11 For your name's sake, O LORD,
        preserve my life.
    In your righteousness bring
        me out of trouble.
12 In your steadfast love cut
        off my enemies,
    and destroy all my adversaries,
        for I am your servant.

PSALM 144

PRAYER FOR NATIONAL
DELIVERANCE AND SECURITY
Of David.

1 Blessed be the LORD, my rock,
        who trains my hands for war,
        and my fingers for battle;
2 my rock[b] and my fortress,
        my stronghold and
        my deliverer,
    my shield, in whom I take
        refuge,
    who subdues the peoples[c]
        under me.

3 O LORD, what are human beings
        that you regard them,
    or mortals that you
        think of them?
4 They are like a breath;
        their days are like a
        passing shadow.

5 Bow your heavens, O LORD,
        and come down;
    touch the mountains so
        that they smoke.
6 Make the lightning flash
        and scatter them;
    send out your arrows
        and rout them.

7 Stretch out your hand
        from on high;
    set me free and rescue me from
        the mighty waters,
    from the hand of aliens,
8 whose mouths speak lies,
    and whose right hands are false.

9 I will sing a new song to
        you, O God;
    upon a ten-stringed harp
        I will play to you,
10 the one who gives victory to kings,
        who rescues his servant David.
11 Rescue me from the cruel sword,
    and deliver me from the
        hand of aliens,
    whose mouths speak lies,
    and whose right hands are false.

12 May our sons in their youth
        be like plants full grown,
    our daughters like corner pillars,
        cut for the building of a palace.
13 May our barns be filled,
        with produce of every kind;
    may our sheep increase
        by thousands,
    by tens of thousands
        in our fields,
14 and may our cattle be
        heavy with young.
    May there be no breach in
        the walls,[d] no exile,
    and no cry of distress
        in our streets.

15 Happy are the people to whom
        such blessings fall;
    happy are the people whose
        God is the LORD.

PSALM 145

THE GREATNESS AND THE
GOODNESS OF GOD
Praise. Of David.

1 I will extol you, my God and King,
        and bless your name
        forever and ever.

[a] 143.9 One Heb Ms Gk: MT *to you I have
hidden* [b] 144.2 With 18.2 and 2 Sam 22.2:
Heb *my steadfast love* [c] 144.2 Heb Mss Syr
Aquila Jerome: MT *my people* [d] 144.14 Heb
lacks *in the walls*

² Every day I will bless you,
    and praise your name
        forever and ever.
³ Great is the LORD, and greatly
        to be praised;
    his greatness is unsearchable.

⁴ One generation shall laud your
        works to another,
    and shall declare your
        mighty acts.
⁵ On the glorious splendor
        of your majesty,
    and on your wondrous
        works, I will meditate.
⁶ The might of your awesome deeds
        shall be proclaimed,
    and I will declare your
        greatness.
⁷ They shall celebrate the fame of
        your abundant goodness,
    and shall sing aloud of
        your righteousness.

⁸ The LORD is gracious
        and merciful,
    slow to anger and abounding
        in steadfast love.
⁹ The LORD is good to all,
    and his compassion is over
        all that he has made.

¹⁰ All your works shall give thanks
        to you, O LORD,
    and all your faithful
        shall bless you.
¹¹ They shall speak of the glory
        of your kingdom,
    and tell of your power,
¹² to make known to all people
        your\ mighty deeds,
    and the glorious splendor
        of your\ kingdom.
¹³ Your kingdom is an everlasting
        kingdom,
    and your dominion
        endures throughout
        all generations.

The LORD is faithful in
    all his words,
    and gracious in all
        his deeds.\
¹⁴ The LORD upholds all who
        are falling,
    and raises up all who are
        bowed down.

¹⁵ The eyes of all look to you,
    and you give them their
        food in due season.
¹⁶ You open your hand,
    satisfying the desire of
        every living thing.
¹⁷ The LORD is just in all his ways,
    and kind in all his doings.
¹⁸ The LORD is near to all who
        call on him,
    to all who call on him in truth.
¹⁹ He fulfills the desire of all
        who fear him;
    he also hears their cry,
        and saves them.
²⁰ The LORD watches over all
        who love him,
    but all the wicked he
        will destroy.

²¹ My mouth will speak the
        praise of the LORD,
    and all flesh will bless his holy
        name forever and ever.

PSALM 146

PRAISE FOR GOD'S HELP

¹ Praise the LORD!
    Praise the LORD, O my soul!
² I will praise the LORD as
        long as I live;
    I will sing praises to my
        God all my life long.

³ Do not put your trust in princes,
    in mortals, in whom
        there is no help.
⁴ When their breath departs, they
        return to the earth;
    on that very day their
        plans perish.

⁵ Happy are those whose help
        is the God of Jacob,
    whose hope is in the
        LORD their God,
⁶ who made heaven and earth,
    the sea, and all that is in them;

ᵃ 145.12 Gk Jerome Syr: Heb *his*
ᵇ 145.12 Heb *his*   ᶜ 145.13 These two lines
supplied by Q Ms Gk Syr

OUR TRUST AND HOPE

Happy are those whose help is the God of Jacob, whose hope is in the LORD their God.

—Psalm 146.5

As we look around us for a foundation on which to build a life, all too often we turn to things we perceive as certain and sure, only to find that they ultimately fail us. It may be a political leader who, we hope, will finally bring about changes that are truly needed in our country. It may be a life goal for us, like the final payment on our home mortgage. It may be a career. In the end, however, all these things will eventually prove to be shifting sand for the foundation of our life.

Who or what, then, can we turn to? The psalmist clearly tells us: our trust and hope is to rest in the Lord, our God, the creator of the universe. The psalmist calls us to trust in the God who gave us life, to whom we owe our very existence, our talents, our feelings, our blessings, our challenges, our achievements. He gives us love itself, and he never changes. He will never die, and one day he will return to take us to be with him in heaven.

But what is this great, omnipotent, unchanging God really like? What kind of God is the psalmist calling us to trust in? Verses 7–9 beautifully describe him as a God who is not primarily interested in power and glory but rather in giving food to the poor, in liberating the oppressed, in protecting the defenseless. He is a God who loves to bring good things to those who most need it and free people from the things that enslave them. In fact, when we look at the life of Jesus, who represents God the Father perfectly for us (see John 14.9–10), what do we see? Someone who desired to be in the company of the rich? Of the powerful? Of the prestigious? No; instead, he sought out the poor, the despised, the physically impaired. If Jesus were living on earth today, he very well might live in a government housing project—or maybe among the oppressed in some nation where people live in great need.

As we place our trust in our powerful, loving, unchanging God, we ourselves gain the strength and ability to carry out Jesus' command to emulate him in our daily lives (see Matthew 16.24). We can work to alleviate the sufferings of those lying on the street under a newspaper or who turn eyes hungry for friendship toward us as we walk by (cf. Luke 10.25–37). We can reach out to children who come from homes where there is little love and nurturing. We can begin to break down the shell of protection that we have built around ourselves and reach out to help others in all kinds of situations. Serving others is one way that we can imitate the psalmist and praise our great God for his goodness to us.

Going Deeper

- What are some things that Jesus did on earth that resemble the psalmist's description of God's care for his people?
- What are some ways you can praise God by serving others?

who keeps faith forever;
7 who executes justice for
the oppressed;
who gives food to the hungry.

The LORD sets the
prisoners free;
8 the LORD opens the eyes
of the blind.
The LORD lifts up those who
are bowed down;
the LORD loves
the righteous.
9 The LORD watches over
the strangers;
he upholds the orphan
and the widow,
but the way of the wicked
he brings to ruin.

10 The LORD will reign forever,
your God, O Zion, for all
generations.
Praise the LORD!

WE ARE EMPOWERED

BY GOD TO MEET ALL OF

LIFE'S CHALLENGES. WE

UNDERESTIMATE OUR OWN

STRENGTH—WITH GOD.

PSALM 147

PRAISE FOR GOD'S CARE
FOR JERUSALEM

1 Praise the LORD!
How good it is to sing
praises to our God;
for he is gracious, and a song
of praise is fitting.
2 The LORD builds up Jerusalem;
he gathers the outcasts
of Israel.
3 He heals the brokenhearted,
and binds up their wounds.
4 He determines the number
of the stars;
he gives to all of them
their names.

5 Great is our Lord, and
abundant in power;
his understanding is
beyond measure.
6 The LORD lifts up the
downtrodden;
he casts the wicked to
the ground.

7 Sing to the LORD with
thanksgiving;
make melody to our God
on the lyre.
8 He covers the heavens
with clouds,
prepares rain for the earth,
makes grass grow on the hills.
9 He gives to the animals
their food,
and to the young ravens
when they cry.
10 His delight is not in the
strength of the horse,
nor his pleasure in the
speed of a runner;[a]
11 but the LORD takes pleasure in
those who fear him,
in those who hope in his
steadfast love.

12 Praise the LORD, O Jerusalem!
Praise your God, O Zion!
13 For he strengthens the bars
of your gates;
he blesses your children
within you.
14 He grants peace[b] within
your borders;
he fills you with the
finest of wheat.
15 He sends out his command
to the earth;
his word runs swiftly.
16 He gives snow like wool;
he scatters frost like ashes.
17 He hurls down hail like crumbs—
who can stand before his cold?
18 He sends out his word, and
melts them;
he makes his wind blow,
and the waters flow.
19 He declares his word to Jacob,
his statutes and ordinances
to Israel.

a **147.10** Heb *legs of a person*   b **147.14** Or
prosperity

20 He has not dealt thus with
    any other nation;
  they do not know his
    ordinances.
  Praise the LORD!

PSALM 148

PRAISE FOR GOD'S
UNIVERSAL GLORY

1 Praise the LORD!
  Praise the LORD from the heavens;
    praise him in the heights!
2 Praise him, all his angels;
    praise him, all his host!

3 Praise him, sun and moon;
    praise him, all you
      shining stars!
4 Praise him, you highest heavens,
    and you waters above
      the heavens!

5 Let them praise the name
    of the LORD,
  for he commanded and
    they were created.
6 He established them forever
    and ever;
  he fixed their bounds, which
    cannot be passed.a

7 Praise the LORD from the earth,
    you sea monsters and all deeps,
8 fire and hail, snow and frost,
  stormy wind fulfilling
    his command!

9 Mountains and all hills,
    fruit trees and all cedars!
10 Wild animals and all cattle,
    creeping things and
      flying birds!

11 Kings of the earth and all peoples,
    princes and all rulers
      of the earth!
12 Young men and women alike,
    old and young together!

13 Let them praise the name
    of the LORD,
  for his name alone is exalted;
    his glory is above earth
      and heaven.

14 He has raised up a horn
    for his people,
  praise for all his faithful,
  for the people of Israel who
    are close to him.
  Praise the LORD!

PSALM 149

PRAISE FOR GOD'S
GOODNESS TO ISRAEL

1 Praise the LORD!
  Sing to the LORD a new song,
    his praise in the assembly
      of the faithful.
2 Let Israel be glad in its Maker;
    let the children of Zion
      rejoice in their King.
3 Let them praise his name
    with dancing,
  making melody to him with
    tambourine and lyre.
4 For the LORD takes pleasure
    in his people;
  he adorns the humble
    with victory.
5 Let the faithful exult in glory;
    let them sing for joy on
      their couches.
6 Let the high praises of God
    be in their throats
  and two-edged swords
    in their hands,
7 to execute vengeance on
    the nations
  and punishment on the peoples,
8 to bind their kings with fetters
    and their nobles with
      chains of iron,
9 to execute on them the
    judgment decreed.
  This is glory for all his
    faithful ones.
  Praise the LORD!

PSALM 150

PRAISE FOR GOD'S
SURPASSING GREATNESS

1 Praise the LORD!

---

a 148.6 Or *he set a law that cannot
pass away*

Praise God in his sanctuary;
   praise him in his mighty
      firmament!ᵃ
2 Praise him for his mighty deeds;
   praise him according to his
      surpassing greatness!

3 Praise him with trumpet sound;
   praise him with lute and harp!
4 Praise him with tambourine
   and dance;

   praise him with strings
      and pipe!
5 Praise him with clanging
   cymbals;
   praise him with loud
      clashing cymbals!
6 Let everything that breathes
   praise the LORD!
Praise the LORD!

ᵃ **150.1** Or *dome*

PROVERBS

Sometimes the deepest truths are contained in simple sayings. The book of Proverbs is like that—simple sentences full of wisdom and truth. Proverbs was written so that its readers might gain wisdom for avoiding some of the most common pitfalls of life. Do you need guidance in making decisions? Are you trying to shape a balanced and fulfilling life? Would you like to understand what it means to "fear the LORD"? Proverbs offers a wealth of practical advice on the art of living—wisdom that works and insights that won't wear out.

1

The proverbs of Solomon son of David, king of Israel:

PROLOGUE

2 For learning about wisdom
and instruction,
for understanding words
of insight,
3 for gaining instruction in
wise dealing,
righteousness, justice,
and equity;
4 to teach shrewdness to
the simple,
knowledge and prudence
to the young—
5 let the wise also hear and
gain in learning,
and the discerning
acquire skill,
6 to understand a proverb
and a figure,
the words of the wise
and their riddles.

7 The fear of the LORD is the
beginning of knowledge;
fools despise wisdom
and instruction.

WARNINGS AGAINST
EVIL COMPANIONS

8 Hear, my child, your father's
instruction,
and do not reject your
mother's teaching;
9 for they are a fair garland
for your head,
and pendants for your neck.
10 My child, if sinners
entice you,
do not consent.
11 If they say, "Come with us, let
us lie in wait for blood;
let us wantonly ambush
the innocent;
12 like Sheol let us swallow
them alive
and whole, like those who
go down to the Pit.
13 We shall find all kinds of
costly things;
we shall fill our houses
with booty.
14 Throw in your lot among us;
we will all have
one purse"—

15 my child, do not walk in
their way,
keep your foot from
their paths;
16 for their feet run to evil,
and they hurry to shed blood.
17 For in vain is the net baited
while the bird is looking on;
18 yet they lie in wait—to
kill themselves!
and set an ambush—for
their own lives!
19 Such is the end[a] of all who
are greedy for gain;
it takes away the life of
its possessors.

GOD IS PERSISTENTLY

OFFERING WISDOM TO ALL

OF US. WE ARE ADMONISHED

NOT TO IGNORE OR

OVERLOOK THE OFFER.

THE CALL OF WISDOM

20 Wisdom cries out
in the street;
in the squares she raises
her voice.
21 At the busiest corner
she cries out;
at the entrance of the city
gates she speaks:
22 "How long, O simple ones, will
you love being simple?
How long will scoffers delight
in their scoffing
and fools hate knowledge?
23 Give heed to my reproof;
I will pour out my thoughts
to you;
I will make my words
known to you.
24 Because I have called and
you refused,
have stretched out my hand
and no one heeded,

---

a 1.19 Gk: Heb *are the ways*

25 and because you have ignored
all my counsel
and would have none
of my reproof,
26 I also will laugh at your calamity;
I will mock when panic
strikes you,
27 when panic strikes you
like a storm,
and your calamity comes
like a whirlwind,
when distress and anguish
come upon you.
28 Then they will call upon me,
but I will not answer;
they will seek me diligently,
but will not find me.
29 Because they hated knowledge
and did not choose the
fear of the LORD,
30 would have none of my counsel,
and despised all my reproof,
31 therefore they shall eat the
fruit of their way
and be sated with their
own devices.
32 For waywardness kills the simple,
and the complacency of
fools destroys them;
33 but those who listen to me
will be secure
and will live at ease, without
dread of disaster."

THE VALUE OF WISDOM

2 My child, if you accept
my words
and treasure up my
commandments
within you,
2 making your ear attentive
to wisdom
and inclining your heart
to understanding;
3 if you indeed cry out for insight,
and raise your voice for
understanding;
4 if you seek it like silver,
and search for it as for
hidden treasures—
5 then you will understand the
fear of the LORD
and find the knowledge of God.
6 For the LORD gives wisdom;
from his mouth come
knowledge and
understanding;

7 he stores up sound wisdom
for the upright;
he is a shield to those who
walk blamelessly,
8 guarding the paths of justice
and preserving the way of
his faithful ones.
9 Then you will understand
righteousness and justice
and equity, every good path;
10 for wisdom will come into
your heart,
and knowledge will be
pleasant to your soul;
11 prudence will watch over you;
and understanding will
guard you.
12 It will save you from the
way of evil,
from those who speak
perversely,
13 who forsake the paths of
uprightness
to walk in the ways
of darkness,
14 who rejoice in doing evil
and delight in the
perverseness of evil;
15 those whose paths are crooked,
and who are devious
in their ways.
16 You will be saved from the
loose[a] woman,
from the adulteress with
her smooth words,
17 who forsakes the partner
of her youth
and forgets her sacred
covenant;
18 for her way[b] leads down to death,
and her paths to the shades;
19 those who go to her never
come back,
nor do they regain the
paths of life.
20 Therefore walk in the way
of the good,
and keep to the paths
of the just.
21 For the upright will abide
in the land,
and the innocent will
remain in it;

a 2.16 Heb strange   b 2.18 Cn: Heb house

22 but the wicked will be cut
       off from the land,
   and the treacherous will
       be rooted out of it.

ADMONITION TO TRUST AND HONOR GOD

3 My child, do not forget
       my teaching,
   but let your heart keep my
       commandments;
2 for length of days and years of life
   and abundant welfare
       they will give you.

3 Do not let loyalty and faithfulness
       forsake you;
   bind them around your neck,
   write them on the tablet
       of your heart.
4 So you will find favor and
       good repute
   in the sight of God and
       of people.

5 Trust in the LORD with
       all your heart,
   and do not rely on your
       own insight.
6 In all your ways acknowledge
       him,
   and he will make straight
       your paths.
7 Do not be wise in your
       own eyes;
   fear the LORD, and turn
       away from evil.
8 It will be a healing for your flesh
   and a refreshment for
       your body.

9 Honor the LORD with
       your substance
   and with the first fruits of
       all your produce;
10 then your barns will be
       filled with plenty,
   and your vats will be
       bursting with wine.

11 My child, do not despise the
       LORD's discipline
   or be weary of his reproof,
12 for the LORD reproves the
       one he loves,
   as a father the son in
       whom he delights.

THE TRUE WEALTH

13 Happy are those who
       find wisdom,
   and those who get
       understanding,
14 for her income is better
       than silver,
   and her revenue better
       than gold.
15 She is more precious than jewels,
   and nothing you desire can
       compare with her.
16 Long life is in her right hand;
   in her left hand are riches
       and honor.
17 Her ways are ways of
       pleasantness,
   and all her paths are peace.
18 She is a tree of life to those
       who lay hold of her;
   those who hold her fast
       are called happy.

PONDER

[Wisdom] is a tree of life to those
who lay hold of her; those who
hold her fast are called happy.
—Proverbs 3.18

PRAY

Lord of all Truth, this book has brought
   home to us that the way of wisdom
   brings sensitivity, human intimacy,
   the open exhibition of emotions such
   as love and grief without restraint.
Teach us wisdom, Lord, so that we can
   have discernment, sound judgment
   and wisdom's blessings. Give us the
   eagerness to teach those who look to
   us for leadership. Help us to experience
   the enlightened liberation and joy that
   come from our ability to say without
   embarrassment, "I am a little Christ,
   and I want to live up to his commands.
   And when I fall short of the glory of
   God and the commands of Jesus,
   I always will be forgiven if I turn to
   God in prayer through my faith in my
   Savior." In his name we pray. Amen.

GOD'S WISDOM IN CREATION

19 The LORD by wisdom
        founded the earth;
    by understanding he
        established the heavens;
20 by his knowledge the deeps
        broke open,
    and the clouds drop
        down the dew.

THE TRUE SECURITY

21 My child, do not let these escape
        from your sight:
    keep sound wisdom
        and prudence,
22 and they will be life for your soul
    and adornment for your neck.
23 Then you will walk on your
        way securely
    and your foot will not stumble.
24 If you sit down,[a] you will
        not be afraid;
    when you lie down, your
        sleep will be sweet.
25 Do not be afraid of sudden panic,
    or of the storm that strikes
        the wicked;
26 for the LORD will be your
        confidence
    and will keep your foot
        from being caught.

27 Do not withhold good from those
        to whom it is due,[b]
    when it is in your power to do it.
28 Do not say to your neighbor,
    "Go, and come again,
    tomorrow I will give it"—when
        you have it with you.
29 Do not plan harm against
        your neighbor
    who lives trustingly beside you.
30 Do not quarrel with anyone
        without cause,
    when no harm has been
        done to you.
31 Do not envy the violent
    and do not choose any
        of their ways;
32 for the perverse are an
        abomination to the LORD,
    but the upright are in
        his confidence.
33 The LORD's curse is on the
        house of the wicked,
    but he blesses the abode
        of the righteous.

34 Toward the scorners he
        is scornful,
    but to the humble he
        shows favor.
35 The wise will inherit honor,
    but stubborn fools, disgrace.

PARENTAL ADVICE

4 Listen, children, to a
        father's instruction,
    and be attentive, that you
        may gain[c] insight;
2 for I give you good precepts:
    do not forsake my teaching.
3 When I was a son
        with my father,
    tender, and my mother's
        favorite,
4 he taught me, and said to me,
    "Let your heart hold fast
        my words;
    keep my commandments,
        and live.
5 Get wisdom; get insight: do not
        forget, nor turn away
    from the words of my mouth.
6 Do not forsake her, and she
        will keep you;
    love her, and she will
        guard you.
7 The beginning of wisdom is
        this: Get wisdom,
    and whatever else you
        get, get insight.
8 Prize her highly, and she
        will exalt you;
    she will honor you if you
        embrace her.
9 She will place on your head
        a fair garland;
    she will bestow on you a
        beautiful crown."

ADMONITION TO KEEP
TO THE RIGHT PATH

10 Hear, my child, and accept
        my words,
    that the years of your life
        may be many.
11 I have taught you the way
        of wisdom;
    I have led you in the paths
        of uprightness.

---

[a] 3.24 Gk: Heb lie down   [b] 3.27 Heb from
its owners   [c] 4.1 Heb know

12 When you walk, your step will
     not be hampered;
   and if you run, you will
     not stumble.
13 Keep hold of instruction;
     do not let go;
   guard her, for she is your life.
14 Do not enter the path of
     the wicked,
   and do not walk in the
     way of evildoers.
15 Avoid it; do not go on it;
   turn away from it and pass on.
16 For they cannot sleep unless
     they have done wrong;
   they are robbed of sleep
     unless they have made
     someone stumble.
17 For they eat the bread of
     wickedness
   and drink the wine of violence.
18 But the path of the righteous is
     like the light of dawn,
   which shines brighter and
     brighter until full day.
19 The way of the wicked is like
     deep darkness;
   they do not know what
     they stumble over.
20 My child, be attentive to
     my words;
   incline your ear to my sayings.
21 Do not let them escape
     from your sight;
   keep them within your heart.
22 For they are life to those
     who find them,
   and healing to all their flesh.
23 Keep your heart with all
     vigilance,
   for from it flow the
     springs of life.
24 Put away from you crooked
     speech,
   and put devious talk
     far from you.
25 Let your eyes look directly
     forward,
   and your gaze be straight
     before you.
26 Keep straight the path
     of your feet,
   and all your ways
     will be sure.
27 Do not swerve to the right
     or to the left;
   turn your foot away from evil.

WARNING AGAINST IMPURITY AND INFIDELITY

5 My child, be attentive
     to my wisdom;
   incline your ear to my
     understanding,
2 so that you may hold on
     to prudence,
   and your lips may guard
     knowledge.
3 For the lips of a loose[a] woman
     drip honey,
   and her speech is
     smoother than oil;
4 but in the end she is bitter
     as wormwood,
   sharp as a two-edged sword.
5 Her feet go down to death;
   her steps follow the
     path to Sheol.
6 She does not keep straight
     to the path of life;
   her ways wander, and she
     does not know it.

7 And now, my child,[b] listen to me,
   and do not depart from the
     words of my mouth.
8 Keep your way far from her,
   and do not go near the
     door of her house;
9 or you will give your honor
     to others,
   and your years to the merciless,
10 and strangers will take their
     fill of your wealth,
   and your labors will go to
     the house of an alien;
11 and at the end of your life
     you will groan,
   when your flesh and body
     are consumed,
12 and you say, "Oh, how I
     hated discipline,
   and my heart
     despised reproof!
13 I did not listen to the voice
     of my teachers
   or incline my ear to my
     instructors.
14 Now I am at the point
     of utter ruin
   in the public assembly."

a 5.3 Heb *strange*   b 5.7 Gk Vg: Heb *children*

15 Drink water from your
own cistern,
flowing water from
your own well.
16 Should your springs be
scattered abroad,
streams of water
in the streets?
17 Let them be for yourself alone,
and not for sharing
with strangers.
18 Let your fountain be blessed,
and rejoice in the wife
of your youth,
19   a lovely deer, a graceful doe.
May her breasts satisfy
you at all times;
may you be intoxicated
always by her love.
20 Why should you be
intoxicated, my son,
by another woman
and embrace the bosom
of an adulteress?
21 For human ways are under
the eyes of the LORD,
and he examines all
their paths.
22 The iniquities of the wicked
ensnare them,
and they are caught in the
toils of their sin.
23 They die for lack of discipline,
and because of their great
folly they are lost.

PRACTICAL ADMONITIONS

6 My child, if you have given your
pledge to your neighbor,
if you have bound yourself
to another,[a]
2 you are snared by the utterance
of your lips,[b]
caught by the words of
your mouth.
3 So do this, my child, and
save yourself,
for you have come into your
neighbor's power:
go, hurry,[c] and plead with
your neighbor.
4 Give your eyes no sleep
and your eyelids no slumber;
5 save yourself like a gazelle
from the hunter,[d]
like a bird from the hand
of the fowler.

6 Go to the ant, you lazybones;
consider its ways, and be wise.
7 Without having any chief
or officer or ruler,
8 it prepares its food in summer,
and gathers its sustenance
in harvest.
9 How long will you lie there,
O lazybones?
When will you rise from
your sleep?
10 A little sleep, a little slumber,
a little folding of the
hands to rest,
11 and poverty will come upon
you like a robber,
and want, like an armed
warrior.

12 A scoundrel and a villain
goes around with
crooked speech,
13 winking the eyes, shuffling
the feet,
pointing the fingers,
14 with perverted mind
devising evil,
continually sowing discord;
15 on such a one calamity will
descend suddenly;
in a moment, damage
beyond repair.

16 There are six things that
the LORD hates,
seven that are an
abomination to him:
17 haughty eyes, a lying tongue,
and hands that shed
innocent blood,
18 a heart that devises wicked plans,
feet that hurry to run to evil,
19 a lying witness who
testifies falsely,
and one who sows discord
in a family.

20 My child, keep your father's
commandment,
and do not forsake your
mother's teaching.

[a] 6.1 Or a stranger [b] 6.2 Cn Compare Gk
Syr: Heb the words of your mouth   [c] 6.3 Or
humble yourself   [d] 6.5 Cn: Heb from
the hand

21 Bind them upon your
     heart always;
  tie them around your neck.
22 When you walk, they[a]
     will lead you;
  when you lie down, they[a]
     will watch over you;
  and when you awake, they[a]
     will talk with you.
23 For the commandment is a lamp
     and the teaching a light,
  and the reproofs of discipline
     are the way of life,
24 to preserve you from the
     wife of another,[b]
  from the smooth tongue
     of the adulteress.
25 Do not desire her beauty
     in your heart,
  and do not let her capture
     you with her eyelashes;
26 for a prostitute's fee is only
     a loaf of bread,[c]
  but the wife of another stalks
     a man's very life.
27 Can fire be carried in the bosom
     without burning one's clothes?
28 Or can one walk on hot coals
     without scorching the feet?
29 So is he who sleeps with his
     neighbor's wife;
  no one who touches her
     will go unpunished.

30 Thieves are not despised
     who steal only
  to satisfy their appetite when
     they are hungry.
31 Yet if they are caught, they
     will pay sevenfold;
  they will forfeit all the
     goods of their house.
32 But he who commits adultery
     has no sense;
  he who does it destroys
     himself.
33 He will get wounds and dishonor,
     and his disgrace will not
     be wiped away.
34 For jealousy arouses a
     husband's fury,
  and he shows no restraint
     when he takes revenge.
35 He will accept no compensation,
     and refuses a bribe no
     matter how great.

THE FALSE ATTRACTIONS OF ADULTERY

7 My child, keep my words
  and store up my
     commandments with you;

[a] **6.22** Heb *it* [b] **6.24** Gk: MT *the evil woman* [c] **6.26** Cn Compare Gk Syr Vg Tg: Heb *for because of a harlot to a piece of bread*

BIBLE IN LIFE

Peacemaking, Not Discord

Proverbs 6.16–19

Many terrible sins, such as lying, envy, and pride, cause problems in relationships. Proverbs 6.19 includes a surprising sin among the list of more obvious ones: stirring up discord in the community. The early church dealt with much dissension among its members. Christians felt competitive over whether their particular gifts or talents were superior to those of others (see 1 Corinthians 12). They disagreed about how to observe the Lord's supper and debated whether meat offered to idols was okay to eat. There were problems between the Jews and Gentiles. The leaders of the early church addressed these conflicts, even assuming personal responsibility for them (see Paul's persuasive appeal in the book of Philemon). These peacemakers reaped a harvest of righteousness (see James 3.18).

We have discord within the church today too—within our own churches, within denominations and between denominations. We argue about issues such as effective leadership, proper forms of worship, the role of women in the church and the separation of church and state. Until Christ returns, we will continue to have our differences, but we need to find ways to smooth over dissension, not stir it up. We need to get along with each other as we focus on the elements that are critical to our faith in Christ.

2 keep my commandments
    and live,
    keep my teachings as the
      apple of your eye;
3 bind them on your fingers,
    write them on the tablet
      of your heart.
4 Say to wisdom, "You are
      my sister,"
    and call insight your
      intimate friend,
5 that they may keep you from
      the loose[a] woman,
    from the adulteress with
      her smooth words.

6 For at the window of my house
    I looked out through
      my lattice,
7 and I saw among
      the simple ones,
    I observed among the youths,
      a young man without sense,
8 passing along the street
      near her corner,
    taking the road to her house
9 in the twilight, in the evening,
      at the time of night
      and darkness.

10 Then a woman comes
      toward him,
    decked out like a prostitute,
      wily of heart.[b]
11 She is loud and wayward;
    her feet do not stay at home;
12 now in the street, now in
      the squares,
    and at every corner she
      lies in wait.
13 She seizes him and kisses him,
    and with impudent face
      she says to him:
14 "I had to offer sacrifices,
    and today I have
      paid my vows;
15 so now I have come out
      to meet you,
    to seek you eagerly, and
      I have found you!
16 I have decked my couch
      with coverings,
    colored spreads of
      Egyptian linen;
17 I have perfumed my bed
      with myrrh,
    aloes, and cinnamon.

18 Come, let us take our fill of
      love until morning;
    let us delight ourselves
      with love.
19 For my husband is not at home;
    he has gone on a long journey.
20 He took a bag of money with him;
    he will not come home
      until full moon."

21 With much seductive speech
      she persuades him;
    with her smooth talk she
      compels him.
22 Right away he follows her,
    and goes like an ox to
      the slaughter,
    or bounds like a stag
      toward the trap[c]
23   until an arrow pierces
      its entrails.
    He is like a bird rushing
      into a snare,
    not knowing that it will
      cost him his life.

24 And now, my children,
      listen to me,
    and be attentive to the
      words of my mouth.
25 Do not let your hearts turn
      aside to her ways;
    do not stray into her paths.
26 For many are those she
      has laid low,
    and numerous are her victims.
27 Her house is the way to Sheol,
    going down to the
      chambers of death.

THE GIFTS OF WISDOM

8 Does not wisdom call,
    and does not understanding
      raise her voice?
2 On the heights, beside the way,
    at the crossroads she
      takes her stand;
3 beside the gates in front
      of the town,
    at the entrance of the
      portals she cries out:
4 "To you, O people, I call,
    and my cry is to all that live.

---

a **7.5** Heb *strange*   b **7.10** Meaning of Heb
uncertain   c **7.22** Cn Compare Gk: Meaning
of Heb uncertain

5 O simple ones, learn prudence;
  acquire intelligence,
    you who lack it.
6 Hear, for I will speak
    noble things,
  and from my lips will
    come what is right;
7 for my mouth will utter truth;
  wickedness is an abomination
    to my lips.
8 All the words of my mouth
    are righteous;
  there is nothing twisted
    or crooked in them.
9 They are all straight to one
    who understands
  and right to those who
    find knowledge.
10 Take my instruction
    instead of silver,
  and knowledge rather
    than choice gold;
11 for wisdom is better than jewels,
  and all that you may desire
    cannot compare with her.
12 I, wisdom, live with prudence,[a]
  and I attain knowledge
    and discretion.
13 The fear of the LORD is
    hatred of evil.
  Pride and arrogance and
    the way of evil
  and perverted speech I hate.
14 I have good advice and
    sound wisdom;
  I have insight, I have strength.
15 By me kings reign,
  and rulers decree
    what is just;
16 by me rulers rule,
  and nobles, all who
    govern rightly.
17 I love those who love me,
  and those who seek me
    diligently find me.
18 Riches and honor are with me,
  enduring wealth and
    prosperity.
19 My fruit is better than gold,
    even fine gold,
  and my yield than choice silver.
20 I walk in the way of
    righteousness,
  along the paths of justice,
21 endowing with wealth those
    who love me,
  and filling their treasuries.

WISDOM'S PART IN CREATION

22 The LORD created me at the
    beginning[b] of his work,[c]
  the first of his acts of long ago.
23 Ages ago I was set up,
  at the first, before the
    beginning of the earth.
24 When there were no depths I
    was brought forth,
  when there were no springs
    abounding with water.
25 Before the mountains had
    been shaped,
  before the hills, I was
    brought forth—
26 when he had not yet made
    earth and fields,[a]
  or the world's first bits of soil.

[a] 8.12,26 Meaning of Heb uncertain
[b] 8.22 Or *me as the beginning*
[c] 8.22 Heb *way*

PONDER

"The LORD created me at the beginning of his work, the first of his acts of long ago. Ages ago I was set up, at the first, before the beginning of the earth."
—Proverbs 8.22–23

PRAY

O Father, we are thankful for the opportunity to study your Word, to be reminded by the ancient proverbs that you do not change. Wisdom existed from the beginning, and a thousand years after Solomon, Jesus Christ came and demonstrated by his own words and actions that your wisdom, your grace and your Word are eternal. Implant your wisdom deep in our hearts. Help us turn away from our sinful ways of negligence and from negative thoughts, inactivity and selfishness. Help us embrace and renew our commitment to exemplify Christ in our own lives. We ask in the name of our Savior. Amen.

27 When he established the
        heavens, I was there,
    when he drew a circle on
        the face of the deep,
28 when he made firm the
        skies above,
    when he established the
        fountains of the deep,
29 when he assigned to the
        sea its limit,
    so that the waters might not
        transgress his command,
    when he marked out the
        foundations of the earth,
30   then I was beside him, like
        a master worker;[a]
    and I was daily his[b] delight,
        rejoicing before him always,
31 rejoicing in his inhabited world
        and delighting in the
        human race.

32 "And now, my children,
        listen to me:
    happy are those who
        keep my ways.
33 Hear instruction and be wise,
        and do not neglect it.
34 Happy is the one who
        listens to me,
    watching daily at my gates,
        waiting beside my doors.
35 For whoever finds me finds life
        and obtains favor from
        the LORD;
36 but those who miss me
        injure themselves;
    all who hate me love death."

WISDOM'S FEAST

9 Wisdom has built her house,
        she has hewn her
        seven pillars.
2   She has slaughtered her animals,
        she has mixed her wine,
        she has also set her table.
3   She has sent out her
        servant-girls, she calls
        from the highest places
        in the town,
4   "You that are simple,
        turn in here!"
    To those without sense
        she says,
5   "Come, eat of my bread
        and drink of the wine
        I have mixed.

6 Lay aside immaturity,[c] and live,
    and walk in the way of insight."

GENERAL MAXIMS

7 Whoever corrects a scoffer
        wins abuse;
    whoever rebukes the
        wicked gets hurt.
8 A scoffer who is rebuked
        will only hate you;
    the wise, when rebuked,
        will love you.
9 Give instruction[d] to the
        wise, and they will
        become wiser still;
    teach the righteous and they
        will gain in learning.
10 The fear of the LORD is the
        beginning of wisdom,
    and the knowledge of the
        Holy One is insight.
11 For by me your days will
        be multiplied,
    and years will be added
        to your life.
12 If you are wise, you are
        wise for yourself;
    if you scoff, you alone
        will bear it.

THE NATURE OF WISDOM IS
CONSTRUCTIVE. THE NATURE
OF FOLLY IS DESTRUCTIVE.

FOLLY'S INVITATION
AND PROMISE

13 The foolish woman is loud;
    she is ignorant and
        knows nothing.
14 She sits at the door of her house,
    on a seat at the high
        places of the town,
15 calling to those who pass by,
    who are going straight
        on their way,

a **8.30** Another reading is *little child*
b **8.30** Gk: Heb lacks *his*   c **9.6** Or
simpleness   d **9.9** Heb lacks *instruction*

16 "You who are simple,
       turn in here!"
   And to those without
       sense she says,
17 "Stolen water is sweet,
       and bread eaten in secret
       is pleasant."
18 But they do not know that
       the dead[a] are there,
   that her guests are in the
       depths of Sheol.

WISE SAYINGS OF SOLOMON

10 The proverbs of Solomon.

   A wise child makes a glad father,
     but a foolish child is a
       mother's grief.
2 Treasures gained by wickedness
       do not profit,
   but righteousness delivers
       from death.
3 The LORD does not let the
       righteous go hungry,
   but he thwarts the craving
       of the wicked.
4 A slack hand causes poverty,
     but the hand of the diligent
       makes rich.
5 A child who gathers in
       summer is prudent,
   but a child who sleeps in
       harvest brings shame.
6 Blessings are on the head
       of the righteous,
   but the mouth of the wicked
       conceals violence.
7 The memory of the righteous
       is a blessing,
   but the name of the
       wicked will rot.
8 The wise of heart will heed
       commandments,
   but a babbling fool will
       come to ruin.
9 Whoever walks in integrity
       walks securely,
   but whoever follows perverse
       ways will be found out.
10 Whoever winks the eye
       causes trouble,
   but the one who rebukes
       boldly makes peace.[b]
11 The mouth of the righteous
       is a fountain of life,
   but the mouth of the wicked
       conceals violence.

12 Hatred stirs up strife,
     but love covers all offenses.
13 On the lips of one who
       has understanding
       wisdom is found,
   but a rod is for the back of
       one who lacks sense.
14 The wise lay up knowledge,
     but the babbling of a fool
       brings ruin near.
15 The wealth of the rich is
       their fortress;
   the poverty of the poor
       is their ruin.
16 The wage of the righteous
       leads to life,
   the gain of the wicked to sin.
17 Whoever heeds instruction is
       on the path to life,
   but one who rejects a
       rebuke goes astray.
18 Lying lips conceal hatred,
     and whoever utters
       slander is a fool.
19 When words are many,
       transgression is
       not lacking,
   but the prudent are
       restrained in speech.
20 The tongue of the righteous
       is choice silver;
   the mind of the wicked
       is of little worth.
21 The lips of the righteous
       feed many,
   but fools die for lack of sense.
22 The blessing of the LORD
       makes rich,
   and he adds no sorrow with it.[c]
23 Doing wrong is like sport
       to a fool,
   but wise conduct is
       pleasure to a person
       of understanding.
24 What the wicked dread will
       come upon them,
   but the desire of the righteous
       will be granted.
25 When the tempest passes, the
       wicked are no more,
   but the righteous are
       established forever.

a 9.18 Heb *shades*   b 10.10 Gk: Heb *but a
babbling fool will come to ruin*   c 10.22 Or
and toil adds nothing to it

26 Like vinegar to the teeth, and
        smoke to the eyes,
    so are the lazy to their
        employers.
27 The fear of the LORD prolongs life,
    but the years of the wicked
        will be short.
28 The hope of the righteous
        ends in gladness,
    but the expectation of the
        wicked comes to nothing.
29 The way of the LORD is
        a stronghold for
        the upright,
    but destruction for evildoers.
30 The righteous will never
        be removed,
    but the wicked will not
        remain in the land.
31 The mouth of the righteous
        brings forth wisdom,
    but the perverse tongue
        will be cut off.
32 The lips of the righteous know
        what is acceptable,
    but the mouth of the wicked
        what is perverse.

11 A false balance is an
        abomination to the LORD,
    but an accurate weight
        is his delight.
2 When pride comes, then
        comes disgrace;
    but wisdom is with
        the humble.
3 The integrity of the upright
        guides them,
    but the crookedness of
        the treacherous
        destroys them.
4 Riches do not profit in the
        day of wrath,
    but righteousness delivers
        from death.
5 The righteousness of the
        blameless keeps their
        ways straight,
    but the wicked fall by their
        own wickedness.
6 The righteousness of the
        upright saves them,
    but the treacherous are taken
        captive by their schemes.
7 When the wicked die, their
        hope perishes,
    and the expectation of the
        godless comes to nothing.

PONDER

The righteousness of the blameless
keeps their ways straight.
—Proverbs 11.5

PRAY

Holy Father, give us the courage to look
at our own lives, not with trepidation, but
with excitement. Let us look deep within
our hearts and minds and ask, "How can I
align my will more closely with yours? How
can I grow in righteousness and straighten
the path I'm walking on? How can I have a
more adventurous, challenging, joyful and
expansive life as I submit my will to yours
and let the Holy Spirit fill my heart and
my soul?" We ask these questions in the
name of our Savior, Jesus Christ. Amen.

8 The righteous are delivered
        from trouble,
    and the wicked get into
        it instead.
9 With their mouths the
        godless would destroy
        their neighbors,
    but by knowledge the
        righteous are delivered.
10 When it goes well with the
        righteous, the city rejoices;
    and when the wicked perish,
        there is jubilation.
11 By the blessing of the upright
        a city is exalted,
    but it is overthrown by the
        mouth of the wicked.
12 Whoever belittles another
        lacks sense,
    but an intelligent person
        remains silent.
13 A gossip goes about telling secrets,
    but one who is trustworthy in
        spirit keeps a confidence.
14 Where there is no guidance,
        a nation[a] falls,
    but in an abundance of
        counselors there is safety.

a 11.14 Or *an army*

15 To guarantee loans for a stranger
    brings trouble,
  but there is safety in
    refusing to do so.
16 A gracious woman gets honor,
  but she who hates virtue is
    covered with shame.[a]
  The timid become destitute,[b]
  but the aggressive
    gain riches.
17 Those who are kind reward
    themselves,
  but the cruel do
    themselves harm.
18 The wicked earn no real gain,
  but those who sow
    righteousness get
    a true reward.
19 Whoever is steadfast in
    righteousness will live,
  but whoever pursues
    evil will die.
20 Crooked minds are an
    abomination to the LORD,
  but those of blameless ways
    are his delight.
21 Be assured, the wicked will
    not go unpunished,
  but those who are righteous
    will escape.
22 Like a gold ring in a pig's snout
  is a beautiful woman
    without good sense.
23 The desire of the righteous
    ends only in good;
  the expectation of the
    wicked in wrath.
24 Some give freely, yet grow
    all the richer;
  others withhold what is due,
    and only suffer want.
25 A generous person will
    be enriched,
  and one who gives water
    will get water.
26 The people curse those who
    hold back grain,
  but a blessing is on the head
    of those who sell it.
27 Whoever diligently seeks
    good seeks favor,
  but evil comes to the one
    who searches for it.
28 Those who trust in their
    riches will wither,[c]
  but the righteous will flourish
    like green leaves.

29 Those who trouble their
    households will
    inherit wind,
  and the fool will be servant
    to the wise.
30 The fruit of the righteous
    is a tree of life,
  but violence[d] takes lives away.
31 If the righteous are repaid
    on earth,
  how much more the wicked
    and the sinner!

12 Whoever loves discipline
    loves knowledge,
  but those who hate to be
    rebuked are stupid.
2 The good obtain favor
    from the LORD,
  but those who devise evil
    he condemns.
3 No one finds security by
    wickedness,
  but the root of the righteous
    will never be moved.
4 A good wife is the crown
    of her husband,
  but she who brings shame
    is like rottenness
    in his bones.
5 The thoughts of the
    righteous are just;
  the advice of the wicked
    is treacherous.
6 The words of the wicked are
    a deadly ambush,
  but the speech of the upright
    delivers them.
7 The wicked are overthrown
    and are no more,
  but the house of the
    righteous will stand.
8 One is commended for
    good sense,
  but a perverse mind
    is despised.
9 Better to be despised and
    have a servant,
  than to be self-important
    and lack food.
10 The righteous know the needs
    of their animals,
  but the mercy of the
    wicked is cruel.

a 11.16 Compare Gk Syr: Heb lacks *but she . . .
shame*   b 11.16 Gk: Heb lacks *The timid . . .
destitute*   c 11.28 Cn: Heb *fall*   d 11.30 Cn
Compare Gk Syr: Heb *a wise man*

11 Those who till their land will
      have plenty of food,
    but those who follow worthless
      pursuits have no sense.
12 The wicked covet the proceeds
      of wickedness,[a]
    but the root of the righteous
      bears fruit.
13 The evil are ensnared by the
      transgression of their lips,
    but the righteous escape
      from trouble.
14 From the fruit of the mouth one
      is filled with good things,
    and manual labor has
      its reward.
15 Fools think their own way is right,
    but the wise listen to advice.
16 Fools show their anger at once,
    but the prudent ignore
      an insult.
17 Whoever speaks the truth gives
      honest evidence,
    but a false witness speaks
      deceitfully.
18 Rash words are like sword thrusts,
    but the tongue of the wise
      brings healing.
19 Truthful lips endure forever,
    but a lying tongue lasts
      only a moment.
20 Deceit is in the mind of those
      who plan evil,
    but those who counsel
      peace have joy.
21 No harm happens to the
      righteous,
    but the wicked are filled
      with trouble.
22 Lying lips are an abomination
      to the LORD,
    but those who act faithfully
      are his delight.
23 One who is clever conceals
      knowledge,
    but the mind of a fool[b]
      broadcasts folly.
24 The hand of the diligent will rule,
    while the lazy will be put
      to forced labor.
25 Anxiety weighs down the
      human heart,
    but a good word cheers it up.
26 The righteous gives good
      advice to friends,[c]
    but the way of the wicked
      leads astray.

27 The lazy do not roast[d]
      their game,
    but the diligent obtain
      precious wealth.[d]
28 In the path of righteousness
      there is life,
    in walking its path there
      is no death.

13 A wise child loves
      discipline,[e]
    but a scoffer does not
      listen to rebuke.
2 From the fruit of their
      words good persons
      eat good things,
    but the desire of the
      treacherous is for
      wrongdoing.
3 Those who guard their mouths
      preserve their lives;
    those who open wide their
      lips come to ruin.
4 The appetite of the lazy craves,
      and gets nothing,
    while the appetite of the
      diligent is richly supplied.
5 The righteous hate falsehood,
    but the wicked act shamefully
      and disgracefully.
6 Righteousness guards one
      whose way is upright,
    but sin overthrows the wicked.
7 Some pretend to be rich,
      yet have nothing;
    others pretend to be poor,
      yet have great wealth.
8 Wealth is a ransom for a
      person's life,
    but the poor get no threats.
9 The light of the righteous rejoices,
    but the lamp of the
      wicked goes out.
10 By insolence the heedless
      make strife,
    but wisdom is with those
      who take advice.
11 Wealth hastily gotten[f]
      will dwindle,
    but those who gather little by
      little will increase it.

a 12.12 Or *covet the catch of the
wicked*   b 12.23 Heb *the heart of fools*
c 12.26 Syr: Meaning of Heb uncertain
d 12.27 Meaning of Heb uncertain
e 13.1 Cn: Heb *A wise child the discipline of
his father*   f 13.11 Gk Vg: Heb *from vanity*

12 Hope deferred makes the
        heart sick,
    but a desire fulfilled is
        a tree of life.
13 Those who despise the word
        bring destruction
        on themselves,
    but those who respect
        the commandment
        will be rewarded.
14 The teaching of the wise is
        a fountain of life,
    so that one may avoid the
        snares of death.
15 Good sense wins favor,
    but the way of the faithless
        is their ruin.[a]
16 The clever do all things
        intelligently,
    but the fool displays folly.
17 A bad messenger
        brings trouble,
    but a faithful envoy,
        healing.
18 Poverty and disgrace are for
        the one who ignores
        instruction,
    but one who heeds reproof
        is honored.
19 A desire realized is sweet
        to the soul,
    but to turn away from evil is
        an abomination to fools.
20 Whoever walks with the wise
        becomes wise,
    but the companion of
        fools suffers harm.
21 Misfortune pursues sinners,
    but prosperity rewards
        the righteous.
22 The good leave an inheritance to
        their children's children,
    but the sinner's wealth is laid
        up for the righteous.
23 The field of the poor may
        yield much food,
    but it is swept away
        through injustice.
24 Those who spare the rod hate
        their children,
    but those who love them
        are diligent to
        discipline them.
25 The righteous have enough to
        satisfy their appetite,
    but the belly of the
        wicked is empty.

14 The wise woman[b]
        builds her house,
    but the foolish tears it down
        with her own hands.
2 Those who walk uprightly
        fear the LORD,
    but one who is devious in
        conduct despises him.
3 The talk of fools is a rod
        for their backs,[c]
    but the lips of the wise
        preserve them.
4 Where there are no oxen,
        there is no grain;
    abundant crops come by the
        strength of the ox.
5 A faithful witness does not lie,
    but a false witness
        breathes out lies.
6 A scoffer seeks wisdom in vain,
    but knowledge is easy for
        one who understands.
7 Leave the presence of a fool,
    for there you do not find
        words of knowledge.
8 It is the wisdom of the
        clever to understand
        where they go,
    but the folly of fools misleads.
9 Fools mock at the guilt offering,[d]
    but the upright enjoy
        God's favor.
10 The heart knows its own
        bitterness,
    and no stranger shares its joy.
11 The house of the wicked
        is destroyed,
    but the tent of the upright
        flourishes.
12 There is a way that seems
        right to a person,
    but its end is the way to death.[e]
13 Even in laughter the heart is sad,
    and the end of joy is grief.
14 The perverse get what their
        ways deserve,
    and the good, what their
        deeds deserve.[f]
15 The simple believe everything,
    but the clever consider
        their steps.

[a] 13.15 Cn Compare Gk Syr Vg Tg:
Heb is enduring   [b] 14.1 Heb Wisdom
of women   [c] 14.3 Cn: Heb a rod of
pride   [d] 14.9 Meaning of Heb uncertain
[e] 14.12 Heb ways of death   [f] 14.14 Cn: Heb
from upon him

16 The wise are cautious and
        turn away from evil,
    but the fool throws off
        restraint and is careless.
17 One who is quick-tempered
        acts foolishly,
    and the schemer is hated.
18 The simple are adorned with[a] folly,
    but the clever are crowned
        with knowledge.
19 The evil bow down before
        the good,
    the wicked at the gates
        of the righteous.
20 The poor are disliked even by
        their neighbors,
    but the rich have many friends.
21 Those who despise their
        neighbors are sinners,
    but happy are those who
        are kind to the poor.
22 Do they not err that plan evil?
    Those who plan good find
        loyalty and faithfulness.
23 In all toil there is profit,
    but mere talk leads only
        to poverty.
24 The crown of the wise is
        their wisdom,[b]
    but folly is the garland[c] of fools.
25 A truthful witness saves lives,
    but one who utters lies
        is a betrayer.
26 In the fear of the LORD one has
        strong confidence,
    and one's children will
        have a refuge.
27 The fear of the LORD is a
        fountain of life,
    so that one may avoid the
        snares of death.
28 The glory of a king is a
        multitude of people;
    without people a prince
        is ruined.
29 Whoever is slow to anger has
        great understanding,
    but one who has a hasty
        temper exalts folly.
30 A tranquil mind gives life
        to the flesh,
    but passion makes the
        bones rot.
31 Those who oppress the poor
        insult their Maker,
    but those who are kind to
        the needy honor him.

32 The wicked are overthrown
        by their evildoing,
    but the righteous find a refuge
        in their integrity.[d]
33 Wisdom is at home in the
        mind of one who has
        understanding,
    but it is not[e] known in
        the heart of fools.
34 Righteousness
        exalts a nation,
    but sin is a reproach
        to any people.
35 A servant who deals wisely
        has the king's favor,
    but his wrath falls on one
        who acts shamefully.

15 A soft answer turns
        away wrath,
    but a harsh word stirs
        up anger.
2 The tongue of the wise
        dispenses knowledge,[f]
    but the mouths of fools
        pour out folly.
3 The eyes of the LORD are
        in every place,
    keeping watch on the evil
        and the good.
4 A gentle tongue is a tree of life,
    but perverseness in it
        breaks the spirit.
5 A fool despises a parent's
        instruction,
    but the one who heeds
        admonition is prudent.
6 In the house of the righteous
        there is much treasure,
    but trouble befalls the
        income of the wicked.
7 The lips of the wise spread
        knowledge;
    not so the minds of fools.
8 The sacrifice of the wicked is an
        abomination to the LORD,
    but the prayer of the upright
        is his delight.
9 The way of the wicked is an
        abomination to the LORD,
    but he loves the one who
        pursues righteousness.

a 14.18 Or inherit   b 14.24 Cn Compare
Gk: Heb riches   c 14.24 Cn: Heb is the
folly   d 14.32 Gk Syr: Heb in their death
e 14.33 Gk Syr: Heb lacks not   f 15.2 Cn:
Heb makes knowledge good

10 There is severe discipline for one
    who forsakes the way,
  but one who hates a
    rebuke will die.
11 Sheol and Abaddon lie open
    before the LORD,
  how much more
    human hearts!
12 Scoffers do not like
    to be rebuked;
  they will not go to the wise.
13 A glad heart makes a cheerful
    countenance,
  but by sorrow of heart the
    spirit is broken.
14 The mind of one who has
    understanding
    seeks knowledge,
  but the mouths of fools
    feed on folly.
15 All the days of the
    poor are hard,
  but a cheerful heart has
    a continual feast.
16 Better is a little with the
    fear of the LORD
  than great treasure and
    trouble with it.
17 Better is a dinner of vegetables
    where love is
  than a fatted ox and
    hatred with it.
18 Those who are hot-tempered
    stir up strife,
  but those who are slow to
    anger calm contention.
19 The way of the lazy is overgrown
    with thorns,
  but the path of the upright
    is a level highway.
20 A wise child makes a glad father,
  but the foolish despise
    their mothers.
21 Folly is a joy to one who
    has no sense,
  but a person of understanding
    walks straight ahead.
22 Without counsel, plans go wrong,
  but with many advisers
    they succeed.
23 To make an apt answer is
    a joy to anyone,
  and a word in season,
    how good it is!
24 For the wise the path of life
    leads upward,
  in order to avoid Sheol below.

25 The LORD tears down the
    house of the proud,
  but maintains the widow's
    boundaries.
26 Evil plans are an abomination
    to the LORD,
  but gracious words are pure.
27 Those who are greedy for unjust
    gain make trouble for
    their households,
  but those who hate
    bribes will live.
28 The mind of the righteous
    ponders how to answer,
  but the mouth of the wicked
    pours out evil.
29 The LORD is far from the wicked,
  but he hears the prayer
    of the righteous.
30 The light of the eyes rejoices
    the heart,
  and good news refreshes
    the body.
31 The ear that heeds wholesome
    admonition
  will lodge among the wise.
32 Those who ignore instruction
    despise themselves,
  but those who heed
    admonition gain
    understanding.
33 The fear of the LORD is
    instruction in wisdom,
  and humility goes before honor.

16 The plans of the mind
    belong to mortals,
  but the answer of the tongue
    is from the LORD.
2 All one's ways may be pure
    in one's own eyes,
  but the LORD weighs the spirit.
3 Commit your work to the LORD,
  and your plans will be
    established.
4 The LORD has made everything
    for its purpose,
  even the wicked for the
    day of trouble.
5 All those who are arrogant are an
    abomination to the LORD;
  be assured, they will not
    go unpunished.
6 By loyalty and faithfulness
    iniquity is atoned for,
  and by the fear of the LORD
    one avoids evil.

PONDER

Commit your work to the LORD, and your plans will be established.
—Proverbs 16.3

PRAY

Eternal Father, we sometimes believe you don't understand the pressures on us; you don't see our needs and those of our families in a competitive environment where we are tempted to cut corners. But we realize that if we commit to you and pattern our priorities after yours, we don't have to cut corners on honesty or truth. We don't have to tear down our neighbors in order to exalt ourselves. We don't have to hold grudges against others. We don't have to ignore the needy people we quite often pass by. We ask that you forgive us and help us start anew with a realization that through your guidance, we can have joyful freedom and integrity. Through the Holy Spirit with our Savior, Jesus Christ. Amen.

7 When the ways of people
        please the LORD,
    he causes even their enemies
        to be at peace with them.
8 Better is a little with
        righteousness
    than large income
        with injustice.
9 The human mind plans the way,
    but the LORD directs
        the steps.
10 Inspired decisions are on
        the lips of a king;
    his mouth does not sin
        in judgment.
11 Honest balances and scales
        are the LORD's;
    all the weights in the
        bag are his work.
12 It is an abomination to
        kings to do evil,
    for the throne is established
        by righteousness.

13 Righteous lips are the
        delight of a king,
    and he loves those who
        speak what is right.
14 A king's wrath is a messenger
        of death,
    and whoever is wise
        will appease it.
15 In the light of a king's face
        there is life,
    and his favor is like the clouds
        that bring the spring rain.
16 How much better to get
        wisdom than gold!
    To get understanding is to be
        chosen rather than silver.
17 The highway of the upright
        avoids evil;
    those who guard their way
        preserve their lives.
18 Pride goes before destruction,
    and a haughty spirit
        before a fall.
19 It is better to be of a lowly
        spirit among the poor
    than to divide the spoil
        with the proud.
20 Those who are attentive to a
        matter will prosper,
    and happy are those who
        trust in the LORD.
21 The wise of heart is called
        perceptive,
    and pleasant speech increases
        persuasiveness.
22 Wisdom is a fountain of life
        to one who has it,
    but folly is the punishment
        of fools.
23 The mind of the wise makes
        their speech judicious,
    and adds persuasiveness
        to their lips.
24 Pleasant words are like a
        honeycomb,
    sweetness to the soul and
        health to the body.
25 Sometimes there is a way that
        seems to be right,
    but in the end it is the
        way to death.
26 The appetite of workers
        works for them;
    their hunger urges them on.
27 Scoundrels concoct evil,
    and their speech is like
        a scorching fire.

28 A perverse person spreads strife,
     and a whisperer separates
          close friends.
29 The violent entice their neighbors,
     and lead them in a way
          that is not good.
30 One who winks the eyes plans[a]
     perverse things;
     one who compresses the lips
          brings evil to pass.
31 Gray hair is a crown of glory;
     it is gained in a righteous life.
32 One who is slow to anger is
          better than the mighty,
     and one whose temper is
          controlled than one
          who captures a city.
33 The lot is cast into the lap,
     but the decision is the
          LORD's alone.

WE TEND TO BELIEVE OUR

DESTINY IS IN OUR OWN

HANDS. IN NOT SEEKING

GOD'S WILL, WE FORFEIT

PARTNERSHIP WITH GOD.

17

Better is a dry morsel
     with quiet
than a house full of feasting
     with strife.
2 A slave who deals wisely will
          rule over a child who
          acts shamefully,
     and will share the inheritance
          as one of the family.
3 The crucible is for silver, and
          the furnace is for gold,
     but the LORD tests the heart.
4 An evildoer listens to wicked lips;
     and a liar gives heed to a
          mischievous tongue.
5 Those who mock the poor
          insult their Maker;
     those who are glad at calamity
          will not go unpunished.
6 Grandchildren are the crown
          of the aged,
     and the glory of children
          is their parents.

7 Fine speech is not becoming
          to a fool;
     still less is false speech
          to a ruler.[b]
8 A bribe is like a magic stone
     in the eyes of those
          who give it;
     wherever they turn
          they prosper.
9 One who forgives an affront
          fosters friendship,
     but one who dwells on disputes
          will alienate a friend.
10 A rebuke strikes deeper into
          a discerning person
     than a hundred blows
          into a fool.
11 Evil people seek only rebellion,
     but a cruel messenger will
          be sent against them.
12 Better to meet a she-bear
          robbed of its cubs
     than to confront a fool
          immersed in folly.
13 Evil will not depart from
          the house
     of one who returns
          evil for good.
14 The beginning of strife is like
          letting out water;
     so stop before the quarrel
          breaks out.
15 One who justifies the wicked
     and one who condemns
          the righteous
     are both alike an abomination
          to the LORD.
16 Why should fools have a
          price in hand
     to buy wisdom, when they
          have no mind to learn?
17 A friend loves at all times,
     and kinsfolk are born to
          share adversity.
18 It is senseless to
          give a pledge,
     to become surety for
          a neighbor.
19 One who loves transgression
          loves strife;
     one who builds a high
          threshold invites
          broken bones.

a 16.30 Gk Syr Vg Tg: Heb to plan   b 17.7 Or
a noble person

20 The crooked of mind do
   not prosper,
   and the perverse of tongue
   fall into calamity.
21 The one who begets a fool
   gets trouble;
   the parent of a fool has no joy.
22 A cheerful heart is a good
   medicine,
   but a downcast spirit dries
   up the bones.
23 The wicked accept a concealed bribe
   to pervert the ways of justice.
24 The discerning person looks
   to wisdom,
   but the eyes of a fool to the
   ends of the earth.
25 Foolish children are a grief
   to their father
   and bitterness to her
   who bore them.
26 To impose a fine on the
   innocent is not right,
   or to flog the noble for
   their integrity.
27 One who spares words is
   knowledgeable;
   one who is cool in spirit
   has understanding.
28 Even fools who keep silent are
   considered wise;
   when they close their lips, they
   are deemed intelligent.

18 The one who lives alone
   is self-indulgent,
   showing contempt for all who
   have sound judgment.[a]
2 A fool takes no pleasure in
   understanding,
   but only in expressing
   personal opinion.

3 When wickedness comes,
   contempt comes also;
   and with dishonor
   comes disgrace.
4 The words of the mouth
   are deep waters;
   the fountain of wisdom is
   a gushing stream.
5 It is not right to be partial
   to the guilty,
   or to subvert the innocent
   in judgment.
6 A fool's lips bring strife,
   and a fool's mouth invites
   a flogging.
7 The mouths of fools are
   their ruin,
   and their lips a snare
   to themselves.
8 The words of a whisperer are
   like delicious morsels;
   they go down into the inner
   parts of the body.
9 One who is slack in work
   is close kin to a vandal.
10 The name of the LORD is
   a strong tower;
   the righteous run into
   it and are safe.
11 The wealth of the rich is
   their strong city;
   in their imagination it is
   like a high wall.
12 Before destruction one's
   heart is haughty,
   but humility goes before honor.
13 If one gives answer before
   hearing,
   it is folly and shame.

[a] 18.1 Meaning of Heb uncertain

BIBLE IN LIFE

Pride

Proverbs 18.12

Pride comes naturally to us; by default, we live self-centered lives. When we think we're self-sufficient, we crowd out God's Spirit. We prevent the Spirit from coming in and giving us the strength to carry out God's work through our lives. We might be important in the eyes of our neighbors, our co-workers or those over whom we have authority, but without the Holy Spirit to inspire and guide us, we are less effective as Christian witnesses. Pride keeps closed the door on which Christ is knocking (see Revelation 3.20). We need to move away from the destruction of self-centeredness and cling to the dependence of Christ-centeredness. When our focus is off ourselves and on Christ, the power of God through the Holy Spirit will move in amazing ways.

14 The human spirit will
        endure sickness;
    but a broken spirit—
        who can bear?
15 An intelligent mind acquires
        knowledge,
    and the ear of the wise
        seeks knowledge.
16 A gift opens doors;
    it gives access to the great.
17 The one who first states a
        case seems right,
    until the other comes and
        cross-examines.
18 Casting the lot puts an
        end to disputes
    and decides between
        powerful contenders.
19 An ally offended is stronger
        than a city;[a]
    such quarreling is like the
        bars of a castle.
20 From the fruit of the mouth one's
        stomach is satisfied;
    the yield of the lips brings
        satisfaction.
21 Death and life are in the
        power of the tongue,
    and those who love it
        will eat its fruits.
22 He who finds a wife finds
        a good thing,
    and obtains favor from
        the LORD.
23 The poor use entreaties,
    but the rich answer roughly.
24 Some[b] friends play
        at friendship[c]
    but a true friend sticks closer
        than one's nearest kin.

19 Better the poor walking
        in integrity
    than one perverse of speech
        who is a fool.
2 Desire without knowledge
        is not good,
    and one who moves too
        hurriedly misses the way.
3 One's own folly leads to ruin,
    yet the heart rages
        against the LORD.
4 Wealth brings many friends,
    but the poor are
        left friendless.
5 A false witness will not go
        unpunished,
    and a liar will not escape.

6 Many seek the favor of
        the generous,
    and everyone is a friend
        to a giver of gifts.
7 If the poor are hated even
        by their kin,
    how much more are they
        shunned by their friends!
    When they call after them,
        they are not there.[d]
8 To get wisdom is to love oneself;
    to keep understanding
        is to prosper.
9 A false witness will not go
        unpunished,
    and the liar will perish.
10 It is not fitting for a fool to
        live in luxury,
    much less for a slave to
        rule over princes.
11 Those with good sense are
        slow to anger,
    and it is their glory to
        overlook an offense.
12 A king's anger is like the
        growling of a lion,
    but his favor is like dew
        on the grass.
13 A stupid child is ruin to a father,
    and a wife's quarreling is a
        continual dripping of rain.
14 House and wealth are inherited
        from parents,
    but a prudent wife is
        from the LORD.
15 Laziness brings on deep sleep;
    an idle person will suffer hunger.
16 Those who keep the
        commandment will live;
    those who are heedless of
        their ways will die.
17 Whoever is kind to the poor
        lends to the LORD,
    and will be repaid in full.
18 Discipline your children while
        there is hope;
    do not set your heart on
        their destruction.
19 A violent tempered person
        will pay the penalty;
    if you effect a rescue, you will
        only have to do it again.[d]

a 18.19 Gk Syr Vg Tg: Meaning of Heb
uncertain   b 18.24 Syr Tg: Heb A man of
c 18.24 Cn Compare Syr Vg Tg: Meaning of
Heb uncertain   d 19.7,19 Meaning of Heb
uncertain

20 Listen to advice and accept
    instruction,
        that you may gain wisdom
        for the future.
21 The human mind may devise
    many plans,
        but it is the purpose of
        the LORD that will
        be established.
22 What is desirable in a
    person is loyalty,
        and it is better to be
        poor than a liar.
23 The fear of the LORD is life indeed;
        filled with it one rests secure
        and suffers no harm.
24 The lazy person buries a
    hand in the dish,
        and will not even bring it
        back to the mouth.
25 Strike a scoffer, and the simple
        will learn prudence;
        reprove the intelligent, and
        they will gain knowledge.
26 Those who do violence to
    their father and chase
        away their mother
    are children who cause shame
        and bring reproach.
27 Cease straying, my child, from
        the words of knowledge,
        in order that you may
        hear instruction.
28 A worthless witness mocks
        at justice,
        and the mouth of the wicked
        devours iniquity.
29 Condemnation is ready
        for scoffers,
        and flogging for the
        backs of fools.

20 Wine is a mocker, strong
        drink a brawler,
    and whoever is led astray
        by it is not wise.
2 The dread anger of a king is like
        the growling of a lion;
    anyone who provokes him to
        anger forfeits life itself.
3 It is honorable to refrain
        from strife,
    but every fool is quick
        to quarrel.
4 The lazy person does not
        plow in season;
    harvest comes, and there is
        nothing to be found.

PONDER

Listen to advice and accept
instruction, that you may gain
wisdom for the future.
—Proverbs 19.20

PRAY

Everlasting God, when we read the
Bible, we are sometimes reluctant to
apply your Word to our lives. We have
a tendency to think that your words
are theoretical, or that they apply to
someone else. Soften our hearts to
accept the discipline that you send
our way and to listen to the advice
of people who are in tune with your
will. We pray that our lives might be
changed, that we might have embedded
in our hearts a realization that our lives
will be counted as wise, not by our
neighbors but by the only One that
counts, Jesus Christ, our Savior and
Judge. In his name we pray. Amen.

5 The purposes in the human mind
        are like deep water,
    but the intelligent will
        draw them out.
6 Many proclaim themselves loyal,
        but who can find one
        worthy of trust?
7 The righteous walk
        in integrity—
    happy are the children
        who follow them!
8 A king who sits on the throne
        of judgment
    winnows all evil with his eyes.
9 Who can say, "I have made
        my heart clean;
    I am pure from my sin"?
10 Diverse weights and diverse
        measures
    are both alike an abomination
        to the LORD.
11 Even children make themselves
    known by their acts,
        by whether what they do
        is pure and right.

12 The hearing ear and the
    seeing eye—
  the LORD has made
    them both.
13 Do not love sleep, or else you
    will come to poverty;
  open your eyes, and you will
    have plenty of bread.
14 "Bad, bad," says the buyer,
    then goes away and boasts.
15 There is gold, and abundance
    of costly stones;
  but the lips informed
    by knowledge are a
    precious jewel.
16 Take the garment of one
    who has given surety
    for a stranger;
  seize the pledge given as
    surety for foreigners.
17 Bread gained by deceit is sweet,
  but afterward the mouth
    will be full of gravel.
18 Plans are established by
    taking advice;
  wage war by following
    wise guidance.
19 A gossip reveals secrets;
  therefore do not associate
    with a babbler.
20 If you curse father or mother,
  your lamp will go out in
    utter darkness.
21 An estate quickly acquired
    in the beginning
  will not be blessed in the end.
22 Do not say, "I will repay evil";
  wait for the LORD, and
    he will help you.
23 Differing weights are an
    abomination to the LORD,
  and false scales are not good.
24 All our steps are ordered
    by the LORD;
  how then can we understand
    our own ways?
25 It is a snare for one to say
    rashly, "It is holy,"
  and begin to reflect only
    after making a vow.
26 A wise king winnows
    the wicked,
  and drives the wheel
    over them.
27 The human spirit is the
    lamp of the LORD,
  searching every inmost part.

28 Loyalty and faithfulness
    preserve the king,
  and his throne is upheld
    by righteousness.[a]
29 The glory of youths is
    their strength,
  but the beauty of the aged
    is their gray hair.
30 Blows that wound cleanse
    away evil;
  beatings make clean the
    innermost parts.

21 The king's heart is a
    stream of water in the
    hand of the LORD;
  he turns it wherever he will.
2 All deeds are right in the
    sight of the doer,
  but the LORD weighs the heart.
3 To do righteousness and justice
  is more acceptable to the
    LORD than sacrifice.
4 Haughty eyes and a
    proud heart—
  the lamp of the wicked—
    are sin.
5 The plans of the diligent lead
    surely to abundance,
  but everyone who is hasty
    comes only to want.
6 The getting of treasures by
    a lying tongue
  is a fleeting vapor and a
    snare[b] of death.
7 The violence of the wicked will
    sweep them away,
  because they refuse to
    do what is just.
8 The way of the guilty is crooked,
  but the conduct of the
    pure is right.
9 It is better to live in a corner
    of the housetop
  than in a house shared with
    a contentious wife.
10 The souls of the wicked
    desire evil;
  their neighbors find no
    mercy in their eyes.
11 When a scoffer is punished, the
    simple become wiser;
  when the wise are instructed,
    they increase in
    knowledge.

a **20.28** Gk: Heb *loyalty*   b **21.6** Gk: Heb *seekers*

12 The Righteous One observes the
        house of the wicked;
    he casts the wicked
        down to ruin.
13 If you close your ear to the
        cry of the poor,
    you will cry out and
        not be heard.
14 A gift in secret averts anger;
    and a concealed bribe in the
        bosom, strong wrath.
15 When justice is done, it is a
        joy to the righteous,
    but dismay to evildoers.
16 Whoever wanders from the
        way of understanding
    will rest in the assembly
        of the dead.
17 Whoever loves pleasure
        will suffer want;
    whoever loves wine and
        oil will not be rich.
18 The wicked is a ransom for
        the righteous,
    and the faithless for
        the upright.
19 It is better to live in a
        desert land
    than with a contentious
        and fretful wife.
20 Precious treasure remains[a] in
        the house of the wise,
    but the fool devours it.
21 Whoever pursues righteousness
        and kindness
    will find life[b] and honor.
22 One wise person went up against
        a city of warriors
    and brought down the
        stronghold in which
        they trusted.
23 To watch over mouth
        and tongue
    is to keep out of trouble.
24 The proud, haughty person,
        named "Scoffer,"
    acts with arrogant pride.
25 The craving of the lazy
        person is fatal,
    for lazy hands refuse to labor.
26 All day long the wicked covet,[c]
    but the righteous give and
        do not hold back.
27 The sacrifice of the wicked is
        an abomination;
    how much more when brought
        with evil intent.

28 A false witness will perish,
    but a good listener will
        testify successfully.
29 The wicked put on a bold face,
    but the upright give thought
        to[d] their ways.
30 No wisdom, no understanding,
        no counsel,
    can avail against the LORD.
31 The horse is made ready for
        the day of battle,
    but the victory belongs
        to the LORD.

22 A good name is to be chosen
        rather than great riches,
    and favor is better than
        silver or gold.
2 The rich and the poor have
        this in common:
    the LORD is the maker
        of them all.
3 The clever see danger and hide;
    but the simple go on,
        and suffer for it.
4 The reward for humility and
        fear of the LORD
    is riches and honor and life.
5 Thorns and snares are in the
        way of the perverse;
    the cautious will keep
        far from them.
6 Train children in the right way,
    and when old, they
        will not stray.
7 The rich rule over the poor,
    and the borrower is the
        slave of the lender.
8 Whoever sows injustice will
        reap calamity,
    and the rod of anger will fail.
9 Those who are generous
        are blessed,
    for they share their bread
        with the poor.
10 Drive out a scoffer, and
        strife goes out;
    quarreling and abuse
        will cease.
11 Those who love a pure heart and
        are gracious in speech
    will have the king as a friend.

a 21.20 Gk: Heb and oil   b 21.21 Gk:
Heb life and righteousness   c 21.26 Gk:
Heb all day long one covets covetously
d 21.29 Another reading is establish

12 The eyes of the LORD keep
    watch over knowledge,
  but he overthrows the words
    of the faithless.
13 The lazy person says, "There
    is a lion outside!
  I shall be killed in
    the streets!"
14 The mouth of a loose[a] woman
    is a deep pit;
  he with whom the LORD is
    angry falls into it.
15 Folly is bound up in the
    heart of a boy,
  but the rod of discipline
    drives it far away.
16 Oppressing the poor in order
    to enrich oneself,
  and giving to the rich, will
    lead only to loss.

SAYINGS OF THE WISE

17   The words of the wise:

Incline your ear and hear
    my words,[b]
and apply your mind to
    my teaching;
18 for it will be pleasant if you
    keep them within you,
  if all of them are ready
    on your lips.
19 So that your trust may be
    in the LORD,
  I have made them known to
    you today—yes, to you.
20 Have I not written for you
    thirty sayings
  of admonition and
    knowledge,

21 to show you what is right
    and true,
  so that you may give a
    true answer to those
    who sent you?

22 Do not rob the poor because
    they are poor,
  or crush the afflicted
    at the gate;
23 for the LORD pleads
    their cause
  and despoils of life those
    who despoil them.
24 Make no friends with those
    given to anger,
  and do not associate
    with hotheads,
25 or you may learn their ways
  and entangle yourself
    in a snare.
26 Do not be one of those who
    give pledges,
  who become surety for debts.
27 If you have nothing with
    which to pay,
  why should your bed be
    taken from under you?
28 Do not remove the ancient
    landmark
  that your ancestors set up.
29 Do you see those who are
    skillful in their work?
  They will serve kings;
  they will not serve
    common people.

a **22.14** Heb *strange*   b **22.17** Cn Compare
Gk: Heb *Incline your ear, and hear the words
of the wise*

BIBLE IN LIFE

The Children We Influence
                                               Proverbs 22.6

Christian men and women are responsible for the formation of the lives of children within their sphere of influence. From their earliest years, children hear all kinds of conflicting, negative voices that shape their lives, and those voices are much broader in their scope than ever before in history. This poses a serious problem in our modern world. Straying from the beneficial influence of Christian families is much easier these days. Children are inundated with the influence of entertainment, news media, marketing, advertising and peer groups. We cannot filter all the multiple voices that try to shape the faith and habits of our children and the children around us. The best way to have a positive influence on children is through prayer and by demonstrating the teachings of Christ in our words and actions.

23

When you sit down to
eat with a ruler,
observe carefully what[a]
is before you,

2 and put a knife to your throat
if you have a big appetite.

3 Do not desire the ruler's[b]
delicacies,
for they are deceptive food.

4 Do not wear yourself out
to get rich;
be wise enough to desist.

5 When your eyes light upon
it, it is gone;
for suddenly it takes
wings to itself,
flying like an eagle
toward heaven.

6 Do not eat the bread of
the stingy;
do not desire their delicacies;

7 for like a hair in the throat,
so are they.[c]
"Eat and drink!" they
say to you;
but they do not mean it.

8 You will vomit up the little
you have eaten,
and you will waste your
pleasant words.

9 Do not speak in the hearing
of a fool,
who will only despise the
wisdom of your words.

10 Do not remove an ancient
landmark
or encroach on the fields
of orphans,

11 for their redeemer is strong;
he will plead their cause
against you.

12 Apply your mind to
instruction
and your ear to words
of knowledge.

13 Do not withhold discipline
from your children;
if you beat them with a rod,
they will not die.

14 If you beat them with the rod,
you will save their lives
from Sheol.

15 My child, if your heart is wise,
my heart too will be glad.

16 My soul will rejoice
when your lips speak
what is right.

17 Do not let your heart
envy sinners,
but always continue in the
fear of the LORD.

18 Surely there is a future,
and your hope will not
be cut off.

19 Hear, my child, and be wise,
and direct your mind
in the way.

20 Do not be among winebibbers,
or among gluttonous
eaters of meat;

21 for the drunkard and the glutton
will come to poverty,
and drowsiness will clothe
them with rags.

22 Listen to your father who
begot you,
and do not despise your
mother when she is old.

23 Buy truth, and do not sell it;
buy wisdom, instruction,
and understanding.

24 The father of the righteous
will greatly rejoice;
he who begets a wise son
will be glad in him.

25 Let your father and
mother be glad;
let her who bore you rejoice.

26 My child, give me your heart,
and let your eyes observe[d]
my ways.

27 For a prostitute is a deep pit;
an adulteress[e] is a narrow well.

28 She lies in wait like a robber
and increases the number
of the faithless.

29 Who has woe? Who has sorrow?
Who has strife? Who has
complaining?
Who has wounds without cause?
Who has redness of eyes?

30 Those who linger late over wine,
those who keep trying
mixed wines.

---

a 23.1 Or *who*   b 23.3 Heb *his*
c 23.7 Meaning of Heb uncertain
d 23.26 Another reading is *delight in*
e 23.27 Heb *an alien woman*

31 Do not look at wine when it is red,
    when it sparkles in the cup
    and goes down smoothly.
32 At the last it bites like a serpent,
    and stings like an adder.
33 Your eyes will see strange things,
    and your mind utter
        perverse things.
34 You will be like one who
        lies down in the
        midst of the sea,
    like one who lies on the
        top of a mast.[a]
35 "They struck me," you will say,[b]
    "but I was not hurt;
    they beat me, but I did
        not feel it.
    When shall I awake?
    I will seek another drink."

24 Do not envy the wicked,
    nor desire to be with them;
2 for their minds devise violence,
    and their lips talk of mischief.

3 By wisdom a house is built,
    and by understanding
        it is established;
4 by knowledge the rooms are filled
    with all precious and
        pleasant riches.
5 Wise warriors are mightier
        than strong ones,[c]
    and those who have
        knowledge than those
        who have strength;
6 for by wise guidance you can
        wage your war,
    and in abundance of counselors
        there is victory.
7 Wisdom is too high for fools;
    in the gate they do not
        open their mouths.

8 Whoever plans to do evil
    will be called a mischief-maker.
9 The devising of folly is sin,
    and the scoffer is an
        abomination to all.

10 If you faint in the day
        of adversity,
    your strength being small;
11 if you hold back from
        rescuing those taken
        away to death,
    those who go staggering
        to the slaughter;

12 if you say, "Look, we did not
        know this"—
    does not he who weighs the
        heart perceive it?
    Does not he who keeps watch
        over your soul know it?
    And will he not repay all
        according to their deeds?

13 My child, eat honey, for it is good,
    and the drippings of the
        honeycomb are sweet
        to your taste.
14 Know that wisdom is such
        to your soul;
    if you find it, you will
        find a future,
    and your hope will not be cut off.

15 Do not lie in wait like an outlaw
        against the home
        of the righteous;
    do no violence to the place
        where the righteous live;
16 for though they fall seven times,
        they will rise again;
    but the wicked are overthrown
        by calamity.

17 Do not rejoice when your
        enemies fall,
    and do not let your heart be
        glad when they stumble,
18 or else the LORD will see it
        and be displeased,
    and turn away his anger
        from them.

19 Do not fret because of evildoers.
    Do not envy the wicked;
20 for the evil have no future;
    the lamp of the wicked
        will go out.

21 My child, fear the LORD
        and the king,
    and do not disobey
        either of them;[d]
22 for disaster comes from
        them suddenly,
    and who knows the ruin
        that both can bring?

a 23.34 Meaning of Heb uncertain
b 23.35 Gk Syr Vg Tg: Heb lacks *you will say*
c 24.5 Gk Compare Syr Tg: Heb *A wise man is
    strength*   d 24.21 Gk: Heb *do not associate
    with those who change*

FURTHER SAYINGS OF THE WISE

23 These also are sayings
of the wise:

Partiality in judging is not good.
24 Whoever says to the wicked,
"You are innocent,"
will be cursed by peoples,
abhorred by nations;
25 but those who rebuke the wicked
will have delight,
and a good blessing will
come upon them.
26 One who gives an honest answer
gives a kiss on the lips.

27 Prepare your work outside,
get everything ready for
you in the field;
and after that build
your house.

28 Do not be a witness against your
neighbor without cause,
and do not deceive
with your lips.
29 Do not say, "I will do to others as
they have done to me;
I will pay them back for
what they have done."

30 I passed by the field of one
who was lazy,
by the vineyard of a
stupid person;
31 and see, it was all overgrown
with thorns;
the ground was covered
with nettles,
and its stone wall was
broken down.
32 Then I saw and considered it;
I looked and received
instruction.
33 A little sleep, a little slumber,
a little folding of the
hands to rest,
34 and poverty will come upon
you like a robber,
and want, like an armed
warrior.

FURTHER WISE SAYINGS
OF SOLOMON

25 These are other proverbs of
Solomon that the officials of
King Hezekiah of Judah copied.

2 It is the glory of God to
conceal things,
but the glory of kings is to
search things out.
3 Like the heavens for height, like
the earth for depth,
so the mind of kings is
unsearchable.
4 Take away the dross from
the silver,
and the smith has material
for a vessel;
5 take away the wicked from the
presence of the king,
and his throne will
be established in
righteousness.
6 Do not put yourself forward in
the king's presence
or stand in the place
of the great;
7 for it is better to be told,
"Come up here,"
than to be put lower in the
presence of a noble.

What your eyes have seen
8 do not hastily bring into court;
for[a] what will you do in the end,
when your neighbor puts
you to shame?
9 Argue your case with your
neighbor directly,
and do not disclose
another's secret;
10 or else someone who hears
you will bring
shame upon you,
and your ill repute will
have no end.

11 A word fitly spoken
is like apples of gold in a
setting of silver.
12 Like a gold ring or an
ornament of gold
is a wise rebuke to a
listening ear.
13 Like the cold of snow in the
time of harvest
are faithful messengers to
those who send them;
they refresh the spirit of
their masters.

a 25.8 Cn: Heb or else

14 Like clouds and wind without rain
  is one who boasts of a
    gift never given.
15 With patience a ruler may
    be persuaded,
  and a soft tongue can
    break bones.
16 If you have found honey, eat
    only enough for you,
  or else, having too much,
    you will vomit it.
17 Let your foot be seldom in your
    neighbor's house,
  otherwise the neighbor
    will become weary of
    you and hate you.
18 Like a war club, a sword, or
    a sharp arrow
  is one who bears false witness
    against a neighbor.
19 Like a bad tooth or a lame foot
  is trust in a faithless person
    in time of trouble.
20 Like vinegar on a wound[a]
  is one who sings songs
    to a heavy heart.
  Like a moth in clothing or
    a worm in wood,
  sorrow gnaws at the
    human heart.[b]
21 If your enemies are hungry,
    give them bread to eat;
  and if they are thirsty, give
    them water to drink;

22 for you will heap coals of fire
    on their heads,
  and the LORD will reward you.
23 The north wind produces rain,
  and a backbiting tongue,
    angry looks.
24 It is better to live in a corner
    of the housetop
  than in a house shared with
    a contentious wife.
25 Like cold water to a thirsty soul,
  so is good news from
    a far country.
26 Like a muddied spring or a
    polluted fountain
  are the righteous who give
    way before the wicked.
27 It is not good to eat much honey,
  or to seek honor on
    top of honor.
28 Like a city breached,
    without walls,
  is one who lacks self-control.

26 Like snow in summer
    or rain in harvest,
  so honor is not fitting for a fool.
2 Like a sparrow in its flitting, like
    a swallow in its flying,
  an undeserved curse
    goes nowhere.

a 25.20 Gk: Heb *Like one who takes off a garment on a cold day, like vinegar on lye*
b 25.20 Gk Syr Tg: Heb lacks *Like a moth ... human heart*

├─┤ BIBLE IN LIFE ▷

Repaying Evil With Good   *Proverbs 25.21–22*

How we respond to good and evil falls into one of three categories. Option one is that we can do evil to people who are good to us, which is a sin of which we are all guilty sometimes. Option two is treating others as they have treated us: If somebody treats us badly, we repay that person with evil, or if someone is good to us, we treat that person kindly. Option three is very difficult: If someone does a bad deed to us, we repay that person with a blessing.

The concept of repaying evil with good goes against human nature and even the traditional teaching of equal retribution that was taught in Old Testament times ("eye for eye, tooth for tooth, hand for hand, foot for foot" [Exodus 21.24]). One of Jesus' revolutionary teachings is that we are to love our enemies (see Matthew 5.43–48). This was difficult for early Christians to practice as they faced persecution for their faith. We also struggle with loving our enemies. Peter tells us, "Do not repay evil for evil or abuse for abuse; but, on the contrary, repay with a blessing. It is for this that you were called—that you might inherit a blessing" (1 Peter 3.9). Why should we repay evil with good? Because it is Jesus' command and likely to bring benefits to us and to our "enemies."

3 A whip for the horse, a bridle
    for the donkey,
  and a rod for the back of fools.
4 Do not answer fools according
    to their folly,
  or you will be a fool yourself.
5 Answer fools according
    to their folly,
  or they will be wise in
    their own eyes.
6 It is like cutting off one's foot and
    drinking down violence,
  to send a message by a fool.
7 The legs of a disabled person
    hang limp;
  so does a proverb in the
    mouth of a fool.
8 It is like binding a
    stone in a sling
  to give honor to a fool.
9 Like a thornbush brandished by
    the hand of a drunkard
  is a proverb in the
    mouth of a fool.
10 Like an archer who wounds
    everybody
  is one who hires a passing
    fool or drunkard.[a]
11 Like a dog that returns
    to its vomit
  is a fool who reverts to his folly.
12 Do you see persons wise in
    their own eyes?
  There is more hope for
    fools than for them.
13 The lazy person says, "There
    is a lion in the road!
  There is a lion in the streets!"
14 As a door turns on its hinges,
  so does a lazy person in bed.
15 The lazy person buries a
    hand in the dish,
  and is too tired to bring it
    back to the mouth.
16 The lazy person is wiser
    in self-esteem
  than seven who can
    answer discreetly.
17 Like somebody who takes a
    passing dog by the ears
  is one who meddles in the
    quarrel of another.
18 Like a maniac who shoots deadly
    firebrands and arrows,
19 so is one who deceives
    a neighbor
  and says, "I am only joking!"

20 For lack of wood the fire goes out,
  and where there is
    no whisperer,
    quarreling ceases.
21 As charcoal is to hot embers
    and wood to fire,
  so is a quarrelsome person
    for kindling strife.
22 The words of a whisperer are
    like delicious morsels;
  they go down into the inner
    parts of the body.
23 Like the glaze[b] covering an
    earthen vessel
  are smooth[c] lips with
    an evil heart.
24 An enemy dissembles in speaking
  while harboring deceit within;
25 when an enemy speaks
    graciously, do not
    believe it,
  for there are seven
    abominations
    concealed within;
26 though hatred is covered
    with guile,
  the enemy's wickedness will be
    exposed in the assembly.
27 Whoever digs a pit will fall into it,
  and a stone will come
    back on the one who
    starts it rolling.
28 A lying tongue hates its victims,
  and a flattering mouth
    works ruin.

27 Do not boast about
    tomorrow,
  for you do not know what
    a day may bring.
2 Let another praise you, and not
    your own mouth—
  a stranger, and not
    your own lips.
3 A stone is heavy, and sand
    is weighty,
  but a fool's provocation is
    heavier than both.
4 Wrath is cruel, anger is
    overwhelming,
  but who is able to stand
    before jealousy?
5 Better is open rebuke
  than hidden love.

[a] 26.10 Meaning of Heb uncertain
[b] 26.23 Cn: Heb silver of dross [c] 26.23 Gk:
Heb burning

⁶ Well meant are the wounds
    a friend inflicts,
  but profuse are the kisses
    of an enemy.
⁷ The sated appetite spurns honey,
    but to a ravenous appetite
      even the bitter is sweet.
⁸ Like a bird that strays
    from its nest
  is one who strays from home.
⁹ Perfume and incense make
    the heart glad,
  but the soul is torn
    by trouble.ᵃ
¹⁰ Do not forsake your friend or the
      friend of your parent;
  do not go to the house of
      your kindred in the
      day of your calamity.
  Better is a neighbor who
      is nearby
  than kindred who
      are far away.
¹¹ Be wise, my child, and make
      my heart glad,
  so that I may answer whoever
      reproaches me.
¹² The clever see danger and hide;
    but the simple go on,
      and suffer for it.
¹³ Take the garment of one
      who has given surety
      for a stranger;
    seize the pledge given as
      surety for foreigners.ᵇ
¹⁴ Whoever blesses a neighbor
      with a loud voice,
    rising early in the morning,
    will be counted as cursing.
¹⁵ A continual dripping on
      a rainy day
    and a contentious wife
      are alike;
¹⁶ to restrain her is to restrain
      the wind
    or to grasp oil in the
      right hand.ᶜ
¹⁷ Iron sharpens iron,
    and one person sharpens
      the witsᵈ of another.
¹⁸ Anyone who tends a fig tree
      will eat its fruit,
    and anyone who takes care of
      a master will be honored.
¹⁹ Just as water reflects the face,
    so one human heart
      reflects another.

²⁰ Sheol and Abaddon are
      never satisfied,
    and human eyes are
      never satisfied.
²¹ The crucible is for silver, and
      the furnace is for gold,
    so a person is testedᵉ by
      being praised.
²² Crush a fool in a mortar
      with a pestle
    along with crushed grain,
    but the folly will not
      be driven out.

²³ Know well the condition
      of your flocks,
    and give attention to
      your herds;
²⁴ for riches do not last forever,
    nor a crown for all generations.
²⁵ When the grass is gone, and
      new growth appears,
    and the herbage of the
      mountains is gathered,
²⁶ the lambs will provide
      your clothing,
    and the goats the price of a field;
²⁷ there will be enough goats'
      milk for your food,
    for the food of your household
    and nourishment for your
      servant-girls.

28 The wicked flee when
      no one pursues,
    but the righteous are as
      bold as a lion.
² When a land rebels
      it has many rulers;
    but with an intelligent ruler
      there is lasting order.ᶜ
³ A rulerᶠ who oppresses the poor
      is a beating rain that
      leaves no food.
⁴ Those who forsake the law
      praise the wicked,
    but those who keep the law
      struggle against them.
⁵ The evil do not understand
      justice,
    but those who seek the LORD
      understand it completely.

ᵃ **27.9** Gk: Heb *the sweetness of a friend is
better than one's own counsel*   ᵇ **27.13** Vg
and 20.16: Heb *for a foreign woman*
ᶜ **27.16; 28.2** Meaning of Heb uncertain
ᵈ **27.17** Heb *face*   ᵉ **27.21** Heb lacks *is tested*
ᶠ **28.3** Cn: Heb *A poor person*

6 Better to be poor and walk
    in integrity
        than to be crooked in one's
        ways even though rich.

7 Those who keep the law are
    wise children,
        but companions of gluttons
        shame their parents.

8 One who augments wealth by
    exorbitant interest
        gathers it for another who
        is kind to the poor.

9 When one will not listen
    to the law,
        even one's prayers are
        an abomination.

10 Those who mislead the upright
    into evil ways
        will fall into pits of their
        own making,
        but the blameless will have
        a goodly inheritance.

11 The rich is wise in
    self-esteem,
        but an intelligent poor person
        sees through the pose.

12 When the righteous triumph,
    there is great glory,
        but when the wicked prevail,
        people go into hiding.

13 No one who conceals
    transgressions
        will prosper,
        but one who confesses
        and forsakes them
        will obtain mercy.

14 Happy is the one who is
    never without fear,
        but one who is hard-hearted
        will fall into calamity.

15 Like a roaring lion or a
    charging bear
        is a wicked ruler over
        a poor people.

16 A ruler who lacks understanding
    is a cruel oppressor;
        but one who hates unjust gain
        will enjoy a long life.

17 If someone is burdened with
    the blood of another,
        let that killer be a fugitive
        until death;
        let no one offer assistance.

18 One who walks in integrity
    will be safe,
        but whoever follows crooked
        ways will fall into the Pit.ᵃ

19 Anyone who tills the land will
    have plenty of bread,
        but one who follows worthless
        pursuits will have
        plenty of poverty.

20 The faithful will abound
    with blessings,
        but one who is in a hurry
        to be rich will not
        go unpunished.

21 To show partiality is not good—
        yet for a piece of bread a
        person may do wrong.

22 The miser is in a
    hurry to get rich
        and does not know that
        loss is sure to come.

23 Whoever rebukes a person will
    afterward find more favor
        than one who flatters
        with the tongue.

24 Anyone who robs father
    or mother
        and says, "That is no crime,"
        is partner to a thug.

25 The greedy person stirs
    up strife,
        but whoever trusts in the
        LORD will be enriched.

26 Those who trust in their
    own wits are fools;
        but those who walk in wisdom
        come through safely.

27 Whoever gives to the poor
    will lack nothing,
        but one who turns a blind eye
        will get many a curse.

28 When the wicked prevail,
    people go into hiding;
        but when they perish, the
        righteous increase.

ᵃ **28.18** Syr: Heb *fall all at once*

A FAMILY NEEDS

PEACEMAKERS—THOSE

WHO WILL BRING ABOUT

RECONCILIATION.

29

One who is often reproved,
   yet remains stubborn,
will suddenly be broken
   beyond healing.
2 When the righteous are
      in authority, the
      people rejoice;
   but when the wicked rule,
      the people groan.
3 A child who loves wisdom
      makes a parent glad,
   but to keep company with
      prostitutes is to squander
      one's substance.
4 By justice a king gives stability
      to the land,
   but one who makes heavy
      exactions ruins it.
5 Whoever flatters a neighbor
   is spreading a net for the
      neighbor's feet.
6 In the transgression of the
      evil there is a snare,
   but the righteous sing
      and rejoice.
7 The righteous know the
      rights of the poor;
   the wicked have no such
      understanding.
8 Scoffers set a city aflame,
   but the wise turn away wrath.
9 If the wise go to law with fools,
   there is ranting and ridicule
      without relief.
10 The bloodthirsty hate the
      blameless,
   and they seek the life of
      the upright.
11 A fool gives full vent to anger,
   but the wise quietly holds it back.
12 If a ruler listens to falsehood,
   all his officials will be wicked.
13 The poor and the oppressor
      have this in common:
   the LORD gives light to
      the eyes of both.
14 If a king judges the poor
      with equity,
   his throne will be
      established forever.
15 The rod and reproof give wisdom,
   but a mother is disgraced
      by a neglected child.
16 When the wicked are in authority,
      transgression increases,
   but the righteous will look
      upon their downfall.

PONDER

The righteous know the rights
of the poor, the wicked have
no such understanding.
—Proverbs 29.7

PRAY

Sovereign Lord, we have been
challenged to look at your undistorted
Holy Word. We ask you for strength
of purpose and wisdom in eliminating
discrimination and the overbearing
power of those in authority, to the
detriment of those who are weak or in
need. Help us remember that Christ
reached out to the most helpless.
Soften our hearts and help us overcome
the differences that arise from
political positions and debates about
interpretation of individual verses, to
remember that the basic teachings of
our Savior are humility, service, justice,
compassion and love. We ask these
things in his precious name. Amen.

17 Discipline your children, and
      they will give you rest;
   they will give delight
      to your heart.
18 Where there is no prophecy, the
      people cast off restraint,
   but happy are those who
      keep the law.
19 By mere words servants are
      not disciplined,
   for though they understand,
      they will not give heed.
20 Do you see someone who is
      hasty in speech?
   There is more hope for a fool
      than for anyone like that.
21 A slave pampered from childhood
   will come to a bad end.[a]
22 One given to anger stirs up strife,
   and the hothead causes
      much transgression.

a 29.21 Vg: Meaning of Heb uncertain

23 A person's pride will bring
        humiliation,
     but one who is lowly in spirit
        will obtain honor.
24 To be a partner of a thief is to
        hate one's own life;
     one hears the victim's curse,
        but discloses nothing.[a]
25 The fear of others[b] lays a snare,
     but one who trusts in the
        LORD is secure.
26 Many seek the favor of a ruler,
     but it is from the LORD that
        one gets justice.
27 The unjust are an abomination
        to the righteous,
     but the upright are an
        abomination to the wicked.

SAYINGS OF AGUR

30 The words of Agur son of Ja-
     keh. An oracle.

Thus says the man: I am
        weary, O God,
I am weary, O God. How
        can I prevail?[c]
2 Surely I am too stupid to
        be human;
     I do not have human
        understanding.
3 I have not learned wisdom,
     nor have I knowledge of
        the holy ones.[d]
4 Who has ascended to heaven
        and come down?
     Who has gathered the wind in
        the hollow of the hand?
     Who has wrapped up the
        waters in a garment?
     Who has established all the
        ends of the earth?
     What is the person's name?
     And what is the name of
        the person's child?
     Surely you know!

5 Every word of God proves true;
     he is a shield to those who
        take refuge in him.
6 Do not add to his words,
     or else he will rebuke you, and
        you will be found a liar.

7 Two things I ask of you;
     do not deny them to me
        before I die:

8 Remove far from me falsehood
        and lying;
     give me neither poverty
        nor riches;
     feed me with the food
        that I need,
9 or I shall be full, and deny you,
     and say, "Who is the LORD?"
     or I shall be poor, and steal,
     and profane the name
        of my God.

10 Do not slander a servant
        to a master,
     or the servant will curse
        you, and you will
        be held guilty.

11 There are those who curse
        their fathers
     and do not bless their mothers.
12 There are those who are pure
        in their own eyes
     yet are not cleansed of
        their filthiness.
13 There are those—how lofty
        are their eyes,
     how high their eyelids lift!—
14 there are those whose teeth
        are swords,
     whose teeth are knives,
     to devour the poor from
        off the earth,
     the needy from among mortals.

15 The leech[a] has two daughters;
     "Give, give," they cry.
     Three things are never satisfied;
     four never say, "Enough":
16 Sheol, the barren womb,
     the earth ever thirsty for water,
     and the fire that never
        says, "Enough."[a]

17 The eye that mocks a father
        and scorns to obey a mother
     will be pecked out by the
        ravens of the valley
     and eaten by the vultures.

18 Three things are too
        wonderful for me;
     four I do not understand:

---

[a] 29.24; 30.15,16 Meaning of Heb uncertain
[b] 29.25 Or human fear   [c] 30.1 Or I am
spent. Meaning of Heb uncertain   [d] 30.3 Or
Holy One

19 the way of an eagle in the sky,
   the way of a snake on a rock,
the way of a ship on the
   high seas,
and the way of a man
   with a girl.

20 This is the way of an adulteress:
   she eats, and wipes her mouth,
and says, "I have done
   no wrong."

21 Under three things the
   earth trembles;
   under four it cannot
   bear up:
22 a slave when he becomes king,
   and a fool when glutted
   with food;
23 an unloved woman when she
   gets a husband,
and a maid when she
   succeeds her mistress.

24 Four things on earth are small,
   yet they are exceedingly wise:
25 the ants are a people
   without strength,
   yet they provide their food
   in the summer;
26 the badgers are a people
   without power,
   yet they make their homes
   in the rocks;
27 the locusts have no king,
   yet all of them march in rank;
28 the lizard[a] can be grasped
   in the hand,
   yet it is found in kings' palaces.

29 Three things are stately
   in their stride;
four are stately in their gait:
30 the lion, which is mightiest
   among wild animals
and does not turn back
   before any;
31 the strutting rooster,[b]
   the he-goat,
and a king striding
   before[c] his people.

32 If you have been foolish,
   exalting yourself,
or if you have been
   devising evil,
put your hand on your mouth.

33 For as pressing milk
   produces curds,
and pressing the nose
   produces blood,
so pressing anger
   produces strife.

THE TEACHING OF KING LEMUEL'S MOTHER

31 The words of King Lemuel. An oracle that his mother taught him:

2 No, my son! No, son of my womb!
   No, son of my vows!
3 Do not give your strength
   to women,
   your ways to those who
   destroy kings.
4 It is not for kings, O Lemuel,
   it is not for kings to
   drink wine,
   or for rulers to desire[d]
   strong drink;
5 or else they will drink and forget
   what has been decreed,
   and will pervert the rights
   of all the afflicted.
6 Give strong drink to one
   who is perishing,
   and wine to those in
   bitter distress;
7 let them drink and forget
   their poverty,
   and remember their
   misery no more.
8 Speak out for those who
   cannot speak,
   for the rights of all the
   destitute.[e]
9 Speak out, judge righteously,
   defend the rights of the
   poor and needy.

ODE TO A CAPABLE WIFE

10 A capable wife who can find?
   She is far more precious
   than jewels.
11 The heart of her husband
   trusts in her,
   and he will have no
   lack of gain.

[a] 30.28 Or *spider*   [b] 30.31 Gk Syr Tg
Compare Vg: Meaning of Heb uncertain
[c] 30.31 Meaning of Heb uncertain
[d] 31.4 Cn: Heb *where*   [e] 31.8 Heb *all children of passing away*

12 She does him good, and
        not harm,
    all the days of her life.
13 She seeks wool and flax,
    and works with willing hands.
14 She is like the ships of
        the merchant,
    she brings her food
        from far away.
15 She rises while it is still night
    and provides food for
        her household
    and tasks for her servant-girls.
16 She considers a field and buys it;
    with the fruit of her hands
        she plants a vineyard.
17 She girds herself with strength,
    and makes her arms strong.
18 She perceives that her
        merchandise is profitable.
    Her lamp does not go
        out at night.
19 She puts her hands
        to the distaff,
    and her hands hold the spindle.
20 She opens her hand to the poor,
    and reaches out her hands
        to the needy.
21 She is not afraid for her
        household when it snows,
    for all her household are
        clothed in crimson.
22 She makes herself coverings;
    her clothing is fine linen
        and purple.

23 Her husband is known in
        the city gates,
    taking his seat among the
        elders of the land.
24 She makes linen garments
        and sells them;
    she supplies the merchant
        with sashes.
25 Strength and dignity are
        her clothing,
    and she laughs at the
        time to come.
26 She opens her mouth
        with wisdom,
    and the teaching of kindness
        is on her tongue.
27 She looks well to the ways
        of her household,
    and does not eat the
        bread of idleness.
28 Her children rise up and
        call her happy;
    her husband too, and
        he praises her:
29 "Many women have done
        excellently,
    but you surpass them all."
30 Charm is deceitful, and
        beauty is vain,
    but a woman who fears the
        LORD is to be praised.
31 Give her a share in the fruit
        of her hands,
    and let her works praise
        her in the city gates.

ECCLESIASTES

Imagine what it would be like to look back over your life and discover that everything you did was meaningless. The writer of Ecclesiastes, most likely Solomon, faced this very situation. Though he enjoyed more knowledge, accomplishments, opulence and pleasure than many of us could even dream of, he concluded that a life without God at its very center is futile. He honestly confessed his struggles with doubt and disillusionment. As we read this book, we can think about our own sense of purpose and how we can cultivate a God-centered life.

REFLECTIONS OF A ROYAL PHILOSOPHER

1 The words of the Teacher,[a] the son of David, king in Jerusalem.

2 Vanity of vanities, says
the Teacher,[a]
vanity of vanities! All is vanity.
3 What do people gain from
all the toil
at which they toil
under the sun?
4 A generation goes, and a
generation comes,
but the earth remains forever.
5 The sun rises and the sun
goes down,
and hurries to the place
where it rises.
6 The wind blows to the south,
and goes around to the north;
round and round goes the wind,
and on its circuits the
wind returns.
7 All streams run to the sea,
but the sea is not full;
to the place where the
streams flow,
there they continue to flow.
8 All things[b] are wearisome;
more than one can express;
the eye is not satisfied
with seeing,
or the ear filled with hearing.
9 What has been is what will be,
and what has been done is
what will be done;
there is nothing new
under the sun.
10 Is there a thing of which it is said,
"See, this is new"?
It has already been,
in the ages before us.
11 The people of long ago are
not remembered,
nor will there be any
remembrance
of people yet to come
by those who come after them.

THE FUTILITY OF SEEKING WISDOM

12 I, the Teacher,[a] when king over Israel in Jerusalem, 13applied my mind to seek and to search out by wisdom all that is done under heaven; it is an unhappy business that God has given to human beings to be busy with. 14I saw all the deeds that are done under the sun; and see, all is vanity and a chasing after wind.[c]
15 What is crooked cannot be
made straight,
and what is lacking cannot
be counted.

16 I said to myself, "I have acquired great wisdom, surpassing all who were over Jerusalem before me; and my mind has had great experience of wisdom and knowledge." 17And I applied my mind to know wisdom and to know madness and folly. I perceived that this also is but a chasing after wind.[c]
18 For in much wisdom is
much vexation,
and those who increase
knowledge increase
sorrow.

THE FUTILITY OF SELF-INDULGENCE

2 I said to myself, "Come now, I will make a test of pleasure; enjoy yourself." But again, this also was vanity. 2I said of laughter, "It is mad," and of pleasure, "What use is it?" 3I searched with my mind how to cheer my body with wine—my mind still guiding me with wisdom—and how to lay hold on folly, until I might see what was good for mortals to do under heaven during the few days of their life. 4I made great works; I built houses and planted vineyards for myself; 5I made myself gardens and parks, and planted in them all kinds of fruit trees. 6I made myself pools from which to water the forest of growing trees. 7I bought male and female slaves, and had slaves who were born in my house; I also had great possessions of herds and flocks, more than any who had been before me in Jerusalem. 8I also gathered for myself silver and gold and the treasure of kings and of the provinces; I got singers, both men and women, and delights of the flesh, and many concubines.[d]

[a] 1.1,2,12 Heb *Qoheleth*, traditionally rendered *Preacher*   [b] 1.8 Or *words*
[c] 1.14,17 Or *a feeding on wind*. See Hos 12.1
[d] 2.8 Meaning of Heb uncertain

9 So I became great and surpassed all who were before me in Jerusalem; also my wisdom remained with me. 10Whatever my eyes desired I did not keep from them; I kept my heart from no pleasure, for my heart found pleasure in all my toil, and this was my reward for all my toil. 11Then I considered all that my hands had done and the toil I had spent in doing it, and again, all was vanity and a chasing after wind,[a] and there was nothing to be gained under the sun.

WISDOM AND JOY GIVEN TO ONE WHO PLEASES GOD

12 So I turned to consider wisdom and madness and folly; for what can the one do who comes after the king? Only what has already been done. 13Then I saw that wisdom excels folly as light excels darkness.

14 The wise have eyes in their head,
　　but fools walk in darkness.

Yet I perceived that the same fate befalls all of them. 15Then I said to myself, "What happens to the fool will happen to me also; why then have I been so very wise?" And I said to myself that this also is vanity. 16For there is no enduring remembrance of the wise or of fools, seeing that in the days to come all will have been long forgotten. How can the wise die just like fools? 17So I hated life, because what is done under the sun was grievous to me; for all is vanity and a chasing after wind.[a]

18 I hated all my toil in which I had toiled under the sun, seeing that I must leave it to those who come after me 19—and who knows whether they will be wise or foolish? Yet they will be master of all for which I toiled and used my wisdom under the sun. This also is vanity. 20So I turned and gave my heart up to despair concerning all the toil of my labors under the sun, 21because sometimes one who has toiled with wisdom and knowledge and skill must leave all to be enjoyed by another who did not toil for it. This also is vanity and a great evil. 22What do mortals get from all the toil and strain with which they toil under the sun? 23For all their days are full of pain, and their work is a vexation; even at night their minds do not rest. This also is vanity.

24 There is nothing better for mortals than to eat and drink, and find enjoyment in their toil. This also, I saw, is from the hand of God; 25for apart from him[b] who can eat or who can have enjoyment? 26For to the one who pleases him God gives wisdom and knowledge and joy; but to the sinner he gives the work of gathering and heaping, only to give to one who pleases God. This also is vanity and a chasing after wind.[a]

EVERYTHING HAS ITS TIME

3 For everything there is a season, and a time for every matter under heaven:
2 　a time to be born, and a
　　　　time to die;

---

[a] 2.11,17,26 Or *a feeding on wind.* See Hos 12.1
[b] 2.25 Gk Syr: Heb *apart from me*

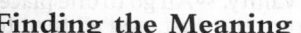

BIBLE IN LIFE

Finding the Meaning
Ecclesiastes 2.16

Approaching death is obviously one of the most troubling aspects of life, even for Christians. Imagine if we shared the view of death espoused by the writer of Ecclesiastes. The Teacher found it unfair that people receive the same fate, no matter what they do. Whether they're good or bad, wise or foolish, respectful or cursing, it doesn't matter; everybody eventually dies and will soon be forgotten. But that doesn't necessarily imply that life and death are meaningless. Jesus came to give meaning to life. He said, "I came that they may have life, and have it abundantly" (John 10.10), now and in eternity. Because of Christ and his resurrection, life can be full of meaning, and our fate in death is not hopeless.

a time to plant, and a time to
 pluck up what is planted;
3 a time to kill, and a time to heal;
a time to break down, and a
 time to build up;
4 a time to weep, and a
 time to laugh;
a time to mourn, and a
 time to dance;
5 a time to throw away stones,
 and a time to gather
 stones together;
a time to embrace, and a time to
 refrain from embracing;
6 a time to seek, and a time to lose;
a time to keep, and a time
 to throw away;
7 a time to tear, and a time to sew;
a time to keep silence, and
 a time to speak;
8 a time to love, and a time to hate;
a time for war, and a time
 for peace.

THE GOD-GIVEN TASK

9 What gain have the workers from their toil? 10 I have seen the business that God has given to everyone to be busy with. 11 He has made everything suitable for its time; moreover he has put a sense of past and future into their minds, yet they cannot find out what God has done from the beginning to the end. 12 I know that there is nothing better for them than to be happy and enjoy themselves as long as they live; 13 moreover, it is God's gift that all should eat and drink and take pleasure in all their toil. 14 I know that whatever God does endures forever; nothing can be added to it, nor anything taken from it; God has done this, so that all should stand in awe before him. 15 That which is, already has been; that which is to be, already is; and God seeks out what has gone by.[a]

JUDGMENT AND THE FUTURE BELONG TO GOD

16 Moreover I saw under the sun that in the place of justice, wickedness was there, and in the place of righteousness, wickedness was there as well. 17 I said in my heart, God will judge the righteous and the

---

PONDER

[God] has made everything suitable for its time; moreover he has put a sense of past and future into their minds, yet they cannot find out what God has done from the beginning to the end.
—Ecclesiastes 3.11

PRAY

Father, it is difficult to understand Ecclesiastes. Give us understanding to apply your wisdom in light of the words and actions of our Savior, Jesus Christ. Teach us your truth; give us a comprehension of things we do not know. We know we cannot wholly understand your nature or your being until we stand before your throne, but until then, we are blessed to look at Christ's life in order to see you, our Creator. Give us compassion to minister in Jesus' name. Discipline us to overcome the temptation to be arrogant and self-satisfied; help us to draw nearer to our loving, gentle, sharing, forgiving, humble Savior, we pray. Amen.

---

wicked, for he has appointed a time for every matter, and for every work. 18 I said in my heart with regard to human beings that God is testing them to show that they are but animals. 19 For the fate of humans and the fate of animals is the same; as one dies, so dies the other. They all have the same breath, and humans have no advantage over the animals; for all is vanity. 20 All go to one place; all are from the dust, and all turn to dust again. 21 Who knows whether the human spirit goes upward and the spirit of animals goes downward to the earth? 22 So I saw that there is nothing better than that all should enjoy their work, for that is their lot; who can bring them to see what will be after them?

---

a 3.15 Heb *what is pursued*

4 Again I saw all the oppressions that are practiced under the sun. Look, the tears of the oppressed—with no one to comfort them! On the side of their oppressors there was power—with no one to comfort them. 2 And I thought the dead, who have already died, more fortunate than the living, who are still alive; 3 but better than both is the one who has not yet been, and has not seen the evil deeds that are done under the sun.

4 Then I saw that all toil and all skill in work come from one person's envy of another. This also is vanity and a chasing after wind.[a]

5 Fools fold their hands
    and consume their own flesh.
6 Better is a handful with quiet
    than two handfuls with toil,
    and a chasing after wind.[a]

7 Again, I saw vanity under the sun: 8 the case of solitary individuals, without sons or brothers; yet there is no end to all their toil, and their eyes are never satisfied with riches. "For whom am I toiling," they ask, "and depriving myself of pleasure?" This also is vanity and an unhappy business.

THE VALUE OF A FRIEND

9 Two are better than one, because they have a good reward for their toil. 10 For if they fall, one will lift up the other; but woe to one who is alone and falls and does not have another to help. 11 Again, if two lie together, they keep warm; but how can one keep warm alone? 12 And though one might prevail against another, two will withstand one. A threefold cord is not quickly broken.

13 Better is a poor but wise youth than an old but foolish king, who will no longer take advice. 14 One can indeed come out of prison to reign, even though born poor in the kingdom. 15 I saw all the living who, moving about under the sun, follow that[b] youth who replaced the king;[c] 16 there was no end to all those people whom he led. Yet those who come later will not rejoice in him. Surely this also is vanity and a chasing after wind.[a]

REVERENCE, HUMILITY, AND CONTENTMENT

5[d] Guard your steps when you go to the house of God; to draw near to listen is better than the sacrifice offered by fools; for they do not know how to keep from doing evil.[e] 2 [f] Never be rash with your mouth, nor let your heart be quick to utter a word before God, for God is in heaven, and you upon earth; therefore let your words be few.

3 For dreams come with many cares, and a fool's voice with many words.

4 When you make a vow to God, do not delay fulfilling it; for he has no pleasure in fools. Fulfill what you vow. 5 It is better that you should not vow than that you should vow and not fulfill it. 6 Do not let your mouth lead you into sin, and do not say before the messenger that it was a

[a] 4.4,6,16 Or *a feeding on wind.* See Hos 12.1 [b] 4.15 Heb *the second* [c] 4.15 Heb *him* [d] 5.1 Ch 4.17 in Heb [e] 5.1 Cn: Heb *they do not know how to do evil* [f] 5.2 Ch 5.1 in Heb

---

⊢⊣ BIBLE IN LIFE ▷

Sharing God's Blessings   *Ecclesiastes 4.7–12*

If you asked most churchgoers whether service to others should be a part of the Christian life, they would probably say "yes." Years of Sunday School lessons and sermons have instilled in our brains that benevolence and love for others are important components of the Christian faith. The writer of Ecclesiastes points out another practical benefit of helping others: the direct advantage we receive by forming a harmonious partnership with other people. He reminds us that "two are better than one" (verse 9) and "a threefold cord is not quickly broken" (verse 12).

mistake; why should God be angry at your words, and destroy the work of your hands?

7 With many dreams come vanities and a multitude of words;[a] but fear God.

8 If you see in a province the oppression of the poor and the violation of justice and right, do not be amazed at the matter; for the high official is watched by a higher, and there are yet higher ones over them. 9But all things considered, this is an advantage for a land: a king for a plowed field.[a]

10 The lover of money will not be satisfied with money; nor the lover of wealth, with gain. This also is vanity.

11 When goods increase, those who eat them increase; and what gain has their owner but to see them with his eyes?

12 Sweet is the sleep of laborers, whether they eat little or much; but the surfeit of the rich will not let them sleep.

13 There is a grievous ill that I have seen under the sun: riches were kept by their owners to their hurt, 14and those riches were lost in a bad venture; though they are parents of children, they have nothing in their hands. 15As they came from their mother's womb, so they shall go again, naked as they came; they shall take nothing for their toil, which they may carry away with their hands. 16This also is a grievous ill: just as they came, so shall they go; and what gain do they have from toiling for the wind? 17Besides, all their days they eat in darkness, in much vexation and sickness and resentment.

18 This is what I have seen to be good: it is fitting to eat and drink and find enjoyment in all the toil with which one toils under the sun the few days of the life God gives us; for this is our lot. 19Likewise all to whom God gives wealth and possessions and whom he enables to enjoy them, and to accept their lot and find enjoyment in their toil— this is the gift of God. 20For they will scarcely brood over the days of their lives, because God keeps them occupied with the joy of their hearts.

EACH LIFE IS A MIXTURE OF GOOD AND EVIL, JOY AND SORROW.

THE FRUSTRATION OF DESIRES

6 There is an evil that I have seen under the sun, and it lies heavy upon humankind: 2those to whom God gives wealth, possessions, and honor, so that they lack nothing of all that they desire, yet God does not enable them to enjoy these things, but a stranger enjoys them. This is vanity; it is a grievous ill. 3A man may beget a hundred children, and live many years; but however many are the days of his years, if he does not enjoy life's good things, or has no burial, I say that a stillborn child is better off than he. 4For it comes into vanity and goes into darkness, and in darkness its name is covered; 5moreover it has not seen the sun or known anything; yet it finds rest rather than he. 6Even though he should live a thousand years twice over, yet enjoy no good—do not all go to one place?

7 All human toil is for the mouth, yet the appetite is not satisfied. 8For what advantage have the wise over fools? And what do the poor have who know how to conduct themselves before the living? 9Better is the sight of the eyes than the wandering of desire; this also is vanity and a chasing after wind.[b]

10 Whatever has come to be has already been named, and it is known what human beings are, and that they are not able to dispute with those who are stronger. 11The more words, the more vanity, so how is one the better? 12For who knows what is good for mortals while they

---

a 5.7,9 Meaning of Heb uncertain   b 6.9 Or *a feeding on wind*. See Hos 12.1

live the few days of their vain life, which they pass like a shadow? For who can tell them what will be after them under the sun?

A DISILLUSIONED VIEW OF LIFE

7 A good name is better than
precious ointment,
and the day of death, than
the day of birth.

2 It is better to go to the house
of mourning
than to go to the house
of feasting;
for this is the end of everyone,
and the living will lay
it to heart.

3 Sorrow is better than laughter,
for by sadness of countenance
the heart is made glad.

4 The heart of the wise is in the
house of mourning;
but the heart of fools is in
the house of mirth.

5 It is better to hear the
rebuke of the wise
than to hear the song of fools.

6 For like the crackling of
thorns under a pot,
so is the laughter of fools;
this also is vanity.

7 Surely oppression makes
the wise foolish,
and a bribe corrupts
the heart.

8 Better is the end of a thing
than its beginning;
the patient in spirit are better
than the proud in spirit.

9 Do not be quick to anger,
for anger lodges in the
bosom of fools.

10 Do not say, "Why were the former
days better than these?"
For it is not from wisdom
that you ask this.

11 Wisdom is as good as an
inheritance,
an advantage to those
who see the sun.

12 For the protection of wisdom
is like the protection
of money,
and the advantage of
knowledge is that
wisdom gives life to the
one who possesses it.

13 Consider the work of God;
who can make straight what
he has made crooked?

14 In the day of prosperity be joyful, and in the day of adversity consider; God has made the one as well as the other, so that mortals may not find out anything that will come after them.

THE RIDDLES OF LIFE

15 In my vain life I have seen everything; there are righteous people who perish in their righteousness, and there are wicked people who prolong their life in their evildoing. 16 Do not be too righteous, and do not act too wise; why should you destroy yourself? 17 Do not be too wicked, and do not be a fool; why should you die before your time? 18 It is good that you should take hold of the one, without letting go of the other; for the one who fears God shall succeed with both.

19 Wisdom gives strength to the wise more than ten rulers that are in a city.

20 Surely there is no one on earth so righteous as to do good without ever sinning.

21 Do not give heed to everything that people say, or you may hear your servant cursing you; 22 your heart knows that many times you have yourself cursed others.

23 All this I have tested by wisdom; I said, "I will be wise," but it was far from me. 24 That which is, is far off, and deep, very deep; who can find it out? 25 I turned my mind to know and to search out and to seek wisdom and the sum of things, and to know that wickedness is folly and that foolishness is madness. 26 I found more bitter than death the woman who is a trap, whose heart is snares and nets, whose hands are fetters; one who pleases God escapes her, but the sinner is taken by her. 27 See, this is what I found, says the Teacher,[a] adding one thing to another to find the sum, 28 which my mind has sought repeatedly, but I

---

a 7.27 *Qoheleth*, traditionally rendered *Preacher*

have not found. One man among a thousand I found, but a woman among all these I have not found. [29]See, this alone I found, that God made human beings straightforward, but they have devised many schemes.

OBEY THE KING AND ENJOY YOURSELF

8 Who is like the wise man?
And who knows the
interpretation of a thing?
Wisdom makes one's face shine,
and the hardness of one's
countenance is changed.

[2]Keep[a] the king's command because of your sacred oath. [3]Do not be terrified; go from his presence, do not delay when the matter is unpleasant, for he does whatever he pleases. [4]For the word of the king is powerful, and who can say to him, "What are you doing?" [5]Whoever obeys a command will meet no harm, and the wise mind will know the time and way. [6]For every matter has its time and way, although the troubles of mortals lie heavy upon them. [7]Indeed, they do not know what is to be, for who can tell them how it will be? [8]No one has power over the wind[b] to restrain the wind,[b] or power over the day of death; there is no discharge from the battle, nor does wickedness deliver those who practice it. [9]All this I observed, applying my mind to all that is done under the sun, while one person exercises authority over another to the other's hurt.

GOD'S WAYS ARE INSCRUTABLE

[10]Then I saw the wicked buried; they used to go in and out of the holy place, and were praised in the city where they had done such things.[c] This also is vanity. [11]Because sentence against an evil deed is not executed speedily, the human heart is fully set to do evil. [12]Though sinners do evil a hundred times and prolong their lives, yet I know that it will be well with those who fear God, because they stand in fear before him, [13]but it will not be well with the wicked, neither will they prolong their days like a shadow, because they do not stand in fear before God.

[14]There is a vanity that takes place on earth, that there are righteous people who are treated according to the conduct of the wicked, and there are wicked people who are treated according to the conduct of the righteous. I said that this also is vanity. [15]So I commend enjoyment, for there is nothing better for people under the sun than to eat, and drink, and enjoy themselves, for this will go with them in their toil through the days of life that God gives them under the sun.

[16]When I applied my mind to know wisdom, and to see the busi-

[a] **8.2** Heb *I keep*   [b] **8.8** Or *breath*
[c] **8.10** Meaning of Heb uncertain

⊣ BIBLE IN LIFE ▷

Life Before Death
Ecclesiastes 8.7–8

Physical death is inevitable, and the afterlife remains something of a mystery to us. We don't know what life after death will really be like or how we will exist in it. However, we do know what life *before* death is like. If we have placed our faith and trust in Jesus Christ, the One who has control over life and death, then we have no need to worry about death. We can let go of the human exigencies that permeate our thoughts and our ambitions. Paul reminds us, "We look not on what can be seen but at what cannot be seen; for what can be seen is temporary, but what cannot be seen is eternal" (2 Corinthians 4.18). What we cannot see are unchanging principles such as peace, justice, truth, service, humility, compassion, understanding and unselfish love. These are the true measures of success; these are permanent ideals because these are the factors that shape life after death. They should shape our lives before death as well.

ness that is done on earth, how one's eyes see sleep neither day nor night, [17]then I saw all the work of God, that no one can find out what is happening under the sun. However much they may toil in seeking, they will not find it out; even though those who are wise claim to know, they cannot find it out.

TAKE LIFE AS IT COMES

9 All this I laid to heart, examining it all, how the righteous and the wise and their deeds are in the hand of God; whether it is love or hate one does not know. Everything that confronts them [2]is vanity,[a] since the same fate comes to all, to the righteous and the wicked, to the good and the evil,[b] to the clean and the unclean, to those who sacrifice and those who do not sacrifice. As are the good, so are the sinners; those who swear are like those who shun an oath. [3]This is an evil in all that happens under the sun, that the same fate comes to everyone. Moreover, the hearts of all are full of evil; madness is in their hearts while they live, and after that they go to the dead. [4]But whoever is joined with all the living has hope, for a living dog is better than a dead lion. [5]The living know that they will die, but the dead know nothing; they have no more reward, and even the memory of them is lost. [6]Their love and their hate and their envy have already perished; never again will they have any share in all that happens under the sun.

[7] Go, eat your bread with enjoyment, and drink your wine with a merry heart; for God has long ago approved what you do. [8]Let your garments always be white; do not let oil be lacking on your head. [9]Enjoy life with the wife whom you love, all the days of your vain life that are given you under the sun, because that is your portion in life and in your toil at which you toil under the sun. [10]Whatever your hand finds to do, do with your might; for there is no work or thought or knowledge or wisdom in Sheol, to which you are going.

[11] Again I saw that under the sun the race is not to the swift, nor the battle to the strong, nor bread to the wise, nor riches to the intelligent, nor favor to the skillful; but time and chance happen to them all. [12]For no one can anticipate the time of disaster. Like fish taken in a cruel net, and like birds caught in a snare, so mortals are snared at a time of calamity, when it suddenly falls upon them.

WISDOM SUPERIOR TO FOLLY

[13] I have also seen this example of wisdom under the sun, and it seemed great to me. [14]There was a little city with few people in it. A great king came against it and besieged it, building great siegeworks against it. [15]Now there was found in it a poor wise man, and he by his wisdom delivered the city. Yet no one remembered that poor man. [16]So I said, "Wisdom is better than might; yet the poor man's wisdom is despised, and his words are not heeded."

[17] The quiet words of the wise are
more to be heeded
than the shouting of a
ruler among fools.
[18] Wisdom is better than
weapons of war,
but one bungler destroys
much good.

MISCELLANEOUS OBSERVATIONS

10 Dead flies make the
perfumer's ointment
give off a foul odor;
so a little folly outweighs
wisdom and honor.
[2] The heart of the wise inclines
to the right,
but the heart of a fool
to the left.
[3] Even when fools walk on the
road, they lack sense,
and show to everyone
that they are fools.
[4] If the anger of the ruler rises
against you, do not
leave your post,
for calmness will undo
great offenses.

[a] **9.2** Syr Compare Gk: Heb *Everything that confronts them* [2]*is everything*   [b] **9.2** Gk Syr Vg: Heb lacks *and the evil*

5 There is an evil that I have seen under the sun, as great an error as if it proceeded from the ruler: **6**folly is set in many high places, and the rich sit in a low place. **7**I have seen slaves on horseback, and princes walking on foot like slaves.

8 Whoever digs a pit will fall into it;
　　and whoever breaks
　　　　through a wall will be
　　　　bitten by a snake.
9 Whoever quarries stones will
　　　　be hurt by them;
　　and whoever splits logs will
　　　　be endangered by them.
10 If the iron is blunt, and one does
　　　　not whet the edge,
　　then more strength
　　　　must be exerted;
　　but wisdom helps one
　　　　to succeed.
11 If the snake bites before
　　　　it is charmed,
　　there is no advantage
　　　　in a charmer.

12 Words spoken by the wise
　　　　bring them favor,
　　but the lips of fools
　　　　consume them.
13 The words of their mouths
　　　　begin in foolishness,
　　and their talk ends in
　　　　wicked madness;
14 yet fools talk on and on.
　　No one knows what
　　　　is to happen,
　　and who can tell anyone
　　　　what the future holds?
15 The toil of fools wears
　　　　them out,
　　for they do not even know
　　　　the way to town.

16 Alas for you, O land, when your
　　　　king is a servant,[a]
　　and your princes feast
　　　　in the morning!
17 Happy are you, O land, when
　　　　your king is a nobleman,
　　and your princes feast at
　　　　the proper time—
　　for strength, and not for
　　　　drunkenness!
18 Through sloth the roof sinks in,
　　and through indolence
　　　　the house leaks.

19 Feasts are made for laughter;
　　wine gladdens life,
　　and money meets every need.
20 Do not curse the king, even
　　　　in your thoughts,
　　or curse the rich, even in
　　　　your bedroom;
　　for a bird of the air may
　　　　carry your voice,
　　or some winged creature
　　　　tell the matter.

THE VALUE OF DILIGENCE

11 Send out your bread
　　　　upon the waters,
　　for after many days you
　　　　will get it back.
2 Divide your means seven
　　　　ways, or even eight,
　　for you do not know
　　　　what disaster may
　　　　happen on earth.
3 When clouds are full,
　　　　they empty rain on the earth;
　　whether a tree falls to the
　　　　south or to the north,
　　in the place where the tree
　　　　falls, there it will lie.
4 Whoever observes the wind
　　　　will not sow;
　　and whoever regards the
　　　　clouds will not reap.
5 Just as you do not know how the breath comes to the bones in the mother's womb, so you do not know the work of God, who makes everything.

A WORTHY LEGACY IS A

LIFELONG PROCESS.

6 In the morning sow your seed, and at evening do not let your hands be idle; for you do not know which will prosper, this or that, or whether both alike will be good.

YOUTH AND OLD AGE

7 Light is sweet, and it is pleasant for the eyes to see the sun.

[a] **10.16** Or *a child*

8 Even those who live many years should rejoice in them all; yet let them remember that the days of darkness will be many. All that comes is vanity.

9 Rejoice, young man, while you are young, and let your heart cheer you in the days of your youth. Follow the inclination of your heart and the desire of your eyes, but know that for all these things God will bring you into judgment.

10 Banish anxiety from your mind, and put away pain from your body; for youth and the dawn of life are vanity.

12 Remember your creator in the days of your youth, before the days of trouble come, and the years draw near when you will say, "I have no pleasure in them"; **2**before the sun and the light and the moon and the stars are darkened and the clouds return with[a] the rain; **3**in the day when the guards of the house tremble, and the strong men are bent, and the women who grind cease working because they are few, and those who look through the windows see dimly; **4**when the doors on the street are shut, and the sound of the grinding is low, and one rises up at the sound of a bird, and all the daughters of song are brought low; **5**when one is afraid of heights, and terrors are in the road; the almond tree blossoms, the grasshopper drags itself along[b] and desire fails; because all must go to their eternal home, and the mourners will go about the streets; **6**before the silver cord is snapped,[c] and the golden bowl is broken, and the pitcher is broken at the fountain, and the wheel broken at the cistern, **7**and the dust returns to the earth as it was, and the breath[d] returns to God who gave it. **8**Vanity of vanities, says the Teacher;[e] all is vanity.

EPILOGUE

9 Besides being wise, the Teacher[e] also taught the people knowledge, weighing and studying and arranging many proverbs. **10**The Teacher[e] sought to find pleasing words, and he wrote words of truth plainly.

11 The sayings of the wise are like goads, and like nails firmly fixed are the collected sayings that are given by one shepherd.[f] **12**Of anything beyond these, my child, beware. Of making many books there is no end, and much study is a weariness of the flesh.

13 The end of the matter; all has been heard. Fear God, and keep his commandments; for that is the whole duty of everyone. **14**For God will bring every deed into judgment, including[g] every secret thing, whether good or evil.

[a] **12.2** Or *after*; Heb *'ahar* [b] **12.5** Or *is a burden* [c] **12.6** Syr Vg Compare Gk: Heb *is removed* [d] **12.7** Or *the spirit* [e] **12.8,9,10** *Qoheleth*, traditionally rendered *Preacher* [f] **12.11** Meaning of Heb uncertain [g] **12.14** Or *into the judgment on*

BIBLE IN LIFE

Take a Chance
Ecclesiastes 11.1–10

We cannot understand the work of God. There's a vast array of knowledge that we'll never absorb in our short lifetime. The writer of Ecclesiastes advises us to sow our seed in the morning (verse 6). But we can't keep waiting and waiting until the temperature and moisture are exactly right or the weather report is favorable. In other words, we build our lives as best we can in the midst of uncertainties and unknowable facts. We know that we are inadequate. We know that we are sinful. We know that we will fail. We know that we will lose loved ones. We know that some of our ambitions will never be realized. If we wait for the perfect time in our lives, for exactly the right moment before we act, we will never act. God knows our lives. He knows the opportunities we have to live out our faith. He knows which opportunities we take and which we reject or postpone. Christ wants us to be bold, to reach out and to take a chance in an uncertain world. Take a chance.

The

SONG OF SOLOMON

Often it seems as though nothing consumes us as much as the desire to experience intimacy with another person. Turn on the television or radio, walk into any bookstore or even down a city street and you'll be inundated with songs, conversation and images about romantic love. So it stands to reason that the God who created us with these desires has something to say about love, intimacy and marriage. Song of Solomon acclaims the passion, delight and allure of married love. Song of Solomon is a celebration of one of God's choicest gifts—the love between a man and a woman.

1

The Song of Songs, which is Solomon's.

COLLOQUY OF BRIDE AND FRIENDS

2 Let him kiss me with the
kisses of his mouth!
For your love is better than wine,
3 your anointing oils
are fragrant,
your name is perfume
poured out;
therefore the maidens
love you.
4 Draw me after you, let us
make haste.
The king has brought me
into his chambers.
We will exult and rejoice in you;
we will extol your love
more than wine;
rightly do they love you.

5 I am black and beautiful,
O daughters of Jerusalem,
like the tents of Kedar,
like the curtains of Solomon.
6 Do not gaze at me because
I am dark,
because the sun has
gazed on me.
My mother's sons were
angry with me;
they made me keeper of
the vineyards,
but my own vineyard I
have not kept!
7 Tell me, you whom my soul loves,
where you pasture your flock,
where you make it lie
down at noon;
for why should I be like one
who is veiled
beside the flocks of your
companions?

8 If you do not know,
O fairest among women,
follow the tracks of the flock,
and pasture your kids
beside the shepherds' tents.

COLLOQUY OF BRIDEGROOM, FRIENDS, AND BRIDE

9 I compare you, my love,
to a mare among Pharaoh's
chariots.

10 Your cheeks are comely
with ornaments,
your neck with strings
of jewels.
11 We will make you ornaments
of gold,
studded with silver.

12 While the king was on his couch,
my nard gave forth its
fragrance.
13 My beloved is to me a
bag of myrrh
that lies between my breasts.
14 My beloved is to me a cluster
of henna blossoms
in the vineyards of En-gedi.

15 Ah, you are beautiful, my love;
ah, you are beautiful;
your eyes are doves.
16 Ah, you are beautiful,
my beloved,
truly lovely.
Our couch is green;
17 the beams of our house
are cedar,
our rafters[a] are pine.

2

I am a rose[b] of Sharon,
a lily of the valleys.

2 As a lily among brambles,
so is my love among maidens.

3 As an apple tree among the
trees of the wood,
so is my beloved among
young men.
With great delight I sat
in his shadow,
and his fruit was sweet
to my taste.
4 He brought me to the
banqueting house,
and his intention toward
me was love.
5 Sustain me with raisins,
refresh me with apples;
for I am faint with love.
6 O that his left hand were
under my head,
and that his right hand
embraced me!

a 1.17 Meaning of Heb uncertain   b 2.1 Heb
crocus

7 I adjure you, O daughters
        of Jerusalem,
    by the gazelles or the wild does:
    do not stir up or awaken love
        until it is ready!

SPRINGTIME RHAPSODY

8 The voice of my beloved!
    Look, he comes,
    leaping upon the mountains,
        bounding over the hills.
9 My beloved is like a gazelle
        or a young stag.
    Look, there he stands
        behind our wall,
    gazing in at the windows,
        looking through the lattice.
10 My beloved speaks and says to me:
    "Arise, my love, my fair one,
        and come away;
11 for now the winter is past,
        the rain is over and gone.
12 The flowers appear on the earth;
        the time of singing has come,
    and the voice of the turtledove
        is heard in our land.
13 The fig tree puts forth its figs,
        and the vines are in blossom;
        they give forth fragrance.
    Arise, my love, my fair one,
        and come away.
14 O my dove, in the clefts
        of the rock,
    in the covert of the cliff,
    let me see your face,
        let me hear your voice;
    for your voice is sweet,
        and your face is lovely.
15 Catch us the foxes,
        the little foxes,
    that ruin the vineyards—
        for our vineyards are
            in blossom."

16 My beloved is mine and I am his;
        he pastures his flock
            among the lilies.
17 Until the day breathes
        and the shadows flee,
    turn, my beloved, be like a gazelle
        or a young stag on the
            cleft mountains.[a]

LOVE'S DREAM

3 Upon my bed at night
    I sought him whom
        my soul loves;

I sought him, but found him not;
    I called him, but he gave
        no answer.[b]
2 "I will rise now and go
        about the city,
    in the streets and in the squares;
    I will seek him whom my
        soul loves."
    I sought him, but found
        him not.
3 The sentinels found me,
        as they went about in the city.
    "Have you seen him whom
        my soul loves?"
4 Scarcely had I passed them,
        when I found him whom
            my soul loves.
    I held him, and would not
        let him go
    until I brought him into
        my mother's house,
    and into the chamber of her
        that conceived me.
5 I adjure you, O daughters
        of Jerusalem,
    by the gazelles or the wild does:
    do not stir up or awaken love
        until it is ready!

THE GROOM AND HIS
PARTY APPROACH

6 What is that coming up from
        the wilderness,
    like a column of smoke,
    perfumed with myrrh and
        frankincense,
    with all the fragrant powders
        of the merchant?
7 Look, it is the litter of Solomon!
    Around it are sixty mighty men
        of the mighty men of Israel,
8 all equipped with swords
        and expert in war,
    each with his sword at his thigh
        because of alarms by night.
9 King Solomon made himself
        a palanquin
    from the wood of Lebanon.
10 He made its posts of silver,
        its back of gold, its seat of purple;
    its interior was inlaid with love.[c]
        Daughters of Jerusalem,
11 come out.

a 2.17 Or on the mountains of Bether;
meaning of Heb uncertain   b 3.1 Gk: Heb
lacks this line   c 3.10 Meaning of Heb
uncertain

Look, O daughters of Zion,
    at King Solomon,
at the crown with which his
        mother crowned him
    on the day of his wedding,
    on the day of the gladness
        of his heart.

THE BRIDE'S BEAUTY EXTOLLED

4 How beautiful you
        are, my love,
    how very beautiful!
Your eyes are doves
        behind your veil.
Your hair is like a flock of goats,
    moving down the slopes
        of Gilead.
2 Your teeth are like a flock
        of shorn ewes
    that have come up from
        the washing,
all of which bear twins,
    and not one among them
        is bereaved.
3 Your lips are like a crimson
        thread,
    and your mouth is lovely.
Your cheeks are like halves
        of a pomegranate
    behind your veil.
4 Your neck is like the tower
        of David,
    built in courses;
on it hang a thousand bucklers,
    all of them shields of warriors.
5 Your two breasts are like
        two fawns,
    twins of a gazelle,
    that feed among the lilies.
6 Until the day breathes
    and the shadows flee,
I will hasten to the mountain
        of myrrh
    and the hill of frankincense.
7 You are altogether beautiful,
        my love;
    there is no flaw in you.
8 Come with me from Lebanon,
        my bride;
    come with me from Lebanon.
Depart[a] from the peak
        of Amana,
    from the peak of Senir
        and Hermon,
from the dens of lions,
    from the mountains
        of leopards.

9 You have ravished my heart,
        my sister, my bride,
    you have ravished my heart
    with a glance of your eyes,
    with one jewel of your
        necklace.
10 How sweet is your love, my
        sister, my bride!
    how much better is your
        love than wine,
    and the fragrance of your
        oils than any spice!
11 Your lips distill nectar, my bride;
    honey and milk are under
        your tongue;
    the scent of your garments is
        like the scent of Lebanon.
12 A garden locked is my
        sister, my bride,
    a garden locked, a
        fountain sealed.
13 Your channel[b] is an orchard
        of pomegranates
    with all choicest fruits,
    henna with nard,
14 nard and saffron, calamus
        and cinnamon,
    with all trees of frankincense,
    myrrh and aloes,
    with all chief spices—
15 a garden fountain, a well
        of living water,
    and flowing streams
        from Lebanon.
16 Awake, O north wind,
    and come, O south wind!
Blow upon my garden
    that its fragrance may be
        wafted abroad.
Let my beloved come to
        his garden,
    and eat its choicest fruits.

5 I come to my garden, my
        sister, my bride;
I gather my myrrh
        with my spice,
I eat my honeycomb
        with my honey,
I drink my wine with my milk.

Eat, friends, drink,
    and be drunk with love.

a 4.8 Or Look   b 4.13 Meaning of Heb
uncertain

ANOTHER DREAM

2 I slept, but my heart was awake.
Listen! my beloved is knocking.
"Open to me, my sister, my love,
my dove, my perfect one;
for my head is wet with dew,
my locks with the drops
of the night."

3 I had put off my garment;
how could I put it on again?
I had bathed my feet;
how could I soil them?

4 My beloved thrust his hand
into the opening,
and my inmost being
yearned for him.

5 I arose to open to my beloved,
and my hands dripped
with myrrh,
my fingers with liquid myrrh,
upon the handles of the bolt.

6 I opened to my beloved,
but my beloved had turned
and was gone.
My soul failed me
when he spoke.
I sought him, but did not find him;
I called him, but he gave
no answer.

7 Making their rounds in the city
the sentinels found me;
they beat me, they wounded me,
they took away my mantle,
those sentinels of the walls.

8 I adjure you, O daughters
of Jerusalem,
if you find my beloved,
tell him this:
I am faint with love.

COLLOQUY OF FRIENDS AND BRIDE

9 What is your beloved more than
another beloved,
O fairest among women?
What is your beloved more than
another beloved,
that you thus adjure us?

10 My beloved is all radiant and ruddy,
distinguished among
ten thousand.

11 His head is the finest gold;
his locks are wavy,
black as a raven.

12 His eyes are like doves
beside springs of water,

bathed in milk,
fitly set.[a]

13 His cheeks are like beds of spices,
yielding fragrance.
His lips are lilies,
distilling liquid myrrh.

14 His arms are rounded gold,
set with jewels.
His body is ivory work,[a]
encrusted with sapphires.[b]

15 His legs are alabaster columns,
set upon bases of gold.
His appearance is like Lebanon,
choice as the cedars.

16 His speech is most sweet,
and he is altogether desirable.
This is my beloved and this
is my friend,
O daughters of Jerusalem.

6 Where has your beloved gone,
O fairest among women?
Which way has your
beloved turned,
that we may seek him
with you?

2 My beloved has gone down
to his garden,
to the beds of spices,
to pasture his flock in the gardens,
and to gather lilies.

3 I am my beloved's and my
beloved is mine;
he pastures his flock
among the lilies.

THE BRIDE'S MATCHLESS BEAUTY

4 You are beautiful as Tirzah,
my love,
comely as Jerusalem,
terrible as an army
with banners.

5 Turn away your eyes from me,
for they overwhelm me!
Your hair is like a flock of goats,
moving down the slopes
of Gilead.

6 Your teeth are like a flock of ewes,
that have come up from
the washing;
all of them bear twins,
and not one among them
is bereaved.

a 5.12,14 Meaning of Heb uncertain
b 5.14 Heb lapis lazuli

7 Your cheeks are like halves
        of a pomegranate
        behind your veil.
8 There are sixty queens and
        eighty concubines,
    and maidens without number.
9 My dove, my perfect one,
        is the only one,
    the darling of her mother,
        flawless to her that bore her.
    The maidens saw her and
        called her happy;
    the queens and concubines
        also, and they praised her.
10 "Who is this that looks forth
        like the dawn,
    fair as the moon, bright
        as the sun,
    terrible as an army
        with banners?"

11 I went down to the nut orchard,
        to look at the blossoms
        of the valley,
    to see whether the vines
        had budded,
    whether the pomegranates
        were in bloom.
12 Before I was aware, my
        fancy set me
    in a chariot beside
        my prince.[a]

13b Return, return, O Shulammite!
    Return, return, that we
        may look upon you.

Why should you look upon
        the Shulammite,
    as upon a dance before
        two armies?[c]

EXPRESSIONS OF PRAISE

7 How graceful are your
        feet in sandals,
    O queenly maiden!
Your rounded thighs are
        like jewels,
    the work of a master hand.
2 Your navel is a rounded bowl
        that never lacks mixed wine.
Your belly is a heap of wheat,
        encircled with lilies.
3 Your two breasts are like
        two fawns,
    twins of a gazelle.
4 Your neck is like an ivory tower.

Your eyes are pools in Heshbon,
    by the gate of Bath-rabbim.
Your nose is like a tower
        of Lebanon,
    overlooking Damascus.
5 Your head crowns you like Carmel,
    and your flowing locks
        are like purple;
    a king is held captive in
        the tresses.[d]

6 How fair and pleasant you are,
    O loved one, delectable maiden![e]
7 You are stately[f] as a palm tree,
    and your breasts are
        like its clusters.
8 I say I will climb the palm tree
    and lay hold of its branches.
O may your breasts be like
        clusters of the vine,
    and the scent of your
        breath like apples,
9 and your kisses[g] like the best wine
        that goes down[h] smoothly,
    gliding over lips and teeth.[i]

10 I am my beloved's,
    and his desire is for me.
11 Come, my beloved,
    let us go forth into the fields,
    and lodge in the villages;
12 let us go out early to the vineyards,
    and see whether the vines
        have budded,
    whether the grape blossoms
        have opened
    and the pomegranates
        are in bloom.
There I will give you my love.
13 The mandrakes give forth
        fragrance,
    and over our doors are
        all choice fruits,
new as well as old,
    which I have laid up for
        you, O my beloved.

8 O that you were like a
        brother to me,
    who nursed at my
        mother's breast!

---

[a] 6.12 Cn: Meaning of Heb uncertain
[b] 6.13 Ch 7.1 in Heb   [c] 6.13 Or *dance
of Mahanaim*   [d] 7.5 Meaning of Heb
uncertain   [e] 7.6 Syr: Heb *in delights*
[f] 7.7 Heb *This your stature is*   [g] 7.9 Heb
palate   [h] 7.9 Heb *down for my lover*
[i] 7.9 Gk Syr Vg: Heb *lips of sleepers*

If I met you outside, I
would kiss you,
and no one would despise me.
2 I would lead you and bring you
into the house of my mother,
and into the chamber of the
one who bore me.[a]
I would give you spiced
wine to drink,
the juice of my pomegranates.
3 O that his left hand were
under my head,
and that his right hand
embraced me!
4 I adjure you, O daughters
of Jerusalem,
do not stir up or awaken love
until it is ready!

HOMECOMING

5 Who is that coming up from
the wilderness,
leaning upon her beloved?

Under the apple tree I
awakened you.
There your mother was in
labor with you;
there she who bore you
was in labor.

6 Set me as a seal upon your heart,
as a seal upon your arm;
for love is strong as death,
passion fierce as the grave.
Its flashes are flashes of fire,
a raging flame.
7 Many waters cannot quench love,
neither can floods drown it.
If one offered for love
all the wealth of one's house,
it would be utterly scorned.

8 We have a little sister,
and she has no breasts.
What shall we do for our sister,
on the day when she
is spoken for?
9 If she is a wall,
we will build upon her a
battlement of silver;
but if she is a door,
we will enclose her with
boards of cedar.
10 I was a wall,
and my breasts were
like towers;

then I was in his eyes
as one who brings[b] peace.
11 Solomon had a vineyard
at Baal-hamon;
he entrusted the vineyard
to keepers;
each one was to bring for
its fruit a thousand
pieces of silver.
12 My vineyard, my very own,
is for myself;
you, O Solomon, may have
the thousand,
and the keepers of the
fruit two hundred!

13 O you who dwell in the gardens,
my companions are listening
for your voice;
let me hear it.

14 Make haste, my beloved,
and be like a gazelle
or a young stag
upon the mountains of spices!

a **8.2** Gk Syr: Heb *my mother; she* (or *you*)
will teach me   b **8.10** Or *finds*

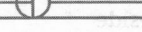

PONDER

Love is strong as death, passion
fierce as the grave. Its flashes are
flashes of fire, a raging flame.
—Song of Solomon 8.6

PRAY

O Father, help us always to open our
hearts and minds and receive the truth
about our lives and relationships with
you and with others. Let our lives blaze
with love that is strong, expansive and
life-giving. Let us face the future with
confidence in and harmony with Jesus
Christ our Savior. Following his perfect
example, we can experience all kinds of
love—abounding, amazing love—God's
love in all our relationships. We ask
these things and offer you all our love
in the name of Jesus your Son. Amen.

ISAIAH

Through the visions God gave him, Isaiah unveiled the full force of God's judgment against sin. The images of destruction and death are difficult to read and even more difficult to think about. But the prophet also painted a picture of comfort, redemption and restoration for those who put their hope in God. Many of Isaiah's most stirring prophecies predict the coming of the Messiah, the One who is to restore and redeem the earth—and the people—to the divine ideal so that the God of Israel will be praised and glorified.

1 The vision of Isaiah son of Amoz, which he saw concerning Judah and Jerusalem in the days of Uzziah, Jotham, Ahaz, and Hezekiah, kings of Judah.

THE WICKEDNESS OF JUDAH

2 Hear, O heavens, and
        listen, O earth;
    for the LORD has spoken:
    I reared children and
        brought them up,
    but they have rebelled
        against me.
3 The ox knows its owner,
    and the donkey its
        master's crib;
    but Israel does not know,
        my people do not understand.

4 Ah, sinful nation,
    people laden with iniquity,
    offspring who do evil,
        children who deal corruptly,
    who have forsaken the LORD,
    who have despised the
        Holy One of Israel,
    who are utterly estranged!

5 Why do you seek further
        beatings?
    Why do you continue to rebel?
    The whole head is sick,
        and the whole heart faint.
6 From the sole of the foot
        even to the head,
        there is no soundness in it,
    but bruises and sores
        and bleeding wounds;
    they have not been drained,
        or bound up,
        or softened with oil.

7 Your country lies desolate,
    your cities are burned
        with fire;
    in your very presence
        aliens devour your land;
    it is desolate, as overthrown
        by foreigners.
8 And daughter Zion is left
    like a booth in a vineyard,
    like a shelter in a
        cucumber field,
    like a besieged city.
9 If the LORD of hosts
    had not left us a few survivors,
    we would have been like Sodom,
        and become like Gomorrah.

10 Hear the word of the LORD,
        you rulers of Sodom!
    Listen to the teaching of our God,
        you people of Gomorrah!
11 What to me is the multitude
        of your sacrifices?
        says the LORD;
    I have had enough of burnt
        offerings of rams
        and the fat of fed beasts;
    I do not delight in the
        blood of bulls,
        or of lambs, or of goats.

12 When you come to appear
        before me,[a]
    who asked this from
        your hand?
    Trample my courts no more;
13 bringing offerings is futile;
    incense is an abomination
        to me.
    New moon and sabbath and
        calling of convocation—
    I cannot endure solemn
        assemblies with iniquity.
14 Your new moons and your
        appointed festivals
        my soul hates;
    they have become a
        burden to me,
    I am weary of bearing them.
15 When you stretch out your hands,
    I will hide my eyes from you;
    even though you make
        many prayers,
        I will not listen;
    your hands are full of blood.
16 Wash yourselves; make
        yourselves clean;
    remove the evil of your doings
        from before my eyes;
    cease to do evil,
17   learn to do good;
    seek justice,
        rescue the oppressed,
    defend the orphan,
        plead for the widow.

18 Come now, let us argue it out,
        says the LORD:

a 1.12 Or *see my face*

PONDER

Come now, let us argue it out, says the LORD: though your sins are like scarlet, they shall be like snow; though they are red like crimson, they shall become like wool.
—Isaiah 1.18

PRAY

Lord, we are thankful that these words of Isaiah, written in ancient times, still apply to us. Help us realize that to the extent that we depart from your law and the profession of Jesus Christ, we are held captive in our own selfishness and sinfulness. But you love us in spite of our sin and have shown the way to be cleansed white as snow. Through faith in Christ, and by your blessings and mercy, you forgive us and make us new as we strive always to live in the presence of our Savior. Amen.

---

though your sins are like scarlet,
they shall be like snow;
though they are red like crimson,
they shall become like wool.
19 If you are willing and obedient,
you shall eat the good
of the land;
20 but if you refuse and rebel,
you shall be devoured
by the sword;
for the mouth of the
LORD has spoken.

THE DEGENERATE CITY

21 How the faithful city
has become a whore!
She that was full of justice,
righteousness lodged in her—
but now murderers!
22 Your silver has become dross,
your wine is mixed with water.
23 Your princes are rebels
and companions of thieves.
Everyone loves a bribe
and runs after gifts.

They do not defend the orphan,
and the widow's cause does
not come before them.
24 Therefore says the Sovereign,
the LORD of hosts, the
Mighty One of Israel:
Ah, I will pour out my wrath
on my enemies,
and avenge myself on my foes!
25 I will turn my hand against you;
I will smelt away your
dross as with lye
and remove all your alloy.
26 And I will restore your judges
as at the first,
and your counselors as at
the beginning.
Afterward you shall be called the
city of righteousness,
the faithful city.

27 Zion shall be redeemed by justice,
and those in her who repent,
by righteousness.
28 But rebels and sinners shall be
destroyed together,
and those who forsake the
LORD shall be consumed.
29 For you shall be ashamed
of the oaks
in which you delighted;
and you shall blush for
the gardens
that you have chosen.
30 For you shall be like an oak
whose leaf withers,
and like a garden
without water.
31 The strong shall become
like tinder,
and their worka like a spark;
they and their work shall
burn together,
with no one to quench them.

THE FUTURE HOUSE OF GOD

2 The word that Isaiah son of Amoz saw concerning Judah and Jerusalem.

2 In days to come
the mountain of the
LORD's house

a 1.31 Or its makers

shall be established as the highest
of the mountains,
and shall be raised
above the hills;
all the nations shall stream to it.
3 Many peoples shall
come and say,
"Come, let us go up to the
mountain of the LORD,
to the house of the
God of Jacob;
that he may teach us his ways
and that we may walk
in his paths."
For out of Zion shall go
forth instruction,
and the word of the LORD
from Jerusalem.
4 He shall judge between
the nations,
and shall arbitrate for
many peoples;
they shall beat their swords
into plowshares,
and their spears into
pruning hooks;
nation shall not lift up sword
against nation,
neither shall they learn
war any more.

JUDGMENT PRONOUNCED ON ARROGANCE

5 O house of Jacob,
come, let us walk
in the light of the LORD!
6 For you have forsaken the
ways of[a] your people,
O house of Jacob.
Indeed they are full of diviners[b]
from the east
and of soothsayers like
the Philistines,
and they clasp hands
with foreigners.
7 Their land is filled with
silver and gold,
and there is no end to
their treasures;
their land is filled with horses,
and there is no end to
their chariots.
8 Their land is filled with idols;
they bow down to the work
of their hands,
to what their own fingers
have made.

9 And so people are humbled,
and everyone is brought low—
do not forgive them!
10 Enter into the rock,
and hide in the dust
from the terror of the LORD,
and from the glory of
his majesty.
11 The haughty eyes of people
shall be brought low,
and the pride of everyone
shall be humbled;
and the LORD alone will be
exalted on that day.
12 For the LORD of hosts has a day
against all that is proud
and lofty,
against all that is lifted
up and high;[c]
13 against all the cedars of Lebanon,
lofty and lifted up;
and against all the oaks
of Bashan;
14 against all the high mountains,
and against all the lofty hills;
15 against every high tower,
and against every
fortified wall;
16 against all the ships of Tarshish,
and against all the
beautiful craft.[d]
17 The haughtiness of people
shall be humbled,
and the pride of everyone
shall be brought low;
and the LORD alone will be
exalted on that day.
18 The idols shall utterly pass away.
19 Enter the caves of the rocks
and the holes of the ground,
from the terror of the LORD,
and from the glory of
his majesty,
when he rises to terrify
the earth.
20 On that day people will
throw away
to the moles and to the bats
their idols of silver and their
idols of gold,
which they made for
themselves to worship,

---

a 2.6 Heb lacks *the ways of*   b 2.6 Cn: Heb
lacks *of diviners*   c 2.12 Cn Compare Gk:
Heb *low*   d 2.16 Compare Gk: Meaning of
Heb uncertain

21 to enter the caverns of the rocks
    and the clefts in the crags,
from the terror of the LORD,
  and from the glory of
    his majesty,
when he rises to terrify
    the earth.
22 Turn away from mortals,
  who have only breath in
    their nostrils,
  for of what account are they?

3 For now the Sovereign,
    the LORD of hosts,
  is taking away from Jerusalem
    and from Judah
support and staff—
  all support of bread,
  and all support of water—
2 warrior and soldier,
  judge and prophet,
  diviner and elder,
3 captain of fifty
  and dignitary,
counselor and skillful magician
  and expert enchanter.
4 And I will make boys
  their princes,
and babes shall rule
  over them.
5 The people will be oppressed,
  everyone by another
  and everyone by a neighbor;
the youth will be insolent
  to the elder,
and the base to
  the honorable.

6 Someone will even seize
  a relative,
a member of the clan, saying,
"You have a cloak;
  you shall be our leader,
and this heap of ruins
  shall be under your rule."
7 But the other will cry out on
    that day, saying,
"I will not be a healer;
  in my house there is neither
    bread nor cloak;
you shall not make me
  leader of the people."
8 For Jerusalem has stumbled
  and Judah has fallen,
because their speech and
  their deeds are
    against the LORD,
defying his glorious presence.

9 The look on their faces bears
    witness against them;
they proclaim their sin
  like Sodom,
they do not hide it.
Woe to them!
  For they have brought evil
    on themselves.
10 Tell the innocent how
    fortunate they are,
for they shall eat the fruit
  of their labors.
11 Woe to the guilty! How
    unfortunate they are,
for what their hands have done
  shall be done to them.
12 My people—children are
  their oppressors,
and women rule over them.
O my people, your leaders
  mislead you,
and confuse the course
  of your paths.

13 The LORD rises to argue his case;
  he stands to judge
    the peoples.
14 The LORD enters into judgment
  with the elders and princes
    of his people:
It is you who have devoured
  the vineyard;
the spoil of the poor is
  in your houses.
15 What do you mean by
    crushing my people,
by grinding the face of
    the poor? says the
    Lord GOD of hosts.

16 The LORD said:
Because the daughters of
    Zion are haughty
and walk with outstretched
    necks,
glancing wantonly with
    their eyes,
mincing along as they go,
  tinkling with their feet;
17 the Lord will afflict with scabs
  the heads of the daughters
    of Zion,
and the LORD will lay bare
    their secret parts.

18 In that day the Lord will take
away the finery of the anklets, the

headbands, and the crescents; ¹⁹the pendants, the bracelets, and the scarfs; ²⁰the headdresses, the armlets, the sashes, the perfume boxes, and the amulets; ²¹the signet rings and nose rings; ²²the festal robes, the mantles, the cloaks, and the handbags; ²³the garments of gauze, the linen garments, the turbans, and the veils.

²⁴ Instead of perfume there
　　will be a stench;
　and instead of a sash, a rope;
　and instead of well-set
　　hair, baldness;
　and instead of a rich robe, a
　　binding of sackcloth;
　instead of beauty, shame.ᵃ
²⁵ Your men shall fall by the sword
　and your warriors in battle.
²⁶ And her gates shall lament
　　and mourn;
　ravaged, she shall sit
　　upon the ground.

4 Seven women shall take hold of one man in that day, saying, "We will eat our own bread and
　　wear our own clothes;
　just let us be called by your name;
　take away our disgrace."

THE CAUSE OF OUR SEPARATION OR ALIENATION FROM GOD IS HAVING GOALS AND PRIORITIES THAT ARE NOT GOD'S.

THE FUTURE GLORY OF THE SURVIVORS IN ZION

2 On that day the branch of the LORD shall be beautiful and glorious, and the fruit of the land shall be the pride and glory of the survivors of Israel. ³Whoever is left in Zion and remains in Jerusalem will be called holy, everyone who has been recorded for life in Jerusalem, ⁴once the Lord has washed away the filth of the daughters of Zion

and cleansed the bloodstains of Jerusalem from its midst by a spirit of judgment and by a spirit of burning. ⁵Then the LORD will create over the whole site of Mount Zion and over its places of assembly a cloud by day and smoke and the shining of a flaming fire by night. Indeed over all the glory there will be a canopy. ⁶It will serve as a pavilion, a shade by day from the heat, and a refuge and a shelter from the storm and rain.

THE SONG OF THE UNFRUITFUL VINEYARD

5 Let me sing for my beloved
　my love-song concerning
　　his vineyard:
My beloved had a vineyard
　on a very fertile hill.
² He dug it and cleared
　　it of stones,
　and planted it with
　　choice vines;
he built a watchtower in
　　the midst of it,
　and hewed out a wine vat in it;
he expected it to yield grapes,
　but it yielded wild grapes.

³ And now, inhabitants
　　of Jerusalem
　and people of Judah,
judge between me
　and my vineyard.
⁴ What more was there to do
　　for my vineyard
　that I have not done in it?
When I expected it to
　　yield grapes,
　why did it yield wild grapes?

⁵ And now I will tell you
　　what I will do to
　　　my vineyard.
I will remove its hedge,
　and it shall be devoured;
I will break down its wall,
　and it shall be trampled down.
⁶ I will make it a waste;
　it shall not be pruned or hoed,
　and it shall be overgrown
　　with briers and thorns;
I will also command the clouds
　that they rain no rain upon it.

ᵃ 3.24 Q Ms: MT lacks *shame*

7 For the vineyard of the
    LORD of hosts
    is the house of Israel,
    and the people of Judah
    are his pleasant planting;
    he expected justice,
        but saw bloodshed;
    righteousness,
        but heard a cry!

THE MORE WE HAVE, THE

LESS WE FEEL THE NEED

TO DEPEND ON GOD FOR

SUPPORT AND GUIDANCE.

SOCIAL INJUSTICE DENOUNCED

8 Ah, you who join house to house,
    who add field to field,
    until there is room for no
        one but you,
    and you are left to live alone
        in the midst of the land!
9 The LORD of hosts has sworn
        in my hearing:
    Surely many houses shall
        be desolate,
    large and beautiful houses,
        without inhabitant.
10 For ten acres of vineyard shall
        yield but one bath,
    and a homer of seed shall
        yield a mere ephah.a

11 Ah, you who rise early in
        the morning
    in pursuit of strong drink,
    who linger in the evening
        to be inflamed by wine,
12 whose feasts consist of
        lyre and harp,
    tambourine and flute and wine,
    but who do not regard the
        deeds of the LORD,
    or see the work of his hands!
13 Therefore my people go into exile
        without knowledge;
    their nobles are dying of hunger,
    and their multitude is
        parched with thirst.

14 Therefore Sheol has enlarged
        its appetite
    and opened its mouth
        beyond measure;
    the nobility of Jerusalemb and
        her multitude go down,
    her throng and all who
        exult in her.
15 People are bowed down, everyone
        is brought low,
    and the eyes of the haughty
        are humbled.
16 But the LORD of hosts is
        exalted by justice,
    and the Holy God shows himself
        holy by righteousness.
17 Then the lambs shall graze
        as in their pasture,
    fatlings and kidsc shall feed
        among the ruins.

18 Ah, you who drag iniquity along
        with cords of falsehood,
    who drag sin along as
        with cart ropes,
19 who say, "Let him make haste,
    let him speed his work
        that we may see it;
    let the plan of the Holy
        One of Israel hasten
            to fulfillment,
    that we may know it!"
20 Ah, you who call evil good
        and good evil,
    who put darkness for light
        and light for darkness,
    who put bitter for sweet
        and sweet for bitter!
21 Ah, you who are wise in
        your own eyes,
    and shrewd in your own sight!
22 Ah, you who are heroes in
        drinking wine
    and valiant at mixing drink,
23 who acquit the guilty for a bribe,
    and deprive the innocent
        of their rights!

FOREIGN INVASION PREDICTED

24 Therefore, as the tongue of fire
        devours the stubble,
    and as dry grass sinks
        down in the flame,

a 5.10 The Heb *bath*, *homer*, and *ephah*
are measures of quantity   b 5.14 Heb *her
nobility*   c 5.17 Cn Compare Gk: Heb *aliens*

so their root will become rotten,
> and their blossom go
> up like dust;
for they have rejected the
> instruction of the
> LORD of hosts,
and have despised the word of
> the Holy One of Israel.

25 Therefore the anger of the
> LORD was kindled
> against his people,
and he stretched out his
> hand against them
> and struck them;
the mountains quaked,
and their corpses were like refuse
> in the streets.
For all this his anger has
> not turned away,
and his hand is stretched
> out still.

26 He will raise a signal for a
> nation far away,
and whistle for a people at
> the ends of the earth;
Here they come, swiftly, speedily!
27 None of them is weary,
> none stumbles,
none slumbers or sleeps,
not a loincloth is loose,
not a sandal-thong broken;
28 their arrows are sharp,
> all their bows bent,
their horses' hoofs seem like flint,
and their wheels like
> the whirlwind.
29 Their roaring is like a lion,
> like young lions they roar;
they growl and seize their prey,
they carry it off, and no
> one can rescue.
30 They will roar over it on that day,
> like the roaring of the sea.
And if one look to the land—
> only darkness and distress;
and the light grows dark
> with clouds.

A VISION OF GOD IN
THE TEMPLE

6 In the year that King Uzziah died, I saw the Lord sitting on a throne, high and lofty; and the hem of his robe filled the temple. 2Seraphs were in attendance above him;

each had six wings: with two they covered their faces, and with two they covered their feet, and with two they flew. 3And one called to another and said:

"Holy, holy, holy is the
> LORD of hosts;
the whole earth is full
> of his glory."

4The pivots[a] on the thresholds shook at the voices of those who called, and the house filled with smoke. 5And I said: "Woe is me! I am lost, for I am a man of unclean lips, and I live among a people of unclean lips; yet my eyes have seen the King, the LORD of hosts!"

6 Then one of the seraphs flew to me, holding a live coal that had

---

a 6.4 Meaning of Heb uncertain

PONDER

"Woe is me! I am lost, for I am a man of unclean lips, and I live among a people of unclean lips; yet my eyes have seen the King, the LORD of hosts!"
—Isaiah 6.5

PRAY

Almighty God, we are grateful to read the words of this great prophet who foretold the coming of our Savior, Jesus Christ, and who committed himself totally to you, turning his life over to completely serve you in accordance with your will. But Isaiah also acknowledged his own sins—his unclean lips—and you purified him when he repented. We pray that you will cleanse us from the sins of speaking with anger, bitterness, envy, dishonesty and disrespect. Help us to apply these scriptures so that we can be more dedicated to our Savior, Jesus Christ. Help us to answer his call for us to espouse truth, peace, justice, benevolence, compassion, forgiveness and love. We ask these things in Jesus' name. Amen.

been taken from the altar with a pair of tongs. [7]The seraph[a] touched my mouth with it and said: "Now that this has touched your lips, your guilt has departed and your sin is blotted out." [8]Then I heard the voice of the Lord saying, "Whom shall I send, and who will go for us?" And I said, "Here am I; send me!" [9]And he said, "Go and say to this people:

'Keep listening, but do not
    comprehend;
keep looking, but do not
    understand.'
[10] Make the mind of this
        people dull,
    and stop their ears,
    and shut their eyes,
so that they may not look
        with their eyes,
    and listen with their ears,
and comprehend with
        their minds,
    and turn and be healed."
[11] Then I said, "How long,
        O Lord?" And he said:
"Until cities lie waste
    without inhabitant,
    and houses without people,
    and the land is utterly desolate;
[12] until the LORD sends
        everyone far away,
    and vast is the emptiness in
        the midst of the land.
[13] Even if a tenth part remain in it,
    it will be burned again,
like a terebinth or an oak
    whose stump remains
        standing
    when it is felled."[b]
The holy seed is its stump.

ISAIAH REASSURES KING AHAZ

7 In the days of Ahaz son of Jotham son of Uzziah, king of Judah, King Rezin of Aram and King Pekah son of Remaliah of Israel went up to attack Jerusalem, but could not mount an attack against it. [2]When the house of David heard that Aram had allied itself with Ephraim, the heart of Ahaz[c] and the heart of his people shook as the trees of the forest shake before the wind.

[3] Then the LORD said to Isaiah, Go out to meet Ahaz, you and your son Shear-jashub,[d] at the end of the conduit of the upper pool on the highway to the Fuller's Field, [4]and say to him, Take heed, be quiet, do not fear, and do not let your heart be faint because of these two smoldering stumps of firebrands, because of the fierce anger of Rezin and Aram and the son of Remaliah. [5]Because Aram—with Ephraim and the son of Remaliah—has plotted evil against you, saying, [6]Let us go up against Judah and cut off Jerusalem[e] and conquer it for ourselves and make the son of Tabeel king in it; [7]therefore thus says the Lord GOD:

It shall not stand,
    and it shall not come to pass.
[8] For the head of Aram is
        Damascus,
    and the head of Damascus
        is Rezin.
(Within sixty-five years Ephraim will be shattered, no longer a people.)
[9] The head of Ephraim is Samaria,
    and the head of Samaria is
        the son of Remaliah.
If you do not stand firm in faith,
    you shall not stand at all.

ISAIAH GIVES AHAZ THE SIGN OF IMMANUEL

[10] Again the LORD spoke to Ahaz, saying, [11]Ask a sign of the LORD your God; let it be deep as Sheol or high as heaven. [12]But Ahaz said, I will not ask, and I will not put the LORD to the test. [13]Then Isaiah[f] said: "Hear then, O house of David! Is it too little for you to weary mortals, that you weary my God also? [14]Therefore the Lord himself will give you a sign. Look, the young woman[g] is with child and shall bear a son, and shall name him Immanuel.[h] [15]He shall eat curds and honey by the time he knows how to refuse the evil and choose the good. [16]For before the child knows how to refuse the evil and choose the good, the land before whose two kings you are in dread will be deserted. [17]The LORD will

[a] 6.7 Heb *He*   [b] 6.13 Meaning of Heb uncertain   [c] 7.2 Heb *his heart*   [d] 7.3 That is *A remnant shall return*   [e] 7.6 Heb *cut it off*   [f] 7.13 Heb *he*   [g] 7.14 Gk *the virgin*   [h] 7.14 That is *God is with us*

bring on you and on your people and on your ancestral house such days as have not come since the day that Ephraim departed from Judah—the king of Assyria."

18 On that day the LORD will whistle for the fly that is at the sources of the streams of Egypt, and for the bee that is in the land of Assyria. 19And they will all come and settle in the steep ravines, and in the clefts of the rocks, and on all the thornbushes, and on all the pastures.

20 On that day the Lord will shave with a razor hired beyond the River—with the king of Assyria—the head and the hair of the feet, and it will take off the beard as well.

21 On that day one will keep alive a young cow and two sheep, 22and will eat curds because of the abundance of milk that they give; for everyone that is left in the land shall eat curds and honey.

23 On that day every place where there used to be a thousand vines, worth a thousand shekels of silver, will become briers and thorns. 24With bow and arrows one will go there, for all the land will be briers and thorns; 25and as for all the hills that used to be hoed with a hoe, you will not go there for fear of briers and thorns; but they will become a place where cattle are let loose and where sheep tread.

ISAIAH'S SON A SIGN OF THE ASSYRIAN INVASION

8 Then the LORD said to me, Take a large tablet and write on it in common characters, "Belonging to Maher-shalal-hash-baz,"[a] 2and have it attested[b] for me by reliable witnesses, the priest Uriah and Zechariah son of Jeberechiah. 3And I went to the prophetess, and she conceived and bore a son. Then the LORD said to me, Name him Maher-shalal-hash-baz; 4for before the child knows how to call "My father" or "My mother," the wealth of Damascus and the spoil of Samaria will be carried away by the king of Assyria.

5 The LORD spoke to me again: 6Because this people has refused the waters of Shiloah that flow gently, and melt in fear before[c] Rezin and the son of Remaliah; 7therefore, the Lord is bringing up against it the mighty flood waters of the River, the king of Assyria and all his glory; it will rise above all its channels and overflow all its banks; 8it will sweep on into Judah as a flood, and, pouring over, it will reach up to the neck; and its outspread wings will fill the breadth of your land, O Immanuel.

a 8.1 That is *The spoil speeds, the prey hastens*   b 8.2 Q Ms Gk Syr: MT *and I caused to be attested*   c 8.6 Cn: Meaning of Heb uncertain

---

⊢ BIBLE IN LIFE ▷

The Virgin Birth   *Isaiah 7.14*

The virgin birth is mentioned only three times in the Bible: as a prophecy here in the book of Isaiah ("young woman" can also be translated "virgin"), in Matthew 1 and in Luke 1. Mary could not grasp the idea of how a virgin could give birth. She asked the angel Gabriel, "How will this be?" Gabriel explained to Mary, "The Holy Spirit will come upon you, and the power of the Most High will overshadow you" (Luke 1.34–35). Her son would be both spirit and human. Imagine a teenage girl trying to comprehend this strange concept.

Some Christians resist the idea of the virgin birth of Jesus. We cannot understand how God did this miracle, yet we believe in other miracles. We can believe that God created the universe, that Jesus healed people who were sick and blind, calmed the seas and changed water into wine. We believe in the resurrection. We cannot explain any of these miracles. God's miraculous nature is something that we accept by faith, even though we don't understand it. The virgin birth shows the uniqueness of Jesus Christ—a Savior both fully human and fully divine. Jesus' birth was designed to be miraculous—that's one of its beauties.

⁹ Band together, you peoples,
    and be dismayed;
  listen, all you far countries;
  gird yourselves and be dismayed;
    gird yourselves and
      be dismayed!
¹⁰ Take counsel together, but it shall
    be brought to naught;
  speak a word, but it
    will not stand,
  for God is with us.ᵃ

11 For the LORD spoke thus to me while his hand was strong upon me, and warned me not to walk in the way of this people, saying: **12**Do not call conspiracy all that this people calls conspiracy, and do not fear what it fears, or be in dread. **13**But the LORD of hosts, him you shall regard as holy; let him be your fear, and let him be your dread. **14**He will become a sanctuary, a stone one strikes against; for both houses of Israel he will become a rock one stumbles over—a trap and a snare for the inhabitants of Jerusalem. **15**And many among them shall stumble; they shall fall and be broken; they shall be snared and taken.

DISCIPLES OF ISAIAH

16 Bind up the testimony, seal the teaching among my disciples. **17**I will wait for the LORD, who is hiding his face from the house of Jacob, and I will hope in him. **18**See, I and the children whom the LORD has given me are signs and portents in Israel from the LORD of hosts, who dwells on Mount Zion. **19**Now if people say to you, "Consult the ghosts and the familiar spirits that chirp and mutter; should not a people consult their gods, the dead on behalf of the living, **20**for teaching and for instruction?" surely, those who speak like this will have no dawn! **21**They will pass through the land,ᵇ greatly distressed and hungry; when they are hungry, they will be enraged and will curseᶜ their king and their gods. They will turn their faces upward, **22**or they will look to the earth, but will see only distress and darkness, the gloom of anguish; and they will be thrust into thick darkness.ᵈ

THE RIGHTEOUS REIGN OF THE COMING KING

9ᵉ But there will be no gloom for those who were in anguish. In the former time he brought into contempt the land of Zebulun and the land of Naphtali, but in the latter time he will make glorious the way

ᵃ **8.10** Heb *immanu el*   ᵇ **8.21** Heb *it*
ᶜ **8.21** Or *curse by*   ᵈ **8.22** Meaning of Heb uncertain   ᵉ **9.1** Ch 8.23 in Heb

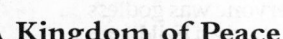

BIBLE IN LIFE

A Kingdom of Peace   *Isaiah 9.2–7*

Being a peacemaker is not simply a matter of persuading ourselves or others to put down our weapons and stop fighting each other, for peace encompasses more than merely eliminating war or open conflict. Being a peacemaker involves promoting true peace, which is the result of genuine harmony among us, our fellow human beings and God. True harmony can only be achieved through a process of reconciliation that starts with each of us (see 2 Corinthians 5.18–20). Through Christ, the Prince of Peace, we have peace with God and are no longer regarded as enemies because of our sin and rebellion (see Romans 5.1). This inner peace between us and God compels us to imitate Christ's example and to seek to bring peace to others as well; we have a direct responsibility in our own limited field of influence—within our communities, within our churches, within our own families—to promote peace. We can be peacemakers in small ways: extending ourselves in loving deeds to others, listening and relating to them, and seeking to right any wrongs that we may have done to them. As we carry out our responsibility to be peacemakers, we reflect God's character more and more, which is what Jesus meant when he said that peacemakers will be called "children of God" (Matthew 5.9).

of the sea, the land beyond the Jordan, Galilee of the nations.

2a The people who walked
        in darkness
    have seen a great light;
    those who lived in a land of
        deep darkness—
    on them light has shined.
3 You have multiplied the nation,
    you have increased its joy;
    they rejoice before you
    as with joy at the harvest,
    as people exult when
        dividing plunder.
4 For the yoke of their burden,
    and the bar across their
        shoulders,
    the rod of their oppressor,
    you have broken as on the
        day of Midian.
5 For all the boots of the
        tramping warriors
    and all the garments
        rolled in blood
    shall be burned as fuel
        for the fire.
6 For a child has been born for us,
    a son given to us;
    authority rests upon his shoulders;
    and he is named
    Wonderful Counselor,
        Mighty God,
    Everlasting Father,
        Prince of Peace.
7 His authority shall grow
        continually,
    and there shall be endless peace
    for the throne of David and
        his kingdom.
    He will establish and uphold it
    with justice and with
        righteousness
    from this time onward
        and forevermore.
    The zeal of the LORD of hosts
        will do this.

JUDGMENT ON ARROGANCE
AND OPPRESSION

8 The Lord sent a word
        against Jacob,
    and it fell on Israel;
9 and all the people knew it—
    Ephraim and the inhabitants
        of Samaria—
    but in pride and arrogance
    of heart they said:

10 "The bricks have fallen,
    but we will build with
        dressed stones;
    the sycamores have been
        cut down,
    but we will put cedars
        in their place."
11 So the LORD raised adversaries[b]
        against them,
    and stirred up their enemies,
12 the Arameans on the east and the
        Philistines on the west,
    and they devoured Israel
        with open mouth.
    For all this his anger has
        not turned away;
    his hand is stretched out still.
13 The people did not turn to him
        who struck them,
    or seek the LORD of hosts.
14 So the LORD cut off from
        Israel head and tail,
    palm branch and reed
        in one day—
15 elders and dignitaries
        are the head,
    and prophets who teach
        lies are the tail;
16 for those who led this people
        led them astray,
    and those who were led by them
        were left in confusion.
17 That is why the Lord did not
        have pity on[c] their
        young people,
    or compassion on their
        orphans and widows;
    for everyone was godless
        and an evildoer,
    and every mouth spoke folly.
    For all this his anger has
        not turned away;
    his hand is stretched out still.
18 For wickedness burned like a fire,
    consuming briers and thorns;
    it kindled the thickets of the forest,
    and they swirled upward in
        a column of smoke.
19 Through the wrath of the
        LORD of hosts
    the land was burned,

a 9.2 Ch 9.1 in Heb   b 9.11 Cn: Heb the
adversaries of Rezin   c 9.17 Q Ms: MT
rejoice over

and the people became like
　　fuel for the fire;
　no one spared another.
20 They gorged on the right, but
　　still were hungry,
　and they devoured on the left,
　　but were not satisfied;
　they devoured the flesh of
　　their own kindred;[a]
21 Manasseh devoured Ephraim,
　　and Ephraim Manasseh,
　and together they were
　　against Judah.
　For all this his anger has
　　not turned away,
　　his hand is stretched out still.

10 Ah, you who make
　　iniquitous decrees,
　who write oppressive statutes,
2 　to turn aside the needy
　　from justice
　and to rob the poor of my
　　people of their right,
　that widows may be your spoil,
　and that you may make the
　　orphans your prey!
3 What will you do on the day
　　of punishment,
　in the calamity that will
　　come from far away?
　To whom will you flee for help,
　and where will you leave
　　your wealth,
4 so as not to crouch among
　　the prisoners
　or fall among the slain?
　For all this his anger has
　　not turned away,
　　his hand is stretched out still.

ARROGANT ASSYRIA
ALSO JUDGED

5 Ah, Assyria, the rod of my anger—
　　the club in their hands
　　is my fury!
6 Against a godless nation
　　I send him,
　and against the people of my
　　wrath I command him,
　to take spoil and seize plunder,
　and to tread them down like
　　the mire of the streets.
7 But this is not what he intends,
　　nor does he have this in mind;
　but it is in his heart to destroy,
　　and to cut off nations not a few.

PONDER

Ah, you who make iniquitous decrees,
who write oppressive statutes, to turn
aside the needy from justice and to rob
the poor of my people of their right, that
widows may be your spoil, and that
you may make the orphans your prey!
　　　　　　　　—Isaiah 10.1–2

PRAY

Father, sometimes we are shaken up
by your words in the Holy Scriptures,
at least for a while. Most of the time,
however, we turn back to that which is
convenient, without risk, self-gratifying
and self-congratulatory. We fail to
use talent, innovation and a spirit of
adventure to serve you, combating
injustice, oppression and poverty. We
don't even feel guilty about it because
we think we are okay. We pray that
we might be courageous enough
and wise enough to seek you daily
and to find eternal joy in our service
to Jesus Christ our Savior and his
kingdom. In his name we pray. Amen.

8 For he says:
　"Are not my commanders all kings?
9 Is not Calno like Carchemish?
　　Is not Hamath like Arpad?
　　Is not Samaria like Damascus?
10 As my hand has reached to the
　　　kingdoms of the idols
　　whose images were greater
　　　than those of Jerusalem
　　　and Samaria,
11 shall I not do to Jerusalem
　　　and her idols
　　what I have done to Samaria
　　　and her images?"

12 When the Lord has finished all
his work on Mount Zion and on Jerusalem, he[b] will punish the arrogant boasting of the king of Assyria
and his haughty pride. 13 For he says:

―――――――――――――――――
[a] 9.20 Or *arm*　[b] 10.12 Heb *I*

"By the strength of my hand
    I have done it,
and by my wisdom, for I
    have understanding;
I have removed the boundaries
    of peoples,
and have plundered
    their treasures;
like a bull I have brought down
    those who sat on thrones.
14 My hand has found, like a nest,
    the wealth of the peoples;
and as one gathers eggs that
    have been forsaken,
so I have gathered all the earth;
and there was none that
    moved a wing,
or opened its mouth,
    or chirped."

15 Shall the ax vaunt itself over
    the one who wields it,
or the saw magnify itself
    against the one
    who handles it?
As if a rod should raise the
    one who lifts it up,
or as if a staff should lift the
    one who is not wood!
16 Therefore the Sovereign, the
    LORD of hosts,
will send wasting sickness
    among his stout warriors,
and under his glory a burning
    will be kindled,
like the burning of fire.
17 The light of Israel will
    become a fire,
    and his Holy One a flame;
and it will burn and devour
    his thorns and briers in one day.
18 The glory of his forest and
    his fruitful land
    the LORD will destroy, both
    soul and body,
and it will be as when an
    invalid wastes away.
19 The remnant of the trees of his
    forest will be so few
    that a child can write
    them down.

THE REPENTANT REMNANT
OF ISRAEL

20 On that day the remnant of Israel and the survivors of the house
of Jacob will no more lean on the
one who struck them, but will lean
on the LORD, the Holy One of Israel,
in truth. 21A remnant will return,
the remnant of Jacob, to the mighty
God. 22For though your people Israel were like the sand of the sea,
only a remnant of them will return.
Destruction is decreed, overflowing
with righteousness. 23For the Lord
GOD of hosts will make a full end, as
decreed, in all the earth.[a]

24 Therefore thus says the Lord
GOD of hosts: O my people, who live
in Zion, do not be afraid of the Assyrians when they beat you with
a rod and lift up their staff against
you as the Egyptians did. 25For in
a very little while my indignation
will come to an end, and my anger
will be directed to their destruction. 26The LORD of hosts will wield
a whip against them, as when he
struck Midian at the rock of Oreb;
his staff will be over the sea, and he
will lift it as he did in Egypt. 27On
that day his burden will be removed
from your shoulder, and his yoke
will be destroyed from your neck.

He has gone up from Rimmon,[b]
28   he has come to Aiath;
he has passed through Migron,
    at Michmash he stores
    his baggage;
29 they have crossed over the pass,
    at Geba they lodge for
    the night;
Ramah trembles,
    Gibeah of Saul has fled.
30 Cry aloud, O daughter Gallim!
    Listen, O Laishah!
    Answer her, O Anathoth!
31 Madmenah is in flight,
    the inhabitants of Gebim
    flee for safety.
32 This very day he will halt at Nob,
    he will shake his fist
    at the mount of daughter Zion,
    the hill of Jerusalem.

33 Look, the Sovereign, the
    LORD of hosts,
will lop the boughs with
    terrifying power;

a 10.23 Or *land*   b 10.27 Cn: Heb *and his
yoke from your neck, and a yoke will be
destroyed because of fatness*

the tallest trees will be cut down,
   and the lofty will be
      brought low.
34 He will hack down the thickets
      of the forest with an ax,
   and Lebanon with its
      majestic trees[a] will fall.

THE PEACEFUL KINGDOM

11 A shoot shall come out
   from the stump of Jesse,
and a branch shall grow
   out of his roots.
2 The spirit of the LORD shall
      rest on him,
   the spirit of wisdom and
      understanding,
   the spirit of counsel and might,
   the spirit of knowledge and
      the fear of the LORD.
3 His delight shall be in the
      fear of the LORD.

He shall not judge by what
      his eyes see,
   or decide by what
      his ears hear;
4 but with righteousness he
      shall judge the poor,
   and decide with equity for
      the meek of the earth;
he shall strike the earth with
      the rod of his mouth,
   and with the breath of his lips
      he shall kill the wicked.
5 Righteousness shall be the belt
      around his waist,
   and faithfulness the belt
      around his loins.

6 The wolf shall live with the lamb,
   the leopard shall lie down
      with the kid,
the calf and the lion and the
      fatling together,
   and a little child shall
      lead them.
7 The cow and the bear shall graze,
   their young shall lie
      down together;
   and the lion shall eat
      straw like the ox.
8 The nursing child shall play over
      the hole of the asp,
   and the weaned child
      shall put its hand on
         the adder's den.

PONDER

The wolf shall live with the lamb, the
leopard shall lie down with the kid,
the calf and the lion and the fatling
together, and a little child shall lead
them . . . They will not hurt or destroy
on all my holy mountain, for the earth
will be full of the knowledge of the
LORD as the waters cover the sea.
—Isaiah 11.6,9

PRAY

Lord, we face here some provocative but
inspiring words. These words, spoken
by Isaiah thousands of years ago, refer
to the day when the resurrected Jesus
brings true peace to this world—which
he also modeled to us during his earthly
ministry. Help us keep our own lives
oriented toward living according to your
commands and the example Jesus set
for us, so that we will always be ready to
meet you. We pray that your kingdom
will come and your will be done. Let us
commit to being peacemakers in our
hearts and in our relationships with
others. Guide us as we promote peace
among all men and women in the name
of our Savior, Jesus Christ. Amen.

9   They will not hurt or destroy
      on all my holy mountain;
   for the earth will be full of the
      knowledge of the LORD
      as the waters cover the sea.

RETURN OF THE REMNANT
OF ISRAEL AND JUDAH

10 On that day the root of Jesse
shall stand as a signal to the peoples;
the nations shall inquire of him, and
his dwelling shall be glorious.

11 On that day the Lord will extend
his hand yet a second time to recover
the remnant that is left of his people, from Assyria, from Egypt, from

---

a **10.34** Cn Compare Gk Vg: Heb *with a*
majestic one

BIBLE IN FOCUS

THE JUDGE OF RIGHTEOUSNESS

He shall not judge by what his eyes see, or decide by what his ears hear; but with righteousness he shall judge the poor, and decide with equity for the meek of the earth.

—Isaiah 11.3–4

The prophet Isaiah used provocative and dramatic words to describe a leader who would bring peace to God's people. Isaiah lived during a time of turmoil in Israel's history. Israel and its leaders were corrupt in social, political and religious affairs. The northern kingdom had fallen to Assyria, a dominant empire in what we today call the Middle East. And God told Isaiah that Judah will also be facing disaster. But in the midst of the turmoil, God sent a message of hope.

From the descendants of Jessie (King David's father) would come a "shoot," a leader who would bring new life to the people who were in despair (verse 1). This leader would be filled with the Spirit of the Lord. He would have a Spirit of wisdom and of counsel and of might, and he would have authority. His "delight [would] be in the fear of the LORD"—a reverence or respect for God—and an acknowledgment that God is all powerful.

This leader would judge with righteousness and equity. He would not seek out the powerful and influential but would pay particular attention to the poor and the meek. He would understand that their lives are dependent upon his sound judgment, his righteousness. And when he would arrive, he would bring peace.

We know from reading the New Testament that Isaiah's description points to the Messiah. We know how Jesus reacted to people who were despised, forlorn, forgotten and condemned—but we don't always think the way he lived applies to us in our time. If we accept that Isaiah's premises describe the character of Jesus Christ, then they should also describe us, because Jesus is the example to be followed by Christians. The appeal of the words of Isaiah and the life and words of Jesus Christ directly apply to us.

We human beings are created in the image of God, and God has given us an element of freedom. We are not puppets controlled by an all-powerful God. We can make decisions. Will we take responsibility for the poor and the meek and those in need? Will we love those who may not love us? Will we be forgiving? As God has given us the free will, he's also given us the wisdom and the presence of his Spirit to live as a follower of Jesus Christ.

Going Deeper

- What words can you use to describe the way you live? What are the similarities between your life and Isaiah's description of Jesus?
- What does the "fear of the LORD" look like in your relationship with God?

Pathros, from Ethiopia,[a] from Elam, from Shinar, from Hamath, and from the coastlands of the sea.
12 He will raise a signal for
      the nations,
   and will assemble the
      outcasts of Israel,
and gather the dispersed of Judah
   from the four corners
      of the earth.
13 The jealousy of Ephraim
      shall depart,
   the hostility of Judah
      shall be cut off;
Ephraim shall not be jealous
      of Judah,
   and Judah shall not be hostile
      towards Ephraim.
14 But they shall swoop down
      on the backs of the
      Philistines in the west,
   together they shall plunder
      the people of the east.
They shall put forth their hand
      against Edom and Moab,
   and the Ammonites shall
      obey them.
15 And the LORD will utterly destroy
      the tongue of the sea of Egypt;
   and will wave his hand
      over the River
   with his scorching wind;
and will split it into seven channels,
   and make a way to cross on foot;
16 so there shall be a highway
      from Assyria
   for the remnant that is
      left of his people,
as there was for Israel
   when they came up from
      the land of Egypt.

THANKSGIVING AND PRAISE

12 You will say in that day:
   I will give thanks to
      you, O LORD,
   for though you were
      angry with me,
your anger turned away,
   and you comforted me.
2 Surely God is my salvation;
   I will trust, and will
      not be afraid,
for the LORD GOD[b] is my
      strength and my might;
   he has become my salvation.

3 With joy you will draw water
from the wells of salvation. 4And
you will say in that day:
   Give thanks to the LORD,
      call on his name;
   make known his deeds
         among the nations;
      proclaim that his name
         is exalted.
5 Sing praises to the LORD, for he
      has done gloriously;
   let this be known[c] in
      all the earth.
6 Shout aloud and sing for
      joy, O royal[d] Zion,
   for great in your midst is the
      Holy One of Israel.

PROCLAMATION
AGAINST BABYLON

13 The oracle concerning Babylon that Isaiah son of Amoz saw.

2 On a bare hill raise a signal,
      cry aloud to them;
   wave the hand for them to enter
      the gates of the nobles.
3 I myself have commanded my
      consecrated ones,
   have summoned my warriors,
      my proudly exulting ones,
   to execute my anger.

4 Listen, a tumult on the
      mountains
   as of a great multitude!
Listen, an uproar of kingdoms,
   of nations gathering together!
The LORD of hosts is mustering
   an army for battle.
5 They come from a distant land,
   from the end of the heavens,
the LORD and the weapons
      of his indignation,
   to destroy the whole earth.

6 Wail, for the day of the
      LORD is near;
   it will come like destruction
      from the Almighty![e]

a 11.11 Or *Nubia;* Heb *Cush*   b 12.2 Heb
for Yah, the LORD   c 12.5 Or *this is
made known*   d 12.6 Or *O inhabitant of*
e 13.6 Traditional rendering of Heb *Shaddai*

7 Therefore all hands will be feeble,
  and every human heart
    will melt,
8   and they will be dismayed.
  Pangs and agony will seize them;
    they will be in anguish like
      a woman in labor.
  They will look aghast at
    one another;
    their faces will be aflame.
9 See, the day of the LORD comes,
    cruel, with wrath and
      fierce anger,
  to make the earth a desolation,
    and to destroy its
      sinners from it.
10 For the stars of the heavens and
      their constellations
    will not give their light;
  the sun will be dark at its rising,
    and the moon will not
      shed its light.
11 I will punish the world for its evil,
    and the wicked for
      their iniquity;
  I will put an end to the pride
      of the arrogant,
    and lay low the insolence
      of tyrants.
12 I will make mortals more
      rare than fine gold,
    and humans than the
      gold of Ophir.
13 Therefore I will make the
      heavens tremble,
    and the earth will be shaken
      out of its place,
  at the wrath of the
    LORD of hosts
  in the day of his fierce anger.

14 Like a hunted gazelle,
    or like sheep with no one
      to gather them,
  all will turn to their own people,
    and all will flee to their
      own lands.
15 Whoever is found will be
      thrust through,
    and whoever is caught will
      fall by the sword.
16 Their infants will be dashed
      to pieces
    before their eyes;
  their houses will be plundered,
    and their wives ravished.
17 See, I am stirring up the
      Medes against them,
    who have no regard for silver
      and do not delight in gold.
18 Their bows will slaughter
      the young men;
    they will have no mercy on
      the fruit of the womb;
    their eyes will not pity children.
19 And Babylon, the glory
      of kingdoms,
    the splendor and pride of
      the Chaldeans,
  will be like Sodom and Gomorrah
    when God overthrew them.
20 It will never be inhabited
    or lived in for all generations;
  Arabs will not pitch their
      tents there,
    shepherds will not make their
      flocks lie down there.
21 But wild animals will lie
      down there,
    and its houses will be full of
      howling creatures;

BIBLE IN LIFE

The Day of the Lord
Isaiah 13.6–16

Jesus borrows this language from Isaiah 13.10 when he describes the end of time to his disciples (see Matthew 24). At the end of time, the heavens will be changed. We don't know how that will happen, but we do know that the God who created us and the earth and the trees and the flowers and the stars and the sun is the same God who will bring the universe under his subjection in the final days. The Bible says that no one knows when the final days will be—neither the angels in heaven nor the Son, Jesus Christ. Only God the Father knows when this will occur. Jesus says, "Therefore you also must be ready, for the Son of Man is coming at an unexpected hour" (Matthew 24.44). Will we be prepared for the second coming of Christ? Will our lives reflect our faith in Jesus at all times?

there ostriches will live,
and there goat-demons
will dance.
²² Hyenas will cry in its towers,
and jackals in the
pleasant palaces;
its time is close at hand,
and its days will not
be prolonged.

RESTORATION OF JUDAH

14 But the LORD will have compassion on Jacob and will
again choose Israel, and will set
them in their own land; and aliens
will join them and attach themselves to the house of Jacob. ² And
the nations will take them and bring
them to their place, and the house
of Israel will possess the nationsª as
male and female slaves in the LORD's
land; they will take captive those
who were their captors, and rule
over those who oppressed them.

DOWNFALL OF THE
KING OF BABYLON

3 When the LORD has given you
rest from your pain and turmoil and
the hard service with which you
were made to serve, ⁴you will take
up this taunt against the king of
Babylon:

How the oppressor has ceased!
How his insolenceᵇ has ceased!
⁵ The LORD has broken the
staff of the wicked,
the scepter of rulers,
⁶ that struck down the
peoples in wrath
with unceasing blows,
that ruled the nations in anger
with unrelenting persecution.
⁷ The whole earth is at rest
and quiet;
they break forth into singing.
⁸ The cypresses exult over you,
the cedars of Lebanon, saying,
"Since you were laid low,
no one comes to cut us down."
⁹ Sheol beneath is stirred up
to meet you when you come;
it rouses the shades to greet you,
all who were leaders of the earth;
it raises from their thrones
all who were kings of
the nations.

¹⁰ All of them will speak
and say to you:
"You too have become as
weak as we!
You have become like us!"
¹¹ Your pomp is brought
down to Sheol,
and the sound of your harps;
maggots are the bed beneath you,
and worms are your covering.

¹² How you are fallen from heaven,
O Day Star, son of Dawn!
How you are cut down to
the ground,
you who laid the nations low!
¹³ You said in your heart,
"I will ascend to heaven;
I will raise my throne
above the stars of God;
I will sit on the mount
of assembly
on the heights of Zaphon;ᶜ
¹⁴ I will ascend to the tops
of the clouds,
I will make myself like
the Most High."
¹⁵ But you are brought down
to Sheol,
to the depths of the Pit.
¹⁶ Those who see you will
stare at you,
and ponder over you:
"Is this the man who made
the earth tremble,
who shook kingdoms,
¹⁷ who made the world like a desert
and overthrew its cities,
who would not let his
prisoners go home?"
¹⁸ All the kings of the nations
lie in glory,
each in his own tomb;
¹⁹ but you are cast out, away
from your grave,
like loathsome carrion,ᵈ
clothed with the dead, those
pierced by the sword,
who go down to the
stones of the Pit,
like a corpse trampled
underfoot.

ª 14.2 Heb *them*   ᵇ 14.4 Q Ms Compare
Gk Syr Vg: Meaning of MT uncertain
ᶜ 14.13 Or *assembly in the far north*
ᵈ 14.19 Cn Compare Gk: Heb *like a loathed
branch*

20 You will not be joined with
    them in burial,
because you have destroyed
    your land,
    you have killed your people.

May the descendants
    of evildoers
    nevermore be named!
21 Prepare slaughter for his sons
    because of the guilt of
    their father.[a]
Let them never rise to
    possess the earth
    or cover the face of the
    world with cities.

22 I will rise up against them,
says the LORD of hosts, and will cut
off from Babylon name and remnant, offspring and posterity, says
the LORD. 23 And I will make it a possession of the hedgehog, and pools
of water, and I will sweep it with the
broom of destruction, says the LORD
of hosts.

AN ORACLE CONCERNING
ASSYRIA

24 The LORD of hosts has sworn:
As I have designed,
    so shall it be;
and as I have planned,
    so shall it come to pass:
25 I will break the Assyrian
    in my land,
and on my mountains trample
    him under foot;
his yoke shall be removed
    from them,
and his burden from
    their shoulders.
26 This is the plan that is planned
    concerning the whole earth;
and this is the hand that
    is stretched out
    over all the nations.
27 For the LORD of hosts
    has planned,
and who will annul it?
His hand is stretched out,
    and who will turn it back?

AN ORACLE CONCERNING
PHILISTIA

28 In the year that King Ahaz died
this oracle came:

29 Do not rejoice, all you Philistines,
    that the rod that struck
    you is broken,
for from the root of the snake
    will come forth an adder,
and its fruit will be a flying
    fiery serpent.
30 The firstborn of the poor
    will graze,
and the needy lie down
    in safety;
but I will make your root
    die of famine,
    and your remnant I[b] will kill.
31 Wail, O gate; cry, O city;
    melt in fear, O Philistia,
    all of you!
For smoke comes out of
    the north,
and there is no straggler
    in its ranks.

32 What will one answer the
    messengers of the nation?
"The LORD has founded Zion,
    and the needy among
    his people
    will find refuge in her."

AN ORACLE CONCERNING MOAB

15 An oracle concerning Moab.

Because Ar is laid waste
    in a night,
    Moab is undone;
because Kir is laid waste
    in a night,
    Moab is undone.
2 Dibon[c] has gone up to the temple,
    to the high places to weep;
over Nebo and over Medeba
    Moab wails.
On every head is baldness,
    every beard is shorn;
3 in the streets they bind
    on sackcloth;
    on the housetops and
    in the squares
everyone wails and
    melts in tears.
4 Heshbon and Elealeh cry out,
    their voices are heard
    as far as Jahaz;

a 14.21 Syr Compare Gk: Heb *fathers*
b 14.30 Q Ms Vg: MT *he*   c 15.2 Cn: Heb *the house and Dibon*

therefore the loins of Moab quiver;[a]
his soul trembles.
5 My heart cries out for Moab;
his fugitives flee to Zoar,
to Eglath-shelishiyah.
For at the ascent of Luhith
they go up weeping;
on the road to Horonaim
they raise a cry of destruction;
6 the waters of Nimrim
are a desolation;
the grass is withered, the
new growth fails,
the verdure is no more.
7 Therefore the abundance
they have gained
and what they have laid up
they carry away
over the Wadi of the Willows.
8 For a cry has gone
around the land of Moab;
the wailing reaches to Eglaim,
the wailing reaches to Beer-elim.
9 For the waters of Dibon[b]
are full of blood;
yet I will bring upon Dibon[b]
even more—
a lion for those of Moab
who escape,
for the remnant of the land.

16 Send lambs
to the ruler of the land,
from Sela, by way of the desert,
to the mount of daughter Zion.
2 Like fluttering birds,
like scattered nestlings,
so are the daughters of Moab
at the fords of the Arnon.
3 "Give counsel,
grant justice;
make your shade like night
at the height of noon;
hide the outcasts,
do not betray the fugitive;
4 let the outcasts of Moab
settle among you;
be a refuge to them
from the destroyer."

When the oppressor is no more,
and destruction has ceased,
and marauders have vanished
from the land,
5 then a throne shall be established
in steadfast love
in the tent of David,
and on it shall sit in faithfulness

a ruler who seeks justice
and is swift to do what is right.
6 We have heard of the
pride of Moab
—how proud he is!—
of his arrogance, his pride,
and his insolence;
his boasts are false.
7 Therefore let Moab wail,
let everyone wail for Moab.
Mourn, utterly stricken,
for the raisin cakes of
Kir-hareseth.

8 For the fields of Heshbon
languish,
and the vines of Sibmah,
whose clusters once made drunk
the lords of the nations,
reached to Jazer
and strayed to the desert;
their shoots once spread abroad
and crossed over the sea.
9 Therefore I weep with the
weeping of Jazer
for the vines of Sibmah;
I drench you with my tears,
O Heshbon and Elealeh;
for the shout over your
fruit harvest
and your grain harvest
has ceased.
10 Joy and gladness are taken away
from the fruitful field;
and in the vineyards no
songs are sung,
no shouts are raised;
no treader treads out wine
in the presses;
the vintage-shout is hushed.[c]
11 Therefore my heart throbs
like a harp for Moab,
and my very soul for Kir-heres.
12 When Moab presents himself,
when he wearies himself upon the
high place, when he comes to his
sanctuary to pray, he will not prevail.

13 This was the word that the
LORD spoke concerning Moab in
the past. 14 But now the LORD says,
In three years, like the years of a

a 15.4 Cn Compare Gk Syr: Heb *the armed
men of Moab cry aloud*   b 15.9 Q Ms Vg
Compare Syr: MT *Dimon*   c 16.10 Gk: Heb *I
have hushed*

hired worker, the glory of Moab will be brought into contempt, in spite of all its great multitude; and those who survive will be very few and feeble.

AN ORACLE CONCERNING DAMASCUS

17 An oracle concerning Damascus.

See, Damascus will cease
   to be a city,
   and will become a
      heap of ruins.
2 Her towns will be deserted
      forever;[a]
   they will be places for flocks,
      which will lie down, and
      no one will make
      them afraid.
3 The fortress will disappear
      from Ephraim,
   and the kingdom from
      Damascus;
   and the remnant of Aram will be
      like the glory of the
      children of Israel,
         says the LORD of hosts.

4 On that day
   the glory of Jacob will
      be brought low,
   and the fat of his flesh
      will grow lean.
5 And it shall be as when reapers
      gather standing grain
   and their arms harvest
      the ears,
   and as when one gleans
      the ears of grain
   in the Valley of Rephaim.
6 Gleanings will be left in it,
   as when an olive tree
      is beaten—
   two or three berries
      in the top of the highest bough,
   four or five
      on the branches of a fruit tree,
         says the LORD God of Israel.

7 On that day people will regard their Maker, and their eyes will look to the Holy One of Israel; 8 they will not have regard for the altars, the work of their hands, and they will not look to what their own fingers have made, either the sacred poles[b] or the altars of incense.

9 On that day their strong cities will be like the deserted places of the Hivites and the Amorites,[c] which they deserted because of the children of Israel, and there will be desolation.

WE NEED A GOOD AWARENESS

OF WORLD EVENTS AND

THE REALIZATION THAT

GOD IS STILL SUPREME.

10 For you have forgotten the God
      of your salvation,
   and have not remembered
      the Rock of your refuge;
   therefore, though you plant
      pleasant plants
   and set out slips of an alien god,
11 though you make them
      grow on the day that
      you plant them,
   and make them blossom in the
      morning that you sow;
   yet the harvest will flee away
      in a day of grief and
      incurable pain.

12 Ah, the thunder of many peoples,
   they thunder like the
      thundering of the sea!
   Ah, the roar of nations,
   they roar like the roaring
      of mighty waters!
13 The nations roar like the roaring
      of many waters,
   but he will rebuke them, and
      they will flee far away,
   chased like chaff on the
      mountains before
      the wind
   and whirling dust before
      the storm.

a 17.2 Cn Compare Gk: Heb *the cities of Aroer are deserted*   b 17.8 Heb *Asherim*
c 17.9 Cn Compare Gk: Heb *places of the wood and the highest bough*

14 At evening time, lo, terror!
Before morning, they
are no more.
This is the fate of those
who despoil us,
and the lot of those who
plunder us.

AN ORACLE CONCERNING ETHIOPIA

18 Ah, land of whirring wings
beyond the rivers
of Ethiopia,[a]
2 sending ambassadors by the Nile
in vessels of papyrus
on the waters!
Go, you swift messengers,
to a nation tall and smooth,
to a people feared near and far,
a nation mighty and
conquering,
whose land the rivers divide.

3 All you inhabitants of the world,
you who live on the earth,
when a signal is raised on the
mountains, look!
When a trumpet is
blown, listen!
4 For thus the LORD said to me:
I will quietly look from
my dwelling
like clear heat in sunshine,
like a cloud of dew in the
heat of harvest.
5 For before the harvest, when
the blossom is over
and the flower becomes
a ripening grape,
he will cut off the shoots with
pruning hooks,
and the spreading branches
he will hew away.
6 They shall all be left
to the birds of prey of
the mountains
and to the animals of the earth.
And the birds of prey will
summer on them,
and all the animals of the earth
will winter on them.

7 At that time gifts will be brought
to the LORD of hosts from[b] a people tall and smooth, from a people
feared near and far, a nation mighty
and conquering, whose land the rivers divide, to Mount Zion, the place
of the name of the LORD of hosts.

AN ORACLE CONCERNING EGYPT

19 An oracle concerning Egypt.

See, the LORD is riding on
a swift cloud
and comes to Egypt;
the idols of Egypt will tremble
at his presence,
and the heart of the Egyptians
will melt within them.
2 I will stir up Egyptians
against Egyptians,
and they will fight, one
against the other,
neighbor against neighbor,
city against city, kingdom
against kingdom;
3 the spirit of the Egyptians within
them will be emptied out,
and I will confound their plans;
they will consult the idols and
the spirits of the dead
and the ghosts and the
familiar spirits;
4 I will deliver the Egyptians
into the hand of a hard master;
a fierce king will rule over them,
says the Sovereign, the
LORD of hosts.

5 The waters of the Nile will
be dried up,
and the river will be
parched and dry;
6 its canals will become foul,
and the branches of Egypt's
Nile will diminish
and dry up,
reeds and rushes will rot away.
7 There will be bare places
by the Nile,
on the brink of the Nile;
and all that is sown by the
Nile will dry up,
be driven away, and
be no more.
8 Those who fish will mourn;
all who cast hooks in the
Nile will lament,
and those who spread nets on
the water will languish.

a **18.1** Or *Nubia*; Heb *Cush*   b **18.7** Q Ms Gk
Vg: MT *of*

9 The workers in flax will
        be in despair,
    and the carders and those at
        the loom will grow pale.
10 Its weavers will be dismayed,
    and all who work for wages
        will be grieved.

11 The princes of Zoan are
        utterly foolish;
    the wise counselors of Pharaoh
        give stupid counsel.
    How can you say to Pharaoh,
    "I am one of the sages,
        a descendant of ancient kings"?
12 Where now are your sages?
    Let them tell you and
        make known
    what the LORD of hosts has
        planned against Egypt.
13 The princes of Zoan have
        become fools,
    and the princes of Memphis
        are deluded;
    those who are the cornerstones
        of its tribes
    have led Egypt astray.
14 The LORD has poured into them[a]
        a spirit of confusion;
    and they have made Egypt
        stagger in all its doings
    as a drunkard staggers
        around in vomit.
15 Neither head nor tail, palm
        branch or reed,
    will be able to do anything
        for Egypt.

16 On that day the Egyptians will be like women, and tremble with fear before the hand that the LORD of hosts raises against them. 17And the land of Judah will become a terror to the Egyptians; everyone to whom it is mentioned will fear because of the plan that the LORD of hosts is planning against them.

EGYPT, ASSYRIA, AND ISRAEL BLESSED

18 On that day there will be five cities in the land of Egypt that speak the language of Canaan and swear allegiance to the LORD of hosts. One of these will be called the City of the Sun.
19 On that day there will be an altar to the LORD in the center of the land of Egypt, and a pillar to the LORD at its border. 20It will be a sign and a witness to the LORD of hosts in the land of Egypt; when they cry to the LORD because of oppressors, he will send them a savior, and will defend and deliver them. 21The LORD will make himself known to the Egyptians; and the Egyptians will know the LORD on that day, and will worship with sacrifice and burnt offering, and they will make vows to the LORD and perform them. 22The LORD will strike Egypt, striking and healing; they will return to the LORD, and he will listen to their supplications and heal them.

23 On that day there will be a highway from Egypt to Assyria, and the Assyrian will come into Egypt, and the Egyptian into Assyria, and the Egyptians will worship with the Assyrians.

24 On that day Israel will be the third with Egypt and Assyria, a blessing in the midst of the earth, 25whom the LORD of hosts has blessed, saying, "Blessed be Egypt my people, and Assyria the work of my hands, and Israel my heritage."

MANY OF US ARE DESPERATELY

AFRAID TO DIE BEFORE WE

HAVE LEARNED HOW TO LIVE.

ISAIAH DRAMATIZES THE CONQUEST OF EGYPT AND ETHIOPIA

20 In the year that the commander-in-chief, who was sent by King Sargon of Assyria, came to Ashdod and fought against it and took it— 2at that time the LORD had spoken to Isaiah son of Amoz, saying, "Go, and loose the sackcloth from your loins and take your sandals off your feet," and he

a 19.14 Gk Compare Tg: Heb it

had done so, walking naked and barefoot. [3]Then the LORD said, "Just as my servant Isaiah has walked naked and barefoot for three years as a sign and a portent against Egypt and Ethiopia,[a] [4]so shall the king of Assyria lead away the Egyptians as captives and the Ethiopians[b] as exiles, both the young and the old, naked and barefoot, with buttocks uncovered, to the shame of Egypt. [5]And they shall be dismayed and confounded because of Ethiopia[a] their hope and of Egypt their boast. [6]In that day the inhabitants of this coastland will say, 'See, this is what has happened to those in whom we hoped and to whom we fled for help and deliverance from the king of Assyria! And we, how shall we escape?' "

ORACLES CONCERNING BABYLON, EDOM, AND ARABIA

21 The oracle concerning the wilderness of the sea.

As whirlwinds in the
    Negeb sweep on,
it comes from the desert,
    from a terrible land.
[2] A stern vision is told to me;
    the betrayer betrays,
    and the destroyer destroys.
Go up, O Elam,
    lay siege, O Media;
all the sighing she has caused
    I bring to an end.
[3] Therefore my loins are filled
    with anguish;
pangs have seized me,
    like the pangs of a
    woman in labor;
I am bowed down so that
    I cannot hear,
I am dismayed so that
    I cannot see.
[4] My mind reels, horror has
    appalled me;
the twilight I longed for
    has been turned for me
    into trembling.
[5] They prepare the table,
    they spread the rugs,
    they eat, they drink.
Rise up, commanders,
    oil the shield!

[6] For thus the Lord said to me:
"Go, post a lookout,
    let him announce what he sees.
[7] When he sees riders,
    horsemen in pairs,
riders on donkeys, riders
    on camels,
let him listen diligently,
    very diligently."
[8] Then the watcher[c] called out:
"Upon a watchtower I
    stand, O Lord,
continually by day,
and at my post I am stationed
    throughout the night.
[9] Look, there they come, riders,
    horsemen in pairs!"
Then he responded,
    "Fallen, fallen is Babylon;
and all the images of her gods
    lie shattered on the ground."
[10] O my threshed and
    winnowed one,
what I have heard from
    the LORD of hosts,
    the God of Israel, I
    announce to you.

[11] The oracle concerning Dumah.

One is calling to me from Seir,
    "Sentinel, what of the night?
    Sentinel, what of the night?"
[12] The sentinel says:
"Morning comes, and
    also the night.
If you will inquire, inquire;
    come back again."

[13] The oracle concerning the desert plain.

In the scrub of the desert
    plain you will lodge,
    O caravans of Dedanites.
[14] Bring water to the thirsty,
    meet the fugitive with bread,
    O inhabitants of the
    land of Tema.
[15] For they have fled from
    the swords,
from the drawn sword,
    from the bent bow,
and from the stress of battle.

[a] 20.3,5 Or Nubia; Heb Cush   [b] 20.4 Or Nubians; Heb Cushites   [c] 21.8 Q Ms: MT a lion

16 For thus the Lord said to me: Within a year, according to the years of a hired worker, all the glory of Kedar will come to an end; **17** and the remaining bows of Kedar's warriors will be few; for the LORD, the God of Israel, has spoken.

A WARNING OF DESTRUCTION OF JERUSALEM

22 The oracle concerning the valley of vision.

What do you mean that you
have gone up,
all of you, to the housetops,
2 you that are full of shoutings,
tumultuous city,
exultant town?
Your slain are not slain
by the sword,
nor are they dead in battle.
3 Your rulers have all fled together;
they were captured without
the use of a bow.[a]
All of you who were found
were captured,
though they had fled far away.[b]
4 Therefore I said:
Look away from me,
let me weep bitter tears;
do not try to comfort me
for the destruction of my
beloved people.

5 For the Lord GOD of hosts
has a day
of tumult and trampling
and confusion
in the valley of vision,
a battering down of walls
and a cry for help to the
mountains.
6 Elam bore the quiver
with chariots and cavalry,[c]
and Kir uncovered the shield.
7 Your choicest valleys were
full of chariots,
and the cavalry took their
stand at the gates.
8 He has taken away the
covering of Judah.

On that day you looked to the weapons of the House of the Forest, **9** and you saw that there were many breaches in the city of David, and you collected the waters of the lower pool. **10** You counted the houses of Jerusalem, and you broke down the houses to fortify the wall. **11** You made a reservoir between the two walls for the water of the old pool. But you did not look to him who did it, or have regard for him who planned it long ago.

12 In that day the Lord GOD of hosts
called to weeping and
mourning,
to baldness and putting
on sackcloth;
13 but instead there was joy
and festivity,
killing oxen and
slaughtering sheep,
eating meat and
drinking wine.
"Let us eat and drink,
for tomorrow we die."
14 The LORD of hosts has revealed
himself in my ears:
Surely this iniquity will not be
forgiven you until you die,
says the Lord GOD of hosts.

DENUNCIATION OF SELF-SEEKING OFFICIALS

15 Thus says the Lord GOD of hosts: Come, go to this steward, to Shebna, who is master of the household, and say to him: **16** What right do you have here? Who are your relatives here, that you have cut out a tomb here for yourself, cutting a tomb on the height, and carving a habitation for yourself in the rock? **17** The LORD is about to hurl you away violently, my fellow. He will seize firm hold on you, **18** whirl you round and round, and throw you like a ball into a wide land; there you shall die, and there your splendid chariots shall lie, O you disgrace to your master's house! **19** I will thrust you from your office, and you will be pulled down from your post.

20 On that day I will call my servant Eliakim son of Hilkiah, **21** and will clothe him with your robe and bind your sash on him. I will com-

---

[a] 22.3 Or *without their bows*   [b] 22.3 Gk Syr Vg: Heb *fled from far away*
[c] 22.6 Meaning of Heb uncertain

mit your authority to his hand, and he shall be a father to the inhabitants of Jerusalem and to the house of Judah. ²²I will place on his shoulder the key of the house of David; he shall open, and no one shall shut; he shall shut, and no one shall open. ²³I will fasten him like a peg in a secure place, and he will become a throne of honor to his ancestral house. ²⁴And they will hang on him the whole weight of his ancestral house, the offspring and issue, every small vessel, from the cups to all the flagons. ²⁵On that day, says the LORD of hosts, the peg that was fastened in a secure place will give way; it will be cut down and fall, and the load that was on it will perish, for the LORD has spoken.

AN ORACLE CONCERNING TYRE

23 The oracle concerning Tyre.

Wail, O ships of Tarshish,
  for your fortress is destroyed.ᵃ
When they came in from Cyprus
  they learned of it.
² Be still, O inhabitants
    of the coast,
  O merchants of Sidon,
your messengers crossed
    over the seaᵇ
³   and were on the mighty
      waters;
your revenue was the
      grain of Shihor,
  the harvest of the Nile;
  you were the merchant
    of the nations.
⁴ Be ashamed, O Sidon, for the
    sea has spoken,
  the fortress of the sea, saying:
"I have neither labored
    nor given birth,
  I have neither reared
    young men
  nor brought up young women."
⁵ When the report comes to Egypt,
  they will be in anguish over
    the report about Tyre.
⁶ Cross over to Tarshish—
  wail, O inhabitants
    of the coast!
⁷ Is this your exultant city
  whose origin is from
    days of old,

whose feet carried her
  to settle far away?
⁸ Who has planned this
  against Tyre, the bestower
    of crowns,
whose merchants were princes,
  whose traders were the
    honored of the earth?
⁹ The LORD of hosts has
    planned it—
  to defile the pride of all glory,
  to shame all the honored
    of the earth.
¹⁰ Cross over to your own land,
    O ships ofᶜ Tarshish;
  this is a harborᵈ no more.
¹¹ He has stretched out his
      hand over the sea,
  he has shaken the kingdoms;
  the LORD has given command
      concerning Canaan
  to destroy its fortresses.
¹² He said:
You will exult no longer,
    O oppressed virgin
      daughter Sidon;
rise, cross over to Cyprus—
    even there you will
      have no rest.

¹³ Look at the land of the Chaldeans! This is the people; it was not Assyria. They destined Tyre for wild animals. They erected their siege towers, they tore down her palaces, they made her a ruin.ᵉ
¹⁴ Wail, O ships of Tarshish,
  for your fortress is destroyed.
¹⁵From that day Tyre will be forgotten for seventy years, the lifetime of one king. At the end of seventy years, it will happen to Tyre as in the song about the prostitute:
¹⁶ Take a harp,
    go about the city,
    you forgotten prostitute!
Make sweet melody,
    sing many songs,
    that you may be remembered.
¹⁷At the end of seventy years, the LORD will visit Tyre, and she will

ᵃ **23.1** Cn Compare verse 14: Heb *for it is destroyed, without houses*   ᵇ **23.2** Q Ms: MT *crossing over the sea, they replenished you*   ᶜ **23.10** Cn Compare Gk: Heb *like the Nile, daughter*   ᵈ **23.10** Cn: Heb *restraint*   ᵉ **23.13** Meaning of Heb uncertain

return to her trade, and will prostitute herself with all the kingdoms of the world on the face of the earth. [18]Her merchandise and her wages will be dedicated to the LORD; her profits[a] will not be stored or hoarded, but her merchandise will supply abundant food and fine clothing for those who live in the presence of the LORD.

IMPENDING JUDGMENT ON THE EARTH

24 Now the LORD is about to lay waste the earth and make it desolate, and he will twist its surface and scatter its inhabitants.

[2] And it shall be, as with the people, so with the priest; as with the slave, so with his master; as with the maid, so with her mistress; as with the buyer, so with the seller; as with the lender, so with the borrower; as with the creditor, so with the debtor.

[3] The earth shall be utterly laid waste and utterly despoiled; for the LORD has spoken this word.

[4] The earth dries up and withers, the world languishes and withers; the heavens languish together with the earth.

[5] The earth lies polluted under its inhabitants; for they have transgressed laws, violated the statutes, broken the everlasting covenant.

[6] Therefore a curse devours the earth, and its inhabitants suffer for their guilt; therefore the inhabitants of the earth dwindled, and few people are left.

[7] The wine dries up, the vine languishes, all the merry-hearted sigh.

[8] The mirth of the timbrels is stilled, the noise of the jubilant has ceased, the mirth of the lyre is stilled.

[9] No longer do they drink wine with singing; strong drink is bitter to those who drink it.

[10] The city of chaos is broken down, every house is shut up so that no one can enter.

[11] There is an outcry in the streets for lack of wine; all joy has reached its eventide; the gladness of the earth is banished.

[12] Desolation is left in the city, the gates are battered into ruins.

[13] For thus it shall be on the earth and among the nations, as when an olive tree is beaten, as at the gleaning when the grape harvest is ended.

[14] They lift up their voices, they sing for joy; they shout from the west over the majesty of the LORD.

[15] Therefore in the east give glory to the LORD; in the coastlands of the sea glorify the name of the LORD, the God of Israel.

[16] From the ends of the earth we hear songs of praise, of glory to the Righteous One. But I say, I pine away, I pine away. Woe is me! For the treacherous deal treacherously, the treacherous deal very treacherously.

[17] Terror, and the pit, and the snare are upon you, O inhabitant of the earth!

[18] Whoever flees at the sound of the terror shall fall into the pit; and whoever climbs out of the pit shall be caught in the snare.

[a] 23.18 Heb it

For the windows of heaven
    are opened,
    and the foundations of
        the earth tremble.
19 The earth is utterly broken,
    the earth is torn asunder,
    the earth is violently shaken.
20 The earth staggers like
        a drunkard,
    it sways like a hut;
    its transgression lies
        heavy upon it,
    and it falls, and will
        not rise again.

21 On that day the LORD will punish
    the host of heaven in heaven,
    and on earth the kings
        of the earth.
22 They will be gathered together
    like prisoners in a pit;
    they will be shut up in a prison,
    and after many days they
        will be punished.
23 Then the moon will be abashed,
    and the sun ashamed;
    for the LORD of hosts will reign
        on Mount Zion and in
            Jerusalem,
    and before his elders he will
        manifest his glory.

PRAISE FOR DELIVERANCE
FROM OPPRESSION

25 O LORD, you are my God;
        I will exalt you, I will
        praise your name;
    for you have done wonderful
        things,
    plans formed of old,
        faithful and sure.
2 For you have made the
        city a heap,
    the fortified city a ruin;
    the palace of aliens is a
        city no more,
    it will never be rebuilt.
3 Therefore strong peoples
        will glorify you;
    cities of ruthless nations
        will fear you.
4 For you have been a refuge
        to the poor,
    a refuge to the needy in
        their distress,
    a shelter from the rainstorm
        and a shade from the heat.

When the blast of the
        ruthless was like a
        winter rainstorm,
5   the noise of aliens like
        heat in a dry place,
    you subdued the heat with
        the shade of clouds;
    the song of the ruthless
        was stilled.

6 On this mountain the LORD
        of hosts will make
    for all peoples
        a feast of rich food, a feast
        of well-aged wines,
    of rich food filled with
        marrow, of well-aged
        wines strained clear.
7 And he will destroy on
        this mountain
    the shroud that is cast
        over all peoples,
    the sheet that is spread
        over all nations;
8   he will swallow up
        death forever.
Then the Lord GOD will
        wipe away the tears
        from all faces,
    and the disgrace of his
        people he will take away
        from all the earth,
    for the LORD has spoken.
9 It will be said on that day,
    Lo, this is our God; we have
        waited for him, so that
        he might save us.
    This is the LORD for whom
        we have waited;
    let us be glad and rejoice
        in his salvation.
10 For the hand of the LORD will
        rest on this mountain.

The Moabites shall be trodden
        down in their place
    as straw is trodden down
        in a dung-pit.
11 Though they spread out their
        hands in the midst of it,
    as swimmers spread out
        their hands to swim,
    their pride will be laid low
        despite the struggle[a]
        of their hands.

[a] 25.11 Meaning of Heb uncertain

12 The high fortifications of his walls
    will be brought down,
  laid low, cast to the ground,
    even to the dust.

JUDAH'S SONG OF VICTORY

26 On that day this song will be
sung in the land of Judah:
We have a strong city;
  he sets up victory
    like walls and bulwarks.
2 Open the gates,
  so that the righteous nation
    that keeps faith
  may enter in.
3 Those of steadfast mind you
    keep in peace—
  in peace because they
    trust in you.
4 Trust in the LORD forever,
  for in the LORD GOD[a]
  you have an everlasting rock.

PONDER

Open the gates so that the
righteous nation that keeps faith
may enter in. Those of steadfast
mind you keep in peace—in peace
because they trust in you.
—Isaiah 26.2–3

PRAY

O Father, your words reveal to us the
simple but profound significance of
being your people. We pray that you
will guide us and give us wisdom and
influence to be faithful citizens in our
nation and influence others to seek
and trust you. Center our hearts and
minds steadfastly in you, so that as
a Christian community, we can build
unity based on our common faith in
Jesus Christ. Thank you for sending
Jesus as our guide: He looked upon
all people as equal before you; he
was a Prince of Peace; he taught us
to love one another; he reached out
to the poor, the sick and the helpless.
In Jesus' name we pray. Amen.

---

5 For he has brought low
  the inhabitants of the height;
  the lofty city he lays low.
He lays it low to the ground,
  casts it to the dust.
6 The foot tramples it,
  the feet of the poor,
  the steps of the needy.

7 The way of the righteous is level;
  O Just One, you make smooth
    the path of the righteous.
8 In the path of your judgments,
  O LORD, we wait for you;
  your name and your renown
  are the soul's desire.
9 My soul yearns for you
  in the night,
  my spirit within me
    earnestly seeks you.
For when your judgments
  are in the earth,
  the inhabitants of the world
  learn righteousness.
10 If favor is shown to the wicked,
  they do not learn
    righteousness;
in the land of uprightness
  they deal perversely
and do not see the majesty
  of the LORD.
11 O LORD, your hand is lifted up,
  but they do not see it.
Let them see your zeal for your
    people, and be ashamed.
Let the fire for
  your adversaries
  consume them.
12 O LORD, you will ordain
    peace for us,
  for indeed, all that we
    have done, you have
    done for us.
13 O LORD our God,
  other lords besides you
    have ruled over us,
  but we acknowledge your
    name alone.
14 The dead do not live;
  shades do not rise—
because you have punished
    and destroyed them,
  and wiped out all
    memory of them.

a **26.4** Heb *in Yah, the LORD*

15 But you have increased the
    nation, O LORD,
    you have increased the nation;
    you are glorified;
    you have enlarged all the
    borders of the land.

16 O LORD, in distress they
    sought you,
    they poured out a prayer[a]
    when your chastening
    was on them.
17 Like a woman with child,
    who writhes and cries
    out in her pangs
    when she is near her time,
so were we because of
    you, O LORD;
18 we were with child,
    we writhed,
    but we gave birth
    only to wind.
We have won no victories
    on earth,
    and no one is born to
    inhabit the world.
19 Your dead shall live, their
    corpses[b] shall rise.
    O dwellers in the dust, awake
    and sing for joy!
For your dew is a radiant dew,
    and the earth will give birth
    to those long dead.[c]

20 Come, my people, enter
    your chambers,
    and shut your doors
    behind you;
hide yourselves for a little while
    until the wrath is past.
21 For the LORD comes out
    from his place
    to punish the inhabitants
    of the earth for
    their iniquity;
the earth will disclose the
    blood shed on it,
    and will no longer
    cover its slain.

ISRAEL'S REDEMPTION

27 On that day the LORD with
his cruel and great and
strong sword will punish Leviathan
the fleeing serpent, Leviathan the
twisting serpent, and he will kill the
dragon that is in the sea.

2 On that day:
    A pleasant vineyard,
        sing about it!
3   I, the LORD, am its keeper;
    every moment I water it.
I guard it night and day
    so that no one can harm it;
4   I have no wrath.
If it gives me thorns and briers,
    I will march to
        battle against it.
    I will burn it up.
5 Or else let it cling to me
    for protection,
    let it make peace with me,
    let it make peace with me.

6 In days to come[d] Jacob
        shall take root,
    Israel shall blossom and
        put forth shoots,
    and fill the whole world
        with fruit.

7 Has he struck them down as
        he struck down those
        who struck them?
    Or have they been killed as
        their killers were killed?
8 By expulsion,[a] by exile you
        struggled against them;
    with his fierce blast he
        removed them in the
        day of the east wind.
9 Therefore by this the guilt of
        Jacob will be expiated,
    and this will be the full fruit
        of the removal of his sin:
when he makes all the stones
        of the altars
    like chalkstones crushed
        to pieces,
    no sacred poles[e] or
        incense altars will
        remain standing.
10 For the fortified city is solitary,
    a habitation deserted
        and forsaken, like
        the wilderness;
the calves graze there,
    there they lie down, and
        strip its branches.

[a] 26.16; 27.8 Meaning of Heb uncertain
[b] 26.19 Cn Compare Syr Tg: Heb my corpse
[c] 26.19 Heb to the shades   [d] 27.6 Heb
Those to come   [e] 27.9 Heb Asherim

11 When its boughs are dry,
    they are broken;
women come and make
    a fire of them.
For this is a people without
    understanding;
therefore he that made
    them will not have
    compassion on them,
he that formed them will
    show them no favor.

12 On that day the LORD will thresh from the channel of the Euphrates to the Wadi of Egypt, and you will be gathered one by one, O people of Israel. 13 And on that day a great trumpet will be blown, and those who were lost in the land of Assyria and those who were driven out to the land of Egypt will come and worship the LORD on the holy mountain at Jerusalem.

JUDGMENT ON CORRUPT RULERS, PRIESTS, AND PROPHETS

28 Ah, the proud garland of the
    drunkards of Ephraim,
and the fading flower of
    its glorious beauty,
which is on the head of those
    bloated with rich food, of
    those overcome with wine!
2 See, the Lord has one who is
    mighty and strong;
like a storm of hail, a
    destroying tempest,
like a storm of mighty,
    overflowing waters;
with his hand he will hurl
    them down to the earth.
3 Trampled under foot will be
    the proud garland of the
    drunkards of Ephraim.
4 And the fading flower of its
    glorious beauty,
which is on the head of those
    bloated with rich food,
will be like a first-ripe fig
    before the summer;
whoever sees it, eats it up
    as soon as it comes to hand.

5 In that day the LORD of hosts will
    be a garland of glory,
and a diadem of beauty, to the
    remnant of his people;

6 and a spirit of justice to the one
    who sits in judgment,
and strength to those who turn
    back the battle at the gate.

7 These also reel with wine
    and stagger with
    strong drink;
the priest and the prophet reel
    with strong drink,
they are confused with wine,
they stagger with
    strong drink;
they err in vision,
    they stumble in giving
    judgment.
8 All tables are covered with
    filthy vomit;
    no place is clean.

9 "Whom will he teach knowledge,
    and to whom will he explain
    the message?
Those who are weaned from milk,
    those taken from the breast?
10 For it is precept upon precept,
    precept upon precept,
    line upon line, line upon line,
    here a little, there a little."[a]

11 Truly, with stammering lip
    and with alien tongue
he will speak to this people,
12   to whom he has said,
"This is rest;
    give rest to the weary;
and this is repose";
    yet they would not hear.
13 Therefore the word of the LORD
    will be to them,
"Precept upon precept,
    precept upon precept,
    line upon line, line upon line,
    here a little, there a little;"[a]
in order that they may go,
    and fall backward,
    and be broken, and
    snared, and taken.

14 Therefore hear the word of the
    LORD, you scoffers
who rule this people
    in Jerusalem.

---

[a] **28.10,13** Meaning of Heb of this verse uncertain

15 Because you have said, "We
        have made a covenant
        with death,
    and with Sheol we have
        an agreement;
    when the overwhelming
        scourge passes through
    it will not come to us;
    for we have made lies our refuge,
        and in falsehood we have
        taken shelter";
16 therefore thus says
        the Lord GOD,
    See, I am laying in Zion a
        foundation stone,
    a tested stone,
    a precious cornerstone, a
        sure foundation:
    "One who trusts will
        not panic."
17 And I will make justice the line,
        and righteousness the
        plummet;
    hail will sweep away the
        refuge of lies,
    and waters will overwhelm
        the shelter.
18 Then your covenant with death
        will be annulled,
    and your agreement with
        Sheol will not stand;
    when the overwhelming
        scourge passes through
    you will be beaten down by it.
19 As often as it passes through,
        it will take you;
    for morning by morning it
        will pass through,
    by day and by night;

    and it will be sheer terror to
        understand the message.
20 For the bed is too short to
        stretch oneself on it,
    and the covering too narrow
        to wrap oneself in it.
21 For the LORD will rise up as
        on Mount Perazim,
    he will rage as in the
        valley of Gibeon
    to do his deed—strange
        is his deed!—
    and to work his work—
        alien is his work!
22 Now therefore do not scoff,
    or your bonds will be
        made stronger;
    for I have heard a decree
        of destruction
    from the Lord GOD of hosts
        upon the whole land.

23 Listen, and hear my voice;
    Pay attention, and hear
        my speech.
24 Do those who plow for sowing
        plow continually?
    Do they continually open and
        harrow their ground?
25 When they have leveled
        its surface,
    do they not scatter dill,
        sow cummin,
    and plant wheat in rows
    and barley in its
        proper place,
    and spelt as the border?
26 For they are well instructed;
    their God teaches them.

✛ BIBLE IN LIFE ▷

Living Stones   *Isaiah 28.16*

In the Old Testament, the Messiah, whom we know as Jesus, is referred to as a "cornerstone" (see Psalm 118.22). Today we generally think of a cornerstone as decorative: a small, inscribed brick ceremonially placed in a building after the steel framework has been finished. The word *stone* used in Isaiah 28.16 describes a cornerstone that has been prepared for use in the foundation of a building and vital to supporting the whole structure. Christ—the living stone—can provide a sure foundation for our entire existence. We are also to be "like living stones." We are to "let [our]selves be built into a spiritual house, to be a holy priesthood" (1 Peter 2.5). As living stones, we help build Christ's kingdom on the foundation of our tested, precious cornerstone, Jesus.

27 Dill is not threshed with a
    threshing sledge,
    nor is a cart wheel rolled
        over cummin;
    but dill is beaten out with a stick,
        and cummin with a rod.
28 Grain is crushed for bread,
        but one does not thresh
            it forever;
    one drives the cart wheel
        and horses over it,
    but does not pulverize it.
29 This also comes from the
        LORD of hosts;
    he is wonderful in counsel,
        and excellent in wisdom.

THE SIEGE OF JERUSALEM

29 Ah, Ariel, Ariel,
    the city where David
        encamped!
Add year to year;
    let the festivals run
        their round.
2 Yet I will distress Ariel,
    and there shall be moaning
        and lamentation,
    and Jerusalem[a] shall be to
        me like an Ariel.[b]
3 And like David[c] I will encamp
        against you;
    I will besiege you
        with towers
    and raise siegeworks
        against you.
4 Then deep from the earth
        you shall speak,
    from low in the dust your
        words shall come;
    your voice shall come from
        the ground like the
        voice of a ghost,
    and your speech shall whisper
        out of the dust.

5 But the multitude of your foes[d]
        shall be like small dust,
    and the multitude of tyrants
        like flying chaff.
    And in an instant, suddenly,
6   you will be visited by the
        LORD of hosts
    with thunder and earthquake
        and great noise,
    with whirlwind and tempest,
        and the flame of a
        devouring fire.

7 And the multitude of all the
        nations that fight
            against Ariel,
    all that fight against her
        and her stronghold,
        and who distress her,
    shall be like a dream, a
        vision of the night.
8 Just as when a hungry person
        dreams of eating
    and wakes up still hungry,
    or a thirsty person dreams
        of drinking
    and wakes up faint,
        still thirsty,
    so shall the multitude of all
        the nations be
    that fight against
        Mount Zion.

9 Stupefy yourselves and
        be in a stupor,
    blind yourselves
        and be blind!
    Be drunk, but not from wine;
    stagger, but not from
        strong drink!
10 For the LORD has poured
        out upon you
    a spirit of deep sleep;
    he has closed your eyes,
        you prophets,
    and covered your heads,
        you seers.

11 The vision of all this has become for you like the words of a sealed document. If it is given to those who can read, with the command, "Read this," they say, "We cannot, for it is sealed." 12 And if it is given to those who cannot read, saying, "Read this," they say, "We cannot read."

13 The Lord said:
    Because these people draw near
        with their mouths
    and honor me with their lips,
        while their hearts are
            far from me,
    and their worship of me is a
        human commandment
        learned by rote;

a 29.2 Heb *she*   b 29.2 Probable
meaning, *altar hearth*; compare Ezek
43.15   c 29.3 Gk: Meaning of Heb uncertain
d 29.5 Cn: Heb *strangers*

14 so I will again do
        amazing things with
            this people,
        shocking and amazing.
The wisdom of their wise
        shall perish,
    and the discernment
        of the discerning
        shall be hidden.

15 Ha! You who hide a plan too
        deep for the LORD,
    whose deeds are in the dark,
    and who say, "Who sees us?
        Who knows us?"
16 You turn things upside down!
    Shall the potter be regarded
        as the clay?
Shall the thing made say
        of its maker,
    "He did not make me";
or the thing formed say of the
        one who formed it,
    "He has no understanding"?

HOPE FOR THE FUTURE

17 Shall not Lebanon in a
        very little while
    become a fruitful field,
    and the fruitful field be
        regarded as a forest?
18 On that day the deaf shall hear
        the words of a scroll,
    and out of their gloom
        and darkness
    the eyes of the blind shall see.
19 The meek shall obtain fresh
        joy in the LORD,
    and the neediest people
        shall exult in the
        Holy One of Israel.
20 For the tyrant shall be no more,
    and the scoffer shall
        cease to be;
    all those alert to do evil
        shall be cut off—
21 those who cause a person
        to lose a lawsuit,
    who set a trap for the
        arbiter in the gate,
    and without grounds
        deny justice to the
        one in the right.

22 Therefore thus says the LORD,
who redeemed Abraham, concerning the house of Jacob:

No longer shall Jacob be ashamed,
    no longer shall his face
        grow pale.
23 For when he sees his children,
    the work of my hands,
        in his midst,
    they will sanctify my name;
they will sanctify the Holy
        One of Jacob,
    and will stand in awe of
        the God of Israel.
24 And those who err in spirit will
        come to understanding,
    and those who grumble will
        accept instruction.

THE FUTILITY OF
RELIANCE ON EGYPT

30 Oh, rebellious children,
        says the LORD,
who carry out a plan,
        but not mine;
who make an alliance, but
        against my will,
    adding sin to sin;
2 who set out to go
        down to Egypt
    without asking for my counsel,
to take refuge in the protection
        of Pharaoh,
    and to seek shelter in the
        shadow of Egypt;
3 Therefore the protection of
        Pharaoh shall become
        your shame,
    and the shelter in the
        shadow of Egypt
        your humiliation.
4 For though his officials
        are at Zoan
    and his envoys reach Hanes,
5 everyone comes to shame
        through a people that
            cannot profit them,
    that brings neither help
            nor profit,
    but shame and disgrace.

6 An oracle concerning the animals of the Negeb.
    Through a land of trouble
            and distress,
        of lioness and roaring[a] lion,
        of viper and flying serpent,

[a] 30.6 Cn: Heb from them

they carry their riches on the
    backs of donkeys,
and their treasures on the
    humps of camels,
to a people that cannot
    profit them.
7 For Egypt's help is worthless
    and empty,
therefore I have called her,
    "Rahab who sits still."[a]

TRUE REPENTANCE COMES

WHEN WE REALIZE THERE IS

MORE JOY AND FULFILLMENT

IN LIVING UNSELFISHLY IN

THE EMBRACE OF A LOVING

AND FORGIVING GOD.

A REBELLIOUS PEOPLE

8 Go now, write it before
    them on a tablet,
and inscribe it in a book,
so that it may be for the
    time to come
    as a witness forever.
9 For they are a
    rebellious people,
    faithless children,
children who will not hear
    the instruction of the LORD;
10 who say to the seers,
    "Do not see";
and to the prophets, "Do
    not prophesy to us
    what is right;
speak to us smooth things,
    prophesy illusions,
11 leave the way, turn aside
    from the path,
let us hear no more about the
    Holy One of Israel."
12 Therefore thus says the Holy
    One of Israel:
Because you reject
    this word,
and put your trust in
    oppression and deceit,
    and rely on them;

13 therefore this iniquity shall
    become for you
like a break in a high wall,
    bulging out, and
    about to collapse,
whose crash comes suddenly,
    in an instant;
14 its breaking is like that of
    a potter's vessel
    that is smashed so ruthlessly
that among its fragments
    not a sherd is found
for taking fire from the hearth,
    or dipping water out
    of the cistern.

15 For thus said the Lord GOD, the
    Holy One of Israel:
In returning and rest you
    shall be saved;
in quietness and in trust
    shall be your strength.
But you refused 16and said,
    "No! We will flee upon horses"—
    therefore you shall flee!
and, "We will ride upon
    swift steeds"—
therefore your pursuers
    shall be swift!
17 A thousand shall flee at the
    threat of one,
at the threat of five
    you shall flee,
until you are left
    like a flagstaff on the top
    of a mountain,
like a signal on a hill.

GOD'S PROMISE TO ZION

18 Therefore the LORD waits to
    be gracious to you;
therefore he will rise up to
    show mercy to you.
For the LORD is a God of justice;
    blessed are all those who
    wait for him.
19 Truly, O people in Zion, inhabitants of Jerusalem, you shall weep no more. He will surely be gracious to you at the sound of your cry; when he hears it, he will answer you. 20Though the Lord may give you the bread of adversity and the water of affliction, yet your Teacher will not hide himself any more, but your eyes

a 30.7 Meaning of Heb uncertain

shall see your Teacher. [21]And when you turn to the right or when you turn to the left, your ears shall hear a word behind you, saying, "This is the way; walk in it." [22]Then you will defile your silver-covered idols and your gold-plated images. You will scatter them like filthy rags; you will say to them, "Away with you!"

[23] He will give rain for the seed with which you sow the ground, and grain, the produce of the ground, which will be rich and plenteous. On that day your cattle will graze in broad pastures; [24]and the oxen and donkeys that till the ground will eat silage, which has been winnowed with shovel and fork. [25]On every lofty mountain and every high hill there will be brooks running with water—on a day of the great slaughter, when the towers fall. [26]Moreover the light of the moon will be like the light of the sun, and the light of the sun will be sevenfold, like the light of seven days, on the day when the LORD binds up the injuries of his people, and heals the wounds inflicted by his blow.

JUDGMENT ON ASSYRIA

[27] See, the name of the LORD
    comes from far away,
    burning with his anger, and
        in thick rising smoke;[a]
his lips are full of indignation,
    and his tongue is like a
        devouring fire;
[28] his breath is like an
        overflowing stream
    that reaches up to the neck—
to sift the nations with the
        sieve of destruction,
    and to place on the jaws of
        the peoples a bridle that
        leads them astray.

[29] You shall have a song as in the night when a holy festival is kept; and gladness of heart, as when one sets out to the sound of the flute to go to the mountain of the LORD, to the Rock of Israel. [30]And the LORD will cause his majestic voice to be heard and the descending blow of his arm to be seen, in furious anger and a flame of devouring fire, with

a cloudburst and tempest and hailstones. [31]The Assyrian will be terrorstricken at the voice of the LORD, when he strikes with his rod. [32]And every stroke of the staff of punishment that the LORD lays upon him will be to the sound of timbrels and lyres; battling with brandished arm he will fight with him. [33]For his burning place[b] has long been prepared; truly it is made ready for the king,[c] its pyre made deep and wide, with fire and wood in abundance; the breath of the LORD, like a stream of sulfur, kindles it.

ALLIANCE WITH EGYPT IS FUTILE

31 Alas for those who go
        down to Egypt for help
and who rely on horses,
who trust in chariots because
        they are many
    and in horsemen because
        they are very strong,
but do not look to the Holy
        One of Israel
    or consult the LORD!
[2] Yet he too is wise and
        brings disaster;
he does not call back his words,
but will rise against the house
        of the evildoers,
    and against the helpers of
        those who work iniquity.
[3] The Egyptians are human,
        and not God;
    their horses are flesh,
        and not spirit.
When the LORD stretches
        out his hand,
    the helper will stumble, and
        the one helped will fall,
    and they will all perish
        together.

[4] For thus the LORD said to me,
As a lion or a young lion
        growls over its prey,
    and—when a band of
        shepherds is called
        out against it—
is not terrified by their shouting
    or daunted at their noise,

---

[a] 30.27 Meaning of Heb uncertain
[b] 30.33 Or *Topheth*   [c] 30.33 Or *Molech*

so the Lord of hosts will
    come down
    to fight upon Mount Zion
    and upon its hill.
5 Like birds hovering overhead,
    so the Lord of hosts
    will protect Jerusalem;
he will protect and deliver it,
    he will spare and rescue it.

6 Turn back to him whom you[a]
have deeply betrayed, O people of Israel. 7For on that day all of you shall
throw away your idols of silver and
idols of gold, which your hands have
sinfully made for you.
8 "Then the Assyrian shall fall by
    a sword, not of mortals;
    and a sword, not of humans,
    shall devour him;
he shall flee from the sword,
    and his young men shall be
    put to forced labor.
9 His rock shall pass away in terror,
    and his officers desert the
    standard in panic,"
says the Lord, whose
    fire is in Zion,
    and whose furnace is
    in Jerusalem.

GOVERNMENT WITH
JUSTICE PREDICTED

32 See, a king will reign
    in righteousness,
    and princes will rule
    with justice.
2 Each will be like a hiding
    place from the wind,
    a covert from the tempest,
like streams of water in
    a dry place,
like the shade of a great
    rock in a weary land.
3 Then the eyes of those who have
    sight will not be closed,
    and the ears of those who
    have hearing will listen.
4 The minds of the rash will
    have good judgment,
    and the tongues of stammerers
    will speak readily
    and distinctly.
5 A fool will no longer be
    called noble,
    nor a villain said to be
    honorable.

6 For fools speak folly,
    and their minds plot iniquity:
to practice ungodliness,
    to utter error concerning
    the Lord,
to leave the craving of the
    hungry unsatisfied,
    and to deprive the
    thirsty of drink.
7 The villainies of villains are evil;
    they devise wicked devices
to ruin the poor with lying words,
    even when the plea of the
    needy is right.
8 But those who are noble
    plan noble things,
    and by noble things they stand.

COMPLACENT WOMEN
WARNED OF DISASTER

9 Rise up, you women who are
    at ease, hear my voice;
    you complacent daughters,
    listen to my speech.
10 In little more than a year
    you will shudder, you
    complacent ones;
for the vintage will fail,
    the fruit harvest will not come.
11 Tremble, you women who
    are at ease,
    shudder, you complacent ones;
strip, and make yourselves bare,
    and put sackcloth on your loins.
12 Beat your breasts for the
    pleasant fields,
    for the fruitful vine,
13 for the soil of my people
    growing up in thorns
    and briers;
yes, for all the joyous houses
    in the jubilant city.
14 For the palace will be forsaken,
    the populous city deserted;
the hill and the watchtower
    will become dens forever,
the joy of wild asses,
    a pasture for flocks;
15 until a spirit from on high is
    poured out on us,
    and the wilderness becomes
    a fruitful field,
    and the fruitful field is
    deemed a forest.

a 31.6 Heb they

THE PEACE OF GOD'S REIGN

16 Then justice will dwell in
        the wilderness,
    and righteousness abide
        in the fruitful field.
17 The effect of righteousness
        will be peace,
    and the result of righteousness,
        quietness and
        trust forever.
18 My people will abide in a
        peaceful habitation,
    in secure dwellings, and in
        quiet resting places.
19 The forest will disappear
        completely,[a]
    and the city will be
        utterly laid low.
20 Happy will you be who sow
        beside every stream,
    who let the ox and the
        donkey range freely.

A PROPHECY OF DELIVERANCE FROM FOES

33 Ah, you destroyer,
    who yourself have not
        been destroyed;
    you treacherous one,
        with whom no one has
            dealt treacherously!
    When you have
        ceased to destroy,
    you will be destroyed;
    and when you have stopped
        dealing treacherously,
    you will be dealt with
        treacherously.

2 O LORD, be gracious to us;
        we wait for you.
    Be our arm every morning,
        our salvation in the
        time of trouble.
3 At the sound of tumult,
        peoples fled;
    before your majesty,
        nations scattered.
4 Spoil was gathered as the
        caterpillar gathers;
    as locusts leap, they
        leaped[b] upon it.
5 The LORD is exalted, he
        dwells on high;
    he filled Zion with justice
        and righteousness;

6 he will be the stability of
        your times,
    abundance of salvation,
        wisdom, and knowledge;
    the fear of the LORD is
        Zion's treasure.[c]

7 Listen! the valiant[b] cry
        in the streets;
    the envoys of peace
        weep bitterly.
8 The highways are deserted,
        travelers have quit the road.
    The treaty is broken,
        its oaths[d] are despised,
        its obligation[e] is disregarded.
9 The land mourns and languishes;
        Lebanon is confounded
            and withers away;
    Sharon is like a desert;
        and Bashan and Carmel
            shake off their leaves.

10 "Now I will arise," says the LORD,
        "now I will lift myself up;
        now I will be exalted.
11 You conceive chaff, you bring
            forth stubble;
    your breath is a fire that
            will consume you.
12 And the peoples will be as
            if burned to lime,
    like thorns cut down, that
            are burned in the fire."

13 Hear, you who are far away,
        what I have done;
    and you who are near,
        acknowledge my might.
14 The sinners in Zion are afraid;
        trembling has seized
            the godless:
    "Who among us can live with
            the devouring fire?
    Who among us can live with
            everlasting flames?"
15 Those who walk righteously
        and speak uprightly,
    who despise the gain
        of oppression,

a 32.19 Cn: Heb *And it will hail when the forest comes down*   b 33.4,7 Meaning of Heb uncertain   c 33.6 Heb *his treasure*; meaning of Heb uncertain   d 33.8 Q Ms: MT *cities*   e 33.8 Or *everyone*

who wave away a bribe instead
of accepting it,
who stop their ears from
hearing of bloodshed
and shut their eyes from
looking on evil,
16 they will live on the heights;
their refuge will be the
fortresses of rocks;
their food will be supplied,
their water assured.

THE LAND OF THE
MAJESTIC KING

17 Your eyes will see the king
in his beauty;
they will behold a land that
stretches far away.
18 Your mind will muse on
the terror:
"Where is the one who
counted?
Where is the one who
weighed the tribute?
Where is the one who
counted the towers?"
19 No longer will you see the
insolent people,
the people of an obscure
speech that you cannot
comprehend,
stammering in a language that
you cannot understand.
20 Look on Zion, the city of our
appointed festivals!
Your eyes will see Jerusalem,
a quiet habitation, an
immovable tent,
whose stakes will never
be pulled up,
and none of whose ropes
will be broken.
21 But there the LORD in majesty
will be for us
a place of broad rivers
and streams,
where no galley with oars can go,
nor stately ship can pass.
22 For the LORD is our judge, the
LORD is our ruler,
the LORD is our king;
he will save us.

23 Your rigging hangs loose;
it cannot hold the mast
firm in its place,
or keep the sail spread out.

Then prey and spoil in abundance
will be divided;
even the lame will fall
to plundering.
24 And no inhabitant will
say, "I am sick";
the people who live there will
be forgiven their iniquity.

JUDGMENT ON THE NATIONS

34 Draw near, O nations,
to hear;
O peoples, give heed!
Let the earth hear, and
all that fills it,
the world, and all that
comes from it.
2 For the LORD is enraged against
all the nations,
and furious against all
their hordes;
he has doomed them, has given
them over for slaughter.
3 Their slain shall be cast out,
and the stench of their
corpses shall rise;
the mountains shall flow
with their blood.
4 All the host of heaven
shall rot away,
and the skies roll up like a scroll.
All their host shall wither
like a leaf withering on a vine,
or fruit withering on a fig tree.

5 When my sword has drunk its
fill in the heavens,
lo, it will descend upon Edom,
upon the people I have
doomed to judgment.
6 The LORD has a sword; it is
sated with blood,
it is gorged with fat,
with the blood of lambs
and goats,
with the fat of the
kidneys of rams.
For the LORD has a sacrifice
in Bozrah,
a great slaughter in the
land of Edom.
7 Wild oxen shall fall with them,
and young steers with
the mighty bulls.
Their land shall be soaked
with blood,
and their soil made rich with fat.

8 For the LORD has a day
of vengeance,
a year of vindication by
Zion's cause.[a]
9 And the streams of Edom[b] shall
be turned into pitch,
and her soil into sulfur;
her land shall become
burning pitch.
10 Night and day it shall not
be quenched;
its smoke shall go up forever.
From generation to generation
it shall lie waste;
no one shall pass through
it forever and ever.
11 But the hawk[c] and the hedgehog[c]
shall possess it;
the owl[c] and the raven
shall live in it.
He shall stretch the line of
confusion over it,
and the plummet of chaos
over[d] its nobles.
12 They shall name it No
Kingdom There,
and all its princes shall
be nothing.
13 Thorns shall grow over its
strongholds,
nettles and thistles in
its fortresses.
It shall be the haunt of jackals,
an abode for ostriches.
14 Wildcats shall meet with hyenas,
goat-demons shall call
to each other;
there too Lilith shall repose,
and find a place to rest.
15 There shall the owl nest
and lay and hatch and
brood in its shadow;
there too the buzzards
shall gather,
each one with its mate.
16 Seek and read from the
book of the LORD:
Not one of these shall
be missing,
none shall be without its mate.
For the mouth of the LORD
has commanded,
and his spirit has
gathered them.
17 He has cast the lot for them,
his hand has portioned it out
to them with the line;

they shall possess it forever,
from generation to generation
they shall live in it.

**TRUE RELIGION EMPHASIZES
LOVE, FORGIVENESS,
EQUALITY, PEACE, A PERSONAL
RELATIONSHIP WITH GOD,
SOLIDARITY WITH THE
POOR AND COURAGE TO
CONFRONT AND REJECT
FALSE OBJECTS OF WORSHIP.**

**THE RETURN OF THE
REDEEMED TO ZION**

35 The wilderness and the
dry land shall be glad,
the desert shall rejoice
and blossom;
like the crocus **2**it shall
blossom abundantly,
and rejoice with joy
and singing.
The glory of Lebanon shall
be given to it,
the majesty of Carmel
and Sharon.
They shall see the glory
of the LORD,
the majesty of our God.

3 Strengthen the weak hands,
and make firm the
feeble knees.
4 Say to those who are of a
fearful heart,
"Be strong, do not fear!
Here is your God.
He will come
with vengeance,
with terrible recompense.
He will come and save you."

a **34.8** Or *of recompense by Zion's
defender*   b **34.9** Heb *her streams*
c **34.11** Identification uncertain   d **34.11** Heb
lacks *over*

⁵ Then the eyes of the blind
    shall be opened,
  and the ears of the deaf
    unstopped;
⁶ then the lame shall leap
    like a deer,
  and the tongue of the
    speechless sing for joy.
For waters shall break forth
    in the wilderness,
  and streams in the desert;
⁷ the burning sand shall
    become a pool,
  and the thirsty ground
    springs of water;
the haunt of jackals shall
    become a swamp,ᵃ
the grass shall become
    reeds and rushes.

⁸ A highway shall be there,
  and it shall be called
    the Holy Way;
the unclean shall not travel on it,ᵇ
  but it shall be for God's people;ᶜ
no traveler, not even fools,
    shall go astray.
⁹ No lion shall be there,
  nor shall any ravenous
    beast come up on it;
they shall not be found there,
  but the redeemed shall
    walk there.
¹⁰ And the ransomed of the
    LORD shall return,
  and come to Zion with singing;
everlasting joy shall be
    upon their heads;
they shall obtain joy
    and gladness,
and sorrow and sighing
    shall flee away.

SENNACHERIB THREATENS JERUSALEM

36 In the fourteenth year of King Hezekiah, King Sennacherib of Assyria came up against all the fortified cities of Judah and captured them. ² The king of Assyria sent the Rabshakeh from Lachish to King Hezekiah at Jerusalem, with a great army. He stood by the conduit of the upper pool on the highway to the Fuller's Field. ³ And there came out to him Eliakim son of Hilkiah, who was in charge of the palace, and

Shebna the secretary, and Joah son of Asaph, the recorder.

4 The Rabshakeh said to them, "Say to Hezekiah: Thus says the great king, the king of Assyria: On what do you base this confidence of yours? ⁵ Do you think that mere words are strategy and power for war? On whom do you now rely, that you have rebelled against me? ⁶ See, you are relying on Egypt, that broken reed of a staff, which will pierce the hand of anyone who leans on it. Such is Pharaoh king of Egypt to all who rely on him. ⁷ But if you say to me, 'We rely on the LORD our God,' is it not he whose high places and altars Hezekiah has removed, saying to Judah and to Jerusalem, 'You shall worship before this altar'? ⁸ Come now, make a wager with my master the king of Assyria: I will give you two thousand horses, if you are able on your part to set riders on them. ⁹ How then can you repulse a single captain among the least of my master's servants, when you rely on Egypt for chariots and for horsemen? ¹⁰ Moreover, is it without the LORD that I have come up against this land to destroy it? The LORD said to me, Go up against this land, and destroy it."

11 Then Eliakim, Shebna, and Joah said to the Rabshakeh, "Please speak to your servants in Aramaic, for we understand it; do not speak to us in the language of Judah within the hearing of the people who are on the wall." ¹² But the Rabshakeh said, "Has my master sent me to speak these words to your master and to you, and not to the people sitting on the wall, who are doomed with you to eat their own dung and drink their own urine?"

13 Then the Rabshakeh stood and called out in a loud voice in the language of Judah, "Hear the words of the great king, the king of Assyria! ¹⁴ Thus says the king: 'Do not let Hezekiah deceive you, for he will not be able to deliver you. ¹⁵ Do not let Hezekiah make you rely on the LORD by

ᵃ **35.7** Cn: Heb *in the haunt of jackals is her resting place* ᵇ **35.8** Or *pass it by*
ᶜ **35.8** Cn: Heb *for them*

saying, The LORD will surely deliver us; this city will not be given into the hand of the king of Assyria.' [16]Do not listen to Hezekiah; for thus says the king of Assyria: 'Make your peace with me and come out to me; then every one of you will eat from your own vine and your own fig tree and drink water from your own cistern, [17]until I come and take you away to a land like your own land, a land of grain and wine, a land of bread and vineyards. [18]Do not let Hezekiah mislead you by saying, The LORD will save us. Has any of the gods of the nations saved their land out of the hand of the king of Assyria? [19]Where are the gods of Hamath and Arpad? Where are the gods of Sepharvaim? Have they delivered Samaria out of my hand? [20]Who among all the gods of these countries have saved their countries out of my hand, that the LORD should save Jerusalem out of my hand?'"

[21] But they were silent and answered him not a word, for the king's command was, "Do not answer him." [22]Then Eliakim son of Hilkiah, who was in charge of the palace, and Shebna the secretary, and Joah son of Asaph, the recorder, came to Hezekiah with their clothes torn, and told him the words of the Rabshakeh.

HEZEKIAH CONSULTS ISAIAH

37 When King Hezekiah heard it, he tore his clothes, covered himself with sackcloth, and went into the house of the LORD. [2]And he sent Eliakim, who was in charge of the palace, and Shebna the secretary, and the senior priests, covered with sackcloth, to the prophet Isaiah son of Amoz. [3]They said to him, "Thus says Hezekiah, This day is a day of distress, of rebuke, and of disgrace; children have come to the birth, and there is no strength to bring them forth. [4]It may be that the LORD your God heard the words of the Rabshakeh, whom his master the king of Assyria has sent to mock the living God, and will rebuke the words that the LORD your God has heard; therefore lift up your prayer for the remnant that is left."

[5] When the servants of King Hezekiah came to Isaiah, [6]Isaiah said to them, "Say to your master, 'Thus says the LORD: Do not be afraid because of the words that you have heard, with which the servants of the king of Assyria have reviled me. [7]I myself will put a spirit in him, so that he shall hear a rumor, and return to his own land; I will cause him to fall by the sword in his own land.'"

[8] The Rabshakeh returned, and found the king of Assyria fighting against Libnah; for he had heard that the king had left Lachish. [9]Now the king[a] heard concerning King Tirhakah of Ethiopia,[b] "He has set out to fight against you." When he heard it, he sent messengers to Hezekiah, saying, [10]"Thus shall you speak to King Hezekiah of Judah: Do not let your God on whom you rely deceive you by promising that Jerusalem will not be given into the hand of the king of Assyria. [11]See, you have heard what the kings of Assyria have done to all lands, destroying them utterly. Shall you be delivered? [12]Have the gods of the nations delivered them, the nations that my predecessors destroyed, Gozan, Haran, Rezeph, and the people of Eden who were in Telassar? [13]Where is the king of Hamath, the king of Arpad, the king of the city of Sepharvaim, the king of Hena, or the king of Ivvah?"

HEZEKIAH'S PRAYER

[14] Hezekiah received the letter from the hand of the messengers and read it; then Hezekiah went up to the house of the LORD and spread it before the LORD. [15]And Hezekiah prayed to the LORD, saying: [16]"O LORD of hosts, God of Israel, who are enthroned above the cherubim, you are God, you alone, of all the kingdoms of the earth; you have made heaven and earth. [17]Incline your ear, O LORD, and hear; open your eyes, O LORD, and see; hear all the words of Sennacherib, which he has sent to mock the living God. [18]Truly, O LORD, the kings of Assyria

[a] **37.9** Heb *he*   [b] **37.9** Or *Nubia*; Heb *Cush*

have laid waste all the nations and their lands, 19and have hurled their gods into the fire, though they were no gods, but the work of human hands—wood and stone—and so they were destroyed. 20So now, O LORD our God, save us from his hand, so that all the kingdoms of the earth may know that you alone are the LORD."

21 Then Isaiah son of Amoz sent to Hezekiah, saying: "Thus says the LORD, the God of Israel: Because you have prayed to me concerning King Sennacherib of Assyria, 22this is the word that the LORD has spoken concerning him:

She despises you, she
    scorns you—
virgin daughter Zion;
she tosses her head—behind
    your back,
    daughter Jerusalem.

23 "Whom have you mocked
    and reviled?
Against whom have you
    raised your voice
and haughtily lifted your eyes?
    Against the Holy
    One of Israel!
24 By your servants you have
    mocked the Lord,
and you have said, 'With
    my many chariots
I have gone up the heights
    of the mountains,
    to the far recesses of Lebanon;
I felled its tallest cedars,
    its choicest cypresses;
I came to its remotest height,
    its densest forest.
25 I dug wells
    and drank waters,
I dried up with the sole of my foot
    all the streams of Egypt.'
26 "Have you not heard
    that I determined it long ago?
I planned from days of old
    what now I bring to pass,
that you should make
    fortified cities
    crash into heaps of ruins,
27 while their inhabitants,
    shorn of strength,
    are dismayed and confounded;

they have become like
    plants of the field
    and like tender grass,
like grass on the housetops,
    blighted[a] before it is grown.

28 "I know your rising up[b] and
    your sitting down,
    your going out and coming in,
    and your raging against me.
29 Because you have raged
    against me
    and your arrogance has
    come to my ears,
I will put my hook in your nose
    and my bit in your mouth;
I will turn you back on the way
    by which you came.

30 "And this shall be the sign for you: This year eat what grows of itself, and in the second year what springs from that; then in the third year sow, reap, plant vineyards, and eat their fruit. 31The surviving remnant of the house of Judah shall again take root downward, and bear fruit upward; 32for from Jerusalem a remnant shall go out, and from Mount Zion a band of survivors. The zeal of the LORD of hosts will do this.

33 "Therefore thus says the LORD concerning the king of Assyria: He shall not come into this city, shoot an arrow there, come before it with a shield, or cast up a siege ramp against it. 34By the way that he came, by the same he shall return; he shall not come into this city, says the LORD. 35For I will defend this city to save it, for my own sake and for the sake of my servant David."

SENNACHERIB'S DEFEAT AND DEATH

36 Then the angel of the LORD set out and struck down one hundred eighty-five thousand in the camp of the Assyrians; when morning dawned, they were all dead bodies. 37Then King Sennacherib of Assyria left, went home, and lived at Nineveh. 38As he was worshiping in the house of his god Nisroch, his sons

---

[a] 37.27 With 2 Kings 19.26: Heb field
[b] 37.28 Q Ms Gk: MT lacks your rising up

Adrammelech and Sharezer killed him with the sword, and they escaped into the land of Ararat. His son Esar-haddon succeeded him.

HEZEKIAH'S ILLNESS

38 In those days Hezekiah became sick and was at the point of death. The prophet Isaiah son of Amoz came to him, and said to him, "Thus says the LORD: Set your house in order, for you shall die; you shall not recover." 2 Then Hezekiah turned his face to the wall, and prayed to the LORD: 3 "Remember now, O LORD, I implore you, how I have walked before you in faithfulness with a whole heart, and have done what is good in your sight." And Hezekiah wept bitterly.

4 Then the word of the LORD came to Isaiah: 5 "Go and say to Hezekiah, Thus says the LORD, the God of your ancestor David: I have heard your prayer, I have seen your tears; I will add fifteen years to your life. 6 I will deliver you and this city out of the hand of the king of Assyria, and defend this city.

7 "This is the sign to you from the LORD, that the LORD will do this thing that he has promised: 8 See, I will make the shadow cast by the declining sun on the dial of Ahaz turn back ten steps." So the sun turned back on the dial the ten steps by which it had declined.[a]

9 A writing of King Hezekiah of Judah, after he had been sick and had recovered from his sickness:
10 I said: In the noontide of my days
    I must depart;
I am consigned to the
      gates of Sheol
    for the rest of my years.
11 I said, I shall not see the LORD
    in the land of the living;
I shall look upon mortals no more
    among the inhabitants
      of the world.
12 My dwelling is plucked up and
      removed from me
    like a shepherd's tent;
like a weaver I have rolled
      up my life;
he cuts me off from the loom;

from day to night you bring
    me to an end;[a]
13 I cry for help[b] until morning;
like a lion he breaks all my bones;
from day to night you bring
    me to an end.[a]

14 Like a swallow or a crane[a]
    I clamor,
I moan like a dove.
My eyes are weary with
    looking upward.
O Lord, I am oppressed;
    be my security!
15 But what can I say? For he
    has spoken to me,
    and he himself has done it.
All my sleep has fled[c]
    because of the bitterness
    of my soul.

PRAYER IS A GREAT UNTAPPED RESOURCE. GOD'S RESPONSES MAY INCLUDE YES, NO, WAIT— OR "YOU MUST BE KIDDING."

16 O Lord, by these things
    people live,
    and in all these is the
      life of my spirit.[a]
Oh, restore me to health
    and make me live!
17 Surely it was for my welfare
    that I had great bitterness;
but you have held back[d] my life
    from the pit of destruction,
for you have cast all my sins
    behind your back.
18 For Sheol cannot thank you,
    death cannot praise you;
those who go down to the
      Pit cannot hope
    for your faithfulness.

---

[a] 38.8,12,13,14,16 Meaning of Heb uncertain
[b] 38.13 Cn: Meaning of Heb uncertain
[c] 38.15 Cn Compare Syr: Heb *I will walk slowly all my years* [d] 38.17 Cn Compare Gk Vg: Heb *loved*

19 The living, the living, they
     thank you,
     as I do this day;
fathers make known to children
     your faithfulness.

20 The LORD will save me,
     and we will sing to stringed
          instruments[a]
all the days of our lives,
     at the house of the LORD.

21 Now Isaiah had said, "Let them
take a lump of figs, and apply it to
the boil, so that he may recover."
22 Hezekiah also had said, "What
is the sign that I shall go up to the
house of the LORD?"

ENVOYS FROM BABYLON
WELCOMED

39 At that time King Merodach-
baladan son of Baladan of
Babylon sent envoys with letters and
a present to Hezekiah, for he heard
that he had been sick and had recovered. 2 Hezekiah welcomed them;
he showed them his treasure house,
the silver, the gold, the spices, the
precious oil, his whole armory, all
that was found in his storehouses.
There was nothing in his house or in
all his realm that Hezekiah did not
show them. 3 Then the prophet Isaiah
came to King Hezekiah and said to
him, "What did these men say? From
where did they come to you?" Hezekiah answered, "They have come
to me from a far country, from Babylon." 4 He said, "What have they seen
in your house?" Hezekiah answered,
"They have seen all that is in my
house; there is nothing in my storehouses that I did not show them."

5 Then Isaiah said to Hezekiah,
"Hear the word of the LORD of hosts:
6 Days are coming when all that is in
your house, and that which your ancestors have stored up until this day,
shall be carried to Babylon; nothing
shall be left, says the LORD. 7 Some
of your own sons who are born to
you shall be taken away; they shall
be eunuchs in the palace of the king
of Babylon." 8 Then Hezekiah said to
Isaiah, "The word of the LORD that
you have spoken is good." For he

thought, "There will be peace and security in my days."

GOD'S PEOPLE ARE COMFORTED

40 Comfort, O comfort
     my people,
     says your God.
2 Speak tenderly to Jerusalem,
     and cry to her
that she has served her term,
     that her penalty is paid,
     that she has received from
          the LORD's hand
     double for all her sins.

3 A voice cries out:
"In the wilderness prepare the
     way of the LORD,
make straight in the desert a
     highway for our God.

a 38.20 Heb *my stringed instruments*

PONDER

Comfort, O comfort my people, says
your God. Speak tenderly to Jerusalem,
and cry to her that she has served
her term, that her penalty is paid.
—Isaiah 40.1–2

PRAY

O Father of compassion, when
we encounter problems, burdens,
disappointment and sorrow, we long for
comfort. Help us grasp the meaning in
these beautiful words through the lens
of knowing our Savior, Jesus Christ,
not only seeking the comfort of your
mercy and love for ourselves, but also
demonstrating among our neighbors
that we, in the name of Jesus, "console
those who are in any affliction with the
consolation with which we ourselves
are consoled by God" (2 Corinthians
1.4). Bless us as we go about the work
you gave us to do for your kingdom, so
that we are equipped to bring the love
of Jesus to those we encounter every
day. We pray in Jesus' name. Amen.

4 Every valley shall be lifted up,
    and every mountain and
        hill be made low;
the uneven ground shall
        become level,
    and the rough places a plain.
5 Then the glory of the LORD
        shall be revealed,
    and all people shall see
        it together,
    for the mouth of the LORD
        has spoken."

6 A voice says, "Cry out!"
    And I said, "What shall I cry?"
All people are grass,
    their constancy is like the
        flower of the field.
7 The grass withers, the
        flower fades,
    when the breath of the
        LORD blows upon it;
    surely the people are grass.
8 The grass withers, the
        flower fades;
    but the word of our God
        will stand forever.
9 Get you up to a high mountain,
    O Zion, herald of good tidings;[a]
lift up your voice with strength,
    O Jerusalem, herald of
        good tidings,[b]
    lift it up, do not fear;

say to the cities of Judah,
    "Here is your God!"
10 See, the Lord GOD comes
        with might,
    and his arm rules for him;
his reward is with him,
    and his recompense
        before him.
11 He will feed his flock like
        a shepherd;
    he will gather the lambs
        in his arms,
and carry them in his bosom,
    and gently lead the
        mother sheep.

12 Who has measured the waters in
        the hollow of his hand
    and marked off the heavens
        with a span,
enclosed the dust of the earth
        in a measure,
    and weighed the mountains
        in scales
    and the hills in a balance?
13 Who has directed the spirit
        of the LORD,
    or as his counselor has
        instructed him?

a **40.9** Or *O herald of good tidings to Zion* b **40.9** Or *O herald of good tidings to Jerusalem*

BIBLE IN LIFE ▷

God's Word Stands Forever

Isaiah 40.1–8

When Isaiah spoke words of comfort to God's people, his message wasn't merely good wishes for a beleaguered people. His words captured the very promises of Almighty God, whose word endures forever. The power and trustworthiness of God's Word can be seen throughout Israel's history. When God spoke, the entire universe was created: the heavens and the earth, human beings, the entire existing order of things. Later, when God spoke again, the Israelites were released from slavery in Egypt and received the land that had been promised to them. God's spoken promises continued to be fulfilled through leaders such as David and Solomon. Although in this passage God's people had recently experienced punishment and exile for their sins, Isaiah was reminding Israel that God's words can always be trusted, and God's promises of hope are sure. The people would indeed experience God's comfort and restoration and could be certain that God would dwell among them again. We too have great promises from God. One of those promises is the hope of redemption through Christ's sacrifice on the cross. Jesus, who himself is the Word of God (see John 1.1), gives eternal life to all who call on him (see Romans 10.13). People may fail us, and human promises will often be broken, but we can rejoice that God's Word stands forever!

14 Whom did he consult for his
      enlightenment,
   and who taught him the
      path of justice?
   Who taught him knowledge,
      and showed him the way
      of understanding?
15 Even the nations are like a
      drop from a bucket,
   and are accounted as dust
      on the scales;
   see, he takes up the isles
      like fine dust.
16 Lebanon would not provide
      fuel enough,
   nor are its animals enough
      for a burnt offering.
17 All the nations are as nothing
      before him;
   they are accounted by him
      as less than nothing
      and emptiness.

18 To whom then will
      you liken God,
   or what likeness compare
      with him?
19 An idol? —A workman casts it,
   and a goldsmith overlays
      it with gold,
   and casts for it silver chains.
20 As a gift one chooses
      mulberry wood[a]
   —wood that will not rot—
   then seeks out a
      skilled artisan
   to set up an image that
      will not topple.

21 Have you not known? Have
      you not heard?
   Has it not been told you
      from the beginning?
   Have you not understood
      from the foundations
      of the earth?
22 It is he who sits above the
      circle of the earth,
   and its inhabitants are
      like grasshoppers;
   who stretches out the heavens
      like a curtain,
   and spreads them like a
      tent to live in;
23 who brings princes to naught,
   and makes the rulers of the
      earth as nothing.

24 Scarcely are they planted,
      scarcely sown,
   scarcely has their stem taken
      root in the earth,
   when he blows upon them,
      and they wither,
   and the tempest carries
      them off like stubble.

25 To whom then will you
      compare me,
   or who is my equal? says
      the Holy One.
26 Lift up your eyes on
      high and see:
   Who created these?

[a] 40.20 Meaning of Heb uncertain

BIBLE IN LIFE

Defining God

Isaiah 40.13–28

Many people try to define God or picture what God looks like. Isaiah asks the question, "To whom then will you liken God, or what likeness compare with him?" (verse 18). We cannot know what God has not chosen to reveal to us. Within some denominations, Christians debate whether God is male or female. When we reduce God to human terms, we take away from the essence of the nature of God. We simply cannot define God in a narrow, human way. We know that God is an omniscient presence—God knows all. God is omnipresent—God is everywhere. God is omnipotent—God has all power. At the same time, God has a personal relationship with human beings through the person of Jesus Christ, who was God in human form. We should not be concerned with limited definitions of who God is. God is concerned about whether or not we know and revere our Creator and obey his commandments, and about people knowing and submitting to Jesus.

He who brings out their host
　　and numbers them,
　　calling them all by name;
because he is great in strength,
　　mighty in power,
　　not one is missing.

27 Why do you say, O Jacob,
　　and speak, O Israel,
"My way is hidden from
　　the LORD,
and my right is disregarded
　　by my God"?
28 Have you not known? Have
　　you not heard?
The LORD is the everlasting God,
　　the Creator of the ends
　　of the earth.
He does not faint or grow weary;
　　his understanding is
　　unsearchable.
29 He gives power to the faint,
　　and strengthens the powerless.
30 Even youths will faint
　　and be weary,
and the young will fall
　　exhausted;
31 but those who wait for the
　　LORD shall renew
　　their strength,
they shall mount up with
　　wings like eagles,
they shall run and not be weary,
　　they shall walk and not faint.

WE MUST ACKNOWLEDGE

OUR OWN INADEQUACY

AND THE SUFFICIENCY OF

GOD, THROUGH CHRIST.

ISRAEL ASSURED OF GOD'S HELP

41 Listen to me in silence,
　　O coastlands;
let the peoples renew
　　their strength;
let them approach, then
　　let them speak;
let us together draw near
　　for judgment.

2 Who has roused a victor
　　from the east,
　　summoned him to his service?
He delivers up nations to him,
　　and tramples kings under foot;
he makes them like dust
　　with his sword,
　　like driven stubble
　　with his bow.
3 He pursues them and
　　passes on safely,
　　scarcely touching the
　　path with his feet.
4 Who has performed and
　　done this,
　　calling the generations
　　from the beginning?
I, the LORD, am first,
　　and will be with the last.
5 The coastlands have seen
　　and are afraid,
　　the ends of the
　　earth tremble;
they have drawn near
　　and come.
6 Each one helps the other,
　　saying to one another,
　　"Take courage!"
7 The artisan encourages
　　the goldsmith,
　　and the one who smooths
　　with the hammer
　　encourages the one
　　who strikes the anvil,
saying of the soldering,
　　"It is good";
and they fasten it with nails so
　　that it cannot be moved.
8 But you, Israel, my servant,
　　Jacob, whom I have chosen,
　　the offspring of Abraham,
　　my friend;
9 you whom I took from the
　　ends of the earth,
　　and called from its
　　farthest corners,
saying to you, "You are
　　my servant,
I have chosen you and
　　not cast you off";
10 do not fear, for I am with you,
　　do not be afraid, for I
　　am your God;
I will strengthen you, I
　　will help you,
I will uphold you with my
　　victorious right hand.

11 Yes, all who are incensed
    against you
        shall be ashamed and disgraced;
    those who strive against you
        shall be as nothing and
            shall perish.
12 You shall seek those who
        contend with you,
    but you shall not find them;
    those who war against you
        shall be as nothing at all.
13 For I, the LORD your God,
        hold your right hand;
    it is I who say to you, "Do not fear,
        I will help you."

14 Do not fear, you worm Jacob,
        you insect[a] Israel!
    I will help you, says the LORD;
        your Redeemer is the Holy
            One of Israel.
15 Now, I will make of you a
        threshing sledge,
    sharp, new, and having teeth;
    you shall thresh the mountains
        and crush them,
    and you shall make the
        hills like chaff.
16 You shall winnow them
        and the wind shall
            carry them away,
    and the tempest shall
        scatter them.
    Then you shall rejoice in the LORD;
        in the Holy One of Israel
            you shall glory.

17 When the poor and needy
        seek water,
    and there is none,
    and their tongue is parched
        with thirst,
    I the LORD will answer them,
    I the God of Israel will
        not forsake them.
18 I will open rivers on the
        bare heights,[b]
    and fountains in the midst
        of the valleys;
    I will make the wilderness
        a pool of water,
    and the dry land springs
        of water.
19 I will put in the wilderness
        the cedar,
    the acacia, the myrtle,
        and the olive;

I will set in the desert the cypress,
    the plane and the pine
        together,
20 so that all may see and know,
    all may consider and
        understand,
    that the hand of the LORD
        has done this,
    the Holy One of Israel
        has created it.

THE FUTILITY OF IDOLS

21 Set forth your case, says
        the LORD;
    bring your proofs, says
        the King of Jacob.
22 Let them bring them, and tell us
        what is to happen.
    Tell us the former things,
        what they are,
    so that we may consider them,
    and that we may know
        their outcome;
    or declare to us the
        things to come.
23 Tell us what is to
        come hereafter,
    that we may know that
        you are gods;
    do good, or do harm,
    that we may be afraid
        and terrified.
24 You, indeed, are nothing
    and your work is nothing at all;
    whoever chooses you is
        an abomination.

25 I stirred up one from the north,
        and he has come,
    from the rising of the sun he
        was summoned by name.[c]
    He shall trample[d] on rulers
        as on mortar,
    as the potter treads clay.
26 Who declared it from the
        beginning, so that
            we might know,
    and beforehand, so that we
        might say, "He is right"?
    There was no one who declared
        it, none who proclaimed,
    none who heard your words.

[a] 41.14 Syr: Heb *men of*   [b] 41.18 Or *trails*
[c] 41.25 Cn Compare Q Ms Gk: MT *and he
shall call on my name*   [d] 41.25 Cn:
Heb *come*

²⁷ I first have declared it to Zion,^a
 and I give to Jerusalem a
  herald of good tidings.
²⁸ But when I look there is no one;
 among these there is
  no counselor
 who, when I ask, gives
  an answer.
²⁹ No, they are all a delusion;
 their works are nothing;
 their images are empty wind.

THE SERVANT, A LIGHT TO THE NATIONS

42 Here is my servant,
 whom I uphold,
 my chosen, in whom my
  soul delights;
I have put my spirit upon him;
 he will bring forth justice
  to the nations.
² He will not cry or lift
 up his voice,
 or make it heard in the street;
³ a bruised reed he will not break,
 and a dimly burning wick
  he will not quench;
 he will faithfully bring
  forth justice.
⁴ He will not grow faint or
 be crushed
 until he has established
  justice in the earth;
 and the coastlands wait
  for his teaching.

⁵ Thus says God, the LORD,
 who created the heavens and
  stretched them out,
 who spread out the earth and
  what comes from it,
 who gives breath to the
  people upon it
 and spirit to those who
  walk in it:
⁶ I am the LORD, I have called
 you in righteousness,
 I have taken you by the
  hand and kept you;
 I have given you as a covenant
  to the people,^b
 a light to the nations,
⁷ to open the eyes that are blind,
to bring out the prisoners
 from the dungeon,
 from the prison those who
  sit in darkness.

PONDER

Here is my servant, whom I uphold,
my chosen, in whom my soul delights;
I have put my spirit upon him; he will
bring forth justice to the nations.
—Isaiah 42.1

PRAY

Father of Life, we are grateful for this
passage from the ancient scriptures
that describes our Savior, Jesus Christ,
in vivid and provocative terms. We are
thankful for his coming with justice,
humility and knowledge to give hope to
those who are hopeless, encouragement
to those who are weak and ambition
to those who are timid. We pray that
you open our eyes to see expanded
horizons of service in your kingdom
in a way that gives us abundant life.
May we turn our hearts and minds to
the Holy Spirit's presence in order to
emulate the words and actions of Jesus
Christ. In his name we pray. Amen.

⁸ I am the LORD, that is my name;
 my glory I give to no other,
 nor my praise to idols.
⁹ See, the former things have
 come to pass,
 and new things I now declare;
before they spring forth,
 I tell you of them.

A HYMN OF PRAISE
¹⁰ Sing to the LORD a new song,
 his praise from the end
  of the earth!
Let the sea roar^c and all
  that fills it,
 the coastlands and their
  inhabitants.

^a **41.27** Cn: Heb *First to Zion—Behold,
behold them* ^b **42.6** Meaning of Heb
uncertain ^c **42.10** Cn Compare Ps 96.11;
98.7: Heb *Those who go down to the sea*

11 Let the desert and its towns
        lift up their voice,
    the villages that Kedar
        inhabits;
    let the inhabitants of Sela
        sing for joy,
    let them shout from the tops
        of the mountains.
12 Let them give glory to the LORD,
    and declare his praise in
        the coastlands.
13 The LORD goes forth like a soldier,
    like a warrior he stirs
        up his fury;
    he cries out, he shouts aloud,
    he shows himself mighty
        against his foes.

14 For a long time I have
        held my peace,
    I have kept still and
        restrained myself;
    now I will cry out like a
        woman in labor,
    I will gasp and pant.
15 I will lay waste mountains
        and hills,
    and dry up all their herbage;
    I will turn the rivers into islands,
    and dry up the pools.
16 I will lead the blind
    by a road they do not know,
    by paths they have not known
        I will guide them.
    I will turn the darkness before
        them into light,
    the rough places into
        level ground.
    These are the things I will do,
    and I will not forsake them.
17 They shall be turned back and
        utterly put to shame—
    those who trust in
        carved images,
    who say to cast images,
        "You are our gods."

18 Listen, you that are deaf;
    and you that are blind,
        look up and see!
19 Who is blind but my servant,
    or deaf like my messenger
        whom I send?
    Who is blind like my
        dedicated one,
    or blind like the servant
        of the LORD?

20 He sees many things, but does[a]
        not observe them;
    his ears are open, but he
        does not hear.

ISRAEL'S DISOBEDIENCE

21 The LORD was pleased, for the
        sake of his righteousness,
    to magnify his teaching and
        make it glorious.
22 But this is a people robbed
        and plundered,
    all of them are trapped in holes
    and hidden in prisons;
    they have become a prey with
        no one to rescue,
    a spoil with no one to
        say, "Restore!"
23 Who among you will give
        heed to this,
    who will attend and listen
        for the time to come?
24 Who gave up Jacob to the spoiler,
    and Israel to the robbers?
    Was it not the LORD, against
        whom we have sinned,
    in whose ways they
        would not walk,
    and whose law they
        would not obey?
25 So he poured upon him the
        heat of his anger
    and the fury of war;
    it set him on fire all around, but
        he did not understand;
    it burned him, but he did
        not take it to heart.

RESTORATION AND
PROTECTION PROMISED

43 But now thus says the LORD,
    he who created you, O Jacob,
    he who formed you, O Israel:
    Do not fear, for I have
        redeemed you;
    I have called you by name,
        you are mine.
2 When you pass through the
        waters, I will be with you;
    and through the rivers, they
        shall not overwhelm you;
    when you walk through fire you
        shall not be burned,
    and the flame shall not
        consume you.

a **42.20** Heb *You see many things but do*

3 For I am the LORD your God,
　　the Holy One of Israel,
　　　your Savior.
　I give Egypt as your ransom,
　　Ethiopia[a] and Seba in
　　　exchange for you.
4 Because you are precious
　　in my sight,
　and honored, and I love you,
　I give people in return for you,
　　nations in exchange for your life.
5 Do not fear, for I am with you;
　I will bring your offspring
　　from the east,
　and from the west I will
　　gather you;
6 I will say to the north,
　　"Give them up,"
　and to the south, "Do
　　not withhold;
　bring my sons from far away
　and my daughters from the
　　end of the earth—
7 everyone who is called by my name,
　　whom I created for my glory,
　　whom I formed and made."

8 Bring forth the people who are
　　blind, yet have eyes,
　who are deaf, yet have ears!
9 Let all the nations gather together,
　　and let the peoples assemble.
　Who among them declared this,
　　and foretold to us the
　　　former things?
　Let them bring their witnesses
　　to justify them,
　and let them hear and
　　say, "It is true."

10 You are my witnesses,
　　says the LORD,
　and my servant whom
　　I have chosen,
　so that you may know
　　and believe me
　and understand that I am he.
　Before me no god was formed,
　　nor shall there be any after me.
11 I, I am the LORD,
　　and besides me there
　　　is no savior.
12 I declared and saved and
　　proclaimed,
　when there was no strange
　　god among you;
　and you are my witnesses,
　　says the LORD.
13 I am God, and also henceforth
　　I am He;
　there is no one who can
　　deliver from my hand;
　I work and who can hinder it?

14 Thus says the LORD,
　　your Redeemer, the Holy
　　　One of Israel:
　For your sake I will send
　　to Babylon
　and break down all the bars,
　and the shouting of the
　　Chaldeans will be turned
　　　to lamentation.[b]
15 I am the LORD, your Holy One,
　　the Creator of Israel, your King.

a 43.3 Or *Nubia*; Heb *Cush*
b 43.14 Meaning of Heb uncertain

─┤ BIBLE IN LIFE ▷

Knowing God   *Isaiah 43.10–13*

How do we learn about God? No one has seen God (see 1 John 4.12). God does not have a physical body that we can see or touch. We don't even know how to describe God, but God reaches out to us through the scriptures. When we read God's Word, we see glimpses of who God is: God created the whole universe; God is omnipotent; God is omnipresent; God is omniscient. Isaiah 43.10–13 describes God as a savior who has revealed and proclaimed that "I, I am the LORD." When we read about God's mighty acts of deliverance, we also learn about God's character and passionate love and protection for us. In the person of Jesus Christ, the Almighty God showcases divine love, compassion, mercy and forgiveness, no matter what we do. Jesus said, "Whoever has seen me has seen the Father" (John 14.9). When we wonder what God is like, we can read the Bible, and we can look closely at the life of Jesus, God in flesh.

16 Thus says the LORD,
    who makes a way in the sea,
    a path in the mighty waters,
17 who brings out chariot and horse,
    army and warrior;
  they lie down, they cannot rise,
    they are extinguished,
    quenched like a wick:
18 Do not remember the
    former things,
    or consider the things of old.
19 I am about to do a new thing;
    now it springs forth, do
    you not perceive it?
  I will make a way in the
    wilderness
  and rivers in the desert.
20 The wild animals will honor me,
    the jackals and the ostriches;
  for I give water in the wilderness,
    rivers in the desert,
  to give drink to my chosen people,
21   the people whom I
    formed for myself
  so that they might declare
    my praise.

22 Yet you did not call upon
    me, O Jacob;
  but you have been weary
    of me, O Israel!
23 You have not brought me your
    sheep for burnt offerings,
  or honored me with
    your sacrifices.
  I have not burdened you
    with offerings,
  or wearied you with
    frankincense.
24 You have not bought me sweet
    cane with money,
  or satisfied me with the fat
    of your sacrifices.
  But you have burdened me
    with your sins;
  you have wearied me with
    your iniquities.

25 I, I am He
  who blots out your
    transgressions for
    my own sake,
  and I will not remember
    your sins.
26 Accuse me, let us go to trial;
  set forth your case, so that you
    may be proved right.

27 Your first ancestor sinned,
    and your interpreters
    transgressed against me.
28 Therefore I profaned the princes
    of the sanctuary,
  I delivered Jacob to utter
    destruction,
  and Israel to reviling.

GOD'S BLESSING ON ISRAEL

44 But now hear, O Jacob
    my servant,
  Israel whom I have chosen!
2 Thus says the LORD who
    made you,
  who formed you in the womb
    and will help you:
  Do not fear, O Jacob my servant,
  Jeshurun whom I have chosen.
3 For I will pour water on
    the thirsty land,
  and streams on
    the dry ground;
  I will pour my spirit upon
    your descendants,
  and my blessing on
    your offspring.
4 They shall spring up like a
    green tamarisk,
  like willows by flowing
    streams.
5 This one will say, "I am
    the LORD's,"
  another will be called by
    the name of Jacob,
  yet another will write on the
    hand, "The LORD's,"
  and adopt the name of Israel.

6 Thus says the LORD, the
    King of Israel,
  and his Redeemer, the
    LORD of hosts:
  I am the first and I am the last;
    besides me there is no god.
7 Who is like me? Let them
    proclaim it,
  let them declare and set
    it forth before me.
  Who has announced from of old
    the things to come?a
  Let them tell usb what
    is yet to be.

a 44.7 Cn: Heb *from my placing an
eternal people and things to come*
b 44.7 Tg: Heb *them*

8 Do not fear, or be afraid;
    have I not told you from of
        old and declared it?
    You are my witnesses!
    Is there any god besides me?
    There is no other rock; I
        know not one.

THE ABSURDITY OF IDOL WORSHIP

9 All who make idols are nothing, and the things they delight in do not profit; their witnesses neither see nor know. And so they will be put to shame. 10Who would fashion a god or cast an image that can do no good? 11Look, all its devotees shall be put to shame; the artisans too are merely human. Let them all assemble, let them stand up; they shall be terrified, they shall all be put to shame.

12 The ironsmith fashions it[a] and works it over the coals, shaping it with hammers, and forging it with his strong arm; he becomes hungry and his strength fails, he drinks no water and is faint. 13The carpenter stretches a line, marks it out with a stylus, fashions it with planes, and marks it with a compass; he makes it in human form, with human beauty, to be set up in a shrine. 14He cuts down cedars or chooses a holm tree or an oak and lets it grow strong among the trees of the forest. He plants a cedar and the rain nourishes it. 15Then it can be used as fuel. Part of it he takes and warms himself; he kindles a fire and bakes bread. Then he makes a god and worships it, makes it a carved image and bows down before it. 16Half of it he burns in the fire; over this half he roasts meat, eats it and is satisfied. He also warms himself and says, "Ah, I am warm, I can feel the fire!" 17The rest of it he makes into a god, his idol, bows down to it and worships it; he prays to it and says, "Save me, for you are my god!"

18 They do not know, nor do they comprehend; for their eyes are shut, so that they cannot see, and their minds as well, so that they cannot understand. 19No one considers, nor is there knowledge or discernment to say, "Half of it I burned in the fire; I also baked bread on its coals, I roasted meat and have eaten. Now shall I make the rest of it an abomination? Shall I fall down before a block of wood?" 20He feeds on ashes; a deluded mind has led him astray, and he cannot save himself or say, "Is not this thing in my right hand a fraud?"

ISRAEL IS NOT FORGOTTEN

21 Remember these things, O Jacob,
    and Israel, for you are
        my servant;
    I formed you, you are my servant;
        O Israel, you will not be
            forgotten by me.
22 I have swept away your
        transgressions
        like a cloud,
    and your sins like mist;
    return to me, for I have
        redeemed you.

23 Sing, O heavens, for the
        LORD has done it;
    shout, O depths of the earth;
    break forth into singing,
        O mountains,
        O forest, and every tree in it!
    For the LORD has redeemed Jacob,
        and will be glorified in Israel.

24 Thus says the LORD, your
        Redeemer,
    who formed you in the womb:
    I am the LORD, who made
        all things,
    who alone stretched out
        the heavens,
    who by myself spread
        out the earth;
25 who frustrates the omens of liars,
    and makes fools of diviners;
    who turns back the wise,
    and makes their
        knowledge foolish;
26 who confirms the word
    of his servant,
    and fulfills the prediction
    of his messengers;
    who says of Jerusalem, "It
        shall be inhabited,"
    and of the cities of Judah,
        "They shall be rebuilt,
    and I will raise up their ruins";

a 44.12 Cn: Heb *an ax*

27 who says to the deep, "Be dry—
    I will dry up your rivers";
28 who says of Cyrus, "He is
        my shepherd,
    and he shall carry out
        all my purpose";
and who says of Jerusalem,
    "It shall be rebuilt,"
    and of the temple, "Your
        foundation shall be laid."

CYRUS, GOD'S INSTRUMENT

45 Thus says the LORD to his
    anointed, to Cyrus,
    whose right hand I
        have grasped
    to subdue nations before him
    and strip kings of their robes,
    to open doors before him—
    and the gates shall not be closed:
2 I will go before you
    and level the mountains,[a]
    I will break in pieces the
        doors of bronze
    and cut through the
        bars of iron,
3 I will give you the treasures
        of darkness
    and riches hidden in
        secret places,
    so that you may know that
        it is I, the LORD,
    the God of Israel, who call
        you by your name.
4 For the sake of my servant Jacob,
    and Israel my chosen,
    I call you by your name,
    I surname you, though you
        do not know me.
5 I am the LORD, and there
        is no other;
    besides me there is no god.
    I arm you, though you
        do not know me,
6 so that they may know, from
        the rising of the sun
    and from the west, that there
        is no one besides me;
    I am the LORD, and there
        is no other.
7 I form light and create darkness,
    I make weal and create woe;
    I the LORD do all these things.

8 Shower, O heavens, from above,
    and let the skies rain down
        righteousness;

let the earth open, that salvation
    may spring up,[b]
    and let it cause righteousness
        to sprout up also;
    I the LORD have created it.

9 Woe to you who strive with
        your Maker,
    earthen vessels with
        the potter![c]
Does the clay say to the one
    who fashions it, "What
        are you making"?
    or "Your work has no handles"?
10 Woe to anyone who says to
        a father, "What are
        you begetting?"
    or to a woman, "With what
        are you in labor?"
11 Thus says the LORD,
    the Holy One of Israel,
        and its Maker:
Will you question me[d] about
        my children,
    or command me concerning
        the work of my hands?
12 I made the earth,
    and created humankind
        upon it;
    it was my hands that stretched
        out the heavens,
    and I commanded all
        their host.
13 I have aroused Cyrus[e] in
        righteousness,
    and I will make all his
        paths straight;
    he shall build my city
    and set my exiles free,
    not for price or reward,
        says the LORD of hosts.
14 Thus says the LORD:
The wealth of Egypt and the
        merchandise of Ethiopia,[f]
    and the Sabeans, tall of stature,
    shall come over to you
        and be yours,
    they shall follow you;
    they shall come over in chains
        and bow down to you.

a 45.2 Q Ms Gk: MT the swellings
b 45.8 Q Ms: MT that they may bring
forth salvation   c 45.9 Cn: Heb with the
potsherds, or with the potters   d 45.11 Cn:
Heb Ask me of things to come   e 45.13 Heb
him   f 45.14 Or Nubia; Heb Cush

They will make supplication
    to you, saying,
"God is with you alone, and
    there is no other;
    there is no god besides him."
15 Truly, you are a God who
    hides himself,
    O God of Israel, the Savior.
16 All of them are put to shame
    and confounded,
    the makers of idols go in
    confusion together.
17 But Israel is saved by the LORD
    with everlasting salvation;
you shall not be put to shame
    or confounded
    to all eternity.

18 For thus says the LORD,
    who created the heavens
    (he is God!),
who formed the earth
    and made it
    (he established it;
he did not create it a chaos,
    he formed it to
    be inhabited!):
I am the LORD, and there
    is no other.
19 I did not speak in secret,
    in a land of darkness;
I did not say to the offspring
    of Jacob,
    "Seek me in chaos."
I the LORD speak the truth,
    I declare what is right.

IDOLS CANNOT SAVE
BABYLON

20 Assemble yourselves and
    come together,
    draw near, you survivors
    of the nations!
They have no knowledge—
    those who carry about
    their wooden idols,
and keep on praying to a god
    that cannot save.
21 Declare and present your case;
    let them take counsel together!
Who told this long ago?
    Who declared it of old?
Was it not I, the LORD?
    There is no other god
    besides me,
a righteous God and a Savior;
    there is no one besides me.

22 Turn to me and be saved,
    all the ends of the earth!
For I am God, and there
    is no other.
23 By myself I have sworn,
    from my mouth has gone
    forth in righteousness
    a word that shall not return:
"To me every knee shall bow,
    every tongue shall swear."

24 Only in the LORD, it shall
    be said of me,
are righteousness and strength;
all who were incensed
    against him
    shall come to him and
    be ashamed.
25 In the LORD all the offspring
    of Israel
    shall triumph and glory.

46 Bel bows down, Nebo stoops,
    their idols are on
    beasts and cattle;
these things you carry are loaded
    as burdens on weary animals.
2 They stoop, they bow
    down together;
    they cannot save the burden,
but themselves go into
    captivity.

3 Listen to me, O house of Jacob,
    all the remnant of the
    house of Israel,
who have been borne by me
    from your birth,
    carried from the womb;
4 even to your old age I am he,
    even when you turn gray
    I will carry you.
I have made, and I will bear;
    I will carry and will save.

5 To whom will you liken me
    and make me equal,
    and compare me, as though
    we were alike?
6 Those who lavish gold
    from the purse,
    and weigh out silver in
    the scales—
they hire a goldsmith, who
    makes it into a god;
then they fall down
    and worship!

7 They lift it to their shoulders,
    they carry it,
    they set it in its place, and
        it stands there;
    it cannot move from its place.
If one cries out to it, it does
        not answer
    or save anyone from trouble.

8 Remember this and consider,ᵃ
    recall it to mind, you
        transgressors,
9 remember the former
        things of old;
for I am God, and there
        is no other;
    I am God, and there is
        no one like me,
10 declaring the end from
        the beginning
    and from ancient times
        things not yet done,
saying, "My purpose shall stand,
    and I will fulfill my intention,"
11 calling a bird of prey
        from the east,
    the man for my purpose
        from a far country.
I have spoken, and I will
        bring it to pass;
    I have planned, and I will do it.

12 Listen to me, you stubborn
        of heart,
    you who are far from
        deliverance:
13 I bring near my deliverance,
        it is not far off,
    and my salvation will not tarry;
I will put salvation in Zion,
    for Israel my glory.

THE HUMILIATION OF BABYLON

47 Come down and sit
        in the dust,
    virgin daughter Babylon!
Sit on the ground without
        a throne,
    daughter Chaldea!
For you shall no more be called
    tender and delicate.
2 Take the millstones and
        grind meal,
    remove your veil,
strip off your robe, uncover
        your legs,
    pass through the rivers.

3 Your nakedness shall be
        uncovered,
    and your shame shall be seen.
I will take vengeance,
    and I will spare no one.
4 Our Redeemer—the LORD of
        hosts is his name—
    is the Holy One of Israel.

5 Sit in silence, and go into
        darkness,
    daughter Chaldea!
For you shall no more be called
    the mistress of kingdoms.
6 I was angry with my people,
    I profaned my heritage;
I gave them into your hand,
    you showed them no mercy;
on the aged you made your yoke
    exceedingly heavy.
7 You said, "I shall be
        mistress forever,"
so that you did not lay these
        things to heart
    or remember their end.

8 Now therefore hear this, you
        lover of pleasures,
    who sit securely,
who say in your heart,
    "I am, and there is no
        one besides me;
I shall not sit as a widow
    or know the loss
        of children"—
9 both these things shall
        come upon you
    in a moment, in one day:
the loss of children and
        widowhood
    shall come upon you in
        full measure,
in spite of your many sorceries
    and the great power of
        your enchantments.

10 You felt secure in your
        wickedness;
    you said, "No one sees me."
Your wisdom and your
        knowledge
    led you astray,
and you said in your heart,
    "I am, and there is no
        one besides me."

ᵃ 46.8 Meaning of Heb uncertain

11 But evil shall come upon you,
      which you cannot charm away;
   disaster shall fall upon you,
      which you will not be
         able to ward off;
   and ruin shall come on
         you suddenly,
      of which you know nothing.

12 Stand fast in your enchantments
      and your many sorceries,
      with which you have labored
         from your youth;
   perhaps you may be able
         to succeed,
      perhaps you may inspire terror.
13 You are wearied with your
         many consultations;
      let those who study[a]
         the heavens
   stand up and save you,
      those who gaze at the stars,
   and at each new moon predict
      what[b] shall befall you.

14 See, they are like stubble,
      the fire consumes them;
   they cannot deliver
         themselves
      from the power of the flame.
   No coal for warming
         oneself is this,
      no fire to sit before!
15 Such to you are those with
         whom you have labored,
   who have trafficked with
         you from your youth;
   they all wander about in
         their own paths;
      there is no one to save you.

GOD THE CREATOR
AND REDEEMER

48 Hear this, O house of Jacob,
      who are called by the
         name of Israel,
   and who came forth from
         the loins[c] of Judah;
   who swear by the name
         of the LORD,
   and invoke the God of Israel,
      but not in truth or right.
2 For they call themselves
         after the holy city,
      and lean on the God of Israel;
         the LORD of hosts
            is his name.

3 The former things I declared
         long ago,
   they went out from my mouth
         and I made them known;
   then suddenly I did them
         and they came to pass.
4 Because I know that you
         are obstinate,
      and your neck is
         an iron sinew
      and your forehead brass,
5 I declared them to you
         from long ago,
   before they came to pass I
         announced them to you,
   so that you would not say,
         "My idol did them,
   my carved image and my cast
         image commanded them."

6 You have heard;
      now see all this;
      and will you not declare it?
   From this time forward I make
         you hear new things,
      hidden things that you
         have not known.
7 They are created now,
         not long ago;
      before today you have never
         heard of them,
   so that you could not say, "I
         already knew them."
8 You have never heard, you
         have never known,
      from of old your ear has
         not been opened.
   For I knew that you would deal
         very treacherously,
      and that from birth you
         were called a rebel.

9 For my name's sake I defer
         my anger,
      for the sake of my praise I
         restrain it for you,
      so that I may not cut you off.
10 See, I have refined you, but
         not like[d] silver;
      I have tested you in the
         furnace of adversity.

---

[a] 47.13 Meaning of Heb uncertain
[b] 47.13 Gk Syr Compare Vg: Heb *from what*
[c] 48.1 Cn: Heb *waters*   [d] 48.10 Cn:
Heb *with*

11 For my own sake, for my
       own sake, I do it,
    for why should my name[a]
       be profaned?
    My glory I will not give
       to another.

12 Listen to me, O Jacob,
       and Israel, whom I called:
    I am He; I am the first,
       and I am the last.
13 My hand laid the foundation
       of the earth,
    and my right hand spread
       out the heavens;
    when I summon them,
       they stand at attention.

14 Assemble, all of you,
       and hear!
    Who among them has
       declared these things?
    The LORD loves him;
    he shall perform his
       purpose on Babylon,
    and his arm shall be against
       the Chaldeans.
15 I, even I, have spoken and
       called him,
    I have brought him, and he
       will prosper in his way.
16 Draw near to me, hear this!
    From the beginning I have
       not spoken in secret,
    from the time it came to be
       I have been there.
    And now the Lord GOD has
       sent me and his spirit.

17 Thus says the LORD,
       your Redeemer, the Holy
       One of Israel:
    I am the LORD your God,
    who teaches you for
       your own good,
    who leads you in the way
       you should go.
18 O that you had paid attention
       to my commandments!
    Then your prosperity would
       have been like a river,
    and your success like the
       waves of the sea;
19 your offspring would have
       been like the sand,
    and your descendants
       like its grains;

their name would never be cut off
    or destroyed from before me.

20 Go out from Babylon, flee
       from Chaldea,
    declare this with a shout
       of joy, proclaim it,
    send it forth to the end of the earth;
    say, "The LORD has redeemed
       his servant Jacob!"
21 They did not thirst when he led
       them through the deserts;
    he made water flow for
       them from the rock;
    he split open the rock and
       the water gushed out.

22 "There is no peace," says the
    LORD, "for the wicked."

THE SERVANT'S MISSION

49 Listen to me, O coastlands,
       pay attention, you peoples
       from far away!
    The LORD called me before
       I was born,
    while I was in my mother's
       womb he named me.
2 He made my mouth like
       a sharp sword,
    in the shadow of his
       hand he hid me;
    he made me a polished arrow,
    in his quiver he hid me away.
3 And he said to me, "You
       are my servant,
    Israel, in whom I will
       be glorified."
4 But I said, "I have labored in vain,
    I have spent my strength for
       nothing and vanity;
    yet surely my cause is
       with the LORD,
    and my reward with my God."

5 And now the LORD says,
    who formed me in the womb
       to be his servant,
    to bring Jacob back to him,
    and that Israel might be
       gathered to him,
    for I am honored in the
       sight of the LORD,
    and my God has become
       my strength—

[a] 48.11 Gk Old Latin: Heb *for why should it*

6 he says,
"It is too light a thing that you
should be my servant
to raise up the tribes of Jacob
and to restore the
survivors of Israel;
I will give you as a light
to the nations,
that my salvation may reach
to the end of the earth."

7 Thus says the LORD,
the Redeemer of Israel
and his Holy One,
to one deeply despised, abhorred
by the nations,
the slave of rulers,
"Kings shall see and stand up,
princes, and they shall
prostrate themselves,
because of the LORD, who
is faithful,
the Holy One of Israel, who
has chosen you."

ZION'S CHILDREN TO BE BROUGHT HOME

8 Thus says the LORD:
In a time of favor I have
answered you,
on a day of salvation I
have helped you;
I have kept you and given you
as a covenant to
the people,ᵃ
to establish the land,
to apportion the desolate
heritages;
9 saying to the prisoners,
"Come out,"
to those who are in darkness,
"Show yourselves."
They shall feed along
the ways,
on all the bare heightsᵇ shall
be their pasture;
10 they shall not hunger or thirst,
neither scorching wind nor sun
shall strike them down,
for he who has pity on them
will lead them,
and by springs of water
will guide them.
11 And I will turn all my
mountains into a road,
and my highways shall
be raised up.

PONDER

In a time of favor I have answered you,
on a day of salvation I have helped
you; I have kept you and given you as
a covenant to the people . . . saying to
the prisoners, "Come out," to those who
are in darkness, "Show yourselves."
—Isaiah 49.8–9

PRAY

Lord, thank you for revealing the shades
of meaning in the ancient words that
you proclaimed through Isaiah, for the
vision of justice and hope they instill in
our spirits. Help us to be courageous
enough to look at our own lives without
fear or trepidation, but rather with hope
and anticipation, so that not only
can we be blessed, but also that we
can be a blessing to others. We take
upon ourselves the responsibility for
establishing justice and promoting
peace in our own communities and
throughout the world, to let all people
know of your saving grace. We pray
in the name of our Savior. Amen.

12 Lo, these shall come from
far away,
and lo, these from the north
and from the west,
and these from the
land of Syene.ᶜ

13 Sing for joy, O heavens, and
exult, O earth;
break forth, O mountains,
into singing!
For the LORD has comforted
his people,
and will have compassion
on his suffering ones.

14 But Zion said, "The LORD
has forsaken me,
my Lord has forgotten me."

ᵃ 49.8 Meaning of Heb uncertain
ᵇ 49.9 Or the trails   ᶜ 49.12 Q Ms: MT Sinim

15 Can a woman forget her
        nursing child,
    or show no compassion for
        the child of her womb?
Even these may forget,
    yet I will not forget you.
16 See, I have inscribed you on the
        palms of my hands;
    your walls are continually
        before me.
17 Your builders outdo your
        destroyers,[a]
    and those who laid you waste
        go away from you.
18 Lift up your eyes all
        around and see;
    they all gather, they
        come to you.
As I live, says the LORD,
    you shall put all of them on
        like an ornament,
    and like a bride you shall
        bind them on.

19 Surely your waste and your
        desolate places
    and your devastated land—
surely now you will be too
        crowded for your
        inhabitants,
    and those who swallowed
        you up will be far away.
20 The children born in the time
        of your bereavement
    will yet say in your hearing:
"The place is too
        crowded for me;
    make room for me to settle."
21 Then you will say
        in your heart,
    "Who has borne me these?
I was bereaved and barren,
    exiled and put away—
    so who has reared these?
I was left all alone—
    where then have these
        come from?"

22 Thus says the Lord GOD:
    I will soon lift up my hand
        to the nations,
    and raise my signal to
        the peoples;
and they shall bring your sons
        in their bosom,
    and your daughters shall be
        carried on their shoulders.

23 Kings shall be your foster fathers,
    and their queens your
        nursing mothers.
With their faces to the
        ground they shall
        bow down to you,
    and lick the dust of your feet.
Then you will know that I
        am the LORD;
    those who wait for me shall
        not be put to shame.

24 Can the prey be taken from
        the mighty,
    or the captives of a tyrant[b]
        be rescued?
25 But thus says the LORD:
Even the captives of the mighty
        shall be taken,
    and the prey of the tyrant
        be rescued;
for I will contend with those
        who contend with you,
    and I will save your children.
26 I will make your oppressors
        eat their own flesh,
    and they shall be drunk
        with their own blood
        as with wine.
Then all flesh shall know
    that I am the LORD
        your Savior,
    and your Redeemer, the
        Mighty One of Jacob.

50 Thus says the LORD:
    Where is your mother's
        bill of divorce
with which I put her away?
Or which of my creditors is it
    to whom I have sold you?
No, because of your sins
        you were sold,
    and for your transgressions
        your mother was
        put away.
2 Why was no one there
        when I came?
    Why did no one answer
        when I called?
Is my hand shortened, that
        it cannot redeem?
Or have I no power to deliver?

---

a 49.17 Or Your children come swiftly; your
destroyers   b 49.24 Q Ms Syr Vg: MT of a
righteous person

By my rebuke I dry up the sea,
   I make the rivers a desert;
their fish stink for lack of water,
   and die of thirst.[a]
3 I clothe the heavens with
     blackness,
   and make sackcloth
     their covering.

THE SERVANT'S HUMILIATION AND VINDICATION

4 The Lord GOD has given me
   the tongue of a teacher,[b]
that I may know how to sustain
   the weary with a word.
Morning by morning he
     wakens—
   wakens my ear
   to listen as those who
     are taught.
5 The Lord GOD has opened my ear,
   and I was not rebellious,
   I did not turn backward.
6 I gave my back to those
     who struck me,
   and my cheeks to those who
     pulled out the beard;
I did not hide my face
   from insult and spitting.

7 The Lord GOD helps me;
   therefore I have not
     been disgraced;
therefore I have set my
     face like flint,
   and I know that I shall not
     be put to shame;
8   he who vindicates me is near.
Who will contend with me?
   Let us stand up together.
Who are my adversaries?
   Let them confront me.
9 It is the Lord GOD
     who helps me;
   who will declare me guilty?
All of them will wear out
     like a garment;
   the moth will eat them up.

10 Who among you fears the LORD
   and obeys the voice of
     his servant,
who walks in darkness
   and has no light,
yet trusts in the name
     of the LORD
   and relies upon his God?

11 But all of you are kindlers of fire,
   lighters of firebrands.[c]
Walk in the flame of your fire,
   and among the brands that
     you have kindled!
This is what you shall have
     from my hand:
   you shall lie down in torment.

BLESSINGS IN STORE FOR GOD'S PEOPLE

51 Listen to me, you that
     pursue righteousness,
   you that seek the LORD.
Look to the rock from which
     you were hewn,
   and to the quarry from
     which you were dug.
2 Look to Abraham your father
   and to Sarah who bore you;
for he was but one when
     I called him,
   but I blessed him and
     made him many.
3 For the LORD will
     comfort Zion;
   he will comfort all her
     waste places,
and will make her wilderness
     like Eden,
   her desert like the garden
     of the LORD;
joy and gladness will be
     found in her,
   thanksgiving and the
     voice of song.

4 Listen to me, my people,
   and give heed to me,
     my nation;
for a teaching will go
     out from me,
   and my justice for a light
     to the peoples.
5 I will bring near my
     deliverance swiftly,
   my salvation has gone out
   and my arms will rule
     the peoples;
the coastlands wait for me,
   and for my arm they hope.
6 Lift up your eyes to the heavens,
   and look at the earth beneath;

[a] 50.2 Or *die on the thirsty ground*
[b] 50.4 Cn: Heb *of those who are taught*
[c] 50.11 Syr: Heb *you gird yourselves with firebrands*

for the heavens will vanish
    like smoke,
  the earth will wear out
    like a garment,
  and those who live on it
    will die like gnats;[a]
but my salvation will be forever,
  and my deliverance will
    never be ended.

7 Listen to me, you who know
    righteousness,
  you people who have my
    teaching in your hearts;
do not fear the reproach of others,
  and do not be dismayed
    when they revile you.
8 For the moth will eat them
    up like a garment,
  and the worm will eat
    them like wool;
but my deliverance will
    be forever,
  and my salvation to all
    generations.

9 Awake, awake, put on strength,
    O arm of the LORD!
Awake, as in days of old,
    the generations of long ago!
Was it not you who cut
    Rahab in pieces,
  who pierced the dragon?
10 Was it not you who dried
    up the sea,
  the waters of the great deep;
who made the depths of
    the sea a way
  for the redeemed
    to cross over?
11 So the ransomed of the
    LORD shall return,
  and come to Zion
    with singing;
everlasting joy shall be
    upon their heads;
  they shall obtain joy
    and gladness,
  and sorrow and sighing
    shall flee away.

12 I, I am he who comforts you;
  why then are you afraid
    of a mere mortal
    who must die,
  a human being who
    fades like grass?

13 You have forgotten the
    LORD, your Maker,
  who stretched out the heavens
  and laid the foundations
    of the earth.
You fear continually all day long
  because of the fury of
    the oppressor,
who is bent on destruction.
  But where is the fury of
    the oppressor?
14 The oppressed shall speedily
    be released;
  they shall not die and go
    down to the Pit,
  nor shall they lack bread.
15 For I am the LORD your God,
  who stirs up the sea so that
    its waves roar—
  the LORD of hosts is his name.
16 I have put my words in
    your mouth,
  and hidden you in the
    shadow of my hand,
stretching out[b] the heavens
  and laying the foundations
    of the earth,
  and saying to Zion, "You
    are my people."

17 Rouse yourself, rouse yourself!
    Stand up, O Jerusalem,
you who have drunk at the
    hand of the LORD
  the cup of his wrath,
who have drunk to the dregs
    the bowl of staggering.
18 There is no one to guide her
  among all the children
    she has borne;
there is no one to take her
    by the hand
  among all the children she
    has brought up.
19 These two things have
    befallen you
  —who will grieve with you?—
devastation and destruction,
    famine and sword—
  who will comfort you?[c]
20 Your children have fainted,
    they lie at the head of
    every street
  like an antelope in a net;

---

a 51.6 Or *in like manner* b 51.16 Syr: Heb
planting c 51.19 Q Ms Gk Syr Vg: MT *how
may I comfort you?*

they are full of the wrath
of the LORD,
the rebuke of your God.

21 Therefore hear this, you who
are wounded,ᵃ
who are drunk, but not
with wine:
22 Thus says your Sovereign,
the LORD,
your God who pleads the
cause of his people:
See, I have taken from your hand
the cup of staggering;
you shall drink no more
from the bowl of my wrath.
23 And I will put it into the hand
of your tormentors,
who have said to you,
"Bow down, that we may
walk on you";
and you have made your back
like the ground
and like the street for
them to walk on.

LET ZION REJOICE

52 Awake, awake,
put on your strength,
O Zion!
Put on your beautiful garments,
O Jerusalem, the holy city;
for the uncircumcised and
the unclean
shall enter you no more.
2 Shake yourself from the
dust, rise up,
O captiveᵇ Jerusalem;
loose the bonds from your neck,
O captive daughter Zion!

3 For thus says the LORD: You
were sold for nothing, and you shall
be redeemed without money. 4For
thus says the Lord GOD: Long ago,
my people went down into Egypt to
reside there as aliens; the Assyrian,
too, has oppressed them without
cause. 5Now therefore what am I doing here, says the LORD, seeing that
my people are taken away without
cause? Their rulers howl, says the
LORD, and continually, all day long,
my name is despised. 6Therefore my
people shall know my name; therefore in that day they shall know that
it is I who speak; here am I.

7 How beautiful upon the
mountains
are the feet of the messenger
who announces peace,
who brings good news,
who announces salvation,
who says to Zion, "Your
God reigns."
8 Listen! Your sentinels lift
up their voices,
together they sing for joy;
for in plain sight they see
the return of the LORD to Zion.
9 Break forth together
into singing,
you ruins of Jerusalem;
for the LORD has comforted
his people,
he has redeemed Jerusalem.

ᵃ **51.21** Or *humbled*   ᵇ **52.2** Cn: Heb *rise up, sit*

BIBLE IN LIFE

Sharing the Good News

Isaiah 52.7

"How beautiful . . . are the feet of the messenger who announces peace." We Christians
have received the Word, and we believe that "Everyone who calls on the name of the
Lord shall be saved" (Romans 10.13). The last admonition we received from Christ before
his ascension into heaven was: "You will be my witnesses in Jerusalem, in all Judea and
Samaria, and to the ends of the earth" (Acts 1.8). Will we obey Christ's exhortation? The
message is for everyone. All that people have to do is believe in Christ and profess faith
in him, and they will be saved. But "how are they to call on one in whom they have not
believed?" (Romans 10.14). We should be prepared whenever an opportunity arises, and
create opportunities if possible, to share this message with others.

10 The LORD has bared his holy arm
    before the eyes of all
        the nations;
    and all the ends of the
        earth shall see
        the salvation of our God.

11 Depart, depart, go out from there!
    Touch no unclean thing;
    go out from the midst of it,
        purify yourselves,
    you who carry the vessels
        of the LORD.
12 For you shall not go out in haste,
    and you shall not go in flight;
    for the LORD will go before you,
    and the God of Israel will
        be your rear guard.

THE SUFFERING SERVANT

13 See, my servant shall prosper;
    he shall be exalted
        and lifted up,
    and shall be very high.
14 Just as there were many who
        were astonished at him[a]
    —so marred was his
        appearance, beyond
        human semblance,
    and his form beyond that
        of mortals—
15 so he shall startle[b]
        many nations;
    kings shall shut their mouths
        because of him;
    for that which had not been told
        them they shall see,
    and that which they had
        not heard they shall
        contemplate.

53 Who has believed what
        we have heard?
    And to whom has the arm of
        the LORD been revealed?
2 For he grew up before him
        like a young plant,
    and like a root out of
        dry ground;
    he had no form or majesty that
        we should look at him,
    nothing in his appearance that
        we should desire him.
3 He was despised and rejected
        by others;
    a man of suffering[c] and
        acquainted with
        infirmity;

and as one from whom others
        hide their faces[d]
    he was despised, and we held
        him of no account.

4 Surely he has borne our
        infirmities
    and carried our diseases;
    yet we accounted him stricken,
        struck down by God,
        and afflicted.
5 But he was wounded for our
        transgressions,
    crushed for our iniquities;
    upon him was the punishment
        that made us whole,
    and by his bruises we
        are healed.
6 All we like sheep have
        gone astray;
    we have all turned to
        our own way,
    and the LORD has laid on him
        the iniquity of us all.

7 He was oppressed, and he
        was afflicted,
    yet he did not open his mouth;
    like a lamb that is led to
        the slaughter,
    and like a sheep that before
        its shearers is silent,
    so he did not open his mouth.
8 By a perversion of justice he
        was taken away.
    Who could have imagined
        his future?
    For he was cut off from the
        land of the living,
    stricken for the transgression
        of my people.
9 They made his grave with
        the wicked
    and his tomb[e] with the rich,[f]
    although he had done
        no violence,
    and there was no deceit
        in his mouth.

10 Yet it was the will of the LORD
        to crush him with pain.[g]

[a] 52.14 Syr Tg: Heb *you*   [b] 52.15 Meaning of
Heb uncertain   [c] 53.3 Or *a man of sorrows*
[d] 53.3 Or *as one who hides his face from us*
[e] 53.9 Q Ms: MT *and in his death*   [f] 53.9 Cn:
Heb *with a rich person*   [g] 53.10 Or *by
disease*; meaning of Heb uncertain

When you make his life an
    offering for sin,[a]
he shall see his offspring, and
    shall prolong his days;
through him the will of the
    LORD shall prosper.

11 Out of his anguish he
    shall see light;[b]
he shall find satisfaction through
    his knowledge.
The righteous one,[c] my
    servant, shall make
    many righteous,
and he shall bear their
    iniquities.

12 Therefore I will allot him a
    portion with the great,
and he shall divide the spoil
    with the strong;
because he poured out
    himself to death,
and was numbered with
    the transgressors;
yet he bore the sin of many,
and made intercession for
    the transgressors.

THE ETERNAL COVENANT
OF PEACE

54 Sing, O barren one
    who did not bear;
burst into song and shout,
you who have not
    been in labor!
For the children of the desolate
    woman will be more
    than the children of
    her that is married,
    says the LORD.

2 Enlarge the site of your tent,
    and let the curtains of
    your habitations be
    stretched out;
do not hold back; lengthen
    your cords
and strengthen your stakes.

3 For you will spread out to the
    right and to the left,
and your descendants will
    possess the nations
and will settle the
    desolate towns.

4 Do not fear, for you will
    not be ashamed;
do not be discouraged, for you
    will not suffer disgrace;
for you will forget the shame
    of your youth,
and the disgrace of your
    widowhood you will
    remember no more.

5 For your Maker is your husband,
    the LORD of hosts is his name;
the Holy One of Israel is
    your Redeemer,
the God of the whole
    earth he is called.

6 For the LORD has called you
    like a wife forsaken and
    grieved in spirit,
like the wife of a man's youth
    when she is cast off,
    says your God.

a 53.10 Meaning of Heb uncertain
b 53.11 Q Mss: MT lacks light   c 53.11 Or
and he shall find satisfaction. Through his
knowledge, the righteous one

┤ BIBLE IN LIFE ▷

The Suffering Servant   Isaiah 53.1–11

A humble, suffering servant—where is the exaltation in this? This description would have sounded incompatible with the Israelites' expectation of the promised, exalted Messiah. Christ came as the revolutionary Son of God Almighty and showed, in effect, "I will not exercise my full power; I will not be punitive; I will not be autocratic." He humbled himself and embraced his role as a suffering servant. What is the image of our own Christianity as compared with Christ's choice of being a suffering servant? He taught that "all who humble themselves will be exalted" (Matthew 23.12). We have the same choice. Christ chose to humble himself and suffer, even to die. He chose servanthood, compassion, truth, justice, humility and sacrificial love. Jesus loved the unlovable and the needy. These choices are incompatible with the pressures of our own worldly lives and may require a transformation in the way we look at ourselves.

7 For a brief moment I
    abandoned you,
  but with great compassion
    I will gather you.
8 In overflowing wrath for
    a moment
  I hid my face from you,
  but with everlasting love I will
    have compassion on you,
  says the Lord, your Redeemer.
9 This is like the days of
    Noah to me:
  Just as I swore that the
    waters of Noah
  would never again go
    over the earth,
  so I have sworn that I will not
    be angry with you
  and will not rebuke you.
10 For the mountains may depart
    and the hills be removed,
  but my steadfast love shall not
    depart from you,
  and my covenant of peace
    shall not be removed,
  says the Lord, who has
    compassion on you.

11 O afflicted one, storm-tossed,
    and not comforted,
  I am about to set your
    stones in antimony,
  and lay your foundations
    with sapphires.ᵃ
12 I will make your pinnacles
    of rubies,
  your gates of jewels,
  and all your wall of
    precious stones.
13 All your children shall be
    taught by the Lord,
  and great shall be the
    prosperity of your
    children.
14 In righteousness you shall
    be established;
  you shall be far from
    oppression, for you
    shall not fear;
  and from terror, for it shall
    not come near you.
15 If anyone stirs up strife,
    it is not from me;
  whoever stirs up
    strife with you
    shall fall because of you.

16 See it is I who have created
    the smith
  who blows the fire of coals,
  and produces a weapon
    fit for its purpose;
  I have also created the
    ravager to destroy.
17 No weapon that is fashioned
    against you shall prosper,
  and you shall confute every
    tongue that rises against
    you in judgment.
  This is the heritage of the
    servants of the Lord
  and their vindication from
    me, says the Lord.

WE ARE INVITED TO GOD'S

FEAST. THIS IS NOT A COVERED-

DISH MEAL, FOR WE HAVE

NOTHING TO BRING. WE

HAVE ONLY TO RESPOND.

AN INVITATION TO
ABUNDANT LIFE

55 Ho, everyone who thirsts,
  come to the waters;
and you that have no money,
  come, buy and eat!
Come, buy wine and milk
  without money and
    without price.
2 Why do you spend your
    money for that which
    is not bread,
  and your labor for that which
    does not satisfy?
Listen carefully to me, and
    eat what is good,
  and delight yourselves
    in rich food.
3 Incline your ear, and come to me;
  listen, so that you may live.
I will make with you an
    everlasting covenant,
  my steadfast, sure love
    for David.

ᵃ 54.11 Or *lapis lazuli*

4 See, I made him a witness
    to the peoples,
  a leader and commander
    for the peoples.
5 See, you shall call nations that
    you do not know,
  and nations that do not know
    you shall run to you,
  because of the LORD your God,
    the Holy One of Israel,
  for he has glorified you.

6 Seek the LORD while he
    may be found,
  call upon him while he is near;
7 let the wicked forsake
    their way,
  and the unrighteous
    their thoughts;
  let them return to the LORD,
    that he may have
    mercy on them,
  and to our God, for he will
    abundantly pardon.
8 For my thoughts are not
    your thoughts,
  nor are your ways my ways,
    says the LORD.
9 For as the heavens are higher
    than the earth,
  so are my ways higher
    than your ways
  and my thoughts than
    your thoughts.

10 For as the rain and the
    snow come down
    from heaven,
  and do not return there
    until they have
    watered the earth,
  making it bring
    forth and sprout,
  giving seed to the sower and
    bread to the eater,
11 so shall my word be that goes
    out from my mouth;
  it shall not return
    to me empty,
  but it shall accomplish that
    which I purpose,
  and succeed in the thing
    for which I sent it.

12 For you shall go out in joy,
    and be led back in peace;
  the mountains and the
    hills before you
  shall burst into song,
  and all the trees of the field
    shall clap their hands.
13 Instead of the thorn shall
    come up the cypress;
  instead of the brier shall
    come up the myrtle;
  and it shall be to the LORD
    for a memorial,
  for an everlasting sign that
    shall not be cut off.

┤ BIBLE IN LIFE ▷

While He May Be Found   *Isaiah 55.6*

When Isaiah tells the people to seek the Lord "while he may be found," he is not saying that God will soon disappear and not be available to us. As long as we live, God is receptive to our cries.

In this verse, Isaiah is not really talking so much about the Creator, but more about us. As we go about our lives, we make decisions that will culminate in either acceptance or rejection of a relationship with God Almighty. Day by day we can postpone the decision to seek God, focusing our attention on other things, just as the people of Judah were inclined to do. Perhaps we think we have plenty of time to make that final decision to surrender to Christ. Perhaps we don't want to turn our lives over to God just yet because we fear that we will miss out on something we want to experience in our "secular life." But one day the time will come when God will finally and eternally give us exactly what we have been choosing all along—no relationship with him. This same message rings consistently through the Bible; Jesus Christ (see Matthew 7.7–8) and the apostles (see 2 Corinthians 6.2) preached about the need to turn to God. We must not postpone any longer the decision to follow God, but seek the Lord while he may be found.

THE COVENANT EXTENDED TO ALL WHO OBEY

56 Thus says the LORD:
Maintain justice, and
do what is right,
for soon my salvation
will come,
and my deliverance
be revealed.

2 Happy is the mortal who
does this,
the one who holds it fast,
who keeps the sabbath,
not profaning it,
and refrains from
doing any evil.

3 Do not let the foreigner joined
to the LORD say,
"The LORD will surely separate
me from his people";
and do not let the eunuch say,
"I am just a dry tree."
4 For thus says the LORD:
To the eunuchs who keep
my sabbaths,
who choose the things
that please me
and hold fast my covenant,
5 I will give, in my house and
within my walls,
a monument and a name
better than sons and
daughters;
I will give them an
everlasting name
that shall not be cut off.

6 And the foreigners who join
themselves to the LORD,
to minister to him, to love
the name of the LORD,
and to be his servants,
all who keep the sabbath, and
do not profane it,
and hold fast my covenant—
7 these I will bring to my
holy mountain,
and make them joyful in
my house of prayer;
their burnt offerings and
their sacrifices
will be accepted on my altar;
for my house shall be called
a house of prayer
for all peoples.

8 Thus says the Lord GOD,
who gathers the outcasts
of Israel,
I will gather others to them
besides those already
gathered.[a]

THE CORRUPTION OF ISRAEL'S RULERS

9 All you wild animals,
all you wild animals in the
forest, come to devour!
10 Israel's[b] sentinels are blind,
they are all without
knowledge;
they are all silent dogs
that cannot bark;
dreaming, lying down,
loving to slumber.
11 The dogs have a
mighty appetite;
they never have enough.
The shepherds also have no
understanding;
they have all turned to
their own way,
to their own gain, one and all.
12 "Come," they say, "let
us[c] get wine;
let us fill ourselves with
strong drink.
And tomorrow will be like today,
great beyond measure."

ISRAEL'S FUTILE IDOLATRY

57 The righteous perish,
and no one takes it to heart;
the devout are taken away,
while no one understands.
For the righteous are taken
away from calamity,
2 and they enter into peace;
those who walk uprightly
will rest on their couches.
3 But as for you, come here,
you children of a sorceress,
you offspring of an adulterer
and a whore.[d]
4 Whom are you mocking?
Against whom do you open
your mouth wide
and stick out your tongue?

---

a 56.8 Heb *besides his gathered ones*
b 56.10 Heb *His*   c 56.12 Q Ms Syr Vg Tg: MT
me   d 57.3 Heb *an adulterer and she plays
the whore*

Are you not children of
    transgression,
    the offspring of deceit—
5 you that burn with lust
        among the oaks,
    under every green tree;
you that slaughter your children
        in the valleys,
    under the clefts of the rocks?
6 Among the smooth stones of the
        valley is your portion;
    they, they, are your lot;
to them you have poured out
        a drink offering,
    you have brought a
        grain offering.
    Shall I be appeased for
        these things?
7 Upon a high and lofty mountain
    you have set your bed,
    and there you went up
        to offer sacrifice.
8 Behind the door and
        the doorpost
    you have set up your symbol;
for, in deserting me,[a] you have
        uncovered your bed,
    you have gone up to it,
    you have made it wide;
and you have made a bargain
        for yourself with them,
    you have loved their bed,
    you have gazed on their
        nakedness.[b]
9 You journeyed to Molech[c]
        with oil,
    and multiplied
        your perfumes;
you sent your envoys far away,
    and sent down even to Sheol.
10 You grew weary from your
        many wanderings,
    but you did not say,
        "It is useless."
You found your desire rekindled,
    and so you did not weaken.

11 Whom did you dread and fear
        so that you lied,
and did not remember me
    or give me a thought?
Have I not kept silent and
        closed my eyes,[d]
    and so you do not fear me?
12 I will concede your righteousness
        and your works,
    but they will not help you.

13 When you cry out, let your
        collection of idols
        deliver you!
    The wind will carry them off,
    a breath will take them away.
But whoever takes refuge in me
        shall possess the land
    and inherit my holy mountain.

A PROMISE OF HELP AND HEALING

14 It shall be said,
    "Build up, build up, prepare
        the way,
    remove every obstruction
        from my people's way."
15 For thus says the high
        and lofty one
    who inhabits eternity,
        whose name is Holy:
I dwell in the high and holy place,
        and also with those who
        are contrite and
        humble in spirit,
    to revive the spirit of the humble,
        and to revive the heart
        of the contrite.
16 For I will not continually accuse,
        nor will I always be angry;
for then the spirits would grow
        faint before me,
    even the souls that I have made.
17 Because of their wicked
        covetousness I was angry;
    I struck them, I hid and
        was angry;
    but they kept turning back
        to their own ways.
18 I have seen their ways, but
        I will heal them;
    I will lead them and repay
        them with comfort,
    creating for their mourners
        the fruit of the lips.[a]
19 Peace, peace, to the far and the
        near, says the LORD;
    and I will heal them.
20 But the wicked are like
        the tossing sea
    that cannot keep still;
    its waters toss up mire
        and mud.

---

[a] 57.8,18 Meaning of Heb uncertain
[b] 57.8 Or *their phallus*; Heb *the hand*
[c] 57.9 Or *the king*   [d] 57.11 Gk Vg: Heb *silent even for a long time*

21 There is no peace, says my
    God, for the wicked.

FALSE AND TRUE WORSHIP

58 Shout out, do not hold back!
    Lift up your voice
      like a trumpet!
Announce to my people
    their rebellion,
to the house of
    Jacob their sins.
2 Yet day after day they seek me
    and delight to know my ways,
as if they were a nation that
      practiced righteousness
and did not forsake the
      ordinance of their God;
they ask of me righteous
      judgments,
they delight to draw
      near to God.
3 "Why do we fast, but you
      do not see?
Why humble ourselves, but
      you do not notice?"
Look, you serve your own
      interest on your fast day,
    and oppress all your workers.
4 Look, you fast only to quarrel
      and to fight
    and to strike with a wicked fist.
Such fasting as you do today
    will not make your voice
      heard on high.
5 Is such the fast that I choose,
    a day to humble oneself?
Is it to bow down the head
    like a bulrush,
and to lie in sackcloth
    and ashes?
Will you call this a fast,
    a day acceptable to the LORD?

6 Is not this the fast that I choose:
    to loose the bonds of injustice,
    to undo the thongs
      of the yoke,
to let the oppressed go free,
    and to break every yoke?
7 Is it not to share your bread
      with the hungry,
and bring the homeless
      poor into your house;
when you see the naked,
    to cover them,
and not to hide yourself
    from your own kin?

8 Then your light shall break
      forth like the dawn,
and your healing shall
      spring up quickly;
your vindicator[a] shall go
      before you,
the glory of the LORD shall
      be your rear guard.
9 Then you shall call, and the
      LORD will answer;
you shall cry for help, and he
      will say, Here I am.

PEOPLE OF GOD MUST

REPRESENT THE CAUSE

OF JUSTICE ON BEHALF

OF THE OPPRESSED.

If you remove the yoke
    from among you,
the pointing of the finger,
    the speaking of evil,
10 if you offer your food to
    the hungry
and satisfy the needs of
    the afflicted,
then your light shall rise
    in the darkness
and your gloom be like
    the noonday.
11 The LORD will guide you
    continually,
and satisfy your needs in
    parched places,
and make your bones strong;
and you shall be like a
    watered garden,
like a spring of water,
    whose waters never fail.
12 Your ancient ruins shall
    be rebuilt;
you shall raise up the
    foundations of many
    generations;
you shall be called the repairer
    of the breach,
the restorer of streets to live in.

a **58.8** Or *vindication*

BIBLE IN FOCUS

REAL WORSHIP

Is not this the fast that I choose: to loose the bonds of injustice, to undo the thongs of the yoke, to let the oppressed go free, and to break every yoke? Is it not to share your bread with the hungry, and bring the homeless poor into your house; when you see the naked, to cover them, and not to hide yourself from your own kin?

—Isaiah 58.6–7

The people of Judah knew how to worship God. They didn't worship idols. They fasted, went to religious services every sabbath day, wore sackcloth and even wallowed in ashes. But they lived in ways that were incompatible with God's commands. They fasted, then quarreled and fought on the same day. They oppressed their workers (see verses 3–4). They were very proud of the fact that they worshiped God, and they were waiting for the wonderful blessings to come to them—but the blessings didn't come.

Isaiah told the people that all their superficial worship of God did nothing but make them self-righteous. They were putting God to the test, saying they'd done their part and were expecting God to make them successful. This kind of worship didn't reach God. Isaiah told the Israelites to reach out to those around them in a spirit of justice, love and compassion—that would demonstrate the essence, the sincerity, of their worship. That is worship that pleases God.

Isaiah 58.7 reminds us of the words of Christ in Matthew 25 when he refers to the sheep and the goats. In the judgment, we will stand before Jesus and give an account of how we shared our food with the hungry, gave water to the thirsty, visited those who were sick or in prison and provided shelter for the homeless. Jesus said, "Just as you did it to one of the least of these who are members of my family, you did it to me" (Matthew 25.40). There are depths to the message of Isaiah—and this message of Jesus—that we don't want to plumb. But these commands are the heart of Christianity, as they were at the heart of proper worship for the people of Judah long before Jesus Christ.

The essence of worship is coming before God as sinners; we ask for forgiveness, acknowledge the sovereignty of God and concentrate, not on ourselves, but on God Almighty, his commands and the teachings of Jesus. Because we love God, we will champion and demonstrate love in justice, humility, service, compassion and generosity. Those are the works that constitute a proper worship of God. In Isaiah 58.8, the people of Judah were told that their "light [would] break forth like the dawn" when they worshiped God with their good deeds. The light that "breaks forth" from us is our worship, the proof of our love for other people through Jesus.

Going Deeper

- When you hear the word *worship*, what activities and attitudes come to mind?
- Does your worship of God extend beyond the walls of a church building? How?

13 If you refrain from trampling
    the sabbath,
    from pursuing your own
        interests on my holy day;
    if you call the sabbath a delight
    and the holy day of the
        LORD honorable;
    if you honor it, not going
        your own ways,
    serving your own interests,
    or pursuing your
        own affairs;[a]
14 then you shall take delight
    in the LORD,
    and I will make you ride upon
        the heights of the earth;
    I will feed you with the heritage
    of your ancestor Jacob,
    for the mouth of the
        LORD has spoken.

INJUSTICE AND OPPRESSION TO BE PUNISHED

59 See, the LORD's hand is
    not too short to save,
    nor his ear too dull to hear.
2 Rather, your iniquities have
        been barriers
    between you and your God,
    and your sins have hidden
        his face from you
    so that he does not hear.
3 For your hands are defiled
        with blood,
    and your fingers with iniquity;
    your lips have spoken lies,
    your tongue mutters
        wickedness.

4 No one brings suit justly,
    no one goes to law honestly;
    they rely on empty pleas,
        they speak lies,
    conceiving mischief and
        begetting iniquity.
5 They hatch adders' eggs,
    and weave the spider's web;
    whoever eats their eggs dies,
    and the crushed egg
        hatches out a viper.
6 Their webs cannot serve
        as clothing;
    they cannot cover themselves
        with what they make.
    Their works are works of iniquity,
    and deeds of violence are
        in their hands.
7 Their feet run to evil,
    and they rush to shed
        innocent blood;
    their thoughts are thoughts
        of iniquity,
    desolation and destruction
        are in their highways.
8 The way of peace they do not know,
    and there is no justice
        in their paths.
    Their roads they have
        made crooked;
    no one who walks in them
        knows peace.

9 Therefore justice is far from us,
    and righteousness does
        not reach us;

a 58.13 Heb or speaking words

▷ BIBLE IN LIFE ⊃

Separated From God

Isaiah 59.2

Our sin separates us from God because God cannot accept sin, and God's judgment is perfect. Sin must be punished. But God loves us in spite of our failures, in spite of our sins, in spite of our omissions, in spite of our mistakes. God is eager to forgive us at any time. Through our Savior, Jesus Christ, who came to earth to live as a human being and who was without sin, we can be forgiven. For a transient moment, Christ was separated from God because he took our sins on himself. During Jesus' crucifixion, he suffered not just from the physical pain of the nails and spear but also from the spiritual and emotional pain of carrying the weight and pain of our guilt and punishment (see Matthew 27.45–53). Second Corinthians 5.21 declares, "For our sake [God] made him to be sin who knew no sin, so that in him we might become the righteousness of God." Because of this, we no longer have to be separated from God. Through faith in Christ as Savior, we can be forgiven and reconciled with God.

we wait for light, and lo!
    there is darkness;
  and for brightness, but
    we walk in gloom.
10 We grope like the blind
    along a wall,
  groping like those who
    have no eyes;
we stumble at noon as in
    the twilight,
  among the vigorous[a] as
    though we were dead.
11 We all growl like bears;
  like doves we moan
    mournfully.
We wait for justice, but
    there is none;
  for salvation, but it is
    far from us.
12 For our transgressions before
    you are many,
  and our sins testify against us.
Our transgressions indeed
    are with us,
  and we know our iniquities:
13 transgressing, and denying
    the LORD,
  and turning away from
    following our God,
talking oppression and revolt,
  conceiving lying words
    and uttering them
    from the heart.
14 Justice is turned back,
  and righteousness stands
    at a distance;
for truth stumbles in the
    public square,
  and uprightness cannot enter.
15 Truth is lacking,
  and whoever turns from
    evil is despoiled.

The LORD saw it, and it
    displeased him
  that there was no justice.
16 He saw that there was no one,
  and was appalled that there
    was no one to intervene;
so his own arm brought
    him victory,
  and his righteousness
    upheld him.
17 He put on righteousness
    like a breastplate,
  and a helmet of salvation
    on his head;

he put on garments of vengeance
    for clothing,
  and wrapped himself in
    fury as in a mantle.
18 According to their deeds,
    so will he repay;
  wrath to his adversaries,
    requital to his enemies;
to the coastlands he will
    render requital.
19 So those in the west shall fear
    the name of the LORD,
  and those in the east,
    his glory;
for he will come like a
    pent-up stream
that the wind of the
    LORD drives on.

20 And he will come to Zion
    as Redeemer,
  to those in Jacob who turn
    from transgression,
    says the LORD.
21 And as for me, this is my covenant with them, says the LORD: my spirit that is upon you, and my words that I have put in your mouth, shall not depart out of your mouth, or out of the mouths of your children, or out of the mouths of your children's children, says the LORD, from now on and forever.

THE INGATHERING OF THE DISPERSED

60 Arise, shine; for your
    light has come,
  and the glory of the LORD
    has risen upon you.
2 For darkness shall cover
    the earth,
  and thick darkness
    the peoples;
but the LORD will arise upon you,
  and his glory will appear
    over you.
3 Nations shall come to your light,
  and kings to the brightness
    of your dawn.

4 Lift up your eyes and look around;
  they all gather together,
    they come to you;

[a] 59.10 Meaning of Heb uncertain

your sons shall come
from far away,
and your daughters shall
be carried on their
nurses' arms.
5 Then you shall see and be radiant;
your heart shall thrill
and rejoice,[a]
because the abundance of the sea
shall be brought to you,
the wealth of the nations
shall come to you.
6 A multitude of camels
shall cover you,
the young camels of
Midian and Ephah;
all those from Sheba
shall come.
They shall bring gold and
frankincense,
and shall proclaim the
praise of the LORD.
7 All the flocks of Kedar shall
be gathered to you,
the rams of Nebaioth shall
minister to you;
they shall be acceptable
on my altar,
and I will glorify my
glorious house.
8 Who are these that fly
like a cloud,
and like doves to their
windows?
9 For the coastlands shall
wait for me,
the ships of Tarshish first,
to bring your children
from far away,
their silver and gold
with them,
for the name of the LORD
your God,
and for the Holy One of Israel,
because he has glorified you.
10 Foreigners shall build up
your walls,
and their kings shall
minister to you;
for in my wrath I struck
you down,
but in my favor I have
had mercy on you.
11 Your gates shall always be open;
day and night they shall
not be shut,

so that nations shall bring
you their wealth,
with their kings led in
procession.
12 For the nation and kingdom
that will not serve you
shall perish;
those nations shall be
utterly laid waste.
13 The glory of Lebanon shall
come to you,
the cypress, the plane,
and the pine,
to beautify the place of
my sanctuary;
and I will glorify where
my feet rest.
14 The descendants of those
who oppressed you
shall come bending low to you,
and all who despised you
shall bow down at your feet;
they shall call you the City
of the LORD,
the Zion of the Holy
One of Israel.
15 Whereas you have been
forsaken and hated,
with no one passing through,
I will make you majestic forever,
a joy from age to age.
16 You shall suck the milk
of nations,
you shall suck the
breasts of kings;
and you shall know that I, the
LORD, am your Savior
and your Redeemer, the
Mighty One of Jacob.

17 Instead of bronze I will
bring gold,
instead of iron I will
bring silver;
instead of wood, bronze,
instead of stones, iron.
I will appoint Peace as
your overseer
and Righteousness as
your taskmaster.
18 Violence shall no more be
heard in your land,
devastation or destruction
within your borders;

a 60.5 Heb be enlarged

you shall call your walls Salvation,
and your gates Praise.

GOD THE GLORY OF ZION

19 The sun shall no longer be
   your light by day,
nor for brightness shall the moon
   give light to you by night;[a]
but the LORD will be your
   everlasting light,
and your God will be
   your glory.
20 Your sun shall no more go down,
   or your moon withdraw itself;
for the LORD will be your
   everlasting light,
and your days of mourning
   shall be ended.
21 Your people shall all be righteous;
   they shall possess the
   land forever.
They are the shoot that I planted,
   the work of my hands,
so that I might be glorified.
22 The least of them shall
   become a clan,
and the smallest one a
   mighty nation;
I am the LORD;
   in its time I will accomplish
   it quickly.

THE GOOD NEWS OF DELIVERANCE

61 The spirit of the Lord
   GOD is upon me,
because the LORD has
   anointed me;
he has sent me to bring good
   news to the oppressed,
to bind up the brokenhearted,
to proclaim liberty to
   the captives,
and release to the prisoners;
2 to proclaim the year of the
   LORD's favor,
and the day of vengeance
   of our God;
to comfort all who mourn;
3 to provide for those who
   mourn in Zion—
to give them a garland
   instead of ashes,
the oil of gladness instead
   of mourning,
the mantle of praise instead
   of a faint spirit.

PONDER

The spirit of the Lord GOD is upon me, because the LORD has anointed me; he has sent me to bring good news to the oppressed, to bind up the brokenhearted, to proclaim liberty to the captives, and release to the prisoners; to proclaim the year of the LORD's favor.

—Isaiah 61.1–2

PRAY

Sovereign Lord, we praise you for these ancient prophecies about our Savior, that foresaw his humble birth. Ignored by some, persecuted by many, and beloved by the faithful, he was gentle, loving, forgiving and generous. He came to mend our hearts, free us from sin and despair, and comfort us when we grieve. He carries our burdens as we struggle in our everyday lives. He taught us what it means to live each day in your kingdom. He gives us abundant life so that our talents, abilities and influences can be maximized to do your will and draw us closer to you. For all this we give you thanks and praise. Amen.

They will be called oaks of
   righteousness,
the planting of the LORD,
   to display his glory.
4 They shall build up the
   ancient ruins,
they shall raise up the
   former devastations;
they shall repair the ruined cities,
   the devastations of many
   generations.

5 Strangers shall stand and
   feed your flocks,
foreigners shall till your land
   and dress your vines;

a 60.19 Q Ms Gk Old Latin Tg: MT lacks *by night*

6 but you shall be called priests
of the LORD,
you shall be named
ministers of our God;
you shall enjoy the wealth
of the nations,
and in their riches you
shall glory.
7 Because their[a] shame
was double,
and dishonor was proclaimed
as their lot,
therefore they shall possess
a double portion;
everlasting joy shall be theirs.

8 For I the LORD love justice,
I hate robbery and
wrongdoing;[b]
I will faithfully give them
their recompense,
and I will make an everlasting
covenant with them.
9 Their descendants shall be known
among the nations,
and their offspring among
the peoples;
all who see them shall
acknowledge
that they are a people whom
the LORD has blessed.
10 I will greatly rejoice in the LORD,
my whole being shall
exult in my God;
for he has clothed me with the
garments of salvation,
he has covered me with the
robe of righteousness,
as a bridegroom decks himself
with a garland,
and as a bride adorns herself
with her jewels.
11 For as the earth brings
forth its shoots,
and as a garden causes what is
sown in it to spring up,
so the Lord GOD will cause
righteousness and praise
to spring up before all
the nations.

THE VINDICATION AND
SALVATION OF ZION

62 For Zion's sake I will
not keep silent,
and for Jerusalem's sake
I will not rest,

until her vindication shines
out like the dawn,
and her salvation like a
burning torch.
2 The nations shall see your
vindication,
and all the kings your glory;
and you shall be called by
a new name
that the mouth of the
LORD will give.
3 You shall be a crown of beauty
in the hand of the LORD,
and a royal diadem in the
hand of your God.

THE HOLY SPIRIT IS NOT
JUST A FORCE, A POWER OR
AN INFLUENCE. THE SPIRIT
IS A DIVINE PERSON, THE
PRESENCE OF GOD, WHO
GAVE JESUS THE POWER FOR
A MINISTRY OF LIBERATION
AND RECONCILIATION.

4 You shall no more be termed
Forsaken,[c]
and your land shall no more
be termed Desolate;[d]
but you shall be called My
Delight Is in Her,[e]
and your land Married;[f]
for the LORD delights in you,
and your land shall be married.
5 For as a young man marries
a young woman,
so shall your builder[g]
marry you,
and as the bridegroom rejoices
over the bride,
so shall your God rejoice
over you.

---

[a] 61.7 Heb your   [b] 61.8 Or robbery with
a burnt offering   [c] 62.4 Heb Azubah
[d] 62.4 Heb Shemamah   [e] 62.4 Heb
Hephzibah   [f] 62.4 Heb Beulah   [g] 62.5 Cn:
Heb your sons

6 Upon your walls, O Jerusalem,
    I have posted sentinels;
all day and all night
    they shall never be silent.
You who remind the LORD,
    take no rest,
7 and give him no rest
    until he establishes Jerusalem
    and makes it renowned
        throughout the earth.
8 The LORD has sworn by
        his right hand
    and by his mighty arm:
I will not again give your grain
    to be food for your enemies,
and foreigners shall not
    drink the wine
    for which you have labored;
9 but those who garner it
        shall eat it
    and praise the LORD,
and those who gather it
        shall drink it
    in my holy courts.

10 Go through, go through
        the gates,
    prepare the way for
        the people;
build up, build up the highway,
    clear it of stones,
    lift up an ensign over
        the peoples.
11 The LORD has proclaimed
    to the end of the earth:
Say to daughter Zion,
    "See, your salvation comes;
his reward is with him,
    and his recompense
        before him."
12 They shall be called, "The
        Holy People,
    The Redeemed of the LORD";
and you shall be called,
    "Sought Out,
    A City Not Forsaken."

VENGEANCE ON EDOM

63 "Who is this that comes
        from Edom,
    from Bozrah in garments
        stained crimson?
Who is this so splendidly robed,
    marching in his great might?"

"It is I, announcing vindication,
    mighty to save."

2 "Why are your robes red,
    and your garments like
        theirs who tread
        the wine press?"

3 "I have trodden the wine
        press alone,
    and from the peoples no
        one was with me;
I trod them in my anger
    and trampled them in
        my wrath;
their juice spattered on
        my garments,
    and stained all my robes.
4 For the day of vengeance
        was in my heart,
    and the year for my redeeming
        work had come.
5 I looked, but there was no helper;
    I stared, but there was no
        one to sustain me;
so my own arm brought
        me victory,
    and my wrath sustained me.
6 I trampled down peoples
        in my anger,
    I crushed them in my wrath,
    and I poured out their
        lifeblood on the earth."

GOD'S MERCY REMEMBERED

7 I will recount the gracious
        deeds of the LORD,
    the praiseworthy acts
        of the LORD,
because of all that the LORD
        has done for us,
    and the great favor to the
        house of Israel
that he has shown them
        according to his mercy,
    according to the abundance
        of his steadfast love.
8 For he said, "Surely they
        are my people,
    children who will not
        deal falsely";
and he became their savior
9   in all their distress.
It was no messenger[a] or angel
    but his presence that
        saved them;[b]

---

a 63.9 Gk: Heb *anguish* b 63.9 Or *savior.*
*9In all their distress he was distressed; the
angel of his presence saved them;*

in his love and in his pity he
    redeemed them;
he lifted them up and carried
    them all the days of old.

10 But they rebelled
    and grieved his holy spirit;
therefore he became their enemy;
    he himself fought
        against them.
11 Then they[a] remembered
    the days of old,
    of Moses his servant.[b]
Where is the one who brought
    them up out of the sea
with the shepherds
    of his flock?
Where is the one who put
    within them
    his holy spirit,
12 who caused his glorious arm
    to march at the right
        hand of Moses,
who divided the waters
    before them
to make for himself an
    everlasting name,
13 who led them through
    the depths?
Like a horse in the desert,
    they did not stumble.
14 Like cattle that go down
    into the valley,
the spirit of the LORD
    gave them rest.
Thus you led your people,
    to make for yourself a
    glorious name.

A PRAYER OF PENITENCE

15 Look down from
    heaven and see,
from your holy and
    glorious habitation.
Where are your zeal and
    your might?
The yearning of your heart
    and your compassion?
They are withheld from me.
16 For you are our father,
    though Abraham does
        not know us
and Israel does not
    acknowledge us;
you, O LORD, are our father;
    our Redeemer from of
        old is your name.

17 Why, O LORD, do you make us
    stray from your ways
and harden our heart, so that
    we do not fear you?
Turn back for the sake of
    your servants,
for the sake of the tribes that
    are your heritage.
18 Your holy people took possession
    for a little while;
but now our adversaries
    have trampled down
    your sanctuary.
19 We have long been like those
    whom you do not rule,
like those not called by
    your name.

64 O that you would tear
    open the heavens
    and come down,
so that the mountains would
    quake at your presence—
2[c] as when fire kindles brushwood
    and the fire causes
    water to boil—
to make your name known to
    your adversaries,
so that the nations might
    tremble at your presence!
3 When you did awesome deeds
    that we did not expect,
you came down, the
    mountains quaked
    at your presence.
4 From ages past no
    one has heard,
    no ear has perceived,
no eye has seen any God
    besides you,
who works for those who
    wait for him.
5 You meet those who
    gladly do right,
those who remember
    you in your ways.
But you were angry, and
    we sinned;
because you hid yourself
    we transgressed.[d]
6 We have all become like one
    who is unclean,
and all our righteous deeds
    are like a filthy cloth.

a 63.11 Heb *he*   b 63.11 Cn: Heb *his people*
c 64.2 Ch 64.1 in Heb   d 64.5 Meaning of
Heb uncertain

We all fade like a leaf,
    and our iniquities, like the
        wind, take us away.
7 There is no one who calls
        on your name,
    or attempts to take hold of you;
for you have hidden your
        face from us,
    and have delivered[a] us into the
        hand of our iniquity.
8 Yet, O LORD, you are our Father;
    we are the clay, and you
        are our potter;
    we are all the work of your hand.
9 Do not be exceedingly
        angry, O LORD,
    and do not remember
        iniquity forever.
    Now consider, we are all
        your people.
10 Your holy cities have become
        a wilderness,
    Zion has become a wilderness,
    Jerusalem a desolation.
11 Our holy and beautiful house,
    where our ancestors praised you,
has been burned by fire,
    and all our pleasant places
        have become ruins.
12 After all this, will you restrain
        yourself, O LORD?
    Will you keep silent, and
        punish us so severely?

WHEN WE ARE RECONCILED

WITH GOD, WE HAVE

EXCITING OPPORTUNITIES

TO EXPAND OUR LIVES.

THE RIGHTEOUSNESS OF
GOD'S JUDGMENT

65 I was ready to be sought out
    by those who did not ask,
to be found by those who
        did not seek me.
I said, "Here I am, here I am,"
    to a nation that did not
        call on my name.

2 I held out my hands all day long
    to a rebellious people,
who walk in a way that
        is not good,
    following their own devices;
3 a people who provoke me
    to my face continually,
sacrificing in gardens
    and offering incense on bricks;
4 who sit inside tombs,
    and spend the night in
        secret places;
who eat swine's flesh,
    with broth of abominable
        things in their vessels;
5 who say, "Keep to yourself,
    do not come near me, for I
        am too holy for you."
These are a smoke in my nostrils,
    a fire that burns all day long.
6 See, it is written before me:
    I will not keep silent,
        but I will repay;
I will indeed repay into their laps
7   their[b] iniquities and
        their[b] ancestors'
            iniquities together,
                says the LORD;
because they offered incense
        on the mountains
    and reviled me on the hills,
I will measure into their laps
    full payment for their actions.
8 Thus says the LORD:
As the wine is found in
        the cluster,
    and they say, "Do not
        destroy it,
    for there is a blessing in it,"
so I will do for my servants' sake,
    and not destroy them all.
9 I will bring forth descendants[c]
        from Jacob,
    and from Judah inheritors[d]
        of my mountains;
my chosen shall inherit it,
    and my servants shall
        settle there.
10 Sharon shall become a
        pasture for flocks,
    and the Valley of Achor a place
        for herds to lie down,
    for my people who have
        sought me.

a **64.7** Gk Syr Old Latin Tg: Heb *melted*
b **65.7** Gk Syr: Heb *your*   c **65.9** Or *a
descendant*   d **65.9** Or *an inheritor*

11 But you who forsake the LORD,
who forget my holy mountain,
who set a table for Fortune
and fill cups of mixed
wine for Destiny;
12 I will destine you to the sword,
and all of you shall bow
down to the slaughter;
because, when I called, you
did not answer,
when I spoke, you did
not listen,
but you did what was evil
in my sight,
and chose what I did
not delight in.
13 Therefore thus says
the Lord GOD:
My servants shall eat,
but you shall be hungry;
my servants shall drink,
but you shall be thirsty;
my servants shall rejoice,
but you shall be put to shame;
14 my servants shall sing for
gladness of heart,
but you shall cry out for
pain of heart,
and shall wail for anguish
of spirit.
15 You shall leave your name to my
chosen to use as a curse,
and the Lord GOD will
put you to death;
but to his servants he will
give a different name.
16 Then whoever invokes a
blessing in the land
shall bless by the God
of faithfulness,
and whoever takes an oath
in the land
shall swear by the God
of faithfulness;
because the former troubles
are forgotten
and are hidden from my sight.

THE GLORIOUS NEW CREATION
17 For I am about to create
new heavens
and a new earth;
the former things shall not
be remembered
or come to mind.
18 But be glad and rejoice forever
in what I am creating;

for I am about to create
Jerusalem as a joy,
and its people as a delight.
19 I will rejoice in Jerusalem,
and delight in my people;
no more shall the sound of
weeping be heard in it,
or the cry of distress.
20 No more shall there be in it
an infant that lives but
a few days,
or an old person who does
not live out a lifetime;
for one who dies at a hundred years
will be considered a youth,
and one who falls short
of a hundred will be
considered accursed.
21 They shall build houses and
inhabit them;
they shall plant vineyards
and eat their fruit.
22 They shall not build and
another inhabit;
they shall not plant and
another eat;
for like the days of a tree shall the
days of my people be,
and my chosen shall long enjoy
the work of their hands.
23 They shall not labor in vain,
or bear children for calamity;[a]
for they shall be offspring
blessed by the LORD—
and their descendants as well.
24 Before they call I will answer,
while they are yet speaking
I will hear.
25 The wolf and the lamb shall
feed together,
the lion shall eat straw
like the ox;
but the serpent—its food
shall be dust!
They shall not hurt or destroy
on all my holy mountain,
says the LORD.

THE WORSHIP GOD DEMANDS
66 Thus says the LORD:
Heaven is my throne
and the earth is my footstool;
what is the house that you
would build for me,
and what is my resting place?

a **65.23** Or *sudden terror*

2 All these things my hand
        has made,
    and so all these things
        are mine,[a]
                says the LORD.
    But this is the one to whom
        I will look,
    to the humble and
        contrite in spirit,
    who trembles at my word.

3 Whoever slaughters an ox
        is like one who kills
        a human being;
    whoever sacrifices a lamb,
        like one who breaks
        a dog's neck;
    whoever presents a grain
        offering, like one who
        offers swine's blood;[b]
    whoever makes a
        memorial offering of
        frankincense, like one
        who blesses an idol.
    These have chosen their
        own ways,
    and in their abominations
        they take delight;
4 I also will choose to mock[c] them,
    and bring upon them
        what they fear;
    because, when I called, no
        one answered,
    when I spoke, they did
        not listen;
    but they did what was evil
        in my sight,
    and chose what did not
        please me.

THE LORD VINDICATES ZION
5 Hear the word of the LORD,
    you who tremble at his word:
    Your own people who hate you
        and reject you for my
        name's sake
    have said, "Let the LORD
        be glorified,
    so that we may see your joy";
    but it is they who shall
        be put to shame.

6 Listen, an uproar from the city!
    A voice from the temple!
    The voice of the LORD,
        dealing retribution to
        his enemies!

7 Before she was in labor
        she gave birth;
    before her pain came upon her
        she delivered a son.
8 Who has heard of such a thing?
    Who has seen such things?
    Shall a land be born in one day?
    Shall a nation be delivered
        in one moment?
    Yet as soon as Zion was in labor
        she delivered her children.
9 Shall I open the womb and
        not deliver?
        says the LORD;
    shall I, the one who delivers,
        shut the womb?
        says your God.

10 Rejoice with Jerusalem, and
        be glad for her,
    all you who love her;
    rejoice with her in joy,
    all you who mourn over her—
11 that you may nurse and
        be satisfied
    from her consoling breast;
    that you may drink deeply
        with delight
    from her glorious bosom.

12 For thus says the LORD:
    I will extend prosperity to
        her like a river,
    and the wealth of the nations
        like an overflowing stream;
    and you shall nurse and be
        carried on her arm,
    and dandled on her knees.
13 As a mother comforts her child,
        so I will comfort you;
    you shall be comforted
        in Jerusalem.

**THE REIGN AND INDIGNATION
OF GOD**
14 You shall see, and your heart
        shall rejoice;
    your bodies[d] shall flourish
        like the grass;
    and it shall be known that the
        hand of the LORD is
        with his servants,
    and his indignation is
        against his enemies.

[a] **66.2** Gk Syr: Heb *these things came to be* [b] **66.3** Meaning of Heb uncertain [c] **66.4** Or *to punish* [d] **66.14** Heb *bones*

15 For the LORD will come in fire,
    and his chariots like the
        whirlwind,
to pay back his anger in fury,
    and his rebuke in flames of fire.
16 For by fire will the LORD
        execute judgment,
    and by his sword, on all flesh;
    and those slain by the
        LORD shall be many.

17 Those who sanctify and purify themselves to go into the gardens, following the one in the center, eating the flesh of pigs, vermin, and rodents, shall come to an end together, says the LORD.

18 For I know[a] their works and their thoughts, and I am[b] coming to gather all nations and tongues; and they shall come and shall see my glory, 19and I will set a sign among them. From them I will send survivors to the nations, to Tarshish, Put,[c] and Lud—which draw the bow—to Tubal and Javan, to the coastlands far away that have not heard of my fame or seen my glory; and they shall declare my glory among the nations. 20They shall bring all your kindred from all the nations as an offering to the LORD, on horses, and in chariots, and in litters, and on mules, and on dromedaries, to my holy mountain Jerusalem, says the LORD, just as the Israelites bring a grain offering in a clean vessel to the house of the LORD. 21And I will also take some of them as priests and as Levites, says the LORD.

22 For as the new heavens and
        the new earth,
    which I will make,
shall remain before me,
        says the LORD;
    so shall your descendants and
        your name remain.
23 From new moon to new moon,
    and from sabbath to sabbath,
all flesh shall come to
        worship before me,
    says the LORD.

24 And they shall go out and look at the dead bodies of the people who have rebelled against me; for their worm shall not die, their fire shall not be quenched, and they shall be an abhorrence to all flesh.

a 66.18 Gk Syr: Heb lacks *know* b 66.18 Gk Syr Vg Tg: Heb *it is* c 66.19 Gk: Heb *Pul*

JEREMIAH

Jeremiah had the grim job of prophesying to people who were indifferent, rebellious and even hostile. Perhaps they characterized him, as we might even today, as a "gloom and doom" prophet because he emphasized sin and judgment. But the book of Jeremiah is not all dark prophecies; the prophet also offered God's people the hope that their sincere repentance will postpone the inevitable, and even that their punishment will end with restoration. The book of Jeremiah pictures God as an incomprehensibly powerful Creator and Judge; at the same time, it reaffirms God's deep concern for each and every one of us.

1 The words of Jeremiah son of Hilkiah, of the priests who were in Anathoth in the land of Benjamin, ²to whom the word of the LORD came in the days of King Josiah son of Amon of Judah, in the thirteenth year of his reign. ³It came also in the days of King Jehoiakim son of Josiah of Judah, and until the end of the eleventh year of King Zedekiah son of Josiah of Judah, until the captivity of Jerusalem in the fifth month.

JEREMIAH'S CALL AND COMMISSION

4 Now the word of the LORD came to me saying,
5 "Before I formed you in the
   womb I knew you,
and before you were born I
   consecrated you;
I appointed you a prophet
   to the nations."
⁶Then I said, "Ah, Lord GOD! Truly I do not know how to speak, for I am only a boy." ⁷But the LORD said to me, "Do not say, 'I am only a boy';
for you shall go to all to
   whom I send you,
and you shall speak whatever
   I command you.
8 Do not be afraid of them,
for I am with you to deliver you,
   says the LORD."
⁹Then the LORD put out his hand and touched my mouth; and the LORD said to me,
"Now I have put my words
   in your mouth.
10 See, today I appoint you
   over nations and
   over kingdoms,
to pluck up and to pull down,
to destroy and to overthrow,
to build and to plant."
11 The word of the LORD came to me, saying, "Jeremiah, what do you see?" And I said, "I see a branch of an almond tree."ᵃ ¹²Then the LORD said to me, "You have seen well, for I am watchingᵇ over my word to perform it." ¹³The word of the LORD came to me a second time, saying, "What do you see?" And I said, "I see a boiling pot, tilted away from the north."
14 Then the LORD said to me: Out of the north disaster shall break out

on all the inhabitants of the land. ¹⁵For now I am calling all the tribes of the kingdoms of the north, says the LORD; and they shall come and all of them shall set their thrones at the entrance of the gates of Jerusalem, against all its surrounding walls and against all the cities of Judah. ¹⁶And I will utter my judgments against them, for all their wickedness in forsaking me; they have made offerings to other gods, and worshiped the works of their own hands. ¹⁷But you, gird up your loins; stand up and tell them everything that I command you. Do not break down before them, or I will break you before them. ¹⁸And I for my part have made you today a fortified city, an iron pillar, and a bronze wall, against the whole

---

ᵃ **1.11** Heb *shaqed*   ᵇ **1.12** Heb *shoqed*

PONDER

But you, gird up your loins; stand up and tell them everything that I command you. Do not break down before them.
—Jeremiah 1.17

PRAY

Sovereign Lord, open our hearts to the message that comes to us from your Holy Word, the life of Jeremiah and the teachings of Jesus Christ. With these words we hear your call to us—to be ready, to be courageous, and most of all, to trust in your love and protection. Let us have a spirit of determination and faith. Teach us to recognize our unique talents and gifts, remembering that our lives are significant. Teach us what to say and do according to your perfect plan for each of us. Let us also realize that the growth of your kingdom on earth is firmly based on the life and teachings of our Savior, Jesus Christ. In his name we pray. Amen.

CALLED

*"Before I formed you in the womb I knew you, and before you were born
I consecrated you; I appointed you a prophet to the nations."*

—Jeremiah 1.5

Jeremiah was the son of an average priest and lived in an obscure town. We don't know whether Jeremiah had extraordinary intelligence or eloquence. But he served as God's spokesman for almost 50 years—longer than any other Biblical prophet—during a major upheaval in the history of his people. Israel had fallen to the Assyrians more than 120 years earlier, and at this time Jeremiah was called by God to warn the Israelites about the impending fall of Judah.

Jeremiah responded to God's call with hesitation: "Truly I do not know how to speak, for I am only a boy" (verse 6). Jeremiah doubted his capabilities of carrying out God's will, to do anything extraordinary. But God twice promised to be with him and rescue him (verses 8,19).

There is a pattern that emerged in the Old Testament when God called people to his service: First of all, there was a great need. Then God would identify and call someone to carry out his purpose. The call would almost always come as a big surprise. And then the person would respond with reluctance. When God wanted Moses to confront the pharaoh, Moses said, "Lord I'm not qualified to do that. I can't talk. I mumble when I try to speak." Both Jeremiah and Moses turned God down, and then God pointed out that he'd provide the way and the will and the capability and the assistance and the support. God promised to be with them.

In the New Testament, Jesus issued a call to his disciples and to all believers in Christ: The Great Commission. We are called to go into the world and tell people about Christ. How do we respond to this call? Most of us have feelings of inadequacy. We don't feel qualified. But how much money does it take to demonstrate our commitment to peace and justice and forgiveness? How many college degrees are required to reach out to help others? It doesn't take an extraordinary person to carry out God's will. God's promise to be with us is the same promise he gave to Jeremiah.

We don't know if there were people that God called in Biblical times who didn't respond. But there were those who did respond, and God's call profoundly affected the lives of other human beings. Will we answer God's call and take a chance on influencing others in the name of Christ? We carry out the Great Commission when we copy the words and actions of Christ in our lives.

Going Deeper

- Do you believe that before you were born, you were set apart by God for special purpose? If so, what might that mean for your life?
- What insecurities prevent you from answering God's call? How do you experience Jesus' promise to be with you always?

land—against the kings of Judah, its princes, its priests, and the people of the land. ¹⁹They will fight against you; but they shall not prevail against you, for I am with you, says the LORD, to deliver you.

GOD PLEADS WITH ISRAEL TO REPENT

2 The word of the LORD came to me, saying: ²Go and proclaim in the hearing of Jerusalem, Thus says the LORD:

I remember the devotion
    of your youth,
your love as a bride,
how you followed me in
    the wilderness,
in a land not sown.
³ Israel was holy to the LORD,
    the first fruits of his harvest.
All who ate of it were
    held guilty;
disaster came upon them,
                        says the LORD.

⁴ Hear the word of the LORD, O house of Jacob, and all the families of the house of Israel. ⁵Thus says the LORD:

What wrong did your
    ancestors find in me
that they went far from me,
and went after worthless
        things, and became
        worthless themselves?
⁶ They did not say, "Where
        is the LORD
who brought us up from
        the land of Egypt,
who led us in the wilderness,
    in a land of deserts and pits,

in a land of drought and
        deep darkness,
in a land that no one
        passes through,
where no one lives?"
⁷ I brought you into a
        plentiful land
to eat its fruits and its
        good things.
But when you entered you
        defiled my land,
and made my heritage
        an abomination.
⁸ The priests did not say, "Where
        is the LORD?"
Those who handle the law
        did not know me;
the rulers[a] transgressed
        against me;
the prophets prophesied
        by Baal,
and went after things
        that do not profit.

⁹ Therefore once more I accuse you,
                        says the LORD,
and I accuse your children's
        children.
¹⁰ Cross to the coasts of
        Cyprus and look,
send to Kedar and examine
        with care;
see if there has ever been
        such a thing.
¹¹ Has a nation changed its gods,
        even though they are no gods?
But my people have changed
        their glory
for something that does
        not profit.

ᵃ **2.8** Heb *shepherds*

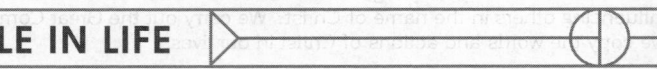

BIBLE IN LIFE

Bride of Christ

Jeremiah 2.1–2

Wedding imagery is woven throughout the Bible. And in the Old Testament, wedding imagery is used to describe the permanent, close aspect of God's relationship with human beings. God is depicted as the husband and the Israelites as the bride. The Old Testament prophets anticipated the marriage of God to the people—that someday there would be a closer relationship between God Almighty and us, provided that we are moving toward reconciliation with God. In the New Testament, Christ is described as the groom and his people as the bride. As Christians who are betrothed to Christ, our ultimate goal is a permanent, faithful, loving marriage with him.

12 Be appalled, O heavens, at this,
    be shocked, be utterly desolate,
        says the LORD,
13 for my people have committed
        two evils:
    they have forsaken me,
the fountain of living water,
    and dug out cisterns for
        themselves,
cracked cisterns
    that can hold no water.

14 Is Israel a slave? Is he a
    homeborn servant?
Why then has he become
    plunder?
15 The lions have roared
        against him,
    they have roared loudly.
They have made his land a waste;
    his cities are in ruins,
        without inhabitant.
16 Moreover, the people of Memphis
        and Tahpanhes
have broken the crown
    of your head.
17 Have you not brought this
        upon yourself
by forsaking the LORD
    your God,
while he led you in the way?
18 What then do you gain by
        going to Egypt,
    to drink the waters of the Nile?
Or what do you gain by
        going to Assyria,
    to drink the waters of
        the Euphrates?
19 Your wickedness will punish you,
    and your apostasies will
        convict you.
Know and see that it is
        evil and bitter
for you to forsake the
        LORD your God;
the fear of me is not in you,
        says the Lord GOD of hosts.

20 For long ago you broke your yoke
    and burst your bonds,
    and you said, "I will not serve!"
On every high hill
    and under every green tree
    you sprawled and played
        the whore.
21 Yet I planted you as a choice vine,
    from the purest stock.

How then did you turn degenerate
    and become a wild vine?
22 Though you wash yourself with lye
    and use much soap,
    the stain of your guilt is
        still before me,
        says the Lord GOD.
23 How can you say, "I am
        not defiled,
    I have not gone after
        the Baals"?
Look at your way in the valley;
    know what you have done—
a restive young camel
        interlacing her tracks,
24   a wild ass at home in
        the wilderness,
in her heat sniffing the wind!
    Who can restrain her lust?
None who seek her need
        weary themselves;
    in her month they will find her.
25 Keep your feet from going unshod
    and your throat from thirst.
But you said, "It is hopeless,
    for I have loved strangers,
    and after them I will go."

26 As a thief is shamed when caught,
    so the house of Israel shall
        be shamed—
they, their kings, their officials,
    their priests, and their
        prophets,
27 who say to a tree, "You
        are my father,"
    and to a stone, "You
        gave me birth."
For they have turned their
        backs to me,
    and not their faces.
But in the time of their
        trouble they say,
    "Come and save us!"
28 But where are your gods
    that you made for yourself?
Let them come, if they
        can save you,
    in your time of trouble;
for you have as many gods
    as you have towns, O Judah.

29 Why do you complain
        against me?
You have all rebelled
        against me,
        says the LORD.

30 In vain I have struck down
    your children;
  they accepted no correction.
Your own sword devoured
    your prophets
  like a ravening lion.
31 And you, O generation, behold
    the word of the LORD![a]
Have I been a wilderness
    to Israel,
  or a land of thick darkness?
Why then do my people
    say, "We are free,
  we will come to you no more"?
32 Can a girl forget her ornaments,
    or a bride her attire?
Yet my people have
    forgotten me,
  days without number.

33 How well you direct your course
    to seek lovers!
So that even to wicked women
  you have taught your ways.
34 Also on your skirts is found
    the lifeblood of the
      innocent poor,
though you did not catch
    them breaking in.
Yet in spite of all these things[a]
35 you say, "I am innocent;
  surely his anger has
    turned from me."
Now I am bringing you
    to judgment
for saying, "I have not sinned."
36 How lightly you gad about,
  changing your ways!
You shall be put to shame
  by Egypt
as you were put to shame
  by Assyria.
37 From there also you will
    come away
with your hands on your head;
for the LORD has rejected those
  in whom you trust,
  and you will not prosper
    through them.

UNFAITHFUL ISRAEL

3 If[b] a man divorces his wife
  and she goes from him
and becomes another man's wife,
  will he return to her?
Would not such a land be
  greatly polluted?

You have played the whore
  with many lovers;
  and would you return to me?
    says the LORD.
2 Look up to the bare
    heights,[c] and see!
Where have you not
    been lain with?
By the waysides you have sat
    waiting for lovers,
  like a nomad in the wilderness.
You have polluted the land
  with your whoring and
    wickedness.
3 Therefore the showers have
    been withheld,
  and the spring rain
    has not come;
yet you have the forehead
  of a whore,
  you refuse to be ashamed.
4 Have you not just now
    called to me,
"My Father, you are the
    friend of my youth—
5 will he be angry forever,
  will he be indignant
    to the end?"
This is how you have spoken,
  but you have done all the
    evil that you could.

A CALL TO REPENTANCE

6 The LORD said to me in the days of King Josiah: Have you seen what she did, that faithless one, Israel, how she went up on every high hill and under every green tree, and played the whore there? 7 And I thought, "After she has done all this she will return to me"; but she did not return, and her false sister Judah saw it. 8 She[d] saw that for all the adulteries of that faithless one, Israel, I had sent her away with a decree of divorce; yet her false sister Judah did not fear, but she too went and played the whore. 9 Because she took her whoredom so lightly, she polluted the land, committing adultery with stone and tree. 10 Yet for all this her false sister Judah did not return to me with her whole heart, but only in pretense, says the LORD.

[a] 2.31,34 Meaning of Heb uncertain
[b] 3.1 Q Ms Gk Syr: MT *Saying, If*   [c] 3.2 Or *the trails*   [d] 3.8 Q Ms Gk Mss Syr: MT *I*

11 Then the LORD said to me: Faithless Israel has shown herself less guilty than false Judah. 12Go, and proclaim these words toward the north, and say:
Return, faithless Israel,
　　　　　says the LORD.
I will not look on you in anger,
　for I am merciful,
　　　　　says the LORD;
I will not be angry forever.
13 Only acknowledge your guilt,
　that you have rebelled against
　　the LORD your God,
　and scattered your favors
　　　among strangers under
　　　every green tree,
　and have not obeyed my voice,
　　　　　says the LORD.
14 Return, O faithless children,
　　　　　says the LORD,
　for I am your master;
　I will take you, one from a city
　　　and two from a family,
　and I will bring you to Zion.

15 I will give you shepherds after my own heart, who will feed you with knowledge and understanding. 16And when you have multiplied and increased in the land, in those days, says the LORD, they shall no longer say, "The ark of the covenant of the LORD." It shall not come to mind, or be remembered, or missed; nor shall another one be made. 17At that time Jerusalem shall be called the throne of the LORD, and all nations shall gather to it, to the presence of the LORD in Jerusalem, and they shall no longer stubbornly follow their own evil will. 18In those days the house of Judah shall join the house of Israel, and together they shall come from the land of the north to the land that I gave your ancestors for a heritage.

19 I thought
　how I would set you among
　　my children,
　and give you a pleasant land,
　　the most beautiful heritage
　　of all the nations.
　And I thought you would
　　　call me, My Father,
　and would not turn from
　　following me.

20 Instead, as a faithless wife
　leaves her husband,
　so you have been faithless to
　　me, O house of Israel,
　　　　　says the LORD.
21 A voice on the bare heights[a]
　　is heard,
　the plaintive weeping of
　　Israel's children,
　because they have perverted
　　their way,
　they have forgotten the
　　LORD their God:
22 Return, O faithless children,
　I will heal your faithlessness.

"Here we come to you;
　for you are the LORD our God.
23 Truly the hills are[b] a delusion,
　the orgies on the mountains.
Truly in the LORD our God
　is the salvation of Israel.
24 "But from our youth the shameful thing has devoured all for which our ancestors had labored, their flocks and their herds, their sons and their daughters. 25Let us lie down in our shame, and let our dishonor cover us; for we have sinned against the LORD our God, we and our ancestors, from our youth even to this day; and we have not obeyed the voice of the LORD our God."

4 If you return, O Israel,
　　　　　says the LORD,
　if you return to me,
　if you remove your abominations
　　from my presence,
　and do not waver,
2　and if you swear, "As the
　　LORD lives!"
　in truth, in justice, and
　　in uprightness,
　then nations shall be
　　blessed[c] by him,
　and by him they shall boast.

3 For thus says the LORD to the people of Judah and to the inhabitants of Jerusalem:
Break up your fallow ground,
　and do not sow among thorns.

[a] 3.21 Or the trails　[b] 3.23 Gk Syr Vg: Heb Truly from the hills is　[c] 4.2 Or shall bless themselves

4 Circumcise yourselves
        to the LORD,
    remove the foreskin of
        your hearts,
    O people of Judah and
        inhabitants of Jerusalem,
    or else my wrath will go
        forth like fire,
    and burn with no one
        to quench it,
    because of the evil of
        your doings.

INVASION AND DESOLATION
OF JUDAH THREATENED

5 Declare in Judah, and proclaim
in Jerusalem, and say:
    Blow the trumpet through
        the land;
    shout aloud[a] and say,
    "Gather together, and let us go
        into the fortified cities!"
6 Raise a standard toward Zion,
        flee for safety, do not delay,
    for I am bringing evil
        from the north,
        and a great destruction.
7 A lion has gone up from
        its thicket,
    a destroyer of nations
        has set out;
    he has gone out from his place
    to make your land a waste;
        your cities will be ruins
        without inhabitant.
8 Because of this put on sackcloth,
        lament and wail:
    "The fierce anger of the LORD
        has not turned away from us."

BEING CALLED BY GOD MEANS

OUR LIVES ARE BLESSED

WITH A SENSE OF PURPOSE.

9 On that day, says the LORD, courage shall fail the king and the officials; the priests shall be appalled
and the prophets astounded. 10 Then
I said, "Ah, Lord GOD, how utterly
you have deceived this people and

Jerusalem, saying, 'It shall be well
with you,' even while the sword is at
the throat!"

11 At that time it will be said to
this people and to Jerusalem: A hot
wind comes from me out of the
bare heights[b] in the desert toward
my poor people, not to winnow or
cleanse— 12a wind too strong for
that. Now it is I who speak in judgment against them.
13 Look! He comes up like clouds,
        his chariots like the whirlwind;
    his horses are swifter
        than eagles—
    woe to us, for we are ruined!
14 O Jerusalem, wash your heart
        clean of wickedness
        so that you may be saved.
    How long shall your evil schemes
        lodge within you?
15 For a voice declares from Dan
        and proclaims disaster from
        Mount Ephraim.
16 Tell the nations, "Here they are!"
        Proclaim against Jerusalem,
    "Besiegers come from a
        distant land;
    they shout against the
        cities of Judah.
17 They have closed in around her
        like watchers of a field,
    because she has rebelled
        against me,
                    says the LORD.
18 Your ways and your doings
        have brought this upon you.
    This is your doom; how bitter it is!
    It has reached your very heart."

SORROW FOR A
DOOMED NATION

19 My anguish, my anguish! I
        writhe in pain!
    Oh, the walls of my heart!
    My heart is beating wildly;
        I cannot keep silent;
    for I[c] hear the sound of
        the trumpet,
        the alarm of war.
20 Disaster overtakes disaster,
        the whole land is laid waste.

a 4.5 Or shout, take your weapons: Heb
shout, fill (your hand)   b 4.11 Or the trails
c 4.19 Another reading is for you, O my soul,

Suddenly my tents are destroyed,
    my curtains in a moment.
21 How long must I see the standard,
    and hear the sound of
        the trumpet?
22 "For my people are foolish,
    they do not know me;
they are stupid children,
    they have no understanding.
They are skilled in doing evil,
    but do not know how
        to do good."

23 I looked on the earth, and lo, it
        was waste and void;
    and to the heavens, and
        they had no light.
24 I looked on the mountains, and
        lo, they were quaking,
    and all the hills moved
        to and fro.
25 I looked, and lo, there was
        no one at all,
    and all the birds of the
        air had fled.
26 I looked, and lo, the fruitful
        land was a desert,
    and all its cities were
        laid in ruins
before the LORD, before
    his fierce anger.
27 For thus says the LORD: The whole land shall be a desolation; yet I will not make a full end.
28 Because of this the earth
        shall mourn,
    and the heavens above
        grow black;
for I have spoken, I have
        purposed;
I have not relented nor
        will I turn back.

29 At the noise of horseman
        and archer
    every town takes to flight;
they enter thickets; they
        climb among rocks;
all the towns are forsaken,
    and no one lives in them.
30 And you, O desolate one,
    what do you mean that you
        dress in crimson,
    that you deck yourself with
        ornaments of gold,
    that you enlarge your
        eyes with paint?

In vain you beautify yourself.
    Your lovers despise you;
    they seek your life.
31 For I heard a cry as of a
        woman in labor,
    anguish as of one bringing
        forth her first child,
the cry of daughter Zion
        gasping for breath,
        stretching out her hands,
"Woe is me! I am fainting
        before killers!"

THE UTTER CORRUPTION OF GOD'S PEOPLE

5 Run to and fro through the
        streets of Jerusalem,
    look around and take note!
Search its squares and see
    if you can find one person
who acts justly
    and seeks truth—
so that I may
        pardon Jerusalem.[a]
2 Although they say, "As
        the LORD lives,"
    yet they swear falsely.
3 O LORD, do your eyes not
        look for truth?
You have struck them,
    but they felt no anguish;
you have consumed them,
    but they refused to take
        correction.
They have made their faces
        harder than rock;
    they have refused
        to turn back.

4 Then I said, "These are
        only the poor,
    they have no sense;
for they do not know the
        way of the LORD,
    the law of their God.
5 Let me go to the rich[b]
    and speak to them;
surely they know the way
        of the LORD,
    the law of their God."
But they all alike had
        broken the yoke,
    they had burst the bonds.

[a] 5.1 Heb *it*   [b] 5.5 Or *the great*

6 Therefore a lion from the
    forest shall kill them,
  a wolf from the desert
    shall destroy them.
A leopard is watching
    against their cities;
everyone who goes out of them
    shall be torn in pieces—
because their transgressions
  are many,
    their apostasies are great.

7 How can I pardon you?
  Your children have
    forsaken me,
  and have sworn by those
    who are no gods.
When I fed them to the full,
  they committed adultery
  and trooped to the houses
    of prostitutes.
8 They were well-fed lusty stallions,
  each neighing for his
    neighbor's wife.
9 Shall I not punish them for
  these things?
            says the LORD;
  and shall I not bring
    retribution
  on a nation such as this?

10 Go up through her vine-rows
    and destroy,
  but do not make a full end;
strip away her branches,
  for they are not the LORD's.
11 For the house of Israel and
    the house of Judah
  have been utterly
    faithless to me,
           says the LORD.
12 They have spoken falsely
    of the LORD,
  and have said, "He will
    do nothing.
No evil will come upon us,
  and we shall not see
    sword or famine."
13 The prophets are nothing
    but wind,
  for the word is not in them.
Thus shall it be done to them!

14 Therefore thus says the LORD,
    the God of hosts:
Because they[a] have spoken
  this word,

I am now making my words
    in your mouth a fire,
  and this people wood, and the
    fire shall devour them.
15 I am going to bring upon you
  a nation from far away,
    O house of Israel,
           says the LORD.
It is an enduring nation,
  it is an ancient nation,
a nation whose language
    you do not know,
  nor can you understand
    what they say.
16 Their quiver is like an open tomb;
  all of them are mighty warriors.
17 They shall eat up your harvest
    and your food;
  they shall eat up your sons
    and your daughters;
  they shall eat up your flocks
    and your herds;
  they shall eat up your vines
    and your fig trees;
  they shall destroy with the sword
    your fortified cities in
    which you trust.

18 But even in those days, says
the LORD, I will not make a full end
of you. 19 And when your people say,
"Why has the LORD our God done all
these things to us?" you shall say to
them, "As you have forsaken me and
served foreign gods in your land, so
you shall serve strangers in a land
that is not yours."

20 Declare this in the house of Jacob,
  proclaim it in Judah:
21 Hear this, O foolish and
    senseless people,
  who have eyes, but do not see,
  who have ears, but do not hear.
22 Do you not fear me? says
    the LORD;
  Do you not tremble before me?
I placed the sand as a boundary
    for the sea,
  a perpetual barrier that
    it cannot pass;
though the waves toss, they
    cannot prevail,
  though they roar, they
    cannot pass over it.

[a] 5.14 Heb *you*

23 But this people has a stubborn
        and rebellious heart;
    they have turned aside
        and gone away.
24 They do not say in their hearts,
    "Let us fear the LORD our God,
    who gives the rain in its season,
        the autumn rain and
        the spring rain,
    and keeps for us
        the weeks appointed for
        the harvest."
25 Your iniquities have turned
        these away,
    and your sins have deprived
        you of good.
26 For scoundrels are found
        among my people;
    they take over the goods
        of others.
    Like fowlers they set a trap;[a]
        they catch human beings.
27 Like a cage full of birds,
        their houses are full
        of treachery;
    therefore they have become
        great and rich,
28   they have grown fat
        and sleek.
    They know no limits in deeds
        of wickedness;
        they do not judge with justice
    the cause of the orphan, to
        make it prosper,
    and they do not defend the
        rights of the needy.
29 Shall I not punish them for
        these things?
                    says the LORD,
    and shall I not bring
        retribution
    on a nation such as this?

30 An appalling and horrible thing
        has happened in the land:
31 the prophets prophesy falsely,
        and the priests rule as the
        prophets direct;[b]
    my people love to have it so,
        but what will you do when
        the end comes?

THE IMMINENCE AND
HORROR OF THE INVASION

6 Flee for safety, O children
        of Benjamin,
    from the midst of Jerusalem!
Blow the trumpet in Tekoa,
    and raise a signal on
        Beth-haccherem;
for evil looms out of the north,
    and great destruction.
2 I have likened daughter Zion
    to the loveliest pasture.[c]
3 Shepherds with their flocks
        shall come against her.
    They shall pitch their
        tents around her;
    they shall pasture, all
        in their places.
4 "Prepare war against her;
    up, and let us attack at noon!"
"Woe to us, for the day declines,
    the shadows of evening
        lengthen!"
5 "Up, and let us attack by night,
    and destroy her palaces!"
6 For thus says the LORD of hosts:
    Cut down her trees;
    cast up a siege ramp
        against Jerusalem.
This is the city that must
    be punished;[d]
    there is nothing but
        oppression within her.
7 As a well keeps its water fresh,
    so she keeps fresh her
        wickedness;
violence and destruction are
    heard within her;
    sickness and wounds are
        ever before me.
8 Take warning, O Jerusalem,
    or I shall turn from you
        in disgust,
and make you a desolation,
    an uninhabited land.

9 Thus says the LORD of hosts:
    Glean[e] thoroughly as a vine
        the remnant of Israel;
    like a grape-gatherer, pass
        your hand again
        over its branches.

10 To whom shall I speak and
        give warning,
    that they may hear?

---

[a] 5.26 Meaning of Heb uncertain   [b] 5.31 Or
rule by their own authority   [c] 6.2 Or *I will
destroy daughter Zion, the loveliest pasture*
[d] 6.6 Or *the city of license*   [e] 6.9 Cn: Heb
They shall glean

See, their ears are closed,[a]
  they cannot listen.
The word of the LORD is to them
  an object of scorn;
  they take no pleasure in it.
11 But I am full of the wrath
  of the LORD;
  I am weary of holding it in.

Pour it out on the children
  in the street,
and on the gatherings of
  young men as well;
both husband and wife
  shall be taken,
  the old folk and the very aged.
12 Their houses shall be turned
  over to others,
  their fields and wives together;
for I will stretch out my hand
  against the inhabitants
  of the land,
      says the LORD.

13 For from the least to the
  greatest of them,
everyone is greedy for
  unjust gain;
and from prophet to priest,
  everyone deals falsely.
14 They have treated the wound of
  my people carelessly,
saying, "Peace, peace,"
  when there is no peace.
15 They acted shamefully, they
  committed abomination;
yet they were not ashamed,
  they did not know
  how to blush.
Therefore they shall fall among
  those who fall;
at the time that I punish them,
  they shall be overthrown,
      says the LORD.
16 Thus says the LORD:
Stand at the crossroads, and look,
  and ask for the ancient paths,
where the good way lies;
  and walk in it,
and find rest for your souls.
But they said, "We will
  not walk in it."
17 Also I raised up sentinels for you:
"Give heed to the sound
  of the trumpet!"
But they said, "We will
  not give heed."

PONDER

Stand at the crossroads, and look,
and ask for the ancient paths, where
the good way lies, and walk in it.
—Jeremiah 6.16

PRAY

Sovereign Lord, give us the courage
to look at our own hearts and lives to
see what kind of people we are. As we
stand at each crossroad of decision,
remind us to ask where the good way
is. Help us strive each day or each hour
to expand our hearts and minds to love
other people, particularly those in need.
Help us remember how Jesus dealt with
the adulterous woman or the despised
people such as the Samaritans, the
sick, the impoverished, the excluded.
Help us apply the teachings of your
words through Jeremiah in light of
the more familiar words that we
heard from our Savior, Jesus Christ.
In his name we pray. Amen.

18 Therefore hear, O nations,
  and know, O congregation,
    what will happen to them.
19 Hear, O earth; I am going
  to bring disaster
  on this people,
the fruit of their schemes,
because they have not given
  heed to my words;
and as for my teaching,
  they have rejected it.
20 Of what use to me is frankincense
  that comes from Sheba,
or sweet cane from a
  distant land?
Your burnt offerings are
  not acceptable,
nor are your sacrifices
  pleasing to me.
21 Therefore thus says the LORD:

[a] 6.10 Heb *are uncircumcised*

See, I am laying before
    this people
    stumbling blocks against
      which they shall stumble;
parents and children together,
    neighbor and friend
    shall perish.

22 Thus says the LORD:
    See, a people is coming from
      the land of the north,
    a great nation is stirring
      from the farthest
      parts of the earth.
23 They grasp the bow and
      the javelin,
    they are cruel and have
      no mercy,
    their sound is like the
      roaring sea;
they ride on horses,
    equipped like a warrior
      for battle,
    against you, O daughter Zion!

24 "We have heard news of them,
    our hands fall helpless;
anguish has taken hold of us,
    pain as of a woman in labor.
25 Do not go out into the field,
    or walk on the road;
for the enemy has a sword,
    terror is on every side."

26 O my poor people, put
    on sackcloth,
    and roll in ashes;
make mourning as for
    an only child,
    most bitter lamentation:

for suddenly the destroyer
    will come upon us.

27 I have made you a tester and a
    refiner[a] among my people
    so that you may know and
    test their ways.
28 They are all stubbornly rebellious,
    going about with slanders;
    they are bronze and iron,
    all of them act corruptly.
29 The bellows blow fiercely,
    the lead is consumed
      by the fire;
in vain the refining goes on,
    for the wicked are not removed.
30 They are called "rejected silver,"
    for the LORD has rejected them.

JEREMIAH PROCLAIMS GOD'S JUDGMENT ON THE NATION

7 The word that came to Jeremiah from the LORD: 2Stand in the gate of the LORD's house, and proclaim there this word, and say, Hear the word of the LORD, all you people of Judah, you that enter these gates to worship the LORD. 3Thus says the LORD of hosts, the God of Israel: Amend your ways and your doings, and let me dwell with you[b] in this place. 4Do not trust in these deceptive words: "This is[c] the temple of the LORD, the temple of the LORD, the temple of the LORD."

5 For if you truly amend your ways and your doings, if you truly

a 6.27 Or *a fortress*   b 7.3 Or *and I will let you dwell*   c 7.4 Heb *They are*

⊣ BIBLE IN LIFE ▷

Dealing With Change   Jeremiah 7.1–10

God demanded change from the hearts of the people of Judah, but they seemed unwilling to budge. They thought they were "safe" in their sin. They were comfortable doing things their own way. In the same manner, it is not easy for us to reexamine our way of life if this might mandate uncomfortable, inconvenient changes in our perspectives or priorities. We become lazy; we don't want to modify our habits, prejudices, goals or purposes. Jesus never advocated comfort or security or self-satisfaction. It's not easy to correlate the selfish way we want to live with the teachings of Jesus Christ. Change feels uncomfortable. It causes us to share what we have instead of keeping it for ourselves, to look beyond our own family to the broader family of Christ and to understand, serve and love others.

Not Too Late

*Thus says the LORD of hosts, the God of Israel: Amend your ways
and your doings, and let me dwell with you in this place.*

—Jeremiah 7.3

When God first called the prophet Jeremiah to preach a very difficult message to his people, the nation of Judah had not yet experienced exile. Over a century earlier, the northern kingdom of Israel, because of its wickedness, had been carried away into captivity, but the southern kingdom of Judah managed to remain intact. By Jeremiah's time, it seems that the people of Judah had come to see themselves as invincible and immune to exile because the temple of the Lord was located in Jerusalem and continued to function as the place of worship for God's people. Apparently, the people of Judah thought they could live however they pleased—oppressing others and even offering sacrifices to other gods—yet they remained confident that God would continue to protect them. But Jeremiah soon made it clear that this was not so.

Jeremiah instructed the people to take a lesson from the town of Shiloh (see Jeremiah 7.1–15). In the days before Jerusalem became the capital of Israel (the undivided kingdom) and the location of the temple, the ark of the covenant and the tabernacle resided in various locations in Israel, including the town of Shiloh, about 20 miles north of Jerusalem. The people used to offer sacrifices there, just as they did later at Jerusalem. One day they took the ark into battle against the Philistines, expecting that it would work like a good luck charm and give them victory. Instead, the Lord allowed the ark to be captured by the Philistines, who also destroyed the town of Shiloh. Through this familiar story, God was telling the people of Judah that possessing the ark or the temple would not protect them. True security requires obedience and devotion to God.

The same lesson applies to us today. We may go to church every week, give our offerings, sing hymns, and tell everybody we are Christians, but what really matters is whether we are truly loving God and our neighbors and demonstrating that love through real action. Jesus made this same point centuries after Jeremiah's time (see Matthew 23.13–24), and the apostle James said that faith without works is dead (see James 2.17).

In the end, the people of Judah failed to heed Jeremiah's warnings. Though God promised to remain with them if they changed their ways and acted justly, they chose to continue in their oppressive ways, and they suffered defeat and exile as a result. But it's not too late for us. We can choose to change our self-satisfied, self-concerned ways of living and instead love God and our neighbors.

Going Deeper

- What is the spiritual danger of talking the talk of Christianity without walking the walk?
- What are some practical ways you can demonstrate your love for God and others?

act justly one with another, 6if you do not oppress the alien, the orphan, and the widow, or shed innocent blood in this place, and if you do not go after other gods to your own hurt, 7then I will dwell with you in this place, in the land that I gave of old to your ancestors forever and ever.

8 Here you are, trusting in deceptive words to no avail. 9Will you steal, murder, commit adultery, swear falsely, make offerings to Baal, and go after other gods that you have not known, 10and then come and stand before me in this house, which is called by my name, and say, "We are safe!"—only to go on doing all these abominations? 11Has this house, which is called by my name, become a den of robbers in your sight? You know, I too am watching, says the LORD. 12Go now to my place that was in Shiloh, where I made my name dwell at first, and see what I did to it for the wickedness of my people Israel. 13And now, because you have done all these things, says the LORD, and when I spoke to you persistently, you did not listen, and when I called you, you did not answer, 14therefore I will do to the house that is called by my name, in which you trust, and to the place that I gave to you and to your ancestors, just what I did to Shiloh. 15And I will cast you out of my sight, just as I cast out all your kinsfolk, all the offspring of Ephraim.

THE PEOPLE'S DISOBEDIENCE

16 As for you, do not pray for this people, do not raise a cry or prayer on their behalf, and do not intercede with me, for I will not hear you. 17Do you not see what they are doing in the towns of Judah and in the streets of Jerusalem? 18The children gather wood, the fathers kindle fire, and the women knead dough, to make cakes for the queen of heaven; and they pour out drink offerings to other gods, to provoke me to anger. 19Is it I whom they provoke? says the LORD. Is it not themselves, to their own hurt? 20Therefore thus says the Lord GOD: My anger and my wrath shall be poured out on this place,

on human beings and animals, on the trees of the field and the fruit of the ground; it will burn and not be quenched.

21 Thus says the LORD of hosts, the God of Israel: Add your burnt offerings to your sacrifices, and eat the flesh. 22For in the day that I brought your ancestors out of the land of Egypt, I did not speak to them or command them concerning burnt offerings and sacrifices. 23But this command I gave them, "Obey my voice, and I will be your God, and you shall be my people; and walk only in the way that I command you, so that it may be well with you." 24Yet they did not obey or incline their ear, but, in the stubbornness of their evil will, they walked in their own counsels, and looked backward rather than forward. 25From the day that your ancestors came out of the land of Egypt until this day, I have persistently sent all my servants the prophets to them, day after day; 26yet they did not listen to me, or pay attention, but they stiffened their necks. They did worse than their ancestors did.

27 So you shall speak all these words to them, but they will not listen to you. You shall call to them, but they will not answer you. 28You shall say to them: This is the nation that did not obey the voice of the LORD their God, and did not accept discipline; truth has perished; it is cut off from their lips.
29 Cut off your hair and
    throw it away;
  raise a lamentation on
    the bare heights,a
  for the LORD has rejected
    and forsaken
  the generation that
    provoked his wrath.

30 For the people of Judah have done evil in my sight, says the LORD; they have set their abominations in the house that is called by my name, defiling it. 31And they go on building the high placeb of Topheth, which is in the valley of the son of

a 7.29 Or the trails   b 7.31 Gk Tg: Heb high places

Hinnom, to burn their sons and their daughters in the fire—which I did not command, nor did it come into my mind. 32 Therefore, the days are surely coming, says the LORD, when it will no more be called Topheth, or the valley of the son of Hinnom, but the valley of Slaughter: for they will bury in Topheth until there is no more room. 33 The corpses of this people will be food for the birds of the air, and for the animals of the earth; and no one will frighten them away. 34 And I will bring to an end the sound of mirth and gladness, the voice of the bride and bridegroom in the cities of Judah and in the streets of Jerusalem; for the land shall become a waste.

8 At that time, says the LORD, the bones of the kings of Judah, the bones of its officials, the bones of the priests, the bones of the prophets, and the bones of the inhabitants of Jerusalem shall be brought out of their tombs; 2 and they shall be spread before the sun and the moon and all the host of heaven, which they have loved and served, which they have followed, and which they have inquired of and worshiped; and they shall not be gathered or buried; they shall be like dung on the surface of the ground. 3 Death shall be preferred to life by all the remnant that remains of this evil family in all the places where I have driven them, says the LORD of hosts.

THE BLIND PERVERSITY
OF THE WHOLE NATION

4 You shall say to them, Thus
    says the LORD:
When people fall, do they
    not get up again?
If they go astray, do they
    not turn back?
5 Why then has this people[a]
    turned away
in perpetual backsliding?
They have held fast to deceit,
    they have refused to return.
6 I have given heed and listened,
    but they do not
    speak honestly;
no one repents of wickedness,
    saying, "What have I done!"

All of them turn to their
    own course,
like a horse plunging
    headlong into battle.
7 Even the stork in the heavens
    knows its times;
and the turtledove, swallow,
    and crane[b]
observe the time of
    their coming;
but my people do not know
    the ordinance of the LORD.

8 How can you say, "We are wise,
    and the law of the LORD
    is with us,"
when, in fact, the false pen
    of the scribes
    has made it into a lie?
9 The wise shall be put to shame,
    they shall be dismayed
    and taken;
since they have rejected the
    word of the LORD,
    what wisdom is in them?
10 Therefore I will give their
    wives to others
    and their fields to conquerors,
because from the least to
    the greatest
everyone is greedy for
    unjust gain;
from prophet to priest
    everyone deals falsely.
11 They have treated the wound of
    my people carelessly,
    saying, "Peace, peace,"
    when there is no peace.
12 They acted shamefully, they
    committed abomination;
yet they were not at
    all ashamed,
    they did not know how to blush.
Therefore they shall fall among
    those who fall;
at the time when I punish them,
    they shall be overthrown,
    says the LORD.
13 When I wanted to gather
    them, says the LORD,
    there are[c] no grapes
    on the vine,
    nor figs on the fig tree;

a 8.5 One Ms Gk: MT this people, Jerusalem,
b 8.7 Meaning of Heb uncertain c 8.13 Or
I will make an end of them, says the LORD.
There are

even the leaves are withered,
and what I gave them has
passed away from them.[a]

14 Why do we sit still?
Gather together, let us go into
the fortified cities
and perish there;
for the LORD our God has
doomed us to perish,
and has given us poisoned
water to drink,
because we have sinned
against the LORD.
15 We look for peace, but
find no good,
for a time of healing, but
there is terror instead.

16 The snorting of their horses
is heard from Dan;
at the sound of the neighing
of their stallions
the whole land quakes.
They come and devour the land
and all that fills it,
the city and those who
live in it.
17 See, I am letting snakes
loose among you,
adders that cannot
be charmed,
and they shall bite you,
says the LORD.

THE PROPHET MOURNS
FOR THE PEOPLE

18 My joy is gone, grief
is upon me,
my heart is sick.
19 Hark, the cry of my poor people
from far and wide in the land:
"Is the LORD not in Zion?
Is her King not in her?"
("Why have they provoked me to
anger with their images,
with their foreign idols?")
20 "The harvest is past, the
summer is ended,
and we are not saved."
21 For the hurt of my poor
people I am hurt,
I mourn, and dismay has
taken hold of me.

22 Is there no balm in Gilead?
Is there no physician there?

Why then has the health of
my poor people
not been restored?

9[b] O that my head were a
spring of water,
and my eyes a fountain of tears,
so that I might weep day
and night
for the slain of my poor people!
2[c] O that I had in the desert
a traveler's lodging place,
that I might leave my people
and go away from them!
For they are all adulterers,
a band of traitors.
3 They bend their tongues
like bows;
they have grown strong in
the land for falsehood,
and not for truth;
for they proceed from evil to evil,
and they do not know me,
says the LORD.

4 Beware of your neighbors,
and put no trust in any
of your kin;[d]
for all your kin[e] are supplanters,
and every neighbor goes
around like a slanderer.
5 They all deceive their neighbors,
and no one speaks the truth;
they have taught their tongues
to speak lies;
they commit iniquity and are
too weary to repent.[f]
6 Oppression upon oppression,
deceit[g] upon deceit!
They refuse to know me,
says the LORD.

7 Therefore thus says the
LORD of hosts:
I will now refine and test them,
for what else can I do with
my sinful people?[h]
8 Their tongue is a deadly arrow;
it speaks deceit through
the mouth.

[a] 8.13 Meaning of Heb uncertain   [b] 9.1 Ch
8.23 in Heb   [c] 9.2 Ch 9.1 in Heb   [d] 9.4 Heb
in a brother   [e] 9.4 Heb for every brother
[f] 9.5 Cn Compare Gk: Heb they weary
themselves with iniquity. 6Your dwelling
[g] 9.6 Cn: Heb Your dwelling in the midst of
deceit   [h] 9.7 Or my poor people

They all speak friendly words
    to their neighbors,
but inwardly are planning
    to lay an ambush.
9 Shall I not punish them for these
    things? says the LORD;
and shall I not bring retribution
    on a nation such as this?

10 Take up[a] weeping and wailing
    for the mountains,
and a lamentation for the
    pastures of the wilderness,
because they are laid waste so that
    no one passes through,
and the lowing of cattle
    is not heard;
both the birds of the air
    and the animals
    have fled and are gone.
11 I will make Jerusalem a
    heap of ruins,
    a lair of jackals;
and I will make the towns of
    Judah a desolation,
    without inhabitant.

12 Who is wise enough to understand this? To whom has the mouth of the LORD spoken, so that they may declare it? Why is the land ruined and laid waste like a wilderness, so that no one passes through? 13And the LORD says: Because they have forsaken my law that I set before them, and have not obeyed my voice, or walked in accordance with it, 14but have stubbornly followed their own hearts and have gone after the Baals, as their ancestors taught them. 15Therefore thus says the LORD of hosts, the God of Israel: I am feeding this people with wormwood, and giving them poisonous water to drink. 16I will scatter them among nations that neither they nor their ancestors have known; and I will send the sword after them, until I have consumed them.

THE PEOPLE MOURN
IN JUDGMENT

17 Thus says the LORD of hosts:
Consider, and call for the
    mourning women
    to come;
send for the skilled
    women to come;

18 let them quickly raise a
    dirge over us,
so that our eyes may run
    down with tears,
and our eyelids flow
    with water.
19 For a sound of wailing is
    heard from Zion:
"How we are ruined!
We are utterly shamed,
because we have left the land,
because they have cast
    down our dwellings."

20 Hear, O women, the word
    of the LORD,
and let your ears receive the
    word of his mouth;
teach to your daughters a dirge,
    and each to her neighbor
    a lament.
21 "Death has come up into
    our windows,
it has entered our palaces,
to cut off the children from
    the streets
and the young men from
    the squares."
22 Speak! Thus says the LORD:
"Human corpses shall fall
    like dung upon the open field,
like sheaves behind the reaper,
    and no one shall gather them."

23 Thus says the LORD: Do not let the wise boast in their wisdom, do not let the mighty boast in their might, do not let the wealthy boast in their wealth; 24but let those who boast boast in this, that they understand and know me, that I am the LORD; I act with steadfast love, justice, and righteousness in the earth, for in these things I delight, says the LORD.

25 The days are surely coming, says the LORD, when I will attend to all those who are circumcised only in the foreskin: 26Egypt, Judah, Edom, the Ammonites, Moab, and all those with shaven temples who live in the desert. For all these nations are uncircumcised, and all the house of Israel is uncircumcised in heart.

---

a **9.10** Gk Syr: Heb *I will take up*

IDOLATRY HAS BROUGHT
RUIN ON ISRAEL

10 Hear the word that the LORD
speaks to you, O house of Israel. ²Thus says the LORD:
Do not learn the way of
    the nations,
  or be dismayed at the signs
    of the heavens;
  for the nations are
    dismayed at them.
³ For the customs of the
    peoples are false:
  a tree from the forest is cut down,
  and worked with an ax by the
    hands of an artisan;
⁴ people deck it with silver
    and gold;
  they fasten it with
    hammer and nails
  so that it cannot move.
⁵ Their idols[a] are like scarecrows
    in a cucumber field,
  and they cannot speak;
  they have to be carried,
    for they cannot walk.
  Do not be afraid of them,
    for they cannot do evil,
    nor is it in them to do good.

⁶ There is none like you, O LORD;
  you are great, and your name
    is great in might.
⁷ Who would not fear you,
    O King of the nations?
  For that is your due;
  among all the wise ones
    of the nations
  and in all their kingdoms
    there is no one like you.
⁸ They are both stupid
    and foolish;
  the instruction given by idols
  is no better than wood![b]
⁹ Beaten silver is brought
    from Tarshish,
  and gold from Uphaz.
  They are the work of the artisan
    and of the hands of
    the goldsmith;
  their clothing is blue
    and purple;
  they are all the product of
    skilled workers.
¹⁰ But the LORD is the true God;
  he is the living God and the
    everlasting King.

At his wrath the earth quakes,
  and the nations cannot
    endure his indignation.

¹¹ Thus shall you say to them: The
gods who did not make the heavens
and the earth shall perish from the
earth and from under the heavens.[c]

WHAT IS AN IDOL? IT'S
ANYTHING THAT USURPS
GOD'S SUPREMACY IN
OUR LIVES. IT'S WHATEVER
WE PRIZE HIGHEST AND
SEEK MOST AVIDLY.

¹² It is he who made the earth
    by his power,
  who established the world
    by his wisdom,
  and by his understanding
    stretched out the heavens.
¹³ When he utters his voice, there
    is a tumult of waters
    in the heavens,
  and he makes the mist rise
    from the ends of the earth.
  He makes lightnings for the rain,
  and he brings out the wind
    from his storehouses.
¹⁴ Everyone is stupid and
    without knowledge;
  goldsmiths are all put to
    shame by their idols;
  for their images are false,
  and there is no breath in them.
¹⁵ They are worthless, a work
    of delusion;
  at the time of their punishment
    they shall perish.
¹⁶ Not like these is the LORD,[d]
    the portion of Jacob,
  for he is the one who
    formed all things,

[a] 10.5 Heb *They* [b] 10.8 Meaning of Heb
uncertain [c] 10.11 This verse is in Aramaic
[d] 10.16 Heb lacks *the LORD*

and Israel is the tribe of
his inheritance;
the LORD of hosts is his name.

THE COMING EXILE

17 Gather up your bundle from
the ground,
O you who live under siege!
18 For thus says the LORD:
I am going to sling out the
inhabitants of the land
at this time,
and I will bring distress on them,
so that they shall feel it.

19 Woe is me because of my hurt!
My wound is severe.
But I said, "Truly this is
my punishment,
and I must bear it."
20 My tent is destroyed,
and all my cords are broken;
my children have gone from me,
and they are no more;
there is no one to spread
my tent again,
and to set up my curtains.
21 For the shepherds are stupid,
and do not inquire
of the LORD;
therefore they have not
prospered,
and all their flock is scattered.

22 Hear, a noise! Listen, it
is coming—
a great commotion from
the land of the north
to make the cities of Judah
a desolation,
a lair of jackals.

23 I know, O LORD, that the way
of human beings is
not in their control,
that mortals as they walk
cannot direct their steps.
24 Correct me, O LORD, but
in just measure;
not in your anger, or you will
bring me to nothing.

25 Pour out your wrath on
the nations that do
not know you,
and on the peoples that do
not call on your name;

PONDER

I know, O LORD, that the way of human beings is not in their control, that mortals as they walk cannot direct their steps. Correct me, O LORD, but in just measure; not in your anger, or you will bring me to nothing.
—Jeremiah 10.23–24

PRAY

Father, we ask you to open our hearts and minds to acknowledge our own departure from your commands and those of Jesus. Discipline us, Lord, but in mercy. We ask you to forgive us when we depart from righteousness, justice, peace, forgiveness, love and generosity toward those who are in need. Open our hearts to receive your guidance on how we can best be living illustrations of Jesus. Help us to remember that Christianity is not just what we believe in but actually what we do. Give us the courage to correct our wrongdoing and to reach for greatness and great achievement as you measure it. We praise your holy name. Amen.

for they have devoured Jacob;
they have devoured him
and consumed him,
and have laid waste his
habitation.

ISRAEL AND JUDAH HAVE BROKEN THE COVENANT

11 The word that came to Jeremiah from the LORD: 2 Hear the words of this covenant, and speak to the people of Judah and the inhabitants of Jerusalem. 3 You shall say to them, Thus says the LORD, the God of Israel: Cursed be anyone who does not heed the words of this covenant, 4 which I commanded your ancestors when I brought them out of the land of Egypt, from the iron-smelter, saying, Listen to my voice, and do all that I command you. So

shall you be my people, and I will be your God, [5]that I may perform the oath that I swore to your ancestors, to give them a land flowing with milk and honey, as at this day. Then I answered, "So be it, LORD."

6 And the LORD said to me: Proclaim all these words in the cities of Judah, and in the streets of Jerusalem: Hear the words of this covenant and do them. [7]For I solemnly warned your ancestors when I brought them up out of the land of Egypt, warning them persistently, even to this day, saying, Obey my voice. [8]Yet they did not obey or incline their ear, but everyone walked in the stubbornness of an evil will. So I brought upon them all the words of this covenant, which I commanded them to do, but they did not.

9 And the LORD said to me: Conspiracy exists among the people of Judah and the inhabitants of Jerusalem. [10]They have turned back to the iniquities of their ancestors of old, who refused to heed my words; they have gone after other gods to serve them; the house of Israel and the house of Judah have broken the covenant that I made with their ancestors. [11]Therefore, thus says the LORD, assuredly I am going to bring disaster upon them that they cannot escape; though they cry out to me, I will not listen to them. [12]Then the cities of Judah and the inhabitants of Jerusalem will go and cry out to the gods to whom they make offerings, but they will never save them in the time of their trouble. [13]For your gods have become as many as your towns, O Judah; and as many as the streets of Jerusalem are the altars to shame you have set up, altars to make offerings to Baal.

14 As for you, do not pray for this people, or lift up a cry or prayer on their behalf, for I will not listen when they call to me in the time of their trouble. [15]What right has my beloved in my house, when she has done vile deeds? Can vows[a] and sacrificial flesh avert your doom? Can you then exult? [16]The LORD once called you, "A green olive tree, fair with goodly fruit"; but with the roar of a great tempest he will set fire to it, and its branches will be consumed. [17]The LORD of hosts, who planted you, has pronounced evil against you, because of the evil that the house of Israel and the house of Judah have done, provoking me to anger by making offerings to Baal.

JEREMIAH'S LIFE THREATENED

[18] It was the LORD who made it
known to me, and I knew;
then you showed me
their evil deeds.
[19] But I was like a gentle lamb
led to the slaughter.
And I did not know it was
against me
that they devised
schemes, saying,
"Let us destroy the tree
with its fruit,
let us cut him off from the
land of the living,
so that his name will no
longer be remembered!"
[20] But you, O LORD of hosts, who
judge righteously,
who try the heart and
the mind,
let me see your retribution
upon them,
for to you I have committed
my cause.

21 Therefore thus says the LORD concerning the people of Anathoth, who seek your life, and say, "You shall not prophesy in the name of the LORD, or you will die by our hand"— [22]therefore thus says the LORD of hosts: I am going to punish them; the young men shall die by the sword; their sons and their daughters shall die by famine; [23]and not even a remnant shall be left of them. For I will bring disaster upon the people of Anathoth, the year of their punishment.

JEREMIAH COMPLAINS TO GOD

12 You will be in the
right, O LORD,
when I lay charges against you;
but let me put my case to you.

---

[a] 11.15 Gk: Heb *Can many*

Why does the way of the
guilty prosper?
Why do all who are
treacherous thrive?
2 You plant them, and they
take root;
they grow and bring
forth fruit;
you are near in their mouths
yet far from their hearts.
3 But you, O LORD, know me;
You see me and test me—
my heart is with you.
Pull them out like sheep for
the slaughter,
and set them apart for the
day of slaughter.
4 How long will the land mourn,
and the grass of every
field wither?
For the wickedness of those
who live in it
the animals and the birds
are swept away,
and because people said, "He
is blind to our ways."[a]

GOD REPLIES TO JEREMIAH

5 If you have raced with
foot-runners and they
have wearied you,
how will you compete
with horses?
And if in a safe land you
fall down,
how will you fare in the
thickets of the Jordan?
6 For even your kinsfolk and
your own family,
even they have dealt
treacherously with you;
they are in full cry after you;
do not believe them,
though they speak friendly
words to you.

7 I have forsaken my house,
I have abandoned
my heritage;
I have given the beloved
of my heart
into the hands of her enemies.
8 My heritage has become to me
like a lion in the forest;
she has lifted up her voice
against me—
therefore I hate her.

9 Is the hyena greedy[b] for my
heritage at my command?
Are the birds of prey all
around her?
Go, assemble all the wild animals;
bring them to devour her.
10 Many shepherds have destroyed
my vineyard,
they have trampled down
my portion,
they have made my
pleasant portion
a desolate wilderness.
11 They have made it a desolation;
desolate, it mourns to me.
The whole land is made desolate,
but no one lays it to heart.
12 Upon all the bare heights[c]
in the desert
spoilers have come;
for the sword of the LORD
devours
from one end of the land
to the other;
no one shall be safe.
13 They have sown wheat and
have reaped thorns,
they have tired themselves
out but profit nothing.
They shall be ashamed of
their[d] harvests
because of the fierce anger
of the LORD.

14 Thus says the LORD concerning all my evil neighbors who touch the heritage that I have given my people Israel to inherit: I am about to pluck them up from their land, and I will pluck up the house of Judah from among them. 15 And after I have plucked them up, I will again have compassion on them, and I will bring them again to their heritage and to their land, every one of them. 16 And then, if they will diligently learn the ways of my people, to swear by my name, "As the LORD lives," as they taught my people to swear by Baal, then they shall be built up in the midst of my people. 17 But if any nation will not listen, then I will completely uproot it and destroy it, says the LORD.

a 12.4 Gk: Heb to our future   b 12.9 Cn: Heb
Is the hyena, the bird of prey   c 12.12 Or the
trails   d 12.13 Heb your

THE LINEN LOINCLOTH

13 Thus said the LORD to me, "Go and buy yourself a linen loincloth, and put it on your loins, but do not dip it in water." ²So I bought a loincloth according to the word of the LORD, and put it on my loins. ³And the word of the LORD came to me a second time, saying, ⁴"Take the loincloth that you bought and are wearing, and go now to the Euphrates,ᵃ and hide it there in a cleft of the rock." ⁵So I went, and hid it by the Euphrates,ᵇ as the LORD commanded me. ⁶And after many days the LORD said to me, "Go now to the Euphrates,ᵃ and take from there the loincloth that I commanded you to hide there." ⁷Then I went to the Euphrates,ᵃ and dug, and I took the loincloth from the place where I had hidden it. But now the loincloth was ruined; it was good for nothing.

8 Then the word of the LORD came to me: ⁹Thus says the LORD: Just so I will ruin the pride of Judah and the great pride of Jerusalem. ¹⁰This evil people, who refuse to hear my words, who stubbornly follow their own will and have gone after other gods to serve them and worship them, shall be like this loincloth, which is good for nothing. ¹¹For as the loincloth clings to one's loins, so I made the whole house of Israel and the whole house of Judah cling to me, says the LORD, in order that they might be for me a people, a name, a praise, and a glory. But they would not listen.

OUR PRAYERS ARE BASED

ON THE CONVICTION THAT

GOD IS FAIR, MERCIFUL AND

WAITING TO HELP US.

SYMBOL OF THE WINE-JARS

12 You shall speak to them this word: Thus says the LORD, the God of Israel: Every wine-jar should be filled with wine. And they will say to you, "Do you think we do not know that every wine-jar should be filled with wine?" ¹³Then you shall say to them: Thus says the LORD: I am about to fill all the inhabitants of this land—the kings who sit on David's throne, the priests, the prophets, and all the inhabitants of Jerusalem—with drunkenness. ¹⁴And I will dash them one against another, parents and children together, says the LORD. I will not pity or spare or have compassion when I destroy them.

EXILE THREATENED

¹⁵ Hear and give ear; do not
    be haughty,
    for the LORD has spoken.
¹⁶ Give glory to the LORD your God
    before he brings darkness,
  and before your feet stumble
    on the mountains at twilight;
  while you look for light,
    he turns it into gloom
    and makes it deep darkness.
¹⁷ But if you will not listen,
    my soul will weep in secret
    for your pride;
  my eyes will weep bitterly and
    run down with tears,
  because the LORD's flock has
    been taken captive.

¹⁸ Say to the king and the
    queen mother:
  "Take a lowly seat,
  for your beautiful crown
    has come down from
    your head."ᶜ
¹⁹ The towns of the Negeb
    are shut up
  with no one to open them;
  all Judah is taken into exile,
    wholly taken into exile.

²⁰ Lift up your eyes and see
    those who come from
    the north.
  Where is the flock that
    was given you,
    your beautiful flock?

ᵃ 13.4,6,7 Or to Parah; Heb perath
ᵇ 13.5 Or by Parah; Heb perath   ᶜ 13.18 Gk
Syr Vg: Meaning of Heb uncertain

21 What will you say when they
        set as head over you
    those whom you have trained
        to be your allies?
    Will not pangs take hold of you,
        like those of a woman in labor?
22 And if you say in your heart,
        "Why have these things
        come upon me?"
    it is for the greatness of
        your iniquity
    that your skirts are lifted up,
        and you are violated.
23 Can Ethiopians[a] change their skin
        or leopards their spots?
    Then also you can do good
        who are accustomed to do evil.
24 I will scatter you[b] like chaff
        driven by the wind from
        the desert.
25 This is your lot,
        the portion I have measured
        out to you, says the LORD,
    because you have forgotten me
        and trusted in lies.
26 I myself will lift up your skirts
        over your face,
    and your shame will be seen.
27 I have seen your abominations,
        your adulteries and neighings,
        your shameless
        prostitutions
    on the hills of the countryside.
    Woe to you, O Jerusalem!
        How long will it be
    before you are made clean?

THE GREAT DROUGHT

14 The word of the LORD that
came to Jeremiah concern-
ing the drought:
2 Judah mourns
        and her gates languish;
    they lie in gloom on the ground,
        and the cry of Jerusalem
        goes up.
3 Her nobles send their
        servants for water;
    they come to the cisterns,
    they find no water,
        they return with their
        vessels empty.
    They are ashamed and dismayed
        and cover their heads,
4 because the ground is cracked.
    Because there has been no
        rain on the land

the farmers are dismayed;
        they cover their heads.
5 Even the doe in the field forsakes
        her newborn fawn
    because there is no grass.
6 The wild asses stand on the
        bare heights,[c]
    they pant for air like jackals;
        their eyes fail
    because there is no herbage.

7 Although our iniquities
        testify against us,
    act, O LORD, for your
        name's sake;
    our apostasies indeed are many,
        and we have sinned
        against you.
8 O hope of Israel,
        its savior in time of trouble,
    why should you be like a
        stranger in the land,
    like a traveler turning
        aside for the night?
9 Why should you be like
        someone confused,
    like a mighty warrior who
        cannot give help?
    Yet you, O LORD, are in
        the midst of us,
    and we are called by
        your name;
    do not forsake us!

10 Thus says the LORD concerning
        this people:
    Truly they have loved to wander,
        they have not restrained
        their feet;
    therefore the LORD does
        not accept them,
    now he will remember
        their iniquity
    and punish their sins.

11 The LORD said to me: Do not
pray for the welfare of this people.
12 Although they fast, I do not hear
their cry, and although they offer
burnt offering and grain offering,
I do not accept them; but by the
sword, by famine, and by pestilence
I consume them.

a 13.23 Or *Nubians*; Heb *Cushites*
b 13.24 Heb *them*   c 14.6 Or *the trails*

DENUNCIATION OF LYING PROPHETS

13 Then I said: "Ah, Lord GOD! Here are the prophets saying to them, 'You shall not see the sword, nor shall you have famine, but I will give you true peace in this place.'" 14And the LORD said to me: The prophets are prophesying lies in my name; I did not send them, nor did I command them or speak to them. They are prophesying to you a lying vision, worthless divination, and the deceit of their own minds. 15Therefore thus says the LORD concerning the prophets who prophesy in my name though I did not send them, and who say, "Sword and famine shall not come on this land": By sword and famine those prophets shall be consumed. 16And the people to whom they prophesy shall be thrown out into the streets of Jerusalem, victims of famine and sword. There shall be no one to bury them—themselves, their wives, their sons, and their daughters. For I will pour out their wickedness upon them.

17 You shall say to them this word:
Let my eyes run down with
tears night and day,
and let them not cease,
for the virgin daughter—my
people—is struck down
with a crushing blow,
with a very grievous wound.
18 If I go out into the field,
look—those killed by the sword!
And if I enter the city,
look—those sick witha famine!
For both prophet and priest
ply their trade
throughout the land,
and have no knowledge.

THE PEOPLE PLEAD FOR MERCY

19 Have you completely
rejected Judah?
Does your heart loathe Zion?
Why have you struck us down
so that there is no
healing for us?
We look for peace, but
find no good;
for a time of healing, but
there is terror instead.

20 We acknowledge our
wickedness, O LORD,
the iniquity of our ancestors,
for we have sinned
against you.
21 Do not spurn us, for your
name's sake;
do not dishonor your
glorious throne;
remember and do not break
your covenant with us.
22 Can any idols of the nations
bring rain?
Or can the heavens
give showers?
Is it not you, O LORD
our God?
We set our hope on you,
for it is you who do all this.

PUNISHMENT IS INEVITABLE

15 Then the LORD said to me: Though Moses and Samuel stood before me, yet my heart would not turn toward this people. Send them out of my sight, and let them go! 2And when they say to you, "Where shall we go?" you shall say to them: Thus says the LORD:
Those destined for pestilence,
to pestilence,
and those destined for the
sword, to the sword;
those destined for famine,
to famine,
and those destined for
captivity, to captivity.
3And I will appoint over them four kinds of destroyers, says the LORD: the sword to kill, the dogs to drag away, and the birds of the air and the wild animals of the earth to devour and destroy. 4I will make them a horror to all the kingdoms of the earth because of what King Manasseh son of Hezekiah of Judah did in Jerusalem.

5 Who will have pity on you,
O Jerusalem,
or who will bemoan you?
Who will turn aside
to ask about your welfare?

a 14.18 Heb look—the sicknesses of

6 You have rejected me,
    says the LORD,
  you are going backward;
so I have stretched out my
    hand against you and
    destroyed you—
  I am weary of relenting.
7 I have winnowed them with
    a winnowing fork
  in the gates of the land;
I have bereaved them, I have
    destroyed my people;
  they did not turn from
    their ways.
8 Their widows became
    more numerous
  than the sand of the seas;
I have brought against the
    mothers of youths
  a destroyer at noonday;
I have made anguish and terror
  fall upon her suddenly.
9 She who bore seven has
    languished;
  she has swooned away;
her sun went down while
    it was yet day;
  she has been shamed
    and disgraced.
And the rest of them I will
  give to the sword
before their enemies,
              says the LORD.

JEREMIAH COMPLAINS AGAIN
AND IS REASSURED

10 Woe is me, my mother, that
you ever bore me, a man of strife and
contention to the whole land! I have
not lent, nor have I borrowed, yet all
of them curse me. 11 The LORD said:
Surely I have intervened in your life[a]
for good, surely I have imposed enemies on you in a time of trouble and
in a time of distress.[b] 12 Can iron and
bronze break iron from the north?

13 Your wealth and your treasures
I will give as plunder, without price,
for all your sins, throughout all your
territory. 14 I will make you serve
your enemies in a land that you do
not know, for in my anger a fire is
kindled that shall burn forever.
15 O LORD, you know;
    remember me and visit me,
    and bring down retribution for
      me on my persecutors.

In your forbearance do not
    take me away;
  know that on your account
    I suffer insult.
16 Your words were found,
    and I ate them,
  and your words became
    to me a joy
  and the delight of my heart;
for I am called by your name,
    O LORD, God of hosts.
17 I did not sit in the company
    of merrymakers,
  nor did I rejoice;
under the weight of your
    hand I sat alone,
  for you had filled me with
    indignation.
18 Why is my pain unceasing,
    my wound incurable,
  refusing to be healed?
Truly, you are to me like a
    deceitful brook,
  like waters that fail.

19 Therefore thus says the LORD:
If you turn back, I will
    take you back,
  and you shall stand before me.
If you utter what is precious, and
    not what is worthless,
  you shall serve as my mouth.
It is they who will turn to you,
  not you who will turn to them.
20 And I will make you to
    this people
  a fortified wall of bronze;
they will fight against you,
    but they shall not prevail
      over you,
for I am with you
  to save you and deliver you,
              says the LORD.
21 I will deliver you out of the
    hand of the wicked,
  and redeem you from the
    grasp of the ruthless.

JEREMIAH'S CELIBACY
AND MESSAGE

16 The word of the LORD came
to me: 2 You shall not take
a wife, nor shall you have sons or
daughters in this place. 3 For thus

---

a 15.11 Heb *intervened with you*
b 15.11 Meaning of Heb uncertain

says the LORD concerning the sons and daughters who are born in this place, and concerning the mothers who bear them and the fathers who beget them in this land: [4]They shall die of deadly diseases. They shall not be lamented, nor shall they be buried; they shall become like dung on the surface of the ground. They shall perish by the sword and by famine, and their dead bodies shall become food for the birds of the air and for the wild animals of the earth.

[5] For thus says the LORD: Do not enter the house of mourning, or go to lament, or bemoan them; for I have taken away my peace from this people, says the LORD, my steadfast love and mercy. [6]Both great and small shall die in this land; they shall not be buried, and no one shall lament for them; there shall be no gashing, no shaving of the head for them. [7]No one shall break bread[a] for the mourner, to offer comfort for the dead; nor shall anyone give them the cup of consolation to drink for their fathers or their mothers. [8]You shall not go into the house of feasting to sit with them, to eat and drink. [9]For thus says the LORD of hosts, the God of Israel: I am going to banish from this place, in your days and before your eyes, the voice of mirth and the voice of gladness, the voice of the bridegroom and the voice of the bride.

[10] And when you tell this people all these words, and they say to you, "Why has the LORD pronounced all this great evil against us? What is our iniquity? What is the sin that we have committed against the LORD our God?" [11]then you shall say to them: It is because your ancestors have forsaken me, says the LORD, and have gone after other gods and have served and worshiped them, and have forsaken me and have not kept my law; [12]and because you have behaved worse than your ancestors, for here you are, every one of you, following your stubborn evil will, refusing to listen to me. [13]Therefore I will hurl you out of this land into a land that neither you nor your ancestors have known,

and there you shall serve other gods day and night, for I will show you no favor.

GOD WILL RESTORE ISRAEL

[14] Therefore, the days are surely coming, says the LORD, when it shall no longer be said, "As the LORD lives who brought the people of Israel up out of the land of Egypt," [15]but "As the LORD lives who brought the people of Israel up out of the land of the north and out of all the lands where he had driven them." For I will bring them back to their own land that I gave to their ancestors.

[16] I am now sending for many fishermen, says the LORD, and they shall catch them; and afterward I will send for many hunters, and they shall hunt them from every mountain and every hill, and out of the clefts of the rocks. [17]For my eyes are on all their ways; they are not hidden from my presence, nor is their iniquity concealed from my sight. [18]And[b] I will doubly repay their iniquity and their sin, because they have polluted my land with the carcasses of their detestable idols, and have filled my inheritance with their abominations.

[19] O LORD, my strength and
   my stronghold,
   my refuge in the
      day of trouble,
to you shall the nations come
   from the ends of the
      earth and say:
Our ancestors have inherited
      nothing but lies,
   worthless things in which
      there is no profit.
[20] Can mortals make for
      themselves gods?
   Such are no gods!

[21] "Therefore I am surely going to teach them, this time I am going to teach them my power and my might, and they shall know that my name is the LORD."

---

[a] **16.7** Two Mss Gk: MT *break for them*
[b] **16.18** Gk: Heb *And first*

JUDAH'S SIN AND PUNISHMENT

17 The sin of Judah is written with an iron pen; with a diamond point it is engraved on the tablet of their hearts, and on the horns of their altars, 2while their children remember their altars and their sacred poles,[a] beside every green tree, and on the high hills, 3on the mountains in the open country. Your wealth and all your treasures I will give for spoil as the price of your sin[b] throughout all your territory. 4By your own act you shall lose the heritage that I gave you, and I will make you serve your enemies in a land that you do not know, for in my anger a fire is kindled[c] that shall burn forever.

5 Thus says the LORD:
Cursed are those who trust
    in mere mortals
and make mere flesh
    their strength,
whose hearts turn away
    from the LORD.
6 They shall be like a shrub
    in the desert,
and shall not see when
    relief comes.
They shall live in the parched
    places of the wilderness,
in an uninhabited salt land.

7 Blessed are those who trust
    in the LORD,
whose trust is the LORD.
8 They shall be like a tree
    planted by water,
sending out its roots
    by the stream.

It shall not fear when heat comes,
    and its leaves shall stay green;
in the year of drought it
    is not anxious,
and it does not cease
    to bear fruit.

9 The heart is devious above all else;
    it is perverse—
who can understand it?
10 I the LORD test the mind
    and search the heart,
to give to all according
    to their ways,
according to the fruit of
    their doings.

11 Like the partridge hatching
    what it did not lay,
so are all who amass
    wealth unjustly;
in mid-life it will leave them,
    and at their end they will
    prove to be fools.

12 O glorious throne, exalted
    from the beginning,
shrine of our sanctuary!
13 O hope of Israel! O LORD!
All who forsake you shall
    be put to shame;
those who turn away from
    you[d] shall be recorded
    in the underworld,[e]
for they have forsaken the
    fountain of living
    water, the LORD.

a 17.2 Heb Asherim   b 17.3 Cn: Heb spoil
your high places for sin   c 17.4 Two Mss
Theodotion: you kindled   d 17.13 Heb me
e 17.13 Or in the earth

├─┤ BIBLE IN LIFE ▷

Confidence in God
Jeremiah 17.7–8

We all face daily challenges and problems. Sometimes they prey on our minds and dominate our thoughts, but we have an accessible, free gift from God that can heal our wounds, answer our questions and alleviate our concerns. By placing our confidence in God, we can transcend the future. As we put our trust in God, we can release our worries. This is wonderful assurance, yet it is news that we tend to forget when we dwell on the troubles or tragedies we face, such as sickness or the loss of loved ones. In the New Testament, Peter says, "Cast all your anxiety on him, because he cares for you" (1 Peter 5.7). When we put our confidence in God, we need not worry about the present or the future.

JEREMIAH PRAYS FOR VINDICATION

14 Heal me, O LORD, and I
    shall be healed;
    save me, and I shall be saved;
    for you are my praise.
15 See how they say to me,
    "Where is the word of
        the LORD?
    Let it come!"
16 But I have not run away from
        being a shepherd[a]
    in your service,
    nor have I desired the fatal day.
    You know what came
        from my lips;
    it was before your face.
17 Do not become a terror to me;
    you are my refuge in the
        day of disaster;
18 Let my persecutors be shamed,
    but do not let me be shamed;
    let them be dismayed,
    but do not let me be dismayed;
    bring on them the day of disaster;
    destroy them with double
        destruction!

HALLOW THE SABBATH DAY

19 Thus said the LORD to me:
Go and stand in the People's Gate,
by which the kings of Judah enter and by which they go out, and
in all the gates of Jerusalem, 20 and
say to them: Hear the word of the
LORD, you kings of Judah, and all
Judah, and all the inhabitants of Jerusalem, who enter by these gates.
21 Thus says the LORD: For the sake of
your lives, take care that you do not
bear a burden on the sabbath day
or bring it in by the gates of Jerusalem. 22 And do not carry a burden
out of your houses on the sabbath or
do any work, but keep the sabbath
day holy, as I commanded your ancestors. 23 Yet they did not listen or
incline their ear; they stiffened their
necks and would not hear or receive
instruction.

24 But if you listen to me, says
the LORD, and bring in no burden
by the gates of this city on the sabbath day, but keep the sabbath day
holy and do no work on it, 25 then
there shall enter by the gates of this
city kings[b] who sit on the throne
of David, riding in chariots and on
horses, they and their officials, the
people of Judah and the inhabitants
of Jerusalem; and this city shall be
inhabited forever. 26 And people
shall come from the towns of Judah
and the places around Jerusalem,
from the land of Benjamin, from the
Shephelah, from the hill country,
and from the Negeb, bringing burnt
offerings and sacrifices, grain offerings and frankincense, and bringing thank offerings to the house of
the LORD. 27 But if you do not listen
to me, to keep the sabbath day holy,
and to carry in no burden through
the gates of Jerusalem on the sabbath day, then I will kindle a fire
in its gates; it shall devour the palaces of Jerusalem and shall not be
quenched.

THE POTTER AND THE CLAY

18 The word that came to Jeremiah from the LORD:
2 "Come, go down to the potter's
house, and there I will let you hear
my words." 3 So I went down to the
potter's house, and there he was
working at his wheel. 4 The vessel he
was making of clay was spoiled in
the potter's hand, and he reworked
it into another vessel, as seemed
good to him.

5 Then the word of the LORD
came to me: 6 Can I not do with you,
O house of Israel, just as this potter
has done? says the LORD. Just like
the clay in the potter's hand, so are
you in my hand, O house of Israel.
7 At one moment I may declare concerning a nation or a kingdom, that
I will pluck up and break down and
destroy it, 8 but if that nation, concerning which I have spoken, turns
from its evil, I will change my mind
about the disaster that I intended to
bring on it. 9 And at another moment
I may declare concerning a nation or
a kingdom that I will build and plant
it, 10 but if it does evil in my sight,
not listening to my voice, then I will
change my mind about the good that
I had intended to do to it. 11 Now,

a 17.16 Meaning of Heb uncertain
b 17.25 Cn: Heb *kings and officials*

therefore, say to the people of Judah and the inhabitants of Jerusalem: Thus says the LORD: Look, I am a potter shaping evil against you and devising a plan against you. Turn now, all of you from your evil way, and amend your ways and your doings.

ISRAEL'S STUBBORN IDOLATRY

12 But they say, "It is no use! We will follow our own plans, and each of us will act according to the stubbornness of our evil will."

13 Therefore thus says the LORD:
   Ask among the nations:
      Who has heard the like of this?
   The virgin Israel has done
      a most horrible thing.
14 Does the snow of Lebanon leave
      the crags of Sirion?[a]
   Do the mountain[b] waters
      run dry,[c]
      the cold flowing streams?
15 But my people have forgotten me,
      they burn offerings to
      a delusion;
   they have stumbled[d] in
      their ways,
      in the ancient roads,
   and have gone into bypaths,
      not the highway,
16 making their land a horror,
      a thing to be hissed at forever.
   All who pass by it are horrified
      and shake their heads.
17 Like the wind from the east,
      I will scatter them before
      the enemy.

   I will show them my back,
      not my face,
   in the day of their calamity.

A PLOT AGAINST JEREMIAH

18 Then they said, "Come, let us make plots against Jeremiah—for instruction shall not perish from the priest, nor counsel from the wise, nor the word from the prophet. Come, let us bring charges against him,[e] and let us not heed any of his words."

19 Give heed to me, O LORD,
      and listen to what my
      adversaries say!
20 Is evil a recompense for good?
      Yet they have dug a
      pit for my life.
   Remember how I stood before you
      to speak good for them,
      to turn away your wrath
      from them.
21 Therefore give their children
      over to famine;
   hurl them out to the power
      of the sword,
   let their wives become childless
      and widowed.
   May their men meet death
      by pestilence,
      their youths be slain by
      the sword in battle.

a **18.14** Cn: Heb *of the field*   b **18.14** Cn: Heb *foreign*   c **18.14** Cn: Heb *Are... plucked up?*   d **18.15** Gk Syr Vg: Heb *they made them stumble*   e **18.18** Heb *strike him with the tongue*

⊢ BIBLE IN LIFE ▷   ⊙

Pliable   *Jeremiah 18.1–12*

Isaiah compares humans to clay—a malleable, pliable substance. Most of us, particularly as we get older, become less willing to change. We've built a comfortable, familiar world within which we operate. We don't venture outside of it much because that's an unpredictable adventure. We choose to live within a world that we carve out for ourselves, and we don't want it populated with people who don't look or act like us or who might demand something of us. But God, the potter, wants to transform our hearts and minds to be like Christ (see 2 Corinthians 3.18). God does not intend for us to be like dried, hardened pots that cannot be transformed for the better. Are we courageous enough to be changed substantially, or are we too proud or too comfortable to admit we need a transformation? We need to be malleable in order to be more effectively used by God to reach out to other people in forgiveness, love and acceptance.

22 May a cry be heard from
their houses,
when you bring the marauder
suddenly upon them!
For they have dug a pit
to catch me,
and laid snares for my feet.
23 Yet you, O LORD, know
all their plotting to kill me.
Do not forgive their iniquity,
do not blot out their sin
from your sight.
Let them be tripped up
before you;
deal with them while
you are angry.

THE BROKEN EARTHENWARE JUG

19 Thus said the LORD: Go and
buy a potter's earthenware
jug. Take with youª some of the elders of the people and some of the
senior priests, 2and go out to the
valley of the son of Hinnom at the
entry of the Potsherd Gate, and proclaim there the words that I tell you.
3You shall say: Hear the word of the
LORD, O kings of Judah and inhabitants of Jerusalem. Thus says the
LORD of hosts, the God of Israel: I am
going to bring such disaster upon
this place that the ears of everyone
who hears of it will tingle. 4Because
the people have forsaken me, and
have profaned this place by making
offerings in it to other gods whom
neither they nor their ancestors nor
the kings of Judah have known, and
because they have filled this place
with the blood of the innocent, 5and
gone on building the high places of
Baal to burn their children in the
fire as burnt offerings to Baal, which
I did not command or decree, nor
did it enter my mind; 6therefore
the days are surely coming, says
the LORD, when this place shall no
more be called Topheth, or the valley
of the son of Hinnom, but the valley of Slaughter. 7And in this place
I will make void the plans of Judah
and Jerusalem, and will make them
fall by the sword before their enemies, and by the hand of those who
seek their life. I will give their dead
bodies for food to the birds of the air
and to the wild animals of the earth.

8And I will make this city a horror, a
thing to be hissed at; everyone who
passes by it will be horrified and
will hiss because of all its disasters.
9And I will make them eat the flesh
of their sons and the flesh of their
daughters, and all shall eat the flesh
of their neighbors in the siege, and
in the distress with which their enemies and those who seek their life
afflict them.

10 Then you shall break the jug in
the sight of those who go with you,
11and shall say to them: Thus says the
LORD of hosts: So will I break this
people and this city, as one breaks a
potter's vessel, so that it can never be
mended. In Topheth they shall bury
until there is no more room to bury.
12Thus will I do to this place, says the
LORD, and to its inhabitants, making this city like Topheth. 13And the
houses of Jerusalem and the houses
of the kings of Judah shall be defiled
like the place of Topheth—all the
houses upon whose roofs offerings
have been made to the whole host
of heaven, and libations have been
poured out to other gods.

14 When Jeremiah came from Topheth, where the LORD had sent
him to prophesy, he stood in the
court of the LORD's house and said to
all the people: 15Thus says the LORD
of hosts, the God of Israel: I am now
bringing upon this city and upon all
its towns all the disaster that I have
pronounced against it, because they
have stiffened their necks, refusing
to hear my words.

JEREMIAH PERSECUTED
BY PASHHUR

20 Now the priest Pashhur son
of Immer, who was chief officer in the house of the LORD, heard
Jeremiah prophesying these things.
2Then Pashhur struck the prophet
Jeremiah, and put him in the stocks
that were in the upper Benjamin
Gate of the house of the LORD. 3The
next morning when Pashhur released Jeremiah from the stocks,
Jeremiah said to him, The LORD has

ª 19.1 Syr Tg Compare Gk: Heb lacks *take
with you*

named you not Pashhur but "Terror-all-around." 4For thus says the LORD: I am making you a terror to yourself and to all your friends; and they shall fall by the sword of their enemies while you look on. And I will give all Judah into the hand of the king of Babylon; he shall carry them captive to Babylon, and shall kill them with the sword. 5I will give all the wealth of this city, all its gains, all its prized belongings, and all the treasures of the kings of Judah into the hand of their enemies, who shall plunder them, and seize them, and carry them to Babylon. 6And you, Pashhur, and all who live in your house, shall go into captivity, and to Babylon you shall go; there you shall die, and there you shall be buried, you and all your friends, to whom you have prophesied falsely.

JEREMIAH DENOUNCES HIS PERSECUTORS

7 O LORD, you have enticed me,
    and I was enticed;
you have overpowered me,
    and you have prevailed.
I have become a laughingstock
    all day long;
    everyone mocks me.
8 For whenever I speak, I
        must cry out,
    I must shout, "Violence
        and destruction!"
For the word of the LORD
    has become for me
    a reproach and derision
    all day long.
9 If I say, "I will not
        mention him,
    or speak any more in
        his name,"
then within me there is
    something like a
        burning fire
    shut up in my bones;
I am weary with holding it in,
    and I cannot.
10 For I hear many whispering:
    "Terror is all around!
    Denounce him! Let us
        denounce him!"
    All my close friends
    are watching for me
        to stumble.

"Perhaps he can be enticed,
    and we can prevail
        against him,
    and take our revenge on him."
11 But the LORD is with me like
        a dread warrior;
    therefore my persecutors
        will stumble,
    and they will not prevail.
They will be greatly shamed,
    for they will not succeed.
Their eternal dishonor
    will never be forgotten.
12 O LORD of hosts, you test
        the righteous,
    you see the heart and
        the mind;
let me see your retribution
        upon them,
    for to you I have committed
        my cause.

13 Sing to the LORD;
    praise the LORD!

⊖

PONDER

O LORD of hosts, you test the righteous, you see the heart and the mind; let me see your retribution upon them, for to you I have committed my cause.
—Jeremiah 20.12

PRAY

O Father, we hardly know how to respond to this somewhat strange lament from Jeremiah, who poured out his anger and hurt in a way that seems almost blasphemous to us. But Lord, we understand that this poetry teaches us that pouring out our hearts to you is really a sign of faith; nevertheless, Jeremiah had confidence that your unlimited power and knowledge were still available to him. Thank you for hearing us when our trials, tribulations, sorrows and fears threaten to overcome us. May we live exemplary lives walking hand in hand with our Savior, Jesus Christ. In his name we pray. Amen.

For he has delivered the
    life of the needy
from the hands of evildoers.

14 Cursed be the day
    on which I was born!
The day when my mother
      bore me,
    let it not be blessed!
15 Cursed be the man
    who brought the news to
      my father, saying,
"A child is born to you, a son,"
    making him very glad.
16 Let that man be like the cities
    that the LORD overthrew
      without pity;
let him hear a cry in the morning
    and an alarm at noon,
17 because he did not kill me
    in the womb;
so my mother would have
      been my grave,
    and her womb forever great.
18 Why did I come forth from
    the womb
    to see toil and sorrow,
    and spend my days in shame?

JERUSALEM WILL FALL TO NEBUCHADREZZAR

21 This is the word that came to Jeremiah from the LORD, when King Zedekiah sent to him Pashhur son of Malchiah and the priest Zephaniah son of Maaseiah, saying, 2"Please inquire of the LORD on our behalf, for King Nebuchadrezzar of Babylon is making war against us; perhaps the LORD will perform a wonderful deed for us, as he has often done, and will make him withdraw from us."

3 Then Jeremiah said to them: 4Thus you shall say to Zedekiah: Thus says the LORD, the God of Israel: I am going to turn back the weapons of war that are in your hands and with which you are fighting against the king of Babylon and against the Chaldeans who are besieging you outside the walls; and I will bring them together into the center of this city. 5I myself will fight against you with outstretched hand and mighty arm, in anger, in fury, and in great wrath. 6And I will strike down the inhabitants of this city, both human beings and animals; they shall die of a great pestilence. 7Afterward, says the LORD, I will give King Zedekiah of Judah, and his servants, and the people in this city—those who survive the pestilence, sword, and famine—into the hands of King Nebuchadrezzar of Babylon, into the hands of their enemies, into the hands of those who seek their lives. He shall strike them down with the edge of the sword; he shall not pity them, or spare them, or have compassion.

8 And to this people you shall say: Thus says the LORD: See, I am setting before you the way of life and the way of death. 9Those who stay in this city shall die by the sword, by famine, and by pestilence; but those who go out and surrender to the Chaldeans who are besieging you shall live and shall have their lives as a prize of war. 10For I have set my face against this city for evil and not for good, says the LORD: it shall be given into the hands of the king of Babylon, and he shall burn it with fire.

MESSAGE TO THE HOUSE OF DAVID

11 To the house of the king of Judah say: Hear the word of the LORD, 12O house of David! Thus says the LORD:

Execute justice in the morning,
    and deliver from the hand
      of the oppressor
anyone who has
      been robbed,
or else my wrath will go
      forth like fire,
and burn, with no one
      to quench it,
because of your evil doings.

13 See, I am against you,
    O inhabitant
      of the valley,
O rock of the plain,
         says the LORD;
you who say, "Who can come
      down against us,
    or who can enter our
      places of refuge?"

14 I will punish you according to
the fruit of your doings,
says the LORD;
I will kindle a fire in its forest,
and it shall devour all
that is around it.

EXHORTATION TO REPENT

22 Thus says the LORD: Go
down to the house of the
king of Judah, and speak there this
word, 2and say: Hear the word of the
LORD, O King of Judah sitting on
the throne of David—you, and your
servants, and your people who enter these gates. 3Thus says the LORD:
Act with justice and righteousness,
and deliver from the hand of the
oppressor anyone who has been
robbed. And do no wrong or violence to the alien, the orphan, and
the widow, or shed innocent blood
in this place. 4For if you will indeed
obey this word, then through the
gates of this house shall enter kings
who sit on the throne of David, riding in chariots and on horses, they,
and their servants, and their people. 5But if you will not heed these
words, I swear by myself, says the
LORD, that this house shall become a
desolation. 6For thus says the LORD
concerning the house of the king of
Judah:

You are like Gilead to me,
like the summit of Lebanon;
but I swear that I will make
you a desert,
an uninhabited city.ᵃ
7 I will prepare destroyers
against you,
all with their weapons;
they shall cut down your
choicest cedars
and cast them into the fire.

8 And many nations will pass by
this city, and all of them will say one
to another, "Why has the LORD dealt
in this way with that great city?"
9And they will answer, "Because
they abandoned the covenant of
the LORD their God, and worshiped
other gods and served them."

10 Do not weep for him
who is dead,
nor bemoan him;

weep rather for him who
goes away,
for he shall return no more
to see his native land.

MESSAGE TO THE SONS OF JOSIAH

11 For thus says the LORD concerning Shallum son of King Josiah
of Judah, who succeeded his father
Josiah, and who went away from
this place: He shall return here no
more, 12but in the place where they
have carried him captive he shall
die, and he shall never see this land
again.

13 Woe to him who builds his house
by unrighteousness,
and his upper rooms
by injustice;
who makes his neighbors
work for nothing,
and does not give them
their wages;
14 who says, "I will build myself
a spacious house
with large upper rooms,"
and who cuts out windows for it,
paneling it with cedar,
and painting it with vermilion.
15 Are you a king
because you compete in cedar?
Did not your father eat and drink
and do justice and
righteousness?
Then it was well with him.
16 He judged the cause of the
poor and needy;
then it was well.
Is not this to know me?
says the LORD.
17 But your eyes and heart
are only on your
dishonest gain,
for shedding innocent blood,
and for practicing oppression
and violence.

18 Therefore thus says the LORD
concerning King Jehoiakim son of
Josiah of Judah:

They shall not lament for
him, saying,
"Alas, my brother!" or
"Alas, sister!"

ᵃ 22.6 Cn: Heb *uninhabited cities*

They shall not lament for
   him, saying,
"Alas, lord!" or "Alas,
   his majesty!"
19 With the burial of a donkey
   he shall be buried—
dragged off and thrown
   out beyond the gates
   of Jerusalem.

20 Go up to Lebanon, and cry out,
   and lift up your voice in Bashan;
cry out from Abarim,
   for all your lovers are crushed.
21 I spoke to you in your prosperity,
   but you said, "I will not listen."
This has been your way
   from your youth,
for you have not obeyed
   my voice.
22 The wind shall shepherd all
   your shepherds,
   and your lovers shall go
      into captivity;
then you will be ashamed
   and dismayed
because of all your wickedness.
23 O inhabitant of Lebanon,
   nested among the cedars,
how you will groan[a] when
      pangs come upon you,
   pain as of a woman in labor!

JUDGMENT ON CONIAH
(JEHOIACHIN)

24 As I live, says the LORD, even if
King Coniah son of Jehoiakim of Judah were the signet ring on my right
hand, even from there I would tear
you off 25and give you into the hands
of those who seek your life, into the
hands of those of whom you are
afraid, even into the hands of King
Nebuchadrezzar of Babylon and into
the hands of the Chaldeans. 26I will
hurl you and the mother who bore
you into another country, where you
were not born, and there you shall
die. 27But they shall not return to the
land to which they long to return.
28 Is this man Coniah a despised
      broken pot,
   a vessel no one wants?
Why are he and his offspring
      hurled out
and cast away in a land that
      they do not know?

29 O land, land, land,
   hear the word of the LORD!
30 Thus says the LORD:
Record this man as childless,
   a man who shall not
      succeed in his days;
for none of his offspring
      shall succeed
in sitting on the throne of David,
   and ruling again in Judah.

RESTORATION AFTER EXILE

23 Woe to the shepherds who
destroy and scatter the
sheep of my pasture! says the LORD.
2Therefore thus says the LORD, the
God of Israel, concerning the shepherds who shepherd my people: It
is you who have scattered my flock,
and have driven them away, and you
have not attended to them. So I will
attend to you for your evil doings,
says the LORD. 3Then I myself will
gather the remnant of my flock out
of all the lands where I have driven
them, and I will bring them back to
their fold, and they shall be fruitful
and multiply. 4I will raise up shepherds over them who will shepherd
them, and they shall not fear any
longer, or be dismayed, nor shall any
be missing, says the LORD.

THE RIGHTEOUS BRANCH
OF DAVID

5 The days are surely coming, says
the LORD, when I will raise up for
David a righteous Branch, and he
shall reign as king and deal wisely,
and shall execute justice and righteousness in the land. 6In his days
Judah will be saved and Israel will
live in safety. And this is the name
by which he will be called: "The
LORD is our righteousness."

7 Therefore, the days are surely
coming, says the LORD, when it shall
no longer be said, "As the LORD lives
who brought the people of Israel up
out of the land of Egypt," 8but "As
the LORD lives who brought out and
led the offspring of the house of Israel out of the land of the north and
out of all the lands where he[b] had

---

[a] 22.23 Gk Vg Syr: Heb *will be pitied*
[b] 23.8 Gk: Heb *I*

driven them." Then they shall live in their own land.

FALSE PROPHETS OF HOPE DENOUNCED

9 Concerning the prophets:
My heart is crushed within me,
    all my bones shake;
I have become like a drunkard,
    like one overcome by wine,
because of the LORD
    and because of his holy words.
10 For the land is full of adulterers;
    because of the curse the
        land mourns,
    and the pastures of the
        wilderness are dried up.
Their course has been evil,
    and their might is not right.
11 Both prophet and priest
        are ungodly;
    even in my house I have found
        their wickedness,
                    says the LORD.
12 Therefore their way shall
        be to them
    like slippery paths in
        the darkness,
    into which they shall be
        driven and fall;
for I will bring disaster upon them
    in the year of their punishment,
                    says the LORD.
13 In the prophets of Samaria
    I saw a disgusting thing:
they prophesied by Baal
    and led my people Israel astray.
14 But in the prophets of Jerusalem
    I have seen a more
        shocking thing:
they commit adultery and
        walk in lies;
they strengthen the hands
        of evildoers,
so that no one turns from
        wickedness;
all of them have become like
        Sodom to me,
    and its inhabitants like
        Gomorrah.
15 Therefore thus says the LORD
    of hosts concerning
        the prophets:
"I am going to make them
        eat wormwood,
    and give them poisoned
        water to drink;

for from the prophets of
        Jerusalem
ungodliness has spread
        throughout the land."

16 Thus says the LORD of hosts: Do not listen to the words of the prophets who prophesy to you; they are deluding you. They speak visions of their own minds, not from the mouth of the LORD. 17 They keep saying to those who despise the word of the LORD, "It shall be well with you"; and to all who stubbornly follow their own stubborn hearts, they say, "No calamity shall come upon you."

18 For who has stood in the
        council of the LORD
    so as to see and to hear
        his word?
Who has given heed to his
        word so as to proclaim it?
19 Look, the storm of the LORD!
    Wrath has gone forth,
a whirling tempest;
    it will burst upon the head
        of the wicked.
20 The anger of the LORD will
        not turn back
    until he has executed and
        accomplished
    the intents of his mind.
In the latter days you will
        understand it clearly.

21 I did not send the prophets,
        yet they ran;
I did not speak to them,
        yet they prophesied.
22 But if they had stood in
        my council,
    then they would have
        proclaimed my words
        to my people,
and they would have turned
        them from their evil way,
    and from the evil of
        their doings.

23 Am I a God near by, says the LORD, and not a God far off? 24 Who can hide in secret places so that I cannot see them? says the LORD. Do I not fill heaven and earth? says the LORD. 25 I have heard what the prophets have said who prophesy

lies in my name, saying, "I have dreamed, I have dreamed!" 26How long? Will the hearts of the prophets ever turn back—those who prophesy lies, and who prophesy the deceit of their own heart? 27They plan to make my people forget my name by their dreams that they tell one another, just as their ancestors forgot my name for Baal. 28Let the prophet who has a dream tell the dream, but let the one who has my word speak my word faithfully. What has straw in common with wheat? says the LORD. 29Is not my word like fire, says the LORD, and like a hammer that breaks a rock in pieces? 30See, therefore, I am against the prophets, says the LORD, who steal my words from one another. 31See, I am against the prophets, says the LORD, who use their own tongues and say, "Says the LORD." 32See, I am against those who prophesy lying dreams, says the LORD, and who tell them, and who lead my people astray by their lies and their recklessness, when I did not send them or appoint them; so they do not profit this people at all, says the LORD.

33 When this people, or a prophet, or a priest asks you, "What is the burden of the LORD?" you shall say to them, "You are the burden,a and I will cast you off, says the LORD." 34And as for the prophet, priest, or the people who say, "The burden of the LORD," I will punish them and their households. 35Thus shall you say to one another, among yourselves, "What has the LORD answered?" or "What has the LORD spoken?" 36But "the burden of the LORD" you shall mention no more, for the burden is everyone's own word, and so you pervert the words of the living God, the LORD of hosts, our God. 37Thus you shall ask the prophet, "What has the LORD answered you?" or "What has the LORD spoken?" 38But if you say, "the burden of the LORD," thus says the LORD: Because you have said these words, "the burden of the LORD," when I sent to you, saying, You shall not say, "the burden of the LORD," 39therefore, I will surely lift you upb

and cast you away from my presence, you and the city that I gave to you and your ancestors. 40And I will bring upon you everlasting disgrace and perpetual shame, which shall not be forgotten.

FALSE PROPHETS ARE
THOSE PEOPLE AND
THINGS THAT SEDUCE US
AWAY FROM CHRIST.

THE GOOD AND THE BAD FIGS

24 The LORD showed me two baskets of figs placed before the temple of the LORD. This was after King Nebuchadrezzar of Babylon had taken into exile from Jerusalem King Jeconiah son of Jehoiakim of Judah, together with the officials of Judah, the artisans, and the smiths, and had brought them to Babylon. 2One basket had very good figs, like first-ripe figs, but the other basket had very bad figs, so bad that they could not be eaten. 3And the LORD said to me, "What do you see, Jeremiah?" I said, "Figs, the good figs very good, and the bad figs very bad, so bad that they cannot be eaten."

4 Then the word of the LORD came to me: 5Thus says the LORD, the God of Israel: Like these good figs, so I will regard as good the exiles from Judah, whom I have sent away from this place to the land of the Chaldeans. 6I will set my eyes upon them for good, and I will bring them back to this land. I will build them up, and not tear them down; I will plant them, and not pluck them up. 7I will give them a heart to know that I am the LORD; and they shall be my people and I will be their God, for they shall return to me with their whole heart.

a 23.33 Gk Vg: Heb *What burden*
b 23.39 Heb Mss Gk Vg: MT *forget you*

8 But thus says the LORD: Like the bad figs that are so bad they cannot be eaten, so will I treat King Zedekiah of Judah, his officials, the remnant of Jerusalem who remain in this land, and those who live in the land of Egypt. 9 I will make them a horror, an evil thing, to all the kingdoms of the earth—a disgrace, a byword, a taunt, and a curse in all the places where I shall drive them. 10 And I will send sword, famine, and pestilence upon them, until they are utterly destroyed from the land that I gave to them and their ancestors.

THE BABYLONIAN CAPTIVITY FORETOLD

25 The word that came to Jeremiah concerning all the people of Judah, in the fourth year of King Jehoiakim son of Josiah of Judah (that was the first year of King Nebuchadrezzar of Babylon), 2 which the prophet Jeremiah spoke to all the people of Judah and all the inhabitants of Jerusalem: 3 For twenty-three years, from the thirteenth year of King Josiah son of Amon of Judah, to this day, the word of the LORD has come to me, and I have spoken persistently to you, but you have not listened. 4 And though the LORD persistently sent you all his servants the prophets, you have neither listened nor inclined your ears to hear 5 when they said, "Turn now, every one of you, from your evil way and wicked doings, and you will remain upon the land that the LORD has given to you and your ancestors from of old and forever; 6 do not go after other gods to serve and worship them, and do not provoke me to anger with the work of your hands. Then I will do you no harm." 7 Yet you did not listen to me, says the LORD, and so you have provoked me to anger with the work of your hands to your own harm.

8 Therefore thus says the LORD of hosts: Because you have not obeyed my words, 9 I am going to send for all the tribes of the north, says the LORD, even for King Nebuchadrezzar of Babylon, my servant, and I will bring them against this land and its inhabitants, and against all these nations around; I will utterly destroy them, and make them an object of horror and of hissing, and an everlasting disgrace.a 10 And I will banish from them the sound of mirth and the sound of gladness, the voice of the bridegroom and the voice of the bride, the sound of the millstones and the light of the lamp. 11 This whole land shall become a ruin and a waste, and these nations shall serve the king of Babylon seventy years. 12 Then after seventy years are

a 25.9 Gk Compare Syr: Heb *and everlasting desolations*

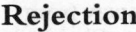

BIBLE IN LIFE

Rejection

Jeremiah 25.4–7

The lives of the prophets of God followed a common pattern: (1) they were anointed by God through visions, dreams or direct words; (2) they delivered a message calling the people to repent; (3) they were rejected by the people to whom they were sent; (4) they suffered. We see a strong correlation between the life and ministry of Jesus Christ and the prophets who preceded him. In Jerusalem, Jesus was overwhelmingly rejected by religious and political leaders, yet Jesus responded to this rejection by deeply loving the Jews who rejected him: "Jerusalem, Jerusalem, the city that kills the prophets and stone those who are sent to it! How often have I desired to gather your children together as a hen gathers her brood under her wings, and you were not willing" (Luke 13.34). All of us can remember instances when we have faced the ordeal of human rejection. How do we respond to those who reject us? By using Christ as our model, we can persist in our ministry and emulate God's love for those who reject our love and our message of the gospel.

completed, I will punish the king of Babylon and that nation, the land of the Chaldeans, for their iniquity, says the LORD, making the land an everlasting waste. 13I will bring upon that land all the words that I have uttered against it, everything written in this book, which Jeremiah prophesied against all the nations. 14For many nations and great kings shall make slaves of them also; and I will repay them according to their deeds and the work of their hands.

THE CUP OF GOD'S WRATH

15 For thus the LORD, the God of Israel, said to me: Take from my hand this cup of the wine of wrath, and make all the nations to whom I send you drink it. 16They shall drink and stagger and go out of their minds because of the sword that I am sending among them.

17 So I took the cup from the LORD's hand, and made all the nations to whom the LORD sent me drink it: 18Jerusalem and the towns of Judah, its kings and officials, to make them a desolation and a waste, an object of hissing and of cursing, as they are today; 19Pharaoh king of Egypt, his servants, his officials, and all his people; 20all the mixed people;a all the kings of the land of Uz; all the kings of the land of the Philistines—Ashkelon, Gaza, Ekron, and the remnant of Ashdod; 21Edom, Moab, and the Ammonites; 22all the kings of Tyre, all the kings of Sidon, and the kings of the coastland across the sea; 23Dedan, Tema, Buz, and all who have shaven temples; 24all the kings of Arabia and all the kings of the mixed peoplesa that live in the desert; 25all the kings of Zimri, all the kings of Elam, and all the kings of Media; 26all the kings of the north, far and near, one after another, and all the kingdoms of the world that are on the face of the earth. And after them the king of Sheshachb shall drink.

27 Then you shall say to them, Thus says the LORD of hosts, the God of Israel: Drink, get drunk and vomit, fall and rise no more, because of the sword that I am sending among you.

28 And if they refuse to accept the cup from your hand to drink, then you shall say to them: Thus says the LORD of hosts: You must drink! 29See, I am beginning to bring disaster on the city that is called by my name, and how can you possibly avoid punishment? You shall not go unpunished, for I am summoning a sword against all the inhabitants of the earth, says the LORD of hosts.

30 You, therefore, shall prophesy against them all these words, and say to them:

The LORD will roar from on high,
   and from his holy habitation
      utter his voice;
he will roar mightily
      against his fold,
   and shout, like those who
      tread grapes,
   against all the inhabitants
      of the earth.

31 The clamor will resound to the
   ends of the earth,
   for the LORD has an indictment
      against the nations;
he is entering into judgment
      with all flesh,
   and the guilty he will
      put to the sword,
         says the LORD.

32 Thus says the LORD of hosts:
See, disaster is spreading
   from nation to nation,
and a great tempest is stirring
   from the farthest parts
      of the earth!

33 Those slain by the LORD on that day shall extend from one end of the earth to the other. They shall not be lamented, or gathered, or buried; they shall become dung on the surface of the ground.

34 Wail, you shepherds, and cry out;
   roll in ashes, you lords
      of the flock,
for the days of your slaughter
      have come—and
      your dispersions,a
   and you shall fall like a
      choice vessel.

---

a 25.20,24,34 Meaning of Heb uncertain
b 25.26 Sheshach is a cryptogram for Babel, Babylon

35 Flight shall fail the shepherds,
　　and there shall be no escape
　　　for the lords of the flock.
36 Hark! the cry of the shepherds,
　　and the wail of the lords
　　　of the flock!
For the LORD is despoiling
　　their pasture,
37 and the peaceful folds
　　are devastated,
because of the fierce anger
　　of the LORD.
38 Like a lion he has left his covert;
　　for their land has
　　become a waste
because of the cruel sword,
　　and because of his fierce anger.

JEREMIAH'S PROPHECIES IN THE TEMPLE

26 At the beginning of the reign of King Jehoiakim son of Josiah of Judah, this word came from the LORD: 2 Thus says the LORD: Stand in the court of the LORD's house, and speak to all the cities of Judah that come to worship in the house of the LORD; speak to them all the words that I command you; do not hold back a word. 3 It may be that they will listen, all of them, and will turn from their evil way, that I may change my mind about the disaster that I intend to bring on them because of their evil doings. 4 You shall say to them: Thus says the LORD: If you will not listen to me, to walk in my law that I have set before you, 5 and to heed the words of my servants the prophets whom I send to you urgently—though you have not heeded— 6 then I will make this house like Shiloh, and I will make this city a curse for all the nations of the earth.

7 The priests and the prophets and all the people heard Jeremiah speaking these words in the house of the LORD. 8 And when Jeremiah had finished speaking all that the LORD had commanded him to speak to all the people, then the priests and the prophets and all the people laid hold of him, saying, "You shall die! 9 Why have you prophesied in the name of the LORD, saying, 'This house shall be like Shiloh, and this city shall be desolate, without inhabitant'?" And all the people gathered around Jeremiah in the house of the LORD.

10 When the officials of Judah heard these things, they came up from the king's house to the house of the LORD and took their seat in the entry of the New Gate of the house of the LORD. 11 Then the priests and the prophets said to the officials and to all the people, "This man deserves the sentence of death because he has prophesied against this city, as you have heard with your own ears."

12 Then Jeremiah spoke to all the officials and all the people, saying, "It is the LORD who sent me to prophesy against this house and this city all the words you have heard. 13 Now therefore amend your ways and your doings, and obey the voice of the LORD your God, and the LORD will change his mind about the disaster that he has pronounced against you. 14 But as for me, here I am in your hands. Do with me as seems good and right to you. 15 Only know for certain that if you put me to death, you will be bringing innocent blood upon yourselves and upon this city and its inhabitants, for in truth the LORD sent me to you to speak all these words in your ears."

16 Then the officials and all the people said to the priests and the prophets, "This man does not deserve the sentence of death, for he has spoken to us in the name of the LORD our God." 17 And some of the elders of the land arose and said to all the assembled people, 18 "Micah of Moresheth, who prophesied during the days of King Hezekiah of Judah, said to all the people of Judah: 'Thus says the LORD of hosts,

Zion shall be plowed as a field;
　Jerusalem shall become
　　a heap of ruins,
　and the mountain of the
　　house a wooded height.'

19 Did King Hezekiah of Judah and all Judah actually put him to death? Did he not fear the LORD and entreat the favor of the LORD, and did not the LORD change his mind about the disaster that he had pronounced against them? But we are about to bring great disaster on ourselves!"

20 There was another man prophesying in the name of the LORD, Uriah son of Shemaiah from Kiriath-jearim. He prophesied against this city and against this land in words exactly like those of Jeremiah. 21And when King Jehoiakim, with all his warriors and all the officials, heard his words, the king sought to put him to death; but when Uriah heard of it, he was afraid and fled and escaped to Egypt. 22Then King Jehoiakim senta Elnathan son of Achbor and men with him to Egypt, 23and they took Uriah from Egypt and brought him to King Jehoiakim, who struck him down with the sword and threw his dead body into the burial place of the common people.

24 But the hand of Ahikam son of Shaphan was with Jeremiah so that he was not given over into the hands of the people to be put to death.

THE SIGN OF THE YOKE

27 In the beginning of the reign of King Zedekiahb son of Josiah of Judah, this word came to Jeremiah from the LORD. 2Thus the LORD said to me: Make yourself a yoke of straps and bars, and put them on your neck. 3Send wordc to the king of Edom, the king of Moab, the king of the Ammonites, the king of Tyre, and the king of Sidon by the hand of the envoys who have come to Jerusalem to King Zedekiah of Judah. 4Give them this charge for their masters: Thus says the LORD of hosts, the God of Israel: This is what you shall say to your masters: 5It is I who by my great power and my outstretched arm have made the earth, with the people and animals that are on the earth, and I give it to whomever I please. 6Now I have given all these lands into the hand of King Nebuchadnezzar of Babylon, my servant, and I have given him even the wild animals of the field to serve him. 7All the nations shall serve him and his son and his grandson, until the time of his own land comes; then many nations and great kings shall make him their slave.

8 But if any nation or kingdom will not serve this king, Nebuchadnezzar of Babylon, and put its neck under the yoke of the king of Babylon, then I will punish that nation with the sword, with famine, and with pestilence, says the LORD, until I have completed itsd destruction by his hand. 9You, therefore, must not listen to your prophets, your diviners, your dreamers,e your soothsayers, or your sorcerers, who are saying to you, "You shall not serve the king of Babylon." 10For they are prophesying a lie to you, with the result that you will be removed far from your land; I will drive you out, and you will perish. 11But any nation that will bring its neck under the yoke of the king of Babylon and serve him, I will leave on its own land, says the LORD, to till it and live there.

12 I spoke to King Zedekiah of Judah in the same way: Bring your necks under the yoke of the king of Babylon, and serve him and his people, and live. 13Why should you and your people die by the sword, by famine, and by pestilence, as the LORD has spoken concerning any nation that will not serve the king of Babylon? 14Do not listen to the words of the prophets who are telling you not to serve the king of Babylon, for they are prophesying a lie to you. 15I have not sent them, says the LORD, but they are prophesying falsely in my name, with the result that I will drive you out and you will perish, you and the prophets who are prophesying to you.

16 Then I spoke to the priests and to all this people, saying, Thus says the LORD: Do not listen to the words of your prophets who are prophesying to you, saying, "The vessels of the LORD's house will soon be brought back from Babylon," for they are prophesying a lie to you. 17Do not listen to them; serve the king of Babylon and live. Why should this city become a desolation? 18If

a 26.22 Heb adds men to Egypt
b 27.1 Another reading is Jehoiakim
c 27.3 Cn: Heb send them d 27.8 Heb their
e 27.9 Gk Syr Vg: Heb dreams

indeed they are prophets, and if the word of the LORD is with them, then let them intercede with the LORD of hosts, that the vessels left in the house of the LORD, in the house of the king of Judah, and in Jerusalem may not go to Babylon. ¹⁹For thus says the LORD of hosts concerning the pillars, the sea, the stands, and the rest of the vessels that are left in this city, ²⁰which King Nebuchadnezzar of Babylon did not take away when he took into exile from Jerusalem to Babylon King Jeconiah son of Jehoiakim of Judah, and all the nobles of Judah and Jerusalem— ²¹thus says the LORD of hosts, the God of Israel, concerning the vessels left in the house of the LORD, in the house of the king of Judah, and in Jerusalem: ²²They shall be carried to Babylon, and there they shall stay, until the day when I give attention to them, says the LORD. Then I will bring them up and restore them to this place.

HANANIAH OPPOSES JEREMIAH AND DIES

28 In that same year, at the beginning of the reign of King Zedekiah of Judah, in the fifth month of the fourth year, the prophet Hananiah son of Azzur, from Gibeon, spoke to me in the house of the LORD, in the presence of the priests and all the people, saying, ²"Thus says the LORD of hosts, the God of Israel: I have broken the yoke of the king of Babylon. ³Within two years I will bring back to this place all the vessels of the LORD's house, which King Nebuchadnezzar of Babylon took away from this place and carried to Babylon. ⁴I will also bring back to this place King Jeconiah son of Jehoiakim of Judah, and all the exiles from Judah who went to Babylon, says the LORD, for I will break the yoke of the king of Babylon."

⁵Then the prophet Jeremiah spoke to the prophet Hananiah in the presence of the priests and all the people who were standing in the house of the LORD; ⁶and the prophet Jeremiah said, "Amen! May the LORD do so; may the LORD fulfill the words that you have prophesied, and bring back to this place from Babylon the vessels of the house of the LORD, and all the exiles. ⁷But listen now to this word that I speak in your hearing and in the hearing of all the people. ⁸The prophets who preceded you and me from ancient times prophesied war, famine, and pestilence against many countries and great kingdoms. ⁹As for the prophet who prophesies peace, when the word of that prophet comes true, then it will be known that the LORD has truly sent the prophet."

¹⁰Then the prophet Hananiah took the yoke from the neck of the prophet Jeremiah, and broke it. ¹¹And Hananiah spoke in the presence of all the people, saying, "Thus says the LORD: This is how I will break the yoke of King Nebuchadnezzar of Babylon from the neck of all the nations within two years." At this, the prophet Jeremiah went his way.

¹²Sometime after the prophet Hananiah had broken the yoke from the neck of the prophet Jeremiah, the word of the LORD came to Jeremiah: ¹³Go, tell Hananiah, Thus says the LORD: You have broken wooden bars only to forge iron bars in place of them! ¹⁴For thus says the LORD of hosts, the God of Israel: I have put an iron yoke on the neck of all these nations so that they may serve King Nebuchadnezzar of Babylon, and they shall indeed serve him; I have even given him the wild animals. ¹⁵And the prophet Jeremiah said to the prophet Hananiah, "Listen, Hananiah, the LORD has not sent you, and you made this people trust in a lie. ¹⁶Therefore thus says the LORD: I am going to send you off the face of the earth. Within this year you will be dead, because you have spoken rebellion against the LORD."

¹⁷In that same year, in the seventh month, the prophet Hananiah died.

JEREMIAH'S LETTER TO THE EXILES IN BABYLON

29 These are the words of the letter that the prophet Jeremiah sent from Jerusalem to the remaining elders among the exiles, and to the priests, the prophets, and all the people, whom Nebuchadnezzar had taken into exile from Jerusalem to Babylon. 2This was after King Jeconiah, and the queen mother, the court officials, the leaders of Judah and Jerusalem, the artisans, and the smiths had departed from Jerusalem. 3The letter was sent by the hand of Elasah son of Shaphan and Gemariah son of Hilkiah, whom King Zedekiah of Judah sent to Babylon to King Nebuchadnezzar of Babylon. It said: 4Thus says the LORD of hosts, the God of Israel, to all the exiles whom I have sent into exile from Jerusalem to Babylon: 5Build houses and live in them; plant gardens and eat what they produce. 6Take wives and have sons and daughters; take wives for your sons, and give your daughters in marriage, that they may bear sons and daughters; multiply there, and do not decrease. 7But seek the welfare of the city where I have sent you into exile, and pray to the LORD on its behalf, for in its welfare you will find your welfare. 8For thus says the LORD of hosts, the God of Israel: Do not let the prophets and the diviners who are among you deceive you, and do not listen to the dreams that they dream,a 9for it is a lie that they are prophesying to you in my name; I did not send them, says the LORD.

10 For thus says the LORD: Only when Babylon's seventy years are completed will I visit you, and I will fulfill to you my promise and bring you back to this place. 11For surely I know the plans I have for you, says the LORD, plans for your welfare and not for harm, to give you a future with hope. 12Then when you call upon me and come and pray to me, I will hear you. 13When you search for me, you will find me; if you seek me with all your heart, 14I will let you find me, says the LORD, and I will restore your fortunes and gather you from all the nations and all the places where I have driven you, says the LORD, and I will bring you back to the place from which I sent you into exile.

PONDER

For surely I know the plans I have for you, says the LORD, plans for your welfare and not for harm, to give you a future with hope.
—Jeremiah 29.11

PRAY

Our Lord, sometimes we have to stretch our hearts and minds to understand what Jeremiah's words to Judah mean to us. But we praise you, Lord, for giving us these words of assurance: whatever happens, you are in control and you will be with us. Help us to remember that your love for us never waivers, your forgiveness for our sin is absolute, and your mercy for us is unswerving. Help us to realign our lives to your will, not someday, but now, through quiet prayer, contemplation and courageous examination of our thoughts and motives—so we may be redeemed and find a joyful, expansive, transcendent and successful way of living in accordance with your Word. Fill us with the presence of your Holy Spirit, we pray. Amen.

15 Because you have said, "The LORD has raised up prophets for us in Babylon,"— 16Thus says the LORD concerning the king who sits on the throne of David, and concerning all the people who live in this city, your kinsfolk who did not go out with you into exile: 17Thus says the LORD of hosts, I am going to let loose on them sword, famine, and pestilence, and I will make them like rotten figs that are so bad they cannot be eaten. 18I will pursue them with the sword, with famine, and with pestilence, and will make them a horror to all the kingdoms of the earth, to be an object of cursing, and horror, and

a 29.8 Cn: Heb your dreams that you cause to dream

BIBLE IN FOCUS

GOD'S GOOD PLAN

For surely I know the plans I have for you, says the LORD, plans for your wel-
fare and not for harm, to give you a future with hope. Then when you call
upon me and come and pray to me, I will hear you. When you search
for me, you will find me; if you seek me with all your heart.

—Jeremiah 29.11–13

After many Judeans (including the king and other members of the royal family) had been taken into exile by Nebuchadnezzar, the king of Babylon, Jeremiah wrote a letter to the exiles instructing them to settle down and make the best of their new life in Babylon. He urged them not to rise up in animosity against Nebuchadnezzar or to listen to the false prophets who were predicting a very short time of exile for these Judeans. Jeremiah made it clear that they would be there for many years, so they should make plans that demonstrated their intent to build a new life there. They should plant gardens, which might take years of cultivation before producing fruit, and expect to eat from them. They were to put down deep roots in that foreign place. He even urged the Judeans to promote the welfare of Babylon, their new country. In essence, Jeremiah was urging the Judeans in Babylon to take advantage of their new situation and capitalize on the opportunities they had even in the midst of their exile in a faraway place.

When we suffer a major setback in life or endure a painful experience, all too often we choose to respond in ways that lead to more pain for ourselves or that effectively sideline us for other good things. Perhaps we blame God for not intervening, and we nurse bitterness toward him. Maybe we retreat into ourselves and live inside a protective cocoon, separated from others, or maybe we simply shut down and wait for God to change our circumstances. But these words from the prophet Jeremiah tell us that in difficult times, God often calls us to look up, reach out, and settle in for the long haul, making the most of the opportunities that God provides for us.

As Jeremiah pointed out to the exiles, it is important to remember that in all things—joyful or painful—God has good plans for us, plans to help us and not harm us, plans to give us hope for the future. We need not wait until our situation improves to move forward. As difficult as it might seem to us, during our struggles we should look for new opportunities to serve God and build a new life of hope and trust in God's care for us.

Going Deeper

- What are some painful or disappointing experiences you have suffered in the past or are suffering now? How have you responded to them?
- What are some ways you can redirect your life and continue to serve God and others in the midst of your pain?

hissing, and a derision among all the nations where I have driven them, [19]because they did not heed my words, says the LORD, when I persistently sent to you my servants the prophets, but they[a] would not listen, says the LORD. [20]But now, all you exiles whom I sent away from Jerusalem to Babylon, hear the word of the LORD: [21]Thus says the LORD of hosts, the God of Israel, concerning Ahab son of Kolaiah and Zedekiah son of Maaseiah, who are prophesying a lie to you in my name: I am going to deliver them into the hand of King Nebuchadrezzar of Babylon, and he shall kill them before your eyes. [22]And on account of them this curse shall be used by all the exiles from Judah in Babylon: "The LORD make you like Zedekiah and Ahab, whom the king of Babylon roasted in the fire," [23]because they have perpetrated outrage in Israel and have committed adultery with their neighbors' wives, and have spoken in my name lying words that I did not command them; I am the one who knows and bears witness, says the LORD.

THE LETTER OF SHEMAIAH

[24]To Shemaiah of Nehelam you shall say: [25]Thus says the LORD of hosts, the God of Israel: In your own name you sent a letter to all the people who are in Jerusalem, and to the priest Zephaniah son of Maaseiah, and to all the priests, saying, [26]The LORD himself has made you priest instead of the priest Jehoiada, so that there may be officers in the house of the LORD to control any madman who plays the prophet, to put him in the stocks and the collar. [27]So now why have you not rebuked Jeremiah of Anathoth who plays the prophet for you? [28]For he has actually sent to us in Babylon, saying, "It will be a long time; build houses and live in them, and plant gardens and eat what they produce."

[29]The priest Zephaniah read this letter in the hearing of the prophet Jeremiah. [30]Then the word of the LORD came to Jeremiah: [31]Send to all the exiles, saying, Thus says the LORD concerning Shemaiah of Nehelam:

Because Shemaiah has prophesied to you, though I did not send him, and has led you to trust in a lie, [32]therefore thus says the LORD: I am going to punish Shemaiah of Nehelam and his descendants; he shall not have anyone living among this people to see[b] the good that I am going to do to my people, says the LORD, for he has spoken rebellion against the LORD.

RESTORATION PROMISED FOR ISRAEL AND JUDAH

30 The word that came to Jeremiah from the LORD: [2]Thus says the LORD, the God of Israel: Write in a book all the words that I have spoken to you. [3]For the days are surely coming, says the LORD, when I will restore the fortunes of my people, Israel and Judah, says the LORD, and I will bring them back to the land that I gave to their ancestors and they shall take possession of it.

[4]These are the words that the LORD spoke concerning Israel and Judah:

[5] Thus says the LORD:
We have heard a cry of panic,
   of terror, and no peace.
[6] Ask now, and see,
   can a man bear a child?
Why then do I see every man
   with his hands on his loins
      like a woman in labor?
Why has every face
   turned pale?
[7] Alas! that day is so great
   there is none like it;
it is a time of distress for Jacob;
   yet he shall be rescued from it.

[8]On that day, says the LORD of hosts, I will break the yoke from off his[c] neck, and I will burst his[c] bonds, and strangers shall no more make a servant of him. [9]But they shall serve the LORD their God and David their king, whom I will raise up for them.

[10] But as for you, have no fear,
      my servant Jacob,
      says the LORD,
   and do not be dismayed,
      O Israel;

---

[a] **29.19** Syr: Heb *you*   [b] **29.32** Gk: Heb *and he shall not see*   [c] **30.8** Cn: Heb *your*

for I am going to save you
from far away,
and your offspring from the
land of their captivity.
Jacob shall return and have
quiet and ease,
and no one shall make
him afraid.
11 For I am with you, says the
LORD, to save you;
I will make an end of all
the nations
among which I scattered you,
but of you I will not
make an end.
I will chastise you in just
measure,
and I will by no means leave
you unpunished.

12 For thus says the LORD:
Your hurt is incurable,
your wound is grievous.
13 There is no one to uphold
your cause,
no medicine for your wound,
no healing for you.
14 All your lovers have
forgotten you;
they care nothing for you;
for I have dealt you the blow
of an enemy,
the punishment of a
merciless foe,
because your guilt is great,
because your sins are
so numerous.
15 Why do you cry out over
your hurt?
Your pain is incurable.
Because your guilt is great,
because your sins are
so numerous,
I have done these
things to you.
16 Therefore all who devour you
shall be devoured,
and all your foes, every
one of them, shall
go into captivity;
those who plunder you shall
be plundered,
and all who prey on you I
will make a prey.
17 For I will restore health to you,
and your wounds I will heal,
says the LORD,

because they have called
you an outcast:
"It is Zion; no one
cares for her!"

NO MATTER WHAT WE SEEK,
WE ARE MORE LIKELY TO
FIND IT WHEN WE MOVE
AWAY FROM PREOCCUPATION
WITH OURSELVES.

18 Thus says the LORD:
I am going to restore the fortunes
of the tents of Jacob,
and have compassion on
his dwellings;
the city shall be rebuilt
upon its mound,
and the citadel set on
its rightful site.
19 Out of them shall come
thanksgiving,
and the sound of
merrymakers.
I will make them many, and
they shall not be few;
I will make them honored,
and they shall not
be disdained.
20 Their children shall
be as of old,
their congregation shall be
established before me;
and I will punish all who
oppress them.
21 Their prince shall be one
of their own,
their ruler shall come
from their midst;
I will bring him near, and he
shall approach me,
for who would otherwise
dare to approach me?
says the LORD.
22 And you shall be my people,
and I will be your God.

23 Look, the storm of the LORD!
Wrath has gone forth,

a whirling[a] tempest;
　　it will burst upon the head
　　　　of the wicked.
24 The fierce anger of the LORD
　　will not turn back
　　until he has executed and
　　　　accomplished
the intents of his mind.
In the latter days you will
　　understand this.

THE JOYFUL RETURN
OF THE EXILES

31 At that time, says the LORD, I will be the God of all the families of Israel, and they shall be my people.
2 Thus says the LORD:
The people who survived
　　the sword
found grace in the wilderness;
when Israel sought for rest,
3　　the LORD appeared to him[b]
　　from far away.[c]
I have loved you with an
　　everlasting love;
therefore I have continued
　　my faithfulness to you.
4 Again I will build you, and
　　you shall be built,
　　O virgin Israel!
Again you shall take[d] your
　　tambourines,
　　and go forth in the dance of
　　　　the merrymakers.
5 Again you shall plant vineyards
　　on the mountains of Samaria;
the planters shall plant,
　　and shall enjoy the fruit.
6 For there shall be a day when
　　sentinels will call
in the hill country of Ephraim:
"Come, let us go up to Zion,
　　to the LORD our God."

7 For thus says the LORD:
Sing aloud with gladness for Jacob,
　　and raise shouts for the
　　　　chief of the nations;
proclaim, give praise, and say,
　　"Save, O LORD, your people,
　　the remnant of Israel."
8 See, I am going to bring
　　them from the land
　　of the north,
and gather them from the
　　farthest parts of the earth,

among them the blind
　　and the lame,
those with child and those
　　in labor, together;
a great company, they
　　shall return here.
9 With weeping they shall come,
　　and with consolations[e] I
　　　　will lead them back,
I will let them walk by
　　brooks of water,
in a straight path in which
　　they shall not stumble;
for I have become a father
　　to Israel,
　　and Ephraim is my firstborn.

10 Hear the word of the LORD,
　　O nations,
　　and declare it in the
　　　　coastlands far away;
say, "He who scattered Israel
　　will gather him,
　　and will keep him as a
　　　　shepherd a flock."
11 For the LORD has ransomed Jacob,
　　and has redeemed him from
　　　　hands too strong for him.
12 They shall come and sing aloud
　　on the height of Zion,
　　and they shall be radiant over
　　　　the goodness of the LORD,
over the grain, the wine,
　　and the oil,
　　and over the young of the
　　　　flock and the herd;
their life shall become like a
　　watered garden,
　　and they shall never
　　　　languish again.
13 Then shall the young women
　　rejoice in the dance,
　　and the young men and the
　　　　old shall be merry.
I will turn their mourning
　　into joy,
　　I will comfort them, and give
　　　　them gladness for sorrow.
14 I will give the priests their
　　fill of fatness,
　　and my people shall be
　　　　satisfied with my bounty,
　　　　　　says the LORD.

a 30.23 One Ms: Meaning of MT uncertain
b 31.3 Gk: Heb me　c 31.3 Or to him
long ago　d 31.4 Or adorn yourself with
e 31.9 Gk Compare Vg Tg: Heb supplications

15 Thus says the LORD:
A voice is heard in Ramah,
    lamentation and bitter
        weeping.
Rachel is weeping for
    her children;
she refuses to be comforted
    for her children,
because they are no more.
16 Thus says the LORD:
Keep your voice from weeping,
    and your eyes from tears;
for there is a reward for
    your work,
                    says the LORD:
they shall come back from
    the land of the enemy;
17 there is hope for your future,
                    says the LORD:
your children shall come back
    to their own country.

18 Indeed I heard Ephraim pleading:
"You disciplined me, and I
    took the discipline;
I was like a calf untrained.
Bring me back, let me come back,
    for you are the LORD my God.
19 For after I had turned away
        I repented;
and after I was discovered,
    I struck my thigh;
I was ashamed, and I
    was dismayed
because I bore the disgrace
    of my youth."
20 Is Ephraim my dear son?
    Is he the child I delight in?
As often as I speak against him,
    I still remember him.
Therefore I am deeply
        moved for him;
I will surely have mercy
    on him,
                    says the LORD.

21 Set up road markers for yourself,
    make yourself signposts;
consider well the highway,
    the road by which you went.
Return, O virgin Israel,
    return to these your cities.
22 How long will you waver,
    O faithless daughter?
For the LORD has created a new
    thing on the earth:
    a woman encompasses[a] a man.

23 Thus says the LORD of hosts,
the God of Israel: Once more
they shall use these words in the land of
Judah and in its towns when I restore their fortunes:
"The LORD bless you, O abode
    of righteousness,
    O holy hill!"
24 And Judah and all its towns shall
live there together, the farmers
and those who wander[b] with their
flocks.
25 I will satisfy the weary,
    and all who are faint I
        will replenish.
26 Thereupon I awoke and looked,
and my sleep was pleasant to me.

INDIVIDUAL RETRIBUTION

27 The days are surely coming,
says the LORD, when I will sow the
house of Israel and the house of Judah with the seed of humans and
the seed of animals. 28 And just as I
have watched over them to pluck up
and break down, to overthrow, destroy, and bring evil, so I will watch
over them to build and to plant, says
the LORD. 29 In those days they shall
no longer say:
"The parents have eaten
        sour grapes,
    and the children's teeth
    are set on edge."
30 But all shall die for their own sins;
the teeth of everyone who eats sour
grapes shall be set on edge.

A NEW COVENANT

31 The days are surely coming,
says the LORD, when I will make a
new covenant with the house of Israel and the house of Judah. 32 It will
not be like the covenant that I made
with their ancestors when I took
them by the hand to bring them out
of the land of Egypt—a covenant
that they broke, though I was their
husband,[c] says the LORD. 33 But this
is the covenant that I will make with
the house of Israel after those days,
says the LORD: I will put my law
within them, and I will write it on
their hearts; and I will be their God,

a 31.22 Meaning of Heb uncertain
b 31.24 Cn Compare Syr Vg Tg: Heb and they
shall wander   c 31.32 Or master

and they shall be my people. ³⁴No longer shall they teach one another, or say to each other, "Know the LORD," for they shall all know me, from the least of them to the greatest, says the LORD; for I will forgive their iniquity, and remember their sin no more.

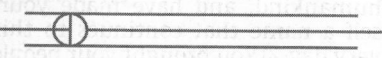

PONDER

This is the covenant that I will make with the house of Israel after those days, says the LORD: I will put my law within them, and I will write it on their hearts; and I will be their God, and they shall be my people.
—Jeremiah 31.33

PRAY

O Father, we come before you searching for your truth and your presence. We are awed that the covenant you made with Abraham, Moses, David and Israel is fulfilled in the covenant you made with us in our Savior, Jesus Christ. You have given us these great promises, to write your law on our minds and hearts. Help us demonstrate in our daily lives that we are children of your covenant with truth, humility, service, forgiveness, generosity, compassion and love. We ask this in the name of our Savior, Jesus Christ. Amen.

³⁵ Thus says the LORD,
who gives the sun for light by day
and the fixed order of the
moon and the stars
for light by night,
who stirs up the sea so that
its waves roar—
the LORD of hosts is his name:
³⁶ If this fixed order were
ever to cease
from my presence, says
the LORD,
then also the offspring of
Israel would cease
to be a nation before
me forever.

³⁷ Thus says the LORD:
If the heavens above can
be measured,
and the foundations of
the earth below
can be explored,
then I will reject all the
offspring of Israel
because of all they
have done,
says the LORD.

JERUSALEM TO BE ENLARGED

³⁸ The days are surely coming, says the LORD, when the city shall be rebuilt for the LORD from the tower of Hananel to the Corner Gate. ³⁹And the measuring line shall go out farther, straight to the hill Gareb, and shall then turn to Goah. ⁴⁰The whole valley of the dead bodies and the ashes, and all the fields as far as the Wadi Kidron, to the corner of the Horse Gate toward the east, shall be sacred to the LORD. It shall never again be uprooted or overthrown.

JEREMIAH BUYS A FIELD DURING THE SIEGE

32 The word that came to Jeremiah from the LORD in the tenth year of King Zedekiah of Judah, which was the eighteenth year of Nebuchadrezzar. ²At that time the army of the king of Babylon was besieging Jerusalem, and the prophet Jeremiah was confined in the court of the guard that was in the palace of the king of Judah, ³where King Zedekiah of Judah had confined him. Zedekiah had said, "Why do you prophesy and say: Thus says the LORD: I am going to give this city into the hand of the king of Babylon, and he shall take it; ⁴King Zedekiah of Judah shall not escape out of the hands of the Chaldeans, but shall surely be given into the hands of the king of Babylon, and shall speak with him face to face and see him eye to eye; ⁵and he shall take Zedekiah to Babylon, and there he shall remain until I attend to him, says the LORD; though you fight against the Chaldeans, you shall not succeed?"

6 Jeremiah said, The word of the LORD came to me: 7Hanamel son of your uncle Shallum is going to come to you and say, "Buy my field that is at Anathoth, for the right of redemption by purchase is yours." 8Then my cousin Hanamel came to me in the court of the guard, in accordance with the word of the LORD, and said to me, "Buy my field that is at Anathoth in the land of Benjamin, for the right of possession and redemption is yours; buy it for yourself." Then I knew that this was the word of the LORD.

9 And I bought the field at Anathoth from my cousin Hanamel, and weighed out the money to him, seventeen shekels of silver. 10I signed the deed, sealed it, got witnesses, and weighed the money on scales. 11Then I took the sealed deed of purchase, containing the terms and conditions, and the open copy; 12and I gave the deed of purchase to Baruch son of Neriah son of Mahseiah, in the presence of my cousin Hanamel, in the presence of the witnesses who signed the deed of purchase, and in the presence of all the Judeans who were sitting in the court of the guard. 13In their presence I charged Baruch, saying, 14Thus says the LORD of hosts, the God of Israel: Take these deeds, both this sealed deed of purchase and this open deed, and put them in an earthenware jar, in order that they may last for a long time. 15For thus says the LORD of hosts, the God of Israel: Houses and fields and vineyards shall again be bought in this land.

JEREMIAH PRAYS FOR UNDERSTANDING

16 After I had given the deed of purchase to Baruch son of Neriah, I prayed to the LORD, saying: 17Ah Lord GOD! It is you who made the heavens and the earth by your great power and by your outstretched arm! Nothing is too hard for you. 18You show steadfast love to the thousandth generation,ᵃ but repay the guilt of parents into the laps of their children after them, O great and mighty God whose name is the LORD of hosts, 19great in counsel and mighty in deed; whose eyes are open to all the ways of mortals, rewarding all according to their ways and according to the fruit of their doings. 20You showed signs and wonders in the land of Egypt, and to this day in Israel and among all humankind, and have made yourself a name that continues to this very day. 21You brought your people Israel out of the land of Egypt with signs and wonders, with a strong hand and outstretched arm, and with great terror; 22and you gave them this land, which you swore to their ancestors to give them, a land flowing with milk and honey; 23and they entered and took possession of it. But they did not obey your voice or follow your law; of all you commanded them to do, they did nothing. Therefore you have made all these disasters come upon them. 24See, the siege ramps have been cast up against the city to take it, and the city, faced with sword, famine, and pestilence, has been given into the hands of the Chaldeans who are fighting against it. What you spoke has happened, as you yourself can see. 25Yet you, O Lord GOD, have said to me, "Buy the field for money and get witnesses"—though the city has been given into the hands of the Chaldeans.

GOD'S ASSURANCE OF THE PEOPLE'S RETURN

26 The word of the LORD came to Jeremiah: 27See, I am the LORD, the God of all flesh; is anything too hard for me? 28Therefore, thus says the LORD: I am going to give this city into the hands of the Chaldeans and into the hand of King Nebuchadrezzar of Babylon, and he shall take it. 29The Chaldeans who are fighting against this city shall come, set it on fire, and burn it, with the houses on whose roofs offerings have been made to Baal and libations have been poured out to other gods, to provoke me to anger. 30For the people of Israel and the

ᵃ 32.18 Or to thousands

PONDER

See, I am the LORD, the God of all flesh; is anything too hard for me?
—Jeremiah 32.27

PRAY

Lord God, we are grateful to learn a little more about Jeremiah, the people of Judah, and perhaps even more about ourselves and how the simplicity of your loving act—giving us Jesus Christ as our Savior—can prevent our feeling unsure of the future or having a sense of helplessness. We know that you are Lord of the universe and are in control.

We know through faith in our Savior that our hope can be strengthened and made secure. We pray that we might go one step further after faith and hope, and learn not only to let you love us, but also to love others unselfishly. Let us learn that with love comes the fulfillment of our faith and hope. We ask these things in the name of our Savior. Amen.

people of Judah have done nothing but evil in my sight from their youth; the people of Israel have done nothing but provoke me to anger by the work of their hands, says the LORD. 31This city has aroused my anger and wrath, from the day it was built until this day, so that I will remove it from my sight 32because of all the evil of the people of Israel and the people of Judah that they did to provoke me to anger—they, their kings and their officials, their priests and their prophets, the citizens of Judah and the inhabitants of Jerusalem. 33They have turned their backs to me, not their faces; though I have taught them persistently, they would not listen and accept correction. 34They set up their abominations in the house that bears my name, and defiled it. 35They built the high places of Baal in the valley of the son of Hinnom, to offer up

their sons and daughters to Molech, though I did not command them, nor did it enter my mind that they should do this abomination, causing Judah to sin.

36 Now therefore thus says the LORD, the God of Israel, concerning this city of which you say, "It is being given into the hand of the king of Babylon by the sword, by famine, and by pestilence": 37See, I am going to gather them from all the lands to which I drove them in my anger and my wrath and in great indignation; I will bring them back to this place, and I will settle them in safety. 38They shall be my people, and I will be their God. 39I will give them one heart and one way, that they may fear me for all time, for their own good and the good of their children after them. 40I will make an everlasting covenant with them, never to draw back from doing good to them; and I will put the fear of me in their hearts, so that they may not turn from me. 41I will rejoice in doing good to them, and I will plant them in this land in faithfulness, with all my heart and all my soul.

42 For thus says the LORD: Just as I have brought all this great disaster upon this people, so I will bring upon them all the good fortune that I now promise them. 43Fields shall be bought in this land of which you are saying, It is a desolation, without human beings or animals; it has been given into the hands of the Chaldeans. 44Fields shall be bought for money, and deeds shall be signed and sealed and witnessed, in the land of Benjamin, in the places around Jerusalem, and in the cities of Judah, of the hill country, of the Shephelah, and of the Negeb; for I will restore their fortunes, says the LORD.

HEALING AFTER PUNISHMENT

33 The word of the LORD came to Jeremiah a second time, while he was still confined in the court of the guard: 2Thus says the LORD who made the earth,[a] the

[a] 33.2 Gk: Heb it

LORD who formed it to establish it—the LORD is his name: ³Call to me and I will answer you, and will tell you great and hidden things that you have not known. ⁴For thus says the LORD, the God of Israel, concerning the houses of this city and the houses of the kings of Judah that were torn down to make a defense against the siege ramps and before the sword:ᵃ ⁵The Chaldeans are coming in to fightᵇ and to fill them with the dead bodies of those whom I shall strike down in my anger and my wrath, for I have hidden my face from this city because of all their wickedness. ⁶I am going to bring it recovery and healing; I will heal them and reveal to them abundanceᵃ of prosperity and security. ⁷I will restore the fortunes of Judah and the fortunes of Israel, and rebuild them as they were at first. ⁸I will cleanse them from all the guilt of their sin against me, and I will forgive all the guilt of their sin and rebellion against me. ⁹And this cityᶜ shall be to me a name of joy, a praise and a glory before all the nations of the earth who shall hear of all the good that I do for them; they shall fear and tremble because of all the good and all the prosperity I provide for it.

¹⁰Thus says the LORD: In this place of which you say, "It is a waste without human beings or animals," in the towns of Judah and the streets of Jerusalem that are desolate, without inhabitants, human or animal, there shall once more be heard ¹¹the voice of mirth and the voice of gladness, the voice of the bridegroom and the voice of the bride, the voices of those who sing, as they bring thank offerings to the house of the LORD:

"Give thanks to the LORD of hosts,
   for the LORD is good,
   for his steadfast love
      endures forever!"

For I will restore the fortunes of the land as at first, says the LORD.

¹²Thus says the LORD of hosts: In this place that is waste, without human beings or animals, and in all its towns there shall again be pasture for shepherds resting their flocks. ¹³In the towns of the hill country, of the Shephelah, and of the Negeb, in the land of Benjamin, the places around Jerusalem, and in the towns of Judah, flocks shall again pass under the hands of the one who counts them, says the LORD.

THE RIGHTEOUS BRANCH AND THE COVENANT WITH DAVID

¹⁴The days are surely coming, says the LORD, when I will fulfill the promise I made to the house of Israel and the house of Judah. ¹⁵In those days and at that time I will cause a

ᵃ 33.4,6 Meaning of Heb uncertain
ᵇ 33.5 Cn: Heb *They are coming in to fight against the Chaldeans*   ᶜ 33.9 Heb *And it*

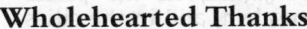

BIBLE IN LIFE

Wholehearted Thanks   *Jeremiah 33.6–11*

"Give thanks to the LORD, for he is good" (Psalm 136.1). These words voice the insurmountable joy and thankfulness that the people of Judah would again feel toward God after their restoration. As people who have been restored to God through Christ, can we recite these words wholeheartedly? We are sometimes uncertain about our own degree of success. We question the purpose of life. We dwell on the little things that aggravate us. We feel jealous of others. We gossip about and resent others. We are sometimes quite unwilling to acknowledge our own need to change, so we tend to compare ourselves with whatever competition we feel is inferior to us. And we think that will make us feel "good." But if we are courageous enough to compare our lives with the perfect life of Christ, we realize that we are in need of God's forgiveness; his grace is available to us because of Christ's death on the cross. And through the process of being forgiven, we find a joyful, sincere attitude toward God, which is thankfulness.

righteous Branch to spring up for David; and he shall execute justice and righteousness in the land. 16In those days Judah will be saved and Jerusalem will live in safety. And this is the name by which it will be called: "The LORD is our righteousness."

17 For thus says the LORD: David shall never lack a man to sit on the throne of the house of Israel, 18and the levitical priests shall never lack a man in my presence to offer burnt offerings, to make grain offerings, and to make sacrifices for all time.

19 The word of the LORD came to Jeremiah: 20Thus says the LORD: If any of you could break my covenant with the day and my covenant with the night, so that day and night would not come at their appointed time, 21only then could my covenant with my servant David be broken, so that he would not have a son to reign on his throne, and my covenant with my ministers the Levites. 22Just as the host of heaven cannot be numbered and the sands of the sea cannot be measured, so I will increase the offspring of my servant David, and the Levites who minister to me.

23 The word of the LORD came to Jeremiah: 24Have you not observed how these people say, "The two families that the LORD chose have been rejected by him," and how they hold my people in such contempt that they no longer regard them as a nation? 25Thus says the LORD: Only if I had not established my covenant with day and night and the ordinances of heaven and earth, 26would I reject the offspring of Jacob and of my servant David and not choose any of his descendants as rulers over the offspring of Abraham, Isaac, and Jacob. For I will restore their fortunes, and will have mercy upon them.

DEATH IN CAPTIVITY
PREDICTED FOR ZEDEKIAH

34 The word that came to Jeremiah from the LORD, when King Nebuchadrezzar of Babylon and all his army and all the king-doms of the earth and all the peoples under his dominion were fighting against Jerusalem and all its cities: 2Thus says the LORD, the God of Israel: Go and speak to King Zedekiah of Judah and say to him: Thus says the LORD: I am going to give this city into the hand of the king of Babylon, and he shall burn it with fire. 3And you yourself shall not escape from his hand, but shall surely be captured and handed over to him; you shall see the king of Babylon eye to eye and speak with him face to face; and you shall go to Babylon. 4Yet hear the word of the LORD, O King Zedekiah of Judah! Thus says the LORD concerning you: You shall not die by the sword; 5you shall die in peace. And as spices were burned[a] for your ancestors, the earlier kings who preceded you, so they shall burn spices[b] for you and lament for you, saying, "Alas, lord!" For I have spoken the word, says the LORD.

6 Then the prophet Jeremiah spoke all these words to Zedekiah king of Judah, in Jerusalem, 7when the army of the king of Babylon was fighting against Jerusalem and against all the cities of Judah that were left, Lachish and Azekah; for these were the only fortified cities of Judah that remained.

TREACHEROUS TREATMENT
OF SLAVES

8 The word that came to Jeremiah from the LORD, after King Zedekiah had made a covenant with all the people in Jerusalem to make a proclamation of liberty to them— 9that all should set free their Hebrew slaves, male and female, so that no one should hold another Judean in slavery. 10And they obeyed, all the officials and all the people who had entered into the covenant that all would set free their slaves, male or female, so that they would not be enslaved again; they obeyed and set them free. 11But afterward they turned around and took back the male and female slaves they had set

---

[a] 34.5 Heb *as there was burning*
[b] 34.5 Heb *shall burn*

free, and brought them again into subjection as slaves. 12The word of the LORD came to Jeremiah from the LORD: 13Thus says the LORD, the God of Israel: I myself made a covenant with your ancestors when I brought them out of the land of Egypt, out of the house of slavery, saying, 14"Every seventh year each of you must set free any Hebrews who have been sold to you and have served you six years; you must set them free from your service." But your ancestors did not listen to me or incline their ears to me. 15You yourselves recently repented and did what was right in my sight by proclaiming liberty to one another, and you made a covenant before me in the house that is called by my name; 16but then you turned around and profaned my name when each of you took back your male and female slaves, whom you had set free according to their desire, and you brought them again into subjection to be your slaves. 17Therefore, thus says the LORD: You have not obeyed me by granting a release to your neighbors and friends; I am going to grant a release to you, says the LORD—a release to the sword, to pestilence, and to famine. I will make you a horror to all the kingdoms of the earth. 18And those who transgressed my covenant and did not keep the terms of the covenant that they made before me, I will make likea the calf when they cut it in two and passed between its parts: 19the officials of Judah, the officials of Jerusalem, the eunuchs, the priests, and all the people of the land who passed between the parts of the calf 20shall be handed over to their enemies and to those who seek their lives. Their corpses shall become food for the birds of the air and the wild animals of the earth. 21And as for King Zedekiah of Judah and his officials, I will hand them over to their enemies and to those who seek their lives, to the army of the king of Babylon, which has withdrawn from you. 22I am going to command, says the LORD, and will bring them back to this city; and they will fight against it, and take it, and burn

it with fire. The towns of Judah I will make a desolation without inhabitant.

THE RECHABITES COMMENDED

35 The word that came to Jeremiah from the LORD in the days of King Jehoiakim son of Josiah of Judah: 2Go to the house of the Rechabites, and speak with them, and bring them to the house of the LORD, into one of the chambers; then offer them wine to drink. 3So I took Jaazaniah son of Jeremiah son of Habazziniah, and his brothers, and all his sons, and the whole house of the Rechabites. 4I brought them to the house of the LORD into the chamber of the sons of Hanan son of Igdaliah, the man of God, which was near the chamber of the officials, above the chamber of Maaseiah son of Shallum, keeper of the threshold. 5Then I set before the Rechabites pitchers full of wine, and cups; and I said to them, "Have some wine." 6But they answered, "We will drink no wine, for our ancestor Jonadab son of Rechab commanded us, 'You shall never drink wine, neither you nor your children; 7nor shall you ever build a house, or sow seed; nor shall you plant a vineyard, or even own one; but you shall live in tents all your days, that you may live many days in the land where you reside.' 8We have obeyed the charge of our ancestor Jonadab son of Rechab in all that he commanded us, to drink no wine all our days, ourselves, our wives, our sons, or our daughters, 9and not to build houses to live in. We have no vineyard or field or seed; 10but we have lived in tents, and have obeyed and done all that our ancestor Jonadab commanded us. 11But when King Nebuchadrezzar of Babylon came up against the land, we said, 'Come, and let us go to Jerusalem for fear of the army of the Chaldeans and the army of the Arameans.' That is why we are living in Jerusalem."

12 Then the word of the LORD came to Jeremiah: 13Thus says the LORD of hosts, the God of Israel: Go

a 34.18 Cn: Heb lacks like

and say to the people of Judah and the inhabitants of Jerusalem, Can you not learn a lesson and obey my words? says the LORD. 14 The command has been carried out that Jonadab son of Rechab gave to his descendants to drink no wine; and they drink none to this day, for they have obeyed their ancestor's command. But I myself have spoken to you persistently, and you have not obeyed me. 15 I have sent to you all my servants the prophets, sending them persistently, saying, "Turn now every one of you from your evil way, and amend your doings, and do not go after other gods to serve them, and then you shall live in the land that I gave to you and your ancestors." But you did not incline your ear or obey me. 16 The descendants of Jonadab son of Rechab have carried out the command that their ancestor gave them, but this people has not obeyed me. 17 Therefore, thus says the LORD, the God of hosts, the God of Israel: I am going to bring on Judah and on all the inhabitants of Jerusalem every disaster that I have pronounced against them; because I have spoken to them and they have not listened, I have called to them and they have not answered.

18 But to the house of the Rechabites Jeremiah said: Thus says the LORD of hosts, the God of Israel: Because you have obeyed the command of your ancestor Jonadab, and kept all his precepts, and done all that he commanded you, 19 therefore thus says the LORD of hosts, the God of Israel: Jonadab son of Rechab shall not lack a descendant to stand before me for all time.

THE SCROLL READ
IN THE TEMPLE

36 In the fourth year of King Jehoiakim son of Josiah of Judah, this word came to Jeremiah from the LORD: 2 Take a scroll and write on it all the words that I have spoken to you against Israel and Judah and all the nations, from the day I spoke to you, from the days of Josiah until today. 3 It may be that when the house of Judah hears of all the disasters that I intend to do to them, all of them may turn from their evil ways, so that I may forgive their iniquity and their sin.

4 Then Jeremiah called Baruch son of Neriah, and Baruch wrote on a scroll at Jeremiah's dictation all the words of the LORD that he had spoken to him. 5 And Jeremiah ordered Baruch, saying, "I am prevented from entering the house of the LORD; 6 so you go yourself, and on a fast day in the hearing of the people in the LORD's house you shall read the words of the LORD from the scroll that you have written at my dictation. You shall read them also in the hearing of all the people of Judah who come up from their towns. 7 It may be that their plea will come before the LORD, and that all of them will turn from their evil ways, for great is the anger and wrath that the LORD has pronounced against this people." 8 And Baruch son of Neriah did all that the prophet Jeremiah ordered him about reading from the scroll the words of the LORD in the LORD's house.

9 In the fifth year of King Jehoiakim son of Josiah of Judah, in the ninth month, all the people in Jerusalem and all the people who came from the towns of Judah to Jerusalem proclaimed a fast before the LORD. 10 Then, in the hearing of all the people, Baruch read the words of Jeremiah from the scroll, in the house of the LORD, in the chamber of Gemariah son of Shaphan the secretary, which was in the upper court, at the entry of the New Gate of the LORD's house.

THE SCROLL READ
IN THE PALACE

11 When Micaiah son of Gemariah son of Shaphan heard all the words of the LORD from the scroll, 12 he went down to the king's house, into the secretary's chamber; and all the officials were sitting there: Elishama the secretary, Delaiah son of Shemaiah, Elnathan son of Achbor, Gemariah son of Shaphan, Zedekiah son of Hananiah, and all the officials. 13 And Micaiah told them all the

words that he had heard, when Baruch read the scroll in the hearing of the people. ¹⁴Then all the officials sent Jehudi son of Nethaniah son of Shelemiah son of Cushi to say to Baruch, "Bring the scroll that you read in the hearing of the people, and come." So Baruch son of Neriah took the scroll in his hand and came to them. ¹⁵And they said to him, "Sit down and read it to us." So Baruch read it to them. ¹⁶When they heard all the words, they turned to one another in alarm, and said to Baruch, "We certainly must report all these words to the king." ¹⁷Then they questioned Baruch, "Tell us now, how did you write all these words? Was it at his dictation?" ¹⁸Baruch answered them, "He dictated all these words to me, and I wrote them with ink on the scroll." ¹⁹Then the officials said to Baruch, "Go and hide, you and Jeremiah, and let no one know where you are."

JEHOIAKIM BURNS THE SCROLL

20 Leaving the scroll in the chamber of Elishama the secretary, they went to the court of the king; and they reported all the words to the king. ²¹Then the king sent Jehudi to get the scroll, and he took it from the chamber of Elishama the secretary; and Jehudi read it to the king and all the officials who stood beside the king. ²²Now the king was sitting in his winter apartment (it was the ninth month), and there was a fire burning in the brazier before him. ²³As Jehudi read three or four columns, the king^a would cut them off with a penknife and throw them into the fire in the brazier, until the entire scroll was consumed in the fire that was in the brazier. ²⁴Yet neither the king, nor any of his servants who heard all these words, was alarmed, nor did they tear their garments. ²⁵Even when Elnathan and Delaiah and Gemariah urged the king not to burn the scroll, he would not listen to them. ²⁶And the king commanded Jerahmeel the king's son and Seraiah son of Azriel and Shelemiah son of Abdeel to arrest the secretary Baruch and the

prophet Jeremiah. But the LORD hid them.

JEREMIAH DICTATES ANOTHER

27 Now, after the king had burned the scroll with the words that Baruch wrote at Jeremiah's dictation, the word of the LORD came to Jeremiah: ²⁸Take another scroll and write on it all the former words that were in the first scroll, which King Jehoiakim of Judah has burned. ²⁹And concerning King Jehoiakim of Judah you shall say: Thus says the LORD, You have dared to burn this scroll, saying, Why have you written in it that the king of Babylon will certainly come and destroy this land, and will cut off from it human beings and animals? ³⁰Therefore thus says the LORD concerning King Jehoiakim of Judah: He shall have no one to sit upon the throne of David, and his dead body shall be cast out to the heat by day and the frost by night. ³¹And I will punish him and his offspring and his servants for their iniquity; I will bring on them, and on the inhabitants of Jerusalem, and on the people of Judah, all the disasters with which I have threatened them—but they would not listen.

32 Then Jeremiah took another scroll and gave it to the secretary Baruch son of Neriah, who wrote on it at Jeremiah's dictation all the words of the scroll that King Jehoiakim of Judah had burned in the fire; and many similar words were added to them.

ZEDEKIAH'S VAIN HOPE

37 Zedekiah son of Josiah, whom King Nebuchadrezzar of Babylon made king in the land of Judah, succeeded Coniah son of Jehoiakim. ²But neither he nor his servants nor the people of the land listened to the words of the LORD that he spoke through the prophet Jeremiah.

3 King Zedekiah sent Jehucal son of Shelemiah and the priest Zephaniah son of Maaseiah to the prophet Jeremiah saying, "Please pray for

a 36.23 Heb *he*

us to the LORD our God." 4Now Jeremiah was still going in and out among the people, for he had not yet been put in prison. 5Meanwhile, the army of Pharaoh had come out of Egypt; and when the Chaldeans who were besieging Jerusalem heard news of them, they withdrew from Jerusalem.

6 Then the word of the LORD came to the prophet Jeremiah: 7Thus says the LORD, God of Israel: This is what the two of you shall say to the king of Judah, who sent you to me to inquire of me: Pharaoh's army, which set out to help you, is going to return to its own land, to Egypt. 8And the Chaldeans shall return and fight against this city; they shall take it and burn it with fire. 9Thus says the LORD: Do not deceive yourselves, saying, "The Chaldeans will surely go away from us," for they will not go away. 10Even if you defeated the whole army of Chaldeans who are fighting against you, and there remained of them only wounded men in their tents, they would rise up and burn this city with fire.

JEREMIAH IS IMPRISONED

11 Now when the Chaldean army had withdrawn from Jerusalem at the approach of Pharaoh's army, 12Jeremiah set out from Jerusalem to go to the land of Benjamin to receive his share of property[a] among the people there. 13When he reached the Benjamin Gate, a sentinel there named Irijah son of Shelemiah son of Hananiah arrested the prophet Jeremiah saying, "You are deserting to the Chaldeans." 14And Jeremiah said, "That is a lie; I am not deserting to the Chaldeans." But Irijah would not listen to him, and arrested Jeremiah and brought him to the officials. 15The officials were enraged at Jeremiah, and they beat him and imprisoned him in the house of the secretary Jonathan, for it had been made a prison. 16Thus Jeremiah was put in the cistern house, in the cells, and remained there many days.

17 Then King Zedekiah sent for him, and received him. The king questioned him secretly in his house, and said, "Is there any word from the LORD?" Jeremiah said, "There is!" Then he said, "You shall be handed over to the king of Babylon." 18Jeremiah also said to King Zedekiah, "What wrong have I done to you or your servants or this people, that you have put me in prison? 19Where are your prophets who prophesied to you, saying, 'The king of Babylon will not come against you and against this land'? 20Now please hear me, my lord king: be good enough to listen to my plea, and do not send me back to the house of the secretary Jonathan to die there." 21So King Zedekiah gave orders, and they committed Jeremiah to the court of the guard; and a loaf of bread was given him daily from the bakers' street, until all the bread of the city was gone. So Jeremiah remained in the court of the guard.

JEREMIAH IN THE CISTERN

38 Now Shephatiah son of Mattan, Gedaliah son of Pashhur, Jucal son of Shelemiah, and Pashhur son of Malchiah heard the words that Jeremiah was saying to all the people, 2Thus says the LORD, Those who stay in this city shall die by the sword, by famine, and by pestilence; but those who go out to the Chaldeans shall live; they shall have their lives as a prize of war, and live. 3Thus says the LORD, This city shall surely be handed over to the army of the king of Babylon and be taken. 4Then the officials said to the king, "This man ought to be put to death, because he is discouraging the soldiers who are left in this city, and all the people, by speaking such words to them. For this man is not seeking the welfare of this people, but their harm." 5King Zedekiah said, "Here he is; he is in your hands; for the king is powerless against you." 6So they took Jeremiah and threw him into the cistern of Malchiah, the king's son, which was in the court of the guard, letting Jeremiah down by ropes. Now there was no water in

[a] 37.12 Meaning of Heb uncertain

the cistern, but only mud, and Jeremiah sank in the mud.

JEREMIAH IS RESCUED BY EBED-MELECH

7 Ebed-melech the Ethiopian,[a] a eunuch in the king's house, heard that they had put Jeremiah into the cistern. The king happened to be sitting at the Benjamin Gate, 8 So Ebed-melech left the king's house and spoke to the king, 9 "My lord king, these men have acted wickedly in all they did to the prophet Jeremiah by throwing him into the cistern to die there of hunger, for there is no bread left in the city." 10 Then the king commanded Ebed-melech the Ethiopian,[a] "Take three men with you from here, and pull the prophet Jeremiah up from the cistern before he dies." 11 So Ebed-melech took the men with him and went to the house of the king, to a wardrobe of[b] the storehouse, and took from there old rags and worn-out clothes, which he let down to Jeremiah in the cistern by ropes. 12 Then Ebed-melech the Ethiopian[a] said to Jeremiah, "Just put the rags and clothes between your armpits and the ropes." Jeremiah did so. 13 Then they drew Jeremiah up by the ropes and pulled him out of the cistern. And Jeremiah remained in the court of the guard.

PROPHETS—AND DISCIPLES—

ARE RESPONSIBLE FOR

DELIVERING THE MESSAGE,

NOT FOR HOW THE

MESSAGE IS RECEIVED.

ZEDEKIAH CONSULTS JEREMIAH AGAIN

14 King Zedekiah sent for the prophet Jeremiah and received him at the third entrance of the temple of the LORD. The king said to Jeremiah, "I have something to ask you; do not hide anything from me." 15 Jeremiah said to Zedekiah, "If I tell you, you will put me to death, will you not? And if I give you advice, you will not listen to me." 16 So King Zedekiah swore an oath in secret to Jeremiah, "As the LORD lives, who gave us our lives, I will not put you to death or hand you over to these men who seek your life."

17 Then Jeremiah said to Zedekiah, "Thus says the LORD, the God of hosts, the God of Israel, If you will only surrender to the officials of the king of Babylon, then your life shall be spared, and this city shall not be burned with fire, and you and your house shall live. 18 But if you do not surrender to the officials of the king of Babylon, then this city shall be handed over to the Chaldeans, and they shall burn it with fire, and you yourself shall not escape from their hand." 19 King Zedekiah said to Jeremiah, "I am afraid of the Judeans who have deserted to the Chaldeans, for I might be handed over to them and they would abuse me." 20 Jeremiah said, "That will not happen. Just obey the voice of the LORD in what I say to you, and it shall go well with you, and your life shall be spared. 21 But if you are determined not to surrender, this is what the LORD has shown me— 22 a vision of all the women remaining in the house of the king of Judah being led out to the officials of the king of Babylon and saying,

'Your trusted friends have
     seduced you
    and have overcome you;
Now that your feet are stuck
     in the mud,
    they desert you.'

23 All your wives and your children shall be led out to the Chaldeans, and you yourself shall not escape from their hand, but shall be seized by the king of Babylon; and this city shall be burned with fire."

24 Then Zedekiah said to Jeremiah, "Do not let anyone else know of this conversation, or you will die.

a 38.7,10,12 Or Nubian; Heb Cushite
b 38.11 Cn: Heb to under

25If the officials should hear that I have spoken with you, and they should come and say to you, 'Just tell us what you said to the king; do not conceal it from us, or we will put you to death. What did the king say to you?' 26then you shall say to them, 'I was presenting my plea to the king not to send me back to the house of Jonathan to die there.' " 27All the officials did come to Jeremiah and questioned him; and he answered them in the very words the king had commanded. So they stopped questioning him, for the conversation had not been overheard. 28And Jeremiah remained in the court of the guard until the day that Jerusalem was taken.

THE FALL OF JERUSALEM

39 In the ninth year of King Zedekiah of Judah, in the tenth month, King Nebuchadrezzar of Babylon and all his army came against Jerusalem and besieged it; 2in the eleventh year of Zedekiah, in the fourth month, on the ninth day of the month, a breach was made in the city. 3When Jerusalem was taken,a all the officials of the king of Babylon came and sat in the middle gate: Nergal-sharezer, Samgar-nebo, Sarsechim the Rabsaris, Nergal-sharezer the Rabmag, with all the rest of the officials of the king of Babylon. 4When King Zedekiah of Judah and all the soldiers saw them, they fled, going out of the city at night by way of the king's garden through the gate between the two walls; and they went toward the Arabah. 5But the army of the Chaldeans pursued them, and overtook Zedekiah in the plains of Jericho; and when they had taken him, they brought him up to King Nebuchadrezzar of Babylon, at Riblah, in the land of Hamath; and he passed sentence on him. 6The king of Babylon slaughtered the sons of Zedekiah at Riblah before his eyes; also the king of Babylon slaughtered all the nobles of Judah. 7He put out the eyes of Zedekiah, and bound him in fetters to take him to Babylon. 8The Chaldeans burned the king's house and the houses of the people,

and broke down the walls of Jerusalem. 9Then Nebuzaradan the captain of the guard exiled to Babylon the rest of the people who were left in the city, those who had deserted to him, and the people who remained. 10Nebuzaradan the captain of the guard left in the land of Judah some of the poor people who owned nothing, and gave them vineyards and fields at the same time.

JEREMIAH, SET FREE, REMEMBERS EBED-MELECH

11 King Nebuchadrezzar of Babylon gave command concerning Jeremiah through Nebuzaradan, the captain of the guard, saying, 12"Take him, look after him well and do him no harm, but deal with him as he may ask you." 13So Nebuzaradan the captain of the guard, Nebushazban the Rabsaris, Nergal-sharezer the Rabmag, and all the chief officers of the king of Babylon sent 14and took Jeremiah from the court of the guard. They entrusted him to Gedaliah son of Ahikam son of Shaphan to be brought home. So he stayed with his own people.

15 The word of the LORD came to Jeremiah while he was confined in the court of the guard: 16Go and say to Ebed-melech the Ethiopian:b Thus says the LORD of hosts, the God of Israel: I am going to fulfill my words against this city for evil and not for good, and they shall be accomplished in your presence on that day. 17But I will save you on that day, says the LORD, and you shall not be handed over to those whom you dread. 18For I will surely save you, and you shall not fall by the sword; but you shall have your life as a prize of war, because you have trusted in me, says the LORD.

JEREMIAH WITH GEDALIAH THE GOVERNOR

40 The word that came to Jeremiah from the LORD after Nebuzaradan the captain of the guard had let him go from Ramah,

a 39.3 This clause has been transposed from 38.28   b 39.16 Or Nubian; Heb Cushite

when he took him bound in fetters along with all the captives of Jerusalem and Judah who were being exiled to Babylon. 2The captain of the guard took Jeremiah and said to him, "The LORD your God threatened this place with this disaster; 3and now the LORD has brought it about, and has done as he said, because all of you sinned against the LORD and did not obey his voice. Therefore this thing has come upon you. 4Now look, I have just released you today from the fetters on your hands. If you wish to come with me to Babylon, come, and I will take good care of you; but if you do not wish to come with me to Babylon, you need not come. See, the whole land is before you; go wherever you think it good and right to go. 5If you remain,ᵃ then return to Gedaliah son of Ahikam son of Shaphan, whom the king of Babylon appointed governor of the towns of Judah, and stay with him among the people; or go wherever you think it right to go." So the captain of the guard gave him an allowance of food and a present, and let him go. 6Then Jeremiah went to Gedaliah son of Ahikam at Mizpah, and stayed with him among the people who were left in the land.

7 When all the leaders of the forces in the open country and their troops heard that the king of Babylon had appointed Gedaliah son of Ahikam governor in the land, and had committed to him men, women, and children, those of the poorest of the land who had not been taken into exile to Babylon, 8they went to Gedaliah at Mizpah—Ishmael son of Nethaniah, Johanan son of Kareah, Seraiah son of Tanhumeth, the sons of Ephai the Netophathite, Jezaniah son of the Maacathite, they and their troops. 9Gedaliah son of Ahikam son of Shaphan swore to them and their troops, saying, "Do not be afraid to serve the Chaldeans. Stay in the land and serve the king of Babylon, and it shall go well with you. 10As for me, I am staying at Mizpah to represent you before the Chaldeans who come to us; but as for you, gather

wine and summer fruits and oil, and store them in your vessels, and live in the towns that you have taken over." 11Likewise, when all the Judeans who were in Moab and among the Ammonites and in Edom and in other lands heard that the king of Babylon had left a remnant in Judah and had appointed Gedaliah son of Ahikam son of Shaphan as governor over them, 12then all the Judeans returned from all the places to which they had been scattered and came to the land of Judah, to Gedaliah at Mizpah; and they gathered wine and summer fruits in great abundance.

13 Now Johanan son of Kareah and all the leaders of the forces in the open country came to Gedaliah at Mizpah 14and said to him, "Are you at all aware that Baalis king of the Ammonites has sent Ishmael son of Nethaniah to take your life?" But Gedaliah son of Ahikam would not believe them. 15Then Johanan son of Kareah spoke secretly to Gedaliah at Mizpah, "Please let me go and kill Ishmael son of Nethaniah, and no one else will know. Why should he take your life, so that all the Judeans who are gathered around you would be scattered, and the remnant of Judah would perish?" 16But Gedaliah son of Ahikam said to Johanan son of Kareah, "Do not do such a thing, for you are telling a lie about Ishmael."

INSURRECTION AGAINST GEDALIAH

41 In the seventh month, Ishmael son of Nethaniah son of Elishama, of the royal family, one of the chief officers of the king, came with ten men to Gedaliah son of Ahikam, at Mizpah. As they ate bread together there at Mizpah, 2Ishmael son of Nethaniah and the ten men with him got up and struck down Gedaliah son of Ahikam son of Shaphan with the sword and killed him, because the king of Babylon had appointed him governor in the land. 3Ishmael also killed all the Judeans who were with Gedaliah at Mizpah,

ᵃ **40.5** Syr: Meaning of Heb uncertain

and the Chaldean soldiers who happened to be there.

4 On the day after the murder of Gedaliah, before anyone knew of it, 5eighty men arrived from Shechem and Shiloh and Samaria, with their beards shaved and their clothes torn, and their bodies gashed, bringing grain offerings and incense to present at the temple of the LORD. 6And Ishmael son of Nethaniah came out from Mizpah to meet them, weeping as he came. As he met them, he said to them, "Come to Gedaliah son of Ahikam." 7When they reached the middle of the city, Ishmael son of Nethaniah and the men with him slaughtered them, and threw them[a] into a cistern. 8But there were ten men among them who said to Ishmael, "Do not kill us, for we have stores of wheat, barley, oil, and honey hidden in the fields." So he refrained, and did not kill them along with their companions.

9 Now the cistern into which Ishmael had thrown all the bodies of the men whom he had struck down was the large cistern[b] that King Asa had made for defense against King Baasha of Israel; Ishmael son of Nethaniah filled that cistern with those whom he had killed. 10Then Ishmael took captive all the rest of the people who were in Mizpah, the king's daughters and all the people who were left at Mizpah, whom Nebuzaradan, the captain of the guard, had committed to Gedaliah son of Ahikam. Ishmael son of Nethaniah took them captive and set out to cross over to the Ammonites.

11 But when Johanan son of Kareah and all the leaders of the forces with him heard of all the crimes that Ishmael son of Nethaniah had done, 12they took all their men and went to fight against Ishmael son of Nethaniah. They came upon him at the great pool that is in Gibeon. 13And when all the people who were with Ishmael saw Johanan son of Kareah and all the leaders of the forces with him, they were glad. 14So all the people whom Ishmael had carried away captive from Mizpah turned around and came back, and went to Johanan son of Kareah. 15But Ishmael son of Nethaniah escaped from Johanan with eight men, and went to the Ammonites. 16Then Johanan son of Kareah and all the leaders of the forces with him took all the rest of the people whom Ishmael son of Nethaniah had carried away captive[c] from Mizpah after he had slain Gedaliah son of Ahikam—soldiers, women, children, and eunuchs, whom Johanan brought back from Gibeon.[d] 17And they set out, and stopped at Geruth Chimham near Bethlehem, intending to go to Egypt 18because of the Chaldeans; for they were afraid of them, because Ishmael son of Nethaniah had killed Gedaliah son of Ahikam, whom the king of Babylon had made governor over the land.

JEREMIAH ADVISES SURVIVORS NOT TO MIGRATE

42 Then all the commanders of the forces, and Johanan son of Kareah and Azariah[e] son of Hoshaiah, and all the people from the least to the greatest, approached 2the prophet Jeremiah and said, "Be good enough to listen to our plea, and pray to the LORD your God for us—for all this remnant. For there are only a few of us left out of many, as your eyes can see. 3Let the LORD your God show us where we should go and what we should do." 4The prophet Jeremiah said to them, "Very well: I am going to pray to the LORD your God as you request, and whatever the LORD answers you I will tell you; I will keep nothing back from you." 5They in their turn said to Jeremiah, "May the LORD be a true and faithful witness against us if we do not act according to everything that the LORD your God sends us through you. 6Whether it is good or bad, we will obey the voice of the LORD our God to whom we are sending you, in order that it may go well

[a] 41.7 Syr: Heb lacks and threw them; compare verse 9   [b] 41.9 Gk: Heb whom he had killed by the hand of Gedaliah   [c] 41.16 Cn: Heb whom he recovered from Ishmael son of Nethaniah   [d] 41.16 Meaning of Heb uncertain   [e] 42.1 Gk: Heb Jezaniah

with us when we obey the voice of the LORD our God."

7 At the end of ten days the word of the LORD came to Jeremiah. 8 Then he summoned Johanan son of Kareah and all the commanders of the forces who were with him, and all the people from the least to the greatest, 9and said to them, "Thus says the LORD, the God of Israel, to whom you sent me to present your plea before him: 10If you will only remain in this land, then I will build you up and not pull you down; I will plant you, and not pluck you up; for I am sorry for the disaster that I have brought upon you. 11Do not be afraid of the king of Babylon, as you have been; do not be afraid of him, says the LORD, for I am with you, to save you and to rescue you from his hand. 12I will grant you mercy, and he will have mercy on you and restore you to your native soil. 13But if you continue to say, 'We will not stay in this land,' thus disobeying the voice of the LORD your God 14and saying, 'No, we will go to the land of Egypt, where we shall not see war, or hear the sound of the trumpet, or be hungry for bread, and there we will stay,' 15then hear the word of the LORD, O remnant of Judah. Thus says the LORD of hosts, the God of Israel: If you are determined to enter Egypt and go to settle there, 16then the sword that you fear shall overtake you there, in the land of Egypt; and the famine that you dread shall follow close after you into Egypt; and there you shall die. 17All the people who have determined to go to Egypt to settle there shall die by the sword, by famine, and by pestilence; they shall have no remnant or survivor from the disaster that I am bringing upon them.

18 "For thus says the LORD of hosts, the God of Israel: Just as my anger and my wrath were poured out on the inhabitants of Jerusalem, so my wrath will be poured out on you when you go to Egypt. You shall become an object of execration and horror, of cursing and ridicule. You shall see this place no more. 19The LORD has said to you, O remnant of Judah, Do not go to Egypt. Be well

aware that I have warned you today 20that you have made a fatal mistake. For you yourselves sent me to the LORD your God, saying, 'Pray for us to the LORD our God, and whatever the LORD our God says, tell us and we will do it.' 21So I have told you today, but you have not obeyed the voice of the LORD your God in anything that he sent me to tell you. 22Be well aware, then, that you shall die by the sword, by famine, and by pestilence in the place where you desire to go and settle."

TAKEN TO EGYPT, JEREMIAH WARNS OF JUDGMENT

43 When Jeremiah finished speaking to all the people all these words of the LORD their God, with which the LORD their God had sent him to them, 2Azariah son of Hoshaiah and Johanan son of Kareah and all the other insolent men said to Jeremiah, "You are telling a lie. The LORD our God did not send you to say, 'Do not go to Egypt to settle there'; 3but Baruch son of Neriah is inciting you against us, to hand us over to the Chaldeans, in order that they may kill us or take us into exile in Babylon." 4So Johanan son of Kareah and all the commanders of the forces and all the people did not obey the voice of the LORD, to stay in the land of Judah. 5But Johanan son of Kareah and all the commanders of the forces took all the remnant of Judah who had returned to settle in the land of Judah from all the nations to which they had been driven— 6the men, the women, the children, the princesses, and everyone whom Nebuzaradan the captain of the guard had left with Gedaliah son of Ahikam son of Shaphan; also the prophet Jeremiah and Baruch son of Neriah. 7And they came into the land of Egypt, for they did not obey the voice of the LORD. And they arrived at Tahpanhes.

8 Then the word of the LORD came to Jeremiah in Tahpanhes: 9Take some large stones in your hands, and bury them in the clay pavement[a] that is at the entrance

---

[a] 43.9 Meaning of Heb uncertain

to Pharaoh's palace in Tahpanhes. Let the Judeans see you do it, [10]and say to them, Thus says the LORD of hosts, the God of Israel: I am going to send and take my servant King Nebuchadrezzar of Babylon, and he[a] will set his throne above these stones that I have buried, and he will spread his royal canopy over them. [11]He shall come and ravage the land of Egypt, giving

those who are destined for
    pestilence, to pestilence,
and those who are destined for
    captivity, to captivity,
and those who are destined for
    the sword, to the sword.

[12]He[b] shall kindle a fire in the temples of the gods of Egypt; and he shall burn them and carry them away captive; and he shall pick clean the land of Egypt, as a shepherd picks his cloak clean of vermin; and he shall depart from there safely. [13]He shall break the obelisks of Heliopolis, which is in the land of Egypt; and the temples of the gods of Egypt he shall burn with fire.

DENUNCIATION OF PERSISTENT IDOLATRY

44 The word that came to Jeremiah for all the Judeans living in the land of Egypt, at Migdol, at Tahpanhes, at Memphis, and in the land of Pathros, [2]Thus says the LORD of hosts, the God of Israel: You yourselves have seen all the disaster that I have brought on Jerusalem and on all the towns of Judah. Look at them; today they are a desolation, without an inhabitant in them, [3]because of the wickedness that they committed, provoking me to anger, in that they went to make offerings and serve other gods that they had not known, neither they, nor you, nor your ancestors. [4]Yet I persistently sent to you all my servants the prophets, saying, "I beg you not to do this abominable thing that I hate!" [5]But they did not listen or incline their ear, to turn from their wickedness and make no offerings to other gods. [6]So my wrath and my anger were poured out and kindled in the towns of Judah and in the streets of Jerusalem; and they became a waste and a desolation, as they still are today. [7]And now thus says the LORD God of hosts, the God of Israel: Why are you doing such great harm to yourselves, to cut off man and woman, child and infant, from the midst of Judah, leaving yourselves without a remnant? [8]Why do you provoke me to anger with the works of your hands, making offerings to other gods in the land of Egypt where you have come to settle? Will you be cut off and become an object of cursing and ridicule among all the nations of the earth? [9]Have you forgotten the crimes of your ancestors, of the kings of Judah, of their[c] wives, your own crimes and those of your wives, which they committed in the land of Judah and in the streets of Jerusalem? [10]They have shown no contrition or fear to this day, nor have they walked in my law and my statutes that I set before you and before your ancestors.

[11] Therefore thus says the LORD of hosts, the God of Israel: I am determined to bring disaster on you, to bring all Judah to an end. [12]I will take the remnant of Judah who are determined to come to the land of Egypt to settle, and they shall perish, everyone; in the land of Egypt they shall fall; by the sword and by famine they shall perish; from the least to the greatest, they shall die by the sword and by famine; and they shall become an object of execration and horror, of cursing and ridicule. [13]I will punish those who live in the land of Egypt, as I have punished Jerusalem, with the sword, with famine, and with pestilence, [14]so that none of the remnant of Judah who have come to settle in the land of Egypt shall escape or survive or return to the land of Judah. Although they long to go back to live there, they shall not go back, except some fugitives.

[15] Then all the men who were aware that their wives had been

---

a [43.10] Gk Syr: Heb *I*   b [43.12] Gk Syr Vg: Heb *I*   c [44.9] Heb *his* making offerings to other gods, and all the women who stood by, a great assembly, all the people who lived in Pathros in the land of Egypt, answered Jeremiah: 16"As for the word that you have spoken to us in the name of the LORD, we are not going to listen to you. 17Instead, we will do everything that we have vowed, make offerings to the queen of heaven and pour out libations to her, just as we and our ancestors, our kings and our officials, used to do in the towns of Judah and in the streets of Jerusalem. We used to have plenty of food, and prospered, and saw no misfortune. 18But from the time we stopped making offerings to the queen of heaven and pouring out libations to her, we have lacked everything and have perished by the sword and by famine." 19And the women said,a "Indeed we will go on making offerings to the queen of heaven and pouring out libations to her; do you think that we made cakes for her, marked with her image, and poured out libations to her without our husbands' being involved?"

20 Then Jeremiah said to all the people, men and women, all the people who were giving him this answer: 21"As for the offerings that you made in the towns of Judah and in the streets of Jerusalem, you and your ancestors, your kings and your officials, and the people of the land, did not the LORD remember them? Did it not come into his mind? 22The LORD could no longer bear the sight of your evil doings, the abominations that you committed; therefore your land became a desolation and a waste and a curse, without inhabitant, as it is to this day. 23It is because you burned offerings, and because you sinned against the LORD and did not obey the voice of the LORD or walk in his law and in his statutes and in his decrees, that this disaster has befallen you, as is still evident today."

24 Jeremiah said to all the people and all the women, "Hear the word of the LORD, all you Judeans who are in the land of Egypt, 25Thus says the LORD of hosts, the God of Israel: You

and your wives have accomplished in deeds what you declared in words, saying, 'We are determined to perform the vows that we have made, to make offerings to the queen of heaven and to pour out libations to her.' By all means, keep your vows and make your libations! 26Therefore hear the word of the LORD, all you Judeans who live in the land of Egypt: Lo, I swear by my great name, says the LORD, that my name shall no longer be pronounced on the lips of any of the people of Judah in all the land of Egypt, saying, 'As the Lord GOD lives.' 27I am going to watch over them for harm and not for good; all the people of Judah who are in the land of Egypt shall perish by the sword and by famine, until not one is left. 28And those who escape the sword shall return from the land of Egypt to the land of Judah, few in number; and all the remnant of Judah, who have come to the land of Egypt to settle, shall know whose words will stand, mine or theirs! 29This shall be the sign to you, says the LORD, that I am going to punish you in this place, in order that you may know that my words against you will surely be carried out: 30Thus says the LORD, I am going to give Pharaoh Hophra, king of Egypt, into the hands of his enemies, those who seek his life, just as I gave King Zedekiah of Judah into the hand of King Nebuchadrezzar of Babylon, his enemy who sought his life."

A WORD OF COMFORT
TO BARUCH

45 The word that the prophet Jeremiah spoke to Baruch son of Neriah, when he wrote these words in a scroll at the dictation of Jeremiah, in the fourth year of King Jehoiakim son of Josiah of Judah: 2Thus says the LORD, the God of Israel, to you, O Baruch: 3You said, "Woe is me! The LORD has added sorrow to my pain; I am weary with my groaning, and I find no rest." 4Thus you shall say to him, "Thus says the

a 44.19 Compare Syr: Heb lacks And the women said

LORD: I am going to break down what I have built, and pluck up what I have planted—that is, the whole land. 5 And you, do you seek great things for yourself? Do not seek them; for I am going to bring disaster upon all flesh, says the LORD; but I will give you your life as a prize of war in every place to which you may go."

GOD IS GRIEVED BY

WICKEDNESS, BICKERING

AMONG BELIEVERS AND

INSINCERE WORSHIP. ALL

THREE RESULT FROM

COMPLACENCY, PRIDE

AND ARROGANCE.

JUDGMENT ON EGYPT

46 The word of the LORD that came to the prophet Jeremiah concerning the nations.

2 Concerning Egypt, about the army of Pharaoh Neco, king of Egypt, which was by the river Euphrates at Carchemish and which King Nebuchadrezzar of Babylon defeated in the fourth year of King Jehoiakim son of Josiah of Judah:

3 Prepare buckler and shield,
   and advance for battle!
4 Harness the horses;
      mount the steeds!
   Take your stations with
         your helmets,
      whet your lances,
      put on your coats of mail!
5 Why do I see them terrified?
   They have fallen back;
   their warriors are beaten down,
      and have fled in haste.
   They do not look back—
      terror is all around!
                     says the LORD.
6 The swift cannot flee away,
   nor can the warrior escape;

in the north by the river Euphrates
   they have stumbled and fallen.

7 Who is this, rising like the Nile,
      like rivers whose waters surge?
8 Egypt rises like the Nile,
      like rivers whose waters surge.
   It said, Let me rise, let me
         cover the earth,
      let me destroy cities and
         their inhabitants.
9 Advance, O horses,
      and dash madly, O chariots!
   Let the warriors go forth:
      Ethiopia[a] and Put who
         carry the shield,
      the Ludim, who draw[b] the bow.
10 That day is the day of the
         Lord GOD of hosts,
      a day of retribution,
      to gain vindication
         from his foes.
   The sword shall devour
         and be sated,
      and drink its fill of their blood.
   For the Lord GOD of hosts
         holds a sacrifice
      in the land of the north by
         the river Euphrates.
11 Go up to Gilead, and take balm,
      O virgin daughter Egypt!
   In vain you have used many
         medicines;
      there is no healing for you.
12 The nations have heard of
         your shame,
      and the earth is full of your cry;
   for warrior has stumbled
         against warrior;
      both have fallen together.

BABYLONIA WILL STRIKE EGYPT

13 The word that the LORD spoke to the prophet Jeremiah about the coming of King Nebuchadrezzar of Babylon to attack the land of Egypt:

14 Declare in Egypt, and
         proclaim in Migdol;
      proclaim in Memphis
         and Tahpanhes;
   Say, "Take your stations
         and be ready,
      for the sword shall devour
         those around you."

a **46.9** Or *Nubia*; Heb *Cush*   b **46.9** Cn: Heb *who grasp, who draw*

¹⁵ Why has Apis fled?^a
Why did your bull not stand?
—because the LORD
thrust him down.
¹⁶ Your multitude stumbled^b
and fell,
and one said to another,^c
"Come, let us go back to
our own people
and to the land of our birth,
because of the destroying
sword."
¹⁷ Give Pharaoh, king of
Egypt, the name
"Braggart who missed
his chance."

¹⁸ As I live, says the King,
whose name is the
LORD of hosts,
one is coming
like Tabor among the
mountains,
and like Carmel by the sea.
¹⁹ Pack your bags for exile,
sheltered daughter Egypt!
For Memphis shall become
a waste,
a ruin, without inhabitant.

²⁰ A beautiful heifer is Egypt—
a gadfly from the north
lights upon her.
²¹ Even her mercenaries in her midst
are like fatted calves;
they too have turned and
fled together,
they did not stand;
for the day of their calamity
has come upon them,
the time of their punishment.

²² She makes a sound like a
snake gliding away;
for her enemies march in force,
and come against her with axes,
like those who fell trees.
²³ They shall cut down her forest,
says the LORD,
though it is impenetrable,
because they are more numerous
than locusts;
they are without number.
²⁴ Daughter Egypt shall be
put to shame;
she shall be handed over to a
people from the north.

²⁵ The LORD of hosts, the God of Israel, said: See, I am bringing punishment upon Amon of Thebes, and Pharaoh, and Egypt and her gods and her kings, upon Pharaoh and those who trust in him. ²⁶ I will hand them over to those who seek their life, to King Nebuchadrezzar of Babylon and his officers. Afterward Egypt shall be inhabited as in the days of old, says the LORD.

GOD WILL SAVE ISRAEL

²⁷ But as for you, have no fear,
my servant Jacob,
and do not be dismayed,
O Israel;
for I am going to save you
from far away,
and your offspring from the
land of their captivity.
Jacob shall return and have
quiet and ease,
and no one shall make
him afraid.
²⁸ As for you, have no fear, my
servant Jacob,
says the LORD,
for I am with you.
I will make an end of all
the nations
among which I have
banished you,
but I will not make an
end of you!
I will chastise you in just measure,
and I will by no means leave
you unpunished.

JUDGMENT ON THE PHILISTINES

47 The word of the LORD that came to the prophet Jeremiah concerning the Philistines, before Pharaoh attacked Gaza:
² Thus says the LORD:
See, waters are rising out
of the north
and shall become an
overflowing torrent;
they shall overflow the land
and all that fills it,
the city and those who
live in it.

^a 46.15 Gk: Heb Why was it swept away
^b 46.16 Gk: Meaning of Heb uncertain
^c 46.16 Gk: Heb and fell one to another and they said

People shall cry out,
and all the inhabitants of
the land shall wail.
3 At the noise of the stamping of
the hoofs of his stallions,
at the clatter of his chariots,
at the rumbling of
their wheels,
parents do not turn back
for children,
so feeble are their hands,
4 because of the day that is coming
to destroy all the Philistines,
to cut off from Tyre and Sidon
every helper that remains.
For the LORD is destroying
the Philistines,
the remnant of the
coastland of Caphtor.
5 Baldness has come upon Gaza,
Ashkelon is silenced.
O remnant of their power!ᵃ
How long will you gash
yourselves?
6 Ah, sword of the LORD!
How long until you are quiet?
Put yourself into your scabbard,
rest and be still!
7 How can itᵇ be quiet,
when the LORD has given
it an order?
Against Ashkelon and against
the seashore—
there he has appointed it.

JUDGMENT ON MOAB

48 Concerning Moab.
Thus says the LORD of hosts, the God
of Israel:
Alas for Nebo, it is laid waste!
Kiriathaim is put to
shame, it is taken;
the fortress is put to shame
and broken down;
2   the renown of Moab is no more.
In Heshbon they planned
evil against her:
"Come, let us cut her off
from being a nation!"
You also, O Madmen, shall be
brought to silence;ᶜ
the sword shall pursue you.

3 Hark! a cry from Horonaim,
"Desolation and great
destruction!"

4 "Moab is destroyed!"
her little ones cry out.
5 For at the ascent of Luhith
they goᵈ up weeping bitterly;
for at the descent of Horonaim
they have heard the distressing
cry of anguish.
6 Flee! Save yourselves!
Be like a wild assᵉ in the desert!

7 Surely, because you trusted
in your strongholdsᶠ
and your treasures,
you also shall be taken;
Chemosh shall go out into exile,
with his priests and his
attendants.
8 The destroyer shall come
upon every town,
and no town shall escape;
the valley shall perish,
and the plain shall be
destroyed,
as the LORD has spoken.

9 Set aside salt for Moab,
for she will surely fall;
her towns shall become
a desolation,
with no inhabitant in them.

10 Accursed is the one who is slack
in doing the work of the LORD; and
accursed is the one who keeps back
the sword from bloodshed.

11 Moab has been at ease
from his youth,
settled like wineᵍ on its dregs;
he has not been emptied from
vessel to vessel,
nor has he gone into exile;
therefore his flavor has remained
and his aroma is unspoiled.
12 Therefore, the time is surely
coming, says the LORD, when I
shall send to him decanters to de-
cant him, and empty his vessels,
and break hisʰ jars in pieces. 13 Then
Moab shall be ashamed of Chemosh,

ᵃ 47.5 Gk: Heb *their valley*   ᵇ 47.7 Gk Vg:
Heb *you*   ᶜ 48.2 The place-name *Madmen*
sounds like the Hebrew verb *to be silent*
ᵈ 48.5 Cn: Heb *he goes*   ᵉ 48.6 Gk Aquila:
Heb *like Aroer*   ᶠ 48.7 Gk: Heb *works*
ᵍ 48.11 Heb lacks *like wine*   ʰ 48.12 Gk
Aquila: Heb *their*

as the house of Israel was ashamed
of Bethel, their confidence.

14 How can you say, "We are heroes
    and mighty warriors"?
15 The destroyer of Moab and his
        towns has come up,
    and the choicest of his
        young men have gone
        down to slaughter,
    says the King, whose name
        is the LORD of hosts.
16 The calamity of Moab is
        near at hand
    and his doom approaches
        swiftly.
17 Mourn over him, all you
        his neighbors,
    and all who know his name;
    say, "How the mighty
        scepter is broken,
        the glorious staff!"
18 Come down from glory,
    and sit on the parched ground,
        enthroned daughter Dibon!
    For the destroyer of Moab has
        come up against you;
    he has destroyed your
        strongholds.
19 Stand by the road and watch,
        you inhabitant of Aroer!
    Ask the man fleeing and the
        woman escaping;
    say, "What has happened?"
20 Moab is put to shame, for it
        is broken down;
    wail and cry!
    Tell it by the Arnon,
        that Moab is laid waste.

21 Judgment has come upon the
tableland, upon Holon, and Jahzah,
and Mephaath, 22and Dibon, and
Nebo, and Beth-diblathaim, 23and
Kiriathaim, and Beth-gamul, and
Beth-meon, 24and Kerioth, and Boz-
rah, and all the towns of the land of
Moab, far and near. 25The horn of
Moab is cut off, and his arm is bro-
ken, says the LORD.

26 Make him drunk, because
he magnified himself against the
LORD; let Moab wallow in his vomit;
he too shall become a laughingstock.
27Israel was a laughingstock for you,
though he was not caught among

thieves; but whenever you spoke of
him you shook your head!

28 Leave the towns, and live
        on the rock,
    O inhabitants of Moab!
    Be like the dove that nests
        on the sides of the mouth
        of a gorge.
29 We have heard of the pride
        of Moab—
    he is very proud—
    of his loftiness, his pride,
        and his arrogance,
        and the haughtiness
        of his heart.
30 I myself know his insolence,
        says the LORD;
    his boasts are false,
        his deeds are false.
31 Therefore I wail for Moab;
    I cry out for all Moab;
        for the people of Kir-heres
        I mourn.
32 More than for Jazer I
        weep for you,
    O vine of Sibmah!
    Your branches crossed
        over the sea,
    reached as far as Jazer;[a]
    upon your summer fruits
        and your vintage
    the destroyer has fallen.
33 Gladness and joy have been
        taken away
    from the fruitful land of Moab;
    I have stopped the wine from
        the wine presses;
    no one treads them with
        shouts of joy;
    the shouting is not the
        shout of joy.

34 Heshbon and Elealeh cry out;[b]
as far as Jahaz they utter their voice,
from Zoar to Horonaim and Eglath-
shelishiyah. For even the waters
of Nimrim have become desolate.
35And I will bring to an end in Moab,
says the LORD, those who offer sacrifice at a high place and make offerings to their gods. 36Therefore my
heart moans for Moab like a flute,
and my heart moans like a flute for

a 48.32 Two Mss and Isa 16.8: MT *the sea
of Jazer*   b 48.34 Cn: Heb *From the cry of
Heshbon to Elealeh*

the people of Kir-heres; for the riches they gained have perished.

37 For every head is shaved and every beard cut off; on all the hands there are gashes, and on the loins sackcloth. 38 On all the housetops of Moab and in the squares there is nothing but lamentation; for I have broken Moab like a vessel that no one wants, says the LORD. 39 How it is broken! How they wail! How Moab has turned his back in shame! So Moab has become a derision and a horror to all his neighbors.

40 For thus says the LORD:
Look, he shall swoop down
  like an eagle,
and spread his wings
  against Moab;
41 the towns[a] shall be taken
  and the strongholds seized.
The hearts of the warriors of
  Moab, on that day,
shall be like the heart of a
  woman in labor.
42 Moab shall be destroyed
  as a people,
because he magnified himself
  against the LORD.
43 Terror, pit, and trap
are before you, O inhabitants
  of Moab!
    says the LORD.
44 Everyone who flees from
  the terror
  shall fall into the pit,
and everyone who climbs
  out of the pit
  shall be caught in the trap.
For I will bring these things[b]
  upon Moab
in the year of their punishment,
    says the LORD.

45 In the shadow of Heshbon
  fugitives stop exhausted;
for a fire has gone out
  from Heshbon,
  a flame from the house
    of Sihon;
it has destroyed the forehead
  of Moab,
  the scalp of the people
    of tumult.[c]
46 Woe to you, O Moab!
  The people of Chemosh
    have perished,

for your sons have been
  taken captive,
and your daughters
  into captivity.
47 Yet I will restore the
  fortunes of Moab
in the latter days, says
  the LORD.
Thus far is the judgment on Moab.

JUDGMENT ON THE AMMONITES

49 Concerning the Ammonites.

Thus says the LORD:
  Has Israel no sons?
    Has he no heir?
  Why then has Milcom
    dispossessed Gad,
  and his people settled
    in its towns?
2 Therefore, the time is
    surely coming,
  says the LORD,
when I will sound the
    battle alarm
  against Rabbah of the
    Ammonites;
it shall become a desolate mound,
  and its villages shall be
    burned with fire;
then Israel shall dispossess those
  who dispossessed him,
    says the LORD.

3 Wail, O Heshbon, for Ai
    is laid waste!
  Cry out, O daughters[d]
    of Rabbah!
Put on sackcloth,
  lament, and slash yourselves
    with whips![e]
For Milcom shall go into exile,
  with his priests and his
    attendants.
4 Why do you boast in your
    strength?
  Your strength is ebbing,
O faithless daughter.
  You trusted in your
    treasures, saying,
  "Who will attack me?"

---

a 48.41 Or *Kerioth* b 48.44 Gk Syr:
Heb *bring upon it* c 48.45 Or *of Shaon*
d 49.3 Or *villages* e 49.3 Cn: Meaning of
Heb uncertain

5 I am going to bring terror
        upon you,
    says the Lord GOD of hosts,
    from all your neighbors,
    and you will be scattered,
        each headlong,
    with no one to gather
        the fugitives.
6 But afterward I will restore the
fortunes of the Ammonites, says the
LORD.

JUDGMENT ON EDOM

7 Concerning Edom.

Thus says the LORD of hosts:
    Is there no longer wisdom
        in Teman?
    Has counsel perished
        from the prudent?
    Has their wisdom vanished?
8 Flee, turn back, get down low,
        inhabitants of Dedan!
    For I will bring the calamity
        of Esau upon him,
        the time when I punish him.
9 If grape-gatherers came to you,
        would they not leave
            gleanings?
    If thieves came by night,
        even they would pillage only
            what they wanted.
10 But as for me, I have stripped
        Esau bare,
    I have uncovered his
        hiding places,
    and he is not able to
        conceal himself.
    His offspring are destroyed,
        his kinsfolk
    and his neighbors; and
        he is no more.
11 Leave your orphans, I will
        keep them alive;
    and let your widows
        trust in me.

12 For thus says the LORD: If those
who do not deserve to drink the cup
still have to drink it, shall you be the
one to go unpunished? You shall not
go unpunished; you must drink it.
13 For by myself I have sworn, says
the LORD, that Bozrah shall become
an object of horror and ridicule,
a waste, and an object of cursing;
and all her towns shall be perpetual
wastes.

14 I have heard tidings from
        the LORD,
    and a messenger has been
        sent among the nations:
    "Gather yourselves together
        and come against her,
    and rise up for battle!"
15 For I will make you least
        among the nations,
    despised by humankind.
16 The terror you inspire
    and the pride of your heart
        have deceived you,
    you who live in the clefts
        of the rock,[a]
    who hold the height of the hill.
    Although you make your nest
        as high as the eagle's,
    from there I will bring
        you down,
                    says the LORD.

17 Edom shall become an object
of horror; everyone who passes by
it will be horrified and will hiss because of all its disasters. 18 As when
Sodom and Gomorrah and their
neighbors were overthrown, says
the LORD, no one shall live there,
nor shall anyone settle in it. 19 Like a
lion coming up from the thickets of
the Jordan against a perennial pasture, I will suddenly chase Edom[b]
away from it; and I will appoint over
it whomever I choose.[c] For who is
like me? Who can summon me? Who
is the shepherd who can stand before me? 20 Therefore hear the plan
that the LORD has made against
Edom and the purposes that he has
formed against the inhabitants of
Teman: Surely the little ones of the
flock shall be dragged away; surely
their fold shall be appalled at their
fate. 21 At the sound of their fall the
earth shall tremble; the sound of
their cry shall be heard at the Red
Sea.[d] 22 Look, he shall mount up
and swoop down like an eagle, and
spread his wings against Bozrah,
and the heart of the warriors of
Edom in that day shall be like the
heart of a woman in labor.

---

[a] 49.16 Or of Sela   [b] 49.19 Heb him
[c] 49.19 Or and I will single out the choicest
of his rams: Meaning of Heb uncertain
[d] 49.21 Or Sea of Reeds

JUDGMENT ON DAMASCUS

23 Concerning Damascus.

Hamath and Arpad are
confounded,
for they have heard bad news;
they melt in fear, they are
troubled like the sea[a]
that cannot be quiet.
24 Damascus has become feeble,
she turned to flee,
and panic seized her;
anguish and sorrows have
taken hold of her,
as of a woman in labor.
25 How the famous city is forsaken,[b]
the joyful town![c]
26 Therefore her young men shall
fall in her squares,
and all her soldiers shall be
destroyed in that day,
says the LORD of hosts.
27 And I will kindle a fire at the
wall of Damascus,
and it shall devour the
strongholds of Ben-hadad.

JUDGMENT ON KEDAR
AND HAZOR

28 Concerning Kedar and the
kingdoms of Hazor that King Nebuchadrezzar of Babylon defeated.

Thus says the LORD:
Rise up, advance against Kedar!
Destroy the people of the east!
29 Take their tents and their flocks,
their curtains and all
their goods;
carry off their camels for
yourselves,
and a cry shall go up: "Terror
is all around!"
30 Flee, wander far away, hide
in deep places,
O inhabitants of Hazor!
says the LORD.
For King Nebuchadrezzar
of Babylon
has made a plan against you
and formed a purpose
against you.

31 Rise up, advance against a
nation at ease,
that lives secure,
says the LORD,

that has no gates or bars,
that lives alone.
32 Their camels shall become booty,
their herds of cattle a spoil.
I will scatter to every wind
those who have shaven
temples,
and I will bring calamity
against them from every side,
says the LORD.
33 Hazor shall become a lair
of jackals,
an everlasting waste;
no one shall live there,
nor shall anyone settle in it.

JUDGMENT ON ELAM

34 The word of the LORD that
came to the prophet Jeremiah concerning Elam, at the beginning of
the reign of King Zedekiah of Judah.
35 Thus says the LORD of hosts: I
am going to break the bow of Elam,
the mainstay of their might; 36and I
will bring upon Elam the four winds
from the four quarters of heaven;
and I will scatter them to all these
winds, and there shall be no nation
to which the exiles from Elam shall
not come. 37I will terrify Elam before their enemies, and before those
who seek their life; I will bring disaster upon them, my fierce anger, says
the LORD. I will send the sword after
them, until I have consumed them;
38and I will set my throne in Elam,
and destroy their king and officials,
says the LORD.
39 But in the latter days I will restore the fortunes of Elam, says the
LORD.

JUDGMENT ON BABYLON

50 The word that the LORD
spoke concerning Babylon,
concerning the land of the Chaldeans, by the prophet Jeremiah:
2 Declare among the nations
and proclaim,
set up a banner and proclaim,
do not conceal it, say:
Babylon is taken,
Bel is put to shame,
Merodach is dismayed.

[a] 49.23 Cn: Heb *there is trouble in the sea*
[b] 49.25 Vg: Heb *is not forsaken*   [c] 49.25 Syr
Vg Tg: Heb *the town of my joy*

Her images are put to shame,
    her idols are dismayed.

3 For out of the north a nation has come up against her; it shall make her land a desolation, and no one shall live in it; both human beings and animals shall flee away.

4 In those days and in that time, says the LORD, the people of Israel shall come, they and the people of Judah together; they shall come weeping as they seek the LORD their God. 5They shall ask the way to Zion, with faces turned toward it, and they shall come and join[a] themselves to the LORD by an everlasting covenant that will never be forgotten.

6 My people have been lost sheep; their shepherds have led them astray, turning them away on the mountains; from mountain to hill they have gone, they have forgotten their fold. 7All who found them have devoured them, and their enemies have said, "We are not guilty, because they have sinned against the LORD, the true pasture, the LORD, the hope of their ancestors."

8 Flee from Babylon, and go out of the land of the Chaldeans, and be like male goats leading the flock. 9For I am going to stir up and bring against Babylon a company of great nations from the land of the north; and they shall array themselves against her; from there she shall be taken. Their arrows are like the arrows of a skilled warrior who does not return empty-handed. 10Chaldea shall be plundered; all who plunder her shall be sated, says the LORD.

11 Though you rejoice, though
    you exult,
    O plunderers of my heritage,
though you frisk about like a
    heifer on the grass,
    and neigh like stallions,
12 your mother shall be utterly
    shamed,
and she who bore you
    shall be disgraced.
Lo, she shall be the last of
    the nations,
    a wilderness, dry land,
    and a desert.

13 Because of the wrath of the LORD
    she shall not be inhabited,
but shall be an utter desolation;
everyone who passes by Babylon
    shall be appalled
    and hiss because of all
      her wounds.
14 Take up your positions
    around Babylon,
all you that bend the bow;
shoot at her, spare no arrows,
    for she has sinned against
      the LORD.
15 Raise a shout against her
    from all sides,
"She has surrendered;
her bulwarks have fallen,
    her walls are thrown down."
For this is the vengeance
    of the LORD:
take vengeance on her,
    do to her as she has done.
16 Cut off from Babylon the sower,
    and the wielder of the sickle
      in time of harvest;
because of the destroying sword
all of them shall return to
    their own people,
and all of them shall flee
    to their own land.

17 Israel is a hunted sheep driven away by lions. First the king of Assyria devoured it, and now at the end King Nebuchadrezzar of Babylon has gnawed its bones. 18Therefore, thus says the LORD of hosts, the God of Israel: I am going to punish the king of Babylon and his land, as I punished the king of Assyria. 19I will restore Israel to its pasture, and it shall feed on Carmel and in Bashan, and on the hills of Ephraim and in Gilead its hunger shall be satisfied. 20In those days and at that time, says the LORD, the iniquity of Israel shall be sought, and there shall be none; and the sins of Judah, and none shall be found; for I will pardon the remnant that I have spared.

21 Go up to the land of Merathaim;[b]
    go up against her,

---

a 50.5 Gk: Heb *toward it. Come! They shall join*   b 50.21 Or *of Double Rebellion*

and attack the inhabitants
of Pekod[a]
and utterly destroy the
last of them,[b]
      says the LORD;
do all that I have
commanded you.
²² The noise of battle is in the land,
and great destruction!
²³ How the hammer of the
whole earth
is cut down and broken!
How Babylon has become
a horror among the nations!
²⁴ You set a snare for yourself
and you were caught,
O Babylon,
but you did not know it;
you were discovered and seized,
because you challenged
the LORD.
²⁵ The LORD has opened
his armory,
and brought out the weapons
of his wrath,
for the Lord GOD of hosts
has a task to do
in the land of the Chaldeans.
²⁶ Come against her from
every quarter;
open her granaries;
pile her up like heaps of grain,
and destroy her utterly;
let nothing be left of her.
²⁷ Kill all her bulls,
let them go down to
the slaughter.
Alas for them, their day
has come,
the time of their punishment!

28 Listen! Fugitives and refugees
from the land of Babylon are coming
to declare in Zion the vengeance of
the LORD our God, vengeance for his
temple.

29 Summon archers against Babylon, all who bend the bow. Encamp
all around her; let no one escape. Repay her according to her deeds; just
as she has done, do to her—for she
has arrogantly defied the LORD, the
Holy One of Israel. ³⁰Therefore her
young men shall fall in her squares,
and all her soldiers shall be destroyed
on that day, says the LORD.

³¹ I am against you, O arrogant one,
says the Lord GOD of hosts;
for your day has come,
the time when I will
punish you.
³² The arrogant one shall
stumble and fall,
with no one to raise him up,
and I will kindle a fire in his cities,
and it will devour everything
around him.

33 Thus says the LORD of hosts:
The people of Israel are oppressed,
and so too are the people of Judah;
all their captors have held them fast
and refuse to let them go. ³⁴Their
Redeemer is strong; the LORD of
hosts is his name. He will surely
plead their cause, that he may give
rest to the earth, but unrest to the
inhabitants of Babylon.

³⁵ A sword against the Chaldeans,
says the LORD,
and against the inhabitants
of Babylon,
and against her officials
and her sages!
³⁶ A sword against the diviners,
so that they may become fools!
A sword against her warriors,
so that they may be destroyed!
³⁷ A sword against her[c] horses and
against her[c] chariots,
and against all the foreign
troops in her midst,
so that they may become
women!
A sword against all her treasures,
that they may be plundered!
³⁸ A drought[d] against her waters,
that they may be dried up!
For it is a land of images,
and they go mad over idols.

39 Therefore wild animals shall
live with hyenas in Babylon,[e] and
ostriches shall inhabit her; she shall
never again be peopled, or inhabited
for all generations. ⁴⁰As when God
overthrew Sodom and Gomorrah
and their neighbors, says the LORD,

a 50.21 Or of Punishment b 50.21 Tg:
Heb destroy after them c 50.37 Cn: Heb
his d 50.38 Another reading is A sword
e 50.39 Heb lacks in Babylon

so no one shall live there, nor shall anyone settle in her.

41 Look, a people is coming
        from the north;
    a mighty nation and many kings
    are stirring from the farthest
        parts of the earth.
42 They wield bow and spear,
        they are cruel and have
        no mercy.
    The sound of them is like
        the roaring sea;
    they ride upon horses,
    set in array as a warrior for battle,
        against you, O daughter
        Babylon!

43 The king of Babylon heard
        news of them,
    and his hands fell helpless;
    anguish seized him,
        pain like that of a woman
        in labor.

44 Like a lion coming up from the thickets of the Jordan against a perennial pasture, I will suddenly chase them away from her; and I will appoint over her whomever I choose.[a] For who is like me? Who can summon me? Who is the shepherd who can stand before me? 45 Therefore hear the plan that the LORD has made against Babylon, and the purposes that he has formed against the land of the Chaldeans: Surely the little ones of the flock shall be dragged away; surely their[b] fold shall be appalled at their fate. 46 At the sound of the capture of Babylon the earth shall tremble, and her cry shall be heard among the nations.

51 Thus says the LORD:
    I am going to stir up a
        destructive wind[c]
    against Babylon
    and against the inhabitants
        of Leb-qamai;[d]
2   and I will send winnowers
        to Babylon,
    and they shall winnow her.
    They shall empty her land
    when they come against
        her from every side
        on the day of trouble.

3 Let not the archer bend his bow,
    and let him not array himself
        in his coat of mail.
   Do not spare her young men;
       utterly destroy her entire army.
4 They shall fall down slain in the
       land of the Chaldeans,
   and wounded in her streets.
5 Israel and Judah have not
       been forsaken
   by their God, the LORD
       of hosts,
   though their land is full of guilt
   before the Holy One of Israel.

6 Flee from the midst of Babylon,
       save your lives, each of you!
   Do not perish because
       of her guilt,
   for this is the time of the
       LORD's vengeance;
   he is repaying her what is due.
7 Babylon was a golden cup in
       the LORD's hand,
   making all the earth drunken;
   the nations drank of her wine,
   and so the nations went mad.
8 Suddenly Babylon has fallen
       and is shattered;
   wail for her!
   Bring balm for her wound;
       perhaps she may be healed.
9 We tried to heal Babylon,
   but she could not be healed.
   Forsake her, and let each of us go
       to our own country;
   for her judgment has reached
       up to heaven
   and has been lifted up
       even to the skies.
10 The LORD has brought forth
       our vindication;
   come, let us declare in Zion
   the work of the LORD our God.

11 Sharpen the arrows!
   Fill the quivers!
The LORD has stirred up the spirit of the kings of the Medes, because his purpose concerning Babylon is to destroy it, for that is the vengeance

---

a 50.44 Or *and I will single out the choicest of her rams*: Meaning of Heb uncertain
b 50.45 Syr Gk Tg Compare 49.20: Heb lacks *their*   c 51.1 Or *stir up the spirit of a destroyer*   d 51.1 *Leb-qamai* is a cryptogram for *Kasdim*, Chaldea

of the LORD, vengeance for his temple.

12 Raise a standard against the
walls of Babylon;
make the watch strong;
post sentinels;
prepare the ambushes;
for the LORD has both
planned and done
what he spoke concerning the
inhabitants of Babylon.
13 You who live by mighty waters,
rich in treasures,
your end has come,
the thread of your life is cut.
14 The LORD of hosts has
sworn by himself:
Surely I will fill you with troops
like a swarm of locusts,
and they shall raise a shout
of victory over you.

15 It is he who made the earth
by his power,
who established the world
by his wisdom,
and by his understanding
stretched out the heavens.
16 When he utters his voice there
is a tumult of waters
in the heavens,
and he makes the mist
rise from the ends
of the earth.
He makes lightnings for the rain,
and he brings out the wind
from his storehouses.
17 Everyone is stupid and
without knowledge;
goldsmiths are all put to
shame by their idols;
for their images are false,
and there is no breath
in them.
18 They are worthless, a work
of delusion;
at the time of their
punishment they
shall perish.
19 Not like these is the LORD,[a]
the portion of Jacob,
for he is the one who
formed all things,
and Israel is the tribe of
his inheritance;
the LORD of hosts is
his name.

ISRAEL THE CREATOR'S INSTRUMENT

20 You are my war club, my
weapon of battle:
with you I smash nations;
with you I destroy kingdoms;
21 with you I smash the horse
and its rider;
with you I smash the chariot
and the charioteer;
22 with you I smash man
and woman;
with you I smash the old
man and the boy;
with you I smash the young
man and the girl;
23 with you I smash shepherds
and their flocks;
with you I smash farmers
and their teams;
with you I smash governors
and deputies.

THE DOOM OF BABYLON

24 I will repay Babylon and all the inhabitants of Chaldea before your very eyes for all the wrong that they have done in Zion, says the LORD.

25 I am against you, O destroying
mountain,
says the LORD,
that destroys the whole earth;
I will stretch out my hand
against you,
and roll you down from
the crags,
and make you a burned-out
mountain.
26 No stone shall be taken from
you for a corner
and no stone for a foundation,
but you shall be a perpetual
waste,
says the LORD.

27 Raise a standard in the land,
blow the trumpet among
the nations;
prepare the nations for
war against her,
summon against her
the kingdoms,
Ararat, Minni, and Ashkenaz;

a 51.19 Heb lacks the LORD

appoint a marshal against her,
    bring up horses like
        bristling locusts.
28 Prepare the nations for war
        against her,
    the kings of the Medes,
        with their governors
        and deputies,
    and every land under
        their dominion.
29 The land trembles and writhes,
    for the LORD's purposes
        against Babylon stand,
    to make the land of Babylon
        a desolation,
    without inhabitant.
30 The warriors of Babylon have
        given up fighting,
    they remain in their strongholds;
    their strength has failed,
        they have become women;
    her buildings are set on fire,
        her bars are broken.
31 One runner runs to meet another,
    and one messenger to
        meet another,
    to tell the king of Babylon
        that his city is taken from
        end to end:
32 the fords have been seized,
    the marshes have been
        burned with fire,
    and the soldiers are in panic.
33 For thus says the LORD of hosts,
        the God of Israel:
Daughter Babylon is like a
        threshing floor
    at the time when it is trodden;
yet a little while
    and the time of her harvest
        will come.

34 "King Nebuchadrezzar of Babylon
        has devoured me,
    he has crushed me;
he has made me an empty vessel,
    he has swallowed me
        like a monster;
he has filled his belly with
        my delicacies,
    he has spewed me out.
35 May my torn flesh be avenged
        on Babylon,"
    the inhabitants of Zion shall say.
"May my blood be avenged on the
        inhabitants of Chaldea,"
    Jerusalem shall say.

36 Therefore thus says the LORD:
I am going to defend your cause
    and take vengeance for you.
I will dry up her sea
    and make her fountain dry;
37 and Babylon shall become
        a heap of ruins,
    a den of jackals,
an object of horror and of hissing,
    without inhabitant.

38 Like lions they shall roar
        together;
    they shall growl like
        lions' whelps.
39 When they are inflamed, I will
        set out their drink
    and make them drunk, until
        they become merry
and then sleep a perpetual sleep
    and never wake, says the LORD.
40 I will bring them down like
        lambs to the slaughter,
    like rams and goats.

41 How Sheshach[a] is taken,
    the pride of the whole
        earth seized!
How Babylon has become
    an object of horror among
        the nations!
42 The sea has risen over Babylon;
    she has been covered by its
        tumultuous waves.
43 Her cities have become an
        object of horror,
    a land of drought and a desert,
a land in which no one lives,
    and through which no
        mortal passes.
44 I will punish Bel in Babylon,
    and make him disgorge what
        he has swallowed.
The nations shall no longer
        stream to him;
    the wall of Babylon has fallen.

45 Come out of her, my people!
    Save your lives, each of you,
    from the fierce anger
        of the LORD!
46 Do not be fainthearted or fearful
    at the rumors heard
        in the land—

a 51.41 *Sheshach* is a cryptogram for *Babel*, Babylon

one year one rumor comes,
    the next year another,
rumors of violence in the land
    and of ruler against ruler.

47 Assuredly, the days are coming
    when I will punish the
        images of Babylon;
her whole land shall be
        put to shame,
    and all her slain shall fall
        in her midst.

48 Then the heavens and
        the earth,
    and all that is in them,
shall shout for joy over Babylon;
    for the destroyers shall
        come against them
        out of the north,
            says the LORD.

49 Babylon must fall for the
        slain of Israel,
    as the slain of all the earth have
        fallen because of Babylon.

50 You survivors of the sword,
    go, do not linger!
Remember the LORD in
        a distant land,
    and let Jerusalem come
        into your mind:

51 We are put to shame, for we
        have heard insults;
    dishonor has covered our face,
for aliens have come
        into the holy places of the
        LORD's house.

52 Therefore the time is surely
        coming, says the LORD,
    when I will punish her idols,
and through all her land
        the wounded shall groan.

53 Though Babylon should
        mount up to heaven,
    and though she should fortify
        her strong height,
from me destroyers would
        come upon her,
            says the LORD.

54 Listen!—a cry from Babylon!
    A great crashing from the
        land of the Chaldeans!

55 For the LORD is laying
        Babylon waste,
    and stilling her loud clamor.

Their waves roar like
        mighty waters,
    the sound of their clamor
        resounds;

56 for a destroyer has come
        against her,
    against Babylon;
her warriors are taken,
    their bows are broken;
for the LORD is a God of
        recompense,
    he will repay in full.

57 I will make her officials and
        her sages drunk,
    also her governors,
        her deputies, and
        her warriors;
they shall sleep a perpetual
        sleep and never wake,
    says the King, whose name
        is the LORD of hosts.

58 Thus says the LORD of hosts:
The broad wall of Babylon
    shall be leveled to the ground,
    and her high gates
        shall be burned with fire.
The peoples exhaust themselves
        for nothing,
    and the nations weary
        themselves only for fire. [a]

JEREMIAH'S COMMAND
TO SERAIAH

59 The word that the prophet Jeremiah commanded Seraiah son of Neriah son of Mahseiah, when he went with King Zedekiah of Judah to Babylon, in the fourth year of his reign. Seraiah was the quartermaster. 60 Jeremiah wrote in a [b] scroll all the disasters that would come on Babylon, all these words that are written concerning Babylon. 61 And Jeremiah said to Seraiah: "When you come to Babylon, see that you read all these words, 62 and say, 'O LORD, you yourself threatened to destroy this place so that neither human beings nor animals shall live in it, and it shall be desolate forever.' 63 When you finish reading this scroll, tie a stone to it, and throw it into the middle of the Euphrates, 64 and say,

a 51.58 Gk Syr Compare Hab 2.13: Heb *and the nations for fire, and they are weary*
b 51.60 Or *one*

'Thus shall Babylon sink, to rise no more, because of the disasters that I am bringing on her.' "[a]

Thus far are the words of Jeremiah.

THE DESTRUCTION OF JERUSALEM REVIEWED

52 Zedekiah was twenty-one years old when he began to reign; he reigned eleven years in Jerusalem. His mother's name was Hamutal daughter of Jeremiah of Libnah. [2] He did what was evil in the sight of the LORD, just as Jehoiakim had done. [3] Indeed, Jerusalem and Judah so angered the LORD that he expelled them from his presence.

Zedekiah rebelled against the king of Babylon. [4] And in the ninth year of his reign, in the tenth month, on the tenth day of the month, King Nebuchadrezzar of Babylon came with all his army against Jerusalem, and they laid siege to it; they built siegeworks against it all around. [5] So the city was besieged until the eleventh year of King Zedekiah. [6] On the ninth day of the fourth month the famine became so severe in the city that there was no food for the people of the land. [7] Then a breach was made in the city wall;[b] and all the soldiers fled and went out from the city by night by the way of the gate between the two walls, by the king's garden, though the Chaldeans were all around the city. They went in the direction of the Arabah. [8] But the army of the Chaldeans pursued the king, and overtook Zedekiah in the plains of Jericho; and all his army was scattered, deserting him. [9] Then they captured the king, and brought him up to the king of Babylon at Riblah in the land of Hamath, and he passed sentence on him. [10] The king of Babylon killed the sons of Zedekiah before his eyes, and also killed all the officers of Judah at Riblah. [11] He put out the eyes of Zedekiah, and bound him in fetters, and the king of Babylon took him to Babylon, and put him in prison until the day of his death.

[12] In the fifth month, on the tenth day of the month—which was the nineteenth year of King Nebuchadrezzar, king of Babylon—Nebuzaradan the captain of the bodyguard who served the king of Babylon, entered Jerusalem. [13] He burned the house of the LORD, the king's house, and all the houses of Jerusalem; every great house he burned down. [14] All the army of the Chaldeans, who were with the captain of the guard, broke down all the walls around Jerusalem. [15] Nebuzaradan the captain of the guard carried into exile some of the poorest of the people and the rest of the people who were left in the city and the deserters who had defected to the king of Babylon, together with the rest of the artisans. [16] But Nebuzaradan the captain of the guard left some of the poorest people of the land to be vinedressers and tillers of the soil.

[17] The pillars of bronze that were in the house of the LORD, and the stands and the bronze sea that were in the house of the LORD, the Chaldeans broke in pieces, and carried all the bronze to Babylon. [18] They took away the pots, the shovels, the snuffers, the basins, the ladles, and all the vessels of bronze used in the temple service. [19] The captain of the guard took away the small bowls also, the firepans, the basins, the pots, the lampstands, the ladles, and the bowls for libation, both those of gold and those of silver. [20] As for the two pillars, the one sea, the twelve bronze bulls that were under the sea, and the stands,[c] which King Solomon had made for the house of the LORD, the bronze of all these vessels was beyond weighing. [21] As for the pillars, the height of the one pillar was eighteen cubits, its circumference was twelve cubits; it was hollow and its thickness was four fingers. [22] Upon it was a capital of bronze; the height of the capital was five cubits; latticework and pomegranates, all of bronze, encircled the top of the capital. And the second pillar had the same, with pomegranates. [23] There were ninety-six pome-

---

[a] 51.64 Gk: Heb *on her. And they shall weary themselves*   [b] 52.7 Heb lacks *wall*
[c] 52.20 Cn: Heb *that were under the stands*

granates on the sides; all the pomegranates encircling the latticework numbered one hundred.

24 The captain of the guard took the chief priest Seraiah, the second priest Zephaniah, and the three guardians of the threshold; 25and from the city he took an officer who had been in command of the soldiers, and seven men of the king's council who were found in the city; the secretary of the commander of the army who mustered the people of the land; and sixty men of the people of the land who were found inside the city. 26Then Nebuzaradan the captain of the guard took them, and brought them to the king of Babylon at Riblah. 27And the king of Babylon struck them down, and put them to death at Riblah in the land of Hamath. So Judah went into exile out of its land.

28 This is the number of the people whom Nebuchadrezzar took into exile: in the seventh year, three thousand twenty-three Judeans; 29in the eighteenth year of Nebuchadrezzar he took into exile from Jerusalem eight hundred thirty-two persons; 30in the twenty-third year of Nebuchadrezzar, Nebuzaradan the captain of the guard took into exile of the Judeans seven hundred forty-five persons; all the persons were four thousand six hundred.

JEHOIACHIN FAVORED IN CAPTIVITY

31 In the thirty-seventh year of the exile of King Jehoiachin of Judah, in the twelfth month, on the twenty-fifth day of the month, King Evil-merodach of Babylon, in the year he began to reign, showed favor to King Jehoiachin of Judah and brought him out of prison; 32he spoke kindly to him, and gave him a seat above the seats of the other kings who were with him in Babylon. 33So Jehoiachin put aside his prison clothes, and every day of his life he dined regularly at the king's table. 34For his allowance, a regular daily allowance was given him by the king of Babylon, as long as he lived, up to the day of his death.

LAMENTATIONS

A lament is a song or poem articulating intense grief, a genre more in vogue in ancient Jewish tradition than today. The book of Lamentations was most likely written by Jeremiah; the tangible agony in the words of the poem suggests that the writer was an eyewitness who wandered among the ruins of Jerusalem and its temple. Lamentations expresses the pain of the conquered people while it acknowledges the judgment of a righteous God. Despite his deep sadness over the plight of his people, Jeremiah rejoices in God's goodness and mercy, "his mercies never come to an end" (Lamentations 3.22).

THE DESERTED CITY

1 How lonely sits the city
    that once was full of people!
How like a widow she
    has become,
    she that was great among
      the nations!
She that was a princess among
      the provinces
    has become a vassal.

2 She weeps bitterly in the night,
    with tears on her cheeks;
among all her lovers
    she has no one to comfort her;
all her friends have dealt
      treacherously with her,
    they have become her enemies.

3 Judah has gone into exile
      with suffering
    and hard servitude;
she lives now among the nations,
    and finds no resting place;
her pursuers have all
      overtaken her
    in the midst of her distress.

4 The roads to Zion mourn,
    for no one comes to
      the festivals;
all her gates are desolate,
    her priests groan;
her young girls grieve,[a]
    and her lot is bitter.

5 Her foes have become
      the masters,
    her enemies prosper,
because the LORD has
      made her suffer
    for the multitude of her
      transgressions;
her children have gone away,
    captives before the foe.

6 From daughter Zion has departed
    all her majesty.
Her princes have become
      like stags
    that find no pasture;
they fled without strength
    before the pursuer.

7 Jerusalem remembers,
    in the days of her affliction
      and wandering,
all the precious things
    that were hers in days of old.
When her people fell into the
      hand of the foe,
    and there was no one
      to help her,
the foe looked on mocking
    over her downfall.

8 Jerusalem sinned grievously,
    so she has become a mockery;
all who honored her despise her,
    for they have seen her
      nakedness;
she herself groans,
    and turns her face away.

9 Her uncleanness was in her skirts;
    she took no thought
      of her future;
her downfall was appalling,
    with none to comfort her.
"O LORD, look at my affliction,
    for the enemy has triumphed!"

10 Enemies have stretched
      out their hands
    over all her precious things;
she has even seen the nations
    invade her sanctuary,
those whom you forbade
    to enter your congregation.

11 All her people groan
    as they search for bread;
they trade their treasures for food
    to revive their strength.
Look, O LORD, and see
    how worthless I have become.

12 Is it nothing to you,[a] all you
      who pass by?
Look and see
if there is any sorrow like
      my sorrow,
    which was brought upon me,
which the LORD inflicted
    on the day of his fierce anger.

13 From on high he sent fire;
    it went deep into my bones;
he spread a net for my feet;
    he turned me back;
he has left me stunned,
    faint all day long.

[a] 1.4,12 Meaning of Heb uncertain

14 My transgressions were
    bound[a] into a yoke;
by his hand they were
    fastened together;
they weigh on my neck,
    sapping my strength;
the Lord handed me over
    to those whom I cannot
    withstand.

15 The LORD has rejected
    all my warriors in the
    midst of me;
he proclaimed a time against me
    to crush my young men;
the Lord has trodden as
    in a wine press
    the virgin daughter Judah.

16 For these things I weep;
    my eyes flow with tears;
for a comforter is far from me,
    one to revive my courage;
my children are desolate,
    for the enemy has prevailed.

17 Zion stretches out her hands,
    but there is no one to
    comfort her;
the LORD has commanded
    against Jacob
    that his neighbors should
    become his foes;
Jerusalem has become
    a filthy thing among them.

18 The LORD is in the right,
    for I have rebelled against
    his word;
but hear, all you peoples,
    and behold my suffering;
my young women and
    young men
    have gone into captivity.

19 I called to my lovers
    but they deceived me;
my priests and elders
    perished in the city
while seeking food
    to revive their strength.

20 See, O LORD, how distressed I am;
    my stomach churns,
my heart is wrung within me,
    because I have been
    very rebellious.
In the street the sword bereaves;
    in the house it is like death.

21 They heard how I was groaning,
    with no one to comfort me.
All my enemies heard of
    my trouble;
they are glad that you
    have done it.
Bring on the day you have
    announced,
    and let them be as I am.

22 Let all their evil doing
    come before you;
    and deal with them
as you have dealt with me
    because of all my
    transgressions;
for my groans are many
    and my heart is faint.

GOD'S WARNINGS FULFILLED

2 How the Lord in his anger
    has humiliated[a] daughter Zion!
He has thrown down from
    heaven to earth
    the splendor of Israel;
he has not remembered
    his footstool
    in the day of his anger.

2 The Lord has destroyed
    without mercy
    all the dwellings of Jacob;
in his wrath he has broken down
    the strongholds of
    daughter Judah;
he has brought down to the
    ground in dishonor
    the kingdom and its rulers.

3 He has cut down in fierce anger
    all the might of Israel;
he has withdrawn his right
    hand from them
    in the face of the enemy;
he has burned like a flaming
    fire in Jacob,
    consuming all around.

4 He has bent his bow like
    an enemy,
    with his right hand
    set like a foe;

a 1.14; 2.1 Meaning of Heb uncertain

he has killed all in whom
we took pride
in the tent of daughter Zion;
he has poured out his
fury like fire.

5 The Lord has become like
an enemy;
he has destroyed Israel.
He has destroyed all its palaces,
laid in ruins its strongholds,
and multiplied in
daughter Judah
mourning and lamentation.

6 He has broken down his
booth like a garden,
he has destroyed his
tabernacle;
the LORD has abolished in Zion
festival and sabbath,
and in his fierce indignation
has spurned
king and priest.

7 The Lord has scorned his altar,
disowned his sanctuary;
he has delivered into the
hand of the enemy
the walls of her palaces;
a clamor was raised in the
house of the LORD
as on a day of festival.

8 The LORD determined to
lay in ruins
the wall of daughter Zion;
he stretched the line;
he did not withhold his hand
from destroying;
he caused rampart and
wall to lament;
they languish together.

9 Her gates have sunk into
the ground;
he has ruined and
broken her bars;
her king and princes are
among the nations;
guidance is no more,
and her prophets obtain
no vision from the LORD.

10 The elders of daughter Zion
sit on the ground in silence;

they have thrown dust
on their heads
and put on sackcloth;
the young girls of Jerusalem
have bowed their heads
to the ground.

11 My eyes are spent with weeping;
my stomach churns;
my bile is poured out on
the ground
because of the destruction
of my people,
because infants and babes faint
in the streets of the city.

12 They cry to their mothers,
"Where is bread and wine?"
as they faint like the wounded
in the streets of the city,
as their life is poured out
on their mothers' bosom.

13 What can I say for you, to
what compare you,
O daughter Jerusalem?
To what can I liken you, that
I may comfort you,
O virgin daughter Zion?
For vast as the sea is your ruin;
who can heal you?

14 Your prophets have
seen for you
false and deceptive visions;
they have not exposed
your iniquity
to restore your fortunes,
but have seen oracles for you
that are false and misleading.

15 All who pass along the way
clap their hands at you;
they hiss and wag their heads
at daughter Jerusalem;
"Is this the city that was called
the perfection of beauty,
the joy of all the earth?"

16 All your enemies
open their mouths
against you;
they hiss, they gnash their teeth,
they cry: "We have
devoured her!
Ah, this is the day we longed for;
at last we have seen it!"

17 The LORD has done what
he purposed,
he has carried out his threat;
as he ordained long ago,
he has demolished
without pity;
he has made the enemy
rejoice over you,
and exalted the might
of your foes.

18 Cry aloud^a to the Lord!
O wall of daughter Zion!
Let tears stream down
like a torrent
day and night!
Give yourself no rest,
your eyes no respite!

19 Arise, cry out in the night,
at the beginning of
the watches!
Pour out your heart like water
before the presence
of the Lord!
Lift your hands to him
for the lives of your children,
who faint for hunger
at the head of every street.

20 Look, O LORD, and consider!
To whom have you done this?
Should women eat their
offspring,
the children they have borne?
Should priest and prophet
be killed
in the sanctuary of the Lord?

21 The young and the
old are lying
on the ground in the streets;
my young women and my
young men
have fallen by the sword;
in the day of your anger you
have killed them,
slaughtering without mercy.

22 You invited my enemies
from all around
as if for a day of festival;
and on the day of the anger
of the LORD
no one escaped or survived;
those whom I bore and reared
my enemy has destroyed.

GOD'S STEADFAST LOVE ENDURES

3 I am one who has seen affliction
under the rod of God's^b wrath;
2 he has driven and brought me
into darkness without
any light;
3 against me alone he turns
his hand,
again and again, all day long.

4 He has made my flesh and my
skin waste away,
and broken my bones;
5 he has besieged and
enveloped me
with bitterness and
tribulation;
6 he has made me sit in darkness
like the dead of long ago.

7 He has walled me about so
that I cannot escape;
he has put heavy chains on me;
8 though I call and cry for help,
he shuts out my prayer;
9 he has blocked my ways
with hewn stones,
he has made my paths crooked.

10 He is a bear lying in wait for me,
a lion in hiding;
11 he led me off my way and
tore me to pieces;
he has made me desolate;
12 he bent his bow and set me
as a mark for his arrow.

13 He shot into my vitals
the arrows of his quiver;
14 I have become the laughingstock
of all my people,
the object of their taunt-songs
all day long.
15 He has filled me with bitterness,
he has sated me with
wormwood.

16 He has made my teeth
grind on gravel,
and made me cower in ashes;
17 my soul is bereft of peace;
I have forgotten what
happiness is;

a 2.18 Cn: Heb Their heart cried
b 3.1 Heb his

18 so I say, "Gone is my glory,
and all that I had hoped
for from the LORD."

19 The thought of my affliction
and my homelessness
is wormwood and gall!
20 My soul continually thinks of it
and is bowed down within me.
21 But this I call to mind,
and therefore I have hope:

22 The steadfast love of the
LORD never ceases,[a]
his mercies never come
to an end;
23 they are new every morning;
great is your faithfulness.
24 "The LORD is my portion,"
says my soul,
"therefore I will hope in him."

25 The LORD is good to those
who wait for him,
to the soul that seeks him.
26 It is good that one should
wait quietly
for the salvation of the LORD.
27 It is good for one to bear
the yoke in youth,
28 to sit alone in silence
when the Lord has imposed it,
29 to put one's mouth to the dust
(there may yet be hope),
30 to give one's cheek to the smiter,
and be filled with insults.

31 For the Lord will not
reject forever.
32 Although he causes grief, he
will have compassion
according to the abundance
of his steadfast love;
33 for he does not willingly afflict
or grieve anyone.

34 When all the prisoners of the land
are crushed under foot,
35 when human rights are perverted
in the presence of the
Most High,
36 when one's case is subverted
—does the Lord not see it?

37 Who can command and
have it done,
if the Lord has not ordained it?

PONDER

The steadfast love of the LORD never ceases, his mercies never come to an end; they are new every morning; great is your faithfulness. "The LORD is my portion," says my soul, "therefore I will hope in him."
—Lamentations 3.22–24

PRAY

Lord of mercy, we praise and thank you that your great love and compassion for us are new every morning. And every day, every morning, may we be faithful in reaching out to you, our Creator, and to our Savior, Jesus Christ, to deepen our relationships with you and our relationships with other human beings. We pray that we might be strengthened with a realization that in partnership with you, there is no limit on how excellent our lives can be in your sight. Help us to look for inspiration and exaltation without the element of pride. Bring us closer as we emulate the life of our Savior, Jesus Christ. In his name we pray. Amen.

38 Is it not from the mouth of
the Most High
that good and bad come?
39 Why should any who draw
breath complain
about the punishment
of their sins?
40 Let us test and examine
our ways,
and return to the LORD.
41 Let us lift up our hearts as
well as our hands
to God in heaven.
42 We have transgressed
and rebelled,
and you have not forgiven.

a 3.22 Syr Tg: Heb LORD, we are not cut off

Never Abandoned

The steadfast love of the LORD never ceases, his mercies never come to an end; they are new every morning; great is your faithfulness.

—Lamentations 3.22–23

The people of Jerusalem were destitute. Jerusalem had been completely conquered by the Babylonians. Some of God's chosen people had been killed, some were taken into captivity, some had escaped into Egypt, and those who remained in Jerusalem and Judah were living in bondage to the conquering Babylonians. At this time of sorrow, grief, disappointment and despair, Jeremiah was still in Jerusalem. Are we surprised, then, by Jeremiah's words in the third chapter of Lamentations? During great despair, Jeremiah turns his thoughts toward God and never loses confidence in him.

When we go outside on a dark night, we can see the stars; the darker the sky is, the more stars we see. It's helpful to remember this contrast between the darkest of nights and the brightest of stars when we read about the despondency of the people in Jerusalem. They certainly contrast with Jeremiah's confidence in the integrity, justice, love and mercy of God. We can extend this situation to our own lives. When we have a death or a terminal illness in the family, we are faced with dark days. It's hard to comprehend why good people have such bad things happen to them. But as Christians, we believe in eternal life for those who profess faith in Jesus Christ. So, although we may look upon death as a tragedy, in the eyes of God it is not. The deaths of believers in Christ have led them to everlasting life.

Death can be compared to a seed. A seed of any kind is not all that beautiful. But within that seed is the potential for becoming a beautiful peanut vine, or a lovely flower, or an enormous oak tree. And when that seed is planted, there is a transformation—out of it comes a luxurious, productive plant that has no resemblance at all to the seed that was planted. That's the image that we have of our hope for eternal life. We have hope in our salvation. Jeremiah had similar hope as he wrote in the midst of his sorrow.

Some people blame God for cancer or for injury or for early death. But the Bible says "For he does not willingly afflict or grieve anyone. When all the prisoners of the land are crushed under foot, when human rights are perverted in the presence of the Most High, when one's case is subverted—does the Lord not see it?" (Lamentations 3.33–36). So we know from these verses that the afflictions of life are not God's doing. We are never abandoned. We want to remember that, in the midst of death or disappointment or sorrow or despair, there is a good foundation for hope with a firm conviction that God's promises will be kept.

Going Deeper

- In what dark moments in your life has God revealed his love and compassion to you?
- How do you perceive death? What are God's promises to Christians regarding death?

43 You have wrapped yourself with
   anger and pursued us,
   killing without pity;
44 you have wrapped yourself
   with a cloud
   so that no prayer can
   pass through.
45 You have made us filth
   and rubbish
   among the peoples.

46 All our enemies
   have opened their mouths
   against us;
47 panic and pitfall have
   come upon us,
   devastation and destruction.
48 My eyes flow with rivers of tears
   because of the destruction
   of my people.

49 My eyes will flow without
   ceasing,
   without respite,
50 until the LORD from heaven
   looks down and sees.
51 My eyes cause me grief
   at the fate of all the young
   women in my city.

52 Those who were my enemies
   without cause
   have hunted me like a bird;
53 they flung me alive into a pit
   and hurled stones on me;
54 water closed over my head;
   I said, "I am lost."

55 I called on your name, O LORD,
   from the depths of the pit;
56 you heard my plea, "Do not
   close your ear
   to my cry for help, but
   give me relief!"
57 You came near when I
   called on you;
   you said, "Do not fear!"

58 You have taken up my
   cause, O Lord,
   you have redeemed my life.
59 You have seen the wrong
   done to me, O LORD;
   judge my cause.
60 You have seen all their malice,
   all their plots against me.

61 You have heard their
   taunts, O LORD,
   all their plots against me.
62 The whispers and murmurs
   of my assailants
   are against me all day long.
63 Whether they sit or rise—see,
   I am the object of their
   taunt-songs.

64 Pay them back for their
   deeds, O LORD,
   according to the work
   of their hands!
65 Give them anguish of heart;
   your curse be on them!
66 Pursue them in anger and
   destroy them
   from under the LORD's
   heavens.

THE PUNISHMENT OF ZION

4 How the gold has grown dim,
   how the pure gold is changed!
The sacred stones lie scattered
   at the head of every street.

2 The precious children of Zion,
   worth their weight in
   fine gold—
how they are reckoned as
   earthen pots,
   the work of a potter's hands!

3 Even the jackals offer the breast
   and nurse their young,
but my people has become cruel,
   like the ostriches in the
   wilderness.

4 The tongue of the infant sticks
   to the roof of its mouth for thirst;
the children beg for food,
   but no one gives them anything.

5 Those who feasted on delicacies
   perish in the streets;
those who were brought
   up in purple
   cling to ash heaps.

6 For the chastisement[a] of my
   people has been greater
   than the punishment[b]
   of Sodom,

a 4.6 Or *iniquity*   b 4.6 Or *sin*

which was overthrown
in a moment,
though no hand was laid on it.[a]

7 Her princes were purer
than snow,
whiter than milk;
their bodies were more
ruddy than coral,
their hair[a] like sapphire.[b]

8 Now their visage is blacker
than soot;
they are not recognized
in the streets.
Their skin has shriveled
on their bones;
it has become as dry as wood.

9 Happier were those pierced
by the sword
than those pierced by hunger,
whose life drains away, deprived
of the produce of the field.

10 The hands of compassionate
women
have boiled their own children;
they became their food
in the destruction of
my people.

11 The LORD gave full vent
to his wrath;
he poured out his hot anger,
and kindled a fire in Zion
that consumed its foundations.

12 The kings of the earth did
not believe,
nor did any of the inhabitants
of the world,
that foe or enemy could enter
the gates of Jerusalem.

13 It was for the sins of her prophets
and the iniquities of
her priests,
who shed the blood of
the righteous
in the midst of her.

14 Blindly they wandered
through the streets,
so defiled with blood
that no one was able
to touch their garments.

15 "Away! Unclean!" people
shouted at them;
"Away! Away! Do not touch!"
So they became fugitives
and wanderers;
it was said among the nations,
"They shall stay here
no longer."

16 The LORD himself has
scattered them,
he will regard them no more;
no honor was shown to
the priests,
no favor to the elders.

17 Our eyes failed, ever watching
vainly for help;
we were watching eagerly
for a nation that could not save.

18 They dogged our steps
so that we could not walk
in our streets;
our end drew near; our days
were numbered;
for our end had come.

19 Our pursuers were swifter
than the eagles in the heavens;
they chased us on the mountains,
they lay in wait for us in
the wilderness.

20 The LORD's anointed, the
breath of our life,
was taken in their pits—
the one of whom we said,
"Under his shadow
we shall live among
the nations."

21 Rejoice and be glad,
O daughter Edom,
you that live in the land of Uz;
but to you also the cup shall pass;
you shall become drunk and
strip yourself bare.

22 The punishment of your
iniquity, O daughter
Zion, is accomplished,
he will keep you in exile
no longer;

a 4.6,7 Meaning of Heb uncertain   b 4.7 Or
lapis lazuli

but your iniquity, O daughter
Edom, he will punish,
he will uncover your sins.

A PLEA FOR MERCY

5 Remember, O LORD, what
has befallen us;
look, and see our disgrace!
2 Our inheritance has been turned
over to strangers,
our homes to aliens.
3 We have become orphans,
fatherless;
our mothers are like widows.
4 We must pay for the water
we drink;
the wood we get must
be bought.
5 With a yoke[a] on our necks
we are hard driven;
we are weary, we are
given no rest.
6 We have made a pact with[b]
Egypt and Assyria,
to get enough bread.
7 Our ancestors sinned; they
are no more,
and we bear their
iniquities.
8 Slaves rule over us;
there is no one to deliver
us from their hand.
9 We get our bread at the
peril of our lives,
because of the sword in
the wilderness.
10 Our skin is black as an oven
from the scorching
heat of famine.
11 Women are raped in Zion,
virgins in the
towns of Judah.

12 Princes are hung up by
their hands;
no respect is shown
to the elders.
13 Young men are compelled
to grind,
and boys stagger under
loads of wood.
14 The old men have left
the city gate,
the young men their music.
15 The joy of our hearts has ceased;
our dancing has been
turned to mourning.
16 The crown has fallen from
our head;
woe to us, for we have sinned!
17 Because of this our hearts
are sick,
because of these things our
eyes have grown dim:
18 because of Mount Zion,
which lies desolate;
jackals prowl over it.

19 But you, O LORD, reign forever;
your throne endures to
all generations.
20 Why have you forgotten
us completely?
Why have you forsaken us
these many days?
21 Restore us to yourself, O LORD,
that we may be restored;
renew our days as of old—
22 unless you have utterly
rejected us,
and are angry with us
beyond measure.

[a] 5.5 Symmachus: Heb lacks *With a yoke*
[b] 5.6 Heb *have given the hand to*

EZEKIEL

Ezekiel, in exile among his people, used words, visions and "mini-dramas" as he communicated God's messages to his people. Even though the book was written when more than 3,000 Jews were in oppressive exile in Babylon, the main theme is hope. Although God had righteously judged Judah and Israel, God didn't forsake them, but promised to remain with them in exile and return with them someday to their home. Through Ezekiel, God told the Jews to "know that I am the LORD" (Ezekiel 6.14). God promises to be with us even in the most remote and unlikely places.

THE VISION OF THE CHARIOT

1 In the thirtieth year, in the fourth month, on the fifth day of the month, as I was among the exiles by the river Chebar, the heavens were opened, and I saw visions of God. 2 On the fifth day of the month (it was the fifth year of the exile of King Jehoiachin), 3 the word of the LORD came to the priest Ezekiel son of Buzi, in the land of the Chaldeans by the river Chebar; and the hand of the LORD was on him there.

4 As I looked, a stormy wind came out of the north: a great cloud with brightness around it and fire flashing forth continually, and in the middle of the fire, something like gleaming amber. 5 In the middle of it was something like four living creatures. This was their appearance: they were of human form. 6 Each had four faces, and each of them had four wings. 7 Their legs were straight, and the soles of their feet were like the sole of a calf's foot; and they sparkled like burnished bronze. 8 Under their wings on their four sides they had human hands. And the four had their faces and their wings thus: 9 their wings touched one another; each of them moved straight ahead, without turning as they moved. 10 As for the appearance of their faces: the four had the face of a human being, the face of a lion on the right side, the face of an ox on the left side, and the face of an eagle; 11 such were their faces. Their wings were spread out above; each creature had two wings, each of which touched the wing of another, while two covered their bodies. 12 Each moved straight ahead; wherever the spirit would go, they went, without turning as they went. 13 In the middle of[a] the living creatures there was something that looked like burning coals of fire, like torches moving to and fro among the living creatures; the fire was bright, and lightning issued from the fire. 14 The living creatures darted to and fro, like a flash of lightning.

15 As I looked at the living creatures, I saw a wheel on the earth beside the living creatures, one for each of the four of them.[b] 16 As for the appearance of the wheels and their construction: their appearance was like the gleaming of beryl; and the four had the same form, their construction being something like a wheel within a wheel. 17 When they moved, they moved in any of the four directions without veering as they moved. 18 Their rims were tall and awesome, for the rims of all four were full of eyes all around. 19 When the living creatures moved, the wheels moved beside them; and when the living creatures rose from the earth, the wheels rose. 20 Wherever the spirit would go, they went, and the wheels rose along with them; for the spirit of the living creatures was in the wheels. 21 When they moved, the others moved; when they stopped, the others stopped; and when they rose from the earth, the wheels rose along with them; for the spirit of the living creatures was in the wheels.

22 Over the heads of the living creatures there was something like a dome, shining like crystal,[c] spread out above their heads. 23 Under the dome their wings were stretched out straight, one toward another; and each of the creatures had two wings covering its body. 24 When they moved, I heard the sound of their wings like the sound of mighty waters, like the thunder of the Almighty,[d] a sound of tumult like the sound of an army; when they stopped, they let down their wings. 25 And there came a voice from above the dome over their heads; when they stopped, they let down their wings.

26 And above the dome over their heads there was something like a throne, in appearance like sapphire;[e] and seated above the likeness of a throne was something that seemed like a human form. 27 Upward from what appeared like the loins I saw something like gleaming amber,

a 1.13 Gk OL: Heb And the appearance of b 1.15 Heb of their faces c 1.22 Gk: Heb like the awesome crystal d 1.24 Traditional rendering of Heb Shaddai e 1.26 Or lapis lazuli

something that looked like fire enclosed all around; and downward from what looked like the loins I saw something that looked like fire, and there was a splendor all around. 28Like the bow in a cloud on a rainy day, such was the appearance of the splendor all around. This was the appearance of the likeness of the glory of the LORD.

When I saw it, I fell on my face, and I heard the voice of someone speaking.

THE VISION OF THE SCROLL

2 He said to me: O mortal,[a] stand up on your feet, and I will speak with you. 2And when he spoke to me, a spirit entered into me and set me on my feet; and I heard him speaking to me. 3He said to me, Mortal, I am sending you to the people of Israel, to a nation[b] of rebels who have rebelled against me; they and their ancestors have transgressed against me to this very day. 4The descendants are impudent and stubborn. I am sending you to them, and you shall say to them, "Thus says the Lord GOD." 5Whether they hear or refuse to hear (for they are a rebellious house), they shall know that there has been a prophet among them. 6And you, O mortal, do not be afraid of them, and do not be afraid of their words, though briers and thorns surround you and you live among scorpions; do not be afraid of their words, and do not be dismayed at their looks, for they are a rebellious house. 7You shall speak my words to them, whether they hear or refuse to hear; for they are a rebellious house.

8 But you, mortal, hear what I say to you; do not be rebellious like that rebellious house; open your mouth and eat what I give you. 9I looked, and a hand was stretched out to me, and a written scroll was in it. 10He spread it before me; it had writing on the front and on the back, and written on it were words of lamentation and mourning and woe.

3 He said to me, O mortal, eat what is offered to you; eat this scroll, and go, speak to the house of Israel. 2So I opened my mouth, and

he gave me the scroll to eat. 3He said to me, Mortal, eat this scroll that I give you and fill your stomach with it. Then I ate it; and in my mouth it was as sweet as honey.

4 He said to me: Mortal, go to the house of Israel and speak my very words to them. 5For you are not sent to a people of obscure speech and difficult language, but to the house of Israel— 6not to many peoples of obscure speech and difficult language, whose words you cannot understand. Surely, if I sent you to them, they would listen to you. 7But the house of Israel will not listen to you, for they are not willing to listen to me; because all the house of Israel have a hard forehead and a stubborn heart. 8See, I have made your face hard against their faces, and your forehead hard against their foreheads. 9Like the hardest stone, harder than flint, I have made your forehead; do not fear them or be dismayed at their looks, for they are a rebellious house. 10He said to me: Mortal, all my words that I shall speak to you receive in your heart and hear with your ears; 11then go to the exiles, to your people, and speak to them. Say to them, "Thus says the Lord GOD"; whether they hear or refuse to hear.

EZEKIEL AT THE RIVER CHEBAR

12 Then the spirit lifted me up, and as the glory of the LORD rose[c] from its place, I heard behind me the sound of loud rumbling; 13it was the sound of the wings of the living creatures brushing against one another, and the sound of the wheels beside them, that sounded like a loud rumbling. 14The spirit lifted me up and bore me away; I went in bitterness in the heat of my spirit, the hand of the LORD being strong upon me. 15I came to the exiles at Tel-abib, who lived by the river Chebar.[d] And

a 2.1 Or son of man; Heb ben adam (and so throughout the book when Ezekiel is addressed)   b 2.3 Syr: Heb to nations   c 3.12 Cn: Heb and blessed be the glory of the LORD   d 3.15 Two Mss Syr: Heb Chebar, and to where they lived. Another reading is Chebar, and I sat where they sat

PONDER

He said to me: Mortal, all my words that I shall speak to you receive in your heart and hear with your ears; then go to the exiles, to your people, and speak to them. Say to them, "Thus says the Lord God"; whether they hear or refuse to hear.
—Ezekiel 3.10–11

PRAY

Sovereign Lord, we encounter another strange event in the Old Testament. This passage is difficult to understand and we don't know how it applies to our lives. We know that this passage in Ezekiel has something to teach us, and we pray that you will give us insight and discernment. We hope to heed Ezekiel's message and share your Word with others in a simple, humble way—not in an arrogant or boastful way, in obedience to your command to preach the gospel. Be with us, and let us be bound closer to you. We pray in the name of our Savior. Amen.

I sat there among them, stunned, for seven days.

16 At the end of seven days, the word of the LORD came to me: **17**Mortal, I have made you a sentinel for the house of Israel; whenever you hear a word from my mouth, you shall give them warning from me. **18**If I say to the wicked, "You shall surely die," and you give them no warning, or speak to warn the wicked from their wicked way, in order to save their life, those wicked persons shall die for their iniquity; but their blood I will require at your hand. **19**But if you warn the wicked, and they do not turn from their wickedness, or from their wicked way, they shall die for their iniquity; but you will have saved your life. **20**Again, if the righteous turn from their righteousness and com-

mit iniquity, and I lay a stumbling block before them, they shall die; because you have not warned them, they shall die for their sin, and their righteous deeds that they have done shall not be remembered; but their blood I will require at your hand. **21**If, however, you warn the righteous not to sin, and they do not sin, they shall surely live, because they took warning; and you will have saved your life.

EZEKIEL ISOLATED AND SILENCED

22 Then the hand of the LORD was upon me there; and he said to me, Rise up, go out into the valley, and there I will speak with you. **23**So I rose up and went out into the valley; and the glory of the LORD stood there, like the glory that I had seen by the river Chebar; and I fell on my face. **24**The spirit entered into me, and set me on my feet; and he spoke with me and said to me: Go, shut yourself inside your house. **25**As for you, mortal, cords shall be placed on you, and you shall be bound with them, so that you cannot go out among the people; **26**and I will make your tongue cling to the roof of your mouth, so that you shall be speechless and unable to reprove them; for they are a rebellious house. **27**But when I speak with you, I will open your mouth, and you shall say to them, "Thus says the Lord GOD"; let those who will hear, hear; and let those who refuse to hear, refuse; for they are a rebellious house.

THE SIEGE OF JERUSALEM PORTRAYED

4 And you, O mortal, take a brick and set it before you. On it portray a city, Jerusalem; **2**and put siege-works against it, and build a siege wall against it, and cast up a ramp against it; set camps also against it, and plant battering rams against it all around. **3**Then take an iron plate and place it as an iron wall between you and the city; set your face toward it, and let it be in a state of siege, and press the siege against it. This is a sign for the house of Israel.

4 Then lie on your left side, and place the punishment of the house of Israel upon it; you shall bear their punishment for the number of the days that you lie there. **5** For I assign to you a number of days, three hundred ninety days, equal to the number of the years of their punishment; and so you shall bear the punishment of the house of Israel. **6** When you have completed these, you shall lie down a second time, but on your right side, and bear the punishment of the house of Judah; forty days I assign you, one day for each year. **7** You shall set your face toward the siege of Jerusalem, and with your arm bared you shall prophesy against it. **8** See, I am putting cords on you so that you cannot turn from one side to the other until you have completed the days of your siege.

9 And you, take wheat and barley, beans and lentils, millet and spelt; put them into one vessel, and make bread for yourself. During the number of days that you lie on your side, three hundred ninety days, you shall eat it. **10** The food that you eat shall be twenty shekels a day by weight; at fixed times you shall eat it. **11** And you shall drink water by measure, one-sixth of a hin; at fixed times you shall drink. **12** You shall eat it as a barley-cake, baking it in their sight on human dung. **13** The LORD said, "Thus shall the people of Israel eat their bread, unclean, among the nations to which I will drive them." **14** Then I said, "Ah Lord GOD! I have never defiled myself; from my youth up until now I have never eaten what died of itself or was torn by animals, nor has carrion flesh come into my mouth." **15** Then he said to me, "See, I will let you have cow's dung instead of human dung, on which you may prepare your bread."

16 Then he said to me, Mortal, I am going to break the staff of bread in Jerusalem; they shall eat bread by weight and with fearfulness; and they shall drink water by measure and in dismay. **17** Lacking bread and water, they will look at one another in dismay, and waste away under their punishment.

A SWORD AGAINST JERUSALEM

5 And you, O mortal, take a sharp sword; use it as a barber's razor and run it over your head and your beard; then take balances for weighing, and divide the hair. **2** One third of the hair you shall burn in the fire inside the city, when the days of the siege are completed; one third you shall take and strike with the sword all around the city;[a] and one

a **5.2** Heb *it*

BIBLE IN LIFE

Speaking God's Truth

Ezekiel 3.1–27

When God commanded Ezekiel to speak to the people of Israel, it was clear that it was not Ezekiel's responsibility to make sure the people actually heeded God's warnings. In fact, God warned him that the people would not listen, but Ezekiel was obligated to tell them anyway. Ezekiel's only responsibility was to be faithful to communicate God's message. Soon after I was defeated for governor in 1966, I felt like I had a call from God to go to Lock Haven, Pennsylvania, where some Christians from State College, PA, had identified 100 families who didn't attend any church. Over one week's time, another man and I visited all 100 families and shared the gospel with them. What a wonderful experience! I didn't feel responsible for how people responded to our message. Some were insulted, others were angered, but still others responded with belief and acceptance of Jesus as their Savior. By the end of the week, 48 people accepted Christ, and we started a new church. I can't say that I've felt as filled with the Holy Spirit since then. We simply shared God's message of salvation and left the results to God. When we sense God leading us to talk to someone about Jesus, we need not be concerned about how that person will respond; we only need to be faithful to do our job. God will handle the rest.

third you shall scatter to the wind, and I will unsheathe the sword after them. ³Then you shall take from these a small number, and bind them in the skirts of your robe. ⁴From these, again, you shall take some, throw them into the fire and burn them up; from there a fire will come out against all the house of Israel.

5 Thus says the Lord GOD: This is Jerusalem; I have set her in the center of the nations, with countries all around her. ⁶But she has rebelled against my ordinances and my statutes, becoming more wicked than the nations and the countries all around her, rejecting my ordinances and not following my statutes. ⁷Therefore thus says the Lord GOD: Because you are more turbulent than the nations that are all around you, and have not followed my statutes or kept my ordinances, but have acted according to the ordinances of the nations that are all around you; ⁸therefore thus says the Lord GOD: I, I myself, am coming against you; I will execute judgments among you in the sight of the nations. ⁹And because of all your abominations, I will do to you what I have never yet done, and the like of which I will never do again. ¹⁰Surely, parents shall eat their children in your midst, and children shall eat their parents; I will execute judgments on you, and any of you who survive I will scatter to every wind. ¹¹Therefore, as I live, says the Lord GOD, surely, because you have defiled my sanctuary with all your detestable things and with all your abominations—therefore I will cut you down;ᵃ my eye will not spare, and I will have no pity. ¹²One third of you shall die of pestilence or be consumed by famine among you; one third shall fall by the sword around you; and one third I will scatter to every wind and will unsheathe the sword after them.

13 My anger shall spend itself, and I will vent my fury on them and satisfy myself; and they shall know that I, the LORD, have spoken in my jealousy, when I spend my fury on them. ¹⁴Moreover I will make you

a desolation and an object of mocking among the nations around you, in the sight of all that pass by. ¹⁵You shall beᵇ a mockery and a taunt, a warning and a horror, to the nations around you, when I execute judgments on you in anger and fury, and with furious punishments—I, the LORD, have spoken— ¹⁶when I loose against youᶜ my deadly arrows of famine, arrows for destruction, which I will let loose to destroy you, and when I bring more and more famine upon you, and break your staff of bread. ¹⁷I will send famine and wild animals against you, and they will rob you of your children; pestilence and bloodshed shall pass through you; and I will bring the sword upon you. I, the LORD, have spoken.

JUDGMENT ON IDOLATROUS ISRAEL

6 The word of the LORD came to me: ²O mortal, set your face toward the mountains of Israel, and prophesy against them, ³and say, You mountains of Israel, hear the word of the Lord GOD! Thus says the Lord GOD to the mountains and the hills, to the ravines and the valleys: I, I myself will bring a sword upon you, and I will destroy your high places. ⁴Your altars shall become desolate, and your incense stands shall be broken; and I will throw down your slain in front of your idols. ⁵I will lay the corpses of the people of Israel in front of their idols; and I will scatter your bones around your altars. ⁶Wherever you live, your towns shall be waste and your high places ruined, so that your altars will be waste and ruined,ᵈ your idols broken and destroyed, your incense stands cut down, and your works wiped out. ⁷The slain shall fall in your midst; then you shall know that I am the LORD.

8 But I will spare some. Some of you shall escape the sword among the nations and be scattered through

---

ᵃ 5.11 Another reading is *I will withdraw*
ᵇ 5.15 Gk Syr Vg Tg: Heb *It shall be*
ᶜ 5.16 Heb *them*   ᵈ 6.6 Syr Vg Tg: Heb *and be made guilty*

the countries. 9Those of you who escape shall remember me among the nations where they are carried captive, how I was crushed by their wanton heart that turned away from me, and their wanton eyes that turned after their idols. Then they will be loathsome in their own sight for the evils that they have committed, for all their abominations. 10And they shall know that I am the LORD; I did not threaten in vain to bring this disaster upon them.

11Thus says the Lord GOD: Clap your hands and stamp your foot, and say, Alas for all the vile abominations of the house of Israel! For they shall fall by the sword, by famine, and by pestilence. 12Those far off shall die of pestilence; those nearby shall fall by the sword; and any who are left and are spared shall die of famine. Thus I will spend my fury upon them. 13And you shall know that I am the LORD, when their slain lie among their idols around their altars, on every high hill, on all the mountain tops, under every green tree, and under every leafy oak, wherever they offered pleasing odor to all their idols. 14I will stretch out my hand against them, and make the land desolate and waste, throughout all their settlements, from the wilderness to Riblah.a Then they shall know that I am the LORD.

IMPENDING DISASTER

7 The word of the LORD came to me: 2You, O mortal, thus says the Lord GOD to the land of Israel:
An end! The end has come
    upon the four corners
    of the land.
3   Now the end is upon you,
    I will let loose my anger
        upon you;
    I will judge you according
        to your ways,
    I will punish you for all
        your abominations.
4   My eye will not spare you, I
        will have no pity.
    I will punish you for your ways,
        while your abominations
        are among you.

Then you shall know that I am the LORD.
5 Thus says the Lord GOD:
Disaster after disaster!
    See, it comes.
6   An end has come, the
        end has come.
    It has awakened against
        you; see, it comes!
7   Your doomb has come to you,
        O inhabitant of the land.
    The time has come, the
        day is near—
    of tumult, not of reveling
        on the mountains.
8   Soon now I will pour out my
        wrath upon you;
    I will spend my anger
        against you.
    I will judge you according
        to your ways,
    and punish you for all your
        abominations.
9   My eye will not spare; I will
        have no pity.
    I will punish you according
        to your ways,
    while your abominations
        are among you.
Then you shall know that it is I the LORD who strike.
10 See, the day! See, it comes!
    Your doomb has gone out.
    The rod has blossomed,
        pride has budded.
11   Violence has grown into a
            rod of wickedness.
    None of them shall remain,
        not their abundance, not
            their wealth;
    no pre-eminence
        among them.b
12 The time has come, the
        day draws near;
    let not the buyer rejoice,
        nor the seller mourn,
    for wrath is upon all
        their multitude.
13For the sellers shall not return to what has been sold as long as they remain alive. For the vision concerns all their multitude; it shall not be revoked. Because of their iniquity, they cannot maintain their lives.b

---

a 6.14 Another reading is *Diblah*
b 7.7,10,11,13 Meaning of Heb uncertain

14 They have blown the horn and
　made everything ready;
　but no one goes to battle,
　for my wrath is upon all
　　their multitude.
15 The sword is outside,
　pestilence and
　　famine are inside;
　those in the field die
　　by the sword;
　those in the city—famine and
　　pestilence devour them.
16 If any survivors escape,
　they shall be found on
　　the mountains
　like doves of the valleys,
　all of them moaning over
　　their iniquity.
17 All hands shall grow feeble,
　all knees turn to water.
18 They shall put on sackcloth,
　horror shall cover them.
　Shame shall be on all faces,
　baldness on all their heads.
19 They shall fling their silver
　　into the streets,
　their gold shall be treated
　　as unclean.

THE POWER AND PRESENCE

OF GOD LET US FACE LIFE

AS IT IS. OUR RESPONSE

SHOULD BE GRATITUDE.

Their silver and gold cannot save
them on the day of the wrath of the
LORD. They shall not satisfy their
hunger or fill their stomachs with
it. For it was the stumbling block of
their iniquity. 20 From their[a] beautiful ornament, in which they took
pride, they made their abominable images, their detestable things;
therefore I will make of it an unclean
thing to them.
21 I will hand it over to
　　strangers as booty,
　to the wicked of the
　　earth as plunder;
　they shall profane it.

22 I will avert my face from them,
　so that they may profane
　　my treasured[b] place;
　the violent shall enter it,
　　they shall profane it.
23 Make a chain![c]
　For the land is full of
　　bloody crimes;
　the city is full of violence.
24 I will bring the worst of
　　the nations
　to take possession of
　　their houses.
　I will put an end to the arrogance
　　of the strong,
　and their holy places
　　shall be profaned.
25 When anguish comes, they
　　will seek peace,
　but there shall be none.
26 Disaster comes upon disaster,
　rumor follows rumor;
　they shall keep seeking a vision
　　from the prophet;
　instruction shall perish
　　from the priest,
　and counsel from the elders.
27 The king shall mourn,
　the prince shall be wrapped
　　in despair,
　and the hands of the people of
　　the land shall tremble.
　According to their way I will
　　deal with them;
　according to their own
　　judgments I will
　　judge them.
And they shall know that I am the
LORD.

ABOMINATIONS IN THE TEMPLE

8 In the sixth year, in the sixth
month, on the fifth day of the
month, as I sat in my house, with
the elders of Judah sitting before
me, the hand of the Lord GOD fell
upon me there. 2 I looked, and there
was a figure that looked like a human being;[d] below what appeared
to be its loins it was fire, and above
the loins it was like the appearance
of brightness, like gleaming amber.
3 It stretched out the form of a hand,
and took me by a lock of my head;

a 7.20 Syr Symmachus: Heb its　b 7.22 Or
secret　c 7.23 Meaning of Heb uncertain
d 8.2 Gk: Heb like fire

and the spirit lifted me up between earth and heaven, and brought me in visions of God to Jerusalem, to the entrance of the gateway of the inner court that faces north, to the seat of the image of jealousy, which provokes to jealousy. 4And the glory of the God of Israel was there, like the vision that I had seen in the valley.

5 Then God[a] said to me, "O mortal, lift up your eyes now in the direction of the north." So I lifted up my eyes toward the north, and there, north of the altar gate, in the entrance, was this image of jealousy. 6He said to me, "Mortal, do you see what they are doing, the great abominations that the house of Israel are committing here, to drive me far from my sanctuary? Yet you will see still greater abominations."

7 And he brought me to the entrance of the court; I looked, and there was a hole in the wall. 8Then he said to me, "Mortal, dig through the wall"; and when I dug through the wall, there was an entrance. 9He said to me, "Go in, and see the vile abominations that they are committing here." 10So I went in and looked; there, portrayed on the wall all around, were all kinds of creeping things, and loathsome animals, and all the idols of the house of Israel. 11Before them stood seventy of the elders of the house of Israel, with Jaazaniah son of Shaphan standing among them. Each had his censer in his hand, and the fragrant cloud of incense was ascending. 12Then he said to me, "Mortal, have you seen what the elders of the house of Israel are doing in the dark, each in his room of images? For they say, 'The LORD does not see us, the LORD has forsaken the land.'" 13He said also to me, "You will see still greater abominations that they are committing."

14 Then he brought me to the entrance of the north gate of the house of the LORD; women were sitting there weeping for Tammuz. 15Then he said to me, "Have you seen this, O mortal? You will see still greater abominations than these."

16 And he brought me into the inner court of the house of the LORD;

there, at the entrance of the temple of the LORD, between the porch and the altar, were about twenty-five men, with their backs to the temple of the LORD, and their faces toward the east, prostrating themselves to the sun toward the east. 17Then he said to me, "Have you seen this, O mortal? Is it not bad enough that the house of Judah commits the abominations done here? Must they fill the land with violence, and provoke my anger still further? See, they are putting the branch to their nose! 18Therefore I will act in wrath; my eye will not spare, nor will I have pity; and though they cry in my hearing with a loud voice, I will not listen to them."

THE SLAUGHTER OF THE IDOLATERS

9 Then he cried in my hearing with a loud voice, saying, "Draw near, you executioners of the city, each with his destroying weapon in his hand." 2And six men came from the direction of the upper gate, which faces north, each with his weapon for slaughter in his hand; among them was a man clothed in linen, with a writing case at his side. They went in and stood beside the bronze altar.

3 Now the glory of the God of Israel had gone up from the cherub on which it rested to the threshold of the house. The LORD called to the man clothed in linen, who had the writing case at his side; 4and said to him, "Go through the city, through Jerusalem, and put a mark on the foreheads of those who sigh and groan over all the abominations that are committed in it." 5To the others he said in my hearing, "Pass through the city after him, and kill; your eye shall not spare, and you shall show no pity. 6Cut down old men, young men and young women, little children and women, but touch no one who has the mark. And begin at my sanctuary." So they began with the elders who were in front of the house. 7Then he said to them, "De-

a 8.5 Heb he

file the house, and fill the courts with the slain. Go!" So they went out and killed in the city. 8 While they were killing, and I was left alone, I fell prostrate on my face and cried out, "Ah Lord GOD! will you destroy all who remain of Israel as you pour out your wrath upon Jerusalem?" 9 He said to me, "The guilt of the house of Israel and Judah is exceedingly great; the land is full of bloodshed and the city full of perversity; for they say, 'The LORD has forsaken the land, and the LORD does not see.' 10 As for me, my eye will not spare, nor will I have pity, but I will bring down their deeds upon their heads."

11 Then the man clothed in linen, with the writing case at his side, brought back word, saying, "I have done as you commanded me."

GOD'S GLORY LEAVES JERUSALEM

10 Then I looked, and above the dome that was over the heads of the cherubim there appeared above them something like a sapphire,ᵃ in form resembling a throne. 2 He said to the man clothed in linen, "Go within the wheelwork underneath the cherubim; fill your hands with burning coals from among the cherubim, and scatter them over the city." He went in as I looked on. 3 Now the cherubim were standing on the south side of the house when the man went in; and a cloud filled the inner court. 4 Then the glory of the LORD rose up from the cherub to the threshold of the house; the house was filled with the cloud, and the court was full of the brightness of the glory of the LORD. 5 The sound of the wings of the cherubim was heard as far as the outer court, like the voice of God Almightyᵇ when he speaks.

6 When he commanded the man clothed in linen, "Take fire from within the wheelwork, from among the cherubim," he went in and stood beside a wheel. 7 And a cherub stretched out his hand from among the cherubim to the fire that was among the cherubim, took some of it and put it into the hands of the

man clothed in linen, who took it and went out. 8 The cherubim appeared to have the form of a human hand under their wings.

9 I looked, and there were four wheels beside the cherubim, one beside each cherub; and the appearance of the wheels was like gleaming beryl. 10 And as for their appearance, the four looked alike, something like a wheel within a wheel. 11 When they moved, they moved in any of the four directions without veering as they moved; but in whatever direction the front wheel faced, the others followed without veering as they moved. 12 Their entire body, their rims, their spokes, their wings, and the wheels—the wheels of the four of them—were full of eyes all around. 13 As for the wheels, they were called in my hearing "the wheelwork." 14 Each one had four faces: the first face was that of the cherub, the second face was that of a human being, the third that of a lion, and the fourth that of an eagle.

15 The cherubim rose up. These were the living creatures that I saw by the river Chebar. 16 When the cherubim moved, the wheels moved beside them; and when the cherubim lifted up their wings to rise up from the earth, the wheels at their side did not veer. 17 When they stopped, the others stopped, and when they rose up, the others rose up with them; for the spirit of the living creatures was in them.

18 Then the glory of the LORD went out from the threshold of the house and stopped above the cherubim. 19 The cherubim lifted up their wings and rose up from the earth in my sight as they went out with the wheels beside them. They stopped at the entrance of the east gate of the house of the LORD; and the glory of the God of Israel was above them.

20 These were the living creatures that I saw underneath the God of Israel by the river Chebar; and I knew that they were cherubim. 21 Each had four faces, each four wings, and

ᵃ 10.1 Or *lapis lazuli*   ᵇ 10.5 Traditional rendering of Heb *El Shaddai* underneath their wings something like human hands. 22 As for what their faces were like, they were the same faces whose appearance I had seen by the river Chebar. Each one moved straight ahead.

JUDGMENT ON WICKED COUNSELORS

11 The spirit lifted me up and brought me to the east gate of the house of the LORD, which faces east. There, at the entrance of the gateway, were twenty-five men; among them I saw Jaazaniah son of Azzur, and Pelatiah son of Benaiah, officials of the people. 2 He said to me, "Mortal, these are the men who devise iniquity and who give wicked counsel in this city; 3 they say, 'The time is not near to build houses; this city is the pot, and we are the meat.' 4 Therefore prophesy against them; prophesy, O mortal."

5 Then the spirit of the LORD fell upon me, and he said to me, "Say, Thus says the LORD: This is what you think, O house of Israel; I know the things that come into your mind. 6 You have killed many in this city, and have filled its streets with the slain. 7 Therefore thus says the Lord GOD: The slain whom you have placed within it are the meat, and this city is the pot; but you shall be taken out of it. 8 You have feared the sword; and I will bring the sword upon you, says the Lord GOD. 9 I will take you out of it and give you over to the hands of foreigners, and execute judgments upon you. 10 You shall fall by the sword; I will judge you at the border of Israel. And you shall know that I am the LORD. 11 This city shall not be your pot, and you shall not be the meat inside it; I will judge you at the border of Israel. 12 Then you shall know that I am the LORD, whose statutes you have not followed, and whose ordinances you have not kept, but you have acted according to the ordinances of the nations that are around you."

13 Now, while I was prophesying, Pelatiah son of Benaiah died. Then I fell down on my face, cried with a loud voice, and said, "Ah Lord GOD! will you make a full end of the remnant of Israel?"

GOD WILL RESTORE ISRAEL

14 Then the word of the LORD came to me: 15 Mortal, your kinsfolk, your own kin, your fellow exiles,[a] the whole house of Israel, all of them, are those of whom the inhabitants of Jerusalem have said, "They have gone far from the LORD; to us this land is given for a possession." 16 Therefore say: Thus says the Lord GOD: Though I removed them far away among the nations, and though I scattered them among the countries, yet I have been a sanctuary to them for a little while[b] in the

_____

a 11.15 Gk Syr: Heb *people of your kindred*
b 11.16 Or *to some extent*

⊣ BIBLE IN LIFE ▷

Setting Priorities

Ezekiel 11.12

The Israelites were not following God's laws. Instead, they were choosing to be just like the pagan nations around them. This held grave consequences for them, and Ezekiel told them they were about to be judged. How many of us set our personal priorities so as to conform to the world around us? We're all tempted to do that to some degree. While it's okay to want a nice home and a padded bank account and security, those things should not be the priorities of our lives. When we don't make Jesus Christ the core commitment of our lives, then we naturally deteriorate into self-centered existences. We become obsessed with what we need, what we want, what is good for us and our families. It becomes easier to go along with the world's standards. When we don't pattern our lives after Christ's life and don't set our priorities in accordance with God's priorities, then we gravitate much more easily toward sin.

countries where they have gone. [17]Therefore say: Thus says the Lord GOD: I will gather you from the peoples, and assemble you out of the countries where you have been scattered, and I will give you the land of Israel. [18]When they come there, they will remove from it all its detestable things and all its abominations. [19]I will give them one[a] heart, and put a new spirit within them; I will remove the heart of stone from their flesh and give them a heart of flesh, [20]so that they may follow my statutes and keep my ordinances and obey them. Then they shall be my people, and I will be their God. [21]But as for those whose heart goes after their detestable things and their abominations,[b] I will bring their deeds upon their own heads, says the Lord GOD.

[22] Then the cherubim lifted up their wings, with the wheels beside them; and the glory of the God of Israel was above them. [23]And the

---

PONDER

I will give them one heart, and put a new spirit within them; I will remove the heart of stone from their flesh and give them a heart of flesh.
—Ezekiel 11.19

PRAY

Sovereign Lord, it has been enlightening to think about Ezekiel, a strange prophet who experienced both ecstasy and despair in his life. As he looked around, he saw that people were departing from your teachings; they were misleading themselves by thinking they were special even while they were abandoning God's laws, the essence of life. Please give us enough courage to open our hearts to God's life-giving Spirit and to orient our hearts, words and actions to those of our Savior, Jesus Christ. In his name we pray. Amen.

glory of the LORD ascended from the middle of the city, and stopped on the mountain east of the city. [24]The spirit lifted me up and brought me in a vision by the spirit of God into Chaldea, to the exiles. Then the vision that I had seen left me. [25]And I told the exiles all the things that the LORD had shown me.

JUDAH'S CAPTIVITY PORTRAYED

12 The word of the LORD came to me: [2]Mortal, you are living in the midst of a rebellious house, who have eyes to see but do not see, who have ears to hear but do not hear; [3]for they are a rebellious house. Therefore, mortal, prepare for yourself an exile's baggage, and go into exile by day in their sight; you shall go like an exile from your place to another place in their sight. Perhaps they will understand, though they are a rebellious house. [4]You shall bring out your baggage by day in their sight, as baggage for exile; and you shall go out yourself at evening in their sight, as those do who go into exile. [5]Dig through the wall in their sight, and carry the baggage through it. [6]In their sight you shall lift the baggage on your shoulder, and carry it out in the dark; you shall cover your face, so that you may not see the land; for I have made you a sign for the house of Israel.

[7] I did just as I was commanded. I brought out my baggage by day, as baggage for exile, and in the evening I dug through the wall with my own hands; I brought it out in the dark, carrying it on my shoulder in their sight.

[8] In the morning the word of the LORD came to me: [9]Mortal, has not the house of Israel, the rebellious house, said to you, "What are you doing?" [10]Say to them, "Thus says the Lord GOD: This oracle concerns the prince in Jerusalem and all the house of Israel in it." [11]Say, "I am a sign for you: as I have done, so shall it be done to them; they shall

[a] 11.19 Another reading is *a new*   [b] 11.21 Cn: Heb *And to the heart of their detestable things and their abominations their heart goes*

go into exile, into captivity." ¹²And the prince who is among them shall lift his baggage on his shoulder in the dark, and shall go out; he[a] shall dig through the wall and carry it through; he shall cover his face, so that he may not see the land with his eyes. ¹³I will spread my net over him, and he shall be caught in my snare; and I will bring him to Babylon, the land of the Chaldeans, yet he shall not see it; and he shall die there. ¹⁴I will scatter to every wind all who are around him, his helpers and all his troops; and I will unsheathe the sword behind them. ¹⁵And they shall know that I am the LORD, when I disperse them among the nations and scatter them through the countries. ¹⁶But I will let a few of them escape from the sword, from famine and pestilence, so that they may tell of all their abominations among the nations where they go; then they shall know that I am the LORD.

JUDGMENT NOT POSTPONED

17 The word of the LORD came to me: ¹⁸Mortal, eat your bread with quaking, and drink your water with trembling and with fearfulness; ¹⁹and say to the people of the land, Thus says the Lord GOD concerning the inhabitants of Jerusalem in the land of Israel: They shall eat their bread with fearfulness, and drink their water in dismay, because their land shall be stripped of all it contains, on account of the violence of all those who live in it. ²⁰The inhabited cities shall be laid waste, and the land shall become a desolation; and you shall know that I am the LORD.

21 The word of the LORD came to me: ²²Mortal, what is this proverb of yours about the land of Israel, which says, "The days are prolonged, and every vision comes to nothing"? ²³Tell them therefore, "Thus says the Lord GOD: I will put an end to this proverb, and they shall use it no more as a proverb in Israel." But say to them, The days are near, and the fulfillment of every vision. ²⁴For there shall no longer be any false vision or flattering divination within

the house of Israel. ²⁵But I the LORD will speak the word that I speak, and it will be fulfilled. It will no longer be delayed; but in your days, O rebellious house, I will speak the word and fulfill it, says the Lord GOD.

26 The word of the LORD came to me: ²⁷Mortal, the house of Israel is saying, "The vision that he sees is for many years ahead; he prophesies for distant times." ²⁸Therefore say to them, Thus says the Lord GOD: None of my words will be delayed any longer, but the word that I speak will be fulfilled, says the Lord GOD.

FALSE PROPHETS CONDEMNED

13 The word of the LORD came to me: ²Mortal, prophesy against the prophets of Israel who are prophesying; say to those who prophesy out of their own imagination: "Hear the word of the LORD!" ³Thus says the Lord GOD, Alas for the senseless prophets who follow their own spirit, and have seen nothing! ⁴Your prophets have been like jackals among ruins, O Israel. ⁵You have not gone up into the breaches, or repaired a wall for the house of Israel, so that it might stand in battle on the day of the LORD. ⁶They have envisioned falsehood and lying divination; they say, "Says the LORD," when the LORD has not sent them, and yet they wait for the fulfillment of their word! ⁷Have you not seen a false vision or uttered a lying divination, when you have said, "Says the LORD," even though I did not speak?

8 Therefore thus says the Lord GOD: Because you have uttered falsehood and envisioned lies, I am against you, says the Lord GOD. ⁹My hand will be against the prophets who see false visions and utter lying divinations; they shall not be in the council of my people, nor be enrolled in the register of the house of Israel, nor shall they enter the land of Israel; and you shall know that I am the Lord GOD. ¹⁰Because, in truth, because they have misled my people, saying, "Peace," when there is no peace; and because, when the people

---

a 12.12 Gk Syr: Heb *they*

build a wall, these prophets[a] smear whitewash on it. [11]Say to those who smear whitewash on it that it shall fall. There will be a deluge of rain,[b] great hailstones will fall, and a stormy wind will break out. [12]When the wall falls, will it not be said to you, "Where is the whitewash you smeared on it?" [13]Therefore thus says the Lord GOD: In my wrath I will make a stormy wind break out, and in my anger there shall be a deluge of rain, and hailstones in wrath to destroy it. [14]I will break down the wall that you have smeared with whitewash, and bring it to the ground, so that its foundation will be laid bare; when it falls, you shall perish within it; and you shall know that I am the LORD. [15]Thus I will spend my wrath upon the wall, and upon those who have smeared it with whitewash; and I will say to you, The wall is no more, nor those who smeared it— [16]the prophets of Israel who prophesied concerning Jerusalem and saw visions of peace for it, when there was no peace, says the Lord GOD.

17 As for you, mortal, set your face against the daughters of your people, who prophesy out of their own imagination; prophesy against them [18]and say, Thus says the Lord GOD: Woe to the women who sew bands on all wrists, and make veils for the heads of persons of every height, in the hunt for human lives! Will you hunt down lives among my people, and maintain your own lives? [19]You have profaned me among my people for handfuls of barley and for pieces of bread, putting to death persons who should not die and keeping alive persons who should not live, by your lies to my people, who listen to lies. [20]Therefore thus says the Lord GOD: I am against your bands with which you hunt lives;[c] I will tear them from your arms, and let the lives go free, the lives that you hunt down like birds. [21]I will tear off your veils, and save my people from your hands; they shall no longer be prey in your hands; and you shall know that I am the LORD. [22]Because you have disheartened the righteous falsely, although I have not disheartened them, and you have encouraged the wicked not to turn from their wicked way and save their lives; [23]therefore you shall no longer see false visions or practice divination; I will save my people from your hand. Then you will know that I am the LORD.

GOD'S JUDGMENTS JUSTIFIED

14 Certain elders of Israel came to me and sat down before me. [2]And the word of the LORD came to me: [3]Mortal, these men have taken their idols into their hearts, and placed their iniquity as a stumbling block before them; shall I let myself be consulted by them? [4]Therefore speak to them, and say to them, Thus says the Lord GOD: Any of those of the house of Israel who take their idols into their hearts and place their iniquity as a stumbling block before them, and yet come to the prophet—I the LORD will answer those who come with the multitude of their idols, [5]in order that I may take hold of the hearts of the house of Israel, all of whom are estranged from me through their idols.

6 Therefore say to the house of Israel, Thus says the Lord GOD: Repent and turn away from your idols; and turn away your faces from all your abominations. [7]For any of those of the house of Israel, or of the aliens who reside in Israel, who separate themselves from me, taking their idols into their hearts and placing their iniquity as a stumbling block before them, and yet come to a prophet to inquire of me by him, I the LORD will answer them myself. [8]I will set my face against them; I will make them a sign and a byword and cut them off from the midst of my people; and you shall know that I am the LORD.

9 If a prophet is deceived and speaks a word, I, the LORD, have deceived that prophet, and I will stretch out my hand against him,

---

[a] 13.10 Heb *they* [b] 13.11 Heb *rain and you*
[c] 13.20 Gk Syr: Heb *lives for birds*

and will destroy him from the midst of my people Israel. [10]And they shall bear their punishment—the punishment of the inquirer and the punishment of the prophet shall be the same— [11]so that the house of Israel may no longer go astray from me, nor defile themselves any more with all their transgressions. Then they shall be my people, and I will be their God, says the Lord GOD.

12 The word of the LORD came to me: [13]Mortal, when a land sins against me by acting faithlessly, and I stretch out my hand against it, and break its staff of bread and send famine upon it, and cut off from it human beings and animals, [14]even if Noah, Daniel,[a] and Job, these three, were in it, they would save only their own lives by their righteousness, says the Lord GOD. [15]If I send wild animals through the land to ravage it, so that it is made desolate, and no one may pass through because of the animals; [16]even if these three men were in it, as I live, says the Lord GOD, they would save neither sons nor daughters; they alone would be saved, but the land would be desolate. [17]Or if I bring a sword upon that land and say, "Let a sword pass through the land," and I cut off human beings and animals from it; [18]though these three men were in it, as I live, says the Lord GOD, they would save neither sons nor daughters, but they alone would be saved. [19]Or if I send a pestilence into that land, and pour out my wrath upon it with blood, to cut off humans and animals from it; [20]even if Noah, Daniel,[a] and Job were in it, as I live, says the Lord GOD, they would save neither son nor daughter; they would save only their own lives by their righteousness.

21 For thus says the Lord GOD: How much more when I send upon Jerusalem my four deadly acts of judgment, sword, famine, wild animals, and pestilence, to cut off humans and animals from it! [22]Yet, survivors shall be left in it, sons and daughters who will be brought out; they will come out to you. When you see their ways and their deeds, you will be consoled for the evil that I have brought upon Jerusalem, for all that I have brought upon it. [23]They shall console you, when you see their ways and their deeds; and you shall know that it was not without cause that I did all that I have done in it, says the Lord GOD.

WE BECOME LIKE THAT
WHICH WE REALLY WORSHIP:
GOD, SELF OR THINGS.

THE USELESS VINE

15 The word of the LORD came to me:

2 O mortal, how does the wood
of the vine surpass
all other wood—
the vine branch that is among
the trees of the forest?
3 Is wood taken from it to
make anything?
Does one take a peg from it on
which to hang any object?
4 It is put in the fire for fuel;
when the fire has consumed
both ends of it
and the middle of it is charred,
is it useful for anything?
5 When it was whole it was
used for nothing;
how much less—when the
fire has consumed it,
and it is charred—
can it ever be used for
anything!

6 Therefore thus says the Lord GOD: Like the wood of the vine among the trees of the forest, which I have given to the fire for fuel, so I will give up the inhabitants of Jerusalem. [7]I will set my face against them; although they escape from the fire, the fire shall still consume them; and you shall know that I am the LORD, when I set my face against them. [8]And I will make the

[a] 14.14,20 Or, as otherwise read, Daniel

land desolate, because they have acted faithlessly, says the Lord GOD.

GOD'S FAITHLESS BRIDE

16 The word of the LORD came to me: ²Mortal, make known to Jerusalem her abominations, ³and say, Thus says the Lord GOD to Jerusalem: Your origin and your birth were in the land of the Canaanites; your father was an Amorite, and your mother a Hittite. ⁴As for your birth, on the day you were born your navel cord was not cut, nor were you washed with water to cleanse you, nor rubbed with salt, nor wrapped in cloths. ⁵No eye pitied you, to do any of these things for you out of compassion for you; but you were thrown out in the open field, for you were abhorred on the day you were born.

6 I passed by you, and saw you flailing about in your blood. As you lay in your blood, I said to you, "Live! ⁷and grow up[a] like a plant of the field." You grew up and became tall and arrived at full womanhood;[b] your breasts were formed, and your hair had grown; yet you were naked and bare.

8 I passed by you again and looked on you; you were at the age for love. I spread the edge of my cloak over you, and covered your nakedness: I pledged myself to you and entered into a covenant with you, says the Lord GOD, and you became mine. ⁹Then I bathed you with water and washed off the blood from you, and anointed you with oil. ¹⁰I clothed you with embroidered cloth and with sandals of fine leather; I bound you in fine linen and covered you with rich fabric.[c] ¹¹I adorned you with ornaments: I put bracelets on your arms, a chain on your neck, ¹²a ring on your nose, earrings in your ears, and a beautiful crown upon your head. ¹³You were adorned with gold and silver, while your clothing was of fine linen, rich fabric,[c] and embroidered cloth. You had choice flour and honey and oil for food. You grew exceedingly beautiful, fit to be a queen. ¹⁴Your fame spread among the nations on account of your beauty, for it was perfect because of my splendor that I had bestowed on you, says the Lord GOD.

15 But you trusted in your beauty, and played the whore because of your fame, and lavished your whorings on any passer-by.[d] ¹⁶You took some of your garments, and made for yourself colorful shrines, and on them played the whore; nothing like this has ever been or ever shall be.[c] ¹⁷You also took your beautiful jewels of my gold and my silver that I had given you, and made for yourself male images, and with them played the whore; ¹⁸and you took your embroidered garments to cover them, and set my oil and my incense before them. ¹⁹Also my bread that I gave you—I fed you with choice flour and oil and honey—you set it before them as a pleasing odor; and so it was, says the Lord GOD. ²⁰You took your sons and your daughters, whom you had borne to me, and these you sacrificed to them to be devoured. As if your whorings were not enough! ²¹You slaughtered my children and delivered them up as an offering to them. ²²And in all your abominations and your whorings you did not remember the days of your youth, when you were naked and bare, flailing about in your blood.

23 After all your wickedness (woe, woe to you! says the Lord GOD), ²⁴you built yourself a platform and made yourself a lofty place in every square; ²⁵at the head of every street you built your lofty place and prostituted your beauty, offering yourself to every passer-by, and multiplying your whoring. ²⁶You played the whore with the Egyptians, your lustful neighbors, multiplying your whoring, to provoke me to anger. ²⁷Therefore I stretched out my hand against you, reduced your rations, and gave you up to the will of your enemies, the daughters of the Philistines, who were ashamed of your lewd behavior. ²⁸You played the

---

[a] 16.7 Gk Syr: Heb Live! I made you a myriad
[b] 16.7 Cn: Heb ornament of ornaments
[c] 16.10,13,16 Meaning of Heb uncertain
[d] 16.15 Heb adds let it be his

whore with the Assyrians, because you were insatiable; you played the whore with them, and still you were not satisfied. ²⁹You multiplied your whoring with Chaldea, the land of merchants; and even with this you were not satisfied.

30 How sick is your heart, says the Lord GOD, that you did all these things, the deeds of a brazen whore; ³¹building your platform at the head of every street, and making your lofty place in every square! Yet you were not like a whore, because you scorned payment. ³²Adulterous wife, who receives strangers instead of her husband! ³³Gifts are given to all whores; but you gave your gifts to all your lovers, bribing them to come to you from all around for your whorings. ³⁴So you were different from other women in your whorings: no one solicited you to play the whore; and you gave payment, while no payment was given to you; you were different.

35 Therefore, O whore, hear the word of the LORD: ³⁶Thus says the Lord GOD, Because your lust was poured out and your nakedness uncovered in your whoring with your lovers, and because of all your abominable idols, and because of the blood of your children that you gave to them, ³⁷therefore, I will gather all your lovers, with whom you took pleasure, all those you loved and all those you hated; I will gather them against you from all around, and will uncover your nakedness to them, so that they may see all your nakedness. ³⁸I will judge you as women who commit adultery and shed blood are judged, and bring blood upon you in wrath and jealousy. ³⁹I will deliver you into their hands, and they shall throw down your platform and break down your lofty places; they shall strip you of your clothes and take your beautiful objects and leave you naked and bare. ⁴⁰They shall bring up a mob against you, and they shall stone you and cut you to pieces with their swords. ⁴¹They shall burn your houses and execute judgments on you in the sight of many women; I will stop you from playing the whore, and you shall also make no more payments. ⁴²So I will satisfy my fury on you, and my jealousy shall turn away from you; I will be calm, and will be angry no longer. ⁴³Because you have not remembered the days of your youth, but have enraged me with all these things; therefore, I have returned your deeds upon your head, says the Lord GOD.

Have you not committed lewdness beyond all your abominations? ⁴⁴See, everyone who uses proverbs will use this proverb about you, "Like mother, like daughter." ⁴⁵You are the daughter of your mother, who loathed her husband and her children; and you are the sister of your sisters, who loathed their husbands and their children. Your mother was a Hittite and your father an Amorite. ⁴⁶Your elder sister is Samaria, who lived with her daughters to the north of you; and your younger sister, who lived to the south of you, is Sodom with her daughters. ⁴⁷You not only followed their ways, and acted according to their abominations; within a very little time you were more corrupt than they in all your ways. ⁴⁸As I live, says the Lord GOD, your sister Sodom and her daughters have not done as you and your daughters have done. ⁴⁹This was the guilt of your sister Sodom: she and her daughters had pride, excess of food, and prosperous ease, but did not aid the poor and needy. ⁵⁰They were haughty, and did abominable things before me; therefore I removed them when I saw it. ⁵¹Samaria has not committed half your sins; you have committed more abominations than they, and have made your sisters appear righteous by all the abominations that you have committed. ⁵²Bear your disgrace, you also, for you have brought about for your sisters a more favorable judgment; because of your sins in which you acted more abominably than they, they are more in the right than you. So be ashamed, you also, and bear your disgrace, for you have made your sisters appear righteous.

53 I will restore their fortunes, the fortunes of Sodom and her daughters and the fortunes of Samaria and her daughters, and I will restore your own fortunes along with theirs, 54in order that you may bear your disgrace and be ashamed of all that you have done, becoming a consolation to them. 55As for your sisters, Sodom and her daughters shall return to their former state, Samaria and her daughters shall return to their former state, and you and your daughters shall return to your former state. 56Was not your sister Sodom a byword in your mouth in the day of your pride, 57before your wickedness was uncovered? Now you are a mockery to the daughters of Aram[a] and all her neighbors, and to the daughters of the Philistines, those all around who despise you. 58You must bear the penalty of your lewdness and your abominations, says the LORD.

AN EVERLASTING COVENANT

59 Yes, thus says the Lord GOD: I will deal with you as you have done, you who have despised the oath, breaking the covenant; 60yet I will remember my covenant with you in the days of your youth, and I will establish with you an everlasting covenant. 61Then you will remember your ways, and be ashamed when I[b] take your sisters, both your elder and your younger, and give them to you as daughters, but not on account of my[c] covenant with you. 62I will establish my covenant with you, and you shall know that I am the LORD, 63in order that you may remember and be confounded, and never open your mouth again because of your shame, when I forgive you all that you have done, says the Lord GOD.

THE TWO EAGLES AND THE VINE

17 The word of the LORD came to me: 2O mortal, propound a riddle, and speak an allegory to the house of Israel. 3Say: Thus says the Lord GOD:

A great eagle, with great wings
    and long pinions,
rich in plumage of many colors,
    came to the Lebanon.

He took the top of the cedar,
4   broke off its topmost shoot;
he carried it to a land of trade,
    set it in a city of merchants.
5 Then he took a seed from
        the land,
    placed it in fertile soil;
a plant[d] by abundant waters,
    he set it like a willow twig.
6 It sprouted and became a vine
    spreading out, but low;
its branches turned toward him,
    its roots remained
        where it stood.
So it became a vine;
    it brought forth branches,
    put forth foliage.

7 There was another great eagle,
    with great wings and
        much plumage.
And see! This vine stretched out
    its roots toward him;
it shot out its branches
        toward him,
    so that he might water it.
From the bed where it
        was planted
8   it was transplanted
to good soil by abundant waters,
    so that it might produce
        branches
    and bear fruit
    and become a noble vine.
9Say: Thus says the Lord GOD:
    Will it prosper?
Will he not pull up its roots,
    cause its fruit to rot[d]
        and wither,
    its fresh sprouting
        leaves to fade?
No strong arm or mighty
        army will be needed
    to pull it from its roots.
10 When it is transplanted,
    will it thrive?
When the east wind strikes it,
    will it not utterly wither,
    wither on the bed
        where it grew?

11 Then the word of the LORD came to me: 12Say now to the rebellious house: Do you not know what these things mean? Tell them: The

a 16.57 Another reading is *Edom*
b 16.61 Syr: Heb *you*   c 16.61 Heb lacks *my*
d 17.5,9 Meaning of Heb uncertain

king of Babylon came to Jerusalem, took its king and its officials, and brought them back with him to Babylon. ¹³He took one of the royal offspring and made a covenant with him, putting him under oath (he had taken away the chief men of the land), ¹⁴so that the kingdom might be humble and not lift itself up, and that by keeping his covenant it might stand. ¹⁵But he rebelled against him by sending ambassadors to Egypt, in order that they might give him horses and a large army. Will he succeed? Can one escape who does such things? Can he break the covenant and yet escape? ¹⁶As I live, says the Lord GOD, surely in the place where the king resides who made him king, whose oath he despised, and whose covenant with him he broke—in Babylon he shall die. ¹⁷Pharaoh with his mighty army and great company will not help him in war, when ramps are cast up and siege walls built to cut off many lives. ¹⁸Because he despised the oath and broke the covenant, because he gave his hand and yet did all these things, he shall not escape. ¹⁹Therefore thus says the Lord GOD: As I live, I will surely return upon his head my oath that he despised, and my covenant that he broke. ²⁰I will spread my net over him, and he shall be caught in my snare; I will bring him to Babylon and enter into judgment with him there for the treason he has committed against me. ²¹All the pick[a] of his troops shall fall by the sword, and the survivors shall be scattered to every wind; and you shall know that I, the LORD, have spoken.

ISRAEL EXALTED AT LAST

22 Thus says the Lord GOD:
I myself will take a sprig
    from the lofty top of a cedar;
    I will set it out.
I will break off a tender one
    from the topmost of its
        young twigs;
I myself will plant it
    on a high and lofty mountain.
²³ On the mountain height of Israel
    I will plant it,

in order that it may produce
    boughs and bear fruit,
    and become a noble cedar.
Under it every kind of
    bird will live;
    in the shade of its
        branches will nest
winged creatures of every kind.
²⁴ All the trees of the field
        shall know
    that I am the LORD.
I bring low the high tree,
    I make high the low tree;
I dry up the green tree
    and make the dry tree flourish.
I the LORD have spoken;
    I will accomplish it.

INDIVIDUAL RETRIBUTION

18 The word of the LORD came to me: ²What do you mean by repeating this proverb concerning the land of Israel, "The parents have eaten sour grapes, and the children's teeth are set on edge"? ³As I live, says the Lord GOD, this proverb shall no more be used by you in Israel. ⁴Know that all lives are mine; the life of the parent as well as the life of the child is mine: it is only the person who sins that shall die.

5 If a man is righteous and does what is lawful and right— ⁶if he does not eat upon the mountains or lift up his eyes to the idols of the house of Israel, does not defile his neighbor's wife or approach a woman during her menstrual period, ⁷does not oppress anyone, but restores to the debtor his pledge, commits no robbery, gives his bread to the hungry and covers the naked with a garment, ⁸does not take advance or accrued interest, withholds his hand from iniquity, executes true justice between contending parties, ⁹follows my statutes, and is careful to observe my ordinances, acting faithfully—such a one is righteous; he shall surely live, says the Lord GOD.

10 If he has a son who is violent, a shedder of blood, ¹¹who does any of these things (though his father[b]

---

a **17.21** Another reading is *fugitives*
b **18.11** Heb *he*

does none of them), who eats upon the mountains, defiles his neighbor's wife, 12oppresses the poor and needy, commits robbery, does not restore the pledge, lifts up his eyes to the idols, commits abomination, 13takes advance or accrued interest; shall he then live? He shall not. He has done all these abominable things; he shall surely die; his blood shall be upon himself.

14 But if this man has a son who sees all the sins that his father has done, considers, and does not do likewise, 15who does not eat upon the mountains or lift up his eyes to the idols of the house of Israel, does not defile his neighbor's wife, 16does not wrong anyone, exacts no pledge, commits no robbery, but gives his bread to the hungry and covers the naked with a garment, 17withholds his hand from iniquity,a takes no advance or accrued interest, observes my ordinances, and follows my statutes; he shall not die for his father's iniquity; he shall surely live. 18As for his father, because he practiced extortion, robbed his brother, and did what is not good among his people, he dies for his iniquity.

19 Yet you say, "Why should not the son suffer for the iniquity of the father?" When the son has done what is lawful and right, and has been careful to observe all my statutes, he shall surely live. 20The person who sins shall die. A child shall not suffer for the iniquity of a parent, nor a parent suffer for the iniquity of a child; the righteousness of the righteous shall be his own, and the wickedness of the wicked shall be his own.

21 But if the wicked turn away from all their sins that they have committed and keep all my statutes and do what is lawful and right, they shall surely live; they shall not die. 22None of the transgressions that they have committed shall be remembered against them; for the righteousness that they have done they shall live. 23Have I any pleasure in the death of the wicked, says the Lord GOD, and not rather that they should turn from their ways and

live? 24But when the righteous turn away from their righteousness and commit iniquity and do the same abominable things that the wicked do, shall they live? None of the righteous deeds that they have done shall be remembered; for the treachery of which they are guilty and the sin they have committed, they shall die.

25 Yet you say, "The way of the Lord is unfair." Hear now, O house of Israel: Is my way unfair? Is it not your ways that are unfair? 26When the righteous turn away from their righteousness and commit iniquity, they shall die for it; for the iniquity that they have committed they shall die. 27Again, when the wicked turn away from the wickedness they have committed and do what is lawful and right, they shall save their life. 28Because they considered and turned away from all the transgressions that they had committed, they shall surely live; they shall not die. 29Yet the house of Israel says, "The way of the Lord is unfair." O house of Israel, are my ways unfair? Is it not your ways that are unfair?

30 Therefore I will judge you, O house of Israel, all of you according to your ways, says the Lord GOD. Repent and turn from all your transgressions; otherwise iniquity will be your ruin.b 31Cast away from you all the transgressions that you have committed against me, and get yourselves a new heart and a new spirit! Why will you die, O house of Israel? 32For I have no pleasure in the death of anyone, says the Lord GOD. Turn, then, and live.

ISRAEL DEGRADED

19 As for you, raise up a lamentation for the princes of Israel, 2and say:

What a lioness was your mother
    among lions!
She lay down among young lions,
    rearing her cubs.
3 She raised up one of her cubs;
    he became a young lion,

a 18.17 Gk: Heb the poor b 18.30 Or so that they shall not be a stumbling block of iniquity to you

PONDER

Therefore I will judge you, O house of Israel, all of you according to your ways, says the Lord GOD. Repent . . . Cast away from you all the transgressions that you have committed against me, and get yourselves a new heart and a new spirit! Why will you die, O house of Israel? For I have no pleasure in the death of anyone, says the Lord GOD. Turn, then, and live.
—Ezekiel 18.30–32

PRAY

Father, we are thankful for words in these Old Testament passages that still apply to us. We are grateful for the words of Ezekiel that illuminate and explain the words and actions of Jesus Christ. We pray that we might have the courage to look at our own hearts and to ask, "How can I be a better Christian? How can I more vividly demonstrate that I have faith in our perfect Savior? How can I make my life more meaningful and successful, measured by the standards of Christ?" Give us a new heart and a new spirit. In Jesus' name we pray. Amen.

and he learned to catch prey;
    he devoured humans.
4 The nations sounded an
        alarm against him;
    he was caught in their pit;
    and they brought him with hooks
        to the land of Egypt.
5 When she saw that she
        was thwarted,
    that her hope was lost,
    she took another of her cubs
        and made him a young lion.
6 He prowled among the lions;
    he became a young lion,
    and he learned to catch prey;
    he devoured people.
7 And he ravaged their
        strongholds,[a]
    and laid waste their towns;

the land was appalled,
    and all in it,
    at the sound of his roaring.
8 The nations set upon him
    from the provinces all around;
    they spread their net over him;
    he was caught in their pit.
9 With hooks they put him
        in a cage,
    and brought him to the
        king of Babylon;
    they brought him into custody,
    so that his voice should be
        heard no more
    on the mountains of Israel.
10 Your mother was like a vine
        in a vineyard[b]
    transplanted by the water,
    fruitful and full of branches
        from abundant water.
11 Its strongest stem became
        a ruler's scepter;[c]
    it towered aloft
        among the thick boughs;
    it stood out in its height
        with its mass of branches.
12 But it was plucked up in fury,
        cast down to the ground;
    the east wind dried it up;
        its fruit was stripped off,
    its strong stem was withered;
        the fire consumed it.
13 Now it is transplanted into
        the wilderness,
    into a dry and thirsty land.
14 And fire has gone out
        from its stem,
    has consumed its branches
        and fruit,
    so that there remains in it
        no strong stem,
        no scepter for ruling.

This is a lamentation, and it is used as a lamentation.

ISRAEL'S CONTINUING REBELLION

20 In the seventh year, in the fifth month, on the tenth day of the month, certain elders of Israel came to consult the LORD, and sat down before me. 2 And the word of the LORD came to me: 3 Mor-

[a] 19.7 Heb his widows   [b] 19.10 Cn: Heb in your blood   [c] 19.11 Heb Its strongest stems became rulers' scepters

tal, speak to the elders of Israel, and say to them: Thus says the Lord GOD: Why are you coming? To consult me? As I live, says the Lord GOD, I will not be consulted by you. 4Will you judge them, mortal, will you judge them? Then let them know the abominations of their ancestors, 5and say to them: Thus says the Lord GOD: On the day when I chose Israel, I swore to the offspring of the house of Jacob—making myself known to them in the land of Egypt—I swore to them, saying, I am the LORD your God. 6On that day I swore to them that I would bring them out of the land of Egypt into a land that I had searched out for them, a land flowing with milk and honey, the most glorious of all lands. 7And I said to them, Cast away the detestable things your eyes feast on, every one of you, and do not defile yourselves with the idols of Egypt; I am the LORD your God. 8But they rebelled against me and would not listen to me; not one of them cast away the detestable things their eyes feasted on, nor did they forsake the idols of Egypt.

Then I thought I would pour out my wrath upon them and spend my anger against them in the midst of the land of Egypt. 9But I acted for the sake of my name, that it should not be profaned in the sight of the nations among whom they lived, in whose sight I made myself known to them in bringing them out of the land of Egypt. 10So I led them out of the land of Egypt and brought them into the wilderness. 11I gave them my statutes and showed them my ordinances, by whose observance everyone shall live. 12Moreover I gave them my sabbaths, as a sign between me and them, so that they might know that I the LORD sanctify them. 13But the house of Israel rebelled against me in the wilderness; they did not observe my statutes but rejected my ordinances, by whose observance everyone shall live; and my sabbaths they greatly profaned.

Then I thought I would pour out my wrath upon them in the wilderness, to make an end of them. 14But I acted for the sake of my name, so that it should not be profaned in the sight of the nations, in whose sight I had brought them out. 15Moreover I swore to them in the wilderness that I would not bring them into the land that I had given them, a land flowing with milk and honey, the most glorious of all lands, 16because they rejected my ordinances and did not observe my statutes, and profaned my sabbaths; for their heart went after their idols. 17Nevertheless my eye spared them, and I did not destroy them or make an end of them in the wilderness.

18 I said to their children in the wilderness, Do not follow the statutes of your parents, nor observe their ordinances, nor defile yourselves with their idols. 19I the LORD am your God; follow my statutes, and be careful to observe my ordinances, 20and hallow my sabbaths that they may be a sign between me and you, so that you may know that I the LORD am your God. 21But the children rebelled against me; they did not follow my statutes, and were not careful to observe my ordinances, by whose observance everyone shall live; they profaned my sabbaths.

Then I thought I would pour out my wrath upon them and spend my anger against them in the wilderness. 22But I withheld my hand, and acted for the sake of my name, so that it should not be profaned in the sight of the nations, in whose sight I had brought them out. 23Moreover I swore to them in the wilderness that I would scatter them among the nations and disperse them through the countries, 24because they had not executed my ordinances, but had rejected my statutes and profaned my sabbaths, and their eyes were set on their ancestors' idols. 25Moreover I gave them statutes that were not good and ordinances by which they could not live. 26I defiled them through their very gifts, in their offering up all their firstborn, in order that I might horrify them, so that they might know that I am the LORD.

27 Therefore, mortal, speak to the house of Israel and say to them, Thus says the Lord GOD: In this again your ancestors blasphemed me, by dealing treacherously with me. 28 For when I had brought them into the land that I swore to give them, then wherever they saw any high hill or any leafy tree, there they offered their sacrifices and presented the provocation of their offering; there they sent up their pleasing odors, and there they poured out their drink offerings. 29 (I said to them, What is the high place to which you go? So it is called Bamah[a] to this day.) 30 Therefore say to the house of Israel, Thus says the Lord GOD: Will you defile yourselves after the manner of your ancestors and go astray after their detestable things? 31 When you offer your gifts and make your children pass through the fire, you defile yourselves with all your idols to this day. And shall I be consulted by you, O house of Israel? As I live, says the Lord GOD, I will not be consulted by you.

32 What is in your mind shall never happen—the thought, "Let us be like the nations, like the tribes of the countries, and worship wood and stone."

GOD WILL RESTORE ISRAEL

33 As I live, says the Lord GOD, surely with a mighty hand and an outstretched arm, and with wrath poured out, I will be king over you. 34 I will bring you out from the peoples and gather you out of the countries where you are scattered, with a mighty hand and an outstretched arm, and with wrath poured out; 35 and I will bring you into the wilderness of the peoples, and there I will enter into judgment with you face to face. 36 As I entered into judgment with your ancestors in the wilderness of the land of Egypt, so I will enter into judgment with you, says the Lord GOD. 37 I will make you pass under the staff, and will bring you within the bond of the covenant. 38 I will purge out the rebels among you, and those who transgress against me; I will bring them out of the land where they reside as aliens, but they shall not enter the land of Israel. Then you shall know that I am the LORD.

39 As for you, O house of Israel, thus says the Lord GOD: Go serve your idols, every one of you now and hereafter, if you will not listen to me; but my holy name you shall no more profane with your gifts and your idols.

40 For on my holy mountain, the mountain height of Israel, says the Lord GOD, there all the house of Israel, all of them, shall serve me in the land; there I will accept them, and there I will require your contributions and the choicest of your gifts, with all your sacred things. 41 As a pleasing odor I will accept you, when I bring you out from the peoples, and gather you out of the countries where you have been scattered; and I will manifest my holiness among you in the sight of the nations. 42 You shall know that I am the LORD, when I bring you into the land of Israel, the country that I swore to give to your ancestors. 43 There you shall remember your ways and all the deeds by which you have polluted yourselves; and you shall loathe yourselves for all the evils that you have committed. 44 And you shall know that I am the LORD, when I deal with you for my name's sake, not according to your evil ways, or corrupt deeds, O house of Israel, says the Lord GOD.

A PROPHECY AGAINST THE NEGEB

45[b] The word of the LORD came to me: 46 Mortal, set your face toward the south, preach against the south, and prophesy against the forest land in the Negeb; 47 say to the forest of the Negeb, Hear the word of the LORD: Thus says the Lord GOD, I will kindle a fire in you, and it shall devour every green tree in you and every dry tree; the blazing flame shall not be quenched, and all faces from south to north shall be scorched by

a 20.29 That is *High Place*   b 20.45 Ch 21.1 in Heb

it. 48All flesh shall see that I the LORD have kindled it; it shall not be quenched. 49Then I said, "Ah Lord GOD! they are saying of me, 'Is he not a maker of allegories?' "

THE DRAWN SWORD OF GOD

21ᵃ The word of the LORD came to me: 2Mortal, set your face toward Jerusalem and preach against the sanctuaries; prophesy against the land of Israel 3and say to the land of Israel, Thus says the LORD: I am coming against you, and will draw my sword out of its sheath, and will cut off from you both righteous and wicked. 4Because I will cut off from you both righteous and wicked, therefore my sword shall go out of its sheath against all flesh from south to north; 5and all flesh shall know that I the LORD have drawn my sword out of its sheath; it shall not be sheathed again. 6Moan therefore, mortal; moan with breaking heart and bitter grief before their eyes. 7And when they say to you, "Why do you moan?" you shall say, "Because of the news that has come. Every heart will melt and all hands will be feeble, every spirit will faint and all knees will turn to water. See, it comes and it will be fulfilled," says the Lord GOD.

8 And the word of the LORD came to me: 9Mortal, prophesy and say: Thus says the Lord; Say:

A sword, a sword is sharpened,
    it is also polished;
10 it is sharpened for slaughter,
    honed to flash like lightning!
How can we make merry?
You have despised the rod,
    and all discipline.ᵇ
11 The swordᶜ is given to
        be polished,
    to be grasped in the hand;
it is sharpened, the sword
    is polished,
to be placed in the
        slayer's hand.
12 Cry and wail, O mortal,
    for it is against my people;
it is against all Israel's princes;
    they are thrown to the sword,
    together with my people.
Ah! Strike the thigh!

13For consider: What! If you despise the rod, will it not happen?ᵇ says the Lord GOD.
14 And you, mortal, prophesy;
    strike hand to hand.
Let the sword fall twice, thrice;
    it is a sword for killing.
A sword for great slaughter—
    it surrounds them;
15 therefore hearts melt
    and many stumble.
At all their gates I have set
    the pointᵇ of the sword.
Ah! It is made for flashing,
    it is polishedᵈ for slaughter.
16 Attack to the right!
    Engage to the left!
    —wherever your edge
        is directed.
17 I too will strike hand to hand,
    I will satisfy my fury;
    I the LORD have spoken.

18 The word of the LORD came to me: 19Mortal, mark out two roads for the sword of the king of Babylon to come; both of them shall issue from the same land. And make a signpost, make it for a fork in the road leading to a city; 20mark out the road for the sword to come to Rabbah of the Ammonites or to Judah and toᵉ Jerusalem the fortified. 21For the king of Babylon stands at the parting of the way, at the fork in the two roads, to use divination; he shakes the arrows, he consults the teraphim,ᶠ he inspects the liver. 22Into his right hand comes the lot for Jerusalem, to set battering rams, to call out for slaughter, for raising the battle cry, to set battering rams against the gates, to cast up ramps, to build siege towers. 23But to them it will seem like a false divination; they have sworn solemn oaths; but he brings their guilt to remembrance, bringing about their capture.

24 Therefore thus says the Lord GOD: Because you have brought your guilt to remembrance, in that your transgressions are uncovered, so that in all your deeds your sins appear—because you have come to

ᵃ 21.1 Ch 21.6 in Heb   ᵇ 21.10,13,15 Meaning of Heb uncertain   ᶜ 21.11 Heb It
ᵈ 21.15 Tg: Heb wrapped up   ᵉ 21.20 Gk Syr: Heb Judah in   ᶠ 21.21 Or the household gods

remembrance, you shall be taken in hand.[a]

25 As for you, vile, wicked
    prince of Israel,
    you whose day has come,
    the time of final punishment,
26 thus says the Lord GOD:
Remove the turban, take
    off the crown;
things shall not remain
    as they are.
Exalt that which is low,
    abase that which is high.
27 A ruin, a ruin, a ruin—
    I will make it!
    (Such has never occurred.)
Until he comes whose right it is;
    to him I will give it.

28 As for you, mortal, prophesy, and say, Thus says the Lord GOD concerning the Ammonites, and concerning their reproach; say:
A sword, a sword! Drawn
    for slaughter,
polished to consume,[b] to
    flash like lightning.
29 Offering false visions for you,
    divining lies for you,
they place you over the necks
    of the vile, wicked ones—
those whose day has come,
    the time of final punishment.
30 Return it to its sheath!
In the place where you
    were created,
    in the land of your origin,
    I will judge you.
31 I will pour out my indignation
    upon you,
with the fire of my wrath
    I will blow upon you.
I will deliver you into
    brutish hands,
    those skillful to destroy.
32 You shall be fuel for the fire,
    your blood shall enter
    the earth;
you shall be remembered
    no more,
for I the LORD have spoken.

THE BLOODY CITY

22 The word of the LORD came to me: 2 You, mortal, will you judge, will you judge the bloody city? Then declare to it all its abominable deeds. 3 You shall say, Thus says the Lord GOD: A city! Shedding blood within itself; its time has come; making its idols, defiling itself. 4 You have become guilty by the blood that you have shed, and defiled by the idols that you have made; you have brought your day near, the appointed time of your years has come. Therefore I have made you a disgrace before the nations, and a mockery to all the countries. 5 Those who are near and those who are far from you will mock you, you infamous one, full of tumult.

6 The princes of Israel in you, everyone according to his power, have been bent on shedding blood. 7 Father and mother are treated with contempt in you; the alien residing within you suffers extortion; the orphan and the widow are wronged in you. 8 You have despised my holy things, and profaned my sabbaths. 9 In you are those who slander to shed blood, those in you who eat upon the mountains, who commit lewdness in your midst. 10 In you they uncover their fathers' nakedness; in you they violate women in their menstrual periods. 11 One commits abomination with his neighbor's wife; another lewdly defiles his daughter-in-law; another in you defiles his sister, his father's daughter. 12 In you, they take bribes to shed blood; you take both advance interest and accrued interest, and make gain of your neighbors by extortion; and you have forgotten me, says the Lord GOD.

13 See, I strike my hands together at the dishonest gain you have made, and at the blood that has been shed within you. 14 Can your courage endure, or can your hands remain strong in the days when I shall deal with you? I the LORD have spoken, and I will do it. 15 I will scatter you among the nations and disperse you through the countries, and I will purge your filthiness out of you. 16 And I[c] shall be profaned through you in the sight of the nations; and you shall know that I am the LORD.

a 21.24 Or be taken captive   b 21.28 Cn: Heb to contain   c 22.16 Gk Syr Vg: Heb you

17 The word of the LORD came to me: **18**Mortal, the house of Israel has become dross to me; all of them, silver,[a] bronze, tin, iron, and lead. In the smelter they have become dross. **19**Therefore thus says the Lord GOD: Because you have all become dross, I will gather you into the midst of Jerusalem. **20**As one gathers silver, bronze, iron, lead, and tin into a smelter, to blow the fire upon them in order to melt them; so I will gather you in my anger and in my wrath, and I will put you in and melt you. **21**I will gather you and blow upon you with the fire of my wrath, and you shall be melted within it. **22**As silver is melted in a smelter, so you shall be melted in it; and you shall know that I the LORD have poured out my wrath upon you.

23 The word of the LORD came to me: **24**Mortal, say to it: You are a land that is not cleansed, not rained upon in the day of indignation. **25**Its princes[b] within it are like a roaring lion tearing the prey; they have devoured human lives; they have taken treasure and precious things; they have made many widows within it. **26**Its priests have done violence to my teaching and have profaned my holy things; they have made no distinction between the holy and the common, neither have they taught the difference between the unclean and the clean, and they have disregarded my sabbaths, so that I am profaned among them. **27**Its officials within it are like wolves tearing the prey, shedding blood, destroying lives to get dishonest gain. **28**Its prophets have smeared whitewash on their behalf, seeing false visions and divining lies for them, saying, "Thus says the Lord GOD," when the LORD has not spoken. **29**The people of the land have practiced extortion and committed robbery; they have oppressed the poor and needy, and have extorted from the alien without redress. **30**And I sought for anyone among them who would repair the wall and stand in the breach before me on behalf of the land, so that I would not destroy it; but I found no one. **31**Therefore I have poured out

my indignation upon them; I have consumed them with the fire of my wrath; I have returned their conduct upon their heads, says the Lord GOD.

OHOLAH AND OHOLIBAH

23 The word of the LORD came to me: **2**Mortal, there were two women, the daughters of one mother; **3**they played the whore in Egypt; they played the whore in their youth; their breasts were caressed there, and their virgin bosoms were fondled. **4**Oholah was the name of the elder and Oholibah the name of her sister. They became mine, and they bore sons and daughters. As for their names, Oholah is Samaria, and Oholibah is Jerusalem.

OUR NEARNESS TO

CHRIST CAN HELP US

AVOID THE INFLUENCE

OF FALSE TEACHING.

5 Oholah played the whore while she was mine; she lusted after her lovers the Assyrians, warriors[c] **6**clothed in blue, governors and commanders, all of them handsome young men, mounted horsemen. **7**She bestowed her favors upon them, the choicest men of Assyria all of them; and she defiled herself with all the idols of everyone for whom she lusted. **8**She did not give up her whorings that she had practiced since Egypt; for in her youth men had lain with her and fondled her virgin bosom and poured out their lust upon her. **9**Therefore I delivered her into the hands of her lovers, into the hands of the Assyrians, for whom she lusted. **10**These uncovered her nakedness; they seized her

---

[a] **22.18** Transposed from the end of the verse; compare verse 20   [b] **22.25** Gk: Heb *indignation*. **25**A conspiracy of its prophets   [c] **23.5** Meaning of Heb uncertain

sons and her daughters; and they killed her with the sword. Judgment was executed upon her, and she became a byword among women.

11 Her sister Oholibah saw this, yet she was more corrupt than she in her lusting and in her whorings, which were worse than those of her sister. 12 She lusted after the Assyrians, governors and commanders, warriors[a] clothed in full armor, mounted horsemen, all of them handsome young men. 13 And I saw that she was defiled; they both took the same way. 14 But she carried her whorings further; she saw male figures carved on the wall, images of the Chaldeans portrayed in vermilion, 15 with belts around their waists, with flowing turbans on their heads, all of them looking like officers—a picture of Babylonians whose native land was Chaldea. 16 When she saw them she lusted after them, and sent messengers to them in Chaldea. 17 And the Babylonians came to her into the bed of love, and they defiled her with their lust; and after she defiled herself with them, she turned from them in disgust. 18 When she carried on her whorings so openly and flaunted her nakedness, I turned in disgust from her, as I had turned from her sister. 19 Yet she increased her whorings, remembering the days of her youth, when she played the whore in the land of Egypt 20 and lusted after her paramours there, whose members were like those of donkeys, and whose emission was like that of stallions. 21 Thus you longed for the lewdness of your youth, when the Egyptians[b] fondled your bosom and caressed[c] your young breasts.

22 Therefore, O Oholibah, thus says the Lord GOD: I will rouse against you your lovers from whom you turned in disgust, and I will bring them against you from every side: 23 the Babylonians and all the Chaldeans, Pekod and Shoa and Koa, and all the Assyrians with them, handsome young men, governors and commanders all of them, officers and warriors,[d] all of them riding on horses. 24 They shall come

against you from the north[e] with chariots and wagons and a host of peoples; they shall set themselves against you on every side with buckler, shield, and helmet, and I will commit the judgment to them, and they shall judge you according to their ordinances. 25 I will direct my indignation against you, in order that they may deal with you in fury. They shall cut off your nose and your ears, and your survivors shall fall by the sword. They shall seize your sons and your daughters, and your survivors shall be devoured by fire. 26 They shall also strip you of your clothes and take away your fine jewels. 27 So I will put an end to your lewdness and your whoring brought from the land of Egypt; you shall not long for them, or remember Egypt any more. 28 For thus says the Lord GOD: I will deliver you into the hands of those whom you hate, into the hands of those from whom you turned in disgust; 29 and they shall deal with you in hatred, and take away all the fruit of your labor, and leave you naked and bare, and the nakedness of your whorings shall be exposed. Your lewdness and your whorings 30 have brought this upon you, because you played the whore with the nations, and polluted yourself with their idols. 31 You have gone the way of your sister; therefore I will give her cup into your hand. 32 Thus says the Lord GOD:

You shall drink your sister's cup,
    deep and wide;
you shall be scorned and derided,
    it holds so much.
33 You shall be filled with
        drunkenness and sorrow.
    A cup of horror and desolation
        is the cup of your sister
        Samaria;
34 you shall drink it and drain it out,
    and gnaw its sherds,
    and tear out your breasts;

a 23.12 Meaning of Heb uncertain
b 23.21 Two Mss: MT *from Egypt*
c 23.21 Cn: Heb *for the sake of*
d 23.23 Compare verses 6 and 12: Heb *officers and called ones* e 23.24 Gk: Meaning of Heb uncertain

for I have spoken, says the Lord GOD. 35Therefore thus says the Lord GOD: Because you have forgotten me and cast me behind your back, therefore bear the consequences of your lewdness and whorings.

36 The LORD said to me: Mortal, will you judge Oholah and Oholibah? Then declare to them their abominable deeds. 37For they have committed adultery, and blood is on their hands; with their idols they have committed adultery; and they have even offered up to them for food the children whom they had borne to me. 38Moreover this they have done to me: they have defiled my sanctuary on the same day and profaned my sabbaths. 39For when they had slaughtered their children for their idols, on the same day they came into my sanctuary to profane it. This is what they did in my house.

40 They even sent for men to come from far away, to whom a messenger was sent, and they came. For them you bathed yourself, painted your eyes, and decked yourself with ornaments; 41you sat on a stately couch, with a table spread before it on which you had placed my incense and my oil. 42The sound of a raucous multitude was around her, with many of the rabble brought in drunken from the wilderness; and they put bracelets on the arms[a] of the women, and beautiful crowns upon their heads.

43 Then I said, Ah, she is worn out with adulteries, but they carry on their sexual acts with her. 44For they have gone in to her, as one goes in to a whore. Thus they went in to Oholah and to Oholibah, wanton women. 45But righteous judges shall declare them guilty of adultery and of bloodshed; because they are adulteresses and blood is on their hands.

46 For thus says the Lord GOD: Bring up an assembly against them, and make them an object of terror and of plunder. 47The assembly shall stone them and with their swords they shall cut them down; they shall kill their sons and their daughters, and burn up their houses. 48Thus will I put an end to lewdness in the

land, so that all women may take warning and not commit lewdness as you have done. 49They shall repay you for your lewdness, and you shall bear the penalty for your sinful idolatry; and you shall know that I am the Lord GOD.

THE BOILING POT

24 In the ninth year, in the tenth month, on the tenth day of the month, the word of the LORD came to me: 2Mortal, write down the name of this day, this very day. The king of Babylon has laid siege to Jerusalem this very day. 3And utter an allegory to the rebellious house and say to them, Thus says the Lord GOD:

Set on the pot, set it on,
    pour in water also;
4 put in it the pieces,
    all the good pieces, the thigh
        and the shoulder;
    fill it with choice bones.
5 Take the choicest one of the flock,
    pile the logs[b] under it;
boil its pieces,[c]
    seethe[d] also its bones in it.

6 Therefore thus says the Lord GOD:
Woe to the bloody city,
    the pot whose rust is in it,
    whose rust has not
        gone out of it!
Empty it piece by piece,
    making no choice at all.[e]
7 For the blood she shed is inside it;
    she placed it on a bare rock;
she did not pour it out on
        the ground,
    to cover it with earth.
8 To rouse my wrath, to take
        vengeance,
    I have placed the blood
        she shed
    on a bare rock,
    so that it may not be covered.
9Therefore thus says the Lord GOD:
Woe to the bloody city!
    I will even make the pile great.

---

a 23.42 Heb *hands*   b 24.5 Compare verse 10: Heb *the bones*   c 24.5 Two Mss: Heb *its boilings*   d 24.5 Cn: Heb *its bones seethe*   e 24.6 Heb *piece, no lot has fallen on it*

10 Heap up the logs, kindle the fire;
    boil the meat well, mix
        in the spices,
    let the bones be burned.
11 Stand it empty upon the coals,
    so that it may become hot,
        its copper glow,
    its filth melt in it, its rust
        be consumed.
12 In vain I have wearied myself;[a]
    its thick rust does not depart.
    To the fire with its rust![b]
13 Yet, when I cleansed you in
        your filthy lewdness,
    you did not become clean
        from your filth;
    you shall not again be cleansed
    until I have satisfied my
        fury upon you.
14 I the LORD have spoken; the time is coming, I will act. I will not refrain, I will not spare, I will not relent. According to your ways and your doings I will judge you, says the Lord GOD.

EZEKIEL'S BEREAVEMENT

15 The word of the LORD came to me: 16 Mortal, with one blow I am about to take away from you the delight of your eyes; yet you shall not mourn or weep, nor shall your tears run down. 17 Sigh, but not aloud; make no mourning for the dead. Bind on your turban, and put your sandals on your feet; do not cover your upper lip or eat the bread of mourners.[c] 18 So I spoke to the people in the morning, and at evening my wife died. And on the next morning I did as I was commanded.

19 Then the people said to me, "Will you not tell us what these things mean for us, that you are acting this way?" 20 Then I said to them: The word of the LORD came to me: 21 Say to the house of Israel, Thus says the Lord GOD: I will profane my sanctuary, the pride of your power, the delight of your eyes, and your heart's desire; and your sons and your daughters whom you left behind shall fall by the sword. 22 And you shall do as I have done; you shall not cover your upper lip or eat the bread of mourners.[c] 23 Your turbans shall be on your heads and your sandals on your feet; you shall not mourn or weep, but you shall pine away in your iniquities and groan to one another. 24 Thus Ezekiel shall be a sign to you; you shall do just as he has done. When this comes, then you shall know that I am the Lord GOD.

25 And you, mortal, on the day when I take from them their stronghold, their joy and glory, the delight of their eyes and their heart's affection, and also[d] their sons and their daughters, 26 on that day, one who has escaped will come to you to report to you the news. 27 On that day your mouth shall be opened to the one who has escaped, and you shall speak and no longer be silent. So you shall be a sign to them; and they shall know that I am the LORD.

PROCLAMATION AGAINST AMMON

25 The word of the LORD came to me: 2 Mortal, set your face toward the Ammonites and prophesy against them. 3 Say to the Ammonites, Hear the word of the Lord GOD: Thus says the Lord GOD, Because you said, "Aha!" over my sanctuary when it was profaned, and over the land of Israel when it was made desolate, and over the house of Judah when it went into exile; 4 therefore I am handing you over to the people of the east for a possession. They shall set their encampments among you and pitch their tents in your midst; they shall eat your fruit, and they shall drink your milk. 5 I will make Rabbah a pasture for camels and Ammon a fold for flocks. Then you shall know that I am the LORD. 6 For thus says the Lord GOD: Because you have clapped your hands and stamped your feet and rejoiced with all the malice within you against the land of Israel, 7 therefore I have stretched out my hand against you, and will hand you over as plunder to the nations. I will cut you off from the peoples

---

a 24.12 Cn: Meaning of Heb uncertain
b 24.12 Meaning of Heb uncertain
c 24.17,22 Vg Tg: Heb of men   d 24.25 Heb lacks and also

and will make you perish out of the countries; I will destroy you. Then you shall know that I am the LORD.

PROCLAMATION AGAINST MOAB

8 Thus says the Lord GOD: Because Moab[a] said, The house of Judah is like all the other nations, 9therefore I will lay open the flank of Moab from the towns[b] on its frontier, the glory of the country, Beth-jeshimoth, Baal-meon, and Kiriathaim. 10I will give it along with Ammon to the people of the east as a possession. Thus Ammon shall be remembered no more among the nations, 11and I will execute judgments upon Moab. Then they shall know that I am the LORD.

PROCLAMATION AGAINST EDOM

12 Thus says the Lord GOD: Because Edom acted revengefully against the house of Judah and has grievously offended in taking vengeance upon them, 13therefore thus says the Lord GOD, I will stretch out my hand against Edom, and cut off from it humans and animals, and I will make it desolate; from Teman even to Dedan they shall fall by the sword. 14I will lay my vengeance upon Edom by the hand of my people Israel; and they shall act in Edom according to my anger and according to my wrath; and they shall know my vengeance, says the Lord GOD.

PROCLAMATION AGAINST PHILISTIA

15 Thus says the Lord GOD: Because with unending hostilities the Philistines acted in vengeance, and with malice of heart took revenge in destruction; 16therefore thus says the Lord GOD, I will stretch out my hand against the Philistines, cut off the Cherethites, and destroy the rest of the seacoast. 17I will execute great vengeance on them with wrathful punishments. Then they shall know that I am the LORD, when I lay my vengeance on them.

PROCLAMATION AGAINST TYRE

26 In the eleventh year, on the first day of the month, the word of the LORD came to me: 2Mortal, because Tyre said concerning Jerusalem,

"Aha, broken is the gateway
of the peoples;
it has swung open to me;
I shall be replenished,
now that it is wasted,"
3therefore, thus says the Lord GOD:
See, I am against you, O Tyre!
I will hurl many nations
against you,
as the sea hurls its waves.
4 They shall destroy the
walls of Tyre
and break down its towers.
I will scrape its soil from it
and make it a bare rock.
5 It shall become, in the
midst of the sea,
a place for spreading nets.
I have spoken, says the Lord GOD.
It shall become plunder
for the nations,
6 and its daughter-towns
in the country
shall be killed by the sword.
Then they shall know that I am the LORD.

7 For thus says the Lord GOD: I will bring against Tyre from the north King Nebuchadrezzar of Babylon, king of kings, together with horses, chariots, cavalry, and a great and powerful army.
8 Your daughter-towns in
the country
he shall put to the sword.
He shall set up a siege wall
against you,
cast up a ramp against you,
and raise a roof of shields
against you.
9 He shall direct the shock of
his battering rams
against your walls
and break down your towers
with his axes.
10 His horses shall be so many
that their dust
shall cover you.
At the noise of cavalry,
wheels, and chariots
your very walls shall shake,

a 25.8 Gk Old Latin: Heb Moab and Seir
b 25.9 Heb towns from its towns

when he enters your gates
  like those entering a
    breached city.
11 With the hoofs of his horses
  he shall trample all
    your streets.
He shall put your people
  to the sword,
and your strong pillars shall
  fall to the ground.
12 They will plunder your riches
  and loot your merchandise;
they shall break down your walls
  and destroy your fine houses.
Your stones and timber and soil
  they shall cast into the water.
13 I will silence the music
  of your songs;
the sound of your lyres shall
  be heard no more.
14 I will make you a bare rock;
  you shall be a place for
    spreading nets.
You shall never again be rebuilt,
  for I the LORD have spoken,
    says the Lord GOD.

15 Thus says the Lord GOD to Tyre: Shall not the coastlands shake at the sound of your fall, when the wounded groan, when slaughter goes on within you? 16 Then all the princes of the sea shall step down from their thrones; they shall remove their robes and strip off their embroidered garments. They shall clothe themselves with trembling, and shall sit on the ground; they shall tremble every moment, and be appalled at you. 17 And they shall raise a lamentation over you, and say to you:

How you have vanished[a]
  from the seas,
O city renowned,
once mighty on the sea,
  you and your inhabitants,[b]
who imposed your[c] terror
  on all the mainland![d]
18 Now the coastlands tremble
  on the day of your fall;
the coastlands by the sea
  are dismayed at your passing.

19 For thus says the Lord GOD: When I make you a city laid waste, like cities that are not inhabited, when I bring up the deep over you, and the great waters cover you,

20 then I will thrust you down with those who descend into the Pit, to the people of long ago, and I will make you live in the world below, among primeval ruins, with those who go down to the Pit, so that you will not be inhabited or have a place[e] in the land of the living. 21 I will bring you to a dreadful end, and you shall be no more; though sought for, you will never be found again, says the Lord GOD.

LAMENTATION OVER TYRE

27 The word of the LORD came to me: 2 Now you, mortal, raise a lamentation over Tyre, 3 and say to Tyre, which sits at the entrance to the sea, merchant of the peoples on many coastlands, Thus says the Lord GOD:

O Tyre, you have said,
  "I am perfect in beauty."
4 Your borders are in the
    heart of the seas;
  your builders made perfect
    your beauty.
5 They made all your planks
  of fir trees from Senir;
they took a cedar from Lebanon
  to make a mast for you.
6 From oaks of Bashan
  they made your oars;
they made your deck of pines[f]
  from the coasts of Cyprus,
    inlaid with ivory.
7 Of fine embroidered linen
    from Egypt
  was your sail,
    serving as your ensign;
blue and purple from the
    coasts of Elishah
  was your awning.
8 The inhabitants of Sidon
    and Arvad
  were your rowers;
skilled men of Zemer[g] were
    within you,
  they were your pilots.

a 26.17 Gk OL Aquila: Heb have vanished, O inhabited one,   b 26.17 Heb it and its inhabitants   c 26.17 Heb their   d 26.17 Cn: Heb its inhabitants   e 26.20 Gk: Heb I will give beauty   f 27.6 Or boxwood   g 27.8 Cn Compare Gen 10.18: Heb your skilled men, O Tyre

9 The elders of Gebal and its
    artisans were within you,
    caulking your seams;
all the ships of the sea with
    their mariners were
    within you,
    to barter for your wares.
10 Paras[a] and Lud and Put
    were in your army,
    your mighty warriors;
they hung shield and
    helmet in you;
    they gave you splendor.
11 Men of Arvad and Helech[b]
    were on your walls all around;
    men of Gamad were at
    your towers.
They hung their quivers all
    around your walls;
    they made perfect your beauty.
12 Tarshish did business with
you out of the abundance of your
great wealth; silver, iron, tin, and
lead they exchanged for your wares.
13 Javan, Tubal, and Meshech traded
with you; they exchanged human
beings and vessels of bronze for your
merchandise. 14 Beth-togarmah exchanged for your wares horses, war
horses, and mules. 15 The Rhodians[c]
traded with you; many coastlands
were your own special markets;
they brought you in payment ivory
tusks and ebony. 16 Edom[d] did business with you because of your abundant goods; they exchanged for your
wares turquoise, purple, embroidered work, fine linen, coral, and
rubies. 17 Judah and the land of Israel
traded with you; they exchanged for
your merchandise wheat from Minnith, millet,[e] honey, oil, and balm.
18 Damascus traded with you for your
abundant goods—because of your
great wealth of every kind—wine
of Helbon, and white wool. 19 Vedan
and Javan from Uzal[e] entered into
trade for your wares; wrought iron,
cassia, and sweet cane were bartered
for your merchandise. 20 Dedan
traded with you in saddlecloths for
riding. 21 Arabia and all the princes
of Kedar were your favored dealers
in lambs, rams, and goats; in these
they did business with you. 22 The
merchants of Sheba and Raamah
traded with you; they exchanged for

your wares the best of all kinds of
spices, and all precious stones, and
gold. 23 Haran, Canneh, Eden, the
merchants of Sheba, Asshur, and
Chilmad traded with you. 24 These
traded with you in choice garments,
in clothes of blue and embroidered
work, and in carpets of colored material, bound with cords and made
secure; in these they traded with
you.[f] 25 The ships of Tarshish traveled for you in your trade.
So you were filled and
    heavily laden
    in the heart of the seas.
26 Your rowers have brought you
    into the high seas.
The east wind has wrecked you
    in the heart of the seas.
27 Your riches, your wares,
    your merchandise,
    your mariners and your pilots,
    your caulkers, your dealers
        in merchandise,
    and all your warriors
        within you,
    with all the company
        that is with you,
    sink into the heart of the seas
        on the day of your ruin.
28 At the sound of the cry
        of your pilots
    the countryside shakes,
29 and down from their ships
    come all that handle the oar.
The mariners and all the
        pilots of the sea
    stand on the shore
30 and wail aloud over you,
    and cry bitterly.
They throw dust on their heads
    and wallow in ashes;
31 they make themselves
        bald for you,
    and put on sackcloth,
    and they weep over you in
        bitterness of soul,
    with bitter mourning.
32 In their wailing they raise a
        lamentation for you,
    and lament over you:

a 27.10 Or Persia   b 27.11 Or and
your army   c 27.15 Gk: Heb The
Dedanites   d 27.16 Another reading is
Aram   e 27.17,19 Meaning of Heb uncertain
f 27.24 Cn: Heb in your market

"Who was ever destroyed[a]
    like Tyre
    in the midst of the sea?
33 When your wares came
    from the seas,
    you satisfied many peoples;
    with your abundant wealth
        and merchandise
    you enriched the kings
        of the earth.
34 Now you are wrecked by the seas,
    in the depths of the waters;
    your merchandise and
        all your crew
    have sunk with you.
35 All the inhabitants of the
        coastlands
    are appalled at you;
    and their kings are
        horribly afraid,
    their faces are convulsed.
36 The merchants among the
        peoples hiss at you;
    you have come to a
        dreadful end
    and shall be no more forever."

PROCLAMATION AGAINST
THE KING OF TYRE

28 The word of the LORD came
to me: 2Mortal, say to the
prince of Tyre, Thus says the Lord
GOD:
    Because your heart is proud
        and you have said, "I am a god;
    I sit in the seat of the gods,
        in the heart of the seas,"
    yet you are but a mortal,
        and no god,
    though you compare
        your mind
    with the mind of a god.
3 You are indeed wiser
        than Daniel;[b]
    no secret is hidden from you;
4 by your wisdom and your
        understanding
    you have amassed wealth
        for yourself,
    and have gathered gold and silver
        into your treasuries.
5 By your great wisdom in trade
    you have increased
        your wealth,
    and your heart has become
        proud in your wealth.
6 Therefore thus says the Lord GOD:

Because you compare your mind
    with the mind of a god,
7 therefore, I will bring strangers
        against you,
    the most terrible of
        the nations;
    they shall draw their swords
    against the beauty
        of your wisdom
    and defile your splendor.
8 They shall thrust you down
        to the Pit,
    and you shall die a
        violent death
    in the heart of the seas.
9 Will you still say, "I am a god,"
        in the presence of those
        who kill you,
    though you are but a mortal,
        and no god,
    in the hands of those
        who wound you?
10 You shall die the death of
        the uncircumcised
    by the hand of foreigners;
    for I have spoken, says
        the Lord GOD.

LAMENTATION OVER
THE KING OF TYRE

11 Moreover the word of the LORD
came to me: 12Mortal, raise a lamentation over the king of Tyre, and say
to him, Thus says the Lord GOD:
    You were the signet of
        perfection,[c]
    full of wisdom and
        perfect in beauty.
13 You were in Eden, the
        garden of God;
    every precious stone was
        your covering,
    carnelian, chrysolite, and
        moonstone,
    beryl, onyx, and jasper,
    sapphire,[d] turquoise,
        and emerald;
    and worked in gold were
        your settings
    and your engravings.[c]
    On the day that you were created
    they were prepared.

---

a 27.32 Tg Vg: Heb like silence   b 28.3 Or, as
otherwise read, Danel   c 28.12,13 Meaning
of Heb uncertain   d 28.13 Or lapis lazuli

14 With an anointed cherub as
        guardian I placed you;[a]
    you were on the holy
        mountain of God;
    you walked among the
        stones of fire.
15 You were blameless in your ways
        from the day that you
        were created,
    until iniquity was
        found in you.
16 In the abundance of your trade
        you were filled with violence,
        and you sinned;
    so I cast you as a profane
        thing from the
        mountain of God,
    and the guardian cherub
        drove you out
    from among the stones of fire.
17 Your heart was proud because
        of your beauty;
    you corrupted your wisdom for
        the sake of your splendor.
    I cast you to the ground;
        I exposed you before kings,
        to feast their eyes on you.
18 By the multitude of your
        iniquities,
    in the unrighteousness
        of your trade,
    you profaned your sanctuaries.
    So I brought out fire from
        within you;
    it consumed you,
    and I turned you to ashes
        on the earth
    in the sight of all who saw you.
19 All who know you among
        the peoples
    are appalled at you;
    you have come to a dreadful end
    and shall be no more forever.

PROCLAMATION AGAINST SIDON

20 The word of the LORD came to
me: 21Mortal, set your face toward
Sidon, and prophesy against it,
22and say, Thus says the Lord GOD:
    I am against you, O Sidon,
        and I will gain glory in
        your midst.
    They shall know that I
        am the LORD
    when I execute
        judgments in it,
    and manifest my holiness in it;

23 for I will send pestilence into it,
        and bloodshed into its streets;
    and the dead shall fall
        in its midst,
    by the sword that is against
        it on every side.
    And they shall know that
        I am the LORD.

24 The house of Israel shall no longer find a pricking brier or a piercing thorn among all their neighbors
who have treated them with contempt. And they shall know that I
am the Lord GOD.

FUTURE BLESSING FOR ISRAEL

25 Thus says the Lord GOD: When
I gather the house of Israel from
the peoples among whom they are
scattered, and manifest my holiness
in them in the sight of the nations,
then they shall settle on their own
soil that I gave to my servant Jacob.
26They shall live in safety in it, and
shall build houses and plant vineyards. They shall live in safety, when
I execute judgments upon all their
neighbors who have treated them
with contempt. And they shall know
that I am the LORD their God.

PROCLAMATION AGAINST EGYPT

29 In the tenth year, in the
tenth month, on the twelfth
day of the month, the word of the
LORD came to me: 2Mortal, set your
face against Pharaoh king of Egypt,
and prophesy against him and
against all Egypt; 3speak, and say,
Thus says the Lord GOD:
    I am against you,
        Pharaoh king of Egypt,
    the great dragon sprawling
        in the midst of its channels,
    saying, "My Nile is my own;
        I made it for myself."
4 I will put hooks in your jaws,
        and make the fish of
        your channels stick
        to your scales.
    I will draw you up from
        your channels,
    with all the fish of
        your channels
    sticking to your scales.

[a] 28.14 Meaning of Heb uncertain

5 I will fling you into the
    wilderness,
  you and all the fish of
    your channels;
  you shall fall in the open field,
    and not be gathered and buried.
  To the animals of the earth and
    to the birds of the air
  I have given you as food.
6 Then all the inhabitants of
    Egypt shall know
  that I am the LORD
  because you[a] were a staff of reed
    to the house of Israel;
7 when they grasped you with
    the hand, you broke,
  and tore all their shoulders;
  and when they leaned on
    you, you broke,
  and made all their legs
    unsteady.[b]

8 Therefore, thus says the Lord
GOD: I will bring a sword upon you,
and will cut off from you human
being and animal; 9and the land
of Egypt shall be a desolation and a
waste. Then they shall know that I
am the LORD.

Because you[c] said, "The Nile is
mine, and I made it," 10therefore, I
am against you, and against your
channels, and I will make the land
of Egypt an utter waste and desolation, from Migdol to Syene, as far as
the border of Ethiopia.[d] 11No human
foot shall pass through it, and no animal foot shall pass through it; it shall
be uninhabited forty years. 12I will
make the land of Egypt a desolation
among desolated countries; and her
cities shall be a desolation forty years
among cities that are laid waste. I
will scatter the Egyptians among the
nations, and disperse them among
the countries.

13 Further, thus says the Lord
GOD: At the end of forty years I will
gather the Egyptians from the peoples among whom they were scattered; 14and I will restore the fortunes of Egypt, and bring them back
to the land of Pathros, the land of
their origin; and there they shall be a
lowly kingdom. 15It shall be the most
lowly of the kingdoms, and never
again exalt itself above the nations;
and I will make them so small that

they will never again rule over the
nations. 16The Egyptians[e] shall never
again be the reliance of the house of
Israel; they will recall their iniquity,
when they turned to them for aid.
Then they shall know that I am the
Lord GOD.

BABYLONIA WILL PLUNDER EGYPT

17 In the twenty-seventh year, in
the first month, on the first day of
the month, the word of the LORD
came to me: 18Mortal, King Nebuchadrezzar of Babylon made his
army labor hard against Tyre; every
head was made bald and every shoulder was rubbed bare; yet neither he
nor his army got anything from Tyre
to pay for the labor that he had ex-
pended against it. 19Therefore thus
says the Lord GOD: I will give the
land of Egypt to King Nebuchadrezzar of Babylon; and he shall carry off
its wealth and despoil it and plunder
it; and it shall be the wages for his
army. 20I have given him the land of
Egypt as his payment for which he
labored, because they worked for me,
says the Lord GOD.

21 On that day I will cause a horn
to sprout up for the house of Israel,
and I will open your lips among
them. Then they shall know that I
am the LORD.

LAMENTATION FOR EGYPT

30 The word of the LORD came
to me: 2Mortal, prophesy,
and say, Thus says the Lord GOD:
  Wail, "Alas for the day!"
3   For a day is near,
    the day of the LORD is near;
  it will be a day of clouds,
    a time of doom[f] for the nations.
4 A sword shall come upon Egypt,
    and anguish shall be
      in Ethiopia,[d]
  when the slain fall in Egypt,
    and its wealth is carried away,
    and its foundations are
      torn down.

a 29.6 Gk Syr Vg: Heb they   b 29.7 Syr: Heb
stand   c 29.9 Gk Syr Vg: Heb he   d 29.10;
30.4 Or Nubia; Heb Cush   e 29.16 Heb It
f 30.3 Heb lacks of doom

⁵Ethiopia,ᵃ and Put, and Lud, and all Arabia, and Libya,ᵇ and the people of the allied landᶜ shall fall with them by the sword.

⁶ Thus says the LORD:
Those who support Egypt shall fall,
and its proud might shall
come down;
from Migdol to Syene
they shall fall within it
by the sword,
says the Lord GOD.
⁷ They shall be desolated among
other desolated countries,
and their cities shall lie among
cities laid waste.
⁸ Then they shall know that
I am the LORD,
when I have set fire to Egypt,
and all who help it are broken.
⁹ On that day, messengers shall go out from me in ships to terrify the unsuspecting Ethiopians;ᵈ and anguish shall come upon them on the day of Egypt's doom;ᵉ for it is coming!

¹⁰ Thus says the Lord GOD:
I will put an end to the
hordes of Egypt,
by the hand of King
Nebuchadrezzar
of Babylon.
¹¹ He and his people with him,
the most terrible
of the nations,
shall be brought in to
destroy the land;
and they shall draw their
swords against Egypt,
and fill the land with the slain.
¹² I will dry up the channels,
and will sell the land into
the hand of evildoers;
I will bring desolation upon the
land and everything in it
by the hand of foreigners;
I the LORD have spoken.

¹³ Thus says the Lord GOD:
I will destroy the idols
and put an end to the
images in Memphis;
there shall no longer be a prince
in the land of Egypt;
so I will put fear in the
land of Egypt.

¹⁴ I will make Pathros a desolation,
and will set fire to Zoan,
and will execute acts of
judgment on Thebes.
¹⁵ I will pour my wrath upon
Pelusium,
the stronghold of Egypt,
and cut off the hordes
of Thebes.
¹⁶ I will set fire to Egypt;
Pelusium shall be in
great agony;
Thebes shall be breached,
and Memphis face
adversaries by day.
¹⁷ The young men of On and
of Pi-beseth shall
fall by the sword;
and the cities themselvesᶠ
shall go into captivity.
¹⁸ At Tehaphnehes the day
shall be dark,
when I break there the
dominion of Egypt,
and its proud might shall
come to an end;
the cityᵍ shall be covered
by a cloud,
and its daughter-towns shall
go into captivity.
¹⁹ Thus I will execute acts of
judgment on Egypt.
Then they shall know that
I am the LORD.

PROCLAMATION AGAINST PHARAOH

20 In the eleventh year, in the first month, on the seventh day of the month, the word of the LORD came to me: ²¹Mortal, I have broken the arm of Pharaoh king of Egypt; it has not been bound up for healing or wrapped with a bandage, so that it may become strong to wield the sword. ²²Therefore thus says the Lord GOD: I am against Pharaoh king of Egypt, and will break his arms, both the strong arm and the one that was broken; and I will make the sword fall from his hand. ²³I will scatter the Egyptians among the

ᵃ 30.5 Or *Nubia*; Heb *Cush* ᵇ 30.5 Compare Gk Syr Vg: Heb *Cub* ᶜ 30.5 Meaning of Heb uncertain ᵈ 30.9 Or *Nubians*; Heb *Cush* ᵉ 30.9 Heb *the day of Egypt* ᶠ 30.17 Heb *and they* ᵍ 30.18 Heb *she*

nations, and disperse them throughout the lands. 24I will strengthen the arms of the king of Babylon, and put my sword in his hand; but I will break the arms of Pharaoh, and he will groan before him with the groans of one mortally wounded. 25I will strengthen the arms of the king of Babylon, but the arms of Pharaoh shall fall. And they shall know that I am the LORD, when I put my sword into the hand of the king of Babylon. He shall stretch it out against the land of Egypt, 26and I will scatter the Egyptians among the nations and disperse them throughout the countries. Then they shall know that I am the LORD.

THE LOFTY CEDAR

31 In the eleventh year, in the third month, on the first day of the month, the word of the LORD came to me: 2Mortal, say to Pharaoh king of Egypt and to his hordes:

Whom are you like in your
    greatness?
3   Consider Assyria, a cedar
        of Lebanon,
    with fair branches and
        forest shade,
    and of great height,
        its top among the clouds.ᵃ
4   The waters nourished it,
        the deep made it grow tall,
    making its rivers flowᵇ
        around the place it
            was planted,
    sending forth its streams
        to all the trees of the field.
5   So it towered high
        above all the trees of the field;
    its boughs grew large
        and its branches long,
    from abundant water
        in its shoots.
6   All the birds of the air
        made their nests in its boughs;
    under its branches all the
            animals of the field
        gave birth to their young;
    and in its shade
        all great nations lived.
7   It was beautiful in its greatness,
        in the length of its branches;
    for its roots went down
        to abundant water.

8   The cedars in the garden of
        God could not rival it,
    nor the fir trees equal
        its boughs;
    the plane trees were as nothing
        compared with its branches;
    no tree in the garden of God
        was like it in beauty.
9   I made it beautiful
        with its mass of branches,
    the envy of all the trees of Eden
        that were in the garden of God.

10Therefore thus says the Lord GOD: Because itᶜ towered high and set its top among the clouds,ᵃ and its heart was proud of its height, 11I gave it into the hand of the prince of the nations; he has dealt with it as its wickedness deserves. I have cast it out. 12Foreigners from the most terrible of the nations have cut it down and left it. On the mountains and in all the valleys its branches have fallen, and its boughs lie broken in all the watercourses of the land; and all the peoples of the earth went away from its shade and left it.
13   On its fallen trunk settle
        all the birds of the air,
    and among its boughs lodge
        all the wild animals.

14All this is in order that no trees by the waters may grow to lofty height or set their tops among the clouds,ᵃ and that no trees that drink water may reach up to them in height.

    For all of them are handed
        over to death,
    to the world below;
    along with all mortals,
        with those who go
            down to the Pit.

15Thus says the Lord GOD: On the day it went down to Sheol I closed the deep over it and covered it; I restrained its rivers, and its mighty waters were checked. I clothed Lebanon in gloom for it, and all the trees of the field fainted because of it. 16I made the nations quake at the sound of its fall, when I cast it down to Sheol with those who go down to the Pit; and all the trees of Eden, the choice and best of Lebanon, all that

ᵃ 31.3,10,14 Gk: Heb *thick boughs*   ᵇ 31.4 Gk: Heb *rivers going*   ᶜ 31.10 Syr Vg: Heb *you* were well watered, were consoled in the world below. [17] They also went down to Sheol with it, to those killed by the sword, along with its allies,[a] those who lived in its shade among the nations.

[18] Which among the trees of Eden was like you in glory and in greatness? Now you shall be brought down with the trees of Eden to the world below; you shall lie among the uncircumcised, with those who are killed by the sword. This is Pharaoh and all his horde, says the Lord GOD.

LAMENTATION OVER PHARAOH AND EGYPT

32 In the twelfth year, in the twelfth month, on the first day of the month, the word of the LORD came to me: [2] Mortal, raise a lamentation over Pharaoh king of Egypt, and say to him:
You consider yourself a lion
among the nations,
but you are like a dragon
in the seas;
you thrash about in your streams,
trouble the water with
your feet,
and foul your[b] streams.
[3] Thus says the Lord GOD:
In an assembly of
many peoples
I will throw my net over you;
and I[c] will haul you up
in my dragnet.
[4] I will throw you on the ground,
on the open field I will
fling you,
and will cause all the birds of
the air to settle on you,
and I will let the wild animals
of the whole earth gorge
themselves with you.
[5] I will strew your flesh on
the mountains,
and fill the valleys with
your carcass.[d]
[6] I will drench the land with
your flowing blood
up to the mountains,
and the watercourses will
be filled with you.
[7] When I blot you out, I will
cover the heavens,
and make their stars dark;

I will cover the sun with a cloud,
and the moon shall not
give its light.
[8] All the shining lights of
the heavens
I will darken above you,
and put darkness on your land,
says the Lord GOD.
[9] I will trouble the hearts of
many peoples,
as I carry you captive[e]
among the nations,
into countries you have
not known.
[10] I will make many peoples
appalled at you;
their kings shall shudder
because of you.
When I brandish my sword
before them,
they shall tremble
every moment
for their lives, each one of them,
on the day of your downfall.
[11] For thus says the Lord GOD:
The sword of the king of Babylon
shall come against you.
[12] I will cause your hordes to fall
by the swords of mighty ones,
all of them most terrible
among the nations.
They shall bring to ruin the
pride of Egypt,
and all its hordes shall perish.
[13] I will destroy all its livestock
from beside abundant waters;
and no human foot shall trouble
them any more,
nor shall the hoofs of cattle
trouble them.
[14] Then I will make their
waters clear,
and cause their streams to run
like oil, says the Lord GOD.
[15] When I make the land of
Egypt desolate
and when the land is stripped
of all that fills it,
when I strike down all
who live in it,
then they shall know that
I am the LORD.

---

[a] **31.17** Heb *its arms* [b] **32.2** Heb *their*
[c] **32.3** Gk Vg: Heb *they* [d] **32.5** Symmachus Syr Vg: Heb *your height* [e] **32.9** Gk: Heb *bring your destruction*

16 This is a lamentation; it
     shall be chanted.
The women of the nations
     shall chant it.
Over Egypt and all its hordes
     they shall chant it,
says the Lord GOD.

DIRGE OVER EGYPT

17 In the twelfth year, in the first month,[a] on the fifteenth day of the month, the word of the LORD came to me: 18 Mortal, wail over the
     hordes of Egypt,
and send them down,
with Egypt[b] and the daughters
     of majestic nations,
to the world below,
with those who go
     down to the Pit.
19 "Whom do you surpass in beauty?
Go down! Be laid to rest with
     the uncircumcised!"
20 They shall fall among those who are killed by the sword. Egypt[c] has been handed over to the sword; carry away both it and its hordes. 21 The mighty chiefs shall speak of them, with their helpers, out of the midst of Sheol: "They have come down, they lie still, the uncircumcised, killed by the sword."

22 Assyria is there, and all its company, their graves all around it, all of them killed, fallen by the sword. 23 Their graves are set in the uttermost parts of the Pit. Its company is all around its grave, all of them killed, fallen by the sword, who spread terror in the land of the living.

24 Elam is there, and all its hordes around its grave; all of them killed, fallen by the sword, who went down uncircumcised into the world below, who spread terror in the land of the living. They bear their shame with those who go down to the Pit. 25 They have made Elam[b] a bed among the slain with all its hordes, their graves all around it, all of them uncircumcised, killed by the sword; for terror of them was spread in the land of the living, and they bear their shame with those who go down to the Pit; they are placed among the slain.

26 Meshech and Tubal are there, and all their multitude, their graves all around them, all of them uncircumcised, killed by the sword; for they spread terror in the land of the living. 27 And they do not lie with the fallen warriors of long ago[d] who went down to Sheol with their weapons of war, whose swords were laid under their heads, and whose shields[e] are upon their bones; for the terror of the warriors was in the land of the living. 28 So you shall be broken and lie among the uncircumcised, with those who are killed by the sword.

29 Edom is there, its kings and all its princes, who for all their might are laid with those who are killed by the sword; they lie with the uncircumcised, with those who go down to the Pit.

30 The princes of the north are there, all of them, and all the Sidonians, who have gone down in shame with the slain, for all the terror that they caused by their might; they lie uncircumcised with those who are killed by the sword, and bear their shame with those who go down to the Pit.

31 When Pharaoh sees them, he will be consoled for all his hordes— Pharaoh and all his army, killed by the sword, says the Lord GOD. 32 For he[f] spread terror in the land of the living; therefore he shall be laid to rest among the uncircumcised, with those who are slain by the sword— Pharaoh and all his multitude, says the Lord GOD.

EZEKIEL, ISRAEL'S SENTRY

33 The word of the LORD came to me: 2 O Mortal, speak to your people and say to them, If I bring the sword upon a land, and the people of the land take one of their number as their sentinel; 3 and if the sentinel sees the sword coming upon the land and blows the trumpet and warns the people; 4 then if any who

a 32.17 Gk: Heb lacks *in the first month*   b 32.18,25 Heb *it*   c 32.20 Heb *It*   d 32.27 Gk Old Latin: Heb *of the uncircumcised*   e 32.27 Cn: Heb *iniquities*   f 32.32 Cn: Heb *I*

hear the sound of the trumpet do not take warning, and the sword comes and takes them away, their blood shall be upon their own heads. 5They heard the sound of the trumpet and did not take warning; their blood shall be upon themselves. But if they had taken warning, they would have saved their lives. 6But if the sentinel sees the sword coming and does not blow the trumpet, so that the people are not warned, and the sword comes and takes any of them, they are taken away in their iniquity, but their blood I will require at the sentinel's hand.

7 So you, mortal, I have made a sentinel for the house of Israel; whenever you hear a word from my mouth, you shall give them warning from me. 8If I say to the wicked, "O wicked ones, you shall surely die," and you do not speak to warn the wicked to turn from their ways, the wicked shall die in their iniquity, but their blood I will require at your hand. 9But if you warn the wicked to turn from their ways, and they do not turn from their ways, the wicked shall die in their iniquity, but you will have saved your life.

GOD'S JUSTICE AND MERCY

10 Now you, mortal, say to the house of Israel, Thus you have said: "Our transgressions and our sins weigh upon us, and we waste away because of them; how then can we live?" 11Say to them, As I live, says the Lord GOD, I have no pleasure in the death of the wicked, but that the wicked turn from their ways and live; turn back, turn back from your evil ways; for why will you die, O house of Israel? 12And you, mortal, say to your people, The righteousness of the righteous shall not save them when they transgress; and as for the wickedness of the wicked, it shall not make them stumble when they turn from their wickedness; and the righteous shall not be able to live by their righteousnessa when they sin. 13Though I say to the righteous that they shall surely live, yet if they trust in their righteousness and commit iniquity,

none of their righteous deeds shall be remembered; but in the iniquity that they have committed they shall die. 14Again, though I say to the wicked, "You shall surely die," yet if they turn from their sin and do what is lawful and right— 15if the wicked restore the pledge, give back what they have taken by robbery, and walk in the statutes of life, committing no iniquity—they shall surely live, they shall not die. 16None of the sins that they have committed shall be remembered against them; they have done what is lawful and right, they shall surely live.

17 Yet your people say, "The way of the Lord is not just," when it is their own way that is not just. 18When the righteous turn from their righteousness, and commit iniquity, they shall die for it.b 19And when the wicked turn from their wickedness, and do what is lawful and right, they shall live by it.b 20Yet you say, "The way of the Lord is not just." O house of Israel, I will judge all of you according to your ways!

THE FALL OF JERUSALEM

21 In the twelfth year of our exile, in the tenth month, on the fifth day of the month, someone who had escaped from Jerusalem came to me and said, "The city has fallen." 22Now the hand of the LORD had been upon me the evening before the fugitive came; but he had opened my mouth by the time the fugitive came to me in the morning; so my mouth was opened, and I was no longer unable to speak.

THE SURVIVORS IN JUDAH

23 The word of the LORD came to me: 24Mortal, the inhabitants of these waste places in the land of Israel keep saying, "Abraham was only one man, yet he got possession of the land; but we are many; the land is surely given us to possess." 25Therefore say to them, Thus says the Lord GOD: You eat flesh with the blood, and lift up your eyes to your idols, and shed blood; shall you then possess

a 33.12 Heb by it   b 33.18,19 Heb them

the land? 26You depend on your swords, you commit abominations, and each of you defiles his neighbor's wife; shall you then possess the land? 27Say this to them, Thus says the Lord GOD: As I live, surely those who are in the waste places shall fall by the sword; and those who are in the open field I will give to the wild animals to be devoured; and those who are in strongholds and in caves shall die by pestilence. 28I will make the land a desolation and a waste, and its proud might shall come to an end; and the mountains of Israel shall be so desolate that no one will pass through. 29Then they shall know that I am the LORD, when I have made the land a desolation and a waste because of all their abominations that they have committed.

30 As for you, mortal, your people who talk together about you by the walls, and at the doors of the houses, say to one another, each to a neighbor, "Come and hear what the word is that comes from the LORD." 31They come to you as people come, and they sit before you as my people, and they hear your words, but they will not obey them. For flattery is on their lips, but their heart is set on their gain. 32To them you are like a singer of love songs,[a] one who has a beautiful voice and plays well on an instrument; they hear what you say, but they will not do it. 33When this comes—and come it will!—then they shall know that a prophet has been among them.

ISRAEL'S FALSE SHEPHERDS

34 The word of the LORD came to me: 2Mortal, prophesy against the shepherds of Israel: prophesy, and say to them—to the shepherds: Thus says the Lord GOD: Ah, you shepherds of Israel who have been feeding yourselves! Should not shepherds feed the sheep? 3You eat the fat, you clothe yourselves with the wool, you slaughter the fatlings; but you do not feed the sheep. 4You have not strengthened the weak, you have not healed the sick, you have not bound up the injured, you have not brought back the strayed,

you have not sought the lost, but with force and harshness you have ruled them. 5So they were scattered, because there was no shepherd; and scattered, they became food for all the wild animals. 6My sheep were scattered, they wandered over all the mountains and on every high hill; my sheep were scattered over all the face of the earth, with no one to search or seek for them.

7 Therefore, you shepherds, hear the word of the LORD: 8As I live, says the Lord GOD, because my sheep have become a prey, and my sheep have become food for all the wild animals, since there was no shepherd; and because my shepherds have not searched for my sheep, but the shepherds have fed themselves, and have not fed my sheep; 9therefore, you shepherds, hear the word of the LORD: 10Thus says the Lord GOD, I am against the shepherds; and I will demand my sheep at their hand, and put a stop to their feeding the sheep; no longer shall the shepherds feed themselves. I will rescue my sheep from their mouths, so that they may not be food for them.

GOD, THE TRUE SHEPHERD

11 For thus says the Lord GOD: I myself will search for my sheep, and will seek them out. 12As shepherds seek out their flocks when they are among their scattered sheep, so I will seek out my sheep. I will rescue them from all the places to which they have been scattered on a day of clouds and thick darkness. 13I will bring them out from the peoples and gather them from the countries, and will bring them into their own land; and I will feed them on the mountains of Israel, by the watercourses, and in all the inhabited parts of the land. 14I will feed them with good pasture, and the mountain heights of Israel shall be their pasture; there they shall lie down in good grazing land, and they shall feed on rich pasture on the mountains of Israel. 15I myself will be the shepherd of my sheep, and I will make them lie

a 33.32 Cn: Heb *like a love song*

down, says the Lord GOD. ¹⁶I will seek the lost, and I will bring back the strayed, and I will bind up the injured, and I will strengthen the weak, but the fat and the strong I will destroy. I will feed them with justice.

17 As for you, my flock, thus says the Lord GOD: I shall judge between sheep and sheep, between rams and goats: ¹⁸Is it not enough for you to feed on the good pasture, but you must tread down with your feet the rest of your pasture? When you drink of clear water, must you foul the rest with your feet? ¹⁹And must my sheep eat what you have trodden with your feet, and drink what you have fouled with your feet?

20 Therefore, thus says the Lord GOD to them: I myself will judge between the fat sheep and the lean sheep. ²¹Because you pushed with flank and shoulder, and butted at all the weak animals with your horns until you scattered them far and wide, ²²I will save my flock, and they shall no longer be ravaged; and I will judge between sheep and sheep.

23 I will set up over them one shepherd, my servant David, and he shall feed them: he shall feed them and be their shepherd. ²⁴And I, the LORD, will be their God, and my servant David shall be prince among them; I, the LORD, have spoken.

25 I will make with them a covenant of peace and banish wild animals from the land, so that they may live in the wild and sleep in the woods securely. ²⁶I will make them and the region around my hill a blessing; and I will send down the showers in their season; they shall be showers of blessing. ²⁷The trees of the field shall yield their fruit, and the earth shall yield its increase. They shall be secure on their soil; and they shall know that I am the LORD, when I break the bars of their yoke, and save them from the hands of those who enslaved them. ²⁸They shall no more be plunder for the nations, nor shall the animals of the land devour them; they shall live in safety, and no one shall make them afraid. ²⁹I will provide for them a splendid vegetation so that they shall no more be consumed with hunger in the land, and no longer suffer the insults of the nations. ³⁰They shall know that I, the LORD their God, am with them, and that they, the house of Israel, are my people, says the Lord GOD. ³¹You are my sheep, the sheep of my pastureᵃ and I am your God, says the Lord GOD.

JUDGMENT ON MOUNT SEIR

35 The word of the LORD came to me: ²Mortal, set your face against Mount Seir, and prophesy against it, ³and say to it, Thus says the Lord GOD:

ᵃ **34.31** Gk OL: Heb *pasture, you are people*

⊢ BIBLE IN LIFE ▷ ─○

Being Vulnerable   *Ezekiel 34.12*

Sheep are known to be vulnerable, weak followers. Like sheep, we are vulnerable to the things that can destroy our lives and turn us away from our shepherd—retaining hatred, resentment and unforgiveness, or being centered on our own needs or ambitions to the exclusion of others. Throughout the Bible, God is depicted as a shepherd, and we human beings desperately need God's guiding presence in our lives. We should look upon ourselves as dependent upon a shepherd, needing to be supported, protected, corrected and led by our Savior, Jesus Christ. There's nothing wrong with being a follower if we follow Christ. There's nothing wrong with admitting our vulnerability so that we don't become prey to temptation, fear, doubt and selfishness. Thus, admitting our own vulnerability and accepting the image of ourselves as sheep protects us. Without Christ we may be vulnerable, weak and afraid, but with Christ as our shepherd, we are protected, strong and reassured.

PONDER

I will set up over them one shepherd, my servant David, and he shall feed them: he shall feed them and be their shepherd. And I, the LORD, will be their God, and my servant David shall be prince among them; I, the LORD, have spoken.
—Ezekiel 34.23–24

PRAY

Lord, we are grateful for a chance to read of Ezekiel, a priest who looked at the plight of his contemporaries and saw a need for a great leader. And a great leader did come almost 600 years later in the person of Jesus Christ, our Savior. Jesus, a descendant of David, was the leader who became our Good Shepherd, who knows us by name and calls us. Give us ears to hear and to follow him wherever he leads us. We ask this in his name. Amen.

I am against you, Mount Seir;
　I stretch out my hand
　　against you
　to make you a desolation
　　and a waste.
4 I lay your towns in ruins;
　you shall become a desolation,
　and you shall know that
　　I am the LORD.
5Because you cherished an ancient enmity, and gave over the people of Israel to the power of the sword at the time of their calamity, at the time of their final punishment; 6therefore, as I live, says the Lord GOD, I will prepare you for blood, and blood shall pursue you; since you did not hate bloodshed, bloodshed shall pursue you. 7I will make Mount Seir a waste and a desolation; and I will cut off from it all who come and go. 8I will fill its mountains with the slain; on your hills and in your valleys and in all your watercourses those killed with the sword shall fall. 9I will make you a perpetual desolation, and your cities shall never be inhabited. Then you shall know that I am the LORD.

10 Because you said, "These two nations and these two countries shall be mine, and we will take possession of them,"—although the LORD was there— 11therefore, as I live, says the Lord GOD, I will deal with you according to the anger and envy that you showed because of your hatred against them; and I will make myself known among you,[a] when I judge you. 12You shall know that I, the LORD, have heard all the abusive speech that you uttered against the mountains of Israel, saying, "They are laid desolate, they are given us to devour." 13And you magnified yourselves against me with your mouth, and multiplied your words against me; I heard it. 14Thus says the Lord GOD: As the whole earth rejoices, I will make you desolate. 15As you rejoiced over the inheritance of the house of Israel, because it was desolate, so I will deal with you; you shall be desolate, Mount Seir, and all Edom, all of it. Then they shall know that I am the LORD.

BLESSING ON ISRAEL

36 And you, mortal, prophesy to the mountains of Israel, and say: O mountains of Israel, hear the word of the LORD. 2Thus says the Lord GOD: Because the enemy said of you, "Aha!" and, "The ancient heights have become our possession," 3therefore prophesy, and say: Thus says the Lord GOD: Because they made you desolate indeed, and crushed you from all sides, so that you became the possession of the rest of the nations, and you became an object of gossip and slander among the people; 4therefore, O mountains of Israel, hear the word of the Lord GOD: Thus says the Lord GOD to the mountains and the hills, the watercourses and the valleys, the desolate wastes and the deserted towns, which have become a source of plunder and an object of derision

a 35.11 Gk: Heb *them*

to the rest of the nations all around; ⁵therefore thus says the Lord GOD: I am speaking in my hot jealousy against the rest of the nations, and against all Edom, who, with whole-hearted joy and utter contempt, took my land as their possession, because of its pasture, to plunder it. ⁶Therefore prophesy concerning the land of Israel, and say to the mountains and hills, to the watercourses and valleys, Thus says the Lord GOD: I am speaking in my jealous wrath, because you have suffered the insults of the nations; ⁷therefore thus says the Lord GOD: I swear that the nations that are all around you shall themselves suffer insults.

8 But you, O mountains of Israel, shall shoot out your branches, and yield your fruit to my people Israel; for they shall soon come home. ⁹See now, I am for you; I will turn to you, and you shall be tilled and sown; ¹⁰and I will multiply your population, the whole house of Israel, all of it; the towns shall be inhabited and the waste places rebuilt; ¹¹and I will multiply human beings and animals upon you. They shall increase and be fruitful; and I will cause you to be inhabited as in your former times, and will do more good to you than ever before. Then you shall know that I am the LORD. ¹²I will lead people upon you—my people Israel—and they shall possess you, and you shall be their inheritance. No longer shall you bereave them of children.

13 Thus says the Lord GOD: Because they say to you, "You devour people, and you bereave your nation of children," ¹⁴therefore you shall no longer devour people and no longer bereave your nation of children, says the Lord GOD; ¹⁵and no longer will I let you hear the insults of the nations, no longer shall you bear the disgrace of the peoples; and no longer shall you cause your nation to stumble, says the Lord GOD.

THE RENEWAL OF ISRAEL

16 The word of the LORD came to me: ¹⁷Mortal, when the house of Israel lived on their own soil, they defiled it with their ways and their deeds; their conduct in my sight was like the uncleanness of a woman in her menstrual period. ¹⁸So I poured out my wrath upon them for the blood that they had shed upon the land, and for the idols with which they had defiled it. ¹⁹I scattered them among the nations, and they were dispersed through the countries; in accordance with their conduct and their deeds I judged them. ²⁰But when they came to the nations, wherever they came, they profaned my holy name, in that it was said of them, "These are the people of the LORD, and yet they had to go out of his land." ²¹But I had concern for my holy name, which the house of Israel had profaned among the nations to which they came.

22 Therefore say to the house of Israel, Thus says the Lord GOD: It is not for your sake, O house of Israel, that I am about to act, but for the sake of my holy name, which you have profaned among the nations to which you came. ²³I will sanctify my great name, which has been profaned among the nations, and which you have profaned among them; and the nations shall know that I am the LORD, says the Lord GOD, when through you I display my holiness before their eyes. ²⁴I will take you from the nations, and gather you from all the countries, and bring you into your own land. ²⁵I will sprinkle clean water upon you, and you shall be clean from all your uncleannesses, and from all your idols I will cleanse you. ²⁶A new heart I will give you, and a new spirit I will put within you; and I will remove from your body the heart of stone and give you a heart of flesh. ²⁷I will put my spirit within you, and make you follow my statutes and be careful to observe my ordinances. ²⁸Then you shall live in the land that I gave to your ancestors; and you shall be my people, and I will be your God. ²⁹I will save you from all your uncleannesses, and I will summon the grain and make it abundant and lay no famine upon you. ³⁰I will make the fruit of the tree and the produce of the field abundant, so that you may never

FOR GOD'S HOLY NAME

It is not for your sake, O house of Israel, that I am about to act, but for the sake of
my holy name, which you have profaned among the nations to which you came.

—Ezekiel 36.22

Anger. Criticism. Condemnation. Judgment. These words describe God's message to the disobedient people of Judah before Babylon destroyed Jerusalem. But in Ezekiel 36, we discover new words and a new message: Favor. Prosper. Cleanse. Rebuild. God chose to bring glory to himself by demonstrating his power and his grace in the restoration of his chosen people to their land.

In restoring his chosen people, God demonstrated his own glory, his omnipotence, his grace, his benevolence, his love, his omniscience—his character. It's important to remember that the character of God's chosen people demonstrated the character of God to the nations around them. We find a similar teaching in Matthew 5.16: "In the same way, let your light shine before others, so that they may see your good works and give glory to your Father in heaven." As far as nonbelievers are concerned, they judge Christ by looking at Christians.

God wanted his people to remember and be ashamed of their sin (see Ezekiel 36.31–32), but he also wanted them to be reconciled to him: "A new heart I will give you, and a new spirit I will put within you; and I will remove from your body the heart of stone and give you a heart of flesh. I will put my spirit within you, and make you follow my statutes and be careful to observe my ordinances" (verses 26–27). God wanted his people to glorify him through the work of his Spirit in their lives. In this way, the surrounding heathen countries would see God's omnipotence and his grace through his chosen people.

We are no more deserving of God's grace than the people of Judah were. We know that we have sinned and fallen short of the glory of God the same way they did. We are saved by God's grace through our faith in Jesus Christ (see Ephesians 2.8–9)—not because we have earned it, not because we're such good people, but because God loves us.

If we have faith in Jesus Christ, we have also been given God's Spirit and the ability to bear fruit—the fruit of the Spirit (see Galatians 5.22–23)—to live our lives as Jesus lived and to display his character to others. We can have lives of fulfillment and joy and peace if we permit God's Spirit to be active in our daily habits and actions. We have that seed of faith and good works within us, but we can either reject it or we can accept and nurture it. Accepting the Spirit means emulating the life of Christ—a life of justice, peace, humility, service, selflessness, forgiveness, compassion, benevolence and self-sacrificial love. God is glorified through the work of his Spirit in our lives.

Going Deeper

- What words can you use to describe God's message for you right now?
- How do you let your "light shine before others"? Do people give God the glory through what they've seen him do in your life?

again suffer the disgrace of famine among the nations. ³¹Then you shall remember your evil ways, and your dealings that were not good; and you shall loathe yourselves for your iniquities and your abominable deeds. ³²It is not for your sake that I will act, says the Lord GOD; let that be known to you. Be ashamed and dismayed for your ways, O house of Israel.

33 Thus says the Lord GOD: On the day that I cleanse you from all your iniquities, I will cause the towns to be inhabited, and the waste places shall be rebuilt. ³⁴The land that was desolate shall be tilled, instead of being the desolation that it was in the sight of all who passed by. ³⁵And they will say, "This land that was desolate has become like the garden of Eden; and the waste and desolate and ruined towns are now inhabited and fortified." ³⁶Then the nations that are left all around you shall know that I, the LORD, have rebuilt the ruined places, and replanted that which was desolate; I, the LORD, have spoken, and I will do it.

37 Thus says the Lord GOD: I will also let the house of Israel ask me to do this for them: to increase their population like a flock. ³⁸Like the flock for sacrifices,ᵃ like the flock at Jerusalem during her appointed festivals, so shall the ruined towns be filled with flocks of people. Then they shall know that I am the LORD.

THE VALLEY OF DRY BONES

37 The hand of the LORD came upon me, and he brought me out by the spirit of the LORD and set me down in the middle of a valley; it was full of bones. ²He led me all around them; there were very many lying in the valley, and they were very dry. ³He said to me, "Mortal, can these bones live?" I answered, "O Lord GOD, you know." ⁴Then he said to me, "Prophesy to these bones, and say to them: O dry bones, hear the word of the LORD. ⁵Thus says the Lord GOD to these bones: I will cause breathᵇ to enter you, and you shall live. ⁶I will lay sinews on you, and will cause flesh to come upon you, and cover you with skin, and put breathᵇ in you, and you shall live; and you shall know that I am the LORD."

7 So I prophesied as I had been commanded; and as I prophesied, suddenly there was a noise, a rattling, and the bones came together, bone to its bone. ⁸I looked, and there were sinews on them, and flesh had come upon them, and skin had covered them; but there was no breath in them. ⁹Then he said to me, "Prophesy to the breath, prophesy, mortal, and say to the breath:ᶜ Thus says the Lord GOD: Come from the four winds, O breath,ᶜ and breathe upon these slain, that they may live." ¹⁰I prophesied as he commanded me, and the breath came into them, and they lived, and stood on their feet, a vast multitude.

11 Then he said to me, "Mortal, these bones are the whole house of Israel. They say, 'Our bones are dried up, and our hope is lost; we are cut off completely.' ¹²Therefore prophesy, and say to them, Thus says the Lord GOD: I am going to open your graves, and bring you up from your graves, O my people; and I will bring you back to the land of Israel. ¹³And you shall know that I am the LORD, when I open your graves, and bring you up from your graves, O my people. ¹⁴I will put my spirit within you, and you shall live, and I will place you on your own soil; then you shall know that I, the LORD, have spoken and will act, says the LORD."

THE TWO STICKS

15 The word of the LORD came to me: ¹⁶Mortal, take a stick and write on it, "For Judah, and the Israelites associated with it"; then take another stick and write on it, "For Joseph (the stick of Ephraim) and all the house of Israel associated with it"; ¹⁷and join them together into one stick, so that they may become one in your hand. ¹⁸And when your people say to you, "Will you not show us what you mean by these?" ¹⁹say

ᵃ **36.38** Heb *flock of holy things*   ᵇ **37.5,6** Or *spirit*   ᶜ **37.9** Or *wind* or *spirit*

PONDER

"And you shall know that I am the LORD . . . I will put my spirit within you, and you shall live, and I will place you on your own soil; then you shall know that I, the LORD, have spoken and will act, says the LORD."

—Ezekiel 37.13–14

PRAY

Lord, you promised that the people who love you and bear the fruit of a relationship with you will inherit the covenant with you—people who obey your commandments and are committed to peace, justice, forgiveness, compassion and love in your name. Let us remember as we follow you and bear fruit, that we all are part of that covenant. Also, Father, let us remember that we are all sinners, that the wages of sin is death, and that you sent your only Son to earth to accept the punishment for our sins and give us new life, eternal life in your Spirit. Give us the confidence and the courage to be bold in sharing the truth about Jesus Christ with others. We ask this in the name of our Savior. Amen.

to them, Thus says the Lord GOD: I am about to take the stick of Joseph (which is in the hand of Ephraim) and the tribes of Israel associated with it; and I will put the stick of Judah upon it,[a] and make them one stick, in order that they may be one in my hand. 20When the sticks on which you write are in your hand before their eyes, 21then say to them, Thus says the Lord GOD: I will take the people of Israel from the nations among which they have gone, and will gather them from every quarter, and bring them to their own land. 22I will make them one nation in the land, on the mountains of Israel; and one king shall be king over them all. Never again shall they be two na-

tions, and never again shall they be divided into two kingdoms. 23They shall never again defile themselves with their idols and their detestable things, or with any of their transgressions. I will save them from all the apostasies into which they have fallen,[b] and will cleanse them. Then they shall be my people, and I will be their God.

24 My servant David shall be king over them; and they shall all have one shepherd. They shall follow my ordinances and be careful to observe my statutes. 25They shall live in the land that I gave to my servant Jacob, in which your ancestors lived; they and their children and their children's children shall live there forever; and my servant David shall be their prince forever. 26I will make a covenant of peace with them; it shall be an everlasting covenant with them; and I will bless[c] them and multiply them, and will set my sanctuary among them forevermore. 27My dwelling place shall be with them; and I will be their God, and they shall be my people. 28Then the nations shall know that I the LORD sanctify Israel, when my sanctuary is among them forevermore.

INVASION BY GOG

38 The word of the LORD came to me: 2Mortal, set your face toward Gog, of the land of Magog, the chief prince of Meshech and Tubal. Prophesy against him 3and say: Thus says the Lord GOD: I am against you, O Gog, chief prince of Meshech and Tubal; 4I will turn you around and put hooks into your jaws, and I will lead you out with all your army, horses and horsemen, all of them clothed in full armor, a great company, all of them with shield and buckler, wielding swords. 5Persia, Ethiopia,[d] and Put are with them, all of them with buckler and helmet; 6Gomer and all its troops; Bethtogarmah from the remotest parts of

a 37.19 Heb I will put them upon it
b 37.23 Another reading is from all the settlements in which they have sinned
c 37.26 Tg: Heb give   d 38.5 Or Nubia; Heb Cush

the north with all its troops—many peoples are with you.

7 Be ready and keep ready, you and all the companies that are assembled around you, and hold yourselves in reserve for them. 8After many days you shall be mustered; in the latter years you shall go against a land restored from war, a land where people were gathered from many nations on the mountains of Israel, which had long lain waste; its people were brought out from the nations and now are living in safety, all of them. 9You shall advance, coming on like a storm; you shall be like a cloud covering the land, you and all your troops, and many peoples with you.

10 Thus says the Lord GOD: On that day thoughts will come into your mind, and you will devise an evil scheme. 11You will say, "I will go up against the land of unwalled villages; I will fall upon the quiet people who live in safety, all of them living without walls, and having no bars or gates"; 12to seize spoil and carry off plunder; to assail the waste places that are now inhabited, and the people who were gathered from the nations, who are acquiring cattle and goods, who live at the center[a] of the earth. 13Sheba and Dedan and the merchants of Tarshish and all its young warriors[b] will say to you, "Have you come to seize spoil? Have you assembled your horde to carry off plunder, to carry away silver and gold, to take away cattle and goods, to seize a great amount of booty?"

14 Therefore, mortal, prophesy, and say to Gog: Thus says the Lord GOD: On that day when my people Israel are living securely, you will rouse yourself[c] 15and come from your place out of the remotest parts of the north, you and many peoples with you, all of them riding on horses, a great horde, a mighty army; 16you will come up against my people Israel, like a cloud covering the earth. In the latter days I will bring you against my land, so that the nations may know me, when through you, O Gog, I display my holiness before their eyes.

JUDGMENT ON GOG

17 Thus says the Lord GOD: Are you he of whom I spoke in former days by my servants the prophets of Israel, who in those days prophesied for years that I would bring you against them? 18On that day, when Gog comes against the land of Israel, says the Lord GOD, my wrath shall be aroused. 19For in my jealousy and in my blazing wrath I declare: On that day there shall be a great shaking in the land of Israel; 20the fish of the sea, and the birds of the air, and the animals of the field, and all creeping things that creep on the ground, and all human beings that are on the face of the earth, shall quake at my presence, and the mountains shall be thrown down, and the cliffs shall fall, and every wall shall tumble to the ground. 21I will summon the sword against Gog[d] in[e] all my mountains, says the Lord GOD; the swords of all will be against their comrades. 22With pestilence and bloodshed I will enter into judgment with him; and I will pour down torrential rains and hailstones, fire and sulfur, upon him and his troops and the many peoples that are with him. 23So I will display my greatness and my holiness and make myself known in the eyes of many nations. Then they shall know that I am the LORD.

GOG'S ARMIES DESTROYED

39 And you, mortal, prophesy against Gog, and say: Thus says the Lord GOD: I am against you, O Gog, chief prince of Meshech and Tubal! 2I will turn you around and drive you forward, and bring you up from the remotest parts of the north, and lead you against the mountains of Israel. 3I will strike your bow from your left hand, and will make your arrows drop out of your right hand. 4You shall fall on the mountains of Israel, you and all your troops and the peoples that are with you; I will give you to birds of prey of every kind and to the wild animals to be devoured. 5You shall

---

[a] 38.12 Heb navel   [b] 38.13 Heb young lions   [c] 38.14 Gk: Heb will you not know?   [d] 38.21 Heb him   [e] 38.21 Heb to or for

fall in the open field; for I have spoken, says the Lord GOD. 6I will send fire on Magog and on those who live securely in the coastlands; and they shall know that I am the LORD.

7 My holy name I will make known among my people Israel; and I will not let my holy name be profaned any more; and the nations shall know that I am the LORD, the Holy One in Israel. 8It has come! It has happened, says the Lord GOD. This is the day of which I have spoken.

9 Then those who live in the towns of Israel will go out and make fires of the weapons and burn them—bucklers and shields, bows and arrows, handpikes and spears—and they will make fires of them for seven years. 10They will not need to take wood out of the field or cut down any trees in the forests, for they will make their fires of the weapons; they will despoil those who despoiled them, and plunder those who plundered them, says the Lord GOD.

THE BURIAL OF GOG

11 On that day I will give to Gog a place for burial in Israel, the Valley of the Travelers[a] east of the sea; it shall block the path of the travelers, for there Gog and all his horde will be buried; it shall be called the Valley of Hamon-gog.[b] 12Seven months the house of Israel shall spend burying them, in order to cleanse the land. 13All the people of the land shall bury them; and it will bring them honor on the day that I show my glory, says the Lord GOD. 14They will set apart men to pass through the land regularly and bury any invaders[c] who remain on the face of the land, so as to cleanse it; for seven months they shall make their search. 15As the searchers[c] pass through the land, anyone who sees a human bone shall set up a sign by it, until the buriers have buried it in the Valley of Hamon-gog.[b] 16(A city Hamonah[d] is there also.) Thus they shall cleanse the land.

17 As for you, mortal, thus says the Lord GOD: Speak to the birds of every kind and to all the wild animals: Assemble and come, gather from all around to the sacrificial feast that I am preparing for you, a great sacrificial feast on the mountains of Israel, and you shall eat flesh and drink blood. 18You shall eat the flesh of the mighty, and drink the blood of the princes of the earth—of rams, of lambs, and of goats, of bulls, all of them fatlings of Bashan. 19You shall eat fat until you are filled, and drink blood until you are drunk, at the sacrificial feast that I am preparing for you. 20And you shall be filled at my table with horses and charioteers,[e] with warriors and all kinds of soldiers, says the Lord GOD.

ISRAEL RESTORED TO THE LAND

21 I will display my glory among the nations; and all the nations shall see my judgment that I have executed, and my hand that I have laid on them. 22The house of Israel shall know that I am the LORD their God, from that day forward. 23And the nations shall know that the house of Israel went into captivity for their iniquity, because they dealt treacherously with me. So I hid my face from them and gave them into the hand of their adversaries, and they all fell by the sword. 24I dealt with them according to their uncleanness and their transgressions, and hid my face from them.

25 Therefore thus says the Lord GOD: Now I will restore the fortunes of Jacob, and have mercy on the whole house of Israel; and I will be jealous for my holy name. 26They shall forget[f] their shame, and all the treachery they have practiced against me, when they live securely in their land with no one to make them afraid, 27when I have brought them back from the peoples and gathered them from their enemies' lands, and through them have displayed my holiness in the

---

[a] 39.11 Or of the Abarim   [b] 39.11,15 That is, the Horde of Gog   [c] 39.14,15 Heb travelers   [d] 39.16 That is The Horde   [e] 39.20 Heb chariots   [f] 39.26 Another reading is They shall bear

sight of many nations. 28Then they shall know that I am the LORD their God because I sent them into exile among the nations, and then gathered them into their own land. I will leave none of them behind; 29and I will never again hide my face from them, when I pour out my spirit upon the house of Israel, says the Lord GOD.

THE VISION OF THE NEW TEMPLE

40 In the twenty-fifth year of our exile, at the beginning of the year, on the tenth day of the month, in the fourteenth year after the city was struck down, on that very day, the hand of the LORD was upon me, and he brought me there. 2He brought me, in visions of God, to the land of Israel, and set me down upon a very high mountain, on which was a structure like a city to the south. 3When he brought me there, a man was there, whose appearance shone like bronze, with a linen cord and a measuring reed in his hand; and he was standing in the gateway. 4The man said to me, "Mortal, look closely and listen attentively, and set your mind upon all that I shall show you, for you were brought here in order that I might show it to you; declare all that you see to the house of Israel."

5 Now there was a wall all around the outside of the temple area. The length of the measuring reed in the man's hand was six long cubits, each being a cubit and a handbreadth in length; so he measured the thickness of the wall, one reed; and the height, one reed. 6Then he went into the gateway facing east, going up its steps, and measured the threshold of the gate, one reed deep.a There were 7recesses, and each recess was one reed wide and one reed deep; and the space between the recesses, five cubits; and the threshold of the gate by the vestibule of the gate at the inner end was one reed deep. 8Then he measured the inner vestibule of the gateway, one cubit. 9Then he measured the vestibule of the gateway, eight cubits; and its pilasters, two cubits; and the vestibule of the

gate was at the inner end. 10There were three recesses on either side of the east gate; the three were of the same size; and the pilasters on either side were of the same size. 11Then he measured the width of the opening of the gateway, ten cubits; and the width of the gateway, thirteen cubits. 12There was a barrier before the recesses, one cubit on either side; and the recesses were six cubits on either side. 13Then he measured the gate from the backb of the one recess to the backb of the other, a width of twenty-five cubits, from wall to wall.c 14He measuredd also the vestibule, twenty cubits; and the gate next to the pilaster on every side of the court.e 15From the front of the gate at the entrance to the end of the inner vestibule of the gate was fifty cubits. 16The recesses and their pilasters had windows, with shutterse on the inside of the gateway all around, and the vestibules also had windows on the inside all around; and on the pilasters were palm trees.

17 Then he brought me into the outer court; there were chambers there, and a pavement, all around the court; thirty chambers fronted on the pavement. 18The pavement ran along the side of the gates, corresponding to the length of the gates; this was the lower pavement. 19Then he measured the distance from the inner front off the lower gate to the outer front of the inner court, one hundred cubits.g

20 Then he measured the gate of the outer court that faced north— its depth and width. 21Its recesses, three on either side, and its pilasters and its vestibule were of the same size as those of the first gate; its depth was fifty cubits, and its width twenty-five cubits. 22Its windows, its vestibule, and its palm trees were of the same size as those of the gate that faced toward the east. Seven

a 40.6 Heb *deep, and one threshold, one reed deep*   b 40.13 Gk: Heb *roof*   c 40.13 Heb *opening facing opening*   d 40.14 Heb *made*   e 40.14,16 Meaning of Heb uncertain   f 40.19 Compare Gk: Heb *from before*   g 40.19 Heb adds *the east and the north*

steps led up to it; and its vestibule was on the inside.[a] 23Opposite the gate on the north, as on the east, was a gate to the inner court; he measured from gate to gate, one hundred cubits.

24 Then he led me toward the south, and there was a gate on the south; and he measured its pilasters and its vestibule; they had the same dimensions as the others. 25There were windows all around in it and in its vestibule, like the windows of the others; its depth was fifty cubits, and its width twenty-five cubits. 26There were seven steps leading up to it; its vestibule was on the inside.[a] It had palm trees on its pilasters, one on either side. 27There was a gate on the south of the inner court; and he measured from gate to gate toward the south, one hundred cubits.

28 Then he brought me to the inner court by the south gate, and he measured the south gate; it was of the same dimensions as the others. 29Its recesses, its pilasters, and its vestibule were of the same size as the others; and there were windows all around in it and in its vestibule; its depth was fifty cubits, and its width twenty-five cubits. 30There were vestibules all around, twenty-five cubits deep and five cubits wide. 31Its vestibule faced the outer court, and palm trees were on its pilasters, and its stairway had eight steps.

32 Then he brought me to the inner court on the east side, and he measured the gate; it was of the same size as the others. 33Its recesses, its pilasters, and its vestibule were of the same dimensions as the others; and there were windows all around in it and in its vestibule; its depth was fifty cubits, and its width twenty-five cubits. 34Its vestibule faced the outer court, and it had palm trees on its pilasters, on either side; and its stairway had eight steps.

35 Then he brought me to the north gate, and he measured it; it had the same dimensions as the others. 36Its recesses, its pilasters, and its vestibule were of the same size as the others;[b] and it had windows all around. Its depth was fifty cubits,

and its width twenty-five cubits. 37Its vestibule[c] faced the outer court, and it had palm trees on its pilasters, on either side; and its stairway had eight steps.

38 There was a chamber with its door in the vestibule of the gate,[d] where the burnt offering was to be washed. 39And in the vestibule of the gate were two tables on either side, on which the burnt offering and the sin offering and the guilt offering were to be slaughtered. 40On the outside of the vestibule[e] at the entrance of the north gate were two tables; and on the other side of the vestibule of the gate were two tables. 41Four tables were on the inside, and four tables on the outside of the side of the gate, eight tables, on which the sacrifices were to be slaughtered. 42There were also four tables of hewn stone for the burnt offering, a cubit and a half long, and one cubit and a half wide, and one cubit high, on which the instruments were to be laid with which the burnt offerings and the sacrifices were slaughtered. 43There were pegs, one handbreadth long, fastened all around the inside. And on the tables the flesh of the offering was to be laid.

44 On the outside of the inner gateway there were chambers for the singers in the inner court, one[f] at the side of the north gate facing south, the other at the side of the east gate facing north. 45He said to me, "This chamber that faces south is for the priests who have charge of the temple, 46and the chamber that faces north is for the priests who have charge of the altar; these are the descendants of Zadok, who alone among the descendants of Levi may come near to the LORD to minister to him." 47He measured the court, one hundred cubits deep, and one hundred cubits wide, a square; and the altar was in front of the temple.

THE TEMPLE

48 Then he brought me to the vestibule of the temple and measured the pilasters of the vestibule, five cubits on either side; and the width of the gate was fourteen cubits; and the sidewalls of the gate were three cubits[a] on either side. 49The depth of the vestibule was twenty cubits, and the width twelve[b] cubits; ten steps led up[c] to it; and there were pillars beside the pilasters on either side.

41 Then he brought me to the nave, and measured the pilasters; on each side six cubits was the width of the pilasters.[d] 2The width of the entrance was ten cubits; and the sidewalls of the entrance were five cubits on either side. He measured the length of the nave, forty cubits, and its width, twenty cubits. 3Then he went into the inner room and measured the pilasters of the entrance, two cubits; and the width of the entrance, six cubits; and the sidewalls[e] of the entrance, seven cubits. 4He measured the depth of the room, twenty cubits, and its width, twenty cubits, beyond the nave. And he said to me, This is the most holy place.

5 Then he measured the wall of the temple, six cubits thick; and the width of the side chambers, four cubits, all around the temple. 6The side chambers were in three stories, one over another, thirty in each story. There were offsets[f] all around the wall of the temple to serve as supports for the side chambers, so that they should not be supported by the wall of the temple. 7The passageway[g] of the side chambers widened from story to story; for the structure was supplied with a stairway all around the temple. For this reason the structure became wider from story to story. One ascended from the bottom story to the uppermost story by way of the middle one. 8I saw also that the temple had a raised platform all around; the foundations of the side chambers measured a full reed of six long cubits. 9The thickness of the outer wall of the side chambers was five cubits; and the free space between the side chambers of the temple 10and the chambers of the court was a width of twenty cubits all around the temple on every side. 11The side chambers opened onto the area left free, one door toward the north, and another door toward the south; and the width of the part that was left free was five cubits all around.

12 The building that was facing the temple yard on the west side was seventy cubits wide; and the wall of the building was five cubits thick all around, and its depth ninety cubits. 13 Then he measured the temple, one hundred cubits deep; and the yard and the building with its walls, one hundred cubits deep; 14also the width of the east front of the temple and the yard, one hundred cubits.

15 Then he measured the depth of the building facing the yard at the west, together with its galleries[h] on either side, one hundred cubits.

The nave of the temple and the inner room and the outer[i] vestibule 16were paneled,[j] and, all around, all three had windows with recessed[k] frames. Facing the threshold the temple was paneled with wood all around, from the floor up to the windows (now the windows were covered), 17to the space above the door, even to the inner room, and on the outside. And on all the walls all around in the inner room and the nave there was a pattern.[l] 18It was formed of cherubim and palm trees, a palm tree between cherub and cherub. Each cherub had two faces: 19a human face turned toward the palm tree on the one side, and the face of a young lion turned toward the palm tree on the other side. They were carved on the whole temple all around; 20from the floor to the area above the door, cherubim and palm trees were carved on the wall.[a]

21 The doorposts of the nave were square. In front of the holy place was something resembling 22an altar of wood, three cubits high, two cubits long, and two cubits wide;[b] its corners, its base,[c] and its walls were of wood. He said to me, "This is the table that stands before the LORD." 23The nave and the holy place had each a double door. 24The doors had two leaves apiece, two swinging leaves for each door. 25On the doors of the nave were carved cherubim and palm trees, such as were carved on the walls; and there was a canopy of wood in front of the vestibule outside. 26And there were recessed windows and palm trees on either side, on the sidewalls of the vestibule.[d]

THE HOLY CHAMBERS AND THE OUTER WALL

42 Then he led me out into the outer court, toward the north, and he brought me to the chambers that were opposite the temple yard and opposite the building on the north. 2The length of the building that was on the north side[e] was[f] one hundred cubits, and the width fifty cubits. 3Across the twenty cubits that belonged to the inner court, and facing the pavement that belonged to the outer court, the chambers rose[g] gallery[h] by gallery[h] in three stories. 4In front of the chambers was a passage on the inner side, ten cubits wide and one hundred cubits deep,[i] and its[j] entrances were on the north. 5Now the upper chambers were narrower, for the galleries[h] took more away from them than from the lower and middle chambers in the building. 6For they were in three stories, and they had no pillars like the pillars of the outer[k] court; for this reason the upper chambers were set back from the ground more than the lower and the middle ones. 7There was a wall outside parallel to the chambers, toward the outer court, opposite the chambers, fifty cubits long. 8For the chambers on the outer court were fifty cubits long, while those oppo-site the temple were one hundred cubits long. 9At the foot of these chambers ran a passage that one entered from the east in order to enter them from the outer court. 10The width of the passage[l] was fixed by the wall of the court.

On the south[m] also, opposite the vacant area and opposite the building, there were chambers 11with a passage in front of them; they were similar to the chambers on the north, of the same length and width, with the same exits[n] and arrangements and doors. 12So the entrances of the chambers to the south were entered through the entrance at the head of the corresponding passage, from the east, along the matching wall.[h]

13 Then he said to me, "The north chambers and the south chambers opposite the vacant area are the holy chambers, where the priests who approach the LORD shall eat the most holy offerings; there they shall deposit the most holy offerings— the grain offering, the sin offering, and the guilt offering—for the place is holy. 14When the priests enter the holy place, they shall not go out of it into the outer court without laying there the vestments in which they minister, for these are holy; they shall put on other garments before they go near to the area open to the people."

15 When he had finished measuring the interior of the temple area, he led me out by the gate that faces east, and measured the temple area all around. 16He measured the east side with the measuring reed, five hundred cubits by the measuring reed. 17Then he turned and mea-

a 41.20 Cn Compare verse 25: Heb and the wall b 41.22 Gk: Heb lacks two cubits wide c 41.22 Gk: Heb length d 41.26 Cn: Heb vestibule. And the side chambers of the temple and the canopies e 42.2 Gk: Heb door f 42.2 Gk: Heb before the length g 42.3 Heb lacks the chambers rose h 42.3,5,12 Meaning of Heb uncertain i 42.4 Gk: Heb a way of one cubit j 42.4 Heb their k 42.6 Gk: Heb lacks outer l 42.10 Heb lacks of the passage m 42.10 Gk: Heb east n 42.11 Heb and all their exits

sured[a] the north side, five hundred cubits by the measuring reed. 18 Then he turned and measured[a] the south side, five hundred cubits by the measuring reed. 19 Then he turned to the west side and measured, five hundred cubits by the measuring reed. 20 He measured it on the four sides. It had a wall around it, five hundred cubits long and five hundred cubits wide, to make a separation between the holy and the common.

THE DIVINE GLORY RETURNS TO THE TEMPLE

43 Then he brought me to the gate, the gate facing east. 2 And there, the glory of the God of Israel was coming from the east; the sound was like the sound of mighty waters; and the earth shone with his glory. 3 The[b] vision I saw was like the vision that I had seen when he came to destroy the city, and[c] like the vision that I had seen by the river Chebar; and I fell upon my face. 4 As the glory of the LORD entered the temple by the gate facing east, 5 the spirit lifted me up, and brought me into the inner court; and the glory of the LORD filled the temple.

6 While the man was standing beside me, I heard someone speaking to me out of the temple. 7 He said to me: Mortal, this is the place of my throne and the place for the soles of my feet, where I will reside among the people of Israel forever. The house of Israel shall no more defile my holy name, neither they nor their kings, by their whoring, and by the corpses of their kings at their death.[d] 8 When they placed their threshold by my threshold and their doorposts beside my doorposts, with only a wall between me and them, they were defiling my holy name by their abominations that they committed; therefore I have consumed them in my anger. 9 Now let them put away their idolatry and the corpses of their kings far from me, and I will reside among them forever.

10 As for you, mortal, describe the temple to the house of Israel, and let them measure the pattern; and let them be ashamed of their iniquities. 11 When they are ashamed of all that they have done, make known to them the plan of the temple, its arrangement, its exits and its entrances, and its whole form—all its ordinances and its entire plan and all its laws; and write it down in their sight, so that they may observe and follow the entire plan and all its ordinances. 12 This is the law of the temple: the whole territory on the top of the mountain all around shall be most holy. This is the law of the temple.

THE ALTAR

13 These are the dimensions of the altar by cubits (the cubit being one cubit and a handbreadth): its base shall be one cubit high,[e] and one cubit wide, with a rim of one span around its edge. This shall be the height of the altar: 14 From the base on the ground to the lower ledge, two cubits, with a width of one cubit; and from the smaller ledge to the larger ledge, four cubits, with a width of one cubit; 15 and the altar hearth, four cubits; and from the altar hearth projecting upward, four horns. 16 The altar hearth shall be square, twelve cubits long by twelve wide. 17 The ledge also shall be square, fourteen cubits long by fourteen wide, with a rim around it half a cubit wide, and its surrounding base, one cubit. Its steps shall face east.

18 Then he said to me: Mortal, thus says the Lord GOD: These are the ordinances for the altar: On the day when it is erected for offering burnt offerings upon it and for dashing blood against it, 19 you shall give to the levitical priests of the family of Zadok, who draw near to me to minister to me, says the Lord GOD, a bull for a sin offering. 20 And you shall take some of its blood, and put it on the four horns of the altar, and on the four corners of the ledge, and

[a] 42.17,18 Gk: Heb measuring reed all around. He measured   [b] 43.3 Gk: Heb Like the vision   [c] 43.3 Syr: Heb and the visions   [d] 43.7 Or on their high places   [e] 43.13 Gk: Heb lacks high

upon the rim all around; thus you shall purify it and make atonement for it. 21 You shall also take the bull of the sin offering, and it shall be burnt in the appointed place belonging to the temple, outside the sacred area.

22 On the second day you shall offer a male goat without blemish for a sin offering; and the altar shall be purified, as it was purified with the bull. 23 When you have finished purifying it, you shall offer a bull without blemish and a ram from the flock without blemish. 24 You shall present them before the LORD, and the priests shall throw salt on them and offer them up as a burnt offering to the LORD. 25 For seven days you shall provide daily a goat for a sin offering; also a bull and a ram from the flock, without blemish, shall be provided. 26 Seven days shall they make atonement for the altar and cleanse it, and so consecrate it. 27 When these days are over, then from the eighth day onward the priests shall offer upon the altar your burnt offerings and your offerings of well-being; and I will accept you, says the Lord GOD.

THE CLOSED GATE

44 Then he brought me back to the outer gate of the sanctuary, which faces east; and it was shut. 2 The LORD said to me: This gate shall remain shut; it shall not be opened, and no one shall enter by it; for the LORD, the God of Israel, has entered by it; therefore it shall remain shut. 3 Only the prince, because he is a prince, may sit in it to eat food before the LORD; he shall enter by way of the vestibule of the gate, and shall go out by the same way.

ADMISSION TO THE TEMPLE

4 Then he brought me by way of the north gate to the front of the temple; and I looked, and lo! the glory of the LORD filled the temple of the LORD; and I fell upon my face. 5 The LORD said to me: Mortal, mark well, look closely, and listen attentively to all that I shall tell you concerning all the ordinances of the temple of the LORD and all its

laws; and mark well those who may be admitted to[a] the temple and all those who are to be excluded from the sanctuary. 6 Say to the rebellious house,[b] to the house of Israel, Thus says the Lord GOD: O house of Israel, let there be an end to all your abominations 7 in admitting foreigners, uncircumcised in heart and flesh, to be in my sanctuary, profaning my temple when you offer to me my food, the fat and the blood. You[c] have broken my covenant with all your abominations. 8 And you have not kept charge of my sacred offerings; but you have appointed foreigners[d] to act for you in keeping my charge in my sanctuary.

9 Thus says the Lord GOD: No foreigner, uncircumcised in heart and flesh, of all the foreigners who are among the people of Israel, shall enter my sanctuary. 10 But the Levites who went far from me, going astray from me after their idols when Israel went astray, shall bear their punishment. 11 They shall be ministers in my sanctuary, having oversight at the gates of the temple, and serving in the temple; they shall slaughter the burnt offering and the sacrifice for the people, and they shall attend on them and serve them. 12 Because they ministered to them before their idols and made the house of Israel stumble into iniquity, therefore I have sworn concerning them, says the Lord GOD, that they shall bear their punishment. 13 They shall not come near to me, to serve me as priest, nor come near any of my sacred offerings, the things that are most sacred; but they shall bear their shame, and the consequences of the abominations that they have committed. 14 Yet I will appoint them to keep charge of the temple, to do all its chores, all that is to be done in it.

THE LEVITICAL PRIESTS

15 But the levitical priests, the descendants of Zadok, who kept the charge of my sanctuary when the people of Israel went astray from me,

a 44.5 Cn: Heb the entrance of b 44.6 Gk: Heb lacks house c 44.7 Gk Syr Vg: Heb They d 44.8 Heb lacks foreigners

shall come near to me to minister to me; and they shall attend me to offer me the fat and the blood, says the Lord GOD. 16It is they who shall enter my sanctuary, it is they who shall approach my table, to minister to me, and they shall keep my charge. 17When they enter the gates of the inner court, they shall wear linen vestments; they shall have nothing of wool on them, while they minister at the gates of the inner court, and within. 18They shall have linen turbans on their heads, and linen undergarments on their loins; they shall not bind themselves with anything that causes sweat. 19When they go out into the outer court to the people, they shall remove the vestments in which they have been ministering, and lay them in the holy chambers; and they shall put on other garments, so that they may not communicate holiness to the people with their vestments. 20They shall not shave their heads or let their locks grow long; they shall only trim the hair of their heads. 21No priest shall drink wine when he enters the inner court. 22They shall not marry a widow, or a divorced woman, but only a virgin of the stock of the house of Israel, or a widow who is the widow of a priest. 23They shall teach my people the difference between the holy and the common, and show them how to distinguish between the unclean and the clean. 24In a controversy they shall act as judges, and they shall decide it according to my judgments. They shall keep my laws and my statutes regarding all my appointed festivals, and they shall keep my sabbaths holy. 25They shall not defile themselves by going near to a dead person; for father or mother, however, and for son or daughter, and for brother or unmarried sister they may defile themselves. 26After he has become clean, they shall count seven days for him. 27On the day that he goes into the holy place, into the inner court, to minister in the holy place, he shall offer his sin offering, says the Lord GOD.

28 This shall be their inheritance: I am their inheritance; and you shall give them no holding in Israel; I am their holding. 29They shall eat the grain offering, the sin offering, and the guilt offering; and every devoted thing in Israel shall be theirs. 30The first of all the first fruits of all kinds, and every offering of all kinds from all your offerings, shall belong to the priests; you shall also give to the priests the first of your dough, in order that a blessing may rest on your house. 31The priests shall not eat of anything, whether bird or animal, that died of itself or was torn by animals.

EVERY SIN HAS ITS
CONSEQUENCE. ALTHOUGH
FORGIVEN, WE LOSE
OPPORTUNITIES, REPUTATIONS,
PEACE OF MIND OR INNER JOY.

THE HOLY DISTRICT

45 When you allot the land as an inheritance, you shall set aside for the LORD a portion of the land as a holy district, twenty-five thousand cubits long and twenty[a] thousand cubits wide; it shall be holy throughout its entire extent. 2Of this, a square plot of five hundred by five hundred cubits shall be for the sanctuary, with fifty cubits for an open space around it. 3In the holy district you shall measure off a section twenty-five thousand cubits long and ten thousand wide, in which shall be the sanctuary, the most holy place. 4It shall be a holy portion of the land; it shall be for the priests, who minister in the sanctuary and approach the LORD to minister to him; and it shall be both a place for their houses and a holy place for the sanctuary. 5Another section, twenty-five thousand cubits

a 45.1 Gk: Heb ten

long and ten thousand cubits wide, shall be for the Levites who minister at the temple, as their holding for cities to live in.[a]

6 Alongside the portion set apart as the holy district you shall assign as a holding for the city an area five thousand cubits wide, and twenty-five thousand cubits long; it shall belong to the whole house of Israel.

7 And to the prince shall belong the land on both sides of the holy district and the holding of the city, alongside the holy district and the holding of the city, on the west and on the east, corresponding in length to one of the tribal portions, and extending from the western to the eastern boundary 8of the land. It is to be his property in Israel. And my princes shall no longer oppress my people; but they shall let the house of Israel have the land according to their tribes.

9 Thus says the Lord GOD: Enough, O princes of Israel! Put away violence and oppression, and do what is just and right. Cease your evictions of my people, says the Lord GOD.

WEIGHTS AND MEASURES

10 You shall have honest balances, an honest ephah, and an honest bath.[b] 11The ephah and the bath shall be of the same measure, the bath containing one-tenth of a homer, and the ephah one-tenth of a homer; the homer shall be the standard measure. 12The shekel shall be twenty gerahs. Twenty shekels, twenty-five shekels, and fifteen shekels shall make a mina for you.

OFFERINGS

13 This is the offering that you shall make: one-sixth of an ephah from each homer of wheat, and one-sixth of an ephah from each homer of barley, 14and as the fixed portion of oil,[c] one-tenth of a bath from each cor (the cor,[d] like the homer, contains ten baths); 15and one sheep from every flock of two hundred, from the pastures of Israel. This is the offering for grain offerings, burnt offerings, and offerings

of well-being, to make atonement for them, says the Lord GOD. 16All the people of the land shall join with the prince in Israel in making this offering. 17But this shall be the obligation of the prince regarding the burnt offerings, grain offerings, and drink offerings, at the festivals, the new moons, and the sabbaths, all the appointed festivals of the house of Israel: he shall provide the sin offerings, grain offerings, the burnt offerings, and the offerings of well-being, to make atonement for the house of Israel.

FESTIVALS

18 Thus says the Lord GOD: In the first month, on the first day of the month, you shall take a young bull without blemish, and purify the sanctuary. 19The priest shall take some of the blood of the sin offering and put it on the doorposts of the temple, the four corners of the ledge of the altar, and the posts of the gate of the inner court. 20You shall do the same on the seventh day of the month for anyone who has sinned through error or ignorance; so you shall make atonement for the temple.

21 In the first month, on the fourteenth day of the month, you shall celebrate the festival of the passover, and for seven days unleavened bread shall be eaten. 22On that day the prince shall provide for himself and all the people of the land a young bull for a sin offering. 23And during the seven days of the festival he shall provide as a burnt offering to the LORD seven young bulls and seven rams without blemish, on each of the seven days; and a male goat daily for a sin offering. 24He shall provide as a grain offering an ephah for each bull, an ephah for each ram, and a hin of oil to each ephah. 25In the seventh month, on the fifteenth day of the month and for the seven days of the festival, he shall make the same provision for sin offerings, burnt

a 45.5 Gk: Heb as their holding, twenty chambers   b 45.10 A Heb measure of volume   c 45.14 Cn: Heb oil, the bath the oil   d 45.14 Vg: Heb homer

offerings, and grain offerings, and for the oil.

MISCELLANEOUS REGULATIONS

46 Thus says the Lord GOD: The gate of the inner court that faces east shall remain closed on the six working days; but on the sabbath day it shall be opened and on the day of the new moon it shall be opened. ²The prince shall enter by the vestibule of the gate from outside, and shall take his stand by the post of the gate. The priests shall offer his burnt offering and his offerings of well-being, and he shall bow down at the threshold of the gate. Then he shall go out, but the gate shall not be closed until evening. ³The people of the land shall bow down at the entrance of that gate before the LORD on the sabbaths and on the new moons. ⁴The burnt offering that the prince offers to the LORD on the sabbath day shall be six lambs without blemish and a ram without blemish; ⁵and the grain offering with the ram shall be an ephah, and the grain offering with the lambs shall be as much as he wishes to give, together with a hin of oil to each ephah. ⁶On the day of the new moon he shall offer a young bull without blemish, and six lambs and a ram, which shall be without blemish; ⁷as a grain offering he shall provide an ephah with the bull and an ephah with the ram, and with the lambs as much as he wishes, together with a hin of oil to each ephah. ⁸When the prince enters, he shall come in by the vestibule of the gate, and he shall go out by the same way.

9 When the people of the land come before the LORD at the appointed festivals, whoever enters by the north gate to worship shall go out by the south gate; and whoever enters by the south gate shall go out by the north gate: they shall not return by way of the gate by which they entered, but shall go out straight ahead. ¹⁰When they come in, the prince shall come in with them; and when they go out, he shall go out.

11 At the festivals and the appointed seasons the grain offering with a young bull shall be an ephah, and with a ram an ephah, and with the lambs as much as one wishes to give, together with a hin of oil to an ephah. ¹²When the prince provides a freewill offering, either a burnt offering or offerings of well-being as a freewill offering to the LORD, the gate facing east shall be opened for him; and he shall offer his burnt offering or his offerings of well-being as he does on the sabbath day. Then he shall go out, and after he has gone out the gate shall be closed.

13 He shall provide a lamb, a yearling, without blemish, for a burnt offering to the LORD daily; morning by morning he shall provide it. ¹⁴And he shall provide a grain offering with it morning by morning regularly, one-sixth of an ephah, and one-third of a hin of oil to moisten the choice flour, as a grain offering to the LORD; this is the ordinance for all time. ¹⁵Thus the lamb and the grain offering and the oil shall be provided, morning by morning, as a regular burnt offering.

16 Thus says the Lord GOD: If the prince makes a gift to any of his sons out of his inheritance,ᵃ it shall belong to his sons, it is their holding by inheritance. ¹⁷But if he makes a gift out of his inheritance to one of his servants, it shall be his to the year of liberty; then it shall revert to the prince; only his sons may keep a gift from his inheritance. ¹⁸The prince shall not take any of the inheritance of the people, thrusting them out of their holding; he shall give his sons their inheritance out of his own holding, so that none of my people shall be dispossessed of their holding.

19 Then he brought me through the entrance, which was at the side of the gate, to the north row of the holy chambers for the priests; and there I saw a place at the extreme western end of them. ²⁰He said to me, "This is the place where the priests shall boil the guilt offering and the sin offering, and where they shall bake the grain offering, in

---

ᵃ **46.16** Gk: Heb *it is his inheritance*

order not to bring them out into the outer court and so communicate holiness to the people."

21 Then he brought me out to the outer court, and led me past the four corners of the court; and in each corner of the court there was a court— 22in the four corners of the court were small[a] courts, forty cubits long and thirty wide; the four were of the same size. 23On the inside, around each of the four courts[b] was a row of masonry, with hearths made at the bottom of the rows all around. 24Then he said to me, "These are the kitchens where those who serve at the temple shall boil the sacrifices of the people."

WATER FLOWING FROM THE TEMPLE

47 Then he brought me back to the entrance of the temple; there, water was flowing from below the threshold of the temple toward the east (for the temple faced east); and the water was flowing down from below the south end of the threshold of the temple, south of the altar. 2Then he brought me out by way of the north gate, and led me around on the outside to the outer gate that faces toward the east;[c] and the water was coming out on the south side.

3 Going on eastward with a cord in his hand, the man measured one thousand cubits, and then led me through the water; and it was ankle-deep. 4Again he measured one thousand, and led me through the water; and it was knee-deep. Again he measured one thousand, and led me through the water; and it was up to the waist. 5Again he measured one thousand, and it was a river that I could not cross, for the water had risen; it was deep enough to swim in, a river that could not be crossed. 6He said to me, "Mortal, have you seen this?"

Then he led me back along the bank of the river. 7As I came back, I saw on the bank of the river a great many trees on the one side and on the other. 8He said to me, "This water flows toward the eastern region and goes down into the Arabah; and when it enters the sea, the sea of stagnant waters, the water will become fresh. 9Wherever the river goes,[d] every living creature that swarms will live, and there will be very many fish, once these waters reach there. It will become fresh; and everything will live where the river goes. 10People will stand fishing beside the sea[e] from En-gedi to En-eglaim; it will be a place for the spreading of nets; its fish will be of a great many kinds, like the fish of the Great Sea. 11But its swamps and marshes will not become fresh; they are to be left for salt. 12On the banks, on both sides of the river, there will grow all kinds of trees for food. Their leaves will not wither nor their fruit fail, but they will bear fresh fruit every month, because the water for them flows from the sanctuary. Their fruit will be for food, and their leaves for healing."

THE NEW BOUNDARIES OF THE LAND

13 Thus says the Lord GOD: These are the boundaries by which you shall divide the land for inheritance among the twelve tribes of Israel. Joseph shall have two portions. 14You shall divide it equally; I swore to give it to your ancestors, and this land shall fall to you as your inheritance.

15 This shall be the boundary of the land: On the north side, from the Great Sea by way of Hethlon to Lebo-hamath, and on to Zedad,[f] 16Berothah, Sibraim (which lies between the border of Damascus and the border of Hamath), as far as Hazer-hatticon, which is on the border of Hauran. 17So the boundary shall run from the sea to Hazar-enon, which is north of the border of Damascus, with the border of Hamath to the north.[c] This shall be the north side.

18 On the east side, between Hauran and Damascus; along the Jor-

a 46.22 Gk Syr Vg: Meaning of Heb uncertain   b 46.23 Heb *the four of them*   c 47.2,17 Meaning of Heb uncertain   d 47.9 Gk Syr Vg Tg: Heb *the two rivers go*   e 47.10 Heb *it*   f 47.15 Gk: Heb *Lebo-zedad*, 16*Hamath*

dan between Gilead and the land of Israel; to the eastern sea and as far as Tamar.[a] This shall be the east side.

19 On the south side, it shall run from Tamar as far as the waters of Meribath-kadesh, from there along the Wadi of Egypt[b] to the Great Sea. This shall be the south side.

20 On the west side, the Great Sea shall be the boundary to a point opposite Lebo-hamath. This shall be the west side.

21 So you shall divide this land among you according to the tribes of Israel. 22 You shall allot it as an inheritance for yourselves and for the aliens who reside among you and have begotten children among you. They shall be to you as citizens of Israel; with you they shall be allotted an inheritance among the tribes of Israel. 23 In whatever tribe aliens reside, there you shall assign them their inheritance, says the Lord GOD.

THE TRIBAL PORTIONS

48 These are the names of the tribes: Beginning at the northern border, on the Hethlon road,[c] from Lebo-hamath, as far as Hazar-enon (which is on the border of Damascus, with Hamath to the north), and[d] extending from the east side to the west,[e] Dan, one portion. 2 Adjoining the territory of Dan, from the east side to the west, Asher, one portion. 3 Adjoining the territory of Asher, from the east side to the west, Naphtali, one portion. 4 Adjoining the territory of Naphtali, from the east side to the west, Manasseh, one portion. 5 Adjoining the territory of Manasseh, from the east side to the west, Ephraim, one portion. 6 Adjoining the territory of Ephraim, from the east side to the west, Reuben, one portion. 7 Adjoining the territory of Reuben, from the east side to the west, Judah, one portion.

8 Adjoining the territory of Judah, from the east side to the west, shall be the portion that you shall set apart, twenty-five thousand cubits in width, and in length equal to one of the tribal portions, from the east side to the west, with the sanc-tuary in the middle of it. 9 The portion that you shall set apart for the LORD shall be twenty-five thousand cubits in length, and twenty[f] thousand in width. 10 These shall be the allotments of the holy portion: the priests shall have an allotment measuring twenty-five thousand cubits on the northern side, ten thousand cubits in width on the western side, ten thousand in width on the eastern side, and twenty-five thousand in length on the southern side, with the sanctuary of the LORD in the middle of it. 11 This shall be for the consecrated priests, the descendants[g] of Zadok, who kept my charge, who did not go astray when the people of Israel went astray, as the Levites did. 12 It shall belong to them as a special portion from the holy portion of the land, a most holy place, adjoining the territory of the Levites. 13 Alongside the territory of the priests, the Levites shall have an allotment twenty-five thousand cubits in length and ten thousand in width. The whole length shall be twenty-five thousand cubits and the width twenty[h] thousand. 14 They shall not sell or exchange any of it; they shall not transfer this choice portion of the land, for it is holy to the LORD.

15 The remainder, five thousand cubits in width and twenty-five thousand in length, shall be for ordinary use for the city, for dwellings and for open country. In the middle of it shall be the city; 16 and these shall be its dimensions: the north side four thousand five hundred cubits, the south side four thousand five hundred, the east side four thousand five hundred, and the west side four thousand five hundred. 17 The city shall have open land: on the north two hundred fifty cubits, on the south two hundred fifty, on the east

---

[a] 47.18 Compare Syr: Heb *you shall measure*
[b] 47.19 Heb lacks *of Egypt*   [c] 48.1 Compare 47.15: Heb *by the side of the way*   [d] 48.1 Cn: Heb *and they shall be his*   [e] 48.1 Gk Compare verses 2–8: Heb *the east side the west*   [f] 48.9 Compare 45.1: Heb *ten*
[g] 48.11 One Ms Gk: Heb *of the descendants*
[h] 48.13 Gk: Heb *ten*

two hundred fifty, on the west two hundred fifty. [18] The remainder of the length alongside the holy portion shall be ten thousand cubits to the east, and ten thousand to the west, and it shall be alongside the holy portion. Its produce shall be food for the workers of the city. [19] The workers of the city, from all the tribes of Israel, shall cultivate it. [20] The whole portion that you shall set apart shall be twenty-five thousand cubits square, that is, the holy portion together with the property of the city.

[21] What remains on both sides of the holy portion and of the property of the city shall belong to the prince. Extending from the twenty-five thousand cubits of the holy portion to the east border, and westward from the twenty-five thousand cubits to the west border, parallel to the tribal portions, it shall belong to the prince. The holy portion with the sanctuary of the temple in the middle of it, [22] and the property of the Levites and of the city, shall be in the middle of that which belongs to the prince. The portion of the prince shall lie between the territory of Judah and the territory of Benjamin.

[23] As for the rest of the tribes: from the east side to the west, Benjamin, one portion. [24] Adjoining the territory of Benjamin, from the east side to the west, Simeon, one portion. [25] Adjoining the territory of Simeon, from the east side to the west, Issachar, one portion. [26] Adjoining the territory of Issachar, from the east side to the west, Zebulun, one portion. [27] Adjoining the territory of Zebulun, from the east side to the west, Gad, one portion. [28] And adjoining the territory of Gad to the south, the boundary shall run from Tamar to the waters of Meribath-kadesh, from there along the Wadi of Egypt[a] to the Great Sea. [29] This is the land that you shall allot as an inheritance among the tribes of Israel, and these are their portions, says the Lord GOD.

[30] These shall be the exits of the city: On the north side, which is to be four thousand five hundred cubits by measure, [31] three gates, the gate of Reuben, the gate of Judah, and the gate of Levi, the gates of the city being named after the tribes of Israel. [32] On the east side, which is to be four thousand five hundred cubits, three gates, the gate of Joseph, the gate of Benjamin, and the gate of Dan. [33] On the south side, which is to be four thousand five hundred cubits by measure, three gates, the gate of Simeon, the gate of Issachar, and the gate of Zebulun. [34] On the west side, which is to be four thousand five hundred cubits, three gates,[b] the gate of Gad, the gate of Asher, and the gate of Naphtali. [35] The circumference of the city shall be eighteen thousand cubits. And the name of the city from that time on shall be, The LORD is There.

---

[a] 48.28 Heb lacks *of Egypt*   [b] 48.34 One Ms Gk Syr: MT *their gates three*

DANIEL

Fiery furnaces and lions' dens, dreams and visions—these are the larger-than-life experiences Daniel recounted. Yet even greater than these events is the God who controlled them. One of the most compelling realities in these stories is that God worked through Daniel and his three friends—Hananiah, Mishael and Azariah—even though they were young. These four lived out their faith in amazing ways that revealed God's power and ability to save them. As we read this book, we can imagine ourselves in their place. How might we respond?

FOUR YOUNG ISRAELITES AT THE BABYLONIAN COURT

1 In the third year of the reign of King Jehoiakim of Judah, King Nebuchadnezzar of Babylon came to Jerusalem and besieged it. ²The Lord let King Jehoiakim of Judah fall into his power, as well as some of the vessels of the house of God. These he brought to the land of Shinar,ᵃ and placed the vessels in the treasury of his gods.

3 Then the king commanded his palace master Ashpenaz to bring some of the Israelites of the royal family and of the nobility, ⁴young men without physical defect and handsome, versed in every branch of wisdom, endowed with knowledge and insight, and competent to serve in the king's palace; they were to be taught the literature and language of the Chaldeans. ⁵The king assigned them a daily portion of the royal rations of food and wine. They were to be educated for three years, so that at the end of that time they could be stationed in the king's court. ⁶Among them were Daniel, Hananiah, Mishael, and Azariah, from the tribe of Judah. ⁷The palace master gave them other names: Daniel he called Belteshazzar, Hananiah he called Shadrach, Mishael he called Meshach, and Azariah he called Abednego.

8 But Daniel resolved that he would not defile himself with the royal rations of food and wine; so he asked the palace master to allow him not to defile himself. ⁹Now God allowed Daniel to receive favor and compassion from the palace master. ¹⁰The palace master said to Daniel, "I am afraid of my lord the king; he has appointed your food and your drink. If he should see you in poorer condition than the other young men of your own age, you would endanger my head with the king." ¹¹Then Daniel asked the guard whom the palace master had appointed over Daniel, Hananiah, Mishael, and Azariah: ¹²"Please test your servants for ten days. Let us be given vegetables to eat and water to drink. ¹³You can then compare our appearance with the appearance of the young men who eat the royal rations, and deal with your servants according to what you observe." ¹⁴So he agreed to this proposal and tested them for ten days. ¹⁵At the end of ten days it was observed that they appeared better and fatter than all the young men who had been eating the royal rations. ¹⁶So the guard continued to withdraw their royal rations and the wine they were to drink, and gave them vegetables. ¹⁷To these four young men God gave knowledge and skill in every aspect of literature and wisdom; Daniel also had insight into all visions and dreams.

PONDER

To these four young men God gave knowledge and skill in every aspect of literature and wisdom; Daniel also had insight into all visions and dreams.
—Daniel 1.17

PRAY

Lord, thank you for this exciting story about Daniel, this intelligent young man who was filled with faith, courage, humility and generosity. Help us to follow his example of serving you with quiet courage as we serve our Savior, Jesus Christ. We ask for knowledge, discernment and wisdom such as you gave Daniel, and the boldness to use these gifts in your kingdom work as he did. We thank you for all the blessings in our lives. In the name of Jesus, we pray. Amen.

---

18 At the end of the time that the king had set for them to be brought in, the palace master brought them into the presence of Nebuchadnezzar, ¹⁹and the king spoke with them. And among them all, no one

ᵃ 1.2 Gk Theodotion: Heb adds *to the house of his own gods* was found to compare with Daniel, Hananiah, Mishael, and Azariah; therefore they were stationed in the king's court. 20 In every matter of wisdom and understanding concerning which the king inquired of them, he found them ten times better than all the magicians and enchanters in his whole kingdom. 21 And Daniel continued there until the first year of King Cyrus.

NEBUCHADNEZZAR'S DREAM

2 In the second year of Nebuchadnezzar's reign, Nebuchadnezzar dreamed such dreams that his spirit was troubled and his sleep left him. 2 So the king commanded that the magicians, the enchanters, the sorcerers, and the Chaldeans be summoned to tell the king his dreams. When they came in and stood before the king, 3 he said to them, "I have had such a dream that my spirit is troubled by the desire to understand it." 4 The Chaldeans said to the king (in Aramaic), a "O king, live forever! Tell your servants the dream, and we will reveal the interpretation." 5 The king answered the Chaldeans, "This is a public decree: if you do not tell me both the dream and its interpretation, you shall be torn limb from limb, and your houses shall be laid in ruins. 6 But if you do tell me the dream and its interpretation, you shall receive from me gifts and rewards and great honor. Therefore tell me the dream and its interpretation." 7 They answered a second time, "Let the king first tell his servants the dream, then we can give its interpretation." 8 The king answered, "I know with certainty that you are trying to gain time, because you see I have firmly decreed: 9 if you do not tell me the dream, there is but one verdict for you. You have agreed to speak lying and misleading words to me until things take a turn. Therefore, tell me the dream, and I shall know that you can give me its interpretation." 10 The Chaldeans answered the king, "There is no one on earth who can reveal what the king demands! In fact no king, however great and powerful, has ever asked such a thing of any magician or enchanter or Chaldean. 11 The thing that the king is asking is too difficult, and no one can reveal it to the king except the gods, whose dwelling is not with mortals."

12 Because of this the king flew into a violent rage and commanded that all the wise men of Babylon be destroyed. 13 The decree was issued, and the wise men were about to be executed; and they looked for Daniel and his companions, to execute them. 14 Then Daniel responded with prudence and discretion to Arioch, the king's chief executioner, who had gone out to execute the wise men of Babylon; 15 he asked Arioch, the royal official, "Why is the decree of the king so urgent?" Arioch then explained the matter to Daniel. 16 So Daniel went in and requested that the king give him time and he would tell the king the interpretation.

GOD REVEALS NEBUCHADNEZZAR'S DREAM

17 Then Daniel went to his home and informed his companions, Hananiah, Mishael, and Azariah, 18 and told them to seek mercy from the God of heaven concerning this mystery, so that Daniel and his companions with the rest of the wise men of Babylon might not perish. 19 Then the mystery was revealed to Daniel in a vision of the night, and Daniel blessed the God of heaven.
20 Daniel said:

"Blessed be the name of God
      from age to age,
   for wisdom and
      power are his.
21 He changes times and seasons,
      deposes kings and sets
         up kings;
   he gives wisdom to the wise
      and knowledge to those who
         have understanding.
22 He reveals deep and
      hidden things;
   he knows what is in
      the darkness,
   and light dwells with him.

---

a 2.4 The text from this point to the end of chapter 7 is in Aramaic

23 To you, O God of my ancestors,
    I give thanks and praise,
for you have given me
    wisdom and power,
and have now revealed to me
    what we asked of you,
for you have revealed to us
    what the king ordered."

DANIEL INTERPRETS THE DREAM

24 Therefore Daniel went to Arioch, whom the king had appointed to destroy the wise men of Babylon, and said to him, "Do not destroy the wise men of Babylon; bring me in before the king, and I will give the king the interpretation."

25 Then Arioch quickly brought Daniel before the king and said to him: "I have found among the exiles from Judah a man who can tell the king the interpretation." 26 The king said to Daniel, whose name was Belteshazzar, "Are you able to tell me the dream that I have seen and its interpretation?" 27 Daniel answered the king, "No wise men, enchanters, magicians, or diviners can show to the king the mystery that the king is asking, 28 but there is a God in heaven who reveals mysteries, and he has disclosed to King Nebuchadnezzar what will happen at the end of days. Your dream and the visions of your head as you lay in bed were these: 29 To you, O king, as you lay in bed, came thoughts of what would be hereafter, and the revealer of mysteries disclosed to you what is to be. 30 But as for me, this mystery has not been revealed to me because of any wisdom that I have more than any other living being, but in order that the interpretation may be known to the king and that you may understand the thoughts of your mind.

31 "You were looking, O king, and lo! there was a great statue. This statue was huge, its brilliance extraordinary; it was standing before you, and its appearance was frightening. 32 The head of that statue was of fine gold, its chest and arms of silver, its middle and thighs of bronze, 33 its legs of iron, its feet partly of iron and partly of clay. 34 As you looked on, a stone was cut out, not by human hands, and it struck the statue on its feet of iron and clay and broke them in pieces. 35 Then the iron, the clay, the bronze, the silver, and the gold, were all broken in pieces and became like the chaff of the summer threshing floors; and the wind carried them away, so that not a trace of them could be found. But the stone that struck the statue became a great mountain and filled the whole earth.

36 "This was the dream; now we will tell the king its interpretation. 37 You, O king, the king of kings—to whom the God of heaven has given the kingdom, the power, the might, and the glory, 38 into whose hand he has given human beings, wherever they live, the wild animals of the field, and the birds of the air, and whom he has established as ruler over them all—you are the head of gold. 39 After you shall arise another kingdom inferior to yours, and yet a third kingdom of bronze, which shall rule over the whole earth. 40 And there shall be a fourth kingdom, strong as iron; just as iron crushes and smashes everything,[a] it shall crush and shatter all these. 41 As you saw the feet and toes partly of potter's clay and partly of iron, it shall be a divided kingdom; but some of the strength of iron shall be in it, as you saw the iron mixed with the clay. 42 As the toes of the feet were part iron and part clay, so the kingdom shall be partly strong and partly brittle. 43 As you saw the iron mixed with clay, so will they mix with one another in marriage,[b] but they will not hold together, just as iron does not mix with clay. 44 And in the days of those kings the God of heaven will set up a kingdom that shall never be destroyed, nor shall this kingdom be left to another people. It shall crush all these kingdoms and bring them to an end, and it shall stand forever; 45 just as you saw that a stone was cut from the mountain not by hands, and that it crushed the iron,

a 2.40 Gk Theodotion Syr Vg: Aram adds *and like iron that crushes*   b 2.43 Aram *by human seed*

the bronze, the clay, the silver, and the gold. The great God has informed the king what shall be hereafter. The dream is certain, and its interpretation trustworthy."

DANIEL AND HIS FRIENDS PROMOTED

46 Then King Nebuchadnezzar fell on his face, worshiped Daniel, and commanded that a grain offering and incense be offered to him. 47The king said to Daniel, "Truly, your God is God of gods and Lord of kings and a revealer of mysteries, for you have been able to reveal this mystery!" 48Then the king promoted Daniel, gave him many great gifts, and made him ruler over the whole province of Babylon and chief prefect over all the wise men of Babylon. 49Daniel made a request of the king, and he appointed Shadrach, Meshach, and Abednego over the affairs of the province of Babylon. But Daniel remained at the king's court.

THE GOLDEN IMAGE

3 King Nebuchadnezzar made a golden statue whose height was sixty cubits and whose width was six cubits; he set it up on the plain of Dura in the province of Babylon. 2Then King Nebuchadnezzar sent for the satraps, the prefects, and the governors, the counselors, the treasurers, the justices, the magistrates, and all the officials of the provinces, to assemble and come to the dedication of the statue that King Nebuchadnezzar had set up. 3So the satraps, the prefects, and the governors, the counselors, the treasurers, the justices, the magistrates, and all the officials of the provinces, assembled for the dedication of the statue that King Nebuchadnezzar had set up. When they were standing before the statue that Nebuchadnezzar had set up, 4the herald proclaimed aloud, "You are commanded, O peoples, nations, and languages, 5that when you hear the sound of the horn, pipe, lyre, trigon, harp, drum, and entire musical ensemble, you are to fall down and worship the golden statue that King Nebuchadnezzar has set

up. 6Whoever does not fall down and worship shall immediately be thrown into a furnace of blazing fire." 7Therefore, as soon as all the peoples heard the sound of the horn, pipe, lyre, trigon, harp, drum, and entire musical ensemble, all the peoples, nations, and languages fell down and worshiped the golden statue that King Nebuchadnezzar had set up.

8 Accordingly, at this time certain Chaldeans came forward and denounced the Jews. 9They said to King Nebuchadnezzar, "O king, live forever! 10You, O king, have made a decree, that everyone who hears the sound of the horn, pipe, lyre, trigon, harp, drum, and entire musical ensemble, shall fall down and worship the golden statue, 11and whoever does not fall down and worship shall be thrown into a furnace of blazing fire. 12There are certain Jews whom you have appointed over the affairs of the province of Babylon: Shadrach, Meshach, and Abednego. These pay no heed to you, O king. They do not serve your gods and they do not worship the golden statue that you have set up."

13 Then Nebuchadnezzar in furious rage commanded that Shadrach, Meshach, and Abednego be brought in; so they brought those men before the king. 14Nebuchadnezzar said to them, "Is it true, O Shadrach, Meshach, and Abednego, that you do not serve my gods and you do not worship the golden statue that I have set up? 15Now if you are ready when you hear the sound of the horn, pipe, lyre, trigon, harp, drum, and entire musical ensemble to fall down and worship the statue that I have made, well and good.a But if you do not worship, you shall immediately be thrown into a furnace of blazing fire, and who is the god that will deliver you out of my hands?"

16 Shadrach, Meshach, and Abednego answered the king, "O Nebuchadnezzar, we have no need to present a defense to you in this matter. 17If our God whom we serve is able

a 3.15 Aram lacks well and good

to deliver us from the furnace of blazing fire and out of your hand, O king, let him deliver us.[a] 18But if not, be it known to you, O king, that we will not serve your gods and we will not worship the golden statue that you have set up."

THE FIERY FURNACE

19 Then Nebuchadnezzar was so filled with rage against Shadrach, Meshach, and Abednego that his face was distorted. He ordered the furnace heated up seven times more than was customary, 20and ordered some of the strongest guards in his army to bind Shadrach, Meshach, and Abednego and to throw them into the furnace of blazing fire. 21So the men were bound, still wearing their tunics,[b] their trousers,[b] their hats, and their other garments, and they were thrown into the furnace of blazing fire. 22Because the king's command was urgent and the furnace was so overheated, the raging flames killed the men who lifted Shadrach, Meshach, and Abednego. 23But the three men, Shadrach, Meshach, and Abednego, fell down, bound, into the furnace of blazing fire.

24 Then King Nebuchadnezzar was astonished and rose up quickly. He said to his counselors, "Was it not three men that we threw bound into the fire?" They answered the king, "True, O king." 25He replied, "But I see four men unbound, walking in the middle of the fire, and they are not hurt; and the fourth has the appearance of a god."[c] 26Nebuchadnezzar then approached the door of the furnace of blazing fire and said, "Shadrach, Meshach, and Abednego, servants of the Most High God, come out! Come here!" So Shadrach, Meshach, and Abednego came out from the fire. 27And the satraps, the prefects, the governors, and the king's counselors gathered together and saw that the fire had not had any power over the bodies of those men; the hair of their heads was not singed, their tunics[b] were not harmed, and not even the smell of fire came from them. 28Nebuchadnezzar said, "Blessed be the God of Shadrach, Meshach, and Abednego, who has sent his angel and delivered his servants who trusted in him. They disobeyed the king's command and yielded up their bodies rather than serve and worship any god except their own God.

a 3.17 Or If our God whom we serve is able to deliver us, he will deliver us from the furnace of blazing fire and out of your hand, O king.
b 3.21,27 Meaning of Aram word uncertain
c 3.25 Aram a son of the gods

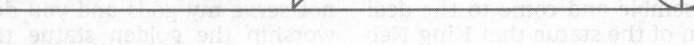

BIBLE IN LIFE

Civil Disobedience

Daniel 3.1–30

Are there times when we Christians are allowed, or perhaps even compelled, to disobey the government in order to follow what we believe is God's will? Yes, I believe so. While the Bible makes it clear that we are to submit to the government in every way that we can without violating the commands of God (see Romans 13.1–7), the stories in the book of Daniel show us that sometimes we simply cannot obey certain demands of the government when they stand in direct opposition to mandates of God. We need to be cautious in how we put this into practice, however, because this can easily be misconstrued as a justification for disregarding any laws with which we simply disagree. In our desire to follow Christ, the misuse of force or other actions is never justified. Civil disobedience is acceptable only when it becomes impossible to obey the law and still obey Christ. If we break a law, however, we also need to be prepared to suffer the consequences, such as being arrested or fined. Our highest allegiance always belongs to Christ. Over time, God may use our actions to help shape the government's laws (and society's thinking) to be more in line with Christ's commands, such as the changes we have seen in the past with issues such as civil rights, opposition to war and environmental concerns.

29 Therefore I make a decree: Any people, nation, or language that utters blasphemy against the God of Shadrach, Meshach, and Abednego shall be torn limb from limb, and their houses laid in ruins; for there is no other god who is able to deliver in this way." 30 Then the king promoted Shadrach, Meshach, and Abednego in the province of Babylon.

NEBUCHADNEZZAR'S SECOND DREAM

4 a King Nebuchadnezzar to all peoples, nations, and languages that live throughout the earth: May you have abundant prosperity! 2 The signs and wonders that the Most High God has worked for me I am pleased to recount.
3 How great are his signs,
   how mighty his wonders!
His kingdom is an everlasting
   kingdom,
   and his sovereignty is from
      generation to generation.
4 b I, Nebuchadnezzar, was living at ease in my home and prospering in my palace. 5 I saw a dream that frightened me; my fantasies in bed and the visions of my head terrified me. 6 So I made a decree that all the wise men of Babylon should be brought before me, in order that they might tell me the interpretation of the dream. 7 Then the magicians, the enchanters, the Chaldeans, and the diviners came in, and I told them the dream, but they could not tell me its interpretation. 8 At last Daniel came in before me—he who was named Belteshazzar after the name of my god, and who is endowed with a spirit of the holy gods c —and I told him the dream: 9 "O Belteshazzar, chief of the magicians, I know that you are endowed with a spirit of the holy gods c and that no mystery is too difficult for you. Hear d the dream that I saw; tell me its interpretation.
10 e Upon my bed this
      is what I saw;
   there was a tree at the
      center of the earth,
   and its height was great.

11 The tree grew great and strong,
   its top reached to heaven,
   and it was visible to the ends
      of the whole earth.
12 Its foliage was beautiful,
   its fruit abundant,
   and it provided food for all.
The animals of the field found
      shade under it,
   the birds of the air nested
      in its branches,
   and from it all living
      beings were fed.

13 "I continued looking, in the visions of my head as I lay in bed, and there was a holy watcher, coming down from heaven. 14 He cried aloud and said:
'Cut down the tree and chop
      off its branches,
   strip off its foliage and
      scatter its fruit.
Let the animals flee from
      beneath it
   and the birds from its
      branches.
15 But leave its stump and roots
      in the ground,
   with a band of iron and bronze,
   in the tender grass of the field.
Let him be bathed with the
      dew of heaven,
   and let his lot be with the
      animals of the field
   in the grass of the earth.
16 Let his mind be changed from
      that of a human,
   and let the mind of an animal
      be given to him.
   And let seven times
      pass over him.
17 The sentence is rendered by
      decree of the watchers,
   the decision is given by order
      of the holy ones,
   in order that all who live
      may know
   that the Most High is
      sovereign over the
         kingdom of mortals;

---

a 4.1 Ch 3.31 in Aram   b 4.4 Ch 4.1 in Aram   c 4.8,9 Or a holy, divine spirit
d 4.9 Theodotion: Aram The visions of
e 4.10 Theodotion Syr Compare Gk: Aram adds The visions of my head

he gives it to whom he will
and sets over it the lowliest
of human beings.'

18 "This is the dream that I, King Nebuchadnezzar, saw. Now you, Belteshazzar, declare the interpretation, since all the wise men of my kingdom are unable to tell me the interpretation. You are able, however, for you are endowed with a spirit of the holy gods."[a]

DANIEL INTERPRETS THE SECOND DREAM

19 Then Daniel, who was called Belteshazzar, was severely distressed for a while. His thoughts terrified him. The king said, "Belteshazzar, do not let the dream or the interpretation terrify you." Belteshazzar answered, "My lord, may the dream be for those who hate you, and its interpretation for your enemies! 20 The tree that you saw, which grew great and strong, so that its top reached to heaven and was visible to the end of the whole earth, 21whose foliage was beautiful and its fruit abundant, and which provided food for all, under which animals of the field lived, and in whose branches the birds of the air had nests— 22it is you, O king! You have grown great and strong. Your greatness has increased and reaches to heaven, and your sovereignty to the ends of the earth. 23 And whereas the king saw a holy watcher coming down from heaven and saying, 'Cut down the tree and destroy it, but leave its stump and roots in the ground, with a band of iron and bronze, in the grass of the field; and let him be bathed with the dew of heaven, and let his lot be with the animals of the field, until seven times pass over him'— 24this is the interpretation, O king, and it is a decree of the Most High that has come upon my lord the king: 25You shall be driven away from human society, and your dwelling shall be with the wild animals. You shall be made to eat grass like oxen, you shall be bathed with the dew of heaven, and seven times shall pass over you, until you have

learned that the Most High has sovereignty over the kingdom of mortals, and gives it to whom he will. 26 As it was commanded to leave the stump and roots of the tree, your kingdom shall be re-established for you from the time that you learn that Heaven is sovereign. 27Therefore, O king, may my counsel be acceptable to you: atone for[b] your sins with righteousness, and your iniquities with mercy to the oppressed, so that your prosperity may be prolonged."

NEBUCHADNEZZAR'S HUMILIATION

28 All this came upon King Nebuchadnezzar. 29At the end of twelve months he was walking on the roof of the royal palace of Babylon, 30and the king said, "Is this not magnificent Babylon, which I have built as a royal capital by my mighty power and for my glorious majesty?" 31While the words were still in the king's mouth, a voice came from heaven: "O King Nebuchadnezzar, to you it is declared: The kingdom has departed from you! 32You shall be driven away from human society, and your dwelling shall be with the animals of the field. You shall be made to eat grass like oxen, and seven times shall pass over you, until you have learned that the Most High has sovereignty over the kingdom of mortals and gives it to whom he will." 33Immediately the sentence was fulfilled against Nebuchadnezzar. He was driven away from human society, ate grass like oxen, and his body was bathed with the dew of heaven, until his hair grew as long as eagles' feathers and his nails became like birds' claws.

NEBUCHADNEZZAR PRAISES GOD

34 When that period was over, I, Nebuchadnezzar, lifted my eyes to heaven, and my reason returned to me.

---

[a] 4.18 Or *a holy, divine spirit*   [b] 4.27 Aram *break off*

I blessed the Most High,
and praised and honored the
one who lives forever.
For his sovereignty is an
everlasting sovereignty,
and his kingdom endures from
generation to generation.
35 All the inhabitants of the earth
are accounted as nothing,
and he does what he wills
with the host of heaven
and the inhabitants
of the earth.
There is no one who can
stay his hand
or say to him, "What are
you doing?"
36 At that time my reason returned to me; and my majesty and splendor were restored to me for the glory of my kingdom. My counselors and my lords sought me out, I was re-established over my kingdom, and still more greatness was added to me. 37 Now I, Nebuchadnezzar, praise and extol and honor the King of heaven,
for all his works are truth,
and his ways are justice;
and he is able to bring low
those who walk in pride.

BELSHAZZAR'S FEAST

5 King Belshazzar made a great festival for a thousand of his lords, and he was drinking wine in the presence of the thousand.

2 Under the influence of the wine, Belshazzar commanded that they bring in the vessels of gold and silver that his father Nebuchadnezzar had taken out of the temple in Jerusalem, so that the king and his lords, his wives, and his concubines might drink from them. 3 So they brought in the vessels of gold and silver[a] that had been taken out of the temple, the house of God in Jerusalem, and the king and his lords, his wives, and his concubines drank from them. 4 They drank the wine and praised the gods of gold and silver, bronze, iron, wood, and stone.

THE WRITING ON THE WALL

5 Immediately the fingers of a human hand appeared and began writing on the plaster of the wall of the royal palace, next to the lampstand. The king was watching the hand as it wrote. 6 Then the king's face turned pale, and his thoughts terrified him. His limbs gave way, and his knees knocked together. 7 The king cried aloud to bring in the enchanters, the Chaldeans, and the diviners; and the king said to the wise men of Babylon, "Whoever can read this writing and tell me its interpretation shall be clothed in purple, have a chain of gold around his neck, and rank third in the kingdom." 8 Then all the king's wise men came in, but they could not read the writing or tell the king the interpretation. 9 Then King Belshazzar became greatly terrified and his face turned pale, and his lords were perplexed.

10 The queen, when she heard the discussion of the king and his lords, came into the banqueting hall. The queen said, "O king, live forever! Do not let your thoughts terrify you or your face grow pale. 11 There is a man in your kingdom who is endowed with a spirit of the holy gods.[b] In the days of your father he was found to have enlightenment, understanding, and wisdom like the wisdom of the gods. Your father, King Nebuchadnezzar, made him chief of the magicians, enchanters, Chaldeans, and diviners,[c] 12 because an excellent spirit, knowledge, and understanding to interpret dreams, explain riddles, and solve problems were found in this Daniel, whom the king named Belteshazzar. Now let Daniel be called, and he will give the interpretation."

THE WRITING ON THE
WALL INTERPRETED

13 Then Daniel was brought in before the king. The king said to Daniel, "So you are Daniel, one of the exiles of Judah, whom my father the king brought from Judah? 14 I have heard of you that a spirit of the gods[d] is in you, and that enlightenment,

a 5.3 Theodotion Vg: Aram lacks and silver
b 5.11 Or a holy, divine spirit   c 5.11 Aram
adds the king your father   d 5.14 Or a
divine spirit

understanding, and excellent wisdom are found in you. ¹⁵Now the wise men, the enchanters, have been brought in before me to read this writing and tell me its interpretation, but they were not able to give the interpretation of the matter. ¹⁶But I have heard that you can give interpretations and solve problems. Now if you are able to read the writing and tell me its interpretation, you shall be clothed in purple, have a chain of gold around your neck, and rank third in the kingdom."

17 Then Daniel answered in the presence of the king, "Let your gifts be for yourself, or give your rewards to someone else! Nevertheless I will read the writing to the king and let him know the interpretation. ¹⁸O king, the Most High God gave your father Nebuchadnezzar kingship, greatness, glory, and majesty. ¹⁹And because of the greatness that he gave him, all peoples, nations, and languages trembled and feared before him. He killed those he wanted to kill, kept alive those he wanted to keep alive, honored those he wanted to honor, and degraded those he wanted to degrade. ²⁰But when his heart was lifted up and his spirit was hardened so that he acted proudly, he was deposed from his kingly throne, and his glory was stripped from him. ²¹He was driven from human society, and his mind was made like that of an animal. His dwelling was with the wild asses, he was fed grass like oxen, and his body was bathed with the dew of heaven, until he learned that the Most High God has sovereignty over the kingdom of mortals, and sets over it whomever he will. ²²And you, Belshazzar his son, have not humbled your heart, even though you knew all this! ²³You have exalted yourself against the Lord of heaven! The vessels of his temple have been brought in before you, and you and your lords, your wives and your concubines have been drinking wine from them. You have praised the gods of silver and gold, of bronze, iron, wood, and stone, which do not see or hear or know; but the God in whose

power is your very breath, and to whom belong all your ways, you have not honored.

24 "So from his presence the hand was sent and this writing was inscribed. ²⁵And this is the writing that was inscribed: MENE, MENE, TEKEL, and PARSIN. ²⁶This is the interpretation of the matter: MENE, God has numbered the days of[a] your kingdom and brought it to an end; ²⁷TEKEL, you have been weighed on the scales and found wanting; ²⁸PERES,[b] your kingdom is divided and given to the Medes and Persians."

29 Then Belshazzar gave the command, and Daniel was clothed in purple, a chain of gold was put around his neck, and a proclamation was made concerning him that he should rank third in the kingdom.

30 That very night Belshazzar, the Chaldean king, was killed. ³¹[c]And Darius the Mede received the kingdom, being about sixty-two years old.

THE PLOT AGAINST DANIEL

6 It pleased Darius to set over the kingdom one hundred twenty satraps, stationed throughout the whole kingdom, ²and over them three presidents, including Daniel; to these the satraps gave account, so that the king might suffer no loss. ³Soon Daniel distinguished himself above all the other presidents and satraps because an excellent spirit was in him, and the king planned to appoint him over the whole kingdom. ⁴So the presidents and the satraps tried to find grounds for complaint against Daniel in connection with the kingdom. But they could find no grounds for complaint or any corruption, because he was faithful, and no negligence or corruption could be found in him. ⁵The men said, "We shall not find any ground for complaint against this Daniel unless we find it in connection with the law of his God."

6 So the presidents and satraps conspired and came to the king and

a 5.26 Aram lacks *the days of*   b 5.28 The singular of *Parsin*   c 5.31 Ch 6.1 in Aram said to him, "O King Darius, live forever! 7All the presidents of the kingdom, the prefects and the satraps, the counselors and the governors are agreed that the king should establish an ordinance and enforce an interdict, that whoever prays to anyone, divine or human, for thirty days, except to you, O king, shall be thrown into a den of lions. 8Now, O king, establish the interdict and sign the document, so that it cannot be changed, according to the law of the Medes and the Persians, which cannot be revoked." 9Therefore King Darius signed the document and interdict.

DANIEL IN THE LIONS' DEN

10 Although Daniel knew that the document had been signed, he continued to go to his house, which had windows in its upper room open toward Jerusalem, and to get down on his knees three times a day to pray to his God and praise him, just as he had done previously. 11The conspirators came and found Daniel praying and seeking mercy before his God. 12Then they approached the king and said concerning the interdict, "O king! Did you not sign an interdict, that anyone who prays to anyone, divine or human, within thirty days except to you, O king, shall be thrown into a den of lions?" The king answered, "The thing stands fast, according to the law of the Medes and Persians, which cannot be revoked." 13Then they responded to the king, "Daniel, one of the exiles from Judah, pays no attention to you, O king, or to the interdict you have signed, but he is saying his prayers three times a day."

14When the king heard the charge, he was very much distressed. He was determined to save Daniel, and until the sun went down he made every effort to rescue him. 15Then the conspirators came to the king and said to him, "Know, O king, that it is a law of the Medes and Persians that no interdict or ordinance that the king establishes can be changed."

16Then the king gave the command, and Daniel was brought and

PONDER

[Daniel] continued . . . to get down on his knees three times a day to pray to his God and praise him, just as he had done previously.
—Daniel 6.10

PRAY

O Father, again we are confronted by these age-old challenges—lessons that are difficult for us. It is easy for us to see how they apply to the characters of the Bible, but it is not easy for us to acknowledge that they also apply to us. The faith of Daniel, who was courageous, dedicated and heroic, shows us what following you really means. So help us copy his faith and courage in our own lives. Teach us to pray faithfully and constantly as Daniel did. Father, we acknowledge that we need to be transformed in your image and in the image of your Son Jesus, through the Holy Spirit. Amen.

thrown into the den of lions. The king said to Daniel, "May your God, whom you faithfully serve, deliver you!" 17A stone was brought and laid on the mouth of the den, and the king sealed it with his own signet and with the signet of his lords, so that nothing might be changed concerning Daniel. 18Then the king went to his palace and spent the night fasting; no food was brought to him, and sleep fled from him.

DANIEL SAVED FROM THE LIONS

19 Then, at break of day, the king got up and hurried to the den of lions. 20When he came near the den where Daniel was, he cried out anxiously to Daniel, "O Daniel, servant of the living God, has your God whom you faithfully serve been able to deliver you from the lions?" 21Daniel then said to the king, "O king, live forever! 22My God sent

his angel and shut the lions' mouths so that they would not hurt me, because I was found blameless before him; and also before you, O king, I have done no wrong." 23Then the king was exceedingly glad and commanded that Daniel be taken up out of the den. So Daniel was taken up out of the den, and no kind of harm was found on him, because he had trusted in his God. 24The king gave a command, and those who had accused Daniel were brought and thrown into the den of lions—they, their children, and their wives. Before they reached the bottom of the den the lions overpowered them and broke all their bones in pieces.

25 Then King Darius wrote to all peoples and nations of every language throughout the whole world: "May you have abundant prosperity! 26I make a decree, that in all my royal dominion people should tremble and fear before the God of Daniel:

For he is the living God,
    enduring forever.
His kingdom shall never
        be destroyed,
    and his dominion has no end.
27 He delivers and rescues,
    he works signs and wonders
        in heaven and on earth;
    for he has saved Daniel
        from the power of the lions."
28So this Daniel prospered during the reign of Darius and the reign of Cyrus the Persian.

OUR LIVES AND OUR

WORDS SHOULD INFLUENCE

OTHERS TO SERVE GOD.

VISIONS OF THE FOUR BEASTS

7 In the first year of King Belshazzar of Babylon, Daniel had a dream and visions of his head as he lay in bed. Then he wrote down the dream:[a] 2I,[b] Daniel, saw in my vision by night the four winds of heaven

stirring up the great sea, 3and four great beasts came up out of the sea, different from one another. 4The first was like a lion and had eagles' wings. Then, as I watched, its wings were plucked off, and it was lifted up from the ground and made to stand on two feet like a human being; and a human mind was given to it. 5Another beast appeared, a second one, that looked like a bear. It was raised up on one side, had three tusks[c] in its mouth among its teeth and was told, "Arise, devour many bodies!" 6After this, as I watched, another appeared, like a leopard. The beast had four wings of a bird on its back and four heads; and dominion was given to it. 7After this I saw in the visions by night a fourth beast, terrifying and dreadful and exceedingly strong. It had great iron teeth and was devouring, breaking in pieces, and stamping what was left with its feet. It was different from all the beasts that preceded it, and it had ten horns. 8I was considering the horns, when another horn appeared, a little one coming up among them; to make room for it, three of the earlier horns were plucked up by the roots. There were eyes like human eyes in this horn, and a mouth speaking arrogantly.

JUDGMENT BEFORE THE ANCIENT ONE

9 As I watched,
    thrones were set in place,
        and an Ancient One[d]
            took his throne,
    his clothing was white
            as snow,
        and the hair of his head
            like pure wool;
    his throne was fiery flames,
        and its wheels were
            burning fire.
10 A stream of fire issued
        and flowed out from
            his presence.

[a] 7.1 Q Ms Theodotion: MT adds *the beginning of the words; he said* [b] 7.2 Theodotion: Aram *Daniel answered and said, I* [c] 7.5 Or *ribs* [d] 7.9 Aram *an Ancient of Days*

A thousand thousands
 served him,
and ten thousand times
 ten thousand stood
 attending him.
The court sat in judgment,
 and the books were opened.

11 I watched then because of the noise of the arrogant words that the horn was speaking. And as I watched, the beast was put to death, and its body destroyed and given over to be burned with fire. **12** As for the rest of the beasts, their dominion was taken away, but their lives were prolonged for a season and a time. **13** As I watched in the night visions,

I saw one like a human being[a]
 coming with the clouds
 of heaven.
And he came to the Ancient One[b]
 and was presented before him.
14 To him was given dominion
 and glory and kingship,
 that all peoples, nations,
  and languages
 should serve him.
His dominion is an everlasting
 dominion
 that shall not pass away,
and his kingship is one
 that shall never be destroyed.

DANIEL'S VISIONS INTERPRETED

15 As for me, Daniel, my spirit was troubled within me,[c] and the visions of my head terrified me. **16** I

approached one of the attendants to ask him the truth concerning all this. So he said that he would disclose to me the interpretation of the matter: **17** "As for these four great beasts, four kings shall arise out of the earth. **18** But the holy ones of the Most High shall receive the kingdom and possess the kingdom forever— forever and ever."

19 Then I desired to know the truth concerning the fourth beast, which was different from all the rest, exceedingly terrifying, with its teeth of iron and claws of bronze, and which devoured and broke in pieces, and stamped what was left with its feet; **20** and concerning the ten horns that were on its head, and concerning the other horn, which came up and to make room for which three of them fell out— the horn that had eyes and a mouth that spoke arrogantly, and that seemed greater than the others. **21** As I looked, this horn made war with the holy ones and was prevailing over them, **22** until the Ancient One[b] came; then judgment was given for the holy ones of the Most High, and the time arrived when the holy ones gained possession of the kingdom.

23 This is what he said: "As for the fourth beast,

[a] 7.13 Aram *one like a son of man*
[b] 7.13,22 Aram *the Ancient of Days*
[c] 7.15 Aram *troubled in its sheath*

⊣╫ BIBLE IN LIFE ▷ ⊕

Heaven

Daniel 7.13

Throughout the Bible, we are given only tiny glimpses of what heaven is like. Heaven is the dwelling place of God (see 1 Kings 8.30); God is seated on a throne in heaven (see 1 Kings 22.19). Christ reigns, as Daniel's vision showed, "like a human being coming with the clouds of heaven" (Daniel 7.13). Heaven is a city with streets made of gold with gates made of pearls (see Revelation 21.18–21). Eventually this city of gold, which is called the New Jerusalem, will come to earth (see Revelation 21.2,10) after our bodies are resurrected (see 1 Corinthians 15). We surmise that we will be identifiable; though we won't look the same, we'll likely recognize each other. We will be more Christlike in heaven; our sinful nature will be totally erased. Because Christ came and lived a sinless life among us, and because he went to the cross and took our punishment for our sins on himself, then through faith in him our sins can be completely forgiven. We don't understand these human concepts of heaven, nor do we have the ability to accurately grasp or envision it. But we can look forward to an indescribable existence with Christ in a resurrected life.

there shall be a fourth
    kingdom on earth
    that shall be different from
        all the other kingdoms;
    it shall devour the whole earth,
    and trample it down, and
        break it to pieces.
24 As for the ten horns,
    out of this kingdom ten
        kings shall arise,
    and another shall arise
        after them.
    This one shall be different from
        the former ones,
    and shall put down
        three kings.
25 He shall speak words against
        the Most High,
    shall wear out the holy ones
        of the Most High,
    and shall attempt to change
        the sacred seasons
        and the law;
    and they shall be given
        into his power
    for a time, two times,[a]
        and half a time.
26 Then the court shall sit
        in judgment,
    and his dominion shall
        be taken away,
    to be consumed and
        totally destroyed.
27 The kingship and dominion
    and the greatness of the
        kingdoms under the
        whole heaven
    shall be given to the people
        of the holy ones of
        the Most High;
    their kingdom shall be an
        everlasting kingdom,
    and all dominions shall
        serve and obey them."

28 Here the account ends. As for
me, Daniel, my thoughts greatly terrified me, and my face turned pale;
but I kept the matter in my mind.

VISION OF A RAM AND A GOAT

8 In the third year of the reign
of King Belshazzar a vision appeared to me, Daniel, after the one
that had appeared to me at first. 2In
the vision I was looking and saw myself in Susa the capital, in the province of Elam,[b] and I was by the river
Ulai.[c] 3I looked up and saw a ram
standing beside the river.[d] It had
two horns. Both horns were long,
but one was longer than the other,
and the longer one came up second.
4I saw the ram charging westward
and northward and southward. All
beasts were powerless to withstand
it, and no one could rescue from its
power; it did as it pleased and became strong.

5 As I was watching, a male goat
appeared from the west, coming
across the face of the whole earth
without touching the ground. The
goat had a horn[e] between its eyes.
6It came toward the ram with the
two horns that I had seen standing
beside the river,[d] and it ran at it with
savage force. 7I saw it approaching
the ram. It was enraged against it
and struck the ram, breaking its two
horns. The ram did not have power
to withstand it; it threw the ram
down to the ground and trampled
upon it, and there was no one who
could rescue the ram from its power.
8Then the male goat grew exceedingly great; but at the height of its
power, the great horn was broken,
and in its place there came up four
prominent horns toward the four
winds of heaven.

9 Out of one of them came another[f] horn, a little one, which grew
exceedingly great toward the south,
toward the east, and toward the
beautiful land. 10It grew as high as
the host of heaven. It threw down to
the earth some of the host and some
of the stars, and trampled on them.
11Even against the prince of the host
it acted arrogantly; it took the regular burnt offering away from him
and overthrew the place of his sanctuary. 12Because of wickedness, the
host was given over to it together
with the regular burnt offering;[g] it
cast truth to the ground, and kept
prospering in what it did. 13Then I

a 7.25 Aram *a time, times*   b 8.2 Gk
Theodotion: MT Q Ms repeat *in the vision
I was looking*   c 8.2 Or *the Ulai Gate*
d 8.3,6 Or *gate*   e 8.5 Theodotion: Gk
one horn; Heb *a horn of vision*   f 8.9 Cn
Compare 7.8: Heb *one*   g 8.12 Meaning of
Heb uncertain

heard a holy one speaking, and another holy one said to the one that spoke, "For how long is this vision concerning the regular burnt offering, the transgression that makes desolate, and the giving over of the sanctuary and host to be trampled?"[a] [14] And he answered him,[b] "For two thousand three hundred evenings and mornings; then the sanctuary shall be restored to its rightful state."

GABRIEL INTERPRETS THE VISION

[15] When I, Daniel, had seen the vision, I tried to understand it. Then someone appeared standing before me, having the appearance of a man, [16] and I heard a human voice by the Ulai, calling, "Gabriel, help this man understand the vision." [17] So he came near where I stood; and when he came, I became frightened and fell prostrate. But he said to me, "Understand, O mortal,[c] that the vision is for the time of the end."

[18] As he was speaking to me, I fell into a trance, face to the ground; then he touched me and set me on my feet. [19] He said, "Listen, and I will tell you what will take place later in the period of wrath; for it refers to the appointed time of the end. [20] As for the ram that you saw with the two horns, these are the kings of Media and Persia. [21] The male goat[d] is the king of Greece, and the great horn between its eyes is the first king. [22] As for the horn that was broken, in place of which four others arose, four kingdoms shall arise from his[e] nation, but not with his power.

[23] At the end of their rule,
    when the transgressions
        have reached their
            full measure,
    a king of bold countenance
        shall arise,
    skilled in intrigue.
[24] He shall grow strong in power,[f]
    shall cause fearful destruction,
    and shall succeed in
        what he does.
He shall destroy the powerful
    and the people of
        the holy ones.

[25] By his cunning
    he shall make deceit prosper
        under his hand,
    and in his own mind he
        shall be great.
Without warning he shall
        destroy many
    and shall even rise up against
        the Prince of princes.
But he shall be broken, and
        not by human hands.
[26] The vision of the evenings and the mornings that has been told is true. As for you, seal up the vision, for it refers to many days from now."

[27] So I, Daniel, was overcome and lay sick for some days; then I arose and went about the king's business. But I was dismayed by the vision and did not understand it.

DANIEL'S PRAYER FOR THE PEOPLE

9 In the first year of Darius son of Ahasuerus, by birth a Mede, who became king over the realm of the Chaldeans— [2] in the first year of his reign, I, Daniel, perceived in the books the number of years that, according to the word of the LORD to the prophet Jeremiah, must be fulfilled for the devastation of Jerusalem, namely, seventy years.

[3] Then I turned to the Lord God, to seek an answer by prayer and supplication with fasting and sackcloth and ashes. [4] I prayed to the LORD my God and made confession, saying,

"Ah, Lord, great and awesome God, keeping covenant and steadfast love with those who love you and keep your commandments, [5] we have sinned and done wrong, acted wickedly and rebelled, turning aside from your commandments and ordinances. [6] We have not listened to your servants the prophets, who spoke in your name to our kings, our princes, and our ancestors, and to all the people of the land.

---

[a] 8.13 Meaning of Heb uncertain [b] 8.14 Gk Theodotion Syr Vg: Heb *me* [c] 8.17 Heb *son of man* [d] 8.21 Or *shaggy male goat* [e] 8.22 Gk Theodotion Vg: Heb *the* [f] 8.24 Theodotion and one Gk Ms: Heb repeats (from 8.22) *but not with his power*

7 "Righteousness is on your side, O Lord, but open shame, as at this day, falls on us, the people of Judah, the inhabitants of Jerusalem, and all Israel, those who are near and those who are far away, in all the lands to which you have driven them, because of the treachery that they have committed against you. 8Open shame, O LORD, falls on us, our kings, our officials, and our ancestors, because we have sinned against you. 9To the Lord our God belong mercy and forgiveness, for we have rebelled against him, 10and have not obeyed the voice of the LORD our God by following his laws, which he set before us by his servants the prophets.

WE PRAY IN THE CONTEXT OF

GOD'S WILL, NOT OUR OWN.

11 "All Israel has transgressed your law and turned aside, refusing to obey your voice. So the curse and the oath written in the law of Moses, the servant of God, have been poured out upon us, because we have sinned against you. 12He has confirmed his words, which he spoke against us and against our rulers, by bringing upon us a calamity so great that what has been done against Jerusalem has never before been done under the whole heaven. 13Just as it is written in the law of Moses, all this calamity has come upon us. We did not entreat the favor of the LORD our God, turning from our iniquities and reflecting on hisa fidelity. 14So the LORD kept watch over this calamity until he brought it upon us. Indeed, the LORD our God is right in all that he has done; for we have disobeyed his voice.

15 "And now, O Lord our God, who brought your people out of the land of Egypt with a mighty hand and made your name renowned even to this day—we have sinned, we have done wickedly. 16O Lord, in view of all your righteous acts, let your anger and wrath, we pray, turn away from your city Jerusalem, your holy mountain; because of our sins and the iniquities of our ancestors, Jerusalem and your people have become a disgrace among all our neighbors. 17Now therefore, O our God, listen to the prayer of your servant and to his supplication, and for your own sake, Lord,b let your face shine upon your desolated sanctuary. 18Incline your ear, O my God, and hear. Open your eyes and look at our desolation and the city that bears your name. We do not present our supplication before you on the ground of our righteousness, but on the ground of your great mercies. 19O Lord, hear; O Lord, forgive; O Lord, listen and act and do not delay! For your own sake, O my God, because your city and your people bear your name!"

THE SEVENTY WEEKS

20 While I was speaking, and was praying and confessing my sin and the sin of my people Israel, and presenting my supplication before the LORD my God on behalf of the holy mountain of my God— 21while I was speaking in prayer, the man Gabriel, whom I had seen before in a vision, came to me in swift flight at the time of the evening sacrifice. 22He camec and said to me, "Daniel, I have now come out to give you wisdom and understanding. 23At the beginning of your supplications a word went out, and I have come to declare it, for you are greatly beloved. So consider the word and understand the vision:

24 "Seventy weeks are decreed for your people and your holy city: to finish the transgression, to put an end to sin, and to atone for iniquity, to bring in everlasting righteousness, to seal both vision and prophet, and to anoint a most holy place.d 25Know therefore and understand: from the time that the word went out to restore and rebuild Jerusalem until the time of an anointed prince,

a 9.13 Heb your   b 9.17 Theodotion Vg
Compare Syr: Heb for the Lord's sake
c 9.22 Gk Syr: Heb He made to understand
d 9.24 Or thing or one

there shall be seven weeks; and for sixty-two weeks it shall be built again with streets and moat, but in a troubled time. 26After the sixty-two weeks, an anointed one shall be cut off and shall have nothing, and the troops of the prince who is to come shall destroy the city and the sanctuary. Its[a] end shall come with a flood, and to the end there shall be war. Desolations are decreed. 27He shall make a strong covenant with many for one week, and for half of the week he shall make sacrifice and offering cease; and in their place[b] shall be an abomination that desolates, until the decreed end is poured out upon the desolator."

CONFLICT OF NATIONS AND HEAVENLY POWERS

10 In the third year of King Cyrus of Persia a word was revealed to Daniel, who was named Belteshazzar. The word was true, and it concerned a great conflict. He understood the word, having received understanding in the vision. 2At that time I, Daniel, had been mourning for three weeks. 3I had eaten no rich food, no meat or wine had entered my mouth, and I had not anointed myself at all, for the full three weeks. 4On the twenty-fourth day of the first month, as I was standing on the bank of the great river (that is, the Tigris), 5I looked up and saw a man clothed in linen, with a belt of gold from Uphaz around his waist. 6His body was like beryl, his face like lightning, his eyes like flaming torches, his arms and legs like the gleam of burnished bronze, and the sound of his words like the roar of a multitude. 7I, Daniel, alone saw the vision; the people who were with me did not see the vision, though a great trembling fell upon them, and they fled and hid themselves. 8So I was left alone to see this great vision. My strength left me, and my complexion grew deathly pale, and I retained no strength. 9Then I heard the sound of his words; and when I heard the sound of his words, I fell into a trance, face to the ground.

10But then a hand touched me and roused me to my hands and knees. 11He said to me, "Daniel, greatly beloved, pay attention to the words that I am going to speak to you. Stand on your feet, for I have now been sent to you." So while he was speaking this word to me, I stood up trembling. 12He said to me, "Do not fear, Daniel, for from the first day that you set your mind to gain understanding and to humble yourself before your God, your words have been heard, and I have come because of your words. 13But the prince of the kingdom of Persia opposed me twenty-one days. So Michael, one of the chief princes, came to help me, and I left him there with the prince of the kingdom of Persia,[c] 14and have come to help you understand what is to happen to your people at the end of days. For there is a further vision for those days."

15While he was speaking these words to me, I turned my face toward the ground and was speechless. 16Then one in human form touched my lips, and I opened my mouth to speak, and said to the one who stood before me, "My lord, because of the vision such pains have come upon me that I retain no strength. 17How can my lord's servant talk with my lord? For I am shaking,[d] no strength remains in me, and no breath is left in me."

18Again one in human form touched me and strengthened me. 19He said, "Do not fear, greatly beloved, you are safe. Be strong and courageous!" When he spoke to me, I was strengthened and said, "Let my lord speak, for you have strengthened me." 20Then he said, "Do you know why I have come to you? Now I must return to fight against the prince of Persia, and when I am through with him, the prince of Greece will come. 21But I am to tell you what is inscribed in the book of

a 9.26 Or His b 9.27 Cn: Meaning of Heb uncertain c 10.13 Gk Theodotion: Heb *I was left there with the kings of Persia* d 10.17 Gk: Heb *from now*

truth. There is no one with me who contends against these princes except Michael, your prince. [1]As for me, in the first year of Darius the Mede, I stood up to support and strengthen him.

2 "Now I will announce the truth to you. Three more kings shall arise in Persia. The fourth shall be far richer than all of them, and when he has become strong through his riches, he shall stir up all against the kingdom of Greece. [3]Then a warrior king shall arise, who shall rule with great dominion and take action as he pleases. [4]And while still rising in power, his kingdom shall be broken and divided toward the four winds of heaven, but not to his posterity, nor according to the dominion with which he ruled; for his kingdom shall be uprooted and go to others besides these.

5 "Then the king of the south shall grow strong, but one of his officers shall grow stronger than he and shall rule a realm greater than his own realm. [6]After some years they shall make an alliance, and the daughter of the king of the south shall come to the king of the north to ratify the agreement. But she shall not retain her power, and his offspring shall not endure. She shall be given up, she and her attendants and her child and the one who supported her.

"In those times [7]a branch from her roots shall rise up in his place. He shall come against the army and enter the fortress of the king of the north, and he shall take action against them and prevail. [8]Even their gods, with their idols and with their precious vessels of silver and gold, he shall carry off to Egypt as spoils of war. For some years he shall refrain from attacking the king of the north; [9]then the latter shall invade the realm of the king of the south, but will return to his own land.

10 "His sons shall wage war and assemble a multitude of great forces, which shall advance like a flood and pass through, and again shall carry the war as far as his fortress. [11]Moved with rage, the king of the south shall go out and do battle against the king of the north, who shall muster a great multitude, which shall, however, be defeated by his enemy. [12]When the multitude has been carried off, his heart shall be exalted, and he shall overthrow tens of thousands, but he shall not prevail. [13]For the king of the north shall again raise a multitude, larger than the former, and after some years[a] he shall advance with a great army and abundant supplies.

14 "In those times many shall rise against the king of the south. The lawless among your own people shall lift themselves up in order to fulfill the vision, but they shall fail. [15]Then the king of the north shall come and throw up siegeworks, and take a well-fortified city. And the forces of the south shall not stand, not even his picked troops, for there shall be no strength to resist. [16]But he who comes against him shall take the actions he pleases, and no one shall withstand him. He shall take a position in the beautiful land, and all of it shall be in his power. [17]He shall set his mind to come with the strength of his whole kingdom, and he shall bring terms of peace[b] and perform them. In order to destroy the kingdom,[c] he shall give him a woman in marriage; but it shall not succeed or be to his advantage. [18]Afterward he shall turn to the coastlands, and shall capture many. But a commander shall put an end to his insolence; indeed,[d] he shall turn his insolence back upon him. [19]Then he shall turn back toward the fortresses of his own land, but he shall stumble and fall, and shall not be found.

20 "Then shall arise in his place one who shall send an official for the glory of the kingdom; but within a few days he shall be broken, though not in anger or in battle. [21]In his place shall arise a contemptible person on whom royal majesty had not been conferred; he shall come in without warning and obtain the

---

[a] 11.13 Heb *and at the end of the times years*
[b] 11.17 Gk: Heb *kingdom, and upright ones with him*   [c] 11.17 Heb *it*   [d] 11.18 Meaning of Heb uncertain

kingdom through intrigue. 22Armies shall be utterly swept away and broken before him, and the prince of the covenant as well. 23And after an alliance is made with him, he shall act deceitfully and become strong with a small party. 24Without warning he shall come into the richest partsa of the province and do what none of his predecessors had ever done, lavishing plunder, spoil, and wealth on them. He shall devise plans against strongholds, but only for a time. 25He shall stir up his power and determination against the king of the south with a great army, and the king of the south shall wage war with a much greater and stronger army. But he shall not succeed, for plots shall be devised against him 26by those who eat of the royal rations. They shall break him, his army shall be swept away, and many shall fall slain. 27The two kings, their minds bent on evil, shall sit at one table and exchange lies. But it shall not succeed, for there remains an end at the time appointed. 28He shall return to his land with great wealth, but his heart shall be set against the holy covenant. He shall work his will, and return to his own land.

29 "At the time appointed he shall return and come into the south, but this time it shall not be as it was before. 30For ships of Kittim shall come against him, and he shall lose heart and withdraw. He shall be enraged and take action against the holy covenant. He shall turn back and pay heed to those who forsake the holy covenant. 31Forces sent by him shall occupy and profane the temple and fortress. They shall abolish the regular burnt offering and set up the abomination that makes desolate. 32He shall seduce with intrigue those who violate the covenant; but the people who are loyal to their God shall stand firm and take action. 33The wise among the people shall give understanding to many; for some days, however, they shall fall by sword and flame, and suffer captivity and plunder. 34When they fall victim, they shall receive a little help, and many shall join them insincerely. 35Some of the wise shall fall, so that they may be refined, purified, and cleansed,b until the time of the end, for there is still an interval until the time appointed.

36 "The king shall act as he pleases. He shall exalt himself and consider himself greater than any god, and shall speak horrendous things against the God of gods. He shall prosper until the period of wrath is completed, for what is determined shall be done. 37He shall pay no respect to the gods of his ancestors, or to the one beloved by women; he shall pay no respect to any other god, for he shall consider himself greater than all. 38He shall honor the god of fortresses instead of these; a god whom his ancestors did not know he shall honor with gold and silver, with precious stones and costly gifts. 39He shall deal with the strongest fortresses by the help of a foreign god. Those who acknowledge him he shall make more wealthy, and shall appoint them as rulers over many, and shall distribute the land for a price.

THE TIME OF THE END

40 "At the time of the end the king of the south shall attack him. But the king of the north shall rush upon him like a whirlwind, with chariots and horsemen, and with many ships. He shall advance against countries and pass through like a flood. 41He shall come into the beautiful land, and tens of thousands shall fall victim, but Edom and Moab and the main part of the Ammonites shall escape from his power. 42He shall stretch out his hand against the countries, and the land of Egypt shall not escape. 43He shall become ruler of the treasures of gold and of silver, and all the riches of Egypt; and the Libyans and the Ethiopiansc shall follow in his train. 44But reports from the east and the north shall alarm him, and he shall go out with great fury to bring ruin

a 11.24 Or among the richest men
b 11.35 Heb made them white   c 11.43 Or Nubians; Heb Cushites

and complete destruction to many. [45]He shall pitch his palatial tents between the sea and the beautiful holy mountain. Yet he shall come to his end, with no one to help him.

THE RESURRECTION
OF THE DEAD

12 "At that time Michael, the great prince, the protector of your people, shall arise. There shall be a time of anguish, such as has never occurred since nations first came into existence. But at that time your people shall be delivered, everyone who is found written in the book. [2]Many of those who sleep in the dust of the earth[a] shall awake, some to everlasting life, and some to shame and everlasting contempt. [3]Those who are wise shall shine like the brightness of the sky,[b] and those who lead many to righteousness, like the stars forever and ever. [4]But you, Daniel, keep the words secret and the book sealed until the time of the end. Many shall be running back and forth, and evil[c] shall increase."

[5] Then I, Daniel, looked, and two others appeared, one standing on this bank of the stream and one on the other. [6]One of them said to the man clothed in linen, who was upstream, "How long shall it be until the end of these wonders?" [7]The man

clothed in linen, who was upstream, raised his right hand and his left hand toward heaven. And I heard him swear by the one who lives forever that it would be for a time, two times, and half a time,[d] and that when the shattering of the power of the holy people comes to an end, all these things would be accomplished. [8]I heard but could not understand; so I said, "My lord, what shall be the outcome of these things?" [9]He said, "Go your way, Daniel, for the words are to remain secret and sealed until the time of the end. [10]Many shall be purified, cleansed, and refined, but the wicked shall continue to act wickedly. None of the wicked shall understand, but those who are wise shall understand. [11]From the time that the regular burnt offering is taken away and the abomination that desolates is set up, there shall be one thousand two hundred ninety days. [12]Happy are those who persevere and attain the thousand three hundred thirty-five days. [13]But you, go your way,[e] and rest; you shall rise for your reward at the end of the days."

---

[a] 12.2 Or *the land of dust*   [b] 12.3 Or *dome*
[c] 12.4 Cn Compare Gk: Heb *knowledge*
[d] 12.7 Heb *a time, times, and a half*
[e] 12.13 Gk Theodotion: Heb adds *to the end*

ONE DAY

"At that time . . . your people shall be delivered, everyone who is found written in the book. Many of those who sleep in the dust of the earth shall awake, some to everlasting life, and some to shame and everlasting contempt. Those who are wise will shine like the brightness of the sky, and those who lead many to righteousness, like the stars forever and ever."

—Daniel 12.1–3

The book of Daniel is often categorized as a type of literature called "apocalyptic," which means "revelation" or "prophecy." That is, it is a revelation of the way things really are and of things that are yet to come. It sometimes may seem that the world is spinning out of control and that God's people are completely at the mercy of others, but in reality, God is sovereign over all things, and ultimately, he has a plan to redeem us from our troubles. That is essentially the message of Daniel, especially in chapters 7–12.

It is possible that this prophecy in Daniel was given for a time of persecution that the Jews experienced under a pagan ruler named Antiochus IV Epiphanes. Antiochus tried to stamp out the Jewish religion by forbidding the Jews to possess or read their scriptures or to practice many of the rituals of their religion, such as circumcision or offering sacrifices. Daniel's prophecies gave the people hope in this dark time when it seemed that God's people were on the brink of extinction and that the wicked would triumph over the righteous.

Part of Daniel's message of hope and assurance is a promise of a final resurrection from the dead. After everyone, righteous and otherwise, is raised from the dead, believers will be granted eternal life with God in heaven. This promise gives the faithful an unshakable assurance that one day all will be made right even if they pass from this earth without yet experiencing God's rescue from their troubles. We need only to rest in God's sovereign care for us and seek to live righteous lives.

Daniel was not the only one in the Bible to foretell the coming resurrection of the dead. Jesus did also in Matthew 22.29–32; 24.1–42). Paul (see 1 Corinthians 15.12–28) and John (see Revelation 20.4–13) taught about the resurrection as others did also. Jesus made it clear, though, that we don't know exactly when the resurrection of the dead and other events of the future will take place, but we can be certain that it will all happen one day just as the Bible has said. Instead of fixating on timing, our focus should be on the assurance that we receive from the promise of the resurrection and other events of the future: God is sovereign and one day will vindicate all who trust in him!

Going Deeper

- What kinds of trouble sometimes cause you to feel hopeless?
- How does the promise of the resurrection give you assurance in times of trouble?

HOSEA

Sometimes God uses unexpected methods to teach us: the prophet Hosea's life was a case in point. God told Hosea to marry a prostitute and then to forgive her unfaithfulness—more than once! Why? Because God wanted to create a vivid living picture of love for the people of Israel. The book of Hosea is a vignette of God as a lover who's been repeatedly abandoned, a vignette that lets us see God's hurt and anger as well as God's unrelenting devotion to God's people and the willingness to forgive them time and again.

1

The word of the LORD that came to Hosea son of Beeri, in the days of Kings Uzziah, Jotham, Ahaz, and Hezekiah of Judah, and in the days of King Jeroboam son of Joash of Israel.

THE FAMILY OF HOSEA

2 When the LORD first spoke through Hosea, the LORD said to Hosea, "Go, take for yourself a wife of whoredom and have children of whoredom, for the land commits great whoredom by forsaking the LORD." 3 So he went and took Gomer daughter of Diblaim, and she conceived and bore him a son.

4 And the LORD said to him, "Name him Jezreel;[a] for in a little while I will punish the house of Jehu for the blood of Jezreel, and I will put an end to the kingdom of the house of Israel. 5 On that day I will break the bow of Israel in the valley of Jezreel."

6 She conceived again and bore a daughter. Then the LORD said to him, "Name her Lo-ruhamah,[b] for I will no longer have pity on the house of Israel or forgive them. 7 But I will have pity on the house of Judah, and I will save them by the LORD their God; I will not save them by bow, or by sword, or by war, or by horses, or by horsemen."

8 When she had weaned Lo-ruhamah, she conceived and bore a son. 9 Then the LORD said, "Name him Lo-ammi,[c] for you are not my people and I am not your God."[d]

THE RESTORATION OF ISRAEL

10[e] Yet the number of the people of Israel shall be like the sand of the sea, which can be neither measured nor numbered; and in the place where it was said to them, "You are not my people," it shall be said to them, "Children of the living God." 11 The people of Judah and the people of Israel shall be gathered together, and they shall appoint for themselves one head; and they shall take possession of[f] the land, for great shall be the day of Jezreel.

2

Say to your brother,[h] Ammi,[i] and to your sister,[j] Ruhamah.[k]

ISRAEL'S INFIDELITY, PUNISHMENT, AND REDEMPTION

2 Plead with your mother, plead—
    for she is not my wife,
    and I am not her husband—
that she put away her whoring
        from her face,
    and her adultery
        from between her breasts,
3 or I will strip her naked
    and expose her as in the
        day she was born,
and make her like a wilderness,
    and turn her into a
        parched land,
    and kill her with thirst.
4 Upon her children also I
        will have no pity,
    because they are children
        of whoredom.
5 For their mother has played
        the whore;
    she who conceived them
        has acted shamefully.
For she said, "I will go
        after my lovers;
    they give me my bread
        and my water,
    my wool and my flax, my
        oil and my drink."
6 Therefore I will hedge up her[l]
        way with thorns;
    and I will build a wall
        against her,
    so that she cannot find
        her paths.
7 She shall pursue her lovers,
    but not overtake them;
and she shall seek them,
    but shall not find them.
Then she shall say, "I will go
    and return to my first husband,
    for it was better with me
        then than now."
8 She did not know
    that it was I who gave her
    the grain, the wine, and the oil,
and who lavished upon her silver
    and gold that they used for Baal.

[a] 1.4 That is *God sows* [b] 1.6 That is *Not pitied* [c] 1.9 That is *Not my people* [d] 1.9 Heb *I am not yours* [e] 1.10 Ch 2.1 in Heb [f] 1.11 Heb *rise up from* [g] 2.1 Ch 2.3 in Heb [h] 2.1 Gk: Heb *brothers* [i] 2.1 That is *My people* [j] 2.1 Gk Vg: Heb *sisters* [k] 2.1 That is *Pitied* [l] 2.6 Gk Syr: Heb *your*

9 Therefore I will take back
   my grain in its time,
   and my wine in its season;
and I will take away my
      wool and my flax,
   which were to cover
      her nakedness.
10 Now I will uncover her shame
   in the sight of her lovers,
   and no one shall rescue her
      out of my hand.
11 I will put an end to all her mirth,
   her festivals, her new
      moons, her sabbaths,
   and all her appointed festivals.
12 I will lay waste her vines
      and her fig trees,
   of which she said,
"These are my pay,
   which my lovers have
      given me."
I will make them a forest,
   and the wild animals shall
      devour them.
13 I will punish her for the festival
      days of the Baals,
   when she offered
      incense to them
and decked herself with her
      ring and jewelry,
   and went after her lovers,
   and forgot me, says
      the LORD.

14 Therefore, I will now allure her,
   and bring her into the
      wilderness,
   and speak tenderly to her.
15 From there I will give her
      her vineyards,
   and make the Valley of
      Achor a door of hope.

There she shall respond as in
      the days of her youth,
   as at the time when she came
      out of the land of Egypt.
16 On that day, says the LORD, you
will call me, "My husband," and no
longer will you call me, "My Baal."[a]
17 For I will remove the names of the
Baals from her mouth, and they shall
be mentioned by name no more. 18 I
will make for you[b] a covenant on that
day with the wild animals, the birds
of the air, and the creeping things of
the ground; and I will abolish[c] the
bow, the sword, and war from the
land; and I will make you lie down in
safety. 19 And I will take you for my
wife forever; I will take you for my
wife in righteousness and in justice,
in steadfast love, and in mercy. 20 I
will take you for my wife in faithfulness; and you shall know the LORD.
21 On that day I will answer,
      says the LORD,
   I will answer the heavens
   and they shall answer the earth;
22 and the earth shall answer
      the grain, the wine,
      and the oil,
   and they shall answer Jezreel;[d]
23   and I will sow him[e] for
      myself in the land.
And I will have pity on
      Lo-ruhamah,[f]
   and I will say to Lo-ammi,[g]
      "You are my people";
   and he shall say, "You
      are my God."

[a] 2.16 That is, "My master"   [b] 2.18 Heb
them   [c] 2.18 Heb break   [d] 2.22 That is
God sows   [e] 2.23 Cn: Heb her   [f] 2.23 That
is Not pitied   [g] 2.23 That is Not my people

BIBLE IN LIFE

Chosen by God   Hosea 2.23

What does it mean to be chosen by God? Who are the lucky ones whom God calls "my people"? Hosea describes how God plants and calls the chosen, and the chosen acknowledge
God. Those who are far from God become God's own. From this side of the cross, God's chosen people pattern their lives after the life of Jesus Christ, and they honor the admonitions
and commands of Jesus. They measure success by commitments to peace, humility, service,
truth, justice, compassion and love. They bind the church into harmony, not fragmentation,
and seek common ground based on the teachings of Christ, not on human-created theolo-
gies. If we belong to God through faith in Jesus Christ, then we are God's chosen people.

REDEMPTION STORY

And I will have pity on Lo-ruhamah, and I will say to Lo-ammi,
"You are my people"; and he shall say, "You are my God."

—Hosea 2.23

The relationship between Hosea and Gomer portrays a beautiful story about the simplicity of redemption. It illustrates the incredible love of Jehovah for his people. Just as Gomer abandoned Hosea and pursued other lovers, the Israelites abandoned God by taking up with false gods. In that particular time, the Israelites' crops were good, they had not been captured and put into exile, and they were fairly prosperous. Yet they attributed their blessings to Baal rather than to God. Like Gomer and the ancient Israelites, we are also unfaithful and in need of God's forgiveness.

In order for someone to be unfaithful, there first has to be an element of commitment; there has to be a promise. If there is no relationship with another person, how can one be unfaithful to them? Christians have entered into a covenant with God through Jesus Christ, and there are many ways we are unfaithful, including disobedience to God's laws and the laws of the land. We might be unfaithful because we cherish too much the convenience of modern technology, the acquisition of wealth, our reputations and anything else that might fascinate us. There's nothing wrong with those things, but when we let them come between us and our commitment to Jesus Christ, then that is unfaithfulness.

In the book of Hosea, Gomer was being pursued by Hosea, just as the Israelites were being pursued by God. God pursues us as well, but how faithful are we to our covenant with God? Do we pursue God in return? Do we seek a more intimate relationship with Christ? When we rise every morning and brush our teeth and comb our hair and put on our clothes, do we think about how we can be closer to Jesus Christ during this day? Do we remember the origin of our blessings and give thanks? Jesus performed miracles to show people who he was, to alleviate suffering, to rescue the lonely and the outcast and the despised. Do we adopt those Christlike attributes—gentleness, humility, service, compassion, justice, truth and love?

Hosea offered total redemption and reconciliation to Gomer, as though she had never been a prostitute, as though she had always been a faithful wife. That's the relationship that we have with our Savior. If we know that Christ is reaching out to us and that he promises forgiveness under any circumstance, we can share our failures with him and know absolutely that our sins will be forgiven. Christ tells us to come back home—because he loves us.

Going Deeper

- Is your work preeminent in your life? Your reputation? What kinds of distractions come between you and your commitment to Jesus Christ?
- How much of your time is devoted to show the love of Jesus Christ to others—rescuing the lonely, the outcast, the despised, the poverty-stricken, the inarticulate and those who suffer prejudice?

FURTHER ASSURANCES OF GOD'S REDEEMING LOVE

3 The LORD said to me again, "Go, love a woman who has a lover and is an adulteress, just as the LORD loves the people of Israel, though they turn to other gods and love raisin cakes." [2] So I bought her for fifteen shekels of silver and a homer of barley and a measure of wine.[a] [3] And I said to her, "You must remain as mine for many days; you shall not play the whore, you shall not have intercourse with a man, nor I with you." [4] For the Israelites shall remain many days without king or prince, without sacrifice or pillar, without ephod or teraphim. [5] Afterward the Israelites shall return and seek the LORD their God, and David their king; they shall come in awe to the LORD and to his goodness in the latter days.

GOD ACCUSES ISRAEL

4 Hear the word of the LORD,
　　O people of Israel;
for the LORD has an
　　　indictment against the
　　　inhabitants of the land.
There is no faithfulness or loyalty,
　　and no knowledge of
　　　God in the land.
[2] Swearing, lying, and murder,
　　and stealing and adultery
　　　break out;
　　bloodshed follows bloodshed.
[3] Therefore the land mourns,
　　and all who live in it languish;
together with the wild animals
　　and the birds of the air,
　　even the fish of the sea
　　　are perishing.

[4] Yet let no one contend,
　　and let none accuse,
　　for with you is my
　　　contention, O priest.[b]
[5] You shall stumble by day;
　　the prophet also shall stumble
　　　with you by night,
　　and I will destroy your mother.
[6] My people are destroyed for
　　　lack of knowledge;
　　because you have rejected
　　　knowledge,
　　I reject you from being
　　　a priest to me.

And since you have forgotten
　　　the law of your God,
　　I also will forget your children.

[7] The more they increased,
　　the more they sinned
　　　against me;
　　they changed[c] their glory
　　　into shame.
[8] They feed on the sin of my people;
　　they are greedy for their iniquity.
[9] And it shall be like people,
　　　like priest;
　　I will punish them for
　　　their ways,
　　and repay them for their deeds.

[a] 3.2 Gk: Heb *a homer of barley and a lethech of barley*　[b] 4.4 Cn: Meaning of Heb uncertain　[c] 4.7 Ancient Heb tradition: MT *I will change*

PONDER

There is no faithfulness or loyalty, and no knowledge of God in the land. Swearing, lying, and murder, and stealing and adultery break out . . . I desire steadfast love and not sacrifice, the knowledge of God rather than burnt offerings.
—Hosea 4.1–2; 6.6

PRAY

Almighty Father, as we study these troubling words of Hosea, help us to decide honestly how they apply to us. We come to you in prayer to ask for enlightenment and courage; help us decide, with a sense of innovation and adventure, how we can use our blessings for others. Forgive our sinfulness, our selfishness, our egocentric thoughts. Teach us to offer what you desire, to offer mercy to others and love toward you. As Jesus impressed on us the virtues of faith and love during his earthly ministry, so help us do the same for others. We pray in his name. Amen.

10 They shall eat, but not
        be satisfied;
    they shall play the whore,
        but not multiply;
    because they have forsaken
        the LORD
    to devote themselves to
        11whoredom.

THE IDOLATRY OF ISRAEL

Wine and new wine
    take away the understanding.
12 My people consult a piece
        of wood,
    and their divining rod
        gives them oracles.
    For a spirit of whoredom has
        led them astray,
    and they have played the
        whore, forsaking
        their God.
13 They sacrifice on the tops of
        the mountains,
    and make offerings
        upon the hills,
    under oak, poplar, and terebinth,
        because their shade is good.

    Therefore your daughters
        play the whore,
    and your daughters-in-law
        commit adultery.
14 I will not punish your
        daughters when they
        play the whore,
    nor your daughters-
        in-law when they
        commit adultery;
    for the men themselves go
        aside with whores,
    and sacrifice with temple
        prostitutes;
    thus a people without
        understanding
        comes to ruin.

15 Though you play the
        whore, O Israel,
    do not let Judah become guilty.
    Do not enter into Gilgal,
        or go up to Beth-aven,
    and do not swear, "As
        the LORD lives."
16 Like a stubborn heifer,
        Israel is stubborn;
    can the LORD now feed them
        like a lamb in a broad pasture?

17 Ephraim is joined to idols—
        let him alone.
18 When their drinking is
        ended, they indulge
        in sexual orgies;
    they love lewdness more
        than their glory.a
19 A wind has wrappedb them
        in its wings,
    and they shall be ashamed
        because of their altars.c

IMPENDING JUDGMENT ON ISRAEL AND JUDAH

5 Hear this, O priests!
    Give heed, O house of Israel!
Listen, O house of the king!
    For the judgment
        pertains to you;
    for you have been a snare
        at Mizpah,
    and a net spread upon Tabor,
2   and a pit dug deep in Shittim;d
    but I will punish all of them.

3   I know Ephraim,
    and Israel is not hidden
        from me;
    for now, O Ephraim, you have
        played the whore;
    Israel is defiled.
4   Their deeds do not permit them
        to return to their God.
    For the spirit of whoredom
        is within them,
    and they do not know
        the LORD.

5   Israel's pride testifies against him;
    Ephraime stumbles in his guilt;
    Judah also stumbles with them.
6   With their flocks and herds
        they shall go
        to seek the LORD,
    but they will not find him;
    he has withdrawn from them.
7   They have dealt faithlessly
        with the LORD;
    for they have borne
        illegitimate children.
    Now the new moon shall
        devour them along
        with their fields.

a 4.18 Cn Compare Gk: Meaning of Heb
uncertain   b 4.19 Heb her   c 4.19 Gk Syr:
Heb sacrifices   d 5.2 Cn: Meaning of Heb
uncertain   e 5.5 Heb Israel and Ephraim

8 Blow the horn in Gibeah,
    the trumpet in Ramah.
Sound the alarm at Beth-aven;
    look behind you, Benjamin!
9 Ephraim shall become
      a desolation
    in the day of punishment;
among the tribes of Israel
    I declare what is sure.
10 The princes of Judah have become
    like those who remove
      the landmark;
on them I will pour out
    my wrath like water.
11 Ephraim is oppressed, crushed
      in judgment,
    because he was determined
      to go after vanity.[a]
12 Therefore I am like maggots
      to Ephraim,
    and like rottenness to the
      house of Judah.
13 When Ephraim saw
      his sickness,
    and Judah his wound,
then Ephraim went to Assyria,
    and sent to the great king.[b]
But he is not able to cure you
    or heal your wound.
14 For I will be like a lion
      to Ephraim,
    and like a young lion to
      the house of Judah.
I myself will tear and go away;
    I will carry off, and no
      one shall rescue.
15 I will return again to my place
    until they acknowledge their
      guilt and seek my face.
In their distress they will
    beg my favor:

A CALL TO REPENTANCE

6 "Come, let us return
      to the LORD;
for it is he who has torn,
    and he will heal us;
he has struck down, and
    he will bind us up.
2 After two days he will revive us;
    on the third day he will
      raise us up,
    that we may live before him.
3 Let us know, let us press on
      to know the LORD;
    his appearing is as sure
      as the dawn;

he will come to us like
      the showers,
    like the spring rains that
      water the earth."

IMPENITENCE OF ISRAEL AND JUDAH

4 What shall I do with you,
      O Ephraim?
What shall I do with
    you, O Judah?
Your love is like a morning cloud,
    like the dew that goes
      away early.
5 Therefore I have hewn them
      by the prophets,
    I have killed them by the
      words of my mouth,
    and my[c] judgment goes
      forth as the light.
6 For I desire steadfast love
      and not sacrifice,
    the knowledge of God rather
      than burnt offerings.
7 But at[d] Adam they transgressed
      the covenant;
    there they dealt faithlessly
      with me.
8 Gilead is a city of evildoers,
    tracked with blood.
9 As robbers lie in wait[e] for someone,
    so the priests are banded
      together;[f]
they murder on the road
    to Shechem,
    they commit a monstrous crime.
10 In the house of Israel I have
      seen a horrible thing;
    Ephraim's whoredom is
      there, Israel is defiled.
11 For you also, O Judah, a harvest
    is appointed.

When I would restore the
      fortunes of my people,
7 ¹when I would heal Israel,
    the corruption of Ephraim
      is revealed,
    and the wicked deeds
      of Samaria;

---

[a] 5.11 Gk: Meaning of Heb uncertain
[b] 5.13 Cn: Heb to a king who will contend
[c] 6.5 Gk Syr: Heb your   [d] 6.7 Cn: Heb like   [e] 6.9 Cn: Meaning of Heb uncertain
[f] 6.9 Syr: Heb are a company

for they deal falsely,
the thief breaks in,
and the bandits raid outside.
2 But they do not consider
that I remember all their
wickedness.
Now their deeds
surround them,
they are before my face.
3 By their wickedness they
make the king glad,
and the officials by
their treachery.
4 They are all adulterers;
they are like a heated oven,
whose baker does not need
to stir the fire,
from the kneading of the
dough until it is leavened.
5 On the day of our king
the officials
became sick with the
heat of wine;
he stretched out his hand
with mockers.
6 For they are kindled[a] like
an oven, their heart
burns within them;
all night their anger smolders;
in the morning it blazes
like a flaming fire.
7 All of them are hot as an oven,
and they devour their rulers.
All their kings have fallen;
none of them calls upon me.

8 Ephraim mixes himself
with the peoples;
Ephraim is a cake not turned.
9 Foreigners devour his strength,
but he does not know it;
gray hairs are sprinkled
upon him,
but he does not know it.
10 Israel's pride testifies
against[b] him;
yet they do not return to
the LORD their God,
or seek him, for all this.

FUTILE RELIANCE ON
THE NATIONS
11 Ephraim has become
like a dove,
silly and without sense;
they call upon Egypt, they
go to Assyria.

12 As they go, I will cast my
net over them;
I will bring them down
like birds of the air;
I will discipline them
according to the report
made to their assembly.[c]
13 Woe to them, for they have
strayed from me!
Destruction to them, for they
have rebelled against me!
I would redeem them,
but they speak lies against me.

14 They do not cry to me
from the heart,
but they wail upon their beds;
they gash themselves for
grain and wine;
they rebel against me.
15 It was I who trained and
strengthened their arms,
yet they plot evil against me.
16 They turn to that which
does not profit;[d]
they have become like a
defective bow;
their officials shall fall
by the sword
because of the rage of
their tongue.
So much for their babbling in
the land of Egypt.

ISRAEL'S APOSTASY
8 Set the trumpet to your lips!
One like a vulture[c] is over the
house of the LORD,
because they have broken
my covenant,
and transgressed my law.
2 Israel cries to me,
"My God, we—Israel—
know you!"
3 Israel has spurned the good;
the enemy shall pursue him.

4 They made kings, but not
through me;
they set up princes, but
without my knowledge.
With their silver and gold
they made idols
for their own destruction.

a 7.6 Gk Syr: Heb *brought near*   b 7.10 Or
humbles   c 7.12; 8.1 Meaning of Heb uncertain
d 7.16 Cn: Meaning of Heb uncertain

5 Your calf is rejected, O Samaria.
My anger burns against them.
How long will they be incapable
of innocence?
6 For it is from Israel,
an artisan made it;
it is not God.
The calf of Samaria
shall be broken to pieces.[a]

7 For they sow the wind,
and they shall reap the
whirlwind.
The standing grain has no heads,
it shall yield no meal;
if it were to yield,
foreigners would devour it.
8 Israel is swallowed up;
now they are among
the nations
as a useless vessel.
9 For they have gone up to Assyria,
a wild ass wandering alone;
Ephraim has bargained
for lovers.
10 Though they bargain with
the nations,
I will now gather them up.
They shall soon writhe
under the burden of kings
and princes.

11 When Ephraim multiplied
altars to expiate sin,
they became to him altars
for sinning.
12 Though I write for him the
multitude of my
instructions,
they are regarded as a
strange thing.
13 Though they offer choice
sacrifices,[b]
though they eat flesh,
the LORD does not accept them.
Now he will remember
their iniquity,
and punish their sins;
they shall return to Egypt.
14 Israel has forgotten his Maker,
and built palaces;
and Judah has multiplied
fortified cities;
but I will send a fire
upon his cities,
and it shall devour his
strongholds.

PUNISHMENT FOR ISRAEL'S SIN

9 Do not rejoice, O Israel!
Do not exult[c] as other
nations do;
for you have played the whore,
departing from your God.
You have loved a
prostitute's pay
on all threshing floors.
2 Threshing floor and wine vat
shall not feed them,
and the new wine shall
fail them.
3 They shall not remain in the
land of the LORD;
but Ephraim shall
return to Egypt,
and in Assyria they shall
eat unclean food.

4 They shall not pour drink
offerings of wine
to the LORD,
and their sacrifices shall
not please him.
Such sacrifices shall be like
mourners' bread;
all who eat of it shall be defiled;
for their bread shall be for
their hunger only;
it shall not come to the
house of the LORD.

5 What will you do on the day
of appointed festival,
and on the day of the
festival of the LORD?
6 For even if they escape
destruction,
Egypt shall gather them,
Memphis shall bury them.
Nettles shall possess their
precious things of silver;[d]
thorns shall be in their tents.

7 The days of punishment
have come,
the days of recompense
have come;
Israel cries,[e]
"The prophet is a fool,
the man of the spirit is mad!"

a 8.6 Or shall go up in flames   b 8.13 Cn:
Meaning of Heb uncertain   c 9.1 Gk: Heb To
exultation   d 9.6 Meaning of Heb uncertain
e 9.7 Cn Compare Gk: Heb shall know

Because of your great iniquity,
    your hostility is great.
8 The prophet is a sentinel for my
       God over Ephraim,
    yet a fowler's snare is on
       all his ways,
    and hostility in the
       house of his God.
9 They have deeply corrupted
       themselves
    as in the days of Gibeah;
    he will remember their iniquity,
    he will punish their sins.

10 Like grapes in the wilderness,
    I found Israel.
    Like the first fruit on the fig tree,
       in its first season,
    I saw your ancestors.
    But they came to Baal-peor,
    and consecrated themselves
       to a thing of shame,
    and became detestable like
       the thing they loved.
11 Ephraim's glory shall fly
       away like a bird—
    no birth, no pregnancy,
       no conception!
12 Even if they bring up children,
    I will bereave them until
       no one is left.
    Woe to them indeed
       when I depart from them!
13 Once I saw Ephraim as a
       young palm planted
       in a lovely meadow,[a]
    but now Ephraim must
       lead out his children
       for slaughter.
14 Give them, O LORD—
    what will you give?
    Give them a miscarrying womb
       and dry breasts.

15 Every evil of theirs began
       at Gilgal;
    there I came to hate them.
    Because of the wickedness
       of their deeds
    I will drive them out
       of my house.
    I will love them no more;
       all their officials are rebels.

16 Ephraim is stricken,
    their root is dried up,
    they shall bear no fruit.

Even though they give birth,
    I will kill the cherished
       offspring of their womb.
17 Because they have not
       listened to him,
    my God will reject them;
    they shall become wanderers
       among the nations.

ISRAEL'S SIN AND CAPTIVITY

10 Israel is a luxuriant vine
    that yields its fruit.
The more his fruit increased
    the more altars he built;
as his country improved,
    he improved his pillars.
2 Their heart is false;
    now they must bear their guilt.
The LORD[b] will break down
       their altars,
    and destroy their pillars.

3 For now they will say:
    "We have no king,
for we do not fear the LORD,
    and a king—what could
       he do for us?"
4 They utter mere words;
    with empty oaths they
       make covenants;
so litigation springs up like
       poisonous weeds
    in the furrows of the field.
5 The inhabitants of Samaria
       tremble
    for the calf[c] of Beth-aven.
Its people shall mourn for it,
    and its idolatrous priests
       shall wail[d] over it,
    over its glory that has
       departed from it.
6 The thing itself shall be
       carried to Assyria
    as tribute to the great king.[e]
Ephraim shall be put to shame,
    and Israel shall be ashamed
       of his idol.[f]

7 Samaria's king shall perish
    like a chip on the face
       of the waters.

---

a 9.13 Meaning of Heb uncertain
b 10.2 Heb *he*   c 10.5 Gk Syr: Heb *calves*
d 10.5 Cn: Heb *exult*   e 10.6 Cn: Heb *to a*
king who will contend   f 10.6 Cn:
Heb *counsel*

8 The high places of Aven,
　　the sin of Israel,
　shall be destroyed.
　Thorn and thistle shall grow up
　　on their altars.
　They shall say to the
　　mountains, Cover us,
　and to the hills, Fall on us.

WHETHER OR NOT WE ARE

BLESSED WITH ABSOLUTE

BELIEF, WE ARE OFTEN MORE

OBSESSED WITH DELAYING

DEATH THAN FULFILLING LIFE.

9 Since the days of Gibeah you
　　have sinned, O Israel;
　there they have continued.
　Shall not war overtake
　　them in Gibeah?
10 I will come[a] against the wayward
　　people to punish them;
　and nations shall be gathered
　　against them
　when they are punished[b] for
　　their double iniquity.

11 Ephraim was a trained heifer
　　that loved to thresh,
　and I spared her fair neck;
　but I will make Ephraim
　　break the ground;
　Judah must plow;
　Jacob must harrow for himself.
12 Sow for yourselves
　　righteousness;
　reap steadfast love;
　break up your fallow ground;
　for it is time to seek the LORD,
　that he may come and rain
　　righteousness upon you.

13 You have plowed wickedness,
　you have reaped injustice,
　you have eaten the fruit of lies.
　Because you have trusted
　　in your power
　and in the multitude of
　　your warriors,

14 therefore the tumult of war shall
　　rise against your people,
　and all your fortresses
　　shall be destroyed,
　as Shalman destroyed Beth-arbel
　　on the day of battle
　when mothers were dashed in
　　pieces with their children.
15 Thus it shall be done to
　　you, O Bethel,
　because of your great
　　wickedness.
　At dawn the king of Israel
　　shall be utterly cut off.

GOD'S COMPASSION DESPITE ISRAEL'S INGRATITUDE

11 When Israel was a
　　child, I loved him,
　and out of Egypt I
　　called my son.
2 The more I[c] called them,
　　the more they went from me;[d]
　they kept sacrificing to the Baals,
　and offering incense to idols.

3 Yet it was I who taught
　　Ephraim to walk,
　I took them up in my[e] arms;
　but they did not know
　　that I healed them.
4 I led them with cords of
　　human kindness,
　with bands of love.
　I was to them like those
　　who lift infants to
　　their cheeks.[f]
　I bent down to them
　　and fed them.

5 They shall return to the
　　land of Egypt,
　and Assyria shall
　　be their king,
　because they have refused
　　to return to me.
6 The sword rages in their cities,
　　it consumes their
　　oracle-priests,
　and devours because of
　　their schemes.

---

a 10.10 Cn Compare Gk: Heb *In my desire*
b 10.10 Gk: Heb *bound*　c 11.2 Gk: Heb *they*
d 11.2 Gk: Heb *them*　e 11.3 Gk Syr Vg: Heb *his*　f 11.4 Or *who ease the yoke on their jaws*

7 My people are bent on turning
away from me.
To the Most High they call,
but he does not raise
them up at all.[a]

8 How can I give you up, Ephraim?
How can I hand you
over, O Israel?
How can I make you like Admah?
How can I treat you
like Zeboiim?
My heart recoils within me;
my compassion grows
warm and tender.
9 I will not execute my fierce anger;
I will not again destroy
Ephraim;
for I am God and no mortal,
the Holy One in your midst,
and I will not come in wrath.[a]

10 They shall go after the LORD,
who roars like a lion;
when he roars,
his children shall come
trembling from the west.
11 They shall come trembling like
birds from Egypt,
and like doves from the
land of Assyria;
and I will return them to their
homes, says the LORD.

12 [b]Ephraim has surrounded
me with lies,
and the house of Israel
with deceit;
but Judah still walks[c] with God,
and is faithful to the Holy One.

12 Ephraim herds the wind,
and pursues the east
wind all day long;
they multiply falsehood
and violence;
they make a treaty
with Assyria,
and oil is carried to Egypt.

THE LONG HISTORY
OF REBELLION

2 The LORD has an indictment
against Judah,
and will punish Jacob
according to his ways,
and repay him according
to his deeds.

3 In the womb he tried to
supplant his brother,
and in his manhood he
strove with God.
4 He strove with the angel
and prevailed,
he wept and sought his favor;
he met him at Bethel,
and there he spoke with him.[d]
5 The LORD the God of hosts,
the LORD is his name!
6 But as for you, return to your God,
hold fast to love and justice,
and wait continually
for your God.

7 A trader, in whose hands
are false balances,
he loves to oppress.
8 Ephraim has said, "Ah, I am rich,
I have gained wealth
for myself;
in all of my gain
no offense has been
found in me
that would be sin."[a]
9 I am the LORD your God
from the land of Egypt;
I will make you live in
tents again,
as in the days of the
appointed festival.

10 I spoke to the prophets;
it was I who multiplied visions,
and through the prophets I
will bring destruction.
11 In Gilead[e] there is iniquity,
they shall surely come
to nothing.
In Gilgal they sacrifice bulls,
so their altars shall be
like stone heaps
on the furrows of the field.
12 Jacob fled to the land of Aram,
there Israel served for a wife,
and for a wife he
guarded sheep.[f]
13 By a prophet the LORD brought
Israel up from Egypt,
and by a prophet he
was guarded.

[a] 11.7,9; 12.8 Meaning of Heb uncertain
[b] 11.12 Ch 12.1 in Heb   [c] 11.12 Heb
roams or *rules*   [d] 12.4 Gk Syr: Heb
us   [e] 12.11 Compare Syr: Heb *Gilead*
[f] 12.12 Heb lacks *sheep*

14 Ephraim has given bitter offense,
     so his Lord will bring his
          crimes down on him
     and pay him back for
          his insults.

RELENTLESS JUDGMENT
ON ISRAEL

13 When Ephraim spoke,
     there was trembling;
he was exalted in Israel;
but he incurred guilt through
     Baal and died.

2 And now they keep on sinning
     and make a cast image
          for themselves,
     idols of silver made according to
          their understanding,
     all of them the work
          of artisans.
"Sacrifice to these," they say.[a]
     People are kissing calves!
3 Therefore they shall be like
          the morning mist
     or like the dew that goes
          away early,
like chaff that swirls from
          the threshing floor
     or like smoke
          from a window.

4 Yet I have been the LORD
          your God
     ever since the land of Egypt;
you know no God but me,
     and besides me there
          is no savior.
5 It was I who fed[b] you in
          the wilderness,
     in the land of drought.
6 When I fed[c] them, they
          were satisfied;
     they were satisfied, and
          their heart was proud;
     therefore they forgot me.
7 So I will become like a
          lion to them,
     like a leopard I will lurk
          beside the way.
8 I will fall upon them like a bear
          robbed of her cubs,
     and will tear open the
          covering of their heart;
there I will devour them
          like a lion,
     as a wild animal would
          mangle them.

9 I will destroy you, O Israel;
     who can help you?[d]
10 Where now is[e] your king, that
          he may save you?
Where in all your cities
     are your rulers,
of whom you said,
     "Give me a king and rulers"?
11 I gave you a king in my anger,
     and I took him away
          in my wrath.

12 Ephraim's iniquity is bound up;
     his sin is kept in store.
13 The pangs of childbirth
          come for him,
     but he is an unwise son;
for at the proper time he does
          not present himself
     at the mouth of the womb.

14 Shall I ransom them from
          the power of Sheol?
     Shall I redeem them
          from Death?
O Death, where are[f] your
          plagues?
     O Sheol, where is[f] your
          destruction?
     Compassion is hidden
          from my eyes.

15 Although he may flourish
          among rushes,[g]
     the east wind shall come, a
          blast from the LORD,
     rising from the wilderness;
and his fountain shall dry up,
     his spring shall be parched.
It shall strip his treasury
     of every precious thing.
16[h] Samaria shall bear her guilt,
     because she has rebelled
          against her God;
they shall fall by the sword,
     their little ones shall be
          dashed in pieces,
     and their pregnant women
          ripped open.

---

[a] 13.2 Cn Compare Gk: Heb *To these they
say sacrifices of people*   [b] 13.5 Gk Syr:
Heb *knew*   [c] 13.6 Cn: Heb *according to
their pasture*   [d] 13.9 Gk Syr: Heb *for in me
is your help*   [e] 13.10 Gk Syr Vg: Heb *I will
be*   [f] 13.14 Gk Syr: Heb *I will be*   [g] 13.15 Or
among brothers   [h] 13.16 Ch 14.1 in Heb

A PLEA FOR REPENTANCE

14 Return, O Israel, to the
LORD your God,
for you have stumbled because
of your iniquity.
2 Take words with you
and return to the LORD;
say to him,
"Take away all guilt;
accept that which is good,
and we will offer
the fruit[a] of our lips.
3 Assyria shall not save us;
we will not ride upon horses;
we will say no more, 'Our God,'
to the work of our hands.
In you the orphan finds mercy."

ASSURANCE OF FORGIVENESS

4 I will heal their disloyalty;
I will love them freely,
for my anger has turned
from them.
5 I will be like the dew to Israel;
he shall blossom like the lily,
he shall strike root like the
forests of Lebanon.[b]
6 His shoots shall spread out;
his beauty shall be like
the olive tree,
and his fragrance like
that of Lebanon.
7 They shall again live beneath
my[c] shadow,
they shall flourish as a garden;[d]
they shall blossom like the vine,
their fragrance shall be like
the wine of Lebanon.

8 O Ephraim, what have I[e]
to do with idols?
It is I who answer and
look after you.[f]
I am like an evergreen cypress;
your faithfulness[g] comes
from me.
9 Those who are wise understand
these things;
those who are discerning
know them.

PONDER

Those who are wise understand these things; those who are discerning know them. For the ways of the LORD are right, and the upright walk in them, but transgressors stumble in them.
—Hosea 14.9

PRAY

Lord, we are grateful for the chance to read the book of Hosea. His life was a strange but provocative picture of your tenacious love. Inspire us to understanding and righteousness, just as Hosea encouraged the people of those ancient times to correct their relationship with you. Open our hearts and fill them with the Holy Spirit. And now that we have the exalted and perfect example set for us by Jesus Christ, inspire us to live within our communities and our homes as you would have us live, knowing that through this commitment we can have your finest blessing. We ask this in the name of Jesus Christ, our Savior. Amen.

For the ways of the LORD
are right,
and the upright
walk in them,
but transgressors
stumble in them.

---

a **14.2** Gk Syr: Heb *bulls*   b **14.5** Cn: Heb *like Lebanon*   c **14.7** Heb *his*   d **14.7** Cn: Heb *they shall grow grain*   e **14.8** Or *What more has Ephraim*   f **14.8** Heb *him*   g **14.8** Heb *your fruit*

JOEL

Have you ever wondered if there is spiritual significance in natural
disasters such as floods, hurricanes and earthquakes? The book of Joel
may give you a clue. Joel views the plague of locusts as a foretaste of
God's catastrophic judgment on people who are cold and indifferent
toward their Lord. Joel warns of the coming judgment for all nations, including the Israelites. He calls the nation to repent and paints a picture of
the restoration and healing that will follow if they do. Consider this as you
read the book of Joel: In God's eyes, the worst disaster is a human heart
that is impermeable to God's love.

1

The word of the LORD that came to Joel son of Pethuel:

LAMENT OVER THE RUIN OF THE COUNTRY

2 Hear this, O elders,
　　give ear, all inhabitants
　　　of the land!
　　Has such a thing happened
　　　in your days,
　　or in the days of your
　　　ancestors?
3 Tell your children of it,
　　and let your children tell
　　　their children,
　　and their children another
　　　generation.

4 What the cutting locust left,
　　the swarming locust has eaten.
　　What the swarming locust left,
　　　the hopping locust has eaten,
　　and what the hopping locust left,
　　　the destroying locust has eaten.

5 Wake up, you drunkards,
　　　and weep;
　　and wail, all you
　　　wine-drinkers,
　　over the sweet wine,
　　　for it is cut off from
　　　　your mouth.
6 For a nation has invaded my land,
　　　powerful and innumerable;
　　its teeth are lions' teeth,
　　　and it has the fangs
　　　　of a lioness.
7 It has laid waste my vines,
　　　and splintered my fig trees;
　　it has stripped off their bark
　　　and thrown it down;
　　　their branches have
　　　　turned white.

8 Lament like a virgin dressed
　　　in sackcloth
　　for the husband of her youth.
9 The grain offering and the drink
　　　offering are cut off
　　from the house of the LORD.
　　The priests mourn,
　　　the ministers of the LORD.
10 The fields are devastated,
　　　the ground mourns;
　　for the grain is destroyed,
　　　the wine dries up,
　　　　the oil fails.

11 Be dismayed, you farmers,
　　　wail, you vinedressers,
　　over the wheat and the barley;
　　　for the crops of the field
　　　　are ruined.
12 The vine withers,
　　　the fig tree droops.
　　Pomegranate, palm, and apple—
　　　all the trees of the field
　　　　are dried up;
　　surely, joy withers away
　　　among the people.

A CALL TO REPENTANCE AND PRAYER

13 Put on sackcloth and lament,
　　　you priests;
　　wail, you ministers of the altar.
　　Come, pass the night in sackcloth,
　　　you ministers of my God!
　　Grain offering and drink offering
　　　are withheld from the
　　　　house of your God.

14 Sanctify a fast,
　　　call a solemn assembly.
　　Gather the elders
　　　and all the inhabitants
　　　　of the land
　　to the house of the LORD
　　　your God,
　　　and cry out to the LORD.

15 Alas for the day!
　　For the day of the LORD is near,
　　　and as destruction from the
　　　　Almighty[a] it comes.
16 Is not the food cut off
　　　before our eyes,
　　joy and gladness
　　　from the house of our God?

17 The seed shrivels under the clods,[b]
　　　the storehouses are desolate;
　　the granaries are ruined
　　　because the grain has failed.
18 How the animals groan!
　　The herds of cattle
　　　wander about
　　because there is no pasture
　　　for them;
　　even the flocks of sheep
　　　are dazed.[c]

a 1.15 Traditional rendering of Heb
Shaddai　　b 1.17 Meaning of Heb uncertain
c 1.18 Compare Gk Syr Vg: Meaning of Heb
uncertain

19 To you, O LORD, I cry.
For fire has devoured
    the pastures of the wilderness,
and flames have burned
    all the trees of the field.
20 Even the wild animals cry to you
    because the watercourses
        are dried up,
and fire has devoured
    the pastures of the wilderness.

2 Blow the trumpet in Zion;
    sound the alarm on my
        holy mountain!
Let all the inhabitants of
    the land tremble,
for the day of the LORD is
    coming, it is near—
2 a day of darkness and gloom,
    a day of clouds and
        thick darkness!
Like blackness spread upon
    the mountains
    a great and powerful
        army comes;
their like has never been
    from of old,
nor will be again after them
    in ages to come.

3 Fire devours in front of them,
    and behind them a
        flame burns.
Before them the land is like
    the garden of Eden,
but after them a desolate
    wilderness,
and nothing escapes them.

4 They have the appearance
    of horses,
and like war-horses
    they charge.
5 As with the rumbling
    of chariots,
they leap on the tops of
    the mountains,
like the crackling of a flame of fire
    devouring the stubble,
like a powerful army
    drawn up for battle.

6 Before them peoples are
    in anguish,
all faces grow pale.[a]
7 Like warriors they charge,
    like soldiers they scale the wall.

Each keeps to its own course,
    they do not swerve from[b]
        their paths.
8 They do not jostle one another,
    each keeps to its own track;
they burst through the weapons
    and are not halted.
9 They leap upon the city,
    they run upon the walls;
they climb up into the houses,
    they enter through the
        windows like a thief.
10 The earth quakes before them,
    the heavens tremble.
The sun and the moon
    are darkened,
and the stars withdraw
    their shining.
11 The LORD utters his voice
    at the head of his army;
how vast is his host!
Numberless are those who
    obey his command.
Truly the day of the
    LORD is great;
terrible indeed—who
    can endure it?

12 Yet even now, says the LORD,
    return to me with all
        your heart,
with fasting, with weeping,
    and with mourning;
13   rend your hearts and not
        your clothing.
Return to the LORD, your God,
    for he is gracious
        and merciful,
slow to anger, and abounding
    in steadfast love,
and relents from punishing.
14 Who knows whether he will
    not turn and relent,
    and leave a blessing
        behind him,
a grain offering and a
    drink offering
for the LORD, your God?

15 Blow the trumpet in Zion;
    sanctify a fast;
call a solemn assembly;
16   gather the people.

a 2.6 Meaning of Heb uncertain   b 2.7 Gk
Syr Vg: Heb *they do not take a pledge along*

Sanctify the congregation;
assemble the aged;
gather the children,
even infants at the breast.
Let the bridegroom leave his room,
and the bride her canopy.
17 Between the vestibule
and the altar
let the priests, the ministers
of the LORD, weep.
Let them say, "Spare your
people, O LORD,
and do not make your
heritage a mockery,
a byword among the nations.
Why should it be said among
the peoples,
'Where is their God?'"

GOD'S RESPONSE AND PROMISE
18 Then the LORD became
jealous for his land,
and had pity on his people.
19 In response to his people
the LORD said:
I am sending you
grain, wine, and oil,
and you will be satisfied;
and I will no more make you
a mockery among the nations.

20 I will remove the northern
army far from you,
and drive it into a parched
and desolate land,
its front into the eastern sea,
and its rear into the western sea;
its stench and foul smell
will rise up.
Surely he has done great things!

21 Do not fear, O soil;
be glad and rejoice,
for the LORD has done
great things!
22 Do not fear, you animals
of the field,
for the pastures of the
wilderness are green;
the tree bears its fruit,
the fig tree and vine give
their full yield.

23 O children of Zion, be glad
and rejoice in the LORD
your God;

for he has given the early rain[a]
for your vindication,
he has poured down for
you abundant rain,
the early and the later
rain, as before.
24 The threshing floors shall
be full of grain,
the vats shall overflow
with wine and oil.

25 I will repay you for the years
that the swarming
locust has eaten,
the hopper, the destroyer,
and the cutter,
my great army, which I
sent against you.

26 You shall eat in plenty and
be satisfied,
and praise the name of the
LORD your God,
who has dealt wondrously
with you.
And my people shall never
again be put to shame.
27 You shall know that I am in
the midst of Israel,
and that I, the LORD, am your
God and there is no other.
And my people shall never
again be put to shame.

GOD'S SPIRIT POURED OUT
28[b] Then afterward
I will pour out my spirit
on all flesh;
your sons and your daughters
shall prophesy,
your old men shall
dream dreams,
and your young men
shall see visions.
29 Even on the male and
female slaves,
in those days, I will pour
out my spirit.

30 I will show portents in the heavens and on the earth, blood and fire and columns of smoke. 31The sun shall be turned to darkness, and the moon to blood, before the great and

[a] 2.23 Meaning of Heb uncertain
[b] 2.28 Ch 3.1 in Heb

terrible day of the LORD comes. ³²Then everyone who calls on the name of the LORD shall be saved; for in Mount Zion and in Jerusalem there shall be those who escape, as the LORD has said, and among the survivors shall be those whom the LORD calls.

PONDER

Then afterward I will pour out my spirit on all flesh; your sons and your daughters shall prophesy, your old men shall dream dreams, and your young men shall see visions.
—Joel 2.28

PRAY

Father, open our hearts to receive the words of the ancient prophets courageously into our own lives. No matter what our circumstances might be, our lives can be expanded and fulfilled to the extent that we make room for the Holy Spirit to work within us. We are tempted go our own ways. But you provide the opportunities and the means to allow the Holy Spirit to guide and counsel us. We are grateful that you forgive us when we fail and that your vision and power are always available to us. We give you the honor and the glory in the name of our Savior, Jesus Christ. Amen.

3 ᵃ For then, in those days and at that time, when I restore the fortunes of Judah and Jerusalem, ²I will gather all the nations and bring them down to the valley of Jehoshaphat, and I will enter into judgment with them there, on account of my people and my heritage Israel, because they have scattered them among the nations. They have divided my land, ³and cast lots for my people, and traded boys for prostitutes, and sold girls for wine, and drunk it down.

4 What are you to me, O Tyre and Sidon, and all the regions of Philistia? Are you paying me back for something? If you are paying me back, I will turn your deeds back upon your own heads swiftly and speedily. ⁵For you have taken my silver and my gold, and have carried my rich treasures into your temples.ᵇ ⁶You have sold the people of Judah and Jerusalem to the Greeks, removing them far from their own border. ⁷But now I will rouse them to leave the places to which you have sold them, and I will turn your deeds back upon your own heads. ⁸I will sell your sons and your daughters into the hand of the people of Judah, and they will sell them to the Sabeans, to a nation far away; for the LORD has spoken.

JUDGMENT IN THE VALLEY OF JEHOSHAPHAT

9 Proclaim this among the nations:
Prepare war,ᶜ
    stir up the warriors.
Let all the soldiers draw near,
    let them come up.
10 Beat your plowshares
        into swords,
    and your pruning hooks
        into spears;
    let the weakling say, "I
        am a warrior."

11 Come quickly,ᵈ
    all you nations all around,
    gather yourselves there.
Bring down your warriors,
    O LORD.
12 Let the nations rouse themselves,
    and come up to the valley
        of Jehoshaphat;
for there I will sit to judge
    all the neighboring nations.

13 Put in the sickle,
    for the harvest is ripe.
Go in, tread,
    for the wine press is full.
The vats overflow,
    for their wickedness is great.

ᵃ 3.1 Ch 4.1 in Heb   ᵇ 3.5 Or *palaces*
ᶜ 3.9 Heb *sanctify war*   ᵈ 3.11 Meaning of Heb uncertain

14 Multitudes, multitudes,
in the valley of decision!
For the day of the LORD is near
in the valley of decision.
15 The sun and the moon
are darkened,
and the stars withdraw
their shining.

16 The LORD roars from Zion,
and utters his voice
from Jerusalem,
and the heavens and the
earth shake.
But the LORD is a refuge
for his people,
a stronghold for the
people of Israel.

THE GLORIOUS FUTURE OF JUDAH

17 So you shall know that I, the
LORD your God,
dwell in Zion, my holy
mountain.
And Jerusalem shall be holy,
and strangers shall never
again pass through it.

18 In that day
the mountains shall drip
sweet wine,
the hills shall flow with milk,
and all the stream
beds of Judah
shall flow with water;
a fountain shall come forth from
the house of the LORD
and water the Wadi Shittim.

19 Egypt shall become a desolation
and Edom a desolate
wilderness,
because of the violence done to
the people of Judah,
in whose land they have
shed innocent blood.
20 But Judah shall be inhabited
forever,
and Jerusalem to all
generations.
21 I will avenge their blood, and I
will not clear the guilty,[a]
for the LORD dwells in Zion.

[a] 3.21 Gk Syr: Heb *I will hold innocent their
blood that I have not held innocent*

AMOS

What is it about prosperity that seems to lead to corruption? Many great nations have accumulated riches and power, only to crumble into vice, economic inequity and social injustice. The prophet Amos is living during such a time. He speaks out against those who made themselves powerful at the expense of the poor, and he urges nations to return to justice. Amos delivers a timeless message of social justice we would do well to heed—and to respond to with compassionate hearts.

1 The words of Amos, who was among the shepherds of Tekoa, which he saw concerning Israel in the days of King Uzziah of Judah and in the days of King Jeroboam son of Joash of Israel, two years[a] before the earthquake.

JUDGMENT ON ISRAEL'S NEIGHBORS

2 And he said:

The LORD roars from Zion,
    and utters his voice
        from Jerusalem;
the pastures of the shepherds
        wither,
    and the top of Carmel
        dries up.

3 Thus says the LORD:
For three transgressions
        of Damascus,
    and for four, I will not revoke
        the punishment;[b]
because they have
        threshed Gilead
    with threshing sledges of iron.
4 So I will send a fire on the
        house of Hazael,
    and it shall devour the
        strongholds of Ben-hadad.
5 I will break the gate bars
        of Damascus,
    and cut off the inhabitants
        from the Valley of Aven,
    and the one who holds the
        scepter from Beth-eden;
and the people of Aram shall
        go into exile to Kir,
            says the LORD.

6 Thus says the LORD:
For three transgressions
        of Gaza,
    and for four, I will not revoke
        the punishment;[b]
because they carried into exile
        entire communities,
    to hand them over to Edom.
7 So I will send a fire on the
        wall of Gaza,
    fire that shall devour its
        strongholds.
8 I will cut off the inhabitants
        from Ashdod,
    and the one who holds the
        scepter from Ashkelon;

I will turn my hand
        against Ekron,
    and the remnant of the
        Philistines shall perish,
            says the Lord GOD.
9 Thus says the LORD:
For three transgressions of Tyre,
    and for four, I will not revoke
        the punishment;[b]
because they delivered
        entire communities
        over to Edom,
    and did not remember the
        covenant of kinship.
10 So I will send a fire on the
        wall of Tyre,
    fire that shall devour its
        strongholds.

11 Thus says the LORD:
For three transgressions of Edom,
    and for four, I will not revoke
        the punishment;[b]
because he pursued his brother
        with the sword
    and cast off all pity;
he maintained his anger
        perpetually,[c]
    and kept his wrath[d] forever.
12 So I will send a fire on Teman,
    and it shall devour the
        strongholds of Bozrah.

13 Thus says the LORD:
For three transgressions of
        the Ammonites,
    and for four, I will not revoke
        the punishment;[b]
because they have ripped
        open pregnant
        women in Gilead
    in order to enlarge
        their territory.
14 So I will kindle a fire against
        the wall of Rabbah,
    fire that shall devour its
        strongholds,
with shouting on the
        day of battle,
    with a storm on the day
        of the whirlwind;

a 1.1 Or *during two years*   b 1.3,6,9,11,13 Heb
cause it to return   c 1.11 Syr Vg: Heb *and
his anger tore perpetually*   d 1.11 Gk Syr Vg:
Heb *and his wrath kept*

15 then their king shall go into exile,
   he and his officials together,
         says the LORD.

2

Thus says the LORD:
For three transgressions
   of Moab,
and for four, I will not revoke
   the punishment;[a]
because he burned to lime
   the bones of the king of Edom.
2 So I will send a fire on Moab,
   and it shall devour the
      strongholds of Kerioth,
and Moab shall die amid uproar,
   amid shouting and the
      sound of the trumpet;
3 I will cut off the ruler
   from its midst,
and will kill all its officials
   with him,
         says the LORD.

JUDGMENT ON JUDAH

4 Thus says the LORD:
For three transgressions of Judah,
   and for four, I will not revoke
   the punishment;[a]
because they have rejected
   the law of the LORD,
and have not kept his statutes,
but they have been led astray
   by the same lies
after which their
   ancestors walked.
5 So I will send a fire on Judah,
   and it shall devour the
      strongholds of Jerusalem.

JUDGMENT ON ISRAEL

6 Thus says the LORD:
For three transgressions of Israel,
   and for four, I will not revoke
   the punishment;[a]
because they sell the
   righteous for silver,
   and the needy for a pair
      of sandals—
7 they who trample the head
   of the poor into the
      dust of the earth,
   and push the afflicted
      out of the way;
father and son go in to
   the same girl,
so that my holy name
   is profaned;

8 they lay themselves down
   beside every altar
on garments taken in pledge;
and in the house of their
   God they drink
wine bought with fines
   they imposed.

9 Yet I destroyed the Amorite
   before them,
whose height was like the
   height of cedars,
and who was as strong as oaks;
I destroyed his fruit above,
   and his roots beneath.
10 Also I brought you up out of
   the land of Egypt,
and led you forty years in
   the wilderness,
to possess the land of
   the Amorite.
11 And I raised up some of your
   children to be prophets
and some of your youths
   to be nazirites.[b]
Is it not indeed so,
   O people of Israel?
         says the LORD.

12 But you made the nazirites[b]
   drink wine,
and commanded the prophets,
   saying, "You shall not
      prophesy."

13 So, I will press you down
   in your place,
just as a cart presses down
   when it is full of sheaves.[c]
14 Flight shall perish
   from the swift,
and the strong shall not
      retain their strength,
nor shall the mighty
   save their lives;
15 those who handle the bow
   shall not stand,
and those who are swift of foot
   shall not save themselves,
nor shall those who ride
   horses save their lives;

---

a 2.1,4,6 Heb *cause it to return*
b 2.11,12 That is, *those separated* or *those consecrated*   c 2.13 Meaning of Heb uncertain

A LESSON ON RIGHTEOUSNESS

Thus says the LORD: For three transgressions of Israel, and for four, I will not revoke the punishment; because they sell the righteous for silver, and the needy for a pair of sandals—they who trample the head of the poor into the dust of the earth, and push the afflicted out of the way.

—Amos 2.6–7

God called Amos to prophesy to the northern kingdom of Israel during a time of their great prosperity. Israel and Judah had split centuries earlier, and up until Amos's time, the people of Israel were faring well and even expanding their territory. They undoubtedly felt that their economic well-being was evidence of their favored standing with God. So, when Amos condemned the Gentile nations around them for their iniquity, the Israelites probably agreed. The same was likely true as Amos moved on to condemn Judah, the southern kingdom, for its spiritual unfaithfulness (verses 4–5). But when Amos began to criticize Israel too, it probably raised the ire of more than a few Israelites.

In this chapter, Amos's condemnation of Judah was essentially about its vertical relationship with God, while his condemnation of Israel was about the Israelites' horizontal relationships with other people (verses 6–7). Amos condemned Israel for injustice—for taking advantage of the poor, the deprived, the afflicted and the helpless. It was primarily a condemnation of the rich and powerful, those who seemed very secure in their resources.

How are we like Israel today? For one, we often deceive ourselves into thinking that our security and economic well-being are direct evidence of our favored status with God. We assume that because we have a nice income, a good job and a growing retirement account, God is pleased with us. Why should we give part of what we have earned to help people who (or so they seem to us) aren't as pleasing to God? We might say, "I worked hard for my money, so why shouldn't they do the same? Why should I make myself less comfortable to reach out to people who can't reciprocate my kindness to them?" We can apply the same words of warning Amos pronounced on Judah and Israel to our own thoughts and attitudes.

Amos condemned Judah and Israel for the two kinds of sins people commit—those against God and those against others—and we still commit them today. But Jesus taught, in a positive sense, about what it means to be righteous. We are called to be faithful and to serve God wholeheartedly, but that should also result in right actions and attitudes. Throughout his teaching and through his example, Jesus has made it clear that we are called to reach out to the needy, the oppressed and the outcast. We are called to go beyond our "duty" and give generously to others. We are to stand up for justice. When we are right with God, it will be evident in our gracious attitudes and actions toward others.

Going Deeper

- What are some specific ways you sin "horizontally"?
- What is one way you can go above the call of duty and reach out to others?

16 and those who are stout of heart
 among the mighty
shall flee away naked
 in that day,
  says the LORD.

SIN, IN TOTALITY, IS A

FAILURE TO LOVE.

ISRAEL'S GUILT AND PUNISHMENT

3 Hear this word that the LORD
has spoken against you, O people of Israel, against the whole family
that I brought up out of the land of
Egypt:
2 You only have I known
 of all the families of the earth;
therefore I will punish you
 for all your iniquities.

3 Do two walk together
 unless they have made
  an appointment?
4 Does a lion roar in the forest,
 when it has no prey?
Does a young lion cry out
 from its den,
if it has caught nothing?
5 Does a bird fall into a snare
 on the earth,
when there is no trap for it?
Does a snare spring up from
 the ground,
when it has taken nothing?
6 Is a trumpet blown in a city,
 and the people are not afraid?
Does disaster befall a city,
 unless the LORD has done it?
7 Surely the Lord GOD does nothing,
 without revealing his secret
to his servants the prophets.
8 The lion has roared;
 who will not fear?
The Lord GOD has spoken;
 who can but prophesy?

9 Proclaim to the strongholds
 in Ashdod,
and to the strongholds in
 the land of Egypt,

and say, "Assemble yourselves
 on Mount[a] Samaria,
and see what great tumults
 are within it,
and what oppressions
 are in its midst."
10 They do not know how to do
 right, says the LORD,
those who store up violence
 and robbery in their
  strongholds.
11 Therefore thus says the Lord GOD:
 An adversary shall surround
  the land,
and strip you of your defense;
and your strongholds shall
 be plundered.

12 Thus says the LORD: As the shepherd rescues from the mouth of the
lion two legs, or a piece of an ear, so
shall the people of Israel who live in
Samaria be rescued, with the corner of
a couch and part[b] of a bed.

13 Hear, and testify against the
 house of Jacob,
 says the Lord GOD, the
  God of hosts:
14 On the day I punish Israel for
 its transgressions,
I will punish the altars of Bethel,
and the horns of the altar
 shall be cut off
and fall to the ground.
15 I will tear down the winter house as
 well as the summer house;
and the houses of ivory
 shall perish,
and the great houses[c] shall
 come to an end,
  says the LORD.

4 Hear this word, you cows
of Bashan
who are on Mount Samaria,
who oppress the poor, who
 crush the needy,
who say to their husbands,
 "Bring something to drink!"
2 The Lord GOD has sworn
 by his holiness:
The time is surely coming
 upon you,

[a] 3.9 Gk Syr: Heb *the mountains of*
[b] 3.12 Meaning of Heb uncertain [c] 3.15 Or
many houses

when they shall take you
away with hooks,
even the last of you
with fishhooks.
3 Through breaches in the wall
you shall leave,
each one straight ahead;
and you shall be flung out
into Harmon,[a]
says the LORD.
4 Come to Bethel—and transgress;
to Gilgal—and multiply
transgression;
bring your sacrifices every
morning,
your tithes every three days;
5 bring a thank offering of
leavened bread,
and proclaim freewill
offerings, publish them;
for so you love to do,
O people of Israel!
says the Lord GOD.

ISRAEL REJECTS CORRECTION

6 I gave you cleanness of teeth
in all your cities,
and lack of bread in all
your places,
yet you did not return to me,
says the LORD.

7 And I also withheld the
rain from you
when there were still three
months to the harvest;
I would send rain on one city,
and send no rain on
another city;
one field would be rained upon,
and the field on which it did
not rain withered;
8 so two or three towns wandered
to one town
to drink water, and were
not satisfied;
yet you did not return to me,
says the LORD.

9 I struck you with blight
and mildew;
I laid waste[b] your gardens
and your vineyards;
the locust devoured your fig
trees and your olive trees;
yet you did not return to me,
says the LORD.

10 I sent among you a pestilence
after the manner of Egypt;
I killed your young men
with the sword;
I carried away your horses;[c]
and I made the stench
of your camp go up
into your nostrils;
yet you did not return to me,
says the LORD.

11 I overthrew some of you,
as when God overthrew
Sodom and Gomorrah,
and you were like a brand
snatched from the fire;
yet you did not return to me,
says the LORD.

12 Therefore thus I will do to
you, O Israel;
because I will do this to you,
prepare to meet your
God, O Israel!

13 For lo, the one who forms
the mountains,
creates the wind,
reveals his thoughts to mortals,
makes the morning darkness,
and treads on the heights
of the earth—
the LORD, the God of
hosts, is his name!

A LAMENT FOR ISRAEL'S SIN

5 Hear this word that I take up
over you in lamentation, O house
of Israel:
2 Fallen, no more to rise,
is maiden Israel;
forsaken on her land,
with no one to raise her up.

3 For thus says the Lord GOD:
The city that marched out
a thousand
shall have a hundred left,
and that which marched
out a hundred
shall have ten left.[d]

---

[a] 4.3 Meaning of Heb uncertain   [b] 4.9 Cn:
Heb *the multitude of*   [c] 4.10 Heb *with the
captivity of your horses*   [d] 5.3 Heb adds *to
the house of Israel*

⁴ For thus says the LORD to
　　the house of Israel:
Seek me and live;
⁵ 　　but do not seek Bethel,
and do not enter into Gilgal
　　or cross over to Beer-sheba;
for Gilgal shall surely go
　　into exile,
and Bethel shall come
　　to nothing.

⁶ Seek the LORD and live,
　　or he will break out against the
　　　house of Joseph like fire,
and it will devour Bethel, with
　　no one to quench it.
⁷ Ah, you that turn justice
　　to wormwood,
and bring righteousness
　　to the ground!

⁸ The one who made the
　　Pleiades and Orion,
and turns deep darkness
　　into the morning,
and darkens the day into night,
who calls for the waters of the sea,
　　and pours them out on the
　　　surface of the earth,
the LORD is his name,
⁹ who makes destruction flash
　　out against the strong,
so that destruction comes
　　upon the fortress.

¹⁰ They hate the one who
　　reproves in the gate,
and they abhor the one who
　　speaks the truth.
¹¹ Therefore because you
　　trample on the poor
and take from them
　　levies of grain,
you have built houses of
　　hewn stone,
but you shall not live in them;
you have planted pleasant
　　vineyards,
but you shall not drink
　　their wine.
¹² For I know how many are
　　your transgressions,
and how great are your sins—
you who afflict the righteous,
　　who take a bribe,
and push aside the needy
　　in the gate.

¹³ Therefore the prudent will keep
　　silent in such a time;
for it is an evil time.

¹⁴ Seek good and not evil,
　　that you may live;
and so the LORD, the God of
　　hosts, will be with you,
just as you have said.
¹⁵ Hate evil and love good,
　　and establish justice
　　in the gate;
it may be that the LORD,
　　the God of hosts,
will be gracious to the
　　remnant of Joseph.

¹⁶ Therefore thus says the LORD, the
　　God of hosts, the Lord:
In all the squares there
　　shall be wailing;
and in all the streets they
　　shall say, "Alas! alas!"
They shall call the farmers
　　to mourning,
and those skilled in
　　lamentation, to wailing;
¹⁷ in all the vineyards there
　　shall be wailing,
for I will pass through
　　the midst of you,
　　　　　says the LORD.

THE DAY OF THE LORD
A DARK DAY

¹⁸ Alas for you who desire the
　　day of the LORD!
Why do you want the
　　day of the LORD?
It is darkness, not light;
¹⁹ 　as if someone fled from a lion,
　　and was met by a bear;
or went into the house and rested
　　a hand against the wall,
and was bitten by a snake.
²⁰ Is not the day of the LORD
　　darkness, not light,
and gloom with no
　　brightness in it?

²¹ I hate, I despise your festivals,
　　and I take no delight in your
　　solemn assemblies.
²² Even though you offer me
　　your burnt offerings
　　and grain offerings,
I will not accept them;

SEEK GOOD

Seek good and not evil, that you may live; and so the LORD, the God of hosts, will be with you, just as you have said. Hate evil and love good, and establish justice in the gate; it may be that the LORD, the God of hosts, will be gracious to the remnant of Joseph.

—Amos 5.14–15

No matter how religious the northern kingdom of Israel appeared by making offerings at pagan shrines and observing sacred festivals, Amos condemned them because in their hearts they had abandoned the Lord. They were respecting rituals, but these pagan ceremonies were not an adequate replacement for a genuine relationship with God. Amos warned the people that one day they would meet their Creator (verses 8–12), as they seemed to want to do through their religiosity, but it would not be the meeting they expected, for God's holiness involves judgment of sinners.

That is not to say that God is not a God of love. Clearly God displays abundant mercy, forgiveness, compassion and grace, and these things form a critical part of God's character. That is the side of God's holiness with which we are most comfortable. But God is also a God of judgment, a God who calls people to account for their actions and attitudes. God's standard of righteousness leads to painful consequences for those who choose to disobey.

God's holiness can be seen in laws we have received, as explained and demonstrated by Jesus Christ. That is, when we obey God's laws, we generally reap good results, evidence of God's love and protection. Yet when we disobey, we often reap painful consequences that naturally stem from our wrong choices, evidence of God's wrath and judgment. Both results display aspects of God's character and holiness.

At times we are like the ancient Israelites of Amos's day. We may think we are walking in God's favor, because we are going through all the motions of spirituality. We go to church, we tithe, we pray before mealtimes. But none of these things, in and of itself, is an adequate substitute for loving God from our hearts. Like the Israelites, we may think we are okay, but as Amos says, we are not. We must love the Lord our God with all our heart, our whole soul and mind, and we must love our neighbors as ourselves (see Matthew 22.37–39). If we are not doing that, we are not pleasing God, and God's righteous judgment surely will follow. But if we seek to follow God in our hearts and love our neighbors as ourselves, we will invariably experience the abundant blessings of God's love.

Going Deeper

- In what ways do you find yourself "going through the motions" of spirituality, yet lacking a real relationship with God?
- What are some visible demonstrations of God's grace and love? What are some visible demonstrations of God's displeasure and judgment?

and the offerings of well-being
of your fatted animals
I will not look upon.
23 Take away from me the noise
of your songs;
I will not listen to the
melody of your harps.
24 But let justice roll down
like waters,
and righteousness like an
ever-flowing stream.

25 Did you bring to me sacrifices
and offerings the forty years in the
wilderness, O house of Israel? 26 You
shall take up Sakkuth your king, and
Kaiwan your star-god, your images,[a]
which you made for yourselves;
27 therefore I will take you into exile
beyond Damascus, says the LORD,
whose name is the God of hosts.

COMPLACENT SELF-INDULGENCE WILL BE PUNISHED

6 Alas for those who are
at ease in Zion,
and for those who feel secure
on Mount Samaria,

◯

PONDER

Alas for those who are at ease
in Zion, and for those who feel
secure on Mount Samaria.
—Amos 6.1

PRAY

Father God, help us see that in many
ways we mirror attitudes of people in
Amos's time. We think, "We are pretty
good. We are fairly well off in the eyes
of God. We worship, so we will be
blessed." Help us to understand how
we can take Amos's warnings to heart.
Give us strength and courage to look
at our shortcomings and fallibilities,
and avail ourselves of your love and
support as we try to improve. Use us to
further your kingdom. We ask you in
the name of our gentle Savior. Amen.

---

the notables of the first
of the nations,
to whom the house of
Israel resorts!
2 Cross over to Calneh, and see;
from there go to Hamath
the great;
then go down to Gath of
the Philistines.
Are you better[b] than these
kingdoms?
Or is your[c] territory greater
than their[d] territory,
3 O you that put far away
the evil day,
and bring near a reign
of violence?

4 Alas for those who lie on
beds of ivory,
and lounge on their couches,
and eat lambs from the flock,
and calves from the stall;
5 who sing idle songs to the
sound of the harp,
and like David improvise on
instruments of music;
6 who drink wine from bowls,
and anoint themselves
with the finest oils,
but are not grieved over
the ruin of Joseph!
7 Therefore they shall now be the
first to go into exile,
and the revelry of the loungers
shall pass away.

8 The Lord GOD has sworn
by himself
(says the LORD, the God of hosts):
I abhor the pride of Jacob
and hate his strongholds;
and I will deliver up the city
and all that is in it.

9 If ten people remain in one
house, they shall die. 10 And if a relative, one who burns the dead,[e] shall
take up the body to bring it out of
the house, and shall say to someone
in the innermost parts of the house,
"Is anyone else with you?" the answer will come, "No." Then the rel-

[a] 5.26 Heb your images, your star-god
[b] 6.2 Or Are they better   [c] 6.2 Heb their
[d] 6.2 Heb your   [e] 6.10 Or who makes a
burning for him

ative[a] shall say, "Hush! We must not mention the name of the LORD."

11 See, the LORD commands,
and the great house shall
be shattered to bits,
and the little house to pieces.
12 Do horses run on rocks?
Does one plow the sea
with oxen?[b]
But you have turned justice
into poison
and the fruit of righteousness
into wormwood—
13 you who rejoice in Lo-debar,[c]
who say, "Have we not by
our own strength
taken Karnaim[d] for ourselves?"
14 Indeed, I am raising up
against you a nation,
O house of Israel, says the
LORD, the God of hosts,
and they shall oppress you
from Lebo-hamath
to the Wadi Arabah.

LOCUSTS, FIRE, AND
A PLUMB LINE

7 This is what the Lord GOD showed me: he was forming locusts at the time the latter growth began to sprout (it was the latter growth after the king's mowings). 2When they had finished eating the grass of the land, I said,
"O Lord GOD, forgive, I beg you!
How can Jacob stand?
He is so small!"
3 The LORD relented
concerning this;
"It shall not be," said the LORD.

4 This is what the Lord GOD showed me: the Lord GOD was calling for a shower of fire,[e] and it devoured the great deep and was eating up the land. 5Then I said,
"O Lord GOD, cease, I beg you!
How can Jacob stand?
He is so small!"
6 The LORD relented
concerning this;
"This also shall not be,"
said the Lord GOD.

7 This is what he showed me: the Lord was standing beside a wall built

with a plumb line, with a plumb line in his hand. 8And the LORD said to me, "Amos, what do you see?" And I said, "A plumb line." Then the Lord said,
"See, I am setting a
plumb line
in the midst of my
people Israel;
I will never again pass
them by;
9 the high places of Isaac shall
be made desolate,
and the sanctuaries of Israel
shall be laid waste,
and I will rise against the
house of Jeroboam
with the sword."

[a] 6.10 Heb *he* [b] 6.12 Or *Does one plow them with oxen* [c] 6.13 Or *in a thing of nothingness* [d] 6.13 Or *horns* [e] 7.4 Or *for a judgment by fire*

PONDER

This is what he showed me: the Lord was standing beside a wall built with a plumb line, with a plumb line in his hand. And the LORD said to me, "Amos, what do you see?" And I said, "A plumb line."
—Amos 7.7–8

PRAY

Father God, we are blessed to read the ancient words of this relatively unknown prophet, Amos, who came out of the fields to declare your will for the people of those days. With the coming of Christ, your will for us was made even more clear to us, the people of the new covenant. Transform us into the likeness of your Son. Remind us to pray constantly, to courageously reassess ourselves and consider, in our remaining years, how we can better reflect the purity and goodness of Jesus. We ask these things in our Savior's name. Amen.

AMAZIAH COMPLAINS
TO THE KING

10 Then Amaziah, the priest of Bethel, sent to King Jeroboam of Israel, saying, "Amos has conspired against you in the very center of the house of Israel; the land is not able to bear all his words. 11For thus Amos has said,

'Jeroboam shall die
    by the sword,
and Israel must go into exile
    away from his land.' "

12And Amaziah said to Amos, "O seer, go, flee away to the land of Judah, earn your bread there, and prophesy there; 13but never again prophesy at Bethel, for it is the king's sanctuary, and it is a temple of the kingdom."

14 Then Amos answered Amaziah, "I am[a] no prophet, nor a prophet's son; but I am[a] a herdsman, and a dresser of sycamore trees, 15and the LORD took me from following the flock, and the LORD said to me, 'Go, prophesy to my people Israel.'
16 "Now therefore hear the
    word of the LORD.
You say, 'Do not prophesy
    against Israel,
and do not preach against
    the house of Isaac.'
17 Therefore thus says the LORD:
'Your wife shall become a
    prostitute in the city,
and your sons and your
    daughters shall fall
    by the sword,
and your land shall be
    parceled out by line;
you yourself shall die in an
    unclean land,
and Israel shall surely go into
    exile away from its land.' "

THE BASKET OF FRUIT

8 This is what the Lord GOD showed me—a basket of summer fruit.[b] 2He said, "Amos, what do you see?" And I said, "A basket of summer fruit."[b] Then the LORD said to me,

"The end[c] has come upon
    my people Israel;
I will never again
    pass them by.

3 The songs of the temple[d]
    shall become wailings
    in that day,"
        says the Lord GOD;
"the dead bodies shall be many,
    cast out in every place.
Be silent!"

4 Hear this, you that trample
    on the needy,
and bring to ruin the
    poor of the land,
5 saying, "When will the new
    moon be over
so that we may sell grain;
and the sabbath,
    so that we may offer
    wheat for sale?
We will make the ephah small
    and the shekel great,
and practice deceit with
    false balances,
6 buying the poor for silver
and the needy for a pair
    of sandals,
and selling the sweepings
    of the wheat."

7 The LORD has sworn by the
    pride of Jacob:
Surely I will never forget
    any of their deeds.
8 Shall not the land tremble
    on this account,
and everyone mourn
    who lives in it,
and all of it rise like the Nile,
    and be tossed about and
    sink again, like the
    Nile of Egypt?

9 On that day, says the Lord GOD,
    I will make the sun go
    down at noon,
and darken the earth in
    broad daylight.
10 I will turn your feasts into
    mourning,
and all your songs into
    lamentation;
I will bring sackcloth
    on all loins,
and baldness on every head;

---

a 7.14 Or was   b 8.1,2 Heb qayits
c 8.2 Heb qets   d 8.3 Or palace

I will make it like the mourning
   for an only son,
and the end of it like
   a bitter day.

11 The time is surely coming,
   says the Lord GOD,
when I will send a famine
   on the land;
not a famine of bread, or a
   thirst for water,
but of hearing the words
   of the LORD.
12 They shall wander
   from sea to sea,
and from north to east;
they shall run to and fro, seeking
   the word of the LORD,
but they shall not find it.

13 In that day the beautiful
   young women and
   the young men
shall faint for thirst.
14 Those who swear by Ashimah
   of Samaria,
and say, "As your god
   lives, O Dan,"
and, "As the way of Beer-sheba
   lives"—
they shall fall, and never
   rise again.

THE DESTRUCTION
OF ISRAEL

9 I saw the LORD standing beside[a]
the altar, and he said:
Strike the capitals until the
   thresholds shake,
and shatter them on the
   heads of all the people;[b]
and those who are left I will
   kill with the sword;
not one of them
   shall flee away,
not one of them shall escape.

2 Though they dig into Sheol,
   from there shall my
   hand take them;
though they climb up to heaven,
   from there I will bring
   them down.
3 Though they hide themselves
   on the top of Carmel,
   from there I will search
   out and take them;

and though they hide from
   my sight at the
   bottom of the sea,
there I will command the
   sea-serpent, and it
   shall bite them.
4 And though they go into captivity
   in front of their enemies,
there I will command
   the sword, and it
   shall kill them;
and I will fix my eyes on them
   for harm and not for good.

5 The Lord, GOD of hosts,
he who touches the earth
   and it melts,
and all who live in it mourn,
and all of it rises like the Nile,
and sinks again, like the
   Nile of Egypt;
6 who builds his upper chambers
   in the heavens,
and founds his vault
   upon the earth;
who calls for the waters of the sea,
and pours them out upon the
   surface of the earth—
the LORD is his name.

7 Are you not like the
   Ethiopians[c] to me,
O people of Israel? says
   the LORD.
Did I not bring Israel up from
   the land of Egypt,
and the Philistines from
   Caphtor and the
   Arameans from Kir?
8 The eyes of the Lord GOD are upon
   the sinful kingdom,
and I will destroy it from
   the face of the earth
   —except that I will not utterly
   destroy the house of Jacob,
   says the LORD.

9 For lo, I will command,
   and shake the house of Israel
   among all the nations
as one shakes with a sieve,
but no pebble shall fall
   to the ground.

[a] 9.1 Or on   [b] 9.1 Heb all of them   [c] 9.7 Or
Nubians; Heb Cushites

10 All the sinners of my people
        shall die by the sword,
    who say, "Evil shall not
        overtake or meet us."

THE RESTORATION OF DAVID'S KINGDOM

11 On that day I will raise up
        the booth of David
        that is fallen,
    and repair its[a] breaches,
        and raise up its[b] ruins,
        and rebuild it as in the
        days of old;
12 in order that they may possess
        the remnant of Edom
    and all the nations who are
        called by my name,
    says the LORD who does this.

13 The time is surely coming,
        says the LORD,
    when the one who plows
        shall overtake the
        one who reaps,

and the treader of grapes the
        one who sows the seed;
    the mountains shall drip
        sweet wine,
    and all the hills shall
        flow with it.
14 I will restore the fortunes of
        my people Israel,
    and they shall rebuild the
        ruined cities and
        inhabit them;
    they shall plant vineyards and
        drink their wine,
    and they shall make gardens
        and eat their fruit.
15 I will plant them upon their land,
    and they shall never again
        be plucked up
    out of the land that I
        have given them,
        says the LORD your God.

a 9.11 Gk: Heb *their*   b 9.11 Gk: Heb *his*

OBADIAH

Remember Jacob and Esau from Genesis? The Edomites (descendants of Esau) still haven't forgiven Jacob for stealing Esau's birthright. So they gloat when Israel (descendants of Jacob) is devastated by foreign powers. Then Obadiah enters the picture, rebuking the Edomites for their pride and announcing that they will be destroyed for their attitude and actions. Obadiah further declares that the Lord will deliver Israel, resulting in victory for the kingdom of God.

PROUD EDOM WILL BE BROUGHT LOW

1 The vision of Obadiah.

Thus says the Lord GOD
   concerning Edom:
We have heard a report
   from the LORD,
and a messenger has been sent
   among the nations:
"Rise up! Let us rise against
   it for battle!"
2 I will surely make you least
   among the nations;
   you shall be utterly despised.
3 Your proud heart has deceived you,
   you that live in the clefts
      of the rock,[a]
   whose dwelling is in the heights.
You say in your heart,
   "Who will bring me down
      to the ground?"
4 Though you soar aloft like the eagle,
   though your nest is set
      among the stars,
   from there I will bring
      you down,
                    says the LORD.

PILLAGE AND SLAUGHTER WILL REPAY EDOM'S CRUELTY

5 If thieves came to you,
   if plunderers by night
   —how you have been
      destroyed!—
   would they not steal only
      what they wanted?

If grape-gatherers came to you,
   would they not leave
      gleanings?
6 How Esau has been pillaged,
   his treasures searched out!
7 All your allies have deceived you,
   they have driven you
      to the border;
your confederates have
      prevailed against you;
   those who ate[b] your bread
      have set a trap for you—
   there is no understanding of it.
8 On that day, says the LORD,
   I will destroy the wise
      out of Edom,
   and understanding out
      of Mount Esau.
9 Your warriors shall be
      shattered, O Teman,
   so that everyone from Mount
      Esau will be cut off.

EDOM MISTREATED HIS BROTHER

10 For the slaughter and
      violence done to your
      brother Jacob,
   shame shall cover you,
   and you shall be cut off forever.
11 On the day that you stood aside,
   on the day that strangers
      carried off his wealth,

[a] 3 Or clefts of Sela   [b] 7 Cn: Heb lacks those who ate

⊣ BIBLE IN LIFE ▷   ⊕

A Need for Change   Obadiah 3–4

Ultimately, God does not allow people to get away with pride. God abhors pride (see Proverbs 8.13; Amos 6.8). The sins of pride and self-satisfaction cause us to think that we've got it made, that we're good enough, and that we are superior to other people, that we're fortunate because God recognizes our special worth. When we are filled with pride, we are blinded to our need for change. But through times of adversity or weakness, we are often stripped of our pride, and we have the opportunity to acknowledge the need for growth in our faith. When we are weak and destitute—when we have failed, when we face a tragedy or deep loss, when we are frustrated with our own lives—then we can look at ourselves and see our need for Christ. Paul says, "Therefore I am content with weaknesses, insults, hardships, persecutions, and calamities for the sake of Christ; for whenever I am weak, then I am strong" (2 Corinthians 12.10). God doesn't just automatically change us; we must have the desire to change and grow. May we not be deceived by our pride into thinking that we are strong and invincible, as the Edomites did. Instead, let us repent of our pride and humble ourselves.

and foreigners entered his gates
and cast lots for Jerusalem,
you too were like
one of them.
12 But you should not
have gloated[a] over[b]
your brother
on the day of his misfortune;
you should not have rejoiced
over the people of Judah
on the day of their ruin;
you should not have boasted
on the day of distress.
13 You should not have entered
the gate of my people
on the day of their calamity;
you should not have joined
in the gloating over
Judah's[c] disaster
on the day of his calamity;
you should not have looted
his goods
on the day of his calamity.
14 You should not have stood
at the crossings
to cut off his fugitives;
you should not have handed
over his survivors
on the day of distress.

15 For the day of the LORD is near
against all the nations.
As you have done, it shall
be done to you;
your deeds shall return on
your own head.
16 For as you have drunk on my
holy mountain,
all the nations around
you shall drink;
they shall drink and gulp down,[d]
and shall be as though they
had never been.

ISRAEL'S FINAL TRIUMPH

17 But on Mount Zion there shall
be those that escape,
and it shall be holy;
and the house of Jacob shall take
possession of those who
dispossessed them.
18 The house of Jacob shall be a fire,
the house of Joseph a flame,
and the house of Esau stubble;
they shall burn them and
consume them,
and there shall be no survivor
of the house of Esau;
for the LORD has spoken.
19 Those of the Negeb shall
possess Mount Esau,
and those of the Shephelah the
land of the Philistines;
they shall possess the land
of Ephraim and the
land of Samaria,
and Benjamin shall
possess Gilead.
20 The exiles of the Israelites
who are in Halah[e]
shall possess[f] Phoenicia as
far as Zarephath;
and the exiles of Jerusalem
who are in Sepharad
shall possess the towns
of the Negeb.
21 Those who have been saved[g] shall
go up to Mount Zion
to rule Mount Esau;
and the kingdom shall
be the LORD's.

---

[a] 12 Heb *But do not gloat* (and similarly through verse 14)   [b] 12 Heb *on the day of*   [c] 13 Heb *his*   [d] 16 Meaning of Heb uncertain   [e] 20 Cn: Heb *in this army*   [f] 20 Cn: Meaning of Heb uncertain   [g] 21 Or *Saviors*

JONAH

Have you ever been in a situation when you knew God wanted you to do something, but instead of obeying, you tried to hide? If so, you and Jonah would connect. Jonah tried to refuse God's call, but later he got angry when God didn't do what he expected. Despite Jonah's resistance, God used him to demonstrate mercy to Nineveh. Through Jonah's story we see that God goes to great lengths to pursue people, and he responds with compassion and forgiveness when they return in repentance and faith.

JONAH TRIES TO RUN AWAY FROM GOD

1 Now the word of the LORD came to Jonah son of Amittai, saying, [2] "Go at once to Nineveh, that great city, and cry out against it; for their wickedness has come up before me." [3] But Jonah set out to flee to Tarshish from the presence of the LORD. He went down to Joppa and found a ship going to Tarshish; so he paid his fare and went on board, to go with them to Tarshish, away from the presence of the LORD.

PONDER

Now the word of the LORD came to Jonah son of Amittai, saying, "Go at once to Nineveh, that great city, and cry out against it; for their wickedness has come up before me."
—Jonah 1.1–2

PRAY

Dear Father, sometimes we have to stretch our souls to comprehend the message that you give us in your Holy Word. Even in strange stories like that of Jonah, we ask that you enlighten us and draw us closer to Jesus Christ. Teach us to follow the teachings in your Word. Convict us of the vestiges of racial discrimination or ethnic distinctions we hold on to and to confess those attitudes that separate us from you and others. As we become more generous and more humble, help us to look upon all people, regardless of their status in life, as equals because they are equal in your eyes. We are thankful to you for your grace, love and forgiveness. We ask all this in the name of our Savior, Jesus Christ. Amen.

---

[4] But the LORD hurled a great wind upon the sea, and such a mighty storm came upon the sea that the ship threatened to break up. [5] Then the mariners were afraid, and each cried to his god. They threw the cargo that was in the ship into the sea, to lighten it for them. Jonah, meanwhile, had gone down into the hold of the ship and had lain down, and was fast asleep. [6] The captain came and said to him, "What are you doing sound asleep? Get up, call on your god! Perhaps the god will spare us a thought so that we do not perish."

[7] The sailors[a] said to one another, "Come, let us cast lots, so that we may know on whose account this calamity has come upon us." So they cast lots, and the lot fell on Jonah. [8] Then they said to him, "Tell us why this calamity has come upon us. What is your occupation? Where do you come from? What is your country? And of what people are you?" [9] "I am a Hebrew," he replied. "I worship the LORD, the God of heaven, who made the sea and the dry land." [10] Then the men were even more afraid, and said to him, "What is this that you have done!" For the men knew that he was fleeing from the presence of the LORD, because he had told them so.

[11] Then they said to him, "What shall we do to you, that the sea may quiet down for us?" For the sea was growing more and more tempestuous. [12] He said to them, "Pick me up and throw me into the sea; then the sea will quiet down for you; for I know it is because of me that this great storm has come upon you." [13] Nevertheless the men rowed hard to bring the ship back to land, but they could not, for the sea grew more and more stormy against them. [14] Then they cried out to the LORD, "Please, O LORD, we pray, do not let us perish on account of this man's life. Do not make us guilty of innocent blood; for you, O LORD, have done as it pleased you." [15] So they picked Jonah up and threw him into the sea; and the sea ceased from its raging. [16] Then the men feared the LORD even more, and they offered a sacrifice to the LORD and made vows.

---

[a] 1.7 Heb *They*

17ª But the LORD provided a large fish to swallow up Jonah; and Jonah was in the belly of the fish three days and three nights.

A PSALM OF THANKSGIVING

2 Then Jonah prayed to the LORD his God from the belly of the fish, ²saying,
"I called to the LORD out
of my distress,
and he answered me;
out of the belly of Sheol I cried,
and you heard my voice.
³ You cast me into the deep,
into the heart of the seas,
and the flood surrounded me;
all your waves and your billows
passed over me.
⁴ Then I said, 'I am driven away
from your sight;
howᵇ shall I look again
upon your holy temple?'
⁵ The waters closed in over me;
the deep surrounded me;
weeds were wrapped
around my head
⁶ at the roots of the mountains.
I went down to the land
whose bars closed upon
me forever;
yet you brought up my life
from the Pit,
O LORD my God.
⁷ As my life was ebbing away,
I remembered the LORD;
and my prayer came to you,
into your holy temple.
⁸ Those who worship vain idols
forsake their true loyalty.
⁹ But I with the voice of
thanksgiving
will sacrifice to you;
what I have vowed I will pay.
Deliverance belongs
to the LORD!"
¹⁰Then the LORD spoke to the fish, and it spewed Jonah out upon the dry land.

CONVERSION OF NINEVEH

3 The word of the LORD came to Jonah a second time, saying,
²"Get up, go to Nineveh, that great city, and proclaim to it the message that I tell you." ³So Jonah set out and went to Nineveh, according to the word of the LORD. Now Nineveh was an exceedingly large city, a three days' walk across. ⁴Jonah began to go into the city, going a day's walk. And he cried out, "Forty days more, and Nineveh shall be overthrown!" ⁵And the people of Nineveh believed God; they proclaimed a fast, and everyone, great and small, put on sackcloth.

⁶When the news reached the king of Nineveh, he rose from his throne, removed his robe, covered himself with sackcloth, and sat in ashes. ⁷Then he had a proclamation made in Nineveh: "By the decree of the king and his nobles: No human being or animal, no herd or flock, shall taste anything. They shall not feed, nor shall they drink water. ⁸Human beings and animals shall be covered with sackcloth, and they shall cry mightily to God. All shall turn from their evil ways and from the violence that is in their hands. ⁹Who knows? God may relent and change his mind; he may turn from his fierce anger, so that we do not perish."

¹⁰When God saw what they did, how they turned from their evil ways, God changed his mind about the calamity that he had said he would bring upon them; and he did not do it.

WE SHOULD NOT CONSIDER
THE FAILURE OF OTHERS AS
FINAL. GOD'S GRACE AND
LOVE ARE FOR ALL PEOPLE.

JONAH'S ANGER

4 But this was very displeasing to Jonah, and he became angry. ²He prayed to the LORD and said, "O LORD! Is not this what I said

ª **1.17** Ch 2.1 in Heb   ᵇ **2.4** Theodotion: Heb *surely*

GRACE AND REDEMPTION

When God saw what they did, how they turned from their evil ways, God changed his mind about the calamity that he had said he would bring upon them; and he did not do it. But this was very displeasing to Jonah, and he became angry.

—Jonah 3.10—4.1

When you ask most people what the story of Jonah is about, they remember the part about the big fish, but few people realize that this element of the drama is really not the focus of the story. It is simply the means God used to save Jonah and give him another chance to carry out the mission for which God had called him. The real meaning of the story has much more to do with God's redemptive grace toward outcast sinners—little of which seemed to be found in Jonah's heart. By the time of Jonah (about 780 years before the time of Jesus), the nation of Assyria had established itself as a fierce and formidable power in the region northeast of Israel. The prophet Nahum later described their capital city of Nineveh as a hotbed of hatred, cruelty and oppression. From the perspective of Israel and of Jonah, Nineveh had no redeeming or redeemable features. It was to these people that the Lord called Jonah to prophesy, and by prophesying to the people of Nineveh, Jonah would actually be giving them a chance to repent and avoid God's wrath.

Jonah refused to obey God's call and chose instead to spend a great deal of money to buy a ticket to Tarshish—the equivalent of the end of the earth in the ancient world. In other words, Jonah was trying to get as far out of God's reach as possible. It seems that the last thing Jonah wanted was to give the Assyrians any opportunity to repent and experience God's forgiveness and grace.

Jonah's response to God's call should not surprise us very much, though, because if we are honest, we will likely find that we are not that much different. We all harbor attitudes of prejudice and we all have a favorite grudge. We want God to be merciful to us but not so much to our enemies. We tend to look down on others because of the color of their skin or because they have AIDS or because they are poor or from another country. We tend to think that we're a little better than those people, that we somehow deserve God's blessing more than they do. Yet these are the kinds of people—despised Samaritans, feared lepers, destitute widows—that Jesus himself specifically reached out to know and to help. The teachings of Jesus and the apostles make it clear that God extends mercy and grace to people from every nation, no matter their color, gender or social stratum; no one person is more deserving of God's grace than another.

Going Deeper

- If God were to call you to reach out to a group of people with whom you felt uncomfortable or actually disliked, what kind of people might that include?
- What makes someone more deserving of God's grace and forgiveness than another? How does this relate to what Jesus and the apostles taught about God's love for people?

while I was still in my own country? That is why I fled to Tarshish at the beginning; for I knew that you are a gracious God and merciful, slow to anger, and abounding in steadfast love, and ready to relent from punishing. ³And now, O LORD, please take my life from me, for it is better for me to die than to live." ⁴And the

---

PONDER

But this was very displeasing to Jonah, and he became angry . . . And the LORD said, "Is it right for you to be angry?"
—Jonah 4.1,4

PRAY

O Father, we sometimes struggle through the books of the Old Testament, and we confess that sometimes we don't pay much attention to what they say. We are thankful for Jonah and for his experiences, which show us your heart of love and compassion. Help us search our minds and hearts in moments of quiet prayer and decide how we can be more Christlike in our own lives, never forgetting that you are reaching to us with forgiveness, reconciliation and love. We ask these things in the name of Jesus Christ, our Savior. Amen.

LORD said, "Is it right for you to be angry?" ⁵Then Jonah went out of the city and sat down east of the city, and made a booth for himself there. He sat under it in the shade, waiting to see what would become of the city.

⁶ The LORD God appointed a bush,ᵃ and made it come up over Jonah, to give shade over his head, to save him from his discomfort; so Jonah was very happy about the bush. ⁷But when dawn came up the next day, God appointed a worm that attacked the bush, so that it withered. ⁸When the sun rose, God prepared a sultry east wind, and the sun beat down on the head of Jonah so that he was faint and asked that he might die. He said, "It is better for me to die than to live."

JONAH IS REPROVED

⁹ But God said to Jonah, "Is it right for you to be angry about the bush?" And he said, "Yes, angry enough to die." ¹⁰Then the LORD said, "You are concerned about the bush, for which you did not labor and which you did not grow; it came into being in a night and perished in a night. ¹¹And should I not be concerned about Nineveh, that great city, in which there are more than a hundred and twenty thousand persons who do not know their right hand from their left, and also many animals?"

ᵃ 4.6 Heb *qiqayon*, possibly *the castor bean plant*

MICAH

Nothing eats away at the fabric of a nation like social injustice and empty spirituality. When the rich get richer at the expense of the less powerful, when political leaders accept bribes, when spiritual leaders lead others astray, God takes notice—and isn't pleased. The prophet Micah lived during a time when the Israelites experienced all these things, and his message to them resounds with judgment. Yet Micah also provides a message of hope—hope of deliverance, comfort and forgiveness through the coming Messiah.

1

The word of the LORD that came to Micah of Moresheth in the days of Kings Jotham, Ahaz, and Hezekiah of Judah, which he saw concerning Samaria and Jerusalem.

JUDGMENT PRONOUNCED AGAINST SAMARIA

2 Hear, you peoples, all of you;
    listen, O earth, and all
        that is in it;
and let the Lord GOD be a
        witness against you,
    the Lord from his holy temple.
3 For lo, the LORD is coming
    out of his place,
    and will come down and
        tread upon the high
        places of the earth.
4 Then the mountains will
        melt under him
    and the valleys will
        burst open,
like wax near the fire,
    like waters poured down
        a steep place.
5 All this is for the transgression
        of Jacob
    and for the sins of the
        house of Israel.
What is the transgression
        of Jacob?
    Is it not Samaria?
And what is the high
        place[a] of Judah?
    Is it not Jerusalem?
6 Therefore I will make Samaria a
        heap in the open country,
    a place for planting vineyards.
I will pour down her stones
        into the valley,
    and uncover her foundations.
7 All her images shall be
        beaten to pieces,
    all her wages shall be
        burned with fire,
    and all her idols I will
        lay waste;
for as the wages of a prostitute
        she gathered them,
and as the wages of a prostitute
        they shall again be used.

THE DOOM OF THE CITIES OF JUDAH

8 For this I will lament and wail;
    I will go barefoot and naked;
I will make lamentation
    like the jackals,
    and mourning like
        the ostriches.
9 For her wound[b] is incurable.
    It has come to Judah;
it has reached to the gate
        of my people,
    to Jerusalem.

10 Tell it not in Gath,
    weep not at all;
in Beth-leaphrah
    roll yourselves in the dust.
11 Pass on your way,
    inhabitants of Shaphir,
    in nakedness and shame;
the inhabitants of Zaanan
    do not come forth;
Beth-ezel is wailing
    and shall remove its
        support from you.
12 For the inhabitants of Maroth
    wait anxiously for good,
yet disaster has come down
        from the LORD
    to the gate of Jerusalem.
13 Harness the steeds to
        the chariots,
    inhabitants of Lachish;
it was the beginning of sin
    to daughter Zion,
for in you were found
    the transgressions
        of Israel.
14 Therefore you shall give
        parting gifts
    to Moresheth-gath;
the houses of Achzib shall
        be a deception
    to the kings of Israel.
15 I will again bring a conqueror
        upon you,
    inhabitants of Mareshah;
the glory of Israel
    shall come to Adullam.
16 Make yourselves bald and
        cut off your hair
    for your pampered
        children;
make yourselves as bald
        as the eagle,
for they have gone from
        you into exile.

[a] 1.5 Heb *what are the high places*   [b] 1.9 Gk Syr Vg: Heb *wounds*

SOCIAL EVILS DENOUNCED

2 Alas for those who devise
    wickedness
and evil deeds[a] on their beds!
When the morning dawns,
    they perform it,
    because it is in their power.
2 They covet fields, and seize them;
    houses, and take them away;
they oppress householder
    and house,
    people and their inheritance.
3 Therefore thus says the LORD:
Now, I am devising against
    this family an evil
from which you cannot
    remove your necks;
and you shall not walk haughtily,
    for it will be an evil time.
4 On that day they shall take up a
    taunt song against you,
    and wail with bitter
        lamentation,
and say, "We are utterly ruined;
    the LORD[b] alters the
        inheritance of my people;
how he removes it from me!
    Among our captors[c] he
        parcels out our fields."
5 Therefore you will have no one
    to cast the line by lot
    in the assembly of the LORD.

6 "Do not preach"—thus
    they preach—
"one should not preach
    of such things;
disgrace will not overtake us."
7 Should this be said, O house
    of Jacob?
    Is the LORD's patience
        exhausted?
    Are these his doings?
Do not my words do good
    to one who walks uprightly?
8 But you rise up against my
    people[d] as an enemy;
    you strip the robe from
        the peaceful,[e]
from those who pass by trustingly
    with no thought of war.
9 The women of my people
    you drive out
    from their pleasant houses;
from their young children
    you take away
    my glory forever.

10 Arise and go;
    for this is no place to rest,
because of uncleanness
    that destroys
    with a grievous destruction.[f]
11 If someone were to go about
    uttering empty
        falsehoods,
saying, "I will preach to you of
    wine and strong drink,"
such a one would be the
    preacher for this people!

A PROMISE FOR THE
REMNANT OF ISRAEL

12 I will surely gather all of
    you, O Jacob,
    I will gather the survivors
        of Israel;
I will set them together
    like sheep in a fold,
like a flock in its pasture;
    it will resound with people.
13 The one who breaks out will
    go up before them;
    they will break through
        and pass the gate,
    going out by it.
Their king will pass on
    before them,
    the LORD at their head.

WICKED RULERS AND PROPHETS

3 And I said:
    Listen, you heads of Jacob
    and rulers of the house
        of Israel!
Should you not know justice?—
2   you who hate the good
        and love the evil,
who tear the skin off my people,[g]
    and the flesh off their bones;
3 who eat the flesh of my people,
    flay their skin off them,
break their bones in pieces,
    and chop them up like
        meat[h] in a kettle,
    like flesh in a caldron.

4 Then they will cry to the LORD,
    but he will not answer them;

a 2.1 Cn: Heb *work evil*   b 2.4 Heb *he*
c 2.4 Cn: Heb *the rebellious*   d 2.8 Cn:
Heb *But yesterday my people rose*
e 2.8 Cn: Heb *from before a garment*
f 2.10 Meaning of Heb uncertain   g 3.2 Heb
from them   h 3.3 Gk: Heb *as*

he will hide his face from
them at that time,
because they have acted
wickedly.

5 Thus says the LORD concerning
the prophets
who lead my people astray,
who cry "Peace"
when they have
something to eat,
but declare war against those
who put nothing into
their mouths.

6 Therefore it shall be night to
you, without vision,
and darkness to you,
without revelation.
The sun shall go down upon
the prophets,
and the day shall be
black over them;

7 the seers shall be disgraced,
and the diviners
put to shame;
they shall all cover their lips,
for there is no answer
from God.

8 But as for me, I am filled
with power,
with the spirit of the LORD,
and with justice and might,
to declare to Jacob his
transgression
and to Israel his sin.

9 Hear this, you rulers of the
house of Jacob
and chiefs of the house
of Israel,
who abhor justice
and pervert all equity,

10 who build Zion with blood
and Jerusalem with wrong!

11 Its rulers give judgment
for a bribe,
its priests teach for a price,
its prophets give oracles
for money;
yet they lean upon the
LORD and say,
"Surely the LORD is with us!
No harm shall
come upon us."

12 Therefore because of you
Zion shall be plowed
as a field;

PONDER

Hear this, you rulers of the house
of Jacob and chiefs of the house
of Israel, who abhor justice and
pervert all equity, who build Zion with
blood and Jerusalem with wrong!
—Micah 3.9–10

PRAY

Holy God, we read of the ancient
prophets and how they condemned
the wickedness in their society. We ask
you for courage to hear their call for
justice, righteousness, compassion, love
and service, for it is the same call Jesus
made so vividly to us. We pray that we
might have the courage to open our
hearts and to incorporate what we've
learned and to see how we might be
closer to you. We worship in the name
of Jesus Christ, our Savior. Amen.

Jerusalem shall become a
heap of ruins,
and the mountain of the
house a wooded height.

PEACE AND SECURITY THROUGH OBEDIENCE

4 In days to come
the mountain of the
LORD's house
shall be established as the highest
of the mountains,
and shall be raised up
above the hills.
Peoples shall stream to it,
2 and many nations shall
come and say:
"Come, let us go up to the
mountain of the LORD,
to the house of the God of Jacob;
that he may teach us his ways
and that we may walk
in his paths."
For out of Zion shall go
forth instruction,
and the word of the LORD
from Jerusalem.

NOT AN INSURANCE POLICY

Its rulers give judgment for a bribe, its priests teach for a price, its prophets give oracles for money; yet they lean upon the LORD and say, "Surely the LORD is with us! No harm shall come upon us."

—Micah 3.11

Like so many other prophets in the days of ancient Israel, Micah was deeply troubled by the sins he saw all around him. There was plenty of religion—that is, plenty of rituals and spiritual practice. But at the same time, people took advantage of each other, and leaders—both spiritual and political—offered their services to the highest bidder. All this was done with the knowledge that it was wrong, but the people didn't seem to care. As Micah says, they reasoned that the Lord was among them, so surely no real harm would ever come to them for their sins.

In essence, God seemed to be regarded by the Israelites as a sort of insurance policy. The people paid the premiums of temple attendance, sacrifices and public prayer, and they expected God to repay them with security, health and material blessing. No examination of their heart's motives was necessary. Sincerity in worship was optional.

Before we condemn the Israelites too harshly, though, we should look at ourselves. How often do we assess our own lives to see how we measure up to the perfect standards of Jesus? We tend to become self-satisfied in our spiritual walk and fail to move out of the cocoon we have built around ourselves. We go to church, give money to charity, and even pray in public now and then, but our spirituality may pretty much stop there. We excuse habitual sins. We don't really seek God in Bible study and personal prayer. We don't reach out to those who are less fortunate than us or stretch ourselves to love those who are different from us. We mistakenly think that since we have accepted Jesus Christ as our Savior, we're pretty much okay with God. No need to worry about God getting upset about a few little indulgences. No need to go to extremes with our faith.

Such flippancy is a grave insult to God. It is as if we believe God can be bribed into acquiescence. It fails to recognize God's true greatness and our ultimate accountability in all things. Instead of using our faith to justify complacency, we should constantly strive to emulate Jesus Christ. We should periodically take time to assess how well our lives match up against his life, our values against his values. Are we befriending the outcast? Are we reaching out to the needy? Are we striving to grow in our understanding of God? We must not treat God like an insurance policy, but rather as the Lord of our lives.

Going Deeper

- Would people who know you well describe you as a person who constantly seeks to grow in your personal faith? Why or why not?
- What are some ways you can help guard against becoming complacent in your faith?

3 He shall judge between
   many peoples,
   and shall arbitrate between
      strong nations far away;
   they shall beat their swords
      into plowshares,
   and their spears into
      pruning hooks;
   nation shall not lift up sword
      against nation,
   neither shall they learn
      war any more;
4 but they shall all sit under their
      own vines and under
      their own fig trees,
   and no one shall make
      them afraid;
   for the mouth of the LORD
      of hosts has spoken.

5 For all the peoples walk,
      each in the name
      of its god,
   but we will walk in the name
      of the LORD our God
      forever and ever.

RESTORATION PROMISED AFTER EXILE

6 In that day, says the LORD,
   I will assemble the lame
   and gather those who have
      been driven away,
   and those whom I
      have afflicted.
7 The lame I will make the
      remnant,
   and those who were cast
      off, a strong nation;
   and the LORD will reign over
      them in Mount Zion
   now and forevermore.

8 And you, O tower
      of the flock,
   hill of daughter Zion,
   to you it shall come,
      the former dominion
      shall come,
   the sovereignty of daughter
      Jerusalem.

9 Now why do you cry aloud?
   Is there no king in you?
   Has your counselor perished,
      that pangs have seized you
      like a woman in labor?

10 Writhe and groan,[a]
      O daughter Zion,
   like a woman in labor;
   for now you shall go forth
      from the city
   and camp in the open country;
      you shall go to Babylon.
   There you shall be rescued,
      there the LORD will
      redeem you
   from the hands of your
      enemies.

11 Now many nations
      are assembled against you,
   saying, "Let her be profaned,
      and let our eyes gaze
      upon Zion."
12 But they do not know
      the thoughts of the LORD;
   they do not understand his plan,
      that he has gathered them
      as sheaves to the
      threshing floor.
13 Arise and thresh,
      O daughter Zion,
   for I will make your horn iron
      and your hoofs bronze;
   you shall beat in pieces
      many peoples,
   and shall[b] devote their
      gain to the LORD,
   their wealth to the Lord
      of the whole earth.

5 [c] Now you are walled around
      with a wall;[d]
   siege is laid against us;
   with a rod they strike the
      ruler of Israel
      upon the cheek.

THE RULER FROM BETHLEHEM

2 [e] But you, O Bethlehem of
      Ephrathah,
   who are one of the little
      clans of Judah,
   from you shall come forth for me
      one who is to rule in Israel,
   whose origin is from of old,
      from ancient days.

a 4.10 Meaning of Heb uncertain   b 4.13 Gk
Syr Tg: Heb *and I will*   c 5.1 Ch 4.14 in
Heb   d 5.1 Cn Compare Gk: Meaning of Heb
uncertain   e 5.2 Ch 5.1 in Heb

PONDER

But you, O Bethlehem of Ephrathah,
who are one of the little clans of Judah,
from you shall come forth for me one
who is to rule in Israel, whose origin
is from of old, from ancient days.
—Micah 5.2

PRAY

Eternal God, you have graciously
given us the words of Micah, Isaiah,
Luke, Matthew, Mark and John, which
all confirm the same true story of
the coming of the Messiah. Let these
stories shape our lives as we celebrate
the human birth of our Savior, Jesus
Christ. Keep these thoughts in our
hearts to remember the exalted and
divine nature of Jesus the Messiah
who came to earth as a child, while
also remembering the humility of
Jesus the Christ, who died for us. We
praise you as we ask these things in
the name of Jesus Christ. Amen.

3 Therefore he shall give them
    up until the time
   when she who is in labor
    has brought forth;
   then the rest of his kindred
    shall return
   to the people of Israel.
4 And he shall stand and feed his
    flock in the strength
    of the LORD,
   in the majesty of the name
    of the LORD his God.
   And they shall live secure, for
    now he shall be great
   to the ends of the earth;
5 and he shall be the
    one of peace.

   If the Assyrians come
    into our land
   and tread upon our soil,ᵃ
   we will raise against them
    seven shepherds
   and eight installed as rulers.

6 They shall rule the land of
    Assyria with the sword,
   and the land of Nimrod with
    the drawn sword;ᵇ
   theyᶜ shall rescue us from
    the Assyrians
   if they come into our land
   or tread within our border.

THE FUTURE ROLE OF
THE REMNANT

7 Then the remnant of Jacob,
   surrounded by many peoples,
   shall be like dew from the LORD,
   like showers on the grass,
   which do not depend upon people
   or wait for any mortal.
8 And among the nations the
    remnant of Jacob,
   surrounded by many peoples,
   shall be like a lion among the
    animals of the forest,
   like a young lion among
    the flocks of sheep,
   which, when it goes through,
    treads down
   and tears in pieces, with
    no one to deliver.
9 Your hand shall be lifted up
    over your adversaries,
   and all your enemies
    shall be cut off.

10 In that day, says the LORD,
   I will cut off your horses
    from among you
   and will destroy your chariots;
11 and I will cut off the cities
    of your land
   and throw down all your
    strongholds;
12 and I will cut off sorceries
    from your hand,
   and you shall have no
    more soothsayers;
13 and I will cut off your images
   and your pillars from
    among you,
   and you shall bow down no more
    to the work of your hands;
14 and I will uproot your sacred
    polesᵈ from among you
   and destroy your towns.

ᵃ 5.5 Gk: Heb in our palaces ᵇ 5.6 Cn: Heb
in its entrances ᶜ 5.6 Heb he ᵈ 5.14 Heb
Asherim

15 And in anger and wrath I will
  execute vengeance
  on the nations that
  did not obey.

GOD CHALLENGES ISRAEL

6 Hear what the LORD says:
  Rise, plead your case before
  the mountains,
  and let the hills hear
  your voice.
2 Hear, you mountains, the
  controversy
  of the LORD,
  and you enduring foundations
  of the earth;
  for the LORD has a controversy
  with his people,
  and he will contend
  with Israel.

3 "O my people, what have
  I done to you?
  In what have I wearied
  you? Answer me!
4 For I brought you up from
  the land of Egypt,
  and redeemed you from
  the house of slavery;
  and I sent before you Moses,
  Aaron, and Miriam.
5 O my people, remember now
  what King Balak of
  Moab devised,
  what Balaam son of Beor
  answered him,

and what happened from
  Shittim to Gilgal,
  that you may know the saving
  acts of the LORD."

WHAT GOD REQUIRES

6 "With what shall I come
  before the LORD,
  and bow myself before
  God on high?
  Shall I come before him with
  burnt offerings,
  with calves a year old?
7 Will the LORD be pleased with
  thousands of rams,
  with ten thousands of
  rivers of oil?
  Shall I give my firstborn for
  my transgression,
  the fruit of my body for
  the sin of my soul?"
8 He has told you, O mortal,
  what is good;
  and what does the LORD
  require of you
  but to do justice, and to
  love kindness,
  and to walk humbly
  with your God?

CHEATING AND VIOLENCE TO BE PUNISHED

9 The voice of the LORD
  cries to the city
  (it is sound wisdom to
  fear your name):

⊢ BIBLE IN LIFE ▷

What God Requires

Micah 6.8

Many of us had parents who expected standards of behavior or achievements we could never meet, which may have led to a breakdown in our relationship with them. Or perhaps we are the demanding parents who have required too much of our children. Sometimes a similar relationship breakdown occurs between God and ourselves, and we may feel that we are alienated from God because we can't meet God's perfect standards of holiness. We know about the sacrifice of Jesus Christ and the support of the Holy Spirit, yet because we feel inadequate, we can't really form an intimate and constant relationship. An element of guilt or shame keeps us from God. Well, what does God expect of us? In my inaugural address as president, I quoted Micah's overriding, transcendent standard for our lives: "To do justice, and to love kindness, and to walk humbly with your God" (verse 8). This crystallizes the essence of our faith and makes it attainable. Are we able to do this? If we live up to these standards, we can live a life pleasing to God.

Hear, O tribe and assembly
of the city!ᵃ
10 Can I forgetᵇ the treasures
of wickedness in the
house of the wicked,
and the scant measure
that is accursed?
11 Can I tolerate wicked scales
and a bag of dishonest
weights?
12 Yourᶜ wealthy are full of violence;
yourᵈ inhabitants speak lies,
with tongues of deceit
in their mouths.
13 Therefore I have begunᵉ to
strike you down,
making you desolate
because of your sins.
14 You shall eat, but not be satisfied,
and there shall be a gnawing
hunger within you;
you shall put away, but not save,
and what you save, I will
hand over to the sword.
15 You shall sow, but not reap;
you shall tread olives, but not
anoint yourselves with oil;
you shall tread grapes, but
not drink wine.
16 For you have kept the
statutes of Omriᶠ
and all the works of the
house of Ahab,
and you have followed
their counsels.
Therefore I will make you
a desolation, and
yourᵍ inhabitants an
object of hissing;
so you shall bear the scorn
of my people.

THE TOTAL CORRUPTION
OF THE PEOPLE

7 Woe is me! For I have become
like one who,
after the summer fruit has
been gathered,
after the vintage has
been gleaned,
finds no cluster to eat;
there is no first-ripe fig for
which I hunger.
2 The faithful have disappeared
from the land,
and there is no one left
who is upright;

they all lie in wait for blood,
and they hunt each
other with nets.
3 Their hands are skilled to do evil;
the official and the judge
ask for a bribe,
and the powerful dictate
what they desire;
thus they pervert justice.ʰ
4 The best of them is like a brier,
the most upright of them
a thorn hedge.
The day of theirⁱ sentinels, of
theirⁱ punishment,
has come;
now their confusion is at hand.
5 Put no trust in a friend,
have no confidence in
a loved one;
guard the doors of your mouth
from her who lies in
your embrace;
6 for the son treats the father
with contempt,
the daughter rises up
against her mother,
the daughter-in-law against
her mother-in-law;
your enemies are members of
your own household.
7 But as for me, I will look
to the LORD,
I will wait for the God
of my salvation;
my God will hear me.

PENITENCE AND TRUST IN GOD
8 Do not rejoice over me,
O my enemy;
when I fall, I shall rise;
when I sit in darkness,
the LORD will be a
light to me.
9 I must bear the indignation
of the LORD,
because I have sinned
against him,
until he takes my side
and executes judgment for me.

ᵃ 6.9 Cn Compare Gk: Heb tribe, and who has appointed it yet? ᵇ 6.10 Cn: Meaning of Heb uncertain ᶜ 6.12 Heb Whose ᵈ 6.12 Heb whose ᵉ 6.13 Gk Syr Vg: Heb have made sick ᶠ 6.16 Gk Syr Vg Tg: Heb the statutes of Omri are kept ᵍ 6.16 Heb its ʰ 7.3 Cn: Heb they weave it ⁱ 7.4 Heb your

He will bring me out to the light;
    I shall see his vindication.
10 Then my enemy will see,
    and shame will cover her
      who said to me,
    "Where is the LORD your God?"
My eyes will see her downfall;[a]
    now she will be trodden down
    like the mire of the streets.

A BISHOP ONCE TOLD ME,

"I HOPE YOU ARE NOT

GOING TO LET COMPASSION

REPLACE JUSTICE." I DON'T

REALLY KNOW WHAT HE

MEANT, BUT TO ME THE

TWO ARE INSEPARABLE.

A PROPHECY OF RESTORATION
11 A day for the building of
    your walls!
    In that day the boundary
      shall be far extended.
12 In that day they will come to you
    from Assyria to[b] Egypt,
    and from Egypt to the River,
    from sea to sea and from
      mountain to mountain.
13 But the earth will be desolate
    because of its inhabitants,
    for the fruit of their doings.

14 Shepherd your people
    with your staff,
    the flock that belongs to you,
which lives alone in a forest
    in the midst of a garden land;
let them feed in Bashan
    and Gilead
    as in the days of old.

15 As in the days when you came
      out of the land of Egypt,
    show us[c] marvelous things.
16 The nations shall see and
      be ashamed
    of all their might;
they shall lay their hands
    on their mouths;
    their ears shall be deaf;
17 they shall lick dust
    like a snake,
    like the crawling things
      of the earth;
they shall come trembling out
    of their fortresses;
they shall turn in dread to
    the LORD our God,
    and they shall stand
      in fear of you.

GOD'S COMPASSION AND STEADFAST LOVE
18 Who is a God like you,
    pardoning iniquity
    and passing over the
      transgression
    of the remnant of your[d]
      possession?
He does not retain his
    anger forever,
    because he delights in
      showing clemency.
19 He will again have compassion
    upon us;
    he will tread our iniquities
      under foot.
You will cast all our[e] sins
    into the depths of the sea.
20 You will show faithfulness
    to Jacob
    and unswerving loyalty
    to Abraham,
as you have sworn to our
    ancestors
    from the days of old.

[a] 7.10 Heb lacks *downfall*   [b] 7.12 One Ms: MT *Assyria and cities of*   [c] 7.15 Cn: Heb *I will show him*   [d] 7.18 Heb *his*   [e] 7.19 Gk Syr Vg Tg: Heb *their*

NAHUM

Nahum (his name means "comfort") prophesies that the Assyrian city of Nineveh will fall. The city of Nineveh was destroyed in 612 BC in fulfillment of this prophecy. Nahum prophesies against the cruelty and wickedness of the Assyrians, and he highlights God's sovereignty, mercy and justice. Nahum comforts the southern kingdom of Judah with the assurance that God is in control of the present as well as the future and will not allow evil to triumph. We too can take comfort that God is the Lord of world events and that the kingdom of God will prevail.

1 An oracle concerning Nineveh. The book of the vision of Nahum of Elkosh.

THE CONSUMING WRATH OF GOD

2 A jealous and avenging
　　God is the LORD,
　　the LORD is avenging
　　　and wrathful;
　　the LORD takes vengeance
　　　on his adversaries
　　and rages against his enemies.
3 The LORD is slow to anger
　　but great in power,
　　and the LORD will by no
　　　means clear the guilty.

　　His way is in whirlwind
　　　and storm,
　　and the clouds are the
　　　dust of his feet.
4 He rebukes the sea and
　　　makes it dry,
　　and he dries up all the rivers;
　　Bashan and Carmel wither,
　　　and the bloom of
　　　Lebanon fades.
5 The mountains quake before him,
　　and the hills melt;
　　the earth heaves before him,
　　　the world and all who live in it.

6 Who can stand before his
　　　indignation?
　　Who can endure the heat
　　　of his anger?
　　His wrath is poured out like fire,
　　and by him the rocks are
　　　broken in pieces.
7 The LORD is good,
　　a stronghold in a day
　　　of trouble;

　　he protects those who take
　　　refuge in him,
8 　even in a rushing flood.
　　He will make a full end of
　　　his adversaries,[a]
　　and will pursue his enemies
　　　into darkness.
9 Why do you plot against
　　　the LORD?
　　He will make an end;
　　no adversary will
　　　rise up twice.
10 Like thorns they are entangled,
　　like drunkards they are drunk;
　　they are consumed like
　　　dry straw.
11 From you one has gone out
　　who plots evil against
　　　the LORD,
　　one who counsels wickedness.

GOOD NEWS FOR JUDAH

12 Thus says the LORD,
　　"Though they are at full
　　　strength and many,[b]
　　they will be cut off and
　　　pass away.
　　Though I have afflicted you,
　　　I will afflict you no more.
13 And now I will break off his
　　　yoke from you
　　and snap the bonds
　　　that bind you."

14 The LORD has commanded
　　　concerning you:
　　"Your name shall be
　　　perpetuated no longer;

---

a 1.8 Gk: Heb *of her place*　b 1.12 Meaning of Heb uncertain

‖ BIBLE IN LIFE ▷

The Wrath of God
Nahum 1.2–3

Many people have the misconception that God is angry, ready to pounce on us whenever we make a mistake. Throughout the Bible, the word *wrath* is used to describe God. But notice that God is also "slow to anger." God is not vindictive. God is not hunting people to punish. Even when we sin, God's nature is one of compassion, grace, forgiveness and love. But God is completely holy and cannot accept immorality, so punishment exists when we bring upon ourselves the consequences of our sins. In a way, wrath reveals the corrective nature of God—not vindictiveness or revenge. Wrath is a consequence of sin, but we are forgiven through our faith in Jesus Christ.

from the house of your gods
    I will cut off
the carved image and
    the cast image.
I will make your grave, for
    you are worthless."

15a Look! On the mountains
    the feet of one
who brings good tidings,
    who proclaims peace!
Celebrate your festivals, O Judah,
    fulfill your vows,
for never again shall the
      wicked invade you;
    they are utterly cut off.

THE DESTRUCTION OF THE WICKED CITY

2 A shatterer[b] has come
    up against you.
    Guard the ramparts;
    watch the road;
gird your loins;
    collect all your strength.

2 (For the LORD is restoring the
      majesty of Jacob,
    as well as the majesty of Israel,
though ravagers have
      ravaged them
    and ruined their branches.)

3 The shields of his warriors
      are red;
    his soldiers are clothed
      in crimson.
The metal on the chariots flashes
    on the day when he
      musters them;
    the chargers[c] prance.
4 The chariots race madly
      through the streets,
    they rush to and fro
      through the squares;
their appearance is like torches,
    they dart like lightning.
5 He calls his officers;
    they stumble as they
      come forward;
they hasten to the wall,
    and the mantelet[d] is set up.
6 The river gates are opened,
    the palace trembles.
7 It is decreed[d] that the
      city[e] be exiled,
    its slave women led away,

moaning like doves
    and beating their breasts.
8 Nineveh is like a pool
    whose waters[f] run away.
"Halt! Halt!"—
    but no one turns back.
9 "Plunder the silver,
    plunder the gold!
There is no end of treasure!
    An abundance of every
      precious thing!"

10 Devastation, desolation,
    and destruction!
Hearts faint and knees tremble,
    all loins quake,
    all faces grow pale!
11 What became of the lions' den,
    the cave[g] of the young lions,
where the lion goes,
    and the lion's cubs, with no
      one to disturb them?
12 The lion has torn enough
    for his whelps
and strangled prey for
      his lionesses;
he has filled his caves with prey
    and his dens with torn flesh.

13 See, I am against you, says the
LORD of hosts, and I will burn your[h]
chariots in smoke, and the sword
shall devour your young lions; I will
cut off your prey from the earth, and
the voice of your messengers shall be
heard no more.

RUIN IMMINENT AND INEVITABLE

3 Ah! City of bloodshed,
    utterly deceitful, full of booty—
    no end to the plunder!
2 The crack of whip and
      rumble of wheel,
    galloping horse and
      bounding chariot!
3 Horsemen charging,
    flashing sword and
      glittering spear,

a 1.15 Ch 2.1 in Heb   b 2.1 Cn: Heb
scatterer   c 2.3 Cn Compare Gk Syr:
Heb *cypresses*   d 2.5,7 Meaning of Heb
uncertain   e 2.7 Heb *it*   f 2.8 Cn Compare
Gk: Heb *a pool, from the days that she has
become, and they*   g 2.11 Cn: Heb *pasture*
h 2.13 Heb *her*

piles of dead,
　　heaps of corpses,
dead bodies without end—
　　they stumble over the bodies!
4 Because of the countless
　　　debaucheries of
　　　the prostitute,
　　gracefully alluring,
　　　mistress of sorcery,
who enslaves[a] nations through
　　　her debaucheries,
　　and peoples through
　　　her sorcery,
5 I am against you,
　　says the LORD of hosts,
　　and will lift up your skirts
　　　over your face;
and I will let nations look on
　　　your nakedness
　　and kingdoms on your shame.
6 I will throw filth at you
　　and treat you with contempt,
　　and make you a spectacle.
7 Then all who see you will shrink
　　　from you and say,
　　"Nineveh is devastated; who
　　　will bemoan her?"
　　Where shall I seek
　　　comforters for you?

8 Are you better than Thebes[b]
　　that sat by the Nile,
　　with water around her,
　　　her rampart a sea,
　　　water her wall?
9 Ethiopia[c] was her strength,
　　Egypt too, and that
　　　without limit;
　　Put and the Libyans were
　　　her[d] helpers.

10 Yet she became an exile,
　　　she went into captivity;
　　even her infants were
　　　dashed in pieces
　　　at the head of every street;
　　lots were cast for her nobles,
　　all her dignitaries were
　　　bound in fetters.
11 You also will be drunken,
　　　you will go into hiding;[e]
　　you will seek
　　　a refuge from the enemy.
12 All your fortresses are
　　　like fig trees
　　　with first-ripe figs—

if shaken they fall
　　into the mouth of the eater.
13 Look at your troops:
　　they are women in your midst.
The gates of your land
　　are wide open to your foes;
　　fire has devoured the bars
　　　of your gates.

14 Draw water for the siege,
　　strengthen your forts;
trample the clay,
　　tread the mortar,
　　take hold of the brick mold!
15 There the fire will devour you,
　　the sword will cut you off.
It will devour you like
　　the locust.

Multiply yourselves like
　　the locust,
　　multiply like the grasshopper!
16 You increased your merchants
　　more than the stars of
　　　the heavens.
　　The locust sheds its skin
　　　and flies away.
17 Your guards are like
　　　grasshoppers,
　　your scribes like swarms[e]
　　　of locusts
settling on the fences
　　on a cold day—
when the sun rises,
　　they fly away;
no one knows where
　　they have gone.

18 Your shepherds are asleep,
　　O king of Assyria;
　　your nobles slumber.
Your people are scattered
　　on the mountains
　　with no one to gather them.
19 There is no assuaging your hurt,
　　your wound is mortal.
All who hear the
　　news about you
　　clap their hands over you.
For who has ever escaped
　　your endless cruelty?

<hr />

a 3.4 Heb sells　b 3.8 Heb No-amon
c 3.9 Or Nubia; Heb Cush　d 3.9 Gk: Heb
your　e 3.11,17 Meaning of Heb uncertain

HABAKKUK

If you could have a Q&A time with God, what would you ask? The prophet Habakkuk had such an opportunity. The book of Habakkuk is like a transcript of his conversation with God. Habakkuk poses two questions that we still wonder about today: 1) Why does God tolerate cruelty and injustice; and 2) why is God silent when wicked people seem to be in control? God answers, declaring that when the time is right, the wicked will be punished and the faithful will be rewarded. As you read this book, you might realize, as Habakkuk did, that God is willing enough and powerful enough to see justice done.

1
The oracle that the prophet Habakkuk saw.

THE PROPHET'S COMPLAINT

2 O LORD, how long shall I
    cry for help,
    and you will not listen?
Or cry to you "Violence!"
    and you will not save?
3 Why do you make me see
    wrongdoing
    and look at trouble?
Destruction and violence
    are before me;
    strife and contention arise.
4 So the law becomes slack
    and justice never prevails.
The wicked surround the
    righteous—
    therefore judgment comes
    forth perverted.

5 Look at the nations, and see!
    Be astonished! Be astounded!
For a work is being done
    in your days
    that you would not believe
    if you were told.
6 For I am rousing the Chaldeans,
    that fierce and impetuous
    nation,
who march through the
    breadth of the earth
    to seize dwellings not their own.
7 Dread and fearsome are they;
    their justice and dignity
    proceed from themselves.
8 Their horses are swifter
    than leopards,
    more menacing than
    wolves at dusk;
    their horses charge.
Their horsemen come
    from far away;
    they fly like an eagle
    swift to devour.
9 They all come for violence,
    with faces pressing[a] forward;
    they gather captives like sand.
10 At kings they scoff,
    and of rulers they make sport.
They laugh at every fortress,
    and heap up earth to take it.
11 Then they sweep by like the wind;
    they transgress and
    become guilty;
    their own might is their god!

12 Are you not from of old,
    O LORD my God, my Holy One?
    You[b] shall not die.
O LORD, you have marked
    them for judgment;
    and you, O Rock, have
    established them
    for punishment.
13 Your eyes are too pure to
    behold evil,
    and you cannot look on
    wrongdoing;
why do you look on the
    treacherous,
    and are silent when the
    wicked swallow
    those more righteous
    than they?
14 You have made people like
    the fish of the sea,
    like crawling things that
    have no ruler.

WE ARE STILL INCLINED

TO HONOR MILITARY

VICTORS RATHER THAN

THOSE WHO SEEK PEACE. WE

TEND TO DEFINE MESSIAH IN

OUR OWN WAY, BASED ON

DOMINATION OVER OTHERS.

15 The enemy[c] brings all of them
    up with a hook;
he drags them out with his net,
    he gathers them in his seine;
    so he rejoices and exults.
16 Therefore he sacrifices to his net
    and makes offerings to his seine;
for by them his portion is lavish,
    and his food is rich.
17 Is he then to keep on
    emptying his net,
    and destroying nations
    without mercy?

---

[a] 1.9 Meaning of Heb uncertain   [b] 1.12 Ancient
Heb tradition: MT We   [c] 1.15 Heb He

GOD'S REPLY TO THE PROPHET'S COMPLAINT

2 I will stand at my watchpost,
and station myself on
the rampart;
I will keep watch to see what
he will say to me,
and what he[a] will answer
concerning my complaint.
2 Then the LORD answered
me and said:
Write the vision;
make it plain on tablets,
so that a runner may read it.
3 For there is still a vision for
the appointed time;
it speaks of the end, and
does not lie.
If it seems to tarry, wait for it;
it will surely come, it
will not delay.
4 Look at the proud!
Their spirit is not right
in them,
but the righteous live
by their faith.[b]
5 Moreover, wealth[c] is treacherous;
the arrogant do not endure.
They open their throats
wide as Sheol;
like Death they never
have enough.
They gather all nations
for themselves,
and collect all peoples
as their own.

INJUSTICE IS NOT IGNORED

BY GOD; IT SHOULD NOT

BE IGNORED BY US.

THE WOES OF THE WICKED

6 Shall not everyone taunt such people and, with mocking riddles, say about them,
"Alas for you who heap up what
is not your own!"
How long will you load
yourselves with goods
taken in pledge?

7 Will not your own creditors
suddenly rise,
and those who make you
tremble wake up?
Then you will be booty
for them.
8 Because you have plundered
many nations,
all that survive of the peoples
shall plunder you—
because of human bloodshed, and
violence to the earth,
to cities and all who
live in them.

9 "Alas for you who get evil
gain for your house,
setting your nest on high
to be safe from the
reach of harm!"
10 You have devised shame
for your house
by cutting off many peoples;
you have forfeited your life.
11 The very stones will cry out
from the wall,
and the plaster[d] will respond
from the woodwork.

12 "Alas for you who build a
town by bloodshed,
and found a city on iniquity!"
13 Is it not from the LORD of hosts
that peoples labor only to
feed the flames,
and nations weary themselves
for nothing?
14 But the earth will be filled
with the knowledge of the
glory of the LORD,
as the waters cover the sea.

15 "Alas for you who make your
neighbors drink,
pouring out your wrath[e]
until they are drunk,
in order to gaze on their
nakedness!"
16 You will be sated with contempt
instead of glory.
Drink, you yourself,
and stagger![f]

---

a 2.1 Syr: Heb *I*   b 2.4 Or *faithfulness*
c 2.5 Other Heb Mss read *wine*   d 2.11 Or
beam   e 2.15 Or *poison*   f 2.16 Q Ms Gk:
MT *be uncircumcised*

The cup in the LORD's right hand
will come around to you,
and shame will come
upon your glory!
17 For the violence done to Lebanon
will overwhelm you;
the destruction of the animals
will terrify you—[a]
because of human bloodshed and
violence to the earth,
to cities and all who
live in them.

18 What use is an idol
once its maker has
shaped it—
a cast image, a teacher of lies?
For its maker trusts in what
has been made,
though the product is only an
idol that cannot speak!
19 Alas for you who say to the
wood, "Wake up!"
to silent stone, "Rouse yourself!"
Can it teach?
See, it is gold and silver plated,
and there is no breath in it at all.

20 But the LORD is in his holy temple;
let all the earth keep
silence before him!

3 A prayer of the prophet Habakkuk according to Shigionoth.

THE PROPHET'S PRAYER
2 O LORD, I have heard of
your renown,
and I stand in awe, O LORD,
of your work.
In our own time revive it;
in our own time make
it known;
in wrath may you
remember mercy.
3 God came from Teman,
the Holy One from Mount
Paran. *Selah*
His glory covered the heavens,
and the earth was full
of his praise.
4 The brightness was like the sun;
rays came forth from his hand,
where his power lay hidden.
5 Before him went pestilence,
and plague followed
close behind.

6 He stopped and shook the earth;
he looked and made the
nations tremble.
The eternal mountains
were shattered;
along his ancient pathways
the everlasting hills sank low.
7 I saw the tents of Cushan
under affliction;
the tent-curtains of the land
of Midian trembled.
8 Was your wrath against the
rivers,[b] O LORD?
Or your anger against
the rivers,[b]
or your rage against the sea,[c]
when you drove your horses,
your chariots to victory?
9 You brandished your naked bow,
sated[d] were the arrows at your
command.[e]   *Selah*
You split the earth with rivers.
10 The mountains saw you,
and writhed;
a torrent of water swept by;
the deep gave forth its voice.
The sun[f] raised high its hands;
11 the moon[g] stood still in its
exalted place,
at the light of your arrows
speeding by,
at the gleam of your
flashing spear.
12 In fury you trod the earth,
in anger you trampled nations.
13 You came forth to save
your people,
to save your anointed.
You crushed the head of the
wicked house,
laying it bare from foundation
to roof.[e]   *Selah*
14 You pierced with their[h] own
arrows the head[i]
of his warriors,[j]
who came like a whirlwind
to scatter us,[k]
gloating as if ready to
devour the poor who
were in hiding.

---

[a] 2.17 Gk Syr: Meaning of Heb uncertain
[b] 3.8 Or *against River*   [c] 3.8 Or *against Sea*
[d] 3.9 Cn: Heb *oaths*   [e] 3.9,13 Meaning of
Heb uncertain   [f] 3.10 Heb *It*   [g] 3.11 Heb
sun, moon   [h] 3.14 Heb *his*   [i] 3.14 Or
leader   [j] 3.14 Vg Compare Gk Syr: Meaning
of Heb uncertain   [k] 3.14 Heb *me*

15 You trampled the sea with
    your horses,
    churning the mighty
      waters.

16 I hear, and I tremble within;
    my lips quiver at the sound.
    Rottenness enters
      into my bones,
    and my steps tremble[a]
      beneath me.
    I wait quietly for the day
      of calamity
    to come upon the people
      who attack us.

**TRUST AND JOY IN THE
MIDST OF TROUBLE**

17 Though the fig tree does
    not blossom,
    and no fruit is on the vines;

though the produce of
    the olive fails,
    and the fields yield no food;
though the flock is cut off
    from the fold,
    and there is no herd
      in the stalls,

18 yet I will rejoice in the LORD;
    I will exult in the God
      of my salvation.

19 GOD, the Lord, is my strength;
    he makes my feet like
      the feet of a deer,
    and makes me tread upon
      the heights.[b]

To the leader: with stringed[c]
    instruments.

[a] 3.16 Cn Compare Gk: Meaning of Heb
uncertain   [b] 3.19 Heb *my heights*
[c] 3.19 Heb *my stringed*

⊢ BIBLE IN LIFE ▷ ⊕

Rejoicing Always   *Habakkuk 3.17–19*

When facing trials in life, how many of us can say, "Yet I will rejoice," as Habakkuk
does here? In the New Testament, Paul instructs the Thessalonians to "Rejoice always"
(1 Thessalonians 5.16), even though many of them were in the midst of opposition and
persecution for their faith. What are some of the constants, the good things that we
always have in life, no matter what happens? Because we have God's love, forgiveness
and grace, we have cause to rejoice despite our tragedies, disappointments or failures.
We have life. We have opportunities, talents, abilities and potential adventures. We have
a continuing relationship with Jesus Christ. Are these things good? Are they an adequate
foundation for joy? Sure, they are! Sometimes we allow our problems to eclipse our
reasons for joy. We obsess over little everyday things that in the scheme of God's world
amount to very little. In those times we forget to rejoice, and we disregard the source of
our legitimate joy: the love of Jesus Christ.

ZEPHANIAH

The "day of the LORD" sounds ominous. Although no one really knows what it will be like, it's a safe bet we won't want to experience it! Zephaniah's prophecy depicts the stark horror of that ordeal, the force of God's anger against sin. But Zephaniah doesn't stop there. While God does punish people for their flagrant and deliberate sin, those who seek the Lord with humility will receive mercy. As you read, look for the note of hope—that judgment will pave the way for a new day when all people will worship the Lord.

1

The word of the LORD that came to Zephaniah son of Cushi son of Gedaliah son of Amariah son of Hezekiah, in the days of King Josiah son of Amon of Judah.

THE COMING JUDGMENT ON JUDAH

2 I will utterly sweep away
    everything
    from the face of the earth,
        says the LORD.
3 I will sweep away humans
        and animals;
    I will sweep away
        birds of the air
    and the fish of the sea.
I will make the wicked stumble.[a]
    I will cut off humanity
    from the face of the earth,
        says the LORD.
4 I will stretch out my hand
        against Judah,
    and against all the inhabitants
        of Jerusalem;
    and I will cut off from this place
        every remnant of Baal
    and the name of the
        idolatrous priests;[b]
5 those who bow down
        on the roofs
    to the host of the heavens;
    those who bow down and
        swear to the LORD,
    but also swear by Milcom;[c]
6 those who have turned back from
        following the LORD,
    who have not sought the LORD
        or inquired of him.

7 Be silent before the Lord GOD!
    For the day of the LORD
        is at hand;
    the LORD has prepared
        a sacrifice,
    he has consecrated his guests.
8 And on the day of the
        LORD's sacrifice
    I will punish the officials
        and the king's sons
    and all who dress themselves
        in foreign attire.
9 On that day I will punish
    all who leap over
        the threshold,
    who fill their master's house
        with violence and fraud.

10 On that day, says the LORD,
    a cry will be heard from
        the Fish Gate,
    a wail from the Second Quarter,
        a loud crash from the hills.
11 The inhabitants of the
        Mortar wail,
    for all the traders have
        perished;
    all who weigh out silver
        are cut off.
12 At that time I will search
        Jerusalem with lamps,
    and I will punish the people
    who rest complacently[d]
        on their dregs,
    those who say in their hearts,
    "The LORD will not do good,
        nor will he do harm."
13 Their wealth shall be plundered,
        and their houses laid waste.
    Though they build houses,
        they shall not inhabit them;
    though they plant vineyards,
        they shall not drink wine
            from them.

THE GREAT DAY OF THE LORD

14 The great day of the LORD is near,
        near and hastening fast;
    the sound of the day of the
            LORD is bitter,
    the warrior cries aloud there.
15 That day will be a day of wrath,
        a day of distress and anguish,
    a day of ruin and devastation,
        a day of darkness and gloom,
    a day of clouds and thick
            darkness,
16   a day of trumpet blast
            and battle cry
    against the fortified cities
        and against the lofty
            battlements.

17 I will bring such distress
        upon people
    that they shall walk
        like the blind;
    because they have sinned
        against the LORD,

---

a 1.3 Cn: Heb *sea, and those who cause the wicked to stumble*   b 1.4 Compare Gk: Heb *the idolatrous priests with the priests*   c 1.5 Gk Mss Syr Vg: Heb *Malcam* (or, *their king*)   d 1.12 Heb *who thicken*

their blood shall be poured
    out like dust,
    and their flesh like dung.
18 Neither their silver nor their gold
    will be able to save them
    on the day of the LORD's wrath;
in the fire of his passion
    the whole earth shall
        be consumed;
for a full, a terrible end
    he will make of all the
        inhabitants of the earth.

JUDGMENT ON ISRAEL'S ENEMIES

2 Gather together, gather,
    O shameless nation,
2 before you are driven away
    like the drifting chaff,[a]
before there comes upon you
    the fierce anger of the LORD,
before there comes upon you
    the day of the LORD's wrath.
3 Seek the LORD, all you
        humble of the land,
    who do his commands;
seek righteousness, seek
        humility;
    perhaps you may be hidden
    on the day of the LORD's wrath.
4 For Gaza shall be deserted,
    and Ashkelon shall become
        a desolation;
Ashdod's people shall be
        driven out at noon,
    and Ekron shall be uprooted.
5 Ah, inhabitants of the seacoast,
    you nation of the
        Cherethites!
The word of the LORD is
        against you,
    O Canaan, land of the
        Philistines;
    and I will destroy you until
        no inhabitant is left.
6 And you, O seacoast, shall
    be pastures,
    meadows for shepherds
    and folds for flocks.
7 The seacoast shall become
        the possession
    of the remnant of the
        house of Judah,
    on which they shall pasture,
and in the houses of Ashkelon
    they shall lie down at evening.

PONDER

Seek the LORD, all you humble of
the land, who do his commands;
seek righteousness, seek humility.
—Zephaniah 2.3

PRAY

O Father, help each one of us to have
the courage to see in ourselves the
complacent and self-satisfied people
of Jerusalem, to realize that you do
not want us to conform to the shaky
moral and ethical standards of our
society, but that you call us to follow
your commands, even though we
may have to stand alone at times.
Let us do this in a spirit of meekness,
humility, truth, dedication and love.
Remind us of these things as we rest
in the benevolent and forgiving arms
of our Savior, Jesus Christ. Amen.

For the LORD their God will
    be mindful of them
    and restore their fortunes.

8 I have heard the taunts of Moab
    and the revilings of the
        Ammonites,
how they have taunted my people
    and made boasts against
        their territory.
9 Therefore, as I live, says the
        LORD of hosts,
    the God of Israel,
Moab shall become like Sodom
    and the Ammonites
        like Gomorrah,
a land possessed by nettles
    and salt pits,
    and a waste forever.
The remnant of my people
    shall plunder them,
    and the survivors of my nation
        shall possess them.

a 2.2 Cn Compare Gk Syr: Heb *before a
decree is born; like chaff a day has
passed away*

10 This shall be their lot in return
        for their pride,
    because they scoffed
        and boasted
    against the people of the
        LORD of hosts.
11 The LORD will be terrible
        against them;
    he will shrivel all the
        gods of the earth,
    and to him shall bow down,
        each in its place,
    all the coasts and islands
        of the nations.

12 You also, O Ethiopians,[a]
        shall be killed by my sword.

13 And he will stretch out his hand
        against the north,
    and destroy Assyria;
    and he will make Nineveh
        a desolation,
    a dry waste like the desert.
14 Herds shall lie down in it,
        every wild animal;[b]
    the desert owl[c] and the
        screech owl[c]
    shall lodge on its capitals;
    the owl[d] shall hoot at
        the window,
    the raven[e] croak on
        the threshold;
    for its cedar work will
        be laid bare.
15 Is this the exultant city
        that lived secure,
    that said to itself,
    "I am, and there is no
        one else"?
    What a desolation it has become,
        a lair for wild animals!
    Everyone who passes by it
        hisses and shakes the fist.

THE WICKEDNESS OF
JERUSALEM

3 Ah, soiled, defiled,
        oppressing city!
2 It has listened to no voice;
        it has accepted no correction.
    It has not trusted in the LORD;
        it has not drawn near
        to its God.

3 The officials within it
        are roaring lions;

its judges are evening wolves
    that leave nothing until
        the morning.
4 Its prophets are reckless,
        faithless persons;
    its priests have profaned
        what is sacred,
    they have done violence
        to the law.
5 The LORD within it is righteous;
        he does no wrong.
    Every morning he renders
        his judgment,
    each dawn without fail;
    but the unjust knows no shame.

6 I have cut off nations;
        their battlements are in ruins;
    I have laid waste their streets
        so that no one walks in them;
    their cities have been
        made desolate,
    without people, without
        inhabitants.
7 I said, "Surely the city[f]
        will fear me,
    it will accept correction;
    it will not lose sight[g]
        of all that I have brought
        upon it."
    But they were the more eager
        to make all their deeds corrupt.

PUNISHMENT AND CONVERSION
OF THE NATIONS

8 Therefore wait for me,
        says the LORD,
    for the day when I arise
        as a witness.
    For my decision is to
        gather nations,
    to assemble kingdoms,
    to pour out upon them my
        indignation,
    all the heat of my anger;
    for in the fire of my passion
        all the earth shall be consumed.

9 At that time I will change the
        speech of the peoples
        to a pure speech,

a 2.12 Or *Nubians*; Heb *Cushites*   b 2.14 Tg
Compare Gk: Heb *nation*   c 2.14 Meaning
of Heb uncertain   d 2.14 Cn: Heb *a voice*
e 2.14 Gk Vg: Heb *desolation*   f 3.7 Heb
it   g 3.7 Gk Syr: Heb *its dwelling will not
be cut off*

PONDER

At that time I will change the speech of the peoples to a pure speech, that all of them may call on the name of the LORD and serve him with one accord.
—Zephaniah 3.9

PRAY

Lord, thank you for Zephaniah, one of your ancient prophets, who brought the same message to the people of Jerusalem that we need to hear today. We need to be reminded of the treatment we owe our fellow human beings. We need to relate to them with love, justice and service, a way of life that isn't just "preferable," but rather is central to our commitment to follow in Christ's footsteps. Grant us humility and courage to change our hearts and our ways, so that perhaps in the final days we can respond with right judgment and understanding. We ask in Jesus' name. Amen.

that all of them may call on
the name of the LORD
and serve him with one accord.

10 From beyond the rivers
of Ethiopiaᵃ
my suppliants, my
scattered ones,
shall bring my offering.

11 On that day you shall not
be put to shame
because of all the deeds
by which you have
rebelled against me;
for then I will remove from
your midst
your proudly exultant ones,
and you shall no longer
be haughty
in my holy mountain.

12 For I will leave in the midst of you
a people humble and lowly.
They shall seek refuge in the
name of the LORD—
13 the remnant of Israel;
they shall do no wrong
and utter no lies,
nor shall a deceitful tongue
be found in their mouths.
Then they will pasture
and lie down,
and no one shall make
them afraid.

A SONG OF JOY
14 Sing aloud, O daughter Zion;
shout, O Israel!

ᵃ **3.10** Or *Nubia*; Heb *Cush*

BIBLE IN LIFE

Humble and Lowly
Zephaniah 3.12

Those who trust in God are "humble and lowly." Jesus modeled humility, not by submitting to authority or domination of others, but through his humble service to God. Being humble and lowly doesn't mean we let everybody beat on us or that we don't struggle for success in achieving important goals. It means that we should have the courage to look within ourselves and ask, "How have I measured up to the standards of my Lord and Savior, Jesus Christ? How does my life look from his perspective? What is the degree of my success?" Christ certainly was rebuffed by many people, but he reached out to the most unsavory of all the people he could possibly find in the Holy Land—the worst ones. Quite often the people whom we consider the most antagonistic or the most rejected might be the ones who are most uncertain and hungry for an element of Christian love. The simple things prove to be a learning process for us as Christians. We should emulate Christ by embracing courage and strength, but with an absence of pride.

Rejoice and exult with all
your heart,
O daughter Jerusalem!
15 The LORD has taken away the
judgments against you,
he has turned away
your enemies.
The king of Israel, the LORD,
is in your midst;
you shall fear disaster
no more.
16 On that day it shall be said
to Jerusalem:
Do not fear, O Zion;
do not let your hands
grow weak.
17 The LORD, your God, is in
your midst,
a warrior who gives victory;
he will rejoice over you
with gladness,
he will renew you[a] in his love;
he will exult over you with
loud singing
18 as on a day of festival.[b]

I will remove disaster from you,[c]
so that you will not bear
reproach for it.
19 I will deal with all your
oppressors
at that time.
And I will save the lame
and gather the outcast,
and I will change their
shame into praise
and renown in all the earth.
20 At that time I will bring
you home,
at the time when I gather you;
for I will make you renowned
and praised
among all the peoples
of the earth,
when I restore your fortunes
before your eyes, says
the LORD.

[a] 3.17 Gk Syr: Heb he will be silent
[b] 3.18 Gk Syr: Meaning of Heb uncertain
[c] 3.18 Cn: Heb I will remove from you;
they were

HAGGAI

"Look, I'd love to help, but I have to study."
"I need time to grow and mature. When I feel more ready, then I'll help."
"I know God's work is important, but I have to think about my career."
Haggai is a book about priorities. He tells his readers that when God's people give priority to building the temple, they are blessed. Haggai instructs them that although they may gain some things by putting their interests before God's, they will miss the very best of what God promises—the encouragement and strength of the Spirit. As you read, notice what God values and ask yourself if God's priorities are also yours.

THE COMMAND TO REBUILD THE TEMPLE

1 In the second year of King Darius, in the sixth month, on the first day of the month, the word of the LORD came by the prophet Haggai to Zerubbabel son of Shealtiel, governor of Judah, and to Joshua son of Jehozadak, the high priest: ²Thus says the LORD of hosts: These people say the time has not yet come to rebuild the LORD's house. ³Then the word of the LORD came by the prophet Haggai, saying: ⁴Is it a time for you yourselves to live in your paneled houses, while this house lies in ruins? ⁵Now therefore thus says the LORD of hosts: Consider how you have fared. ⁶You have sown much, and harvested little; you eat, but you never have enough; you drink, but you never have your fill; you clothe yourselves, but no one is warm; and you that earn wages earn wages to put them into a bag with holes.

7 Thus says the LORD of hosts: Consider how you have fared. ⁸Go up to the hills and bring wood and build the house, so that I may take pleasure in it and be honored, says the LORD. ⁹You have looked for much, and, lo, it came to little; and when you brought it home, I blew it away. Why? says the LORD of hosts. Because my house lies in ruins, while all of you hurry off to your own houses. ¹⁰Therefore the heavens above you have withheld the dew, and the earth has withheld its produce. ¹¹And I have called for a drought on the land and the hills, on the grain, the new wine, the oil, on what the soil produces, on human beings and animals, and on all their labors.

12 Then Zerubbabel son of Shealtiel, and Joshua son of Jehozadak, the high priest, with all the remnant of the people, obeyed the voice of the LORD their God, and the words of the prophet Haggai, as the LORD their God had sent him; and the people feared the LORD. ¹³Then Haggai, the messenger of the LORD, spoke to the people with the LORD's message, saying, I am with you, says the LORD. ¹⁴And the LORD stirred up

PONDER

Now therefore thus says the LORD of hosts: Consider how you have fared. You have sown much, and harvested little; you eat, but you never have enough; you drink, but you never have your fill.
—Haggai 1.5–6

PRAY

O Father, today we read about what happened thousands of years ago when the people came back to Jerusalem, immediately forgot about you and set goals that left your will out of their lives. We know that we have that same self-centered, myopic nature. Give us the insight and courage to look at our own lives. Help us to remember the words and actions of our Savior, Jesus Christ, so that we can apply his truth to our own lives. You said to the Israelites, "I am with you." We know that you are with us, too, and we are grateful for it. In praise and thanksgiving to you, through Jesus Christ, our Lord. Amen.

the spirit of Zerubbabel son of Shealtiel, governor of Judah, and the spirit of Joshua son of Jehozadak, the high priest, and the spirit of all the remnant of the people; and they came and worked on the house of the LORD of hosts, their God, ¹⁵on the twenty-fourth day of the month, in the sixth month.

THE FUTURE GLORY OF THE TEMPLE

2 In the second year of King Darius, ¹in the seventh month, on the twenty-first day of the month, the word of the LORD came by the prophet Haggai, saying: ²Speak now to Zerubbabel son of Shealtiel, governor of Judah, and to Joshua son of Jehozadak, the high priest, and to the remnant of the people, and say, ³Who is left among you that saw this house in its former glory? How

BIBLE IN FOCUS

Careful Thought

Now therefore thus says the Lord of hosts: "Consider how you have fared."

—Haggai 1.5

What must it have been like to receive a message from a prophet like Haggai? He prophesied 15 years after the people of Judah had returned from exile in Babylon. Those who were among the first to return worked hard to clear the foundation of the temple and set up the altar, but 15 years later, no further progress had been made towards its reconstruction. So God raised up the prophet Haggai and gave him several messages for the people.

In fairness, it's not as if the people rebelled outright against God and refused to build the temple. Instead, it seems that they became preoccupied with their own affairs soon after the foundation was cleared. They had businesses and homes of their own to attend to, and they were also facing some opposition from the Samaritans to the north. They may have gotten used to worshiping without a temple in Babylon and may not have seen much need to rebuild it. They may also have been unmotivated to work on a temple that was clearly going to be less glorious than the original. Perhaps they were thinking there was still plenty of time to complete the work, since the prophet Jeremiah had foretold that the people would be in exile for 70 years, and some of the people had only been in exile for about 51 years when they returned.

In any case, once Haggai began giving the people messages from the Lord, they immediately responded by getting back to work on the temple. The text makes it clear that they got everyone together and started the work again only 23 days after Haggai gave his first message from God.

Many of us resemble the inhabitants of Jerusalem during Haggai's time. We have many things that occupy our daily lives, like going to school or working at our jobs or raising our kids. None of these things are bad, but how often do we consider what else needs to be done to promote God's work in the world? We shouldn't be fooled into thinking we need to wait until we receive some special message from God, like the people of Haggai's day. The truth is that we have already received a special message from God through Jesus Christ. We have been called to follow Christ's example of reaching out to others, of loving those who don't love us, of promoting justice and concern for the oppressed. These additional adventures will not be sacrifices but blessings to our lives. Christ did not call us to a one-time task but to lifelong service for God. Let's respond with the same enthusiasm as the people of Jerusalem and get to work!

Going Deeper

- What kinds of concerns tend to occupy your mind and time the most?
- What are some things you can be doing, in the name of Christ, during the next week?

does it look to you now? Is it not in your sight as nothing? 4Yet now take courage, O Zerubbabel, says the LORD; take courage, O Joshua, son of Jehozadak, the high priest; take courage, all you people of the land, says the LORD; work, for I am with you, says the LORD of hosts, 5according to the promise that I made you when you came out of Egypt. My spirit abides among you; do not fear. 6For thus says the LORD of hosts: Once again, in a little while, I will shake the heavens and the earth and the sea and the dry land; 7and I will shake all the nations, so that the treasure of all nations shall come, and I will fill this house with splendor, says the LORD of hosts. 8The silver is mine, and the gold is mine, says the LORD of hosts. 9The latter splendor of this house shall be greater than the former, says the LORD of hosts; and in this place I will give prosperity, says the LORD of hosts.

A REBUKE AND A PROMISE

10 On the twenty-fourth day of the ninth month, in the second year of Darius, the word of the LORD came by the prophet Haggai, saying: 11Thus says the LORD of hosts: Ask the priests for a ruling: 12If one carries consecrated meat in the fold of one's garment, and with the fold touches bread, or stew, or wine, or oil, or any kind of food, does it become holy? The priests answered, "No." 13Then Haggai said, "If one who is unclean by contact with a dead body touches any of these, does it become unclean?" The priests answered, "Yes, it becomes unclean." 14Haggai then said, So is it with this people, and with this nation before me, says the LORD; and so with every work of their hands; and what they offer there is unclean. 15But now, consider what will come to pass from this day on. Before a stone was placed upon a stone in the LORD's temple, 16how did you fare?a When one came to a heap of twenty measures, there were but ten; when one came to the wine vat to draw fifty measures, there were but twenty.

17I struck you and all the products of your toil with blight and mildew and hail; yet you did not return to me, says the LORD. 18Consider from this day on, from the twenty-fourth day of the ninth month. Since the day that the foundation of the LORD's temple was laid, consider: 19Is there any seed left in the barn? Do the vine, the fig tree, the pomegranate, and the olive tree still yield nothing? From this day on I will bless you.

GOD'S PROMISE TO ZERUBBABEL

20 The word of the LORD came a second time to Haggai on the twenty-fourth day of the month: 21Speak to Zerubbabel, governor of Judah, saying, I am about to shake

a 2.16 Gk: Heb since they were

the heavens and the earth, 22and to overthrow the throne of kingdoms; I am about to destroy the strength of the kingdoms of the nations, and overthrow the chariots and their riders; and the horses and their riders shall fall, every one by the sword of a comrade. 23On that day, says the LORD of hosts, I will take you, O Zerubbabel my servant, son of Shealtiel, says the LORD, and make you like a signet ring; for I have chosen you, says the LORD of hosts.

ZECHARIAH

You may notice that the book of Zechariah conveys a sense of urgency and anticipation. Maybe it's because Zechariah was concerned about the rebuilding of the temple or because he really wanted people to experience spiritual renewal. Perhaps it's because God gave Zechariah so many prophecies concerning the coming Messiah. To a people discouraged about the gargantuan task of building a temple, Zechariah's prophecy encourages the Jews as they return to their homeland and restores to them a renewed vision of God's ultimate purposes.

ISRAEL URGED TO REPENT

1 In the eighth month, in the second year of Darius, the word of the LORD came to the prophet Zechariah son of Berechiah son of Iddo, saying: 2The LORD was very angry with your ancestors. 3Therefore say to them, Thus says the LORD of hosts: Return to me, says the LORD of hosts, and I will return to you, says the LORD of hosts. 4Do not be like your ancestors, to whom the former prophets proclaimed, "Thus says the LORD of hosts, Return from your evil ways and from your evil deeds." But they did not hear or heed me, says the LORD. 5Your ancestors, where are they? And the prophets, do they live forever? 6But my words and my statutes, which I commanded my servants the prophets, did they not overtake your ancestors? So they repented and said, "The LORD of hosts has dealt with us according to our ways and deeds, just as he planned to do."

FIRST VISION: THE HORSEMEN

7 On the twenty-fourth day of the eleventh month, the month of Shebat, in the second year of Darius, the word of the LORD came to the prophet Zechariah son of Berechiah son of Iddo; and Zechariah[a] said, 8In the night I saw a man riding on a red horse! He was standing among the myrtle trees in the glen; and behind him were red, sorrel, and white horses. 9Then I said, "What are these, my lord?" The angel who talked with me said to me, "I will show you what they are." 10So the man who was standing among the myrtle trees answered, "They are those whom the LORD has sent to patrol the earth." 11Then they spoke to the angel of the LORD who was standing among the myrtle trees, "We have patrolled the earth, and lo, the whole earth remains at peace." 12Then the angel of the LORD said, "O LORD of hosts, how long will you withhold mercy from Jerusalem and the cities of Judah, with which you have been angry these seventy years?" 13Then the LORD replied with gracious and comforting words to the angel who talked with me. 14So the angel who talked with me said to me, Proclaim this message: Thus says the LORD of hosts; I am very jealous for Jerusalem and for Zion. 15And I am extremely angry with the nations that are at ease; for while I was only a little angry, they made the disaster worse. 16Therefore, thus says the LORD, I have returned to Jerusalem with compassion; my house shall be built in it, says the LORD of hosts, and the measuring line shall be stretched out over Jerusalem. 17Proclaim further: Thus says the LORD of hosts: My cities shall again overflow with prosperity; the LORD will again comfort Zion and again choose Jerusalem.

SECOND VISION: THE HORNS AND THE SMITHS

18[b] And I looked up and saw four horns. 19I asked the angel who talked with me, "What are these?" And he answered me, "These are the horns that have scattered Judah, Israel, and Jerusalem." 20Then the LORD showed me four blacksmiths. 21And I asked, "What are they coming to do?" He answered, "These are the horns that scattered Judah, so that no head could be raised; but these have come to terrify them, to strike down the horns of the nations that lifted up their horns against the land of Judah to scatter its people."[c]

THIRD VISION: THE MAN WITH A MEASURING LINE

2[d] I looked up and saw a man with a measuring line in his hand. 2Then I asked, "Where are you going?" He answered me, "To measure Jerusalem, to see what is its width and what is its length." 3Then the angel who talked with me came forward, and another angel came forward to meet him, 4and said to him, "Run, say to that young man: Jerusalem shall be inhabited like villages without walls, because of the multitude of people and animals in it. 5For I will be a wall of fire all around

---

a 1.7 Heb *and he*   b 1.18 Ch 2.1 in Heb
c 1.21 Heb *it*   d 2.1 Ch 2.5 in Heb

it, says the LORD, and I will be the glory within it."

INTERLUDE: AN APPEAL TO THE EXILES

6 Up, up! Flee from the land of the north, says the LORD; for I have spread you abroad like the four winds of heaven, says the LORD. 7 Up! Escape to Zion, you that live with daughter Babylon. 8 For thus said the LORD of hosts (after his glory[a] sent me) regarding the nations that plundered you: Truly, one who touches you touches the apple of my eye.[b] 9 See now, I am going to raise[c] my hand against them, and they shall become plunder for their own slaves. Then you will know that the LORD of hosts has sent me. 10 Sing and rejoice, O daughter Zion! For lo, I will come and dwell in your midst, says the LORD. 11 Many nations shall join themselves to the LORD on that day, and shall be my people; and I will dwell in your midst. And you shall know that the LORD of hosts has sent me to you. 12 The LORD will inherit Judah as his portion in the holy land, and will again choose Jerusalem.

REPENTANCE IS NOT AN

EMBARRASSMENT, BUT A

JOYFUL AND LIBERATING

GIFT OF RECONCILIATION

WITH GOD.

13 Be silent, all people, before the LORD; for he has roused himself from his holy dwelling.

FOURTH VISION: JOSHUA AND SATAN

3 Then he showed me the high priest Joshua standing before the angel of the LORD, and Satan[d] standing at his right hand to accuse him. 2 And the LORD said to Satan,[d]

"The LORD rebuke you, O Satan![d] The LORD who has chosen Jerusalem rebuke you! Is not this man a brand plucked from the fire?" 3 Now Joshua was dressed with filthy clothes as he stood before the angel. 4 The angel said to those who were standing before him, "Take off his filthy clothes." And to him he said, "See, I have taken your guilt away from you, and I will clothe you with festal apparel." 5 And I said, "Let them put a clean turban on his head." So they put a clean turban on his head and clothed him with the apparel; and the angel of the LORD was standing by.

6 Then the angel of the LORD assured Joshua, saying 7 "Thus says the LORD of hosts: If you will walk in my ways and keep my requirements, then you shall rule my house and have charge of my courts, and I will give you the right of access among those who are standing here. 8 Now listen, Joshua, high priest, you and your colleagues who sit before you! For they are an omen of things to come: I am going to bring my servant the Branch. 9 For on the stone that I have set before Joshua, on a single stone with seven facets, I will engrave its inscription, says the LORD of hosts, and I will remove the guilt of this land in a single day. 10 On that day, says the LORD of hosts, you shall invite each other to come under your vine and fig tree."

FIFTH VISION: THE LAMPSTAND AND OLIVE TREES

4 The angel who talked with me came again, and wakened me, as one is wakened from sleep. 2 He said to me, "What do you see?" And I said, "I see a lampstand all of gold, with a bowl on the top of it; there are seven lamps on it, with seven lips on each of the lamps that are on the top of it. 3 And by it there are two olive trees, one on the right of the bowl and the other on its left." 4 I said to the angel who talked with me, "What are these, my lord?" 5 Then

a 2.8 Cn: Heb *after glory he*   b 2.8 Heb *his eye*   c 2.9 Or *wave*   d 3.1,2 Or *the Accuser*; Heb *the Adversary*

the angel who talked with me answered me, "Do you not know what these are?" I said, "No, my lord." [6]He said to me, "This is the word of the LORD to Zerubbabel: Not by might, nor by power, but by my spirit, says the LORD of hosts. [7]What are you, O great mountain? Before Zerubbabel you shall become a plain; and he shall bring out the top stone amid shouts of 'Grace, grace to it!'"

[8] Moreover the word of the LORD came to me, saying, [9]"The hands of Zerubbabel have laid the foundation of this house; his hands shall also complete it. Then you will know that the LORD of hosts has sent me to you. [10]For whoever has despised the day of small things shall rejoice, and shall see the plummet in the hand of Zerubbabel.

"These seven are the eyes of the LORD, which range through the whole earth." [11]Then I said to him, "What are these two olive trees on the right and the left of the lampstand?" [12]And a second time I said to him, "What are these two branches of the olive trees, which pour out the oil[a] through the two golden pipes?" [13]He said to me, "Do you not know what these are?" I said, "No, my lord." [14]Then he said, "These are the two anointed ones who stand by the Lord of the whole earth."

SIXTH VISION: THE FLYING SCROLL

5 Again I looked up and saw a flying scroll. [2]And he said to me, "What do you see?" I answered, "I see a flying scroll; its length is twenty cubits, and its width ten cubits." [3]Then he said to me, "This is the curse that goes out over the face of the whole land; for everyone who steals shall be cut off according to the writing on one side, and everyone who swears falsely[b] shall be cut off according to the writing on the other side. [4]I have sent it out, says the LORD of hosts, and it shall enter the house of the thief, and the house of anyone who swears falsely by my name; and it shall abide in that house and consume it, both timber and stones."

SEVENTH VISION: THE WOMAN IN A BASKET

[5] Then the angel who talked with me came forward and said to me, "Look up and see what this is that is coming out." [6]I said, "What is it?" He said, "This is a basket[c] coming out." And he said, "This is their iniquity[d] in all the land." [7]Then a leaden cover was lifted, and there was a woman sitting in the basket![c] [8]And he said, "This is Wickedness." So he thrust her back into the basket,[c] and pressed the leaden weight down on its mouth. [9]Then I looked up and saw two women coming forward. The wind was in their wings; they had wings like the wings of a stork, and they lifted up the basket[c] between earth and sky. [10]Then I said to the angel who talked with me, "Where are they taking the basket?"[c] [11]He said to me, "To the land of Shinar, to build a house for it; and when this is prepared, they will set the basket[c] down there on its base."

EIGHTH VISION: FOUR CHARIOTS

6 And again I looked up and saw four chariots coming out from between two mountains—mountains of bronze. [2]The first chariot had red horses, the second chariot black horses, [3]the third chariot white horses, and the fourth chariot dappled gray[e] horses. [4]Then I said to the angel who talked with me, "What are these, my lord?" [5]The angel answered me, "These are the four winds[f] of heaven going out, after presenting themselves before the Lord of all the earth. [6]The chariot with the black horses goes toward the north country, the white ones go toward the west country,[g] and the dappled ones go toward the south country." [7]When the steeds came out, they were impatient to get out and patrol the earth. And he said, "Go, patrol the earth." So they patrolled the earth. [8]Then he cried out

a 4.12 Cn: Heb *gold*   b 5.3 The word *falsely* added from verse 4   c 5.6,7,8,9,10,11 Heb *ephah*   d 5.6 Gk Compare Syr: Heb *their eye*   e 6.3 Compare Gk: Meaning of Heb uncertain   f 6.5 Or *spirits*   g 6.6 Cn: Heb *go after them*

to me, "Lo, those who go toward the north country have set my spirit at rest in the north country."

THE CORONATION OF THE BRANCH

9 The word of the LORD came to me: [10]Collect silver and gold[a] from the exiles—from Heldai, Tobijah, and Jedaiah—who have arrived from Babylon; and go the same day to the house of Josiah son of Zephaniah. [11]Take the silver and gold and make a crown,[b] and set it on the head of the high priest Joshua son of Jehozadak; [12]say to him: Thus says the LORD of hosts: Here is a man whose name is Branch: for he shall branch out in his place, and he shall build the temple of the LORD. [13]It is he that shall build the temple of the LORD; he shall bear royal honor, and shall sit upon his throne and rule. There shall be a priest by his throne, with peaceful understanding between the two of them. [14]And the crown[c] shall be in the care of Heldai,[d] Tobijah, Jedaiah, and Josiah[e] son of Zephaniah, as a memorial in the temple of the LORD.

15 Those who are far off shall come and help to build the temple of the LORD; and you shall know that the LORD of hosts has sent me to you. This will happen if you diligently obey the voice of the LORD your God.

HYPOCRITICAL FASTING CONDEMNED

7 In the fourth year of King Darius, the word of the LORD came to Zechariah on the fourth day of the ninth month, which is Chislev. [2]Now the people of Bethel had sent Sharezer and Regem-melech and their men, to entreat the favor of the LORD, [3]and to ask the priests of the house of the LORD of hosts and the prophets, "Should I mourn and practice abstinence in the fifth month, as I have done for so many years?" [4]Then the word of the LORD of hosts came to me: [5]Say to all the people of the land and the priests: When you fasted and lamented in the fifth month and in the seventh, for these seventy years, was it for me

that you fasted? [6]And when you eat and when you drink, do you not eat and drink only for yourselves? [7]Were not these the words that the LORD proclaimed by the former prophets, when Jerusalem was inhabited and in prosperity, along with the towns around it, and when the Negeb and the Shephelah were inhabited?

PUNISHMENT FOR REJECTING GOD'S DEMANDS

8 The word of the LORD came to Zechariah, saying: [9]Thus says the LORD of hosts: Render true judgments, show kindness and mercy to one another; [10]do not oppress the widow, the orphan, the alien, or the poor; and do not devise evil in your hearts against one another. [11]But

[a] 6.10 Cn Compare verse 11: Heb lacks *silver and gold*   [b] 6.11 Gk Mss Syr Tg: Heb *crowns*   [c] 6.14 Gk Syr: Heb *crowns*   [d] 6.14 Syr Compare verse 10: Heb *Helem*   [e] 6.14 Syr Compare verse 10: Heb *Hen*

PONDER

Thus says the LORD of hosts: Render true judgments, show kindness and mercy to one another; do not oppress the widow, the orphan, the alien, or the poor; and do not devise evil in your hearts against one another.

—Zechariah 7.9–10

PRAY

O Father, help us resolve in our hearts to absorb the words Zechariah directed to these folk, but that are also addressed to us. Help us to love one another. Help us to love peace, justice and truth and to serve with humility and compassion. Teach us to realize that doing so does not constrain us but rather liberates as it opens up to us a much more adventurous and interesting and satisfying life. We are thankful for your Word in the name of our Savior, Jesus Christ. Amen.

they refused to listen, and turned a stubborn shoulder, and stopped their ears in order not to hear. [12] They made their hearts adamant in order not to hear the law and the words that the LORD of hosts had sent by his spirit through the former prophets. Therefore great wrath came from the LORD of hosts. [13] Just as, when I[a] called, they would not hear, so, when they called, I would not hear, says the LORD of hosts, [14] and I scattered them with a whirlwind among all the nations that they had not known. Thus the land they left was desolate, so that no one went to and fro, and a pleasant land was made desolate.

WE MUST NOT STAGNATE IN "COMPASSIONATE CONCERN." OUR ROLE IS TO TAKE COMPASSIONATE ACTION, IN JESUS' NAME.

GOD'S PROMISES TO ZION

8 The word of the LORD of hosts came to me, saying: [2] Thus says the LORD of hosts: I am jealous for Zion with great jealousy, and I am jealous for her with great wrath. [3] Thus says the LORD: I will return to Zion, and will dwell in the midst of Jerusalem; Jerusalem shall be called the faithful city, and the mountain of the LORD of hosts shall be called the holy mountain. [4] Thus says the LORD of hosts: Old men and old women shall again sit in the streets of Jerusalem, each with staff in hand because of their great age. [5] And the streets of the city shall be full of boys and girls playing in its streets. [6] Thus says the LORD of hosts: Even though it seems impossible to the remnant of this people in these days, should it also seem impossible to me, says the LORD of hosts? [7] Thus says the LORD of hosts: I will save my peo-

ple from the east country and from the west country; [8] and I will bring them to live in Jerusalem. They shall be my people and I will be their God, in faithfulness and in righteousness.

[9] Thus says the LORD of hosts: Let your hands be strong—you that have recently been hearing these words from the mouths of the prophets who were present when the foundation was laid for the rebuilding of the temple, the house of the LORD of hosts. [10] For before those days there were no wages for people or for animals, nor was there any safety from the foe for those who went out or came in, and I set them all against one another. [11] But now I will not deal with the remnant of this people as in the former days, says the LORD of hosts. [12] For there shall be a sowing of peace; the vine shall yield its fruit, the ground shall give its produce, and the skies shall give their dew; and I will cause the remnant of this people to possess all these things. [13] Just as you have been a cursing among the nations, O house of Judah and house of Israel, so I will save you and you shall be a blessing. Do not be afraid, but let your hands be strong.

[14] For thus says the LORD of hosts: Just as I purposed to bring disaster upon you, when your ancestors provoked me to wrath, and I did not relent, says the LORD of hosts, [15] so again I have purposed in these days to do good to Jerusalem and to the house of Judah; do not be afraid. [16] These are the things that you shall do: Speak the truth to one another, render in your gates judgments that are true and make for peace, [17] do not devise evil in your hearts against one another, and love no false oath; for all these are things that I hate, says the LORD.

JOYFUL FASTING

[18] The word of the LORD of hosts came to me, saying: [19] Thus says the LORD of hosts: The fast of the fourth month, and the fast of the fifth, and the fast of the seventh, and the fast

<hr />

[a] 7.13 Heb *he*

of the tenth, shall be seasons of joy and gladness, and cheerful festivals for the house of Judah: therefore love truth and peace.

MANY PEOPLES DRAWN TO JERUSALEM

20 Thus says the LORD of hosts: Peoples shall yet come, the inhabitants of many cities; 21the inhabitants of one city shall go to another, saying, "Come, let us go to entreat the favor of the LORD, and to seek the LORD of hosts; I myself am going." 22Many peoples and strong nations shall come to seek the LORD of hosts in Jerusalem, and to entreat the favor of the LORD. 23Thus says the LORD of hosts: In those days ten men from nations of every language shall take hold of a Jew, grasping his garment and saying, "Let us go with you, for we have heard that God is with you."

JUDGMENT ON ISRAEL'S ENEMIES

9 An Oracle.

The word of the LORD is against
the land of Hadrach
and will rest upon Damascus.
For to the LORD belongs the
capital[a] of Aram,[b]
as do all the tribes of Israel;
2 Hamath also, which borders on it,
Tyre and Sidon, though
they are very wise.
3 Tyre has built itself a rampart,
and heaped up silver like dust,
and gold like the dirt
of the streets.
4 But now, the Lord will strip
it of its possessions
and hurl its wealth
into the sea,
and it shall be
devoured by fire.
5 Ashkelon shall see it and
be afraid;
Gaza too, and shall writhe
in anguish;
Ekron also, because its
hopes are withered.
The king shall perish from Gaza;
Ashkelon shall be uninhabited;

6 a mongrel people shall
settle in Ashdod,
and I will make an end of
the pride of Philistia.
7 I will take away its blood
from its mouth,
and its abominations from
between its teeth;
it too shall be a remnant
for our God;
it shall be like a clan in Judah,
and Ekron shall be like
the Jebusites.
8 Then I will encamp at my
house as a guard,
so that no one shall
march to and fro;
no oppressor shall again
overrun them,
for now I have seen with
my own eyes.

WE NEED TO COMPREHEND

THE ABSOLUTE STRENGTH

OF JESUS CHRIST AND HIS

AVAILABILITY TO US.

THE COMING RULER OF GOD'S PEOPLE

9 Rejoice greatly, O daughter Zion!
Shout aloud, O daughter
Jerusalem!
Lo, your king comes to you;
triumphant and victorious is he,
humble and riding on a donkey,
on a colt, the foal of a donkey.
10 He[c] will cut off the chariot
from Ephraim
and the war-horse from
Jerusalem;
and the battle bow shall be cut off,
and he shall command
peace to the nations;
his dominion shall be
from sea to sea,
and from the River to the
ends of the earth.

a 9.1 Heb eye   b 9.1 Cn: Heb of Adam (or of humankind)   c 9.10 Gk: Heb I

11 As for you also, because
of the blood of my
covenant with you,
I will set your prisoners free
from the waterless pit.
12 Return to your stronghold,
O prisoners of hope;
today I declare that I will
restore to you double.
13 For I have bent Judah
as my bow;
I have made Ephraim
its arrow.
I will arouse your sons,
O Zion,
against your sons, O Greece,
and wield you like a
warrior's sword.

14 Then the LORD will appear
over them,
and his arrow go forth
like lightning;
the Lord GOD will sound
the trumpet
and march forth in the
whirlwinds of the south.
15 The LORD of hosts will
protect them,
and they shall devour and
tread down the slingers;[a]
they shall drink their
blood[b] like wine,
and be full like a bowl,
drenched like the corners
of the altar.

16 On that day the LORD their
God will save them
for they are the flock
of his people;
for like the jewels of a crown
they shall shine on his land.
17 For what goodness and
beauty are his!
Grain shall make the young
men flourish,
and new wine the
young women.

RESTORATION OF JUDAH AND ISRAEL

10 Ask rain from the LORD
in the season of the
spring rain,
from the LORD who makes
the storm clouds,
who gives showers of
rain to you,[c]
the vegetation in the
field to everyone.
2 For the teraphim[d]
utter nonsense,
and the diviners see lies;
the dreamers tell false dreams,
and give empty consolation.
Therefore the people wander
like sheep;
they suffer for lack of
a shepherd.

a 9.15 Cn: Heb the slingstones   b 9.15 Gk:
Heb shall drink   c 10.1 Heb them
d 10.2 Or household gods

⊢ BIBLE IN LIFE ▷

Jesus the Messiah   Zechariah 9.9

In Bible times, riding a donkey symbolized royalty. When Prince Solomon entered Jerusalem to inherit the crown from his father, King David, he rode on David's favorite mule (see 1 Kings 1.38). Zechariah predicted that the Son of God would enter Jerusalem riding on a colt, a young donkey (see Zechariah 9.9). This prophecy is clearly fulfilled in the New Testament (see Matthew 21; Mark 11; Luke 19; John 12). During the three years of Jesus' ministry, we only see evidence of Jesus walking with his disciples and followers. But when Jesus rode a donkey while his disciples and followers all walked down the road toward Jerusalem, he made a unique statement. In addition to the historical significance of his action was the practical significance: Jesus had visibly elevated his stature with respect to the people who knew and loved him. By fulfilling prophecy and accepting the people's praise, he acknowledged that he was indeed the Messiah. Who is Jesus to us? Is he someone with whom we talk once in a while? Do we merely "walk along" with him? Or is he our Lord and Savior, God's Son, the Messiah, whom we worship and adore?

3 My anger is hot against
    the shepherds,
    and I will punish the leaders;[a]
for the LORD of hosts
    cares for his flock, the
    house of Judah,
    and will make them like his
    proud war-horse.
4 Out of them shall come the
    cornerstone,
    out of them the tent peg,
out of them the battle bow,
    out of them every commander.
5 Together they shall be like
    warriors in battle,
    trampling the foe in the
    mud of the streets;
they shall fight, for the LORD
    is with them,
and they shall put to shame
    the riders on horses.

6 I will strengthen the
    house of Judah,
    and I will save the house
    of Joseph.
I will bring them back because
    I have compassion
    on them,
and they shall be as though I
    had not rejected them;
for I am the LORD their God
    and I will answer them.
7 Then the people of Ephraim shall
    become like warriors,
    and their hearts shall be
    glad as with wine.
Their children shall see
    it and rejoice,
    their hearts shall exult
    in the LORD.

8 I will signal for them and
    gather them in,
    for I have redeemed them,
and they shall be as numerous
    as they were before.
9 Though I scattered them
    among the nations,
    yet in far countries they
    shall remember me,
and they shall rear their
    children and return.
10 I will bring them home from
    the land of Egypt,
    and gather them
    from Assyria;

I will bring them to the land of
    Gilead and to Lebanon,
    until there is no room for them.
11 They[b] shall pass through the
    sea of distress,
    and the waves of the sea
    shall be struck down,
and all the depths of the
    Nile dried up.
The pride of Assyria shall
    be laid low,
    and the scepter of Egypt
    shall depart.
12 I will make them strong
    in the LORD,
    and they shall walk
    in his name,
             says the LORD.

11 Open your doors,
    O Lebanon,
    so that fire may devour
    your cedars!
2 Wail, O cypress, for the
    cedar has fallen,
    for the glorious trees
    are ruined!
Wail, oaks of Bashan,
    for the thick forest has
    been felled!
3 Listen, the wail of the shepherds,
    for their glory is despoiled!
Listen, the roar of the lions,
    for the thickets of the Jordan
    are destroyed!

TWO KINDS OF SHEPHERDS

4 Thus said the LORD my God: Be a shepherd of the flock doomed to slaughter. 5 Those who buy them kill them and go unpunished; and those who sell them say, "Blessed be the LORD, for I have become rich"; and their own shepherds have no pity on them. 6 For I will no longer have pity on the inhabitants of the earth, says the LORD. I will cause them, every one, to fall each into the hand of a neighbor, and each into the hand of the king; and they shall devastate the earth, and I will deliver no one from their hand.

7 So, on behalf of the sheep merchants, I became the shepherd of the flock doomed to slaughter. I took

---

[a] 10.3 Or *male goats*   [b] 10.11 Gk: Heb *He*

two staffs; one I named Favor, the other I named Unity, and I tended the sheep. ⁸In one month I disposed of the three shepherds, for I had become impatient with them, and they also detested me. ⁹So I said, "I will not be your shepherd. What is to die, let it die; what is to be destroyed, let it be destroyed; and let those that are left devour the flesh of one another!" ¹⁰I took my staff Favor and broke it, annulling the covenant that I had made with all the peoples. ¹¹So it was annulled on that day, and the sheep merchants, who were watching me, knew that it was the word of the LORD. ¹²I then said to them, "If it seems right to you, give me my wages; but if not, keep them." So they weighed out as my wages thirty shekels of silver. ¹³Then the LORD said to me, "Throw it into the treasury"ᵃ—this lordly price at which I was valued by them. So I took the thirty shekels of silver and threw them into the treasuryᵃ in the house of the LORD. ¹⁴Then I broke my second staff Unity, annulling the family ties between Judah and Israel.

15 Then the LORD said to me: Take once more the implements of a worthless shepherd. ¹⁶For I am now raising up in the land a shepherd who does not care for the perishing, or seek the wandering,ᵇ or heal the maimed, or nourish the healthy,ᶜ but devours the flesh of the fat ones, tearing off even their hoofs.

¹⁷ Oh, my worthless shepherd,
    who deserts the flock!
May the sword strike his arm
    and his right eye!
Let his arm be completely
        withered,
    his right eye utterly blinded!

JERUSALEM'S VICTORY

12   An Oracle.

The word of the LORD concerning Israel: Thus says the LORD, who stretched out the heavens and founded the earth and formed the human spirit within: ²See, I am about to make Jerusalem a cup of reeling for all the surrounding peoples; it will be against Judah also in the siege against Jerusalem. ³On that day I will make Jerusalem a heavy stone for all the peoples; all who lift it shall grievously hurt themselves. And all the nations of the earth shall come together against it. ⁴On that day, says the LORD, I will strike every horse with panic, and its rider with madness. But on the house of Judah I will keep a watchful eye, when I strike every horse of the peoples with blindness. ⁵Then the clans of Judah shall say to themselves, "The inhabitants of Jerusalem have strength through the LORD of hosts, their God."

6 On that day I will make the clans of Judah like a blazing pot on a pile of wood, like a flaming torch among sheaves; and they shall devour to the right and to the left all the surrounding peoples, while Jerusalem shall again be inhabited in its place, in Jerusalem.

7 And the LORD will give victory to the tents of Judah first, that the glory of the house of David and the glory of the inhabitants of Jerusalem may not be exalted over that of Judah. ⁸On that day the LORD will shield the inhabitants of Jerusalem so that the feeblest among them on that day shall be like David, and the house of David shall be like God, like the angel of the LORD, at their head. ⁹And on that day I will seek to destroy all the nations that come against Jerusalem.

MOURNING FOR THE PIERCED ONE

10 And I will pour out a spirit of compassion and supplication on the house of David and the inhabitants of Jerusalem, so that, when they look on the oneᵈ whom they have pierced, they shall mourn for him, as one mourns for an only child, and weep bitterly over him, as one weeps over a firstborn. ¹¹On that day the mourning in Jerusalem will be as great as the mourning for Hadad-

ᵃ 11.13 Syr: Heb *it to the potter*
ᵇ 11.16 Syr Compare Gk Vg: Heb *the youth*   ᶜ 11.16 Meaning of Heb uncertain
ᵈ 12.10 Heb *on me*

rimmon in the plain of Megiddo. 12The land shall mourn, each family by itself; the family of the house of David by itself, and their wives by themselves; the family of the house of Nathan by itself, and their wives by themselves; 13the family of the house of Levi by itself, and their wives by themselves; the family of the Shimeites by itself, and their wives by themselves; 14and all the families that are left, each by itself, and their wives by themselves.

13

On that day a fountain shall be opened for the house of David and the inhabitants of Jerusalem, to cleanse them from sin and impurity.

IDOLATRY CUT OFF

2 On that day, says the LORD of hosts, I will cut off the names of the idols from the land, so that they shall be remembered no more; and also I will remove from the land the prophets and the unclean spirit. 3And if any prophets appear again, their fathers and mothers who bore them will say to them, "You shall not live, for you speak lies in the name of the LORD"; and their fathers and their mothers who bore them shall pierce them through when they prophesy. 4On that day the prophets will be ashamed, every one, of their visions when they prophesy; they will not put on a hairy mantle in order to deceive, 5but each of them will say, "I am no prophet, I am a tiller of the soil; for the land has been my possession[a] since my youth." 6And if anyone asks them, "What are these wounds on your chest?"[b] the answer will be "The wounds I received in the house of my friends."

THE ONLY CURE FOR

PRIDE IS TO CONFESS SIN,

ASK FORGIVENESS AND

LET GOD RE-CREATE US.

THE SHEPHERD STRUCK, THE FLOCK SCATTERED

7 "Awake, O sword, against
    my shepherd,
   against the man who is
    my associate,"
      says the LORD of hosts.
  Strike the shepherd, that the
    sheep may be scattered;
  I will turn my hand against
    the little ones.
8 In the whole land, says the LORD,
    two-thirds shall be cut
      off and perish,
  and one-third shall be left alive.
9 And I will put this third
      into the fire,
  refine them as one
      refines silver,
  and test them as gold is tested.
  They will call on my name,
    and I will answer them.
  I will say, "They are my people";
    and they will say, "The
    LORD is our God."

FUTURE WARFARE AND FINAL VICTORY

14

See, a day is coming for the LORD, when the plunder taken from you will be divided in your midst. 2For I will gather all the nations against Jerusalem to battle, and the city shall be taken, and the houses looted and the women raped; half the city shall go into exile, but the rest of the people shall not be cut off from the city. 3Then the LORD will go forth and fight against those nations as when he fights on a day of battle. 4On that day his feet shall stand on the Mount of Olives, which lies before Jerusalem on the east; and the Mount of Olives shall be split in two from east to west by a very wide valley; so that one half of the Mount shall withdraw northward, and the other half southward. 5And you shall flee by the valley of the LORD's mountain,[c] for the valley between the mountains shall reach to Azal;[d] and you shall flee as you fled from the earthquake in the days of King

[a] 13.5 Cn: Heb *for humankind has caused me to possess*   [b] 13.6 Heb *wounds between your hands*   [c] 14.5 Heb *my mountains*
[d] 14.5 Meaning of Heb uncertain

Uzziah of Judah. Then the LORD my God will come, and all the holy ones with him.

6 On that day there shall not be[a] either cold or frost.[b] 7 And there shall be continuous day (it is known to the LORD), not day and not night, for at evening time there shall be light.

8 On that day living waters shall flow out from Jerusalem, half of them to the eastern sea and half of them to the western sea; it shall continue in summer as in winter.

9 And the LORD will become king over all the earth; on that day the LORD will be one and his name one.

10 The whole land shall be turned into a plain from Geba to Rimmon south of Jerusalem. But Jerusalem shall remain aloft on its site from the Gate of Benjamin to the place of the former gate, to the Corner Gate, and from the Tower of Hananel to the king's wine presses. 11 And it shall be inhabited, for never again shall it be doomed to destruction; Jerusalem shall abide in security.

12 This shall be the plague with which the LORD will strike all the peoples that wage war against Jerusalem: their flesh shall rot while they are still on their feet; their eyes shall rot in their sockets, and their tongues shall rot in their mouths. 13 On that day a great panic from the LORD shall fall on them, so that each will seize the hand of a neighbor, and the hand of the one will be raised against the hand of the other; 14 even Judah will fight at Jerusalem. And the wealth of all the surrounding nations shall be collected— gold, silver, and garments in great abundance. 15 And a plague like this plague shall fall on the horses, the mules, the camels, the donkeys, and whatever animals may be in those camps.

16 Then all who survive of the nations that have come against Jerusalem shall go up year after year to worship the King, the LORD of hosts, and to keep the festival of booths.[c] 17 If any of the families of the earth do not go up to Jerusalem to worship the King, the LORD of hosts, there will be no rain upon them. 18 And if the family of Egypt do not go up and present themselves, then on them shall[d] come the plague that the LORD inflicts on the nations that do not go up to keep the festival of booths.[c] 19 Such shall be the punishment of Egypt and the punishment of all the nations that do not go up to keep the festival of booths.[c]

20 On that day there shall be inscribed on the bells of the horses, "Holy to the LORD." And the cooking pots in the house of the LORD shall be as holy as[e] the bowls in front of the altar; 21 and every cooking pot in Jerusalem and Judah shall be sacred to the LORD of hosts, so that all who sacrifice may come and use them to boil the flesh of the sacrifice. And there shall no longer be traders[f] in the house of the LORD of hosts on that day.

a 14.6 Cn: Heb *there shall not be light*
b 14.6 Compare Gk Syr Vg Tg: Meaning of Heb uncertain   c 14.16,18,19 Or *tabernacles*; Heb *succoth*   d 14.18 Gk Syr: Heb *shall not*   e 14.20 Heb *shall be like*   f 14.21 Or *Canaanites*

MALACHI

How do you feel when someone breaks faith with you? Perhaps they lie to you or just go through the motions of loving you. In Malachi, we witness God's wrenching grief when the people of Israel break faith with their Lord; they rob God of the proper tithes, break God's laws for marriage and perpetuate injustice. Malachi announces that the Lord will send a messenger to refine and purify the people. Malachi implores them to return to God and remain faithful, to be God's "special possession" (Malachi 3:17).

1
An oracle. The word of the LORD to Israel by Malachi.[a]

ISRAEL PREFERRED TO EDOM

2 I have loved you, says the LORD. But you say, "How have you loved us?" Is not Esau Jacob's brother? says the LORD. Yet I have loved Jacob 3but I have hated Esau; I have made his hill country a desolation and his heritage a desert for jackals. 4If Edom says, "We are shattered but we will rebuild the ruins," the LORD of hosts says: They may build, but I will tear down, until they are called the wicked country, the people with whom the LORD is angry forever. 5Your own eyes shall see this, and you shall say, "Great is the LORD beyond the borders of Israel!"

CORRUPTION OF THE PRIESTHOOD

6 A son honors his father, and servants their master. If then I am a father, where is the honor due me? And if I am a master, where is the respect due me? says the LORD of hosts to you, O priests, who despise my name. You say, "How have we despised your name?" 7By offering polluted food on my altar. And you say, "How have we polluted it?"[b] By thinking that the LORD's table may be despised. 8When you offer blind animals in sacrifice, is that not wrong? And when you offer those that are lame or sick, is that not wrong? Try presenting that to your governor; will he be pleased with you or show you favor? says the LORD of hosts. 9And now implore the favor of God, that he may be gracious to us. The fault is yours. Will he show favor to any of you? says the LORD of hosts. 10Oh, that someone among you would shut the temple[c] doors, so that you would not kindle fire on my altar in vain! I have no pleasure in you, says the LORD of hosts, and I will not accept an offering from your hands. 11For from the rising of the sun to its setting my name is great among the nations, and in every place incense is offered to my name, and a pure offering; for my name is great among the nations, says the LORD of hosts. 12But you profane it when you say that the Lord's table is polluted, and the food for it[d] may be despised. 13"What a weariness this is," you say, and you sniff at me,[e] says the LORD of hosts. You bring what has been taken by violence or is lame or sick, and this you bring as your offering! Shall I accept that from your hand? says the LORD. 14Cursed be the cheat who has a male in the flock and vows to give it, and yet sacrifices to the Lord what is blemished; for I am a great King, says the LORD of hosts, and my name is reverenced among the nations.

2
And now, O priests, this command is for you. 2If you will not listen, if you will not lay it to heart to give glory to my name, says the LORD of hosts, then I will send the curse on you and I will curse your blessings; indeed I have already cursed them,[f] because you do not lay it to heart. 3I will rebuke your offspring, and spread dung on your faces, the dung of your offerings, and I will put you out of my presence.[g]

4 Know, then, that I have sent this command to you, that my covenant with Levi may hold, says the LORD of hosts. 5My covenant with him was a covenant of life and well-being, which I gave him; this called for reverence, and he revered me and stood in awe of my name. 6True instruction was in his mouth, and no wrong was found on his lips. He walked with me in integrity and uprightness, and he turned many from iniquity. 7For the lips of a priest should guard knowledge, and people should seek instruction from his mouth, for he is the messenger of the LORD of hosts. 8But you have turned aside from the way; you have caused many to stumble by your instruction; you have corrupted the covenant of Levi, says the LORD of

---

a 1.1 Or by my messenger b 1.7 Gk: Heb you
c 1.10 Heb lacks temple d 1.12 Compare Syr
Tg: Heb its fruit, its food e 1.13 Another
reading is at it f 2.2 Heb it g 2.3 Cn
Compare Gk Syr: Heb and he shall bear
you to it

hosts, [9]and so I make you despised and abased before all the people, inasmuch as you have not kept my ways but have shown partiality in your instruction.

THE COVENANT PROFANED BY JUDAH

10 Have we not all one father? Has not one God created us? Why then are we faithless to one another, profaning the covenant of our ancestors? [11]Judah has been faithless, and abomination has been committed in Israel and in Jerusalem; for Judah has profaned the sanctuary of the LORD, which he loves, and has married the daughter of a foreign god. [12]May the LORD cut off from the tents of Jacob anyone who does this—any to witness[a] or answer, or to bring an offering to the LORD of hosts.

13 And this you do as well: You cover the LORD's altar with tears, with weeping and groaning because he no longer regards the offering or accepts it with favor at your hand. [14]You ask, "Why does he not?" Because the LORD was a witness between you and the wife of your youth, to whom you have been faithless, though she is your companion and your wife by covenant. [15]Did not one God make her?[b] Both flesh and spirit are his.[c] And what does the one God[d] desire? Godly off-spring. So look to yourselves, and do not let anyone be faithless to the wife of his youth. [16]For I hate[e] divorce, says the LORD, the God of Israel, and covering one's garment with violence, says the LORD of hosts. So take heed to yourselves and do not be faithless.

17 You have wearied the LORD with your words. Yet you say, "How have we wearied him?" By saying, "All who do evil are good in the sight of the LORD, and he delights in them." Or by asking, "Where is the God of justice?"

THE COMING MESSENGER

3 See, I am sending my messenger to prepare the way before me, and the Lord whom you seek will suddenly come to his temple. The messenger of the covenant in whom you delight—indeed, he is coming, says the LORD of hosts. [2]But who can endure the day of his coming, and who can stand when he appears?

For he is like a refiner's fire and like fullers' soap; [3]he will sit as a refiner and purifier of silver, and he will purify the descendants of Levi and refine them like gold and silver, until they present offerings to the

[a] **2.12** Cn Compare Gk: Heb *arouse*
[b] **2.15** Or *Has he not made one?* [c] **2.15** Cn: Heb *and a remnant of spirit was his*
[d] **2.15** Heb *he* [e] **2.16** Cn: Heb *he hates*

⊢ BIBLE IN LIFE ▷

Humble Service
Malachi 3.1

Malachi prophesied about the coming of John the Baptist, who would "go before the Lord to prepare his ways, to give knowledge of salvation to his people the by the forgiveness of their sins" (Luke 1.76–77). John the Baptist proclaimed a baptism of repentance for the forgiveness of sins. People from all over the Judean countryside and from Jerusalem went out to the wilderness to confess their sins and be baptized by John in the Jordan River. John proclaimed the powerful One who would come after him: Jesus. John said, "I baptize you with water; but one who is more powerful than I is coming; I am not worthy to untie the thong of his sandals. He will baptize you with the Holy Spirit and fire" (Luke 3.16). Though John spoke to hundreds, perhaps thousands, of people, and though Jesus praised John above all other people (see Luke 7.28), John never exalted himself. He took no credit for the forgiveness of sin. Humbly John the Baptist served as a precursor to Christ by preparing the people's hearts for their Savior. How do we prepare our hearts to accept Christ? How do we humbly prepare the way for Jesus in the lives of others?

Not What They Asked For

I am sending my messenger to prepare the way before me . . . But who can endure the day of his coming, and who can stand when he appears? For he is like a refiner's fire and like fullers' soap.

Malachi 3.1-2

The people living in the time of Malachi were calling on God, asking him to uphold justice—that is, to give them what they deserved (Malachi 1.2; 2.13–14,17). They believed they ought to have much better than what they were getting, having recently returned to Judah from exile in Babylon and working to rebuild the temple. Nevertheless, they were still experiencing hardship and living under foreign domination. Why wasn't God rewarding them for their efforts and granting them justice? The truth was that real justice was the last thing these people wanted to face.

The words of Malachi warned that God would send a messenger soon to prepare the way and to uphold justice, but God's justice would be something entirely different from what they expected. God would judge the people for offering sacrifices of blind and crippled animals, ones that were not worthy sacrifices on the part of the giver. God would condemn the priests and Levites for being corrupt in their judgments. Justice would not be a pat on the back or material blessings for the people of Judah; it would mean punishment for all their wrongdoing. By punishing them, though, God would refine the people like gold or silver, burning off the dross of sin and making them pure once again.

What about us today? We often think we want God to give us justice, to rescue us from the wrongs that are being done to us or from the difficult circumstances we are facing. In reality, we would not be able to endure God's justice because it would fall on us just as heavily as it would fall on anyone else. As Paul says in Romans 3.23, we all have sinned and deserve God's wrath. Instead of justice, what we really want—and need—is mercy. Thankfully, that is exactly what God offers us in Jesus Christ. We are offered forgiveness and mercy—not punishment as we deserve, but eternal life and reconciliation with God. The first step, though, is recognizing that we need God's mercy and grace. As we repent of our sin, we are graciously refined; our hearts and our actions are transformed. At the same time, we will find that our concerns will become less focused on ourselves and more focused on how we can extend God's love to others, just as Jesus did.

Going Deeper

- Describe a time when you wished for God's justice to be meted out on someone who wronged you.
- If God were truly to give you total justice, what might that look like? How would God's mercy and forgiveness be a better gift to you?

PONDER

But who can endure the day of his coming, and who can stand when he appears? For he is like a refiner's fire and like fullers' soap; he will sit as a refiner and purifier of silver, and he will purify the descendants of Levi and refine them like gold and silver, until they present offerings to the LORD in righteousness.
—Malachi 3.2–3

PRAY

Father, we know that in the scriptures of the Old Testament you sometimes address your people in harsh terms. We realize, after some contemplation, that our service to Jesus Christ is all too often lukewarm. We realize that we could be subject to condemnation but instead are saved by the refining fire of a loving Savior, Jesus Christ. Give us the courage to look at ourselves and to stoke the fires of our zeal for him. Let us realize that the blessings of a Christlike life are the finest rewards we can have, not only in the final days and the hereafter, but also today. Let us always remember that if we open the door of our hearts, the presence of Jesus Christ and the Holy Spirit will come and be within us. Amen.

LORD in righteousness.[a] 4 Then the offering of Judah and Jerusalem will be pleasing to the LORD as in the days of old and as in former years.

5 Then I will draw near to you for judgment; I will be swift to bear witness against the sorcerers, against the adulterers, against those who swear falsely, against those who oppress the hired workers in their wages, the widow and the orphan, against those who thrust aside the alien, and do not fear me, says the LORD of hosts.

6 For I the LORD do not change; therefore you, O children of Jacob, have not perished. 7 Ever since the days of your ancestors you have turned aside from my statutes and have not kept them. Return to me, and I will return to you, says the LORD of hosts. But you say, "How shall we return?"

DO NOT ROB GOD

8 Will anyone rob God? Yet you are robbing me! But you say, "How are we robbing you?" In your tithes and offerings! 9 You are cursed with a curse, for you are robbing me— the whole nation of you! 10 Bring the full tithe into the storehouse, so that there may be food in my house, and thus put me to the test, says the LORD of hosts; see if I will not open the windows of heaven for you and pour down for you an overflowing blessing. 11 I will rebuke the locust[b] for you, so that it will not destroy the produce of your soil; and your vine in the field shall not be barren, says the LORD of hosts. 12 Then all nations will count you happy, for you will be a land of delight, says the LORD of hosts.

13 You have spoken harsh words against me, says the LORD. Yet you say, "How have we spoken against you?" 14 You have said, "It is vain to serve God. What do we profit by keeping his command or by going about as mourners before the LORD of hosts? 15 Now we count the arrogant happy; evildoers not only prosper, but when they put God to the test they escape."

THE REWARD OF
THE FAITHFUL

16 Then those who revered the LORD spoke with one another. The LORD took note and listened, and a book of remembrance was written before him of those who revered the LORD and thought on his name. 17 They shall be mine, says the LORD of hosts, my special possession on the day when I act, and I will spare them as parents spare their children who serve them. 18 Then once more you shall see the difference between

a 3.3 Or right offerings to the LORD
b 3.11 Heb devourer

the righteous and the wicked, between one who serves God and one who does not serve him.

THE GREAT DAY OF THE LORD

4 [a] See, the day is coming, burning like an oven, when all the arrogant and all evildoers will be stubble; the day that comes shall burn them up, says the LORD of hosts, so that it will leave them neither root nor branch. 2 But for you who revere my name the sun of righteousness shall rise, with healing in its wings. You shall go out leaping like calves from the stall. 3 And you shall tread down the wicked, for they will be ashes under the soles of your feet, on the day when I act, says the LORD of hosts.

4 Remember the teaching of my servant Moses, the statutes and ordinances that I commanded him at Horeb for all Israel.

5 Lo, I will send you the prophet Elijah before the great and terrible day of the LORD comes. 6 He will turn the hearts of parents to their children and the hearts of children to their parents, so that I will not come and strike the land with a curse. [b]

[a] 4.1 Ch 4.1–6 are Ch 3.19–24 in Heb
[b] 4.6 Or a ban of utter destruction

PONDER

But for you who revere my name the sun of righteousness shall rise, with healing in its wings. You shall go out leaping like calves from the stall. And you shall tread down the wicked, for they will be ashes under the soles of your feet, on the day when I act, says the LORD of hosts.
—Malachi 4.2–3

PRAY

Father, we read from these intriguing prophets, all of whom were very different. But you gave all of them the responsibility to tell other people the truth about you, a responsibility you also give us. But first we have to know the truth ourselves. Teach us your truth and give us the courage to look within our own hearts, to repent of our sins and correct our mistakes and failures. We praise and thank you as we realize the blessings of grace, mercy and forgiveness that you give us through your Son, Jesus Christ. In his name we pray. Amen.

THE NEW TESTAMENT

The Gospel According to
MATTHEW

Have you ever read a sequel to a novel without having read the original story? The book of Matthew picks up the story line between the Old and New Testaments, helping us to understand how the life and teachings of Jesus build upon God's centuries-old promises. The Jewish people in Jesus' day had been waiting for the promised Messiah to inaugurate God's kingdom on earth. Matthew draws heavily on material from the Old Testament, offering proof that Jesus is the One that Israel has been waiting for.

THE GENEALOGY OF JESUS THE MESSIAH

1 An account of the genealogy[a] of Jesus the Messiah,[b] the son of David, the son of Abraham.

2 Abraham was the father of Isaac, and Isaac the father of Jacob, and Jacob the father of Judah and his brothers, 3 and Judah the father of Perez and Zerah by Tamar, and Perez the father of Hezron, and Hezron the father of Aram, 4 and Aram the father of Aminadab, and Aminadab the father of Nahshon, and Nahshon the father of Salmon, 5 and Salmon the father of Boaz by Rahab, and Boaz the father of Obed by Ruth, and Obed the father of Jesse, 6 and Jesse the father of King David.

And David was the father of Solomon by the wife of Uriah, 7 and Solomon the father of Rehoboam, and Rehoboam the father of Abijah, and Abijah the father of Asaph,[c] 8 and Asaph[c] the father of Jehoshaphat, and Jehoshaphat the father of Joram, and Joram the father of Uzziah, 9 and Uzziah the father of Jotham, and Jotham the father of Ahaz, and Ahaz the father of Hezekiah, 10 and Hezekiah the father of Manasseh, and Manasseh the father of Amos,[d] and Amos[d] the father of Josiah, 11 and Josiah the father of Jechoniah and his brothers, at the time of the deportation to Babylon.

12 And after the deportation to Babylon: Jechoniah was the father of Salathiel, and Salathiel the father of Zerubbabel, 13 and Zerubbabel the father of Abiud, and Abiud the father of Eliakim, and Eliakim the father of Azor, 14 and Azor the father of Zadok, and Zadok the father of Achim, and Achim the father of Eliud, 15 and Eliud the father of Eleazar, and Eleazar the father of Matthan, and Matthan the father of Jacob, 16 and Jacob the father of Joseph the husband of Mary, of whom Jesus was born, who is called the Messiah.[e]

17 So all the generations from Abraham to David are fourteen generations; and from David to the deportation to Babylon, fourteen generations; and from the deportation to Babylon to the Messiah,[e] fourteen generations.

THE BIRTH OF JESUS THE MESSIAH

18 Now the birth of Jesus the Messiah[b] took place in this way. When his mother Mary had been engaged to Joseph, but before they lived together, she was found to be with child from the Holy Spirit. 19 Her husband Joseph, being a righteous man and unwilling to expose her to public disgrace, planned to dismiss her quietly. 20 But just when he had resolved to do this, an angel of the Lord appeared to him in a dream and said, "Joseph, son of David, do not be afraid to take Mary as your wife, for the child conceived in her is from the Holy Spirit. 21 She will bear a son, and you are to name him Jesus, for he will save his people from their sins." 22 All this took place to fulfill what had been spoken by the Lord through the prophet:

23 "Look, the virgin shall conceive
    and bear a son,
and they shall name him
    Emmanuel,"

which means, "God is with us." 24 When Joseph awoke from sleep, he did as the angel of the Lord commanded him; he took her as his wife, 25 but had no marital relations with her until she had borne a son;[f] and he named him Jesus.

THE VISIT OF THE WISE MEN

2 In the time of King Herod, after Jesus was born in Bethlehem of Judea, wise men[g] from the East came to Jerusalem, 2 asking, "Where is the child who has been born king of the Jews? For we observed his star at its rising,[h] and have come to pay him homage." 3 When King Herod heard this, he was frightened, and all Jerusalem with him; 4 and calling together all the chief priests and scribes of the people, he inquired of them where the Messiah[e] was to be born. 5 They told him, "In Bethlehem

a 1.1 Or birth   b 1.1,18 Or Jesus Christ
c 1.7,8 Other ancient authorities read Asa
d 1.10 Other ancient authorities read Amon
e 1.16,17; 2.4 Or the Christ   f 1.25 Other ancient authorities read her firstborn son
g 2.1 Or astrologers; Gk magi   h 2.2 Or in the East

PONDER

When Joseph awoke from sleep, he did as the angel of the Lord commanded him; he took [Mary] as his wife.
—Matthew 1.24

PRAY

Lord, when we read of Jesus' birth, we usually think about Mary, the shepherds, the angels and the wise men. But we are also thankful for this story about Joseph, who obeyed you without questioning. Joseph's inspired decision to take Mary for his wife is instructive for us because he trusted you. We pray that we might allow righteousness such as Joseph's to guide our daily decisions. May your righteousness prevail in our dealings toward one another and in our roles as citizens of a great nation. We ask you in the name of our Savior. Amen.

of Judea; for so it has been written by the prophet:
6 'And you, Bethlehem, in
the land of Judah,
are by no means least among
the rulers of Judah;
for from you shall come a ruler
who is to shepherd[a] my
people Israel.' "
7 Then Herod secretly called for the wise men[b] and learned from them the exact time when the star had appeared. 8Then he sent them to Bethlehem, saying, "Go and search diligently for the child; and when you have found him, bring me word so that I may also go and pay him homage." 9When they had heard the king, they set out; and there, ahead of them, went the star that they had seen at its rising,[c] until it stopped over the place where the child was. 10When they saw that the star had stopped,[d] they were overwhelmed with joy. 11On entering the house, they saw the child with Mary his

mother; and they knelt down and paid him homage. Then, opening their treasure chests, they offered him gifts of gold, frankincense, and myrrh. 12And having been warned in a dream not to return to Herod, they left for their own country by another road.

THE ESCAPE TO EGYPT

13 Now after they had left, an angel of the Lord appeared to Joseph in a dream and said, "Get up, take the child and his mother, and flee to Egypt, and remain there until I tell you; for Herod is about to search for the child, to destroy him." 14Then Joseph[e] got up, took the child and his mother by night, and went to Egypt, 15and remained there until the death of Herod. This was to fulfill what had been spoken by the Lord through the prophet, "Out of Egypt I have called my son."

THE MASSACRE OF THE INFANTS

16 When Herod saw that he had been tricked by the wise men,[b] he was infuriated, and he sent and killed all the children in and around Bethlehem who were two years old or under, according to the time that he had learned from the wise men.[b] 17Then was fulfilled what had been spoken through the prophet Jeremiah:
18 "A voice was heard in Ramah,
wailing and loud lamentation,
Rachel weeping for her children;
she refused to be consoled,
because they are no more."

THE RETURN FROM EGYPT

19 When Herod died, an angel of the Lord suddenly appeared in a dream to Joseph in Egypt and said, 20"Get up, take the child and his mother, and go to the land of Israel, for those who were seeking the child's life are dead." 21Then Joseph[e] got up, took the child and his mother, and went to the land of Israel. 22But when he heard that Archelaus was ruling over Judea in place of his father Herod, he was

a 2.6 Or rule   b 2.7,16 Or astrologers; Gk magi   c 2.9 Or in the East   d 2.10 Gk saw the star   e 2.14,21 Gk he

afraid to go there. And after being warned in a dream, he went away to the district of Galilee. 23There he made his home in a town called Nazareth, so that what had been spoken through the prophets might be fulfilled, "He will be called a Nazorean."

THE PROCLAMATION OF JOHN THE BAPTIST

3 In those days John the Baptist appeared in the wilderness of Judea, proclaiming, 2"Repent, for the kingdom of heaven has come near."[a] 3This is the one of whom the prophet Isaiah spoke when he said,

"The voice of one crying out
in the wilderness:

PONDER

Then Joseph got up, took the child and his mother by night, and went to Egypt, and remained there until the death of Herod. This was to fulfill what had been spoken by the Lord through the prophet, "Out of Egypt I have called my son."
—Matthew 2.14–15

PRAY

Father, we are thankful for this vivid, intriguing story told by Matthew—an exciting and dramatic story that holds many mysteries about what is going to happen next. That is the way our lives are—sometimes very quiet and private, sometimes very loud and publicized. All of us are going to face vicissitudes, disappointments, sorrows, challenges and temptations. Help us, as we go through these times, to remember that you are our strong Savior and ally. Help us to hear your Word through study and prayer. Let it be our foundation, our inspiration and our source of strength. Help us, each in our unique way, to turn constantly to you through our Savior, Jesus Christ. In his name we pray. Amen.

'Prepare the way of the Lord,
make his paths straight.' "
4Now John wore clothing of camel's hair with a leather belt around his waist, and his food was locusts and wild honey. 5Then the people of Jerusalem and all Judea were going out to him, and all the region along the Jordan, 6and they were baptized by him in the river Jordan, confessing their sins.

7 But when he saw many Pharisees and Sadducees coming for baptism, he said to them, "You brood of vipers! Who warned you to flee from the wrath to come? 8Bear fruit worthy of repentance. 9Do not presume to say to yourselves, 'We have Abraham as our ancestor'; for I tell you, God is able from these stones to raise up children to Abraham. 10Even now the ax is lying at the root of the trees; every tree therefore that does not bear good fruit is cut down and thrown into the fire.

11 "I baptize you with[b] water for repentance, but one who is more powerful than I is coming after me; I am not worthy to carry his sandals. He will baptize you with[b] the Holy Spirit and fire. 12His winnowing fork is in his hand, and he will clear his threshing floor and will gather his wheat into the granary; but the chaff he will burn with unquenchable fire."

THE BAPTISM OF JESUS

13 Then Jesus came from Galilee to John at the Jordan, to be baptized by him. 14John would have prevented him, saying, "I need to be baptized by you, and do you come to me?" 15But Jesus answered him, "Let it be so now; for it is proper for us in this way to fulfill all righteousness." Then he consented. 16And when Jesus had been baptized, just as he came up from the water, suddenly the heavens were opened to him and he saw the Spirit of God descending like a dove and alighting on him. 17And a voice from heaven said, "This is my Son, the Beloved,[c] with whom I am well pleased."

[a] 3.2 Or is at hand   [b] 3.11 Or in   [c] 3.17 Or my beloved Son

SEEKING THE KINGDOM

In those days John the Baptist appeared in the wilderness of Judea, proclaiming, "Repent, for the kingdom of heaven has come near."

—Matthew 3.1–2

Pause for a moment and consider what John meant by the words *kingdom of heaven*. The Pharisees and Sadducees distinguished God's kingdom as something far in the distance or something with elements of punishment for sins. So here John the Baptist uses *kingdom of heaven* as a phrase designed to alert the people. He wanted them to see that they needed to repent in the present because the kingdom of heaven was already in their midst.

We live in the midst of the kingdom of heaven now, just as John did in the time of Christ. The kingdom of heaven is a continuing history of human beings and our relationship and reconciliation with God through faith in Jesus Christ. Everything now and in days past and in years ahead is under the sovereignty of God. Human beings are designed to live in God's kingdom. And we can be part of the kingdom of heaven if we separate ourselves from the morals and customs and demands of the secular world and align ourselves with God through faith in Jesus.

Seeking the kingdom is a highly personal endeavor. Each of us has an individual relationship with God through personal faith in Jesus Christ. We are responsible to accept the place we've been given in the kingdom of heaven by repenting of sin and having faith in him.

The kingdom of heaven is like a flood that encompasses the whole world and is comprised of the people who accept faith in Jesus Christ. It is a community of Christians that should be intimately bound to each other as brothers and sisters. It is also a community that should always be expanding. That's the Great Commission of Jesus Christ (see Matthew 28.16–20).

The degree of our commitment to our relationship with God, through our faith in Jesus Christ and our desire to emulate the perfect example set for us by Jesus, establishes our place in the kingdom of heaven. How well do our lives demonstrate that God's kingdom is within us? Are we living in the present kingdom of heaven as a community of Christians, repenting of our sin and allowing Jesus to make us more like him? Or are we living—like the Pharisees and Sadducees—as if the kingdom of heaven is a distant event, out of our reach and the reach of those around us?

Going Deeper

- What activities and behaviors in your life give evidence that the kingdom of heaven is within you?
- How would you describe your level of participation in the kingdom of heaven?

THE TEMPTATION OF JESUS

4 Then Jesus was led up by the Spirit into the wilderness to be tempted by the devil. ²He fasted forty days and forty nights, and afterwards he was famished. ³The tempter came and said to him, "If you are the Son of God, command these stones to become loaves of bread." ⁴But he answered, "It is written,

'One does not live by bread alone,
    but by every word that comes
        from the mouth of God.'"

5 Then the devil took him to the holy city and placed him on the pinnacle of the temple, ⁶saying to him, "If you are the Son of God, throw yourself down; for it is written,

'He will command his angels
    concerning you,'
and 'On their hands they
    will bear you up,
so that you will not dash your
    foot against a stone.'"

⁷Jesus said to him, "Again it is written, 'Do not put the Lord your God to the test.'"

8 Again, the devil took him to a very high mountain and showed him all the kingdoms of the world and their splendor; ⁹and he said to him, "All these I will give you, if you will fall down and worship me."

¹⁰Jesus said to him, "Away with you, Satan! for it is written,

'Worship the Lord your God,
    and serve only him.'"

¹¹Then the devil left him, and suddenly angels came and waited on him.

JESUS BEGINS HIS MINISTRY IN GALILEE

12 Now when Jesusª heard that John had been arrested, he withdrew to Galilee. ¹³He left Nazareth and made his home in Capernaum by the sea, in the territory of Zebulun and Naphtali, ¹⁴so that what had been spoken through the prophet Isaiah might be fulfilled:

15 "Land of Zebulun, land
        of Naphtali,
    on the road by the sea, across
        the Jordan, Galilee
        of the Gentiles—
16 the people who sat in darkness
        have seen a great light,
    and for those who sat in
        the region and
        shadow of death
    light has dawned."

¹⁷From that time Jesus began to proclaim, "Repent, for the kingdom of heaven has come near."ᵇ

ª 4.12 Gk *he*   ᵇ 4.17 Or *is at hand*

BIBLE IN LIFE ▷

No Shortcuts   Matthew 4.1–11

It is interesting to note that when the devil tempted Jesus near the start of his ministry, the things Satan offered were not sinful in and of themselves. It was not wrong for Jesus to desire food, nor was it wrong for him to desire safety from physical harm. It was not even wrong for him to desire to rule over all the kingdoms of the world—after all, they were rightfully his. The sin that the devil dangled before Jesus lay in the means he would have used to attain each of those things. In short, the devil offered him shortcuts to gaining legitimate desires, rather than patiently following the perfect will of his Father in heaven.

Do we ever attempt to take sinful shortcuts to reach legitimate goals in life? Do we students cheat on tests to help earn better grades or get into good schools? Do we business workers spend important work time making personal phone calls? Do we business executives fail to pay adequate wages to employees? Do we young people compromise moral convictions about sexual purity in order to please others? Goals that may not be sinful can quickly become sources of sin if we try to attain them in ways that circumvent God's means. As Jesus showed us, the path we need to follow is to trust God to help us bring about all the good things he has for us in his will and in his way and in his time.

JESUS CALLS THE FIRST DISCIPLES

18 As he walked by the Sea of Galilee, he saw two brothers, Simon, who is called Peter, and Andrew his brother, casting a net into the sea— for they were fishermen. 19 And he said to them, "Follow me, and I will make you fish for people." 20 Immediately they left their nets and followed him. 21 As he went from there, he saw two other brothers, James son of Zebedee and his brother John, in the boat with their father Zebedee, mending their nets, and he called them. 22 Immediately they left the boat and their father, and followed him.

JESUS MINISTERS TO CROWDS OF PEOPLE

23 Jesus[a] went throughout Galilee, teaching in their synagogues and proclaiming the good news[b] of the kingdom and curing every disease and every sickness among the people. 24 So his fame spread throughout all Syria, and they brought to him all the sick, those who were afflicted with various diseases and pains, demoniacs, epileptics, and paralytics, and he cured them. 25 And great crowds followed him from Galilee, the Decapolis, Jerusalem, Judea, and from beyond the Jordan.

THE BEATITUDES

5 When Jesus[c] saw the crowds, he went up the mountain; and after he sat down, his disciples came to him. 2 Then he began to speak, and taught them, saying:

3 "Blessed are the poor in spirit, for theirs is the kingdom of heaven.

4 "Blessed are those who mourn, for they will be comforted.

5 "Blessed are the meek, for they will inherit the earth.

6 "Blessed are those who hunger and thirst for righteousness, for they will be filled.

7 "Blessed are the merciful, for they will receive mercy.

8 "Blessed are the pure in heart, for they will see God.

9 "Blessed are the peacemakers, for they will be called children of God.

10 "Blessed are those who are persecuted for righteousness' sake, for theirs is the kingdom of heaven.

11 "Blessed are you when people revile you and persecute you and utter all kinds of evil against you falsely[d] on my account. 12 Rejoice and be glad, for your reward is great in heaven, for in the same way they persecuted the prophets who were before you.

SALT AND LIGHT

13 "You are the salt of the earth; but if salt has lost its taste, how can

a 4.23 Gk He   b 4.23 Gk gospel   c 5.1 Gk he
d 5.11 Other ancient authorities lack falsely

its saltiness be restored? It is no longer good for anything, but is thrown out and trampled under foot.

14 "You are the light of the world. A city built on a hill cannot be hid. 15No one after lighting a lamp puts it under the bushel basket, but on the lampstand, and it gives light to all in the house. 16In the same way, let your light shine before others, so that they may see your good works and give glory to your Father in heaven.

THE LAW AND THE PROPHETS

17 "Do not think that I have come to abolish the law or the prophets; I have come not to abolish but to fulfill. 18For truly I tell you, until heaven and earth pass away, not one letter,[a] not one stroke of a letter, will pass from the law until all is accomplished. 19Therefore, whoever breaks[b] one of the least of these commandments, and teaches others to do the same, will be called least in the kingdom of heaven; but whoever does them and teaches them will be called great in the kingdom of heaven. 20For I tell you, unless your righteousness exceeds that of the scribes and Pharisees, you will never enter the kingdom of heaven.

CONCERNING ANGER

21 "You have heard that it was said to those of ancient times, 'You shall not murder'; and 'whoever murders shall be liable to judgment.' 22But I say to you that if you are angry with a brother or sister,[c] you will be liable to judgment; and if you insult[d] a brother or sister,[e] you will be liable to the council; and if you say, 'You fool,' you will be liable to the hell[f] of fire. 23So when you are offering your gift at the altar, if you remember that your brother or sister[g] has something against you, 24leave your gift there before the altar and go; first be reconciled to your brother or sister,[g] and then come and offer your gift. 25Come to terms quickly with your accuser while you are on the way to court[h] with him, or your accuser

may hand you over to the judge, and the judge to the guard, and you will be thrown into prison. 26Truly I tell you, you will never get out until you have paid the last penny.

CONCERNING ADULTERY

27 "You have heard that it was said, 'You shall not commit adultery.' 28But I say to you that everyone who looks at a woman with lust has already committed adultery with her in his heart. 29If your right eye causes you to sin, tear it out and throw it away; it is better for you to lose one of your members than for your whole body to be thrown into hell.[f] 30And if your right hand causes you to sin, cut it off and throw it away; it is better for you to lose one of your members than for your whole body to go into hell.[f]

CONCERNING DIVORCE

31 "It was also said, 'Whoever divorces his wife, let him give her a certificate of divorce.' 32But I say to you that anyone who divorces his wife, except on the ground of unchastity, causes her to commit adultery; and whoever marries a divorced woman commits adultery.

CONCERNING OATHS

33 "Again, you have heard that it was said to those of ancient times, 'You shall not swear falsely, but carry out the vows you have made to the Lord.' 34But I say to you, Do not swear at all, either by heaven, for it is the throne of God, 35or by the earth, for it is his footstool, or by Jerusalem, for it is the city of the great King. 36And do not swear by your head, for you cannot make one hair white or black. 37Let your word be 'Yes, Yes' or 'No, No'; anything more than this comes from the evil one.[i]

---

a 5.18 Gk one iota   b 5.19 Or annuls
c 5.22 Gk a brother; other ancient authorities add without cause   d 5.22 Gk say Raca to (an obscure term of abuse)
e 5.22 Gk a brother   f 5.22,29,30 Gk Gehenna   g 5.23,24 Gk your brother
h 5.25 Gk lacks to court   i 5.37 Or evil

CONCERNING RETALIATION

38 "You have heard that it was said, 'An eye for an eye and a tooth for a tooth.' 39But I say to you, Do not resist an evildoer. But if anyone strikes you on the right cheek, turn the other also; 40and if anyone wants to sue you and take your coat, give your cloak as well; 41and if anyone forces you to go one mile, go also the second mile. 42Give to everyone who begs from you, and do not refuse anyone who wants to borrow from you.

LOVE FOR ENEMIES

43 "You have heard that it was said, 'You shall love your neighbor and hate your enemy.' 44But I say to you, Love your enemies and pray for those who persecute you, 45so that you may be children of your Father in heaven; for he makes his sun rise on the evil and on the good, and sends rain on the righteous and on the unrighteous. 46For if you love those who love you, what reward do you have? Do not even the tax collectors do the same? 47And if you greet only your brothers and sisters,ᵃ what more are you doing than others? Do not even the Gentiles do the same? 48Be perfect, therefore, as your heavenly Father is perfect.

CONCERNING ALMSGIVING

6 "Beware of practicing your piety before others in order to be seen by them; for then you have no reward from your Father in heaven.

2 "So whenever you give alms, do not sound a trumpet before you, as the hypocrites do in the synagogues and in the streets, so that they may be praised by others. Truly I tell you, they have received their reward. 3But when you give alms, do not let your left hand know what your right hand is doing, 4so that your alms may be done in secret; and your Father who sees in secret will reward you.ᵇ

CONCERNING PRAYER

5 "And whenever you pray, do not be like the hypocrites; for they love to stand and pray in the synagogues and at the street corners, so that they may be seen by others. Truly I tell you, they have received their reward. 6But whenever you pray, go into your room and shut the door and pray to your Father who is in secret; and your Father who sees in secret will reward you.ᵇ

7 "When you are praying, do not heap up empty phrases as the Gentiles do; for they think that they will be heard because of their many words. 8Do not be like them, for your Father knows what you need before you ask him.

9 "Pray then in this way:

ᵃ 5.47 Gk your brothers ᵇ 6.4,6 Other ancient authorities add openly

BIBLE IN LIFE

Humble Servanthood
Matthew 6.2–4

Christ tells us that we shouldn't do our good deeds in public. While there's nothing wrong with a Christlike act being recognized by others, we should not be kind or generous for the sole purpose of being recognized. We don't have to broadcast our service to others; in fact, God especially rewards our secret, unrecognized acts of service. How do we exhibit a genuine Christian attitude? By finding simple ways to reach out and serve others in the name of Christ: spending time with an elderly person down the street, sitting down for a cup of coffee with a lonely neighbor, including and befriending those who are unattractive, loving people who don't love us back—finding ways in our modern, fast-paced society to demonstrate the love of Jesus through our actions.

Our Father in heaven,
    hallowed be your name.
10   Your kingdom come.
    Your will be done,
      on earth as it is in heaven.
11   Give us this day our
      daily bread.[a]
12   And forgive us our debts,
      as we also have forgiven
      our debtors.
13   And do not bring us to
      the time of trial,[b]
      but rescue us from
      the evil one.[c]

14 For if you forgive others their trespasses, your heavenly Father will also forgive you; 15 but if you do not forgive others, neither will your Father forgive your trespasses.

CONCERNING FASTING

16 "And whenever you fast, do not look dismal, like the hypocrites, for they disfigure their faces so as to show others that they are fasting. Truly I tell you, they have received their reward. 17 But when you fast, put oil on your head and wash your face, 18 so that your fasting may be seen not by others but by your Father who is in secret; and your Father who sees in secret will reward you.[d]

CONCERNING TREASURES

19 "Do not store up for yourselves treasures on earth, where moth and rust[e] consume and where thieves break in and steal; 20 but store up for yourselves treasures in heaven, where neither moth nor rust[e] consumes and where thieves do not break in and steal. 21 For where your treasure is, there your heart will be also.

THE SOUND EYE

22 "The eye is the lamp of the body. So, if your eye is healthy, your whole body will be full of light; 23 but if your eye is unhealthy, your whole body will be full of darkness. If then the light in you is darkness, how great is the darkness!

SERVING TWO MASTERS

24 "No one can serve two masters; for a slave will either hate the one

PONDER

"Do not store up for yourselves treasures on earth, where moth and rust consume and where thieves break in and steal; but store up for yourselves treasures in heaven, where neither moth nor rust consumes and where thieves do not break in and steal. For where your treasure is, there your heart will be also."
—Matthew 6.19–21

PRAY

Lord, we are thankful for these provocative words, but we don't want to analyze them too deeply. The Sermon on the Mount is intimidating to us because it asks so much of us. It can make us feel inadequate and sometimes even embarrassed by our own faults and failures, so we turn away from it. But help us to realize these words are there for our sustenance, our strengthening, our happiness, our freedom. Teach us to invest our hearts—our treasures—in your kingdom. We ask these things in the name of our Savior, Jesus Christ. Amen.

and love the other, or be devoted to the one and despise the other. You cannot serve God and wealth.[f]

DO NOT WORRY

25 "Therefore I tell you, do not worry about your life, what you will eat or what you will drink,[g] or about your body, what you will wear. Is not life more than food, and the body more than clothing? 26 Look at the birds of the air; they neither sow nor reap nor gather into barns,

a 6.11 Or our bread for tomorrow   b 6.13 Or us into temptation   c 6.13 Or from evil. Other ancient authorities add, in some form, For the kingdom and the power and the glory are yours forever. Amen.   d 6.18 Other ancient authorities add openly   e 6.19,20 Gk eating   f 6.24 Gk mammon   g 6.25 Other ancient authorities lack or what you will drink

and yet your heavenly Father feeds them. Are you not of more value than they? [27]And can any of you by worrying add a single hour to your span of life?[a] [28]And why do you worry about clothing? Consider the lilies of the field, how they grow; they neither toil nor spin, [29]yet I tell you, even Solomon in all his glory was not clothed like one of these. [30]But if God so clothes the grass of the field, which is alive today and tomorrow is thrown into the oven, will he not much more clothe you—you of little faith? [31]Therefore do not worry, saying, 'What will we eat?' or 'What will we drink?' or 'What will we wear?' [32]For it is the Gentiles who strive for all these things; and indeed your heavenly Father knows that you need all these things. [33]But strive first for the kingdom of God[b] and his[c] righteousness, and all these things will be given to you as well.

[34]"So do not worry about tomorrow, for tomorrow will bring worries of its own. Today's trouble is enough for today.

THERE'S ALWAYS TENSION BETWEEN GOD'S SOVEREIGNTY AND HUMAN FREEDOM: OUR SAYING, "YOUR WILL BE DONE," OR GOD'S SAYING, "YOUR WILL BE DONE."

JUDGING OTHERS

7 "Do not judge, so that you may not be judged. [2]For with the judgment you make you will be judged, and the measure you give will be the measure you get. [3]Why do you see the speck in your neighbor's[d] eye, but do not notice the log in your own eye? [4]Or how can you say to your neighbor,[e] 'Let me take the speck out of your eye,' while the log is in your own eye? [5]You hypo-crite, first take the log out of your own eye, and then you will see clearly to take the speck out of your neighbor's[d] eye.

PROFANING THE HOLY

[6]"Do not give what is holy to dogs; and do not throw your pearls before swine, or they will trample them under foot and turn and maul you.

ASK, SEARCH, KNOCK

[7]"Ask, and it will be given you; search, and you will find; knock, and the door will be opened for you. [8]For everyone who asks receives, and everyone who searches finds, and for everyone who knocks, the door will be opened. [9]Is there anyone among you who, if your child asks for bread, will give a stone? [10]Or if the child asks for a fish, will give a snake? [11]If you then, who are evil, know how to give good gifts to your children, how much more will your Father in heaven give good things to those who ask him!

THE GOLDEN RULE

[12]"In everything do to others as you would have them do to you; for this is the law and the prophets.

THE NARROW GATE

[13]"Enter through the narrow gate; for the gate is wide and the road is easy[f] that leads to destruction, and there are many who take it. [14]For the gate is narrow and the road is hard that leads to life, and there are few who find it.

A TREE AND ITS FRUIT

[15]"Beware of false prophets, who come to you in sheep's clothing but inwardly are ravenous wolves. [16]You will know them by their fruits. Are grapes gathered from thorns, or figs from thistles? [17]In the same way, every good tree bears good fruit, but the bad tree bears bad fruit. [18]A

[a] 6.27 Or add one cubit to your height
[b] 6.33 Other ancient authorities lack of God
[c] 6.33 Or its   [d] 7.3,5 Gk brother's   [e] 7.4 Gk brother   [f] 7.13 Other ancient authorities read for the road is wide and easy

good tree cannot bear bad fruit, nor can a bad tree bear good fruit. 19Every tree that does not bear good fruit is cut down and thrown into the fire. 20Thus you will know them by their fruits.

CONCERNING SELF-DECEPTION

21 "Not everyone who says to me, 'Lord, Lord,' will enter the kingdom of heaven, but only the one who does the will of my Father in heaven. 22On that day many will say to me, 'Lord, Lord, did we not prophesy in your name, and cast out demons in your name, and do many deeds of power in your name?' 23Then I will declare to them, 'I never knew you; go away from me, you evildoers.'

HEARERS AND DOERS

24 "Everyone then who hears these words of mine and acts on them will be like a wise man who built his house on rock. 25The rain fell, the floods came, and the winds blew and beat on that house, but it did not fall, because it had been founded on rock. 26And everyone who hears these words of mine and does not act on them will be like a foolish man who built his house on sand. 27The rain fell, and the floods came, and the winds blew and beat against that house, and it fell—and great was its fall!"

28 Now when Jesus had finished saying these things, the crowds were astounded at his teaching, 29for he taught them as one having authority, and not as their scribes.

JESUS CLEANSES A LEPER

8 When Jesus[a] had come down from the mountain, great crowds followed him; 2and there was a leper[b] who came to him and knelt before him, saying, "Lord, if you choose, you can make me clean." 3He stretched out his hand and touched him, saying, "I do choose. Be made clean!" Immediately his leprosy[b] was cleansed. 4Then Jesus said to him, "See that you say nothing to anyone; but go, show yourself to the priest, and offer the gift that Moses commanded, as a testimony to them."

JESUS HEALS A CENTURION'S SERVANT

5When he entered Capernaum, a centurion came to him, appealing to him 6and saying, "Lord, my servant is lying at home paralyzed, in terrible distress." 7And he said to him, "I will come and cure him." 8The centurion answered, "Lord, I am not worthy to have you come under my roof; but only speak the word, and my servant will be healed. 9For I also am a man under authority, with soldiers under me; and I say to one, 'Go,' and

[a] 8.1 Gk *he*   [b] 8.2,3 The terms *leper* and *leprosy* can refer to several diseases

---

┤ BIBLE IN LIFE ▷   ⊕

A Hard Road   Matthew 7.13–14

Too often we take the convenient path in life. We walk down the "easy" road, as Christ said, but the way to salvation is a "hard" road, not a easy highway on which everyone else is walking. It takes a special effort, beyond what comes naturally, to say to ourselves routinely or in incisive moments of our lives, "As a Christian, how do I measure up to the standards of the life and teaching of Jesus Christ?" This is a very disturbing question, and it's easy to turn away from the answer because it might be inconvenient to take the narrow road of imitating Christ and act as a modern-day Christian. It's not easy to find out how we can get to know a poor person, a sick person, a despised person or an unloving person. It's uncomfortable to break down the barriers that exist between us and them. Christ gives us a very high calling: We must be willing to take a chance on being rejected and emulate the principles modeled for us by Jesus Christ as we walk down the "hard" road of life.

he goes, and to another, 'Come,' and he comes, and to my slave, 'Do this,' and the slave does it." ¹⁰When Jesus heard him, he was amazed and said to those who followed him, "Truly I tell you, in no one^a in Israel have I found such faith. ¹¹I tell you, many will come from east and west and will eat with Abraham and Isaac and Jacob in the kingdom of heaven, ¹²while the heirs of the kingdom will be thrown into the outer darkness, where there will be weeping and gnashing of teeth." ¹³And to the centurion Jesus said, "Go; let it be done for you according to your faith." And the servant was healed in that hour.

JESUS HEALS MANY AT PETER'S HOUSE

¹⁴When Jesus entered Peter's house, he saw his mother-in-law lying in bed with a fever; ¹⁵he touched her hand, and the fever left her, and she got up and began to serve him. ¹⁶That evening they brought to him many who were possessed with demons; and he cast out the spirits with a word, and cured all who were sick. ¹⁷This was to fulfill what had been spoken through the prophet Isaiah, "He took our infirmities and bore our diseases."

WOULD-BE FOLLOWERS OF JESUS

¹⁸Now when Jesus saw great crowds around him, he gave orders to go over to the other side. ¹⁹A scribe then approached and said, "Teacher, I will follow you wherever you go." ²⁰And Jesus said to him, "Foxes have holes, and birds of the air have nests; but the Son of Man has nowhere to lay his head." ²¹Another of his disciples said to him, "Lord, first let me go and bury my father." ²²But Jesus said to him, "Follow me, and let the dead bury their own dead."

JESUS STILLS THE STORM

²³And when he got into the boat, his disciples followed him. ²⁴A windstorm arose on the sea, so great that the boat was being swamped by the waves; but he was asleep. ²⁵And they went and woke him up, saying, "Lord, save us! We are perishing!" ²⁶And he said to them, "Why are you afraid, you of little faith?" Then he got up and rebuked the winds and the sea; and there was a dead calm. ²⁷They were amazed, saying, "What sort of man is this, that even the winds and the sea obey him?"

JESUS HEALS THE GADARENE DEMONIACS

²⁸When he came to the other side, to the country of the Gadarenes,^b two demoniacs coming out of the tombs met him. They were so fierce that no one could pass that way. ²⁹Suddenly they shouted, "What have you to do with us, Son of God? Have you come here to torment us before the time?" ³⁰Now a large herd of swine was feeding at some distance from them. ³¹The demons

^a 8.10 Other ancient authorities read *Truly I tell you, not even* ^b 8.28 Other ancient authorities read *Gergesenes*; others, *Gerasenes*

┤├ **BIBLE IN LIFE** ▷ ─────────────── ⊕

Loving the Unlovable
Matthew 8.1–4

It is very difficult to train ourselves to love people who are different from us. They might be unattractive. We might see them lying on a city street, under a sheet of plastic to fend off the rain. They might have a different color skin. They may not share our citizenship rights. How can we love the unlovable? Christ encountered lepers, who were commonly regarded as sinners condemned by God. Christ encountered Samaritans, who were despised by the Jews. Christ encountered tax collectors and prostitutes. But he loved them all! He reached out to them. He healed the sick and befriended the outcast. He went out of his way to find opportunities to encompass all people with God's love. We can learn from the scriptures about how Christ lived, and then we can go and do the same.

begged him, "If you cast us out, send us into the herd of swine." [32]And he said to them, "Go!" So they came out and entered the swine; and suddenly, the whole herd rushed down the steep bank into the sea and perished in the water. [33]The swineherds ran off, and on going into the town, they told the whole story about what had happened to the demoniacs. [34]Then the whole town came out to meet Jesus; and when they saw him, they begged him to leave their neighborhood. [1]And after getting into a boat he crossed the sea and came to his own town.

JESUS HEALS A PARALYTIC

[2]And just then some people were carrying a paralyzed man lying on a bed. When Jesus saw their faith, he said to the paralytic, "Take heart, son; your sins are forgiven." [3]Then some of the scribes said to themselves, "This man is blaspheming." [4]But Jesus, perceiving their thoughts, said, "Why do you think evil in your hearts? [5]For which is easier, to say, 'Your sins are forgiven,' or to say, 'Stand up and walk'? [6]But so that you may know that the Son of Man has authority on earth to forgive sins"—he then said to the paralytic—"Stand up, take your bed and go to your home." [7]And he stood up and went to his home. [8]When the crowds saw it, they were filled with awe, and they glorified God, who had given such authority to human beings.

THE CALL OF MATTHEW

[9]As Jesus was walking along, he saw a man called Matthew sitting at the tax booth; and he said to him, "Follow me." And he got up and followed him.

[10]And as he sat at dinner[a] in the house, many tax collectors and sinners came and were sitting[b] with him and his disciples. [11]When the Pharisees saw this, they said to his disciples, "Why does your teacher eat with tax collectors and sinners?" [12]But when he heard this, he said, "Those who are well have no need of a physician, but those who are sick. [13]Go and learn what this means, 'I desire mercy, not sacrifice.' For I have come to call not the righteous but sinners."

THE QUESTION ABOUT FASTING

[14]Then the disciples of John came to him, saying, "Why do we and the Pharisees fast often,[c] but your disciples do not fast?" [15]And Jesus said to them, "The wedding guests cannot mourn as long as the bridegroom is with them, can they? The days will come when the bridegroom is taken away from them, and then they will fast. [16]No one sews a piece of unshrunk cloth on an old cloak, for the patch pulls away from the cloak, and a worse tear is made. [17]Neither is new wine put into old wineskins; otherwise, the skins burst, and the wine is

[a] 9.10 Gk *reclined*   [b] 9.10 Gk *were reclining*
[c] 9.14 Other ancient authorities lack *often*

⊨ BIBLE IN LIFE ▷   ○⊐

Underestimating the Power of God   *Matthew 8.23–27*

The disciples had their individual reasons for following Jesus. He had called each of them under different circumstances. But faced with a terrifying storm, they were all in the same boat—figuratively and literally! They thought they were going to die, and they felt skeptical as to whether or not Jesus cared enough for them to save them. The disciples had seen other people benefit from the healing miracles of Christ, but up until this point, they had not had that personal, profound, shocking, life-changing experience that the blind man or the leper had. In this storm, the disciples came to see that the all-encompassing power of God through Jesus Christ transcends anything that they could possibly fear. They had underestimated Jesus and his power as the Son of God. We need not make the same mistake.

spilled, and the skins are destroyed; but new wine is put into fresh wineskins, and so both are preserved."

A GIRL RESTORED TO LIFE AND A WOMAN HEALED

18 While he was saying these things to them, suddenly a leader of the synagogue[a] came in and knelt before him, saying, "My daughter has just died; but come and lay your hand on her, and she will live." 19 And Jesus got up and followed him, with his disciples. 20 Then suddenly a woman who had been suffering from hemorrhages for twelve years came up behind him and touched the fringe of his cloak, 21 for she said to herself, "If I only touch his cloak, I will be made well." 22 Jesus turned, and seeing her he said, "Take heart, daughter; your faith has made you well." And instantly the woman was made well. 23 When Jesus came to the leader's house and saw the flute players and the crowd making a commotion, 24 he said, "Go away; for the girl is not dead but sleeping." And they laughed at him. 25 But when the crowd had been put outside, he went in and took her by the hand, and the girl got up. 26 And the report of this spread throughout that district.

JESUS HEALS TWO BLIND MEN

27 As Jesus went on from there, two blind men followed him, crying loudly, "Have mercy on us, Son of David!" 28 When he entered the house, the blind men came to him; and Jesus said to them, "Do you believe that I am able to do this?" They said to him, "Yes, Lord." 29 Then he touched their eyes and said, "According to your faith let it be done to you." 30 And their eyes were opened. Then Jesus sternly ordered them, "See that no one knows of this." 31 But they went away and spread the news about him throughout that district.

JESUS HEALS ONE WHO WAS MUTE

32 After they had gone away, a demoniac who was mute was brought to him. 33 And when the demon had been cast out, the one who had been mute spoke; and the crowds were amazed and said, "Never has anything like this been seen in Israel." 34 But the Pharisees said, "By the ruler of the demons he casts out the demons."[b]

THE HARVEST IS GREAT, THE LABORERS FEW

35 Then Jesus went about all the cities and villages, teaching in their synagogues, and proclaiming the good news of the kingdom, and curing every disease and every sickness. 36 When he saw the crowds, he had compassion for them, because they were harassed and helpless, like sheep without a shepherd. 37 Then he said to his disciples, "The harvest is plentiful, but the laborers are few; 38 therefore ask the Lord of the harvest to send out laborers into his harvest."

THE TWELVE APOSTLES

10 Then Jesus[c] summoned his twelve disciples and gave them authority over unclean spirits, to cast them out, and to cure every disease and every sickness. 2 These are the names of the twelve apostles: first, Simon, also known as Peter, and his brother Andrew; James son of Zebedee, and his brother John; 3 Philip and Bartholomew; Thomas and Matthew the tax collector; James son of Alphaeus, and Thaddaeus;[d] 4 Simon the Cananaean, and Judas Iscariot, the one who betrayed him.

THE MISSION OF THE TWELVE

5 These twelve Jesus sent out with the following instructions: "Go nowhere among the Gentiles, and enter no town of the Samaritans, 6 but go rather to the lost sheep of the house of Israel. 7 As you go, proclaim the good news, 'The kingdom of heaven has come near.'[e] 8 Cure the

---

[a] 9.18 Gk lacks of the synagogue
[b] 9.34 Other ancient authorities lack this verse   [c] 10.1 Gk he   [d] 10.3 Other ancient authorities read Lebbaeus, or Lebbaeus called Thaddaeus   [e] 10.7 Or is at hand

sick, raise the dead, cleanse the lepers,[a] cast out demons. You received without payment; give without payment. 9Take no gold, or silver, or copper in your belts, 10no bag for your journey, or two tunics, or sandals, or a staff; for laborers deserve their food. 11Whatever town or village you enter, find out who in it is worthy, and stay there until you leave. 12As you enter the house, greet it. 13If the house is worthy, let your peace come upon it; but if it is not worthy, let your peace return to you. 14If anyone will not welcome you or listen to your words, shake off the dust from your feet as you leave that house or town. 15Truly I tell you, it will be more tolerable for the land of Sodom and Gomorrah on the day of judgment than for that town.

COMING PERSECUTIONS

16 "See, I am sending you out like sheep into the midst of wolves; so be wise as serpents and innocent as doves. 17Beware of them, for they will hand you over to councils and flog you in their synagogues; 18and you will be dragged before governors and kings because of me, as a testimony to them and the Gentiles. 19When they hand you over, do not worry about how you are to speak or what you are to say; for what you are to say will be given to you at that time; 20for it is not you who speak, but the Spirit of your Father speaking through you. 21Brother will betray brother to death, and a father his child, and children will rise against parents and have them put to death; 22and you will be hated by all because of my name. But the one who endures to the end will be saved. 23When they persecute you in one town, flee to the next; for truly I tell you, you will not have gone through all the towns of Israel before the Son of Man comes.

24 "A disciple is not above the teacher, nor a slave above the master; 25it is enough for the disciple to be like the teacher, and the slave like the master. If they have called the master of the house Beelzebul, how much more will they malign those of his household!

WHOM TO FEAR

26 "So have no fear of them; for nothing is covered up that will not be uncovered, and nothing secret that will not become known. 27What I say to you in the dark, tell in the light; and what you hear whispered, proclaim from the housetops. 28Do not fear those who kill the body but cannot kill the soul; rather fear him who can destroy both soul and body

[a] 10.8 The terms *leper* and *leprosy* can refer to several diseases

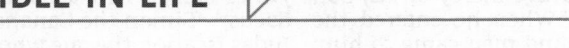

BIBLE IN LIFE

Being Hated
Matthew 10.22

Jesus was born into a complacent religious world where people prided themselves on their adherence to God's laws. Jesus shook the establishment by saying things such as, "Blessed are the meek," and "Turn the other [cheek]" and "Love your enemies" (Matthew 5.5,39,44). Jesus set a higher standard for what is right and acceptable in God's eyes, creating conflict around him and in the lives of his disciples. Ultimately, he was crucified because of it. Most of his apostles also lost their lives because they believed in Christ despite the condemnation and hatred they experienced. We don't experience as much conflict for our faith, largely because we conform too much to the world. We only want to hear the parts of the Bible and follow the parts of Christ's teachings that are compatible with the way we want to live. When we modify the standards of God to suit our own lives, we are complacent Christians, but we can only go so far with complacency. Eventually we must either accept Christ's teachings or turn away from them. When we adhere faithfully to Christ's pure principles and center our lives on him, we must be prepared to experience conflict.

in hell.[a] 29 Are not two sparrows sold for a penny? Yet not one of them will fall to the ground apart from your Father. 30 And even the hairs of your head are all counted. 31 So do not be afraid; you are of more value than many sparrows.

32 "Everyone therefore who acknowledges me before others, I also will acknowledge before my Father in heaven; 33 but whoever denies me before others, I also will deny before my Father in heaven.

NOT PEACE, BUT A SWORD

34 "Do not think that I have come to bring peace to the earth; I have not come to bring peace, but a sword.

35 For I have come to set a man
    against his father,
and a daughter against
    her mother,
and a daughter-in-law against
    her mother-in-law;
36 and one's foes will be members
    of one's own household.

37 Whoever loves father or mother more than me is not worthy of me; and whoever loves son or daughter more than me is not worthy of me; 38 and whoever does not take up the cross and follow me is not worthy of me. 39 Those who find their life will lose it, and those who lose their life for my sake will find it.

REWARDS

40 "Whoever welcomes you welcomes me, and whoever welcomes me welcomes the one who sent me. 41 Whoever welcomes a prophet in the name of a prophet will receive a prophet's reward; and whoever welcomes a righteous person in the name of a righteous person will receive the reward of the righteous; 42 and whoever gives even a cup of cold water to one of these little ones in the name of a disciple—truly I tell you, none of these will lose their reward."

11 Now when Jesus had finished instructing his twelve disciples, he went on from there to teach and proclaim his message in their cities.

MESSENGERS FROM JOHN THE BAPTIST

2 When John heard in prison what the Messiah[b] was doing, he sent word by his[c] disciples 3 and said to him, "Are you the one who is to come, or are we to wait for another?" 4 Jesus answered them, "Go and tell John what you hear and see: 5 the blind receive their sight, the lame walk, the lepers[d] are cleansed, the

a 10.28 Gk *Gehenna*   b 11.2 Or *the Christ*
c 11.2 Other ancient authorities read *two of his*   d 11.5 The terms *leper* and *leprosy* can refer to several diseases

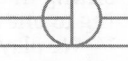

─┤ BIBLE IN LIFE ▷──────────⊕

Everyday Ministry   Matthew 10.42

Often when we think of doing ministry in the name of Jesus, we mistakenly assume that it requires a person with great talent, resources or time. We tend to think of high-profile people like pastors, evangelists, gifted musicians or worship leaders. But what example did Jesus give to describe ministry that he will most certainly reward? Giving "a cup of cold water" in his name. It's that simple, which means that all of us are capable of ministering in Jesus' name. We do not need to be able to preach to hundreds, to donate thousands of dollars to a charity or to take part in grand musical performances in order to minister (though there is certainly nothing wrong with those types of ministry either). Our simple ministry may take the form of calling lonely, elderly neighbors, volunteering in the nursery at church or serving meals at a homeless shelter. The important thing is not how noteworthy the act is but the motivation behind the act: a desire to serve Jesus. If no one ever knows what you are doing to help others, that's even better; God knows, and God's reward matters (see Matthew 6.1–4). You may also find that simple acts of kindness may eventually open the door to even greater ministry with the befriended persons.

deaf hear, the dead are raised, and the poor have good news brought to them. 6And blessed is anyone who takes no offense at me."

JESUS PRAISES JOHN
THE BAPTIST

7 As they went away, Jesus began to speak to the crowds about John: "What did you go out into the wilderness to look at? A reed shaken by the wind? 8What then did you go out to see? Someonea dressed in soft robes? Look, those who wear soft robes are in royal palaces. 9What then did you go out to see? A prophet?b Yes, I tell you, and more than a prophet. 10This is the one about whom it is written,
'See, I am sending my messenger
        ahead of you,
who will prepare your
        way before you.'
11Truly I tell you, among those born of women no one has arisen greater than John the Baptist; yet the least in the kingdom of heaven is greater than he. 12From the days of John the Baptist until now the kingdom of heaven has suffered violence,c and the violent take it by force. 13For all the prophets and the law prophesied until John came; 14and if you are willing to accept it, he is Elijah who is to come. 15Let anyone with earsd listen!

16 "But to what will I compare this generation? It is like children sitting in the marketplaces and calling to one another,
17 'We played the flute for you,
        and you did not dance;
we wailed, and you did
        not mourn.'
18For John came neither eating nor drinking, and they say, 'He has a demon'; 19the Son of Man came eating and drinking, and they say, 'Look, a glutton and a drunkard, a friend of tax collectors and sinners!' Yet wisdom is vindicated by her deeds."e

WOES TO UNREPENTANT CITIES

20 Then he began to reproach the cities in which most of his deeds of power had been done, because they did not repent. 21"Woe to you, Chorazin! Woe to you, Bethsaida! For if the

deeds of power done in you had been done in Tyre and Sidon, they would have repented long ago in sackcloth and ashes. 22But I tell you, on the day of judgment it will be more tolerable for Tyre and Sidon than for you. 23And you, Capernaum,
will you be exalted to heaven?
        No, you will be brought
                down to Hades.
For if the deeds of power done in you had been done in Sodom, it would have remained until this day. 24But I tell you that on the day of judgment it will be more tolerable for the land of Sodom than for you."

JESUS THANKS HIS FATHER

25 At that time Jesus said, "I thankf you, Father, Lord of heaven and earth, because you have hidden these things from the wise and the intelligent and have revealed them to infants; 26yes, Father, for such was your gracious will.g 27All things have been handed over to me by my Father; and no one knows the Son except the Father, and no one knows the Father except the Son and anyone to whom the Son chooses to reveal him.

28 "Come to me, all you that are weary and are carrying heavy burdens, and I will give you rest. 29Take my yoke upon you, and learn from me; for I am gentle and humble in heart, and you will find rest for your souls. 30For my yoke is easy, and my burden is light."

PLUCKING GRAIN ON
THE SABBATH

12 At that time Jesus went through the grainfields on the sabbath; his disciples were hungry, and they began to pluck heads of grain and to eat. 2When the Pharisees saw it, they said to him, "Look,

---

a 11.8 Or Why then did you go out? To see someone   b 11.9 Other ancient authorities read Why then did you go out? To see a prophet?   c 11.12 Or has been coming violently   d 11.15 Other ancient authorities add to hear   e 11.19 Other ancient authorities read children   f 11.25 Or praise   g 11.26 Or for so it was well-pleasing in your sight

your disciples are doing what is not lawful to do on the sabbath." ³He said to them, "Have you not read what David did when he and his companions were hungry? ⁴He entered the house of God and ate the bread of the Presence, which it was not lawful for him or his companions to eat, but only for the priests. ⁵Or have you not read in the law that on the sabbath the priests in the temple break the sabbath and yet are guiltless? ⁶I tell you, something greater than the temple is here. ⁷But if you had known what this means, 'I desire mercy and not sacrifice,' you would not have condemned the guiltless. ⁸For the Son of Man is lord of the sabbath."

THE MAN WITH A WITHERED HAND

9 He left that place and entered their synagogue; ¹⁰a man was there with a withered hand, and they asked him, "Is it lawful to cure on the sabbath?" so that they might accuse him. ¹¹He said to them, "Suppose one of you has only one sheep and it falls into a pit on the sabbath; will you not lay hold of it and lift it out? ¹²How much more valuable is a human being than a sheep! So it is lawful to do good on the sabbath." ¹³Then he said to the man, "Stretch out your hand." He stretched it out, and it was restored, as sound as the other. ¹⁴But the Pharisees went out and conspired against him, how to destroy him.

GOD'S CHOSEN SERVANT

15 When Jesus became aware of this, he departed. Many crowds[a] followed him, and he cured all of them, ¹⁶and he ordered them not to make him known. ¹⁷This was to fulfill what had been spoken through the prophet Isaiah:
¹⁸ "Here is my servant, whom
　　I have chosen,
　my beloved, with whom my
　　soul is well pleased.
I will put my Spirit upon him,
　and he will proclaim justice
　　to the Gentiles.
¹⁹ He will not wrangle or cry aloud,
　nor will anyone hear his
　　voice in the streets.
²⁰ He will not break a bruised reed
　or quench a smoldering wick
until he brings justice to victory.
²¹ 　And in his name the
　　Gentiles will hope."

JESUS AND BEELZEBUL

22 Then they brought to him a demoniac who was blind and mute; and he cured him, so that the one who had been mute could speak and see. ²³All the crowds were amazed and said, "Can this be the Son of David?" ²⁴But when the Pharisees heard it, they said, "It is only by Beelzebul, the ruler of the demons, that this fellow casts out the demons." ²⁵He knew what they were thinking and said to them, "Every kingdom

a **12.15** Other ancient authorities lack *crowds*

├─ BIBLE IN LIFE ▷

The Message of Scripture   *Matthew 12.1–14*

The Pharisees and teachers of the law of Jesus' time were so concerned about exactly what could and could not be done on the sabbath that they lost sight of the Lord of the sabbath, the Creator of the original purpose of the sabbath. They forgot that the same God who instituted a holy day of rest is also filled with love and grace and forgiveness. They became so absorbed with the details of individual, little rules that they completely lost the essence of God's intention. We too can easily focus on details, rules, regulations and legalities of special verses of scripture, but how can we find out how to act on an everyday basis? We can follow the example that Jesus set before us when he walked on this earth. When Christ came to earth, he embraced God's idea of the sabbath but refused to honor the legalistic regulations and prohibitions because they were standing in the way of loving others. When love and legalism conflicted, Jesus chose to love.

divided against itself is laid waste, and no city or house divided against itself will stand. 26If Satan casts out Satan, he is divided against himself; how then will his kingdom stand? 27If I cast out demons by Beelzebul, by whom do your own exorcists[a] cast them out? Therefore they will be your judges. 28But if it is by the Spirit of God that I cast out demons, then the kingdom of God has come to you. 29Or how can one enter a strong man's house and plunder his property, without first tying up the strong man? Then indeed the house can be plundered. 30Whoever is not with me is against me, and whoever does not gather with me scatters. 31Therefore I tell you, people will be forgiven for every sin and blasphemy, but blasphemy against the Spirit will not be forgiven. 32Whoever speaks a word against the Son of Man will be forgiven, but whoever speaks against the Holy Spirit will not be forgiven, either in this age or in the age to come.

A TREE AND ITS FRUIT

33 "Either make the tree good, and its fruit good; or make the tree bad, and its fruit bad; for the tree is known by its fruit. 34You brood of vipers! How can you speak good things, when you are evil? For out of the abundance of the heart the mouth speaks. 35The good person brings good things out of a good treasure, and the evil person brings evil things out of an evil treasure. 36I tell you, on the day of judgment you will have to give an account for every careless word you utter; 37for by your words you will be justified, and by your words you will be condemned."

THE SIGN OF JONAH

38 Then some of the scribes and Pharisees said to him, "Teacher, we wish to see a sign from you." 39But he answered them, "An evil and adulterous generation asks for a sign, but no sign will be given to it except the sign of the prophet Jonah. 40For just as Jonah was three days and three nights in the belly of the sea monster, so for three days and three nights the Son of Man will be in the heart of the earth. 41The people of Nineveh will rise up at the judgment with this generation and condemn it, because they repented at the proclamation of Jonah, and see, something greater than Jonah is here! 42The queen of the South will rise up at the judgment with this generation and condemn it, because she came from the ends of the earth to listen to the wisdom of Solomon, and see, something greater than Solomon is here!

THE RETURN OF THE UNCLEAN SPIRIT

43 "When the unclean spirit has gone out of a person, it wanders through waterless regions looking for a resting place, but it finds none. 44Then it says, 'I will return to my house from which I came.' When it comes, it finds it empty, swept, and put in order. 45Then it goes and brings along seven other spirits more evil than itself, and they enter and live there; and the last state of that person is worse than the first. So will it be also with this evil generation."

THE TRUE KINDRED OF JESUS

46 While he was still speaking to the crowds, his mother and his brothers were standing outside, wanting to speak to him. 47Someone told him, "Look, your mother and your brothers are standing outside, wanting to speak to you."[b] 48But to the one who had told him this, Jesus[c] replied, "Who is my mother, and who are my brothers?" 49And pointing to his disciples, he said, "Here are my mother and my brothers! 50For whoever does the will of my Father in heaven is my brother and sister and mother."

THE PARABLE OF THE SOWER

13 That same day Jesus went out of the house and sat beside the sea. 2Such great crowds

---

a 12.27 Gk *sons*   b 12.47 Other ancient authorities lack verse 47   c 12.48 Gk *he* gathered around him that he got into a boat and sat there, while the whole crowd stood on the beach. 3And he told them many things in parables, saying: "Listen! A sower went out to sow. 4And as he sowed, some seeds fell on the path, and the birds came and ate them up. 5Other seeds fell on rocky ground, where they did not have much soil, and they sprang up quickly, since they had no depth of soil. 6But when the sun rose, they were scorched; and since they had no root, they withered away. 7Other seeds fell among thorns, and the thorns grew up and choked them. 8Other seeds fell on good soil and brought forth grain, some a hundredfold, some sixty, some thirty. 9Let anyone with ears[a] listen!"

THE PURPOSE OF THE PARABLES

10 Then the disciples came and asked him, "Why do you speak to them in parables?" 11He answered, "To you it has been given to know the secrets[b] of the kingdom of heaven, but to them it has not been given. 12For to those who have, more will be given, and they will have an abundance; but from those who have nothing, even what they have will be taken away. 13The reason I speak to them in parables is that 'seeing they do not perceive, and hearing they do not listen, nor do they understand.' 14With them indeed is fulfilled the prophecy of Isaiah that says:
'You will indeed listen, but
    never understand,
and you will indeed look,
    but never perceive.
15 For this people's heart has
    grown dull,
and their ears are hard
    of hearing,
and they have shut
    their eyes;
so that they might not
    look with their eyes,
and listen with their ears,
and understand with their
    heart and turn—
and I would heal them.'
16But blessed are your eyes, for they see, and your ears, for they hear.

17Truly I tell you, many prophets and righteous people longed to see what you see, but did not see it, and to hear what you hear, but did not hear it.

THE PARABLE OF THE
SOWER EXPLAINED

18 "Hear then the parable of the sower. 19When anyone hears the word of the kingdom and does not understand it, the evil one comes and snatches away what is sown in the heart; this is what was sown on the path. 20As for what was sown on rocky ground, this is the one who hears the word and immediately receives it with joy; 21yet such a person has no root, but endures only for a while, and when trouble or persecution arises on account of the word, that person immediately falls away.[c] 22As for what was sown among thorns, this is the one who hears the word, but the cares of the world and the lure of wealth choke the word, and it yields nothing. 23But as for what was sown on good soil, this is the one who hears the word and understands it, who indeed bears fruit and yields, in one case a hundredfold, in another sixty, and in another thirty."

THE PARABLE OF WEEDS
AMONG THE WHEAT

24 He put before them another parable: "The kingdom of heaven may be compared to someone who sowed good seed in his field; 25but while everybody was asleep, an enemy came and sowed weeds among the wheat, and then went away. 26So when the plants came up and bore grain, then the weeds appeared as well. 27And the slaves of the householder came and said to him, 'Master, did you not sow good seed in your field? Where, then, did these weeds come from?' 28He answered, 'An enemy has done this.' The slaves said to him, 'Then do you want us to go and gather them?' 29But he replied, 'No; for in gathering the

a 13.9 Other ancient authorities add to hear   b 13.11 Or mysteries   c 13.21 Gk stumbles

weeds you would uproot the wheat along with them. 30 Let both of them grow together until the harvest; and at harvest time I will tell the reapers, Collect the weeds first and bind them in bundles to be burned, but gather the wheat into my barn.' "

THE PARABLE OF THE MUSTARD SEED

31 He put before them another parable: "The kingdom of heaven is like a mustard seed that someone took and sowed in his field; 32 it is the smallest of all the seeds, but when it has grown it is the greatest of shrubs and becomes a tree, so that the birds of the air come and make nests in its branches."

THE PARABLE OF THE YEAST

33 He told them another parable: "The kingdom of heaven is like yeast that a woman took and mixed in with[a] three measures of flour until all of it was leavened."

THE USE OF PARABLES

34 Jesus told the crowds all these things in parables; without a parable he told them nothing. 35 This was to fulfill what had been spoken through the prophet:[b]

"I will open my mouth to
　　speak in parables;
I will proclaim what has
　　been hidden from the
　　foundation of the world."[c]

JESUS EXPLAINS THE PARABLE OF THE WEEDS

36 Then he left the crowds and went into the house. And his disciples approached him, saying, "Explain to us the parable of the weeds of the field." 37 He answered, "The one who sows the good seed is the Son of Man; 38 the field is the world, and the good seed are the children of the kingdom; the weeds are the children of the evil one, 39 and the enemy who sowed them is the devil; the harvest is the end of the age, and the reapers are angels. 40 Just as the weeds are collected and burned up with fire, so will it be at the end of the age. 41 The Son of Man will send

his angels, and they will collect out of his kingdom all causes of sin and all evildoers, 42 and they will throw them into the furnace of fire, where there will be weeping and gnashing of teeth. 43 Then the righteous will shine like the sun in the kingdom of their Father. Let anyone with ears[d] listen!

IN EACH DAY OF OUR EXISTENCE, THERE IS CONFLICT BETWEEN THE MUNDANE AND THE EXALTED: BETWEEN OUR HUMAN FALLIBILITY AND A LIFE FOUNDED ON THE ROCK OF FAITH IN JESUS CHRIST.

THREE PARABLES

44 "The kingdom of heaven is like treasure hidden in a field, which someone found and hid; then in his joy he goes and sells all that he has and buys that field.

45 "Again, the kingdom of heaven is like a merchant in search of fine pearls; 46 on finding one pearl of great value, he went and sold all that he had and bought it.

47 "Again, the kingdom of heaven is like a net that was thrown into the sea and caught fish of every kind; 48 when it was full, they drew it ashore, sat down, and put the good into baskets but threw out the bad. 49 So it will be at the end of the age. The angels will come out and separate the evil from the righteous 50 and throw them into the furnace of fire, where there will be weeping and gnashing of teeth.

---

[a] 13.33 Gk hid in　[b] 13.35 Other ancient authorities read the prophet Isaiah
[c] 13.35 Other ancient authorities lack of the world　[d] 13.43 Other ancient authorities add to hear

TREASURES NEW AND OLD

51 "Have you understood all this?" They answered, "Yes." **52** And he said to them, "Therefore every scribe who has been trained for the kingdom of heaven is like the master of a household who brings out of his treasure what is new and what is old." **53** When Jesus had finished these parables, he left that place.

THE REJECTION OF JESUS AT NAZARETH

54 He came to his hometown and began to teach the people[a] in their synagogue, so that they were astounded and said, "Where did this man get this wisdom and these deeds of power? **55** Is not this the carpenter's son? Is not his mother called Mary? And are not his brothers James and Joseph and Simon and Judas? **56** And are not all his sisters with us? Where then did this man get all this?" **57** And they took offense at him. But Jesus said to them, "Prophets are not without honor except in their own country and in their own house." **58** And he did not do many deeds of power there, because of their unbelief.

THE DEATH OF JOHN THE BAPTIST

14 At that time Herod the ruler[b] heard reports about Jesus; **2** and he said to his servants, "This is John the Baptist; he has been raised from the dead, and for this reason these powers are at work in him." **3** For Herod had arrested John, bound him, and put him in prison on account of Herodias, his brother Philip's wife,[c] **4** because John had been telling him, "It is not lawful for you to have her." **5** Though Herod[d] wanted to put him to death, he feared the crowd, because they regarded him as a prophet. **6** But when Herod's birthday came, the daughter of Herodias danced before the company, and she pleased Herod **7** so much that he promised on oath to grant her whatever she might ask. **8** Prompted by her mother, she said, "Give me the head of John the Baptist here on a platter." **9** The king was grieved, yet out of regard for his oaths and for the guests, he commanded it to be given; **10** he sent and had John beheaded in the prison. **11** The head was brought on a platter and given to the girl, who brought it to her mother. **12** His disciples came and took the body and buried it; then they went and told Jesus.

FEEDING THE FIVE THOUSAND

13 Now when Jesus heard this, he withdrew from there in a boat to a deserted place by himself. But when the crowds heard it, they followed him on foot from the towns. **14** When he went ashore, he saw a great crowd; and he had compassion for them and cured their sick. **15** When it was evening, the disciples came to him and said, "This is a deserted place, and the hour is now late; send the crowds away so that they may go into the villages and buy food for themselves." **16** Jesus said to them, "They need not go away; you give them something to eat." **17** They replied, "We have nothing here but five loaves and two fish." **18** And he said, "Bring them here to me." **19** Then he ordered the crowds to sit down on the grass. Taking the five loaves and the two fish, he looked up to heaven, and blessed and broke the loaves, and gave them to the disciples, and the disciples gave them to the crowds. **20** And all ate and were filled; and they took up what was left over of the broken pieces, twelve baskets full. **21** And those who ate were about five thousand men, besides women and children.

JESUS WALKS ON THE WATER

22 Immediately he made the disciples get into the boat and go on ahead to the other side, while he dismissed the crowds. **23** And after he had dismissed the crowds, he went up the mountain by himself to pray. When evening came, he was there alone, **24** but by this time the boat, battered by the waves, was far from the land,[e] for the wind was against

---

[a] **13.54** Gk *them*   [b] **14.1** Gk *tetrarch*
[c] **14.3** Other ancient authorities read *his brother's wife*   [d] **14.5** Gk *he*   [e] **14.24** Other ancient authorities read *was out on the sea*

them. 25And early in the morning he came walking toward them on the sea. 26But when the disciples saw him walking on the sea, they were terrified, saying, "It is a ghost!" And they cried out in fear. 27But immediately Jesus spoke to them and said, "Take heart, it is I; do not be afraid."

28 Peter answered him, "Lord, if it is you, command me to come to you on the water." 29He said, "Come." So Peter got out of the boat, started walking on the water, and came toward Jesus. 30But when he noticed the strong wind,[a] he became frightened, and beginning to sink, he cried out, "Lord, save me!" 31Jesus immediately reached out his hand and caught him, saying to him, "You of little faith, why did you doubt?" 32When they got into the boat, the wind ceased. 33And those in the boat worshiped him, saying, "Truly you are the Son of God."

JESUS HEALS THE SICK IN GENNESARET

34 When they had crossed over, they came to land at Gennesaret. 35After the people of that place recognized him, they sent word throughout the region and brought all who were sick to him, 36and begged him that they might touch even the fringe of his cloak; and all who touched it were healed.

THE TRADITION OF THE ELDERS

15 Then Pharisees and scribes came to Jesus from Jerusalem and said, 2"Why do your disciples break the tradition of the elders? For they do not wash their hands before they eat." 3He answered them, "And why do you break the commandment of God for the sake of your tradition? 4For God said,[b] 'Honor your father and your mother,' and, 'Whoever speaks evil of father or mother must surely die.' 5But you say that whoever tells father or mother, 'Whatever support you might have had from me is given to God,'[c] then that person need not honor the father.[d] 6So, for the sake of your tradition, you make void the word[e] of

God. 7You hypocrites! Isaiah prophesied rightly about you when he said:

8 'This people honors me
　　with their lips,
but their hearts are
　　far from me;
9 in vain do they worship me,
　　teaching human precepts
　　　　as doctrines.' "

THINGS THAT DEFILE

10 Then he called the crowd to him and said to them, "Listen and understand: 11it is not what goes into the mouth that defiles a person, but it is what comes out of the mouth that defiles." 12Then the disciples approached and said to him, "Do you know that the Pharisees took offense when they heard what you said?" 13He answered, "Every plant that my heavenly Father has not planted will be uprooted. 14Let them alone; they are blind guides of the blind.[f] And if one blind person guides another, both will fall into a pit." 15But Peter said to him, "Explain this parable to us." 16Then he said, "Are you also still without understanding? 17Do you not see that whatever goes into the mouth enters the stomach, and goes out into the sewer? 18But what comes out of the mouth proceeds from the heart, and this is what defiles. 19For out of the heart come evil intentions, murder, adultery, fornication, theft, false witness, slander. 20These are what defile a person, but to eat with unwashed hands does not defile."

THE CANAANITE WOMAN'S FAITH

21 Jesus left that place and went away to the district of Tyre and Sidon. 22Just then a Canaanite woman from that region came out and started shouting, "Have mercy on

a **14.30** Other ancient authorities read *the wind*　b **15.4** Other ancient authorities read *commanded, saying*　c **15.5** Or *is an offering*　d **15.5** Other ancient authorities add *or the mother*　e **15.6** Other ancient authorities read *law*; others, *commandment*　f **15.14** Other ancient authorities lack *of the blind*

me, Lord, Son of David; my daughter is tormented by a demon." 23But he did not answer her at all. And his disciples came and urged him, saying, "Send her away, for she keeps shouting after us." 24He answered, "I was sent only to the lost sheep of the house of Israel." 25But she came and knelt before him, saying, "Lord, help me." 26He answered, "It is not fair to take the children's food and throw it to the dogs." 27She said, "Yes, Lord, yet even the dogs eat the crumbs that fall from their masters' table." 28Then Jesus answered her, "Woman, great is your faith! Let it be done for you as you wish." And her daughter was healed instantly.

JESUS CURES MANY PEOPLE

29 After Jesus had left that place, he passed along the Sea of Galilee, and he went up the mountain, where he sat down. 30Great crowds came to him, bringing with them the lame, the maimed, the blind, the mute, and many others. They put them at his feet, and he cured them, 31so that the crowd was amazed when they saw the mute speaking, the maimed whole, the lame walking, and the blind seeing. And they praised the God of Israel.

FEEDING THE FOUR THOUSAND

32 Then Jesus called his disciples to him and said, "I have compassion for the crowd, because they have been with me now for three days and have nothing to eat; and I do not want to send them away hungry, for they might faint on the way." 33The disciples said to him, "Where are we to get enough bread in the desert to feed so great a crowd?" 34Jesus asked them, "How many loaves have you?" They said, "Seven, and a few small fish." 35Then ordering the crowd to sit down on the ground, 36he took the seven loaves and the fish; and after giving thanks he broke them and gave them to the disciples, and the disciples gave them to the crowds. 37And all of them ate and were filled; and they took up the broken pieces left over, seven baskets full. 38Those who had eaten were four thousand

men, besides women and children. 39After sending away the crowds, he got into the boat and went to the region of Magadan.[a]

THE DEMAND FOR A SIGN

16 The Pharisees and Sadducees came, and to test Jesus[b] they asked him to show them a sign from heaven. 2He answered them, "When it is evening, you say, 'It will be fair weather, for the sky is red.' 3And in the morning, 'It will be stormy today, for the sky is red and threatening.' You know how to interpret the appearance of the sky, but you cannot interpret the signs of the times.[c] 4An evil and adulterous generation asks for a sign, but no sign will be given to it except the sign of Jonah." Then he left them and went away.

THE YEAST OF THE PHARISEES AND SADDUCEES

5 When the disciples reached the other side, they had forgotten to bring any bread. 6Jesus said to them, "Watch out, and beware of the yeast of the Pharisees and Sadducees." 7They said to one another, "It is because we have brought no bread." 8And becoming aware of it, Jesus said, "You of little faith, why are you talking about having no bread? 9Do you still not perceive? Do you not remember the five loaves for the five thousand, and how many baskets you gathered? 10Or the seven loaves for the four thousand, and how many baskets you gathered? 11How could you fail to perceive that I was not speaking about bread? Beware of the yeast of the Pharisees and Sadducees!" 12Then they understood that he had not told them to beware of the yeast of bread, but of the teaching of the Pharisees and Sadducees.

PETER'S DECLARATION ABOUT JESUS

13 Now when Jesus came into the district of Caesarea Philippi, he

---

[a] 15.39 Other ancient authorities read *Magdala* or *Magdalan* [b] 16.1 Gk *him*
[c] 16.3 Other ancient authorities lack *2When it is ... of the times*

asked his disciples, "Who do people say that the Son of Man is?" [14]And they said, "Some say John the Baptist, but others Elijah, and still others Jeremiah or one of the prophets." [15]He said to them, "But who do you say that I am?" [16]Simon Peter answered, "You are the Messiah,[a] the Son of the living God." [17]And Jesus answered him, "Blessed are you, Simon son of Jonah! For flesh and blood has not revealed this to you, but my Father in heaven. [18]And I tell you, you are Peter,[b] and on this rock[c] I will build my church, and the gates of Hades will not prevail against it. [19]I will give you the keys of the kingdom of heaven, and whatever you bind on earth will be bound in heaven, and whatever you loose on earth will be loosed in heaven." [20]Then he sternly ordered the disciples not to tell anyone that he was[d] the Messiah.[a]

JESUS FORETELLS HIS DEATH AND RESURRECTION

[21] From that time on, Jesus began to show his disciples that he must go to Jerusalem and undergo great suffering at the hands of the elders and chief priests and scribes, and be killed, and on the third day be raised. [22]And Peter took him aside and began to rebuke him, saying, "God forbid it, Lord! This must never happen to you." [23]But he turned and said to Peter, "Get behind me, Satan! You are a stumbling block to me; for you are setting your mind not on divine things but on human things."

THE CROSS AND SELF-DENIAL

[24] Then Jesus told his disciples, "If any want to become my followers, let them deny themselves and take up their cross and follow me. [25]For those who want to save their life will lose it, and those who lose their life for my sake will find it. [26]For what will it profit them if they gain the whole world but forfeit their life? Or what will they give in return for their life?

[27] "For the Son of Man is to come with his angels in the glory of his Father, and then he will repay everyone for what has been done. [28]Truly I tell you, there are some standing here who will not taste death before they see the Son of Man coming in his kingdom."

THE TRANSFIGURATION

17 Six days later, Jesus took with him Peter and James and his brother John and led them up a high mountain, by themselves. [2]And he was transfigured before

[a] 16.16,20 Or the Christ   [b] 16.18 Gk Petros
[c] 16.18 Gk petra   [d] 16.20 Other ancient authorities add Jesus

---

⊣ BIBLE IN LIFE ▷

Belief in the Resurrection   Matthew 16.21–22

Human beings struggle to grasp how someone who is dead can live again. There is no scientific proof that there is a second life. Because they saw it, Jesus' disciples knew that he had been arrested, tortured and humiliated. They believed he had been crucified and buried, but when it came to the empty tomb, they felt bewildered. Even though Jesus had told them in very clear language that it would happen, they could not comprehend it. Because of this, Jesus' followers did not recognize him after the resurrection (Luke 24.13–35).

We Christians accept the fact of Jesus' resurrection as the basis for our belief. We accept the logic-defying, supernatural resurrection of our Lord, yet we go through everyday life acknowledging the presence of Christ only when it's convenient for us—on special occasions or in times of prayer or crisis. If we agree that the resurrection is the most important event in the history of the universe, and that because of the resurrection Christ is alive today, here and now, then why do we rarely acknowledge the presence of Christ? His presence should permeate our entire existence.

them, and his face shone like the sun, and his clothes became dazzling white. ³Suddenly there appeared to them Moses and Elijah, talking with him. ⁴Then Peter said to Jesus, "Lord, it is good for us to be here; if you wish, I[a] will make three dwellings[b] here, one for you, one for Moses, and one for Elijah." ⁵While he was still speaking, suddenly a bright cloud overshadowed them, and from the cloud a voice said, "This is my Son, the Beloved;[c] with him I am well pleased; listen to him!" ⁶When the disciples heard this, they fell to the ground and were overcome by fear. ⁷But Jesus came and touched them, saying, "Get up and do not be afraid." ⁸And when they looked up, they saw no one except Jesus himself alone.

9 As they were coming down the mountain, Jesus ordered them, "Tell no one about the vision until after the Son of Man has been raised from the dead." ¹⁰And the disciples asked him, "Why, then, do the scribes say that Elijah must come first?" ¹¹He replied, "Elijah is indeed coming and will restore all things; ¹²but I tell you that Elijah has already come, and they did not recognize him, but they did to him whatever they pleased. So also the Son of Man is about to suffer at their hands." ¹³Then the disciples understood that he was speaking to them about John the Baptist.

JESUS CURES A BOY WITH A DEMON

14 When they came to the crowd, a man came to him, knelt before him, ¹⁵and said, "Lord, have mercy on my son, for he is an epileptic and he suffers terribly; he often falls into the fire and often into the water. ¹⁶And I brought him to your disciples, but they could not cure him." ¹⁷Jesus answered, "You faithless and perverse generation, how much longer must I be with you? How much longer must I put up with you? Bring him here to me." ¹⁸And Jesus rebuked the demon,[d] and it[e] came out of him, and the boy was cured instantly. ¹⁹Then the disciples came to Jesus privately and said, "Why could we not cast it

out?" ²⁰He said to them, "Because of your little faith. For truly I tell you, if you have faith the size of a[f] mustard seed, you will say to this mountain, 'Move from here to there,' and it will move; and nothing will be impossible for you."[g]

JESUS AGAIN FORETELLS HIS DEATH AND RESURRECTION

22 As they were gathering[h] in Galilee, Jesus said to them, "The Son of Man is going to be betrayed into human hands, ²³and they will kill him, and on the third day he will be raised." And they were greatly distressed.

JESUS AND THE TEMPLE TAX

24 When they reached Capernaum, the collectors of the temple tax[i] came to Peter and said, "Does your teacher not pay the temple tax?"[i] ²⁵He said, "Yes, he does." And when he came home, Jesus spoke of it first, asking, "What do you think, Simon? From whom do kings of the earth take toll or tribute? From their children or from others?" ²⁶When Peter[j] said, "From others," Jesus said to him, "Then the children are free. ²⁷However, so that we do not give offense to them, go to the sea and cast a hook; take the first fish that comes up; and when you open its mouth, you will find a coin;[k] take that and give it to them for you and me."

TRUE GREATNESS

18 At that time the disciples came to Jesus and asked, "Who is the greatest in the kingdom of heaven?" ²He called a child, whom he put among them, ³and said, "Truly I tell you, unless you change and become like children, you will never enter the kingdom of heaven. ⁴Whoever becomes humble like this

[a] 17.4 Other ancient authorities read *we*
[b] 17.4 Or *tents*   [c] 17.5 Or *my beloved Son*
[d] 17.18 Gk *it or him*   [e] 17.18 Gk *the demon*
[f] 17.20 Gk *faith as a grain of*   [g] 17.20 Other ancient authorities add verse 21, *But this kind does not come out except by prayer and fasting*   [h] 17.22 Other ancient authorities read *living*   [i] 17.24 Gk *didrachma*
[j] 17.26 Gk *he*   [k] 17.27 Gk *stater*; the stater was worth two didrachmas

child is the greatest in the kingdom of heaven. 5Whoever welcomes one such child in my name welcomes me.

TEMPTATIONS TO SIN

6 "If any of you put a stumbling block before one of these little ones who believe in me, it would be better for you if a great millstone were fastened around your neck and you were drowned in the depth of the sea. 7Woe to the world because of stumbling blocks! Occasions for stumbling are bound to come, but woe to the one by whom the stumbling block comes!

8 "If your hand or your foot causes you to stumble, cut it off and throw it away; it is better for you to enter life maimed or lame than to have two hands or two feet and to be thrown into the eternal fire. 9And if your eye causes you to stumble, tear it out and throw it away; it is better for you to enter life with one eye than to have two eyes and to be thrown into the hell[a] of fire.

THE PARABLE OF THE LOST SHEEP

10 "Take care that you do not despise one of these little ones; for, I tell you, in heaven their angels continually see the face of my Father in heaven.[b] 12What do you think? If a shepherd has a hundred sheep, and one of them has gone astray, does he not leave the ninety-nine on the mountains and go in search of the one that went astray? 13And if he finds it, truly I tell you, he rejoices over it more than over the ninety-nine that never went astray. 14So it is not the will of your[c] Father in heaven that one of these little ones should be lost.

REPROVING ANOTHER WHO SINS

15 "If another member of the church[d] sins against you,[e] go and point out the fault when the two of you are alone. If the member listens to you, you have regained that one.[f] 16But if you are not listened to, take one or two others along with you, so that every word may be confirmed by the evidence of two or three witnesses. 17If the member refuses to listen to them, tell it to the church; and if the offender refuses to listen even to the church, let such a one be to you as a Gentile and a tax collector. 18Truly I tell you, whatever you bind on earth will be bound in heaven, and whatever you loose on earth will be loosed in heaven. 19Again, truly I tell you, if two of you agree on earth about anything you ask, it will be done for you by my Father in heaven. 20For where two or three are gathered in my name, I am there among them."

FORGIVENESS

21 Then Peter came and said to him, "Lord, if another member of the church[g] sins against me, how often should I forgive? As many as seven times?" 22Jesus said to him, "Not seven times, but, I tell you, seventy-seven[h] times.

THE PARABLE OF THE UNFORGIVING SERVANT

23 "For this reason the kingdom of heaven may be compared to a king who wished to settle accounts with his slaves. 24When he began the reckoning, one who owed him ten thousand talents[i] was brought to him; 25and, as he could not pay, his lord ordered him to be sold, together with his wife and children and all his possessions, and payment to be made. 26So the slave fell on his knees before him, saying, 'Have patience with me, and I will pay you everything.' 27And out of pity for him, the lord of that slave released him and forgave him the debt. 28But that same slave, as he went out, came upon one of his fellow slaves who owed him a hundred denarii;[j] and

a 18.9 Gk Gehenna   b 18.10 Other ancient authorities add verse 11, For the Son of Man came to save the lost   c 18.14 Other ancient authorities read my   d 18.15 Gk If your brother   e 18.15 Other ancient authorities lack against you   f 18.15 Gk the brother   g 18.21 Gk if my brother   h 18.22 Or seventy times seven   i 18.24 A talent was worth more than fifteen years' wages of a laborer   j 18.28 The denarius was the usual day's wage for a laborer

seizing him by the throat, he said, 'Pay what you owe.' 29 Then his fellow slave fell down and pleaded with him, 'Have patience with me, and I will pay you.' 30 But he refused; then he went and threw him into prison until he would pay the debt. 31 When his fellow slaves saw what had happened, they were greatly distressed, and they went and reported to their lord all that had taken place. 32 Then his lord summoned him and said to him, 'You wicked slave! I forgave you all that debt because you pleaded with me. 33 Should you not have had mercy on your fellow slave, as I had mercy on you?' 34 And in anger his lord handed him over to be tortured until he would pay his entire debt. 35 So my heavenly Father will also do to every one of you, if you do not forgive your brother or sister[a] from your heart."

TEACHING ABOUT DIVORCE

19 When Jesus had finished saying these things, he left Galilee and went to the region of Judea beyond the Jordan. 2 Large crowds followed him, and he cured them there.

3 Some Pharisees came to him, and to test him they asked, "Is it lawful for a man to divorce his wife for any cause?" 4 He answered, "Have you not read that the one who made them at the beginning 'made them male and female,' 5 and said, 'For this reason a man shall leave his father and mother and be joined to his wife, and the two shall become one flesh'? 6 So they are no longer two, but one flesh. Therefore what God has joined together, let no one separate." 7 They said to him, "Why then did Moses command us to give a certificate of dismissal and to divorce her?" 8 He said to them, "It was because you were so hard-hearted that Moses allowed you to divorce your wives, but from the beginning it was not so. 9 And I say to you, whoever divorces his wife, except for unchastity, and marries another commits adultery."[b]

10 His disciples said to him, "If such is the case of a man with his wife, it is better not to marry." 11 But he said to them, "Not everyone can accept this teaching, but only those to whom it is given. 12 For there are eunuchs who have been so from birth, and there are eunuchs who have been made eunuchs by others, and there are eunuchs who have made themselves eunuchs for the sake of the kingdom of heaven. Let anyone accept this who can."

JESUS BLESSES LITTLE CHILDREN

13 Then little children were being brought to him in order that he

[a] 18.35 Gk brother   [b] 19.9 Other ancient authorities read except on the ground of unchastity, causes her to commit adultery; others add at the end of the verse and he who marries a divorced woman commits adultery

---

┤├ BIBLE IN LIFE ▷

Forgive and Be Forgiven   *Matthew 18.21–35*

How often should we forgive? Jesus answered, "Not seven times, but, I tell you, seventy-seven times" (Matthew 18.22). Jesus' words tie back to a strange passage in Genesis in which Lamech, one of the earliest humans who lived, told his two wives that he had killed a man who injured him. He said, "If Cain is avenged sevenfold, truly Lamech seventy-sevenfold" (Genesis 4.24). Jesus played off the words of Lamech to apply not to vengeance, but to forgiveness. Human forgiveness must be considered in the context of God's forgiveness. We owe God a debt that is immeasurable, a debt that we could never repay. By the grace of God and through the sacrifice of Jesus Christ, we are forgiven our crippling debt! But Christ says if we don't forgive those who owe us, who sin against us, then we will not be forgiven, and we'll have to pay the debt that we owe. This gives us great motivation to forgive.

might lay his hands on them and pray. The disciples spoke sternly to those who brought them; ¹⁴but Jesus said, "Let the little children come to me, and do not stop them; for it is to such as these that the kingdom of heaven belongs." ¹⁵And he laid his hands on them and went on his way.

THE RICH YOUNG MAN

16 Then someone came to him and said, "Teacher, what good deed must I do to have eternal life?" ¹⁷And he said to him, "Why do you ask me about what is good? There is only one who is good. If you wish to enter into life, keep the commandments." ¹⁸He said to him, "Which ones?" And Jesus said, "You shall not murder; You shall not commit adultery; You shall not steal; You shall not bear false witness; ¹⁹Honor your father and mother; also, You shall love your neighbor as yourself." ²⁰The young man said to him, "I have kept all these;ª what do I still lack?" ²¹Jesus said to him, "If you wish to be perfect, go, sell your possessions, and give the moneyᵇ to the poor, and you will have treasure in heaven; then come, follow me." ²²When the young man heard this word, he went away grieving, for he had many possessions.

BOTH CONFRONTATION

AND ACCOMMODATION ARE

IMPORTANT. FORGIVENESS

IS NECESSARY FOR THE SAKE

OF THE OFFENDER, THE

OFFENDED, THE CHURCH

AND JESUS CHRIST.

23 Then Jesus said to his disciples, "Truly I tell you, it will be hard for a rich person to enter the kingdom of heaven. ²⁴Again I tell you, it is easier for a camel to go through the eye of a needle than for someone who is rich to enter the kingdom of God." ²⁵When the disciples heard this, they were greatly astounded and said, "Then who can be saved?" ²⁶But Jesus looked at them and said, "For mortals it is impossible, but for God all things are possible."

27 Then Peter said in reply, "Look, we have left everything and followed you. What then will we have?" ²⁸Jesus said to them, "Truly I tell you, at the renewal of all things, when the Son of Man is seated on the throne of his glory, you who have followed me will also sit on twelve thrones, judging the twelve tribes of Israel. ²⁹And everyone who has left houses or brothers or sisters or father or mother or children or fields, for my name's sake, will receive a hundredfold,ᶜ and will inherit eternal life. ³⁰But many who are first will be last, and the last will be first.

THE LABORERS IN THE VINEYARD

20 "For the kingdom of heaven is like a landowner who went out early in the morning to hire laborers for his vineyard. ²After agreeing with the laborers for the usual daily wage,ᵈ he sent them into his vineyard. ³When he went out about nine o'clock, he saw others standing idle in the marketplace; ⁴and he said to them, 'You also go into the vineyard, and I will pay you whatever is right.' So they went. ⁵When he went out again about noon and about three o'clock, he did the same. ⁶And about five o'clock he went out and found others standing around; and he said to them, 'Why are you standing here idle all day?' ⁷They said to him, 'Because no one has hired us.' He said to them, 'You also go into the vineyard.' ⁸When evening came, the owner of the vineyard said to his manager, 'Call the laborers and give them their

---

ª **19.20** Other ancient authorities add *from my youth*   ᵇ **19.21** Gk lacks *the money*   ᶜ **19.29** Other ancient authorities read *manifold*   ᵈ **20.2** Gk *a denarius*

pay, beginning with the last and then going to the first.' ⁹When those hired about five o'clock came, each of them received the usual daily wage.ᵃ ¹⁰Now when the first came, they thought they would receive more; but each of them also received the usual daily wage.ᵃ ¹¹And when they received it, they grumbled against the landowner, ¹²saying, 'These last worked only one hour, and you have made them equal to us who have borne the burden of the day and the scorching heat.' ¹³But he replied to one of them, 'Friend, I am doing you no wrong; did you not agree with me for the usual daily wage?ᵃ ¹⁴Take what belongs to you and go; I choose to give to this last the same as I give to you. ¹⁵Am I not allowed to do what I choose with what belongs to me? Or are you envious because I am generous?'ᵇ ¹⁶So the last will be first, and the first will be last."ᶜ

A THIRD TIME JESUS FORETELLS HIS DEATH AND RESURRECTION

¹⁷While Jesus was going up to Jerusalem, he took the twelve disciples aside by themselves, and said to them on the way, ¹⁸"See, we are going up to Jerusalem, and the Son of Man will be handed over to the chief priests and scribes, and they will condemn him to death; ¹⁹then they will hand him over to the Gentiles to be mocked and flogged and crucified; and on the third day he will be raised."

THE REQUEST OF THE MOTHER OF JAMES AND JOHN

²⁰Then the mother of the sons of Zebedee came to him with her sons, and kneeling before him, she asked a favor of him. ²¹And he said to her, "What do you want?" She said to him, "Declare that these two sons of mine will sit, one at your right hand and one at your left, in your kingdom." ²²But Jesus answered, "You do not know what you are asking. Are you able to drink the cup that I am about to drink?"ᵈ They said to him, "We are able." ²³He said to them, "You will indeed drink my cup, but to sit at my right hand and at my

PONDER

"So the last will be first, and the first will be last."
—Matthew 20.16

PRAY

O Father, sometimes we have a hard time accepting your will, which sometimes seems to us complex, wearisome and difficult. But we realize, as we listen to the startling and provocative words of Jesus Christ, that it is the truth. It is the truth that in your power and love we can reach out to others in a spirit of genuine love, humility, forgiveness and peace. We are thankful for Matthew 20; we pray that through Jesus' teaching, we will learn more about the importance of humility and service. Forgive our many sins, and join our hearts together, so that we can demonstrate the true measure of success in your kingdom— love. We ask in Jesus' name. Amen.

left, this is not mine to grant, but it is for those for whom it has been prepared by my Father."

²⁴When the ten heard it, they were angry with the two brothers. ²⁵But Jesus called them to him and said, "You know that the rulers of the Gentiles lord it over them, and their great ones are tyrants over them. ²⁶It will not be so among you; but whoever wishes to be great among you must be your servant, ²⁷and whoever wishes to be first among you must be your slave; ²⁸just as the Son of Man came not to be served but to serve, and to give his life a ransom for many."

ᵃ **20.9,10,13** Gk *a denarius*   ᵇ **20.15** Gk *is your eye evil because I am good?*
ᶜ **20.16** Other ancient authorities add *for many are called but few are chosen*
ᵈ **20.22** Other ancient authorities add *or to be baptized with the baptism that I am baptized with?*

EQUAL GRACE

"But he replied to one of them, 'Friend, I am doing you no wrong; did you not agree with me for the usual daily wage? Take what belongs to you and go; I choose to give to this last the same as I give to you.'"

—Matthew 20.13

In Jesus' parable of the workers in the vineyard, the landowner behaved in a radical, shocking way. Normally the intention of a landowner, or of someone running a farm, would be to get as much work as possible out of whoever is in his field. The benefits that would come to the farmer depended on the productivity of the workers who were shaking peanuts or picking cotton or plowing or whatever. Yet the prime consideration of the landowner in this parable was the well-being of the workers. His intention was to give all his workers the same opportunity to make a living.

This parable gives us a glimpse of the kingdom of heaven. The landowner represents God Almighty. Whether people have led a life faithful to Christ for 80 years or led a very sinful life for 79 years then repented and turned to Christ before their death, God's grace is offered to all equally. We who are already participating in the kingdom of heaven should accept the grace we've been given and that it has been given to others.

Our ultimate goal in life should be to serve others and be willing to sacrifice our own well-being for their benefit. This is difficult for us to do because we set our priorities in our lives based on our ideas of success. We all define success in different ways: attaining financial stability, living in nice communities, gaining the respect of neighbors, earning educational degrees, achieving professional maturity. There's nothing wrong with any of these but they ought not to be our highest ambitions. Instead, our priorities were spelled out by Christ—to be servant leaders, to be meek but not weak, to mourn for the sins of the world and to confront and combat evil whenever we can, to use our talents and abilities for the service of others.

Our highest priorities as members of the kingdom of heaven should be to orient our character, our habits, our achievements, our purposes to those of Jesus Christ. And these radical ideas that Christ presented are not irrational. They're not impractical. Any of us can be a servant of others. Any of us can put aside superiority, which is pride, and treat people as equals, as the landowner did as he hired the workers during the day.

Going Deeper

- Is it difficult for you to accept that God has extended the same grace that was given to you to others, regardless of what they've done or who they are? Why?
- In what areas of your life have you been successful in putting aside your own benefits for the well-being of someone else? In what areas do you still struggle with this?

JESUS HEALS TWO BLIND MEN

29 As they were leaving Jericho, a large crowd followed him. [30] There were two blind men sitting by the roadside. When they heard that Jesus was passing by, they shouted, "Lord,[a] have mercy on us, Son of David!" [31] The crowd sternly ordered them to be quiet; but they shouted even more loudly, "Have mercy on us, Lord, Son of David!" [32] Jesus stood still and called them, saying, "What do you want me to do for you?" [33] They said to him, "Lord, let our eyes be opened." [34] Moved with compassion, Jesus touched their eyes. Immediately they regained their sight and followed him.

JESUS' TRIUMPHAL ENTRY INTO JERUSALEM

21 When they had come near Jerusalem and had reached Bethphage, at the Mount of Olives, Jesus sent two disciples, [2] saying to them, "Go into the village ahead of you, and immediately you will find a donkey tied, and a colt with her; untie them and bring them to me. [3] If anyone says anything to you, just say this, 'The Lord needs them.' And he will send them immediately."[b] [4] This took place to fulfill what had been spoken through the prophet, saying,
[5] "Tell the daughter of Zion,

Look, your king is coming to you,
    humble, and mounted
        on a donkey,
    and on a colt, the foal
        of a donkey."
[6] The disciples went and did as Jesus had directed them; [7] they brought the donkey and the colt, and put their cloaks on them, and he sat on them. [8] A very large crowd[c] spread their cloaks on the road, and others cut branches from the trees and spread them on the road. [9] The crowds that went ahead of him and that followed were shouting,
"Hosanna to the Son of David!
Blessed is the one who comes
    in the name of the Lord!
Hosanna in the highest heaven!"
[10] When he entered Jerusalem, the whole city was in turmoil, asking, "Who is this?" [11] The crowds were saying, "This is the prophet Jesus from Nazareth in Galilee."

JESUS CLEANSES THE TEMPLE

12 Then Jesus entered the temple[d] and drove out all who were selling and buying in the temple, and he overturned the tables of the money changers and the seats of those who

a **20.30** Other ancient authorities lack Lord
b **21.3** Or 'The Lord needs them and will send them back immediately.'   c **21.8** Or Most of the crowd   d **21.12** Other ancient authorities add of God

---

BIBLE IN LIFE

Dedicated to Christ   Matthew 21.1–11

The crowds that surrounded Jesus during his entrance into Jerusalem knew about this controversial teacher. Some of them had probably seen Jesus heal people. Some of them may have heard the Sermon on the Mount. However, they had also heard from their own religious and political leaders that Jesus was a subversive rebel and a blasphemer. He had violated the sabbath laws, claimed an ascendant relationship with God and even forgiven sins. Thus, the people felt torn. To their disappointment, Jesus didn't come to them as a powerful king or military conqueror riding on a beautiful white horse. Just days later, they would abandon him and shout, "Crucify him!" They had welcomed Christ when it was convenient for them, but they deserted him when it meant some sacrifice on their part. Does this description resonate with us? Are we dedicated to Christ when it's convenient—when we pray that our sorrow might be lessened, our sickness healed or our troubles overcome? Do we prove ourselves to be Christians only when we want to convey that we're good, honest and truthful? Or do we follow Christ when it means some dedication or sacrifice on our part?

sold doves. 13He said to them, "It is written,

'My house shall be called a
house of prayer';
but you are making it a
den of robbers.'"

14 The blind and the lame came to him in the temple, and he cured them. 15But when the chief priests and the scribes saw the amazing things that he did, and heard[a] the children crying out in the temple, "Hosanna to the Son of David," they became angry 16and said to him, "Do you hear what these are saying?" Jesus said to them, "Yes; have you never read,

'Out of the mouths of infants
and nursing babies
you have prepared praise
for yourself'?"

17He left them, went out of the city to Bethany, and spent the night there.

JESUS CURSES THE FIG TREE

18 In the morning, when he returned to the city, he was hungry. 19And seeing a fig tree by the side of the road, he went to it and found nothing at all on it but leaves. Then he said to it, "May no fruit ever come from you again!" And the fig tree withered at once. 20When the disciples saw it, they were amazed, saying, "How did the fig tree wither at once?" 21Jesus answered them, "Truly I tell you, if you have faith and do not doubt, not only will you do what has been done to the fig tree, but even if you say to this mountain, 'Be lifted up and thrown into the sea,' it will be done. 22Whatever you ask for in prayer with faith, you will receive."

THE AUTHORITY OF JESUS QUESTIONED

23 When he entered the temple, the chief priests and the elders of the people came to him as he was teaching, and said, "By what authority are you doing these things, and who gave you this authority?" 24Jesus said to them, "I will also ask you one question; if you tell me the answer, then I will also tell you by what au-

thority I do these things. 25Did the baptism of John come from heaven, or was it of human origin?" And they argued with one another, "If we say, 'From heaven,' he will say to us, 'Why then did you not believe him?' 26But if we say, 'Of human origin,' we are afraid of the crowd; for all regard John as a prophet." 27So they answered Jesus, "We do not know." And he said to them, "Neither will I tell you by what authority I am doing these things.

THE PARABLE OF THE TWO SONS

28 "What do you think? A man had two sons; he went to the first and said, 'Son, go and work in the vineyard today.' 29He answered, 'I will not'; but later he changed his mind and went. 30The father[b] went to the second and said the same; and he answered, 'I go, sir'; but he did not go. 31Which of the two did the will of his father?" They said, "The first." Jesus said to them, "Truly I tell you, the tax collectors and the prostitutes are going into the kingdom of God ahead of you. 32For John came to you in the way of righteousness and you did not believe him, but the tax collectors and the prostitutes believed him; and even after you saw it, you did not change your minds and believe him.

THE PARABLE OF THE WICKED TENANTS

33 "Listen to another parable. There was a landowner who planted a vineyard, put a fence around it, dug a wine press in it, and built a watchtower. Then he leased it to tenants and went to another country. 34When the harvest time had come, he sent his slaves to the tenants to collect his produce. 35But the tenants seized his slaves and beat one, killed another, and stoned another. 36Again he sent other slaves, more than the first; and they treated them in the same way. 37Finally he sent his son to them, saying, 'They will respect my son.' 38But when the tenants saw the son, they said to

a 21.15 Gk lacks *heard*   b 21.30 Gk *He*

themselves, 'This is the heir; come, let us kill him and get his inheritance.' 39So they seized him, threw him out of the vineyard, and killed him. 40Now when the owner of the vineyard comes, what will he do to those tenants?" 41They said to him, "He will put those wretches to a miserable death, and lease the vineyard to other tenants who will give him the produce at the harvest time."

42 Jesus said to them, "Have you never read in the scriptures:

'The stone that the builders
   rejected
has become the cornerstone;[a]
this was the Lord's doing,
   and it is amazing in our eyes'?

43Therefore I tell you, the kingdom of God will be taken away from you and given to a people that produces the fruits of the kingdom.[b] 44The one who falls on this stone will be broken to pieces; and it will crush anyone on whom it falls."[c]

45 When the chief priests and the Pharisees heard his parables, they realized that he was speaking about them. 46They wanted to arrest him, but they feared the crowds, because they regarded him as a prophet.

THE PARABLE OF THE WEDDING BANQUET

22 Once more Jesus spoke to them in parables, saying: 2"The kingdom of heaven may be compared to a king who gave a wedding banquet for his son. 3He sent his slaves to call those who had been invited to the wedding banquet, but they would not come. 4Again he sent other slaves, saying, 'Tell those who have been invited: Look, I have prepared my dinner, my oxen and my fat calves have been slaughtered, and everything is ready; come to the wedding banquet.' 5But they made light of it and went away, one to his farm, another to his business, 6while the rest seized his slaves, mistreated them, and killed them. 7The king was enraged. He sent his troops, destroyed those murderers, and burned their city. 8Then he said to his slaves, 'The wedding is ready, but those invited were not worthy. 9Go therefore into the main streets, and invite everyone you find to the wedding banquet.' 10Those slaves went out into the streets and gathered all whom they found, both good and bad; so the wedding hall was filled with guests.

11 "But when the king came in to see the guests, he noticed a man there who was not wearing a wedding robe, 12and he said to him, 'Friend, how did you get in here without a wedding robe?' And he was speechless. 13Then the king said to the attendants, 'Bind him hand and foot, and throw him into the outer darkness, where there will be weeping and gnashing of teeth.' 14For many are called, but few are chosen."

THE QUESTION ABOUT PAYING TAXES

15 Then the Pharisees went and plotted to entrap him in what he said. 16So they sent their disciples to him, along with the Herodians, saying, "Teacher, we know that you are sincere, and teach the way of God in accordance with truth, and show deference to no one; for you do not regard people with partiality. 17Tell us, then, what you think. Is it lawful to pay taxes to the emperor, or not?" 18But Jesus, aware of their malice, said, "Why are you putting me to the test, you hypocrites? 19Show me the coin used for the tax." And they brought him a denarius. 20Then he said to them, "Whose head is this, and whose title?" 21They answered, "The emperor's." Then he said to them, "Give therefore to the emperor the things that are the emperor's, and to God the things that are God's." 22When they heard this, they were amazed; and they left him and went away.

THE QUESTION ABOUT THE RESURRECTION

23 The same day some Sadducees came to him, saying there is no resurrection;[d] and they asked him a question, saying, 24"Teacher, Moses

---

[a] 21.42 Or keystone   [b] 21.43 Gk the fruits of it   [c] 21.44 Other ancient authorities lack verse 44   [d] 22.23 Other ancient authorities read who say that there is no resurrection

said, 'If a man dies childless, his brother shall marry the widow, and raise up children for his brother.' 25Now there were seven brothers among us; the first married, and died childless, leaving the widow to his brother. 26The second did the same, so also the third, down to the seventh. 27Last of all, the woman herself died. 28In the resurrection, then, whose wife of the seven will she be? For all of them had married her."

29 Jesus answered them, "You are wrong, because you know neither the scriptures nor the power of God. 30For in the resurrection they neither marry nor are given in marriage, but are like angels[a] in heaven. 31And as for the resurrection of the dead, have you not read what was said to you by God, 32'I am the God of Abraham, the God of Isaac, and the God of Jacob'? He is God not of the dead, but of the living." 33And when the crowd heard it, they were astounded at his teaching.

THE GREATEST COMMANDMENT

34 When the Pharisees heard that he had silenced the Sadducees, they gathered together, 35and one of them, a lawyer, asked him a question to test him. 36"Teacher, which commandment in the law is the greatest?" 37He said to him, " 'You shall love the Lord your God with all your heart, and with all your soul, and with all your mind.' 38This is the greatest and first commandment. 39And a second is like it: 'You shall love your neighbor as yourself.' 40On these two commandments hang all the law and the prophets."

THE QUESTION ABOUT DAVID'S SON

41 Now while the Pharisees were gathered together, Jesus asked them this question: 42"What do you think of the Messiah?[b] Whose son is he?" They said to him, "The son of David." 43He said to them, "How is it then that David by the Spirit[c] calls him Lord, saying,

44 'The Lord said to my Lord,

"Sit at my right hand,
until I put your enemies
under your feet" '?
45If David thus calls him Lord, how can he be his son?" 46No one was able to give him an answer, nor from that day did anyone dare to ask him any more questions.

JESUS DENOUNCES SCRIBES AND PHARISEES

23 Then Jesus said to the crowds and to his disciples, 2"The scribes and the Pharisees sit on Moses' seat; 3therefore, do whatever they teach you and follow it; but do not do as they do, for they do not practice what they teach. 4They tie up heavy burdens, hard to bear,[d] and lay them on the shoulders of others; but they themselves are unwilling to lift a finger to move them. 5They do all their deeds to be seen by others; for they make their phylacteries broad and their fringes long. 6They love to have the place of honor at banquets and the best seats in the synagogues, 7and to be greeted with respect in the marketplaces, and to have people call them rabbi. 8But you are not to be called rabbi, for you have one teacher, and you are all students.[e] 9And call no one your father on earth, for you have one Father— the one in heaven. 10Nor are you to be called instructors, for you have one instructor, the Messiah.[f] 11The greatest among you will be your servant. 12All who exalt themselves will be humbled, and all who humble themselves will be exalted.

13 "But woe to you, scribes and Pharisees, hypocrites! For you lock people out of the kingdom of heaven. For you do not go in yourselves, and when others are going in, you stop them.[g] 15Woe to you, scribes and

a 22.30 Other ancient authorities add of God   b 22.42 Or Christ   c 22.43 Gk in spirit   d 23.4 Other ancient authorities lack hard to bear   e 23.8 Gk brothers   f 23.10 Or the Christ   g 23.13 Other authorities add here (or after verse 12) verse 14, Woe to you, scribes and Pharisees, hypocrites! For you devour widows' houses and for the sake of appearance you make long prayers; therefore you will receive the greater condemnation

Pharisees, hypocrites! For you cross sea and land to make a single convert, and you make the new convert twice as much a child of hell[a] as yourselves.

16 "Woe to you, blind guides, who say, 'Whoever swears by the sanctuary is bound by nothing, but whoever swears by the gold of the sanctuary is bound by the oath.' 17You blind fools! For which is greater, the gold or the sanctuary that has made the gold sacred? 18And you say, 'Whoever swears by the altar is bound by nothing, but whoever swears by the gift that is on the altar is bound by the oath.' 19How blind you are! For which is greater, the gift or the altar that makes the gift sacred? 20So whoever swears by the altar, swears by it and by everything on it; 21and whoever swears by the sanctuary, swears by it and by the one who dwells in it; 22and whoever swears by heaven, swears by the throne of God and by the one who is seated upon it.

23 "Woe to you, scribes and Pharisees, hypocrites! For you tithe mint, dill, and cummin, and have neglected the weightier matters of the law: justice and mercy and faith. It is these you ought to have practiced without neglecting the others. 24You blind guides! You strain out a gnat but swallow a camel!

25 "Woe to you, scribes and Pharisees, hypocrites! For you clean the outside of the cup and of the plate, but inside they are full of greed and self-indulgence. 26You blind Pharisee! First clean the inside of the cup,[b] so that the outside also may become clean.

27 "Woe to you, scribes and Pharisees, hypocrites! For you are like whitewashed tombs, which on the outside look beautiful, but inside they are full of the bones of the dead and of all kinds of filth. 28So you also on the outside look righteous to others, but inside you are full of hypocrisy and lawlessness.

29 "Woe to you, scribes and Pharisees, hypocrites! For you build the tombs of the prophets and decorate the graves of the righteous, 30and you say, 'If we had lived in the days of our ancestors, we would not have taken part with them in shedding the blood of the prophets.' 31Thus you testify against yourselves that you are descendants of those who murdered the prophets. 32Fill up, then, the measure of your ancestors. 33You snakes, you brood of vipers! How can you escape being sentenced to hell?[a] 34Therefore I send you prophets, sages, and scribes, some of whom you will kill and crucify, and some you will flog in your synagogues and pursue from town

a 23.15,33 Gk *Gehenna*   b 23.26 Other ancient authorities add *and of the plate*

⊣├ BIBLE IN LIFE ▷──────⊕

Pharisaic Superiority   *Matthew 23.1–39*

Matthew 23 clearly indicates what Christ thought of the Pharisees. The Pharisees were separatists—they thought it was sinful for them to associate with people who fit their definition of sinners, and they condemned Christ for befriending and eating with those very same people. They concocted very narrow definitions of what was acceptable and unacceptable in God's eyes. They were traditionalists—they looked back on their study of God's Word and tried to preserve it, while also adding their own human interpretation to it. They defined, in effect, the proper relationship with God. In order for someone to be accepted by God in their eyes and in the eyes of the religious establishment, that person had to comply with their human definitions. The Pharisees were devout and sincere, but the personal aspect of God's love was secondary to them. We may also be devout and sincere in our devotion to God, but when we reject people because of their sinfulness or because they are different from us, we yield to the same temptations that afflicted the Pharisees.

to town, 35so that upon you may come all the righteous blood shed on earth, from the blood of righteous Abel to the blood of Zechariah son of Barachiah, whom you murdered between the sanctuary and the altar. 36Truly I tell you, all this will come upon this generation.

THE LAMENT OVER JERUSALEM

37 "Jerusalem, Jerusalem, the city that kills the prophets and stones those who are sent to it! How often have I desired to gather your children together as a hen gathers her brood under her wings, and you were not willing! 38See, your house is left to you, desolate.[a] 39For I tell you, you will not see me again until you say, 'Blessed is the one who comes in the name of the Lord.'"

THE DESTRUCTION OF THE TEMPLE FORETOLD

24 As Jesus came out of the temple and was going away, his disciples came to point out to him the buildings of the temple. 2Then he asked them, "You see all these, do you not? Truly I tell you, not one stone will be left here upon another; all will be thrown down."

SIGNS OF THE END OF THE AGE

3When he was sitting on the Mount of Olives, the disciples came to him privately, saying, "Tell us, when will this be, and what will be the sign of your coming and of the end of the age?" 4Jesus answered them, "Beware that no one leads you astray. 5For many will come in my name, saying, 'I am the Messiah!'[b] and they will lead many astray. 6And you will hear of wars and rumors of wars; see that you are not alarmed; for this must take place, but the end is not yet. 7For nation will rise against nation, and kingdom against kingdom, and there will be famines[c] and earthquakes in various places: 8all this is but the beginning of the birth pangs.

PERSECUTIONS FORETOLD

9 "Then they will hand you over to be tortured and will put you to death, and you will be hated by all nations because of my name. 10Then many will fall away,[d] and they will betray one another and hate one another. 11And many false prophets will arise and lead many astray. 12And because of the increase of lawlessness, the love of many will grow cold. 13But the one who endures to the end will be saved. 14And this good news[e] of the kingdom will be proclaimed throughout the world, as a testimony to all the nations; and then the end will come.

THE DESOLATING SACRILEGE

15 "So when you see the desolating sacrilege standing in the holy place, as was spoken of by the prophet Daniel (let the reader understand), 16then those in Judea must flee to the mountains; 17the one on the housetop must not go down to take what is in the house; 18the one in the field must not turn back to get a coat. 19Woe to those who are pregnant and to those who are nursing infants in those days! 20Pray that your flight may not be in winter or on a sabbath. 21For at that time there will be great suffering, such as has not been from the beginning of the world until now, no, and never will be. 22And if those days had not been cut short, no one would be saved; but for the sake of the elect those days will be cut short. 23Then if anyone says to you, 'Look! Here is the Messiah!'[b] or 'There he is!'—do not believe it. 24For false messiahs[f] and false prophets will appear and produce great signs and omens, to lead astray, if possible, even the elect. 25Take note, I have told you beforehand. 26So, if they say to you, 'Look! He is in the wilderness,' do not go out. If they say, 'Look! He is in the inner rooms,' do not believe it. 27For as the lightning comes from the east and flashes as far as the west, so will be the coming of the Son of Man. 28Wherever the corpse is, there the vultures will gather.

---

a 23.38 Other ancient authorities lack desolate   b 24.5,23 Or the Christ
c 24.7 Other ancient authorities add and pestilences   d 24.10 Or stumble
e 24.14 Or gospel   f 24.24 Or christs

THE COMING OF THE
SON OF MAN

29 "Immediately after the suffering of those days

the sun will be darkened,
and the moon will not
give its light;
the stars will fall from heaven,
and the powers of heaven
will be shaken.

30 Then the sign of the Son of Man will appear in heaven, and then all the tribes of the earth will mourn, and they will see 'the Son of Man coming on the clouds of heaven' with power and great glory. 31 And he will send out his angels with a loud trumpet call, and they will gather his elect from the four winds, from one end of heaven to the other.

THE LESSON OF THE FIG TREE

32 "From the fig tree learn its lesson: as soon as its branch becomes tender and puts forth its leaves, you know that summer is near. 33 So also, when you see all these things, you know that he[a] is near, at the very gates. 34 Truly I tell you, this generation will not pass away until all these things have taken place. 35 Heaven and earth will pass away, but my words will not pass away.

THE NECESSITY FOR
WATCHFULNESS

36 "But about that day and hour no one knows, neither the angels of heaven, nor the Son,[b] but only the Father. 37 For as the days of Noah were, so will be the coming of the Son of Man. 38 For as in those days before the flood they were eating and drinking, marrying and giving in marriage, until the day Noah entered the ark, 39 and they knew nothing until the flood came and swept them all away, so too will be the coming of the Son of Man. 40 Then two will be in the field; one will be taken and one will be left. 41 Two women will be grinding meal together; one will be taken and one will be left. 42 Keep awake therefore, for you do not know on what day[c] your Lord is coming. 43 But understand this: if the owner of the house had known in what part

of the night the thief was coming, he would have stayed awake and would not have let his house be broken into. 44 Therefore you also must be ready, for the Son of Man is coming at an unexpected hour.

THE FAITHFUL OR THE
UNFAITHFUL SLAVE

45 "Who then is the faithful and wise slave, whom his master has put in charge of his household, to give the other slaves[d] their allowance of food at the proper time? 46 Blessed is that slave whom his master will find at work when he arrives. 47 Truly I tell you, he will put that one in

a 24.33 Or it   b 24.36 Other ancient authorities lack *nor the Son*   c 24.42 Other ancient authorities read *at what hour*
d 24.45 Gk *to give them*

PONDER

"Who then is the faithful and wise slave, whom his master has put in charge of his household, to give the other slaves their allowance of food at the proper time? Blessed is that slave whom his master will find at work when he arrives."
—Matthew 24.45–46

PRAY

Heavenly Father, like many other parts of the Bible, this passage shakes us. It proposes profound life-changing truth in very simple terms. We too are commissioned as your servants, to work in and for your kingdom. Give us the will to be faithful as Jesus was faithful: He came as a son over your household and was a diligent steward of all you gave him; he healed sick people and gave new life to those who were forlorn, lifted up the outcasts as worthy human beings and cared for those in need. We pray that this message will inspire us to pattern our lives more closely after his perfect life. We ask these things in your name. Amen.

charge of all his possessions. [48]But if that wicked slave says to himself, 'My master is delayed,' [49]and he begins to beat his fellow slaves, and eats and drinks with drunkards, [50]the master of that slave will come on a day when he does not expect him and at an hour that he does not know. [51]He will cut him in pieces[a] and put him with the hypocrites, where there will be weeping and gnashing of teeth.

THE PARABLE OF THE TEN BRIDESMAIDS

25 "Then the kingdom of heaven will be like this. Ten bridesmaids[b] took their lamps and went to meet the bridegroom.[c] [2]Five of them were foolish, and five were wise. [3]When the foolish took their lamps, they took no oil with them; [4]but the wise took flasks of oil with their lamps. [5]As the bridegroom was delayed, all of them became drowsy and slept. [6]But at midnight there was a shout, 'Look! Here is the bridegroom! Come out to meet him.' [7]Then all those bridesmaids[b] got up and trimmed their lamps. [8]The foolish said to the wise, 'Give us some of your oil, for our lamps are going out.' [9]But the wise replied, 'No! there will not be enough for you and for us; you had better go to the dealers and buy some for yourselves.' [10]And while they went to buy it, the bridegroom

came, and those who were ready went with him into the wedding banquet; and the door was shut. [11]Later the other bridesmaids[b] came also, saying, 'Lord, lord, open to us.' [12]But he replied, 'Truly I tell you, I do not know you.' [13]Keep awake therefore, for you know neither the day nor the hour.[d]

THE PARABLE OF THE TALENTS

[14] "For it is as if a man, going on a journey, summoned his slaves and entrusted his property to them; [15]to one he gave five talents,[e] to another two, to another one, to each according to his ability. Then he went away. [16]The one who had received the five talents went off at once and traded with them, and made five more talents. [17]In the same way, the one who had the two talents made two more talents. [18]But the one who had received the one talent went off and dug a hole in the ground and hid his master's money. [19]After a long time the master of those slaves came and settled accounts with them. [20]Then the one who had received the five talents came forward, bringing five more talents, saying, 'Master, you

[a] 24.51 Or cut him off   [b] 25.1,7,11 Gk virgins
[c] 25.1 Other ancient authorities add and the bride   [d] 25.13 Other ancient authorities add in which the Son of Man is coming
[e] 25.15 A talent was worth more than fifteen years' wages of a laborer

---

⊣ BIBLE IN LIFE ▷ ⊕

Using Our Talents   Matthew 25.14–30

All of us have talents that God gave us, and we can use these talents to serve God and others as well as to enhance our own lives. One person may be a gifted speaker or have musical ability. Another may be skilled in medicine, good with finances or a compassionate listener. Whatever talents and resources God has given us, we need to make sure we are not wasting them during our short time on earth. Some people waste their resources by using them solely for their own benefit, never reaching out to others and blessing them. Others waste their resources by never even using them at all. They are satisfied with the narrow life they have carved out for themselves and never stretch beyond that. The things we do for God don't have to be headline news. They don't have to be dramatic, but they have to be specific: acts of kindness, gifts of forgiveness, simple visits, building houses for homeless families, serving meals to poor people or visiting lonely persons in prison. When we use our talents to serve God and others, we are emulating the selfless character of our Savior, Jesus Christ . . . and we ourselves are greatly blessed.

handed over to me five talents; see, I have made five more talents.' 21His master said to him, 'Well done, good and trustworthy slave; you have been trustworthy in a few things, I will put you in charge of many things; enter into the joy of your master.' 22And the one with the two talents also came forward, saying, 'Master, you handed over to me two talents; see, I have made two more talents.' 23His master said to him, 'Well done, good and trustworthy slave; you have been trustworthy in a few things, I will put you in charge of many things; enter into the joy of your master.' 24Then the one who had received the one talent also came forward, saying, 'Master, I knew that you were a harsh man, reaping where you did not sow, and gathering where you did not scatter seed; 25so I was afraid, and I went and hid your talent in the ground. Here you have what is yours.' 26But his master replied, 'You wicked and lazy slave! You knew, did you, that I reap where I did not sow, and gather where I did not scatter? 27Then you ought to have invested my money with the bankers, and on my return I would have received what was my own with interest. 28So take the talent from him, and give it to the one with the ten talents. 29For to all those who have, more will be given, and they will have an abundance; but from those who have nothing, even what they have will be taken away. 30As for this worthless slave, throw him into the outer darkness, where there will be weeping and gnashing of teeth.'

THE JUDGMENT OF THE NATIONS

31 "When the Son of Man comes in his glory, and all the angels with him, then he will sit on the throne of his glory. 32All the nations will be gathered before him, and he will separate people one from another as a shepherd separates the sheep from the goats, 33and he will put the sheep at his right hand and the goats at the left. 34Then the king will say to those at his right hand, 'Come, you that are blessed by my Father,

inherit the kingdom prepared for you from the foundation of the world; 35for I was hungry and you gave me food, I was thirsty and you gave me something to drink, I was a stranger and you welcomed me, 36I was naked and you gave me clothing, I was sick and you took care of me, I was in prison and you visited me.' 37Then the righteous will answer him, 'Lord, when was it that we saw you hungry and gave you food, or thirsty and gave you something to drink? 38And when was it that we saw you a stranger and welcomed you, or naked and gave you clothing? 39And when was it that we saw you sick or in prison and visited you?' 40And the king will answer them, 'Truly I tell you, just as you did it to one of the least of these who are members of my family,ª you did it to me.' 41Then he will say to those at his left hand, 'You that are accursed, depart from me into the eternal fire prepared for the devil and his angels; 42for I was hungry and you gave me no food, I was thirsty and you gave me nothing to drink, 43I was a stranger and you did not welcome me, naked and you did not give me clothing, sick and in prison and you did not visit me.' 44Then they also will answer, 'Lord, when was it that we saw you hungry or thirsty or a stranger or naked or sick or in prison, and did not take care of you?' 45Then he will answer them, 'Truly I tell you, just as you did not do it to one of the least of these, you did not do it to me.' 46And these will go away into eternal punishment, but the righteous into eternal life."

THE PLOT TO KILL JESUS

26 When Jesus had finished saying all these things, he said to his disciples, 2"You know that after two days the Passover is coming, and the Son of Man will be handed over to be crucified."

3 Then the chief priests and the elders of the people gathered in the palace of the high priest, who was

ª 25.40 Gk these my brothers

called Caiaphas, 4and they conspired to arrest Jesus by stealth and kill him. 5But they said, "Not during the festival, or there may be a riot among the people."

THE ANOINTING AT BETHANY

6 Now while Jesus was at Bethany in the house of Simon the leper,[a] 7a woman came to him with an alabaster jar of very costly ointment, and she poured it on his head as he sat at the table. 8But when the disciples saw it, they were angry and said, "Why this waste? 9For this ointment could have been sold for a large sum, and the money given to the poor." 10But Jesus, aware of this, said to them, "Why do you trouble the woman? She has performed a good service for me. 11For you always have the poor with you, but you will not always have me. 12By pouring this ointment on my body she has prepared me for burial. 13Truly I tell you, wherever this good news[b] is proclaimed in the whole world, what she has done will be told in remembrance of her."

JUDAS AGREES TO BETRAY JESUS

14 Then one of the twelve, who was called Judas Iscariot, went to the chief priests 15and said, "What will you give me if I betray him to you?" They paid him thirty pieces of silver. 16And from that moment he began to look for an opportunity to betray him.

THE PASSOVER WITH THE DISCIPLES

17 On the first day of Unleavened Bread the disciples came to Jesus, saying, "Where do you want us to make the preparations for you to eat the Passover?" 18He said, "Go into the city to a certain man, and say to him, 'The Teacher says, My time is near; I will keep the Passover at your house with my disciples.' " 19So the disciples did as Jesus had directed them, and they prepared the Passover meal.

20 When it was evening, he took his place with the twelve;[c] 21and while they were eating, he said,

"Truly I tell you, one of you will betray me." 22And they became greatly distressed and began to say to him one after another, "Surely not I, Lord?" 23He answered, "The one who has dipped his hand into the bowl with me will betray me. 24The Son of Man goes as it is written of him, but woe to that one by whom the Son of Man is betrayed! It would have been better for that one not to have been born." 25Judas, who betrayed him, said, "Surely not I, Rabbi?" He replied, "You have said so."

THE INSTITUTION OF THE LORD'S SUPPER

26 While they were eating, Jesus took a loaf of bread, and after blessing it he broke it, gave it to the disciples, and said, "Take, eat; this is my body." 27Then he took a cup, and after giving thanks he gave it to them, saying, "Drink from it, all of you; 28for this is my blood of the[d] covenant, which is poured out for many for the forgiveness of sins. 29I tell you, I will never again drink of this fruit of the vine until that day when I drink it new with you in my Father's kingdom."

30 When they had sung the hymn, they went out to the Mount of Olives.

PETER'S DENIAL FORETOLD

31 Then Jesus said to them, "You will all become deserters because of me this night; for it is written,

'I will strike the shepherd,
    and the sheep of the flock
        will be scattered.'

32But after I am raised up, I will go ahead of you to Galilee." 33Peter said to him, "Though all become deserters because of you, I will never desert you." 34Jesus said to him, "Truly I tell you, this very night, before the cock crows, you will deny me three times." 35Peter said to him, "Even though I must die with you, I will not deny you." And so said all the disciples.

---

[a] 26.6 The terms *leper* and *leprosy* can refer to several diseases   [b] 26.13 Or *gospel*
[c] 26.20 Other ancient authorities add *disciples*   [d] 26.28 Other ancient authorities add *new*

JESUS PRAYS IN GETHSEMANE

36 Then Jesus went with them to a place called Gethsemane; and he said to his disciples, "Sit here while I go over there and pray." **37** He took with him Peter and the two sons of Zebedee, and began to be grieved and agitated. **38** Then he said to them, "I am deeply grieved, even to death; remain here, and stay awake with me." **39** And going a little farther, he threw himself on the ground and prayed, "My Father, if it is possible, let this cup pass from me; yet not what I want but what you want." **40** Then he came to the disciples and found them sleeping; and he said to Peter, "So, could you not stay awake with me one hour? **41** Stay awake and pray that you may not come into the time of trial;[a] the spirit indeed is willing, but the flesh is weak." **42** Again he went away for the second time and prayed, "My Father, if this cannot pass unless I drink it, your will be done." **43** Again he came and found them sleeping, for their eyes were heavy. **44** So leaving them again, he went away and prayed for the third time, saying the same words. **45** Then he came to the disciples and said to them, "Are you still sleeping and taking your rest? See, the hour is at hand, and the Son of Man is betrayed into the hands of sinners. **46** Get up, let us be going. See, my betrayer is at hand."

THE BETRAYAL AND ARREST OF JESUS

47 While he was still speaking, Judas, one of the twelve, arrived; with him was a large crowd with swords and clubs, from the chief priests and the elders of the people. **48** Now the betrayer had given them a sign, saying, "The one I will kiss is the man; arrest him." **49** At once he came up to Jesus and said, "Greetings, Rabbi!" and kissed him. **50** Jesus said to him, "Friend, do what you are here to do." Then they came and laid hands on Jesus and arrested him. **51** Suddenly, one of those with Jesus put his hand on his sword, drew it, and struck the slave of the high priest, cutting off his ear. **52** Then Jesus said to him, "Put your sword back into its place; for all who take the sword will perish by the sword. **53** Do you think that I cannot appeal to my Father, and he will at once send me more than twelve legions of angels? **54** But how then would the scriptures be fulfilled, which say it must happen in this way?" **55** At that hour Jesus said to the crowds, "Have you come out with swords and clubs to arrest me as though I were a bandit? Day after day I sat in the temple teaching, and you did not arrest me. **56** But all this has taken place, so that the scriptures of the prophets may be fulfilled." Then all the disciples deserted him and fled.

JESUS BEFORE THE HIGH PRIEST

57 Those who had arrested Jesus took him to Caiaphas the high priest, in whose house the scribes and the elders had gathered. **58** But

a **26.41** Or *into temptation*

BIBLE IN LIFE

Convenient Faith
Matthew 26.56

Where were the disciples after Jesus was arrested? Gone. They had been his closest friends, dedicated to him when it was convenient, when it didn't interfere with their other priorities, such as survival and safety. On the night of Jesus' trial and arrest, Peter didn't even want to be associated with him. He was afraid of being crucified with Jesus; he wanted to blend in with the crowd (see John 18.25). Although Peter was convinced that Christ was the Son of God (see Matthew 16.16), he chose his own well-being instead of identifying himself with Christ. How are we like Peter and the rest of the disciples? Do we believe wholeheartedly that Jesus is the Son of God, yet abandon being associated with Christ when it's unsafe or inconvenient for us?

Peter was following him at a distance, as far as the courtyard of the high priest; and going inside, he sat with the guards in order to see how this would end. 59Now the chief priests and the whole council were looking for false testimony against Jesus so that they might put him to death, 60but they found none, though many false witnesses came forward. At last two came forward 61and said, "This fellow said, 'I am able to destroy the temple of God and to build it in three days.'" 62The high priest stood up and said, "Have you no answer? What is it that they testify against you?" 63But Jesus was silent. Then the high priest said to him, "I put you under oath before the living God, tell us if you are the Messiah,[a] the Son of God." 64Jesus said to him, "You have said so. But I tell you,

From now on you will see
the Son of Man
seated at the right
hand of Power
and coming on the clouds
of heaven."

65Then the high priest tore his clothes and said, "He has blasphemed! Why do we still need witnesses? You have now heard his blasphemy. 66What is your verdict?" They answered, "He deserves death." 67Then they spat in his face and struck him; and some slapped him, 68saying, "Prophesy to us, you Messiah![a] Who is it that struck you?"

PETER'S DENIAL OF JESUS

69 Now Peter was sitting outside in the courtyard. A servant-girl came to him and said, "You also were with Jesus the Galilean." 70But he denied it before all of them, saying, "I do not know what you are talking about." 71When he went out to the porch, another servant-girl saw him, and she said to the bystanders, "This man was with Jesus of Nazareth."[b] 72Again he denied it with an oath, "I do not know the man." 73After a little while the bystanders came up and said to Peter, "Certainly you are also one of them, for your accent betrays you." 74Then he be-

gan to curse, and he swore an oath, "I do not know the man!" At that moment the cock crowed. 75Then Peter remembered what Jesus had said: "Before the cock crows, you will deny me three times." And he went out and wept bitterly.

LIKE THE DISCIPLES, WE ARE

LIKELY TO PROFESS OUR

LOYALTY, BUT RESIST THE

ESSENCE OF JESUS' LIFE.

JESUS BROUGHT BEFORE PILATE

27 When morning came, all the chief priests and the elders of the people conferred together against Jesus in order to bring about his death. 2They bound him, led him away, and handed him over to Pilate the governor.

THE SUICIDE OF JUDAS

3When Judas, his betrayer, saw that Jesus[c] was condemned, he repented and brought back the thirty pieces of silver to the chief priests and the elders. 4He said, "I have sinned by betraying innocent[d] blood." But they said, "What is that to us? See to it yourself." 5Throwing down the pieces of silver in the temple, he departed; and he went and hanged himself. 6But the chief priests, taking the pieces of silver, said, "It is not lawful to put them into the treasury, since they are blood money." 7After conferring together, they used them to buy the potter's field as a place to bury foreigners. 8For this reason that field has been called the Field of Blood to this day. 9Then was fulfilled what had been spoken through the prophet Jeremiah,[e] "And they

a 26.63,68 Or Christ b 26.71 Gk the
Nazorean c 27.3 Gk he d 27.4 Other
ancient authorities read righteous
e 27.9 Other ancient authorities read
Zechariah or Isaiah

took[a] the thirty pieces of silver, the price of the one on whom a price had been set,[b] on whom some of the people of Israel had set a price, [10]and they gave[c] them for the potter's field, as the Lord commanded me."

PILATE QUESTIONS JESUS

11 Now Jesus stood before the governor; and the governor asked him, "Are you the King of the Jews?" Jesus said, "You say so." [12]But when he was accused by the chief priests and elders, he did not answer. [13]Then Pilate said to him, "Do you not hear how many accusations they make against you?" [14]But he gave him no answer, not even to a single charge, so that the governor was greatly amazed.

BARABBAS OR JESUS?

15 Now at the festival the governor was accustomed to release a prisoner for the crowd, anyone whom they wanted. [16]At that time they had a notorious prisoner, called Jesus[d] Barabbas. [17]So after they had gathered, Pilate said to them, "Whom do you want me to release for you, Jesus[d] Barabbas or Jesus who is called the Messiah?"[e] [18]For he realized that it was out of jealousy that they had handed him over. [19]While he was sitting on the judgment seat, his wife sent word to him, "Have nothing to do with that innocent man, for today I have suffered a great deal because of a dream about him." [20]Now the chief priests and the elders persuaded the crowds to ask for Barabbas and to have Jesus killed. [21]The governor again said to them, "Which of the two do you want me to release for you?" And they said, "Barabbas." [22]Pilate said to them, "Then what should I do with Jesus who is called the Messiah?"[e] All of them said, "Let him be crucified!" [23]Then he asked, "Why, what evil has he done?" But they shouted all the more, "Let him be crucified!"

PILATE HANDS JESUS OVER TO BE CRUCIFIED

24 So when Pilate saw that he could do nothing, but rather that a riot was beginning, he took some water and washed his hands before the crowd, saying, "I am innocent of this man's blood;[f] see to it yourselves." [25]Then the people as a whole answered, "His blood be on us and on our children!" [26]So he released Barabbas for them; and after flogging Jesus, he handed him over to be crucified.

THE SOLDIERS MOCK JESUS

27 Then the soldiers of the governor took Jesus into the governor's headquarters,[g] and they gathered the whole cohort around him. [28]They stripped him and put a scarlet robe on him, [29]and after twisting some thorns into a crown, they put it on his head. They put a reed in his right hand and knelt before him and mocked him, saying, "Hail, King of the Jews!" [30]They spat on him, and took the reed and struck him on the head. [31]After mocking him, they stripped him of the robe and put his own clothes on him. Then they led him away to crucify him.

THE CRUCIFIXION OF JESUS

32 As they went out, they came upon a man from Cyrene named Simon; they compelled this man to carry his cross. [33]And when they came to a place called Golgotha (which means Place of a Skull), [34]they offered him wine to drink, mixed with gall; but when he tasted it, he would not drink it. [35]And when they had crucified him, they divided his clothes among themselves by casting lots;[h] [36]then they sat down there and kept watch over him. [37]Over his head they put the charge against him, which read, "This is Jesus, the King of the Jews." 38 Then two bandits were crucified with him, one on his right

[a] 27.9 Or I took   [b] 27.9 Or the price of the precious One   [c] 27.10 Other ancient authorities read I gave   [d] 27.16,17 Other ancient authorities lack Jesus   [e] 27.17,22 Or the Christ   [f] 27.24 Other ancient authorities read this righteous blood, or this righteous man's blood   [g] 27.27 Gk the praetorium   [h] 27.35 Other ancient authorities add in order that what had been spoken through the prophet might be fulfilled, "They divided my clothes among themselves, and for my clothing they cast lots."

and one on his left. 39Those who passed by derided[a] him, shaking their heads 40and saying, "You who would destroy the temple and build it in three days, save yourself! If you are the Son of God, come down from the cross." 41In the same way the chief priests also, along with the scribes and elders, were mocking him, saying, 42"He saved others; he cannot save himself.[b] He is the King of Israel; let him come down from the cross now, and we will believe in him. 43He trusts in God; let God deliver him now, if he wants to; for he said, 'I am God's Son.' " 44The bandits who were crucified with him also taunted him in the same way.

THE DEATH OF JESUS

45 From noon on, darkness came over the whole land[c] until three in the afternoon. 46And about three o'clock Jesus cried with a loud voice, "Eli, Eli, lema sabachthani?" that is, "My God, my God, why have you forsaken me?" 47When some of the bystanders heard it, they said, "This man is calling for Elijah." 48At once one of them ran and got a sponge, filled it with sour wine, put it on a stick, and gave it to him to drink. 49But the others said, "Wait, let us see whether Elijah will come to save him."[d] 50Then Jesus cried again with a loud voice and breathed his last.[e] 51At that moment the curtain of the temple was torn in two, from top to bottom. The earth shook, and the rocks were split. 52The tombs also were opened, and many bodies of the saints who had fallen asleep were raised. 53After his resurrection they came out of the tombs and entered the holy city and appeared to many. 54Now when the centurion and those with him, who were keeping watch over Jesus, saw the earthquake and what took place, they were terrified and said, "Truly this man was God's Son!"[f]

55 Many women were also there, looking on from a distance; they had followed Jesus from Galilee and had provided for him. 56Among them were Mary Magdalene, and Mary the mother of James and Joseph, and the mother of the sons of Zebedee.

PONDER

The angel said to the women, "Do not be afraid; I know that you are looking for Jesus who was crucified. He is not here; for he has been raised, as he said." —Matthew 28.5–6

PRAY

O Father, we are thankful for the heroes of the faith, particularly the women and the disciples and those who believed in our Savior: those who offered their lives, those who have inspired us throughout history. Most of all we thank you for the glorious resurrection of your Son, whom you raised from the dead to open the way to eternal life. We praise you for the realization that we need not be afraid of death but can embrace that life that lasts forever. We thank you for the truly transcendent and expanded lives you give us in Jesus Christ. Be with us and strengthen our faith in our Savior, Jesus Christ. We ask in his name. Amen.

THE BURIAL OF JESUS

57 When it was evening, there came a rich man from Arimathea, named Joseph, who was also a disciple of Jesus. 58He went to Pilate and asked for the body of Jesus; then Pilate ordered it to be given to him. 59So Joseph took the body and wrapped it in a clean linen cloth 60and laid it in his own new tomb, which he had hewn in the rock. He then rolled a great stone to the door of the tomb and went away. 61Mary Magdalene and the other Mary were there, sitting opposite the tomb.

THE GUARD AT THE TOMB

62 The next day, that is, after the day of Preparation, the chief priests

a 27.39 Or blasphemed   b 27.42 Or is he unable to save himself?   c 27.45 Or earth
d 27.49 Other ancient authorities add And another took a spear and pierced his side, and out came water and blood   e 27.50 Or gave up his spirit   f 27.54 Or a son of God

and the Pharisees gathered before Pilate [63]and said, "Sir, we remember what that impostor said while he was still alive, 'After three days I will rise again.' [64]Therefore command the tomb to be made secure until the third day; otherwise his disciples may go and steal him away, and tell the people, 'He has been raised from the dead,' and the last deception would be worse than the first." [65]Pilate said to them, "You have a guard[a] of soldiers; go, make it as secure as you can."[b] [66]So they went with the guard and made the tomb secure by sealing the stone.

THE RESURRECTION OF JESUS

28 After the sabbath, as the first day of the week was dawning, Mary Magdalene and the other Mary went to see the tomb. [2]And suddenly there was a great earthquake; for an angel of the Lord, descending from heaven, came and rolled back the stone and sat on it. [3]His appearance was like lightning, and his clothing white as snow. [4]For fear of him the guards shook and became like dead men. [5]But the angel said to the women, "Do not be afraid; I know that you are looking for Jesus who was crucified. [6]He is not here; for he has been raised, as he said. Come, see the place where he[a] lay. [7]Then go quickly and tell his disciples, 'He has been raised from the dead,[b] and indeed he is going ahead of you to Galilee; there you will see him.' This is my message for you." [8]So they left the tomb quickly with fear and great joy, and ran to tell his disciples. [9]Suddenly Jesus met them and said, "Greetings!" And they came to him, took hold of his feet, and worshiped him. [10]Then Jesus said to them, "Do not be afraid; go and tell my brothers to go to Galilee; there they will see me."

THE REPORT OF THE GUARD

[11]While they were going, some of the guard went into the city and told the chief priests everything that had happened. [12]After the priests[c] had assembled with the elders, they devised a plan to give a large sum of money to the soldiers, [13]telling them, "You must say, 'His disciples came by night and stole him away while we were asleep.' [14]If this comes to the governor's ears, we will satisfy him and keep you out of trouble." [15]So they took the money and did as

[a] **27.65** Or *Take a guard*   [b] **27.65** Gk *you know how*   [c] **28.6** Other ancient authorities read *the Lord*   [d] **28.7** Other ancient authorities lack *from the dead*   [e] **28.12** Gk *they*

⊢ BIBLE IN LIFE ▷

Be Like Jesus   *Matthew 28.18–20*

One of the very last instructions Jesus gave his disciples was to go and teach people to follow him—that is, to do the same things he himself had done on earth. Go and speak as I have spoken, go and act as I have acted and do this in my name. Where should we go: to the neighbor next door, to the person in our church, to a family member, to all nations by supporting missions or serving in other countries? Where will our strength come from to do this? From the presence of Jesus Christ. Jesus promised that he will always be with us as we carry out his work and act in his name; he will never leave us to do this work alone. The exact way each of us should carry out Jesus' command may differ, for we are all given different talents, resources and circumstances in which to operate. We all need to be expansive, transcendent, aggressive, ambitious and adventurous in how we demonstrate that we are "little Christs," which is one meaning of the term "Christian." With that commitment and that demonstration, we will find fulfillment in our lives. We often think that following Christ means we give up things, but in reality, we are gaining real, abundant life. In Christ we gain freedom, joy and peace that transcend anything we could possibly know on our own.

they were directed. And this story is still told among the Jews to this day.

THE COMMISSIONING OF THE DISCIPLES

16 Now the eleven disciples went to Galilee, to the mountain to which Jesus had directed them. 17When they saw him, they worshiped him; but some doubted. 18And Jesus came and said to them, "All authority in heaven and on earth has been given to me. 19Go therefore and make disciples of all nations, baptizing them in the name of the Father and of the Son and of the Holy Spirit, 20and teaching them to obey everything that I have commanded you. And remember, I am with you always, to the end of the age."[a]

---

[a] 28.20 Other ancient authorities add *Amen*

The Gospel According to

MARK

"Just the facts" is what Mark gives us in his fast-paced Gospel—the highlights of Jesus' life and ministry told succinctly. The shortest and probably the oldest of the four Gospels, the book of Mark is detailed and action-oriented. It explains Jewish customs for the benefit of non-Jewish readers, records the high points of Jesus' miracles and describes the weeks before his crucifixion. Mark's Gospel describes Jesus' ministry in active terms: Jesus calls people, heals them, prays to the Father, teaches the crowds, appoints disciples, drives out unclean spirits, serves others and gives his life for us (see Mark 10.45).

THE PROCLAMATION OF JOHN THE BAPTIST

1 The beginning of the good news[a] of Jesus Christ, the Son of God.[b] 2 As it is written in the prophet Isaiah,[c]

"See, I am sending my messenger
ahead of you,[d]
who will prepare your way;
3 the voice of one crying out
in the wilderness:
'Prepare the way of the Lord,
make his paths straight,'"

4 John the baptizer appeared[e] in the wilderness, proclaiming a baptism of repentance for the forgiveness of sins. 5 And people from the whole Judean countryside and all the people of Jerusalem were going out to him, and were baptized by him in the river Jordan, confessing their sins. 6 Now John was clothed with camel's hair, with a leather belt around his waist, and he ate locusts and wild honey. 7 He proclaimed, "The one who is more powerful than I is coming after me; I am not worthy to stoop down and untie the thong of his sandals. 8 I have baptized you with[f] water; but he will baptize you with[f] the Holy Spirit."

THE BAPTISM OF JESUS

9 In those days Jesus came from Nazareth of Galilee and was baptized by John in the Jordan. 10 And just as he was coming up out of the water, he saw the heavens torn apart and the Spirit descending like a dove on him. 11 And a voice came from heaven, "You are my Son, the Beloved;[g] with you I am well pleased."

THE TEMPTATION OF JESUS

12 And the Spirit immediately drove him out into the wilderness. 13 He was in the wilderness forty days, tempted by Satan; and he was with the wild beasts; and the angels waited on him.

THE BEGINNING OF THE GALILEAN MINISTRY

14 Now after John was arrested, Jesus came to Galilee, proclaiming the good news[h] of God,[i] 15 and saying, "The time is fulfilled, and the kingdom of God has come near;[j] repent, and believe in the good news."[h]

PONDER

Just as [Jesus] was coming up out of the water, he saw the heavens torn apart and the Spirit descending like a dove on him. And a voice came from heaven, "You are my Son, the Beloved; with you I am well pleased."
—Mark 1.10–11

PRAY

O Father, we are grateful to learn about the anointing of your Son as the One you sent to reveal yourself in human form. It is heartening to witness the love you showed him, the love you expressed openly, even though he had not yet begun to do the work you sent him to do. This passage makes us realize the enormity of the sacrifice you made: You became like us to show us the way back to you, our Father in heaven. Through our Savior, Jesus, you made it possible to call you Father as well as Lord. We give you praise. Amen.

JESUS CALLS THE FIRST DISCIPLES

16 As Jesus passed along the Sea of Galilee, he saw Simon and his brother Andrew casting a net into the sea—for they were fishermen. 17 And Jesus said to them, "Follow me and I will make you fish for people." 18 And immediately they left their nets and followed him. 19 As he went a little farther, he saw James son of Zebedee and his brother John, who were in their boat mending the

[a] 1.1 Or gospel   [b] 1.1 Other ancient authorities lack the Son of God   [c] 1.2 Other ancient authorities read in the prophets   [d] 1.2 Gk before your face   [e] 1.4 Other ancient authorities read John was baptizing   [f] 1.8 Or in   [g] 1.11 Or my beloved Son   [h] 1.14,15 Or gospel   [i] 1.14 Other ancient authorities read of the kingdom   [j] 1.15 Or is at hand

nets. 20Immediately he called them; and they left their father Zebedee in the boat with the hired men, and followed him.

THE MAN WITH AN UNCLEAN SPIRIT

21 They went to Capernaum; and when the sabbath came, he entered the synagogue and taught. 22They were astounded at his teaching, for he taught them as one having authority, and not as the scribes. 23Just then there was in their synagogue a man with an unclean spirit, 24and he cried out, "What have you to do with us, Jesus of Nazareth? Have you come to destroy us? I know who you are, the Holy One of God." 25But Jesus rebuked him, saying, "Be silent, and come out of him!" 26And the unclean spirit, convulsing him and crying with a loud voice, came out of him. 27They were all amazed, and they kept on asking one another, "What is this? A new teaching—with authority! He[a] commands even the unclean spirits, and they obey him." 28At once his fame began to spread throughout the surrounding region of Galilee.

JESUS HEALS MANY AT SIMON'S HOUSE

29 As soon as they[b] left the synagogue, they entered the house of Simon and Andrew, with James and John. 30Now Simon's mother-in-law was in bed with a fever, and they told him about her at once. 31He came and took her by the hand and lifted her up. Then the fever left her, and she began to serve them.

32 That evening, at sunset, they brought to him all who were sick or possessed with demons. 33And the whole city was gathered around the door. 34And he cured many who were sick with various diseases, and cast out many demons; and he would not permit the demons to speak, because they knew him.

A PREACHING TOUR IN GALILEE

35 In the morning, while it was still very dark, he got up and went out to a deserted place, and there he prayed. 36And Simon and his companions hunted for him. 37When they found him, they said to him, "Everyone is searching for you." 38He answered, "Let us go on to the neighboring towns, so that I may proclaim the message there also; for that is what I came out to do." 39And he went throughout Galilee, proclaiming the message in their synagogues and casting out demons.

JESUS CLEANSES A LEPER

40 A leper[c] came to him begging him, and kneeling[d] he said to him, "If you choose, you can make me clean." 41Moved with pity,[e] Jesus[f] stretched out his hand and touched him, and said to him, "I do choose. Be made clean!" 42Immediately the leprosy[c] left him, and he was made clean. 43After sternly warning him he sent him away at once, 44saying to him, "See that you say nothing to anyone; but go, show yourself to the priest, and offer for your cleansing what Moses commanded, as a testimony to them." 45But he went out and began to proclaim it freely, and to spread the word, so that Jesus[f] could no longer go into a town openly, but stayed out in the country; and people came to him from every quarter.

JESUS HEALS A PARALYTIC

2 When he returned to Capernaum after some days, it was reported that he was at home. 2So many gathered around that there was no longer room for them, not even in front of the door; and he was speaking the word to them. 3Then some people[g] came, bringing to him a paralyzed man, carried by four of them. 4And when they could not bring him to Jesus because of the crowd, they removed the roof above him; and after having dug through

---

[a] 1.27 Or A new teaching! With authority he [b] 1.29 Other ancient authorities read he [c] 1.40,42 The terms leper and leprosy can refer to several diseases [d] 1.40 Other ancient authorities lack kneeling [e] 1.41 Other ancient authorities read anger [f] 1.41,45 Gk he [g] 2.3 Gk they

it, they let down the mat on which the paralytic lay. 5When Jesus saw their faith, he said to the paralytic, "Son, your sins are forgiven." 6Now some of the scribes were sitting there, questioning in their hearts, 7"Why does this fellow speak in this way? It is blasphemy! Who can forgive sins but God alone?" 8At once Jesus perceived in his spirit that they were discussing these questions among themselves; and he said to them, "Why do you raise such questions in your hearts? 9Which is easier, to say to the paralytic, 'Your sins are forgiven,' or to say, 'Stand up and take your mat and walk'? 10But so that you may know that the Son of Man has authority on earth to forgive sins"—he said to the paralytic— 11"I say to you, stand up, take your mat and go to your home." 12And he stood up, and immediately took the mat and went out before all of them; so that they were all amazed and glorified God, saying, "We have never seen anything like this!"

JESUS CALLS LEVI

13 Jesus[a] went out again beside the sea; the whole crowd gathered around him, and he taught them.

14As he was walking along, he saw Levi son of Alphaeus sitting at the tax booth, and he said to him, "Follow me." And he got up and followed him.

15 And as he sat at dinner[b] in Levi's[c] house, many tax collectors and sinners were also sitting[d] with Jesus and his disciples—for there were many who followed him. 16When the scribes of[e] the Pharisees saw that he was eating with sinners and tax collectors, they said to his disciples, "Why does he eat[f] with tax collectors and sinners?" 17When Jesus heard this, he said to them, "Those who are well have no need of a physician, but those who are sick; I have come to call not the righteous but sinners."

THE QUESTION ABOUT FASTING

18 Now John's disciples and the Pharisees were fasting; and people[g] came and said to him, "Why do John's disciples and the disciples of the Pharisees fast, but your disciples

a 2.13 Gk He   b 2.15 Gk reclined   c 2.15 Gk his   d 2.15 Gk reclining   e 2.16 Other ancient authorities read and   f 2.16 Other ancient authorities add and drink   g 2.18 Gk they

---

⊢ BIBLE IN LIFE ▷

Despising Others   Mark 2.15–17

In Jesus' time, tax collectors were regarded as betrayers of the people of Israel because they collected taxes from the Jews on behalf of the Romans. They were outcasts, yet Jesus had no qualms about going to Levi's house and eating with him. This signifies Christ's care for those who are despised.

How does the church today respond to those who are despised? Some of us tend to think that outcasts in our society somehow deserve it. We may pity the drug addict, the alcoholic, the prisoner, but we often think we're better, and we thank God that we're not like them. We have a tendency to despise—perhaps not actively but passively—people who are different from us. The poor are quite often looked upon as less valuable or worthy. We may think that if they had worked as hard as we had or studied as much as we had, then they wouldn't be poor. In our Carter Center's work among the poorest people in Africa, we find that they are just as intelligent, hardworking and ambitious and have family values equal to ours. When given a chance, they succeed. Christ said, "I have come to call not the righteous but sinners" (Mark 2.17). He saw that deprivation in people's lives was harmful and needed to be corrected. Human afflictions—being deprived of education, nourishment, health, equal treatment, justice or freedom—were a reason for Christ's ministry, and they should be a reason for ours.

do not fast?" ¹⁹Jesus said to them, "The wedding guests cannot fast while the bridegroom is with them, can they? As long as they have the bridegroom with them, they cannot fast. ²⁰The days will come when the bridegroom is taken away from them, and then they will fast on that day.

21 "No one sews a piece of unshrunk cloth on an old cloak; otherwise, the patch pulls away from it, the new from the old, and a worse tear is made. ²²And no one puts new wine into old wineskins; otherwise, the wine will burst the skins, and the wine is lost, and so are the skins; but one puts new wine into fresh wineskins."ᵃ

PRONOUNCEMENT ABOUT THE SABBATH

23 One sabbath he was going through the grainfields; and as they made their way his disciples began to pluck heads of grain. ²⁴The Pharisees said to him, "Look, why are they doing what is not lawful on the sabbath?" ²⁵And he said to them, "Have you never read what David did when he and his companions were hungry and in need of food? ²⁶He entered the house of God, when Abiathar was high priest, and ate the bread of the Presence, which it is not lawful for any but the priests to eat, and he gave some to his companions." ²⁷Then he said to them, "The sabbath was made for humankind, and not humankind for the sabbath; ²⁸so the Son of Man is lord even of the sabbath."

THE MAN WITH A WITHERED HAND

3 Again he entered the synagogue, and a man was there who had a withered hand. ²They watched him to see whether he would cure him on the sabbath, so that they might accuse him. ³And he said to the man who had the withered hand, "Come forward." ⁴Then he said to them, "Is it lawful to do good or to do harm on the sabbath, to save life or to kill?" But they were silent. ⁵He looked around at them with anger;

he was grieved at their hardness of heart and said to the man, "Stretch out your hand." He stretched it out, and his hand was restored. ⁶The Pharisees went out and immediately conspired with the Herodians against him, how to destroy him.

A MULTITUDE AT THE SEASIDE

7 Jesus departed with his disciples to the sea, and a great multitude from Galilee followed him; ⁸hearing all that he was doing, they came to him in great numbers from Judea, Jerusalem, Idumea, beyond the Jordan, and the region around Tyre and Sidon. ⁹He told his disciples to have a boat ready for him because of the crowd, so that they would not crush him; ¹⁰for he had cured many, so that all who had diseases pressed upon him to touch him. ¹¹Whenever the unclean spirits saw him, they fell down before him and shouted, "You are the Son of God!" ¹²But he sternly ordered them not to make him known.

JESUS APPOINTS THE TWELVE

13 He went up the mountain and called to him those whom he wanted, and they came to him. ¹⁴And he appointed twelve, whom he also named apostles,ᵇ to be with him, and to be sent out to proclaim the message, ¹⁵and to have authority to cast out demons. ¹⁶So he appointed the twelve:ᶜ Simon (to whom he gave the name Peter); ¹⁷James son of Zebedee and John the brother of James (to whom he gave the name Boanerges, that is, Sons of Thunder); ¹⁸and Andrew, and Philip, and Bartholomew, and Matthew, and Thomas, and James son of Alphaeus, and Thaddaeus, and Simon the Cananaean, ¹⁹and Judas Iscariot, who betrayed him.

JESUS AND BEELZEBUL

Then he went home; ²⁰and the crowd came together again, so that

ᵃ 2.22 Other ancient authorities lack *but one puts new wine into fresh wineskins*
ᵇ 3.14 Other ancient authorities lack *whom he also named apostles*   ᶜ 3.16 Other ancient authorities lack *So he appointed the twelve*

they could not even eat. 21When his family heard it, they went out to restrain him, for people were saying, "He has gone out of his mind." 22And the scribes who came down from Jerusalem said, "He has Beelzebul, and by the ruler of the demons he casts out demons." 23And he called them to him, and spoke to them in parables, "How can Satan cast out Satan? 24If a kingdom is divided against itself, that kingdom cannot stand. 25And if a house is divided against itself, that house will not be able to stand. 26And if Satan has risen up against himself and is divided, he cannot stand, but his end has come. 27But no one can enter a strong man's house and plunder his property without first tying up the strong man; then indeed the house can be plundered.

28 "Truly I tell you, people will be forgiven for their sins and whatever blasphemies they utter; 29but whoever blasphemes against the Holy Spirit can never have forgiveness, but is guilty of an eternal sin"— 30for they had said, "He has an unclean spirit."

THE TRUE KINDRED OF JESUS

31 Then his mother and his brothers came; and standing outside, they sent to him and called him. 32A crowd was sitting around him; and they said to him, "Your mother and your brothers and sisters[a] are outside, asking for you." 33And he replied, "Who are my mother and my brothers?" 34And looking at those who sat around him, he said, "Here are my mother and my brothers! 35Whoever does the will of God is my brother and sister and mother."

THE PARABLE OF THE SOWER

4 Again he began to teach beside the sea. Such a very large crowd gathered around him that he got into a boat on the sea and sat there, while the whole crowd was beside the sea on the land. 2He began to teach them many things in parables, and in his teaching he said to them: 3"Listen! A sower went out to sow.

4And as he sowed, some seed fell on the path, and the birds came and ate it up. 5Other seed fell on rocky ground, where it did not have much soil, and it sprang up quickly, since it had no depth of soil. 6And when the sun rose, it was scorched; and since it had no root, it withered away. 7Other seed fell among thorns, and the thorns grew up and choked it, and it yielded no grain. 8Other seed fell into good soil and brought forth grain, growing up and increasing and yielding thirty and sixty and a hundredfold." 9And he said, "Let anyone with ears to hear listen!"

THE PURPOSE OF THE PARABLES

10 When he was alone, those who were around him along with the twelve asked him about the parables. 11And he said to them, "To you has been given the secret[b] of the kingdom of God, but for those outside, everything comes in parables; 12in order that

'they may indeed look, but
  not perceive,
and may indeed listen, but
  not understand;
so that they may not turn again
  and be forgiven.' "

13 And he said to them, "Do you not understand this parable? Then how will you understand all the parables? 14The sower sows the word. 15These are the ones on the path where the word is sown: when they hear, Satan immediately comes and takes away the word that is sown in them. 16And these are the ones sown on rocky ground: when they hear the word, they immediately receive it with joy. 17But they have no root, and endure only for a while; then, when trouble or persecution arises on account of the word, immediately they fall away.[c] 18And others are those sown among the thorns: these are the ones who hear the word, 19but the cares of the world, and the lure of wealth, and the desire for other things come in and choke the word, and it yields nothing. 20And

a 3.32 Other ancient authorities lack *and sisters* b 4.11 Or *mystery* c 4.17 Or *stumble*

these are the ones sown on the good soil: they hear the word and accept it and bear fruit, thirty and sixty and a hundredfold."

A LAMP UNDER A BUSHEL BASKET

21 He said to them, "Is a lamp brought in to be put under the bushel basket, or under the bed, and not on the lampstand? 22 For there is nothing hidden, except to be disclosed; nor is anything secret, except to come to light. 23 Let anyone with ears to hear listen!" 24 And he said to them, "Pay attention to what you hear; the measure you give will be the measure you get, and still more will be given you. 25 For to those who have, more will be given; and from those who have nothing, even what they have will be taken away."

THE PARABLE OF THE GROWING SEED

26 He also said, "The kingdom of God is as if someone would scatter seed on the ground, 27 and would sleep and rise night and day, and the seed would sprout and grow, he does not know how. 28 The earth produces of itself, first the stalk, then the head, then the full grain in the head. 29 But when the grain is ripe, at once he goes in with his sickle, because the harvest has come."

THE PARABLE OF THE MUSTARD SEED

30 He also said, "With what can we compare the kingdom of God, or what parable will we use for it? 31 It is like a mustard seed, which, when sown upon the ground, is the smallest of all the seeds on earth; 32 yet when it is sown it grows up and becomes the greatest of all shrubs, and puts forth large branches, so that the birds of the air can make nests in its shade."

THE USE OF PARABLES

33 With many such parables he spoke the word to them, as they were able to hear it; 34 he did not speak to them except in parables, but he explained everything in private to his disciples.

JESUS STILLS A STORM

35 On that day, when evening had come, he said to them, "Let us go across to the other side." 36 And leaving the crowd behind, they took him with them in the boat, just as he was. Other boats were with him. 37 A great windstorm arose, and the waves beat into the boat, so that the boat was already being swamped. 38 But he was in the stern, asleep on the cushion; and they woke him up and said to him, "Teacher, do you not care that we are perishing?" 39 He woke up and rebuked the wind, and said to the sea, "Peace! Be still!"

⊢⊢ BIBLE IN LIFE ▷

Personal Witness

Mark 4.33–34

Jesus could draw a crowd, but he also knew how to leave a crowd. Jesus differentiated between teaching a crowd and relating more intimately with a small group. He created opportunities to have more personal discussions with his disciples. Our relationships are strengthened and deepened when we can share our own experiences, reveal our innermost thoughts, admit our failures and be honest about our faith, but we cannot do these things in a crowd. Quite often we are able to live our personal witness more effectively in a small group, where an element of trust exists. In the context of a small group, Christ strengthened his relationship with and witnessed to a few people on whom he would be depending to establish his church after his departure from the earthly scene. Christ relied on the disciples. Do we follow Jesus' example? Do we have more intimate relationships with a small group of people on whom we rely and trust? Do we seek opportunities to get to know people at a more personal faith level?

Then the wind ceased, and there was a dead calm. [40]He said to them, "Why are you afraid? Have you still no faith?" [41]And they were filled with great awe and said to one another, "Who then is this, that even the wind and the sea obey him?"

JESUS HEALS THE
GERASENE DEMONIAC

5 They came to the other side of the sea, to the country of the Gerasenes.[a] [2]And when he had stepped out of the boat, immediately a man out of the tombs with an unclean spirit met him. [3]He lived among the tombs; and no one could restrain him any more, even with a chain; [4]for he had often been restrained with shackles and chains, but the chains he wrenched apart, and the shackles he broke in pieces; and no one had the strength to subdue him. [5]Night and day among the tombs and on the mountains he was always howling and bruising himself with stones. [6]When he saw Jesus from a distance, he ran and bowed down before him; [7]and he shouted at the top of his voice, "What have you to do with me, Jesus, Son of the Most High God? I adjure you by God, do not torment me." [8]For he had said to him, "Come out of the man, you unclean spirit!" [9]Then Jesus[b] asked him, "What is your name?" He replied, "My name is Legion; for we are many." [10]He begged him earnestly not to send them out of the country. [11]Now there on the hillside a great herd of swine was feeding; [12]and the unclean spirits[c] begged him, "Send us into the swine; let us enter them." [13]So he gave them permission. And the unclean spirits came out and entered the swine; and the herd, numbering about two thousand, rushed down the steep bank into the sea, and were drowned in the sea.

14 The swineherds ran off and told it in the city and in the country. Then people came to see what it was that had happened. [15]They came to Jesus and saw the demoniac sitting there, clothed and in his right mind, the very man who had had the legion; and they were afraid. [16]Those who had seen what had happened to the demoniac and to the swine reported it. [17]Then they began to beg Jesus[d] to leave their neighborhood. [18]As he was getting into the boat, the man who had been possessed by demons begged him that he might be with him. [19]But Jesus[b] refused, and said to him, "Go home to your friends, and tell them how much the Lord has done for you, and what mercy he has shown you." [20]And he went away and began to proclaim in the Decapolis how much Jesus had done for him; and everyone was amazed.

A GIRL RESTORED TO LIFE
AND A WOMAN HEALED

21 When Jesus had crossed again in the boat[e] to the other side, a great crowd gathered around him; and he was by the sea. [22]Then one of the leaders of the synagogue named Jairus came and, when he saw him, fell at his feet [23]and begged him repeatedly, "My little daughter is at the point of death. Come and lay your hands on her, so that she may be made well, and live." [24]So he went with him.

And a large crowd followed him and pressed in on him. [25]Now there was a woman who had been suffering from hemorrhages for twelve years. [26]She had endured much under many physicians, and had spent all that she had; and she was no better, but rather grew worse. [27]She had heard about Jesus, and came up behind him in the crowd and touched his cloak, [28]for she said, "If I but touch his clothes, I will be made well." [29]Immediately her hemorrhage stopped; and she felt in her body that she was healed of her disease. [30]Immediately aware that power had gone forth from him, Jesus turned about in the crowd and said, "Who touched my clothes?" [31]And his disciples said to him, "You see the crowd pressing in on you; how can you say, 'Who touched

a 5.1 Other ancient authorities read *Gergesenes*; others, *Gadarenes*   b 5.9,19 Gk *he*   c 5.12 Gk *they*   d 5.17 Gk *him*
e 5.21 Other ancient authorities lack *in the boat*

me?' " ³²He looked all around to see who had done it. ³³But the woman, knowing what had happened to her, came in fear and trembling, fell down before him, and told him the whole truth. ³⁴He said to her, "Daughter, your faith has made you well; go in peace, and be healed of your disease."

35 While he was still speaking, some people came from the leader's house to say, "Your daughter is dead. Why trouble the teacher any further?" ³⁶But overhearing^a what they said, Jesus said to the leader of the synagogue, "Do not fear, only believe." ³⁷He allowed no one to follow him except Peter, James, and John, the brother of James. ³⁸When they came to the house of the leader of the synagogue, he saw a commotion, people weeping and wailing loudly. ³⁹When he had entered, he said to them, "Why do you make a commotion and weep? The child is not dead but sleeping." ⁴⁰And they laughed at him. Then he put them all outside, and took the child's father and mother and those who were with him, and went in where the child was. ⁴¹He took her by the hand and said to her, "Talitha cum," which means, "Little girl, get up!" ⁴²And immediately the girl got up and began to walk about (she was twelve years of age). At this they were overcome with amazement. ⁴³He strictly ordered them that no

one should know this, and told them to give her something to eat.

THE REJECTION OF JESUS AT NAZARETH

6 He left that place and came to his hometown, and his disciples followed him. ²On the sabbath he began to teach in the synagogue, and many who heard him were astounded. They said, "Where did this man get all this? What is this wisdom that has been given to him? What deeds of power are being done by his hands! ³Is not this the carpenter, the son of Mary^b and brother of James and Joses and Judas and Simon, and are not his sisters here with us?" And they took offense^c at him. ⁴Then Jesus said to them, "Prophets are not without honor, except in their hometown, and among their own kin, and in their own house." ⁵And he could do no deed of power there, except that he laid his hands on a few sick people and cured them. ⁶And he was amazed at their unbelief.

THE MISSION OF THE TWELVE

Then he went about among the villages teaching. ⁷He called the twelve and began to send them out two by two, and gave them authority

^a 5.36 Or *ignoring*; other ancient authorities read *hearing* ^b 6.3 Other ancient authorities read *son of the carpenter and of Mary* ^c 6.3 Or *stumbled*

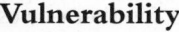

BIBLE IN LIFE

Vulnerability   Mark 5.24–34

One of the most difficult things that we do in life is to let people really know us. We all have a strong inclination to hide our deepest feelings and needs. When we live transparent lives, we make ourselves vulnerable. Most of us tend to build shells around ourselves. We put on a happy face, a devout expression of our faith, and we try to give others the impression that we are okay in the eyes of Christ. The woman who had been subject to bleeding for 12 years was willing to take a chance by revealing her most embarrassing secret in order to touch Jesus and be healed. Her faith was so profoundly deep that she thought if she just touched his clothes, she would be healed. All of us know that Jesus Christ has the ability to heal whatever is wrong with us. With faith in Christ, we can confront ourselves as we are, with a full realization that Jesus accepts us, and we will not be injured, weakened or rejected by him. We will be strengthened, loved and forgiven, just as the vulnerable woman was.

over the unclean spirits. ⁸He ordered them to take nothing for their journey except a staff; no bread, no bag, no money in their belts; ⁹but to wear sandals and not to put on two tunics. ¹⁰He said to them, "Wherever you enter a house, stay there until you leave the place. ¹¹If any place will not welcome you and they refuse to hear you, as you leave, shake off the dust that is on your feet as a testimony against them." ¹²So they went out and proclaimed that all should repent. ¹³They cast out many demons, and anointed with oil many who were sick and cured them.

THE DEATH OF JOHN THE BAPTIST

14 King Herod heard of it, for Jesus'ᵃ name had become known. Some wereᵇ saying, "John the baptizer has been raised from the dead; and for this reason these powers are at work in him." ¹⁵But others said, "It is Elijah." And others said, "It is a prophet, like one of the prophets of old." ¹⁶But when Herod heard of it, he said, "John, whom I beheaded, has been raised."

17 For Herod himself had sent men who arrested John, bound him, and put him in prison on account of Herodias, his brother Philip's wife, because Herodᶜ had married her. ¹⁸For John had been telling Herod, "It is not lawful for you to have your brother's wife." ¹⁹And Herodias had a grudge against him, and wanted to kill him. But she could not, ²⁰for Herod feared John, knowing that he was a righteous and holy man, and he protected him. When he heard him, he was greatly perplexed;ᵈ and yet he liked to listen to him. ²¹But an opportunity came when Herod on his birthday gave a banquet for his courtiers and officers and for the leaders of Galilee. ²²When his daughter Herodiasᵉ came in and danced, she pleased Herod and his guests; and the king said to the girl, "Ask me for whatever you wish, and I will give it." ²³And he solemnly swore to her, "Whatever you ask me, I will give you, even half of my kingdom." ²⁴She went out and said to her mother, "What should I ask for?" She replied, "The head of John the baptizer." ²⁵Immediately she rushed back to the king and requested, "I want you to give me at once the head of John the Baptist on a platter." ²⁶The king was deeply grieved; yet out of regard for his oaths and for the guests, he did not want to refuse her. ²⁷Immediately the king sent a soldier of the guard with orders to bring John'sᵃ head. He went and beheaded him in the prison, ²⁸brought his head on a platter, and gave it to the girl. Then the girl gave it to her mother. ²⁹When his disciples heard about it, they came and took his body, and laid it in a tomb.

FEEDING THE FIVE THOUSAND

30 The apostles gathered around Jesus, and told him all that they had done and taught. ³¹He said to them, "Come away to a deserted place all by yourselves and rest a while." For many were coming and going, and they had no leisure even to eat. ³²And they went away in the boat to a deserted place by themselves. ³³Now many saw them going and recognized them, and they hurried there on foot from all the towns and arrived ahead of them. ³⁴As he went ashore, he saw a great crowd; and he had compassion for them, because they were like sheep without a shepherd; and he began to teach them many things. ³⁵When it grew late, his disciples came to him and said, "This is a deserted place, and the hour is now very late; ³⁶send them away so that they may go into the surrounding country and villages and buy something for themselves to eat." ³⁷But he answered them, "You give them something to eat." They said to him, "Are we to go and buy two hundred denariiᶠ worth of bread, and give it to them to eat?" ³⁸And he said to them, "How many

---

ᵃ 6.14,27 Gk *his*   ᵇ 6.14 Other ancient authorities read *He was*   ᶜ 6.17 Gk *he*
ᵈ 6.20 Other ancient authorities read *he did many things*   ᵉ 6.22 Other ancient authorities read *the daughter of Herodias herself*   ᶠ 6.37 The denarius was the usual day's wage for a laborer

loaves have you? Go and see." When they had found out, they said, "Five, and two fish." 39Then he ordered them to get all the people to sit down in groups on the green grass. 40So they sat down in groups of hundreds and of fifties. 41Taking the five loaves and the two fish, he looked up to heaven, and blessed and broke the loaves, and gave them to his disciples to set before the people; and he divided the two fish among them all. 42And all ate and were filled; 43and they took up twelve baskets full of broken pieces and of the fish. 44Those who had eaten the loaves numbered five thousand men.

PONDER

"Come away to a deserted place all by yourselves and rest a while."
—Mark 6.31

PRAY

Father, your Son Jesus needed to get away from the crowds to commune with you and encouraged his disciples to do so as well. It is sobering but encouraging to realize that our Savior grew tired and hungry, that he sometimes needed to be alone with you. How can we think we can live in our own strength? Help us to realize that you are always with us; the presence of the Holy Spirit is with us. Help us to resolve that sometime during this coming week we will find one hour, just one hour in our busy lives, to be alone with you—in the woods or behind a closed door—and kneel down, be patient and let your message come to us so that we can be renewed by your Spirit and have a glorious new life, a future in the presence of our Savior. In his name we pray. Amen.

JESUS WALKS ON THE WATER

45 Immediately he made his disciples get into the boat and go on ahead to the other side, to Bethsaida, while he dismissed the crowd. 46After saying farewell to them, he went up on the mountain to pray.

47 When evening came, the boat was out on the sea, and he was alone on the land. 48When he saw that they were straining at the oars against an adverse wind, he came towards them early in the morning, walking on the sea. He intended to pass them by. 49But when they saw him walking on the sea, they thought it was a ghost and cried out; 50for they all saw him and were terrified. But immediately he spoke to them and said, "Take heart, it is I; do not be afraid." 51Then he got into the boat with them and the wind ceased. And they were utterly astounded, 52for they did not understand about the loaves, but their hearts were hardened.

HEALING THE SICK IN GENNESARET

53 When they had crossed over, they came to land at Gennesaret and moored the boat. 54When they got out of the boat, people at once recognized him, 55and rushed about that whole region and began to bring the sick on mats to wherever they heard he was. 56And wherever he went, into villages or cities or farms, they laid the sick in the marketplaces, and begged him that they might touch even the fringe of his cloak; and all who touched it were healed.

THE TRADITION OF THE ELDERS

7 Now when the Pharisees and some of the scribes who had come from Jerusalem gathered around him, 2they noticed that some of his disciples were eating with defiled hands, that is, without washing them. 3(For the Pharisees, and all the Jews, do not eat unless they thoroughly wash their hands,[a] thus observing the tradition of the elders; 4and they do not eat anything from the market unless they wash it;[b] and there are also many

[a] 7.3 Meaning of Gk uncertain [b] 7.4 Other ancient authorities read and when they come from the marketplace, they do not eat unless they purify themselves

other traditions that they observe, the washing of cups, pots, and bronze kettles.[a]) [5]So the Pharisees and the scribes asked him, "Why do your disciples not live[b] according to the tradition of the elders, but eat with defiled hands?" [6]He said to them, "Isaiah prophesied rightly about you hypocrites, as it is written,

'This people honors me
    with their lips,
but their hearts are
    far from me;
[7] in vain do they worship me,
    teaching human precepts
        as doctrines.'

[8]You abandon the commandment of God and hold to human tradition."

[9]Then he said to them, "You have a fine way of rejecting the commandment of God in order to keep your tradition! [10]For Moses said, 'Honor your father and your mother'; and, 'Whoever speaks evil of father or mother must surely die.' [11]But you say that if anyone tells father or mother, 'Whatever support you might have had from me is Corban' (that is, an offering to God[c])— [12]then you no longer permit doing anything for a father or mother, [13]thus making void the word of God through your tradition that you have handed on. And you do many things like this."

[14]Then he called the crowd again and said to them, "Listen to me, all of you, and understand: [15]there is nothing outside a person that by going in can defile, but the things that come out are what defile."[d]

[17]When he had left the crowd and entered the house, his disciples asked him about the parable. [18]He said to them, "Then do you also fail to understand? Do you not see that whatever goes into a person from outside cannot defile, [19]since it enters, not the heart but the stomach, and goes out into the sewer?" (Thus he declared all foods clean.) [20]And he said, "It is what comes out of a person that defiles. [21]For it is from within, from the human heart, that evil intentions come: fornication, theft, murder, [22]adultery, avarice, wickedness, deceit, licentiousness,

envy, slander, pride, folly. [23]All these evil things come from within, and they defile a person."

THE SYROPHOENICIAN WOMAN'S FAITH

[24]From there he set out and went away to the region of Tyre.[e] He entered a house and did not want anyone to know he was there. Yet he could not escape notice, [25]but a woman whose little daughter had an unclean spirit immediately heard about him, and she came and bowed down at his feet. [26]Now the woman was a Gentile, of Syrophoenician origin. She begged him to cast the demon out of her daughter. [27]He said to her, "Let the children be fed first, for it is not fair to take the children's food and throw it to the dogs." [28]But she answered him, "Sir,[f] even the dogs under the table eat the children's crumbs." [29]Then he said to her, "For saying that, you may go— the demon has left your daughter." [30]So she went home, found the child lying on the bed, and the demon gone.

JESUS CURES A DEAF MAN

[31]Then he returned from the region of Tyre, and went by way of Sidon towards the Sea of Galilee, in the region of the Decapolis. [32]They brought to him a deaf man who had an impediment in his speech; and they begged him to lay his hand on him. [33]He took him aside in private, away from the crowd, and put his fingers into his ears, and he spat and touched his tongue. [34]Then looking up to heaven, he sighed and said to him, "Ephphatha," that is, "Be opened." [35]And immediately his ears were opened, his tongue was released, and he spoke plainly. [36]Then Jesus[g] ordered them to tell no one; but the more he ordered them, the more zealously they proclaimed it.

[a] 7.4 Other ancient authorities add *and beds* [b] 7.5 Gk *walk* [c] 7.11 Gk lacks *to God* [d] 7.15 Other ancient authorities add verse 16, *"Let anyone with ears to hear listen"* [e] 7.24 Other ancient authorities add *and Sidon* [f] 7.28 Or *Lord*; other ancient authorities prefix *Yes* [g] 7.36 Gk *he*

By the Word

"Isaiah prophesied rightly about you hypocrites, as it is written, 'This people honors me with their lips, but their hearts are far from me; in vain do they worship me, teaching human precepts as doctrines.'"

—Mark 7.6–7

The Pharisees were traditionalists who had taken the law of Moses, pulled it apart and reinterpreted it into minute shades and subtleties. Pharisees imposed on the people more than 600 different little rules and regulations derived from the scriptures. They believed that a person would have to follow all these rules in order to have a proper relationship with God. But Jesus brought a revolutionary approach to God's law.

In Mark 7 Jesus speaks out, contradicting the Pharisees after they accused his disciples of being unworthy of God's blessing because they violated the tradition of the ceremonial washing of hands. Jesus tells the Pharisees that Isaiah had been referring to others like them. The Pharisees were overemphasizing the washing of hands while ignoring the basic premises of God's word. Jesus later explains to the crowd that there is nothing that goes into a person's mouth that can defile them, but rather what comes out—their words and actions, driven by their evil thoughts. The Pharisees and religious leaders saw God as a judge, concerned only with strict adherence to rules and regulations. Jesus Christ came to earth and pictured for humankind a different and more accurate image of God. God was incarnate in Jesus. God does judge and condemn evil but is also filled with grace and forgiveness and love. God is not remote and separated from us by religious authorities, but rather he is someone with whom we can relate personally and individually, to whom we can bare our hearts and minds, to whom we can worship directly.

The message that Christ brought to us is that God is our Father, our "Abba," who loves us just as Jesus did. Jesus Christ, the Son of God, set an example for us in reaching out to those who are deemed unworthy by their culture, such as the lepers, tax collectors, Samaritans and Gentiles. Every day of our lives we are constrained to ask: What words and actions of Christ can I take to heart in the way I relate to God Almighty and my fellow human beings? The word "Christian" can mean "little Christ," one who has accepted Christ as Savior and whose life is patterned after the perfect example set by Jesus.

We are not defined by a set of rules we follow. Instead, we adhere to the essence of the Word of God—in justice, peace, humility, service, forgiveness, compassion, sharing, generosity and sacrificial love.

Going Deeper

- What "defiles" you? What comes out of you that hinders your relationship with God?
- How can you pattern your life more closely to the example set by Jesus and further away from the example set by the Pharisees?

PONDER

"Sir, even the dogs under the table eat the children's crumbs." Then he said to her, "For saying that, you may go—the demon has left your daughter."
—Mark 7.28–29

PRAY

O Father, we are grateful for these words from Mark's Gospel, sometimes humorous, sometimes perplexing, that describe Jesus' interactions with the people who asked much of him. It is encouraging to see how he alleviated the woman's concerns and frustrations and met her needs. And we know that you can help us in our need. Help us to be eager to turn to Jesus at every moment of our lives for strength and provision. And let us realize that the most important elements of our existence are your love and provision for us, even as you give us eternal life. In our Savior's name we pray. Amen.

37 They were astounded beyond measure, saying, "He has done everything well; he even makes the deaf to hear and the mute to speak."

FEEDING THE FOUR THOUSAND

8 In those days when there was again a great crowd without anything to eat, he called his disciples and said to them, 2 "I have compassion for the crowd, because they have been with me now for three days and have nothing to eat. 3 If I send them away hungry to their homes, they will faint on the way—and some of them have come from a great distance." 4 His disciples replied, "How can one feed these people with bread here in the desert?" 5 He asked them, "How many loaves do you have?" They said, "Seven." 6 Then he ordered the crowd to sit down on the ground; and he took the seven loaves, and after giving thanks he broke them and gave them to his disciples to distribute; and they distributed them to the crowd. 7 They had also a few small fish; and after blessing them, he ordered that these too should be distributed. 8 They ate and were filled; and they took up the broken pieces left over, seven baskets full. 9 Now there were about four thousand people. And he sent them away. 10 And immediately he got into the boat with his disciples and went to the district of Dalmanutha.[a]

THE DEMAND FOR A SIGN

11 The Pharisees came and began to argue with him, asking him for a sign from heaven, to test him. 12 And he sighed deeply in his spirit and said, "Why does this generation ask for a sign? Truly I tell you, no sign will be given to this generation." 13 And he left them, and getting into the boat again, he went across to the other side.

THE YEAST OF THE PHARISEES AND OF HEROD

14 Now the disciples[b] had forgotten to bring any bread; and they had only one loaf with them in the boat. 15 And he cautioned them, saying, "Watch out—beware of the yeast of the Pharisees and the yeast of Herod."[c] 16 They said to one another, "It is because we have no bread." 17 And becoming aware of it, Jesus said to them, "Why are you talking about having no bread? Do you still not perceive or understand? Are your hearts hardened? 18 Do you have eyes, and fail to see? Do you have ears, and fail to hear? And do you not remember? 19 When I broke the five loaves for the five thousand, how many baskets full of broken pieces did you collect?" They said to him, "Twelve." 20 "And the seven for the four thousand, how many baskets full of broken pieces did you collect?" And they said to him, "Seven." 21 Then he said to them, "Do you not yet understand?"

a 8.10 Other ancient authorities read *Mageda* or *Magdala*   b 8.14 Gk *they*
c 8.15 Other ancient authorities read *the Herodians*

JESUS CURES A BLIND MAN AT BETHSAIDA

22 They came to Bethsaida. Some people[a] brought a blind man to him and begged him to touch him. 23 He took the blind man by the hand and led him out of the village; and when he had put saliva on his eyes and laid his hands on him, he asked him, "Can you see anything?" 24 And the man[b] looked up and said, "I can see people, but they look like trees, walking." 25 Then Jesus[b] laid his hands on his eyes again; and he looked intently and his sight was restored, and he saw everything clearly. 26 Then he sent him away to his home, saying, "Do not even go into the village."[c]

PONDER

[Jesus] took the seven loaves, and after giving thanks he broke them and gave them to his disciples to distribute; and they distributed them to the crowd.
—Mark 8.6

PRAY

O Father, it is not always easy for us to put ourselves in the disciples' shoes. They were able to look at Jesus' face, share a loaf of bread with him, and talk with him. They learned from you, and in community they shared opportunities to see him work and shared obligations to work with him. We pray that you will help us to participate in the same way in a community of believers, looking beyond the daily preoccupations that take up our time. Expand our sphere of influence to reach people that we otherwise wouldn't get to know. Give us the desire to learn more about your world and reach out with love to an ever-wider circle of new friends and in so doing, demonstrate our Christian faith. We pray in the name of our Savior. Amen.

PETER'S DECLARATION ABOUT JESUS

27 Jesus went on with his disciples to the villages of Caesarea Philippi; and on the way he asked his disciples, "Who do people say that I am?" 28 And they answered him, "John the Baptist; and others, Elijah; and still others, one of the prophets." 29 He asked them, "But who do you say that I am?" Peter answered him, "You are the Messiah."[d] 30 And he sternly ordered them not to tell anyone about him.

JESUS FORETELLS HIS DEATH AND RESURRECTION

31 Then he began to teach them that the Son of Man must undergo great suffering, and be rejected by the elders, the chief priests, and the scribes, and be killed, and after three days rise again. 32 He said all this quite openly. And Peter took him aside and began to rebuke him. 33 But turning and looking at his disciples, he rebuked Peter and said, "Get behind me, Satan! For you are setting your mind not on divine things but on human things."

34 He called the crowd with his disciples, and said to them, "If any want to become my followers, let them deny themselves and take up their cross and follow me. 35 For those who want to save their life will lose it, and those who lose their life for my sake, and for the sake of the gospel,[e] will save it. 36 For what will it profit them to gain the whole world and forfeit their life? 37 Indeed, what can they give in return for their life? 38 Those who are ashamed of me and of my words[f] in this adulterous and sinful generation, of them the Son of Man will also be ashamed when he comes in the glory of his Father

9 with the holy angels." 1 And he said to them, "Truly I tell you,

a 8.22 Gk *They*   b 8.24,25 Gk *he*
c 8.26 Other ancient authorities add *or tell anyone in the village*   d 8.29 Or *the Christ*   e 8.35 Other ancient authorities read *lose their life for the sake of the gospel*
f 8.38 Other ancient authorities read *and of mine*

there are some standing here who will not taste death until they see that the kingdom of God has come with[a] power."

THE TRANSFIGURATION

2 Six days later, Jesus took with him Peter and James and John, and led them up a high mountain apart, by themselves. And he was transfigured before them, 3and his clothes became dazzling white, such as no one[b] on earth could bleach them. 4And there appeared to them Elijah with Moses, who were talking with Jesus. 5Then Peter said to Jesus, "Rabbi, it is good for us to be here; let us make three dwellings,[c] one for you, one for Moses, and one for Elijah." 6He did not know what to say, for they were terrified. 7Then a cloud overshadowed them, and from the cloud there came a voice, "This is my Son, the Beloved;[d] listen to him!" 8Suddenly when they looked around, they saw no one with them any more, but only Jesus.

THE COMING OF ELIJAH

9 As they were coming down the mountain, he ordered them to tell no one about what they had seen, until after the Son of Man had risen from the dead. 10So they kept the matter to themselves, questioning what this rising from the dead could mean. 11Then they asked him, "Why do the scribes say that Elijah must come first?" 12He said to them, "Elijah is indeed coming first to restore all things. How then is it written about the Son of Man, that he is to go through many sufferings and be treated with contempt? 13But I tell you that Elijah has come, and they did to him whatever they pleased, as it is written about him."

THE HEALING OF A BOY WITH A SPIRIT

14 When they came to the disciples, they saw a great crowd around them, and some scribes arguing with them. 15When the whole crowd saw him, they were immediately overcome with awe, and they ran forward to greet him. 16He asked them, "What are you arguing about with them?" 17Someone from the crowd answered him, "Teacher, I brought you my son; he has a spirit that makes him unable to speak; 18and whenever it seizes him, it dashes him down; and he foams and grinds his teeth and becomes rigid; and I asked your disciples to cast it out, but they could not do so." 19He answered them, "You faithless generation, how much longer must I be among you? How much longer must I put up with you? Bring him to me." 20And they brought the boy[e] to him. When the spirit saw him, immediately it convulsed the boy,[e] and he fell on the ground and rolled about, foaming at the mouth. 21Jesus[f] asked the father, "How long has this been happening to him?" And he said, "From childhood. 22It has often cast him into the fire and into the water, to destroy him; but if you are able to do anything, have pity on us and help us." 23Jesus said to him, "If you are able!—All things can be done for the one who believes." 24Immediately the father of the child cried out,[g] "I believe; help my unbelief!" 25When Jesus saw that a crowd came running together, he rebuked the unclean spirit, saying to it, "You spirit that keeps this boy from speaking and hearing, I command you, come out of him, and never enter him again!" 26After crying out and convulsing him terribly, it came out, and the boy was like a corpse, so that most of them said, "He is dead." 27But Jesus took him by the hand and lifted him up, and he was able to stand. 28When he had entered the house, his disciples asked him privately, "Why could we not cast it out?" 29He said to them, "This kind can come out only through prayer."[h]

JESUS AGAIN FORETELLS HIS DEATH AND RESURRECTION

30 They went on from there and passed through Galilee. He did not

[a] 9.1 Or in   [b] 9.3 Gk no fuller   [c] 9.5 Or tents   [d] 9.7 Or my beloved Son   [e] 9.20 Gk him   [f] 9.21 Gk He   [g] 9.24 Other ancient authorities add with tears   [h] 9.29 Other ancient authorities add and fasting

PONDER

When [Jesus] had entered the house,
his disciples asked him privately,
"Why could we not cast it out?"
He said to them, "This kind can
come out only through prayer."
—Mark 9.28–29

PRAY

Father, we are thankful for this scripture
about the disciples, whom you used to
build your kingdom, even though they
faltered and failed. We see how after
the resurrection they were empowered
by the Holy Spirit, their faith grew, and
they played significant roles in the
birth of the Christian church. We are
grateful to see their human fallibilities
because quite often their mistakes
show us our own mistakes. But we
also see how you lifted them up. Help
us learn from them and apply the
essence of their experiences to our
own. Give us quiet space in our hearts
for contemplation and sustained,
devoted and sincere prayer, and bless
our continued relationship with you.
We ask this in Jesus' name. Amen.

want anyone to know it; [31]for he
was teaching his disciples, saying to
them, "The Son of Man is to be betrayed into human hands, and they
will kill him, and three days after being killed, he will rise again." [32]But
they did not understand what he
was saying and were afraid to ask
him.

WHO IS THE GREATEST?

33 Then they came to Capernaum;
and when he was in the house he
asked them, "What were you arguing about on the way?" [34]But they
were silent, for on the way they had
argued with one another who was
the greatest. [35]He sat down, called
the twelve, and said to them, "Whoever wants to be first must be last of
all and servant of all." [36]Then he took
a little child and put it among them;
and taking it in his arms, he said
to them, [37]"Whoever welcomes one
such child in my name welcomes
me, and whoever welcomes me welcomes not me but the one who sent
me."

ANOTHER EXORCIST

38 John said to him, "Teacher, we
saw someone[a] casting out demons
in your name, and we tried to stop
him, because he was not following
us." [39]But Jesus said, "Do not stop
him; for no one who does a deed
of power in my name will be able
soon afterward to speak evil of me.
[40]Whoever is not against us is for us.
[41]For truly I tell you, whoever gives
you a cup of water to drink because
you bear the name of Christ will by
no means lose the reward.

TEMPTATIONS TO SIN

42 "If any of you put a stumbling
block before one of these little ones
who believe in me,[b] it would be better for you if a great millstone were
hung around your neck and you
were thrown into the sea. [43]If your
hand causes you to stumble, cut it
off; it is better for you to enter life
maimed than to have two hands
and to go to hell,[c] to the unquenchable fire.[d] [45]And if your foot causes
you to stumble, cut it off; it is better for you to enter life lame than to
have two feet and to be thrown into
hell.[c,d] [47]And if your eye causes you
to stumble, tear it out; it is better
for you to enter the kingdom of God
with one eye than to have two eyes
and to be thrown into hell,[c] [48]where
their worm never dies, and the fire
is never quenched.

49 "For everyone will be salted
with fire.[e] [50]Salt is good; but if salt

[a] **9.38** Other ancient authorities add *who
does not follow us* [b] **9.42** Other ancient
authorities lack *in me* [c] **9.43,45,47** Gk
Gehenna [d] **9.43,45** Verses 44 and 46
(which are identical with verse 48) are
lacking in the best ancient authorities
[e] **9.49** Other ancient authorities either add
or substitute *and every sacrifice will be
salted with salt*

has lost its saltiness, how can you season it?[a] Have salt in yourselves, and be at peace with one another."

TEACHING ABOUT DIVORCE

10 He left that place and went to the region of Judea and[b] beyond the Jordan. And crowds again gathered around him; and, as was his custom, he again taught them.

2 Some Pharisees came, and to test him they asked, "Is it lawful for a man to divorce his wife?" 3 He answered them, "What did Moses command you?" 4 They said, "Moses allowed a man to write a certificate of dismissal and to divorce her." 5 But Jesus said to them, "Because of your hardness of heart he wrote this commandment for you. 6 But from the beginning of creation, 'God made them male and female.' 7 'For this reason a man shall leave his father and mother and be joined to his wife,[c] 8 and the two shall become one flesh.' So they are no longer two, but one flesh. 9 Therefore what God has joined together, let no one separate."

10 Then in the house the disciples asked him again about this matter. 11 He said to them, "Whoever divorces his wife and marries another commits adultery against her; 12 and if she divorces her husband and marries another, she commits adultery."

JESUS BLESSES LITTLE CHILDREN

13 People were bringing little children to him in order that he might touch them; and the disciples spoke sternly to them. 14 But when Jesus saw this, he was indignant and said to them, "Let the little children come to me; do not stop them; for it is to such as these that the kingdom of God belongs. 15 Truly I tell you, whoever does not receive the kingdom of God as a little child will never enter it." 16 And he took them up in his arms, laid his hands on them, and blessed them.

THE RICH MAN

17 As he was setting out on a journey, a man ran up and knelt before him, and asked him, "Good Teacher, what must I do to inherit eternal life?" 18 Jesus said to him, "Why do you call me good? No one is good but God alone. 19 You know the commandments: 'You shall not murder; You shall not commit adultery; You shall not steal; You shall not bear false witness; You shall not defraud; Honor your father and mother.' " 20 He said to him, "Teacher, I have kept all these since my youth." 21 Jesus, looking at him, loved him and said, "You lack one thing; go, sell what you own, and give the money[d] to the poor, and you will have treasure in heaven; then come, follow me." 22 When he heard this, he was

[a] 9.50 Or how can you restore its saltiness?
[b] 10.1 Other ancient authorities lack and
[c] 10.7 Other ancient authorities lack and be joined to his wife
[d] 10.21 Gk lacks the money

⊦ BIBLE IN LIFE ▷

Selfishness

Mark 9.33–35

Our goals and ambitions are no different from those of Jesus' disciples. We are selfish. We want to be the greatest. We tend to focus on ourselves. These are natural human traits that Christ recognized in his close friends. At the Last Supper, in the last few hours Jesus had with his disciples, he got down on his hands and knees and washed their dirty feet (see John 13). Through his actions, Jesus communicated that greatness lies in our service to other people. Like the disciples, we should not be proud, seek an ascendant position or argue about who's the greatest among us. We're not any better than other people simply because we know we are sinful and that through our faith in Jesus our sins are forgiven. In fact, because we know Jesus and that our sins are forgiven, we are called to respect and serve others with the same love that Christ has shown to us.

shocked and went away grieving, for he had many possessions.

23 Then Jesus looked around and said to his disciples, "How hard it will be for those who have wealth to enter the kingdom of God!" 24 And the disciples were perplexed at these words. But Jesus said to them again, "Children, how hard it is[a] to enter the kingdom of God! 25 It is easier for a camel to go through the eye of a needle than for someone who is rich to enter the kingdom of God." 26 They were greatly astounded and said to one another,[b] "Then who can be saved?" 27 Jesus looked at them and said, "For mortals it is impossible, but not for God; for God all things are possible."

⊕

PONDER

[The disciples] were greatly astounded and said to one another, "Then who can be saved?" Jesus looked at them and said, "For mortals it is impossible, but not for God; for God all things are possible."
—Mark 10.26–27

PRAY

Our Father, in this scripture we read about a young man who was ambitious and eager to approach Jesus Christ. Jesus then showed the young man what it would cost to be his disciple, but the young man wasn't willing to make the sacrifice. All of us should be asking of our own lives: What should be the ultimate goal of my life? What is Jesus demanding of me? How can I change my life to follow more closely Jesus Christ in whom I have complete faith? Help us have the courage to look within and see what our priorities are. What drives our lives? If we made the commitment to predicate our whole lives on faith in Jesus Christ, how great could the benefits be? Help us to ask these questions, Father, and answer them honestly, we ask in Jesus' name. Amen.

28 Peter began to say to him, "Look, we have left everything and followed you." 29 Jesus said, "Truly I tell you, there is no one who has left house or brothers or sisters or mother or father or children or fields, for my sake and for the sake of the good news,[c] 30 who will not receive a hundredfold now in this age—houses, brothers and sisters, mothers and children, and fields, with persecutions—and in the age to come eternal life. 31 But many who are first will be last, and the last will be first."

A THIRD TIME JESUS FORETELLS HIS DEATH AND RESURRECTION

32 They were on the road, going up to Jerusalem, and Jesus was walking ahead of them; they were amazed, and those who followed were afraid. He took the twelve aside again and began to tell them what was to happen to him, 33 saying, "See, we are going up to Jerusalem, and the Son of Man will be handed over to the chief priests and the scribes, and they will condemn him to death; then they will hand him over to the Gentiles; 34 they will mock him, and spit upon him, and flog him, and kill him; and after three days he will rise again."

THE REQUEST OF JAMES AND JOHN

35 James and John, the sons of Zebedee, came forward to him and said to him, "Teacher, we want you to do for us whatever we ask of you." 36 And he said to them, "What is it you want me to do for you?" 37 And they said to him, "Grant us to sit, one at your right hand and one at your left, in your glory." 38 But Jesus said to them, "You do not know what you are asking. Are you able to drink the cup that I drink, or be baptized with the baptism that I am baptized with?" 39 They replied, "We are able." Then Jesus said to them, "The cup that I drink you will drink; and with

a **10.24** Other ancient authorities add *for those who trust in riches*   b **10.26** Other ancient authorities read *to him*   c **10.29** Or *gospel*

╱╲

the baptism with which I am baptized, you will be baptized; ⁴⁰but to sit at my right hand or at my left is not mine to grant, but it is for those for whom it has been prepared."

41 When the ten heard this, they began to be angry with James and John. ⁴²So Jesus called them and said to them, "You know that among the Gentiles those whom they recognize as their rulers lord it over them, and their great ones are tyrants over them. ⁴³But it is not so among you; but whoever wishes to become great among you must be your servant, ⁴⁴and whoever wishes to be first among you must be slave of all. ⁴⁵For the Son of Man came not to be served but to serve, and to give his life a ransom for many."

THE HEALING OF BLIND BARTIMAEUS

46 They came to Jericho. As he and his disciples and a large crowd were leaving Jericho, Bartimaeus son of Timaeus, a blind beggar, was sitting by the roadside. ⁴⁷When he heard that it was Jesus of Nazareth, he began to shout out and say, "Jesus, Son of David, have mercy on me!" ⁴⁸Many sternly ordered him to be quiet, but he cried out even more loudly, "Son of David, have mercy on me!" ⁴⁹Jesus stood still and said, "Call him here." And they called the blind man, saying to him, "Take heart; get up, he is calling you." ⁵⁰So throwing off his cloak, he sprang up and came to Jesus. ⁵¹Then Jesus said to him, "What do you want me to do for you?" The blind man said to him, "My teacher,ᵃ let me see again." ⁵²Jesus said to him, "Go; your faith has made you well." Immediately he regained his sight and followed him on the way.

JESUS' TRIUMPHAL ENTRY INTO JERUSALEM

11 When they were approaching Jerusalem, at Bethphage and Bethany, near the Mount of Olives, he sent two of his disciples ²and said to them, "Go into the village ahead of you, and immediately as you enter it, you will find tied there a colt that has never been ridden; untie it and bring it. ³If anyone says to you, 'Why are you doing this?' just say this, 'The Lord needs it and will send it back here immediately.'" ⁴They went away and found a colt tied near a door, outside in the street. As they were untying it, ⁵some of the bystanders said to them, "What are you doing, untying the colt?" ⁶They told them what Jesus had said; and they allowed them to take it. ⁷Then they brought the colt to Jesus and threw their cloaks on it; and he sat on it. ⁸Many people spread their cloaks on the road, and others spread leafy branches that they had cut in the fields. ⁹Then those who went ahead and those who followed were shouting,

"Hosanna!
    Blessed is the one who comes
        in the name of the Lord!
10   Blessed is the coming kingdom
        of our ancestor David!
Hosanna in the highest heaven!"

11 Then he entered Jerusalem and went into the temple; and when he had looked around at everything, as it was already late, he went out to Bethany with the twelve.

JESUS CURSES THE FIG TREE

12 On the following day, when they came from Bethany, he was hungry. ¹³Seeing in the distance a fig tree in leaf, he went to see whether perhaps he would find anything on it. When he came to it, he found nothing but leaves, for it was not the season for figs. ¹⁴He said to it, "May no one ever eat fruit from you again." And his disciples heard it.

JESUS CLEANSES THE TEMPLE

15 Then they came to Jerusalem. And he entered the temple and began to drive out those who were selling and those who were buying in the temple, and he overturned the tables of the money changers and the seats of those who sold doves; ¹⁶and he would not allow anyone to carry anything through the temple.

ᵃ 10.51 Aramaic *Rabbouni*

[17] He was teaching and saying, "Is it not written,

'My house shall be called a
house of prayer for
all the nations'?
But you have made it a
den of robbers.'"

[18] And when the chief priests and the scribes heard it, they kept looking for a way to kill him; for they were afraid of him, because the whole crowd was spellbound by his teaching. [19] And when evening came, Jesus and his disciples[a] went out of the city.

THE LESSON FROM THE WITHERED FIG TREE

[20] In the morning as they passed by, they saw the fig tree withered away to its roots. [21] Then Peter remembered and said to him, "Rabbi, look! The fig tree that you cursed has withered." [22] Jesus answered them, "Have[b] faith in God. [23] Truly I tell you, if you say to this mountain, 'Be taken up and thrown into the sea,' and if you do not doubt in your heart, but believe that what you say will come to pass, it will be done for you. [24] So I tell you, whatever you ask for in prayer, believe that you have received[c] it, and it will be yours.

[25] "Whenever you stand praying, forgive, if you have anything against anyone; so that your Father in heaven may also forgive you your trespasses."[d]

JESUS' AUTHORITY IS QUESTIONED

[27] Again they came to Jerusalem. As he was walking in the temple, the chief priests, the scribes, and the elders came to him [28] and said, "By what authority are you doing these things? Who gave you this authority to do them?" [29] Jesus said to them, "I will ask you one question; answer me, and I will tell you by what authority I do these things. [30] Did the baptism of John come from heaven, or was it of human origin? Answer me." [31] They argued with one another, "If we say, 'From heaven,' he will say, 'Why then did you not believe him?' [32] But shall we say, 'Of human origin'?"—they were afraid of the crowd, for all regarded John as truly a prophet. [33] So they answered Jesus, "We do not know." And Jesus said to them, "Neither will I tell you by what authority I am doing these things."

PONDER

"So I tell you, whatever you ask for in prayer, believe that you have received it, and it will be yours. Whenever you stand praying, forgive, if you have anything against anyone; so that your Father in heaven may also forgive you your trespasses."
—Mark 11.24–25

PRAY

Our Father, these accounts of the early ministry of Jesus demonstrate to us that he was indeed the promised Messiah; that he is indeed your Son; that he acted on your authority; that he was a humble lover of peace, justice, forgiveness, humility, service, compassion and love—characteristics that should exemplify our own lives as Christians. We ask for your favor on us, your forgiveness of our sin, your power to grow our faith and your harmony among us as we worship the Prince of Peace, Jesus Christ. Amen.

THE PARABLE OF THE WICKED TENANTS

12 Then he began to speak to them in parables. "A man planted a vineyard, put a fence around it, dug a pit for the wine press, and built a watchtower; then he leased it to tenants and went to

---

[a] **11.19** Gk *they*: other ancient authorities read *he*   [b] **11.22** Other ancient authorities read "*If you have*   [c] **11.24** Other ancient authorities read *are receiving*   [d] **11.25** Other ancient authorities add verse 26, "*But if you do not forgive, neither will your Father in heaven forgive your trespasses.*"

another country. 2When the season came, he sent a slave to the tenants to collect from them his share of the produce of the vineyard. 3But they seized him, and beat him, and sent him away empty-handed. 4And again he sent another slave to them; this one they beat over the head and insulted. 5Then he sent another, and that one they killed. And so it was with many others; some they beat, and others they killed. 6He had still one other, a beloved son. Finally he sent him to them, saying, 'They will respect my son.' 7But those tenants said to one another, 'This is the heir; come, let us kill him, and the inheritance will be ours.' 8So they seized him, killed him, and threw him out of the vineyard. 9What then will the owner of the vineyard do? He will come and destroy the tenants and give the vineyard to others. 10Have you not read this scripture:

'The stone that the builders
    rejected
has become the cornerstone;a
11 this was the Lord's doing,
    and it is amazing in our eyes'?"

12When they realized that he had told this parable against them, they wanted to arrest him, but they feared the crowd. So they left him and went away.

THE QUESTION ABOUT PAYING TAXES

13 Then they sent to him some Pharisees and some Herodians to trap him in what he said. 14And they came and said to him, "Teacher, we know that you are sincere, and show deference to no one; for you do not regard people with partiality, but teach the way of God in accordance with truth. Is it lawful to pay taxes to the emperor, or not? 15Should we pay them, or should we not?" But knowing their hypocrisy, he said to them, "Why are you putting me to the test? Bring me a denarius and let me see it." 16And they brought one. Then he said to them, "Whose head is this, and whose title?" They answered, "The emperor's." 17Jesus said to them, "Give to the emperor the things that are the emperor's, and to

God the things that are God's." And they were utterly amazed at him.

THE QUESTION ABOUT THE RESURRECTION

18 Some Sadducees, who say there is no resurrection, came to him and asked him a question, saying, 19"Teacher, Moses wrote for us that if a man's brother dies, leaving a wife but no child, the manb shall marry the widow and raise up children for his brother. 20There were seven brothers; the first married and, when he died, left no children; 21and the second married the widowc and died, leaving no children; and the third likewise; 22none of the seven left children. Last of all the woman herself died. 23In the resurrectiond whose wife will she be? For the seven had married her."

24 Jesus said to them, "Is not this the reason you are wrong, that you know neither the scriptures nor the power of God? 25For when they rise from the dead, they neither marry nor are given in marriage, but are like angels in heaven. 26And as for the dead being raised, have you not read in the book of Moses, in the story about the bush, how God said to him, 'I am the God of Abraham, the God of Isaac, and the God of Jacob'? 27He is God not of the dead, but of the living; you are quite wrong."

THE FIRST COMMANDMENT

28 One of the scribes came near and heard them disputing with one another, and seeing that he answered them well, he asked him, "Which commandment is the first of all?" 29Jesus answered, "The first is, 'Hear, O Israel: the Lord our God, the Lord is one; 30you shall love the Lord your God with all your heart, and with all your soul, and with all your mind, and with all your strength.' 31The second is this, 'You shall love your neighbor as yourself.' There is no other commandment greater than these." 32Then the scribe said to him, "You are right,

---

a 12.10 Or keystone   b 12.19 Gk his brother
c 12.21 Gk her   d 12.23 Other ancient
authorities add when they rise

Teacher; you have truly said that 'he is one, and besides him there is no other'; 33and 'to love him with all the heart, and with all the understanding, and with all the strength,' and 'to love one's neighbor as oneself,'— this is much more important than all whole burnt offerings and sacrifices." 34When Jesus saw that he answered wisely, he said to him, "You are not far from the kingdom of God." After that no one dared to ask him any question.

THE QUESTION ABOUT DAVID'S SON

35 While Jesus was teaching in the temple, he said, "How can the scribes say that the Messiah[a] is the son of David? 36David himself, by the Holy Spirit, declared,

'The Lord said to my Lord,
"Sit at my right hand,
   until I put your enemies
      under your feet." '

37David himself calls him Lord; so how can he be his son?" And the large crowd was listening to him with delight.

JESUS DENOUNCES THE SCRIBES

38 As he taught, he said, "Beware of the scribes, who like to walk around in long robes, and to be greeted with respect in the mar-

ketplaces, 39and to have the best seats in the synagogues and places of honor at banquets! 40They devour widows' houses and for the sake of appearance say long prayers. They will receive the greater condemnation."

THE WIDOW'S OFFERING

41 He sat down opposite the treasury, and watched the crowd putting money into the treasury. Many rich people put in large sums. 42A poor widow came and put in two small copper coins, which are worth a penny. 43Then he called his disciples and said to them, "Truly I tell you, this poor widow has put in more than all those who are contributing to the treasury. 44For all of them have contributed out of their abundance; but she out of her poverty has put in everything she had, all she had to live on."

THE DESTRUCTION OF THE TEMPLE FORETOLD

13 As he came out of the temple, one of his disciples said to him, "Look, Teacher, what large stones and what large buildings!" 2Then Jesus asked him, "Do you see these great buildings? Not one stone

a 12.35 Or the Christ

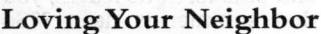

BIBLE IN LIFE ▷

Loving Your Neighbor   Mark 12.29–34

What does it mean to love one's neighbor as oneself? One of my great friends was a Cuban pastor with whom I did missionary work in Massachusetts, and he said you only need two loves in your life: God and the person who happens to be in front of you at any particular time. Although I realize we have to love other people, this simple perspective really transformed my concept of love, because a lot of the people in front of me do not seem very lovable or interesting, they can't even thank me for my love, or they may not even feel inclined to respond to my love. These folks sit beside us on an airplane or bus or ride an elevator with us, or they work in our office. Our goal is to engender within our own hearts a feeling of genuine, unselfish love—love for the unlovable, love that won't be repaid, love for unsavory people, love for lonely people whom others are ignoring because of their low stature in life. That's the kind of love that Christ tells us to show others. This love leads to a truly abundant life, a life in which we reach out to others and search for opportunities to expand our hearts, our lives and our minds to learn more about God's world and to meet different people. It's the kind of love that makes an investment in the future of others.

will be left here upon another; all will be thrown down."

3 When he was sitting on the Mount of Olives opposite the temple, Peter, James, John, and Andrew asked him privately, 4"Tell us, when will this be, and what will be the sign that all these things are about to be accomplished?" 5Then Jesus began to say to them, "Beware that no one leads you astray. 6Many will come in my name and say, 'I am he!'ᵃ and they will lead many astray. 7When you hear of wars and rumors of wars, do not be alarmed; this must take place, but the end is still to come. 8For nation will rise against nation, and kingdom against kingdom; there will be earthquakes in various places; there will be famines. This is but the beginning of the birth pangs.

PERSECUTION FORETOLD

9 "As for yourselves, beware; for they will hand you over to councils; and you will be beaten in synagogues; and you will stand before governors and kings because of me, as a testimony to them. 10And the good newsᵇ must first be proclaimed to all nations. 11When they bring you to trial and hand you over, do not worry beforehand about what you are to say; but say whatever is given you at that time, for it is not you who speak, but the Holy Spirit. 12Brother will betray brother to death, and a father his child, and children will rise against parents and have them put to death; 13and you will be hated by all because of my name. But the one who endures to the end will be saved.

THE DESOLATING SACRILEGE

14 "But when you see the desolating sacrilege set up where it ought not to be (let the reader understand), then those in Judea must flee to the mountains; 15the one on the housetop must not go down or enter the house to take anything away; 16the one in the field must not turn back to get a coat. 17Woe to those who are pregnant and to those who are nursing infants in those days! 18Pray

that it may not be in winter. 19For in those days there will be suffering, such as has not been from the beginning of the creation that God created until now, no, and never will be. 20And if the Lord had not cut short those days, no one would be saved; but for the sake of the elect, whom he chose, he has cut short those days. 21And if anyone says to you at that time, 'Look! Here is the Messiah!'ᶜ or 'Look! There he is!'—do not believe it. 22False messiahsᵈ and false prophets will appear and produce signs and omens, to lead astray, if possible, the elect. 23But be alert; I have already told you everything.

THE COMING OF THE SON OF MAN

24 "But in those days, after that suffering,
    the sun will be darkened,
        and the moon will not
            give its light,
25 and the stars will be falling
        from heaven,
    and the powers in the heavens
        will be shaken.
26Then they will see 'the Son of Man coming in clouds' with great power and glory. 27Then he will send out the angels, and gather his elect from the four winds, from the ends of the earth to the ends of heaven.

THE LESSON OF THE FIG TREE

28 "From the fig tree learn its lesson: as soon as its branch becomes tender and puts forth its leaves, you know that summer is near. 29So also, when you see these things taking place, you know that heᵉ is near, at the very gates. 30Truly I tell you, this generation will not pass away until all these things have taken place. 31Heaven and earth will pass away, but my words will not pass away.

THE NECESSITY FOR WATCHFULNESS

32 "But about that day or hour no one knows, neither the angels in

ᵃ 13.6 Gk I am   ᵇ 13.10 Gk gospel
ᶜ 13.21 Or the Christ   ᵈ 13.22 Or christs
ᵉ 13.29 Or it

heaven, nor the Son, but only the Father. [33]Beware, keep alert;[a] for you do not know when the time will come. [34]It is like a man going on a journey, when he leaves home and puts his slaves in charge, each with his work, and commands the doorkeeper to be on the watch. [35]Therefore, keep awake—for you do not know when the master of the house will come, in the evening, or at midnight, or at cockcrow, or at dawn, [36]or else he may find you asleep when he comes suddenly. [37]And what I say to you I say to all: Keep awake."

THE PLOT TO KILL JESUS

14 It was two days before the Passover and the festival of Unleavened Bread. The chief priests and the scribes were looking for a way to arrest Jesus[b] by stealth and kill him; [2]for they said, "Not during the festival, or there may be a riot among the people."

THE ANOINTING AT BETHANY

[3]While he was at Bethany in the house of Simon the leper,[c] as he sat at the table, a woman came with an alabaster jar of very costly ointment of nard, and she broke open the jar and poured the ointment on his head. [4]But some were there who said to one another in anger, "Why was the ointment wasted in this way? [5]For this ointment could have been sold for more than three hun-

dred denarii,[d] and the money given to the poor." And they scolded her. [6]But Jesus said, "Let her alone; why do you trouble her? She has performed a good service for me. [7]For you always have the poor with you, and you can show kindness to them whenever you wish; but you will not always have me. [8]She has done what she could; she has anointed my body beforehand for its burial. [9]Truly I tell you, wherever the good news[e] is proclaimed in the whole world, what she has done will be told in remembrance of her."

JUDAS AGREES TO BETRAY JESUS

[10]Then Judas Iscariot, who was one of the twelve, went to the chief priests in order to betray him to them. [11]When they heard it, they were greatly pleased, and promised to give him money. So he began to look for an opportunity to betray him.

THE PASSOVER WITH THE DISCIPLES

[12]On the first day of Unleavened Bread, when the Passover lamb is sacrificed, his disciples said to him, "Where do you want us to go and make the preparations for you to eat the Passover?" [13]So he sent two

[a] 13.33 Other ancient authorities add and pray [b] 14.1 Gk him [c] 14.3 The terms leper and leprosy can refer to several diseases [d] 14.5 The denarius was the usual day's wage for a laborer [e] 14.9 Or gospel

---

⊢─┤ **BIBLE IN LIFE** ▷ ─────────── ⊂⊃

Extraordinary Acts

Mark 14.3–9

This story may make us uncomfortable. If we had been present in the room, how would we have reacted when the woman broke the jar of expensive perfume? Embarrassed by the strangeness of the act? Outraged that someone would waste something so valuable? Jesus responded in a surprising way, saying, "She has performed a good service for me." She wanted to show her love for her Savior in a humble, worshipful, loving, beautiful way. She was not left destitute after breaking the jar; she had the richness of the love of Christ. As we show kindness to others in the name of Christ in ways that are unusual or unpredictable, our own lives will be enriched. What we do doesn't have to be grandiose or publicized. We may simply reach out in the name of Christ to people who are estranged from us or with whom we're not acquainted. Just as this woman, in essence, said, "I want to do something extraordinary for my Savior," so we have that same opportunity.

of his disciples, saying to them, "Go into the city, and a man carrying a jar of water will meet you; follow him, 14and wherever he enters, say to the owner of the house, 'The Teacher asks, Where is my guest room where I may eat the Passover with my disciples?' 15He will show you a large room upstairs, furnished and ready. Make preparations for us there." 16So the disciples set out and went to the city, and found everything as he had told them; and they prepared the Passover meal.

17 When it was evening, he came with the twelve. 18And when they had taken their places and were eating, Jesus said, "Truly I tell you, one of you will betray me, one who is eating with me." 19They began to be distressed and to say to him one after another, "Surely, not I?" 20He said to them, "It is one of the twelve, one who is dipping bread[a] into the bowl[b] with me. 21For the Son of Man goes as it is written of him, but woe to that one by whom the Son of Man is betrayed! It would have been better for that one not to have been born."

THE INSTITUTION OF
THE LORD'S SUPPER

22 While they were eating, he took a loaf of bread, and after blessing it he broke it, gave it to them, and said, "Take; this is my body." 23Then he took a cup, and after giving thanks he gave it to them, and all of them drank from it. 24He said to them, "This is my blood of the[c] covenant, which is poured out for many. 25Truly I tell you, I will never again drink of the fruit of the vine until that day when I drink it new in the kingdom of God."

PETER'S DENIAL FORETOLD

26When they had sung the hymn, they went out to the Mount of Olives. 27And Jesus said to them, "You will all become deserters; for it is written,

'I will strike the shepherd,
    and the sheep will be scattered.'
28But after I am raised up, I will go before you to Galilee." 29Peter

said to him, "Even though all become deserters, I will not." 30Jesus said to him, "Truly I tell you, this day, this very night, before the cock crows twice, you will deny me three times." 31But he said vehemently, "Even though I must die with you, I will not deny you." And all of them said the same.

JESUS PRAYS IN GETHSEMANE

32 They went to a place called Gethsemane; and he said to his disciples, "Sit here while I pray." 33He took with him Peter and James and John, and began to be distressed and agitated. 34And he said to them, "I am deeply grieved, even to death; remain here, and keep awake." 35And going a little farther, he threw himself on the ground and prayed that, if it were possible, the hour might pass from him. 36He said, "Abba,[d] Father, for you all things are possible; remove this cup from me; yet, not what I want, but what you want." 37He came and found them sleeping; and he said to Peter, "Simon, are you asleep? Could you not keep awake one hour? 38Keep awake and pray that you may not come into the time of trial;[e] the spirit indeed is willing, but the flesh is weak." 39And again he went away and prayed, saying the same words. 40And once more he came and found them sleeping, for their eyes were very heavy; and they did not know what to say to him. 41He came a third time and said to them, "Are you still sleeping and taking your rest? Enough! The hour has come; the Son of Man is betrayed into the hands of sinners. 42Get up, let us be going. See, my betrayer is at hand."

THE BETRAYAL AND
ARREST OF JESUS

43 Immediately, while he was still speaking, Judas, one of the twelve, arrived; and with him there was a crowd with swords and clubs, from

a 14.20 Gk lacks bread   b 14.20 Other ancient authorities read same bowl
c 14.24 Other ancient authorities add new   d 14.36 Aramaic for Father   e 14.38 Or into temptation

the chief priests, the scribes, and the elders. 44Now the betrayer had given them a sign, saying, "The one I will kiss is the man; arrest him and lead him away under guard." 45So when he came, he went up to him at once and said, "Rabbi!" and kissed him. 46Then they laid hands on him and arrested him. 47But one of those who stood near drew his sword and struck the slave of the high priest, cutting off his ear. 48Then Jesus said to them, "Have you come out with swords and clubs to arrest me as though I were a bandit? 49Day after day I was with you in the temple teaching, and you did not arrest me. But let the scriptures be fulfilled." 50All of them deserted him and fled.

51 A certain young man was following him, wearing nothing but a linen cloth. They caught hold of him, 52but he left the linen cloth and ran off naked.

JESUS BEFORE THE COUNCIL

53 They took Jesus to the high priest; and all the chief priests, the elders, and the scribes were assembled. 54Peter had followed him at a distance, right into the courtyard of the high priest; and he was sitting with the guards, warming himself at the fire. 55Now the chief priests and the whole council were looking for testimony against Jesus to put him to death; but they found none. 56For many gave false testimony against him, and their testimony did not agree. 57Some stood up and gave false testimony against him, saying, 58"We heard him say, 'I will destroy this temple that is made with hands, and in three days I will build another, not made with hands.' " 59But even on this point their testimony did not agree. 60Then the high priest stood up before them and asked Jesus, "Have you no answer? What is it that they testify against you?" 61But he was silent and did not answer. Again the high priest asked him, "Are you the Messiah,ᵃ the Son of the Blessed One?" 62Jesus said, "I am; and 'you will see the Son of Man

seated at the right hand
of the Power,'
and 'coming with the clouds
of heaven.' "
63Then the high priest tore his clothes and said, "Why do we still need witnesses? 64You have heard his blasphemy! What is your decision?" All of them condemned him as deserving death. 65Some began to spit on him, to blindfold him, and to strike him, saying to him, "Prophesy!" The guards also took him over and beat him.

PONDER

But he was silent and did not answer.
Again the high priest asked him,
"Are you the Messiah, the Son of the
Blessed One?" Jesus said, "I am; and
'you will see the Son of Man seated
at the right hand of the Power,' and
'coming with the clouds of heaven.'"
—Mark 14.61–62

PRAY

Almighty God, this scripture reminds us of all that Jesus Christ—your Son, the promised Messiah—means to us. This scripture brings home to us the extraordinary life of Christ: his words, miracles, suffering and his betrayal, punishment and resurrection. Absorbing this truth should be a vital life experience and lesson for us. Give us the courage to look at ourselves and the wisdom to apply this scripture in a personal way for the rest of our lives. We ask in the name of Jesus. Amen.

PETER DENIES JESUS

66 While Peter was below in the courtyard, one of the servant-girls of the high priest came by. 67When she saw Peter warming himself, she stared at him and said, "You also were with Jesus, the man from Nazareth."

ᵃ 14.61 Or the Christ

68 But he denied it, saying, "I do not know or understand what you are talking about." And he went out into the forecourt.[a] Then the cock crowed.[b] 69 And the servant-girl, on seeing him, began again to say to the bystanders, "This man is one of them." 70 But again he denied it. Then after a little while the bystanders again said to Peter, "Certainly you are one of them; for you are a Galilean." 71 But he began to curse, and he swore an oath, "I do not know this man you are talking about." 72 At that moment the cock crowed for the second time. Then Peter remembered that Jesus had said to him, "Before the cock crows twice, you will deny me three times." And he broke down and wept.

JESUS BEFORE PILATE

15 As soon as it was morning, the chief priests held a consultation with the elders and scribes and the whole council. They bound Jesus, led him away, and handed him over to Pilate. 2 Pilate asked him, "Are you the King of the Jews?" He answered him, "You say so." 3 Then the chief priests accused him of many things. 4 Pilate asked him again, "Have you no answer? See how many charges they bring against you." 5 But Jesus made no further reply, so that Pilate was amazed.

PILATE HANDS JESUS OVER TO BE CRUCIFIED

6 Now at the festival he used to release a prisoner for them, anyone for whom they asked. 7 Now a man called Barabbas was in prison with the rebels who had committed murder during the insurrection. 8 So the crowd came and began to ask Pilate to do for them according to his custom. 9 Then he answered them, "Do you want me to release for you the King of the Jews?" 10 For he realized that it was out of jealousy that the chief priests had handed him over. 11 But the chief priests stirred up the crowd to have him release Barabbas for them instead. 12 Pilate spoke to them again, "Then what do you wish me to do[c] with the man you call[d] the King of the Jews?" 13 They shouted back, "Crucify him!" 14 Pilate asked them, "Why, what evil has he done?" But they shouted all the more, "Crucify him!" 15 So Pilate, wishing to satisfy the crowd, released Barabbas for them; and after flogging Jesus, he handed him over to be crucified.

THE SOLDIERS MOCK JESUS

16 Then the soldiers led him into the courtyard of the palace (that is, the governor's headquarters[e]); and they called together the whole cohort. 17 And they clothed him in a purple cloak; and after twisting some thorns into a crown, they put it on him. 18 And they began saluting him, "Hail, King of the Jews!" 19 They struck his head with a reed, spat upon him, and knelt down in homage to him. 20 After mocking him, they stripped him of the purple cloak and put his own clothes on him. Then they led him out to crucify him.

THE CRUCIFIXION OF JESUS

21 They compelled a passer-by, who was coming in from the country, to carry his cross; it was Simon of Cyrene, the father of Alexander and Rufus. 22 Then they brought Jesus[f] to the place called Golgotha (which means the place of a skull). 23 And they offered him wine mixed with myrrh; but he did not take it. 24 And they crucified him, and divided his clothes among them, casting lots to decide what each should take.

25 It was nine o'clock in the morning when they crucified him. 26 The inscription of the charge against him read, "The King of the Jews." 27 And with him they crucified two bandits, one on his right and one on his left.[g] 29 Those who passed by

a 14.68 Or *gateway*   b 14.68 Other ancient authorities lack *Then the cock crowed*   c 15.12 Other ancient authorities read *what should I do*   d 15.12 Other ancient authorities lack *the man you call*   e 15.16 Gk *the praetorium*   f 15.22 Gk *him*   g 15.27 Other ancient authorities add verse 28, *And the scripture was fulfilled that says, "And he was counted among the lawless."*

derided[a] him, shaking their heads and saying, "Aha! You who would destroy the temple and build it in three days, 30save yourself, and come down from the cross!" 31In the same way the chief priests, along with the scribes, were also mocking him among themselves and saying, "He saved others; he cannot save himself. 32Let the Messiah,[b] the King of Israel, come down from the cross now, so that we may see and believe." Those who were crucified with him also taunted him.

THE DEATH OF JESUS

33When it was noon, darkness came over the whole land[c] until three in the afternoon. 34At three o'clock Jesus cried out with a loud voice, "Eloi, Eloi, lema sabachthani?" which means, "My God, my God, why have you forsaken me?"[d] 35When some of the bystanders heard it, they said, "Listen, he is calling for Elijah." 36And someone ran, filled a sponge with sour wine, put it on a stick, and gave it to him to drink, saying, "Wait, let us see whether Elijah will come to take him down." 37Then Jesus gave a loud cry and breathed his last. 38And the curtain of the temple was torn in two, from top to bottom. 39Now when the centurion, who stood facing him, saw that in this way he[e] breathed his last, he said, "Truly this man was God's Son!"[f]

40There were also women looking on from a distance; among them were Mary Magdalene, and Mary the mother of James the younger and of Joses, and Salome. 41These used to follow him and provided for him when he was in Galilee; and there were many other women who had come up with him to Jerusalem.

THE BURIAL OF JESUS

42When evening had come, and since it was the day of Preparation, that is, the day before the sabbath, 43Joseph of Arimathea, a respected member of the council, who was also himself waiting expectantly for the kingdom of God, went boldly to Pilate and asked for the body of Jesus.

44Then Pilate wondered if he were already dead; and summoning the centurion, he asked him whether he had been dead for some time. 45When he learned from the centurion that he was dead, he granted the body to Joseph. 46Then Joseph[g] bought a linen cloth, and taking down the body,[h] wrapped it in the linen cloth, and laid it in a tomb that had been hewn out of the rock. He then rolled a stone against the door of the tomb. 47Mary Magdalene and Mary the mother of Joses saw where the body[h] was laid.

WE ARE NOT CALLED TO PROVE EASTER, BUT TO WITNESS TO IT.

THE RESURRECTION OF JESUS

16 When the sabbath was over, Mary Magdalene, and Mary the mother of James, and Salome bought spices, so that they might go and anoint him. 2And very early on the first day of the week, when the sun had risen, they went to the tomb. 3They had been saying to one another, "Who will roll away the stone for us from the entrance to the tomb?" 4When they looked up, they saw that the stone, which was very large, had already been rolled back. 5As they entered the tomb, they saw a young man, dressed in a white robe, sitting on the right side; and they were alarmed. 6But he said to them, "Do not be alarmed; you are looking for Jesus of Nazareth, who was crucified. He has been raised; he is not here. Look, there is the place they laid him. 7But go, tell his disciples and Peter that he is going ahead of you to Galilee; there you will see

[a] 15.29 Or blasphemed [b] 15.32 Or the Christ [c] 15.33 Or earth [d] 15.34 Other ancient authorities read made me a reproach [e] 15.39 Other ancient authorities add cried out and [f] 15.39 Or a son of God [g] 15.46 Gk he [h] 15.46,47 Gk it

him, just as he told you." [8]So they went out and fled from the tomb, for terror and amazement had seized them; and they said nothing to anyone, for they were afraid.[a]

THE SHORTER ENDING OF MARK

⟦And all that had been commanded them they told briefly to those around Peter. And afterward Jesus himself sent out through them, from east to west, the sacred and imperishable proclamation of eternal salvation.[b]⟧

THE LONGER ENDING OF MARK

JESUS APPEARS TO MARY MAGDALENE

[9]⟦Now after he rose early on the first day of the week, he appeared first to Mary Magdalene, from whom he had cast out seven demons. [10]She went out and told those who had been with him, while they were mourning and weeping. [11]But when they heard that he was alive and had been seen by her, they would not believe it.

JESUS APPEARS TO TWO DISCIPLES

[12]After this he appeared in another form to two of them, as they were walking into the country.

[13]And they went back and told the rest, but they did not believe them.

JESUS COMMISSIONS THE DISCIPLES

[14]Later he appeared to the eleven themselves as they were sitting at the table; and he upbraided them for their lack of faith and stubbornness, because they had not believed those who saw him after he had risen.[c] [15]And he said to them, "Go into all the world and proclaim the good news[d] to the whole creation.

[a] 16.8 Some of the most ancient authorities bring the book to a close at the end of verse 8. One authority concludes the book with the shorter ending; others include the shorter ending and then continue with verses 9–20. In most authorities verses 9–20 follow immediately after verse 8, though in some of these authorities the passage is marked as being doubtful. [b] 16.8 Other ancient authorities add *Amen* [c] 16.14 Other ancient authorities add, in whole or in part, *And they excused themselves, saying, "This age of lawlessness and unbelief is under Satan, who does not allow the truth and power of God to prevail over the unclean things of the spirits. Therefore reveal your righteousness now"—thus they spoke to Christ. And Christ replied to them, "The term of years of Satan's power has been fulfilled, but other terrible things draw near. And for those who have sinned I was handed over to death, that they may return to the truth and sin no more, that they may inherit the spiritual and imperishable glory of righteousness that is in heaven."* [d] 16.15 Or *gospel*

⊦──── BIBLE IN LIFE ▷────

Courageous Witnessing   Mark 16.1–11

Who were the courageous ones who stuck with Christ during his trial, crucifixion, burial and resurrection? The women. They never abandoned him. Mary, the sister of Martha and Lazarus, anointed Jesus' feet the week before his crucifixion (see John 12.1–8). On the resurrection morning, Peter, John and the rest of the disciples were hiding, but not the women. They went to the tomb and saw that the stone was rolled away. Mary Magdalene was the first to see Jesus after the resurrection. If the ancient writers had wanted to mislead people, they would not have featured women in the story. At that time, women had no standing in court, so the testimony of a woman was assumed to be meaningless. If someone wanted to write a story to convince people that Jesus had risen, they wouldn't have included a bunch of women. This lends enormous credibility to the truth of the resurrection. Sometimes we may feel that our words have no meaning to others. We may feel afraid or inferior, but we can learn a lesson from the women who courageously stood by Jesus and proclaimed the truth to those around them.

16 The one who believes and is baptized will be saved; but the one who does not believe will be condemned. 17 And these signs will accompany those who believe: by using my name they will cast out demons; they will speak in new tongues; 18 they will pick up snakes in their hands,[a] and if they drink any deadly thing, it will not hurt them; they will lay their hands on the sick, and they will recover."

THE ASCENSION OF JESUS

19 So then the Lord Jesus, after he had spoken to them, was taken up into heaven and sat down at the right hand of God. 20 And they went out and proclaimed the good news everywhere, while the Lord worked with them and confirmed the message by the signs that accompanied it.[b]]]

[a] 16.18 Other ancient authorities lack *in their hands*   [b] 16.20 Other ancient authorities add *Amen*

The Gospel According to

LUKE

The Gospel of Luke is like a richly textured portrait that captures the depth of Jesus' identity. This Gospel gives the fullest account of Jesus' life. The physician Luke highlights Jesus' warmth and humanity, his love for all people—Jew and Gentile alike—as well as his power as God's Son. We glimpse Jesus' childhood, observe his gentleness toward the poor and oppressed, his smile as he welcomes little children. But the power of his teaching and miracles proclaim that he also is God. More than any other Gospel, Luke demonstrates that Jesus is both God and human.

DEDICATION TO THEOPHILUS

1 Since many have undertaken to set down an orderly account of the events that have been fulfilled among us, ²just as they were handed on to us by those who from the beginning were eyewitnesses and servants of the word, ³I too decided, after investigating everything carefully from the very first,ᵃ to write an orderly account for you, most excellent Theophilus, ⁴so that you may know the truth concerning the things about which you have been instructed.

THE BIRTH OF JOHN THE BAPTIST FORETOLD

5 In the days of King Herod of Judea, there was a priest named Zechariah, who belonged to the priestly order of Abijah. His wife was a descendant of Aaron, and her name was Elizabeth. ⁶Both of them were righteous before God, living blamelessly according to all the commandments and regulations of the Lord. ⁷But they had no children, because Elizabeth was barren, and both were getting on in years.

8 Once when he was serving as priest before God and his section was on duty, ⁹he was chosen by lot, according to the custom of the priesthood, to enter the sanctuary of the Lord and offer incense. ¹⁰Now at the time of the incense offering, the whole assembly of the people was praying outside. ¹¹Then there appeared to him an angel of the Lord, standing at the right side of the altar of incense. ¹²When Zechariah saw him, he was terrified; and fear overwhelmed him. ¹³But the angel said to him, "Do not be afraid, Zechariah, for your prayer has been heard. Your wife Elizabeth will bear you a son, and you will name him John. ¹⁴You will have joy and gladness, and many will rejoice at his birth, ¹⁵for he will be great in the sight of the Lord. He must never drink wine or strong drink; even before his birth he will be filled with the Holy Spirit. ¹⁶He will turn many of the people of Israel to the Lord their God. ¹⁷With the spirit and power of Elijah he will go before him, to turn the hearts of parents to their children, and the disobedient to the wisdom of the righteous, to make ready a people prepared for the Lord." ¹⁸Zechariah said to the angel, "How will I know that this is so? For I am an old man, and my wife is getting on in years." ¹⁹The angel replied, "I am Gabriel. I stand in the presence of God, and I have been sent to speak to you and to bring you this good news. ²⁰But now, because you did not believe my words, which will be fulfilled in their time, you will become mute, unable to speak, until the day these things occur."

ᵃ 1.3 Or *for a long time*

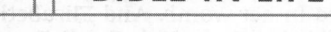

BIBLE IN LIFE

Unexpected Birth Announcements
Luke 1.5–38

In Luke 1, we are given the details of two very different reactions to two birth announcements. First, we meet Zechariah, a priest and a powerful, influential man. He had prayed for a child. Second, we meet Mary, a teenage girl with no influence whatsoever, a common, unknown girl who was betrothed to Joseph. Having a child out of wedlock could have led to her death by stoning. Zechariah and Mary had completely opposite reactions to Gabriel's announcements to them: Zechariah, who should have had faith, had doubts because of his age, and God struck him mute. Mary, who should have feared for her life, praised God in song. When Mary found out what God wanted from her, she was wholly obedient; she responded in faith to God's call to do something that she didn't understand and that endangered her very life. How do we react to God's surprises in our lives? Like Zechariah, do we have doubts when a prayer is answered? Or like Mary, do we praise God even when we have zero understanding of our circumstances?

21 Meanwhile the people were waiting for Zechariah, and wondered at his delay in the sanctuary. 22When he did come out, he could not speak to them, and they realized that he had seen a vision in the sanctuary. He kept motioning to them and remained unable to speak. 23When his time of service was ended, he went to his home.

24 After those days his wife Elizabeth conceived, and for five months she remained in seclusion. She said, 25"This is what the Lord has done for me when he looked favorably on me and took away the disgrace I have endured among my people."

THE BIRTH OF JESUS FORETOLD

26 In the sixth month the angel Gabriel was sent by God to a town in Galilee called Nazareth, 27to a virgin engaged to a man whose name was Joseph, of the house of David. The virgin's name was Mary. 28And he came to her and said, "Greetings, favored one! The Lord is with you."[a] 29But she was much perplexed by his words and pondered what sort of greeting this might be. 30The angel said to her, "Do not be afraid, Mary, for you have found favor with God. 31And now, you will conceive in your womb and bear a son, and you will name him Jesus. 32He will be great, and will be called the Son of the Most High, and the Lord God will give to him the throne of his ancestor David. 33He will reign over the house of Jacob forever, and of his kingdom there will be no end." 34Mary said to the angel, "How can this be, since I am a virgin?"[b] 35The angel said to her, "The Holy Spirit will come upon you, and the power of the Most High will overshadow you; therefore the child to be born[c] will be holy; he will be called Son of God. 36And now, your relative Elizabeth in her old age has also conceived a son; and this is the sixth month for her who was said to be barren. 37For nothing will be impossible with God." 38Then Mary said, "Here am I, the servant of the Lord; let it be with me according to your word." Then the angel departed from her.

PONDER

The angel said to her, "Do not be afraid, Mary, for you have found favor with God. And now, you will conceive in your womb and bear a son, and you will name him Jesus. He will be great, and will be called the Son of the Most High."
—Luke 1.30–32

PRAY

O Father, as we reflect on the Christmas story, may our minds be particularly open to receive the message that resonates down through the centuries, that Jesus is the Messiah, your Son; that he humbled himself and was born a helpless infant into a world of hardship and pain. For that we give you praise and thanksgiving. Make these stories about Mary, Joseph and Jesus, Simeon and Anna come to life in our hearts. Make our joy as profound as theirs. Increase our desire to be about your work, regardless of the cost. In Jesus' name we pray. Amen.

MARY VISITS ELIZABETH

39 In those days Mary set out and went with haste to a Judean town in the hill country, 40where she entered the house of Zechariah and greeted Elizabeth. 41When Elizabeth heard Mary's greeting, the child leaped in her womb. And Elizabeth was filled with the Holy Spirit 42and exclaimed with a loud cry, "Blessed are you among women, and blessed is the fruit of your womb. 43And why has this happened to me, that the mother of my Lord comes to me? 44For as soon as I heard the sound of your greeting, the child in my womb leaped for joy. 45And blessed is she who believed that there would be[d]

a 1.28 Other ancient authorities add Blessed are you among women   b 1.34 Gk I do not know a man   c 1.35 Other ancient authorities add of you   d 1.45 Or believed, for there will be a fulfillment of what was spoken to her by the Lord."

MARY'S SONG OF PRAISE

46 And Mary[a] said,

"My soul magnifies the Lord,
47   and my spirit rejoices in
         God my Savior,
48 for he has looked with favor
         on the lowliness
         of his servant.
   Surely, from now on all
         generations will
         call me blessed;
49 for the Mighty One has done
         great things for me,
   and holy is his name.
50 His mercy is for those
         who fear him
   from generation to generation.
51 He has shown strength
         with his arm;
   he has scattered the proud
         in the thoughts of
         their hearts.
52 He has brought down the
         powerful from
         their thrones,
   and lifted up the lowly;
53 he has filled the hungry
         with good things,
   and sent the rich away empty.
54 He has helped his servant Israel,
   in remembrance of his mercy,
55 according to the promise he
         made to our ancestors,
   to Abraham and to his
         descendants forever."

56 And Mary remained with her about three months and then returned to her home.

THE BIRTH OF JOHN
THE BAPTIST

57 Now the time came for Elizabeth to give birth, and she bore a son. 58 Her neighbors and relatives heard that the Lord had shown his great mercy to her, and they rejoiced with her.

59 On the eighth day they came to circumcise the child, and they were going to name him Zechariah after his father. 60 But his mother said, "No; he is to be called John." 61 They said to her, "None of your relatives has this name." 62 Then they began

motioning to his father to find out what name he wanted to give him. 63 He asked for a writing tablet and wrote, "His name is John." And all of them were amazed. 64 Immediately his mouth was opened and his tongue freed, and he began to speak, praising God. 65 Fear came over all their neighbors, and all these things were talked about throughout the entire hill country of Judea. 66 All who heard them pondered them and said, "What then will this child become?" For, indeed, the hand of the Lord was with him.

ZECHARIAH'S PROPHECY

67 Then his father Zechariah was filled with the Holy Spirit and spoke this prophecy:
68 "Blessed be the Lord God of Israel,
         for he has looked favorably
         on his people and
         redeemed them.
69 He has raised up a mighty
         savior[b] for us
   in the house of his
         servant David,
70 as he spoke through the
         mouth of his holy
         prophets from of old,
71   that we would be saved from
         our enemies and from the
         hand of all who hate us.
72 Thus he has shown the mercy
         promised to our ancestors,
   and has remembered his
         holy covenant,
73 the oath that he swore to our
         ancestor Abraham,
   to grant us 74 that we, being
         rescued from the hands
         of our enemies,
   might serve him without
         fear, 75 in holiness
         and righteousness
   before him all our days.
76 And you, child, will be called the
         prophet of the Most High;
   for you will go before the Lord
         to prepare his ways,
77 to give knowledge of salvation
         to his people
   by the forgiveness of their sins.

78 By the tender mercy
    of our God,
the dawn from on high
    will break upon[a] us,
79 to give light to those who sit
    in darkness and in the
    shadow of death,
to guide our feet into the
    way of peace."

80 The child grew and became strong in spirit, and he was in the wilderness until the day he appeared publicly to Israel.

THE BIRTH OF JESUS

2 In those days a decree went out from Emperor Augustus that all the world should be registered. ²This was the first registration and was taken while Quirinius was governor of Syria. ³All went to their own towns to be registered. ⁴Joseph also went from the town of Nazareth in Galilee to Judea, to the city of David called Bethlehem, because he was descended from the house and family of David. ⁵He went to be registered with Mary, to whom he was engaged and who was expecting a child. ⁶While they were there, the time came for her to deliver her child. ⁷And she gave birth to her firstborn son and wrapped him in bands of cloth, and laid him in a manger, because there was no place for them in the inn.

THE SHEPHERDS AND THE ANGELS

8 In that region there were shepherds living in the fields, keeping watch over their flock by night. ⁹Then an angel of the Lord stood before them, and the glory of the Lord shone around them, and they were terrified. ¹⁰But the angel said to them, "Do not be afraid; for see—I am bringing you good news of great joy for all the people: ¹¹to you is born this day in the city of David a Savior, who is the Messiah,[b] the Lord. ¹²This will be a sign for you: you will find a child wrapped in bands of cloth and lying in a manger." ¹³And suddenly there was with the angel a multitude of the heavenly host,[c] praising God and saying,

14 "Glory to God in the
    highest heaven,
and on earth peace among
    those whom he favors!"[d]

15 When the angels had left them and gone into heaven, the shepherds said to one another, "Let us go now to Bethlehem and see this thing that has taken place, which the Lord has made known to us." ¹⁶So they went with haste and found Mary and Joseph, and the child lying in the manger. ¹⁷When they saw this, they made known what had been told them about this child; ¹⁸and all who heard it were amazed at what the shepherds told them. ¹⁹But Mary treasured all these words and pondered them in her heart. ²⁰The shepherds returned, glorifying and praising God for all they had heard and seen, as it had been told them.

a 1.78 Other ancient authorities read *has broken upon* b 2.11 Or *the Christ* c 2.13 Gk *army* d 2.14 Other ancient authorities read *peace, goodwill among people*

PONDER

When they saw this, they made known what had been told them about this child; and all who heard it were amazed at what the shepherds told them. But Mary treasured all these words and pondered them in her heart.
—Luke 2.17–19

PRAY

Father, implant more deeply in our own hearts and minds the lessons we learn about the birth of our Savior, Jesus Christ, an event that transformed the world—and transforms us individually. Teach us how to live lives of peace, compassion, forgiveness, service, humility and love, the characteristics of a person filled with your grace and wisdom. Help us to emulate the life of our Savior, Jesus Christ. We ask these things in his name. Amen.

JESUS IS NAMED

21 After eight days had passed, it was time to circumcise the child; and he was called Jesus, the name given by the angel before he was conceived in the womb.

JESUS IS PRESENTED IN THE TEMPLE

22 When the time came for their purification according to the law of Moses, they brought him up to Jerusalem to present him to the Lord 23(as it is written in the law of the Lord, "Every firstborn male shall be designated as holy to the Lord"), 24and they offered a sacrifice according to what is stated in the law of the Lord, "a pair of turtledoves or two young pigeons."

25 Now there was a man in Jerusalem whose name was Simeon;[a] this man was righteous and devout, looking forward to the consolation of Israel, and the Holy Spirit rested on him. 26It had been revealed to him by the Holy Spirit that he would not see death before he had seen the Lord's Messiah.[b] 27Guided by the Spirit, Simeon[c] came into the temple; and when the parents brought in the child Jesus, to do for him what was customary under the law, 28Simeon[d] took him in his arms and praised God, saying,

29 "Master, now you are dismissing
    your servant[e] in peace,
    according to your word;

30 for my eyes have seen
    your salvation,
31 which you have prepared in
    the presence of all peoples,
32 a light for revelation to
    the Gentiles
    and for glory to your
    people Israel."

33 And the child's father and mother were amazed at what was being said about him. 34Then Simeon[a] blessed them and said to his mother Mary, "This child is destined for the falling and the rising of many in Israel, and to be a sign that will be opposed 35so that the inner thoughts of many will be revealed— and a sword will pierce your own soul too."

36 There was also a prophet, Anna[f] the daughter of Phanuel, of the tribe of Asher. She was of a great age, having lived with her husband seven years after her marriage, 37then as a widow to the age of eighty-four. She never left the temple but worshiped there with fasting and prayer night and day. 38At that moment she came, and began to praise God and to speak about the child[g] to all who were looking for the redemption of Jerusalem.

a 2.25,34 Gk *Symeon*   b 2.26 Or *the Lord's Christ*   c 2.27 Gk *In the Spirit, he*   d 2.28 Gk *he*   e 2.29 Gk *slave*   f 2.36 Gk *Hanna*   g 2.38 Gk *him*

⊢ BIBLE IN LIFE ▷

Convenient Faith

Luke 2.38

In the Old Testament, we read prophesies about the Messiah who would redeem Israel— and the Messiah did redeem Israel, but not in the way the people expected. The Jews believed that the Messiah would be a temporal, political leader who would overthrow the Romans' yoke of oppression on the Jewish people and liberate Israel as a nation. Immediately after Jesus' death and resurrection, his disciples felt disappointed (see Luke 24.21). They had hoped that Jesus would be the messiah, the redeemer and leader who would overthrow Rome. They didn't fully comprehend the scriptures but interpreted them selectively. Like the disciples, we tend to read the scriptures with a lens that accommodates our personal, human ambitions. We select those things that we want to remember and that are comfortable for us. We like to deal with people who are just like us. We don't really want to stretch our hearts or minds or confront new challenges that might put a burden on us. We prefer a convenient faith.

THE RETURN TO NAZARETH

39 When they had finished everything required by the law of the Lord, they returned to Galilee, to their own town of Nazareth. 40 The child grew and became strong, filled with wisdom; and the favor of God was upon him.

THE BOY JESUS IN THE TEMPLE

41 Now every year his parents went to Jerusalem for the festival of the Passover. 42 And when he was twelve years old, they went up as usual for the festival. 43 When the festival was ended and they started to return, the boy Jesus stayed behind in Jerusalem, but his parents did not know it. 44 Assuming that he was in the group of travelers, they went a day's journey. Then they started to look for him among their relatives and friends. 45 When they did not find him, they returned to Jerusalem to search for him. 46 After three days they found him in the temple, sitting among the teachers, listening to them and asking them questions. 47 And all who heard him were amazed at his understanding and his answers. 48 When his parents[a] saw him they were astonished; and his mother said to him, "Child, why have you treated us like this? Look, your father and I have been searching for you in great anxiety." 49 He said to them, "Why were you searching for me? Did you not know that I must be in my Father's house?"[b] 50 But they did not understand what he said to them. 51 Then he went down with them and came to Nazareth, and was obedient to them. His mother treasured all these things in her heart.

52 And Jesus increased in wisdom and in years,[c] and in divine and human favor.

THE PROCLAMATION OF JOHN THE BAPTIST

3 In the fifteenth year of the reign of Emperor Tiberius, when Pontius Pilate was governor of Judea, and Herod was ruler[d] of Galilee, and his brother Philip ruler[d] of the region of Ituraea and Trachonitis, and Lysanias ruler[d] of Abilene, 2 during the high priesthood of Annas and Caiaphas, the word of God came to John son of Zechariah in the wilderness. 3 He went into all the region around the Jordan, proclaiming a baptism of repentance for the forgiveness of sins, 4 as it is written in the book of the words of the prophet Isaiah,

"The voice of one crying out
    in the wilderness:
'Prepare the way of the Lord,
    make his paths straight.
5 Every valley shall be filled,
    and every mountain and hill
        shall be made low,
    and the crooked shall be
        made straight,
    and the rough ways
        made smooth;
6 and all flesh shall see the
    salvation of God.' "

7 John said to the crowds that came out to be baptized by him, "You brood of vipers! Who warned you to flee from the wrath to come? 8 Bear fruits worthy of repentance. Do not begin to say to yourselves, 'We have Abraham as our ancestor'; for I tell you, God is able from these stones to raise up children to Abraham. 9 Even now the ax is lying at the root of the trees; every tree therefore that does not bear good fruit is cut down and thrown into the fire."

10 And the crowds asked him, "What then should we do?" 11 In reply he said to them, "Whoever has two coats must share with anyone who has none; and whoever has food must do likewise." 12 Even tax collectors came to be baptized, and they asked him, "Teacher, what should we do?" 13 He said to them, "Collect no more than the amount prescribed for you." 14 Soldiers also asked him, "And we, what should we do?" He said to them, "Do not extort money from anyone by threats or false accusation, and be satisfied with your wages."

15 As the people were filled with expectation, and all were questioning

a 2.48 Gk they   b 2.49 Or be about my Father's interests?   c 2.52 Or in stature
d 3.1 Gk tetrarch

in their hearts concerning John, whether he might be the Messiah,[a] [16]John answered all of them by saying, "I baptize you with water; but one who is more powerful than I is coming; I am not worthy to untie the thong of his sandals. He will baptize you with[b] the Holy Spirit and fire. [17]His winnowing fork is in his hand, to clear his threshing floor and to gather the wheat into his granary; but the chaff he will burn with unquenchable fire."

[18] So, with many other exhortations, he proclaimed the good news to the people. [19]But Herod the ruler,[c] who had been rebuked by him because of Herodias, his brother's wife, and because of all the evil things that Herod had done, [20]added to them all by shutting up John in prison.

THE BAPTISM OF JESUS

[21] Now when all the people were baptized, and when Jesus also had been baptized and was praying, the heaven was opened, [22]and the Holy Spirit descended upon him in bodily form like a dove. And a voice came from heaven, "You are my Son, the Beloved;[d] with you I am well pleased."[e]

THE ANCESTORS OF JESUS

[23] Jesus was about thirty years old when he began his work. He was the son (as was thought) of Joseph son of Heli, [24]son of Matthat, son of Levi, son of Melchi, son of Jannai, son of Joseph, [25]son of Mattathias, son of Amos, son of Nahum, son of Esli, son of Naggai, [26]son of Maath, son of Mattathias, son of Semein, son of Josech, son of Joda, [27]son of Joanan, son of Rhesa, son of Zerubbabel, son of Shealtiel,[f] son of Neri, [28]son of Melchi, son of Addi, son of Cosam, son of Elmadam, son of Er, [29]son of Joshua, son of Eliezer, son of Jorim, son of Matthat, son of Levi, [30]son of Simeon, son of Judah, son of Joseph, son of Jonam, son of Eliakim, [31]son of Melea, son of Menna, son of Mattatha, son of Nathan, son of David, [32]son of Jesse, son of Obed, son of Boaz, son of Sala,[g] son of Nahshon, [33]son of Amminadab, son of Admin, son of Arni,[h] son of Hezron, son of Perez, son of Judah, [34]son of Jacob, son of Isaac, son of Abraham, son of Terah, son of Nahor, [35]son of Serug, son of Reu, son of Peleg, son of Eber, son of Shelah, [36]son of Cainan,

[a] 3.15 Or *the Christ*   [b] 3.16 Or *in*   [c] 3.19 Gk *tetrarch*   [d] 3.22 Or *my beloved Son*
[e] 3.22 Other ancient authorities read *You are my Son, today I have begotten you*
[f] 3.27 Gk *Salathiel*   [g] 3.32 Other ancient authorities read *Salmon*   [h] 3.33 Other ancient authorities read *Amminadab, son of Aram*; others vary widely

---

 BIBLE IN LIFE

Self-Examination

Luke 3.7–14

John the Baptist did not mince words about what God expected from people. His words cut like a knife into the hearts of his original hearers; if we are willing to apply John's message to ourselves, it cuts us to the core as well. John's message was straightforward: Don't think that your heritage gives you special status with God; God's true people are those who demonstrate their repentance by right deeds. If we take John's message seriously, then we will inevitably be led to do some careful self-examination. "Am I proud of my religiosity?" "Do I consider myself superior to others?" "Have I truly repented of my wrong ways and sought to be different?" Perhaps we need to set aside 15 minutes periodically to ask ourselves how well our lives measure up to the mandates of Christ. If we are honest and courageous enough, we'll see that there are many elements of our lives that can be improved. We might harbor some blatant sin, or some sins of omission, or some sins of timidity or dormancy or self-satisfaction, when all we want is to guarantee that our own lives are secure and pleasant. We might list these things on a piece of paper and then ask God to begin to change them, to help stretch our minds and hearts to encompass what God is calling us to do.

son of Arphaxad, son of Shem, son of Noah, son of Lamech, ³⁷son of Methuselah, son of Enoch, son of Jared, son of Mahalaleel, son of Cainan, ³⁸son of Enos, son of Seth, son of Adam, son of God.

THE TEMPTATION OF JESUS

4 Jesus, full of the Holy Spirit, returned from the Jordan and was led by the Spirit in the wilderness, ²where for forty days he was tempted by the devil. He ate nothing at all during those days, and when they were over, he was famished. ³The devil said to him, "If you are the Son of God, command this stone to become a loaf of bread." ⁴Jesus answered him, "It is written, 'One does not live by bread alone.'"

5 Then the devilᵃ led him up and showed him in an instant all the kingdoms of the world. ⁶And the devilᵃ said to him, "To you I will give their glory and all this authority; for it has been given over to me, and I give it to anyone I please. ⁷If you, then, will worship me, it will all be yours." ⁸Jesus answered him, "It is written,

'Worship the Lord your God,
    and serve only him.'"

9 Then the devilᵃ took him to Jerusalem, and placed him on the pinnacle of the temple, saying to him, "If you are the Son of God, throw yourself down from here, ¹⁰for it is written,

'He will command his angels
        concerning you,
    to protect you,'

¹¹and
'On their hands they will
        bear you up,
    so that you will not dash your
        foot against a stone.'"

¹²Jesus answered him, "It is said, 'Do not put the Lord your God to the test.'" ¹³When the devil had finished every test, he departed from him until an opportune time.

THE BEGINNING OF THE GALILEAN MINISTRY

14 Then Jesus, filled with the power of the Spirit, returned to Galilee, and a report about him spread through all the surrounding country. ¹⁵He began to teach in their synagogues and was praised by everyone.

THE REJECTION OF JESUS AT NAZARETH

16 When he came to Nazareth, where he had been brought up, he went to the synagogue on the sabbath day, as was his custom. He stood up to read, ¹⁷and the scroll of the prophet Isaiah was given to him. He unrolled the scroll and found the place where it was written:
¹⁸ "The Spirit of the Lord
        is upon me,
    because he has anointed me
        to bring good news
        to the poor.

ᵃ **4.5,6,9** Gk *he*

⊣├─ **BIBLE IN LIFE** ▷──────────────⊂○⊢

Facing Temptation   Luke 4.1–13

The devil packages his temptations so that they appear quite attractive. Sin is appealing, and we can invent all kinds of rationalizations to take care of our own needs. Yet nothing in Christianity says that faithful believers will be immune from suffering, self-doubt, disappointment, failure, illness or even early death. There's no promise that we'll be more powerful, more influential, more exalted socially, more financially prosperous if we accept Christ as our Savior. Jesus knew this, and he rejected the temptations to alleviate ordinary suffering and to gain political power. During his temptation, Jesus chose to be a suffering, humble servant (see Isaiah 53). Luke 4.1 tells us that Jesus was "full of the Holy Spirit." As we are filled with the Holy Spirit, we can also find the courage to resist the temptations of the devil.

He has sent me to proclaim
    release to the captives
and recovery of sight
    to the blind,
    to let the oppressed go free,
19 to proclaim the year of the
    Lord's favor."

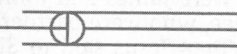

PONDER

"The Spirit of the Lord is upon me,
because he has anointed me to
bring good news to the poor. He has
sent me to proclaim release to the
captives and recovery of sight to the
blind, to let the oppressed go free, to
proclaim the year of the Lord's favor."
—Luke 4.18–19

PRAY

Father, we see the opening of the public
ministry of Christ as he declared that
he was the Messiah and proclaimed
the mission you gave him. Implant in
us the desire to continue his mission
in our own area of ministry. Help us
to avail ourselves of his promises, to
share this message with others and
to allow the presence of the Holy
Spirit to dwell in us. We resolve this
day to accept the mission that you
have given to us, to identify it clearly
and to ever expand it as we grow in
Christ. In his name we pray. Amen.

20 And he rolled up the scroll, gave
it back to the attendant, and sat
down. The eyes of all in the synagogue were fixed on him. 21 Then he
began to say to them, "Today this
scripture has been fulfilled in your
hearing." 22 All spoke well of him
and were amazed at the gracious
words that came from his mouth.
They said, "Is not this Joseph's son?"
23 He said to them, "Doubtless you
will quote to me this proverb, 'Doctor, cure yourself!' And you will say,
'Do here also in your hometown the
things that we have heard you did at
Capernaum.'" 24 And he said, "Truly
I tell you, no prophet is accepted in
the prophet's hometown. 25 But the
truth is, there were many widows in
Israel in the time of Elijah, when the
heaven was shut up three years and
six months, and there was a severe
famine over all the land; 26 yet Elijah was sent to none of them except
to a widow at Zarephath in Sidon.
27 There were also many lepers[a] in
Israel in the time of the prophet Elisha, and none of them was cleansed
except Naaman the Syrian." 28 When
they heard this, all in the synagogue
were filled with rage. 29 They got up,
drove him out of the town, and led
him to the brow of the hill on which
their town was built, so that they
might hurl him off the cliff. 30 But he
passed through the midst of them
and went on his way.

THE MAN WITH AN
UNCLEAN SPIRIT

31 He went down to Capernaum,
a city in Galilee, and was teaching
them on the sabbath. 32 They were
astounded at his teaching, because
he spoke with authority. 33 In the
synagogue there was a man who
had the spirit of an unclean demon,
and he cried out with a loud voice,
34 "Let us alone! What have you to
do with us, Jesus of Nazareth? Have
you come to destroy us? I know who
you are, the Holy One of God." 35 But
Jesus rebuked him, saying, "Be silent, and come out of him!" When
the demon had thrown him down
before them, he came out of him
without having done him any harm.
36 They were all amazed and kept
saying to one another, "What kind
of utterance is this? For with authority and power he commands the
unclean spirits, and out they come!"
37 And a report about him began to
reach every place in the region.

HEALINGS AT SIMON'S HOUSE

38 After leaving the synagogue
he entered Simon's house. Now Simon's mother-in-law was suffering

[a] 4.27 The terms *leper* and *leprosy* can refer
to several diseases

from a high fever, and they asked him about her. 39 Then he stood over her and rebuked the fever, and it left her. Immediately she got up and began to serve them.

40 As the sun was setting, all those who had any who were sick with various kinds of diseases brought them to him; and he laid his hands on each of them and cured them. 41 Demons also came out of many, shouting, "You are the Son of God!" But he rebuked them and would not allow them to speak, because they knew that he was the Messiah.[a]

JESUS PREACHES IN THE SYNAGOGUES

42 At daybreak he departed and went into a deserted place. And the crowds were looking for him; and when they reached him, they wanted to prevent him from leaving them. 43 But he said to them, "I must proclaim the good news of the kingdom of God to the other cities also; for I was sent for this purpose." 44 So he continued proclaiming the message in the synagogues of Judea.[b]

JESUS CALLS THE FIRST DISCIPLES

5 Once while Jesus[c] was standing beside the lake of Gennesaret, and the crowd was pressing in on him to hear the word of God, 2 he saw two boats there at the shore of the lake; the fishermen had gone out of them and were washing their nets. 3 He got into one of the boats, the one belonging to Simon, and asked him to put out a little way from the shore. Then he sat down and taught the crowds from the boat. 4 When he had finished speaking, he said to Simon, "Put out into the deep water and let down your nets for a catch." 5 Simon answered, "Master, we have worked all night long but have caught nothing. Yet if you say so, I will let down the nets." 6 When they had done this, they caught so many fish that their nets were beginning to break. 7 So they signaled their partners in the other boat to come and help them. And they came and

filled both boats, so that they began to sink. 8 But when Simon Peter saw it, he fell down at Jesus' knees, saying, "Go away from me, Lord, for I am a sinful man!" 9 For he and all who were with him were amazed at the catch of fish that they had taken; 10 and so also were James and John, sons of Zebedee, who were partners with Simon. Then Jesus said to Simon, "Do not be afraid; from now on you will be catching people." 11 When they had brought their boats to shore, they left everything and followed him.

JESUS CLEANSES A LEPER

12 Once, when he was in one of the cities, there was a man covered with leprosy.[d] When he saw Jesus, he bowed with his face to the ground and begged him, "Lord, if you choose, you can make me clean." 13 Then Jesus[c] stretched out his hand, touched him, and said, "I do choose. Be made clean." Immediately the leprosy[d] left him. 14 And he ordered him to tell no one. "Go," he said, "and show yourself to the priest, and, as Moses commanded, make an offering for your cleansing, for a testimony to them." 15 But now more than ever the word about Jesus[e] spread abroad; many crowds would gather to hear him and to be cured of their diseases. 16 But he would withdraw to deserted places and pray.

JESUS HEALS A PARALYTIC

17 One day, while he was teaching, Pharisees and teachers of the law were sitting near by (they had come from every village of Galilee and Judea and from Jerusalem); and the power of the Lord was with him to heal.[f] 18 Just then some men came, carrying a paralyzed man on a bed. They were trying to bring him in and lay him before Jesus;[e] 19 but finding no way to bring him in

---

[a] 4.41 Or the Christ [b] 4.44 Other ancient authorities read Galilee [c] 5.1,13 Gk he [d] 5.12,13 The terms leper and leprosy can refer to several diseases [e] 5.15,18 Gk him [f] 5.17 Other ancient authorities read was present to heal them

because of the crowd, they went up on the roof and let him down with his bed through the tiles into the middle of the crowd[a] in front of Jesus. 20When he saw their faith, he said, "Friend,[b] your sins are forgiven you." 21Then the scribes and the Pharisees began to question, "Who is this who is speaking blasphemies? Who can forgive sins but God alone?" 22When Jesus perceived their questionings, he answered them, "Why do you raise such questions in your hearts? 23Which is easier, to say, 'Your sins are forgiven you,' or to say, 'Stand up and walk'? 24But so that you may know that the Son of Man has authority on earth to forgive sins"—he said to the one who was paralyzed—"I say to you, stand up and take your bed and go to your home." 25Immediately he stood up before them, took what he had been lying on, and went to his home, glorifying God. 26Amazement seized all of them, and they glorified God and were filled with awe, saying, "We have seen strange things today."

JESUS CALLS LEVI

27 After this he went out and saw a tax collector named Levi, sitting at the tax booth; and he said to him, "Follow me." 28And he got up, left everything, and followed him.

29 Then Levi gave a great banquet for him in his house; and there was a large crowd of tax collectors and others sitting at the table[c] with them. 30The Pharisees and their scribes were complaining to his disciples, saying, "Why do you eat and drink with tax collectors and sinners?" 31Jesus answered, "Those who are well have no need of a physician, but those who are sick; 32I have come to call not the righteous but sinners to repentance."

THE QUESTION ABOUT FASTING

33 Then they said to him, "John's disciples, like the disciples of the Pharisees, frequently fast and pray, but your disciples eat and drink." 34Jesus said to them, "You cannot make wedding guests fast while the bridegroom is with them, can you? 35The days will come when the bridegroom will be taken away from them, and then they will fast in those days." 36He also told them a parable: "No one tears a piece from a new garment and sews it on an old garment; otherwise the new will be torn, and the piece from the new will not match the old. 37And no one puts new wine into old wineskins; otherwise the new wine will burst the skins and will be spilled, and the skins will be destroyed. 38But new wine must be put into fresh wineskins. 39And no one after drinking old wine desires new wine, but says, 'The old is good.'"[d]

THE QUESTION ABOUT THE SABBATH

6 One sabbath[e] while Jesus[f] was going through the grainfields, his disciples plucked some heads of grain, rubbed them in their hands, and ate them. 2But some of the Pharisees said, "Why are you doing what is not lawful[g] on the sabbath?" 3Jesus answered, "Have you not read what David did when he and his companions were hungry? 4He entered the house of God and took and ate the bread of the Presence, which it is not lawful for any but the priests to eat, and gave some to his companions?" 5Then he said to them, "The Son of Man is lord of the sabbath."

THE MAN WITH A WITHERED HAND

6 On another sabbath he entered the synagogue and taught, and there was a man there whose right hand was withered. 7The scribes and the Pharisees watched him to see whether he would cure on the sabbath, so that they might find an accusation against him. 8Even though he knew what they were thinking, he said to the man who had the withered hand, "Come and stand

---

[a] 5.19 Gk into the midst   [b] 5.20 Gk Man
[c] 5.29 Gk reclining   [d] 5.39 Other ancient authorities read better; others lack verse 39   [e] 6.1 Other ancient authorities read On the second first sabbath   [f] 6.1 Gk he
[g] 6.2 Other ancient authorities add to do

here." He got up and stood there. 9 Then Jesus said to them, "I ask you, is it lawful to do good or to do harm on the sabbath, to save life or to destroy it?" 10 After looking around at all of them, he said to him, "Stretch out your hand." He did so, and his hand was restored. 11 But they were filled with fury and discussed with one another what they might do to Jesus.

JESUS CHOOSES THE TWELVE APOSTLES

12 Now during those days he went out to the mountain to pray; and he spent the night in prayer to God. 13 And when day came, he called his disciples and chose twelve of them, whom he also named apostles: 14 Simon, whom he named Peter, and his brother Andrew, and James, and John, and Philip, and Bartholomew, 15 and Matthew, and Thomas, and James son of Alphaeus, and Simon, who was called the Zealot, 16 and Judas son of James, and Judas Iscariot, who became a traitor.

JESUS TEACHES AND HEALS

17 He came down with them and stood on a level place, with a great crowd of his disciples and a great multitude of people from all Judea, Jerusalem, and the coast of Tyre and Sidon. 18 They had come to hear him and to be healed of their diseases; and those who were troubled with unclean spirits were cured. 19 And all in the crowd were trying to touch him, for power came out from him and healed all of them.

BLESSINGS AND WOES

20 Then he looked up at his disciples and said:
"Blessed are you who are poor,
for yours is the kingdom
of God.
21 "Blessed are you who are
hungry now,
for you will be filled.
"Blessed are you who weep now,
for you will laugh.
22 "Blessed are you when people hate you, and when they exclude you, revile you, and defame you[a] on

account of the Son of Man. 23 Rejoice in that day and leap for joy, for surely your reward is great in heaven; for that is what their ancestors did to the prophets.
24 "But woe to you who are rich,
for you have received
your consolation.
25 "Woe to you who are full now,
for you will be hungry.
"Woe to you who are
laughing now,
for you will mourn and weep.
26 "Woe to you when all speak well of you, for that is what their ancestors did to the false prophets.

LOVE FOR ENEMIES

27 "But I say to you that listen, Love your enemies, do good to those who hate you, 28 bless those who curse you, pray for those who abuse you. 29 If anyone strikes you on the cheek, offer the other also; and from anyone who takes away your coat do not withhold even your shirt. 30 Give to everyone who begs from you; and if anyone takes away your goods, do not ask for them again. 31 Do to others as you would have them do to you.
32 "If you love those who love you, what credit is that to you? For even sinners love those who love them. 33 If you do good to those who do good to you, what credit is that to you? For even sinners do the same. 34 If you lend to those from whom you hope to receive, what credit is that to you? Even sinners lend to sinners, to receive as much again. 35 But love your enemies, do good, and lend, expecting nothing in return.[b] Your reward will be great, and you will be children of the Most High; for he is kind to the ungrateful and the wicked. 36 Be merciful, just as your Father is merciful.

JUDGING OTHERS

37 "Do not judge, and you will not be judged; do not condemn, and you will not be condemned. Forgive, and you will be forgiven; 38 give, and it

a 6.22 Gk cast out your name as evil
b 6.35 Other ancient authorities read despairing of no one

will be given to you. A good measure, pressed down, shaken together, running over, will be put into your lap; for the measure you give will be the measure you get back."

39 He also told them a parable: "Can a blind person guide a blind person? Will not both fall into a pit? 40 A disciple is not above the teacher, but everyone who is fully qualified will be like the teacher. 41 Why do you see the speck in your neighbor's[a] eye, but do not notice the log in your own eye? 42 Or how can you say to your neighbor,[b] 'Friend,[b] let me take out the speck in your eye,' when you yourself do not see the log in your own eye? You hypocrite, first take the log out of your own eye, and then you will see clearly to take the speck out of your neighbor's[a] eye.

JESUS COMMANDS US
TO EXAMINE OURSELVES
AND NOT OTHERS.

A TREE AND ITS FRUIT
43 "No good tree bears bad fruit, nor again does a bad tree bear good fruit; 44 for each tree is known by its own fruit. Figs are not gathered from thorns, nor are grapes picked from a bramble bush. 45 The good person out of the good treasure of the heart produces good, and the evil person out of evil treasure produces evil; for it is out of the abundance of the heart that the mouth speaks.

THE TWO FOUNDATIONS
46 "Why do you call me 'Lord, Lord,' and do not do what I tell you? 47 I will show you what someone is like who comes to me, hears my words, and acts on them. 48 That one is like a man building a house, who dug deeply and laid the foundation on rock; when a flood arose, the river burst against that house but could not shake it, because it had been well built.[c] 49 But the one who hears and does not act is like a man who built a house on the ground without a foundation. When the river burst against it, immediately it fell, and great was the ruin of that house."

JESUS HEALS A CENTURION'S SERVANT
7 After Jesus[d] had finished all his sayings in the hearing of the

[a] 6.41,42 Gk brother's   [b] 6.42 Gk brother
[c] 6.48 Other ancient authorities read founded upon the rock   [d] 7.1 Gk he

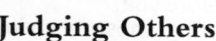

BIBLE IN LIFE

Judging Others
Luke 6.37

One of the things Jesus is known for saying is, "Do not judge, and you will not be judged." That's a very difficult thing for us to apply. We have a tendency to judge others, viewing them almost always as inferior to us. It's a natural human trait of which we're all guilty. We each say to ourselves something like, "The way I do things is the proper way, and the way someone else does something is inferior to me." Christ tells us not to do that. This statement of Jesus' closely correlates with Romans 3.23, which reads, "All have sinned and fall short of the glory of God." All of us are sinners—we can't say someone else is more sinful than we are. We are to let God be the judge of that. Instead, we can carefully evaluate our own position: We are all sinners, and God cannot accept sinfulness. But through Christ's grace and truth, we can be forgiven and become children of God. As children, we share Christ's righteousness and equality with others, which ought to eliminate all the discrimination that sometimes is endorsed by the church. We discriminate against women in the church, against people who are African American or against folks who are foreigners—even though Christ says all of us are equal as children of God.

people, he entered Capernaum. ²A centurion there had a slave whom he valued highly, and who was ill and close to death. ³When he heard about Jesus, he sent some Jewish elders to him, asking him to come and heal his slave. ⁴When they came to Jesus, they appealed to him earnestly, saying, "He is worthy of having you do this for him, ⁵for he loves our people, and it is he who built our synagogue for us." ⁶And Jesus went with them, but when he was not far from the house, the centurion sent friends to say to him, "Lord, do not trouble yourself, for I am not worthy to have you come under my roof; ⁷therefore I did not presume to come to you. But only speak the word, and let my servant be healed. ⁸For I also am a man set under authority, with soldiers under me; and I say to one, 'Go,' and he goes, and to another, 'Come,' and he comes, and to my slave, 'Do this,' and the slave does it." ⁹When Jesus heard this he was amazed at him, and turning to the crowd that followed him, he said, "I tell you, not even in Israel have I found such faith." ¹⁰When those who had been sent returned to the house, they found the slave in good health.

JESUS RAISES THE WIDOW'S SON AT NAIN

11 Soon afterwards[a] he went to a town called Nain, and his disciples and a large crowd went with him. ¹²As he approached the gate of the town, a man who had died was being carried out. He was his mother's only son, and she was a widow; and with her was a large crowd from the town. ¹³When the Lord saw her, he had compassion for her and said to her, "Do not weep." ¹⁴Then he came forward and touched the bier, and the bearers stood still. And he said, "Young man, I say to you, rise!" ¹⁵The dead man sat up and began to speak, and Jesus[b] gave him to his mother. ¹⁶Fear seized all of them; and they glorified God, saying, "A great prophet has risen among us!" and "God has looked favorably on his people!" ¹⁷This word about him spread throughout Judea and all the surrounding country.

MESSENGERS FROM JOHN THE BAPTIST

18 The disciples of John reported all these things to him. So John summoned two of his disciples ¹⁹and sent them to the Lord to ask, "Are you the one who is to come, or are we to wait for another?" ²⁰When the men had come to him, they said, "John the Baptist has sent us to you to ask, 'Are you the one who is to come, or are we to wait for another?'" ²¹Jesus[c] had just then cured many people of diseases, plagues, and evil spirits, and had given sight to many who were blind. ²²And he answered them, "Go and tell John what you have seen and heard: the blind receive their sight, the lame walk, the lepers[d] are cleansed, the deaf hear, the dead are raised, the poor have good news brought to them. ²³And blessed is anyone who takes no offense at me."

24 When John's messengers had gone, Jesus[b] began to speak to the crowds about John:[e] "What did you go out into the wilderness to look at? A reed shaken by the wind? ²⁵What then did you go out to see? Someone[f] dressed in soft robes? Look, those who put on fine clothing and live in luxury are in royal palaces. ²⁶What then did you go out to see? A prophet? Yes, I tell you, and more than a prophet. ²⁷This is the one about whom it is written,

'See, I am sending my messenger
        ahead of you,
who will prepare your
        way before you.'

²⁸I tell you, among those born of women no one is greater than John; yet the least in the kingdom of God is greater than he." ²⁹(And all the people who heard this, including the tax collectors, acknowledged the justice of God,[g] because they had been baptized with John's baptism. ³⁰But by refusing to be baptized by him,

a 7.11 Other ancient authorities read Next day   b 7.15,24 Gk he   c 7.21 Gk He   d 7.22 The terms leper and leprosy can refer to several diseases   e 7.24 Gk him   f 7.25 Or Why then did you go out? To see someone   g 7.29 Or praised God

the Pharisees and the lawyers rejected God's purpose for themselves.) 31 "To what then will I compare the people of this generation, and what are they like? 32 They are like children sitting in the marketplace and calling to one another,

'We played the flute for you,
and you did not dance;
we wailed, and you
did not weep.'

33 For John the Baptist has come eating no bread and drinking no wine, and you say, 'He has a demon'; 34 the Son of Man has come eating and drinking, and you say, 'Look, a glutton and a drunkard, a friend of tax collectors and sinners!' 35 Nevertheless, wisdom is vindicated by all her children."

A SINFUL WOMAN FORGIVEN

36 One of the Pharisees asked Jesus[a] to eat with him, and he went into the Pharisee's house and took his place at the table. 37 And a woman in the city, who was a sinner, having learned that he was eating in the Pharisee's house, brought an alabaster jar of ointment. 38 She stood behind him at his feet, weeping, and began to bathe his feet with her tears and to dry them with her hair. Then she continued kissing his feet and anointing them with the ointment. 39 Now when the Pharisee who had invited him saw it, he said to himself, "If this man were a prophet, he would have known who and what kind of woman this is who is touching him—that she is a sinner." 40 Jesus spoke up and said to him, "Simon, I have something to say to you." "Teacher," he replied, "speak." 41 "A certain creditor had two debtors; one owed five hundred denarii,[b] and the other fifty. 42 When they could not pay, he canceled the debts for both of them. Now which of them will love him more?" 43 Simon answered, "I suppose the one for whom he canceled the greater debt." And Jesus[c] said to him, "You have judged rightly." 44 Then turning toward the woman, he said to Simon, "Do you see this woman? I entered your house; you gave me no water for my feet, but she has bathed my feet with her tears and dried them with her hair. 45 You gave me no kiss, but from the time I came in she has not stopped kissing my feet. 46 You did not anoint my head with oil, but she has anointed my feet with ointment. 47 Therefore, I tell you, her sins, which were many, have been forgiven; hence she has shown great love. But the one to whom little is forgiven, loves little." 48 Then he said to her, "Your sins are forgiven." 49 But those who were at the table with him began to say among themselves, "Who is this who even forgives sins?" 50 And he said to the woman, "Your faith has saved you; go in peace."

SOME WOMEN ACCOMPANY JESUS

8 Soon afterwards he went on through cities and villages,

[a] 7.36 Gk him [b] 7.41 The denarius was the usual day's wage for a laborer [c] 7.43 Gk he

PONDER

"Therefore, I tell you, her sins, which were many, have been forgiven; hence she has shown great love. But the one to whom little is forgiven, loves little." Then he said to her, "Your sins are forgiven."
—Luke 7.47–48

PRAY

O Father, as we read this vivid story given to us by Luke about our Savior, Jesus Christ, his human nature, and the interesting things that he said and did, this account brings to our hearts and minds the true meaning of a Christian faith—a faith based on love, generosity and forgiveness. Help us to love Jesus freely as this woman did; we honor you and thank you that we are forgiven through our faith in Jesus Christ. In his name we pray. Amen.

proclaiming and bringing the good news of the kingdom of God. The twelve were with him, 2as well as some women who had been cured of evil spirits and infirmities: Mary, called Magdalene, from whom seven demons had gone out, 3and Joanna, the wife of Herod's steward Chuza, and Susanna, and many others, who provided for them[a] out of their resources.

THE PARABLE OF THE SOWER

4 When a great crowd gathered and people from town after town came to him, he said in a parable: 5"A sower went out to sow his seed; and as he sowed, some fell on the path and was trampled on, and the birds of the air ate it up. 6Some fell on the rock; and as it grew up, it withered for lack of moisture. 7Some fell among thorns, and the thorns grew with it and choked it. 8Some fell into good soil, and when it grew, it produced a hundredfold." As he said this, he called out, "Let anyone with ears to hear listen!"

THE PURPOSE OF THE PARABLES

9 Then his disciples asked him what this parable meant. 10He said, "To you it has been given to know the secrets[b] of the kingdom of God; but to others I speak[c] in parables, so that

'looking they may not perceive,
and listening they may
not understand.'

THE PARABLE OF THE SOWER EXPLAINED

11 "Now the parable is this: The seed is the word of God. 12The ones on the path are those who have heard; then the devil comes and takes away the word from their hearts, so that they may not believe and be saved. 13The ones on the rock are those who, when they hear the word, receive it with joy. But these have no root; they believe only for a while and in a time of testing fall away. 14As for what fell among the thorns, these are the ones who hear; but as they go on their way, they are choked by the cares and riches

and pleasures of life, and their fruit does not mature. 15But as for that in the good soil, these are the ones who, when they hear the word, hold it fast in an honest and good heart, and bear fruit with patient endurance.

A LAMP UNDER A JAR

16 "No one after lighting a lamp hides it under a jar, or puts it under a bed, but puts it on a lampstand, so that those who enter may see the light. 17For nothing is hidden that will not be disclosed, nor is anything secret that will not become known and come to light. 18Then pay attention to how you listen; for to those who have, more will be given; and from those who do not have, even what they seem to have will be taken away."

THE TRUE KINDRED OF JESUS

19 Then his mother and his brothers came to him, but they could not reach him because of the crowd. 20And he was told, "Your mother and your brothers are standing outside, wanting to see you." 21But he said to them, "My mother and my brothers are those who hear the word of God and do it."

JESUS CALMS A STORM

22 One day he got into a boat with his disciples, and he said to them, "Let us go across to the other side of the lake." So they put out, 23and while they were sailing he fell asleep. A windstorm swept down on the lake, and the boat was filling with water, and they were in danger. 24They went to him and woke him up, shouting, "Master, Master, we are perishing!" And he woke up and rebuked the wind and the raging waves; they ceased, and there was a calm. 25He said to them, "Where is your faith?" They were afraid and amazed, and said to one another, "Who then is this, that he commands even the winds and the water, and they obey him?"

a 8.3 Other ancient authorities read him
b 8.10 Or mysteries c 8.10 Gk lacks I speak

JESUS HEALS THE
GERASENE DEMONIAC

26 Then they arrived at the country of the Gerasenes,[a] which is opposite Galilee. 27 As he stepped out on land, a man of the city who had demons met him. For a long time he had worn[b] no clothes, and he did not live in a house but in the tombs. 28 When he saw Jesus, he fell down before him and shouted at the top of his voice, "What have you to do with me, Jesus, Son of the Most High God? I beg you, do not torment me"— 29 for Jesus[c] had commanded the unclean spirit to come out of the man. (For many times it had seized him; he was kept under guard and bound with chains and shackles, but he would break the bonds and be driven by the demon into the wilds.) 30 Jesus then asked him, "What is your name?" He said, "Legion"; for many demons had entered him. 31 They begged him not to order them to go back into the abyss.

32 Now there on the hillside a large herd of swine was feeding; and the demons[d] begged Jesus[e] to let them enter these. So he gave them permission. 33 Then the demons came out of the man and entered the swine, and the herd rushed down the steep bank into the lake and was drowned.

34 When the swineherds saw what had happened, they ran off and told it in the city and in the country. 35 Then people came out to see what had happened, and when they came to Jesus, they found the man from whom the demons had gone sitting at the feet of Jesus, clothed and in his right mind. And they were afraid. 36 Those who had seen it told them how the one who had been possessed by demons had been healed. 37 Then all the people of the surrounding country of the Gerasenes[a] asked Jesus[e] to leave them; for they were seized with great fear. So he got into the boat and returned. 38 The man from whom the demons had gone begged that he might be with him; but Jesus[c] sent him away, saying, 39 "Return to your home, and declare how much God has done for you." So he went away, proclaiming throughout the city how much Jesus had done for him.

A GIRL RESTORED TO LIFE
AND A WOMAN HEALED

40 Now when Jesus returned, the crowd welcomed him, for they were all waiting for him. 41 Just then there came a man named Jairus, a leader of the synagogue. He fell at Jesus' feet and begged him to come to his house, 42 for he had an only daughter, about twelve years old, who was dying.

As he went, the crowds pressed in on him. 43 Now there was a woman who had been suffering from hemorrhages for twelve years; and though she had spent all she had on physicians,[f] no one could cure her. 44 She came up behind him and touched the fringe of his clothes, and immediately her hemorrhage stopped. 45 Then Jesus asked, "Who touched me?" When all denied it, Peter[g] said, "Master, the crowds surround you and press in on you." 46 But Jesus said, "Someone touched me; for I noticed that power had gone out from me." 47 When the woman saw that she could not remain hidden, she came trembling; and falling down before him, she declared in the presence of all the people why she had touched him, and how she had been immediately healed. 48 He said to her, "Daughter, your faith has made you well; go in peace."

49 While he was still speaking, someone came from the leader's house to say, "Your daughter is dead; do not trouble the teacher any longer." 50 When Jesus heard this, he replied, "Do not fear. Only believe, and she will be saved." 51 When he came to the house, he did not allow anyone to enter with him, except Peter, John, and James, and the child's father and

---

a 8.26,37 Other ancient authorities read *Gadarenes*; others, *Gergesenes* b 8.27 Other ancient authorities read *a man of the city who had had demons for a long time met him. He wore* c 8.29,38 Gk *he* d 8.32 Gk *they* e 8.32,37 Gk *him* f 8.43 Other ancient authorities lack *and though she had spent all she had on physicians* g 8.45 Other ancient authorities add *and those who were with him*

mother. 52They were all weeping and wailing for her; but he said, "Do not weep; for she is not dead but sleeping." 53And they laughed at him, knowing that she was dead. 54But he took her by the hand and called out, "Child, get up!" 55Her spirit returned, and she got up at once. Then he directed them to give her something to eat. 56Her parents were astounded; but he ordered them to tell no one what had happened.

THE MISSION OF THE TWELVE

9 Then Jesus[a] called the twelve together and gave them power and authority over all demons and to cure diseases, 2and he sent them out to proclaim the kingdom of God and to heal. 3He said to them, "Take nothing for your journey, no staff, nor bag, nor bread, nor money— not even an extra tunic. 4Whatever house you enter, stay there, and leave from there. 5Wherever they do not welcome you, as you are leaving that town shake the dust off your feet as a testimony against them." 6They departed and went through the villages, bringing the good news and curing diseases everywhere.

HEROD'S PERPLEXITY

7 Now Herod the ruler[b] heard about all that had taken place, and he was perplexed, because it was said by some that John had been raised from the dead, 8by some that Elijah had appeared, and by others that one of the ancient prophets had arisen. 9Herod said, "John I beheaded; but who is this about whom I hear such things?" And he tried to see him.

FEEDING THE FIVE THOUSAND

10 On their return the apostles told Jesus[c] all they had done. He took them with him and withdrew privately to a city called Bethsaida. 11When the crowds found out about it, they followed him; and he welcomed them, and spoke to them about the kingdom of God, and healed those who needed to be cured.

12 The day was drawing to a close, and the twelve came to him and said, "Send the crowd away, so that they may go into the surrounding villages and countryside, to lodge and get provisions; for we are here in a deserted place." 13But he said to them, "You give them something to eat." They said, "We have no more than five loaves and two fish— unless we are to go and buy food for

a 9.1 Gk he   b 9.7 Gk tetrarch
c 9.10 Gk him

┼ BIBLE IN LIFE ▷

Responding to Christ   Luke 8.40–56

Three stigmas separated a devout Jew from the temple and from worship: leprosy, contact with a dead person and an issue of blood. The woman who had suffered from menstrual bleeding for 12 years was an outcast, prohibited from worshiping with her own people, even alienated from all her friends and acquaintances, because if anyone touched her, that person would become unclean too. By even being in the crowd surrounding Jesus, she was violating the law of that time, because she was not supposed to touch anybody. This desperate woman knew about Jesus, had a tremendous amount of faith and desired a personal encounter with Christ, believing in his healing power. She came to Christ in faith, and her life was transformed. How will we respond to Christ? We may not be overt outcasts or lawbreakers, but we all have sin in our lives that separates us from God. Will we humble ourselves enough to admit that we're sinful, and will we approach Christ in faith for healing? No matter what our sins may be, if we have faith in Christ, he will take the punishment, making us as white as snow (see Isaiah 1.18), as though we had never sinned. And we will have life abundant on this earth and life eternal in the presence of Christ who heals us.

all these people." [14]For there were about five thousand men. And he said to his disciples, "Make them sit down in groups of about fifty each." [15]They did so and made them all sit down. [16]And taking the five loaves and the two fish, he looked up to heaven, and blessed and broke them, and gave them to the disciples to set before the crowd. [17]And all ate and were filled. What was left over was gathered up, twelve baskets of broken pieces.

TO BE A "LIVING SACRIFICE"

IS TO ORIENT OURSELVES

CONSTANTLY TO JESUS CHRIST.

IT IS NOT AN ACHIEVEMENT,

BUT A DAILY WORK.

PETER'S DECLARATION ABOUT JESUS

[18]Once when Jesus[a] was praying alone, with only the disciples near him, he asked them, "Who do the crowds say that I am?" [19]They answered, "John the Baptist; but others, Elijah; and still others, that one of the ancient prophets has arisen." [20]He said to them, "But who do you say that I am?" Peter answered, "The Messiah[b] of God."

JESUS FORETELLS HIS DEATH AND RESURRECTION

[21]He sternly ordered and commanded them not to tell anyone, [22]saying, "The Son of Man must undergo great suffering, and be rejected by the elders, chief priests, and scribes, and be killed, and on the third day be raised."

[23]Then he said to them all, "If any want to become my followers, let them deny themselves and take up their cross daily and follow me. [24]For those who want to save their life will lose it, and those who lose their life

for my sake will save it. [25]What does it profit them if they gain the whole world, but lose or forfeit themselves? [26]Those who are ashamed of me and of my words, of them the Son of Man will be ashamed when he comes in his glory and the glory of the Father and of the holy angels. [27]But truly I tell you, there are some standing here who will not taste death before they see the kingdom of God."

THE TRANSFIGURATION

[28]Now about eight days after these sayings Jesus[a] took with him Peter and John and James, and went up on the mountain to pray. [29]And while he was praying, the appearance of his face changed, and his clothes became dazzling white. [30]Suddenly they saw two men, Moses and Elijah, talking to him. [31]They appeared in glory and were speaking of his departure, which he was about to accomplish at Jerusalem. [32]Now Peter and his companions were weighed down with sleep; but since they had stayed awake,[c] they saw his glory and the two men who stood with him. [33]Just as they were leaving him, Peter said to Jesus, "Master, it is good for us to be here; let us make three dwellings,[d] one for you, one for Moses, and one for Elijah"—not knowing what he said. [34]While he was saying this, a cloud came and overshadowed them; and they were terrified as they entered the cloud. [35]Then from the cloud came a voice that said, "This is my Son, my Chosen;[e] listen to him!" [36]When the voice had spoken, Jesus was found alone. And they kept silent and in those days told no one any of the things they had seen.

JESUS HEALS A BOY WITH A DEMON

[37]On the next day, when they had come down from the mountain, a great crowd met him. [38]Just then a man from the crowd shouted,

[a] 9.18,28 Gk he   [b] 9.20 Or The Christ
[c] 9.32 Or but when they were fully awake
[d] 9.33 Or tents   [e] 9.35 Other ancient authorities read my Beloved

"Teacher, I beg you to look at my son; he is my only child. 39Suddenly a spirit seizes him, and all at once he[a] shrieks. It convulses him until he foams at the mouth; it mauls him and will scarcely leave him. 40I begged your disciples to cast it out, but they could not." 41Jesus answered, "You faithless and perverse generation, how much longer must I be with you and bear with you? Bring your son here." 42While he was coming, the demon dashed him to the ground in convulsions. But Jesus rebuked the unclean spirit, healed the boy, and gave him back to his father. 43And all were astounded at the greatness of God.

JESUS AGAIN FORETELLS HIS DEATH

While everyone was amazed at all that he was doing, he said to his disciples, 44"Let these words sink into your ears: The Son of Man is going to be betrayed into human hands." 45But they did not understand this saying; its meaning was concealed from them, so that they could not perceive it. And they were afraid to ask him about this saying.

TRUE GREATNESS

46 An argument arose among them as to which one of them was the greatest. 47But Jesus, aware of their inner thoughts, took a little child and put it by his side, 48and said to them, "Whoever welcomes this child in my name welcomes me, and whoever welcomes me welcomes the one who sent me; for the least among all of you is the greatest."

ANOTHER EXORCIST

49 John answered, "Master, we saw someone casting out demons in your name, and we tried to stop him, because he does not follow with us." 50But Jesus said to him, "Do not stop him; for whoever is not against you is for you."

A SAMARITAN VILLAGE REFUSES TO RECEIVE JESUS

51When the days drew near for him to be taken up, he set his face to go to Jerusalem. 52And he sent messengers ahead of him. On their way they entered a village of the Samaritans to make ready for him; 53but they did not receive him, because his face was set toward Jerusalem. 54When his disciples James and John saw it, they said, "Lord, do you want us to command fire to come down from heaven and consume them?"[b] 55But he turned and rebuked them. 56Then[c] they went on to another village.

WOULD-BE FOLLOWERS OF JESUS

57 As they were going along the road, someone said to him, "I will follow you wherever you go." 58And Jesus said to him, "Foxes have holes, and birds of the air have nests; but the Son of Man has nowhere to lay his head." 59To another he said, "Follow me." But he said, "Lord, first let me go and bury my father." 60But Jesus[d] said to him, "Let the dead bury their own dead; but as for you, go and proclaim the kingdom of God." 61Another said, "I will follow you, Lord; but let me first say farewell to those at my home." 62Jesus said to him, "No one who puts a hand to the plow and looks back is fit for the kingdom of God."

THE MISSION OF THE SEVENTY

10 After this the Lord appointed seventy[e] others and sent them on ahead of him in pairs to every town and place where he himself intended to go. 2He said to them, "The harvest is plentiful, but the laborers are few; therefore ask the Lord of the harvest to send out laborers into his harvest. 3Go on your way. See, I am sending you out like lambs into the midst of wolves. 4Carry no purse, no bag, no sandals; and greet no one on the road. 5Whatever house you enter, first say, 'Peace to this house!' 6And if anyone is there who

a 9.39 Or it   b 9.54 Other ancient authorities add as Elijah did   c 9.56 Other ancient authorities read rebuked them, and said, "You do not know what spirit you are of, 56for the Son of Man has not come to destroy the lives of human beings but to save them." Then   d 9.60 Gk he   e 10.1 Other ancient authorities read seventy-two

shares in peace, your peace will rest on that person; but if not, it will return to you. ⁷Remain in the same house, eating and drinking whatever they provide, for the laborer deserves to be paid. Do not move about from house to house. ⁸Whenever you enter a town and its people welcome you, eat what is set before you; ⁹cure the sick who are there, and say to them, 'The kingdom of God has come near to you.'ᵃ ¹⁰But whenever you enter a town and they do not welcome you, go out into its streets and say, ¹¹'Even the dust of your town that clings to our feet, we wipe off in protest against you. Yet know this: the kingdom of God has come near.'ᵇ ¹²I tell you, on that day it will be more tolerable for Sodom than for that town.

WOES TO UNREPENTANT CITIES

13 "Woe to you, Chorazin! Woe to you, Bethsaida! For if the deeds of power done in you had been done in Tyre and Sidon, they would have repented long ago, sitting in sackcloth and ashes. ¹⁴But at the judgment it will be more tolerable for Tyre and Sidon than for you. ¹⁵And you, Capernaum,
will you be exalted to heaven?
No, you will be brought
down to Hades.
16 "Whoever listens to you listens to me, and whoever rejects you rejects me, and whoever rejects me rejects the one who sent me."

THE RETURN OF THE SEVENTY

17 The seventyᶜ returned with joy, saying, "Lord, in your name even the demons submit to us!" ¹⁸He said to them, "I watched Satan fall from heaven like a flash of lightning. ¹⁹See, I have given you authority to tread on snakes and scorpions, and over all the power of the enemy; and nothing will hurt you. ²⁰Nevertheless, do not rejoice at this, that the spirits submit to you, but rejoice that your names are written in heaven."

JESUS REJOICES

21 At that same hour Jesusᵈ rejoiced in the Holy Spiritᵉ and said, "I thankᶠ you, Father, Lord of heaven and earth, because you have hidden these things from the wise and the intelligent and have revealed them to infants; yes, Father, for such was your gracious will.ᵍ ²²All things have been handed over to me by my Father; and no one knows who the Son is except the Father, or who the Father is except the Son and

---

ᵃ 10.9 Or is at hand for you   ᵇ 10.11 Or is at hand   ᶜ 10.17 Other ancient authorities read seventy-two   ᵈ 10.21 Gk he   ᵉ 10.21 Other authorities read in the spirit   ᶠ 10.21 Or praise   ᵍ 10.21 Or for so it was well-pleasing in your sight

---

BIBLE IN LIFE

Jesus' Standards for Success   Luke 9.58

It is virtually a universal trait of human beings to measure ourselves and our success by the world's standards. We ask these questions of ourselves: What has been the purpose of my life? How do my achievements measure up to others'? What has distinguished me from others in life? How am I faring financially? Yet these kinds of questions are all rooted in human measurements for success. If we are followers of Christ, our lives should constantly be assessed by Jesus' standards. We should be striving to make his priorities our priorities and to value what he values. How large was Jesus' bank account while he was on earth? What kind of house did he have? How was he regarded by the leaders and other people of influence and power? If we assessed Jesus' life by the same standards that we tend to use for ourselves, he wouldn't fare well. Yet, of course, his life was infinitely successful because he carried out his Father's will perfectly and revolutionized human history. How can we begin to live by Jesus' standards for success? The first step is to understand his priorities and values. We internalize his standards by reading scripture, praying, and learning about him from other believers. The second step is to examine consciously our standards and values and then ask God to help us adopt Jesus' standards instead.

anyone to whom the Son chooses to reveal him."

23 Then turning to the disciples, Jesus[a] said to them privately, "Blessed are the eyes that see what you see! **24** For I tell you that many prophets and kings desired to see what you see, but did not see it, and to hear what you hear, but did not hear it."

THE PARABLE OF THE GOOD SAMARITAN

25 Just then a lawyer stood up to test Jesus.[b] "Teacher," he said, "what must I do to inherit eternal life?" **26** He said to him, "What is written in the law? What do you read there?" **27** He answered, "You shall love the Lord your God with all your heart, and with all your soul, and with all your strength, and with all your mind; and your neighbor as yourself." **28** And he said to him, "You have given the right answer; do this, and you will live."

29 But wanting to justify himself, he asked Jesus, "And who is my neighbor?" **30** Jesus replied, "A man was going down from Jerusalem to Jericho, and fell into the hands of robbers, who stripped him, beat him, and went away, leaving him half dead. **31** Now by chance a priest was going down that road; and when he saw him, he passed by on the other side. **32** So likewise a Levite, when he came to the place and saw him, passed by on the other side. **33** But a Samaritan while traveling came near him; and when he saw him,

he was moved with pity. **34** He went to him and bandaged his wounds, having poured oil and wine on them. Then he put him on his own animal, brought him to an inn, and took care of him. **35** The next day he took out two denarii,[c] gave them to the innkeeper, and said, 'Take care of him; and when I come back, I will repay you whatever more you spend.' **36** Which of these three, do you think, was a neighbor to the man who fell into the hands of the robbers?" **37** He said, "The one who showed him mercy." Jesus said to him, "Go and do likewise."

JESUS VISITS MARTHA AND MARY

38 Now as they went on their way, he entered a certain village, where a woman named Martha welcomed him into her home. **39** She had a sister named Mary, who sat at the Lord's feet and listened to what he was saying. **40** But Martha was distracted by her many tasks; so she came to him and asked, "Lord, do you not care that my sister has left me to do all the work by myself? Tell her then to help me." **41** But the Lord answered her, "Martha, Martha, you are worried and distracted by many things; **42** there is need of only one thing.[d] Mary has chosen the better part, which will not be taken away from her."

a **10.23** Gk *he*   b **10.25** Gk *him*   c **10.35** The denarius was the usual day's wage for a laborer   d **10.42** Other ancient authorities read *few things are necessary, or only one*

⊢ BIBLE IN LIFE ▷

A Relationship With Christ   *Luke 10.38–42*

Most of us would consider Martha quite admirable—a hardworking housekeeper, good cook, gracious hostess. If we didn't know Jesus' answer to Martha, we might perceive Mary as lazy. But Martha was distracted by her preparations while Mary savored something that would last forever—a close, personal relationship with Jesus Christ. This relationship later brought Mary to do something good and lovely for Christ when she anointed his feet with perfume prior to his death and burial (see John 12.3). Mary had her priorities straight. Most of us do not. We spend too much time and consideration on material things, even things that are good in moderation. We want to be successful. We want to have adequate bank accounts and nice homes. We might read the Bible on occasion. We might pray when we're in trouble or when we want something. We might go to church. We profess to be Christians. But we establish priorities in our lives that relegate Jesus to the periphery of our existence. An intimate relationship with Christ should instead be the driving force of our lives.

DOING EVERYTHING
JESUS COMMANDS IS THE
ESSENCE OF DISCIPLESHIP.

THE LORD'S PRAYER

11 He was praying in a certain place, and after he had finished, one of his disciples said to him, "Lord, teach us to pray, as John taught his disciples." ²He said to them, "When you pray, say:

Father,ᵃ hallowed be your name.
Your kingdom come.ᵇ
3   Give us each day our
        daily bread.ᶜ
4   And forgive us our sins,
        for we ourselves forgive
            everyone indebted to us.
        And do not bring us to
            the time of trial."ᵈ

PERSEVERANCE IN PRAYER

5 And he said to them, "Suppose one of you has a friend, and you go to him at midnight and say to him, 'Friend, lend me three loaves of bread; ⁶for a friend of mine has arrived, and I have nothing to set before him.' ⁷And he answers from within, 'Do not bother me; the door has already been locked, and my children are with me in bed; I cannot get up and give you anything.' ⁸I tell you, even though he will not get up and give him anything because he is his friend, at least because of his persistence he will get up and give him whatever he needs.

9 "So I say to you, Ask, and it will be given you; search, and you will find; knock, and the door will be opened for you. ¹⁰For everyone who asks receives, and everyone who searches finds, and for everyone who knocks, the door will be opened. ¹¹Is there anyone among you who, if your child asks forᵉ a fish, will give a snake instead of a fish? ¹²Or if the child asks for an egg, will give a scorpion? ¹³If you then, who are

evil, know how to give good gifts to your children, how much more will the heavenly Father give the Holy Spiritᶠ to those who ask him!"

JESUS AND BEELZEBUL

14 Now he was casting out a demon that was mute; when the demon had gone out, the one who had been mute spoke, and the crowds were amazed. ¹⁵But some of them said, "He casts out demons by Beelzebul, the ruler of the demons." ¹⁶Others, to test him, kept demanding from him a sign from heaven. ¹⁷But he knew what they were thinking and said to them, "Every kingdom divided against itself becomes a desert, and house falls on house. ¹⁸If Satan also is divided against himself, how will his kingdom stand? —for you say that I cast out the demons by Beelzebul. ¹⁹Now if I cast out the demons by Beelzebul, by whom do your exorcistsᵍ cast them out? Therefore they will be your judges. ²⁰But if it is by the finger of God that I cast out the demons, then the kingdom of God has come to you. ²¹When a strong man, fully armed, guards his castle, his property is safe. ²²But when one stronger than he attacks him and overpowers him, he takes away his armor in which he trusted and divides his plunder. ²³Whoever is not with me is against me, and whoever does not gather with me scatters.

THE RETURN OF THE
UNCLEAN SPIRIT

24 "When the unclean spirit has gone out of a person, it wanders

---

ᵃ 11.2 Other ancient authorities read *Our Father in heaven*   ᵇ 11.2 A few ancient authorities read *Your Holy Spirit come upon us and cleanse us.* Other ancient authorities add *Your will be done, on earth as in heaven*   ᶜ 11.3 Or *our bread for tomorrow*   ᵈ 11.4 Or *us into temptation.* Other ancient authorities add *but rescue us from the evil one (or from evil)*   ᵉ 11.11 Other ancient authorities add *bread, will give a stone; or if your child asks for*   ᶠ 11.13 Other ancient authorities read *the Father give the Holy Spirit from heaven*   ᵍ 11.19 Gk *sons*

through waterless regions looking for a resting place, but not finding any, it says, 'I will return to my house from which I came.' 25When it comes, it finds it swept and put in order. 26Then it goes and brings seven other spirits more evil than itself, and they enter and live there; and the last state of that person is worse than the first."

TRUE BLESSEDNESS

27While he was saying this, a woman in the crowd raised her voice and said to him, "Blessed is the womb that bore you and the breasts that nursed you!" 28But he said, "Blessed rather are those who hear the word of God and obey it!"

THE SIGN OF JONAH

29 When the crowds were increasing, he began to say, "This generation is an evil generation; it asks for a sign, but no sign will be given to it except the sign of Jonah. 30For just as Jonah became a sign to the people of Nineveh, so the Son of Man will be to this generation. 31The queen of the South will rise at the judgment with the people of this generation and condemn them, because she came from the ends of the earth to listen to the wisdom of Solomon, and see, something greater than Solomon is here! 32The people of Nineveh will rise up at the judgment with this generation and condemn it, because they repented at the proclamation of Jonah, and see, something greater than Jonah is here!

THE LIGHT OF THE BODY

33 "No one after lighting a lamp puts it in a cellar,ᵃ but on the lampstand so that those who enter may see the light. 34Your eye is the lamp of your body. If your eye is healthy, your whole body is full of light; but if it is not healthy, your body is full of darkness. 35Therefore consider whether the light in you is not darkness. 36If then your whole body is full of light, with no part of it in darkness, it will be as full of light as when a lamp gives you light with its rays."

JESUS DENOUNCES PHARISEES AND LAWYERS

37While he was speaking, a Pharisee invited him to dine with him; so he went in and took his place at the table. 38The Pharisee was amazed to see that he did not first wash before dinner. 39Then the Lord said to him, "Now you Pharisees clean the outside of the cup and of the dish, but inside you are full of greed and wickedness. 40You fools! Did not the one who made the outside make the inside also? 41So give for alms those things that are within; and see, everything will be clean for you.

42 "But woe to you Pharisees! For you tithe mint and rue and herbs of all kinds, and neglect justice and the love of God; it is these you ought to have practiced, without neglecting the others. 43Woe to you Pharisees! For you love to have the seat of honor in the synagogues and to be greeted with respect in the marketplaces. 44Woe to you! For you are like unmarked graves, and people walk over them without realizing it."

45 One of the lawyers answered him, "Teacher, when you say these things, you insult us too." 46And he said, "Woe also to you lawyers! For you load people with burdens hard to bear, and you yourselves do not lift a finger to ease them. 47Woe to you! For you build the tombs of the prophets whom your ancestors killed. 48So you are witnesses and approve of the deeds of your ancestors; for they killed them, and you build their tombs. 49Therefore also the Wisdom of God said, 'I will send them prophets and apostles, some of whom they will kill and persecute,' 50so that this generation may be charged with the blood of all the prophets shed since the foundation of the world, 51from the blood of Abel to the blood of Zechariah, who perished between the altar and the sanctuary. Yes, I tell you, it will be charged against this generation. 52Woe to you lawyers! For you have taken away the key of knowledge;

ᵃ 11.33 Other ancient authorities add *or under the bushel basket*

you did not enter yourselves, and you hindered those who were entering."

53 When he went outside, the scribes and the Pharisees began to be very hostile toward him and to cross-examine him about many things, **54** lying in wait for him, to catch him in something he might say.

A WARNING AGAINST HYPOCRISY

12 Meanwhile, when the crowd gathered by the thousands, so that they trampled on one another, he began to speak first to his disciples, "Beware of the yeast of the Pharisees, that is, their hypocrisy. **2** Nothing is covered up that will not be uncovered, and nothing secret that will not become known. **3** Therefore whatever you have said in the dark will be heard in the light, and what you have whispered behind closed doors will be proclaimed from the housetops.

EXHORTATION TO FEARLESS CONFESSION

4 "I tell you, my friends, do not fear those who kill the body, and after that can do nothing more. **5** But I will warn you whom to fear: fear him who, after he has killed, has authority[a] to cast into hell.[b] Yes, I tell you, fear him! **6** Are not five sparrows sold for two pennies? Yet not one of them is forgotten in God's sight.

7 But even the hairs of your head are all counted. Do not be afraid; you are of more value than many sparrows.

8 "And I tell you, everyone who acknowledges me before others, the Son of Man also will acknowledge before the angels of God; **9** but whoever denies me before others will be denied before the angels of God. **10** And everyone who speaks a word against the Son of Man will be forgiven; but whoever blasphemes against the Holy Spirit will not be forgiven. **11** When they bring you before the synagogues, the rulers, and the authorities, do not worry about how[c] you are to defend yourselves or what you are to say; **12** for the Holy Spirit will teach you at that very hour what you ought to say."

THE PARABLE OF THE RICH FOOL

13 Someone in the crowd said to him, "Teacher, tell my brother to divide the family inheritance with me." **14** But he said to him, "Friend, who set me to be a judge or arbitrator over you?" **15** And he said to them, "Take care! Be on your guard against all kinds of greed; for one's life does not consist in the abundance of possessions." **16** Then he told them a parable: "The land of a rich man produced abundantly. **17** And he thought to himself, 'What should I do, for I have no place to store my crops?' **18** Then he

a **12.5** Or *power*   b **12.5** Gk *Gehenna*
c **12.11** Other ancient authorities add *or what*

BIBLE IN LIFE ▷

Greed

Luke 12.13–21

The rich man in this parable wouldn't give anything away, and then, abruptly, he died. His life was by no means a success. We are all approaching the end of our own earthly lives, and we must wonder whether our lives are a success. This story reminds us that the avenue to true success leads us away from a self-centered existence. We should invest what we have and what God has given us in the well-being of others, becoming rich toward God. Like the rich man in the story, most of us say, "I have to get enough for myself first, while the getting's good. Once I get all I 'need,' then I'll start thinking about others. Then I'll start being generous and unselfish." Generosity is incompatible with our greedy human nature. We tend to think that we'll deprive ourselves or our families of something that we really need if we are too generous. We think we won't be successful if we give to others, but Jesus teaches us by word and example that generosity is the way to success.

said, 'I will do this: I will pull down my barns and build larger ones, and there I will store all my grain and my goods. 19 And I will say to my soul, Soul, you have ample goods laid up for many years; relax, eat, drink, be merry.' 20 But God said to him, 'You fool! This very night your life is being demanded of you. And the things you have prepared, whose will they be?' 21 So it is with those who store up treasures for themselves but are not rich toward God."

DO NOT WORRY

22 He said to his disciples, "Therefore I tell you, do not worry about your life, what you will eat, or about your body, what you will wear. 23 For life is more than food, and the body more than clothing. 24 Consider the ravens: they neither sow nor reap, they have neither storehouse nor barn, and yet God feeds them. Of how much more value are you than the birds! 25 And can any of you by worrying add a single hour to your span of life?[a] 26 If then you are not able to do so small a thing as that, why do you worry about the rest? 27 Consider the lilies, how they grow: they neither toil nor spin;[b] yet I tell you, even Solomon in all his glory was not clothed like one of these. 28 But if God so clothes the grass of the field, which is alive today and tomorrow is thrown into the oven, how much more will he clothe you—you of little faith! 29 And do not keep striving for what you are to eat and what you are to drink, and do not keep worrying. 30 For it is the nations of the world that strive after all these things, and your Father knows that you need them. 31 Instead, strive for his[c] kingdom, and these things will be given to you as well.

32 "Do not be afraid, little flock, for it is your Father's good pleasure to give you the kingdom. 33 Sell your possessions, and give alms. Make purses for yourselves that do not wear out, an unfailing treasure in heaven, where no thief comes near and no moth destroys. 34 For where your treasure is, there your heart will be also.

WATCHFUL SLAVES

35 "Be dressed for action and have your lamps lit; 36 be like those who are waiting for their master to return from the wedding banquet, so that they may open the door for him as soon as he comes and knocks. 37 Blessed are those slaves whom the master finds alert when he comes; truly I tell you, he will fasten his belt and have them sit down to eat, and he will come and serve them. 38 If he comes during the middle of the night, or near dawn, and finds them so, blessed are those slaves.

39 "But know this: if the owner of the house had known at what hour the thief was coming, he[d] would not have let his house be broken into. 40 You also must be ready, for the Son of Man is coming at an unexpected hour."

THE FAITHFUL OR THE UNFAITHFUL SLAVE

41 Peter said, "Lord, are you telling this parable for us or for everyone?" 42 And the Lord said, "Who then is the faithful and prudent manager whom his master will put in charge of his slaves, to give them their allowance of food at the proper time? 43 Blessed is that slave whom his master will find at work when he arrives. 44 Truly I tell you, he will put that one in charge of all his possessions. 45 But if that slave says to himself, 'My master is delayed in coming,' and if he begins to beat the other slaves, men and women, and to eat and drink and get drunk, 46 the master of that slave will come on a day when he does not expect him and at an hour that he does not know, and will cut him in pieces,[e] and put him with the unfaithful. 47 That slave who knew what his master wanted, but did not prepare himself or do what was wanted, will receive a severe beating. 48 But

a 12.25 Or add a cubit to your stature
b 12.27 Other ancient authorities read Consider the lilies; they neither spin nor weave   c 12.31 Other ancient authorities read God's   d 12.39 Other ancient authorities add would have watched and   e 12.46 Or cut him off

the one who did not know and did what deserved a beating will receive a light beating. From everyone to whom much has been given, much will be required; and from the one to whom much has been entrusted, even more will be demanded.

JESUS THE CAUSE OF DIVISION

49 "I came to bring fire to the earth, and how I wish it were already kindled! 50I have a baptism with which to be baptized, and what stress I am under until it is completed! 51Do you think that I have come to bring peace to the earth? No, I tell you, but rather division! 52From now on five in one household will be divided, three against two and two against three; 53they will be divided:

father against son
    and son against father,
mother against daughter
    and daughter against mother,
mother-in-law against her
        daughter-in-law
    and daughter-in-law against
        mother-in-law."

INTERPRETING THE TIME

54 He also said to the crowds, "When you see a cloud rising in the west, you immediately say, 'It is going to rain'; and so it happens. 55And when you see the south wind blowing, you say, 'There will be scorching heat'; and it happens. 56You hypocrites! You know how to interpret the appearance of earth and sky, but why do you not know how to interpret the present time?

SETTLING WITH YOUR OPPONENT

57 "And why do you not judge for yourselves what is right? 58Thus, when you go with your accuser before a magistrate, on the way make an effort to settle the case,ᵃ or you may be dragged before the judge, and the judge hand you over to the officer, and the officer throw you in prison. 59I tell you, you will never get out until you have paid the very last penny."

REPENT OR PERISH

13 At that very time there were some present who told him about the Galileans whose blood Pilate had mingled with their sacrifices. 2He asked them, "Do you think that because these Galileans suffered in this way they were worse sinners than all other Galileans? 3No, I tell you; but unless you repent, you will all perish as they did. 4Or those eighteen who were killed when the tower of Siloam fell on them—do you think that they were worse offenders than all the others living in Jerusalem? 5No, I tell you; but unless you repent, you will all perish just as they did."

THE PARABLE OF THE BARREN FIG TREE

6 Then he told this parable: "A man had a fig tree planted in his vineyard; and he came looking for fruit on it and found none. 7So he said to the gardener, 'See here! For three years I have come looking for fruit on this fig tree, and still I find none. Cut it down! Why should it be wasting the soil?' 8He replied, 'Sir, let it alone for one more year, until I dig around it and put manure on it. 9If it bears fruit next year, well and good; but if not, you can cut it down.'"

JESUS HEALS A CRIPPLED WOMAN

10 Now he was teaching in one of the synagogues on the sabbath. 11And just then there appeared a woman with a spirit that had crippled her for eighteen years. She was bent over and was quite unable to stand up straight. 12When Jesus saw her, he called her over and said, "Woman, you are set free from your ailment." 13When he laid his hands on her, immediately she stood up straight and began praising God. 14But the leader of the synagogue, indignant because Jesus had cured on the sabbath, kept saying to the crowd, "There are six days on which work ought to be done; come on

ᵃ 12.58 Gk settle with him

those days and be cured, and not on the sabbath day." 15But the Lord answered him and said, "You hypocrites! Does not each of you on the sabbath untie his ox or his donkey from the manger, and lead it away to give it water? 16And ought not this woman, a daughter of Abraham whom Satan bound for eighteen long years, be set free from this bondage on the sabbath day?" 17When he said this, all his opponents were put to shame; and the entire crowd was rejoicing at all the wonderful things that he was doing.

THE PARABLE OF THE MUSTARD SEED

18 He said therefore, "What is the kingdom of God like? And to what should I compare it? 19It is like a mustard seed that someone took and sowed in the garden; it grew and became a tree, and the birds of the air made nests in its branches."

THE PARABLE OF THE YEAST

20 And again he said, "To what should I compare the kingdom of God? 21It is like yeast that a woman took and mixed in with[a] three measures of flour until all of it was leavened."

THE NARROW DOOR

22 Jesus[b] went through one town and village after another, teaching as he made his way to Jerusalem. 23Someone asked him, "Lord, will only a few be saved?" He said to them, 24"Strive to enter through the narrow door; for many, I tell you, will try to enter and will not be able. 25When once the owner of the house has got up and shut the door, and you begin to stand outside and to knock at the door, saying, 'Lord, open to us,' then in reply he will say to you, 'I do not know where you come from.' 26Then you will begin to say, 'We ate and drank with you, and you taught in our streets.' 27But he will say, 'I do not know where you come from; go away from me, all you evildoers!' 28There will be weeping and gnashing of teeth when you see Abraham and Isaac and Jacob and

all the prophets in the kingdom of God, and you yourselves thrown out. 29Then people will come from east and west, from north and south, and will eat in the kingdom of God. 30Indeed, some are last who will be first, and some are first who will be last."

WE TAKE JESUS' KIND OF
RISK WHEN WE OPEN REAL
TIES TO OTHER PEOPLE,
THEN DISCUSS AND
DEMONSTRATE OUR FAITH.

THE LAMENT OVER JERUSALEM

31 At that very hour some Pharisees came and said to him, "Get away from here, for Herod wants to kill you." 32He said to them, "Go and tell that fox for me,[c] 'Listen, I am casting out demons and performing cures today and tomorrow, and on the third day I finish my work. 33Yet today, tomorrow, and the next day I must be on my way, because it is impossible for a prophet to be killed outside of Jerusalem.' 34Jerusalem, Jerusalem, the city that kills the prophets and stones those who are sent to it! How often have I desired to gather your children together as a hen gathers her brood under her wings, and you were not willing! 35See, your house is left to you. And I tell you, you will not see me until the time comes when[d] you say, 'Blessed is the one who comes in the name of the Lord.' "

JESUS HEALS THE MAN WITH DROPSY

14 On one occasion when Jesus[e] was going to the house of a leader of the Pharisees to eat a meal

---

a 13.21 Gk hid in   b 13.22 Gk He   c 13.32 Gk lacks for me   d 13.35 Other ancient authorities lack the time comes when   e 14.1 Gk he on the sabbath, they were watching him closely. 2Just then, in front of him, there was a man who had dropsy. 3And Jesus asked the lawyers and Pharisees, "Is it lawful to cure people on the sabbath, or not?" 4But they were silent. So Jesus[a] took him and healed him, and sent him away. 5Then he said to them, "If one of you has a child[b] or an ox that has fallen into a well, will you not immediately pull it out on a sabbath day?" 6And they could not reply to this.

HUMILITY AND HOSPITALITY

7 When he noticed how the guests chose the places of honor, he told them a parable. 8"When you are invited by someone to a wedding banquet, do not sit down at the place of honor, in case someone more distinguished than you has been invited by your host; 9and the host who invited both of you may come and say to you, 'Give this person your place,' and then in disgrace you would start to take the lowest place. 10But when you are invited, go and sit down at the lowest place, so that when your host comes, he may say to you, 'Friend, move up higher'; then you will be honored in the presence of all who sit at the table with you. 11For all who exalt themselves will be humbled, and those who humble themselves will be exalted."

12 He said also to the one who had invited him, "When you give a luncheon or a dinner, do not invite your friends or your brothers or your relatives or rich neighbors, in case they may invite you in return, and you would be repaid. 13But when you give a banquet, invite the poor, the crippled, the lame, and the blind. 14And you will be blessed, because they cannot repay you, for you will be repaid at the resurrection of the righteous."

THE PARABLE OF THE GREAT DINNER

15 One of the dinner guests, on hearing this, said to him, "Blessed is anyone who will eat bread in the kingdom of God!" 16Then Jesus[a] said to him, "Someone gave a great dinner and invited many. 17At the time

for the dinner he sent his slave to say to those who had been invited, 'Come; for everything is ready now.' 18But they all alike began to make excuses. The first said to him, 'I have bought a piece of land, and I must go out and see it; please accept my regrets.' 19Another said, 'I have bought five yoke of oxen, and I am going to try them out; please accept my regrets.' 20Another said, 'I have just been married, and therefore I cannot come.' 21So the slave returned and reported this to his master. Then the owner of the house became angry and said to his slave, 'Go out at once into the streets and lanes of the town and bring in the poor, the crippled, the blind, and the lame.' 22And the slave said, 'Sir, what you ordered has been done, and there is still room.' 23Then the master said to the slave, 'Go out into the roads and lanes, and compel people to come in, so that my house may be filled. 24For I tell you,[c] none of those who were invited will taste my dinner.' "

THE COST OF DISCIPLESHIP

25 Now large crowds were traveling with him; and he turned and said to them, 26"Whoever comes to me and does not hate father and mother, wife and children, brothers and sisters, yes, and even life itself, cannot be my disciple. 27Whoever does not carry the cross and follow me cannot be my disciple. 28For which of you, intending to build a tower, does not first sit down and estimate the cost, to see whether he has enough to complete it? 29Otherwise, when he has laid a foundation and is not able to finish, all who see it will begin to ridicule him, 30saying, 'This fellow began to build and was not able to finish.' 31Or what king, going out to wage war against another king, will not sit down first and consider whether he is able with ten thousand to oppose the one who comes against him with twenty thousand? 32If he cannot, then, while the other is still far away, he sends a delegation and asks for the

[a] 14.4,16 Gk *he*   [b] 14.5 Other ancient authorities read *a donkey*   [c] 14.24 The Greek word for *you* here is plural

terms of peace. 33So therefore, none of you can become my disciple if you do not give up all your possessions.

ABOUT SALT

34 "Salt is good; but if salt has lost its taste, how can its saltiness be restored?[a] 35It is fit neither for the soil nor for the manure pile; they throw it away. Let anyone with ears to hear listen!"

WE ALWAYS HAVE AN

OPPORTUNITY TO COME

BACK TO GOD.

THE PARABLE OF THE LOST SHEEP

15 Now all the tax collectors and sinners were coming near to listen to him. 2And the Pharisees and the scribes were grumbling and saying, "This fellow welcomes sinners and eats with them."

3 So he told them this parable: 4"Which one of you, having a hundred sheep and losing one of them, does not leave the ninety-nine in the wilderness and go after the one that is lost until he finds it? 5When he has found it, he lays it on his shoulders and rejoices. 6And when he comes home, he calls together his friends and neighbors, saying to them, 'Rejoice with me, for I have found my sheep that was lost.' 7Just so, I tell you, there will be more joy in heaven over one sinner who repents than over ninety-nine righteous persons who need no repentance.

THE PARABLE OF THE LOST COIN

8 "Or what woman having ten silver coins,[b] if she loses one of them, does not light a lamp, sweep the house, and search carefully until she finds it? 9When she has found it, she calls together her friends and neighbors, saying, 'Rejoice with me, for I have found the coin that I had lost.' 10Just so, I tell you, there is joy in the

presence of the angels of God over one sinner who repents."

THE PARABLE OF THE PRODIGAL AND HIS BROTHER

11 Then Jesus[c] said, "There was a man who had two sons. 12The younger of them said to his father, 'Father, give me the share of the property that will belong to me.' So he divided his property between them. 13A few days later the younger son gathered all he had and traveled to a distant country, and there he squandered his property in dissolute living. 14When he had spent everything, a severe famine took place throughout that country, and he began to be in need. 15So he went and hired himself out to one of the citizens of that country, who sent him to his fields to feed the pigs. 16He would gladly have filled himself with[d] the pods that the pigs were eating; and no one gave him anything. 17But when he came to himself he said, 'How many of my father's hired hands have bread enough and to spare, but here I am dying of hunger! 18I will get up and go to my father, and I will say to him, "Father, I have sinned against heaven and before you; 19I am no longer worthy to be called your son; treat me like one of your hired hands."' 20So he set off and went to his father. But while he was still far off, his father saw him and was filled with compassion; he ran and put his arms around him and kissed him. 21Then the son said to him, 'Father, I have sinned against heaven and before you; I am no longer worthy to be called your son.'[e] 22But the father said to his slaves, 'Quickly, bring out a robe—the best one—and put it on him; put a ring on his finger and sandals on his feet. 23And get the fatted calf and kill it, and let us eat and celebrate; 24for this son of mine was dead and is alive again; he was lost and is found!' And they began to celebrate.

a 14.34 Or how can it be used for seasoning? b 15.8 Gk drachmas, each worth about a day's wage for a laborer   c 15.11 Gk he   d 15.16 Other ancient authorities read filled his stomach with e 15.21 Other ancient authorities add Treat me like one of your hired servants

25 "Now his elder son was in the field; and when he came and approached the house, he heard music and dancing. **26** He called one of the slaves and asked what was going on. **27** He replied, 'Your brother has come, and your father has killed the fatted calf, because he has got him back safe and sound.' **28** Then he became angry and refused to go in. His father came out and began to plead with him. **29** But he answered his father, 'Listen! For all these years I have been working like a slave for you, and I have never disobeyed your command; yet you have never given me even a young goat so that I might celebrate with my friends. **30** But when this son of yours came back, who has devoured your property with prostitutes, you killed the fatted calf for him!' **31** Then the father[a] said to him, 'Son, you are always with me, and all that is mine is yours. **32** But we had to celebrate and rejoice, because this brother of yours was dead and has come to life; he was lost and has been found.'"

THE PARABLE OF THE DISHONEST MANAGER

16 Then Jesus[a] said to the disciples, "There was a rich man who had a manager, and charges were brought to him that this man was squandering his property. **2** So he summoned him and said to him, 'What is this that I hear about you? Give me an accounting of your management, because you cannot be my manager any longer.' **3** Then the manager said to himself, 'What will I do, now that my master is taking the position away from me? I am not strong enough to dig, and I am ashamed to beg. **4** I have decided what to do so that, when I am dismissed as manager, people may welcome me into their homes.' **5** So, summoning his master's debtors one by one, he asked the first, 'How much do you owe my master?' **6** He answered, 'A hundred jugs of olive oil.' He said to him, 'Take your bill, sit down quickly, and make it fifty.' **7** Then he asked another, 'And how much do you owe?' He replied, 'A

PONDER

"Then the father said to him, 'Son, you are always with me, and all that is mine is yours. But we had to celebrate and rejoice, because this brother of yours was dead and has come to life; he was lost and has been found.'"
—Luke 15.31–32

PRAY

Father, we pray that we will always see fresh meaning in this familiar parable. We appreciate the fact that you did not wrap your profound messages in theological terms; instead you delivered them through simple stories—so that we can envision this young man coming home in disgrace to his father, who receives him with open arms and with total forgiveness. We are thankful for this story that illustrates your generous heart, and pray that this parable will renew our faith in Christ and our commitment to you. We pray in the name of our Savior. Amen.

hundred containers of wheat.' He said to him, 'Take your bill and make it eighty.' **8** And his master commended the dishonest manager because he had acted shrewdly; for the children of this age are more shrewd in dealing with their own generation than are the children of light. **9** And I tell you, make friends for yourselves by means of dishonest wealth[b] so that when it is gone, they may welcome you into the eternal homes.[c] **10** "Whoever is faithful in a very little is faithful also in much; and whoever is dishonest in a very little is dishonest also in much. **11** If then you have not been faithful with the dishonest wealth,[b] who will entrust to you the true riches? **12** And if you

[a] 15.31; 16.1 Gk *he* [b] 16.9,11 Gk *mammon* [c] 16.9 Gk *tents*

have not been faithful with what belongs to another, who will give you what is your own? 13No slave can serve two masters; for a slave will either hate the one and love the other, or be devoted to the one and despise the other. You cannot serve God and wealth."ᵃ

THE LAW AND THE KINGDOM OF GOD

14 The Pharisees, who were lovers of money, heard all this, and they ridiculed him. 15So he said to them, "You are those who justify yourselves in the sight of others; but God knows your hearts; for what is prized by human beings is an abomination in the sight of God.

16 "The law and the prophets were in effect until John came; since then the good news of the kingdom of God is proclaimed, and everyone tries to enter it by force.ᵇ 17But it is easier for heaven and earth to pass away, than for one stroke of a letter in the law to be dropped.

18 "Anyone who divorces his wife and marries another commits adultery, and whoever marries a woman divorced from her husband commits adultery.

THE RICH MAN AND LAZARUS

19 "There was a rich man who was dressed in purple and fine linen and who feasted sumptuously every day. 20And at his gate lay a poor man named Lazarus, covered with sores, 21who longed to satisfy his hunger with what fell from the rich man's table; even the dogs would come and lick his sores. 22The poor man died and was carried away by the angels to be with Abraham.ᶜ The rich man also died and was buried. 23In Hades, where he was being tormented, he looked up and saw Abraham far away with Lazarus by his side.ᵈ 24He called out, 'Father Abraham, have mercy on me, and send Lazarus to dip the tip of his finger in water and cool my tongue; for I am in agony in these flames.' 25But Abraham said, 'Child, remember that during your lifetime you received your good things, and Lazarus in like manner

evil things; but now he is comforted here, and you are in agony. 26Besides all this, between you and us a great chasm has been fixed, so that those who might want to pass from here to you cannot do so, and no one can cross from there to us.' 27He said, 'Then, father, I beg you to send him to my father's house— 28for I have five brothers—that he may warn them, so that they will not also come into this place of torment.' 29Abraham replied, 'They have Moses and the prophets; they should listen to them.' 30He said, 'No, father Abraham; but if someone goes to them from the dead, they will repent.' 31He said to him, 'If they do not listen to Moses and the prophets, neither will they be convinced even if someone rises from the dead.'"

TO ENJOY LUXURY AT

THE EXPENSE OF OTHERS

LEADS TO FAILURE.

SOME SAYINGS OF JESUS

17 Jesusᵉ said to his disciples, "Occasions for stumbling are bound to come, but woe to anyone by whom they come! 2It would be better for you if a millstone were hung around your neck and you were thrown into the sea than for you to cause one of these little ones to stumble. 3Be on your guard! If another discipleᶠ sins, you must rebuke the offender, and if there is repentance, you must forgive. 4And if the same person sins against you seven times a day, and turns back to you seven times and says, 'I repent,' you must forgive."

5 The apostles said to the Lord, "Increase our faith!" 6The Lord replied,

ᵃ 16.13 Gk mammon   ᵇ 16.16 Or everyone is strongly urged to enter it   ᶜ 16.22 Gk to Abraham's bosom   ᵈ 16.23 Gk in his bosom   ᵉ 17.1 Gk He   ᶠ 17.3 Gk your brother

"If you had faith the size of a[a] mustard seed, you could say to this mulberry tree, 'Be uprooted and planted in the sea,' and it would obey you.

7 "Who among you would say to your slave who has just come in from plowing or tending sheep in the field, 'Come here at once and take your place at the table'? 8 Would you not rather say to him, 'Prepare supper for me, put on your apron and serve me while I eat and drink; later you may eat and drink'? 9 Do you thank the slave for doing what was commanded? 10 So you also, when you have done all that you were ordered to do, say, 'We are worthless slaves; we have done only what we ought to have done!'"

JESUS CLEANSES TEN LEPERS

11 On the way to Jerusalem Jesus[b] was going through the region between Samaria and Galilee. 12 As he entered a village, ten lepers[c] approached him. Keeping their distance, 13 they called out, saying, "Jesus, Master, have mercy on us!" 14 When he saw them, he said to them, "Go and show yourselves to the priests." And as they went, they were made clean. 15 Then one of them, when he saw that he was healed, turned back, praising God with a loud voice. 16 He prostrated himself at Jesus'[d] feet and thanked him. And he was a Samaritan. 17 Then Jesus asked, "Were not ten made clean? But the other nine, where are they? 18 Was none of them found to return and give praise to God except this foreigner?" 19 Then he said to him, "Get up and go on your way; your faith has made you well."

THE COMING OF THE KINGDOM

20 Once Jesus[b] was asked by the Pharisees when the kingdom of God was coming, and he answered, "The kingdom of God is not coming with things that can be observed; 21 nor will they say, 'Look, here it is!' or 'There it is!' For, in fact, the kingdom of God is among[e] you."

22 Then he said to the disciples, "The days are coming when you will long to see one of the days of the Son of Man, and you will not see it. 23 They will say to you, 'Look there!' or 'Look here!' Do not go, do not set off in pursuit. 24 For as the lightning flashes and lights up the sky from one side to the other, so will the Son of Man be in his day.[f] 25 But first he must endure much suffering and be rejected by this generation. 26 Just as it was in the days of Noah, so too it will be in the days of the Son of Man. 27 They were eating and drinking, and marrying and being given in marriage, until the day Noah entered the ark, and the flood came and destroyed all of them. 28 Likewise, just as it was in the days of Lot: they were eating and drinking, buying and selling, planting and

[a] 17.6 Gk faith as a grain of [b] 17.11,20 Gk he [c] 17.12 The terms leper and leprosy can refer to several diseases [d] 17.16 Gk his [e] 17.21 Or within [f] 17.24 Other ancient authorities lack in his day

---

⊢ BIBLE IN LIFE ▷

Prejudice

Luke 17.11–19

All of us have a natural tendency toward prejudice. We don't have many lepers in our society now, but we have a lot of outcasts. Many of us regard those with AIDS in the same way people in Jesus' time regarded lepers. What Christ showed his disciples in this particular episode is that the mercy of God, the love of God, the forgiveness of God, the healing power of God—these are freely available to everyone. An element of courage and a reminder of the essence of Christ's character have to be implemented in our hearts and minds before we can treat people equally. As Christ did, we must equate them with the ones we love most, who are the same color as ourselves, who are healthy or who live in our own country.

building, 29but on the day that Lot left Sodom, it rained fire and sulfur from heaven and destroyed all of them 30—it will be like that on the day that the Son of Man is revealed. 31On that day, anyone on the housetop who has belongings in the house must not come down to take them away; and likewise anyone in the field must not turn back. 32Remember Lot's wife. 33Those who try to make their life secure will lose it, but those who lose their life will keep it. 34I tell you, on that night there will be two in one bed; one will be taken and the other left. 35There will be two women grinding meal together; one will be taken and the other left."a 37Then they asked him, "Where, Lord?" He said to them, "Where the corpse is, there the vultures will gather."

THE PARABLE OF THE WIDOW AND THE UNJUST JUDGE

18 Then Jesusb told them a parable about their need to pray always and not to lose heart. 2He said, "In a certain city there was a judge who neither feared God nor had respect for people. 3In that city there was a widow who kept coming to him and saying, 'Grant me justice against my opponent.' 4For a while he refused; but later he said to himself, 'Though I have no fear of God and no respect for anyone, 5yet because this widow keeps bothering me, I will grant her justice, so that she may not wear me out by continually coming.' "c 6And the Lord said, "Listen to what the unjust judge says. 7And will not God grant justice to his chosen ones who cry to him day and night? Will he delay long in helping them? 8I tell you, he will quickly grant justice to them. And yet, when the Son of Man comes, will he find faith on earth?"

THE PARABLE OF THE PHARISEE AND THE TAX COLLECTOR

9 He also told this parable to some who trusted in themselves that they were righteous and regarded others with contempt: 10"Two men went up to the temple to pray, one a Phar-

PONDER

"And will not God grant justice to his chosen ones who cry to him day and night? Will he delay long in helping them? I tell you, he will quickly grant justice to them. And yet, when the Son of Man comes, will he find faith on earth?"
—Luke 18.7–8

PRAY

Heavenly Father, we pray that, having heard about this widow's persistence in asking for things that were best for her, we might learn this lesson and constantly turn to you in prayer. Help us look at our own lives and consider all the times in our daily existence when we should ask you for guidance for our lives: How can I live a transcendent life regardless of my income and social status? How can I live a life in which I can be satisfied and that serves the purposes of my Savior? We should ask you for guidance about each encounter with our loved ones: How can I commit to this relationship more intimately? How can I fill the relationship with more love? How can I forgive those who may have hurt me in the past? We ask these things in the name of Jesus. Amen.

isee and the other a tax collector. 11The Pharisee, standing by himself, was praying thus, 'God, I thank you that I am not like other people: thieves, rogues, adulterers, or even like this tax collector. 12I fast twice a week; I give a tenth of all my income.' 13But the tax collector, standing far off, would not even look up to heaven, but was beating his breast and saying, 'God, be merciful to me, a sinner!' 14I tell you, this man went

---

a 17.35 Other ancient authorities add verse 36, "Two will be in the field; one will be taken and the other left."   b 18.1 Gk he   c 18.5 Or so that she may not finally come and slap me in the face

down to his home justified rather than the other; for all who exalt themselves will be humbled, but all who humble themselves will be exalted."

JESUS BLESSES LITTLE CHILDREN

15 People were bringing even infants to him that he might touch them; and when the disciples saw it, they sternly ordered them not to do it. 16But Jesus called for them and said, "Let the little children come to me, and do not stop them; for it is to such as these that the kingdom of God belongs. 17Truly I tell you, whoever does not receive the kingdom of God as a little child will never enter it."

THE RICH RULER

18 A certain ruler asked him, "Good Teacher, what must I do to inherit eternal life?" 19Jesus said to him, "Why do you call me good? No one is good but God alone. 20You know the commandments: 'You shall not commit adultery; You shall not murder; You shall not steal; You shall not bear false witness; Honor your father and mother.'" 21He replied, "I have kept all these since my youth." 22When Jesus heard this, he said to him, "There is still one thing lacking. Sell all that you own and distribute the moneyᵃ to the poor, and you will have treasure in heaven; then come, follow me." 23But when he heard this, he became sad; for he was very rich. 24Jesus looked at him and said, "How hard it is for those who have wealth to enter the kingdom of God! 25Indeed, it is easier for a camel to go through the eye of a needle than for someone who is rich to enter the kingdom of God."

26 Those who heard it said, "Then who can be saved?" 27He replied, "What is impossible for mortals is possible for God."

28 Then Peter said, "Look, we have left our homes and followed you." 29And he said to them, "Truly I tell you, there is no one who has left house or wife or brothers or parents or children, for the sake of the kingdom of God, 30who will not get back very much more in this age, and in the age to come eternal life."

A THIRD TIME JESUS FORETELLS HIS DEATH AND RESURRECTION

31 Then he took the twelve aside and said to them, "See, we are going up to Jerusalem, and everything that is written about the Son of Man by the prophets will be accomplished. 32For he will be handed over to the Gentiles; and he will be mocked and insulted and spat upon. 33After they have flogged him, they will kill him, and on the third day he will rise again." 34But they understood nothing about all these things; in fact, what he said was hidden from them, and they did not grasp what was said.

JESUS HEALS A BLIND BEGGAR NEAR JERICHO

35 As he approached Jericho, a blind man was sitting by the roadside begging. 36When he heard a crowd going by, he asked what was happening. 37They told him, "Jesus of Nazarethᵇ is passing by." 38Then he shouted, "Jesus, Son of David, have mercy on me!" 39Those who were in front sternly ordered him to be quiet; but he shouted even more loudly, "Son of David, have mercy on me!" 40Jesus stood still and ordered the man to be brought to him; and when he came near, he asked him, 41"What do you want me to do for you?" He said, "Lord, let me see again." 42Jesus said to him, "Receive your sight; your faith has saved you." 43Immediately he regained his sight and followed him, glorifying God; and all the people, when they saw it, praised God.

JESUS AND ZACCHAEUS

19 He entered Jericho and was passing through it. 2A man was there named Zacchaeus; he was a chief tax collector and was rich. 3He was trying to see who Jesus was, but on account of the crowd he could

---

ᵃ 18.22 Gk lacks the money ᵇ 18.37 Gk the Nazorean

not, because he was short in stature. 4So he ran ahead and climbed a sycamore tree to see him, because he was going to pass that way. 5When Jesus came to the place, he looked up and said to him, "Zacchaeus, hurry and come down; for I must stay at your house today." 6So he hurried down and was happy to welcome him. 7All who saw it began to grumble and said, "He has gone to be the guest of one who is a sinner." 8Zacchaeus stood there and said to the Lord, "Look, half of my possessions, Lord, I will give to the poor; and if I have defrauded anyone of anything, I will pay back four times as much." 9Then Jesus said to him, "Today salvation has come to this house, because he too is a son of Abraham. 10For the Son of Man came to seek out and to save the lost."

THE PARABLE OF THE
TEN POUNDS

11 As they were listening to this, he went on to tell a parable, because he was near Jerusalem, and because they supposed that the kingdom of God was to appear immediately. 12So he said, "A nobleman went to a distant country to get royal power for himself and then return. 13He summoned ten of his slaves, and gave them ten pounds,a and said to them, 'Do business with these until I come back.' 14But the citizens of his country hated him and sent a delegation after him, saying, 'We do not want this man to rule over us.' 15When he returned, having received royal power, he ordered these slaves, to whom he had given the money, to be summoned so that he might find out what they had gained by trading. 16The first came forward and said, 'Lord, your pound has made ten more pounds.' 17He said to him, 'Well done, good slave! Because you have been trustworthy in a very small thing, take charge of ten cities.' 18Then the second came, saying, 'Lord, your pound has made five pounds.' 19He said to him, 'And you, rule over five cities.' 20Then the other came, saying, 'Lord, here is your pound. I wrapped it up in a piece of cloth, 21for I was afraid of you, because you are a harsh man; you take what you did not deposit, and reap what you did not sow.' 22He said to him, 'I will judge you by your own words, you wicked slave! You knew, did you, that I was a harsh man, taking what I did not deposit and reaping what I did not sow? 23Why then did you not put my money into the bank? Then when I returned, I could have collected it with interest.' 24He said to the bystanders, 'Take the pound from him and give it to the one who has ten pounds.' 25(And they said to him, 'Lord, he has ten

a 19.13 The mina, rendered here by pound, was about three months' wages for a laborer

BIBLE IN LIFE

Through Trial to Salvation

Luke 18.35–43

Through the inevitable difficulties of life, we can find ways to grow closer to Christ through faith in him. Someone who experienced salvation through trial was the man who was blind. This man had very limited influence. He was despised and considered sinful and alienated from God. But from hearing a few rumors about Jesus, he recognized that Jesus was the Messiah. With absolute faith, he became a follower of Christ, and Christ made him whole in more ways than one. In contrast, we know much more about Jesus than the blind beggar did, yet we often find it hard to see through our trials and to look to Jesus for salvation. We lose sight of the fact that what we should be requesting is humility and an opportunity to serve others, a chance to reach out to those who are despised or in need, a chance to emulate the words and actions of our Savior, Jesus Christ. Even during difficult times, with faith in Jesus we can emerge from despair and helplessness with gratitude, joy and success.

pounds!') 26'I tell you, to all those who have, more will be given; but from those who have nothing, even what they have will be taken away. 27But as for these enemies of mine who did not want me to be king over them—bring them here and slaughter them in my presence.'"

JESUS' TRIUMPHAL ENTRY INTO JERUSALEM

28 After he had said this, he went on ahead, going up to Jerusalem.

29 When he had come near Bethphage and Bethany, at the place called the Mount of Olives, he sent two of the disciples, 30saying, "Go into the village ahead of you, and as you enter it you will find tied there a colt that has never been ridden. Untie it and bring it here. 31If anyone asks you, 'Why are you untying it?' just say this, 'The Lord needs it.'" 32So those who were sent departed and found it as he had told them. 33As they were untying the colt, its owners asked them, "Why are you untying the colt?" 34They said, "The Lord needs it." 35Then they brought it to Jesus; and after throwing their cloaks on the colt, they set Jesus on it. 36As he rode along, people kept spreading their cloaks on the road. 37As he was now approaching the path down from the Mount of Olives, the whole multitude of the disciples began to praise God joyfully with a loud voice for all the deeds of power that they had seen, 38saying,

"Blessed is the king
    who comes in the name
        of the Lord!
Peace in heaven,
    and glory in the highest
        heaven!"

39Some of the Pharisees in the crowd said to him, "Teacher, order your disciples to stop." 40He answered, "I tell you, if these were silent, the stones would shout out."

JESUS WEEPS OVER JERUSALEM

41 As he came near and saw the city, he wept over it, 42saying, "If you, even you, had only recognized on this day the things that make for peace! But now they are hidden from your eyes. 43Indeed, the days will come upon you, when your enemies will set up ramparts around you and surround you, and hem you in on every side. 44They will crush you to the ground, you and your children within you, and they will not leave within you one stone upon another; because you did not recognize the time of your visitation from God."[a]

JESUS CLEANSES THE TEMPLE

45 Then he entered the temple and began to drive out those who were selling things there; 46and he said, "It is written,

'My house shall be a house
    of prayer';
but you have made it a
    den of robbers."

47 Every day he was teaching in the temple. The chief priests, the scribes, and the leaders of the people kept looking for a way to kill him; 48but they did not find anything they could do, for all the people were spellbound by what they heard.

THE AUTHORITY OF JESUS QUESTIONED

20 One day, as he was teaching the people in the temple and telling the good news, the chief priests and the scribes came with the elders 2and said to him, "Tell us, by what authority are you doing these things? Who is it who gave you this authority?" 3He answered them, "I will also ask you a question, and you tell me: 4Did the baptism of John come from heaven, or was it of human origin?" 5They discussed it with one another, saying, "If we say, 'From heaven,' he will say, 'Why did you not believe him?' 6But if we say, 'Of human origin,' all the people will stone us; for they are convinced that John was a prophet." 7So they answered that they did not know where it came from. 8Then Jesus said to them, "Neither will I tell you by what authority I am doing these things."

---

[a] 19.44 Gk lacks from God

THE PARABLE OF THE WICKED TENANTS

9 He began to tell the people this parable: "A man planted a vineyard, and leased it to tenants, and went to another country for a long time. 10When the season came, he sent a slave to the tenants in order that they might give him his share of the produce of the vineyard; but the tenants beat him and sent him away empty-handed. 11Next he sent another slave; that one also they beat and insulted and sent away empty-handed. 12And he sent still a third; this one also they wounded and threw out. 13Then the owner of the vineyard said, 'What shall I do? I will send my beloved son; perhaps they will respect him.' 14But when the tenants saw him, they discussed it among themselves and said, 'This is the heir; let us kill him so that the inheritance may be ours.' 15So they threw him out of the vineyard and killed him. What then will the owner of the vineyard do to them? 16He will come and destroy those tenants and give the vineyard to others." When they heard this, they said, "Heaven forbid!" 17But he looked at them and said, "What then does this text mean:

'The stone that the builders
    rejected
    has become the cornerstone'?[a]

18Everyone who falls on that stone will be broken to pieces; and it will crush anyone on whom it falls." 19When the scribes and chief priests realized that he had told this parable against them, they wanted to lay hands on him at that very hour, but they feared the people.

THE QUESTION ABOUT PAYING TAXES

20 So they watched him and sent spies who pretended to be honest, in order to trap him by what he said, so as to hand him over to the jurisdiction and authority of the governor. 21So they asked him, "Teacher, we know that you are right in what you say and teach, and you show deference to no one, but teach the way of God in accordance with truth. 22Is it lawful for us to pay taxes to the emperor, or not?" 23But he perceived their craftiness and said to them, 24"Show me a denarius. Whose head and whose title does it bear?" They said, "The emperor's." 25He said to them, "Then give to the emperor the things that are the emperor's, and to God the things that are God's." 26And they were not able in the presence of the people to trap him by what he said; and being amazed by his answer, they became silent.

THE QUESTION ABOUT THE RESURRECTION

27 Some Sadducees, those who say there is no resurrection, came to him 28and asked him a question, "Teacher, Moses wrote for us that if a man's brother dies, leaving a wife but no children, the man[b] shall marry the widow and raise up children for his brother. 29Now there were seven brothers; the first married, and died childless; 30then the second 31and the third married her, and so in the same way all seven died childless. 32Finally the woman also died. 33In the resurrection, therefore, whose wife will the woman be? For the seven had married her."

34 Jesus said to them, "Those who belong to this age marry and are given in marriage; 35but those who are considered worthy of a place in that age and in the resurrection from the dead neither marry nor are given in marriage. 36Indeed they cannot die anymore, because they are like angels and are children of God, being children of the resurrection. 37And the fact that the dead are raised Moses himself showed, in the story about the bush, where he speaks of the Lord as the God of Abraham, the God of Isaac, and the God of Jacob. 38Now he is God not of the dead, but of the living; for to him all of them are alive." 39Then some of the scribes answered, "Teacher, you have spoken well." 40For they no longer dared to ask him another question.

[a] 20.17 Or keystone   [b] 20.28 Gk his brother

THE QUESTION ABOUT DAVID'S SON

41 Then he said to them, "How can they say that the Messiah[a] is David's son? 42For David himself says in the book of Psalms,

'The Lord said to my Lord,
"Sit at my right hand,
43   until I make your enemies
        your footstool." '

44David thus calls him Lord; so how can he be his son?"

JESUS DENOUNCES THE SCRIBES

45 In the hearing of all the people he said to the[b] disciples, 46"Beware of the scribes, who like to walk around in long robes, and love to be greeted with respect in the marketplaces, and to have the best seats in the synagogues and places of honor at banquets. 47They devour widows' houses and for the sake of appearance say long prayers. They will receive the greater condemnation."

WORSHIP IS OUR

NATURAL EXPRESSION OF

GRATITUDE TO GOD.

THE WIDOW'S OFFERING

21 He looked up and saw rich people putting their gifts into the treasury; 2he also saw a poor widow put in two small copper coins. 3He said, "Truly I tell you, this poor widow has put in more than all of them; 4for all of them have contributed out of their abundance, but she out of her poverty has put in all she had to live on."

THE DESTRUCTION OF THE TEMPLE FORETOLD

5 When some were speaking about the temple, how it was adorned with beautiful stones and gifts dedicated to God, he said, 6"As for these things that you see, the days will come when not one stone will be left upon another; all will be thrown down."

SIGNS AND PERSECUTIONS

7 They asked him, "Teacher, when will this be, and what will be the sign that this is about to take place?" 8And he said, "Beware that you are not led astray; for many will come in my name and say, 'I am he!'[c] and, 'The time is near!'[d] Do not go after them.

9 "When you hear of wars and insurrections, do not be terrified; for these things must take place first, but the end will not follow immediately." 10Then he said to them, "Nation will rise against nation, and kingdom against kingdom; 11there will be great earthquakes, and in various places famines and plagues; and there will be dreadful portents and great signs from heaven.

12 "But before all this occurs, they will arrest you and persecute you; they will hand you over to synagogues and prisons, and you will be brought before kings and governors because of my name. 13This will give you an opportunity to testify. 14So make up your minds not to prepare your defense in advance; 15for I will give you words[e] and a wisdom that none of your opponents will be able to withstand or contradict. 16You will be betrayed even by parents and brothers, by relatives and friends; and they will put some of you to death. 17You will be hated by all because of my name. 18But not a hair of your head will perish. 19By your endurance you will gain your souls.

THE DESTRUCTION OF JERUSALEM FORETOLD

20 "When you see Jerusalem surrounded by armies, then know that its desolation has come near.[f] 21Then those in Judea must flee to the mountains, and those inside the city must leave it, and those out in the country must not enter it; 22for these are days of vengeance, as a fulfillment of all that is written. 23Woe to those who are pregnant and to those who are nursing infants in those

[a] 20.41 Or the Christ [b] 20.45 Other ancient authorities read his [c] 21.8 Gk I am [d] 21.8 Or at hand [e] 21.15 Gk a mouth [f] 21.20 Or is at hand

days! For there will be great distress on the earth and wrath against this people; 24they will fall by the edge of the sword and be taken away as captives among all nations; and Jerusalem will be trampled on by the Gentiles, until the times of the Gentiles are fulfilled.

THE COMING OF THE SON OF MAN

25 "There will be signs in the sun, the moon, and the stars, and on the earth distress among nations confused by the roaring of the sea and the waves. 26People will faint from fear and foreboding of what is coming upon the world, for the powers of the heavens will be shaken. 27Then they will see 'the Son of Man coming in a cloud' with power and great glory. 28Now when these things begin to take place, stand up and raise your heads, because your redemption is drawing near."

THE LESSON OF THE FIG TREE

29 Then he told them a parable: "Look at the fig tree and all the trees; 30as soon as they sprout leaves you can see for yourselves and know that summer is already near. 31So also, when you see these things taking place, you know that the kingdom of God is near. 32Truly I tell you, this generation will not pass away until all things have taken place. 33Heaven and earth will pass away, but my words will not pass away.

EXHORTATION TO WATCH

34 "Be on guard so that your hearts are not weighed down with dissipation and drunkenness and the worries of this life, and that day does not catch you unexpectedly, 35like a trap. For it will come upon all who live on the face of the whole earth. 36Be alert at all times, praying that you may have the strength to escape all these things that will take place, and to stand before the Son of Man."

37 Every day he was teaching in the temple, and at night he would go out and spend the night on the Mount of Olives, as it was called.

38And all the people would get up early in the morning to listen to him in the temple.

THE PLOT TO KILL JESUS

22 Now the festival of Unleavened Bread, which is called the Passover, was near. 2The chief priests and the scribes were looking for a way to put Jesus[a] to death, for they were afraid of the people.

3 Then Satan entered into Judas called Iscariot, who was one of the twelve; 4he went away and conferred with the chief priests and officers of the temple police about how he might betray him to them. 5They were greatly pleased and agreed to give him money. 6So he consented and began to look for an opportunity to betray him to them when no crowd was present.

THE PREPARATION OF THE PASSOVER

7 Then came the day of Unleavened Bread, on which the Passover lamb had to be sacrificed. 8So Jesus[b] sent Peter and John, saying, "Go and prepare the Passover meal for us that we may eat it." 9They asked him, "Where do you want us to make preparations for it?" 10"Listen," he said to them, "when you have entered the city, a man carrying a jar of water will meet you; follow him into the house he enters 11and say to the owner of the house, 'The teacher asks you, "Where is the guest room, where I may eat the Passover with my disciples?" ' 12He will show you a large room upstairs, already furnished. Make preparations for us there." 13So they went and found everything as he had told them; and they prepared the Passover meal.

THE INSTITUTION OF THE LORD'S SUPPER

14 When the hour came, he took his place at the table, and the apostles with him. 15He said to them, "I have eagerly desired to eat this Passover with you before I suffer; 16for I

a 22.2 Gk him   b 22.8 Gk he

tell you, I will not eat it[a] until it is fulfilled in the kingdom of God." [17]Then he took a cup, and after giving thanks he said, "Take this and divide it among yourselves; [18]for I tell you that from now on I will not drink of the fruit of the vine until the kingdom of God comes." [19]Then he took a loaf of bread, and when he had given thanks, he broke it and gave it to them, saying, "This is my body, which is given for you. Do this in remembrance of me." [20]And he did the same with the cup after supper, saying, "This cup that is poured out for you is the new covenant in my blood.[b] [21]But see, the one who betrays me is with me, and his hand is on the table. [22]For the Son of Man is going as it has been determined,

---

PONDER

Then he took a loaf of bread, and when he had given thanks, he broke it and gave it to them, saying, "This is my body, which is given for you. Do this in remembrance of me." And he did the same with the cup after the supper, saying, "This cup that is poured out for you is the new covenant in my blood."
—Luke 22.19–20

PRAY

O Father, we bless you for this scripture passage in which Jesus lovingly met with his own disciples, even one who betrayed him, to have supper, to offer you thanksgiving and to commemorate his coming death and resurrection. As we contemplate, in an incisive and personal way, the importance of this Last Supper, we witness the deep love Jesus had for you and his fervent desire to follow you. We confess our sin and repent of our sometimes-superficial allegiance. Give us the will, throughout the moments of our lives, to emulate the perfect life of our Savior, in whose name we pray. Amen.

---

but woe to that one by whom he is betrayed!" [23]Then they began to ask one another which one of them it could be who would do this.

THE DISPUTE ABOUT GREATNESS

[24]A dispute also arose among them as to which one of them was to be regarded as the greatest. [25]But he said to them, "The kings of the Gentiles lord it over them; and those in authority over them are called benefactors. [26]But not so with you; rather the greatest among you must become like the youngest, and the leader like one who serves. [27]For who is greater, the one who is at the table or the one who serves? Is it not the one at the table? But I am among you as one who serves.

[28]"You are those who have stood by me in my trials; [29]and I confer on you, just as my Father has conferred on me, a kingdom, [30]so that you may eat and drink at my table in my kingdom, and you will sit on thrones judging the twelve tribes of Israel.

JESUS PREDICTS PETER'S DENIAL

[31]"Simon, Simon, listen! Satan has demanded[c] to sift all of you like wheat, [32]but I have prayed for you that your own faith may not fail; and you, when once you have turned back, strengthen your brothers." [33]And he said to him, "Lord, I am ready to go with you to prison and to death!" [34]Jesus[d] said, "I tell you, Peter, the cock will not crow this day, until you have denied three times that you know me."

PURSE, BAG, AND SWORD

[35]He said to them, "When I sent you out without a purse, bag, or sandals, did you lack anything?" They said, "No, not a thing." [36]He said to them, "But now, the one who has a purse must take it, and likewise a bag. And the one who has no

[a] **22.16** Other ancient authorities read *never eat it again*   [b] **22.20** Other ancient authorities lack, in whole or in part, verses 19b–20 (*which is given... in my blood*)   [c] **22.31** Or *has obtained permission*   [d] **22.34** Gk *He*

sword must sell his cloak and buy one. 37For I tell you, this scripture must be fulfilled in me, 'And he was counted among the lawless'; and indeed what is written about me is being fulfilled." 38They said, "Lord, look, here are two swords." He replied, "It is enough."

JESUS PRAYS ON THE MOUNT OF OLIVES

39 He came out and went, as was his custom, to the Mount of Olives; and the disciples followed him. 40When he reached the place, he said to them, "Pray that you may not come into the time of trial."[a] 41Then he withdrew from them about a stone's throw, knelt down, and prayed, 42"Father, if you are willing, remove this cup from me; yet, not my will but yours be done." [[43Then an angel from heaven appeared to him and gave him strength. 44In his anguish he prayed more earnestly, and his sweat became like great drops of blood falling down on the ground.]][b] 45When he got up from prayer, he came to the disciples and found them sleeping because of grief, 46and he said to them, "Why are you sleeping? Get up and pray that you may not come into the time of trial."[a]

THE BETRAYAL AND ARREST OF JESUS

47 While he was still speaking, suddenly a crowd came, and the one called Judas, one of the twelve, was leading them. He approached Jesus to kiss him; 48but Jesus said to him, "Judas, is it with a kiss that you are betraying the Son of Man?" 49When those who were around him saw what was coming, they asked, "Lord, should we strike with the sword?" 50Then one of them struck the slave of the high priest and cut off his right ear. 51But Jesus said, "No more of this!" And he touched his ear and healed him. 52Then Jesus said to the chief priests, the officers of the temple police, and the elders who had come for him, "Have you come out with swords and clubs as if I were a bandit? 53When I was with you day

after day in the temple, you did not lay hands on me. But this is your hour, and the power of darkness!"

PETER DENIES JESUS

54 Then they seized him and led him away, bringing him into the high priest's house. But Peter was following at a distance. 55When they had kindled a fire in the middle of the courtyard and sat down together, Peter sat among them. 56Then a servant-girl, seeing him in the firelight, stared at him and said, "This man also was with him." 57But he denied it, saying, "Woman, I do not know him." 58A little later someone else, on seeing him, said, "You also are one of them." But Peter said, "Man, I am not!" 59Then about an hour later still another kept insisting, "Surely this man also was with him; for he is a Galilean." 60But Peter said, "Man, I do not know what you are talking about!" At that moment, while he was still speaking, the cock crowed. 61The Lord turned and looked at Peter. Then Peter remembered the word of the Lord, how he had said to him, "Before the cock crows today, you will deny me three times." 62And he went out and wept bitterly.

THE MOCKING AND BEATING OF JESUS

63 Now the men who were holding Jesus began to mock him and beat him; 64they also blindfolded him and kept asking him, "Prophesy! Who is it that struck you?" 65They kept heaping many other insults on him.

JESUS BEFORE THE COUNCIL

66 When day came, the assembly of the elders of the people, both chief priests and scribes, gathered together, and they brought him to their council. 67They said, "If you are the Messiah,[c] tell us." He replied, "If I tell you, you will not believe; 68and if I question you, you will not answer. 69But from now on the Son

a 22.40,46 Or into temptation
b 22.44 Other ancient authorities lack verses 43 and 44   c 22.67 Or the Christ

of Man will be seated at the right hand of the power of God." [70]All of them asked, "Are you, then, the Son of God?" He said to them, "You say that I am." [71]Then they said, "What further testimony do we need? We have heard it ourselves from his own lips!"

JESUS BEFORE PILATE

23 Then the assembly rose as a body and brought Jesus[a] before Pilate. [2]They began to accuse him, saying, "We found this man perverting our nation, forbidding us to pay taxes to the emperor, and saying that he himself is the Messiah, a king."[b] [3]Then Pilate asked him, "Are you the king of the Jews?" He answered, "You say so." [4]Then Pilate said to the chief priests and the crowds, "I find no basis for an accusation against this man." [5]But they were insistent and said, "He stirs up the people by teaching throughout all Judea, from Galilee where he began even to this place."

JESUS BEFORE HEROD

[6]When Pilate heard this, he asked whether the man was a Galilean. [7]And when he learned that he was under Herod's jurisdiction, he sent him off to Herod, who was himself in Jerusalem at that time. [8]When Herod saw Jesus, he was very glad, for he had been wanting to see him for a long time, because he had heard about him and was hoping to see him perform some sign. [9]He questioned him at some length, but Jesus[c] gave him no answer. [10]The chief priests and the scribes stood by, vehemently accusing him. [11]Even Herod with his soldiers treated him with contempt and mocked him; then he put an elegant robe on him, and sent him back to Pilate. [12]That same day Herod and Pilate became friends with each other; before this they had been enemies.

JESUS SENTENCED TO DEATH

[13]Pilate then called together the chief priests, the leaders, and the people, [14]and said to them, "You brought me this man as one who was perverting the people; and here I have examined him in your presence and have not found this man guilty of any of your charges against him. [15]Neither has Herod, for he sent him back to us. Indeed, he has done nothing to deserve death. [16]I will therefore have him flogged and release him."[d]

[18]Then they all shouted out together, "Away with this fellow! Release Barabbas for us!" [19](This was a man who had been put in prison for an insurrection that had taken place in the city, and for murder.) [20]Pilate, wanting to release Jesus, addressed them again; [21]but they kept shouting, "Crucify, crucify him!" [22]A third time he said to them, "Why, what evil has he done? I have found in him no ground for the sentence of death; I will therefore have him flogged and then release him." [23]But they kept urgently demanding with loud shouts that he should be crucified; and their voices prevailed. [24]So Pilate gave his verdict that their demand should be granted. [25]He released the man they asked for, the one who had been put in prison for insurrection and murder, and handed Jesus over as they wished.

THE CRUCIFIXION OF JESUS

[26]As they led him away, they seized a man, Simon of Cyrene, who was coming from the country, and they laid the cross on him, and made him carry it behind Jesus. [27]A great number of the people followed him, and among them were women who were beating their breasts and wailing for him. [28]But Jesus turned to them and said, "Daughters of Jerusalem, do not weep for me, but weep for yourselves and for your children. [29]For the days are surely coming when they will say, 'Blessed are the barren, and the wombs that never bore, and the breasts that never nursed.' [30]Then they will begin to say to the mountains, 'Fall on us';

[a] 23.1 Gk him   [b] 23.2 Or is an anointed king
[c] 23.9 Gk he   [d] 23.16 Here, or after verse 19, other ancient authorities add verse 17, Now he was obliged to release someone for them at the festival

and to the hills, 'Cover us.' [31]For if they do this when the wood is green, what will happen when it is dry?"

[32] Two others also, who were criminals, were led away to be put to death with him. [33]When they came to the place that is called The Skull, they crucified Jesus[a] there with the criminals, one on his right and one on his left. [[[34]Then Jesus said, "Father, forgive them; for they do not know what they are doing."]][b] And they cast lots to divide his clothing. [35]And the people stood by, watching; but the leaders scoffed at him, saying, "He saved others; let him save himself if he is the Messiah[c] of God, his chosen one!" [36]The soldiers also mocked him, coming up and offering him sour wine, [37]and saying, "If you are the King of the Jews, save yourself!" [38]There was also an inscription over him,[d] "This is the King of the Jews."

[39] One of the criminals who were hanged there kept deriding[e] him and saying, "Are you not the Messiah?[c] Save yourself and us!" [40]But the other rebuked him, saying, "Do you not fear God, since you are under the same sentence of condemnation? [41]And we indeed have been condemned justly, for we are getting what we deserve for our deeds, but this man has done nothing wrong." [42]Then he said, "Jesus, remember me when you come into[f] your kingdom." [43]He replied, "Truly I tell you, today you will be with me in Paradise."

THE DEATH OF JESUS

[44] It was now about noon, and darkness came over the whole land[g] until three in the afternoon, [45]while the sun's light failed;[h] and the curtain of the temple was torn in two. [46]Then Jesus, crying with a loud voice, said, "Father, into your hands I commend my spirit." Having said this, he breathed his last. [47]When the centurion saw what had taken place, he praised God and said, "Certainly this man was innocent."[i] [48]And when all the crowds who had gathered there for this spectacle saw what had taken place, they returned

PONDER

Then Jesus, crying with a loud voice, said, "Father, into your hands I commend my spirit." Having said this, he breathed his last.
—Luke 23.46

PRAY

Lord Jesus, though we have heard since we were children this story about your death on the cross, we are deeply moved by your words. In spite of your terrible suffering, you entrusted your spirit to your Father. Inspire us, even in our loneliest moments, by the memory of what you did for us. Help us to realize that you paid the price for our sinfulness. Thank you that we can come to you in prayer and entrust our spirits, our hearts and our lives to you. Thank you that despite our trials and tribulations, our fears and doubts, our failures and our sorrows, we can speak directly with you, the Source of unlimited power and wisdom. With praise and gratitude we pray. Amen.

home, beating their breasts. [49]But all his acquaintances, including the women who had followed him from Galilee, stood at a distance, watching these things.

THE BURIAL OF JESUS

[50] Now there was a good and righteous man named Joseph, who, though a member of the council, [51]had not agreed to their plan and action. He came from the Jewish town of Arimathea, and he was

[a] **23.33** Gk *him*   [b] **23.34** Other ancient authorities lack the sentence *Then Jesus... what they are doing*   [c] **23.35,39** Or *the Christ*   [d] **23.38** Other ancient authorities add *written in Greek and Latin and Hebrew* (that is, *Aramaic*)   [e] **23.39** Or *blaspheming*   [f] **23.42** Other ancient authorities read *in*   [g] **23.44** Or *earth*   [h] **23.45** Or *the sun was eclipsed.* Other ancient authorities read *the sun was darkened*   [i] **23.47** Or *righteous*

waiting expectantly for the kingdom of God. 52 This man went to Pilate and asked for the body of Jesus. 53 Then he took it down, wrapped it in a linen cloth, and laid it in a rock-hewn tomb where no one had ever been laid. 54 It was the day of Preparation, and the sabbath was beginning.[a] 55 The women who had come with him from Galilee followed, and they saw the tomb and how his body was laid. 56 Then they returned, and prepared spices and ointments.

On the sabbath they rested according to the commandment.

THE RESURRECTION OF JESUS

24 But on the first day of the week, at early dawn, they came to the tomb, taking the spices that they had prepared. 2 They found the stone rolled away from the tomb, 3 but when they went in, they did not find the body.[b] 4 While they were perplexed about this, suddenly two men in dazzling clothes stood beside them. 5 The women[c] were terrified and bowed their faces to the ground, but the men[d] said to them, "Why do you look for the living among the dead? He is not here, but has risen.[e] 6 Remember how he told you, while he was still in Galilee, 7 that the Son of Man must be handed over to sinners, and be crucified, and on the third day rise again." 8 Then they remembered his words, 9 and returning from the tomb, they told all this to the eleven and to all the rest. 10 Now it was Mary Magdalene, Joanna, Mary the mother of James, and the other women with them who told this to the apostles. 11 But these words seemed to them an idle tale, and they did not believe them. 12 But Peter got up and ran to the tomb; stooping and looking in, he saw the linen cloths by themselves; then he went home, amazed at what had happened.[f]

THE WALK TO EMMAUS

13 Now on that same day two of them were going to a village called Emmaus, about seven miles[g] from Jerusalem, 14 and talking with each other about all these things that had

happened. 15 While they were talking and discussing, Jesus himself came near and went with them, 16 but their eyes were kept from recognizing him. 17 And he said to them, "What are you discussing with each other while you walk along?" They stood still, looking sad.[h] 18 Then one of them, whose name was Cleopas, answered him, "Are you the only stranger in Jerusalem who does not know the things that have taken place there in these days?" 19 He

[a] **23.54** Gk *was dawning*   [b] **24.3** Other ancient authorities add *of the Lord Jesus*   [c] **24.5** Gk *They*   [d] **24.5** Gk *but they*   [e] **24.5** Other ancient authorities lack *He is not here, but has risen*   [f] **24.12** Other ancient authorities lack verse 12   [g] **24.13** Gk *sixty stadia; other ancient authorities read a hundred sixty stadia*   [h] **24.17** Other ancient authorities read *walk along, looking sad?"*

asked them, "What things?" They replied, "The things about Jesus of Nazareth,[a] who was a prophet mighty in deed and word before God and all the people, 20and how our chief priests and leaders handed him over to be condemned to death and crucified him. 21But we had hoped that he was the one to redeem Israel.[b] Yes, and besides all this, it is now the third day since these things took place. 22Moreover, some women of our group astounded us. They were at the tomb early this morning, 23and when they did not find his body there, they came back and told us that they had indeed seen a vision of angels who said that he was alive. 24Some of those who were with us went to the tomb and found it just as the women had said; but they did not see him." 25Then he said to them, "Oh, how foolish you are, and how slow of heart to believe all that the prophets have declared! 26Was it not necessary that the Messiah[c] should suffer these things and then enter into his glory?" 27Then beginning with Moses and all the prophets, he interpreted to them the things about himself in all the scriptures.

28 As they came near the village to which they were going, he walked ahead as if he were going on. 29But they urged him strongly, saying, "Stay with us, because it is almost evening and the day is now nearly over." So he went in to stay with them. 30When he was at the table with them, he took bread, blessed and broke it, and gave it to them. 31Then their eyes were opened, and they recognized him; and he vanished from their sight. 32They said to each other, "Were not our hearts burning within us[d] while he was talking to us on the road, while he was opening the scriptures to us?" 33That same hour they got up and returned to Jerusalem; and they found the eleven and their companions gathered together. 34They were saying, "The Lord has risen indeed, and he has appeared to Simon!" 35Then they told what had happened on the road, and how he had been made known to them in the breaking of the bread.

JESUS APPEARS TO HIS DISCIPLES

36 While they were talking about this, Jesus himself stood among them and said to them, "Peace be with you."[e] 37They were startled and terrified, and thought that they were seeing a ghost. 38He said to them, "Why are you frightened, and why do doubts arise in your

[a] 24.19 Other ancient authorities read *Jesus the Nazorean* [b] 24.21 Or *to set Israel free* [c] 24.26 Or *the Christ* [d] 24.32 Other ancient authorities lack *within us* [e] 24.36 Other ancient authorities lack *and said to them, "Peace be with you."*

⊢ BIBLE IN LIFE ▷

Hope
Luke 24.13–49

To experience the presence of Christ, people need both faith and hope. The disciples, including the two believers whom Jesus met on the road to Emmaus, had hoped that Jesus would be the one to redeem Israel, yet they had not believed what Jesus had told them about his resurrection. They did not have faith in the scriptures that pointed to the Messiah's death and resurrection. They had even discounted the good news told to them by the women who had been to the empty tomb. They were left without hope. However, the risen Jesus revealed himself to them, and these hopeless, fearful, uneducated disciples were empowered with a new hope. Their faith in the resurrected Christ led them to become heroic, brave, courageous, ambitious people who spread the gospel and formed churches. Because of the resurrection of Christ, hope is available to every one of us. No matter how frustrated or inadequate we might feel, we can do great things in the name of Christ and can share that hope with others.

hearts? [39]Look at my hands and my feet; see that it is I myself. Touch me and see; for a ghost does not have flesh and bones as you see that I have." [40]And when he had said this, he showed them his hands and his feet.[a] [41]While in their joy they were disbelieving and still wondering, he said to them, "Have you anything here to eat?" [42]They gave him a piece of broiled fish, [43]and he took it and ate in their presence.

[44] Then he said to them, "These are my words that I spoke to you while I was still with you—that everything written about me in the law of Moses, the prophets, and the psalms must be fulfilled." [45]Then he opened their minds to understand the scriptures, [46]and he said to them, "Thus it is written, that the Messiah[b] is to suffer and to rise from the dead on the third day, [47]and that repentance and forgiveness of sins is to be proclaimed in his name to all nations, beginning from Jerusalem. [48]You are witnesses[c] of these things. [49]And see, I am sending upon you what my Father promised; so stay here in the city until you have been clothed with power from on high."

THE ASCENSION OF JESUS

[50] Then he led them out as far as Bethany, and, lifting up his hands, he blessed them. [51]While he was blessing them, he withdrew from them and was carried up into heaven.[d] [52]And they worshiped him, and[e] returned to Jerusalem with great joy; [53]and they were continually in the temple blessing God.[f]

[a] **24.40** Other ancient authorities lack verse 40   [b] **24.46** Or *the Christ*
[c] **24.48** Or *nations. Beginning from Jerusalem* [48]*you are witnesses*
[d] **24.51** Other ancient authorities lack *and was carried up into heaven*   [e] **24.52** Other ancient authorities lack *worshiped him, and*
[f] **24.53** Other ancient authorities add *Amen*

The Gospel According to

JOHN

Knowing about Jesus involves acquiring information about him. But knowing Jesus means to embrace him with eager belief, as the Son of God. John writes this Gospel to prompt this second response to Jesus. John's Gospel highlights the rich symbolic language Jesus himself uses to show that he is from the Father and "the way, and the truth, and the life" (John 14.6). As you read this book, meditate on the many facets of Jesus as the source of life: He is the Lamb of God (1.29), the living water (4.10), the bread of life (6.35), the light of the world (8.12), the good shepherd (10.14).

THE WORD BECAME FLESH

1 In the beginning was the Word, and the Word was with God, and the Word was God. ²He was in the beginning with God. ³All things came into being through him, and without him not one thing came into being. What has come into being ⁴in him was life,ᵃ and the life was the light of all people. ⁵The light shines in the darkness, and the darkness did not overcome it.

6 There was a man sent from God, whose name was John. ⁷He came as a witness to testify to the light, so that all might believe through him. ⁸He himself was not the light, but he came to testify to the light. ⁹The true light, which enlightens everyone, was coming into the world.ᵇ

THE HUMANITY OF CHRIST

HELPS US TO KNOW HIM

AND OURSELVES.

10 He was in the world, and the world came into being through him; yet the world did not know him. ¹¹He came to what was his own,ᶜ and his own people did not accept him. ¹²But to all who received him, who believed in his name, he gave power to become children of God, ¹³who were born, not of blood or of the will of the flesh or of the will of man, but of God.

14 And the Word became flesh and lived among us, and we have seen his glory, the glory as of a father's only son,ᵈ full of grace and truth. ¹⁵(John testified to him and cried out, "This was he of whom I said, 'He who comes after me ranks ahead of me because he was before me.' ") ¹⁶From his fullness we have all received, grace upon grace. ¹⁷The law indeed was given through Moses; grace and truth came through Jesus Christ. ¹⁸No one has ever seen God. It is God the only Son,ᵉ who is close to the Father's heart,ᶠ who has made him known.

THE TESTIMONY OF JOHN THE BAPTIST

19 This is the testimony given by John when the Jews sent priests and Levites from Jerusalem to ask him, "Who are you?" ²⁰He confessed and did not deny it, but confessed, "I am not the Messiah."ᵍ ²¹And they asked him, "What then? Are you Elijah?" He said, "I am not." "Are you the prophet?" He answered, "No." ²²Then they said to him, "Who are you? Let us have an answer for those who sent us. What do you say about yourself?" ²³He said,

"I am the voice of one crying
out in the wilderness,
'Make straight the way
of the Lord,' "

as the prophet Isaiah said.

24 Now they had been sent from the Pharisees. ²⁵They asked him, "Why then are you baptizing if you are neither the Messiah,ᵍ nor Elijah, nor the prophet?" ²⁶John answered them, "I baptize with water. Among you stands one whom you do not know, ²⁷the one who is coming after me; I am not worthy to untie the thong of his sandal." ²⁸This took place in Bethany across the Jordan where John was baptizing.

THE LAMB OF GOD

29 The next day he saw Jesus coming toward him and declared, "Here is the Lamb of God who takes away the sin of the world! ³⁰This is he of whom I said, 'After me comes a man who ranks ahead of me because he was before me.' ³¹I myself did not know him; but I came baptizing with water for this reason, that he might be revealed to Israel." ³²And John testified, "I saw the Spirit descending from heaven like a dove, and it remained on him. ³³I myself did not know him, but the one who sent me to baptize with water said to

ᵃ 1.4 Or ³through him. And without him not one thing came into being that has come into being. ⁴In him was life ᵇ 1.9 Or He was the true light that enlightens everyone coming into the world ᶜ 1.11 Or to his own home ᵈ 1.14 Or the Father's only Son ᵉ 1.18 Other ancient authorities read It is an only Son, God, or It is the only Son ᶠ 1.18 Gk bosom ᵍ 1.20,25 Or the Christ

BIBLE IN FOCUS

Grace and More Grace

From his fullness we have all received, grace upon grace.

—John 1.16

The first chapter of John is one of the most beautiful parts of the Bible. Look at the words used to describe Jesus' entry into the world: God Almighty "became flesh and lived among us, and we have seen his glory, the glory as of a father's only son, full of grace and truth" (verse 14). It was through Jesus, the Word, that God gave us his unlimited riches and blessings.

There's another beautiful picture painted in John 1.16: From the fullness of his grace we have all received one blessing after another. God's grace is unlimited, unbounded, unfathomable, unexplainable and inexhaustible. Here's Jesus, a human being who personifies and epitomizes unlimited love, service, compassion, peace, truth and grace.

John continues to try and get us to stretch our minds. He wants us to consider the significance of Jesus Christ: God's Son, who shares God's deity and was present when the universe was created. As a man, Jesus walked as flesh and blood. He hurt when people whipped him and drove nails through his hands and feet and when thorns penetrated his brow or his skull. He felt abandoned at the cross when he took our sins upon himself.

Through Jesus' sacrifice, God extends forgiveness to us that we do not deserve. He doesn't treat us the way we often treat others by saying, "I'll forgive you this time, but if you do anything wrong again, then you're gone." But he continues to extend grace to us as long as we acknowledge Jesus as the Son of God.

What should we get out of this most beautiful of passages? We should take a look at Jesus' life—how he acted, what he did, what he said, how he related to others—and apply it in our own lives.

That is not an easy thing to do, because when we get back to the mundane living in the modern, fast-changing, technologically advanced world, it's hard for us to believe that Jesus' teaching 2,000 years ago really can apply to life today, but it does. We should contemplate our lives and measure ourselves against the example that John has given us in this beautiful first chapter of his book.

How do our lives compare with that of Christ? In what ways can we closer emulate how Christ lived? How can we accept the grace and truth we've received and extend it to others? Our lives should be more compatible with the teaching of God, to whom we have pledged on our word of honor to revere and to have as core to our own human existence. That's what John is telling us to do.

Going Deeper

- Why do you suppose forgiveness is so difficult to extend to others?
- How would your immediate family or community look different if you more closely emulated the grace and love of Christ?

me, 'He on whom you see the Spirit descend and remain is the one who baptizes with the Holy Spirit.' 34 And I myself have seen and have testified that this is the Son of God."[a]

THE FIRST DISCIPLES OF JESUS

35 The next day John again was standing with two of his disciples, 36 and as he watched Jesus walk by, he exclaimed, "Look, here is the Lamb of God!" 37 The two disciples heard him say this, and they followed Jesus. 38 When Jesus turned and saw them following, he said to them, "What are you looking for?" They said to him, "Rabbi" (which translated means Teacher), "where are you staying?" 39 He said to them, "Come and see." They came and saw where he was staying, and they remained with him that day. It was about four o'clock in the afternoon. 40 One of the two who heard John speak and followed him was Andrew, Simon Peter's brother. 41 He first found his brother Simon and said to him, "We have found the Messiah" (which is translated Anointed[b]). 42 He brought Simon[c] to Jesus, who looked at him and said, "You are Simon son of John. You are to be called Cephas" (which is translated Peter[d]).

JESUS CALLS PHILIP AND NATHANAEL

43 The next day Jesus decided to go to Galilee. He found Philip and said to him, "Follow me." 44 Now Philip was from Bethsaida, the city of Andrew and Peter. 45 Philip found Nathanael and said to him, "We have found him about whom Moses in the law and also the prophets wrote, Jesus son of Joseph from Nazareth." 46 Nathanael said to him, "Can anything good come out of Nazareth?" Philip said to him, "Come and see." 47 When Jesus saw Nathanael coming toward him, he said of him, "Here is truly an Israelite in whom there is no deceit!" 48 Nathanael asked him, "Where did you get to know me?" Jesus answered, "I saw you under the fig tree before Philip called you." 49 Nathan-

ael replied, "Rabbi, you are the Son of God! You are the King of Israel!" 50 Jesus answered, "Do you believe because I told you that I saw you under the fig tree? You will see greater things than these." 51 And he said to him, "Very truly, I tell you,[e] you will see heaven opened and the angels of God ascending and descending upon the Son of Man."

THE WEDDING AT CANA

2 On the third day there was a wedding in Cana of Galilee, and the mother of Jesus was there. 2 Jesus and his disciples had also been invited to the wedding. 3 When the wine gave out, the mother of Jesus said to him, "They have no wine." 4 And Jesus said to her, "Woman, what concern is that to you and to me? My hour has not yet come." 5 His mother said to the servants, "Do whatever he tells you." 6 Now standing there were six stone water jars for the Jewish rites of purification, each holding twenty or thirty gallons. 7 Jesus said to them, "Fill the jars with water." And they filled them up to the brim. 8 He said to them, "Now draw some out, and take it to the chief steward." So they took it. 9 When the steward tasted the water that had become wine, and did not know where it came from (though the servants who had drawn the water knew), the steward called the bridegroom 10 and said to him, "Everyone serves the good wine first, and then the inferior wine after the guests have become drunk. But you have kept the good wine until now." 11 Jesus did this, the first of his signs, in Cana of Galilee, and revealed his glory; and his disciples believed in him.

12 After this he went down to Capernaum with his mother, his brothers, and his disciples; and they remained there a few days.

---

[a] 1.34 Other ancient authorities read is God's chosen one   [b] 1.41 Or Christ   [c] 1.42 Gk him   [d] 1.42 From the word for rock in Aramaic (kepha) and Greek (petra), respectively   [e] 1.51 Both instances of the Greek word for you in this verse are plural

JESUS CLEANSES THE TEMPLE

13 The Passover of the Jews was near, and Jesus went up to Jerusalem. 14 In the temple he found people selling cattle, sheep, and doves, and the money changers seated at their tables. 15 Making a whip of cords, he drove all of them out of the temple, both the sheep and the cattle. He also poured out the coins of the money changers and overturned their tables. 16 He told those who were selling the doves, "Take these things out of here! Stop making my Father's house a marketplace!" 17 His disciples remembered that it was written, "Zeal for your house will consume me." 18 The Jews then said to him, "What sign can you show us for doing this?" 19 Jesus answered them, "Destroy this temple, and in three days I will raise it up." 20 The Jews then said, "This temple has been under construction for forty-six years, and will you raise it up in three days?" 21 But he was speaking of the temple of his body. 22 After he was raised from the dead, his disciples remembered that he had said this; and they believed the scripture and the word that Jesus had spoken.

23 When he was in Jerusalem during the Passover festival, many believed in his name because they saw the signs that he was doing. 24 But Jesus on his part would not entrust himself to them, because he knew all people 25 and needed no one to testify about anyone; for he himself knew what was in everyone.

NICODEMUS VISITS JESUS

3 Now there was a Pharisee named Nicodemus, a leader of the Jews. 2 He came to Jesus[a] by night and said to him, "Rabbi, we know that you are a teacher who has come from God; for no one can do these signs that you do apart from the presence of God." 3 Jesus answered him, "Very truly, I tell you, no one can see the kingdom of God without being born from above."[b] 4 Nicodemus said to him, "How can anyone be born after having grown old? Can one enter a second time into the mother's womb and be born?" 5 Jesus answered, "Very truly, I tell you, no one can enter the kingdom of God without being born of water and Spirit. 6 What is born of the flesh is flesh, and what is born of the Spirit is spirit.[c] 7 Do not be astonished that I said to you, 'You[d] must be born from above.'[e] 8 The wind[c] blows where it chooses, and you hear the sound of it, but you do not know where it comes from or where it goes. So it is with everyone who is born of the Spirit." 9 Nicodemus said to him, "How can these things be?"

---

[a] 3.2 Gk *him*   [b] 3.3 Or *born anew*
[c] 3.6,8 The same Greek word means both *wind* and *spirit*   [d] 3.7 The Greek word for *you* here is plural   [e] 3.7 Or *anew*

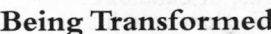

BIBLE IN LIFE

Being Transformed
John 2.1–11

In the Old Testament, we read about plagues inflicted upon the Egyptians, waters parting, an ax head floating, lions' mouths remaining shut. All those miracles create consternation and wonder in us as we see the glory of God. With God's ordainment, miracles occur. In Jesus' first miracle, recorded in John 2, we see a human touch. Here is God in human form, the Christ, the Messiah. What happened to the disciples after this event? They were still human beings. They still made mistakes. They still left Jesus in times of crisis. But because of the transforming power of Jesus' turning water into wine, the disciples believed in Jesus. In the same way, even though we believe in Jesus, we continue to make mistakes. At times we turn away from Christ. We might even have doubts about our faith, but as we observe the miracles of Christ, we, too, can experience transformation and become more like Christ.

10 Jesus answered him, "Are you a teacher of Israel, and yet you do not understand these things?

11 "Very truly, I tell you, we speak of what we know and testify to what we have seen; yet you[a] do not receive our testimony. 12 If I have told you about earthly things and you do not believe, how can you believe if I tell you about heavenly things? 13 No one has ascended into heaven except the one who descended from heaven, the Son of Man.[b] 14 And just as Moses lifted up the serpent in the wilderness, so must the Son of Man be lifted up, 15 that whoever believes in him may have eternal life.[c]

WITH CHRIST, WE "PUT OFF THE OLD PERSON," "MAKE ALL THINGS NEW" AND ARE "BORN AGAIN." THESE WORDS CAN BE GLIB EXPRESSIONS OR LIFE TRANSFORMING.

16 "For God so loved the world that he gave his only Son, so that everyone who believes in him may not perish but may have eternal life. 17 "Indeed, God did not send the Son into the world to condemn the world, but in order that the world might be saved through him. 18 Those who believe in him are not condemned; but those who do not believe are condemned already, because they have not believed in the name of the only Son of God. 19 And this is the judgment, that the light has come into the world, and people loved darkness rather than light because their deeds were evil. 20 For all who do evil hate the light and do not come to the light, so that their deeds may not be exposed. 21 But those who do what is true come to the light, so that it may be clearly seen that their deeds have been done in God."[c]

JESUS AND JOHN THE BAPTIST

22 After this Jesus and his disciples went into the Judean countryside, and he spent some time there with them and baptized. 23 John also was baptizing at Aenon near Salim because water was abundant there; and people kept coming and were being baptized 24 —John, of course, had not yet been thrown into prison. 25 Now a discussion about purification arose between John's disciples and a Jew.[d] 26 They came to John and said to him, "Rabbi, the one who was with you across the Jordan, to whom you testified, here he is baptizing, and all are going to him." 27 John answered, "No one can receive anything except what has been given from heaven. 28 You yourselves are my witnesses that I said, 'I am not the Messiah,[e] but I have been sent ahead of him.' 29 He who has the bride is the bridegroom. The friend of the bridegroom, who stands and hears him, rejoices greatly at the bridegroom's voice. For this reason my joy has been fulfilled. 30 He must increase, but I must decrease."[f]

THE ONE WHO COMES FROM HEAVEN

31 The one who comes from above is above all; the one who is of the earth belongs to the earth and speaks about earthly things. The one who comes from heaven is above all. 32 He testifies to what he has seen and heard, yet no one accepts his testimony. 33 Whoever has accepted his testimony has certified[g] this, that God is true. 34 He whom God has sent speaks the words of God, for he gives the Spirit without measure. 35 The Father loves the Son and has placed all things in his hands. 36 Whoever believes in the Son has eternal life; whoever disobeys the Son will

[a] 3.11 The Greek word for you here and in verse 12 is plural   [b] 3.13 Other ancient authorities add who is in heaven   [c] 3.15,21 Some interpreters hold that the quotation concludes with verse 15   [d] 3.25 Other ancient authorities read the Jews   [e] 3.28 Or the Christ   [f] 3.30 Some interpreters hold that the quotation continues through verse 36   [g] 3.33 Gk set a seal to

not see life, but must endure God's wrath.

JESUS AND THE WOMAN OF SAMARIA

4 Now when Jesus[a] learned that the Pharisees had heard, "Jesus is making and baptizing more disciples than John" 2—although it was not Jesus himself but his disciples who baptized— 3he left Judea and started back to Galilee. 4But he had to go through Samaria. 5So he came to a Samaritan city called Sychar, near the plot of ground that Jacob had given to his son Joseph. 6Jacob's well was there, and Jesus, tired out by his journey, was sitting by the well. It was about noon.

7 A Samaritan woman came to draw water, and Jesus said to her, "Give me a drink." 8(His disciples had gone to the city to buy food.) 9The Samaritan woman said to him, "How is it that you, a Jew, ask a drink of me, a woman of Samaria?" (Jews do not share things in common with Samaritans.)[b] 10Jesus answered her, "If you knew the gift of God, and who it is that is saying to you, 'Give me a drink,' you would have asked him, and he would have given you living water." 11The woman said to him, "Sir, you have no bucket, and the well is deep. Where do you get that living water? 12Are you greater than our ancestor Jacob, who gave us the well, and with his sons and his flocks drank from it?" 13Jesus said to her, "Everyone who drinks of this water will be thirsty again, 14but those who drink of the water that I will give them will never be thirsty. The water that I will give will become in them a spring of water gushing up to eternal life." 15The woman said to him, "Sir, give me this water, so that I may never be thirsty or have to keep coming here to draw water."

16 Jesus said to her, "Go, call your husband, and come back." 17The woman answered him, "I have no husband." Jesus said to her, "You are right in saying, 'I have no husband'; 18for you have had five husbands, and the one you have now is not your husband. What you have said is true!" 19The woman said to him, "Sir, I see that you are a prophet. 20Our ancestors worshiped on this mountain, but you[c] say that the place where people must worship is in Jerusalem." 21Jesus said to her, "Woman, believe me, the hour is coming when you will worship the Father neither on this mountain nor in Jerusalem. 22You worship what you do not know; we worship what we know, for salvation is from the Jews. 23But the hour is coming, and is now here, when the true worshipers will worship the Father in spirit and truth, for the Father seeks such as these to worship him. 24God is spirit, and those who worship him must worship in spirit and truth." 25The woman said to him, "I know that Messiah is coming" (who is called Christ). "When he comes, he will proclaim all things to us." 26Jesus said to her, "I am he,[d] the one who is speaking to you."

27 Just then his disciples came. They were astonished that he was speaking with a woman, but no one said, "What do you want?" or, "Why are you speaking with her?" 28Then the woman left her water jar and went back to the city. She said to the people, 29"Come and see a man who told me everything I have ever done! He cannot be the Messiah,[e] can he?" 30They left the city and were on their way to him.

31 Meanwhile the disciples were urging him, "Rabbi, eat something." 32But he said to them, "I have food to eat that you do not know about." 33So the disciples said to one another, "Surely no one has brought him something to eat?" 34Jesus said to them, "My food is to do the will of him who sent me and to complete his work. 35Do you not say, 'Four months more, then comes the harvest'? But I tell you, look around you, and see how the fields are ripe for harvesting. 36The reaper is already

---

a 4.1 Other ancient authorities read the Lord   b 4.9 Other ancient authorities lack this sentence   c 4.20 The Greek word for you here and in verses 21 and 22 is plural   d 4.26 Gk I am   e 4.29 Or the Christ

receiving[a] wages and is gathering fruit for eternal life, so that sower and reaper may rejoice together. [37]For here the saying holds true, 'One sows and another reaps.' [38]I sent you to reap that for which you did not labor. Others have labored, and you have entered into their labor."

39 Many Samaritans from that city believed in him because of the woman's testimony, "He told me everything I have ever done." [40]So when the Samaritans came to him, they asked him to stay with them; and he stayed there two days. [41]And many more believed because of his word. [42]They said to the woman, "It is no longer because of what you said that we believe, for we have heard for ourselves, and we know that this is truly the Savior of the world."

JESUS RETURNS TO GALILEE

43 When the two days were over, he went from that place to Galilee [44](for Jesus himself had testified that a prophet has no honor in the prophet's own country). [45]When he came to Galilee, the Galileans welcomed him, since they had seen all that he had done in Jerusalem at the festival; for they too had gone to the festival.

JESUS HEALS AN OFFICIAL'S SON

46 Then he came again to Cana in Galilee where he had changed the water into wine. Now there was a royal official whose son lay ill in Capernaum. [47]When he heard that Jesus had come from Judea to Galilee, he went and begged him to come down and heal his son, for he was at the point of death. [48]Then Jesus said to him, "Unless you[b] see signs and wonders you will not believe." [49]The official said to him, "Sir, come down before my little boy dies." [50]Jesus said to him, "Go; your son will live." The man believed the word that Jesus spoke to him and started on his way. [51]As he was going down, his slaves met him and told him that his child was alive. [52]So he asked them the hour when he began to recover, and they said to him, "Yesterday at one in the afternoon the fever left him." [53]The father realized that this was the hour when Jesus had said to him, "Your son will live." So he himself believed, along with his whole household. [54]Now this was the second sign that Jesus did after coming from Judea to Galilee.

JESUS HEALS ON THE SABBATH

5 After this there was a festival of the Jews, and Jesus went up to Jerusalem.

2 Now in Jerusalem by the Sheep Gate there is a pool, called in Hebrew[a]

---

[a] 4.36 Or [35]... the fields are already ripe for harvesting. [36]The reaper is receiving
[b] 4.48 Both instances of the Greek word for you in this verse are plural

---

BIBLE IN LIFE

Breaking Down Barriers   John 4.1–42

There was an intense hatred between the Jews and the Samaritans. When Jews traveled from Galilee to Jerusalem, they would ordinarily cross the Jordan River, journey down the eastern bank of it and then cross back toward Jerusalem, just to keep from going through Samaria. The disciples were shocked that Jesus wanted to travel through Samaria. It was even more disturbing that Jesus spoke to a Samaritan woman, for it was strictly forbidden that any religious Jew speak to a woman in public, much less an immoral woman. Jesus broke down the barriers that separated them by talking with her and asking for a drink from her water jar. He accepted her just as she was. Some of us will live out the rest of our lives and never break through the barriers that separate us from those to whom Christ sends us. But when we confront our own sins and remember that those who don't know Christ are equally sinful but equally loved by God, we can break down the barriers and witness to them.

PONDER

The father realized that this was the hour when Jesus had said to him, "Your son will live." So he himself believed, along with his whole household.

—John 4.53

PRAY

O Father, help us to learn from the faith of the father of this little boy. Help us remember the miraculous way that Christ answered his entreaty. As we witness this miracle, let us not simply wonder about the medical reasons for the child's recovery but see the life-giving power of Jesus. May we all believe as the father and his household believed. We pray these things in Jesus' name. Amen.

Beth-zatha,ᵇ which has five porticoes. ³In these lay many invalids—blind, lame, and paralyzed.ᶜ ⁵One man was there who had been ill for thirty-eight years. ⁶When Jesus saw him lying there and knew that he had been there a long time, he said to him, "Do you want to be made well?" ⁷The sick man answered him, "Sir, I have no one to put me into the pool when the water is stirred up; and while I am making my way, someone else steps down ahead of me." ⁸Jesus said to him, "Stand up, take your mat and walk." ⁹At once the man was made well, and he took up his mat and began to walk.

Now that day was a sabbath. ¹⁰So the Jews said to the man who had been cured, "It is the sabbath; it is not lawful for you to carry your mat." ¹¹But he answered them, "The man who made me well said to me, 'Take up your mat and walk.'" ¹²They asked him, "Who is the man who said to you, 'Take it up and walk'?" ¹³Now the man who had been healed did not know who it was, for Jesus had disappeared inᵈ the crowd that was there. ¹⁴Later Jesus found him in the temple and said to him, "See, you have been made well! Do not sin any more, so that nothing worse happens to you." ¹⁵The man went away and told the Jews that it was Jesus who had made him well. ¹⁶Therefore the Jews started persecuting Jesus, because he was doing such things on the sabbath. ¹⁷But Jesus answered them, "My Father is still working, and I also am working." ¹⁸For this reason the Jews were seeking all the more to kill him, because he was not only breaking the sabbath, but was also calling God his own Father, thereby making himself equal to God.

THE AUTHORITY OF THE SON

19 Jesus said to them, "Very truly, I tell you, the Son can do nothing on his own, but only what he sees the Father doing; for whatever the Fatherᵉ does, the Son does likewise. ²⁰The Father loves the Son and shows him all that he himself is doing; and he will show him greater works than these, so that you will be astonished. ²¹Indeed, just as the Father raises the dead and gives them life, so also the Son gives life to whomever he wishes. ²²The Father judges no one but has given all judgment to the Son, ²³so that all may honor the Son just as they honor the Father. Anyone who does not honor the Son does not honor the Father who sent him. ²⁴Very truly, I tell you, anyone who hears my word and believes him who sent me has eternal life, and does not come under judgment, but has passed from death to life.

25 "Very truly, I tell you, the hour is coming, and is now here, when

ᵃ 5.2 That is, *Aramaic*   ᵇ 5.2 Other ancient authorities read *Bethesda*, others *Bethsaida*   ᶜ 5.3 Other ancient authorities add, wholly or in part, *waiting for the stirring of the water;* ⁴*for an angel of the Lord went down at certain seasons into the pool, and stirred up the water; whoever stepped in first after the stirring of the water was made well from whatever disease that person had.* ᵈ 5.13 Or *had left because of*   ᵉ 5.19 Gk *that one*

⊕

PONDER

Jesus said to him, "Stand up, take your mat and walk." At once the man was made well, and he took up his mat and began to walk.
—John 5.8–9

PRAY

Father, as we read about the miracles of Jesus, help us also to look with wonder at the events in our daily lives. If we look, we can see you among us, healing and giving new life. Give us insight to apply your Word to our lives in the spirit of humility and dedication to our Savior. Give us the courage to reach toward the perfect standard set for us by Jesus. We know that when we inevitably fall short, your forgiveness is unlimited, for your grace is not bound by our human perceptions. May your love and unity, Triune God, be the pattern for unity among us, your people. Amen.

the dead will hear the voice of the Son of God, and those who hear will live. 26For just as the Father has life in himself, so he has granted the Son also to have life in himself; 27and he has given him authority to execute judgment, because he is the Son of Man. 28Do not be astonished at this; for the hour is coming when all who are in their graves will hear his voice 29and will come out—those who have done good, to the resurrection of life, and those who have done evil, to the resurrection of condemnation.

WITNESSES TO JESUS

30 "I can do nothing on my own. As I hear, I judge; and my judgment is just, because I seek to do not my own will but the will of him who sent me. 31 "If I testify about myself, my testimony is not true. 32There is another who testifies on my behalf,

and I know that his testimony to me is true. 33You sent messengers to John, and he testified to the truth. 34Not that I accept such human testimony, but I say these things so that you may be saved. 35He was a burning and shining lamp, and you were willing to rejoice for a while in his light. 36But I have a testimony greater than John's. The works that the Father has given me to complete, the very works that I am doing, testify on my behalf that the Father has sent me. 37And the Father who sent me has himself testified on my behalf. You have never heard his voice or seen his form, 38and you do not have his word abiding in you, because you do not believe him whom he has sent.

39 "You search the scriptures because you think that in them you have eternal life; and it is they that testify on my behalf. 40Yet you refuse to come to me to have life. 41I do not accept glory from human beings. 42But I know that you do not have the love of God in[a] you. 43I have come in my Father's name, and you do not accept me; if another comes in his own name, you will accept him. 44How can you believe when you accept glory from one another and do not seek the glory that comes from the one who alone is God? 45Do not think that I will accuse you before the Father; your accuser is Moses, on whom you have set your hope. 46If you believed Moses, you would believe me, for he wrote about me. 47But if you do not believe what he wrote, how will you believe what I say?"

FEEDING THE FIVE THOUSAND

6 After this Jesus went to the other side of the Sea of Galilee, also called the Sea of Tiberias.[b] 2A large crowd kept following him, because they saw the signs that he was doing for the sick. 3Jesus went up the mountain and sat down there with his disciples. 4Now the Passover, the festival of the Jews, was near. 5When he looked up and saw a large crowd

[a] 5.42 Or among   [b] 6.1 Gk of Galilee of Tiberias

coming toward him, Jesus said to Philip, "Where are we to buy bread for these people to eat?" [6]He said this to test him, for he himself knew what he was going to do. [7]Philip answered him, "Six months' wages[a] would not buy enough bread for each of them to get a little." [8]One of his disciples, Andrew, Simon Peter's brother, said to him, [9]"There is a boy here who has five barley loaves and two fish. But what are they among so many people?" [10]Jesus said, "Make the people sit down." Now there was a great deal of grass in the place; so they[b] sat down, about five thousand in all. [11]Then Jesus took the loaves, and when he had given thanks, he distributed them to those who were seated; so also the fish, as much as they wanted. [12]When they were satisfied, he told his disciples, "Gather up the fragments left over, so that nothing may be lost." [13]So they gathered them up, and from the fragments of the five barley loaves, left by those who had eaten, they filled twelve baskets. [14]When the people saw the sign that he had done, they began to say, "This is indeed the prophet who is to come into the world."

[15]When Jesus realized that they were about to come and take him by force to make him king, he withdrew again to the mountain by himself.

JESUS WALKS ON THE WATER

[16]When evening came, his disciples went down to the sea, [17]got into a boat, and started across the sea to Capernaum. It was now dark, and Jesus had not yet come to them. [18]The sea became rough because a strong wind was blowing. [19]When they had rowed about three or four miles,[c] they saw Jesus walking on the sea and coming near the boat, and they were terrified. [20]But he said to them, "It is I;[d] do not be afraid." [21]Then they wanted to take him into the boat, and immediately the boat reached the land toward which they were going.

THE BREAD FROM HEAVEN

[22]The next day the crowd that had stayed on the other side of the sea saw that there had been only one boat there. They also saw that Jesus had not got into the boat with his disciples, but that his disciples had gone away alone. [23]Then some boats from Tiberias came near the place where they had eaten the bread after the Lord had given thanks.[e] [24]So when the crowd saw that neither Jesus nor his disciples were there, they themselves got into the boats and went to Capernaum looking for Jesus.

[25]When they found him on the other side of the sea, they said to him, "Rabbi, when did you come here?" [26]Jesus answered them, "Very truly, I tell you, you are looking for me, not because you saw signs, but because you ate your fill of the loaves. [27]Do not work for the food that perishes, but for the food that endures for eternal life, which the Son of Man will give you. For it is on him that God the Father has set his seal." [28]Then they said to him, "What must we do to perform the works of God?" [29]Jesus answered them, "This is the work of God, that you believe in him whom he has sent." [30]So they said to him, "What sign are you going to give us then, so that we may see it and believe you? What work are you performing? [31]Our ancestors ate the manna in the wilderness; as it is written, 'He gave them bread from heaven to eat.' " [32]Then Jesus said to them, "Very truly, I tell you, it was not Moses who gave you the bread from heaven, but it is my Father who gives you the true bread from heaven. [33]For the bread of God is that which[f] comes down from heaven and gives life to the world." [34]They said to him, "Sir, give us this bread always."

[35]Jesus said to them, "I am the bread of life. Whoever comes to me will never be hungry, and whoever believes in me will never be

[a] 6.7 Gk Two hundred denarii; the denarius was the usual day's wage for a laborer
[b] 6.10 Gk the men   [c] 6.19 Gk about twenty-five or thirty stadia   [d] 6.20 Gk I am   [e] 6.23 Other ancient authorities lack after the Lord had given thanks   [f] 6.33 Or he who

thirsty. 36But I said to you that you have seen me and yet do not believe. 37Everything that the Father gives me will come to me, and anyone who comes to me I will never drive away; 38for I have come down from heaven, not to do my own will, but the will of him who sent me. 39And this is the will of him who sent me, that I should lose nothing of all that he has given me, but raise it up on the last day. 40This is indeed the will of my Father, that all who see the Son and believe in him may have eternal life; and I will raise them up on the last day."

41 Then the Jews began to complain about him because he said, "I am the bread that came down from heaven." 42They were saying, "Is not this Jesus, the son of Joseph, whose father and mother we know? How can he now say, 'I have come down from heaven'?" 43Jesus answered them, "Do not complain among yourselves. 44No one can come to me unless drawn by the Father who sent me; and I will raise that person up on the last day. 45It is written in the prophets, 'And they shall all be taught by God.' Everyone who has heard and learned from the Father comes to me. 46Not that anyone has seen the Father except the one who is from God; he has seen the Father. 47Very truly, I tell you, whoever believes has eternal life. 48I am the bread of life. 49Your ancestors ate the manna in the wilderness, and they died. 50This is the bread that comes down from heaven, so that one may eat of it and not die. 51I am the living bread that came down from heaven. Whoever eats of this bread will live forever; and the bread that I will give for the life of the world is my flesh."

52 The Jews then disputed among themselves, saying, "How can this man give us his flesh to eat?" 53So Jesus said to them, "Very truly, I tell you, unless you eat the flesh of the Son of Man and drink his blood, you have no life in you. 54Those who eat my flesh and drink my blood have eternal life, and I will raise them up on the last day; 55for my flesh is true food and my blood is true drink. 56Those who eat my flesh and drink my blood abide in me, and I in them. 57Just as the living Father sent me, and I live because of the Father, so whoever eats me will live because of me. 58This is the bread that came down from heaven, not like that which your ancestors ate, and they died. But the one who eats this bread will live forever." 59He said these things while he was teaching in the synagogue at Capernaum.

THE WORDS OF ETERNAL LIFE

60 When many of his disciples heard it, they said, "This teaching is difficult; who can accept it?" 61But Jesus, being aware that his disciples were complaining about it, said to them, "Does this offend you? 62Then what if you were to see the Son of Man ascending to where he was before? 63It is the spirit that gives life; the flesh is useless. The words that I have spoken to you are spirit and life. 64But among you there are some who do not believe." For Jesus knew from the first who were the ones that did not believe, and who was the one that would betray him. 65And he said, "For this reason I have told you that no one can come to me unless it is granted by the Father."

66 Because of this many of his disciples turned back and no longer went about with him. 67So Jesus asked the twelve, "Do you also wish to go away?" 68Simon Peter answered him, "Lord, to whom can we go? You have the words of eternal life. 69We have come to believe and know that you are the Holy One of God."a 70Jesus answered them, "Did I not choose you, the twelve? Yet one of you is a devil." 71He was speaking of Judas son of Simon Iscariot,b for he, though one of the twelve, was going to betray him.

a 6.69 Other ancient authorities read the Christ, the Son of the living God
b 6.71 Other ancient authorities read Judas Iscariot son of Simon; others, Judas son of Simon from Karyot (Kerioth)

THE UNBELIEF OF JESUS' BROTHERS

7 After this Jesus went about in Galilee. He did not wish[a] to go about in Judea because the Jews were looking for an opportunity to kill him. 2 Now the Jewish festival of Booths[b] was near. 3 So his brothers said to him, "Leave here and go to Judea so that your disciples also may see the works you are doing; 4 for no one who wants[c] to be widely known acts in secret. If you do these things, show yourself to the world." 5 (For not even his brothers believed in him.) 6 Jesus said to them, "My time has not yet come, but your time is always here. 7 The world cannot hate you, but it hates me because I testify against it that its works are evil. 8 Go to the festival yourselves. I am not[d] going to this festival, for my time has not yet fully come." 9 After saying this, he remained in Galilee.

JESUS AT THE FESTIVAL OF BOOTHS

10 But after his brothers had gone to the festival, then he also went, not publicly but as it were[e] in secret. 11 The Jews were looking for him at the festival and saying, "Where is he?" 12 And there was considerable complaining about him among the crowds. While some were saying, "He is a good man," others were saying, "No, he is deceiving the crowd." 13 Yet no one would speak openly about him for fear of the Jews.

14 About the middle of the festival Jesus went up into the temple and began to teach. 15 The Jews were astonished at it, saying, "How does this man have such learning,[f] when he has never been taught?" 16 Then Jesus answered them, "My teaching is not mine but his who sent me. 17 Anyone who resolves to do the will of God will know whether the teaching is from God or whether I am speaking on my own. 18 Those who speak on their own seek their own glory; but the one who seeks the glory of him who sent him is true, and there is nothing false in him. 19 "Did not Moses give you the law? Yet none of you keeps the law.

Why are you looking for an opportunity to kill me?" 20 The crowd answered, "You have a demon! Who is trying to kill you?" 21 Jesus answered them, "I performed one work, and all of you are astonished. 22 Moses gave you circumcision (it is, of course, not from Moses, but from the patriarchs), and you circumcise a man on the sabbath. 23 If a man receives circumcision on the sabbath in order that the law of Moses may not be broken, are you angry with me because I healed a man's whole body on the sabbath? 24 Do not judge by appearances, but judge with right judgment."

IS THIS THE CHRIST?

25 Now some of the people of Jerusalem were saying, "Is not this the man whom they are trying to kill? 26 And here he is, speaking openly, but they say nothing to him! Can it be that the authorities really know that this is the Messiah?[g] 27 Yet we know where this man is from; but when the Messiah[g] comes, no one will know where he is from." 28 Then Jesus cried out as he was teaching in the temple, "You know me, and you know where I am from. I have not come on my own. But the one who sent me is true, and you do not know him. 29 I know him, because I am from him, and he sent me." 30 Then they tried to arrest him, but no one laid hands on him, because his hour had not yet come. 31 Yet many in the crowd believed in him and were saying, "When the Messiah[g] comes, will he do more signs than this man has done?"[h]

OFFICERS ARE SENT TO ARREST JESUS

32 The Pharisees heard the crowd muttering such things about him, and the chief priests and Pharisees sent temple police to arrest him.

[a] 7.1 Other ancient authorities read *was not at liberty*   [b] 7.2 Or *Tabernacles*   [c] 7.4 Other ancient authorities read *wants it*   [d] 7.8 Other ancient authorities add *yet*   [e] 7.10 Other ancient authorities lack *as it were*   [f] 7.15 Or *this man know his letters*   [g] 7.26,27,31 Or *the Christ*   [h] 7.31 Other ancient authorities read *is doing*

[33]Jesus then said, "I will be with you a little while longer, and then I am going to him who sent me. [34]You will search for me, but you will not find me; and where I am, you cannot come." [35]The Jews said to one another, "Where does this man intend to go that we will not find him? Does he intend to go to the Dispersion among the Greeks and teach the Greeks? [36]What does he mean by saying, 'You will search for me and you will not find me' and 'Where I am, you cannot come'?"

RIVERS OF LIVING WATER

[37] On the last day of the festival, the great day, while Jesus was standing there, he cried out, "Let anyone who is thirsty come to me, [38]and let the one who believes in me drink. As[a] the scripture has said, 'Out of the believer's heart[b] shall flow rivers of living water.' " [39]Now he said this about the Spirit, which believers in him were to receive; for as yet there was no Spirit,[c] because Jesus was not yet glorified.

DIVISION AMONG THE PEOPLE

[40] When they heard these words, some in the crowd said, "This is really the prophet." [41]Others said, "This is the Messiah."[d] But some asked, "Surely the Messiah[d] does not come from Galilee, does he? [42]Has not the scripture said that the Messiah[d] is descended from David and comes from Bethlehem, the village where David lived?" [43]So there was a division in the crowd because of him. [44]Some of them wanted to arrest him, but no one laid hands on him.

THE UNBELIEF OF THOSE IN AUTHORITY

[45] Then the temple police went back to the chief priests and Pharisees, who asked them, "Why did you not arrest him?" [46]The police answered, "Never has anyone spoken like this!" [47]Then the Pharisees replied, "Surely you have not been deceived too, have you? [48]Has any one of the authorities or of the Pharisees believed in him? [49]But this crowd, which does not know the law—they are accursed." [50]Nicodemus, who had gone to Jesus[e] before, and who was one of them, asked, [51]"Our law does not judge people without first giving them a hearing to find out what they are doing, does it?" [52]They replied, "Surely you are not also from Galilee, are you? Search and you will see that no prophet is to arise from Galilee."

THE WOMAN CAUGHT IN ADULTERY

8 ⟦[53]Then each of them went home, [1]while Jesus went to the Mount of Olives. [2]Early in the morning he came again to the temple. All

---

PONDER

"Let anyone who is thirsty come to me, and let the one who believes in me drink. As the scripture has said, 'Out of the believer's heart shall flow rivers of living water.'"
—John 7.37–38

PRAY

Lord Jesus, you have given us an incentive to stretch our hearts and minds to encompass the truths that are difficult. It is hard to understand how we can come to you and drink. It is hard for us to visualize you as a humbled, suffering human who lived among us, but we know it is true. It is hard to look at our own existence in light of the grace, justice, peace, compassion, understanding and love that you showed us. But as we face the future, fill us with the Holy Spirit so that we can follow you. Bring us nearer to you, our Savior. Amen.

---

[a] 7.38 Or come to me and drink. [38]The one who believes in me, as   [b] 7.38 Gk out of his belly   [c] 7.39 Other ancient authorities read for as yet the Spirit (others, Holy Spirit) had not been given   [d] 7.41,42 Or the Christ   [e] 7.50 Gk him

the people came to him and he sat down and began to teach them. 3The scribes and the Pharisees brought a woman who had been caught in adultery; and making her stand before all of them, 4they said to him, "Teacher, this woman was caught in the very act of committing adultery. 5Now in the law Moses commanded us to stone such women. Now what do you say?" 6They said this to test him, so that they might have some charge to bring against him. Jesus bent down and wrote with his finger on the ground. 7When they kept on questioning him, he straightened up and said to them, "Let anyone among you who is without sin be the first to throw a stone at her." 8And once again he bent down and wrote on the ground.a 9When they heard it, they went away, one by one, beginning with the elders; and Jesus was left alone with the woman standing before him. 10Jesus straightened up and said to her, "Woman, where are they? Has no one condemned you?" 11She said, "No one, sir."b And Jesus said, "Neither do I condemn you. Go your way, and from now on do not sin again."]]c

JESUS THE LIGHT OF THE WORLD

12 Again Jesus spoke to them, saying, "I am the light of the world. Whoever follows me will never walk in darkness but will have the light of life." 13Then the Pharisees said to him, "You are testifying on your own behalf; your testimony is not valid." 14Jesus answered, "Even if I testify on my own behalf, my testimony is valid because I know where I have come from and where I am going, but you do not know where I come from or where I am going. 15You judge by human standards;d I judge no one. 16Yet even if I do judge, my judgment is valid; for it is not I alone who judge, but I and the Fathere who sent me. 17In your law it is written that the testimony of two witnesses is valid. 18I testify on my own behalf, and the Father who sent me testifies on my behalf." 19Then they said to him, "Where is your Father?" Jesus answered, "You know neither me nor my Father. If you knew me, you would know my Father also." 20He spoke these words while he was teaching in the treasury of the temple, but no one arrested him, because his hour had not yet come.

JESUS FORETELLS HIS DEATH

21 Again he said to them, "I am going away, and you will search for me, but you will die in your sin. Where I am going, you cannot come." 22Then the Jews said, "Is he going to kill himself? Is that what he means by saying, 'Where I am going, you cannot come'?" 23He said to them, "You are from below, I am from above; you are of this world, I am not of this world. 24I told you that you would die in your sins, for you will die in your sins unless you believe that I am he."f 25They said to him, "Who are you?" Jesus said to them, "Why do I speak to you at all?g 26I have much to say about you and much to condemn; but the one who sent me is true, and I declare to the world what I have heard from him." 27They did not understand that he was speaking to them about the Father. 28So Jesus said, "When you have lifted up the Son of Man, then you will realize that I am he,f and that I do nothing on my own, but I speak these things as the Father instructed me. 29And the one who sent me is with me; he has not left me alone, for I always do what is pleasing to him." 30As he was saying these things, many believed in him.

TRUE DISCIPLES

31 Then Jesus said to the Jews who had believed in him, "If you continue in my word, you are truly my disciples; 32and you will know the

a 8.8 Other ancient authorities add the sins of each of them   b 8.11 Or Lord   c 8.11 The most ancient authorities lack 7.53–8.11; other authorities add the passage here or after 7.36 or after 21.25 or after Luke 21.38, with variations of text; some mark the passage as doubtful.   d 8.15 Gk according to the flesh   e 8.16 Other ancient authorities read he   f 8.24,28 Gk I am   g 8.25 Or What I have told you from the beginning

truth, and the truth will make you free." 33They answered him, "We are descendants of Abraham and have never been slaves to anyone. What do you mean by saying, 'You will be made free'?"

34 Jesus answered them, "Very truly, I tell you, everyone who commits sin is a slave to sin. 35The slave does not have a permanent place in the household; the son has a place there forever. 36So if the Son makes you free, you will be free indeed. 37I know that you are descendants of Abraham; yet you look for an opportunity to kill me, because there is no place in you for my word. 38I declare what I have seen in the Father's presence; as for you, you should do what you have heard from the Father."a

JESUS AND ABRAHAM

39 They answered him, "Abraham is our father." Jesus said to them, "If you were Abraham's children, you would be doingb what Abraham did, 40but now you are trying to kill me, a man who has told you the truth that I heard from God. This is not what Abraham did. 41You are indeed doing what your father does." They said to him, "We are not illegitimate children; we have one father, God himself." 42Jesus said to them, "If God were your Father, you would love me, for I came from God and now I am here. I did not come on my own, but he sent me. 43Why do you not understand what I say? It is because you cannot accept my word. 44You are from your father the devil, and you choose to do your father's desires. He was a murderer from the beginning and does not stand in the truth, because there is no truth in him. When he lies, he speaks according to his own nature, for he is a liar and the father of lies. 45But because I tell the truth, you do not believe me. 46Which of you convicts me of sin? If I tell the truth, why do you not believe me? 47Whoever is from God hears the words of God. The reason you do not hear them is that you are not from God."

48 The Jews answered him, "Are we not right in saying that you are a Samaritan and have a demon?" 49Jesus answered, "I do not have a demon; but I honor my Father, and you dishonor me. 50Yet I do not seek my own glory; there is one who seeks it and he is the judge. 51Very truly, I tell you, whoever keeps my word will never see death." 52The Jews said to him, "Now we know that you have a demon. Abraham died, and so did the prophets; yet you say, 'Whoever keeps my word will never taste death.' 53Are you greater than our father Abraham, who died? The prophets also died. Who do you claim to be?" 54Jesus answered, "If I glorify myself, my glory is nothing. It is my Father who glorifies me, he of whom you say, 'He is our God,' 55though you do not know him. But I know him; if I would say that I do not know him, I would be a liar like you. But I do know him and I keep his word. 56Your ancestor Abraham rejoiced that he would see my day; he saw it and was glad." 57Then the Jews said to him, "You are not yet fifty years old, and have you seen Abraham?"c 58Jesus said to them, "Very truly, I tell you, before Abraham was, I am." 59So they picked up stones to throw at him, but Jesus hid himself and went out of the temple.

A MAN BORN BLIND RECEIVES SIGHT

9 As he walked along, he saw a man blind from birth. 2His disciples asked him, "Rabbi, who sinned, this man or his parents, that he was born blind?" 3Jesus answered, "Neither this man nor his parents sinned; he was born blind so that God's works might be revealed in him. 4Wed must work the works of him who sent mee while it is day; night is coming when no one can work. 5As long as I am in the

---

a 8.38 Other ancient authorities read *you do what you have heard from your father* b 8.39 Other ancient authorities read *If you are Abraham's children, then do* c 8.57 Other ancient authorities read *has Abraham seen you?* d 9.4 Other ancient authorities read *I* e 9.4 Other ancient authorities read *us*

world, I am the light of the world." ⁶When he had said this, he spat on the ground and made mud with the saliva and spread the mud on the man's eyes, ⁷saying to him, "Go, wash in the pool of Siloam" (which means Sent). Then he went and washed and came back able to see. ⁸The neighbors and those who had seen him before as a beggar began to ask, "Is this not the man who used to sit and beg?" ⁹Some were saying, "It is he." Others were saying, "No, but it is someone like him." He kept saying, "I am the man." ¹⁰But they kept asking him, "Then how were your eyes opened?" ¹¹He answered, "The man called Jesus made mud, spread it on my eyes, and said to me, 'Go to Siloam and wash.' Then I went and washed and received my sight." ¹²They said to him, "Where is he?" He said, "I do not know."

THE PHARISEES INVESTIGATE THE HEALING

13 They brought to the Pharisees the man who had formerly been blind. ¹⁴Now it was a sabbath day when Jesus made the mud and opened his eyes. ¹⁵Then the Pharisees also began to ask him how he had received his sight. He said to them, "He put mud on my eyes. Then I washed, and now I see." ¹⁶Some of the Pharisees said, "This man is not from God, for he does not observe the sabbath." But others said, "How can a man who is a sinner perform such signs?" And they were divided. ¹⁷So they said again to the blind man, "What do you say about him?

It was your eyes he opened." He said, "He is a prophet."

18 The Jews did not believe that he had been blind and had received his sight until they called the parents of the man who had received his sight ¹⁹and asked them, "Is this your son, who you say was born blind? How then does he now see?" ²⁰His parents answered, "We know that this is our son, and that he was born blind; ²¹but we do not know how it is that now he sees, nor do we know who opened his eyes. Ask him; he is of age. He will speak for himself." ²²His parents said this because they were afraid of the Jews; for the Jews had already agreed that anyone who confessed Jesusᵃ to be the Messiahᵇ would be put out of the synagogue. ²³Therefore his parents said, "He is of age; ask him."

24 So for the second time they called the man who had been blind, and they said to him, "Give glory to God! We know that this man is a sinner." ²⁵He answered, "I do not know whether he is a sinner. One thing I do know, that though I was blind, now I see." ²⁶They said to him, "What did he do to you? How did he open your eyes?" ²⁷He answered them, "I have told you already, and you would not listen. Why do you want to hear it again? Do you also want to become his disciples?" ²⁸Then they reviled him, saying, "You are his disciple, but we are disciples of Moses. ²⁹We know that God has spoken to Moses, but as for this man, we do not know

ᵃ **9.22** Gk *him*   ᵇ **9.22** Or *the Christ*

⊢ BIBLE IN LIFE ▷

Limited Time   *John 9.3–5*

Jesus did not say, "*I* must work the works." He said, "*We* must work the works." The word *we* refers to Jesus, his disciples and all of us together. We have an allotted span of life, a limited period of time, in which to do God's works. We display God's works by following the example Jesus set for us. Christ is the light through which our own lives become significant, and Jesus said we shouldn't delay. We shouldn't start "someday" when it's more convenient. Today, right now, we have the opportunity to make our lives more expansive and more gratifying, to utilize the brief period that we have remaining on earth to do God's work.

PONDER

[The man] answered, "I do not know whether he is a sinner. One thing I do know, that though I was blind, now I see."
—John 9.25

PRAY

Lord, so many of the things that we read or study about you shake us. They force us to our knees to seek guidance, courage and enlightenment. In this scripture, we see how in healing this blind beggar you used his affliction for your glory. We pray that you will use our experiences, good or bad, for your glory. Fill us with your Holy Spirit who teaches us, guides us and advocates for us before the Father. Inspire us to lead greater lives according to the perfect commands of our Savior. In your name we pray. Amen.

where he comes from." 30The man answered, "Here is an astonishing thing! You do not know where he comes from, and yet he opened my eyes. 31We know that God does not listen to sinners, but he does listen to one who worships him and obeys his will. 32Never since the world began has it been heard that anyone opened the eyes of a person born blind. 33If this man were not from God, he could do nothing." 34They answered him, "You were born entirely in sins, and are you trying to teach us?" And they drove him out.

SPIRITUAL BLINDNESS

35 Jesus heard that they had driven him out, and when he found him, he said, "Do you believe in the Son of Man?"a 36He answered, "And who is he, sir?b Tell me, so that I may believe in him." 37Jesus said to him, "You have seen him, and the one speaking with you is he." 38He said, "Lord,b I believe." And he worshiped

him. 39Jesus said, "I came into this world for judgment so that those who do not see may see, and those who do see may become blind." 40Some of the Pharisees near him heard this and said to him, "Surely we are not blind, are we?" 41Jesus said to them, "If you were blind, you would not have sin. But now that you say, 'We see,' your sin remains.

JESUS THE GOOD SHEPHERD

10 "Very truly, I tell you, anyone who does not enter the sheepfold by the gate but climbs in by another way is a thief and a bandit. 2The one who enters by the gate is the shepherd of the sheep. 3The gatekeeper opens the gate for him, and the sheep hear his voice. He calls his own sheep by name and leads them out. 4When he has brought out all his own, he goes ahead of them, and the sheep follow him because they know his voice. 5They will not follow a stranger, but they will run from him because they do not know the voice of strangers." 6Jesus used this figure of speech with them, but they did not understand what he was saying to them.

7 So again Jesus said to them, "Very truly, I tell you, I am the gate for the sheep. 8All who came before me are thieves and bandits; but the sheep did not listen to them. 9I am the gate. Whoever enters by me will be saved, and will come in and go out and find pasture. 10The thief comes only to steal and kill and destroy. I came that they may have life, and have it abundantly.

11 "I am the good shepherd. The good shepherd lays down his life for the sheep. 12The hired hand, who is not the shepherd and does not own the sheep, sees the wolf coming and leaves the sheep and runs away— and the wolf snatches them and scatters them. 13The hired hand runs away because a hired hand does not care for the sheep. 14I am the good shepherd. I know my own and my own know me, 15just as the Father

a 9.35 Other ancient authorities read the Son of God   b 9.36,38 Sir and Lord translate the same Greek word

knows me and I know the Father. And I lay down my life for the sheep. ¹⁶I have other sheep that do not belong to this fold. I must bring them also, and they will listen to my voice. So there will be one flock, one shepherd. ¹⁷For this reason the Father loves me, because I lay down my life in order to take it up again. ¹⁸No one takesᵃ it from me, but I lay it down of my own accord. I have power to lay it down, and I have power to take it up again. I have received this command from my Father."

19 Again the Jews were divided because of these words. ²⁰Many of them were saying, "He has a demon and is out of his mind. Why listen to him?" ²¹Others were saying, "These are not the words of one who has a demon. Can a demon open the eyes of the blind?"

JESUS IS REJECTED BY THE JEWS

22 At that time the festival of the Dedication took place in Jerusalem. It was winter, ²³and Jesus was walking in the temple, in the portico of Solomon. ²⁴So the Jews gathered around him and said to him, "How long will you keep us in suspense? If you are the Messiah,ᵇ tell us plainly." ²⁵Jesus answered, "I have told you, and you do not believe. The works that I do in my Father's name testify to me; ²⁶but you do not believe, because you do not belong to my sheep. ²⁷My sheep hear my voice. I know them, and they follow me. ²⁸I give them eternal life, and they will never perish. No one will snatch them out of my hand. ²⁹What my Father has given me is greater than all else, and no one can snatch it out of the Father's hand.ᶜ ³⁰The Father and I are one."

31 The Jews took up stones again to stone him. ³²Jesus replied, "I have shown you many good works from the Father. For which of these are you going to stone me?" ³³The Jews answered, "It is not for a good work that we are going to stone you, but for blasphemy, because you, though only a human being, are making yourself God." ³⁴Jesus answered, "Is it not written in your law,ᵈ 'I said, you are gods'? ³⁵If those to whom the word of God came were called 'gods'—and the scripture cannot be annulled— ³⁶can you say that the one whom the Father has sanctified and sent into the world is blaspheming because I said, 'I am God's Son'? ³⁷If I am not doing the works of my Father, then do not believe me. ³⁸But if I do them, even though you

---

ᵃ **10.18** Other ancient authorities read *has taken*   ᵇ **10.24** Or *the Christ*   ᶜ **10.29** Other ancient authorities read *My Father who has given them to me is greater than all, and no one can snatch them out of the Father's hand*   ᵈ **10.34** Other ancient authorities read *in the law*

⊢ BIBLE IN LIFE ▷

Hearing Jesus' Voice
John 10.27

In the culture of Old and New Testament times, people understood the habits of sheep. When different flocks of sheep came to a central watering hole, they would all mix together as they drank water from a stream or a trough. When the sheep were done, the shepherds would stand aside and call or whistle in a certain way. Every shepherd's sheep would come only to their master. There was a distinct relationship between the sheep and their particular shepherd.

Jesus describes himself as our shepherd. We need to train ourselves to listen for and recognize his voice. It doesn't come naturally to ignore the conflicting voices we hear—the enticements and temptations we face. Or we might choose a lot of good voices but, in the process, ignore the one excellent voice. How can we discern the voice of Christ amidst all the other noise in our lives? We can read the Bible and pray; we can look at our lives and strive to be more compatible with Christ. In these ways we can train ourselves to hear the voice of our Savior.

do not believe me, believe the works, so that you may know and understand[a] that the Father is in me and I am in the Father." 39Then they tried to arrest him again, but he escaped from their hands.

40 He went away again across the Jordan to the place where John had been baptizing earlier, and he remained there. 41Many came to him, and they were saying, "John performed no sign, but everything that John said about this man was true." 42And many believed in him there.

THE DEATH OF LAZARUS

11 Now a certain man was ill, Lazarus of Bethany, the village of Mary and her sister Martha. 2Mary was the one who anointed the Lord with perfume and wiped his feet with her hair; her brother Lazarus was ill. 3So the sisters sent a message to Jesus,[b] "Lord, he whom you love is ill." 4But when Jesus heard it, he said, "This illness does not lead to death; rather it is for God's glory, so that the Son of God may be glorified through it." 5Accordingly, though Jesus loved Martha and her sister and Lazarus, 6after having heard that Lazarus[c] was ill, he stayed two days longer in the place where he was.

7 Then after this he said to the disciples, "Let us go to Judea again." 8The disciples said to him, "Rabbi, the Jews were just now trying to stone you, and are you going there again?" 9Jesus answered, "Are there not twelve hours of daylight? Those who walk during the day do not stumble, because they see the light of this world. 10But those who walk at night stumble, because the light is not in them." 11After saying this, he told them, "Our friend Lazarus has fallen asleep, but I am going there to awaken him." 12The disciples said to him, "Lord, if he has fallen asleep, he will be all right." 13Jesus, however, had been speaking about his death, but they thought that he was referring merely to sleep. 14Then Jesus told them plainly, "Lazarus is dead. 15For your sake I am glad I was not there, so that you may believe. But let us go to him." 16Thomas, who was

called the Twin,[d] said to his fellow disciples, "Let us also go, that we may die with him."

JESUS THE RESURRECTION AND THE LIFE

17 When Jesus arrived, he found that Lazarus[c] had already been in the tomb four days. 18Now Bethany was near Jerusalem, some two miles[e] away, 19and many of the Jews had come to Martha and Mary to console them about their brother. 20When Martha heard that Jesus was coming, she went and met him, while Mary stayed at home. 21Martha said to Jesus, "Lord, if you had been here, my brother would not have died. 22But even now I know that God will give you whatever you ask of him." 23Jesus said to her, "Your brother will rise again." 24Martha said to him, "I know that he will rise again in the resurrection on the last day." 25Jesus said to her, "I am the resurrection and the life.[f] Those who believe in me, even though they die, will live, 26and everyone who lives and believes in me will never die. Do you believe this?" 27She said to him, "Yes, Lord, I believe that you are the Messiah,[g] the Son of God, the one coming into the world."

JESUS WEEPS

28 When she had said this, she went back and called her sister Mary, and told her privately, "The Teacher is here and is calling for you." 29And when she heard it, she got up quickly and went to him. 30Now Jesus had not yet come to the village, but was still at the place where Martha had met him. 31The Jews who were with her in the house, consoling her, saw Mary get up quickly and go out. They followed her because they thought that she was going to the tomb to weep there. 32When Mary came where Jesus was and saw him, she knelt at his feet and said

---

[a] 10.38 Other ancient authorities lack and understand; others read and believe
[b] 11.3 Gk him   [c] 11.6,17 Gk he   [d] 11.16 Gk Didymus   [e] 11.18 Gk fifteen stadia
[f] 11.25 Other ancient authorities lack and the life   [g] 11.27 Or the Christ

to him, "Lord, if you had been here, my brother would not have died." ³³When Jesus saw her weeping, and the Jews who came with her also weeping, he was greatly disturbed in spirit and deeply moved. ³⁴He said, "Where have you laid him?" They said to him, "Lord, come and see." ³⁵Jesus began to weep. ³⁶So the Jews said, "See how he loved him!" ³⁷But some of them said, "Could not he who opened the eyes of the blind man have kept this man from dying?"

JESUS RAISES LAZARUS TO LIFE

38 Then Jesus, again greatly disturbed, came to the tomb. It was a cave, and a stone was lying against it. ³⁹Jesus said, "Take away the stone." Martha, the sister of the dead man, said to him, "Lord, already there is a stench because he has been dead four days." ⁴⁰Jesus said to her, "Did I not tell you that if you believed, you would see the glory of God?" ⁴¹So they took away the stone. And Jesus looked upward and said, "Father, I thank you for having heard me. ⁴²I knew that you always hear me, but I have said this for the sake of the crowd standing here, so that they may believe that you sent me." ⁴³When he had said this, he cried with a loud voice, "Lazarus, come out!" ⁴⁴The dead man came out, his hands and feet bound with strips of cloth, and his face wrapped in a cloth. Jesus said to them, "Unbind him, and let him go."

THE PLOT TO KILL JESUS

45 Many of the Jews therefore, who had come with Mary and had seen what Jesus did, believed in him. ⁴⁶But some of them went to the Pharisees and told them what he had done. ⁴⁷So the chief priests and the Pharisees called a meeting of the council, and said, "What are we to do? This man is performing many signs. ⁴⁸If we let him go on like this, everyone will believe in him, and the Romans will come and destroy both our holy placeᵃ and our nation." ⁴⁹But one of them, Caiaphas, who was high priest that year, said to them, "You know nothing at all! ⁵⁰You do not understand that it is better for you to have one man die for the people than to have the whole nation destroyed." ⁵¹He did not say this on his own, but being high priest that year he prophesied that Jesus was about to die for the nation, ⁵²and not for the nation only, but to gather into one the dispersed children of God. ⁵³So from that day on they planned to put him to death.

54 Jesus therefore no longer walked about openly among the Jews, but went from there to a town called Ephraim in the region near the wilderness; and he remained there with the disciples.

55 Now the Passover of the Jews was near, and many went up from the country to Jerusalem before the Passover to purify themselves. ⁵⁶They were looking for Jesus and were asking one another as they stood in the temple, "What do you think? Surely he will not come to the festival, will he?" ⁵⁷Now the chief

ᵃ 11.48 Or our temple; Greek our place

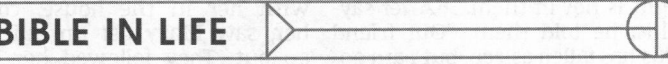

BIBLE IN LIFE

Showing Emotion   John 11.35

Jesus Christ, the Son of God, wept. One lesson we can derive from this text is that it's healthy for us to exhibit human emotion; it's all right for us to cry if we feel like it, especially over a deep loss, such as the death of a loved one. Grief is good. We don't have to pretend to be immune to sorrow just because we are Christians and believe in the resurrection. We still feel pain and sadness. As Christ brought Lazarus out of the tomb after he had been dead for four days, Christ showed that he has power over death. He also demonstrated that he has very real human emotions with which we can identify.

priests and the Pharisees had given orders that anyone who knew where Jesus[a] was should let them know, so that they might arrest him.

MARY ANOINTS JESUS

12 Six days before the Passover Jesus came to Bethany, the home of Lazarus, whom he had raised from the dead. [2]There they gave a dinner for him. Martha served, and Lazarus was one of those at the table with him. [3]Mary took a pound of costly perfume made of pure nard, anointed Jesus' feet, and wiped them[b] with her hair. The house was filled with the fragrance of the perfume. [4]But Judas Iscariot, one of his disciples (the one who was about to betray him), said, [5]"Why was this perfume not

PONDER

Mary took a pound of costly perfume made of pure nard, anointed Jesus' feet, and wiped them with her hair. The house was filled with the fragrance of the perfume.
—John 12.3

PRAY

O Father, this story and Jesus' reaction to it leads us to consider how we can emulate Mary's actions and do something extravagant, something that will show you how much we love you. Perhaps we can break through our shells, reaching out to another human being, and in the name of our Savior do something that is good and lovely. We ask that you forgive our insensitivity and coldness to you and to others. Forgive our underestimation of the resources, the talents and the abilities you have given us. Help us realize that with you, with the presence of the Holy Spirit, with the grace of Jesus Christ, the only limit we have is the one we impose on ourselves. In your name we pray. Amen.

sold for three hundred denarii[c] and the money given to the poor?" [6](He said this not because he cared about the poor, but because he was a thief; he kept the common purse and used to steal what was put into it.) [7]Jesus said, "Leave her alone. She bought it[d] so that she might keep it for the day of my burial. [8]You always have the poor with you, but you do not always have me."

THE PLOT TO KILL LAZARUS

[9]When the great crowd of the Jews learned that he was there, they came not only because of Jesus but also to see Lazarus, whom he had raised from the dead. [10]So the chief priests planned to put Lazarus to death as well, [11]since it was on account of him that many of the Jews were deserting and were believing in Jesus.

JESUS' TRIUMPHAL ENTRY INTO JERUSALEM

[12]The next day the great crowd that had come to the festival heard that Jesus was coming to Jerusalem. [13]So they took branches of palm trees and went out to meet him, shouting, "Hosanna!

Blessed is the one who comes in
the name of the Lord—
the King of Israel!"

[14]Jesus found a young donkey and sat on it; as it is written:
[15] "Do not be afraid, daughter
of Zion.
Look, your king is coming,
sitting on a donkey's colt!"
[16]His disciples did not understand these things at first; but when Jesus was glorified, then they remembered that these things had been written of him and had been done to him. [17]So the crowd that had been with him when he called Lazarus out of the tomb and raised him from the dead continued to testify.[e] [18]It was also because they heard

[a] 11.57 Gk *he*   [b] 12.3 Gk *his feet*
[c] 12.5 Three hundred denarii would be nearly a year's wages for a laborer
[d] 12.7 Gk lacks *She bought it*   [e] 12.17 Other ancient authorities read *with him began to testify that he had called ... from the dead*

that he had performed this sign that the crowd went to meet him. 19 The Pharisees then said to one another, "You see, you can do nothing. Look, the world has gone after him!"

SOME GREEKS WISH TO SEE JESUS

20 Now among those who went up to worship at the festival were some Greeks. 21 They came to Philip, who was from Bethsaida in Galilee, and said to him, "Sir, we wish to see Jesus." 22 Philip went and told Andrew; then Andrew and Philip went and told Jesus. 23 Jesus answered them, "The hour has come for the Son of Man to be glorified. 24 Very truly, I tell you, unless a grain of wheat falls into the earth and dies, it remains just a single grain; but if it dies, it bears much fruit. 25 Those who love their life lose it, and those who hate their life in this world will keep it for eternal life. 26 Whoever serves me must follow me, and where I am, there will my servant be also. Whoever serves me, the Father will honor.

JESUS SPEAKS ABOUT HIS DEATH

27 "Now my soul is troubled. And what should I say—'Father, save me from this hour'? No, it is for this reason that I have come to this hour. 28 Father, glorify your name." Then a voice came from heaven, "I have glorified it, and I will glorify it again." 29 The crowd standing there heard it and said that it was thunder. Others said, "An angel has spoken to him." 30 Jesus answered, "This voice has come for your sake, not for mine. 31 Now is the judgment of this world; now the ruler of this world will be driven out. 32 And I, when I am lifted up from the earth, will draw all people[a] to myself." 33 He said this to indicate the kind of death he was to die. 34 The crowd answered him, "We have heard from the law that the Messiah[b] remains forever. How can you say that the Son of Man must be lifted up? Who is this Son of Man?" 35 Jesus said to them, "The light is with you for a little longer. Walk while you have the light, so

that the darkness may not overtake you. If you walk in the darkness, you do not know where you are going. 36 While you have the light, believe in the light, so that you may become children of light."

THE UNBELIEF OF THE PEOPLE

After Jesus had said this, he departed and hid from them. 37 Although he had performed so many signs in their presence, they did not believe in him. 38 This was to fulfill the word spoken by the prophet Isaiah:

"Lord, who has believed
    our message,
and to whom has the arm of
    the Lord been revealed?"

39 And so they could not believe, because Isaiah also said,

40 "He has blinded their eyes
    and hardened their heart,
so that they might not look
    with their eyes,
and understand with their
    heart and turn—
and I would heal them."

41 Isaiah said this because[c] he saw his glory and spoke about him. 42 Nevertheless many, even of the authorities, believed in him. But because of the Pharisees they did not confess it, for fear that they would be put out of the synagogue; 43 for they loved human glory more than the glory that comes from God.

SUMMARY OF JESUS' TEACHING

44 Then Jesus cried aloud: "Whoever believes in me believes not in me but in him who sent me. 45 And whoever sees me sees him who sent me. 46 I have come as light into the world, so that everyone who believes in me should not remain in the darkness. 47 I do not judge anyone who hears my words and does not keep them, for I came not to judge the world, but to save the world. 48 The one who rejects me and does not receive my word has a judge; on the last day the word that I have spoken will serve as judge, 49 for I have not

a 12.32 Other ancient authorities read all things   b 12.34 Or the Christ   c 12.41 Other ancient witnesses read when

spoken on my own, but the Father who sent me has himself given me a commandment about what to say and what to speak. ⁵⁰And I know that his commandment is eternal life. What I speak, therefore, I speak just as the Father has told me."

JESUS WASHES THE DISCIPLES' FEET

13 Now before the festival of the Passover, Jesus knew that his hour had come to depart from this world and go to the Father. Having loved his own who were in the world, he loved them to the end. ²The devil had already put it into the heart of Judas son of Simon Iscariot to betray him. And during supper ³Jesus, knowing that the Father had given all things into his hands, and that he had come from God and was going to God, ⁴got up from the table,ᵃ took off his outer robe, and tied a towel around himself. ⁵Then he poured water into a basin and began to wash the disciples' feet and to wipe them with the towel that was tied around him. ⁶He came to Simon Peter, who said to him, "Lord, are you going to wash my feet?" ⁷Jesus answered, "You do not know now what I am doing, but later you will understand." ⁸Peter said to him, "You will never wash my feet." Jesus answered, "Un-less I wash you, you have no share with me." ⁹Simon Peter said to him, "Lord, not my feet only but also my hands and my head!" ¹⁰Jesus said to him, "One who has bathed does not need to wash, except for the feet,ᵇ but is entirely clean. And youᶜ are clean, though not all of you." ¹¹For he knew who was to betray him; for this reason he said, "Not all of you are clean."

¹² After he had washed their feet, had put on his robe, and had returned to the table, he said to them, "Do you know what I have done to you? ¹³You call me Teacher and Lord—and you are right, for that is what I am. ¹⁴So if I, your Lord and Teacher, have washed your feet, you also ought to wash one another's feet. ¹⁵For I have set you an example, that you also should do as I have done to you. ¹⁶Very truly, I tell you, servantsᵈ are not greater than their master, nor are messengers greater than the one who sent them. ¹⁷If you know these things, you are blessed if you do them. ¹⁸I am not speaking of all of you; I know whom I have chosen. But it is to fulfill the scripture, 'The one who ate my breadᵉ has

ᵃ 13.4 Gk *from supper*   ᵇ 13.10 Other ancient authorities lack *except for the feet* ᶜ 13.10 The Greek word for *you* here is plural ᵈ 13.16 Gk *slaves*   ᵉ 13.18 Other ancient authorities read *ate bread with me*

├─── BIBLE IN LIFE ▷ ───┤

Aggressive Servanthood   John 13.3–17

When Jesus commanded his disciples to follow his example and wash each other's feet, what exactly did he mean? The dirty task of washing a person's feet was the work of a lowly servant, so it seems that Jesus' point was to demonstrate true servanthood and humility for his disciples and to command them to do the same for each other. How do we do this for each other today? Does humility mean we are dormant and passive? Does being a servant preclude our doing anything ambitious or great? Washing each other's feet means we actively look for ways we can help others, and we do it with an attitude of humility rather than superiority. Are we aggressive, excited, determined servants of others? If not, then we are failing to carry out Christ's mandate. How do we demonstrate the love of Christ? By going to church every Sunday, wearing nice clothes, exclusively associating with people just like us, singing hymns, giving a small percent of our income for ministries at home or overseas, developing the reputation of good Christians in the community? These things are not as significant as we'd like to think. When Christ called his disciples to serve each other, he presented them with a truly challenging concept of life, for it calls us to change both our hearts and our actions toward others.

lifted his heel against me.' [19]I tell you this now, before it occurs, so that when it does occur, you may believe that I am he.[a] [20]Very truly, I tell you, whoever receives one whom I send receives me; and whoever receives me receives him who sent me."

JESUS FORETELLS HIS BETRAYAL

[21]After saying this Jesus was troubled in spirit, and declared, "Very truly, I tell you, one of you will betray me." [22]The disciples looked at one another, uncertain of whom he was speaking. [23]One of his disciples—the one whom Jesus loved—was reclining next to him; [24]Simon Peter therefore motioned to him to ask Jesus of whom he was speaking. [25]So while reclining next to Jesus, he asked him, "Lord, who is it?" [26]Jesus answered, "It is the one to whom I give this piece of bread when I have dipped it in the dish."[b] So when he had dipped the piece of bread, he gave it to Judas son of Simon Iscariot.[c] [27]After he received the piece of bread,[d] Satan entered into him. Jesus said to him, "Do quickly what you are going to do." [28]Now no one at the table knew why he said this to him. [29]Some thought that, because Judas had the common purse, Jesus was telling him, "Buy what we need for the festival"; or, that he should give something to the poor. [30]So, after receiving the piece of bread, he immediately went out. And it was night.

THE NEW COMMANDMENT

[31]When he had gone out, Jesus said, "Now the Son of Man has been glorified, and God has been glorified in him. [32]If God has been glorified in him,[e] God will also glorify him in himself and will glorify him at once. [33]Little children, I am with you only a little longer. You will look for me; and as I said to the Jews so now I say to you, 'Where I am going, you cannot come.' [34]I give you a new commandment, that you love one another. Just as I have loved you, you also should love one another. [35]By this everyone will know that you are my disciples, if you have love for one another."

JESUS FORETELLS PETER'S DENIAL

[36]Simon Peter said to him, "Lord, where are you going?" Jesus answered, "Where I am going, you cannot follow me now; but you will follow afterward." [37]Peter said to him, "Lord, why can I not follow you now? I will lay down my life for you." [38]Jesus answered, "Will you lay down your life for me? Very truly, I tell you, before the cock crows, you will have denied me three times.

JESUS THE WAY TO THE FATHER

14 "Do not let your hearts be troubled. Believe[f] in God, believe also in me. [2]In my Father's house there are many dwelling places. If it were not so, would I have told you that I go to prepare a place for you?[g] [3]And if I go and prepare a place for you, I will come again and will take you to myself, so that where I am, there you may be also. [4]And you know the way to the place where I am going."[h] [5]Thomas said to him, "Lord, we do not know where you are going. How can we know the way?" [6]Jesus said to him, "I am the way, and the truth, and the life. No one comes to the Father except through me. [7]If you know me, you will know[i] my Father also. From now on you do know him and have seen him."

[8]Philip said to him, "Lord, show us the Father, and we will be satisfied." [9]Jesus said to him, "Have I been with you all this time, Philip, and you still do not know me? Whoever has seen me has seen the Father. How can you say, 'Show us the Father'? [10]Do you not believe that I am in the Father and the Father is

[a] 13.19 Gk I am   [b] 13.26 Gk dipped it
[c] 13.26 Other ancient authorities read Judas Iscariot son of Simon; others, Judas son of Simon from Karyot (Kerioth)   [d] 13.27 Gk After the piece of bread   [e] 13.32 Other ancient authorities lack If God has been glorified in him   [f] 14.1 Or You believe
[g] 14.2 Or If it were not so, I would have told you; for I go to prepare a place for you
[h] 14.4 Other ancient authorities read Where I am going you know, and the way you know
[i] 14.7 Other ancient authorities read If you had known me, you would have known

in me? The words that I say to you I do not speak on my own; but the Father who dwells in me does his works. ¹¹Believe me that I am in the Father and the Father is in me; but if you do not, then believe me because of the works themselves. ¹²Very truly, I tell you, the one who believes in me will also do the works that I do and, in fact, will do greater works than these, because I am going to the Father. ¹³I will do whatever you ask in my name, so that the Father may be glorified in the Son. ¹⁴If in my name you ask me[a] for anything, I will do it.

THE PROMISE OF THE HOLY SPIRIT

15 "If you love me, you will keep[b] my commandments. ¹⁶And I will ask the Father, and he will give you another Advocate,[c] to be with you forever. ¹⁷This is the Spirit of truth, whom the world cannot receive, because it neither sees him nor knows him. You know him, because he abides with you, and he will be in[d] you.

18 "I will not leave you orphaned; I am coming to you. ¹⁹In a little while the world will no longer see me, but you will see me; because I live, you also will live. ²⁰On that day you will know that I am in my Father, and you in me, and I in you. ²¹They who have my commandments and keep them are those who love me; and those who love me will be loved by my Father, and I will love them and reveal myself to them." ²²Judas (not

Iscariot) said to him, "Lord, how is it that you will reveal yourself to us, and not to the world?" ²³Jesus answered him, "Those who love me will keep my word, and my Father will love them, and we will come to them and make our home with them. ²⁴Whoever does not love me does not keep my words; and the word that you hear is not mine, but is from the Father who sent me.

25 "I have said these things to you while I am still with you. ²⁶But the Advocate,[c] the Holy Spirit, whom the Father will send in my name, will teach you everything, and remind you of all that I have said to you. ²⁷Peace I leave with you; my peace I give to you. I do not give to you as the world gives. Do not let your hearts be troubled, and do not let them be afraid. ²⁸You heard me say to you, 'I am going away, and I am coming to you.' If you loved me, you would rejoice that I am going to the Father, because the Father is greater than I. ²⁹And now I have told you this before it occurs, so that when it does occur, you may believe. ³⁰I will no longer talk much with you, for the ruler of this world is coming. He has no power over me; ³¹but I do as the Father has commanded me, so that the world may know that I love the Father. Rise, let us be on our way.

[a] 14.14 Other ancient authorities lack *me*
[b] 14.15 Other ancient authorities read *me, keep*   [c] 14.16,26 Or *Helper*   [d] 14.17 Or *among*

BIBLE IN LIFE

The Holy Spirit   John 14.25–27

Christ's time on earth was limited. Knowing that Jesus was facing death, his disciples, who loved him, felt bereft of consolation. They feared that they were going to be abandoned. Christ reassured them that God would send the Holy Spirit to comfort them and be with them as God's redemptive presence on earth. Christ's influence would not wane when his physical presence on earth ended. In his love and grace, God has sent his Spirit to dwell with us permanently. And where did Christ say that the Holy Spirit would dwell? In all of us. The Holy Spirit is a personal reality who lives in the followers of Christ and lets the Word of Christ continue and prevail through us. The Spirit is not intangible. The tangibility of the Spirit exists in our receptivity, our willingness to accept the gift of God's presence.

JESUS THE TRUE VINE

15 "I am the true vine, and my Father is the vinegrower. ²He removes every branch in me that bears no fruit. Every branch that bears fruit he prunes[a] to make it bear more fruit. ³You have already been cleansed[a] by the word that I have spoken to you. ⁴Abide in me as I abide in you. Just as the branch cannot bear fruit by itself unless it abides in the vine, neither can you unless you abide in me. ⁵I am the vine, you are the branches. Those who abide in me and I in them bear much fruit, because apart from me you can do nothing. ⁶Whoever does not abide in me is thrown away like a branch and withers; such branches are gathered, thrown into the fire, and burned. ⁷If you abide in me, and my words abide in you, ask for whatever you wish, and it will be done for you. ⁸My Father is glorified by this, that you bear much fruit and become[b] my disciples. ⁹As the Father has loved me, so I have loved you; abide in my love. ¹⁰If you keep my commandments, you will abide in my love, just as I have kept my Father's commandments and abide in his love. ¹¹I have said these things to you so that my joy may be in you, and that your joy may be complete.

¹²"This is my commandment, that you love one another as I have loved you. ¹³No one has greater love than this, to lay down one's life for one's friends. ¹⁴You are my friends if you do what I command you. ¹⁵I do not call you servants[c] any longer, because the servant[d] does not know what the master is doing; but I have called you friends, because I have made known to you everything that I have heard from my Father. ¹⁶You did not choose me but I chose you. And I appointed you to go and bear fruit, fruit that will last, so that the Father will give you whatever you ask him in my name. ¹⁷I am giving you these commands so that you may love one another.

THE WORLD'S HATRED

18 "If the world hates you, be aware that it hated me before it hated you. ¹⁹If you belonged to the world,[e] the world would love you as its own. Because you do not belong to the world, but I have chosen you out of the world—therefore the world hates you. ²⁰Remember the word that I said to you, 'Servants[f] are not greater than their master.' If they persecuted me, they will persecute you; if they kept my word, they will keep yours also. ²¹But they will do all these things to you on account of my name, because they do not know him who sent me. ²²If I had not come and spoken to them, they would not have sin; but now

---

[a] 15.2,3 The same Greek root refers to pruning and cleansing   [b] 15.8 Or be   [c] 15.15 Gk *slaves*   [d] 15.15 Gk *slave*   [e] 15.19 Gk *were of the world*   [f] 15.20 Gk *Slaves*

BIBLE IN LIFE

Not of This World

John 15.18–27

What's the distinction between those who are of the world and those who are not of the world? Those who are of the world blend into the world, while those who are not of the world build their lives around Christ. Jesus chose us "out of the world" (verse 19). When we're of the world, we fit in with our neighbors, but when we're not of the world, we may be hated, despised, cast out or even killed. Christ said, "If they persecuted me, they will persecute you" (verse 20). This sounds hopeless! But Jesus promised that we will be strengthened by the presence of the Holy Spirit, who will help us testify about our relationship with Christ (verses 26–27). We are to stand firm in our faith, and our voice will be heard as we tell others about their need for repentance and forgiveness. We may suffer physically, we may be outcasts, we may be despised and we may be lonely, but we won't be alone, because we have the Holy Spirit within us.

they have no excuse for their sin. 23Whoever hates me hates my Father also. 24If I had not done among them the works that no one else did, they would not have sin. But now they have seen and hated both me and my Father. 25It was to fulfill the word that is written in their law, 'They hated me without a cause.'

26 "When the Advocate[a] comes, whom I will send to you from the Father, the Spirit of truth who comes from the Father, he will testify on my behalf. 27You also are to testify because you have been with me from the beginning.

16 "I have said these things to you to keep you from stumbling. 2They will put you out of the synagogues. Indeed, an hour is coming when those who kill you will think that by doing so they are offering worship to God. 3And they will do this because they have not known the Father or me. 4But I have said these things to you so that when their hour comes you may remember that I told you about them.

THE WORK OF THE SPIRIT

"I did not say these things to you from the beginning, because I was with you. 5But now I am going to him who sent me; yet none of you asks me, 'Where are you going?' 6But because I have said these things to you, sorrow has filled your hearts. 7Nevertheless I tell you the truth: it is to your advantage that I go away, for if I do not go away, the Advocate[a] will not come to you; but if I go, I will send him to you. 8And when he comes, he will prove the world wrong about[b] sin and righteousness and judgment: 9about sin, because they do not believe in me; 10about righteousness, because I am going to the Father and you will see me no longer; 11about judgment, because the ruler of this world has been condemned.

12 "I still have many things to say to you, but you cannot bear them now. 13When the Spirit of truth comes, he will guide you into all the truth; for he will not speak on his own, but will speak whatever

he hears, and he will declare to you the things that are to come. 14He will glorify me, because he will take what is mine and declare it to you. 15All that the Father has is mine. For this reason I said that he will take what is mine and declare it to you.

SORROW WILL TURN INTO JOY

16 "A little while, and you will no longer see me, and again a little while, and you will see me." 17Then some of his disciples said to one another, "What does he mean by saying to us, 'A little while, and you will no longer see me, and again a little while, and you will see me'; and 'Because I am going to the Father'?" 18They said, "What does he mean by this 'a little while'? We do not know what he is talking about." 19Jesus knew that they wanted to ask him, so he said to them, "Are you discussing among yourselves what I meant when I said, 'A little while, and you will no longer see me, and again a little while, and you will see me'? 20Very truly, I tell you, you will weep and mourn, but the world will rejoice; you will have pain, but your pain will turn into joy. 21When a woman is in labor, she has pain, because her hour has come. But when her child is born, she no longer remembers the anguish because of the joy of having brought a human being into the world. 22So you have pain now; but I will see you again, and your hearts will rejoice, and no one will take your joy from you. 23On that day you will ask nothing of me.[c] Very truly, I tell you, if you ask anything of the Father in my name, he will give it to you.[d] 24Until now you have not asked for anything in my name. Ask and you will receive, so that your joy may be complete.

PEACE FOR THE DISCIPLES

25 "I have said these things to you in figures of speech. The hour is coming when I will no longer speak to you in figures, but will tell you

---

[a] 15.26; 16.7 Or *Helper* [b] 16.8 Or *convict the world of* [c] 16.23 Or *will ask me no question* [d] 16.23 Other ancient authorities read *Father, he will give it to you in my name*

plainly of the Father. 26On that day you will ask in my name. I do not say to you that I will ask the Father on your behalf; 27for the Father himself loves you, because you have loved me and have believed that I came from God.ᵃ 28I came from the Father and have come into the world; again, I am leaving the world and am going to the Father."

29 His disciples said, "Yes, now you are speaking plainly, not in any figure of speech! 30Now we know that you know all things, and do not need to have anyone question you; by this we believe that you came from God." 31Jesus answered them, "Do you now believe? 32The hour is coming, indeed it has come, when you will be scattered, each one to his home, and you will leave me alone. Yet I am not alone because the Father is with me. 33I have said this to you, so that in me you may have peace. In the world you face persecution. But take courage; I have conquered the world!"

JESUS PRAYS FOR HIS DISCIPLES

17 After Jesus had spoken these words, he looked up to heaven and said, "Father, the hour has come; glorify your Son so that the Son may glorify you, 2since you have given him authority over all people,ᵇ to give eternal life to all whom you have given him. 3And this is eternal life, that they may know you, the only true God, and Jesus Christ whom you have sent. 4I glorified you on earth by finishing the work that you gave me to do. 5So now, Father, glorify me in your own presence with the glory that I had in your presence before the world existed.

6 "I have made your name known to those whom you gave me from the world. They were yours, and you gave them to me, and they have kept your word. 7Now they know that everything you have given me is from you; 8for the words that you gave to me I have given to them, and they have received them and know in truth that I came from you; and they have believed that you sent me. 9I

am asking on their behalf; I am not asking on behalf of the world, but on behalf of those whom you gave me, because they are yours. 10All mine are yours, and yours are mine; and I have been glorified in them. 11And now I am no longer in the world, but they are in the world, and I am coming to you. Holy Father, protect them in your name that you have given me, so that they may be one, as we are one. 12While I was with them, I protected them in your name thatᶜ you have given me. I guarded them, and not one of them was lost except the one destined to be lost,ᵈ so that the scripture might be fulfilled. 13But now I am coming to you, and I speak these things in the world so that they may have my joy made complete in themselves.ᵉ 14I have given them your word, and the world has hated them because they do not belong to the world, just as I do not belong to the world. 15I am not asking you to take them out of the world, but I ask you to protect them from the evil one.ᶠ 16They do not belong to the world, just as I do not belong to the world. 17Sanctify them in the truth; your word is truth. 18As you have sent me into the world, so I have sent them into the world. 19And for their sakes I sanctify myself, so that they also may be sanctified in truth.

20 "I ask not only on behalf of these, but also on behalf of those who will believe in me through their word, 21that they may all be one. As you, Father, are in me and I am in you, may they also be in us,ᵍ so that the world may believe that you have sent me. 22The glory that you have given me I have given them, so that they may be one, as we are one, 23I in them and you in me, that they may become completely one, so that the world may know that you have

ᵃ **16.27** Other ancient authorities read *the Father* ᵇ **17.2** Gk *flesh* ᶜ **17.12** Other ancient authorities read *protected in your name those whom* ᵈ **17.12** Gk *except the son of destruction* ᵉ **17.13** Or *among themselves* ᶠ **17.15** Or *from evil* ᵍ **17.21** Other ancient authorities read *be one in us*

Take Heart

"I have said this to you, so that in me you may have peace. In the world you face persecution. But take courage; I have conquered the world!"

—John 16.33

Jesus warns in John 15 that when he chose the disciples out of the world, it ensured that they would be hated, cast out, even killed. What's the distinction between those who are of the world and those who are not of the world? Those who are of the world build their lives around themselves. Those who are not of the world build their lives around Christ. The world hated Christ and rejoiced in his death. And almost all of Jesus' disciples lost their lives because they believed in Christ and were willing to express their beliefs in spite of the condemnation and the hatred of the world around them. We must also be willing to suffer for Christ, but we must not be without hope.

Is there a more vivid description of Christ's crucifixion and resurrection than an image of a woman in childbirth? "When a woman is in labor, she has pain, because her hour has come. But when her child is born, she no longer remembers the anguish because of the joy of having brought a human being into the world" (John 16.21). The physical discomfort of labor is almost unbearable. But after the baby is born and a new life is created, there's a flood of joy. The pain is remembered, not with rejection, but as part of the love. Through the pain of Christ's death, we can experience the joy of his resurrection and our salvation. We are given hope.

Before Jesus' death, he told his disciples, "You will weep and mourn, but the world will rejoice; you will have pain, but your pain will turn into joy" (verse 20). The world triumphed in Christ's death, proclaiming, "This radical has been destroyed!" But Jesus' disciples were cast into the depths of despondency and sorrow. And then what happened? Christ was raised, and the disciples rejoiced. Their faltering faith was strengthened, and their hope was renewed.

The disciples were sinners; so are we. Other people listened to the disciples and saw them make mistakes. People listen to us as Christians and watch us make mistakes. But as the Holy Spirit sustained and strengthened the disciples, so he will sustain and strengthen us. We may suffer, we may be outcasts, we may be despised, and we may be alienated and lonely among our neighbors, but we won't be alone—because Jesus said he would be with us through the Holy Spirit. With the Holy Spirit permeating our souls and our hearts, we'll be strengthened; we won't be abandoned. With his presence in our lives, we can speak the words of Christ to others as the disciples did. And we can do so without fear because of the hope we have in the resurrection of our Savior, Jesus Christ.

Going Deeper

- What experiences of alienation or even suffering have you had because of your faith in Christ? Do you tend to keep silent about your faith for fear of confrontation with those who are opposed to Christianity?
- Does anything within you keep the Holy Spirit from strengthening your faith?

sent me and have loved them even as you have loved me. 24Father, I desire that those also, whom you have given me, may be with me where I am, to see my glory, which you have given me because you loved me before the foundation of the world.

25 "Righteous Father, the world does not know you, but I know you; and these know that you have sent me. 26I made your name known to them, and I will make it known, so that the love with which you have loved me may be in them, and I in them."

THE BETRAYAL AND ARREST OF JESUS

18 After Jesus had spoken these words, he went out with his disciples across the Kidron valley to a place where there was a garden, which he and his disciples entered. 2Now Judas, who betrayed him, also knew the place, because Jesus often met there with his disciples. 3So Judas brought a detachment of soldiers together with police from the chief priests and the Pharisees, and they came there with lanterns and torches and weapons. 4Then Jesus, knowing all that was to happen to him, came forward and asked them, "Whom are you looking for?" 5They answered, "Jesus of Nazareth."ª Jesus replied, "I am he."ᵇ Judas, who betrayed him, was standing with them. 6When Jesusᶜ said to them, "I am he,"ᵇ they stepped back and fell to the ground. 7Again he asked them, "Whom are you looking for?" And they said, "Jesus of Nazareth."ª 8Jesus answered, "I told you that I am he.ᵇ So if you are looking for me, let these men go." 9This was to fulfill the word that he had spoken, "I did not lose a single one of those whom you gave me." 10Then Simon Peter, who had a sword, drew it, struck the high priest's slave, and cut off his right ear. The slave's name was Malchus. 11Jesus said to Peter, "Put your sword back into its sheath. Am I not to drink the cup that the Father has given me?"

JESUS BEFORE THE HIGH PRIEST

12 So the soldiers, their officer, and the Jewish police arrested Jesus

and bound him. 13First they took him to Annas, who was the father-in-law of Caiaphas, the high priest that year. 14Caiaphas was the one who had advised the Jews that it was better to have one person die for the people.

PETER DENIES JESUS

15 Simon Peter and another disciple followed Jesus. Since that disciple was known to the high priest, he went with Jesus into the courtyard of the high priest, 16but Peter was standing outside at the gate. So the other disciple, who was known to the high priest, went out, spoke to the woman who guarded the gate, and brought Peter in. 17The woman said to Peter, "You are not also one of this man's disciples, are you?" He said, "I am not." 18Now the slaves and the police had made a charcoal fire because it was cold, and they were standing around it and warming themselves. Peter also was standing with them and warming himself.

THE HIGH PRIEST QUESTIONS JESUS

19 Then the high priest questioned Jesus about his disciples and about his teaching. 20Jesus answered, "I have spoken openly to the world; I have always taught in synagogues and in the temple, where all the Jews come together. I have said nothing in secret. 21Why do you ask me? Ask those who heard what I said to them; they know what I said." 22When he had said this, one of the police standing nearby struck Jesus on the face, saying, "Is that how you answer the high priest?" 23Jesus answered, "If I have spoken wrongly, testify to the wrong. But if I have spoken rightly, why do you strike me?" 24Then Annas sent him bound to Caiaphas the high priest.

PETER DENIES JESUS AGAIN

25 Now Simon Peter was standing and warming himself. They

ª 18.5,7 Gk *the Nazorean*   ᵇ 18.5,6,8 Gk *I am*   ᶜ 18.6 Gk *he* asked him, "You are not also one of his disciples, are you?" He denied it and said, "I am not." 26One of the slaves of the high priest, a relative of the man whose ear Peter had cut off, asked, "Did I not see you in the garden with him?" 27Again Peter denied it, and at that moment the cock crowed.

JESUS BEFORE PILATE

28 Then they took Jesus from Caiaphas to Pilate's headquarters.[a] It was early in the morning. They themselves did not enter the headquarters,[a] so as to avoid ritual defilement and to be able to eat the Passover. 29So Pilate went out to them and said, "What accusation do you bring against this man?" 30They answered, "If this man were not a criminal, we would not have handed him over to you." 31Pilate said to them, "Take him yourselves and judge him according to your law." The Jews replied, "We are not permitted to put anyone to death." 32(This was to fulfill what Jesus had said when he indicated the kind of death he was to die.)

33 Then Pilate entered the headquarters[a] again, summoned Jesus, and asked him, "Are you the King of the Jews?" 34Jesus answered, "Do you ask this on your own, or did others tell you about me?" 35Pilate replied, "I am not a Jew, am I? Your own nation and the chief priests have handed you over to me. What have you done?" 36Jesus answered, "My kingdom is not from this world. If my kingdom were from this world, my followers would be fighting to keep me from being handed over to the Jews. But as it is, my kingdom is not from here." 37Pilate asked him, "So you are a king?" Jesus answered, "You say that I am a king. For this I was born, and for this I came into the world, to testify to the truth. Everyone who belongs to the truth listens to my voice." 38Pilate asked him, "What is truth?"

JESUS SENTENCED TO DEATH

After he had said this, he went out to the Jews again and told them,

"I find no case against him. 39But you have a custom that I release someone for you at the Passover. Do you want me to release for you the King of the Jews?" 40They shouted in reply, "Not this man, but Barabbas!" Now Barabbas was a bandit.

19 Then Pilate took Jesus and had him flogged. 2And the soldiers wove a crown of thorns and put it on his head, and they dressed him in a purple robe. 3They kept coming up to him, saying, "Hail, King of the Jews!" and striking him on the face. 4Pilate went out again and said to them, "Look, I am bringing him out to you to let you know that I find no case against him." 5So

---

[a] 18.28,33 Gk the praetorium

Jesus came out, wearing the crown of thorns and the purple robe. Pilate said to them, "Here is the man!" 6When the chief priests and the police saw him, they shouted, "Crucify him! Crucify him!" Pilate said to them, "Take him yourselves and crucify him; I find no case against him." 7The Jews answered him, "We have a law, and according to that law he ought to die because he has claimed to be the Son of God."

8 Now when Pilate heard this, he was more afraid than ever. 9He entered his headquarters[a] again and asked Jesus, "Where are you from?" But Jesus gave him no answer. 10Pilate therefore said to him, "Do you refuse to speak to me? Do you not know that I have power to release you, and power to crucify you?" 11Jesus answered him, "You would have no power over me unless it had been given you from above; therefore the one who handed me over to you is guilty of a greater sin." 12From then on Pilate tried to release him, but the Jews cried out, "If you release this man, you are no friend of the emperor. Everyone who claims to be a king sets himself against the emperor."

13 When Pilate heard these words, he brought Jesus outside and sat[b] on the judge's bench at a place called The Stone Pavement, or in Hebrew[c] Gabbatha. 14Now it was the day of Preparation for the Passover; and it was about noon. He said to the Jews, "Here is your King!" 15They cried out, "Away with him! Away with him! Crucify him!" Pilate asked them, "Shall I crucify your King?" The chief priests answered, "We have no king but the emperor." 16Then he handed him over to them to be crucified.

THE CRUCIFIXION OF JESUS

So they took Jesus; 17and carrying the cross by himself, he went out to what is called The Place of the Skull, which in Hebrew[c] is called Golgotha. 18There they crucified him, and with him two others, one on either side, with Jesus between them. 19Pilate also had an inscription written and put on the cross. It read, "Jesus of Nazareth,[d] the King of the Jews." 20Many of the Jews read this inscription, because the place where Jesus was crucified was near the city; and it was written in Hebrew,[c] in Latin, and in Greek. 21Then the chief priests of the Jews said to Pilate, "Do not write, 'The King of the Jews,' but, 'This man said, I am King of the Jews.' " 22Pilate answered, "What I have written I have written." 23When the soldiers had crucified Jesus, they took his clothes and divided them into four parts, one for each soldier. They also took his tunic; now the tunic was seamless, woven in one piece from the top. 24So they said to one another, "Let us not tear it, but cast lots for it to see who will get it." This was to fulfill what the scripture says,

"They divided my clothes
    among themselves,
and for my clothing
        they cast lots."

25And that is what the soldiers did.

Meanwhile, standing near the cross of Jesus were his mother, and his mother's sister, Mary the wife of Clopas, and Mary Magdalene. 26When Jesus saw his mother and the disciple whom he loved standing beside her, he said to his mother, "Woman, here is your son." 27Then he said to the disciple, "Here is your mother." And from that hour the disciple took her into his own home.

28 After this, when Jesus knew that all was now finished, he said (in order to fulfill the scripture), "I am thirsty." 29A jar full of sour wine was standing there. So they put a sponge full of the wine on a branch of hyssop and held it to his mouth. 30When Jesus had received the wine, he said, "It is finished." Then he bowed his head and gave up his spirit.

JESUS' SIDE IS PIERCED

31 Since it was the day of Preparation, the Jews did not want the bodies left on the cross during the sabbath, especially because that

a 19.9 Gk the praetorium b 19.13 Or seated him c 19.13,17,20 That is, Aramaic d 19.19 Gk the Nazorean

sabbath was a day of great solemnity. So they asked Pilate to have the legs of the crucified men broken and the bodies removed. ³²Then the soldiers came and broke the legs of the first and of the other who had been crucified with him. ³³But when they came to Jesus and saw that he was already dead, they did not break his legs. ³⁴Instead, one of the soldiers pierced his side with a spear, and at once blood and water came out. ³⁵(He who saw this has testified so that you also may believe. His testimony is true, and he knows[a] that he tells the truth.) ³⁶These things occurred so that the scripture might be fulfilled, "None of his bones shall be broken." ³⁷And again another passage of scripture says, "They will look on the one whom they have pierced."

THE BURIAL OF JESUS

38 After these things, Joseph of Arimathea, who was a disciple of Jesus, though a secret one because of his fear of the Jews, asked Pilate to let him take away the body of Jesus. Pilate gave him permission; so he came and removed his body. ³⁹Nicodemus, who had at first come to Jesus by night, also came, bringing a mixture of myrrh and aloes, weighing about a hundred pounds. ⁴⁰They took the body of Jesus and wrapped it with the spices in linen cloths, according to the burial custom of the Jews. ⁴¹Now there was a garden in the place where he was crucified, and in the garden there was a new tomb in which no one had ever been laid. ⁴²And so, because it was the Jewish day of Preparation, and the tomb was nearby, they laid Jesus there.

THE RESURRECTION OF JESUS

20 Early on the first day of the week, while it was still dark, Mary Magdalene came to the tomb and saw that the stone had been removed from the tomb. ²So she ran and went to Simon Peter and the other disciple, the one whom Jesus loved, and said to them, "They have taken the Lord out of the tomb, and we do not know where they have laid him." ³Then Peter and the other disciple set out and went toward the tomb. ⁴The two were running together, but the other disciple outran Peter and reached the tomb first. ⁵He bent down to look in and saw the linen wrappings lying there, but he did not go in. ⁶Then Simon Peter came, following him, and went into the tomb. He saw the linen wrappings lying there, ⁷and the cloth that had been on Jesus' head, not lying with the linen wrappings but rolled up in a place by itself. ⁸Then the other disciple, who reached the

[a] **19.35** Or *there is one who knows*

BIBLE IN LIFE

Recognizing Jesus
John 20.1–18

The first person to go to Jesus' tomb was Mary Magdalene. Filled with sorrow, she went there, but when the tomb was empty, she refused to leave that place without an explanation. When Jesus said to her, "Mary," she responded by saying, "Rabbouni!" (Aramaic for "Teacher"). When Jesus called her name, it created a tie between them that let her recognize Christ in a totally different way. Some people consider this exchange to provide one of the more profound theological lessons in the Bible. At that moment, Mary recognized not Jesus, her human friend, but Jesus, the resurrected Lord. It may be that we have the same inability to accept the miracle of the resurrection unless we have a personal tie with Christ—unless Jesus has, in effect, called our names. In Revelation 3.20, Jesus says, "I am standing at the door, knocking; if you hear my voice and open the door, I will come in to you and eat with you, and you with me." As long as Christ is calling our names and we don't respond, it's like a ringing doorbell that no one answers. Mary was extremely receptive. Will we be?

tomb first, also went in, and he saw and believed; 9for as yet they did not understand the scripture, that he must rise from the dead. 10Then the disciples returned to their homes.

JESUS APPEARS TO MARY MAGDALENE

11 But Mary stood weeping outside the tomb. As she wept, she bent over to look[a] into the tomb; 12and she saw two angels in white, sitting where the body of Jesus had been lying, one at the head and the other at the feet. 13They said to her, "Woman, why are you weeping?" She said to them, "They have taken away my Lord, and I do not know where they have laid him." 14When she had said this, she turned around and saw Jesus standing there, but she did not know that it was Jesus. 15Jesus said to her, "Woman, why are you weeping? Whom are you looking for?" Supposing him to be the gardener, she said to him, "Sir, if you have carried him away, tell me where you have laid him, and I will take him away." 16Jesus said to her, "Mary!" She turned and said to him in Hebrew,[b] "Rabbouni!" (which means Teacher). 17Jesus said to her, "Do not hold on to me, because I have not yet ascended to the Father. But go to my brothers and say to them, 'I am ascending to my Father and your Father, to my God and your God.' " 18Mary Magdalene went and announced to the disciples, "I have seen the Lord"; and she told them that he had said these things to her.

JESUS APPEARS TO THE DISCIPLES

19 When it was evening on that day, the first day of the week, and the doors of the house where the disciples had met were locked for fear of the Jews, Jesus came and stood among them and said, "Peace be with you." 20After he said this, he showed them his hands and his side. Then the disciples rejoiced when they saw the Lord. 21Jesus said to them again, "Peace be with you. As the Father has sent me, so I send you." 22When he had said this, he breathed on them and said to them, "Receive the Holy Spirit. 23If you forgive the sins of any, they are forgiven them; if you retain the sins of any, they are retained."

JESUS AND THOMAS

24 But Thomas (who was called the Twin[c]), one of the twelve, was not with them when Jesus came. 25So the other disciples told him, "We have seen the Lord." But he said to them, "Unless I see the mark of the nails in his hands, and put my finger in the mark of the nails and my hand in his side, I will not believe."

26 A week later his disciples were again in the house, and Thomas was with them. Although the doors were shut, Jesus came and stood among them and said, "Peace be with you." 27Then he said to Thomas, "Put your finger here and see my hands. Reach out your hand and put it in my side. Do not doubt but believe." 28Thomas answered him, "My Lord and my God!" 29Jesus said to him, "Have you believed because you have seen me? Blessed are those who have not seen and yet have come to believe."

THE PURPOSE OF THIS BOOK

30 Now Jesus did many other signs in the presence of his disciples, which are not written in this book. 31But these are written so that you may come to believe[d] that Jesus is the Messiah,[e] the Son of God, and that through believing you may have life in his name.

JESUS APPEARS TO SEVEN DISCIPLES

21 After these things Jesus showed himself again to the disciples by the Sea of Tiberias; and he showed himself in this way. 2Gathered there together were Simon Peter, Thomas called the Twin,[c] Nathanael of Cana in Galilee, the sons of Zebedee, and two others of his disciples. 3Simon Peter said to

---

a 20.11 Gk lacks *to look*   b 20.16 That is, *Aramaic*   c 20.24; 21.2 Gk *Didymus*
d 20.31 Other ancient authorities read *may continue to believe*   e 20.31 Or *the Christ*

them, "I am going fishing." They said to him, "We will go with you." They went out and got into the boat, but that night they caught nothing.

4 Just after daybreak, Jesus stood on the beach; but the disciples did not know that it was Jesus. 5 Jesus said to them, "Children, you have no fish, have you?" They answered him, "No." 6 He said to them, "Cast the net to the right side of the boat, and you will find some." So they cast it, and now they were not able to haul it in because there were so many fish. 7 That disciple whom Jesus loved said to Peter, "It is the Lord!" When Simon Peter heard that it was the Lord, he put on some clothes, for he was naked, and jumped into the sea. 8 But the other disciples came in the boat, dragging the net full of fish, for they were not far from the land, only about a hundred yards[a] off.

9 When they had gone ashore, they saw a charcoal fire there, with fish on it, and bread. 10 Jesus said to them, "Bring some of the fish that you have just caught." 11 So Simon Peter went aboard and hauled the net ashore, full of large fish, a hundred fifty-three of them; and though there were so many, the net was not torn. 12 Jesus said to them, "Come and have breakfast." Now none of the disciples dared to ask him, "Who are you?" because they knew it was the Lord. 13 Jesus came and took the bread and gave it to them, and did the same with the fish. 14 This was now the third time that Jesus appeared to the disciples after he was raised from the dead.

JESUS AND PETER

15 When they had finished breakfast, Jesus said to Simon Peter, "Simon son of John, do you love me more than these?" He said to him, "Yes, Lord; you know that I love you." Jesus said to him, "Feed my lambs." 16 A second time he said to him, "Simon son of John, do you love me?" He said to him, "Yes, Lord; you know that I love you." Jesus said to him, "Tend my sheep." 17 He said to him the third time, "Simon son of John, do you love me?" Peter felt hurt because he said to him the third time, "Do you love me?" And he said to him, "Lord, you know everything; you know that I love you." Jesus said to him, "Feed my sheep. 18 Very truly, I tell you, when you were younger, you used to fasten your own belt and to go wherever you wished. But when you grow old, you will stretch out your hands, and someone else will fasten a belt around you and take you where you do not wish to go." 19 (He said this to indicate the kind of death by which he would glorify God.) After this he said to him, "Follow me."

JESUS AND THE BELOVED DISCIPLE

20 Peter turned and saw the disciple whom Jesus loved following them; he was the one who had reclined next to Jesus at the supper and had said, "Lord, who is it that is going to betray you?" 21 When Peter saw him, he said to Jesus, "Lord, what about him?" 22 Jesus said to him, "If it is my will that he remain until I come, what is that to you? Follow me!" 23 So the rumor spread in the community[b] that this disciple would not die. Yet Jesus did not say to him that he would not die, but, "If it is my will that he remain until I come, what is that to you?"[c]

24 This is the disciple who is testifying to these things and has written them, and we know that his testimony is true. 25 But there are also many other things that Jesus did; if every one of them were written down, I suppose that the world itself could not contain the books that would be written.

a 21.8 Gk two hundred cubits   b 21.23 Gk among the brothers   c 21.23 Other ancient authorities lack what is that to you

The

ACTS

of the Apostles

The book of Acts picks up the story of the embryonic church where the Gospel of Luke ends—with Jesus' ascension. In Acts, Luke compresses a broad range of information about the development of the church after Jesus' ascension. He begins with the centerpiece event: the awe-inspiring descent of the Holy Spirit on the believers assembled at Jerusalem. Luke goes on to narrate the ministries of Peter and Paul and the outreach of the early Christian community. The book of Acts is much more than a record of historical events—each chapter is illuminated with the power and grace of the Holy Spirit.

THE PROMISE OF THE HOLY SPIRIT

1 In the first book, Theophilus, I wrote about all that Jesus did and taught from the beginning ²until the day when he was taken up to heaven, after giving instructions through the Holy Spirit to the apostles whom he had chosen. ³After his suffering he presented himself alive to them by many convincing proofs, appearing to them during forty days and speaking about the kingdom of God. ⁴While staying[a] with them, he ordered them not to leave Jerusalem, but to wait there for the promise of the Father. "This," he said, "is what you have heard from me; ⁵for John baptized with water, but you will be baptized with[b] the Holy Spirit not many days from now."

THE ASCENSION OF JESUS

6 So when they had come together, they asked him, "Lord, is this the time when you will restore the kingdom to Israel?" ⁷He replied, "It is not for you to know the times or periods that the Father has set by his own authority. ⁸But you will receive power when the Holy Spirit has come upon you; and you will be my witnesses in Jerusalem, in all Judea and Samaria, and to the ends of the earth." ⁹When he had said this, as they were watching, he was lifted up, and a cloud took him out of their sight. ¹⁰While he was going and they were gazing up toward heaven, suddenly two men in white robes stood by them. ¹¹They said, "Men of Galilee, why do you stand looking up toward heaven? This Jesus, who has been taken up from you into heaven, will come in the same way as you saw him go into heaven."

MATTHIAS CHOSEN TO REPLACE JUDAS

12 Then they returned to Jerusalem from the mount called Olivet, which is near Jerusalem, a sabbath day's journey away. ¹³When they had entered the city, they went to the room upstairs where they were staying, Peter, and John, and James, and Andrew, Philip and Thomas, Bartholomew and Matthew, James son of Alphaeus, and Simon the Zealot, and Judas son of[c] James. ¹⁴All these were constantly devoting themselves to prayer, together with certain women, including Mary the mother of Jesus, as well as his brothers.

15 In those days Peter stood up among the believers[d] (together the crowd numbered about one hundred twenty persons) and said, ¹⁶"Friends,[e] the scripture had to be fulfilled, which the Holy Spirit through David foretold concerning Judas, who became a guide for those who arrested Jesus— ¹⁷for he was numbered among us and was allotted his share in this ministry." ¹⁸(Now this man acquired a field with the reward of his wickedness; and falling headlong,[f] he burst open in the middle and all his bowels gushed out. ¹⁹This became known to all the residents of Jerusalem, so that the field was called in their language Hakeldama, that is, Field of Blood.) ²⁰"For it is written in the book of Psalms,

'Let his homestead become
    desolate,
and let there be no one
    to live in it';
and
'Let another take his position
    of overseer.'

²¹So one of the men who have accompanied us during all the time that the Lord Jesus went in and out among us, ²²beginning from the baptism of John until the day when he was taken up from us—one of these must become a witness with us to his resurrection." ²³So they proposed two, Joseph called Barsabbas, who was also known as Justus, and Matthias. ²⁴Then they prayed and said, "Lord, you know everyone's heart. Show us which one of these two you have chosen ²⁵to take the place[g] in this ministry and apostleship from which Judas turned

[a] 1.4 Or eating   [b] 1.5 Or by   [c] 1.13 Or the brother of   [d] 1.15 Gk brothers   [e] 1.16 Gk Men, brothers   [f] 1.18 Or swelling up   [g] 1.25 Other ancient authorities read the share

aside to go to his own place." 26 And they cast lots for them, and the lot fell on Matthias; and he was added to the eleven apostles.

THE COMING OF THE HOLY SPIRIT

2 When the day of Pentecost had come, they were all together in one place. 2 And suddenly from heaven there came a sound like the rush of a violent wind, and it filled the entire house where they were sitting. 3 Divided tongues, as of fire, appeared among them, and a tongue rested on each of them. 4 All of them were filled with the Holy Spirit and began to speak in other languages, as the Spirit gave them ability.

5 Now there were devout Jews from every nation under heaven living in Jerusalem. 6 And at this sound the crowd gathered and was bewildered, because each one heard them speaking in the native language of each. 7 Amazed and astonished, they asked, "Are not all these who are speaking Galileans? 8 And how is it that we hear, each of us, in our own native language? 9 Parthians, Medes, Elamites, and residents of Mesopotamia, Judea and Cappadocia, Pontus and Asia, 10 Phrygia and Pamphylia, Egypt and the parts of Libya belonging to Cyrene, and visitors from Rome, both Jews and proselytes, 11 Cretans and Arabs—in our own languages we hear them speaking about God's deeds of power." 12 All were amazed and perplexed, saying to one another, "What does this mean?" 13 But others sneered and said, "They are filled with new wine."

PETER ADDRESSES THE CROWD

14 But Peter, standing with the eleven, raised his voice and addressed them, "Men of Judea and all who live in Jerusalem, let this be known to you, and listen to what I say. 15 Indeed, these are not drunk, as you suppose, for it is only nine o'clock in the morning. 16 No, this is what was spoken through the prophet Joel:

PONDER

All of them were filled with the Holy Spirit and began to speak in other languages, as the Spirit gave them ability.
—Acts 2.4

PRAY

O Father, we are thankful to be faced with this exciting, if sometimes incomprehensible, event that happened just a few days after Jesus' ascension. A group of his disciples, in a spirit of expectation, demonstrated to thousands of people what it meant for your Spirit to come upon them and into them. Help us remember that your Spirit lives in us also, just as thoroughly as he did in the early disciples. Help us to dedicate ourselves as they did to carry out your will. In Jesus' name we pray. Amen.

17 'In the last days it will be,
        God declares,
    that I will pour out my Spirit
        upon all flesh,
    and your sons and your
            daughters shall prophesy,
    and your young men shall
            see visions,
    and your old men shall
            dream dreams.
18 Even upon my slaves, both
            men and women,
    in those days I will pour
            out my Spirit;
        and they shall prophesy.
19 And I will show portents in
            the heaven above
    and signs on the earth below,
        blood, and fire, and
            smoky mist.
20 The sun shall be turned
        to darkness
    and the moon to blood,
        before the coming of
            the Lord's great and
            glorious day.

21 Then everyone who calls on
    the name of the Lord
    shall be saved.'

22 "You that are Israelites,[a] listen to what I have to say: Jesus of Nazareth,[b] a man attested to you by God with deeds of power, wonders, and signs that God did through him among you, as you yourselves know— 23this man, handed over to you according to the definite plan and foreknowledge of God, you crucified and killed by the hands of those outside the law. 24But God raised him up, having freed him from death,[c] because it was impossible for him to be held in its power. 25For David says concerning him,
    'I saw the Lord always before me,
    for he is at my right hand so
      that I will not be shaken;
26 therefore my heart was glad,
    and my tongue rejoiced;
    moreover my flesh will
      live in hope.
27 For you will not abandon
    my soul to Hades,
    or let your Holy One
      experience corruption.
28 You have made known to
    me the ways of life;
    you will make me full
      of gladness with
      your presence.'

29 "Fellow Israelites,[d] I may say to you confidently of our ancestor David that he both died and was buried, and his tomb is with us to this day. 30Since he was a prophet, he knew that God had sworn with an oath to him that he would put one of his descendants on his throne. 31Foreseeing this, David[e] spoke of the resurrection of the Messiah,[f] saying,
    'He was not abandoned to Hades,
    nor did his flesh experience
      corruption.'
32This Jesus God raised up, and of that all of us are witnesses. 33Being therefore exalted at[g] the right hand of God, and having received from the Father the promise of the Holy Spirit, he has poured out this that you both see and hear. 34For David did not ascend into the heavens, but he himself says,
    'The Lord said to my Lord,
    "Sit at my right hand,
35   until I make your enemies
      your footstool." '
36Therefore let the entire house of Israel know with certainty that God has made him both Lord and Messiah,[h] this Jesus whom you crucified."

THE FIRST CONVERTS

37 Now when they heard this, they were cut to the heart and said to Peter and to the other apostles, "Brothers,[d] what should we do?" 38Peter said to them, "Repent, and be baptized every one of you in the name of Jesus Christ so that your sins may be forgiven; and you will receive the gift of the Holy Spirit. 39For the promise is for you, for your children, and for all who are far away, everyone whom the Lord our God calls to him." 40And he testified with many other arguments and exhorted them, saying, "Save yourselves from this corrupt generation." 41So those who welcomed his message were baptized, and that day about three thousand persons were added. 42They devoted themselves to the apostles' teaching and fellowship, to the breaking of bread and the prayers.

LIFE AMONG THE BELIEVERS

43 Awe came upon everyone, because many wonders and signs were being done by the apostles. 44All who believed were together and had all things in common; 45they would sell their possessions and goods and distribute the proceeds[i] to all, as any had need. 46Day by day, as they spent much time together in the temple, they broke bread at home[j] and ate their food with glad and generous[k] hearts, 47praising God and having the goodwill of all the people. And day by day the Lord added to their number those who were being saved.

[a] 2.22 Gk Men, Israelites   [b] 2.22 Gk the Nazorean   [c] 2.24 Gk the pains of death [d] 2.29,37 Gk Men, brothers   [e] 2.31 Gk he   [f] 2.31 Or the Christ   [g] 2.33 Or by [h] 2.36 Or Christ   [i] 2.45 Gk them   [j] 2.46 Or from house to house   [k] 2.46 Or sincere

PETER HEALS A CRIPPLED BEGGAR

3 One day Peter and John were going up to the temple at the hour of prayer, at three o'clock in the afternoon. ² And a man lame from birth was being carried in. People would lay him daily at the gate of the temple called the Beautiful Gate so that he could ask for alms from those entering the temple. ³ When he saw Peter and John about to go into the temple, he asked them for alms. ⁴ Peter looked intently at him, as did John, and said, "Look at us." ⁵ And he fixed his attention on them, expecting to receive something from them. ⁶ But Peter said, "I have no silver or gold, but what I have I give you; in the name of Jesus Christ of Nazareth,ᵃ stand up and walk." ⁷ And he took him by the right hand and raised him up; and immediately his feet and ankles were made strong. ⁸ Jumping up, he stood and began to walk, and he entered the temple with them, walking and leaping and praising God. ⁹ All the people saw him walking and praising God, ¹⁰ and they recognized him as the one who used to sit and ask for alms at the Beautiful Gate of the temple; and they were filled with wonder and amazement at what had happened to him.

PETER SPEAKS IN SOLOMON'S PORTICO

¹¹ While he clung to Peter and John, all the people ran together to them in the portico called Solomon's Portico, utterly astonished. ¹² When Peter saw it, he addressed the people, "You Israelites,ᵇ why do you wonder at this, or why do you stare at us, as though by our own power or piety we had made him walk? ¹³ The God of Abraham, the God of Isaac, and the God of Jacob, the God of our ancestors has glorified his servantᶜ Jesus, whom you handed over and rejected in the presence of Pilate, though he had decided to release him. ¹⁴ But you rejected the Holy and Righteous One and asked to have a murderer given to you, ¹⁵ and you killed the Author of life, whom God raised from the dead. To this we are witnesses. ¹⁶ And by faith in his name, his name itself has made this man strong, whom you see and know; and the faith that is through Jesusᵈ has given him this perfect health in the presence of all of you.

¹⁷ "And now, friends,ᵉ I know that you acted in ignorance, as did also your rulers. ¹⁸ In this way God ful-

ᵃ 3.6 Gk *the Nazorean* ᵇ 3.12 Gk *Men, Israelites* ᶜ 3.13 Or *child* ᵈ 3.16 Gk *him* ᵉ 3.17 Gk *brothers*

BIBLE IN LIFE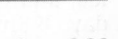

The Good News

Acts 2.38

For many people, the gospel's call to repent and turn to Christ sounds like a predominantly sorrowful ordeal, as if becoming a Christian is a matter of surrendering the life we *really* want for the life we feel we *ought* to be living. But repentance is not self-effacement. It's not embarrassment. It's not an acknowledgement of inferiority, the tedious recounting of our sins or the somber recognition that we ought to be living differently. Instead, the gospel is Good News for our lives—for life in eternity and for life here and now. In fact, that is exactly what the word *gospel* means: Good News. It's not a sorrowful thing; it's a joyful thing. It's not self-effacement; it's exaltation in Christ. It's not a life of restriction or imprisonment; it's a life of freedom and vitality. Christ says that if we stay connected to him, we will experience fruitful, abundant lives for God's glory; we will be filled with joy (see John 15.1–11). In addition to our sins being forgiven, our hearts will be constantly expanding, and our minds will be ever more aware of God's world around us. This is the path to true adventure, real achievement and lasting peace. What a wonderful opportunity God gives us in repentance! How could we choose instead to keep ourselves imprisoned in our old lives, focusing on ourselves and gratifying our dead-end desires? We can embrace the gospel of Jesus Christ as Good News!

filled what he had foretold through all the prophets, that his Messiah[a] would suffer. 19Repent therefore, and turn to God so that your sins may be wiped out, 20so that times of refreshing may come from the presence of the Lord, and that he may send the Messiah[b] appointed for you, that is, Jesus, 21who must remain in heaven until the time of universal restoration that God announced long ago through his holy prophets. 22Moses said, 'The Lord your God will raise up for you from your own people[c] a prophet like me. You must listen to whatever he tells you. 23And it will be that everyone who does not listen to that prophet will be utterly rooted out of the people.' 24And all the prophets, as many as have spoken, from Samuel and those after him, also predicted these days. 25You are the descendants of the prophets and of the covenant that God gave to your ancestors, saying to Abraham, 'And in your descendants all the families of the earth shall be blessed.' 26When God raised up his servant,[d] he sent him first to you, to bless you by turning each of you from your wicked ways."

WE CAN BE ORDINARY

PEOPLE, IN ORDINARY PLACES,

DOING EXTRAORDINARY

THINGS—IN JESUS' NAME.

PETER AND JOHN BEFORE THE COUNCIL

4 While Peter and John[e] were speaking to the people, the priests, the captain of the temple, and the Sadducees came to them, 2much annoyed because they were teaching the people and proclaiming that in Jesus there is the resurrection of the dead. 3So they arrested them and put them in custody until the next day, for it was already eve-

ning. 4But many of those who heard the word believed; and they numbered about five thousand.

5 The next day their rulers, elders, and scribes assembled in Jerusalem, 6with Annas the high priest, Caiaphas, John,[f] and Alexander, and all who were of the high-priestly family. 7When they had made the prisoners[g] stand in their midst, they inquired, "By what power or by what name did you do this?" 8Then Peter, filled with the Holy Spirit, said to them, "Rulers of the people and elders, 9if we are questioned today because of a good deed done to someone who was sick and are asked how this man has been healed, 10let it be known to all of you, and to all the people of Israel, that this man is standing before you in good health by the name of Jesus Christ of Nazareth,[h] whom you crucified, whom God raised from the dead. 11This Jesus[i] is

'the stone that was rejected
    by you, the builders;
it has become the cornerstone.'[j]

12There is salvation in no one else, for there is no other name under heaven given among mortals by which we must be saved."

13 Now when they saw the boldness of Peter and John and realized that they were uneducated and ordinary men, they were amazed and recognized them as companions of Jesus. 14When they saw the man who had been cured standing beside them, they had nothing to say in opposition. 15So they ordered them to leave the council while they discussed the matter with one another. 16They said, "What will we do with them? For it is obvious to all who live in Jerusalem that a notable sign has been done through them; we cannot deny it. 17But to keep it from spreading further among the people, let us warn them to speak no more to anyone in this name." 18So

---

[a] 3.18 Or *his Christ*   [b] 3.20 Or *the Christ*
[c] 3.22 Gk *brothers*   [d] 3.26 Or *child*
[e] 4.1 Gk *While they*   [f] 4.6 Other ancient authorities read *Jonathan*   [g] 4.7 Gk *them*
[h] 4.10 Gk *the Nazorean*   [i] 4.11 Gk *This*
[j] 4.11 Or *keystone*

they called them and ordered them not to speak or teach at all in the name of Jesus. [19]But Peter and John answered them, "Whether it is right in God's sight to listen to you rather than to God, you must judge; [20]for we cannot keep from speaking about what we have seen and heard." [21]After threatening them again, they let them go, finding no way to punish them because of the people, for all of them praised God for what had happened. [22]For the man on whom this sign of healing had been performed was more than forty years old.

THE BELIEVERS PRAY FOR BOLDNESS

[23]After they were released, they went to their friends[a] and reported what the chief priests and the elders had said to them. [24]When they heard it, they raised their voices together to God and said, "Sovereign Lord, who made the heaven and the earth, the sea, and everything in them, [25]it is you who said by the Holy Spirit through our ancestor David, your servant:[b]

'Why did the Gentiles rage,
     and the peoples imagine
        vain things?
[26] The kings of the earth took
        their stand,
     and the rulers have
        gathered together
     against the Lord and
        against his Messiah.'[c]

[27]For in this city, in fact, both Herod and Pontius Pilate, with the Gentiles and the peoples of Israel, gathered together against your holy servant[b] Jesus, whom you anointed, [28]to do whatever your hand and your plan had predestined to take place. [29]And now, Lord, look at their threats, and grant to your servants[d] to speak your word with all boldness, [30]while you stretch out your hand to heal, and signs and wonders are performed through the name of your holy servant[b] Jesus." [31]When they had prayed, the place in which they were gathered together was shaken; and they were all filled with the Holy Spirit and spoke the word of God with boldness.

PONDER

When they had prayed, the place in which they were gathered together was shaken; and they were all filled with the Holy Spirit and spoke the word of God with boldness.
—Acts 4.31

PRAY

O Father, we are reminded that the early disciples were not well-educated, not very powerful and not very eloquent. They were filled with timidity and fear, and they even denied Jesus Christ in his moments of trial. But filled with the Holy Spirit, they were transformed from disciples who were learners into apostles who were leaders and teachers. Help us, Father to be imbued with the Holy Spirit so we can boldly demonstrate with our words and actions that we are disciples of Jesus Christ, fulfilling the Great Commission. Be with us as we go about our lives. Bind our hearts in Christian love. We ask in the name of our Savior, Jesus Christ. Amen.

THE BELIEVERS SHARE THEIR POSSESSIONS

[32] Now the whole group of those who believed were of one heart and soul, and no one claimed private ownership of any possessions, but everything they owned was held in common. [33]With great power the apostles gave their testimony to the resurrection of the Lord Jesus, and great grace was upon them all. [34]There was not a needy person among them, for as many as owned lands or houses sold them and brought the proceeds of what was sold. [35]They laid it at the apostles' feet, and it was distributed to each as any had need. [36]There was a Levite, a native of Cyprus, Joseph,

---

[a] 4.23 Gk their own   [b] 4.25,27,30 Or child
[c] 4.26 Or his Christ   [d] 4.29 Gk slaves

to whom the apostles gave the name Barnabas (which means "son of encouragement"). ³⁷He sold a field that belonged to him, then brought the money, and laid it at the apostles' feet.

ANANIAS AND SAPPHIRA

5 But a man named Ananias, with the consent of his wife Sapphira, sold a piece of property; ²with his wife's knowledge, he kept back some of the proceeds, and brought only a part and laid it at the apostles' feet. ³"Ananias," Peter asked, "why has Satan filled your heart to lie to the Holy Spirit and to keep back part of the proceeds of the land? ⁴While it remained unsold, did it not remain your own? And after it was sold, were not the proceeds at your disposal? How is it that you have contrived this deed in your heart? You did not lie to us[a] but to God!" ⁵Now when Ananias heard these words, he fell down and died. And great fear seized all who heard of it. ⁶The young men came and wrapped up his body,[b] then carried him out and buried him.

7 After an interval of about three hours his wife came in, not knowing what had happened. ⁸Peter said to her, "Tell me whether you and your husband sold the land for such and such a price." And she said, "Yes, that was the price." ⁹Then Peter said to her, "How is it that you have agreed together to put the Spirit of the Lord to the test? Look, the feet of those who have buried your husband are at the door, and they will carry you out." ¹⁰Immediately she fell down at his feet and died. When the young men came in they found her dead, so they carried her out and buried her beside her husband. ¹¹And great fear seized the whole church and all who heard of these things.

THE APOSTLES HEAL MANY

12 Now many signs and wonders were done among the people through the apostles. And they were all together in Solomon's Portico. ¹³None of the rest dared to join them, but the people held them in high esteem. ¹⁴Yet more than ever believers were added to the Lord, great numbers of both men and women, ¹⁵so that they even carried out the sick into the streets, and laid them on cots and mats, in order that Peter's shadow might fall on some of them as he came by. ¹⁶A great number of people would also gather from the towns around Jerusalem, bringing the sick and those tormented by unclean spirits, and they were all cured.

THERE IS NO SUCH THING

AS SECRET DISCIPLESHIP.

THE APOSTLES ARE PERSECUTED

17 Then the high priest took action; he and all who were with him (that is, the sect of the Sadducees), being filled with jealousy, ¹⁸arrested the apostles and put them in the public prison. ¹⁹But during the night an angel of the Lord opened the prison doors, brought them out, and said, ²⁰"Go, stand in the temple and tell the people the whole message about this life." ²¹When they heard this, they entered the temple at daybreak and went on with their teaching.

When the high priest and those with him arrived, they called together the council and the whole body of the elders of Israel, and sent to the prison to have them brought. ²²But when the temple police went there, they did not find them in the prison; so they returned and reported, ²³"We found the prison securely locked and the guards standing at the doors, but when we opened them, we found no one inside." ²⁴Now when the captain of the temple and the chief priests heard these words, they were perplexed about them, wondering what

[a] 5.4 Gk to men [b] 5.6 Meaning of Gk uncertain

might be going on. 25Then someone arrived and announced, "Look, the men whom you put in prison are standing in the temple and teaching the people!" 26Then the captain went with the temple police and brought them, but without violence, for they were afraid of being stoned by the people.

27 When they had brought them, they had them stand before the council. The high priest questioned them, 28saying, "We gave you strict orders not to teach in this name,ᵃ yet here you have filled Jerusalem with your teaching and you are determined to bring this man's blood on us." 29But Peter and the apostles answered, "We must obey God rather than any human authority.ᵇ 30The God of our ancestors raised up Jesus, whom you had killed by hanging him on a tree. 31God exalted him at his right hand as Leader and Savior that he might give repentance to Israel and forgiveness of sins. 32And we are witnesses to these things, and so is the Holy Spirit whom God has given to those who obey him."

33 When they heard this, they were enraged and wanted to kill them. 34But a Pharisee in the council named Gamaliel, a teacher of the law, respected by all the people, stood up and ordered the men to be put outside for a short time. 35Then he said to them, "Fellow Israelites,ᶜ consider carefully what you propose to do to these men. 36For some time ago Theudas rose up, claiming to be somebody, and a number of men, about four hundred, joined him; but he was killed, and all who followed him were dispersed and disappeared. 37After him Judas the Galilean rose up at the time of the census and got people to follow him; he also perished, and all who followed him were scattered. 38So in the present case, I tell you, keep away from these men and let them alone; because if this plan or this undertaking is of human origin, it will fail; 39but if it is of God, you will not be able to overthrow them—in that case you may even be found fighting against God!"

They were convinced by him, 40and when they had called in the apostles, they had them flogged. Then they ordered them not to speak in the name of Jesus, and let them go. 41As they left the council, they rejoiced that they were considered worthy to suffer dishonor for the sake of the name. 42And every day in the temple and at homeᵈ they did not cease to teach and proclaim Jesus as the Messiah.ᵉ

ᵃ 5.28 Other ancient authorities read *Did we not give you strict orders not to teach in this name?* ᵇ 5.29 Gk *than men* ᶜ 5.35 Gk *Men, Israelites* ᵈ 5.42 Or *from house to house* ᵉ 5.42 Or *the Christ*

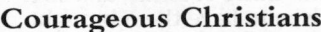

BIBLE IN LIFE

Courageous Christians   Acts 5.17–42

The disciples no longer hid in fear and shame after the crucifixion but boldly proclaimed the gospel of Jesus Christ. What made the difference? The Holy Spirit was with them. When they were ordered not to preach in the name of Jesus, they did not quit. They felt honored to be punished in the name of Christ. Their actions, attitudes and level of commitment to Christ cause us to assess our own relatively superficial dedication to Christ. For most of us, our relationship with Christ is fairly casual, our commitment to Christ is partial and our sense of the presence of the Holy Spirit is not total. We are filled with doubt and often lack courage. It's sometimes more difficult for us as Christians to make the small daily decisions to follow Christ's teachings than it would be to make a single, dramatic, publicized commitment to Christ. When a choice arises to be loyal to our Savior, we can be loyal not only with our words but also with our actions. How many times during a day do we make a courageous choice to sacrifice our own well-being for the well-being of others in the name of Christ?

SEVEN CHOSEN TO SERVE

6 Now during those days, when the disciples were increasing in number, the Hellenists complained against the Hebrews because their widows were being neglected in the daily distribution of food. ²And the twelve called together the whole community of the disciples and said, "It is not right that we should neglect the word of God in order to wait on tables.ᵃ ³Therefore, friends,ᵇ select from among yourselves seven men of good standing, full of the Spirit and of wisdom, whom we may appoint to this task, ⁴while we, for our part, will devote ourselves to prayer and to serving the word." ⁵What they said pleased the whole community, and they chose Stephen, a man full of faith and the Holy Spirit, together with Philip, Prochorus, Nicanor, Timon, Parmenas, and Nicolaus, a proselyte of Antioch. ⁶They had these men stand before the apostles, who prayed and laid their hands on them.

7 The word of God continued to spread; the number of the disciples increased greatly in Jerusalem, and a great many of the priests became obedient to the faith.

THE ARREST OF STEPHEN

8 Stephen, full of grace and power, did great wonders and signs among the people. ⁹Then some of those who belonged to the synagogue of the Freedmen (as it was called), Cyrenians, Alexandrians, and others of those from Cilicia and Asia, stood up and argued with Stephen. ¹⁰But they could not withstand the wisdom and the Spiritᶜ with which he spoke. ¹¹Then they secretly instigated some men to say, "We have heard him speak blasphemous words against Moses and God." ¹²They stirred up the people as well as the elders and the scribes; then they suddenly confronted him, seized him, and brought him before the council. ¹³They set up false witnesses who said, "This man never stops saying things against this holy place and the law; ¹⁴for we have heard him say that this Jesus of Nazarethᵈ will

---

PONDER

The word of God continued to spread; the number of the disciples increased greatly in Jerusalem, and a great many of the priests became obedient to the faith.
—Acts 6.7

PRAY

O Father, we are thankful for a reminder of the struggles of the early church. We have been reminded that we have differences among ourselves. Christians are all over the world. We argue with one another; we debate theology; we have disputes just as those early Christians did. But we see how the early church worked out their problems peaceably and with order, and the church grew. Fill us also with your Holy Spirit, so that we can heal our differences and present a common front as Christian believers to the rest of the world so that your Name will be praised. Bind us together in the spirit of forgiveness and compassion, we ask in Jesus' name. Amen.

---

destroy this place and will change the customs that Moses handed on to us." ¹⁵And all who sat in the council looked intently at him, and they saw that his face was like the face of an angel.

STEPHEN'S SPEECH TO THE COUNCIL

7 Then the high priest asked him, "Are these things so?" ²And Stephen replied:

"Brothersᵉ and fathers, listen to me. The God of glory appeared to our ancestor Abraham when he was in Mesopotamia, before he lived in Haran, ³and said to him, 'Leave your country and your relatives and go to the land that I will show you.' ⁴Then

ᵃ **6.2** Or *keep accounts*   ᵇ **6.3** Gk *brothers*
ᶜ **6.10** Or *spirit*   ᵈ **6.14** Gk *the Nazorean*
ᵉ **7.2** Gk *Men, brothers*

he left the country of the Chaldeans and settled in Haran. After his father died, God had him move from there to this country in which you are now living. ⁵He did not give him any of it as a heritage, not even a foot's length, but promised to give it to him as his possession and to his descendants after him, even though he had no child. ⁶And God spoke in these terms, that his descendants would be resident aliens in a country belonging to others, who would enslave them and mistreat them during four hundred years. ⁷'But I will judge the nation that they serve,' said God, 'and after that they shall come out and worship me in this place.' ⁸Then he gave him the covenant of circumcision. And so Abraham[a] became the father of Isaac and circumcised him on the eighth day; and Isaac became the father of Jacob, and Jacob of the twelve patriarchs.

9 "The patriarchs, jealous of Joseph, sold him into Egypt; but God was with him, ¹⁰and rescued him from all his afflictions, and enabled him to win favor and to show wisdom when he stood before Pharaoh, king of Egypt, who appointed him ruler over Egypt and over all his household. ¹¹Now there came a famine throughout Egypt and Canaan, and great suffering, and our ancestors could find no food. ¹²But when Jacob heard that there was grain in Egypt, he sent our ancestors there on their first visit. ¹³On the second visit Joseph made himself known to his brothers, and Joseph's family became known to Pharaoh. ¹⁴Then Joseph sent and invited his father Jacob and all his relatives to come to him, seventy-five in all; ¹⁵so Jacob went down to Egypt. He himself died there as well as our ancestors, ¹⁶and their bodies[b] were brought back to Shechem and laid in the tomb that Abraham had bought for a sum of silver from the sons of Hamor in Shechem.

17 "But as the time drew near for the fulfillment of the promise that God had made to Abraham, our people in Egypt increased and multiplied ¹⁸until another king who had not known Joseph ruled over Egypt. ¹⁹He dealt craftily with our race and forced our ancestors to abandon their infants so that they would die. ²⁰At this time Moses was born, and he was beautiful before God. For three months he was brought up in his father's house; ²¹and when he was abandoned, Pharaoh's daughter adopted him and brought him up as her own son. ²²So Moses was instructed in all the wisdom of the Egyptians and was powerful in his words and deeds.

23 "When he was forty years old, it came into his heart to visit his relatives, the Israelites.[c] ²⁴When he saw one of them being wronged, he defended the oppressed man and avenged him by striking down the Egyptian. ²⁵He supposed that his kinsfolk would understand that God through him was rescuing them, but they did not understand. ²⁶The next day he came to some of them as they were quarreling and tried to reconcile them, saying, 'Men, you are brothers; why do you wrong each other?' ²⁷But the man who was wronging his neighbor pushed Moses[d] aside, saying, 'Who made you a ruler and a judge over us? ²⁸Do you want to kill me as you killed the Egyptian yesterday?' ²⁹When he heard this, Moses fled and became a resident alien in the land of Midian. There he became the father of two sons.

30 "Now when forty years had passed, an angel appeared to him in the wilderness of Mount Sinai, in the flame of a burning bush. ³¹When Moses saw it, he was amazed at the sight; and as he approached to look, there came the voice of the Lord: ³²'I am the God of your ancestors, the God of Abraham, Isaac, and Jacob.' Moses began to tremble and did not dare to look. ³³Then the Lord said to him, 'Take off the sandals from your feet, for the place where you are standing is holy ground. ³⁴I have surely seen the mistreatment of my people who are in Egypt and have

---

[a] 7.8 Gk he [b] 7.16 Gk they [c] 7.23 Gk his brothers, the sons of Israel [d] 7.27 Gk him

heard their groaning, and I have come down to rescue them. Come now, I will send you to Egypt.'

35 "It was this Moses whom they rejected when they said, 'Who made you a ruler and a judge?' and whom God now sent as both ruler and liberator through the angel who appeared to him in the bush. 36 He led them out, having performed wonders and signs in Egypt, at the Red Sea, and in the wilderness for forty years. 37 This is the Moses who said to the Israelites, 'God will raise up a prophet for you from your own people[a] as he raised me up.' 38 He is the one who was in the congregation in the wilderness with the angel who spoke to him at Mount Sinai, and with our ancestors; and he received living oracles to give to us. 39 Our ancestors were unwilling to obey him; instead, they pushed him aside, and in their hearts they turned back to Egypt, 40 saying to Aaron, 'Make gods for us who will lead the way for us; as for this Moses who led us out from the land of Egypt, we do not know what has happened to him.' 41 At that time they made a calf, offered a sacrifice to the idol, and reveled in the works of their hands. 42 But God turned away from them and handed them over to worship the host of heaven, as it is written in the book of the prophets:

'Did you offer to me slain
        victims and sacrifices
    forty years in the wilderness,
        O house of Israel?
43 No; you took along the
        tent of Moloch,
    and the star of your
        god Rephan,
    the images that you
        made to worship;
so I will remove you beyond
        Babylon.'

44 "Our ancestors had the tent of testimony in the wilderness, as God[b] directed when he spoke to Moses, ordering him to make it according to the pattern he had seen. 45 Our ancestors in turn brought it in with Joshua when they dispossessed the nations that God drove out before our ancestors. And it was there un-til the time of David, 46 who found favor with God and asked that he might find a dwelling place for the house of Jacob.[c] 47 But it was Solomon who built a house for him. 48 Yet the Most High does not dwell in houses made with human hands;[d] as the prophet says,

49 'Heaven is my throne,
        and the earth is my footstool.
    What kind of house will you build
        for me, says the Lord,
    or what is the place of my rest?
50 Did not my hand make all
        these things?'

51 "You stiff-necked people, uncircumcised in heart and ears, you are forever opposing the Holy Spirit, just as your ancestors used to do. 52 Which of the prophets did your ancestors not persecute? They killed those who foretold the coming of the Righteous One, and now you have become his betrayers and murderers. 53 You are the ones that received the law as ordained by angels, and yet you have not kept it."

THE STONING OF STEPHEN

54 When they heard these things, they became enraged and ground their teeth at Stephen.[e] 55 But filled with the Holy Spirit, he gazed into heaven and saw the glory of God and Jesus standing at the right hand of God. 56 "Look," he said, "I see the heavens opened and the Son of Man standing at the right hand of God!" 57 But they covered their ears, and with a loud shout all rushed together against him. 58 Then they dragged him out of the city and began to stone him; and the witnesses laid their coats at the feet of a young man named Saul. 59 While they were stoning Stephen, he prayed, "Lord Jesus, receive my spirit." 60 Then he knelt down and cried out in a loud voice, "Lord, do not hold this sin against them." When he had said this, he died.[f] 1 And Saul approved of their killing him.

---

[a] 7.37 Gk your brothers [b] 7.44 Gk he
[c] 7.46 Other ancient authorities read for the God of Jacob [d] 7.48 Gk with hands
[e] 7.54 Gk him [f] 7.60 Gk fell asleep

PONDER

But filled with the Holy Spirit,
[Stephen] gazed into heaven and
saw the glory of God and Jesus
standing at the right hand of God.
—Acts 7.55

PRAY

Father, here we have learned about
one of the early Christian heroes,
and we pray that we might possess
even a small portion of his devotion
to you. We pray that his example
will inspire us to greater boldness to
proclaim your kingship in our lives,
and we ask you to use our human
weakness and limitations to expand
the kingdom of our Savior, Jesus
Christ. In his name we pray. Amen.

SAUL PERSECUTES THE CHURCH

That day a severe persecution began against the church in Jerusalem, and all except the apostles were
scattered throughout the countryside of Judea and Samaria. 2Devout
men buried Stephen and made loud
lamentation over him. 3But Saul
was ravaging the church by entering house after house; dragging off
both men and women, he committed them to prison.

PHILIP PREACHES IN SAMARIA

4 Now those who were scattered
went from place to place, proclaiming the word. 5Philip went down to
the city[a] of Samaria and proclaimed
the Messiah[b] to them. 6The crowds
with one accord listened eagerly to
what was said by Philip, hearing
and seeing the signs that he did, 7for
unclean spirits, crying with loud
shrieks, came out of many who were
possessed; and many others who
were paralyzed or lame were cured.
8So there was great joy in that city.
9 Now a certain man named Simon had previously practiced magic

in the city and amazed the people of Samaria, saying that he was
someone great. 10All of them, from
the least to the greatest, listened
to him eagerly, saying, "This man
is the power of God that is called
Great." 11And they listened eagerly to
him because for a long time he had
amazed them with his magic. 12But
when they believed Philip, who was
proclaiming the good news about
the kingdom of God and the name
of Jesus Christ, they were baptized,
both men and women. 13Even Simon himself believed. After being
baptized, he stayed constantly with
Philip and was amazed when he saw
the signs and great miracles that
took place.
14 Now when the apostles at Jerusalem heard that Samaria had
accepted the word of God, they sent
Peter and John to them. 15The two
went down and prayed for them
that they might receive the Holy
Spirit 16(for as yet the Spirit had not
come[c] upon any of them; they had
only been baptized in the name of
the Lord Jesus). 17Then Peter and
John[d] laid their hands on them, and
they received the Holy Spirit. 18Now
when Simon saw that the Spirit
was given through the laying on of
the apostles' hands, he offered them
money, 19saying, "Give me also this
power so that anyone on whom I
lay my hands may receive the Holy
Spirit." 20But Peter said to him,
"May your silver perish with you,
because you thought you could obtain God's gift with money! 21You
have no part or share in this, for
your heart is not right before God.
22Repent therefore of this wickedness of yours, and pray to the Lord
that, if possible, the intent of your
heart may be forgiven you. 23For I
see that you are in the gall of bitterness and the chains of wickedness."
24Simon answered, "Pray for me to
the Lord, that nothing of what you[e]
have said may happen to me."

a 8.5 Other ancient authorities read a
city   b 8.5 Or the Christ   c 8.16 Gk fallen
d 8.17 Gk they   e 8.24 The Greek word for
you and the verb pray are plural

25 Now after Peter and John[a] had testified and spoken the word of the Lord, they returned to Jerusalem, proclaiming the good news to many villages of the Samaritans.

LOVE CAN BE COSTLY:

JESUS DIED ON THE CROSS

BECAUSE HE LOVES US.

PHILIP AND THE ETHIOPIAN EUNUCH

26 Then an angel of the Lord said to Philip, "Get up and go toward the south[b] to the road that goes down from Jerusalem to Gaza." (This is a wilderness road.) **27** So he got up and went. Now there was an Ethiopian eunuch, a court official of the Candace, queen of the Ethiopians, in charge of her entire treasury. He had come to Jerusalem to worship **28** and was returning home; seated in his chariot, he was reading the prophet Isaiah. **29** Then the Spirit said to Philip, "Go over to this chariot and join it." **30** So Philip ran up to it and heard him reading the prophet Isaiah. He asked, "Do you understand what you are reading?" **31** He replied, "How can I, unless someone guides me?" And he invited Philip to get in and sit beside him. **32** Now the passage of the scripture that he was reading was this:

"Like a sheep he was led to
    the slaughter,
and like a lamb silent
    before its shearer,
so he does not open
    his mouth.
33 In his humiliation justice
    was denied him.
Who can describe his
    generation?
For his life is taken away
    from the earth."

34 The eunuch asked Philip, "About whom, may I ask you, does the prophet say this, about himself or

PONDER

Then Philip began to speak, and starting with this scripture, he proclaimed to him the good news about Jesus.
—Acts 8.35

PRAY

Father, it is remarkable to read about the first missionary, Philip. It is remarkable how through persecution you sent him, as well as Paul and other apostles, to various countries to preach in the name of Jesus. We can learn from Philip, who was bold and obedient and alert to your guidance. Father, bind us more closely to our Savior, Jesus Christ, and teach us, through fervent prayer, to listen for your voice and obey your directions.

Give us hearts to love our fellow human beings, many of whom we are inclined to ignore or forget, and give us grace to follow more closely in Jesus' footsteps. In his name we pray. Amen.

about someone else?" **35** Then Philip began to speak, and starting with this scripture, he proclaimed to him the good news about Jesus. **36** As they were going along the road, they came to some water; and the eunuch said, "Look, here is water! What is to prevent me from being baptized?"[c] **38** He commanded the chariot to stop, and both of them, Philip and the eunuch, went down into the water, and Philip[d] baptized him. **39** When they came up out of the water, the Spirit of the Lord snatched Philip away; the eunuch saw him no more, and went on his way rejoicing. **40** But Philip found himself at Azotus, and as he was passing through the region, he proclaimed

[a] **8.25** Gk *after they*   [b] **8.26** Or *go at noon*
[c] **8.36** Other ancient authorities add all or most of verse 37, *And Philip said, "If you believe with all your heart, you may." And he replied, "I believe that Jesus Christ is the Son of God."*   [d] **8.38** Gk *he*

the good news to all the towns until he came to Caesarea.

THE CONVERSION OF SAUL

9 Meanwhile Saul, still breathing threats and murder against the disciples of the Lord, went to the high priest ²and asked him for letters to the synagogues at Damascus, so that if he found any who belonged to the Way, men or women, he might bring them bound to Jerusalem. ³Now as he was going along and approaching Damascus, suddenly a light from heaven flashed around him. ⁴He fell to the ground and heard a voice saying to him, "Saul, Saul, why do you persecute me?" ⁵He asked, "Who are you, Lord?" The reply came, "I am Jesus, whom you are persecuting. ⁶But get up and enter the city, and you will be told what you are to do." ⁷The men who were traveling with him stood speechless because they heard the voice but saw no one. ⁸Saul got up from the ground, and though his eyes were open, he could see nothing; so they led him by the hand and brought him into Damascus. ⁹For three days he was without sight, and neither ate nor drank.

10 Now there was a disciple in Damascus named Ananias. The Lord said to him in a vision, "Ananias." He answered, "Here I am, Lord." ¹¹The Lord said to him, "Get up and go to the street called Straight, and at the house of Judas look for a man of Tarsus named Saul. At this moment he is praying, ¹²and he has seen in a vision[a] a man named Ananias come in and lay his hands on him so that he might regain his sight." ¹³But Ananias answered, "Lord, I have heard from many about this man, how much evil he has done to your saints in Jerusalem; ¹⁴and here he has authority from the chief priests to bind all who invoke your name." ¹⁵But the Lord said to him, "Go, for he is an instrument whom I have chosen to bring my name before Gentiles and kings and before the people of Israel; ¹⁶I myself will show him how much he must suffer for the sake of my name." ¹⁷So Ananias went and

entered the house. He laid his hands on Saul[b] and said, "Brother Saul, the Lord Jesus, who appeared to you on your way here, has sent me so that you may regain your sight and be filled with the Holy Spirit." ¹⁸And immediately something like scales fell from his eyes, and his sight was restored. Then he got up and was baptized, ¹⁹and after taking some food, he regained his strength.

PONDER

"Go, for he is an instrument whom I have chosen to bring my name before Gentiles and kings and before the people of Israel; I myself will show him how much he must suffer for the sake of my name." —Acts 9.15–16

PRAY

O Lord, help us, as we read about your dramatic call to Paul and your quieter call to Ananias, to be alert to the ways in which you are calling us. Teach us to see that our lives are shaped by our responses to those calls. Too often we respond too late, or not at all, and we ask your forgiveness for that. We ask for your strength to look at ourselves, the courage to address our shortcomings, and the humility to realize how we need to increase our dedication to our Savior. In his name we pray. Amen.

SAUL PREACHES IN DAMASCUS

For several days he was with the disciples in Damascus, ²⁰and immediately he began to proclaim Jesus in the synagogues, saying, "He is the Son of God." ²¹All who heard him were amazed and said, "Is not this the man who made havoc in Jerusalem among those who invoked this name? And has he not come here for

[a] 9.12 Other ancient authorities lack *in a vision* [b] 9.17 Gk *him*

CALL AND RESPONSE

"Go, for [Saul] is an instrument whom I have chosen to bring my name before Gentiles and kings and before the people of Israel"... So Ananias went and entered the house.

—Acts 9.15,17

How many of us have been called by God to do something specific? There are dramatic ways of being called: a vision, a dream, a crisis in one's life, or a powerful sermon. We've had those experiences. But there are other times when God calls and we are presented with a choice: whether to be generous to those who are in need; to reach out a hand of help or compassion or love or partnership to those who are unattractive or different; to improve a situation in the name of Christ; to heal an unpleasant relationship with another human being; to forgive someone who might have hurt us in some fashion. As Christians, our responses to those calls determine the character of our lives.

After the resurrection of Jesus, Saul took it upon himself to go from house to house arresting anyone who was alleged to be a follower of Christ. And he had no aversion to having them executed. Saul was accustomed to all the good things of life: he had the authority of religious and even semi-secular power; he was esteemed by the other Pharisees and admired because of his fervent religious faith. But Jesus' call to him had a dramatic impact on him. At his conversion, he became helplessly blind in the midst of strangers. We can imagine the abject humility forced on this proud man.

Ananias was called to make a choice. We can imagine his fear—he knew Saul's reputation. But he didn't argue with the Lord very long and responded positively to God's call. It's quite remarkable that when Ananias first touched this hated and feared man, Saul, he said, "Brother." Ananias believed Paul had actually had an encounter with Jesus Christ. He went and knelt with Paul, who had been praying. And immediately afterward, Paul was baptized. Paul (formerly Saul) would go on to convert kings and spread the gospel among the Gentiles throughout the Roman Empire.

Jesus Christ's call to Paul was blazing, dramatic, unforgettable. His call to Ananias was quiet and private. We might be called either way. But we will make choices each day and each week whether or not to respond to Jesus' call. We can go to the end of our existence pleasing ourselves, or we can answer God's call and, in the name of Jesus, do things that are mind-boggling in their significance. Success in the eyes of Jesus Christ is found in supplying drinking water to those without, visiting the sick or someone in prison, or sharing our wealth with somebody else. If we decide to be compassionate in Jesus' name, God will make it possible. God prepared the way for Paul and Ananias to answer his call, and he'll prepare the way for us, too.

Going Deeper

- What have you recently been called by God to do?
- When have you hesitated in answering God's call to get involved with people who might be very different from you? How does Ananias's response to God's call encourage you to put your fears of serving aside?

the purpose of bringing them bound before the chief priests?" 22Saul became increasingly more powerful and confounded the Jews who lived in Damascus by proving that Jesus[a] was the Messiah.[b]

SAUL ESCAPES FROM THE JEWS

23 After some time had passed, the Jews plotted to kill him, 24but their plot became known to Saul. They were watching the gates day and night so that they might kill him; 25but his disciples took him by night and let him down through an opening in the wall,[c] lowering him in a basket.

SAUL IN JERUSALEM

26When he had come to Jerusalem, he attempted to join the disciples; and they were all afraid of him, for they did not believe that he was a disciple. 27But Barnabas took him, brought him to the apostles, and described for them how on the road he had seen the Lord, who had spoken to him, and how in Damascus he had spoken boldly in the name of Jesus. 28So he went in and out among them in Jerusalem, speaking boldly in the name of the Lord. 29He spoke and argued with the Hellenists; but they were attempting to kill him. 30When the believers[d] learned of it, they brought him down to Caesarea and sent him off to Tarsus.

31 Meanwhile the church throughout Judea, Galilee, and Samaria had peace and was built up. Living in the fear of the Lord and in the comfort of the Holy Spirit, it increased in numbers.

THE HEALING OF AENEAS

32 Now as Peter went here and there among all the believers,[e] he came down also to the saints living in Lydda. 33There he found a man named Aeneas, who had been bedridden for eight years, for he was paralyzed. 34Peter said to him, "Aeneas, Jesus Christ heals you; get up and make your bed!" And immediately he got up. 35And all the residents of Lydda and Sharon saw him and turned to the Lord.

PETER IN LYDDA AND JOPPA

36 Now in Joppa there was a disciple whose name was Tabitha, which in Greek is Dorcas.[f] She was devoted to good works and acts of charity. 37At that time she became ill and died. When they had washed her, they laid her in a room upstairs. 38Since Lydda was near Joppa, the disciples, who heard that Peter was there, sent two men to him with the request, "Please come to us without delay." 39So Peter got up and went with them; and when he arrived, they took him to the room upstairs. All the widows stood beside him, weeping and showing tunics and other clothing that Dorcas had made while she was with them. 40Peter put all of them outside, and then he knelt down and prayed. He turned to the body and said, "Tabitha, get up." Then she opened her eyes, and seeing Peter, she sat up. 41He gave her his hand and helped her up. Then calling the saints and widows, he showed her to be alive. 42This became known throughout Joppa, and many believed in the Lord. 43Meanwhile he stayed in Joppa for some time with a certain Simon, a tanner.

PETER AND CORNELIUS

10 In Caesarea there was a man named Cornelius, a centurion of the Italian Cohort, as it was called. 2He was a devout man who feared God with all his household; he gave alms generously to the people and prayed constantly to God. 3One afternoon at about three o'clock he had a vision in which he clearly saw an angel of God coming in and saying to him, "Cornelius." 4He stared at him in terror and said, "What is it, Lord?" He answered, "Your prayers and your alms have ascended as a memorial before God. 5Now send men to Joppa for a certain Simon who is called Peter; 6he is lodging with Simon, a tanner, whose house is by the seaside." 7When the angel

---

[a] 9.22 Gk that this   [b] 9.22 Or the Christ
[c] 9.25 Gk through the wall   [d] 9.30 Gk brothers   [e] 9.32 Gk all of them   [f] 9.36 The name Tabitha in Aramaic and the name Dorcas in Greek mean a gazelle

who spoke to him had left, he called two of his slaves and a devout soldier from the ranks of those who served him, 8and after telling them everything, he sent them to Joppa.

9 About noon the next day, as they were on their journey and approaching the city, Peter went up on the roof to pray. 10He became hungry and wanted something to eat; and while it was being prepared, he fell into a trance. 11He saw the heaven opened and something like a large sheet coming down, being lowered to the ground by its four corners. 12In it were all kinds of four-footed creatures and reptiles and birds of the air. 13Then he heard a voice saying, "Get up, Peter; kill and eat." 14But Peter said, "By no means, Lord; for I have never eaten anything that is profane or unclean." 15The voice said to him again, a second time, "What God has made clean, you must not call profane." 16This happened three times, and the thing was suddenly taken up to heaven.

17 Now while Peter was greatly puzzled about what to make of the vision that he had seen, suddenly the men sent by Cornelius appeared. They were asking for Simon's house and were standing by the gate. 18They called out to ask whether Simon, who was called Peter, was staying there. 19While Peter was still thinking about the vision, the Spirit said to him, "Look, threea men are searching for you. 20Now get up, go down, and go with them without hesitation; for I have sent them." 21So Peter went down to the men and said, "I am the one you are looking for; what is the reason for your coming?" 22They answered, "Cornelius, a centurion, an upright and God-fearing man, who is well spoken of by the whole Jewish nation, was directed by a holy angel to send for you to come to his house and to hear what you have to say." 23So Peterb invited them in and gave them lodging.

The next day he got up and went with them, and some of the believersc from Joppa accompanied him.

24The following day they came to Caesarea. Cornelius was expecting them and had called together his relatives and close friends. 25On Peter's arrival Cornelius met him, and falling at his feet, worshiped him. 26But Peter made him get up, saying, "Stand up; I am only a mortal." 27And as he talked with him, he went in and found that many had assembled; 28and he said to them, "You yourselves know that it is unlawful for a Jew to associate with or to visit a Gentile; but God has shown me that I should not call anyone profane or unclean. 29So when I was sent for, I came without objection. Now may I ask why you sent for me?"

GOD USES PEOPLE OF ALL

AGES AND NATIONALITIES

IN HIS SERVICE.

30 Cornelius replied, "Four days ago at this very hour, at three o'clock, I was praying in my house when suddenly a man in dazzling clothes stood before me. 31He said, 'Cornelius, your prayer has been heard and your alms have been remembered before God. 32Send therefore to Joppa and ask for Simon, who is called Peter; he is staying in the home of Simon, a tanner, by the sea.' 33Therefore I sent for you immediately, and you have been kind enough to come. So now all of us are here in the presence of God to listen to all that the Lord has commanded you to say."

GENTILES HEAR THE GOOD NEWS

34 Then Peter began to speak to them: "I truly understand that God shows no partiality, 35but in every

a 10.19 One ancient authority reads two; others lack the word   b 10.23 Gk he
c 10.23 Gk brothers

PONDER

"I truly understand that God shows no partiality, but in every nation anyone who fears him and does what is right is acceptable to him."
—Acts 10.34–35

PRAY

O Father, this scripture shows us that your love and grace have no national or racial boundaries just as our love and compassion should have no boundaries. With your Spirit, break us out of the cocoon we tend to spin around ourselves, excluding others. Help us to see all people as you do and look beyond race, color, nationality and other distinctions and see just people—people like us—who need you. Help us to follow Jesus' footsteps and to reach out with enthusiasm, determination and innovation to those who are in need, excluded, forgotten or just different from us. We ask these things in the name of our Savior. Amen.

nation anyone who fears him and does what is right is acceptable to him. 36 You know the message he sent to the people of Israel, preaching peace by Jesus Christ—he is Lord of all. 37 That message spread throughout Judea, beginning in Galilee after the baptism that John announced: 38 how God anointed Jesus of Nazareth with the Holy Spirit and with power; how he went about doing good and healing all who were oppressed by the devil, for God was with him. 39 We are witnesses to all that he did both in Judea and in Jerusalem. They put him to death by hanging him on a tree; 40 but God raised him on the third day and allowed him to appear, 41 not to all the people but to us who were chosen by God as witnesses, and who ate and drank with him after he rose from the dead. 42 He commanded us to preach to the people and to testify that he is the one ordained by God as judge of the living and the dead. 43 All the prophets testify about him that everyone who believes in him receives forgiveness of sins through his name."

GENTILES RECEIVE THE HOLY SPIRIT

44 While Peter was still speaking, the Holy Spirit fell upon all who heard the word. 45 The circumcised believers who had come with Peter were astounded that the gift of the Holy Spirit had been poured out even on the Gentiles, 46 for they heard them speaking in tongues and extolling God. Then Peter said, 47 "Can anyone withhold the water for baptizing these people who have received the Holy Spirit just as we have?" 48 So he ordered them to be baptized in the name of Jesus Christ. Then they invited him to stay for several days.

PETER'S REPORT TO THE CHURCH AT JERUSALEM

11 Now the apostles and the believers[a] who were in Judea heard that the Gentiles had also accepted the word of God. 2 So when Peter went up to Jerusalem, the circumcised believers[b] criticized him, 3 saying, "Why did you go to uncircumcised men and eat with them?" 4 Then Peter began to explain it to them, step by step, saying, 5 "I was in the city of Joppa praying, and in a trance I saw a vision. There was something like a large sheet coming down from heaven, being lowered by its four corners; and it came close to me. 6 As I looked at it closely I saw four-footed animals, beasts of prey, reptiles, and birds of the air. 7 I also heard a voice saying to me, 'Get up, Peter; kill and eat.' 8 But I replied, 'By no means, Lord; for nothing profane or unclean has ever entered my mouth.' 9 But a second time the voice answered from heaven, 'What God has made clean, you must not call profane.' 10 This happened three

[a] 11.1 Gk brothers   [b] 11.2 Gk lacks believers

times; then everything was pulled up again to heaven. ¹¹At that very moment three men, sent to me from Caesarea, arrived at the house where we were. ¹²The Spirit told me to go with them and not to make a distinction between them and us.ᵃ These six brothers also accompanied me, and we entered the man's house. ¹³He told us how he had seen the angel standing in his house and saying, 'Send to Joppa and bring Simon, who is called Peter; ¹⁴he will give you a message by which you and your entire household will be saved.' ¹⁵And as I began to speak, the Holy Spirit fell upon them just as it had upon us at the beginning. ¹⁶And I remembered the word of the Lord, how he had said, 'John baptized with water, but you will be baptized with the Holy Spirit.' ¹⁷If then God gave them the same gift that he gave us when we believed in the Lord Jesus Christ, who was I that I could hinder God?" ¹⁸When they heard this, they were silenced. And they praised God, saying, "Then God has given even to the Gentiles the repentance that leads to life."

THE CHURCH IN ANTIOCH

19 Now those who were scattered because of the persecution that took place over Stephen traveled as far as Phoenicia, Cyprus, and Antioch, and they spoke the word to no one except Jews. ²⁰But among them were some men of Cyprus and Cyrene who, on coming to Antioch, spoke to the Hellenistsᵇ also, proclaiming the Lord Jesus. ²¹The hand of the Lord was with them, and a great number became believers and turned to the Lord. ²²News of this came to the ears of the church in Jerusalem, and they sent Barnabas to Antioch. ²³When he came and saw the grace of God, he rejoiced, and he exhorted them all to remain faithful to the Lord with steadfast devotion; ²⁴for he was a good man, full of the Holy Spirit and of faith. And a great many people were brought to the Lord. ²⁵Then Barnabas went to Tarsus to look for Saul, ²⁶and when he had found him, he brought him to Antioch. So it was that for an entire year they met withᶜ the church and taught a great many people, and it was in Antioch that the disciples were first called "Christians."

27 At that time prophets came down from Jerusalem to Antioch. ²⁸One of them named Agabus stood up and predicted by the Spirit that there would be a severe famine over all the world; and this took place during the reign of Claudius. ²⁹The disciples determined that according

ᵃ **11.12** Or *not to hesitate*   ᵇ **11.20** Other ancient authorities read *Greeks*   ᶜ **11.26** Or *were guests of*

BIBLE IN LIFE

The Light of God's Glory   *Acts 11.26*

Our commitment to be "little Christs," or "Christians," brings us liberation: it opens the door to a life that is far better than anything we've known before. We must be innovative and aggressive and look for opportunities to let God's light shine brightly through us to the world. We cannot all go to Peru, India or the Philippines or build homes for Habitat for Humanity, but we can ascertain, among those around us, who is lonely, suffering or even despised and minister to them in a spirit of friendship, equality and sharing. Perhaps we can honor God by forgiving those who have wronged us in the past. We can strive to open up a new spirit of friendship and love with them. God's light is always shining in us. Whether we are eight years old or 80 years old, our relationship with God through Christ can sustain us and change whatever blackness, darkness, fear or disappointment is in us, and bring us light, hope and joy with Jesus Christ. As the light of God's glory shines ever more brightly in us, this glory will become increasingly more evident to those around us, and people will see God at work.

to their ability, each would send relief to the believers[a] living in Judea; 30this they did, sending it to the elders by Barnabas and Saul.

JAMES KILLED AND PETER IMPRISONED

12 About that time King Herod laid violent hands upon some who belonged to the church. 2He had James, the brother of John, killed with the sword. 3After he saw that it pleased the Jews, he proceeded to arrest Peter also. (This was during the festival of Unleavened Bread.) 4When he had seized him, he put him in prison and handed him over to four squads of soldiers to guard him, intending to bring him out to the people after the Passover. 5While Peter was kept in prison, the church prayed fervently to God for him.

PONDER

While Peter was kept in prison, the church prayed fervently to God for him.
—Acts 12.5

PRAY

Father, today we understand a little more about this early phase in the Christian experience: when these heroes of the Bible showed faith though they were fearful, when they turned to you in prayer in times of stress and doubt, when they strengthened one another, and when they sought your will. Remind us to eagerly and regularly turn to you in prayer for guidance to help us overcome doubt, fear, disappointment, sorrow and failure, knowing that our relationship with you through Christ is all in all, that you are our strength and our freedom. We pray in Jesus' name. Amen.

PETER DELIVERED FROM PRISON

6 The very night before Herod was going to bring him out, Peter, bound with two chains, was sleeping between two soldiers, while guards in front of the door were keeping watch over the prison. 7Suddenly an angel of the Lord appeared and a light shone in the cell. He tapped Peter on the side and woke him, saying, "Get up quickly." And the chains fell off his wrists. 8The angel said to him, "Fasten your belt and put on your sandals." He did so. Then he said to him, "Wrap your cloak around you and follow me." 9Peter[b] went out and followed him; he did not realize that what was happening with the angel's help was real; he thought he was seeing a vision. 10After they had passed the first and the second guard, they came before the iron gate leading into the city. It opened for them of its own accord, and they went outside and walked along a lane, when suddenly the angel left him. 11Then Peter came to himself and said, "Now I am sure that the Lord has sent his angel and rescued me from the hands of Herod and from all that the Jewish people were expecting."

12 As soon as he realized this, he went to the house of Mary, the mother of John whose other name was Mark, where many had gathered and were praying. 13When he knocked at the outer gate, a maid named Rhoda came to answer. 14On recognizing Peter's voice, she was so overjoyed that, instead of opening the gate, she ran in and announced that Peter was standing at the gate. 15They said to her, "You are out of your mind!" But she insisted that it was so. They said, "It is his angel." 16Meanwhile Peter continued knocking; and when they opened the gate, they saw him and were amazed. 17He motioned to them with his hand to be silent, and described for them how the Lord had brought him out of the prison. And he added, "Tell this to James and to the believers."[a] Then he left and went to another place.

[a] 11.29; 12.17 Gk brothers   [b] 12.9 Gk He

18 When morning came, there was no small commotion among the soldiers over what had become of Peter. **19** When Herod had searched for him and could not find him, he examined the guards and ordered them to be put to death. Then he went down from Judea to Caesarea and stayed there.

THE DEATH OF HEROD

20 Now Herod[a] was angry with the people of Tyre and Sidon. So they came to him in a body; and after winning over Blastus, the king's chamberlain, they asked for a reconciliation, because their country depended on the king's country for food. **21** On an appointed day Herod put on his royal robes, took his seat on the platform, and delivered a public address to them. **22** The people kept shouting, "The voice of a god, and not of a mortal!" **23** And immediately, because he had not given the glory to God, an angel of the Lord struck him down, and he was eaten by worms and died.

24 But the word of God continued to advance and gain adherents. **25** Then after completing their mission Barnabas and Saul returned to[b] Jerusalem and brought with them John, whose other name was Mark.

BARNABAS AND SAUL COMMISSIONED

13 Now in the church at Antioch there were prophets and teachers: Barnabas, Simeon who was called Niger, Lucius of Cyrene, Manaen a member of the court of Herod the ruler,[c] and Saul. **2** While they were worshiping the Lord and fasting, the Holy Spirit said, "Set apart for me Barnabas and Saul for the work to which I have called them." **3** Then after fasting and praying they laid their hands on them and sent them off.

THE APOSTLES PREACH IN CYPRUS

4 So, being sent out by the Holy Spirit, they went down to Seleucia; and from there they sailed to Cyprus. **5** When they arrived at Salamis, they

proclaimed the word of God in the synagogues of the Jews. And they had John also to assist them. **6** When they had gone through the whole island as far as Paphos, they met a certain magician, a Jewish false prophet, named Bar-Jesus. **7** He was with the proconsul, Sergius Paulus, an intelligent man, who summoned Barnabas and Saul and wanted to hear the word of God. **8** But the magician Elymas (for that is the translation of his name) opposed them and tried to turn the proconsul away from the faith. **9** But Saul, also known as Paul, filled with the Holy Spirit, looked intently at him **10** and said, "You son of the devil, you enemy of all righteousness, full of all deceit and villainy, will you not stop making crooked the straight paths of the Lord? **11** And now listen—the hand of the Lord is against you, and you will be blind for a while, unable

[a] **12.20** Gk *he* [b] **12.25** Other ancient authorities read *from* [c] **13.1** Gk *tetrarch*

to see the sun." Immediately mist and darkness came over him, and he went about groping for someone to lead him by the hand. 12When the proconsul saw what had happened, he believed, for he was astonished at the teaching about the Lord.

PAUL AND BARNABAS IN ANTIOCH OF PISIDIA

13 Then Paul and his companions set sail from Paphos and came to Perga in Pamphylia. John, however, left them and returned to Jerusalem; 14but they went on from Perga and came to Antioch in Pisidia. And on the sabbath day they went into the synagogue and sat down. 15After the reading of the law and the prophets, the officials of the synagogue sent them a message, saying, "Brothers, if you have any word of exhortation for the people, give it." 16So Paul stood up and with a gesture began to speak: "You Israelites,ᵃ and others who fear God, listen. 17The God of this people Israel chose our ancestors and made the people great during their stay in the land of Egypt, and with uplifted arm he led them out of it. 18For about forty years he put up withᵇ them in the wilderness. 19After he had destroyed seven nations in the land of Canaan, he gave them their land as an inheritance 20for about four hundred fifty years. After that he gave them judges until the time of the prophet Samuel. 21Then they asked for a king; and God gave them Saul son of Kish, a man of the tribe of Benjamin, who reigned for forty years. 22When he had removed him, he made David their king. In his testimony about him he said, 'I have found David, son of Jesse, to be a man after my heart, who will carry out all my wishes.' 23Of this man's posterity God has brought to Israel a Savior, Jesus, as he promised; 24before his coming John had already proclaimed a baptism of repentance to all the people of Israel. 25And as John was finishing his work, he said, 'What do you suppose that I am? I am not he. No, but one is coming after me; I am not worthy to untie the thong of the sandalsᶜ on his feet.'

26 "My brothers, you descendants of Abraham's family, and others who fear God, to usᵈ the message of this salvation has been sent. 27Because the residents of Jerusalem and their leaders did not recognize him or understand the words of the prophets that are read every sabbath, they fulfilled those words by condemning him. 28Even though they found no cause for a sentence of death, they asked Pilate to have him killed. 29When they had carried out everything that was written about him, they took him down from the tree and laid him in a tomb. 30But God raised him from the dead; 31and for many days he appeared to those who came up with him from Galilee to Jerusalem, and they are now his witnesses to the people. 32And we bring you the good news that what God promised to our ancestors 33he has fulfilled for us, their children, by raising Jesus; as also it is written in the second psalm,

'You are my Son;
    today I have begotten you.'

34As to his raising him from the dead, no more to return to corruption, he has spoken in this way,

'I will give you the holy promises
    made to David.'

35Therefore he has also said in another psalm,

'You will not let your Holy One
    experience corruption.'

36For David, after he had served the purpose of God in his own generation, died,ᵉ was laid beside his ancestors, and experienced corruption; 37but he whom God raised up experienced no corruption. 38Let it be known to you therefore, my brothers, that through this man forgiveness of sins is proclaimed to you; 39by this Jesusᶠ everyone who believes is set free from all those sinsᵍ from which you could not be freed by the law of Moses. 40Beware, therefore, that what the prophets said does not happen to you:

ᵃ 13.16 Gk Men, Israelites   ᵇ 13.18 Other ancient authorities read cared for
ᶜ 13.25 Gk untie the sandals   ᵈ 13.26 Other ancient authorities read you   ᵉ 13.36 Gk fell asleep   ᶠ 13.39 Gk this   ᵍ 13.39 Gk all

[41] 'Look, you scoffers!
Be amazed and perish,
for in your days I am
doing a work,
a work that you will
never believe, even if
someone tells you.'"
[42] As Paul and Barnabas[a] were going out, the people urged them to speak about these things again the next sabbath. [43] When the meeting of the synagogue broke up, many Jews and devout converts to Judaism followed Paul and Barnabas, who spoke to them and urged them to continue in the grace of God.

[44] The next sabbath almost the whole city gathered to hear the word of the Lord.[b] [45] But when the Jews saw the crowds, they were filled with jealousy; and blaspheming, they contradicted what was spoken by Paul. [46] Then both Paul and Barnabas spoke out boldly, saying, "It was necessary that the word of God should be spoken first to you. Since you reject it and judge yourselves to be unworthy of eternal life, we are now turning to the Gentiles. [47] For so the Lord has commanded us, saying,
'I have set you to be a light
for the Gentiles,
so that you may bring
salvation to the ends
of the earth.'"
[48] When the Gentiles heard this, they were glad and praised the word of the Lord; and as many as had been destined for eternal life became believers. [49] Thus the word of the Lord spread throughout the region. [50] But the Jews incited the devout women of high standing and the leading men of the city, and stirred up persecution against Paul and Barnabas, and drove them out of their region. [51] So they shook the dust off their feet in protest against them, and went to Iconium. [52] And the disciples were filled with joy and with the Holy Spirit.

PAUL AND BARNABAS IN ICONIUM

14 The same thing occurred in Iconium, where Paul and Barnabas[c] went into the Jewish synagogue and spoke in such a way that a great number of both Jews and Greeks became believers. [2] But the unbelieving Jews stirred up the Gentiles and poisoned their minds against the brothers. [3] So they remained for a long time, speaking boldly for the Lord, who testified to the word of his grace by granting signs and wonders to be done through them. [4] But the residents of the city were divided; some sided with the Jews, and some with the apostles. [5] And when an attempt was made by both Gentiles and Jews, with their rulers, to mistreat them and to stone them, [6] the apostles[c] learned of it and fled to Lystra and Derbe, cities of Lycaonia, and to the surrounding country; [7] and there they continued proclaiming the good news.

[a] 13.42 Gk *they*   [b] 13.44 Other ancient authorities read *God*   [c] 14.1,6 Gk *they*

PONDER

So [Paul and Barnabas] remained for a long time, speaking boldly for the Lord, who testified to the word of his grace by granting signs and wonders to be done through them.
—Acts 14.3

PRAY

Father God, when we compare ourselves with those who followed Jesus in the early years of the church, this example of the early Christians may challenge us. It inspires us to take a look at ourselves, whether we are 20 or 90 years old, and ask, "How can I draw closer to Jesus Christ and demonstrate my faith in him?" We ask to be filled with the same Spirit that filled Paul and Barnabas with the boldness to proclaim the Gospel in the face of opposition and persecution, for we know that the boldness you gave them, the power of your spirit, doesn't fade with time. In the name of our Savior we pray. Amen.

PAUL AND BARNABAS IN LYSTRA AND DERBE

8 In Lystra there was a man sitting who could not use his feet and had never walked, for he had been crippled from birth. 9He listened to Paul as he was speaking. And Paul, looking at him intently and seeing that he had faith to be healed, 10said in a loud voice, "Stand upright on your feet." And the man[a] sprang up and began to walk. 11When the crowds saw what Paul had done, they shouted in the Lycaonian language, "The gods have come down to us in human form!" 12Barnabas they called Zeus, and Paul they called Hermes, because he was the chief speaker. 13The priest of Zeus, whose temple was just outside the city,[b] brought oxen and garlands to the gates; he and the crowds wanted to offer sacrifice. 14When the apostles Barnabas and Paul heard of it, they tore their clothes and rushed out into the crowd, shouting, 15"Friends,[c] why are you doing this? We are mortals just like you, and we bring you good news, that you should turn from these worthless things to the living God, who made the heaven and the earth and the sea and all that is in them. 16In past generations he allowed all the nations to follow their own ways; 17yet he has not left himself without a witness in doing good—giving you rains from heaven and fruitful seasons, and filling you with food and your hearts with joy." 18Even with these words, they scarcely restrained the crowds from offering sacrifice to them.

19 But Jews came there from Antioch and Iconium and won over the crowds. Then they stoned Paul and dragged him out of the city, supposing that he was dead. 20But when the disciples surrounded him, he got up and went into the city. The next day he went on with Barnabas to Derbe.

THE RETURN TO ANTIOCH IN SYRIA

21 After they had proclaimed the good news to that city and had made many disciples, they returned to Lystra, then on to Iconium and Antioch. 22There they strengthened the souls of the disciples and encouraged them to continue in the faith, saying, "It is through many persecutions that we must enter the kingdom of God." 23And after they had appointed elders for them in each church, with prayer and fasting they entrusted them to the Lord in whom they had come to believe.

24 Then they passed through Pisidia and came to Pamphylia. 25When they had spoken the word in Perga, they went down to Attalia. 26From there they sailed back to Antioch, where they had been commended to the grace of God for the work[d] that they had completed. 27When they arrived, they called the church together and related all that God had done with them, and how he had opened a door of faith for the Gentiles. 28And they stayed there with the disciples for some time.

THE COUNCIL AT JERUSALEM

15 Then certain individuals came down from Judea and were teaching the brothers, "Unless you are circumcised according to the custom of Moses, you cannot be saved." 2And after Paul and Barnabas had no small dissension and debate with them, Paul and Barnabas and some of the others were appointed to go up to Jerusalem to discuss this question with the apostles and the elders. 3So they were sent on their way by the church, and as they passed through both Phoenicia and Samaria, they reported the conversion of the Gentiles, and brought great joy to all the believers.[e] 4When they came to Jerusalem, they were welcomed by the church and the apostles and the elders, and they reported all that God had done with them. 5But some believers who belonged to the sect of the Pharisees stood up and said, "It is necessary for them to be circumcised and ordered to keep the law of Moses."

a 14.10 Gk he   b 14.13 Or The priest of Zeus-Outside-the-City   c 14.15 Gk Men
d 14.26 Or committed in the grace of God to the work   e 15.3 Gk brothers

6 The apostles and the elders met together to consider this matter. **7** After there had been much debate, Peter stood up and said to them, "My brothers,[a] you know that in the early days God made a choice among you, that I should be the one through whom the Gentiles would hear the message of the good news and become believers. **8** And God, who knows the human heart, testified to them by giving them the Holy Spirit, just as he did to us; **9** and in cleansing their hearts by faith he has made no distinction between them and us. **10** Now therefore why are you putting God to the test by placing on the neck of the disciples a yoke that neither our ancestors nor we have been able to bear? **11** On the contrary, we believe that we will be saved through the grace of the Lord Jesus, just as they will."

12 The whole assembly kept silence, and listened to Barnabas and Paul as they told of all the signs and wonders that God had done through them among the Gentiles. **13** After they finished speaking, James replied, "My brothers,[a] listen to me. **14** Simeon has related how God first looked favorably on the Gentiles, to take from among them a people for his name. **15** This agrees with the words of the prophets, as it is written,

16 'After this I will return,

and I will rebuild the dwelling of
     David, which has fallen;
from its ruins I will rebuild it,
     and I will set it up,
17 so that all other peoples may
     seek the Lord—
even all the Gentiles over
     whom my name
     has been called.
Thus says the Lord, who has
     been making these things
     18 known from long ago.'[b]

19 Therefore I have reached the decision that we should not trouble those Gentiles who are turning to God, **20** but we should write to them to abstain only from things polluted by idols and from fornication and from whatever has been strangled[c] and from blood. **21** For in every city, for generations past, Moses has had those who proclaim him, for he has been read aloud every sabbath in the synagogues."

THE COUNCIL'S LETTER TO GENTILE BELIEVERS

22 Then the apostles and the elders, with the consent of the whole church, decided to choose men from among their members[d] and to send them to Antioch with Paul and Barnabas.

[a] **15.7,13** Gk *Men, brothers*   [b] **15.18** Other ancient authorities read *things.* *18Known to God from of old are all his works.'*
[c] **15.20** Other ancient authorities lack *and from whatever has been strangled*
[d] **15.22** Gk *from among them*

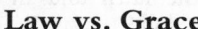 **BIBLE IN LIFE** ▷ ⊕

Law vs. Grace   Acts 15.1–11

It was startling for the early Jewish Christians to depart from the long list of requirements they had always followed to earn God's acceptance (rules such as being circumcised and following every detail of the law of Moses). It was an adjustment to embrace a simplified definition of salvation—*to believe in Jesus Christ*—and to grasp that faith alone was enough for God to accept them. We too can become exclusive in our definition of what it means to be a Christian. We may wonder, "How could God be so gracious that he would allow these people, who are so different from me, to be Christians? How could God be so openhearted? There must be something more to it than that." The truth, though, is that a person who is a Christian is one who is saved by placing their faith solely on God's free gift of grace. We don't have to work for it. We don't have to meet certain standards. We just need faith in Jesus Christ. Period.

They sent Judas called Barsabbas, and Silas, leaders among the brothers, [23]with the following letter: "The brothers, both the apostles and the elders, to the believers[a] of Gentile origin in Antioch and Syria and Cilicia, greetings. [24]Since we have heard that certain persons who have gone out from us, though with no instructions from us, have said things to disturb you and have unsettled your minds,[b] [25]we have decided unanimously to choose representatives[c] and send them to you, along with our beloved Barnabas and Paul, [26]who have risked their lives for the sake of our Lord Jesus Christ. [27]We have therefore sent Judas and Silas, who themselves will tell you the same things by word of mouth. [28]For it has seemed good to the Holy Spirit and to us to impose on you no further burden than these essentials: [29]that you abstain from what has been sacrificed to idols and from blood and from what is strangled[d] and from fornication. If you keep yourselves from these, you will do well. Farewell."

[30] So they were sent off and went down to Antioch. When they gathered the congregation together, they delivered the letter. [31]When its members[e] read it, they rejoiced at the exhortation. [32]Judas and Silas, who were themselves prophets, said much to encourage and strengthen the believers.[f] [33]After they had been there for some time, they were sent off in peace by the believers[f] to those who had sent them.[g] [35]But Paul and Barnabas remained in Antioch, and there, with many others, they taught and proclaimed the word of the Lord.

PAUL AND BARNABAS SEPARATE

[36] After some days Paul said to Barnabas, "Come, let us return and visit the believers[f] in every city where we proclaimed the word of the Lord and see how they are doing." [37]Barnabas wanted to take with them John called Mark. [38]But Paul decided not to take with them one who had deserted them in Pamphylia and had not accompanied

them in the work. [39]The disagreement became so sharp that they parted company; Barnabas took Mark with him and sailed away to Cyprus. [40]But Paul chose Silas and set out, the believers[f] commending him to the grace of the Lord. [41]He went through Syria and Cilicia, strengthening the churches.

CHRIST DOES NOT ISSUE
CONFLICTING ORDERS.
DISSENSION IS PROOF THAT
WE ARE IGNORING THE BASIC
MESSAGES OF CHRIST.

TIMOTHY JOINS PAUL AND SILAS

16 Paul[h] went on also to Derbe and to Lystra, where there was a disciple named Timothy, the son of a Jewish woman who was a believer; but his father was a Greek. [2]He was well spoken of by the believers[f] in Lystra and Iconium. [3]Paul wanted Timothy to accompany him; and he took him and had him circumcised because of the Jews who were in those places, for they all knew that his father was a Greek. [4]As they went from town to town, they delivered to them for observance the decisions that had been reached by the apostles and elders who were in Jerusalem. [5]So the churches were strengthened in the faith and increased in numbers daily.

PAUL'S VISION OF THE MAN OF MACEDONIA

[6] They went through the region of Phrygia and Galatia, having been

a 15.23 Gk brothers   b 15.24 Other ancient authorities add saying, 'You must be circumcised and keep the law,'   c 15.25 Gk men   d 15.29 Other ancient authorities lack and from what is strangled   e 15.31 Gk When they   f 15.32,33,36,40; 16.2 Gk brothers   g 15.33 Other ancient authorities add verse 34, But it seemed good to Silas to remain there   h 16.1 Gk He

forbidden by the Holy Spirit to speak
the word in Asia. 7When they had
come opposite Mysia, they attempted to go into Bithynia, but the Spirit
of Jesus did not allow them; 8so,
passing by Mysia, they went down
to Troas. 9During the night Paul had
a vision: there stood a man of Macedonia pleading with him and saying, "Come over to Macedonia and
help us." 10When he had seen the vision, we immediately tried to cross
over to Macedonia, being convinced
that God had called us to proclaim
the good news to them.

PONDER

During the night Paul had a vision: there stood a man of Macedonia pleading with him and saying, "Come over to Macedonia and help us."
—Acts 16.9

PRAY

O Father, we pray that you will open our hearts to receive the messages that you send us regarding the direction of our lives. The Holy Spirit stopped Paul from going some places and told him to go elsewhere. We know that sometimes you tell us to go somewhere or do something. We know that sometimes you tell us not to go somewhere. Sometimes you direct us to people who give us a message from the Holy Spirit about the shape of our lives. Sometimes through prayer you inspire us to be more courageous and adventurous. We pray for the ears to hear your voice regardless of the means you use. In the name of Jesus we pray. Amen.

THE CONVERSION OF LYDIA

11 We set sail from Troas and took
a straight course to Samothrace,
the following day to Neapolis, 12and
from there to Philippi, which is a
leading city of the district[a] of Macedonia and a Roman colony. We remained in this city for some days.
13On the sabbath day we went outside the gate by the river, where we
supposed there was a place of prayer;
and we sat down and spoke to the
women who had gathered there. 14A
certain woman named Lydia, a worshiper of God, was listening to us;
she was from the city of Thyatira and
a dealer in purple cloth. The Lord
opened her heart to listen eagerly to
what was said by Paul. 15When she
and her household were baptized,
she urged us, saying, "If you have
judged me to be faithful to the Lord,
come and stay at my home." And she
prevailed upon us.

PAUL AND SILAS IN PRISON

16 One day, as we were going to
the place of prayer, we met a slave-
girl who had a spirit of divination
and brought her owners a great deal
of money by fortune-telling. 17While
she followed Paul and us, she would
cry out, "These men are slaves of the
Most High God, who proclaim to
you[b] a way of salvation." 18She kept
doing this for many days. But Paul,
very much annoyed, turned and
said to the spirit, "I order you in the
name of Jesus Christ to come out of
her." And it came out that very hour.
19 But when her owners saw that
their hope of making money was
gone, they seized Paul and Silas and
dragged them into the marketplace
before the authorities. 20When they
had brought them before the magistrates, they said, "These men are disturbing our city; they are Jews 21and
are advocating customs that are not
lawful for us as Romans to adopt or
observe." 22The crowd joined in attacking them, and the magistrates
had them stripped of their clothing
and ordered them to be beaten with
rods. 23After they had given them
a severe flogging, they threw them
into prison and ordered the jailer
to keep them securely. 24Follow-
ing these instructions, he put them
in the innermost cell and fastened
their feet in the stocks.

[a] 16.12 Other authorities read *a city of the first district* [b] 16.17 Other ancient authorities read *to us*

25 About midnight Paul and Silas were praying and singing hymns to God, and the prisoners were listening to them. 26Suddenly there was an earthquake, so violent that the foundations of the prison were shaken; and immediately all the doors were opened and everyone's chains were unfastened. 27When the jailer woke up and saw the prison doors wide open, he drew his sword and was about to kill himself, since he supposed that the prisoners had escaped. 28But Paul shouted in a loud voice, "Do not harm yourself, for we are all here." 29The jailer[a] called for lights, and rushing in, he fell down trembling before Paul and Silas. 30Then he brought them outside and said, "Sirs, what must I do to be saved?" 31They answered, "Believe on the Lord Jesus, and you will be saved, you and your household." 32They spoke the word of the Lord[b] to him and to all who were in his house. 33At the same hour of the night he took them and washed their wounds; then he and his entire family were baptized without delay. 34He brought them up into the house and set food before them; and he and his entire household rejoiced that he had become a believer in God.

35 When morning came, the magistrates sent the police, saying, "Let those men go." 36And the jailer reported the message to Paul, saying, "The magistrates sent word to let you go; therefore come out now and go in peace." 37But Paul replied, "They have beaten us in public, uncondemned, men who are Roman citizens, and have thrown us into prison; and now are they going to discharge us in secret? Certainly not! Let them come and take us out themselves." 38The police reported these words to the magistrates, and they were afraid when they heard that they were Roman citizens; 39so they came and apologized to them. And they took them out and asked them to leave the city. 40After leaving the prison they went to Lydia's home; and when they had seen and encouraged the brothers and sisters[c] there, they departed.

THE UPROAR IN THESSALONICA

17 After Paul and Silas[d] had passed through Amphipolis and Apollonia, they came to Thessalonica, where there was a synagogue of the Jews. 2And Paul went in, as was his custom, and on three sabbath days argued with them from the scriptures, 3explaining and proving that it was necessary for the Messiah[e] to suffer and to rise from the dead, and saying, "This is the Messiah,[e] Jesus whom I am proclaiming to you." 4Some of them were persuaded and joined Paul and Silas, as did a great many of the devout Greeks and not a few of the leading women. 5But the Jews became jealous, and with the help of some ruffians in the marketplaces they formed a mob and set the city in an uproar. While they were searching for Paul and Silas to bring them out to the assembly, they attacked Jason's house. 6When they could not find them, they dragged Jason and some believers[c] before the city authorities,[f] shouting, "These people who have been turning the world upside down have come here also, 7and Jason has entertained them as guests. They are all acting contrary to the decrees of the emperor, saying that there is another king named Jesus." 8The people and the city officials were disturbed when they heard this, 9and after they had taken bail from Jason and the others, they let them go.

PAUL AND SILAS IN BEROEA

10 That very night the believers[c] sent Paul and Silas off to Beroea; and when they arrived, they went to the Jewish synagogue. 11These Jews were more receptive than those in Thessalonica, for they welcomed the message very eagerly and examined the scriptures every day to see whether these things were so. 12Many of them therefore believed, including not a few Greek women and men of high standing. 13But when the Jews

a 16.29 Gk He   b 16.32 Other ancient authorities read word of God
c 16.40; 17.6,10 Gk brothers   d 17.1 Gk they
e 17.3 Or the Christ   f 17.6 Gk politarchs

of Thessalonica learned that the word of God had been proclaimed by Paul in Beroea as well, they came there too, to stir up and incite the crowds. [14]Then the believers[a] immediately sent Paul away to the coast, but Silas and Timothy remained behind. [15]Those who conducted Paul brought him as far as Athens; and after receiving instructions to have Silas and Timothy join him as soon as possible, they left him.

PAUL IN ATHENS

[16]While Paul was waiting for them in Athens, he was deeply distressed to see that the city was full of idols. [17]So he argued in the synagogue with the Jews and the devout persons, and also in the marketplace[b] every day with those who happened to be there. [18]Also some Epicurean and Stoic philosophers debated with him. Some said, "What does this babbler want to say?" Others said, "He seems to be a proclaimer of foreign divinities." (This was because he was telling the good news about Jesus and the resurrection.) [19]So they took him and brought him to the Areopagus and asked him, "May we know what this new teaching is that you are presenting? [20]It sounds rather strange to us, so we would like to know what it means." [21]Now all the Athenians and the foreigners living there would spend their time in nothing but telling or hearing something new.

[22]Then Paul stood in front of the Areopagus and said, "Athenians, I see how extremely religious you are in every way. [23]For as I went through the city and looked carefully at the objects of your worship, I found among them an altar with the inscription, 'To an unknown god.' What therefore you worship as unknown, this I proclaim to you. [24]The God who made the world and everything in it, he who is Lord of heaven and earth, does not live in shrines made by human hands, [25]nor is he served by human hands, as though he needed anything, since he himself gives to all mortals life and breath and all things. [26]From one ancestor[c] he made all nations to inhabit the whole earth, and he allotted the times of their existence and the boundaries of the places where they would live, [27]so that they would search for God[d] and perhaps grope for him and find him—though indeed he is not far from each one of us. [28]For 'In him we live and move and have our being'; as even some of your own poets have said,

'For we too are his offspring.'

[a] 17.14 Gk brothers   [b] 17.17 Or civic center; Gk agora   [c] 17.26 Gk From one; other ancient authorities read From one blood   [d] 17.27 Other ancient authorities read the Lord

---

╫ **BIBLE IN LIFE** ▷ ─────────────── ⊕

Honest Inquiry

Acts 17.10–12

The Bereans were admirable. They were curious, courageous and willing to question anything that might conflict with the scriptures. They doggedly sought truth, just as Nicodemus had done (see John 3). Nicodemus was a learned man, a member of the high Jewish council (a ruling body under the Romans) who courageously came to Jesus during the night to question him. Because Nicodemus was a respected leader, visiting the troublesome teacher, Jesus, was risky. Like Nicodemus, we should be courageous in approaching Jesus and the scriptures with open minds and a willingness to question and explore things we can't understand. We're not going to disturb God by asking a question. If we live with questions that trouble us about the nature of God or what Christ meant, and if we never ask or explore, then we're needlessly circumscribing our lives. We're denying ourselves available knowledge about God and the created world—about science and history and astronomy and paleontology and the earth's truths. Like the Bereans, we have been given freedom to think and question and ask and learn and stretch our minds.

29Since we are God's offspring, we ought not to think that the deity is like gold, or silver, or stone, an image formed by the art and imagination of mortals. 30While God has overlooked the times of human ignorance, now he commands all people everywhere to repent, 31because he has fixed a day on which he will have the world judged in righteousness by a man whom he has appointed, and of this he has given assurance to all by raising him from the dead."

WE WITNESS BEST WHEN WE IDENTIFY WITH THE UNSAVED.

32When they heard of the resurrection of the dead, some scoffed; but others said, "We will hear you again about this." 33At that point Paul left them. 34But some of them joined him and became believers, including Dionysius the Areopagite and a woman named Damaris, and others with them.

PAUL IN CORINTH

18 After this Paul[a] left Athens and went to Corinth. 2There he found a Jew named Aquila, a native of Pontus, who had recently come from Italy with his wife Priscilla, because Claudius had ordered all Jews to leave Rome. Paul[b] went to see them, 3and, because he was of the same trade, he stayed with them, and they worked together— by trade they were tentmakers. 4Every sabbath he would argue in the synagogue and would try to convince Jews and Greeks.

5 When Silas and Timothy arrived from Macedonia, Paul was occupied with proclaiming the word,[c] testifying to the Jews that the Messiah[d] was Jesus. 6When they opposed and reviled him, in protest he shook the dust from his clothes[e] and said to them, "Your blood be on your own

heads! I am innocent. From now on I will go to the Gentiles." 7Then he left the synagogue[f] and went to the house of a man named Titius[g] Justus, a worshiper of God; his house was next door to the synagogue. 8Crispus, the official of the synagogue, became a believer in the Lord, together with all his household; and many of the Corinthians who heard Paul became believers and were baptized. 9One night the Lord said to Paul in a vision, "Do not be afraid, but speak and do not be silent; 10for I am with you, and no one will lay a hand on you to harm you, for there are many in this city who are my people." 11He stayed there a year and six months, teaching the word of God among them.

12 But when Gallio was proconsul of Achaia, the Jews made a united attack on Paul and brought him before the tribunal. 13They said, "This man is persuading people to worship God in ways that are contrary to the law." 14Just as Paul was about to speak, Gallio said to the Jews, "If it were a matter of crime or serious villainy, I would be justified in accepting the complaint of you Jews; 15but since it is a matter of questions about words and names and your own law, see to it yourselves; I do not wish to be a judge of these matters." 16And he dismissed them from the tribunal. 17Then all of them[h] seized Sosthenes, the official of the synagogue, and beat him in front of the tribunal. But Gallio paid no attention to any of these things.

PAUL'S RETURN TO ANTIOCH

18 After staying there for a considerable time, Paul said farewell to the believers[i] and sailed for Syria, accompanied by Priscilla and Aquila. At Cenchreae he had his hair cut, for he was under a vow. 19When they reached Ephesus, he left them

a 18.1 Gk he   b 18.2 Gk He   c 18.5 Gk with the word   d 18.5 Or the Christ   e 18.6 Gk reviled him, he shook out his clothes   f 18.7 Gk left there   g 18.7 Other ancient authorities read Titus   h 18.17 Other ancient authorities read all the Greeks   i 18.18 Gk brothers

there, but first he himself went into the synagogue and had a discussion with the Jews. 20When they asked him to stay longer, he declined; 21but on taking leave of them, he said, "I[a] will return to you, if God wills." Then he set sail from Ephesus.

22 When he had landed at Caesarea, he went up to Jerusalem[b] and greeted the church, and then went down to Antioch. 23After spending some time there he departed and went from place to place through the region of Galatia[c] and Phrygia, strengthening all the disciples.

MINISTRY OF APOLLOS

24 Now there came to Ephesus a Jew named Apollos, a native of Alexandria. He was an eloquent man, well-versed in the scriptures. 25He had been instructed in the Way of the Lord; and he spoke with burning enthusiasm and taught accurately the things concerning Jesus, though he knew only the baptism of John. 26He began to speak boldly in the synagogue; but when Priscilla and Aquila heard him, they took him aside and explained the Way of God to him more accurately. 27And when he wished to cross over to Achaia, the believers[d] encouraged him and wrote to the disciples to welcome him. On his arrival he greatly helped those who through grace had become believers, 28for he powerfully refuted the Jews in public, showing by the scriptures that the Messiah[e] is Jesus.

PAUL IN EPHESUS

19 While Apollos was in Corinth, Paul passed through the interior regions and came to Ephesus, where he found some disciples. 2He said to them, "Did you receive the Holy Spirit when you became believers?" They replied, "No, we have not even heard that there is a Holy Spirit." 3Then he said, "Into what then were you baptized?" They answered, "Into John's baptism." 4Paul said, "John baptized with the baptism of repentance, telling the people to believe in the one who was to come after him, that is, in Jesus."

5On hearing this, they were baptized in the name of the Lord Jesus. 6When Paul had laid his hands on them, the Holy Spirit came upon them, and they spoke in tongues and prophesied— 7altogether there were about twelve of them.

8 He entered the synagogue and for three months spoke out boldly, and argued persuasively about the kingdom of God. 9When some stubbornly refused to believe and spoke evil of the Way before the congregation, he left them, taking the disciples with him, and argued daily in the lecture hall of Tyrannus.[f] 10This continued for two years, so that all the residents of Asia, both Jews and Greeks, heard the word of the Lord.

THE EARLY CHRISTIAN COMMUNITY, THOUGH TORN APART BY FUNDAMENTAL DIFFERENCES, HEALED THE DIVISIONS BY COMING TOGETHER, PUTTING ASIDE THE EXTRANEOUS (BUT IMPORTANT) ISSUES AND FORGING A COHESIVE FORCE BASED ON THE MESSAGE OF JESUS CHRIST.

THE SONS OF SCEVA

11 God did extraordinary miracles through Paul, 12so that when the handkerchiefs or aprons that had touched his skin were brought to the

a 18.21 Other ancient authorities read I must at all costs keep the approaching festival in Jerusalem, but I   b 18.22 Gk went up   c 18.23 Gk the Galatian region   d 18.27 Gk brothers   e 18.28 Or the Christ   f 19.9 Other ancient authorities read of a certain Tyrannus, from eleven o'clock in the morning to four in the afternoon

sick, their diseases left them, and the evil spirits came out of them. [13]Then some itinerant Jewish exorcists tried to use the name of the Lord Jesus over those who had evil spirits, saying, "I adjure you by the Jesus whom Paul proclaims." [14]Seven sons of a Jewish high priest named Sceva were doing this. [15]But the evil spirit said to them in reply, "Jesus I know, and Paul I know; but who are you?" [16]Then the man with the evil spirit leaped on them, mastered them all, and so overpowered them that they fled out of the house naked and wounded. [17]When this became known to all residents of Ephesus, both Jews and Greeks, everyone was awestruck; and the name of the Lord Jesus was praised. [18]Also many of those who became believers confessed and disclosed their practices. [19]A number of those who practiced magic collected their books and burned them publicly; when the value of these books[a] was calculated, it was found to come to fifty thousand silver coins. [20]So the word of the Lord grew mightily and prevailed.

THE RIOT IN EPHESUS

[21] Now after these things had been accomplished, Paul resolved in the Spirit to go through Macedonia and Achaia, and then to go on to Jerusalem. He said, "After I have gone there, I must also see Rome." [22]So he sent two of his helpers, Timothy and Erastus, to Macedonia, while he himself stayed for some time longer in Asia.

[23] About that time no little disturbance broke out concerning the Way. [24]A man named Demetrius, a silversmith who made silver shrines of Artemis, brought no little business to the artisans. [25]These he gathered together, with the workers of the same trade, and said, "Men, you know that we get our wealth from this business. [26]You also see and hear that not only in Ephesus but in almost the whole of Asia this Paul has persuaded and drawn away a considerable number of people by saying that gods made with hands are not gods. [27]And there is danger not only

that this trade of ours may come into disrepute but also that the temple of the great goddess Artemis will be scorned, and she will be deprived of her majesty that brought all Asia and the world to worship her."

[28] When they heard this, they were enraged and shouted, "Great is Artemis of the Ephesians!" [29]The city was filled with the confusion; and people[b] rushed together to the theater, dragging with them Gaius and Aristarchus, Macedonians who were Paul's travel companions. [30]Paul wished to go into the crowd, but the disciples would not let him; [31]even some officials of the province of Asia,[c] who were friendly to him, sent him a message urging him not to venture into the theater. [32]Meanwhile, some were shouting one thing, some another; for the assembly was in confusion, and most of them did not know why they had come together. [33]Some of the crowd gave instructions to Alexander, whom the Jews had pushed forward. And Alexander motioned for silence and tried to make a defense before the people. [34]But when they recognized that he was a Jew, for about two hours all of them shouted in unison, "Great is Artemis of the Ephesians!" [35]But when the town clerk had quieted the crowd, he said, "Citizens of Ephesus, who is there that does not know that the city of the Ephesians is the temple keeper of the great Artemis and of the statue that fell from heaven?[d] [36]Since these things cannot be denied, you ought to be quiet and do nothing rash. [37]You have brought these men here who are neither temple robbers nor blasphemers of our[e] goddess. [38]If therefore Demetrius and the artisans with him have a complaint against anyone, the courts are open, and there are proconsuls; let them bring charges there against one another. [39]If there is anything further[f]

[a] 19.19 Gk *them* [b] 19.29 Gk
they [c] 19.31 Gk *some of the Asiarchs*
[d] 19.35 Meaning of Gk uncertain
[e] 19.37 Other ancient authorities read *your*
[f] 19.39 Other ancient authorities read *about
other matters*

you want to know, it must be settled in the regular assembly. ⁴⁰For we are in danger of being charged with rioting today, since there is no cause that we can give to justify this commotion." ⁴¹When he had said this, he dismissed the assembly.

PAUL GOES TO MACEDONIA AND GREECE

20 After the uproar had ceased, Paul sent for the disciples; and after encouraging them and saying farewell, he left for Macedonia. ²When he had gone through those regions and had given the believersᵃ much encouragement, he came to Greece, ³where he stayed for three months. He was about to set sail for Syria when a plot was made against him by the Jews, and so he decided to return through Macedonia. ⁴He was accompanied by Sopater son of Pyrrhus from Beroea, by Aristarchus and Secundus from Thessalonica, by Gaius from Derbe, and by Timothy, as well as by Tychicus and Trophimus from Asia. ⁵They went ahead and were waiting for us in Troas; ⁶but we sailed from Philippi after the days of Unleavened Bread, and in five days we joined them in Troas, where we stayed for seven days.

PAUL'S FAREWELL VISIT TO TROAS

⁷On the first day of the week, when we met to break bread, Paul was holding a discussion with them; since he intended to leave the next day, he continued speaking until midnight. ⁸There were many lamps in the room upstairs where we were meeting. ⁹A young man named Eutychus, who was sitting in the window, began to sink off into a deep sleep while Paul talked still longer. Overcome by sleep, he fell to the ground three floors below and was picked up dead. ¹⁰But Paul went down, and bending over him took him in his arms, and said, "Do not be alarmed, for his life is in him." ¹¹Then Paul went upstairs, and after he had broken bread and eaten, he continued to converse with them

until dawn; then he left. ¹²Meanwhile they had taken the boy away alive and were not a little comforted.

GOD CALLS AND ANOINTS

EVERY CHRISTIAN TO THE

MINISTRY OF PROCLAIMING

THE GOOD NEWS OF

SALVATION AND HOPE

IN JESUS CHRIST.

THE VOYAGE FROM TROAS TO MILETUS

¹³We went ahead to the ship and set sail for Assos, intending to take Paul on board there; for he had made this arrangement, intending to go by land himself. ¹⁴When he met us in Assos, we took him on board and went to Mitylene. ¹⁵We sailed from there, and on the following day we arrived opposite Chios. The next day we touched at Samos, andᵇ the day after that we came to Miletus. ¹⁶For Paul had decided to sail past Ephesus, so that he might not have to spend time in Asia; he was eager to be in Jerusalem, if possible, on the day of Pentecost.

PAUL SPEAKS TO THE EPHESIAN ELDERS

¹⁷From Miletus he sent a message to Ephesus, asking the elders of the church to meet him. ¹⁸When they came to him, he said to them:

"You yourselves know how I lived among you the entire time from the first day that I set foot in Asia, ¹⁹serving the Lord with all humility and with tears, enduring the trials that came to me through the plots of the Jews. ²⁰I did not shrink from doing anything helpful, proclaiming the message to you and teaching

ᵃ **20.2** Gk *given them* ᵇ **20.15** Other ancient authorities add *after remaining at Trogyllium* you publicly and from house to house, 21as I testified to both Jews and Greeks about repentance toward God and faith toward our Lord Jesus. 22And now, as a captive to the Spirit,a I am on my way to Jerusalem, not knowing what will happen to me there, 23except that the Holy Spirit testifies to me in every city that imprisonment and persecutions are waiting for me. 24But I do not count my life of any value to myself, if only I may finish my course and the ministry that I received from the Lord Jesus, to testify to the good news of God's grace.

25 "And now I know that none of you, among whom I have gone about proclaiming the kingdom, will ever see my face again. 26Therefore I declare to you this day that I am not responsible for the blood of any of you, 27for I did not shrink from declaring to you the whole purpose of God. 28Keep watch over yourselves and over all the flock, of which the Holy Spirit has made you overseers, to shepherd the church of Godb that he obtained with the blood of his own Son.c 29I know that after I have gone, savage wolves will come in among you, not sparing the flock. 30Some even from your own group will come distorting the truth in order to entice the disciples to follow them. 31Therefore be alert, remembering that for three years I did not cease night or day to warn everyone with tears. 32And now I commend you to God and to the message of his grace, a message that is able to build you up and to give you the inheritance among all who are sanctified. 33I coveted no one's silver or gold or clothing. 34You know for yourselves that I worked with my own hands to support myself and my companions. 35In all this I have given you an example that by such work we must support the weak, remembering the words of the Lord Jesus, for he himself said, 'It is more blessed to give than to receive.' "

36When he had finished speaking, he knelt down with them all and prayed. 37There was much weeping among them all; they embraced

Paul and kissed him, 38grieving especially because of what he had said, that they would not see him again. Then they brought him to the ship.

PAUL'S JOURNEY TO JERUSALEM

21 When we had parted from them and set sail, we came by a straight course to Cos, and the next day to Rhodes, and from there to Patara.d 2When we found a ship bound for Phoenicia, we went on board and set sail. 3We came in sight of Cyprus; and leaving it on our left, we sailed to Syria and landed at Tyre, because the ship was to unload its cargo there. 4We looked up the disciples and stayed there for seven days. Through the Spirit they told Paul not to go on to Jerusalem. 5When our days there were ended, we left and proceeded on our journey; and all of them, with wives and children, escorted us outside the city. There we knelt down on the beach and prayed 6and said farewell to one another. Then we went on board the ship, and they returned home.

7When we had finishede the voyage from Tyre, we arrived at Ptolemais; and we greeted the believersf and stayed with them for one day. 8The next day we left and came to Caesarea; and we went into the house of Philip the evangelist, one of the seven, and stayed with him. 9He had four unmarried daughtersg who had the gift of prophecy. 10While we were staying there for several days, a prophet named Agabus came down from Judea. 11He came to us and took Paul's belt, bound his own feet and hands with it, and said, "Thus says the Holy Spirit, 'This is the way the Jews in Jerusalem will bind the man who owns this belt and will hand him over to the Gentiles.' " 12When we heard this, we and the people there urged him not to go up to Jerusalem. 13Then Paul answered, "What

a 20.22 Or And now, bound in the spirit
b 20.28 Other ancient authorities read of the Lord   c 20.28 Or with his own blood; Gk with the blood of his Own   d 21.1 Other ancient authorities add and Myra   e 21.7 Or continued   f 21.7 Gk brothers   g 21.9 Gk four daughters, virgins,

are you doing, weeping and breaking my heart? For I am ready not only to be bound but even to die in Jerusalem for the name of the Lord Jesus." ¹⁴Since he would not be persuaded, we remained silent except to say, "The Lord's will be done."

¹⁵ After these days we got ready and started to go up to Jerusalem. ¹⁶Some of the disciples from Caesarea also came along and brought us to the house of Mnason of Cyprus, an early disciple, with whom we were to stay.

PAUL VISITS JAMES AT JERUSALEM

¹⁷When we arrived in Jerusalem, the brothers welcomed us warmly. ¹⁸The next day Paul went with us to visit James; and all the elders were present. ¹⁹After greeting them, he related one by one the things that God had done among the Gentiles through his ministry. ²⁰When they heard it, they praised God. Then they said to him, "You see, brother, how many thousands of believers there are among the Jews, and they are all zealous for the law. ²¹They have been told about you that you teach all the Jews living among the Gentiles to forsake Moses, and that you tell them not to circumcise their children or observe the customs. ²²What then is to be done? They will certainly hear that you have come. ²³So

do what we tell you. We have four men who are under a vow. ²⁴Join these men, go through the rite of purification with them, and pay for the shaving of their heads. Thus all will know that there is nothing in what they have been told about you, but that you yourself observe and guard the law. ²⁵But as for the Gentiles who have become believers, we have sent a letter with our judgment that they should abstain from what has been sacrificed to idols and from blood and from what is strangled[a] and from fornication." ²⁶Then Paul took the men, and the next day, having purified himself, he entered the temple with them, making public the completion of the days of purification when the sacrifice would be made for each of them.

PAUL ARRESTED IN THE TEMPLE

²⁷When the seven days were almost completed, the Jews from Asia, who had seen him in the temple, stirred up the whole crowd. They seized him, ²⁸shouting, "Fellow Israelites, help! This is the man who is teaching everyone everywhere against our people, our law, and this place; more than that, he has actually brought Greeks into the temple and has defiled this holy place."

[a] 21.25 Other ancient authorities lack *and from what is strangled*

BIBLE IN LIFE

Willing to Suffer

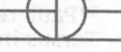

Acts 21.13

The Christians were under harsh attack in Jerusalem. They were being criticized by their fellow Jews who had not accepted Christ and his teachings. Paul was warned not to go to Jerusalem, but he was willing to be bound with chains and even to give his life for Christ (Acts 21.13). When Paul arrived in Jerusalem, he could have retreated and lived as a quiet, dormant, safe, admired, non-witnessing Christian—a description that would apply to many of us. But he didn't. He was a man who believed deeply, taught openly and lived boldly. Paul was destined to be perhaps the greatest Christian witness of all time; part of his ability to witness was that he was willing to suffer. Paul paid a severe price because he witnessed for Christ, but the cost was worth it. The church was strengthened and grew because of Paul's witness, and Paul surely earned a high reward from Jesus. Are we afraid of what might happen to us if we witness for Christ? As Paul told his protégé Timothy: "God did not give us a spirit of cowardice, but rather a spirit of power and of love and of self-discipline" (2 Timothy 1.7).

29For they had previously seen Trophimus the Ephesian with him in the city, and they supposed that Paul had brought him into the temple. 30Then all the city was aroused, and the people rushed together. They seized Paul and dragged him out of the temple, and immediately the doors were shut. 31While they were trying to kill him, word came to the tribune of the cohort that all Jerusalem was in an uproar. 32Immediately he took soldiers and centurions and ran down to them. When they saw the tribune and the soldiers, they stopped beating Paul. 33Then the tribune came, arrested him, and ordered him to be bound with two chains; he inquired who he was and what he had done. 34Some in the crowd shouted one thing, some another; and as he could not learn the facts because of the uproar, he ordered him to be brought into the barracks. 35When Paula came to the steps, the violence of the mob was so great that he had to be carried by the soldiers. 36The crowd that followed kept shouting, "Away with him!"

PAUL DEFENDS HIMSELF

37 Just as Paul was about to be brought into the barracks, he said to the tribune, "May I say something to you?" The tribuneb replied, "Do you know Greek? 38Then you are not the Egyptian who recently stirred up a revolt and led the four thousand assassins out into the wilderness?" 39Paul replied, "I am a Jew, from Tarsus in Cilicia, a citizen of an important city; I beg you, let me speak to the people." 40When he had given him permission, Paul stood on the steps and motioned to the people for silence; and when there was a great hush, he addressed them in the Hebrewc language, saying:

22 "Brothers and fathers, listen to the defense that I now make before you."

2 When they heard him addressing them in Hebrew,c they became even more quiet. Then he said:

3 "I am a Jew, born in Tarsus in Cilicia, but brought up in this city at the feet of Gamaliel, educated strictly according to our ancestral law, being zealous for God, just as all of you are today. 4I persecuted this Way up to the point of death by binding both men and women and putting them in prison, 5as the high priest and the whole council of elders can testify about me. From them I also received letters to the brothers in Damascus, and I went there in order to bind those who were there and to bring them back to Jerusalem for punishment.

PAUL TELLS OF HIS CONVERSION

6 "While I was on my way and approaching Damascus, about noon a great light from heaven suddenly shone about me. 7I fell to the ground and heard a voice saying to me, 'Saul, Saul, why are you persecuting me?' 8I answered, 'Who are you, Lord?' Then he said to me, 'I am Jesus of Nazarethd whom you are persecuting.' 9Now those who were with me saw the light but did not hear the voice of the one who was speaking to me. 10I asked, 'What am I to do, Lord?' The Lord said to me, 'Get up and go to Damascus; there you will be told everything that has been assigned to you to do.' 11Since I could not see because of the brightness of that light, those who were with me took my hand and led me to Damascus.

12 "A certain Ananias, who was a devout man according to the law and well spoken of by all the Jews living there, 13came to me; and standing beside me, he said, 'Brother Saul, regain your sight!' In that very hour I regained my sight and saw him. 14Then he said, 'The God of our ancestors has chosen you to know his will, to see the Righteous One and to hear his own voice; 15for you will be his witness to all the world of what you have seen and heard. 16And now why do you delay? Get up, be baptized, and have your sins washed away, calling on his name.'

a 21.35 Gk he   b 21.37 Gk He
c 21.40; 22.2 That is, Aramaic
d 22.8 Gk the Nazorean

PAUL SENT TO THE GENTILES

17 "After I had returned to Jerusalem and while I was praying in the temple, I fell into a trance [18]and saw Jesus[a] saying to me, 'Hurry and get out of Jerusalem quickly, because they will not accept your testimony about me.' [19]And I said, 'Lord, they themselves know that in every synagogue I imprisoned and beat those who believed in you. [20]And while the blood of your witness Stephen was shed, I myself was standing by, approving and keeping the coats of those who killed him.' [21]Then he said to me, 'Go, for I will send you far away to the Gentiles.' "

PAUL AND THE ROMAN TRIBUNE

22 Up to this point they listened to him, but then they shouted, "Away with such a fellow from the earth! For he should not be allowed to live." [23]And while they were shouting, throwing off their cloaks, and tossing dust into the air, [24]the tribune directed that he was to be brought into the barracks, and ordered him to be examined by flogging, to find out the reason for this outcry against him. [25]But when they had tied him up with thongs,[b] Paul said to the centurion who was standing by, "Is it legal for you to flog a Roman citizen who is uncondemned?" [26]When the centurion heard that, he went to the tribune and said to him, "What are you about to do? This man is a Roman citizen." [27]The tribune came and asked Paul,[a] "Tell me, are you a Roman citizen?" And he said, "Yes." [28]The tribune answered, "It cost me a large sum of money to get my citizenship." Paul said, "But I was born a citizen." [29]Immediately those who were about to examine him drew back from him; and the tribune also was afraid, for he realized that Paul was a Roman citizen and that he had bound him.

PAUL BEFORE THE COUNCIL

30 Since he wanted to find out what Paul[c] was being accused of by the Jews, the next day he released him and ordered the chief priests and the entire council to meet. He brought Paul down and had him stand before them.

23 While Paul was looking intently at the council he said, "Brothers,[d] up to this day I have lived my life with a clear conscience before God." [2]Then the high priest Ananias ordered those standing near him to strike him on the mouth. [3]At this Paul said to him, "God will strike you, you whitewashed wall! Are you sitting there to judge me according to the law, and yet in violation of the law you order me to be struck?" [4]Those standing nearby said, "Do you dare to insult God's high priest?" [5]And Paul said, "I did not realize, brothers, that he was high priest; for it is written, 'You shall not speak evil of a leader of your people.' "

6 When Paul noticed that some were Sadducees and others were Pharisees, he called out in the council, "Brothers, I am a Pharisee, a son of Pharisees. I am on trial concerning the hope of the resurrection[e] of the dead." [7]When he said this, a dissension began between the Pharisees and the Sadducees, and the assembly was divided. [8](The Sadducees say that there is no resurrection, or angel, or spirit; but the Pharisees acknowledge all three.) [9]Then a great clamor arose, and certain scribes of the Pharisees' group stood up and contended, "We find nothing wrong with this man. What if a spirit or an angel has spoken to him?" [10]When the dissension became violent, the tribune, fearing that they would tear Paul to pieces, ordered the soldiers to go down, take him by force, and bring him into the barracks.

11 That night the Lord stood near him and said, "Keep up your courage! For just as you have testified for me in Jerusalem, so you must bear witness also in Rome."

THE PLOT TO KILL PAUL

12 In the morning the Jews joined in a conspiracy and bound themselves by an oath neither to eat nor

---

[a] 22.18,27 Gk him   [b] 22.25 Or up for the lashes   [c] 22.30 Gk he   [d] 23.1 Gk Men, brothers   [e] 23.6 Gk concerning hope and resurrection

PONDER

That night the Lord stood near him and said, "Keep up your courage! For just as you have testified for me in Jerusalem, so you must bear witness also in Rome."
—Acts 23.11

PRAY

Lord, we are thankful for this message about the early church; it has endured for more than two thousand years. It is our story and our inheritance. We pray that you might open our hearts to look at the early church and ask, "What can we learn from this history?" Help us remember its simple but profound nature. Help us to form strong Christian communities that support its members, even as the early church supported its own. We pray in the name of our Savior. Amen.

drink until they had killed Paul. 13There were more than forty who joined in this conspiracy. 14They went to the chief priests and elders and said, "We have strictly bound ourselves by an oath to taste no food until we have killed Paul. 15Now then, you and the council must notify the tribune to bring him down to you, on the pretext that you want to make a more thorough examination of his case. And we are ready to do away with him before he arrives."

16 Now the son of Paul's sister heard about the ambush; so he went and gained entrance to the barracks and told Paul. 17Paul called one of the centurions and said, "Take this young man to the tribune, for he has something to report to him." 18So he took him, brought him to the tribune, and said, "The prisoner Paul called me and asked me to bring this young man to you; he has something to tell you." 19The tribune took him by the hand, drew him aside privately, and asked, "What is it that you have to report to me?" 20He answered, "The Jews have agreed to ask you to bring Paul down to the council tomorrow, as though they were going to inquire more thoroughly into his case. 21But do not be persuaded by them, for more than forty of their men are lying in ambush for him. They have bound themselves by an oath neither to eat nor drink until they kill him. They are ready now and are waiting for your consent." 22So the tribune dismissed the young man, ordering him, "Tell no one that you have informed me of this."

PAUL SENT TO FELIX THE GOVERNOR

23 Then he summoned two of the centurions and said, "Get ready to leave by nine o'clock tonight for Caesarea with two hundred soldiers, seventy horsemen, and two hundred spearmen. 24Also provide mounts for Paul to ride, and take him safely to Felix the governor." 25He wrote a letter to this effect:

26 "Claudius Lysias to his Excellency the governor Felix, greetings. 27This man was seized by the Jews and was about to be killed by them, but when I had learned that he was a Roman citizen, I came with the guard and rescued him. 28Since I wanted to know the charge for which they accused him, I had him brought to their council. 29I found that he was accused concerning questions of their law, but was charged with nothing deserving death or imprisonment. 30When I was informed that there would be a plot against the man, I sent him to you at once, ordering his accusers also to state before you what they have against him."[a]

31 So the soldiers, according to their instructions, took Paul and brought him during the night to Antipatris. 32The next day they let the horsemen go on with him, while they returned to the barracks. 33When they came to Caesarea and

[a] 23.30 Other ancient authorities add *Farewell*

delivered the letter to the governor, they presented Paul also before him. [34]On reading the letter, he asked what province he belonged to, and when he learned that he was from Cilicia, [35]he said, "I will give you a hearing when your accusers arrive." Then he ordered that he be kept under guard in Herod's headquarters.[a]

PAUL BEFORE FELIX AT CAESAREA

24 Five days later the high priest Ananias came down with some elders and an attorney, a certain Tertullus, and they reported their case against Paul to the governor. [2]When Paul[b] had been summoned, Tertullus began to accuse him, saying:

"Your Excellency,[c] because of you we have long enjoyed peace, and reforms have been made for this people because of your foresight. [3]We welcome this in every way and everywhere with utmost gratitude. [4]But, to detain you no further, I beg you to hear us briefly with your customary graciousness. [5]We have, in fact, found this man a pestilent fellow, an agitator among all the Jews throughout the world, and a ringleader of the sect of the Nazarenes.[d] [6]He even tried to profane the temple, and so we seized him.[e] [8]By examining him yourself you will be able to learn from him concerning everything of which we accuse him." [9]The Jews also joined in the charge by asserting that all this was true.

PAUL'S DEFENSE BEFORE FELIX

[10]When the governor motioned to him to speak, Paul replied:

"I cheerfully make my defense, knowing that for many years you have been a judge over this nation. [11]As you can find out, it is not more than twelve days since I went up to worship in Jerusalem. [12]They did not find me disputing with anyone in the temple or stirring up a crowd either in the synagogues or throughout the city. [13]Neither can they prove to you the charge that they now bring against me. [14]But this I admit to you, that according to the Way, which they call a sect, I worship the God of our ancestors, believing everything laid down according to the law or written in the prophets. [15]I have a hope in God—a hope that they themselves also accept—that there will be a resurrection of both[f] the righteous and the unrighteous. [16]Therefore I do my best always to have a clear conscience toward God and all people. [17]Now after some years I came to bring alms to my nation and to offer sacrifices. [18]While I was doing this, they found me in the temple, completing the rite of purification, without any crowd or disturbance. [19]But there were some Jews from Asia—they ought to be here before you to make an accusation, if they have anything against me. [20]Or let these men here tell what crime they had found when I stood before the council, [21]unless it was this one sentence that I called out while standing before them, 'It is about the resurrection of the dead that I am on trial before you today.' "

[22]But Felix, who was rather well informed about the Way, adjourned the hearing with the comment, "When Lysias the tribune comes down, I will decide your case." [23]Then he ordered the centurion to keep him in custody, but to let him have some liberty and not to prevent any of his friends from taking care of his needs.

PAUL HELD IN CUSTODY

[24]Some days later when Felix came with his wife Drusilla, who was Jewish, he sent for Paul and heard him speak concerning faith in Christ Jesus. [25]And as he discussed justice, self-control, and the coming judgment, Felix became frightened and said, "Go away for the present; when I have an opportunity, I will

[a] 23.35 Gk *praetorium*   [b] 24.2 Gk *he*
[c] 24.2 Gk lacks *Your Excellency*   [d] 24.5 Gk *Nazoreans*   [e] 24.6 Other ancient authorities add *and we would have judged him according to our law.* [7]*But the chief captain Lysias came and with great violence took him out of our hands,* [8]*commanding his accusers to come before you.*   [f] 24.15 Other ancient authorities read *of the dead, both of*

send for you." 26 At the same time he hoped that money would be given him by Paul, and for that reason he used to send for him very often and converse with him.

27 After two years had passed, Felix was succeeded by Porcius Festus; and since he wanted to grant the Jews a favor, Felix left Paul in prison.

PAUL APPEALS TO THE EMPEROR

25 Three days after Festus had arrived in the province, he went up from Caesarea to Jerusalem 2 where the chief priests and the leaders of the Jews gave him a report against Paul. They appealed to him 3 and requested, as a favor to them against Paul,ᵃ to have him transferred to Jerusalem. They were, in fact, planning an ambush to kill him along the way. 4 Festus replied that Paul was being kept at Caesarea, and that he himself intended to go there shortly. 5 "So," he said, "let those of you who have the authority come down with me, and if there is anything wrong about the man, let them accuse him."

6 After he had stayed among them not more than eight or ten days, he went down to Caesarea; the next day he took his seat on the tribunal and ordered Paul to be brought. 7 When he arrived, the Jews who had gone down from Jerusalem surrounded him, bringing many serious charges against him, which they could not prove. 8 Paul said in his defense, "I have in no way committed an offense against the law of the Jews, or against the temple, or against the emperor." 9 But Festus, wishing to do the Jews a favor, asked Paul, "Do you wish to go up to Jerusalem and be tried there before me on these charges?" 10 Paul said, "I am appealing to the emperor's tribunal; this is where I should be tried. I have done no wrong to the Jews, as you very well know. 11 Now if I am in the wrong and have committed something for which I deserve to die, I am not trying to escape death; but if there is nothing to their charges against me, no one can turn me over to them. I appeal to the emperor."

12 Then Festus, after he had conferred with his council, replied, "You have appealed to the emperor; to the emperor you will go."

FESTUS CONSULTS
KING AGRIPPA

13 After several days had passed, King Agrippa and Bernice arrived at Caesarea to welcome Festus. 14 Since they were staying there several days, Festus laid Paul's case before the king, saying, "There is a man here who was left in prison by Felix. 15 When I was in Jerusalem, the chief priests and the elders of the Jews informed me about him and asked for a sentence against him. 16 I told them that it was not the custom of the Romans to hand over anyone before the accused had met the accusers face to face and had been given an opportunity to make a defense against the charge. 17 So when they met here, I lost no time, but on the next day took my seat on the tribunal and ordered the man to be brought. 18 When the accusers stood up, they did not charge him with any of the crimesᵇ that I was expecting. 19 Instead they had certain points of disagreement with him about their own religion and about a certain Jesus, who had died, but whom Paul asserted to be alive. 20 Since I was at a loss how to investigate these questions, I asked whether he wished to go to Jerusalem and be tried there on these charges.ᶜ 21 But when Paul had appealed to be kept in custody for the decision of his Imperial Majesty, I ordered him to be held until I could send him to the emperor." 22 Agrippa said to Festus, "I would like to hear the man myself." "Tomorrow," he said, "you will hear him."

PAUL BROUGHT BEFORE
AGRIPPA

23 So on the next day Agrippa and Bernice came with great pomp, and they entered the audience hall with the military tribunes and the

ᵃ 25.3 Gk him   ᵇ 25.18 Other ancient authorities read with anything   ᶜ 25.20 Gk on them

prominent men of the city. Then Festus gave the order and Paul was brought in. 24 And Festus said, "King Agrippa and all here present with us, you see this man about whom the whole Jewish community petitioned me, both in Jerusalem and here, shouting that he ought not to live any longer. 25 But I found that he had done nothing deserving death; and when he appealed to his Imperial Majesty, I decided to send him. 26 But I have nothing definite to write to our sovereign about him. Therefore I have brought him before all of you, and especially before you, King Agrippa, so that, after we have examined him, I may have something to write— 27 for it seems to me unreasonable to send a prisoner without indicating the charges against him."

PAUL DEFENDS HIMSELF BEFORE AGRIPPA

26 Agrippa said to Paul, "You have permission to speak for yourself." Then Paul stretched out his hand and began to defend himself:

2 "I consider myself fortunate that it is before you, King Agrippa, I am to make my defense today against all the accusations of the Jews, 3 because you are especially familiar with all the customs and controversies of the Jews; therefore I beg of you to listen to me patiently.

4 "All the Jews know my way of life from my youth, a life spent from the beginning among my own people and in Jerusalem. 5 They have known for a long time, if they are willing to testify, that I have belonged to the strictest sect of our religion and lived as a Pharisee. 6 And now I stand here on trial on account of my hope in the promise made by God to our ancestors, 7 a promise that our twelve tribes hope to attain, as they earnestly worship day and night. It is for this hope, your Excellency,ᵃ that I am accused by Jews! 8 Why is it thought incredible by any of you that God raises the dead?

9 "Indeed, I myself was convinced that I ought to do many things against the name of Jesus of Nazareth.ᵇ 10 And that is what I did in Jerusalem; with authority received from the chief priests, I not only locked up many of the saints in prison, but I also cast my vote against them when they were being condemned to death. 11 By punishing them often in all the synagogues I tried to force them to blaspheme; and since I was so furiously enraged at them, I pursued them even to foreign cities.

PAUL TELLS OF HIS CONVERSION

12 "With this in mind, I was traveling to Damascus with the authority and commission of the chief priests, 13 when at midday along the road, your Excellency,ᵃ I saw a light

ᵃ 26.7,13 Gk O king   ᵇ 26.9 Gk the Nazorean

BIBLE IN LIFE

Testify   Acts 26.2–27

When Paul gained an audience with King Agrippa, he didn't preach theology to him. What was his message? In effect, Paul said, "Let me tell you what happened to me: There I was, a successful Pharisee, persecuting Christians. There I was, on the road to Damascus. There I was, stricken blind. There I was, debased and ashamed. There I was, mistrusted. There I was, with my life changed. There I was, side by side with Jesus. There I was, beaten and imprisoned. There I was, protected by God." Paul simply told Agrippa what had happened to him. Our message can be just as simple: "There I was . . . and here's what God did." Are we able to tell people what happened to us? Does anything happen to us during a week that we could share if we had an opportunity to talk face to face with someone about God's work in our lives? Paul's mission was to testify to what God had accomplished in his life, and we can do the same.

from heaven, brighter than the sun, shining around me and my companions. ¹⁴When we had all fallen to the ground, I heard a voice saying to me in the Hebrew[a] language, 'Saul, Saul, why are you persecuting me? It hurts you to kick against the goads.' ¹⁵I asked, 'Who are you, Lord?' The Lord answered, 'I am Jesus whom you are persecuting. ¹⁶But get up and stand on your feet; for I have appeared to you for this purpose, to appoint you to serve and testify to the things in which you have seen me[b] and to those in which I will appear to you. ¹⁷I will rescue you from your people and from the Gentiles—to whom I am sending you ¹⁸to open their eyes so that they may turn from darkness to light and from the power of Satan to God, so that they may receive forgiveness of sins and a place among those who are sanctified by faith in me.'

PAUL TELLS OF HIS PREACHING

19 "After that, King Agrippa, I was not disobedient to the heavenly vision, ²⁰but declared first to those in Damascus, then in Jerusalem and throughout the countryside of Judea, and also to the Gentiles, that they should repent and turn to God and do deeds consistent with repentance. ²¹For this reason the Jews seized me in the temple and tried to kill me. ²²To this day I have had help from God, and so I stand here, testifying to both small and great, saying nothing but what the prophets and Moses said would take place: ²³that the Messiah[c] must suffer, and that, by being the first to rise from the dead, he would proclaim light both to our people and to the Gentiles."

PAUL APPEALS TO AGRIPPA TO BELIEVE

24 While he was making this defense, Festus exclaimed, "You are out of your mind, Paul! Too much learning is driving you insane!" ²⁵But Paul said, "I am not out of my mind, most excellent Festus, but I am speaking the sober truth. ²⁶Indeed the king knows about these things, and to him I speak freely; for I am

certain that none of these things has escaped his notice, for this was not done in a corner. ²⁷King Agrippa, do you believe the prophets? I know that you believe." ²⁸Agrippa said to Paul, "Are you so quickly persuading me to become a Christian?"[d] ²⁹Paul replied, "Whether quickly or not, I pray to God that not only you but also all who are listening to me today might become such as I am— except for these chains."

30 Then the king got up, and with him the governor and Bernice and those who had been seated with them; ³¹and as they were leaving, they said to one another, "This man is doing nothing to deserve death or imprisonment." ³²Agrippa said to Festus, "This man could have been set free if he had not appealed to the emperor."

PAUL SAILS FOR ROME

27 When it was decided that we were to sail for Italy, they transferred Paul and some other prisoners to a centurion of the Augustan Cohort, named Julius. ²Embarking on a ship of Adramyttium that was about to set sail to the ports along the coast of Asia, we put to sea, accompanied by Aristarchus, a Macedonian from Thessalonica. ³The next day we put in at Sidon; and Julius treated Paul kindly, and allowed him to go to his friends to be cared for. ⁴Putting out to sea from there, we sailed under the lee of Cyprus, because the winds were against us. ⁵After we had sailed across the sea that is off Cilicia and Pamphylia, we came to Myra in Lycia. ⁶There the centurion found an Alexandrian ship bound for Italy and put us on board. ⁷We sailed slowly for a number of days and arrived with difficulty off Cnidus, and as the wind was against us, we sailed under the lee of Crete off Salmone. ⁸Sailing past it with difficulty, we came to a place called Fair Havens, near the city of Lasea.

[a] 26.14 That is, Aramaic [b] 26.16 Other ancient authorities read the things that you have seen [c] 26.23 Or the Christ [d] 26.28 Or Quickly you will persuade me to play the Christian

9 Since much time had been lost and sailing was now dangerous, because even the Fast had already gone by, Paul advised them, **10**saying, "Sirs, I can see that the voyage will be with danger and much heavy loss, not only of the cargo and the ship, but also of our lives." **11**But the centurion paid more attention to the pilot and to the owner of the ship than to what Paul said. **12**Since the harbor was not suitable for spending the winter, the majority was in favor of putting to sea from there, on the chance that somehow they could reach Phoenix, where they could spend the winter. It was a harbor of Crete, facing southwest and northwest.

"SEND ME" IS THE SPIRIT OF A

TRUE CHRISTIAN SERVANT. BUT

WHEN WE GO, WE MUST HAVE

THOUGHTFUL PREPARATION.

WE MUST EXPECT OPPOSITION

AND DISCOURAGEMENT

AND SEEK THE ASSISTANCE

THAT WILL HELP US RECEIVE

COURAGE AND STRENGTH

ADEQUATE FOR THE WORK.

THE STORM AT SEA

13 When a moderate south wind began to blow, they thought they could achieve their purpose; so they weighed anchor and began to sail past Crete, close to the shore. **14**But soon a violent wind, called the northeaster, rushed down from Crete.[a] **15**Since the ship was caught and could not be turned head-on into the wind, we gave way to it and were driven. **16**By running under the lee of a small island called Cauda[b] we were scarcely able to get the ship's boat under control. **17**After hoisting

it up they took measures[c] to undergird the ship; then, fearing that they would run on the Syrtis, they lowered the sea anchor and so were driven. **18**We were being pounded by the storm so violently that on the next day they began to throw the cargo overboard, **19**and on the third day with their own hands they threw the ship's tackle overboard. **20**When neither sun nor stars appeared for many days, and no small tempest raged, all hope of our being saved was at last abandoned.

21 Since they had been without food for a long time, Paul then stood up among them and said, "Men, you should have listened to me and not have set sail from Crete and thereby avoided this damage and loss. **22**I urge you now to keep up your courage, for there will be no loss of life among you, but only of the ship. **23**For last night there stood by me an angel of the God to whom I belong and whom I worship, **24**and he said, 'Do not be afraid, Paul; you must stand before the emperor; and indeed, God has granted safety to all those who are sailing with you.' **25**So keep up your courage, men, for I have faith in God that it will be exactly as I have been told. **26**But we will have to run aground on some island."

27 When the fourteenth night had come, as we were drifting across the sea of Adria, about midnight the sailors suspected that they were nearing land. **28**So they took soundings and found twenty fathoms; a little farther on they took soundings again and found fifteen fathoms. **29**Fearing that we might run on the rocks, they let down four anchors from the stern and prayed for day to come. **30**But when the sailors tried to escape from the ship and had lowered the boat into the sea, on the pretext of putting out anchors from the bow, **31**Paul said to the centurion and the soldiers, "Unless these men stay in the ship, you cannot be saved." **32**Then the soldiers cut away the ropes of the boat and set it adrift.

33 Just before daybreak, Paul urged all of them to take some food, saying, "Today is the fourteenth day that you have been in suspense and remaining without food, having eaten nothing. **34** Therefore I urge you to take some food, for it will help you survive; for none of you will lose a hair from your heads." **35** After he had said this, he took bread; and giving thanks to God in the presence of all, he broke it and began to eat. **36** Then all of them were encouraged and took food for themselves. **37** (We were in all two hundred seventy-six[a] persons in the ship.) **38** After they had satisfied their hunger, they lightened the ship by throwing the wheat into the sea.

THE SHIPWRECK

39 In the morning they did not recognize the land, but they noticed a bay with a beach, on which they planned to run the ship ashore, if they could. **40** So they cast off the anchors and left them in the sea. At the same time they loosened the ropes that tied the steering-oars; then hoisting the foresail to the wind, they made for the beach. **41** But striking a reef,[b] they ran the ship aground; the bow stuck and remained immovable, but the stern was being broken up by the force of the waves. **42** The soldiers' plan was to kill the prisoners, so that none might swim away and escape; **43** but the centurion, wishing to save Paul, kept them from carrying out their plan. He ordered those who could swim to jump overboard first and make for the land, **44** and the rest to follow, some on planks and others on pieces of the ship. And so it was that all were brought safely to land.

PAUL ON THE ISLAND OF MALTA

28 After we had reached safety, we then learned that the island was called Malta. **2** The natives showed us unusual kindness. Since it had begun to rain and was cold, they kindled a fire and welcomed all of us around it. **3** Paul had gathered a bundle of brushwood and was putting it on the fire, when a viper, driven out by the heat, fastened itself on his hand. **4** When the natives saw the creature hanging from his hand, they said to one another, "This man must be a murderer; though he has escaped from the sea, justice has not allowed him to live." **5** He, however, shook off the creature into the fire and suffered no harm. **6** They were expecting him to swell up or drop dead, but after they had waited a long time and saw that nothing unusual had happened to him, they changed their minds and began to say that he was a god.

7 Now in the neighborhood of that place were lands belonging to the leading man of the island, named Publius, who received us and entertained us hospitably for three days. **8** It so happened that the father of Publius lay sick in bed with fever and dysentery. Paul visited him and cured him by praying and putting his hands on him. **9** After this happened, the rest of the people on the island who had diseases also came and were cured. **10** They bestowed many honors on us, and when we were about to sail, they put on board all the provisions we needed.

PAUL ARRIVES AT ROME

11 Three months later we set sail on a ship that had wintered at the island, an Alexandrian ship with the Twin Brothers as its figurehead. **12** We put in at Syracuse and stayed there for three days; **13** then we weighed anchor and came to Rhegium. After one day there a south wind sprang up, and on the second day we came to Puteoli. **14** There we found believers[c] and were invited to stay with them for seven days. And so we came to Rome. **15** The believers[c] from there, when they heard of us, came as far as the Forum of Appius and Three Taverns to meet us. On seeing them, Paul thanked God and took courage.

---

[a] **27.37** Other ancient authorities read *seventy-six*; others, *about seventy-six*
[b] **27.41** Gk *place of two seas*   [c] **28.14,15** Gk *brothers*

16 When we came into Rome, Paul was allowed to live by himself, with the soldier who was guarding him.

PAUL AND JEWISH LEADERS IN ROME

17 Three days later he called together the local leaders of the Jews. When they had assembled, he said to them, "Brothers, though I had done nothing against our people or the customs of our ancestors, yet I was arrested in Jerusalem and handed over to the Romans. **18** When they had examined me, the Romans[a] wanted to release me, because there was no reason for the death penalty in my case. **19** But when the Jews objected, I was compelled to appeal to the emperor—even though I had no charge to bring against my nation. **20** For this reason therefore I have asked to see you and speak with you,[b] since it is for the sake of the hope of Israel that I am bound with this chain." **21** They replied, "We have received no letters from Judea about you, and none of the brothers coming here has reported or spoken anything evil about you. **22** But we would like to hear from you what you think, for with regard to this sect we know that everywhere it is spoken against."

PAUL PREACHES IN ROME

23 After they had set a day to meet with him, they came to him at his lodgings in great numbers. From morning until evening he explained the matter to them, testifying to the kingdom of God and trying to convince them about Jesus both from the law of Moses and from the prophets. **24** Some were convinced by what he had said, while others refused to believe. **25** So they disagreed with each other; and as they were leaving, Paul made one further statement: "The Holy Spirit was right in saying to your ancestors through the prophet Isaiah,
26 'Go to this people and say,
You will indeed listen, but
never understand,
and you will indeed look,
but never perceive.
27 For this people's heart has
grown dull,
and their ears are hard
of hearing,
and they have shut
their eyes;
so that they might not
look with their eyes,
and listen with their ears,
and understand with their
heart and turn—
and I would heal them.'
28 Let it be known to you then that this salvation of God has been sent to the Gentiles; they will listen."[c]

30 He lived there two whole years at his own expense[d] and welcomed all who came to him, **31** proclaiming the kingdom of God and teaching about the Lord Jesus Christ with all boldness and without hindrance.

---

[a] **28.18** Gk *they*   [b] **28.20** Or *I have asked you to see me and speak with me*
[c] **28.28** Other ancient authorities add verse 29, *And when he had said these words, the Jews departed, arguing vigorously among themselves*   [d] **28.30** Or *in his own hired dwelling*

The Letter of Paul to the
ROMANS

"Why do some people accept Jesus as Savior and Lord but others don't?" "Why do I struggle with sin, even though I'm a Christian?" "How can a gracious and loving God judge and punish people?" If you've ever wanted answers for questions like these, you'll find a clear expression of Christian belief in lively, practical terms in the book of Romans. But be prepared! Reading this book has been a turning point for many, including Martin Luther and John Wesley. If you're hungry for spiritual renewal, read Romans—it's a great place to begin.

SALUTATION

1 Paul, a servant[a] of Jesus Christ, called to be an apostle, set apart for the gospel of God, ²which he promised beforehand through his prophets in the holy scriptures, ³the gospel concerning his Son, who was descended from David according to the flesh ⁴and was declared to be Son of God with power according to the spirit[b] of holiness by resurrection from the dead, Jesus Christ our Lord, ⁵through whom we have received grace and apostleship to bring about the obedience of faith among all the Gentiles for the sake of his name, ⁶including yourselves who are called to belong to Jesus Christ,

7 To all God's beloved in Rome, who are called to be saints:

Grace to you and peace from God our Father and the Lord Jesus Christ.

PRAYER OF THANKSGIVING

8 First, I thank my God through Jesus Christ for all of you, because your faith is proclaimed throughout the world. ⁹For God, whom I serve with my spirit by announcing the gospel[c] of his Son, is my witness that without ceasing I remember you always in my prayers, ¹⁰asking that by God's will I may somehow at last succeed in coming to you. ¹¹For I am longing to see you so that I may share with you some spiritual gift to strengthen you— ¹²or rather so that we may be mutually encouraged by each other's faith, both yours and mine. ¹³I want you to know, brothers and sisters,[d] that I have often intended to come to you (but thus far have been prevented), in order that I may reap some harvest among you as I have among the rest of the Gentiles. ¹⁴I am a debtor both to Greeks and to barbarians, both to the wise and to the foolish ¹⁵—hence my eagerness to proclaim the gospel to you also who are in Rome.

THE POWER OF THE GOSPEL

16 For I am not ashamed of the gospel; it is the power of God for salvation to everyone who has faith, to the Jew first and also to the Greek. ¹⁷For in it the righteousness of God is revealed through faith for faith; as it is written, "The one who is righteous will live by faith."[e]

THE GUILT OF HUMANKIND

18 For the wrath of God is revealed from heaven against all ungodliness and wickedness of those who by their wickedness suppress the truth. ¹⁹For what can be known about God is plain to them, because God has shown it to them. ²⁰Ever since the creation of the world his eternal power and divine nature, invisible though they are, have been

[a] 1.1 Gk *slave*   [b] 1.4 Or *Spirit*   [c] 1.9 Gk *my spirit in the gospel*   [d] 1.13 Gk *brothers*   [e] 1.17 Or *The one who is righteous through faith will live*

┤├ BIBLE IN LIFE ▷

Encountering God in Creation
Romans 1.18–32

In the early days of the church, Christians debated how people who never hear about God Almighty are supposed to know about God. Paul said that "what can be known about God is plain to them, because God has shown it to them" (verse 19). People are without excuse. We can't see God, but we are aware of God's presence through what has been created. We are aware of God through unexplainable facets or miracles of the world—whether they're in the vast reaches of space or in the minutia of microscopic particles or in the human brain or in the bloodstream or in the birth of a baby. Some think that the creation is a lucky accident; the universe with all its mysteries was not shaped by a superior being—God. But Paul says that all we have to do is look around us to see adequate proof of the existence of God. That's a foundation on which we can begin to grow. Natural revelation plants the seed of religious faith. So how many people on earth should know about God? Everyone, Paul said.

understood and seen through the things he has made. So they are without excuse; 21for though they knew God, they did not honor him as God or give thanks to him, but they became futile in their thinking, and their senseless minds were darkened. 22Claiming to be wise, they became fools; 23and they exchanged the glory of the immortal God for images resembling a mortal human being or birds or four-footed animals or reptiles.

24 Therefore God gave them up in the lusts of their hearts to impurity, to the degrading of their bodies among themselves, 25because they exchanged the truth about God for a lie and worshiped and served the creature rather than the Creator, who is blessed forever! Amen.

26 For this reason God gave them up to degrading passions. Their women exchanged natural intercourse for unnatural, 27and in the same way also the men, giving up natural intercourse with women, were consumed with passion for one another. Men committed shameless acts with men and received in their own persons the due penalty for their error.

28 And since they did not see fit to acknowledge God, God gave them up to a debased mind and to things that should not be done. 29They were filled with every kind of wickedness, evil, covetousness, malice. Full of envy, murder, strife, deceit, craftiness, they are gossips, 30slanderers, God-haters,a insolent, haughty, boastful, inventors of evil, rebellious toward parents, 31foolish, faithless, heartless, ruthless. 32They know God's decree, that those who practice such things deserve to die—yet they not only do them but even applaud others who practice them.

THE RIGHTEOUS
JUDGMENT OF GOD

2 Therefore you have no excuse, whoever you are, when you judge others; for in passing judgment on another you condemn yourself, because you, the judge, are doing the very same things. 2You

say,b "We know that God's judgment on those who do such things is in accordance with truth." 3Do you imagine, whoever you are, that when you judge those who do such things and yet do them yourself, you will escape the judgment of God? 4Or do you despise the riches of his kindness and forbearance and patience? Do you not realize that God's kindness is meant to lead you to repentance? 5But by your hard and impenitent heart you are storing up wrath for yourself on the day of wrath, when God's righteous judgment will be revealed. 6For he will repay according to each one's deeds: 7to those who by patiently doing good seek for glory and honor and immortality, he will give eternal life; 8while for those who are self-seeking and who obey not the truth but wickedness, there will be wrath and fury. 9There will be anguish and distress for everyone who does evil, the Jew first and also the Greek, 10but glory and honor and peace for everyone who does good, the Jew first and also the Greek. 11For God shows no partiality.

12 All who have sinned apart from the law will also perish apart from the law, and all who have sinned under the law will be judged by the law. 13For it is not the hearers of the law who are righteous in God's sight, but the doers of the law who will be justified. 14When Gentiles, who do not possess the law, do instinctively what the law requires, these, though not having the law, are a law to themselves. 15They show that what the law requires is written on their hearts, to which their own conscience also bears witness; and their conflicting thoughts will accuse or perhaps excuse them 16on the day when, according to my gospel, God, through Jesus Christ, will judge the secret thoughts of all.

THE JEWS AND THE LAW

17 But if you call yourself a Jew and rely on the law and boast of your relation to God 18and know his will and determine what is best because

a 1.30 Or God-hated   b 2.2 Gk lacks You say

you are instructed in the law, ¹⁹and if you are sure that you are a guide to the blind, a light to those who are in darkness, ²⁰a corrector of the foolish, a teacher of children, having in the law the embodiment of knowledge and truth, ²¹you, then, that teach others, will you not teach yourself? While you preach against stealing, do you steal? ²²You that forbid adultery, do you commit adultery? You that abhor idols, do you rob temples? ²³You that boast in the law, do you dishonor God by breaking the law? ²⁴For, as it is written, "The name of God is blasphemed among the Gentiles because of you."

25 Circumcision indeed is of value if you obey the law; but if you break the law, your circumcision has become uncircumcision. ²⁶So, if those who are uncircumcised keep the requirements of the law, will not their uncircumcision be regarded as circumcision? ²⁷Then those who are physically uncircumcised but keep the law will condemn you that have the written code and circumcision but break the law. ²⁸For a person is not a Jew who is one outwardly, nor is true circumcision something external and physical. ²⁹Rather, a person is a Jew who is one inwardly, and real circumcision is a matter of the heart—it is spiritual and not literal. Such a person receives praise not from others but from God.

3 Then what advantage has the Jew? Or what is the value of circumcision? ²Much, in every way. For in the first place the Jews[a] were entrusted with the oracles of God. ³What if some were unfaithful? Will their faithlessness nullify the faithfulness of God? ⁴By no means! Although everyone is a liar, let God be proved true, as it is written,

"So that you may be justified
    in your words,
    and prevail in your judging."[b]

⁵But if our injustice serves to confirm the justice of God, what should we say? That God is unjust to inflict wrath on us? (I speak in a human way.) ⁶By no means! For then how could God judge the world? ⁷But if through my falsehood God's truth-

fulness abounds to his glory, why am I still being condemned as a sinner? ⁸And why not say (as some people slander us by saying that we say), "Let us do evil so that good may come"? Their condemnation is deserved!

NONE IS RIGHTEOUS

9 What then? Are we any better off?[c] No, not at all; for we have already charged that all, both Jews and Greeks, are under the power of sin, ¹⁰as it is written:

"There is no one who is
    righteous, not even one;
¹¹ there is no one who has
    understanding,
    there is no one who
    seeks God.
¹² All have turned aside,
    together they have
    become worthless;
    there is no one who
    shows kindness,
    there is not even one."
¹³ "Their throats are opened graves;
    they use their tongues
    to deceive."
    "The venom of vipers is
    under their lips."
¹⁴   "Their mouths are full of
    cursing and bitterness."
¹⁵ "Their feet are swift to shed blood;
¹⁶ ruin and misery are in
    their paths,
¹⁷ and the way of peace they
    have not known."
¹⁸ "There is no fear of God
    before their eyes."

19 Now we know that whatever the law says, it speaks to those who are under the law, so that every mouth may be silenced, and the whole world may be held accountable to God. ²⁰For "no human being will be justified in his sight" by deeds prescribed by the law, for through the law comes the knowledge of sin.

RIGHTEOUSNESS THROUGH FAITH

21 But now, apart from law, the righteousness of God has been disclosed,

a 3.2 Gk they   b 3.4 Gk when you are being judged   c 3.9 Or at any disadvantage?

and is attested by the law and the prophets, 22the righteousness of God through faith in Jesus Christ[a] for all who believe. For there is no distinction, 23since all have sinned and fall short of the glory of God; 24they are now justified by his grace as a gift, through the redemption that is in Christ Jesus, 25whom God put forward as a sacrifice of atonement[b] by his blood, effective through faith. He did this to show his righteousness, because in his divine forbearance he had passed over the sins previously committed; 26it was to prove at the present time that he himself is righteous and that he justifies the one who has faith in Jesus.[c]

27 Then what becomes of boasting? It is excluded. By what law? By that of works? No, but by the law of faith. 28For we hold that a person is justified by faith apart from works prescribed by the law. 29Or is God the God of Jews only? Is he not the God of Gentiles also? Yes, of Gentiles also, 30since God is one; and he will justify the circumcised on the ground of faith and the uncircumcised through that same faith. 31Do we then overthrow the law by this faith? By no means! On the contrary, we uphold the law.

THE EXAMPLE OF ABRAHAM

4 What then are we to say was gained by[d] Abraham, our ancestor according to the flesh? 2For if Abraham was justified by works, he has something to boast about, but not before God. 3For what does the scripture say? "Abraham believed God, and it was reckoned to him as righteousness." 4Now to one who works, wages are not reckoned as a gift but as something due. 5But to one who without works trusts him who justifies the ungodly, such faith is reckoned as righteousness. 6So also David speaks of the blessedness of those to whom God reckons righteousness apart from works:

7 "Blessed are those whose
      iniquities are forgiven,
   and whose sins are covered;
8 blessed is the one against
      whom the Lord will
      not reckon sin."

9 Is this blessedness, then, pronounced only on the circumcised, or also on the uncircumcised? We say, "Faith was reckoned to Abraham as righteousness." 10How then was it reckoned to him? Was it before or after he had been circumcised? It was not after, but before he was circumcised. 11He received the sign of circumcision as a seal of the righteousness that he had by faith while he was still uncircumcised. The purpose was to make him the ancestor of all who believe without being circumcised and who thus have righteousness reckoned to them, 12and likewise the ancestor of the circumcised who are not only circumcised but who also follow the example of the faith that our ancestor Abraham had before he was circumcised.

GOD'S PROMISE REALIZED THROUGH FAITH

13 For the promise that he would inherit the world did not come to Abraham or to his descendants through the law but through the righteousness of faith. 14If it is the adherents of the law who are to be the heirs, faith is null and the promise is void. 15For the law brings wrath; but where there is no law, neither is there violation.

16 For this reason it depends on faith, in order that the promise may rest on grace and be guaranteed to all his descendants, not only to the adherents of the law but also to those who share the faith of Abraham (for he is the father of all of us, 17as it is written, "I have made you the father of many nations")—in the presence of the God in whom he believed, who gives life to the dead and calls into existence the things that do not exist. 18Hoping against hope, he believed that he would become "the father of many nations," according to what was said, "So numerous shall your descendants be." 19He did not weaken in faith when he considered his own body, which was already[e] as good as dead (for he was

[a] 3.22 Or *through the faith of Jesus Christ*
[b] 3.25 Or *a place of atonement*   [c] 3.26 Or *who has the faith of Jesus*   [d] 4.1 Other ancient authorities read *say about*
[e] 4.19 Other ancient authorities lack *already*

about a hundred years old), or when he considered the barrenness of Sarah's womb. [20]No distrust made him waver concerning the promise of God, but he grew strong in his faith as he gave glory to God, [21]being fully convinced that God was able to do what he had promised. [22]Therefore his faith[a] "was reckoned to him as righteousness." [23]Now the words, "it was reckoned to him," were written not for his sake alone, [24]but for ours also. It will be reckoned to us who believe in him who raised Jesus our Lord from the dead, [25]who was handed over to death for our trespasses and was raised for our justification.

RESULTS OF JUSTIFICATION

5 Therefore, since we are justified by faith, we[b] have peace with God through our Lord Jesus Christ, [2]through whom we have obtained access[c] to this grace in which we stand; and we[d] boast in our hope of sharing the glory of God. [3]And not only that, but we[d] also boast in our sufferings, knowing that suffering produces endurance, [4]and endurance produces character, and character produces hope, [5]and hope does not disappoint us, because God's love has been poured into our hearts through the Holy Spirit that has been given to us.

[6] For while we were still weak, at the right time Christ died for the ungodly. [7]Indeed, rarely will anyone die for a righteous person— though perhaps for a good person someone might actually dare to die. [8]But God proves his love for us in that while we still were sinners Christ died for us. [9]Much more surely then, now that we have been justified by his blood, will we be saved through him from the wrath of God.[e] [10]For if while we were enemies, we were reconciled to God through the death of his Son, much more surely, having been reconciled, will we be saved by his life. [11]But more than that, we even boast in God through our Lord Jesus Christ, through whom we have now received reconciliation.

ADAM AND CHRIST

[12] Therefore, just as sin came into the world through one man, and death came through sin, and so death spread to all because all have sinned— [13]sin was indeed in the world before the law, but sin is not reckoned when there is no law. [14]Yet death exercised dominion from Adam to Moses, even over those whose sins were not like the transgression of Adam, who is a type of the one who was to come.

PEACE IS THE WHOLENESS

OF LIFE AVAILABLE TO US

THROUGH CHRIST.

[15] But the free gift is not like the trespass. For if the many died through the one man's trespass, much more surely have the grace of God and the free gift in the grace of the one man, Jesus Christ, abounded for the many. [16]And the free gift is not like the effect of the one man's sin. For the judgment following one trespass brought condemnation, but the free gift following many trespasses brings justification. [17]If, because of the one man's trespass, death exercised dominion through that one, much more surely will those who receive the abundance of grace and the free gift of righteousness exercise dominion in life through the one man, Jesus Christ.

[18] Therefore just as one man's trespass led to condemnation for all, so one man's act of righteousness leads to justification and life for all. [19]For just as by the one man's disobedience the many were made sinners, so by the one man's obedience the many will be made righteous. [20]But law came in, with the result that the trespass multiplied; but where sin

a 4.22 Gk *Therefore it*   b 5.1 Other ancient authorities read *let us*   c 5.2 Other ancient authorities add *by faith*   d 5.2,3 Or *let us*   e 5.9 Gk *the wrath*

increased, grace abounded all the more, [21]so that, just as sin exercised dominion in death, so grace might also exercise dominion through justification[a] leading to eternal life through Jesus Christ our Lord.

DYING AND RISING WITH CHRIST

6 What then are we to say? Should we continue in sin in order that grace may abound? [2]By no means! How can we who died to sin go on living in it? [3]Do you not know that all of us who have been baptized into Christ Jesus were baptized into his death? [4]Therefore we have been buried with him by baptism into death, so that, just as Christ was raised from the dead by the glory of the Father, so we too might walk in newness of life.

[5] For if we have been united with him in a death like his, we will certainly be united with him in a resurrection like his. [6]We know that our old self was crucified with him so that the body of sin might be destroyed, and we might no longer be enslaved to sin. [7]For whoever has died is freed from sin. [8]But if we have died with Christ, we believe that we will also live with him. [9]We know that Christ, being raised from the dead, will never die again; death no longer has dominion over him. [10]The death he died, he died to sin, once for all; but the life he lives, he lives to God. [11]So you also must consider yourselves dead to sin and alive to God in Christ Jesus.

[12] Therefore, do not let sin exercise dominion in your mortal bodies, to make you obey their passions. [13]No longer present your members to sin as instruments[b] of wickedness, but present yourselves to God as those who have been brought from death to life, and present your members to God as instruments[b] of righteousness. [14]For sin will have no dominion over you, since you are not under law but under grace.

SLAVES OF RIGHTEOUSNESS

[15] What then? Should we sin because we are not under law but under grace? By no means! [16]Do you not know that if you present yourselves to anyone as obedient slaves, you are slaves of the one whom you obey, either of sin, which leads to death, or of obedience, which leads to righteousness? [17]But thanks be to God that you, having once been slaves of sin, have become obedient from the heart to the form of teaching to which you were entrusted, [18]and that you, having been set free from sin, have become slaves of righteousness. [19]I am speaking in human terms because of your natural limitations.[c] For just as you once presented your members as slaves to impurity and to greater and greater iniquity, so now present your members as slaves to righteousness for sanctification.

[a] 5.21 Or *righteousness*   [b] 6.13 Or *weapons*
[c] 6.19 Gk *the weakness of your flesh*

BIBLE IN LIFE

Slaves to Righteousness

Romans 6.18

If we become a slave to a master, then by definition (and to avoid punishment) we must obey that master. Paul says that when we accept the grace of God and salvation through our faith in Jesus Christ, we become slaves to righteousness. That means that we should be attuning our entire hearts, souls and minds—our daily habits, priorities and attitudes—to the perfect life of Jesus Christ. It's not an easy thing to do, but it's not oppressive. It gives us infinite enjoyment of life, and we are no longer bogged down with the troubles of human aspirations. When we elevate our earthly ambitions to the top priority of our lives, we are abandoning the teachings of Christ. Jesus, who set a perfect example for us, was a servant. By accepting God's gift of salvation, we accept a partnership with God Almighty, and in that process, we become servants of God and slaves to righteousness.

20 When you were slaves of sin, you were free in regard to righteousness. **21**So what advantage did you then get from the things of which you now are ashamed? The end of those things is death. **22**But now that you have been freed from sin and enslaved to God, the advantage you get is sanctification. The end is eternal life. **23**For the wages of sin is death, but the free gift of God is eternal life in Christ Jesus our Lord.

AN ANALOGY FROM MARRIAGE

7 Do you not know, brothers and sisters[a]—for I am speaking to those who know the law—that the law is binding on a person only during that person's lifetime? **2**Thus a married woman is bound by the law to her husband as long as he lives; but if her husband dies, she is discharged from the law concerning the husband. **3**Accordingly, she will be called an adulteress if she lives with another man while her husband is alive. But if her husband dies, she is free from that law, and if she marries another man, she is not an adulteress.

4 In the same way, my friends,[a] you have died to the law through the body of Christ, so that you may belong to another, to him who has been raised from the dead in order that we may bear fruit for God. **5**While we were living in the flesh, our sinful passions, aroused by the law, were at work in our members to bear fruit for death. **6**But now we are discharged from the law, dead to that which held us captive, so that we are slaves not under the old written code but in the new life of the Spirit.

THE LAW AND SIN

7 What then should we say? That the law is sin? By no means! Yet, if it had not been for the law, I would not have known sin. I would not have known what it is to covet if the law had not said, "You shall not covet." **8**But sin, seizing an opportunity in the commandment, produced in me all kinds of covetousness. Apart from the law sin lies dead. **9**I was once alive apart from the law, but when the commandment came, sin revived **10**and I died, and the very commandment that promised life proved to be death to me. **11**For sin, seizing an opportunity in the commandment, deceived me and through it killed me. **12**So the law is holy, and the commandment is holy and just and good.

13 Did what is good, then, bring death to me? By no means! It was sin, working death in me through what is good, in order that sin might be shown to be sin, and through the commandment might become sinful beyond measure.

LIVING FOR JESUS IS A CHALLENGE, BUT NOT HARD WORK AT ALL. BY DOING WHAT GOD WANTS—BECOMING SUBSERVIENT TO CHRIST—WE ATTAIN FREEDOM AND JOY.

THE INNER CONFLICT

14 For we know that the law is spiritual; but I am of the flesh, sold into slavery under sin.[b] **15**I do not understand my own actions. For I do not do what I want, but I do the very thing I hate. **16**Now if I do what I do not want, I agree that the law is good. **17**But in fact it is no longer I that do it, but sin that dwells within me. **18**For I know that nothing good dwells within me, that is, in my flesh. I can will what is right, but I cannot do it. **19**For I do not do the good I want, but the evil I do not want is what I do. **20**Now if I do what I do not want, it is no longer I that do it, but sin that dwells within me.

21 So I find it to be a law that when I want to do what is good, evil lies

---

[a] **7.1,4** Gk *brothers*   [b] **7.14** Gk *sold under sin*

close at hand. 22For I delight in the law of God in my inmost self, 23but I see in my members another law at war with the law of my mind, making me captive to the law of sin that dwells in my members. 24Wretched man that I am! Who will rescue me from this body of death? 25Thanks be to God through Jesus Christ our Lord!

So then, with my mind I am a slave to the law of God, but with my flesh I am a slave to the law of sin.

LIFE IN THE SPIRIT

8 There is therefore now no condemnation for those who are in Christ Jesus. 2For the law of the Spirit[a] of life in Christ Jesus has set you[b] free from the law of sin and of death. 3For God has done what the law, weakened by the flesh, could not do: by sending his own Son in the likeness of sinful flesh, and to deal with sin,[c] he condemned sin in the flesh, 4so that the just requirement of the law might be fulfilled in us, who walk not according to the flesh but according to the Spirit.[a] 5For those who live according to the flesh set their minds on the things of the flesh, but those who live according to the Spirit[a] set their minds on the things of the Spirit.[a] 6To set the mind on the flesh is death, but to set the mind on the Spirit[a] is life and peace. 7For this reason the mind that is set on the flesh is hostile to God; it does not submit to God's law—indeed it cannot, 8and those who are in the flesh cannot please God.

9 But you are not in the flesh; you are in the Spirit,[a] since the Spirit of God dwells in you. Anyone who does not have the Spirit of Christ does not belong to him. 10But if Christ is in you, though the body is dead because of sin, the Spirit[a] is life because of righteousness. 11If the Spirit of him who raised Jesus from the dead dwells in you, he who raised Christ[d] from the dead will give life to your mortal bodies also through[e] his Spirit that dwells in you.

12 So then, brothers and sisters,[f] we are debtors, not to the flesh, to live according to the flesh— 13for if you live according to the flesh, you will die; but if by the Spirit you put to death the deeds of the body, you will live. 14For all who are led by the Spirit of God are children of God. 15For you did not receive a spirit of slavery to fall back into fear, but you have received a spirit of adoption. When we cry, "Abba![g] Father!" 16it is that very Spirit bearing

[a] 8.2,4,5,6,9,10 Or *spirit*   [b] 8.2 Here the Greek word *you* is singular number; other ancient authorities read *me* or *us*   [c] 8.3 Or *and as a sin offering*   [d] 8.11 Other ancient authorities read *the Christ* or *Christ Jesus* or *Jesus Christ*   [e] 8.11 Other ancient authorities read *on account of*   [f] 8.12 Gk *brothers*   [g] 8.15 Aramaic for *Father*

⊢ BIBLE IN LIFE ▷

Repentance

Romans 7.24–25

Paul made here the same kind of confession that every one of us should make if we are courageous enough and introspective enough to confess. We have a natural inclination to think, "Well, I'm not as bad as most other folks." But Paul—by human standards a very good man—was filled with anguish and despair over his sin against God.

When we look at ourselves, we see the law of the Spirit, which is a description of allowing Christ to live his life through us in the power of the Holy Spirit. But the law of sin and death tends to prevail. We should imagine ourselves on trial: "Are you guilty under the law?" We must confess: "Yes, I'm guilty. I'm guilty of not always promoting peace, of discriminating against other people, of not sharing as much as I should with others. I'm guilty of gossip that hurts someone else. I'm guilty, and I stand here ready to be condemned." But if we repent and Christ lives in us, we are not condemned but are set free (see Romans 8.1).

witness[a] with our spirit that we are children of God, [17]and if children, then heirs, heirs of God and joint heirs with Christ—if, in fact, we suffer with him so that we may also be glorified with him.

FUTURE GLORY

[18] I consider that the sufferings of this present time are not worth comparing with the glory about to be revealed to us. [19]For the creation waits with eager longing for the revealing of the children of God; [20]for the creation was subjected to futility, not of its own will but by the will of the one who subjected it, in hope [21]that the creation itself will be set free from its bondage to decay and will obtain the freedom of the glory of the children of God. [22]We know that the whole creation has been groaning in labor pains until now; [23]and not only the creation, but we ourselves, who have the first fruits of the Spirit, groan inwardly while we wait for adoption, the redemption of our bodies. [24]For in[b] hope we were saved. Now hope that is seen is not hope. For who hopes[c] for what is seen? [25]But if we hope for what we do not see, we wait for it with patience.

[26] Likewise the Spirit helps us in our weakness; for we do not know how to pray as we ought, but that very Spirit intercedes[d] with sighs too deep for words. [27]And God,[e] who searches the heart, knows what is the mind of the Spirit, because the Spirit[f] intercedes for the saints according to the will of God.[g]

[28] We know that all things work together for good[h] for those who love God, who are called according to his purpose. [29]For those whom he foreknew he also predestined to be conformed to the image of his Son, in order that he might be the firstborn within a large family.[i] [30]And those whom he predestined he also called; and those whom he called he also justified; and those whom he justified he also glorified.

GOD'S LOVE IN CHRIST JESUS

[31] What then are we to say about these things? If God is for us, who is against us? [32]He who did not withhold his own Son, but gave him up for all of us, will he not with him also give us everything else? [33]Who will bring any charge against God's elect? It is God who justifies. [34]Who is to condemn? It is Christ Jesus, who died, yes, who was raised, who

[a] 8.16 Or [15]a spirit of adoption, by which we cry, "Abba! Father!" [16]The Spirit itself bears witness   [b] 8.24 Or by   [c] 8.24 Other ancient authorities read awaits   [d] 8.26 Other ancient authorities add for us   [e] 8.27 Gk the one   [f] 8.27 Gk he or it   [g] 8.27 Gk according to God   [h] 8.28 Other ancient authorities read God makes all things work together for good, or in all things God works for good   [i] 8.29 Gk among many brothers

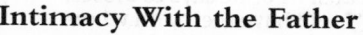

BIBLE IN LIFE

Intimacy With the Father
Romans 8.14–17

What does *Abba* mean in modern-day language? Daddy! If we are really children of God, if we absorb in our hearts and souls the Holy Spirit, then we can be as intimate with God Almighty as with the best earthly dad. Instead of addressing God as "Reverend Creator and remote Father in heaven," we can call God "Daddy." This intimacy of relating to God Almighty is available to us through Jesus Christ. No matter what our trials, doubts, fears, concerns, sorrows or failures might be, we can find strength and assurance by forming a partnership with God Almighty, who knows everything and who has all power. This partnership requires from us a commitment. We make many insignificant choices in life, but the cumulative effect of all those thousands of decisions that we make shapes who we are. Paul extends the offer to us: We can be a child of God, a brother or sister of Jesus Christ, depending upon the choices that we make. It's a beautiful but very sobering promise because the responsibility to choose is on us.

is at the right hand of God, who indeed intercedes for us.[a] 35Who will separate us from the love of Christ? Will hardship, or distress, or persecution, or famine, or nakedness, or peril, or sword? 36As it is written,

"For your sake we are being
    killed all day long;
we are accounted as sheep
    to be slaughtered."

37No, in all these things we are more than conquerors through him who loved us. 38For I am convinced that neither death, nor life, nor angels, nor rulers, nor things present, nor things to come, nor powers, 39nor height, nor depth, nor anything else in all creation, will be able to separate us from the love of God in Christ Jesus our Lord.

GOD'S ELECTION OF ISRAEL

9 I am speaking the truth in Christ—I am not lying; my conscience confirms it by the Holy Spirit— 2I have great sorrow and unceasing anguish in my heart. 3For I could wish that I myself were accursed and cut off from Christ for the sake of my own people,[b] my kindred according to the flesh. 4They are Israelites, and to them belong the adoption, the glory, the covenants, the giving of the law, the worship, and the promises; 5to them belong the patriarchs, and from them, according to the flesh, comes the Messiah,[c] who is over all, God blessed forever.[d] Amen.

6 It is not as though the word of God had failed. For not all Israelites truly belong to Israel, 7and not all of Abraham's children are his true descendants; but "It is through Isaac that descendants shall be named for you." 8This means that it is not the children of the flesh who are the children of God, but the children of the promise are counted as descendants. 9For this is what the promise said, "About this time I will return and Sarah shall have a son." 10Nor is that all; something similar happened to Rebecca when she had conceived children by one husband, our ancestor Isaac. 11Even before they had been born or had done anything

good or bad (so that God's purpose of election might continue, 12not by works but by his call) she was told, "The elder shall serve the younger." 13As it is written,

"I have loved Jacob,
    but I have hated Esau."

14 What then are we to say? Is there injustice on God's part? By no means! 15For he says to Moses,

"I will have mercy on whom
    I have mercy,
and I will have compassion
    on whom I have
    compassion."

16So it depends not on human will or exertion, but on God who shows mercy. 17For the scripture says to Pharaoh, "I have raised you up for

[a] 8.34 Or Is it Christ Jesus... for us?
[b] 9.3 Gk my brothers   [c] 9.5 Or the Christ
[d] 9.5 Or Messiah, who is God over all, blessed forever; or Messiah. May he who is God over all be blessed forever

---

PONDER

This means that it is not the children of the flesh who are the children of God, but the children of the promise are counted as descendants.
    —Romans 9.8

PRAY

We are thankful for the blessings of the covenant, Father, which you gave Abraham in ages past and that are still valid through your Son, Jesus. You love us as your children, and through your grace you forgive us. But we know that with this grace, with this forgiveness, with this love comes an obligation of demonstrable proof through our words and actions that we have been saved, that we reflect you, our Father. Help us to show that we are children of your covenant by reaching out in a spirit of love, service, humility and dedication to others. In the name of our Savior, Jesus Christ, we pray. Amen.

the very purpose of showing my power in you, so that my name may be proclaimed in all the earth." [18]So then he has mercy on whomever he chooses, and he hardens the heart of whomever he chooses.

GOD'S WRATH AND MERCY

[19] You will say to me then, "Why then does he still find fault? For who can resist his will?" [20]But who indeed are you, a human being, to argue with God? Will what is molded say to the one who molds it, "Why have you made me like this?" [21]Has the potter no right over the clay, to make out of the same lump one object for special use and another for ordinary use? [22]What if God, desiring to show his wrath and to make known his power, has endured with much patience the objects of wrath that are made for destruction; [23]and what if he has done so in order to make known the riches of his glory for the objects of mercy, which he has prepared beforehand for glory— [24]including us whom he has called, not from the Jews only but also from the Gentiles? [25]As indeed he says in Hosea,

"Those who were not my people
    I will call 'my people,'
and her who was not beloved
    I will call 'beloved.' "
[26] "And in the very place where it
        was said to them, 'You
        are not my people,'
    there they shall be called
        children of the
        living God."

[27] And Isaiah cries out concerning Israel, "Though the number of the children of Israel were like the sand of the sea, only a remnant of them will be saved; [28]for the Lord will execute his sentence on the earth quickly and decisively."[a] [29]And as Isaiah predicted,

"If the Lord of hosts had not
        left survivors[b] to us,
    we would have fared
        like Sodom
    and been made like Gomorrah."

ISRAEL'S UNBELIEF

[30] What then are we to say? Gentiles, who did not strive for righ-

teousness, have attained it, that is, righteousness through faith; [31]but Israel, who did strive for the righteousness that is based on the law, did not succeed in fulfilling that law. [32]Why not? Because they did not strive for it on the basis of faith, but as if it were based on works. They have stumbled over the stumbling stone, [33]as it is written,

"See, I am laying in Zion a stone
        that will make people
        stumble, a rock that
        will make them fall,
and whoever believes in him[c]
        will not be put to shame."

10 Brothers and sisters,[d] my heart's desire and prayer to God for them is that they may be saved. [2]I can testify that they have a zeal for God, but it is not enlightened. [3]For, being ignorant of the righteousness that comes from God, and seeking to establish their own, they have not submitted to God's righteousness. [4]For Christ is the end of the law so that there may be righteousness for everyone who believes.

SALVATION IS FOR ALL

[5] Moses writes concerning the righteousness that comes from the law, that "the person who does these things will live by them." [6]But the righteousness that comes from faith says, "Do not say in your heart, 'Who will ascend into heaven?' " (that is, to bring Christ down) [7]"or 'Who will descend into the abyss?' " (that is, to bring Christ up from the dead). [8]But what does it say?

"The word is near you,
    on your lips and in your heart"
(that is, the word of faith that we proclaim); [9]because[e] if you confess with your lips that Jesus is Lord and believe in your heart that God raised him from the dead, you will be saved. [10]For one believes with

---

[a] **9.28** Other ancient authorities read *for he will finish his work and cut it short in righteousness, because the Lord will make the sentence shortened on the earth* [b] **9.29** Or *descendants*; Gk *seed* [c] **9.33** Or *trusts in it* [d] **10.1** Gk *Brothers* [e] **10.9** Or *namely, that*

the heart and so is justified, and one confesses with the mouth and so is saved. ¹¹The scripture says, "No one who believes in him will be put to shame." ¹²For there is no distinction between Jew and Greek; the same Lord is Lord of all and is generous to all who call on him. ¹³For, "Everyone who calls on the name of the Lord shall be saved."

14 But how are they to call on one in whom they have not believed? And how are they to believe in one of whom they have never heard? And how are they to hear without someone to proclaim him? ¹⁵And how are they to proclaim him unless they are sent? As it is written, "How beautiful are the feet of those who bring good news!" ¹⁶But not all have obeyed the good news;ᵃ for Isaiah says, "Lord, who has believed our message?" ¹⁷So faith comes from what is heard, and what is heard comes through the word of Christ.ᵇ

18 But I ask, have they not heard? Indeed they have; for

"Their voice has gone out
    to all the earth,
and their words to the
    ends of the world."

¹⁹Again I ask, did Israel not understand? First Moses says,

"I will make you jealous of those
    who are not a nation;
with a foolish nation I will
    make you angry."

²⁰Then Isaiah is so bold as to say,

"I have been found by those
    who did not seek me;
I have shown myself to those
    who did not ask for me."

²¹But of Israel he says, "All day long I have held out my hands to a disobedient and contrary people."

ISRAEL'S REJECTION IS NOT FINAL

11 I ask, then, has God rejected his people? By no means! I myself am an Israelite, a descendant of Abraham, a member of the tribe of Benjamin. ²God has not rejected his people whom he foreknew. Do you not know what the scripture says of Elijah, how he pleads with God against Israel? ³"Lord, they have killed your prophets, they have demolished your altars; I alone am left, and they are seeking my life." ⁴But what is the divine reply to him? "I have kept for myself seven thousand who have not bowed the knee to Baal." ⁵So too at the present time there is a remnant, chosen by grace. ⁶But if it is by grace, it is no longer on the basis of works, otherwise grace would no longer be grace.ᶜ

7 What then? Israel failed to obtain what it was seeking. The elect

---

ᵃ 10.16 Or gospel ᵇ 10.17 Or about Christ; other ancient authorities read of God
ᶜ 11.6 Other ancient authorities add But if it is by works, it is no longer on the basis of grace, otherwise work would no longer be work

---

BIBLE IN LIFE ▷

Christ, the Culmination of the Law   Romans 10.4

Before Christ, people believed that if they kept the ten commandments and observed all the details of the law, they would be accepted by God as righteous and receive salvation. However, by Jesus' day, the Pharisees had delineated about 600 laws that had to be kept—concerning exactly what a person could do on the sabbath day, for example, or exactly how one had to bathe before worshiping. But how do we relate to the law? In Romans 8, Paul says the law is important, but not the way to salvation. We don't earn salvation through compliance with the law. We receive salvation because Christ took the punishment for our sins. Our faith in Christ gives us forgiveness for our sins and reconciliation with God. But because of our faith, we should be more deeply committed to the observance of God's laws as demonstrated by the life of Jesus—peace, justice, truth, humility, service, patience, forgiveness, thanksgiving to God, compassion for others, sharing what we have and love for the unlovable.

obtained it, but the rest were hardened, [8]as it is written,

"God gave them a sluggish spirit,
　eyes that would not see
　and ears that would not hear,
　down to this very day."
[9]And David says,
"Let their table become a
　　snare and a trap,
　a stumbling block and a
　　retribution for them;
[10] let their eyes be darkened so
　　that they cannot see,
　and keep their backs
　　forever bent."

THE SALVATION OF
THE GENTILES

[11] So I ask, have they stumbled so as to fall? By no means! But through their stumbling[a] salvation has come to the Gentiles, so as to make Israel[b] jealous. [12]Now if their stumbling[a] means riches for the world, and if their defeat means riches for Gentiles, how much more will their full inclusion mean!

[13] Now I am speaking to you Gentiles. Inasmuch then as I am an apostle to the Gentiles, I glorify my ministry [14]in order to make my own people[c] jealous, and thus save some of them. [15]For if their rejection is the reconciliation of the world, what will their acceptance be but life from the dead! [16]If the part of the dough offered as first fruits is holy, then the whole batch is holy; and if the root is holy, then the branches also are holy.

[17] But if some of the branches were broken off, and you, a wild olive shoot, were grafted in their place to share the rich root[d] of the olive tree, [18]do not boast over the branches. If you do boast, remember that it is not you that support the root, but the root that supports you. [19]You will say, "Branches were broken off so that I might be grafted in." [20]That is true. They were broken off because of their unbelief, but you stand only through faith. So do not become proud, but stand in awe. [21]For if God did not spare the natural branches, perhaps he will not spare you.[e] [22]Note then the kindness and the severity of God: severity toward those who have fallen, but God's kindness toward you, provided you continue in his kindness; otherwise you also will be cut off. [23]And even those of Israel,[f] if they do not persist in unbelief, will be grafted in, for God has the power to graft them in again. [24]For if you have been cut from what is by nature a wild olive tree and grafted, contrary to nature, into a cultivated olive tree, how much more will these natural branches be grafted back into their own olive tree.

ALL ISRAEL WILL BE SAVED

[25] So that you may not claim to be wiser than you are, brothers and sisters,[g] I want you to understand this mystery: a hardening has come upon part of Israel, until the full number of the Gentiles has come in. [26]And so all Israel will be saved; as it is written,
"Out of Zion will come
　　the Deliverer;
　he will banish ungodliness
　　from Jacob."
[27] "And this is my covenant
　　with them,
　when I take away their sins."
[28]As regards the gospel they are enemies of God[h] for your sake; but as regards election they are beloved, for the sake of their ancestors; [29]for the gifts and the calling of God are irrevocable. [30]Just as you were once disobedient to God but have now received mercy because of their disobedience, [31]so they have now been disobedient in order that, by the mercy shown to you, they too may now[i] receive mercy. [32]For God has imprisoned all in disobedience so that he may be merciful to all.

[33] O the depth of the riches and wisdom and knowledge of God! How unsearchable are his judgments and how inscrutable his ways!

[a] 11.11,12 Gk transgression　[b] 11.11 Gk them
[c] 11.14 Gk my flesh　[d] 11.17 Other ancient
authorities read the richness　[e] 11.21 Other
ancient authorities read neither will
he spare you　[f] 11.23 Gk lacks of Israel
[g] 11.25 Gk brothers　[h] 11.28 Gk lacks of God
[i] 11.31 Other ancient authorities lack now

34 "For who has known the
mind of the Lord?
Or who has been his
counselor?"
35 "Or who has given a gift to him,
to receive a gift in return?"
36For from him and through him
and to him are all things. To him be
the glory forever. Amen.

THE NEW LIFE IN CHRIST

12 I appeal to you therefore,
brothers and sisters,ᵃ by the
mercies of God, to present your bodies as a living sacrifice, holy and acceptable to God, which is your spiri-
tualᵇ worship. 2Do not be conformed
to this world,ᶜ but be transformed by
the renewing of your minds, so that
you may discern what is the will of
God—what is good and acceptable
and perfect.ᵈ

3 For by the grace given to me I
say to everyone among you not to
think of yourself more highly than
you ought to think, but to think
with sober judgment, each according to the measure of faith that God
has assigned. 4For as in one body
we have many members, and not all
the members have the same function, 5so we, who are many, are one
body in Christ, and individually we
are members one of another. 6We
have gifts that differ according to
the grace given to us: prophecy, in
proportion to faith; 7ministry, in
ministering; the teacher, in teaching; 8the exhorter, in exhortation;
the giver, in generosity; the leader,
in diligence; the compassionate, in
cheerfulness.

MARKS OF THE TRUE CHRISTIAN

9 Let love be genuine; hate what is
evil, hold fast to what is good; 10love
one another with mutual affection;
outdo one another in showing honor.
11Do not lag in zeal, be ardent in spirit,
serve the Lord.ᵉ 12Rejoice in hope,
be patient in suffering, persevere in
prayer. 13Contribute to the needs of the
saints; extend hospitality to strangers.

14 Bless those who persecute you;
bless and do not curse them. 15Rejoice
with those who rejoice, weep with
those who weep. 16Live in harmony
with one another; do not be haughty,
but associate with the lowly;ᶠ do not
claim to be wiser than you are. 17Do
not repay anyone evil for evil, but take
thought for what is noble in the sight
of all. 18If it is possible, so far as it depends on you, live peaceably with all.
19Beloved, never avenge yourselves,
but leave room for the wrath of God;ᵍ
for it is written, "Vengeance is mine,
I will repay, says the Lord." 20No, "if
your enemies are hungry, feed them; if
they are thirsty, give them something
to drink; for by doing this you will
heap burning coals on their heads."
21Do not be overcome by evil, but overcome evil with good.

BEING SUBJECT TO AUTHORITIES

13 Let every person be subject
to the governing authorities;

ᵃ **12.1** Gk *brothers*   ᵇ **12.1** Or *reasonable*
ᶜ **12.2** Gk *age*   ᵈ **12.2** Or *what is the
good and acceptable and perfect will of
God*   ᵉ **12.11** Other ancient authorities read
serve the opportune time   ᶠ **12.16** Or *give
yourselves to humble tasks*   ᵍ **12.19** Gk *the
wrath*

┤ BIBLE IN LIFE ▷

New Creation   Romans 12.2

What does it mean to be a Christian? It means we have received Christ as our Savior and
have become a new creation in him. It means in everyday life, we try to walk as Jesus
walked. Being a Christian—a new creation—requires us constantly to renew our minds
in order not to be constrained and shaped by the world around us (see Romans 12:2).
Sometimes in religious circles we don't want to think too much about the mind. We prefer to think about the heart or the soul, but Paul says we are to renew our minds. How do
we think? What are our priorities? How confidently can we say that we are new creations,
transformed by the renewal of our minds?

for there is no authority except from God, and those authorities that exist have been instituted by God. ²Therefore whoever resists authority resists what God has appointed, and those who resist will incur judgment. ³For rulers are not a terror to good conduct, but to bad. Do you wish to have no fear of the authority? Then do what is good, and you will receive its approval; ⁴for it is God's servant for your good. But if you do what is wrong, you should be afraid, for the authorityᵃ does not bear the sword in vain! It is the servant of God to execute wrath on the wrongdoer. ⁵Therefore one must be subject, not only because of wrath but also because of conscience. ⁶For the same reason you also pay taxes, for the authorities are God's servants, busy with this very thing. ⁷Pay to all what is due them—taxes to whom taxes are due, revenue to whom revenue is due, respect to whom respect is due, honor to whom honor is due.

LOVE FOR ONE ANOTHER

8 Owe no one anything, except to love one another; for the one who loves another has fulfilled the law. ⁹The commandments, "You shall not commit adultery; You shall not murder; You shall not steal; You shall not covet"; and any other commandment, are summed up in this word, "Love your neighbor as yourself." ¹⁰Love does no wrong to a

neighbor; therefore, love is the fulfilling of the law.

CHRISTIAN LOVE IS NOT INITIATED BY US, BUT IS AN OVERFLOW OF WHAT GOD HAS ALREADY DONE FOR US.

AN URGENT APPEAL

11 Besides this, you know what time it is, how it is now the moment for you to wake from sleep. For salvation is nearer to us now than when we became believers; ¹²the night is far gone, the day is near. Let us then lay aside the works of darkness and put on the armor of light; ¹³let us live honorably as in the day, not in reveling and drunkenness, not in debauchery and licentiousness, not in quarreling and jealousy. ¹⁴Instead, put on the Lord Jesus Christ, and make no provision for the flesh, to gratify its desires.

DO NOT JUDGE ANOTHER

14 Welcome those who are weak in faith,ᵇ but not for the

ᵃ 13.4 Gk *it* ᵇ 14.1 Or *conviction*

BIBLE IN LIFE

Agape Love

Romans 12.9–21

When Paul speaks of love, he is describing agape love, which is self-sacrificial love committed to the service of others. It means loving somebody who may not love us back or who doesn't deserve our affection. It means a commitment in advance to perform properly, even when we know something bad is going to happen to us at the hands of another person. It comes from so deeply immersing ourselves in Jesus Christ and his teachings that our spirit is strengthened and we do not succumb to temptations when they arise for hatred, animosity, condemnation and lies about others. This is not something that we can make up our minds to do after a crisis arises and we already have that bad feeling toward somebody else. Paul is telling us to be prepared for it, to commit ourselves in advance to love. We must strengthen our inner feelings with the constant presence of the Holy Spirit, so we are able to emulate what Jesus Christ would do under the same circumstances.

WHOSE AUTHORITY?

*Let every person be subject to the governing authorities; for there is no authority ex-
cept from God, and those authorities that exist have been instituted by God.*

—**Romans 13.1**

Reading Romans 13.1–7 might give us a queasy feeling. Must we always submit to
authority? What would that have meant if we lived in Germany when the authority was
Adolph Hitler? How do we reconcile what Paul is saying in Romans 13 with the realities
of corrupt government and imperfect authorities in the world?

First of all, let's go back and look at the time when Paul wrote this. The authority
was Rome. And Rome was headed by Caesar, who for Romans was both the emperor,
the head of state and, at least to the Romans, a deity. What did this mean as far as
the application of Roman law? The Romans were very wise in that when they took
over a country or a region, they let the local people retain their own God and their own
system of worship provided that they pay their taxes and abide by Roman law. The
Jewish religious leaders operated the temple and synagogues without any interference
from the Romans.

But in Acts 5.27–29, when Peter and other apostles were ordered to stop preaching,
they answered the religious authorities by saying, "We must obey God rather than any
human authority." Does this mean that Paul and Peter disagree? No. There is no conflict between Paul's words and Peter's. Rather, we are to interpret each passage within
its context. Peter was willing to give his life in order to continue to preach the Word
of Christ, even though the authorities said not to preach. Paul did most of his writing
from prison. He complied with all the laws of Caesar, and he's telling the Romans to
do so as well. But Paul also reserved the right to abide by the ultimate laws of God.

Paul never said not to try to change government policies that are contrary to God's
Word. The United States was founded on the right of people to seek redress from an
abusive government. And that is certainly not contrary to what Paul is writing, although
it seems to be if we just look at a few verses by themselves. In 1776, American citizens
rose up against the king of England and established this nation. And our country has
evolved because people exerted influence based upon Christian principles of equality.

We are to respect the law and accommodate the authorities, as Paul said. But we
must not be afraid to try to change a law if it is in direct violation of God's Word. Our
priority as Christians should be to influence the shaping of our government's policies
to comply with the teachings of Jesus Christ: teachings of love and peace and understanding and compassion and service and justice and truth and freedom. We are to
influence society in a way that will further God's kingdom.

Going Deeper

- How do you shape your priorities as far as authority is concerned?
- How should you act as a Christian as a citizen of your country? When should you
  challenge the laws of your country?

purpose of quarreling over opinions. ²Some believe in eating anything, while the weak eat only vegetables. ³Those who eat must not despise those who abstain, and those who abstain must not pass judgment on those who eat; for God has welcomed them. ⁴Who are you to pass judgment on servants of another? It is before their own lord that they stand or fall. And they will be upheld, for the Lord[a] is able to make them stand.

5 Some judge one day to be better than another, while others judge all days to be alike. Let all be fully convinced in their own minds. ⁶Those who observe the day, observe it in honor of the Lord. Also those who eat, eat in honor of the Lord, since they give thanks to God; while those who abstain, abstain in honor of the Lord and give thanks to God.

7 We do not live to ourselves, and we do not die to ourselves. ⁸If we live, we live to the Lord, and if we die, we die to the Lord; so then, whether we live or whether we die, we are the Lord's. ⁹For to this end Christ died and lived again, so that he might be Lord of both the dead and the living.

10 Why do you pass judgment on your brother or sister?[b] Or you, why do you despise your brother or sister?[b] For we will all stand before the judgment seat of God.[c] ¹¹For it is written,

"As I live, says the Lord, every
   knee shall bow to me,
and every tongue shall
   give praise to[d] God."

¹²So then, each of us will be accountable to God.[e]

DO NOT MAKE ANOTHER STUMBLE

13 Let us therefore no longer pass judgment on one another, but resolve instead never to put a stumbling block or hindrance in the way of another.[f] ¹⁴I know and am persuaded in the Lord Jesus that nothing is unclean in itself; but it is unclean for anyone who thinks it unclean. ¹⁵If your brother or sister[b] is being injured by what you eat, you are no longer walking in love. Do not let what you eat cause the ruin of one for whom Christ died. ¹⁶So do not let your good be spoken of as evil. ¹⁷For the kingdom of God is not food and drink but righteousness and peace and joy in the Holy Spirit. ¹⁸The one who thus serves Christ is acceptable to God and has human approval. ¹⁹Let us then pursue what makes for peace and for mutual upbuilding. ²⁰Do not, for the sake of food, destroy the work of God. Everything is indeed clean, but

[a] 14.4 Other ancient authorities read *for God*   [b] 14.10,15 Gk *brother*   [c] 14.10 Other ancient authorities read *of Christ*   [d] 14.11 Or *confess*   [e] 14.12 Other ancient authorities lack *to God*   [f] 14.13 Gk *of a brother*

BIBLE IN LIFE ▷

Clean and Unclean   Romans 14.1–3

The early church was sharply divided about what could and could not be eaten. Certain types of food had always been considered unclean by the Jews. The Jewish converts with a weaker faith were the ones who might not dare to eat unclean meat or meat donated to idols. Those who were stronger or bolder might eat without constraint. Basically, Paul is saying that devout Christians may have different interpretations of the scriptures, but we should not let these differences separate us from one another. Neither believer should take a position of superiority or condemn the other, but all should continue to love and forgive, as did Jesus. If we believe that our salvation does not depend on what we do or don't do, but that our salvation depends on our faith in Christ, then we can understand what Paul is saying here: Despite inevitable differences among Christians on some issues, we must love, respect and work together in the name of Christ.

PONDER

Let us therefore no longer pass judgment on one another, but resolve instead never to put a stumbling block or hindrance in the way of another.
—Romans 14.13

PRAY

O Father, this was a troubling admonition for the early church; we hardly know how to apply it. We recognize that it tells us to be aware of the practices and traditions that divide us, and to focus instead on doing that which most benefits a brother or sister. It is also a warning to us: we will stand before you to answer for the times when we judge others or stand in the way of their worship. Give us strength to resist this temptation and to live in accordance with the teachings of Christ. We ask these things in the name of our Savior. Amen.

it is wrong for you to make others fall by what you eat; [21]it is good not to eat meat or drink wine or do anything that makes your brother or sister[a] stumble.[b] [22]The faith that you have, have as your own conviction before God. Blessed are those who have no reason to condemn themselves because of what they approve. [23]But those who have doubts are condemned if they eat, because they do not act from faith;[c] for whatever does not proceed from faith[c] is sin.[d]

PLEASE OTHERS, NOT YOURSELVES

15 We who are strong ought to put up with the failings of the weak, and not to please ourselves. [2]Each of us must please our neighbor for the good purpose of building up the neighbor. [3]For Christ did not please himself; but, as it is written, "The insults of those who insult you have fallen on me."

[4]For whatever was written in former days was written for our instruction, so that by steadfastness and by the encouragement of the scriptures we might have hope. [5]May the God of steadfastness and encouragement grant you to live in harmony with one another, in accordance with Christ Jesus, [6]so that together you may with one voice glorify the God and Father of our Lord Jesus Christ.

THE GOSPEL FOR JEWS AND GENTILES ALIKE

[7]Welcome one another, therefore, just as Christ has welcomed you, for the glory of God. [8]For I tell you that Christ has become a servant of the circumcised on behalf of the truth of God in order that he might confirm the promises given to the patriarchs, [9]and in order that the Gentiles might glorify God for his mercy. As it is written,

"Therefore I will confess[e] you
        among the Gentiles,
    and sing praises to your name";
[10]and again he says,
    "Rejoice, O Gentiles, with
        his people";
[11]and again,
    "Praise the Lord, all you Gentiles,
        and let all the peoples
            praise him";
[12]and again Isaiah says,
    "The root of Jesse shall come,
        the one who rises to rule
            the Gentiles;
    in him the Gentiles shall hope."
[13]May the God of hope fill you with all joy and peace in believing, so that you may abound in hope by the power of the Holy Spirit.

PAUL'S REASON FOR WRITING SO BOLDLY

14 I myself feel confident about you, my brothers and sisters,[f] that you yourselves are full of goodness, filled with all knowledge, and able to instruct one another. [15]Nevertheless

[a] 14.21 Gk brother   [b] 14.21 Other ancient authorities add or be upset or be weakened   [c] 14.23 Or conviction   [d] 14.23 Other authorities, some ancient, add here 16.25–27   [e] 15.9 Or thank   [f] 15.14 Gk brothers

on some points I have written to you rather boldly by way of reminder, because of the grace given me by God [16]to be a minister of Christ Jesus to the Gentiles in the priestly service of the gospel of God, so that the offering of the Gentiles may be acceptable, sanctified by the Holy Spirit. [17]In Christ Jesus, then, I have reason to boast of my work for God. [18]For I will not venture to speak of anything except what Christ has accomplished[a] through me to win obedience from the Gentiles, by word and deed, [19]by the power of signs and wonders, by the power of the Spirit of God,[b] so that from Jerusalem and as far around as Illyricum I have fully proclaimed the good news[c] of Christ. [20]Thus I make it my ambition to proclaim the good news,[c] not where Christ has already been named, so that I do not build on someone else's foundation, [21]but as it is written,

"Those who have never been
        told of him shall see,
and those who have never
        heard of him shall
        understand."

PAUL'S PLAN TO VISIT ROME

[22] This is the reason that I have so often been hindered from coming to you. [23]But now, with no further place for me in these regions, I desire, as I have for many years, to come to you [24]when I go to Spain. For I do hope to see you on my journey and to be sent on by you, once I have enjoyed your company for a little while. [25]At present, however, I am going to Jerusalem in a ministry to the saints; [26]for Macedonia and Achaia have been pleased to share their resources with the poor among the saints at Jerusalem. [27]They were pleased to do this, and indeed they owe it to them; for if the Gentiles have come to share in their spiritual blessings, they ought also to be of service to them in material things. [28]So, when I have completed this, and have delivered to them what has been collected,[d] I will set out by way of you to Spain; [29]and I know that when I come to you, I will come in the fullness of the blessing[e] of Christ.

[30] I appeal to you, brothers and sisters,[f] by our Lord Jesus Christ and by the love of the Spirit, to join me in earnest prayer to God on my behalf, [31]that I may be rescued from the unbelievers in Judea, and that my ministry[g] to Jerusalem may be acceptable to the saints, [32]so that by God's will I may come to you with joy and be refreshed in your company. [33]The God of peace be with all of you.[h] Amen.

PERSONAL GREETINGS

16 I commend to you our sister Phoebe, a deacon[i] of the church at Cenchreae, [2]so that you may welcome her in the Lord as is fitting for the saints, and help her in whatever she may require from you, for she has been a benefactor of many and of myself as well.

[3] Greet Prisca and Aquila, who work with me in Christ Jesus, [4]and who risked their necks for my life, to whom not only I give thanks, but also all the churches of the Gentiles. [5]Greet also the church in their house. Greet my beloved Epaenetus, who was the first convert[j] in Asia for Christ. [6]Greet Mary, who has worked very hard among you. [7]Greet Andronicus and Junia,[k] my relatives[l] who were in prison with me; they are prominent among the apostles, and they were in Christ before I was. [8]Greet Ampliatus, my beloved in the Lord. [9]Greet Urbanus, our co-worker in Christ, and my beloved Stachys. [10]Greet Apelles, who is approved in Christ. Greet those who belong to the family of Aristobulus. [11]Greet my relative[m] Herodion. Greet those in the Lord who belong to the family

[a] 15.18 Gk *speak of those things that Christ has not accomplished* [b] 15.19 Other ancient authorities read *of the Spirit* or *of the Holy Spirit* [c] 15.19,20 Or *gospel* [d] 15.28 Gk *have sealed to them this fruit* [e] 15.29 Other ancient authorities add *of the gospel* [f] 15.30 Gk *brothers* [g] 15.31 Other ancient authorities read *my bringing of a gift* [h] 15.33 One ancient authority adds 16.25–27 here [i] 16.1 Or *minister* [j] 16.5 Gk *first fruits* [k] 16.7 Or *Junias;* other ancient authorities read *Julia* [l] 16.7 Or *compatriots* [m] 16.11 Or *compatriot*

of Narcissus. 12Greet those workers in the Lord, Tryphaena and Tryphosa. Greet the beloved Persis, who has worked hard in the Lord. 13Greet Rufus, chosen in the Lord; and greet his mother—a mother to me also. 14Greet Asyncritus, Phlegon, Hermes, Patrobas, Hermas, and the brothers and sistersᵃ who are with them. 15Greet Philologus, Julia, Nereus and his sister, and Olympas, and all the saints who are with them. 16Greet one another with a holy kiss. All the churches of Christ greet you.

FINAL INSTRUCTIONS

17 I urge you, brothers and sisters,ᵃ to keep an eye on those who cause dissensions and offenses, in opposition to the teaching that you have learned; avoid them. 18For such people do not serve our Lord Christ, but their own appetites,ᵇ and by smooth talk and flattery they deceive the hearts of the simple-minded. 19For while your obedience is known to all, so that I rejoice over you, I want you to be wise in what is good and guileless in what is evil. 20The God of peace will shortly crush Satan under your feet. The grace of our Lord Jesus Christ be with you.ᶜ

21 Timothy, my co-worker, greets you; so do Lucius and Jason and Sosipater, my relatives.ᵈ

22 I Tertius, the writer of this letter, greet you in the Lord.ᵉ

23 Gaius, who is host to me and to the whole church, greets you. Erastus, the city treasurer, and our brother Quartus, greet you.ᶠ

FINAL DOXOLOGY

25 Now to Godᵍ who is able to strengthen you according to my gospel and the proclamation of Jesus Christ, according to the revelation of the mystery that was kept secret for long ages 26but is now disclosed, and through the prophetic writings is made known to all the Gentiles, according to the command of the eternal God, to bring about the obedience of faith— 27to the only wise God, through Jesus Christ, to whomʰ be the glory forever! Amen.ⁱ

ᵃ 16.14,17 Gk brothers   ᵇ 16.18 Gk their own belly   ᶜ 16.20 Other ancient authorities lack this sentence   ᵈ 16.21 Or compatriots   ᵉ 16.22 Or I Tertius, writing this letter in the Lord, greet you   ᶠ 16.23 Other ancient authorities add verse 24, The grace of our Lord Jesus Christ be with all of you. Amen.   ᵍ 16.25 Gk the one   ʰ 16.27 Other ancient authorities lack to whom. The verse then reads, to the only wise God be the glory through Jesus Christ forever. Amen.   ⁱ 16.27 Other ancient authorities lack 16.25–27 or include it after 14.23 or 15.33; others put verse 24 after verse 27

The First Letter of Paul to the

CORINTHIANS

There's a good chance that Corinth might have ranked first on a "Top 10" list for "The Ancient World's Most Wicked Cities." The Corinthian Christians faced the difficulty of following Jesus Christ in the midst of a contaminated culture. The church had to deal with problems such as sexual immorality, dissension among various groups, Christians suing Christians and misuse of spiritual gifts. Paul's letter addresses these issues, but it also tackles some underlying spiritual issues—inspiring readers with a few words on agape love (chapter 13) and the resurrection (chapter 15). Let this book inspire you to renew your efforts to follow Jesus while living in a sinful world.

SALUTATION

1 Paul, called to be an apostle of Christ Jesus by the will of God, and our brother Sosthenes,

2 To the church of God that is in Corinth, to those who are sanctified in Christ Jesus, called to be saints, together with all those who in every place call on the name of our Lord Jesus Christ, both their Lord[a] and ours:

3 Grace to you and peace from God our Father and the Lord Jesus Christ.

4 I give thanks to my[b] God always for you because of the grace of God that has been given you in Christ Jesus, 5for in every way you have been enriched in him, in speech and knowledge of every kind— 6just as the testimony of[c] Christ has been strengthened among you— 7so that you are not lacking in any spiritual gift as you wait for the revealing of our Lord Jesus Christ. 8He will also strengthen you to the end, so that you may be blameless on the day of our Lord Jesus Christ. 9God is faithful; by him you were called into the fellowship of his Son, Jesus Christ our Lord.

DIVISIONS IN THE CHURCH

10 Now I appeal to you, brothers and sisters,[d] by the name of our Lord Jesus Christ, that all of you be in agreement and that there be no divisions among you, but that you be united in the same mind and the same purpose. 11For it has been reported to me by Chloe's people that there are quarrels among you, my brothers and sisters.[e] 12What I mean is that each of you says, "I belong to Paul," or "I belong to Apollos," or "I belong to Cephas," or "I belong to Christ." 13Has Christ been divided? Was Paul crucified for you? Or were you baptized in the name of Paul? 14I thank God[f] that I baptized none of you except Crispus and Gaius, 15so that no one can say that you were baptized in my name. 16(I did baptize also the household of Stephanas; beyond that, I do not know whether I baptized anyone else.) 17For Christ did not send me to baptize but to proclaim the gospel, and not with eloquent wisdom, so that the cross of Christ might not be emptied of its power.

CHRIST THE POWER AND WISDOM OF GOD

18 For the message about the cross is foolishness to those who are perishing, but to us who are being saved it is the power of God. 19For it is written,
"I will destroy the wisdom
    of the wise,
and the discernment of the
    discerning I will thwart."

---

a 1.2 Gk theirs   b 1.4 Other ancient authorities lack my   c 1.6 Or to   d 1.10 Gk brothers   e 1.11 Gk my brothers   f 1.14 Other ancient authorities read I am thankful

---

BIBLE IN LIFE

Leadership Disputes   1 Corinthians 1.10–13

In the early church, some believers were following different leaders and identifying their faith with that leader. They were elevating or idolizing their favorite preacher or whoever founded their church. Some said they "belonged to Apollos" or "belonged to Paul" or "belonged to Peter." These loyalties caused divisions within the early church. Within the modern-day church, we continue to have that same kind of problem. Some believers argue about the power or authority of pastors as compared to the power and authority of the general congregation. Church members idolize well-known pastors and television preachers, identifying their faith with a fallen human instead of with the perfect Savior, Jesus Christ. All of us—including our leaders—are servants of Christ. Exclusively, we "belong to Jesus Christ."

²⁰Where is the one who is wise? Where is the scribe? Where is the debater of this age? Has not God made foolish the wisdom of the world? ²¹For since, in the wisdom of God, the world did not know God through wisdom, God decided, through the foolishness of our proclamation, to save those who believe. ²²For Jews demand signs and Greeks desire wisdom, ²³but we proclaim Christ crucified, a stumbling block to Jews and foolishness to Gentiles, ²⁴but to those who are the called, both Jews and Greeks, Christ the power of God and the wisdom of God. ²⁵For God's foolishness is wiser than human wisdom, and God's weakness is stronger than human strength.

²⁶ Consider your own call, brothers and sisters:[a] not many of you were wise by human standards,[b] not many were powerful, not many were of noble birth. ²⁷But God chose what is foolish in the world to shame the wise; God chose what is weak in the world to shame the strong; ²⁸God chose what is low and despised in the world, things that are not, to reduce to nothing things that are, ²⁹so that no one[c] might boast in the presence of God. ³⁰He is the source of your life in Christ Jesus, who became for us wisdom from God, and righteousness and sanctification and redemption, ³¹in order that, as it is written, "Let the one who boasts, boast in[d] the Lord."

PROCLAIMING CHRIST CRUCIFIED

2 When I came to you, brothers and sisters,[a] I did not come proclaiming the mystery[e] of God to you in lofty words or wisdom. ²For I decided to know nothing among you except Jesus Christ, and him crucified. ³And I came to you in weakness and in fear and in much trembling. ⁴My speech and my proclamation were not with plausible words of wisdom,[f] but with a demonstration of the Spirit and of power, ⁵so that your faith might rest not on human wisdom but on the power of God.

PONDER

God chose what is foolish in the world to shame the wise; God chose what is weak in the world to shame the strong.
—1 Corinthians 1.27

PRAY

O Father, there are "Christians" who don't believe there is a miracle in the New Testament that actually happened. There are those who try to analyze ancient scriptures and carefully select things that can only be explained in human terms, even though the totality of human understanding makes small strides in understanding the extreme complexity of your universe. The wise of the world are not really wise. But we are thankful that your Son came to earth to show us, in relatively plain terms, the two simple admonitions of Jesus: to love God with all our hearts and souls and to love our fellow human beings as we do ourselves. We pray that we will be among those who "foolishly" believe in these simple truths. Amen.

THE TRUE WISDOM OF GOD

6 Yet among the mature we do speak wisdom, though it is not a wisdom of this age or of the rulers of this age, who are doomed to perish. ⁷But we speak God's wisdom, secret and hidden, which God decreed before the ages for our glory. ⁸None of the rulers of this age understood this; for if they had, they would not have crucified the Lord of glory. ⁹But, as it is written,

"What no eye has seen,
    nor ear heard,
    nor the human heart
        conceived,

---

[a] **1.26; 2.1** Gk brothers   [b] **1.26** Gk according to the flesh   [c] **1.29** Gk no flesh   [d] **1.31** Or of   [e] **2.1** Other ancient authorities read testimony   [f] **2.4** Other ancient authorities read the persuasiveness of wisdom

what God has prepared for
those who love him"—
[10] these things God has revealed to us through the Spirit; for the Spirit searches everything, even the depths of God. [11] For what human being knows what is truly human except the human spirit that is within? So also no one comprehends what is truly God's except the Spirit of God. [12] Now we have received not the spirit of the world, but the Spirit that is from God, so that we may understand the gifts bestowed on us by God. [13] And we speak of these things in words not taught by human wisdom but taught by the Spirit, interpreting spiritual things to those who are spiritual.[a]

[14] Those who are unspiritual[b] do not receive the gifts of God's Spirit, for they are foolishness to them, and they are unable to understand them because they are spiritually discerned. [15] Those who are spiritual discern all things, and they are themselves subject to no one else's scrutiny.

[16] "For who has known the
mind of the Lord
so as to instruct him?"
But we have the mind of Christ.

ON DIVISIONS IN THE CORINTHIAN CHURCH

3 And so, brothers and sisters,[c] I could not speak to you as spiritual people, but rather as people of the flesh, as infants in Christ. [2] I fed you with milk, not solid food, for you were not ready for solid food. Even now you are still not ready, [3] for you are still of the flesh. For as long as there is jealousy and quarreling among you, are you not of the flesh, and behaving according to human inclinations? [4] For when one says, "I belong to Paul," and another, "I belong to Apollos," are you not merely human?

[5] What then is Apollos? What is Paul? Servants through whom you came to believe, as the Lord assigned to each. [6] I planted, Apollos watered, but God gave the growth. [7] So neither the one who plants nor the one who waters is anything, but only

God who gives the growth. [8] The one who plants and the one who waters have a common purpose, and each will receive wages according to the labor of each. [9] For we are God's servants, working together; you are God's field, God's building.

[10] According to the grace of God given to me, like a skilled master builder I laid a foundation, and someone else is building on it. Each builder must choose with care how to build on it. [11] For no one can lay any foundation other than the one that has been laid; that foundation is Jesus Christ. [12] Now if anyone builds on the foundation with gold, silver, precious stones, wood, hay, straw— [13] the work of each builder will become visible, for the Day will disclose it, because it will be revealed

[a] 2.13 Or interpreting spiritual things in spiritual language, or comparing spiritual things with spiritual   [b] 2.14 Or natural   [c] 3.1 Gk brothers

with fire, and the fire will test what sort of work each has done. [14]If what has been built on the foundation survives, the builder will receive a reward. [15]If the work is burned up, the builder will suffer loss; the builder will be saved, but only as through fire.

[16]Do you not know that you are God's temple and that God's Spirit dwells in you?[a] [17]If anyone destroys God's temple, God will destroy that person. For God's temple is holy, and you are that temple.

[18]Do not deceive yourselves. If you think that you are wise in this age, you should become fools so that you may become wise. [19]For the wisdom of this world is foolishness with God. For it is written,

"He catches the wise in
        their craftiness,"
[20]and again,
"The Lord knows the thoughts
        of the wise,
    that they are futile."

[21]So let no one boast about human leaders. For all things are yours, [22]whether Paul or Apollos or Cephas or the world or life or death or the present or the future—all belong to you, [23]and you belong to Christ, and Christ belongs to God.

THE MINISTRY OF THE APOSTLES

4 Think of us in this way, as servants of Christ and stewards of God's mysteries. [2]Moreover, it is required of stewards that they be found trustworthy. [3]But with me it is a very small thing that I should be judged by you or by any human court. I do not even judge myself. [4]I am not aware of anything against myself, but I am not thereby acquitted. It is the Lord who judges me. [5]Therefore do not pronounce judgment before the time, before the Lord comes, who will bring to light the things now hidden in darkness and will disclose the purposes of the heart. Then each one will receive commendation from God.

[6]I have applied all this to Apollos and myself for your benefit, brothers and sisters,[b] so that you may learn through us the meaning of the say-

ing, "Nothing beyond what is written," so that none of you will be puffed up in favor of one against another. [7]For who sees anything different in you?[c] What do you have that you did not receive? And if you received it, why do you boast as if it were not a gift?

[8]Already you have all you want! Already you have become rich! Quite apart from us you have become kings! Indeed, I wish that you had become kings, so that we might be kings with you! [9]For I think that God has exhibited us apostles as last of all, as though sentenced to death, because we have become a spectacle to the world, to angels and to mortals. [10]We are fools for the sake of Christ, but you are wise in Christ. We are weak, but you are strong. You are held in honor, but we in disrepute. [11]To the present hour we are hungry and thirsty, and we are poorly clothed and beaten and homeless, [12]and we grow weary from the work of our own hands. When reviled, we bless; when persecuted, we endure; [13]when slandered, we speak kindly. We have become like the rubbish of the world, the dregs of all things, to this very day.

FATHERLY ADMONITION

14 I am not writing this to make you ashamed, but to admonish you as my beloved children. [15]For though you might have ten thousand guardians in Christ, you do not have many fathers. Indeed, in Christ Jesus I became your father through the gospel. [16]I appeal to you, then, be imitators of me. [17]For this reason I sent[d] you Timothy, who is my beloved and faithful child in the Lord, to remind you of my ways in Christ Jesus, as I teach them everywhere in every church. [18]But some of you, thinking that I am not coming to you, have become arrogant. [19]But I will come to you soon, if the Lord wills, and I will find out not the talk of these arrogant people but their power. [20]For

[a] 3.16 In verses 16 and 17 the Greek word for *you* is plural   [b] 4.6 Gk *brothers*   [c] 4.7 Or *Who makes you different from another?*   [d] 4.17 Or *am sending*

PONDER

For this reason I sent you Timothy, who is my beloved and faithful child in the Lord, to remind you of my ways in Christ Jesus, as I teach them everywhere in every church.

—1 Corinthians 4.17

PRAY

Father, we are thankful for this message from Paul, one of the greatest men who ever lived, who dedicated his life, talent and abilities to your service. Paul sent Timothy to the Corinthians to teach them his "ways in Christ Jesus." Help us to draw strength and inspiration from this reality Paul learned from his Savior: Jesus said, "I am the way." If we're looking for the truth about life, Jesus said, "I am the truth." If we are looking for life itself, the meaning of life, Jesus said, "I am the life." That is the life Paul taught us to live, and we pray in the name of Jesus that we can remember this always. Amen.

the kingdom of God depends not on talk but on power. ²¹What would you prefer? Am I to come to you with a stick, or with love in a spirit of gentleness?

SEXUAL IMMORALITY DEFILES THE CHURCH

5 It is actually reported that there is sexual immorality among you, and of a kind that is not found even among pagans; for a man is living with his father's wife. ²And you are arrogant! Should you not rather have mourned, so that he who has done this would have been removed from among you?

3 For though absent in body, I am present in spirit; and as if present I have already pronounced judgment ⁴in the name of the Lord Jesus on the man who has done such a thing.ᵃ When you are assembled, and my

spirit is present with the power of our Lord Jesus, ⁵you are to hand this man over to Satan for the destruction of the flesh, so that his spirit may be saved in the day of the Lord.ᵇ

6 Your boasting is not a good thing. Do you not know that a little yeast leavens the whole batch of dough? ⁷Clean out the old yeast so that you may be a new batch, as you really are unleavened. For our paschal lamb, Christ, has been sacrificed. ⁸Therefore, let us celebrate the festival, not with the old yeast, the yeast of malice and evil, but with the unleavened bread of sincerity and truth.

SEXUAL IMMORALITY MUST BE JUDGED

9 I wrote to you in my letter not to associate with sexually immoral persons— ¹⁰not at all meaning the immoral of this world, or the greedy and robbers, or idolaters, since you would then need to go out of the world. ¹¹But now I am writing to you not to associate with anyone who bears the name of brother or sisterᶜ who is sexually immoral or greedy, or is an idolater, reviler, drunkard, or robber. Do not even eat with such a one. ¹²For what have I to do with judging those outside? Is it not those who are inside that you are to judge? ¹³God will judge those outside. "Drive out the wicked person from among you."

LAWSUITS AMONG BELIEVERS

6 When any of you has a grievance against another, do you dare to take it to court before the unrighteous, instead of taking it before the saints? ²Do you not know that the saints will judge the world? And if the world is to be judged by you, are you incompetent to try trivial cases? ³Do you not know that we are to judge angels—to say nothing of ordinary matters? ⁴If you have ordinary cases, then, do you appoint as judges those who have no standing in the church?

ᵃ **5.4** Or on the man who has done such a thing in the name of the Lord Jesus
ᵇ **5.5** Other ancient authorities add Jesus
ᶜ **5.11** Gk brother

[5]I say this to your shame. Can it be that there is no one among you wise enough to decide between one believer[a] and another, [6]but a believer[a] goes to court against a believer[a]—and before unbelievers at that?

[7] In fact, to have lawsuits at all with one another is already a defeat for you. Why not rather be wronged? Why not rather be defrauded? [8]But you yourselves wrong and defraud—and believers[b] at that.

[9] Do you not know that wrongdoers will not inherit the kingdom of God? Do not be deceived! Fornicators, idolaters, adulterers, male prostitutes, sodomites, [10]thieves, the greedy, drunkards, revilers, robbers—none of these will inherit the kingdom of God. [11]And this is what some of you used to be. But you were washed, you were sanctified, you were justified in the name of the Lord Jesus Christ and in the Spirit of our God.

THE SMART PERSON IS NOT

THE ONE WHO KNOWS ALL

THE ANSWERS, BUT THE ONE

WHO CONTINUES TO ASK

THE RIGHT QUESTIONS.

GLORIFY GOD IN BODY AND SPIRIT

[12] "All things are lawful for me," but not all things are beneficial. "All things are lawful for me," but I will not be dominated by anything. [13]"Food is meant for the stomach and the stomach for food,"[c] and God will destroy both one and the other. The body is meant not for fornication but for the Lord, and the Lord for the body. [14]And God raised the Lord and will also raise us by his power. [15]Do you not know that your bodies are members of Christ? Should I therefore take the members of Christ and make them members of a prostitute? Never! [16]Do you not know that whoever is united to a prostitute becomes one body with her? For it is said, "The two shall be one flesh." [17]But anyone united to the Lord becomes one spirit with him. [18]Shun fornication! Every sin that a person commits is outside the body; but the fornicator sins against the body itself. [19]Or do you not know that your body is a temple[d] of the Holy Spirit within you, which you have from God, and that you are not your own? [20]For you were bought with a price; therefore glorify God in your body.

DIRECTIONS CONCERNING MARRIAGE

7 Now concerning the matters about which you wrote: "It is well for a man not to touch a woman." [2]But because of cases of sexual immorality, each man should have his own wife and each woman her own husband. [3]The husband should give to his wife her conjugal rights, and likewise the wife to her husband. [4]For the wife does not have authority over her own body, but the husband does; likewise the husband does not have authority over his own body, but the wife does. [5]Do not deprive one another except perhaps by agreement for a set time, to devote yourselves to prayer, and then come together again, so that Satan may not tempt you because of your lack of self-control. [6]This I say by way of concession, not of command. [7]I wish that all were as I myself am. But each has a particular gift from God, one having one kind and another a different kind.

[8] To the unmarried and the widows I say that it is well for them to remain unmarried as I am. [9]But if they are not practicing self-control, they should marry. For it is better to marry than to be aflame with passion.

[10] To the married I give this command—not I but the Lord—that the wife should not separate from her husband [11](but if she does separate, let her remain unmarried or else be

[a] 6.5,6 Gk *brother* [b] 6.8 Gk *brothers*
[c] 6.13 The quotation may extend to the word *other* [d] 6.19 Or *sanctuary*

reconciled to her husband), and that the husband should not divorce his wife.

12 To the rest I say—I and not the Lord—that if any believer[a] has a wife who is an unbeliever, and she consents to live with him, he should not divorce her. 13 And if any woman has a husband who is an unbeliever, and he consents to live with her, she should not divorce him. 14 For the unbelieving husband is made holy through his wife, and the unbelieving wife is made holy through her husband. Otherwise, your children would be unclean, but as it is, they are holy. 15 But if the unbelieving partner separates, let it be so; in such a case the brother or sister is not bound. It is to peace that God has called you.[b] 16 Wife, for all you know, you might save your husband. Husband, for all you know, you might save your wife.

THE LIFE THAT THE LORD HAS ASSIGNED

17 However that may be, let each of you lead the life that the Lord has assigned, to which God called you. This is my rule in all the churches. 18 Was anyone at the time of his call already circumcised? Let him not seek to remove the marks of circumcision. Was anyone at the time of his call uncircumcised? Let him not seek circumcision. 19 Circumcision is nothing, and uncircumcision is nothing; but obeying the commandments of God is everything. 20 Let each of you remain in the condition in which you were called.

21 Were you a slave when called? Do not be concerned about it. Even if you can gain your freedom, make use of your present condition now more than ever.[c] 22 For whoever was called in the Lord as a slave is a freed person belonging to the Lord, just as whoever was free when called is a slave of Christ. 23 You were bought with a price; do not become slaves of human masters. 24 In whatever condition you were called, brothers and sisters,[d] there remain with God.

THE UNMARRIED AND THE WIDOWS

25 Now concerning virgins, I have no command of the Lord, but I give my opinion as one who by the Lord's mercy is trustworthy. 26 I think that, in view of the impending[e] crisis, it is well for you to remain as you are. 27 Are you bound to a wife? Do not seek to be free. Are you free from a wife? Do not seek a wife. 28 But if you marry, you do not sin, and if a virgin marries, she does not sin. Yet those who marry will experience distress in this life,[f] and I would spare you that. 29 I mean, brothers and sisters,[d] the appointed time has grown short; from now on, let even those who have wives be as though they had none, 30 and those who mourn as though they were not mourning, and those who rejoice as though they were not rejoicing, and those who buy as though they had no possessions, 31 and those who deal with the world as though they had no dealings with it. For the present form of this world is passing away.

KNOWLEDGE THAT PUFFS

UP AND FREEDOM THAT

DESTROYS HARMONY ARE

NOT FRUITS OF THE GOSPEL.

WE MUST BALANCE WHAT

WE KNOW AND BELIEVE

AGAINST HOW THIS AFFECTS

OTHER CHRISTIANS. WE

MUST ASK: IS THIS THE

LOVING THING TO DO?

32 I want you to be free from anxieties. The unmarried man is anxious about the affairs of the Lord, how to please the Lord; 33 but the married man is anxious about the affairs of the world, how to please his wife, 34 and his

a 7.12 Gk brother   b 7.15 Other ancient authorities read us   c 7.21 Or avail yourself of the opportunity   d 7.24,29 Gk brothers   e 7.26 Or present   f 7.28 Gk in the flesh

interests are divided. And the unmarried woman and the virgin are anxious about the affairs of the Lord, so that they may be holy in body and spirit; but the married woman is anxious about the affairs of the world, how to please her husband. 35I say this for your own benefit, not to put any restraint upon you, but to promote good order and unhindered devotion to the Lord.

36 If anyone thinks that he is not behaving properly toward his fiancée,[a] if his passions are strong, and so it has to be, let him marry as he wishes; it is no sin. Let them marry. 37But if someone stands firm in his resolve, being under no necessity but having his own desire under control, and has determined in his own mind to keep her as his fiancée,[a] he will do well. 38So then, he who marries his fiancée[a] does well; and he who refrains from marriage will do better.

39 A wife is bound as long as her husband lives. But if the husband dies,[b] she is free to marry anyone she wishes, only in the Lord. 40But in my judgment she is more blessed if she remains as she is. And I think that I too have the Spirit of God.

FOOD OFFERED TO IDOLS

8 Now concerning food sacrificed to idols: we know that "all of us possess knowledge." Knowledge puffs up, but love builds up. 2Anyone who claims to know something does not yet have the necessary knowledge; 3but anyone who loves God is known by him.

4 Hence, as to the eating of food offered to idols, we know that "no idol in the world really exists," and that "there is no God but one." 5Indeed, even though there may be so-called gods in heaven or on earth—as in fact there are many gods and many lords— 6yet for us there is one God, the Father, from whom are all things and for whom we exist, and one Lord, Jesus Christ, through whom are all things and through whom we exist.

7 It is not everyone, however, who has this knowledge. Since some have become so accustomed to idols until now, they still think of the food they eat as food offered to an idol; and their conscience, being weak, is defiled. 8"Food will not bring us close to God."[c] We are no worse off if we do not eat, and no better off if we do. 9But take care that this liberty of yours does not somehow become a stumbling block to the weak. 10For if others see you, who possess knowledge, eating in the temple of an idol, might they not, since their conscience is weak, be encouraged to the point of eating food sacrificed to idols? 11So by your knowledge those weak believers for whom Christ died are destroyed.[d] 12But when you thus sin against members of your family,[e] and wound their conscience when it is weak, you sin against Christ.

[a] 7.36,37,38 Gk *virgin*   [b] 7.39 Gk *falls asleep*
[c] 8.8 The quotation may extend to the end of the verse   [d] 8.11 Gk *the weak brother…is destroyed*   [e] 8.12 Gk *against the brothers*

┤ BIBLE IN LIFE ▷

Our Differences   *1 Corinthians 8.1–13*

We may not struggle with food choices, as the Jewish converts to Christianity in Paul's day did, but there are many issues that divide Christians and other denominations worldwide. When we think we are right about an issue, we tend to spiritualize our own beliefs and imply that anyone who disagrees with us is not only wrong but separate from God. It's tempting for us to think, "I am superior; you are inferior." Paul is saying here, once again, that these differences in our beliefs should not come between us; we should love those with differing opinions. Christ taught us that forgiveness, love, compassion, service, humility, truth and justice are the transcendent things, the things that matter—not the lesser issues of what we eat, the style in which we worship, whether or not we have prayer in school or allow women to be elders and pastors.

13Therefore, if food is a cause of their falling,[a] I will never eat meat, so that I may not cause one of them[b] to fall.

THE RIGHTS OF AN APOSTLE

9 Am I not free? Am I not an apostle? Have I not seen Jesus our Lord? Are you not my work in the Lord? 2If I am not an apostle to others, at least I am to you; for you are the seal of my apostleship in the Lord.

3 This is my defense to those who would examine me. 4Do we not have the right to our food and drink? 5Do we not have the right to be accompanied by a believing wife,[c] as do the other apostles and the brothers of the Lord and Cephas? 6Or is it only Barnabas and I who have no right to refrain from working for a living? 7Who at any time pays the expenses for doing military service? Who plants a vineyard and does not eat any of its fruit? Or who tends a flock and does not get any of its milk?

8 Do I say this on human authority? Does not the law also say the same? 9For it is written in the law of Moses, "You shall not muzzle an ox while it is treading out the grain." Is it for oxen that God is concerned? 10Or does he not speak entirely for our sake? It was indeed written for our sake, for whoever plows should plow in hope and whoever threshes should thresh in hope of a share in the crop. 11If we have sown spiritual good among you, is it too much if we reap your material benefits? 12If others share this rightful claim on you, do not we still more?

Nevertheless, we have not made use of this right, but we endure anything rather than put an obstacle in the way of the gospel of Christ. 13Do you not know that those who are employed in the temple service get their food from the temple, and those who serve at the altar share in what is sacrificed on the altar? 14In the same way, the Lord commanded that those who proclaim the gospel should get their living by the gospel.

15 But I have made no use of any of these rights, nor am I writing this so that they may be applied in my case. Indeed, I would rather die than that—no one will deprive me of my ground for boasting! 16If I proclaim the gospel, this gives me no ground for boasting, for an obligation is laid on me, and woe to me if I do not proclaim the gospel! 17For if I do this of my own will, I have a reward; but if not of my own will, I am entrusted with a commission. 18What then is my reward? Just this: that in my proclamation I may make the gospel free of charge, so as not to make full use of my rights in the gospel.

19 For though I am free with respect to all, I have made myself a slave to all, so that I might win more of them. 20To the Jews I became as a Jew, in order to win Jews. To those under the law I became as one under the law (though I myself am not

[a] 8.13 Gk my brother's falling [b] 8.13 Gk cause my brother [c] 9.5 Gk a sister as wife

---

├─ BIBLE IN LIFE ▷────────────────○

Connecting With Others

1 Corinthians 9.19–20

What does Paul mean by saying, "To the Jews I became as a Jew," and "To those under the law I became as one under the law"? Paul answers this himself; he does these things in order to win as many as possible. He was 100 percent Jew when he was in the temple going through purification rites. He was 100 percent Christian Jew when he met with James and delivered the gifts to the church in Jerusalem (see Acts 21). He was 100 percent Roman citizen when he was about to be flogged (see Acts 22). He never violated his commitment to Christ. He knew that when we identify ourselves with other people, they will be more likely to listen to us. This is an important attribute of human life—defining common ground on which to communicate better. The most important things that can draw people together are shared, deep experiences. What can tie us to those who need to hear about their need for Jesus Christ?

under the law) so that I might win those under the law. 21To those outside the law I became as one outside the law (though I am not free from God's law but am under Christ's law) so that I might win those outside the law. 22To the weak I became weak, so that I might win the weak. I have become all things to all people, that I might by all means save some. 23I do it all for the sake of the gospel, so that I may share in its blessings.

24 Do you not know that in a race the runners all compete, but only one receives the prize? Run in such a way that you may win it. 25Athletes exercise self-control in all things; they do it to receive a perishable wreath, but we an imperishable one. 26So I do not run aimlessly, nor do I box as though beating the air; 27but I punish my body and enslave it, so that after proclaiming to others I myself should not be disqualified.

⊖

PONDER

Athletes exercise self-control in all things; they do it to receive a perishable wreath, but we an imperishable one.
—1 Corinthians 9.25

PRAY

Father, we need to hear these words of Paul, who faced not only challenges and difficulties, but also experienced great transformation in his life. Most of us never expect to have such a transformation, but then few of us enter the strict training that such transformation requires. Help us listen to Paul's words of inspiration, obligation, and opportunity, so that we can also earn the "imperishable wreath," so that within our own small spheres of influence we can "run the race," demonstrating the power of Jesus Christ and our faith in him. Amen.

WARNINGS FROM ISRAEL'S HISTORY

10 I do not want you to be unaware, brothers and sisters,[a] that our ancestors were all under the cloud, and all passed through the sea, 2and all were baptized into Moses in the cloud and in the sea, 3and all ate the same spiritual food, 4and all drank the same spiritual drink. For they drank from the spiritual rock that followed them, and the rock was Christ. 5Nevertheless, God was not pleased with most of them, and they were struck down in the wilderness.

6 Now these things occurred as examples for us, so that we might not desire evil as they did. 7Do not become idolaters as some of them did; as it is written, "The people sat down to eat and drink, and they rose up to play." 8We must not indulge in sexual immorality as some of them did, and twenty-three thousand fell in a single day. 9We must not put Christ[b] to the test, as some of them did, and were destroyed by serpents. 10And do not complain as some of them did, and were destroyed by the destroyer. 11These things happened to them to serve as an example, and they were written down to instruct us, on whom the ends of the ages have come. 12So if you think you are standing, watch out that you do not fall. 13No testing has overtaken you that is not common to everyone. God is faithful, and he will not let you be tested beyond your strength, but with the testing he will also provide the way out so that you may be able to endure it.

14 Therefore, my dear friends,[c] flee from the worship of idols. 15I speak as to sensible people; judge for yourselves what I say. 16The cup of blessing that we bless, is it not a sharing in the blood of Christ? The bread that we break, is it not a sharing in the body of Christ? 17Because there is one bread, we who are many are one body, for we all partake of the one bread. 18Consider the people of

---

[a] 10.1 Gk brothers   [b] 10.9 Other ancient authorities read the Lord   [c] 10.14 Gk my beloved

Israel;[a] are not those who eat the sacrifices partners in the altar? 19What do I imply then? That food sacrificed to idols is anything, or that an idol is anything? 20No, I imply that what pagans sacrifice, they sacrifice to demons and not to God. I do not want you to be partners with demons. 21You cannot drink the cup of the Lord and the cup of demons. You cannot partake of the table of the Lord and the table of demons. 22Or are we provoking the Lord to jealousy? Are we stronger than he?

DO ALL TO THE GLORY OF GOD

23 "All things are lawful," but not all things are beneficial. "All things are lawful," but not all things build up. 24Do not seek your own advantage, but that of the other. 25Eat whatever is sold in the meat market without raising any question on the ground of conscience, 26for "the earth and its fullness are the Lord's." 27If an unbeliever invites you to a meal and you are disposed to go, eat whatever is set before you without raising any question on the ground of conscience. 28But if someone says to you, "This has been offered in sacrifice," then do not eat it, out of consideration for the one who informed you, and for the sake of conscience— 29I mean the other's conscience, not your own. For why should my liberty be subject to the judgment of someone else's conscience? 30If I partake with thankfulness, why should I be denounced because of that for which I give thanks?

FOR WHAT PURPOSES ARE

WE USING OUR GOD-

GIVEN FREEDOM?

31 So, whether you eat or drink, or whatever you do, do everything for the glory of God. 32Give no offense to Jews or to Greeks or to the church of God, 33just as I try to please everyone in everything I do, not seeking my own advantage, but that of many, so that they may be saved. 11 1Be imitators of me, as I am of Christ.

HEAD COVERINGS

2 I commend you because you remember me in everything and maintain the traditions just as I handed them on to you. 3But I want you to understand that Christ is the head of every man, and the husband[b] is the head of his wife,[c] and God is the head of Christ. 4Any man who prays or prophesies with something on his head disgraces his head, 5but any woman who prays or prophesies with her head unveiled disgraces her head—it is one and the same thing as having her head shaved. 6For if a woman will not veil herself, then she should cut off her hair; but if it is disgraceful for a woman to have her hair cut off or to be shaved, she should wear a veil. 7For a man ought not to have his head veiled, since he is the image and reflection[d] of God; but woman is the reflection[d] of man. 8Indeed, man was not made from woman, but woman from man. 9Neither was man created for the sake of woman, but woman for the sake of man. 10For this reason a woman ought to have a symbol of[e] authority on her head,[f] because of the angels. 11Nevertheless, in the Lord woman is not independent of man or man independent of woman. 12For just as woman came from man, so man comes through woman; but all things come from God. 13Judge for yourselves: is it proper for a woman to pray to God with her head unveiled? 14Does not nature itself teach you that if a man wears long hair, it is degrading to him, 15but if a woman has long hair, it is her glory? For her hair is given to her for a covering. 16But if anyone is disposed to

---

a 10.18 Gk *Israel according to the flesh*
b 11.3 The same Greek word means *man or husband*   c 11.3 Or *head of the woman*
d 11.7 Or *glory*   e 11.10 Gk lacks *a symbol of*
f 11.10 Or *have freedom of choice regarding her head*

be contentious—we have no such custom, nor do the churches of God.

ABUSES AT THE LORD'S SUPPER

17 Now in the following instructions I do not commend you, because when you come together it is not for the better but for the worse. 18For, to begin with, when you come together as a church, I hear that there are divisions among you; and to some extent I believe it. 19Indeed, there have to be factions among you, for only so will it become clear who among you are genuine. 20When you come together, it is not really to eat the Lord's supper. 21For when the time comes to eat, each of you goes ahead with your own supper, and one goes hungry and another becomes drunk. 22What! Do you not have homes to eat and drink in? Or do you show contempt for the church of God and humiliate those who have nothing? What should I say to you? Should I commend you? In this matter I do not commend you!

THE INSTITUTION OF THE LORD'S SUPPER

23 For I received from the Lord what I also handed on to you, that the Lord Jesus on the night when he was betrayed took a loaf of bread, 24and when he had given thanks, he broke it and said, "This is my body that is fora you. Do this in remembrance of me." 25In the same way he took the cup also, after supper, saying, "This cup is the new covenant

in my blood. Do this, as often as you drink it, in remembrance of me." 26For as often as you eat this bread and drink the cup, you proclaim the Lord's death until he comes.

PARTAKING OF THE SUPPER UNWORTHILY

27 Whoever, therefore, eats the bread or drinks the cup of the Lord in an unworthy manner will be answerable for the body and blood of the Lord. 28Examine yourselves, and only then eat of the bread and drink of the cup. 29For all who eat and drinkb without discerning the body,c eat and drink judgment against themselves. 30For this reason many of you are weak and ill, and some have died.d 31But if we judged ourselves, we would not be judged. 32But when we are judged by the Lord, we are disciplinede so that we may not be condemned along with the world.

33 So then, my brothers and sisters,f when you come together to eat, wait for one another. 34If you are hungry, eat at home, so that when you come together, it will not be for your condemnation. About the other things I will give instructions when I come.

a 11.24 Other ancient authorities read *is broken for* b 11.29 Other ancient authorities add *in an unworthy manner,* c 11.29 Other ancient authorities read *the Lord's body* d 11.30 Gk *fallen asleep* e 11.32 Or *When we are judged, we are being disciplined by the Lord* f 11.33 Gk *brothers*

⊢ BIBLE IN LIFE ▷

Spiritual Gifts

1 Corinthians 12.1–11

The totality of our potential—our talents, our abilities, our opportunities in life—comes from the Holy Spirit. Paul says there are varieties of gifts, but the same Spirit; there are varieties of services, but the same Lord; there are varieties of activities, but the same God who activates all of them. What do we do with our talents and opportunities? The responsibility for the gifts we are given falls on us. Do we accept what the Spirit has given to us and joyfully use our talents? Or do we brag that our gifts are superior to the gifts of others? Paul warns against that pride: "so that there may be no dissension within the body, but [that] the members may have the same care for one another" (verse 25). In manifesting our gifts, we should all strive for the "common good" (verse 7), which is the expansion and enrichment of Christ's kingdom.

PONDER

Now there are varieties of gifts,
but the same Spirit; and there are
varieties of services, but the same
Lord; and there are varieties of
activities, but it is the same God who
activates all of them in everyone.
—1 Corinthians 12.4–6

PRAY

Father, sometimes our appearance,
natural gifts, and abilities can be a
source of contention among us. We
might be jealous of someone else's
gift of service or feel superior about
our own intellect. But through Paul
you show us that the gifts of your
Spirit are meant to bring us together
in unity. Help us to understand that
we each have gifts given to us by the
same God that work for one purpose,
one standard of living, one set of
principles. These gifts are given to
us by our Savior, Jesus Christ, who
promised us the presence and strength
of the Holy Spirit, available to us on
a daily basis. Give us the grace and
love to see that together we have more
abundant life in you, our Savior. Amen.

SPIRITUAL GIFTS

12 Now concerning spiritual
gifts,[a] brothers and sisters,[b] I
do not want you to be uninformed.
²You know that when you were
pagans, you were enticed and led
astray to idols that could not speak.
³Therefore I want you to understand
that no one speaking by the Spirit of
God ever says "Let Jesus be cursed!"
and no one can say "Jesus is Lord"
except by the Holy Spirit.

4 Now there are varieties of gifts,
but the same Spirit; ⁵and there are
varieties of services, but the same
Lord; ⁶and there are varieties of activities, but it is the same God who
activates all of them in everyone. ⁷To
each is given the manifestation of

the Spirit for the common good. ⁸To
one is given through the Spirit the
utterance of wisdom, and to another
the utterance of knowledge according to the same Spirit, ⁹to another
faith by the same Spirit, to another
gifts of healing by the one Spirit, ¹⁰to
another the working of miracles, to
another prophecy, to another the discernment of spirits, to another various kinds of tongues, to another the
interpretation of tongues. ¹¹All these
are activated by one and the same
Spirit, who allots to each one individually just as the Spirit chooses.

ONE BODY WITH MANY MEMBERS

12 For just as the body is one and
has many members, and all the
members of the body, though many,
are one body, so it is with Christ.
¹³For in the one Spirit we were all
baptized into one body—Jews or
Greeks, slaves or free—and we were
all made to drink of one Spirit.

14 Indeed, the body does not consist of one member but of many. ¹⁵If
the foot would say, "Because I am
not a hand, I do not belong to the
body," that would not make it any
less a part of the body. ¹⁶And if the
ear would say, "Because I am not an
eye, I do not belong to the body," that
would not make it any less a part of
the body. ¹⁷If the whole body were an
eye, where would the hearing be? If
the whole body were hearing, where
would the sense of smell be? ¹⁸But
as it is, God arranged the members
in the body, each one of them, as he
chose. ¹⁹If all were a single member,
where would the body be? ²⁰As it is,
there are many members, yet one
body. ²¹The eye cannot say to the
hand, "I have no need of you," nor
again the head to the feet, "I have no
need of you." ²²On the contrary, the
members of the body that seem to
be weaker are indispensable, ²³and
those members of the body that
we think less honorable we clothe
with greater honor, and our less respectable members are treated with

a **12.1** Or *spiritual persons*   b **12.1** Gk
brothers

greater respect; 24whereas our more respectable members do not need this. But God has so arranged the body, giving the greater honor to the inferior member, 25that there may be no dissension within the body, but the members may have the same care for one another. 26If one member suffers, all suffer together with it; if one member is honored, all rejoice together with it.

27 Now you are the body of Christ and individually members of it. 28And God has appointed in the church first apostles, second prophets, third teachers; then deeds of power, then gifts of healing, forms of assistance, forms of leadership, various kinds of tongues. 29Are all apostles? Are all prophets? Are all teachers? Do all work miracles? 30Do all possess gifts of healing? Do all speak in tongues? Do all interpret? 31But strive for the greater gifts. And I will show you a still more excellent way.

THE GIFT OF LOVE

13 If I speak in the tongues of mortals and of angels, but do not have love, I am a noisy gong or a clanging cymbal. 2And if I have prophetic powers, and understand all mysteries and all knowledge, and if I have all faith, so as to remove mountains, but do not have love, I am nothing. 3If I give away all my possessions, and if I hand over my body so that I may boast,[a] but do not have love, I gain nothing.

4 Love is patient; love is kind; love is not envious or boastful or arrogant 5or rude. It does not insist on its own way; it is not irritable or resentful; 6it does not rejoice in wrongdoing, but rejoices in the truth. 7It bears all things, believes all things, hopes all things, endures all things.

8 Love never ends. But as for prophecies, they will come to an end; as for tongues, they will cease; as for knowledge, it will come to an end. 9For we know only in part, and we prophesy only in part; 10but when the complete comes, the partial will come to an end. 11When I was a child, I spoke like a child, I thought like a child, I reasoned like a child; when I became an adult, I

put an end to childish ways. 12For now we see in a mirror, dimly,[b] but then we will see face to face. Now I know only in part; then I will know fully, even as I have been fully known. 13And now faith, hope, and love abide, these three; and the greatest of these is love.

GIFTS OF PROPHECY AND TONGUES

14 Pursue love and strive for the spiritual gifts, and especially that you may prophesy. 2For those who speak in a tongue do not speak to other people but to God; for nobody understands them, since they are speaking mysteries in the Spirit. 3On the other hand, those who prophesy speak to other people for their upbuilding and encouragement and consolation. 4Those who speak in a tongue build up themselves, but those who prophesy build up the church. 5Now I would like all of you

a 13.3 Other ancient authorities read *body to be burned*   b 13.12 Gk *in a riddle*

BIBLE IN FOCUS

THE GREATEST IS LOVE

And now faith, hope, and love abide, these three; and the greatest of these is love.

—1 Corinthians 13.13

An old friend of mine once told me, "You just have to have two loves in your life: Love for God and love for the person who happens to be in front of you at any particular time." I have never been able to forget that. It's a beautiful thought and compatible with what Paul is telling us about love in 1 Corinthians 13.

As Christians, we should engender in our hearts a love for others, even for those who may be totally unlovable. It isn't enough to just help someone in need or engage in acts of kindness. Paul says, "If I have all faith, so as to remove mountains, but do not have love, I am nothing. If I give away all my possessions . . . but do not have love, I gain nothing" (1 Corinthians 13.2–3). We Christians like to measure our achievement in God's kingdom by good deeds. Yet they have no value if they are done without love.

What does it mean for us when we say love is patient and kind? Paul is saying that love, agape love, is perfectly patient. So, to be patient with someone is a very difficult thing. Each of us is deeply individualistic. And just as we understand our own faults and inadequacies, at least to some degree, we are to understand and allow others to have their own. Love is also perfectly kind; it means always showing others that we care for them, always trying to ascertain their needs and assuage their hurts.

Although 1 Corinthians 13 is often read at weddings, patience and kindness don't just apply to two people who are in love. That's the easy part. Paul is also talking about a greater challenge—showing patience and kindness to people who are not very attractive to us or who might aggravate us. How do we reach out to them with a patient or kind love? Paul says that agape, Christlike, love permits us to do this.

"[Love] does not rejoice in wrongdoing." This is a strange phrase that means that we should never rejoice in an enemy's wrongdoing or rejoice when someone that we despise falls down.

"[Love] rejoices with the truth," including the truth about ourselves. When we face the truth about ourselves, we can correct what we see and move to a more intimate harmony with our Savior. We consider in our hearts and minds what we can do to be complete, to be free, to be close to Christ. We find the answers in this thirteenth chapter of 1 Corinthians and how it relates to our comprehension of the Creator of the universe and of his Son, Jesus Christ. "For God so loved the world that he gave his only Son, so that everyone who believes in him may not perish but may have eternal life" (John 3.16). That's what love is.

Going Deeper

- How can you apply the definition of love to your daily existence?
- How can you love God and love that person, whoever it might be, who happens to be in front of you at any particular time?

to speak in tongues, but even more to prophesy. One who prophesies is greater than one who speaks in tongues, unless someone interprets, so that the church may be built up.

6 Now, brothers and sisters,[a] if I come to you speaking in tongues, how will I benefit you unless I speak to you in some revelation or knowledge or prophecy or teaching? 7It is the same way with lifeless instruments that produce sound, such as the flute or the harp. If they do not give distinct notes, how will anyone know what is being played? 8And if the bugle gives an indistinct sound, who will get ready for battle? 9So with yourselves; if in a tongue you utter speech that is not intelligible, how will anyone know what is being said? For you will be speaking into the air. 10There are doubtless many different kinds of sounds in the world, and nothing is without sound. 11If then I do not know the meaning of a sound, I will be a foreigner to the speaker and the speaker a foreigner to me. 12So with yourselves; since you are eager for spiritual gifts, strive to excel in them for building up the church.

13 Therefore, one who speaks in a tongue should pray for the power to interpret. 14For if I pray in a tongue, my spirit prays but my mind is unproductive. 15What should I do then? I will pray with the spirit, but I will pray with the mind also; I will sing praise with the spirit, but I will sing praise with the mind also. 16Otherwise, if you say a blessing with the spirit, how can anyone in the position of an outsider say the "Amen" to your thanksgiving, since the outsider does not know what you are saying? 17For you may give thanks well enough, but the other person is not built up. 18I thank God that I speak in tongues more than all of you; 19nevertheless, in church I would rather speak five words with my mind, in order to instruct others also, than ten thousand words in a tongue.

20 Brothers and sisters,[a] do not be children in your thinking; rather, be infants in evil, but in thinking be adults. 21In the law it is written,
"By people of strange tongues
    and by the lips of foreigners
I will speak to this people;
    yet even then they will
        not listen to me,"
says the Lord. 22Tongues, then, are a sign not for believers but for unbelievers, while prophecy is not for unbelievers but for believers. 23If, therefore, the whole church comes together and all speak in tongues, and outsiders or unbelievers enter, will they not say that you are out of your mind? 24But if all prophesy, an unbeliever or outsider who enters is reproved by all and called to account by all. 25After the secrets of the unbeliever's heart are disclosed, that person will bow down before God

a 14.6,20 Gk brothers

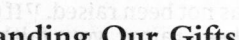

BIBLE IN LIFE

Expanding Our Gifts   *1 Corinthians 14.12*

God gives Christians a diversity of spiritual gifts. Sometimes those gifts must be nurtured and developed. Just as we're not born with the automatic ability to play a sport or an instrument, we're also not born with the immediate ability to build up the church with our spiritual gifts. They must be cultivated over time. With courage we should analyze our own character, interests, motivations and talents. Sadly, many of us stumble through life without ever searching to grow the gifts, talents or opportunities that we've been given. We are too easily satisfied by a minimal life. We don't want to stretch ourselves or be challenged, fearing we might fail or embarrass ourselves by trying something new. No matter what age we might be, we shouldn't be satisfied with the present state of our gifts. What additional gifts do we have within us that might be nurtured in the name of Christ so that we might excel in serving and building up the church?

and worship him, declaring, "God is really among you."

ORDERLY WORSHIP

26 What should be done then, my friends?[a] When you come together, each one has a hymn, a lesson, a revelation, a tongue, or an interpretation. Let all things be done for building up. 27If anyone speaks in a tongue, let there be only two or at most three, and each in turn; and let one interpret. 28But if there is no one to interpret, let them be silent in church and speak to themselves and to God. 29Let two or three prophets speak, and let the others weigh what is said. 30If a revelation is made to someone else sitting nearby, let the first person be silent. 31For you can all prophesy one by one, so that all may learn and all be encouraged. 32And the spirits of prophets are subject to the prophets, 33for God is a God not of disorder but of peace.

(As in all the churches of the saints, 34women should be silent in the churches. For they are not permitted to speak, but should be subordinate, as the law also says. 35If there is anything they desire to know, let them ask their husbands at home. For it is shameful for a woman to speak in church.[b] 36Or did the word of God originate with you? Or are you the only ones it has reached?)

37 Anyone who claims to be a prophet, or to have spiritual powers, must acknowledge that what I am writing to you is a command of the Lord. 38Anyone who does not recognize this is not to be recognized. 39So, my friends,[c] be eager to prophesy, and do not forbid speaking in tongues; 40but all things should be done decently and in order.

THE RESURRECTION OF CHRIST

15 Now I would remind you, brothers and sisters,[a] of the good news[d] that I proclaimed to you, which you in turn received, in which also you stand, 2through which also you are being saved, if you hold firmly to the message that I proclaimed to you—unless you have come to believe in vain.

3 For I handed on to you as of first importance what I in turn had received: that Christ died for our sins in accordance with the scriptures, 4and that he was buried, and that he was raised on the third day in accordance with the scriptures, 5and that he appeared to Cephas, then to the twelve. 6Then he appeared to more than five hundred brothers and sisters[a] at one time, most of whom are still alive, though some have died.[e] 7Then he appeared to James, then to all the apostles. 8Last of all, as to one untimely born, he appeared also to me. 9For I am the least of the apostles, unfit to be called an apostle, because I persecuted the church of God. 10But by the grace of God I am what I am, and his grace toward me has not been in vain. On the contrary, I worked harder than any of them— though it was not I, but the grace of God that is with me. 11Whether then it was I or they, so we proclaim and so you have come to believe.

THE RESURRECTION OF THE DEAD

12 Now if Christ is proclaimed as raised from the dead, how can some of you say there is no resurrection of the dead? 13If there is no resurrection of the dead, then Christ has not been raised; 14and if Christ has not been raised, then our proclamation has been in vain and your faith has been in vain. 15We are even found to be misrepresenting God, because we testified of God that he raised Christ—whom he did not raise if it is true that the dead are not raised. 16For if the dead are not raised, then Christ has not been raised. 17If Christ has not been raised, your faith is futile and you are still in your sins. 18Then those also who have died[e] in Christ have perished. 19If for this life only we have hoped in Christ, we are of all people most to be pitied.

20 But in fact Christ has been raised from the dead, the first fruits of those who have died.[e] 21For since

a 14.26; 15.1,6 Gk brothers   b 14.35 Other ancient authorities put verses 34–35 after verse 40   c 14.39 Gk my brothers   d 15.1 Or gospel   e 15.6,18,20 Gk fallen asleep

death came through a human being, the resurrection of the dead has also come through a human being; 22for as all die in Adam, so all will be made alive in Christ. 23But each in his own order: Christ the first fruits, then at his coming those who belong to Christ. 24Then comes the end,ª when he hands over the kingdom to God the Father, after he has destroyed every ruler and every authority and power. 25For he must reign until he has put all his enemies under his feet. 26The last enemy to be destroyed is death. 27For "Godᵇ has put all things in subjection under his feet." But when it says, "All things are put in subjection," it is plain that this does not include the one who put all things in subjection under him. 28When all things are subjected to him, then the Son himself will also be subjected to the one who put all things in subjection under him, so that God may be all in all.

29 Otherwise, what will those people do who receive baptism on behalf of the dead? If the dead are not raised at all, why are people baptized on their behalf?

30 And why are we putting ourselves in danger every hour? 31I die every day! That is as certain, brothers and sisters,ᶜ as my boasting of you—a boast that I make in Christ Jesus our Lord. 32If with merely human hopes I fought with wild animals at Ephesus, what would I have gained by it? If the dead are not raised,

"Let us eat and drink,
    for tomorrow we die."

33Do not be deceived:
"Bad company ruins
    good morals."

34Come to a sober and right mind, and sin no more; for some people have no knowledge of God. I say this to your shame.

THE RESURRECTION BODY

35 But someone will ask, "How are the dead raised? With what kind of body do they come?" 36Fool! What you sow does not come to life unless it dies. 37And as for what you sow, you do not sow the body that is to be, but a bare seed, perhaps of wheat or of some other grain. 38But God gives it a body as he has chosen, and to each kind of seed its own body. 39Not all flesh is alike, but there is one flesh for human beings, another for animals, another for birds, and another for fish. 40There are both heavenly bodies and earthly bodies, but the glory of the heavenly is one thing, and that of the earthly is another. 41There is one glory of the sun, and another glory of the moon, and another glory of the stars; indeed, star differs from star in glory.

ª 15.24 Or Then come the rest   ᵇ 15.27 Gk he   ᶜ 15.31 Gk brothers

---

⊣ BIBLE IN LIFE ▷

Belief in the Resurrection
1 Corinthians 15.1–34

The resurrection is the foundation of the Christian faith. Because most of us prefer to have empirical proof of something, we struggle to grasp this difficult concept. In essence, Paul says to the Corinthian church, "If you don't believe in this, there is no Christian faith, and we—I, the 12 disciples, the 500 people who saw the risen Jesus—are all nothing but liars." Each of four gospel accounts of the resurrection includes different details, such as who went to the tomb first, who first discovered Jesus' body, the disciples' reactions and the appearance of angels. These differences should reassure us. Because the stories are slightly different, we can have more faith in the authenticity of the gospel. Writers who wanted to deceive their audience would have collaborated to make sure all the details of their stories were exactly the same. Permeating all four Gospels and Paul's writings is the fact of the risen Christ. What are our doubts? Do we truly believe in the resurrection? Without the resurrection, we have no hope.

42 So it is with the resurrection of the dead. What is sown is perishable, what is raised is imperishable. **43**It is sown in dishonor, it is raised in glory. It is sown in weakness, it is raised in power. **44**It is sown a physical body, it is raised a spiritual body. If there is a physical body, there is also a spiritual body. **45**Thus it is written, "The first man, Adam, became a living being"; the last Adam became a life-giving spirit. **46**But it is not the spiritual that is first, but the physical, and then the spiritual. **47**The first man was from the earth, a man of dust; the second man is[a] from heaven. **48**As was the man of dust, so are those who are of the dust; and as is the man of heaven, so are those who are of heaven. **49**Just as we have borne the image of the man of dust, we will[b] also bear the image of the man of heaven.

50 What I am saying, brothers and sisters,[c] is this: flesh and blood cannot inherit the kingdom of God, nor does the perishable inherit the imperishable. **51**Listen, I will tell you a mystery! We will not all die,[d] but we will all be changed, **52**in a moment, in the twinkling of an eye, at the last trumpet. For the trumpet will sound, and the dead will be raised imperishable, and we will be changed. **53**For this perishable body must put on imperishability, and this mortal body must put on immortality. **54**When this perishable body puts on imperishability, and this mortal body puts on immortality, then the saying that is written will be fulfilled:

"Death has been swallowed
    up in victory."
55 "Where, O death, is your victory?
    Where, O death, is your sting?"
56The sting of death is sin, and the power of sin is the law. **57**But thanks be to God, who gives us the victory through our Lord Jesus Christ.

58 Therefore, my beloved,[e] be steadfast, immovable, always excelling in the work of the Lord, because you know that in the Lord your labor is not in vain.

THE COLLECTION FOR THE SAINTS

16 Now concerning the collection for the saints: you

PONDER

The sting of death is sin, and the power of sin is the law. But thanks be to God, who gives us the victory through our Lord Jesus Christ.
—1 Corinthians 15.56–57

PRAY

Father, we hardly have the words to give you praise and thanksgiving for the victory over death that you have given us through Jesus. We spend time and energy avoiding death, worrying about death, preparing for death, but it is amazing to know that Jesus overcame death to open the door to us—the door to eternal life. We pray that, given this victory, we can stop obsessing about death but instead prepare for a resurrected, imperishable life with you. May your kingdom come and your will be done on heaven and earth. Amen.

should follow the directions I gave to the churches of Galatia. **2**On the first day of every week, each of you is to put aside and save whatever extra you earn, so that collections need not be taken when I come. **3**And when I arrive, I will send any whom you approve with letters to take your gift to Jerusalem. **4**If it seems advisable that I should go also, they will accompany me.

PLANS FOR TRAVEL

5 I will visit you after passing through Macedonia—for I intend to pass through Macedonia— **6**and perhaps I will stay with you or even spend the winter, so that you may send me on my way, wherever I go. **7**I do not want to see you now just in passing, for I hope to spend some time with you, if the Lord permits.

[a] **15.47** Other ancient authorities add *the Lord* [b] **15.49** Other ancient authorities read *let us* [c] **15.50** Gk *brothers* [d] **15.51** Gk *fall asleep* [e] **15.58** Gk *beloved brothers*

⁸But I will stay in Ephesus until Pentecost, ⁹for a wide door for effective work has opened to me, and there are many adversaries.

10 If Timothy comes, see that he has nothing to fear among you, for he is doing the work of the Lord just as I am; ¹¹therefore let no one despise him. Send him on his way in peace, so that he may come to me; for I am expecting him with the brothers.

12 Now concerning our brother Apollos, I strongly urged him to visit you with the other brothers, but he was not at all willingᵃ to come now. He will come when he has the opportunity.

FINAL MESSAGES AND GREETINGS

13 Keep alert, stand firm in your faith, be courageous, be strong. ¹⁴Let all that you do be done in love.

15 Now, brothers and sisters,ᵇ you know that members of the household of Stephanas were the first converts in Achaia, and they have devoted themselves to the service of the saints; ¹⁶I urge you to put yourselves at the service of such people, and of everyone who works and toils with them. ¹⁷I rejoice at the coming of Stephanas and Fortunatus and Achaicus, because they have made up for your absence; ¹⁸for they refreshed my spirit as well as yours. So give recognition to such persons.

19 The churches of Asia send greetings. Aquila and Prisca, together with the church in their house, greet you warmly in the Lord. ²⁰All the brothers and sistersᵇ send greetings. Greet one another with a holy kiss.

GIVE FOR HIS GLORY, NOT

OUR OWN. GIVE, TRUSTING

THAT SACRIFICES WILL

BECOME REWARDS.

21 I, Paul, write this greeting with my own hand. ²²Let anyone be accursed who has no love for the Lord. Our Lord, come!ᶜ ²³The grace of the Lord Jesus be with you. ²⁴My love be with all of you in Christ Jesus.ᵈ

ᵃ 16.12 Or it was not at all God's will for him
ᵇ 16.15,20 Gk brothers   ᶜ 16.22 Gk Marana tha. These Aramaic words can also be read Maran atha, meaning Our Lord has come
ᵈ 16.24 Other ancient authorities add Amen

The Second Letter of Paul to the

CORINTHIANS

"Wait a minute! That's not what I said—and that's not who I am."
Thoughts like these must have raced through Paul's mind after his character
and ministry were attacked in Corinth. Among other things, false teachers
were challenging Paul's authority as an apostle and accusing him of stealing church collection money. It's not surprising that Paul gets emotional
and seesaws between despair and joy as he writes. Yet even as he defends
himself, he challenges the Corinthians—and readers today—to let themselves be controlled by Jesus' love when they face conflict and to rely on his
grace when they're weak.

SALUTATION

1 Paul, an apostle of Christ Jesus by the will of God, and Timothy our brother,

To the church of God that is in Corinth, including all the saints throughout Achaia:

2 Grace to you and peace from God our Father and the Lord Jesus Christ.

PAUL'S THANKSGIVING AFTER AFFLICTION

3 Blessed be the God and Father of our Lord Jesus Christ, the Father of mercies and the God of all consolation, **4** who consoles us in all our affliction, so that we may be able to console those who are in any affliction with the consolation with which we ourselves are consoled by God. **5** For just as the sufferings of Christ are abundant for us, so also our consolation is abundant through Christ. **6** If we are being afflicted, it is for your consolation and salvation; if we are being consoled, it is for your consolation, which you experience when you patiently endure the same sufferings that we are also suffering. **7** Our hope for you is unshaken; for we know that as you share in our sufferings, so also you share in our consolation.

DO WE HAVE AN OBLIGATION

TO SUFFER FOR CHRIST?

A STRANGE QUESTION,

BUT ONE PERTINENT TO

THE CHRISTIAN LIFE.

8 We do not want you to be unaware, brothers and sisters,[a] of the affliction we experienced in Asia; for we were so utterly, unbearably crushed that we despaired of life itself. **9** Indeed, we felt that we had received the sentence of death so that we would rely not on ourselves but on God who raises the dead. **10** He who rescued us from so deadly a peril will continue to rescue us; on him we have set our hope that he will rescue us again, **11** as you also join in helping us by your prayers, so that many will give thanks on our[b] behalf for the blessing granted us through the prayers of many.

THE POSTPONEMENT OF PAUL'S VISIT

12 Indeed, this is our boast, the testimony of our conscience: we have behaved in the world with frankness[c] and godly sincerity, not by earthly wisdom but by the grace of God—and all the more toward you. **13** For we write you nothing other than what you can read and also understand; I hope you will understand until the end— **14** as you have already understood us in part—that on the day of the Lord Jesus we are your boast even as you are our boast.

15 Since I was sure of this, I wanted to come to you first, so that you might have a double favor;[d] **16** I wanted to visit you on my way to Macedonia, and to come back to you from Macedonia and have you send me on to Judea. **17** Was I vacillating when I wanted to do this? Do I make my plans according to ordinary human standards,[e] ready to say "Yes, yes" and "No, no" at the same time? **18** As surely as God is faithful, our word to you has not been "Yes and No." **19** For the Son of God, Jesus Christ, whom we proclaimed among you, Silvanus and Timothy and I, was not "Yes and No"; but in him it is always "Yes." **20** For in him every one of God's promises is a "Yes." For this reason it is through him that we say the "Amen," to the glory of God. **21** But it is God who establishes us with you in Christ and has anointed us, **22** by putting his seal on us and giving us his Spirit in our hearts as a first installment.

---

[a] **1.8** Gk *brothers*   [b] **1.11** Other ancient authorities read *your*   [c] **1.12** Other ancient authorities read *holiness*   [d] **1.15** Other ancient authorities read *pleasure*   [e] **1.17** Gk *according to the flesh*

23 But I call on God as witness against me: it was to spare you that I did not come again to Corinth. 24I do not mean to imply that we lord it over your faith; rather, we are workers with you for your joy, because you 2 stand firm in the faith. 1So I made up my mind not to make you another painful visit. 2For if I cause you pain, who is there to make me glad but the one whom I have pained? 3And I wrote as I did, so that when I came, I might not suffer pain from those who should have made me rejoice; for I am confident about all of you, that my joy would be the joy of all of you. 4For I wrote you out of much distress and anguish of heart and with many tears, not to cause you pain, but to let you know the abundant love that I have for you.

FORGIVENESS FOR THE OFFENDER

5 But if anyone has caused pain, he has caused it not to me, but to some extent—not to exaggerate it—to all of you. 6This punishment by the majority is enough for such a person; 7so now instead you should forgive and console him, so that he may not be overwhelmed by excessive sorrow. 8So I urge you to reaffirm your love for him. 9I wrote for this reason: to test you and to know whether you are obedient in everything. 10Anyone whom you forgive, I also forgive. What I have forgiven, if I have forgiven anything, has been for your sake in the presence of Christ. 11And we do this so that we may not be outwitted by Satan; for we are not ignorant of his designs.

PAUL'S ANXIETY IN TROAS

12 When I came to Troas to proclaim the good news of Christ, a door was opened for me in the Lord; 13but my mind could not rest because I did not find my brother Titus there. So I said farewell to them and went on to Macedonia.

14 But thanks be to God, who in Christ always leads us in triumphal procession, and through us spreads in every place the fragrance that comes from knowing him. 15For we are the aroma of Christ to God among those who are being saved and among those who are perishing; 16to the one a fragrance from death to death, to the other a fragrance from life to life. Who is sufficient for these things? 17For we are not peddlers of God's word like so many;[a] but in Christ we speak as persons of

a 2.17 Other ancient authorities read *like the others*

⊢ BIBLE IN LIFE ▷

Forgiving One Another
2 Corinthians 2.1–11

Forgiving one another is not always easy, but it is critical to maintaining good relationships. Rosalynn and I have been married for more than sixty-five years, and we have had some difficult times and sharp differences between us. We usually alternate reading the Bible aloud to each other every night, but there have been times when we were so angry with each other that we just read it by ourselves and went to bed. One time we had a very serious argument, and finally I went out to my woodshop and sliced off, with my finest saw, a very thin piece of beautiful walnut. I wrote this message on it: "To Rosalynn, each evening forever, this is good for an apology or forgiveness as you desire." She's used it several times since then, and so far I've been able to honor it, either with an apology when I'm wrong or forgiveness where Rosalynn has been wrong. Over the years, that symbol has helped us make sure we reconcile with each other before we go to bed at night. As we strive to maintain good relationships in life, we can't underestimate the importance of forgiveness. We are often quick to accept God's forgiveness of our sins, but we need to make sure we extend forgiveness to those who wrong us too. We must not let unresolved anger and resentment destroy our relationship with another person.

sincerity, as persons sent from God and standing in his presence.

MINISTERS OF THE NEW COVENANT

3 Are we beginning to commend ourselves again? Surely we do not need, as some do, letters of recommendation to you or from you, do we? [2]You yourselves are our letter, written on our[a] hearts, to be known and read by all; [3]and you show that you are a letter of Christ, prepared by us, written not with ink but with the Spirit of the living God, not on tablets of stone but on tablets of human hearts.

4 Such is the confidence that we have through Christ toward God. [5]Not that we are competent of ourselves to claim anything as coming from us; our competence is from God, [6]who has made us competent to be ministers of a new covenant, not of letter but of spirit; for the letter kills, but the Spirit gives life.

7 Now if the ministry of death, chiseled in letters on stone tablets,[b] came in glory so that the people of Israel could not gaze at Moses' face because of the glory of his face, a glory now set aside, [8]how much more will the ministry of the Spirit come in glory? [9]For if there was glory in the ministry of condemnation, much more does the ministry of justification abound in glory! [10]Indeed, what once had glory has lost its glory because of the greater glory; [11]for if what was set aside came through glory, much more has the permanent come in glory!

12 Since, then, we have such a hope, we act with great boldness, [13]not like Moses, who put a veil over his face to keep the people of Israel from gazing at the end of the glory that[c] was being set aside. [14]But their minds were hardened. Indeed, to this very day, when they hear the reading of the old covenant, that same veil is still there, since only in Christ is it set aside. [15]Indeed, to this very day whenever Moses is read, a veil lies over their minds; [16]but when one turns to the Lord, the veil is removed. [17]Now the Lord is the Spirit, and where the Spirit of the Lord is, there is freedom. [18]And all of us, with unveiled faces, seeing the glory of the Lord as though reflected in a mirror, are being transformed into the same image from one degree of glory to another; for this comes from the Lord, the Spirit.

TREASURE IN CLAY JARS

4 Therefore, since it is by God's mercy that we are engaged in this ministry, we do not lose heart. [2]We have renounced the shameful things that one hides; we refuse to practice cunning or to falsify God's word; but by the open statement of the truth we commend ourselves to the conscience of everyone in the sight of God. [3]And even if our gospel is veiled, it is veiled to those who are perishing. [4]In their case the god of this world has blinded the minds of the unbelievers, to keep

---

[a] 3.2 Other ancient authorities read *your*
[b] 3.7 Gk *on stones*   [c] 3.13 Gk *of what*

⊣⊢ BIBLE IN LIFE ▷

Spiritual Freedom
2 Corinthians 3.12–18

God has given us the gift of freedom to make our own choices, which is one of the disturbing mysteries of life. We can choose to sin and say, "I don't need to burden myself with people who are different from me or who may be desperately in need. I will walk past them and not acknowledge their existence, because if I get entangled with them it might put a burden on me." Or we can choose to emulate more vividly and persistently in our lives the essence of Christ. Our spiritual lives are embedded in our relationship with Christ and our relationship with the Holy Spirit. Our spiritual lives also involve our relationships with others and how our ties to Christ affect them. Jesus' example gives us a higher standard of peace, truth, justice, compassion, service, humility and forgiveness. As we choose to freely become more like Christ, we fulfill the expectation of our Creator.

them from seeing the light of the gospel of the glory of Christ, who is the image of God. ⁵For we do not proclaim ourselves; we proclaim Jesus Christ as Lord and ourselves as your slaves for Jesus' sake. ⁶For it is the God who said, "Let light shine out of darkness," who has shone in our hearts to give the light of the knowledge of the glory of God in the face of Jesus Christ.

7 But we have this treasure in clay jars, so that it may be made clear that this extraordinary power belongs to God and does not come from us. ⁸We are afflicted in every way, but not crushed; perplexed, but not driven to despair; ⁹persecuted, but not forsaken; struck down, but not destroyed; ¹⁰always carrying in the body the death of Jesus, so that the life of Jesus may also be made visible in our bodies. ¹¹For while we live, we are always being given up to death for Jesus' sake, so that the life of Jesus may be made visible in our mortal flesh. ¹²So death is at work in us, but life in you.

13 But just as we have the same spirit of faith that is in accordance with scripture—"I believed, and so I spoke"—we also believe, and so we speak, ¹⁴because we know that the one who raised the Lord Jesus will raise us also with Jesus, and will bring us with you into his presence. ¹⁵Yes, everything is for your sake, so that grace, as it extends to more and more people, may increase thanksgiving, to the glory of God.

LIVING BY FAITH

16 So we do not lose heart. Even though our outer nature is wasting away, our inner nature is being re-

PONDER

We have this treasure in clay jars, so that it may be made clear that this extraordinary power belongs to God and does not come from us.
—2 Corinthians 4.7

PRAY

Father God, in our daily lives we are tortured sometimes by a struggle between what is wrong and what is right. We struggle with how we should behave and how we should look upon others. We struggle to draw nearer to you. But we forget that through your love— through Jesus' death and resurrection— we are reconciled with you. In ourselves we are weak, but your power is great. We are "clay jars," but you fill us with power to do the tasks you have set for us. Implant this truth in our hearts and minds, we pray in Jesus' name. Amen.

newed day by day. ¹⁷For this slight momentary affliction is preparing us for an eternal weight of glory beyond all measure, ¹⁸because we look not at what can be seen but at what cannot be seen; for what can be seen is temporary, but what cannot be seen is eternal.

5 For we know that if the earthly tent we live in is destroyed, we have a building from God, a house not made with hands, eternal in the heavens. ²For in this tent we groan,

BIBLE IN LIFE ▷

Things Unseen
2 Corinthians 4.18

Paul said that the things that are most important, the things that last forever, are the things we cannot see, such as peace and justice. These are the things we should set as our top priorities as Christians in this secular, mundane human existence. As we look at our lives, and as we assess what is fair, right and just in God's eyes, we must move away from our human standards of excellence and achievement. What are the important things in our lives as measured by Jesus Christ?

longing to be clothed with our heavenly dwelling— [3]if indeed, when we have taken it off[a] we will not be found naked. [4]For while we are still in this tent, we groan under our burden, because we wish not to be unclothed but to be further clothed, so that what is mortal may be swallowed up by life. [5]He who has prepared us for this very thing is God, who has given us the Spirit as a guarantee.

[6]So we are always confident; even though we know that while we are at home in the body we are away from the Lord— [7]for we walk by faith, not by sight. [8]Yes, we do have confidence, and we would rather be away from the body and at home with the Lord. [9]So whether we are at home or away, we make it our aim to please him. [10]For all of us must appear before the judgment seat of Christ, so that each may receive recompense for what has been done in the body, whether good or evil.

THE MINISTRY OF RECONCILIATION

[11]Therefore, knowing the fear of the Lord, we try to persuade others; but we ourselves are well known to God, and I hope that we are also well known to your consciences. [12]We are not commending ourselves to you again, but giving you an opportunity to boast about us, so that you may be able to answer those who boast in outward appearance and not in the heart. [13]For if we are beside ourselves, it is for God; if we are in our right mind, it is for you. [14]For the love of Christ urges us on, because we are convinced that one has died for all; therefore all have died. [15]And he died for all, so that those who live might live no longer for themselves, but for him who died and was raised for them.

[16]From now on, therefore, we regard no one from a human point of view;[b] even though we once knew Christ from a human point of view,[b] we know him no longer in that way. [17]So if anyone is in Christ, there is a new creation: everything old has passed away; see, everything has become new! [18]All this is from God, who reconciled us to himself through Christ, and has given us the ministry of reconciliation; [19]that is, in Christ God was reconciling the world to himself,[c] not counting their trespasses against them, and entrusting the message of reconciliation to us. [20]So we are ambassadors for Christ, since God is making his appeal through us; we entreat you on behalf of Christ, be reconciled to God. [21]For our sake he made him to be sin who knew no sin, so that in him we might become the righteousness of God.

OUR DOING GOOD MAY

REDUCE CRITICISM OF

CHRISTIANITY AND LEAD

OTHERS TO CHRIST.

6 As we work together with him,[d] we urge you also not to accept the grace of God in vain. [2]For he says,

"At an acceptable time I have
listened to you,
and on a day of salvation
I have helped you."

See, now is the acceptable time; see, now is the day of salvation! [3]We are putting no obstacle in anyone's way, so that no fault may be found with our ministry, [4]but as servants of God we have commended ourselves in every way: through great endurance, in afflictions, hardships, calamities, [5]beatings, imprisonments, riots, labors, sleepless nights, hunger; [6]by purity, knowledge, patience, kindness, holiness of spirit, genuine love, [7]truthful speech, and the power of God; with the weapons of righteousness for the right hand and for the left; [8]in honor and dishonor,

[a] 5.3 Other ancient authorities read *put it on*
[b] 5.16 Gk *according to the flesh*   [c] 5.19 Or *God was in Christ reconciling the world to himself*   [d] 6.1 Gk *As we work together*

PONDER

So if anyone is in Christ,
there is a new creation.
—2 Corinthians 5.17

PRAY

O Father, you have given each of us the opportunity to embark on a new life, to become a new creation. We praise you for your life-giving Spirit, the new work you have begun in us. We pray for more hope, joy, peace, adventure and demonstrations of unselfish love. Help us forgive those who might have hurt us and reach out to those around us who are in need, those who might become the most precious friends we will ever have in life. Help us to reach these goals in the name of our gentle Savior, Jesus Christ. Amen.

in ill repute and good repute. We are treated as impostors, and yet are true; 9as unknown, and yet are well known; as dying, and see—we are alive; as punished, and yet not killed; 10as sorrowful, yet always rejoicing; as poor, yet making many rich; as having nothing, and yet possessing everything.

11 We have spoken frankly to you Corinthians; our heart is wide open to you. 12There is no restriction in our affections, but only in yours. 13In return—I speak as to children— open wide your hearts also.

THE TEMPLE OF THE LIVING GOD

14 Do not be mismatched with unbelievers. For what partnership is there between righteousness and lawlessness? Or what fellowship is there between light and darkness? 15What agreement does Christ have with Beliar? Or what does a believer share with an unbeliever? 16What agreement has the temple of God with idols? For wea are the temple of the living God; as God said,

"I will live in them and walk
among them,
and I will be their God,
and they shall be my people.
17 Therefore come out from
them,
and be separate from them,
says the Lord,
and touch nothing unclean;
then I will welcome you,
18 and I will be your father,
and you shall be my sons
and daughters,
says the Lord Almighty."

7 Since we have these promises, beloved, let us cleanse ourselves from every defilement of body and of spirit, making holiness perfect in the fear of God.

PAUL'S JOY AT THE CHURCH'S REPENTANCE

2 Make room in your heartsb for us; we have wronged no one, we have corrupted no one, we have taken advantage of no one. 3I do not say this to condemn you, for I said before that you are in our hearts, to die together and to live together. 4I often boast about you; I have great pride in you; I am filled with consolation; I am overjoyed in all our affliction.

5 For even when we came into Macedonia, our bodies had no rest, but we were afflicted in every way— disputes without and fears within. 6But God, who consoles the downcast, consoled us by the arrival of Titus, 7and not only by his coming, but also by the consolation with which he was consoled about you, as he told us of your longing, your mourning, your zeal for me, so that I rejoiced still more. 8For even if I made you sorry with my letter, I do not regret it (though I did regret it, for I see that I grieved you with that letter, though only briefly). 9Now I rejoice, not because you were grieved, but because your grief led to repentance; for you felt a godly grief, so that you were not harmed in any way by us. 10For godly grief

a 6.16 Other ancient authorities read you
b 7.2 Gk lacks in your hearts

⊕

PONDER

For even when we came into
Macedonia, our bodies had no rest,
but we were afflicted in every way—
disputes without and fears within.
But God, who consoles the downcast,
consoled us by the arrival of Titus.
—2 Corinthians 7.5–6

PRAY

O Father, we are grateful for the
teaching of the apostle Paul, words
that tell us the story of your love and
provision for your disciples as they
brought the Good News to people
in many lands. We know that your
comfort and provision are available
to your people, to those who profess
your name and seek you with all their
hearts. Help us realize that you love us
all equally. Still, we have an obligation
as Christians—endowed with a treasure
of knowledge about our Savior, Jesus
Christ—to share not just our money with
others but our knowledge about truth,
humility, generosity, compassion and
love. In Jesus' name we pray. Amen.

produces a repentance that leads to
salvation and brings no regret, but
worldly grief produces death. ¹¹For
see what earnestness this godly grief
has produced in you, what eagerness to clear yourselves, what indignation, what alarm, what longing,
what zeal, what punishment! At
every point you have proved yourselves guiltless in the matter. ¹²So
although I wrote to you, it was not
on account of the one who did the
wrong, nor on account of the one
who was wronged, but in order
that your zeal for us might be made
known to you before God. ¹³In this
we find comfort.

In addition to our own consolation, we rejoiced still more at the
joy of Titus, because his mind has
been set at rest by all of you. ¹⁴For if I

have been somewhat boastful about
you to him, I was not disgraced; but
just as everything we said to you
was true, so our boasting to Titus
has proved true as well. ¹⁵And his
heart goes out all the more to you,
as he remembers the obedience of all
of you, and how you welcomed him
with fear and trembling. ¹⁶I rejoice,
because I have complete confidence
in you.

ENCOURAGEMENT TO
BE GENEROUS

8 We want you to know, brothers
and sisters,ᵃ about the grace of
God that has been granted to the
churches of Macedonia; ²for during
a severe ordeal of affliction, their
abundant joy and their extreme
poverty have overflowed in a wealth
of generosity on their part. ³For, as I
can testify, they voluntarily gave according to their means, and even beyond their means, ⁴begging us earnestly for the privilegeᵇ of sharing
in this ministry to the saints— ⁵and
this, not merely as we expected; they
gave themselves first to the Lord
and, by the will of God, to us, ⁶so
that we might urge Titus that, as he
had already made a beginning, so he
should also complete this generous
undertakingᶜ among you. ⁷Now as
you excel in everything—in faith, in
speech, in knowledge, in utmost eagerness, and in our love for youᵈ—so
we want you to excel also in this
generous undertaking.ᶜ

⁸ I do not say this as a command,
but I am testing the genuineness of
your love against the earnestness
of others. ⁹For you know the generous actᵉ of our Lord Jesus Christ,
that though he was rich, yet for
your sakes he became poor, so that
by his poverty you might become
rich. ¹⁰And in this matter I am giving my advice: it is appropriate for
you who began last year not only to
do something but even to desire to
do something— ¹¹now finish doing
it, so that your eagerness may be

ᵃ **8.1** Gk brothers   ᵇ **8.4** Gk grace
ᶜ **8.6,7** Gk this grace   ᵈ **8.7** Other ancient
authorities read your love for us   ᵉ **8.9** Gk
the grace

matched by completing it according to your means. [12]For if the eagerness is there, the gift is acceptable according to what one has—not according to what one does not have. [13]I do not mean that there should be relief for others and pressure on you, but it is a question of a fair balance between [14]your present abundance and their need, so that their abundance may be for your need, in order that there may be a fair balance. [15]As it is written,

"The one who had much did
	not have too much,
and the one who had little
	did not have too little."

WE NEED TO UNDERSTAND

THE RELATIONSHIP

BETWEEN PRIVILEGE

AND RESPONSIBILITY,

PROSPERITY AND HELPING

THE POOR, LOVE AND

ACTION, FAITH AND WORKS.

COMMENDATION OF TITUS

[16] But thanks be to God who put in the heart of Titus the same eagerness for you that I myself have. [17]For he not only accepted our appeal, but since he is more eager than ever, he is going to you of his own accord. [18]With him we are sending the brother who is famous among all the churches for his proclaiming the good news;[a] [19]and not only that, but he has also been appointed by the churches to travel with us while we are administering this generous undertaking[b] for the glory of the Lord himself[c] and to show our goodwill. [20]We intend that no one should blame us about this generous gift that we are administering, [21]for we intend to do what is right not only in the Lord's sight but also in the sight of others. [22]And with them we

are sending our brother whom we have often tested and found eager in many matters, but who is now more eager than ever because of his great confidence in you. [23]As for Titus, he is my partner and co-worker in your service; as for our brothers, they are messengers[d] of the churches, the glory of Christ. [24]Therefore openly before the churches, show them the proof of your love and of our reason for boasting about you.

THE COLLECTION FOR CHRISTIANS AT JERUSALEM

9 Now it is not necessary for me to write you about the ministry to the saints, [2]for I know your eagerness, which is the subject of my boasting about you to the people of Macedonia, saying that Achaia has been ready since last year; and your zeal has stirred up most of them. [3]But I am sending the brothers in order that our boasting about you may not prove to have been empty in this case, so that you may be ready, as I said you would be; [4]otherwise, if some Macedonians come with me and find that you are not ready, we would be humiliated—to say nothing of you—in this undertaking.[e] [5]So I thought it necessary to urge the brothers to go on ahead to you, and arrange in advance for this bountiful gift that you have promised, so that it may be ready as a voluntary gift and not as an extortion.

[6]The point is this: the one who sows sparingly will also reap sparingly, and the one who sows bountifully will also reap bountifully. [7]Each of you must give as you have made up your mind, not reluctantly or under compulsion, for God loves a cheerful giver. [8]And God is able to provide you with every blessing in abundance, so that by always having enough of everything, you may share abundantly in every good work. [9]As it is written,

---

[a] 8.18 Or *the gospel*   [b] 8.19 Gk *this grace*
[c] 8.19 Other ancient authorities lack *himself*
[d] 8.23 Gk *apostles*   [e] 9.4 Other ancient authorities add *of boasting*

PONDER

The one who sows sparingly will also reap sparingly, and the one who sows bountifully will also reap bountifully. Each of you must give as you have made up your mind, not reluctantly or under compulsion, for God loves a cheerful giver.

—2 Corinthians 9.6–7

PRAY

O Father, this scripture may be troubling to some of us, but it is also one that offers us expanded lives of righteousness, thanksgiving and security. It offers each of us a transcendent life, not measured by human terms, but measured by the standards of our Savior—achievement based not on the accumulation of things but on justice, humility, service, compassion and love. Give us the will and the means to bless others as God has blessed us. We have so much to be thankful for; we desire to share but sometimes we are reluctant to let go of our wealth, our security. Help us to embrace these principles Paul gave us: to sow generously, to give cheerfully. Inspire us to do these things in the spirit of humility without publicity, without attention to ourselves, in order to strengthen your kingdom on earth. We ask in the name of our Savior. Amen.

"He scatters abroad, he
    gives to the poor;
his righteousness[a]
    endures forever."

[10] He who supplies seed to the sower and bread for food will supply and multiply your seed for sowing and increase the harvest of your righteousness.[a] [11] You will be enriched in every way for your great generosity, which will produce thanksgiving to God through us; [12] for the rendering of this ministry not only supplies the needs of the saints but also over-flows with many thanksgivings to God. [13] Through the testing of this ministry you glorify God by your obedience to the confession of the gospel of Christ and by the generosity of your sharing with them and with all others, [14] while they long for you and pray for you because of the surpassing grace of God that he has given you. [15] Thanks be to God for his indescribable gift!

PAUL DEFENDS HIS MINISTRY

10 I myself, Paul, appeal to you by the meekness and gentleness of Christ—I who am humble when face to face with you, but bold toward you when I am away!— [2] I ask that when I am present I need not show boldness by daring to oppose those who think we are acting according to human standards.[b] [3] Indeed, we live as human beings,[c] but we do not wage war according to human standards;[b] [4] for the weapons of our warfare are not merely human,[d] but they have divine power to destroy strongholds. We destroy arguments [5] and every proud obstacle raised up against the knowledge of God, and we take every thought captive to obey Christ. [6] We are ready to punish every disobedience when your obedience is complete.

[7] Look at what is before your eyes. If you are confident that you belong to Christ, remind yourself of this, that just as you belong to Christ, so also do we. [8] Now, even if I boast a little too much of our authority, which the Lord gave for building you up and not for tearing you down, I will not be ashamed of it. [9] I do not want to seem as though I am trying to frighten you with my letters. [10] For they say, "His letters are weighty and strong, but his bodily presence is weak, and his speech contemptible." [11] Let such people understand that what we say by letter when absent, we will also do when present.

[12] We do not dare to classify or compare ourselves with some of

---

[a] 9.9,10 Or *benevolence*   [b] 10.2,3 Gk *according to the flesh*   [c] 10.3 Gk *in the flesh*
[d] 10.4 Gk *fleshly*

those who commend themselves. But when they measure themselves by one another, and compare themselves with one another, they do not show good sense. 13We, however, will not boast beyond limits, but will keep within the field that God has assigned to us, to reach out even as far as you. 14For we were not overstepping our limits when we reached you; we were the first to come all the way to you with the good news[a] of Christ. 15We do not boast beyond limits, that is, in the labors of others; but our hope is that, as your faith increases, our sphere of action among you may be greatly enlarged, 16so that we may proclaim the good news[a] in lands beyond you, without boasting of work already done in someone else's sphere of action. 17"Let the one who boasts, boast in the Lord." 18For it is not those who commend themselves that are approved, but those whom the Lord commends.

WE TEND TO EXPEND OUR
GOOD WORKS THROUGH AN
EYEDROPPER, CONCERNED
ABOUT HANGING ON TO
EVERYTHING POSSIBLE
AND NOT APPEARING
OVERLY GENEROUS.

PAUL AND THE FALSE APOSTLES

11 I wish you would bear with me in a little foolishness. Do bear with me! 2I feel a divine jealousy for you, for I promised you in marriage to one husband, to present you as a chaste virgin to Christ. 3But I am afraid that as the serpent deceived Eve by its cunning, your thoughts will be led astray from a sincere and pure[b] devotion to Christ. 4For if someone comes and proclaims another Jesus than the one

we proclaimed, or if you receive a different spirit from the one you received, or a different gospel from the one you accepted, you submit to it readily enough. 5I think that I am not in the least inferior to these super-apostles. 6I may be untrained in speech, but not in knowledge; certainly in every way and in all things we have made this evident to you.

7 Did I commit a sin by humbling myself so that you might be exalted, because I proclaimed God's good news[c] to you free of charge? 8I robbed other churches by accepting support from them in order to serve you. 9And when I was with you and was in need, I did not burden anyone, for my needs were supplied by the friends[d] who came from Macedonia. So I refrained and will continue to refrain from burdening you in any way. 10As the truth of Christ is in me, this boast of mine will not be silenced in the regions of Achaia. 11And why? Because I do not love you? God knows I do!

12 And what I do I will also continue to do, in order to deny an opportunity to those who want an opportunity to be recognized as our equals in what they boast about. 13For such boasters are false apostles, deceitful workers, disguising themselves as apostles of Christ. 14And no wonder! Even Satan disguises himself as an angel of light. 15So it is not strange if his ministers also disguise themselves as ministers of righteousness. Their end will match their deeds.

PAUL'S SUFFERINGS AS AN APOSTLE

16 I repeat, let no one think that I am a fool; but if you do, then accept me as a fool, so that I too may boast a little. 17What I am saying in regard to this boastful confidence, I am saying not with the Lord's authority, but as a fool; 18since many boast according to human standards,[e] I will also boast. 19For you gladly put up

a 10.14,16 Or the gospel   b 11.3 Other ancient authorities lack and pure   c 11.7 Gk the gospel of God   d 11.9 Gk brothers   e 11.18 Gk according to the flesh

with fools, being wise yourselves! ²⁰For you put up with it when someone makes slaves of you, or preys upon you, or takes advantage of you, or puts on airs, or gives you a slap in the face. ²¹To my shame, I must say, we were too weak for that!

But whatever anyone dares to boast of—I am speaking as a fool—I also dare to boast of that. ²²Are they Hebrews? So am I. Are they Israelites? So am I. Are they descendants of Abraham? So am I. ²³Are they ministers of Christ? I am talking like a madman—I am a better one: with far greater labors, far more imprisonments, with countless floggings, and often near death. ²⁴Five times I have received from the Jews the forty lashes minus one. ²⁵Three times I was beaten with rods. Once I received a stoning. Three times I was shipwrecked; for a night and a day I was adrift at sea; ²⁶on frequent journeys, in danger from rivers, danger from bandits, danger from my own people, danger from Gentiles, danger in the city, danger in the wilderness, danger at sea, danger from false brothers and sisters;ᵃ ²⁷in toil and hardship, through many a sleepless night, hungry and thirsty, often without food, cold and naked. ²⁸And, besides other things, I am under daily pressure because of my anxiety for all the churches. ²⁹Who is weak, and I am not weak? Who is made to stumble, and I am not indignant?

³⁰If I must boast, I will boast of the things that show my weakness. ³¹The God and Father of the Lord Jesus (blessed be he forever!) knows that I do not lie. ³²In Damascus, the governorᵇ under King Aretas guarded the city of Damascus in order toᶜ seize me, ³³but I was let down in a basket through a window in the wall,ᵈ and escaped from his hands.

PAUL'S VISIONS AND
REVELATIONS

12 It is necessary to boast; nothing is to be gained by it, but I will go on to visions and revelations of the Lord. ²I know a person in Christ who fourteen years ago

was caught up to the third heaven—whether in the body or out of the body I do not know; God knows. ³And I know that such a person—whether in the body or out of the body I do not know; God knows—⁴was caught up into Paradise and heard things that are not to be told, that no mortal is permitted to repeat. ⁵On behalf of such a one I will boast, but on my own behalf I will not boast, except of my weaknesses. ⁶But if I wish to boast, I will not be a fool, for I will be speaking the truth. But I refrain from it, so that no one may think better of me than what is seen in me or heard from me, ⁷even considering the exceptional character of the revelations. Therefore, to keepᵉ me from being too elated, a thorn was given me in the flesh, a messenger of Satan to torment me, to keep me from being too elated.ᶠ ⁸Three times I appealed to the Lord about this, that it would leave me, ⁹but he said to me, "My grace is sufficient for you, for powerᵍ is made perfect in weakness." So, I will boast all the more gladly of my weaknesses, so that the power of Christ may dwell in me. ¹⁰Therefore I am content with weaknesses, insults, hardships, persecutions, and calamities for the sake of Christ; for whenever I am weak, then I am strong.

PEACE IS NOT THE ABSENCE
OF CONFLICT, BUT GOD'S GIFT
AMID THE STRUGGLES OF LIFE.

PAUL'S CONCERN FOR THE
CORINTHIAN CHURCH

11 I have been a fool! You forced me to it. Indeed you should have

---

ᵃ 11.26 Gk *brothers*   ᵇ 11.32 Gk *ethnarch*
ᶜ 11.32 Other ancient authorities read *and wanted to*   ᵈ 11.33 Gk *through the wall*
ᵉ 12.7 Other ancient authorities read *To keep*
ᶠ 12.7 Other ancient authorities lack *to keep me from being too elated*   ᵍ 12.9 Other ancient authorities read *my power*

PONDER

But he said to me, "My grace is sufficient for you, for power is made perfect in weakness."
—2 Corinthians 12.9

PRAY

Almighty Father, we are often confronted by phrases in your Holy Book that are difficult to understand— like how we are the strongest at the weakest times of our lives. How can we overcome the handicaps that we quite often like to talk about? We like to make vivid in the minds of friends the problems we have, the suffering that we have withstood, in order to prove our own personal strength. But such behavior results in a torturous existence; we never quite feel that our lives are as they should be. We are grateful for the message Paul has given us with a simple answer: we are to put our faith in Jesus—in the love, humility, service, compassion and inclination to forgive others that he established as a perfect example. Help us to remember these things and carry them in our hearts. That is what we pray. Amen.

been the ones commending me, for I am not at all inferior to these super-apostles, even though I am nothing. 12The signs of a true apostle were performed among you with utmost patience, signs and wonders and mighty works. 13How have you been worse off than the other churches, except that I myself did not burden you? Forgive me this wrong!

14 Here I am, ready to come to you this third time. And I will not be a burden, because I do not want what is yours but you; for children ought not to lay up for their parents, but parents for their children. 15I will most gladly spend and be spent for you. If I love you more, am I to be loved less? 16Let

it be assumed that I did not burden you. Nevertheless (you say) since I was crafty, I took you in by deceit. 17Did I take advantage of you through any of those whom I sent to you? 18I urged Titus to go, and sent the brother with him. Titus did not take advantage of you, did he? Did we not conduct ourselves with the same spirit? Did we not take the same steps?

19 Have you been thinking all along that we have been defending ourselves before you? We are speaking in Christ before God. Everything we do, beloved, is for the sake of building you up. 20For I fear that when I come, I may find you not as I wish, and that you may find me not as you wish; I fear that there may perhaps be quarreling, jealousy, anger, selfishness, slander, gossip, conceit, and disorder. 21I fear that when I come again, my God may humble me before you, and that I may have to mourn over many who previously sinned and have not repented of the impurity, sexual immorality, and licentiousness that they have practiced.

FURTHER WARNING

13 This is the third time I am coming to you. "Any charge must be sustained by the evidence of two or three witnesses." 2I warned those who sinned previously and all the others, and I warn them now while absent, as I did when present on my second visit, that if I come again, I will not be lenient— 3since you desire proof that Christ is speaking in me. He is not weak in dealing with you, but is powerful in you. 4For he was crucified in weakness, but lives by the power of God. For we are weak in him,[a] but in dealing with you we will live with him by the power of God.

5 Examine yourselves to see whether you are living in the faith. Test yourselves. Do you not realize that Jesus Christ is in you?—unless, indeed, you fail to meet the test! 6I

a 13.4 Other ancient authorities read with him

hope you will find out that we have not failed. [7]But we pray to God that you may not do anything wrong—not that we may appear to have met the test, but that you may do what is right, though we may seem to have failed. [8]For we cannot do anything against the truth, but only for the truth. [9]For we rejoice when we are weak and you are strong. This is what we pray for, that you may become perfect. [10]So I write these things while I am away from you, so that when I come, I may not have to be severe in using the authority that the Lord has given me for building up and not for tearing down.

FINAL GREETINGS AND BENEDICTION

[11]Finally, brothers and sisters,[a] farewell.[b] Put things in order, listen to my appeal,[c] agree with one another, live in peace; and the God of love and peace will be with you. [12]Greet one another with a holy kiss. All the saints greet you.

[13]The grace of the Lord Jesus Christ, the love of God, and the communion of[d] the Holy Spirit be with all of you.

[a] 13.11 Gk brothers   [b] 13.11 Or rejoice   [c] 13.11 Or encourage one another   [d] 13.13 Or and the sharing in

The Letter of Paul to the

GALATIANS

What is essential for salvation? Circle one.

A. Faith + keeping the Sabbath.

B. Faith + having daily quiet times.

C. Faith in Jesus Christ alone.

D. Faith + attending every church service.

C is the right answer, but we often live as if A, B and D are the required responses. Paul wrote to the Galatians to remind them of the right answer, for false teachers were adding their own requirements to the gospel. Galatians is a clear explanation of what it means to be saved by faith.

SALUTATION

1 Paul an apostle—sent neither by human commission nor from human authorities, but through Jesus Christ and God the Father, who raised him from the dead— [2]and all the members of God's family[a] who are with me,

To the churches of Galatia:

3 Grace to you and peace from God our Father and the Lord Jesus Christ, [4]who gave himself for our sins to set us free from the present evil age, according to the will of our God and Father, [5]to whom be the glory forever and ever. Amen.

THERE IS NO OTHER GOSPEL

6 I am astonished that you are so quickly deserting the one who called you in the grace of Christ and are turning to a different gospel— [7]not that there is another gospel, but there are some who are confusing you and want to pervert the gospel of Christ. [8]But even if we or an angel[b] from heaven should proclaim to you a gospel contrary to what we proclaimed to you, let that one be accursed! [9]As we have said before, so now I repeat, if anyone proclaims to you a gospel contrary to what you received, let that one be accursed!

10 Am I now seeking human approval, or God's approval? Or am I trying to please people? If I were still pleasing people, I would not be a servant[c] of Christ.

PAUL'S VINDICATION OF HIS APOSTLESHIP

11 For I want you to know, brothers and sisters,[d] that the gospel that was proclaimed by me is not of human origin; [12]for I did not receive it from a human source, nor was I taught it, but I received it through a revelation of Jesus Christ.

13 You have heard, no doubt, of my earlier life in Judaism. I was violently persecuting the church of God and was trying to destroy it. [14]I advanced in Judaism beyond many among my people of the same age, for I was far more zealous for the traditions of my ancestors. [15]But when God, who had set me apart before I

PONDER

For I want you to know, brothers and sisters, that the gospel that was proclaimed by me is not of human origin; for I did not receive it from a human source, nor was I taught it, but I received it through a revelation of Jesus Christ.

—Galatians 1.11–12

PRAY

O Father, we are grateful to read the inspired words of Paul. He had a remarkable way of expressing himself, explaining in clear ways how he came to preach the messages that you have for us. Help us open our hearts to receive this message, to let it sink deep into our hearts. Teach us how we can live in accordance with the gospel, and to cherish the good news we received through our Savior, Jesus Christ. We ask in the name of our Savior. Amen.

was born and called me through his grace, was pleased [16]to reveal his Son to me,[e] so that I might proclaim him among the Gentiles, I did not confer with any human being, [17]nor did I go up to Jerusalem to those who were already apostles before me, but I went away at once into Arabia, and afterwards I returned to Damascus.

18 Then after three years I did go up to Jerusalem to visit Cephas and stayed with him fifteen days; [19]but I did not see any other apostle except James the Lord's brother. [20]In what I am writing to you, before God, I do not lie! [21]Then I went into the regions of Syria and Cilicia, [22]and I was still unknown by sight to the churches of Judea that are in Christ; [23]they only heard it said, "The one who formerly was persecuting us is now proclaiming the faith he once

a **1.2** Gk *all the brothers*   b **1.8** Or *a messenger*   c **1.10** Gk *slave*   d **1.11** Gk *brothers*   e **1.16** Gk *in me*

tried to destroy." ²⁴And they glorified God because of me.

PAUL AND THE OTHER APOSTLES

2 Then after fourteen years I went up again to Jerusalem with Barnabas, taking Titus along with me. ²I went up in response to a revelation. Then I laid before them (though only in a private meeting with the acknowledged leaders) the gospel that I proclaim among the Gentiles, in order to make sure that I was not running, or had not run, in vain. ³But even Titus, who was with me, was not compelled to be circumcised, though he was a Greek. ⁴But because of false believersᵃ secretly brought in, who slipped in to spy on the freedom we have in Christ Jesus, so that they might enslave us— ⁵we did not submit to them even for a moment, so that the truth of the gospel might always remain with you. ⁶And from those who were supposed to be acknowledged leaders (what they actually were makes no difference to me; God shows no partiality)—those leaders contributed nothing to me. ⁷On the contrary, when they saw that I had been entrusted with the gospel for the uncircumcised, just as Peter had been entrusted with the gospel for the circumcised ⁸(for he who worked through Peter making him an apostle to the circumcised also worked through me in sending me to the Gentiles), ⁹and when James and Cephas and John, who were acknowledged pillars, recognized the grace that had been given to me, they gave to Barnabas and me the right hand of fellowship, agreeing that we should go to the Gentiles and they to the circumcised. ¹⁰They asked only one thing, that we remember the poor, which was actually what I wasᵇ eager to do.

PAUL REBUKES PETER AT ANTIOCH

¹¹ But when Cephas came to Antioch, I opposed him to his face, because he stood self-condemned; ¹²for until certain people came from James, he used to eat with the Gentiles. But after they came, he drew back and kept himself separate for fear of the circumcision faction. ¹³And the other Jews joined him in this hypocrisy, so that even Barnabas was led astray by their hypocrisy. ¹⁴But when I saw that they were not acting consistently with the truth of the gospel, I said to Cephas before them all, "If you, though a Jew, live like a Gentile and not like a Jew, how can you compel the Gentiles to live like Jews?"ᶜ

FAITH AND WORKS ARE
INSEPARABLE PARTNERS,
APPLIED THROUGH
FORGIVENESS AND LOVE
FOR OTHERS AND IN THE
DAILY EXPERIENCES OF
A CHRISTIAN LIFE.

JEWS AND GENTILES ARE SAVED BY FAITH

¹⁵ We ourselves are Jews by birth and not Gentile sinners; ¹⁶yet we know that a person is justifiedᵈ not by the works of the law but through faith in Jesus Christ.ᵉ And we have come to believe in Christ Jesus, so that we might be justified by faith in Christ,ᶠ and not by doing the works of the law, because no one will be justified by the works of the law. ¹⁷But if, in our effort to be justified in Christ, we ourselves have been found to be sinners, is Christ then a servant of sin? Certainly not! ¹⁸But if I build up again the very things that I once tore down, then I demonstrate that I am a transgressor.

ᵃ 2.4 Gk *false brothers*   ᵇ 2.10 Or *had been*   ᶜ 2.14 Some interpreters hold that the quotation extends into the following paragraph   ᵈ 2.16 Or *reckoned as righteous;* and so elsewhere   ᵉ 2.16 Or *the faith of Jesus Christ*   ᶠ 2.16 Or *the faith of Christ*

19For through the law I died to the law, so that I might live to God. I have been crucified with Christ; 20and it is no longer I who live, but it is Christ who lives in me. And the life I now live in the flesh I live by faith in the Son of God,ᵃ who loved me and gave himself for me. 21I do not nullify the grace of God; for if justificationᵇ comes through the law, then Christ died for nothing.

LAW OR FAITH

3 You foolish Galatians! Who has bewitched you? It was before your eyes that Jesus Christ was publicly exhibited as crucified! 2The only thing I want to learn from you is this: Did you receive the Spirit by doing the works of the law or by believing what you heard? 3Are you so foolish? Having started with the Spirit, are you now ending with the flesh? 4Did you experience so much for nothing?—if it really was for nothing. 5Well then, does Godᶜ supply you with the Spirit and work miracles among you by your doing the works of the law, or by your believing what you heard?

6 Just as Abraham "believed God, and it was reckoned to him as righteousness," 7so, you see, those who believe are the descendants of Abraham. 8And the scripture, foreseeing that God would justify the Gentiles by faith, declared the gospel beforehand to Abraham, saying, "All the Gentiles shall be blessed in you." 9For this reason, those who believe are blessed with Abraham who believed.

10 For all who rely on the works of the law are under a curse; for it is written, "Cursed is everyone who does not observe and obey all the things written in the book of the law." 11Now it is evident that no one is justified before God by the law; for "The one who is righteous will live by faith."ᵈ 12But the law does not rest on faith; on the contrary, "Whoever does the works of the lawᵉ will live by them." 13Christ redeemed us from the curse of the law by becoming a curse for us—for it is written, "Cursed is everyone who hangs on

a tree"— 14in order that in Christ Jesus the blessing of Abraham might come to the Gentiles, so that we might receive the promise of the Spirit through faith.

THE PROMISE TO ABRAHAM

15 Brothers and sisters,ᶠ I give an example from daily life: once a person's willᵍ has been ratified, no one adds to it or annuls it. 16Now the promises were made to Abraham and to his offspring;ʰ it does not say, "And to offsprings,"ⁱ as of many; but it says, "And to your offspring,"ʰ that is, to one person, who is Christ. 17My point is this: the law, which came four hundred thirty years later, does not annul a covenant previously ratified by God, so as to nullify the promise. 18For if the inheritance comes from the law, it no longer comes from the promise; but God granted it to Abraham through promise.

THE PURPOSE OF THE LAW

19 Why then the law? It was added because of transgressions, until the offspringʰ would come to whom the promise had been made; and it was ordained through angels by a mediator. 20Now a mediator involves more than one party; but God is one.

21 Is the law then opposed to the promises of God? Certainly not! For if a law had been given that could make alive, then righteousness would indeed come through the law. 22But the scripture has imprisoned all things under the power of sin, so that what was promised through faith in Jesus Christʲ might be given to those who believe.

23 Now before faith came, we were imprisoned and guarded under the law until faith would be revealed. 24Therefore the law was our disciplinarian until Christ came, so

ᵃ 2.20 Or by the faith of the Son of God ᵇ 2.21 Or righteousness ᶜ 3.5 Gk he ᵈ 3.11 Or The one who is righteous through faith will live ᵉ 3.12 Gk does them ᶠ 3.15 Gk Brothers ᵍ 3.15 Or covenant (as in verse 17) ʰ 3.16,19 Gk seed ⁱ 3.16 Gk seeds ʲ 3.22 Or through the faith of Jesus Christ

that we might be justified by faith. ²⁵But now that faith has come, we are no longer subject to a disciplinarian, ²⁶for in Christ Jesus you are all children of God through faith. ²⁷As many of you as were baptized into Christ have clothed yourselves with Christ. ²⁸There is no longer Jew or Greek, there is no longer slave or free, there is no longer male and female; for all of you are one in Christ Jesus. ²⁹And if you belong to Christ, then you are Abraham's offspring,ᵃ heirs according to the promise.

4 My point is this: heirs, as long as they are minors, are no better than slaves, though they are the owners of all the property; ²but they remain under guardians and trustees until the date set by the father. ³So with us; while we were minors, we were enslaved to the elemental spiritsᵇ of the world. ⁴But when the fullness of time had come, God sent his Son, born of a woman, born under the law, ⁵in order to redeem those who were under the law, so that we might receive adoption as children. ⁶And because you are children, God has sent the Spirit of his Son into ourᶜ hearts, crying, "Abba!ᵈ Father!" ⁷So you are no longer a slave but a child, and if a child then also an heir, through God.ᵉ

PAUL REPROVES THE GALATIANS

8 Formerly, when you did not know God, you were enslaved to beings that by nature are not gods.

⁹Now, however, that you have come to know God, or rather to be known by God, how can you turn back again to the weak and beggarly elemental spirits?ᶠ How can you want to be enslaved to them again? ¹⁰You are observing special days, and months, and seasons, and years. ¹¹I am afraid that my work for you may have been wasted.

12 Friends,ᵍ I beg you, become as I am, for I also have become as you are. You have done me no wrong. ¹³You know that it was because of a physical infirmity that I first announced the gospel to you; ¹⁴though my condition put you to the test, you did not scorn or despise me, but welcomed me as an angel of God, as Christ Jesus. ¹⁵What has become of the goodwill you felt? For I testify that, had it been possible, you would have torn out your eyes and given them to me. ¹⁶Have I now become your enemy by telling you the truth? ¹⁷They make much of you, but for no good purpose; they want to exclude you, so that you may make much of them. ¹⁸It is good to be made much of for a good purpose at all times, and not only when I am present with you. ¹⁹My little children, for whom I am again in the pain of

---

ᵃ **3.29** Gk *seed*   ᵇ **4.3** Or *the rudiments*
ᶜ **4.6** Other ancient authorities read *your*
ᵈ **4.6** Aramaic for *Father*   ᵉ **4.7** Other ancient authorities read *an heir of God through Christ*   ᶠ **4.9** Or *beggarly rudiments*   ᵍ **4.12** Gk *Brothers*

BIBLE IN LIFE

One in Christ   Galatians 3.28–29

A heated argument almost split the early church. The Jews wondered how Gentiles (non-Jews) could be given a share in God's covenant with Abraham (see Genesis 22.17–18). Many Jews claimed that a Gentile had first to become a Jew in order to then become a Christian. Paul took strong issue with this position, saying that it's not a matter of ethnicity that invites a person into the covenant that God made with Abraham. *Faith* includes a person in God's blessing. Because of faith in God through Christ, both Jews and Gentiles share in Abraham's covenant. Particularly among some of the church leaders in Jerusalem, a stigma was still attached to Gentiles, who were Paul's primary audience. Consider the church today: Are certain types of people still stigmatized? How do we cause divisions within the church today because of our differences? We can learn this liberating truth from Paul: we are all "one in Christ Jesus."

CHILDREN OF GOD

For in Christ Jesus you are all children of God through faith . . . And if you belong to Christ, then you are Abraham's offspring, heirs according to the promise.

—Galatians 3.26,29

What makes people children of God? Are only the Jews, God's chosen people, the true children of God? Before faith in Christ, the only thing that bound God's chosen people together was the law handed down by Moses. The only way that the Jews felt they could reach salvation was to meticulously honor every single detail of the law: they had to wash their hands in a certain fashion, wear a certain kind of clothes and so forth. There were restrictions on what they could do on the sabbath day. During one of Jesus' frequent confrontations with the leaders concerning what to do on the sabbath, he said, "The sabbath was made for humankind, and not humankind for the sabbath" (Mark 2.27). A meticulous attempt to honor every detail of the law is not the essence of Christianity or the essence of faith in God.

Paul is much more specific about this. He says in the book of Romans that Abraham was not given the blessing of God because he was a Jew or because he was circumcised, but he was given the blessing of God because of his faith. Paul says that if we have faith in Christ, we are subject to the covenant made between God Almighty and our father Abraham.

Until Christ came, Paul says, we were imprisoned by the law. What he tells us in Galatians 3 is that discipline under the law was replaced by faith in Jesus. We are all children of God who have faith in Jesus Christ—not just those who adopt the Jewish law. Our faith is now what binds us together. And Paul is saying that through faith, Christ has brought all of us, Jews and non-Jews alike, equality.

And because we are all children of God, there is no room in our Christian communities to discriminate among people. To exalt some as superior in some way because they are of a certain race, gender, nationality, social class or denomination is a sin which Christ preached against more than any other subject. We should look on all human beings as equal in the eyes of God because that's the way Christ addressed all people. Paul says that through Christ, "There is no longer Jew or Greek, there is no longer slave or free, there is no longer male and female; for all of you are one in Christ Jesus" (Galatians 3.28). This is a leveling of society's false distinctions and a warning to those who try to look upon themselves as somehow superior or privileged.

Going Deeper

- How have issues of discrimination and inequality improved in the church over the years? What are some inequality issues that the church still struggles with today?
- Does your pride ever get in the way of your love and service to someone who is different than you? How would your relationship with that person change if you truly viewed him or her as your equal?

childbirth until Christ is formed in you, 20I wish I were present with you now and could change my tone, for I am perplexed about you.

THE ALLEGORY OF HAGAR AND SARAH

21 Tell me, you who desire to be subject to the law, will you not listen to the law? 22For it is written that Abraham had two sons, one by a slave woman and the other by a free woman. 23One, the child of the slave, was born according to the flesh; the other, the child of the free woman, was born through the promise. 24Now this is an allegory: these women are two covenants. One woman, in fact, is Hagar, from Mount Sinai, bearing children for slavery. 25Now Hagar is Mount Sinai in Arabia[a] and corresponds to the present Jerusalem, for she is in slavery with her children. 26But the other woman corresponds to the Jerusalem above; she is free, and she is our mother. 27For it is written,

"Rejoice, you childless one, you
  who bear no children,
burst into song and shout,
  you who endure
  no birth pangs;
for the children of the
  desolate woman are
  more numerous
than the children of the one
  who is married."

28Now you,[b] my friends,[c] are children of the promise, like Isaac. 29But just as at that time the child who was born according to the flesh perse-cuted the child who was born according to the Spirit, so it is now also. 30But what does the scripture say? "Drive out the slave and her child; for the child of the slave will not share the inheritance with the child of the free woman." 31So then, friends,[c] we are children, not of the slave but of

5 the free woman. 1For freedom Christ has set us free. Stand firm, therefore, and do not submit again to a yoke of slavery.

THE NATURE OF CHRISTIAN FREEDOM

2 Listen! I, Paul, am telling you that if you let yourselves be circumcised, Christ will be of no benefit to you. 3Once again I testify to every man who lets himself be circumcised that he is obliged to obey the entire law. 4You who want to be justified by the law have cut yourselves off from Christ; you have fallen away from grace. 5For through the Spirit, by faith, we eagerly wait for the hope of righteousness. 6For in Christ Jesus neither circumcision nor uncircumcision counts for anything; the only thing that counts is faith working[d] through love.

7 You were running well; who prevented you from obeying the truth? 8Such persuasion does not come from the one who calls you. 9A little yeast leavens the whole batch of dough. 10I am confident

[a] 4.25 Other ancient authorities read *For Sinai is a mountain in Arabia* [b] 4.28 Other ancient authorities read *we* [c] 4.28,31 Gk *brothers* [d] 5.6 Or *made effective*

⊢ BIBLE IN LIFE ▷

Freedom in Christ
Galatians 5.1

Some of us tend to think that when we follow Christ, he will require us to forfeit some of our freedoms. On the contrary, this relationship is actually a liberating experience. The more deeply we commit ourselves to Christ and shape our lives according to his example and words, the freer we become. Free from what? Free from our sin and its hold on us. Free from the fears of life, such as doubts about our status, the fear of the future or the fear of judgment. Most of our fears relate to human achievements, but when we have an intimate relationship with Christ, those fears fade and become relatively inconsequential. We are free to live without fear, without uncertainty, without excessive guilt—and with that freedom comes the gift of peace.

about you in the Lord that you will not think otherwise. But whoever it is that is confusing you will pay the penalty. 11But my friends,[a] why am I still being persecuted if I am still preaching circumcision? In that case the offense of the cross has been removed. 12I wish those who unsettle you would castrate themselves!

13 For you were called to freedom, brothers and sisters;[a] only do not use your freedom as an opportunity for self-indulgence,[b] but through love become slaves to one another. 14For the whole law is summed up in a single commandment, "You shall love your neighbor as yourself." 15If, however, you bite and devour one another, take care that you are not consumed by one another.

THE WORKS OF THE FLESH
16 Live by the Spirit, I say, and do not gratify the desires of the flesh. 17For what the flesh desires is opposed to the Spirit, and what the Spirit desires is opposed to the flesh; for these are opposed to each other, to prevent you from doing what you want. 18But if you are led by the Spirit, you are not subject to the law. 19Now the works of the flesh are obvious: fornication, impurity, licentiousness, 20idolatry, sorcery, enmities, strife, jealousy, anger, quarrels, dissensions, factions, 21envy,[c] drunkenness, carousing, and things like these. I am warning you, as I warned you before: those who do such things will not inherit the kingdom of God.

THE FRUIT OF THE SPIRIT
22 By contrast, the fruit of the Spirit is love, joy, peace, patience, kindness, generosity, faithfulness, 23gentleness, and self-control. There is no law against such things. 24And those who belong to Christ Jesus have crucified the flesh with its passions and desires. 25If we live by the Spirit, let us also be guided by the Spirit. 26Let us not become conceited, competing against one another, envying one another.

BEAR ONE ANOTHER'S BURDENS
6 My friends,[d] if anyone is detected in a transgression, you who

PONDER

Live by the Spirit, I say, and do not gratify the desires of the flesh. For what the flesh desires is opposed to the Spirit, and what the Spirit desires is opposed to the flesh; for these are opposed to each other, to prevent you from doing what you want.
—Galatians 5.16–17

PRAY

O Father, as is always the case when we open the Holy Scriptures and consider them, there are some disturbing things that we learn—disturbing in that we have to reexamine our own lives and decide if we measure up to the standards of our Savior. We ask, "Have I opened my heart completely to the presence of the Holy Spirit? Am I reconciled to the God who created me? Can I honestly call myself a Christ-follower?" We are thankful that Paul has given us these words about the importance of opening ourselves to the constant presence of the Holy Spirit, and we pray that we will make a determination to do so with our lives. Amen.

have received the Spirit should restore such a one in a spirit of gentleness. Take care that you yourselves are not tempted. 2Bear one another's burdens, and in this way you will fulfill[e] the law of Christ. 3For if those who are nothing think they are something, they deceive themselves. 4All must test their own work; then that work, rather than their neighbor's work, will become a cause for pride. 5For all must carry their own loads.

6 Those who are taught the word must share in all good things with their teacher.

[a] 5.11,13 Gk *brothers*   [b] 5.13 Gk *the flesh*
[c] 5.21 Other ancient authorities add *murder*
[d] 6.1 Gk *Brothers*   [e] 6.2 Other ancient authorities read *in this way fulfill*

7 Do not be deceived; God is not mocked, for you reap whatever you sow. 8If you sow to your own flesh, you will reap corruption from the flesh; but if you sow to the Spirit, you will reap eternal life from the Spirit. 9So let us not grow weary in doing what is right, for we will reap at harvest time, if we do not give up. 10So then, whenever we have an opportunity, let us work for the good of all, and especially for those of the family of faith.

FINAL ADMONITIONS AND BENEDICTION

11 See what large letters I make when I am writing in my own hand! 12It is those who want to make a good showing in the flesh that try to compel you to be circumcised—only that they may not be persecuted for the cross of Christ. 13Even

the circumcised do not themselves obey the law, but they want you to be circumcised so that they may boast about your flesh. 14May I never boast of anything except the cross of our Lord Jesus Christ, by which[a] the world has been crucified to me, and I to the world. 15For[b] neither circumcision nor uncircumcision is anything; but a new creation is everything! 16As for those who will follow this rule—peace be upon them, and mercy, and upon the Israel of God.

17 From now on, let no one make trouble for me; for I carry the marks of Jesus branded on my body.

18 May the grace of our Lord Jesus Christ be with your spirit, brothers and sisters.[c] Amen.

[a] 6.14 Or through whom [b] 6.15 Other ancient authorities add in Christ Jesus [c] 6.18 Gk brothers

The Letter of Paul to the

EPHESIANS

Sometimes the hardest thing in the world is to love other Christians and live in unity with them. At times the only thing we have in common with another believer is that we're both followers of Jesus. But a key message of Ephesians is that the love and grace we've received in Jesus are the means by which we live in unity with each other as well as the reason we do so. Notice that Paul emphasizes God's grace before encouraging the Ephesians to "live in love" (Ephesians 5.2); it is only by mirroring God's grace that we can really live in peace with each other.

SALUTATION

1 Paul, an apostle of Christ Jesus by the will of God,
To the saints who are in Ephesus and are faithful[a] in Christ Jesus:

2 Grace to you and peace from God our Father and the Lord Jesus Christ.

SPIRITUAL BLESSINGS IN CHRIST

3 Blessed be the God and Father of our Lord Jesus Christ, who has blessed us in Christ with every spiritual blessing in the heavenly places, 4just as he chose us in Christ[b] before the foundation of the world to be holy and blameless before him in love. 5He destined us for adoption as his children through Jesus Christ, according to the good pleasure of his will, 6to the praise of his glorious grace that he freely bestowed on us in the Beloved. 7In him we have redemption through his blood, the forgiveness of our trespasses, according to the riches of his grace 8that he lavished on us. With all wisdom and insight 9he has made known to us the mystery of his will, according to his good pleasure that he set forth in Christ, 10as a plan for the fullness of time, to gather up all things in him, things in heaven and things on earth. 11In Christ we have also obtained an inheritance,[c] having been destined according to the purpose of him who accomplishes all things according to his counsel and will, 12so that we, who were the first to set our hope on Christ, might live for the praise of his glory. 13In him you also, when you had heard the word of truth, the gospel of your salvation, and had believed in him, were marked with the seal of the promised Holy Spirit; 14this[d] is the pledge of our inheritance toward redemption as God's own people, to the praise of his glory.

PAUL'S PRAYER

15 I have heard of your faith in the Lord Jesus and your love[e] toward all the saints, and for this reason 16I do not cease to give thanks for you as I remember you in my prayers. 17I pray that the God of our Lord Jesus Christ, the Father of glory, may give

---

PONDER

With all wisdom and insight [God] has made known to us the mystery of his will, according to his good pleasure that he set forth in Christ.
—Ephesians 1.8–9

PRAY

O Father, each one of us—no matter how proud or humble, rich or poor, influential or not—struggles to have a proper relationship with you. Some of us push you aside, missing a tremendous opportunity for fullness and peace and for the grace you make available. Help us to have inquisitive minds, using the full extent of our wisdom to search for the truth about our identity, why we are here, what the world means and what defines success. Help us to see, clearly and decisively, the work you would have each of us do. We ask this in the name of our Savior, Jesus Christ. Amen.

---

you a spirit of wisdom and revelation as you come to know him, 18so that, with the eyes of your heart enlightened, you may know what is the hope to which he has called you, what are the riches of his glorious inheritance among the saints, 19and what is the immeasurable greatness of his power for us who believe, according to the working of his great power. 20God[f] put this power to work in Christ when he raised him from the dead and seated him at his right hand in the heavenly places, 21far above all rule and authority and power and dominion, and above every name that is named, not only in this age but also in the age to come. 22And he has put all things under his feet and has

---

[a] 1.1 Other ancient authorities lack *in Ephesus*, reading *saints who are also faithful* [b] 1.4 Gk *in him* [c] 1.11 Or *been made a heritage* [d] 1.14 Other ancient authorities read *who* [e] 1.15 Other ancient authorities lack *and your love* [f] 1.20 Gk *He*

made him the head over all things for the church, [23]which is his body, the fullness of him who fills all in all.

FROM DEATH TO LIFE

2 You were dead through the trespasses and sins [2]in which you once lived, following the course of this world, following the ruler of the power of the air, the spirit that is now at work among those who are disobedient. [3]All of us once lived among them in the passions of our flesh, following the desires of flesh and senses, and we were by nature children of wrath, like everyone else. [4]But God, who is rich in mercy, out of the great love with which he loved us [5]even when we were dead through our trespasses, made us alive together with Christ[a]—by grace you have been saved— [6]and raised us up with him and seated us with him in the heavenly places in Christ Jesus, [7]so that in the ages to come he might show the immeasurable riches of his grace in kindness toward us in Christ Jesus. [8]For by grace you have been saved through faith, and this is not your own doing; it is the gift of God— [9]not the result of works, so that no one may boast. [10]For we are what he has made us, created in Christ Jesus for good works, which God prepared beforehand to be our way of life.

ONE IN CHRIST

[11]So then, remember that at one time you Gentiles by birth,[b] called "the uncircumcision" by those who are called "the circumcision"—a physical circumcision made in the flesh by human hands— [12]remember that you were at that time without Christ, being aliens from the commonwealth of Israel, and strangers to the covenants of promise, having no hope and without God in the world. [13]But now in Christ Jesus you who once were far off have been brought near by the blood of Christ. [14]For he is our peace; in his flesh he has made both groups into one and has broken down the dividing wall, that is, the hostility between us. [15]He has abolished the law with its commandments and ordinances, that he might create in himself one new humanity in place of the two, thus making peace, [16]and might reconcile both groups to God in one body[c] through the cross, thus putting to death that hostility through it.[d] [17]So he came and proclaimed peace to you who were far off and peace to those who were near; [18]for through him both of us have access in one Spirit to the Father. [19]So then you are no longer strangers and aliens, but you are citizens with the saints and also members of the household of God, [20]built upon the foundation of the apostles and prophets, with Christ Jesus himself as the cornerstone.[e] [21]In him the whole structure is joined together and grows into a holy temple in the Lord; [22]in whom you also are built together spiritually[f] into a dwelling place for God.

PAUL'S MINISTRY TO THE GENTILES

3 This is the reason that I Paul am a prisoner for[g] Christ Jesus for the sake of you Gentiles— [2]for surely you have already heard of the commission of God's grace that was given me for you, [3]and how the mystery was made known to me by revelation, as I wrote above in a few words, [4]a reading of which will enable you to perceive my understanding of the mystery of Christ. [5]In former generations this mystery[h] was not made known to humankind, as it has now been revealed to his holy apostles and prophets by the Spirit: [6]that is, the Gentiles have become fellow heirs, members of the same body, and sharers in the promise in Christ Jesus through the gospel.

[7]Of this gospel I have become a servant according to the gift of God's grace that was given me by the working of his power. [8]Although I am the very least of all the saints, this grace was given to me to bring to the Gentiles the news of

---

[a] 2.5 Other ancient authorities read *in Christ*
[b] 2.11 Gk *in the flesh*   [c] 2.16 Or *reconcile both of us in one body for God*   [d] 2.16 Or *in him*, or *in himself*   [e] 2.20 Or *keystone*   [f] 2.22 Gk *in the Spirit*   [g] 3.1 Or *of*   [h] 3.5 Gk *it*

BIBLE IN FOCUS

CREATED TO DO GOOD

But God, who is rich in mercy, out of the great love with which he loved us even when we were dead through our trespasses, made us alive together with Christ ... by grace you have been saved.

—Ephesians 2.4–5

God created human beings with the ideal of perfection demonstrated by our Savior, Jesus Christ: justice, peace, humility, service, compassion, love. But Adam and Eve were seduced by the temptations of Satan and fell away from that ideal. We've all inherited their fallen condition. But because God loves us so much—through his grace, through his mercy, through his forgiveness and through his love—he gives us the chance to be reconciled to him. Without any recompense required, God forgives our sins through Christ, who took the punishment for our sins upon himself.

When humans depart from God's perfect concept of worthy lives, there is a division between them and God. Paul's letter to the Ephesians emphasizes the reconciliation that results from our redemption in Jesus—the result is that we could once more be intimate with God. It is as though we had never sinned; we are offered the opportunity of living in harmony with our Creator. He's not only restored us to his original intention for us, he's exceeded that in the presence of Jesus Christ. Through Jesus, we have assurance that in the future our existence, our peace, our joy and our success as measured by God's standards will be above and beyond what we have envisioned.

In these verses, God promises us a future in heaven alongside our Savior, Jesus Christ, in the presence of our Creator—not because of our own good works or because we deserve it, but because we're loved with an indescribable love, and we're forgiven without any strings attached. It seems to be too good to be true. All we have to do is have faith. We are saved by God's grace through his love for us through Christ, not because of our good works.

But "we are what he has made us, created in Christ Jesus for good works, which God prepared beforehand to be our way of life" (verse 10). Good works are not accomplished by our own power, but by being like branches connected to a vine. Jesus said, "I am the vine, you are the branches. Those who abide in me and I in them bear much fruit, because apart from me you can do nothing" (John 15.5).

What kind of fruit do we bear? What are the good works for which we were created? God has given us a perfect example of the pattern for our own creation: the life of Jesus. Showing love for others, Christ reached out to the unlovable, the afflicted, the outcasts, the destitute, the sinners, the despised, to many who didn't even appreciate it. We must love as Jesus did.

Going Deeper

- What is your response to God's grace?
- How can you become more connected to the vine? How can you pattern your life now that you have received his free gift of God's grace?

the boundless riches of Christ, 9and to make everyone see[a] what is the plan of the mystery hidden for ages in[b] God who created all things; 10so that through the church the wisdom of God in its rich variety might now be made known to the rulers and authorities in the heavenly places. 11This was in accordance with the eternal purpose that he has carried out in Christ Jesus our Lord, 12in whom we have access to God in boldness and confidence through faith in him.[c] 13I pray therefore that you[d] may not lose heart over my sufferings for you; they are your glory.

JESUS ACCEPTS US AS WE

ARE, WHICH FREES US

FROM THE NECESSITY OF

BOOSTING OURSELVES.

PRAYER FOR THE READERS

14 For this reason I bow my knees before the Father,[e] 15from whom every family[f] in heaven and on earth takes its name. 16I pray that, according to the riches of his glory, he may grant that you may be strengthened in your inner being with power through his Spirit, 17and that Christ may dwell in your hearts through faith, as you are being rooted and grounded in love. 18I pray that you may have the power to comprehend, with all the saints, what is the breadth and length and height and depth, 19and to know the love of Christ that surpasses knowledge, so that you may be filled with all the fullness of God.

20 Now to him who by the power at work within us is able to accomplish abundantly far more than all we can ask or imagine, 21to him be glory in the church and in Christ Jesus to all generations, forever and ever. Amen.

UNITY IN THE BODY OF CHRIST

4 I therefore, the prisoner in the Lord, beg you to lead a life wor-

thy of the calling to which you have been called, 2with all humility and gentleness, with patience, bearing with one another in love, 3making every effort to maintain the unity of the Spirit in the bond of peace. 4There is one body and one Spirit, just as you were called to the one hope of your calling, 5one Lord, one faith, one baptism, 6one God and Father of all, who is above all and through all and in all.

7 But each of us was given grace according to the measure of Christ's gift. 8Therefore it is said,

"When he ascended on high
    he made captivity
        itself a captive;
    he gave gifts to his people."

9(When it says, "He ascended," what does it mean but that he had also descended[g] into the lower parts of the earth? 10He who descended is the same one who ascended far above all the heavens, so that he might fill all things.) 11The gifts he gave were that some would be apostles, some prophets, some evangelists, some pastors and teachers, 12to equip the saints for the work of ministry, for building up the body of Christ, 13until all of us come to the unity of the faith and of the knowledge of the Son of God, to maturity, to the measure of the full stature of Christ. 14We must no longer be children, tossed to and fro and blown about by every wind of doctrine, by people's trickery, by their craftiness in deceitful scheming. 15But speaking the truth in love, we must grow up in every way into him who is the head, into Christ, 16from whom the whole body, joined and knit together by every ligament with which it is equipped, as each part is working properly, promotes the body's growth in building itself up in love.

THE OLD LIFE AND THE NEW

17 Now this I affirm and insist on in the Lord: you must no longer live

[a] 3.9 Other ancient authorities read to bring to light   [b] 3.9 Or by   [c] 3.12 Or the faith of him   [d] 3.13 Or I   [e] 3.14 Other ancient authorities add of our Lord Jesus Christ   [f] 3.15 Gk fatherhood   [g] 4.9 Other ancient authorities add first

as the Gentiles live, in the futility of their minds. [18]They are darkened in their understanding, alienated from the life of God because of their ignorance and hardness of heart. [19]They have lost all sensitivity and have abandoned themselves to licentiousness, greedy to practice every kind of impurity. [20]That is not the way you learned Christ! [21]For surely you have heard about him and were taught in him, as truth is in Jesus. [22]You were taught to put away your former way of life, your old self, corrupt and deluded by its lusts, [23]and to be renewed in the spirit of your minds, [24]and to clothe yourselves with the new self, created according to the likeness of God in true righteousness and holiness.

RULES FOR THE NEW LIFE

[25]So then, putting away falsehood, let all of us speak the truth to our neighbors, for we are members of one another. [26]Be angry but do not sin; do not let the sun go down on your anger, [27]and do not make room for the devil. [28]Thieves must give up stealing; rather let them labor and work honestly with their own hands, so as to have something to share with the needy. [29]Let no evil talk come out of your mouths, but only what is useful for building up,[a] as there is need, so that your words may give grace to those who hear. [30]And do not grieve the Holy Spirit of God, with which you were marked with a seal for the day of redemption. [31]Put away from you all bitterness and wrath and anger and wrangling and slander, together with all malice, [32]and be kind to one another, tenderhearted, forgiving one another, as God in Christ has forgiven you.[b] [1]Therefore be imitators of God, as beloved children, [2]and live in love, as Christ loved us[c] and gave himself up for us, a fragrant offering and sacrifice to God.

RENOUNCE PAGAN WAYS

3 But fornication and impurity of any kind, or greed, must not even be mentioned among us, as is proper among saints. [4]Entirely out of place is obscene, silly, and vulgar talk; but instead, let there be thanksgiving. [5]Be sure of this, that no fornicator or impure person, or one who is greedy (that is, an idolater), has any inheritance in the kingdom of Christ and of God.

6 Let no one deceive you with empty words, for because of these things the wrath of God comes on those who are disobedient. [7]Therefore do not be associated with them. [8]For once you were darkness, but now in the Lord you are light. Live as children of light— [9]for the fruit of the light is found in all that is good and right and true. [10]Try to find out what is pleasing to the Lord. [11]Take

[a] 4.29 Other ancient authorities read *building up faith*   [b] 4.32 Other ancient authorities read *us*   [c] 5.2 Other ancient authorities read *you*

⊣ BIBLE IN LIFE ▷ ⊕

Defining Christianity
Ephesians 4.32

"Be kind to one another, tenderhearted, forgiving one another, as God in Christ has forgiven you." Along with John 3.16, this verse encapsulates the essence of Christianity. Christianity is not about philosophical dissertations or the structure of complicated moral laws written by human beings. Christianity is the assurance of God's forgiveness to those of us who acknowledge and repent of our sins because we believe in Christ. Christianity is the reconciliation between sinful people and God, through Christ's love. Permeating this reconciliation is the worth of an individual human being. If we want to find a definition for those who claim Christianity as their own, we should look no further than the words that epitomize Christ's life—words that should describe the lives of those who follow him: peace, love, compassion, concern, forgiveness, understanding and humility.

no part in the unfruitful works of darkness, but instead expose them. ¹²For it is shameful even to mention what such people do secretly; ¹³but everything exposed by the light becomes visible, ¹⁴for everything that becomes visible is light. Therefore it says,

"Sleeper, awake!
    Rise from the dead,
and Christ will shine on you."

¹⁵Be careful then how you live, not as unwise people but as wise, ¹⁶making the most of the time, because the days are evil. ¹⁷So do not be foolish, but understand what the will of the Lord is. ¹⁸Do not get drunk with wine, for that is debauchery; but be filled with the Spirit, ¹⁹as you sing psalms and hymns and spiritual songs among yourselves, singing and making melody to the Lord in your hearts, ²⁰giving thanks to God the Father at all times and for everything in the name of our Lord Jesus Christ.

THE CHRISTIAN HOUSEHOLD

²¹Be subject to one another out of reverence for Christ.

²²Wives, be subject to your husbands as you are to the Lord. ²³For the husband is the head of the wife just as Christ is the head of the church, the body of which he is the Savior. ²⁴Just as the church is subject to Christ, so also wives ought to be, in everything, to their husbands.

²⁵Husbands, love your wives, just as Christ loved the church and gave himself up for her, ²⁶in order to make her holy by cleansing her with the washing of water by the word, ²⁷so as to present the church

to himself in splendor, without a spot or wrinkle or anything of the kind—yes, so that she may be holy and without blemish. ²⁸In the same way, husbands should love their wives as they do their own bodies. He who loves his wife loves himself. ²⁹For no one ever hates his own body, but he nourishes and tenderly cares for it, just as Christ does for the church, ³⁰because we are members of his body.^a ³¹"For this reason a man will leave his father and mother and be joined to his wife, and the two will become one flesh." ³²This is a great mystery, and I am applying it to Christ and the church. ³³Each of you, however, should love his wife as himself, and a wife should respect her husband.

CHILDREN AND PARENTS

6 Children, obey your parents in the Lord,^b for this is right. ²"Honor your father and mother"—this is the first commandment with a promise: ³"so that it may be well with you and you may live long on the earth."

⁴And, fathers, do not provoke your children to anger, but bring them up in the discipline and instruction of the Lord.

SLAVES AND MASTERS

⁵Slaves, obey your earthly masters with fear and trembling, in singleness of heart, as you obey Christ; ⁶not only while being watched, and in order to please them, but as slaves of Christ, doing the will of God from

^a 5.30 Other ancient authorities add *of his flesh and of his bones* ^b 6.1 Other ancient authorities lack *in the Lord*

⊢ BIBLE IN LIFE ▷ ⊕

Children

Ephesians 5.1

The New Testament frequently describes believers in Jesus Christ as *children*. We might resist that image, wanting to perceive ourselves as mature and independent, yet as children, we are given the status of sons and daughters of God and brothers and sisters of Christ (see Romans 8). No one sibling is superior to another; all believers in God through Christ are on a level field. We're all brothers and sisters with Christ, which also makes us heirs of the promises of God and of eternal life (see Revelation 21.7).

the heart. [7]Render service with enthusiasm, as to the Lord and not to men and women, [8]knowing that whatever good we do, we will receive the same again from the Lord, whether we are slaves or free.

[9]And, masters, do the same to them. Stop threatening them, for you know that both of you have the same Master in heaven, and with him there is no partiality.

THE WHOLE ARMOR OF GOD

[10]Finally, be strong in the Lord and in the strength of his power. [11]Put on the whole armor of God, so that you may be able to stand against the wiles of the devil. [12]For our[a] struggle is not against enemies of blood and flesh, but against the rulers, against the authorities, against the cosmic powers of this present darkness, against the spiritual forces of evil in the heavenly places. [13]Therefore take up the whole armor of God, so that you may be able to withstand on that evil day, and having done everything, to stand firm. [14]Stand therefore, and fasten the belt of truth around your waist, and put on the breastplate of righteousness. [15]As shoes for your feet put on whatever will make you ready to proclaim the gospel of peace. [16]With all of these,[b] take the shield of faith, with which you will be able to quench all the flaming arrows of the evil one. [17]Take the helmet of salvation, and the sword of the Spirit, which is the word of God.

[18]Pray in the Spirit at all times in every prayer and supplication. To that end keep alert and always persevere in supplication for all the saints. [19]Pray also for me, so that when I speak, a message may be given to me to make known with boldness the mystery of the gospel,[c] [20]for which I am an ambassador in chains. Pray that I may declare it boldly, as I must speak.

PERSONAL MATTERS AND BENEDICTION

[21]So that you also may know how I am and what I am doing, Tychicus will tell you everything. He is a dear brother and a faithful minister in the Lord. [22]I am sending him to you for this very purpose, to let you know how we are, and to encourage your hearts.

[23]Peace be to the whole community,[d] and love with faith, from God the Father and the Lord Jesus Christ. [24]Grace be with all who have an undying love for our Lord Jesus Christ.[e]

[a] 6.12 Other ancient authorities read *your*
[b] 6.16 Or *In all circumstances* [c] 6.19 Other ancient authorities lack *of the gospel*
[d] 6.23 Gk *to the brothers* [e] 6.24 Other ancient authorities add *Amen*

BIBLE IN LIFE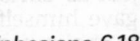

Praying in the Spirit
Ephesians 6.18

We're instructed to "pray in the Spirit at all times." Yet prayer can be frustrating. During a time of trial or temptation or need or sorrow, it can be hard for us to express ourselves in a direct encounter with God Almighty. But God did not leave us to fend for ourselves when it comes to prayer: "We do not know how to pray as we ought, but that very Spirit intercedes with sighs too deep for words. And God, who searches the heart, knows what is the mind of the Spirit, because the Spirit intercedes for the saints according to the will of God" (Romans 8.26–27). The Holy Spirit helps us with our prayers. We can have confidence that God will hear the words of our hearts when we pray.

The Letter of Paul to the

PHILIPPIANS

WARNING: Taking on the attitude of Jesus Christ leads to radical behavior. A relationship with Jesus produces symptoms such as humility, peace and generosity. The patient may exhibit the tendency to "shine like [a star] in the world" (Philippians 2.15), and to "stand firm in the Lord" (4.1). Prognosis: Eventual citizenship in heaven with the Lord Jesus Christ.

Even though Paul wasn't a doctor, he could have included this warning label on his letter to the Philippians. The heart of this book is joy—true joy—that comes from knowing Jesus Christ and living in him. It's powerful and it's contagious.

SALUTATION

1 Paul and Timothy, servants[a] of Christ Jesus,

To all the saints in Christ Jesus who are in Philippi, with the bishops[b] and deacons:[c]

2 Grace to you and peace from God our Father and the Lord Jesus Christ.

PAUL'S PRAYER FOR THE PHILIPPIANS

3 I thank my God every time I remember you, 4constantly praying with joy in every one of my prayers for all of you, 5because of your sharing in the gospel from the first day until now. 6I am confident of this, that the one who began a good work among you will bring it to completion by the day of Jesus Christ. 7It is right for me to think this way about all of you, because you hold me in your heart,[d] for all of you share in God's grace[e] with me, both in my imprisonment and in the defense and confirmation of the gospel. 8For God is my witness, how I long for all of you with the compassion of Christ Jesus. 9And this is my prayer, that your love may overflow more and more with knowledge and full insight 10to help you to determine what is best, so that in the day of Christ you may be pure and blameless, 11having produced the harvest of righteousness that comes through Jesus Christ for the glory and praise of God.

PAUL'S PRESENT CIRCUMSTANCES

12 I want you to know, beloved,[f] that what has happened to me has actually helped to spread the gospel, 13so that it has become known throughout the whole imperial guard[g] and to everyone else that my imprisonment is for Christ; 14and most of the brothers and sisters,[f] having been made confident in the Lord by my imprisonment, dare to speak the word[h] with greater boldness and without fear.

15 Some proclaim Christ from envy and rivalry, but others from goodwill. 16These proclaim Christ out of love, knowing that I have been put here for the defense of the gospel; 17the others proclaim Christ out of selfish ambition, not sincerely but intending to increase my suffering in my imprisonment. 18What does it matter? Just this, that Christ is proclaimed in every way, whether out of false motives or true; and in that I rejoice.

WE HAVE THE HOPE TO LIVE WELL WHEN CONFRONTED BY LIFE'S UNCERTAINTIES AND TO DIE WELL WHEN CONFRONTED BY THE CERTAINTY OF DEATH. THAT HOPE IS NOT BASED WITHIN US, BUT IN JESUS CHRIST.

Yes, and I will continue to rejoice, 19for I know that through your prayers and the help of the Spirit of Jesus Christ this will turn out for my deliverance. 20It is my eager expectation and hope that I will not be put to shame in any way, but that by my speaking with all boldness, Christ will be exalted now as always in my body, whether by life or by death. 21For to me, living is Christ and dying is gain. 22If I am to live in the flesh, that means fruitful labor for me; and I do not know which I prefer. 23I am hard pressed between the two: my desire is to depart and be with Christ, for that is far better; 24but to remain in the flesh is more necessary for you. 25Since I am convinced of this, I know that I will remain and continue with all of you

a 1.1 Gk *slaves*   b 1.1 Or *overseers*   c 1.1 Or *overseers and helpers*   d 1.7 Or *because I hold you in my heart*   e 1.7 Gk *in grace*   f 1.12,14 Gk *brothers*   g 1.13 Gk *whole praetorium*   h 1.14 Other ancient authorities read *word of God*

for your progress and joy in faith, [26]so that I may share abundantly in your boasting in Christ Jesus when I come to you again.

[27] Only, live your life in a manner worthy of the gospel of Christ, so that, whether I come and see you or am absent and hear about you, I will know that you are standing firm in one spirit, striving side by side with one mind for the faith of the gospel, [28]and are in no way intimidated by your opponents. For them this is evidence of their destruction, but of your salvation. And this is God's doing. [29]For he has graciously granted you the privilege not only of believing in Christ, but of suffering for him as well— [30]since you are having the same struggle that you saw I had and now hear that I still have.

IMITATING CHRIST'S HUMILITY

2 If then there is any encouragement in Christ, any consolation from love, any sharing in the Spirit, any compassion and sympathy, [2]make my joy complete: be of the same mind, having the same love, being in full accord and of one mind. [3]Do nothing from selfish ambition or conceit, but in humility regard others as better than yourselves. [4]Let each of you look not to your own interests, but to the interests of others. [5]Let the same mind be in you that was[a] in Christ Jesus,

[6] who, though he was in the
form of God,
did not regard equality
with God
as something to be exploited,
[7] but emptied himself,
taking the form of a slave,
being born in human likeness.
And being found in human form,
[8] he humbled himself
and became obedient to
the point of death—
even death on a cross.

[9] Therefore God also highly
exalted him
and gave him the name
that is above every name,
[10] so that at the name of Jesus
every knee should bend,
in heaven and on earth and
under the earth,
[11] and every tongue should confess
that Jesus Christ is Lord,
to the glory of God the Father.

SHINING AS LIGHTS
IN THE WORLD

[12] Therefore, my beloved, just as you have always obeyed me, not only in my presence, but much more now in my absence, work out your own salvation with fear and trembling; [13]for it is God who is at work in you, enabling you both to will and to work for his good pleasure.

[a] 2.5 Or *that you have*

BIBLE IN LIFE

Attitude of Superiority   *Philippians 2.2–4*

Some Christians in the early church were overly concerned about how they compared to one another. Some wanted exalted positions. Others thought that their particular spiritual gifts or their talents made them superior and thus favored by God. Paul saw these comparisons as a serious threat to the unity of the church.

All of us like to exalt our own favorable attributes but cover up our negative characteristics. It is a natural human tendency to think, even subconsciously, that our color, our social status, our nation, our language, our habits, our songs, our intelligence, our family values are better than those of others, and when we do recognize that pride in ourselves, we tend to cover it up quickly. We rationalize our deficiencies and exaggerate our strengths. As Christians, though, we are not to nurture attitudes of superiority or compare ourselves with others. We are to be like-minded and unselfish in how we interact with other Christians.

14 Do all things without murmuring and arguing, 15so that you may be blameless and innocent, children of God without blemish in the midst of a crooked and perverse generation, in which you shine like stars in the world. 16It is by your holding fast to the word of life that I can boast on the day of Christ that I did not run in vain or labor in vain. 17But even if I am being poured out as a libation over the sacrifice and the offering of your faith, I am glad and rejoice with all of you— 18and in the same way you also must be glad and rejoice with me.

TIMOTHY AND EPAPHRODITUS

19 I hope in the Lord Jesus to send Timothy to you soon, so that I may be cheered by news of you. 20I have no one like him who will be genuinely concerned for your welfare. 21All of them are seeking their own interests, not those of Jesus Christ. 22But Timothy's[a] worth you know, how like a son with a father he has served with me in the work of the gospel. 23I hope therefore to send him as soon as I see how things go with me; 24and I trust in the Lord that I will also come soon.

25 Still, I think it necessary to send to you Epaphroditus—my brother and co-worker and fellow soldier, your messenger[b] and minister to my need; 26for he has been longing for[c] all of you, and has been distressed because you heard that he was ill. 27He was indeed so ill that he nearly died. But God had mercy on him,

and not only on him but on me also, so that I would not have one sorrow after another. 28I am the more eager to send him, therefore, in order that you may rejoice at seeing him again, and that I may be less anxious. 29Welcome him then in the Lord with all joy, and honor such people, 30because he came close to death for the work of Christ,[d] risking his life to make up for those services that you could not give me.

3 Finally, my brothers and sisters,[e] rejoice[f] in the Lord.

BREAKING WITH THE PAST

To write the same things to you is not troublesome to me, and for you it is a safeguard.

2 Beware of the dogs, beware of the evil workers, beware of those who mutilate the flesh![g] 3For it is we who are the circumcision, who worship in the Spirit of God[h] and boast in Christ Jesus and have no confidence in the flesh— 4even though I, too, have reason for confidence in the flesh.

If anyone else has reason to be confident in the flesh, I have more: 5circumcised on the eighth day, a member of the people of Israel, of the tribe of Benjamin, a Hebrew born of Hebrews; as to the law, a

a 2.22 Gk *his*   b 2.25 Gk *apostle*
c 2.26 Other ancient authorities read *longing to see*   d 2.30 Other ancient authorities read *of the Lord*   e 3.1 Gk *my brothers*   f 3.1 Or *farewell*   g 3.2 Gk *the mutilation*   h 3.3 Other ancient authorities read *worship God in spirit*

⊢   **BIBLE IN LIFE** ▷

Flesh vs. Spirit   *Philippians 3.2–4*

When everyday activities, no matter how worthy they seem, become an obsession for Christians, then those self-gratifying things are of the flesh. Paul says they lead to death (see Romans 8.5–11). The mind that is set on the flesh is hostile to God. It does not submit to God's law. But "[we] who worship the Spirit of God and boast in Christ Jesus and have no confidence in the flesh" understand the character of Christ. We understand how Christ related to the stricken, the poor, the bereft, the inarticulate, the blind, the lepers, the prisoners, the hungry, the thirsty, the excluded, the condemned and those who felt the ravages of discrimination. Do we embody the essence of Christianity? Or are we too obsessed with "nice" things such as income, clothes or even how many years we live?

Pharisee; 6as to zeal, a persecutor of the church; as to righteousness under the law, blameless.

7 Yet whatever gains I had, these I have come to regard as loss because of Christ. 8More than that, I regard everything as loss because of the surpassing value of knowing Christ Jesus my Lord. For his sake I have suffered the loss of all things, and I regard them as rubbish, in order that I may gain Christ 9and be found in him, not having a righteousness of my own that comes from the law, but one that comes through faith in Christ,ᵃ the righteousness from God based on faith. 10I want to know Christᵇ and the power of his resurrection and the sharing of his sufferings by becoming like him in his death, 11if somehow I may attain the resurrection from the dead.

PRESSING TOWARD THE GOAL

12 Not that I have already obtained this or have already reached the goal;ᶜ but I press on to make it my own, because Christ Jesus has made me his own. 13Beloved,ᵈ I do not consider that I have made it my own;ᵉ but this one thing I do: forgetting what lies behind and straining forward to what lies ahead, 14I press on toward the goal for the prize of the heavenlyᶠ call of God in Christ Jesus. 15Let those of us then who are mature be of the same mind; and if you think differently about anything, this too God will reveal to you.

16Only let us hold fast to what we have attained.

17 Brothers and sisters,ᵈ join in imitating me, and observe those who live according to the example you have in us. 18For many live as enemies of the cross of Christ; I have often told you of them, and now I tell you even with tears. 19Their end is destruction; their god is the belly; and their glory is in their shame; their minds are set on earthly things. 20But our citizenshipᵍ is in heaven, and it is from there that we are expecting a Savior, the Lord Jesus Christ. 21He will transform the body of our humiliationʰ that it may be conformed to the body of his glory,ⁱ by the power that also enables him to make all things subject to himself. 1Therefore, my brothers and sisters,ʲ whom I love and long for, my joy and crown, stand firm in the Lord in this way, my beloved.

EXHORTATIONS

2 I urge Euodia and I urge Syntyche to be of the same mind in the Lord. 3Yes, and I ask you also, my loyal companion,ᵏ help these

ᵃ 3.9 Or through the faith of Christ
ᵇ 3.10 Gk him   ᶜ 3.12 Or have already been made perfect   ᵈ 3.13,17 Gk Brothers
ᵉ 3.13 Other ancient authorities read my own yet   ᶠ 3.14 Gk upward   ᵍ 3.20 Or commonwealth   ʰ 3.21 Or our humble bodies   ⁱ 3.21 Or his glorious body
ʲ 4.1 Gk my brothers   ᵏ 4.3 Or loyal Syzygus

BIBLE IN LIFE ▷

Worry   Philippians 4.6–7

We tend to think that tension and worry are unique to our fast-paced, modern lifestyles, but as we read Paul's letter to the Philippians, we see how he dealt with this problem of worry and the tensions, pressures and divisions in the lives of those he loved. Undoubtedly, the people to whom Paul was writing lived in fear because they were Christians in a time when it was not an acceptable thing to be. Paul also recognized in the Philippians other causes of uncontrollable fear and tension that afflict us all—doubts about the future, uncertainty, and financial problems. Often our worries are rooted in comparing ourselves with our neighbors, thus creating problems for ourselves. People may look at worrying Christians and ask, "How could people wring their hands and mourn over transient circumstances in their lives if they believe in Christ?" When our problems seem too great, we need to turn to God in prayer. He has promised to send us his peace.

women, for they have struggled beside me in the work of the gospel, together with Clement and the rest of my co-workers, whose names are in the book of life.

4 Rejoice[a] in the Lord always; again I will say, Rejoice.[a] 5Let your gentleness be known to everyone. The Lord is near. 6Do not worry about anything, but in everything by prayer and supplication with thanksgiving let your requests be made known to God. 7And the peace of God, which surpasses all understanding, will guard your hearts and your minds in Christ Jesus.

8 Finally, beloved,[b] whatever is true, whatever is honorable, whatever is just, whatever is pure, whatever is pleasing, whatever is commendable, if there is any excellence and if there is anything worthy of praise, think about[c] these things. 9Keep on doing the things that you have learned and received and heard and seen in me, and the God of peace will be with you.

ACKNOWLEDGMENT OF THE PHILIPPIANS' GIFT

10 I rejoice[d] in the Lord greatly that now at last you have revived your concern for me; indeed, you were concerned for me, but had no opportunity to show it.[e] 11Not that I am referring to being in need; for I have learned to be content with whatever I have. 12I know what it is to have little, and I know what it is to have plenty. In any and all circumstances I have learned the secret of being well-fed and of going hungry, of having plenty and of being in need. 13I can do all things through him who strengthens me. 14In any case, it was kind of you to share my distress.

15 You Philippians indeed know that in the early days of the gospel, when I left Macedonia, no church shared with me in the matter of giving and receiving, except you alone. 16For even when I was in Thessalonica, you sent me help for my needs more than once. 17Not that I seek the gift, but I seek the profit that accumulates to your account. 18I have

been paid in full and have more than enough; I am fully satisfied, now that I have received from Epaphroditus the gifts you sent, a fragrant offering, a sacrifice acceptable and pleasing to God. 19And my God will fully satisfy every need of yours according to his riches in glory in Christ Jesus. 20To our God and Father be glory forever and ever. Amen.

FINAL GREETINGS AND BENEDICTION

21 Greet every saint in Christ Jesus. The friends[f] who are with me greet you. 22All the saints greet you, especially those of the emperor's household.

23 The grace of the Lord Jesus Christ be with your spirit.[g]

[a] 4.4 Or Farewell   [b] 4.8 Gk brothers
[c] 4.8 Gk take account of   [d] 4.10 Gk I rejoiced   [e] 4.10 Gk lacks to show it
[f] 4.21 Gk brothers   [g] 4.23 Other ancient authorities add Amen

The Letter of Paul to the

COLOSSIANS

Jesus means different things to different people. Some regard him as a good man or a prophet. Some think him a magician or a fraud. The book of Colossians addresses the questions of who Jesus is and how he should affect us. Paul writes to the Colossians to refute teachings that relied on human philosophy and knowledge; he argued that only Jesus Christ is necessary for salvation. To this end, Paul asserts that Jesus is supreme over creation, sin, the church and even our relationships. As you read Colossians, ask yourself what difference it would make in your life if you lived in the light of Jesus' supremacy.

SALUTATION

1 Paul, an apostle of Christ Jesus by the will of God, and Timothy our brother,

2 To the saints and faithful brothers and sisters[a] in Christ in Colossae:

Grace to you and peace from God our Father.

PAUL THANKS GOD FOR THE COLOSSIANS

3 In our prayers for you we always thank God, the Father of our Lord Jesus Christ, [4]for we have heard of your faith in Christ Jesus and of the love that you have for all the saints, [5]because of the hope laid up for you in heaven. You have heard of this hope before in the word of the truth, the gospel [6]that has come to you. Just as it is bearing fruit and growing in the whole world, so it has been bearing fruit among yourselves from the day you heard it and truly comprehended the grace of God. [7]This you learned from Epaphras, our beloved fellow servant.[b] He is a faithful minister of Christ on your[c] behalf, [8]and he has made known to us your love in the Spirit.

9 For this reason, since the day we heard it, we have not ceased praying for you and asking that you may be filled with the knowledge of God's[d] will in all spiritual wisdom and understanding, [10]so that you may lead lives worthy of the Lord, fully pleasing to him, as you bear fruit in every good work and as you grow in the knowledge of God. [11]May you be made strong with all the strength that comes from his glorious power, and may you be prepared to endure everything with patience, while joyfully [12]giving thanks to the Father, who has enabled[e] you[f] to share in the inheritance of the saints in the light. [13]He has rescued us from the power of darkness and transferred us into the kingdom of his beloved Son, [14]in whom we have redemption, the forgiveness of sins.[g]

THE SUPREMACY OF CHRIST

15 He is the image of the invisible God, the firstborn of all creation; [16]for in[h] him all things in heaven and on earth were created, things visible and invisible, whether thrones or dominions or rulers or powers—all things have been created through him and for him. [17]He himself is before all things, and in[h] him all things hold together. [18]He is the head of the body, the church; he is the beginning, the firstborn from the dead, so that he might come to have first place in everything. [19]For in him all the fullness of God was pleased to dwell, [20]and through him God was pleased to reconcile to himself all things, whether on earth or in heaven, by making peace through the blood of his cross.

21 And you who were once estranged and hostile in mind, doing evil deeds, [22]he has now reconciled[i] in his fleshly body[j] through death, so as to present you holy and blameless and irreproachable before

---

[a] 1.2 Gk brothers   [b] 1.7 Gk slave
[c] 1.7 Other ancient authorities read our   [d] 1.9 Gk his   [e] 1.12 Other ancient authorities read called   [f] 1.12 Other ancient authorities read us   [g] 1.14 Other ancient authorities add through his blood   [h] 1.16,17 Or by   [i] 1.22 Other ancient authorities read you have now been reconciled   [j] 1.22 Gk in the body of his flesh

---

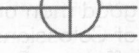

BIBLE IN LIFE

God's People
Colossians 1.4

A saint . . . me? Many people who hear the word saint think that it means a perfect person. It's not a word we hear or use very often in the church today. We hesitate to call ourselves saints because we don't want to come across as braggarts or as thinking we are better than others. The scriptures say that all followers of Christ are saints; we're dedicated to the service of Christ. Even though we know we sin, fall short of the glory of God, deserve punishment and need to repent and change our ways, we are still saints. We are set aside, in effect, for the service of our Savior, Jesus Christ.

PONDER

[The Son] is the image of the invisible God, the firstborn of all creation; for in him all things in heaven and on earth were created, things visible and invisible, whether thrones or dominions or rulers or powers—all things have been created through him and for him.
—Colossians 1.15–16

PRAY

O Father, we know that the church members in Colossae were bombarded with all kinds of conflicting ideas, and that sometimes their faith slipped and was distorted by other teaching. Paul wrote this letter from a distance to remind them of who Jesus Christ is, that he is both God and man, that he is the exalted Savior who suffered and died for us. Paul reminds his readers that Jesus has led them through faith to be completely reconciled to him, a simple but remarkable blessing to which all of us have access. We pray we might be strengthened in our faith in Jesus Christ. Amen.

him— 23provided that you continue securely established and steadfast in the faith, without shifting from the hope promised by the gospel that you heard, which has been proclaimed to every creature under heaven. I, Paul, became a servant of this gospel.

PAUL'S INTEREST IN THE COLOSSIANS

24 I am now rejoicing in my sufferings for your sake, and in my flesh I am completing what is lacking in Christ's afflictions for the sake of his body, that is, the church. 25I became its servant according to God's commission that was given to me for you, to make the word of God fully known, 26the mystery that has been hidden throughout the ages and generations but has now been revealed to his saints. 27To them God chose to make known how great among the Gentiles are the riches of the glory of this mystery, which is Christ in you, the hope of glory. 28It is he whom we proclaim, warning everyone and teaching everyone in all wisdom, so that we may present everyone mature in Christ. 29For this I toil and struggle with all the energy that he powerfully inspires within me.

2 For I want you to know how much I am struggling for you, and for those in Laodicea, and for all who have not seen me face to face. 2I want their hearts to be encouraged and united in love, so that they may have all the riches of assured understanding and have the knowledge of God's mystery, that is, Christ himself,a 3in whom are hidden all the treasures of wisdom and knowledge. 4I am saying this so that no one may deceive you with plausible arguments. 5For though I am absent in body, yet I am with you in spirit, and I rejoice to see your morale and the firmness of your faith in Christ.

FULLNESS OF LIFE IN CHRIST

6 As you therefore have received Christ Jesus the Lord, continue to live your livesb in him, 7rooted and built up in him and established in the faith, just as you were taught, abounding in thanksgiving.

8 See to it that no one takes you captive through philosophy and empty deceit, according to human tradition, according to the elemental spirits of the universe,c and not according to Christ. 9For in him the whole fullness of deity dwells bodily, 10and you have come to fullness in him, who is the head of every ruler and authority. 11In him also you were circumcised with a spiritual circumcision,d by putting off the body of the flesh in the circumcision

a 2.2 Other ancient authorities read of the mystery of God, both of the Father and of Christ   b 2.6 Gk to walk   c 2.8 Or the rudiments of the world   d 2.11 Gk a circumcision made without hands

of Christ; [12]when you were buried with him in baptism, you were also raised with him through faith in the power of God, who raised him from the dead. [13]And when you were dead in trespasses and the uncircumcision of your flesh, God[a] made you[b] alive together with him, when he forgave us all our trespasses, [14]erasing the record that stood against us with its legal demands. He set this aside, nailing it to the cross. [15]He disarmed[c] the rulers and authorities and made a public example of them, triumphing over them in it.

[16] Therefore do not let anyone condemn you in matters of food and drink or of observing festivals, new moons, or sabbaths. [17]These are only a shadow of what is to come, but the substance belongs to Christ. [18]Do not let anyone disqualify you, insisting on self-abasement and worship of angels, dwelling[d] on visions,[e] puffed up without cause by a human way of thinking,[f] [19]and not holding fast to the head, from whom the whole body, nourished and held together by its ligaments and sinews, grows with a growth that is from God.

WARNINGS AGAINST FALSE TEACHERS

[20] If with Christ you died to the elemental spirits of the universe,[g] why do you live as if you still belonged to the world? Why do you submit to regulations, [21]"Do not handle, Do not taste, Do not touch"? [22]All these regulations refer to things that perish with use; they are simply human commands and teachings. [23]These have indeed an appearance of wisdom in promoting self-imposed piety, humility, and severe treatment of the body, but they are of no value in checking self-indulgence.[h]

THE NEW LIFE IN CHRIST

3 So if you have been raised with Christ, seek the things that are above, where Christ is, seated at the right hand of God. [2]Set your minds on things that are above, not on things that are on earth, [3]for you have died, and your life is hidden with Christ in God. [4]When Christ who is your[i] life

is revealed, then you also will be revealed with him in glory.

[5] Put to death, therefore, whatever in you is earthly: fornication, impurity, passion, evil desire, and greed (which is idolatry). [6]On account of these the wrath of God is coming on those who are disobedient.[j] [7]These are the ways you also once followed, when you were living that life.[k] [8]But now you must get rid of all such things—anger, wrath, malice, slander, and abusive[l] language from your mouth. [9]Do not lie to one another, seeing that you have stripped off the old self with its practices [10]and have clothed yourselves with the new self, which is being renewed in knowledge according to the image of its creator. [11]In that renewal[m] there is no longer Greek and Jew, circumcised and uncircumcised, barbarian, Scythian, slave and free; but Christ is all and in all!

HOW WE USE OUR

OPPORTUNITIES REFLECTS

ON BOTH US AND GOD.

[12] As God's chosen ones, holy and beloved, clothe yourselves with compassion, kindness, humility, meekness, and patience. [13]Bear with one another and, if anyone has a complaint against another, forgive each other; just as the Lord[n] has

[a] 2.13 Gk *he* [b] 2.13 Other ancient authorities read *made us*; others, *made* [c] 2.15 Or *divested himself of* [d] 2.18 Other ancient authorities read *not dwelling* [e] 2.18 Meaning of Gk uncertain [f] 2.18 Gk *by the mind of his flesh* [g] 2.20 Or the *rudiments of the world* [h] 2.23 Or *are of no value, serving only to indulge the flesh* [i] 3.4 Other authorities read *our* [j] 3.6 Other ancient authorities lack *on those who are disobedient* (Gk *the children of disobedience*) [k] 3.7 Or *living among such people* [l] 3.8 Or *filthy* [m] 3.11 Gk *its creator,* [n]*where* [n] 3.13 Other ancient authorities read *just as Christ*

forgiven you, so you also must forgive. [14]Above all, clothe yourselves with love, which binds everything together in perfect harmony. [15]And let the peace of Christ rule in your hearts, to which indeed you were called in the one body. And be thankful. [16]Let the word of Christ[a] dwell in you richly; teach and admonish one another in all wisdom; and with gratitude in your hearts sing psalms, hymns, and spiritual songs to God.[b] [17]And whatever you do, in word or deed, do everything in the name of the Lord Jesus, giving thanks to God the Father through him.

RULES FOR CHRISTIAN HOUSEHOLDS

18 Wives, be subject to your husbands, as is fitting in the Lord. [19]Husbands, love your wives and never treat them harshly.

20 Children, obey your parents in everything, for this is your acceptable duty in the Lord. [21]Fathers, do not provoke your children, or they may lose heart. [22]Slaves, obey your earthly masters[c] in everything, not only while being watched and in order to please them, but wholeheartedly, fearing the Lord.[b] [23]Whatever your task, put yourselves into it, as done for the Lord and not for your masters,[d] [24]since you know that from the Lord you will receive the inheritance as your reward; you serve[e] the Lord Christ. [25]For the wrongdoer will be paid back for whatever wrong has been done, and

4 there is no partiality. [1]Masters, treat your slaves justly and fairly, for you know that you also have a Master in heaven.

FURTHER INSTRUCTIONS

2 Devote yourselves to prayer, keeping alert in it with thanksgiving. [3]At the same time pray for us as well that God will open to us a door for the word, that we may declare the mystery of Christ, for which I am in prison, [4]so that I may reveal it clearly, as I should.

5 Conduct yourselves wisely toward outsiders, making the most of the time.[f] [6]Let your speech always be gracious, seasoned with salt, so that you may know how you ought to answer everyone.

FINAL GREETINGS AND BENEDICTION

7 Tychicus will tell you all the news about me; he is a beloved brother, a faithful minister, and a fellow servant[g] in the Lord. [8]I have sent him to you for this very purpose, so that you may know how we are[h] and that he may encourage your hearts; [9]he is coming with Onesimus, the faithful and beloved

[a] **3.16** Other ancient authorities read *of God,* or *of the Lord*   [b] **3.16** Other ancient authorities read *to the Lord*   [c] **3.22** In Greek the same word is used for *master* and *Lord*   [d] **3.23** Gk *not for men*   [e] **3.24** Or *you are slaves of,* or *be slaves of*   [f] **4.5** Or *opportunity*   [g] **4.7** Gk *slave*   [h] **4.8** Other authorities read *that I may know how you are*

BIBLE IN LIFE

Worship God Alone

Colossians 3.1–17

Some of us fail to maintain a total dependence on God. We neglect to set our "minds on things that are above" (verse 2). We hunger for material things, leisure and pleasure, a sense of power, social status and knowledge. When we exalt anything above our intimate relationship with God Almighty, we commit idolatry. Idolatry is revering something other than God or ordering life's priorities in a way that excludes God or relegates God to an inferior position. For example, some people worship the knowledge they have about this universe rather than the One who created it. When we succumb to idolatry, we naturally suppress the truth about ourselves. We don't want to confront who we really are. But inside the heart of every person, Christ asks us to look at ourselves and ask, "For what was I created? What is my highest priority? What do I think about most? What is my obsessive ambition?"

brother, who is one of you. They will tell you about everything here.

10 Aristarchus my fellow prisoner greets you, as does Mark the cousin of Barnabas, concerning whom you have received instructions—if he comes to you, welcome him. 11And Jesus who is called Justus greets you. These are the only ones of the circumcision among my co-workers for the kingdom of God, and they have been a comfort to me. 12Epaphras, who is one of you, a servant[a] of Christ Jesus, greets you. He is always wrestling in his prayers on your behalf, so that you may stand mature and fully assured in everything that God wills. 13For I testify for him that he has worked hard for you and for those in Laodicea and in Hierapolis.

14Luke, the beloved physician, and Demas greet you. 15Give my greetings to the brothers and sisters[b] in Laodicea, and to Nympha and the church in her house. 16And when this letter has been read among you, have it read also in the church of the Laodiceans; and see that you read also the letter from Laodicea. 17And say to Archippus, "See that you complete the task that you have received in the Lord."

18 I, Paul, write this greeting with my own hand. Remember my chains. Grace be with you.[c]

a 4.12 Gk *slave*   b 4.15 Gk *brothers*
c 4.18 Other ancient authorities add *Amen*

⊢ BIBLE IN LIFE ▷

Ministers   *Colossians 4.7*

In the Old Testament, spiritual work was reserved exclusively for the priests and Levites, who were God's chosen ministers. They tended to the work of the tabernacle and cared for the spiritual needs of the people. Who are the ministers in a church today? Pastors, teachers, deacons and elders certainly fit the description of a minister, but *all* of us are called to be ministers in a church. We are to be humble ministers of God's grace, love, forgiveness and compassion—God's work. A minister demonstrates those characteristics of God's work that are personified by the words and actions of Jesus Christ. With our lives and actions, we demonstrate the meaning of Christianity: the teachings of Christ, the actions of Jesus and what they mean today.

The First Letter of Paul to the

THESSALONIANS

Though centuries old, 1 Thessalonians was written for times like ours. It speaks to a culture filled with seductive images and sexual pressures. It brings eternal perspective to discussions of material things. It questions the secular values that undermine God's ways. As you read, watch for practical ways that Christians can live holy lives in a hostile culture. Overshadowing all this is a perspective on life that is shaped by eternity. And you'll find exciting clues about the end times and Jesus' second coming.

SALUTATION

1 Paul, Silvanus, and Timothy,
To the church of the Thessalonians in God the Father and the Lord Jesus Christ:

Grace to you and peace.

THE THESSALONIANS' FAITH AND EXAMPLE

2 We always give thanks to God for all of you and mention you in our prayers, constantly ³remembering before our God and Father your work of faith and labor of love and steadfastness of hope in our Lord Jesus Christ. ⁴For we know, brothers and sistersᵃ beloved by God, that he has chosen you, ⁵because our message of the gospel came to you not in word only, but also in power and in the Holy Spirit and with full conviction; just as you know what kind of persons we proved to be among you for your sake. ⁶And you became im-

PONDER

For we know, brothers and sisters beloved by God, that he has chosen you, because our message of the gospel came to you not in word only, but also in power and in the Holy Spirit and with full conviction.
—1 Thessalonians 1.4–5

PRAY

O Father, we are thankful for Paul's ministry and his explanation to us about our faith in Jesus Christ, your Son, the promised Messiah, the perfect human being, who set an example that all of us should attempt to emulate. We thank you, Lord, for convicting us in the Holy Spirit and calling us to yourself. Give us strength to reshape our lives and to demonstrate vividly what it means to be Christians in our own environments, in our own families, in our own communities. We ask in the name of our Savior. Amen.

itators of us and of the Lord, for in spite of persecution you received the word with joy inspired by the Holy Spirit, ⁷so that you became an example to all the believers in Macedonia and in Achaia. ⁸For the word of the Lord has sounded forth from you not only in Macedonia and Achaia, but in every place your faith in God has become known, so that we have no need to speak about it. ⁹For the people of those regionsᵇ report about us what kind of welcome we had among you, and how you turned to God from idols, to serve a living and true God, ¹⁰and to wait for his Son from heaven, whom he raised from the dead—Jesus, who rescues us from the wrath that is coming.

PAUL'S MINISTRY IN THESSALONICA

2 You yourselves know, brothers and sisters,ᵃ that our coming to you was not in vain, ²but though we had already suffered and been shamefully mistreated at Philippi, as you know, we had courage in our God to declare to you the gospel of God in spite of great opposition. ³For our appeal does not spring from deceit or impure motives or trickery, ⁴but just as we have been approved by God to be entrusted with the message of the gospel, even so we speak, not to please mortals, but to please God who tests our hearts. ⁵As you know and as God is our witness, we never came with words of flattery or with a pretext for greed; ⁶nor did we seek praise from mortals, whether from you or from others, ⁷though we might have made demands as apostles of Christ. But we were gentleᶜ among you, like a nurse tenderly caring for her own children. ⁸So deeply do we care for you that we are determined to share with you not only the gospel of God but also our own selves, because you have become very dear to us.

9 You remember our labor and toil, brothers and sisters;ᵃ we worked night and day, so that we

---

ᵃ **1.4; 2.1,9** Gk *brothers*   ᵇ **1.9** Gk *For they*
ᶜ **2.7** Other ancient authorities read *infants*

might not burden any of you while we proclaimed to you the gospel of God. [10]You are witnesses, and God also, how pure, upright, and blameless our conduct was toward you believers. [11]As you know, we dealt with each one of you like a father with his children, [12]urging and encouraging you and pleading that you lead a life worthy of God, who calls you into his own kingdom and glory.

[13]We also constantly give thanks to God for this, that when you received the word of God that you heard from us, you accepted it not as a human word but as what it really is, God's word, which is also at work in you believers. [14]For you, brothers and sisters,[a] became imitators of the churches of God in Christ Jesus that are in Judea, for you suffered the same things from your own compatriots as they did from the Jews, [15]who killed both the Lord Jesus and the prophets,[b] and drove us out; they displease God and oppose everyone [16]by hindering us from speaking to the Gentiles so that they may be saved. Thus they have constantly been filling up the measure of their sins; but God's wrath has overtaken them at last.[c]

PAUL'S DESIRE TO VISIT THE THESSALONIANS AGAIN

[17]As for us, brothers and sisters,[a] when, for a short time, we were made orphans by being separated from you—in person, not in heart—we longed with great eagerness to see you face to face. [18]For we wanted to come to you—certainly I, Paul, wanted to again and again—but Satan blocked our way. [19]For what is our hope or joy or crown of boasting before our Lord Jesus at his coming? Is it not you? [20]Yes, you are our glory and joy!

3 Therefore when we could bear it no longer, we decided to be left alone in Athens; [2]and we sent Timothy, our brother and co-worker for God in proclaiming[d] the gospel of Christ, to strengthen and encourage you for the sake of your faith, [3]so that no one would be shaken by these persecutions. Indeed, you yourselves know that this is what we are destined for. [4]In fact, when we were with you, we told you beforehand that we were to suffer persecution; so it turned out, as you know. [5]For this reason, when I could bear it no longer, I sent to find out about your faith; I was afraid that somehow the tempter had tempted you and that our labor had been in vain.

TIMOTHY'S ENCOURAGING REPORT

[6]But Timothy has just now come to us from you, and has brought us the good news of your faith and love. He has told us also that you always remember us kindly and long to see us—just as we long to see you. [7]For this reason, brothers and sisters,[a] during all our distress and persecution we have been encouraged about you through your faith. [8]For we now live, if you continue to stand firm in the Lord. [9]How can we thank God enough for you in return for all the joy that we feel before our God because of you? [10]Night and day we pray most earnestly that we may see you face to face and restore whatever is lacking in your faith.

[11]Now may our God and Father himself and our Lord Jesus direct our way to you. [12]And may the Lord make you increase and abound in love for one another and for all, just as we abound in love for you. [13]And may he so strengthen your hearts in holiness that you may be blameless before our God and Father at the coming of our Lord Jesus with all his saints.

A LIFE PLEASING TO GOD

4 Finally, brothers and sisters,[a] we ask and urge you in the Lord Jesus that, as you learned from us how you ought to live and to please God (as, in fact, you are doing), you should do so more and more. [2]For you know what instructions we gave you through the Lord Jesus. [3]For

[a] 2.14,17; 3.7; 4.1 Gk *brothers*   [b] 2.15 Other ancient authorities read *their own prophets*   [c] 2.16 Or *completely* or *forever*   [d] 3.2 Gk lacks *proclaiming*

this is the will of God, your sanctification: that you abstain from fornication; [4]that each one of you know how to control your own body[a] in holiness and honor, [5]not with lustful passion, like the Gentiles who do not know God; [6]that no one wrong or exploit a brother or sister[b] in this matter, because the Lord is an avenger in all these things, just as we have already told you beforehand and solemnly warned you. [7]For God did not call us to impurity but in holiness. [8]Therefore whoever rejects this rejects not human authority but God, who also gives his Holy Spirit to you.

[9]Now concerning love of the brothers and sisters,[c] you do not need to have anyone write to you, for you yourselves have been taught

---

⊕

PONDER

Now concerning love of the brothers and sisters, you do not need to have anyone write to you, for you yourselves have been taught by God to love one another.

—1 Thessalonians 4.9

PRAY

Father, help us remember that you've given us every moment of this existence on earth. We want it to be meaningful. We want it to be significant. We want our lives to be good, not as measured by the standards of a constantly changing society, but excellent as measured by your Word, as expressed to us by our Savior, Jesus Christ, who not only taught with words but with deeds. He taught us what it means to love and continues to teach us through your grace by the Holy Spirit. We want to live in love, in a spirit of humility, not in arrogance or superiority. We want to reach out to others in the name of Christ. More and more, help us be like our Savior. In his name we pray. Amen.

---

by God to love one another; [10]and indeed you do love all the brothers and sisters[c] throughout Macedonia. But we urge you, beloved,[c] to do so more and more, [11]to aspire to live quietly, to mind your own affairs, and to work with your hands, as we directed you, [12]so that you may behave properly toward outsiders and be dependent on no one.

THE COMING OF THE LORD

[13]But we do not want you to be uninformed, brothers and sisters,[c] about those who have died,[d] so that you may not grieve as others do who have no hope. [14]For since we believe that Jesus died and rose again, even so, through Jesus, God will bring with him those who have died.[d] [15]For this we declare to you by the word of the Lord, that we who are alive, who are left until the coming of the Lord, will by no means precede those who have died.[d] [16]For the Lord himself, with a cry of command, with the archangel's call and with the sound of God's trumpet, will descend from heaven, and the dead in Christ will rise first. [17]Then we who are alive, who are left, will be caught up in the clouds together with them to meet the Lord in the air; and so we will be with the Lord forever. [18]Therefore encourage one another with these words.

5 Now concerning the times and the seasons, brothers and sisters,[c] you do not need to have anything written to you. [2]For you yourselves know very well that the day of the Lord will come like a thief in the night. [3]When they say, "There is peace and security," then sudden destruction will come upon them, as labor pains come upon a pregnant woman, and there will be no escape! [4]But you, beloved,[c] are not in darkness, for that day to surprise you like a thief; [5]for you are all children of light and children of the day; we are not of the night or of darkness. [6]So then let us not fall asleep as others do, but let us keep awake and be

---

[a] 4.4 Or *how to take a wife for himself*
[b] 4.6 Gk *brother*   [c] 4.9,10,13; 5.1,4 Gk *brothers*   [d] 4.13,14,15 Gk *fallen asleep*

THE HOLY LIFE

God did not call us to impurity but in holiness.

—1 Thessalonians 4.7

In 1 Thessalonians 4.7, Paul calls us to live holy lives. Holiness implies purity, transcendence, going a little bit further than is expected of us. How can we go further with our forgiveness, generosity, compassion, service or concern for others? By turning to Christ. After all, God is love. Jesus defined it for us. We ought not to say, "I've loved enough." How far, then, should we go with our love?

Paul says in 1 Thessalonians 4.1 that we must love "more and more." Love is not just a matter of passionate feeling. Love is a matter of action. Jesus didn't walk up and down the street saying, "I love those lepers over there; I don't want to get leprosy myself." Or, "I love those tax collectors. I don't want to have anything to do with them, but I'll say a prayer for them." Jesus went among them. He embraced the lepers. He had supper with the tax collectors. And that's what we are called upon by Paul to do—reach for greatness in the love that Jesus taught us.

It doesn't matter where we live, where we travel or what our economic or social circumstances might be. There is a way to break down the barriers that we create around ourselves to exclude people who are not like us. It is not easy to become reconciled with, or even acquainted with, people who are unfriendly, poverty-stricken, homeless, imprisoned, addicted or terminally ill. But sometimes the breaking down of those barriers, the deliberate reaching out is one of the most difficult and one of the most courageous things that a Christian can possibly do.

As Christians, we're supposed to be set apart from the world in a transcendent way. There needs to be a group of resolute human beings whose moral standards do not change, because the teachings and admonitions of Jesus Christ do not change. And in our adherence to Christ's teachings, we are called to promote and emphasize truth and justice, have unselfish love for others, and encompass people within the bounds of our hearts and minds—more and more. In this way, our lives will be blessed. As we turn to Christ, we are liberated from the things that restrain us. Christ says that through the presence of the Holy Spirit, we can be reconciled with God. Our burdens will be shared by God Almighty. The Holy Spirit will fill our hearts. And Christ has promised us peace that passes understanding and joy beyond belief.

Going Deeper

- What are the things that limit your life or that keep you from being truly joyful, truly happy? How can you be liberated from those things?
- In what areas of your life do you need to be more courageous in loving others?

sober; [7]for those who sleep sleep at night, and those who are drunk get drunk at night. [8]But since we belong to the day, let us be sober, and put on the breastplate of faith and love, and for a helmet the hope of salvation. [9]For God has destined us not for wrath but for obtaining salvation through our Lord Jesus Christ, [10]who died for us, so that whether we are awake or asleep we may live with him. [11]Therefore encourage one another and build up each other, as indeed you are doing.

FINAL EXHORTATIONS, GREETINGS, AND BENEDICTION

[12] But we appeal to you, brothers and sisters,[a] to respect those who labor among you, and have charge of you in the Lord and admonish you; [13]esteem them very highly in love because of their work. Be at peace among yourselves. [14]And we urge you, beloved,[a] to admonish the idlers, encourage the fainthearted, help the weak, be patient with all of them. [15]See that none of you repays evil for evil, but always seek to do good to one another and to all. [16]Rejoice always, [17]pray without ceasing, [18]give thanks in all circumstances; for this is the will of God in Christ Jesus for you. [19]Do not quench the Spirit. [20]Do not despise the words of prophets,[b] [21]but test everything;

hold fast to what is good; [22]abstain from every form of evil.

[23] May the God of peace himself sanctify you entirely; and may your spirit and soul and body be kept sound[c] and blameless at the coming of our Lord Jesus Christ. [24]The one who calls you is faithful, and he will do this.

PRAYER SHOULD BE

THE CENTER OF ALL LIFE

EXPERIENCES: SICKNESS,

SINFULNESS, FAILURE,

TRAGEDY—AND HAPPINESS.

[25] Beloved,[d] pray for us.

[26] Greet all the brothers and sisters[a] with a holy kiss. [27]I solemnly command you by the Lord that this letter be read to all of them.[e]

[28] The grace of our Lord Jesus Christ be with you.[f]

[a] 5.12,14,26 Gk brothers   [b] 5.20 Gk despise prophecies   [c] 5.23 Or complete   [d] 5.25 Gk Brothers   [e] 5.27 Gk to all the brothers   [f] 5.28 Other ancient authorities add Amen

---

BIBLE IN LIFE

Church Leadership   1 Thessalonians 5.12–13

During the earliest days of the church, there were no clergy, no pastors, no stewards and no deacons as we know them today. In Paul's final instructions here, he gave the Thessalonians an idea of how to identify and treat leaders in the church. Paul made it clear to them that the leaders in the church are the ones who serve others—the ones who do the work. Leaders are those who get down and do the nitty-gritty, who visit people who are ill, who mow the lawn around the church building, who play music for the services. They're not anointed because of their stature; they have stature because they are dedicated to the service of Christ. With their lives, they set an example of following the teachings of Christ. These are our true leaders, the kinds of people to whom we should listen, the kind of people we should respect.

The Second Letter of Paul to the

THESSALONIANS

Have you ever been puzzled by what's going on in the world around you? This letter provides something stable—an eternal perspective—with which to evaluate society's shifting views. It reminds us that this world is terminal—careening toward its conclusion. But it also reminds us that Christians have a hope for eternity that enables them to live day today in an anti-Christian environment. This letter, along with 1 Thessalonians, tells us much of what we know about the end times.

SALUTATION

1 Paul, Silvanus, and Timothy,
To the church of the Thessalonians in God our Father and the Lord Jesus Christ:

2 Grace to you and peace from God our[a] Father and the Lord Jesus Christ.

THANKSGIVING

3 We must always give thanks to God for you, brothers and sisters,[b] as is right, because your faith is growing abundantly, and the love of every one of you for one another is increasing. 4Therefore we ourselves boast of you among the churches of God for your steadfastness and faith during all your persecutions and the afflictions that you are enduring.

THE JUDGMENT AT CHRIST'S COMING

5 This is evidence of the righteous judgment of God, and is intended to make you worthy of the kingdom of God, for which you are also suffering. 6For it is indeed just of God to repay with affliction those who afflict you, 7and to give relief to the afflicted as well as to us, when the Lord Jesus is revealed from heaven with his mighty angels 8in flaming fire, inflicting vengeance on those who do not know God and on those who do not obey the gospel of our Lord Jesus. 9These will suffer the punishment of eternal destruction, separated from the presence of the Lord and from the glory of his might, 10when he comes to be glorified by his saints and to be marveled at on that day among all who have believed, because our testimony to you was believed. 11To this end we always pray for you, asking that our God will make you worthy of his call and will fulfill by his power every good resolve and work of faith, 12so that the name of our Lord Jesus may be glorified in you, and you in him, according to the grace of our God and the Lord Jesus Christ.

THE MAN OF LAWLESSNESS

2 As to the coming of our Lord Jesus Christ and our being gathered together to him, we beg you,

PONDER

We always pray for you, asking that our God will make you worthy of his call and will fulfill by his power every good resolve and work of faith.
—2 Thessalonians 1.11

PRAY

Father of all, help us to realize that your forgiveness, grace and love are offered to us unconditionally. But also let us realize we have an obligation to live worthy lives, called by God. We know that we bear fruit through your power and by our prayers for ourselves and each other. So Father, make us fruitful and faithful, and bless our attempts to live according to your commands. Forgive our sins, and let us be inspired by the knowledge of your power to sustain us as we attempt to emulate with our own lives the life of our Savior, Jesus Christ, in whose name we pray. Amen.

brothers and sisters,[b] 2not to be quickly shaken in mind or alarmed, either by spirit or by word or by letter, as though from us, to the effect that the day of the Lord is already here. 3Let no one deceive you in any way; for that day will not come unless the rebellion comes first and the lawless one[c] is revealed, the one destined for destruction.[d] 4He opposes and exalts himself above every so-called god or object of worship, so that he takes his seat in the temple of God, declaring himself to be God. 5Do you not remember that I told you these things when I was still with you? 6And you know what is now restraining him, so that he may be revealed when his time

[a] 1.2 Other ancient authorities read *the*
[b] 1.3; 2.1 Gk *brothers* [c] 2.3 Gk *the man of lawlessness*; other ancient authorities read *the man of sin* [d] 2.3 Gk *the son of destruction*

comes. [7]For the mystery of lawlessness is already at work, but only until the one who now restrains it is removed. [8]And then the lawless one will be revealed, whom the Lord Jesus[a] will destroy[b] with the breath of his mouth, annihilating him by the manifestation of his coming. [9]The coming of the lawless one is apparent in the working of Satan, who uses all power, signs, lying wonders, [10]and every kind of wicked deception for those who are perishing, because they refused to love the truth and so be saved. [11]For this reason God sends them a powerful delusion, leading them to believe what is false, [12]so that all who have not believed the truth but took pleasure in unrighteousness will be condemned.

CHOSEN FOR SALVATION

[13]But we must always give thanks to God for you, brothers and sisters[c] beloved by the Lord, because God chose you as the first fruits[d] for salvation through sanctification by the Spirit and through belief in the truth. [14]For this purpose he called you through our proclamation of the good news,[e] so that you may obtain the glory of our Lord Jesus Christ. [15]So then, brothers and sisters,[c] stand firm and hold fast to the traditions that you were taught by us, either by word of mouth or by our letter.

[16]Now may our Lord Jesus Christ himself and God our Father, who loved us and through grace gave us eternal comfort and good hope, [17]comfort your hearts and strengthen them in every good work and word.

REQUEST FOR PRAYER

3 Finally, brothers and sisters,[c] pray for us, so that the word of the Lord may spread rapidly and be glorified everywhere, just as it is among you, [2]and that we may be rescued from wicked and evil people; for not all have faith. [3]But the Lord is faithful; he will strengthen you and guard you from the evil one.[f] [4]And we have confidence in the Lord concerning you, that you are doing and will go on doing the things that we command. [5]May the Lord direct your hearts to the love of God and to the steadfastness of Christ.

WARNING AGAINST IDLENESS

6 Now we command you, beloved,[c] in the name of our Lord Jesus Christ, to keep away from believers who are[g] living in idleness and not according to the tradition that they[h] received from us. [7]For you yourselves know how you ought to imitate us; we were not idle when we were with you, [8]and we did not eat anyone's bread without paying for it; but with toil and labor we worked night and day, so that we might not burden any of you. [9]This was not because we do not have that right, but in order to give you an example to imitate. [10]For even when we were with you, we gave you this command: Anyone unwilling to work should not eat. [11]For we hear that some of you are living in idleness, mere busybodies, not doing any

WE HAVE TIME TO DO

THE MOST IMPORTANT

THINGS. WE MUST MAKE

CHOICES ABOUT HOW WE

USE THE TIME WE HAVE.

work. [12]Now such persons we command and exhort in the Lord Jesus Christ to do their work quietly and to earn their own living. [13]Brothers and sisters,[i] do not be weary in doing what is right.

[a] 2.8 Other ancient authorities lack *Jesus* [b] 2.8 Other ancient authorities read *consume* [c] 2.13,15; 3.1,6 Gk *brothers* [d] 2.13 Other ancient authorities read *from the beginning* [e] 2.14 Or *through our gospel* [f] 3.3 Or *from evil* [g] 3.6 Gk *from every brother who is* [h] 3.6 Other ancient authorities read *you* [i] 3.13 Gk *Brothers*

14 Take note of those who do not obey what we say in this letter; have nothing to do with them, so that they may be ashamed. **15** Do not regard them as enemies, but warn them as believers.[a]

FINAL GREETINGS AND BENEDICTION

16 Now may the Lord of peace himself give you peace at all times in all ways. The Lord be with all of you.

17 I, Paul, write this greeting with my own hand. This is the mark in every letter of mine; it is the way I write. **18** The grace of our Lord Jesus Christ be with all of you.[b]

[a] 3.15 Gk *a brother* [b] 3.18 Other ancient authorities add *Amen*

The First Letter of Paul to

TIMOTHY

If you learn to play a musical instrument, you'll probably learn to play that instrument with others. Christians are not solo instrumentalists. They're called to harmonize with others in a group called the church. What you're about to read is like a conductor's handbook. This nitty-gritty wisdom offers practical help to believers in their relationships with each other, with church leaders and with the world around them. Look for the underlying principles. Though specific problems and answers might never be exactly duplicated, the principles of God's Word never change.

SALUTATION

1 Paul, an apostle of Christ Jesus by the command of God our Savior and of Christ Jesus our hope,

2 To Timothy, my loyal child in the faith:

Grace, mercy, and peace from God the Father and Christ Jesus our Lord.

WARNING AGAINST FALSE TEACHERS

3 I urge you, as I did when I was on my way to Macedonia, to remain in Ephesus so that you may instruct certain people not to teach any different doctrine, 4and not to occupy themselves with myths and endless genealogies that promote speculations rather than the divine training[a] that is known by faith. 5But the aim of such instruction is love that comes from a pure heart, a good conscience, and sincere faith. 6Some people have deviated from these and turned to meaningless talk, 7desiring to be teachers of the law, without understanding either what they are saying or the things about which they make assertions.

8 Now we know that the law is good, if one uses it legitimately. 9This means understanding that the law is laid down not for the innocent but for the lawless and disobedient, for the godless and sinful, for the unholy and profane, for those who kill their father or mother, for murderers, 10fornicators, sodomites, slave traders, liars, perjurers, and whatever else is contrary to the sound teaching 11that conforms to the glorious gospel of the blessed God, which he entrusted to me.

GRATITUDE FOR MERCY

12 I am grateful to Christ Jesus our Lord, who has strengthened me, because he judged me faithful and appointed me to his service, 13even though I was formerly a blasphemer, a persecutor, and a man of violence. But I received mercy because I had acted ignorantly in unbelief, 14and the grace of our Lord overflowed for me with the faith and love that are in Christ Jesus. 15The saying is sure and worthy of full acceptance, that Christ Jesus came into the world to save sinners—of whom I am the foremost. 16But for that very reason I received mercy, so that in me, as the foremost, Jesus Christ might display the utmost patience, making me an example to those who would come to believe in him for eternal life. 17To the King of the ages, immortal, invisible, the only God, be honor and glory forever and ever.[b] Amen.

18 I am giving you these instructions, Timothy, my child, in accordance with the prophecies made earlier about you, so that by following them you may fight the good fight, 19having faith and a good conscience. By rejecting conscience, certain persons have suffered shipwreck in the faith; 20among them are Hymenaeus and Alexander, whom I have turned over to Satan, so that they may learn not to blaspheme.

INSTRUCTIONS CONCERNING PRAYER

2 First of all, then, I urge that supplications, prayers, intercessions, and thanksgivings be made for everyone, 2for kings and all who are in high positions, so that we may lead a quiet and peaceable life in all godliness and dignity. 3This is right and is acceptable in the sight of God our Savior, 4who desires everyone to be saved and to come to the knowledge of the truth. 5For

there is one God;
   there is also one mediator
      between God and
      humankind,
Christ Jesus, himself human,
6   who gave himself a
      ransom for all

—this was attested at the right time. 7For this I was appointed a herald and an apostle (I am telling the truth,[c] I am not lying), a teacher of the Gentiles in faith and truth.

8 I desire, then, that in every place the men should pray, lifting up holy hands without anger or argument; 9also that the women

---

[a] **1.4** Or *plan*   [b] **1.17** Gk *to the ages of the ages*   [c] **2.7** Other ancient authorities add *in Christ*

PONDER

First of all, then, I urge that supplications, prayers, intercessions, and thanksgivings be made for everyone, for kings and all who are in high positions, so that we may lead a quiet and peaceable life in all godliness and dignity.
—1 Timothy 2.1–2

PRAY

Father, we are grateful to be reminded by Paul's inspired words how each of us can immerse our lives in prayer. As we weld ourselves to your Son, Jesus Christ our Savior, make us effective in our prayers as we intercede for all people, including the leaders and others who have authority over our lives. Having the ability to bless others through prayer, give us also the ability to pray through our own setbacks, vicissitudes, disappointments and frustrations. Expand our existence in exemplary, dynamic and peaceful ways, as you have promised. In the name of our Savior, Jesus Christ. Amen.

should dress themselves modestly and decently in suitable clothing, not with their hair braided, or with gold, pearls, or expensive clothes, [10]but with good works, as is proper for women who profess reverence for God. [11]Let a woman[a] learn in silence with full submission. [12]I permit no woman[a] to teach or to have authority over a man;[b] she is to keep silent. [13]For Adam was formed first, then Eve; [14]and Adam was not deceived, but the woman was deceived and became a transgressor. [15]Yet she will be saved through childbearing, provided they continue in faith and love and holiness, with modesty.

QUALIFICATIONS OF BISHOPS

3 The saying is sure:[c] whoever aspires to the office of bishop[d]

desires a noble task. [2]Now a bishop[e] must be above reproach, married only once,[f] temperate, sensible, respectable, hospitable, an apt teacher, [3]not a drunkard, not violent but gentle, not quarrelsome, and not a lover of money. [4]He must manage his own household well, keeping his children submissive and respectful in every way— [5]for if someone does not know how to manage his own household, how can he take care of God's church? [6]He must not be a recent convert, or he may be puffed up with conceit and fall into the condemnation of the devil. [7]Moreover, he must be well thought of by outsiders, so that he may not fall into disgrace and the snare of the devil.

QUALIFICATIONS OF DEACONS

[8]Deacons likewise must be serious, not double-tongued, not indulging in much wine, not greedy for money; [9]they must hold fast to the mystery of the faith with a clear conscience. [10]And let them first be tested; then, if they prove themselves blameless, let them serve as deacons. [11]Women[g] likewise must be serious, not slanderers, but temperate, faithful in all things. [12]Let deacons be married only once,[h] and let them manage their children and their households well; [13]for those who serve well as deacons gain a good standing for themselves and great boldness in the faith that is in Christ Jesus.

THE MYSTERY OF OUR RELIGION

[14]I hope to come to you soon, but I am writing these instructions to you so that, [15]if I am delayed, you may know how one ought to behave in the household of God, which is the church of the living God, the pillar

[a] 2.11,12 Or *wife* [b] 2.12 Or *her husband*
[c] 3.1 Some interpreters place these words at the end of the previous paragraph. Other ancient authorities read *The saying is commonly accepted* [d] 3.1 Or *overseer*
[e] 3.2 Or *an overseer* [f] 3.2 Gk *the husband of one wife* [g] 3.11 Or *Their wives, or Women deacons* [h] 3.12 Gk *be husbands of one wife*

and bulwark of the truth. ¹⁶Without any doubt, the mystery of our religion is great:

He[a] was revealed in flesh,
　vindicated[b] in spirit,[c]
　　seen by angels,
　proclaimed among Gentiles,
　believed in throughout
　　the world,
　　taken up in glory.

FALSE ASCETICISM

4 Now the Spirit expressly says that in later[d] times some will renounce the faith by paying attention to deceitful spirits and teachings of demons, ²through the hypocrisy of liars whose consciences are seared with a hot iron. ³They forbid marriage and demand abstinence from foods, which God created to be received with thanksgiving by those who believe and know the truth. ⁴For everything created by God is good, and nothing is to be rejected, provided it is received with thanksgiving; ⁵for it is sanctified by God's word and by prayer.

A GOOD MINISTER OF JESUS CHRIST

6 If you put these instructions before the brothers and sisters,[e] you will be a good servant[f] of Christ Jesus, nourished on the words of the faith and of the sound teaching that you have followed. ⁷Have nothing to do with profane myths and old wives' tales. Train yourself in godliness, ⁸for, while physical training is of some value, godliness is valuable in every way, holding promise for both the present life and the life to come. ⁹The saying is sure and worthy of full acceptance. ¹⁰For to this end we toil and struggle,[g] because we have our hope set on the living God, who is the Savior of all people, especially of those who believe.

11 These are the things you must insist on and teach. ¹²Let no one despise your youth, but set the believers an example in speech and conduct, in love, in faith, in purity. ¹³Until I arrive, give attention to the public reading of scripture,[h] to

PONDER

Have nothing to do with profane myths and old wives' tales. Train yourself in godliness, for, while physical training is of some value, godliness is valuable in every way, holding promise for both the present life and the life to come.
—1 Timothy 4.7–8

PRAY

Father God, remind us daily of the advice about life that Paul gave to Timothy, that becoming godly is not something that comes to us naturally, but that we have to work at it, to train ourselves through reading the Word and prayer. We ask you for the determination to dedicate ourselves every day to acquire the hallmarks of godliness: honorable speech, right conduct, love, faith and purity. Strengthen us in this commitment. We ask this in the name of our Savior. Amen.

exhorting, to teaching. ¹⁴Do not neglect the gift that is in you, which was given to you through prophecy with the laying on of hands by the council of elders.[i] ¹⁵Put these things into practice, devote yourself to them, so that all may see your progress. ¹⁶Pay close attention to yourself and to your teaching; continue in these things, for in doing this you will save both yourself and your hearers.

DUTIES TOWARD BELIEVERS

5 Do not speak harshly to an older man,[j] but speak to him as to a

a **3.16** Gk *Who*; other ancient authorities read *God*; others, *Which*　b **3.16** Or *justified*
c **3.16** Or *by the Spirit*　d **4.1** Or *the last*　e **4.6** Gk *brothers*　f **4.6** Or *deacon*
g **4.10** Other ancient authorities read *suffer reproach*　h **4.13** Gk *to the reading*
i **4.14** Gk *by the presbytery*　j **5.1** Or *an elder*, or *a presbyter*

father, to younger men as brothers, ²to older women as mothers, to younger women as sisters—with absolute purity.

3 Honor widows who are really widows. ⁴If a widow has children or grandchildren, they should first learn their religious duty to their own family and make some repayment to their parents; for this is pleasing in God's sight. ⁵The real widow, left alone, has set her hope on God and continues in supplications and prayers night and day; ⁶but the widowᵃ who lives for pleasure is dead even while she lives. ⁷Give these commands as well, so that they may be above reproach. ⁸And whoever does not provide for relatives, and especially for family members, has denied the faith and is worse than an unbeliever.

9 Let a widow be put on the list if she is not less than sixty years old and has been married only once;ᵇ ¹⁰she must be well attested for her good works, as one who has brought up children, shown hospitality, washed the saints' feet, helped the afflicted, and devoted herself to doing good in every way. ¹¹But refuse to put younger widows on the list; for when their sensual desires alienate them from Christ, they want to marry, ¹²and so they incur condemnation for having violated their first pledge. ¹³Besides that, they learn to be idle, gadding about from house to house; and they are not merely idle, but also gossips and busybodies, saying what they should not say. ¹⁴So I would have younger widows marry, bear children, and manage their households, so as to give the adversary no occasion to revile us. ¹⁵For some have already turned away to follow Satan. ¹⁶If any believing womanᶜ has relatives who are really widows, let her assist them; let the church not be burdened, so that it can assist those who are real widows.

17 Let the elders who rule well be considered worthy of double honor,ᵈ especially those who labor in preaching and teaching; ¹⁸for the scripture says, "You shall not muzzle an ox while it is treading out the grain," and, "The laborer deserves to be paid." ¹⁹Never accept any accusation against an elder except on the evidence of two or three witnesses. ²⁰As for those who persist in sin, rebuke them in the presence of all, so that the rest also may stand in fear. ²¹In the presence of God and of Christ Jesus and of the elect angels, I warn you to keep these instructions without prejudice, doing nothing on the basis of partiality. ²²Do not ordainᵉ anyone hastily, and do not participate in the sins of others; keep yourself pure.

23 No longer drink only water, but take a little wine for the sake of your stomach and your frequent ailments.

24 The sins of some people are conspicuous and precede them to judgment, while the sins of others follow them there. ²⁵So also good works are conspicuous; and even when they are not, they cannot remain hidden.

6 Let all who are under the yoke of slavery regard their masters as worthy of all honor, so that the name of God and the teaching may not be blasphemed. ²Those who have believing masters must not be disrespectful to them on the ground that they are members of the church;ᶠ rather they must serve them all the more, since those who benefit by their service are believers and beloved.ᵍ

FALSE TEACHING AND TRUE RICHES

Teach and urge these duties. ³Whoever teaches otherwise and does not agree with the sound words of our Lord Jesus Christ and the teaching that is in accordance with godliness, ⁴is conceited, understanding nothing, and has a

---

ᵃ 5.6 Gk *she*   ᵇ 5.9 Gk *the wife of one husband*   ᶜ 5.16 Other ancient authorities read *believing man or woman*; others, *believing man*   ᵈ 5.17 Or *compensation*   ᵉ 5.22 Gk *Do not lay hands on*   ᶠ 6.2 Gk *are brothers*   ᵍ 6.2 Or *since they are believers and beloved, who devote themselves to good deeds*

morbid craving for controversy and for disputes about words. From these come envy, dissension, slander, base suspicions, 5and wrangling among those who are depraved in mind and bereft of the truth, imagining that godliness is a means of gain.[a] 6Of course, there is great gain in godliness combined with contentment; 7for we brought nothing into the world, so that[b] we can take nothing out of it; 8but if we have food and clothing, we will be content with these. 9But those who want to be rich fall into temptation and are trapped by many senseless and harmful desires that plunge people into ruin and destruction. 10For the love of money is a root of all kinds of evil, and in their eagerness to be rich some have wandered away from the faith and pierced themselves with many pains.

THE GOOD FIGHT OF FAITH

11 But as for you, man of God, shun all this; pursue righteousness, godliness, faith, love, endurance, gentleness. 12Fight the good fight of the faith; take hold of the eternal life, to which you were called and for which you made[c] the good confession in the presence of many witnesses. 13In the presence of God, who gives life to all things, and of Christ Jesus, who in his testimony before Pontius Pilate made the good confession, I charge you 14to keep the commandment without spot or blame until the manifestation of our Lord Jesus Christ, 15which he will bring about at the right time—he who is the blessed and only Sovereign, the King of kings and Lord of lords. 16It is he alone who has immortality and dwells in unapproachable light, whom no one has ever seen or can see; to him be honor and eternal dominion. Amen.

17 As for those who in the present age are rich, command them not to be haughty, or to set their hopes on the uncertainty of riches, but rather on God who richly provides us with everything for our enjoyment. 18They are to do good, to be rich in good works, generous, and ready to

PONDER

There is great gain in godliness combined with contentment; for we brought nothing into the world, so that we can take nothing out of it; but if we have food and clothing, we will be content with these.
—1 Timothy 6.6–8

PRAY

Father, with gratitude and thanksgiving we acknowledge that everything we have comes to us from your hand. We work, but you give us meaningful work. We use our talents, but you give us those talents and abilities. Teach us how to be content with the blessings you have already given us. Help us to use all of our gifts wisely, being discerning and careful in the ways we use our gifts so that we do not dishonor you. Come, Holy Spirit, to live within us, to teach, guide and comfort us as Jesus promised you would. And help us to emulate the life, the teaching, and the words of our Savior, Jesus Christ. In his name we pray. Amen.

share, 19thus storing up for themselves the treasure of a good foundation for the future, so that they may take hold of the life that really is life.

PERSONAL INSTRUCTIONS AND BENEDICTION

20 Timothy, guard what has been entrusted to you. Avoid the profane chatter and contradictions of what is falsely called knowledge; 21by professing it some have missed the mark as regards the faith.

Grace be with you.[d]

a 6.5 Other ancient authorities add *Withdraw yourself from such people*
b 6.7 Other ancient authorities read *world—it is certain that* c 6.12 Gk *confessed*
d 6.21 The Greek word for *you* here is plural; in other ancient authorities it is singular. Other ancient authorities add *Amen*

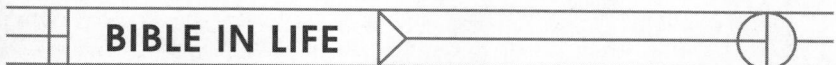

BIBLE IN LIFE

Excluding Others

1 Timothy 6.17–18

When we define ourselves as individuals, we often identify with certain subsets of people. For example, someone might say, "I am a Baptist" or "I am an American." We include ourselves in those groups even though we are unique, self-reliant, independent individuals. But identifying ourselves with certain groups can breed attitudes of superiority. When we take special pride in our nationality or our denomination, we risk excluding people of other nationalities or denominations. If we are proud of our wealth, our self-reliance or our independence, then we exclude those who are unemployed, poor, homeless or dependent on others. There is a temptation for us to be arrogant, to be selfish, to be exclusive—to build a wall around ourselves, including only those just like us. Jesus Christ was different. He certainly did not advocate arrogance; he was meek and humble. He did not condone selfishness; he selflessly shared. Jesus reached out to those who were excluded—the lepers, the poverty-stricken, the homeless and those afflicted with disease—and loved them. We should do the same.

The Second Letter of Paul to

TIMOTHY

If you knew your life was about to end and you wanted to pass on your values to someone close to you, what would you say? Second Timothy offers a look at Paul's answer to this question. Languishing in a cold Roman dungeon, chained like a common criminal and realizing he is about to die, Paul attempts to pull together the wisdom of a lifetime of service to God. His words, forged in the crucible of life-threatening experiences, point to the hope that belongs to all of us in Jesus Christ.

SALUTATION

1 Paul, an apostle of Christ Jesus by the will of God, for the sake of the promise of life that is in Christ Jesus,

2 To Timothy, my beloved child:

Grace, mercy, and peace from God the Father and Christ Jesus our Lord.

THANKSGIVING AND ENCOURAGEMENT

3 I am grateful to God—whom I worship with a clear conscience, as my ancestors did—when I remember you constantly in my prayers night and day. 4Recalling your tears, I long to see you so that I may be filled with joy. 5I am reminded of your sincere faith, a faith that lived first in your grandmother Lois and your mother Eunice and now, I am sure, lives in you. 6For this reason I remind you to rekindle the gift of God that is within you through the laying on of my hands; 7for God did not give us a spirit of cowardice, but rather a spirit of power and of love and of self-discipline.

8 Do not be ashamed, then, of the testimony about our Lord or of me his prisoner, but join with me in suffering for the gospel, relying on the power of God, 9who saved us and called us with a holy calling, not according to our works but according to his own purpose and grace. This grace was given to us in Christ Jesus before the ages began, 10but it has now been revealed through the appearing of our Savior Christ Jesus, who abolished death and brought life and immortality to light through the gospel. 11For this gospel I was appointed a herald and an apostle and a teacher,a 12and for this reason I suffer as I do. But I am not ashamed, for I know the one in whom I have put my trust, and I am sure that he is able to guard until that day what I have entrusted to him.b 13Hold to the standard of sound teaching that you have heard from me, in the faith and love that are in Christ Jesus. 14Guard the good treasure entrusted to you, with the help of the Holy Spirit living in us.

PONDER

Guard the good treasure entrusted to you, with the help of the Holy Spirit living in us.
—2 Timothy 1.14

PRAY

Father, help us to realize our own relative insignificance, our weakness, our need to turn our lives to you. Teach us to be worthy guardians of your truth, able to speak gently and wisely about you to others, discerning and careful in our ways so that we do not dishonor you. Come, Holy Spirit, to live within us, to teach, guide, and comfort us as Jesus promised you would. Help us to be courageous enough to assess what we have accomplished in your eyes in light of the opportunities you have given us. And help us to emulate the life, the teaching, and the words of our Savior, Jesus Christ. In his name we pray. Amen.

15 You are aware that all who are in Asia have turned away from me, including Phygelus and Hermogenes. 16May the Lord grant mercy to the household of Onesiphorus, because he often refreshed me and was not ashamed of my chain; 17when he arrived in Rome, he eagerlyc searched for me and found me 18—may the Lord grant that he will find mercy from the Lord on that day! And you know very well how much service he rendered in Ephesus.

A GOOD SOLDIER OF CHRIST JESUS

2 You then, my child, be strong in the grace that is in Christ Jesus; 2and what you have heard from me through many witnesses entrust to

a 1.11 Other ancient authorities add of the Gentiles   b 1.12 Or what has been entrusted to me   c 1.17 Or promptly

faithful people who will be able to teach others as well. 3Share in suffering like a good soldier of Christ Jesus. 4No one serving in the army gets entangled in everyday affairs; the soldier's aim is to please the enlisting officer. 5And in the case of an athlete, no one is crowned without competing according to the rules. 6It is the farmer who does the work who ought to have the first share of the crops. 7Think over what I say, for the Lord will give you understanding in all things.

8 Remember Jesus Christ, raised from the dead, a descendant of David—that is my gospel, 9for which I suffer hardship, even to the point of being chained like a criminal. But the word of God is not chained. 10Therefore I endure everything for the sake of the elect, so that they may also obtain the salvation that is in Christ Jesus, with eternal glory. 11The saying is sure:

If we have died with him, we
    will also live with him;
12 if we endure, we will also
        reign with him;
    if we deny him, he will
        also deny us;
13 if we are faithless, he
        remains faithful—
    for he cannot deny himself.

A WORKER APPROVED BY GOD

14 Remind them of this, and warn them before God[a] that they are to avoid wrangling over words, which does no good but only ruins those who are listening. 15Do your best to present yourself to God as one approved by him, a worker who has no need to be ashamed, rightly explaining the word of truth. 16Avoid profane chatter, for it will lead people into more and more impiety, 17and their talk will spread like gangrene. Among them are Hymenaeus and Philetus, 18who have swerved from the truth by claiming that the resurrection has already taken place. They are upsetting the faith of some. 19But God's firm foundation stands, bearing this inscription: "The Lord knows those who are his," and, "Let everyone who calls on the name of

the Lord turn away from wickedness."

20 In a large house there are utensils not only of gold and silver but also of wood and clay, some for special use, some for ordinary. 21All who cleanse themselves of the things I have mentioned[b] will become special utensils, dedicated and useful to the owner of the house, ready for every good work. 22Shun youthful passions and pursue righteousness, faith, love, and peace, along with those who call on the Lord from a pure heart. 23Have nothing to do with stupid and senseless controversies; you know that they breed quarrels. 24And the Lord's servant[c] must not be quarrelsome but kindly to everyone, an apt teacher, patient, 25correcting opponents with gentleness. God may perhaps grant that they will repent and come to know the truth, 26and that they may escape from the snare of the devil, having been held captive by him to do his will.[d]

GODLESSNESS IN THE LAST DAYS

3 You must understand this, that in the last days distressing times will come. 2For people will be lovers of themselves, lovers of money, boasters, arrogant, abusive, disobedient to their parents, ungrateful, unholy, 3inhuman, implacable, slanderers, profligates, brutes, haters of good, 4treacherous, reckless, swollen with conceit, lovers of pleasure rather than lovers of God, 5holding to the outward form of godliness but denying its power. Avoid them! 6For among them are those who make their way into households and captivate silly women, overwhelmed by their sins and swayed by all kinds of desires, 7who are always being instructed and can never arrive at a knowledge of the truth. 8As Jannes and Jambres opposed Moses, so these people, of corrupt mind and counterfeit faith, also oppose the

<hr>

[a] 2.14 Other ancient authorities read *the Lord*   [b] 2.21 Gk *of these things*   [c] 2.24 Gk *slave*   [d] 2.26 Or *by him, to do his* (that is, God's) *will*

truth. 9But they will not make much progress, because, as in the case of those two men,[a] their folly will become plain to everyone.

PAUL'S CHARGE TO TIMOTHY

10 Now you have observed my teaching, my conduct, my aim in life, my faith, my patience, my love, my steadfastness, 11my persecutions, and my suffering the things that happened to me in Antioch, Iconium, and Lystra. What persecutions I endured! Yet the Lord rescued me from all of them. 12Indeed, all who want to live a godly life in Christ Jesus will be persecuted. 13But wicked people and impostors will go from bad to worse, deceiving others and being deceived. 14But as for you, continue in what you have learned and firmly believed, knowing from whom you learned it, 15and how from childhood you have known the sacred writings that are able to instruct you for salvation through faith in Christ Jesus. 16All scripture is inspired by God and is[b] useful for teaching, for reproof, for correction, and for training in righteousness, 17so that everyone who belongs to God may be proficient, equipped for every good work.

4 In the presence of God and of Christ Jesus, who is to judge the living and the dead, and in view of his appearing and his kingdom, I

solemnly urge you: 2proclaim the message; be persistent whether the time is favorable or unfavorable; convince, rebuke, and encourage, with the utmost patience in teaching. 3For the time is coming when people will not put up with sound doctrine, but having itching ears, they will accumulate for themselves teachers to suit their own desires, 4and will turn away from listening to the truth and wander away to myths. 5As for you, always be sober, endure suffering, do the work of an evangelist, carry out your ministry fully.

6As for me, I am already being poured out as a libation, and the time of my departure has come. 7I have fought the good fight, I have finished the race, I have kept the faith. 8From now on there is reserved for me the crown of righteousness, which the Lord, the righteous judge, will give me on that day, and not only to me but also to all who have longed for his appearing.

PERSONAL INSTRUCTIONS

9 Do your best to come to me soon, 10for Demas, in love with this present world, has deserted me and gone to Thessalonica; Crescens has gone

[a] 3.9 Gk lacks two men   [b] 3.16 Or Every scripture inspired by God is also

---

╫ **BIBLE IN LIFE** ▷ ─────────────

Valuing Scripture

2 Timothy 3.16–17

When we read the scriptures, we can find answers to the profound questions of life: Who laid the foundation of my existence? What is the meaning of my life? What are the constants that never change? How can I grow and change? This book describes life itself—the meaning of our very existence, our relationship with God and our relationships with fellow human beings—yet it often lies on a shelf gathering dust. When we neglect to read it, we close off a major portion of our minds and voluntarily restrict the expansion of our hearts. The scriptures are inspired, or "God-breathed." God has breathed truths into the totality of scripture for the guidance of our lives. We may find slight variations in wording among translations, and the meaning of individual verses can be twisted out of context, but the basic message that God ordained for us in the Old and New Testaments is inspired. By reading God's Word, we are trained "in righteousness," meaning that we are given the necessary tools to become more like Christ and to live in accordance with God's will.

PONDER

I have fought the good fight, I have finished the race, I have kept the faith. From now on there is reserved for me the crown of righteousness, which the Lord, the righteous judge, will give me on that day, and not only to me but also to all who have longed for his appearing.
—2 Timothy 4.7–8

PRAY

O Father, we open ourselves to your Word through these words of Paul. Inspire each of us to go about our day with a new dedication, searching our consciences in prayer so that you can renew our spirits and our lives and give us greater commitment, greater courage, greater dedication and greater adventure. Plant your Word in us so that we will be open to new ways to serve you and reach out to other people. Help us to invest our talents, abilities and opportunities in your kingdom on earth as demonstrated to us by our Savior, Jesus Christ. In his name we pray. Amen.

to Galatia,ª Titus to Dalmatia. ¹¹Only Luke is with me. Get Mark and bring him with you, for he is useful in my ministry. ¹²I have sent Tychicus to Ephesus. ¹³When you come, bring the cloak that I left with Carpus at Troas, also the books, and above all the parchments. ¹⁴Alexander the coppersmith did me great harm; the Lord will pay him back for his deeds. ¹⁵You also must beware of him, for he strongly opposed our message.

16 At my first defense no one came to my support, but all deserted me. May it not be counted against them! ¹⁷But the Lord stood by me and gave me strength, so that through me the message might be fully proclaimed and all the Gentiles might hear it. So I was rescued from the lion's mouth. ¹⁸The Lord will rescue me from every evil attack and save me for his heavenly kingdom. To him be the glory forever and ever. Amen.

FINAL GREETINGS AND BENEDICTION

19 Greet Prisca and Aquila, and the household of Onesiphorus. ²⁰Erastus remained in Corinth; Trophimus I left ill in Miletus. ²¹Do your best to come before winter. Eubulus sends greetings to you, as do Pudens and Linus and Claudia and all the brothers and sisters.ᵇ

22 The Lord be with your spirit. Grace be with you.ᶜ

ª 4.10 Other ancient authorities read *Gaul*
ᵇ 4.21 Gk *all the brothers* ᶜ 4.22 The Greek word for *you* here is plural. Other ancient authorities add *Amen*

The Letter of Paul to
TITUS

Like Timothy, Titus was a son in the faith to Paul. Paul expresses confidence in Titus, but he also gives Titus instructions about how to lead the troubled and argumentative church in Crete. Even with God's Spirit at work, church life means hard work and a lot of giving. Putting church difficulties in perspective, Paul offers Titus guidelines for a godly life—including successful relationships between family, friends and society—with an emphasis on faith that overcomes division and disharmony among believers.

SALUTATION

1 Paul, a servant[a] of God and an apostle of Jesus Christ, for the sake of the faith of God's elect and the knowledge of the truth that is in accordance with godliness, [2]in the hope of eternal life that God, who never lies, promised before the ages began— [3]in due time he revealed his word through the proclamation with which I have been entrusted by the command of God our Savior,

[4] To Titus, my loyal child in the faith we share:

Grace[b] and peace from God the Father and Christ Jesus our Savior.

TITUS IN CRETE

[5] I left you behind in Crete for this reason, so that you should put in order what remained to be done, and should appoint elders in every town, as I directed you: [6]someone who is blameless, married only once,[c] whose children are believers, not accused of debauchery and not rebellious. [7]For a bishop,[d] as God's steward, must be blameless; he must not be arrogant or quick-tempered or addicted to wine or violent or greedy for gain; [8]but he must be hospitable, a lover of goodness, prudent, upright, devout, and self-controlled. [9]He must have a firm grasp of the word that is trustworthy in accordance with the teaching, so that he may be able both to preach with sound doctrine and to refute those who contradict it.

[10] There are also many rebellious people, idle talkers and deceivers, especially those of the circumcision; [11]they must be silenced, since they are upsetting whole families by teaching for sordid gain what it is not right to teach. [12]It was one of them, their very own prophet, who said,

"Cretans are always liars, vicious
  brutes, lazy gluttons."

[13]That testimony is true. For this reason rebuke them sharply, so that they may become sound in the faith, [14]not paying attention to Jewish myths or to commandments of those who reject the truth. [15]To the pure all things are pure, but to the corrupt and unbelieving nothing is pure. Their very minds and consciences are corrupted. [16]They profess to know God, but they deny him by their actions. They are detestable, disobedient, unfit for any good work.

TEACH SOUND DOCTRINE

2 But as for you, teach what is consistent with sound doctrine. [2]Tell the older men to be temperate, serious, prudent, and sound in faith, in love, and in endurance.

[3] Likewise, tell the older women to be reverent in behavior, not to be slanderers or slaves to drink; they are to teach what is good, [4]so that they

a **1.1** Gk *slave*   b **1.4** Other ancient authorities read *Grace, mercy*,   c **1.6** Gk *husband of one wife*   d **1.7** Or *an overseer*

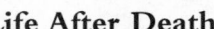

BIBLE IN LIFE

Life After Death   *Titus 1.1–3*

We have legitimate reasons to look upon death with fear, doubt, discomfort and sorrow. We don't understand exactly what will happen after we die, and we don't have any scientific proof of life after death. However, if we believe in Jesus Christ and have faith in his promises, then we can hope that life after death will be realized and that it will be fulfilling. Hope reassures us, tempers our fears and overcomes our sorrows. Jesus said, "In my Father's house there are many dwelling places. If it were not so, would I have told you that I go to prepare a place for you?" (John 14.2). We can envision a comfortable place in which our loved ones are waiting for us. There is nothing wrong with picturing comforting images to help us welcome the unknown. While we don't know exactly what the afterlife will be like, we can joyfully live our lives resting "in the hope of eternal life that God, who never lies, promised before the ages began" (Titus 1.2).

may encourage the young women to love their husbands, to love their children, 5to be self-controlled, chaste, good managers of the household, kind, being submissive to their husbands, so that the word of God may not be discredited.

6 Likewise, urge the younger men to be self-controlled. 7Show yourself in all respects a model of good works, and in your teaching show integrity, gravity, 8and sound speech that cannot be censured; then any opponent will be put to shame, having nothing evil to say of us.

<hr>

PONDER

Show yourself in all respects a model of good works, and in your teaching show integrity, gravity, and sound speech that cannot be censured; then any opponent will be put to shame, having nothing evil to say of us.
—Titus 2.7–8

PRAY

O Father, we are grateful for a message that is both stimulating and troubling because it requires us to consider carefully how we conduct ourselves each day. We pray that our hearts be opened to your words so we can present ourselves proudly as ambassadors of our Savior, Jesus Christ. Based on his message of reconciliation, help us to push aside arguments, debates and self-interpretations that exclude others or prevent them from seeking the kingdom of God, and instead speak gently, truthfully and graciously so that others will come to you. We ask in Jesus' name. Amen.

<hr>

9 Tell slaves to be submissive to their masters and to give satisfaction in every respect; they are not to talk back, 10not to pilfer, but to show complete and perfect fidelity, so that in everything they may be an orna-

ment to the doctrine of God our Savior.

11 For the grace of God has appeared, bringing salvation to all,[a] 12training us to renounce impiety and worldly passions, and in the present age to live lives that are self-controlled, upright, and godly, 13while we wait for the blessed hope and the manifestation of the glory of our great God and Savior,[b] Jesus Christ. 14He it is who gave himself for us that he might redeem us from all iniquity and purify for himself a people of his own who are zealous for good deeds.

15 Declare these things; exhort and reprove with all authority.[c] Let no one look down on you.

MAINTAIN GOOD DEEDS

3 Remind them to be subject to rulers and authorities, to be obedient, to be ready for every good work, 2to speak evil of no one, to avoid quarreling, to be gentle, and to show every courtesy to everyone. 3For we ourselves were once foolish, disobedient, led astray, slaves to various passions and pleasures, passing our days in malice and envy, despicable, hating one another. 4But when the goodness and loving kindness of God our Savior appeared, 5he saved us, not because of any works of righteousness that we had done, but according to his mercy, through the water[d] of rebirth and renewal by the Holy Spirit. 6This Spirit he poured out on us richly through Jesus Christ our Savior, 7so that, having been justified by his grace, we might become heirs according to the hope of eternal life. 8The saying is sure.

I desire that you insist on these things, so that those who have come to believe in God may be careful to devote themselves to good works; these things are excellent and profitable to everyone. 9But avoid stupid controversies, genealogies, dissensions, and quarrels about the law, for they are unprofitable and worthless.

[a] 2.11 Or has appeared to all, bringing salvation   [b] 2.13 Or of the great God and our Savior   [c] 2.15 Gk commandment   [d] 3.5 Gk washing

10 After a first and second admonition, have nothing more to do with anyone who causes divisions, 11 since you know that such a person is perverted and sinful, being self-condemned.

FINAL MESSAGES AND BENEDICTION

12 When I send Artemas to you, or Tychicus, do your best to come to me at Nicopolis, for I have decided to spend the winter there. 13 Make every effort to send Zenas the lawyer and Apollos on their way, and see that they lack nothing. 14 And let people learn to devote themselves to good works in order to meet urgent needs, so that they may not be unproductive.

15 All who are with me send greetings to you. Greet those who love us in the faith.

Grace be with all of you.[a]

---

[a] 3.15 Other ancient authorities add *Amen*

The Letter of Paul to
PHILEMON

Forgiveness is not always easy to ask for or to give. Someone has to swallow the hurt. Philemon is a case study in the cost of asking for forgiveness and of granting it. Writing from prison near the end of his life, Paul writes to ask Philemon, a friend and brother in Christ, to forgive and take back Onesimus, a runaway slave. Most runaway slaves, if caught, faced harsh punishment or even death. But Paul pleads with Philemon to become a living illustration of the grace Onesimus had already received through Jesus Christ.

SALUTATION

1 Paul, a prisoner of Christ Jesus, and Timothy our brother,[a]

To Philemon our dear friend and co-worker, 2to Apphia our sister,[b] to Archippus our fellow soldier, and to the church in your house:

3 Grace to you and peace from God our Father and the Lord Jesus Christ.

PHILEMON'S LOVE AND FAITH

4 When I remember you[c] in my prayers, I always thank my God 5because I hear of your love for all the saints and your faith toward the Lord Jesus. 6I pray that the sharing of your faith may become effective when you perceive all the good that we[d] may do for Christ. 7I have indeed received much joy and encouragement from your love, because the hearts of the saints have been refreshed through you, my brother.

PAUL'S PLEA FOR ONESIMUS

8 For this reason, though I am bold enough in Christ to command you to do your duty, 9yet I would rather appeal to you on the basis of love—and I, Paul, do this as an old man, and now also as a prisoner of Christ Jesus.[e] 10I am appealing to you for my child, Onesimus, whose father I have become during my imprisonment. 11Formerly he was useless to you, but now he is indeed useful[f] both to you and to me. 12I am sending him, that is, my own heart, back to you. 13I wanted to keep him with me, so that he might be of service to me in your place during my imprisonment for the gospel; 14but I preferred to do nothing without your consent, in order that your good deed might be voluntary and not something forced. 15Perhaps this is the reason he was separated from you for a while, so that you might have him back forever, 16no longer as a slave but more than a slave, a beloved brother—especially to me but how much more to you, both in the flesh and in the Lord.

17 So if you consider me your partner, welcome him as you would welcome me. 18If he has wronged you

in any way, or owes you anything, charge that to my account. 19I, Paul, am writing this with my own hand: I will repay it. I say nothing about your owing me even your own self. 20Yes, brother, let me have this benefit from you in the Lord! Refresh my heart in Christ. 21Confident of your obedience, I am writing to you, knowing that you will do even more than I say.

PONDER

I pray that the sharing of your faith may become effective when you perceive all the good that we may do for Christ. I have indeed received much joy and encouragement from your love, because the hearts of the saints have been refreshed through you, my brother.
—Philemon 6–7

PRAY

Lord God, we give you praise and thanksgiving for the love that we share in our Christian communities, love that builds us up, that gives us fellowship, support, comfort and acceptance. We know that you are the source of that love. Because you are the source of love, you sent your Son, Jesus Christ, to be our Savior, so that we are completely forgiven and reconciled to you, our Creator. Help us to adopt anew the characteristics of Jesus' sacrificial love: peace, compassion, humility, as well as service to all people. Remove from among us the barriers that keep us apart and the sins that divide us, and let our lives be attuned more closely every day to the perfect life of our Savior, in whose name we pray. Amen.

---

a 1 Gk *the brother*   b 2 Gk *the sister*
c 4 From verse 4 through verse 21, *you* is singular   d 6 Other ancient authorities read *you* (plural)   e 9 Or *as an ambassador of Christ Jesus, and now also his prisoner*
f 11 The name Onesimus means *useful* or (compare verse 20) *beneficial*

LOVE AS EQUALS

Perhaps this is the reason [Onesimus] was separated from you for a while, so that you might have him back forever, no longer as a slave but more than a slave, a beloved brother—especially to me but how much more to you, both in the flesh and in the Lord.

—Philemon 15–17

Paul's letter to Philemon may be short, but it conveys a very important message. While Paul was in prison, he had come to know a slave named Onesimus who had run away from his master Philemon, a member of the church at Colossae. Paul apparently led Onesimus to Christ, then directed him to return to Philemon and submit to him once again. Paul sent this letter with Onesimus to give to Philemon, urging him to regard Onesimus as a fellow Christian and brother and not simply as his slave. Paul also appears, indirectly, to urge Philemon to release Onesimus from his bondage, both as a favor to Paul and out of their mutual love of Christ.

Based on Paul's appeal to Philemon, one can gather that slavery is incompatible with Christian belief. In any case, it is clear from the letter that Christians should always be careful to regard all people with dignity and respect, even when they have done something against us or are indebted to us in some way. Our attitude should be the same as Christ, who showed respect and love for all people. He reached out in love equally to fellow Jews, to Samaritans and to Roman officers. He responded graciously to wealthy people like Zacchaeus and to poor people like the widow of Nain. He reached out to lepers, the lame and the blind, and even spent time with "sinners" and tax collectors.

Today we sometimes treat people as inferior if they are on welfare, grew up on the wrong side of town, are not yet citizens, or spent time in prison. We see ourselves as better somehow, and we avoid having to interact with them in a meaningful way. We are inclined to want to be with people like ourselves. We need to heed Paul's letter to Philemon and see others as God sees them, not just through our skewed lens of assessment. We need to ask God to help us overcome our feelings of self-importance and instead stretch our hearts and minds to include such people in our circle of friends and associates. After all, who are we to look down on others when we are so deeply dependent on God's forgiveness and grace? God loved us enough to come and live among us. Out of that same mercy we have received, we should freely extend mercy to others.

Going Deeper

- Describe a time when you held a negative attitude toward someone until you got to know that person better. What was it exactly that caused you to change your opinion?
- What group of people do you find hardest to love? Why? How do Paul's words to Philemon apply to your regard for them?

22 One thing more—prepare a guest room for me, for I am hoping through your prayers to be restored to you.

FINAL GREETINGS AND BENEDICTION

23 Epaphras, my fellow prisoner in Christ Jesus, sends greetings to you,[a] **24** and so do Mark, Aristarchus, Demas, and Luke, my fellow workers.

25 The grace of the Lord Jesus Christ be with your spirit.[b]

[a] **23** Here you is singular   [b] **25** Other ancient authorities add *Amen*

The Letter to the

HEBREWS

How would it feel to lose your job or your car because you follow Jesus Christ? How would it feel to lose the approval of your friends? This kind of loss is what the audience of Hebrews faced. They needed to be reminded that Jesus is sufficient to meet their needs and to represent them before God. They needed to hear the dangers of drifting from the faith; they needed to hear about the saints before them who had lived by faith. As you read, allow the writer of Hebrews to motivate you, as he did the early church, to look "to Jesus, the pioneer and perfecter of our faith" (Hebrews 12.2).

GOD HAS SPOKEN BY HIS SON

1 Long ago God spoke to our an-cestors in many and various ways by the prophets, ²but in these last days he has spoken to us by a Son,ᵃ whom he appointed heir of all things, through whom he also cre-ated the worlds. ³He is the reflection of God's glory and the exact imprint of God's very being, and he sustainsᵇ all things by his powerful word. When he had made purification for sins, he sat down at the right hand of the Majesty on high, ⁴having be-come as much superior to angels as the name he has inherited is more excellent than theirs.

THE SON IS SUPERIOR TO ANGELS

5 For to which of the angels did God ever say,

"You are my Son;
    today I have begotten you"?
Or again,
"I will be his Father,
    and he will be my Son"?
⁶And again, when he brings the firstborn into the world, he says,
"Let all God's angels worship him."
⁷Of the angels he says,
"He makes his angels winds,
    and his servants flames of fire."
⁸But of the Son he says,
"Your throne, O God, isᶜ
    forever and ever,
and the righteous scepter is the
    scepter of yourᵈ kingdom.
9 You have loved righteousness
    and hated wickedness;
therefore God, your God,
    has anointed you
with the oil of gladness beyond
    your companions."
¹⁰And,
"In the beginning, Lord, you
    founded the earth,
and the heavens are the
    work of your hands;
¹¹ they will perish, but you remain;
    they will all wear out
    like clothing;
¹² like a cloak you will roll them up,
    and like clothingᵉ they
    will be changed.
But you are the same,
    and your years will never end."

⊖

PONDER

[The Son] is the reflection of God's glory and the exact imprint of God's very being, and he sustains all things by his powerful word. When he had made purification for sins, he sat down at the right hand of the Majesty on high.
—Hebrews 1.3

PRAY

Heavenly Father, we confess that sometimes we forget to orient our lives toward our Savior, Jesus Christ—the one who is divine, eternal, and who lives forever at your right hand with total knowledge and power. Remind us daily to turn our faces to you, to ask for guidance and help from the One who is always with us. Help us to absorb this lesson, plant it deeply into our hearts and minds, and remember as we go through the remaining days of our existence here on earth. We are thankful for our Savior and for a chance to learn increasingly, and sometimes surprisingly, more about the One we have chosen to worship. In his name we pray. Amen.

⊠

¹³But to which of the angels has he ever said,
"Sit at my right hand
    until I make your enemies a
        footstool for your feet"?
¹⁴Are not all angelsᶠ spirits in the divine service, sent to serve for the sake of those who are to inherit sal-vation?

WARNING TO PAY ATTENTION

2 Therefore we must pay greater attention to what we have heard, so that we do not drift away from it. ²For if the message declared

ᵃ 1.2 Or the Son   ᵇ 1.3 Or bears along
ᶜ 1.8 Or God is your throne   ᵈ 1.8 Other ancient authorities read his   ᵉ 1.12 Other ancient authorities lack like clothing
ᶠ 1.14 Gk all of them

through angels was valid, and every transgression or disobedience received a just penalty, ³how can we escape if we neglect so great a salvation? It was declared at first through the Lord, and it was attested to us by those who heard him, ⁴while God added his testimony by signs and wonders and various miracles, and by gifts of the Holy Spirit, distributed according to his will.

EXALTATION THROUGH ABASEMENT

5 Now Godᵃ did not subject the coming world, about which we are speaking, to angels. ⁶But someone has testified somewhere,

"What are human beings that
> you are mindful of them,ᵇ
or mortals, that you
> care for them?ᶜ
7 You have made them for a
> little while lowerᵈ
> than the angels;
> you have crowned them with
> glory and honor,ᵉ
8 subjecting all things
> under their feet."

Now in subjecting all things to them, Godᵃ left nothing outside their control. As it is, we do not yet see everything in subjection to them, ⁹but we do see Jesus, who for a little while was made lowerᶠ than the angels, now crowned with glory and honor because of the suffering of death, so that by the grace of Godᵍ he might taste death for everyone. 10 It was fitting that God,ᵃ for whom and through whom all things exist, in bringing many children to glory, should make the pioneer of their salvation perfect through sufferings. ¹¹For the one who sanctifies and those who are sanctified all have one Father.ʰ For this reason Jesusᵃ is not ashamed to call them brothers and sisters,ⁱ ¹²saying,

"I will proclaim your name to
> my brothers and sisters,ⁱ
in the midst of the
> congregation I will
> praise you."

13 And again,
"I will put my trust in him."
And again,

"Here am I and the children
> whom God has given me."

14 Since, therefore, the children share flesh and blood, he himself likewise shared the same things, so that through death he might destroy the one who has the power of death, that is, the devil, ¹⁵and free those who all their lives were held in slavery by the fear of death. ¹⁶For it is clear that he did not come to help angels, but the descendants of Abraham. ¹⁷Therefore he had to become like his brothers and sistersⁱ in every respect, so that he might be a merciful and faithful high priest in the service of God, to make a sacrifice of atonement for the sins of the people. ¹⁸Because he himself was tested by what he suffered, he is able to help those who are being tested.

MOSES A SERVANT, CHRIST A SON

3 Therefore, brothers and sisters,ⁱ holy partners in a heavenly calling, consider that Jesus, the apostle and high priest of our confession, ²was faithful to the one who appointed him, just as Moses also "was faithful in allʲ God'sᵏ house." ³Yet Jesusˡ is worthy of more glory than Moses, just as the builder of a house has more honor than the house itself. ⁴(For every house is built by someone, but the builder of all things is God.) ⁵Now Moses was faithful in all God'sᵏ house as a servant, to testify to the things that would be spoken later. ⁶Christ, however, was faithful over God'sᵏ house as a son, and we are his house if we hold firmᵐ the confidence and the pride that belong to hope.

ᵃ 2.5,8,10,11 Gk *he*   ᵇ 2.6 Gk *What is man that you are mindful of him?*   ᶜ 2.6 Gk *or the son of man that you care for him?* In the Hebrew of Psalm 8.4–6 both *man* and *son of man* refer to all humankind   ᵈ 2.7 Or *them only a little lower*   ᵉ 2.7 Other ancient authorities add *and set them over the works of your hands*   ᶠ 2.9 Or *who was made a little lower*   ᵍ 2.9 Other ancient authorities read *apart from God*   ʰ 2.11 Gk *are all of one*   ⁱ 2.11,12,17; 3.1 Gk *brothers*   ʲ 3.2 Other ancient authorities lack *all*   ᵏ 3.2,5,6 Gk *his*   ˡ 3.3 Gk *this one*   ᵐ 3.6 Other ancient authorities add *to the end*

WARNING AGAINST UNBELIEF

7 Therefore, as the Holy Spirit says,

"Today, if you hear his voice,
8 do not harden your hearts
       as in the rebellion,
       as on the day of testing
           in the wilderness,
9 where your ancestors put
       me to the test,
   though they had seen my
       works 10 for forty years.
Therefore I was angry with
       that generation,
and I said, 'They always go
       astray in their hearts,
   and they have not known
       my ways.'
11 As in my anger I swore,
   'They will not enter my rest.' "

12 Take care, brothers and sisters,ᵃ that none of you may have an evil, unbelieving heart that turns away from the living God. 13 But exhort one another every day, as long as it is called "today," so that none of you may be hardened by the deceitfulness of sin. 14 For we have become partners of Christ, if only we hold our first confidence firm to the end. 15 As it is said,

"Today, if you hear his voice,
   do not harden your hearts as
       in the rebellion."

16 Now who were they who heard and yet were rebellious? Was it not all those who left Egypt under the leadership of Moses? 17 But with whom was he angry forty years? Was it not those who sinned, whose bodies fell in the wilderness? 18 And to whom did he swear that they would not enter his rest, if not to those who were disobedient? 19 So we see that they were unable to enter because of unbelief.

THE REST THAT GOD PROMISED

4 Therefore, while the promise of entering his rest is still open, let us take care that none of you should seem to have failed to reach it. 2 For indeed the good news came to us just as to them; but the message they heard did not benefit them, because they were not united by faith with those who listened.ᵇ 3 For we

who have believed enter that rest, just as Godᶜ has said,

"As in my anger I swore,
   'They shall not enter my rest,' "

though his works were finished at the foundation of the world. 4 For in one place it speaks about the seventh day as follows, "And God rested on the seventh day from all his works." 5 And again in this place it says, "They shall not enter my rest." 6 Since therefore it remains open for some to enter it, and those who formerly received the good news failed to enter because of disobedience, 7 again he sets a certain day—"today"—saying through David much later, in the words already quoted,

"Today, if you hear his voice,
   do not harden your hearts."

8 For if Joshua had given them rest, Godᶜ would not speak later about another day. 9 So then, a sabbath rest still remains for the people of God; 10 for those who enter God's rest also cease from their labors as God did from his. 11 Let us therefore make every effort to enter that rest, so that no one may fall through such disobedience as theirs.

12 Indeed, the word of God is living and active, sharper than any two-edged sword, piercing until it divides soul from spirit, joints from marrow; it is able to judge the thoughts and intentions of the heart. 13 And before him no creature is hidden, but all are naked and laid bare to the eyes of the one to whom we must render an account.

JESUS THE GREAT HIGH PRIEST

14 Since, then, we have a great high priest who has passed through the heavens, Jesus, the Son of God, let us hold fast to our confession. 15 For we do not have a high priest who is unable to sympathize with our weaknesses, but we have one who in every respect has been testedᵈ as we are, yet without sin. 16 Let us therefore approach the throne of grace with boldness, so that we may

ᵃ 3.12 Gk brothers   ᵇ 4.2 Other ancient authorities read it did not meet with faith in those who listened   ᶜ 4.3,8 Gk he   ᵈ 4.15 Or tempted

⊕

PONDER

Let us therefore approach the throne of grace with boldness, so that we may receive mercy and find grace to help in time of need.
—Hebrews 4.16

PRAY

O Father, we aren't really accustomed to thinking about Jesus as the great high priest, or about approaching you with boldness. But it is good to be reminded every now and then of this wonderful, exalted, and exciting relationship that we have with you, our Creator, through our perfect Savior, Jesus Christ. We are so grateful that we need not be hesitant to approach you with our questions, our problems, our needs, or to share our joys. We praise you for your mercy and grace, available to us when we need you. Amen.

receive mercy and find grace to help in time of need.

5 Every high priest chosen from among mortals is put in charge of things pertaining to God on their behalf, to offer gifts and sacrifices for sins. ²He is able to deal gently with the ignorant and wayward, since he himself is subject to weakness; ³and because of this he must offer sacrifice for his own sins as well as for those of the people. ⁴And one does not presume to take this honor, but takes it only when called by God, just as Aaron was.

5 So also Christ did not glorify himself in becoming a high priest, but was appointed by the one who said to him,
"You are my Son,
today I have begotten you";
⁶as he says also in another place,
"You are a priest forever,
according to the order of
Melchizedek."

7 In the days of his flesh, Jesusª offered up prayers and supplications, with loud cries and tears, to the one who was able to save him from death, and he was heard because of his reverent submission. ⁸Although he was a Son, he learned obedience through what he suffered; ⁹and having been made perfect, he became the source of eternal salvation for all who obey him, ¹⁰having been designated by God a high priest according to the order of Melchizedek.

WARNING AGAINST FALLING AWAY

11 About thisᵇ we have much to say that is hard to explain, since you have become dull in understanding. ¹²For though by this time you ought to be teachers, you need someone to teach you again the basic elements of the oracles of God. You need milk, not solid food; ¹³for everyone who lives on milk, being still an infant, is unskilled in the word of righteousness. ¹⁴But solid food is for the mature, for those whose faculties have been trained by practice to distinguish good from evil.

THE PERIL OF FALLING AWAY

6 Therefore let us go on toward perfection,ᶜ leaving behind the basic teaching about Christ, and not laying again the foundation: repentance from dead works and faith toward God, ²instruction about baptisms, laying on of hands, resurrection of the dead, and eternal judgment. ³And we will doᵈ this, if God permits. ⁴For it is impossible to restore again to repentance those who have once been enlightened, and have tasted the heavenly gift, and have shared in the Holy Spirit, ⁵and have tasted the goodness of the word of God and the powers of the age to come, ⁶and then have fallen away, since on their own they are crucifying again the Son of God and are holding him up to contempt. ⁷Ground that drinks up the rain falling on it repeatedly, and that produces a crop useful to those for whom it is cultivated,

ª 5.7 Gk he   ᵇ 5.11 Or him   ᶜ 6.1 Or toward maturity   ᵈ 6.3 Other ancient authorities read let us do

receives a blessing from God. 8But if it produces thorns and thistles, it is worthless and on the verge of being cursed; its end is to be burned over.

9 Even though we speak in this way, beloved, we are confident of better things in your case, things that belong to salvation. 10For God is not unjust; he will not overlook your work and the love that you showed for his sake[a] in serving the saints, as you still do. 11And we want each one of you to show the same diligence so as to realize the full assurance of hope to the very end, 12so that you may not become sluggish, but imitators of those who through faith and patience inherit the promises.

THE CERTAINTY OF GOD'S PROMISE

13 When God made a promise to Abraham, because he had no one greater by whom to swear, he swore by himself, 14saying, "I will surely bless you and multiply you." 15And thus Abraham,[b] having patiently endured, obtained the promise. 16Human beings, of course, swear by someone greater than themselves, and an oath given as confirmation puts an end to all dispute. 17In the same way, when God desired to show even more clearly to the heirs of the promise the unchangeable character of his purpose, he guaranteed it by an oath, 18so that through two unchangeable things, in which it is impossible that God would prove false,

we who have taken refuge might be strongly encouraged to seize the hope set before us. 19We have this hope, a sure and steadfast anchor of the soul, a hope that enters the inner shrine behind the curtain, 20where Jesus, a forerunner on our behalf, has entered, having become a high priest forever according to the order of Melchizedek.

THE PRIESTLY ORDER OF MELCHIZEDEK

7 This "King Melchizedek of Salem, priest of the Most High God, met Abraham as he was returning from defeating the kings and blessed him"; 2and to him Abraham apportioned "one-tenth of everything." His name, in the first place, means "king of righteousness"; next he is also king of Salem, that is, "king of peace." 3Without father, without mother, without genealogy, having neither beginning of days nor end of life, but resembling the Son of God, he remains a priest forever.

4 See how great he is! Even[c] Abraham the patriarch gave him a tenth of the spoils. 5And those descendants of Levi who receive the priestly office have a commandment in the law to collect tithes[d] from the people, that is, from their kindred,[e] though these also are descended from Abraham. 6But this man, who

a 6.10 Gk *for his name*   b 6.15 Gk *he*   c 7.4 Other ancient authorities lack *Even*   d 7.5 Or *a tenth*   e 7.5 Gk *brothers*

BIBLE IN LIFE

Christian Maturity   *Hebrews 5.13–14*

Our spiritual goal is maturity, which means coming "to the measure of the full stature of Christ" (Ephesians 4.13). In our careers we need more than just textbook learning; we also need apprenticeships and practical experience. So too in our faith we need more than knowledge acquired from the words of others. We also need experiential knowledge, which leads to maturity. We may hear dynamic sermons, sing songs rich in meaning, recite a creed or say the Lord's Prayer, but those things don't give us the experience—the "solid food"—of being a Christian or leading a Christlike life. Growth requires faith experiences such as exploring our gifts, thinking and questioning and seeking the truth, and serving marginalized people—the prisoners, the sick, the poor and lonely, the homeless and the unattractive. Maturity requires us to relate more intimately with Jesus, our Savior, and actively seek to be more like him.

does not belong to their ancestry, collected tithes[a] from Abraham and blessed him who had received the promises. 7It is beyond dispute that the inferior is blessed by the superior. 8In the one case, tithes are received by those who are mortal; in the other, by one of whom it is testified that he lives. 9One might even say that Levi himself, who receives tithes, paid tithes through Abraham, 10for he was still in the loins of his ancestor when Melchizedek met him.

WE HAVE HOPE THAT DEATH
IS NOT THE END OF LIFE.
THIS HOPE IS A CHRISTIAN'S
ANCHOR IN THE MIDST
OF FEAR AND SORROW.

ANOTHER PRIEST, LIKE MELCHIZEDEK

11 Now if perfection had been attainable through the levitical priesthood—for the people received the law under this priesthood—what further need would there have been to speak of another priest arising according to the order of Melchizedek, rather than one according to the order of Aaron? 12For when there is a change in the priesthood, there is necessarily a change in the law as well. 13Now the one of whom these things are spoken belonged to another tribe, from which no one has ever served at the altar. 14For it is evident that our Lord was descended from Judah, and in connection with that tribe Moses said nothing about priests.

15 It is even more obvious when another priest arises, resembling Melchizedek, 16one who has become a priest, not through a legal requirement concerning physical descent, but through the power of an indestructible life. 17For it is attested of him,

"You are a priest forever,
    according to the order
        of Melchizedek."

18There is, on the one hand, the abrogation of an earlier commandment because it was weak and ineffectual 19(for the law made nothing perfect); there is, on the other hand, the introduction of a better hope, through which we approach God.

20 This was confirmed with an oath; for others who became priests took their office without an oath, 21but this one became a priest with an oath, because of the one who said to him,

"The Lord has sworn
    and will not change his mind,
'You are a priest forever' "—

22accordingly Jesus has also become the guarantee of a better covenant.

23 Furthermore, the former priests were many in number, because they were prevented by death from continuing in office; 24but he holds his priesthood permanently, because he continues forever. 25Consequently he is able for all time to save[b] those who approach God through him, since he always lives to make intercession for them.

26 For it was fitting that we should have such a high priest, holy, blameless, undefiled, separated from sinners, and exalted above the heavens. 27Unlike the other[c] high priests, he has no need to offer sacrifices day after day, first for his own sins, and then for those of the people; this he did once for all when he offered himself. 28For the law appoints as high priests those who are subject to weakness, but the word of the oath, which came later than the law, appoints a Son who has been made perfect forever.

MEDIATOR OF A BETTER COVENANT

8 Now the main point in what we are saying is this: we have such a high priest, one who is seated at the right hand of the throne of the Majesty in the heavens, 2a minister

---

[a] 7.6 Or *a tenth*   [b] 7.25 Or *able to save completely*   [c] 7.27 Gk lacks *other*

in the sanctuary and the true tent[a] that the Lord, and not any mortal, has set up. [3]For every high priest is appointed to offer gifts and sacrifices; hence it is necessary for this priest also to have something to offer. [4]Now if he were on earth, he would not be a priest at all, since there are priests who offer gifts according to the law. [5]They offer worship in a sanctuary that is a sketch and shadow of the heavenly one; for Moses, when he was about to erect the tent,[a] was warned, "See that you make everything according to the pattern that was shown you on the mountain." [6]But Jesus[b] has now obtained a more excellent ministry, and to that degree he is the mediator of a better covenant, which has been enacted through better promises. [7]For if that first covenant had been faultless, there would have been no need to look for a second one.

[8]God[c] finds fault with them when he says:
"The days are surely coming,
    says the Lord,
when I will establish a
    new covenant with
    the house of Israel
and with the house of Judah;
[9] not like the covenant that I made
    with their ancestors,
on the day when I took them
    by the hand to lead them
    out of the land of Egypt;
for they did not continue
    in my covenant,
and so I had no concern for
    them, says the Lord.
[10] This is the covenant that I
    will make with the
    house of Israel
after those days, says the Lord:
I will put my laws in
    their minds,
and write them on their hearts,
and I will be their God,
    and they shall be my people.
[11] And they shall not teach
    one another
or say to each other,
    'Know the Lord,'
for they shall all know me,
    from the least of them
    to the greatest.

[12] For I will be merciful toward
    their iniquities,
    and I will remember their
    sins no more."
[13]In speaking of "a new covenant," he has made the first one obsolete. And what is obsolete and growing old will soon disappear.

THE EARTHLY AND THE HEAVENLY SANCTUARIES

9 Now even the first covenant had regulations for worship and an earthly sanctuary. [2]For a tent[a] was constructed, the first one, in which were the lampstand, the table, and the bread of the Presence;[d] this is called the Holy Place. [3]Behind the second curtain was a tent[a] called the Holy of Holies. [4]In it stood the golden altar of incense and the ark of the covenant overlaid on all sides with gold, in which there were a golden urn holding the manna, and Aaron's rod that budded, and the tablets of the covenant; [5]above it were the cherubim of glory overshadowing the mercy seat.[e] Of these things we cannot speak now in detail.

[6] Such preparations having been made, the priests go continually into the first tent[a] to carry out their ritual duties; [7]but only the high priest goes into the second, and he but once a year, and not without taking the blood that he offers for himself and for the sins committed unintentionally by the people. [8]By this the Holy Spirit indicates that the way into the sanctuary has not yet been disclosed as long as the first tent[a] is still standing. [9]This is a symbol[f] of the present time, during which gifts and sacrifices are offered that cannot perfect the conscience of the worshiper, [10]but deal only with food and drink and various baptisms, regulations for the body imposed until the time comes to set things right.

[11] But when Christ came as a high priest of the good things that have come,[g] then through the greater and

[a] 8.2,5; 9.2,3,6,8 Or *tabernacle*   [b] 8.6 Gk *he*
[c] 8.8 Gk *He*   [d] 9.2 Gk *the presentation of the loaves*   [e] 9.5 Or *the place of atonement*
[f] 9.9 Gk *parable*   [g] 9.11 Other ancient authorities read *good things to come*

perfect[a] tent[b] (not made with hands, that is, not of this creation), [12]he entered once for all into the Holy Place, not with the blood of goats and calves, but with his own blood, thus obtaining eternal redemption. [13]For if the blood of goats and bulls, with the sprinkling of the ashes of a heifer, sanctifies those who have been defiled so that their flesh is purified, [14]how much more will the blood of Christ, who through the eternal Spirit[c] offered himself without blemish to God, purify our[d] conscience from dead works to worship the living God!

[15] For this reason he is the mediator of a new covenant, so that those who are called may receive the promised eternal inheritance, because a death has occurred that redeems them from the transgressions under the first covenant.[e] [16]Where a will[e] is involved, the death of the one who made it must be established. [17]For a will[e] takes effect only at death, since it is not in force as long as the one who made it is alive. [18]Hence not even the first covenant was inaugurated without blood. [19]For when every commandment had been told to all the people by Moses in accordance with the law, he took the blood of calves and goats,[f] with water and scarlet wool and hyssop, and sprinkled both the scroll itself and all the people, [20]saying, "This is the blood of the covenant that God has ordained for you." [21]And in the same way he sprinkled with the blood both the tent[b] and all the vessels used in worship. [22]Indeed, under the law almost everything is purified with blood, and without the shedding of blood there is no forgiveness of sins.

CHRIST'S SACRIFICE TAKES AWAY SIN

[23] Thus it was necessary for the sketches of the heavenly things to be purified with these rites, but the heavenly things themselves need better sacrifices than these. [24]For Christ did not enter a sanctuary made by human hands, a mere copy of the true one, but he entered into

PONDER

How much more will the blood of Christ, who through the eternal Spirit offered himself without blemish to God, purify our conscience from dead works to worship the living God!
—Hebrews 9.14

PRAY

Lord, we are confronted again with a somewhat disturbing message because your role as our mediator intrudes on our self-satisfied existence. It causes us to think for a few minutes about the worth of our lives, the standards we set for ourselves, and the priorities we hope to achieve. We realize that most of us are not really searching out the clear voice of perfection, the voice of truth, the voice of love. We are missing a lot. We are missing the promise from Christ himself of an abundant life. Convict us of the sin we tend to hang on to, the sin we hide. Help us to confess our sin, so that our consciences can be cleansed in the blood of Jesus, and so that we can serve you, the living God! In your name we pray. Amen.

heaven itself, now to appear in the presence of God on our behalf. [25]Nor was it to offer himself again and again, as the high priest enters the Holy Place year after year with blood that is not his own; [26]for then he would have had to suffer again and again since the foundation of the world. But as it is, he has appeared once for all at the end of the age to remove sin by the sacrifice of himself. [27]And just as it is appointed for mortals to die once, and after that

[a] 9.11 Gk more perfect [b] 9.11,21 Or tabernacle [c] 9.14 Other ancient authorities read Holy Spirit [d] 9.14 Other ancient authorities read your [e] 9.15,16,17 The Greek word used here means both covenant and will [f] 9.19 Other ancient authorities lack and goats

the judgment, 28so Christ, having been offered once to bear the sins of many, will appear a second time, not to deal with sin, but to save those who are eagerly waiting for him.

CHRIST'S SACRIFICE ONCE FOR ALL

10 Since the law has only a shadow of the good things to come and not the true form of these realities, it[a] can never, by the same sacrifices that are continually offered year after year, make perfect those who approach. 2Otherwise, would they not have ceased being offered, since the worshipers, cleansed once for all, would no longer have any consciousness of sin? 3But in these sacrifices there is a reminder of sin year after year. 4For it is impossible for the blood of bulls and goats to take away sins. 5Consequently, when Christ[b] came into the world, he said,

"Sacrifices and offerings you
    have not desired,
but a body you have
    prepared for me;
6 in burnt offerings and
    sin offerings
you have taken no pleasure.
7 Then I said, 'See, God, I have come
    to do your will, O God'
(in the scroll of the book[c] it
    is written of me)."

8When he said above, "You have neither desired nor taken pleasure in sacrifices and offerings and burnt offerings and sin offerings" (these are offered according to the law), 9then he added, "See, I have come to do your will." He abolishes the first in order to establish the second. 10And it is by God's will[d] that we have been sanctified through the offering of the body of Jesus Christ once for all.

11And every priest stands day after day at his service, offering again and again the same sacrifices that can never take away sins. 12But when Christ[e] had offered for all time a single sacrifice for sins, "he sat down at the right hand of God," 13and since then has been waiting "until his enemies would be made a footstool for his feet." 14For by a single offering he has perfected for all time those who are sanctified. 15And the Holy Spirit also testifies to us, for after saying,

16 "This is the covenant that I
    will make with them
    after those days, says the Lord:
I will put my laws in their hearts,
    and I will write them on
        their minds,"
17he also adds,
"I will remember[f] their sins
        and their lawless
        deeds no more."

18Where there is forgiveness of these, there is no longer any offering for sin.

---

a 10.1 Other ancient authorities read they   b 10.5 Gk he   c 10.7 Meaning of Gk uncertain   d 10.10 Gk by that will   e 10.12 Gk this one   f 10.17 Gk on their minds and I will remember

---

BIBLE IN LIFE

Holy

Hebrews 10.9–10

Among the Israelites, offering a sacrifice was a form of worship. They sacrificed an unblemished animal to God for the atonement of sins and as an expression of their faith. In Romans 12.1, Paul says to "present your bodies as a living sacrifice, holy and acceptable to God, which is your spiritual worship." We are to present our entire beings as holy before God. The word holy may shake us up because we don't consider ourselves to be acceptable to God. Paul said he was the worst of sinners, the least deserving to be forgiven (see 1 Timothy 1.15), but he was forgiven by God. If we have also been forgiven, then we can't look back on our own sinfulness and failures, give up or say we're not worthy to be Christians. We can offer our lives before God, as Paul did, because we are made holy through Christ's ultimate sacrifice on the cross.

A CALL TO PERSEVERE

19 Therefore, my friends,[a] since we have confidence to enter the sanctuary by the blood of Jesus, **20** by the new and living way that he opened for us through the curtain (that is, through his flesh), **21** and since we have a great priest over the house of God, **22** let us approach with a true heart in full assurance of faith, with our hearts sprinkled clean from an evil conscience and our bodies washed with pure water. **23** Let us hold fast to the confession of our hope without wavering, for he who has promised is faithful. **24** And let us consider how to provoke one another to love and good deeds, **25** not neglecting to meet together, as is the habit of some, but encouraging one another, and all the more as you see the Day approaching.

26 For if we willfully persist in sin after having received the knowledge of the truth, there no longer remains a sacrifice for sins, **27** but a fearful prospect of judgment, and a fury of fire that will consume the adversaries. **28** Anyone who has violated the law of Moses dies without mercy "on the testimony of two or three witnesses." **29** How much worse punishment do you think will be deserved by those who have spurned the Son of God, profaned the blood of the covenant by which they were sanctified, and outraged the Spirit of grace? **30** For we know the one who said, "Vengeance is mine, I will repay." And again, "The Lord will judge his people." **31** It is a fearful thing to fall into the hands of the living God.

32 But recall those earlier days when, after you had been enlightened, you endured a hard struggle with sufferings, **33** sometimes being publicly exposed to abuse and persecution, and sometimes being partners with those so treated. **34** For you had compassion for those who were in prison, and you cheerfully accepted the plundering of your possessions, knowing that you yourselves possessed something better and more lasting. **35** Do not, therefore, abandon that confidence of yours; it brings a great reward. **36** For you need endurance, so that when you have done the will of God, you may receive what was promised. **37** For yet

"in a very little while,
    the one who is coming will
        come and will not delay;
38 but my righteous one will
        live by faith.
My soul takes no pleasure in
        anyone who shrinks back."

39 But we are not among those who shrink back and so are lost, but among those who have faith and so are saved.

THE MEANING OF FAITH

11 Now faith is the assurance of things hoped for, the conviction of things not seen. **2** Indeed, by faith[b] our ancestors received approval. **3** By faith we understand that the worlds were prepared by the word of God, so that what is seen was made from things that are not visible.[c]

THE EXAMPLES OF ABEL, ENOCH, AND NOAH

4 By faith Abel offered to God a more acceptable[d] sacrifice than Cain's. Through this he received approval as righteous, God himself giving approval to his gifts; he died, but through his faith[e] he still speaks. **5** By faith Enoch was taken so that he did not experience death; and "he was not found, because God had taken him." For it was attested before he was taken away that "he had pleased God." **6** And without faith it is impossible to please God, for whoever would approach him must believe that he exists and that he rewards those who seek him. **7** By faith Noah, warned by God about events as yet unseen, respected the warning and built an ark to save his household; by this he condemned the world and became an heir to the righteousness that is in accordance with faith.

a **10.19** Gk *Therefore, brothers*   b **11.2** Gk *by this*   c **11.3** Or *was not made out of visible things*   d **11.4** Gk *greater*   e **11.4** Gk *through it*

THE FAITH OF ABRAHAM

8 By faith Abraham obeyed when he was called to set out for a place that he was to receive as an inheritance; and he set out, not knowing where he was going. 9By faith he stayed for a time in the land he had been promised, as in a foreign land, living in tents, as did Isaac and Jacob, who were heirs with him of the same promise. 10For he looked forward to the city that has foundations, whose architect and builder is God. 11By faith he received power of procreation, even though he was too old—and Sarah herself was barren—because he considered him faithful who had promised.a 12Therefore from one person, and this one as good as dead, descendants were born, "as many as the stars of heaven and as the innumerable grains of sand by the seashore."

GOD DOES NOT REQUIRE

SUPERSTARS TO FULFILL

HIS KINGDOM'S PROMISE.

13 All of these died in faith without having received the promises, but from a distance they saw and greeted them. They confessed that they were strangers and foreigners on the earth, 14for people who speak in this way make it clear that they are seeking a homeland. 15If they had been thinking of the land that they had left behind, they would have had opportunity to return. 16But as it is, they desire a better country, that is, a heavenly one. Therefore God is not ashamed to be called their God; indeed, he has prepared a city for them.

17 By faith Abraham, when put to the test, offered up Isaac. He who had received the promises was ready to offer up his only son, 18of whom he had been told, "It is through Isaac that descendants shall be named for you." 19He considered the fact that God is able even to raise someone

from the dead—and figuratively speaking, he did receive him back. 20By faith Isaac invoked blessings for the future on Jacob and Esau. 21By faith Jacob, when dying, blessed each of the sons of Joseph, "bowing in worship over the top of his staff." 22By faith Joseph, at the end of his life, made mention of the exodus of the Israelites and gave instructions about his burial.b

THE FAITH OF MOSES

23 By faith Moses was hidden by his parents for three months after his birth, because they saw that the child was beautiful; and they were not afraid of the king's edict.c 24By faith Moses, when he was grown up, refused to be called a son of Pharaoh's daughter, 25choosing rather to share ill-treatment with the people of God than to enjoy the fleeting pleasures of sin. 26He considered abuse suffered for the Christd to be greater wealth than the treasures of Egypt, for he was looking ahead to the reward. 27By faith he left Egypt, unafraid of the king's anger; for he persevered as thoughe he saw him who is invisible. 28By faith he kept the Passover and the sprinkling of blood, so that the destroyer of the firstborn would not touch the firstborn of Israel.f

THE FAITH OF OTHER
ISRAELITE HEROES

29 By faith the people passed through the Red Sea as if it were dry land, but when the Egyptians attempted to do so they were drowned. 30By faith the walls of Jericho fell after they had been encircled for seven days. 31By faith Rahab the prostitute did not perish with those who were disobedient,g because she had received the spies in peace.

a 11.11 Or By faith Sarah herself, though barren, received power to conceive, even when she was too old, because she considered him faithful who had promised. b 11.22 Gk his bones c 11.23 Other ancient authorities add By faith Moses, when he was grown up, killed the Egyptian, because he observed the humiliation of his people (Gk brothers) d 11.26 Or the Messiah e 11.27 Or because f 11.28 Gk would not touch them g 11.31 Or unbelieving

32 And what more should I say? For time would fail me to tell of Gideon, Barak, Samson, Jephthah, of David and Samuel and the prophets— **33** who through faith conquered kingdoms, administered justice, obtained promises, shut the mouths of lions, **34** quenched raging fire, escaped the edge of the sword, won strength out of weakness, became mighty in war, put foreign armies to flight. **35** Women received their dead by resurrection. Others were tortured, refusing to accept release, in order to obtain a better resurrection. **36** Others suffered mocking and flogging, and even chains and imprisonment. **37** They were stoned to death, they were sawn in two,[a] they were killed by the sword; they went about in skins of sheep and goats, destitute, persecuted, tormented— **38** of whom the world was not worthy. They wandered in deserts and mountains, and in caves and holes in the ground.

39 Yet all these, though they were commended for their faith, did not receive what was promised, **40** since God had provided something better so that they would not, apart from us, be made perfect.

THE EXAMPLE OF JESUS

12 Therefore, since we are surrounded by so great a cloud of witnesses, let us also lay aside every weight and the sin that clings so closely,[b] and let us run with perseverance the race that is set before us, **2** looking to Jesus the pioneer and perfecter of our faith, who for the sake of[c] the joy that was set before him endured the cross, disregarding its shame, and has taken his seat at the right hand of the throne of God.

3 Consider him who endured such hostility against himself from sinners,[d] so that you may not grow weary or lose heart. **4** In your struggle against sin you have not yet resisted to the point of shedding your blood. **5** And you have forgotten the exhortation that addresses you as children—

"My child, do not regard lightly
    the discipline of the Lord,
or lose heart when you are
    punished by him;

6 for the Lord disciplines those
        whom he loves,
    and chastises every child
        whom he accepts."
7 Endure trials for the sake of discipline. God is treating you as children; for what child is there whom a parent does not discipline? **8** If you do not have that discipline in which all children share, then you are illegitimate and not his children. **9** Moreover, we had human parents to discipline us, and we respected them. Should we not be even more willing to be subject to the Father of spirits and live? **10** For they disciplined us for a short time as seemed best to them, but he disciplines us for our good, in order that we may share his holiness. **11** Now, discipline always seems painful rather than pleasant at the time, but later it yields the peaceful fruit of righteousness to those who have been trained by it.

---

[a] **11.37** Other ancient authorities add *they were tempted*   [b] **12.1** Other ancient authorities read *sin that easily distracts*   [c] **12.2** Or *who instead of*   [d] **12.3** Other ancient authorities read *such hostility from sinners against themselves*

⊕

PONDER

[God] disciplines us for our good, in order that we may share his holiness. Now, discipline always seems painful rather than pleasant at the time, but later it yields the peaceful fruit of righteousness to those who have been trained by it.
—Hebrews 12.10–11

PRAY

Father, it's difficult to ask you to discipline us for our good. We don't know what that will mean for us, and we know that discipline can be painful. But we also know from this word that it is necessary. Just as we train our children, you train us, shape us and prepare us for the work you have given us to do. We thank you for the promise of peace that is the result of your loving hand on us. Amen.

---

12 Therefore lift your drooping hands and strengthen your weak knees, 13and make straight paths for your feet, so that what is lame may not be put out of joint, but rather be healed.

WARNINGS AGAINST REJECTING GOD'S GRACE

14 Pursue peace with everyone, and the holiness without which no one will see the Lord. 15See to it that no one fails to obtain the grace of God; that no root of bitterness springs up and causes trouble, and through it many become defiled. 16See to it that no one becomes like Esau, an immoral and godless person, who sold his birthright for a single meal. 17You know that later, when he wanted to inherit the blessing, he was rejected, for he found no chance to repent,a even though he sought the blessingb with tears.

18 You have not come to something c that can be touched, a blazing fire, and darkness, and gloom, and a tempest, 19and the sound of a trumpet, and a voice whose words made the hearers beg that not another word be spoken to them. 20(For they could not endure the order that was given, "If even an animal touches the mountain, it shall be stoned to death." 21Indeed, so terrifying was the sight that Moses said, "I tremble with fear.") 22But you have come to Mount Zion and to the city of the living God, the heavenly Jerusalem, and to innumerable angels in festal gathering, 23and to the assemblyd of the firstborn who are enrolled in heaven, and to God the judge of all, and to the spirits of the righteous made perfect, 24and to Jesus, the mediator of a new covenant, and to the sprinkled blood that speaks a better word than the blood of Abel.

25 See that you do not refuse the one who is speaking; for if they did not escape when they refused the one who warned them on earth, how much less will we escape if we reject the one who warns from heaven! 26At that time his voice shook the earth; but now he has promised, "Yet once more I will shake not only the earth but also the heaven." 27This phrase, "Yet once more," indicates the removal of what is shaken—that is, created things—so that what cannot be shaken may remain. 28Therefore, since we are receiving a kingdom that cannot be shaken, let us give thanks, by which we offer to God an acceptable worship with reverence and awe; 29for indeed our God is a consuming fire.

SERVICE WELL-PLEASING TO GOD

13 Let mutual love continue. 2Do not neglect to show hospitality to strangers, for by doing that some have entertained angels without knowing it. 3Remember those who are in prison, as though you were in prison with them; those who are being tortured, as though you yourselves were being tortured.e 4Let marriage be held in honor by all, and let the marriage bed be kept undefiled; for God will judge fornicators and adulterers. 5Keep your lives free from the love of money, and be content with what you have; for he has said, "I will never leave you or forsake you." 6So we can say with confidence,

"The Lord is my helper;
  I will not be afraid.
What can anyone do to me?"

7 Remember your leaders, those who spoke the word of God to you; consider the outcome of their way of life, and imitate their faith. 8Jesus Christ is the same yesterday and to-day and forever. 9Do not be carried away by all kinds of strange teachings; for it is well for the heart to be strengthened by grace, not by regulations about food,f which have not benefited those who observe them. 10We have an altar from which those who officiate in the tentg have no right to eat. 11For the bodies of those animals whose blood is brought into

a 12.17 Or no chance to change his father's mind   b 12.17 Gk it   c 12.18 Other ancient authorities read a mountain   d 12.23 Or angels, and to the festal gathering 23and assembly   e 13.3 Gk were in the body   f 13.9 Gk not by foods   g 13.10 Or tabernacle

the sanctuary by the high priest as a sacrifice for sin are burned outside the camp. 12Therefore Jesus also suffered outside the city gate in order to sanctify the people by his own blood. 13Let us then go to him outside the camp and bear the abuse he endured. 14For here we have no lasting city, but we are looking for the city that is to come. 15Through him, then, let us continually offer a sacrifice of praise to God, that is, the fruit of lips that confess his name. 16Do not neglect to do good and to share what you have, for such sacrifices are pleasing to God.

17 Obey your leaders and submit to them, for they are keeping watch over your souls and will give an account. Let them do this with joy and not with sighing—for that would be harmful to you.

18 Pray for us; we are sure that we have a clear conscience, desiring to act honorably in all things. 19I urge you all the more to do this, so that I may be restored to you very soon.

BENEDICTION

20 Now may the God of peace, who brought back from the dead our Lord Jesus, the great shepherd of the sheep, by the blood of the eternal covenant, 21make you complete in everything good so that you may do his will, working among us[a] that which is pleasing in his sight, through Jesus Christ, to whom be the glory forever and ever. Amen.

FINAL EXHORTATION AND GREETINGS

22 I appeal to you, brothers and sisters,[b] bear with my word of exhortation, for I have written to you briefly. 23I want you to know that our brother Timothy has been set free; and if he comes in time, he will be with me when I see you. 24Greet all your leaders and all the saints. Those from Italy send you greetings. 25Grace be with all of you.[c]

[a] 13.21 Other ancient authorities read *you*
[b] 13.22 Gk *brothers*   [c] 13.25 Other ancient authorities add *Amen*

The Letter of

JAMES

How should I respond when I face hard times? How can I learn to control my temper—and my mouth? How do I find real wisdom? The book of James is loaded with straightforward advice for everyday life. The refreshing feature about this book is that James takes a no-nonsense approach to hypocrisy. He describes real situations and offers hard-hitting and practical solutions. James shows that it's possible to believe the right things, yet live the wrong way. This book will show you how to turn right doctrine into right living.

SALUTATION

1 James, a servant[a] of God and of the Lord Jesus Christ,

To the twelve tribes in the Dispersion:

Greetings.

FAITH AND WISDOM

2 My brothers and sisters,[b] whenever you face trials of any kind, consider it nothing but joy, ³because you know that the testing of your faith produces endurance; ⁴and let endurance have its full effect, so that you may be mature and complete, lacking in nothing.

5 If any of you is lacking in wisdom, ask God, who gives to all generously and ungrudgingly, and it will be given you. ⁶But ask in faith, never doubting, for the one who doubts is like a wave of the sea, driven and tossed by the wind; ⁷,⁸for the doubter, being double-minded and unstable in every way, must not expect to receive anything from the Lord.

PONDER

If any of you is lacking in wisdom, ask God, who gives to all generously and ungrudgingly, and it will be given you. But ask in faith, never doubting.
—James 1.5–6

PRAY

Father God, we all lack wisdom. We live in complicated times, in frightening times, in troubled times, and we need your wisdom each moment to navigate through our days. We pray for your blessing of wisdom, for knowledge and insight that comes from knowing you. We praise you for your generosity and kindness to us in guiding us. But we also ask that you make our faith grow, that you implant in us the constant reminder that you are available at every turn. We believe—help our unbelief. In the name of our Savior, Jesus Christ, we pray. Amen.

POVERTY AND RICHES

9 Let the believer[c] who is lowly boast in being raised up, ¹⁰and the rich in being brought low, because the rich will disappear like a flower in the field. ¹¹For the sun rises with its scorching heat and withers the field; its flower falls, and its beauty perishes. It is the same way with the rich; in the midst of a busy life, they will wither away.

TRIAL AND TEMPTATION

12 Blessed is anyone who endures temptation. Such a one has stood the test and will receive the crown of life that the Lord[d] has promised to those who love him. ¹³No one, when tempted, should say, "I am being tempted by God"; for God cannot be tempted by evil and he himself tempts no one. ¹⁴But one is tempted by one's own desire, being lured and enticed by it; ¹⁵then, when that desire has conceived, it gives birth to sin, and that sin, when it is fully grown, gives birth to death. ¹⁶Do not be deceived, my beloved.[e]

17 Every generous act of giving, with every perfect gift, is from above, coming down from the Father of lights, with whom there is no variation or shadow due to change.[f] ¹⁸In fulfillment of his own purpose he gave us birth by the word of truth, so that we would become a kind of first fruits of his creatures.

HEARING AND DOING THE WORD

19 You must understand this, my beloved:[g] let everyone be quick to listen, slow to speak, slow to anger; ²⁰for your anger does not produce God's righteousness. ²¹Therefore rid yourselves of all sordidness and rank growth of wickedness, and welcome with meekness the implanted word that has the power to save your souls.

22 But be doers of the word, and not merely hearers who deceive

[a] 1.1 Gk *slave*   [b] 1.2 Gk *brothers*   [c] 1.9 Gk *brother*   [d] 1.12 Gk *he*; other ancient authorities read *God*   [e] 1.16 Gk *my beloved brothers*   [f] 1.17 Other ancient authorities read *variation due to a shadow of turning*   [g] 1.19 Gk *my beloved brothers*

CONSIDER IT PURE JOY

My brothers and sisters, whenever you face trials of any kind, consider it nothing but joy.

—James 1.2

How do we deal with life's accidents, life's unpredictability, life's inevitabilities? And what is one of life's inevitabilities that we all face? Trials. Trials are the problems over which we have no control. In the first chapter of his book, James instructs us in how to face the trials that come our way.

The trials many of us face may be limitations on our own talents and abilities. We may have had ambitions when we were younger—to be a concert violinist, a famous scientist or a great mathematician—but we have had to temper our ambitions to match our abilities or to match our family's income. Tragedy inflicts grief on us—we lose loved ones. Failures and disappointments enter our lives; we might strive for something that's great and then just totally fail at it.

These trials are inevitable, but how are we to react to them? With patience, valor, determination and courage? Surprisingly, James says we are to face the trials of life with joy (see James 1.2). Joy can turn us away from complacency. It can make us take a new look at life.

Health changes. Friends change. Careers change. Finances change. But there are some things in life that don't change, and our trials can make us ask: What foundation can we build our futures on? How can we overcome this setback and set new goals? We experience joy in knowing that a trial can be an invigorating, eye-opening experience. It can build our courage and make us depend upon things that don't change.

There's nothing wrong with asking God to take trials away from us, but we shouldn't expect God to spare us from all trials. As we face the inevitable, we should ask God for wisdom: "The testing of your faith produces endurance; and let endurance have its full effect, so that you may be mature and complete, lacking in nothing. If any of you is lacking in wisdom, ask God, who gives to all generously and ungrudgingly, and it will be given you" (verses 3–5). Each of us should ask ourselves these questions: How should I deal with this crisis in my life wisely? How can I let Christ be within me and deal with this crisis? How can I look at the permanent, the things that don't change?

When we ask for wisdom, we must "ask in faith, never doubting, for the one who doubts is like a wave of the sea, driven and tossed by the wind; for the doubter, being double-minded and unstable in every way, must not expect to receive anything from the Lord" (verses 6–8). Pray, and ask God for wisdom with confidence. Our faith in God, the unchanging foundation in our lives, will see us through each and every trial.

Going Deeper

- What are the things in your life that never change? How can you depend on those things when you are experiencing a trial?
- When faced with a trial, what is your typical response? How does that affect your outlook on life and your influence on those around you?

themselves. 23For if any are hearers of the word and not doers, they are like those who look at themselves[a] in a mirror; 24for they look at themselves and, on going away, immediately forget what they were like. 25But those who look into the perfect law, the law of liberty, and persevere, being not hearers who forget but doers who act—they will be blessed in their doing.

26 If any think they are religious, and do not bridle their tongues but deceive their hearts, their religion is worthless. 27Religion that is pure and undefiled before God, the Father, is this: to care for orphans and widows in their distress, and to keep oneself unstained by the world.

WARNING AGAINST PARTIALITY

2 My brothers and sisters,[b] do you with your acts of favoritism really believe in our glorious Lord Jesus Christ?[c] 2For if a person with gold rings and in fine clothes comes into your assembly, and if a poor person in dirty clothes also comes in, 3and if you take notice of the one wearing the fine clothes and say, "Have a seat here, please," while to the one who is poor you say, "Stand there," or, "Sit at my feet,"[d] 4have you not made distinctions among yourselves, and become judges with

evil thoughts? 5Listen, my beloved brothers and sisters.[e] Has not God chosen the poor in the world to be rich in faith and to be heirs of the kingdom that he has promised to those who love him? 6But you have dishonored the poor. Is it not the rich who oppress you? Is it not they who drag you into court? 7Is it not they who blaspheme the excellent name that was invoked over you?

8 You do well if you really fulfill the royal law according to the scripture, "You shall love your neighbor as yourself." 9But if you show partiality, you commit sin and are convicted by the law as transgressors. 10For whoever keeps the whole law but fails in one point has become accountable for all of it. 11For the one who said, "You shall not commit adultery," also said, "You shall not murder." Now if you do not commit adultery but if you murder, you have become a transgressor of the law. 12So speak and so act as those who are to be judged by the law of liberty. 13For judgment will be without mercy to anyone who has shown no mercy; mercy triumphs over judgment.

[a] 1.23 Gk *at the face of his birth* [b] 2.1 Gk *My brothers* [c] 2.1 Or *hold the faith of our glorious Lord Jesus Christ without acts of favoritism* [d] 2.3 Gk *Sit under my footstool* [e] 2.5 Gk *brothers*

⊢ BIBLE IN LIFE ▷

Reaching Out to the Rejected   James 2.1–13

Who were the people with whom Jesus spent time while he was on earth? The religious leaders? The rich and influential? The attractive and well-liked? Much of the time, Jesus focused his attention on the outcasts of society. He touched lepers, he healed the blind, he showed compassion for those who were despised and rejected, including Samaritans and even hated tax collectors who betrayed their own people and collected money for the occupying Romans. How much of our lives are focused on people like that? How much time do we spend with people who are different from us? To how many people do we reach out who are homeless or in prison or who simply irritate us? We don't want to get involved with them because they are a strain on us. It's more comfortable to be with people just like us, who talk the same language, drive the same kind of cars, live in the same kind of houses, attend the same kind of church. It's a natural human tendency to prefer the company of our own kind, but Christ calls us to reach beyond natural inclinations to show compassion for those who stretch our hearts in different ways. This may even take some deliberate steps on our part to break out of our social cocoons and be with people who differ from us. When you read these descriptions, who comes to mind?

FAITH WITHOUT WORKS IS DEAD

14 What good is it, my brothers and sisters,[a] if you say you have faith but do not have works? Can faith save you? 15If a brother or sister is naked and lacks daily food, 16and one of you says to them, "Go in peace; keep warm and eat your fill," and yet you do not supply their bodily needs, what is the good of that? 17So faith by itself, if it has no works, is dead.

18 But someone will say, "You have faith and I have works." Show me your faith apart from your works, and I by my works will show you my faith. 19You believe that God is one; you do well. Even the demons believe—and shudder. 20Do you want to be shown, you senseless person, that faith apart from works is barren? 21Was not our ancestor Abraham justified by works when he offered his son Isaac on the altar? 22You see that faith was active along with his works, and faith was brought to completion by the works. 23Thus the scripture was fulfilled that says, "Abraham believed God, and it was reckoned to him as righteousness," and he was called the friend of God. 24You see that a person is justified by works and not by faith alone. 25Likewise, was not Rahab the prostitute also justified by works when she welcomed the messengers and sent them out by another road? 26For just as the body without the spirit is dead, so faith without works is also dead.

TAMING THE TONGUE

3 Not many of you should become teachers, my brothers and sisters,[a] for you know that we who teach will be judged with greater strictness. 2For all of us make many mistakes. Anyone who makes no mistakes in speaking is perfect, able to keep the whole body in check with a bridle. 3If we put bits into the mouths of horses to make them obey us, we guide their whole bodies. 4Or look at ships: though they are so large that it takes strong winds to drive them, yet they are guided by a very small rudder wherever the will of the pilot directs. 5So also the tongue is a small member, yet it boasts of great exploits.

How great a forest is set ablaze by a small fire! 6And the tongue is a fire. The tongue is placed among our members as a world of iniquity; it stains the whole body, sets on fire the cycle of nature,[b] and is itself set on fire by hell.[c] 7For every species of beast and bird, of reptile and sea creature, can be tamed and has been tamed by the human species, 8but no one can tame the tongue—a restless evil, full of deadly poison. 9With it we bless the Lord and Father, and with it we curse those who are made in the likeness of God. 10From the same mouth come blessing and cursing. My brothers and sisters,[d]

[a] 2.14; 3.1 Gk brothers   [b] 3.6 Or wheel of birth   [c] 3.6 Gk Gehenna   [d] 3.10 Gk My brothers

---

⊣ BIBLE IN LIFE ▷ ⊖⊃

Gossip

James 3.5–8

We humans have an almost uncontrollable tendency to speak ill of others. We have an inclination to find satisfaction in bad news about people whom we don't like much. Gossip appeals to us, assuages our insecurities and makes us feel better about ourselves. Gossip is one of the most cowardly actions of a human being because 1) it's done in secret; 2) we try to pretend that what we're saying isn't really gossip; 3) it can destroy or damage the reputation of another person in our family, community or church.

But Paul says that in Christ we ought to be kind to one another and forgive one another (see Ephesians 4.32). If we sincerely love other people, as God loves us, we squelch our desire for gossip. We swallow or ignore vicious comments about our children or our spouses rather than air them. Gossip tears apart the body of Christ, but love binds us together.

this ought not to be so. ¹¹Does a spring pour forth from the same opening both fresh and brackish water? ¹²Can a fig tree, my brothers and sisters,ᵃ yield olives, or a grapevine figs? No more can salt water yield fresh.

TWO KINDS OF WISDOM

13 Who is wise and understanding among you? Show by your good life that your works are done with gentleness born of wisdom. ¹⁴But if you have bitter envy and selfish ambition in your hearts, do not be boastful and false to the truth. ¹⁵Such wisdom does not come down from above, but is earthly, unspiritual, devilish. ¹⁶For where there is envy and selfish ambition, there will also be disorder and wickedness of every kind. ¹⁷But the wisdom from above is first pure, then peaceable, gentle, willing to yield, full of mercy and good fruits, without a trace of partiality or hypocrisy. ¹⁸And a harvest of righteousness is sown in peace forᵇ those who make peace.

FRIENDSHIP WITH THE WORLD

4 Those conflicts and disputes among you, where do they come from? Do they not come from your cravings that are at war within you? ²You want something and do not have it; so you commit murder. And you covetᶜ something and cannot obtain it; so you engage in disputes and conflicts. You do not have, because you do not ask. ³You ask and do not receive, because you ask wrongly, in order to spend what you get on your pleasures. ⁴Adulterers! Do you not know that friendship with the world is enmity with God? Therefore whoever wishes to be a friend of the world becomes an enemy of God. ⁵Or do you suppose that it is for nothing that the scripture says, "Godᵈ yearns jealously for the spirit that he has made to dwell in us"? ⁶But he gives all the more grace; therefore it says,

"God opposes the proud,
    but gives grace to the humble."
⁷Submit yourselves therefore to God. Resist the devil, and he will flee from you. ⁸Draw near to God, and he will draw near to you. Cleanse your hands, you sinners, and purify your hearts, you double-minded. ⁹Lament and mourn and weep. Let your laughter be turned into mourning and your joy into dejection. ¹⁰Humble yourselves before the Lord, and he will exalt you.

PONDER

Submit yourselves therefore to God. Resist the devil, and he will flee from you. Draw near to God, and he will draw near to you.
—James 4.7–8

PRAY

O Father, sometimes the Holy Scriptures are disturbing to us; sometimes we like to take issue with them and pretend that we know more about our own lives than James could have comprehended. We are not naturally inclined to submit to anyone, but help us to realize that submitting to you is not giving up, but gaining in blessing, peace and hope. We do want to be near to you; alert us to the devil's temptation and draw us nearer and nearer to your heart. In the precious name of Jesus, we pray. Amen.

WARNING AGAINST JUDGING ANOTHER

11 Do not speak evil against one another, brothers and sisters.ᵉ Whoever speaks evil against another or judges another, speaks evil against the law and judges the law; but if you judge the law, you are not a doer of the law but a judge. ¹²There is one lawgiver and judge who is able to save and to destroy. So who, then, are you to judge your neighbor?

ᵃ 3.12 Gk *my brothers*   ᵇ 3.18 Or *by*   ᶜ 4.2 Or *you murder and you covet*   ᵈ 4.5 Gk *He*   ᵉ 4.11 Gk *brothers*

BOASTING ABOUT TOMORROW

13 Come now, you who say, "To-day or tomorrow we will go to such and such a town and spend a year there, doing business and making money." **14** Yet you do not even know what tomorrow will bring. What is your life? For you are a mist that appears for a little while and then vanishes. **15** Instead you ought to say, "If the Lord wishes, we will live and do this or that." **16** As it is, you boast in your arrogance; all such boasting is evil. **17** Anyone, then, who knows the right thing to do and fails to do it, commits sin.

WARNING TO RICH OPPRESSORS

5 Come now, you rich people, weep and wail for the miseries that are coming to you. **2** Your riches have rotted, and your clothes are moth-eaten. **3** Your gold and silver have rusted, and their rust will be evidence against you, and it will eat your flesh like fire. You have laid up treasure[a] for the last days. **4** Listen! The wages of the laborers who mowed your fields, which you kept back by fraud, cry out, and the cries of the harvesters have reached the ears of the Lord of hosts. **5** You have lived on the earth in luxury and in pleasure; you have fattened your hearts in a day of slaughter. **6** You have condemned and murdered the righteous one, who does not resist you.

PATIENCE IN SUFFERING

7 Be patient, therefore, beloved,[b] until the coming of the Lord. The farmer waits for the precious crop from the earth, being patient with it until it receives the early and the late rains. **8** You also must be patient. Strengthen your hearts, for the coming of the Lord is near.[c] **9** Beloved,[d] do not grumble against one another, so that you may not be judged. See, the Judge is standing at the doors! **10** As an example of suffering and patience, beloved,[b] take the prophets who spoke in the name of the Lord. **11** Indeed we call blessed those who showed endurance. You have heard of the endurance of Job, and you have seen the purpose of the Lord, how the Lord is compassionate and merciful.

12 Above all, my beloved,[b] do not swear, either by heaven or by earth or by any other oath, but let your "Yes" be yes and your "No" be no, so that you may not fall under condemnation.

THE PRAYER OF FAITH

13 Are any among you suffering? They should pray. Are any cheerful? They should sing songs of praise. **14** Are any among you sick? They should call for the elders of the church and have them pray over them, anointing them with oil in the name of the Lord. **15** The prayer of faith will save the sick, and the Lord will raise them up; and anyone who has committed sins will be forgiven. **16** Therefore confess your sins to one another, and pray for one another, so that you may be healed. The prayer of the righteous is powerful and effective. **17** Elijah was a human being like us, and he prayed fervently that it might not rain, and for three years and six months it did not rain on the earth. **18** Then he prayed again, and the heaven gave rain and the earth yielded its harvest.

19 My brothers and sisters,[e] if anyone among you wanders from the truth and is brought back by another, **20** you should know that whoever brings back a sinner from wandering will save the sinner's[f] soul from death and will cover a multitude of sins.

[a] 5.3 Or *will eat your flesh, since you have stored up fire* [b] 5.7,10,12 Gk *brothers* [c] 5.8 Or *is at hand* [d] 5.9 Gk *Brothers* [e] 5.19 Gk *My brothers* [f] 5.20 Gk *his*

The First Letter of

PETER

Peter addresses this letter to Christians scattered throughout the Roman world. His readers were suffering because of the culture's fading tolerance of Christianity. Sound familiar? Peter's letter is as relevant now as the day he wrote it. The apostle poses some hard challenges: Rugged times require disciplined Christian living. There are no platitudes or easy answers here. But Peter's tough advice is gift-wrapped in the language of hope: "You have had to suffer various trials, so that the genuineness of your faith—being more precious than gold that, though perishable, is tested by fire—may be found to result in praise and glory and honor when Jesus Christ is revealed" (1 Peter 1.6–7).

SALUTATION

1 Peter, an apostle of Jesus Christ,
To the exiles of the Dispersion in Pontus, Galatia, Cappadocia, Asia, and Bithynia, ²who have been chosen and destined by God the Father and sanctified by the Spirit to be obedient to Jesus Christ and to be sprinkled with his blood:

May grace and peace be yours in abundance.

A LIVING HOPE

3 Blessed be the God and Father of our Lord Jesus Christ! By his great mercy he has given us a new birth into a living hope through the resurrection of Jesus Christ from the dead, ⁴and into an inheritance that is imperishable, undefiled, and unfading, kept in heaven for you, ⁵who are being protected by the power of God through faith for a salvation ready to be revealed in the last time. ⁶In this you rejoice,ᵃ even if now for a little while you have had to suffer various trials, ⁷so that the genuineness of your faith—being more precious than gold that, though perishable, is tested by fire—may be found to result in praise and glory and honor when Jesus Christ is revealed. ⁸Although you have not seenᵇ him, you love him; and even though you do not see him now, you believe in him and rejoice with an indescribable and glorious joy, ⁹for you are receiving the outcome of your faith, the salvation of your souls.

10 Concerning this salvation, the prophets who prophesied of the grace that was to be yours made careful search and inquiry, ¹¹inquiring about the person or time that the Spirit of Christ within them indicated when it testified in advance to the sufferings destined for Christ and the subsequent glory. ¹²It was revealed to them that they were serving not themselves but you, in regard to the things that have now been announced to you through those who brought you good news by the Holy Spirit sent from heaven—things into which angels long to look!

A CALL TO HOLY LIVING

13 Therefore prepare your minds for action;ᶜ discipline yourselves; set all your hope on the grace that Jesus Christ will bring you when he is revealed. ¹⁴Like obedient children, do not be conformed to the desires that you formerly had in ignorance. ¹⁵Instead, as he who called you is holy, be holy yourselves in all your conduct; ¹⁶for it is written, "You shall be holy, for I am holy."

17 If you invoke as Father the one who judges all people impartially according to their deeds, live in reverent fear during the time of your exile. ¹⁸You know that you were ransomed from the futile ways inherited from your ancestors, not with perishable things like silver or gold, ¹⁹but with the precious blood of Christ, like that of a lamb without

ᵃ **1.6** Or *Rejoice in this*   ᵇ **1.8** Other ancient authorities read *known*   ᶜ **1.13** Gk *gird up the loins of your mind*

PONDER

Like obedient children, do not be conformed to the desires that you formerly had in ignorance. Instead, as he who called you is holy, be holy yourselves in all your conduct; for it is written, "You shall be holy, for I am holy."
—1 Peter 1.14–16

PRAY

O Father, we are grateful for these inspiring and challenging words of Peter, who is one of the most interesting characters in your kingdom. Help us heed Peter's call to holiness, your call to holiness. Teach us what this means in every aspect of our lives. Help us be courageous enough to examine ourselves and pledge repeatedly through prayer that we pattern our lives after the perfect example set by Jesus Christ. In his name we pray. Amen.

defect or blemish. 20He was destined before the foundation of the world, but was revealed at the end of the ages for your sake. 21Through him you have come to trust in God, who raised him from the dead and gave him glory, so that your faith and hope are set on God.

22 Now that you have purified your souls by your obedience to the truth[a] so that you have genuine mutual love, love one another deeply[b] from the heart.[c] 23You have been born anew, not of perishable but of imperishable seed, through the living and enduring word of God.[d] 24For

"All flesh is like grass
　and all its glory like the
　　flower of grass.
The grass withers,
　and the flower falls,
25 but the word of the Lord
　endures forever."
That word is the good news that was announced to you.

THE LIVING STONE AND A CHOSEN PEOPLE

2 Rid yourselves, therefore, of all malice, and all guile, insincerity, and envy, and all slander. 2Like newborn infants, long for the pure, spiritual milk, so that by it you may grow into salvation— 3if indeed you have tasted that the Lord is good.

4 Come to him, a living stone, though rejected by mortals yet chosen and precious in God's sight, and 5like living stones, let yourselves be built[e] into a spiritual house, to be a holy priesthood, to offer spiritual sacrifices acceptable to God through Jesus Christ. 6For it stands in scripture:

"See, I am laying in
　Zion a stone,
　a cornerstone chosen
　　and precious;
and whoever believes in him[f] will
　not be put to shame."

7To you then who believe, he is precious; but for those who do not believe,

"The stone that the builders
　rejected
　has become the very head
　　of the corner,"

8and

"A stone that makes them
　stumble,
　and a rock that makes
　　them fall."

They stumble because they disobey the word, as they were destined to do.

9 But you are a chosen race, a royal priesthood, a holy nation, God's own people,[g] in order that you may proclaim the mighty acts of him who called you out of darkness into his marvelous light. 10 Once you were not a people,

　but now you are God's people;
once you had not received mercy,
　but now you have
　　received mercy.

[a] 1.22 Other ancient authorities add *through the Spirit*　[b] 1.22 Or *constantly*　[c] 1.22 Other ancient authorities read *a pure heart*　[d] 1.23 Or *through the word of the living and enduring God*　[e] 2.5 Or *you yourselves are being built*　[f] 2.6 Or *it*　[g] 2.9 Gk *a people for his possession*

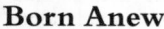 **BIBLE IN LIFE** ▷

Born Anew

1 Peter 1.22–24

What does it mean to be "born anew"? Jesus explained this term to a Pharisee named Nicodemus, who thought it meant to literally emerge one more time from a mother's womb. Jesus said, "Very truly, I tell you, no one can enter the kingdom of God without being born of water and Spirit" (John 3.5). In order to enter God's kingdom, we have to be spiritually born to the Spirit of God. The Pharisees believed that a person could only enter the kingdom of God by keeping the law. Jesus completely reversed that. He taught that it's not what we do that brings us into a proper relationship with God; it's our faith in Christ that aligns us, which leads to a new birth through the Spirit.

LIVE AS SERVANTS OF GOD

11 Beloved, I urge you as aliens and exiles to abstain from the desires of the flesh that wage war against the soul. **12** Conduct yourselves honorably among the Gentiles, so that, though they malign you as evildoers, they may see your honorable deeds and glorify God when he comes to judge.[a]

13 For the Lord's sake accept the authority of every human institution,[b] whether of the emperor as supreme, **14** or of governors, as sent by him to punish those who do wrong and to praise those who do right. **15** For it is God's will that by doing right you should silence the ignorance of the foolish. **16** As servants[c] of God, live as free people, yet do not use your freedom as a pretext for evil. **17** Honor everyone. Love the family of believers.[d] Fear God. Honor the emperor.

THE EXAMPLE OF CHRIST'S SUFFERING

18 Slaves, accept the authority of your masters with all deference, not only those who are kind and gentle but also those who are harsh. **19** For it is a credit to you if, being aware of God, you endure pain while suffering unjustly. **20** If you endure when you are beaten for doing wrong, what credit is that? But if you endure when you do right and suffer for it, you have God's approval. **21** For to this you have been called, because Christ also suffered for you, leaving you an example, so that you should follow in his steps.

22 "He committed no sin,
    and no deceit was found
        in his mouth."

23 When he was abused, he did not return abuse; when he suffered, he did not threaten; but he entrusted himself to the one who judges justly. **24** He himself bore our sins in his body on the cross,[e] so that, free from sins, we might live for righteousness; by his wounds[f] you have been healed. **25** For you were going astray like sheep, but now you have returned to the shepherd and guardian of your souls.

WIVES AND HUSBANDS

3 Wives, in the same way, accept the authority of your husbands, so that, even if some of them do not obey the word, they may be won over without a word by their wives' conduct, **2** when they see the purity and reverence of your lives. **3** Do not adorn yourselves outwardly by braiding your hair, and by wearing gold ornaments or fine clothing; **4** rather, let your adornment be the inner self with the lasting beauty of a gentle and quiet spirit, which is

[a] **2.12** Gk *God on the day of visitation*
[b] **2.13** Or *every institution ordained for human beings* [c] **2.16** Gk *slaves* [d] **2.17** Gk *Love the brotherhood* [e] **2.24** Or *carried up our sins in his body to the tree* [f] **2.24** Gk *bruise*

┤├ BIBLE IN LIFE ▷◁

Spiritual Growth   1 Peter 2.1–3

In the first month after conception, a human embryo increases in size one hundred thousand times. In the second month, it increases in size seven times, and in the third month, it only increases in size by 30 percent. Christians often follow this pattern in spiritual growth: When we first accept Christ, life takes on an entirely new meaning, and we spurt and bloom and blossom. Then, unfortunately, our enthusiasm wanes and eventually dissipates. Peter says we are to "long for the pure, spiritual milk" so we will continue to grow in our salvation (verse 2). Jesus said, "Blessed are those who hunger and thirst for righteousness, for they will be filled" (Matthew 5.6). If we want to grow as Christians, we must yearn to learn more about Christlike living. We must recognize our need to grow and then stretch our hearts and minds. We are to encompass more people with our Christian love and seek to know more about God's world and ways.

BIBLE IN FOCUS

LOVE AND SUBMISSION

Wives, in the same way, accept the authority of your husbands, so that, even if some of them do not obey the word, they may be won over without a word by their wives' conduct, when they see the purity and reverence of your lives.

—1 Peter 3.1–2

How do we react when we read verses about a wife submitting to her husband? We can't just dismiss Peter's words as troubling and say that the principle only applied two thousand years ago. The essence of what Peter is telling us is really understood better by the definition of a Greek word: *hupotasso*. It is generally interpreted to mean submission: our submission to the authority of the government, slaves' submission to their masters, a wife's submission to her husband. It is important to put this into context in order to understand Peter's teaching.

Submission means the willing acceptance of a societal order as it exists, with a meaningful motivation. We have to live within that order. And whatever our circumstances, we have to understand how to correlate them with our faith in God. Submission does not mean, however, that we submit to domination without an assessment of the command. It doesn't mean that we obey a command contrary to our faith or our beliefs.

In the days of Peter, a woman who was married was looked upon as the property of her husband and not his equal. She had to walk behind him. A woman was forbidden to play any leading role in society. We know from Christ's life that there were many instances when he exalted women. Jesus never said that women must always be subordinate to their husbands as property. Peter, Paul and Christ all were saying that there had to be an equality—among men and women, husbands and wives—that the world had never seen before (see Ephesians 5.21–33). In a society of male dominance, Peter was telling the women and the men to build their relationships within the family based on a new principle—that all people are equal in the eyes of God. This was a transforming concept: women—in the name of Christ and before God—were equal to men. This was a quantum movement toward the liberation of women.

With the strength of our submission to Jesus Christ, we can accept the facts of our lives and make the most of them. We shouldn't look upon our gender or our income or our fame as a measuring rod for what we are in the eyes of God or what we can accomplish in the name of Christ. We must look upon the entire Bible and especially the teachings of Jesus as liberating because the ultimate submission for all of us is to our Savior, Jesus Christ.

Going Deeper

- Do you ever find yourself in situations where you are unable to submit due to the sinful nature of the commands or laws? How do you respond?
- How does your submission to Christ carry over into the circumstances of your life? Do you accept and have peace regarding others' authority over you?

very precious in God's sight. 5It was in this way long ago that the holy women who hoped in God used to adorn themselves by accepting the authority of their husbands. 6Thus Sarah obeyed Abraham and called him lord. You have become her daughters as long as you do what is good and never let fears alarm you.

7 Husbands, in the same way, show consideration for your wives in your life together, paying honor to the woman as the weaker sex,[a] since they too are also heirs of the gracious gift of life—so that nothing may hinder your prayers.

SUFFERING FOR DOING RIGHT

8 Finally, all of you, have unity of spirit, sympathy, love for one another, a tender heart, and a humble mind. 9Do not repay evil for evil or abuse for abuse; but, on the contrary, repay with a blessing. It is for this that you were called—that you might inherit a blessing. 10For

"Those who desire life
    and desire to see good days,
let them keep their tongues
        from evil
    and their lips from
        speaking deceit;
11 let them turn away from
        evil and do good;
    let them seek peace
        and pursue it.
12 For the eyes of the Lord are
        on the righteous,
    and his ears are open
        to their prayer.

But the face of the Lord is against
    those who do evil."

13 Now who will harm you if you are eager to do what is good? 14But even if you do suffer for doing what is right, you are blessed. Do not fear what they fear,[b] and do not be intimidated, 15but in your hearts sanctify Christ as Lord. Always be ready to make your defense to anyone who demands from you an accounting for the hope that is in you; 16yet do it with gentleness and reverence.[c] Keep your conscience clear, so that, when you are maligned, those who abuse you for your good conduct in Christ may be put to shame. 17For it is better to suffer for doing good, if suffering should be God's will, than to suffer for doing evil. 18For Christ also suffered[d] for sins once for all, the righteous for the unrighteous, in order to bring you[e] to God. He was put to death in the flesh, but made alive in the spirit, 19in which also he went and made a proclamation to the spirits in prison, 20who in former times did not obey, when God waited patiently in the days of Noah, during the building of the ark, in which a few, that is, eight persons, were saved through water. 21And baptism, which this prefigured, now saves you—not as a removal of dirt from the body, but as an appeal to God for[f] a good conscience, through

[a] 3.7 Gk vessel [b] 3.14 Gk their fear [c] 3.16 Or respect [d] 3.18 Other ancient authorities read died [e] 3.18 Other ancient authorities read us [f] 3.21 Or a pledge to God from

---

⊣├ BIBLE IN LIFE ▷━━━━━━━━━━⊐

Suffering for Christ   1 Peter 3.13–17

The early church endured terrible persecution. Because the Christians were growing in number and strength, the Jewish and Roman authorities felt threatened. In his letter, Peter encouraged Christians by reminding them that their suffering was part of the ministry of Christ and that it's better to suffer for good than evil.

When we live boldly, as Jesus did, and proclaim the gospel, we may come under attack. So we have a choice: We can choose to assimilate passively into the world and not stand out, or we can actively set ourselves apart for Christ and be willing to face oppression and persecution for our faith. If we do suffer persecution for following Christ's example, then we should recognize that our spiritual blessings far exceed the temporal pain of suffering.

the resurrection of Jesus Christ, [22]who has gone into heaven and is at the right hand of God, with angels, authorities, and powers made subject to him.

GOOD STEWARDS OF GOD'S GRACE

4 Since therefore Christ suffered in the flesh,[a] arm yourselves also with the same intention (for whoever has suffered in the flesh has finished with sin), [2]so as to live for the rest of your earthly life[b] no longer by human desires but by the will of God. [3]You have already spent enough time in doing what the Gentiles like to do, living in licentiousness, passions, drunkenness, revels, carousing, and lawless idolatry. [4]They are surprised that you no longer join them in the same excesses of dissipation, and so they blaspheme.[c] [5]But they will have to give an accounting to him who stands ready to judge the living and the dead. [6]For this is the reason the gospel was proclaimed even to the dead, so that, though they had been judged in the flesh as everyone is judged, they might live in the spirit as God does.

[7]The end of all things is near;[d] therefore be serious and discipline yourselves for the sake of your prayers. [8]Above all, maintain constant love for one another, for love covers a multitude of sins. [9]Be hospitable to one another without complaining. [10]Like good stewards of the manifold grace of God, serve one another with whatever gift each of you has received. [11]Whoever speaks must do so as one speaking the very words of God; whoever serves must do so with the strength that God supplies, so that God may be glorified in all things through Jesus Christ. To him belong the glory and the power forever and ever. Amen.

SUFFERING AS A CHRISTIAN

[12]Beloved, do not be surprised at the fiery ordeal that is taking place among you to test you, as though something strange were happening to you. [13]But rejoice insofar as you are sharing Christ's sufferings, so

PONDER

Above all, maintain constant love for one another, for love covers a multitude of sins. Be hospitable to one another without complaining. Like good stewards of the manifold grace of God, serve one another with whatever gift each of you has received.
—1 Peter 4.8–10

PRAY

Lord, we need to hear what Peter had to say about the intensity and constancy of love being the most important thing of all. Help us to apply this to our own individual and diverse lives. Let each one of us take from this passage a spark of inspiration; let us find ten minutes later today to talk to you in private and with sincerity and courage say, "This is what I am, Lord, show me your will so I can serve you no matter what my income might be, no matter what my bank account might be, no matter what my gifts are. Help me to understand that success in life is measured by the only standards that count— the standards of my Savior, Jesus Christ." In his name we pray. Amen.

that you may also be glad and shout for joy when his glory is revealed. [14]If you are reviled for the name of Christ, you are blessed, because the spirit of glory,[e] which is the Spirit of God, is resting on you.[f] [15]But let none of you suffer as a murderer, a thief, a criminal, or even as a mischief maker. [16]Yet if any of you suffers as a Christian, do not consider it a disgrace, but glorify God because you bear this name. [17]For the time

[a] 4.1 Other ancient authorities add *for us;* others, *for you*   [b] 4.2 Gk *rest of the time in the flesh*   [c] 4.4 Or *they malign you*   [d] 4.7 Or *is at hand*   [e] 4.14 Other ancient authorities add *and of power*   [f] 4.14 Other ancient authorities add *On their part he is blasphemed, but on your part he is glorified*

has come for judgment to begin with the household of God; if it begins with us, what will be the end for those who do not obey the gospel of God? 18 And

"If it is hard for the righteous
     to be saved,
what will become of the
     ungodly and the sinners?"

19 Therefore, let those suffering in accordance with God's will entrust themselves to a faithful Creator, while continuing to do good.

TENDING THE FLOCK OF GOD

5 Now as an elder myself and a witness of the sufferings of Christ, as well as one who shares in the glory to be revealed, I exhort the elders among you 2 to tend the flock of God that is in your charge, exercising the oversight,a not under compulsion but willingly, as God would have you do itb—not for sordid gain but eagerly. 3 Do not lord it over those in your charge, but be examples to the flock. 4 And when the chief shepherd appears, you will win the crown of glory that never fades away. 5 In the same way, you who are younger must accept the authority of the elders.c And all of you must clothe yourselves with humility in your dealings with one another, for

"God opposes the proud,
     but gives grace to the humble."

6 Humble yourselves therefore under the mighty hand of God, so that he may exalt you in due time. 7 Cast all your anxiety on him, because he cares for you. 8 Discipline yourselves, keep alert.d Like a roaring lion your adversary the devil prowls around, looking for someone to devour. 9 Resist him, steadfast in your faith, for you know that your brothers and sisterse in all the world are undergoing the same kinds of suffering. 10 And after you have suffered for a little while, the God of all grace, who has called you to his eternal glory in Christ, will himself restore, support, strengthen, and establish you. 11 To him be the power forever and ever. Amen.

FINAL GREETINGS AND BENEDICTION

12 Through Silvanus, whom I consider a faithful brother, I have written this short letter to encourage you and to testify that this is the true grace of God. Stand fast in it. 13 Your sister churchf in Babylon, chosen together with you, sends you greetings; and so does my son Mark. 14 Greet one another with a kiss of love.

Peace to all of you who are in Christ.g

a 5.2 Other ancient authorities lack *exercising the oversight*   b 5.2 Other ancient authorities lack *as God would have you do it*   c 5.5 Or *of those who are older*   d 5.8 Or *be vigilant*   e 5.9 Gk *your brotherhood*   f 5.13 Gk *She who is*   g 5.14 Other ancient authorities add *Amen*

⊣├─ BIBLE IN LIFE ▷─│⊢

Preoccupied

1 Peter 5.7

Jesus didn't rub balm on us to make us impervious to tragedy or disappointment. He knew we would suffer trials, hardships, persecutions and anxieties, but he also knew that those trials, tribulations and testing would bring us closer to God, closer to the reality of life, closer to personal fulfillment, closer to joy, closer to real peace. Jesus said, "Peace I leave with you; my peace I give to you . . . Do not let your hearts be troubled and do not let them be afraid" (John 14.27). We often forget the words of Christ and the reassurance of 1 Peter 5.7; instead we focus on everything around us. We become distracted and preoccupied with technology and the information we learn each day through the news media. We worry about how we fit into the world and how we compare to others. We tend to measure failure by human standards and forget about the fact that God's standards for a Christian are quite different. But if the Holy Spirit is in our hearts, those things we worry about become inconsequential.

The Second Letter of

PETER

Peter's second letter addresses four concerns: 1) the need to develop Christian character; 2) the importance of holding to the truth; 3) warnings against false teachers; and 4) admonitions on how to live in view of the Lord's coming. As you read 2 Peter, consider how you would live if you knew Jesus Christ would return next year . . . next month . . . next week . . . or tomorrow.

SALUTATION

1 Simeon[a] Peter, a servant[b] and apostle of Jesus Christ,

To those who have received a faith as precious as ours through the righteousness of our God and Savior Jesus Christ:[c]

2 May grace and peace be yours in abundance in the knowledge of God and of Jesus our Lord.

THE CHRISTIAN'S CALL AND ELECTION

3 His divine power has given us everything needed for life and godliness, through the knowledge of him who called us by[d] his own glory and goodness. 4 Thus he has given us, through these things, his precious and very great promises, so that through them you may escape from the corruption that is in the world because of lust, and may become participants of the divine nature. 5 For this very reason, you must make every effort to support your faith with goodness, and goodness with knowledge, 6 and knowledge with self-control, and self-control with endurance, and endurance with godliness, 7 and godliness with mutual[e] affection, and mutual[e] affection with love. 8 For if these things are yours and are increasing among you, they keep you from being ineffective and unfruitful in the knowledge of our Lord Jesus Christ. 9 For anyone who lacks these things is short-sighted and blind, and is forgetful of the cleansing of past sins. 10 Therefore, brothers and sisters,[f] be all the more eager to confirm your call and election, for if you do this, you will never stumble. 11 For in this way, entry into the eternal kingdom of our Lord and Savior Jesus Christ will be richly provided for you.

12 Therefore I intend to keep on reminding you of these things, though you know them already and are established in the truth that has come to you. 13 I think it right, as long as I am in this body,[g] to refresh your memory, 14 since I know that my death[h] will come soon, as indeed our Lord Jesus Christ has made clear to me. 15 And I will make every effort so that after my departure you may be able at any time to recall these things.

EYEWITNESSES OF CHRIST'S GLORY

16 For we did not follow cleverly devised myths when we made known to you the power and coming of our Lord Jesus Christ, but we had been eyewitnesses of his majesty. 17 For he received honor and glory from God the Father when that voice was conveyed to him by the Majestic Glory, saying, "This is

[a] 1.1 Other ancient authorities read *Simon* [b] 1.1 Gk *slave* [c] 1.1 Or *of our God and the Savior Jesus Christ* [d] 1.3 Other ancient authorities read *through* [e] 1.7 Gk *brotherly* [f] 1.10 Gk *brothers* [g] 1.13 Gk *tent* [h] 1.14 Gk *the putting off of my tent*

⊣⊢ BIBLE IN LIFE ▷────────⊂⊃

Underestimating Ourselves   2 Peter 1.3

We know that harboring pride in our hearts is sinful, but the opposite is an equally troublesome characteristic that many of us battle: *underestimating ourselves*. We may use our apparent lack of special qualifications as an excuse for not acting as Christians should. When we underestimate our own talents and abilities and opportunities—we think we're not good evangelists or we can't sing or we don't have much money to give away—we may avoid doing anything in the name of Jesus. When we think this way, we are measuring our worth and skill against the world's standards. God wants us to be involved in the kind things, the gentle things, the just things, the fair things, the loving things, the compassionate things, the humble things, the things that any one of us can do that draw us closer to Christ and closer to the people around us. God has given each of us everything we need to live godly lives.

my Son, my Beloved,[a] with whom I am well pleased." [18]We ourselves heard this voice come from heaven, while we were with him on the holy mountain.

[19] So we have the prophetic message more fully confirmed. You will do well to be attentive to this as to a lamp shining in a dark place, until the day dawns and the morning star rises in your hearts. [20]First of all you must understand this, that no prophecy of scripture is a matter of one's own interpretation, [21]because no prophecy ever came by human will, but men and women moved by the Holy Spirit spoke from God.[b]

FALSE PROPHETS AND THEIR PUNISHMENT

2 But false prophets also arose among the people, just as there will be false teachers among you, who will secretly bring in destructive opinions. They will even deny the Master who bought them— bringing swift destruction on themselves. [2]Even so, many will follow their licentious ways, and because of these teachers[c] the way of truth will be maligned. [3]And in their greed they will exploit you with deceptive words. Their condemnation, pronounced against them long ago, has not been idle, and their destruction is not asleep.

[4] For if God did not spare the angels when they sinned, but cast them into hell[d] and committed them to chains[e] of deepest darkness to be kept until the judgment; [5]and if he did not spare the ancient world, even though he saved Noah, a herald of righteousness, with seven others, when he brought a flood on a world of the ungodly; [6]and if by turning the cities of Sodom and Gomorrah to ashes he condemned them to extinction[f] and made them an example of what is coming to the ungodly;[g] [7]and if he rescued Lot, a righteous man greatly distressed by the licentiousness of the lawless [8](for that righteous man, living among them day after day, was tormented in his righteous soul by their lawless deeds that he saw and heard), [9]then the Lord knows how to rescue the godly from trial, and to keep the unrighteous under punishment until the day of judgment [10]—especially those who indulge their flesh in depraved lust, and who despise authority.

Bold and willful, they are not afraid to slander the glorious ones,[h] [11]whereas angels, though greater in might and power, do not bring against them a slanderous judgment from the Lord.[i] [12]These people, however, are like irrational animals, mere creatures of instinct, born to be caught and killed. They slander what they do not understand, and when those creatures are destroyed,[j] they also will be destroyed, [13]suffering[k] the penalty for doing wrong. They count it a pleasure to revel in the daytime. They are blots and blemishes, reveling in their dissipation[l] while they feast with you. [14]They have eyes full of adultery, insatiable for sin. They entice unsteady souls. They have hearts trained in greed. Accursed children! [15]They have left the straight road and have gone astray, following the road of Balaam son of Bosor,[m] who loved the wages of doing wrong, [16]but was rebuked for his own transgression; a speechless donkey spoke with a human voice and restrained the prophet's madness.

[17] These are waterless springs and mists driven by a storm; for them the deepest darkness has been reserved. [18]For they speak bombastic nonsense, and with licentious desires of the flesh they entice people who have just[n] escaped from those

[a] 1.17 Other ancient authorities read *my beloved Son* [b] 1.21 Other ancient authorities read *but moved by the Holy Spirit saints of God spoke* [c] 2.2 Gk *because of them* [d] 2.4 Gk *Tartaros* [e] 2.4 Other ancient authorities read *pits* [f] 2.6 Other ancient authorities lack *to extinction* [g] 2.6 Other ancient authorities read *an example to those who were to be ungodly* [h] 2.10 Or *angels*; Gk *glories* [i] 2.11 Other ancient authorities read *before the Lord*; others lack the phrase [j] 2.12 Gk *in their destruction* [k] 2.13 Other ancient authorities read *receiving* [l] 2.13 Other ancient authorities read *love-feasts* [m] 2.15 Other ancient authorities read *Beor* [n] 2.18 Other ancient authorities read *actually*

who live in error. 19They promise them freedom, but they themselves are slaves of corruption; for people are slaves to whatever masters them. 20For if, after they have escaped the defilements of the world through the knowledge of our Lord and Savior Jesus Christ, they are again entangled in them and overpowered, the last state has become worse for them than the first. 21For it would have been better for them never to have known the way of righteousness than, after knowing it, to turn back from the holy commandment that was passed on to them. 22It has happened to them according to the true proverb,

"The dog turns back to its
own vomit,"

and,

"The sow is washed only to
wallow in the mud."

THE PROMISE OF THE LORD'S COMING

3 This is now, beloved, the second letter I am writing to you; in them I am trying to arouse your sincere intention by reminding you 2that you should remember the words spoken in the past by the holy prophets, and the commandment of the Lord and Savior spoken through your apostles. 3First of all you must understand this, that in the last days scoffers will come, scoffing and indulging their own lusts 4and saying, "Where is the promise of his coming? For ever since our ancestors died,[a] all things continue as they were from the beginning of creation!" 5They deliberately ignore this fact, that by the word of God heavens existed long ago and an earth was formed out of water and by means of water, 6through which the world of that time was deluged with water and perished. 7But by the same word of the present heavens and earth have been reserved for fire, being kept until the day of judgment and destruction of the godless.

8 But do not ignore this one fact, beloved, that with the Lord one day is like a thousand years, and a thousand years are like one day. 9The

Lord is not slow about his promise, as some think of slowness, but is patient with you,[b] not wanting any to perish, but all to come to repentance. 10But the day of the Lord will come like a thief, and then the heavens will pass away with a loud noise, and the elements will be dissolved with fire, and the earth and everything that is done on it will be disclosed.[c]

PONDER

But do not ignore this one fact, beloved, that with the Lord one day is like a thousand years, and a thousand years are like one day. The Lord is not slow about his promise, as some think of slowness, but is patient with you, not wanting any to perish, but all to come to repentance.
—2 Peter 3.8–9

PRAY

Lord, we thank you for all your promises. We are grateful that you are a God who is forbearing and patient, that you wait for your people to turn to you, that you promise your forgiveness when we do. We pray that every heart in doubt will turn to you through faith in Jesus Christ and that those of us who have not done so will make a public profession: "I believe in Jesus Christ; I know that I have been and I am a sinner; I know that Christ took the punishment for my sin for himself, and through my faith in him I will be saved." We pray that all those you call will listen and answer you, in the name of Jesus we pray. Amen.

11 Since all these things are to be dissolved in this way, what sort of persons ought you to be in leading lives of holiness and godliness,

[a] 3.4 Gk our fathers fell asleep   [b] 3.9 Other ancient authorities read on your account   [c] 3.10 Other ancient authorities read will be burned up

12waiting for and hastening[a] the coming of the day of God, because of which the heavens will be set ablaze and dissolved, and the elements will melt with fire? 13But, in accordance with his promise, we wait for new heavens and a new earth, where righteousness is at home.

FINAL EXHORTATION AND DOXOLOGY

14 Therefore, beloved, while you are waiting for these things, strive to be found by him at peace, without spot or blemish; 15and regard the patience of our Lord as salvation. So also our beloved brother Paul wrote to you according to the wisdom given him, 16speaking of this as he does in all his letters. There are some things in them hard to understand, which the ignorant and unstable twist to their own destruction, as they do the other scriptures. 17You therefore, beloved, since you are forewarned, beware that you are not carried away with the error of the lawless and lose your own stability. 18But grow in the grace and knowledge of our Lord and Savior Jesus Christ. To him be the glory both now and to the day of eternity. Amen.[b]

[a] 3.12 Or *earnestly desiring*   [b] 3.18 Other ancient authorities lack *Amen*

The First Letter of

JOHN

Many people hold views that run counter to Jesus' teachings. That's why 1 John is such a relevant book for us. The apostle John writes to correct a false world view that claimed that Jesus was not both God and human. Though written to correct dangerous heresy, his letter is anything but dry. Instead it is a beautiful treatise on the love of God. John stresses that we are to walk in the light of God's love and to love others with the same love we have received, to love "in truth and action" (1 John 3.18).

THE WORD OF LIFE

1 We declare to you what was from the beginning, what we have heard, what we have seen with our eyes, what we have looked at and touched with our hands, concerning the word of life— [2]this life was revealed, and we have seen it and testify to it, and declare to you the eternal life that was with the Father and was revealed to us— [3]we declare to you what we have seen and heard so that you also may have fellowship with us; and truly our fellowship is with the Father and with his Son Jesus Christ. [4]We are writing these things so that our[a] joy may be complete.

GOD IS LIGHT

[5]This is the message we have heard from him and proclaim to you, that God is light and in him there is no darkness at all. [6]If we say that we have fellowship with him while we are walking in darkness, we lie and do not do what is true; [7]but if we walk in the light as he himself is in the light, we have fellowship with one another, and the blood of Jesus his Son cleanses us from all sin. [8]If we say that we have no sin, we deceive ourselves, and the truth is not in us. [9]If we confess our sins, he who is faithful and just will forgive us our sins and cleanse us from all unrighteousness. [10]If we say that we have not sinned, we make him a liar, and his word is not in us.

CHRIST OUR ADVOCATE

2 My little children, I am writing these things to you so that you may not sin. But if anyone does sin, we have an advocate with the Father, Jesus Christ the righteous; [2]and he is the atoning sacrifice for our sins, and not for ours only but also for the sins of the whole world.

[3] Now by this we may be sure that we know him, if we obey his commandments. [4]Whoever says, "I have come to know him," but does not obey his commandments, is a liar, and in such a person the truth does not exist; [5]but whoever obeys his word, truly in this person the love of

God has reached perfection. By this we may be sure that we are in him: [6]whoever says, "I abide in him," ought to walk just as he walked.

A NEW COMMANDMENT

[7] Beloved, I am writing you no new commandment, but an old commandment that you have had from the beginning; the old commandment is the word that you have heard. [8]Yet I am writing you a new commandment that is true in him and in you, because[b] the darkness is passing away and the true light is already shining. [9]Whoever says, "I am in the light," while hating a brother or sister,[c] is still in the darkness. [10]Whoever loves a brother or sister[d] lives in the light, and in such a person[e] there is no cause for stumbling. [11]But whoever hates another believer[f] is in the darkness, walks in the darkness, and does not know the way to go, because the darkness has brought on blindness.

[12] I am writing to you, little children,
because your sins are forgiven
on account of his name.
[13] I am writing to you, fathers,
because you know him who
is from the beginning.
I am writing to you,
young people,
because you have conquered
the evil one.
[14] I write to you, children,
because you know the Father.
I write to you, fathers,
because you know him who
is from the beginning.
I write to you, young people,
because you are strong
and the word of God
abides in you,
and you have overcome
the evil one.

[15] Do not love the world or the things in the world. The love of the Father is not in those who love the world; [16]for all that is in the world— the desire of the flesh, the desire of

[a] 1.4 Other ancient authorities read *your*
[b] 2.8 Or *that*   [c] 2.9 Gk *hating a brother*
[d] 2.10 Gk *loves a brother*   [e] 2.10 Or *in it*
[f] 2.11 Gk *hates a brother*

the eyes, the pride in riches—comes not from the Father but from the world. [17]And the world and its desire[a] are passing away, but those who do the will of God live forever.

WARNING AGAINST ANTICHRISTS

[18] Children, it is the last hour! As you have heard that antichrist is coming, so now many antichrists have come. From this we know that it is the last hour. [19]They went out from us, but they did not belong to us; for if they had belonged to us, they would have remained with us. But by going out they made it plain that none of them belongs to us. [20]But you have been anointed by the Holy One, and all of you have knowledge.[b] [21]I write to you, not because you do not know the truth, but because you know it, and you know that no lie comes from the truth. [22]Who is the liar but the one who denies that Jesus is the Christ?[c] This is the antichrist, the one who denies the Father and the Son. [23]No one who denies the Son has the Father; everyone who confesses the Son has the Father also. [24]Let what you heard from the beginning abide in you. If what you heard from the beginning abides in you, then you will abide in the Son and in the Father. [25]And this is what he has promised us,[d] eternal life.

[26] I write these things to you concerning those who would deceive you. [27]As for you, the anointing that you received from him abides in you, and so you do not need anyone to teach you. But as his anointing teaches you about all things, and is true and is not a lie, and just as it has taught you, abide in him.[e]

[28] And now, little children, abide in him, so that when he is revealed we may have confidence and not be put to shame before him at his coming.

CHILDREN OF GOD

[29] If you know that he is righteous, you may be sure that everyone who does right has been born of him. 3 [1]See what love the Father has given us, that we should be called children of God; and that is what we are. The reason the world does not know us is that it did not know him. [2]Beloved, we are God's children now; what we will be has not yet been revealed. What we do know is this: when he[e] is revealed, we will be like him, for we will see him as he is. [3]And all who have this hope in him purify themselves, just as he is pure.

[4] Everyone who commits sin is guilty of lawlessness; sin is lawlessness. [5]You know that he was revealed to take away sins, and in him there is no sin. [6]No one who abides

[a] 2.17 Or *the desire for it*   [b] 2.20 Other ancient authorities read *you know all things*   [c] 2.22 Or *the Messiah*   [d] 2.25 Other ancient authorities read *you*   [e] 2.27; 3.2 Or *it*

⊢ BIBLE IN LIFE ▷

Resurrected Bodies
1 John 3.2

Someday, John assures us, we will be like Christ. We will have resurrected bodies and flawless spiritual vision. After Jesus' resurrection, his new body was still in human form, but it had changed. He walked through doors (see John 20.19–26). He disappeared (see Luke 24). But he still had scars on his hands and a side for Thomas to touch (see John 20.24–29). We don't know exactly what form Jesus took, "and what we will be has not yet been revealed." Much of the afterlife remains a mystery to us, but God has ordained that we will be resurrected and that we will have eternal life in the kingdom of God. That eternal life begins now, however, not when we're on our deathbeds or even when our souls depart from our bodies. In Jesus, the kingdom came near to us. With faith in Christ and the resurrection, our eternal life has already commenced. Just as our bodies will be transformed to be like Christ's, so our lives should also be transformed into his likeness.

in him sins; no one who sins has either seen him or known him. 7Little children, let no one deceive you. Everyone who does what is right is righteous, just as he is righteous. 8Everyone who commits sin is a child of the devil; for the devil has been sinning from the beginning. The Son of God was revealed for this purpose, to destroy the works of the devil. 9Those who have been born of God do not sin, because God's seed abides in them;[a] they cannot sin, because they have been born of God. 10The children of God and the children of the devil are revealed in this way: all who do not do what is right are not from God, nor are those who do not love their brothers and sisters.[b]

LOVE ONE ANOTHER

11 For this is the message you have heard from the beginning, that we should love one another. 12We must not be like Cain who was from the evil one and murdered his brother. And why did he murder him? Because his own deeds were evil and his brother's righteous. 13Do not be astonished, brothers and sisters,[c] that the world hates you. 14We know that we have passed from death to life because we love one another. Whoever does not love abides in death. 15All who hate a brother or sister[b] are murderers, and you know that murderers do not have eternal life abiding in them. 16We know love by this, that he laid down his life for us—and we ought to lay down our lives for one another. 17How does God's love abide in anyone who has the world's goods and sees a brother or sister[d] in need and yet refuses help? 18 Little children, let us love, not in word or speech, but in truth and action. 19And by this we will know that we are from the truth and will reassure our hearts before him 20whenever our hearts condemn us; for God is greater than our hearts, and he knows everything. 21Beloved, if our hearts do not condemn us, we have boldness before God; 22and we receive from him whatever we ask,

because we obey his commandments and do what pleases him. 23 And this is his commandment, that we should believe in the name of his Son Jesus Christ and love one another, just as he has commanded us. 24All who obey his commandments abide in him, and he abides in them. And by this we know that he abides in us, by the Spirit that he has given us.

PONDER

Beloved, if our hearts do not condemn us, we have boldness before God; and we receive from him whatever we ask, because we obey his commandments and do what pleases him . . . love one another, just as he has commanded us. —1 John 3.21–23

PRAY

O Father, we are thankful for the words of John. Many years after the death of Christ, he restated this message to Christians who, like us, were sometimes divided from one another due to selfishness, inadequate knowledge of the scriptures, or failure to commune with you. We ask you to forgive our sinfulness and our inability to keep your commands. We pray for this message to be especially embedded in our hearts so that we can ambitiously demonstrate love as defined by our Savior, Jesus Christ. In his name we pray. Amen.

TESTING THE SPIRITS

4 Beloved, do not believe every spirit, but test the spirits to see whether they are from God; for many false prophets have gone out into the world. 2By this you know the Spirit of God: every spirit that confesses that Jesus Christ has come in the flesh is from God, 3and every

---

[a] 3.9 Or *because the children of God abide in him* [b] 3.10,15 Gk *his brother* [c] 3.13 Gk *brothers* [d] 3.17 Gk *brother*

spirit that does not confess Jesus[a] is not from God. And this is the spirit of the antichrist, of which you have heard that it is coming; and now it is already in the world. [4]Little children, you are from God, and have conquered them; for the one who is in you is greater than the one who is in the world. [5]They are from the world; therefore what they say is from the world, and the world listens to them. [6]We are from God. Whoever knows God listens to us, and whoever is not from God does not listen to us. From this we know the spirit of truth and the spirit of error.

GOD IS LOVE

[7]Beloved, let us love one another, because love is from God; everyone who loves is born of God and knows God. [8]Whoever does not love does not know God, for God is love. [9]God's love was revealed among us in this way: God sent his only Son into the world so that we might live through him. [10]In this is love, not that we loved God but that he loved us and sent his Son to be the atoning sacrifice for our sins. [11]Beloved, since God loved us so much, we also ought to love one another. [12]No one has ever seen God; if we love one another, God lives in us, and his love is perfected in us.

[13]By this we know that we abide in him and he in us, because he has given us of his Spirit. [14]And we have seen and do testify that the Father has sent his Son as the Savior of the world. [15]God abides in those who confess that Jesus is the Son of God, and they abide in God. [16]So we have known and believe the love that God has for us.

God is love, and those who abide in love abide in God, and God abides in them. [17]Love has been perfected among us in this: that we may have boldness on the day of judgment, because as he is, so are we in this world. [18]There is no fear in love, but perfect love casts out fear; for fear has to do with punishment, and whoever fears has not reached perfection in love. [19]We love[b] because he first loved us. [20]Those who say, "I love God," and hate their brothers or sisters,[c] are liars; for those who do not love a brother or sister[d] whom they have seen, cannot love God whom they have not seen. [21]The commandment we have from him is this: those who love God must love their brothers and sisters[c] also.

[a] 4.3 Other ancient authorities read *does away with Jesus* (Gk *dissolves Jesus*)
[b] 4.19 Other ancient authorities add *him*; others add *God*   [c] 4.20,21 Gk *brothers*
[d] 4.20 Gk *brother*

┤├ BIBLE IN LIFE ▷

God Is Love

1 John 4.7–21

Throughout history, God has revealed various aspects of the divine, but in Jesus, God has revealed himself to us most fully and perfectly. What do we learn about God's character by looking at Jesus? Is God simply a stern judge? Is God the Creator of the world who has left us alone like a windup clock? No. Jesus shows us that *God is love* (verse 8). In his description of God, the term John used for love is the Greek word *agape*. This term refers to love that is transcendent, forgiving, sacrificial and constant, a love that endures even though it is not reciprocated. This is the love of a parent for a child, a love that is willing to suffer for the good of another. What greater love could God display for us than Jesus' sacrifice on the cross for our sins? Though we rebelled and sinned, God reached out to us and paid the price so that we could be saved from sin and its effects (see John 3.16). We are called to show this same love to others. It might be through a simple act of kindness to a stranger. It could require willingness to forgive a deep hurt. It might be demonstrated by an unrelenting commitment to another person's good. However we choose to show God's love to others, we can find our model of perfect love in Jesus.

FAITH CONQUERS THE WORLD

5 Everyone who believes that Jesus is the Christ[a] has been born of God, and everyone who loves the parent loves the child. [2]By this we know that we love the children of God, when we love God and obey his commandments. [3]For the love of God is this, that we obey his commandments. And his commandments are not burdensome, [4]for whatever is born of God conquers the world. And this is the victory that conquers the world, our faith. [5]Who is it that conquers the world but the one who believes that Jesus is the Son of God?

TESTIMONY CONCERNING THE SON OF GOD

[6] This is the one who came by water and blood, Jesus Christ, not with the water only but with the water and the blood. And the Spirit is the one that testifies, for the Spirit is the truth. [7]There are three that testify:[b] [8]the Spirit and the water and the blood, and these three agree. [9]If we receive human testimony, the testimony of God is greater; for this is the testimony of God that he has testified to his Son. [10]Those who believe in the Son of God have the testimony in their hearts. Those who do not believe in God[c] have made him a liar by not believing in the testimony that God has given concerning his Son. [11]And this is the testimony: God gave us eternal life, and this life is in

PONDER

And this is the boldness we have in him, that if we ask anything according to his will, he hears us. And if we know that he hears us in whatever we ask, we know that we have obtained the requests made of him. —1 John 5.14–15

PRAY

Lord of all, John in his wisdom imparts to us your message and reminds us that the answers to our prayers are predicated on our asking you according to your will. Strengthen our faith; give each of us the courage to examine our own hearts and minds and to ask you first and foremost, what your will is for our lives. We praise you that we can come before you in the name of Jesus to ask you for what we need, just as a child asks a father. We pray for that confidence and blessing. In the name of the Savior. Amen.

[a] **5.1** Or *the Messiah*   [b] **5.7** A few other authorities read (with variations) [7]*There are three that testify in heaven, the Father, the Word, and the Holy Spirit, and these three are one.* [8]*And there are three that testify on earth:*   [c] **5.10** Other ancient authorities read *in the Son*

BIBLE IN LIFE

Eternal Life   1 John 5.10–12

John says that God *has* given us eternal life. He does not say that God *will* give us eternal life. For Christians, eternal life begins the moment we put our faith in Jesus Christ. Eternal life is a transformed life of peace, love, unselfishness and closeness to Jesus that begins now and continues through eternity. Physical death, the burial of a human body and the funeral service commemorating earthly life are just steps in the continuum of our total existence. If we will accept this transformational approach to eternal life, then our fears of death will be minimized, and our lives will be enriched. We won't wait until we're at the grave to live eternally, when we can no longer reach out to a poor person and assuage their hunger, their sorrow or their loneliness. Instead, we can start living in eternity now, opening our arms to the poor, the deprived, the inarticulate, the suffering, the dirty, the sinful and the imprisoned, just as Christ did.

his Son. ¹²Whoever has the Son has life; whoever does not have the Son of God does not have life.

EPILOGUE

13 I write these things to you who believe in the name of the Son of God, so that you may know that you have eternal life.

14 And this is the boldness we have in him, that if we ask anything according to his will, he hears us. ¹⁵And if we know that he hears us in whatever we ask, we know that we have obtained the requests made of him. ¹⁶If you see your brother or sister[a] committing what is not a mortal sin, you will ask, and God[b] will give life to such a one—to those whose sin is not mortal. There is sin that is mortal; I do not say that you should pray about that. ¹⁷All wrong-doing is sin, but there is sin that is not mortal.

18 We know that those who are born of God do not sin, but the one who was born of God protects them, and the evil one does not touch them. ¹⁹We know that we are God's children, and that the whole world lies under the power of the evil one. ²⁰And we know that the Son of God has come and has given us understanding so that we may know him who is true;[c] and we are in him who is true, in his Son Jesus Christ. He is the true God and eternal life.

21 Little children, keep yourselves from idols.[d]

[a] 5.16 Gk *your brother* [b] 5.16 Gk *he*
[c] 5.20 Other ancient authorities read *know the true God* [d] 5.21 Other ancient authorities add *Amen*

The Second Letter of

JOHN

After reading 2 John, you may think you've read a summary of 1 John. While this letter was written for a different purpose, it returns to many of the same themes. In this second letter, John warns Christians to be certain of their beliefs so they can resist the efforts of false teachers. As you read, think about how you can stay on target spiritually. This book will challenge you to "be on your guard" (2 John 8) and be certain about what you believe and how you live out your faith.

SALUTATION

1 The elder to the elect lady and her children, whom I love in the truth, and not only I but also all who know the truth, 2because of the truth that abides in us and will be with us forever:

3 Grace, mercy, and peace will be with us from God the Father and from[a] Jesus Christ, the Father's Son, in truth and love.

TRUTH AND LOVE

4 I was overjoyed to find some of your children walking in the truth, just as we have been commanded by the Father. 5But now, dear lady, I ask you, not as though I were writing you a new commandment, but one we have had from the beginning, let us love one another. 6And this is love, that we walk according to his commandments; this is the commandment just as you have heard it from the beginning—you must walk in it.

7 Many deceivers have gone out into the world, those who do not confess that Jesus Christ has come in the flesh; any such person is the deceiver and the antichrist! 8Be on your guard, so that you do not lose what we[b] have worked for, but may receive a full reward. 9Everyone who does not abide in the teaching of Christ, but goes beyond it, does not have God; whoever abides in the teaching has both the Father and the Son. 10Do not receive into the house or welcome anyone who comes to you and does not bring this teaching; 11for to welcome is to participate in the evil deeds of such a person.

FINAL GREETINGS

12 Although I have much to write to you, I would rather not use paper and ink; instead I hope to come to you and talk with you face to face, so that our joy may be complete.

13 The children of your elect sister send you their greetings.[c]

a 3 Other ancient authorities add the Lord
b 8 Other ancient authorities read you
c 13 Other ancient authorities add Amen

⊨ BIBLE IN LIFE ▷ ⊕

Common Ground   2 John 5

The command to love one another is not easy for us. We have a tendency to depersonalize those whom we do not understand or with whom we have differences. That alienates us from others and from God. But if we remember that God forgives us and loves us despite all our faults, that's a perfect pattern to use as we relate to other people. As we get to know someone, we should seek some common basis on which to build and grow an understanding relationship. That common ground, John is saying, can be our faith in Jesus Christ and our belief that God forgives and loves us. Therefore, we should forgive and love other human beings—not in a dormant way but in an active, reaching-out way. This common ground on which we can build will increase our affection for people as we get to know them. If we love one another, God lives in us, and his love is perfected in us.

The Third Letter of

JOHN

What's the correct way to handle opposition to godly leadership, especially when the opposition comes from someone who is arrogant or unreasonable? Third John provides some insight. It seems that Diotrephes had rejected the itinerant teachers John sent to his church and alienated those believers who were trying to be hospitable. John commends his friend Gaius for his faithfulness and his love for the traveling teachers. John doesn't avoid the problem, but deals with it honestly and directly, a great example for leaders then and now.

SALUTATION

1 The elder to the beloved Gaius, whom I love in truth.

GAIUS COMMENDED FOR HIS HOSPITALITY

2 Beloved, I pray that all may go well with you and that you may be in good health, just as it is well with your soul. **3** I was overjoyed when some of the friends[a] arrived and testified to your faithfulness to the truth, namely how you walk in the truth. **4** I have no greater joy than this, to hear that my children are walking in the truth.

5 Beloved, you do faithfully whatever you do for the friends,[a] even though they are strangers to you; **6** they have testified to your love before the church. You will do well to send them on in a manner worthy of God; **7** for they began their journey for the sake of Christ,[b] accepting no support from non-believers.[c] **8** Therefore we ought to support such people, so that we may become co-workers with the truth.

DIOTREPHES AND DEMETRIUS

9 I have written something to the church; but Diotrephes, who likes to put himself first, does not acknowledge our authority. **10** So if I come, I will call attention to what he is doing in spreading false charges against us. And not content with those charges, he refuses to welcome the friends,[a] and even prevents those who want to do so and expels them from the church.

11 Beloved, do not imitate what is evil but imitate what is good. Whoever does good is from God; whoever does evil has not seen God. **12** Everyone has testified favorably about Demetrius, and so has the truth itself. We also testify for him,[d] and you know that our testimony is true.

FINAL GREETINGS

13 I have much to write to you, but I would rather not write with pen and ink; **14** instead I hope to see you soon, and we will talk together face to face.

15 Peace to you. The friends send you their greetings. Greet the friends there, each by name.

[a] **3,5,10** Gk *brothers*   [b] **7** Gk *for the sake of the name*   [c] **7** Gk *the Gentiles*   [d] **12** Gk *lacks for him*

The Letter of
JUDE

Sometimes a slight variation of the truth is like a small spark of error that starts an inferno of heresy. Jude understood this, which is why he wrote this letter. Immoral men in the church were trying to convince believers that being saved by God's grace gave them freedom to sin. You can imagine what these men said: "Our sins are forgiven by grace and we are no longer under the law; go ahead and sin because it doesn't matter." Jude's answer sounds a fire alarm that demands a response of unwavering faith.

SALUTATION

1 Jude,[a] a servant[b] of Jesus Christ and brother of James,

To those who are called, who are beloved[c] in[d] God the Father and kept safe for[d] Jesus Christ:

2 May mercy, peace, and love be yours in abundance.

OCCASION OF THE LETTER

3 Beloved, while eagerly preparing to write to you about the salvation we share, I find it necessary to write and appeal to you to contend for the faith that was once for all entrusted to the saints. 4For certain intruders have stolen in among you, people who long ago were designated for this condemnation as ungodly, who pervert the grace of our God into licentiousness and deny our only Master and Lord, Jesus Christ.[e]

JUDGMENT ON FALSE TEACHERS

5 Now I desire to remind you, though you are fully informed, that the Lord, who once for all saved[f] a people out of the land of Egypt, afterward destroyed those who did not believe. 6And the angels who did not keep their own position, but left their proper dwelling, he has kept in eternal chains in deepest darkness for the judgment of the great day. 7Likewise, Sodom and Gomorrah and the surrounding cities, which, in the same manner as they, indulged in sexual immorality and pursued unnatural lust,[g] serve as an example by undergoing a punishment of eternal fire.

8 Yet in the same way these dreamers also defile the flesh, reject authority, and slander the glorious ones.[h] 9But when the archangel Michael contended with the devil and disputed about the body of Moses, he did not dare to bring a condemnation of slander[i] against him, but said, "The Lord rebuke you!" 10But these people slander whatever they do not understand, and they are destroyed by those things that, like irrational animals, they know by instinct. 11Woe to them! For they go the way of Cain, and abandon themselves to Balaam's error for the sake of gain, and perish in Korah's rebellion. 12These are blemishes[j] on your love-feasts, while they feast with you without fear, feeding themselves.[k] They are waterless clouds carried along by the winds; autumn trees without fruit, twice dead, uprooted; 13wild waves of the sea, casting up the foam of their own shame; wandering stars, for whom the deepest darkness has been reserved forever.

14 It was also about these that Enoch, in the seventh generation from Adam, prophesied, saying, "See, the Lord is coming[l] with ten thousands of his holy ones, 15to execute judgment on all, and to convict everyone of all the deeds of ungodliness that they have committed in such an ungodly way, and of all the harsh things that ungodly sinners have spoken against him." 16These are grumblers and malcontents; they indulge their own lusts; they are bombastic in speech, flattering people to their own advantage.

WARNINGS AND EXHORTATIONS

17 But you, beloved, must remember the predictions of the apostles of our Lord Jesus Christ; 18for they said to you, "In the last time there will be scoffers, indulging their own ungodly lusts." 19It is these worldly people, devoid of the Spirit, who are causing divisions. 20But you, beloved, build yourselves up on your most holy faith; pray in the Holy Spirit; 21keep yourselves in the love of God; look forward to the mercy of our Lord Jesus Christ that leads to[m] eternal life. 22And have mercy on some who are wavering; 23save others by snatching them out of the fire; and have mercy on still others with

a 1 Gk *Judas*   b 1 Gk *slave*   c 1 Other ancient authorities read *sanctified*   d 1 Or *by*   e 4 Or *the only Master and our Lord Jesus Christ*   f 5 Other ancient authorities read *though you were once for all fully informed, that Jesus* (or *Joshua*) *who saved*   g 7 Gk *went after other flesh*   h 8 Or *angels;* Gk *glories*   i 9 Or *condemnation for blasphemy*   j 12 Or *reefs*   k 12 Or *without fear. They are shepherds who care only for themselves*   l 14 Gk *came*   m 21 Gk *Christ to*

fear, hating even the tunic defiled by their bodies.[a]

BENEDICTION

24 Now to him who is able to keep you from falling, and to make you stand without blemish in the presence of his glory with rejoicing, 25 to the only God our Savior, through Jesus Christ our Lord, be glory, majesty, power, and authority, before all time and now and forever. Amen.

[a] 23 Gk *by the flesh*. The Greek text of verses 22–23 is uncertain at several points

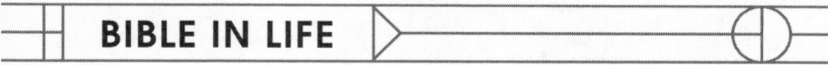

BIBLE IN LIFE

Doubting

Jude 22–23

We are called to "have mercy on some who are wavering." When we hear the word *wavering* or *doubt*, most of us automatically think of Jesus' disciple Thomas (see John 20.19–29). One of the staunch and loyal followers of Christ, Thomas was inclined to ask questions. Jesus showed Thomas mercy by giving him all the proof he needed to believe that Jesus was resurrected. God used Thomas's honest expression of doubt to strengthen his faith in Christ. In his reaction to seeing Jesus, Thomas uttered one of the most profound statements of belief that we could imagine: "My Lord and my God!" (John 20.28). Thomas didn't call Jesus "my friend" or "my prophet." From Thomas's point of view, Christ was transformed from a miracle worker and wonderful companion into the exalted Son of God.

Being merciful with the doubtful applies to us as well. At times we all struggle with doubt. It's okay to have doubts about what we believe; it's okay to question God; it's okay to bare our souls in our prayers, saying, "I believe; help my unbelief!" (Mark 9.24).

The

REVELATION

to John

Seven stars, seven lampstands and seven bowls. The book of life. The mark of the beast. It's tempting to get caught up in the symbolism and prophecies we find in Revelation. But if we focus on these things, we'll miss the point. God gave the apostle John these visions to reassure Christians everywhere that God's kingdom will ultimately prevail. What's more, John's vision unfolds an awesome depiction of the return of Jesus Christ as victorious Savior, resplendent in light and beauty. As you read the final pages of this wonderful, challenging book, be sure to add your own assent: "Amen. Come, Lord Jesus" (Revelation 22.20).

INTRODUCTION AND SALUTATION

1 The revelation of Jesus Christ, which God gave him to show his servants[a] what must soon take place; he made[b] it known by sending his angel to his servant[c] John, 2who testified to the word of God and to the testimony of Jesus Christ, even to all that he saw.

3 Blessed is the one who reads aloud the words of the prophecy, and blessed are those who hear and who keep what is written in it; for the time is near.

4 John to the seven churches that are in Asia:

Grace to you and peace from him who is and who was and who is to come, and from the seven spirits who are before his throne, 5and from Jesus Christ, the faithful witness, the firstborn of the dead, and the ruler of the kings of the earth.

To him who loves us and freed[d] us from our sins by his blood, 6and made[e] us to be a kingdom, priests serving[f] his God and Father, to him be glory and dominion forever and ever. Amen.

7 Look! He is coming with
   the clouds;
   every eye will see him,
   even those who pierced him;
   and on his account all the tribes
      of the earth will wail.
So it is to be. Amen.

8 "I am the Alpha and the Omega," says the Lord God, who is and who was and who is to come, the Almighty.

A VISION OF CHRIST

9 I, John, your brother who share with you in Jesus the persecution and the kingdom and the patient endurance, was on the island called Patmos because of the word of God and the testimony of Jesus.[g] 10I was in the spirit[h] on the Lord's day, and I heard behind me a loud voice like a trumpet 11saying, "Write in a book what you see and send it to the seven churches, to Ephesus, to Smyrna, to Pergamum, to Thyatira, to Sardis, to Philadelphia, and to Laodicea."

12 Then I turned to see whose voice it was that spoke to me, and on turning I saw seven golden lampstands, 13and in the midst of the lampstands I saw one like the Son of Man, clothed with a long robe and with a golden sash across his chest. 14His head and his hair were white as white wool, white as snow; his eyes were like a flame of fire, 15his feet were like burnished bronze, refined as in a furnace, and his voice was like the sound of many waters.

a 1.1 Gk *slaves*   b 1.1 Gk *and he made*
c 1.1 Gk *slave*   d 1.5 Other ancient
authorities read *washed*   e 1.6 Gk *and
he made*   f 1.6 Gk *priests to*   g 1.9 Or
testimony to Jesus   h 1.10 Or *in the Spirit*

⊕

PONDER

His head and his hair were white
as white wool, white as snow; his
eyes were like a flame of fire, his feet
were like burnished bronze, refined
as in a furnace, and his voice was
like the sound of many waters.
—Revelation 1.14–15

PRAY

O Father, as we try to absorb the meaning of this remarkable vision that you showed to John, we praise you for the glorious, transcendent glimpse of the Living One, the First and the Last. It is a vision we should always keep in our hearts and our minds as we go about some of the more mundane tasks we encounter and fulfill the purpose for which you made us. It is a vision that sheds light on our everyday life and shows us that a different kind of kingdom is all around us, that there is more than we see, touch, taste and feel. Help us immerse ourselves in faith in the resurrected Christ, to demonstrate the reality of his being in our daily lives as we model what it means to be a Christian. In the name of the risen Lord we pray. Amen.

16In his right hand he held seven stars, and from his mouth came a sharp, two-edged sword, and his face was like the sun shining with full force.

17 When I saw him, I fell at his feet as though dead. But he placed his right hand on me, saying, "Do not be afraid; I am the first and the last, 18and the living one. I was dead, and see, I am alive forever and ever; and I have the keys of Death and of Hades. 19Now write what you have seen, what is, and what is to take place after this. 20As for the mystery of the seven stars that you saw in my right hand, and the seven golden lampstands: the seven stars are the angels of the seven churches, and the seven lampstands are the seven churches.

THE MESSAGE TO EPHESUS

2 "To the angel of the church in Ephesus write: These are the words of him who holds the seven stars in his right hand, who walks among the seven golden lampstands:

2 "I know your works, your toil and your patient endurance. I know that you cannot tolerate evildoers; you have tested those who claim to be apostles but are not, and have found them to be false. 3I also know that you are enduring patiently and bearing up for the sake of my name, and that you have not grown weary.

4But I have this against you, that you have abandoned the love you had at first. 5Remember then from what you have fallen; repent, and do the works you did at first. If not, I will come to you and remove your lampstand from its place, unless you repent. 6Yet this is to your credit: you hate the works of the Nicolaitans, which I also hate. 7Let anyone who has an ear listen to what the Spirit is saying to the churches. To everyone who conquers, I will give permission to eat from the tree of life that is in the paradise of God.

THE MESSAGE TO SMYRNA

8 "And to the angel of the church in Smyrna write: These are the words of the first and the last, who was dead and came to life:

9 "I know your affliction and your poverty, even though you are rich. I know the slander on the part of those who say that they are Jews and are not, but are a synagogue of Satan. 10Do not fear what you are about to suffer. Beware, the devil is about to throw some of you into prison so that you may be tested, and for ten days you will have affliction. Be faithful until death, and I will give you the crown of life. 11Let anyone who has an ear listen to what the Spirit is saying to the churches. Whoever conquers will not be harmed by the second death.

⊨ BIBLE IN LIFE ▷ ─────── ⊖⊐

The Fear of Death

Revelation 2.10–11

What is our reaction to the words "Do not be fear what you are about to suffer" and "Be faithful until death"? Few of us in developed countries would be expected to give our lives, though many of our brothers and sisters around the world experience suffering and martyrdom as an everyday reality. For most of us, persecution and martyrdom are abstract, distant concepts, yet many of the early disciples and Christian leaders were martyred. Tradition holds that Peter requested to be crucified upside down because he didn't consider himself worthy to be executed the same way Jesus was. The apostle Paul could have renounced his Christian faith, but he spent the last part of his life in prison and presumably was beheaded in Rome. The other disciples showed a similar willingness to give their lives, their freedom, their success and everything they had for faith in Christ. They clung to the hope of resurrection and the promise of eternal life with Jesus. Many of us fear the pain and uncertainty of dying and value the length of our lives instead of the fruits of our existence. We need not fear death. Those who believe in Christ have the promise of everlasting life

THE MESSAGE TO PERGAMUM

12 "And to the angel of the church in Pergamum write: These are the words of him who has the sharp two-edged sword:

13 "I know where you are living, where Satan's throne is. Yet you are holding fast to my name, and you did not deny your faith in me[a] even in the days of Antipas my witness, my faithful one, who was killed among you, where Satan lives. 14But I have a few things against you: you have some there who hold to the teaching of Balaam, who taught Balak to put a stumbling block before the people of Israel, so that they would eat food sacrificed to idols and practice fornication. 15So you also have some who hold to the teaching of the Nicolaitans. 16Repent then. If not, I will come to you soon and make war against them with the sword of my mouth. 17Let anyone who has an ear listen to what the Spirit is saying to the churches. To everyone who conquers I will give some of the hidden manna, and I will give a white stone, and on the white stone is written a new name that no one knows except the one who receives it.

THE MESSAGE TO THYATIRA

18 "And to the angel of the church in Thyatira write: These are the words of the Son of God, who has eyes like a flame of fire, and whose feet are like burnished bronze:

19 "I know your works—your love, faith, service, and patient endurance. I know that your last works are greater than the first. 20But I have this against you: you tolerate that woman Jezebel, who calls herself a prophet and is teaching and beguiling my servants[b] to practice fornication and to eat food sacrificed to idols. 21I gave her time to repent, but she refuses to repent of her fornication. 22Beware, I am throwing her on a bed, and those who commit adultery with her I am throwing into great distress, unless they repent of her doings; 23and I will strike her children dead. And all the churches will know that I am the one who searches minds and hearts,

and I will give to each of you as your works deserve. 24But to the rest of you in Thyatira, who do not hold this teaching, who have not learned what some call 'the deep things of Satan,' to you I say, I do not lay on you any other burden; 25only hold fast to what you have until I come. 26To everyone who conquers and continues to do my works to the end,
I will give authority over
    the nations;
27 to rule[c] them with an iron rod,
    as when clay pots are
        shattered—
28even as I also received authority from my Father. To the one who conquers I will also give the morning star. 29Let anyone who has an ear listen to what the Spirit is saying to the churches.

THE MESSAGE TO SARDIS

3 "And to the angel of the church in Sardis write: These are the words of him who has the seven spirits of God and the seven stars:

"I know your works; you have a name of being alive, but you are dead. 2Wake up, and strengthen what remains and is on the point of death, for I have not found your works perfect in the sight of my God. 3Remember then what you received and heard; obey it, and repent. If you do not wake up, I will come like a thief, and you will not know at what hour I will come to you. 4Yet you have still a few persons in Sardis who have not soiled their clothes; they will walk with me, dressed in white, for they are worthy. 5If you conquer, you will be clothed like them in white robes, and I will not blot your name out of the book of life; I will confess your name before my Father and before his angels. 6Let anyone who has an ear listen to what the Spirit is saying to the churches.

THE MESSAGE TO PHILADELPHIA

7 "And to the angel of the church in Philadelphia write:

---

a 2.13 Or *deny my faith*   b 2.20 Gk *slaves*
c 2.27 Or *to shepherd*

These are the words of the holy
one, the true one,
who has the key of David,
who opens and no one will shut,
who shuts and no one opens:

WE ARE MOST LIKELY

TO BE LUKEWARM WHEN

EVERYTHING IS GOING WELL

FOR US, WHEN WE FEEL

THAT WE ARE EITHER SELF-

SUFFICIENT OR WORTHY OF

ALL OUR BLESSINGS. WHY

SHOULD WE ATTEMPT TO

CHANGE THE STATUS QUO?

8 "I know your works. Look, I have set before you an open door, which no one is able to shut. I know that you have but little power, and yet you have kept my word and have not denied my name. 9I will make those of the synagogue of Satan who say that they are Jews and are not, but are lying—I will make them come and bow down before your feet, and they will learn that I have loved you. 10Because you have kept my word of patient endurance, I will keep you from the hour of trial that is coming on the whole world to test the inhabitants of the earth. 11I am coming soon; hold fast to what you have, so that no one may seize your crown. 12If you conquer, I will make you a pillar in the temple of my God; you will never go out of it. I will write on you the name of my God, and the name of the city of my God, the new Jerusalem that comes down from my God out of heaven, and my own new name. 13Let anyone who has an ear listen to what the Spirit is saying to the churches.

THE MESSAGE TO LAODICEA

14 "And to the angel of the church in Laodicea write: The words of the

Amen, the faithful and true witness, the origin[a] of God's creation:

15 "I know your works; you are neither cold nor hot. I wish that you were either cold or hot. 16So, because you are lukewarm, and neither cold nor hot, I am about to spit you out of my mouth. 17For you say, 'I am rich, I have prospered, and I need nothing.' You do not realize that you are wretched, pitiable, poor, blind, and naked. 18Therefore I counsel you to buy from me gold refined by fire so that you may be rich; and white robes to clothe you and to keep the shame of your nakedness from being seen; and salve to anoint your eyes so that you may see. 19I reprove and discipline those whom I love. Be earnest, therefore, and repent. 20Listen! I am standing at the door, knocking; if you hear my voice and open the door, I will come in to you and eat with you, and you with me. 21To the one who conquers I will give a place with me on my throne, just as I myself conquered and sat down with my Father on his throne. 22Let anyone who has an ear listen to what the Spirit is saying to the churches."

THE HEAVENLY WORSHIP

4 After this I looked, and there in heaven a door stood open! And the first voice, which I had heard speaking to me like a trumpet, said, "Come up here, and I will show you what must take place after this." 2At once I was in the spirit,[b] and there in heaven stood a throne, with one seated on the throne! 3And the one seated there looks like jasper and carnelian, and around the throne is a rainbow that looks like an emerald. 4Around the throne are twenty-four thrones, and seated on the thrones are twenty-four elders, dressed in white robes, with golden crowns on their heads. 5Coming from the throne are flashes of lightning, and rumblings and peals of thunder, and in front of the throne burn seven flaming torches, which are the seven spirits of God; 6and in front of the throne there is something like a sea of glass, like crystal.

PONDER

"Come up here, and I will show you
what must take place after this."
—Revelation 4.1

PRAY

O Father, we pray, as we study the
difficult book of Revelation, that you
will enlighten us and give us insight
into John's writings. We pray that these
scriptures might immerse us ever more
deeply into individual commitments
to you. Help us to adopt principles
in our lives that will make us more
like you: justice, not persecution;
peace instead of war; humility, not
arrogance or pride; service to others,
not selfishness; compassion and
generous love, not hate and apathy.
We ask these things in the name of our
precious Savior, Jesus Christ. Amen.

Around the throne, and on each
side of the throne, are four living
creatures, full of eyes in front and behind: [7]the first living creature like a
lion, the second living creature like
an ox, the third living creature with
a face like a human face, and the
fourth living creature like a flying
eagle. [8]And the four living creatures,
each of them with six wings, are full
of eyes all around and inside. Day
and night without ceasing they sing,
"Holy, holy, holy,
    the Lord God the Almighty,
        who was and is and is to come."
[9]And whenever the living creatures
give glory and honor and thanks to
the one who is seated on the throne,
who lives forever and ever, [10]the
twenty-four elders fall before the
one who is seated on the throne and
worship the one who lives forever
and ever; they cast their crowns before the throne, singing,
[11] "You are worthy, our Lord and God,
    to receive glory and honor
        and power,

for you created all things,
    and by your will they existed
        and were created."

THE SCROLL AND THE LAMB

5 Then I saw in the right hand of
the one seated on the throne a
scroll written on the inside and on
the back, sealed[a] with seven seals;
[2]and I saw a mighty angel proclaiming with a loud voice, "Who is worthy to open the scroll and break its
seals?" [3]And no one in heaven or on
earth or under the earth was able
to open the scroll or to look into it.
[4]And I began to weep bitterly because no one was found worthy
to open the scroll or to look into it.
[5]Then one of the elders said to me,
"Do not weep. See, the Lion of the
tribe of Judah, the Root of David,
has conquered, so that he can open
the scroll and its seven seals."

6 Then I saw between the throne
and the four living creatures and
among the elders a Lamb standing
as if it had been slaughtered, having
seven horns and seven eyes, which
are the seven spirits of God sent out
into all the earth. [7]He went and took
the scroll from the right hand of the
one who was seated on the throne.
[8]When he had taken the scroll, the
four living creatures and the twenty-
four elders fell before the Lamb, each
holding a harp and golden bowls full
of incense, which are the prayers of
the saints. [9]They sing a new song:
"You are worthy to take the scroll
    and to open its seals,
for you were slaughtered and
    by your blood you
        ransomed for God
    saints from[b] every tribe
        and language and
            people and nation;
[10] you have made them to be a
        kingdom and priests
    serving[c] our God,
    and they will reign on earth."
11 Then I looked, and I heard the
voice of many angels surrounding the
throne and the living creatures and
the elders; they numbered myriads

---

[a] 5.1 Or *written on the inside, and sealed on
the back*   [b] 5.9 Gk *ransomed for God from*
[c] 5.10 Gk *priests to*

of myriads and thousands of thousands, [12]singing with full voice,

"Worthy is the Lamb that
was slaughtered
to receive power and wealth and
wisdom and might
and honor and glory and
blessing!"

[13]Then I heard every creature in heaven and on earth and under the earth and in the sea, and all that is in them, singing,

"To the one seated on the throne
and to the Lamb
be blessing and honor and
glory and might
forever and ever!"

[14]And the four living creatures said, "Amen!" And the elders fell down and worshiped.

THE SEVEN SEALS

6 Then I saw the Lamb open one of the seven seals, and I heard one of the four living creatures call out, as with a voice of thunder, "Come!"[a] [2]I looked, and there was a white horse! Its rider had a bow; a crown was given to him, and he came out conquering and to conquer.

[3]When he opened the second seal, I heard the second living creature call out, "Come!"[a] [4]And out came[b] another horse, bright red; its rider was permitted to take peace from the earth, so that people would slaughter one another; and he was given a great sword.

[5]When he opened the third seal, I heard the third living creature call out, "Come!"[a] I looked, and there was a black horse! Its rider held a pair of scales in his hand, [6]and I heard what seemed to be a voice in the midst of the four living creatures saying, "A quart of wheat for a day's pay,[c] and three quarts of barley for a day's pay,[c] but do not damage the olive oil and the wine!"

[7]When he opened the fourth seal, I heard the voice of the fourth living creature call out, "Come!"[a] [8]I looked and there was a pale green horse! Its rider's name was Death, and Hades followed with him; they were given authority over a fourth of the earth, to kill with sword, famine, and pestilence, and by the wild animals of the earth.

[9]When he opened the fifth seal, I saw under the altar the souls of those who had been slaughtered for the word of God and for the testimony they had given; [10]they cried out with a loud voice, "Sovereign Lord, holy and true, how long will it be before you judge and avenge our blood on the inhabitants of the earth?" [11]They were each given a white robe and told to rest a little longer, until the number would be complete both of their fellow servants[d] and of their brothers and sisters,[e] who were soon to be killed as they themselves had been killed.

LIFE WITH CHRIST

TRANSCENDS ANYTHING

THAT WE HAVE TO GIVE UP.

[12]When he opened the sixth seal, I looked, and there came a great earthquake; the sun became black as sackcloth, the full moon became like blood, [13]and the stars of the sky fell to the earth as the fig tree drops its winter fruit when shaken by a gale. [14]The sky vanished like a scroll rolling itself up, and every mountain and island was removed from its place. [15]Then the kings of the earth and the magnates and the generals and the rich and the powerful, and everyone, slave and free, hid in the caves and among the rocks of the mountains, [16]calling to the mountains and rocks, "Fall on us and hide us from the face of the one seated on the throne and from the wrath of the Lamb; [17]for the great day of their wrath has come, and who is able to stand?"

---

[a] 6.1,3,5,7 Or "Go!" [b] 6.4 Or went
[c] 6.6 Gk *a denarius* [d] 6.11 Gk *slaves*
[e] 6.11 Gk *brothers*

THE 144,000 OF ISRAEL
SEALED

7 After this I saw four angels standing at the four corners of the earth, holding back the four winds of the earth so that no wind could blow on earth or sea or against any tree. ²I saw another angel ascending from the rising of the sun, having the seal of the living God, and he called with a loud voice to the four angels who had been given power to damage earth and sea, ³saying, "Do not damage the earth or the sea or the trees, until we have marked the servants[a] of our God with a seal on their foreheads."

4 And I heard the number of those who were sealed, one hundred forty-four thousand, sealed out of every tribe of the people of Israel:
5 From the tribe of Judah twelve
        thousand sealed,
    from the tribe of Reuben
        twelve thousand,
    from the tribe of Gad twelve
        thousand,
6 from the tribe of Asher
        twelve thousand,
    from the tribe of Naphtali
        twelve thousand,
    from the tribe of Manasseh
        twelve thousand,
7 from the tribe of Simeon
        twelve thousand,
    from the tribe of Levi
        twelve thousand,
    from the tribe of Issachar
        twelve thousand,
8 from the tribe of Zebulun
        twelve thousand,
    from the tribe of Joseph
        twelve thousand,
    from the tribe of Benjamin
        twelve thousand sealed.

THE MULTITUDE FROM
EVERY NATION

9 After this I looked, and there was a great multitude that no one could count, from every nation, from all tribes and peoples and languages, standing before the throne and before the Lamb, robed in white, with palm branches in their hands. ¹⁰They cried out in a loud voice, saying,

"Salvation belongs to our God
    who is seated on the
        throne, and to the Lamb!"
¹¹And all the angels stood around the throne and around the elders and the four living creatures, and they fell on their faces before the throne and worshiped God, ¹²singing,
"Amen! Blessing and glory
        and wisdom
and thanksgiving and honor
        and power and might
be to our God forever and
        ever! Amen."

13 Then one of the elders addressed me, saying, "Who are these, robed in white, and where have they come from?" ¹⁴I said to him, "Sir, you are the one that knows." Then he said to me, "These are they who have come out of the great ordeal; they have washed their robes and made them white in the blood of the Lamb.
15 For this reason they are before
        the throne of God,
    and worship him day and
        night within his temple,
    and the one who is seated
        on the throne will
        shelter them.
16 They will hunger no more,
        and thirst no more;
    the sun will not strike them,
        nor any scorching heat;
17 for the Lamb at the center
        of the throne will be
        their shepherd,
    and he will guide them to
        springs of the water of life,
and God will wipe away every
        tear from their eyes."

THE SEVENTH SEAL AND
THE GOLDEN CENSER

8 When the Lamb opened the seventh seal, there was silence in heaven for about half an hour. ²And I saw the seven angels who stand before God, and seven trumpets were given to them.

3 Another angel with a golden censer came and stood at the altar; he was given a great quantity of incense to offer with the prayers of all the saints on the golden altar that is

---

a **7.3** Gk *slaves*

before the throne. 4And the smoke of the incense, with the prayers of the saints, rose before God from the hand of the angel. 5Then the angel took the censer and filled it with fire from the altar and threw it on the earth; and there were peals of thunder, rumblings, flashes of lightning, and an earthquake.

THE SEVEN TRUMPETS

6 Now the seven angels who had the seven trumpets made ready to blow them.

7 The first angel blew his trumpet, and there came hail and fire, mixed with blood, and they were hurled to the earth; and a third of the earth was burned up, and a third of the trees were burned up, and all green grass was burned up.

8 The second angel blew his trumpet, and something like a great mountain, burning with fire, was thrown into the sea. 9A third of the sea became blood, a third of the living creatures in the sea died, and a third of the ships were destroyed.

10 The third angel blew his trumpet, and a great star fell from heaven, blazing like a torch, and it fell on a third of the rivers and on the springs of water. 11The name of the star is Wormwood. A third of the waters became wormwood, and many died from the water, because it was made bitter.

12 The fourth angel blew his trumpet, and a third of the sun was struck, and a third of the moon, and a third of the stars, so that a third of their light was darkened; a third of the day was kept from shining, and likewise the night.

13 Then I looked, and I heard an eagle crying with a loud voice as it flew in midheaven, "Woe, woe, woe to the inhabitants of the earth, at the blasts of the other trumpets that the three angels are about to blow!"

9 And the fifth angel blew his trumpet, and I saw a star that had fallen from heaven to earth, and he was given the key to the shaft of the bottomless pit; 2he opened the shaft of the bottomless pit, and from the shaft rose smoke like the smoke of a great furnace, and the sun and the air were darkened with the smoke from the shaft. 3Then from the smoke came locusts on the earth, and they were given authority like the authority of scorpions of the earth. 4They were told not to damage the grass of the earth or any green growth or any tree, but only those people who do not have the seal of God on their foreheads. 5They were allowed to torture them for five months, but not to kill them, and their torture was like the torture of a scorpion when it stings someone. 6And in those days people will seek death but will not find it; they will long to die, but death will flee from them.

7 In appearance the locusts were like horses equipped for battle. On their heads were what looked like crowns of gold; their faces were like human faces, 8their hair like women's hair, and their teeth like lions' teeth; 9they had scales like iron breastplates, and the noise of their wings was like the noise of many chariots with horses rushing into battle. 10They have tails like scorpions, with stingers, and in their tails is their power to harm people for five months. 11They have as king over them the angel of the bottomless pit; his name in Hebrew is Abaddon,a and in Greek he is called Apollyon.b

12 The first woe has passed. There are still two woes to come.

13 Then the sixth angel blew his trumpet, and I heard a voice from the fourc horns of the golden altar before God, 14saying to the sixth angel who had the trumpet, "Release the four angels who are bound at the great river Euphrates." 15So the four angels were released, who had been held ready for the hour, the day, the month, and the year, to kill a third of humankind. 16The number of the troops of cavalry was two hundred million; I heard their number. 17And this was how I saw the horses in my vision: the riders wore breastplates the color of fire and of sapphired and

a 9.11 That is, Destruction   b 9.11 That is, Destroyer   c 9.13 Other ancient authorities lack four   d 9.17 Gk hyacinth of sulfur; the heads of the horses were like lions' heads, and fire and smoke and sulfur came out of their mouths. 18 By these three plagues a third of humankind was killed, by the fire and smoke and sulfur coming out of their mouths. 19 For the power of the horses is in their mouths and in their tails; their tails are like serpents, having heads; and with them they inflict harm.

20 The rest of humankind, who were not killed by these plagues, did not repent of the works of their hands or give up worshiping demons and idols of gold and silver and bronze and stone and wood, which cannot see or hear or walk. 21 And they did not repent of their murders or their sorceries or their fornication or their thefts.

THE ANGEL WITH THE LITTLE SCROLL

10 And I saw another mighty angel coming down from heaven, wrapped in a cloud, with a rainbow over his head; his face was like the sun, and his legs like pillars of fire. 2 He held a little scroll open in his hand. Setting his right foot on the sea and his left foot on the land, 3 he gave a great shout, like a lion roaring. And when he shouted, the seven thunders sounded. 4 And when the seven thunders had sounded, I was about to write, but I heard a voice from heaven saying, "Seal up what the seven thunders have said, and do not write it down." 5 Then the angel whom I saw standing on the sea and the land

raised his right hand to heaven
6   and swore by him who lives
        forever and ever,
who created heaven and what is in it, the earth and what is in it, and the sea and what is in it: "There will be no more delay, 7 but in the days when the seventh angel is to blow his trumpet, the mystery of God will be fulfilled, as he announced to his servants[a] the prophets."

8 Then the voice that I had heard from heaven spoke to me again, saying, "Go, take the scroll that is

PONDER

Then the angel whom I saw standing on the sea and the land raised his right hand to heaven and swore by him who lives forever and ever . . ."There will be no more delay, but in the days when the seventh angel is to blow his trumpet, the mystery of God will be fulfilled."
—Revelation 10.5–7

PRAY

Lord, the words apocalyptic and eschatology have always been a concern to us, particularly to those of us who are not scholars of the Bible. We appreciate the opportunity to learn about these scripture passages in which you have shown us a glimpse of the mysteries you still hold in store for your people. We know it is good for us that we don't know when you are coming or when our final day is, because you want us to be prepared every day to meet you. Teach us to live soberly and courageously so that we are ready to do so. We praise you for the glory and perfection of your will for the earth and for our existence here. In Jesus' name, we pray. Amen.

open in the hand of the angel who is standing on the sea and on the land." 9 So I went to the angel and told him to give me the little scroll; and he said to me, "Take it, and eat; it will be bitter to your stomach, but sweet as honey in your mouth." 10 So I took the little scroll from the hand of the angel and ate it; it was sweet as honey in my mouth, but when I had eaten it, my stomach was made bitter.

11 Then they said to me, "You must prophesy again about many peoples and nations and languages and kings."

a 10.7 Gk slaves

THE TWO WITNESSES

11 Then I was given a measuring rod like a staff, and I was told, "Come and measure the temple of God and the altar and those who worship there, ²but do not measure the court outside the temple; leave that out, for it is given over to the nations, and they will trample over the holy city for forty-two months. ³And I will grant my two witnesses authority to prophesy for one thousand two hundred sixty days, wearing sackcloth."

4 These are the two olive trees and the two lampstands that stand before the Lord of the earth. ⁵And if anyone wants to harm them, fire pours from their mouth and consumes their foes; anyone who wants to harm them must be killed in this manner. ⁶They have authority to shut the sky, so that no rain may fall during the days of their prophesying, and they have authority over the waters to turn them into blood, and to strike the earth with every kind of plague, as often as they desire.

7 When they have finished their testimony, the beast that comes up from the bottomless pit will make war on them and conquer them and kill them, ⁸and their dead bodies will lie in the street of the great city that is prophetically[a] called Sodom and Egypt, where also their Lord was crucified. ⁹For three and a half days members of the peoples and tribes and languages and nations will gaze at their dead bodies and refuse to let them be placed in a tomb; ¹⁰and the inhabitants of the earth will gloat over them and celebrate and exchange presents, because these two prophets had been a torment to the inhabitants of the earth.

11 But after the three and a half days, the breath[b] of life from God entered them, and they stood on their feet, and those who saw them were terrified. ¹²Then they[c] heard a loud voice from heaven saying to them, "Come up here!" And they went up to heaven in a cloud while their enemies watched them. ¹³At that moment there was a great earthquake, and a tenth of the city fell; seven thousand people were killed in the earthquake, and the rest were terrified and gave glory to the God of heaven.

14 The second woe has passed. The third woe is coming very soon.

THE SEVENTH TRUMPET

15 Then the seventh angel blew his trumpet, and there were loud voices in heaven, saying,

"The kingdom of the world
      has become the
      kingdom of our Lord
and of his Messiah,[d]
and he will reign forever
      and ever."

16 Then the twenty-four elders who sit on their thrones before God fell on their faces and worshiped God, ¹⁷singing,

"We give you thanks, Lord
      God Almighty,
who are and who were,
for you have taken your
      great power
and begun to reign.
18 The nations raged,
      but your wrath has come,
      and the time for judging
            the dead,
for rewarding your servants,[e]
      the prophets
and saints and all who
            fear your name,
both small and great,
and for destroying those who
      destroy the earth."

19 Then God's temple in heaven was opened, and the ark of his covenant was seen within his temple; and there were flashes of lightning, rumblings, peals of thunder, an earthquake, and heavy hail.

THE WOMAN AND THE DRAGON

12 A great portent appeared in heaven: a woman clothed with the sun, with the moon under her feet, and on her head a crown of twelve stars. ²She was pregnant and was crying out in birth pangs,

a 11.8 Or *allegorically*; Gk *spiritually*
b 11.11 Or *the spirit*   c 11.12 Other ancient authorities read *I*   d 11.15 Gk *Christ*
e 11.18 Gk *slaves*

in the agony of giving birth. ³Then another portent appeared in heaven: a great red dragon, with seven heads and ten horns, and seven diadems on his heads. ⁴His tail swept down a third of the stars of heaven and threw them to the earth. Then the dragon stood before the woman who was about to bear a child, so that he might devour her child as soon as it was born. ⁵And she gave birth to a son, a male child, who is to rule[a] all the nations with a rod of iron. But her child was snatched away and taken to God and to his throne; ⁶and the woman fled into the wilderness, where she has a place prepared by God, so that there she can be nourished for one thousand two hundred sixty days.

MICHAEL DEFEATS THE DRAGON

7 And war broke out in heaven; Michael and his angels fought against the dragon. The dragon and his angels fought back, ⁸but they were defeated, and there was no longer any place for them in heaven. ⁹The great dragon was thrown down, that ancient serpent, who is called the Devil and Satan, the deceiver of the whole world—he was thrown down to the earth, and his angels were thrown down with him.

10 Then I heard a loud voice in heaven, proclaiming,

"Now have come the salvation
     and the power
and the kingdom of our God
and the authority of
     his Messiah,[b]
for the accuser of our comrades[c]
     has been thrown down,
who accuses them day and
     night before our God.
¹¹ But they have conquered him by
     the blood of the Lamb
and by the word of their
     testimony,
for they did not cling to life even
     in the face of death.
¹² Rejoice then, you heavens
     and those who dwell in them!
But woe to the earth and the sea,
     for the devil has come
          down to you

with great wrath,
     because he knows that
          his time is short!"

THE DRAGON FIGHTS AGAIN ON EARTH

13 So when the dragon saw that he had been thrown down to the earth, he pursued[d] the woman who had given birth to the male child. ¹⁴But the woman was given the two wings of the great eagle, so that she could fly from the serpent into the wilderness, to her place where she is nourished for a time, and times, and half a time. ¹⁵Then from his mouth the serpent poured water like a river after the woman, to sweep her away with the flood. ¹⁶But the earth came to the help of the woman; it opened its mouth and swallowed the river that the dragon had poured from his mouth. ¹⁷Then the dragon was angry with the woman, and went off to make war on the rest of her children, those who keep the commandments of God and hold the testimony of Jesus.

THE FIRST BEAST

18 Then the dragon[e] took his stand on the sand of the seashore. **13** ¹And I saw a beast rising out of the sea, having ten horns and seven heads; and on its horns were ten diadems, and on its heads were blasphemous names. ²And the beast that I saw was like a leopard, its feet were like a bear's, and its mouth was like a lion's mouth. And the dragon gave it his power and his throne and great authority. ³One of its heads seemed to have received a death-blow, but its mortal wound[f] had been healed. In amazement the whole earth followed the beast. ⁴They worshiped the dragon, for he had given his authority to the beast, and they worshiped the beast, saying, "Who is like the beast, and who can fight against it?"

---

[a] 12.5 Or to shepherd [b] 12.10 Gk Christ
[c] 12.10 Gk brothers [d] 12.13 Or persecuted
[e] 12.18 Gk Then he; other ancient authorities read Then I stood [f] 13.3 Gk the plague of its death

5 The beast was given a mouth uttering haughty and blasphemous words, and it was allowed to exercise authority for forty-two months. 6 It opened its mouth to utter blasphemies against God, blaspheming his name and his dwelling, that is, those who dwell in heaven. 7 Also it was allowed to make war on the saints and to conquer them.[a] It was given authority over every tribe and people and language and nation, 8 and all the inhabitants of the earth will worship it, everyone whose name has not been written from the foundation of the world in the book of life of the Lamb that was slaughtered.[b]

9 Let anyone who has an ear listen:

10 If you are to be taken captive,
    into captivity you go;
    if you kill with the sword,
    with the sword you
        must be killed.

Here is a call for the endurance and faith of the saints.

THE SECOND BEAST

11 Then I saw another beast that rose out of the earth; it had two horns like a lamb and it spoke like a dragon. 12 It exercises all the authority of the first beast on its behalf, and it makes the earth and its inhabitants worship the first beast, whose mortal wound[c] had been healed. 13 It performs great signs, even making fire come down from heaven to earth in the sight of all; 14 and by the signs that it is allowed to perform on behalf of the beast, it deceives the inhabitants of earth, telling them to make an image for the beast that had been wounded by the sword[d] and yet lived; 15 and it was allowed to give breath[e] to the image of the beast so that the image of the beast could even speak and cause those who would not worship the image of the beast to be killed. 16 Also it causes all, both small and great, both rich and poor, both free and slave, to be marked on the right hand or the forehead, 17 so that no one can buy or sell who does not have the mark, that is, the name of the beast or the number of its name. 18 This calls for

wisdom: let anyone with understanding calculate the number of the beast, for it is the number of a person. Its number is six hundred sixty-six.[f]

THE LAMB AND THE 144,000

14 Then I looked, and there was the Lamb, standing on Mount Zion! And with him were one hundred forty-four thousand who had his name and his Father's name written on their foreheads. 2 And I heard a voice from heaven like the sound of many waters and like the sound of loud thunder; the voice I heard was like the sound of harpists playing on their harps; 3 and they sing a new song before the throne and before the four living creatures and before the elders. No one could learn that song except the one hundred forty-four thousand who have been redeemed from the earth. 4 It is these who have not defiled themselves with women, for they are virgins; these follow the Lamb wherever he goes. They have been redeemed from humankind as first fruits for God and the Lamb, 5 and in their mouth no lie was found; they are blameless.

THE MESSAGES OF THE THREE ANGELS

6 Then I saw another angel flying in midheaven, with an eternal gospel to proclaim to those who live[g] on the earth—to every nation and tribe and language and people. 7 He said in a loud voice, "Fear God and give him glory, for the hour of his judgment has come; and worship him who made heaven and earth, the sea and the springs of water."

8 Then another angel, a second, followed, saying, "Fallen, fallen is Babylon the great! She has made

a 13.7 Other ancient authorities lack this sentence   b 13.8 Or written in the book of life of the Lamb that was slaughtered from the foundation of the world   c 13.12 Gk whose plague of its death   d 13.14 Or that had received the plague of the sword   e 13.15 Or spirit   f 13.18 Other ancient authorities read six hundred sixteen g 14.6 Gk sit

all nations drink of the wine of the wrath of her fornication."

9 Then another angel, a third, followed them, crying with a loud voice, "Those who worship the beast and its image, and receive a mark on their foreheads or on their hands, 10 they will also drink the wine of God's wrath, poured unmixed into the cup of his anger, and they will be tormented with fire and sulfur in the presence of the holy angels and in the presence of the Lamb. 11 And the smoke of their torment goes up forever and ever. There is no rest day or night for those who worship the beast and its image and for anyone who receives the mark of its name."

12 Here is a call for the endurance of the saints, those who keep the commandments of God and hold fast to the faith of[a] Jesus.

13 And I heard a voice from heaven saying, "Write this: Blessed are the dead who from now on die in the Lord." "Yes," says the Spirit, "they will rest from their labors, for their deeds follow them."

PONDER

"Fear God and give him glory, for the hour of his judgment has come; and worship him who made heaven and earth, the sea and the springs of water."
—Revelation 14.7

PRAY

O Father, although it is tempting for us to skip over some of the most difficult parts of the Bible, we appreciate the discipline that is required of us to look more deeply into mysterious and complicated verses. We pray for the endurance to study and take to heart the messages from you written in these difficult passages and to let them show us your will and your ways. In Jesus' name, we pray. Amen.

REAPING THE EARTH'S HARVEST

14 Then I looked, and there was a white cloud, and seated on the cloud was one like the Son of Man, with a golden crown on his head, and a sharp sickle in his hand! 15 Another angel came out of the temple, calling with a loud voice to the one who sat on the cloud, "Use your sickle and reap, for the hour to reap has come, because the harvest of the earth is fully ripe." 16 So the one who sat on the cloud swung his sickle over the earth, and the earth was reaped.

17 Then another angel came out of the temple in heaven, and he too had a sharp sickle. 18 Then another angel came out from the altar, the angel who has authority over fire, and he called with a loud voice to him who had the sharp sickle, "Use your sharp sickle and gather the clusters of the vine of the earth, for its grapes are ripe." 19 So the angel swung his sickle over the earth and gathered the vintage of the earth, and he threw it into the great wine press of the wrath of God. 20 And the wine press was trodden outside the city, and blood flowed from the wine press, as high as a horse's bridle, for a distance of about two hundred miles.[b]

THE ANGELS WITH THE SEVEN LAST PLAGUES

15 Then I saw another portent in heaven, great and amazing: seven angels with seven plagues, which are the last, for with them the wrath of God is ended.

2 And I saw what appeared to be a sea of glass mixed with fire, and those who had conquered the beast and its image and the number of its name, standing beside the sea of glass with harps of God in their hands. 3 And they sing the song of Moses, the servant[c] of God, and the song of the Lamb:

"Great and amazing are
    your deeds,
Lord God the Almighty!
Just and true are your ways,
King of the nations![d]

[a] 14.12 Or to their faith in   [b] 14.20 Gk one thousand six hundred stadia   [c] 15.3 Gk slave   [d] 15.3 Other ancient authorities read the ages

4 Lord, who will not fear
    and glorify your name?
For you alone are holy.
    All nations will come
    and worship before you,
    for your judgments have
        been revealed."

5 After this I looked, and the temple of the tent[a] of witness in heaven was opened, 6and out of the temple came the seven angels with the seven plagues, robed in pure bright linen,[b] with golden sashes across their chests. 7Then one of the four living creatures gave the seven angels seven golden bowls full of the wrath of God, who lives forever and ever; 8and the temple was filled with smoke from the glory of God and from his power, and no one could enter the temple until the seven plagues of the seven angels were ended.

THE BOWLS OF GOD'S WRATH

16 Then I heard a loud voice from the temple telling the seven angels, "Go and pour out on the earth the seven bowls of the wrath of God."

2 So the first angel went and poured his bowl on the earth, and a foul and painful sore came on those who had the mark of the beast and who worshiped its image.

3 The second angel poured his bowl into the sea, and it became like the blood of a corpse, and every living thing in the sea died.

4 The third angel poured his bowl into the rivers and the springs of water, and they became blood. 5And I heard the angel of the waters say,

"You are just, O Holy One,
    who are and were,
    for you have judged
        these things;
6 because they shed the blood of
        saints and prophets,
    you have given them
        blood to drink.
It is what they deserve!"
7And I heard the altar respond,
"Yes, O Lord God, the Almighty,
    your judgments are
        true and just!"

8 The fourth angel poured his bowl on the sun, and it was allowed to scorch people with fire; 9they were scorched by the fierce heat, but they cursed the name of God, who had authority over these plagues, and they did not repent and give him glory.

10 The fifth angel poured his bowl on the throne of the beast, and its kingdom was plunged into darkness; people gnawed their tongues in agony, 11and cursed the God of heaven because of their pains and sores, and they did not repent of their deeds.

12 The sixth angel poured his bowl on the great river Euphrates, and its water was dried up in order to prepare the way for the kings from the east. 13And I saw three foul spirits like frogs coming from the mouth of the dragon, from the mouth of the beast, and from the mouth of the false prophet. 14These are demonic spirits, performing signs, who go abroad to the kings of the whole world, to assemble them for battle on the great day of God the Almighty. 15("See, I am coming like a thief! Blessed is the one who stays awake and is clothed,[c] not going about naked and exposed to shame.") 16And they assembled them at the place that in Hebrew is called Harmagedon.

17 The seventh angel poured his bowl into the air, and a loud voice came out of the temple, from the throne, saying, "It is done!" 18And there came flashes of lightning, rumblings, peals of thunder, and a violent earthquake, such as had not occurred since people were upon the earth, so violent was that earthquake. 19The great city was split into three parts, and the cities of the nations fell. God remembered great Babylon and gave her the wine-cup of the fury of his wrath. 20And every island fled away, and no mountains were to be found; 21and huge hailstones, each weighing about a hundred pounds,[d] dropped from heaven

[a] 15.5 Or *tabernacle* [b] 15.6 Other ancient authorities read *stone* [c] 16.15 Gk *and keeps his robes* [d] 16.21 Gk *weighing about a talent*

on people, until they cursed God for the plague of the hail, so fearful was that plague.

THE GREAT WHORE AND THE BEAST

17 Then one of the seven angels who had the seven bowls came and said to me, "Come, I will show you the judgment of the great whore who is seated on many waters, ²with whom the kings of the earth have committed fornication, and with the wine of whose fornication the inhabitants of the earth have become drunk." ³So he carried me away in the spirit[a] into a wilderness, and I saw a woman sitting on a scarlet beast that was full of blasphemous names, and it had seven heads and ten horns. ⁴The woman was clothed in purple and scarlet, and adorned with gold and jewels and pearls, holding in her hand a golden cup full of abominations and the impurities of her fornication; ⁵and on her forehead was written a name, a mystery: "Babylon the great, mother of whores and of earth's abominations." ⁶And I saw that the woman was drunk with the blood of the saints and the blood of the witnesses to Jesus.

When I saw her, I was greatly amazed. ⁷But the angel said to me, "Why are you so amazed? I will tell you the mystery of the woman, and of the beast with seven heads and ten horns that carries her. ⁸The beast that you saw was, and is not, and is about to ascend from the bottomless pit and go to destruction. And the inhabitants of the earth, whose names have not been written in the book of life from the foundation of the world, will be amazed when they see the beast, because it was and is not and is to come.

⁹ "This calls for a mind that has wisdom: the seven heads are seven mountains on which the woman is seated; also, they are seven kings, ¹⁰of whom five have fallen, one is living, and the other has not yet come; and when he comes, he must remain only a little while. ¹¹As for the beast that was and is not, it is an

PONDER

"This calls for a mind that has wisdom."
—Revelation 17.9

PRAY

Almighty Father, give us open hearts and open minds to encompass these strange images and to comprehend not only what they meant for the early church, but also what they mean in our own times and in the world most of us characterize as troubled or challenging. As we read them, help us to focus on the transcendence of your kingdom. Remind us that, no matter what our challenges or fears may be, they fade into relative insignificance compared to the reassurance of your grace and love through our faith in Christ. We ask these things in the name of our Savior. Amen.

eighth but it belongs to the seven, and it goes to destruction. ¹²And the ten horns that you saw are ten kings who have not yet received a kingdom, but they are to receive authority as kings for one hour, together with the beast. ¹³These are united in yielding their power and authority to the beast; ¹⁴they will make war on the Lamb, and the Lamb will conquer them, for he is Lord of lords and King of kings, and those with him are called and chosen and faithful."

15 And he said to me, "The waters that you saw, where the whore is seated, are peoples and multitudes and nations and languages. ¹⁶And the ten horns that you saw, they and the beast will hate the whore; they will make her desolate and naked; they will devour her flesh and burn her up with fire. ¹⁷For God has put it into their hearts to carry out his purpose by agreeing to give their kingdom to the beast, until the words of God will be fulfilled. ¹⁸The woman

[a] 17.3 Or in the Spirit

you saw is the great city that rules over the kings of the earth."

THE FALL OF BABYLON

18 After this I saw another angel coming down from heaven, having great authority; and the earth was made bright with his splendor. ²He called out with a mighty voice,

"Fallen, fallen is Babylon
    the great!
It has become a dwelling
    place of demons,
a haunt of every foul spirit,
a haunt of every foul bird,
a haunt of every foul and
    hateful beast.ᵃ

3 For all the nations
    have drunkᵇ
of the wine of the wrath
    of her fornication,
and the kings of the earth
    have committed
    fornication with her,
and the merchants of the earth
    have grown rich from the
    powerᶜ of her luxury."

4 Then I heard another voice from heaven saying,

"Come out of her, my people,
    so that you do not take
    part in her sins,
and so that you do not share
    in her plagues;
5 for her sins are heaped
    high as heaven,
and God has remembered
    her iniquities.
6 Render to her as she herself
    has rendered,
and repay her double
    for her deeds;
mix a double draught for her
    in the cup she mixed.
7 As she glorified herself and
    lived luxuriously,
so give her a like measure
    of torment and grief.
Since in her heart she says,
'I rule as a queen;
I am no widow,
    and I will never see grief,'
8 therefore her plagues will come
    in a single day—
pestilence and mourning
    and famine—

and she will be burned with fire;
    for mighty is the Lord God
    who judges her."

9 And the kings of the earth, who committed fornication and lived in luxury with her, will weep and wail over her when they see the smoke of her burning; ¹⁰they will stand far off, in fear of her torment, and say,

"Alas, alas, the great city,
    Babylon, the mighty city!
For in one hour your judgment
    has come."

11 And the merchants of the earth weep and mourn for her, since no one buys their cargo anymore, ¹²cargo of gold, silver, jewels and pearls, fine linen, purple, silk and scarlet, all kinds of scented wood, all articles of ivory, all articles of costly wood, bronze, iron, and marble, ¹³cinnamon, spice, incense, myrrh, frankincense, wine, olive oil, choice flour and wheat, cattle and sheep, horses and chariots, slaves—and human lives.ᵈ

14 "The fruit for which your
    soul longed
has gone from you,
and all your dainties and
    your splendor
are lost to you,
    never to be found again!"

¹⁵The merchants of these wares, who gained wealth from her, will stand far off, in fear of her torment, weeping and mourning aloud,

16 "Alas, alas, the great city,
    clothed in fine linen,
    in purple and scarlet,
    adorned with gold,
with jewels, and with pearls!
17 For in one hour all this wealth
    has been laid waste!"

And all shipmasters and seafarers, sailors and all whose trade is on the sea, stood far off ¹⁸and cried out as they saw the smoke of her burning,

---

ᵃ 18.2 Other ancient authorities lack the words *a haunt of every foul beast* and attach the words *and hateful* to the previous line so as to read *a haunt of every foul and hateful bird*   ᵇ 18.3 Other ancient authorities read *She has made all nations drink*   ᶜ 18.3 Or *resources*   ᵈ 18.13 Or *chariots, and human bodies and souls*

"What city was like the
    great city?"
19 And they threw dust on their heads,
as they wept and mourned, crying out,
"Alas, alas, the great city,
    where all who had ships at sea
    grew rich by her wealth!
For in one hour she has
    been laid waste."
20 Rejoice over her, O heaven, you
saints and apostles and prophets!
For God has given judgment for you
against her.

21 Then a mighty angel took up a
stone like a great millstone and threw
it into the sea, saying,
"With such violence Babylon
    the great city
    will be thrown down,
    and will be found no more;
22 and the sound of harpists and
        minstrels and of flutists
        and trumpeters
    will be heard in you no more;
and an artisan of any trade
    will be found in you no more;
and the sound of the millstone
    will be heard in you no more;
23 and the light of a lamp
    will shine in you no more;
    and the voice of bridegroom
        and bride
    will be heard in you no more;
for your merchants were the
        magnates of the earth,
    and all nations were deceived
        by your sorcery.
24 And in you[a] was found the blood
    of prophets and of saints,
    and of all who have been
        slaughtered on earth."

THE REJOICING IN HEAVEN

19 After this I heard what
seemed to be the loud voice
of a great multitude in heaven, saying,
"Hallelujah!
Salvation and glory and
        power to our God,
2   for his judgments are
        true and just;
he has judged the great whore
    who corrupted the earth
        with her fornication,
and he has avenged on her the
    blood of his servants."[b]

3 Once more they said,
"Hallelujah!
The smoke goes up from her
    forever and ever."
4 And the twenty-four elders and the
four living creatures fell down and
worshiped God who is seated on the
throne, saying,
"Amen. Hallelujah!"
5 And from the throne came a
voice saying,
"Praise our God,
    all you his servants,[b]
and all who fear him,
    small and great."
6 Then I heard what seemed to be the
voice of a great multitude, like the
sound of many waters and like the
sound of mighty thunderpeals, crying out,
"Hallelujah!
For the Lord our God
    the Almighty reigns.
7   Let us rejoice and exult
    and give him the glory,
    for the marriage of the
        Lamb has come,
    and his bride has made
        herself ready;
8   to her it has been granted
        to be clothed
    with fine linen, bright
        and pure"—
for the fine linen is the righteous
deeds of the saints.

9 And the angel said[c] to me,
"Write this: Blessed are those who
are invited to the marriage supper of the Lamb." And he said to
me, "These are true words of God."
10 Then I fell down at his feet to worship him, but he said to me, "You
must not do that! I am a fellow servant[d] with you and your comrades[e]
who hold the testimony of Jesus.[f]
Worship God! For the testimony of
Jesus[f] is the spirit of prophecy."

THE RIDER ON THE
WHITE HORSE

11 Then I saw heaven opened, and
there was a white horse! Its rider
is called Faithful and True, and in
righteousness he judges and makes

a 18.24 Gk her   b 19.2,5 Gk slaves
c 19.9 Gk he said   d 19.10 Gk slave
e 19.10 Gk brothers   f 19.10 Or to Jesus

PONDER

"Hallelujah! For the Lord our God the Almighty reigns. Let us rejoice and exult and give him the glory, for the marriage of the Lamb has come, and his bride has made herself ready; to her it has been granted to be clothed with fine linen, bright and pure."
—Revelation 19.6–8

PRAY

O Father, we thank you for the hope that you give us at the end of the mysterious book of Revelation. We praise you for the vision of the church in its ultimate perfection. Give us the will and the wisdom to strengthen this church that is our heritage, our future and the glorious bride of the Lamb, our Lord, Jesus Christ, in whose name we pray. Amen.

---

war. 12His eyes are like a flame of fire, and on his head are many diadems; and he has a name inscribed that no one knows but himself. 13He is clothed in a robe dipped in[a] blood, and his name is called The Word of God. 14And the armies of heaven, wearing fine linen, white and pure, were following him on white horses. 15From his mouth comes a sharp sword with which to strike down the nations, and he will rule[b] them with a rod of iron; he will tread the wine press of the fury of the wrath of God the Almighty. 16On his robe and on his thigh he has a name inscribed, "King of kings and Lord of lords."

THE BEAST AND ITS ARMIES DEFEATED

17 Then I saw an angel standing in the sun, and with a loud voice he called to all the birds that fly in midheaven, "Come, gather for the great supper of God, 18to eat the flesh of kings, the flesh of captains, the flesh of the mighty, the flesh of horses and their riders—flesh of all, both free and slave, both small and great." 19Then I saw the beast and the kings of the earth with their armies gathered to make war against the rider on the horse and against his army. 20And the beast was captured, and with it the false prophet who had performed in its presence the signs by which he deceived those who had received the mark of the beast and those who worshiped its image. These two were thrown alive into the lake of fire that burns with sulfur. 21And the rest were killed by the sword of the rider on the horse, the sword that came from his mouth; and all the birds were gorged with their flesh.

THE THOUSAND YEARS

20 Then I saw an angel coming down from heaven, holding in his hand the key to the bottomless pit and a great chain. 2He seized the dragon, that ancient serpent, who is the Devil and Satan, and bound him for a thousand years, 3and threw him into the pit, and locked and sealed it over him, so that he would deceive the nations no more, until the thousand years were ended. After that he must be let out for a little while.

4 Then I saw thrones, and those seated on them were given authority to judge. I also saw the souls of those who had been beheaded for their testimony to Jesus[c] and for the word of God. They had not worshiped the beast or its image and had not received its mark on their foreheads or their hands. They came to life and reigned with Christ a thousand years. 5(The rest of the dead did not come to life until the thousand years were ended.) This is the first resurrection. 6Blessed and holy are those who share in the first resurrection. Over these the second death has no power, but they will be priests of God and of Christ, and they will reign with him a thousand years.

[a] 19.13 Other ancient authorities read sprinkled with   [b] 19.15 Or will shepherd   [c] 20.4 Or for the testimony of Jesus

SATAN'S DOOM

7 When the thousand years are ended, Satan will be released from his prison 8 and will come out to deceive the nations at the four corners of the earth, Gog and Magog, in order to gather them for battle; they are as numerous as the sands of the sea. 9 They marched up over the breadth of the earth and surrounded the camp of the saints and the beloved city. And fire came down from heaven[a] and consumed them. 10 And the devil who had deceived them was thrown into the lake of fire and sulfur, where the beast and the false prophet were, and they will be tormented day and night forever and ever.

THE DEAD ARE JUDGED

11 Then I saw a great white throne and the one who sat on it; the earth and the heaven fled from his presence, and no place was found for them. 12 And I saw the dead, great and small, standing before the throne, and books were opened. Also another book was opened, the book of life. And the dead were judged according to their works, as recorded in the books. 13 And the sea gave up the dead that were in it, Death and Hades gave up the dead that were in them, and all were judged according to what they had done. 14 Then Death and Hades were thrown into the lake of fire. This is the second death, the lake of fire; 15 and anyone whose name was not found written in the book of life was thrown into the lake of fire.

THE NEW HEAVEN AND
THE NEW EARTH

21 Then I saw a new heaven and a new earth; for the first heaven and the first earth had passed away, and the sea was no more. 2 And I saw the holy city, the new Jerusalem, coming down out of heaven from God, prepared as a bride adorned for her husband. 3 And I heard a loud voice from the throne saying,

"See, the home[b] of God is
     among mortals.

He will dwell[c] with them;
     they will be his peoples,[d]
and God himself will be
     with them;[e]
4   he will wipe every tear
          from their eyes.
Death will be no more;
     mourning and crying and
          pain will be no more,
for the first things have
          passed away."

5 And the one who was seated on the throne said, "See, I am making all things new." Also he said, "Write this, for these words are trustworthy and true." 6 Then he said to me, "It is done! I am the Alpha and the Omega, the beginning and the end. To the thirsty I will give water as a gift from the spring of the water of life. 7 Those who conquer will inherit these things, and I will be their God and they will be my children. 8 But as for the cowardly, the faithless,[f] the polluted, the murderers, the fornicators, the sorcerers, the idolaters, and all liars, their place will be in the lake that burns with fire and sulfur, which is the second death."

VISION OF THE NEW JERUSALEM

9 Then one of the seven angels who had the seven bowls full of the seven last plagues came and said to me, "Come, I will show you the bride, the wife of the Lamb." 10 And in the spirit[g] he carried me away to a great, high mountain and showed me the holy city Jerusalem coming down out of heaven from God. 11 It has the glory of God and a radiance like a very rare jewel, like jasper, clear as crystal. 12 It has a great, high wall with twelve gates, and at the gates twelve angels, and on the gates are inscribed the names of the twelve tribes of the Israelites; 13 on the east three gates, on the north three gates, on the south three gates, and on the

---

[a] 20.9 Other ancient authorities read *from God, out of heaven,* or *out of heaven from God*   [b] 21.3 Gk *the tabernacle*   [c] 21.3 Gk *will tabernacle*   [d] 21.3 Other ancient authorities read *people*   [e] 21.3 Other ancient authorities add *and be their God*   [f] 21.8 Or *the unbelieving*   [g] 21.10 Or *in the Spirit*

BIBLE IN FOCUS

A NEW HEAVEN, A NEW EARTH

Then I saw a new heaven and a new earth; for the first heaven and the first earth had passed away, and the sea was no more.

—Revelation 21.1

In the book of Revelation, which describes the culmination of world history as we know it and the glorious future that awaits believers, John speaks of God creating a new heaven and a new earth. The Greek word he used for *new* (*kainos*) did not simply mean another heaven and earth to replace the old, much like someone buys a new vase to replace a broken one. Instead the Greek word refers to something of a distinctly different, even innovative, quality. It is completely unlike the old.

What will this new heaven and earth be like? First, it will be a place where God lives in the midst of all people. There will no longer be a separation between us and God. We won't look on God as a mysterious being, and the barriers between us will be broken down. We'll understand who God is, what God is, and what is expected of us, and we will experience reconciliation, a merging and an intimacy between ourselves and God.

Second, in the new heaven and earth God will wipe every tear from our eyes. There will be no more suffering or death, no more mourning and sadness. We will live in complete harmony with other human beings. Interestingly, John also notes that "the sea was no more." For sailors like me who have spent a significant amount of time on the sea, this may not sound like a good thing. But for John and many of his readers, the sea was probably regarded as a fearsome thing. It was marked by roaring waves, unpredictability, and even destruction. Perhaps too, John was thinking of the sea as something that confines, since he wrote the book of Revelation after he had been exiled to the island of Patmos by the Romans. In any event, the sea, with all its potentially negative connotations, will not be a part of the new heaven and earth. The new heaven and earth will be a place of pure joy and goodness, with no fear of trouble. For all eternity, this will be the home of all who have placed their faith in Jesus.

John's description of the wonderful future that lies in store for all believers should give us great assurance and security. It should fill us with hope to carry us through anything that we will face in this life, because we know what good things ultimately await us. It should inspire us to serve God all the more earnestly now as we anticipate our future intimacy.

Going Deeper

- What are some things you are experiencing now that you will be glad to leave behind when God creates the new heaven and earth?
- In what ways can the hope of God's promises about the future enable you to live differently now?

west three gates. ¹⁴And the wall of the city has twelve foundations, and on them are the twelve names of the twelve apostles of the Lamb.

15 The angelᵃ who talked to me had a measuring rod of gold to measure the city and its gates and walls. ¹⁶The city lies foursquare, its length the same as its width; and he measured the city with his rod, fifteen hundred miles;ᵇ its length and width and height are equal. ¹⁷He also measured its wall, one hundred forty-four cubitsᶜ by human measurement, which the angel was using. ¹⁸The wall is built of jasper, while the city is pure gold, clear as glass. ¹⁹The foundations of the wall of the city are adorned with every jewel; the first was jasper, the second sapphire, the third agate, the fourth emerald, ²⁰the fifth onyx, the sixth carnelian, the seventh chrysolite, the eighth beryl, the ninth topaz, the tenth chrysoprase, the eleventh jacinth, the twelfth amethyst. ²¹And the twelve gates are twelve pearls, each of the gates is a single pearl, and the street of the city is pure gold, transparent as glass.

22 I saw no temple in the city, for its temple is the Lord God the Almighty and the Lamb. ²³And the city has no need of sun or moon to shine on it, for the glory of God is its light, and its lamp is the Lamb. ²⁴The nations will walk by its light, and the kings of the earth will bring their glory into it. ²⁵Its gates will never be shut by day—and there will be no night there. ²⁶People will bring into it the glory and the honor of the nations. ²⁷But nothing unclean will enter it, nor anyone who practices abomination or falsehood, but only those who are written in the Lamb's book of life.

THE RIVER OF LIFE

22 Then the angelᵈ showed me the river of the water of life, bright as crystal, flowing from the throne of God and of the Lamb ²through the middle of the street of the city. On either side of the river is the tree of lifeᵉ with its twelve kinds of fruit, producing its fruit each

month; and the leaves of the tree are for the healing of the nations. ³Nothing accursed will be found there any more. But the throne of God and of the Lamb will be in it, and his servantsᶠ will worship him; ⁴they will see his face, and his name will be on their foreheads. ⁵And there will be no more night; they need no light of lamp or sun, for the Lord God will be their light, and they will reign forever and ever.

6 And he said to me, "These words are trustworthy and true, for the Lord, the God of the spirits of the prophets, has sent his angel to show his servantsᶠ what must soon take place."

ᵃ **21.15** Gk *He*   ᵇ **21.16** Gk *twelve thousand stadia*   ᶜ **21.17** That is, almost seventy-five yards   ᵈ **22.1** Gk *he*   ᵉ **22.2** Or *the Lamb*.   ²*In the middle of the street of the city, and on either side of the river, is the tree of life*   ᶠ **22.3,6** Gk *slaves*

PONDER

The city has no need of sun or moon to shine on it, for the glory of God is its light, and its lamp is the Lamb. The nations will walk by its light, and the kings of the earth will bring their glory into it.
—Revelation 21.23–24

PRAY

Lord, help us, as we conclude this final book of scripture, to realize that we represent Jesus Christ in our troubled world. Help us to have the courage to speak as Christ would speak. He is the Prince of peace, not war; he is humble, not proud; he is forgiving, not resentful or filled with hatred. Fill us with your love and compassion. Thank you for the assurance, by your grace and through our faith in Jesus Christ, that you love us and have saved us to live in your presence and in the presence of our Savior. In his name we pray. Amen.

7 "See, I am coming soon! Blessed is the one who keeps the words of the prophecy of this book."

EPILOGUE AND BENEDICTION

8 I, John, am the one who heard and saw these things. And when I heard and saw them, I fell down to worship at the feet of the angel who showed them to me; **9**but he said to me, "You must not do that! I am a fellow servant[a] with you and your comrades[b] the prophets, and with those who keep the words of this book. Worship God!"

10 And he said to me, "Do not seal up the words of the prophecy of this book, for the time is near. **11**Let the evildoer still do evil, and the filthy still be filthy, and the righteous still do right, and the holy still be holy."

12 "See, I am coming soon; my reward is with me, to repay according to everyone's work. **13**I am the Alpha and the Omega, the first and the last, the beginning and the end."

14 Blessed are those who wash their robes,[c] so that they will have the right to the tree of life and may enter the city by the gates. **15**Outside are the dogs and sorcerers and fornicators and murderers and idolaters, and everyone who loves and practices falsehood.

16 "It is I, Jesus, who sent my angel to you with this testimony for the churches. I am the root and the descendant of David, the bright morning star."

17 The Spirit and the bride
say, "Come."
And let everyone who hears
say, "Come."
And let everyone who is
thirsty come.
Let anyone who wishes take the
water of life as a gift.

18 I warn everyone who hears the words of the prophecy of this book: if anyone adds to them, God will add to that person the plagues described in this book; **19**if anyone takes away from the words of the book of this prophecy, God will take away that person's share in the tree of life and in the holy city, which are described in this book.

20 The one who testifies to these things says, "Surely I am coming soon."

Amen. Come, Lord Jesus!

21 The grace of the Lord Jesus be with all the saints. Amen.[d]

---

[a] 22.9 Gk *slave*   [b] 22.9 Gk *brothers*
[c] 22.14 Other ancient authorities read *do his commandments*   [d] 22.21 Other ancient authorities lack *all*; others lack *the saints*; others lack *Amen*

A NOTE REGARDING THE TYPE

This Bible was set in the Zondervan NRSV Typeface, commissioned by Zondervan, a division of HarperCollins Christian Publishing, and designed in Aarhus, Denmark, by Klaus E. Krogh and Heidi Rand Sørensen of 2K/DENMARK. The design takes inspiration from the vision of the New Revised Standard Version (NRSV) to be a modern, ecumenical translation that serves the church in personal spiritual formation, in the liturgy, and in the academy. The designers of the Zondervan NRSV Typeface sought to reflect the rich heritage of the New Revised Standard Version and its tradition of being renowned for its beautiful balance of scholarship and readability. The result is a distinctive Bible typeface that is uncompromisingly beautiful, clear, and readable at any size, and will faithfully serve a broad range of Bible readers now and in years to come.